## Contents/Indice

KU-151-553

CANCELLED 1 4 AUG 2024

1 5 DEC 2000

### Editors/Redazione

Debora Mazza          Jane Goldie

Donatella Boi     Francesca Logi     Peter Terrell

Sonia Tinagli-Baxter          Carla Zipoli

Allan Cameron     Michela Masci     Ilaria Panuccio

### Copy editors/Segreteria di redazione

Alice Grandison     Mary Rigby     Daphne Trotter

### Project management by/A cura di
LEXUS

# Preface

This new addition to the Oxford range of Italian dictionaries has been designed to meet the needs of students, tourists and all those who require quick and reliable answers to their translation questions. It provides clear guidance on selecting the most appropriate translation, illustrative examples to help with construction and usage, and precise information on grammar and style.

Focussing on everyday, idiomatic Italian and English, both spoken and written, this easy-to-use dictionary also offers generous treatment of business and computing vocabulary. Its up-to-the-minute coverage and wealth of accurate translations make it an ideal reference tool and study aid.

# Prefazione

Questo nuovo dizionario, che viene ad aggiungersi alla serie dei dizionari inglese-italiano della Oxford, è stato creato per soddisfare le esigenze degli studenti, dei turisti e di tutti coloro che hanno bisogno di risposte rapide e sicure ai problemi di traduzione. Il lettore viene guidato con chiarezza nella scelta del termine più appropriato, con esempi di uso della lingua e con indicazioni precise di grammatica e di stile.

Basandosi sull'uso dell'inglese e dell'italiano contemporaneo, sia scritto che parlato, questo dizionario di facile consultazione dedica particolare attenzione al lessico dell'informatica e degli affari. Estremamente attuale e aggiornato, e grazie all'abbondante e precisa terminologia, rappresenta uno strumento di consultazione ideale e un valido sussidio didattico.

### Proprietary terms

This dictionary includes some words which are, or are asserted to be, proprietary names or trademarks. Their inclusion does not imply that they have acquired for legal purposes a non-proprietary or general significance, nor is any other judgment implied concerning their legal status. In cases where the editor has some evidence that a word is used as a proprietary name or trademark this is indicated by the symbol ®, but no judgment concerning the legal status of such words is made or implied thereby.

### Marche depositate

Questo dizionario include alcune parole che sono o vengono considerate nomi di marche depositate. La loro presenza non implica che abbiano acquisito legalmente un significato generale, né si suggerisce alcun altro giudizio riguardo il loro stato giuridico. Qualora il redattore abbia trovato testimonianza dell'uso di una parola come marca depositata, quest'ultima è stata contrassegnata dal simbolo ®, ma nessun giudizio riguardo lo stato giuridico di tale parola viene espresso o suggerito in tal modo.

# Introduction

Here is some basic information on the way the entries in this dictionary are organized.

A swung dash ~ is used to replace the headword within the entry.

Compounds are listed in alphabetical order. Remember this when looking for a word. The entry 'password', for example, is entered alphabetically – at some distance from the entry 'pass'. Likewise 'paintbrush' and 'paintpot' will have 'painter', 'pain threshold' and 'painting' entered in between.

Indicators are provided to guide the user to the best translation for a specific sense of a word. Types of indicator are:

field labels (see the list on pp viii-ix), which indicate a general area of usage (commercial, computing, photography etc);

sense indicators, eg: **bore** n (of gun) calibro m; (person) seccatore, -trice mf;

typical subjects of verbs, eg: **bond** vt (glue:) attaccare;

typical objects of verbs, placed after the translation of the verb, eg: **boost** vt stimolare (sales); sollevare (morale):

nouns that typically go together with certain adjectives, eg: **rich** a ricco; (food) pesante.

A solid black circle means that the same word is being translated as a different part of speech, eg. **partition** n ... ● vt ...

A solid black square is used to identify phrasal verbs, eg ■ **strip down** vt ... Phrasal verbs are listed in alphabetical order directly after the main verb. So 'strip down' comes after 'strip' and before 'strip cartoon'.

English pronunciation is given for the Italian user in the International Phonetic Alphabet (see p vii).

Italian stress is shown by a ' placed in front of the stressed syllable in a word.

Square brackets are used around parts of an expression which can be omitted without altering the sense.

# Introduzione

Ecco le informazioni essenziali su come sono organizzate le voci nel dizionario.

Un trattino ondulato ~ è utilizzato al posto del lemma all'interno della voce.

I vocaboli composti sono in ordine alfabetico. È importante ricordarlo quando si cerca la parola che interessa. La voce 'password', ad esempio, essendo in ordine alfabetico, compare a una certa distanza dopo la voce 'pass'. Per la stessa ragione fra 'paintbrush' and 'paintpot' compaiono 'painter', 'pain threshold' e 'painting'.

Degli indicatori vengono forniti per indirizzare l'utente verso la traduzione corrispondente al senso voluto di una parola. I tipi di indicatori sono:

etichette semantiche (vedi la lista a pp viii-ix), indicanti l'ambito specifico in cui la parola viene generalmente usata in quel senso (commercio, informatica, fotografia ecc);

indicatori di significato, es.: **redazione** nf (ufficio) editorial office; (di testi) editing;

soggetti tipici di verbi, es.: **trovarsi** vr (luogo:) be;

complementi oggetti tipici di verbi, collocati dopo la traduzione dello stesso verbo, es: **superare** vt overtake (veicolo); pass (esame);

sostantivi che ricorrono tipicamente con certi aggettivi, es.: **solare** a (energia, raggi) solar; (crema) sun.

Un pallino nero indica che la stessa parola viene tradotta come una diversa parte del discorso, es. **calcolatore** a ... ● nm ...

Un quadratino nero viene utilizzato per indicare i phrasal verbs, ad esempio: ■ **strip down** vt ... I phrasal verbs si trovano in ordine alfabetico immediatamente dopo il verbo principale. Così 'strip down' viene subito dopo 'strip' e subito prima di 'strip cartoon'.

La pronuncia inglese è data usando l'Alfabetico Fonetico Internazionale (vedi p vii).

L'accento tonico nelle parole italiane è indicato dal segno ' collocato davanti alla sillaba accentata.

Delle parentesi quadre racchiudono parti di espressioni che possono essere omesse senza alterazioni di senso.

# Pronunciation of Italian

## Vowels:

| | |
|---|---|
| **a** | is broad like *a* in *father*: **casa**. |
| **e** | has two sounds: closed like *ey* in *they*: **sera**; open like *e* in *egg*: **sette**. |
| **i** | is like *ee* in *feet*: **venire**. |
| **o** | has two sounds: closed like *o* in *show*: **bocca**; open like *o* in *dog*: **croma**. |
| **u** | is like *oo* in *moon*: **luna**. |

When two or more vowels come together each vowel is pronounced separately: **buono**; **baia**.

## Consonants:

**b**, **d**, **f**, **l**, **m**, **n**, **p**, **t**, **v** are pronounced as in English. When these are double they are sounded distinctly: **bello**.

| | |
|---|---|
| **c** | before **a**, **o** or **u** and before consonants is like *k* in *king*: **cane**. |
| | before **e** or **i** is like *ch* in *church*: **cena**. |
| **ch** | is also like *k* in *king*: **chiesa**. |
| **g** | before **a**, **o**, or **u** is hard like *g* in *got*: **gufo**. |
| | before **e** or **i** is like *j* in *jelly*: **gentile**. |
| **gh** | is like *g* in *gun*: **ghiaccio**. |
| **gl** | when followed by **a**, **e**, **o**, **u** is like *gl* in *glass*: **gloria**. |
| **gli** | is like *lli* in *million*: **figlio**. |
| **gn** | is like *ni* in *onion*: **bagno**. |
| **h** | is silent. |
| **ng** | is like *ng* in *finger* (not *singer*): **ringraziare**. |
| **r** | is pronounced distinctly. |
| **s** | between two vowels is like *s* in *rose*: **riso**. |
| | at the beginning of a word it is like *s* in *soap*: **sapone**. |
| **sc** | before **e** or **i** is like *sh* in *shell*: **scienza**. |
| **z** | sounds like *ts* within a word: **fazione**; like *dz* at the beginning: **zoo**. |

The stress is shown by the sign ' printed before the stressed syllable.

# Pronuncia Inglese

SIMBOLI FONETICI

## Vocali e dittonghi

| | | |
|---|---|---|
| æ bad | ʊ put | aʊ now |
| ɑ: ah | u: too | aʊə flour |
| e wet | ə ago | ɔɪ coin |
| ɪ sit | ɜ: work | ɪə here |
| i: see | eɪ made | eə hair |
| ɒ got | əʊ home | ʊə poor |
| ɔ: door | aɪ five | |
| ʌ cup | aɪə fire | |

## Consonanti

| | | |
|---|---|---|
| b boy | l leg | t ten |
| d day | m man | tʃ chip |
| dʒ page | n new | θ three |
| f foot | ŋ sing | ð this |
| g go | p pen | v verb |
| h he | r run | w wet |
| j yes | s speak | z his |
| k coat | ʃ ship | ʒ pleasure |

*Note*: ' precede la sillaba accentata.
La vocale nasale in parole quali *nuance* è indicata nella trascrizione fonetica come õ: njuːõs.

# Abbreviations/Abbreviazioni

| | | |
|---|---|---|
| adjective | *a* | aggettivo |
| abbreviation | *abbr* | abbreviazione |
| administration | *Admin* | amministrazione |
| adverb | *adv* | avverbio |
| aeronautics | *Aeron* | aeronautica |
| American | *Am* | americano |
| anatomy | *Anat* | anatomia |
| archaeology | *Archaeol* | archeologia |
| architecture | *Archit* | architettura |
| attributive | *attrib* | attributo |
| astrology, astronomy | *Astr* | astrologia, astronomia |
| automobiles | *Auto* | automobile |
| auxiliary | *aux* | ausiliario |
| biology | *Biol* | biologia |
| botany | *Bot* | botanica |
| British English | *Br* | inglese britannico |
| Chemistry | *Chem* | chimica |
| commerce | *Comm* | commercio |
| computers | *Comput* | informatica |
| conjunction | *conj* | congiunzione |
| cooking | *Culin* | cucina |
| definite article | *def art* | articolo determinativo |
| | *ecc* | eccetera |
| economics | *Econ* | economia |
| electricity | *Electr* | elettricità |
| et cetera | *etc* | |
| feminine | *f* | femminile |
| familiar | *fam* | familiare |
| figurative | *fig* | figurato |
| finance | *Fin* | finanza |
| formal | *fml* | formale |
| geography | *Geog* | geografia |
| geology | *Geol* | geologia |
| grammar | *Gram* | grammatica |
| humorous | *hum* | umoristico |
| indefinite article | *indef art* | articolo indeterminativo |
| interjection | *int* | interiezione |
| interrogative | *inter* | interrogativo |
| invariable | *inv* | invariabile |
| (*no plural form*) | | |
| journalism | *Journ* | giornalismo |
| law | *Jur* | legge/giuridico |
| literary | *liter* | letterario |
| masculine | *m* | maschile |
| mathematics | *Math* | matematica |
| mechanics | *Mech* | meccanica |

| | | |
|---|---|---|
| medicine | *Med* | medicina |
| meteorology | *Metereol* | meteorologia |
| masculine or feminine | *mf* | maschile o femminile |
| military | *Mil* | militare |
| music | *Mus* | musica |
| noun | *n* | sostantivo |
| nautical | *Naut* | nautica |
| old use | *old* | antiquato |
| pejorative | *pej* | peggiorativo |
| personal | *pers* | personale |
| photography | *Phot* | fotografia |
| physics | *Phys* | fisica |
| plural | *pl* | plurale |
| politics | *Pol* | politica |
| possessive | *poss* | possessivo |
| past participle | *pp* | participio passato |
| prefix | *pref* | prefisso |
| preposition | *prep* | preposizione |
| present tense | *pres* | presente |
| pronoun | *pron* | pronome |
| psychology | *Psych* | psicologia |
| past tense | *pt* | tempo passato |
| | *qcno* | qualcuno |
| | *qcsa* | qualcosa |
| proprietary term | ® | marca depositata |
| rail | *Rail* | ferrovia |
| reflexive | *refl* | riflessivo |
| religion | *Relig* | religione |
| relative pronoun | *rel pron* | pronome relativo |
| somebody | *sb* | |
| school | *Sch* | scuola |
| singular | *sg* | singolare |
| slang | *sl* | gergo |
| something | *sth* | |
| suffix | *suff* | suffisso |
| technical | *Techn* | tecnico |
| telephone | *Teleph* | telefono |
| theatrical | *Theat* | teatrale |
| television | *TV* | televisione |
| typography | *Typ* | tipografia |
| university | *Univ* | università |
| auxiliary verb | *v aux* | verbo ausiliare |
| intransitive verb | *vi* | verbo intransitivo |
| reflexive verb | *vr* | verbo riflessivo |
| transitive verb | *vt* | verbo transitivo |
| transitive and intransitive | *vt/i* | verbo transitivo e intransitivo |
| vulgar | *vulg* | volgare |
| cultural equivalent | ≈ | equivalenza culturale |

# Aa

**a** (**ad** *before vowel*) *prep* to; (*stato in luogo, tempo, età*) at; (*con mese, città*) in; (*mezzo, modo*) by; **dire qcsa a qcno** tell sb sth; **alle tre** at three o'clock; **a vent'anni** at the age of twenty; **a Natale** at Christmas; **a dicembre** in December; **ero al cinema** I was at the cinema; **vivo a Londra** I live in London; **a due a due** two by two; **a piedi** on *o* by foot; **maglia a maniche lunghe** long-sleeved sweater; **casa a tre piani** house with three floors; **giocare a tennis** play tennis; **50 km all'ora** 50 km an hour; **2 000 lire al chilo** 2,000 lire a kilo; **al mattino/alla sera** in the morning/evening; **a venti chilometri/due ore da qui** twenty kilometres/two hours away

**'abaco** *nm* abacus

**a'bate** *nm* abbot

**abbacchia'mento** *nm fam* dejection

**abbacchi'ato** *a fam* dejected, downhearted

**ab'bacchio** *nm* [young] lamb. **~ alla romana** spring lamb

**abbaci'nare** *vt* dazzle, blind; *fig* deceive

**abbagli'ante** *a* dazzling ● *nm* headlight; **mettere gli abbaglianti** put the headlights on full beam

**abbagli'are** *vt* dazzle

**ab'baglio** *nm* blunder; **prendere un ~** make a blunder

**abbaia'mento** *nm* barking

**abbai'are** *vi* bark

**abba'ino** *nm* dormer window; (*mansarda*) loft

**abbando'nare** *vt* abandon; leave (*luogo*); give up (*piani ecc*); **~ il campo** *Mil* desert in the face of the enemy

**abbando'narsi** *vr* let oneself go; **~ a** give oneself up to (*ricordi ecc*)

**abbando'nato** *a* abandoned

**abban'dono** *nm* abandoning; *fig* abandon; (*stato*) neglect

**abbarbi'carsi** *vr* **~ a** cling to

**abbassa'mento** *nm* (*di temperatura, acqua, prezzi*) drop

**abbas'sare** *vt* lower; turn down (*radio, TV*); **~ i fari** dip the headlights

**abbas'sarsi** *vr* stoop; (*sole ecc:*) sink; *fig* demean oneself

**ab'basso** *adv* below ● *int* down with

**abba'stanza** *adv* enough; (*alquanto*) quite; **~ nuovo** newish; **ne ho ~!** I've had enough!, I'm fed up!

**ab'battere** *vt* demolish; shoot down (*aereo*); put down (*animale*); topple (*regime*); (*fig: demoralizzare*) dishearten

**ab'battersi** *vr* (*cadere*) fall; *fig* be discouraged. **~ a terra/al suolo** fall down

**abbatti'mento** *nm* (*morale*) despondency

**abbat'tuto** *a* despondent, down-in-the-mouth

**abba'zia** *nf* abbey

**abbelli'mento** *nm* embellishment

**abbel'lire** *vt* embellish

**abbel'lirsi** *vr* adorn oneself

**abbeve'rare** *vt* water

**abbevera'toio** *nm* drinking trough

**abbiccì** *nm inv fig* rudiments *pl*; **l'~ di** the ABC of

**abbi'ente** *a* well-to-do

**abbi'etto** *a* despicable, abject

**abbiglia'mento** *nm* clothes *pl*; (*industria*) clothing industry, rag trade. **~ da bambino** children's wear. **~ da donna** ladies' wear. **~ per uomo** menswear

**abbigli'are** *vt* dress

**abbigli'arsi** *vr* dress up

**abbina'mento** *nm* combining

**abbi'nare** *vt* combine; match (*colori*)

**abbindo'lare** *vt* cheat

**abbocca'mento** *nm* interview; (*conversazione*) talk

**abboc'care** *vi* bite; (*tubi:*) join; *fig* swallow the bait

**abboc'cato** *a* (*vino*) fairly sweet

**abbof'farsi** *= abbuffarsi*

**abbona'mento** *nm* subscription; (*ferroviario ecc*) season-ticket; **fare l'~** take out a subscription. **~ all'autobus** bus pass. **~ mensile** monthly ticket. **~ alla televisione** television licence

**abbo'nare** *vt* make a subscriber

**abbo'narsi** *vr* subscribe (**a** to); take out a season-ticket (**a** for) (*teatro, stadio*)

**abbo'nato, -a** *nmf* subscriber

**abbon'dante** *a* abundant; (*quantità*) copious; (*nevicata*) heavy; (*vestiario*) roomy; **~ di** abounding in

**abbondante'mente** *adv* (*mangiare*) copiously

**abbon'danza** *nf* abundance

**abbon'dare** *vi* abound

**abbor'dabile** *a* (*persona*) approachable; (*prezzo*) reasonable

**abbor'daggio** *nm Mil* boarding

**abbor'dare** *vt* board (*nave*); approach (*persona*); (*fam: attaccar bottone a*) chat up; tackle (*compito ecc*)

**abbotto'nare** *vt* button up

**abbotto'nato** *a fig* tight-lipped

**abbottona'tura** *nf* [row of] buttons; **con ~**

da donna/uomo ⟨*giacca*⟩ that buttons on the left/right

**abboz'zare** *vt* sketch [out]; **~ un sorriso** give a little smile ● *vi fam* ⟨*rassegnarsi*⟩ resign oneself

**ab'bozzo** *nm* sketch

**abbracci'are** *vt* embrace; hug, embrace ⟨*persona*⟩; take up ⟨*professione*⟩; *fig* include

**ab'braccio** *nm* hug

**abbrevi'are** *vt* shorten; ⟨*ridurre*⟩ curtail; abbreviate ⟨*parola*⟩

**abbreviazi'one** *nf* abbreviation

**abbron'zante** *nm* suntan lotion

**abbron'zare** *vt* bronze; tan ⟨*pelle*⟩

**abbron'zarsi** *vr* get a tan

**abbron'zato** *a* tanned

**abbronza'tura** *nf* [sun]tan

**abbrusto'lire** *vt* toast; roast ⟨*caffè ecc*⟩

**abbruti'mento** *nm* brutalization

**abbru'tire** *vt* brutalize; ⟨*lavoro:*⟩ stultify

**abbru'tirsi** *vr* become brutalized

**abbuf'farsi** *vr fam* stuff oneself

**abbuf'fata** *nf fam* blowout

**abbuo'nare** *vt* reduce; *fig* overlook ⟨*mancanza, errore*⟩

**abbu'ono** *nm* allowance; *Sport* handicap

**abdi'care** *vi* abdicate

**abdicazi'one** *nf* abdication

**aber'rante** *a* aberrant

**aberrazi'one** *nf* aberration

**abe'taia** *nf* wood of fir trees

**a'bete** *nm* fir

**abi'etto** *a* despicable

**abiezi'one** *nf* degradation

**abige'ato** *nm Jur* cattle-stealing, rustling

**'abile** *a* able; ⟨*idoneo*⟩ fit; ⟨*astuto*⟩ clever

**abilità** *nf inv* ability; ⟨*idoneità*⟩ fitness; ⟨*astuzia*⟩ cleverness

**abili'tante** *a* **corso ~** [officially recognized] training course

**abili'tare** *vt* qualify

**abili'tato** *a* qualified

**abilitazi'one** *nf* qualification; ⟨*titolo*⟩ diploma

**abil'mente** *adv* ably; ⟨*con astuzia*⟩ cleverly

**abis'sale** *a* abysmal

**a'bisso** *nm* abyss

**abi'tabile** *a* inhabitable

**abitabilità** *nf* fitness for human habitation; **licenza di ~** *document certifying that a building is fit for human habitation*

**abi'tacolo** *nm Auto* passenger compartment

**abi'tante** *nmf* inhabitant

**abi'tare** *vi* live

**abi'tato** *a* inhabited ● *nm* built-up area

**abitazi'one** *nf* house; **crisi delle abitazioni** housing problem

**abi'tino** *nm Relig* scapular

**'abito** *nm* ⟨*da donna*⟩ dress; ⟨*da uomo*⟩ suit; **abiti** *pl* clothes. **~ da ballo** ball dress. **~ da cerimonia** formal dress. **~ da cocktail** cocktail dress. **~ mentale** mentality. **'~ scuro'** ⟨*su inviti*⟩ 'black tie'. **~ da sera** evening dress. **~ talare** cassock. **~ da uomo** suit

**abitu'ale** *a* usual, habitual

**abitual'mente** *adv* usually

**abitu'are** *vt* accustom

**abitu'arsi** *vr* **~ a** get used to

**abitu'ato** *a* **~ a** used to

**abitudi'nario, -a** *a* of fixed habits ● *nmf* person of fixed habits

**abi'tudine** *nf* habit; **d'~** usually; **per ~** out of habit; **avere l'~ di fare qcsa** be in the habit of doing sth; **abitudini** *pl* customs

**abiu'rare** *vt* renounce

**abla'tivo** *nm* ablative

**abluzi'oni** *nfpl* **fare le ~** wash

**abnegazi'one** *nf* self-sacrifice

**ab'norme** *a* abnormal

**abo'lire** *vt* abolish; repeal ⟨*legge*⟩

**abolizi'one** *nf* abolition; ⟨*di legge*⟩ repeal

**abolizio'nismo** *nm* abolitionism

**abolizio'nista** *a & nmf* abolitionist

**abomi'nevole** *a* abominable

**abo'rigeno, -a** *a & nmf* aboriginal

**abor'rire** *vt* abhor

**abor'tire** *vi* miscarry; ⟨*volontariamente*⟩ have an abortion; *fig* fail

**abor'tista** *a* pro-choice

**abor'tivo** *a* abortive

**a'borto** *nm* miscarriage; ⟨*volontario*⟩ abortion

**abrasi'one** *nf* abrasion

**abra'sivo** *a & nm* abrasive

**abro'gare** *vt* repeal

**abroga'tivo** *a* **referendum ~** referendum to repeal a law

**abrogazi'one** *nf* repeal

**abruz'zese** *a* Abruzzi *attrib* ● *nmf* person from the Abruzzi ● *nm* Abruzzi dialect

**'abside** *nf* apse

**abu'lia** *nf* apathy

**a'bulico** *a* apathetic

**abu'sare** *vi* **~ di** abuse; over-indulge in ⟨*alcol*⟩; ⟨*approfittare di*⟩ take advantage of; ⟨*violentare*⟩ rape

**abusi'vismo** *nm* large-scale abuse; **~ edilizio** building without planning permission

**abu'sivo** *a* illegal

**a'buso** *nm* abuse; **'ogni ~ sarà punito'** 'penalty for misuse'. **~ di confidenza** breach of confidence

**a.C.** *abbr* (**avanti Cristo**) BC

**a'cacia** *nf* acacia

**'acaro** *nm Zool* mite

**'acca** *nf fam* **non ho capito un'~** I understood damn all

**acca'demia** *nf* academy. **A~ di Belle Arti** Academy of Fine Arts. **~ militare** military academy

**acca'demico, -a** *a* academic ● *nmf* academician

**acca'dere** *vi* happen; **accada quel che accada** come what may

**acca'duto** *nm* event

**accalappia'cani** *nm inv* dog-catcher

**accalappi'are** *vt* catch; *fig* allure

**accal'care** *vt* cram together

**accal'carsi** *vr* crowd

**accal'darsi** *vr* get overheated; (*per fatica*) get hot; *fig* get excited

**accal'dato** *a* overheated; (*per fatica*) hot; *fig* excited

**accalo'rarsi** *vr* get excited

**accampa'mento** *nm* camp

**accam'pare** *vt fig* put forth

**accam'parsi** *vr* camp

**accani'mento** *nm* tenacity; (*odio*) rage

**acca'nirsi** *vr* persist; (*infierire*) rage

**accanita'mente** *adv* (*odiare*) fiercely; (*insistere*) persistently; (*lavorare*) assiduously

**acca'nito** *a* persistent; (*odio*) fierce; (*fumatore*) inveterate; (*lavoratore*) assiduous

**ac'canto** *adv* near; **~ a** *prep* next to; **la ragazza della porta ~** the girl next door

**accanto'nare** *vt* set aside; *Mil* billet

**accaparra'mento** *nm* hoarding; *Comm* cornering

**accapar'rare** *vt* hoard

**accapar'rarsi** *vr* grab; corner (*mercato*)

**accaparra|'tore, -'trice** *nmf* hoarder

**accapigli'arsi** *vr* scuffle; (*litigare*) squabble

**accappa'toio** *nm* bathrobe; (*per spiaggia*) beachrobe

**accappo'nare** *vt* **fare ~ la pelle a qcno** make sb's flesh creep

**accarez'zare** *vt* caress, stroke; *fig* cherish

**accartocci'are** *vt* scrunch up

**accartocci'arsi** *vr* curl up

**acca'sarsi** *vr* get married

**accasci'arsi** *vr* flop down; *fig* lose heart

**accata'stare** *vt* pile up

**accatti'vante** *a* beguiling

**accatti'varsi** *vr* **~ le simpatie/la stima/ l'affetto di qcno** gain sb's sympathy/respect/affection

**accatto'naggio** *nm* begging

**accat'tone, -a** *nmf* beggar

**accaval'lare** *vt* cross (*gambe*)

**accaval'larsi** *vr* pile up; *fig* overlap

**acce'cante** *a* (*luce*) blinding

**acce'care** *vt* blind ● *vi* go blind

**ac'cedere** *vi* access; **~ a** enter; (*acconsentire*) comply with; *Comput* access

**accele'rare** *vi* accelerate ● *vt* speed up, accelerate; **~ il passo** quicken one's pace

**accele'rata** *nf* sudden acceleration

**accele'rato** *a* rapid

**accelera'tore** *nm* accelerator. **~ grafico** *Comput* graphics accelerator

**accelerazi'one** *nf* acceleration

**ac'cendere** *vt* light; turn on, switch on (*luce, TV ecc*); *fig* inflame; **ha da ~?** have you got a light?

**ac'cendersi** *vr* catch fire; (*illuminarsi*) light up; *fig* become inflamed; (*tv, computer:*) turn on, switch on

**accendi'gas** *nm inv* gas lighter; (*su cucina*) automatic ignition

**accen'dino** *nm* lighter

**accendi'sigari** *nm* cigar-lighter

**accen'nare** *vt* indicate; *hum* (*melodia*): give a hint of (*sorriso*) ● *vi* **~ a** beckon to; *fig* hint at; (*far l'atto di*) make as if to: **accenna a piovere** it looks like rain

**ac'cenno** *nm* gesture; (*con il capo*) nod; *fig* hint

**accensi'one** *nf* lighting; (*di motore*) ignition

**accen'tare** *vt* accent; (*con accento tonico*) stress

**accentazi'one** *nf* accentuation

**ac'cento** *nm* accent; (*tonico*) stress. **~ acuto** acute [accent]. **~ circonflesso** circumflex [accent]. **~ grave** grave [accent]

**accentra'mento** *nm* centralizing

**accen'trare** *vt* centralize

**accentra'tore** *a* (*persona*) who refuses to delegate; (*politica*) of centralization

**accentu'are** *vt* accentuate

**accentu'arsi** *vr* become more noticeable

**accentu'ato** *a* marked

**accerchia'mento** *nm* surrounding

**accerchi'are** *vt* surround

**accerchi'ato** *a* surrounded

**accer'tabile** *a* ascertainable

**accerta'mento** *nm* check; **accertamenti** *pl* [**medici**] tests

**accer'tare** *vt* ascertain; (*controllare*) check; assess (*reddito*)

**ac'ceso** *a* lighted; (*radio, TV ecc*) on; (*colore*) bright

**acces'sibile** *a* accessible; (*persona*) approachable; (*spesa*) reasonable

**ac'cesso** *nm* access; (*Med: di rabbia*) fit; **'vietato l'~'** 'no entry'; **'~ riservato a...'** 'access restricted to...'. **~ diretto** *Comput* direct access. **~ multiplo** *Comput* multi-access. **~ di pazzia** fit of madness. **~ remoto** *Comput* remote access

**accessori'ato** *a* accessorized

**acces'sorio** *a* accessory; (*secondario*) of secondary importance ● *nm* accessory; **accessori** *pl* (*rifiniture*) fittings. **accessori** *pl* **per il bagno** bathroom fittings. **accessori** *pl* **moda** fashion accessories

**ac'cetta** *nf* hatchet

**accet'tabile** *a* acceptable

**accet'tare** *vt* accept; (*aderire a*) agree to

**accettazi'one** *nf* acceptance; (*luogo*) reception; [**banco**] **~** check-in [desk]. **~** [**bagagli**] check-in

**ac'cetto** *a* agreeable; **essere bene ~** be very welcome

**accezi'one** *nf* meaning

**acchiap'pare** *vt* catch

**+acchiotto** *suff* **lupacchiotto** *nm* wolf cub; (*affettuoso*) baby wolf; **orsacchiotto** *nm* teddy bear; **fessacchiotto** *nm* nitwit

**ac'chito** *nm* **di primo ~** at first

**acciac'care** *vt* crush; *fig* prostrate

**acciac'cato, -a** *a* **essere ~** ache all over

**acci'acco** *nm* infirmity; **acciacchi** (*pl: afflizioni*) aches and pains

**acciaie'ria** *nf* steelworks

**acci'aio** *nm* steel: ~ **inossidabile** stainless steel

**acciambel'larsi** *vr* curl up

**acciden'tale** *a* accidental

**acciden'talmente** *adv* accidentally

**acciden'tato** *a* ⟨*terreno*⟩ uneven

**acci'dente** *nm* accident; *Med* stroke; **non capisce/non vede un ~** *fam* he doesn't understand/can't see a damn thing; **mandare un ~ a qcno** *fam* tell sb to go to hell

**acci'denti** *int fam* damn!; **~ a te!** damn you!, blast you!

**ac'cidia** *nf* sloth

**accigli'arsi** *vr* frown

**accigli'ato** *a* a frowning

**ac'cingersi** *vr* ~ **a** be about to

**+accio** *suff* **erbaccia** *nf* weed; **donnaccia** *nf* tart; **faticaccia** *nf* hard slog; **lavoraccio** *nm* ⟨*lavoro faticoso*⟩ helluva job *fam*; ⟨*lavoro malfatto*⟩ botched job; **parolaccia** *nf* swear word; **avaraccio** *nm* skinflint

**acciotto'lato** *nm* cobbled paving, cobblestones *pl*

**acci'picchia** *int* good Lord!

**acciuf'fare** *vt* catch

**acci'uga** *nf* anchovy

**accla'mare** *vt* applaud; ⟨*eleggere*⟩ acclaim

**acclamazi'one** *nf* applause

**acclima'tare** *vt* acclimatize

**acclima'tarsi** *vr* get acclimatized

**acclimatazi'one** *nf* acclimatization

**ac'cludere** *vt* enclose

**ac'cluso** *a* enclosed

**accocco'larsi** *vr* squat

**acco'darsi** *vr* tag along

**accogli'ente** *a* welcoming; ⟨*confortevole*⟩ cosy

**accogli'enza** *nf* welcome

**ac'cogliere** *vt* receive; ⟨*conpiacere*⟩ welcome; ⟨*contenere*⟩ hold

**accol'lare** *vt* ~ **qcsa a qcno** *fig* saddle sb with sth

**accol'larsi** *vr* take on ⟨*responsabilità, debiti, doveri*⟩

**accol'lato** *a* ⟨*maglia*⟩ high-necked

**accoltel'lare** *vt* knife

**accoman'dante** *nmf Jur* sleeping partner

**accomanda'tario, -a** *nmf Jur* general partner

**accoman'dita** *nf Jur* limited partnership. **~ per azioni** limited partnership based on shares

**accomia'tare** *vt* dismiss

**accomia'tarsi** *vr* take one's leave ⟨**da** of⟩

**accomoda'mento** *nm* arrangement

**accomo'dante** *a* accommodating

**accomo'dare** *vt* ⟨*riparare*⟩ mend; ⟨*disporre*⟩ arrange

**accomo'darsi** *vr* make oneself at home; **si accomodi!** come in!; ⟨*si sieda*⟩ take a seat!

**accompagna'mento** *nm* accompaniment; ⟨*seguito*⟩ retinue

**accompa'gnare** *vt* accompany; ~ **qcno a casa** see sb home; ~ **qcno alla porta** show sb to the door; ~ **qcno con lo sguardo** follow sb with one's eyes

**accompa'gnarsi** *vr* ⟨*cibi, colori ecc*⟩ go [well] together; ~ **con** *o* **a qcno** accompany sb

**accompagna|'tore, -'trice** *nmf* companion; ⟨*di comitiva*⟩ escort; *Mus* accompanist. ~ **turistico** tour guide

**accomu'nare** *vt* pool

**acconci'are** *vt* arrange

**acconci'arsi** *vr* do one's hair

**acconcia'tura** *nf* hair-style; ⟨*ornamento*⟩ head-dress; **'acconciature'** 'ladies' hairdresser'

**accondiscen'dente** *a* too obliging

**accondiscen'denza** *nf* excessive desire to please

**accondi'scendere** *vi* ~ **a** condescend; comply with ⟨*desiderio*⟩; ⟨*acconsentire*⟩ consent to

**acconsen'tire** *vi* consent

**acconten'tare** *vt* satisfy

**acconten'tarsi** *vr* be content ⟨**di** with⟩

**ac'conto** *nm* deposit; **in ~** on account; **lasciare un ~** leave a deposit. ~ **di dividendo** interim dividend

**accop'pare** *vt fam* bump off

**accoppia'mento** *nm* coupling; ⟨*di animali*⟩ mating

**accoppi'are** *vt* couple; mate ⟨*animali*⟩

**accoppi'arsi** *vr* pair off; ⟨*animali*⟩ mate

**accoppi'ata** *nf* ⟨*scommessa*⟩ bet placed on two horses for first and second place; **sono una strana ~** they make strange bedfellows; ~ **vincente** *fig* winning combination

**accoppia'tore** *nm* ~ **acustico** *Comput* acoustic coupler

**acco'rato** *a* sorrowful

**accorci'are** *vt* shorten

**accorci'arsi** *vr* get shorter

**accor'dare** *vt* concede; match ⟨*colori ecc*⟩; *Mus* tune

**accor'darsi** *vr* agree

**accorda|'tore, -'trice** *nmf Mus* tuner

**ac'cordo** *nm* agreement; *Mus* chord; ⟨*armonia*⟩ harmony; **andare d'~** get on well; **d'~!** agreed!; **essere d'~** agree; **in ~ con** in collusion with; **prendere accordi con qcno** make arrangements with sb. ~ **collettivo** joint agreement

**ac'corgersi** *vr* ~ **di** notice; ⟨*capire*⟩ realize

**accorgi'mento** *nm* shrewdness; ⟨*espediente*⟩ device

**accorpa'mento** *nm* amalgamation

**accor'pare** *vt* amalgamate

**ac'correre** *vi* hasten

**accorta'mente** *adv* astutely

**accor'tezza** *nf* ⟨*previdenza*⟩ forethought

**ac'corto** *a* shrewd; **mal ~** incautious

**accosta'mento** *nm* ⟨*di colori*⟩ combination

**acco'stare** *vt* draw close to; approach ⟨*persona*⟩; put ajar ⟨*porta ecc*⟩

**acco'starsi** *vr* ~ **a** come near to

**accovacci'arsi** *vr* crouch, squat down

**accovacci'ato** *a* squatting

**accoz'zaglia** *nf* jumble: (*di persone*) mob

**accoz'zare** *vt* ~ **colori** mix colours that clash

**accredi'tabile** *a* reliable

**accredita'mento** *nm* credit. ~ **tramite bancogiro** Bank Giro Credit

**accredi'tare** *vt* confirm ‹*notizia*›; *Comm* credit

**accredi'tato** *a* accredited; ‹*notizia*› reliable

**ac'crescere** *vt* increase

**ac'crescersi** *vr* grow larger

**accresci'mento** *nm* increase

**accresci'tivo** *a* augmentative

**accucci'arsi** *vr* ‹*cane:*› lie down; ‹*persona:*› crouch

**accu'dire** *vi* ~ **a** attend to

**accumu'lare** *vt* accumulate

**accumu'larsi** *vr* pile up, accumulate

**accumula'tore** *nm* accumulator; *Auto, Comput* battery

**accumulazi'one** *nf* accumulation

**ac'cumulo** *nm* (*di merce*) build-up

**accurata'mente** *adv* carefully

**accura'tezza** *nf* care

**accu'rato** *a* careful

**ac'cusa** *nf* accusation; *Jur* charge; **essere in stato di ~** *Jur* have been charged; **mettere qcno sotto ~** *Jur* charge sb; **la Pubblica A~** *Jur* the public prosecutor

**accu'sare** *vt* accuse; *Jur* charge; complain of ‹*dolore*›; ~ **ricevuta di** *Comm* acknowledge receipt of

**accusa'tivo** *nm* *Gram* accusative

**accu'sato, -a** *nmf* accused

**accusa'tore** *a* accusing ● *nm* *Jur* prosecutor

**a'cerbo** *a* sharp; (*non maturo*) unripe

**'acero** *nm* maple

**a'cerrimo** *a* implacable

**ace'tato** *nm* acetate

**a'ceto** *nm* vinegar

**ace'tone** *nm* nail polish remover

**ace'tosa** *nf* *Culin* [edible] sorrel

**aceto'sella** *nf* *Bot* sorrel

**A.C.I.** *nf abbr* (**Automobile Club d'Italia**) Italian Automobile Association

**acidità** *nf* acidity. ~ **di stomaco** acid stomach

**'acido** *a* acid; ‹*persona*› sour ● *nm* acid. ~ **cloridrico** hydrochloric acid

**a'cidulo** *a* slightly sour

**'acino** *nm* berry; (*chicco*) grape

**'acme** *nf* acme

**'acne** *nf* acne

**'acqua** *nf* water; **fare ~** *Naut* leak; ~ **in bocca!** *fig* mum's the word!; **avere l'~ alla gola, essere con l'~ alla gola** *fig* be pushed for time; **ho fatto un buco nell'~** *fig* I had no luck whatsoever; **in cattive acque** in deep water; **navigare in cattive acque** be in financial difficulties. ~ **calda** hot water. ~ **di Colonia** eau de Cologne. ~ **corrente** running water. ~ **dolce** fresh water. ~ **minerale** mineral water. ~ **minerale gassata** fizzy mineral water. ~ **naturale** still mineral water. ~ **potabile** drinking water. ~ **del rubinetto** tap water. ~ **salata** salt water. ~ **saponata** suds. ~ **tonica** tonic water

**acqua'forte** *nf* etching

**ac'quaio** *nm* sink

**acquama'rina** *a* aquamarine

**acqua'plano** *nm* hydroplane

**acqua'rello** *nm* water-colour

**a'cquario** *nm* aquarium; *Astr* Aquarius

**acquartie'rare** *vt* *Mil* billet

**acqua'santa** *nf* holy water

**acquasanti'era** *nf* font

**acqua'scooter** *nm inv* water-scooter

**a'cquata** *nf fam* downpour

**a'cquatico** *a* aquatic; **sport** ~ water sport

**acquat'tarsi** *vr* crouch

**acqua'vite** *nf* brandy

**acquaz'zone** *nm* downpour

**acque'dotto** *nm* aqueduct

**'acqueo** *a* **vapore** ~ water vapour

**acque'rello** *nm* water-colour

**acquicol'tura** *nf* aquaculture

**acquie'scente** *a* acquiescent

**acquie'tare** *vt* appease; calm ‹*dolore*›

**acquie'tarsi** *vr* calm down

**acqui'rente** *nmf* purchaser

**acqui'sire** *vt* acquire

**acqui'sito** *a* acquired

**acquisizi'one** *nf* attainment

**acqui'stare** *vt* purchase; (*ottenere*) acquire; ~ **in** ‹*prestigio, bellezza*› gain in

**a'cquisto** *nm* purchase; ~ **rateale** hire purchase, HP, installment plan *Am*; **uscire per acquisti** go shopping; **fare acquisti** shop; **ufficio acquisti** purchasing department. ~ **per impulso** impulse buy. ~ **a termine** *Fin* forward buying

**acqui'trino** *nm* marsh

**acquo'lina** *nf* **far venire l'~ in bocca a qcno** make sb's mouth water; **ho l'~ in bocca** my mouth is watering

**a'cquoso** *a* watery

**'acre** *a* acrid; (*al gusto*) sour; *fig* harsh

**a'credine** *nf* acridness; (*al gusto*) sourness; *fig* harshness

**acre'mente** *adv* acridly

**a'crilico** *nm* acrylic

**a'critico** *a* acritical

**a'crobata** *nmf* acrobat

**acro'batico** *a* acrobatic

**acroba'zia** *nf* acrobatics *pl*

**acroba'zie** *nfpl* acrobatics; **fare ~** *fig* do acrobatics

**a'cronimo** *nm* acronym

**a'cropoli** *nf* acropolis

**acu'ire** *vt* sharpen

**acu'irsi** *vr* become more intense

**a'culeo** *nm* sting; *Bot* prickle

**a'cume** *nm* acumen

**acumi'nato** *a* pointed

**a'custica** *nf* acoustics *pl*

**acustica'mente** *adv* acoustically

**a'custico** *a* acoustic

**acuta'mente** *adv* shrewdly

**acu'tezza** *nf* acuteness; *fig* shrewdness; (*di suoni*) shrillness

**acutiz'zare** *vt* aggravate ‹*dolore*›

**acutiz'zarsi** *vr* become worse

**a'cuto** *a* sharp; ‹*suono*› shrill; ‹*freddo, odore*› intense; *Gram, Math, Med* acute ● *nm Mus* high note

**ad** (*before vowel*) *prep* = **a**

**A.D.** *abbr Pol* (**Alleanza Democratica**) Democratic Alliance

**adagi'are** *vt* lay down

**adagi'arsi** *vr* lie down

**a'dagio** *adv* slowly ● *nm Mus* adagio; (*proverbio*) adage

**ada'mitico** *a* **in costume ~** in one's birth-day suit, stark naked

**adat'tabile** *a* adaptable

**adattabilità** *nf* adaptability

**adatta'mento** *nm* adaptation; **avere spirito di ~** be adaptable. **~ cinematografico** film adaptation, adaptation for the cinema

**adat'tare** *vt* adapt; (*aggiustare*) fit

**adat'tarsi** *vr* adapt

**adatta'tore** *nm* adaptor

**a'datto** *a* suitable (**a** for); (*giusto*) right

**addi** *adv* **~ 15 settembre 1995** on 15th September 1995

**addebita'mento** *nm* debit. **~ diretto** direct debit

**addebi'tare** *vt* debit; *fig* ascribe ‹*colpa*›

**ad'debito** *nm* charge

**addensa'mento** *nm* thickening; (*di persone*) gathering

**adden'sare** *vt* thicken

**adden'sarsi** *vr* thicken; (*affollarsi*) gather

**adden'tare** *vt* bite

**adden'trarsi** *vr* penetrate

**ad'dentro** *adv* deeply; **essere ~ in** be in on

**addestra'mento** *nm* training. **~ iniziale** basic training

**adde'strare** *vt* train

**adde'strarsi** *vr* train

**addestra|'tore, -'trice** *nmf* trainer

**ad'detto, -a** *a* assigned ● *nmf* employee; (*diplomatico*) attaché. **~ commerciale** salesman. **adetti** *pl* **ai lavori** persons involved in the work; **'vietato l'ingresso ai non addetti ai lavori** 'staff only'. **~ culturale** cultural attaché. **~ stampa** information officer, press officer. **~ ai traslochi** removal man

**addi'accio** *nm* **dormire all'~** sleep in the open

**addi'etro** *adv* (*indietro*) back; (*nel passato*) before

**ad'dio** *nm & int* goodbye. **~ al celibato** stag night, stag party. **cena d'~** farewell dinner

**addirit'tura** *adv* (*perfino*) even; (*assolutamente*) absolutely; **~!** really!

**ad'dirsi** *vr* **~ a** suit

**addi'tare** *vt* point at; (*per identificare*) point out; *fig* point to

**addi'tivo** *a & nm* additive

**addizio'nale** *a* additional ● *nf* (*imposta*) surtax

**addizional'mente** *adv* additionally

**addizio'nare** *vt* add [up]

**addiziona'trice** *nf* adding machine

**addizi'one** *nf* addition

**addob'bare** *vt* decorate

**ad'dobbo** *nm* decoration

**addol'cire** *vt* sweeten; tone down ‹*colore*›; *fig* soften

**addol'cirsi** *vr fig* mellow

**addolo'rare** *vt* grieve

**addolo'rarsi** *vr* be upset (**per** by)

**addolo'rato** *a* pained, distressed

**ad'dome** *nm* abdomen

**addomesti'care** *vt* tame

**addomestica'tore** *nm* tamer

**addomi'nale** *a* abdominal ● *nmpl* **addominali** abdominals

**addormen'tare** *vt* put to sleep

**addormen'tarsi** *vr* go to sleep

**addormen'tato** *a* asleep; *fig* slow

**addos'sare** *vt* **~ a** (*appoggiare*) lean against; (*attribuire*) lay on

**addos'sarsi** *vr* (*ammassarsi*) crowd; shoulder ‹*responsabilità ecc*›

**ad'dosso** *adv* on; **~ a** *prep* on: (*molto vicino*) right next to; **andare/venire ~** qcno run into sb; **mettere gli occhi ~ a** qcno/qcsa hanker after sb/sth; **non mettermi le mani ~!** keep your hands off me!; **stare ~ a** qcno *fig* be on sb's back; **farsela ~** (*fam: bisogni corporali*) dirty oneself; (*pipì*) wet oneself

**ad'durre** *vt* produce ‹*prova, documento*›; give ‹*pretesto, esempio*›

**adegua'mento** *nm* adjustment

**adegu'are** *vt* adjust

**adegu'arsi** *vr* conform

**adegua'tamente** *adv* suitably

**adegua'tezza** *nf* suitability

**adegu'ato** *a* suitable; **~ a** suited to, suitable for

**a'dempiere** *vt* fulfil

**adempi'mento** *nm* fulfilment

**adem'pire** *vt* fulfil

**ade'noidi** *nfpl* adenoids

**a'depto, -a** *nmf* adherent

**ade'rente** *a* adhesive; ‹*vestito*› tight ● *nmf* follower

**ade'renza** *nf* adhesion; **aderenze** *pl* connections

**ade'rire** *vi* **~ a** stick to, adhere to; support ‹*sciopero, petizione*›; agree to ‹*richiesta*›

**adesca'mento** *nm Jur* soliciting

**ade'scare** *vt* bait; *fig* entice

**adesca'trice** *nf* fille de joie

**adesi'one** *nf* adhesion; *fig* agreement

**ade'sivo** *a* adhesive ● *nm* sticker; *Auto* bumper sticker

**a'desso** *adv* now; (*poco fa*) just now; (*tra poco*) any moment now; **da ~ in poi** from now on; **per ~** for the moment; **fino ~** up till now

**adia'cente** *a* adjacent; **~ a** next to

**adia'cenze** *nfpl* adjacent areas

**adi'bire** *vt* **~ a** put to use as

**'adipe** *nm* adipose tissue
**adi'poso** *a* adipose
**adi'rarsi** *vr* get irate
**adi'rato** *a* irate
**a'dire** *vt* resort to; **~ le vie legali** take legal proceedings. **~ la successione** *Jur* take possession of an inheritance
**'adito** *nm* dare **~ a** give rise to
**adocchi'are** *vt* eye; (*con desiderio*) covet
**adole'scente** *a* & *nmf* adolescent *attrib*
**adole'scenza** *nf* adolescence
**adolescenzi'ale** *a* adolescent
**adombra'mento** *nm* darkening
**adom'brare** *vt* darken; *fig* veil
**adom'brarsi** *vr* (*offendersi*) take offence
**adope'rare** *vt* use
**adope'rarsi** *vr* take trouble
**ado'rabile** *a* adorable
**ado'rare** *vt* adore
**adorazi'one** *nf* adoration; **in ~** adoring
**ador'nare** *vt* adorn
**a'dorno** *a* adorned (**di** with)
**adot'tare** *vt* adopt
**adot'tivo** *a* adoptive
**adozi'one** *nf* adoption
**adrena'lina** *nf* adrenalin
**adri'atico** *a* Adriatic ● *nm* **l'A~** the Adriatic
**adu'lare** *vt* flatter
**adula'tore, -'trice** *nmf* flatterer
**adula'torio** *a* sycophantic
**adulazi'one** *nf* flattery
**a'dultera** *nf* adulteress
**adulte'rare** *vt* adulterate
**adulte'rato** *a* adulterated
**adulte'rino** *a* adulterous
**adul'terio** *nm* adultery
**a'dultero** *a* adulterous ● *nm* adulterer
**a'dulto, -a** *a* & *nmf* adult; (*maturo*) mature
**adu'nanza** *nf* assembly
**adu'nare** *vt* gather
**adu'nata** *nf* *Mil* parade
**a'dunco** *a* hooked
**adunghi'are** *vt* claw
**ae'rare** *vt* air ⟨*stanza*⟩
**aera'tore** *nm* ventilator
**aerazi'one** *nf* ventilation
**a'ereo** *a* aerial; (*dell'aviazione*) air ● *nm* aeroplane, plane; **andare in ~** fly. **~ da carico** cargo plane. **~ da guerra** warplane. **~ di linea** airliner. **~ navetta** shuttle. **~ a reazione** jet [plane]
**ae'robica** *nf* aerobics
**ae'robico** *a* aerobic
**aerodi'namica** *nf* aerodynamics *sg*
**aerodi'namico** *a* aerodynamic
**aero'grafo** *nm* airbrush
**aero'gramma** *nm* aerogram[me]
**aero'linea** *nf* airline
**aero'mobile** *nm* aircraft
**aeromo'dello** *nm* model aircraft
**aero'nautica** *nf* aeronautics; *Mil* Air Force
**aero'nautico** *a* aeronautical
**aerona'vale** *a* air and sea *attrib*
**aero'plano** *nm* aeroplane

**aero'porto** *nm* airport
**aeroportu'ale** *a* airport *attrib*
**aero'scalo** *nm* cargo and servicing area
**aero'sol** *nm* *inv* aerosol
**aerospazi'ale** *a* aerospace *attrib*
**aero'statico** *a* **pallone ~** aerostat
**ae'rostato** *nm* aerostat
**aerostazi'one** *nf* air terminal
**aerosti'ere** *nm* balloonist
**aero'via** *nf* air-corridor
**A.F.** *abbr* (**alta frequenza**) HF
**'afa** *nf* sultriness
**af'fabile** *a* affable
**affabilità** *nf* affability
**affaccen'darsi** *vr* busy oneself (**a** with)
**affacci'arsi** *vr* show oneself; **~ alla finestra** appear at the window
**affacen'dato** *a* busy
**affa'mare** *vt* starve [out]
**affa'mato** *a* starving
**affan'nare** *vt* leave breathless
**affan'narsi** *vr* busy oneself; (*agitarsi*) get worked up
**affan'nato** *a* breathless; **dal respiro ~** wheezy
**af'fanno** *nm* breathlessness; *fig* worry; **essere in ~ per** be anxious about
**affannosa'mente** *adv* breathlessly
**affan'noso** *a* exhausting; **respiro ~** heavy breathing
**af'fare** *nm* matter; (*occasione*) bargain; *Comm* transaction, deal; **pensa agli affari tuoi** mind your own business; **non sono affari tuoi** *fam* it's none of your business; **fare affari d'oro** have a field day; **af'fari** *pl* business; **d'affari** ⟨*uomo, cena, viaggio*⟩ business. **ministro degli affari esteri** Foreign Secretary *Br*, Secretary of State *Am*
**affa'rismo** *nm* *pej* wheeling and dealing
**affa'rista** *nmf* wheeler-dealer
**affasci'nante** *a* fascinating; ⟨*persona, sorriso*⟩ bewitching
**affasci'nare** *vt* bewitch; *fig* charm
**affastel'lare** *vt* tie up in bundles
**affatica'mento** *nm* fatigue
**affati'care** *vt* tire; (*sfinire*) exhaust
**affati'carsi** *vr* tire oneself out; (*affannarsi*) strive
**affati'cato** *a* fatigued, suffering from fatigue
**af'fatto** *adv* completely; **non... ~** not... at all; **niente ~!** not at all!
**affer'mare** *vt* affirm; (*sostenere*) assert
**affer'marsi** *vr* establish oneself
**affermativa'mente** *adv* in the affirmative
**afferma'tivo** *a* affirmative
**affer'mato** *a* established
**affermazi'one** *nf* assertion; (*successo*) achievement
**affer'rare** *vt* seize; catch ⟨*oggetto*⟩; (*capire*) grasp; **~ al volo** *fig* be quick on the uptake
**affer'rarsi** *vr* **~ a** grasp at, clutch at

**affet'tare** vt slice; (ostentare) affect

**affet'tato** a sliced; (sorriso, maniere) affected ● nm cold meat, sliced meat

**affetta'trice** nf bacon-slicer

**affettazi'one** nf affectation

**affet'tivo** a affective; **rapporto ~** emotional tie

**af'fetto**[1] nm affection; **con ~** affectionately; **gli affetti familiari** family ties

**af'fetto**[2] a **~ da** suffering from

**affettuosa'mente** adv affectionately

**affettuosità** nf inv (gesto) affectionate gesture

**affettu'oso** a affectionate

**affezio'narsi** vr **~ a** grow fond of

**affezio'nato** a devoted (a to)

**affezi'one** nf affection; Med ailment

**affian'care** vt put side by side; Mil flank; fig support

**affian'carsi** vr come side by side; fig stand together, stand shoulder to shoulder; **~ a qcno** fig help sb out

**affiata'mento** nm harmony

**affia'tarsi** vr get on well together

**affia'tato** a close-knit; **una coppia affiatata** a very close couple

**affibbi'are** vt **~ qcsa a qcno** saddle sb with sth; **~ un pugno a qcno** let fly at sb

**affi'dabile** a reliable, dependable

**affidabilità** nf reliability, dependability

**affida'mento** nm (Jur: dei minori) custody; **fare ~ su qcno** rely on sb; **non dare ~ (a qcno)** not inspire confidence (in sb)

**affi'dare** vt entrust

**affi'darsi** vr **~ a** rely on

**affievoli'mento** nm weakening

**affievo'lirsi** vr grow weak

**af'figgere** vt affix

**affilacol'telli** nm inv knife sharpener

**affi'lare** vt sharpen

**affili'are** vt affiliate

**affili'arsi** vr become affiliated

**affiliazi'one** nf affiliation

**affi'nare** vt sharpen; (perfezionare) refine

**affinché** conj so that, in order that

**af'fine** a similar

**affinità** nf inv affinity

**affiora'mento** nm emergence; Naut surfacing

**affio'rare** vi emerge; fig come to light

**affissi'one** nf bill-posting; **'divieto di ~'** 'stick no bills'

**af'fisso** nm bill; Gram affix

**affitta'camere** nm inv landlord ● nf inv landlady

**affit'tare** vt (dare in affitto) let; (prendere in affitto) rent. **af'fittasi** to let, for rent

**af'fitto** nm rent; **contratto d'~** lease; **dare in ~** let; **prendere in ~** rent

**affittu'ario, -a** nmf Jur lessee

**af'fliggere** vt torment

**af'fliggersi** vr distress oneself

**af'flitto** a distressed

**afflizi'one** nf distress; fig affliction

**afflosci'are** vt la pioggia ha afflosciato

**le foglie** the rain has made the leaves go all limp; **mi hai afflosciato il morale** you've demoralized me

**afflosci'arsi** vr become floppy; (accasciarsi) flop down; (morale) decline

**afflu'ente** a & nm tributary

**afflu'enza** nf flow; (di gente) crowd

**afflu'ire** vi flow; fig pour in

**af'flusso** nm influx

**affoga'mento** nm drowning

**affo'gare** vt/i drown; Culin poach; **~ in** fig be swamped with

**affo'garsi** vr (suicidarsi) drown oneself

**affo'gato** a (persona) drowned; (uova) poached ● nm **~ al caffè** ice cream with hot espresso poured over it

**affolla'mento** nm crowd

**affol'lare** vt crowd

**affol'larsi** vr crowd

**affol'lato** a crowded

**affonda'mento** nm sinking

**affon'dare** vt/i sink

**affon'darsi** vr sink

**affossa'mento** nm (avvallamento) pothole; fig burial

**affran'care** vt redeem (bene); stamp (lettera); free (schiavo)

**affran'carsi** vr free oneself

**affran'cato** a (lettera) stamped; (schiavo) freed; **già ~** (lettera) prepaid

**affranca'trice** nf franking machine, franker

**affranca'tura** nf stamping; (di spedizione) postage. **~ per l'estero** postage abroad

**af'franto** a prostrate with grief, grief-stricken; (esausto) worn out

**affre'scare** vt paint a fresco on

**af'fresco** nm fresco

**affret'tare** vt speed up

**affret'tarsi** vr hurry

**affrettata'mente** adv hastily

**affret'tato** a (passo) fast; (decisione) hasty; (lavoro) rushed

**affron'tare** vt face; confront (nemico); meet (spese)

**affron'tarsi** vr clash

**af'fronto** nm affront, insult; **fare un ~ a qcno** insult sb

**affumi'care** vt fill with smoke; Culin smoke

**affumi'cato** a (prosciutto, formaggio) smoked; (lenti, vetro) tinted

**affuso'lare** vt taper [off]

**affuso'lato** a tapering

**Af'ganistan** nm Afghanistan

**af'gano** a & nmf Afghani, Afghan

**AFI** nm abbr (**Alfabeto Fonetico Internazionale**) IPA

**aficio'nado, -a** nmf aficionado

**'afide** nm aphid

**'afono** a (senza voce) unvoiced

**afo'risma** nm aphorism

**a'foso** a sultry

**'Africa** nf Africa. **~ orientale** East Africa. **~ nera** Black Africa. **~ del Nord** North Africa

**afri'cano, -a** *a & nmf* African
**afri'kaans** *nm* Afrikaans
**afroameri'cano** *a* Afro-American
**afroasi'atico** *a* Afro-Asian
**afroca'ribico** *a* Afro-Caribbean
**afrocu'bano** *a* Afro-Cuban
**afrodi'siaco** *a & nm* aphrodisiac
**a'genda** *nf* diary. **~ elettronica** personal organizer. **~ da tavolo** desk diary
**agen'dina** *nf* pocket-diary
**a'gente** *nm* agent; **agenti** *pl* **atmosferici** atmospheric agents. **~ di cambio** stockbroker. **~ di custodia** prison warder. **~ del fisco** assessor. **~ immobiliare** estate agent, realtor *Am*. **~ marittimo** shipping agent. **~ di polizia** police officer. **~ segreto** secret agent. **~ teatrale** theatrical agent; *(di compagnia)* impresario. **~ di viaggio** travel agent
**agen'zia** *nf* agency; *(filiale)* branch office; *(di banca)* branch. **~ di collocamento** employment exchange. **~ immobiliare** estate agency, realtor *Am*. **~ matrimoniale** dating agency. **~ pubblicitaria** advertising agency. **~ di recupero crediti** debt collection agency. **~ di stampa** news agency, press agency. **~ di viaggi** travel agency
**agevo'lare** *vt* facilitate
**agevolazi'one** *nf* facilitation. **agevolazioni** *pl* **fiscali** tax breaks **a'gevole** *a* easy; *(strada)* smooth
**agevol'mente** *adv* easily
**agganci'are** *vt* hook up; *Rail* couple
**aggan'ci'arsi** *vr* *(vestito:)* hook up; **~ a** *(maglia:)* catch on; *(rimorchio:)* hook onto
**ag'gancio** *nm* Aeron docking
**ag'geggio** *nm* gadget
**agget'tivo** *nm* adjective
**agghiacci'ante** *a* terrifying
**agghiacci'are** *vt fig* **~ qcno** make sb's blood run cold
**agghiacci'arsi** *vr* freeze
**agghin'dare** *vt fam* dress up
**agghin'darsi** *vr fam* doll oneself up
**agghin'dato** *a* dressed up; *(sala)* decorated; *(fig: stile)* stilted
**aggiornabilità** *nf Comput* upgradability
**aggiorna'mento** *nm* update; *(azione)* updating; **corso di ~** refresher course
**aggior'nare** *vt* *(rinviare)* postpone; *(mettere a giorno)* bring up to date, update
**aggior'narsi** *vr* get up to date
**aggior'nato** *a* up-to-date; *(versione)* updated
**aggio'taggio** *nm Jur* manipulation of the market
**aggira'mento** *nm Mil* outflanking
**aggi'rare** *vt* surround; *(fig: ingannare)* trick
**aggi'rarsi** *vr* hang about; **~ su** *(discorso ecc:)* be about; *(somma:)* be around
**aggiudi'care** *vt* award; *(all'asta)* knock down
**aggiudi'carsi** *vr* win
**aggi'ungere** *vt* add
**aggi'unta** *nf* addition; **in ~** in addition

**aggiun'tivo** *a* supplementary
**aggi'unto** *a* added ● *a & nm (assistente)* assistant
**aggiu'stare** *vt* mend; *(sistemare)* settle; *(fam: mettere a posto)* fix; **ora l'aggiusto io** *fig* I'll sort him out
**aggiu'starsi** *vr* adapt; *(mettersi in ordine)* tidy oneself up; *(decidere)* sort things out; *(tempo:)* clear up
**aggiusta'tina** *nf* **dare un'~** a neaten
**agglomera'mento** *nm* conglomeration
**agglome'rante** *nm* binder
**agglome'rato** *nm* built-up area
**aggrap'pare** *vt* grasp
**aggrap'parsi** *vr* **~ a** cling to
**aggrava'mento** *nm* worsening; *(di pena)* increase
**aggra'vante** *Jur nf* aggravation ● *a* aggravating; **circostanza ~** aggravation
**aggra'vare** *vt* *(peggiorare)* make worse; increase *(pena)*; *(appesantire)* weigh down
**aggra'varsi** *vr* worsen
**ag'gravio** *nm* **~ fiscale** tax burden
**aggrazi'ato** *a* graceful
**aggre'dire** *vt* attack
**aggre'gare** *vt* add; *(associare a un gruppo ecc)* admit
**aggre'garsi** *vr* **~ a** join
**aggre'gato** *a* associated ● *nm* aggregate; *(di case)* block
**aggregazi'one** *nf* *(di persone)* gathering
**aggressi'one** *nf* aggression; *(atto)* attack. **~ a mano armata** armed assault
**aggressività** *nf* aggressiveness
**aggres'sivo** *a* aggressive
**aggres'sore** *nm* aggressor
**aggrin'zare, aggrin'zire** *vt* wrinkle
**aggrin'zirsi** *vr* wrinkle
**aggrot'tare** *vt* **~ le ciglia/la fronte** frown
**aggrovigli'are** *vt* tangle
**aggrovigli'arsi** *vr* get entangled; *fig* get complicated
**aggrovigli'ato** *a* entangled; *fig* confused
**agguan'tare** *vt* catch
**agguan'tarsi** *vr* **~ a** grasp
**aggu'ato** *nm* ambush; *(tranello)* trap; **stare in ~** lie in wait; **tendere un ~ a qcno** set an ambush for sb
**agguer'rito** *a* fierce
**agiata'mente** *adv* comfortably
**agia'tezza** *nf* comfort
**agi'ato** *a* *(persona)* well off; *(vita)* comfortable
**a'gibile** *a* *(palazzo)* fit for human habitation
**agibilità** *nf* fitness for human habitation
**'agile** *a* agile
**agilità** *nf* agility
**agil'mente** *adv* agilely
**'agio** *nm* ease; **mettersi a proprio ~** make oneself at home
**a'gire** *vi* act; *(comportarsi)* behave; *(funzionare)* work; **~ su** affect
**agi'tare** *vt* shake; wave *(mano)*; *(fig: turbare)* trouble; **'~ prima dell'uso'** 'shake before using'

**agi'tarsi** *vr* toss about; *(essere inquieto)* be restless; ⟨*mare:*⟩ get rough

**agi'tato** *a* restless; ⟨*mare*⟩ rough

**agita|'tore, -'trice** *nmf (persona)* agitator

**agitazi'one** *nf* agitation; **mettere in ~ qcno** send sb into a flat spin

**'agli** = a + gli

**'aglio** *nm* garlic

**a'gnello** *nm* lamb

**agno'lotti** *nmpl* ravioli *sg*

**a'gnostico, -a** *a & nmf* agnostic

**'ago** *nm* needle; **a 9 aghi** ⟨*stampante*⟩ 9-pin. **~ di pino** pine-needle

**ago'gnare** *vt liter* yearn for, thirst for

**ago'nia** *nf* agony

**ago'nismo** *nm* competitiveness

**ago'nistica** *nf* competition

**ago'nistico** *a* competitive

**agoniz'zante** *a* in one's death throes

**agoniz'zare** *vi* be on one's deathbed

**agopun|'tore, -'trice** *nmf* acupuncturist

**agopun'tura** *nf* acupuncture

**agorafo'bia** *nf* agoraphobia

**ago'rafobo, -a** *nmf* agoraphobic

**agostini'ano, -a** *a & nmf* Augustinian

**a'gosto** *nm* August

**a'graria** *nf* agriculture

**a'grario** *a* agricultural ● *nm* landowner

**a'greste** *a* rustic

**a'gricolo** *a* agricultural

**agricol'tore** *nm* farmer

**agricol'tura** *nf* agriculture. **~ biologica** organic farming

**agri'foglio** *nm* holly

**agrimen'sore** *nm* land-surveyor

**agritu'rismo** *nm* farm holidays, agro-tourism

**'agro¹** *a* sour; **all'~** *Culin* pickled

**'agro²** *nm* countryside around a town

**agroalimen'tare** *a* food *attrib*

**agro'dolce** *a* bitter-sweet; *Culin* sweet-and-sour; **in ~** sweet and sour

**agrono'mia** *nf* agronomy

**a'gronomo, -a** *nmf* agriculturalist

**agropasto'rale** *a* based on farming

**a'grume** *nm* citrus fruit; *(pianta)* citrus tree

**agru'meto** *nm* citrus plantation

**aguz'zare** *vt* sharpen; **~ le orecchie** prick up one's ears; **~ la vista** look hard

**aguz'zino** *nm* slave-driver; *(carceriere)* jailer

**a'guzzo** *a* pointed

**ah** *int* ah!; **ah, davvero?** oh really?

**ahi** *int* ow!

**ahimè** *int* alas!

**'ai** = a + i

**'aia** *nf* threshing-floor

**'Aia** *nf* L'**~** The Hague

**Aids** *nm* Aids

**AIE** *abbr* (**Associazione Italiana degli Editori**) association of Italian publishers

**air bag** *nm inv* Auto air bag

**ai'rone** *nm* heron

**air terminal** *nm inv* air terminal

**ai'tante** *a* sturdy

**aiu'ola** *nf* flower-bed

**aiu'tante** *nmf* assistant ● *nm* Mil adjutant. **~ di campo** aide-de-camp

**aiu'tare** *vt* help

**ai'uto** *nm* help, aid; *(assistente)* assistant. **dare un ~** lend a hand; **venire in ~ a qcno** come to sb's rescue; **~!** help!. **~ chirurgo** assistant surgeon. **~ domestico** mother's help. **~ infermiere** nursing auxiliary. **~ in linea** Comput on-line help

**aiz'zare** *vt* incite; **~ contro** set on

**al** = a + il

**'ala** *nf* wing; **fare ~** make way; **avere le ali ai piedi** *fig* run like the wind; **tarpare le ali a qcno** *fig* clip sb's wings. **~ destra/sinistra** *(in calcio)* right/left wing

**ala'bastro** *nm* alabaster

**'alacre** *a* brisk

**alam'bicco** *nm* alembic

**a'lano** *nm* Great Dane

**a'lare** *nm* firedog; **apertura ~** wingspan

**'alba** *nf* dawn

**alba'nese** *a & nmf* Albanian

**Alba'nia** *nf* Albania

**al'batro** *nm* albatross

**albeggi'are** *vi* dawn

**albe'rare** *vt* line with trees ⟨*strada*⟩

**albe'rato** *a* wooded; ⟨*viale*⟩ tree-lined

**albera'tura** *nf* Naut masts *pl*

**albe'rello** *nm* sapling

**alber'gare** *vt* ⟨*edificio:*⟩ accommodate ● *vi liter* lodge

**alberga|'tore, -'trice** *nmf* hotel-keeper

**alberghi'ero** *a* hotel *attrib*

**al'bergo** *nm* hotel; **~ diurno** hotel where rooms are rented during the daytime; **~ a 3 stelle** 3-star hotel

**'albero** *nm* tree; *Naut* mast; *Mech* shaft. **~ a camme** camshaft. **~ a foglie caduche** deciduous tree. **~ da frutto** fruit tree. **~ genealogico** family tree. **~ a gomiti** crankshaft. **~ maestro** Naut mainmast. **~ di Natale** Christmas tree. **~ di trasmissione** Mech transmission shaft, prop shaft

**albi'cocca** *nf* apricot

**albi'cocco** *nm* apricot-tree

**al'bino** *nm* albino

**'albo** *nm* register; *(libro ecc)* album; *(per avvisi)* notice board **'album** *nm inv* album. **~ da colorare** colouring book. **~ da disegno** sketch-book

**al'bume** *nm* albumen

**albu'mina** *nf* albumin

**alca'lino** *a* alkaline

**'alce** *nm* elk

**alchi'mia** *nf* alchemy

**alchi'mista** *nm* alchemist

**'alcol** *nm* alcohol; *Med* spirit; *(liquori forti)* spirits *pl*; **darsi all'~** take to drink. **~ denaturato** meths. **~ etilico** ethyl alcohol

**alcolicità** *nf* alcohol content

**al'colico** *a* alcoholic ● *nm* alcoholic drink

**alco'lismo** *nm* alcoholism

**alco'lista** *nmf* alcoholic

**alcoliz'zato, -a** *a & nmf* alcoholic

**alco'test®** *nm inv* Breathalyser<sup>R</sup>

**al'cova** *nf* alcove

**al'cun, al'cuno** *a & pron* any; **non ha ~ amico** he hasn't any friends. he has no friends. **alcuni** *pl* some, a few; **~i suoi amici** some of his friends

**aldilà** *nm* next world, hereafter

**alea'torio** *a* unpredictable; *Jur* aleatory

**aleggi'are** *vi* ⟨*brezza:*⟩ blow gently; ⟨*profumo:*⟩ waft

**a'letta** *nf Mech* fin

**alet'tone** *nm Aeron* aileron: *Auto* stabilizer

**'alfa** *nf inv* alpha

**alfa'betico** *a* alphabetical

**alfabetizzazi'one** *nf* **~ della popolazione** teaching people to read and write; **tasso di ~** literacy rate

**alfa'beto** *nm* alphabet. **A~ Fonetico Internazionale** International Phonetic Alphabet. **~ Morse** Morse code

**alfanu'merico** *a* alphanumeric

**alfi'ere** *nm* ⟨*negli scacchi*⟩ bishop

**al'fine** *adv* eventually, in the end

**'alga** *nf* weed. **alghe** *pl* marine seaweed

**'algebra** *nf* algebra

**Al'geri** *nf* Algiers

**Alge'ria** *nf* Algeria

**alge'rino, -a** *a & nmf* Algerian

**algocol'tura** *nf* seaweed farming

**algo'ritmo** *nm* algorithm

**ali'ante** *nm* glider

**'alibi** *nm inv* alibi

**a'lice** *nf* anchovy

**alie'nabile** *a Jur* alienable

**alie'nare** *vt* alienate

**alie'narsi** *vr* become estranged; **~ le simpatie di qcno** lose sb's good will

**ali'enato, -a** *a* alienated ● *nmf* lunatic

**alienazi'one** *nf* alienation

**a'lieno, -a** *nmf* alien ● *a* **è ~ da invidia** envy is foreign *or* alien to him

**alimen'tare** *vt* feed; *fig* foment ● *a* food *attrib*; ⟨*abitudine*⟩ dietary ● *nm* **alimentari** *pl* food-stuffs

**alimenta'tore** *nm* power unit. **~ automatico di documenti** automatic paper feed

**alimentazi'one** *nf* feeding; ⟨*cibo*⟩ food; ⟨*elettrica, a gas ecc*⟩ supply

**ali'mento** *nm* food. **alimenti** *pl* food; *Jur* alimony

**a'liquota** *nf* share; ⟨*di imposta*⟩ rate. **~ minima** basic rate. **ad ~ zero** zero-rated

**ali'scafo** *nm* hydrofoil

**'alito** *nm* breath; **~ cattivo** bad breath

**ali'tosi** *nf inv* halitosis

**all.** *abbr* (**allegato**) encl

**'alla** = **a** + **la**

**allaccia'mento** *nm* connection

**allacci'are** *vt* fasten ⟨*cintura*⟩; lace up ⟨*scarpe*⟩; do up ⟨*vestito*⟩; ⟨*collegare*⟩ connect; form ⟨*amicizia*⟩

**allacci'arsi** *vr* do up, fasten ⟨*vestito, cintura*⟩

**allaga'mento** *nm* flooding

**alla'gare** *vt* flood

**alla'garsi** *vr* to become flooded

**allampa'nato** *a* lanky

**allarga'mento** *nm* ⟨*di strada, ricerche*⟩ widening

**allar'gare** *vt* widen; open ⟨*braccia, gambe*⟩; let out ⟨*vestito ecc*⟩; *fig* extend

**allar'garsi** *vr* to widen

**allar'mante** *a* alarming

**allar'mare** *vt* alarm

**allar'mato** *a* panicky

**al'larme** *nm* alarm; **dare l'~** raise the alarm; **mettere in ~ qcno** alarm sb; **far scattare il campanello d'~** set the alarm bells ringing; **falso ~** *fig* false alarm. **~ aereo** air-raid siren; ⟨*suono*⟩ air-raid warning. **~ antincendio** fire alarm

**allar'mismo** *nm* alarmism

**allar'mista** *nmf* alarmist

**allatta'mento** *nm* ⟨*di animale*⟩ suckling; ⟨*di neonato*⟩ feeding

**allat'tare** *vt* suckle ⟨*animale*⟩; feed ⟨*neonato*⟩; **~ artificialmente** bottle feed

**'alle** = **a** + **le**

**alle'anza** *nf* alliance. **A~ Democratica** *Pol* Democratic Alliance. **A~ Nazionale** *Pol* National Alliance

**alle'are** *vt* unite

**alle'arsi** *vr* form an alliance

**alle'ato, -a** *a* allied ● *nmf* ally

**alle'gare¹** *vt Jur* allege

**alle'gare²** *vt* ⟨*accludere*⟩ enclose; set on edge ⟨*denti*⟩

**alle'gato** *a* enclosed ● *nm* enclosure; **in ~** attached, appended

**allegazi'one** *nf Jur* allegation

**allegeri'mento** *nm* alleviation

**allegge'rire** *vt* lighten; *fig* alleviate

**allegge'rirsi** *vr* become lighter; ⟨*vestirsi leggero*⟩ put on lighter clothes

**allego'ria** *nf* allegory

**alle'gorico** *a* allegorical

**allegra'mente** *adv* breezily

**alle'gria** *nf* gaiety

**al'legro** *a* cheerful; ⟨*colore*⟩ bright; ⟨*brillo*⟩ tipsy ● *nm Mus* allegro

**alle'luia** *int* hallelujah

**allena'mento** *nm* training

**alle'nare** *vt* train

**alle'narsi** *vr* train

**allena|'tore, -'trice** *nmf* trainer, coach

**allen'tare** *vt* loosen; *fig* relax

**allen'tarsi** *vr* become loose; *Mech* work loose

**aller'gia** *nf* allergy

**al'lergico** *a* allergic

**aller'gologo, -a** *nmf* allergist

**al'lerta** *nf* **stare ~** be alert, be on the alert; **essere in stato di ~** *Mil* be in a state of alert; **mettere in stato di ~** put on the alert

**allesti'mento** *nm* preparation; **in ~** in preparation; **~ scenico** *Theat* set

**alle'stire** *vt* prepare; stage ⟨*spettacolo*⟩; *Naut* fit out

**allet'tante** *a* alluring; **poco ~** unattractive

**allet'tare** *vt* entice

**alleva'mento** *nm* breeding; (*processo*) bringing up; (*luogo*) farm; (*per piante*) nursery; **pollo di ~** battery chicken. **~ in batteria** battery farming

**alle'vare** *vt* bring up ‹bambini›; breed ‹animali›; grow ‹piante›

**alleva|'tore, -'trice** *nmf* breeder

**allevia'mento** *nm* alleviation

**allevi'are** *vt* alleviate; *fig* lighten

**alli'bito** *a* astounded; **rimanere ~** be astounded

**allibra'tore** *nm* bookmaker

**allie'tare** *vt* gladden

**allie'tarsi** *vr* rejoice

**alli'evo, -a** *nmf* pupil ● *nm* Mil cadet

**alliga'tore** *nm* alligator

**allinea'mento** *nm* alignment

**alline'are** *vt* line up; *Typ* align; *Fin* adjust

**alline'arsi** *vr* line up; *fig* fall into line; **~ con qcno** *fig* align oneself with sb

**alline'ato** *a* lined up; **i paesi non allineati** the non-aligned states

**'allo** = a + lo

**allo'care** *vt* allocate

**al'locco** *nm* tawny owl

**al'locco, -a** *nmf fig* idiot

**allocuzi'one** *nf* speech

**al'lodola** *nf* [sky]lark

**alloggi'are** *vt* ‹persona:› put up; ‹casa:› provide accommodation for; *Mil* billet ● *vi* put up, stay; *Mil* be billeted

**al'loggio** *nm* (*appartamento*) flat, apartment *Am*; *Mil* billet. **~ popolare** council flat

**allontana'mento** *nm* removal

**allonta'nare** *vt* move away; (*licenziare*) dismiss; avert ‹pericolo›

**allonta'narsi** *vr* go away

**allopa'tia** *nf Med* allopathy

**al'lora** *adv* then; (*in quel tempo*) at that time; (*in tal caso*) in that case; **~ ~** just then; **d'~ in poi** from then on; **e ~?** what now?; (*e con ciò?*) so what?; **fino ~** until then

**allorchè** *conj* when, as soon as

**al'loro** *nm* laurel; *Culin* bay; **dormire sugli allori** rest on one's laurels

**'alluce** *nm* big toe

**alluci'nante** *a fam* incredible; **sostanza ~** hallucinogen

**alluci'nato, -a** *nmf* person who suffers from hallucinations; *fam* space cadet

**allucina'torio** *a* hallucinatory

**allucinazi'one** *nf* hallucination

**allucino'geno** *a* ‹sostanza› hallucinatory

**al'ludere** *vi* **~ a** allude to

**allu'minio** *nm* aluminium

**allu'naggio** *nm* moon-landing

**allu'nare** *vi* land on the moon

**allun'gabile** *a* ‹tavolo› extending

**allun'gare** *vt* lengthen; stretch out ‹mano›; stretch ‹gamba›; extend ‹tavolo›; (*diluire*) dilute; **~ il collo** crane one's neck; **~ il muso** pull a long face; **~ il passo** quicken one's step; **~ le mani su qcno** touch sb up; (*picchiare*) start fighting with sb; **~ uno schiaffo a qcno** slap sb

**allun'garsi** *vr* grow longer; (*crescere*) grow taller; (*sdraiarsi*) lie down, stretch out

**al'lungo** *nm* (*nel calcio*) pass; (*nella corsa*) spurt; (*nel pugilato*) lunge

**allusi'one** *nf* allusion

**allu'sivo** *a* allusive

**alluvi'onale** *a* alluvial

**alluvio'nato** *a* ‹popolazione› flooded out; ‹territorio› flooded

**alluvi'one** *nf* flood

**alma'nacco** *nm* almanac. **~ nobiliare** peerage

**al'meno** *adv* at least; **[se] ~ venisse il sole!** if only the sun would come out!

**a'logena** *nf* halogen lamp

**a'logeno** *nm* halogen ● *a* **lampada alogena** halogen lamp

**a'lone** *nm* halo

**alo'pecia** *nf Med* alopecia

**al'paca** *nm inv* alpaca

**al'pestre** *a* Alpine

**'Alpi** *nfpl* **le ~** the Alps

**alpi'nismo** *nm* mountaineering

**alpi'nista** *nmf* mountaineer

**alpi'nistico** *a* mountaineering *attrib*

**al'pino** *a* Alpine ● *nm Mil* **gli alpini** the Alpine troops

**al'quanto** *a* a certain amount of ● *adv* rather

**Al'sazia** *nf* Alsace

**alt** *int* stop; **intimare l'~** give the order to halt

**alta'lena** *nf* swing; (*tavola in bilico*) see-saw

**altale'nare** *vi fig* vacillate

**alta'mente** *adv* highly

**al'tare** *nm* altar

**alta'rino** *nm* **scoprire gli altarini di qcno** reveal sb's guilty secrets

**alte'rabile** *a* which can be changed, alterable

**alte'rare** *vt* alter; adulterate ‹vino›; (*falsificare*) falsify

**alte'rarsi** *vr* be altered; ‹cibo:› go bad; ‹merci:› deteriorate; (*arrabbiarsi*) get angry

**alte'rato** *a* ‹suono› distorted; ‹viso› careworn; ‹cibo› spoilt; ‹vino› adulterated; (*arrabbiato*) angry

**alterazi'one** *nf* alteration; (*di vino*) adulteration

**al'terco** *nm* altercation

**alte'rigia** *nf* haughtiness

**alter'nanza** *nf* alternation; (*in agricoltura*) rotation; *Pol* regular change in government

**alter'nare** *vt* alternate

**alter'narsi** *vr* alternate

**alterna'tiva** *nf* alternative

**alterna'tivo** *a* alternate; **medicina alternativa** alternative medicine

**alter'nato** *a* alternating

**alterna'tore** *nm Electr* alternator

**al'terno** *a* alternate; **a giorni alterni** every other day

**al'tero** *a* haughty

**al'tezza** *nf* height; (*profondità*) depth;

⟨*suono*⟩ pitch; ⟨*di tessuto*⟩ width; ⟨*titolo*⟩ Highness; **essere all'~ di** be on a level with; *fig* be up to. **~ libera di passaggio** headroom

**altezzosa'mente** *adv* haughtily

**altezzosità** *nf* haughtiness

**altez'zoso** *a* haughty

**al'ticcio** *a* tipsy, merry

**al'timetro** *nm* altimeter

**altipi'ano** *nm* plateau

**altiso'nante** *a* high-sounding

**alti'tudine** *nf* altitude

**'alto** *a* high; ⟨*di statura*⟩ tall; ⟨*profondo*⟩ deep; ⟨*suono*⟩ high-pitched; ⟨*tessuto*⟩ wide; *Geog* northern; **a notte alta** in the middle of the night; **avere degli alti e bassi** have some ups and downs; **di ~ bordo** high-class; **di ~ rango** high-ranking; **ad alta definizione** high-definition; **ad alta fedeltà** high-fidelity; **ad ~ livello** high-level; **a voce alta, ad alta voce** in a loud voice; ⟨*leggere*⟩ aloud; **essere in ~ mare** be on the high seas; *fig* be all at sea. **alta borghesia** *nf* gentry. **~ commissariato** *nm* High Commission. **alta finanza** *nf* high finance. **alta frequenza** *nf* high frequency. **~ medioevo** *nm* Dark Ages. **alta moda** *nf* high fashion. **alta pressione** *nf* ⟨*metereologica*⟩ high pressure. **alta società** *nf* high society. **alta tensione** *nf* high voltage. **~ tradimento** *nm* high treason ● *adv* high; **in ~** ⟨*essere*⟩ at the top; ⟨*guardare*⟩ up; **mani in ~!** hands up!; **dall'~** from above; **guardare qcno dall'~ ~ in basso** look down on sb

**altoate'sino** *a* South Tirolese

**alto'forno** *nm* blast-furnace

**altolà** *int* halt there!

**altolo'cato** *a* highly placed

**altopar'lante** *nm* loudspeaker

**altopi'ano** *nm* plateau

**altret'tanto** *a & pron* as much; ⟨*pl*⟩ as many ● *adv* likewise; **buona fortuna! – grazie, ~** good luck! – thank you, the same to you

**altri'menti** *adv* otherwise

**'altro** *a* other; **un ~, un'altra** another; **l'altr'anno** last year; **l'~ ieri** the day before yesterday; **domani l'~** the day after tomorrow; **l'ho visto l'~ giorno** I saw him the other day ● *pron* other [one]; **un ~, un'altra** another [one]; **ne vuoi dell'~?** would you like some more?; **l'un l'~** one another; **nessun ~** nobody else; **gli altri** ⟨*la gente*⟩ other people ● *nm* something else; **non fa ~ che lavorare** he does nothing but work; **desidera ~?** ⟨*in negozio*⟩ anything else?; **più che ~, sono stanco** I'm tired more than anything; **se non ~** at least; **senz'~** certainly; **tra l'~** what's more; **~ che!** absolutely!

**altrochè** *adv* absolutely!

**altroi'eri** *nm* **l'~** the day before yesterday

**al'tronde**: **d'~** *adv* on the other hand

**al'trove** *adv* elsewhere

**al'trui** *a* other people's ● *nm* other people's belongings *pl*

**altru'ismo** *nm* altruism

**altru'ista** *nmf* altruist

**al'tura** *nf* high ground; *Naut* deep sea

**a'lunno, -a** *nmf* pupil

**alve'are** *nm* hive

**'alveo** *nm* bed

**alzabandi'era** *nm inv* flag-raising

**alzacri'stallo** *nm Auto* window winder

**al'zare** *vt* lift, raise; ⟨*costruire*⟩ build; *Naut* hoist; **~ le spalle** shrug one's shoulders; **~ i tacchi** *fig* take to one's heels; **~ la voce** raise one's voice; **~ il volume** turn up the volume

**al'zarsi** *vr* ⟨*in piedi*⟩ stand up; ⟨*da letto*⟩ get up; ⟨*vento, temperatura:*⟩ rise

**al'zata** *nf* lifting; ⟨*aumento*⟩ rise; ⟨*da letto*⟩ getting up; *Archit* elevation. **~ di spalle** shrug of the shoulders

**alza'taccia** *nf fam* **fare un'~** get up at the crack of dawn

**al'zato** *a* up

**A.M.** *abbr* (**aeronautica militare**) Air Force

**a'mabile** *a* lovable; ⟨*vino*⟩ sweet

**amabilità** *nf* kindness

**amabil'mente** *adv* kindly

**a'maca** *nf* hammock

**a'malgama** *nm* amalgam

**amalga'mare** *vt* amalgamate

**amalga'marsi** *vr* amalgamate

**ama'nita** *nf Bot* amanita

**a'mante** *a* **~ di** fond of ● *nm* lover. **~ degli animali** animal lover ● *nf* mistress. **~ della lettura** book lover

**amara'mente** *adv* bitterly

**ama'ranto** *nm Bot* amarant[h]us; ⟨*colore*⟩ rich purple ● *a* rich purple

**a'mare** *vt* love; be fond of ⟨*musica, sport ecc*⟩

**amareggia'mento** *nm* bitterness

**amareggi'are** *vt* embitter

**amareggi'arsi** *vr* become embittered

**amareggi'ato** *a* embittered

**ama'rena** *nf* sour black cherry

**ama'retto** *nm* macaroon

**ama'rezza** *nf* bitterness; ⟨*dolore*⟩ sorrow

**a'maro** *a* bitter ● *nm* bitterness; ⟨*liquore*⟩ bitters *pl*

**ama'rognolo** *a* rather bitter

**a'mato, -a** *a* loved ● *nmf* beloved

**ama|'tore, -'trice** *nmf* lover

**a'mazzone** *nf* ⟨*in mitologia*⟩ Amazon; **all'~** side saddle

**Amaz'zonia** *nf* Amazonia

**amaz'zonico** *a* Amazonian

**ambasce'ria** *nf* diplomatic mission

**ambasci'ata** *nf* embassy; ⟨*messaggio*⟩ message

**ambascia|'tore, -'trice** *nm* ambassador ● *nf* ambassadress

**ambe'due** *a & pron* both

**ambi'destro** *a* ambidextrous

**ambien'tale** *a* environmental

**ambienta'lismo** *nm* environmentalism

**ambienta'lista** *a & nmf* environmentalist

**ambienta'mento** *nm* acclimatization

**ambien'tare** *vt* acclimatize; set ⟨*personaggio, film ecc*⟩

**ambien'tarsi** *vr* get acclimatized

**ambi'ente** *nm* environment; (*stanza*) room

**ambiguità** *nf inv* ambiguity; (*di persona*) shadiness

**am'biguo** *a* ambiguous; (*persona*) shady

**am'bire** *vi* ~ **a** aspire to

**am'bito** *a* (*lavoro, incarico*) much sought-after

**'ambito** *nm* sphere

**ambiva'lente** *a* ambivalent

**ambiva'lenza** *nf* ambivalence

**ambizi'one** *nf* ambition

**ambizi'oso** *a* ambitious

**amblio'pia** *nf* lazy eye

**'ambo** *a inv* both ● *nm* (*in tombola, lotto*) double

**'ambra** *nf* amber

**am'brato** *a* amber

**ambu'lante** *a* wandering; **venditore** ~ hawker

**ambu'lanza** *nf* ambulance

**ambulatori'ale** *a* **essere trattato con intervento** ~ have day surgery

**ambula'torio** *nm* (*di medico*) surgery; (*di ospedale*) out-patients' [department]. ~ **dentistico** dental clinic

**Am'burgo** *nf* Hamburg

**a'meba** *nf* amoeba

**a'mebico** *a* amoebic

**'amen** *int* amen; **e allora** ~**!** well, so be it!

**amenità** *nf inv* (*facezia*) pleasantry

**a'meno** *a* pleasant

**amenor'rea** *nf Med* amenorrhoea

**A'merica** *nf* America. ~ **centrale** Central America. ~ **Latina** Latin America. ~ **del nord/sud** North/South America

**america'nata** *nf* (*pej: film*) American rubbish

**america'nismo** *nm* Americanism; (*patriottismo*) flag-waving

**americaniz'zarsi** *vr* become Americanized

**ameri'cano, -a** *a & nmf* American

**ame'rindio** *a* Native American

**ame'tista** *nf* amethyst

**ami'anto** *nm* asbestos

**ami'chevole** *a* friendly

**ami'cizia** *nf* friendship; **fare** ~ **con qcno** make friends with sb; **amicizie** *pl* (*amici*) friends

**a'mico, -a** *a* (*parola, persona*) friendly ● *nmf* friend; ~ **del cuore** bosom friend. ~ **d'infanzia** childhood friend. ~ **intimo** close friend. ~ **di penna** penfriend, penpal

**'amido** *nm* starch

**ammac'care** *vt* dent (*metallo*); bruise (*frutto*)

**ammac'carsi** *vr* (*metallo:*) get dented; (*frutto:*) bruise

**ammac'cato** *a* (*metallo*) dented; (*frutto*) bruised

**ammacca'tura** *nf* dent; (*livido*) bruise

**ammaestra'mento** *nm* training

**ammae'strare** *vt* (*istruire*) teach; train (*animale*)

**ammae'strato** *a* trained

**ammaestra'tore, -'trice** *nmf* trainer

**ammainabandi'era** *nm inv* flag-lowering

**ammai'nare** *vt* lower (*bandiera*); furl (*vele*)

**amma'larsi** *vr* fall ill

**amma'lato, -a** *a* ill ● *nmf* sick person (*paziente*) patient

**ammali'are** *vt* bewitch

**ammali'ato** *a* bewitched

**ammalia|'tore, -'trice** *a* bewitching ● *nm* enchanter ● *nf* enchantress

**am'manco** *nm* deficit

**ammanet'tare** *vt* handcuff

**ammani'carsi** *vr fig* acquire connections

**ammani'cato** *a* **essere** ~ have connections

**ammanigli'arsi** *vr fig* = **ammanicarsi**

**ammanigli'ato** *a fig* = **ammanicato**

**amman'sire** *vt* tame, domesticate (*animali*); *fig* pacify, placate

**amman'sirsi** *vr* (*animali:*) become tame; *fig* calm down

**amman'tarsi** *vr* (*persona:*) wrap oneself up in a cloak; ~ **di** *fig* feign (*virtù*)

**amma'raggio** *nm* splashdown

**amma'rare** *vi* put down on the sea; (*nave spaziale:*) splash down

**ammassa'mento** *nm Mil* build-up

**ammas'sare** *vt* amass

**ammas'sarsi** *vr* crowd together

**am'masso** *nm* mass; (*mucchio*) pile

**ammat'tire** *vi* go mad

**ammazzacaffè** *nm inv* liqueur

**ammazza'fame** *nm inv* stodge

**ammaz'zare** *vt* kill

**ammaz'zarsi** *vr* (*suicidarsi, fig*) kill oneself; (*rimanere ucciso*) be killed

**am'menda** *nf* amends *pl*; (*multa*) fine; **fare** ~ **di qcsa** make amends for sth

**am'messo** *pp di* **ammettere** ● *conj* ~ **che** supposing that

**am'mettere** *vt* admit; (*riconoscere*) acknowledge; (*supporre*) suppose; **ammettiamo che...** let's suppose [that]...

**ammez'zato** *nm* (*piano ammezzato*) mezzanine

**ammic'care** *vi* wink

**ammini'strare** *vt* administer; (*gestire*) run

**ammini'strarsi** *vr fig* manage one's finances

**amministra'tivo** *a* administrative

**amministra|'tore, -'trice** *nmf* administrator; (*di azienda*) manager; (*di società*) director; ~ **aggiunto** associate director. ~ **del condominio** property manger. ~ **delegato** managing director. ~ **unico** sole director

**amministrazi'one** *nf* administration; **fatti di ordinaria** ~ *fig* routine matters. ~ **aziendale** (*studi*) business studies. ~ **comunale** local council. ~ **controllata** receivership. ~ **pubblica** civil service. ~ **regionale** regional council

**ammino'acido** *nm* amino acid

**ammi'rabile** *a* admirable

**ammi'raglia** *nf* flag-ship

15

**ammiragli'ato** | **analcolico**

**ammiragli'ato** *nm* admiralty
**ammi'raglio** *nm* admiral
**ammi'rare** *vt* admire
**ammi'rato** *a* **restare/essere ~** be full of admiration
**ammira'tore, -'trice** *nmf* admirer
**ammirazi'one** *nf* admiration
**ammi'revole** *a* admirable
**ammis'sibile** *a* admissible
**ammissibilità** *nf* acceptability
**ammissi'one** *nf* admission; (approvazione) acknowledgement
**ammobili'are** *vt* furnish
**ammobili'ato** *a* furnished; **stanza ammobiliata** furnished room
**ammoderna'mento** *nm* modernization
**ammoder'nare** *vt* modernize
**ammoder'narsi** *vr* move with the times
**am'modo** *a* proper ● *adv* properly
**ammogli'are** *vt* marry off
**ammogli'arsi** *vr* get married
**ammogli'ato** *a* married ● *nm* married man
**am'mollo** *nm* **in ~** soaking; **mettere in ~** pre-soak
**ammo'niaca** *nf* ammonia
**ammoni'mento** *nm* warning; (di rimprovero) admonishment
**ammo'nire** *vt* warn; (rimproverare) admonish
**ammoni'tore** *a* admonishing
**ammonizi'one** *nf* Sport warning; (rimprovero) admonishment
**ammon'tare** *vi* **~ a** amount to ● *nm* amount
**ammonticchi'are** *vt* heap up, pile up
**ammonticchi'arsi** *vr* pile up
**ammor'bare** *vt* (con odore) pollute; (con malattie) infect
**ammorbi'dente** *nm* (per panni) softener
**ammorbi'dire** *vt* soften
**ammorbi'dirsi** *vr* soften
**ammorta'mento** *nm* Comm amortization
**ammor'tare** *vt* pay off (spesa); Comm amortize (debito)
**ammortiz'zare** *vt* Comm = **ammortare**; Mech damp
**ammortizza'tore** *nm* shock-absorber
**ammosci'are** *vt* make flabby
**ammosci'arsi** *vi* get flabby
**ammucchi'are** *vt* pile up
**ammucchi'arsi** *vr* pile up
**ammucchi'ata** *nf* (sl: orgia) orgy; **un'~ di** (fam: ammasso) loads of
**ammuf'fire** *vi* go mouldy
**ammuf'firsi** *vr* go mouldy
**ammuf'fito** *a* mouldy; fig stuffy
**ammutina'mento** *nm* mutiny
**ammuti'narsi** *vr* mutiny
**ammuti'nato** *a* mutinous ● *nm* mutineer
**ammuto'lire** *vi* be struck dumb
**ammuto'lirsi** *vr* fall silent
**amne'sia** *nf* amnesia
**amni'stia** *nf* amnesty
**amnisti'are** *vt* amnesty
**'amo** *nm* hook; fig bait

**amo'rale** *a* amoral
**amoralità** *nf* amorality
**a'more** *nm* love; **d'~** (canzone, film) love; **fare l'~** make love; **per l'amor di Dio/del cielo!** for heaven's sake!; **andare d'~ e d'accordo** get on like a house on fire; **amor proprio** self-respect; **amor cortese** courtly love; **è un ~** (persona:) he's/she's a darling; **per ~ di** for the sake of; **amori** *pl* love affairs
**amoreggi'are** *vi* flirt
**amo'revole** *a* loving
**amorevol'mente** *adv* lovingly
**a'morfo** *a* shapeless; (persona) colourless, grey
**amo'rino** *nm* cherub
**amorosa'mente** *adv* lovingly
**amo'roso** *a* loving, (sguardo ecc) amorous; (lettera, relazione) love attrib
**am'pere** *nm inv* ampere; **da 15 ~** 15-amp
**ampe'rometro** *nm* ammeter
**ampia'mente** *adv* widely
**ampi'ezza** *nf* (di esperienza) breadth; (di stanza) spaciousness; (di gonna) fullness; (importanza) scale. **~ di vedute** broad-mindedness
**'ampio** *a* ample; (esperienza) wide; (stanza) spacious; (vestito) loose; (gonna, descrizione) full; (pantaloni) baggy; **~ di vedute** broadminded
**am'plesso** *nm* embrace
**amplia'mento** *nm* (di casa, porto) enlargement; (di strada, conoscenze) broadening
**ampli'are** *vt* broaden, widen (strada, conoscenze); enlarge (casa)
**ampli'arsi** *vr* broaden, grow wider
**amplifi'care** *vt* amplify; fig magnify
**amplifica'tore** *nm* amplifier
**amplificazi'one** *nf* amplification
**am'polla** *nf* cruet
**ampol'loso** *a* pompous
**ampu'tare** *vt* amputate
**amputazi'one** *nf* amputation
**amu'leto** *nm* amulet
**A.N.** *abbr* Pol (**Alleanza Nazionale**) National Alliance (right-wing party)
**anabbagli'ante** *a* Auto dipped ● *nm* **anabbaglianti** *pl* dipped headlights
**anaboliz'zante** *nm* anabolic steroid
**ana'cardi** *nmpl* cashew nuts
**ana'cardio** *nm* cashew
**ana'conda** *nf* Zool anaconda
**anacro'nismo** *nm* anachronism
**anacro'nistico** *a* anachronistic; **essere ~** be an anachronism
**anae'robico** *a* anaerobic
**anafi'lattico** *a* **shock ~** Med anaphylactic shock
**a'nagrafe** *nf* (ufficio) registry office; (registro) register of births, marriages and deaths
**ana'grafico** *a* **dati** *pl* **anagrafici** personal data
**ana'gramma** *nm* anagram
**anal'colico** *a* non-alcoholic ● *nm* soft drink, non-alcoholic drink

**a'nale** *a* anal

**analfa'beta** *a & nmf* illiterate

**analfabe'tismo** *nm* illiteracy

**anal'gesico** *nm* painkiller

**a'nalisi** *nf inv* analysis; *Med* test; **in ultima ~** in the final analysis. **~ grammaticale/del periodo/logica** parsing. **~ di mercato** market research. **~ del percorso critico** critical path analysis. **~ del sangue** blood test

**ana'lista** *nmf* analyst. **~ economico** economic analyst. **~ finanziario** business analyst

**ana'litico** *a* analytical

**analiz'zabile** *a* analysable

**analiz'zare** *vt* analyse; *Med* test, analyse

**anal'lergico** *a* hypoallergenic

**analoga'mente** *adv* analogously

**analo'gia** *nf* analogy

**ana'logico** *a* analogue

**analo'gismo** *nm* reasoning by analogy

**a'nalogo** *a* analogous

**anam'nesi** *nf inv* medical history

**'ananas** *nm inv* pineapple

**anar'chia** *nf* anarchy

**a'narchico, -a** *a* anarchic ● *nmf* anarchist

**anar'chismo** *nm* anarchism

**A.N.A.S.** *nf abbr* (Azienda Nazionale Autonoma delle Strade) *national road maintenance authority*

**ana'tema** *nm* anathema

**anato'mia** *nf* anatomy

**ana'tomico** *a* anatomical; ‹sedia› contoured, ergonomic

**'anatra** *nf* duck. **~ selvatica** mallard

**ana'troccolo** *nm* duckling

**'anca** *nf* hip; (di animale) flank

**ance'strale** *a* ancestral

**'anche** *conj* also, too, as well; (persino) even; **parla ~ francese** he also speaks French, he speaks French too, he speaks French as well; **~ se** even if

**ancheggi'are** *vi* wiggle one's hips

**anchilo'sarsi** *vr fig* stiffen up

**anchilo'sato** *a fig* stiff

**an'cora** *adv* still; (con negazione) yet; (di nuovo) again; (di più) some more; **~ una volta** once more; **non ~** not yet; **~ esistente** extant; **~ più bello** even more beautiful; **~ una birra** another beer, one more beer

**'ancora** *nf* anchor; **gettare l'~** drop anchor. **~ di salvezza** last hope

**anco'raggio** *nm* anchorage

**anco'rare** *vt* anchor

**anco'rarsi** *vr* anchor, drop anchor; **~ a** *fig* cling to

**Andalu'sia** *nf* Andalusia

**anda'luso, -a** *a & nmf* Andalusian

**anda'mento** *nm* (del mercato, degli affari) trend

**an'dante** *a* (corrente) current; (di poco valore) cheap ● *nm Mus* andante

**an'dare** *vi* go; (funzionare) work; (essere di moda) be in; **~ via** (partire) leave; ‹macchia:› come out; **~ a piedi** walk; **~ a sciare** go skiing: **~ [bene]** (confarsi) suit; ‹taglia:› fit; **ti va bene alle tre?** does three o'clock suit you?; **non mi va di mangiare** I don't feel like eating; **~ di fretta** be in a hurry; **~ fiero di** be proud of; **~ di moda** be in fashion; **va per i 20 anni** he's nearly 20; **ma va'** [là]! come on!; **come va?** how are things?; **~ a male** go off; **~ a fuoco** go up in flames; **~ perduto** be lost; **va spedito** [entro] **stamattina** it must be sent this morning; **ne va del mio lavoro** my job is at stake; **come è andata a finire?** how did it turn out?; **cosa vai dicendo?** what are you talking about?; **andarsene** go away; (morire) pass away ● *nm* going; **~ e venire** (andirivieni) comings and goings *pl*; **a lungo** eventually; **a tutto ~** at full speed; **con l'~ del tempo** with the passing of time

**an'data** *nf* going; (viaggio) outward journey; **biglietto di sola ~/di ~ e ritorno** single/return [ticket]

**anda'tura** *nf* walk; (portamento) bearing; *Naut* tack; *Sport* pace

**an'dazzo** *nm fam* turn of events; **prendere un brutto ~** turn nasty

**'Ande** *nfpl* **le ~** the Andes

**an'dino** *a* Andean

**andirivi'eni** *nm inv* comings and goings *pl*

**'andito** *nm* passage

**An'dorra** *nf* Andorra

**an'drone** *nm* entrance

**andro'pausa** *nf hum* male menopause

**a'neddoto** *nm* anecdote

**ane'lare** *vt* **~ a** long for

**a'nelito** *nm* longing

**a'nello** *nm* ring; (di catena) link. **~ di fidanzamento** engagement ring. **~ d'oro** gold ring

**ane'mia** *nf* anaemia

**a'nemico** *a* anaemic

**a'nemone** *nm* anemone

**aneste'sia** *nf* anaesthesia; (sostanza) anaesthetic. **~ epidurale** epidural

**aneste'sista** *nmf* anaesthetist

**ane'stetico** *a & nm* anaesthetic

**anestetiz'zare** *vt* anaesthetize

**a'neto** *nm* dill

**anfeta'mina** *nf* amphetamine

**an'fibi** *nmpl* (stivali) army boots

**an'fibio** *nm* amphibian ● *a* amphibious

**anfite'atro** *nm* amphitheatre

**'anfora** *nf* amphora

**an'fratto** *nm* ravine

**an'gelico** *a* angelic

**'angelo** *nm* angel. **~ custode** guardian angel

**anghe'ria** *nf* harassment

**an'gina** *nf inv* **~** [pectoris] angina [pectoris]

**angi'ologo, -a** *nmf Med* angiologist

**anglica'nesimo** *nm Relig* Anglicanism

**angli'cano, -a** *a & nmf Relig* Anglican

**angli'cismo** *nm* Anglicism

**angliciz'zare** *vt* anglicize

**anglo+** *pref* Anglo+

**angloameri'cano, -a** *nmf* Anglo-American

**an'glofilo, -a** *a & nmf* Anglophile

**an'glofono, -a** *nmf* English-speaker

**anglofran'cese** *a* Anglo-French

**anglo'sassone** *a & nmf* Anglo-Saxon

**An'gola** *nf* Angola

**ango'lano, -a** *a & nmf* Angolan

**ango'lare** *a* angular

**angolazi'one** *nf* angle shot; *fig* point of view

**angoli'era** *nf* (*mobile*) corner cupboard

**'angolo** *nm* corner; *Math* angle; **dietro l'~** round the corner; **fare ~ con** ‹*negozio, casa:*› be on the corner of. **~ acuto** acute angle. **~ [di] cottura** kitchenette. **~ retto** right angle

**ango'loso** *a* angular; ‹*carattere*› difficult to get on with

**'angora** *nf* [**lana d'**]**~** angora

**an'goscia** *nf* anguish

**angosci'are** *vt* torment

**angosci'arsi** *vr* (*preoccuparsi*) worry oneself sick, torment oneself

**angosci'ato** *a* agonized

**angosci'oso** *a* (*disperato*) anguished; (*che dà angoscia*) distressing

**angu'illa** *nf* eel

**an'guria** *nf* water-melon

**an'gustia** *nf* (*ansia*) anxiety; (*penuria*) poverty

**angusti'are** *vt* distress

**angusti'arsi** *vr* be distressed (**per** about)

**angusti'ato** *a* distressed

**an'gusto** *a* narrow

**'anice** *nm* anise; *Culin* aniseed; (*liquore*) anisette

**ani'cino** *nm* (*biscotto*) aniseed biscuit

**ani'dride** *nf* **~ carbonica** carbon dioxide. **~ solforosa** sulphur dioxide

**'anima** *nf* soul; **non c'era ~ viva** there was not a soul about; **all'~!** good grief!; **mi fa dannare l'~!** he'll be the death of me!; **l'~ della festa** the life and soul of the party; **un'~ in pena** a soul in torment; **volere un bene dell'~ a** qcno love sb to death; **la buon'~ della zia** my late aunt, God rest her soul. **~ gemella** soul mate

**ani'male** *a & nm* animal. **animali** *pl* **domestici** pets. **animali** *pl* **selvatici** wild animals

**anima'lesco** *a* animal

**anima'lista** *nmf* animal activist

**ani'mare** *vt* give life to; (*ravvivare*) enliven; (*incoraggiare*) encourage

**ani'marsi** *vr* come to life; (*accalorarsi*) become animated

**ani'mato** *a* animate; ‹*discussione*› animated; ‹*strada, paese*› lively

**anima'tore, -'trice** *nmf* leading spirit; *Cinema* animator

**animazi'one** *nf* animation; **con ~** animatedly

**ani'melle** *nfpl* (*di agnello, vitello*) sweetbread

**'animo** *nm* (*mente*) mind; (*indole*) disposition; (*cuore*) heart; **perdersi d'~** lose heart; **farsi ~** take heart

**animosa'mente** *adv* boldly

**animosità** *nf* animosity

**ani'moso** *a* brave; (*ostile*) hostile

**ani'setta** *nf* anisette

**'anitra** *nf* duck

**annacqua'mento** *nm fig* watering down, dilution

**annac'quare** *vt anche fig* water down

**annac'quato** *a* watered down; ‹*colore, resoconto*› insipid

**annaffi'are** *vt* water

**annaffia'toio** *nm* watering-can

**an'nali** *nmpl* annals; **restare negli ~** go down in history

**anna'spare** *vi* flounder

**an'nata** *nf* year; (*importo annuale*) annual amount; (*di vino*) vintage; **vino d'~** vintage wine

**annebbia'mento** *nm* fog build-up; *fig* clouding

**annebbi'are** *vt* cloud ‹*vista, mente*›

**annebbi'arsi** *vr* get misty; (*in città, su autostrada*) get foggy; ‹*vista, mente:*› grow dim

**annega'mento** *nm* drowning

**anne'gare** *vt/i* drown

**anne'rire** *vt/i* blacken

**anne'rirsi** *vr* become black

**an'nessi** *nmpl* (*costruzioni*) outbuildings; **tutti gli ~ e i connessi** all the appurtenances

**annessi'one** *nf* (*di nazione*) annexation

**an'nesso** *pp di* **annettere** ● *a* attached; ‹*Stato*› annexed

**an'nettere** *vt* add; (*accludere*) enclose; annex ‹*Stato*›

**annichi'lire** *vt* annihilate

**anni'darsi** *vr* nest

**annienta'mento** *nm* annihilation

**annien'tare** *vt* annihilate

**annien'tarsi** *vr* abase oneself

**anniver'sario** *a & nm* anniversary. **~ di matrimonio** wedding anniversary

**'anno** *nm* year; **Buon A~!** Happy New Year!; **quanti anni ha?** how old are you?; **Tommaso ha dieci anni** Thomas is ten [years old]; **gli anni '30** the '30s. **~ accademico** academic year. **~ bisestile** leap year. **~ civile** calendar year. **~ giudiziario** law year. **~ luce** light year. **~ nuovo** New Year. **~ sabbatico** *Univ* sabbatical. **anni** *pl* **verdi** salad days

**anno'dare** *vt* knot; do up ‹*cintura*›; *fig* form

**anno'darsi** *vr* become knotted

**annoi'are** *vt* bore; (*recare fastidio*) annoy

**annoi'arsi** *vr* get bored; (*condizione*) be bored

**annoi'ato** *a* bored

**an'noso** *a* ‹*questione*› age-old

**anno'tare** *vt* note down; annotate ‹*testo*›

**annotazi'one** *nf* note

**annove'rare** *vt* number

**annu'ale** *a* annual, yearly

**annual'mente** *adv* annually

**annu'ario** *nm* year-book

**annu'ire** *vi* nod; (*acconsentire*) agree

**annulla'mento** *nm* annulment: (*di appuntamento*) cancellation

**annul'lare** *vt* annul: cancel 〈*appuntamento*〉: (*togliere efficacia a*) undo; disallow 〈*gol*〉; (*distruggere*) destroy

**annul'larsi** *vr* cancel each other out

**an'nullo** *nm* (*timbro*) franking

**annunci'are** *vt* announce; (*preannunciare*) foretell

**annuncia|'tore, -'trice** *nmf* announcer

**annunciazi'one** *nf* Annunciation

**an'nuncio** *nm* announcement; (*pubblicitario*) advertisement; (*notizia*) news. **annunci** *pl* **economici** classified advertisements. **annunci** *pl* **mortuari** obituaries, death notices. **~ pubblicitario** advertisement

**'annuo** *a* annual, yearly

**annu'sare** *vt* sniff

**annu'sata** *nf* **dare un'~ a** have a sniff at

**annuvola'mento** *nm* clouding over

**annuvo'lare** *vt* cloud

**annuvo'larsi** *vr* cloud over

**'ano** *nm* anus

**a'nodino** *a* anodyne

**'anodo** *nm* anode

**anoma'lia** *nf* anomaly

**a'nomalo** *a* anomalous

**a'nonima** *nf* **A~ Alcolisti** Alcoholics Anonymous. **~ sequestri** *Italian criminal organization specializing in kidnapping*

**anoni'mato** *nm* **mantenere l'~** remain anonymous

**anonimità** *nf* anonymity

**a'nonimo, -a** *a* anonymous ● *nmf* unknown person; (*pittore, scrittore*) anonymous painter/writer

**anores'sia** *nf Med* anorexia

**ano'ressico, -a** *a nmf* anorexic

**anor'male** *a* abnormal ● *nmf* deviant, abnormal person

**anormalità** *nf inv* abnormality

**ANSA** *nf abbr* (**Agenzia Nazionale Stampa Associata**) *Italian press agency*

**'ansa** *nf* handle; (*di fiume*) bend

**an'sante** *a* panting

**an'sare** *vi* pant

**'ansia, ansietà** *nf* anxiety; **stare/essere in ~ per** be anxious about

**ansi'mante** *a* breathless

**ansi'mare** *vi* gasp for breath

**ansio'litico** *nm* tranquillizer

**ansi'oso** *a* anxious

**'anta** *nf* (*di finestra*) shutter; (*di armadio*) door

**antago'nismo** *nm* antagonism

**antago'nista** *nmf* antagonist

**antago'nistico** *a* antagonistic

**an'tartico** *a & nm* Antarctic

**An'tartide** *nf* Antarctica

**ante'bellico** *a* pre-war

**antece'dente** *a* preceding ● *nm* precedent

**ante'fatto** *nm* prior event

**ante'guerra** *a* pre-war ● *nm* pre-war period

**ante'nato, -a** *nmf* ancestor

**an'tenna** *nf Radio, TV* aerial; (*di animale*) antenna; *Naut* yard; **rizzare le antenne** *fig* prick up one's ears. **~ parabolica** satellite dish. **~ radar** radar scanner

**ante'porre** *vt* put before

**ante'prima** *nf* preview; **vedere qcsa in ~** have a sneak preview of sth

**anteri'ore** *a* front *attrib*; (*nel tempo*) previous

**anterior'mente** *adv* (*nel tempo*) previously; (*nello spazio*) in front

**antesi'gnano, -a** *nmf fig* forerunner

**anti+** *pref* anti+

**antiabor'tista** *nmf* antiabortionist ● *a* antiabortion *attrib*

**anti'acido** *nm* antacid

**antiade'rente** *a* 〈*padella*〉 nonstick

**antia'ereo** *a* anti-aircraft *attrib*

**antial'lergico** *a* hypoallergenic

**antia'partheid** *a inv* antiapartheid

**antia'tomico** *a* anti-nuclear; **rifugio ~** fall-out shelter

**antibat'terico** *a* antibacterial

**antibi'otico** *a & nm* antibiotic

**antibloc'caggio** *a inv* antilock *attrib*

**anti'caglia** *nf* (*oggetto*) piece of old junk

**anti-cal'care** *nm* softener

**antica'mente** *adv* in ancient times, long ago

**anti'camera** *nf* ante-room; **fare ~** be kept waiting

**antichità** *nf inv* antiquity; (*oggetto*) antique

**anti'clone** *nm* anticyclone

**antici'clonico** *a* 〈*area*〉 anti-cyclonic

**antici'pare** *vt* advance; *Comm* pay in advance; (*prevedere*) anticipate; (*prevenire*) forestall ● *vi* be early

**anticipata'mente** *adv* in advance

**antici'pato** *a* upfront; **pagamento ~** advance payment

**anticipazi'one** *nf* anticipation; (*notizia*) advance news

**an'ticipo** *nm* advance; (*caparra*) deposit; **in ~** early; (*nel lavoro*) ahead of schedule; **giocare d'~** *Sport, fig* anticipate the next move

**an'tico** *a* ancient; 〈*mobile ecc*〉 antique; (*vecchio*) old; **all'antica** old-fashioned ● *nm* **gli antichi** the ancients

**anticomu'nista** *a & nmf* anti-communist

**anticoncezio'nale** *a & nm* contraceptive

**anticonfor'mismo** *nm* unconventionality

**anticonfor'mista** *nmf* nonconformist

**anticonfor'mistico** *a* unconventional, nonconformist

**anticonge'lante** *a & nm* anti-freeze

**anticonsu'mismo** *nm* anti-consumerism

**anti'corpo** *nm* antibody

**anticostituzio'nale** *a* unconstitutional

**anti'crimine** *a inv* 〈*squadra*〉 crime *attrib*

**antidemo'cratico** *a* undemocratic
**antidepres'sivo** *nm* antidepressant
**antidiluvi'ano** *a fig* antediluvian
**antidolo'rifico** *nm* painkiller
**anti'doping** *nm inv Sport* dope test
**an'tidoto** *nm* antidote
**anti'droga** *a* ⟨campagna⟩ anti-drugs:
⟨squadra⟩ drug *attrib*
**antie'stetico** *a* ugly
**antifa'scismo** *nm* anti-fascism
**antifa'scista** *a & nmf* anti-fascist
**an'tifona** *nf fig* dull and repetitive speech;
capire l'~ take the hint; **sempre la stessa**
~ always the same old story
**anti'forfora** *a inv* dandruff *attrib*
**anti'fumo** *a inv* anti-smoking
**anti'furto** *a inv* anti-theft device; ⟨allarme⟩
alarm ●*a inv* ⟨sistema⟩ anti-theft
**anti'gelo** *a inv* anti-freeze ●*nm* antifreeze;
⟨parabrezza⟩ defroster
**anti'gene** *nm* antigen
**antigi'enico** *a* unhygienic
**anti-inflazi'one** *a inv* anti-inflation
**An'tille** *nfpl* le ~ the West Indies
**an'tilope** *nf* antelope
**anti'mafia** *a inv* anti-Mafia
**antimilita'rista** *a inv* anti-militaristic
●*nmf* anti-militarist
**antin'cendio** *a inv* allarme ~ fire alarm;
porta ~ fire door
**anti'nebbia** *a inv* [faro] ~ *Auto* foglamp,
foglight
**antine'vralgico** *a* pain-killing ●*nm* painkiller
**antinfiamma'torio** *a & nm* anti-inflammatory
**antinflazio'nistico** *a* anti-inflationary
**antinquina'mento** *a inv* anti-pollution
**antinucle'are** *a* anti-nuclear
**antio'rario** *a* anti-clockwise
**antiparassi'tario** *nm* insecticide
**antiparlamen'tare** *a* unparliamentary
**antipasti'era** *nf* hors d'oeuvre dish
**anti'pasto** *nm* hors d'oeuvre, starter.
**antipasti** *pl* **caldi** hot starters. **antipasti** *pl*
**freddi** cold starters. **antipasti** *pl* **misti** variety of starters
**antipa'tia** *nf* antipathy
**anti'patico** *a* unpleasant
**an'tipodi** *nmpl* Antipodes: **essere agli** ~
*fig* be poles apart
**anti'polio** *nf inv* ⟨vaccino⟩ polio vaccine;
**fare l'~** have a polio injection ●*a* ⟨siero,
vaccino⟩ polio *attrib*
**antipopo'lare** *a* anti-working-class
**antiprobizio'nismo** *nm* anti-
prohibitionism
**antiproibizio'nista** *a & nmf* anti-prohibi-
tionist
**antiproi'ettile** *a inv* bullet-proof
**antiquari'ato** *nm* antique trade; **pezzo d'~**
antique
**anti'quario, -a** *nmf* antique dealer
**anti'quato** *a* antiquated
**antiraz'zismo** *nm* antiracism

**antireu'matico** *a & nm* anti-rheumatic
**antiri'flesso** *a inv* antiglare
**anti'ruggine** *nm inv* rust-inhibitor ●*a*
anti-rust
**anti'rughe** *a inv* anti-wrinkle *attrib*
**anti'scasso** *a inv* ⟨porta⟩ burglar-proof
**antisci'opero** *a inv* anti-strike
**anti'scippo** *a inv* theft-proof
**anti'scivolo** *a inv* nonskid
**antise'mita** *a* anti-Semitic
**antisemi'tismo** *nm* anti-Semitism
**anti'settico** *a & nm* antiseptic
**antisinda'cale** *a* ⟨comportamento⟩ anti-
trade-union
**anti'sismico** *a* earthquake-proof
**antisoci'ale** *a* anti-social
**antiso'lare** *a & nm* suntan
**antisommer'gibile** *a inv* anti-submarine
●*nm* submarine hunter
**antista'minico** *nm* antihistamine
**anti'stante** *prep* ~ **a** in front of
**anti'tarlo** *nm inv* woodworm treatment
**anti'tarmico** *a* mothproof
**antiterro'rismo** *nm* counter-terrorism
**antiterro'rista** *a* antiterrorist
**antiterro'ristico** *a* antiterrorist
**an'titesi** *nf inv* antithesis
**antite'tanica** *nf* tetanus injection
**antite'tanico** *a* tetanus *attrib*
**anti'tetico** *a* antithetical
**anti'trust** *a* antitrust
**antitumo'rale** *a* which stops the growth of
tumours
**anti'urto** *a* shockproof
**antivaio'losa** *nf* smallpox injection
**anti'vipera** *a* siero ~ snakebite antidote
**antivi'rale** *a* anti-viral
**antolo'gia** *nf* anthology
**an'tonimo** *nm* antonym
**antono'masia: per** ~ **a** ⟨poeta⟩ quintessential
**antra'cite** *nf* anthracite; ⟨colore⟩ charcoal
[grey]
**'antro** *nm* cavern
**antro'pofago** *a* man-eating, cannibalistic
**antropolo'gia** *nf* anthropology
**antropo'logico** *a* anthropological
**antro'pologo, -a** *nmf* anthropologist
**anu'lare** *nm* ring-finger
**An'versa** *nf* Antwerp
**'anzi** *conj* in fact; ⟨o meglio⟩ or better still; ⟨al
contrario⟩ on the contrary
**anzianità** *nf* old age; ⟨di servizio⟩ seniority
**anzi'ano, -a** *a* old, elderly; ⟨di grado ecc⟩ senior ●*nmf* elderly person
**anziché** *conj* rather than
**anzi'tempo** *adv* prematurely
**anzi'tutto** *adv* first of all
**a'orta** *nf* aorta
**A'pache** *mf inv* Apache
**apar'theid** *nf* apartheid
**apar'titico** *a* unaligned
**apa'tia** *nf* apathy
**a'patico** *a* apathetic
**'ape** *nf* bee. ~ **regina** queen bee

aperi'tivo *nm* aperitif

aperta'mente *adv* openly

a'perto *a* open; **all'aria aperta** in the open air; **all'~** ⟨*piscina, teatro*⟩ open-air. **~ a tutti** open to all comers. **rimanere a bocca aperta** be dumbfounded

aper'tura *nf* opening; (*inizio*) beginning; (*ampiezza*) spread; (*di arco*) span; *Pol* overtures *pl: Phot* aperture. **~ alare** wing span. **~ di credito** loan agreement. **~ mentale** openness

api'ario *nm* apiary

'apice *nm* apex; **l'~ di** the acme of

apicol|'tore, -'trice *nmf* beekeeper

apicol'tura *nf* beekeeping

a'plomb *nm inv* (*di un abito*) hang; *fig* aplomb, self-assuredness

ap'nea *nf* **immersione in ~** free diving

Apoca'lisse *nf* **l'~** the Apocalypse

apoca'littico *a* apocalyptic

a'pocrifo *a* apocryphal

apo'geo *nm* apogee

a'polide *a* stateless ● *nmf* stateless person

apo'litico *a* apolitical

A'pollo *nm* Apollo

apolo'geta *nmf* apologist (**di** for)

apolo'gia *nf* apologia; (*celebrazione*) eulogy. **~ di reato** condoning of a criminal act

apoples'sia *nf* apoplexy

apo'plettico *a* apoplectic

a'postolo *nm* apostle

apostro'fare *vt* (*mettere un apostrofo a*) write with an apostrophe; reprimand ⟨*persona*⟩

a'postrofo *nm* apostrophe

apote'osi *nf* apotheosis

appaga'mento *nm* fulfilment

appa'gare *vt* satisfy

appa'garsi *vr* **~ di** be satisfied with

appa'gato *a* sated

appai'are *vt* pair; mate ⟨*animali*⟩

appallotto'lare *vt* roll into a ball

appallotto'larsi *vr* ⟨*gatto:*⟩ curl up in a ball; ⟨*farina:*⟩ become lumpy

appalta'tore *nm* contractor

ap'palto *nm* contract; **dare in ~** contract out; **gara di ~** call for tenders

appan'naggio *nm* (*in denaro*) annuity; *fig* prerogative

appan'nare *vt* mist ⟨*vetro*⟩; dim ⟨*vista*⟩

appan'narsi *vr* mist over; ⟨*vista:*⟩ grow dim

appa'rato *nm* apparatus; (*apparecchiamento*) array; (*pompa*) display. **~ digerente** digestive system. **~ scenico** set

apparecchi'are *vt* prepare ● *vi* lay the table *Br*, set the table

apparecchia'tura *nf* (*impianti*) equipment

appa'recchio *nm* apparatus; (*congegno*) device; (*radio, tv ecc*) set; (*aeroplano*) aircraft; (*telefono*) phone. **~ acustico** hearing aid

appa'rente *a* apparent

apparente'mente *adv* apparently

appa'renza *nf* appearance; **in ~** apparently

appa'rire *vi* appear; (*sembrare*) look

appari'scente *a* striking; *pej* gaudy

apparizi'one *nf* apparition

apparta'mento *nm* flat, apartment *Am*. **~ ammobiliato** furnished flat. **~ in multiproprietà** timeshare

appar'tarsi *vr* withdraw

appar'tato *a* secluded

apparte'nente *a* **~ a** belonging to

apparte'nenza *nf* membership

apparte'nere *vi* belong

appassio'nante *a* ⟨*storia, argomento*⟩ exciting

appassio'nare *vt* excite; (*commuovere*) move

appassio'narsi *vr* **~ a** become excited by

appassio'nato *a* passionate; **~ di** (*entusiastico*) fond of

appas'sire *vi* wither

appas'sirsi *vr* fade

appas'sito *a* faded

appel'larsi *vr* **~ a** appeal to

ap'pello *nm* appeal; (*chiamata per nome*) rollcall; (*esami*) exam session; **fare l'~** call the roll

ap'pena *adv* just; (*a fatica*) hardly ● *conj* [**non**] **~** as soon as, no sooner... than; **~ prima di** just before

ap'pendere *vt* hang [up]

appendi'abiti *nm inv* hat-stand, hallstand

appen'dice *nf* appendix; **romanzo d'~** novel serialized in a magazine or newspaper

appendi'cite *nf* appendicitis

Appen'nini *nmpl* **gli ~** the Apennines

appen'ninico *a* Apennine

appesan'tire *vt* weigh down

appesan'tirsi *vr* become heavy

ap'peso *pp di* **appendere** ● *a* hanging; (*impiccato*) hanged

appe'tito *nm* appetite; **aver ~** be hungry; **buon ~!** enjoy your meal!

appeti'toso *a* appetizing; *fig* tempting

appezza'mento *nm* plot of land

appia'nare *vt* level; *fig* smooth over

appia'narsi *vr* improve

appiat'tire *vt* flatten

appiat'tirsi *vr* flatten oneself; *fig* level out

appic'care *vt* **~ fuoco a** set fire to

appicci'care *vt* stick; **~ a** (*fig: appioppare*) palm off on ● *vi* be sticky

appicci'carsi *vr* stick; ⟨*cose:*⟩ stick together; **~ a qcno** *fig* stick to sb like glue

appiccica'ticcio *a* sticky; *fig* clingy

appicci'cato *a* **stare ~ a qcno** be all over sb

appicci'coso *a* sticky; *fig* clingy

appie'dato *a* **sono ~** I don't have the car; **sono rimasto ~** I was stranded

appi'eno *adv* fully

appigli'arsi *vr* **~ a** get hold of; *fig* stick to

ap'piglio *nm* fingerhold; (*per piedi*) foothold; *fig* pretext

appiop'pare *vt* **~ a** palm off on; (*fam: dare*) give; **~ un ceffone a qcno** slap sb

appiso'larsi *vr* doze off

applau'dire *vt/i* applaud

**ap'plauso** *nm* applause

**appli'cabile** *a* applicable

**appli'care** *vt* apply; enforce ⟨*legge ecc*⟩

**appli'carsi** *vr* apply oneself

**appli'cato** *nmf* (*impiegato*) senior clerk ● *a* (*nel ricamo*) appliqué; **matematica applicata** applied mathematics

**applica'tore** *nm* applicator

**applicazi'one** *nf* application; (*di legge*) enforcement. **applicazioni** *pl* **tecniche** handicrafts

**appoggi'are** *vt* lean (**a** against): (*mettere*) put; (*sostenere*) back

**appoggi'arsi** *vr* ~ **a** lean against; *fig* rely on

**appoggi'ato** *a* leaning (**su** on; **contro, a** against)

**ap'poggio** *nm* support; **appoggi** *pl fig* influential contacts

**appollai'arsi** *vr fig* perch

**ap'porre** *vt* affix

**appor'tare** *vt* bring; (*causare*) cause; ~ **delle modifiche a qcsa** modify sth

**ap'porto** *nm* contribution

**apposita'mente** *adv* (*specialmente*) especially; **fatto** ~ purpose-made

**ap'posito** *a* proper

**apposizi'one** *nf* apposition

**ap'posta** *adv* on purpose; (*espressamente*) specially; **neanche a farlo** ~! what a coincidence!

**apposta'mento** *nm* ambush; (*caccia*) lying in wait

**appo'stare** *vt* post ⟨*soldati*⟩

**appo'starsi** *vr* lie in wait

**ap'prendere** *vt* understand; (*imparare*) learn

**apprendi'mento** *nm* learning

**appren'dista** *nmf* apprentice

**apprendi'stato** *nm* apprenticeship

**apprensi'one** *nf* apprehension; **essere in** ~ **per** be anxious about

**appren'sivo** *a* apprehensive

**ap'presso** *adv & prep* (*vicino*) near; (*dietro*) behind; **come** ~ as follows

**appre'stare** *vt* prepare

**appre'starsi** *vr* get ready

**apprez'zabile** *a* appreciable

**apprezza'mento** *nm* appreciation; (*giudizio*) opinion

**apprez'zare** *vt* appreciate

**apprez'zato** *a* appreciated

**ap'proccio** *nm* approach

**appro'dare** *vi* land; ~ **a** *fig* come to; **non** ~ **a nulla** come to nothing

**ap'prodo** *nm* landing; (*luogo*) landing-stage

**approfit'tare** *vi* take advantage (**di** of), profit (**di** by)

**approfitta|'tore, -'trice** *nmf* chancer

**approfondi'mento** *nm* deepening; **di** ~ ⟨*corso*⟩ advanced

**approfon'dire** *vt* broaden, widen ⟨*indagine, conoscenze*⟩

**approfon'dirsi** *vr* ⟨*divario:*⟩ widen

**approfon'dito** *a* ⟨*studio, ricerca*⟩ in-depth

**appron'tare** *vt* get ready, prepare

**appropri'arsi** *vr* ~ **a** (*essere adatto a*) suit; ~ **di** take possession of; ~ **indebitamente di** embezzle, misappropriate

**appropri'ato** *a* appropriate

**appropriazi'one** *nf* Jur appropriation. ~ **indebita** Jur embezzlement

**approssi'mare** *vt* ~ **per eccesso/difetto** round up/down

**approssi'marsi** *vr* draw near

**approssimativa'mente** *adv* approximately

**approssima'tivo** *a* approximate

**approssimazi'one** *nf* approximation

**appro'vare** *vt* approve of; approve ⟨*legge*⟩

**approvazi'one** *nf* approval

**approvvigiona'mento** *nm* supplying; **approvvigionamenti** *pl* provisions

**approvvigio'nare** *vt* supply

**approvvigio'narsi** *vr* stock up

**appunta'mento** *nm* appointment; *fam* date; **fissare un** ~, **prendere un** ~ make an appointment; **darsi** ~ decide to meet

**appun'tare** *vt* (*annotare*) take notes; (*fissare*) fix; (*con spillo*) pin; (*appuntire*) sharpen

**appun'tarsi** *vr* ~ **su** ⟨*teoria:*⟩ be based on

**appun'tato** *nm* (*carabiniere*) lowest rank in the carabinieri

**appuntel'larsi** *vr* (*sostenersi*) support oneself

**appun'tino** *adv* meticulously

**appun'tire** *vt* sharpen

**appun'tito** *a* ⟨*matita*⟩ sharp; ⟨*mento*⟩ pointed

**ap'punto¹** *nm* note; (*piccola critica*) niggle

**ap'punto²** *adv* exactly; **per l'**~! exactly!; **stavo** ~ **dicendo...** I was just saying...

**appura'mento** *nm* verification

**appu'rare** *vt* verify

**a'pribile** *a* that can be opened; **tettuccio** ~ Auto sun roof

**apribot'tiglie** *nm inv* bottle-opener

**a'prile** *nm* April; **primo d'**~ April Fool's Day

**aprio'ristico** *a* a priori

**a'prire** *vt* open; turn on ⟨*luce, acqua ecc*⟩; (*con chiave*) unlock; open up ⟨*ferita ecc*⟩; ~ **le ostilità** Mil commence hostilities; **apriti cielo!** heavens above!

**a'prirsi** *vr* open; (*spaccarsi*) split; (*confidarsi*) confide (**con** in)

**apri'scatole** *nf inv* tin opener Br, can opener

**APT** *abbr* (**Azienda di Promozione Turistica**) Tourist Board

**aqua'planing** *nm* **andare in** ~ aquaplane

**'aquila** *nf* eagle; **non è un'** ~! *fig* he's no genius!

**aqui'lino** *a* aquiline

**aqui'lone** *nm* (*giocattolo*) kite

**aqui'lotto** *nm* (*piccolo dell'aquila*) eaglet

**AR** *abbr* (**andata e ritorno**) return [ticket];

*abbr* (**avviso di ricevimento**) return receipt for registered letters

**ara'besco** *nm* arabesque; *hum* scribble

**A'rabia** *nf* Arabia. **l'~ Saudita** Saudi Arabia

**'arabo, -a** *a* Arab; ⟨*lingua*⟩ Arabic ● *nmf* Arab ● *nm* (*lingua*) Arabic

**arabo-israeli'ano** *a* Arab-Israeli

**a'rachide** *nf* peanut

**arago'nese** *a* Aragonese

**ara'gosta** *nf* lobster

**a'raldica** *nf* heraldry

**a'raldico** *nm* herald ● *a* heraldic

**aran'ceto** *nm* orange grove

**a'rancia** *nf* orange; **succo d'~** orange juice

**aranci'ata** *nf* orangeade

**a'rancio** *nm* orange-tree; (*colore*) orange

**aranci'one** *a & nm* orange

**a'rare** *vt* plough

**ara'tore** *nm* ploughman

**a'ratro** *nm* plough

**ara'tura** *nf* ploughing

**a'razzo** *nm* tapestry

**arbi'traggio** *nm Comm* arbitrage; *Sport* refereeing; *Jur* arbitration

**arbi'trare** *vt* arbitrate in; *Sport* referee

**arbitrarietà** *nf* arbitrariness

**arbi'trario** *a* arbitrary

**arbi'trato** *nm* arbitration

**ar'bitrio** *nm* will: **è un ~** it's very high-handed

**'arbitro** *nm* arbiter; *Sport* referee; (*nel baseball*) umpire

**arboricol'tura** *nf* arboriculture

**ar'busto** *nm* shrub

**'arca** *nf* ark; (*cassa*) chest. **l'~ di Noè** Noah's Ark

**ar'caico** *a* archaic

**arca'ismo** *nm* archaism

**ar'cangelo** *nm* archangel

**ar'cano** *a* mysterious ● *nm* mystery

**ar'cata** *nf* arch; (*serie di archi*) arcade

**archeolo'gia** *nf* archaeology

**archeo'logico** *a* archaeological

**arche'ologo, -a** *nmf* archaeologist

**ar'chetipo** *nm* archetype

**ar'chetto** *nm Mus* bow

**architet'tare** *vt fig* devise; **cosa state architettando?** *fig* what are you plotting?

**archi'tetto** *nm* architect. **~ d'interni** interior designer

**architet'tonico** *a* architectural

**architet'tura** *nf anche Comput* architecture

**archi'trave** *nm* lintel

**archivi'abile** *a* that can be filed

**archivi'are** *vt* file; *Jur* close

**archiviazi'one** *nf* filing; (*Jur: di caso*) closing. **~ dati** data storage

**ar'chivio** *nm* archives *pl*; *Comput* file

**archi'vista** *nmf* filing clerk

**archi'vistica** *nf rules governing the keeping of archives and records*

**ARCI** *nf abbr* (**Associazione Ricreativa Culturale Italiana**) *Italian cultural and leisure association*

**arci'duca** *nm* archduke

**arcidu'chessa** *nf* archduchess

**arci'ere** *nm* archer

**ar'cigno** *a* grim

**arci'one** *nm* saddle

**arci'pelago** *nm* archipelago

**arci'vescovo** *nm* archbishop

**'arco** *nm* arch; *Math* arc; (*arma, Mus*) bow; **nell'~ di una giornata/due mesi** in the space of a day/two months. **~ rampante** flying buttress

**arcoba'leno** *nm* rainbow

**arcu'are** *vt* bend: **~ la schiena** ⟨*gatto:*⟩ arch its back

**arcu'arsi** *vr* bend

**arcu'ato** *a* bent; ⟨*schiena di gatto*⟩ arched

**ar'dente** *a* burning; *fig* ardent; **camera ~** chapel of rest

**ardente'mente** *adv* ardently

**'ardere** *vt/i* burn; **legna da ~** fire-wood

**ar'desia** *nf* slate

**ardi'mento** *nm* boldness

**ar'dire** *vi* dare ● *nm* (*coraggio*) daring, boldness; (*sfrontatezza*) impudence

**ar'dito** *a* daring; (*coraggioso*) bold; (*sfacciato*) impudent

**ar'dore** *nm* (*calore*) heat; *fig* ardour

**'arduo** *a* arduous; (*ripido*) steep

**'area** *nf* area; (*superficie*) surface. **~ fabbricabile** building land. **~ di rigore** (*in calcio*) penalty area, penalty box. **~ di servizio** service area

**a'rena** *nf* arena

**are'naria** *nf* sandstone

**are'narsi** *vr* run aground; ⟨*fig: trattative*⟩ reach deadlock; **mi sono arenato** I'm stuck

**are'nile** *nm* stretch of sand

**areo'plano** *nm* aeroplane

**'argano** *nm* winch

**argen'tato** *a* silver-plated

**ar'genteo** *a* silvery

**argente'ria** *nf* silver[ware]

**argenti'ere** *nm* silversmith

**Argen'tina** *nf* Argentina

**argen'tina** *nf* (*maglia*) round-necked pullover

**argen'tino** *a* silvery

**argen'tino, -a** *a & nmf* Argentinian

**ar'gento** *nm* silver; **d'~** silver. **~ vivo** *Chem* quicksilver

**ar'gilla** *nf* clay

**argil'loso** *a* ⟨*terreno*⟩ clayey; (*simile all'argilla*) clay-like

**argi'nare** *vt* embank; *fig* hold in check, contain

**'argine** *nm* embankment; (*diga*) dike; **fare ~ a** *fig* hold in check, contain

**argomen'tare** *vi* argue

**argo'mento** *nm* argument; (*motivo*) reason; (*soggetto*) subject

**argu'ire** *vt* deduce

**arguta'mente** *adv* (*con astuzia*) shrewdly; (*con facezia*) wittily

**ar'guto** *a* witty; (*astuto*) shrewd

**ar'guzia** *nf* wit; (*battuta*) witticism; (*astuzia*) shrewdness '**aria** *nf* air; *(aspetto)* appearance; *Mus* tune; **avere l'~...** look...; **corrente d'~** draught; **mandare all'~ qcsa** *fig* ruin sth; **andare all'~** *fig* fall through; **a tenuta d'~** draughtproof; **avere la testa per ~** *fig* be absent-minded, have one's head in the clouds; **che ~ tirava?** *fig* what was the atmosphere like?; **cambiare ~** *fig* have a change of scene; **cambia ~!** *hum* get out of here!. **~-~** *a inv Mil* air-to-air. **~ conditionata** air-conditioning. **~-terra** *a inv* air-to-ground

**ari'ano** *a* Aryan

**arida'mente** *adv* without emotion

**aridità** *nf* aridity

'**arido** *a* arid

**arieggi'are** *vt* air; **~ una stanza** give a room an airing

**arieggi'ato** *a* airy

**ari'ete** *nm* ram; *(strumento)* battering-ram; **A~** *Astr* Aries

**ari'etta** *nf* *(brezza)* breeze

**a'ringa** *nf* herring

**ari'oso** *a* ⟨*locale:*⟩ light and airy

'**arista** *nf* chine of pork

**aristo'cratico, -a** *a* aristocratic ● *nmf* aristocrat

**aristocra'zia** *nf* aristocracy

**arit'metica** *nf* arithmetic

**arit'metico** *a* arithmetical

**arlec'chino** *nm* Harlequin; *fig* buffoon

'**arma** *nf* weapon; *(forze armate)* [armed] forces; **armi** *pl* arms; **chiamare alle armi** call up; **sotto le armi** in the army; **alle prime armi** *fig* inexperienced, fledg[e]ling; **prendere/deporre le armi** take up arms/ put down one's arms; **passare qcno per le armi** execute sb; **confrontarsi ad armi pari** compete on an equal footing. **~ bianca** knife. **~ a doppio taglio** *fig* double-edged sword. **~ da fuoco** firearm. **~ impropria** makeshift weapon. **armi** *pl* **nucleari** nuclear weapons

**armadi'etto** *nm* locker, cupboard; *(in aereo)* overhead locker. **~ del bagno** bathroom cabinet. **~ dei medicinali** medicine cabinet

**arma'dillo** *nm* armadillo

**ar'madio** *nm* cupboard; *(guardaroba)* wardrobe. **~ a muro** fitted cupboard

**armamen'tario** *nm* tools *pl*; *fig* paraphernalia

**arma'mento** *nm* armament; *Naut* fitting out

**ar'mare** *vt* arm; *(equipaggiare)* fit out; *Archit* reinforce

**ar'marsi** *vr* arm oneself (**di** with)

**ar'mata** *nf* army; *(flotta)* fleet

**ar'mato** *a* armed; **rapina a mano armata** armed robbery

**arma'tore** *nm* shipowner

**arma'tura** *nf* framework; *(impalcatura)* scaffolding; *(di guerriero)* armour

**armeggi'are** *vi fig* manoeuvre

**Ar'menia** *nf* Armenia

**ar'meno, -a** *a & nmf* Armenian

**arme'ria** *nf Mil* armoury

**armi'stizio** *nm* armistice

**armo'nia** *nf* harmony

**ar'monica** *nf* **~ [a bocca]** mouth-organ

**ar'monico** *a* harmonic

**armoniosa'mente** *adv* harmoniously

**armoni'oso** *a* harmonious

**armoniz'zare** *vt* harmonize ● *vi* match

**armoniz'zarsi** *vr* ⟨*colori:*⟩ go together, match

**ar'nese** *nm* tool; *(oggetto)* thing; *(congegno)* gadget; **male in ~** in bad condition

'**arnia** *nf* beehive

**a'roma** *nm* aroma; **aromi** *pl* herbs; **aromi** *pl* **naturali/artificiali** natural/artificial flavourings

**aromatera'pia** *nf* aromatherapy

**aro'matico** *a* aromatic

**aromatiz'zare** *vt* flavour

'**arpa** *nf* harp

**ar'peggio** *nm* arpeggio

**ar'pia** *nf* harpy

**arpi'one** *nm* hook; *(pesca)* harpoon

**ar'pista** *nmf* harpist

**arrabat'tarsi** *vr* do all one can

**arrabbi'arsi** *vr* get angry

**arrabbi'ato** *a* angry

**arrabbia'tura** *nf* rage; **prendersi un'~** fly into a rage

**arraf'fare** *vt* grab

**arraf'fone** *nmf fam* thief

**arrampi'carsi** *vr* climb [up]; **~ sugli specchi** *fig* clutch at straws

**arrampi'cata** *nf* climb

**arrampica'tore, -'trice** *nmf* climber. **~ sociale** social climber

**arran'care** *vi* limp, hobble; *fig* struggle, limp along

**arrangia'mento** *nm* arrangement

**arrangi'are** *vt* arrange

**arrangi'arsi** *vr* manage; **~ alla meglio** get by; **ar'rangiati!** get on with it!

**arrangia'tore, -'trice** *nmf Mus* arranger

**arra'parsi** *vr vulg* get randy

**arre'care** *vt* bring; *(causare)* cause

**arreda'mento** *nm* interior decoration; *(l'arredare)* furnishing; *(mobili ecc)* furnishings *pl*

**arre'dare** *vt* furnish

**arreda'tore, -'trice** *nmf* interior designer

**ar'redo** *nm* furnishings *pl*

**arrem'baggio** *nm* **buttarsi all'~** *fig* stampede

**ar'rendersi** *vr* surrender; **~ all'evidenza dei fatti** face facts

**arren'devole** *a* ⟨*persona*⟩ yielding

**arrendevo'lezza** *nf* softness

**arre'stare** *vt* arrest; *(fermare)* stop

**arre'starsi** *vr* halt

**ar'resto** *nm* stop; *Jur* arrest; **la dichiaro in [stato d']~** you are under arrest; **mandato di ~** warrant. **~ cardiaco** heart failure, cardiac arrest. **arresti** *pl* **domiciliari** *Jur* house arrest

**arretra'mento** *nm* withdrawal

**arre'trare** *vt* withdraw: pull back ⟨*giocatore*⟩ ● *vi* withdraw

**arre'trato** *a* ⟨*paese ecc*⟩ backward: ⟨*Mil: posizione*⟩ rear: **numero ~** ⟨*di rivista*⟩ back number: **del lavoro ~** a backlog of work ● *nm* ⟨*di stipendio*⟩ back pay; **essere in ~** be behind schedule; **arretrati** *pl* arrears. **arretrati** *pl* **di paga** back pay

**arricchi'mento** *nm* enrichment

**arric'chire** *vt* enrich

**arric'chirsi** *vr* get rich

**arric'chito, -a** *nmf* nouveau riche

**arricciaca'pelli** *nm inv* tongs

**arricci'are** *vt* curl; **~ il naso** turn up one's nose

**ar'ridere** *vi* **~ a qcno** ⟨*sorte:*⟩ smile on sb

**ar'ringa** *nf* Jur closing address

**arrin'gare** *vt* harangue

**arrischi'arsi** *vr* dare

**arrischi'ato** *a* risky; ⟨*imprudente*⟩ rash

**arri'vare** *vi* arrive; **~ a** ⟨*raggiungere*⟩ reach; ⟨*ridursi*⟩ be reduced to

**arri'vato, -a** *a* successful: **il primo/ secondo ~** ⟨*in gare*⟩: **ben ~!** welcome! ● *nmf* successful person

**arrive'derci** *int* goodbye; **~ a domani** see you tomorrow

**arri'vismo** *nm* social climbing; ⟨*nel lavoro*⟩ careerism

**arri'vista** *nmf* social climber; ⟨*nel lavoro*⟩ careerist

**ar'rivo** *nm* arrival; *Sport* finish; **~ previsto per le ore...** expected time of arrival...

**arro'gante** *a* arrogant

**arro'ganza** *nf* arrogance

**arro'garsi** *vr* **~ il diritto di fare qcsa** take it upon oneself to do sth; **~ il merito** take the credit

**arrossa'mento** *nm* reddening

**arros'sare** *vt* make red, redden ⟨*occhi*⟩

**arros'sarsi** *vr* go red

**arros'sire** *vi* blush, go red

**arro'stire** *vt* roast; toast ⟨*pane*⟩; ⟨*ai ferri*⟩ grill

**arro'stirsi** *vr fig* broil

**ar'rosto** *a & nm* roast; **molto fumo e niente ~** *fig* all show and no substance. **~ d'agnello** roast lamb

**arro'tare** *vt* sharpen; ⟨*fam: investire*⟩ run over

**arro'tino** *nm* knife-sharpener

**arroto'lare** *vt* roll up

**arroton'dare** *vt* round; *Math ecc* round off; **~ lo stipendio** supplement one's income

**arroton'darsi** *vr* become round; ⟨*persona:*⟩ get plump

**arrovel'larsi** *vr* **~ il cervello** rack one's brains

**arroven'tare** *vt* make red-hot

**arroven'tarsi** *vr* become red-hot

**arroven'tato** *a* red-hot; ⟨*fig: discorso*⟩ fiery

**arruf'fare** *vt* ruffle; *fig* confuse

**arruf'farsi** *vr* become ruffled

**arruf'fato** *a* ⟨*capelli*⟩ dishevelled

**arruffia'narsi** *vr* **~ [con] qcno** *fig* butter sb up

**arruggi'nire** *vt* rust

**arruggi'nirsi** *vr* go rusty; *fig* ⟨*fisicamente*⟩ stiffen up; ⟨*conoscenze:*⟩ go rusty

**arruggi'nito** *a* rusty

**arruola'mento** *nm* enlistment

**arruo'lare** *vt/i* enlist

**arruo'larsi** *vr* enlist

**arse'nale** *nm* arsenal; ⟨*cantiere*⟩ [naval] dockyard

**ar'senico** *nm* arsenic

**'arso** *pp di* ardere ● *a* burnt; ⟨*arido*⟩ dry

**ar'sura** *nf* burning heat: ⟨*sete*⟩ parching thirst

**art déco** *nf* art deco

**'arte** *nf* art; ⟨*abilità*⟩ craftsmanship; **senza ~ né parte** incapable; **nome d'~** professional name. **~ drammatica** dramatics. **le belle arti** *pl* the fine arts. **arti** *pl* figurative figurative arts. **arti** *pl* **dello spettacolo** performing arts

**arte'fare** *vt* adulterate ⟨*vino*⟩; disguise ⟨*voce*⟩

**arte'fatto** *a* fake; ⟨*vino*⟩ adulterated

**ar'tefice** *nm* craftsman; *fig* author ● *nf* craftswoman

**ar'teria** *nf* artery. **~ [stradale]** arterial road

**arterio'sclerosi** *nf* arteriosclerosis, hardening of the arteries

**arterioscle'rotico** *a* senile

**arteri'oso** *a* Anat arterial

**'Artico** *nm* **l'~** the Arctic

**'artico** *a* Arctic

**artico'lare** *a* articular ● *vt* articulate; ⟨*suddividere*⟩ divide

**artico'larsi** *vr fig* **~ in** consist of

**artico'lato** *a* Auto articulated; *fig* well-constructed

**articolazi'one** *nf* Anat articulation

**ar'ticolo** *nm* article. **articoli** *pl* **per la casa** household goods. **~ civetta** Comm loss leader. **articoli** *pl* **per la cucina** kitchenware. **~ determinativo** Gram definite article. **~ di fondo** leader, leading article. **~ indeterminativo** Gram indefinite article. **articoli** *pl* **di marca** brand name goods. **~ di prima pagina** Journ cover story. **articoli** *pl* **da regalo** gifts. **articoli** *pl* **da spiaggia** things for the beach. **articoli** *pl* **sportivi** sports gear; **negozio di ~ ~** sports shop

**'Artide** *nf* **l'~** the Arctic [region]

**artifici'ale** *a* artificial

**artifici'ere** *nm* Mil explosives expert, bomb disposal expert

**arti'ficio** *nm* artifice; ⟨*affettazione*⟩ affectation

**artificiosità** *nf* artificiality

**artifici'oso** *a* artful; ⟨*affettato*⟩ affected

**artigi'ana** *nf* craftswoman

**artigia'nale** *a* made by hand; *hum* amateurish

**artigianal'mente** *adv* with craftsmanship; *hum* amateurishly

**artigia'nato** *nm* craftsmanship; *(ceto)* craftsmen *pl*

**artigi'ano** *nm* craftsman

**artigli'ato** *a* with claws

**artigli'ere** *nm* artilleryman

**artiglie'ria** *nf* artillery. **~ antiaerea** flak

**ar'tiglio** *nm* claw; *fig* clutch; **sfoderare gli artigli** *fig* show one's claws

**ar'tista** *nmf* artist

**artistica'mente** *adv* artistically

**ar'tistico** *a* artistic

**arti'stoide** *a* arty

**art nouveau** *nf* art nouveau

**'arto** *nm* limb

**ar'trite** *nf* arthritis

**ar'tritico, -a** *nmf* arthritic

**ar'trosi** *nf* rheumatism

**arzigogo'lato** *a* fantastic, bizarre

**ar'zillo** *a* sprightly

**a'scella** *nf* armpit

**ascen'dente** *a* ascending ● *nm* *(antenato)* ancestor; *(influenza)* ascendancy; *Astr* ascendant

**ascen'denza** *nf* ancestry

**a'scendere** *vi* ascend

**ascensi'one** *nf* ascent; **l'A~** the Ascension

**ascen'sore** *nm* lift, elevator *Am*

**a'scesa** *nf* ascent; *(al trono)* accession; *(al potere)* rise

**a'scesi** *nf* asceticism

**a'scesso** *nm* abscess

**a'sceta** *nmf* ascetic

**a'scetico** *a* ascetic

**'ascia** *nf* axe

**asciugabianche'ria** *nm inv* *(stenditoio)* clothes horse; *(macchina)* tumble dryer

**asciuga'pelli** *nm inv* hair dryer, hairdrier

**asciuga'mano** *nm* towel. **~ di carta** paper towel

**asciu'gare** *vt* dry; **~ le stoviglie** do the drying-up

**asciu'garsi** *vr* dry oneself; *(diventare asciutto)* dry up; **~ le mani** dry one's hands

**asciuga'trice** *nf* tumble dryer

**asci'utto** *a* dry; *(magro)* wiry; *(risposta)* curt; **essere all'~** *fig* be hard up

**ascol'tare** *vt* listen to ● *vi* listen

**ascolta|'tore, -'trice** *nmf* listener

**a'scolto** *nm* listening; **dare ~ a** listen to; **essere in ~** *Radio* be listening; **mettersi in ~** *Radio* tune in; **prestare ~** listen

**a'scrivere** *vt* *(attribuire)* ascribe; **~ a** *(annoverare)* number among

**asessu'ato** *a* asexual

**a'settico** *a* aseptic

**asfal'tare** *vt* asphalt

**asfal'tato** *a* tarmac

**a'sfalto** *nm* asphalt

**asfis'sia** *nf* asphyxia

**asfissi'ante** *a* *(caldo)* oppressive; *(fig: persona)* annoying

**asfissi'are** *vt* asphyxiate; *fig* annoy

**'Asia** *nf* Asia. **~ Minore** Asia Minor

**asi'ago** *nm* *full-fat white cheese*

**asi'atico, -a** *a & nmf* Asian

**a'silo** *nm* shelter; *(d'infanzia)* nursery school. **~ infantile** day nursery. **~ nido** day nursery. **~ politico** political asylum

**asim'metrico** *a* asymmetric[al]

**a'sincrono** *a* asynchronous

**'asino** *nm* donkey; *(fig: persona stupida)* ass; *Sch* dunce; **qui casca l'~!** *fig* that's where it falls down!

**'asma** *nf* asthma

**a'smatico** *a* asthmatic

**asoci'ale** *a* asocial

**'asola** *nf* buttonhole

**a'sparagi** *nmpl* asparagus *sg*

**aspara'gina** *nf* *Bot* asparagus fern

**a'sparago** *nm* asparagus

**a'spergere** *vt* **~ con/di** sprinkle with

**asperità** *nf inv* harshness; *(di terreno)* roughness

**asper'sorio** *nm* aspergillum, holy-water sprinkler

**aspet'tare** *vt* wait for; *(prevedere)* expect; **~ un bambino** be expecting [a baby]; **fare ~ qcno** keep sb waiting ● *vi* wait

**aspet'tarsi** *vr* expect

**aspet'tativa** *nf* expectation; *(nel lavoro)* leave of absence; **all'altezza delle aspettative** up to expectations; **inferiore alle aspettative** not up to expectations. **~ per malattia** sick leave. **~ per maternità** maternity leave

**a'spetto**[1] *nm* look; *(di problema)* aspect; **di bell'~** good-looking

**a'spetto**[2] *nm* **sala d'~** waiting room

**aspi'rante** *a* aspiring; *(pompa)* suction attrib ● *nmf* *(a un posto)* applicant; *(al trono)* aspirant; **gli aspiranti al titolo** the contenders for the title

**aspira'polvere** *nm inv* vacuum cleaner; **passare l'~** vacuum, hoover

**aspi'rare** *vt* inhale; *Mech* suck in; *(con elettrodomestici)* vacuum, hoover ● *vi* **~ a** aspire to

**aspi'rato** *a* aspirate

**aspira'tore** *nm* extractor fan

**aspirazi'one** *nf* inhalation; *Mech* suction; *(ambizione)* ambition

**aspi'rina** *nf* aspirin

**aspor'tare** *vt* take away

**aspra'mente** *adv* *(duramente)* severely

**a'sprezza** *nf* *(al gusto)* sourness; *(di clima)* severity; *(di carattere, parole, suono)* harshness; *(di odore)* pungency; *(di litigio)* bitterness

**a'sprigno** *a* slightly sour

**'aspro** *a* *(al gusto)* sour; *(clima)* severe; *(suono, parole)* harsh; *(odore)* pungent; *(litigio)* bitter

**assaggi'are** *vt* taste

**assaggia|'tore, -'trice** *nmf* taster

**assag'gini** *nmpl* *Culin* samples

**as'saggio** *nm* tasting; *(piccola quantità)* taste; *(fig: campione)* sample

**as'sai** *adv* very; *(moltissimo)* very much; *(abbastanza)* enough

**assa'lire** *vt* attack

**assali|'tore, -'trice** *nmf* assailant

**assal'tare** *vt Mil* attack, charge; hold up ‹*banca, treno*›

**assalta'tore** *nm* hold-up man

**as'salto** *nm* attack; **d'~** ‹*giornalismo*› aggressive; **prendere d'~** storm ‹*città*›: *fig* mob ‹*persona*›; hold up ‹*banca*›

**assapo'rare** *vt* savour

**assas'sina** *nf* murderess

**assassi'nare** *vt* murder, assassinate: *fig* murder

**assas'sinio** *nm* murder, assassination

**assas'sino** *a* murderous ● *nm* murderer

**'asse** *nf* board ● *nm Techn* axle; *Math* axis. **~ da stiro** ironing board

**assecon'dare** *vt* satisfy; (*favorire*) support; **~ i capricci di qcno** indulge sb's every whim; **~ i desideri di qcno** comply with sb's wishes

**assedi'are** *vt* besiege

**assedi'ato** *a* besieged

**as'sedio** *nm* siege

**assegna'mento** *nm* allotment; **fare ~ su** rely on

**asse'gnare** *vt* allot; award ‹*premio*›

**assegna'tario, -a** *nmf* recipient

**assegnazi'one** *nf* (*di alloggio, denaro, borsa di studio*) allocation; (*di premio*) award

**as'segno** *nm* allowance; (*bancario*) cheque; **contro ~** cash on delivery; **pagare con un ~** pay by cheque. **~ circolare** bank draft. **assegni** *pl* **familiari** family allowance, child benefit. **~ post-datato** post-dated cheque. **~ sbarrato** crossed cheque. **~ non trasferibile** cheque made out to "account payee only". **~ turistico** traveller's cheque. **~ a vuoto** bad cheque, dud cheque

**assem'blaggio** *nm* assemblage

**assem'blare** *vt* assemble

**assem'blea** *nf* assembly; (*adunanza*) gathering. **~ generale annuale** Annual General Meeting, AGM

**assembra'mento** *nm* gathering

**assem'brare** *vt* gather

**assen'nato** *a* sensible

**as'senso** *nm* assent

**assen'tarsi** *vr* go away; (*da stanza*) leave the room

**as'sente** *a* absent; (*distratto*) absent-minded ● *nmf* absentee

**assente'ismo** *nm* absenteeism

**assente'ista** *nmf* frequent absentee

**assen'tire** *vi* acquiesce (**a** in)

**as'senza** *nf* absence; (*mancanza*) lack. **~ di gravità** zero gravity

**asse'rire** *vt* assert

**asserragli'arsi** *vr* barricade oneself

**asser'tivo** *a* assertive

**asser|'tore, -'trice** *nmf* supporter

**asservi'mento** *nm* subservience

**asser'vire** *vt fig* enslave

**asser'virsi** *vr fig* be subservient

**asserzi'one** *nf* assertion

**assesso'rato** *nm* [council] department

**asses'sore** *nm* councillor

**assesta'mento** *nm* settlement

**asse'stare** *vt* arrange; **~ un colpo** deal a blow

**asse'starsi** *vr* settle oneself

**asse'stato** *a* **ben ~** well-judged

**asse'tato** *a* parched

**as'setto** *nm* order; *Naut, Aeron* trim; **in ~ di guerra** on a war footing; **cambiare l'~ territoriale dell'Europa** change the map of Europe

**assi'cella** *nf* lath

**assicu'rabile** *a* insurable

**assicu'rare** *vt* assure; *Comm* insure; register ‹*posta*›; (*fissare*) secure; (*accertare*) ensure

**assicu'rarsi** *vr* (*con contratto*) insure oneself; (*legarsi*) fasten oneself; **~ che** make sure that

**assicu'rata** *nf* registered letter

**assicura'tivo** *a* insurance *attrib*

**assicu'rato** *a* insured; **lettera assicurata** registered letter

**assicura|'tore, -'trice** *nmf* insurance agent ● *a* insurance; **società assicuratrice** insurance company

**assicurazi'one** *nf* assurance; (*contratto*) insurance; **fare un'~** take out insurance. **~ multirischi** blanket cover. **~ sanitaria** medical insurance. **~ di viaggio** travel insurance

**assidera'mento** *nm* exposure

**asside'rarsi** *vr fam* be frozen; *Med* be suffering from exposure

**asside'rato** *a Med* suffering from exposure; *fam* frozen

**assidua'mente** *adv* assiduously

**assidu'ità** *nf* assiduity

**as'siduo** *a* assiduous; ‹*cliente*› regular

**assi'eme** *a* [together] with

**assil'lante** *a* ‹*persona, pensiero*› nagging

**assil'lare** *vt* pester

**assil'larsi** *vr* torment oneself

**as'sillo** *nm* worry

**assimi'lare** *vt* assimilate

**assimilazi'one** *nf* assimilation

**assi'oma** *nm* axiom

**assio'matico** *a* axiomatic

**As'siria** *nf* Assyria

**as'sise** *nfpl* assizes; **Corte d'A~** Court of Assize[s]

**assi'stente** *nmf* assistant. **~ sociale** social worker. **~ universitario** assistant lecturer. **~ di volo** flight attendant

**assi'stenza** *nf* assistance; (*presenza*) presence. **~ medica** medical care. **~ ospedaliera** hospital treatment. **~ sanitaria** health care. **~ sociale** social work

**assistenzi'ale** *a* welfare

**assistenzia'lismo** *nm* abuse of the welfare state

**as'sistere** *vt* assist; (*curare*) nurse ● *vi* **~ a** (*essere presente*) be present at; watch ‹*spettacolo ecc*›

**assi'stito** *a* **~ da computer** computer-aided

**'asso** *nm* ace; **piantare in ~** leave in the lurch. **~ nella manica** trump card

**associ'are** *vt* join; (*collegare*) associate

**associ'arsi** *vr* join forces; *Comm* enter into partnership. **~ a** join; subscribe to (*giornale ecc*)

**associ'ato, -a** *a* associate ● *nmf* partner

**associazi'one** *nf* association. **~ di categoria** trade-union. **~ per delinquere** criminal organization. **A~ Europea di Libero Scambio** European Free Trade Association. **~ in partecipazione** *Comm* joint venture

**associazio'nismo** *nm* *Pol* excessive tendency to form associations; *Psych* associationism

**asso'dare** *vt* ascertain (*verità*)

**assogget'tare** *vt* subject

**assogget'tarsi** *vr* submit

**asso'lato** *a* sunny

**assol'dare** *vt* recruit

**as'solo** *nm Mus* solo

**as'solto** *pp di* **assolvere**

**assoluta'mente** *adv* absolutely

**assolu'tismo** *nm* absolutism

**assolu'tista** *nmf* absolutist

**assolu'tistico** *a* absolutist

**asso'luto** *a* absolute

**assolu'torio** *a* **formula assolutoria** acquittal

**assoluzi'one** *nf* acquittal; *Relig* absolution

**as'solvere** *vt* perform (*compito*); *Jur* acquit; *Relig* absolve

**assolvi'mento** *nm* performance

**assomigli'are** *vi* **~ a** be like, resemble

**assomigli'arsi** *vr* resemble each other

**assom'marsi** *vr* combine; **~ a qcsa** add to sth

**asso'nanza** *nf* assonance

**asson'nato** *a* drowsy

**asso'pirsi** *vr* doze off

**assor'bente** *a & nm* absorbent. **~ igienico** sanitary towel

**assor'bire** *vt* absorb

**assor'dante** *a* deafening

**assor'dare** *vt* deafen

**assorti'mento** *nm* assortment

**assor'tire** *vt* match (*colori*)

**assor'tito** *a* assorted; (*colori, persone*) matched

**as'sorto** *a* engrossed

**assottiglia'mento** *nm* thinning; (*aguzzamento*) sharpening

**assottigli'are** *vt* make thin; (*aguzzare*) sharpen; (*ridurre*) reduce

**assottigli'arsi** *vr* grow thin; (*finanze:*) be whittled away

**assue'fare** *vt* accustom

**assue'farsi** *vr* **~ a** get used to

**assue'fatto** *a* (*a caffè, aspirina*) immune to the effects; (*a droga*) addicted

**assuefazi'one** *nf* (*a caffè, aspirina*) immunity to the effects; (*a droga*) addiction

**as'sumere** *vt* assume; take on (*impiegato*); **~ informazioni** make inquiries

**as'sunto** *pp di* **assumere** ● *nm* task

**assunzi'one** *nf* (*di impiegato*) employment; **l'A~** Assumption

**assurdità** *nf inv* absurdity; **dire delle ~** talk nonsense

**as'surdo** *a* absurd

**'asta** *nf* pole; *Mech* bar; *Comm* auction; **a mezz'~** at half-mast. **~ di livello** [**dell'olio**] *Auto* dip-stick

**a'stemio** *a* abstemious

**aste'nersi** *vr* abstain (**da** from)

**astensi'one** *nf* abstention

**astensio'nismo** *nm* persistent abstention

**astensio'nista** *nmf* persistent abstainer

**astensio'nistico** *a* **tendenza astensionistica** tendency to abstain

**aste'nuto, -a** *nmf* abstainer

**aste'risco** *nm* asterisk

**aste'roide** *nm* asteroid

**'astice** *nm* crayfish

**asti'cella** *nf* stick; (*in salto in alto*) bar

**astig'matico** *a* astigmatic

**astigma'tismo** *nm* astigmatism

**asti'nenza** *nf* abstinence; **crisi di ~** withdrawal symptoms

**'astio** *nm* rancour; **avere ~ contro qcno** bear sb a grudge

**asti'oso** *a* resentful

**a'stragalo** *nm* anklebone

**'astrakan** *nm* astrakhan

**astrat'tezza** *nf* abstractness

**astrat'tismo** *nm* abstractionism

**a'stratto** *a* abstract

**astrin'gente** *a & nm* astringent

**'astro** *nm* star

**+astro** *suff* **giovinastro** *nm* lout; **giallastro** *a* yellowish; **dolciastro** *a* sweetish; **fattaccio** *nm hum* foul deed

**astro'fisica** *nf* astrophysics

**astro'fisico, -a** *a* astrophysical ● *nmf* astrophysicist

**astrolo'gia** *nf* astrology

**astro'logico** *a* astrological

**a'strologo, -a** *nmf* astrologer

**astro'nauta** *nmf* astronaut

**astro'nautica** *nf* astronautics

**astro'nave** *nf* spaceship

**astrono'mia** *nf* astronomy

**astro'nomico** *a* (*anche fig*) astronomic, astronomical

**a'stronomo** *nm* astronomer

**astrusità** *nf* abstruseness

**a'struso** *a* abstruse

**a'stuccio** *nm* case

**a'stuto** *a* shrewd; (*furbo*) cunning

**a'stuzia** *nf* shrewdness; (*azione*) trick

**a'tavico** *a* atavistic

**ate'ismo** *nm* atheism

**ate'lier** *nm inv* (*di alta moda*) atelier; (*di artista*) [artist's] studio

**A'tene** *nf* Athens

**ate'neo** *nm* university

**ateni'ese** *a & nmf* Athenian

**'ateo, -a** *a & nmf* atheist

**a'tipico** *a* atypical

at'lante *nm* atlas: **i monti dell'A~** the Atlas Mountains

at'lantico *a* Atlantic; **l'[Oceano] A~** the Atlantic [Ocean]

at'leta *nmf* athlete

a'tletica *nf* athletics *sg.* **~ leggera** track and field events. **~ pesante** *weight-lifting, boxing, wrestling, etc*

a'tletico *a* athletic

atle'tismo *nm* athleticism

atmo'sfera *nf* atmosphere

atmo'sferico *a* atmospheric

a'tollo *nm* atoll

a'tomica *nf* atom bomb

a'tomico *a* atomic

atomiz'zare *vt* atomize

atomizza'tore *nm* atomizer

'atomo *nm* atom

'atono *a* unstressed

'atrio *nm* entrance hall, lobby

a'troce *a* atrocious; (*terrible*) dreadful

atroce'mente *adv* atrociously

atrocità *nf inv* atrocity

atro'fia *nf* atrophy

atrofiz'zare *vt* atrophy

atrofiz'zarsi *vr Med, fig* atrophy

attac'cabile *a* attachable

attaccabot'toni *nmf inv* [crashing] bore

attacca'brighe *nmf inv* troublemaker

attacca'mento *nm* attachment

attac'cante *a* attacking ● *nm Sport* forward

attacca'panni *nm inv* [coat-]hanger; (*a muro*) [clothes-]hook

attac'care *vt* attach; (*legare*) tie; (*appendere*) hang; (*cucire*) sew on; (*contagiare*) pass on; (*assalire*) attack; (*iniziare*) start ● *vi* stick; (*diffondersi*) catch on

attac'carsi *vr* cling; (*affezionarsi*) become attached; (*litigare*) quarrel

attacca'ticcio *a* sticky; *fig* clinging and tiresome

attac'cato *a* stuck

attacca'tura *nf* junction. **~ dei capelli** hairline

attac'chino *nm* billposter

at'tacco *nm* attack; (*punto d'unione*) junction; (*accesso*) fit. **~ cardiaco** heart attack. **~ epilettico** epileptic fit

attanagli'are *vt* (*fig: tormentare*) haunt

attar'darsi *vr* stay late; (*indugiare*) linger

attec'chire *vt* take; (*moda ecc*) catch on

atteggia'mento *nm* attitude

atteggi'are *vt* assume

atteggi'arsi *vr* **~ a** pose as

attem'pato *a* elderly

atten'darsi *vr* camp, pitch camp

atten'dente *nm Mil* batman

at'tendere *vt* wait for ● *vi* **~ a** attend to

at'tendersi *vr* expect

atten'dibile *a* reliable

attendibilità *nf* reliability

atte'nersi *vr* **~ a** stick to

attenta'mente *adv* attentively

atten'tare *vi* **~ a** make an attempt on

atten'tato *nm* act of violence; (*contro politico ecc*) assassination attempt; **~ alla vita di** attempted murder of. **~ dinamitardo** bombing

attenta'tore, -'trice *nmf* attacker; (*a scopo politico*) terrorist

at'tento *a* attentive; (*accurato*) careful; **~!** look out!; **stare ~** pay attention; **'attenti al cane'** 'beware of the dog'

attenu'ante *nf* extenuating circumstance

attenu'are *vt* attenuate; (*minimizzare*) minimize; subdue (*colori ecc*); calm (*dolore*); soften (*colpo*)

attenu'arsi *vr* diminish

attenuazi'one *nf* lessening

attenzi'one *nf* attention; (*cura*) care; **fare ~** be careful; **~!** watch out!; **~, prego** your attention, please; **coprire di attenzioni** lavish attention on

atter'raggio *nm* landing. **~ di fortuna** emergency landing

atter'rare *vt* knock down ● *vi* land

atter'rire *vt* terrorize

atter'rirsi *vr* be terrified

at'tesa *nf* waiting; (*aspettativa*) expectation; **in ~ di** waiting for

at'teso *pp di* attendere

atte'stabile *a* certifiable

atte'stare *vt* state; (*certificare*) certify

atte'stato *nm* certificate

attestazi'one *nf* certificate; (*dichiarazione*) declaration

'Attica *nf* Attica

'attico[1] *nm* (*lingua*) Attic

'attico[2] *nm* (*appartamento*) penthouse

at'tiguo *a* adjacent

attil'lato *a* (*vestito*) close-fitting

'attimo *nm* second; **un ~!** just a sec!; **in un ~** in double-quick time; **non ho avuto un ~ di respiro** I haven't had time to draw breath

atti'nente *a* **~ a** pertaining to

at'tingere *vt* draw; *fig* obtain

atti'rare *vt* attract

atti'rarsi *vr* draw (*attenzione*); incur (*odio*)

attitudi'nale *nm* **test ~** aptitude test

atti'tudine *nf* (*disposizione*) aptitude; (*atteggiamento*) attitude

atti'vare *vt* activate

attivazi'one *nf* setting in motion, turning on; *Phys, Chem* activation

atti'vismo *nm* activism

atti'vista *nmf* activist

attività *nf inv* activity; *Comm* assets *pl.* **~ pl fisse** fixed assets. **~ pl liquide** *Comm* liquid assets

at'tivo *a* active; *Comm* productive ● *nm* assets *pl*

attiz'zare *vt* poke; *fig* stir up

attizza'toio *nm* poker

'atto *nm* act; (*azione*) action; *Comm, Jur* deed; (*certificato*) certificate; **fare ~ di presenza** put in an appearance; **mettere in ~** put into action; **atti** *pl* (*di società ecc*) proceedings. **atti** *pl* **di libidine violenta** inde-

cent assault. **atti** pl **osceni** gross indecency.
~ **di vendita** bill of sale

**+attolo** suff **vermiciattolo** nm slimy individual

**at'tonito** a astonished

**attorcigli'are** vt twist

**attorcigli'arsi** vr get twisted

**at'tore** nm actor

**attorni'are** vt surround

**attorni'arsi** vr ~ **di** surround oneself with

**at'torno** adv around, about ● prep ~ **a** around, about

**attrac'care** vt/i dock

**attra'ente** a attractive

**at'trarre** vt attract

**at'trarsi** vr be attracted to each other

**attrat'tiva** nf charm, attraction

**attraversa'mento** nm (di strada) crossing. ~ **pedonale** pedestrian crossing, crosswalk Am

**attraver'sare** vt cross; (passare) go through

**attra'verso** prep through; (obliquamente) across

**attrazi'one** nf attraction. **attrazioni** pl **turistiche** tourist attractions

**attrez'zare** vt equip; Naut rig

**attrez'zarsi** vr kit oneself out

**attrezza'tura** nf equipment; Naut rigging. ~ **da campeggio** camping equipment

**at'trezzo** nm tool. **at'trezzi** pl equipment; Sport appliances pl

**attribu'ibile** a attributable

**attribu'ire** vt attribute

**attribu'irsi** vr ascribe to oneself; ~ **il merito di** claim credit for

**attri'buto** nm attribute

**attribuzi'one** nf attribution

**at'trice** nf actress

**at'trito** nm friction

**attrup'pare** vt assemble

**attrup'parsi** vr gather

**attu'abile** a feasible

**attuabilità** nf viability

**attu'ale** a present; (di attualità) topical; (effettivo) actual

**attualità** nf inv topicality; (avvenimento) news; **programma di** ~ current affairs programme

**attualiz'zare** vt update

**attual'mente** adv at present

**attu'are** vt carry out

**attu'ario, -a** nmf actuary

**attu'arsi** vr be realized

**attua'tore** nm Techn actuator

**attuazi'one** nf carrying out

**attuti'mento** nm (di colpo) softening; (di suoni) muffling

**attu'tire** vt deaden; ~ **il colpo** soften the blow

**au'dace** a daring, bold; (insolente) audacious

**au'dacia** nf daring, boldness; (insolenza) audacity

**audiapprendi'mento** nm audio-based learning

**'audience** nf inv (telespettatori) audience

**'audio** nm audio

**audiocas'setta** nf audio cassette

**audio'leso** a hearing-impaired

**audio'libro** nm audiobook

**audio'metrico** a Med aural

**audiovi'sivo** a audiovisual

**'auditing** nm auditing

**audi'torio** nm auditorium

**audizi'one** nf audition; Jur hearing

**'auge** nm height; **essere in** ~ be popular

**augu'rare** vt wish

**augu'rarsi** vr hope

**au'gurio** nm wish; (presagio) omen; **auguri!** all the best!; (a Natale) Happy Christmas!; **tanti auguri** best wishes

**au'gusto** a august

**'aula** nf classroom; Univ lecture-hall; (sala) hall; **silenzio in** ~! silence in court!. ~ **bunker** (in tribunale) secure courtroom. ~ **magna** Univ great hall. ~ **del tribunale** courtroom

**aumen'tare** vt/i increase; ~ **di peso** gain weight

**au'mento** nm increase; (di stipendio) [pay] rise. ~ **di prezzo** price increase

**'aureo** a golden

**au'reola** nf halo

**au'rora** nf dawn. ~ **boreale** aurora borealis, Northern Lights

**auscul'tare** vt Med auscultate

**ausili'are** a & nmf auxiliary

**auspi'cabile** a **è** ~ **che...** it is to be hoped that...

**auspi'care** vt hope for

**au'spicio** nm omen; **auspici** pl (protezione) auspices; **è di buon** ~ it is a good omen

**austerità** nf austerity

**au'stero** a austere

**Austra'lasia** nf Australasia

**au'strale** a southern

**Au'stralia** nf Australia

**australi'ano, -a** a & nmf Australian

**'Austria** nf Austria

**au'striaco, -a** a & nmf Austrian

**austroun'garico** a Austro-Hungarian

**autar'chia** nf autarchy

**au'tarchico** a autarchic

**aut aut** nm inv either-or [choice]

**autenti'care** vt authenticate

**autenticità** nf authenticity

**au'tentico** a authentic; (vero) true

**au'tismo** nm autism

**au'tista** nm driver

**au'tistico** a autistic

**'auto** nf inv car; **viaggiare in** ~ travel by car. ~ **blindata** armour-plated car. ~ **a quattro ruote motrici** four-wheel drive car. ~ **sportiva** sports car. ~ **a trazione anteriore** front-wheel drive car. ~ **usata** second-hand car

**auto+** pref self+

**autoabbron'zante** nm self-tan ● a self-tanning

**autoaccesso'rista** *nmf* car accessory supplier

**autoade'sivo** *a* self-adhesive ● *nm* sticker

**autoaffermazi'one** *nf* self-assertion

**autoambu'lanza** *nf* ambulance

**autoa'nalisi** *nf* self-analysis

**autoartico'lato** *nm* articulated lorry

**autobiogra'fia** *nf* autobiography

**autobio'grafico** *a* autobiographical

**auto'blinda** *nf* armoured car

**auto'bomba** *nf* car-bomb

**auto'botte** *nf* tanker

**'autobus** *nm inv* bus

**auto'carro** *nm* lorry

**autocertificazi'one** *nf* self-certification

**autoci'sterna** *nf* tanker

**auto'clave** *nf* (*contenitore ad alta pressione*) autoclave; (*idraulica*) surge tank

**autocombusti'one** *nf* spontaneous combustion

**autocommiserazi'one** *nf* self-pity

**autocompiaci'mento** *nm* smugness, self-satisfaction

**autocompiaci'uto** *a* smug, self-satisfied

**autoconcessio'nario** *nm* car dealer

**autocon'trollo** *nm* self-control

**au'tocrate** *nm* autocrat

**auto'cratico** *a* autocratic

**auto'critica** *nf* self-criticism

**au'toctono** *a* native, aboriginal

**autodemolizi'one** *nf* self-destruction

**autode'nuncia** *nf* spontaneous confession

**autodeterminazi'one** *nf* self-determination

**autodi'datta** *a* self-taught ● *nmf* self-educated person, autodidact

**autodi'fesa** *nf* self-defence

**autodisci'plina** *nf* self-discipline

**autodi'struggersi** *vr* self-destruct

**autoferrotranvi'ario** *a* public-transport *attrib*

**autoferrotranvi'eri** *nmpl* public-transport workers

**autoffi'cina** *nf* garage

**autofinanzia'mento** *nm* self-financing

**autofinanzi'arsi** *vr* be self-financing; (*persona:*) use one's own finance

**autogesti'one** *nf* self-management

**autoge'stirsi** *vr* (*operai, studenti*) be self-managing; **mio figlio si autogestisce** my son can cope by himself

**autoge'stito** *a* self-managed

**auto'gol** *nm inv Sport* own goal

**au'tografo** *a & nm* autograph

**auto'grill** *nm inv* motorway café

**autogrù** *nf inv* breakdown truck

**autogui'dato** *a* homing *attrib*

**autoim'mune** *a* autoimmune

**autoiro'nia** *nf* self-mockery

**autola'vaggio** *nm* car wash

**autolesi'one** *nf* self-inflicted wound

**autolesio'nismo** *nm fig* self-destruction

**autolesio'nistico** *a* self-destructive

**auto'linea** *nf* bus line

**au'toma** *nm* robot

**automatica'mente** *adv* automatically

**auto'matico** *a* automatic; **auto con il cambio** ~ automatic ● *nm* (*bottone*) press-stud; (*fucile*) automatic

**automatiz'zare** *vt* automate

**automatizzazi'one** *nf* automation

**automazi'one** *nf* automation

**auto'mezzo** *nm* motor vehicle; **uscita automezzi** motor vehicles exit

**auto'mobile** *nf* [motor] car. ~ **da corsa** racing car

**automobi'lina** *nf* toy car

**automobi'lismo** *nm* motoring

**automobi'lista** *nmf* motorist

**automobi'listico** *a* (*industria*) automobile *attrib*

**automodel'lismo** *nm* model car making; (*collezione*) model car collecting

**autono'leggio** *nm* car-rental

**autonoma'mente** *adv* autonomously

**autono'mia** *nf* autonomy; *Auto* range; (*di laptop, cellulare*) battery life

**au'tonomo** *a* autonomous

**auto'parco** *nm* (*insieme di auto*) fleet of cars

**autopat'tuglia** *nf* patrol car

**auto'pista** *nf* [fairground] race track

**auto'pompa** *nf* fire engine

**auto'psia** *nf* autopsy

**autopunizi'one** *nf* self-punishment

**auto'radio** *nf inv* car radio; (*veicolo*) radio car

**au'tore, -'trice** *nmf* author; (*di pitture*) painter; (*di furto ecc*) perpetrator; **quadro d'~** genuine master

**autoregolamentazi'one** *nf* self-regulation

**autore'parto** *nm Mil* mechanized unit

**auto'revole** *a* authoritative; (*che ha influenza*) influential

**autorevo'lezza** *nf* authority

**autoriduzi'one** *nf* protest which takes the form of paying less than the requisite amount

**autori'messa** *nf* garage

**autoriparazi'oni** *nfpl* '~' 'car repairs', 'auto repairs'

**autorità** *nf inv* authority

**autori'tario** *a* autocratic

**autorita'rismo** *nm* authoritarianism

**autori'tratto** *nm* self-portrait

**autoriz'zare** *vt* authorize

**autorizzazi'one** *nf* authorization

**auto'scatto** *nm Phot* automatic shutter release

**auto'scontro** *nm inv* bumper car

**autoscu'ola** *nf* driving school

**autosno'dato** *nm* articulated bus

**autosoc'corso** *nm* breakdown service; (*veicolo*) breakdown van, breakdown truck

**auto'starter** *nm inv Auto* self-starter

**auto'stop** *nm* hitch-hiking, hitching; **fare l'~** hitch-hike, hitch

**autostop'pista** *nmf* hitch-hiker

**auto'strada** *nf* motorway, highway *Am*. **A~ del Sole** Highway of the Sun (*connecting Milan and Reggio Calabria*)

**autostra'dale** *a* motorway *attrib*, highway *attrib Am*

**autosuffici'ente** *a* self-sufficient

**autosuffici'enza** *nf* self-sufficiency

**autosuggesti'one** *nf* autosuggestion

**autotrasporta|'tore, -'trice** *nmf* haulier, carrier

**autotra'sporto** *nm* road haulage

**auto'treno** *nm* articulated lorry, roadtrain

**autove'icolo** *nm* motor vehicle

**auto'velox** *nm inv* speed camera

**autovet'tura** *nf* motor vehicle

**autun'nale** *a* autumnal; ⟨*giornata, vestiti*⟩ autumn *attrib*

**au'tunno** *nm* autumn

**aval'lare** *vt* endorse, back ⟨*cambiale*⟩; *fig* endorse

**a'vallo** *nm* endorsement

**avam'braccio** *nm* forearm

**avam'posto** *nm Mil* forward position

**A'vana** *nf* Havana

**a'vana** *nm inv* (*sigaro*) Havana [cigar]; (*colore*) tobacco, dark brown ● *a inv* ⟨*colore*⟩ tobacco-coloured, dark brown

**avangu'ardia** *nf* vanguard; *fig* avant-garde; **essere all'~** be in the forefront; *Techn* be at the leading edge; **d'~** avant-garde

**avansco'perta** *nf* reconnaissance; **andare in ~** reconnoitre

**avanspet'tacolo** *nm* **da ~** in poor taste

**a'vanti** *adv* (*in avanti*) forward; (*davanti*) in front; (*prima*) before; **~!** (*entrate*) come in!; (*suvvia*) come on!; '**~**' (*su semaforo*) 'cross now', 'walk' *Am*: **~ diritto** straight ahead; **più ~** further on; **va' ~!** go ahead!; **andare ~** (*precedere*) go ahead; ⟨*orologio:*⟩ be fast; **~ e indietro** backwards and forwards ● *a* (*precedente*) before ● *prep* **~ a** before; (*in presenza di*) in the presence of

**avanti'eri** *adv* the day before yesterday

**avan'treno** *nm* front axle assembly

**avanza'mento** *nm* progress; (*promozione*) promotion

**avan'zare** *vi* advance; (*progredire*) progress; (*essere d'avanzo*) be left [over] ● *vt* advance; (*superare*) surpass; (*promuovere*) promote

**avan'zarsi** *vr* advance; (*avvicinarsi*) approach

**avan'zata** *nf* advance

**avan'zato** *a* advanced; (*nella notte*) late; **in età avanzata** elderly

**a'vanzo** *nm* remainder; *Comm* surplus; **avanzi** *pl* (*rovine*) remains; (*di cibo*) leftovers. **~ di galera** jailbird

**ava'raccio** *nm* Scrooge

**ava'ria** *nf* (*di motore*) engine failure

**avari'arsi** *vr* spoil

**avari'ato** *a* ⟨*frutta, verdura*⟩ rotten; ⟨*carne*⟩ tainted

**ava'rizia** *nf* avarice

**a'varo, -a** *a* stingy ● *nmf* miser

**a'vena** *nf* oats *pl*

**a'vere** *vt* have; (*ottenere*) get; (*indossare*) wear; (*provare*) feel; **ho trent'anni** I'm thirty; **ha avuto il posto** he got the job; **~ fame/ freddo** be hungry/cold; **ho mal di denti** I've got toothache; **cos'ha a che fare con lui?** what has it got to do with him?; **~ da fare** be busy; **~ luogo** take place; **che hai?** what's the matter with you?; **nei hai per molto?** will you be long?; **quanti ne abbiamo oggi?** what date is it today?; **avercela con qcno** have it in for sb ● *v aux* have; **non l'ho visto** I haven't seen him; **lo hai visto?** have you seen him?; **l'ho visto ieri** I saw him yesterday ● *nm* **averi** *pl* wealth *sg*

**avia|'tore, -'trice** *nmf* aviator

**aviazi'one** *nf* aviation; *Mil* Air Force

**avicol'tura** *nm* poultry farming

**avida'mente** *adv* avidly

**avidità** *nf* avidness

**'avido** *a* avid

**avi'ere** *nm* aircraft[s]man

**avio'getto** *nm* jet [plane]

**avio'linea** *nf* airline

**aviotraspor'tato** *a* airborne

**avitami'nosi** *nf* vitamin deficiency

**a'vito** *a* ancestral

**'avo, -a** *nmf* ancestor

**avo'cado** *nm inv* avocado

**a'vorio** *nm* ivory

**a'vulso** *a* **~ dal contesto** *fig* taken out of context

**Avv.** *abbr* avvocato

**avva'lersi** *vr* avail oneself (**of** di)

**avvalla'mento** *nm* depression

**avvalo'rare** *vt* bear out ⟨*tesi*⟩; endorse ⟨*documento*⟩; (*accrescere*) enhance

**avvam'pare** *vi* flare up; (*arrossire*) blush

**avvantaggi'are** *vt* favour

**avvantaggi'arsi** *vr* **~ di** benefit from; (*approfittare*) take advantage of

**avve'dersi** *vr* (*accorgersi*) notice; (*capire*) realize

**avve'duto** *a* shrewd

**avvelena'mento** *nm* poisoning

**avvele'nare** *vt* poison

**avvele'narsi** *vr* poison oneself

**avvele'nato** *a* poisoned

**avve'nente** *a* attractive

**avve'nenza** *nf* attraction, charm

**avveni'mento** *nm* event

**avve'nire** *vi* happen; (*aver luogo*) take place ● *nm* future

**avveni'rismo** *nm* excessive confidence in the future

**avveni'ristico** *a* futuristic

**avven'tarsi** *vr* fling oneself

**avventata'mente** *adv* recklessly

**avven'tato** *a* ⟨*decisione*⟩ rash

**avven'tizio** *a* (*personale*) temporary; (*guadagno*) casual

**av'vento** *nm* advent; *Relig* Advent

**avven'tore** *nm* regular customer

**avven'tura** *nf* adventure; (*amorosa*) affair; **d'~** ⟨*film*⟩ adventure *attrib*

**avventu'rarsi** *vr* venture

**avventuri'ero, -a** *nm* adventurer ● *nf* adventuress

**avventu'rismo** *nm* adventurism

**avventu'ristico** *a* adventurist

**avventu'roso** *a* adventurous

**avve'rabile** *a* ⟨*previsione*⟩ that may come true

**avve'rarsi** *vr* come true

**av'verbio** *nm* adverb

**avver'sare** *vt* oppose

**avver'sario, -a** *a* opposing ● *nmf* opponent

**avversi'one** *nf* aversion

**avversità** *nf inv* adversity

**av'verso** *a* ⟨*sfavorevole*⟩ adverse; ⟨*contrario*⟩ averse

**avver'tenza** *nf* ⟨*cura*⟩ care; ⟨*avvertimento*⟩ warning; ⟨*avviso*⟩ notice; ⟨*premessa*⟩ foreword; **avvertenze** *pl* ⟨*istruzioni*⟩ instructions

**avver'tibile** *a* ⟨*disagio*⟩ perceptible

**avverti'mento** *nm* warning

**avver'tire** *vt* warn; ⟨*informare*⟩ inform; ⟨*sentire*⟩ feel

**avvertita'mente** *adv* deliberately

**avvez'zare** *vt* accustom

**avvez'zarsi** *vr* accustom oneself

**av'vezzo** *a* ~ **a** used to

**avvia'mento** *nm* starting; *Comm* goodwill

**avvi'are** *vt* start

**avvi'arsi** *vr* set out

**avvi'ato** *a* under way; **bene** ~ thriving

**avvicenda'mento** *nm* ⟨*in agricoltura*⟩ rotation; ⟨*nel lavoro*⟩ replacement; ⟨*delle stagioni*⟩ change

**avvicen'dare** *vt* rotate

**avvicen'darsi** *vr* take turns, alternate

**avvicina'mento** *nm* approach

**avvici'nare** *vt* bring near; approach ⟨*persona*⟩

**avvici'narsi** *vr* come nearer, approach; **avvicinarsi a** come nearer to, approach

**avvi'lente** *a* demoralizing; ⟨*umiliante*⟩ humiliating

**avvili'mento** *nm* despondency; ⟨*degradazione*⟩ degradation

**avvi'lire** *vt* dishearten; ⟨*degradare*⟩ degrade

**avvi'lirsi** *vr* lose heart; ⟨*degradarsi*⟩ degrade oneself

**avvi'lito** *a* disheartened; ⟨*degradato*⟩ degraded

**avvilup'pare** *vt* envelop

**avvilup'parsi** *vr* wrap oneself up; ⟨*aggrovigliarsi*⟩ get entangled

**avvinaz'zato** *a* drunk

**avvin'cente** *a* ⟨*libro ecc*⟩ enthralling

**av'vincere** *vt* enthral

**avvinghi'are** *vt* clutch

**avvinghi'arsi** *vr* cling

**av'vio** *nm* start-up; **dare l'~ a qcsa** get sth under way; **prendere l'~** get under way

**avvi'saglia** *nf* ⟨*di malattia*⟩ first sign

**avvi'sare** *vt* inform; ⟨*mettere in guardia*⟩ warn

**av'viso** *nm* notice; ⟨*annuncio*⟩ announcement; ⟨*avvertimento*⟩ warning; ⟨*pubblicitario*⟩ advertisement; **a mio** ~ in my opinion. ~ **di garanzia** *Jur* notification that one is to be the subject of a legal enquiry

**avvista'mento** *nm* sighting

**avvi'stare** *vt* catch sight of: ~ **terra** make landfall

**avvi'tare** *vt* screw in; screw down ⟨*coperchio*⟩

**avvi'tarsi** *vr* ⟨*aereo:*⟩ go into a spin

**avvi'tata** *nf* ⟨*di aereo*⟩ spin

**avviz'zire** *vi* wither

**avviz'zito** *a* withered

**avvo'cato** *nm* lawyer; *fig* advocate. ~ **del diavolo** devil's advocate

**avvoca'tura** *nf* legal profession; ⟨*insieme di avvocati*⟩ lawyers

**av'volgere** *vt* wrap [up]

**av'volgersi** *vr* wrap oneself up

**avvol'gibile** *nm* roller blind

**avvolgi'mento** *nm* winding

**av'volto** *a* ~ **in** wrapped in

**avvol'toio** *nm* vulture

**aza'lea** *nf* azalea

**Azerbaigi'an** *nm* Azerbaijan

**azerbaigi'ano, -a** *a* & *nmf* Azerbaijani

**azi'enda** *nf* business, firm. ~ **agricola** farm. ~ **elettrica** electricity board. ~ **a partecipazioni statali** enterprise in which the government has a shareholding. ~ **di soggiorno** tourist bureau

**azien'dale** *a* ⟨*politica, dirigente*⟩ company *attrib*; ⟨*giornale*⟩ in-house

**azienda'listico** *a* company *attrib*

**azio'nabile** *a* which can be operated

**aziona'mento** *nm* operation

**azio'nare** *vt* operate

**azio'nario** *a* share *attrib*; **mercato** ~ share market

**azi'one** *nf* action; *Fin* share; **d'~** ⟨*romanzo, film*⟩ action[-packed]; **ad** ~ **ritardata** delayed action. ~ **sindacale** industrial action

**azio'nista** *nmf* shareholder

**a'zoto** *nm* nitrogen

**az'teco, -a** *a* & *nmf* Aztec

**azzan'nare** *vt* seize with its teeth; sink its teeth into ⟨*gamba*⟩

**azzar'dare** *vt* risk

**azzar'darsi** *vr* dare

**azzar'dato** *a* risky; ⟨*precipitoso*⟩ rash

**az'zardo** *nm* hazard; **gioco d'~** game of chance

**azzec'care** *vt* hit; ⟨*fig: indovinare*⟩ guess

**azzera'mento** *nm* setting to zero; *fig* **corso di** ~ remedial classes *pl*

**azze'rare** *vt* reset

**azzi'mato** *a* dapper

**'azzimo** *a* unleavened

**azzit'tirsi** *vr* go quiet, fall silent

**azzit'tire** *vt* silence, hush

**azzop'pare** *vt* lame

**Az'zorre** *nfpl* **le** ~ the Azores

**azzuf'farsi** *vr* come to blows

**azzur'rato** *a* ⟨*lenti*⟩ blue-tinted

**az'zurro** *a* & *nm* blue; **principe** ~ Prince Charming; **gli azzurri** the Italian national team

**azzur'rognolo** *a* bluish

# Bb

**babà** *nm inv* ~ **al rum** rum baba

**bab'beo** *a* foolish ● *nm* idiot

**'babbo** *nm fam* dad, daddy. **B~ Natale** Father Christmas

**bab'buccia** *nf* slipper

**babbu'ino** *nm* baboon

**ba'bordo** *nm Naut* port side

**baby boom** *nm* baby boom

**baby'sitter** *nmf inv* baby-sitter; **fare il/la ~** babysit, do baby-sitting

**ba'cato** *a* wormeaten; **avere il cervello ~** have a slate loose

**'bacca** *nf* berry

**baccalà** *nm inv* dried salted cod

**bac'cano** *nm* din

**bac'cello** *nm* pod

**bac'chetta** *nf* rod; (*magica*) wand; (*di direttore d'orchestra*) baton; (*di tamburo*) drumstick

**ba'checa** *nf* showcase; (*in ufficio*) notice board. **~ elettronica** *Comput* bulletin board

**bacia'mano** *nm* kiss on the hand; **fare il ~ a qcno** kiss sb's hand

**baci'are** *vt* kiss

**baci'arsi** *vr* kiss [each other]

**ba'cillo** *nm* bacillus

**baci'nella** *nf* basin; (*contenuto*) basinful

**ba'cino** *nm* basin; *Anat* pelvis; (*di porto*) dock; (*di minerali*) field. **~ d'utenza** catchment area

**'bacio** *nm* kiss; **~ sulla bocca** kiss on the lips

**backgammon** *nm* backgammon

**'baco** *nm* worm. **~ da seta** silkworm

**'bacon** *nm* bacon

**ba'cucco** *a* **un vecchio ~** a senile old man

**'bada** *nf* **tenere qcno a ~** keep sb at bay

**ba'dare** *vi* take care (**a** of); (*fare attenzione*) look out; **bada ai fatti tuoi!** mind your own business!

**ba'dia** *nf* abbey

**ba'dile** *nm* shovel

**'badminton** *nm* badminton

**'baffi** *nmpl* moustache *sg*; (*di animale*) whiskers; **mi fa un baffo** I don't give a damn; **ridere sotto i ~** laugh up one's sleeve

**baf'futo** *a* moustached

**ba'gagli** *nmpl* luggage, baggage; **ritiro bagagli** baggage claim

**bagagli'aio** *nm Rail* luggage van, baggage car *Am*; *Auto* boot

**ba'gaglio** *nm* luggage, baggage; *Mil* kit; **un ~** a piece of luggage. **~ a mano** hand-luggage, hand-baggage. **~ in eccesso, ~ eccedente** excess baggage

**baga'rino** *nm* ticket tout

**baga'tella** *nf* trifle; *Mus* bagatelle

**baggia'nata** *nf* piece of nonsense; **non dire baggianate** don't talk nonsense

**Bagh'dad** *nf* Baghdad

**bagli'ore** *nm* glare; (*improvviso*) flash; (*fig: di speranza*) glimmer

**bagna'cauda** *nf* vegetables (*especially raw*) in an oil, garlic and anchovy sauce

**ba'gnante** *nmf* bather

**ba'gnare** *vt* wet; (*inzuppare*) soak; (*immergere*) dip; (*innaffiare*) water; (*mare, lago:*) wash; (*fiume:*) flow through

**ba'gnarsi** *vr* get wet; (*al mare ecc*) swim, bathe; **'vietato ~'** 'no bathing'

**bagnasci'uga** *nm inv* edge of the water, waterline

**ba'gnato** *a* wet; **~ fradicio** soaked

**ba'gnino, -a** *nmf* life guard

**'bagno** *nm* bath; (*stanza*) bathroom; (*gabinetto*) toilet; (*al mare*) swim, bathe; **bagni** *pl* (*stabilimento*) lido; **fare il ~** have a bath; (*nel mare ecc*) [have a] swim, bathe; **andare in ~** go to the bathroom, go to the toilet; **mettere a ~** soak; **con ~** (*camera*) en suite. **~ oculare** eyebath. **~ rivelatore** *Phot* developing bath. **~ di sangue** bloodbath. **~ di sviluppo** *Phot* developing bath. **~ turco** Turkish bath

**bagnoma'ria** *nm* **cuocere a ~** cook in a double saucepan

**bagnoschi'uma** *nm inv* bubble bath

**ba'guette** *nf inv* French loaf, baguette

**Ba'hamas** *nfpl* **le ~** the Bahamas

**Bah'rain** *nm* Bahrain, Bahrein

**'baia** *nf* bay

**baio'netta** *nf* bayonet

**'baita** *nf* mountain chalet

**bala'ustra, balau'strata** *nf* balustrade

**balbet'tare** *vt/i* stammer; (*bambino:*) babble

**balbet'tio** *nm* stammering; (*di bambino*) babble

**bal'buzie** *nf* stutter

**balbuzi'ente** *a* stuttering ● *nmf* stutterer

**Bal'cani** *nmpl* Balkans

**bal'canico** *a* Balkan

**balco'nata** *nf Theat* balcony, dress circle

**balon'cino** *nm* **reggiseno a ~** underwired bra

**bal'cone** *nm* balcony

**baldac'chino** *nm* canopy; **letto a ~** four-poster bed

**bal'danza** *nf* boldness
**baldan'zoso** *a* bold
**bal'doria** *nf* revelry; **far ~** have a riotous time
**Bale'ari** *nfpl* **le [isole] ~** the Balearics, the Balearic Islands
**ba'lena** *nf* whale
**bale'nare** *vi* lighten; *fig* flash; **mi è balenata un'idea** I've just had an idea
**bale'niera** *nf* whaler
**ba'leno** *nm* **in un ~** in a flash
**balenot'tera** *nf* **~ azzurra** blue whale
**ba'lera** *nf* dance hall
**ba'lestra** *nf* crossbow
**'balia** *nf* wetnurse
**ba'lia** *nf* **in ~ di** at the mercy of
**ba'listico** *a* ballistic; **perito ~** ballistics expert
**'balla** *nf* bale; (*fam: frottola*) tall story
**bal'labile** *a* **essere ~** be good for dancing to
**bal'lare** *vi* dance; **andare a ~** go dancing
**bal'lata** *nf* ballad
**balla'toio** *nm* (*nelle scale*) landing
**balle'rino, -a** *nmf* dancer; (*classico*) ballet dancer ● *nf nf* (*classica*) ballet dancer, ballerina
**bal'letto** *nm* ballet
**bal'lista** *nmf fam* bull-shitter
**'ballo** *nm* dance; (*il ballare*) dancing; **sala da ~** ballroom; **essere in ~** (*lavoro, vita:*) be at stake; (*persona:*) be committed; **tirare qcno in ~** involve sb. **~ liscio** ballroom dancing. **~ in maschera** masked ball
**ballonzo'lare** *vi* skip about
**ballot'taggio** *nm* second count [of votes]
**balne'are** *a* bathing *attrib*; **stagione ~** swimming season; **stazione ~** seaside resort
**balneazi'one** *nf* '**divieto di ~**' 'no bathing'
**ba'lordo** *a* foolish; (*stordito*) stunned; **tempo ~** nasty weather
**bal'samico** *a* (*aria*) balmy
**'balsamo** *nm* balsam; (*per capelli*) conditioner; (*lenimento*) remedy
**'baltico** *a* Baltic. **il [mar] B~** The Baltic [Sea]
**balu'ardo** *nm* bulwark
**'balza** *nf* crag; (*di abito*) flounce
**bal'zano** *a* (*idea*) weird
**bal'zare** *vi* bounce; (*saltare*) jump; **~ in piedi** leap to one's feet
**'balzo** *nm* bounce; (*salto*) jump; **prendere la palla al ~** *fig* seize an opportunity
**bam'bagia** *nf* cotton wool; **vivere nella ~** *fig* be in clover
**bam'bina** *nf* little girl; (*piccola*) baby; **ha avuto una ~** she had a [baby] girl
**bambi'naia** *nf* nursemaid, nanny
**bambi'nata** *nf* childish thing to do/say
**bam'bino** *nm* child; (*appena nato*) baby; **avere un ~** have a baby; (*maschio*) have a [baby] boy; **bambini** *pl* children, kids; (*piccoli*) babies. **~ prodigio** child prodigy
**bambi'none, -a** *nmf pej* big or overgrown child

**bam'boccio** *nm* chubby child; (*sciocco*) simpleton; (*fantoccio*) rag doll
**'bambola** *nf* doll
**bambo'lotto** *nm* male doll
**bambù** *nm* bamboo
**ba'nale** *a* banal
**banalità** *nf inv* banality
**banaliz'zare** *vt* trivialize
**ba'nana** *nf* banana
**ba'nano** *nm* banana-tree
**'banca** *nf* bank. **~ d'affari** merchant bank, investment bank. **~ [di] dati** databank. **B~ Europea per la Ricostruzione e lo Sviluppo** European Bank for Reconstruction and Development. **~ degli occhi** eye bank. **~ del sangue** blood bank. **~ dello sperma** sperm bank
**banca'rella** *nf* stall
**bancarel'lista** *nmf* stallholder
**ban'cario, -a** *a* banking *attrib*; **trasferimento ~** bank transfer ● *nmf* bank employee
**banca'rotta** *nf* bankruptcy; **fare ~** go bankrupt
**banchet'tare** *vi* banquet
**ban'chetto** *nm* banquet
**banchi'ere** *nm* banker
**ban'china** *nf Naut* quay; (*in stazione*) platform; (*di strada*) path. **~ spartitraffico** central reservation, median strip *Am*. **~ non transitabile** soft verge
**ban'chisa** *nf* floe
**'banco** *nm* (*di scuola*) desk; (*di negozio*) counter; (*di officina*) bench; (*di gioco, banca*) bank; (*di mercato*) stall; (*degli imputati*) dock; **sotto ~** under the counter; **medicinale da ~** over the counter medicines. **~ dei formaggi** (*in supermercato*) cheese counter; (*in mercato*) cheese stall. **~ di ghiaccio** ice floe. **~ informazioni** information desk. **~ di nebbia** fog bank. **~ di sabbia** sandbank
**'bancomat®** *nm inv* autobank, cashpoint; (*carta*) bank card, cash card
**ban'cone** *nm* counter; (*in bar*) bar
**banco'nota** *nf* banknote, bill *Am*; **banco'note** *pl* paper currency
**'banda** *nf* band; (*di delinquenti*) gang. **~ d'atterraggio** *Aeron* landing strip. **~ passante** bandwidth. **~ rumorosa** rumble strip
**banderu'ola** *nf* weathercock; *Naut* pennant
**bandi'era** *nf* flag; **cambiare ~** change sides, switch allegiances
**bandie'rina** *nf* (*nel calcio*) corner flag
**bandie'rine** *nfpl* bunting
**ban'dire** *vt* banish; (*pubblicare*) publish; *fig* dispense with (*formalità, complimenti*)
**ban'dista** *nmf* bandsman
**bandi'tismo** *nm* banditry
**ban'dito** *nm* bandit
**bandi'tore** *nm* (*di aste*) auctioneer
**'bando** *nm* proclamation; **~ di concorso** job advertisement (*published in an official gazette for a job for which a competitive examination has to be sat*)

**bang** *nm inv* wham. ~ **sonico** sonic boom
**Bangla'desh** *nm* Bangladesh
**bar** *nm inv* bar
**'bara** *nf* coffin
**ba'racca** *nf* hut; *(catapecchia)* hovel: **mandare avanti la** ~ keep the ship afloat
**barac'cato, -a** *a* living in a shanty town ● *nmf* shanty town dweller
**barac'chino** *nm (di gelati. giornali)* kiosk: *Radio* CB radio
**barac'cone** *nm (roulotte)* circus caravan; *(in luna park)* booth; *(fig: organizzazione)* lumbering great dinosaur of an organization
**barac'copoli** *nf inv* shanty town
**bara'onda** *nf* chaos; **non fare** ~ don't make a mess
**ba'rare** *vi* cheat
**'baratro** *nm* chasm
**barat'tare** *vt* barter
**ba'ratto** *nm* barter
**ba'rattolo** *nm* jar; *(di latta)* tin
**'barba** *nf* beard; *(fam: noia)* bore; **farsi la** ~ shave: **in** ~ **a** in spite of; **è una** ~ *(noia)* it's boring
**barbabi'etola** *nf* beetroot; **barbabietole** *pl* beetroot. ~ **da zucchero** sugar-beet
**Bar'bados** *nfpl* **le** ~ Barbados
**barbagi'anni** *nm inv* barn owl
**bar'barico** *a* barbaric
**bar'barie** *nf inv* barbarity
**barba'rismo** *nm* barbarism
**'barbaro** *a* barbarous ● *nm* barbarian
**'barbecue** *nm inv* barbecue
**bar'betta** *nf Naut* painter
**barbi'ere** *nm* barber; *(negozio)* barber's
**bar'biglio** *nm* barb
**barbi'turico** *nm* barbiturate
**bar'bone, -a** *nm (vagabondo)* vagrant; *(cane)* poodle ● *nf* bag lady
**bar'boso** *a fam* boring
**barbu'gliare** *vi* mumble
**bar'buto** *a* bearded
**'barca** *nf* boat; **una** ~ **di** *fig* a lot of. ~ **a motore** motorboat. ~ **da pesca** fishing boat. ~ **a remi** rowing boat, rowboat *Am*. ~ **di salvataggio** lifeboat. ~ **a vela** sailing boat, sailboat *Am*
**barcai'olo** *nm* boatman
**barcame'narsi** *vr* manage
**barca'rola** *nf Mus* barcarolle
**Barcel'lona** *nf* Barcelona
**barcol'lare** *vi* stagger
**barcol'loni** *adv* **camminare** ~ stagger
**bar'cone** *nm* barge; *(di ponte)* pontoon
**bar'dare** *vt* harness
**bar'darsi** *vr hum* dress up
**barda'tura** *nf (per cavallo)* harness
**ba'rella** *nf* stretcher
**barelli'ere** *nm* stretcher-bearer
**'Barents: mare di** ~ Barents S
**ba'rese** *a* from Bari
**bari'centro** *nm* centre of gravi
**ba'rile** *nm* barrel
**bari'lotto** *nm fig* tub of lard
**ba'rista** *nm* barman ● *nf* barmaid

**ba'ritono** *nm* baritone
**bar'lume** *nm* glimmer: **un** ~ **di speranza** a glimmer of hope
**'barman** *nm inv* barman
**'baro** *nm* cardsharper
**ba'rocco** *a & nm* baroque
**ba'rometro** *nm* barometer
**baro'nale** *a* baronial
**ba'rone** *nm* baron; **i baroni** *fig* the top brass
**baro'nessa** *nf* baroness
**'barra** *nf* bar; *(lineetta)* oblique; *Naut* tiller. ~ **retroversa** backslash. ~ **di rimorchio** tow bar. ~ **spazio** space bar. ~ **di stato** *Comput* status bar. ~ **strumenti** *Comput* tool bar
**bar'rage** *nm inv Sport* jump-off
**bar'rare** *vt* block off *(strada)*
**barri'care** *vt* barricade
**barri'cata** *nf* barricade
**barri'era** *nf* barrier; *(stradale)* road-block; *Geol* reef. ~ **corallina** coral reef. ~ **linguistica** language barrier. ~ **razziale** colour bar. ~ **del suono** sound barrier
**bar'rire** *vi* trumpet
**bar'rito** *nm* trumpeting
**ba'ruffa** *nf* scuffle. **far** ~ quarrel
**barzel'letta** *nf* joke; ~ **sporca** *o* **spinta** dirty joke
**basa'mento** *nm* base; *Geol* bedrock
**ba'sare** *vt* base
**ba'sarsi** *vr* ~ **su** be based on; **mi baso su ciò che ho visto** I'm going on [the basis of] what I saw
**'basco, -a** *a & nmf* Basque ● *nm (copricapo)* beret
**'base** *nf* basis; *(fondamento)* foundation; *Mil* base; *Pol* rank and file; **a** ~ **di** containing; **in** ~ **a** on the basis of. ~ **di controllo** ground control. ~ **[di] dati** database. ~ **d'intesa** common ground. ~ **logica** logical basis. ~ **navale** naval base
**'baseball** *nm* baseball
**ba'setta** *nf* sideburn
**basi'lare** *a* basic
**ba'silica** *nf* basilica
**Basili'cata** *nf* Basilicata
**ba'silico** *nm* basil
**ba'sista** *nm* grass roots politician; *(di un crimine)* mastermind
**'basket** *nm* basketball
**bas'sezza** *nf* lowness; *(di statura)* shortness; *(viltà)* vileness
**bas'sista** *nmf* bassist
**'basso** *a* low; *(di statura)* short; *(acqua)* shallow; *(televisione)* quiet; *(vile)* despicable; **parlare a bassa voce** speak quietly, speak in a low voice. **la bassa Italia** southern Italy ● *nm* lower part; *Mus* bass; **guardare in** ~ look down
**basso'fondo** *nm (pl bassifondi)* shallows: **bassifondi** *pl (quartieri poveri)* slums
**bassorili'evo** *nm* bas-relief
**bas'sotto** *nm* dachshund
**ba'stardo, -a** *a* bastard; *(di animale)* mongrel ● *nmf* bastard; *(animale)* mongrel
**ba'stare** *vi* be enough; *(durare)* last; **basta!**

that's enough!. that'll do!: **basta che** (*purchè*) provided that: **basta cosi** that's enough: **basta cosí?** is that enough?. will that do?: (*in negozio*) will there be anything else?: **basta andare alla posta** you only have to go to the post office; **basta che tu lo faccia bene** make sure you do it well

**Basti'an con'trario** *nm* contrary old so-and-so

**basti'mento** *nm* ship: (*carico*) cargo

**basti'one** *nm* bastion

**basto'nare** *vt* beat

**basto'nata** *nf* **dare una ~ a** beat with a stick

**baston'cino** *nm* (*da sci*) ski pole. **~ di pesce** fish finger; fish stick *Am*

**ba'stone** *nm* stick; (*da golf*) club; (*da passeggio*) walking stick. **~ da hockey** hockey stick

**ba'tosta** *nf* blow

**bat'tage** *nm inv* **~ pubblicitario** media hype

**bat'taglia** *nf* battle; (*lotta*) fight

**battagli'are** *vi* battle; *fig* fight

**bat'taglio** *nm* (*di campana*) clapper; (*di porta*) knocker

**battagli'one** *nm* battalion

**bat'tello** *nm* boat; (*motonave*) steamer

**bat'tente** *nm* (*di porta*) wing; (*di finestra*) shutter; (*battaglio*) knocker

**'battere** *vt* beat; hit, knock ‹*testa, spalla*›; (*percorrere*) scour; thresh ‹*grano*›; break ‹*record*› ● *vi* (*bussare, urtare*) knock; ‹*cuore:*› beat; ‹*ali ecc:*› flap; *Tennis* serve; **~ a macchina** type; **~ gli occhi** blink; **~ il piede** tap one's foot; **~ le mani** clap [one's hands]; **~ le ore** strike the hours

**bat'teri** *nmpl* bacteria

**batte'ria** *nf* battery; *Mus* drums *pl*; (*Sport: eliminatoria*) heat

**bat'terico** *a* bacterial

**bat'terio** *nm* bacterium

**batteriolo'gia** *nf* bacteriology

**batterio'logico** *a* bacteriological

**batte'rista** *nmf* drummer

**'battersi** *vr* fight

**bat'tesimo** *nm* baptism. christening

**battez'zare** *vt* baptize, christen

**battiba'leno** *nm* **in un ~** in a flash

**batti'becco** *nm* squabble

**batticu'ore** *nm* palpitation; **mi venne il ~** I was scared

**bat'tigia** *nf* water's edge

**batti'mano** *nm* applause

**batti'panni** *nm inv* carpetbeater

**batti'scopa** *nm inv* skirting board

**batti'stero** *nm* baptistery

**batti'strada** *nm inv* outrider; (*di pneumatico*) tread; *Sport* pacesetter

**battitap'peto** *nm inv* carpet sweeper

**'battito** *nm* (*alle tempie*) throbbing; (*di orologio*) ticking; (*della pioggia*) beating. **~ cardiaco** heartbeat

**batti‖'tore, -'trice** *nmf Sport* batsman

**bat'tuta** *nf* beat; (*colpo*) knock; (*spirito-*

*saggine*) wisecrack; (*osservazione*) remark; *Mus* bar; *Tennis* service; *Theat* cue; (*dattilografia*) stroke. **~ d'arresto** setback

**ba'tuffolo** *nm* flock

**ba'ule** *nm* trunk

**bau'xite** *nf* bauxite

**'bava** *nf* dribble; (*di cane ecc*) slobber; **aver la ~ alla bocca** foam at the mouth

**bava'glino** *nm* bib

**ba'vaglio** *nm* gag

**bava'rese** *nf* ice-cream cake with milk, eggs and cream

**'bavero** *nm* collar

**ba'zar** *nm inv* bazaar

**ba'zooka** *nm inv* bazooka

**baz'zecola** *nf* trifle

**bazzi'care** *vt/i* haunt

**baz'zotto** *a* softboiled

**be'arsi** *vr* delight (**di** in)

**beata'mente** *adv* blissfully

**beatifi'care** *vt* beatify

**beati'tudine** *nf* bliss

**be'ato** *a* blissful; *Relig* blessed; **~ te!** lucky you!

**beauty-'case** *nm inv* toilet bag

**bebè** *nm inv* baby

**bec'caccia** *nf* woodcock

**bec'care** *vt* peck; *fig* catch

**bec'carsi** *vr* (*litigare*) quarrel

**bec'cata** *nf* beakful; (*colpo*) peck

**beccheggi'are** *vi* pitch

**bec'chime** *nm* birdseed

**bec'chino** *nm* grave-digger

**'becco** *nm* beak; (*di caffettiera ecc*) spout; **chiudi il ~** *fam* shut your trap; **non ha il ~ di un quattrino** *fam* he's skint; **restare a ~ asciutto** *fam* end up with nothing. **~ Bunsen** Bunsen [burner]. **~ a gas** gas burner

**bec'cuccio** *nm* spout

**'beeper** *nm inv* beeper

**be'fana** *nf* legendary old woman who brings presents to children on Twelfth Night; (*giorno*) Twelfth Night; (*donna brutta*) old witch

**'beffa** *nf* hoax; **farsi beffe di qcno** mock sb

**bef'fardo** *a* derisory; ‹*persona*› mocking

**bef'fare** *vt* mock

**bef'farsi** *vr* **~ di** make fun of

**beffeggi'are** *vt* taunt

**'bega** *nf* quarrel; **è una bella ~** it's really annoying

**be'gonia** *nf* begonia

**beh** *int* well

**'beige** *a & nm* beige

**Bei'rut** *nf* Beirut

**be'lare** *vi* bleat

**be'lato** *nm* bleating

**'belga** *a & nmf* Belgian

**'Belgio** *nm* Belgium

**Bel'grado** *nf* Belgrade

**Be'lize** *nm* Belize

**'bella** *nf* (*in carte, Sport*) decider; (*innamorata*) sweetheart. **~ di giorno** *Bot* morning glory. **~ di notte** *fig* lady of the night

**bel'lezza** *nf* beauty: **che ~!** how lovely!: **per ~** (*per decorazione*) for decoration; **chiudere/finire in ~** end on a high note; **la ~ di tre mesi/200 000 lire** all of three months/200.000 lire

**belli'cismo** *nm* warmongering

**belli'cistico** *a* warmongering

**'bellico** *a* war *attrib*: **periodo ~** wartime

**bellicosità** *nf* belligerence

**belli'coso** *a* warlike

**bellige'rante** *a & nmf* belligerent

**bellige'ranza** *nf* belligerence

**bellim'busto** *nm* dandy

**'bello** *a* nice; (*di aspetto*) beautiful; ⟨*uomo*⟩ handsome; (*moralmente*) good; **cosa fai di ~ stasera?** what are you up to tonight?; **oggi fa ~** it's a nice day: **una bella cifra** a lot; **un bel piatto di pasta** a big plate of pasta; **nel bel mezzo** right in the middle; **un bel niente** absolutely nothing; **bell'e fatto** over and done with; **bell'amico!** fine friend he is/ you are!: **questa è bella!** that's a good one!; **bel voto** good mark; **il bel mondo** the beautiful people; **le belle arti** the fine arts; **bella lì!** *sl* hi!: (*arrivederci*) bye!, see you! ● *nm* (*bellezza*) beauty; (*innamorato*) sweetheart; **sul più ~** at the crucial moment; **il ~ è che...** the funny thing is that...

**beltà** *nf liter* beauty

**'belva** *nf* wild beast

**be'molle** *nm Mus* flat

**ben** *vedi* **bene**

**benché** *conj* though, although

**'benda** *nf* bandage; (*per occhi*) blindfold

**ben'dare** *vt* bandage; blindfold ⟨*occhi*⟩

**bendi'sposto** *a* **essere ~ verso** be well-disposed towards

**'bene** *adv* well; **ben ~** thoroughly; **~!** good!; **star ~** (*di salute*) be well; (*vestito, stile:*) suit; (*finanziariamente*) be well off; **non sta ~** (*non è educato*) it's not nice; **sta/va ~!** all right!; **ti sta ~!** [it] serves you right!; **ti auguro ~** I wish you well; **voler ~ a** love; **di ~ in meglio** better and better; **fare ~** (*aver ragione*) do the right thing; **fare ~ a** ⟨*cibo:*⟩ be good for; **una persona per ~** a good person; **per ~** ⟨*fare*⟩ properly; **è ben difficile** it's very difficult; **ben cotto** well done; **come tu ben sai** as you well know; **lo credo ~!** I can well believe it! ● *nm* good; **per il tuo ~** for your own good. **beni** *pl* (*averi*) property *sg*; **un ~ di famiglia** a family heirloom. **beni** *pl* **ambientali** environment. **beni** *pl* **di consumo** consumer products, consumer goods. **beni** *pl* **culturali** cultural heritage. **beni** *pl* **immobili** real estate, realty *Am*. **beni** *pl* **mobili** movables

**benedet'tino** *a & nm* Benedictine

**bene'detto** *a* blessed

**bene'dire** *vt* bless; **mandare qcno a farsi ~** *fam* tell sb to get lost

**benedizi'one** *nf* blessing

**benedu'cato** *a* well-mannered

**benefat|'tore, -'trice** *nmf* benefactor; benefactress

**benefi'care** *vt* help

**benefi'cenza** *nf* charity

**benefici'are** *vi* **~ di** profit by

**benefici'ario, -a** *a & nmf* beneficiary

**bene'ficio** *nm* benefit;·**con ~ di inventario** with reservations. **~ accessorio** perquisite

**be'nefico** *a* beneficial; (*di beneficenza*) charitable

**'Benelux** *nm* Benelux

**beneme'renza** *nf* benevolence

**bene'merito** *a* worthy

**bene'placito** *nm* consent, approval

**be'nessere** *nm* well-being

**bene'stante** *a* well off ● *nmf* well-off person

**bene'stare** *nm* consent

**benevo'lenza** *nf* benevolence

**be'nevolo** *a* benevolent

**ben'fatto** *a* well-made

**Ben'gala** *nm* Bengal

**ben'godi** *nm* **il paese di ~** a land of plenty

**'beni** *nmpl* property *sg; Fin* assets; **~ di consumo** consumer goods

**benia'mino** *nm* favourite

**be'nigno** *a* kindly; *Med* benign

**Be'nin** *nm* Benin

**beninfor'mato** *a* well-informed ● *npl* **i beninformati** those in the know

**benintenzio'nato, -a** *a* well-meaning ● *nmf* well-meaning person

**benin'teso** *adv* needless to say, of course; **~ che...** of course,...

**be'nissimo** *int* fine

**benpen'sante** *a & nmf* self-righteous

**benser'vito** *nm* **dare il ~ a qcno** give sb the sack

**bensì** *conj* but rather

**benve'nuto** *a & nm* welcome; **benvenuta!** welcome!

**ben'visto** *a* **essere ~** (*da qcno*) go down well (with sb)

**benvo'lere** *vt* **farsi ~ da qcno** win sb's affection; **prendere qcno in ~** take a liking to sb; **essere benvoluto da tutti** be well-liked by everyone

**benvo'luto** *a* well-liked

**ben'zene** *nm* benzene

**ben'zina** *nf* petrol, gas *Am*; **far ~** get petrol. **~ senza piombo** leadfree petrol. **~ super** four-star petrol, premium gas *Am*. **~ verde** unleaded petrol

**benzi'naio, -a** *nmf* petrol station attendant, gas station attendant *Am*

**be'one, -a** *nmf fam* boozer

**'berbero, -a** *a & nmf* Berber

**'bere** *vt* drink; (*assorbire*) absorb; *fig* swallow; **~ una tazza di tè** have a cup of tea ● *nm* drinking; **da ~ e da mangiare** food and drink

**berga'motto** *nm* bergamot

**'Bering il mare di ~** the Bering Sea: **lo stretto di ~** the Bering Straits

**ber'lina** *nf Auto* saloon: **mettere alla ~ qcno** ridicule sb

**berli'nese** *nmf* Berliner ● *a* Berlin *attrib*

**Ber'lino** *nm* Berlin. **~ Est** East Berlin

**Ber'muda** *nfpl* **le ~** the Bermudas

**ber'muda** *nfpl* (*pantaloni*) Bermuda shorts

**'Berna** *nf* Berne

**ber'noccolo** *nm* bump; (*disposizione*) flair

**ber'retto** *nm* beret, cap. **~ a pompòn** bobble hat

**bersagli'are** *vt fig* bombard

**ber'saglio** *nm* target

**bescia'mella** *nf* béchamel, white sauce

**be'stemmia** *nf* swear-word; (*maledizione*) oath; (*sproposito*) blasphemy

**bestemmi'are** *vi* swear

**'bestia** *nf* animal; (*persona brutale*) beast; (*persona sciocca*) fool; **andare in ~** *fam* blow one's top; **lavorare come una ~** slave away

**besti'ale** *a* bestial; (*espressione, violenza*) brutal; (*fam: freddo, fame*) terrible; **fa un caldo/freddo ~** it's dreadfully hot/cold

**bestialità** *nf inv* bestiality; *fig* nonsense

**besti'ame** *nm* livestock

**betabloc'cante** *nm* betablocker

**Be'tlemme** *nf* Bethlehem

**betoni'era** *nf* concrete mixer

**'bettola** *nf fig* dive

**be'tulla** *nf* birch

**be'vanda** *nf* drink. **~ alcolica** alcoholic drink

**bevi|'tore, -'trice** *nmf* drinker

**be'vuta** *nf* drink

**be'vuto** *pp di* bere

**Bhu'tan** *nm* Bhutan

**bi+** *pref* bi+

**bi'ada** *nf* fodder

**bianche'ria** *nf* linen. **~ per la casa** white goods, household linen. **~ intima** underwear; (*da donna*) lingerie. **~ da letto** bed linen

**bian'chetto** *nm* whitener

**bi'anco, -a** *a* white; (*foglio*) blank; **voce bianca** treble voice ● *nmf* white ● *nm* white; **mangiare in ~** eat bland food; **andare in ~** *fam* not score; **in ~ e nero** (*film, fotografia*) black and white, monochrome; **passare una notte in ~** have a sleepless night. **~ sporco** off white. **~ d'uovo** egg white

**biancomangi'are** *nm* blancmange

**bian'core** *nm* (*bianchezza*) whiteness

**bianco'segno** *nm Jur blank document bearing a signature*

**bianco'spino** *nm* hawthorn

**biasci'care** *vt* (*mangiare*) eat noisily; (*parlare*) mumble

**biasi'mare** *vt* blame

**biasi'mevole** *a* blameworthy

**bi'asimo** *nm* blame

**'Bibbia** *nf* Bible

**bibe'ron** *nm inv* [baby's] bottle

**'bibita** *nf* [soft] drink. **~ gasata** fizzy drink

**'biblico** *a* biblical

**bibliogra'fia** *nf* bibliography

**biblio'grafico** *a* bibliographical

**biblio'teca** *nf* library; (*mobile*) bookcase

**bibliote'cario, -a** *nmf* librarian

**bicame'rale** *a* two-chamber *attrib*. bicameral

**bicarbo'nato** *nm* bicarbonate. **~ di sodio** bicarbonate of soda

**bicchie'rata** *nf* glassful

**bicchi'ere** *nm* glass

**bicchie'rino** *nm fam* tipple

**bicente'nario** *nm* bicentenary

**bici'cletta** *nf* bicycle, bike; **andare in ~** cycle, go by bike; (*sapere*) ride a bicycle. **~ da corsa** racer

**bi'cipite** *nm* biceps

**bi'cocca** *nf* hovel

**bico'lore** *a* two-coloured

**bidè** *nm inv* bidet

**bi'dello, -a** *nmf* janitor, [school] caretaker

**bidirezio'nale** *a* bidirectional

**bido'nare** *vt* con, swindle; **farsi ~** be conned

**bido'nata** *nf fam* swindle

**bi'done** *nm* bin; (*fam: truffa*) swindle; **fare un ~ a qcno** *fam* stand sb up. **~ dell'immondizia, ~ della spazzatura** rubbish bin, trash can *Am*

**bidon'ville** *nf inv* shantytown

**bi'eco** *a* callous

**bi'ella** *nf* connecting rod

**Bielo'russia** *nf* Belarus

**bielo'russo, -a** *a & nmf* Belorussian

**bien'nale** *a* biennial

**bi'ennio** *nm* two-year period

**bi'erre** *nfpl* (*Brigate Rosse*) Red Brigades

**bi'etola** *nf* beet

**bifo'cale** *a* bifocal

**bi'folco, -a** *nmf fig* boor

**bifor'carsi** *vr* fork

**biforcazi'one** *nf* fork

**bifor'cuto** *a* forked

**biga'mia** *nf* bigamy

**'bigamo, -a** *a* bigamous ● *nmf* bigamist

**big bang** *nm* big bang

**bighello'nare** *vi* loaf around

**bighel'lone** *nm* loafer

**bigiotte'ria** *nf* costume jewellery; (*negozio*) jeweller's

**bigliet'taio** *nm* booking clerk; (*sui treni*) ticket-collector

**bigliette'ria** *nf* ticket-office; *Theat* box-office. **~ automatica** ticket vending machine

**bigli'etto** *nm* ticket; (*lettera breve*) note; (*cartoncino*) card; (*di banca*) banknote. **~ di sola andata** single [ticket]. **~ di andata e ritorno** return [ticket]. **~ di auguri** card. **~ chilometrico** *ticket allowing travel up to a maximum specified distance*. **~ collettivo** group ticket. **~ giornaliero** day pass. **~ d'ingresso** entrance ticket. **~ della lotteria** lottery ticket. **~ da visita** business card

**bigliet'tone** *nm* (*fam: soldi*) big one

**bignè** *nm inv* puff. **~ alla crema** cream puff

**bigo'dino** *nm* roller

**bi'gotto** *nm* bigot

**bi'kini** *nm inv* bikini

**bi'lancia** *nf* scales *pl*; (*di orologio, Comm*) balance; **B~** *Astr* Libra. **~ commerciale** balance of trade. **~ da cucina** kitchen scales.

**~ dei pagamenti** balance of payments. **~ pesapersone** scales

**bilanci'are** vt balance; fig weigh

**bilancia'tura** nf **~ gomme** wheel-balancing

**bilanci'ere** nm (in sollevamento pesi) barbell; (di orologio) balance wheel

**bi'lancio** nm budget; Comm balance [sheet]; **fare il ~** balance the books; fig take stock; **chiudere il ~ in attivo/passivo** to end the financial year in profit/with a loss. **~ preventivo** budget

**bilate'rale** a bilateral

**'bile** nf bile; fig rage

**bili'ardo** nm billiards sg

**'bilico** nm equilibrium; **in ~** in the balance

**bi'lingue** a bilingual

**bilingu'ismo** nm bilingualism

**bili'one** nm billion

**bili'oso** a bilious

**bilo'cale** a two-room ● nm two-room flat

**'bimbo, -a** nmf child. **~ in fasce** babe in arms

**bimen'sile** a fortnightly Br, twice-monthly

**bime'strale** a bimonthly

**bi'mestre** nm two months

**bi'nario** nm track; (piattaforma) platform

**bi'nocolo** nm binoculars pl

**bi'nomio** nm binomial

**bio+** pref bio+

**bioagricol'tore** nm organic farmer

**bioagricol'tura** nf organic farming

**bio'chimica** nf biochemistry

**bio'chimico, -a** nmf biochemist ● a biochemical

**biodegra'dabile** a biodegradable

**biodiversità** nf biodiversity

**bio'etica** nf bioethics

**bio'fisica** nf biophysics

**biogra'fia** nf biography

**bio'grafico** a biographical

**bi'ografo, -a** nmf biographer

**bioingegne'ria** nf bioengineering

**biolo'gia** nf biology

**biologica'mente** adv biologically

**bio'logico** a biological

**bi'ologo, -a** nmf biologist

**bi'onda** nf blonde. **~ ossigenata** peroxide blonde

**bi'ondo** a blond ● nm fair colour; (uomo) fair-haired man. **~ cenere** ash blond. **~ platino** platinum blonde

**bi'onico** a bionic

**bio'psia** nf biopsy

**bio'ritmo** nm biorhythm

**bio'sfera** nf biosphere

**bi'ossido** nm dioxide. **~ di carbonio** carbon dioxide

**biotecnolo'gia** nf biotechnology

**bip** nm inv blip

**bipar'titico** a bipartisan

**biparti'tismo** nm two-party system

**bipar'tito** a bipartite, two-party attrib ● nm two-party coalition

**bipartizi'one** nf division into two parts

**bipo'lare** a Electr bipolar; Pol dominated by two large parties

**bipola'rismo** nm Pol system in which the numerous parties line up behind two main parties

**bipolarizazzi'one** nf Pol tendency towards 'bipolarismo'

**bi'posto** a inv & nm inv two-seater

**'birba** nf, **bir'bante** nm rascal, rogue

**birbo'nata** nf trick

**bir'bone** a wicked

**birdie** nm inv (golf) birdie

**biri'chino, -a** a naughty ● nmf little devil

**bi'rillo** nm skittle

**Bir'mania** nf Burma

**bir'mano, -a** a & nmf Burmese

**'birra** nf beer; **a tutta ~** fig flat out. **~ chiara** lager. **~ grande** ≈ pint. **~ piccola** ≈ half-pint. **~ scura** dark beer, brown ale Br

**birre'ria** nf beer-house; (fabbrica) brewery

**bis** nm inv encore

**bi'saccia** nf haversack

**bi'sbetica** nf shrew

**bi'sbetico** a bad-tempered

**bisbigli'are** vt/i whisper

**bi'sbiglio** nm whisper

**bi'sboccia** nf **fare ~** make merry

**'bisca** nf gambling-house

**Bi'scaglia** nf **il golfo di ~** the Bay of Biscay

**'biscia** nf snake

**biscotti'era** nf biscuit barrel, biscuit tin

**bi'scotto** nm biscuit. **~ per cani** dog-biscuit

**bisessu'ale** a & nmf bisexual

**bise'stile** a **anno ~** leap year

**bisettima'nale** a twice-weekly

**biset'trice** nf bisector

**bisezi'one** nf bisection

**bisil'labico** a two-syllable attrib, bisyllabic

**bi'slacco** a peculiar

**bi'slungo** a oblong

**bi'snonno, -a** nm great-grandfather ● nf great-grandmother

**biso'gnare** vi **bisogna agire subito** we must act at once; **bisogna farlo** it is necessary to do it; **non bisogna venire** you don't have to come

**bi'sogno** nm need; (povertà) poverty; **aver ~ di** need

**biso'gnoso** a needy; (povero) poor; **~ di** in need of

**bi'sonte** nm bison

**bi'stecca** nf steak. **~ di cavallo** horsemeat steak. **~ ai ferri** grilled steak. **~ alla fiorentina** large grilled beef steak

**bi'sticci** nmpl bickering

**bisticci'are** vi quarrel

**bi'sticcio** nm quarrel; (gioco di parole) pun

**bistrat'tare** vt mistreat

**bistrò** nm inv bistro

**'bisturi** nm inv scalpel

**bi'sunto** a very greasy

**bit** nm inv bit

**bito'nale** a two-tone

**bi'torzolo** nm lump

'**bitter** nm inv bitter aperitif
**bi'tume** nm bitumen
**bivac'care** vi bivouac
**bi'vacco** nm bivouac
'**bivio** nm crossroads; (di strada) fork
**bizan'tino** a Byzantine
'**bizza** nf tantrum; **fare le bizze** ⟨bambini:⟩ play up
**bizzar'ria** nf eccentricity
**biz'zarro** a bizarre
**biz'zeffe** adv **a ~** galore
'**blackjack** nm blackjack
**blan'dire** vt soothe; (allettare) flatter
'**blando** a mild
**bla'sfemo** a blasphemous
**bla'sone** nm coat of arms
**blate'rare** vi blether, blather; **~ di qcsa** burble on about sth
'**blatta** nf cockroach
'**bleso** a lisping
**blin'dare** vt armour-plate
**blin'dato** a armoured
'**blinker** nm inv blinker
'**blister** nm inv blister pack
**blitz** nm inv blitz
**bloc'care** vt block; (isolare) cut off; Mil blockade; Comm freeze; stop ⟨assegno⟩; **~ l'accesso** a seal off
**bloc'carsi** vr Mech jam
**blocca'sterzo** nm steering lock
**bloc'cato** a blocked
**bloc'chetto** nm **~ per appunti** memo pad. **~ di biglietti** book of tickets
'**blocco** nm block; Mil blockade; (dei fitti) restriction; (di carta) pad; (unione) coalition; **in ~** Comm in bulk. **~ per appunti** notepad. **~ psicologico** mental block. **~ stradale** roadblock
**block-notes** nm inv memo pad
**blu** a & nm blue
**blu'astro** a bluish
**blue chip** nf inv Fin blue chip
**blue-'jeans** nmpl jeans
**bluff** nm inv (carte, fig) bluff
**bluf'fare** vi (carte, fig) bluff
'**blusa** nf blouse
'**boa** nm boa [constrictor]; (sciarpa) [feather] boa ● nf Naut buoy
**bo'ato** nm rumbling
**bo'bina** nf spool; (di film) reel; Electr coil
**bobi'nare** vt spool
'**bocca** nf mouth; **a ~ aperta** fig dumbfounded; **in ~ al lupo!** fam break a leg!; **fare la respirazione ~ a ~ a qcno** give sb mouth to mouth resuscitation, give sb the kiss of life; **essere di ~ buona** eat anything; fig be easily satisfied; **essere sulla ~ di tutti** be the talk of the town. **~ del camino** chimneybreast. **~ di leone** snapdragon
**boccac'cesco** a licentious
**boc'caccia** nf grimace; **far boccacce** make faces
**boc'caglio** nm nozzle
**boc'cale** nm jug; (da birra) mug
**bocca'porto** nm Naut hatch

**bocca'scena** nm inv proscenium
**boc'cata** nf (di fumo) puff; **prendere una ~ d'aria** get a breath of fresh air
**boc'cetta** nf small bottle
**bocchegi'are** vi gasp
**boc'chino** nm cigarette holder; (di pipa, Mus) mouthpiece
'**boccia** nf (palla) bowl; **bocce** pl (gioco) bowls sg; **giocare a bocce** play bowls
**bocci'are** vt (agli esami) fail; (respingere) reject; (alle bocce) hit; **essere bocciato** fail; (ripetere) repeat a year
**boccia'tura** nf failure
**bocci'olo** nm bud
'**boccolo** nm ringlet
**boccon'cino** nm morsel
**boc'cone** nm mouthful; (piccolo pasto) snack
**boc'coni** adv face down[wards]
**Bo'emia** nf Bohemia
**bo'emo, -a** a & nmf Bohemian
**bo'ero, -a** nmf Afrikaner
**bofonchi'are** vi grumble
**boh** int dunno
'**boia** nm executioner; **fa un freddo ~** fam it's brass-monkey weather; **ho un sonno ~** fam I can't keep my eyes open
**boi'ata** nf fam rubbish
**boicot'taggio** nm boycotting
**boicot'tare** vt boycott
**bo'lero** nm bolero
'**bolgia** nf (caos) bedlam
'**bolide** nm meteor; **passare come un ~** shoot past [like a rocket]
**Bo'livia** nf Bolivia
**bolivi'ano, -a** a & nmf Bolivian
'**bolla** nf bubble; (vescica, in tappezzeria) blister; **finire in una ~ di sapone** go up in smoke. **~ di accompagnamento** packing list. **~ d'aria** (in acqua) air bubble. **~ di consegna** packing list
**bol'lare** vt stamp; fig brand
**bol'lato** a fig branded; **carta bollata** paper with stamp showing payment of duty
**bol'lente** a boiling [hot]
**bol'letta** nf bill; **essere in ~** be hard up
**bollet'tino** nm bulletin; Comm list. **~ d'informazione** fact sheet. **~ meteorologico** weather report. **~ ufficiale** gazette
**bolli'latte** nm milk pan
**bol'lino** nm coupon
**bol'lire** vt/i boil
**bol'lito** nm boiled meat
**bolli'tore** nm boiler; (per l'acqua) kettle
**bolli'tura** nf boiling
'**bollo** nm stamp; Auto tax disc
**bol'lore** nm boil; (caldo) intense heat; fig ardour
**Bo'logna** nf Bologna
**bolo'gnese** nmf person from Bologna; **spaghetti alla ~** spaghetti bolognese
'**bomba** nf bomb; **a prova di ~** bomb-proof; **tornare a ~** get back to the point. **~ atomica** nuclear bomb. **~ a mano** hand gre-

nade. ~ **molotov** petrol bomb. ~ **ad orologeria** time bomb

**bombarda'mento** *nm* shelling; (*con aerei*) bombing; *fig* bombardment. ~ **aereo** air raid

**bombar'dare** *vt* shell; (*con aerei*) bomb; *fig* bombard

**bombardi'ere** *nm* bomber

**bom'bato** *a* domed

'**bomber** *nm inv* bomber jacket

**bom'betta** *nf* bowler [hat]

'**bombo** *nm* bumblebee

'**bombola** *nf* cylinder. ~ **di gas** gas bottle, gas cylinder

**bcmbo'lone** *nm* doughnut

**bomboni'era** *nf* wedding keep-sake

**bo'naccia** *nf Naut* calm

**bonacci'one, -a** *nmf* good-natured person ● *a* good-natured

**bo'nario** *a* kindly

**bo'nifica** *nf* land reclamation

**bonifi'care** *vt* reclaim

**bo'nifico** *nm Comm* discount; ~ [**bancario**] [credit] transfer

**bontà** *nf* goodness; (*gentilezza*) kindness

'**bonus-'malus** *nm inv Auto* car-insurance policy with no claims bonus clause

'**boogie** *nm* boogie

'**bookmaker** *nm inv* bookmaker

'**boomerang** *nm inv* boomerang

**boot** *nm Comput* boot-up; **eseguire il** ~ boot up

'**bora** *nf cold north-east wind in the upper Adriatic*

**borbot'tare** *vi* mumble; ⟨*stomaco:*⟩ rumble

**borbot'tio** *nm* mumbling; (*di stomaco*) rumbling

'**borchia** *nf* stud

**borchi'ato** *a* studded

**bor'dare** *vt* border

**bor'data** *nf Naut* broadside

**borda'tura** *nf* border

**bor'deaux** *nm inv* (*vino*) claret, Bordeaux ● *a inv* (*colore*) claret

**bor'dello** *nm* brothel; *fig* bedlam; (*disordine*) mess

**bor'dino** *nm* narrow border

'**bordo** *nm* border; (*estremità*) edge; **a** ~ *Aeron, Naut* on board; **d'alto** ~ ⟨*prostituta*⟩ high-class. ~ **d'attacco** *Aeron* leading edge

**bor'dura** *nf* border

**bor'gata** *nf* hamlet

**bor'ghese** *a* bourgeois; ⟨*abito*⟩ civilian; **in** ~ in civilian dress; ⟨*poliziotto*⟩ in plain clothes

**borghe'sia** *nf* middle classes *pl*

'**borgo** *nm* village; (*quartiere*) district

'**boria** *nf* conceit

**bori'oso** *a* conceited

**bor'lotto** *nm* [**fagiolo**] ~ borlotto bean

'**Borneo** *nm* Borneo

**boro'talco** *nm* talcum powder

**bor'raccia** *nf* flask

'**Borsa** *nf* ~ [**valori**] Stock Exchange

'**borsa** *nf* bag; (*borsetta*) handbag. ~ **dell'acqua calda** hot-water bottle. ~ **frigo**

cool-box. ~ **della spesa** shopping bag. ~ **di studio** scholarship. ~ **termica** cool bag. ~ **da viaggio** travel bag

**borsai'olo** *nm* pickpocket

**bor'seggio** *nm* pickpocketing

**borsel'lino** *nm* purse

**bor'sello** *nm* (*portamonete*) purse; (*borsetto*) man's handbag

**bor'setta** *nf* handbag

**bor'setto** *nm* man's handbag

**bor'sino** *nm Fin* dealing room

**bor'sista** *nmf Fin* speculator; *Sch* scholarship holder

**bo'scaglia** *nf* woodlands *pl*

**boscai'olo** *nm* woodman; (*guardaboschi*) forester

**bo'schetto** *nm* grove

'**bosco** *nm* wood

**bo'scoso** *a* wooded

'**Bosnia** *nf* Bosnia

**bos'niaco, -a** *a & nmf* Bosnian

**Bosnia-Erzego'vina** *nf* Bosnia-Herzegovina

**boss** *nm inv* ~ **mafioso** Mafia boss

'**bosso** *nm* boxwood

'**bossolo** *nm* cartridge case

**Bot** *nm abbr* (**Buoni Ordinari Del Tesoro**) T-bills

**bo'tanica** *nf* botany

**bo'tanico** *a* botanical ● *nm* botanist

'**botola** *nf* trapdoor

**Bot'swana** *nm* Botswana

'**botta** *nf* blow; (*rumore*) bang; **fare a botte** come to blows. ~ **e risposta** *fig* thrust and counter-thrust

**botta'trice** *nf* monkfish

'**botte** *nf* barrel

**bot'tega** *nf* shop; (*di artigiano*) workshop

**botte'gaio, -a** *nmf* shopkeeper

**botte'ghino** *nm Theatr* box-office; (*del lotto*) lottery-shop

**bot'tiglia** *nf* bottle; **in** ~ bottled

**bottiglie'ria** *nf* wine shop

**bot'tino** *nm* loot; *Mil* booty

'**botto** *nm* bang. **di** ~ all of a sudden

**bot'tone** *nm* button; *Bot* bud. ~ **di carica** winder

**botu'lismo** *nm* botulism

'**bourbon** *nm inv* bourbon

**bo'vini** *nmpl* cattle

**bo'vino** *a* bovine

'**bowling** *nm* bowling

**box** *nm inv* (*per cavalli*) loosebox; (*recinto per bambini*) play-pen

'**boxe** *nf* boxing

'**bozza** *nf* draft; *Typ* proof; (*bernoccolo*) bump; ~ **in colonna** galley [proof]. ~ **definitiva** page proof. ~ **impaginata** page proof. ~ **di stampa** page proofs

**boz'zetto** *nm* sketch

'**bozzolo** *nm* cocoon

**BR** *nfpl abbr* (**Brigate Rosse**) Red Brigades

**brac'care** *vt* hunt

**brac'cetto** *nm* **a** ~ arm in arm

**bracci'ale** *nm* bracelet; (*fascia*) armband

**braccia'letto** *nm* bracelet; *(di orologio)* watch-strap

**bracci'ante** *nm* day labourer

**bracci'ata** *nf (nel nuoto)* stroke

**'braccio** *nm (pl nf* **braccia)** arm; *(di fiume, pl* **bracci)** arm. ~ **di ferro** arm wrestling

**bracci'olo** *nm (di sedia)* arm[rest]; *(da nuoto)* armband

**'bracco** *nm* hound

**bracconi'ere** *nm* poacher

**'brace** *nf* embers *pl*; **alla** ~ char-grilled

**'brache** *nfpl (fam: pantaloni)* britches; **calare le** ~ *fig* chicken out

**braci'ere** *nm* brazier

**braci'ola** *nf* chop. ~ **di maiale** pork chop

**'brado** *a* **allo stato** ~ in the wild

**braille** *nm* Braille

**brain-'storming** *nm inv* brainstorming

**'brama** *nf* longing

**bra'mare** *vt* long for

**bra'mino** *nm* Brahmin

**bramo'sia** *nf* yearning

**'branca** *nf* branch

**'branchia** *nf* gill

**'branco** *nm (di cani)* pack; *(pej: di persone)* gang

**branco'lare** *vi* grope

**'branda** *nf* camp-bed

**bran'dello** *nm* scrap; **a brandelli** in tatters

**bran'dina** *nf* cot

**bran'dire** *vt* brandish

**'brandy** *nm inv* brandy

**'brano** *nm* piece; *(di libro)* passage

**bran'zino** *nm* sea bass

**bra'sare** *vt* braise

**bra'sato** *nm braised beef with herbs*

**Bra'sile** *nm* Brazil

**brasili'ano, -a** *a & nmf* Brazilian

**bra'vata** *nf* bragging

**'bravo** *a* good; *(abile)* clever; *(coraggioso)* brave; ~! well done!

**bra'vura** *nf* skill

**'breccia** *nf* breach; **sulla** ~ *fig* very successful, at the top

**brecci'ame** *nm* loose chippings *pl*

**bre'saola** *nf dried, salted beef sliced thinly and eaten cold*

**Bre'tagna** *nf* Brittany

**bre'tella** *nf* shoulder-strap; *Mech* brace; **bretelle** *pl (di calzoni)* braces, suspenders *Am*

**'bretone** *a & nmf* Breton

**'breve** *a* brief, short; **in** ~ briefly; **tra** ~ shortly

**brevet'tare** *vt* patent

**bre'vetto** *nm* patent; *(attestato)* licence

**brevità** *nf* shortness

**'brezza** *nf* breeze

**'bricco** *nm* jug. ~ **del latte** milk jug

**bricco'nata** *nf* dirty trick

**bric'cone** *nm* blackguard; *hum* rascal

**'briciola** *nf* crumb; *fig* grain

**'briciolo** *nm* fragment; **non hai un** ~ **di cervello!** you don't have an ounce of common sense!

**bridge** *nm inv (carte)* bridge

**'briga** *nf (fastidio)* trouble; *(lite)* quarrel; **attaccar** ~ pick a quarrel; **prendersi la** ~ **di fare qcsa** go to the trouble of doing sth

**brigadi'ere** *nm (dei carabinieri)* sergeant

**brigan'taggio** *nm* highway robbery

**bri'gante** *nm* bandit; *hum* rogue

**bri'gare** *vi* to intrigue

**bri'gata** *nf* brigade; *(gruppo)* group

**briga'tista** *nmf* Pol member of the Red Brigades

**'briglia** *nf* rein; **a** ~ **sciolta** at full gallop; *fig* at breakneck speed

**bril'lante** *a* brilliant; *(scintillante)* sparkling ● *nm* diamond

**brillan'tina** *nf* brilliantine

**bril'lare** *vi* shine; *(metallo:)* glitter; *(scintillare)* sparkle

**'brillo** *a* tipsy

**'brina** *nf* hoar-frost

**brin'dare** *vi* toast; ~ **a qcno** drink a toast to sb

**'brindisi** *nm inv* toast

**'brio** *nm* vivacity

**bri'oche** *nf inv* croissant

**bri'oso** *a* vivacious

**'briscola** *nf (seme)* trumps

**bri'tannico** *a* British

**'brivido** *nm* shiver; *(di paura ecc)* shudder; *(di emozione)* thrill; **avere i brividi** have the shivers; **dare i brividi a qcno** give sb the shivers

**brizzo'lato** *a (capelli, barba)* greying

**'brocca** *nf* jug

**broc'cato** *nm* brocade

**'broccoli** *nmpl* broccoli

**bro'daglia** *nf pej* dishwater

**'brodo** *nm* broth; *(per cucinare)* stock. ~ **di manzo** beef tea. ~ **di pollo** chicken broth; *(per cucinare)* chicken stock. ~ **ristretto** consommé. ~ **vegetale** clear broth; *(per cucinare)* vegetable stock

**'broglio** *nm* ~ **elettorale** gerrymandering

**'broker** *nmf inv* broker; ~ **d'assicurazioni** insurance broker

**'bromo** *nm* Chem bromine

**bro'muro** *nm* bromide

**bronchi'ale** *a* bronchial

**bron'chite** *nf* bronchitis

**bron'chitico** *a* chesty

**'broncio** *nm* sulk; **fare il** ~ sulk

**bronto'lare** *vi* grumble; *(tuono ecc:)* rumble; ~ **contro qcno/qcsa** grumble *or* grouch about sb/sth

**bronto'lio** *nm* grumbling; *(di tuono, stomaco)* rumbling

**bronto'lone, -a** *nmf* grumbler

**'bronzo** *nm* bronze; **una faccia di** ~ *fam* a brass neck

**bros'sura** *nf* **edizione in** ~ paperback

**bru'care** *vt (pecora:)* graze

**bruciacchi'are** *vt* scorch

**bruci'ante** *a* burning

**brucia'pelo** *adv* **a** ~ point-blank

**bruci'are** vt burn: (scottare) scald; (incendiare) set fire to ● vi burn; (scottare) scald

**bruci'arsi** vr burn oneself

**bruci'ato** a burnt; fig burnt-out

**brucia'tore** nm burner

**brucia'tura** nf burn

**bruci'ore** nm burning sensation

**'bruco** nm grub

**'brufolo** nm spot

**brughi'era** nf heath

**bruli'care** vi swarm

**bruli'chio** nm swarming

**'brullo** a bare

**'bruma** nf mist

**Bru'nei** nm Brunei

**'bruno** a brown; ⟨occhi, capelli⟩ dark

**brusca'mente** adv (di colpo) suddenly

**bru'schetta** nf toasted bread rubbed with garlic and sprinkled with olive oil

**'brusco** a sharp; ⟨persona⟩ brusque, abrupt; ⟨improvviso⟩ sudden

**bru'sio** nm buzzing

**bru'tale** a brutal

**brutalità** nf brutality

**brutaliz'zare** vt brutalize

**'bruto** a & nm brute

**brut'tezza** nf ugliness

**'brutto** a ugly; ⟨tempo, tipo, situazione, affare⟩ nasty; (cattivo) bad. **brutta copia** nf rough copy. ~ **tiro** nm dirty trick

**brut'tura** nf ugly thing

**bub'bone** nm Med swelling

**'buca** nf hole; (avvallamento) hollow. ~ **delle lettere** letter-box

**buca'neve** nm inv snowdrop

**bucani'ere** nm buccaneer

**bu'care** vt make a hole in; (pungere) prick; punch ⟨biglietti⟩ ● vi have a puncture

**'Bucarest** nf Bucharest

**bu'carsi** vr prick oneself; (con droga) shoot up

**buca'tini** nmpl pasta similar to spaghetti but thicker and hollow

**bu'cato** nm washing; **fare il ~** do the washing

**'buccia** nf peel, skin; **bucce** pl (di frutta) parings. ~ **di banana** banana skin

**bucherel'lare** vt riddle

**bucherel'lato** a pitted

**'buco** nm hole. ~ **della serratura** keyhole

**bu'colica** nf bucolic

**bu'colico** nm bucolic

**'Budda** nm Buddha

**bud'dista** nmf Buddhist

**bu'dello** nm (pl nf **budella**) bowel

**'budget** nm inv budget; ~ **provvisorio** minibudget

**budge'tario** a budgetary

**bu'dino** nm pudding

**'bue** nm (pl **buoi**) ox; **carne di ~** beef

**'bufalo** nm buffalo

**bu'fera** nf storm; (di neve) blizzard

**bufferiz'zato** a Comput buffered

**buf'fet** nm inv snack bar; (mobile) sideboard; (pasto) buffet

**buf'fetto** nm cuff

**'buffo** a funny; Theat comic ● nm funny thing

**buffo'nata** nf (scherzo) joke

**buf'fone** nm buffoon; **fare il ~** play the fool

**bu'gia** nf lie; ~ **pietosa** white lie

**bugi'ardo, -a** a lying ● nmf liar

**bugi'gattolo** nm cubby-hole

**'buio** a dark ● nm darkness; **al ~** in the dark; ~ **pesto** pitch dark

**'bulbo** nm bulb; (dell'occhio) eyeball

**Bulga'ria** nf Bulgaria

**'bulgaro, -a** a & nmf Bulgarian

**buli'mia** nf bulimia

**bu'limico** nmf bulimic

**'bullo** nm bully

**bul'lone** nm bolt

**'bunker** nm inv bunker

**buona'fede** nf good faith

**buo'nanima** nf **quella ~ di mio zio** my late uncle, God rest his soul

**buona'notte** int good night

**buona'sera** int good evening

**buonco'stume** nf Vice Squad

**buondì** int good day!

**buon'giorno** int good morning; (di pomeriggio) good afternoon

**buon'grado** nm **di ~** willingly

**buongu'staio, -a** nmf gourmet

**buon'gusto** nm good taste

**bu'ono** a good; ⟨momento⟩ right; **dar ~** (convalidare) accept; **alla buona** easy-going; ⟨cena⟩ informal; **buona fortuna!** good luck!; **buona notte/sera** good night/evening; **buon compleanno/Natale!** happy birthday/merry Christmas!; **buon viaggio!** have a good trip!; **buon appetito!** enjoy your meal!; ~ **senso** common sense; **di buon'ora** early; **a buon mercato** cheap; **una buona volta** once and for all; **buona parte di** the best part of; **tre ore buone** three good hours ● nm good; (in film) goody; (tagliando) voucher; (titolo) bond; **con le buone** gently. ~ **acquisto** gift token. ~ **sconto** money-off-coupon ● nmf **buono, -a a nulla** dead loss

**buontem'pone, -a** nmf happy-go-lucky person

**buonu'more** nm good temper

**buonu'scita** nf retirement bonus; (di dirigente) golden handshake

**buratti'naio** nm puppeteer

**burat'tino** nm puppet

**'burbero** a surly; (nei modi) rough

**bu'rino, -a** nmf hick

**'burla** nf joke; **fare una ~ a** play a trick on; **per ~** for fun

**bur'lare** vt make a fool of

**bur'larsi** vr ~ **di** make fun of

**buro'crate** nm bureaucrat

**burocra'tese** nm gobbledygook

**buro'cratico** a bureaucratic

**burocra'zia** nf bureaucracy

**bu'rotica** nf office automation

**bur'rasca** nf storm

**burra'scoso** a stormy

**'burro** nm butter. ~ **di arachidi** peanut butter

**bur'rone** *nm* ravine
**Bu'rundi** *nm* Burundi
**bus** *nmt inv Comput* bus. **~ locale** local bus
**bu'scare** *vt* catch; **buscarle** *fam* get a hiding
**bu'scarsi** *vr* catch
**bus'sare** *vt* knock
**'bussola** *nf* compass; **perdere la ~** lose one's bearings
**'busta** *nf* envelope; *(astuccio)* case. **~ affrancata** business reply envelope. **~ a finestra** window envelope. **~ imbottita** Jiffy bag®, padded envelope. **~ paga** pay packet
**busta'rella** *nf* bribe

**bu'stina** *nf (di tè)* tea bag; *(per medicine)* sachet
**'busto** *nm* bust; *(indumento)* girdle; **a mezzo ~** half-length
**bu'tano** *nm* Calor gas®
**buttafu'ori** *nm inv* bouncer
**but'tare** *vt* throw; **~ giù** *(demolire)* knock down; *(inghiottire)* gulp down; scribble down *(scritto)*; *fam* put on *(pasta)*; *(scoraggiare)* dishearten; **~ via** throw away
**but'tarsi** *vr* throw oneself; *(saltare)* jump
**butte'rato** *a* pitted
**buz'zurro** *nm fam* yokel
**byte** *nm inv Comput* byte

# Cc

**ca.** *abbr* **(circa)** c.
**caba'ret** *nm inv* cabaret
**cabaret'tisco** *a* cabaret *attrib*
**ca'bina** *nf Naut, Aeron* cabin; *(al mare)* beach hut; *(di funivia)* [cable] car. **~ elettorale** polling booth. **~ di pilotaggio** cockpit; *(di aereo di linea)* flight deck. **~ di prova** fitting room. **~ telefonica** telephone box *Br*, phone booth
**cabi'nato** *nm* cabin cruiser
**ca'blaggio** *nm Electr* wiring
**ca'blato** *a (messaggio)* cable *attrib*
**cablo'gramma** *nm* cablegram
**cabo'taggio** *nm Naut* coastal navigation
**cabrio'let** *nm inv Auto* convertible
**ca'cao** *nm* cocoa
**ca'care** *vi vulg* have a crap
**caca'toa** *nm inv* cockatoo
**'cacca** *nf fam* poo, number two
**'cacchio** *nm fam* hell; **ma che ~ fai/dici?** *fam* what the hell are you doing/saying?
**'caccia** *nf* hunt; *(con fucile)* shooting; *(inseguimento)* chase; *(selvaggina)* game ● *nm inv Aeron* fighter; *Naut* destroyer; **andare a ~** go hunting. **~ grossa** big game. **~ all'uomo** man-hunt
**cacciabombardi'ere** *nm Aeron* fighter-bomber
**cacciagi'one** *nf* game
**cacci'are** *vt* hunt; *(mandar via)* chase away; *(scacciare)* drive out; *(ficcare)* shove; **caccia [fuori] i soldi!** *fam* out with the money!; **~ un urlo** *fam* let out a yell ● *vi* go hunting
**cacci'arsi** *vr (nascondersi)* hide; *(andare a finire)* get to; **~ nei guai** get into trouble
**caccia'tora: alla ~** *a Culin* chasseur
**caccia|'tore, -'trice** *nmf* hunter. **~ di dote** gold digger. **~ di frodo** poacher. **~ di taglie** bounty hunter. **~ di teste** *Comm* head-hunter

**cacciatorpedini'ere** *nm inv* destroyer
**caccia'vite** *nm inv* screwdriver
**cacci'ucco** *nm* **~ alla livornese** soup of seafood, tomato and wine served with bread
**cache-'sexe** *nm inv* thong
**ca'chet** *nm inv Med* capsule; *(colorante)* colour rinse; *(stile)* cachet
**'cachi** *nm inv* persimmon ● *a inv (colore)* khaki
**'cacio** *nm (formaggio)* cheese
**caci'otta** *nf* creamy, fairly soft cheese
**'caco** *nm fam* persimmon
**cacofo'nia** *nf* cacophony
**'cactus** *nm inv* cactus
**cada'uno** *a* each
**ca'davere** *nm* corpse
**cada'verico** *a fig* deathly pale
**ca'dente** *a* falling; *(casa)* crumbling
**ca'denza** *nf* cadence; *(ritmo)* rhythm; *Mus* cadenza
**caden'zare** *vt* give rhythm to
**caden'zato** *a* measured
**ca'dere** *vi* fall; *(capelli ecc.)* fall out; *(capitombolare)* tumble; *(vestito ecc.)* hang; **far ~** *(di mano)* drop; **~ dal sonno** feel very sleepy; **lasciar ~** drop; **~ dalle nuvole** *fig* be taken aback; **~ dalla finestra** fall out of the window
**ca'detto** *nm* cadet
**ca'duta** *nf* fall; *fig* downfall. **~ dei capelli** hair loss. **~ libera** freefall. **~ massi** falling rocks
**ca'duto** *nm* **i caduti** the dead; **monumento ai caduti** war memorial
**caffè** *nm inv* coffee; *(locale)* café. **~ corretto** espresso with a dash of liqueur. **~ lungo** weak black coffee. **~ macchiato** coffee with a dash of milk. **~ ristretto** extra-strong espresso coffee. **~ solubile** instant coffee

**caffe'ina** *nf* caffeine
**caffel'latte** *nm inv* white coffee
**caffette'ria** *nf* coffee bar
**caffetti'era** *nf* coffee-pot
**cafo'naggine** *nf* boorishness
**cafo'nata** *nf* boorishness
**ca'fone, -a** *nmf* boor
**cafone'ria** *nf* (*comportamento*) boorishness: è stata una ~ it was boorish
**ca'gare** *vi vulg* crap; **va' a ~!** go and get stuffed!
**cagio'nare** *vt* cause
**cagio'nevole** *a* delicate
**cagli'are** *vi* curdle
**cagli'arsi** *vr* curdle
**cagli'ata** *nf* curd cheese
**caglia'tura** *nf* curdling
**'cagna** *nf* bitch
**ca'gnara** *nf fam* din
**ca'gnesco** *a* **guardare qcno in ~** scowl at sb
**ca'gnetto** *nm* lapdog
**C.A.I.** *nm abbr* (**Club Alpino Italiano**) *Italian mountain sports association*
**cai'mano** *nm* cayman
**'caio** *nm* so-and-so
**'Cairo** *nm* **il ~** Cairo
**'cala** *nf* creek
**cala'brese** *a* & *nmf* Calabrian
**Ca'labria** *nf* Calabria
**cala'brone** *nm* hornet
**Cala'hari** *nm* **il ~** the Kalahari [Desert]
**cala'maio** *nm* inkpot
**cala'maretto** *nm* small squid
**cala'mari** *nmpl* squid *sg*
**cala'maro** *nm* squid
**cala'mita** *nf* magnet
**calamità** *nf inv* calamity. ~ **pl naturali** natural disasters
**calami'tare** *vt* draw (*attenzione*)
**ca'lante** *a* waning
**ca'lare** *vi* come down; (*vento:*) drop; (*diminuire*) fall; (*tramontare*) set; ~ **di peso** lose weight; ~ **di tono** *fig* drag ● *vt* (*abbassare*) lower; (*nei lavori a maglia*) decrease ● *nm* (*di luna*) waning
**ca'larsi** *vr* lower oneself
**ca'lata** *nf* (*invasione*) invasion
**'calca** *nf* throng
**cal'cagno** *nm* (*pl f* **calcagna**) heel; **stare alle calcagna di qcno** *fig* follow sb around
**cal'care**[1] *nm* limestone
**cal'care**[2] *vt* tread; (*premere*) press [down]; ~ **la mano** *fig* exaggerate; ~ **le orme di qcno** *fig* follow in sb's footsteps; ~ **le scene** *fig* tread the boards
**'calce**[1] *nf* lime. ~ **viva** quicklime
**'calce**[2] *nm* **in ~** at the foot of the page
**calce'struzzo** *nm* concrete
**cal'cetto** *nm* *Sport* five-a-side [football]; (*da tavolo*) table football
**calci'are** *vt* kick
**calcia'tore** *nm* footballer
**calcifi'carsi** *vr* calcify
**calcificazi'one** *nf* calcification

**cal'cina** *nf* mortar
**calci'naccio** *nm* (*pezzo di intonaco*) flake of plaster; (*pezzo di muro*) piece of rubble
**'calcio**[1] *nm* kick; *Sport* football; (*di arma da fuoco*) butt; **dare un ~** a kick; **giocare a ~** play football. ~ **d'angolo** corner [kick]. ~ **di punizione** free kick. ~ **di rigore** penalty [kick]
**'calcio**[2] *nm* *Chem* calcium
**calcio-mer'cato** *nm inv* transfer market
**'calco** *nm* (*con carta*) tracing; (*arte*) cast
**calco'lare** *vt* calculate; (*considerare*) consider
**calco'lato** *a* calculated
**calcola'tore** *a* calculating ● *nm* calculator; (*macchina elettronica*) computer. ~ **digitale** (*calcolatrice*) calculator
**calcola'trice** *nf* calculating machine
**'calcolo** *nm* calculation; *Med* stone; **per ~** *fig* out of self-interest; **mi sono fatto i calcoli** *fig* I've weighed up the pros and cons. ~ **approssimativo** guesstimate. ~ **biliare** gallstone. ~ **renale** kidney stone
**cal'daia** *nf* boiler
**caldar'rosta** *nf* roast chestnut
**caldeggi'are** *vt* support
**'caldo** *a* warm; (*molto caldo*) hot; (*situazione, zona*) dangerous; (*notizie*) latest; **non gli fa né ~ né freddo** *fig* he doesn't give a damn; **ondata di ~** heatwave; **tavola calda** snack bar ● *nm* heat; **avere ~** be warm, be hot; **fa ~** it's warm, it's hot
**caleido'scopio** *nm* kaleidoscope
**calen'dario** *nm* calendar. ~ **sportivo** sporting calendar
**ca'lesse** *nm* gig
**cali'brare** *vt* calibrate
**cali'brato** *a* calibrated; *fig* balanced; **taglie pl calibrate** clothes for non-standard sizes
**'calibro** *nm* calibre; (*strumento*) callipers *pl*; **di grosso ~** (*persona*) top *attrib*
**'calice** *nm* goblet; *Relig* chalice
**californi'ano, -a** *a* & *nmf* Californian
**ca'ligine** *nm* fog; (*industriale*) smog
**call-girl** *nf inv* call girl
**calligra'fia** *nf* handwriting; (*cinese*) calligraphy
**calli'grafico** *a* **perizia calligrafica** handwriting analysis
**cal'ligrafo, -a** *nmf* calligrapher
**cal'lista** *nmf* chiropodist
**'callo** *nm* corn; **fare il ~ a** become hardened to
**cal'loso** *a* callous
**'calma** *nf* calm; **mantenere la ~** keep calm; **prendersela con ~** *fig* take it easy; **fare qcsa con ~** take one's time doing sth
**cal'mante** *a* calming ● *nm* sedative
**cal'mare** *vt* calm [down]; (*lenire*) soothe
**cal'marsi** *vr* calm down; (*vento:*) drop; (*dolore:*) die down
**calmie'rare** *vt* control the prices of
**calmi'ere** *nm* price control

'**calmo** *a* calm

'**calo** *nm Comm* fall; (*di volume*) shrinkage; (*di peso*) loss: **in ~** dwindling

ca'**lore** *nm* heat; (*moderato*) warmth; **in ~** (*di animale*) on heat

calo'**ria** *nf* calorie

ca'**lorico** *a* calorific

calo'**rifero** *nm* radiator

calorosa'**mente** *adv* warmly

calorosità *nf fig* warmth

calo'**roso** *a* warm

ca'**lotta** *nf* **~ cranica** skullcap. **~ glaciale** icecap. **~ polare** polar icecap

calpe'**stare** *vt* trample [down]; *fig* trample on (*diritti, sentimenti*); '**vietato ~ l'erba**' 'keep off the grass'

calpe'**stio** *nm* (*passi*) footsteps *pl*; (*rumore*) stamping

ca'**lunnia** *nf* slander

calunni'**are** *vt* slander

calunni'**oso** *a* slanderous

ca'**lura** *nf* heat

cal'**vario** *nm* Calvary; *fig* trial

calvi'**nismo** *nm* Calvinism

calvi'**nista** *nmf* Calvinist

cal'**vizie** *nf* baldness

'**calvo** *a* bald

'**calza** *nf* (*da reggicalze*) stocking; (*da uomo*) sock. **~ della befana** ≈ Christmas stocking

calza'**maglia** *nf* tights *pl*; (*per danza*) leotard

cal'**zante** *a fig* fitting

cal'**zare** *vt* (*indossare*) wear; (*mettersi*) put on ● *vi* fit; **~ a pennello** (*indumenti:*) fit like a glove

calza'**scarpe** *nm inv* shoehorn

calza'**tura** *nf* footwear; **calzature** *pl* footwear *sg*

calzaturi'**ficio** *nm* shoe factory

cal'**zetta** *nf* ankle sock; **è una mezza ~** *fig* he's no use

calzet'**tone** *nm* knee-length woollen sock

cal'**zino** *nm* sock

calzo'**laio** *nm* shoe mender

calzole'**ria** *nf* (*negozio*) shoe shop

calzon'**cini** *nmpl* shorts. **~ da bagno** swimming trunks

cal'**zone** *nm* Culin folded pizza with tomato, mozzarella etc inside

cal'**zoni** *nmpl* trousers, pants *Am*. **~ alla cavallerizza** jodhpurs

camale'**onte** *nm* chameleon

cambi'**ale** *nf Comm* bill of exchange

cambia'**mento** *nm* change

cambi'**are** *vt* change; move (*casa*); (*fare cambio di*) exchange; **~ canale** *TV* switch over; **~ rotta** *Naut* alter course; **~ l'aria in una stanza** air a room ● *vi* change; (*fare cambio*) exchange

cambi'**arsi** *vr* change

cambiava'**lute** *nm* bureau de change

'**cambio** *nm* change; (*Comm, scambio*) exchange; *Mech* gear; **dare il ~ a qcno** relieve sb; **in ~ di** in exchange for. **~ della guardia** changeover. **~ dell'olio** oil change

Cam'**bogia** *nf* Cambodia

cambogi'**ano** *a & nmf* Cambodian

cam'**busa** *nf* pantry

ca'**melia** *nf* camellia

'**camera** *nf* room; (*mobili*) [bedroom] suite; *Phot* camera; **C~** *Pol, Comm* Chamber. **~ ammobiliata** bedsit. **~ ardente** chapel of rest. **~ d'aria** inner tube. **~ blindata** strong room. **C~ di Commercio** Chamber of Commerce. **C~ dei Comuni** House of Commons. **C~ dei Deputati** *Pol* ≈ House of Commons. **~ doppia** double room. **~ a gas** gas chamber. **~ da letto** bedroom. **~ a due letti** twin room. **~ matrimoniale** double room. **~ oscura** darkroom. **~ degli ospiti** guest room. **~ singola** single room

came'**rata**[1] *nf* (*dormitorio*) dormitory; *Mil* barrack room

came'**rata**[2] *nmf* mate

camera'**tesco** *a* comradely

camera'**tismo** *nm* comradeship

cameri'**era** *nf* maid; (*di ristorante*) waitress; (*in albergo*) chamber-maid

cameri'**ere** *nm* manservant; (*di ristorante*) waiter

came'**rino** *nm* dressing-room

came'**ristico** *a Mus* chamber

'**Camerun** *nm* il **~** Cameroon

'**camice** *nm* overall

camice'**ria** *nf* shirt shop

cami'**cetta** *nf* blouse

ca'**micia** *nf* shirt; **essere nato con la ~** *fig* be born lucky; **uovo in ~** poached egg. **~ di forza** strait-jacket. **~ nera** Blackshirt. **~ da notte** nightdress; (*da uomo*) nightshirt

camici'**aio** *nm* (*venditore*) shirtseller; (*sarto*) shirtmaker

camici'**ola** *nf* vest

cami'**netto** *nm* fireplace

ca'**mino** *nm* chimney; (*focolare*) fireplace, hearth

'**camion** *nm inv* lorry *Br*, truck

camion'**cino** *nm* van

camio'**netta** *nf* jeep

camio'**nista** *nmf* lorry driver *Br*, truck driver

'**camma** *nf* cam; **albero a camme** *Auto* camshaft

cam'**mello** *nm* camel; (*tessuto*) camel-hair ● *a inv* (*colore*) camel

cam'**meo** *nm* cameo

cammi'**nare** *vi* walk; (*auto, orologio:*) go; **~ avanti e indietro** pace up and down

cammi'**nata** *nf* walk; **fare una ~** go for a walk

cam'**mino** *nm* way; **essere in ~** be on the way; **mettersi in ~** set out; **cammin facendo** on the way

camo'**milla** *nf* camomile; (*bevanda*) camomile tea

camo'**millarsi** *vr sl* **camomillati!** don't get your knickers in a twist!, cool it!

Ca'**morra** *nf* local mafia

camor'**rista** *nmf* member of the 'Camorra'

ca'**moscio** *nm* chamois; (*pelle*) suede

**cam'pagna** *nf* country: (*paesaggio*) countryside: *Comm, Mil* campaign; **in ~** in the country. **~ elettorale** election campaign. **~ promozionale** promotional campaign, marketing campaign. **~ pubblicitaria** publicity campaign

**campa'gnola** *nf Auto* cross-country vehicle

**campa'gnolo, -a** *a* rustic ● *nm* countryman ● *nf* countrywoman

**cam'pale** *a* field *attrib*; **giornata ~** *fig* strenuous day

**cam'pana** *nf* bell; (*di vetro*) belljar; **a ~** bell-shaped; **essere sordo come una ~** be as deaf as a doorpost; **sentire anche l'altra ~** *fig* hear the other side of the story; **vivere sotto una ~ di vetro** *fig* be mollycoddled. **campane** *pl* **a morto** death knell

**campa'naccio** *nm* cowbell

**campa'naro** *nm* bell-ringer

**campa'nella** *nf* (*di tenda*) curtain ring

**campa'nello** *nm* door-bell; (*cicalino*) buzzer

**Cam'pania** *nf* Campania

**campa'nile** *nm* bell tower

**campani'lismo** *nm* parochialism

**campani'lista** *nmf* person with a parochial outlook

**campani'listico** *a* parochial

**cam'panula** *nf Bot* campanula

**cam'pare** *vi* live; (*a stento*) get by; **tirare a ~** *fig* live from day to day

**cam'pato** *a* **~ in aria** unfounded

**campeggi'are** *vi* camp; (*spiccare*) stand out; **'vietato ~'** 'no camping'

**campeggia|'tore, -'trice** *nmf* camper

**cam'peggio** *nm* camping; (*terreno*) campsite; **andare in ~** go camping; **fare ~ libero** camp in the wild. **~ per roulotte** caravan site

**cam'pestre** *a* rural

**Campi'doglio** *nm* Capitol

**'camping** *nm inv* campsite

**campiona'mento** *nm* sampling

**campio'nario** *nm* [set of] samples ● *a* **fiera campionaria** trade fair

**campio'nato** *nm* championship. **C~ Mondiale di Calcio** World Cup

**campiona'tura** *nf* (*di merce*) range of samples; (*in statistica*) sampling. **~ casuale** random sample

**campi'one** *nm* champion; *Comm* sample; (*esemplare*) specimen; **indagine ~** (*in statistica*) sample. **~ gratuito** free sample. **'~ senza valore'** 'sample, no commercial value'

**campio'nessa** *nf* ladies' champion

**'campo** *nm* field; (*accampamento*) camp; *Mil* encampment; **abbandonare il ~** *Mil* desert in the face of the enemy; *fig* throw in the towel; **a tutto ~** *fig* wide-ranging; **avere ~ libero** *fig* have a free hand; **giocare a tutto ~** *Sport* cover the entire pitch. **~ base** base camp. **~ di battaglia** battlefield. **~ da calcio** football pitch. **~ di concentramento** concentration camp. **~ da golf** golf course. **~ di grano** cornfield. **~ da hockey** hockey field. **~ di mais** cornfield. **~**

**sportivo** sports ground. **~ di sterminio** death camp. **~ da tennis** tennis court

**campo'santo** *nm* cemetery

**'campus** *nm inv* (*di università*) campus

**camuf'fare** *vt* disguise

**camuf'farsi** *vr* disguise oneself

**ca'muso** *a* **naso ~** snub nose

**'Canada** *nm* Canada

**cana'dese** *a & nmf* Canadian

**ca'naglia** *nf* scoundrel; (*plebaglia*) rabble

**ca'nale** *nm* channel; (*artificiale*) canal. **Canal Grande** Gran Canal. **~ della Manica** English Channel. **~ di scolo** dyke

**canaliz'zare** *vt* channel (*acque, energie*)

**canalizzazi'one** *nf* channelling; (*rete*) pipes *pl*

**'canapa** *nf* hemp. **~ indiana** (*droga*) cannabis

**Ca'narie** *nfpl* **le ~** the Canaries

**cana'rino** *nm* canary

**ca'nasta** *nf* (*gioco*) canasta

**cancel'labile** *a* erasable; (*impegno, incontro*) which can be cancelled

**cancel'lare** *vt* cross out; (*con la gomma*) rub out; *fig* wipe out; (*annullare*) cancel; *Comput* delete, erase

**cancel'larsi** *vr* be erased, be wiped out

**cancel'lata** *nf* railings *pl*

**cancel'lato** *a* cancelled

**cancella'tura** *nf* erasure

**cancellazi'one** *nf* cancellation; *Comput* deletion

**cancelle'ria** *nf* chancellery; (*articoli per scrivere*) stationery

**cancelli'ere** *nm* chancellor; (*di tribunale*) clerk

**cancel'lino** *nm* duster

**can'cello** *nm* gate

**cance'rogeno** *nm* carcinogen ● *a* carcinogenic

**cance'roso** *a* cancerous

**can'crena** *nf* gangrene; **andare in ~** become gangrenous

**cancre'noso** *a* gangrenous

**'cancro** *nm* cancer. **C~** *Astr* Cancer; **tropico del C~** Tropic of Cancer

**candeggi'are** *vt* bleach

**candeg'gina** *nf* bleach

**can'deggio** *nm* bleaching

**can'dela** *nf* candle; *Auto* spark plug; **a lume di ~** by candle-light; (*cena*) candlelit; **tenere la ~** *fig* play gooseberry; **il gioco non vale la ~** the game is not worth the candle

**cande'labro** *nm* candelabra

**cande'letta** *nf Med* pessary

**candeli'ere** *nm* candlestick

**cande'line** *nfpl* candles

**cande'lotto** *nm* (*di dinamite*) stick. **~ lacrimogeno** tear gas grenade

**candida'mente** *adv* innocently

**candi'dare** *vt* put forward as a candidate

**candi'darsi** *vr* stand as a candidate

**candi'dato, -a** *nmf* candidate

**candida'tura** *nf Pol* candidacy; (*per lavoro*) application

**'candido** *a* snow-white: (*sincero*) candid; (*puro*) pure

**can'dito** *a* candied ● *nm* piece of candied fruit

**can'dore** *nm* whiteness; *fig* innocence

**'cane** *nm* dog; (*di arma da fuoco*) cock; **un tempo da cani** foul weather; **fa un freddo ~** it's bitterly cold; **non c'era un ~** *fig* there wasn't a soul about; **solo come un ~** *fig* all on one's own; **essere come ~ e gatto** *fig* fight like cat and dog; **essere un ~** ⟨*attore, cantante*⟩ be appalling, be a dog *sl*; **fatto da cani** *fig* ⟨*lavoro*⟩ botched; **mangiare da cani** *fig* eat very badly; **figlio di un ~** *fam* son of a bitch. **~ da caccia** hunting dog. **~ per ciechi** guide-dog. **~ da corsa** greyhound. **~ da guardia** guard-dog. **~ lupo** alsatian. **~ poliziotto** police dog. **~ da salotto** lapdog. **~ sciolto** *fig* maverick

**ca'nestro** *nm* basket; **fare ~** score a basket

**'canfora** *nf* camphor

**cangi'ante** *a* iridescent; **seta ~** shot silk

**can'guro** *nm* kangaroo

**ca'nicola** *nf* scorching heat

**ca'nile** *nm* kennel; (*di allevamento*) kennels *pl*. **~ municipale** dog pound

**ca'nino** *a & nm* canine

**ca'nizie** *nm* white hair

**'canna** *nf* reed; (*da zucchero*) cane; (*di fucile*) barrel; (*bastone*) stick; (*di bicicletta*) crossbar; (*asta*) rod; (*fam: hascish*) joint; **povero in ~** destitute. **~ fumaria** flue. **~ da pesca** fishing-rod

**'cannabis** *nm inv* cannabis

**can'nella** *nf* cinnamon

**cannel'loni** *nmpl* **~ al forno** rolls of pasta stuffed with meat and baked in the oven

**can'neto** *nm* bed of reeds

**can'nibale** *nm* cannibal

**canniba'lismo** *nm* cannibalism

**cannocchi'ale** *nm* telescope

**can'noli** *nmpl* **~ alla siciliana** cylindrical pastries filled with ricotta and candied fruit

**canno'nata** *nf* cannon shot; **è una ~** *fig* it's brilliant

**cannon'cino** *nm* (*dolce*) cream horn

**can'none** *nm* cannon; *fig* ace

**cannoneggia'mento** *nm* cannonade

**canoni'era** *nf* gunboat

**cannoni'ere** *nm* (*soldato*) gunner; (*calciatore*) top goal scorer

**can'nuccia** *nf* [drinking] straw; (*di pipa*) stem

**ca'noa** *nf* canoe

**'canone** *nm* canon; (*affitto*) rent; **equo ~** rent set by law

**ca'nonica** *nf* manse

**ca'nonico** *nm* canon

**canoniz'zare** *vt* canonize

**canonizzazi'one** *nf* canonization

**ca'noro** *a* melodious

**ca'notta** *nf* (*estiva*) vest top

**canot'taggio** *nm* canoeing; (*voga*) rowing

**canotti'era** *nf* vest

**canotti'ere** *nm* oarsman

**ca'notto** *nm* [rubber] dinghy

**cano'vaccio** *nm* (*trama*) plot; (*straccio*) duster; (*per ricamo*) canvas

**can'tante** *nmf* singer. **~ lirico** opera-singer

**can'tare** *vt/i* sing; **~ vittoria** *fig* crow; **fare ~ qcno** *sl* make sb talk; **me le ha cantate** *fam* he told me off

**canta'storie** *nmf inv* story-teller

**can'tata** *nf Mus* cantata

**can'tato** *a* sung

**cantau'tore, -'trice** *nmf* singer-song-writer

**canticchi'are** *vt* sing softly; (*a bocca chiusa*) hum

**'cantico** *nm* hymn

**canti'ere** *nm* yard; *Naut* shipyard; (*di edificio*) construction site. **~ navale** naval dockyard; (*per piccole imbarcazioni*) boatyard

**cantie'ristica** *nf* construction

**canti'lena** *nf* singsong; (*ninna-nanna*) lullaby

**can'tina** *nf* cellar; (*osteria*) wine shop

**'canto**[1] *nm* singing; (*canzone*) song; *Relig* chant; (*poesia*) poem. **~ di Natale, ~ natalizio** Christmas carol. **~ degli uccelli** birdsong

**'canto**[2] *nm* (*angolo*) corner; (*lato*) side; **dal ~ mio** for my part; **d'altro ~** on the other hand

**canto'nale** *a* cantonal

**canto'nata** *nf* **prendere una ~** *fig* be sadly mistaken

**can'tone** *nm* canton; (*angolo*) corner

**can'tore** *nm* chorister

**can'tuccio** *nm* nook; **stare in un ~** *fig* hold oneself aloof

**ca'nuto** *a liter* whitehaired

**canzo'nare** *vt* tease

**canzona'torio** *a* teasing

**canzona'tura** *nf* teasing

**can'zone** *nf* song. **~ d'amore** love song

**canzo'netta** *nf fam* pop song

**canzoni'ere** *nm* songbook

**'caos** *nm* chaos

**ca'otico** *a* chaotic

**C.A.P.** *nm abbr* (**Codice di Avviamento Postale**) post code, zip code *Am*

**cap.** *abbr* (**capitolo**) chap

**ca'pace** *a* able; (*esperto*) skilled; ⟨*stadio, contenitore*⟩ big; **~ di** (*disposto a*) capable of; **è ~ a cantare?** can he sing?

**capacità** *nf inv* ability; (*attitudine*) skill; (*capienza*) capacity. **~ d'assorbimento** absorbency. **~ di credito** creditworthiness. **~ di memorizzazione** retentiveness. **~ produttiva** production capacity. **~ di resistenza** staying power

**capaci'tarsi** *vr* **~ di** (*rendersi conto*) understand; (*accorgersi*) realize

**ca'panna** *nf* hut

**capan'nello** *nm* knot of people; **fare ~ intorno a qcno/qcsa** gather round sb/sth

**ca'panno** *nm* **~ degli attrezzi** garden shed. **~ da spiaggia** beach hut, cabana

**capan'none** *nm* shed; *Aeron* hangar

**caparbietà** *nf* obstinacy

**ca'parbio** *a* obstinate

**ca'parra** *nf* deposit

**capa'tina** *nf* short visit; **fare una ~ in città/da qcno** pop into town/in on sb

**ca'pello** *nm* hair: **non torcere un ~ a qcno** *fig* not lay a finger on sb; **capelli** *pl (capigliatura)* hair *sg*: **asciugarsi/lavarsi i capelli** dry/wash one's hair; **avere i capelli a spazzola** have a crew-cut; **spaccare il ~ in quattro** split hairs; **averne fin sopra i capelli** *fig* be fed up to the back teeth; **mettersi le mani nei capelli** *fig* tear one's hair out. **capelli** *pl* **d'angelo** vermicelli

**capel'lone** *nm* long-haired type, hippie

**capel'luto** *a* hairy; **cuoio ~** scalp

**ca'pestro** *nm* noose; **contratto ~** strait-jacket of a contract

**capez'zale** *nm* bolster; *fig* bedside

**ca'pezzolo** *nm* nipple

**capi'ente** *a* capacious

**capi'enza** *nf* capacity

**capiglia'tura** *nf* hair

**capil'lare** *a* capillary

**ca'pire** *vt* understand; **non capisco** I don't understand; **~ male** misunderstand; **si capisce!** naturally!; **sì, ho capito** yes, I see

**capi'tale** *a Jur* capital; *(principale)* main ● *nf (città)* capital ● *nm Comm* capital. **~ di avviamento** start-up capital. **~ azionario** *Fin* equity capital, share capital. **~ di investimento** investment capital. **~ di rischio** venture capital. **~ sociale** *Fin* share capital

**capita'lismo** *nm* capitalism

**capita'lista** *nmf* capitalist

**capita'listico** *a* capitalist

**capitaliz'zare** *vt* capitalize

**capitalizzazi'one** *nf* capitalization

**capita'nare** *vt* lead ‹rivolta›; *Sport* captain

**capitane'ria** *nf* **~ di porto** port authorities *pl*

**capi'tano** *nm* captain. **~ di lungo corso** *Naut* captain

**capi'tare** *vi (giungere per caso)* come; *(accadere)* happen

**'capite**: **pro ~** *adv* per capita

**capi'tello** *nm Archit* capital

**capito'lare** *vi* capitulate

**capitolazi'one** *nf* capitulation

**ca'pitolo** *nm* chapter

**capi'tombolo** *nm* headlong fall; **fare un ~** tumble down

**'capo** *nm* head; *(chi comanda)* boss *fam*; *(di vestiario)* item: *Geog* cape; *(in tribù)* chief; *(parte estrema)* top; **a ~** *(in dettato)* new paragraph; **da ~** over again; **giramento di ~** dizziness; **mal di ~** headache; **in ~ a un mese** within a month; **non ha né ~ né coda** ‹discorso, ragionamento›: I can't make head nor tail of it. **~ d'abbigliamento** item of clothing. **~ d'accusa** *Jur* charge, count. **~ di bestiame** head of cattle. **C~ di Buona Speranza** Cape of Good Hope. **~ reparto** head of department. **il C~ Verde** Cape Verde

**capo'banda** *nm Mus* band-master: *(di delinquenti)* ringleader

**capocameri'ere, -a** *nm* head waiter ● *nf* head waitress

**ca'pocchia** *nf* **~ di spillo** pinhead

**ca'poccia** *nm (fam: testa)* nut

**capocci'one, -a** *nm fam* brainbox

**capo'classe** *nmf* ≈ form captain

**capocor'data** *nmf (alpinista)* leader

**capocu'oco, -a** *nmf* headcook

**capo'danno** *nm* New Year's Day

**capofa'miglia** *nm* head of the family

**capo'fitto** *nm* **a ~** headlong

**capo'giro** *nm* giddiness

**capo'gruppo** *nm* group leader

**capola'voro** *nm* masterpiece

**capo'linea** *nm* terminus

**capo'lino** *nm* **fare ~** peep in

**capo'lista** *nmf Sport* league leaders *pl*; *Pol* candidate whose name appears first on the list

**capolu'ogo** *nm* main town

**capo'mafia** *nm* Mafia boss

**capo'mastro** *nm* master builder

**capo'rale** *nm* lance-corporal

**capore'parto** *nmf* department head, head of department

**capo'sala** *nf inv Med* ward sister

**capo'saldo** *nm* stronghold

**capo'scalo** *nm* airline manager

**capo'squadra** *nm inv* foreman; *Sport* team captain

**capostazi'one** *nm inv* stationmaster

**capo'stipite** *nmf (di famiglia)* progenitor; *(di esemplare)* archetype

**capo'tavola** *nmf (persona)* head of the table; **sedere a ~** sit at the head of the table

**capo'treno** *nm* guard

**ca'potta** *nf* top

**capot'tare** *vi* somersault

**capouf'ficio** *nmf* department head

**capo'verso** *nm* first line; *Jur* paragraph

**capo'volgere** *vt* overturn; *fig* reverse

**capo'volgersi** *vr* overturn; ‹barca:› capsize; *fig* be reversed

**capovolgi'mento** *nm* turnaround

**capo'volto** *pp di* **capovolgere** ● *a* upside-down

**'cappa** *nf* cloak; *(di camino)* cowl; *(di cucina)* hood

**cappa'santa** *nf Culin* scallop

**cap'pella** *nf* chapel. **la C~ Sistina** the Sistine Chapel

**cappel'lano** *nm* chaplain

**cappel'letti** *nmpl small filled pasta parcels*

**cappelli'era** *nf* hatbox

**cappel'lino** *nm* **~ di carta** party hat

**cap'pello** *nm* hat; **tanto di ~!** I take my hat off to you!. **~ a cilindro** top hat. **~ da cow boy** stetson, cowboy hat. **~ di feltro** homburg. **~ di paglia** straw hat. **~ da sole** sun hat

**'cappero** *nm* caper; **capperi!** *fam* gosh!

**'cappio** *nm* noose; **avere il ~ al collo** *fig* have a millstone round one's neck; ‹marito:› be henpecked cap'pone *nm* capon

cap'potto *nm* [over|coat

cappuc'cino *nm* (*frate*) Capuchin [friar]; (*bevanda*) white coffee

cap'puccio *nm* hood; (*di penna stilografica*) cap

'capra *nf* goat; **salvare ~ e cavoli** *fig* run with the hare and hunt with the hounds

ca'pretto *nm* kid

ca'priccio *nm* whim: (*bizzarria*) freak; **fare i capricci** have tantrums

capricci'oso *a* capricious; (*bambino*) naughty

Capri'corno *nm* Astr Capricorn

capri'foglio *nm* honeysuckle

ca'prino *nm* goat's cheese

capri'ola *nf* somersault

capri'olo *nm* roe-deer

'capro *nm* [billy-]goat. **~ espiatorio** scapegoat

ca'prone *nm* [billy-]goat

'capsula *nf* capsule; (*di proiettile*) cap; (*di dente*) crown

cap'tare *vt* Radio, TV pick up; catch (*attenzione*)

**C.A.R.** *nm abbr* (**Centro Addestramento Reclute**) basic training camp

cara'bina *nf* carbine

carabini'ere *nm* carabiniere; **carabini'eri** *pl Italian police force (which is a branch of the army)*

ca'raffa *nf* carafe

Ca'raibi *nmpl* (*zona*) Caribbean *sg*; (*isole*) Caribbean Islands; **il mar dei ~** the Caribbean [Sea]

cara'ibico *a* Caribbean

cara'mella *nf* sweet. **~ alla menta** mint

cara'mello *nm* caramel

ca'rato *nm* carat

ca'rattere *nm* character; (*caratteristica*) characteristic; **di buon ~** good-natured; **in ~ con** (*intonato*) in keeping with; **è una persona di ~** (*deciso*) he's got character. **~ jolly** *Comput* wild card. **~ tipografico** typeface

caratte'rino *nm* difficult nature

caratte'rista *nm* character actor ● *nf* character actress

caratte'ristico, -a *a* characteristic; (*pittoresco*) quaint ● *nf* characteristic

caratteriz'zare *vt* characterize

caratterizzazi'one *nf* characterization

cara'tura *nf* carats; *Comm* part-ownership

'caravan *nm inv* caravan

carboi'drato *nm* carbohydrate

car'bonchio *nm* anthrax

carbon'cino *nm* (*per disegno*) charcoal

car'bone *nm* coal; **stare sui carboni ardenti** *fig* be on tenterhooks. **~ fossile** anthracite

carbo'nifero *a* carboniferous

car'bonio *nm* carbon. **~ 14** carbon-14

carboniz'zare *vt* burn to a cinder, burn to a crisp; **è morto carbonizzato** he was burned to death

carbu'rante *nm* fuel

carbu'rare *vt* carburize ● *vi fig* be firing on all four cylinders: **il motore carbura male** the mixture is wrong

carbura'tore *nm* carburettor

carburazi'one *nf* carburation

car'cassa *nf* carcass; *fig* old wreck

carce'rario *a* prison *attrib*

carce'rato, -a *nmf* prisoner

carcerazi'one *nf* imprisonment. **~ preventiva** preventive detention

'carcere *nm* prison; (*punizione*) imprisonment. **~ di massima sicurezza** maximum-security prison

carceri'ere, -a *nmf* gaoler

carci'noma *nm* carcinoma

carcio'fino *nm* baby artichoke

carci'ofo *nm* artichoke

cardel'lino *nm* goldfinch

car'diaco *a* cardiac; **disturbo ~** heart disease

'cardigan *nm inv* cardigan

cardi'nale *a & nm* cardinal

'cardine *nm* hinge

cardiochi'rurgo *nm* heart surgeon

cardiolo'gia *nf* cardiology

cardi'ologo *nm* heart specialist

cardio'patico *nmf* person suffering from a heart complaint

cardio'tonico *nm* heart stimulant

cardiovasco'lare *a* cardiovascular

'cardo *nm* thistle

ca'rena *nf Naut* bottom

care'naggio *nm* **bacino di ~** dry dock

ca'rente *a* **~ di** lacking in

ca'renza *nf* lack; (*scarsità*) scarcity

care'stia *nf* famine; (*mancanza*) dearth

ca'rezza *nf* stroke; (*di madre, amante*) caress; **fare una ~ a** stroke; (*madre, amante:*) caress

carez'zare *vt* stroke; (*madre, amante:*) caress

carez'zevole *a fig* sweet

'cargo *nm inv* (*nave*) cargo boat, freighter; (*aereo*) cargo plane, freight plane

cari'are *vt* decay

cari'arsi *vi* decay

cari'ato *a* decayed

'carica *nf* office; *Mil, Electr* charge; *fig* drive; **dotato di una forte ~ di simpatia** really likeable. **~ esplosiva** payload

caricabatte'ria *nm inv* battery charger

cari'care *vt* load (*camion, software*); *Mil, Electr* charge; wind up (*orologio*)

cari'carsi *vr Electr* charge [up]; **~ di lavoro** take on too much work

cari'cato *a fig* affected

carica'tore *nm* (*per proiettile*) magazine; (*per diapositive*) carousel

carica'tura *nf* caricature

caricatu'rale *a* grotesque

caricatu'rista *nmf* caricaturist

'carico *a* loaded (**di** with); (*colore*) strong; (*orologio*) wound [up]; (*batteria*) charged ● *nm* load; (*di nave*) cargo; (*il caricare*) loading; **avere un ~ di lavoro** have a heavy workload; **testimone a** ~ *Jur* witness for the prosecution; **a** ~ **di** *Comm* to be charged to; ⟨*persona*⟩ dependent on. ~ **utile** payload

'**carie** *nf* [tooth] decay

**caril'lon** *nm inv* musical box

ca'**rino** *a* pretty; (*piacevole*) agreeable

ca'**risma** *nm* charisma

cari'**smatico** *a* charismatic

**carità** *nf* charity; **per ~!** (*come rifiuto*) God forbid!

**carita'tevole** *a* charitable

car'**linga** *nf* fuselage

car'**lino** *nm* pug

**carnagi'one** *nf* complexion

car'**naio** *nm fig* shambles

car'**nale** *a* carnal; **cugino ~** first cousin

'**carne** *nf* flesh; (*alimento*) meat; **di** ~ meaty. ~ **macinata** mince, ground beef *Am*. ~ **di maiale** pork. ~ **di manzo** beef. ~ **di vitello** veal

car'**nefice** *nm* executioner

carnefi'**cina** *nf* slaughter

carne'**vale** *nm* carnival

carneva'**lesco** *a* carnival

car'**nivoro** *nm* carnivore ● *a* carnivorous

car'**noso** *a* fleshy

'**caro, -a** *a* dear; **cari saluti** kind regards ● *nmf fam* darling, dear; **i miei cari** my nearest and dearest

ca'**rogna** *nf* carcass; *fig* bastard

caro'**sello** *nm* merry-go-round

ca'**rota** *nf* carrot

caro'**vana** *nf* caravan; (*di veicoli*) convoy

caro'**vita** *nm* high cost of living

'**carpa** *nf* carp

car'**paccio** *nm finely sliced raw beef with oil, lemon and grated Parmesan*

Car'**pazi** *nmpl* **i** ~ the Carpathians

carpenti'**ere** *nm* carpenter

car'**pire** *vt* seize; (*con difficoltà*) extort

car'**pone, car'poni** *adv* on all fours; **camminare** ~ crawl

car'**rabile** *a* suitable for vehicles; **passo ~ = passo carraio**

car'**raio** *a* **passo** ~ entrance to driveway, garage etc where parking is forbidden

carreggi'**ata** *nf* roadway; **doppia** ~ dual carriageway, divided highway *Am*; **rimettersi in** ~ *fig* straighten oneself out

carrel'**lata** *nf* TV pan; (*fig: di notizie*) round-up

car'**rello** *nm* trolley; (*di macchina da scrivere*) carriage; *Aeron* undercarriage; *Cinema, TV* dolly. ~ **d'atterraggio** *Aeron* landing gear. ~ **dei dolci** dessert trolley. ~ **portabagagli** luggage trolley, baggage cart *Am*

car'**retta** *nf* (*veicolo vecchio*) old banger; **tirare la** ~ *fig* plod along

car'**retto** *nm* cart

carri'**era** *nf* career; **di gran** ~ at full speed; **fare** ~ get on

carrie'**rismo** *nm* careerism

carrie'**rista** *nmf* **è un** ~ his career is all that matters

carri'**ola** *nf* wheelbarrow

'**carro** *nm* cart. ~ **armato** tank. ~ **attrezzi** breakdown vehicle, wrecker *Am*. ~ **funebre** hearse. ~ **merci** truck

car'**rozza** *nf* carriage; *Rail* coach, car. ~ **bagagliaio** *Rail* guard's van. ~ **belvedere** *Rail* observation car. ~ **cuccette** sleeping car. ~ **fumatori** *Rail* smoker. ~ **letti** *Rail* sleeping car. ~ **ristorante** *Rail* restaurant car, buffet car

carroz'**zella** *nf* (*per bambini*) pram; (*per invalidi*) wheelchair

carrozze'**ria** *nf* bodywork; (*officina*) body-shop

carrozzi'**ere** *nm* panel beater

carroz'**zina** *nf* pram; (*pieghevole*) push-chair, stroller *Am*

carroz'**zone** *nm* (*di circo*) caravan; (*fig: organizzazione*) slow-moving great monster of an organization

car'**ruba** *nf* carob

car'**rubo** *nm* carob

car'**rucola** *nf* pulley

'**carta** *nf* paper; (*da gioco*) card; (*statuto*) charter; *Geog* map. ~ **di addebito** charge card, debit card. ~ **d'argento** senior citizens' railcard. ~ **assegni** cheque card. ~ **assorbente** blotting-paper. ~ **carbone** carbon paper. ~ **di credito** credit card. ~ **crespata** crepe paper. ~ **geografica** map. ~ **d'identità** identity card. ~ **igienica** toilet-paper. ~ **d'imbarco** boarding pass, boarding card. ~ **intelligente** smart card. ~ **da lettere** writing-paper. ~ **millimetrata** graph paper. ~ **da pacchi** wrapping paper. ~ **da parati** wallpaper. ~ **da regali** giftwrap. ~ **di riso** rice paper. ~ **smerigliata** emery paper. ~ **stagnola** silver paper; *Culin* aluminium foil. ~ **straccia** waste paper. ~ **stradale** road map. ~ **termica** thermal paper. ~ **topografica** ≈ Ordnance Survey Map. ~ **velina** tissue-paper. ~ **verde** *Auto* green card. ~ **vetrata** sandpaper. ~ **dei vini** wine-list

cartacar'**bone** *nf* carbon paper

car'**taccia** *nf* waste paper

car'**taceo** *a* paper

carta'**modello** *nm* pattern

cartamo'**neta** *nf* paper money

carta'**pecora** *nf* vellum

carta'**pesta** *nf* papier mâché

carta'**straccia** *nf* waste paper

carteg'**gio** *nm* correspondence

car'**tella** *nf* (*per documenti ecc*) briefcase; (*di cartone*) folder; (*di scolaro*) satchel. ~ **clinica** medical record

carte'**llina** *nf* document wallet, folder

carte'**llino** *nm* (*etichetta*) label; (*dei prezzi*) price-tag; (*di presenza*) time-card; **timbrare il** ~ clock in; (*all'uscita*) clock out

car'**tello** *nm* sign; (*pubblicitario*) poster; (*stradale*) road sign; (*di protesta*) placard; (*Comm, di droga*) cartel

cartel'**lone** *nm* poster; *Theat* bill. ~ **pubblicitario** billboard

**cartello'nista** *nmf* poster designer

**cartello'nistica** *nf* poster designing

**carti'era** *nf* paper-mill

**carti'lagine** *nf* cartilage

**car'tina** *nf* map. ~ **di tornasole** litmus paper

**car'toccio** *nm* paper bag; **al ~** *Culin* baked in foil

**cartogra'fia** *nf* cartography

**car'tografo** *nm* cartographer

**carto'laio, -a** *nmf* stationer

**cartole'ria** *nf* stationer's [shop]

**cartolibre'ria** *nf* stationer's and book shop

**carto'lina** *nf* postcard. ~ **postale** postcard. ~ **[precetto]** call-up papers

**carto'mante** *nmf* fortune-teller

**carton'cino** *nm* (*materiale*) card; (*biglietto*) card

**car'tone** *nm* cardboard; (*arte*) cartoon. ~ **animato** [animated] cartoon. ~ **ondulato** corrugated cardboard. ~ **di uova** egg box

**car'tuccia** *nf* cartridge; **mezza ~** *fig* weakling. ~ **d'inchiostro** ink cartridge

**'casa** *nf* house; (*abitazione propria*) home; (*ditta*) firm; **amico di ~** family friend; **andare a ~** go home; **uscire di ~** leave the house; **essere di ~** be like one of the family; **fatto in ~** home-made. ~ **di correzione** ≈ reform school. ~ **di cura** nursing home. ~ **del custode** gatehouse. ~ **madre** *Comm* parent company. ~ **di moda** fashion house. ~ **in multiproprietà** timeshare. ~ **popolare** council house. ~ **di riposo** old people's home. ~ **di sartoria** fashion house. ~ **dello studente** hall of residence. ~ **per le vacanze** holiday home

**ca'sacca** *nf* military coat; (*giacca*) jacket

**ca'saccio** *adv* **a ~** at random; **sparare a ~ su qcno/qcsa** take a potshot at sb/sth

**ca'sale** *nm* (*gruppo di case*) hamlet; (*casolare*) farmhouse

**casa'linga** *nf* housewife

**casa'lingo** *a* domestic; (*fatto in casa*) home-made; (*amante della casa*) home-loving; (*semplice*) homely ● *nm* **casalinghi** *pl* household goods

**casa'nova** *nm inv* (*donnaiolo*) Casanova

**ca'sata** *nf* family

**ca'sato** *nm* family name

**ca'scante** *a* falling; (*floscio*) flabby

**ca'scare** *vi* fall [down]

**ca'scata** *nf* (*di acqua*) waterfall

**casca|'tore, -'trice** *nm* stuntman ● *nf* stuntwoman

**cas'chetto** *nm* [capelli a] ~ bob

**ca'scina** *nf* farm building

**casci'nale** *nf* farmhouse

**'casco** *nm* crash-helmet; (*asciuga-capelli*) [hair-]drier. ~ **di banane** bunch of bananas. **Caschi** *pl* **blu** *Mil* Blue Helmets, Blue Berets

**caseggi'ato** *nm* block of flats *Br*, apartment block

**casei'ficio** *nm* dairy

**ca'sella** *nf* pigeon-hole. ~ **postale** post office box, PO box; (*elettronica*) mailbox

**casel'lante** *nmf* (*per treni*) signalman; (*in autostrada*) toll collector

**casel'lario** *nm* (*mobile*) filing cabinet; (*di documenti*) file. ~ **giudiziario** record of convictions; **avere il ~ giudiziario vuoto** have no criminal record

**ca'sello** *nm* (*di autostrada*) [motorway] toll booth

**case'reccio** *a* home-made

**ca'serma** *nf* barracks *pl*; (*dei carabinieri*) [police] station; **da ~** (*linguaggio*) barrack room *attrib.* ~ **dei carabinieri** military police station. ~ **dei pompieri, ~ dei vigili del fuoco** fire station

**caser'mone** *nm pej* barracks *pl*

**cash and carry** *nm inv* cash-and-carry

**casi'nista** *nmf fam* muddler

**ca'sino** *nm fam* (*bordello*) brothel; (*fig sl: confusione*) racket; (*disordine*) mess; **un ~ di** loads of; **è un ~** (*complicato*) it's too complicated

**casinò** *nm inv* casino

**ca'sistica** *nf* (*classificazione*) record of occurrences

**'caso** *nm* chance; (*fatto, circostanza, Med, Gram*) case; **a ~** at random; **~ mai** if need be; **far ~ a** pay attention to; **non far ~ a** take no account of; **per ~** by chance. ~ **[giudiziario]** [legal] case. ~ **urgente** *Med* emergency case

**caso'lare** *nm* farmhouse

**'caspita** *int* good gracious

**'cassa** *nf* till; (*di legno*) crate; *Comm* cash; (*luogo di pagamento*) cash desk; (*mobile*) chest; (*istituto bancario*) bank. ~ **automatica prelievi** cash dispenser, automatic teller. ~ **comune** kitty ~ **continua** autobank. ~ **da morto** coffin. ~ **di risparmio** savings bank. ~ **toracica** ribcage

**cassa'forte** *nf* safe

**cassa'panca** *nf* linen chest

**cas'sata** *nf* ice-cream cake

**cas'sero** *nm Naut* quarterdeck

**casseru'ola** *nf* saucepan

**cas'setta** *nf* case; (*per registratore*) cassette. **far buona ~** *Theatr* be good box-office. ~ **degli attrezzi** toolbox. ~ **delle lettere** postbox, letterbox. ~ **delle offerte** charity box. ~ **portapane** breadbin. ~ **portavalori** cash box. ~ **del pronto soccorso** first-aid kit. ~ **di sicurezza** strong-box

**cas'setto** *nm* drawer; (*di fotocopiatrice ecc*) tray. ~ **di inserimento** [dei] **fogli** paper feed tray

**casset'tone** *nm* chest of drawers

**cassi'ere, -a** *nmf* cashier; (*di supermercato*) checkout assistant, checkout operator; (*di banca*) teller

**cassinte'grato** *nmf* person who has been laid off

**cas'sone** *nm* (*cassa*) chest; (*per acqua*) cofferdam

**casso'netto** *nm* rubbish bin, trash can *Am*

**'casta** *nf* caste

**ca'stagna** *nf* chestnut; **prendere qcno in**

~ *fig* catch sb in the act. ~ **d'India** horse chestnut

**casta'gnaccio** *nm tart from Tuscany made with chestnut flour*

**casta'gneto** *nm* chestnut grove

**ca'stagno** *nm* chestnut[-tree]

**casta'gnola** *nf (petardo)* firecracker

**ca'stano** *a* chestnut; ‹*occhi, capelli*› brown

**ca'stello** *nm* castle; *(impalcatura)* scaffold. ~ **incantato** enchanted castle. ~ **di sabbia** sandcastle

**casti'gare** *vt* punish

**casti'gato** *a (casto)* chaste; ‹*abito, atteggiamento*› prim and proper

**ca'stigo** *nm* punishment

**castità** *nf* chastity

**'casto** *a* chaste

**ca'storo** *nm* beaver

**ca'strante** *a fig* frustrating

**ca'strare** *vt* castrate

**ca'strato** *a* castrated; *(inibito)* inhibited; *(cantante)* castrato

**castrazi'one** *nf* gelding

**ca'strone** *nm* gelding

**castrone'ria** *nf fam* rubbish

**'casual** *nm inv* casual wear

**casu'ale** *a* chance *attrib*

**casual'mente** *adv* by chance

**ca'supola** *nf* little house

**cata'clisma** *nm fig* upheaval

**cata'comba** *nf* catacomb

**cata'falco** *nm* catafalque

**cata'fascio** *nm* **andare a** ~ go to rack and ruin

**cata'litico** *a* **marmitta catalitica** *Auto* catalytic converter

**cataliz'zare** *vt fig* heighten

**cataliz'zato** *a Auto* fitted with a catalytic converter

**catalizza'tore** *a Phys* catalysing; **centro** ~ *fig* catalyst ● *nm Auto* catalytic converter; *fig* catalyst

**catalo'gabile** *a* which can be listed

**catalo'gare** *vt* catalogue

**catalogazi'one** *nf* cataloguing

**cata'logna** *nf type of chicory with large leaves*

**ca'talogo** *nm* catalogue

**catama'rano** *nm (da diporto)* catamaran

**cata'pecchia** *nf* hovel; *fam* dump

**cata'pulta** *nf* catapult

**catapul'tare** *vt (scaraventare fuori)* eject

**catapul'tarsi** *vr (precipitarsi)* dive

**catarifran'gente** *nm* reflector

**ca'tarro** *nm* catarrh

**catar'roso** *a* ‹*voce*› catarrhal

**ca'tarsi** *nf inv* catharsis

**ca'tartico** *a* cathartic

**ca'tasta** *nf* pile

**cata'stale** *a* **registro** ~ land registry; **rendita** ~ revenue from landed property

**ca'tasto** *nm* land register

**ca'tastrofe** *nf* catastrophe

**cata'strofico** *a* catastrophic

**catastro'fismo** *nm* catastrophe theory

**catch** *nm* all-in wrestling

**cate'chismo** *nm* catechism

**catego'ria** *nf* category

**cate'gorico** *a* categorical

**ca'tena** *nf* chain. ~ **montuosa** mountain range. **catene** *pl* **da neve** [snow] chains

**cate'naccio** *nm* bolt

**cate'nella** *nf (collana)* chain; *(di orologio)* watch chain; **tirare la** ~ *(del gabinetto)* flush, pull the plug

**cate'nina** *nf* chain

**cate'ratta** *nf* cataract

**ca'terva** *nf* **una** ~ **di** heaps of, loads of

**ca'tetere** *nm* catheter

**'catgut** *nm inv* catgut

**cati'nella** *nf* basin; **piovere a catinelle** bucket down

**ca'tino** *nm* basin

**ca'todico** *a* cathode; **raggi catodici** cathode rays

**ca'torcio** *nm fam* old wreck

**catra'mare** *vt* tar

**ca'trame** *nm* tar

**'cattedra** *nf (tavolo di insegnante)* desk; *(di università)* chair

**catte'drale** *nf* cathedral

**catte'dratico, -a** *nmf* professor ● *a* ‹*pedante*› pedantic; ‹*insegnamento*› university *attrib*

**catti'veria** *nf* wickedness; *(azione)* wicked action; **fare una** ~ **a qcno** be nasty to sb

**cattività** *nf* captivity

**cat'tivo** *a* bad; ‹*bambino*› naughty

**cattocomu'nista** *nmf* Catholic-communist

**cattoli'cesimo** *nm* Catholicism

**cat'tolico, -a** *a & nmf* [Roman] Catholic

**cat'tura** *nf* capture

**cattu'rare** *vt* capture

**cau'casico, -a** *nmf* Caucasian

**'Caucaso** *nm* **il** ~ the Caucasus

**caucciù** *nm* rubber

**'causa** *nf* cause; *Jur* lawsuit; **far** ~ **a qcno** sue sb; ~ **di forza maggiore** circumstances beyond one's control; *(in assicurazione)* act of God

**cau'sale** *a* causal

**cau'sare** *vt* cause

**'caustico** *a* caustic

**cauta'mente** *adv* cautiously

**cau'tela** *nf* caution

**caute'lare** *vt* protect

**caute'larsi** *vr* take precautions

**cauteriz'zare** *vt* cauterize

**cauterizzazi'one** *nf* cauterization

**'cauto** *a* cautious

**cauzi'one** *nf* security; *(per libertà provvisoria)* bail; *(deposito)* deposit

**cav.** *abbr* **(cavaliere)** Kt, Knight

**'cava** *nf* quarry; *fig* mine

**caval'care** *vt* ride; *(stare a cavalcioni)* sit astride

**caval'cata** *nf* ride; *(corteo)* cavalcade

**cavalca'via** *nm* flyover

**cavalci'oni: a** ~ *adv* astride

**cavali'ere** *nm* rider: (*titolo*) knight; (*accompagnatore*) escort; (*al ballo*) partner

**cavalle'resco** *a* chivalrous

**cavalle'ria** *nf* chivalry; *Mil* cavalry

**cavalle'rizzo, -a** *nm* horseman ● *nf* horse-woman ¶

**caval'letta** *nf* grasshopper

**caval'letto** *nm* trestle; (*di macchina fotografica*) tripod; (*di pittore*) easel

**caval'lina** *nf* (*ginnastica*) horse; (*gioco*) leap-frog; **correre la ~** *fig* pursue a life of pleasure

**caval'lino** *a* equine

**ca'vallo** *nm* horse; (*misura di potenza*) horsepower: (*scacchi*) knight; (*dei pantaloni*) crotch; **a ~** on horseback; **andare a ~** go horse-riding. **~ di battaglia** war horse. **~ a dondolo** rocking-horse. **~ da tiro** carthorse. **~ di Troia** Trojan horse

**caval'lona** *nf pej* ungainly female

**caval'lone** *nm* (*ondata*) roller

**caval'luccio** *nm* **~ marino** sea horse

**ca'vare** *vt* take out; (*di dosso*) take off; **cavarsela** get away with it; **se la cava bene** he's/she's doing all right

**cavasti'vali** *nm inv* bootjack

**cava'tappi** *nm inv* corkscrew

**ca'veau** *nm inv* (*di banca*) vault

**ca'verna** *nf* cave

**caver'nicolo, -a** *nmf* cave dweller

**caver'noso** *a* ‹*voce*› deep

**ca'vetto** *nm Electr* lead

**ca'vezza** *nf* halter; **mettere la ~ al collo a qcno** put sb on a tight rein

**'cavia** *nf* guinea-pig

**cavi'ale** *nm* caviar

**ca'viglia** *nf* ankle

**cavil'lare** *vi* quibble

**ca'villo** *nm* quibble

**cavil'loso** *a* pettifogging

**cavità** *nf inv* cavity

**'cavo** *a* hollow ● *nm* cavity; (*di metallo*) cable; *Naut* rope; **televisione via ~** cable TV. **~ di collegamento** [connecting] cable. **~ seriale** serial cable. **~ di spiegamento** rip-cord

**cavo'lata** *nf fam* rubbish; **non dire cavolate** *fam* don't talk rubbish; **non fare cavolate** *fam* don't act like an idiot

**cavo'letto** *nm* **~ di Bruxelles** Brussels sprout

**cavolfi'ore** *nm* cauliflower

**'cavolo** *nm* cabbage; **~!** *fam* sugar!; **non ho capito un ~** *fam* I understood bugger-all; **che ~ succede?** what the heck is going on?. **~ cappuccio** spring cabbage

**caz'zata** *nf vulg* shit; **non dire cazzate** don't talk shit; **non fare cazzate** don't fuck things up

**'cazzo** *vulg nm* prick ● *int* fuck!; **non capisce un ~** he doesn't understand a fucking thing; **non me ne importa un ~!** I don't give a fuck!; **sono cazzi miei!** it's my fucking business!

**caz'zotto** *nm* punch: **prendere qcno a cazzotti** beat sb up

**cazzu'ola** *nf* trowel

**CB** *nf abbr* (**banda cittadina**) CB

**cc** *abbr* (**centimetri cubi**) cc

**c/c** *abbr* (**conto corrente**) c/a

**CCT** *nm abbr* (**Certificato di Credito del Tesoro**) T-bill

**CD** *nm inv* CD

**CD-ROM** *nm inv* CD-Rom

**ce** *pers pron* (*a noi*) us; **ce lo ha dato** he gave it to us ● *adv* there; **ce ne sono molti** there are many; **ce ne vuole!** it takes some doing!

**cec'chino** *nm* sniper; *Pol* MP who votes against his own party

**'cece** *nm* chick-pea

**cecità** *nf* blindness

**ceco, -a** *a & nmf* Czech; **la Repubblica Ceca** the Czech Republic

**Cecoslo'vacchia** *nf* Czechoslovakia

**cecoslo'vacco, -a** *a & nmf* Czechoslovak

**'cedere** *vi* (*arrendersi*) surrender; (*concedere*) yield; (*sprofondare*) subside ● *vt* give up; make over ‹*proprietà ecc*›

**ce'devole** *a* ‹*terreno ecc*› soft; *fig* yielding

**ce'diglia** *nf* cedilla

**cedi'mento** *nm* (*di terreno*) subsidence

**'cedola** *nf* coupon

**'cedro** *nm* (*albero*) cedar; (*frutto*) citron

**C.E.E.** *nf abbr* (**Comunità Economica Europea**) E[E]C

**cefa'lea** *nf* headache

**ce'falo** *nm* mullet

**'ceffo** *nm* (*muso*) snout; (*pej: persona*) mug

**cef'fone** *nm* slap

**ce'lare** *vt* conceal

**ce'larsi** *vr* conceal oneself

**ce'lato** *a* concealed

**cele'brare** *vt* celebrate, observe ‹*festività*›

**celebra'tivo** *a* celebratory

**celebrazi'one** *nf* celebration

**'celebre** *a* famous

**celebrità** *nf inv* celebrity

**'celere** *a* swift; **corso ~** crash course ● *nf* (*polizia*) flying squad

**celerità** *nf* speed; **con ~** speedily

**ce'leste** *a* (*divino*) heavenly ● *a & nm* (*colore*) pale blue

**celesti'ale** *a* celestial

**celi'bato** *nm* celibacy

**'celibe** *a* single ● *nm* bachelor

**'cella** *nf* cell. **~ frigorifera** cold store. **~ di isolamento** solitary confinement

**+cello** *suff* **monticello** *nm* mound; **praticello** *nm* small meadow

**'cellofan** *nm inv* cellophane; *Culin* cling film

**cellofa'nare** *vt* wrap in cling film

**'cellula** *nf* cell. **~ fotoelettrica** electronic eye

**cellu'lare** *nm* (*telefono*) cellular [phone] ● *a* **furgone ~** police van; **telefono ~** cellular [phone]

**cellu'lite** *nf* cellulite

**cellu'litico** *a* full of cellulite

**cellu'loide** *a* celluloid: **il mondo della ~** *fig* the celluloid world

**cellu'losa** *nf* cellulose

'**Celsius** *a inv* Celsius

'**celta** *nm* Celt

'**celtico** *a* Celtic

'**cembalo** *nm Mus* cembalo, harpsichord

**cemen'tare** *vt* cement

**cementifi'care** *vt* turn into a cement jungle

**cementificazi'one** *nf* turning into a cement jungle

**cementi'ficio** *nm* cement factory

**ce'mento** *nm* cement. **~ armato** reinforced concrete

'**cena** *nf* dinner; (*leggera*) supper; (*festa*) dinner party

**ce'nacolo** *nm* circle

**ce'nare** *vi* have dinner: **~ fuori** eat out

'**cencio** *nm* rag; (*per spolverare*) duster; **bianco come un ~** white as a sheet

**cenci'oso** *a* in rags

'**cenere** *nf* ash; (*di carbone ecc*) cinders *pl*; **Ceneri** *pl* Ash Wednesday

**Cene'rentola** *nf* Cinderella

**ce'netta** *nf* (*cena semplice*) informal dinner; (*cena intima*) romantic dinner

'**cenno** *nm* sign; (*col capo*) nod; (*con la mano*) wave; (*allusione*) hint; (*breve resoconto*) mention; **far ~ di sì** nod

**ce'none** *nm* **il ~ di Capodanno/Natale** *special New Year's Eve/Christmas Eve dinner*

**ceno'tafio** *nm* cenotaph

**censi'mento** *nm* census

**cen'sire** *vt* take a census of

**CENSIS** *nm abbr* (**Centro Studi Investimenti Sociali**) *national opinion research institute*

**cen'sore** *nm* censor

**cen'sura** *nf* censorship

**censu'rare** *vt* censor

**centelli'nare** *vt* sip; *fig* measure out carefully

**cente'nario, -a** *a & nmf* centenarian ● *nm* (*commemorazione*) centenary

**centen'nale** *a* centennial

**cen'tesimo** *a* hundredth ● *nm* hundredth; (*di dollaro*) cent; **non avere un ~** be penniless

**cen'tigrado** *a* centigrade

**cen'tilitro** *nm* centilitre

**cen'timetro** *nm* centimetre

**centi'naia** *nfpl* hundreds

**centi'naio** *nm* hundred

'**cento** *a & nm* a or one hundred; **per ~** per cent

**centodi'eci** *nm* a or one hundred and ten; **~ e lode** *Univ* ≈ first class honours

**centome'trista** *nmf Sport* one hundred metres runner

**cento'mila** *nm* a or one hundred thousand

**cen'trale** *a* central ● *nf* (*di società ecc*) head office. **~ atomica** atomic power station. **~ elettrica** power station. **~ idroelettrica** hydroelectric power station. **~ nucleare** nuclear power station. **~ operativa** (*di polizia*)

operations room. **~ telefonica** [telephone] exchange

**centra'lina** *nf Teleph* switchboard: (*apparecchiatura*) junction box

**centrali'nista** *nmf* [switchboard] operator

**centra'lino** *nm Teleph* exchange: (*di albergo ecc*) switchboard

**centra'lismo** *nm* centralism

**centraliz'zare** *vt* centralize

**cen'trare** *vt* **~ qcsa** hit sth in the centre; (*fissare nel centro*) centre; *fig* hit on the head ⟨*idea*⟩

**cen'trato** *a* ⟨*tiro, colpo*⟩ well-aimed: ⟨*fig: osservazione*⟩ right on target

**centrat'tacco** *nm Sport* centre forward

**centra'vanti** *nm Sport* centre forward

**cen'trifuga** *nf* spin-drier. **~** [**asciugaverdure**] shaker. **~ elettrica** juice extractor

**centrifu'gare** *vt Techn* centrifuge; ⟨*lavatrice:*⟩ spin

**cen'trino** *nm* doily

**cen'trismo** *nm Pol* centrism

**cen'trista** *a Pol* centrist

'**centro** *nm* centre; **in ~** ⟨*essere*⟩ in town; ⟨*andare*⟩ into town. **~ di accoglienza** reception centre. **~ di attrazione** focal point. **~ città** city centre. **~ commerciale** shopping centre, mall. **~ di costi** *Comm* cost centre. **~ culturale** arts centre. **~ di gravità** centre of gravity. **~ di informazioni turistiche** tourist information office. **~ operativo** *Mil* operations room. **~ di riabilitazione** halfway house. **~ sociale** community centre. **~ sportivo** leisure centre. **~ storico** old town

**centrocam'pista** *nm Sport* midfield player, midfielder

**centro'campo** *nm* midfield

**centro'destra** *nm inv Pol* centre right

**centromedi'ano** *nm Sport* centre half

**centrosi'nistra** *nm inv Pol* centre left

**centro'tavola** *nm inv* centre-piece

**centupli'care** *vt fig* multiply

'**ceppo** *nm* (*di albero*) stump; (*da ardere*) log; (*fig: gruppo*) stock

'**cera** *nf* wax; (*aspetto*) look. **~ d'api** beeswax. **~ per auto** car wax. **~ per il pavimento** floor-polish

**cera'lacca** *nf* sealing-wax

**ce'ramica** *nf* (*arte*) ceramics; (*materia*) pottery; (*oggetto*) piece of pottery

**cera'mista** *nmf* ceramicist

**ce'rato** *a* ⟨*tela*⟩ waxed

**cerbi'atto** *nm* fawn

**cerbot'tana** *nf* blowpipe

'**cerca** *nf* **andare in ~ di** look for

**cercaper'sone** *nm inv* beeper; **chiamare con il ~** beep

**cer'care** *vt* look for ● *vi* **~ di** try to

**cerca'|tore, -'trice** *nmf* **~ d'oro** gold seeker

'**cerchia** *nf* circle. **~ familiare** family circle

**cerchi'are** *vt* circle, draw a circle around ⟨*parola*⟩

**cerchi'ato** *a* ⟨*occhi*⟩ black-ringed

**cerchi'etto** *nm* (*per capelli*) hairband
**'cerchio** *nm* circle: (*giocattolo*) hoop
**cerchi'one** *nm* alloy wheel
**cere'ale** *nm* cereal
**cerea'licolo** *a* grain *attrib*, cereal *attrib*
**cere'brale** *a* cerebral
**'cereo** *a* waxen
**ce'retta** *nf* depilatory wax; **fare la ~** wax
**cer'foglio** *nm* chervil
**ceri'monia** *nf* ceremony. **~ inaugurale** induction ceremony. **~ nuziale** marriage ceremony. **~ di premiazione** awards ceremony
**cerimoni'ale** *nm* ceremonial
**cerimoni'ere** *nm* master of ceremonies
**cerimoni'oso** *a* ceremonious
**ce'rino** *nm* [wax] match
**cerni'era** *nf* hinge: (*di borsa*) clasp. **~ lampo** zip[-fastener], zipper *Am*
**'cernita** *nf* selection
**'cero** *nm* candle
**ce'rone** *nm* greasepaint
**ce'rotto** *nm* [sticking] plaster. **~ callifugo** corn plaster
**certa'mente** *adv* certainly
**cer'tezza** *nf* certainty
**certifi'care** *vt* certify
**certifi'cato** *nm* certificate. **~ medico** doctor's note. **~ di morte** death certificate
**certificazi'one** *nf* certification. **~ di bilancio** *Fin* auditors' report
**'certo** *a* certain; (*notizia*) definite; (*indeterminativo*) some; **sono ~ di riuscire** I am certain to succeed; **a una certa età** at a certain age; **certi giorni** some days; **un ~ signor Giardini** a Mr Giardini; **una certa Anna** somebody called Anna; **certa gente** *pej* some people; **ho certi dolori!** I'm in such pain!. **certi** *pron pl* some; (*alcune persone*) some people ● *adv* of course; **sapere per ~** know for certain, know for sure; **di ~** surely; **~ che…** surely…
**cer'tosa** *nf* Carthusian monastery
**certo'sino** *nm* Carthusian [monk]; **pazienza certosina** exceptional patience
**cer'tuni** *pron* some
**ce'rume** *nm* earwax
**cer'vello** *nm* brain; **avere un ~ da gallina** be a bird-brain
**cervel'lone, -a** *nmf hum* brainbox
**cervel'lotico** *a* (*macchinoso*) over-elaborate
**cervi'cale** *a* cervical
**'cervice** *nf* cervix
**'cervo** *nm* deer
**ce'sareo** *a Med* Caesarean; **parto ~** Caesarean
**cesel'lare** *vt* chisel
**cesel'lato** *a* chiselled
**cesella'tura** *nf* chiselling
**ce'sello** *nm* chisel
**ce'soie** *nfpl* shears
**'cespite** *nm* source of income
**ce'spuglio** *nm* bush
**cespugli'oso** *a* (*terreno*) bushy
**ces'sare** *vi* stop, cease ● *vt* stop
**ces'sate** *nm* **~ il fuoco** ceasefire

**ces'sato** *a* **~ allarme/pericolo** all clear
**cessazi'one** *nf* cessation. **~ d'esercizio** closing down
**cessi'one** *nf* handover
**'cesso** *nm sl* (*gabinetto*) bog, john *Am*: (*fig: locale, luogo*) dump
**'cesta** *nf* [large] basket
**ce'stello** *nm* (*per lavatrice*) drum
**cesti'nare** *vt* throw away; bin (*lettera*): turn down (*proposta*)
**ce'stino** *nm* [small] basket: (*per la carta straccia*) waste-paper basket
**'cesto** *nm* basket. **~ della biancheria** linen basket
**ce'sura** *nf* caesura
**ce'taceo** *nm* cetacean
**'ceto** *nm* [social] class
**'cetra** *nf* lyre
**cetrio'lino** *nm* gherkin
**cetri'olo** *nm* cucumber
**cfr** *abbr* (**confronta**) cf
**C.G.I.L.** *nf abbr* (**Confederazione Generale Italiana del Lavoro**) *trades union organization*
**cha'let** *nm inv* chalet
**cham'pagne** *nm inv* champagne
**'chance** *nf inv* chance
**char'lotte** *nf ice-cream cake with fresh cream, biscuits and fruit*
**'charter** *nm inv* charter plane; **volo ~** charter flight
**che** *rel pron* (*persona: soggetto*) who; (*persona: oggetto*) whom; (*cosa, animale*) which; **questa è la casa ~ ho comprato** this is the house [that] I've bought; **il ~ mi sorprende** which surprises me; **dai ~ deduco che…** from which I gather that…; **avere di ~ vivere** have enough to live on; **grazie! – non c'è di che!** thank you – don't mention it; **il giorno ~ ti ho visto** *fam* the day I saw you ● *inter a* what; (*esclamativo: con aggettivo*) how; (*con nome*) what a; **~ macchina prendiamo, la tua o la mia?** which car are we taking, yours or mine?; **~ bello!** how nice!; **~ idea!** what an idea!; **~ bella giornata!** what a lovely day! ● *inter pron* what; **a ~ pensi?** what are you thinking about? ● *conj* that; (*con comparazioni*): **credo ~ abbia ragione** I think [that] he is right; **era così commosso ~ non riusciva a parlare** he was so moved, [that] he couldn't speak; **aspetto ~ telefoni** I'm waiting for him to phone; **è da un po' ~ non lo vedo** it's been a while since I saw him; **mi piace più Roma ~ Milano** I like Rome better than Milan; **~ ti piaccia o no** whether you like it or not; **~ io sappia** as far as I know
**'checca** *nf fam* queen
**checché** *pron* whatever
**check-'in** *nm inv* check-in; **fare il ~** check in
**check-'up** *nm inv Med* check-up; **fare un ~** have a check-up
**cheese'burger** *nm inv* cheeseburger
**'chef** *nm inv* chef

'**chela** *nf* nipper

**chemiotera'pia** *nf* chemotherapy, chemo *fam*

**chemisi'er** *nm inv* chemise

**chero'sene** *nm* paraffin

**cheru'bino** *nm* cherub

**che'tare** *vt* quieten

**che'tarsi** *vr* quieten down

**cheti'chella**: **alla ~** *adv* silently

'**cheto** *a* quiet

**chi** *rel pron* whoever; (*coloro che*) people who; **ho trovato ~ ti può aiutare** I found somebody who can help you; **c'è ~ dice che...** some people say that...; **senti ~ parla!** listen to who's talking! ● *inter pron* (*soggetto*) who; (*oggetto, con preposizione*) whom; (*possessivo*) **di ~** whose; **~ sei?** who are you?; **~ hai incontrato?** who did you meet?, whom did you meet? *fml*; **di ~ sono questi libri?** whose books are these?; **con ~ parli?** who are you talking to?, to whom are you talking? *fml*; **a ~ lo dici!** tell me about it!

**chi'acchiera** *nf* chat; (*pettegolezzo*) gossip; **chiacchiere** *pl* chitchat; **far quattro chiacchiere** have a chat

**chiacchie'rare** *vi* chat; (*far pettegolezzi*) gossip

**chiacchie'rato** *a* **essere ~** (*persona:*) be the subject of gossip

**chi'acchiere** *nfpl* (*dolci*) *sweet pastries fried and sprinkled with fine sugar*

**chiacchie'rone, -a** *a* talkative ● *nmf* chatterer

**chia'mare** *vt* call; (*far venire*) send for; **come ti chiami?** what's your name?; **mi chiamo Roberto** my name is Robert; **~ alle armi** call up; **mandare a ~** send for; **~ a rapporto** debrief

**chia'marsi** *vr* be called

**chia'mata** *nf* call; *Mil* call-up. **~ a carico del destinatario** reverse charge call. **~ interurbana** long-distance call. **~ in teleselezione** direct dialling. **~ urbana** local call

**chi'appa** *nf fam* cheek

**chiara'mente** *adv* clearly

**chia'rezza** *nf* clarity; (*limpidezza*) clearness

**chiarifi'care** *vt* clarify

**chiarifica'tore** *a* clarificatory

**chiarificazi'one** *nf* clarification

**chiari'mento** *nm* clarification

**chia'rire** *vt* make clear; (*spiegare*) clear up

**chia'rirsi** *vr* become clear

**chi'aro** *a* clear; (*luminoso*) bright; (*colore*) light

**chia'rore** *nm* glimmer

**chiaro'scuro** *nm* (*tecnica*) chiaroscuro

**chiaroveg'gente** *a* clear-sighted ● *nmf* clairvoyant

**chi'asso** *nm* din

**chiassosa'mente** *adv* (*rumorosamente*) rowdily; (*vistosamente*) gaudily

**chias'soso** *a* (*rumoroso*) rowdy; (*vistoso*) gaudy

**chi'atta** *nf* canal boat, canal barge

**chi'ave** *nf* key; **chiudere a ~** lock. **~ dell'accensione** ignition key. **~ di basso** *Mus* bass clef. **~ inglese** monkey-wrench. **~ [inglese] a rullino** adjustable spanner

**chia'vetta** *nf* (*in tubi*) key

**chiavi'stello** *nm* latch

**chi'azza** *nf* stain. **~ di petrolio** oil-slick

**chiaz'zare** *vt* stain

**chiaz'zato** *a* dappled

**chic** *a inv* chic

**chicches'sia** *pron* anybody

**chicchirichi** *nm inv* cock-a-doodle-doo

'**chicco** *nm* grain: (*di caffè*) bean; (*d'uva*) grape. **~ di caffè** coffee bean. **~ di grandine** hailstone. **~ d'orzo** barleycorn

**chi'edere** *vt* ask; (*per avere*) ask for; (*esigere*) demand; **~ notizie di** ask after

**chi'edersi** *vr* wonder

**chieri'chetto** *nm* altar boy

**chi'erico** *nm* cleric

**chi'esa** *nf* church

**chi'esto** *pp di* **chiedere**

**chif'fon** *nm* chiffon

'**chiglia** *nf* keel

**chi'gnon** *nm inv* bun

'**chilo** *nm* kilo

**chilo'grammo** *nm* kilogram[me]

**chilo'hertz** *nm inv* kilohertz

**chilome'traggio** *nm* *Auto* ≈ mileage

**chilo'metrico** *a* in kilometres; *fig* endless

**chi'lometro** *nm* kilometre

'**chilowatt** *nm inv* kilowatt

**chilowat'tora** *nm inv* kilowatt hour

**chi'mera** *nf fig* illusion

'**chimica** *nf* chemistry. **~ organica** organic chemistry

'**chimico, -a** *a* chemical ● *nmf* chemist

**chi'mono** *nm* kimono

'**china** *nf* (*declivio*) slope; **inchiostro di ~** Indian ink

**chi'nare** *vt* lower

**chi'narsi** *vr* stoop

**chincaglie'rie** *nfpl* knick-knacks

**chinesitera'pia** *nf* physiotherapy

**chi'nino** *nm* quinine

'**chino** *a* bent

**chi'notto** *nm* *sparkling soft drink*

**chintz** *nm* chintz

**chi'occia** *nf* sitting hen

**chi'occiola** *nf* snail; **scala a ~** spiral staircase

**chio'dato** *a* **pneumatici chiodati** snow tyres; **scarpe chiodate** shoes with crampons

**chi'odo** *nm* nail; (*idea fissa*) obsession. **~ di garofano** clove

**chi'oma** *nf* [head of] hair; (*fogliame*) foliage

**chi'osco** *nm* kiosk; (*per giornali*) newsstand

**chi'ostro** *nm* cloister

**chip** *nm inv* **~ [di silicio]** chip

'**chipset** *nm inv* chipset

**chiro'mante** *nmf* fortune teller, palmist

**chiroman'zia** *nf* palmistry

**chirur'gia** *nf* surgery. ~ **estetica** cosmetic surgery

**chirurgica'mente** *adv* surgically

**chi'rurgico** *a* surgical

**chi'rurgo** *nm* surgeon

**chissà** *adv* who knows; ~ **quando arriverà** I wonder when he will arrive

**chi'tarra** *nf* guitar. ~ **acustica** acoustic guitar

**chitar'rista** *nmf* guitarist

**chi'udere** *vt* shut, close; (*con chiave*) lock; turn off, switch off ‹*luce ecc*›; turn off ‹*acqua*›; (*per sempre*) close down ‹*negozio, fabbrica ecc*›; (*recingere*) enclose; **chiudi il becco!** shut up! ● *vi* shut, close; (*con chiave*) lock up

**chi'udersi** *vr* shut; ‹*tempo:*› cloud over; ‹*ferita:*› heal over; *fig* withdraw into oneself

**chi'unque** *pron* anyone, anybody ● *rel pron* whoever

**chi'usa** *nf* enclosure; (*di canale*) lock; (*conclusione*) close

**chi'uso** *pp di* **chiudere** ● *a* closed, shut; ‹*tempo*› overcast; ‹*persona*› reserved; '~ **per turno**' 'closing day'

**chiu'sura** *nf* closing; (*sistema*) lock; (*allacciatura*) fastener; '~ **settimanale il lunedì**' 'closed on Mondays'. ~ **centralizzata** *Auto* central locking. ~ **lampo** zip, zipper *Am*

**ci** *pron* (*personale*) us; (*riflessivo*) ourselves; (*reciproco*) each other; (*a ciò, di ciò ecc*) about it; **non ci disturbare** don't disturb us; **aspettateci** wait for us; **ci ha detto tutto** he told us everything; **ci consideriamo...** we consider ourselves...; **ci laviamo le mani** we wash our hands; **ci odiamo** we hate each other; **non ci penso mai** I never think about it; **pensaci!** think about it! ● *adv* (*qui*) here; (*lì*) there; (*moto per luogo*) through it; **ci siamo** here we are; **ci siete?** are you there?; **ci siamo passati tutti** we all went through it; **c'è** there is; **ci vuole pazienza** it takes patience; **non ci vedo/sento** I can't see/hear

**C.ia** *abbr* (*compagnia*) Co.

**cia'batta** *nf* slipper

**ciabat'tare** *vi* shuffle

**ciabat'tino** *nm* cobbler

**ci'ac** *nm inv* *Cinema* ~ **si gira!** action!

**ci'alda** *nf* wafer

**cial'trone** *nm* (*mascalzone*) scoundrel; (*fannullone*) wastrel

**ciam'bella** *nf* *Culin* ring-shaped cake; (*salvagente*) lifebelt; (*gonfiabile*) rubber ring

**ci'ance** *nfpl* yapping

**cianci'are** *vi* gossip

**cianfru'saglie** *nfpl* knick-knacks

**cia'notico** *a* ‹*viso*› puce

**cia'nuro** *nm* cyanide

**ci'ao** *int fam* (*all'arrivo*) hello!, hi!; (*alla partenza*) bye-bye!, cheerio!

**ciar'lare** *vi* chat

**ciarla'tano** *nm* charlatan

**ciarli'ero** *a* (*loquace*) talkative

**cia'scuno** *a* each ● *pron* everyone, everybody; (*distributivo*) each [one]; **per** ~ each

**ci'bare** *vt* feed

**ci'barie** *nfpl* provisions

**ci'barsi** *vr* eat: ~ **di** live on

**ciber'netica** *nf* cybernetics

**ciber'netico** *a* cybernetic

**ciber'spazio** *nm* cyberspace

**'cibo** *nm* food; **non toccare** ~ leave one's food untouched; **non ha toccato** ~ **da ieri** he hasn't had a bite to eat since yesterday. **cibi** *pl* **precotti** ready meals

**ci'cala** *nf* cicada

**cica'lino** *nm* buzzer

**cica'trice** *nf* scar

**cicatriz'zante** *nm* ointment

**cicatriz'zare** *vi* heal [up]

**cicatriz'zarsi** *vr* heal [up]

**cicatrizzazi'one** *nf* healing

**'cicca** *nf* cigarette end; (*fam: sigaretta*) fag; (*fam: gomma*) [chewing] gum

**cic'chetto** *nm fam* (*bicchierino*) nip; (*rimprovero*) telling-off

**'ciccia** *nf fam* fat, flab

**cicci'one, -a** *nmf fam* fatty, fatso

**cice'rone** *nm* guide

**cicla'mino** *nm* cyclamen

**ciclica'mente** *adv* cyclically

**'ciclico** *a* cyclical

**ci'clismo** *nm* cycling

**ci'clista** *nmf* cyclist

**'ciclo** *nm* cycle; (*di malattia*) course. ~ **economico** business cycle

**ciclo'cross** *nm inv* cyclo-cross

**ciclomo'tore** *nm* moped

**ci'clone** *nm* cyclone

**ci'clonico** *a* cyclonic

**ciclosti'lare** *vt* duplicate

**ciclosti'lato** *nm* duplicate [copy] ● *a* duplicate

**ci'cogna** *nf* stork

**ci'coria** *nf* chicory

**ci'cuta** *nf* hemlock

**ci'eco, -a** *a* blind ● *nmf* blind man; blind woman; **i parzialmente ciechi** the partially sighted

**ciel'lino** *nmf Pol* member of the *Comunione e Liberazione movement*

**ci'elo** *nm* sky; *Relig* heaven; **al settimo** ~ in seventh heaven; **santo** ~! good heavens!

**'cifra** *nf* figure; (*somma*) sum; (*monogramma*) monogram; (*codice*) code; **una** ~ *sl* like crazy

**ci'frare** *vt* embroider with a monogram; (*codificare*) code

**ci'frato** *a* monogrammed; (*codificato*) coded

**'ciglio** *nm* (*bordo*) edge; (*degli occhi*) eyelash; **ciglia** *pl* eyelashes

**'cigno** *nm* swan

**cigo'lante** *a* squeaky

**cigo'lare** *vt* squeak

**cigo'lio** *nm* squeak

**'Cile** *nm* Chile

**ci'lecca** *nf* far ~ miss

**ci'leno, -a** *a & nmf* Chilean

**cili'egia** *nf* cherry

**cili'egio** *nm* cherry[-tree]
**cilin'drata** *nf* cubic capacity, c.c.; **macchina di alta ~** highpowered car
**ci'lindro** *nm* cylinder; (*cappello*) top hat, topper
**'cima** *nf* top; (*fig: persona*) genius; **in ~** at the top of; **da ~ a fondo** from top to bottom. **~ alla genovese** baked veal stuffed with chicken and chopped vegetables, served cold.
**cime** *pl* **di rapa** turnip greens
**ci'melio** *nm* relic; **cimeli** *pl* memorabilia
**cimen'tare** *vt* put to the test
**cimen'tarsi** *vr* (*provare*) try one's hand; **~ in** (*arrischiarsi*) venture into
**'cimice** *nf* bug; (*puntina*) drawing pin, thumbtack *Am*
**cimini'era** *nf* chimney; *Naut* funnel
**cimi'tero** *nm* cemetery. **~ delle macchine** breaker's yard
**ci'mosa** *nf* selvage, selvedge
**ci'murro** *nm* distemper
**'Cina** *nf* China
**cincial'legra** *nf* great tit
**cincia'rella** *nf* blue tit
**cincillà** *nm inv* chinchilla
**cin cin** *int* cheers!
**cincischi'are** *vi* fiddle
**cincischi'arsi** *vr* mess around
**'cine** *nm fam* film
**cine'asta** *nmf* film maker
**Cinecittà** *nf* (*stabilimento*) film complex in the suburbs of Rome
**cine'club** *nm inv* film club
**ci'nefilo, -a** *nmf* cinemagoer
**cinegior'nale** *nm* newsreel
**'cinema** *nm inv* cinema. **~ d'essai** arts cinema
**cine'matica** *nf* kinematics
**cinematogra'fare** *vt* film
**cinematogra'fia** *nf* cinematography
**cinemato'grafico** *a* film *attrib*
**cinema'tografo** *nm* cinema
**cine'presa** *nf* cine-camera
**ci'nereo** *a* ashen
**ci'nese** *a* & *nmf* Chinese
**cinese'rie** *nfpl* chinoiserie
**cine'teca** *nf* (*raccolta*) film collection
**ci'netico** *a* kinetic
**'cingere** *vt* (*circondare*) surround
**'cinghia** *nf* strap; (*cintura*) belt. **~ del ventilatore** fanbelt. **~ della ventola** fanbelt
**cinghi'ale** *nm* wild boar; **pelle di ~** pigskin
**cinghi'ata** *nf* lash
**cingo'lato** *a* (*mezzi*) caterpillar *attrib* ● *nm* caterpillar
**'cingolo** *nm Mech* belt
**cinguet'tare** *vi* twitter
**cinguet'tio** *nm* twittering
**cinica'mente** *adv* cynically
**'cinico** *a* cynical
**ci'niglia** *nf* (*tessuto*) chenille
**ci'nismo** *nm* cynicism
**ci'nofilo** *a* (*unità*) dog-loving
**cin'quanta** *a* & *nm* fifty
**cinquanten'nale** *nm* fiftieth anniversary

**cinquan'tenne** *a* & *nmf* fifty-year-old
**cinquan'tesimo** *a* & *nm* fiftieth
**cinquan'tina** *nf* **una ~ di** about fifty
**'cinque** *a* & *nm* five
**cinquecen'tesco** *a* sixteenth-century
**cinque'cento** *a* five hundred ● *nm* **il C~** the sixteenth century
**cinque'mila** *a* & *nm* five thousand
**cin'quina** *nf* (*in tombola*) five in a row
**'cinta** *nf* (*di pantaloni*) belt; **muro di ~** [boundary] wall
**cin'tare** *vt* enclose
**'cintola** *nf* (*di pantaloni*) belt
**cin'tura** *nf* belt. **~ nera** black belt. **~ di salvataggio** lifebelt. **~ di sicurezza** *Aeron, Auto* seat belt
**cintu'rato** *nm Auto* radial tyre
**cintu'rino** *nm* **~ [dell'orologio]** watch-strap; (*di metallo*) bracelet
**ciò** *pron* this; that; **~ che** what; **~ nondimeno** nevertheless
**ci'occa** *nf* lock
**ciocco'lata** *nf* chocolate; (*bevanda*) [hot] chocolate. **~ in polvere** drinking chocolate
**cioccola'tino** *nm* chocolate
**ciocco'lato** *nm* chocolate. **~ fondente** plain chocolate, dark chocolate. **~ al latte** milk chocolate. **~ da pasticceria** cooking chocolate
**cioè** *adv* that is
**ciondo'lare** *vi* dangle
**ciondo'lio** *nm* dangling
**ci'ondolo** *nm* pendant
**ciondo'loni** *adv fig* hanging about
**cionono'stante** *adv* nonetheless
**ci'otola** *nf* bowl
**ci'ottolo** *nm* pebble; **ciottoli** *pl* (*in spiaggia*) shingle
**ci'piglio** *nm* frown; **con ~** with a frown
**ci'polla** *nf* onion; (*bulbo*) bulb
**ci'presso** *nm* cypress
**'cipria** *nf* [face] powder
**cipri'ota** *a* & *nmf* Cypriot
**'Cipro** *nm* Cyprus
**'circa** *adv* & *prep* about
**cir'cense** *a* circus *attrib*
**'circo** *nm* circus
**circo'lare** *a* circular ● *nf* circular; (*di metropolitana*) circle line ● *vi* circulate
**circola'torio** *a Med* circulatory
**circolazi'one** *nf* circulation; (*traffico*) traffic
**'circolo** *nm* circle; (*società*) club. **~ del golf** golf-club. **C~ polare antartico** Antarctic Circle. **C~ polare artico** Arctic Circle
**circon'cidere** *vt* circumcise
**circoncisi'one** *nf* circumcision
**circon'dare** *vt* surround
**circon'dario** *nm* (*amministrativo*) administrative district; (*vicinato*) neighbourhood
**circon'darsi** *vr* **~ di** surround oneself with
**circonfe'renza** *nf* circumference. **~ del**

**collo** collar size. **~ dei fianchi** hip measurement. **~ [della] vita** waist measurement
**circon'flesso** a e con l'accento ~ circumflex e
**circonvallazi'one** nf ring road
**circo'scritto** pp di **circoscrivere** ● a limited
**circo'scrivere** vt circumscribe
**circoscrizio'nale** a area
**circoscrizi'one** nf area. **~ elettorale** constituency
**circo'spetto** a wary
**circospezi'one** nf **con ~** warily
**circo'stante** a surrounding
**circo'stanza** nf circumstance; (occasione) occasion
**circostanzi'ato** a circumstantial
**circu'ire** vt (ingannare) trick
**circuite'ria** nf circuitry
**cir'cuito** nm circuit
**circumnavi'gare** vt circumnavigate
**circumnavigazi'one** nf circumnavigation
**ci'rillico** a Cyrillic
**cir'ripede** nm barnacle
**cir'rosi** nf cirrhosis
**Cisgior'dania** nf West Bank
**C.I.S.L.** nf abbr (**Confederazione Italiana Sindacati Lavoratori**) trades union organization
**C.I.S.N.A.L.** nf abbr (**Confederazione Italiana Sindacati Nazionali dei Lavoratori**) trades union organization
**'cispa** nf (nell'occhio) sleep
**ci'sposo** a bleary-eyed
**'ciste** nf inv cyst
**ci'sterna** nf cistern; (serbatoio) tank
**'cisti** nf cyst
**cisti'fellea** nf gall bladder
**ci'stite** nf cystitis
**C.I.T.** nm abbr (**Compagnia Italiana Turismo**) Italian tourist organization
**ci'tare** vt (riportare brani ecc) quote; (come esempio) cite; Jur summons
**citazi'one** nf quotation; Jur summons sg
**citofo'nare** vt buzz
**ci'tofono** nm entry phone; (in ufficio, su aereo ecc) intercom
**cito'logico** a cytological
**'citrico** a citric
**ci'trullo** nmf fam dimwit
**città** nf inv town; (grande) city. **C~ del Capo** Cape Town. **~ fantasma** ghost town. **~ giardino** garden city. **C~ del Vaticano** Vatican City
**citta'della** nf citadel
**citta'dina** nf town
**cittadi'nanza** nf citizenship; (popolazione) citizens pl
**citta'dino, -a** nmf citizen; (abitante di città) city dweller
**ciuci'are** vt fam suck
**ci'uccio** nm fam dummy
**ci'uco** nm ass
**ci'uffo** nm tuft

**ci'urma** nf Naut crew
**ciur'maglia** nf (gentaglia) rabble
**ci'vetta** nf owl; (fig: donna) flirt; [auto] ~ unmarked police car
**civet'tare** vi flirt
**civette'ria** nf flirtatiousness, coquettishness
**civettu'olo** a flirtatious, coquettish
**'civico** a civic
**ci'vile** a civil ● nm civilian
**civi'lista** nmf (avvocato) specialist in civil law
**civiliz'zare** vt civilize
**civiliz'zarsi** vr become civilized
**civiliz'zato** a (paese) civilized
**civilizzazi'one** nf civilization
**civil'mente** adv civilly
**civiltà** nf civilization; (cortesia) civility
**ci'vismo** nm public spirit
**CL** nf abbr (**Comunione e Liberazione**) young Catholics association
**cl** abbr (**centilitri**) centilitre(s)
**'clacson** nm inv horn
**clacso'nare** vi beep the horn, hoot
**cla'more** nm clamour; **fare ~** cause a sensation
**clamorosa'mente** adv (sbagliare) sensationally
**clamo'roso** a noisy; (sbaglio) sensational
**clan** nm inv clan; fig clique
**clandestina'mente** adv secretly
**clandestinità** nf secrecy; **vivere nella ~** live underground
**clande'stino** a clandestine; **movimento ~** underground movement; **passeggero ~** stowaway
**claque** nf inv claque
**clarinet'tista** nmf clarinettist
**clari'netto** nm clarinet
**'classe** nf class; (aula) classroom; **di prima ~** first-class. **~ economica** economy class. **~ operaia** working class. **~ turistica** tourist class
**classicheggi'ante** a classical
**classi'cismo** nm classicism
**classi'cista** nmf classicist
**'classico** a classical; (tipico) classic ● nm classic
**clas'sifica** nf classification; Sport results pl
**classifi'cabile** a classifiable
**classifi'care** vt classify
**classifi'carsi** vr be placed
**classifica'tore** nm (cartella) folder; (mobile) filing cabinet
**classificazi'one** nf classification
**clas'sista** a class-conscious ● nmf class-conscious person
**claudi'cante** a lame
**'clausola** nf clause. **~ penale** Jur, Comm penalty clause. **~ di recesso** Jur, Comm escape clause
**claustrofo'bia** nf claustrophobia
**claustro'fobico** a claustrophobic

**clau'sura** *nf Relig* cloistered life: **di ~** ‹*suora*› cloistered: **essere in ~** *fig* shut oneself up: **vivere in ~** *fig* live like a hermit

**'clava** *nf* club

**clavicemba'lista** *nmf* harpsichord player

**clavi'cembalo** *nm* harpsichord

**cla'vicola** *nf* collar-bone

**clavi'cordo** *nm* clavichord

**cle'mente** *a* merciful: ‹*tempo*› mild

**cle'menza** *nf* mercy, clemency

**clep'tomane** *nmf* kleptomaniac

**cleptoma'nia** *nf* kleptomania

**cleri'cale** *a* clerical

**'clero** *nm* clergy

**cles'sidra** *nf* hourglass

**clic** *nm inv Comput* click; **fare ~ su** click on

**clic'care** *vi Comput* click; **~ su** click on

**cliché** *nm inv* cliché

**click** = **clic**

**cli'ente** *nmf* client; (*di negozio*) customer

**clien'tela** *nf* customers *pl*, clientèle: (*di avvocato*) clientèle

**cliente'lare** *a Pol* nepotistic

**cliente'lismo** *nm* nepotism

**'clima** *nm* climate

**clima'terio** *nm* climacteric

**climatica'mente** *adv* climatically

**cli'matico** *a* climatic; **stazione climatica** health resort

**climatizza'tore** *nm* air conditioner

**climatizzazi'one** *nf* air conditioning

**'clinica** *nf* clinic. **~ odontoiatrica** dental clinic. **~ ostetrica** maternity hospital. **~ psichiatrica** mental hospital

**'clinico** *a* clinical ● *nm* clinician

**clip** *nf inv* paper-clip; (*di orecchino*) clip

**cli'stere** *nm Med* enema

**clo'aca** *nf* sewer

**cloche** *nf inv* cloche hat

**clo'nare** *vt* clone

**'clone** *nm* clone

**clo'rato** *a* chlorate

**'cloro** *nm* chlorine

**cloro'filla** *nf* chlorophyll

**clorofluorocar'buro** *nm* chlorofluorocarbon, CFC

**cloro'formio** *nm* chloroform

**clou** *a inv* **momenti ~** highlights

**club-'sandwich** *nm inv* club sandwich

**cm** *abbr* (**centimetro**) cm

**CNR** *nm abbr* (**Consiglio Nazionale delle Ricerche**) national research council

**Co.** *abbr* (**compagnia**) Co

**coabi'tare** *vi* live together

**coabitazi'one** *nf* (*di razze*) coexistence

**coadiu'|tore, -'trice** *nmf* (*in ufficio*) assistant

**coadiu'vare** *vt* cooperate with

**coagu'lante** *nm* coagulant

**coagu'lare** *vt* coagulate

**coagu'larsi** *vr* coagulate

**coagulazi'one** *nf* coagulation

**coalizi'one** *nf* coalition

**coaliz'zare** *vt fig* unite

**coaliz'zarsi** *vr* unite

**co'atto** *a Jur* compulsory

**co'balto** *nm* cobalt: (*colore*) cobalt blue

**COBAS** *nmpl abbr* (**Comitati di Base**) independent trade unions

**'cobra** *nm inv* cobra

**'Coca®** *nf* Coke®

**Coca 'cola®** *nf* Coca Cola

**coca'ina** *nf* cocaine

**cocai'nomane** *nmf* cocaine addict

**coc'carda** *nf* rosette

**cocchi'ere** *nm* coachman

**coc'chio** *nm* coach

**coc'cige** *nm* coccyx

**cocci'nella** *nf* ladybird

**'coccio** *nm* earthenware; (*frammento*) fragment

**cocciu'taggine** *nf* stubbornness

**cocciuta'mente** *adv* stubbornly

**cocci'uto** *a* stubborn

**'cocco** *nm* coconut palm: *fam* love; **noce di ~** coconut

**coccodè** *nm inv* cluck

**cocco'drillo** *nm* crocodile

**cocco'lare** *vt* cuddle

**co'cente** *a* ‹*sole*› burning; ‹*lacrime, delusione*› bitter

**'cocker** *nm inv* **~ [spaniel]** cocker spaniel

**'cocktail** *nm inv* (*ricevimento*) cocktail party

**co'comero** *nm* watermelon

**co'cuzzolo** *nm* top; (*di testa, cappello*) crown

**'coda** *nf* tail; (*di abito*) train; (*fila*) queue; (*di traffico*) tailback; **fare la ~** queue [up], stand in line *Am*. **~ di cavallo** (*acconciatura*) pony tail. **~ dell'occhio** corner of one's eye. **~ di paglia** guilty conscience

**co'dardo, -a** *a* cowardly ● *nmf* coward

**co'dazzo** *nm* train

**code'ina** *nf* codeine

**co'desto** *a* that

**'codice** *nm* code; **in ~** ‹*messaggio*› coded, in code; **mettere in ~** encode. **~ di avviamento postale** postal code, zip code *Am*. **~ a barre** bar-code. **~ civile** civil code. **~ fiscale** tax code. **~ penale** penal code. **~ segreto** (*di carta di credito*) PIN. **~ della strada** highway code

**codi'cillo** *nm* codicil

**co'difica** *nf* coding

**codifi'care** *vt* encode; codify ‹*legge*›

**codifica'|tore, -'trice** *nmf Comput* encoder

**codificazi'one** *nf* encoding: (*di legge*) codification

**co'dini** *nmpl* bunches

**coeffici'ente** *nm* coefficient

**coercizi'one** *nf* coercion

**coe'rente** *a* consistent

**coe'renza** *nf* consistency

**coesi'one** *nf* cohesion

**coe'sistere** *vi* coexist

**coe'sivo** *a* cohesive

**coe'taneo, -a** *a & nmf* contemporary

**cofa'netto** *nm* casket

**'cofano** *nm* (*forziere*) chest: *Auto* bonnet. hood *Am*

**cofirma'tario, -a** *nmf* cosignatory

**coge'stire** *vt* co-manage

**cogi'tare** *vi* ponder

**'cogliere** *vt* pick: (*sorprendere*) catch: (*afferrare*) seize: (*colpire*) hit; ~ **la palla al balzo** seize the opportunity; ~ **di sorpresa** take by surprise

**co'glione** *nm vulg* ball: (*sciocco*) dickhead; **rompere i coglioni a qcno** get on sb's tits

**'Cognac** *nm* cognac

**co'gnato, -a** *nm* brother-in-law ● *nf* sister-in-law

**cognizi'one** *nf* knowledge: **con ~ di causa** on an informed basis

**co'gnome** *nm* surname. ~ **da ragazza/da nubile** maiden name

**cogu'aro** *nm* cougar

**'coi = con + i**

**coi'bente** *a* insulating

**coinci'denza** *nf* coincidence; (*di treno ecc*) connection

**coin'cidere** *vi* coincide

**coinqui'lino** *nm* flatmate

**coin'volgere** *vt* involve

**coinvolgi'mento** *nm* involvement

**coin'volto** *a* involved

**'coito** *nm* coitus

**col = con + il**

**colà** *adv* there

**cola'brodo** *nm inv* strainer: **ridotto a un ~** *fam* full of holes

**cola'pasta** *nm inv* colander

**co'lare** *vt* strain; (*versare lentamente*) drip ● *vi* (*gocciolare*) drip: (*perdere*) leak; ~ **a picco** *Naut* sink

**co'lata** *nf* (*di metallo*) casting; (*di lava*) flow

**colazi'one** *nf* (*del mattino*) breakfast; (*di mezzogiorno*) lunch; **prima ~** breakfast; **far ~** have breakfast/lunch. ~ **di lavoro** working lunch. ~ **al sacco** packed lunch

**col'bacco** *nm* fur hat

**co'lei** *pron f* the one

**co'lera** *nm* cholera

**coleste'rolo** *nm* cholesterol

**colf** *nf abbr* (**collaboratrice familiare**) home help

**colibri** *nm inv* humming-bird

**'colica** *nf* colic

**co'lino** *nm* [tea] strainer

**'colla** *nf* glue: (*di farina*) paste. ~ **di pesce** gelatine

**collabo'rare** *vi* collaborate; ~ **con** (*polizia*) co-operate with; ~ **a** (*rivista*) contribute to

**collabora|'tore, -'trice** *nmf* collaborator; (*di rivista*) contributor. ~ **familiare** domestic help

**collaborazi'one** *nf* collaboration: (*con polizia*) co-operation

**collaborazio'nista** *nmf* collaborator

**col'lage** *nm inv* collage

**col'lana** *nf* necklace: (*serie*) series. ~ **di perle** pearl necklace

**col'lant** *nmpl* tights. ~ **velati** sheer tights

**col'lante** *a* adhesive

**col'lare** *nm* collar

**colla'rino** *nm* dog collar

**col'lasso** *nm* collapse. ~ **cardiaco** syncope. ~ **renale** kidney failure

**collate'rale** *a* collateral

**collau'dare** *vt* test

**collauda|'tore, -'trice** *nmf* tester

**col'laudo** *nm* test

**collazio'nare** *vt* collate

**'colle** *nm* hill: (*passo*) pass

**col'lega** *nmf* colleague

**colle'gabile** *a* compatible (**a** with)

**collega'mento** *nm* connection; *Mil* liaison; *Radio ecc* link. ~ **dati** data link. ~ **in rete** networking

**colle'gare** *vt* connect

**colle'garsi** *vr TV, Radio* link up (**a** with); (*Comput: a una rete ecc*) go on line (**a** to)

**collegi'ale** *nmf* boarder ● *a* (*responsabilità, decisione*) collective

**col'legio** *nm* (*convitto*) boarding-school. ~ **elettorale** constituency

**'collera** *nf* anger; **andare in ~** get angry

**col'lerico** *a* irascible

**col'letta** *nf* collection

**collettività** *nf inv* community

**collet'tivo** *a* collective; (*interesse*) general; **biglietto ~** group ticket ● *nm* (*studentesco, femminista*) collective

**col'letto** *nm* collar

**collet'tore** *nm* (*di fognatura*) main sewer. ~ **delle imposte** collector of taxes

**collezio'nare** *vt* collect

**collezi'one** *nf* collection. ~ **invernale** winter collection

**collezio'nismo** *nm* collecting

**collezio'nista** *nmf* collector. ~ **di franco-bolli** stamp collector

**colli'mare** *vi* coincide

**col'lina** *nf* hill

**colli'nare** *a* hill *attrib*

**colli'netta** *nf* knoll

**colli'noso** *a* hilly

**col'lirio** *nm* eyewash

**collisi'one** *nf* collision

**'collo** *nm* neck; (*pacco*) package; **a ~ alto** high-necked; **a rotta di ~** breakneck. ~ **del piede** instep

**colloca'mento** *nm* placing; (*impiego*) employment

**collo'care** *vt* place

**collo'carsi** *vr* take one's place

**collocazi'one** *nf* placing

**colloqui'ale** *a* (*termine*) colloquial; (*tono*) informal

**col'loquio** *nm* conversation: (*udienza ecc*) interview; (*esame*) oral [exam]

**col'loso** *a* glutinous

**col'lottola** *nf* nape

**collusi'one** *nf* collusion

**colluttazi'one** *nf* scuffle

**col'mare** *vt* fill; bridge (*divario*); ~ **qcno di gentilezze** overwhelm sb with kindness '**colmo** *a* full ● *nm* top; *fig* height: **al ~ della disperazione** in the depths of despair: **questo è il ~!** (*con indignazione*) this is the last straw!; (*con stupore*) I don't believe it!: **per ~ di sfortuna** to crown it all

+**colo** *suff* poetucolo second rate poet

**co'lomba** *nf* dove. **~ pasquale** *dove-shaped cake with candied fruit eaten at Easter*

**colom'baccio** *nm* wood pigeon

**colom'baia** *nf* dovecote

**Co'lombia** *nf* Colombia

**colombi'ano** *a & nmf* Colombian

**co'lombo** *nm* pigeon; **colombi** *pl* (*innamorati*) lovebirds

**Co'lonia** *nf* Cologne: [**acqua di**] **c~** [eau de] Cologne

**co'lonia** *nf* colony: (*per bambini*) holiday camp

**coloni'ale** *a* colonial

**co'lonico** *a* (*terreno, casa*) farm *attrib*

**coloniz'zare** *vt* colonize

**colonizza'|tore, -'trice** *nmf* colonizer

**co'lonna** *nf* column; (*di auto*) tailback. **~ sonora** sound-track. **~ vertebrale** spine

**colon'nato** *nm* colonnade

**colon'nello** *nm* colonel

**colon'nina** *nf* (*distributore*) petrol pump, gas pump *Am*

**co'lono** *nm* tenant farmer

**colo'rante** *nm* colouring. **~ alimentare** food colouring

**colo'rare** *vt* colour; colour in (*disegno*)

**co'lore** *nm* colour; (*carte*) suit; **a colori** in colour; **di ~** coloured; **farne di tutti i colori** get up to all sorts of mischief; **passarne di tutti i colori** go through hell. **diventare di tutti i colori** *fig* turn scarlet. **~ a olio** oil paint

**colori'ficio** *nm* paint and dyes shop

**colo'rito** *a* coloured; (*viso*) rosy; (*racconto, linguaggio*) colourful ● *nm* complexion

**co'loro** *pron pl* the ones

**colos'sale** *a* colossal

**Colos'seo** *nm* Coliseum

**co'losso** *nm* colossus

'**colpa** *nf* fault; (*biasimo*) blame; (*colpevolezza*) guilt; (*peccato*) sin; **dare la ~ a** blame; **essere in ~** be at fault; **per ~ di** because of; **è ~ mia** it's my fault

**col'pevole** *a* guilty ● *nmf* culprit

**col'pire** *vt* hit, strike; *fig* strike; **~ nel segno** hit the nail on the head

'**colpo** *nm* blow; (*di arma da fuoco*) shot; (*urto*) knock; (*emozione*) shock; *Med, Sport* stroke; (*furto*) robbery; **di ~** suddenly; **far ~** make a strong impression; **far venire un ~ a qcno** *fig* give sb a fright; **perdere colpi** (*motore:*) keep missing; **a ~ d'occhio** at a glance; **a ~ sicuro** for certain. **~ d'aria** chill. **~ basso** blow below the belt. **~ di frusta** *Med* whiplash injury. **~ di grazia** kiss of death. **~ da maestro** masterstroke. **~ di scena** sensational development. **~ di sole** sunstroke. **colpi** *pl* **di sole** (*su capelli*) highlights. **~ di Stato** coup [d'état]. **~ di**

**telefono** ring, call; **dare un ~ di telefono a qn** give sb a ring *or* call. **~ di testa** [sudden] impulse. **~ di vento** gust of wind

**col'poso** *a omicidio* ~ manslaughter

**coltel'lata** *nf* stab

**coltelle'ria** *nf* cutlery shop

**col'tello** *nm* knife; **avere il ~ dalla parte del manico** have the upper hand. **~ per il pane** breadknife. **~ a serramanico** jack-knife

**colti'vare** *vt* cultivate

**coltiva'|tore, -'trice** *nmf* farmer

**coltivazi'one** *nf* farming; (*di piante*) growing. **~ intensiva** intensive farming

'**colto** *pp di* cogliere ● *a* cultured

'**coltre** *nf* blanket

**col'tura** *nf* cultivation. **~ alternata** crop rotation

**co'lui** *pron m* the one

'**colza** *nf Bot* rape

'**coma** *nm inv* coma; **in ~** in a coma; **in ~ irreversibile** brain dead

**comanda'mento** *nm* commandment

**coman'dante** *nm* commander: *Naut, Aeron* captain

**coman'dare** *vt* command; *Mech* control; **~ a qcno di fare qcsa** order sb to do sth ● *vi* be in charge

**co'mando** *nm* command; (*di macchina*) control

**co'mare** *nf* (*pettegola*) gossip

**coma'toso** *a Med* comatose

**combaci'are** *vi* fit together; (*testimonianze:*) concur

**combat'tente** *a* fighting ● *nm* combatant. **ex ~** ex-serviceman

**com'battere** *vt/i* fight

**combatti'mento** *nm* fight; *Mil* battle; **fuori ~** (*pugilato*) knocked out

**combat'tuto** *a* (*gara*) hard fought; (*tormentato*) torn; (*discussione*) heated

**combi'nare** *vt/i* arrange; (*mettere insieme*) combine; (*fam: fare*) do: **cosa stai combinando?** what are you doing?

**combi'narsi** *vr* combine; (*mettersi d'accordo*) come to an agreement

**combinazi'one** *nf* combination; (*caso*) coincidence; **per ~** by chance

**com'briccola** *nf* gang

**combu'stibile** *a* combustible ● *nm* fuel

**combusti'one** *nf* combustion

**com'butta** *nf* gang; **in ~** in league

'**come** *adv* like; (*in qualità di*) as; (*interrogativo, esclamativo*) how; **questo vestito è ~ il tuo** this dress is like yours; **~?** pardon?; **~ stai?** how are you?; **~ va?** how are things?; **~ mai?** how come?; **~?** what?; **non sa ~ fare** he doesn't know what to do; **~ sta bene!** how well he looks!; **~ no!** that will be right!; **~ tu sai** as you know: **fa ~ vuoi** do as you like: **~ se** as if ● *conj* (*non appena*) as soon as

**come'done** *nm* blackhead

**co'meta** *nf* comet

**'comfort** *nm inv* comfort; **con tutti i ~** with all mod cons

**'comico** *a* comical; ‹*teatro, attore*› comic ● *nm* funny side; (*attore*) comic actor, comedian ● *nf* comedienne; (*attrice*) comic actress, comedienne; (*a torte in faccia*) slapstick sketch

**co'mignolo** *nm* chimney-pot

**cominci'are** *vt/i* begin, start; **a ~ da oggi** from today; **per ~ to** begin with; **cominciamo bene!** we're off to a fine start!

**comi'tato** *nm* committee. **~ consultivo** advisory committee. **~ direttivo** steering committee. **~ esecutivo** executive committee. **~ di gestione** management committee

**comi'tiva** *nf* party, group

**co'mizio** *nm* meeting. **~ elettorale** election rally

**'comma** *nm* (*capoverso*) paragraph

**com'mando** *nm inv* commando

**com'media** *nf* comedy; (*opera teatrale*) play; *fig* sham. **~ musicale** musical

**commedi'ante** *nm* comic actor; *fig pej* phoney ● *nf* comic actress; *fig pej* phoney

**commedi'ografo, -a** *nmf* playwright

**commemo'rare** *vt* commemorate

**commemorazi'one** *nf* commemoration. **~ dei defunti** (*2 novembre*) All Souls' Day

**commenda'tore** *nm* commander

**commen'sale** *nmf* fellow diner

**commen'tare** *vt* comment on; (*annotare*) annotate

**commen'tario** *nm* commentary

**commenta|'tore, -'trice** *nmf* commentator

**com'mento** *nm* comment; *TV, Radio* commentary. **~ musicale** music

**commerci'ale** *a* commercial; ‹*relazioni, trattative*› trade; ‹*attività*› business; **centro ~** shopping centre

**commercia'lista** *nmf* business consultant; (*contabile*) accountant

**commercializ'zare** *vt* market; *pej* commercialize

**commercializzazi'one** *nf* marketing; *pej* commercialization

**commerci'ante** *nmf* trader, merchant; (*negoziante*) shopkeeper. **~ all'ingrosso** wholesaler. **~ di oggetti d'arte** art dealer

**commerci'are** *vi* **~ in** deal in

**com'mercio** *nm* commerce; (*internazionale*) trade; (*affari*) business; **in ~** ‹*prodotto*› on sale. **~ all'ingrosso** wholesale trade. **~ al minuto** retail trade

**com'messo, -a** *pp di* **commettere** ● *nmf* shop assistant; **commessi** *pl* counter staff. **~ viaggiatore** commercial traveller ● *nf* (*ordine*) order

**comme'stibile** *a* edible ● *nm* **commestibili** *pl* groceries

**com'mettere** *vt* commit; make ‹*sbaglio*›; **~ un reato** commit an offence

**commi'ato** *nm* leave; **prendere ~ da** take leave of

**commise'rare** *vt* commiserate

**commise'rarsi** *vr* feel sorry for oneself

**commissari'ato** *nm* (*di polizia*) police sta tion

**commis'sario** *nm* ≈ [police] superintend ent; (*membro di commissione*) commissioner *Sport* steward; *Comm* commission agent. **~ di bordo** purser. **~ capo** chief superintend ent. **~ d'esame** examiner. **~ di gara** rac official, steward. **~ tecnico** (*della nazio nale*) national team manager

**commissi'one** *nf* (*incarico*) errand (*comitato, percentuale*) commission; (*Comm di merce*) order; **commissioni** *pl* (*acquisti* **fare commissioni** go shopping. **~ d'esame** board of examiners. **C~ Europea** European Commission. **~ d'inchiesta** court of inquiry

**commit'tente** *nmf* purchaser

**com'mosso** *pp di* **commuovere** ● *a* move

**commo'vente** *a* moving

**commozi'one** *nf* emotion. **~ cerebrale** concussion

**commu'overe** *vt* touch, move

**commu'oversi** *vr* be touched

**commu'tare** *vt* change; *Jur* commute

**commuta'tore** *nm Electr* commutator

**commutazi'one** *nf* (*di pena*) commutation

**comò** *nm inv* chest of drawers

**comoda'mente** *adv* comfortably

**como'dino** *nm* bedside table

**comodità** *nf inv* comfort; (*convenienza*) con venience

**'comodo** *a* comfortable; (*conveniente*) con venient; (*spazioso*) roomy; (*facile*) easy; **stia comodo!** don't get up!; **far ~** be useful ● *nm* comfort; **fare il proprio ~** do as one pleases **prendila con ~!** take it easy!

**'compact disc** *nm inv* compact disc

**compae'sano, -a** *nm* fellow countryman ● *nf* fellow countrywoman

**com'pagine** *nf* (*squadra*) team

**compa'gnia** *nf* company; (*gruppo*) party; **fare ~ a qcno** keep sb company; **essere di ~** be sociable. **~ aerea** airline. **~ di bandiera** (*aerea*) national airline

**com'pagno, -a** *nmf* companion; (*Comm, Sport, in coppia*) partner; *Pol* comrade. **~ di classe** classmate. **~ di scuola** schoolmate. **~ di squadra** team-mate. **~ di viaggio** fel low traveller

**compa'rabile** *a* comparable

**compa'rare** *vt* compare

**compara'tivo** *a & nm* comparative

**comparazi'one** *nf* comparison

**com'pare** *nm* sidekick

**compa'rire** *vi* appear; (*spiccare*) stand out. **~ in giudizio** appear in court

**com'parso, -a** *pp di* **comparire** ● *nf* ap pearance; *Cinema* extra; *Theat* walk-on

**compartecipazi'one** *nf* sharing; (*quota*) share

**comparti'mento** *nm* compartment; (*am ministrativo*) department

**compas'sato** *a* calm and collected

**compassi'one** *nf* compassion; **aver ~ per** feel pity for; **far ~** arouse pity

**compassio'nevole** *a* compassionate

**com'passo** *nm* [pair of] compasses *pl*

**compa'tibile** *a* (*conciliabile*) compatible; (*scusabile*) excusable

**compatibilità** *nf* compatibility

**compatibil'mente** *adv* **~ con i miei impegni** if my commitments allow

**compati'mento** *nm* **un'aria di ~** air of condescension

**compa'tire** *vt* pity; (*scusare*) make allowances for

**compatri'ota** *nmf* compatriot

**compat'tezza** *nf* (*di materia*) compactness; (*fig: di partito*) solidarity

**com'patto** *a* compact; (*denso*) dense; (*solido*) solid; *fig* united

**compendi'are** *vt* (*fare un sunto*) summarize

**com'pendio** *nm* outline; (*sunto*) synopsis; (*libro*) compendium

**compene'trare** *vt* pervade

**compen'sare** *vt* compensate; (*supplire*) make up for

**compen'sarsi** *vr* balance each other out

**compen'sato** *nm* (*legno*) plywood

**compensazi'one** *nf* compensation

**com'penso** *nm* compensation; (*retribuzione*) remuneration; **in compenso** (*in cambio*) in return; (*d'altra parte*) on the other hand; (*invece*) instead

**'compera** *nf* purchase; **far compere** do some shopping

**compe'rare** *vt* buy

**compe'tente** *a* competent; (*ufficio*) appropriate

**compe'tenza** *nf* competence; (*responsabilità*) responsibility; **competenze** *pl* (*onorari*) fees

**com'petere** *vi* compete; **~ a** (*compito:*) be the responsibility of

**competitività** *nf* competitiveness

**competi'tivo** *a* (*prezzo, carattere*) competitive

**competi|'tore, -'trice** *nmf* competitor

**competizi'one** *nf* competition

**compia'cente** *a* obliging

**compia'cenza** *nf* obligingness; **avere la ~ di...** be so obliging as to...

**compia'cere** *vt/i* please

**compia'cersi** *vr* (*congratularsi*) congratulate; **~ di** (*degnarsi*) condescend to

**compiaci'mento** *nm* satisfaction; *pej* smugness

**compiaci'uto** *a* satisfied; (*aria, sorriso*) smug

**compi'angere** *vt* pity; (*per lutto ecc*) sympathize with

**'compiere** *vt* (*concludere*) complete; commit (*delitto*); **~ gli anni** have one's birthday

**'compiersi** *vr* end; (*avverarsi*) come true

**compi'lare** *vt* compile; fill in (*modulo*)

**compila|'tore, -'trice** *nmf* compiler

**compilazi'one** *nf* compilation

**compi'mento** *nm* completion; **portare a ~ qcsa** conclude sth

**com'pire** *vt* = **compiere**

**compi'tare** *vt* spell

**'compito**[1] *nm* task; (*dovere*) duty; *Sch* homework; **fare i compiti** do one's homework

**com'pito**[2] *a* polite

**compiu'tezza** *nf* completeness

**compi'uto** *a* **avere 30 anni compiuti** be over 30

**comple'anno** *nm* birthday

**complemen'tare** *a* complementary; (*secondario*) subsidiary

**comple'mento** *nm* complement; *Mil* draft. **~ oggetto** *Gram* direct object

**comples'sato** *a* hung-up

**complessità** *nf* complexity

**complessiva'mente** *adv* on the whole; (*in totale*) altogether

**comples'sivo** *a* comprehensive; (*totale*) total

**com'plesso** *a* complex; (*difficile*) complicated ● *nm* complex, hang up *fam*; *Psych* complex; (*di cantanti ecc*) group; (*di circostanze, fattori*) combination; **in ~** on the whole; (*in totale*) altogether. **~ di inferiorità** inferiority complex

**completa'mente** *adv* completely

**completa'mento** *nm* completion

**comple'tare** *vt* complete

**comple'tezza** *nf* completeness

**com'pleto** *a* complete; (*pieno*) full [up]; **al ~** (*teatro:*) sold out; (*albergo*) full; **'~'** 'no vacancies'; **la famiglia al ~** the whole family ● *nm* (*vestito*) suit; (*insieme di cose*) set

**compli'care** *vt* complicate

**compli'carsi** *vr* become complicated

**compli'cato** complicated

**complicazi'one** *nf* complication; **salvo complicazioni** all being well

**'complice** *nmf* accomplice ● *a* (*sguardo*) knowing

**complicità** *nf* complicity

**complimen'tare** *nm* compliment ● *vt* compliment

**complimen'tarsi** *vr* **~ con** congratulate

**compli'mento** *nm* compliment. **complimenti** *pl* (*ossequi*) regards; (*congratulazioni*) congratulations; **far complimenti** stand on ceremony

**complot'tare** *vi* plot

**com'plotto** *nm* plot

**compo'nente** *a & nm* component ● *nmf* member

**componen'tistica** *nf* (*per auto, elettronica*) accessories *pl*

**compo'nibile** *a* (*cucina*) fitted; (*mobili*) modular

**componi'mento** *nm* composition; (*letterario*) work

**com'porre** *vt* compose; (*sistemare*) put in order; *Typ* set; lay out (*salma*); settle (*lite*)

**com'porsi** *vr* **~ di** be made up of

**comportamen'tale** *a* behavioural

**comporta'mento** *nm* behaviour
**compor'tare** *vt* (*implicare*) involve
**compor'tarsi** *vr* behave
**com'posito** *a* Chem. Phot composite
**composi'|tore, -'trice** *nmf* composer; Typ compositor
**composizi'one** *nf* composition. **~ florea-le** flower arrangement
**com'posta** *nf* stewed fruit; (*concime*) compost
**compo'stezza** *nf* composure
**com'posto** *pp di* **comporre** ● *a* ⟨*parola*⟩ compound; **essere ~ da** consist of, comprise; **stai ~!** sit properly! ● *nm* Chem compound; *Culin* mixture
**com'prare** *vt* buy; (*fig: corrompere*) buy off, bribe
**compra'|tore, -'trice** *nmf* buyer
**compra'vendita** *nf* buying and selling; **atto di ~** deed of sale
**com'prendere** *vt* understand; (*includere*) comprise
**compren'donio** *nm* **essere duro di ~** be slow on the uptake
**compren'sibile** *a* understandable
**comprensibil'mente** *adv* understandably
**comprensi'one** *nf* understanding
**compren'sivo** *a* understanding; (*che include*) inclusive
**com'preso** *pp di* **comprendere** ● *a* included; **tutto ~** ⟨*prezzo*⟩ all-in; **da lunedì a venerdì ~** Monday to Friday inclusive
**com'pressa** *nf* compress; (*pastiglia*) tablet
**compressi'one** *nf* compression. **~ dati** *Comput* data compression
**com'presso** *pp di* **comprimere** ● *a* compressed
**compres'sore** *nm* (*rullo*) steamroller
**compri'mario** *nm* Theat supporting actor ● *nf* supporting actress
**com'primere** *vt* press; (*reprimere*) repress
**compro'messo** *pp di* **compromettere** ● *nm* compromise; (*contratto*) *preliminary but binding agreement*
**compromet'tente** *a* compromising
**compro'mettere** *vt* compromise
**comproprietà** *nf* multiple ownership
**comproprie'tario, -a** *nmf* joint owner
**compro'vare** *vt* prove
**com'punto** *a* contrite
**compunzi'one** *nf* compunction
**compu'tare** *vt* calculate; (*addebitare*) estimate
**com'puter** *nm inv* computer. **~ da casa** home computer
**computeriz'zare** *vt* computerize
**computeriz'zato** *a* computerized
**computerizzazi'one** *nf* computerization
**computiste'ria** *nf* book-keeping
**'computo** *nm* calculation
**comu'nale** *a* municipal
**co'mune** *a* common; ⟨*parti*⟩ communal,

common; ⟨*amico*⟩ mutual; (*ordinario*) ordinary ● *nm* municipality; **fuori del ~** out of the ordinary; **avere qcsa in ~** have sth in common ● *nf* collective farm
**comu'nella** *nf* **fare ~** form a clique
**comune'mente** *adv* commonly
**comuni'cante** *a* interconnecting
**comuni'care** *vt* communicate; pass on ⟨*malattia*⟩; *Relig* administer Communion to
**comuni'carsi** *vr* receive Communion
**comunica'tiva** *nf* communicativeness
**comunica'tivo** *a* communicative
**comuni'cato** *nm* communiqué. **~ commerciale** *Radio* commercial. **~ stampa** press release
**comunicazi'one** *nf* communication; *Teleph* [phone] call; **avere la ~** get through; **dare la ~ a qcno** put sb through. **~ dati** *Comput* data communications
**comuni'one** *nf* communion; *Relig* [Holy] Communion
**comu'nismo** *nm* communism
**comu'nista** *a* & *nmf* communist
**comunità** *nf inv* community. **C~ [Economica] Europea** European [Economic] Community. **C~ degli Stati indipendenti** Commonwealth of Independent States. **~ terapeutica** residential therapy group
**co'munque** *conj* however ● *adv* anyhow
**con** *prep* with; (*mezzo*) by; **~ facilità** easily; **~ mia grande gioia** to my great delight; **è gentile ~ tutti** he is kind to everyone; **col treno** by train; **~ questo tempo** in this weather
**co'nato** *nm* **~ di vomito** retching
**'conca** *nf* basin; (*valle*) dell
**concate'nare** *vt* link together
**concate'narsi** *vr* ⟨*idee:*⟩ be connected
**concatenazi'one** *nf* connection
**'concavo** *a* concave
**con'cedere** *vt* grant; award ⟨*premio*⟩; (*ammettere*) admit
**con'cedersi** *vr* allow oneself ⟨*pausa*⟩; treat oneself to ⟨*lusso, vacanza*⟩
**concentra'mento** *nm* concentration
**concen'trare** *vt* concentrate
**concen'trarsi** *vr* concentrate
**concen'trato** *a* concentrated ● *nm* concentrate. **~ di pomodoro** tomato pureé
**concentrazi'one** *nf* concentration
**con'centrico** *a* concentric
**concepi'mento** *nm* conception
**conce'pire** *vt* conceive ⟨*bambino*⟩; (*capire*) understand; (*figurarsi*) conceive of; devise ⟨*piano ecc*⟩
**con'cernere** *vt* concern
**concer'tare** *vt* Mus harmonize; (*organizzare*) arrange
**concer'tarsi** *vr* agree
**concer'tista** *nmf* concert performer
**con'certo** *nm* concert; (*composizione*) concerto. **~ rock** rock concert
**concessio'nario** *nm* agent
**concessi'one** *nf* concession

**con'cesso** pp di **concedere**

**con'cetto** nm concept; (opinione) opinion

**concet'toso** a cerebral

**concezi'one** nf conception; (idea) concept

**con'chiglia** nf [sea] shell. **~ del pellegrino**, **~ di san Giacomo** scallop shell

'**concia** nf tanning; (di tabacco) curing

**conci'are** vt tan; cure ‹tabacco›; **~ qcno per le feste** give sb a good hiding

**conci'arsi** vr (sporcarsi) get dirty; (vestirsi male) dress badly

**conci'ato** a ‹pelle, cuoio› tanned; **essere ~ come un barbone** look like something the cat dragged in

**concili'abile** a compatible

**concili'abolo** nm private meeting

**concili'ante** a conciliatory

**concili'are** vt reconcile; pay ‹contravvenzione›; (favorire) induce

**concili'arsi** vr go together; (mettersi d'accordo) become reconciled

**conciliazi'one** nf reconciliation; Jur settlement

**con'cilio** nm Relig council; (riunione) assembly

**conci'maia** nf dunghill

**conci'mare** vt feed ‹pianta›

**con'cime** nm manure; (chimico) fertilizer

**concisi'one** nf conciseness

**con'ciso** a concise

**conci'tato** a excited

**concitta'dino, -a** nmf fellow citizen

**concla'mato** a Med full blown

**con'clave** nm conclave

**con'cludere** vt conclude; (finire con successo) successfully complete

**con'cludersi** vr come to an end

**conclusi'one** nf conclusion; **in ~** (insomma) in short

**conclu'sivo** a conclusive

**con'cluso** pp di **concludere**

**concomi'tante** a contributory

**concomi'tanza** nf (di circostanze, fatti) combination; **in ~ con** combined with, in conjunction with

**concor'danza** nf agreement

**concor'dare** vt agree [on]; Gram make agree ● vi (sul prezzo) agree

**concor'dato** nm agreement; Jur, Comm composition

**con'corde** a in agreement; (unanime) unanimous

**con'cordia** nf concord

**concor'rente** a concurrent; (rivale) competing ● nmf Comm, Sport competitor; (candidato) candidate; (a quiz, concorso di bellezza) contestant

**concor'renza** nf competition. **~ sleale** unfair competition

**concorrenzi'ale** a competitive

**con'correre** vi (contribuire) combine; (andare insieme) go together; (competere) compete

**con'corso** pp di **concorrere** ● nm competition; **fuori ~** not in the official competition.

**~ di bellezza** beauty contest. **~ di circostanze** combination of circumstances. **~ di colpa** contributory negligence. **~ ippico** showjumping event. **~ a premi** prizewinning competition. **~ in reato** Jur complicity. **~ per titoli** competition in which exam results are not the sole criterion

**concreta'mente** adv concretely

**concre'tare, concretiz'zare** vt put into concrete form

**con'creto** a concrete; **in ~** in concrete terms

**concu'bina** nf concubine

**concussi'one** nf acceptance of a bribe

**con'danna** nf sentence; **pronunziare una ~** hand down a sentence. **~ a morte** death sentence. **~ penale** prison sentence

**condan'nare** vt (disapprovare) condemn; Jur sentence

**condan'nato, -a** a (destinato) forced ● nmf prisoner

**con'densa** nf condensation

**conden'sare** vt condense

**conden'sarsi** vr condense

**condensa'tore** nm Electr condenser

**condensazi'one** nf condensation

**condi'mento** nm seasoning; (salsa) dressing. **~ per insalata** salad dressing

**con'dire** vt flavour; dress ‹insalata›

**condiscen'dente** a indulgent; pej condescending; (arrendevole) compliant

**condiscen'denza** nf indulgence; pej condescension; (arrendevolezza) compliance

**con'dito** a Culin seasoned

**condi'videre** vt share

**condizio'nale** a & nm conditional ● nf Jur suspended sentence

**condiziona'mento** nm Psych conditioning

**condizio'nare** vt condition

**condizionata'mente** adv conditionally

**condizio'nato** a conditional (**da** on); **aria condizionata** air-conditioning

**condiziona'tore** nm air conditioner

**condizi'one** nf condition; **a ~ che** on condition that. **condizioni** pl di credito credit terms. **~ imprescindibile** precondition

**condogli'anze** nfpl condolences; **fare le ~ a** offer one's condolences to

'**condom** nm inv condom

**condomini'ale** a ‹spese› common; ‹riunione› tenants' attrib

**condo'minio** nm joint ownership; (edificio) condominium

**condo'mino, -a** nmf joint owner

**condo'nare** vt remit

**con'dono** nm remission

**con'dotta** nf conduct, (circoscrizione di medico) country practice; (di gara ecc) management; (tubazione) pipe

**con'dotto** pp di **condurre** ● a medico **~** country doctor ● nm pipe; Anat duct. **~ dell'aria** air duct. **~ sotterraneo** culvert

**condu'cente** nm driver. **~ di autobus** bus driver

**con'durre** vt lead; drive ‹veicoli›; (accompagnare) take; conduct ‹gas, elettricità ecc›; (gestire) run; ~ **a termine** complete; ~ **delle indagini** carry out an investigation

**con'dursi** vr behave

**condut'tore** a **filo** ~ leitmotif

**condut|'tore, -'trice** nmf TV presenter; (di veicolo) driver ● nm Electr conductor

**condut'tura** nf duct. ~ **del gas** gas main

**conduzi'one** nf conduction

**confabu'lare** vi have a confab

**confa'cente** a suitable

**con'farsi** vr confarsi a suit

**confederazi'one** nf confederation. **C~ elvetica** Swiss Confederation

**confe'renza** nf (discorso) lecture; (congresso) conference. ~ **stampa** press conference, news conference

**conferenzi'ere, -a** nmf lecturer, speaker

**confe'rire** vt (donare) confer ● vi (consultarsi) confer

**con'ferma** nf confirmation; **dare** ~ confirm

**confer'mare** vt confirm

**confes'sare** vt confess

**confes'sarsi** vr confess

**confessio'nale** a ‹segreto› of the confession ● nm confessional

**confessi'one** nf confession

**confes'sore** nm confessor

**con'fetto** nm (di mandorla) sugared almond

**confet'tura** nf jam

**confezio'nare** vt manufacture; make ‹abiti›; package ‹merci›

**confezio'nato** a ‹vestiti› off-the-peg; ‹gelato› wrapped

**confezi'one** nf manufacture; (di abiti) making; (di pacchi) packaging; **di** ~ ‹abiti› off-the-peg; **confezioni** pl clothes. ~ **economica** economy pack, economy size. ~ **famiglia** family size. ~ **regalo** gift set. ~ **da sei** (di bottiglie, lattine) six-pack

**confic'care** vt thrust

**confic'carsi** vr lodge

**confic'cato** a ~ **in** lodged in, embedded in

**confi'dare** vt confide ● vi ~ **in** trust

**confi'darsi** vr ~ **con** confide in

**confi'dente** a confident ● nmf confidant; (informatore) informer

**confi'denza** nf confidence; (familiarità) familiarity; **prendersi delle confidenze** take liberties

**confidenzi'ale** a confidential; ‹tono› familiar; **in via** ~ confidentially

**configu'rare** vt Comput configure

**configurazi'one** nf configuration

**confi'nante** a neighbouring

**confi'nare** vt (relegare) confine ● vi ~ **con** border on

**confi'narsi** vr (ritirarsi) withdraw

**confi'nato** a confined ● nm prisoner

**con'fine** nm border; (tra terreni) boundary

**con'fino** nm political exile

**confi'sca** nf (di proprietà) confiscation

**confi'scare** vt confiscate

**conflagrazi'one** nf conflagration

**con'flitto** nm conflict

**conflittu'ale** a adversarial

**conflittualità** nf adversarial nature

**conflu'enza** nf confluence; (di strade) junction

**conflu'ire** vi ‹fiumi:› flow together; ‹strade:› meet

**con'fondere** vt confuse; (imbarazzare) embarrass

**con'fondersi** vr (mescolarsi) mingle; (sbagliarsi) be mistaken

**confor'mare** vt standardize (**a** in line with)

**confor'marsi** vr conform

**conformazi'one** nf conformity (**a** with); (del terreno) nature

**con'forme** a standard

**conforme'mente** adv accordingly

**confor'mismo** nm conformity

**confor'mista** nmf conformist

**conformità** nf (a norma) conformity (**a** with); **in** ~ **a** in accordance with, in conformity with

**confor'tante** a comforting

**confor'tare** vt comfort

**confor'tevole** a (comodo) comfortable

**con'forto** nm comfort; **a** ~ **di** ‹una tesi› in support of; **conforti** pl **religiosi** last rites

**confra'telli** nmpl brethren

**confra'ternita** nf brotherhood

**confron'tare** vt compare

**con'fronto** nm comparison; **in** ~ **a** by comparison with; **nei tuoi confronti** towards you; **senza** ~ far and away, by far. ~ **diretto** head to head

**confusio'nario** a ‹persona› muddle-headed

**confusi'one** nf confusion; (baccano) racket; (disordine) mess; (imbarazzo) embarrassment

**con'fuso** pp di **confondere** ● a confused; (indistinto) indistinct; (imbarazzato) embarrassed

**confu'tare** vt confute

**conge'dare** vt dismiss; Mil discharge

**conge'darsi** vr take one's leave

**con'gedo** nm leave; **essere in** ~ be on leave. ~ **malattia** sick leave. ~ **[di] maternità** maternity leave. ~ **[di] paternità** paternity leave

**conge'gnare** vt devise; (mettere insieme) assemble

**con'gegno** nm device

**congela'mento** nm freezing; Med frostbite

**conge'lare** vt freeze

**conge'lato** a ‹cibo› deep-frozen

**congela'tore** nm freezer

**congeni'ale** a congenial

**con'genito** a congenital

**congestio'nare** vt congest

**congestio'nato** a ‹traffico› congested; ‹viso› flushed

**congesti'one** nf congestion

**conget'tura** *nf* conjecture

**congi'ungere** *vt* join, connect; join ⟨*mani*⟩; combine ⟨*sforzi*⟩

**congi'ungersi** *vr* join, connect

**congiunti'vite** *nf* conjunctivitis

**congiun'tivo** *nm* subjunctive

**congi'unto** *pp di* **congiungere** ● *a* joined; ⟨*azione*⟩ joint; ⟨*forze, sforzo*⟩ combined ● *nm* relative

**congiun'tura** *nf* junction; ⟨*situazione*⟩ situation

**congiuntu'rale** *a* economic

**congiunzi'one** *nf Gram* conjunction

**congi'ura** *nf* conspiracy

**congiu'rare** *vi* conspire

**conglome'rato** *nm* conglomerate; *fig* conglomeration; ⟨*da costruzione*⟩ concrete

**'Congo** *nm* Congo

**congo'lese** *a & nmf* Congolese

**congratu'larsi** *vr* ~ **con qcno per** congratulate sb on

**congratulazi'oni** *nfpl* congratulations

**con'grega** *nf* band

**congre'gare** *vt* gather

**congre'garsi** *vr* congregate

**congregazi'one** *nf* congregation

**congres'sista** *nmf* convention participant

**con'gresso** *nm* congress, convention; ⟨*americano*⟩ Congress. **C~ Nazionale Africano** African National Congress

**'congrua** *nf* stipend

**'congruo** *a* proper; ⟨*giusto*⟩ fair

**conguagli'are** *vt* balance

**congu'aglio** *nm* balance

**coni'are** *vt* coin

**conia'tura** *nf* coinage

**coniazi'one** *nf* coinage

**'conico** *a* conical

**co'nifera** *nf* conifer

**co'niglia** *nf* female rabbit, doe

**conigli'era** *nf* rabbit hutch

**conigli'etta** *nf* bunny girl

**conigli'etto** *nm* bunny

**co'niglio** *nm* rabbit

**coniu'gale** *a* marital; ⟨*vita*⟩ married

**coniu'gare** *vt* conjugate

**coniu'garsi** *vr* get married; *Gram* conjugate

**coniu'gato** *a* ⟨*sposato*⟩ married

**coniugazi'one** *nf* conjugation

**'coniuge** *nmf* spouse

**connazio'nale** *nmf* compatriot

**connessi'one** *nf* connection

**con'nesso** *pp di* **connettere**

**con'nettere** *vt* connect ● *vi* think rationally

**con'nettersi** *vr* ⟨*Comput: a bacheca elettronica*⟩ log on (**a** to)

**connet'tore** *nm* connector

**conni'vente** *a* conniving

**conno'tare** *vt* connote

**conno'tato** *nm* distinguishing feature; **connotati** *pl* description; **rispondere ai connotati** fit the description; **cambiare i connotati a qcno** *hum* re-arrange sb's face

**con'nubio** *nm fig* union

**'cono** *nm* cone

**cono'scente** *nmf* acquaintance

**cono'scenza** *nf* knowledge; ⟨*persona*⟩ acquaintance; ⟨*sensi*⟩ consciousness; **perdere ~** lose consciousness; **riprendere ~** regain consciousness, come to. **~ di lavoro** business contact

**co'noscere** *vt* know; ⟨*essere a conoscenza di*⟩ be acquainted with; ⟨*fare la conoscenza di*⟩ meet; **~ qcsa a fondo** know sth inside out

**conosci'tore, -'trice** *nmf* connoisseur

**conosci'uto** *pp di* **conoscere** ● *a* well-known

**con'quista** *nf* conquest

**conqui'stare** *vt* conquer; *fig* win

**conquista'tore** *nm* conqueror; *fig* lady-killer

**consa'crare** *vt* consecrate; ordain ⟨*sacerdote*⟩; ⟨*dedicare*⟩ dedicate

**consa'crarsi** *vr* devote oneself

**consa'crato** *a* ⟨*suolo*⟩ hallowed

**consacrazi'one** *nf* consecration

**consangu'ineo, -a** *nmf* blood-relation

**consa'pevole** *a* conscious

**consapevo'lezza** *nf* consciousness

**consapevol'mente** *adv* consciously

**conscia'mente** *adv* consciously

**'conscio** *a* conscious

**consecu'tivo** *a* consecutive; ⟨*seguente*⟩ next

**con'segna** *nf* delivery; ⟨*merce*⟩ consignment; ⟨*custodia*⟩ care; ⟨*di prigioniero*⟩ handover; ⟨*Mil: ordine*⟩ orders *pl*; ⟨*Mil: punizione*⟩ confinement to barracks; **pagamento alla ~** cash on delivery. **~ della posta** mail delivery

**conse'gnare** *vt* deliver; *Mil* confine to barracks; hand over ⟨*prigioniero, chiavi*⟩

**consegna'tario** *nm* consignee

**consegu'ente** *a* consequent

**consegu'enza** *nf* consequence; **di ~** ⟨*perciò*⟩ consequently; ⟨*agire, comportarsi*⟩ accordingly

**consegui'mento** *nm* achievement

**consegu'ire** *vt* achieve ● *vi* follow

**con'senso** *nm* consent; ⟨*della popolazione*⟩ consensus

**consensu'ale** *a* consensus-based

**consen'tire** *vi* consent ● *vt* allow

**consenzi'ente** *a* consenting

**con'serto** *a* **a braccia conserte** with one's arms folded

**con'serva** *nf* preserve; ⟨*di frutta*⟩ jam; ⟨*di agrumi*⟩ marmalade. **~ di pomodoro** tomato sauce

**conser'vare** *vt* preserve; ⟨*mantenere*⟩ keep; **~ in frigo** keep refrigerated; **~ in luogo asciutto** keep dry

**conser'varsi** *vr* keep; **~ in salute** keep well

**conserva'tore, -'trice** *a & nmf Pol* conservative; **partito ~** Conservative Party, Tory Party *Br*

**conserva'torio** *nm* conservatory, school of music

**conservato'rismo** *nm* conservatism
**conservazi'one** *nf* preservation: **a lunga ~** long-life
**con'sesso** *nm* assembly
**conside'rare** *vt* consider; (*stimare*) regard
**conside'rato** *a* (*stimato*) esteemed
**considerazi'one** *nf* consideration; (*osservazione, riflessione*) remark; (*stima*) respect
**conside'revole** *a* considerable
**consigli'abile** *a* advisable
**consigli'are** *vt* advise; (*raccomandare*) recommend
**consigli'arsi** *vr* **~ con qcno** ask sb's advice
**consigli'ere, -a** *nmf* adviser; (*membro di un consiglio*) councillor. **~ d'amministrazione** board member. **~ delegato** managing director
**con'siglio** *nm* advice; (*ente*) council; **un ~** a piece of advice. **~ d'amministrazione** board of directors. **~ di guerra** war cabinet. **~ d'istituto** parent-teacher association. **~ dei ministri** Cabinet. **~ scolastico** education committee. **C~ di Sicurezza** (*dell'ONU*) Security Council. **C~ Superiore della Magistratura** *body responsible for ensuring the independence of the judiciary*
**con'simile** *a* similar
**consi'stente** *a* substantial; (*spesso*) thick; (*fig: argomento*) solid
**consi'stenza** *nf* consistency; (*spessore*) thickness; (*fig: di argomento*) solidity
**con'sistere** *vi* **~ in** consist of
**consoci'arsi** *vr* go into partnership
**consoci'ata** *nf* (*azienda*) subsidiary
**consociati'vismo** *nm* excessive tendency to form associations
**consoci'ato** *nm* associate
**con'socio, -a** *nmf* fellow-member
**conso'lante** *a* consoling
**conso'lare**[1] *a* consular
**conso'lare**[2] *vt* console
**conso'larsi** *vr* console oneself
**conso'lato** *nm* consulate
**consolazi'one** *nf* consolation
**'console** *nm* consul
**con'sole** *nf inv* (*tastiera*) console
**consolida'mento** *nm* consolidation
**consoli'dare** *vt* consolidate
**consoli'darsi** *vr* consolidate
**consommé** *nm inv* consommé
**conso'nante** *nf* consonant
**conso'nanza** *nf* consonance
**'consono** *a* appropriate (**a** to), suitable (**a** for)
**con'sorte** *nmf* consort
**con'sorzio** *nm* consortium
**con'stare** *vi* **~ di** consist of; (*risultare*) appear; **a quanto mi consta** as far as I know; **mi consta che...** seemingly,....
**consta'tare** *vt* ascertain
**constatazi'one** *nf* statement of fact
**consu'eto** *a* usual ● *nm* **più del ~** more than usual

**consuetudi'nario** *a* (*diritto*) commo (*persona*) set in one's ways
**consue'tudine** *nf* habit; (*usanza*) custom
**consu'lente** *nmf* consultant. **~ aziendal** management consultant; (*azienda*) manag ment consultancy. **~ matrimoniale** ma riage guidance counsellor
**consu'lenza** *nf* consultancy
**consul'tare** *vt* consult
**consul'tarsi** *vr* **~ con** consult with
**consultazi'one** *nf* consultation
**consul'tivo** *a* consultative
**con'sulto** *nm* consultation
**consul'torio** *nm* free clinic providing trea ment for sexual problems and advice
**consu'mare** *vt* (*usare*) consume; wear o (*abito, scarpe*); consummate (*matrimonio* commit (*delitto*)
**consu'marsi** *vr* consume; (*abito, scarpe* wear out; (*struggersi*) pine; **'da preferibilmente entro il...'** 'best before...'
**consu'mato** *a* (*politico*) consummat (*scarpe, tappeto*) worn [out]
**consuma'tore, -'trice** *nmf* consumer
**consumazi'one** *nf* consumption; (*bibit* drink; (*spuntino*) snack; (*di matrimonio*) co summation; (*di delitto*) commission
**consu'mismo** *nm* consumerism
**consu'mista** *nmf* consumerist
**con'sumo** *nm* consumption; (*uso*) us **generi di ~** consumer goods. **~ [di carb rante]** [fuel] consumption
**consun'tivo** *nm* **bilancio ~** balance shee **fare il ~ di** *fig* take stock of
**con'sunto** *a* well-worn
**conta'balle** *nmf fam* storyteller
**con'tabile** *a* book-keeping ● *nmf* accoun ant
**contabilità** *nf inv* accounting; (*ufficio*) a counts department; **tenere la ~** keep the a counts. **~ di gestione** management a counts. **~ in partita doppia** double entr book-keeping
**contachi'lometri** *nm inv* mileomete odometer *Am*
**conta'dino, -a** *nmf* farm-worker, agricu tural labourer; (*proprietario*) farme (*medievale*) peasant
**contagi'are** *vt* infect; **la sua allegri contagia tutti** his cheerfulness is very cor tagious
**contagi'ato** *a* infected
**con'tagio** *nm* contagion
**contagi'oso** *a* contagious
**conta'giri** *nm inv* rev counter
**conta'gocce** *nm inv* dropper; **dare qcs col ~** *fig* dole sth out in dribs and drabs
**contami'nare** *vt* contaminate
**contaminazi'one** *nf* contamination
**contami'nuti** *nm inv* timer
**con'tante** *nm* cash; **pagare in contant** pay cash
**con'tare** *vt* count; (*tenere conto di*) take int

account; **devi ~ un'ora per il viaggio** you have to allow an hour for the journey ● *vi* count; **~ di fare qcsa** plan to do sth

**conta'scatti** *nm inv Teleph* time-unit counter

**con'tato** *a* ⟨*giorni, ore*⟩ numbered

**conta'tore** *nm* meter. **~ del gas** gas meter

**contat'tare** *vt* contact

**con'tatto** *nm* contact; **essere in ~ con** be in touch *or* contact with; **mettersi in ~ con** contact, get in touch with

**'conte** *nm* count, earl *Br*

**con'tea** *nf* county

**conteggi'are** *vt* include ● *vi* calculate

**con'teggio** *nm* calculation. **~ alla rovescia** countdown

**con'tegno** *nm* behaviour; (*atteggiamento*) attitude; **darsi un ~** pull oneself together

**conte'gnoso** *a* dignified

**contem'plare** *vt* contemplate; (*fissare*) gaze at

**contempla'tivo** *a* contemplative

**contemplazi'one** *nf* contemplation

**con'tempo** *nm* **nel ~** in the meantime

**contemporanea'mente** *adv* at the same time

**contempo'raneo, -a** *a* & *nmf* contemporary

**conten'dente** *nmf* competitor

**con'tendere** *vi* compete; (*litigare*) quarrel ● *vt* dispute

**con'tendersi** *vr* **~ qcsa** compete for sth

**conte'nere** *vt* contain; (*reprimere*) repress

**conte'nersi** *vr* contain oneself

**conteni'tore** *nm* container

**conten'tabile** *a* **facilmente ~** easy to please

**conten'tare** *vt* please

**conten'tarsi** *vr* **~ di** be content with

**conten'tezza** *nf* happiness

**conten'tino** *nm* placebo

**con'tento** *a* glad; (*soddisfatto*) happy

**conte'nuto** *nm* contents *pl*; (*di libro, testo*) content

**contenzi'oso** *a* contentious ● *nm* dispute; (*ufficio*) legal department

**con'tesa** *nf* disagreement; *Sport* contest

**con'teso** *pp di* **contendere** ● *a* contested

**con'tessa** *nf* countess

**conte'stare** *vt* contest; *Jur* give notification of ⟨*contravvenzione*⟩; **~ un reato a qcno** charge sb with an offence

**contesta|'tore, -'trice** *nmf* person who is anti-authority ● *a* anti-authority

**contestazi'one** *nf* (*disputa*) dispute; (*protesta*) protest; (*di contravvenzione*) notification

**con'testo** *nm* context

**con'tiguo** *a* adjacent

**continen'tale** *a* continental

**conti'nente** *nm* continent

**conti'nenza** *nf* continence

**contin'gente** *nm* contingent; (*quota*) quota

**contin'genza** *nf* contingency

**continua'mente** *adv* (*senza interruzione*) continuously; (*frequentemente*) continually

**continu'are** *vt/i* continue; (*riprendere*) resume; **~ gli studi** stay on at school

**continuazi'one** *nf* continuation

**continu'ità** *nf* continuity

**con'tinuo** *a* continuous; (*molto frequente*) continual; **di ~** continuously; (*frequentemente*) continually; **corrente continua** direct current

**con'tinuum** *nm inv* continuum

**'conto** *nm* calculation; (*in banca, negozio*) account; (*di ristorante ecc*) bill; (*stima*) consideration; **a conti fatti** all things considered; **ad ogni buon ~** in any case; **di poco/nessun ~** of little/no importance; **in fin dei conti** when all's said and done; **per ~ di** on behalf of; **per ~ mio** (*a mio parere*) in my opinion; (*da solo*) on my own; **per ~ terzi** for a third party; **sul ~ di qcno** ⟨*voci, informazioni*⟩ about sb; **far ~ di** (*supporre*) suppose; (*proporsi*) intend; **far ~ su** rely on; **fare i propri conti** do one's accounts; **fare i conti con qcno** *fig* sort sb out; **fare i conti in tasca a qcno** estimate how much sb is worth; **fare i conti senza l'oste** forget the most important thing; **render ~ a qcno di qcsa** be accountable to sb for sth; **rendersi ~ di qcsa** realize sth; **starsene per ~ proprio** be on one's own; **tener ~ di qcsa** take sth into account; **tenere da ~ qcsa** look after sth. **~ in banca** bank account. **~ congiunto** joint account. **~ corrente** current account, checking account *Am.* **~ [corrente] comune** joint account. **~ corrente postale** Giro account. **~ profitti e perdite** profit and loss account. **~ alla rovescia** countdown. **~ spese** expense account

**con'torcere** *vt* twist

**con'torcersi** *vr* twist about

**contor'nare** *vt* surround

**con'torno** *nm* contour; *Culin* vegetables *pl*

**contorsi'one** *nf* contortion

**contorsio'nista** *nmf* contortionist

**con'torto** *pp di* **contorcere** ● *a* twisted

**contrabban'dare** *vt* smuggle

**contrabbandi'ere, -a** *nmf* smuggler

**contrab'bando** *nm* contraband

**contrabbas'sista** *nmf* double bass player

**contrab'basso** *nm* double bass

**contraccambi'are** *vt* return

**contrac'cambio** *nm* return

**contraccet'tivo** *nm* contraceptive

**contraccezi'one** *nf* contraception

**contrac'colpo** *nm* rebound; (*di arma da fuoco*) recoil; *fig* repercussion

**con'trada** *nf* (*rione*) district

**contrad'detto** *pp di* **contraddire**

**contrad'dire** *vt* contradict

**contraddi'stinguere** *vt* differentiate, distinguish

**contraddi'stinto** *pp di* **distinguere** ● *a* ~ **da** distinguished by

**contraddit'torio** *a* contradictory

**contraddizi'one** *nf* contradiction

**contra'ente** *nmf* contracting party

**contra'ereo** *a* anti-aircraft

**contraf'fare** *vt* disguise

**contraf'fatto** *pp di* **contraffare** ● *a* disguised

**contraffazi'one** *nf* disguising

**contraf'forte** *nm* buttress

**con'tralto** *nm* countertenor ● *nf* contralto

**contrap'peso** *nm* counterbalance

**contrap'porre** *vt* (*confrontare*) compare; ~ **A a B** counter B with A

**contrap'porsi** *vr* be in opposition; ~ **a** contrast with; (*opporsi a*) be opposed to

**contrap'punto** *nm Mus* counterpoint

**contraria'mente** *adv* ~ **a** contrary to; ~ **a me** unlike me

**contrari'are** *vt* oppose; (*infastidire*) annoy

**contrari'arsi** *vr* get annoyed

**contrarietà** *nf* adversity; (*ostacolo*) setback

**con'trario** *a* contrary, opposite; (*direzione*) opposite; (*esito, vento*) unfavourable ● *nm* contrary, opposite; **al** ~ on the contrary

**con'trarre** *vt* contract

**contrasse'gnare** *vt* mark

**contras'segno** *nm* mark; **[in]** ~ (*spedizione*) cash on delivery, COD. ~ **IVA** VAT receipt

**contra'stante** *a* contrasting

**contra'stare** *vt* oppose; (*contestare*) contest ● *vi* contrast; (*colori:*) clash

**con'trasto** *nm* contrast; (*di colori*) clash; (*litigio*) dispute

**contrattac'care** *vt* counter-attack

**contrat'tacco** *nm* counter-attack

**contrat'tare** *vt/i* negotiate; (*mercanteggiare*) bargain

**contrattazi'one** *nf* contravention; (*multa*) fine; (*salariale*) bargaining. ~ **di azioni** share dealing

**contrat'tempo** *nm* hitch

**con'tratto** *pp di* **contrarre** ● *nm* contract. ~ **di lavoro** employment contract. ~ **a termine** fixed-term contract. **contratti** *pl* **a termine** *Fin* futures

**contrattu'ale** *a* contractual

**contravve'nire** *vi* contravene a law

**contrazi'one** *nf* contraction; (*di prezzi*) reduction

**contribu'ente** *nmf* contributor; (*del fisco*) taxpayer

**contribu'ire** *vi* contribute

**contribu'tivo** *a* contributory

**contri'buto** *nm* contribution. **contributi** *pl* **pensionistici** pension contributions

**con'trito** *a* contrite

**'contro** *prep* against; ~ **di me** against me ● *nm* **il pro e il** ~ the pros and cons *pl*

**contro'battere** *vt* counter

**controbilanci'are** *vt* counterbalance

**controcor'rente** *a* (*idee, persona*) non-conformist ● *adv* upriver; *fig* upstream; **andar** ~ *fig* swim against the tide

**controcul'tura** *nf* counterculture

**contro'curva** *nf* second bend

**contro'esodo** *nm* massive return from holiday

**controfa'gotto** *nm* double bassoon

**controffen'siva** *nf* counter-offensive

**controfi'gura** *nf* stand-in

**controfi'letto** *nm* sirloin

**controfir'mare** *vt* countersign

**controindicazi'one** *nf Med* contra indication

**controinterroga'torio** *nm* cross examination

**control'labile** *a* (*emozione*) controllable, *Tech* which can be monitored

**control'lare** *vt* control; (*verificare*) check

**control'larsi** *vr* control oneself

**control'lato** *a* controlled

**con'troller** *nm inv Fin* controller

**con'trollo** *nm* control; (*verifica*) check; *Med* check-up; **perdere il** ~ **di** lose control of. ~ **degli armamenti** arms control. ~ **automatico della velocità** automatic speed check. ~ **bagagli** baggage control. ~ **biglietti** ticket inspection. ~ **dei cambi** exchange control. ~ **del credito** credit control. ~ **medico** check-up. ~ **delle nascite** birth control. ~ **passaporti** passport control. ~ **[di] qualità** quality control. ~ **radar della velocità** radar speed check

**control'lore** *nm* controller; (*sui treni ecc*) [ticket] inspector. ~ **di volo** air-traffic controller

**contro'luce** *nf* **in** ~ against the light

**contro'mano** *adv* in the wrong direction

**contromi'sura** *nf* countermeasure

**contropar'tita** *nf* compensation; **in** ~ in return

**contropi'ede** *nm Sport* breakaway; **prendere in** ~ *fig* catch off guard

**controprodu'cente** *a* counter-productive

**contro'prova** *nf* cross-check; **fare la** ~ **di qcsa** cross-check sth

**con'trordine** *nm* counter order; **salvo contrordini** unless I/you hear to the contrary

**contro'senso** *nm* contradiction in terms

**controspio'naggio** *nm* counterespionage

**controten'denza** *nf* countertrend

**controva'lore** *nm* equivalent

**contro'vento** *adv* against the wind

**contro'versia** *nf* controversy; *Jur* dispute

**contro'verso** *a* controversial

**contro'voglia** *adv* unwillingly

**contu'mace** *a Jur* in default, absent

**contu'macia** *nf* default; **in** ~ in one's absence

**contun'dente** *a* (*corpo, arma*) blunt

**contur'bante** *a* perturbing

**contur'bare** *vt* perturb

**contusi'one** *nf* bruise

**con'tuso** *nm* person suffering from cuts and bruises

**convale'scente** a & nmf convalescent

**convale'scenza** nf convalescence; **essere in ~** be convalescing

**con'valida** nf ratification; (di nomina) confirmation; (di biglietto) validation

**convali'dare** vt ratify; confirm (nomina); validate (atto, biglietto)

**con'vegno** nm meeting; (congresso) convention, congress

**conve'nevole** a suitable

**conve'nevoli** nmpl pleasantries

**conveni'ente** a convenient; (vantaggioso) advantageous; (prezzo) attractive

**conveni'enza** nf convenience; (interesse) advantage; (di prezzo) attractiveness

**conve'nire** vi agree; (riunirsi) gather; (essere opportuno) be convenient; **ci conviene andare** it's better to go; **non mi conviene stancarmi** I'd better not tire myself out ● vt agree [on]

**conven'ticola** nf clique

**con'vento** nm (di suore) convent; (di frati) monastery

**conve'nuto** a agreed

**convenzio'nale** a conventional

**convenzio'nato** a (prezzo) controlled

**convenzi'one** nf convention

**conver'gente** a converging

**conver'genza** nf convergence

**con'vergere** vi converge

**con'versa** nf lay sister

**conver'sare** vi converse

**conversa|'tore, -'trice** nmf conversationalist

**conversazi'one** nf conversation

**conversi'one** nf conversion

**con'verso** pp di **convergere**

**conver'tibile** nf Auto convertible

**conver'tire** vt convert

**conver'tirsi** vr convert

**conver'tito, -a** a converted ● nmf convert

**converti'tore** nm converter

**con'vesso** a convex

**convezi'one** nf convection

**convin'cente** a convincing

**con'vincere** vt convince

**con'vinto** a convinced

**convinzi'one** nf conviction

**convi'tato** nm guest

**con'vitto** nm boarding school

**convi'vente** nm common-law husband ● nf common-law wife

**convi'venza** nf cohabitation

**con'vivere** vi live together

**convivi'ale** a convivial

**convo'care** vt summon; Jur summons; convene (riunione)

**convocazi'one** nf summoning; Jur summonsing; (atto) summons; (riunione) meeting

**convogli'are** vt convey; (navi:) convoy

**con'voglio** nm convoy; (ferroviario) train

**convo'lare** vi ~ **a giuste nozze** hum tie the knot

**convulsa'mente** adv convulsively

**convulsi'one** nf convulsion; fig fit

**convul'sivo** a Med convulsive; (riso) hysterical

**coope'rare** vi co-operate

**coopera'tiva** nf co-operative

**cooperazi'one** nf co-operation

**coordina'mento** nm co-ordination

**coordi'nare** vt co-ordinate

**coordi'nata** nf Math co-ordinate; **coordinate** pl (su mappa) grid reference. **coordinate** pl **bancarie** [bank] sort code

**coordi'nato** a co-ordinated

**coordina|'tore, -'trice** nmf co-ordinator

**coordinazi'one** nf co-ordination

**co'perchio** nm lid; (copertura) cover

**co'perta** nf blanket; (copertura) cover; Naut deck. **~ elettrica** electric blanket

**coper'tina** nf cover; (di libro) dust-jacket

**co'perto** pp di **coprire** ● a covered; (vestito) wrapped up; (cielo) overcast; (piscina) indoor ● nm (a tavola) place; (prezzo del coperto) cover charge; **al ~** under cover

**coper'tone** nm tarpaulin; (gomma) tyre

**coper'tura** nf cover; (azione) covering; (di strada) surfacing; (di malefatta) cover-up. **~ globale** blanket coverage

**'copia** nf copy; **bella/brutta ~** fair/rough copy; **essere la ~ spiccicata di qcno** be the spitting image of sb. **~ su carta** hardcopy. **~ pirata** pirate copy. **~ di riserva** Comput backup copy

**copi'are** vt copy

**copia'trice** nf copier

**copi'lota** nmf co-pilot; (di auto) co-driver

**copi'one** nm Cinema, TV script

**copi'oso** a copious

**'coppa** nf (calice) goblet; (bicchiere) glass; (per gelato ecc) dish; Sport cup. **~ [di] gelato** ice-cream (served in a dish). **~ del mondo** World Cup

**cop'petta** nf (di ceramica, vetro) bowl; (di gelato) small tub

**'coppia** nf couple; (in carte, voga) pair

**co'prente** a (cipria, vernice) thick; (collant) opaque

**copri'capo** nm head covering

**coprifu'oco** nm curfew

**copri'letto** nm bedspread

**copri'mozzo** nm hub-cap

**copripiu'mino** nm duvet cover

**co'prire** vt cover; drown [out] (suono); hold (carica)

**co'prirsi** vr (vestirsi) cover oneself up; (vestirsi pesante) dress warmly; fig cover up; (proteggersi) cover oneself; (cielo:) become overcast

**copritei'era** nm tea cosy

**co-protago'nista** nmf Cinema co-star

**'coque: alla ~** a (uovo) soft-boiled

**co'raggio** nm bravery, courage; (sfacciataggine) nerve; **~!** chin up!

**coraggiosa'mente** adv bravely, courageously

**coraggi'oso** a brave, courageous

**co'rale** a choral

co'rallo *nm* coral

co'rano *nm* Koran

co'razza *nf* armour; (*di animali*) shell

coraz'zata *nf* battleship

coraz'zato *a* ‹nave› armour-plated

corazza'tura *nf* armour plate, armour plating

corazzi'ere *nm* cuirassier

corbelle'ria *nf* piece of nonsense; **dire corbellerie** talk nonsense

'corda *nf* cord; (*spago, Mus*) string; (*fune*) rope; (*cavo*) cable; **essere giù di ~** be down; **dare ~ a qcno** encourage sb; **tagliare la ~** cut and run; **tenere qcno sulla ~** keep sb on tenterhooks. **corde** *pl* **vocali** vocal cords

cor'data *nf* roped party

cordi'ale *a* cordial ● *nm* (*bevanda*) cordial; **cordiali saluti** best wishes

cordialità *nf* cordiality; **~** *pl* (*saluti*) best wishes

cor'doglio *nm* grief; (*lutto*) mourning

cor'done *nm* cord; (*schieramento*) cordon. **~ ombelicale** umbilical cord. **~ sanitario** cordon sanitaire

Co'rea *nf* Korea

core'ano, -a *a* & *nmf* Korean

coreogra'fia *nf* choreography; **fare la ~ di** choreograph

core'ografo, -a *nmf* choreographer

Corfù *nf* Corfu

cori'aceo *a* tough

cori'andoli *nmpl* (*di carta*) confetti *sg*

cori'andolo *nm* (*spezia*) coriander

cori'care *vt* put to bed

cori'carsi *vr* go to bed

Co'rinto *nf* Corinth

co'rista *nmf* choir member

'corna *vedi* corno

cor'nacchia *nf* crow

corna'musa *nf* bagpipes *pl*

'cornea *nf* cornea

'corner *nm inv* corner; **salvarsi in ~** *fig* have a lucky escape

cor'netta *nf* *Mus* cornet; (*del telefono*) receiver

cor'netto *nm* (*brioche*) croissant. **~ acustico** ear trumpet

cor'nice *nf* frame

cornici'one *nm* cornice

cornifi'care *vt fam* cheat on

'corno *nm* (*pl f* **corna**) horn; **fare le corna a qcno** *fam* cheat on sb; **fare le corna** (*per scongiuro*) ≈ touch wood; **un ~!** you must be joking!; (*per niente*) nonsense!. **~ da caccia** French horn

Corno'vaglia *nf* Cornwall

cornu'copia *nf* cornucopia

cor'nuto *a* horned ● *nm* (*fam: marito tradito*) cuckold; (*insulto*) bastard

'coro *nm* chorus; *Relig* choir

co'rolla *nf* corolla

corol'lario *nm* corollary

co'rona *nf* crown; (*di fiori*) wreath; (*rosario* rosary

corona'mento *nm* (*di sogno*) fulfilment; (*d carriera*) crowning achievement

coro'nare *vt* fulfil ‹sogno›

coro'nario *a* ‹arteria› coronary

cor'petto *nm* bodice

'corpo *nm* body; (*Mil, diplomatico*) corps *in* [a] **~ a ~** *Mil* hand to hand; **lottare** [a] **~ ~** have a punch-up, slug it out; **dare ~ qcsa** give substance to sth; **buttarsi a ~ morto in qcsa** throw oneself desperatel into sth; **andare di ~** move one's bowels. **di ballo** corps de ballet. **~ insegnante** teaching staff. **~ del reato** incriminatin piece of evidence

corpo'rale *a* corporal

corporati'vismo *nm* corporatism

corpora'tura *nf* build

corporazi'one *nf* corporation

cor'poreo *a* bodily

cor'poso *a* full-bodied

'corpus *nm inv* corpus

cor'puscolo *nm* corpuscle

corre'dare *vt* (*di note*) supply (**di** with) **corredato di curriculum** accompanied by CV

corre'dino *nm* (*per neonato*) layette

cor'redo *nm* (*nuziale*) trousseau; (*d informazioni ecc*) set

cor'reggere *vt* correct; lace ‹bevanda›

corre'lare *vt* correlate

cor'rente *a* running; (*in vigore*) current (*frequente*) everyday; ‹inglese ecc› fluent ● *n* current; (*d'aria*) draught; **essere al ~ d qcsa** be aware of sth; **tenersi al ~** keep up t date (**di** with). **~ continua** direct current. **~ trasversale** cross current

corrente'mente *adv* ‹parlare› fluently (*comunemente*) commonly

'correre *vi* run; (*affrettarsi*) hurry; *Spor* race; ‹notizie:› circulate; **lascia ~!** let it go! **~ dietro a** run after; **tra loro non corre buon sangue** there is bad blood between them ● *vt* run; **~ un pericolo** run a risk **corre voce che...** there's a rumour that...

correspon'sabile *nmf* person jointly re sponsible

corresponsi'one *nf* payment

corretta'mente *adv* correctly; ‹sedersi mangiare› properly; ‹trattare, fare qcsa› righ

corret'tivo *nm* corrective

cor'retto *pp di* **correggere** ● *a* correct ‹caffè› with a drop of alcohol

corret'tore, -'trice *nmf* **~ di bozze** proof-reader ● *nm* **~ grammaticale** *Compu* grammar checker. **~ ortografico** *Compu* spellcheck[er]

correzi'one *nf* correction. **~ di bozze** proof-reading. **~ errori** *Comput* error correc tion

cor'rida *nf* bullfight

corri'doio *nm* corridor; *Aeron* aisle

**corri'dore, -'trice** *nmf* (*automobilistico*) driver; (*ciclista*) cyclist: (*a piedi*) runner

**corri'era** *nf* coach, bus

**corri'ere** *nm* courier: (*posta*) mail: (*spedizioniere*) carrier

**corri'mano** *nm* banister

**corrispet'tivo** *nm* amount due

**corrispon'dente** *a* corresponding ● *nmf* correspondent

**corrispon'denza** *nf* correspondence; **tenersi in ~ con** correspond with; **per ~** ‹*fare un corso*› by correspondence; **corso per ~** correspondence course; **vendite per ~** mail-order [shopping]

**corri'spondere** *vi* correspond; ‹*stanza:*› communicate; **~ a** (*contraccambiare*) return

**corri'sposto** *a* ‹*amore*› reciprocated

**corrobo'rare** *vt* strengthen; *fig* corroborate

**cor'rodere** *vt* corrode

**cor'rodersi** *vr* corrode

**cor'rompere** *vt* corrupt; (*con denaro*) bribe

**corrosi'one** *nf* corrosion

**corro'sivo** *a* corrosive

**cor'roso** *pp di* **corrodere**

**cor'rotto** *pp di* **corrompere** ● *a* corrupt

**corrucci'arsi** *vr* be vexed

**corrucci'ato** *a* vexed

**corru'gare** *vt* wrinkle; **~ la fronte** knit one's brows

**corrut'tela** *nf* depravity

**corruzi'one** *nf* corruption; (*con denaro*) bribery

**'corsa** *nf* running; (*rapida*) dash; *Sport* race: (*di treno ecc*) journey; **di ~** at a run; **di gran ~** in a great hurry; **fare una ~** ‹*sbrigarsi*› run, hurry. **~ agli armamenti** arms race. **~ ciclistica** cycle race. **~ a ostacoli** obstacle race. **~ piana** flat racing. **~ semplice** one way [ticket]

**cor'sia** *nf* gangway; (*di ospedale*) ward; *Auto* lane; (*di supermercato*) aisle. **~ autobus** bus lane. **~ d'emergenza** *Auto* hard shoulder. **~ di sorpasso** fast lane, outside lane

**'Corsica** *nf* Corsica

**cor'sivo** *nm* italics *pl*; **in ~** in italics

**'corso** *pp di* **correre** ● *nm* course; (*strada*) main street; *Comm* circulation; (*in borsa*) price, quotation; **essere in ~** be underway; **lavori in ~** work in progress; **nel ~ di** during; **avere ~ legale** be legal tender. **~ d'acqua** waterway. **~ per corrispondenza** correspondence course; **~ di formazione professionale** training course. **~ del giorno** current daily price. **~ di laurea** degree course. **~ serale** evening class

**'corso, -a** *a & nmf* (*della Corsica*) Corsican

**'corte** *nf* [court]yard; (*Jur, regale*) court; **fare la ~ a qcno** court sb. **~ d'appello** court of appeal. **~ d'assise** ≈ crown court. **C~ di cassazione** supreme court of appeal. **C~ dei conti** ≈ National Audit Office. **C~ europea per i diritti dell'uomo** European Court of Human Rights. **C~ europea di giustizia** European Court of Justice. **~ di giustizia** court of law

**cor'teccia** *nf* bark

**corteggia'mento** *nm* courtship

**corteggi'are** *vt* court

**corteggia'tore** *nm* admirer

**cor'teo** *nm* procession. **~ di auto** motorcade. **~ funebre** funeral cortège. **~ nuziale** bridal party

**cor'tese** *a* courteous

**corte'sia** *nf* courtesy; **per ~** please

**cortigi'ano, -a** *nmf* courtier ● *nf* courtesan

**cor'tile** *nm* courtyard

**cor'tina** *nf* curtain; (*schermo*) screen

**'corto** *a* short; **per farla corta** to cut a long story short; **a ~ di** short of, hard up for. **~ circuito** *nm* short [circuit]

**corto'metraggio** *nm* *Cinema* short

**cor'vino** *a* jet-black

**'corvo** *nm* raven

**'cosa** *nf* thing; (*faccenda*) matter; *inter, rel* what; [**che**] **~** what; **nessuna ~** nothing; **ogni ~** everything; **per prima ~** first of all; **tante cose** [so] many things; (*augurio*) all the best; **~?** what?; **~ hai detto?** what did you say?; **le cose le vanno bene** she's doing all right

**'cosca** *nf* clan

**'coscia** *nf* thigh; *Culin* leg; **cosce** *pl* **di rana** frogs' legs

**cosci'ente** *a* conscious

**cosci'enza** *nf* conscience; (*consapevolezza*) consciousness; **mettersi la ~ a posto** salve one's conscience

**coscienziosa'mente** *adv* conscientiously

**coscienzi'oso** *a* conscientious

**cosci'otto** *nm* leg

**co'scritto** *nm* conscript

**coscrizi'one** *nf* conscription

**co'sì** *adv* so; (*in questo modo*) like this, like that; (*perciò*) therefore; **le cose stanno ~** that's how things stand; **fermo ~!** hold it; **proprio ~!** exactly!; **basta ~!** that will do!; **ah, è ~?** it's like that, is it?; **~ ~** so-so; **e ~ via** and so on; **per ~ dire** so to speak; **più di ~** any more; **una ~ cara ragazza!** such a nice girl!; **è stato ~ generoso da aiutarti** he was kind enough to help you ● *conj* (*allora*) so ● *a inv* (*tale*) like that, such; **una ragazza ~** a girl like that, such a girl

**cosicché** *conj* and so

**cosid'detto** *a* so-called

**co'smesi** *nf* beauty treatment

**co'smetico** *a* cosmetic ● *nm* **cosmetici** *pl* cosmetics; (*trucchi*) make-up

**'cosmico** *a* cosmic

**'cosmo** *nm* cosmos

**cosmo'nauta** *nmf* cosmonaut

**cosmopo'lita** *a* cosmopolitan

**co'spargere** *vt* sprinkle; (*disseminare*) scatter; **~ il pavimento di cera** spread wax on the floor

**co'spetto** *nm* **al ~ di** in the presence of

**co'spicuo** *a* conspicuous; ‹*somma ecc*› considerable

**cospi'rare** *vi* conspire, plot

**cospira|'tore, -'trice** *nmf* conspirator, plotter

**cospirazi'one** *nf* conspiracy, plot

**'costa** *nf* coast, coastline; **sotto ~ inshore**. **C~ d'Avorio** Ivory Coast. **C~ Azzurra** Côte d'Azur. **C~ Smeralda** Emerald coast (*in Sardinia*)

**costà** *adv* there

**co'stante** *a & nf* constant

**co'stanza** *nf* constancy

**co'stare** *vi* cost; **quanto costa?** how much is it?; **costi quel che costi** whatever the cost

**co'stata** *nf* chop. **~ [di manzo]** rib steak

**co'stato** *nm* ribs *pl*

**costeggi'are** *vt* (*per mare*) coast; (*per terra*) skirt

**co'stei** *pers pron* (*soggetto*) she; (*complemento*) her

**costellazi'one** *nf* constellation

**coster'nato** *a* dismayed

**costernazi'one** *nf* consternation

**costi'era** *nf* stretch of coast

**costi'ero** *a* coastal

**co'stine** *nfpl* (*di maiale*) spare ribs

**'costing** *nm inv* costing

**costi'pato** *a* constipated; **essere ~** (*raffreddato*) have a bad cold

**costipazi'one** *nf* constipation; (*raffreddore*) bad cold

**costitu'ire** *vt* constitute; (*essere*) be; (*formare*) form; (*nominare*) appoint

**costitu'irsi** *vr* (*criminale*) give oneself up

**costituzio'nale** *a* constitutional

**costituzional'mente** *adv* Pol constitutionally

**costituzi'one** *nf* constitution; (*formazione*) formation

**'costo** *nm* cost; **a nessun ~** on no account; **a ~ di perdere la salute** at the cost of one's health; **sotto ~** at less than cost price. **~ del denaro** Fin cost of money. **costi** *pl* **di gestione** administration costs. **costi** *pl* **di spedizione** freight charges. **~ unitario** unit cost. **~ della vita** cost of living

**'costola** *nf* rib; (*di libro*) spine; **stare alle costole di qcno** follow sb around

**costo'letta** *nf* cutlet

**co'storo** *pron* (*soggetto*) they; (*complemento*) them

**co'stoso** *a* costly

**co'stretto** *pp di* **costringere**

**co'stringere** *vt* force, compel

**costrit'tivo** *a* coercive

**costrizi'one** *nf* compulsion

**costru'ire** *vt* build, construct

**costrut'tivo** *a* constructive

**costruzi'one** *nf* building, construction; (*edificio*) building

**co'stui** *pers pron* (*soggetto*) he; (*complemento*) him

**co'stume** *nm* (*usanza*) custom; (*indumento*) costume; **buon ~** vice squad; **costumi** *pl* (*morale*) morals. **~ da bagno** swim-suit; (*da uomo*) swimming trunks. **~ tradizionale** traditional costume

**costu'mista** *nmf* wardrobe assistant

**cote'chino** *nm* spiced pork sausage

**co'tenna** *nf* pigskin; (*della pancetta*) rind. **~ arrostita** crackling

**co'togna** *nf* quince

**coto'letta** *nf* cutlet. **~ alla milanese** veal cutlet in breadcrumbs

**coto'nato** *a* (*capelli*) back-combed

**co'tone** *nm* cotton. **~ idrofilo** cotton wool, absorbent cotton *Am*

**coto'nificio** *nm* cotton mill

**'cotta** *nf* Relig surplice; (*fam: innamoramento*) crush; **prendere una ~ per qcno** fam have a crush on sb

**'cottimo** *nm* piece-work

**'cotto** *pp di* **cuocere** ●*a* done; (*fam: innamorato*) in love; (*sbronzo*) drunk; **ben ~** well cooked; (*carne*) well done; **poco ~** undercooked; (*carne*) underdone; **troppo ~** overcooked; (*carne*) overdone

**'cotton fi'oc®** *nm inv* cotton bud

**cot'tura** *nf* cooking

**'country** *nm inv* country and western

**cou'pon** *nm inv* coupon

**cou'scous** *nm inv* couscous

**co'vare** *vt* hatch; sicken for (*malattia*); harbour (*rancore*)

**co'vata** *nf* brood

**'covo** *nm* den

**co'vone** *nm* sheaf

**cow-'boy** *nm inv* cowboy

**'cozza** *nf* mussel. **cozze** *pl* **alla marinara** moules marinière

**coz'zare** *vi* **~ contro** bump into

**'cozzo** *nm fig* clash

**C.P.** *abbr* (**Casella Postale**) PO Box

**crac** *nm inv* crack; (*di tessuto*) rip

**crack** *nm* (*droga*) crack

**Cra'covia** *nf* Cracow

**'crafen** *nm inv* cream doughnut

**'crampo** *nm* cramp

**'cranio** *nm* skull

**cra'tere** *nm* crater

**cra'vatta** *nf* tie; (*a farfalla*) bow-tie

**cre'anza** *nf* manners; **mala ~** bad manners

**cre'are** *vt* create; **~ assuefazione** be habit-forming

**creatività** *nf* creativity

**crea'tivo** *a* creative

**cre'ato** *nm* creation

**crea|'tore, -'trice** *nmf* creator; **andare al ~** go to meet one's maker

**crea'tura** *nf* creature; (*bambino*) baby; **povera ~!** poor thing!

**creazi'one** *nf* creation

**cre'dente** *nmf* believer

**cre'denza** *nf* belief; Comm credit; (*mobile*) sideboard

**credenzi'ali** *nfpl* credentials

**'credere** *vt* believe; (*pensare*) think ●*vi* **~ in** believe in; **credo di sì** I think so; **non ti credo** I don't believe you; **non posso crederci!** I can't believe it!

'**credersi** *vr* think oneself to be: **si crede uno scrittore** he flatters himself he is a writer

**cre'dibile** *a* credible. believable

**credibilità** *nf* credibility

**credi'tizio** *a* credit *attrib*

'**credito** *nm* credit; (*stima*) esteem; **comprare a ~** buy on credit; **dare ~ a qcsa** give credence to sth; **fare ~** give credit. **~ all'esportazione** export credit. **~ inesigibile** bad debt

**credi|'tore, -'trice** *nmf* creditor

'**credo** *nm inv* credo

**credulità** *nf* credulity

'**credulo** *a* credulous

**credu'lone, -a** *nmf* simpleton

'**crema** *nf* cream; (*di uova e latte*) custard. **~ base per il trucco** vanishing cream. **~ depilatoria** depilatory [cream]. **~ detergente** cleansing cream. **~ idratante** moisturizer. **~ per le mani** hand cream. **~ pasticciera** confectioner's custard. **~ per la pelle** skin cream. **~ protettiva** barrier cream. **~ solare** suntan lotion. **~ per il viso** face cream

**cremagli'era** *nf* ratchet

**cre'mare** *vt* cremate

**crema'torio** *nm* crematorium

**cremazi'one** *nf* cremation

**crème cara'mel** *nf* crème caramel

**creme'ria** *nf* dairy (*also selling ice cream and cakes*)

**Crem'lino** *nm* Kremlin

**cre'moso** *a* creamy

**cren** *nm* horseradish

'**crepa** *nf* crack

**cre'paccio** *nm* cleft; (*di ghiacciaio*) crevasse

**crepacu'ore** *nm* heart-break

**crepa'pelle: a ~** *adv* fit to burst

**cre'pare** *vi* crack; (*fam: morire*) kick the bucket; **~ dal ridere** laugh fit to burst

**crepa'tura** *nf* crevice

**crêpe** *nf inv* pancake

**crepi'tare** *vi* crackle

**crepi'tio** *nm* crackling

**cre'puscolo** *nm* twilight

**cre'scendo** *nm* crescendo

**cre'scenza** *nf creamy white cheese*

'**crescere** *vi* grow; (*aumentare*) increase, grow ● *vt* (*allevare*) bring up; (*aumentare*) increase

**cresci'one** *nm* watercress

'**crescita** *nf* growth; (*aumento*) increase, growth

**cresci'uto** *pp di* **crescere**

'**cresima** *nf* confirmation

**cresi'mare** *vt* confirm

**cre'spato** *a* crinkly

**cre'spella** *nf* pancake

'**crespo** *a* ‹*capelli*› frizzy ● *nm* crêpe

'**cresta** *nf* crest; (*cima*) peak; **abbassare la ~** become less cocky; **alzare la ~** become cocky; **sulla ~ dell'onda** on the crest of a wave

'**creta** *nf* clay

'**Creta** *nf* Crete

**cre'tese** *a & nmf* Cretan

**creti'nata** *nf* something stupid: **dire cretinate** talk nonsense

**cre'tino, -a** *a* stupid ● *nmf* idiot

**C.R.I.** *abbr* (**Croce Rossa Italiana**) Italian Red Cross

'**cribbio** *int* gosh!, golly!

**cric** *nm inv* jack

'**cricca** *nf* gang

'**cricco** *nm* jack

**cri'ceto** *nm* hamster

'**cricket** *nm* cricket

**crimi'nale** *a & nmf* criminal

**criminalità** *nf* crime. **~ organizzata** organized crime

'**crimine** *nm* crime

**criminolo'gia** *nf* criminology

**crimi'nologo, -a** *nmf* criminologist

**crimi'noso** *a* criminal

'**crine** *nm* horsehair

**crini'era** *nf* mane

**crino'lina** *nf* crinoline

'**cripta** *nf* crypt

**crisan'temo** *nm* chrysanthemum

'**crisi** *nf inv* crisis; *Med* fit; **essere in ~ di astinenza** be having withdrawal symptoms, be cold turkey *fam*. **~ di nervi** hysterics. **~ del settimo anno** seven-year itch

**cristal'lino** *a* crystal clear ● *nm* crystalline lens

**cristalliz'zare** *vt* crystallize

**cristalliz'zarsi** *vr* crystallize; ‹*fig: parola, espressione:*› become part of the language

**cri'stallo** *nm* crystal

**Cristia'nesimo** *nm* Christianity

**cristianità** *nf* Christendom

**cristi'ano, -a** *a & nmf* Christian

'**Cristo** *nm* Christ; **avanti ~** BC; **dopo ~** AD; **un povero c~** a poor beggar

**cri'terio** *nm* criterion; (*buon senso*) [common] sense

'**critica** *nf* criticism; (*recensione*) review; **fare la ~ di** review ‹*film, libro*›

**criti'care** *vt* criticize

'**critico** *a* critical ● *nm* critic. **~ letterario** literary critic

**criti'cone, -a** *nmf* fault finder

**crittazi'one** *nf* **~ [dei] dati** *Comput* data encryption

**crivel'lare** *vt* riddle (**di** with)

**cri'vello** *nm* sieve

**cro'ato, -a** *a & nmf* Croatian, Croat

**Cro'azia** *nf* Croatia

**croc'cante** *a* crisp ● *nm type of crunchy nut biscuit*

**croc'chetta** *nf* croquette

'**crocchia** *nf* bun

'**crocchio** *nm* cluster

'**croce** *nf* cross; **a occhio e ~** roughly; **fare testa e ~** toss a coin; **fare o mettere una ~ sopra qcsa** *fig* forget about sth; **mettere in ~** (*criticare*) crucify; (*tormentare*) nag nonstop. **C~ Rossa** Red Cross

**crocero's'sina** *nf* Red Cross nurse

**croce'via** *nm inv* crossroads *sg*

**croci'ata** *nf* crusade

croci'ato *a* cruciform ● *nm* crusader

cro'cicchio *nm* crossroads *sg*

croci'era *nf* cruise; **velocità di ~** cruising speed

croci'figgere *vt* crucify

crocifissi'one *nf* crucifixion

croci'fisso *pp di* **crocifiggere** ● *a* crucified ● *nm* crucifix

crogi'olo *nm* crucible: *fig* melting pot

crogio'larsi *vr* bask

crogiu'olo *nm* = **crogiolo**

crois'sant *nm inv* croissant

crol'lare *vi* collapse; ⟨*prezzi*⟩ slump

'crollo *nm* collapse: ⟨*dei prezzi*⟩ slump

'croma *nf* quaver

cro'mato *a* chromium-plated

'cromo *nm* chrome

cromo'soma *nm* chromosome

'cronaca *nf* chronicle; ⟨*di giornale*⟩ news; *TV, Radio* commentary; **fatto di ~** news item. **~ mondana** gossip column. **~ nera** crime news

'cronico *a* chronic

cro'nista *nmf* reporter; ⟨*di partita*⟩ commentator

croni'storia *nf* chronicle

cro'nografo *nm* chronograph

cronolo'gia *nf* chronology

cronologica'mente *adv* chronologically

crono'logico *a* chronological

cronome'traggio *nm* timing

cronome'trare *vt* time

cronome'trista *nmf Sport* timekeeper

cro'nometro *nm* chronometer; *Sport* stopwatch

cross *nm* ⟨*corsa campestre*⟩ cross-country; ⟨*motocross*⟩ motocross

cros'sista *nmf* scrambler; ⟨*a piedi*⟩ cross-country runner

'crosta *nf* crust; ⟨*di formaggio*⟩ rind; ⟨*di ferita*⟩ scab; ⟨*quadro*⟩ daub

cro'staceo *nm* shellfish

cro'stata *nf* tart. **~ di frutta** fruit tart. **~ di mele** apple pie

cro'stino *nm* croûton; **crostini** *pl* pieces of toasted bread served as a starter

croupi'er *nmf inv* croupier

crucci'are *vt* torment

crucci'arsi *vr* torment oneself

'cruccio *nm* torment

cruci'ale *a* crucial

cruci'verba *nm inv* crossword [puzzle]

cru'dele *a* cruel

crudel'mente *adv* cruelly

crudeltà *nf* cruelty

'crudo *a* raw; ⟨*linguaggio*⟩ crude

cru'ento *a* bloody

cru'miro *nm* blackleg, scab

'crusca *nf* bran

cru'scotto *nm* dashboard

C.S.I. *nf abbr* (**Comunità degli Stati Indipendenti**) CIS

'Cuba *nf* Cuba

cu'bano, -a *a & nmf* Cuban

cu'betto *nm* **~ di ghiaccio** ice cube

'cubico *a* cubic

cu'bismo *nm* cubism

cu'bista *a & nmf* cubist

cubi'tale *a* **a caratteri cubitali** in enormous letters

'cubo *nm* cube

cuc'cagna *nf* abundance; ⟨*baldoria*⟩ merry-making; **paese della ~** land of plenty

cuc'cetta *nf* ⟨*su un treno*⟩ couchette; *Naut* berth

cucchiai'ata *nf* spoonful

cucchia'ino *nm* teaspoon; ⟨*contenuto*⟩ teaspoon[ful]

cuc'chiaio *nm* spoon; **un ~** a spoon[ful] ⟨**di** of⟩; **al ~** ⟨*dolce*⟩ creamy. **~ di legno** wooden spoon. **~ da minestra** soup-spoon. **~ tavola** tablespoon; ⟨*contenuto*⟩ tablespoon[ful]

cucchiai'one *nm* serving spoon

'cuccia *nf* basket; ⟨*in giardino*⟩ kennel; [**fa' la**] **~!** down!

cuccio'lata *nf* litter

'cucciolo *nm* puppy

cu'cina *nf* kitchen; ⟨*il cucinare*⟩ cooking; ⟨*cibo*⟩ food; ⟨*apparecchio*⟩ cooker; **far da ~** cook; **libro di ~** cook[ery] book. **~ a gas** gas cooker. **~ componibile** fitted kitchen. **~ economica** cooker

cuci'nare *vt* cook

cuci'nino *nm* kitchenette

cu'cire *vt* sew; **macchina per ~** sewing-machine; **cucilo a macchina** do it on the machine

cu'cito *nm* sewing

cuci'tura *nf* seam

cucù *nm inv* cuckoo; **~!** peekaboo!

'cuculo *nm* cuckoo

'cuffia *nf* bonnet; ⟨*ricevitore*⟩ headphones *pl*. **~ da bagno** bathing cap

cu'gino, -a *nmf* cousin

'cui *pron rel* ⟨*persona: con prep*⟩ who[m]; ⟨*cose, animali: con prep*⟩ which; ⟨*tra articolo e nome*⟩ whose; **la persona con ~ ho parlato** the person I spoke to, the person to whom I spoke *fml*; **la ditta per ~ lavoro** the company I work for, the company for which I work; **l'amico il ~ libro è stato pubblicato** the friend whose book was published; **in ~** ⟨*dove*⟩ where; ⟨*quando*⟩ that; **per ~** ⟨*perciò*⟩ so; **la città in ~ vivo** the city I live in, the city where I live; **il giorno in ~ l'ho visto** the day [that] I saw him

cu'latta *nf* breech

culi'naria *nf* cookery

culi'nario *a* culinary

'culla *nf* cradle

cul'lare *vt* rock; *fig* cherish ⟨*sogno, speranza*⟩

cul'larsi *vr* **~ nella speranza di** *liter* cherish the fond hope that

culmi'nante *a* culminating

culmi'nare *vi* culminate

cul'mine *nm* peak

'culo *nm vulg* arse; ⟨*fortuna*⟩ luck; **prendere qcno per il ~** take the piss out of sb

'culto *nm* cult; *Relig* religion; ⟨*adorazione*⟩ worship

**cul'tura** *nf* culture. ~ **generale** general knowledge. ~ **di massa** mass culture

**cultu'rale** *a* cultural

**cultu'rismo** *nm* body-building

**cultu'rista** *nmf* body-builder

**cu'mino** *nm* ~ **nero** cumin

**cumula'tivo** *a* cumulative; ⟨*prezzo*⟩ all-in, all-inclusive; **biglietto** ~ group ticket

**'cumulo** *nm* pile; (*mucchio*) heap; (*nuvola*) cumulus

**'cuneo** *nm* wedge

**cu'netta** *nf* gutter

**cu'nicolo** *nm* tunnel

**cu'ocere** *vt* cook; fire ⟨*ceramica*⟩ ● *vi* cook; ⟨*ceramica*⟩ fire

**cu'oco, -a** *nmf* cook

**cu'oia** *nfpl* **tirare le** ~ *fam* kick the bucket

**cu'oio** *nm* leather. ~ **capelluto** scalp

**cu'ore** *nm* heart; **cuori** *pl* (*carte*) hearts; **di [buon]** ~ ⟨*persona*⟩ kind-hearted; **di tutto** ~ wholeheartedly; **ti ringrazio di tutto** ~ many thanks; **nel profondo del** ~ in one's heart of hearts; **nel** ~ **della notte** in the middle of the night; **senza** ~ heartless; **mettersi il** ~ **in pace** come to terms with it; **parlare a** ~ **aperto** have a heart-to-heart (**con** with); **stare a** ~ **a qcno** be very important to sb. ~ **tenero** (*persona*) softy

**cupa'mente** *adv* darkly

**cupi'digia** *nf* greed

**Cu'pido** *nm* Cupid

**'cupo** *a* gloomy; ⟨*voce*⟩ deep

**'cupola** *nf* dome; **a** ~ domed

**'cura** *nf* care; (*amministrazione*) management; *Med* treatment; **aver** ~ **di** look after; **a** ~ **di** ⟨*libro*⟩ edited by; **in** ~ under treatment; **fare delle cure termali** take the waters. ~ **dimagrante** diet

**cu'rabile** *a* curable

**cu'rante** *a* **medico** ~ GP, doctor

**cu'rare** *vt* take care of, look after; *Med* treat; (*guarire*) cure; edit ⟨*testo*⟩

**cu'rarsi** *vr* take care of oneself, look after oneself; ~ **dei fatti propri** mind one's own business

**cu'rato** *nm* parish priest

**cura|'tore, -'trice** *nmf* trustee; (*di testo*) editor. ~ **fallimentare** official receiver

**'curcuma** *nf* turmeric

**curcu'mina** *nf* turmeric

**'curdo, -a** *nmf* Kurd ● *a* Kurdish

**'curia** *nf* curia

**curio'saggine** *nf* nosiness

**curio'sare** *vi* be curious; (*mettere il naso*) pry (**in** into); (*nei negozi*) look around

**curiosità** *nf inv* curiosity

**curi'oso** *a* curious; (*strano*) odd, curious ● *nm* busybody

**'curling** *nm inv Sport* curling

**cur'ricolo** *nm* curriculum

**cur'riculum** *nm inv* curriculum

**'curry** *nm inv* curry. ~ **in polvere** curry powder

**cur'sore** *nm Comput* cursor

**'curva** *nf* curve; (*stradale*) bend. ~ **a gomito** dogleg. ~ **di apprendimento** learning curve

**cur'vare** *vt/i* bend, curve

**cur'varsi** *vr* bend, curve

**'curvo** *a* curved; (*piegato*) bent

**cusci'netto** *nm* pad; *Mech* bearing. ~ **puntaspilli** pincushion. ~ **a sfere** ball bearing

**cu'scino** *nm* cushion; (*guanciale*) pillow. ~ **gonfiabile** air cushion

**cu'scus** *nm inv* couscous

**'cuspide** *nf* spire

**cu'stode** *nm* caretaker; (*di abitazione*) concierge; (*di fabbrica*) guard; (*di museo*) custodian. ~ **giudiziario** official receiver

**cu'stodia** *nf* care; *Jur* custody; (*astuccio*) case; **ottenere la** ~ **di** get custody of. ~ **cautelare** remand

**custo'dire** *vt* keep; (*badare*) look after

**cu'taneo** *a* skin *attrib*

**'cute** *nf* skin

**cu'ticola** *nf* cuticle

**'cutter** *nm inv* cutter

**CV** *abbr* (**cavallo vapore**) hp

**cyber'spazio** *nm* cyberspace

**cy'clette®** *nf inv* exercise bicycle

# Dd

**da** *prep* from; (*con verbo passivo*) by; (*moto a luogo*) to; (*moto per luogo*) through; (*stato in luogo*) at; (*temporale*) since; (*continuativo*) for; (*causale*) with; (*in qualità di*) as; (*con caratteristica*) with; (*come*) like; **da Roma a Milano** from Rome to Milan; **staccare un quadro dalla parete** take a picture off the wall; **i bambini dai 5 ai 10 anni** children between 5 and 10; **vedere qcsa da vicino/lontano** see sth from up close/from a distance; **amato da tutti** loved by everybody; **scritto da** written by; **andare dal panettiere** go to the baker's; **passo da te più tardi** I'll come over to your place later; **passiamo da qui** let's go this way; **un appuntamento dal dentista** an appointment at the dentist's; **il treno passa da Venezia** the train goes through Venice; **dall'anno scorso** since last year; **vivo qui da due anni** I've been living here for two years; **da domani** from tomorrow; **piangere dal dolore** cry with pain; **ho molto da fare** I have a lot to do; **occhiali da sole** sunglasses; **qualcosa da mangiare** something to eat; **un uomo dai capelli scuri** a man with dark hair; **è un oggetto da poco** it's not worth much; **da solo** alone; **l'ho fatto da solo** I did it by myself; **si è fatto da sé** he is a self-made man; **vive da re** he lives like a king; **non è da lui** it's not like him

**dab'bene** a honest

**dac'capo** adv again; (dall'inizio) from the beginning

**dacché** conj since

**dada'ismo** nm (arte) Dadaism

**dada'ista** a & nmf Dadaist

**'dado** nm dice; Culin stock cube; Techn nut. ~ **ad alette** wing nut

**daf'fare** nm work

**'dagli** = da + gli

**'dai**[1] = da + i

**'dai**[2] int come on!; ~, **non fare così!** come on, don't be like that!; ~, **sbrigati!** come on, get a move on!

**'daino** nm deer; (pelle) buckskin

**dal** = da + il

**'dalla** = da + la

**'dalle** = da + le

**'dallo** = da + lo

**'dalia** nf dahlia

**'dalmata** nmf (cane) Dalmatian

**Dal'mazia** nf Dalmatia

**dal'tonico** a colour-blind

**'dama** nf lady; (nei balli) partner; (gioco) draughts. ~ **di compagnia** lady's companion. ~ **di corte** lady-in-waiting

**dama'scato** a damask

**da'masco** nm (tessuto) damask

**dame'rino** nm (bellimbusto) dandy

**dami'gella** nf (di sposa) bridesmaid

**damigi'ana** nf demijohn

**dam'meno** adv **non essere** ~ be no less good (**di** than)

**DAMS** nm abbr (Discipline delle Arti, della Musica e dello Spettacolo) (corso di laurea) degree in fine art, music and drama

**da'naro** nm = **denaro**

**dana'roso** a (fam: ricco) loaded

**da'nese** a Danish ● nmf Dane ● nm (lingua) Danish

**Dani'marca** nf Denmark

**dan'nare** vt damn; **far** ~ **qcno** drive sb mad

**dan'narsi** vr fig wear oneself out; ~ **l'anima (a fare qcsa)** wear oneself out (doing sth)

**dan'nato, -a** a damned, damn fam ● nmf damned person; **lavorare/studiare come un** ~ fig work/study like mad

**dannazi'one** nf damnation

**danneggia'mento** nm damage

**danneggi'are** vt damage; (nuocere) harm

**danneggi'ato** a Jur injured

**'danno** nm damage; (a persona) harm; **danni** pl damage

**dan'noso** a harmful

**dan'tesco** a Dantean, Dantesque

**danubi'ano** a Danubian

**Da'nubio** nm Danube

**'danza** nf dance; (il danzare) dancing. ~ **folcloristica** country dancing

**dan'zante** a **serata** ~ dance

**dan'zare** vi dance

**danza|'tore, -'trice** nmf dancer. **danza-trice del ventre** belly dancer

**dapper'tutto** adv everywhere

**dap'poco** a worthless

**dap'prima** adv at first

**Darda'nelli** nmpl **i** ~ the Dardanelles

**'dardo** nm dart

**'dare** vt give; sit (esame); have (festa); ~ **qcsa a qcno** give sb sth; ~ **da mangiare a qcno** give sb something to eat; ~ **fuoco a qcsa** set fire to sth; ~ **il benvenuto a qcno** welcome sb; ~ **la buonanotte a qcno** say good night to sb; ~ **del tu/del lei a qcno** address sb "tu"/"lei"; ~ **del cretino a qcno** call sb an idiot; ~ **qcsa per scontato** take sth for granted; ~ **fastidio a** annoy; ~ **cosa danno alla TV stasera?** what's on TV tonight?; **darle a qcno** (picchiare) give sb a walloping ● vi ~ **nell'occhio** be conspicuous; ~ **alla testa** go to one's head; ~ **su** (finestra, casa:) look on to; ~ **sui** o **ai nervi a qcno** get on sb's nerves ● nm Comm debit

**dar'sena** nf dock

**'darsi** vr (scambiarsi) give each other; ~ **da fare** get down to it; **si è dato tanto da fare!** he went to so much trouble!; ~ **a** (cominciare) take up; ~ **al bere** take to drink; ~ **per** (malato) pretend to be; ~ **per vinto** give up; **può** ~ maybe

**darvini'ano** a Darwinian

**darvi'nista** nmf Darwinist

**'data** nf date; **di lunga** ~ old-established. ~ **di emissione** date of issue. ~ **di nascita** date of birth. ~ **di scadenza** expiry date; (su cibo) best before date

**data'base** nm inv database. ~ **relazionale** relational database

**da'tabile** a dateable

**da'tare** vt date; **a** ~ **da** as from

**da'tario** nm (su orologio) calendar

**da'tato** a dated

**da'tivo** nm dative

**'dato** a given; (dedito) addicted; ~ **che** seeing that, given that ● nm datum; **dati** pl data. ~ **di fatto** well established fact

**da'tore** nm giver. ~ **di lavoro** employer

**'dattero** nm date

**dattilogra'fare** vt/i type; ~ **a tastiera cieca** touch-type

**dattilogra'fia** nf typing. ~ **a tastiera cieca** touch-typing

**datti'lografo, -a** nmf typist

**dattilo'scritto** a (copia) typewritten, typed

**dat'torno** adv **togliersi** ~ clear off

**da'vanti** adv before; (dirimpetto) opposite; (di fronte) in front ● a inv front ● nm front; ~ **di dietro** (maglia) back-to-front · ~ **a** prep before, in front of; **passare** ~ **a** pass, go past

**davan'zale** nm window sill

**da'vanzo** *adv* **ce n'è** ~ there is more than
enough
**dav'vero** *adv* really: **per** ~ in earnest; **dici**
~? honestly?
**dazi'ario** *a* excise
'**dazio** *nm* duty; (*ufficio*) customs *pl.* **dazi** *pl*
**doganali** customs duties. ~ **d'importa-**
**zione** import duty
**D.C.** *nf abbr* (**Democrazia Cristiana**) Christian Democratic Party
**d.C.** *abbr* (**dopo Cristo**) AD
**D.D.T.** *nm* (*insetticida*) DDT
'**dea** *nf* goddess
**deambula'torio** *a* ambulatory
**debel'lare** *vt* defeat
**debili'tante** *a* weakening
**debili'tare** *vt* weaken
**debili'tarsi** *vr* become debilitated
**debilitazi'one** *nf* debilitation
**debita'mente** *adv* duly
'**debito** *a* due; **a tempo** ~ in due course
● *nm* debt. ~ **pubblico** national debt
**debi|'tore, -'trice** *nmf* debtor
'**debole** *a* weak; (*luce*) dim; (*suono*) faint
● *nm* weak point; **avere un** ~ **per qcno** have
a soft spot for sb; **avere un** ~ **per qcsa** have
a weakness for sth
**debo'lezza** *nf* weakness
**debor'dare** *vi* overflow
**debosci'ato** *a* debauched
**debrai'ata** *nf Auto* declutching
**debut'tante** *a* beginner ● *nmf* beginner;
(*attore*) actor/actress making his/her début
**debut'tare** *vi* make one's début
**de'butto** *nm* début
'**decade** *nf* period of ten days
**deca'dente** *a* decadent
**decaden'tismo** *nm* decadence
**deca'denza** *nf* decline; *Jur* loss
**deca'dere** *vi* lapse
**decadi'mento** *nm* (*delle arti*) decline
**deca'duto** *a* (*persona*) impoverished;
(*decreto, norma*) no longer in force
**decaffei'nato** *a* decaffeinated ● *nm* decaffeinated coffee, decaf *fam*
**deca'grammo** *nm* decagram
**decal'care** *vt* trace
**decalcifi'carsi** *vr* become brittle
**decalcificazi'one** *nf* (*condizione*) brittle
bones
**decalcoma'nia** *nf* transfer
**de'calitro** *nm* decalitre
**de'calogo** *nm fig* rule book
**de'cametro** *nm* decametre
**de'cano** *nm* dean
**decan'tare** *vt* (*lodare*) praise
**decapi'tare** *vt* decapitate; behead (*condan-*
*nato*)
**decapitazi'one** *nf* decapitation; beheading
**decappot'tabile** *a* convertible
**decappot'tare** *vt* take down the hood of
'**decathlon** *nm inv* decathlon
**de'cedere** *vi* (*morire*) die
**dece'duto** *a* deceased
**decele'rare** *vt/i* slow down, decelerate

**decelerazi'one** *nf* deceleration
**decen'nale** *a* ten-yearly ● *nm* (*anniver-*
*sario*) tenth anniversary
**de'cenne** *a* (*bambino*) ten-year-old
**de'cennio** *nm* decade
**de'cente** *a* decent
**decente'mente** *adv* decently
**decentraliz'zare** *vt* decentralize
**decentra'mento** *nm* decentralization
**decen'trare** *vt* decentralize
**de'cenza** *nf* decency
**de'cesso** *nm* death, decease *fml*; **atto di** ~
death certificate
'**decibel** *nm inv* decibel
**de'cidere** *vt* decide; settle (*questione*)
**de'cidersi** *vr* make up one's mind
**deci'frabile** *a* decipherable
**deci'frare** *vt* decipher; (*documenti cifrati*)
decode
**decifrazi'one** *nf* deciphering
**de'cigrado** *nm* tenth of a degree
**deci'grammo** *nm* decigram[me]
**de'cilitro** *nm* decilitre
**deci'male** *a* decimal
**deci'mare** *vt* decimate
**de'cimetro** *nm* decimetre
'**decimo** *a & nm* tenth
**de'cina** *nf Math* ten; **una** ~ **di** (*circa dieci*)
about ten
**decisa'mente** *adv* definitely, decidedly
**decisio'nale** *a* decision-making
**decisi'one** *nf* decision; **prendere una** ~
make *or* take a decision; **con** ~ decisively
**decisio'nismo** *nm tendency to make deci-*
*sions without consulting others*
**decisio'nista** *nmf person who does not con-*
*sult others before making decisions*
**deci'sivo** *a* decisive
**de'ciso** *pp di* **decidere** ● *a* decided
**decla'mare** *vt/i* declaim
**declama'torio** *a* (*stile*) declamatory
**declas'sare** *vt* downgrade
**decli'nabile** *a Gram* declinable; (*offerta*)
that can be refused
**decli'nare** *vt* decline; turn down, refuse
(*invito*); ~ **ogni responsabilità** disclaim all
responsibility ● *vi* go down; (*tramontare*) set
**declinazi'one** *nf Gram* declension
**de'clino** *nm* decline; **in** ~ (*popolarità*) on
the decline
**de'clivio** *nm* downward slope
**dé'co** *a inv* Art Deco
**deco'difica** *nf* decoding
**decodifi'care** *vt* decode
**decodifica'tore** *nm TV* descrambler
**decodificazi'one** *nf* decoding
**decol'lare** *vi* take off
**décolle'té** *a inv* low cut ● *nm inv* low neckline
**de'collo** *nm* take-off
**decolonizzazi'one** *nf* decolonization
**decolo'rante** *nm* bleach
**decolo'rare** *vt* bleach
**decolorazi'one** *nf* bleaching
**decom'porre** *vt* decompose

**decom'porsi** vr decompose
**decomposizi'one** nf decomposition
**decompressi'one** nf decompression
**deconcen'trarsi** vr become distracted
**deconge'lare** vt defrost
**decongestio'nare** vt Med. fig relieve congestion in
**decontami'nare** vt Techn decontaminate
**decontaminazi'one** nf decontamination
**decontrazi'one** nf relaxation
**deco'rare** vt decorate
**deco'rato** a (ornato) decorated
**decora|'tore, -'trice** nmf decorator
**decorazi'one** nf decoration. ~ **floreale** flower arranging
**de'coro** nm decorum
**decorosa'mente** adv decorously
**deco'roso** a dignified
**decor'renza** nf ~ **dal...** with effect from..., effective...
**de'correre** vi pass; **a ~ da** with effect from
**de'corso** pp di decorrere ● nm passing; Med course
**decre'mento** nm decrease
**de'crepito** a decrepit
**decre'scente** a decreasing
**de'crescere** vi decrease; (prezzi:) go down; (acque:) subside
**decre'tare** vt decree; ~ **lo stato d'emergenza** declare a state of emergency
**de'creto** nm decree. ~ **ingiuntivo** decree. ~ **legge** decree which has the force of law. ~ **legislativo** decree requiring the approval of Parliament
**decre'tone** nm Pol portmanteau bill
**de'cubito** nm **piaghe da ~** bedsores
**decur'tare** vt reduce
**decurtazi'one** nf reduction
**'dedalo** nm maze
**'dedica** nf dedication
**dedi'care** vt dedicate
**dedi'carsi** vr dedicate oneself
**'dedito** a ~ **a** given to; (assorto) engrossed in; addicted to (vizi)
**dedizi'one** nf dedication
**de'dotto** pp di dedurre ● a deduced
**dedu'cibile** a (tassa) allowable
**de'durre** vt deduce; (sottrarre) deduct
**dedut'tivo** a deductive
**deduzi'one** nf deduction
**défail'lance** nf inv (cedimento) collapse
**defal'care** vt deduct
**defalcazi'one** nf deduction
**defe'care** vi defecate
**defecazi'one** nf defecation
**defene'strare** vt fig remove from office
**defe'rente** a deferential
**defe'renza** nf deference
**deferi'mento** nm referral
**defe'rire** vt Jur remit
**defezio'nare** vi (abbandonare) defect
**defezi'one** nf defection
**defezio'nista** nmf defector
**defici'ente** a (mancante) deficient; Med

mentally deficient ● nmf mental defective; pej half-wit
**defici'enza** nf deficiency; (lacuna) gap; Med mental deficiency
**'deficit** nm inv deficit, shortfall; **essere in ~** be in deficit
**defici'tario** a (bilancio) deficit attrib; (sviluppo) insufficient
**defi'larsi** vr (scomparire) slip away; ~ **da qcsa** sneak away from sth
**défi'lé** nm inv fashion show
**defi'nibile** a definable; ~ **dall'utente** Comput user-definable
**defi'nire** vt define: (risolvere) settle
**definitiva'mente** adv for good
**defini'tivo** a definitive
**defi'nito** a definite
**definizi'one** nf definition; (soluzione) settlement
**defiscaliz'zare** vt abolish the tax on
**defiscalizzazi'one** nf abolition of tax
**defla'grare** vt (esplodere) explode
**deflagrazi'one** nf (esplosione) explosion
**deflazio'nare** vt deflate
**deflazi'one** nf deflation
**deflazio'nistico** a deflationary
**deflet'tore** nm Auto quarterlight
**deflu'ire** vi (liquidi:) flow away; (persone:) stream out
**de'flusso** nm (di marea) ebb
**defogli'ante** a defoliating ● nm defoliant
**deforestazi'one** nf deforestation
**defor'mante** a artrite ~ acute arthritis
**defor'mare** vt deform (arto); fig distort
**defor'marsi** vr lose its shape
**defor'mato** a warped
**deformazi'one** nf (di fatti) distortion; **è una ~ professionale** put it down to the job
**de'forme** a deformed
**deformità** nf inv deformity
**defrau'dare** vt defraud
**de'funto, -a** a & nmf deceased
**degene'rare** vi degenerate
**degenera'tivo** a (processo) degenerative
**degene'rato** a degenerate
**degenerazi'one** nf degeneration
**de'genere** a degenerate
**de'gente** a bedridden ● nmf patient
**de'genza** nf confinement. ~ **ospedaliera** stay in hospital
**'degli** = di + gli
**deglu'tire** vt swallow
**deglutizi'one** nf swallowing
**de'gnare** vt ~ **qcno/qcsa di uno sguardo** deign or condescend to look at sb/sth
**de'gnarsi** vr deign, condescend
**'degno** a worthy; (meritevole) deserving. ~ **di lode** praiseworthy. ~ **di nota** noteworthy
**degrada'mento** nm degradation
**degra'dante** a demeaning
**degra'dare** vt degrade
**degra'darsi** vr lower oneself; (città:) fall into a state of disrepair
**degradazi'one** nf degradation
**de'grado** nm deterioration; ~ **ambientale**

environmental damage. **~ urbano** urban blight, urban decay

**degu'stare** *vt* taste

**degustazi'one** *nf* tasting. **~ di vini** wine tasting

**'dei** = di + i

**deindiciz'zare** *vt* deindex

**déjà vu** *nm inv* déjà vu

**del** = di + il

**dela|'tore, -'trice** *nmf* [police] informer

**delazi'one** *nf* informing

**'delega** *nf* proxy; **legge ~** *law that does not require Parliamentary approval*

**dele'gante** *nmf Jur* representative

**dele'gare** *vt* delegate

**dele'gato** *nm* delegate

**delegazi'one** *nf* delegation

**dele'terio** *a* harmful

**del'fino** *nm* dolphin; ⟨stile di nuoto⟩ butterfly [stroke]; **nuotare a ~** do the butterfly

**de'libera** *nf* bylaw

**delibe'rante** *a* ⟨organo⟩ decision making

**delibe'rare** *vt/i* deliberate; **~ su/in** rule on/in

**deliberata'mente** *adv* deliberately

**delibe'rato** *a* ⟨intenzionale⟩ deliberate

**delicata'mente** *adv* delicately

**delica'tezza** *nf* delicacy; ⟨fragilità⟩ frailty; ⟨tatto⟩ tact

**deli'cato** *a* delicate; ⟨salute⟩ frail; ⟨suono, colore⟩ soft

**deligitti'mare** *vt* delegitimize

**delimi'tare** *vt* define

**delimita'tivo** *a* defining

**delimitazi'one** *nf* definition

**deline'are** *vt* outline

**deline'arsi** *vr* be outlined; *fig* take shape

**deline'ato** *a* outlined

**delineazi'one** *nf* outline

**delinqu'ente** *nmf* delinquent. **~ minorenne** young offender

**delinqu'enza** *nf* delinquency. **~ minorile** juvenile crime

**delinquenzi'ale** *a* criminal

**de'linquere** *vi* commit a criminal act; **associazione per ~** conspiracy [to commit a crime]; **istigazione a ~** incitement to crime

**de'liquio** *nm* **cadere in ~** swoon

**deli'rante** *a Med* delirious; ⟨assurdo⟩ insane; ⟨sfrenato⟩ frenzied

**deli'rare** *vi* be delirious

**de'lirio** *nm* delirium; *fig* frenzy; **mandare/andare in ~** *fig* send/go into a frenzy

**de'litto** *nm* crime. **~ passionale** crime of passion

**delittu'oso** *a* criminal

**de'lizia** *nf* delight

**delizi'are** *vt* delight

**delizi'arsi** *vr* **~ di** delight in

**delizi'oso** *a* delightful; ⟨cibo⟩ delicious

**'della** = di + la

**'delle** = di + le

**'dello** = di + lo

**'delta** *nm inv* delta

**delta'piano** *nm* hang-glider; **fare ~** go hang-gliding

**deluci'dare** *vt fig* clarify

**delucidazi'one** *nf* clarification

**delu'dente** *a* disappointing

**de'ludere** *vt* disappoint

**delusi'one** *nf* disappointment

**de'luso** *a* disappointed; **essere ~ di qcsa/qcno** be disillusioned with sth/sb

**dema'gogico** *a* popularity-seeking, demagogic

**dema'gogo** *nm* demagogue

**deman'dare** *vt* entrust

**demani'ale** *a* ⟨proprietà⟩ government *attrib*

**de'manio** *nm* government property

**demar'care** *vt* demarcate

**demarcazi'one** *nf* demarcation; **linea di ~** demarcation line

**de'mente** *a* demented

**de'menza** *nf* dementia. **~ senile** senile dementia

**demenzi'ale** *a* ⟨assurdo⟩ zany

**de'merito** *nm* **nota di ~** demerit mark

**demilitariz'zare** *vt* demilitarize

**demilitarizzazi'one** *nf* demilitarization

**demistifi'care** *vt* debunk

**demistifica|'tore, -'trice** *nmf* debunker

**demistifica'torio** *a* debunking

**demistificazi'one** *nf* debunking

**demitiz'zare** *vt* demythologize

**demitizzazi'one** *nf* demythologization

**democratica'mente** *adv* democratically

**demo'cratico** *a* democratic

**democratiz'zare** *vt* democratize

**democra'zia** *nf* democracy

**democristi'ano, -a** *a & nmf* Christian Democrat

**'demodisk** *nm inv Comput* demo disk

**demogra'fia** *nf* demography

**demo'grafico** *a* demographic; **incremento ~** increase in population

**demo'lire** *vt* demolish

**demo'lito** *a* demolished

**demolizi'one** *nf* demolition

**'demone** *nm* demon

**demo'niaco** *a* demonic

**de'monio** *nm* demon

**demoniz'zare** *vt* demonize

**demonizzazi'one** *nf* demonization

**demoraliz'zante** *a* demoralizing

**demoraliz'zare** *vt* demoralize

**demoraliz'zarsi** *vr* become demoralized

**demoraliz'zato** *a* demoralized

**de'mordere** *vi* give up

**demoti'vare** *vt* demotivate

**demoti'varsi** *vr* become demotivated

**demoti'vato** *a* demotivated

**demotivazi'one** *nf* demotivation

**de'nari** *nmpl* ⟨nelle carte⟩ diamonds

**de'naro** *nm* money

**denatu'rato** *a* **alcol ~** methylated spirits

**denazionaliz'zare** *vt* denationalize

**deni'grare** *vt* denigrate

**denigra|'tore, -'trice** *a* denigrating ● *nmf* denigrator

**denigra'torio** *a* denigratory
**denigrazi'one** *nf* denigration
**denomi'nare** *vt* name
**denomi'narsi** *vr* be named
**denomina'tivo** *a* denominative
**denomina'tore** *nm* denominator
**denominazi'one** *nf* denomination. ~ **di origine controllata** *mark guaranteeing the quality of a wine*
**deno'tare** *vt* denote
**denotazi'one** *nf* denotation
**densa'mente** *adv* densely
**densità** *nf* density. **ad alta/bassa ~ di popolazione** densely/sparsely populated
**'denso** *a* thick, dense
**den'tale** *a* dental
**den'tario** *a* dental
**den'tata** *nf* bite
**den'tato** *a* ⟨*lama*⟩ serrated
**denta'tura** *nf* teeth *pl*; *Techn* serration
**'dente** *nm* tooth; (*di forchetta*) prong; (*di montagna*) jagged peak; **al ~** *Culin* just slightly firm; **lavarsi i denti** brush one's teeth. **~ del giudizio** wisdom tooth. **~ di latte** milk tooth. **~ di leone** *Bot* dandelion
**'dentice** *nm* dentex (*type of sea bream*)
**denti'era** *nf* dentures *pl*, false teeth *pl*; **metterla la ~** put one's false teeth in
**denti'fricio** *nm* toothpaste
**den'tista** *nmf* dentist
**'dentro** *adv* in, inside; (*in casa*) indoors; **da ~** from within; **qui ~** in here; **metter ~** (*fam: in prigione*) lock up, put inside ● *prep* in, inside; (*di tempo*) within, by ● *nm* inside
**denucleariz'zare** *vt* denuclearize
**denucleariz'zato** *a* nuclear-free, denuclearized
**denuclearizzazi'one** *nf* denuclearization
**denu'dare** *vt* bare
**denu'darsi** *vr* strip
**de'nuncia** *nf* denunciation; (*alla polizia*) reporting; **fare una ~** draw up a report. **~ dei redditi** income tax return
**denunci'are** *vt* denounce; (*accusare*) report
**de'nunzia** = **denuncia**
**denu'trito** *a* underfed
**denutrizi'one** *nf* malnutrition
**deodo'rante** *a* & *nm* deodorant. **~ antitraspirante** antiperspirant. **~ a sfera** roll-on
**deodo'rare** *vt* deodorize
**deontolo'gia** *nf* (*etica professionale*) code of conduct
**depenaliz'zare** *vt* decriminalize
**depenalizzazi'one** *nf* decriminalization
**depen'dance** *nf inv* outbuilding
**depe'ribile** *a* perishable
**deperi'mento** *nm* wasting away; (*di merci*) deterioration
**depe'rire** *vi* waste away
**depe'rito** *a* wasted
**depi'lare** *vt* depilate
**depi'larsi** *vr* shave ⟨*gambe*⟩; pluck ⟨*sopracciglia*⟩

**depila'tore** *a* depilatory ● *nm* (*apparecchio*) hair remover
**depila'torio** *nm* depilatory
**depilazi'one** *nf* hair removal. **~ diatermica** electrolysis
**depi'staggio** *nm fig* diversionary manoeuvre
**depi'stare** *vt fig* throw off the track
**dépli'ant** *nm inv* brochure, leaflet
**deplo'rabile** *a* deplorable
**deplo'rare** *vt* deplore; (*dolersi di*) grieve over
**deplo'revole** *a* deplorable
**depoliticiz'zare** *vt* depoliticize
**de'porre** *vt* put down; lay down ⟨*armi*⟩; lay ⟨*uova*⟩; (*togliere da una carica*) depose; (*testimoniare*) testify
**depor'tare** *vt* deport
**depor'tato, -a** *nmf* deportee
**deportazi'one** *nf* deportation
**deposi'tante** *nmf Fin* depositor
**deposi'tare** *vt* deposit; (*lasciare in custodia*) leave; (*in magazzino*) store
**deposi'tario, -a** *nmf* (*di segreto*) repository
**deposi'tarsi** *vr* settle
**de'posito** *nm* deposit; (*luogo*) warehouse; *Mil* depot. **~ d'armi** arms dump. **~ bagagli** left-luggage office, baggage checkroom *Am*. **~ bancario** deposit account. **~ bancario vincolato** fixed term deposit account
**deposizi'one** *nf* deposition; (*da una carica*) removal
**de'posto** *a* deposed
**depotenzi'are** *vt* weaken
**depra'vare** *vt* deprave
**depra'vato** *a* depraved
**depravazi'one** *nf* depravity
**depre'cabile** *a* appalling
**depre'care** *vt* deprecate
**depre'dare** *vt* plunder
**depressio'nario** *a* **area depressionaria** *Meteorol* area of low pressure
**depressi'one** *nf* depression; **area di ~** *Meteorol* area of low pressure; *Econ* depressed area
**depres'sivo** *a* depressive
**de'presso** *pp di* **deprimere** ● *a* depressed
**depressuriz'zare** *vt* depressurize
**depressurizzazi'one** *nf* depressurization
**deprezza'mento** *nm* depreciation
**deprez'zare** *vt* depreciate
**deprez'zarsi** *vr* depreciate
**depri'mente** *a* depressing
**de'primere** *vt* depress
**de'primersi** *vr* get depressed
**deprivazi'one** *nf* deprivation
**depu'rare** *vt* purify
**depu'rarsi** *vr* be purified
**depura'tore** *nm* purifier
**depurazi'one** *nf* purification; (*di detriti*) effluent
**depu'tare** *vt* delegate
**depu'tato, -a** *nmf* ≈ Member of Parliament, MP
**deputazi'one** *nf* deputation

**dequalifi'care** *vt* disqualify

**dequalifi'carsi** *vr* disqualify oneself

**dequalificazi'one** *nf* disqualification

**deraglia'mento** *nm* derailment

**deragli'are** *vi* go off the lines; **far ~** derail

**deraglia'tore** *nm* derailleur gears *pl*

**dera'pare** *vi Auto* skid; ⟨*sciatore:*⟩ sideslip

**derattiz'zare** *vt* clear of rats

**derattizzazi'one** *nf* rodent control

'**derby** *nm inv Sport* local Derby

**deregolamen'tare** *vt Comm* deregulate

**deregolamentazi'one** *nf* deregulation

**dere'litto** *a* derelict

**deresponsabiliz'zare** *vt* deprive of responsibility

**deresponsabiliz'zarsi** *vr* abdicate responsibility

**deresponsabilizzazi'one** *nf* depriving of responsibility

**dere'tano** *nm* backside, bottom

**de'ridere** *vt* deride

**derisi'one** *nf* derision

**deri'sorio** *a* derisory

**de'riva** *nf* drift; **andare alla ~** drift

**deri'vabile** *a* derivable

**deri'vare** *vi* **~ da** ⟨*provenire*⟩ derive from ● *vt* derive; ⟨*sviare*⟩ divert

**deri'vata** *nf Math* derivative

**deri'vato** *a* derived ● *nm* by-product

**derivazi'one** *nf* derivation; ⟨*di fiume*⟩ diversion

**derma'tite** *nf* dermatitis

**dermatolo'gia** *nf* dermatology

**dermato'logico** *a* dermatological

**derma'tologo, -a** *nmf* dermatologist

**derma'tosi** *nf* dermatosis

**dermoprotet'tivo** *a* ⟨*crema*⟩ skin *attrib*; ⟨*azione*⟩ protective

'**deroga** *nf* dispensation

**dero'gare** *vi* **~ a** depart from

**deroga'torio** *a* derogatory

**der'rata** *nf* merchandise. **derrate** *pl* **alimentari** foodstuffs

**deru'bare** *vt* rob

**deru'bato** *a* robbed

**desaliniz'zare** *vt* desalinate

**desalinizzazi'one** *nf* desalination

**desapare'cido** *nmf* (*pl* **~s**) disappeared man/woman, desaparecido

**descolarizzazi'one** *nf* deschooling

**descrit'tivo** *a* descriptive

**de'scritto** *pp di* descrivere

**de'scrivere** *vt* describe

**descri'vibile** *a* describable

**descrizi'one** *nf* description

**desensibiliz'zare** *vt* desensitize

**desensibilizzazi'one** *nf* desensitization

**de'sertico** *a* desert

**de'serto** *a* uninhabited ● *nm* desert

**deside'rabile** *a* desirable

**deside'rare** *vt* wish; ⟨*volere*⟩ want; ⟨*intensamente*⟩ long for; ⟨*bramare*⟩ desire; **desidera?** what would you like?, can I help you?; **lasciare a ~** leave a lot to be desired

**deside'rato** *a* intended

**desi'derio** *nm* wish; ⟨*brama*⟩ desire; ⟨*intenso*⟩ longing

**deside'roso** *a* desirous; ⟨*bramoso*⟩ longing

**desi'gnare** *vt* appoint, designate; ⟨*fissare*⟩ fix

**desi'gnato** *a* designate *attrib*

**designazi'one** *nf* appointment

**de'signer** *nmf inv* designer

**desi'nare** *vi* dine ● *nm* dinner

**desi'nenza** *nf* ending

**de'sistere** *vi* **~ da** desist from

'**desktop 'publishing** *nm inv* desktop publishing, DTP

**deso'lante** *a* distressing

**deso'lare** *vt* distress

**deso'lato** *a* desolate; ⟨*spiacente*⟩ sorry; **siamo desolati di dovervi comunicare che...** ⟨*in lettere*⟩ we are sorry to have to inform you that...

**desolazi'one** *nf* desolation

'**despota** *nm* despot

**desqua'marsi** *vr* flake off

**desquamazi'one** *nf* flaking off

**destabiliz'zante** *a* destabilizing

**destabiliz'zare** *vt* destabilize

**destabilizzazi'one** *nf* destabilization

**de'stare** *vt* waken; *fig* awaken

**de'starsi** *vr* waken; *fig* awaken

**desti'nare** *vt* destine; ⟨*nominare*⟩ appoint; ⟨*assegnare*⟩ assign; ⟨*indirizzare*⟩ address

**destina'tario** *nm* ⟨*di lettera, pacco*⟩ addressee

**desti'nato** *a* **essere ~ a fare qcsa** be destined *or* fated to do sth

**destinazi'one** *nf* destination; *fig* purpose; **con ~ Parigi** ⟨*aereo, treno*⟩ destined for Paris

**de'stino** *nm* destiny; ⟨*fato*⟩ fate

**destitu'ire** *vt* dismiss

**destitu'ito** *a* **~ di** devoid of

**destituzi'one** *nf* dismissal

'**desto** *a liter* awake

'**destra** *nf* ⟨*parte*⟩ right; ⟨*mano*⟩ right hand; **prendere a ~** turn right; **a ~** ⟨*essere*⟩ on the right; ⟨*andare*⟩ to the right; **la prima a ~** the first on the right; **di ~** *Pol* right wing; **la ~** *Pol* the Right

**destreggi'are** *vi* manoeuvre

**destreggi'arsi** *vr* manoeuvre

**de'strezza** *nf* dexterity; ⟨*abilità*⟩ skill

'**destro** *a* right; ⟨*abile*⟩ skilful

**de'stroide** *a Pol* right-wing

**destruttu'rato** *a* ⟨*incoerente*⟩ unstructured

**desu'eto** *a* obsolete

**de'sumere** *vt* ⟨*congetturare*⟩ infer; ⟨*ricavare*⟩ obtain

**desu'mibile** *a* inferable

**detas'sare** *vt* abolish the tax on

**detassazi'one** *nf* abolition of tax

**detei'nato** *a* tannin free

**dete'nere** *vt* hold; ⟨*polizia:*⟩ detain

**deten'tivo** *a* **pena detentiva** custodial sentence

**deten|'tore, -'trice** *nmf* holder. **~ del titolo** title-holder

**dete'nuto, -a** *nmf* prisoner

**detenzi'one** *nf* detention

**deter'gente** *a* cleaning; ⟨*latte, crema*⟩ cleansing ●*nm* detergent; (*per la pelle*) cleanser

**deteriora'mento** *nm* deterioration

**deterio'rare** *vt* cause to deteriorate ⟨*cibo, relazione*⟩

**deterio'rarsi** *vr* deteriorate

**determi'nabile** *a* determinable

**determinabilità** *nf* determinability

**determi'nante** *a* decisive

**determi'nare** *vt* determine

**determi'narsi** *vr* ~ **a** resolve to

**determina'tezza** *nf* determination

**determina'tivo** *a* ⟨*articolo*⟩ definite; **pronome** ~ determiner

**determi'nato** *a* (*risoluto*) determined; (*particolare*) specific; (*stabilito*) certain

**determinazi'one** *nf* determination; (*decisione*) decision

**determi'nismo** *nm* determinism

**deter'rente** *a* & *nm* deterrent

**deter'sivo** *nm* detergent. ~ **biologico** biological powder. ~ **per bucato** washing powder. ~ **per i piatti** washing-up liquid, dishwashing liquid *Am*

**dete'stare** *vt* detest, hate

**dete'starsi** *vr* hate oneself

**deto'nare** *vi* detonate

**detona'tore** *nm* detonator

**detonazi'one** *nf* detonation

**detra'ibile** *a* deductible

**de'trarre** *vt* deduct (**da** from)

**de'tratto** *pp di* **detrarre** ●*a* deducted

**detrat'tore, -'trice** *nmf* detractor

**detrazi'one** *nf* deduction; (*da tasse*) tax allowance

**detri'mento** *nm* detriment; **a** ~ **di** to the detriment of

**de'trito** *nm* debris; **detriti** *pl* (*di fiume*) detritus. ~ **di falda** scree

**detroniz'zare** *vt* dethrone

**'detta** *nf* **a** ~ **di** according to

**dettagli'ante** *nmf Comm* retailer

**dettagli'are** *vt* detail

**dettagliata'mente** *adv* in detail

**det'taglio** *nm* detail; **al** ~ *Comm* retail

**det'tame** *nm* dictate; **i dettami della moda** the dictates of fashion

**det'tare** *vt* dictate; ~ **legge** *fig* lay down the law

**det'tato** *nm Sch* dictation

**detta'tura** *nf* dictation

**'detto** *a* said; (*chiamato*) called; (*soprannominato*) nicknamed; ~ **fatto** no sooner said than done ●*nm* ~ [**popolare**] saying

**detur'pare** *vt* disfigure

**deturpazi'one** *nf* disfigurement

**deumidifi'care** *vt* dehumidify

**deumidifica'tore** *nm* dehumidifier

**deumidificazi'one** *nf* dehumidification

**devalutazi'one** *nf* devaluation

**deva'stante** *a* devastating

**deva'stare** *vt* devastate

**deva'stato** *a* devastated

**devasta'tore, -'trice** *a* destructive: *fig* devastating ●*nmf* destroyer

**devastazi'one** *nf* devastation: *fig* ravages *pl*

**devi'ante** *a* deviant

**devi'anza** *nf* deviance

**devi'are** *vi* deviate ●*vt* divert

**devi'ato** *a* ⟨*mente*⟩ warped

**deviazi'one** *nf* deviation; (*stradale*) diversion; **fare una** ~ *Auto* make a detour

**devitaliz'zare** *vt* kill the nerve of, devitalize *fml*

**devitalizzazi'one** *nf* killing of the nerve, devitalization *fml*

**devo'luto** *pp di* **devolvere** ●*a* devolved

**devoluzi'one** *nf* devolution

**de'volvere** *vt* devolve; ~ **qcsa in beneficenza** give sth to charity

**devota'mente** *adv* devoutly

**de'voto** *a* devout; (*affezionato*) devoted

**devozi'one** *nf* devotion

**dg** *abbr* (**decigrammi**) decigrams

**di** *prep* of; (*partitivo*) some; (*scritto da*) by; ⟨*parlare, pensare ecc*⟩ about; (*con causa, mezzo*) with; (*con provenienza*) from; (*in comparazioni*) than; (*con infinito*) to; **la casa di mio padre/dei miei genitori** my father's house/my parents' house; **compra del pane** buy some bread; **hai del pane?** do you have any bread?; **un film di guerra** a war film; **piangere di dolore** cry with pain; **coperto di neve** covered with snow; **sono di Genova** I'm from Genoa; **uscire di casa** leave one's house; **mi è uscito di mente** it slipped my mind; **più alto di te** taller than you; **è ora di partire** it's time to go; **crede di aver ragione** he thinks he's right; **dire di sì** say yes; **di domenica** on Sundays; **di sera** in the evening; **una pausa di un'ora** an hour's break; **un corso di due mesi** a two-month course

**dia'bete** *nm* diabetes

**dia'betico, -a** *a* & *nmf* diabetic

**diabolica'mente** *adv* devilishly

**dia'bolico** *a* diabolic[al]

**di'acono** *nm* deacon

**dia'critico** *a* diacritic

**dia'dema** *nm* diadem; (*di donna*) tiara

**di'afano** *a* diaphanous

**dia'framma** *nm* diaphragm; (*divisione*) screen

**di'agnosi** *nf inv* diagnosis

**dia'gnostica** *nf Med* diagnostics

**diagnosti'care** *vt* diagnose

**dia'gnostici** *nmpl Comput* diagnostics

**dia'gnostico** *a* diagnostic

**diago'nale** *a* & *nf* diagonal

**diagonal'mente** *adv* diagonally

**dia'gramma** *nm* diagram. ~ **a barre** bar chart. ~ **di flusso** flowchart

**dialet'tale** *a* dialect *attrib*; **poesia** ~ poetry in dialect

**dialettaleggi'ante** *a* dialect *attrib*

**dia'lettica** *nf* dialectics

**dia'lettico** *a* dialectic

**dia'letto** *nm* dialect

**di'alisi** *nf* dialysis

**dialo'gante** *a* **unità ~** *Comput* interactive terminal

**dialo'gare** *vt* write the dialogue for ‹*scena*› ● *vi* **~ con** converse with

**dialo'gato** *a* in dialogue

**dialo'ghista** *nmf* (*scrittore*) dialogue writer

**di'alogo** *nm* dialogue

**dia'mante** *nm* diamond

**diaman'tifero** *a* diamond bearing

**diametral'mente** *adv* diametrically

**di'ametro** *nm* diameter

**di'amine** *int* **che ~...** what on earth...

**di'apason** *nm inv* (*per accordatura*) tuning fork

**diaposi'tiva** *nf* slide

**di'aria** *nf* daily allowance

**di'ario** *nm* diary. **~ di bordo** logbook. **~ di classe** class register

**dia'rista** *nmf* (*scrittore*) diarist

**diar'rea** *nf* diarrhoea

**di'aspora** *nf* Diaspora

**dia'triba** *nf* diatribe

**diavole'ria** *nf* (*azione*) devilment; (*marchingegno*) weird contraption

**diavo'letto** *nm* imp; (*hum: bambino*) little devil

**di'avolo** *nm* devil; **va' al ~!** *fam* go to hell!; **che ~ fai?** *fam* what the hell are you doing?

**di'battere** *vt* debate

**di'battersi** *vr* struggle

**dibattimen'tale** *a Jur* of the hearing

**dibatti'mento** *nm* (*discussione*) debate; *Jur* hearing

**di'battito** *nm* debate; (*meno formale*) discussion

**dica'stero** *nm* office

**di'cembre** *nm* December

**dice'ria** *nf* rumour

**dichia'rare** *vt* state; (*ufficialmente*) declare; **~ colpevole** *Jur* convict; **niente da ~?** anything to declare?

**dichia'rarsi** *vr* (*in amore*) declare one's love; **~ soddisfatto** declare oneself satisfied; **si dichiara innocente** he says he's innocent; **~ a favore di qcsa** declare oneself in favour of sth; **si dichiara che...** (*in documenti*) it is hereby declared that...; **~ vinto** acknowledge defeat

**dichia'rato** *a* avowed

**dichiarazi'one** *nf* statement; (*documento, di guerra, d'amore*) declaration; **fare una ~** (*ufficialmente*) make a statement. **~ dei diritti** *Pol* bill of rights. **~ doganale** customs declaration. **~ dei redditi** [income] tax return

**dician'nove** *a & nm* nineteen

**dicianno'venne** *a & nmf* nineteen-year-old

**dicianno'vesimo** *a & nm* nineteenth

**dicias'sette** *a & nm* seventeen

**diciasset'tenne** *a & nmf* seventeen-year-old

**diciasset'tesimo** *a & nm* seventeenth

**diciot'tenne** *a & nmf* eighteen-year-old

**diciot'tesimo** *a & nm* eighteenth

**dici'otto** *a & nm* eighteen

**dici'tura** *nf* wording

**dicoto'mia** *nf* dichotomy

**didasca'lia** *nf* (*di film*) subtitle; (*di illustrazione*) caption; *Theat* stage direction

**dida'scalico** *a* ‹*letteratura*› didactic

**di'dattica** *nf* didactics

**didattica'mente** *adv* didactically

**di'dattico** *a* didactic; ‹*televisione*› educational

**di'dentro** *adv* inside

**didi'etro** *adv* behind ● *nm hum* hindquarters *pl*

**di'eci** *a & nm* ten

**dieci'mila** *a & nm* ten thousand

**die'cina** = **decina**

**di'eresi** *nf* diaeresis

**'diesel** *a & nm inv* diesel

**di'esis** *nm inv* sharp

**di'eta** *nf* diet; **a ~ on** a diet

**die'tetica** *nf* dietetics

**die'tetico** *a* diet

**die'tista** *nmf* dietician

**die'tologo** *nmf* dietician

**di'etro** *adv* behind ● *prep* behind; (*dopo*) after ● *a* back; (*di zampe*) hind ● *nm* back; **le stanze di ~** the back rooms; **le zampe di ~** the hind legs

**dietro'front** *nm inv* about-turn; *fig* U-turn; **~!** about turn!

**dietrolo'gia** *nf* investigative journalism

**di'fatti** *adv* in fact

**di'fendere** *vt* defend

**di'fendersi** *vr* defend oneself; (*fam: cavarsela*) get by

**difen'dibile** *a* defendable, defensible

**difen'siva** *nf* **stare sulla ~** be on the defensive

**difen'sivo** *a* defensive

**difen'sore** *a* **avvocato ~** defence counsel ● *nm* defender. **~ civico** ombudsman

**di'fesa** *nf* defence; **prendere le difese di qcno** come to sb's defence. **~ civile** Civil Defence

**di'feso** *pp di* **difendere** ● *a* defended; ‹*luogo*› sheltered

**difet'tare** *vi* be defective; **~ di** lack

**difet'tivo** *a* defective

**di'fetto** *nm* defect; (*morale*) fault, flaw; (*mancanza*) lack; (*in tessuto, abito*) flaw; **essere in ~** be at fault; **far ~** be lacking

**difet'toso** *a* defective; ‹*abito*› flawed

**diffa'mare** *vt* (*con parole*) slander; (*per iscritto*) libel

**diffama|'tore, -'trice** *nmf* slanderer; (*per iscritto*) libeller

**diffama'torio** *a* slanderous; (*per iscritto*) libellous

**diffamazi'one** *nf* slander; (*scritta*) libel

**diffe'rente** *a* different

**differente'mente** *adv* differently

**diffe'renza** *nf* difference; **a ~ di** unlike; **non fare ~** make no distinction (**fra** between)

**differenzi'abile** *a* differentiable

**differenzi'ale** *a* & *nm* differential

**differenzi'are** *vt* differentiate

**differenzi'arsi** *vr* **~ da** differ from

**differenzi'ato** *a* differentiated

**differenziazi'one** *nf* differentiation

**diffe'ribile** *a* postponable

**diffe'rire** *vt* postpone ● *vi* be different

**diffe'rita** *nf* **in ~** *TV* prerecorded

**dif'ficile** *a* difficult; (*duro*) hard; (*improbabile*) unlikely ● *nm* difficulty

**difficil'mente** *adv* with difficulty

**difficoltà** *nf* difficulty; **trovarsi in ~** be in trouble; **mettere qcno in ~** put sb on the spot

**dif'fida** *nf* warning

**diffi'dare** *vi* **~ di** distrust ● *vt* warn

**diffi'dente** *a* mistrustful

**diffi'denza** *nf* mistrust

**dif'fondere** *vt* spread; diffuse (*calore, luce ecc*)

**dif'fondersi** *vr* spread

**difformità** *nf inv* deformation; (*di opinioni*) difference of opinion

**diffusa'mente** *adv* at length

**diffusi'one** *nf* diffusion; (*di giornale*) circulation

**dif'fuso** *pp di* **diffondere** ● *a* common; (*malattia*) widespread; (*luce*) diffuse

**diffu'sore** *nm* (*per asciugacapelli*) diffuser

**difi'lato** *adv* straight; (*subito*) straightaway

**di'fronte** *a inv* & *adv* opposite; **~ all'ingresso** in front of the entrance; (*dall'altro lato della strada*) opposite the entrance

**difte'rite** *nf* diphtheria

**'diga** *nf* dam; (*argine*) dike

**dige'rente** *a* alimentary

**dige'ribile** *a* digestible

**digeribilità** *nf* digestibility

**dige'rire** *vt* digest; *fam* stomach

**digesti'one** *nf* digestion

**dige'stivo** *a* digestive ● *nm* digestive; (*dopo cena*) liqueur

**Digi'one** *nf* Dijon

**digi'tale** *a* digital; (*delle dita*) finger *attrib* ● *nf* (*fiore*) foxglove

**digitalizzazi'one** *nf* digitalizing

**digi'tare** *vt* key in (*dati*)

**digiu'nare** *vi* fast

**digi'uno** *a* essere **~** have an empty stomach ● *nm* fast; **a ~** (*bere ecc*) on an empty stomach

**dignità** *nf* dignity

**digni'tario** *nm* dignitary

**dignitosa'mente** *adv* with dignity

**digni'toso** *a* dignified

**DIGOS** *nf abbr* (**Divisione Investigazioni Generali e Operazioni Speciali**) ≈ riot police

**digressi'one** *nf* digression

**digri'gnare** *vi* **~ i denti** grind one's teeth

**digros'sare** *vt fig* impart basic concepts to

**dik'tat** *nm inv* (*trattato*) diktat

**dila'gare** *vi* flood; *fig* spread

**dilani'are** *vt* tear to pieces

**dilapi'dare** *vt* squander

**dilapidazi'one** *nf* squandering

**dila'tare** *vt* dilate

**dila'tarsi** *vr* dilate; (*legno*) swell; (*metallo, gas*) expand

**dila'tato** *a* dilated; (*legno*) swollen; (*metallo, gas*) expanded

**dilatazi'one** *nf* dilation; (*di legno*) swelling; (*di metallo, gas*) expansion

**dilazio'nabile** *a* postponable

**dilazio'nare** *vt* delay

**dilazi'one** *nf* delay

**dileggi'are** *vt* mock

**dilegu'are** *vt* disperse

**dilegu'arsi** *vr* disappear

**di'lemma** *nm* dilemma

**dilet'tante** *nmf* amateur

**dilettan'tesco** *a* amateurish

**dilettan'tismo** *nm* amateurism

**dilettan'tistico** *a* amateurish

**dilet'tare** *vt* delight

**dilet'tarsi** *vr* **~ di** delight in

**dilet'tevole** *a* delightful

**di'letto, -a** *a* beloved ● *nm* (*piacere*) delight ● *nmf* (*persona*) beloved

**dili'gente** *a* diligent; (*lavoro*) accurate

**dili'genza** *nf* diligence

**dilu'ente** *nm* diluent

**dilu'ire** *vt* dilute

**diluizi'one** *nf* dilution

**dilun'gare** *vt* prolong

**dilun'garsi** *vr* **~ su** dwell on (*argomento*)

**diluvi'are** *vi* pour [down]

**di'luvio** *nm* downpour; *fig* flood. **il ~ universale** the Flood

**dima'grante** *a* slimming, diet

**dimagri'mento** *nm* loss of weight

**dima'grire** *vi* lose weight

**dima'grirsi** *vr* lose weight

**dime'nare** *vt* wave; wag (*coda*)

**dime'narsi** *vr* be agitated

**dimensio'nare** *vt fig* get into proportion

**dimensi'one** *nf* dimension; (*misura*) size

**dimenti'canza** *nf* forgetfulness; (*svista*) oversight; **per ~** accidentally

**dimenti'care** *vt* forget; **l'ho dimenticato a casa** I left it at home

**dimenti'carsi** *vr* **~ [di]** forget

**dimentica'toio** *nm* **andare/finire nel ~** *hum* fall into oblivion

**di'mentico** *a* **~ di** (*che non ricorda*) forgetful of; (*non curante*) oblivious of

**dimessa'mente** *adv* modestly

**di'messo** *pp di* **dimettere** ● *a* humble; (*trasandato*) shabby; (*voce*) low

**dimesti'chezza** *nf* familiarity

**di'mettere** *vt* dismiss; (*da ospedale ecc*) discharge

**di'mettersi** *vr* resign

**dimez'zare** *vt* halve

**diminu'ire** *vt/i* diminish; (*in maglia*) decrease

**diminu'ito** *a Mus* diminished
**diminu'tivo** *a* & *nm* diminutive
**diminuzi'one** *nf* decrease; (*riduzione*) reduction: **in ~** dwindling
**dimissio'nario** *a* outgoing ● *nmf* outgoing chairman/president etc
**dimissi'oni** *nfpl* resignation *sg*; **dare le ~** resign
**di'mora** *nf* residence
**dimo'rare** *vi* reside
**dimo'strabile** *a* demonstrable
**dimostrabilità** *nf* demonstrability
**dimo'strante** *nmf* demonstrator
**dimo'strare** *vt* demonstrate; (*provare*) prove; (*mostrare*) show
**dimo'strarsi** *vr* prove [to be]
**dimostra'tivo** *a* demonstrative
**dimostrazi'one** *nf* demonstration; *Math* proof
**di'namica** *nf* dynamics; **~ dei fatti** sequence of events
**di'namico** *a* dynamic
**dina'mismo** *nm* dynamism
**dinami'tardo** *a* **attentato ~** bomb attack ● *nmf* bomber
**dina'mite** *nf* dynamite
**'dinamo** *nf inv* dynamo
**di'nanzi** *adv* in front ● *prep* **~ a** in front of
**'dinaro** *nm* (*moneta*) dinar
**dina'stia** *nf* dynasty
**di'nastico** *a* dynastic
**din'don** *nm inv* dingdong
**'dingo** *nm* (*cane*) dingo
**dini'ego** *nm* denial
**dinocco'lato** *a* lanky
**dino'sauro** *nm* dinosaur
**din'torni** *nmpl* outskirts: **nei ~ di** in the vicinity of
**din'torno** *adv* around
**'dio** *nm* (*pl* **'dei**) god; **D~** God; **D~ mio!** my God!
**dioce'sano** *a* diocesan
**di'ocesi** *nf inv* diocese
**dioni'siaco** *a* Dionysian
**dios'sina** *nf* dioxin
**diot'tria** *nf* dioptre
**dipa'nare** *vt* wind into a ball; *fig* unravel
**diparti'mento** *nm* department
**dipen'dente** *a* depending ● *nmf* employee
**dipen'denza** *nf* dependence; (*edificio*) annexe
**di'pendere** *vi* **~ da** depend on; (*provenire*) derive from; **dipende** it depends
**di'pingere** *vt* paint; (*descrivere*) describe
**di'pinto** *pp di* **dipingere** ● *a* painted ● *nm* painting
**di'ploma** *nm* diploma
**diplo'mare** *vt* graduate
**diplo'marsi** *vr* graduate
**diplomatica'mente** *adv* diplomatically
**diplo'matico** *a* diplomatic ● *nm* diplomat; (*pasticcino*) millefeuille (*with alcohol*)
**diplo'mato** *nmf* person with school qualification ● *a* qualified
**diploma'zia** *nf* diplomacy

**di'porto** *nm* **imbarcazione da ~** pleasure craft
**dirada'mento** *nf* thinning out
**dira'dare** *vt* thin out; make less frequent (*visite*)
**dira'darsi** *vr* thin out; ⟨nebbia:⟩ clear
**dira'mare** *vt* issue
**dira'marsi** *vr* branch out
**diramazi'one** *nf* (*di strada, fiume*) fork; (*di albero, impresa*) branch; (*di ordine*) issuing
**'dire** *vt* say; (*raccontare, riferire*) tell; **~ quello che si pensa** speak one's mind; **voler ~** mean; **volevo ben ~!** I wondered!; **~ di sì/no** say yes/no; **si dice che...** rumour has it that...; **come si dice "casa" in inglese?** what's the English for "casa"?; **questo nome mi dice qualcosa** the name rings a bell; **che ne dici di...?** how about...?; **non c'è che ~** there's no disputing that; **e ~ che...** to think that...; **a dir poco/tanto** at least/most ● *vi* **~ bene/male di** speak highly/ill of sb; **dica pure** (*in negozio*) how can I help you?; **dici sul serio?** are you serious?; **per modo di ~** as it were
**di'retta** *nf TV* live broadcast; **in ~** live
**diretta'mente** *adv* directly
**diret'tissima** *nf* (*strada*) main route; **per ~** *Jur* (*processare*) without going through the normal procedures
**diret'tissimo** *nm* fast train
**diret'tiva** *nf* directive; **direttive** *pl* (*indicazioni*) guidelines
**diret'tivo** *a* (*dirigente*) management *attrib*, managerial ● *nm Pol* executive
**di'retto** *pp di* **dirigere** ● *a* direct; **il mio ~ superiore** my immediate superior; **~ a** (*inteso*) meant for; **essere ~ a** be heading for; **in diretta** (*trasmissione*) live ● *nm* (*treno*) through train
**diret'tore** *nm* manager; (*più in alto nella gerarchia*) director; (*di scuola*) headmaster. **~ amministrativo** company secretary. **~ artistico** artistic director. **~ del carcere** prison governor. **~ di filiale** branch manager. **~ di gara** referee. **~ generale** managing director, chief executive officer. **~ di giornale** newspaper editor. **~ d'istituto** *Univ* department head. **~ d'orchestra** conductor. **~ del personale** personnel manager/director. **~ di produzione** production manager/director. **~ spirituale** spiritual advisor. **~ sportivo** team manager. **~ tecnico** *Sport* manager. **~ di zona** area manager; regional director
**diret'trice** *nf* manageress; (*di scuola*) headmistress; (*indirizzo*) guiding principle
**direzio'nale** *a* directional
**direzio'nare** *vt* direct
**direzi'one** *nf* direction; (*di società*) management; *Sch* headmaster's/headmistress's office (*primary school*); **in ~ nord** (*traffico*) northbound; **'tutte le direzioni'** *Auto* 'all routes'
**diri'gente** *a* ruling ● *nmf* executive. **~ di partito** *Pol* party leader

**diri'genza** *nf* management; *Pol* leadership.
~ **aziendale** business management

**dirigenzi'ale** *a* management *attrib*, managerial

**di'rìgere** *vt* direct; conduct ⟨*orchestra*⟩; run ⟨*impresa*⟩

**di'rigersi** *vr* ~ **verso** head for

**diri'gìbile** *nm* airship

**dirim'petto** *adv* opposite ● *prep* ~ **a** facing

**di'ritto¹** *a* straight; (*destro*) right ● *adv* straight; **andare** ~ go straight on; **sempre** ~ straight ahead, straight on ● *nm* right side: *Tennis* forehand; **fare un** ~ (*a maglia*) knit one

**di'ritto²** *nm* right; *Jur* law. **diritti** *pl* **d'autore** royalties. ~ **civile** civil law. **diritti** *pl* **civili** civil rights. ~ **commerciale** commercial law. ~ **penale** criminal law. **diritti** *pl* **di prelievo** *Fin* drawing rights. **diritti** *pl* **umani** human rights. ~ **di voto** right to vote, suffrage

**dirit'tura** *nf* straight line; *fig* honesty. ~ **d'arrivo** *Sport, fig* home straight

**diroc'cato** *a* tumbledown

**dirom'pente** *a anche fig* explosive

**dirotta'mento** *nm* hijacking

**dirot'tare** *vt* reroute ⟨*treno, aereo*⟩; (*illegalmente*) hijack; divert ⟨*traffico*⟩ ● *vi* alter course

**dirotta|'tore, -'trice** *nmf* hijacker

**di'rotto** *a* ⟨*pioggia*⟩ pouring; ⟨*pianto*⟩ uncontrollable; **piovere a** ~ rain heavily

**di'rupo** *nm* precipice

**di'sàbile** *a* disabled ● *nmf* disabled person

**disabili'tare** *vt* disable

**disabi'tato** *a* uninhabited

**disabitu'arsi** *vr* ~ **a** get out of the habit of

**disac'cordo** *nm* disagreement

**disadatta'mento** *nm* maladjustment

**disadat'tato, -a** *a* maladjusted ● *nmf* misfit

**disa'dorno** *a* unadorned

**disaffezi'one** *nf* disaffection

**disa'gevole** *a* (*scomodo*) uncomfortable; (*difficile*) inconvenient

**disagi'ato** *a* poor; ⟨*vita*⟩ hard; (*scomodo*) uncomfortable

**di'sagio** *nm* discomfort; (*difficoltà*) inconvenience; (*imbarazzo*) embarrassment; **sentirsi a** ~ feel uncomfortable; **disagi** *pl* (*privazioni*) hardships

**di'samina** *nf* close examination

**disamora'mento** *nm* estrangement

**disanco'rare** *vt Fin* de-link

**disappro'vare** *vt* disapprove of

**disapprovazi'one** *nf* disapproval

**disap'punto** *nm* disappointment; **con suo grande** ~ [much] to his chagrin

**disarcio'nare** *vt* unseat

**disar'mante** *a fig* disarming

**disar'mare** *vt/i* disarm

**disar'mato** *a* disarmed; *fig* defenceless

**di'sarmo** *nm* disarmament

**disartico'lato** *a fig* disjointed

**disa'strato, -a** *a* devastated ● *nmf* victim (*of flood, earthquake ecc*)

**di'sastro** *nm* disaster; (*fam: grande confusione*) mess; (*fam: persona*) disaster area

**disastrosa'mente** *adv* disastrously

**disa'stroso** *a* disastrous

**disat'tento** *a* inattentive

**disattenzi'one** *nf* inattention; (*svista*) oversight

**disatti'vare** *vt* de-activate

**disa'vanzo** *nm* deficit

**disavve'duto** *a* thoughtless

**disavven'tura** *nf* misadventure

**disavver'tenza** *nf* inadvertence

**di'sbrigo** *nm* dispatch

**di'scapito** *nm* **a** ~ **di** to the detriment of

**di'scarica** *nf* scrap-yard

**di'scarico** *nm* (*di merce*) unloading; **prova a** ~ evidence for the defence; **testimone a** ~ witness for the defence

**discen'dente** *a* descending ● *nmf* descendant

**discen'denza** *nf* descent; (*discendenti*) descendants *pl*

**di'scendere** *vi* (*dal treno*) get off; (*da cavallo*) dismount; (*sbarcare*) land. ~ **da** (*trarre origine da*) be a descendant of ● *vt* descend

**discen'sore** *nm* (*attrezzo*) karabiner

**di'scepolo, -a** *nmf* disciple

**di'scernere** *vt* discern

**discerni'mento** *nm* discernment

**di'scesa** *nf* descent; (*pendio*) slope; ~ **in picchiata** (*di aereo*) nosedive; **essere in** ~ ⟨*strada:*⟩ go downhill. ~ **libera** (*in sci*) downhill race

**disce'sista** *nmf* (*sciatore*) downhill skier

**di'sceso** *pp di* **discendere**

**di'schetto** *nm Comput* diskette

**dischi'udere** *vt* open; (*svelare*) disclose

**dischi'udersi** *vr* open up

**di'scinto** *a* scantily dressed

**disci'ogliere** *vt* dissolve; thaw ⟨*neve*⟩; (*fondere*) melt

**disci'ogliersi** *vr* dissolve; ⟨*neve:*⟩ thaw; (*fondersi*) melt

**disci'olto** *pp di* **disciogliere**

**disci'plina** *nf* discipline

**discipli'nare** *a* disciplinary ● *vt* discipline

**discipli'nato** *a* disciplined

**disc-'jockey** *nm inv* disc jockey, DJ

**'disco** *nm* disc; *Sport* discus; *Mus* record; **ernia del** ~ slipped disc. ~ **a 33 giri** LP. ~ **a 45 giri** single. ~ **fisso** *Comput* fixed disk, hard disk. ~ **dei freni** brake disc. ~ **master** *Comput* master disk. ~ **rigido** *Comput* hard disk. ~ **volante** flying saucer

**discogra'fia** *nf* (*insieme di incisioni*) discography; (*industria*) record industry

**disco'grafico** *a* ⟨*industria*⟩ record *attrib*, recording; ⟨*mercato, raccolta*⟩ record *attrib*; **casa discografica** record company, recording company ● *nmf* record producer

**'discolo** *nmf* rascal ● *a* unruly

**di'scolpa** *nf* clearing; **a sua ~ si deve dire che...** in his defence it must be said that...

**discol'pare** *vt* clear

**discol'parsi** *vr* clear oneself

**disco'noscere** *vt* deny; disown ⟨*figlio*⟩

**discontinuità** *nf inv* ⟨*nel lavoro*⟩ irregularity; ⟨*di stile*⟩ unevenness

**discon'tinuo** *a* intermittent; ⟨*fig: impegno, rendimento*⟩ uneven

**discopa'tia** *nf* disc problems *pl*

**discor'dante** *a* discordant

**discor'danza** *nf* discordance; **essere in ~** clash

**discor'dare** *vi* ⟨*opinioni:*⟩ conflict

**di'scorde** *a* clashing

**di'scordia** *nf* discord; ⟨*dissenso*⟩ dissension

**di'scorrere** *vi* talk (**di** about)

**discor'sivo** *a* colloquial

**di'scorso** *pp di* **discorrere** ● *nm* speech; ⟨*conversazione*⟩ talk. **~ di ringraziamento** vote of thanks

**di'scosto** *a* distant ● *adv* far away; **stare ~** stand apart

**disco'teca** *nf* disco; ⟨*raccolta*⟩ record library

**discote'caro** *nmf pej* disco freak

**di'scount** *nm inv* discount store

**discredi'tare** *vt* discredit

**di'scredito** *nm* discredit

**discre'pante** *a* contradictory

**discre'panza** *nf* discrepancy

**di'screto** *a* discreet; ⟨*moderato*⟩ moderate; ⟨*abbastanza buono*⟩ fairly good

**discrezionalità** *nf* discretion

**discrezi'one** *nf* discretion; ⟨*giudizio*⟩ judgement; **a ~ di** at the discretion of

**discrimi'nante** *a* extenuating ● *nf Jur* extenuating circumstances *pl*

**discrimi'nare** *vt* discriminate

**discrimina'tivo** *a* ⟨*provvedimento*⟩ discriminatory

**discrimina'torio** *a* ⟨*atteggiamento*⟩ discriminatory

**discriminazi'one** *nf* discrimination

**discussi'one** *nf* discussion; ⟨*alterco*⟩ argument; **messa in ~** questioning

**di'scusso** *pp di* **discutere** ● *a* controversial

**di'scutere** *vt* discuss; ⟨*formale*⟩ debate; ⟨*litigare*⟩ argue ● *vi* **~ su qcsa** discuss sth

**discu'tibile** *a* debatable; ⟨*gusto*⟩ questionable

**disde'gnare** *vt* disdain

**di'sdegno** *nm* disdain

**disde'gnoso** *a* disdainful

**di'sdetta** *nf* retraction; ⟨*sfortuna*⟩ bad luck; *Comm* cancellation

**di'sdetto** *pp di* **disdire**

**disdi'cevole** *a* unbecoming

**di'sdire** *vt* retract; ⟨*annullare*⟩ cancel

**disedu'care** *vt* have a bad effect on

**diseduca'tivo** *a* bad for children

**dise'gnare** *vt* draw; ⟨*progettare*⟩ design

**disegna|'tore, -'trice** *nmf* designer. **~ di moda** fashion designer

**di'segno** *nm* drawing; ⟨*progetto, linea*⟩ design. **~ di legge** bill

**diser'bante** *nm* herbicide, weed-killer ● *a* herbicidal, weed-killing

**diser'bare** *vt* weed

**disere'dare** *vt* disinherit

**disere'dato** *a* dispossessed ● *nmf* **i diseredati** the dispossessed

**diser'tare** *vt/i* desert; **~ la scuola** stay away from school

**diser'tore** *nm* deserter

**diserzi'one** *nf* desertion

**disfaci'mento** *nm* decay; *fig* decline; **in ~** decaying; *fig* in decline

**di'sfare** *vt* undo; strip ⟨*letto*⟩; ⟨*smantellare*⟩ take down; ⟨*annientare*⟩ defeat; **~ le valigie** unpack [one's bags]

**di'sfarsi** *vr* fall to pieces; ⟨*sciogliersi*⟩ melt; **~ di** ⟨*liberarsi di*⟩ get rid of; **~ in lacrime** dissolve into tears

**di'sfatta** *nf* defeat

**disfat'tismo** *nm* defeatism

**disfat'tista** *a & nmf* defeatist

**di'sfatto** *a fig* worn out

**disfunzi'one** *nf* disorder

**disge'lare** *vt/i* thaw

**disge'larsi** *vr* thaw

**di'sgelo** *nm* thaw

**disgi'ungere** *vt* disconnect

**disgi'unto** *a* ⟨*firme*⟩ separate

**di'sgrazia** *nf* misfortune; ⟨*incidente*⟩ accident; ⟨*sfavore*⟩ disgrace

**disgraziata'mente** *adv* unfortunately

**disgrazi'ato, -a** *a* unfortunate ● *nmf* wretch

**disgrega'mento** *nm* disintegration

**disgre'gare** *vt* break up

**disgre'garsi** *vr* disintegrate

**disgrega'tivo** *a* disintegrating

**disgrega'tore** *a* disintegrating

**disgregazi'one** *nf* ⟨*di società*⟩ break-up

**disgu'ido** *nm* **~ postale** mistake in delivery

**disgu'stare** *vt* disgust

**disgu'starsi** *vr* **~ di** be disgusted by

**di'sgusto** *nm* disgust

**disgustosa'mente** *adv* disgustingly; **~ dolce** nauseatingly sweet

**disgu'stoso** *a* disgusting

**disidra'tante** *a* dehydrating

**disidra'tare** *vt* dehydrate

**disidra'tarsi** *vr* become dehydrated

**disidra'tato** *a* dehydrated

**disidratazi'one** *nf* dehydration

**disil'ludere** *vt* disenchant, disillusion

**disil'ludersi** *vr* become disenchanted, become disillusioned

**disillusi'one** *nf* disenchantment, disillusionment

**disil'luso** *a* disenchanted, disillusioned

**disimbal'laggio** *nm* unpacking

**disimbal'lare** *vt* unpack

**disimpa'rare** *vt* forget

**disimpe'gnare** *vt* release; ⟨*compiere*⟩ fulfil; redeem ⟨*oggetto dato in pegno*⟩

**disimpe'gnarsi** *vr* disengage oneself: (*cavarsela*) manage

**disim'pegno** *nm* (*locale*) vestibule; (*disinteresse*) lack of interest

**disimpi'ego** *nm* re-allocation: (*di truppe*) re-assignment

**disincagli'are** *vt Naut* refloat

**disincagli'arsi** *vr Naut* float off

**disincan'tato** *a* (*disilluso*) disillusioned

**disincar'nato** *a* disembodied

**disincenti'vante** *a* demotivating

**disincenti'vare** *vt* demotivate

**disincen'tivo** *nm* disincentive

**disincroci'are** *vt* uncross

**disinfe'stare** *vt* disinfest

**disinfestazi'one** *nf* disinfestation

**disinfet'tante** *a & nm* disinfectant

**disinfet'tare** *vt* disinfect

**disinfezi'one** *nf* disinfection

**disinfiam'marsi** *vr* become less inflamed

**disinflazio'nare** *vt* disinflate

**disinflazi'one** *nf* disinflation

**disinflazio'nistico** *a* disinflationary

**disinfor'mato** *a* uninformed

**disinformazi'one** *nf* lack of information; (*informazione erronea*) misinformation

**disingan'nare** *vt* disabuse

**disin'ganno** *nm* disillusion

**disini'birsi** *vr* lose one's inhibitions

**disini'bito** *a* uninhibited

**disinne'scare** *vt* defuse

**disin'nesco** *nm* (*di bomba*) bomb disposal

**disinne'stare** *vt* disengage

**disinne'starsi** *vr* disengage

**disin'nesto** *nm* disengagement

**disinquina'mento** *nm* cleaning up

**disinqui'nare** *vt* clean up

**disinse'rire** *vt* disconnect

**disinse'rito** *a* disconnected

**disinte'grare** *vt* disintegrate

**disinte'grarsi** *vr* disintegrate

**disintegrazi'one** *nf* disintegration

**disinteressa'mento** *nm* lack of interest

**disinteres'sarsi** *vr* ~ **di** take no interest in

**disinteressata'mente** *adv* without interest; (*senza secondo fine*) disinterestedly

**disinteres'sato** *a* uninterested; (*senza secondo fine*) disinterested

**disinte'resse** *nm* indifference; (*oggettività*) disinterestedness

**disintossi'care** *vt* detoxify

**disintossi'carsi** *vr* come off drugs; ‹*alcolizzato:*› dry out

**disintossicazi'one** *nf* giving up alcohol/drugs; **programma di** ~ detox programme

**disinvolta'mente** *adv* in a relaxed way

**disin'volto** *a* relaxed

**disinvol'tura** *nf* confidence

**disi'stima** *nf* lack of respect

**disles'sia** *nf* dyslexia

**di'slessico** *a* dyslexic

**disli'vello** *nm* difference in height; *fig* inequality

**disloca'mento** *nm Mil* posting

**dislo'care** *vt Mil* post

**dismenor'rea** *nf* dysmenorrhoea

**dismi'sura** *nf* excess; **a** ~ excessively

**disobbedi'ente** *a* disobedient

**disobbe'dire** *vt* disobey

**disoccu'pato, -a** *a* unemployed ● *nmf* unemployed person

**disoccupazi'one** *nf* unemployment

**disonestà** *nf* dishonesty

**diso'nesto** *a* dishonest

**disono'rare** *vt* dishonour

**disono'rato** *a* dishonoured

**diso'nore** *nm* dishonour

**di'sopra** *adv* above ● *a* upper ● *nm* top

**disordi'nare** *vt* disarrange

**disordinata'mente** *adv* untidily

**disordi'nato** *a* untidy; (*sregolato*) immoderate

**di'sordine** *nm* disorder, untidiness; (*sregolatezza*) debauchery

**disores'sia** *nf* eating disorder

**disor'ganico** *a* inconsistent

**disorganiz'zare** *vt* disorganize

**disorganiz'zato** *a* disorganized

**disorganizzazi'one** *nf* disorganization

**disorienta'mento** *nm* disorientation

**disorien'tare** *vt* disorientate

**disorien'tarsi** *vr* lose one's bearings

**disorien'tato** *a fig* bewildered

**disos'sare** *vt* bone

**disos'sato** *a* boned

**di'sotto** *adv* below ● *a* lower ● *nm* bottom

**di'spaccio** *nm* dispatch

**dispa'rato** *a* disparate

**'dispari** *a* odd, uneven

**dispa'rire** *vi* disappear

**disparità** *nf inv* disparity

**di'sparte** *adv* **in** ~ apart; **stare in** ~ stand aside

**di'spendio** *nm* expenditure; *pej* waste

**dispendiosa'mente** *adv* extravagantly

**dispendi'oso** *a* expensive

**di'spensa** *nf* pantry; (*distribuzione*) distribution; (*mobile*) cupboard; *Jur* exemption; *Relig* dispensation; (*pubblicazione periodica*) number

**dispen'sare** *vt* distribute; (*esentare*) exonerate

**dispen'sario** *nm* dispensary

**di'spenser** *nm inv* display rack; (*confezione*) dispenser

**dispe'rare** *vi* despair (**di** of)

**dispe'rarsi** *vr* despair

**disperata'mente** *adv* ‹*piangere*› desperately; ‹*studiare*› like mad

**dispe'rato** *a* desperate

**disperazi'one** *nf* despair

**di'sperdere** *vt* scatter, disperse

**di'sperdersi** *vr* scatter, disperse

**dispersi'one** *nf* dispersion; (*di truppe*) dispersal

**disper'sivo** *a* disorganized

**di'sperso** *pp di* **disperdere** ● *a* scattered; (*smarrito*) lost ● *nm* missing soldier

**di'spetto** *nm* spite; **a** ~ **di** in spite of; **fare un** ~ **a qcno** spite sb

**dispet'toso** *a* spiteful

**dispia'cere** *nm* upset; (*rammarico*) regret; (*dolore*) sorrow; (*preoccupazione*) worry ● *vi* **mi dispiace** I'm sorry; **non mi dispiace** I don't dislike it; **se non ti dispiace** if you don't mind

**dispiaci'uto** *a* sorry

**dispie'gare** *vt* unfold

**dispie'garsi** *vr* unfurl

**dispo'nibile** *a* available; (*gentile*) helpful

**disponibilità** *nf* availability; (*gentilezza*) helpfulness. **~ pl correnti** *Fin* current assets

**di'sporre** *vt* arrange ● *vi* dispose; (*stabilire*) order; **~ di** have at one's disposal

**di'sporsi** *vr* (*in fila*) line up

**disposi'tivo** *nm* device. **~ di emergenza** emergency button/handle. **~ di puntamento** *Comput* pointing device

**disposizi'one** *nf* disposition; (*ordine*) order; (*libera disponibilità*) disposal

**di'sposto** *pp di* **disporre** ● *a* ready; (*incline*) disposed; **essere ben disposto verso** be favourably disposed towards

**dispotica'mente** *adv* despotically

**di'spotico** *a* despotic

**dispo'tismo** *nm* despotism

**dispregia'tivo** *a* disparaging

**disprez'zabile** *a* despicable

**disprez'zare** *vt* despise

**di'sprezzo** *nm* contempt

**'disputa** *nf* dispute

**dispu'tare** *vi* dispute; (*gareggiare*) compete

**dispu'tarsi** *vr* **~ qcsa** contend for sth

**disqui'sire** *vi* discourse

**disquisizi'one** *nf* disquisition

**dissa'crante** *a* debunking

**dissa'crare** *vt* debunk

**dissacra|'tore, -'trice** *nmf* debunker

**dissacra'torio** *a* debunking

**dissacrazi'one** *nf* debunking

**dissangua'mento** *nm* loss of blood; *fig* impoverishment

**dissangua're** *vt* bleed; *fig* bleed dry

**dissangu'arsi** *vr* bleed; *fig* become impoverished

**dissangu'ato** *a* bloodless; *fig* impoverished

**dissa'pore** *nm* disagreement

**dissec'care** *vt* dry up

**dissec'carsi** *vr* dry up

**dissemi'nare** *vt* disseminate; (*notizie*) spread

**dissen'nato** *a* (*politica*) senseless

**dis'senso** *nm* dissent; (*disaccordo*) disagreement

**dissente'ria** *nf* dysentery

**dissen'tire** *vi* disagree (**da** with)

**dissepelli'mento** *nm* exhumation

**dissepel'lire** *vt* exhume (*cadavere*); disinter (*rovine*); *fig* unearth

**dissertazi'one** *nf* dissertation

**disser'vizio** *nm* poor service

**disse'stare** *vt* upset; *Comm* damage

**disse'stato** *a* (*strada*) uneven; (*azienda*) shaky

**dis'sesto** *nm* ruin

**disse'tante** *a* thirst-quenching

**disse'tare** *vt* **~ qcno** quench sb's thirst

**disse'tarsi** *vr* quench one's thirst

**dissezio'nare** *vr* dissect

**dissezi'one** *nf* dissection

**dissi'dente** *a & nmf* dissident

**dissi'denza** *nf* dissidence

**dis'sidio** *nm* disagreement

**dis'simile** *a* unlike, dissimilar

**dissimu'lare** *vt* conceal

**dissimu'lato** *a* concealed

**dissimula|'tore, -'trice** *nmf* dissembler

**dissimulazi'one** *nf* concealment

**dissi'pare** *vt* dissipate; (*sperperare*) squander

**dissi'parsi** *vr* (*nebbia:*) clear; (*dubbio:*) disappear

**dissipa'tezza** *nf* dissipation

**dissi'pato** *a* dissipated

**dissipa'tore** *nm* **~ termico** heat sink

**dissipazi'one** *nf* squandering

**dissoci'abile** *a* separable

**dissoci'are** *vt* dissociate

**dissoci'arsi** *vr* dissociate oneself

**dissoci'ato, -a** *a Pol* dissenting ● *nmf Pol* dissenter

**dissociazi'one** *nf Pol* dissociation

**dissoda'mento** *nm* tillage

**disso'dare** *vt* till

**dis'solto** *pp di* **dissolvere**

**disso'lubile** *a* dissoluble

**dissolu'tezza** *nf* dissoluteness

**dissolu'tivo** *a* divisive

**disso'luto** *a* dissolute

**dissol'venza** *nf* (*di immagine*) fade-out, dissolve

**dis'solvere** *vt* dissolve; (*disperdere*) dispel

**dis'solversi** *vr* dissolve; (*disperdersi*) clear

**disso'nante** *a* dissonant

**disso'nanza** *nf* dissonance

**dissotterra'mento** *nm* disinterment

**dissotter'rare** *vt* disinter (*bara*); *fig* resurrect (*rancore*)

**dissua'dere** *vt* dissuade

**dissuasi'one** *nf* dissuasion

**dissua'sivo** *a* dissuasive

**distacca'mento** *nm Mil* detachment

**distac'care** *vt* detach; *Sport* leave behind

**distac'carsi** *vr* be detached

**distac'cato** *a* (*tono, voce*) expressionless

**di'stacco** *nm* detachment; (*separazione*) separation; *Sport* lead

**di'stante** *a* far away; (*fig: person*) detached ● *adv* far away

**di'stanza** *nf* distance

**distanzia'mento** *nm* spacing [out]; *Sport* outdistancing

**distanzi'are** *vt* space out; *Sport* outdistance

**di'stare** *vi* be distant; **quanto dista?** how far is it?; **Roma dista 20 chilometri da qui** Rome is 20 kilometres away, Rome is 20 kilometres from here

**di·'stendere** vt stretch out ⟨parte del corpo⟩; ⟨spiegare⟩ spread; ⟨deporre⟩ lay

**di·'stendersi** vr stretch; ⟨sdraiarsi⟩ lie down; ⟨rilassarsi⟩ relax

**disten·si'one** nf stretching; ⟨rilassamento⟩ relaxation; Pol détente

**disten·'sivo** a relaxing

**di·'stesa** nf expanse

**di·'steso** pp di **distendere**

**distil·'lare** vt/i distil

**distil·'lato** a distilled ● nm distillate

**distillazi·'one** nf distillation

**distille·'ria** nf distillery

**di·'stinguere** vt distinguish

**di·'stinguersi** vr ⟨per bravura ecc⟩ distinguish oneself; **si distingue dagli altri per...** it is distinguished from the others by...

**distin·'guibile** a distinguishable

**di·'stinguo** nm inv distinction

**di·'stinta** nf Comm list. **~ di pagamento** receipt. **~ di versamento** paying-in slip

**distinta·'mente** adv ⟨separatamente⟩ individually, separately; ⟨chiaramente⟩ clearly; ⟨in modo elegante⟩ in a distinguished way; **vi saluto ~** yours truly

**distin·'tivo** a distinctive ● nm badge

**di·'stinto** pp di **distinguere** ● a distinct; ⟨signorile⟩ distinguished; **distinti saluti** Yours faithfully

**distinzi·'one** nf distinction

**di·'stogliere** vt **~ da** ⟨allontanare⟩ remove from; ⟨dissuadere⟩ dissuade from

**di·'stolto** pp di **distogliere**

**di·'storcere** vt twist; distort ⟨suono⟩

**di·'storcersi** vr sprain ⟨la caviglia⟩

**distorsi·'one** nf Med sprain; ⟨alterazione⟩ distortion

**di·'storto** a warped; ⟨suono⟩ distorted

**di·'strarre** vt distract; ⟨divertire⟩ amuse

**di·'strarsi** vr ⟨deconcentrarsi⟩ be distracted; ⟨svagarsi⟩ amuse oneself; **non ti distrarre!** pay attention!

**distratta·'mente** adv absently

**di·'stratto** pp di **distrarre** ● a absent-minded; ⟨disattento⟩ inattentive

**distrazi·'one** nf absent-mindedness; ⟨errore⟩ inattention; ⟨svago⟩ amusement; **errore di ~** absent-minded mistake

**di·'stretto** nm district

**distrettu·'ale** a district attrib

**distribu·'ire** vt distribute; ⟨disporre⟩ arrange; deal ⟨carte⟩

**distribu·'tore** nm distributor; ⟨di benzina⟩ petrol pump, gas pump Am; ⟨automatico⟩ slot-machine. **~ automatico di biglietti** ticket machine. **~ di bevande** drinks dispenser. **~ di monete** change machine

**distribuzi·'one** nf distribution

**distri·'care** vt disentangle

**distri·'carsi** vr fig get out of it

**distro·'fia** nf **~ muscolare** muscular dystrophy

**di·'strofico** a dystrophic

**di·'struggere** vt destroy

**di·'struggersi** vr **si distrugge col bere** he

is destroying himself with drink; **la macchina si è distrutta** the car has been written off

**distruttività** nf destructiveness

**distrut·'tivo** a destructive; ⟨critica⟩ negative

**di·'strutto** pp di **distruggere** ● a destroyed; **un uomo ~** a broken man

**distrut·'tore** nm **~ di documenti** paper shredder

**distruzi·'one** nf destruction

**distur·'bare** vt disturb; ⟨sconvolgere⟩ upset

**distur·'barsi** vr trouble oneself; **non si disturbi** please don't trouble yourself

**distur·'bato** a ⟨Med: mente⟩ disordered; ⟨intestino⟩ upset

**di·'sturbo** nm bother; ⟨indisposizione⟩ trouble; Med problem; Radio, TV interference; **disturbi** pl Radio, TV static. **disturbi** pl di **stomaco** stomach trouble

**disubbidi·'ente** a disobedient

**disubbidi·'enza** nf disobedience

**disubbi·'dire** vi **~ a** disobey

**disuguagli·'anza** nf disparity; ⟨eterogeneità⟩ irregularity

**disugu·'ale** a unequal; ⟨eterogeneo⟩ irregular

**disumanità** nf inhumanity

**disu·'mano** a inhuman

**disuni·'one** nf disunity

**disu·'nire** vt divide

**di·'suso** nm **cadere in ~** fall into disuse

**di·'tale** nm thimble

**di·'tata** nf poke; ⟨impronta⟩ finger-mark

**'dito** nm ⟨pl nf **dita**⟩ finger; ⟨di vino, acqua⟩ finger. **~ del piede** toe

**'ditta** nf firm. **~ di vendita per corrispondenza** mail order firm

**dit·'tafono** nm dictaphone

**ditta·'tore** nm dictator

**dittatori·'ale** a dictatorial

**ditta·'tura** nf dictatorship

**dit·'tongo** nm diphthong

**diu·'retico** a diuretic

**di·'urno** a daytime; **spettacolo ~** matinée

**'diva** nf diva

**diva·'gare** vi digress

**divagazi·'one** nf digression. **~ sul tema** digression

**divam·'pare** vi burst into flames; fig spread like wildfire

**di·'vano** nm settee, sofa. **~ letto** sofa bed

**divari·'care** vt open

**divari·'carsi** vr splay

**divari·'cata** nf splits pl

**divari·'cato** a ⟨gambe, braccia⟩ splayed

**di·'vario** nm discrepancy; **un ~ di opinioni** a difference of opinion

**di·'vellere** vt ⟨sradicare⟩ uproot

**di·'velto** pp di **divellere**

**dive·'nire** vi = **diventare**

**diven·'tare** vi become; ⟨lentamente⟩ grow; ⟨rapidamente⟩ turn

**dive·'nuto** pp di **divenire**

**di·'verbio** nm squabble

**diver'gente** *a* divergent

**diver'genza** *nf* divergence; **~ di opinioni** difference of opinion

**di'vergere** *vi* diverge

**diversa'mente** *adv* (*altrimenti*) otherwise; (*in modo diverso*) differently

**di'versi** *a & pron* (*parecchi*) several

**diversifi'care** *vt* diversify

**diversifi'carsi** *vr* differ, be different

**diversifi'cato** *a* broad-based

**diversificazi'one** *nf* diversification

**diversi'one** *nf* diversion

**diversità** *nf inv* diversity; **ci sono molte ~** there are many differences

**diver'sivo** *a* diversionary ● *nm* diversion

**di'verso** *a* different ● *nm* (*omosessuale*) deviant

**diver'tente** *a* amusing

**diver'ticolo** *nm* digression

**diverti'mento** *nm* fun, amusement; **buon ~!** enjoy yourself!, have fun!

**diver'tire** *vt* amuse

**diver'tirsi** *vr* enjoy oneself, have fun

**diver'tito** *a* amused

**divi'dendo** *nm* dividend

**di'videre** *vt* divide; (*condividere*) share

**di'vidersi** *vr* (*separarsi*) separate

**divi'eto** *nm* prohibition; '**~ di pesca**' 'fishing prohibited'; '**~ di sosta**' 'no parking'

**divina'mente** *adv* divinely

**divinco'larsi** *vr* wriggle

**divinità** *nf inv* divinity

**di'vino** *a* divine

**di'visa** *nf* uniform; *Comm* currency

**divi'sibile** *a* divisible

**divisi'one** *nf* division

**divisio'nismo** *nm* (*in arte*) pointillism

**di'vismo** *nm* worship; (*atteggiamento*) superstar mentality

**di'viso** *pp di* **dividere** ● *a* divided

**divi'sore** *nm* divisor

**divi'sorio** *a* dividing; **muro ~** partition wall

**'divo, -a** *nmf/a* star

**divo'rare** *vt* devour

**divo'rarsi** *vr* **~ da** be consumed with

**divorzi'are** *vi* divorce

**divorzi'ato, -a** *nmf* divorcee

**di'vorzio** *nm* divorce

**divul'gare** *vt* divulge; (*rendere popolare*) popularize

**divul'garsi** *vr* spread

**divulga'tivo** *a* popular

**divulgazi'one** *nf* spread; (*di cultura, scienza*) popularization

**dizio'nario** *nm* dictionary. **~ dei sinonimi** thesaurus

**dizi'one** *nf* diction

**DJ** *nm inv* DJ

**DNA** *nm inv* DNA

**do** *nm Mus* (*chiave, nota*) C

**'doccia** *nf* shower; (*grondaia*) gutter; **fare la ~** have a shower, shower

**doccia'tura** *nf Med* douche

**D.O.C.** *abbr* (**Denominazione di Origine Controllata**) *mark guaranteeing the quality of a wine*

**do'cente** *a* teaching ● *nmf* teacher; (*di università*) lecturer

**do'cenza** *nf* university teacher's qualification

**D.O.C.G.** *abbr* (**Denominazione di Origine Controllata e Garantita**) *mark guaranteeing the high quality of a wine*

**'docile** *a* docile

**docilità** *nf* docility

**documen'tare** *vt* document

**documen'tario** *a & nm* documentary

**documen'tarsi** *vr* gather information (**su** about)

**documen'tato** *a* well-documented; (*persona*) well-informed

**documentazi'one** *nf* documentation

**docu'mento** *nm* document; **documenti** *pl* papers. **~ d'identità** ID

**dodeca'fonico** *a Mus* dodecaphonic

**Dodeca'neso** *nm* **il ~** the Dodecanese

**dodi'cenne** *a & nmf* twelve-year-old

**dodi'cesimo** *a & nm* twelfth

**'dodici** *a & nm* twelve

**do'gana** *nf* customs *pl*; (*dazio*) duty. **~ merci** customs for freight. **~ passeggeri** passenger customs

**doga'nale** *a* customs *attrib*

**dogani'ere** *nm* customs officer

**'doglie** *nfpl* labour pains

**'dogma** *nm* dogma

**dog'matico** *a* dogmatic

**dogma'tismo** *nm* dogmatism

**'dolce** *a* sweet; (*clima*) mild; (*voce, consonante*) soft; (*acqua*) fresh ● *nm* (*portata*) dessert; (*torta*) cake; **non mangio dolci** I don't eat sweet things; **dolci** *pl* **della casa** (*in menu*) home-made cakes

**dolce'mente** *adv* sweetly

**dolce'vita** *a inv* (*maglione*) rollneck

**dol'cezza** *nf* sweetness; (*di clima*) mildness

**dolci'ario** *a* confectionery

**dolci'astro** *a* sweetish

**dolcifi'cante** *nm* sweetener ● *a* sweetening

**dolcifica'tore** *nm* (*per acqua*) softener

**dolci'umi** *nmpl* sweets

**do'lente** *a* painful; (*spiacente*) sorry; **punto ~** sore point

**do'lere** *vi* ache, hurt; (*dispiacere*) regret

**do'lersi** *vr* regret; (*protestare*) complain; **~ di** be sorry for

**'dollaro** *nm* dollar

**'dolly** *nm inv Cinema, TV* dolly

**'dolmen** *nm inv* dolmen

**'dolo** *nm Jur* malice; (*truffa*) fraud

**Dolo'miti** *nfpl* **le ~** the Dolomites

**dolo'mitico** *a* Dolomite, of the Dolomites

**dolo'rante** *a* aching

**do'lore** *nm* pain; (*morale*) sorrow; **avere dei dolori** be in pain. **dolori** *pl* **post-partum** after-pains

**dolorosa'mente** *adv* painfully

**dolo'roso** *a* painful

**do'loso** *a* malicious

**do'manda** *nf* question; (*richiesta*) request; (*scritta*) application; *Comm* demand; **~ e offerta** supply and demand: **fare una ~ (a qcno)** ask (sb) a question. **~ di impiego** job application. **~ riconvenzionale** counterclaim

**doman'dare** *vt* ask; (*esigere*) demand; **~ qcsa a qcno** ask sb for sth

**doman'darsi** *vr* wonder

**do'mani** *adv* tomorrow; **~ sera** tomorrow evening; **a ~** see you tomorrow ● *nm* **il ~** the future

**do'mare** *vt* tame; *fig* control ‹*emozioni*›

**doma'tore, -'trice** *nmf* tamer. **~ di cavalli** horsebreaker

**domat'tina** *adv* tomorrow morning

**doma'tura** *nf* (*di cavallo*) breaking

**do'menica** *nf* Sunday; **di ~** on Sundays. **~ delle palme** Palm Sunday

**domeni'cale** *a* Sunday *attrib*

**domeni'cano** *a* Dominican

**do'mestico, -a** *a* domestic: **le pareti domestiche** one's own four walls ● *nm* servant ● *nf* maid

**domicili'are** *a* **arresti domiciliari** *Jur* house arrest; **perquisizione ~** *Jur* house search

**domicili'arsi** *vr* settle

**domi'cilio** *nm* domicile; (*abitazione*) home; **recapitiamo a ~** we do home deliveries

**domi'nante** *a* ‹*nazione, colore*› dominant; ‹*caratteri*› chief; ‹*opinione*› prevailing; ‹*motivo*› main

**domi'nanza** *nf* *Biol, Zool* dominance

**domi'nare** *vt* dominate; (*controllare*) control ● *vi* rule over; (*prevalere*) be dominant

**domi'narsi** *vr* control oneself

**domina'tore, -'trice** *a* domineering ● *nmf* ruler

**dominazi'one** *nf* domination

**domini'cano** *a* **la Repubblica Dominicana** the Dominican Republic

**do'minio** *nm* control; *Pol* dominion; (*ambito*) field; **di ~ pubblico** common knowledge

**'domino** *nm* (*gioco*) dominoes

**don** *nm inv* (*ecclesiastico*) Father

**do'nare** *vt* give; donate ‹*sangue, organo*› ● *vi* **~ a** (*giovare esteticamente*) suit

**do'narsi** *vr* dedicate oneself

**dona'tore, -'trice** *nmf* donor. **~ di organi** organ donor

**donazi'one** *nf* donation

**dondo'lare** *vt* swing; (*cullare*) rock ● *vi* sway

**dondo'larsi** *vr* swing

**dondo'lio** *nm* rocking

**'dondolo** *nm* swing; **cavallo/sedia a ~** rocking-horse/chair

**dongio'vanni** *nm inv* Romeo, Don Juan

**'donna** *nf* woman; **fare la prima ~** act like a prima donna; **'donne'** 'ladies'. **~ d'affari** businesswoman. **~ delle pulizie** cleaner. **~ di servizio** domestic help. **~ di vita** (*prostituta*) lady of the night

**don'naccia** *nf pej* hussy

**donnai'olo** *nm* womanizer

**donnicci'ola** *nf fig* old woman

**'donnola** *nf* weasel

**'dono** *nm* gift

**'doping** *nm inv Sport* drug-taking; **fa uso di ~** he takes drugs

**'dopo** *prep* after; (*a partire da*) since ● *adv* after, afterwards; (*più tardi*) later; (*in seguito*) later on; **~ di me** after me

**dopo'barba** *nm inv* aftershave

**dopo'cena** *nm inv* evening

**dopodiché** *adv* after which

**dopodo'mani** *adv* the day after tomorrow

**dopogu'erra** *nm inv* post-war period

**dopola'voro** *nm inv* working man's club

**dopo'pranzo** *nm inv* afternoon

**dopo'sci** *a & nm inv* après-ski

**doposcu'ola** *nm inv* after-school activities *pl*

**dopo-'shampoo** *nm inv* conditioner ● *a inv* conditioning

**dopo'sole** *nm inv* aftersun cream ● *a inv* aftersun

**dopo'tutto** *adv* after all

**doppi'aggio** *nm* dubbing

**doppia'mente** *adv* (*in misura doppia*) doubly

**doppi'are** *vt Naut* double; *Sport* lap; *Cinema* dub

**doppia'tore, -'trice** *nmf* dubber

**doppi'etta** *nf* (*fucile*) double-barrelled shotgun; *Auto* double-declutch; (*in calcio*) two goals; (*in pugilato*) one-two

**doppi'ezza** *nf* duplicity

**'doppio** *a & adv* double. **~ clic** *Comput* double click; **fare un ~ su** double-click on. **~ fallo** *nm Tennis* double fault. **~ gioco** *nm* double-dealing. **~ mento** *nm* double chin. **~ senso** *nm* double entendre. **doppi vetri** *nmpl* double glazing ● *nm* double, twice the quantity; *Tennis* doubles *pl*. **~ misto** *Tennis* mixed doubles

**doppio'fondo** *nm Naut* double hull; (*in valigia*) false bottom

**doppiogio'chista** *nmf* double-dealer

**doppi'one** *nm* duplicate

**doppio'petto** *a* double-breasted

**dop'pista** *nmf Tennis* doubles player

**do'rare** *vt* gild; *Culin* brown

**do'rato** *a* gilt; (*color oro*) golden

**dora'tura** *nf* gilding

**'dorico** *a Archit* Doric

**do'rifora** *nf* Colorado beetle

**dormicchi'are** *vi* doze

**dormigli'one, -a** *nmf* sleepyhead; *fig* lazybones

**dor'mire** *vi* sleep; (*essere addormentato*) be asleep; *fig* be asleep; **andare a ~** go to bed; **~ come un ghiro** sleep like a log; **~ in piedi** *fig* be half asleep; (*essere stanco*) be dead tired; **dormirci sopra** sleep on it

**dor'mita** *nf* good sleep; **fare una bella ~** have a good sleep

**dormi'tina** *nf* nap

**dormi'torio** *nm* dormitory. **~ pubblico** night shelter

**dormi'veglia** *nm* **essere nel ~** be half asleep

**dor'sale** *a* dorsal ● *nf* (*di monte*) ridge

**dor'sista** *nmf* backstroke swimmer

**'dorso** *nm* back; (*di libro*) spine; (*di monte*) crest; (*nel nuoto*) backstroke; **a ~ di cavallo** on horseback

**do'saggio** *nm* dosage; *fig* weighing; **sbagliare il ~** get the amount wrong

**do'sare** *vt* dose; *fig* measure; **~ le parole** weigh one's words

**do'sato** *a* measured

**dosa'tore** *nm* measuring jug

**'dose** *nf* dose; **~ eccessiva** overdose; **in buona ~** *fig* in good measure

**dos'sier** *nm inv* (*raccolta di dati, fascicolo*) file

**'dosso** *nm* (*dorso*) back; **levarsi di ~ gli abiti** take off one's clothes

**do'tare** *vt* endow; (*di accessori*) equip

**do'tato** *a* ⟨*persona*⟩ gifted; (*fornito*) equipped

**dotazi'one** *nf* (*attrezzatura*) equipment; (*mezzi finanziari*) endowment; **avere qcsa in ~** be equipped with sth

**'dote** *nf* dowry; (*qualità*) gift

**dott.** *abbr* (**dottore**) Dr.

**'dotto** *a* learned ● *nm* scholar; *Anat* duct

**dotto'rale** *a* doctoral; *pej* pedantic

**dotto'rando, -a** *nmf* postgraduate student

**dotto'rato** *nm* doctorate

**dot'tor|e, ~'essa** *nmf* doctor

**dot'trina** *nf* doctrine

**dott.ssa** *abbr* (**dottoressa**) Dr.

**'dove** *adv* where; **di ~ sei?** where do you come from; **fin ~?** how far?; **per ~?** which way?

**do'vere** *vi* (*obbligo*) have to, must; **devo andare** I have to go, I must go; **devo venire anch'io?** do I have to come too?; **avresti dovuto dirmelo** you should have told me, you ought to have told me; **devo sedermi un attimo** I must sit down for a minute, I need to sit down for a minute; **dev'essere successo qualcosa** something must have happened; **come si deve** properly ● *vt* (*essere debitore di, derivare*) owe; **essere dovuto a** be due to ● *nm* duty; **per ~** out of duty; **rivolgersi a chi di ~** apply to the appropriate authorities

**dove'roso** *a* right and proper, only right

**do'vizia** *nf* **con ~ di particolari** in great detail

**do'vunque** *adv* (*dappertutto*) everywhere; (*in qualsiasi luogo*) anywhere ● *conj* wherever

**dovuta'mente** *adv* duly

**do'vuto** *a* due; (*debito*) proper; **essere ~ a** be attributable to; **ha fatto più del ~** he did more than he had to

**Down: sindrome di ~** *Med* Down's syndrome

**doz'zina** *nf* **una ~ di uova** a dozen eggs; **mezza ~ di uova** half a dozen eggs

**dozzi'nale** *a* cheap

**'draga** *nf* (*scavatrice*) dredger

**draga'mine** *nf* minesweeper

**dra'gare** *vt* dredge

**'drago** *nm* dragon

**'dramma** *nm* drama; **fare un ~ di qcsa** *fig* make a drama out of sth

**drammatica'mente** *adv* dramatically

**drammaticità** *nf* dramatic force

**dram'matico** *a* dramatic

**drammatiz'zare** *vt* dramatize

**drammatizzazi'one** *nf* dramatization

**drammatur'gia** *nf* (*genere*) drama

**dramma'turgo** *nm* playwright

**dram'mone** *nm* (*film*) tear-jerker, weepy

**drappeggi'are** *vt* drape

**drap'peggio** *nm* drapery

**drap'pello** *nm* *Mil* squad; (*gruppo*) band

**'drappo** *nm* (*tessuto*) cloth

**drastica'mente** *adv* drastically

**'drastico** *a* drastic

**dre'naggio** *nm* drainage. **~ di capitali** transfer of capital. **~ fiscale** fiscal drag

**dre'nare** *vt* drain

**'Dresda** *nf* Dresden

**dres'sage** *nm inv* (*gara*) dressage

**drib'blare** *vt* (*in calcio*) dribble; *fig* dodge

**'dribbling** *nm inv* (*in calcio*) dribble

**'dritta** *nf* (*mano destra*) right hand; *Naut* starboard; (*informazione*) pointer, tip; **a ~ e a manca** (*dappertutto*) left, right and centre

**dritta'mente** *adv* (*furbescamente*) craftily

**'dritto** *a* = **diritto**[1] ● *nmf fam* crafty so-and-so

**drive** *nm inv Comput* drive

**drive-in** *nm inv* drive-in

**driz'zare** *vt* straighten; (*rizzare*) prick up

**driz'zarsi** *vr* straighten [up]; (*alzarsi*) raise; **mi sono drizzati i capelli** *fig* my hair stood on end

**'droga** *nf* drug. **~ leggera** soft drug. **~ pesante** hard drug

**dro'gare** *vt* drug

**dro'garsi** *vr* take drugs

**dro'gato, -a** *nmf* drug addict

**droghe'ria** *nf* grocery

**droghi'ere, -a** *nmf* grocer

**drome'dario** *nm* dromedary

**'druso** *nmf* Druse

**dua'lismo** *nm* dualism; (*contrasto*) conflict

**'dubbio** *a* doubtful; (*ambiguo*) dubious ● *nm* doubt; (*sospetto*) suspicion; **mettere in ~** doubt; **essere fuori ~** be beyond doubt; **essere in ~** be doubtful

**dubbiosa'mente** *adv* doubtfully

**dubbi'oso, dubi'tante** *a* doubtful

**dubi'tare** *vi* doubt; **~ di** doubt; (*diffidare*) mistrust; **dubito che venga** I doubt whether he'll come

**dubita'tivo** *a* (*ambiguo*) ambiguous

**duble-'face** *a inv* reversible

**Du'blino** *nf* Dublin

**'duca** *nm* duke

**du'cale** *a* ducal

**'duce** *nm* (*capo del fascismo*) Duce

**du'chessa** *nf* duchess

**'due** *a & nm* two

**duecen'tesco** *a* thirteenth-century

**duecen'tesimo** two hundredth

**due'cento** *a & nm* two hundred

**duel'lante** *nmf* dueller

**duel'lare** *vi* duel

**du'ello** *nm* duel

**due'mila** *a & nm* two thousand

**due'pezzi** *nm inv* *(bikini)* bikini; *(vestito)* two-piece suit

**du'etto** *nm* duo; *Mus* duet

**'dumping** *nm inv Fin* dumping

**'duna** *nf* dune

**dune 'buggy** *nm inv* beach buggy

**'dunque** *conj* therefore; *(allora)* well [then]; **arrivare al ~** get down to the nitty-gritty

**'duo** *nm inv* duo; *Mus* duet

**duodeci'male** *a* duodecimal

**duode'nale** *a* **ulcera ~** duodenal ulcer

**duo'deno** *nm* duodenum

**du'omo** *nm* cathedral

**'duplex** *nm Teleph* party line

**dupli'care** *vt* duplicate

**dupli'cato** *nm* duplicate

**duplicazi'one** *nf* duplication

**'duplice** *a* double; **in ~** in duplicate

**duplicità** *nf* duplicity

**dura'mente** *adv* *(lavorare)* hard; *(rimproverare)* harshly

**du'rante** *prep* during

**du'rare** *vi* last; *(cibo:)* keep; *(resistere)* hold out; **così non può ~** this can't go on any longer; **~ in carica** remain in office; **finché dura** as long as it lasts ● *vt* **~ fatica** sweat blood

**du'rata** *nf* duration. **~ del collegamento** on-line time. **~ di conservazione** shelflife. **~ della vita** life span

**dura'turo** *a* lasting

**du'revole** *a* *(pace)* lasting, enduring

**du'rezza** *nf* hardness; *(di carne)* toughness; *(di voce, padre)* harshness

**'duro, -a** *a* hard; *(persona, carne)* tough; *(voce)* harsh; *(pane)* stale; **tieni ~!** *(resistere)* hang in there!; **~ d'orecchio** hard of hearing ● *nmf* *(persona)* tough person, toughie *fam*

**du'rone** *nm* hardened skin

**'duttile** *a* *(materiale)* ductile; *(carattere, persona)* malleable

**duttilità** *nf* *(di materiale)* ductility; *(di individuo)* malleability

**'duty free** *nm inv* duty-free shop

# Ee

**e** *conj* and

**eba'nista** *nmf* cabinet-maker

**'ebano** *nm* ebony

**eb'bene** *conj* well [then]

**eb'brezza** *nf* inebriation; *(euforia)* elation; **guida in stato di ~** drink-driving; **l'~ della velocità** the thrill of speed

**'ebbro** *a* inebriated; **~ di gioia** delirious with joy

**'ebete** *a* stupid

**ebollizi'one** *nf* boiling

**e'braico** *a & nm* Hebrew

**ebra'ismo** *nm* Judaism

**e'breo, -a** *a* Jewish ● *nm* Jew ● *nf* Jewess

**'Ebridi** *nfpl* **le ~** the Hebrides

**eca'tombe** *nf* **fare un'~** wreak havoc

**ecc** *abbr* **(eccetera)** etc

**ecce'dente** *a* *(peso, bagaglio)* excess

**ecce'denza** *nf* excess; *(d'avanzo)* surplus; **avere qcsa in ~** have an excess of sth; **bagagli in ~** excess baggage. **~ di cassa** surplus. **~ di peso** excess weight

**ec'cedere** *vt* exceed ● *vi* go too far; **~ nel bere** drink to excess; **~ nel mangiare** overeat

**eccel'lente** *a* excellent

**eccel'lenza** *nf* excellence; *(titolo)* Excellency; **per ~** par excellence

**ec'cellere** *vi* excel **(in** at)

**eccentricità** *nf* eccentricity

**ec'centrico, -a** *a & nmf* eccentric

**ecce'pire** *vt* object to

**eccessiva'mente** *adv* excessively

**ecces'sivo** *a* excessive

**ec'cesso** *nm* excess; **andare agli eccessi** go to extremes; **dare in eccessi** fly into a temper; **all'~** to excess. **~ di personale** overmanning. **~ di peso** excess weight. **~ di velocità** speeding

**ec'cetera** *adv* et cetera

**ec'cetto** *prep* except; **~ che** *(a meno che)* unless

**eccettu'are** *vt* except

**eccezio'nale** *a* exceptional; **in via [del tutto] ~** as an exception

**eccezional'mente** *adv* exceptionally; *(contrariamente alla regola)* as an exception

**eccezi'one** *nf* exception; *Jur* objection; **a ~ di** with the exception of; **d'~** exceptional

**ec'chimosi** *nf inv* bruising

**'ecci** *int* atishoo

**ec'cidio** *nm* massacre

**ecci'tabile** *a* *(persona, carattere)* excitable

**ecci'tamento** *nm* excitement

**ecci'tante** *a* exciting; *(sostanza)* stimulant ● *nm* stimulant

**ecci'tare** *vt* excite; *(sessualmente)* excite, arouse

**ecci'tarsi** *vr* get excited; *(sessualmente)* become aroused *or* excited

**ecci'tato** *a* excited; *(sessulamente)* excited, aroused; ~ **da** flushed with

**eccitazi'one** *nf* excitement; *(sessuale)* arousal, excitement

**ecclesi'astico** *a* ecclesiastical ● *nm* priest

'**ecco** *adv (qui)* here; *(là)* there; ~**!** *(con approvazione)* that's right!; ~ **qua!** *(dando qcsa)* here you are!; ~ **la tua borsa** here is your bag; ~ **mio figlio** there is my son; **eccomi** here I am; ~ **fatto** there we are; ~ **perché** this is why; ~ **tutto** that is all

**ec'come** *adv & int* and how!

**ECG** *abbr* (**elettrocardiogramma**) ECG

**echeggi'are** *vi* echo

**e'clettico** *a* eclectic

**eclet'tismo** *nm* eclecticism

**eclis'sare** *vt fig* eclipse

**eclis'sarsi** *vr (sparire)* disappear

**e'clissi** *nf inv* eclipse

'**eco** *nmf* (*pl m* **echi**) echo; **ha suscitato una vasta** ~ it caused a great stir

**eco+** *pref* eco+

**ecogra'fia** *nf* scan

**ecolo'gia** *nf* ecology

**eco'logico** *a* ecological; *(prodotto)* environmentally friendly, eco-friendly

**e'cologo, -a** *nmf* ecologist

**e commerci'ale** *nf* ampersand

**econo'mia** *nf* economy; *(scienza)* economics; **fare** ~ economize (**di** on); [**fatto**] **in** ~ [done] on the cheap; **senza** ~ unstintingly; **fare qcsa senza** ~ spare no expense doing sth. ~ **aziendale** business administration. ~ **domestica** *Sch* home economics. ~ **di mercato** market economy. ~ **mista** mixed economy. ~ **sommersa** black economy

**economicità** *nf* economy

**eco'nomico** *a* economic; *(a buon prezzo)* cheap; *(con pochi costi)* economical; **difficoltà economiche** financial difficulties; **classe economica** economy class; **edizione economica** paperback

**econo'mie** *nfpl (risparmi)* savings

**econo'mista** *nmf* economist

**economiz'zare** *vt* save *(tempo, denaro)* ● *vi* economize (**su** on)

**economizza'tore** *nm Auto* fuel economizer

**e'conomo, -a** *a* thrifty ● *nmf (di collegio)* bursar

**ecosi'stema** *nm* ecosystem

**é'cru** *a inv* fawn

'**Ecu** *nm inv* ECU, ecu

**Ecua'dor** *nm* Ecuador

**ecuadori'ano, -a** *a & nmf* Ecuadorian

**ecu'menico** *a* ecumenical

**ec'zema** *nm* eczema

**ed** *conj vedi* **e**

**e'dema** *nm* oedema

'**Eden** *nm* Eden

'**edera** *nf* ivy

**e'dicola** *nf* [newspaper] kiosk

**edifi'cabile** *a (area, terreno)* classified as suitable for development

**edifi'cante** *a* edifying

**edifi'care** *vt* build; *(indurre al bene)* edify

**edi'ficio** *nm* building; *fig* structure

**e'dile** *a* building *attrib* ● *nm* **edili** *pl* construction workers

**edi'lizia** *nf* building trade

**edi'lizio** *a* building *attrib*

**Edim'burgo** *nf* Edinburgh

**E'dipo** *nm* Oedipus; **complesso di** ~ Oedipus complex

**edi'tare** *vt* edit

'**editing** *nm* editing

'**edito** *a* published

**edi|'tore, -'trice** *a* publishing ● *nmf* publisher; *(curatore)* editor

**edito'ria** *nf* publishing. ~ **elettronica** desktop publishing. ~ **telematica** online publishing

**editori'ale** *a* publishing ● *nm (articolo)* editorial, leader

**e'ditto** *nm* edict

**edizi'one** *nf* edition; *(di manifestazione)* performance; **in** ~ **italiana** *(film)* dubbed into Italian. ~ **ridotta** abridgement, abridged version. ~ **della sera** *(di telegiornale)* evening news

**edo'nismo** *nm* hedonism

**edo'nistico** *a* hedonistic

**educagi'oco** *nm* edutainment

**edu'canda** *nf* [convent school] boarder; *fig* prim and proper girl

**edu'care** *vt* educate; *(allevare)* bring up

**educa'tivo** *a* educational

**edu'cato** *a* polite

**educa|'tore, -'trice** *nmf* educator

**educazi'one** *nf* education; *(di bambini)* upbringing; *(buone maniere)* [good] manners *pl*; **bella** ~**!** what manners!. ~ **fisica** physical education

**edulco'rare** *vt* ~ **la pillola** sweeten the pill

**e'felide** *nf* freckle

**effemi'nato** *a* effeminate

**effe'rato** *a* brutal

**efferve'scente** *a* effervescent; *(frizzante)* fizzy; *(aspirina)* soluble

**effettiva'mente** *adv* **è troppo tardi** – ~ it's too late – so it is

**effet'tivo** *a* actual; *(efficace)* effective; *(personale)* permanent; *Mil* regular ● *nm (somma totale)* sum total

**ef'fetto** *nm* effect; *(impressione)* impression; *(cambiale)* bill; **fare** ~ *(medicina:)* take effect; **fare** ~ **su** have an effect on, affect; **in effetti** in fact; **a tutti gli effetti** to all intents and purposes; **ad effetto** *(frase)* catchy; **la vista del sangue mi fa** ~ I can't stand the sight of blood; **tiro con** ~ spin. ~ **boomerang** boomerang effect. ~ **di luce** trick of the light. **effetti** *pl* **personali** personal belongings, personal effects *fml*. ~ **ritardato** delayed effect. ~ **serra** greenhouse effect. ~

**sonoro** sound effect. **~ speciale** *Cinema,
TV* special effect

**effettu'are** *vt* effect: carry out ⟨*controllo,
sondaggio*⟩

**effettu'arsi** *vr* take place; **'si effettua dal...
al...'** 'this service is available from... till...'

**effi'cace** *a* effective

**effi'cacia** *nf* effectiveness

**effici'ente** *a* efficient

**effici'enza** *nf* efficiency; **in piena ~** in full
swing

**ef'figie** *nf* effigy

**ef'fimero** *a* ephemeral

**ef'flusso** *nm* outflow

**ef'fluvio** *nm* stink

**effondersi** *vr* **~ in ringraziamenti** be
profusive in one's thanks

**effrazi'one** *nf* **~ con scasso** *Jur* breaking
and entering

**effusi'one** *nf* effusion

**'Egadi** *nfpl* **le [isole] ~** the Egadi Islands

**egemo'nia** *nf* hegemony

**E'geo** *nm* **l'~** the Aegean [Sea]

**e'gida** *nf* **sotto l'~ di** under the aegis of

**E'gitto** *nm* Egypt

**egizi'ano, -a** *a & nmf* Egyptian

**e'gizio, -a** *a & nmf* Ancient Egyptian

**'egli** *pers pron* he; **~ stesso** he himself

**ego'centrico, -a** *a* egocentric ● *nmf* egocentric person

**egocen'trismo** *nm* egocentricity

**ego'ismo** *nm* selfishness

**ego'ista** *a* selfish ● *nmf* selfish person

**egoistica'mente** *adv* selfishly

**ego'istico** *a* selfish

**Egr.** *abbr* (**egregio**) **~ Sig.** (*su busta*) Mr.

**e'gregio** *a* distinguished; **E~ Signore** Dear
Sir

**eguali'tario** *a & nm* egalitarian

**eh** *int* huh!

**'ehi** *int* hey!

**ehilà** *int* hi!

**ehm** *int* um

**eiacu'lare** *vi* ejaculate

**eiaculazi'one** *nf* ejaculation

**eiet'tabile** *a* ⟨*sedile*⟩ ejector

**eiezi'one** *nf Aeron* ejection

**'Eire** *nf* Eire

**elabo'rare** *vt* elaborate; process ⟨*dati*⟩

**elabo'rato** *a* elaborate ● *nm* (*tabulato*) pre-
printed form

**elabora'tore** *nm* **~ [di testi]** word processor

**elaborazi'one** *nf* elaboration; (*di dati*)
processing. **~ [dei] dati** data processing. **~
sequenziale** *Comput* batch processing. **~
[di] testi** word processing

**elar'gire** *vt* lavish

**elasticità** *nf* elasticity. **~ mentale** mental
agility. **~ di movimento** litheness

**elasticiz'zato** *a* ⟨*stoffa*⟩ elasticated

**e'lastico** *a* elastic; ⟨*tessuto*⟩ stretch; ⟨*passo*⟩
springy; ⟨*orario, mente*⟩ flexible; ⟨*persona*⟩
easy-going; ⟨*morale*⟩ lax; **collant** *pl* **elastici**
support tights ● *nm* elastic; (*fascia*) rubber
band

**'Elba** *nf* Elba

**eldo'rado** *nm* eldorado

**ele'fante** *nm* elephant; **avere una
memoria da ~** have a memory like an elephant; **fare passi da ~** thump about. **~
marino** sea-elephant

**elefan'tesco** *a* elephantine

**elefan'tessa** *nf* cow[-elephant]

**elefan'tiaco** *a* (*enorme*) elephantine

**ele'gante** *a* elegant

**elegante'mente** *adv* elegantly

**ele'ganza** *nf* elegance

**e'leggere** *vt* elect

**eleg'gibile** *a* eligible

**ele'gia** *nf* elegy

**elemen'tare** *a* elementary; **scuola ~** primary school

**ele'mento** *nm* element; (*componente*) part;
**trovarsi nel proprio ~** be in one's element;
**elementi** *pl* (*fatti*) data; (*rudimenti*) elements

**ele'mosina** *nf* charity; **chiedere l'~** beg.
**vivere d'~** live on charity; **fare l'~** give
money to beggars

**elemosi'nare** *vt/i* beg

**elen'care** *vt* list

**e'lenco** *nm* list. **~ [degli] abbonati** *Teleph*
telephone directory. **~ telefonico** telephone
directory

**elet'tivo** *a* ⟨*carica*⟩ elective

**e'letto, -a** *pp di* **eleggere** ● *a* chosen ● *nmf*
(*nominato*) elected member; **per pochi eletti**
*fig* for the chosen few

**eletto'rale** *a* electoral

**elettora'lismo** *nm* electioneering

**eletto'rato** *nm* electorate

**elet'tore, -'trice** *nmf* voter

**elet'trauto** *nm* electrics garage

**elettri'cista** *nm* electrician

**elettricità** *nf* electricity; **togliere l'~** cut
the electricity off; **è mancata l'~** there was a
power cut

**e'lettrico** *a* electric

**elettriz'zante** *a* ⟨*notizia, gara*⟩ electrifying

**elettriz'zare** *vt fig* electrify

**elettriz'zato** *a fig* electrified

**elettro+** *pref* electro+

**elettrocardio'gramma** *nm* electrocardiogram, ECG

**elettrocuzi'one** *nf* electrocution

**e'lettrodo** *nm* electrode

**elettrodo'mestico** *nm* [electrical] household appliance

**elettroencefalo'gramma** *nm* electroen-
cephalogram

**elettroesecuzi'one** *nf* electrocution

**elet'trogeno** *a* **gruppo ~** generator

**elet'trolisi** *nf* electrolysis

**elettromo'tore** *nm* electric motor

**elettromo'trice** *nf* electric train

**elet'trone** *nm* electron

**elet'tronico, -a** *a* electronic ● *nf* electronics

**elettroshockera'pia** *nf* electroshock therapy, electroshock treatment. EST

**elettro'tecnica** *nf* electrical engineering

**elettro'tecnico** *nm* electrical engineer

**elettro'treno** *nm* electric train

**ele'vare** *vt* raise: (*promuovere*) promote; (*erigere*) erect; (*fig: migliorare*) better; ~ al quadrato/cubo square/cube

**ele'varsi** *vr* rise: (*edificio:*) stand

**ele'vato** *a* high; (*fig: sentimento*) lofty; ~ al cubo/al quadrato cubed/squared; ~ a dieci raised to the power of ten

**eleva'tore** *nm* fork-lift truck

**elevazi'one** *nf* elevation

**elezi'one** *nf* election. **elezioni** *pl* **amministrative** local council elections. **elezioni** *pl* **politiche** general election

**eliambu'lanza** *nf* air ambulance

**'elica** *nf* *Naut* screw, propeller; *Aeron* propeller; (*del ventilatore*) blade

**eli'cottero** *nm* helicopter

**elimi'nabile** *a* which can be eliminated

**elimi'nare** *vt* eliminate

**elimina'toria** *nf Sport* [preliminary] heat

**eliminazi'one** *nf* elimination

**'elio** *nm* (*gas*) helium

**eli'porto** *nm* heliport

**elisabetti'ano** *a* & *nmf* Elizabethan

**é'lite** *nf inv* élite

**eli'tista** *a* elitist

**'ella** *pers pron liter* she; ~ **stessa** she herself

**el'lenico** *a* Hellenic

**elle'nistico** *a* Hellenistic

**ellepi** *nm inv* LP

**+ellino** *suff* **campanellino** *nm* [small] bell; **fiorellino** *nm* [little] flower; **gonnellina** *nf* short skirt

**el'lisse** *nf* ellipse

**el'lissi** *nf inv* ellipsis

**el'littico** *a* elliptical

**+ello** *suff* **finestrella** *nf* little window; **pecorella** *nf* woolly sheep; **saltello** *nm* skip

**el'metto** *nm* helmet

**elogi'are** *vt* praise

**elogia'tivo** *a* laudatory

**e'logio** *nm* praise; (*discorso, scritto*) eulogy; **degno di** ~ laudable, praiseworthy; **ti faccio i miei elogi per** congratulations on. ~ **funebre** funeral oration

**elo'quente** *a* eloquent; *fig* tell-tale

**elo'quenza** *nf* eloquence

**El Salva'dor** *nm* El Salvador; **nel Salvador** in El Salvador

**e'ludere** *vt* elude; evade (*sorveglianza, controllo*)

**elusi'one** *nf* ~ **fiscale** tax avoidance

**elu'sivo** *a* elusive

**el'vetico** *a* Swiss; **Confederazione Elvetica** Swiss Confederation

**emaci'ato** *a* emaciated

**'E-mail** *nf* e-mail; **mandare per** ~ e-mail, send by e-mail

**ema'nare** *vt* give off; pass (*legge*) ● *vi* emanate

**emanazi'one** *nf* giving off: (*di legge*) enactment

**emanci'pare** *vt* emancipate

**emanci'parsi** *vr* become emancipated

**emanci'pato** *a* emancipated

**emancipazi'one** *nf* emancipation

**emargi'nato** *nm* marginalized person

**emarginazi'one** *nf* marginalization

**ema'toma** *nm* haematoma

**em'bargo** *nm* embargo

**em'blema** *nm* emblem

**emble'matico** *a* emblematic

**embo'lia** *nf* embolism

**'embolo** *nm* embolus

**embrio'nale** *a Biol, fig* embryonic; **allo stato** ~ (*progetto, idea*) embryonic

**embri'one** *nm* embryo

**emenda'mento** *nm* amendment

**emen'dare** *vt* amend

**emen'darsi** *vr* reform

**emer'gente** *a* emergent

**emer'genza** *nf* emergency; **in caso di** ~ in an emergency; **di** ~ (*di riserva*) stand-by; **uscita d'**~ emergency exit. ~ **sanitaria** ambulance

**e'mergere** *vi* emerge; (*sottomarino:*) surface; (*distinguersi*) stand out

**e'merito** *a* (*professore*) emeritus; **un** ~ **imbecille** a prize idiot

**e'merso** *pp di* **emergere**

**e'messo** *pp di* **emettere**

**e'metico** *a* emetic

**e'mettere** *vt* emit; give out (*luce, suono*); let out (*grido*); (*mettere in circolazione*) issue

**emi'crania** *nf* migraine

**emi'grare** *vi* emigrate

**emi'grato, -a** *nmf* immigrant

**emigrazi'one** *nf* emigration

**emi'nente** *a* eminent

**emi'nenza** *nf* eminence; **Sua E**~ His/Your Eminence. ~ **grigia** éminence grise

**emi'rato** *nm* emirate; **Emirati** *pl* **Arabi Uniti** United Arab Emirates

**e'miro** *nm* emir

**emi'sfero** *nm* hemisphere

**emis'sario** *nm* emissary; (*fiume*) effluent

**emissi'one** *nf* emission; (*di denaro, francobolli*) issue; (*trasmissione*) broadcast; '~ **del biglietto**' 'take your ticket here'

**emit'tente** *a* issuing; (*trasmittente*) broadcasting ● *nf Radio* transmitter

**'emmental** *nm* Emmenthal

**emofi'lia** *nf* haemophilia

**emofi'liaco, -a** *nmf* haemophiliac

**emoglo'bina** *nf* haemoglobin

**emorra'gia** *nf* haemorrhage; **avere un'**~ haemorrhage

**emor'roidi** *nfpl* haemorrhoids, piles

**emo'statico** *a* haemostatic

**emotività** *nf* emotional make-up

**emo'tivo** *a* emotional

**emozio'nante** *a* exciting; (*commovente*) moving

**emozio'nare** *vt* excite; (*commuovere*) move

**emozio'narsi** *vr* become excited; (*commuoversi*) be moved

**emozio'nato** *a* excited; (*commosso*) moved

**emozi'one** *nf* emotion; (*agitazione*) excitement

**empietà** *nf* impiety

**'empio** *a* impious; (*spietato*) pitiless; (*malvagio*) wicked

**em'pirico** *a* empirical

**empi'rismo** *nm* empiricism

**empi'rista** *nmf* empiricist

**em'porio** *nm* emporium; (*negozio*) general store

**emù** *nm inv* emu

**emu'lare** *vt* emulate

**emulazi'one** *nf* emulation. **~ di terminale** terminal emulation

**emulsio'nare** *vt* emulsify

**emulsio'narsi** *vr* emulsify

**emulsi'one** *nf* emulsion

**ena'lotto** *nm* weekly lottery

**encefa'lite** *nf* **~ bovina spongiforme** Bovine Spongiform Encephalopathy, BSE

**encefalo'gramma** *nm* encephalogram

**en'ciclica** *nf* encyclical

**enciclope'dia** *nf* encyclopaedia

**enciclo'pedico** *a* (*mente, cultura, dizionario*) encyclopaedic

**encomi'are** *vt* commend

**en'comio** *nm* commendation

**ende'mia** *nf* (*situazione*) endemic

**en'demico** *a* endemic

**en'divia** *nf* Belgian endive

**endocrinolo'gia** *nf* endocrinology

**endo'vena** *nf* intravenous injection ● *adv* intravenously

**endove'noso** *a* intravenous; **per via endovenosa** intravenously

**ener'getico** *a* (*risorse, crisi*) energy *attrib*; (*alimento*) energy-giving

**ener'gia** *nf* energy; **pieno di ~** full of energy. **~ atomica** atomic energy. **~ elettrica** electricity. **~ eolica** wind power. **~ nucleare** nuclear energy, nuclear power. **~ solare** solar energy, solar power

**energica'mente** *adv* energetically

**e'nergico** *a* energetic; (*efficace*) strong

**ener'gumeno** *nm* Neanderthal

**'enfasi** *nf* emphasis

**en'fatico** *a* emphatic

**enfatiz'zare** *vt* emphasize

**enfi'sema** *nm* emphysema

**e'nigma** *nm* enigma

**enig'matico** *a* enigmatic

**enig'mistica** *nf* puzzles *pl*

**E.N.I.T.** *nm abbr* (**Ente Nazionale Italiano per il Turismo**) Italian State Tourist Office

**en'nesimo** *a* Math nth; *fam* umpteenth; **all'ennesima potenza** Math, *fig* to the nth power/degree

**eno'logico** *a* wine *attrib*

**e'norme** *a* enormous; **è un'ingiustizia** it's enormously unfair

**enorme'mente** *adv* massively

**enormità** *nf inv* enormity; (*assurdità*) absurdity

**eno'teca** *nf* wine-tasting shop

**eno'tera** *nf* evening primrose

**en pas'sant** *adv* in passing

**'ente** *nm* board; (*società*) company; (*in filosofia*) being

**ente'rite** *nf* enteritis

**entero'clisma** *nm* Med enema

**entità** *nf inv* (*filosofia*) entity; (*gravità*) seriousness; (*dimensione*) extent

**entomolo'gia** *nf* entomology

**entou'rage** *nm inv* entourage

**en'trambi** *a & pron* both

**en'trare** *vi* go in, enter; **~ in** go into; (*stare in, trovar posto in*) fit into; (*arruolarsi*) join; **entrarci** (*avere a che fare*) have to do with; **tu che c'entri?** what has it got to do with you?; **da che parte si entra?** how do you get in?; **fallo ~** (*in ufficio, dal medico ecc*) show him in; **'vietato ~'** 'no entry'

**en'trata** *nf* entry, entrance; **~ libera** admission free; **en'trate** *pl Comm* takings; (*reddito*) income *sg*

**entre'côte** *nf* beef entrecote

**'entro** *prep* (*tempo*) within; **~ oggi** by the end of today

**entro'bordo** *nm* (*motore*) inboard motor; (*motoscafo*) speedboat

**entro'terra** *nm inv* hinterland

**entusia'smante** *a* fascinating, exciting

**entusia'smare** *vt* arouse enthusiasm in

**entusia'smarsi** *vr* be enthusiastic (**per** about)

**entusi'asmo** *nm* enthusiasm

**entusi'asta** *a* enthusiastic ● *nmf* enthusiast

**entusi'astico** *a* enthusiastic

**enucle'are** *vt* define

**enume'rare** *vt* enumerate

**enumerazi'one** *nf* enumeration

**enunci'are** *vt* enunciate

**enunciazi'one** *nf* enunciation

**E'olie** *nfpl* **le ~** the Aeolian Islands

**epa'tite** *nf* hepatitis

**epi'centro** *nm* epicentre

**'epico** *a* epic

**epide'mia** *nf* epidemic

**epi'dermide** *nf* epidermis

**epidu'rale** *a* (*Med: anestesia*) epidural

**Epifa'nia** *nf* Epiphany

**epi'gramma** *nm* epigram

**epiles'sia** *nf* epilepsy

**epi'lettico, -a** *a & nmf* epileptic

**e'pilogo** *nm* epilogue

**episco'pato** *nm* episcopacy

**epi'sodico** *a* episodic; **caso ~** one-off case

**epi'sodio** *nm* episode

**e'pistola** *nf* epistle

**episto'lare** *a* epistolary

**episto'lario** *nm* correspondence, letters *pl*

**epi'taffio** *nm* epitaph

**e'piteto** *nm* epithet

**'epoca** *nf* age; (*periodo*) period; **a quell'~** in those days; **un avvenimento che ha fatto**

~ an epoch-making event; **auto d'**~ vintage car; **mobile d'**~ period furniture

**e'ponimo** *a* eponymous

**epo'pea** *nf* epic

**ep'pure** *conj* [and] yet

**E.P.T.** *abbr* (**Ente Provinciale per il Turismo**) *Italian local tourist board*

**epu'rare** *vt* purge; purify ⟨acqua⟩

**epura'tore** *nm* water purifier

**epurazi'one** *nf* purging; (*di acqua*) purification. ~ **etnica** ethnic cleansing

**equalizza'tore** *nm* equalizer

**e'quanime** *a* level-headed; (*imparziale*) impartial

**equa'tore** *nm* equator

**equatori'ale** *a* equatorial

**equazi'one** *nf* equation

**e'questre** *a* equestrian; **circo** ~ circus

**equidi'stante** *a* equidistant

**equi'latero** *a* equilateral

**equili'brare** *vt* balance

**equili'brato** *a* ⟨persona⟩ well-balanced

**equi'librio** *nm* balance; (*buon senso*) common sense; (*di bilancia*) equilibrium

**equili'brismo** *nm* **fare** ~ do a balancing act

**equili'brista** *nmf* tightrope walker

**e'quino** *a* horse *attrib*

**equi'nozio** *nm* equinox

**equipaggia'mento** *nm* equipment

**equipaggi'are** *vt* equip; (*di persone*) man

**equi'paggio** *nm* crew; *Aeron* cabin crew. ~ **di volo** aircrew

**equipa'rare** *vt* make equal

**equipa'rato** *a* equal

**é'quipe** *nf inv* team

**equità** *nf* equity

**equitazi'one** *nf* riding

**equiva'lente** *a & nm* equivalent

**equiva'lenza** *nf* equivalence

**equiva'lere** *vi* ~ **a** be equivalent to

**equivo'care** *vi* misunderstand

**e'quivoco** *a* equivocal; (*sospetto*) suspicious; **un tipo** ~ a shady character ● *nm* misunderstanding; **a scanso di equivoci** to avoid any misunderstandings; **giocare sull'**~ equivocate

**'equo** *a* fair, just

**'era** *nf* era. ~ **glaciale** Ice Age

**'erba** *nf* grass; (*aromatica, medicinale*) herb; **in** ~ ⟨atleta, attore⟩ budding. ~ **cipollina** chives

**er'baccia** *nf* weed

**er'baceo** *a* herbaceous

**erbi'cida** *nm* weed-killer

**erbi'voro** *a* herbivorous ● *nm* herbivore

**erbo'rista** *nmf* herbalist

**erboriste'ria** *nf* herbalist's shop

**er'boso** *a* grassy

**Erco'lano** *nf* Herculaneum

**'Ercole** *nm* Hercules

**er'culeo** *a* ⟨forza⟩ herculean

**e'rede** *nm* heir ● *nf* heiress

**eredità** *nf inv* inheritance; *Biol* heredity

**eredi'tare** *vt* inherit

**ereditarietà** *nf* heredity

**eredi'tario** *a* hereditary

**erediti'era** *nf* heiress

**+erello** *suff* **furterello** *nm* petty theft; **pioggerella** *nf* drizzle

**ere'mita** *nm* hermit

**'eremo** *nm* isolated place; *fig* retreat

**ere'sia** *nf* heresy

**e'retico, -a** *a* heretical ● *nmf* heretic

**e'retto** *pp di* **erigere** ● *a* erect

**erezi'one** *nf* erection; (*costruzione*) building

**ergasto'lano, -a** *nmf* prisoner serving a life sentence, lifer *fam*

**er'gastolo** *nm* life sentence; (*luogo*) prison

**ergono'mia** *nf* ergonomics

**ergo'nomico** *a* ergonomic

**ergotera'pia** *nf* occupational therapy

**ergotera'pista** *nmf* occupational therapist

**'erica** *nf* heather

**e'rigere** *vt* erect; (*fig: fondare*) found

**eri'tema** *nm* (*cutaneo*) inflammation; (*solare*) sunburn; ~ **da pannolini** nappy rash

**Eri'trea** *nf* Eritrea

**eri'treo, -a** *a & nmf* Eritrean

**ermafro'dito** *a & nm* hermaphrodite

**ermel'lino** *nm* ermine

**ermetica'mente** *adv* hermetically

**er'metico** *a* hermetic; (*a tenuta d'aria*) airtight

**'ernia** *nf* hernia

**e'rodere** *vi* erode

**e'roe** *nm* hero

**ero'gare** *vt* distribute; (*fornire*) supply

**erogazi'one** *nf* supply

**e'rogeno** *a* erogenous

**eroica'mente** *adv* heroically

**e'roico** *a* heroic

**ero'ina** *nf* heroine; (*droga*) heroin

**ero'ismo** *nm* heroism

**'eros** *nm* Eros

**erosi'one** *nf* erosion

**e'rotico** *a* erotic

**ero'tismo** *nm* eroticism

**'erpice** *nm* harrow

**er'rante** *a* wandering

**er'rare** *vi* (*vagare*) wander; (*sbagliare*) be mistaken

**er'rato** *a* (*sbagliato*) mistaken; **se non vado** ~ if I'm not mistaken

**'erre** *nf* ~ **moscia** burr

**erronea'mente** *adv* mistakenly

**er'rore** *nm* error, mistake; (*di stampa*) misprint; **essere in** ~ be wrong. ~ **giudiziario** miscarriage of justice. ~ **di stampa** printing error, typo

**'erta** *nf* **stare all'**~ be on the alert

**eru'dirsi** *vr* get educated

**eru'dito** *a* learned

**erut'tare** *vt* ⟨vulcano:⟩ erupt ● *vi* (*ruttare*) belch

**eruzi'one** *nf* eruption; *Med* rash

**Es** *nm Psych* **l'**~ the id

**es.** *abbr* (**esempio**) eg.

**esacer'bare** *vt* exacerbate

**esage'rare** *vt* exaggerate; ~ **le cose** exaggerate things, go over the top ● *vi* exaggerate; (*nel comportamento*) go over the top; ~ **nel mangiare** eat too much

**esagerata'mente** *adv* excessively

**esage'rato** *a* exaggerated; (*prezzo*) exorbitant ● **n'n è un** ~ he exaggerates

**esagerazi'one** *nf* exaggeration; **è costato un'**~ it cost the earth; **senza** ~ with no exaggeration

**esago'nale** *a* hexagonal

**e'sagono** *nm* hexagon

**esa'lare** *vt* give off; ~ **l'ultimo respiro** breathe one's last ● *vi* emanate

**esalazi'one** *nf* emission; **esalazioni** *pl* fumes

**esal'tare** *vt* exalt; (*entusiasmare*) elate

**esal'tarsi** *vr* (*entusiasmarsi*) get excited (**per** about)

**esal'tato** *a* (*fanatico*) fanatical ● *nm* fanatic

**esaltazi'one** *nf* exaltation; (*in discorso*) fervour

**e'same** *nm* examination, exam; **dare un** ~ take *or* sit an exam; **prendere in** ~ examine. ~ **di ammissione** *Sch* entrance examination. ~ **di coscienza** soul-searching. ~ **di guida** driving test. **esami** *pl* **di maturità** ≈ A-levels. ~ **orale** *Sch*, *Univ* viva. ~ **del sangue** blood test. ~ **della vista** eye test

**esami'nando, -a** *nmf* examinee

**esami'nare** *vt* examine

**esamina|'tore, -'trice** *nmf* examiner

**e'sangue** *a* bloodless

**e'sanime** *a* lifeless

**esaspe'rante** *a* exasperating

**esaspe'rare** *vt* exasperate

**esaspe'rarsi** *vr* get exasperated

**esasperazi'one** *nf* exasperation

**esatta'mente** *adv* exactly

**esat'tezza** *nf* exactness; (*precisione*) precision; (*di risposta, risultato*) accuracy

**e'satto** *pp di* **esigere** ● *a* exact; (*risposta, risultato*) correct; (*orologio*) right; **hai l'ora** ~? do you have the right time?; **sono le due esatte** it's two o'clock exactly

**esat'tore** *nm* collector. ~ **dei crediti** *Fin* debt collector. ~ **delle imposte** tax collector, tax man

**esau'dire** *vt* grant; fulfil (*speranze*)

**esauri'ente** *a* exhaustive

**esauri'mento** *nm* exhaustion; **'fino ad** ~ **delle scorte'** 'subject to availability'. ~ **nervoso** nervous breakdown

**esau'rire** *vt* exhaust

**esau'rirsi** *vr* exhaust oneself; (*merci ecc*) run out

**esau'rito** *a* exhausted; (*merci*) sold out; (*libro*) out of print; **fare il tutto** ~ (*spettacolo*) play to a full house

**esazi'one** *nf* collection. ~ **crediti** debt collection

**'esca** *nf* bait

**escande'scenza** *nf* outburst; **dare in escandescenze** lose one's temper

**escava'tore** *nm* excavator

**escava'trice** *nf* excavator

**escla'mare** *vi* exclaim

**esclama'tivo** *a* exclamatory

**esclamazi'one** *nf* exclamation

**e'scludere** *vt* exclude; rule out (*possibilità, ipotesi*)

**esclusi'one** *nf* exclusion; **senza** ~ **di colpi** (*attacco*) all-out

**esclu'siva** *nf* exclusive right, sole right; **in** ~ exclusive

**esclusiva'mente** *adv* exclusively

**esclusi'vista** *nmf* exclusive agent

**esclu'sivo** *a* exclusive

**e'scluso** *pp di* **escludere** ● *a* **non è** ~ **che ci sia** it's not out of the question that he'll be there; **esclusi i presenti** with the exception of those present; **esclusi sabati e festivi** except Saturdays and Sundays/holidays ● *nm* outcast

**escogi'tare** *vt* contrive

**escoriazi'one** *nf* graze

**escre'mento** *nm* excrement; **escrementi** *pl* excrement

**escursi'one** *nf* excursion; (*scorreria*) raid; ~ **termica** difference between the lowest and the highest temperature in a 24 hours period

**ese'crabile** *a* abominable

**ese'crare** *vt* abhor

**esecu'tivo** *a* & *nm* executive

**esecu|'tore, -'trice** *nmf* executor; *Mus* performer

**esecuzi'one** *nf* execution; *Mus* performance. ~ **capitale** capital punishment

**esegu'ibile** *nm* *Comput* executable file

**esegu'ire** *vt* carry out; *Jur* execute; *Mus* perform

**e'sempio** *nm* example; **ad** *o* **per** ~ for example; **dare l'**~ **a qcno** set sb an example; **fare un** ~ give an example

**esem'plare** *a* examplary ● *nm* specimen; (*di libro*) copy

**esemplifi'care** *vt* exemplify

**esen'tare** *vt* exempt

**esen'tarsi** *vr* free oneself

**esen'tasse** *a* tax-free

**e'sente** *a* exempt. ~ **da imposta** duty-free. ~ **da IVA** VAT exempt

**e'sequie** *nfpl* funeral rites

**eser'cente** *nmf* shopkeeper

**eserci'tare** *vt* exercise; (*addestrare*) train; (*fare uso di*) exert; (*professione*) practise

**eserci'tarsi** *vr* practise; ~ **nella danza** practise dancing

**eserci'tato** *a* (*occhio*) practised; **tenere la memoria esercitata** give one's memory some exercise

**esercitazi'one** *nf* exercise; *Mil* drill; (*di musica, chimica*) practical class

**e'sercito** *nm* army. **E**~ **della Salvezza** Salvation Army

**eser'cizio** *nm* exercise; (*pratica*) practice; *Comm* financial year; (*azienda*) business; **essere fuori** ~ be out of practice; **nell'**~ **delle proprie funzioni** in the line of duty. ~

**finanziario** financial year. **~ fiscale** fiscal year, tax year. **esercizi** *pl* **a terra** floor exercises. **~ tributario** fiscal year, tax year

**esi'bire** *vt* show off; produce ⟨*documenti*⟩

**esi'birsi** *vr Theat* perform; *fig* show off

**esibizi'one** *nf Theat* performance; (*di documenti*) production

**esibizio'nismo** *nm* showing off

**esibizio'nista** *nmf* exhibitionist

**esi'gente** *a* exacting; (*pignolo*) fastidious

**esi'genza** *nf* demand; (*bisogno*) need

**e'sigere** *vt* demand; (*riscuotere*) collect

**e'siguo** *a* meagre

**esila'rante** *a* exhilarating

**esila'rare** *vt* exhilarate

**'esile** *a* slender; ⟨*voce*⟩ thin

**esili'are** *vt* exile

**esili'arsi** *vr* go into exile

**esili'ato, -a** *a* exiled ● *nmf* exile

**e'silio** *nm* exile

**e'simere** *vt* release

**e'simersi** *vr* **~ da** get out of

**e'simio** *a* distinguished

**esi'stente** *a* existing

**esi'stenza** *nf* existence

**esistenzi'ale** *a* existential

**esistenzia'lismo** *nm* existentialism

**esi'stere** *vi* exist

**esi'tante** *a* hesitating; ⟨*voce*⟩ faltering

**esi'tare** *vi* hesitate

**esitazi'one** *nf* hesitation

**'esito** *nm* result; **avere buon ~** be a success

**'esodo** *nm* exodus

**e'sofago** *nm* oesophagus

**esone'rare** *vt* exempt

**e'sonero** *nm* exemption

**esorbi'tante** *a* exorbitant

**esorbi'tare** *vi* **~ da** exceed

**esor'cismo** *nm* exorcism

**esor'cista** *nmf* exorcist

**esorciz'zare** *vt* exorcize

**esordi'ente** *nmf* person making his/her début

**e'sordio** *nm* opening; (*di attore*) début

**esor'dire** *vi* début

**esor'tare** *vt* (*pregare*) beg; (*incitare*) urge

**eso'terico** *a* esoteric

**e'sotico** *a* exotic

**espa'drillas** *nfpl* espadrilles

**e'spandere** *vt* expand

**e'spandersi** *vr* expand; (*diffondersi*) extend

**espan'dibile** *a Comput* upgradeable

**espandibilità** *nf inv Comput* upgradeability

**espansi'one** *nf* expansion; **in ~** expanding

**espansio'nista** *nmf* expansionist

**espansio'nistico** *a* expansionist

**espan'sivo** *a* expansive; ⟨*persona*⟩ friendly

**espatri'are** *vi* leave one's country

**espatri'ato, -a** *nmf* expatriate, expat *fam*

**e'spatrio** *nm* expatriation

**espedi'ente** *nm* expedient; **vivere di espedienti** live by one's wits

**e'spellere** *vt* expel; send off ⟨*calciatore*⟩

**esperi'enza** *nf* experience; **per ~** ⟨*sapere, parlare*⟩ from experience; **non ha ~** he doesn't have any experience

**esperi'mento** *nm* experiment

**e'sperto, -a** *a* & *nmf* expert. **~ di computer** computer expert

**espi'are** *vt* atone for

**espia'torio** *a* expiatory

**espi'rare** *vt/i* breathe out

**espirazi'one** *nf* exhalation; (*scadenza*) expiry

**espli'care** *vt* carry on

**esplicita'mente** *adv* explicitly

**e'splicito** *a* explicit

**e'splodere** *vi* explode ● *vt* ⟨*arma:*⟩ fire

**esplo'rare** *vt* explore

**esplora|'tore, -'trice** *nmf* explorer; **giovane ~** boy scout; **giovane esploratrice** girl guide

**esplorazi'one** *nf* exploration

**esplosi'one** *nf* explosion

**esplo'sivo** *a* & *nm* explosive

**espo'nente** *nm* exponent; **2 all'~** superscript 2

**esponenzi'ale** *a* exponential

**e'sporre** *vt* expose; display ⟨*merci*⟩; (*spiegare*) expound; exhibit ⟨*quadri ecc*⟩

**e'sporsi** *vr* (*compromettersi*) compromise oneself; (*al sole*) expose oneself; (*alle critiche*) lay oneself open

**espor'tare** *vt Comm, Comput* export

**esporta|'tore, -'trice** *nmf* exporter

**esportazi'one** *nf* export

**espo'simetro** *nm* light meter

**esposi|'tore, -'trice** *nmf* exhibitor ● *nm* display rack

**esposizi'one** *nf* (*mostra*) exhibition; (*in vetrina*) display; (*spiegazione ecc*) exposition; (*posizione, fotografia*) exposure; **con ~ a nord/sud** north-/south-facing

**e'sposto** *pp di* **esporre** ● *a* exposed; ⟨*merce*⟩ on show; ⟨*spiegato*⟩ set out; **~ a nord/sud** north-/south-facing ● *nm* submission

**espressa'mente** *adv* expressly; **non l'ha detto ~** he didn't put it in so many words

**espressi'one** *nf* expression

**espressio'nismo** *nm* expressionism

**espressio'nista** *a* & *nmf* expressionist

**espressio'nistico** *a* expressionistic

**espres'sivo** *a* expressive

**e'spresso** *pp di* **esprimere** ● *a* express ● *nm* (*lettera*) special delivery; (*treno*) express train; (*caffè*) espresso; **per ~** ⟨*spedire*⟩ [by] express [post]; **piatto ~** meal made to order

**e'sprimere** *vt* express

**e'sprimersi** *vr* express oneself

**espropri'are** *vt* dispossess

**espropriazi'one** *nf Jur* expropriation

**e'sproprio** *nm* expropriation

**espulsi'one** *nf* expulsion

**e'spulso** *pp di* **espellere**

**esqui'mese** *a* & *nmf* Eskimo

**es'senza** *nf* essence

**essenzi'ale** *a* essential ● *nm* important thing: **l'~** (*di teoria ecc*) the bare bones; **l'~ è...** (*la cosa più importante*) the main thing is...

**essenzial'mente** *adv* essentially

**'essere** *vi* be; **c'è** there is; **ci sono** there are; **ci sono!** (*ho capito*) I've got it!; **ci siamo!** (*siamo arrivati*) here we are at last!; **non ce n'è più** there's none left; **c'è di che essere contenti** there's a lot to be happy about; **che ora è? – sono le dieci** what time is it? – it's ten o'clock; **chi è? – sono io** who is it? – it's me; **è stato detto che** it has been said that; **siamo in due** there are two of us; **questa camicia è da lavare** this shirt is to be washed; **non è da te** it's not like you; **~ di** belong to; (*provenire da*) be from; **~ per** (*favorevole*) be in favour of; **se fossi in te,...** if I were you,...; **sarà!** if you say so!; **come sarebbe a dire?** what are you getting at? ● *v aux* have; (*in passivi*) be; **siamo arrivati** we have arrived; **ci sono stato ieri** I was there yesterday; **sono nato a Torino** I was born in Turin; **è riconosciuto come...** he is recognized as... ● *nm* being. **~ umano** human being; **~ vivente** living creature

**essic'care** *vt* dry

**essic'cato** *a* dried; (*noce di cocco*) desiccated

**'esso, -a** *pers pron* he, she; (*cosa, animale*) it

**est** *nm* east; **l'E~ europeo** Eastern Europe

**'estasi** *nf* ecstasy; **andare in ~ per** go into raptures over

**estasi'are** *vt* enrapture

**estasi'arsi** *vr* go into raptures

**e'state** *nf* summer

**e'statico** *a* ecstatic

**estempo'raneo** *a* impromptu

**e'stendere** *vt* extend

**e'stendersi** *vr* spread; (*allungarsi*) stretch

**estensi'one** *nf* extension; (*ampiezza*) expanse; *Mus* range

**esten'sivo** *a* extensive

**estenu'ante** *a* exhausting

**estenu'are** *vt* exhaust

**estenu'arsi** *vr* exhaust oneself

**'estere** *nm* ester

**esteri'ore** *a & nm* exterior

**esteriorità** *nf inv* outward appearance; **badare all'~** judge by appearances

**esterioriz'zare** *vt* externalize

**esterior'mente** *adv* externally; (*di persone*) outwardly

**esterna'mente** *adv* on the outside

**ester'nare** *vt* express, show

**e'sterno, -a** *a* external; (*scala*) outside; **per uso ~** for external use only ● *nm Archit* exterior; (*in film*) location shot ● *nmf* day-pupil

**'estero** *a* foreign ● *nm* foreign countries *pl*; **all'~** abroad; **ministero degli esteri** ≈ Foreign Office *Br*, State Department *Am*

**esterofi'lia** *nf* xenophilia

**este'rofilo** *a* xenophile

**esterre'fatto** *a* horrified

**e'steso** *pp di* **estendere** ● *a* extensive; (*diffuso*) widespread; **per ~** (*scrivere*) in full

**e'steta** *nmf* aesthete

**e'stetica** *nf* aesthetics

**estetica'mente** *adv* aesthetically

**esteticità** *nf* aestheticism

**e'stetico** *a* aesthetic; (*chirurgia, chirurgo*) plastic

**este'tismo** *nm* (*dottrina, carattere*) aestheticism

**este'tista** *nmf* beautician

**estima'tore, -'trice** *nmf* fan

**'estimo** *nm* estimate

**e'stinguere** *vt* extinguish; close (*conto*)

**e'stinguersi** *vr* die out

**e'stinto, -a** *pp di* **estinguere** ● *nmf* deceased

**estin'tore** *nm* [fire] extinguisher

**estinzi'one** *nf* extinction; (*di incendio*) putting out

**estir'pare** *vt* uproot; extract (*dente*); *fig* eradicate (*crimine, malattia*)

**estirpazi'one** *nf* eradication; (*di dente*) extraction

**e'stivo** *a* summer *attrib*

**e'stone** *a & nm* Estonian

**E'stonia** *nf* Estonia

**e'storcere** *vt* extort

**estorsi'one** *nf* extortion

**e'storto** *pp di* **estorcere**

**estradizi'one** *nf* extradition

**estra'gone** *nm* tarragon

**estra'ibile** *a* removeable

**e'straneo, -a** *a* extraneous; (*straniero*) foreign ● *nmf* stranger

**estrani'are** *vt* estrange

**estrani'arsi** *vr* become estranged

**estrapo'lare** *vt* extrapolate

**e'strarre** *vt* extract; (*sorteggiare*) draw

**e'stratto** *pp di* **estrarre** ● *nm* extract; (*brano*) excerpt; (*documento*) abstract. **~ conto** statement [of account], bank statement

**estrazi'one** *nf* extraction; (*a sorte*) draw

**estrema'mente** *adv* extremely

**estre'mismo** *nm* extremism

**estre'mista** *nmf* extremist

**estremità** *nf inv* extremity; (*di una corda*) end; **~ pl** *Anat* extremities

**e'stremo** *a* extreme; (*ultimo*) last; **misure estreme** drastic measures; **fare un ~ tentativo** make one last try; **l'E~ Oriente** the Far East; **~ saluto** *Mil* military funeral; **l'estrema unzione** last rites ● *nm* (*limite*) extreme; **all'~** in the extreme; **passare da un ~ all'altro** go from one extreme to the other; **estremi** *pl* (*di documento*) main points; (*di reato*) essential elements; **essere agli estremi** be at the end of one's tether; **andare agli estremi** go to extremes; **essere all'~ delle forze** have no strength left

**'estro** *nm* (*disposizione artistica*) talent; (*ispirazione*) inspiration; (*capriccio*) whim

**e'strogeno** *nm* oestrogen

**estro'mettere** *vt* expel

**estromissi'one** *nf* ejection

**e'stroso** *a* talented; (*capriccioso*) unpredictable

**estro'verso** *a* extroverted ● *nm* extrovert
**estu'ario** *nm* estuary
**esube'rante** *a* exuberant
**esube'ranza** *nf* exuberance
**e'subero** *nm* ~ **cassa integrazione** voluntary redundancy
**esu'lare** *vt* ~ **da** be beyond the scope of
**'esule** *nmf* exile
**esul'tante** *a* exultant
**esul'tanza** *nf* exultation
**esul'tare** *vi* rejoice
**esu'mare** *vt* exhume
**età** *nf* age; **raggiungere la maggiore** ~ come of age; **un uomo di mezz'** ~ a middle-aged man; **avere la stessa** ~ be the same age; **che** ~ **gli daresti?** how old would you say he was?; **fin dalla più tenera** ~ from his/her etc earliest years; **in** ~ **avanzata** of advanced years; **è senza** ~ it's hard to tell his age. ~ **del Bronzo** Bronze Age. ~ **della pensione** retirement age
**e'tano** *nm* ethane
**eta'nolo** *nm* ethanol
**'etere** *nm* ether. ~ **etilico** ether
**e'tereo** *a* ethereal
**eterna'mente** *adv* eternally
**eternità** *nf* eternity; **è un'** ~ **che non la vedo** I haven't seen her for ages
**e'terno** *a* eternal; ⟨*questione, problema*⟩ age-old; ⟨*fig: dicorso, conferenza*⟩ never-ending; **in** ~ *fam* for ever; **giurare** ~ **amore** swear undying love; **un** ~ **bambino** a child
**etero'geneo** *a* diverse, heterogeneous
**eterosessu'ale** *a* & *nmf* heterosexual
**eterosessualità** *nf* heterosexuality
**'etica** *nf* ethics
**eti'chetta¹** *nf* label; ⟨con il prezzo⟩ price-tag
**eti'chetta²** *nf* ⟨cerimoniale⟩ etiquette
**etichet'tare** *vt* label
**etichetta'trice** *nf* labelling machine
**etichetta'tura** *nf* ⟨operazione⟩ labelling
**'etico** *a* ethical
**eti'lometro** *nm* Breathalyzer ᴿ˙
**etimolo'gia** *nf* etymology
**e'tiope** *a* & *nmf* Ethiopian
**Eti'opia** *nf* Ethiopia
**eti'opico** *a* Ethiopian
**'Etna** *nm* Etna
**et'nia** *nf* ethnic group
**'etnico** *a* ethnic
**etnolo'gia** *nf* ethnology
**e'trusco** *a* & *nmf* Etruscan
**'ettaro** *nm* hectare
**+ettino** *suff* **cosettina** *nf* small thing; **è una cosettina da niente** it's nothing
**'etto, etto'grammo** *nm* hundred grams, quarter pound
**+etto** *suff* **cameretta** *nf* little bedroom; **scherzetto** *nf* prank; **piccoletto** *nm pej* shorty
**et'tolitro** *nm* hectolitre
**euca'lipto** *nm* eucalyptus
**eucari'stia** *nf* Eucharist
**eufe'mismo** *nm* euphemism
**eufe'mistico** *a* euphemistic

**eufo'ria** *nf* elation; *Med* euphoria
**eu'forico** *a* elated; *Med* euphoric
**euge'netica** *nf* eugenics
**eu'nuco** *nm* eunuch
**Eur'asia** *nf* Eurasia
**eurasi'atico** *a* Eurasian
**'EURATOM** *nf abbr* (**Comunità Europea dell'Energia Atomica**) EURATOM
**euro+** *pref* Euro+
**eurobbligazi'one** *nf* Eurobond
**euro'cheque** *nm inv* Eurocheque
**Euro'city** *nm inv Rail* international Intercity
**eurodepu'tato** *nm* Euro MP, MEP
**eurodi'visa** *nf* Eurocurrency
**euro'dollaro** *nm* Eurodollar
**Eu'ropa** *nf* Europe
**europe'ismo** *nm* Europeanism
**euro'peo, -a** *a* & *nmf* European
**euro'scettico** *nm* eurosceptic
**eutana'sia** *nf* euthanasia
**evacu'are** *vt* evacuate
**evacuazi'one** *nf* evacuation
**e'vadere** *vt* evade; ⟨sbrigare⟩ deal with ● *vi* ~ **da** escape from
**evane'scente** *a* vanishing
**evan'gelico** *a* evangelical
**evange'lista** *nm* evangelist
**evan'gelo** *nm* = **vangelo**
**evapo'rare** *vi* evaporate
**evaporazi'one** *nf* evaporation
**evasi'one** *nf* escape; ⟨fiscale⟩ evasion; *fig* escapism
**evasiva'mente** *adv* evasively
**eva'sivo** *a* evasive
**e'vaso, -a** *pp di* **evadere** ● *nmf* fugitive
**eva'sore** *nm* ~ **fiscale** tax evader
**eveni'enza** *nf* eventuality; **in ogni** ~ if need be
**e'vento** *nm* event
**eventu'ale** *a* possible
**eventualità** *nf inv* eventuality; **in ogni** ~ at all events; **nell'** ~ **che** in the event that
**eventual'mente** *adv* if necessary
**ever'sivo** *a* subversive
**evi'dente** *a* evident
**evidente'mente** *adv* evidently
**evi'denza** *nf* evidence; **mettere in** ~ emphasize; **mettersi in** ~ make oneself conspicuous; **arrendersi all'** ~ face the facts
**evidenzi'are** *vt* highlight
**evidenzia'tore** *nm* ⟨penna⟩ highlighter
**evi'rare** *vt* emasculate
**evi'tare** *vt* avoid; ⟨risparmiare⟩ spare
**'evo** *nm* age
**evo'care** *vt* evoke
**evolu'tivo** *a* evolutionary
**evo'luto** *pp di* **evolvere** ● *a* evolved; ⟨progredito⟩ progressive; ⟨civiltà, nazione⟩ advanced; **una donna evoluta** a modern woman
**evoluzi'one** *nf* evolution; ⟨di ⁱⁱginnasta, aereo⟩ circle
**e'volvere** *vt* develop
**e'volversi** *vr* evolve
**ev'viva** *int* hurray; ~ **il Papa!** long live the

Pope!: **gridare** ~ cheer; ~ **la modestia!** what modesty!

**ex** *prep* ex, former; **ex moglie** ex-wife

**ex 'aequo** *adv* **arrivare** ~ ~ come in joint first

**ex-Jugo|slavia** *nf* ex-Yugoslavia

**ex-jugo'slavo** *a & nmf* ex-Yugoslav

**ex 'libris** *nm inv* bookplate

**ex'ploit** *nm inv* feat, exploit

**'extra** *a inv* extra; ⟨qualità⟩ first-class ● *nm*

*inv* extra

**extracomuni'tario** *a* non-EC, non-EU

**extraconiu'gale** *a* extramarital

**extraeuro'peo** *a* non-European

**extraparlamen'tare** *a* extraparliamentary

**extrasco'lastico** *a* extra-curricular

**extrasensori'ale** *a* extrasensory

**extrater'restre** *nmf* extra-terrestrial

**extrauniversi'tario** *a* extramural

**ex 'voto** *nm inv* ex voto

# Ff

**fa¹** *nm inv* Mus (chiave, nota) F

**fa²** *adv* ago; **due mesi** ~ two months ago

**fabbi'sogno** *nm* requirements pl, needs pl. ~ **dello Stato** government spending estimates

**'fabbrica** *nf* factory

**fabbri'cabile** *a* ⟨area, terreno⟩ that can be built on

**fabbri'cante** *nm* manufacturer. ~ **d'armi** arms manufacturer

**fabbri'care** *vt* build; (produrre) manufacture; (fig: inventare) fabricate

**fabbri'cato** *nm* building

**fabbricazi'one** *nf* manufacturing; (costruzione) building

**'fabbro** *nm* blacksmith

**fac'cenda** *nf* matter; **faccende** pl **domestiche** housework sg

**faccendi'ere** *nm* wheeler-dealer

**fac'chino** *nm* porter

**'faccia** *nf* face; (di foglio) side; ~ **a** ~ face to face; ~ **tosta** cheek; **voltar** ~ change sides; **di** ~ ⟨palazzo⟩ opposite; **alla** ~ **di** ⟨fam: a dispetto di⟩ in spite of; **alla** ~! ⟨stupore⟩ bloody hell!

**facci'ata** *nf* façade; (di foglio) side; (fig: esteriorità) outward appearance

**fa'cente** *nmf* ~ **funzioni** deputy

**fa'ceto** *a* facetious; **tra il serio e il** ~ half joking

**fa'cezia** *nf* (battuta) witticism

**fa'chiro** *nm* fakir

**'facile** *a* easy; (affabile) easy-going; **essere** ~ **alle critiche** be quick to criticize; **essere** ~ **al riso** laugh a lot; **è** ~ **a farsi** easy to do; **è** ~ **che piova** it's likely to rain

**facilità** *nf inv* ease; (disposizione) aptitude; **avere** ~ **di parola** express oneself well. ~ **d'uso** ease of use, user-friendliness

**facili'tare** *vt* facilitate

**facilitazi'one** *nf* facility; **facilitazioni** pl Fin special terms; **facilitazioni** pl **di pagamento** Fin easy terms

**facil'mente** *adv* (con facilità) easily; (probabilmente) probably

**faci'lone** *a* slapdash

**facilone'ria** *nf* slapdash attitude

**facino'roso** *a* violent

**facoltà** *nf inv* faculty; (potere) power; **essere nel pieno possesso delle proprie** ~ be compos mentis

**facolta'tivo** *a* optional; **fermata facoltativa** request stop

**facol'toso** *a* wealthy

**fac'simile** *nm* facsimile

**fac'totum** *nm inv* man Friday ● *nf inv* girl Friday

**'faggio** *nm* beech

**fagi'ano** *nm* pheasant

**fagio'lino** *nm* French bean

**fagi'olo** *nm* bean; **a** ~ ⟨arrivare, capitare⟩ at the right time. ~ **borlotto** borlotti bean. ~ **di Spagna** runner bean, string bean

**fagoci'tare** *vt* gobble up ⟨società⟩

**fa'gotto** *nm* bundle; Mus bassoon

**Fahren'heit** *a* Fahrenheit

**'faida** *nf* feud

**fai da te** *nm* do-it-yourself, DIY

**fa'ina** *nf* weasel

**fa'lange** *nf* (dito, Mil) phalanx

**fal'cata** *nf* stride

**'falce** *nf* scythe; ~ **e martello** (simbolo) the hammer and sickle

**fal'cetto** *nm* sickle

**falci'are** *vt* cut; fig mow down

**falci'ata** *nf* (quantità d'erba) swathe

**falcia'trice** *nf* [lawn-]mower

**'falco** *nm* hawk

**fal'cone** *nm* falcon

**'falda** *nf* stratum; (di neve) flake; (di cappello) brim; (di cappotto, frac) coat-tails; (pendio) slope. ~ **freatica** water table

**fale'gname** *nm* carpenter

**falegname'ria** *nf* carpentry

**fa'lena** *nf* moth

**'Falkland** *nfpl* **le** [**isole**] ~ the Falklands

**'falla** *nf* leak

**fal'lace** *a* deceptive

**'fallico** *a* phallic

**fallimen'tare** *a* disastrous; *Jur* bankruptcy

**falli'mento** *nm Comm* bankruptcy; *fig* failure

**fal'lire** *vi Comm* go bankrupt; *fig* fail ● *vt* miss ⟨*colpo*⟩

**fal'lito** *a* unsuccessful ● *a & nm* bankrupt

**'fallo** *nm* fault; (*errore*) mistake; *Sport* foul; (*imperfezione*) flaw: **senza ~** without fail; **cogliere in ~** catch red-handed; **mettere un piede in ~** slip. **~ di mano** (*in calcio*) handball

**falò** *nm inv* bonfire

**fal'sare** *vt* alter; (*falsificare*) falsify

**falsa'riga** *nf* **sulla ~ di** along the same lines as

**fal'sario, -a** *nmf* forger; (*di documenti*) counterfeiter

**fal'setto** *nm* falsetto

**falsifi'care** *vt* fake; (*contraffare*) forge

**falsificazi'one** *nf* (*di documento*) falsification

**falsità** *nf* falseness

**'falso** *a* false; (*sbagliato*) wrong; ⟨*opera d'arte ecc*⟩ fake; (*gioielli, oro*) imitation; **essere un ~ magro** be fatter than one looks ● *nm* forgery; **giurare il ~** commit perjury. **~ in atto pubblico** forgery of a legal document

**'fama** *nf* fame; (*reputazione*) reputation

**'fame** *nf* hunger; **aver ~** be hungry; **fare la ~** barely scrape a living; **da ~** ⟨*stipendio*⟩ miserly; **avere una ~ da lupo** be ravenous

**fa'melico** *a* ravenous

**famige'rato** *a* infamous

**fa'miglia** *nf* family

**famili'are** *a* family *attrib*; (*ben noto*) familiar; (*senza cerimonie*) informal ● *nm* relative, relation

**familiarità** *nf* familiarity; (*informalità*) informality

**familiariz'zarsi** *vr* familiarize oneself

**fa'moso** *a* famous

**fa'nale** *nm* lamp; *Auto ecc* light. **fanali** *pl* **posteriori** *Auto* rear lights

**fana'lino** *nm* **~ di coda** *Auto* tail light; **essere il ~ di coda** *fig* bring up the rear, be the back marker

**fa'natico, -a** *a* fanatical; **essere ~ di calcio/cinema** be a football/cinema fanatic ● *nmf* fanatic

**fana'tismo** *nm* fanaticism

**fanciul'lezza** *nf* childhood

**fanci'ullo, -a** *nmf* young boy; young girl

**fan'donia** *nf* lie; **fandonie!** nonsense!

**fan'fara** *nf* fanfare; (*complesso*) brass band

**fanfaro'nata** *nf* brag; **fanfaronate** *pl* bragging

**fanfa'rone, -a** *nmf* braggart

**fan'ghiglia** *nf* mud

**'fango** *nm* mud

**fan'goso** *a* muddy

**fannul'lone, -a** *nmf* idler

**fantasci'enza** *nf* science fiction

**fanta'sia** *nf* fantasy; (*immaginazione*) imagination; (*capriccio*) fancy; (*di tessuto*) pattern; **fantasie** *pl* (*sciocchezze*) moonshine

**fantasi'oso** *a* ⟨*stilista, ragazzo*⟩ imaginative; ⟨*resoconto*⟩ improbable, fanciful

**fan'tasma** *nm* ghost; **essere il ~ di se stesso** be a shadow of one's former self: **città ~** ghost town; **governo ~** shadow cabinet

**fantasti'care** *vi* day-dream, fantasize

**fantasti'cheria** *nf* day-dream, fantasy

**fan'tastico** *a* fantastic; ⟨*racconto*⟩ fantasy *attrib*

**'fante** *nm* infantryman; (*nelle carte*) jack

**fante'ria** *nm* infantry

**fan'tino** *nm* jockey

**fan'toccio** *nm* puppet

**fanto'matico** *a* (*inafferrabile*) phantom *attrib*; (*immaginario*) mythical

**fara'butto** *nm* trickster

**fara'ona** *nf* (*uccello*) guinea-fowl

**'farcia** *nf* stuffing; (*di torta*) filling

**far'cire** *vt* stuff; fill ⟨*torta*⟩

**far'cito** *a* stuffed; ⟨*dolce*⟩ filled

**fard** *nm inv* blusher

**far'dello** *nm* bundle; *fig* burden

**'fare** *vt* do; make ⟨*dolce, letto, ecc*⟩; (*recitare la parte di*) play; (*trascorrere*) spend; **~ una pausa/un sogno** have a break/a dream; **~ colpo su** impress; **~ paura a** frighten; **~ piacere a** please; **farla finita** put an end to it; **~ l'insegnante** be a teacher; **~ lo scemo** play the idiot; **~ una settimana al mare** spend a week at the seaside; **3 più 3 fa 6** 3 and 3 makes 6; **quanto fa? – fanno 10 000 lire** how much is it? – it's 10,000 lire; **far ~ qcsa a qcno** get sb to do sth; (*costringere*) make sb do sth; **~ vedere** show; **fammi parlare** let me speak; **niente a che ~ con** nothing to do with; **non c'è niente da ~** (*per problema*) there is nothing we/you etc can do; **fa caldo/buio** it's warm/dark; **non fa niente** it doesn't matter; **strada facendo** on the way. **farcela** (*riuscire*) manage ● *vi* **fai in modo di venire** try and come; **~ da** act as; **~ per** make as if to; **~ presto** be quick; **non fa per me** it's not for me ● *nm* (*comportamento*) manner; **sul far del giorno** at daybreak

**fa'retto** *nm* spot[light]

**far'falla** *nf* butterfly

**farfal'lino** *nm* (*cravatta*) bow tie

**farfugli'are** *vt* mutter

**fa'rina** *nf* flour. **~ di ceci** chickpea flour, gram flour. **~ gialla** maize flour. **~ integrale** wholemeal flour. **~ lattea** powdered milk for babies. **~ d'ossa** bonemeal

**fari'nacei** *nmpl* starchy food *sg*

**fa'ringe** *nf* pharynx

**farin'gite** *nf* pharyngitis

**fari'noso** *a* ⟨*neve*⟩ powdery; ⟨*mela*⟩ soft; ⟨*patata*⟩ floury

**farma'ceutico** *a* pharmaceutical; **industria farmaceutica** pharmaceuticals industry

**farma'cia** *nf* pharmacy; (*negozio*) chemist's [shop]. **~ di turno** duty pharmacy

**farma'cista** *nmf* chemist, pharmacist

**'farmaco** nm drug; **essere sotto farmaci** be on medication

**'faro** nm Auto headlight; Aeron beacon; (costruzione) lighthouse; **abbassare i fari** dip one's headlights; **accendere i fari** switch on one's lights. **fari** pl **antinebbia** fog lamps. **fari** pl **posteriori** rear lights

**farragi'noso** a confused

**'farsa** nf farce

**far'sesco** a farcical

**'farsi** vr (diventare) get; (sl: drogarsi) shoot up: **~ avanti** come forward; **~ i fatti propri** mind one's own business; **~ la barba** shave; **~ la villa** fam buy a villa; **~ il ragazzo** fam find a boyfriend; **~ due risate** have a laugh; **~ male** hurt oneself; **~ un nome** make a name for oneself; **farsela sotto** fam wet oneself

**Far 'west** nm Wild West

**fa'scetta** nf strip; (per capelli) hair band; (di giornale) wrapper

**'fascia** nf band; (zona) area; (ufficiale) sash; (benda) bandage; (di smoking) cummerbund; (in statistica) bracket. **~ per capelli** hair band. **~ elastica** crepe bandage; (ventriera) girdle. **~ d'età** age bracket, age group. **~ d'ozono** ozone layer. **~ di reddito** income bracket

**fasci'are** vt bandage; cling to (fianchi)

**fasci'arsi** vr bandage; **~ la testa prima di rompersela** worry about something that might never happen

**fascia'tura** nf dressing; (azione) bandaging

**fascicola|'tore, -'trice** nmf sorter

**fa'scicolo** nm file; (di rivista) issue; (libretto) booklet

**fa'scina** nf faggot

**'fascino** nm fascination

**fasci'noso** a charming

**'fascio** nm bundle; (di fiori) bunch. **~ di luce** beam of light

**fa'scismo** nm fascism

**fa'scista** a & nmf fascist

**'fase** nf phase; **il motore è fuori ~** the timing is wrong; **sono fuori ~** I'm not firing on all four cylinders; **essere in ~ di miglioramento** be on the mend, be recovering; **essere in ~ di espansione** be expanding

**fast 'food** nm inv fast food; (ristorante) fast food restaurant

**fa'stidio** nm nuisance; (scomodo) inconvenience. **~** pl (preoccupazioni) worries; (disturbi) troubles; **dar ~ a qcno** bother sb

**fastidi'oso** a tiresome

**'fasto** nm pomp

**fa'stoso** a sumptuous

**fa'sullo** a bogus

**'fata** nf fairy

**fa'tale** a fatal; (inevitabile) fated; **donna ~** femme fatale

**fata'lismo** nm fatalism

**fata'lista** nmf fatalist ● a fatalistic

**fatalità** nf inv fate; (caso sfortunato) misfortune

**fatal'mente** adv inevitably

**fa'tato** a (anello, bacchetta) magic

**fa'tica** nf effort; (lavoro faticoso) hard work; (stanchezza, di metalli) fatigue; **a ~** with great difficulty; **è ~ sprecata** it's a waste of time; **fare ~ a fare qcsa** find it difficult to do sth; **senza [nessuna] ~** without [any] effort; **fare ~ a finire qcsa** struggle to finish sth; **uomo di ~** odd-job man

**fati'caccia** nf pain

**fati'care** vi toil; **~ a** (stentare) find it difficult to

**fati'cata** nf effort; (sfacchinata) grind

**fati'coso** a tiring; (difficile) difficult

**fati'scente** a crumbling

**'fato** nm fate

**fat'taccio** nm hum foul deed

**fat'tezze** nfpl features

**fat'tibile** a feasible

**fatti'specie** nf **nella ~** in this case

**'fatto** pp di fare; **ormai è fatta!** what's done is done ● a made; **~ a mano/in casa** handmade/home-made; **essere ben ~** (persona) have a nice figure; **un uomo ~** a grown man ● nm fact; (azione) action; (avvenimento) event; (faccenda) business, matter; **sa il ~ suo** he knows his business; **le ho detto il ~ suo** I told him what I thought of him; **di ~** in fact; **in ~ di** as regards; **~ sta che** the fact remains that; **mettere di fronte al ~ compiuto** present with a fait accompli

**fat'tore** nm (causa, Math) factor; (di fattoria) farm manager

**fatto'ria** nf farm; (casa) farmhouse

**fatto'rino** nm messenger [boy]. **~ d'albergo** bellboy

**fattucchi'era** nf witch

**fat'tura** nf (stile) cut; (lavorazione) workmanship; Comm invoice. **~ di acquisto** purchase invoice. **~ pro-forma** pro forma [invoice]. **~ di vendita** sales invoice

**fattu'rare** vt invoice; (adulterare) adulterate

**fattu'rato** nm turnover, sales pl

**fatturazi'one** nf invoicing, billing

**'fatuo** a fatuous

**'fauci** nfpl (di leone) maw sg

**'fauna** nf fauna

**'fausto** a propitious

**fau'tore** nm supporter

**'fava** nf broad bean

**fa'vella** nf speech

**fa'villa** nf spark

**'favo** nm honeycomb

**'favola** nf fable; (fiaba) story; (oggetto di pettegolezzi) laughing-stock; **è una ~!** (meraviglia) it's divine!

**favo'loso** a fabulous

**fa'vore** nm favour; **essere a ~ di** be in favour of; **per ~** please; **di ~** (condizioni, trattamento) preferential; **col ~ delle tenebre** under cover of darkness

**favoreggia'mento** nm Jur aiding and abetting

**favo'revole** a favourable

**favorevol'mente** adv favourably

**favo'rire** *vt* favour; (*promuovere*) promote; **vuol ~?** (*a cena, pranzo*) will you have some?; (*entrare*) will you come in?; **favorisca alla cassa** please pay at the cash-desk; **favorisca i documenti** your papers please

**favo'rito, -a** *a & nmf* favourite

**fax** *nm inv* fax; **inviare via ~** fax, send by fax. **~ a carta comune** plain paper fax

**fa'xare** *vt* fax

**fazi'one** *nf* faction

**faziosità** *nf* bias

**fazi'oso** *nm* sectarian

**fazzolet'tino** *nm* **~ [di carta]** [paper] tissue

**fazzo'letto** *nm* handkerchief: (*da testa*) headscarf

**feb'braio** *nm* February

**'febbre** *nf* fever; **avere la ~** have *o* run a temperature; **~ da fieno** hay fever

**febbrici'tante** *a* fevered

**feb'brile** *a* feverish

**febbril'mente** *adv* feverishly

**'feccia** *nf* dregs *pl*

**'fecola** *nf* potato flour

**fecon'dare** *vt* fertilize

**feconda'tore** *nm* fertilizer

**fecondazi'one** *nf* fertilization; **~ artificiale** artificial insemination. **~ in vitro** in vitro fertilization, IVF

**fe'condo** *a* fertile

**'fede** *nf* faith; (*fiducia*) trust; (*anello*) wedding ring; **in buona/mala ~** in good/bad faith; **prestar ~ a** believe; **tener ~ alla parola** keep one's word; **aver ~ in qcno** have faith in sb, believe in sb; **degno di ~** reliable; **in ~** Yours faithfully

**fe'dele** *a* faithful ● *nmf* believer; (*seguace*) follower; **i fedeli** the faithful

**fedel'mente** *adv* faithfully

**fedeltà** *nf* faithfulness; **alta ~** high fidelity

**'federa** *nf* pillowcase

**fede'rale** *a* federal

**federa'lismo** *nm* federalism

**federa'lista** *a* federalist

**fede'rato** *a* federate

**federazi'one** *nf* federation

**fe'difrago, -a** *a* faithless; *hum* two-timing ● *nm* faithless wretch; *hum* two-timer

**fe'dina** *nf* **avere la ~ penale sporca/pulita** have a/no criminal record

**fega'telli** *nmpl* (*di maiale*) pork liver

**fega'tino** *nm* **fegatini** *pl* **di pollo** chicken livers

**'fegato** *nm* liver; *fig* guts *pl*; **mangiarsi il ~, rodersi il ~** be consumed with rage

**'felce** *nf* fern

**fe'lice** *a* happy; (*fortunato*) lucky; **~ come una Pasqua** blissfully happy

**felice'mente** *adv* happily; (*con successo*) successfully

**felicità** *nf* happiness

**felici'tarsi** *vr* **~ con** congratulate

**felicitazi'oni** *nfpl* congratulations

**fe'lino** *a* feline

**'felpa** *nf* (*indumento*) sweatshirt; (*stoffa*) felt

**fel'pato** *a* brushed; (*passo*) stealthy

**'feltro** *nm* felt; (*cappello*) felt hat

**'femmina** *nf* female

**femmi'nile** *a* feminine; (*rivista, abbigliamento*) women's; (*sesso*) female ● *nm* feminine

**femminilità** *nf* femininity

**femmi'nismo** *nm* feminism

**'femore** *nm* femur

**'fendere** *vt* split

**fendi'nebbia** *nm inv* fog lamp

**fendi'tura** *nf* split; (*in roccia*) crack

**fe'nice** *nf* phoenix

**feni'cottero** *nm* flamingo

**fenome'nale** *a* phenomenal

**fe'nomeno** *nm* phenomenon

**'feretro** *nm* coffin

**feri'ale** *a* weekday; **giorno ~** weekday

**'ferie** *nfpl* holidays; (*di università, tribunale ecc*) vacation *sg*; **andare in ~** go on holiday; **prendere le ~** go on holiday; **prendere delle ~** take time off; **prendere un giorno di ~** take a day off

**feri'mento** *nm* wounding

**fe'rire** *vt* wound; (*in incidente*) injure; *fig* hurt

**fe'rirsi** *vr* injure oneself

**fe'rita** *nf* wound

**fe'rito** *a* wounded ● *nm* wounded person; *Mil* casualty; **~ grave** seriously injured person

**feri'toia** *nf* loophole; **feritoie** *pl* **per le schede di espansione** *Comput* expansion slots

**'ferma** *nf Mil* period of service

**fermacal'zoni** *nm inv* cycle clip

**fermaca'pelli** *nm inv* hair slide

**ferma'carte** *nm inv* paperweight

**fermacra'vatta** *nm inv* tiepin

**ferma'fogli** *nm inv* bulldog clip

**fer'maglio** *nm* clasp; (*spilla*) brooch; (*per capelli*) hair slide

**ferma'mente** *adv* firmly

**ferma'porta** *nm inv* doorstop

**fer'mare** *vt* stop; (*fissare*) fix; *Jur* detain ● *vi* stop

**fer'marsi** *vr* stop

**fer'mata** *nf* stop; '**~ prenotata**' 'bus stopping'; **senza fermate** (*tragitto*) non-stop. **~ dell'autobus** bus stop. **~ obbligatoria** compulsory stop. **~ a richiesta** request stop

**fermen'tare** *vi* ferment

**fermentazi'one** *nf* fermentation

**fer'mento** *nm* ferment; (*lievito*) yeast; **essere in ~** be in/get into a tizzy

**fer'mezza** *nf* firmness

**'fermo** *a* still; (*veicolo*) stationary; (*stabile*) steady; (*orologio*) not working; **~!** don't move!; **~ restando che...** it being understood that... ; '**~ per manutenzione**' 'closed for repairs' ● *nm Jur* detention; *Mech* catch; **in stato di ~** in custody. **~ immagine** *TV* freeze frame. **~ posta** poste restante, general delivery *Am*

**fer'net®** *nm inv* bitter digestive liqueur

**fe'roce** *a* fierce, ferocious: ‹*bestia*› wild; ‹*freddo, dolore*› unbearable

**fero'ce'mente** *adv* fiercely, ferociously

**fe'rocia** *nf* ferocity

**fer'raglia** *nf* scrap iron

**ferra'gosto** *nm* 15 August (*bank holiday in Italy*); (*periodo*) August holidays *pl*

**ferra'menta** *nfpl* ironmongery *sg*; **negozio di ~** ironmonger's

**fer'rare** *vt* shoe ‹*cavallo*›

**fer'rato** *a* **~ in** (*preparato in*) well up in

**'ferreo** *a* iron

**'ferro** *nm* iron; (*attrezzo*) tool; (*di chirurgo*) instrument; **di ~** ‹*memoria*› excellent; ‹*alibi*› cast-iron; **salute di ~** ‹ iron constitution; **ai ferri** ‹*bistecca*› grilled; **essere ai ferri corti** be at daggers drawn; **mettere il paese a ~ e fuoco** put a country to the sword; **i ferri del mestiere** the tools of the trade. **~ battuto** wrought iron. **~ da calza** knitting needle. **~ di cavallo** horseshoe. **~ da stiro** iron. **~ a vapore** steam iron

**fer'roso** *a* ferrous

**ferro'vecchio** *nm* scrap merchant

**ferro'via** *nf* railway, railroad *Am*; **Ferrovie pl dello Stato** Italian State Railways

**ferrovi'ario** *a* railway *attrib*, railroad *Am attrib*

**ferrovi'ere** *nm* railwayman, railroad worker *Am*

**'fertile** *a* fertile

**fertilità** *nf* fertility

**fertiliz'zante** *nm* fertilizer

**fertilizzazi'one** *nf* fertilization

**fer'vente** *a* blazing; *fig* fervent

**fervente'mente** *adv* fervently

**'fervere** *vi* ‹*preparativi:*› be well under way

**fervida'mente** *adv* fervently

**'fervido** *a* fervent; **fervidi auguri** best wishes

**fer'vore** *nm* fervour; (*di discussione*) heat

**'fesa** *nf* (*carne*) rump

**fesse'ria** *nf* dire/fare una **~** *fam* say/do something stupid

**'fesso** *pp di fendere* ● *a* cracked; (*fam: sciocco*) foolish ● *nm* (*fam: idiota*) fool; **far ~ qcno** *fam* con sb

**fes'sura** *nf* crack; (*per gettone ecc*) slot. **~ [per la scheda] di espansione** *Comput* expansion slot

**'festa** *nf* feast; (*giorno festivo*) holiday; (*compleanno*) birthday; (*ricevimento*) party; *fig* joy; **fare ~ a qcno** welcome sb; **essere in ~** be on holiday; **far ~** celebrate; **della ~** ‹*vestito, tovaglia*› best; **conciare qcno per le feste** give sb a sound thrashing; **le feste** (*Natale, Capodanno ecc*) the holidays. **~ di compleanno** birthday party. **~ della mamma** Mother's Day, Mothering Sunday. **~ nazionale** public holiday. **~ del papà** Father's Day

**festai'olo** *a* festive

**festeggia'mento** *nm* celebration; (*mani-*

*festazione*) festivity; **festeggiamenti** *pl* celebrations

**festeggi'are** *vt* celebrate; (*accogliere festosamente*) give a hearty welcome to

**fe'stino** *nm* party

**festività** *nfpl* festivities

**fe'stivo** *a* holiday; (*lieto*) festive; **festivi** *pl* public holidays

**fe'stone** *nm* (*nel cucito*) scallop, scollop; (*di carta*) paper chain

**fe'stoso** *a* merry

**fe'tente** *a* evil smelling; *fig* revolting ● *nmf fam* bastard

**fe'ticcio** *nm* fetish

**'feto** *nm* foetus

**fe'tore** *nm* stench

**'fetta** *nf* slice; **a fette** sliced. **~ biscottata** slices of crispy toast-like bread

**fet'tina** *nf* thin slice

**fet'tuccia** *nf* tape; (*con nome*) name tape

**fettuc'cine** *nfpl* ribbon-shaped pasta

**feu'dale** *a* feudal

**'feudo** *nm* feud

**fez** *nm inv* fez

**FFSS** *abbr* (**Ferrovie dello Stato**) Italian State Railways

**fi'aba** *nf* fairy-tale

**fia'besco** *a* fairy-tale *attrib*

**fi'acca** *nf* weariness; (*indolenza*) laziness; **battere la ~** be sluggish

**fiac'care** *vt* weaken

**fi'acco** *a* weak; (*indolente*) slack; (*stanco*) weary; ‹*partita*› dull

**fi'accola** *nf* torch

**fiacco'lata** *nf* torchlight procession

**fi'ala** *nf* phial

**fia'letta** *nf* phial; **~ puzzolente** stink bomb

**fi'amma** *nf* flame; *Naut* pennant; **in fiamme** in flames; **andare in fiamme** go up in flames; **dare alle fiamme** commit to the flames; **alla ~** *Culin* flambé. **le Fiamme Gialle** body responsible for border control and investigating fraud. **~ ossidrica** blowtorch

**fiam'mante** *a* flaming; **nuovo ~** brand new

**fiam'mata** *nf* blaze

**fiammeggi'are** *vi* blaze ● *vt* singe ‹*pollo*›

**fiam'mifero** *nm* match

**fiam'mingo, -a** *a & nm* Flemish ● *nmf* Fleming

**fian'cata** *nf* wing

**fiancheggi'are** *vt* border; *fig* support

**fi'anco** *nm* side; (*di persona*) hip; (*di animale*) flank; *Mil* wing; **al mio ~** by my side; **~ a ~** ‹*lavorare*› side by side

**Fi'andre** *nfpl* **le ~** Flanders

**fia'schetta** *nf* hip flask

**fiaschette'ria** *nf* wine shop

**fi'asco** *nm* flask; *fig* fiasco; **fare ~** be a fiasco

**fia'tare** *vi* breathe; (*parlare*) breathe a word

**fi'ato** *nm* breath; (*vigore*) stamina; **strumenti a ~** wind instruments; **avere il ~ corto** be short of breath; **senza ~** breathlessly; **tutto d'un ~** ‹*bere, leggere*› all in one go

**'fibbia** *nf* buckle

**'fibra** *nf* fibre; **fibre** *pl* (*alimentari*) roughage. **fibre** *pl* **artificiali** man-made fibres. ~ **ottica** optical fibre; **a fibre ottiche** ⟨*cavo*⟩ fibre optic. ~ **sintetica** man-made fibre. synthetic. ~ **di vetro** fibreglass

**fi'broma** *nm* fibroid

**fi'broso** *a* fibrous

**ficca'naso** *nmf* nosey parker

**fic'care** *vt* thrust; drive ⟨*chiodo ecc*⟩; (*fam: mettere*) shove

**fic'carsi** *vr* thrust oneself; (*nascondersi*) hide: ~ **nei guai** get oneself into trouble

**'fiche** *nf inv* (*gettone*) chip

**'fico** *nm* (*albero*) fig-tree; (*frutto*) fig. ~ **d'India** prickly pear; **non me ne importa un** ~ [**secco**] *fam* I don't give a damn; **non capisce un** ~ [**secco**] *fam* he doesn't understand a bloody thing; **non vale un** ~ [**secco**] *fam* it's totally worthless

**'fico, -a** *fam nmf* cool sort ● *a* cool

**fidanza'mento** *nm* engagement; **rompere il** ~ break off one's engagement, break it off

**fidan'zarsi** *vr* get engaged

**fidan'zata** *nf* (*ufficiale*) fiancée; (*innamorata*) girlfriend

**fidan'zato** *nm* (*ufficiale*) fiancé; (*innamorato*) boyfriend

**fi'darsi** *vr* ~ **di** trust

**fi'dato** *a* trustworthy

**'fido** *a* ⟨*compagno*⟩ loyal ● *nm* devoted follower; *Comm* credit

**fi'ducia** *nf* confidence; **degno di** ~ trustworthy; **persona di** ~ reliable person; **di** ~ ⟨*fornitore, banca*⟩ regular, usual; **avere** ~ **in se stessi** believe in oneself; **incarico di** ~ important job

**fiduci'ario, -a** *a* ⟨*rapporto, transazione*⟩ based on trust ● *nmf* trustee

**fiduci'oso** *a* hopeful

**fi'ele** *nm* bile; *fig* bitterness; **amaro come il** ~ bitter

**fienagi'one** *nf* haymaking

**fie'nile** *nm* barn

**fi'eno** *nm* hay

**fi'era** *nf* fair. ~ **commerciale** trade fair. ~ **del libro** book fair

**fie'rezza** *nf* ⟨*dignità*⟩ pride

**fi'ero** *a* proud

**fi'evole** *a* faint; ⟨*luce*⟩ dim

**'fifa** *nf fam* jitters; **aver** ~ have the jitters

**fi'fone, -a** *nmf fam* chicken, yellowbelly

**FIGC** *nf abbr* (**Federazione Italiana Gioco Calcio**) Italian Football Association

**'figli** *nmpl* children

**'figlia** *nf* daughter; ~ **unica** only child

**figli'are** *vi* ⟨*animale:*⟩ calve

**figli'astra** *nf* stepdaughter

**figli'astro** *nm* stepson

**'figlio** *nm* son; (*generico*) child: **è** ~ **d'arte** he was born in a trunk. ~ **adottivo** adopted child. ~ **di papà** spoilt brat. ~ **di puttana** *vulg* son of a bitch. ~ **unico** only child

**figli'occia** *nf* goddaughter

**figli'occio** *nm* godson

**figli'ola** *nf* girl

**figlio'lanza** *nf* offspring

**figli'olo** *nm* boy; **figlioli** *pl* children

**'figo, -a** *a vedi* **fico, -a**

**fi'gura** *nf* figure; (*aspetto esteriore*) shape; (*illustrazione*) illustration; **far bella/brutta** ~ make a good/bad impression; **mi hai fatto fare una brutta** ~ you made me look a fool; **che** ~! how embarrassing!. ~ **paterna** father figure. ~ **retorica** figure of speech

**figu'raccia** *nf* bad impression

**figu'rare** *vt* represent; (*simboleggiare*) symbolize; (*immaginare*) imagine ● *vi* (*far figura*) cut a fine figure; (*in lista*) appear, figure; ~ **in testa al cartellone** *Theat* get top billing

**figu'rarsi** *vr* (*immaginarsi*) imagine; **figurati!** imagine that!; **posso?** – [**ma**] **figurati!** may I? – of course!

**figura'tivo** *a* figurative

**figu'rina** *nf* (*da raccolta*) cigarette card; (*statuetta*) figurine

**figuri'nista** *nmf* dress designer

**figu'rino** *nm* fashion sketch

**figu'rone** *nm* **fare un** ~ make an excellent impression

**fi'guro** *nm* **un losco** ~ a shady character

**fil** *nm* ~ **di ferro** wire

**'fila** *nf* line; (*di soldati ecc*) file; (*di oggetti*) row; (*coda*) queue; **di** ~ in succession; **fare la** ~ queue [up], stand in line *Am*; **in** ~ **indiana** single file

**fila'mento** *nm* filament

**fi'lanca®** *nf type of synthetic stretch fabric*

**fi'lante** *a* ⟨*formaggio*⟩ stringy; **stella** ~ (*di carta*) streamer

**filantro'pia** *nf* philanthropy

**filan'tropico** *a* philanthropic

**fi'lantropo, -a** *nmf* philanthropist

**fi'lare** *vt* spin; *Naut* pay out ● *vi* (*andarsene*) run away; (*liquido:*) trickle; **fila!** *fam* scram!; ~ **con** (*fam: amoreggiare*) go out with; ~ **dritto** toe the line ● *vi* (*ragionamento:*) hang together ● *nm* (*di viti, di alberi*) row

**filar'monica** *nf* (*orchestra*) orchestra

**filar'monico** *a* philharmonic

**fila'strocca** *nf* rigmarole; (*per bambini*) nursery rhyme

**filate'lia** *nf* philately, stamp collecting

**fila'telico, -a** *nmf* philatelist

**fi'lato** *a* spun; (*ininterrotto*) running; (*continuato*) uninterrupted; **di** ~ (*subito*) immediately; **andare dritto** ~ **a** go straight to ● *nm* yarn

**fila'tore, -'trice** *nmf* spinner

**fila'tura** *nf* spinning; (*filanda*) spinning mill

**file** *nm inv Comput* file

**filetta'tura** *nf* (*di vite*) thread

**fi'letto** *nm* (*bordo*) border; (*di vite*) thread; *Culin* fillet. ~ **ai ferri** grilled fillet of beef

**fili'ale** *a* filial ● *nf Comm* branch

**filibusti'ere** *nm* rascal

**fili'forme** *a* stringy

**fili'grana** *nf* filigree; (*su carta*) watermark

**fi'lippica** *nf* invective

**Filip'pine** *nfpl* **le** ~ the Philippines

**filip'pino, -a** *a & nmf* Filipino
**film** *nm inv* film. **~ comico** comedy. **~ drammatico** drama. **~ di fantascienza** science fiction film. **~ giallo** thriller. **~ a lungo metraggio** feature film. **~ dell'orrore** horror film. **~ poliziesco** detective film
**fil'mare** *vt* film
**fil'mato** *a* filmed ● *nm* short film
**fil'mina** *nf* film strip
**fil'mino** *nm* cine film
**'filo** *nm* thread; *(tessile)* yarn; *(metallico)* wire; *(di lama)* edge; *(venatura)* grain; *(di perle)* string; *(d'erba)* blade; *(di luce)* ray; **un ~ di** *(poco)* a drop of; **con un ~ di voce** in a whisper; **per ~ e per segno** in detail; **fare il ~ a qcno** fancy sb; **perdere il ~** lose the thread; **essere appeso a un ~** be hanging by a thread; **essere sul ~ del rasoio** be on a knife-edge; **un ~ d'aria** a breath of air; **un ~ di speranza** a glimmer of hope. **~ interdentale** dental floss. **~ a piombo** plumb-line. **~ spinato** barbed wire
**filo+** *pref* philo+
**filoameri'cano** *a* pro-American
**'filobus** *nm inv* trolleybus
**filocomu'nista** *a* pro-communist
**filodiffusi'one** *nf* rediffusion
**filodram'matica** *nf* amateur dramatic society
**filolo'gia** *nf* philology
**filo'logico** *a* philological
**fi'lologo, -a** *nmf* philologist
**filon'cino** *nm* ≈ French stick
**fi'lone** *nm* vein; *(di pane)* long loaf, Vienna loaf
**fi'loso** *a* stringy
**filoso'fia** *nf* philosophy
**fi'losofo, -a** *nmf* philosopher
**fil'traggio** *nm* filtering
**fil'trare** *vt* filter
**'filtro** *nm* filter. **~ dell'olio** oil filter
**'filza** *nf* string
**fin** *vedi* **fine, fino¹**
**fi'nale** *a* final ● *nm* end ● *nf* Sport final
**fina'lista** *nmf* finalist
**finalità** *nf inv* finality; *(scopo)* aim
**final'mente** *adv* at last; *(in ultimo)* finally
**fi'nanza** *nf* finance
**finanzia'mento** *nm* funding
**finanzi'are** *vt* fund, finance
**finanzi'aria** *nf* investment company; *(holding)* holding company; *Jur* finance bill
**finanzi'ario** *a* financial
**finanzia'tore, -'trice** *nmf* backer
**finanzi'ere** *nm* financier; *(guardia di finanza)* customs officer
**finché** *conj* until; *(per tutto il tempo che)* as long as
**'fine** *a* fine; *(sottile)* thin; *(udito, vista)* keen; *(raffinato)* refined ● *nf* end; **alla ~** in the end; **alla fin ~** after all; **in fin dei conti** when all's said and done; **andare a buon ~** be successful; **te lo dico a fin di bene** I'm telling you for your own good; **che ~ ha fatto Anna?** what became of Anna?; **che ~**

**hanno fatto le chiavi?** where have the keys got to?; **senza ~** endless ● *nm* aim. **~ settimana** weekend
**fi'nestra** *nf* window. **~ a battenti** casement window
**fine'strella** *nf* **~ di aiuto** *Comput* help window. **~ di dialogo** *Comput* dialog box
**fine'strino** *nm* Rail, Auto window
**fi'nezza** *nf* fineness; *(sottigliezza)* thinness; *(raffinatezza)* refinement
**'fingere** *vt* pretend; feign *(affetto ecc)*
**'fingersi** *vr* pretend to be
**fini'menti** *nmpl* finishing touches; *(per cavallo)* harness *sg*
**fini'mondo** *nm* end of the world; *fig* pandemonium
**fi'nire** *vt/i* finish, end; *(smettere)* stop; *(diventare, andare a finire)* end up; **finiscila!** stop it!
**fi'nito** *a* finished; *(abile)* accomplished
**fini'tura** *nf* finish
**finlan'dese** *a* Finnish ● *nmf* Finn ● *nm (lingua)* Finnish
**Fin'landia** *nf* Finland
**'fino¹** *prep* **~ a** till, until; *(spazio)* as far as; **~ all'ultimo** to the last; **~ alla nausea** *(ripetere, leggere)* ad nauseam; **fin da** *(tempo)* since; *(spazio)* from; **fin dall'inizio** from the beginning; **fin qui** as far as here; **fin troppo** too much; **~ a che punto** how far
**'fino²** *a* fine; *(acuto)* subtle; *(puro)* pure
**fi'nocchio** *nm* fennel; *(fam: omosessuale)* poof
**fi'nora** *adv* so far, up till now
**'finta** *nf* pretence, sham; *Sport* feint; **far ~ di** pretend to; **far ~ di niente** act as if nothing had happened; **per ~** *(per scherzo)* for a laugh
**'finto, -a** *pp di* **fingere** ● *a* false; *(artificiale)* artificial; **finta pelle** fake leather; **fare il ~ tonto** act dumb
**finzi'one** *nf* pretence
**fi'occo** *nm* bow; *(di neve)* flake; *(nappa)* tassel; *Naut* jib; **coi fiocchi** *fig* excellent; **fiocchi** *pl* **di avena** oatmeal; *(cotti)* porridge; **fiocchi** *pl* **di granoturco** cornflakes. **fiocchi** *pl* **di latte** cottage cheese. **~ di neve** snowflake
**fi'ocina** *nf* harpoon
**fi'oco** *a* weak; *(luce)* dim
**fi'onda** *nf* catapult
**fio'raio, -a** *nmf* florist
**fiorda'liso** *nm* cornflower
**fi'ordo** *nm* fiord
**fi'ore** *nm* flower; *(parte scelta)* cream; **a fior d'acqua** on the surface of the water; **a fiori** flowery; **in ~** flowering; **fior di** *(abbondanza)* a lot of; **il fior ~ di** the cream of; **ha i nervi a fior di pelle** his nerves are on edge; **nel ~ degli anni** in one's prime; **è il suo ~ all'occhiello** that's a feather in his cap; **suo figlio è il suo ~ all'occhiello** his son is his pride and joy. **fiori** *pl* **d'arancio** orange blossom. **~ di campo** wild flower. **fior di latte** *(formaggio)* soft cheese. **~ selvatico** wild

flower. **fiori** pl **di zucca fritti** fried pumpkin flowers

**fio'rente** a ⟨industria⟩ booming

**fioren'tina** nf ⟨bistecca⟩ T-bone steak

**fioren'tino** a Florentine

**fio'retto** nm ⟨scherma⟩ foil; Relig act of mortification

**fi'ori** nmpl ⟨nelle carte⟩ clubs

**fiori'era** nf container

**fio'rino** nm ~ **olandese** guilder

**fio'rire** vi flower; ⟨albero:⟩ blossom; fig flourish

**fio'rista** nmf florist; ⟨negozio⟩ florist's

**fiori'tura** nf flowering; ⟨di albero⟩ blossoming; ⟨insieme di fiori⟩ flowers pl

**fio'rone** nm ⟨fico⟩ early fig

**fi'otto** nm ⟨di sangue⟩ spurt; **scorrere a fiotti** pour out; **piove a fiotti** the rain is pouring down

**Fi'renze** nf Florence

**'firma** nf signature; ⟨nome⟩ name

**firma'mento** nm firmament

**fir'mare** vt sign

**firma'tario, -a** nmf signatory

**fir'mato** a ⟨quadro, lettera⟩ signed; ⟨abito, borsa⟩ designer attrib

**fisar'monica** nf accordion

**fi'scale** a fiscal

**fisca'lista** nmf tax consultant

**fiscaliz'zare** vt finance with government funds

**fischi'are** vi whistle ● vt whistle; ⟨in segno di disapprovazione⟩ boo; **mi fischiano le orecchie** I've got a ringing noise in my ears; fig my ears are burning

**fischi'ata** nf whistle

**fischiet'tare** vt whistle

**fischiet'tio** nm whistling

**fischi'etto** nm whistle

**'fischio** nm whistle; **fischi** pl Theat booing; **prendere fischi per fiaschi** get hold of the wrong end of the stick

**'fisco** nm treasury; ⟨tasse⟩ taxation; **il** ~ the taxman

**fisica'mente** adv physically

**'fisico, -a** a physical ● nmf physicist. ~ **nucleare** atomic scientist ● nm physique ● nf physics. ~ **nucleare** nuclear physics

**'fisima** nf whim

**fisiolo'gia** nf physiology

**fisio'logico** a physiological

**fisi'ologo, -a** nmf physiologist

**fisiono'mia** nf features pl, face; ⟨di paesaggio⟩ appearance

**fisiotera'pia** nf physiotherapy

**fisiotera'pista** nmf physiotherapist, physio fam

**fissa'mente** adv fixedly; ⟨permanentemente⟩ steadily

**fis'sare** vt fix, fasten; ⟨guardare fissamente⟩ stare at; arrange ⟨appuntamento, ora⟩

**fis'sarsi** vr ⟨stabilirsi⟩ settle; ⟨fissare lo sguardo⟩ stare; ~ **su** ⟨ostinarsi⟩ set one's mind on; ~ **di fare qcsa** become obsessed with doing sth

**fissa'tivo** nm Phot fixative

**fis'sato, -a** a ⟨al muro⟩ fixed; ⟨prezzo⟩ agreed ● nm ⟨persona⟩ person with an obsession

**fissa'tore** nm hair spray

**fissazi'one** nf fixation; ⟨ossessione⟩ obsession

**'fisso** a fixed; **un lavoro** ~ a regular job; **senza fissa dimora** of no fixed abode; **avere una ragazza fissa** have a steady girlfriend ● adv fixedly; **guardare** ~ **negli occhi qcno** stare at sb; ⟨innamorato:⟩ gaze into sb's eyes

**fitotera'pia** nf herbalism; ⟨per piante⟩ plant health

**'fitta** nf sharp pain

**fit'tavolo** nm tenant

**fit'tizio** a fictitious

**'fitto¹** a thick; ~ **di** full of ● nm depth

**'fitto²** nm ⟨affitto⟩ rent; **dare a** ~ let; **prendere a** ~ rent; ⟨noleggiare⟩ hire

**fiu'mana** nf swollen river; fig stream

**fi'ume** nm river; fig stream ● a inv ⟨discussione⟩ endless. never-ending; **romanzo** ~ roman-fleuve

**fiu'tare** vt smell; ⟨animale:⟩ scent; snort ⟨cocaina⟩

**fi'uto** nm [sense of] smell; fig nose

**'flaccido** a flabby

**fla'cone** nm bottle

**flagel'lare** vt flog

**flagellazi'one** nf flagellation

**fla'gello** nm scourge

**fla'grante** a flagrant; **in** ~ in the act

**fla'menco** nm flamenco

**flan** nm inv baked custard

**fla'nella** nf flannel

**'flangia** nf ⟨su ruota⟩ flange

**flash** nm inv Journ newsflash

**flau'tista** nmf flautist

**'flauto** nm flute. ~ **diritto** recorder. ~ **traverso** flute

**'flebile** a feeble

**fle'bite** nf phlebitis

**flebo'clisi** nf drip

**'flemma** nf calm; Med phlegm

**flem'matico** a phlegmatic

**fles'sibile** a flexible

**flessibilità** nf flexibility

**flessi'one** nf ⟨del busto in avanti⟩ forward bend; ⟨a terra⟩ sit-up; ⟨delle ginocchia⟩ knee-bend; ⟨di vendite, produzione⟩ drop, fall

**fles'sivo** a Gram inflected

**'flesso** pp di **flettere** ● a Gram inflected

**flessu'oso** a supple

**'flettere** vt bend

**flip-'flop** nm inv flip flop

**flir'tare** vi flirt

**F.lli** abbr ⟨fratelli⟩ Bros.

**'floppy disk** nm inv floppy disk

**'flora** nf flora

**'florido** a flourishing

**floroviva'istica** nf ⟨attività⟩ growing under glass

**'floscio** a limp; ⟨flaccido⟩ flabby

# flotta | fondue

**'flotta** *nf* fleet

**flot'tiglia** *nf* flotilla

**flu'ente** *a* fluent

**fluidità** *nf* fluidity: (*nel parlare*) fluency

**flu'ido** *nm* fluid

**flu'ire** *vi* flow

**fluore'scente** *a* fluorescent

**fluore'scenza** *nf* fluorescence

**flu'oro** *nm* fluorine

**fluo'ruro** *nm* fluoride

**'flusso** *nm* flow; *Med* flux: (*del mare*) floodtide; **~ e riflusso** ebb and flow. **~ di cassa** cash flow

**'flutti** *nmpl* billows

**fluttu'ante** *a* fluctuating

**fluttu'are** *vi* (*prezzi:*) fluctuate; (*moneta:*) float

**fluttuazi'one** *nf* fluctuation; (*di moneta*) floating

**fluvi'ale** *a* river

**fo'bia** *nf* phobia

**'fobico** *a* phobic

**'foca** *nf* seal

**fo'caccia** *nf* (*pane*) flat bread; (*dolce*) ≈ raisin bread

**fo'cale** *a* (*distanza, punto*) focal

**focaliz'zare** *vt* get into focus (*fotografia*); focus (*attenzione*); define (*problema*)

**'foce** *nf* mouth

**fo'chista** *nm* stoker

**foco'laio** *nm Med* focus; *fig* centre

**foco'lare** *nm* hearth; (*caminetto*) fireplace; *Techn* furnace

**fo'coso** *a* fiery

**'fodera** *nf* lining; (*di libro*) dust-jacket; (*di poltrona ecc*) loose cover

**fode'rare** *vt* line; cover (*libro*)

**fode'rato** *a* lined; (*libro*) covered

**'foga** *nf* impetuosity

**'foggia** *nf* fashion; (*maniera*) manner; (*forma*) shape

**foggi'are** *vt* mould

**'foglia** *nf* leaf; (*di metallo*) foil; **mangiare la ~** catch on. **~ di alloro** bay leaf

**fogli'ame** *nm* foliage

**fogli'et'tino** *nm* **~ igienico** (*per pannolini*) nappy liner

**fogli'etto** *nm* (*pezzetto di carta*) piece of paper

**'foglio** *nm* sheet; (*pagina*) leaf; (*di domanda, di iscrizione*) form. **~ di carta** sheet of paper. **~ elettronico** *Comput* spreadsheet. **~ illustrativo** instruction leaflet. **~ protocollo** foolscap. **~ rosa** provisional driving licence. **~ di via** expulsion order

**'fogna** *nf* sewer

**fogna'tura** *nf* sewerage

**fohn** *nm inv* hair dryer

**fo'lata** *nf* gust

**fol'clore** *nm* folklore

**folclo'ristico** *a* folk; (*bizzarro*) weird

**folgo'rante** *a* (*idea*) brilliant

**folgo'rare** *vi* (*splendere*) shine ● *vt* (*con un fulmine*) strike

**folgo'rato** *a fig* thunderstruck

**folgorazi'one** *nf* (*da fulmine, elettrica*) electrocution: (*fig: idea*) brainwave

**'folgore** *nf* thunderbolt

**'folio: in ~** *a* folio

**'folla** *nf* crowd

**'folle** *a* mad: (*velocità*) breakneck; **in ~ Auto** in neutral; **andare in ~** *Auto* coast

**folleggi'are** *vi* paint the town red

**folle'mente** *adv* madly

**fol'letto** *nm* elf

**fol'lia** *nf* madness; **alla ~** (*amare*) to distraction; **costare una ~** cost the earth; **fare una ~** go mad; **farei follie per lei** I'd do anything for her

**'folto** *a* thick

**fomen'tare** *vt* stir up

**fond'ale** *nm Theat* backcloth. **~ marino** sea bed

**fonda'menta** *nfpl* foundations

**fondamen'tale** *a* fundamental

**fondamenta'lismo** *nm* fundamentalism

**fondamenta'lista** *nmf* fundamentalist

**fonda'mento** *nm* (*di principio, teoria*) foundation: **privo di ~** groundless, without foundation

**fon'dant** *nm inv* fondant

**fon'dare** *vt* establish; base (*ragionamento, accusa*)

**fon'darsi** *vr* be based (**su** on)

**fon'dato** *a* (*ragionamento*) well-founded; **~ su** based on

**fondazi'one** *nf* establishment; **fondazioni** *pl* (*di edificio*) foundations

**fon'delli** *nmpl* **prendere qcno per i ~** *fam* pull sb's leg

**fon'dente** *a* (*cioccolato*) dark

**'fondere** *vt* melt; fuse (*metallo*) ● *vi* melt; (*metallo:*) fuse; (*colori:*) blend

**fonde'ria** *nf* foundry

**'fondersi** *vr* melt; *Comm* merge

**'fondo** *a* deep; **è notte fonda** it's the middle of the night ● *nm* bottom; (*fine*) end; (*sfondo*) background; (*indole*) nature; (*somma di denaro*) fund; (*feccia*) dregs *pl*; (*terreno*) land; [**sci di**] **~** cross-country skiing; **andare a ~** (*nave:*) sink; **in ~** after all; **in ~ a** at the end/ bottom of; **in ~ in ~** deep down; **fino in ~** right to the end; (*capire*) thoroughly; **andare fino in ~ a qcsa** get to the bottom of sth; **dar ~ a** use up; **a doppio ~** false bottomed; **toccare il ~** touch bottom; *fig* hit rock bottom; **senza ~** bottomless; **articolo di ~** (*in giornale*) editorial; **fondi** *pl* (*denaro*) funds; (*di caffè*) grounds. **~ fiduciario** trust fund. **~ [comune] di investimento** investment trust. **fondi** *pl* **di magazzino** old stock. **F~ Monetario Internazionale** International Monetary Fund. **fondi** *pl* **neri** slush funds. **~ pensione** pension fund. **~ per la ricostruzione** disaster fund. **~ sopravvenienze passive** contingency fund. **~ stradale** road surface

**fondo'tinta** *nm inv* foundation [cream]

**fon'due** *nf* (*di formaggio*) fondue

**fon'duta** *nf* fondue

**fo'nema** *nm* phoneme

**fo'netica** *nf* phonetics

**fo'netico** *a* phonetic

**fonolo'gia** *nf* phonology

**fon'tana** *nf* fountain; (*di farina*) well

**fonta'nella** *nf* drinking fountain; *Anat* fontanelle

**'fonte** *nf* spring; *fig* source ● *nm* font

**fon'tina** *nf* soft, mature cheese often used in cooking

**'football** *nm* ~ **americano** American football

**foraggi'are** *vt* fodder

**fo'raggio** *nm* forage

**fo'rare** *vt* pierce; punch ⟨*biglietto*⟩ ● *vi* puncture

**fo'rarsi** *vr* ⟨*gomma, pallone:*⟩ go soft

**fora'tura** *nf* puncture

**'forbici** *nfpl* scissors; **un paio di** ~ a pair of scissors. ~ **da siepe** garden shears. ~ **a zigzag** pinking shears. pinking scissors

**forbi'cina** *nf* earwig; **forbicine** *pl* (*per le unghie*) nail scissors

**for'bito** *a* erudite

**'forca** *nf* fork; (*patibolo*) gallows *pl*

**for'cella** *nf* fork; (*per capelli*) hairpin

**for'chetta** *nf* fork; **essere una buona** ~ enjoy one's food

**forchet'tata** *nf* (*quantità*) forkful

**forchet'tone** *nm* carving fork

**for'cina** *nf* hairpin

**'forcipe** *nm* forceps *pl*

**for'cone** *nm* pitchfork

**fo'rense** *a* forensic

**fo'resta** *nf* forest. ~ **equatoriale** rain forest. **F~ Nera** Black Forest

**fore'stale** *a* forest *attrib*; **la F~** *branch of the police with responsibility for national forests*

**foreste'ria** *nf* guest rooms *pl*

**foresti'ero, -a** *a* foreign ● *nmf* foreigner.

**for'fait** *nm inv* fixed price; **dare** ~ (*abbandonare*) give up; **prezzo [a]** ~ all-in price; **contratto [a]** ~ lump-sum contract

**forfe'tario** *a* flat rate

**'forfora** *nf* dandruff

**'forgia** *nf* forge

**forgi'are** *vt* forge

**'forma** *nf* form; (*sagoma*) shape; *Culin* mould; (*per scarpe*) shoe tree; (*di calzolaio*) last; **essere in** ~ be in good form; **in (gran)** ~ (very) fit, on (top) form; **a** ~ **di** in the shape of; **sotto** ~ **di** in the form of; **forme** *pl* (*del corpo*) curves; (*convenzioni*) appearances

**formag'gera** *nf* [covered] cheese board

**formag'gino** *nm* processed cheese

**for'maggio** *nm* cheese

**for'male** *a* formal

**forma'lina** *nf* formalin

**forma'lismo** *nm* formalism

**forma'lista** *nmf* formalist

**formalità** *nf inv* formality

**formaliz'zare** *vt* formalize

**formaliz'zarsi** *vr* stand on ceremony, be formal

**formal'mente** *adv* formally

**'forma 'mentis** *nf inv* way of thinking, mindset

**for'mare** *vt* form; dial ⟨*numero di telefono*⟩

**for'marsi** *vr* form; (*svilupparsi*) develop

**for'mato** *nm* size; (*di libro, dischetto*) format; ~ **famiglia** economy pack, economy size; ~ **tessera** ⟨*fotografia*⟩ passport-size

**format'tare** *vt* format

**formattazi'one** *nf* formatting

**formazi'one** *nf* formation; *Sport* line-up; **in** ~ in the process of being formed. ~ **professionale** vocational training

**for'mella** *nf* tile

**for'mica** *nf* ant

**'formica®** *nf* Formica

**formi'caio** *nm* anthill

**formichi'ere** *nm* anteater

**formico'lare** *vi* ⟨*braccio ecc:*⟩ tingle; ~ **di** be swarming with: **mi formicola la mano** I have pins and needles in my hand

**formico'lio** *nm* swarming; (*di braccio ecc*) pins and needles *pl*

**formi'dabile** *a* (*tremendo*) formidable; (*eccezionale*) tremendous

**for'mina** *nf* mould

**for'moso** *a* curvy

**'formula** *nf* formula; **assolvere con** ~ **piena** acquit. ~ **di cortesia** polite form of address

**formu'lare** *vt* formulate; (*esprimere*) express

**formulazi'one** *nf* formulation

**for'nace** *nf* furnace; (*per laterizi*) kiln

**for'naio, -a** *nmf* baker; (*negozio*) bakery

**fornel'letto** *nm* ~ **da campeggio** camping stove. ~ **a gas** gas stove

**for'nello** *nm* stove; (*di pipa*) bowl. ~ **da campeggio** camping stove

**fornicazi'one** *nf* fornication

**for'nire** *vt* supply (**di** with); ~ **qcsa a qcno** supply sb with sth

**for'nirsi** *vr* ~ **di** provide oneself with

**forni'tore** *nm* supplier. ~ **di servizi** service provider

**forni'tura** *nf* supply; **forniture** *pl* **per ufficio** office supplies

**'forno** *nm* oven; (*panetteria*) bakery; **al** ~ roast; **da** ~ ⟨*stoviglie*⟩ ovenproof. ~ **crematorio** cremator. ~ **elettrico** electric oven. ~ **a gas** gas oven. ~ **a microonde** microwave [oven]

**'foro** *nm* hole; (*romano*) forum; (*tribunale*) [law] court

**'forse** *adv* perhaps, maybe; **essere in** ~ be in doubt

**forsen'nato, -a** *a* mad ● *nmf* madman; madwoman

**'forte** *a* strong; ⟨*colore*⟩ bright; ⟨*suono*⟩ loud; (*resistente*) tough; ⟨*spesa*⟩ considerable; ⟨*dolore*⟩ severe; ⟨*pioggia*⟩ heavy; (*fam: simpatico*) great; ⟨*taglia*⟩ large; **essere** ~ **in qcsa**

be good at sth ● *adv* strongly; ⟨*parlare*⟩ loudly; ⟨*velocemente*⟩ fast; ⟨*piovere*⟩ heavily ● *nm* ⟨*fortezza*⟩ fort; ⟨*specialità*⟩ strong point

**for'tezza** *nf* fortress; ⟨*forza morale*⟩ fortitude

**fortifi'care** *vt* fortify

**fortifi'cato** *a* ⟨*città*⟩ walled

**for'tino** *nm Mil* blockhouse

**for'tissimo** *a* ⟨*caffè, liquore*⟩ extra-strong

**for'tuito** *a* fortuitous; **incontro** ~ chance encounter

**for'tuna** *nf* fortune; ⟨*successo*⟩ success; ⟨*buona sorte*⟩ luck; **atterraggio di** ~ forced landing; **aver** ~ be lucky; **buona** ~! good luck!; **di** ~ makeshift; **per** ~ luckily; **hai una** ~ **sfacciata!** *fam* you lucky blighter!

**fortu'nale** *nm* storm

**fortunata'mente** *adv* fortunately

**fortu'nato** *a* lucky, fortunate; ⟨*impresa*⟩ successful

**fortu'noso** *a* ⟨*giornata*⟩ eventful

**fo'runcolo** *nm* pimple; ⟨*grosso*⟩ boil

**forunco'loso** *a* spotty

**'forza** *nf* strength; ⟨*potenza*⟩ power; ⟨*fisica*⟩ force; **di** ~ by force; **a** ~ **di** by dint of; **con** ~ hard; ~! come on!; **in** ~ **di** under, in accordance with; ~ **maggiore** circumstances beyond one's control; **la** ~ **pubblica** the police; **le forze armate** the armed forces; **per** ~ against one's will; ⟨*naturalmente*⟩ of course; **farsi** ~ bear up; **mare** ~ 8 force 8 gale; **bella** ~! *fam* big deal!; **che** ~! ⟨*che simpatico, divertente*⟩ cool eh?. ~ **di gravità** [force of] gravity. ~ **lavoro** workforce. **forze** *pl* **di mercato** market forces. ~ **di volontà** willpower

**for'zare** *vt* force; ⟨*scassare*⟩ break open; ⟨*sforzare*⟩ strain

**for'zato** *a* forced; ⟨*sorriso*⟩ strained ● *nm* convict

**forza'tura** *nf* ⟨*di cassaforte*⟩ forcing; **sostenere che... è una** ~ to maintain that... is forcing things

**forzi'ere** *nm* coffer

**for'zuto** *a* strong

**fo'schia** *nf* haze

**'fosco** *a* dark

**fo'sfato** *nm* phosphate

**'fosforo** *nm* phosphorus

**'fossa** *nf* pit; ⟨*tomba*⟩ grave. ~ **biologica** cesspool. ~ **comune** mass grave. ~ **dell'orchestra** orchestra pit

**fos'sato** *nm* ⟨*di fortificazione*⟩ moat

**fos'setta** *nf* ⟨*di guancia*⟩ dimple

**'fossile** *nm* fossil

**'fosso** *nm* ditch; *Mil* trench

**'foto** *nf inv fam* photo; **fare delle** ~ take some photos

**foto'cellula** *nf* photocell

**fotocomposi'tore, -'trice** *nmf* filmsetter

**fotocomposizi'one** *nf* filmsetting, photocomposition

**foto'copia** *nf* photocopy

**fotocopi'are** *vt* photocopy

**fotocopia'trice** *nf* photocopier

**foto'finish** *nm inv* photo finish

**foto'genico** *a* photogenic

**fotogiorna'lista** *nmf* photojournalist

**fotogra'fare** *vt* photograph

**fotogra'fia** *nf* ⟨*arte*⟩ photography; ⟨*immagine*⟩ photograph; **fare fotografie** take photographs

**foto'grafico** *a* photographic; **macchina fotografica** camera

**fo'tografo, -a** *nmf* photographer; ⟨*negozio*⟩ photographer's

**foto'gramma** *nm* frame

**fotoincisi'one** *nf* photoengraving

**fotomo'dello, -a** *nmf* [photographer's] model

**fotomon'taggio** *nm* photomontage

**foto'ottica** *nf* camera shop and optician's

**fotorepor'tage** *nm inv* photo essay

**fotore'porter** *nmf inv* newspaper photographer; ⟨*di rivista*⟩ magazine photographer

**fotori'tocco** *nm* retouching

**fotoro'manzo** *nm* photo story

**foto'sintesi** *nf* photosynthesis

**'fottere** *vt* ⟨*sl: rubare*⟩ nick; ⟨*sl: imbrogliare*⟩ screw; *vulg* fuck, screw

**'fottersene** *vr vulg* not give a fuck; **va' a farti** ~! *vulg* fuck off!

**fot'tuto** *a* ⟨*sl: maledetto*⟩ bloody

**fou'lard** *nm inv* scarf

**'foxhound** *nm inv* foxhound

**fox-'terrier** *nm inv* fox terrier

**fo'yer** *nm inv* foyer

**fra** *prep* ⟨*in mezzo a due*⟩ between; ⟨*in un insieme*⟩ among; ⟨*tempo, distanza*⟩ in; **detto** ~ **noi** between you and me; ~ **sé e sé** to oneself; ~ **l'altro** what's more; ~ **breve** soon; ~ **quindici giorni** in two weeks' time; ~ **tutti, siamo in venti** there are twenty of us altogether

**fracas'sare** *vt* smash

**fracas'sarsi** *vr* shatter

**fracas'sato** *a* smashed

**fra'casso** *nm* din; ⟨*di cose che cadono*⟩ crash

**fracas'sone, -a** *nmf* clumsy person

**'fradicio** *a* ⟨*bagnato*⟩ soaked; **ubriaco** ~ blind drunk

**'fragile** *a* fragile; *fig* frail

**fragilità** *nf* fragility; *fig* frailty

**'fragola** *nf* strawberry

**fra'gore** *nm* uproar; ⟨*di cose rotte*⟩ clatter; ⟨*tuono*⟩ rumble

**frago'roso** *a* uproarious; ⟨*tuono*⟩ rumbling; ⟨*suono*⟩ clanging

**fra'grante** *a* fragrant

**fra'granza** *nf* fragrance

**frain'tendere** *vt* misunderstand

**frain'tendersi** *vr* be at cross-purposes

**frain'teso** *pp di* fraintendere

**frammen'tario** *a* fragmentary

**fram'mento** *nm* fragment

**fram'misto** *a* ~ **di** interspersed with

**'frana** *nf* landslide; ⟨*fam: persona*⟩ walking disaster area

**fra'nare** *vi* slide down

**franca'mente** *adv* frankly

**france'scano** *a & nm* Franciscan

**fran'cese** *a* French ●*nm* Frenchman; (*lingua*) French ●*nf* Frenchwoman

**france'sina** *nf* (*scarpa*) brogue

**fran'chezza** *nf* frankness; **in tutta ~** in all honesty

**fran'chigia** *nf* **~ bagaglio** (*per aereo*) baggage allowance

**'Francia** *nf* France

**'franco**[1] *a* frank; *Comm* free; **farla franca** get away with sth; **parlare ~** speak frankly. **~ a bordo** free on board. **~ domicilio** delivered free of charge. **~ fabbrica** ex-works; **~ di porto** carriage free, carriage paid

**'franco**[2] *nm* (*moneta*) franc

**franco'bollo** *nm* stamp

**franco-cana'dese** *a & nmf* French Canadian

**fran'cofono** *a* Francophone

**Franco'forte** *nf* Frankfurt

**fran'gente** *nm* (*onda*) breaker; (*scoglio*) reef; (*fig: momento difficile*) crisis; **in quel ~** in the circumstances

**fran'getta** *nf* fringe

**'frangia** *nf* fringe

**frangi'flutti** *nm inv* bulwark

**frangi'vento** *nm* windbreak

**fra'noso** *a* subject to landslides

**fran'toio** *nm* olive-press

**frantu'mare** *vt* shatter

**frantu'marsi** *vr* shatter

**fran'tumi** *nmpl* splinters; **in ~** smashed; **andare in ~** be smashed to smithereens

**frappé** *nm inv* milkshake

**frap'porre** *vt* interpose

**frap'porsi** *vr* intervene

**fra'sario** *nm* vocabulary; (*libro*) phrase book

**'frasca** *nf* [leafy] branch; **saltare di palo in ~** jump from subject to subject

**'frase** *nf* sentence; (*espressione*) phrase. **~ fatta** cliché

**fraseolo'gia** *nf* phrases *pl*

**'frassino** *nm* ash[-tree]

**frastagli'are** *vt* make jagged

**frastagli'ato** *a* jagged

**frastor'nare** *vt* daze

**frastor'nato** *a* dazed

**frastu'ono** *nm* racket

**'frate** *nm* friar; (*monaco*) monk

**fratel'lanza** *nf* brotherhood

**fratel'lastro** *nm* half-brother

**fratel'lino** *nm* little brother

**fra'tello** *nm* brother; **fratelli** *pl* (*fratello e sorella*) brother and sister; *Relig* brethren. **~ gemello** twin brother. **~ di sangue** blood brother

**fraternità** *nf* brotherhood

**fraterniz'zare** *vi* fraternize

**fra'terno** *a* brotherly

**fratri'cida** *a* fratricidal ●*nm* fratricide

**frat'taglie** *nfpl* (*di pollo ecc*) giblets

**frat'tanto** *adv* in the meantime

**frat'tura** *nf* fracture

**frattu'rare** *vt* break

**frattu'rarsi** *vr* break

**fraudo'lento** *a* fraudulent

**frazi'one** *nf* fraction; (*borgata*) hamlet; (*paese*) administrative division of a municipality

**'freccia** *nf* arrow; *Auto* indicator

**frecci'ata** *nf* (*osservazione pungente*) cutting remark

**fredda'mente** *adv* coldly

**fred'dare** *vt* cool; (*fig: con sguardo, battuta*) cut down; (*uccidere*) kill

**fred'dezza** *nf* coldness

**'freddo** *a & nm* cold; **aver ~** be cold; **fa ~** it's cold; **a ~** (*sparare*) in cold blood; (*lavare*) in cold water

**freddo'loso** *a* sensitive to cold, chilly

**fred'dura** *nf* pun

**fre'gare** *vt* rub; (*fam: truffare*) cheat; (*fam: rubare*) swipe; **fregarsene** *fam* not give a damn; **me ne frego!** I don't give a damn!; **chi se ne frega!** what the heck!

**fre'garsi** *vr* rub (*occhi, mani*)

**fre'gata** *nf* rub; (*nave*) frigate

**frega'tura** *nf fam* (*truffa*) swindle; (*delusione*) letdown

**'fregio** *nm Archit* frieze; (*ornamento*) decoration

**'fregola** *nf* rutting; **avere la ~ di fare qcsa** *fam* have a craze for doing sth

**fre'mente** *a* quivering

**'fremere** *vi* quiver

**'fremito** *nm* quiver

**fre'nare** *vt* brake; *fig* restrain; hold back (*lacrime, impazienza*) ●*vi* brake

**fre'narsi** *vr* check oneself

**fre'nata** *nf* **fare una ~ brusca** hit the brakes

**frene'sia** *nf* frenzy; (*desiderio smodato*) craze

**frenetica'mente** *adv* frantically

**fre'netico** *a* frantic

**'freno** *nm* brake; *fig* check; **togliere il ~** release the brake; **usare il ~** apply the brake; **tenere a ~** restrain; **tenere a ~ la lingua** hold one's tongue; **porre un ~ a** *fig* rein in. **freni** *pl* **a disco** disc brakes. **~ a mano** handbrake. **~ a pedale** footbrake

**frequen'tare** *vt* frequent; attend (*scuola ecc*); mix with (*persone*); **non ci frequentiamo più** we don't see each other any more

**fre'quente** *a* frequent; **di ~** frequently

**fre'quenza** *nf* frequency; (*assiduità*) attendance

**'fresa** *nf* mill

**fre'sare** *vt* mill

**fre'schezza** *nf* freshness; (*di temperatura*) coolness

**'fresco** *a* fresh; (*temperatura*) cool; **~ di studi** fresh out of school; **stai ~!** *fam* you're for it!; **se ti vede, stai ~** *fam* you're done for if he sees you ●*nm* coolness; **far ~** be cool; **mettere/tenere in ~** put/keep in a cool place; **al ~** (*fam: in prigione*) inside

**fre'scura** *nf* cool

**'fresia** *nf* freesia

**'fretta** *nf* hurry, haste; **aver ~** be in a hurry; **far ~ a qcno** hurry sb; **in ~ e furia** in a great hurry: **andarsene in** ~ rush away; **senza [nessuna]** ~ at your/his etc leisure

**frettolósa'mente** adv hurriedly

**fretto'loso** a ⟨persona⟩ hasty; ⟨lavoro⟩ rushed, hurried

**fri'abile** a crumbly

**fricas'sea** nf stewed meat served with an egg and lemon sauce

**'friggere** vt fry: **vai a farti** ~! get lost! • vi sizzle; ~ **di impazienza** be on tenterhooks

**friggi'trice** nf electric chip pan

**frigidità** nf frigidity

**'frigido** a frigid

**fri'gnare** vi whine

**fri'gnone, -a** nmf whiner

**'frigo** nm inv fridge

**frigo'bar** nm inv minibar

**frigo'rifero** a refrigerating; ⟨camion⟩ refrigerated • nm refrigerator

**fringu'ello** nm chaffinch

**'frisbee®** nm inv frisbee

**frit'tata** nf omelette

**frit'tella** nf fritter; (fam: macchia d'unto) grease stain

**'fritto** pp di **friggere** • a fried; **essere** ~ be done for • nm fried food. ~ **misto** mixed fried fish/vegetables

**frit'tura** nf (pietanza) fried dish. ~ **di pesce** variety of fried fish

**frivo'lezza** nf frivolity

**'frivolo** a frivolous

**frizio'nare** vt rub

**frizi'one** nf friction; Mech clutch; (di pelle) rub

**friz'zante** a fizzy; ⟨vino⟩ sparkling; ⟨aria⟩ bracing

**'frizzo** nm gibe

**fro'dare** vt defraud

**'frode** nf fraud. ~ **fiscale** tax evasion; **con la** ~ Jur under false pretences

**frol'lino** nm (biscotto) ≈ shortbread biscuit

**'frollo** a tender; ⟨selvaggina⟩ high; ⟨persona⟩ spineless; **pasta frolla** short[crust] pastry

**'fronda** nf [leafy] branch; fig rebellion

**fron'doso** a leafy

**fron'tale** a frontal; ⟨scontro⟩ head-on

**'fronte** nf forehead; (di edificio) front • nm Mil, Pol front; **di** ~ opposite; **di** ~ **a** opposite, facing; (a paragone) compared with; **far** ~ **a** face

**fronteggi'are** vt face

**fronte'spizio** nm title page

**fronti'era** nf frontier, border

**fron'tone** nm pediment

**'fronzolo** nm frill

**'frotta** nf swarm; (di animali) flock

**'frottola** nf fib; **frottole** pl nonsense sg

**fru'gale** a frugal

**fru'gare** vi rummage • vt search

**fru'ire** vi ~ **di** make use of, take advantage of

**frul'lare** vt Culin whisk • vi ⟨ali:⟩ whirr

**frul'lato** nm ~ **di frutta** fruit drink with milk and crushed ice

**frulla'tore** nm [electric] mixer

**frul'lino** nm whisk

**fru'mento** nm wheat

**frusci'are** vi rustle

**fru'scio** nm rustle; (radio, giradischi) ground noise; (di acque) murmur

**'frusta** nf whip; (frullino) whisk

**fru'stare** vt whip

**fru'stata** nf lash

**fru'stino** nm riding crop

**fru'strare** vt frustrate

**fru'strato** a frustrated

**frustrazi'one** nf frustration

**'frutta** nf fruit; **negozio di** ~ **e verdura** greengrocer's. ~ **esotica** exotic fruit, tropical fruit. ~ **fresca di stagione** seasonal fruit. ~ **secca** nuts pl

**frut'tare** vi bear fruit; Comm give a return • vt yield

**frut'teto** nm orchard

**frutticol'tore** nm fruit farmer

**frutticol'tura** nf fruit farming, fruit growing

**frutti'era** nf fruit bowl

**frut'tifero** a ⟨albero⟩ fruit-bearing; ⟨Fin: deposito⟩ interest-bearing

**frutti'vendolo, -a** nmf greengrocer

**'frutto** nm anche fig fruit; Fin yield. **frutti** pl **di bosco** fruits of the forest. **frutti** pl **di mare** seafood sg. ~ **della passione** passion fruit

**fruttu'oso** a profitable

**FS** abbr (**Ferrovie dello Stato**) Italian State Railways

**f.to** abbr (**firmato**) signed

**fu** a (defunto) late; **il fu signor Rossi** the late Mr Rossi

**fuci'lare** vt shoot, execute by firing squad

**fucilazi'one** nf execution [by firing squad]

**fu'cile** nm rifle. ~ **ad aria compressa** air rifle

**fucil'lata** nf shot

**fu'cina** nf forge

**'fuco** nm kelp

**'fucsia** nf fuchsia

**'fuga** nf escape; (perdita) leak; (di ciclisti) breakaway; Mus fugue; **darsi alla** ~ take to flight; **mettere qcno in** ~ put sb to flight. ~ **di cervelli** brain drain. ~ **di gradini** flight of steps. ~ **di notizie** leak. ~ **romantica** elopement

**fu'gace** a fleeting

**fug'gevole** a short-lived

**fuggi'asco, -a** nmf fugitive

**fuggi'fuggi** nm stampede

**fug'gire** vi flee; ⟨innamorati:⟩ elope; fig fly

**fuggi'tivo, -a** nmf fugitive

**'fulcro** nm fulcrum

**ful'gore** nm splendour

**fu'liggine** nf soot

**fuliggi'noso** a sooty

**full** nm inv (nel poker) full house

**fulmi'nante** a ⟨sguardo⟩ withering; **è morto di leucemia** ~ he died very soon after contracting leukaemia

**fulmi'nare** vt strike by lightning; (con sguardo) look daggers at; (con scarica elettrica) electrocute

**fulmi'narsi** *vr* burn out

**fulmi'nato** *a* **rimanere ~** electrocute oneself

**'fulmine** *nm* lightning; **colpo di ~** *fig* love at first sight; **un ~ a ciel sereno** a bolt from the blue

**ful'mineo** *a* rapid; ⟨*sguardo*⟩ withering

**'fulvo** *a* tawny

**fumai'olo** *nm* funnel; (*di casa*) chimney

**fu'mante** *a* ⟨*minestra, tazza*⟩ steaming

**fu'mare** *vt/i* smoke; (*in ebollizione*) steam; **'vietato ~'** 'no smoking'

**fu'mario** *a* ⟨*canna*⟩ flue

**fu'mata** *nf* (*segnale*) smoke signal

**fuma|'tore, -'trice** *nmf* smoker; **non fumatori** ⟨*Rail: scompartimento*⟩ non-smoker, non-smoking

**fu'metto** *nm* comic strip; **fumetti** *pl* comics

**'fumo** *nm* smoke; (*vapore*) steam; *fig* hot air; **andare in ~** vanish; **vendere ~** put on an act; **cercava di vendere ~** it was all hot air; **fumi** *pl* (*industriali*) fumes; **sotto i fumi dell'alcol** under the influence of alcohol. **~ passivo** passive smoking

**fu'mogeno** *a* **cortina fumogena** smoke screen

**fu'moso** *a* ⟨*ambiente*⟩ smoky; ⟨*discorso*⟩ vague

**funambo'lesco** *a* acrobatic

**fu'nambolo, -a** *nmf* tightrope walker

**'fune** *nf* rope; (*cavo*) cable

**'funebre** *a* funeral; (*cupa*) gloomy

**fune'rale** *nm* funeral

**fu'nereo** *a* ⟨*aria*⟩ funereal

**fu'nesto** *a* sad

**'fungere** *vi* **~ da** act as

**'fungo** *nm* mushroom; *Bot, Med* fungus; **funghi** *pl Bot* fungi. **~ atomico** mushroom cloud. **~ commestibile** edible mushroom

**funico'lare** *nf* funicular [railway]

**funi'via** *nf* cableway

**funzio'nale** *a* functional

**funzionalità** *nf* functionality

**funziona'mento** *nm* functioning

**funzio'nare** *vi* work, function; **~ da** (*fungere da*) act as

**funzio'nario** *nm* official. **~ statale** civil servant

**funzi'one** *nf* function; (*carica*) office; *Relig* service; **entrare in ~** take up office; **mettere in ~** ⟨*motore*⟩ start up; **vivere in ~ di** live for

**fu'oco** *nm* fire; (*fisica, fotografia*) focus; **far ~ fire**; **dar ~ a** set fire to; **andare a ~** go up in flames; **prendere ~** catch fire; **a ~ vivo** ⟨*cuocere*⟩ on a high heat; **a ~ lento** ⟨*cuocere*⟩ on a low heat; **'vietato accendere fuochi'** 'no campfires'. **fuochi** *pl* **d'artificio** fireworks. **~ di paglia** nine-days' wonder. **fuochi** *pl* **pirotecnici** pyrotechnics

**fuorché** *prep* except

**fu'ori** *adv* out; (*all'esterno*) outside; (*all'aperto*) outdoors; **~!** *fam* get out!; **~ i soldi!** fork up!; **andare di ~** (*traboccare*)

spill over; **essere ~ di sé** be beside oneself; **essere in ~** (*sporgere*) stick out; **far ~** *fam* get rid of; **~ commercio** not for sale; **~ luogo** (*inopportuno*) out of place; **~ mano** out of the way; **~ moda** old-fashioned; **~ pasto** between meals; **~ pericolo** out of danger; **~ programma** unscheduled; **~ questione** out of the question; **~ uso** out of use ● *nm* outside

**fuori'bordo** *nm* speedboat (*with outboard motor*)

**fuori'campo** *a inv* ⟨*Cinema: voce*⟩ off-screen

**fuori'classe** *nmf inv* champion

**fuoricombatti'mento** *nm* knockout

**fuorigi'oco** *nm & adv* offside

**fuori'legge** *nmf* outlaw

**fuori'pista** *nm inv* (*sci*) off-piste skiing

**fuori'serie** *a* custom-made ● *nf Auto* custom-built model

**fuori'strada** *nm inv* off-road vehicle

**fuoriu'scita** *nf* (*perdita*) leak

**fuoriu'scito, -a** *nmf* exile

**fuorvi'are** *vt* lead astray ● *vi* go astray

**furbacchi'one** *nm* crafty old devil

**fur'bastro, -a** *nmf* crafty devil

**furbe'ria** *nf* cunning

**fur'besco** *a* sly, cunning

**fur'bizia** *nf* cunning

**'furbo** *a* sly, cunning; (*intelligente*) clever; (*astuto*) shrewd; **bravo ~!** nice one!; **fare il ~** try to be clever

**fu'rente** *a* furious

**fur'fante** *nm* scoundrel

**furgon'cino** *nm* delivery van

**fur'gone** *nm* van. **~ postale** mail van

**'furia** *nf* fury; (*fretta*) haste; **a ~ di** by dint of; **andare su tutte le furie** fly into a rage

**furi'bondo** *a* furious

**furi'ere** *nm Mil* quartermaster

**furiosa'mente** *adv* furiously

**furi'oso** *a* furious; ⟨*litigio*⟩ violent

**fu'rore** *nm* fury; (*veemenza*) frenzy; **far ~** be all the rage

**furoreggi'are** *vi* be a great success

**furtiva'mente** *adv* covertly

**fur'tivo** *a* furtive

**'furto** *nm* theft; **commettere un ~** steal; **è un ~!** *fig* it's daylight robbery!. **~ con scasso** burglary

**'fusa** *nfpl* **fare le ~** purr

**fu'scello** *nm* (*di legno*) twig; (*di paglia*) straw; **sei un ~** you're as light as a feather

**fu'seaux** *mpl* leggings

**fu'sibile** *nm* fuse

**fu'silli** *nmpl* pasta twirls

**fusi'one** *nf* fusion; *Comm* merger

**'fuso** *pp di* **fondere** ● *a* melted ● *nm* spindle; **a ~** spindle-shaped. **~ orario** time zone

**fuso'liera** *nf* fuselage

**fu'stagno** *nm* corduroy

**fu'stella** *nf* (*talloncino*) part of packaging on prescribed medicine returned by the pharmacist to claim a refund

**fusti'gare** *vt* flog; *fig* castigate

**fu'stino** *nm* (*di detersivo*) box

**'fusto** *nm* stem; (*tronco*) trunk: (*recipiente di metallo*) drum; (*di legno*) barrel. ~ **del letto** bedstead
**'futile** *a* futile
**futilità** *nf* futility

**futu'rismo** *nm* futurism
**futu'rista** *nmf* futurist
**fu'turo** *a* & *nm* future; **predire il** ~ tell fortunes, foretell. ~ **anteriore** *Gram* future perfect

# Gg

**gabar'dine** *nf* (*tessuto*) gabardine
**gab'bare** *vt* cheat
**gab'barsi** *vr* ~ **di** make fun of
**'gabbia** *nf* cage; (*da imballaggio*) crate. ~ **dell'ascensore** lift cage. ~ **degli imputati** dock. ~ **toracica** rib cage
**gabbi'ano** *nm* [sea]gull. ~ **comune** common gull
**gabi'netto** *nm* (*di medico*) consulting room; *Pol* cabinet; (*toletta*) toilet; (*laboratorio*) laboratory; **andare al** ~ go to the toilet. **gabinetti** *pl* **pubblici** public convenience
**'Gabon** *nm* Gabon
**ga'elico** *nm* Gaelic
**'gaffa** *nf* boathook
**'gaffe** *nf inv* blunder
**gagli'ardo** *a* vigorous
**gai'ezza** *nf* gaiety
**'gaio** *a* cheerful
**'gala** *nf* gala
**ga'lante** *a* gallant
**galante'ria** *nf* gallantry
**galantu'omo** *nm* (*pl* **galantuomini**) gentleman
**ga'lassia** *nf* galaxy
**gala'teo** *nm* [good] manners *pl*; (*trattato*) book of etiquette
**gale'otto** *nm* (*rematore*) galley-slave; (*condannato*) convict
**ga'lera** *nf* (*nave*) galley; *fam* slammer
**'galla** *nf Bot* gall; **a** ~ afloat; **venire a** ~ surface
**galleggi'ante** *a* floating ● *nm* craft; (*boa*) float
**galleggi'are** *vi* float
**galle'ria** *nf* (*traforo*) tunnel; (*d'arte*) gallery; *Theat* circle; (*arcata*) arcade; **prima** ~ dress circle. ~ **aerodinamica** wind tunnel. ~ **d'arte** art gallery
**'Galles** *nm* Wales
**gal'lese** *a* Welsh ● *nm* Welshman; (*lingua*) Welsh ● *nf* Welshwoman
**gal'letta** *nf* cracker
**gal'letto** *nm* cockerel; **fare il** ~ show off, impress the girls
**'gallico** *a* Gallic
**gal'lina** *nf* hen
**galli'nella** *nf* ~ **d'acqua** moorhen
**gal'lismo** *nm* machismo
**'gallo** *nm* cock. ~ **cedrone** capercaillie

**gal'lone** *nm* stripe; (*misura*) gallon
**galop'pante** *a* galloping
**galop'pare** *vi* gallop
**galop'pino** *nm* **fare da** ~ **a qcno** *fam* be sb's gopher
**ga'loppo** *nm* gallop; **al** ~ at a gallop
**galvaniz'zare** *vt* galvanize
**'gamba** *nf* leg; (*di lettera*) stem; **a quattro gambe** on all fours; **darsela a gambe** take to one's heels; **essere in** ~ (*essere forte*) be strong; (*capace*) be smart
**gam'bale** *nm* leg; **gambali** *pl* (*calzamaglia*) leggings
**gamba'letto** *nm* pop sock
**gambe'retti** *nmpl* shrimps. ~ **in salsa rosa** prawn cocktail
**'gambero** *nm* prawn; (*di fiume*) crayfish
**gambe'roni** *nmpl* king prawns
**'Gambia** *nf* the Gambia
**gambiz'zare** *vt* kneecap
**'gambo** *nm* stem; (*di pianta*) stalk
**ga'mella** *nf* billy
**game point** *nm inv* game point
**ga'mete** *nm* gamete
**'gamma** *nf Mus* scale; *fig* range. ~ **d'onda** waveband. ~ **di prezzi** price range. ~ **di prodotti** product range
**ga'nascia** *nf* jaw; **ganasce** *pl* **del freno** brake shoes
**'gancio** *nm* hook
**'Gange** *nm* Ganges
**'ganghero** *nm* **uscire dai gangheri** *fig* get into a temper
**'gangster** *nm inv* gangster
**'gara** *nf* competition; (*di velocità*) race; **fare a** ~ compete. ~ **d'appalto** call for tenders. ~ **a cronometro** time-trial
**ga'rage** *nm inv* garage
**gara'gista** *nmf* garage owner
**ga'rante** *nmf* guarantor
**garan'tire** *vt* guarantee; (*rendersi garante*) vouch for; (*assicurare*) assure
**garan'tirsi** *vr* ~ **contro,** ~ **da** guard against, insure against
**garan'tismo** *nm* protection of civil liberties
**garan'tito** *a* guaranteed
**garan'zia** *nf* guarantee; **in** ~ under guarantee. ~ **collaterale** collateral. ~ **di rimborso** money-back guarantee. ~ **a vita** lifetime guarantee

gar'bare *vi* like; **non mi garba** I don't like it
gar'bato *a* courteous
'garbo *nm* courtesy; (*grazia*) grace; **con ~** graciously
gar'buglio *nm* muddle
gar'denia *nf* gardenia
gareggi'are *vi* compete
garga'nella *nf* a **~** from the bottle
garga'rismo *nm* gargle; **fare i gargarismi** gargle
ga'ritta *nf* sentry box
ga'rofano *nm* carnation; **chiodo di ~** clove
gar'retto *nm* shank
gar'rire *vi* chirp
gar'rotta *nf* garrotte
'garrulo *a* garrulous
'garza *nf* gauze
gar'zone *nm* boy. **~ di stalla** stable-boy
gas *nm inv* gas; **dare ~** *Auto* accelerate; **a ~** gas-fired; **a tutto ~** flat out. **~ asfissiante** poisonous gas. **~ esilarante** laughing gas. **~ lacrimogeno** tear gas. **~ nobile** inert gas. **~ propellente** propellant. **~ pl di scarico** exhaust fumes
gas'dotto *nm* natural gas pipeline
ga'solio *nm* diesel oil. **~ invernale** diesel containing anti-freeze
ga'sometro *nm* gasometer
gas'sare *vt* aerate; (*uccidere col gas*) gas
gas'sato *a* gassy
gas'soso, -a *a* gassy; ⟨*bevanda*⟩ fizzy ●*nf* lemonade
'gastrico *a* gastric
ga'strite *nf* gastritis
gastroente'rite *nf* gastro-enteritis
gastrono'mia *nf* gastronomy
gastro'nomico *a* gastronomic[al]
ga'stronomo, -a *nmf* gourmet
'gatta *nf* una **~ da pelare** a headache
gatta'buia *nf hum* clink
gatta'iola *nf* catflap
gat'tino, -a *nmf* kitten
'gatto, -a *nmf* cat; **c'erano solo quattro gatti** there weren't many. **~ delle nevi** snowmobile. **~ a nove code** cat-o'-nine-tails. **~ selvatico** wildcat
gat'toni *adv* on all fours
gat'tuccio *nm* dogfish
gau'dente *a* pleasure-loving
'gaudio *nm* joy
ga'vetta *nf* mess tin; **fare la ~** rise through the ranks
gay *a inv* gay
ga'zebo *nm inv* gazebo
'gazza *nf* magpie
gaz'zarra *nf* racket; **fare ~** make a racket
gaz'zella *nf* gazelle; *Auto* police car
gaz'zetta *nf* gazette. **G~ Ufficiale** official journal
gazzet'tino *nm* (*titolo*) title page; (*rubrica*) page
gaz'zosa *nf* clear lemonade
GB *abbr* (**Gran Bretagna**) GB

'geco *nm* gecko
ge'lare *vt/i* freeze; **far ~ il sangue** make sb's blood run cold
ge'lata *nf* frost
gela'taio, -a *nmf* ice-cream seller ●*nm* (*negozio*) ice-cream shop
gelate'ria *nf* ice-cream parlour
gelati'era *nf* ice-cream maker
gela'tina *nf* gelatine; (*dolce*) jelly. **~ di frutta** fruit jelly
gelati'noso *a* gelatinous
ge'lato *a* frozen ●*nm* ice-cream. **~ alla vaniglia** vanilla ice-cream
'gelido *a* freezing
'gelo *nm* (*freddo intenso*) freezing cold; (*brina*) frost; *fig* chill
ge'lone *nm* chilblain
gelosa'mente *adv* jealously
gelo'sia *nf* jealousy
ge'loso *a* jealous
'gelso *nm* mulberry[-tree]
gelso'mino *nm* jasmine
gemel'laggio *nm* twinning
gemel'lare *vt* twin ●*a* twin
ge'mello, -a *a & nmf* twin; **gemelli** *pl* (*di polsino*) cuff-link; **Gemelli** *pl Astr* Gemini *sg*
'gemere *vi* groan
'gemito *nm* groan
'gemma *nf* gem; *Bot* bud
gemmolo'gia *nf* gemology
gen'darme *nm* gendarme
'gene *nm* gene
genealo'gia *nf* genealogy
genea'logico *a* genealogical
gene'rale[1] *a* general; **in ~** (*tutto sommato*) in general, on the whole; **parlando in ~** generally speaking
gene'rale[2] *nm Mil* general. **~ di divisione** major-general
generalità *nf inv* (*qualità*) generality, general nature; (*maggior parte*) majority; **~ pl** (*dati*) particulars *pl*
generaliz'zare *vt* generalize
generalizzazi'one *nf* generalization
general'mente *adv* generally
gene'rare *vt* give birth to; (*causare*) breed; *Techn* generate
genera'tore *nm Techn* generator
generazio'nale *a* generation
generazi'one *nf* generation; **di ~ in ~** from generation to generation
'genere *nm* kind; *Biol* genus; *Gram* gender; (*letterario, artistico*) genre; (*prodotto*) product; **cose del ~** such things; **il ~ umano** mankind; **in ~** generally. **generi** *pl* **alimentari** provisions. **generi** *pl* **di prima necessità** essentials
generica'mente *adv* generically
ge'nerico *a* generic; **medico ~** general practitioner
'genero *nm* son-in-law
generosa'mente *adv* generously
generosità *nf* generosity
gene'roso *a* generous
'genesi *nf* genesis

**genetica'mente** adv genetically

**ge'netico, -a** a genetic ● nf genetics

**gene'tista** nmf geneticist

**gen'giva** nf gum

**geni'ale** a ingenious; (congeniale) congenial

**geni'ere** nm Mil sapper

'**genio** nm genius; **andare a ~** be to one's taste. **~ civile** civil engineering. **~ incompreso** misunderstood genius. **~ [militare]** Engineers

**geni'tale** a genital ● nm **genitali** pl genitals

**geni'tore** nm parent

**gen'naio** nm January

**geno'cidio** nm genocide

'**Genova** nf Genoa

**geno'vese** a Genoese

**gen'taglia** nf rabble

'**gente** nf people pl

**gen'tile** a kind; **G~ Signore** (in lettere) Dear Sir

**genti'lezza** nf kindness; **per ~** (per favore) please

**gentil'mente** adv kindly

**gentilu'omo** (pl **gentil'uomini**) nm gentleman

**genu'flettersi** vr kneel down

**genuina'mente** adv genuinely

**genu'ino** a genuine; (cibo, prodotto) natural

**genzi'ana** nf gentian

**geo'fisica** nf geophysics

**geo'fisico, -a** nmf geophysician

**geogra'fia** nf geography

**geo'grafico** a geographical

**ge'ografo, -a** nmf geographer

**geolo'gia** nf geology

**geo'logico** a geological

**ge'ologo, -a** nmf geologist

**ge'ometra** nmf surveyor

**geome'tria** nf geometry

**geometrica'mente** adv geometrically

**geo'metrico** a geometric[al]

**geopo'litico** a geopolitical

**geo'termico** a geothermal, geothermic

**ge'ranio** nm geranium

**gerar'chia** nf hierarchy

**gerarchica'mente** adv hierarchically

**ge'rarchico** a hierarchic[al]

**ger'billo** nm gerbil

**ge'rente** nm manager ● nf manageress

'**gergo** nm jargon; (dei giovani) slang. **~ burocratico** bureaucratic jargon

**geri'atra** nmf geriatrician

**geria'tria** nf geriatrics

**geri'atrico** a geriatric

'**gerla** nf wicker basket

**Ger'mania** nf Germany. **~ [dell']Est** East Germany. **~ [dell']Ovest** West Germany

**ger'manico** a Germanic

'**germe** nm germ; (fig: principio) seed. **~ di grano** seedcorn

**germogli'are** vi sprout

**ger'moglio** nm sprout; **in ~** Bot sprouting. **germogli** pl **di soia** beansprouts

**gero'glifico** nm hieroglyph

**geron'tologo, -a** nmf gerontologist

**ge'rundio** nm gerund

**Gerusa'lemme** nf Jerusalem

**ges'setto** nm chalk

'**gesso** nm chalk; (Med, scultura) plaster

**ge'staccio** nm V-sign

**gestazi'one** nf gestation

**gestico'lare** vi gesticulate

**gestio'nale** a management attrib

**gesti'one** nf management. **~ aziendale** business management. **~ dei dati** Comput data management. **~ disco** Comput disk management. **~ dell'energia** energy resource management. **~ del flusso di cassa** cashflow management. **~ patrimoniale** financial mangement

**ge'stire** vi manage; **~ male** mishandle

**ge'stirsi** vr budget one's time and money

'**gesto** nm gesture; (azione: pl f **gesta**) deed

**ge'store** nm manager

**Gesù** nm Jesus. **~ bambino** baby Jesus

**gesu'ita** nm Jesuit

**gesu'itico** a Jesuit attrib

**get'tare** vt throw; (scagliare) fling; (emettere) spout; Techn, fig cast; **~ via** throw away

**get'tarsi** vr throw oneself; **~ in** (fiume:) flow into

**get'tata** nf throw; Techn casting

'**gettito** nm **~ fiscale** tax revenue

'**getto** nm throw; (di liquidi, gas) jet; **a ~ continuo** in a continuous stream; **di ~** straight off

**getto'nato** a (canzone) popular

**get'tone** nm token; (per giochi) counter

**gettoni'era** nf coin box

'**geyser** nm inv geyser

'**Ghana** nm Ghana

**ghe'pardo** nm cheetah

'**gheppio** nm kestrel

**gher'mire** vt grasp

'**ghette** nfpl (per neonato) leggings

**ghettiz'zare** vt ghettoize

'**ghetto** nm ghetto

**ghiacci'aia** nf glacier

**ghiacci'aio** nm glacier

**ghiacci'are** vt/i freeze

**ghiacci'ato** a frozen; (freddissimo) ice-cold

**ghi'accio** nm ice; Auto black ice. **~ secco** dry ice

**ghiacci'olo** nm icicle; (gelato) ice lolly

**ghi'aia** nf gravel

**ghiai'oso** a gritty

**ghi'anda** nf acorn

**ghi'andola** nf gland. **~ pituitaria** pituitary gland. **~ sudoripara** sweat gland. **~ surrenale** adrenal gland

**ghigliot'tina** nf guillotine

**ghi'gnare** vi sneer

'**ghigno** nm sneer

**ghi'otto** a greedy, gluttonous; (appetitoso) appetizing

**ghiot'tone, -a** nmf glutton

**ghiotto'neria** nf (caratteristica) gluttony; (cibo) tasty morsel

**ghiri'goro** nm flourish

**ghir'landa** *nf* (*corona*) wreath: (*di fiori*) garland

**'ghiro** *nm* dormouse: **dormire come un ~** sleep like a log

**'ghisa** *nf* cast iron

**già** *adv* already: (*un tempo*) formerly: **~!** indeed!: **~ da ieri** since yesterday

**gi'acca** *nf* jacket. **~ a vento** wind-cheater

**giacché** *conj* since

**giac'cone** *nm* jacket

**gia'cenza** *nf* **giacenze** *pl* **di magazzino** unsold stock

**gia'cere** *vi* lie

**giaci'mento** *nm* deposit. **~ di petrolio** oil deposit

**gia'cinto** *nm* hyacinth

**gi'ada** *nf* jade

**giaggi'olo** *nm* iris

**giagu'aro** *nm* jaguar

**gial'lastro** *a* yellowish

**gi'allo** *a* & *nm* yellow: [**libro**] **~** crime novel: [**film**] **~** thriller. **~ dell'uovo** egg yolk

**Gia'maica** *nf* Jamaica

**giamai'cano, -a** *a* & *nmf* Jamaican

**Giap'pone** *nm* Japan

**giappo'nese** *a* & *nmf* Japanese

**gi'ara** *nf* jar

**giardi'naggio** *nm* gardening

**giardini'era** *nf* **~ di verdure** *diced, mixed vegetables, cooked and pickled*

**giardini'ere, -a** *nmf* gardener ● *nf* Auto estate car; (*sottaceti*) pickles *pl*

**giar'dino** *nm* garden. **~ d'infanzia** kindergarten. **~ pensile** roof-garden. **giardini** *pl* **pubblici** park. **~ zoologico** zoo

**giarretti'era** *nf* garter

**giavel'lotto** *nm* javelin

**gi'gante** *nm* giant

**gigan'tesco** *a* gigantic

**gigantogra'fia** *nf* blow-up

**'giglio** *nm* lily

**gilè** *nm inv* waistcoat

**gin** *nm inv* gin

**gin'cana** *nf* gymkhana

**ginecolo'gia** *nf* gynaecology

**gineco'logico** *a* gynaecological

**gine'cologo, -a** *nmf* gynaecologist

**gi'nepro** *nm* juniper

**gi'nestra** *nf* broom

**Gi'nevra** *nf* Geneva

**gingil'larsi** *vr* fiddle; (*perder tempo*) potter

**gin'gillo** *nm* plaything; (*ninnolo*) knick-knack

**gin'nasio** *nm* (*scuola*) grammar school

**gin'nasta** *nmf* gymnast

**gin'nastica** *nf* gymnastics; (*esercizi*) exercises *pl*. **~ ritmica** eurhythmics

**ginocchi'ata** *nf* **prendere una ~** bang one's knee

**ginocchi'era** *nf* knee-pad

**gi'nocchio** *nm* (*pl m* **ginocchi** *o f* **ginocchia**) knee; **in ~** on one's knees, kneeling; **mettersi in ~** kneel down; (*per supplicare*) go down on one's knees; **al ~** (*gonna*) knee-length

**ginocchi'oni** *adv* kneeling

**gio'care** *vt/i* play; (*giocherellare*) toy; (*d'azzardo*) gamble; (*puntare*) stake; (*ingannare*) trick: **~ a calcio/a pallavolo** play football/volleyball: **~ d'astuzia** be crafty; **~ d'azzardo** gamble; **~ in Borsa** speculate on the Stock Exchange; **~ in casa** *Sport, fig* play on one's home ground, play at home

**gio'carsi** *vr* **~ la carriera** throw one's career away

**gioca|'tore, -'trice** *nmf* player; (*d'azzardo*) gambler

**gio'cattolo** *nm* toy

**giocherel'lare** *vi* toy; (*nervosamente*) fiddle

**giocherel'lone** *a* skittish

**gi'oco** *nm* game; (*di bambini, Techn*) play; (*d'azzardo*) gambling; (*scherzo*) joke; (*insieme di pezzi ecc*) set; **essere in ~** be at stake; **fare il doppio ~ con qcno** double-cross sb; **è un ~ da ragazzi** *fam* it's a cinch. **~ elettronico** computer game. **giochi** *pl* **della gioventù** *nation-wide sports tournament for children.* **~ dell'oca** snakes and ladders. **Giochi** *pl* **Olimpici** Olympic Games. **~ di parole** play on words. **~ di pazienza** game of manual skill. **~ di prestigio** conjuring trick. **~ di società** board game

**giocoli'ere** *nm* juggler

**gio'coso** *a* playful

**gi'ogo** *nm* yoke

**gi'oia** *nf* joy; (*gioiello*) jewel; (*appellativo*) sweetie

**gioielle'ria** *nf* jeweller's [shop]

**gioi'elli** *nmpl* jewellery

**gioielli'ere, -a** *nmf* jeweller; (*negozio*) jeweller's

**gioi'ello** *nm* jewel

**gioiosa'mente** *adv* joyfully

**gioi'oso** *a* joyful

**gio'ire** *vi* **~ per** rejoice at

**Gior'dania** *nf* Jordan

**gior'dano, -a** *a* & *nmf* Jordanian

**giorna'laio, -a** *nmf* newsagent, newsdealer

**gior'nale** *nm* [news]paper; (*diario*) journal. **~ di bordo** logbook. **~ gratuito** freebie. **~ del mattino** morning paper. **~ radio** radio news. **~ della sera** evening paper

**giornali'ero** *a* daily ● *nm* (*per sciare*) day pass

**giorna'lino** *nm* comic

**giorna'lismo** *nm* journalism

**giorna'lista** *nmf* journalist

**giornal'mente** *adv* daily

**gior'nata** *nf* day; **buona ~!** have a good day!; **in ~** today; **a ~** (*essere pagato*) on a day-to-day basis; **vivere alla ~** live from day to day. **~ lavorativa** working day

**gi'orno** *nm* day; **al ~** per day; **al ~ d'oggi** nowadays; **di ~** by day; **in pieno ~** in broad daylight; **un ~ sì, un ~ no** every other day; **~ per ~** day by day. **~ di chiusura** closing day. **~ fatidico** (*importante*) D-day. **~ feriale** weekday. **~ festivo** public holiday. **~ del giudizio** Judgement Day

**gi'ostra** *nf* merry-go-round

**gio'strarsi** *vr* manage

**giova'mento** *nm* **trarre ~ da** derive benefit from

**gi'ovane** *a* young; *(giovanile)* youthful ● *nm* youth; young man ● *nf* girl, young woman; **giovani** *pl* young people

**giova'nile** *a* youthful; *(scritto)* early

**giova'notto** *nm* young man

**gio'vare** *vi* **~ a** be useful to; *(far bene a)* be good for

**gio'varsi** *vr* **~ di** avail oneself of

**giovedì** *nm inv* Thursday; **di ~** on Thursdays. **~ grasso** *last Thursday before Lent*. **~ santo** Maundy Thursday

**Gi'ove** *nm* Jupiter, Jove

**gioventù** *nf* youth; *(i giovani)* young people *pl*. **~ bruciata** young drop-outs *pl*

**giovi'ale** *a* jovial

**giovi'nezza** *nf* youth

**gi'rabile** *a* ‹assegno› endorsable

**gira'dischi** *nm inv* record-player

**gi'raffa** *nf* giraffe; *Cinema* boom

**gira'mondo** *nmf inv* globetrotter; **da ~** globetrotting

**gi'randola** *nf* *(fuoco d'artificio)* Catherine wheel; *(giocattolo)* windmill; *(banderuola)* weathercock

**gi'rare** *vt* turn; *(andare intorno, visitare)* go round; *Comm* endorse; *Cinema* shoot ● *vi* turn; ‹aerei, uccelli:› circle; *(andare in giro)* wander; **~ sotto...** *Comput* run under...; **mi gira la testa** I feel dizzy; **far ~ la testa a qcno** make sb's head spin; **far ~ le scatole a qcno** *fam* drive sb round the twist; **~ al largo** steer clear

**girar'rosto** *nm* spit

**gi'rarsi** *vr* turn [round]

**gira'sole** *nm* sunflower

**gi'rata** *nf* turn; *Comm* endorsement; *(in macchina ecc)* ride; **fare una ~** *(a piedi)* go for a walk; *(in macchina)* go for a ride

**gira'volta** *nf* spin; *fig* U-turn

**gi'rello** *nm* *(per bambini)* babywalker; *Culin* topside

**gi'revole** *a* revolving; **ponte ~** swing bridge

**gi'rino** *nm* tadpole

**'giro** *nm* turn; *(circolo)* circle; *(percorso)* round; *(viaggio)* tour; *(passeggiata)* short walk; *(in macchina)* drive; *(in bicicletta)* ride; *(circolazione di denaro)* circulation; **andare a fare un ~** *(a piedi)* go for a stroll; *(in macchina)* go for a drive; *(in bicicletta)* go for a cycle ride; **fare il ~ di** go round; **nel ~ di un mese/anno** within a month/year; **prendere in ~ qcno** pull sb's leg; **sentir dire in ~ qcsa** hear sth on the grapevine; **a ~ di posta** by return mail. **~ d'affari** *Comm* turnover. **~ in barca** boat trip. **~ guidato** guided tour. **~ [della] manica** armhole. **giri** *pl* **al minuto** revs per minute, rpm. **~ d'onore** lap of honour. **giri** *pl* **di parole** beating about the bush. **~ di pista** lap. **~ di prova** trial lap. **~ turistico** sightseeing tour. **~ vita** waist measurement

**giro'collo** *nm* choker; **a ~** roundneck

**gi'rone** *nm* round. **~ di andata** first half of the season. **~ di ritorno** second half of the season

**gironzo'lare** *vi* wander about

**giro'tondo** *nm* ring-a-ring-o'-roses

**girova'gare** *vi* wander about

**gi'rovago** *nm* wanderer

**'gita** *nf* trip; **andare in ~** go on a trip. **~ organizzata** package tour. **~ in pullman** coach trip. **~ scolastica** school trip

**gi'tano, -a** *nmf* gipsy

**gi'tante** *nmf* tripper

**giù** *adv* down; *(sotto)* below; *(dabbasso)* downstairs; **a testa in ~** *(a capofitto)* headlong; **essere ~** *(di morale)* be down, be depressed; *(di salute)* be run down; **~ di corda** down; **~ di lì, su per ~** more or less; **non andare ~ a qcno** stick in sb's craw

**gi'ubba** *nf* jacket; *Mil* tunic

**giub'botto** *nm* bomber jacket, jerkin. **~ antiproiettile** bulletproof vest. **~ di pelle** leather jacket. **~ di salvataggio** lifejacket

**gi'ubilo** *nm* rejoicing

**giudi'care** *vt* judge; *(ritenere)* consider

**gi'udice** *nm* judge. **~ conciliatore** justice of the peace. **~ di gara** umpire. **~ di linea** linesman

**giudizi'ario** *a* legal, judicial

**giu'dizio** *nm* judg[e]ment; *(opinione)* opinion; *(senno)* wisdom; *(processo)* trial; *(sentenza)* sentence; **mettere ~** become wise. **~ universale** Last Judgement

**giudizi'oso** *a* sensible

**gi'ugno** *nm* June

**giugu'lare** *nf* jugular

**giul'lare** *nm* jester

**giu'menta** *nf* mare

**giun'chiglia** *nf* jonquil

**gi'unco** *nm* reed

**gi'ungere** *vi* arrive; **~ a** *(riuscire)* succeed in; **mi giunge nuovo** it's news to me ● *vt* *(unire)* join

**gi'ungla** *nf* jungle. **~ d'asfalto** concrete jungle

**gi'unta** *nf* addition; *Mil* junta; **per ~** in addition. **~ comunale** district council. **~ [militare]** [military] junta

**gi'unto** *pp di* **giungere** ● *nm* *Mech* joint. **~ sferico** ball-and-socket joint

**giun'tura** *nf* joint

**giuo'care, giu'oco** = **giocare, gioco**

**giura'mento** *nm* oath; **sotto ~** under oath; **prestare ~** take the oath. **~ d'Ippocrate** Hippocratic oath

**giu'rare** *vt/i* swear

**giu'rato, -a** *a* sworn ● *nmf* juror

**giu'ria** *nf* jury

**giu'ridico** *a* legal

**giurisdizi'one** *nf* jurisdiction

**giurispru'denza** *nf* jurisprudence

**giu'rista** *nmf* jurist

**giu'stezza** *nf* justness

**giustifi'care** *vt* justify

**giustifi'carsi** *vr* justify oneself; ~ **di** *o* **per qcsa** give an explanation for sth
**giustificazi'one** *nf* justification
**giu'stizia** *nf* justice; **farsi** ~ **da sé** take the law into one's own hands
**giustizi'are** *vt* execute
**giustizi'ere** *nm* executioner
**gi'usto** *a* just, fair; (*adatto*) right; (*esatto*) exact ● *nm* (*uomo retto*) just man; (*cosa giusta*) right ● *adv* exactly; ~ **ora** just now
**glaci'ale** *a* glacial
**gladia'tore** *nm* gladiator
**gla'diolo** *nm* gladiolus
**'glassa** *nf Culin* icing
**glau'coma** *nm* glaucoma
**gli** *def art m pl* the; *vedi* **il** ● *pers pron* (*a lui*) [to] him; (*a esso*) [to] it; (*a loro*) [to] them; **non** ~ **credo** I don't believe him/them
**glice'mia** *nf* glycaemia
**glice'rina** *nf* glycerine
**'glicine** *nm* wisteria
**gli'elo** *pron* (*a lui*) to him; (*a lei*) to her; (*a loro*) to them; (*a Lei, forma di cortesia*) to you: ~ **prestai** I lent it to him/her etc; **gliel'ho chiesto** I've asked him/her etc
**glie'ne** *pron* (*di ciò*) of it; ~ **ho dato un po'** I gave him/her/them/you some [of it]; ~ **ho parlato** I've talked to him/her etc about it
**glis'sare** *vi* avoid the issue; ~ **su qcsa** skate over sth
**glo'bale** *a* global; *fig* overall
**global'mente** *adv* globally
**'globo** *nm* globe. ~ **oculare** eyeball. ~ **terrestre** globe
**'globulo** *nm* globule; *Med* corpuscle. ~ **bianco** white cell, white corpuscle. ~ **rosso** red cell, red corpuscle
**'gloria** *nf* glory
**glori'arsi** *vr* ~ **di** be proud of
**glorifi'care** *vt* glorify
**gloriosa'mente** *adv* gloriously
**glori'oso** *a* glorious
**'glossa** *nf* gloss
**glos'sario** *nm* glossary
**glottolo'gia** *nf* linguistics
**glu'cosio** *nm* glucose
**glutam'mato** *nm* ~ **di sodio** monosodium glutamate
**'gluteo** *nm* buttock
**'gnocchi** *nmpl* small flour and potato dumplings
**'gnomo** *nm* gnome
**'gnorri** *nm* **fare lo** ~ play dumb
**goal** *nm inv* goal; **fare un** ~ score *or* get a goal
**'gobba** *nf* hump
**'gobbo, -a** *a* hunchbacked ● *nmf* hunchback
**goc'cetto** *nm* pick-me-up
**'goccia** *nf* drop; (*di sudore*) bead; **è stata l'ultima** ~ it was the last straw. ~ **di pioggia** raindrop. ~ **di rugiada** dewdrop
**goccio'lare** *vi* drip
**goccio'lio** *nm* dripping
**go'dere** *vi* (*sl: sessualmente*) come; ~ **di qcsa** enjoy sth, make the most of sth

**go'dersi** *vr* ~ **qcsa** enjoy sth; **godersela** have a good time
**godi'mento** *nm* enjoyment
**gof'faggine** *nf* awkwardness
**goffa'mente** *adv* awkwardly
**'goffo** *a* awkward
**go-'kart** *nm inv* go-kart
**'gola** *nf* throat; (*ingordigia*) gluttony; *Geog* gorge; (*di camino*) flue; **avere mal di** ~ have a sore throat; **far** ~ **a qcno** tempt sb
**go'letta** *nf* schooner
**golf** *nm inv* jersey; *Sport* golf
**gol'fino** *nm* jumper
**'golfo** *nm* gulf
**goli'ardico** *a* student *attrib*
**golosità** *nf inv* greediness; (*cibo*) tasty morsel
**go'loso** *a* greedy
**'golpe** *nm inv* coup
**go'mena** *nf* painter
**gomi'tata** *nf* nudge; **dare una** ~ **a qcno** elbow sb
**'gomito** *nm* elbow; **alzare il** ~ (*fam: bere*) raise one's elbow; ~ **a** ~ (*lavorare*) side by side
**go'mitolo** *nm* ball
**'gomma** *nf* rubber; (*colla, da masticare*) gum; (*pneumatico*) tyre; **avere una** ~ **a terra** have a flat. ~ **arabica** gum arabic. ~ **da masticare** chewing gum. ~ **di scorta** spare tyre
**gommapi'uma®** *nf* foam rubber
**gom'mino** *nm* rubber tip
**gom'mista** *nm* tyre specialist
**gom'mone** *nm* [rubber] dinghy
**gom'moso** *a* chewy
**'gondola** *nf* gondola
**gondoli'ere** *nm* gondolier
**gonfa'lone** *nm* banner
**gonfi'abile** *a* inflatable
**gonfi'are** *vi* swell ● *vt* blow up; pump up (*pneumatico*); (*esagerare*) exaggerate
**gonfi'arsi** *vr* swell; (*acque:*) rise
**'gonfio** *a* swollen; (*pneumatico*) inflated
**gonfi'ore** *nm* swelling
**gongo'lante** *a* overjoyed
**gongo'lare** *vi* be overjoyed
**goni'ometro** *nm* protractor
**'gonna** *nf* skirt. ~ **pantalone** culottes *pl.* ~ **a pieghe** pleated skirt. ~ **a portafoglio** wrapover skirt
**gonor'rea** *nf* gonorrh[o]ea
**'gonzo** *nm* simpleton
**gorgheggi'are** *vi* warble
**gor'gheggio** *nm* warble
**'gorgo** *nm* whirlpool
**gorgogli'ante** *a* burbling, gurgling
**gorgogli'are** *vi* gurgle
**gor'goglio** *nm* burble
**gorgon'zola** *nf* strong, soft blue cheese
**go'rilla** *nm inv* gorilla; (*guardia del corpo*) bodyguard, minder
**'gota** *nf* cheek
**'gotico** *a & nm* Gothic
**'gotta** *nf* gout

**gover'nante** *nf* housekeeper

**gover'nare** *vt* govern; (*dominare*) rule; (*dirigere*) manage; (*curare*) look after

**governa'tivo** *a* government

**governa'tore** *nm* governor

**go'verno** *nm* government; (*dominio*) rule; **al ~** in power. **~ ombra** shadow government

**'gozzo** *nm* (*di animale*) crop; *Med* goitre; *fam* throat

**gozzovigli'are** *vi* eat, drink and be merry

**gracchi'are** *vi* caw; (*fig: persona:*) screech

**'gracchio** *nm* caw

**graci'dare** *vi* croak

**'gracile** *a* delicate

**gra'dasso** *nm* braggart

**gradata'mente** *adv* gradually

**gradazi'one** *nf* gradation. **~ alcoolica** alcohol[ic] content

**gra'devole** *a* agreeable

**gradevol'mente** *adv* pleasantly, agreeably

**gradi'ente** *nm* gradient

**gradi'mento** *nm* liking; **indice di ~** *Radio*, *TV* popularity rating; **non è di mio ~** it's not to my liking

**gradi'nata** *nf* flight of steps; (*di stadio*, *teatro*) tiers *pl*

**gra'dino** *nm* step

**gra'dire** *vt* like; (*desiderare*) wish

**gra'dito** *a* pleasant; (*bene accetto*) welcome

**'grado** *nm* degree; (*rango*) rank; **di buon ~** willingly; **essere in ~ di fare qcsa** be in a position to do sth; (*essere capace a*) be able to do sth; **per gradi** (*procedere*) by degrees

**gradu'ale** *a* gradual

**gradual'mente** *adv* gradually

**gradu'are** *vt* graduate

**gradu'ato** *a* graded; (*provvisto di scala graduata*) graduated ● *nm Mil* noncommissioned officer

**gradua'toria** *nf* list

**graduazi'one** *nf* graduation

**'graffa** *nf* clip; (*segno grafico*) brace

**graf'fetta** *nf* staple

**graffi'are** *vt* scratch

**graffia'tura** *nf* scratch

**'graffio** *nm* scratch

**gra'fia** *nf* [hand]writing; (*ortografia*) spelling

**'grafica** *nf* graphics; (*disciplina*) graphics, graphic design. **~ pubblicitaria** commercial art

**grafica'mente** *adv* in graphics, graphically

**'grafico** *a* graphic ● *nm* graph; (*persona*) graphic designer. **~ a torta** pie chart

**gra'fite** *nf* graphite

**gra'fologo, -a** *nmf* graphologist

**gra'migna** *nf* weed

**gram'matica** *nf* grammar

**grammati'cale** *a* grammatical

**grammatical'mente** *adv* grammatically

**gram'matico** *nm* grammarian

**'grammo** *nm* gram[me]

**gram'mofono** *nm* gramophone

**gran** *vedi* **grande**

**'grana** *nf* grain; (*formaggio*) parmesan; (*fam: seccatura*) trouble; (*fam: soldi*) readies *pl*

**gra'naio** *nm* barn

**gra'nata** *nf Mil* grenade; (*frutto*) pomegranate

**granati'ere** *nm Mil* grenadier

**gra'nato** *nm* garnet

**Gran Bre'tagna** *nf* Great Britain

**gran'cassa** *nf* bass drum

**gran'cevola** *nf* spiny spider crab

**'granchio** *nm* crab; (*fig: errore*) blunder; **prendere un ~** make a blunder

**grandango'lare** *nm* wide-angle lens

**gran'dangolo** *nm* wide-angle lens

**'grande** (*a volte* **gran**) *a* (*ampio*) large; (*grosso*) big; (*alto*) tall; (*largo*) wide; (*fig: senso morale*) great; (*grandioso*) grand; (*adulto*) grown-up; **~ e grosso** beefy; **ho una gran fame** I'm very hungry; **fa un gran caldo** it is very hot; **in ~** on a large scale; **in gran parte** to a great extent; **in gran che** it is nothing much; **di gran carriera** hotfoot; **un gran ballo** a grand ball; **alla ~** *sl* in a big way ● *nmf* (*persona adulta*) grown-up; (*persona eminente*) great man/woman

**grandeggi'are** *vi* **~ su** tower over; (*darsi arie*) show off

**gran'dezza** *nf* greatness; (*ampiezza*) largeness; (*larghezza*) width, breadth; (*dimensione*) size; (*fasto*) grandeur; (*prodigalità*) lavishness; **a ~ naturale** life-size

**grandi'nare** *vi* hail; **grandina** it's hailing

**'grandine** *nf* hail

**grandiosità** *nf* grandeur

**grandi'oso** *a* grand

**gran'duca** *nm* grand duke

**grandu'cato** *nm* grand duchy

**grandu'chessa** *nf* grand duchess

**gra'nello** *nm* grain; (*di frutta*) pip

**gra'nita** *nf* crushed ice drink

**gra'nito** *nm* granite

**'grano** *nm* grain; (*frumento*) wheat. **~ di pepe** peppercorn. **~ saraceno** buckwheat

**gran[o]'turco** *nm* corn

**'granulo** *nm* granule

**'grappa** *nf* very strong, clear spirit distilled from grapes; (*morsa*) cramp

**'grappolo** *nm* bunch. **~ d'uva** bunch of grapes

**gras'setto** *nm* bold [type]

**gras'sezza** *nf* fatness; (*untuosità*) greasiness

**'grasso** *a* fat; ⟨*cibo*⟩ fatty; (*unto*) greasy; ⟨*terreno*⟩ rich; (*grossolano*) coarse ● *nm* fat; (*sostanza*) grease; **a basso contenuto di grassi** low-fat; **senza grassi** nonfat, fat-free

**gras'soccio** *a* plump

**gras'sone, -a** *nmf* dumpling

**'grata** *nf* grating

**gra'tella** *nf Culin* grill

**gra'ticcio** *nm* (*per piante*) trellis; (*stuoia*) rush matting

**gra'ticola** *nf Culin* grill

**gra'tifica** *nf* bonus

**gratificazi'one** *nf* satisfaction

**gra'tin** *nm inv* gratin. ~ **di patate** *potatoes with grated cheese*
**grati'nare** *vt* cook au gratin
**grati'nato** *a* au gratin
**'gratis** *adv* free
**grati'tudine** *nf* gratitude
**'grato** *a* grateful; (*gradito*) pleasant
**gratta'capo** *nm* trouble
**grattaci'elo** *nm* skyscraper
**grat'tare** *vt* scratch; (*raschiare*) scrape; (*grattugiare*) grate; (*fam: rubare*) pinch ● *vi* grate
**grat'tarsi** *vr* scratch oneself
**grat'tugia** *nf* grater
**grattugi'are** *vt* grate
**gratuita'mente** *adv* free [of charge]
**gra'tuito** *a* free [of charge]; (*ingiustificato*) gratuitous
**gra'vare** *vt* burden ● *vi* ~ **su** weigh on
**'grave** *a* (*pesante*) heavy; (*serio*) serious; (*difficile*) hard; ⟨*voce, suono*⟩ low; (*fonetica*) grave; **essere** ~ (*gravemente ammalato*) be seriously ill
**grave'mente** *adv* seriously, gravely
**gravi'danza** *nf* pregnancy. ~ **extrauterina** ectopic pregnancy. ~ **indesiderata** unwanted pregnancy
**'gravido** *a* pregnant
**gravità** *nf* seriousness; *Phys* gravity
**gravi'tare** *vi* gravitate
**gra'voso** *a* onerous
**'grazia** *nf* grace; (*favore*) favour; *Jur* pardon; **entrare nelle grazie di qcno** get into sb's good books; **ministero di** ~ **e giustizia** Ministry of Justice
**grazi'are** *vt* pardon
**'grazie** *int* thank you!, thanks!; ~ **mille!** many thanks!, thanks a lot!; ~ **a Dio/al cielo!** thank God/goodness!; ~ **a** thanks to
**grazi'oso** *a* charming; (*carino*) pretty
**'Grecia** *nf* Greece
**greco, -a** *a & nmf* Greek; ~ **antico** (*lingua*) classical Greek
**gre'gario** *a* gregarious ● *nm* (*ciclismo*) supporting rider
**'gregge** *nm* flock
**'greggio** *a* raw ● *nm* (*petrolio*) crude [oil]
**grembi'ale, grembi'ule** *nm* apron
**'grembo** *nm* lap; (*utero*) womb; *fig* bosom
**gre'mire** *vt* pack
**gre'mirsi** *vr* become crowded (**di** with)
**gre'mito** *a* packed
**'gretto** *a* stingy; (*di vedute ristrette*) narrow-minded
**'greve** *a* heavy
**'grezzo** *a* = **greggio**
**gri'dare** *vi* shout; (*di dolore*) scream; ⟨*animale:*⟩ cry ● *vt* shout; ~ **qcsa ai quattro venti** shout sth from the rooftops
**'grido** *nm* (*pl m* **gridi** *o pl f* **grida**) shout, cry; (*di animale*) cry; **all'ultimo** ~ the latest fashion; **scrittore di** ~ celebrated writer. ~ **d'aiuto** cry for help. ~ **di battaglia** battle cry
**'grigio** *a & nm* grey. ~ **perla** pearl grey

**'griglia** *nf* grill; **alla** ~ grilled; **cuocere alla** ~ grill
**grigli'ata** *nf* barbecue. ~ **mista** mixed grill. ~ **di pesce** grilled fish
**gril'letto** *nm* trigger
**'grillo** *nm* cricket; (*fig: capriccio*) whim
**grimal'dello** *nm* picklock
**'grinfia** *nf fig* clutch
**'grinta** *nf* grit
**grin'toso** *a* determined
**'grinza** *nf* wrinkle; (*di stoffa*) crease; **non fare una** ~ ⟨*fig: ragionamento:*⟩ be flawless
**grip'pare** *vi Mech* seize up
**gri'sou** *nm* firedamp
**gris'sino** *nm* bread-stick
**'grizzly** *nm inv* grizzly
**groenlan'dese** *a* of Greenland ● *nmf* Greenlander
**Groen'landia** *nf* Greenland
**'groggy** *a inv* punch-drunk
**'gronda** *nf* eaves *pl*
**gron'daia** *nf* gutter
**gron'dare** *vi* pour; (*essere bagnato fradicio*) be dripping wet
**'groppa** *nf* back
**'groppo** *nm* knot; **avere un** ~ **alla gola** have a lump in one's throat
**gros'sezza** *nf* size; (*spessore*) thickness
**gros'sista** *nmf* wholesaler
**'grosso** *a* big, large; (*spesso*) thick; (*grossolano*) coarse; (*grave*) serious ● *nm* big part; (*massa*) bulk; **farla grossa** do a stupid thing
**grossolanità** *nf inv* (*qualità*) coarseness; (*di errore*) grossness; (*gesto*) boorishness
**grosso'lano** *a* coarse; ⟨*errore*⟩ gross; ⟨*comportamento*⟩ boorish
**grosso'modo** *adv* roughly
**'grotta** *nf* cave, grotto
**grot'tesco** *a & nm* grotesque
**grovi'era** *nmf* Gruyère
**gro'viglio** *nm* tangle; *fig* muddle
**gru** *nf inv* (*uccello, edilizia*) crane
**'gruccia** *nf* (*stampella*) crutch; (*per vestito*) hanger
**gru'gnire** *vi* grunt
**gru'gnito** *nm* grunt
**'grugno** *nm* snout
**'grullo** *a* silly
**'grumo** *nm* clot; (*di farina ecc*) lump
**gru'moso** *a* lumpy
**grunge** *nm inv* grunge
**'gruppo** *nm* group; (*comitiva*) party. ~ **pop** pop group. ~ **sanguigno** blood group
**gruvi'era** *nmf* = **groviera**
**'gruzzolo** *nm* nest-egg
**guada'gnare** *vt* earn; gain ⟨*tempo, forza ecc*⟩
**guada'gnarsi** *vr* ~ **da vivere** earn a living
**gua'dagno** *nm* gain; (*profitto*) profit; (*entrate*) earnings *pl*. **guadagni** *pl* **illeciti** ill-gotten gains
**gu'ado** *nm* ford; **passare a** ~ ford
**gua'ina** *nf* sheath; (*busto*) girdle
**gu'aio** *nm* trouble; **che** ~! that's just bril-

liant!; **essere nei guai** be in a fix; **guai a te se lo tocchi!** don't you dare touch it!

**gua'ire** vi yelp

**gua'ito** nm yelp; **guaiti** pl yelping

**gu'ancia** nf cheek

**guanci'ale** nm pillow

**gu'anto** nm glove. ~ **da forno** oven glove. ~ **di spugna** face cloth

**guan'tone** nm mitt. **guantoni** pl [da boxe] boxing gloves

**guarda'boschi** nm inv forester

**guarda'caccia** nm inv gamekeeper

**guarda'coste** nm inv coastguard

**guarda'linee** nm inv Sport linesman

**guarda'macchine** nmf car-park attendant

**guarda'parco** nm inv park ranger

**guar'dare** vt look at; (osservare) watch; (badare a) look after; (finestra:) look out on: ~ **la televisione** watch television ● vi look; (essere orientato verso) face; ~ **in su** look up

**guarda'roba** nm inv wardrobe; (di locale pubblico) cloakroom

**guardarobi'ere, -a** nmf cloakroom attendant

**guar'darsi** vr look at oneself; ~ **da** beware of; (astenersi) refrain from

**gu'ardia** nf guard; (poliziotto) policeman; (vigilanza) watch; **essere di** ~ be on guard; (medico:) be on duty; **fare la** ~ a keep guard over; **mettere in** ~ qcno warn sb; **stare in** ~ be on one's guard. ~ **carceraria** prison warder. ~ **del corpo** bodyguard, minder. ~ **di finanza** body responsible for border control and for investigating fraud. ~ **forestale** forest ranger. ~ **medica** duty doctor

**guardi'ano, -a** nmf caretaker. ~ **notturno** night watchman

**guar'dingo** a cautious

**guardi'ola** nf gatekeeper's lodge

**guarigi'one** nf recovery

**gua'rire** vt cure ● vi recover; (ferita:) heal [up]

**gua'rito** a cured

**guari|'tore, -'trice** nmf healer

**guarnigi'one** nf garrison

**guar'nire** vt trim; Culin garnish

**guarnizi'one** nf trimming; Culin garnish; Mech gasket. ~ **del freno** brake lining

**guasta'feste** nmf inv spoilsport

**gua'stare** vt spoil; (rovinare) ruin; break (meccanismo)

**gua'starsi** vr spoil; (andare a male) go bad; (tempo:) change for the worse; (meccanismo:) break down

**gu'asto** a broken: (ascensore, telefono) out of order; (auto) broken down; (cibo, dente) bad ● nm breakdown; (danno) damage; **ho un** ~ **alla macchina** my car's not working. ~ **al motore** engine failure

**guazza'buglio** nm muddle

**guaz'zare** vi wallow

**gu'ercio** a cross-eyed

**gu'erra** nf war; (tecnica bellica) warfare. ~ **batteriologica** germ warfare. ~ **biologica** biological warfare. ~ **civile** civil war. ~ **fredda** Cold War. ~ **del Golfo** Gulf War. ~ **lampo** blitzkrieg. ~ **mondiale** world war. ~ **dei prezzi** price war. ~ **di secessione** American Civil War

**guerrafon'daio, -a** nmf warmonger

**guerreggi'are** vi wage war

**guer'resco** a (di guerra) war; (bellicoso) warlike

**guerri'ero** nm warrior

**guer'riglia** nf guerrilla warfare

**guerrigli'ero, -a** nmf guerrilla

**'gufo** nm owl

**'guglia** nf spire

**gu'ida** nf guide; (direzione) guidance; (comando) leadership; (elenco) directory; Auto driving; (tappeto) runner; **chi era alla** ~? who was driving?; **essere alla** ~ **di** fig be the head of; **fare da** ~ be a guide (a to). ~ **commerciale** trade directory. ~ **a destra** right-hand drive. ~ **a sinistra** left-hand drive. ~ **telefonica** phone book, telephone directory. ~ **turistica** tourist guide

**gui'dare** vt guide; Auto drive; steer (nave); ~ **a passo d'uomo** drive at walking speed

**guida|'tore, -'trice** nmf driver. ~ **della domenica** Sunday driver

**guin'zaglio** nm leash

**gu'isa** nf a ~ **di** like

**guiz'zare** vi dart; (luce:) flash

**gu'izzo** nm dart; (di luce) flash

**'gulag** nm inv Gulag

**'gulasch** nm inv goulash

**'guru** nm inv high priest

**'guscio** nm shell

**gu'stare** vt taste ● vi like

**'gusto** nm taste; (piacere) liking; **mangiare di** ~ eat heartily; **prenderci** ~ come to enjoy it, develop a taste for it; **al** ~ **di pistacchio** pistachio flavoured. **buon** ~ good taste

**gu'stoso** a tasty; fig delightful

**guttu'rale** a guttural

# Hh

'**habitat** *nm inv* habitat
**habitué** *nmf inv* regular [customer]
'**hacker** *nmf inv Comput* hacker
**Ha'iti** *nf* Haiti
**haiti'ano, -a** *a & nmf* Haitian
**hall** *nf inv* foyer; (*di stazione*) concourse
**ham'burger** *nm inv* hamburger
'**handicap** *nm inv* handicap
**handicap'pare** *vt* handicap
**handicap'pato, -a** *a* disabled ● *nmf* disabled person. **~ mentale** mentally handicapped person
'**hangar** *nm inv* hangar
**hard[-core]** *a* hard core
**hard disk** *nm inv* hard disk
**hard rock** *nm* hard rock
'**hardware** *nm inv Comput* hardware
'**harem** *nm inv* harem
'**hascish** *nm* hashish
**hawai'ano, -a** *a & nmf* Hawaiian

**Ha'waii** *nfpl* le ~ Hawaii
'**heavy 'metal** *nm Mus* heavy metal
**henné** *nm* henna
'**herpes** *nm inv* herpes; (*su labbra*) cold sore. ~ **zoster** shingles
**hi-fi** *nm inv* hi-fi
**high tech** *nf* high tech
**Hima'laia** *nm* Himalayas *pl*
'**hinterland** *nm inv* hinterland
'**hippy** *a & nmf* hippy
'**hit parade** *nf* hit parade, charts *pl*
**HIV** *nm* HIV
'**hockey** *nm* hockey. ~ **su ghiaccio** ice hockey. ~ **su prato** field hockey
'**holding** *nf inv* holding company
**hollywoodi'ano** *a* Hollywood
**Hong Kong** *nf* Hong Kong
'**hostess** *nf inv* stewardess
**hot dog** *nm inv* hot dog
**ho'tel** *nm inv* hotel
'**humus** *nm* humus

# Ii

**i** *def art mpl* the; *vedi* il
**i'ato** *nm* hiatus
**i'berico** *a* Iberian
**iber'nare** *vi* hibernate
**ibernazi'one** *nf* hibernation
**i'bisco** *nm* hibiscus
**ibri'dare** *vt* interbreed
**ibridazi'one** *nf* interbreeding
'**ibrido** *a & nm* hybrid
'**iceberg** *nm inv* iceberg; **la punta dell'**~ *fig* the tip of the iceberg
**i'cona** *nf* icon
**icono'clasta** *a & nmf* iconoclast
**icono'clastico** *a* iconoclastic
**Id'dio** *nm* God
**i'dea** *nf* idea; (*opinione*) opinion; (*ideale*) ideal; (*indizio*) inkling; (*piccola quantità*) hint; (*intenzione*) intention; **cambiare ~** change one's mind; **neanche per ~!** not on your life!; **chiarirsi le idee** get one's ideas straight; **dare l'~ di...** give the impression that...; **essere dell'~ che...** be of the opinion that...; **non ne ho ~!** I've no idea!. **~ fissa** obsession
**ide'ale** *a & nm* ideal

**idea'lista** *nmf* idealist
**idealiz'zare** *vt* idealize
**ide'are** *vt* conceive
**idea|'tore, -'trice** *nmf* originator
'**idem** *adv* the same
**identica'mente** *adv* identically
**i'dentico** *a* identical
**identifi'cabile** *a* identifiable
**identifi'care** *vt* identify
**identificazi'one** *nf* identification
**identi'kit** *nm inv* identikit
**identità** *nf inv* identity
**ideo'gramma** *nm* ideogram
**ideolo'gia** *nf* ideology
**ideologica'mente** *adv* ideologically
**ideo'logico** *a* ideological
**idillica'mente** *adv* idyllically
**i'dillico** *a* idyllic
**i'dillio** *nm* idyll
**idi'oma** *nm* language
**idio'matico** *a* idiomatic; **espressione idiomatica** idiom, idiomatic expression
**idiosincra'sia** *nf fig* aversion; *Med* allergy
**idi'ota** *a* idiotic ● *nmf* idiot
**idio'zia** *nf* idiocy; **dire/fare un'**~ do/say

# idolatrare | imbandito

something stupid: **dire idiozie** talk nonsense; **non fare idiozie!** don't act daft!
**idola'trare** *vt* worship
**idoleggi'are** *vt* idolize
**'idolo** *nm* idol
**idoneità** *nf* suitability; *Mil* fitness; **esame di ~** qualifying examination
**i'doneo** *a* **~ a** suitable for; *Mil* fit for
**i'drante** *nm* hydrant; *(tubo)* hose
**idra'tante** *a* *(crema)* moisturizing
**idra'tare** *vt* hydrate; *(cosmetico:)* moisturize
**idratazi'one** *nf* moisturizing
**i'draulico** *a* hydraulic ● *nm* plumber
**'idrico** *a* water *attrib*
**idrocar'buro** *nm* hydrocarbon
**idroelettricità** *nf* hydroelectricity
**idroe'lettrico** *a* hydroelectric
**i'drofilo** *a* **cotone ~** cotton wool, absorbent cotton *Am*
**idrofo'bia** *nf* rabies *sg*
**i'drofobo** *a* rabid; *fig* furious
**i'drofugo** *a* water-repellent
**i'drogeno** *nm* hydrogen
**idrogra'fia** *nf* hydrography
**i'drolisi** *nf* hydrolysis
**idromas'saggio** *nm* *(sistema)* whirlpool bath
**idro'mele** *nm* mead
**idrorepel'lente** *a & nm* water-repellent
**idroso'lubile** *a* water-soluble
**idrotera'pia** *nf* hydrotherapy
**idrovo'lante** *nm* seaplane
**i'druro** *nm* hydride
**i'ella** *nf fam* bad luck; **portare ~** be bad luck
**iel'lato** *a fam* jinxed, plagued by bad luck
**i'ena** *nf* hyena
**i'eri** *adv* yesterday; **~ l'altro, l'altro ~** the day before yesterday; **il giornale di ~** yesterday's paper; **~ mattina** yesterday morning; **~ notte** last night; **~ pomeriggio** yesterday afternoon; **~ sera** yesterday evening
**ietta**|**'tore, -'trice** *nmf* jinx
**ietta'tura** *nf* *(sfortuna)* bad luck
**igi'ene** *nf* hygiene; **ufficio d'~** ≈ Public Health Service. **~ mentale** mental health. **~ personale** personal hygiene. **~ pubblica** public health
**igienica'mente** *adv* hygienically
**igi'enico** *a* hygienic
**igie'nista** *nmf* hygienist
**ig'loo** *nm inv* igloo
**i'gname** *nm* yam
**i'gnaro** *a* unaware
**i'gnifugo** *a* flame-retardant
**i'gnobile** *a* despicable
**ignobil'mente** *adv* despicably
**igno'minia** *nf* disgrace
**igno'rante** *a* ignorant ● *nmf* ignoramus
**igno'ranza** *nf* ignorance; **~ crassa** crass ignorance
**igno'rare** *vt* *(non sapere)* be unaware of; *(trascurare)* ignore; **essere ignorato** go unheeded
**i'gnoto** *a* unknown
**i'guana** *nf* iguana

**il** *def art m* the; **il latte fa bene** milk is good for you; **il signor Magnetti** Mr Magnetti; **il dottor Piazza** Doctor Piazza; **ha il naso grosso** he's got a big nose; **ha gli occhi azzurri** he's got blue eyes; **mettiti il cappello** put your hat on; **il lunedì** on Mondays; **il 1986** 1986; **5 000 lire il chilo** it costs 5,000 lire a kilo
**'ilare** *a* merry
**ilarità** *nf* hilarity
**i'leo** *nm* hipbone
**illangui'dire** *vi* grow weak
**illazi'one** *nf* inference
**illecita'mente** *adv* illicitly
**il'lecito** *a* illicit
**ille'gale** *a* illegal
**illegalità** *nf* illegality
**illegal'mente** *adv* illegally
**illeg'gibile** *a* illegible; *(libro)* unreadable
**illegittimità** *nf* illegitimacy
**ille'gittimo** *a* illegitimate
**il'leso** *a* unhurt
**illette'rato, -a** *a & nmf* illiterate
**illi'bato** *a* chaste
**illimitata'mente** *adv* indefinitely
**illimi'tato** *a* unlimited
**illivi'dire** *vt* bruise ● *vi* *(per rabbia)* turn livid
**illogica'mente** *adv* illogically
**il'logico** *a* illogical
**il'ludere** *vt* deceive
**il'ludersi** *vr* deceive oneself
**illumi'nare** *vt* light up; *fig* enlighten; **~ a giorno** floodlight
**illumi'narsi** *vr* light up
**illuminazi'one** *nf* lighting; *fig* enlightenment. **~ a gas** gas lighting
**illumi'nismo** *nm* Enlightenment
**illusi'one** *nf* illusion; **farsi illusioni** delude oneself. **~ ottica** optical illusion
**illusio'nismo** *nm* conjuring
**illusio'nista** *nmf* conjurer
**il'luso, -a** *pp di* **illudere** ● *a* deluded ● *nmf* day-dreamer
**illu'sorio** *a* illusory
**illu'strare** *vt* illustrate
**illustra'tivo** *a* illustrative
**illustra**|**'tore, -'trice** *nmf* illustrator
**illustrazi'one** *nf* illustration. **~ a colori/in bianco e nero** colour/black and white illustration
**il'lustre** *a* distinguished
**imbacuc'care** *vt* wrap up
**imbacuc'carsi** *vr* wrap up
**imbacuc'cato** *a* wrapped up
**imbal'laggio** *nm* packing
**imbal'lare** *vt* pack; *Auto* race
**imballa**|**'tore, -'trice** *nmf* packer
**imbalsa'mare** *vt* embalm; stuff *(animale)*
**imbalsa'mato** *a* embalmed; *(animale)* stuffed
**imbambo'lato** *a* vacant
**imban'dito** *a* *(tavolo)* covered with food

**imbaraz'zante** *a* embarrassing

**imbaraz'zare** *vt* embarrass; (*ostacolare*) encumber

**imbaraz'zato** *a* embarrassed

**imba'razzo** *nm* embarrassment; (*ostacolo*) hindrance; **trarre qcno d'~** help sb out of a difficulty; **avere l'~ della scelta** be spoilt for choice. **~ di stomaco** indigestion.

**imbarba'rire** *vt* barbarize

**imbarba'rirsi** *vr* become barbarized

**imbarca'dero** *nm* landing-stage

**imbar'care** *vt* embark; (*fam: rimorchiare*) score; **~ acqua** ship water

**imbar'carsi** *vr* go on board; *fig* embark (**in** on)

**imbarcazi'one** *nf* boat. **~ da pesca** fishing boat. **~ di salvataggio** lifeboat

**im'barco** *nm* boarding; (*banchina*) landing-stage. **'~ immediato'** 'now boarding'

**imbastar'dire** *vt* debase

**imbastar'dirsi** *vr* become debased

**imba'stire** *vt* tack, baste; *fig* sketch

**imbasti'tura** *nf* tacking, basting

**im'battersi** *vr* **~ in** run into

**imbat'tibile** *a* unbeatable

**imbat'tuto** *a* unbeaten

**imbavagli'are** *vt* gag

**imbec'cata** *nf Theat* prompt

**imbe'cille** *a* stupid ● *nmf Med* imbecile

**imbellet'tarsi** *vr hum* doll oneself up

**imbel'lire** *vt* embellish

**im'berbe** *a* beardless; *fig* inexperienced

**imbestia'lire** *vi* fly into a rage; **far ~ qcno** drive sb crazy

**imbestia'lirsi** *vr* fly into a rage

**imbestia'lito** *a* enraged

**im'bevere** *vt* imbue (**di** with)

**im'beversi** *vr* absorb

**imbe'vibile** *a* undrinkable

**imbe'vuto** *a* **~ di** (*acqua*) soaked in; (*nozioni*) imbued with

**imbian'care** *vt* whiten ● *vi* turn white

**imbian'chino** *nm* [house] painter

**imbion'dire** *vt* bleach ● *vi* become bleached

**imbion'dirsi** *vr* become bleached

**imbizzar'rire** *vi* become restless; (*arrabbiarsi*) become angry

**imbizzar'rirsi** *vr* become restless; (*arrabbiarsi*) become angry

**imboc'care** *vt* feed; (*entrare*) enter; *fig* prompt

**imbocca'tura** *nf* opening; (*ingresso*) entrance; (*Mus: di strumento*) mouthpiece

**im'bocco** *nm* entrance

**imboni'mento** *nm* spiel

**imboni'tore** *nm* clever talker

**imborghe'sire** *vi* become middle class

**imborghe'sirsi** *vr* become middle class

**imbo'scare** *vt* hide

**imbo'scarsi** *vr Mil* shirk military service

**imbo'scata** *nf* ambush

**imbo'scato** *nm* draft dodger

**imbottiglia'mento** *nm* traffic jam

**imbottigli'are** *vt* bottle

**imbottigli'arsi** *vr* get snarled up in a traffic jam

**imbottigli'ato** *a* (*vino, acqua*) bottled; (*auto*) stuck in a traffic jam, snarled up; **nave imbottigliata** ship in a bottle

**imbot'tire** *vt* stuff; pad (*giacca*); *Culin* fill

**imbot'tirsi** *vr* **~ di** (*fig: di pasticche*) stuff oneself with

**imbot'tita** *nf* quilt

**imbot'tito** *a* (*spalle*) padded; (*cuscino*) stuffed; (*panino*) filled

**imbotti'tura** *nf* stuffing; (*di giacca*) padding; *Culin* filling

**imbraca'tura** *nf* harness

**imbracci'are** *vt* shoulder (*fucile*); grasp (*scudo*)

**imbra'nato** *a* clumsy

**imbrat'tare** *vt* mark

**imbrat'tarsi** *vr* dirty oneself

**imbrigli'are** *vt* bridle (*cavallo*); dam (*acque*)

**imbroc'care** *vt* hit; **imbroccarla giusta** hit the nail on the head

**imbrogli'are** *vt* muddle; (*raggirare*) cheat. **~ le carte** *fig* confuse the issue

**imbrogli'arsi** *vr* get tangled; (*confondersi*) get confused

**im'broglio** *nm* tangle; (*pasticcio*) mess; (*inganno*) trick

**imbrogli'one, -a** *nmf* cheat

**imbronci'are** *vi* sulk

**imbronci'arsi** *vr* sulk

**imbronci'ato** *a* sulky

**imbru'nire** *vi* get dark; **all'~** at dusk

**imbrut'tire** *vt* make ugly ● *vi* become ugly

**imbu'care** *vt* post, mail; (*nel biliardo*) pot

**imbu'cato** *a fam* **è ~** he only got the job because of who he knows

**imbufa'lirsi** *vr* hit the roof

**imbur'rare** *vt* butter

**im'buto** *nm* funnel

**i'mene** *nm* hymen

**imi'tare** *vt* imitate

**imita'tore, -'trice** *nmf* imitator, impersonator

**imitazi'one** *nf* imitation; **'diffidare delle imitazioni'** 'beware of imitations'

**immaco'lato** *a* spotless, immaculate; **l'Immacolata Concezione** the Immaculate Conception

**immagazzi'nare** *vt* store

**immagi'nare** *vt* imagine; (*supporre*) suppose; **s'immagini!** imagine that!

**immagi'nario** *a* imaginary

**immaginazi'one** *nf* imagination; **è frutto della tua ~** it's a figment of your imagination

**im'magine** *nf* image; (*rappresentazione, idea*) picture. **~ aziendale** corporate image. **~ della marca** brand image. **~ speculare** mirror image

**immagi'noso** *a* full of imagery

**immalinco'nire** *vt* sadden

**immalinco'nirsi** *vr* grow melancholy

**imman'cabile** *a* unfailing

**immancabil'mente** *adv* without fail

**im'mane** a huge; (orribile) terrible
**imma'nente** a immanent
**immangi'abile** a inedible
**immatrico'lare** vt register
**immatrico'larsi** vr ⟨studente:⟩ matriculate
**immatricolazi'one** nf registration; (di studente) matriculation
**immaturità** nf immaturity
**imma'turo** a unripe; ⟨persona⟩ immature: (-precoce) premature
**immedesi'marsi** vr ~ **in** identify oneself with
**immedesimazi'one** nf identification
**immediata'mente** adv immediately
**immedia'tezza** nf immediacy
**immedi'ato** a immediate; **nell'~ futuro** in the immediate future
**immemo'rabile** a immemorial
**im'memore** a oblivious
**immensa'mente** adv enormously
**immensità** nf immensity
**im'menso** a immense
**immensu'rabile** a immeasurable
**im'mergere** vt immerse
**im'mergersi** vr plunge; ⟨sommergibile:⟩ dive; ~ **in** immerse oneself in
**immerata'mente** adv undeservedly
**immeri'tato** a undeserved
**immeri'tevole** a undeserving
**immersi'one** nf immersion; (di sommergibile, palombaro) dive. ~ **[subacquea]** skin diving, scuba diving
**im'merso** pp di **immergere**
**im'mettere** vt introduce
**im'mettersi** vr introduce oneself
**immi'grante** a & nmf immigrant
**immi'grare** vi immigrate
**immi'grato, -a** nmf immigrant
**immigrazi'one** nf immigration. ~ **interna** migration
**immi'nente** a imminent
**immi'nenza** nf imminence
**immischi'are** vt involve
**immischi'arsi** vr ~ **in** meddle in
**immi'scibile** a immiscible
**immis'sario** nm tributary
**immissi'one** nf insertion; Techn intake; (introduzione) introduction. ~ **[di] dati** data entry
**im'mobile** a motionless
**im'mobili** nmpl real estate
**immobili'are** a società ~ building society, savings and loan Am
**immobilità** nf immobility
**immobiliz'zare** vt immobilize; Comm tie up
**immobiliz'zato** a immobilized. ~ **a letto** confined to bed
**immobilizzazi'one** nf immobilization; Fin fixed asset; **spese d'~** capital expenditure
**immoderata'mente** adv immoderately
**immode'rato** a immoderate
**immo'destia** nf immodesty
**immo'desto** a immodest
**immo'lare** vt sacrifice

**immo'larsi** vr sacrifice oneself
**immondez'zaio** nm rubbish tip
**immon'dizia** nf filth: (spazzatura) rubbish
**im'mondo** a filthy
**immo'rale** a immoral
**immoral'mente** adv immorally
**immorta'lare** vt immortalize
**immor'tale** a immortal
**immortalità** nf immortality
**immoti'vato** a unjustified
**im'moto** a motionless
**im'mune** a exempt; Med immune
**immunità** nf immunity. ~ **diplomatica** diplomatic immunity. ~ **parlamentare** parliamentary privilege
**immuniz'zare** vt immunize
**immunizzazi'one** nf immunization
**immunodefici'enza** nf immunodeficiency
**immunolo'gia** nf immunology
**immuno'logico** a immunological
**immuso'nirsi** vr sulk
**immuso'nito** a sulky
**immu'tabile** a unchangeable
**immu'tato** a unchanging
**impacchet'tare** vt wrap up
**impacci'are** vt hamper; (disturbare) inconvenience; (imbarazzare) embarrass
**impacciata'mente** adv awkwardly
**impacci'ato** a embarrassed; (goffo) awkward
**im'paccio** nm embarrassment; (ostacolo) hindrance; (situazione difficile) awkward situation; **trarsi d'~** get out of an awkward situation
**im'pacco** nm compress
**impadro'nirsi** vr ~ **di** take possession of; (fig: imparare) master
**impa'gabile** a priceless
**impagi'nare** vt paginate
**impaginazi'one** nf pagination
**impagli'are** vt stuff ⟨animale⟩
**impa'lare** vt impale
**impa'lato** a fig stiff
**impalca'tura** nf scaffolding; fig structure
**impal'lare** vt snooker
**impalli'dire** vi turn pale; (fig: perdere d'importanza) pale into insignificance
**impalli'nare** vt riddle with bullets
**impal'pabile** a impalpable; ⟨tessuto⟩ gossamer-like
**impa'nare** vt Culin bread
**impa'nato** a breaded
**impanta'narsi** vr get bogged down
**impape'rarsi** vr falter, stammer
**impappi'narsi** vr falter, stammer
**impa'rare** vt learn; ~ **a propie spese** learn to one's cost
**impara'ticcio** nm half-baked
**impareggi'abile** a incomparable
**imparen'tarsi** vr ~ **con** become related to
**imparen'tato** a related
**'impari** a unequal; (dispari) odd
**impar'tire** vt impart
**imparzi'ale** a impartial

**imparzialità** *nf* impartiality
**im'passe** *nf inv* impasse
**impas'sibile** *a* impassive; **con aria ~** impassively
**impa'stare** *vt Culin* knead; blend ⟨*colori*⟩
**impasta'tura** *nf* kneading
**impastic'carsi** *vr* pop pills
**impasticci'are** *vt* make a mess of
**im'pasto** *nm Culin* dough; (*miscuglio*) mixture
**im'patto** *nm* impact. **~ ambientale** environmental impact
**impau'rire** *vt* frighten
**impau'rirsi** *vr* get frightened
**im'pavido** *a* fearless
**impazi'ente** *a* impatient; **~ di fare qcsa** eager to do sth
**impazien'tirsi** *vr* lose patience
**impazi'enza** *nf* impatience
**impaz'zata** *nf* **all'~** at breakneck speed
**impaz'zire** *vi* go mad; ⟨*maionese:*⟩ separate; **far ~ qcno** drive sb mad; **~ per** be crazy about; **da ~** ⟨*mal di testa*⟩ blinding
**impaz'zito** *a* crazed
**impec'cabile** *a* impeccable
**impeccabil'mente** *adv* impeccably
**impedi'mento** *nm* hindrance; (*ostacolo*) obstacle
**impe'dire** *vt* (*impacciare*) hinder; (*ostruire*) obstruct; **~ di** prevent from; **~ a qcno di fare qcsa** prevent sb [from] doing sth
**impe'gnare** *vt* (*dare in pegno*) pawn; (*vincolare*) bind; (*prenotare*) reserve; (*assorbire*) take up
**impe'gnarsi** *vr* apply oneself; **~ a fare qcsa** commit oneself to doing sth
**impegna'tiva** *nf* referral
**impegna'tivo** *a* binding; ⟨*lavoro*⟩ demanding
**impe'gnato** *a* politically committed
**im'pegno** *nm* engagement; *Comm* commitment; (*zelo*) care; **con ~** with dedication; **ho un ~** I'm doing something
**impego'larsi** *vr* **~ in** become enmeshed in
**impel'lente** *a* pressing
**impene'trabile** *a* impenetrable
**impen'narsi** *vr* ⟨*cavallo:*⟩ rear; *fig* bristle
**impen'nata** *nf* (*di prezzi*) sharp rise; (*di cavallo*) rearing; (*di moto*) wheelie; (*di aereo*) climb
**impen'sabile** *a* unthinkable
**impen'sato** *a* unexpected
**impensie'rire** *vt* worry
**impensie'rirsi** *vr* worry
**impe'rante** *a* prevailing
**impe'rare** *vi* reign
**impera'tivo** *a & nm* imperative
**impera|'tore, -'trice** *nm* emperor ● *nf* empress
**impercet'tibile** *a* imperceptible
**impercettibil'mente** *adv* imperceptibly
**imperdo'nabile** *a* unforgivable
**imperfetta'mente** *adv* imperfectly
**imper'fetto** *a & nm* imperfect
**imperfezi'one** *nf* imperfection

**imperi'ale** *a* imperial
**imperia'lismo** *nm* imperialism
**imperia'lista** *a & nmf* imperialist
**imperia'listico** *a* imperialistic
**imperi'oso** *a* imperious; (*impellente*) urgent
**imperi'turo** *a* immortal
**impe'rizia** *nf* lack of skill
**imper'lare** *vt* bead
**imperma'lire** *vt* offend
**imperma'lirsi** *vr* take offence
**imperme'abile** *a* ⟨*orologio*⟩ waterproof; ⟨*terreno*⟩ impermeable ● *nm* raincoat
**imperni'are** *vt* pivot; (*fondare*) base
**imperni'arsi** *vr* **~ su** be based on
**im'pero** *nm* empire; (*potere*) rule; **stile ~** empire style
**imperscru'tabile** *a* inscrutable
**imperso'nale** *a* impersonal
**imperso'nare** *vt* personify; (*interpretare*) act [the part of]
**imper'territo** *a* undaunted
**imperti'nente** *a* impertinent
**imperti'nenza** *nf* impertinence
**impertur'babile** *a* imperturbable
**impertur'bato** *a* unperturbed
**imperver'sare** *vi* rage
**im'pervio** *a* inaccessible
**'impeto** *nm* impetus; (*impulso*) impulse; (*slancio*) transport
**impet'tito** *a* stiff
**impetuosa'mente** *adv* impetuously
**impetu'oso** *a* impetuous; ⟨*vento*⟩ blustering
**impiallacci'are** *vt* veneer
**impiallacci'ato** *a* veneered
**impian'tare** *vt* install; set up ⟨*azienda*⟩
**impi'anto** *nm* plant; (*sistema*) system; (*operazione*) installation. **~ di amplificazione** public address system, PA system. **~ audio** sound system. **~ elettrico** electrical system. **impianti** *pl* **fissi** fixtures and fittings. **~ radio** *Auto* car stereo system. **~ di riscaldamento** heating system. **~ stereo** hi-fi
**impia'strare** *vt* plaster; (*sporcare*) dirty
**impia'strarsi** *vr* get dirty; **~ le mani** get one's hands dirty
**impi'astro** *nm* poultice; (*persona noiosa*) bore; (*pasticcione*) cack-handed person
**impiccagi'one** *nf* hanging
**impic'care** *vt* hang
**impic'carsi** *vr* hang oneself
**impic'cato, -a** *nm* hanged man ● *nf* hanged woman
**impicci'arsi** *vr* meddle
**im'piccio** *nm* hindrance; (*seccatura*) bother
**impicci'one, -a** *nmf* nosey parker
**impie'gare** *vt* employ; (*usare*) use; spend ⟨*tempo, denaro*⟩; *Fin* invest; **l'autobus ha impiegato un'ora** it took the bus an hour
**impie'garsi** *vr* get [oneself] a job
**impiega'tizio** *a* clerical
**impie'gato, -a** *nmf* employee; (*di* ufficio) office worker. **~ di banca** bank clerk. **~ di concetto** administrative employee. **~ in prova** probationer. **~ statale** civil servant
**impi'ego** *nm* employment; (*posto*) job; *Fin*

investment; **pubblico** ~ public sector. ~ **fisso** permanent job. **impieghi** *pl* **saltuari** odd jobs, casual employment. ~ **temporaneo** temporary job

**impieto'sire** *vt* move to pity

**impieto'sirsi** *vr* be moved to pity

**impie'toso** *a* pitiless

**impie'trito** *a* petrified

**impigli'are** *vt* entangle

**impigli'arsi** *vr* get entangled

**impi'grire** *vt* make lazy

**impi'grirsi** *vr* get lazy

**impi'lare** *vt* stack

**impingu'are** *vt fig* fill

**impiom'bare** *vt* seal ‹cassa, porta›

**impla'cabile** *a* implacable

**implemen'tare** *vt* implement

**impli'care** *vt* implicate; (*sottintendere*) imply

**impli'carsi** *vr* become involved

**implicazi'one** *nf* implication

**implicita'mente** *adv* implicitly

**im'plicito** *a* implicit

**implo'rante** *a* imploring

**implo'rare** *vt* implore

**implorazi'one** *nf* entreaty

**implosi'one** *nf* implosion

**impolli'nare** *vt* pollinate

**impollinazi'one** *nf* pollination

**impoltro'nire** *vt* make lazy

**impoltro'nirsi** *vr* become lazy

**impolve'rare** *vt* cover with dust

**impolve'rarsi** *vr* get covered with dust

**impolve'rato** *a* dusty

**impoma'tare** *vt* put brilliantine on

**impoma'tarsi** *vr* put brilliantine on ‹capelli›

**imponde'rabile** *a* imponderable; ‹causa, evento› unpredictable

**impo'nente** *a* imposing

**impo'nenza** *nf* impressiveness

**impo'nibile** *a* taxable ● *nm* taxable income

**impopo'lare** *a* unpopular

**impopolarità** *nf* unpopularity

**imporpo'rarsi** *vr* turn red

**im'porre** *vt* impose; (*ordinare*) order

**im'porsi** *vr* assert oneself; (*aver successo*) be successful; ~ **di** (*prefiggersi di*) set oneself the task of

**impor'tante** *a* important ● *nm* important thing

**impor'tanza** *nf* importance; **di vitale ~** crucially important

**impor'tare** *vt Comm, Comput* import; (*comportare*) cause ● *vi* matter; (*essere necessario*) be necessary. **non importa!** it doesn't matter!; **non me ne importa niente!** I couldn't care less!

**importa**‖**'tore, -'trice** *a* importing ● *nmf* importer

**importazi'one** *nf* importation; (*merce importata*) import

**import-'export** *nm inv* import-export

**im'porto** *nm* amount

**importu'nare** *vt* pester; ~ **qcno per qcsa** pester sb for sth

**impor'tuno** *a* troublesome; (*inopportuno*) untimely

**imposizi'one** *nf* imposition; (*imposta*) tax

**imposses'sarsi** *vr* ~ **di** seize

**impos'sibile** *a* impossible ● *nm* **fare l'**~ do absolutely all one can

**impossibilità** *nf* impossibility

**im'posta¹** *nf* tax. ~ **fondiaria** land tax. ~ **patrimoniale** property tax. ~ **sul reddito** income tax. ~ **sui redditi di capitale** capital gains tax. ~ **sulle società** corporation tax. ~ **supplementare** surtax. ~ **sul valore aggiunto** value added tax

**im'posta²** *nf* (*di finestra*) shutter

**impo'stare** *vt* (*progettare*) plan; (*basare*) base; *Mus* pitch; (*imbucare*) post, mail; set out ‹domanda, problema›

**impostazi'one** *nf* planning; (*di voce*) pitching

**im'posto** *pp di* **imporre**

**impo'store, -a** *nmf* impostor

**impo'stura** *nf* imposture

**impo'tente** *a* powerless; *Med* impotent

**impo'tenza** *nf* powerlessness; *Med* impotence

**impoveri'mento** *nm* impoverishment

**impove'rire** *vt* impoverish

**impove'rirsi** *vr* become poor; ‹risorse:› become depleted; ‹linguaggio:› become impoverished

**imprati'cabile** *a* impracticable; ‹strada› impassable

**impraticabilità** *nf* **per ~ del terreno/delle strade** because of the state of the pitch/roads

**imprati'chire** *vt* train

**imprati'chirsi** *vr* ~ **in** *o* **a** get practice in

**impre'care** *vi* curse

**imprecazi'one** *nf* curse

**impreci'sabile** *a* indeterminable

**impreci'sato** *a* indeterminate

**imprecisi'one** *nf* inaccuracy

**impre'ciso** *a* inaccurate

**impre'gnare** *vt* impregnate; (*imbevere*) soak; *fig* imbue

**impre'gnarsi** *vr* become impregnated with

**imprendi**‖**'tore, -'trice** *nmf* entrepreneur

**imprenditori'ale** *a* entrepreneurial

**imprepa'rato** *a* unprepared

**im'presa** *nf* undertaking; (*gesta*) exploit; (*azienda*) firm. ~ **edile** property developer. ~ **familiare** family business. ~ **di pompe funebri** undertakers, funeral directors. ~ **pubblica** state-owned company. ~ **di traslochi** furniture remover

**impre'sario** *nm* impresario; (*appaltatore*) contractor. ~ **di pompe funebri** undertaker, funeral director, mortician *Am*. ~ **teatrale** theatre manager

**imprescin'dibile** *a* inescapable

**impressio'nabile** *a* impressionable

**impressio'nante** *a* impressive; (*spaventoso*) frightening

**impressio'nare** *vt* impress; (*spaventare*) frighten; expose ‹foto›

**impressio'narsi** *vi* be affected; *(spaventarsi)* be frightened

**impressi'one** *nf* impression; *(sensazione)* sensation; *(impronta)* mark: **far ~ a qcno** upset sb: **dare l'~ di essere...** give the impression of being...

**impressio'nismo** *nm* impressionism

**impressio'nista** *a & nmf* impressionist

**impressio'nistico** *a* impressionistic

**im'presso** *pp di* **imprimere** ● *a* printed

**impre'stare** *vt* lend

**impreve'dibile** *a* unforeseeable; *(persona)* unpredictable

**imprevedibil'mente** *adv* unexpectedly

**imprevi'dente** *a* improvident

**impre'visto** *a* unforeseen ● *nm* unforeseen event; **salvo imprevisti** all being well

**imprigiona'mento** *nm* imprisonment

**imprigio'nare** *vt* imprison

**im'primere** *vt* impress; *(stampare)* print; *(comunicare)* impart; **rimanere impresso a qcno** stick in sb's mind

**impro'babile** *a* unlikely, improbable; **è ~ che ci sia** he is unlikely to be there

**improbabilità** *nf* improbability

**improdut'tivo** *a* unproductive

**im'pronta** *nf* impression; *fig* mark. **~ digitale** fingerprint. **impronte** *pl* **genetiche** genetic fingerprinting. **~ del piede** footprint

**impron'tato** *a* **~ all'ironia** tinged with irony

**impronunci'abile** *a* unpronounceable

**impro'perio** *nm* insult; **improperi** *pl* abuse *sg*

**impropo'nibile** *a* unrealistic

**im'proprio** *a* improper

**improro'gabile** *a* which cannot be extended

**improvvisa'mente** *adv* suddenly

**improvvi'sare** *vt/i* improvise

**improvvi'sarsi** *vr* turn oneself into a

**improvvi'sata** *nf* surprise

**improvvi'sato** *a* *(discorso)* unrehearsed

**improvvisazi'one** *nf* improvisation

**improv'viso** *a* unexpected, sudden; **all'~** unexpectedly, suddenly

**impru'dente** *a* imprudent

**imprudente'mente** *adv* imprudently

**impru'denza** *nf* imprudence

**impu'dente** *a* impudent

**impudente'mente** *adv* impudently

**impu'denza** *nf* impudence

**impu'dico** *a* immodest

**impu'gnare** *vt* grasp; *Jur* contest

**impugna'tura** *nf* grip; *(manico)* handle. **~ a due mani** two-handed grip

**impulsiva'mente** *adv* impulsively

**impulsività** *nf* impulsiveness

**impul'sivo** *a* impulsive

**im'pulso** *nm* impulse; **agire d'~** act on impulse

**impune'mente** *adv* with impunity

**impunità** *nf* impunity

**impu'nito** *a* unpunished

**impun'tarsi** *vr* *fig* dig one's heels in

**impun'tura** *nf* stitching

**impuntu'rare** *vt* backstitch

**impurità** *nf inv* impurity

**im'puro** *a* impure

**impu'tabile** *a* attributable (**a** to); *Jur* indictable

**impu'tare** *vt* attribute; *Jur* charge

**impu'tato, -a** *nmf* accused

**imputazi'one** *nf* charge. **~ di omicidio** murder charge

**imputri'dire** *vi* putrefy

**imputri'dito** *a* putrefied

**in** *prep* in; *(moto a luogo)* to; *(su)* on; *(dentro)* within; *(mezzo)* by; *(con materiale)* made of; **essere in casa/ufficio** be at home/at the office; **in mano/tasca** in one's hand/pocket; **in fondo alla strada/borsa** at the bottom of the street/bag; **andare in Francia/campagna** go to France/the country; **salire in treno** get on the train; **versa la birra nel bicchiere** pour the beer into the glass; **in alto** up there; **in giornata** within the day; **nel 1997** in 1997; **una borsa in pelle** a bag made of leather, a leather bag; **alzarsi in piedi** stand up; **in macchina** *(viaggiare, venire)* by car; **in contanti** [in] cash; **in vacanza** on holiday; **di giorno in giorno** from day to day; **se fossi in te** if I were you; **siamo in sette** there are seven of us

**inabbor'dabile** *a* unapproachable

**i'nabile** *a* incapable; *(fisicamente)* unfit

**inabilità** *nf* incapacity

**inabi'tabile** *a* uninhabitable

**inacces'sibile** *a* inaccessible; *(persona)* unapproachable

**inaccet'tabile** *a* unacceptable

**inaccettabilità** *nf* unacceptability

**inacer'barsi** *vr* grow bitter

**inacer'bire** *vt* embitter; exacerbate *(rapporto)*

**inaci'dire** *vt* turn sour

**inaci'dirsi** *vr* go sour; *(persona:)* become embittered

**ina'datto** *a* unsuitable

**inadegua'tezza** *nf* inadequacy

**inadegu'ato** *a* inadequate

**inadempi'ente** *nmf* defaulter

**inadempi'enza** *nf* nonfulfilment (**a** of). **~ contrattuale** breach of contract

**inadempi'mento** *nm* nonfulfilment

**inaffer'rabile** *a* elusive

**inaffon'dabile** *a* unsinkable

**ina'lare** *vt* inhale

**inala'tore** *nm* inhaler

**inalazi'one** *nf* inhalation

**inalbe'rare** *vt* hoist

**inalbe'rarsi** *vr* *(cavallo:)* rear [up]; *(adirarsi)* lose one's temper

**inalie'nabile** *a* inalienable

**inalte'rabile** *a* unchanging; *(colore)* fast

**inalte'rato** *a* unchanged

**inami'dare** *vt* starch

**inami'dato** *a* starched

**inammis'sibile** *a* inadmissible

**inamovi'bile** *a* *(disco ecc)* non-removable

**inanel'lato** *a* bejewelled

**inani'mato** *a* inanimate; ⟨*senza vita*⟩ lifeless

**inappa'gabile** *a* unsatisfiable

**inappaga'mento** *nm* nonfulfilment

**inappa'gato** *a* unfulfilled

**inappel'labile** *a* final

**inappe'tenza** *nf* lack of appetite

**inappli'cabile** *a* inapplicable

**inappropri'ato** *a* inapt

**inappun'tabile** *a* faultless

**inar'care** *vt* arch; raise ⟨*sopracciglia*⟩

**inar'carsi** *vr* ⟨*legno:*⟩ warp; ⟨*ripiano:*⟩ sag; ⟨*linea:*⟩ curve

**inari'dire** *vt* parch; empty of feelings ⟨*persona*⟩

**inari'dirsi** *vr* dry up; ⟨*persona:*⟩ become empty of feelings

**inarre'stabile** *a* unstoppable

**inartico'lato** *a* inarticulate

**inascol'tato** *a* unheard

**inaspettata'mente** *adv* unexpectedly

**inaspet'tato** *a* unexpected

**inaspri'mento** *nm* ⟨*di carattere*⟩ embitterment; ⟨*di conflitto*⟩ worsening

**ina'sprire** *vt* embitter

**ina'sprirsi** *vr* become embittered

**inattac'cabile** *a* unassailable; ⟨*irreprensibile*⟩ irreproachable

**inatten'dibile** *a* unreliable

**inat'teso** *a* unexpected

**inattività** *nf* inactivity

**inat'tivo** *a* inactive

**inattu'abile** *a* impracticable

**inau'dito** *a* unheard of

**inaugu'rale** *a* inaugural; cerimonia ~ official opening; viaggio ~ maiden voyage

**inaugu'rare** *vt* inaugurate; open ⟨*mostra*⟩; unveil ⟨*statua*⟩; christen ⟨*lavastoviglie ecc*⟩

**inaugurazi'one** *nf* inauguration; ⟨*di mostro*⟩ opening; ⟨*di statua*⟩ unveiling

**inavve'duto** *a* inadvertent; ⟨*sbadato*⟩ careless

**inavver'tenza** *nf* inadvertence

**inavvertita'mente** *adv* inadvertently

**inavvici'nabile** *a* unapproachable

**in'breeding** *nm inv* inbreeding

**incagli'are** *vi* ground ● *vt* hinder

**incagli'arsi** *vr* run aground

**in'caglio** *nm* running aground; *fig* obstacle

**'inca** *a & nmf* (*pl* inca *o* incas) Inca

**incalco'labile** *a* incalculable

**incal'lirsi** *vr* grow callous; ⟨*abituarsi*⟩ become hardened

**incal'lito** *a* callous; ⟨*abituato*⟩ hardened

**incal'zante** *a* ⟨*ritmo*⟩ driving; ⟨*richiesta*⟩ urgent; ⟨*crisi*⟩ imminent

**incal'zare** *vt* pursue; *fig* press

**incame'rare** *vt* appropriate

**incammi'nare** *vt* get going; ⟨*fig: guidare*⟩ set off

**incammi'narsi** *vr* set out

**incanala'mento** *nm* canalization; *fig* channelling

**incana'lare** *vt* canalize; *fig* channel

**incana'larsi** *vr* converge on

**incancel'labile** *a* indelible

**incande'scente** *a* incandescent; ⟨*discussione*⟩ burning

**incande'scenza** *nf* incandescence

**incan'tare** *vt* enchant

**incan'tarsi** *vr* stand spellbound; ⟨*incepparsi*⟩ jam

**incanta|'tore, -'trice** *nmf* enchanter; enchantress. ~ **di serpenti** snake charmer

**incan'tesimo** *nm* spell

**incan'tevole** *a* enchanting

**in'canto** *nm* spell; *fig* delight; ⟨*asta*⟩ auction; come per ~ as if by magic

**incanu'tire** *vt* turn white

**incanu'tito** *a* white

**inca'pace** *a* incapable; ~ **d'intendere e di volere** *Jur* unfit to plead

**incapacità** *nf* incapability

**incapo'nirsi** *vr* be set

**incap'pare** *vi* ~ **in** run into

**incappucci'arsi** *vr* wrap up

**incapretta'mento** *nm* method of trussing up a victim by the ankles

**incapricci'arsi** *vr* ~ **di** take a fancy to

**incapsu'lare** *vt* seal; crown ⟨*dente*⟩

**incarce'rare** *vt* imprison

**incarcerazi'one** *nf* imprisonment

**incari'care** *vt* charge

**incari'carsi** *vr* take upon oneself; **me ne incarico io** I will see to it

**incari'cato, -a** *a* in charge ● *nmf* representative. ~ **d'affari** chargé d'affaires

**in'carico** *nm* charge; **per ~ di** on behalf of

**incar'nare** *vt* embody

**incar'narsi** *vr* become incarnate

**incarnazi'one** *nf* incarnation

**incarta'mento** *nm* documents *pl*

**incartapeco'rito** *a* shrivelled up

**incar'tare** *vt* wrap [in paper]

**incasel'lare** *vt* pigeonhole

**incasi'nato** *a fam* ⟨*vita*⟩ screwed up; ⟨*stanza*⟩ messed up

**incas'sare** *vt* pack; *Mech* embed; ⟨*incastonare*⟩ set; ⟨*riscuotere*⟩ cash; take ⟨*colpo*⟩

**incas'sato** *a* set; ⟨*fiume*⟩ deeply embanked

**in'casso** *nm* collection; ⟨*introito*⟩ takings *pl*

**incasto'nare** *vt* set

**incasto'nato** *a* embedded; ⟨*anello*⟩ inset ⟨**di** with⟩

**incastona'tura** *nf* setting

**inca'strare** *vt* fit in; ⟨*fam: in situazione*⟩ corner

**inca'strarsi** *vr* fit

**in'castro** *nm* joint; **a ~** ⟨*pezzi*⟩ interlocking. ~ **a coda di rondine** dovetail joint

**incate'nare** *vt* chain

**incatra'mare** *vt* tar

**incatti'vire** *vt* turn nasty

**incauta'mente** *adv* imprudently

**in'cauto** *a* imprudent

**inca'vare** *vt* hollow out

**inca'vato** *a* hollow

**incava'tura** *nf* hollow

**in'cavo** *nm* hollow; ⟨*scanalatura*⟩ groove

**incavo'larsi** *vr fam* get shirty
**incavo'lato** *a fam* shirty
**in'cedere** *fml vi* advance solemnly ● *nm* solemn gait
**incendi'are** *vt* set fire to; *fig* inflame
**incendi'ario, -a** *a* incendiary; ⟨*fig: discorso*⟩ inflammatory; ⟨*fig: bellezza*⟩ sultry ● *nmf* arsonist
**incendi'arsi** *vr* catch fire
**in'cendio** *nm* fire. **~ doloso** arson; **incendi** *pl* **dolosi** cases of arson
**inceneri'mento** *nm* incineration; ⟨*cremazione*⟩ cremation
**incene'rire** *vt* burn to ashes; ⟨*cremare*⟩ cremate
**incene'rirsi** *vr* be burnt to ashes
**inceneri'tore** *nm* incinerator
**in'censo** *nm* incense
**incensu'rabile** *a* irreproachable
**incensu'rato** *a* blameless; **essere ~** *Jur* have a clean record
**incenti'vare** *vt* motivate
**incen'tivo** *nm* incentive. **~ fiscale** tax incentive
**incen'trarsi** *vr* **~ su** centre on
**incep'pare** *vt* block; *fig* hamper
**incep'parsi** *vr* jam
**ince'rata** *nf* oilcloth
**incerot'tato** *a* with a plaster on
**incer'tezza** *nf* uncertainty
**in'certo** *a* uncertain ● *nm* uncertainty; **sono gli incerti del mestiere** that's the way it goes in this business
**incespi'care** *vi* ⟨*inciampare*⟩ stumble
**inces'sante** *a* unceasing
**incessante'mente** *adv* incessantly
**in'cesto** *nm* incest
**incestu'oso** *a* incestuous
**in'cetta** *nf* buying up; **fare ~ di** stockpile
**inchi'esta** *nf* investigation; **fare un'~** conduct an inquiry. **~ giudiziaria** criminal investigation. **~ parlamentare** parliamentary inquiry
**inchi'nare** *vt* bow
**inchi'narsi** *vr* bow
**in'chino** *nm* bow; ⟨*di donna*⟩ curtsy
**inchio'dare** *vt* nail; nail down ⟨*coperchio*⟩; **~ a letto** ⟨*malattia:*⟩ confine to bed
**inchi'ostro** *nm* ink. **~ di china** Indian ink. **~ simpatico** invisible ink. **~ di stampa** newsprint
**inciam'pare** *vi* stumble; **~ in** trip over; ⟨*imbattersi*⟩ run into
**inci'ampo** *nm* hindrance
**inciden'tale** *a* incidental
**inci'dente** *nm* ⟨*episodio*⟩ incident; ⟨*infortunio*⟩ accident. **~ aereo** plane crash. **~ d'auto** car accident. **~ sul lavoro** industrial accident. **~ stradale** road accident
**inci'denza** *nf* incidence
**in'cidere** *vt* cut; ⟨*arte*⟩ engrave; ⟨*registrare*⟩ record ● *vi* **~ su** ⟨*gravare*⟩ weigh upon
**in'cinta** *a* pregnant
**incipi'ente** *a* incipient
**incipri'are** *vt* powder

**incipri'arsi** *vr* powder one's face
**in'circa** *adv* **all'~** more or less
**incisi'one** *nf* incision; ⟨*arte*⟩ engraving; ⟨*acquaforte*⟩ etching; ⟨*registrazione*⟩ recording
**inci'sivo** *a* incisive ● *nm* ⟨*dente*⟩ incisor
**in'ciso** *nm* **per ~** incidentally
**inci'sore** *nm* engraver
**incita'mento** *nm* incitement
**inci'tare** *vt* incite
**inci'vile** *a* uncivilized; ⟨*maleducato*⟩ impolite
**inciviltà** *nf* barbarism; ⟨*maleducazione*⟩ rudeness
**inclassifi'cabile** *adv* unclassifiable
**incle'mente** *a* harsh
**incle'menza** *nf* harshness
**incli'nabile** *a* reclining
**incli'nare** *vt* tilt ● *vi* **~ a** be inclined to
**incli'narsi** *vr* list
**incli'nato** *a* tilted; ⟨*terreno*⟩ sloping
**inclinazi'one** *nf* slope, inclination
**in'cline** *a* inclined
**in'cludere** *vt* include; ⟨*allegare*⟩ enclose
**inclusi'one** *nf* inclusion
**inclu'sivo** *a* inclusive
**in'cluso** *pp di* **includere** ● *a* included; ⟨*compreso*⟩ inclusive; ⟨*allegato*⟩ enclosed
**incoe'rente** *a* ⟨*contraddittorio*⟩ inconsistent
**incoerente'mente** *adv* inconsistently
**incoe'renza** *nf* inconsistency
**in'cognita** *nf* unknown quantity
**in'cognito** *a* unknown ● *nm* **in ~** incognito
**incol'lare** *vt* stick; ⟨*con colla liquida*⟩ glue; *Comput* paste
**incol'larsi** *vr* stick to; **~ a qcno** stick close to sb
**incolla'tura** *nf* ⟨*nell'ippica*⟩ neck
**incolle'rirsi** *vr* lose one's temper
**incolle'rito** *a* enraged
**incol'mabile** *a* ⟨*differenza*⟩ unbridgeable; ⟨*vuoto*⟩ unfillable
**incolon'nare** *vt* line up
**inco'lore** *a* colourless
**incol'pare** *vt* blame
**in'colto** *a* uncultivated; ⟨*persona*⟩ uneducated
**in'colume** *a* unhurt
**incom'bente** *a* impending
**incom'benza** *nf* task
**in'combere** *vi* **~ su** hang over; **~ a** ⟨*spettare*⟩ be incumbent on
**incombu'stibile** *a* noncombustible
**incominci'are** *vt/i* begin, start
**incommensu'rabile** *a* immeasurable
**incomo'dare** *vt* inconvenience
**incomo'darsi** *vr* trouble
**in'comodo** *a* uncomfortable; ⟨*inopportuno*⟩ inconvenient ● *nm* inconvenience: **fare il terzo ~** play gooseberry
**incompa'rabile** *a* incomparable
**incompa'tibile** *a* incompatible
**incompatibilità** *nf inv* incompatibility. **~ di carattere** incompatibility

**incompe'tente** *a* incompetent
**incompe'tenza** *nf* incompetence
**incompi'uto** *a* unfinished
**incom'pleto** *a* incomplete
**incompren'sibile** *a* incomprehensible
**incomprensibil'mente** *adv* incomprehensibly
**incomprensi'one** *nf* lack of understanding; (*malinteso*) misunderstanding
**incom'preso** *a* misunderstood
**inconce'pibile** *a* inconceivable
**inconcili'abile** *a* irreconcilable
**inconclu'dente** *a* inconclusive; ⟨*persona*⟩ ineffectual
**incondizionata'mente** *adv* unconditionally
**incondizio'nato** *a* unconditional
**inconfes'sabile** *a* unmentionable
**inconfon'dibile** *a* unmistakable
**inconfondibil'mente** *adv* unmistakably
**inconfu'tabile** *a* irrefutable
**inconfutabil'mente** *adv* irrefutably
**incongru'ente** *a* inconsistent
**incongru'enza** *nf* incongruity
**in'congruo** *a* inadequate
**inconsa'pevole** *a* unaware; (*inconscio*) unconscious
**inconsapevol'mente** *adv* unwittingly
**inconscia'mente** *adv* unconsciously
**in'conscio** *a & nm Psych* unconscious
**inconsegu'ente** *a* **essere ~** be a non sequitur
**inconside'rabile** *a* negligible
**inconside'rato** *a* inconsiderate
**inconsi'stente** *a* insubstantial; ⟨*notizia ecc*⟩ unfounded
**inconsi'stenza** *nf* ⟨*di ragionamento, prove*⟩ flimsiness
**inconso'labile** *a* inconsolable
**inconsu'eto** *a* unusual
**incon'sulto** *a* rash
**incontami'nato** *a* uncontaminated
**inconte'nibile** *a* irrepressible
**inconten'tabile** *a* insatiable; (*esigente*) hard to please
**inconte'stabile** *a* indisputable
**inconte'stato** *a* unchallenged
**inconti'nente** *a* incontinent
**inconti'nenza** *nf* incontinence
**incon'trare** *vt* meet; encounter, meet with ⟨*difficoltà*⟩
**incon'trario: all'~** *adv* the other way around; (*in modo sbagliato*) the wrong way around
**incon'trarsi** *vr* meet (**con qcno** sb)
**incontra'stabile** *a* incontrovertible
**incontra'stato** *a* undisputed
**in'contro** *nm* meeting; (*casuale*) encounter; (*di calcio, rugby*) match; (*di tennis*) game; (*di pugilato*) fight. **~ al vertice** summit meeting ● *prep* **~ a** towards; **andare ~ a qcno** go to meet sb; *fig* meet sb half way
**incontrol'labile** *a* uncontrollable
**incontrollata'mente** *adv* uncontrollably
**inconveni'ente** *nm* drawback

**incoraggia'mento** *nm* encouragement
**incoraggi'ante** *a* encouraging
**incoraggi'are** *vt* encourage
**incor'nare** *vt* gore
**incornici'are** *vt* frame
**incornici'atura** *nf* framing
**incoro'nare** *vt* crown
**incoronazi'one** *nf* coronation
**incorpo'rare** *vt* incorporate; (*mescolare*) blend
**incorpo'rarsi** *vr* blend; ⟨*territori:*⟩ merge
**incorreg'gibile** *a* incorrigible
**in'correre** *vt* **~ in** incur; **~ nel pericolo di...** run the risk of...
**incorrut'tibile** *a* incorruptible
**incosci'ente** *a* unconscious; (*irresponsabile*) reckless ● *nmf* irresponsible person
**incosci'enza** *nf* unconsciousness; (*irresponsabilità*) recklessness
**inco'stante** *a* changeable; ⟨*persona*⟩ fickle
**inco'stanza** *nf* changeableness; (*di persona*) fickleness
**incostituzio'nale** *a* unconstitutional
**incostituzionalità** *nf* unconstitutionality
**incre'dibile** *a* incredible, unbelievable
**incredibil'mente** *adv* incredibly, unbelievably
**incredulità** *nf* incredulity
**in'credulo** *a* incredulous
**incremen'tale** *a Comput, Math* incremental
**incremen'tare** *vt* increase; (*intensificare*) step up
**incre'mento** *nm* increase. **~ demografico** population growth. **~ produttivo** increase in production
**incresci'oso** *a* regrettable
**incre'spare** *vt* ruffle; wrinkle ⟨*tessuto*⟩; make frizzy ⟨*capelli*⟩; **~ la fronte** frown
**incre'sparsi** *vr* ⟨*acqua:*⟩ ripple; ⟨*tessuto:*⟩ wrinkle; ⟨*capelli:*⟩ go frizzy
**incrimi'nabile** *a* indictable
**incrimi'nare** *vt* indict; *fig* incriminate
**incriminazi'one** *nf* indictment
**incri'nare** *vt* crack; *fig* affect ⟨*amicizia*⟩
**incri'narsi** *vr* crack; ⟨*amicizia:*⟩ be affected
**incrina'tura** *nf* crack
**incroci'are** *vt* cross ● *vi Naut, Aeron* cruise
**incroci'arsi** *vr* cross; ⟨*razze:*⟩ interbreed
**incroci'ato** *a* crossover
**incrocia'tore** *nm* cruiser
**in'crocio** *nm* crossing; (*di strade*) crossroads *sg*
**incrol'labile** *a* indestructible
**incro'stare** *vt* encrust
**incrostazi'one** *nf* encrustation
**incuba'trice** *nf* incubator
**incubazi'one** *nf* incubation
**'incubo** *nm* nightmare; **da ~** nightmarish
**in'cudine** *nf* anvil
**incul'care** *vt* inculcate
**incune'are** *vt* wedge
**incune'arsi** *vr* slot in
**incune'ato** *a Med* impacted
**incu'pirsi** *vr fig* darken

**incu'rabile** *a* incurable

**incu'rante** *a* careless

**in'curia** *nf* negligence

**incurio'sire** *vt* make curious

**incurio'sirsi** *vr* become curious

**incursi'one** *nf* raid. **~ aerea** air raid

**incurva'mento** *nm* bending

**incur'vare** *vt* bend

**incur'varsi** *vr* bend

**incurva'tura** *nf* bending

**in'cusso** *pp di* incutere

**incusto'dito** *a* unguarded

**in'cutere** *vt* arouse: **~ spavento a qcno** strike fear into sb

**'indaco** *nm* indigo

**indaffa'rato** *a* busy

**inda'gare** *vt/i* investigate

**in'dagine** *nf* research; (*giudiziaria*) investigation. **~ demoscopica** public opinion poll. **~ di mercato** market survey

**indebi'tare** *vt* get into debt

**indebi'tarsi** *vr* get into debt

**in'debito** *a* undue

**indeboli'mento** *nm* weakening

**indebo'lire** *vt* weaken

**indebo'lirsi** *vr* weaken

**inde'cente** *a* indecent

**indecente'mente** *adv* indecently

**inde'cenza** *nf* indecency; (*vergogna*) disgrace

**indeci'frabile** *a* indecipherable

**indecisi'one** *nf* indecision

**inde'ciso** *a* undecided

**indecli'nabile** *a* indeclinable

**indeco'roso** *a* indecorous

**inde'fesso** *a* tireless

**indefi'nibile** *a* indefinable

**indefi'nito** *a* indefinite

**indefor'mabile** *a* crushproof

**in'degno** *a* unworthy

**inde'lebile** *a* indelible

**indelebil'mente** *adv* indelibly

**indelicata'mente** *adv* indiscreetly

**indelica'tezza** *nf* indelicacy; (*azione*) tactless act

**indeli'cato** *a* indiscreet; (*grossolano*) indelicate

**indemagli'abile** *a* ladderproof

**indemoni'ato** *a* possessed

**in'denne** *a* uninjured; (*da malattia*) unaffected

**inden'nità** *nf inv* allowance; (*per danni*) compensation. **~ di accompagnamento** mobility allowance. **~ di contingenza** cost-of-living allowance. **~ di fine rapporto** severance payment. **~ parlamentare** MP's salary. **~ di trasferimento** relocation allowance. **~ di trasferta** travel allowance

**indenniz'zare** *vt* compensate

**inden'nizzo** *nm* compensation

**indepen'denza** *nf* independence

**indero'gabile** *a* binding

**indescri'vibile** *a* indescribable

**indescrivibil'mente** *adv* indescribably

**indeside'rabile** *a* undesirable

**indeside'rato** *a* (*figlio, ospite*) unwanted

**indetermi'nabile** *a* indeterminable

**indetermina'tezza** *nf* vagueness

**indetermina'tivo** *a* indefinite

**indetermi'nato** *a* indeterminate

**'India** *nf* India

**indi'ano, -a** *a & nmf* Indian; **in fila indiana** in single file. **~ d'America** American Indian

**indiavo'lato** *a* possessed; (*vivace*) wild

**indi'care** *vt* show, indicate; (*col dito*) point at; (*far notare*) point out; (*consigliare*) advise

**indicativa'mente** *adv* as an idea; **può dirmi quanto costa ~?** can you give me an idea of the price?

**indica'tivo** *a* indicative; (*prezzo, cifra*) rough ● *nm* Gram indicative

**indica'tore** *nm* indicator; *Techn* gauge; (*prontuario*) directory. **~ di direzione** indicator light. **~ economico** economic indicator. **~ [del livello] dell'olio** oil gauge. **~ di velocità** speedometer

**indicazi'one** *nf* indication; (*istruzione*) direction. **~ stradale** road sign

**'indice** *nm* (*dito*) forefinger; (*lancetta*) pointer; (*di libro, statistica*) index; (*fig: segno*) sign. **~ di ascolto** audience rating. **~ azionario** share index. **~ di gradimento** popularity rating. **~ di mortalità** death rate. **~ di natalità** birth rate

**indi'cibile** *a* inexpressible

**indiciz'zare** *vt* index-link

**indiciz'zato** *a* index-linked

**indicizzazi'one** *nf* indexing

**indietreggi'are** *vi* draw back; *Mil* withdraw

**indi'etro** *adv* back, behind; **all'~** backwards; **essere ~** be behind; (*mentalmente*) be backward; (*con pagamenti*) be in arrears; (*di orologio*) be slow; **fare marcia ~** reverse; **rimandare ~** send back; **rimanere ~** be left behind; **torna ~!** come back!

**indifen'dibile** *a* indefensible

**indi'feso** *a* undefended; (*inerme*) helpless

**indiffe'rente** *a* indifferent; **mi è ~** it's all the same to me

**indifferente'mente** *adv* (*senza fare distinzioni*) without distinction; (*con indifferenza*) indifferently; **funziona ~ con i due programmi** it works equally well with either program

**indiffe'renza** *nf* indifference

**in'digeno, -a** *a* indigenous ● *nmf* native

**indi'gente** *a* needy

**indi'genza** *nf* poverty

**indigesti'one** *nf* indigestion

**indi'gesto** *a* indigestible

**indi'gnare** *vt* make indignant

**indi'gnarsi** *vr* be indignant

**indi'gnato** *a* indignant

**indignazi'one** *nf* indignation

**indimenti'cabile** *a* unforgettable

**'indio, -a** *a* Indian ● *nmf* (*mpl* **indii** *o* **indios**) Indian

**indipen'dente** *a* independent; (*economicamente*) self-supporting

**indipendente'mente** adv independently; **~ da** regardless of

**in'dire** vt announce

**indiretta'mente** adv indirectly

**indi'retto** a indirect

**indiriz'zare** vt address; (mandare) send; (dirigere) direct

**indiriz'zario** nm mailing list

**indiriz'zarsi** vr direct one's steps

**indi'rizzo** nm address; (direzione) direction. **~ di consegna** delivery address. **'~ del destinatario'** 'addressee'. **~ di memoria** Comput memory address. **'~ del mittente'** 'sender's address'. **~ di posta elettronica** e-mail address

**indisci'plina** nf lack of discipline

**indiscipli'nato** a undisciplined

**indi'screto** a indiscreet; **in modo ~** indiscreetly

**indiscrezi'one** nf indiscretion

**indiscriminata'mente** adv indiscriminately

**indiscrimi'nato** a indiscriminate

**indi'scusso** a unquestioned

**indiscu'tibile** a unquestionable

**indiscutibil'mente** adv unquestionably

**indispen'sabile** a essential; ⟨persona⟩ indispensable

**indispet'tire** vt irritate

**indispet'tirsi** vr get irritated

**indi'sporre** vt anger

**indisposizi'one** nf indisposition

**indi'sposto** pp di **indisporre** ● a indisposed

**indisso'lubile** a indissoluble

**indissolubil'mente** adv indissolubly

**indistin'guibile** a indiscernible

**indistinta'mente** adv without exception

**indi'stinto** a indistinct

**indistrut'tibile** a indestructible

**indistur'bato** a undisturbed

**in'divia** nf endive

**individu'abile** a detectable

**individu'ale** a individual

**individua'lista** nmf individualist

**individua'listico** a individualistic

**individualità** nf individuality

**individu'are** vt individualize; (localizzare) locate; (riconoscere) single out

**indi'viduo** nm individual

**indivi'sibile** a indivisible

**indivisibilità** nf indivisibility

**indi'viso** a undivided

**indizi'are** vt throw suspicion on

**indizi'ario** a circumstantial

**indizi'ato, -a** a suspected ● nmf suspect

**in'dizio** nm sign; Jur circumstantial evidence

**Indo'cina** nf Indochina

**indoeuro'peo** a Indo-European

**'indole** nf nature

**indo'lente** a indolent

**indo'lenza** nf indolence

**indolenzi'mento** nm stiffness, ache

**indolen'zire** vt stiffen up

**indolen'zirsi** vr stiffen up, go stiff

**indolen'zito** a stiff

**indo'lore** a painless

**indo'mabile** a untameable

**indo'mani** nm l'**~** the following day

**in'domito** a untamed

**Indo'nesia** nf Indonesia

**indonesi'ano, -a** a & nmf Indonesian

**indo'rare** vt gild; **~ la pillola** sugar the pill

**indos'sare** vt wear; (mettere addosso) put on

**indossa|'tore, -'trice** nm [male] model ● nf model

**in'dotto** pp di **indurre**

**indottri'nare** vt indoctrinate

**indovi'nare** vt guess; (predire) foretell

**indovi'nato** a successful; (scelta) well-chosen

**indovi'nello** nm riddle

**indo'vino, -a** nmf fortune-teller

**indù** a inv & nmf inv Hindu

**indubbia'mente** adv undoubtedly

**in'dubbio** a undoubted

**indubi'tabile** a indubitable

**indubitabil'mente** adv indubitably

**indugi'are** vi linger

**indugi'arsi** vr linger

**in'dugio** nm delay

**indu'ismo** nm Hinduism

**indul'gente** a indulgent

**indul'genza** nf indulgence

**in'dulgere** vi **~ a** indulge in

**in'dulto** pp di **indulgere** ● nm Jur pardon

**indu'mento** nm garment; **indumenti** pl clothes. **indumenti** pl **intimi** underwear

**induri'mento** nm hardening

**indu'rire** vt harden

**indu'rirsi** vr harden

**in'durre** vt induce; **~ qcno a fare** induce sb to do; **~ in tentazione** lead into temptation

**in'dustria** nf industry. **~ dell'abbigliamento** clothing industry, rag trade fam. **~ leggera** light industry. **~ pesante** heavy industry. **~ dello spettacolo** show business, showbiz fam. **~ terziaria** service industry. **~ tessile** textile industry, textiles

**industri'ale** a industrial; **zona ~** industrial estate ● nmf industrialist

**industrializ'zare** vt industrialize

**industrializ'zato** a industrialized

**industrializzazi'one** nf industrialization

**industrial'mente** adv industrially

**industri'arsi** vr **~ per guadagnare qualcosa** set to and earn some money

**industriosa'mente** adv industriously

**industri'oso** a industrious

**indut'tivo** a inductive

**indut'tore** nm inductor

**induzi'one** nf induction

**inebe'tire** vt daze

**inebe'tito** a stunned

**inebri'ante** a intoxicating, exciting

**inebri'are** vt intoxicate

**inebri'arsi** vr become inebriated

**inecce'pibile** a unexceptionable

**i'nedia** nf starvation

**i'nedito** *a* unpublished

**inedu'cato** *a* impolite

**inef'fabile** *a* inexpressible

**ineffi'cace** *a* ineffective

**ineffici'ente** *a* inefficient

**ineffici'enza** *nf* inefficiency

**ineguagli'abile** *a* incomparable

**ineguagli'ato** *a* unequalled

**inegu'ale** *a* unequal; ⟨*superficie*⟩ uneven

**inelut'tabile** *a* inescapable

**inenar'rabile** *a* indescribable

**inequivo'cabile** *a* unequivocal

**inequivocabil'mente** *adv* unequivocally

**ine'rente** *a* ~ **a** inherent in

**inerente'mente** *adv* ~ **a** concerning

**i'nerme** *a* unarmed; *fig* defenceless

**inerpi'carsi** *vr* ~ **su** clamber up

**i'nerte** *a* inactive; *Phys* inert

**i'nerzia** *nf* inactivity; *Phys* inertia

**inesat'tezza** *nf* inaccuracy

**ine'satto** *a* inaccurate; ⟨*erroneo*⟩ incorrect; ⟨*non riscosso*⟩ uncollected

**inesau'ribile** *a* inexhaustible

**inesi'stente** *a* non-existent

**inesi'stenza** *nf* non-existence

**ineso'rabile** *a* inexorable

**inesorabil'mente** *adv* inexorably

**inesperi'enza** *nf* inexperience

**ine'sperto** *a* inexperienced

**inespli'cabile** *a* inexplicable

**inesplicabil'mente** *adv* inexplicably

**inesplo'rato** *a* undiscovered

**ine'sploso** *a* unexploded

**inespres'sivo** *a* expressionless

**inespri'mibile** *a* inexpressible

**inespu'gnabile** *a* impregnable

**ineste'tismo** *nm* blemish

**inesti'mabile** *a* inestimable

**inestin'guibile** *a* ⟨*sete*⟩ insatiable; ⟨*odio*⟩ undying

**inestir'pabile** *a* impossible to eradicate

**inestri'cabile** *a* inextricable

**inestricabil'mente** *adv* inextricably

**inetti'tudine** *nf* ineptitude

**i'netto** *a* inept. ~ **a** unsuited to

**ine'vaso** *a* ⟨*pratiche, corrispondenza*⟩ pending

**inevi'tabile** *a* inevitable

**inevitabil'mente** *adv* inevitably

**in ex'tremis** *adv* ⟨*segnare un gol*⟩ in the nick of time; ⟨*prima di morire*⟩ in extremis

**i'nezia** *nf* trifle

**infagot'tare** *vt* wrap up

**infagot'tarsi** *vr* wrap [oneself] up

**infal'libile** *a* infallible

**infa'mante** *a* defamatory

**infa'mare** *vt* defame

**infama'torio** *a* defamatory

**in'fame** *a* infamous; ⟨*fam: orrendo*⟩ awful, shocking

**in'famia** *nf* infamy

**infan'gare** *vt* cover with mud; *fig* sully

**infan'garsi** *vr* get muddy

**infanti'cida** *nmf* infanticide

**infanti'cidio** *nm* infanticide

**infan'tile** *a* ⟨*letteratura, abbigliamento*⟩ children's *attrib*; ⟨*ingenuità*⟩ childlike; *pej* childish

**in'fanzia** *nf* childhood; ⟨*bambini*⟩ children *pl*; **prima** ~ infancy

**infar'cire** *vt* stuff (**di** with)

**infari'nare** *vt* flour; ~ **di** sprinkle with

**infarina'tura** *nf fig* smattering

**in'farto** *nm* coronary

**infasti'dire** *vt* irritate

**infasti'dirsi** *vr* get irritated

**infati'cabile** *a* untiring

**infaticabil'mente** *adv* tirelessly

**in'fatti** *conj* as a matter of fact; ⟨*veramente*⟩ indeed

**infatu'arsi** *vr* ~ **di** become infatuated with

**infatu'ato** *a* infatuated

**infatuazi'one** *nf* infatuation

**in'fausto** *a* ill-omened

**infecondità** *nf* infertility

**infe'condo** *a* infertile

**infe'dele** *a* unfaithful

**infedeltà** *nf* unfaithfulness

**infe'lice** *a* unhappy; ⟨*inappropriato*⟩ unfortunate; ⟨*cattivo*⟩ bad

**infelicità** *nf* unhappiness

**infel'trire** *vi* matt

**infel'trirsi** *vr* matt

**infel'trito** *a* matted

**inferi'ore** *a* ⟨*più basso*⟩ lower; ⟨*qualità*⟩ inferior ● *nmf* inferior

**inferiorità** *nf* inferiority

**infe'rire** *vt* infer; strike ⟨*colpo*⟩

**inferme'ria** *nf* infirmary; ⟨*di nave*⟩ sick-bay

**infermi'ere, -a** *nm* [male] nurse ● *nf* nurse

**infermità** *nf* sickness. ~ **mentale** mental illness

**in'fermo, -a** *a* sick ● *nmf* invalid

**infer'nale** *a* infernal; ⟨*spaventoso*⟩ hellish

**in'ferno** *nm* hell; **va' all'~!** go to hell!

**infero'cirsi** *vr* become fierce

**inferri'ata** *nf* grating

**infervo'rare** *vt* arouse enthusiasm in

**infervo'rarsi** *vr* get excited

**infe'stare** *vt* infest

**infestazi'one** *nf* infestation

**infet'tare** *vt* infect

**infet'tarsi** *vr* become infected

**infet'tivo** *a* infectious

**in'fetto** *a* infected

**infezi'one** *nf* infection

**infiac'chire** *vt/i* weaken

**infiac'chirsi** *vr* weaken

**infiam'mabile** *a* [in]flammable

**infiam'mare** *vt* set on fire; *Med, fig* inflame

**infiam'marsi** *vr* catch fire; *Med* become inflamed

**infiammazi'one** *nf Med* inflammation

**infia'scare** *vt* bottle

**infici'are** *vt Jur* invalidate

**in'fido** *a* treacherous

**infie'rire** *vi* ⟨*imperversare*⟩ rage; ~ **su** attack furiously

**in'figgere** *vt* drive

**in'figgersi** *vr* ~ **in** penetrate

**infi'lare** vt thread; (mettere) insert; (indossare) put on

**infi'larsi** vr slip on ‹vestito›: ~ **in** (introdursi) slip into

**infil'trarsi** vr infiltrate

**infil'trato, -a** nmf infiltrator

**infiltrazi'one** nf infiltration; (d'acqua) seepage; (Med: iniezione) injection

**infil'zare** vt pierce; (infilare) string; (conficcare) stick

**'infimo** a lowest

**in'fine** adv finally; (insomma) in short

**infin'gardo** a slothful

**infinità** nf infinity; **un'~ di** masses of

**infinita'mente** adv infinitely

**infinitesi'male** a infinitesimal

**infi'nito** a infinite; Gram infinitive ● nm infinite; Gram infinitive; Math infinity; **all'~** endlessly

**infinocchi'are** vt fam hoodwink

**infiocchet'tare** vt tie up with ribbons

**infiore'scenza** nf inflorescence

**infischi'arsi** vr ~ **di** not care about; **me ne infischio** fam I couldn't care less

**in'fisso** pp di **infiggere** ● nm fixture; (di porta, finestra) frame

**infit'tire** vt/i thicken

**infit'tirsi** vr thicken

**inflazi'one** nf inflation. ~ **galoppante** galloping inflation. ~ **strisciante** creeping inflation

**inflazio'nistico** a inflationary

**infles'sibile** a inflexible

**inflessibilità** nf inflexibility

**inflessi'one** nf inflection, inflexion

**in'fliggere** vt inflict

**in'flitto** pp di **infliggere**

**influ'ente** a influential

**influ'enza** nf influence; Med influenza; **prendere l'~** catch the flu. ~ **gastro-intestinale** gastric flu

**influen'zabile** a ‹mente, opinione› impressionable

**influen'zare** vt influence

**influen'zato** a essere ~ (con febbre) have the flu

**influ'ire** vi ~ **su** influence

**in'flusso** nm influence

**info'carsi** vr catch fire; ‹viso:› go red; ‹discussione:› become heated

**info'gnarsi** vr fam get into a mess

**infol'tire** vt/i thicken

**infon'dato** a unfounded

**in'fondere** vt instil

**infor'care** vt fork ‹fieno›; get on ‹bici›; put on ‹occhiali›

**inforca'tura** nf crotch

**infor'male** a informal

**infor'mare** vt inform

**infor'marsi** vr inquire (**di** about)

**infor'matica** nf information technology, IT

**infor'matico** a computer attrib

**informa'tivo** a informative

**infor'mato** a informed; **male ~** ill-informed

**informa|'tore, -'trice** nmf (di polizia) informer. ~ **medico scientifico** representative of a pharmaceutical company

**informazi'one** nf information; **un'~** a piece of information; **informazioni** pl information; **servizio informazioni** enquiries. ~ **genetica** genetic code. ~ **riservata** confidential information. **informazioni** pl **sbagliate** misinformation

**in'forme** a shapeless

**infor'nare** vt put into the oven

**infortu'narsi** vr have an accident

**infortu'nato, -a** a injured ● nmf injured person; **gli infortunati** the injured

**infor'tunio** nm accident. ~ **sul lavoro** industrial accident

**infortu'nistica** nf study of industrial accidents

**infos'sarsi** vr sink; ‹guance, occhi:› become hollow

**infos'sato** a sunken, hollow

**infradici'are** vt drench

**infradici'arsi** vr get drenched; (diventare marcio) rot

**infra'dito** nmpl (scarpe) flip-flops

**in'frangere** vt break; (in mille pezzi) shatter

**in'frangersi** vr break; (in mille pezzi) shatter

**infran'gibile** a unbreakable

**in'franto** pp di **infrangere** ● a shattered; ‹fig: cuore› broken

**infra'rosso** a infra-red

**infrasettima'nale** a midweek

**infrastrut'tura** nf infrastructure

**infrazi'one** nf offence. ~ **al codice della strada** traffic offence

**infredda'tura** nf cold

**infreddo'lirsi** vr feel cold

**infreddo'lito** a cold

**infre'quente** a infrequent

**infruttu'oso** a fruitless

**infuo'care** vt make red-hot

**infuo'cato** a burning

**infu'ori** adv **all'~** outwards; **all'~ di** except; **denti ~** buck teeth

**infuri'are** vi rage

**infuri'arsi** vr fly into a rage

**infuri'ato** a blustering

**infusi'one** nf infusion

**in'fuso** pp di **infondere** ● nm infusion

**Ing.** abbr **ingegnere**

**ingabbi'are** vt cage; (fig: mettere in prigione) jail

**ingaggi'are** vt engage; sign up ‹calciatori ecc›; begin ‹lotta, battaglia›

**in'gaggio** nm engagement; (di calciatore) signing [up]

**ingan'nare** vt deceive; (essere infedele a) be unfaithful to; ~ **l'attesa** kill time

**ingan'narsi** vr deceive oneself; **se non m'inganno** if I am not mistaken

**ingan'nevole** a deceptive

**in'ganno** nm deceit; (frode) fraud; **trarre in ~** deceive

**ingarbugli'are** vt entangle; (confondere) confuse

**ingarbugli'arsi** *vr* get entangled; (*confondersi*) become confused

**ingarbu'gliato** *a* confused

**inge'gnarsi** *vr* do one's best; **~ per vivere** try to scrape a living

**inge'gnere** *nm* engineer. **~ aeronautico** aeronautical engineer. **~ civile** civil engineer. **~ edile** structural engineer. **~ meccanico** mechanical engineer. **~ minerario** mining engineer. **~ navale** marine engineer

**ingegne'ria** *nf* engineering. **~ aeronautica** aeronautical engineering. **~ civile** civil engineering. **~ edile** structural engineering. **~ genetica** genetic engineering. **~ meccanica** mechanical engineering

**in'gegno** *nm* brains *pl*; (*genio*) genius; (*abilità*) ingenuity

**ingegnosa'mente** *adv* ingeniously

**ingegnosità** *nf* ingenuity

**inge'gnoso** *a* ingenious

**ingelo'sire** *vt* make jealous

**ingelo'sirsi** *vr* become jealous

**in'gente** *a* huge

**ingenua'mente** *adv* artlessly

**ingenuità** *nf* ingenuousness

**in'genuo** *a* ingenuous; (*credulone*) naïve

**inge'renza** *nf* interference

**inge'rire** *vt* swallow

**inges'sare** *vt* put in plaster

**ingessa'tura** *nf* plaster

**Inghil'terra** *nf* England

**inghiot'tire** *vt* swallow

**in'ghippo** *nm* trick

**ingial'lire** *vi* turn yellow

**ingial'lirsi** *vr* turn yellow

**ingial'lito** *a* yellowed

**ingigan'tire** *vt* magnify; blow up out of proportion (*problema*) ● *vi* take on gigantic proportions

**ingigan'tirsi** *vr* take on gigantic proportions

**inginocchi'arsi** *vr* kneel [down]

**inginocchi'ato** *a* kneeling

**inginocchia'toio** *nm* prie-dieu

**ingioiel'larsi** *vr* put on one's jewels

**ingioiel'lato** *a* bejewelled

**ingiù** *adv* down; **all'~** downwards; **a testa ~** head downwards

**ingi'ungere** *vt* order

**ingiunzi'one** *nf* injunction, court order. **~ di pagamento** final demand

**ingi'uria** *nf* insult; (*torto*) wrong; (*danno*) damage

**ingiuri'are** *vt* insult; (*fare un torto a*) wrong

**ingiuri'oso** *a* insulting

**ingiusta'mente** *adv* unjustly

**ingiustifi'cabile** *a* unjustifiable; (*comportamento*) indefensible

**ingiustifi'cato** *a* unjustified

**ingiu'stizia** *nf* unjustice

**ingi'usto** *a* unjust

**in'glese** *a* English ● *nm* Englishman; (*lingua*) English; **gli inglesi** the English ● *nf* Englishwoman

**inglori'oso** *a* inglorious

**ingob'bire** *vi* become stooped

**ingoi'are** *vt* swallow

**ingol'fare** *vt* flood (*motore*)

**ingol'farsi** *vr fig* get involved; (*motore:*) flood

**ingol'lare** *vt* gulp down

**ingom'brante** *a* cumbersome

**ingom'brare** *vt* clutter up; *fig* cram (*mente*)

**in'gombro** *nm* encumbrance; **essere d'~** be in the way

**ingor'digia** *nf* greed

**in'gordo** *a* greedy

**ingor'gare** *vt* block

**ingor'garsi** *vr* be blocked [up]

**in'gorgo** *nm* blockage; (*del traffico*) jam

**ingoz'zare** *vt* gobble up; (*nutrire eccessivamente*) stuff; fatten (*animali*)

**ingoz'zarsi** *vr* stuff oneself (**di** with)

**ingra'naggio** *nm* gear; *fig* mechanism

**ingra'nare** *vt* engage ● *vi* be in gear

**ingrandi'mento** *nm* enlargement

**ingran'dire** *vt* enlarge; (*esagerare*) magnify

**ingran'dirsi** *vr* become larger; (*aumentare*) increase

**ingrandi'tore** *nm Phot* enlarger

**ingras'saggio** *nm* greasing, lubrication

**ingras'sare** *vt* fatten [up]; *Mech* lubricate, grease ● *vi* put on weight

**ingras'sarsi** *vr* put on weight

**in'grasso** *nm* **mettere all'~** force-feed

**ingrati'tudine** *nf* ingratitude

**in'grato** *a* ungrateful; (*sgradevole*) thankless

**ingrazi'arsi** *vr* ingratiate oneself with

**ingredi'ente** *nm* ingredient

**in'gresso** *nm* entrance; (*accesso*) admittance; (*sala*) hall; *Comput* input **~ gratuito** *o* **libero** admission free; **'vietato l'~'** 'no entry; no admittance'. **~ degli artisti** stage door. **~ principale** main entrance. **~ di servizio** tradesmen's entrance. **~/uscita** *Comput* input/output. **~ video** *Techn* video input

**ingros'sare** *vt* make big; (*gonfiare*) swell ● *vi* grow big; (*gonfiare*) swell

**ingros'sarsi** *vr* grow big; (*gonfiare*) swell

**in'grosso** **all'~** *adv* wholesale; (*pressappoco*) roughly

**inguai'arsi** *vr* get into trouble

**inguai'nare** *vt* sheathe

**ingual'cibile** *a* crease-resistant

**ingua'ribile** *a* incurable

**inguaribil'mente** *adv* incurably

**'inguine** *nm* groin

**ingurgi'tare** *vt* gulp down

**ini'bire** *vt* inhibit; (*vietare*) forbid

**ini'bito** *a* inhibited

**inibi'tore** *nm* suppressant

**inibizi'one** *nf* inhibition; (*divieto*) prohibition

**iniet'tare** *vt* inject

**iniet'tarsi** *vr* **~ di sangue** (*occhi:*) become bloodshot

**iniezi'one** *nf* injection. **~ endovenosa** intravenous injection. **~ intramuscolare** intramuscular injection

**inimic'arsi** vr ~ **qcno** make an enemy of sb
**inimi'cizia** nf enmity
**inimi'tabile** a inimitable
**inimmagi'nabile** a unimaginable
**ininfiam'mabile** a nonflammable
**inintelli'gibile** a unintelligible
**ininterrotta'mente** adv continuously
**ininter'rotto** a continuous
**iniquità** nf inv iniquity
**i'niquo** a iniquitous
**inizi'ale** a & nf initial
**inizial'mente** adv initially
**inizi'are** vt begin; (avviare) open; ~ **a fare qcsa** begin doing sth; ~ **qcno a qcsa** initiate sb in sth ● vi begin
**inizia'tiva** nf initiative; **prendere l'**~ take the initiative. ~ **privata** private enterprise
**inizi'ato, -a** nmf initiated
**inizia|'tore, -'trice** nmf initiator
**iniziazi'one** nf initiation
**i'nizio** nm beginning; **dare** ~ **a** a start; **avere** ~ get under way
**innaffi'are** vt water
**innaffia'toio** nm watering-can
**innal'zare** vt raise; (erigere) erect
**innal'zarsi** vr rise
**innamo'rarsi** vr fall in love (di with)
**innamo'rato** a in love ● nm boyfriend
**in'nanzi** adv (stato in luogo) in front; (di tempo) ahead; (avanti) forward; (prima) before; **d'ora** ~ from now on ● prep (prima) before; ~ **a** in front of; ~ **tutto** = **innanzitutto**
**innanzi'tutto** adv (soprattutto) above all; (per prima cosa) first of all
**in'nato** a innate
**innatu'rale** a unnatural
**inne'gabile** a undeniable
**innegabil'mente** adv undeniably
**inneggi'are** vi praise
**innervo'sire** vt make nervous
**innervo'sirsi** vr get irritated
**inne'scare** vt prime
**in'nesco** nm primer
**inne'stare** vt graft; Mech engage; (inserire) insert
**in'nesto** nm graft; Mech clutch; Electr connection
**inneva'mento** nm snowfall. ~ **artificiale** snow-making
**inne'vato** a covered in snow
**'inno** nm hymn. ~ **nazionale** national anthem
**inno'cente** a innocent; Jur not guilty
**innocente'mente** adv innocently
**inno'cenza** nf innocence
**in'nocuo** a innocuous
**inno'vare** vt update
**innova'tivo** a innovative
**innova'tore** a trail-blazing
**innovazi'one** nf innovation
**innume'revole** a innumerable
**+ino** suff **fratellino** nm little brother; **sorellina** nf little sister; **freddino** (piuttosto freddo) chilly; **bellino** a (abbastanza bello) pretty; **benino** adv (così così) not bad;

**pochino** a (troppo poco) not enough; **un pochino** a little bit
**inocu'lare** vt inoculate
**ino'doro** a odourless
**inoffen'sivo** a inoffensive, harmless: ⟨animale⟩ harmless
**inol'trare** vt forward
**inol'trarsi** vr advance
**inol'trato** a late
**i'noltre** adv besides
**i'noltro** nm forwarding
**inon'dare** vt flood
**inondazi'one** nf flood
**inope'roso** a idle
**inopi'nabile** a unimaginable
**inoppor'tuno** a untimely
**inor'ganico** a inorganic
**inorgo'glire** vt make proud
**inorgo'glirsi** vr become proud
**inorri'dire** vt horrify ● vi be horrified
**inospi'tale** a inhospitable
**inosser'vato** a unobserved; (non rispettato) disregarded; **passare** ~ go unobserved
**inossi'dabile** a stainless
**'inox** a inv ⟨acciaio⟩ stainless; ⟨pentole⟩ stainless steel
**'input** nm inv ~ **dati** data input
**inqua'drare** vt frame; fig set
**inqua'drarsi** vr ~ **in** fit into
**inquadra'tura** nf framing
**inqualifi'cabile** a unspeakable
**inquie'tante** a unnerving
**inquie'tare** vt worry
**inquie'tarsi** vr get worried; (impazientirsi) get cross
**inqui'eto** a restless; (preoccupato) worried
**inquie'tudine** nf anxiety
**inqui'lino, -a** nmf tenant
**inquina'mento** nm pollution. ~ **acustico** noise pollution. ~ **atmosferico** air pollution. ~ **delle prove** Jur tampering with the evidence
**inqui'nare** vt pollute
**inqui'nato** a polluted
**inqui'rente** a Jur ⟨magistrato⟩ examining; ⟨commissione⟩ of investigation
**inqui'sire** vt/i investigate
**inqui'sito** a under investigation ● nm person under investigation
**inquisi|'tore, -'trice** a inquiring ● nmf inquisitor
**inquisi'torio** a questioning
**inquisizi'one** nf inquisition
**insabbi'are** vt bury
**insabbi'arsi** vr run aground
**insa'lata** nf salad. ~ **belga** Belgian endive. ~ **di mare** seafood salad. ~ **mista** mixed salad. ~ **di riso** rice salad. ~ **russa** Russian salad
**insalati'era** nf salad bowl
**insa'lubre** a unhealthy
**insa'nabile** a incurable
**insangui'nare** vt stain with blood
**insangui'nato** a blood-stained
**insapo'nare** vt soap

**insapo'narsi** vr soap oneself
**insapo'nata** nf soaping
**insa'pore** a tasteless
**insapo'rire** vt flavour
**insa'puta** nf all'~ di unknown to
**in'saturo** a unsaturated
**insazi'abile** a insatiable
**inscato'lare** vt can
**inscatola'trice** nf canning machine
**insce'nare** vt stage
**inscin'dibile** a inseparable
**in'scrivere** vt Math inscribe
**insec'chire** vt/i wither
**insedia'mento** nm installation
**insedi'are** vt install
**insedi'arsi** vr install oneself
**in'segna** nf sign; (bandiera) flag; (decorazione) decoration; (emblema) insignia pl; (stemma) symbol. ~ **luminosa** neon sign
**insegna'mento** nm teaching
**inse'gnante** a teaching ● nmf teacher. ~ **di matematica** maths teacher. ~ **di sostegno** tutor
**inse'gnare** vt/i teach; ~ **qcsa a qcno** teach sb sth
**insegui'mento** nmf pursuit
**insegu'ire** vt pursue
**insegui'tore, -'trice** nmf pursuer
**inselvati'chire** vt make wild ● vi grow wild
**inselvati'chirsi** vr grow wild
**insemi'nare** vt inseminate
**inseminazi'one** nf insemination. ~ **artificiale** artificial insemination
**insena'tura** nf inlet
**insensata'mente** adv senselessly
**insen'sato** a senseless; (folle) crazy
**insen'sibile** a fig insensitive; **avere le gambe insensibili** have no feeling in one's legs
**insensibilità** nf lack of feeling; fig insensitivity
**insepa'rabile** a inseparable
**inseri'mento** nm insertion
**inse'rire** vt insert; place (annuncio); Electr connect
**inse'rirsi** vr ~ **in** get into
**inseri'tore** nm inv ~ **fogli (singoli)** (single) sheetfeed
**in'serto** nm file; (in un film ecc) insert
**inservi'ente** nmf attendant
**inserzi'one** nf insertion; (avviso) advertisement; **inserzioni** pl classified ads
**inserzio'nista** nmf advertiser
**insetti'cida** nm insecticide
**insetti'fugo** nm insect repellent
**in'setto** nm insect
**insicu'rezza** nf insecurity
**insi'curo** a insecure
**in'sidia** nf trick; (tranello) snare
**insidi'are** vt/i lay a trap for
**insidi'oso** a insidious
**insi'eme** adv together; (contemporaneamente) at the same time ● prep ~ **a** [together] with ● nm whole; (completo) outfit; Theat ensemble; Math set; **nell'~** as a whole; **tutto ~** (in una volta) at one go
**insie'mistica** nf set theory
**in'signe** a renowned
**insignifi'cante** a insignificant
**insi'gnire** vt decorate
**insin'cero** a insincere
**insinda'cabile** a final
**insinu'ante** a insinuating
**insinu'are** vt insinuate
**insinu'arsi** vr penetrate; ~ **in** fig creep into
**insinuazi'one** nf insinuation
**in'sipido** a insipid
**insi'stente** a insistent
**insistente'mente** adv repeatedly
**insi'stenza** nf insistence
**in'sistere** vi insist; (perseverare) persevere
**'insito** a inherent
**insoddisfa'cente** a unsatisfactory
**insoddi'sfatto** a unsatisfied; (scontento) dissatisfied
**insoddisfazi'one** nf dissatisfaction
**insoffe'rente** a intolerant
**insoffe'renza** nf intolerance
**insolazi'one** nf sunstroke
**inso'lente** a rude, insolent
**insolente'mente** adv insolently
**inso'lenza** nf rudeness, insolence; (commento) insolent remark
**insolita'mente** adv unusually
**in'solito** a unusual
**inso'lubile** a insoluble
**inso'luto** a unsolved; (non pagato) unpaid
**insol'vente** a Jur insolvent
**insol'venza** nf insolvency
**insol'vibile** a insolvent
**in'somma** adv in short; ~**!** well!
**inson'dabile** a unfathomable
**in'sonne** a sleepless
**in'sonnia** nf insomnia
**insonno'lito** a sleepy
**insonoriz'zare** vt soundproof
**insonoriz'zato** a soundproofed
**insoppor'tabile** a unbearable
**insoppri'mibile** a unsuppressible
**insor'genza** nf onset
**in'sorgere** vi revolt, rise up; (problema:) arise
**insormon'tabile** a (ostacolo, difficoltà) insurmountable
**in'sorto** pp di **insorgere** ● a rebellious ● nm rebel
**insospet'tabile** a unsuspected
**insospet'tire** vt make suspicious ● vi become suspicious
**insospet'tirsi** vr become suspicious
**insoste'nibile** a untenable; (insopportabile) unbearable
**insostitu'ibile** a irreplaceable
**insoz'zare** vt dirty
**inspe'rabile** a hopeless; (insperato) unhoped-for
**inspe'rato** a unhoped-for
**inspie'gabile** a inexplicable
**inspiegabil'mente** adv inexplicably

**inspi'rare** *vt* breathe in

**in'stabile** *a* unstable; (*variabile*) unsettled

**instabilità** *nf* instability; (*di tempo*) change-ability

**instal'lare** *vt* install

**instal'larsi** *vr* (*in casa, lavoro*) settle in

**installa|'tore, -'trice** *nmf* fitter

**installazi'one** *nf* installation. **installazioni** *pl* **di bordo** on-board equipment

**instan'cabile** *a* untiring

**instancabil'mente** *adv* tirelessly

**instau'rare** *vt* found

**instau'rarsi** *vr* become established

**instaurazi'one** *nf* foundation

**instra'dare** *vt* direct

**insù: all'~** *adv* upwards; **naso all'~** turned-up nose

**insubordi'nato** *a* insubordinate

**insubordinazi'one** *nf* insubordination

**insuc'cesso** *nm* failure

**insudici'are** *vt* dirty

**insudici'arsi** *vr* get dirty

**insuffici'ente** *a* insufficient; (*inadeguato*) inadequate ● *nf Sch* fail

**insufficiente'mente** *adv* insufficiently

**insuffici'enza** *nf* insufficiency; (*inadeguatezza*) inadequacy; *Sch* fail. **~ cardiaca** cardiac insufficiency. **~ di prove** lack of evidence

**insu'lare** *a* insular

**insu'lina** *nf* insulin

**in'sulso** *a* insipid; (*sciocco*) silly

**insul'tare** *vt* insult

**in'sulto** *nm* insult; **coprire qcno di insulti** heap abuse on sb

**insupe'rabile** *a* insuperable; (*eccezionale*) incomparable

**insurrezi'one** *nf* insurrection

**insussi'stente** *a* groundless

**intac'cabile** *a* subject to corrosion; *fig* open to criticism

**intac'care** *vt* nick; (*corrodere*) corrode; draw on (*capitale*); (*danneggiare*) damage

**intagli'are** *vt* carve

**in'taglio** *nm* carving

**intan'gibile** *a* untouchable

**in'tanto** *adv* meanwhile; (*per ora*) for the moment; (*avversativo*) but; **~ che** while

**intarsi'are** *vt* inlay

**intarsi'ato** *a* **~ di** inset with

**in'tarsio** *nm* inlay

**intasa'mento** *nm* (*ostruzione*) blockage; (*ingorgo*) traffic jam

**inta'sare** *vt* block, clog

**inta'sarsi** *vr* become blocked

**inta'sato** *a* blocked

**inta'scare** *vt* pocket

**in'tatto** *a* intact

**intavo'lare** *vt* start

**inte'gerrimo** *a* of integrity

**inte'grale** *a* whole; **edizione ~** unabridged edition; **pane ~** wholemeal bread; **versione ~** (*di film*) uncut version; (*di romanzo*) unabridged version

**integra'lista** *nmf* fundamentalist

**integral'mente** *adv* fully

**inte'grante** *a* integral

**inte'grare** *vt* integrate; (*aggiungere*) supplement

**inte'grarsi** *vr* integrate

**integra'tivo** *a* supplementary, additional; **esame ~** test taken by pupil wishing to transfer from arts to a scientific stream etc

**integra'tore** *nm* **~ alimentare** dietary supplement

**integrazi'one** *nf* integration

**integrità** *nf* integrity

**'integro** *a* complete; (*retto*) upright

**intelaia'tura** *nf* framework

**intellet'tivo** *a* intellectual

**intel'letto** *nm* intellect

**intellettu'ale** *a & nmf* intellectual

**intellettual'mente** *adv* intellectually

**intelli'gente** *a* intelligent

**intelligente'mente** *adv* intelligently

**intelli'genza** *nf* intelligence. **~ artificiale** artificial intelligence

**intelli'ghenzia** *nf* intelligentsia

**intelli'gibile** *a* intelligible

**intelligibil'mente** *adv* intelligibly

**intelli'oco** *nm* computer game

**intempe'rante** *a* intemperate

**intempe'ranza** *nf* intemperance; **intemperanze** *pl* excesses

**intem'perie** *nfpl* bad weather

**intempe'stivo** *a* untimely

**inten'dente** *nm* superintendent

**inten'denza** *nf* **~ di finanza** inland revenue office

**in'tendere** *vt* (*comprendere*) understand; (*udire*) hear; (*avere intenzione*) intend; (*significare*) mean; **[siamo] intesi?** is that clear?

**in'tendersi** *vr* (*capirsi*) understand each other; **~ di** (*essere esperto in*) have a good knowledge of; **intendersela con** (*fam: avere una relazione con*) have it off with

**intendi'mento** *nm* understanding; (*intenzione*) intention

**intendi|'tore, -'trice** *nmf* connoisseur; **intenditori** *pl* cognoscenti

**intene'rire** *vt* soften; (*commuovere*) touch

**intene'rirsi** *vr* be touched

**intensa'mente** *adv* intensely

**intensifi'care** *vt* intensify

**intensifi'carsi** *vr* intensify

**intensità** *nf* intensity

**intensiva'mente** *adv* intensively

**inten'sivo** *a* intensive

**in'tenso** *a* intense

**inten'tare** *vt* start up; **~ causa contro qcno** bring *o* institute proceedings against sb

**inten'tato** *a* **non lasciare nulla di ~** try everything

**in'tento** *a* engrossed (**a** in) ● *nm* purpose

**intenzio'nale** *a* intentional

**intenzio'nato** *a* **essere ~ a fare qcsa** have the intention of doing sth

**intenzi'one** *nf* intention; **senza ~** unintentionally; **avere ~ di fare qcsa** intend to do sth, have the intention of doing sth

**intera'gire** *vi* interact

**intera'mente** *adv* completely, entirely

**interat'tivo** *a* interactive

**interazi'one** *nf* interaction

**interca'lare** *nm* stock phrase ● *vt* insert ‹*esclamazione*›

**intercambi'abile** *a* interchangeable

**interca'pedine** *nf* cavity

**inter'cedere** *vi* intercede

**intercessi'one** *nf* intercession

**intercet'tare** *vt* intercept; tap ‹*telefono*›

**intercettazi'one** *nf* interception. **~ telefonica** telephone tapping

**inter'city** *nm inv* inter-city

**intercomuni'cante** *a* [inter]communicating

**interconfessio'nale** *a* interdenominational

**intercon'nettere** *vt* interconnect

**intercontinen'tale** *a* intercontinental

**inter'correre** *vi* ‹*tempo:*› elapse; (*esistere*) exist

**interco'stale** *a* intercostal; **dolori intercostali** *fam* growing pains

**interden'tale** *a* between the teeth; **filo ~** dental floss

**inter'detto** *pp di* **interdire** ● *a* astonished; (*proibito*) forbidden; **rimanere ~** be taken aback; **lasciare qcno ~** astonish sb, dumbfound sb ● *nm Relig* interdict

**interdipartimen'tale** *a* interdepartmental

**interdipen'dente** *a* interdependent

**interdipen'denza** *nf* interdependence

**inter'dire** *vt* ban; (*nel calcio*) intercept; *Jur* deprive of civil rights; *Relig* interdict; **~ a qcno di fare qcsa** forbid sb to do sth

**interdiscipli'nare** *a* interdisciplinary

**interdizi'one** *nf* ban; (*nel calcio*) interception; *Relig* interdict. **~ giudiziale** *appointment of a legal guardian to a minor of unsound mind*. **~ legale** *legally imposed ban*. **~ dai pubblici uffici** *ban on taking public office*

**interessa'mento** *nm* interest

**interes'sante** *a* interesting; **essere in stato ~** be pregnant

**interes'sare** *vt* interest; (*riguardare*) concern ● *vi* **~ a** interest; **non mi interessa** I'm not interested; (*non mi importa*) I don't care, it doesn't matter to me

**interes'sarsi** *vr* **~ a** take an interest in; **~ di** take care of

**interes'sato** *a* (*attento*) interested; *pej* self-interested; **diretto ~** person concerned

**inte'resse** *nm* interest; **fare qcsa per ~** do sth out of self-interest; **essere nell'~ di qcno** be in sb's interest; **un ~ del 4%** 4% interest. **~ attivo** interest charge. **~ maturato** accrued interest. **~ privato in atti di ufficio** abuse of public office. **~ a tasso variabile** floating rate interest

**interes'senza** *nf Econ* profit-sharing

**inter'faccia** *nf* interface. **~ uomo/macchina** man/machine interface. **~ utente** user interface

**interfacci'are** *vt* interface

**interfacci'arsi** *vr* interface

**interfe'renza** *nf* interference

**interfe'rire** *vi* interfere

**inter'fono** *nm* intercom

**interga'lattico** *a* intergalactic

**interiet'tivo** *a* interjectory

**interiezi'one** *nf* interjection

**'interim** *nm inv* (*incarico*) temporary appointment; (*periodo*) interim; **ad ~** on a temporary basis; ‹*presidente*› acting

**interi'ora** *nfpl* entrails

**interi'ore** *a* inner

**interioriz'zare** *vt* internalize

**interior'mente** *adv* (*nella parte interiore*) internally; (*emotivamente*) inwardly

**inter'linea** *nf* line spacing; *Typ* leading. **~ doppia** double spacing

**interline'are** *vt* space out ● *a* line *attrib*

**interlocu'|tore, -'trice** *nmf* speaker, interlocutor *fml*; **il mio ~** the person I am/was speaking to

**inter'ludio** *nm* interlude

**intermedi'ario, -a** *a* & *nmf* intermediary; *Econ* middleman

**intermediazi'one** *nf* (*intervento*) mediation

**inter'medio** *a* in-between

**inter'mezzo** *nm Theat, Mus* intermezzo

**intermi'nabile** *a* interminable

**interministeri'ale** *a* interdepartmental

**intermissi'one** *nf* intermission

**intermit'tente** *a* intermittent; ‹*vulcano*› dormant

**intermit'tenza** *nf* **a ~** intermittent

**interna'mente** *adv* internally

**interna'mento** *nm* internment; (*in manicomio*) committal

**inter'nare** *vt* intern; (*in manicomio*) commit [to a mental institution]

**inter'nato, -a** *a* interned ● *nmf* internee ● *nm* boarding school

**internazio'nale** *a* international

**internazional'mente** *adv* internationally

**'Internet** *nm* Internet; **in ~** on the Internet; **via ~** through the Internet

**inter'nista** *nmf* internist

**in'terno** *a* internal; *Geog* inland; (*interiore*) inner; ‹*politica*› national; **alunno ~** boarder ● *nm* interior; (*di condominio*) flat; *Teleph* extension; *Cinema* interior shot; **all'~** inside; **ministero degli interni** Ministry of the Interior, ≈ Home Office

**in'tero** *a* whole, entire; *Math* whole; (*intatto*) intact; (*completo*) complete; **per ~** in full ● *nm* (*totalità*) whole

**interparlamen'tare** *a* interparliamentary

**interpel'lanza** *nf* parliamentary question

**interpel'lare** *vt* consult

**interpel'lato, -a** *nmf* person being questioned

**interperso'nale** *a* interpersonal
**interplane'tario** *a* interplanetary
**interpo'lare** *vt* interpolate
**inter'porre** *vt* interpose; use ⟨*influenza*⟩; ~ **ostacoli a** put obstacles in the way of
**inter'porsi** *vr* intervene; ~ **tra** come between
**inter'posto** *a* **per interposta persona** through a third party
**interpre'tare** *vt* interpret; *Mus* perform; ~ **male** misinterpret
**interpretari'ato** *nm* interpreting
**interpretazi'one** *nf* interpretation; *Mus* performance
**in'terprete** *nmf* interpreter; *Mus* performer
**interpunzi'one** *nf* punctuation
**inter'rare** *vt* ⟨*seppellire*⟩ bury; ⟨*riempire*⟩ fill in; lay underground ⟨*cavo, tubo*⟩; plant ⟨*pianta, seme*⟩
**inter'rato** *nm* basement
**interregio'nale** *nm* long-distance train, stopping at all stations
**interro'gante** *nmf* questioner
**interro'gare** *vt* question; *Sch* examine
**interrogativa'mente** *adv* ⟨*guardare*⟩ inquiringly
**interroga'tivo** *a* interrogative; ⟨*sguardo*⟩ questioning ● *nm* question
**interro'gato** *a* ⟨*studente*⟩ examinee; *Jur* person questioned
**interroga'torio** *a & nm* questioning
**interrogazi'one** *nf* question; *Sch* oral [test]. ~ **ciclica** polling. ~ **parlamentare** parliamentary question
**inter'rompere** *vt* interrupt; ⟨*sospendere*⟩ stop; cut off ⟨*collegamento*⟩
**inter'rompersi** *vr* break off
**interrut'tore** *nm* switch. ~ **a reostato** dimmer
**interruzi'one** *nf* interruption; **senza** ~ non-stop. ~ **della corrente** power cut. ~ **di gravidanza** termination of pregnancy
**interscambi'abile** *a* interchangeable
**inter'scambio** *nm* import-export trade
**interse'care** *vt* intersect
**interse'carsi** *vr* intersect
**intersezi'one** *nf* intersection
**inter'stizio** *nm* interstice
**interur'bana** *nf* long-distance call
**interur'bano** *a* inter-city; **telefonata interurbana** long-distance call
**interval'lare** *vt* space out
**inter'vallo** *nm* interval; ⟨*spazio*⟩ space; ⟨*in ufficio*⟩ tea/coffee break; *TV, Sch* break; **fare un** ~ have a break; **a intervalli regolari** at regular intervals. ~ **del pranzo** lunch hour, lunch break. ~ **pubblicitario** commercial break
**interve'nire** *vi* intervene; ⟨*Med: operare*⟩ operate; ~ **a** take part in
**inter'vento** *nm* intervention; ⟨*presenza*⟩ presence; ⟨*chirurgico*⟩ operation; **pronto** ~ emergency services. **un** ~ **a cuore aperto** open-heart surgery
**inter'vista** *nf* interview. ~ **esclusiva** exclusive interview

**intervi'stare** *vt* interview
**intervi'stato, -a** *nmf* interviewee
**intervista'tore, -'trice** *nmf* interviewer
**in'tesa** *nf* understanding; **d'**~ ⟨*cenno*⟩ of acknowledgment
**in'teso, -a** *pp di* **intendere** ● **a resta** ~ **che...** needless to say,...; ~ **a** meant to; [**siamo**] **intesi!** agreed! ● *nf* understanding
**in'tessere** *vt* weave together
**inte'stare** *vt* head; write one's name and address at the top of ⟨*lettera*⟩; *Comm* register
**inte'starsi** *vr* ~ **a fare qcsa** take it into one's head to do sth
**intesta'tario, -a** *nmf* holder
**intestazi'one** *nf* heading; ⟨*su carta da lettere*⟩ letterhead
**intesti'nale** *a* intestinal
**inte'stino** *a* ⟨*lotte*⟩ internal ● *nm* intestine. ~ **crasso** large intestine. ~ **tenue** small intestine
**intiepi'dire** *vt* ⟨*scaldare*⟩ warm; cool ⟨*passione, desiderio*⟩
**intiepi'dirsi** *vr* cool [down]; ⟨*scaldarsi*⟩ warm [up]; ⟨*fede:*⟩ wane
**intima'mente** *adv* ⟨*conoscere*⟩ intimately
**inti'mare** *vt* order; ~ **l'alt** give the order to halt; ~ **l'alt a qcno** order sb to stop
**intimazi'one** *nf* order. ~ **di sfratto** eviction notice
**intimida'torio** *a* threatening
**intimidazi'one** *nf* intimidation
**intimi'dire** *vt* intimidate
**intimi'dirsi** *vr* be overwhelmed with shyness
**intimità** *nf* cosiness
**'intimo** *a* intimate; ⟨*interno*⟩ innermost; ⟨*amico*⟩ close ● *nm* ⟨*amico*⟩ close friend; ⟨*dell'animo*⟩ heart
**intimo'rire** *vt* frighten
**intimo'rirsi** *vr* get frightened
**intimo'rito** *a* frightened
**in'tingere** *vt* dip
**in'tingolo** *nm* sauce; ⟨*pietanza*⟩ stew
**intiriz'zire** *vt* numb
**intiriz'zirsi** *vr* grow numb
**intiriz'zito** *a* **essere** ~ ⟨*dal freddo*⟩ be perished
**intito'lare** *vt* entitle; ⟨*dedicare*⟩ dedicate
**intito'larsi** *vr* be called
**intolle'rabile** *a* intolerable
**intolle'rante** *a* intolerant
**intona'care** *vt* plaster
**intonaca'tore** *nm* plasterer
**in'tonaco** *nm* plaster. ~ **a pinocchino** pebbledash
**into'nare** *vt* start to sing; tune ⟨*strumento*⟩; ⟨*accordare*⟩ match
**into'narsi** *vr* match
**into'nato** *a* ⟨*persona*⟩ able to sing in tune; ⟨*voce, strumento*⟩ in tune; ⟨*colore*⟩ matching
**intonazi'one** *nf* ⟨*inflessione*⟩ intonation; ⟨*ironica*⟩ tone; ⟨*cantando*⟩ ability to sing in tune
**in'tonso** *a* ⟨*libro*⟩ untouched
**inton'tire** *vt* ⟨*botta:*⟩ stun, daze; ⟨*gas:*⟩ make dizzy; *fig* stun ● *vi* go ga-ga

**inton'tito** *a* dazed; *fig* stunned; (*con l'età*) ga-ga

**intop'pare** *vi* ~ **in** run into

**in'toppo** *nm* **c'è un** ~ something's come up

**in'torno** *adv* around ● *prep* ~ **a** around; (*circa*) about

**intorpi'dire** *vt* numb

**intorpi'dirsi** *vr* become numb

**intorpi'dito** *a* torpid

**intossi'care** *vt* poison

**intossi'carsi** *vr* be poisoned

**intossicazi'one** *nf* poisoning. ~ **alimentare** food poisoning

**intra-azien'dale** *a* in-house

**intradu'cibile** *a* untranslatable

**intralci'are** *vt* hamper

**in'tralcio** *nm* hitch; **essere d'**~ **(a qcno/qcsa)** be a hindrance (to sb/sth)

**intrallaz'zare** *vi* intrigue

**intral'lazzo** *nm* racket

**intramon'tabile** *a* timeless

**intramusco'lare** *a* intramuscular

**intransi'gente** *a* intransigent, uncompromising

**intransi'genza** *nf* intransigence

**intransi'tivo** *a* intransitive

**intrappo'lato** *a* **rimanere** ~ be trapped

**intrapren'dente** *a* enterprising

**intrapren'denza** *nf* initiative

**intra'prendere** *vt* undertake

**intrat'tabile** *a* very difficult

**intratte'nere** *vt* entertain

**intratte'nersi** *vr* linger

**intratteni'mento** *nm* entertainment

**intrave'dere** *vt* catch a glimpse of; (*presagire*) foresee

**intrecci'are** *vt* interweave; plait ⟨*capelli, corda*⟩; ~ **le mani** clasp one's hands

**intrecci'are** *vt* interweave

**intrecci'arsi** *vr* intertwine; (*aggrovigliarsi*) become tangled

**in'treccio** *nm* (*trama*) plot; (*di nastri, strade*) tangle

**in'trepido** *a* intrepid

**intri'cato** *a* tangled

**intri'gante** *a* intriguing ● *nmf* schemer

**intri'gare** *vt* entangle; (*incuriosire*) intrigue ● *vi* be intriguing

**intri'garsi** *vr* become entangled; (*immischiarsi*) meddle

**in'trigo** *nm* plot; **intrighi** *pl* plotting; (*di corte*) intrigues

**intrinseca'mente** *adv* intrinsically

**in'trinseco** *a* intrinsic

**in'triso** *a* ~ **di** soaked with; *fig* imbued with

**intri'stire** *vt* sadden

**intri'stirsi** *vr* grow sad

**intro'durre** *vt* introduce; (*inserire*) insert; ~ **a** (*iniziare a*) introduce to

**intro'dursi** *vr* get in; ~ **in** get into

**introdut'tivo** *a* ⟨*pagine, discorso*⟩ introductory

**introduzi'one** *nf* introduction

**in'troito** *nm* income, revenue; (*incasso*) takings *pl*

**intro'mettere** *vt* introduce

**intro'mettersi** *vr* interfere; (*interporsi*) intervene

**intromissi'one** *nf* intervention

**introspet'tivo** *a* introspective

**intro'vabile** *a* unobtainable

**intro'verso, -a** *a* introverted ● *nmf* introvert

**intrufo'larsi** *vr* sneak in

**in'truglio** *nm* concoction

**intrusi'one** *nf* intrusion

**in'truso, -a** *nmf* intruder

**intu'ibile** *a* deducible

**intu'ire** *vt* perceive

**intuitiva'mente** *adv* intuitively

**intui'tivo** *a* intuitive

**in'tuito** *nm* intuition

**intuizi'one** *nf* intuition

**inuguagli'anza** *nf* inequality

**inu'mano** *a* inhuman

**inu'mare** *vt* inter

**inumi'dire** *vt* dampen; moisten ⟨*labbra*⟩

**inumi'dirsi** *vr* become damp

**i'nutile** *a* useless; (*superfluo*) unnecessary

**inutilità** *nf* uselessness

**inutiliz'zabile** *a* unusable

**inutiliz'zato** *a* unused

**inutil'mente** *adv* fruitlessly

**inva'dente** *a* intrusive

**in'vadere** *vt* invade; (*affollare*) overrun

**inva'ghirsi** *vr* ~ **di** take a fancy to

**invali'cabile** *a* impassable; **'limite ~'** *Mil* 'no access beyond this point'

**invali'dare** *vt* invalidate

**invalidità** *nf* disability; *Jur* invalidity

**in'valido, -a** *a* invalid; (*handicappato*) disabled ● *nmf* disabled person; **gli invalidi** the handicapped. ~ **di guerra** disabled ex-serviceman. ~ **del lavoro** industrial accident victim

**in'vano** *adv* in vain

**invari'abile** *a* invariable

**invariabil'mente** *adv* invariably

**invari'ato** *a* unchanged

**invasi'one** *nf* invasion

**in'vaso** *pp di* **invadere**

**inva'sore** *a* invading ● *nm* invader

**invecchia'mento** *nm* (*di vino*) maturation

**invecchi'are** *vt/i* age

**in'vece** *adv* instead; (*anzi*) but; ~ **di** instead of

**inve'ire** *vi* ~ **contro** inveigh against

**invele'nito** *a* embittered

**inven'dibile** *a* unsaleable

**inven'duto** *a* unsold

**inven'tare** *vt* invent

**inventari'are** *vt* make an inventory of

**inven'tario** *nm* inventory

**inven'tato** *a* made-up

**inven'tiva** *nf* inventiveness

**inven'tivo** *a* inventive

**inven|'tore, -'trice** *nmf* inventor

**invenzi'one** *nf* invention

**inver'nale** *a* wintry; **sport** *pl* **invernali** winter sports

**in'verno** *nm* winter
**invero'simile** *a* improbable
**inverosimil'mente** *adv* incredibly
**inversa'mente** *adv* inversely; **~ proporzionale** in inverse proportion
**inversi'one** *nf* inversion; *Mech* reversal; **fare un'~ a U** do a U-turn. **~ di fondo** *Comput* reverse video. **~ di tendenza** turnaround
**in'verso** *a* inverse; (*opposto*) opposite ● *nm* opposite
**inverte'brato** *a & nm* invertebrate
**inver'tire** *vt* reverse; (*capovolgere*) turn upside-down
**inver'tito, -a** *nmf* homosexual
**investi'gare** *vt* investigate
**investiga|'tore, -'trice** *nmf* investigator. **~ privato** private investigator
**investigazi'one** *nf* investigation
**investi'mento** *nm* investment; (*incidente*) crash
**inve'stire** *vt* invest; (*urtare*) collide with; (*travolgere*) run over; **~ qcno di** invest sb with
**investi'tura** *nf* investiture
**invete'rato** *a* inveterate
**invet'tiva** *nf* invective
**invi'are** *vt* send
**invi'ato, -a** *nmf* envoy; (*di giornale*) correspondent. **~ di pace** peace envoy
**in'vidia** *nf* envy
**invidi'are** *vt* envy
**invidi'oso** *a* envious
**invigo'rire** *vt* invigorate
**invigo'rirsi** *vr* become strong
**invin'cibile** *a* invincible
**in'vio** *nm* dispatch; *Comput* enter
**invio'labile** *a* inviolable
**invipe'rirsi** *vr* get nasty
**invipe'rito** *a* furious
**invischi'arsi** *vr* get involved (**in** in)
**invi'sibile** *a* invisible
**invisibilità** *nf* invisibility
**invi'tante** *a* (*piatto, profumo*) enticing
**invi'tare** *vt* invite
**invi'tato, -a** *nmf* guest
**in'vito** *nm* invitation
**invo'care** *vt* invoke; (*implorare*) beg
**invocazi'one** *nf* invocation
**invogli'are** *vt* tempt; (*indurre*) induce
**invogli'arsi** *vr* **~ di** take a fancy to
**involga'rire** *vt* vulgarize
**involontaria'mente** *adv* involuntarily
**involon'tario** *a* involuntary
**invol'tini** *nmpl* stuffed rolls (*of meat, pastry*)
**in'volto** *nm* parcel; (*fagotto*) bundle
**in'volucro** *nm* wrapping
**invo'luto** *a* involved
**invulne'rabile** *a* invulnerable
**inzacche'rare** *vt* splash with mud
**inzup'pare** *vt* soak; (*intingere*) dip
**inzup'parsi** *vr* get soaked
**'io** *pers pron* I; **sono io** it's me; **l'ho fatto io [stesso]** I did it myself ● *nm* **l'io** the ego
**i'odio** *nm* iodine

**i'one** *nm* ion
**i'onico** *a* Ionic
**l'onio** *nm* **lo ~** the Ionian [Sea]
**iono'sfera** *nf* ionosphere
**i'osa: a iosa** *adv* in abundance
**iperattività** *nf* hyperactivity
**iperat'tivo** *a* hyperactive
**i'perbole** *nf* hyperbole
**iper'critico** *a* hypercritical
**ipermer'cato** *nm* hypermarket
**iper'metrope** *a* long-sighted
**ipersen'sibile** *a* hypersensitive
**ipertensi'one** *nf* high blood pressure
**iper'testo** *nm Comput* hypertext
**iperventi'lare** *vi* hyperventilate
**ip'nosi** *nf* hypnosis
**ipnotera'pia** *nf* hypnotherapy
**ip'notico** *a* hypnotic
**ipno'tismo** *nm* hypnotism
**ipnotiz'zare** *vt* hypnotize
**ipoaller'genico** *a* hypoallergenic
**ipoca'lorico** *a* low-calorie
**ipo'centro** *nm* focus
**ipocon'dria** *nf* hypochondria
**ipocon'driaco, -a** *a & nmf* hypochondriac
**ipocri'sia** *nf* hypocrisy
**i'pocrita** *a* hypocritical ● *nmf* hypocrite
**ipocrita'mente** *adv* hypocritically
**ipo'dermico** *a* hypodermic
**i'pofisi** *nf inv* pituitary gland
**ipo'teca** *nf* mortgage
**ipote'cabile** *a* mortgageable
**ipote'care** *vt* mortgage
**ipote'cario** *a* mortgage *attrib*
**ipote'nusa** *nf* hypotenuse
**ipo'termia** *nf* hypothermia
**i'potesi** *nf inv* hypothesis; (*caso, eventualità*) eventuality; **nella migliore delle ~** at best; **nella peggiore delle ~** if the worst comes to the worst
**ipo'tetico** *a* hypothetical
**ipotiz'zare** *vt* hypothesize
**'ippico, -a** *a* horse *attrib* ● *nf* riding
**ippoca'stano** *nm* horse-chestnut
**ip'podromo** *nm* racecourse
**ippo'potamo** *nm* hippopotamus
**'ipsilon** *nf inv* [the letter] y
**'ira** *nf* anger
**ira'scibile** *a* irascible
**i'rato** *a* irate
**'iride** *nf Anat* iris; (*arcobaleno*) rainbow
**'iris** *nm inv Bot* iris
**Ir'landa** *nf* Ireland. **~ del Nord** Northern Ireland
**irlan'dese** *a* Irish ● *nm* Irishman; (*lingua*) Irish ● *nf* Irishwoman
**iro'nia** *nf* irony
**i'ronico** *a* ironic[al]
**irradi'are** *vt/i* radiate
**irradiazi'one** *nf* radiation
**irraggiun'gibile** *a* unattainable
**irragio'nevole** *a* unreasonable; (*speranza, timore*) irrational; (*assurdo*) absurd
**irranci'dire** *vi* go rancid
**irrazio'nale** *a* irrational

**irrazionalità** *a* irrationality
**irrazional'mente** *adv* irrationally
**irre'ale** *a* unreal
**irrea'listico** *a* unrealistic
**irrealiz'zabile** *a* unattainable
**irrealtà** *nf* unreality
**irrecupe'rabile** *a* irrecoverable
**irrecu'sabile** *a* incontrovertible
**irredi'mibile** *a* irredeemable
**irrefre'nabile** *a* uncontrollable
**irrefu'tabile** *a* irrefutable
**irrego'lare** *a* irregular
**irregolarità** *nf inv* irregularity; *(di terreno)* unevenness; *Sport* foul
**irregolar'mente** *adv* *(frequentare)* irregularly; *(comportarsi)* erratically; *(disporre)* unevenly
**irremo'vibile** *a fig* adamant
**irrepa'rabile** *a* irreparable
**irrepe'ribile** *a* *(persona)* not to be found; **sarò irreperibile** I'm not going to be contactable
**irrepren'sibile** *a* irreproachable
**irrepri'mibile** *a* irrepressible
**irrequi'eto** *a* restless
**irresi'stibile** *a* irresistible
**irresistibil'mente** *adv* irresistibly
**irreso'luto** *a* irresolute
**irrespon'sabile** *a* irresponsible
**irresponsabilità** *nf* irresponsibility
**irrestrin'gibile** *a* preshrunk
**irre'tire** *vt* seduce
**irrever'sibile** *a* irreversible
**irreversibil'mente** *adv* irreversibly
**irrevo'cabile** *a* irrevocable
**irrevocabil'mente** *adv* irrevocably
**irricono'scibile** *a* unrecognizable
**irridu'cibile** *a* irreducible
**irri'gare** *vt* irrigate; *(fiume:)* flow through
**irrigazi'one** *nf* irrigation
**irrigidi'mento** *nm* *(di muscoli)* stiffening; *(di disciplina)* tightening
**irrigi'dire** *vt* stiffen up
**irrigi'dirsi** *vr* stiffen up
**irrile'vante** *a* unimportant
**irrimedi'abile** *a* irreparable
**irrimediabil'mente** *adv* irreparably
**irripe'tibile** *a* unrepeatable
**irri'solto** *a* unresolved
**irri'sorio** *a* derisive; *(insignificante)* derisory
**irri'tabile** *a* irritable
**irri'tante** *a* aggravating
**irri'tare** *vt* irritate
**irri'tarsi** *vr* get annoyed
**irri'tato** *a* irritated; *(gola)* sore
**irritazi'one** *nf* irritation
**irrive'renza** *nf* *(qualità)* irreverence; *(azione)* irreverent action
**irrobu'stire** *vt* fortify
**irrobu'stirsi** *vr* get stronger
**ir'rompere** *vi* burst **(in** into)
**irro'rare** *vt* sprinkle
**irrorazi'one** *nf* *(di piante)* crop spraying
**irru'ente** *a* impetuous

**irruvi'dire** *vt* roughen
**irruvi'dirsi** *vr* become rough
**irruzi'one** *nf* raid; *fig* eruption: **fare ~ in** burst into
**ir'suto** *a* shaggy
**'irto** *a* bristly
**i'scritto, -a** *pp di* **iscrivere** ● *a* registered ● *nmf* member; **per ~** in writing
**i'scrivere** *vt* register
**i'scriversi** *vr* ~ **a** register at, enrol at *(scuola)*; join *(circolo ecc)*
**iscrizi'one** *nf* registration; *(epigrafe)* inscription
**i'slamico** *a* Islamic
**isla'mismo** *nm* Islam
**l'slanda** *nf* Iceland
**islan'dese** *a* Icelandic ● *nmf* Icelander
**'ismi** *nmpl* isms
**i'sobara** *nf* isobar
**'isola** *nf* island. **le isole britanniche** the British Isles. **~ deserta** desert island. **~ pedonale** traffic island. **~ spartitraffico** traffic island
**iso'lano, -a** *a* insular ● *nmf* islander
**iso'lante** *a* insulating ● *nm* insulator
**iso'lare** *vt* isolate; *Mech, Electr* insulate; *(acusticamente)* soundproof
**iso'lato** *a* isolated ● *nm* *(di appartamenti)* block
**isolazio'nismo** *nm* isolationism
**iso'metrico** *a* isometric
**i'soscele** *a* isosceles
**is'panico** *a* Hispanic
**ispessi'mento** *nm* thickening
**ispes'sire** *vt* thicken
**ispes'sirsi** *vr* thicken
**ispetto'rato** *nm* inspectorate
**ispet'tore** *nm* inspector. **~ capo** chief inspector. **~ di polizia** police inspector. **~ scolastico** inspector of schools. **~ di zona** *Comm* area manager
**ispezio'nare** *vt* inspect
**ispezi'one** *nf* inspection; *(di nave)* boarding
**'ispido** *a* bristly
**ispi'rare** *vt* inspire; suggest *(idea, soluzione)*
**ispi'rarsi** *vr* ~ **a** be based on
**ispi'rato** *a* inspired
**ispirazi'one** *nf* inspiration; *(idea)* idea
**lsra'ele** *nm* Israel
**israeli'ano, -a** *a & nmf* Israeli
**is'sare** *vt* hoist
**ist.** *abbr* **(istituto)** dept
**istan'taneo, -a** *a* instantaneous ● *nf* snapshot
**i'stante** *nm* instant; **all'~** instantly
**i'stanza** *nf* petition. **~ di divorzio** petition for divorce
**isterecto'mia** *nf* hysterectomy
**i'sterico** *a* hysterical; **attacco ~** hysterics *pl*
**iste'rismo** *nm* hysteria. **~ di massa** mass hysteria
**isti'gare** *vt* instigate; **~ qcno al male** incite sb to evil
**istiga|'tore, -'trice** *nmf* instigator

**istigazi'one** *nf* instigation. ~ **a delinquere** incitement to crime

**istintiva'mente** *adv* instinctively

**istin'tivo** *a* instinctive

**i'stinto** *nm* instinct; **d'~** instinctively. ~ **di conservazione** instinct of self-preservation. ~ **materno** maternal instinct

**istitu'ire** *vt* institute; (*fondare*) found; initiate (*manifestazione*)

**isti'tuto** *nm* institute; *Sch* secondary school; *Univ* department. ~ **di bellezza** beauty salon. ~ **commerciale** business college. ~ **di credito** bank. ~ **per l'infanzia** children's home

**istitu'tore, -'trice** *nmf* (*insegnante*) tutor; (*fondatore*) founder

**istituzio'nale** *a* institutional

**istituzionaliz'zare** *vt* institutionalize

**istituzionaliz'zarsi** *vr* become an institution

**istituzionalizzazi'one** *nf* institutionalization

**istituzi'one** *nf* institution; **le istituzioni** state institutions

**'istmo** *nm* isthmus

**isto'gramma** *nm* bar chart

**istolo'gia** *nf* histology

**istra'dare** *vt* divert; *fig* guide (**a** towards)

**'istrice** *nm* porcupine

**istri'one** *nm* clown; *Theat sl* ham

**istru'ire** *vt* instruct; (*addestrare*) train; (*informare*) inform; *Jur* prepare

**istru'ito** *a* well-educated

**istrut'tivo** *a* instructive

**istrut|'tore, -'trice** *nmf* instructor; **giudice ~** examining magistrate. ~ **di guida** driving instructor. ~ **di nuoto** swimming instructor

**istrut'toria** *nf Jur* investigation

**istruzi'one** *nf* instruction; *Sch* education; **ministero della pubblica ~** Department of Education. **istruzioni** *pl* **per l'uso** instructions for use

**istupi'dire** *vt* stupefy

**l'talia** *nf* Italy

**itali'ano, -a** *a & nmf* Italian

**itine'rante** *a* wandering

**itine'rario** *nm* route, itinerary. ~ **turistico** tourist route

**itte'rizia** *nf* jaundice

**'ittico** *a* fishing *attrib*

**i'uta** *nf* jute

**I.V.A.** *nf abbr* (**imposta sul valore aggiunto**) VAT; ~ **compresa** inclusive of VAT, VAT inclusive

**'ivi** *adv* (*linguaggio burocratico*) therein

# Jj

**ja'bot** *nm inv* jabot

**jack** *nm inv* jack

**jac'quard** *a inv* (*nella maglia*) jacquard

**'jais** *nm* jet

**jam-session** *nf inv* jam-session

**jazz** *nm* jazz

**jaz'zista** *nmf* jazz player

**jeep** *nf inv* jeep

**'jersey** *nm* jersey

**jet** *nm inv* jet. ~ **privato** private jet

**jet-set** *nm* jet set

**'jingle** *nm inv* jingle

**'jodel** *nm inv* yodel

**'jogging** *nm* jogging

**joint venture** *nf inv Comm* joint venture

**'jolly** *nm inv* (*carta da gioco*) joker ● *a Comput* **carattere ~** wildcard [character]

**'joystick** *nm inv* joystick

**Jugo'slavia** *nf* Yugoslavia

**jugo'slavo, -a** *a & nmf* Yugoslav[ian]

**juke box** *nm inv* juke box

**jumbo-'jet** *nm inv* jumbo jet

**junghi'ano, -a** *a & nmf* Jungian

**'junior** *a inv* junior ● *nm* (*pl* **juniores**) junior

**'juta** *nf* jute

# Kk

**kafki'ano** *a* Kafkan, Kafkaesque
**ka'jal** *nm inv* kohl
**'kaki** *a inv* khaki ● *nm inv* persimmon
**ka'pok** *nm* kapok
**ka'putt** *a inv* kaput
**kara'kiri** *nm* fare ~ commit hara-kiri
**kara'oke** *nm inv* karaoke
**kara'te** *nm* karate
**kart** *nm inv* go-kart
**kar'tismo** *nm* go-karting; **fare del ~** go go-karting
**'kasher** *a inv* kosher
**'Kashmir** *nm* Kashmir
**ka'yak** *nm inv* kayak
**KB** *Comput abbr* (**kilobyte**) K, KB
**Kbyte** *Comput abbr* (**kilobyte**) kbyte
**ker'messe** *nf inv* fair; *fig* rowdy celebration
**kero'sene** *nm* paraffin
**'ketchup** *nm* ketchup
**kg** *abbr* (**chilogrammo**) kg

**kib'butz** *nm inv* kibbutz
**'killer** *mf inv* assassin, hit man
**'kilo** *nm* kilo
**kilt** *nm inv* kilt
**ki'mono** *nm inv* kimono
**kinesitera'pia** *nf* physiotherapy
**kit** *nm inv* ~ **di aggiornamento** upgrade kit. ~ **multimediale** multimedia kit
**kitsch** *a inv* kitschy
**'kleenex®** *nm inv* Kleenex
**km** *abbr* (**chilometro**) km
**km/h** *abbr* (**chilometri all'ora**) kph
**kmq** *abbr* (**chilometro quadrato**) km²
**ko'ala** *nm inv* koala
**'krapfen** *nm inv* doughnut
**'kripton** *nm* krypton
**'Kurdistan** *nm* Kurdistan
**kuwaiti'ano** *nm* Kuwaiti
**kW** *abbr* (**kilowatt**) kW
**K-'way®** *nm inv* cagoule
**kWh** *abbr* (**kilowatt all'ora**) kWh

# Ll

**l'** *def art mf* (*before vowel*) the; *vedi* **il**
**la** *def art f* the; *vedi* **il** ● *pron* (*oggetto, riferito a persona*) her; (*riferito a cosa, animale*) it; (*forma di cortesia*) you ● *nm inv Mus* (*chiave, nota*) A
**là** *adv* there; **di là** (*in quel luogo*) in there; (*da quella parte*) that way; **eccolo là!** there he is!; **farsi più in là** (*far largo*) make way; **là dentro** in there; **là fuori** out there; [**ma**] **va là!** come off it!; **più in là** (*nel tempo*) later on; (*nello spazio*) further on
**'labbro** *nm* (*pl nf* **labbra**) lip; **pendere dalle labbra di qcno** hang on sb's every word. ~ **leporino** harelip
**labi'ale** *a & nf* labial
**'labile** *a* fleeting
**labiolet'tura** *nf* lip-reading
**labi'rinto** *nm* labyrinth; (*di sentieri ecc*) maze
**labora'torio** *nm* laboratory; (*di negozio, officina ecc*) workshop. ~ **linguistico** language lab
**laboriosa'mente** *adv* laboriously
**labori'oso** *a* (*operoso*) industrious; (*faticoso*) laborious

**labra'dor** *nm inv* labrador
**labu'rista** *a* Labour ● *nmf* member of the Labour Party
**'lacca** *nf* lacquer; (*per capelli*) hairspray
**lac'care** *vt* lacquer
**lacchè** *nm inv* lackey
**'laccio** *nm* noose; (*lazo*) lasso; (*trappola*) snare; (*stringa*) lace. ~ **emostatico** tourniquet
**lace'rante** *a* (*grido*) earsplitting
**lace'rare** *vt* tear; lacerate (*carne*)
**lace'rarsi** *vr* tear
**lacerazi'one** *nf* laceration
**'lacero** *a* torn; (*cencioso*) ragged
**la'conico** *a* laconic
**'lacrima** *nf* tear; (*goccia*) drop
**lacri'male** *a* (*condotto, ghiandola*) tear *attrib*
**lacri'mare** *vi* weep
**lacri'mevole** *a* tear-jerking
**lacri'mogeno** *a* gas ~ tear gas
**lacri'moso** *a* tearful
**la'cuna** *nf* gap
**lacu'noso** *a* (*preparazione, resoconto*) incomplete

**la'custre** *a* lake *attrib*

**lad'dove** *conj* whereas

**'ladro, -a** *a* thieving ● *nmf* thief; **al ~!** stop thief!

**ladro'cinio** *nm* theft

**la'druncolo** *nm* petty thief

**'lager** *nm inv* concentration camp

**laggiù** *adv* down there: (*lontano*) over there

**'lagna** *nf* (*fam: persona*) moaning Minnie; (*film*) bore

**la'gnanza** *nf* complaint

**la'gnarsi** *vr* moan; (*protestare*) complain (**di** about)

**la'gnoso** *a* 〈*persona*〉 moaning; 〈*film*〉 weepy

**'lago** *nm* lake. **~ di Garda** Lake Garda. **~ di sangue** pool of blood

**la'guna** *nf* lagoon

**lagu'nare** *a* lagoon *attrib*

**laiciz'zare** *vt* laicize

**'laico, -a** *a* lay; 〈*vita*〉 secular ● *nm* layman ● *nf* laywoman

**'lama** *nf* blade; **a doppia ~** 〈*rasoio*〉 twin-blade ● *nm inv* (*animale*) llama

**lambic'carsi** *vr* **~ il cervello** rack one's brains

**lam'bire** *vt* lap

**lamé** *nm inv* lamé

**la'mella** *nf* (*di fungo*) lamella; (*di metallo, plastica*) sheet

**lamen'tare** *vt* lament

**lamen'tarsi** *vr* moan; **~ di** (*lagnarsi*) complain about

**lamen'tela** *nf* complaint

**lamen'tevole** *a* mournful; (*pietoso*) pitiful

**la'mento** *nm* moan

**la'metta** *nf* **~ [da barba]** razor blade

**lami'era** *nf* sheet metal. **~ ondulata** corrugated iron

**'lamina** *nf* foil. **~ d'oro** gold leaf

**lami'nare** *vt* laminate

**lami'naria** *nf* kelp

**lami'nato** *a* laminated ● *nm* laminate; (*tessuto*) lamé

**'lampada** *nf* lamp. **~ abbronzante** sunlamp. **~ alogena** halogen lamp. **~ da comodino** bedside lamp. **~ a gas** gas lamp. **~ a olio** oil lamp. **~ a pila** torch. **~ da soffitto** overhead light. **~ da tavolo** table lamp

**lampa'dario** *nm* chandelier

**lampa'dato** *nm sl* sun-bed freak

**lampa'dina** *nf* light bulb

**lam'pante** *a* clear

**lam'para** *nf* light used when fishing at night

**lampeggi'are** *vi* flash

**lampeggia'tore** *nm* Auto indicator

**lampi'one** *nm* street lamp

**'lampo** *nm* flash of lightning; (*luce*) flash; **lampi** *pl* lightning *sg*; **cerniera ~** zip [fastener], zipper *Am*. **~ di genio** stroke of genius. **~ al magnesio** magnesium flash

**lam'pone** *nm* raspberry

**'lana** *nf* wool; **di ~** woollen. **~ d'acciaio** steel wool. **~ grossa** double knitting [wool]. **~ merino** botany wool. **~ vergine** new wool. **~ di vetro** glass wool

**lan'cetta** *nf* pointer; (*di orologio*) hand. **~ dei minuti** minute hand. **~ delle ore** hour hand. **~ dei secondi** second hand

**'lancia** *nf* (*arma*) spear, lance; *Naut* launch. **~ di salvataggio** lifeboat

**lanciafi'amme** *nm inv* flamethrower

**lancia'missili** *nm inv* missile launcher

**lancia'palle** *a inv* **macchina ~** ball launcher for tennis practice

**lancia'razzi** *a inv* **pistola ~** Very pistol ● *nm inv* rocket launcher

**lanci'are** *vt* throw; (*da un aereo*) drop; launch 〈*missile, prodotto, attacco*〉; give 〈*grido*〉; *Comput* run 〈*file*〉; **~ uno sguardo a** glance at; **~ in alto** throw up

**lanci'arsi** *vr* fling oneself; (*intraprendere*) launch out

**lanci'nante** *a* piercing

**'lancio** *nm* throwing; (*da aereo*) drop; (*di missile, prodotto*) launch; (*Comput: di file*) running. **~ del disco** discus [throwing]. **~ del giavellotto** javelin [throwing]. **~ con paracadute** airdrop. **~ del peso** putting the shot

**'landa** *nf* moor

**languida'mente** *adv* languidly

**'languido** *a* languid; (*debole*) feeble

**langu'ore** *nm* languor; (*spossatezza*) listlessness; **~ di stomaco** hunger pangs *pl*

**lani'ero** *a* wool; **industria laniera** wool industry

**lani'ficio** *nm* woollen mill

**lano'lina** *nf* lanolin

**la'noso** *a* woolly

**lan'terna** *nf* lantern; (*faro*) lighthouse

**la'nugine** *nf* down

**lapalissi'ano** *a* obvious

**laparosco'pia** *nf* laparoscopy

**lapi'dare** *vt* stone; *fig* demolish

**lapi'dario** *a* (*conciso*) terse; **arte lapidaria** stone carving

**'lapide** *nf* tombstone; (*commemorativa*) memorial tablet

**'lapis** *nm inv* pencil

**lapi'slazzuli** *nm inv* lapis lazuli

**'lappa** *nf* Bot burr

**Lap'ponia** *nf* Lapland

**'lapsus** *nm inv* lapse, error. **~ freudiano** Freudian slip

**'laptop** *nm inv* laptop

**lardel'lare** *vt* Culin lard

**'lardo** *nm* lard

**larga'mente** *adv* (*ampiamente*) widely

**largheggi'are** *vi* **~ in** be free with

**lar'ghezza** *nf* width; (*di spalle*) breadth; *fig* liberality. **~ di vedute** broad-mindedness

**'largo** *a* wide; (*ampio*) broad; 〈*abito*〉 loose; (*liberale*) liberal; (*abbondante*) generous; **stare alla larga** keep away; **~ di manica** *fig* generous; **~ di spalle/vedute** broad-shouldered/-minded; **a gambe larghe** with one's legs wide apart; **di larghe vedute** broad-minded ● *nm* width; **andare al ~** *Naut* go out to sea; **fare ~** make room; **farsi ~** make one's way; **al ~ di** off the coast of

**'larice** *nm* larch
**la'ringe** *nf* larynx
**larin'gite** *nf* laryngitis
**'larva** *nf* larva; (*persona emaciata*) shadow. ~ **di pidocchio** nit
**la'sagne** *nfpl* lasagna
**'lasca** *nf* roach
**lasciapas'sare** *nm inv* pass
**lasci'are** *vt* leave; (*rinunciare*) give up; (*rimetterci*) lose; (*smettere di tenere*) let go [of]; (*concedere*) let; ~ **a desiderare** leave a lot to be desired; ~ **di fare qcsa** (*smettere*) stop doing sth; **lascia perdere!** forget it!; **lascialo venire, lascia che venga** let him come
**lasci'arsi** *vr* (*reciproco*) leave each other, split up; ~ **andare** let oneself go
**'lascito** *nm* legacy
**la'scivo** *a* lascivious
**'laser** *a & nm inv* [**raggio**] ~ laser [beam]
**lassa'tivo** *a & nm* laxative
**las'sismo** *nm* laxity
**'lasso** *nm* ~ **di tempo** period of time
**lassù** *adv* up there
**'lastra** *nf* slab; (*di ghiaccio*) sheet; (*di metallo, Phot*) plate; (*radiografia*) X-ray [plate]. ~ **di pietra** paving slab, paving stone
**lastri'care** *vt* pave
**lastri'cato** *nm* pavement
**'lastrico** *nm* paving; **sul** ~ on one's beam-ends
**la'tente** *a* latent
**late'rale** *a* side *attrib*; *Med, Techn ecc* lateral; **via** ~ side street
**lateral'mente** *adv* sideways
**late'rizi** *nmpl* bricks
**'latice** *nm* latex
**latifon'dista** *nm* big landowner
**lati'fondo** *nm* large estate
**lati'nismo** *nm* Latinism
**la'tino** *a & nm* Latin
**latino-ameri'cano, -a** *a & nmf* Latin American
**lati'tante** *a* in hiding ● *nmf* fugitive [from justice]
**lati'tanza** *nf* **darsi alla** ~ go into hiding
**lati'tudine** *nf* latitude
**'lato** *a* (*ampio*) broad; **in senso** ~ broadly speaking ● *nm* side; (*aspetto*) aspect; **a** ~ **di** beside; **dal** ~ **mio** (*punto di vista*) for my part; **d'altro** ~ *fig* on the other hand. ~ **B** B side
**la'tore, -'trice** *nmf Comm* bearer
**la'trare** *vi* bark
**la'trato** *nm* barking
**la'trina** *nf* latrine
**'latta** *nf* tin, can
**lat'taio, -a** *nm* milkman ● *nf* milkwoman
**lat'tante** *a* breast-fed ● *nmf* suckling
**'latte** *nm* milk. ~ **acido** sour milk. ~ **condensato** condensed milk. ~ **detergente** cleansing milk. ~ **di gallina** eggnog. ~ **intero** whole milk. ~ **a lunga conservazione** long-life milk. ~ **materno** mother's milk, breast milk. ~ **parzialmente scremato** semi-skimmed milk. ~ **in pol-**

**vere** powdered milk. ~ **scremato** skimmed milk. ~ **di soia** soya milk
**lat'teo** *a* milky; **dieta lattea** milk diet. **la Via Lattea** the Milky Way
**latte'ria** *nf* dairy
**'lattice** *nm* latex
**latti'cello** *nm* buttermilk
**latti'cini** *nmpl* dairy products
**latti'era** *nf* milk jug
**lattigi'noso** *a* milky
**lat'tina** *nf* can
**lat'tosio** *nm* lactose
**lat'tuga** *nf* lettuce. ~ **romana** cos lettuce
**'laudano** *nm* laudanum
**'laurea** *nf* degree; **prendere la** ~ graduate. ~ **breve** *degree that takes less than the standard period of time*. ~ **in Lettere** arts degree
**laure'ando, -a** *nmf* final-year student
**laure'are** *vt* confer a degree on
**laure'arsi** *vr* graduate
**laure'ato, -a** *a & nmf* graduate
**'lauro** *nm* laurel
**'lauto** *a* lavish; ~ **guadagno** handsome profit
**'lava** *nf* lava
**la'vabile** *a* washable
**la'vabo** *nm* wash-basin
**lavacri'stallo** *nm* windscreen wiper
**la'vaggio** *nm* washing. ~ **automatico** (*per auto*) carwash. ~ **del cervello** brainwashing. ~ **a secco** dry-cleaning
**la'vagna** *nf* slate; *Sch* blackboard. ~ **a fogli mobili** flipchart. ~ **luminosa** overhead projector
**lava'macchine** *nmf inv* car washer
**la'vanda** *nf* wash; *Bot* lavender; **gli hanno fatto la** ~ **gastrica** he had his stomach pumped
**lavan'daia** *nf* washerwoman
**lavande'ria** *nf* laundry. ~ **automatica** launderette
**lavan'dino** *nm* sink; (*hum: persona*) bottomless pit
**lavapi'atti** *nmf inv* dishwasher
**la'vare** *vt* wash; ~ **i piatti** wash up; ~ **a secco** dry-clean; ~ **a mano** wash by hand; ~ **i panni** do the washing
**la'varsi** *vr* wash, have a wash; ~ **i denti** brush one's teeth; ~ **le mani/il viso** wash one's hands/face; ~ **la testa** *o* **i capelli** wash one's hair
**lava'secco** *nmf inv* dry-cleaner's
**lavasto'viglie** *nf inv* dishwasher
**la'vata** *nf* wash; **darsi una** ~ have a wash; ~ **di capo** *fig* scolding
**lava'tivo, -a** *nmf* idler
**lava'trice** *nf* washing-machine
**lava'vetri** *nm inv* squeegee
**la'vello** *nm* kitchen sink
**'lavico** *a* formed by lava
**la'vina** *nf* snowslide
**lavo'rante** *nmf* worker

**lavo'rare** *vi* work; ~ **di fantasia** (*sognare*) day-dream ● *vt* work; knead (*pasta ecc*); till (*la terra*); ~ **a maglia** knit; ~ **troppo** overwork

**lavora'tivo** *a* working; **giorno** ~ workday; **settimana lavorativa** working week

**lavo'rato** *a* (*pietra, legno*) carved; (*cuoio*) tooled; (*metallo*) wrought; (*golf*) patterned; (*terra*) cultivated

**lavora|'tore, -'trice** *nmf* worker. ~ **a domicilio** outworker, homeworker ● *a* working

**lavorazi'one** *nf* manufacture; (*di terra*) working; (*del terreno*) cultivation. ~ [**artigianale**] workmanship. ~ **del metallo** metalwork. ~ **in serie** mass production

**lavo'rio** *nm* intense activity

**la'voro** *nm* work; (*faticoso, sociale*) labour; (*impiego*) job; *Theat* play; **andare al** ~ go to work; **essere senza** ~ be out of work; **mettersi al** ~ (*su qcsa*) set to work (on sth); **ministero del** ~ Department of Employment; **ministero dei lavori pubblici** Department of Public Works. **lavori** *pl* **di casa** housework. **lavori** *pl* **in corso** roadworks. **lavori** *pl* **forzati** hard labour *sg*. ~ **di gruppo** *Sch* working in groups, group work. ~ **a maglia** knitting. ~ **nero** moonlighting. ~ **part time** part-time job. **lavori** *pl* **stradali** roadworks. ~ **straordinario** overtime. ~ **teatrale** play. ~ **a tempo pieno** full-time job

**lazza'rone** *nm* rascal

**le** *def art fpl* the; *vedi* **il** ● *pers pron* (*oggetto*) them; (*a lei*) her; (*forma di cortesia*) you

**'leader** *nm inv* leader. ~ **della marca** brand leader ● *a inv* leading; **prodotto** ~ market leader

**le'ale** *a* loyal

**leal'mente** *adv* loyally

**lealtà** *nf* loyalty

**'leasing** *nm inv* lease-purchase

**'lebbra** *nf* leprosy

**lecca 'lecca** *nm inv* lollipop

**leccapi'edi** *nmf inv pej* bootlicker

**lec'care** *vt* lick; *fig* suck up to

**lec'carsi** *vr* lick; (*fig: agghindarsi*) doll oneself up; **da** ~ **i baffi** mouth-watering

**lec'cata** *nf* lick

**lec'cato** *a* (*persona*) dressed to kill

**'leccio** *nm* holm oak

**leccor'nia** *nf* delicacy

**lecita'mente** *adv* lawfully

**'lecito** *a* lawful; (*permesso*) permissible

**'ledere** *vt* damage; *Med* injure

**'lega** *nf* league; (*di metalli*) alloy; **far** ~ **con qcno** take up with sb. ~ **doganale** customs union

**le'gaccio** *nm* string; (*delle scarpe*) shoelace

**le'gale** *a* legal ● *nm* lawyer

**legalità** *nf* legality

**legaliz'zare** *vt* authenticate; (*rendere legale*) legalize

**legalizzazi'one** *nf* legalization

**legal'mente** *adv* legally

**le'game** *nm* tie; (*amoroso*) liaison; (*connes-*

*sione*) link. ~ **di parentela** family relationship. ~ **di sangue** blood relationship. ~ **sentimentale** emotional relationship

**lega'mento** *nm Med* ligament

**le'gare** *vt* tie; tie up (*persona*); tie together (*due cose*); (*unire, rilegare*) bind; alloy (*metalli*); (*connettere*) connect; **legarsela al dito** *fig* bear a grudge ● *vi* (*far lega*) get on well

**le'garsi** *vr* bind oneself; ~ **a qcno** become attached to sb

**lega'tario, -a** *nmf* legatee

**le'gato** *nm* legacy; *Relig* legate

**lega'tura** *nf* tying; (*di libro*) binding

**legazi'one** *nf* legation

**le'genda** *nf* legend

**'legge** *nf* law; (*parlamentare*) act; **a norma di** ~ by law. ~ **marziale** martial law

**leg'genda** *nf* legend; (*didascalia*) caption

**leggen'dario** *a* legendary

**'leggere** *vt/i* read; ~ **male** (*sbagliato*) misread

**legge'rezza** *nf* lightness; (*frivolezza*) frivolity; (*incostanza*) fickleness

**legger'mente** *adv* slightly

**leg'gero** *a* light; (*bevanda*) weak; (*lieve*) slight; (*frivolo*) frivolous; (*incostante*) fickle; ~ **come una piuma** [as] light as a feather; **alla leggera** lightly

**leggi'adro** *a* liter graceful

**leg'gibile** *a* (*scrittura*) legible; (*stile*) readable

**leg'gio** *nm* lectern; *Mus* music stand

**legife'rare** *vi* legislate

**legio'nario** *nm* legionary

**legi'one** *nf* legion

**legisla'tivo** *a* legislative

**legisla'tore** *nm* legislator

**legisla'tura** *nf* legislature

**legislazi'one** *nf* legislation

**legittima'mente** *adv* legitimately

**legittimità** *nf* legitimacy

**le'gittimo** *a* legitimate; (*giusto*) proper; **legittima difesa** self-defence

**'legna** *nf* firewood

**le'gnaia** *nf* woodshed

**le'gname** *nm* timber

**le'gnata** *nf* blow with a stick

**'legno** *nm* wood; **di** ~ wooden; **legni** *pl Mus* woodwind. ~ **compensato** plywood

**le'gnoso** *a* woody; (*di legno*) wooden; (*gambe*) stiff; (*movimento*) wooden

**le'gume** *nm* pod

**'lei** *pers pron* (*soggetto*) she; (*oggetto, con prep*) her; (*forma di cortesia*) you; **lo ha fatto** ~ **stessa** she did it herself

**'lembo** *nm* edge; (*di terra*) strip

**'lemma** *nm* headword

**'lemming** *nm inv* lemming

**'lena** *nf* vigour

**'lendine** *nm* nit

**le'nire** *vt* soothe

**lenta'mente** *adv* slowly

**'lente** *nf* lens. ~ **a contatto** contact lens; **mettersi le lenti a contatto** put in one's contact lenses. **~ a contatto morbida** soft lens. **~ a contatto rigida** hard lens. **~ d'ingrandimento** magnifying glass. **~ semi-rigida** gas-permeable lens

**len'tezza** *nf* slowness

**len'ticchia** *nf* lentil

**len'tiggine** *nf* freckle

**'lento** *a* slow; (*allentato*) slack; ‹*abito*› loose

**'lenza** *nf* fishing-line

**len'zuolo** *nm* sheet; **le lenzuola** the sheets. **~ con gli angoli** fitted sheet. **~ funebre** shroud

**leon'cino** *nm* lion cub

**le'one** *nm* lion; *Astr* Leo. **~ marino** sea lion

**leo'nessa** *nf* lioness

**leo'pardo** *nm* leopard

**lepo'rino** *a* **labbro ~** hare-lip

**'lepre** *nf* hare

**le'protto** *nm* leveret

**'lercio** *a* filthy

**lerci'ume** *nm* filth

**'lesbica** *nf* lesbian

**'lesbico** *a* lesbian

**lesi'nare** *vt* grudge ● *vi* be stingy

**lesio'nare** *vt* damage

**lesi'one** *nf* lesion; (*danno*) damage. **~ cerebrale** brain damage. **~ interna** internal injury. **lesioni** *pl* **personali** grievous bodily harm, GBH

**'leso** *pp di* **ledere** ● *a* injured; **lesa maestà** high treason

**les'sare** *vt* boil

**lessi'cale** *a* lexical

**'lessico** *nm* vocabulary

**lessicogra'fia** *nf* lexicography

**lessi'cografo, -a** *nmf* lexicographer

**'lesso** *a* boiled ● *nm* boiled meat

**'lesto** *a* quick; ‹*mente*› sharp. **~ di mano** light-fingered

**le'tale** *a* lethal

**leta'maio** *nm* dunghill; *fig* pigsty

**le'tame** *nm* dung

**le'targico** *a* lethargic

**le'targo** *nm* lethargy; (*di animali*) hibernation

**le'tizia** *nf* joy

**'lettera** *nf* letter; **alla ~** literally; **eseguire qcsa alla ~** carry out sth to the letter; **lettere** *pl* (*letteratura*) literature *sg*; *Univ* Arts; **dottore in lettere** BA, Bachelor of Arts. **~ d'accompagnamento** covering letter. **~ d'amore** love letter. **~ assicurata** registered letter. **~ di cambio** bill of exchange. **~ di credito** letter of credit. **~ maiuscola** capital [letter]. **~ minuscola** small letter. **~ di presentazione** letter of introduction. **~ raccomandata** recorded delivery letter. **~ di scuse** letter of apology. **~ di trasporto aereo** air waybill

**lette'rale** *a* literal

**letteral'mente** *adv* literally

**lette'rario** *a* literary

**lette'rato** *a* well-read ● *nm* scholar; **letterati** *pl* literati

**lettera'tura** *nf* literature

**letti'era** *nf* (*per gatto*) litter

**let'tiga** *nf* stretcher

**let'tino** *nm* cot; *Med* couch. **~ [pieghevole]** camp bed

**'letto** *nm* bed; **andare a ~** go to bed; **[ri]fare il ~** make the bed. **~ a castello** bunkbed. **~ di fiume** river bed. **letti** *pl* **gemelli** twin beds. **~ matrimoniale** double bed. **~ a una piazza** single bed. **~ a due piazze** double bed. **~ singolo** single bed

**Let'tonia** *nf* Latvia

**letto'rato** *nm* (*corso*) tutorial

**let|'tore, -'trice** *nmf* reader; *Univ* language assistant ● *nm* *Comput* disk drive. **~ di CD** CD player, CD system. **~ [di] CD-ROM** CD-Rom drive. **~ di codice a barre** barcode reader, scanner. **~ di compact disc** compact disc player. **~ di disco** disk drive. **~ di floppy** floppy [disk] drive

**let'tura** *nf* reading

**leuce'mia** *nf* leukaemia

**'leva** *nf* lever; *Mil* call-up; **nuove leve** *pl* new blood, young blood; **far ~** lever. **~ del cambio** gear lever. **~ di comando** control lever

**le'vante** *nm* East; (*vento*) east wind

**leva'punti** *nm inv* staple remover

**le'vare** *vt* (*alzare*) raise; (*togliere*) take away; (*rimuovere*) take off; (*estrarre*) pull out; lift, abolish ‹*divieto, tassa*›. **~ di mezzo qcsa** get sth out of the way

**le'varsi** *vr* move (**da** away from); ‹*vento:*› get up; ‹*sole:*› rise; **~ di mezzo** get out of the way

**le'vata** *nf* rising; (*di posta*) collection

**leva'taccia** *nf* **fare una ~** get up at the crack of dawn

**leva'toio** *a* **ponte ~** drawbridge

**leva'trice** *nf* midwife

**leva'tura** *nf* intelligence

**levi'gare** *vt* smooth; (*con carta vetro*) rub down

**levi'gato** *a* ‹*superficie*› polished; ‹*pelle*› smooth

**leviga'trice** *nf* sander

**levi'tare** *vi* levitate

**levitazi'one** *nf* levitation

**Le'vitico** *nm* Leviticus

**levri'ero** *nm* greyhound. **~ afgano** Afghan hound

**lezi'one** *nf* lesson; *Univ* lecture; (*rimprovero*) rebuke. **~ di guida** driving lesson. **~ di italiano** Italian lesson, Italian class

**lezi'oso** *a* ‹*stile, modi*› affected

**'lezzo** *nm* stench

**li** *pers pron mpl* them

**lì** *adv* there; **fin lì** as far as there; **giù di lì** thereabouts; **lì per lì** there and then; **la cosa è finita lì** that was the end of it

**li'ana** *nf* liana

**liba'nese** *a & nmf* Lebanese

**Li'bano** *nm* Lebanon

**'libbra** *nf* (*peso*) pound

**li'beccio** *nm* south-west wind

**li'bello** *nm* libel

**li'bellula** *nf* dragon-fly

**libe'rale** *a* liberal; (*generoso*) generous ● *nmf* liberal

**libera'lismo** *nm* ~ [**economico**] economic liberalism

**liberalità** *nf* generosity

**liberal'mente** *adv* liberally

**libe'rare** *vt* free; release ⟨*prigioniero*⟩; vacate ⟨*stanza*⟩; (*salvare*) rescue

**libe'rarsi** *vr* ⟨*stanza*:⟩ become vacant; *Teleph* become free; (*da impegno*) get out of it; ~ **.di** get rid of

**libera|'tore, -'trice** *a* liberating ● *nmf* liberator

**libera'torio** *a* liberating; **pagamento** ~ full and final payment

**liberazi'one** *nf* liberation; **la L~** (*ricorrenza*) Liberation Day. ~ **della donna** women's liberation, women's lib

**libe'rismo** *nm* free trade

**'libero** *a* free; ⟨*strada*⟩ clear; ~ **come l'aria** free as a bird. ~ **arbitrio** *nm* free will. ~ **docente** *nm* qualified university lecturer. ~ **professionista** *nm* self-employed person

**libertà** *nf* freedom; (*di prigioniero*) release; ~ *pl* (*confidenze*) liberties; **prendersi la ~ di fare qcsa** take the liberty of doing sth. ~ **di espressione** freedom of speech. ~ **di pensiero** freedom of thought. ~ **provvisoria** *Jur* bail. ~ **di stampa** freedom of the press. ~ **vigilata** probation

**liber'tino, -a** *a* dissolute, libertine ● *nmf* libertine

**'liberty** *nm & a inv* Art Nouveau

**'Libia** *nf* Libya

**'libico, -a** *a & nmf* Libyan

**li'bidine** *nf* lust

**libidi'noso** *a* lustful

**li'bido** *nf* libido

**li'braio** *nm* bookseller

**libre'ria** *nf* (*biblioteca*) library; (*negozio*) bookshop; (*mobile*) bookcase

**li'bretto** *nm* booklet; *Mus* libretto. ~ **degli assegni** cheque book. ~ **di circolazione** logbook. ~ **d'istruzioni** instruction booklet. ~ **di risparmio** savings account; (*documento*) passbook, savings book. ~ **universitario** *book held by students which records details of their exam performances*

**'libro** *nm* book. ~ **bianco** White Paper. ~ **dei canti** hymn-book. ~ **contabile** account book. ~ **di esercizi** workbook. ~ **di fumetti** comic book. ~ **giallo** crime novel. ~ **mastro** *Comm* ledger. ~ **paga** payroll. ~ **di ricette** cookbook, recipe book. **libri** *pl* **sociali** company's books. ~ **tascabile** paperback. ~ **di testo** course book

**li'cantropo** *nm* werewolf

**lice'ale** *nmf* secondary-school student ● *a* secondary-school *attrib*

**li'cenza** *nf* licence; (*permesso*) permission; *Mil* leave; *Sch* school-leaving certificate; **essere in** ~ be on leave. ~ **di caccia** hunting licence. ~ **di esportazione** export licence. ~ **matrimoniale** marriage licence. ~

**di pesca** fishing licence. ~ **poetica** poetic licence. ~ **di porto d'armi** gun licence

**licenzia'mento** *nm* dismissal

**licenzi'are** *vt* dismiss, sack *fam*; (*conferire un diploma*) grant a school-leaving certificate to

**licenzi'arsi** *vr* (*da un impiego*) resign; (*accomiatarsi*) take one's leave

**licenzi'oso** *a* licentious

**li'ceo** *nm* secondary school, high school. ~ **classico** *secondary school with an emphasis on humanities*. ~ **scientifico** *secondary school with an emphasis on sciences*

**li'chene** *nm* lichen

**'lido** *nm* beach

**'Liechtenstein** *nm* Liechtenstein

**lieta'mente** *adv* happily

**li'eto** *a* glad; ⟨*evento*⟩ happy; **molto** ~! pleased to meet you!

**li'eve** *a* light; (*debole*) faint; (*trascurabile*) slight

**lievi'tare** *vi* rise ● *vt* leaven

**li'evito** *nm* yeast. ~ **in polvere** baking powder

**lift** *nm inv* liftboy

**'lifting** *nm inv* face-lift

**'ligio** *a* **essere** ~ **al dovere** have a sense of duty

**li'gnaggio** *nm* lineage

**'ligneo** *a* wooden

**'lilla** *nf Bot* lilac ● *nm* (*colore*) lilac

**'lima** *nf* file

**limacci'oso** *a* slimy

**li'manda** *nf* dab

**li'mare** *vt* file

**lima'tura** *nf* (*atto*) filing; (*residui*) filings *pl*

**'limbo** *nm* limbo

**li'metta** *nf* ~ [**da unghie**] nail file; (*di carta*) emery board

**limi'tare** *nm* threshold ● *vt* limit

**limi'tarsi** *vr* ~ **a fare qcsa** restrict oneself to doing sth; ~ **in qcsa** cut down on sth

**limitata'mente** *adv* to a limited extent

**limita'tivo** *a* limiting

**limi'tato** *a* limited

**limitazi'one** *nf* limitation

**'limite** *a* ⟨*caso*⟩ extreme ● *nm* limit; (*confine*) boundary; **entro certi limiti** within certain limits. ~ **di credito** credit limit, credit ceiling. ~ **di sopportazione** breaking point. ~ **di sosta** 'restricted parking'. ~ **di tempo** time limit. ~ **di velocità** speed limit; **rispettare il** ~ ~ ~ keep to the speed limit

**li'mitrofo** *a* neighbouring

**'limo** *nm* slime

**limo'nata** *nf* (*bibita*) lemonade; (*succo*) lemon juice. ~ **amara** bitter lemon

**li'mone** *nm* lemon; (*albero*) lemon tree

**'limpido** *a* clear; ⟨*occhi*⟩ limpid

**'lince** *nf* lynx

**linci'are** *vt* lynch

**'lindo** *a* neat; (*pulito*) clean

**'linea** *nf* line; (*di autobus, aereo*) route; (*di metro*) line; (*di abito*) cut; (*di auto, mobile*) design; (*fisico*) figure; **in** ~ **d'aria** as the crow flies: **è caduta la ~** I've been cut off; **in ~ di massima** as a rule; **a grandi linee** in outline; **mantenere la ~** keep one's figure; **in ~** *Comput* on-line; **in prima ~** in the front line; **mettersi in ~** line up; **nave di ~** liner; **volo di ~** scheduled flight. **~ aerea** airline. **~ d'arrivo** *Sport* finishing line. **~ commutata** *Teleph* switched line. **~ di confine** boundary. **~ continua** unbroken line. **~ dedicata** dedicated line. **~ di demarcazione** border line. **~ ferroviaria** railway line. **~ di fondo** baseline. **~ d'immersione** water line. **~ laterale** *Sport* touch line. **linee** *pl* **della mano** lines of the hand. **~ di marea** tidemark. **~ mediana** *Sport* halfway line. **~ di partenza** *Sport* starting line. **~ principale** *Rail* main line. **~ punteggiata** dotted line. **~ secondaria** *Rail* branch line. **~ di tiro** line of fire. **~ tratteggiata** broken line

**linea'menti** *nmpl* features

**line'are** *a* linear; ⟨*discorso*⟩ to the point; ⟨*ragionamento*⟩ consistent

**line'etta** *nf* (*tratto lungo*) dash; (*d'unione*) hyphen

**'linfa** *nf Anat* lymph; *Bot* sap. **~ vitale** *fig* life blood

**lin'fatico** *a Anat* lymphatic

**linfoghi'andola** *nf* lymph gland

**linfo'nodo** *nm* lymph node

**linge'rie** *nf* lingerie

**lin'gotto** *nm* ingot

**'lingua** *nf* tongue; (*linguaggio*) language; **avere la ~ lunga** *fig* have a big mouth. **~ moderna** modern language. **~ morta** dead language. **~ straniera** foreign language

**lingu'accia** *nf* (*persona*) backbiter; **fare le linguacce** put one's tongue out (**a a**)

**lingu'aggio** *nm* language. **~ infantile** baby-talk. **~ dei segni** sign language

**lingu'etta** *nf* (*di scarpa*) tongue; (*di strumento*) reed; (*di busta*) flap; *Mus* reed; (*per tirare*) tab

**lingu'ista** *nmf* linguist

**lingu'istica** *nf* linguistics

**lingu'istico** *a* linguistic

**'lino** *nm Bot* flax; (*tessuto*) linen

**li'noleum** *nm* linoleum

**liofiliz'zare** *vt* freeze-dry

**liofiliz'zato** *a* freeze dried

**li'pide** *nm* lipid

**liposuzi'one** *nf* liposuction

**li'quame** *nm* slurry

**lique'fare** *vt* liquefy; (*sciogliere*) melt

**lique'farsi** *vr* liquefy; (*sciogliersi*) melt

**liqui'dare** *vt* liquidate; settle ⟨*conto*⟩; pay off ⟨*debiti*⟩; clear ⟨*merce*⟩; (*fam: uccidere*) get rid of

**liquida'tore** *nm* liquidator

**liquidazi'one** *nf* liquidation; (*di conti*) settling; (*di merce*) clearance sale. **~ totale [per cessata attività]** closing-down sale

**'liquido** *a & nm* liquid. **~ dei freni** brake fluid. **~ scongelante** *Auto* de-icer. **~ tergicristallo** screen wash

**liqui'gas**® *nm inv* Calor gas ᴿ

**liqui'rizia** *nf* liquorice

**li'quore** *nm* liqueur; **liquori** *pl* (*bevande alcooliche*) liquors

**'lira** *nf* lira; *Mus* lyre. **~ sterlina** pound sterling

**'lirico, -a** *a* lyrical; ⟨*poesia*⟩ lyric; ⟨*cantante, musica*⟩ opera *attrib* ● *nf* lyric poetry; *Mus* opera

**li'rismo** *nm* lyricism

**'lisca** *nf* fishbone; **avere la ~** (*fam: nel parlare*) have a lisp

**lisci'are** *vt* smooth; (*accarezzare*) stroke

**'liscio** *a* smooth; ⟨*capelli*⟩ straight; ⟨*liquore*⟩ neat, straight; ⟨*acqua minerale*⟩ still; **passarla liscia** get away with it

**li'seuse** *nf inv* bed jacket, liseuse

**'liso** *a* worn [out]

**'lista** *nf* list; (*striscia*) strip; **fare una ~** make out a list. **~ di attesa** waiting list; **in ~ ~ ~** on the waiting list; *Aeron* on stand-by. **~ elettorale** list of candidates. **~ degli invitati** guest list. **~ nera** blacklist. **~ di nozze** wedding list. **~ della spesa** shopping list. **~ dei vini** wine list

**li'stare** *vt* edge; *Comput* list

**li'stino** *nm* list. **~ di borsa** Stock-Exchange list. **~ dei cambi** exchange rates *pl*. **~ [dei] prezzi** price list

**Lit.** *abbr* (**lire italiane**) Italian lire

**lita'nia** *nf* litany

**'litchi** *nm inv* lychee

**'lite** *nf* quarrel; (*baruffa*) row; *Jur* lawsuit

**liti'gante** *nmf Jur* litigant

**liti'gare** *vi* quarrel; *Jur* litigate

**li'tigio** *nm* quarrel

**litigi'oso** *a* quarrelsome

**'litio** *nm* lithium

**litogra'fia** *nf* (*procedimento*) lithography; (*stampa*) lithograph

**li'tografo, -a** *nmf* lithographer

**lito'rale** *a* coastal ● *nm* coast

**lito'raneo** *a* coastal

**'litro** *nm* litre

**Litu'ania** *nf* Lithuania

**litu'ano, -a** *a & nmf* Lithuanian

**litur'gia** *nf* liturgy

**li'turgico** *a* liturgical

**li'uto** *nm* lute

**li'vella** *nf* level. **~ a bolla d'aria** spirit level

**livella'mento** *nm* levelling out, levelling off

**livel'lare** *vt* level

**livel'larsi** *vr* level out

**livella'tore** *a* levelling

**livella'trice** *nf* bulldozer

**li'vello** *nm* level; **passaggio a ~** level crossing; **sotto/sul ~ del mare** below/above sea level; **ad alto ~** ⟨*conferenza, trattative*⟩ top-level, high-level; **a più livelli** multilevel. **~ di guardia** danger level. **~ di magazzino** stock level. **~ occupazionale** level of employment

**'livido** *a* livid; (*per il freddo*) blue; ⟨*per una botta*⟩ black and blue; **~ di rabbia** livid ● *nm* bruise

**li'vore** *nm* spite

**Li'vorno** *nf* Leghorn

**li'vrea** *nf* livery

**'lizza** *nf* lists *pl*; **essere in ~ per qcsa** be in the running for sth

**lo** *def art m* (*before s + consonant, gn, ps, z*) the; *vedi il* ● *pron* (*riferito a persona*) him; (*riferito a cosa*) it; **non lo so** I don't know

**'lobbia** *nf* Homburg [hat]

**lob'bista** *nmf* lobbyist

**'lobby** *nf inv* lobby

**lo'belia** *nf* lobelia

**'lobo** *nm* lobe

**loboto'mia** *nf* lobotomy

**lo'cale** *a* local ● *nm* (*stanza*) room; (*treno*) local train; **locali** *pl* (*edifici*) premises. **~ notturno** night-club

**località** *nf* locality. **~ balneare** seaside resort. **~ turistica** tourist resort. **~ di villeggiatura** holiday resort

**localiz'zare** *vt* localize; (*reperire*) locate

**localiz'zarsi** *vr* **~ in** be located in

**localiz'zato** *a* localized

**localizzazi'one** *nf* localization; (*reperimento*) location

**local'mente** *adv* locally

**lo'canda** *nf* inn

**locandi'ere, -a** *nmf* innkeeper

**locan'dina** *nf* bill, poster

**loca'tario, -a** *nmf* tenant. **~ residente** sitting tenant

**loca'tivo** *a Gram* locative; *Jur* rental

**loca|'tore, -'trice** *nm* landlord ● *nf* landlady

**locazi'one** *nf* tenancy

**locomo'tiva** *nf* locomotive. **~ a vapore** steam engine

**locomo'tore** *nm* locomotive, engine

**locomozi'one** *nf* locomotion; **mezzi di ~** means of transport

**'loculo** *nm* burial niche

**lo'custa** *nf* locust

**locuzi'one** *nf* expression

**lo'dare** *vt* praise

**'lode** *nf* praise; **degno di ~** praiseworthy; **laurea con ~** first-class degree

**'loden** *nm inv* (*cappotto*) loden [coat]; (*stoffa*) loden

**lo'devole** *a* praiseworthy

**'lodola** *nf* lark

**loga'ritmo** *nm* logarithm

**'loggia** *nf* loggia; (*massonica*) lodge

**loggi'one** *nm* gallery, gods *pl*

**'logica** *nf* logic

**logica'mente** *adv* (*in modo logico*) logically; (*ovviamente*) of course

**logicità** *nf* logic

**'logico** *a* logical

**lo'gistica** *nf* logistics

**lo'gistico** *a* logistic[al]

**'logo** *nm inv* logo

**logope'dia** *nf* speech therapy

**logope'dista** *nmf* speech therapist

**logo'rante** *a* (*attesa, esperienza*) wearing

**logo'rare** *vt* wear out; (*sciupare*) waste

**logo'rarsi** *vr* wear out; (*persona:*) wear oneself out

**logo'rio** *nm* wear and tear; (*stress*) stress

**'logoro** *a* worn-out

**logor'roico** *a* loquacious

**lom'baggine** *nf* lumbago

**Lombar'dia** *nf* Lombardy

**lom'bardo** *a* Lombardy *attrib*

**lom'bare** *a* lumbar

**lom'bata** *nf* loin. **~ di manzo** sirloin

**'lombo** *nm Anat* loin

**lom'brico** *nm* earthworm

**londi'nese** *a* London *attrib* ● *nmf* Londoner

**'Londra** *nf* London

**long-'drink** *nm inv* long drink

**longevità** *nf* longevity

**lon'gevo** *a* long-lived

**longhe'rone** *nm* strut

**longi'lineo** *a* rangy

**longitudi'nale** *a* lengthwise

**longitudinal'mente** *adv* lengthwise

**longi'tudine** *nf* longitude

**long 'playing** *nm inv* LP, long-playing record

**lontana'mente** *adv* distantly; (*vagamente*) vaguely; **neanche ~** not for a moment

**lonta'nanza** *nf* distance; (*separazione*) separation; **in ~** in the distance

**lon'tano** *a* far; (*distante*) distant; (*nel tempo*) far-off, distant; (*parente*) distant; (*vago*) vague; (*assente*) absent; **più ~** further; **è ~ un paio di chilometri** it is a couple of kilometres away ● *adv* far [away]; **da ~** from a distance; **tenersi ~ da** keep away from; **andare ~** (*allontanarsi*) go away; (*avere successo*) go far

**'lontra** *nf* otter

**'lonza** *nf* (*lombata*) loin

**lo'quace** *a* talkative

**'lordo** *a* dirty; (*somma, peso*) gross; **al ~ di imposte** pre-tax

**'loro**[1] *pers pron pl* (*soggetto*) they; (*oggetto*) them; (*forma di cortesia*) you; **sta a ~** it is up to them

**'loro**[2] (**il ~** *m*, **la ~** *f*, **i ~** *mpl*, **le ~** *fpl*) *poss a* their; (*forma di cortesia*) your; **un ~ amico** a friend of theirs; (*forma di cortesia*) a friend of yours ● *poss pron* theirs; (*forma di cortesia*) yours; **i ~** (*famiglia*) their folk

**lo'sanga** *nf* lozenge; **a losanghe** diamond-shaped

**losca'mente** *adv* suspiciously

**'losco** *a* suspicious

**'loto** *nm* lotus

**'lotta** *nf* fight, struggle; (*contrasto*) conflict; *Sport* wrestling. **~ di classe** class struggle. **~ libera** all-in wrestling

**lot'tare** *vi* fight, struggle; *Sport, fig* wrestle

**lotta|'tore, -'trice** *nmf* wrestler

**lotte'ria** *nf* lottery

**lottiz'zare** *vt* divide up (*terreno*); *fig* parcel out

**lottizzazi'one** *nf* (*di terreno*) division into lots; *fig* parcelling out

**'lotto** *nm* [state] lottery; (*porzione*) lot; (*di terreno*) plot

**lozi'one** *nf* lotion. **~ idratante** moisturizer. **~ solare** suntan lotion

**lubrifi'cante** *a* lubricating ● *nm* lubricant

**lubrifi'care** *vt* lubricate

**luc'chetto** *nm* padlock

**lucci'cante** *a* sparkling

**lucci'care** *vi* sparkle

**lucci'chio** *nm* sparkle

**lucci'cone** *nm* far venire i lucciconi bring tears to the eyes

**'luccio** *nm* pike

**'lucciola** *nf* glow-worm; (*prostituta*) lady of the night

**'luce** *nf* light; *Auto* highlight; **accendere/ spegnere la** ~ switch the light on/off; **far** ~ **su** *fig* shed light on; **dare alla** ~ give birth to; **venire alla** ~ come to light. **luci** *pl* **di arresto** *Auto* stop lights. **luci** *pl* **d'atterraggio** landing lights. **luci** *pl* **d'emergenza** *Auto* hazard [warning] lights, hazards. ~ **della luna** moonlight. **luci** *pl* **di posizione** *Auto* sidelights. **luci** *pl* **posteriori** *Auto* rear-lights. **luci** *pl* **di retromarcia** *Auto* reversing lights. ~ **del sole** sunlight. ~ **stroboscopica** strobe

**lu'cente** *a* shining

**lucen'tezza** *nf* shine

**lucer'nario** *nm* skylight

**lu'certola** *nf* lizard

**lucida'labbra** *nm inv* lip gloss

**luci'dare** *vt* polish

**lucida'trice** *nf* [floor-]polisher

**'lucido** *a* shiny; (*pavimento, scarpe*) polished; (*chiaro*) clear; (*persona, mente*) lucid; (*occhi*) watery ● *nm* shine. ~ [**da scarpe**] [shoe] polish

**lucra'tivo** *a* lucrative

**'lucro** *nm* lucre; **senza fini di** ~ non-profit-making, not-for-profit *Am*

**luculli'ano** *a* (*pranzo*) lavish

**ludo'teca** *nf* playroom

**'luglio** *nm* July

**'lugubre** *a* gloomy

**'lui** *pers pron* (*soggetto*) he; (*oggetto, con prep*) him; **lo ha fatto** ~ **stesso** he did it himself

**lu'maca** *nf* (*mollusco*) snail; *fig* slowcoach

**'lume** *nm* lamp; (*luce*) light; **a** ~ **di candela** by candlelight; **perdere il** ~ **della ragione** be beside oneself with rage

**lumi'nare** *nmf* luminary

**lumi'narie** *nfpl* illuminations

**lumine'scente** *a* luminescent

**lumine'scenza** *nf* luminescence

**lu'mino** *nm* ~ **da notte** nightlight

**luminosa'mente** *adv* luminously

**luminosità** *nf* brightness

**lumi'noso** *a* luminous; (*stanza, cielo ecc*) bright; **idea luminosa** brain wave

**'luna** *nf* moon; **chiaro di** ~ moonlight; **avere la** ~ **storta** be in a bad mood. ~ **di miele** honeymoon. ~ **piena** full moon

**'luna park** *nm inv* fairground

**lu'nare** *a* lunar

**lu'naria** *nf* moonstone

**lu'nario** *nm* almanac; **sbarcare il** ~ make

[both] ends meet

**lu'natico** *a* moody

**lunedì** *nm inv* Monday; **di** ~ on Mondays

**lu'netta** *nf* half-moon [shape]

**lun'gaggine** *nf* slowness

**lunga'mente** *adv* at great length

**lun'ghezza** *nf* length; **di** ~ **media** medium-length. ~ **d'onda** wavelength

**'lungi** *adv* ero [ben] ~ **dall'immaginare che...** I never dreamt for a moment that...

**lungimi'rante** *a* far-seeing

**lungimi'ranza** *nf* far-sightedness

**'lungo** *a* long; (*diluito*) weak; (*lento*) slow; **a** ~ **andare** in the long run; **saperla lunga** be shrewd ● *nm* length; **andare per le lunghe** drag on; **di gran lunga** by far ● *prep* (*durante*) throughout; (*per la lunghezza di*) along

**lungofi'ume** *nm* riverside

**lungo'lago** *nm* lakeside

**lungo'mare** *nm inv* sea front

**lungome'traggio** *nm* feature film

**lu'notto** *nm* rear window. ~ **termico** heated rear window

**'lunula** *nf* half-moon

**lu'ogo** *nm* place; (*punto preciso*) spot; (*passo d'autore*) passage; **aver** ~ take place; **dar** ~ **a** give rise to; **fuori** ~ out of place; **del** (*usanze*) local. ~ **comune** cliché. ~ **di nascita** birth-place. ~ **natale** birthplace. ~ **pubblico** public place. ~ **di villeggiatura** holiday resort

**luogote'nente** *nm Mil* lieutenant

**'lupa** *nf* she-wolf

**lu'para** *nf* sawn-off shotgun

**lu'petto** *nm* Cub [Scout]

**'lupo** *nm* wolf. ~ **mannaro** werewolf

**'luppolo** *nm* hop

**'lurido** *a* filthy

**luri'dume** *nm* filth

**lu'singa** *nf* flattery

**lusin'gare** *vt* flatter

**lusin'garsi** *vr* flatter oneself; (*illudersi*) fool oneself

**lusinghi'ero** *a* flattering

**lus'sare** *vt* dislocate

**lus'sarsi** *vr* dislocate

**lussazi'one** *nf* dislocation

**Lussem'burgo** *nm* Luxembourg

**'lusso** *nm* luxury; **di** ~ luxury *attrib*

**lussuosa'mente** *adv* luxuriously

**lussu'oso** *a* luxurious

**lussureggi'ante** *a* luxuriant

**lus'suria** *nf* lust

**lussuri'oso** *a* dissolute

**lu'strare** *vt* polish

**lu'strino** *nm* sequin

**'lustro** *a* shiny ● *nm* sheen; *fig* prestige; (*quinquennio*) five-year period

**lute'rano** *a & nmf* Lutheran

**'lutto** *nm* mourning; **parato a** ~ draped in black; ~ **stretto** deep mourning

**luttu'oso** *a* mournful

# Mm

**m** *abbr* (**metro**) m

**ma** *conj* but; (*eppure*) yet; **ma!** (*dubbio*) I don't know; (*indignazione*) really!; **ma davvero?** really?; **ma va?** really?; **ma si!** why not!; (*certo che sì*) of course!

**'macabro** *a* macabre

**macché** *int* of course not!

**macche'roni** *nmpl* macaroni *sg*

**macche'ronico** *a* (*italiano*) broken

**'macchia¹** *nf* stain; (*di diverso colore*) spot; (*piccola*) speck; **senza ~** spotless; **spargersi a ~ d'olio** spread rapidly. **~ di colore** splash of colour. **~ d'inchiostro** ink stain. **~ di sangue** bloodstain

**'macchia²** *nf* (*boscaglia*) scrub; **darsi alla ~** take to the woods

**macchi'are** *vt* stain

**macchi'arsi** *vr* stain

**macchi'ato** *a* (*caffè*) with a dash of milk; (*pelo*) spotted; **~ di** (*sporco*) stained with; **~ d'inchiostro** ink-stained, inky. ●*nm* (*caffè*) espresso with a dash of milk

**macchi'etta** *nf* spot

**'macchina** *nf* machine; (*motore*) engine; (*automobile*) car; **in ~** by car; **giro in ~** drive; **cimitero delle macchine** scrapyard. **~ del caffè** coffee-maker. **~ da cucire** sewing machine. **~ per l'espresso** coffee machine. **~ fotografica** camera. **~ obliteratrice** ticket-stamping machine. **~ da presa** cine camera. **~ da scrivere** typewriter. **~ sverniciante** paint stripper. **~ utensile** machine tool. **~ della verità** lie detector

**macchinal'mente** *adv* mechanically

**macchi'nare** *vt* plot

**macchi'nario** *nm* machinery

**macchinazi'oni** *nfpl* machinations, scheming

**macchi'netta** *nf* (*per i denti*) brace; (*per il caffè*) espresso coffee maker; (*accendino*) lighter

**macchi'nista** *nm* Rail engine driver; Naut engineer; Theat stagehand

**macchi'noso** *a* complicated

**Mace'donia** *nf* Macedonia

**mace'donia** *nf* fruit salad

**macel'laio** *nm* butcher

**macel'lare** *vt* slaughter

**macellazi'one** *nf* slaughtering

**macelle'ria** *nf* butcher's [shop]

**ma'cello** *nm* (*mattatoio*) slaughterhouse; *fig* shambles *sg*; **andare al ~** *fig* go to the slaughter; **mandare al ~** *fig* send to his/her death

**mace'rare** *vt* macerate; *fig* distress

**mace'rarsi** *vr* be consumed

**macerazi'one** *nf* maceration

**ma'cerie** *nfpl* rubble *sg*; (*rottami*) debris *sg*

**'macero** *nm* pulping; (*stabilimento*) pulping mill

**Mach** *nm inv* Mach

**ma'chete** *nm inv* machete

**machia'vellico** *a* Machiavellian

**ma'chismo** *nm* machismo

**'macho** *a* macho

**ma'cigno** *nm* boulder

**maci'lento** *a* emaciated

**'macina** *nf* millstone

**macinacaffè** *nm inv* coffee mill

**macina'pepe** *nm inv* pepper mill

**maci'nare** *vt* mill

**maci'nato** *a* ground ●*nm* (*carne*) mince

**maci'nino** *nm* mill; (*hum: macchina*) old banger

**maciul'lare** *vt* (*stritolare*) crush

**'macro** *nf inv* Comput macro

**macrobi'otica** *nf* **negozio di ~** health-food shop

**macrobi'otico** *a* macrobiotic

**macro'clima** *nm* macroclimate

**macro'cosmo** *nm* macrocosm

**macrofotogra'fia** *nf* macrophotography

**macro'scopico** *a* macroscopic

**macu'lato** *a* spotted

**Madaga'scar** *nm* Madagascar

**madami'gella** *nf* young lady

**'madia** *nf* cupboard with a covered trough on top for making bread

**'madido** *a* **~ di** damp with (*sudore*)

**Ma'donna** *nf* Our Lady

**mador'nale** *a* gross

**'madre** *nf* mother

**madre'lingua** *a inv* **inglese ~** English native speaker

**madre'patria** *nf* native land

**madre'perla** *nf* mother-of-pearl

**ma'drepora** *nf* madrepore

**madri'gale** *nm* madrigal

**ma'drina** *nf* godmother

**maestà** *nf* majesty

**maestosa'mente** *adv* majestically

**maestosità** *nf* majesty

**mae'stoso** *a* majestic

**ma'estra** *nf* teacher; *Sch* primary school teacher. **~ d'asilo** kindergarten teacher. **~ di canto** singing teacher. **~ di piano** piano teacher. **~ di sci** ski instructor

**mae'strale** *nm* northwest wind

**mae'stranza** *nf* workers *pl*

**mae'stria** *nf* mastery

**ma'estro** *nm* teacher; *Sch* primary school teacher; *Mus* maestro; (*esperto*) master. **colpo da ~** masterstroke. **~ d'asilo** kindergarten teacher. **~ di canto** singing teacher. **~ di cerimonie** master of ceremonies. **~ di piano** piano teacher. **~ di sci** ski instructor ● *a* (*principale*) main; (*di grande abilità*) skilful

**'mafia** *nf* Mafia

**mafi'oso** *a* of the Mafia ● *nm* member of the Mafia, Mafioso

**'maga** *nf* sorceress, magician

**ma'gagna** *nf* fault

**ma'gari** *adv* (*forse*) maybe ● *int* I wish! ● *conj* (*per esprimere desiderio*) if only; (*anche se*) even if

**magazzini'ere** *nm* storeman, warehouse-man

**magaz'zino** *nm* warehouse; (*emporio*) shop; **grande ~** department store. **magazzini** *pl* **portuali** naval stores

**Magg.** *abbr* (**maggiore**) Maj

**mag'gese** *nm* field lying fallow

**'maggio** *nm* May

**maggio'lino** *nm* May bug

**maggio'rana** *nf* marjoram

**maggio'ranza** *nf* majority

**maggio'rare** *vt* increase

**maggior'domo** *nm* butler

**maggi'ore** *a* (*di dimensioni, numero*) bigger, larger; (*superlativo*) biggest, largest; (*di età*) older; (*superlativo*) oldest; (*di importanza, Mus*) major; (*superlativo*) greatest; **la maggior parte** *di* most; **la maggior parte del tempo** most of the time ● *pron* (*di dimensioni*) the bigger, the larger; (*superlativo*) the biggest, the largest; (*di età*) the older; (*superlativo*) the oldest; (*di importanza*) the major; (*superlativo*) the greatest ● *nm Mil* major; *Aeron* squadron leader

**maggio'renne** *a* of age ● *nmf* adult

**maggiori'tario** *a* (*della maggioranza*) majority; (*sistema*) first-past-the-post *attrib*

**maggior'mente** *adv* [all] the more; (*più di tutto*) most

**'Magi** *nmpl* **i re ~** the Magi

**ma'gia** *nf* magic; (*trucco*) magic trick

**magica'mente** *adv* magically

**'magico** *a* magic

**magi'stero** *nm* (*insegnamento*) teaching; (*maestria*) skill; **facoltà di ~** arts faculty

**magi'strale** *a* masterly; **istituto ~** teacher-training college

**magistral'mente** *adv* in a masterly fashion

**magi'strato** *nm* magistrate

**magistra'tura** *nf* magistrature. **la ~** the Bench

**'maglia** *nf* stitch; (*lavoro ai ferri*) knitting; (*tessuto*) jersey; (*di rete*) mesh; (*di catena*) link; (*indumento*) vest; **fare la ~** knit. **~ diritta** knit. **~ rosa** (*ciclismo*) ≈ yellow jersey. **~ rovescia** purl

**magli'aia** *nf* knitter

**maglie'ria** *nf* knitwear

**magli'etta** *nf* **~** [**a maniche corte**] tee-shirt

**magli'ficio** *nm* knitwear factory

**ma'glina** *nf* (*tessuto*) jersey

**'maglio** *nm* mallet

**magli'one** *nm* sweater, jumper. **~ dolcevita** polo neck [jumper]. **~ a girocollo** crew neck [sweater]. **~ a V** V-neck [sweater]

**'magma** *nm* magma

**ma'gnaccia** *nm inv fam* pimp

**ma'gnanimo** *a* magnanimous

**ma'gnate** *nm* magnate

**ma'gnesia** *nf* magnesia

**ma'gnesio** *nm* magnesium

**ma'gnete** *nm* magnet

**magnetica'mente** *adv* magnetically

**ma'gnetico** *a* magnetic

**magne'tismo** *nm* magnetism

**magne'tofono** *nm* tape recorder

**magnifica'mente** *adv* magnificently

**magnifi'cenza** *nf* magnificence; (*generosità*) munificence

**ma'gnifico** *a* magnificent; (*generoso*) munificent

**magni'tudine** *nf Astr* magnitude

**'magno** *a* **aula magna** main hall

**ma'gnolia** *nf* magnolia

**'magnum** *nm inv* (*bottiglia*) magnum ● *nf inv* (*pistola*) magnum

**'mago** *nm* magician

**ma'gone** *nm* **avere il ~** be down; **mi è venuto il ~** I've got a lump in my throat

**'magra** *nf* low water

**ma'grezza** *nf* thinness

**'magro** *a* thin; (*carne*) lean; (*scarso*) meagre; **magra consolazione** cold comfort

**'mai** *adv* never; (*inter, talvolta*) ever; **caso ~** if anything; **caso ~ tornasse** in case he comes back; **come ~?** why?; **cosa ~?** what on earth?; **~ più** never again; **più che ~** more than ever; **quando ~?** whenever?; **quasi ~** hardly ever

**mai'ale** *nm* pig; (*carne*) pork. **~ arrosto** roast pork

**maia'lino** *nm* piglet

**mai'olica** *nf* majolica

**maio'nese** *nf* mayonnaise

**'mais** *nm* maize

**mai'uscola** *nf* capital [letter]

**mai'uscolo** *a* capital

**mai'zena** [R] *nf* cornflour

**mal** *vedi* **male**

**'mala** *nf sl* **la ~** the underworld

**malac'corto** *a* unwise

**mala'fede** *nf* bad faith

**malaf'fare** *nm* **gente di ~** shady characters *pl*

**mala'lingua** *nf* backbiter

**mala'mente** *adv* (*ridotto*) badly; (*rispondere*) rudely

**malan'dato** *a* in bad shape; (*di salute*) in poor health

**ma'lanimo** *nm* ill will

**ma'lanno** *nm* misfortune; (*malattia*) illness; **prendersi un ~** catch something

**mala'pena** *adv* a ~ hardly

**ma'laria** *nf* malaria

**mala'ticcio** *a* sickly

**ma'lato, -a** *a* ill, sick; ⟨*pianta*⟩ diseased ● *nmf* sick person. ~ **di mente** mentally ill person

**malat'tia** *nf* disease, illness; **ho preso due giorni di** ~ I had two days off sick; **essere in** ~ be on sick leave. ~ **nervosa** nervous disease. ~ **venerea** venereal disease, VD

**malaugurata'mente** *adv* unfortunately

**malaugu'rato** *a* ill-omened

**malau'gurio** *nm* bad *o* ill omen

**mala'vita** *nf* underworld

**malavi'toso, -a** *nmf* gangster

**mala'voglia** *nf* unwillingness; **di** ~ unwillingly

**malcapi'tato** *a* wretched

**malce'lato** *a* ill-concealed

**mal'concio** *a* battered

**malcon'tento** *nm* discontent

**malco'stume** *nm* immorality

**mal'destro** *a* awkward; (*inesperto*) inexperienced

**maldi'cente** *a* slanderous

**maldi'cenza** *nf* slander

**maldi'sposto** *a* ill-disposed

**'male** *adv* badly; **funzionare** ~ not work properly; **star** ~ be ill; **star** ~ **a qcno** ⟨*vestito ecc.*⟩ not suit sb; **rimanerci** ~ be hurt; **ho dormito** ~ I didn't sleep well; **non c'è** ~! not bad at all! ● *nm* evil; (*dolore*) pain, ache; (*malattia*) illness; (*danno*) harm. **distinguere il bene dal** ~ know right from wrong; **andare a** ~ go off; **aver** ~ **a** have a pain in; **dove hai** ~? where does it hurt?, where is the pain?; **far** ~ **a qcno** (*provocare dolore*) hurt sb; ⟨*cibo:*⟩ be bad for sb; **le cipolle mi fanno** ~ onions don't agree with me; **mi fa** ~ **la schiena** my back is hurting; **farsi** ~ **alla schiena** hurt one's back. **mal d'aereo** airsickness. **mal d'aria** airsickness; **soffrire il** ~ ~ be airsick. **mal d'auto** carsickness. **mal di denti** toothache. **mal di gola** sore throat. **mal di mare** seasickness; **avere il** ~ ~ ~ be seasick. **mal d'orecchi** earache. **mal di pancia** stomach-ache. **mal di testa** headache

**maledetta'mente** *adv* flipping

**male'detto** *a* cursed; (*orribile*) awful

**male'dire** *vt* curse

**maledizi'one** *nf* curse; ~! damn!

**maleducata'mente** *adv* rudely

**maledu'cato** *a* ill-mannered

**maleducazi'one** *nf* rudeness

**male'fatta** *nf* misdeed

**male'ficio** *nm* witchcraft

**ma'lefico** *a* ⟨*azione*⟩ evil; (*nocivo*) harmful

**maleodo'rante** *a* foul-smelling

**ma'lese** *a* & *nmf* Malaysian

**Ma'lesia** *nf* Malaysia

**ma'lessere** *nm* indisposition; *fig* uneasiness

**ma'levolo** *a* malevolent

**malfa'mato** *a* of ill repute

**mal'fatto** *a* badly done; (*malformato*) ill-shaped

**malfat'tore** *nm* wrongdoer

**mal'fermo** *a* unsteady; ⟨*salute*⟩ poor

**malfor'mato** *a* misshapen

**malformazi'one** *nf* malformation

**mal'gascio, -a** *a* & *nmf* Malagasy

**malgo'verno** *nm* misgovernment

**mal'grado** *prep* in spite of ● *conj* although

**'Mali** *nm* Mali

**ma'lia** *nf* spell

**maligna'mente** *adv* maliciously

**mali'gnare** *vi* malign

**malignità** *nf* malice; *Med* malignancy

**ma'ligno** *a* malicious; (*perfido*) evil; *Med* malignant

**malinco'nia** *nf* melancholy

**malinconica'mente** *adv* melancholically

**malin'conico** *a* melancholy

**malincu'ore: a** ~ *adv* unwillingly, reluctantly

**malinfor'mato** *a* misinformed

**malintenzio'nato, -a** *nmf* miscreant

**malin'teso** *a* mistaken ● *nm* misunderstanding

**ma'lizia** *nf* malice; (*astuzia*) cunning; (*espediente*) trick

**maliziosa'mente** *adv* mischievously, naughtily

**maliziosità** *nf* naughtiness

**malizi'oso** *a* (*birichino*) mischievous, naughty

**malle'abile** *a* malleable

**mal'leolo** *nm Anat* malleolus

**malleva'dore** *nm* guarantor

**'mallo** *nm* husk

**mal'loppo** *nm fam* loot

**malme'nare** *vt* ill-treat

**mal'messo** *a* (*vestito male*) shabbily dressed; ⟨*casa*⟩ poorly furnished; (*fig: senza soldi*) hard up

**malnu'trito** *a* undernourished

**malnutrizi'one** *nf* malnutrition

**'malo** *a* in ~ **modo** badly

**ma'locchio** *nm* evil eye

**ma'lora** *nf* ruin; **della** ~ awful; **andare in** ~ go to ruin

**ma'lore** *nm* illness; **essere colto da** ~ be suddenly taken ill

**malri'dotto** *a* ⟨*persona*⟩ in a sorry state; ⟨*auto, casa*⟩ dilapidated, in a sorry state

**mal'sano** *a* unhealthy

**malsi'curo** *a* unsafe; (*incerto*) uncertain

**'malta** *nf* mortar

**mal'tempo** *nm* bad weather

**mal'tese** *a* & *nmf* Maltese

**'malto** *nm* malt

**mal'tosio** *nm* maltose

**maltratta'mento** *nm* ill-treatment

**maltrat'tare** *vt* ill-treat

**malu'more** *nm* bad mood; **di** ~ in a bad mood

**'malva** *a inv* mauve

**mal'vagio** *a* wicked

**malvagità** *nf* wickedness

**malva'sia** *nf* type of dessert wine
**malversazi'one** *nf* embezzlement
**mal'visto** *a* unpopular (**da** with)
**malvi'vente** *nm* criminal
**malvolenti'eri** *adv* unwillingly
**malvo'lere** *vt* **farsi ~** make oneself unpopular; **prendere qcno a ~** take a dislike to sb
**'mamma** *nf* mummy, mum; **~ mia!** good gracious!
**mam'mario** *a* mammary
**mam'mella** *nf* breast
**mam'mifero** *nm* mammal
**mam'mismo** *nm* (del figlio) dependency on the mother figure; (della madre) excessive motherliness
**mammogra'fia** *nf* mammograph
**'mammola** *nf* violet
**mammo'letta** *nf* shrinking violet
**mam'mone** *nm* mummy's boy
**mam'mut** *nm inv* mammoth
**ma'nata** *nf* handful; (colpo) slap
**'manca** *nf* vedi manco
**manca'mento** *nm* **avere un ~** faint
**man'cante** *a* missing
**man'canza** *nf* lack; (assenza) absence; (insufficienza) shortage; (fallo) fault; (imperfezione) defect; **in ~ d'altro** failing all else; **sento la sua ~** I miss him. **~ di tatto** lack of tact, indelicacy
**man'care** *vi* be lacking; (essere assente) be missing; (venir meno) fail; (morire) pass away; **~ di** be lacking in; **~ a** fail to keep (promessa); **mi manca casa** I miss home; **mi manchi** I miss you; **mi è mancato il tempo** I didn't have [the] time; **mi mancano 1000 lire** I'm 1,000 lire short; **quanto manca alla partenza?** how long before we leave?; **è mancata la corrente** there was a power failure; **sentirsi ~** feel faint; **sentirsi ~ il respiro** be unable to breathe [properly] ● *vt* miss (bersaglio); **è mancato poco che cadesse** he nearly fell
**man'cato** *a* (appuntamento) missed; (tentativo) unsuccessful; (occasione) wasted
**'manche** *nf inv* heat
**man'chevole** *a* defective
**'mancia** *nf* tip. **~ competente** reward
**manci'ata** *nf* handful
**man'cino** *a* left-handed
**'manco, -a** *a* left ● *nf* left hand ● *adv* (nemmeno) not even
**man'dante** *nmf* (di delitto) instigator; Jur principal
**manda'rancio** *nm* clementine
**man'dare** *vt* send; (emettere) give off; utter (suono); **~ a chiamare** send for; **~ avanti la casa** run the house; **~ giù** (ingoiare) swallow
**manda'rino** *nm* Bot mandarin
**man'data** *nf* consignment; (di serratura) turn; **chiudere a doppia ~** double lock
**manda'tario** *nm* Jur agent
**man'dato** *nm* (incarico) mandate; Jur warrant; (di pagamento) money order. **~ di comparizione [in giudizio]** subpoena. **~ di**
**pagamento** money order. **~ di perquisizione** search warrant
**man'dibola** *nf* jaw
**mando'lino** *nm* mandolin
**'mandorla** *nf* almond; **a ~** (occhi) almond-shaped. **~ amara** bitter almond
**mandor'lato** *nm* nut brittle (type of nougat)
**'mandorlo** *nm* almond[-tree]
**man'dragola** *nf* mandrake
**'mandria** *nf* herd
**mandri'ano** *nm* cowherd
**man'drillo** *nm* (scimmia) mandrill; (attrezzo) mandrel; fig fam goat
**maneg'gevole** *a* easy to handle
**maneggi'are** *vt* handle
**ma'neggio** *nm* handling; (intrigo) plot; (scuola di equitazione) riding school
**ma'nesco** *a* quick to hit out
**ma'netta** *nf* lever; **a tutta ~** flat out; **manette** *pl* handcuffs
**man'forte** *nm* **dare ~ a qcno** support sb
**manga'nello** *nm* truncheon
**manga'nese** *nm* manganese
**mange'reccio** *a* edible
**mangiacas'sette** *nm inv* cassette player
**mangia'dischi**[R] *nm inv* portable record player
**mangia'fumo** *a inv* **candela ~** air-purifying candle
**mangia'nastri** *nm inv* cassette player
**mangi'are** *vt/i* eat; (consumare) eat up; (corrodere) eat away; take (scacchi, carte ecc) ● *nm* eating; (cibo) food; (pasto) meal; **dar da ~ al gatto/cane** feed the cat/dog
**mangi'arsi** *vr* **~ le parole** mumble; **~ le unghie** bite one's nails
**mangia'soldi** *a inv* **macchinetta ~** one-armed bandit
**mangi'ata** *nf* big meal; **farsi una bella ~ di...** feast on...
**mangia'toia** *nf* manger
**mangia|'tore, -'trice** *nmf* eater. **~ di fuoco** fire-eater. **mangiatrice di uomini** man-eater
**man'gime** *nm* fodder. **~ per i polli** chicken feed
**mangi'one, -a** *nmf fam* glutton
**mangiucchi'are** *vt* nibble
**'mango** *nm* mango
**man'grovia** *nf* mangrove
**man'gusta** *nf* mongoose
**ma'nia** *nf* mania. **~ di grandezza** delusions of grandeur. **~ di persecuzione** persecution complex
**mania'cale** *a* manic
**ma'niaco, -a** *a* maniacal ● *nmf* maniac. **~ sessuale** sex maniac
**ma'niaco-depres'sivo** *a & nmf* manic-depressive
**'Manica** *nf* **la ~** the [English] Channel
**'manica** *nf* sleeve; (fam: gruppo) band; **a maniche lunghe** long-sleeved; **senza maniche** sleeveless; **essere in maniche di camicia** be in shirt sleeves; **essere di ~ larga** be generous; **essere di ~ stretta** be strict. **~ a vento** wind sock

**manica'retto** nm tasty dish

**maniche'ismo** nm Manicheism

**mani'chetta** nf hose

**mani'chino** nm (da sarto, vetrina) dummy

**'manico** nm handle: Mus neck. **~ di scopa** broom handle

**mani'comio** nm mental home; (fam: confusione) tip

**mani'cotto** nm muff; Mech sleeve

**mani'cure** nf manicure ● nmf inv (persona) manicurist

**mani'era** nf manner; **in ~ che** so that

**manie'rato** a affected; (stile) mannered

**manie'rismo** nm mannerism

**mani'ero** nm manor

**manifat'tura** nf manufacture; (fabbrica) factory

**manifatturi'ero** a manufacturing

**manifesta'mente** adv demonstrably, manifestly

**manife'stante** nmf demonstrator

**manife'stare** vt show; (esprimere) express ● vi demonstrate

**manifes'tarsi** vr show oneself

**manifestazi'one** nf show; (espressione) expression; (sintomo) manifestation; (dimostrazione pubblica) demonstration

**mani'festo** a evident ● nm poster; (dichiarazione pubblica) manifesto

**ma'niglia** nf handle; (sostegno, in autobus ecc) strap

**manipo'lare** vt handle; (massaggiare) massage; (alterare) adulterate; fig manipulate

**manipola|'tore, -'trice** nmf manipulator

**manipolazi'one** nf handling; (massaggio) massage; (alterazione) adulteration; fig manipulation

**mani'scalco** nm smith

**'manna** nf **~ dal cielo** manna from heaven

**man'naia** nf (scure) axe; (da macellaio) cleaver

**man'naro** a **lupo ~** werewolf

**'mano** nf hand; (strato di vernice ecc) coat; **alla ~** informal; **fuori ~** out of the way; **man ~** little by little; **man ~ che** as; **sotto ~** to hand; **di seconda ~** secondhand; **a mani vuote** empty-handed; **a ~** (scritto, ricamato, fatto) by hand; (trapano ecc) hand[-held]; **dare una ~ a qcno** give or lend sb a hand; **ha le mani di pastafrolla** he is a butterfingers

**mano'dopera** nf labour

**ma'nometro** nm manometer, pressure gauge

**mano'mettere** vt tamper with; (violare) violate

**ma'nopola** nf (di apparecchio) knob; (guanto) mitten; (su pullman) handle

**mano'scritto** a handwritten ● nm manuscript

**mano'vale** nm labourer

**mano'vella** nf handle; Techn crank. **~ alzacristalli** winder

**ma'novra** nf manoeuvre; Rail shunting;

**fare le manovre** Auto manoeuvre. **manovre** pl **di corridoio** lobbying

**mano'vrabile** a manoeuvrable; (fig: persona) easy to manipulate

**mano'vrare** vt (azionare) operate; fig manipulate (persona) ● vi manoeuvre

**manro'vescio** nm slap

**man'sarda** nf attic

**mansio'nario** nm job description

**mansi'one** nf task; (dovere) duty

**mansu'eto** a meek; (animale) docile

**'manta** nf Zool manta

**mante'cato** nm soft ice cream ● a creamy

**man'tella** nf cape

**man'tello** nm cloak; (soprabito, di animale) coat; (di neve) mantle

**mante'nere** vt (conservare) keep; (in buono stato, sostentare) maintain

**mante'nersi** vr **~ in forma** keep fit

**manteni'mento** nm maintenance. **~ della pace** Mil, Pol peacekeeping

**mante'nuta** nf kept woman

**'mantice** nm bellows pl; (di automobile) hood, top

**'mantide** nf mantis

**man'tiglia** nf mantilla

**'manto** nm cloak; (coltre) mantle

**'Mantova** nf Mantua

**manto'vana** nf (di tende) pelmet

**manu'ale** a & nm manual. **~ di conversazione** phrasebook. **~ d'uso** user manual

**manual'mente** adv manually

**ma'nubrio** nm handle; (di bicicletta) handlebars pl; (per ginnastica) dumb-bell

**manu'fatto** a manufactured

**manutenzi'one** nf maintenance

**'manzo** nm steer; (carne) beef

**maomet'tano** a & nm Muslim

**ma'ori** a inv & nm Maori

**'mappa** nf map

**mappa'mondo** nm globe

**mar** vedi **mare**

**mara'chella** nf prank

**maragià** nm inv maharajah

**maran'tacea** nf Bot arrowroot

**mara'schino** nm maraschino, sweet liqueur

**ma'rasma** nm fig decline

**mara'tona** nf marathon

**marato'neta** nmf marathon runner

**'marca** nf mark; Comm brand; (fabbricazione) make; (scontrino) ticket. **~ da bollo** stamp showing that the necessary duties have been paid

**mar'care** vt mark; Sport score

**marcata'mente** adv markedly

**mar'cato** a (tratto, accento) strong, marked

**marca'tore** nm (nel calcio) scorer; (chi marca un avversario) marker; (pennarello) marker pen

**'Marche** nfpl Marches

**mar'chese, -a** nm marquis ● nf marchioness

**mar'chetta** nf (assicurativa) National In-

169

**marchiare | maschera**

surance stamp; **fare marchette** *fam* be on the game

**marchi'are** *vt* brand

'**marchio** *nm* brand; (*caratteristica*) mark. ~ **depositato** registered trademark. ~ **di fabbrica** trademark. ~ **registrato** registered trademark

'**marcia** *nf* march; *Auto* gear; *Sport* walk; **mettere in** ~ put into gear; **mettersi in** ~ start off; **cambiare** ~ change gear; ~ **a senso unico alternato** temporary one way system in operation. ~ **forzata** forced march. ~ **funebre** funeral march. ~ **indietro** reverse gear; **fare** ~ ~ reverse; *fig* back-pedal. ~ **nuziale** wedding march

**marcia'longa** *nf* (*di sci*) cross-country skiing race; (*a piedi*) long-distance race

**marciapi'ede** *nm* pavement, sidewalk *Am*; (*di stazione*) platform

**marci'are** *vi* march; (*funzionare*) go, work

**marcia|'tore, -'trice** *nmf* walker

'**marcio** *a* rotten ● *nm* rotten part; *fig* corruption

**mar'cire** *vi* go bad, rot

**mar'cita** *nf* water meadow

'**marco** *nm* (*moneta*) mark

**marco'nista** *nmf* radio operator

'**mare** *nm* sea; (*luogo di mare*) seaside; **sul** ~ ⟨*casa*⟩ at the seaside; ⟨*città*⟩ on the sea; **andare al** ~ go to the sea; **in alto** ~ on the high seas; **d'alto** ~ ocean-going; **essere in alto** ~ *fig* not know which way to turn. ~ **Adriatico** Adriatic Sea. **mar Cinese** China Sea. **mar Ionio** Ionian Sea. **mar Mediterraneo** Mediterranean. **mar Morto** Dead Sea. **mar Nero** Black Sea. ~ **del Nord** North Sea. **mar Tirreno** Tyrrhenian Sea

**ma'rea** *nf* tide; **una** ~ **di** hundreds of; **alta/bassa** ~ high/low tide. ~ **montante** flood tide

**mareggi'ata** *nf* [sea] storm

**mare'moto** *nm* tidal wave, seaquake

**maresci'allo** *nm* (*ufficiale*) marshal; (*sottufficiale*) warrant-officer

**ma'retta** *nf* choppiness; *fig* tension

**marga'rina** *nf* margarine

**marghe'rita** *nf* marguerite. ~ **settembrina** Michaelmas daisy

**margheri'tina** *nf* daisy

**margi'nale** *a* marginal

**marginal'mente** *adv* marginally

'**margine** *nm* margin; (*orlo*) brink; (*bordo*) border. ~ **di errore** margin of error. ~ **di sicurezza** safety margin. ~ **di vendita** mark-up

**mari'ano** *a Relig* Marian

**ma'rina** *nf* navy; (*costa*) seashore; (*quadro*) seascape. ~ **mercantile** merchant navy. ~ **militare** navy

**mari'naio** *nm* sailor. ~ **d'acqua dolce** landlubber

**mari'nare** *vt* marinate; ~ **la scuola** play truant

**mari'naro** *a* seafaring

**mari'nata** *nf* marinade

**mari'nato** *a Culin* marinated

**ma'rino** *a* sea *attrib*, marine

**mario'netta** *nf* puppet

**mari'tare** *vt* marry

**mari'tarsi** *vr* get married

**ma'rito** *nm* husband

**mari'tozzo** *nm* currant bun

**ma'rittimo** *a* maritime

**mar'maglia** *nf* rabble

**marmel'lata** *nf* jam; (*di agrumi*) marmalade

**mar'mitta** *nf* pot; *Auto* silencer. ~ **catalitica** catalytic converter

'**marmo** *nm* marble

**mar'mocchio** *nm fam* brat

**mar'moreo** *a* marble

**marmoriz'zato** *a* marbled

**mar'motta** *nf* marmot

**maroc'chino** *a & nmf* Moroccan

**Ma'rocco** *nm* Morocco

**ma'roso** *nm* breaker

**mar'rone** *a* brown ● *nm* brown; (*castagna*) chestnut. **marroni** *pl* **canditi** marrons glacés

**mar'sina** *nf* tails *pl*

**marsupi'ale** *nm* marsupial

**mar'supio** *nm* (*borsa*) bumbag

**martedì** *nm* Tuesday; **di** ~ on Tuesdays. ~ **grasso** Shrove Tuesday

**martel'lante** *a* ⟨*mal di testa*⟩ pounding; **hanno fatto una pubblicità** ~ they hyped the product, they bombarded the market with publicity

**martel'lare** *vt* hammer ● *vi* throb

**martel'lata** *nf* hammer blow

**martel'letto** *nm* (*di giudice*) gavel; (*di pianoforte*) hammer; (*di medico*) percussion hammer

**martel'lio** *nm* hammering

**mar'tello** *nm* hammer; (*di battente*) knocker. ~ **pneumatico** pneumatic drill

**marti'netto** *nm Mech* jack

**martin pesca'tore** *nm inv* kingfisher

'**martire** *nmf* martyr

**mar'tirio** *nm* martyrdom

'**martora** *nf* marten

**martori'are** *vt* torment

**mar'xismo** *nm* Marxism

**mar'xista** *a & nmf* Marxist

**marza'pane** *nm* marzipan

**marzi'ale** *a* martial

**marzi'ano, -a** *a & nmf* Martian

'**marzo** *nm* March

**mascal'zone** *nm* rascal

**ma'scara** *nm inv* mascara

**mascar'pone** *nm full-fat cream cheese often used for desserts*

**ma'scella** *nf* jaw

'**maschera** *nf* mask; (*costume*) fancy dress; *Cinema, Theat* usher *m*, usherette *f*; (*nella commedia dell'arte*) stock character. ~ **antigas** gas mask. ~ **di bellezza** face pack. ~ **mortuaria** death mask. ~ **ad ossigeno** oxygen mask

# mascheramento | maturazione

170

**maschera'mento** *nm* masking; *Mil* camouflage

**masche'rare** *vt* mask; *fig* camouflage

**masche'rarsi** *vr* put on a mask; **~ da** dress up as

**masche'rata** *nf* masquerade

**maschi'accio** *nm* (*ragazza*) tomboy

**ma'schile** *a* masculine: ‹*sesso*› male ● *nm* masculine [gender]

**maschi'lista** *a* sexist

**'maschio** *a* male; (*virile*) manly ● *nm* male; (*figlio*) son

**masco'lino** *a* masculine

**ma'scotte** *nf inv* mascot

**maso'chismo** *nm* masochism

**maso'chista** *a & nmf* masochist

**'massa** *nf* mass; *Electr* earth, ground *Am*; **communicazioni di ~** mass media; **una ~** [**di gente**] a crowd [of people]

**massa'crante** *a* gruelling

**massa'crare** *vt* massacre

**mas'sacro** *nm* massacre; *fig* mess

**massaggi'are** *vt* massage

**massaggia'|tore, -'trice** *nm* masseur ● *nf* masseuse

**mas'saggio** *nm* massage. **~ cardiaco** heart massage

**mas'saia** *nf* housewife

**mas'sello** *nm* (*metallo*) ingot ● *a* ‹*legno*› solid

**masse'rizie** *nfpl* household effects

**massiccia'mente** *adv* on a big scale

**massicci'ata** *nf* hard core

**mas'siccio** *a* massive; ‹*oro ecc*› solid; ‹*corporatura*› heavy ● *nm* massif

**massifi'care** *vt* de-individualize ‹*società*›

**massificazi'one** *nf* de-individualization

**'massima** *nf* maxim; (*temperatura*) maximum

**massi'male** *nm* (*assicurazione*) limit of indemnity

**massimizzazi'one** *nf* maximization

**'massimo** *a* greatest; ‹*quantità*› maximum, greatest ● *nm* **il ~** the maximum; **al ~** at [the] most, as a maximum. **~ storico** all-time high

**'masso** *nm* rock

**mas'sone** *nm* [Free]mason

**massone'ria** *nf* Freemasonry

**mastecto'mia** *nf* mastectomy

**ma'stello** *nm* wooden box for the grape or olive harvest

**masti'care** *vt* chew; (*borbottare*) mumble

**'mastice** *nm* mastic; (*per vetri*) putty

**ma'stino** *nm* mastiff

**masto'dontico** *a* gigantic

**ma'stoide** *nm* mastoid

**'mastro** *nm* master; **libro ~** ledger

**mastur'barsi** *vr* masturbate

**masturbazi'one** *nf* masturbation

**ma'tassa** *nf* skein

**match 'point** *nm inv Tennis* match point

**matelassé** *nm inv* quilting

**mate'matica** *nf* mathematics, maths, math *Am*. **~ pura** pure mathematics

**mate'matico, -a** *a* mathematical ● *nmf* mathematician

**materas'sino** *nm* small mattress. **~ gonfiabile** air bed, lilo ᴿ

**mate'rasso** *nm* mattress. **~ ad acqua** water bed. **~ di gommapiuma** foam mattress. **~ a molle** spring mattress

**ma'teria** *nf* matter; (*materiale*) material; (*di studio*) subject. **~ grigia** grey matter. **~ prima** raw material

**materi'ale** *a* material; (*grossolano*) coarse ● *nm* material. **~ da costruzione** building material. **~ pubblicitario** publicity material. **~ di scarto** waste material

**materia'lismo** *nm* materialism

**materia'lista** *a* materialistic; **non ~** unworldly ● *nmf* materialist

**materializ'zarsi** *vr* materialize

**material'mente** *adv* physically

**materna'mente** *adv* maternally

**maternità** *nf* motherhood; **è alla prima ~** it's her first baby; **ospedale di ~** maternity hospital

**ma'terno** *a* maternal; **lingua materna** mother tongue

**ma'tita** *nf* pencil. **matite** *pl* **colorate** colour[ed] pencils. **~ emostatica** styptic pencil. **~ per gli occhi** eyeliner pencil

**matriar'cale** *a* matriarchal

**ma'trice** *nf* matrix; (*origini*) roots *pl*; *Comm* counterfoil. **~ attiva** *Comput* active matrix. **~ passiva** *Comput* passive matrix

**ma'tricola** *nf* (*registro*) register; *Univ* fresher; **numero di ~** (*di studente*) matriculation number

**ma'trigna** *nf* stepmother

**matrimoni'ale** *a* matrimonial; **vita ~** married life

**matri'monio** *nm* marriage; (*cerimonia*) wedding. **~ in bianco** white wedding. **~ civile** civil wedding. **~ di convenienza** marriage of convenience

**ma'trona** *nf* matron

**'matta** *nf* (*nelle carte*) joker

**mattacchi'one, -a** *nmf* rascal

**mat'tanza** *nf* (*di tonni*) tuna fishing; *fig* killings *pl*

**matta'toio** *nm* slaughterhouse

**matta'tore** *nm* (*artista*) star performer

**matte'rello** *nm* rolling-pin

**mat'tina** *nf* morning; **la ~, alla ~** in the morning; **domani ~** tomorrow morning; **ieri ~** yesterday morning

**matti'nata** *nf* morning; *Theat* matinée

**mattini'ero** *a* **essere ~** be an early riser

**mat'tino** *nm* morning

**'matto, -a** *a* mad, crazy; *Med* insane; (*falso*) false; (*opaco*) matt; **~ da legare** barking mad; **avere una voglia matta di...** be dying for... ● *nm* madman ● *nf* madwoman

**mat'tone** *nm* brick; (*libro*) bore

**matto'nella** *nf* tile

**mattu'tino** *a* morning *attrib*

**matu'rare** *vt* ripen; *Fin* mature

**maturazi'one** *nf* ripening; *Fin* maturity;

(*fig: di idea ecc*) gestation; **arrivare a ~** ⟨*frutta:*⟩ ripen; ⟨*polizza:*⟩ mature
**maturità** *nf* maturity; *Sch* school-leaving certificate
**ma'turo** *a* mature; ⟨*frutto*⟩ ripe
**ma'tusa** *nm* old fogey
**Mau'rizio** *nf* [isola di] ~ Mauritius
**mauso'leo** *nm* mausoleum
**maxi+** *pref* maxi+
**'mayday** *nm inv Radio* Mayday
**'mazza** *nf* club; (*martello*) hammer; (*da baseball, cricket*) bat. **~ da golf** golf-club
**maz'zata** *nf* blow
**maz'zetta** *nf* (*di banconote*) bundle; (*tangente*) bribe
**'mazzo** *nm* bunch; (*carte da gioco*) pack
**Mb** *nm abbr* (**megabyte**) *Comput* Mb
**me** *pers pron* me; **me lo ha dato** he gave it to me; **secondo me** in my opinion; **fai come me** do as I do; **è più veloce di me** he is faster than me *o* faster than I am
**me'andro** *nm* meander
**M.E.C.** *nm abbr* (**Mercato Comune Europeo**) EEC
**'Mecca** *nf* **La ~** Mecca
**mec'canica** *nf* mechanics. **~ quantistica** quantum mechanics
**meccanica'mente** *adv* mechanically
**mec'canico** *a* mechanical ● *nm* mechanic. **~ laser** laser engine
**mecca'nismo** *nm* mechanism
**meccanogra'fia** *nf* data processing
**meccano'grafico** *a* data processing *attrib*
**mece'nate** *nmf* patron
**mèche** *nfpl* highlights; **[farsi] fare le ~** have highlights put in, have one's hair streaked
**me'daglia** *nf* medal. **~ al valore** medal for valour
**medagli'ere** *nm* medal collection
**medagli'one** *nm* medallion; (*gioiello*) locket. **medaglioni** *pl* **di vitello** *Culin* medallions of veal
**me'desimo** *a* same
**'media** *nf* average; *Sch* average mark; *Math* mean; **essere nella ~** be in the mid-range
**medi'ano** *a* middle ● *nm* (*calcio*) half-back. **~ di mischia** scrum half
**medi'ante** *prep* by
**medi'are** *vt* act as intermediary in
**media|'tore, -'trice** *nmf* mediator; *Comm* middleman. **~ d'affari** business agent
**mediazi'one** *nf* mediation
**medica'mento** *nm* medicine
**medi'care** *vt* treat; dress ⟨*ferita*⟩
**medi'cato** *a* ⟨*shampoo*⟩ medicated
**medicazi'one** *nf* medication; (*di ferita*) dressing
**me'diceo** *a* from the period of the Medici, Medicean
**medi'cina** *nf* medicine. **~ alternativa** alternative medicine. **~ del lavoro** occupational health. **~ legale** forensic medicine. **~ popolare** folk medicine
**medici'nale** *a* medicinal ● *nm* medicine

**'medico** *a* medical ● *nm* doctor. **~ di base** general practitioner, GP. **~ di famiglia** family doctor. **~ generico** general practitioner, GP. **~ legale** forensic scientist. **~ di turno** duty doctor
**medie'vale** *a* medieval
**'medio** *a* average; ⟨*punto*⟩ middle; ⟨*statura*⟩ medium; **scuola media** secondary school ● *nm* (*dito*) middle finger. **M~ Oriente** Middle East
**medi'ocre** *a* mediocre; (*scadente*) poor
**mediocre'mente** *adv* indifferently
**medio'evo** *nm* Middle Ages *pl*
**medita'bondo** *a* meditative
**medi'tare** *vt* meditate; (*progettare*) plan; (*considerare attentamente*) think over ● *vi* meditate
**medita'tivo** *a* meditative
**meditazi'one** *nf* meditation
**mediter'raneo** *a* Mediterranean; **il [mar] M~** the Mediterranean [Sea]
**me'dusa** *nf* jellyfish
**'megabyte** *nm inv Comput* megabyte
**mega'fono** *nm* megaphone
**megaga'lattico** *a* gigantic
**mega'lite** *nm* megalith
**mega'lomane** *nmf* megalomaniac
**me'gera** *nf* hag
**'meglio** *adv* better; **tanto ~, ~ così** so much the better ● *a* better; (*superlativo*) best ● *nmf* best ● *nf* **avere la ~ su** have the better of; **fare qcsa alla [bell'e] ~** do sth as best one can ● *nm* **fare del proprio ~** do one's best; **fare qcsa il ~ possibile** make an excellent job of sth; **al ~** to the best of one's ability; **per il ~** for the best
**'mela** *nf* apple; **succo di ~** apple juice. **~ cotogna** quince
**mela'grana** *nf* pomegranate
**mé'lange** *nm inv* flecked wool ● *a inv* ⟨*lana*⟩ flecked
**mela'nina** *nf* melanin
**melan'zana** *nf* aubergine, eggplant *Am*. **melanzane** *pl* **alla parmigiana** *baked layers of aubergine, tomato and cheese*
**me'lassa** *nf* molasses *sg*
**me'lenso** *a* ⟨*persona, film*⟩ dull
**me'leto** *nm* apple orchard
**mel'lifluo** *a* ⟨*parole*⟩ honeyed; ⟨*voce*⟩ sugary
**'melma** *nf* slime
**mel'moso** *a* slimy
**'melo** *nm* apple[-tree]
**melo'dia** *nf* melody
**me'lodico** *a* melodic
**melodi'oso** *a* melodious
**melo'dramma** *nm* melodrama
**melodrammatica'mente** *adv* melodramatically
**melodram'matico** *a* melodramatic
**melo'grano** *nm* pomegranate tree
**me'lone** *nm* melon
**mem'brana** *nf* membrane
**'membro** *nm* member; (*pl nf* **membra** *Anat*) limb
**memo'rabile** *a* memorable

'**memore** *a* mindful; *(riconoscente)* grateful

me'**moria** *nf* memory; *(oggetto ricordo)* souvenir; **imparare a ~** learn by heart; **memorie** *pl* *(biografiche)* memoirs. **~ cache** *Comput* cache memory. **~ collettiva** folk memory. **~ dinamica** *Comput* RAM. **~ di massa** *Comput* mass storage. **~ permanente** *Comput* non-volatile memory; **~ di sola lettura** *Comput* read-only memory, ROM. **~ a tampone** *Comput* buffer [memory]. **~ volatile** *Comput* volatile memory

memori'**ale** *nm* memorial

memoriz'**zare** *vt* memorize; *Comput* save, store

mena'**dito**: **a ~** *adv* perfectly

me'**nare** *vt* lead; *(fam: picchiare)* hit; **~ la coda** *(cane:)* wag its tail; **~ qcno per il naso** pull sb's leg

mendi'**cante** *nmf* beggar

mendi'**care** *vt/i* beg

menefre'**ghista** *a* devil-may-care

mene'**strello** *nm* minstrel

me'**ningi** *nfpl* **spremersi le ~** rack one's brains

menin'**gite** *nf* meningitis

me'**nisco** *nm* meniscus

'**meno** *adv* less; *(superlativo)* least; *(in operazioni, con temperatura)* minus; **~ di** less than; **di ~** less; **~ moderno** less modern; **il ~ moderno di tutti** the least modern of all; **far qcsa alla ~ peggio** do sth as best one can; **fare a ~ di qcsa** do without sth; **non posso fare a ~ di ridere** I can't help laughing; **~ male!** thank goodness!; **sempre ~** less and less; **venir ~** *(svenire)* faint; **venir ~ a qcno** *(coraggio:)* fail sb; **sono le tre ~ un quarto** it's a quarter to three; **che tu venga o ~** whether you're coming or not; **quanto ~** at least ● *a inv* less; *(con nomi plurali)* fewer ● *nm* least; *Math* minus sign; **il ~ possibile** as little as possible; **per lo ~** at least ● *prep* except [for] ● *conj* **a ~ che** unless

meno'**mare** *vt* *(incidente:)* maim

meno'**mato** *a* disabled ● *nmf* disabled person

meno'**pausa** *nf* menopause

'**mensa** *nf* table; *Mil* mess; *Sch, Univ* refectory

men'**sile** *a* monthly ● *nm* *(stipendio)* [monthly] salary; *(rivista)* monthly

mensilità *nf inv* monthly salary

mensil'**mente** *adv* monthly

'**mensola** *nf* bracket; *(scaffale)* shelf

'**menta** *nf* mint; **al gusto di ~** mint-flavoured. **~ peperita** peppermint. **~ verde** spearmint

men'**tale** *a* mental

mentalità *nf inv* mentality

'**mente** *nf* mind; **a ~ fredda** in cold blood; **cosa ti è saltato in ~?** what possessed you?; **venire in ~ a qcno** occur to sb

men'**tina** *nf* mint

men'**tire** *vi* lie

'**mento** *nm* chin

men'**tolo** *nm* menthol; **al ~** mentholated

'**mentre** *conj* *(temporale)* while; *(invece)* whereas

me'**nu** *nm inv* menu. **~ a discesa** *Comput* pull-down menu. **~ fisso** set menu. **~ a tendina** *Comput* pull-down menu. **~ turistico** tourist menu

menzio'**nare** *vt* mention

menzi'**one** *nf* mention. **~ speciale** special mention

men'**zogna** *nf* lie

mera'**viglia** *nf* wonder; **a ~** marvellously; **che ~!** how wonderful!; **con mia grande ~** much to my amazement; **mi fa ~ che...** I am surprised that...

meravigli'**are** *vt* surprise

meravigli'**arsi** *vr* **~ di** be surprised at

meravigliosa'**mente** *adv* marvellously

meravigli'**oso** *a* marvellous, wonderful

mer'**cante** *nm* merchant. **~ d'arte** art dealer. **~ di schiavi** slave trader

mercanteggi'**are** *vi* trade; *(sul prezzo)* bargain

mercan'**tile** *a* mercantile ● *nm* merchant ship

mercan'**zia** *nf* merchandise, goods *pl*

merca'**tino** *nm* *(di quartiere)* local street market; *Fin* unlisted securities market

mer'**cato** *nm* market; *Fin* market[place]. **a buon ~** *(comprare)* cheap[ly]; *(articolo)* cheap. **~ aperto** *Econ* open market. **~ azionario** *Fin* equity market, share market. **~ dei cambi** foreign exchange market. **M~ Comune [Europeo]** [European] Common Market. **~ coperto** covered market, indoor market. **~ dell'eurovaluta** eurocurrency market. **~ immobiliare** property market. **~ libero** free market. **~ di massa** mass market. **~ nero** black market. **~ di prova** test market. **~ al rialzo** *Fin* bull market. **~ al ribasso** *Fin* bear market. **~ specializzato** niche market. **~ unico** Single Market

'**merce** *nf* goods *pl*, merchandise; **la ~ venduta non si cambia senza lo scontrino** goods will not be exchanged without a receipt. **~ in conto vendita** sale or return goods. **~ deperibile** perishable goods

mercé *nf* **alla ~ di** at the mercy of

merce'**nario** *a & nm* mercenary

merceolo'**gia** *nf* study of commodities

merce'**ria** *nf* haberdashery; *(negozio)* haberdasher's

mercifi'**care** *vt* commercialize

mercificazi'**one** *nf* commercialization

mercoledì *nm inv* Wednesday; **di ~** on Wednesdays. **~ delle Ceneri** Ash Wednesday

mer'**curio** *nm* mercury

me'**renda** *nf* afternoon snack; **far ~** have an afternoon snack

meridi'**ana** *nf* sundial

meridi'**ano** *a* midday ● *nm* meridian

meridio'**nale** *a* southern ● *nmf* southerner

meridi'**one** *nm* south

me'**ringa** *nf* meringue

merin'**gata** *nf* meringue pie

meri'**tare** *vt* deserve

meri'tato *a* deserved

meri'tevole *a* deserving

'merito *nm* merit; (*valore*) worth; in ~ a as to; per ~ di thanks to

merito'cratico *a* meritocratic

meri'torio *a* meritorious

merla'tura *nf* battlements *pl*

merlet'taia *nf* lacemaker

mer'letto *nm* lace

'merlo *nm* blackbird; bravo ~! you fool!

mer'luzzo *nm* cod

'mero *a* mere

mesca'lina *nf* mescaline

'mescere *vt* pour out

meschine'ria *nf* meanness

me'schino *a* wretched; (*gretto*) mean ● *nm* wretch

'mescita *nf* wine shop

mescola'mento *nm* mixing

mesco'lanza *nf* mixture

mesco'lare *vt* mix; shuffle ⟨carte⟩; (*confondere*) mix up; blend ⟨tè, tabacco ecc⟩

mesco'larsi *vr* mix; (*immischiarsi*) meddle

mesco'lata *nf* (*a carte*) shuffle; Culin stir

'mese *nm* month. ~ civile calendar month

me'setto *nm* un ~ about a month, a month or so

'messa[1] *nf* Mass. ~ nera black mass. ~ da requiem requiem mass. ~ solenne High Mass

'messa[2] *nf* (*il mettere*) putting. ~ in moto Auto starting. ~ in piega (*di capelli*) set; farsi fare la ~ ~ ~ have one's hair set. ~ a punto adjustment. ~ in scena production; *fig* production number. ~ a terra earthing, grounding *Am*

messag'gero *nm* messenger

mes'saggio *nm* message. ~ di errore *Comput* error message

mes'sale *nm* missal

'messe *nf* harvest

Mes'sia *nm* Messiah

messi'cano, -a *a & nmf* Mexican

'Messico *nm* Mexico

messin'scena *nf* staging; *fig* act

'messo *pp di* mettere ● *nm* messenger

mesti'ere *nm* trade; (*lavoro*) job; essere del ~ be an expert, know one's trade

'mesto *a* sad

'mestola *nf* (*di cuoco*) ladle; (*di muratore*) trowel

mestru'ale *a* menstrual

mestruazi'one *nf* menstruation; mestruazioni *pl* period

'meta *nf* destination; *fig* aim

metà *nf inv* half; (*centro*) middle; ~ prezzo half price; a ~ strada half-way; a ~ serata half-way through the evening; fare a ~ con qcno go halves with sb; a ~ con sb; fare [a] ~ e ~ go fifty-fifty, go halves

metabo'lismo *nm* metabolism

meta'carpo *nm* metacarpus

meta'done *nm* methadone

meta'fisica *n* metaphysics

meta'fisico *a* metaphysical

me'tafora *nf* metaphor

metaforica'mente *adv* metaphorically

meta'forico *a* metaphorical

me'tallico *a* metallic

metalliz'zato *a* ⟨grigio⟩ metallic

me'tallo *nm* metal. ~ vile base metal

metal'loide *nm* metalloid

metallur'gia *nf* metallurgy

metal'lurgico *a* metallurgical

metalmec'canico *a* engineering ● *nm* engineering worker

meta'morfosi *nf* metamorphosis

me'tano *nm* methane

metano'dotto *nm* methane pipeline

meta'nolo *nm* methanol

me'tastasi *nf inv* metastasis

meta'tarso *nm* metatarsus

me'teora *nf* meteor

meteo'rite *nm* meteorite

meteorolo'gia *nf* meteorology

meteoro'logico *a* meteorological

meteo'rologo *nm* meteorologist

me'ticcio, -a *nmf* half-caste

meticolosa'mente *adv* meticulously

metico'loso *a* meticulous

me'tile *nm* methyl

me'todico *a* methodical

meto'dista *a & nmf* Methodist

'metodo *nm* method

metodolo'gia *nf* methodology

metodo'logico *a* methodological

me'traggio *nm* length (*in metres*); vendere a ~ sell by the metre

'metrico, -a *a* metric; (*in poesia*) metrical ● *nf* metrics

'metro *nm* metre; (*nastro*) tape measure. ~ cubo cubic metre. ~ quadrato square metre

'metro *nf inv fam* underground, subway *Am*

me'tronomo *nm* metronome

metro'notte *nmf inv* night security guard

me'tropoli *nf inv* metropolis

metropoli'tana *nf* underground, subway *Am*

metropoli'tano *a* metropolitan

'mettere *vt* put; (*indossare*) put on; (*fam: installare*) put in; ~ al mondo bring into the world; ~ da parte set aside; ~ fiducia inspire trust; ~ qcsa in chiaro make sth clear; ~ in mostra display; ~ a posto tidy up; ~ in vendita put up for sale; ~ su set up ⟨casa, azienda⟩; metter su famiglia start a family; ci ho messo un'ora it took me an hour; mettiamo che... let's suppose that...

'mettersi *vr* (*indossare*) put on; (*diventare*) turn out; ~ a start to; ~ con qcno (*fam: formare una coppia*) start to go out with sb; ~ a letto go to bed; ~ a sedere sit down; ~ in viaggio set out

metti'foglio *nm* feeder

'mezza *nf* è la ~ it's half past twelve; sono le quattro e ~ it's half past four

mez'zadria *nf* sharecropping

mezza'luna *nf* half moon; (*simbolo islamico*) crescent; (*coltello*) two-handled chopping knife; a ~ half-moon

**mezza'manica** *nf* a ~ ⟨maglia⟩ short-sleeved; **mezzemaniche** *pl pej* lowest grade of clerks, pen-pushers

**mezza'nino** *nm* mezzanine

**mez'zano, -a** *a* middle

**mezza'notte** *nf* midnight; **aspettare la ~** see in the New Year

**mezz'asta: a ~** at half mast

**mezze'ria** *nf* centre line

**'mezzo** *a* half; **di mezza età** middle aged; ~ **bicchiere** half a glass; **una mezza idea** a vague idea; **siamo mezzi morti** we're half dead; **sono le quattro e ~** it's half past four. **mezza cartuccia** *nf* runt. **mezza dozzina** *nf* half-dozen. **mezza età** *nf* midlife. **mezza giornata** *nf* half day. ~ **guanto** *nm* mitt. ~ **litro** *nm* half a litre. **mezz'ora** *nf* half an hour. **mezza pensione** *nf* half board. **mezza stagione** *nf* **una giacca di ~ ~** a spring/autumn jacket. **mezza verità** *nf* half-truth ● *adv* (a metà) half; ~ **addormentato** half asleep; ~ **morto** half-dead; ~ **morto di paura** petrified; ~ **e ~** (così così) so so ● *nm* (metà) half; (centro) middle; (per raggiungere un fine) means *sg*; **uno e ~** one and a half; **tre anni e ~** three and a half years; **in ~ a** in the middle of; **levare di ~** clear away; **per ~ di** by means of; **a ~ posta** by mail; **via di ~** *fig* halfway house; (soluzione) middle way; **mezzi** *pl* (denaro) means *pl*. **mezzi** *pl* **di comunicazione di massa** mass media. **mezzi** *pl* **pubblici** public transport. **mezzi** *pl* **di trasporto** [means of] transport

**mezzo'busto** *nm* (statua) bust; *TV* talking head; **a ~** ⟨foto, ritratto⟩ half-length

**mezzo'fondo** *nm* middle-distance running

**mezzogi'orno** *nm* midday, noon; (sud) South. **il M~** Southern Italy. ~ **in punto** high noon

**mezzo'sangue** *nmf* crossbreed

**mezzo'servizio** *nm* **lavorare a ~** do part-time cleaning work

**mi** *pers pron* me; (refl) myself; **mi ha dato un libro** he gave me a book; **mi lavo le mani** I wash my hands; **eccomi** here I am ● *nm Mus* (chiave, nota) E

**mia** *vedi* **mio**

**miago'lare** *vi* miaow

**miago'lio** *nm* miaowing

**mi'ao** *nm* miaow

**'mica¹** *nf* mica

**'mica²** *adv fam* (per caso) by any chance; **hai ~ visto Paolo?** have you seen Paul, by any chance?; **non è ~ bello** it is not at all nice; ~ **male** not bad

**'miccia** *nf* fuse

**micidi'ale** *a* deadly

**'micio** *nm* pussy-cat

**mi'cosi** *nf* athlete's foot

**mi'cotico** *a* fungal

**microbiolo'gia** *nf* microbiology

**'microbo** *nm* microbe

**microchirur'gia** *nf* microsurgery

**micro'clima** *nm* microclimate

**microcom'puter** *nm inv* microcomputer

**micro'cosmo** *nm* microcosm

**micro'fiche** *nf inv* microfiche

**micro'film** *nm inv* microfilm

**micro'fisica** *nf* microphysics

**mi'crofono** *nm* microphone. ~ **con la clip** clip-on microphone. ~ **spia** bugging device, bug. ~ **a stelo** boom microphone

**microfotogra'fia** *nf Phot* micrograph; (tecnica) micrography

**microinfor'matica** *nf* microcomputing

**micro'onda** *nf* microwave

**microorga'nismo** *nm* microorganism

**microproces'sore** *nm* microprocessor

**micro'scheda** *nf* microfiche

**micro'scopico** *a* microscopic

**micro'scopio** *nm* microscope; **passare qcsa al ~** *fig* examine sth in microscopic detail

**microse'condo** *nm* microsecond

**micro'solco** *nm* (disco) long-playing record

**micro'spia** *nf* bug

**mi'dollo** *nm* (pl nf **midolla**, *Anat*) marrow; **fino al ~** ⟨bagnato⟩ through and through; ⟨corrotto⟩ to the core. ~ **osseo** bone marrow. ~ **spinale** spinal cord

**'mie** *vedi* **mio**

**mi'ei** *vedi* **mio**

**mi'ele** *nm* honey. ~ **d'acacia** acacia honey

**mi'etere** *vt* reap

**mietitrebbia'trice** *nf* combine harvester

**mieti'trice** *nf* harvester

**mieti'tura** *nf* harvest

**migli'aia** *nfpl* thousands

**migli'aio** *nm* (pl nf **migliaia**) thousand. **a migliaia** in thousands

**'miglio** *nm Bot* millet; (misura: pl f **miglia**) mile. ~ **nautico** nautical mile. **miglia** *pl* **all'ora** miles per hour, mph. ~ **terrestre** mile

**migliora'mento** *nm* improvement

**miglio'rare** *vt/i* improve

**migli'ore** *a* better; (superlativo) the best; ~ **amico** best friend; **i migliori auguri** best wishes ● *nmf* **il/la ~** the best

**miglio'ria** *nf* improvement

**mi'gnatta** *nf* leech

**'mignolo** *nm* little finger, pinkie *fam*; (del piede) little toe

**mi'gnon** *a inv* (bottiglie) miniature

**mi'grare** *vi* migrate

**migra'tore** *a* migratory

**migra'torio** *a* migratory

**migrazi'one** *nf* migration

**'mila** *vedi* **mille**

**mila'nese** *a & nmf* Milanese

**Mi'lano** *nf* Milan

**miliar'dario, -a** *nm* millionaire; (pluri-miliardario) billionaire ● *nf* millionairess; billionairess

**mili'ardo** *nm* billion

**mili'are a pietra** ~ milestone

**milio'nario, -a** *nm* millionaire ● *nf* millionairess

**mili'one** *nm* million

**milio'nesimo** *a & nm* millionth
**mili'tante** *a & nmf* militant
**mili'tanza** *nf* militancy
**mili'tare** *vi* ~ **in** be a member of ⟨*un partito ecc*⟩ ●*a* military ●*nm* soldier; **fare il** ~ do one's military service. ~ **di carriera** regular [soldier]. ~ **di leva** National Serviceman
**milita'rismo** *nm* militarism
**milita'rista** *a* militaristic
**militariz'zare** *vt* militarize
**militas'solto** *a* having done National Service
**'milite** *nm* soldier
**milite'sente** *a* exempt from National Service
**mil'izia** *nf* militia
**millanta'|tore, -'trice** *nmf* boaster
**'mille** *a & nm* (*pl* **mila**) a *o* one thousand; **due/tre mila** two/three thousand; ~ **grazie!** thanks a lot!; **millenovecentonovanta-quattro** *nm* nineteen ninety-four
**mille'foglie** *nm inv Culin* vanilla slice
**mil'lennio** *nm* millennium
**millepi'edi** *nm inv* centipede
**mil'lesimo** *a & nm* thousandth
**milli'bar** *nm inv* millibar
**milli'grammo** *nm* milligram
**milli'litro** *nm* millilitre
**mil'limetro** *nm* millimetre
**'milza** *nf* spleen
**mi'mare** *vt* mimic ⟨*persona*⟩ ●*vi* mime
**mi'metico** *a* **tuta** *f* **mimetica** camouflage; **animale** ~ animal which has the ability to camouflage itself; **vernice mimetica** camouflage paint
**mime'tismo** *nm* ability to camouflage itself; ~ **politico** chameleon-like political traits
**mimetiz'zare** *vt* camouflage
**mimetiz'zarsi** *vr* camouflage oneself
**'mimica** *nf* mime. ~ **facciale** facial expressions *pl*
**'mimico** *a* mimic
**'mimo** *nm* mime
**mi'mosa** *nf* mimosa
**'mina** *nf* mine; (*di matita*) lead
**mi'naccia** *nf* threat. **avere una** ~ **di aborto** come close to having a miscarriage. ~ **di morte** death threat
**minacci'are** *vt* threaten
**minacciosa'mente** *adv* threateningly, menacingly
**minacci'oso** *a* threatening; ⟨*onde*⟩ menacing
**mi'nare** *vt* mine; *fig* undermine
**mina'reto** *nm* minaret
**mina'tore** *nm* miner
**mina'torio** *a* threatening
**mine'rale** *a & nm* mineral
**mineralo'gia** *nf* mineralogy
**mine'rario** *a* mining *attrib*
**mi'nestra** *nf* soup. ~ **in brodo** noodle soup. ~ **di verdure** vegetable soup
**mine'strone** *nm* minestrone (*vegetable soup*); (*fam: insieme confuso*) hotchpotch

**mingher'lino** *a* skinny
**'mini** *nf inv* (*gonna*) mini ●*a inv* mini
**mini+** *pref* mini+
**miniapparta'mento** *nm* studio flat *Br*, studio apartment
**minia'tura** *nf* miniature
**miniaturiz'zato** *a* miniaturized
**mini'bus** *nm inv* minibus
**mini'disco** *nm* minidiskette
**mini'era** *nf* mine; **una** ~ **di notizie** a mine of information; **è una** ~ **di idee** he's full of ideas. ~ **a cielo aperto** opencast mine. ~ **d'oro** gold-mine
**mini'golf** *nm* minigolf, miniature golf
**mini'gonna** *nf* miniskirt, mini
**'minima** *nf* (*atmosferica*) minimum temperature; *Med* minimum blood-pressure level; *Mus* minim
**minima'lista** *nmf* minimalist
**minima'mente** *adv* minimally
**mini'market** *nm inv* minimarket
**minimiz'zare** *vt* minimize
**'minimo** *a* least, slightest; (*il più basso*) lowest; ⟨*salario, quantità ecc*⟩ minimum ●*nm* minimum; **girare al** ~ *Auto* idle; **toccare il** ~ **storico** be at an all-time low; **come** ~ at least, as a minimum
**'minio** *nm* red lead
**ministeri'ale** *a* (*di ministero*) ministerial; (*di governo*) government
**mini'stero** *nm* ministry; (*governo*) government. ~ **degli [affari] esteri** Foreign Office, State Department *Am*. ~ **della difesa** Department of Defence. ~ **della pubblica istruzione** Department of Education. ~ **della sanità** Department of Health
**mi'nistro** *nm* minister. ~ **della difesa** Defence Minister, Defense Secretary *Am*. ~ **degli esteri** Foreign Secretary, Secretary of State *Am*. ~ **di grazia e giustizia** ≈ Attorney General. ~ **dell'interno** Home Secretary, Secretary of the Interior *Am*. ~ **del lavoro** Employment Minister, Employment Secretary. ~ **del tesoro** Chancellor of the Exchequer, Secretary of the Treasury *Am*
**mini'tower** *nm Comput* minitower
**mino'ranza** *nf* minority
**mino'rato, -a** *a* disabled ●*nmf* disabled person
**Mi'norca** *nf* Menorca
**mi'nore** *a* ⟨*gruppo, numero*⟩ smaller; (*superlativo*) smallest; ⟨*distanza*⟩ shorter; (*superlativo*) shortest; ⟨*prezzo*⟩ lower; (*superlativo*) lowest; (*di età*) younger; (*superlativo*) youngest; (*di importanza*) minor; (*superlativo*) least important ●*nmf* younger; (*superlativo*) youngest; *Jur* minor; **il** ~ **dei mali** the lesser of two evils; **i minori di 14 anni** children under 14
**mino'renne** *a* under age ●*nmf* minor
**minori'tario** *a* minority *attrib*
**minu'etto** *nm* minuet
**mi'nuscolo, -a** *a* tiny ●*nf* small letter
**mi'nuta** *nf* rough copy

**minuta'mente** *adv* ⟨*esaminato*⟩ in minute detail. minutely; ⟨*lavorato. tritato*⟩ finely
**mi'nuto**[1] *a* minute; ⟨*persona*⟩ delicate; ⟨*ricerca*⟩ detailed; ⟨*pioggia, neve*⟩ fine; **al ~** *Comm* retail
**mi'nuto**[2] *nm* ⟨*di tempo*⟩ minute; **spaccare il ~** be dead on time. **minuti** *pl* **di recupero** *Sport* injury time
**mi'nuzia** *nf* trifle; **minuzie** *pl* minutiae
**minuziosa'mente** *adv* minutely
**minuzi'oso** *a* minute, detailed; ⟨*persona*⟩ meticulous
**'mio** (il mio *m*, la mia *f*, i miei *mpl*, le mie *fpl*) *poss a* my; **questa macchina è mia** this car is mine; **~ padre** my father; **un ~ amico** a friend of mine ● *poss pron* mine; **i miei** ⟨*genitori ecc*⟩ my folks
**'miope** *a* short-sighted
**mio'pia** *nf* short-sightedness
**'mira** *nf* aim; ⟨*bersaglio*⟩ target; **prendere la ~** take aim; **prendere di ~ qcno** *fig* have it in for sb
**mi'rabile** *a* admirable
**miraco'lato** *a* ⟨*malato*⟩ miraculously cured
**mi'racolo** *nm* miracle
**miracolosa'mente** *adv* miraculously
**miraco'loso** *a* miraculous
**mi'raggio** *nm* mirage
**mi'rare** *vi* [take] aim; **~ alto** aim high
**mi'rarsi** *vr* ⟨*guardarsi*⟩ look at oneself
**mi'riade** *nf* myriad
**mi'rino** *nm* sight; *Phot* view-finder
**'mirra** *nf* myrrh
**mir'tillo** *nm* blueberry
**'mirto** *nm* myrtle
**mi'santropo, -a** *nmf* misanthropist
**mi'scela** *nf* mixture; ⟨*di caffè, tabacco ecc*⟩ blend
**misce'lare** *vt* mix
**miscela'tore** *nm* ⟨*apparecchio*⟩ blender; ⟨*di acqua*⟩ mixer tap
**miscel'lanea** *nf* miscellany
**'mischia** *nf* scuffle; ⟨*nel rugby*⟩ scrum
**mischi'are** *vt* mix; shuffle ⟨*carte da gioco*⟩
**mischi'arsi** *vr* mix; ⟨*immischiarsi*⟩ interfere
**misco'noscere** *vt* not appreciate
**miscre'dente** *nmf* heretic
**mi'scuglio** *nm* mixture; *fig* medley
**mise'rabile** *a* wretched
**misera'mente** *adv* ⟨*finire*⟩ miserably; ⟨*vivere*⟩ in abject poverty; ⟨*vestito*⟩ shabbily
**mi'seria** *nf* poverty; ⟨*infelicità*⟩ misery; **guadagnare una ~** earn a pittance; **miserie** *pl* ⟨*disgrazie*⟩ misfortunes; **porca ~!** *fam* hell!
**miseri'cordia** *nf* mercy
**misericordi'oso** *a* merciful
**'misero** *a* ⟨*miserabile*⟩ wretched; ⟨*povero*⟩ poor; ⟨*scarso*⟩ paltry
**mi'sfatto** *nm* misdeed
**mi'sogino** *nm* misogynist
**mis'saggio** *nm* vision mixer
**'missile** *nm* missile. **~ cruise** cruise missile. **~ terra-aria** surface-to-air missile
**missi'listico** *a* missile *attrib*

**missio'nario, -a** *nmf* missionary
**missi'one** *nf* mission. **~ di pace** peace mission
**misteriosa'mente** *adv* mysteriously
**misteri'oso** *a* mysterious
**mi'stero** *nm* mystery
**'mistica** *nf* mysticism
**misti'cismo** *nm* mysticism
**'mistico** *a* mystic[al] ● *nm* mystic
**mistifi'care** *vt* distort ⟨*verità*⟩
**mistificazi'one** *nf* ⟨*della verità*⟩ distortion
**'misto** *a* mixed; **scuola mista** mixed *o* co-educational school ● *nm* mixture; ⟨*di oggetti*⟩ miscellany. **~ lana** wool mixture; **~ lana/cotone** wool/cotton mix
**mi'sura** *nf* measure; ⟨*dimensione*⟩ measurement; ⟨*taglia*⟩ size; ⟨*limite*⟩ limit; **su ~** ⟨*abiti*⟩ made to measure; ⟨*mobile*⟩ custom-made; **a ~** ⟨*andare, calzare*⟩ perfectly; **a ~ che** as; **nella ~ in cui** insofar as. **~ di sicurezza** safety measure. **~ di capacità** unit of capacity. **~ di lunghezza** unit of length. **~ profilattica** prophylactic
**misu'rare** *vt* measure; try on ⟨*indumenti*⟩; ⟨*limitare*⟩ limit
**misu'rarsi** *vr* **~ con** ⟨*gareggiare*⟩ compete with
**misu'rato** *a* measured
**misu'rino** *nm* measuring spoon
**'mite** *a* mild; ⟨*prezzo*⟩ moderate
**'mitico** *a* mythical
**miti'gare** *vt* mitigate
**miti'garsi** *vr* calm down; ⟨*clima:*⟩ become mild
**'mitilo** *nm* mussel
**mitiz'zare** *vt* mythicize
**'mito** *nm* myth
**mitolo'gia** *nf* mythology
**mito'logico** *a* mythological
**mi'tomane** *nmf* compulsive liar
**'mitra** *nf* *Relig* mitre ● *nm inv Mil* machine-gun
**mitragli'are** *vt* machine-gun; **~ di domande** fire questions at
**mitraglia'trice** *nf* machine-gun
**mitt.** *abbr* (**mittente**) sender
**mitteleuro'peo** *a* Central European
**mit'tente** *nmf* sender
**'mixer** *nm inv* mixer
**mne'monico** *a* mnemonic; **frase mnemonica** mnemonic
**mo'** *nm* **a mo' di** by way of ⟨*esempio, consolazione*⟩
**'mobile**[1] *a* mobile; ⟨*volubile*⟩ fickle; ⟨*che si può muovere*⟩ movable; **beni** *pl* **mobili** movable personal estate; **squadra ~** flying squad
**'mobile**[2] *nm* piece of furniture; **mobili** *pl* furniture *sg*. **~ bar** drinks cabinet. **mobili** *pl* **da giardino** garden furniture. **mobili** *pl* **in stile** reproduction furniture
**mo'bilia** *nf* furniture
**mobili'are** *a* ⟨*capitale*⟩ movable; ⟨*credito*⟩ medium-term; ⟨*mercato*⟩ share *attrib*; **patrimonio ~** non-property assets
**mobili'ere** *nm* furniture dealer

**mobili'ficio** *nm* furniture factory
**mo'bilio** *nm* furniture
**mobilità** *nf* mobility
**mobili'tare** *vt* mobilize
**mobilitazi'one** *nf* mobilization
**'moca** *nm inv* mocha
**mocas'sino** *nm* moccasin
**mocci'coso, -a** *a* snotty ● *nmf* snotty-nosed kid, brat
**'moccolo** *nm* (*di candela*) candle-end; (*moccio*) snot
**'moda** *nf* fashion; **di ~** in fashion; **andare di ~** be in fashion; **alla ~** ⟨*musica, vestiti*⟩ up-to-date; **fuori ~** unfashionable
**mo'dale** *a* ⟨*verbo*⟩ modal
**modalità** *nf inv* formality; **~ d'uso** instruction
**modana'tura** *nf* moulding
**mo'della** *nf* model
**model'lare** *vt* model
**model'lino** *nm* model
**model'lismo** *nm* model-making; (*collezionismo*) collecting models
**model'lista** *nmf* model-maker; (*moda*) [fashion] designer
**mo'dello** *nm* model; (*stampo*) mould; (*di carta*) pattern; (*modulo*) form; (*moda*) male model. **~ in scala** scale model
**'modem** *nm inv* modem; **mandare per ~** modem, send by modem
**'modem-fax** *nm* fax-modem
**mode'rare** *vt* moderate; (*diminuire*) reduce
**mode'rarsi** *vr* control oneself
**moderata'mente** *adv* moderately
**mode'rato** *a* moderate
**modera|'tore, -'trice** *nmf* (*in tavola rotonda*) moderator ● *a* moderating
**moderazi'one** *nf* moderation
**moderna'mente** *adv* (*in modo moderno*) in a modern style
**modernari'ato** *nm* collecting 20th-century art and products
**moder'nismo** *nm* modernism
**modernità** *nf* modernity
**moderniz'zare** *vt* modernize
**modernizzazi'one** *nf* modernization
**mo'derno** *a* modern
**mo'destia** *nf* modesty
**mo'desto** *a* modest
**'modico** *a* reasonable
**mo'difica** *nf* modification
**modifi'care** *vt* modify
**modifica'tore** *nm* modifier
**modificazi'one** *nf* modification
**mo'dista** *nf* milliner
**'modo** *nm* way; (*garbo*) manners *pl*; (*occasione*) chance; *Gram* mood; **ad ogni ~** anyhow; **di ~ che** so that; **fare in ~ di** try to; **in che ~** (*inter*) how; **in qualche ~** somehow; **in questo ~** like this; **~ di dire** idiom; **per ~ di dire** so to speak; **in ~ ottimistico/pessimistico/anormale** optimistically/pessimistically/abnormally
**modu'lare** *vt* modulate

**modula'tore** *nm* modulator. **~ di frequenza** frequency modulator
**modulazi'one** *nf* modulation. **~ di frequenza** frequency modulation
**'modulo** *nm* form; (*lunare, di comando*) module. **~ continuo** continuous paper. **~ di domanda** application form. **~ di iscrizione** enrolment form. **~ di ordinazione** order form
**'modus ope'randi** *nm inv* modus operandi
**'modus vi'vendi** *nm inv* modus vivendi
**mof'fetta** *nf* skunk
**'mogano** *nm* mahogany
**'mogio** *a* dejected
**'moglie** *nf* wife
**moi'cano** *a* **taglio [di capelli] alla moicana** mohican [haircut]
**mo'ine** *nfpl* **fare le ~** behave in an affected way
**'mola** *nf* millstone; *Mech* grindstone
**mo'lare** *nm* molar
**mo'lato** *a* ⟨*vetro*⟩ cut
**mola'trice** *nf Mech* grinder
**'mole** *nf* mass; (*dimensione*) size
**mo'lecola** *nf* molecule
**moleco'lare** *a* molecular
**mole'stare** *vt* bother; (*più forte*) molest
**molesta|'tore, -'trice** *nmf* molester
**mo'lestia** *nf* nuisance. **molestie** *pl* **sessuali** sexual harassment *sg*
**mo'lesto** *a* bothersome
**Mo'lise** *nm* Molise
**'molla** *nf* spring; **molle** *pl* tongs; **prendere qcno con le molle** handle sb with kid gloves
**mol'lare** *vt* let go; (*fam: lasciare*) leave; *fam* give ⟨*ceffone*⟩; *Naut* cast off ● *vi* cease; **mollala!** *fam* stop that!
**'molle** *a* soft; (*bagnato*) wet
**molleggi'are** *vi* be springy ● *vt* spring
**molleggi'arsi** *vr* bend at the knees
**molleggi'ato** *a* bouncy
**mol'leggio** *nm* (*di auto*) suspension; (*di letto*) springs *pl*; (*esercizio*) knee-bends *pl*
**mol'letta** *nf* (*per capelli*) hairgrip, barrette *Am*; (*per bucato*) clothes-peg; **mollette** *pl* (*per ghiaccio ecc*) tongs. **~ da bucato** clothes peg
**mollet'tone** *nm* (*per tavolo*) padded table cloth
**mol'lezza** *nf* softness; **mollezze** *pl fig* luxury
**mol'lica** *nf* crumb
**mol'liccio** *a* squidgy
**mol'lusco** *nm* mollusc
**'molo** *nm* pier; (*banchina*) dock
**'molotov** *a inv* **bottiglia ~** Molotov cocktail
**mol'teplice** *a* manifold; (*numeroso*) numerous
**molteplicità** *nf* multiplicity
**mol'tiplica** *nf* (*di bicicletta*) gear ratio
**moltipli'care** *vt* multiply
**moltipli'carsi** *vr* multiply
**moltiplica'tore** *nm* multiplier
**moltiplica'trice** *nf* calculating machine
**moltiplicazi'one** *nf* multiplication
**molti'tudine** *nf* multitude

'**molto** *a* a lot of: (*con negazione e interrogazione*) much. a lot of; (*con nomi plurali*) many. a lot of; **non ~ tempo** not much time. not a lot of time; **molte grazie** thank you very much ● *adv* very; (*con verbi*) a lot; (*con avverbi*) much; ~ **stupido** very stupid; ~ **bene, grazie** very well. thank you; **mangiare** ~ eat a lot; ~ **più veloce** much faster; **non mangiare** ~ not eat a lot, not eat much ● *pron* a lot; (*molto tempo*) a lot of time; (*con negazione e interrogazione*) much, a lot; (*plurale*) many; **non ne ho** ~ I don't have much, I don't have a lot; **non ne ho molti** I don't have many, I don't have a lot; **non ci metterò** ~ I won't be long; **fra non** ~ before long; **molti** (*persone*) a lot of people; **eravamo in molti** there were a lot of us

**momentanea'mente** *adv* momentarily; **è ~ assente** he's not here at the moment

**momen'taneo** *a* momentary

**mo'mento** *nm* moment; **a momenti** (*a volte*) sometimes; (*fra un momento*) in a moment; **dal ~ che** since; **per il ~** for the time being; **al ~** at the moment; **da un ~ all'altro** ⟨*cambiare idea ecc*⟩ from one moment to the next; ⟨*aspettare qcno ecc*⟩ at any moment

'**monaca** *nf* nun

'**Monaco** *nm* Monaco ● *nf* (*di Baviera*) Munich

'**monaco** *nm* monk

**mo'narca** *nm* monarch

**monar'chia** *nf* monarchy

**mo'narchico, -a** *a* monarchic ● *nmf* monarchist

**mona'stero** *nm* (*di monaci*) monastery; (*di monache*) convent

**mo'nastico** *a* monastic

**monche'rino** *nm* stump

'**monco** *a* maimed; (*fig: troncato*) truncated; ~ **di un braccio** one-armed

**mon'dana** *nf* lady of the night

**mondanità** *nf* (*gente*) beau monde; ~ *pl* pleasures of the world

**mon'dano** *a* worldly; **vita mondana** social life

**mon'dare** *vt* (*sbucciare*) peel; shell ⟨*piselli*⟩; (*pulire*) clean

**mondi'ale** *a* world *attrib*; ⟨*scala*⟩ worldwide; (*fam: fantastico*) fantastic; **di fama ~** world-famous

**mondi'ali** *nmpl* World Cup

**mondial'mente** *adv* ⟨*operare*⟩ worldwide; ~ **noto** world-famous

**mon'dina** *nf* seasonal worker in the rice fields

'**mondo** *nm* world; **il bel ~** fashionable society; **un ~** (*molto*) a lot. **non è la fine del ~** it's not the end of the world; **è la fine del ~** (*fam: fantastico*) it's out of this world; ~ **cane!** *fam* damn!. ~ **accademico** academia. ~ **del lavoro** world of work. ~ **dei sogni** never-never land. ~ **dello spettacolo** show biz

**mondovisi'one** *nf* **in ~** transmitted worldwide

**monelle'ria** *nf* prank

**mo'nello, -a** *nmf* urchin

**mo'neta** *nf* coin: (*denaro*) money; (*denaro spicciolo*) [small] change. ~ **estera** foreign currency. ~ [**a corso**] **legale** legal tender. ~ **unica** single currency

**mone'tario** *a* monetary

**mongolfi'era** *nf* hot air balloon

'**mongolo** *a* Mongol; *Med* mongol

**mo'nile** *nm* jewel

'**monito** *nm* warning

'**monitor** *nm inv* monitor

**monito'raggio** *nm* monitoring

**moni'tore** *nm* monitor

**mono'albero** *a inv* single-camshaft *attrib*

**mono'blocco** *nm Auto* cylinder block ● *a inv* ⟨*cucina*⟩ fitted

**mo'nocolo** *nm* monocle

**monoco'lore** *a Pol* one-party

**monocro'matico** *a* monochrome

**mono'dose** *a inv* individually packaged

**monoga'mia** *nf* monogamy

**mo'nogamo** *a* monogamous

**monogra'fia** *nf* monograph

**mono'gramma** *nm* monogram

**mono'kini** *nm inv* monokini

**mono'lingue** *a* monolingual

**mono'lito** *nm* monolith

**monolo'cale** *nm* studio flat *Br*, studio apartment

**mo'nologo** *nm* monologue

**monoma'nia** *nf* monomania

**mononucle'osi** *nf inv* ~ **infettiva** glandular fever

**mono'pattino** *nm* [child's] scooter

**mono'petto** *a* single-breasted

**mono'plano** *nm* monoplane

**mono'polio** *nm* monopoly. ~ **di Stato** state monopoly

**monopoliz'zare** *vt* monopolize

**mono'posto** *nm* single-seater

**mono'reddito** *a* single-income *attrib*

**monosac'caride** *nm* monosaccharide

**mono'sci** *nm inv* monoski

**monosil'labico** *a* monosyllabic

**mono'sillabo** *nm* monosyllable ● *a* monosyllabic

**mo'nossido** *nm* ~ **di carbonio** carbon monoxide

**monote'istico** *a* monotheistic

**monotona'mente** *adv* monotonously

**mono'tonia** *nf* monotony

**mo'notono** *a* monotonous

**mono'uso** *a* disposable

**monou'tente** *a inv* single-user *attrib*

**monsi'gnore** *nm* monsignor

**mon'sone** *nm* monsoon

'**monta** *nf Zool* covering; (*modo di cavalcare*) riding style; **stallone da ~** stud horse

**monta'carichi** *nm inv* hoist

**mon'taggio** *nm Mech* assembly; *Cinema* editing; **scatola di ~** assembly kit; **catena di ~** production line

**mon'tagna** *nf* mountain; (*zona*) mountains *pl*; **montagne** *pl* **russe** roller coaster, big dipper

**monta'gnoso** *a* mountainous

**monta'naro**, *-a nmf* highlander

**mon'tano** *a* mountain *attrib*

**mon'tante** *nm* (*di finestra, porta*) upright; *Fin* total amount; (*nel pugilato*) upper cut

**mon'tare** *vt/i* mount; get on (*veicolo*); (*aumentare*) rise; *Mech* assemble; frame (*quadro*); *Culin* whip; edit (*film*); (*a cavallo*) ride; *fig* blow up

**mon'tarsi** *vr* ~ **la testa** get big-headed

**mon'tato**, *-a nmf fam* poser

**monta|'tore**, **-'trice** *nmf* assembler

**monta'tura** *nf Mech* assembling; (*di occhiali*) frame; (*di gioiello*) mounting; *fig* exaggeration

**'monte** *nm anche fig* mountain; **a** ~ upstream; **andare a** ~ be ruined; **mandare a** ~ **qcsa** ruin sth. **M~ Bianco** Mont Blanc. ~ **di pietà** pawnshop

**monte'premi** *nm inv* jackpot

**mont'gomery** *nm inv* duffle coat

**mon'tone** *nm* ram; **carne di** ~ mutton

**montu'oso** *a* mountainous

**monumen'tale** *a* monumental

**monu'mento** *nm* monument. ~ **ai caduti** war memorial. ~ **commemorativo** memorial. ~ **nazionale** national monument

**mo'plen**ᴿ *nm* moulded plastic

**mo'quette** *nf* (*tappeto*) fitted carpet

**'mora** *nf* (*del gelso*) mulberry; (*del rovo*) blackberry

**mo'rale** *a* moral ● *nf* morals *pl*; (*di storia*) moral ● *nm* morale

**mora'lista** *nmf* moralist

**mora'listico** *a* moralistic

**moralità** *nf inv* morality; (*condotta*) morals *pl*

**moraliz'zare** *vt/i* moralize

**moral'mente** *adv* morally

**mora'toria** *nf* moratorium

**morbida'mente** *adv* softly

**morbi'dezza** *nf* softness

**'morbido** *a* soft

**mor'billo** *nm* measles *sg*

**'morbo** *nm* disease. ~ **della mucca pazza** mad cow disease

**morbosa'mente** *adv* morbidly

**morbosità** *nf* (*qualità*) morbidity

**mor'boso** *a* morbid

**'morchia** *nf* sludge

**mor'dace** *a* cutting

**mor'dente** *a* biting

**'mordere** *vt* bite; (*corrodere*) bite into

**mordicchi'are** *vt* gnaw

**mo'rello** *nm* black horse ● *a* blackish

**mo'rena** *nf* moraine

**mo'rente** *a* dying

**mo'resco** *a* Moorish

**mor'fina** *nf* morphine

**morfi'nomane** *nmf* morphine addict

**morfolo'gia** *nf* morphology

**morfo'logico** *a* morphological

**mori'bondo** *a* dying; (*istituzione*) moribund

**morige'rato** *a* moderate

**mo'rire** *vi* die; *fig* die out; **fa un freddo da** ~ it's freezing cold, it's perishing; ~ **di noia** be bored to death; **c'era da** ~ **dal ridere** it was hilariously funny; **morir di fame** starve to death; *fig* starve

**mor'mone** *nmf* Mormon

**mormo'rare** *vt/i* murmur; (*brontolare*) mutter

**mormo'rio** *nm* murmuring; (*lamentela*) grumbling

**'moro** *a* dark ● *nm* Moor; (*negro*) black

**mo'roso** *a* in arrears

**'morra** *nf* game for two players where each shouts a number at the same time as showing a number of fingers

**'morsa** *nf* vice; *fig* grip

**'morse** *a* **alfabeto** ~ Morse code

**mor'setto** *nm* clamp; (*stringinaso*) nose clip. ~ **per batteria** battery lead connection

**morsi'care** *vt* bite

**morsica'tura** *nf* [snake] bite

**'morso** *nm* bite; (*di cibo, briglia*) bit; **i morsi della fame** hunger pangs

**morta'della** *nf* mortadella (*type of salted pork*)

**mor'taio** *nm* mortar

**mor'tale** *a* mortal; (*simile a morte*) deadly; **di una noia** ~ deadly

**mortalità** *nf* mortality

**mortal'mente** *adv* (*ferito*) fatally; (*offeso*) mortally; (*annoiato*) to death. ~ **stanco** *fam* dead tired

**morta'retto** *nm* firecracker

**'morte** *nf* death; **non è la** ~ **di nessuno** it's not the end of the world; **lo odia a** ~ *fam* she can't stand the sight of him; **annoiarsi a** ~ *fam* be bored to death. ~ **cerebrale** brain death

**mortifi'cante** *a* mortifying

**mortifi'care** *vt* mortify

**mortifi'carsi** *vr* be mortified

**mortifi'cato** *a* mortified

**mortificazi'one** *nf* mortification

**'morto**, **-a** *pp di* **morire** ● *a* dead; ~ **di freddo** frozen to death; **stanco** ~ dead tired ● *nm* dead man ● *nf* dead woman

**mor'torio** *nm* funeral

**mo'saico** *nm* mosaic

**'Mosca** *nf* Moscow

**'mosca** *nf* fly; (*barba*) goatee; **cadere come le mosche** be dropping like flies; **essere una** ~ **bianca** be a rarity; **non si sentiva volare una** ~ you could have heard a pin drop. ~ **cieca** blindman's buff

**mo'scato** *a* muscat. **noce moscata** nutmeg ● *nm* muscatel

**mosce'rino** *nm* midge; (*fam: persona*) midget

**mo'schea** *nf* mosque

**moschetti'ere** *nm* musketeer

**mo'schetto** *nm* musket

**moschet'tone** *nm* (*in alpinismo*) snaplink; (*gancio*) spring clip

**moschi'cida** *a inv* **carta ~** flypaper; **liquido ~** fly spray

**'moscio** *a* limp: **avere l'erre moscia** not be able to say one's r's properly

**mo'scone** *nm* bluebottle; *(barca)* pedalo

**Mosè** *nm* Moses

**'mossa** *nf* movement; *(passo)* move

**'mosso** *pp di* **muovere** ● *a* *(mare)* rough; *(capelli)* wavy; *(fotografia)* blurred

**mo'starda** *nf* mustard. **~ di Cremona** preserve made from candied fruit in grape must or sugar with mustard

**'mostra** *nf* show; *(d'arte)* exhibition; **far ~ di** pretend; **in ~** on show; **mettersi in ~** make oneself conspicuous; **far ~ di sé** show off; **far bella ~ di sé** look impressive

**'mostra-mer'cato** *nf* trade fair

**mo'strare** *vt* show; *(indicare)* point out; *(spiegare)* explain; **~ di** *(sembrare)* seem; *(fingere)* pretend

**mos'trarsi** *vr* show oneself; *(apparire)* appear

**mo'strina** *nf* flash

**'mostro** *nm* monster; *(fig: persona)* genius; **~ sacro** *fig* sacred cow

**mostruosa'mente** *adv* tremendously

**mostru'oso** *a* monstrous; *(incredibile)* enormous

**mo'tel** *nm inv* motel

**moti'vare** *vt* cause; *Jur* justify

**moti'vato** *a* *(persona)* motivated; *(azione)* justified

**motivazi'one** *nf* motivation; *(giustificazione)* justification

**mo'tivo** *nm* reason; *(movente)* motive; *(in musica, letteratura)* theme; *(disegno)* pattern, motif; **senza ~** for no reason; **~ a scacchi** chequered pattern

**'moto** *nm* motion; *(esercizio)* exercise; *(gesto)* movement; *(sommossa)* rising. **~ ondoso** swell. **~ perpetuo** perpetual motion ● *nf inv* *(motocicletta)* motor bike; **mettere in ~** start *(motore)*

**moto'carro** *nm* three-wheeler

**motoci'cletta** *nf* motor cycle. **~ da corsa** racing motorbike, racer

**motoci'clismo** *nm* motorcycling

**motoci'clista** *nmf* motorcyclist

**moto'cross** *nm* motocross

**motocros'sista** *nmf* scrambler

**moto'lancia** *nf* motor launch

**moto'nautica** *nf* speedboat racing

**moto'nave** *nf* motor vessel

**mo'tore** *a* motor *attrib* ● *nm* motor, engine; **con ~ turbo** turbocharged. . **~ diesel** diesel engine. **~ a iniezione** fuel injection engine. **~ raffreddato ad aria** air-cooled engine. **~ a reazione** jet [engine]. **~ a scoppio** internal combustion engine

**moto'retta** *nf* motor scooter

**moto'rino** *nm* moped. **~ d'avviamento** starter motor

**mo'torio** *a* motor *attrib*

**moto'rista** *mf* **~ di bordo** flight engineer

**motoriz'zare** *vt* motorize

**motoriz'zato** *a* *Mil* motorized

**motorizzazi'one** *nf* *(ufficio)* vehicle licensing office

**moto'scafo** *nm* motorboat

**moto'sega** *nf* chain saw

**motove'detta** *nf* patrol vessel

**mo'trice** *nf* engine

**'motto** *nm* motto; *(facezia)* witticism; *(massima)* saying

**'mountain bike** *nf inv* mountain bike

**mouse** *nm inv Comput* mouse

**mousse** *nf inv Culin* mousse. **~ al cioccolato** chocolate mousse

**mo'vente** *nm* motive

**mo'venze** *nfpl* movements

**movimen'tare** *vt* enliven

**movimen'tato** *a* lively

**movi'mento** *nm* movement; **essere sempre in ~** be always on the go. **~ passeggeri e merci** passenger and freight traffic

**mozi'one** *nf* motion. **~ d'ordine** point of order

**mozzafi'ato** *a inv* nail-biting

**moz'zare** *vt* cut off; dock *(coda)*; **~ il fiato a qcno** take sb's breath away

**mozza'rella** *nf* mozzarella *(mild, white cheese)*

**mozzi'cone** *nm* *(di sigaretta)* stub

**'mozzo** *nm Mech* hub; *Naut* ship's boy ● *a* *(coda)* truncated; *(testa)* severed

**ms** *abbr* **(manoscritto)** MS

**'mucca** *nf* cow; **morbo della ~ pazza** mad cow disease

**'mucchio** *nm* heap, pile; **un ~ di** *fig* lots of

**mucil'lagine** *nf Bot* mucilage

**'muco** *nm* mucus

**'muffa** *nf* mould; **fare la ~** go mouldy

**muf'fire** *vi* go mouldy

**muf'fola** *nf* mitt

**mu'flone** *nm Zool* mouflon

**mugghi'are** *vi* *(vento, mare:)* roar

**mug'gire** *vi* *(mucca:)* moo, low; *(toro:)* bellow

**mug'gito** *nm* *(di mucca)* moo; *(di toro)* bellow; *(azione)* mooing; bellowing

**mu'ghetto** *nm* lily of the valley

**mugo'lare** *vi* whine; *(persona:)* moan

**mugo'lio** *nm* whining

**mugu'gnare** *vt fam* mumble

**mulatti'era** *nf* mule track

**mu'latto, -a** *nmf* mulatto

**mu'leta** *nf inv* muleta

**muli'ebre** *a liter* feminine

**muli'nare** *vi* whirl

**muli'nello** *nm* *(d'acqua)* whirlpool; *(di vento)* eddy; *(giocattolo)* windmill

**mu'lino** *nm* mill. **~ a vento** windmill

**'mulo** *nm* mule

**'multa** *nf* fine. **~ per divieto di sosta** parking ticket

**mul'tare** *vt* fine

**multico'lore** *a* multicoloured

**multicultu'rale** *a* multicultural

**multifunzio'nale** *a* multifunction[al]
**multilate'rale** *a* multilateral
**multi'lingue** *a* multilingual
**multi'media** *mpl* multimedia
**multimedi'ale** *a* multimedia *attrib*
**multimedialità** *nf* multimedia
**multimiliar'dario, -a** *nmf* multi-million-aire
**multinazio'nale** *a* & *nf* multinational
**'multiplo** *a* & *nm* multiple
**multiproprietà** *nf inv* time-share; **una casa in ~** a time-share
**multi'sale** *a inv* **cinema ~** multiplex [cinema]
**multi'tasking** *nm Comput* multitasking
**multi'uso** *a* ‹*utensile*› all-purpose
**'mummia** *nf* mummy; (*fig: persona*) old fogey
**mummifi'care** *vt* mummify
**'mungere** *vt* milk
**mungi'tura** *nf* milking
**munici'pale** *a* municipal
**municipalità** *nf inv* town council
**muni'cipio** *nm* town hall
**munifi'cenza** *nf* munificence, bounty
**mu'nifico** *a* munificent
**mu'nire** *vt* fortify; **~ di** (*provvedere*) supply with; **munitevi di un carrello/cestino** please take a trolley/basket
**munizi'oni** *nfpl* ammunition *sg*
**'munto** *pp di* **mungere**
**mu'overe** *vt* move; (*suscitare*) arouse
**mu'oversi** *vr* move; **muoviti!** hurry up!, come on!
**'mura** *nfpl* (*cinta di città*) walls
**mu'raglia** *nf* wall
**mu'rale** *a* mural; ‹*pittura*› wall *attrib*
**mur'are** *vt* wall up
**mu'rario** *a* masonry *attrib*; **cinta muraria** walls *pl*; **opera muraria** masonry
**mura'tore** *nm* bricklayer; (*con pietre*) mason; (*operaio edile*) builder
**mura'tura** *nf* (*di pietra*) masonry, stonework; (*di mattoni*) brickwork
**mu'rena** *nf* moray eel
**'muro** *nm* wall; (*di nebbia*) bank; **a ~** ‹*armadio*› built-in. **~ di gomma** *fig* wall of indifference. **~ a intercapedine** cavity wall. **M~ del pianto** Wailing Wall. **~ portante** load-bearing wall. **~ del suono** sound barrier
**'musa** *nf anche fig* muse
**muschi'ato** *a* musky
**'muschio** *nm Bot* moss

**musco'lare** *a* muscular
**muscola'tura** *nf* muscles *pl*
**'muscolo** *nm* muscle
**musco'loso** *a* muscular
**mu'seo** *nm* museum
**museru'ola** *nf* muzzle
**'musica** *nf* music
**musica folk** *nf* folk [music]
**'musical** *nm inv* musical
**musi'cale** *a* musical
**musi'care** *vt* set to music
**musicas'setta** *nf* cassette
**musi'cista** *nmf* musician
**musicolo'gia** *nf* musicology
**'muso** *nm* muzzle; (*pej: di persona*) mug; (*di aeroplano*) nose; **fare il ~** sulk
**mu'sone, -a** *nmf* sulker
**'mussola** *nf* muslin
**mussul'mano, -a** *a* & *nmf* Muslim, Moslem
**'muta** *nf* (*cambio*) change; (*di penne*) moult; (*di cani*) pack; (*per immersione subacquea*) wetsuit
**muta'mento** *nm* change
**mu'tande** *nfpl* pants
**mutan'dine** *nfpl* panties; **~ da bagno** bathing trunks; (*da donna*) bikini bottom
**mutan'doni** *nmpl* (*da uomo*) long johns; (*da donna*) bloomers
**mu'tante** *nmf* mutant
**mu'tare** *vt* change
**mutazi'one** *nf* mutation
**mu'tevole** *a* changeable
**muti'lare** *vt* mutilate
**muti'lato, -a** *a* crippled ● *nmf* disabled person. **~ di guerra** disabled ex-serviceman. **~ del lavoro** person disabled at work
**mutilazi'one** *nf* mutilation
**mu'tismo** *nm* dumbness; *fig* obstinate silence
**'muto** *a* dumb; (*silenzioso*) silent; (*fonetica*) mute
**'mutua** *nf* [**cassa**] **~** sickness benefit fund
**mutu'abile** *a* ‹*farmaco*› prescribable on the NHS
**mutu'are** *vt* borrow ‹*teoria, parola*›
**mutua'tario, -a** *nmf Fin* borrower
**mutu'ato, -a** *nmf* ≈ NHS patient
**'mutuo**[1] *a* mutual
**'mutuo**[2] *nm* loan; (*per la casa*) mortgage; **fare un ~** take out a mortgage; **società di ~ soccorso** friendly society. **~ per la casa** home loan. **~ ipotecario** mortgage

# Nn

**na'babbo** *nm* nabob; **vivere come un ~** live in the lap of luxury

**'nacchera** *nf* castanet

**na'dir** *nm* nadir

**'nafta** *nf* naphtha; *(per motori)* diesel oil; **a ~** *(bruciatore)* oil-burning

**'naia** *nf* cobra; *(sl: servizio militare)* national service

**'nailon** *nm* nylon

**Na'mibia** *nf* Namibia

**na'nismo** *nm* dwarfism

**'nanna** *nf (sl: infantile)* byebyes; **andare a ~** go byebyes; **fare la ~** sleep

**'nano, -a** *a & nmf* dwarf

**napalm** *nm* napalm

**napole'tana** *nf (caffettiera)* Neapolitan coffee maker

**napole'tano, -a** *a & nmf* Neapolitan

**'Napoli** *nf* Naples

**'nappa** *nf* tassel; *(pelle)* soft leather

**narci'sismo** *nm* narcissism

**narci'sista** *a & nmf* narcissist

**nar'ciso** *nm* narcissus

**nar'cosi** *nf* general anaesthesia

**nar'cotici** *nf* Drug Squad

**nar'cotico** *a & nm* narcotic

**na'rice** *nf* nostril

**nar'rare** *vt* tell

**narra'tivo, -a** *a* narrative ● *nf* fiction

**narra|'tore, -'trice** *nmf* narrator

**narrazi'one** *nf* narration; *(racconto)* story

**na'sale** *a* nasal

**na'scente** *a* budding

**'nascere** *vi (venire al mondo)* be born; *(germogliare)* sprout; *(sorgere)* rise; **~ da** *fig* arise from

**'nascita** *nf* birth

**nasci'turo** *nm* unborn child

**na'scondere** *vt* hide

**na'scondersi** *vr* hide

**nascon'diglio** *nm* hiding-place

**nascon'dino** *nm* hide-and-seek

**na'scosto** *pp di* nascondere ● *a* hidden; **di ~** secretly

**na'sello** *nm (pesce)* hake

**'naso** *nm* nose

**na'sone** *nm* big nose, hooter *fam*

**'nassa** *nf* lobster pot

**'nastro** *nm* ribbon; *(di registratore ecc)* tape. **~ adesivo** adhesive tape. **~ isolante** insulating tape. **~ magnetico** magnetic tape, mag tape *fam*. **~ trasportatore** conveyor belt

**Na'tale** *nm* Christmas

**na'tale** *a (giorno, paese)* of one's birth

**na'tali** *nmpl* parentage

**natalità** *nf* [number of] births, birthrate

**nata'lizio** *a (del Natale)* Christmas *attrib*; *(di nascita)* of one's birth

**na'tante** *a* floating ● *nm* craft

**'natica** *nf* buttock

**na'tio** *a* native

**Nativà** *nf* Nativity

**na'tivo, -a** *a & nmf* native

**NATO** *nf* Nato, NATO

**'nato** *pp di* nascere ● *a* born; **uno scrittore ~** a born writer; **nata Rossi** née Rossi

**na'tura** *nf* nature; **pagare in ~** pay in kind; **di ~ politica** of a political nature. **~ morta** still life

**natu'rale** *a* natural; **al ~** *(alimento)* plain, natural; **~!** naturally, of course

**natura'lezza** *nf* naturalness

**naturaliz'zare** *vt* naturalize

**natural'mente** *adv (ovviamente)* naturally, of course

**natu'rista** *nmf* naturalist

**natu'ristico** *a* a naturist

**naufra'gare** *vi* be wrecked; *(persona:)* be shipwrecked

**nau'fragio** *nm* shipwreck; *fig* wreck

**'naufrago, -a** *nmf* survivor

**'nausea** *nf* nausea; **avere la ~** feel sick

**nausea'bondo** *a* nauseating

**nause'ante** *a* nauseating

**nause'are** *vt* nauseate

**'nautica** *nf* navigation

**'nautico** *a* nautical

**na'vale** *a* naval

**na'vata** *nf (centrale)* nave; *(laterale)* aisle

**'nave** *nf* ship. **~ ammiraglia** flagship. **~ da carico** cargo boat. **~ cisterna** tanker. **~ da crociera** cruise liner. **~ fattoria** factory ship. **~ da guerra** warship. **~ di linea** liner. **~ passeggeri** passenger ship. **~ porta-container** container ship. **~ spaziale** spaceship. **~ traghetto** ferry

**na'vetta** *nf* shuttle

**navi'cella** *nf* **~ spaziale** nose cone

**navi'gabile** *a* navigable

**navi'gare** *vi* sail; **~ in Internet** surf the Net

**naviga|'tore, -'trice** *mf* navigator; *(in Internet)* surfer; **~ solitario** lone yachtsman. **~ spaziale** spaceman

**navigazi'one** *nf* navigation; **della ~** navigational

**na'viglio** *nm* fleet; *(canale)* canal

**nazifa'scismo** *nm* Nazi fascism

**nazifa'scista** *nmf* Nazi fascist

**nazio'nale** *a* national ● *nf* *Sport* national team

**naziona'lismo** *nm* nationalism

**naziona'lista** *nmf* nationalist

**nazionalità** *nf inv* nationality

**nazionaliz'zare** *vt* nationalize

**nazi'one** *nf* nation. **Nazioni** *pl* **Unite** United Nations

**na'zista** *a* & *nmf* Nazi

**N.B.** *abbr* (**nota bene**) NB

**n.d.r.** *abbr* (**nota del redattore**) editor's note

**'n'drangheta** *nf* Calabrian Mafia

**n.d.t.** *abbr* (**nota del traduttore**) translator's note

**NE** *abbr* (**nord-est**) NE

**ne** *pron* (*di lui*) about him; (*di lei*) about her; (*di loro*) about them; (*di ciò*) about it; (*da ciò*) from that; (*di un insieme*) of it; (*di un gruppo*) of them; **ne sono contento** I'm happy about it; **non ne conosco nessuno** I don't know any of them; **ne ho** I have some; **non ne ho più** I don't have any left ● *adv* from there; **ne vengo ora** I've just come from there; **me ne vado** I'm off; **ne va della mia reputazione** my reputation is at stake

**né** *conj* **né... né...** neither... nor...; **non ne ho il tempo né la voglia** I don't have either the time or the inclination; **né tu né io vogliamo andare** neither you nor I want to go; **né l'uno né l'altro** neither [of them/us]

**ne'anche** *adv* (*neppure*) not even; (*senza neppure*) without even ● *conj* (*e neppure*) neither... nor; **non parlo inglese, e lui ~** I don't speak English, neither does he *o* and he doesn't either

**'nebbia** *nf* mist; (*in città, autostrada*) fog

**nebbi'oso** *a* misty; (*in città, autostrada*) foggy

**nebuliz'zare** *vt* atomize

**nebulizza'tore** *nm* atomizer; (*per il naso*) nasal spray

**nebulizzazi'one** *nf* atomizing; **fare delle nebulizzazioni** take nasal sprays

**nebulosità** *nf* vagueness

**nebu'loso** *a* hazy; ⟨*teoria*⟩ nebulous; ⟨*discorso*⟩ woolly

**necessaria'mente** *adv* necessarily

**neces'sario** *a* necessary ● *nm* **fare il ~ do** the necessary, do the needful

**necessità** *nf inv* necessity; (*bisogno*) need

**necessi'tare** *vi* **~ di** need; (*essere necessario*) be necessary

**necro'logio** *nm* obituary

**ne'cropoli** *nf inv* necropolis

**ne'crosi** *nf* necrosis

**ne'fando** *a* wicked

**ne'fasto** *a* ill-omened

**ne'frite** *nf* nephritis

**nefrolo'gia** *nf* nephrology

**ne'frologo, -a** *nmf* nephrologist

**ne'gabile** *a* deniable

**ne'gare** *vt* deny; (*rifiutare*) refuse; **essere negato per qcsa** be no good at sth

**nega'tiva** *nf* negative

**nega'tivo** *a* negative

**negazi'one** *nf* negation; (*diniego*) denial; *Gram* negative; **essere la ~ per** know nothing about

**ne'gletto** *a* neglected

**'negli** = **in** + **gli**

**negli'gente** *a* negligent

**negli'genza** *nf* negligence

**negozi'abile** *a* negotiable

**negozi'ante** *nmf* dealer; (*bottegaio*) shopkeeper

**negozi'are** *vt* negotiate ● *vi* **~ in** trade in, deal in

**negozi'ati** *nmpl* negotiations

**ne'gozio** *nm* shop. **~ di abbigliamento** fashion boutique. **~ di alimentari** grocer's. **~ di antiquariato** antique shop. **~ duty free** duty-free shop. **~ giuridico** legal transaction

**'negro, -a** *a* Negro, black ● *nmf* Negro, black; (*scrittore*) ghost writer; **come un ~** ⟨*lavorare*⟩ like a slave

**negro'mante** *nmf* necromancer

**'nei** = **in** + **i**

**nel** = **in** + **il**

**'nella** = **in** + **la**

**'nelle** = **in** + **le**

**'nello** = **in** + **lo**

**'nembo** *nm* nimbus

**ne'mesi** *nf* nemesis

**ne'mico, -a** *a* hostile ● *nmf* enemy

**nem'meno** *conj* not even

**'nenia** *nf* dirge; (*per bambini*) lullaby; (*piagnucolio*) wail

**'neo** *nm* mole; (*applicato*) beauty spot

**neo+** *pref* neo+

**neo'classico** *a* neoclassical

**neocolonia'lismo** *nm* neocolonialism

**neofa'scismo** *nm* neofascism

**neola'tino** *a* Romance

**neolaure'ato, -a** *nmf* recent graduate

**neo'litico** *a* Neolithic

**neolo'gismo** *nm* neologism

**'neon** *nm* neon

**neo'nato, -a** *a* newborn ● *nmf* newborn baby

**neona'zismo** *nm* Neonazism

**neona'zista** *a* & *nmf* Neonazi

**neozelan'dese** *a* New Zealand *attrib* ● *nmf* New Zealander

**nep'pure** *conj* not even

**ne'rastro** *a* blackish

**'nerbo** *nm* (*forza*) strength; *fig* backbone; **senza ~** effete

**nerbo'ruto** *a* brawny

**ne'retto** *nm* *Typ* bold [type]

**'nero** *a* black; (*fam: arrabbiato*) fuming ● *nm* black; **l'ho visto ~ su bianco** I've seen it in black and white; **mettere ~ su bianco** put in writing. **~ pieno** *Typ* solid. **~ di seppia** sepia

**nerva'tura** *nf* nerves *pl*; *Bot* veining; (*di libro*) band

**ner'vetti** *nmpl* chopped beef and veal with onions

**ner'vino** *a* ⟨*gas*⟩ nerve *attrib*

'**nervo** *nm* nerve; *Bot* vein; **avere i nervi** be bad-tempered; **dare ai nervi a qcno** get on sb's nerves

**nervo'sismo** *nm* nerviness

**ner'voso** *a* nervous; (*irritabile*) bad-tempered; **avere il ~** be irritable; **esaurimento ~** nervous breakdown

'**nespola** *nf* medlar

'**nespolo** *nm* medlar[-tree]

'**nesso** *nm* link, connection

**nes'suno** *a* no, not... any; (*qualche*) any; **non ho nessun problema** I don't have any problems, I have no problems; **non ha nessun valore** it hasn't any value, it has no value; **da nessuna parte** nowhere; **non lo trovo da nessuna parte** I can't find it anywhere; **in nessun modo** on no account; **per nessun motivo** for no reason; **nessuna notizia?** any news? ● *pron* nobody, no one, not ... anybody, not... anyone; (*qualcuno*) anybody, anyone; **hai delle domande? – nessuna** do you have any questions? – none; **~ di voi** none of you; **~ dei due** (*di voi due*) neither of you; **non ho visto ~ dei tuoi amici** I haven't seen any of your friends; **c'è ~?** is anybody there?

'**nesting** *nm inv Comput* nesting

**net** *nm inv Tennis* net cord

'**nettare** *nm* nectar

**net'tare** *vt* clean

**net'tezza** *nf* cleanliness. **~ urbana** cleansing department

'**netto** *a* clean; (*chiaro*) clear; *Comm* net; **di ~** just like that

**Net'tuno** *nm* Neptune

**nettur'bino** *nm* dustman

'**neuro** *nf* neurological clinic

**neuro+** *pref* neuro+

**neurochirur'gia** *nf* brain surgery

**neurochi'rurgo** *nm* brain surgeon

**neurolo'gia** *nf* neurology

**neurologico** *a* neurological

**neuropsichi'atra** *nm* neuropsychiatry

**neuropsichia'tria** *nf* neuropsychiatrist

**neu'trale** *a & nm* neutral

**neutralità** *nf* neutrality

**neutraliz'zare** *vt* neutralize

'**neutro** *a* neutral; *Gram* neuter ● *nm Gram* neuter

**neu'trone** *nm* neutron

**ne'vaio** *nm* snow-field

'**neve** *nf* snow

**nevi'care** *vi* snow; **nevica** it is snowing

**nevi'cata** *nf* snowfall

**ne'vischio** *nm* sleet

**ne'voso** *a* snowy

**nevral'gia** *nf* neuralgia

**ne'vralgico** *a* neuralgic; **punto ~** nerve centre; (*di questione ecc*) crucial point

**nevraste'nia** *nf* neurasthenia

**nevra'stenico** *a* neurasthenic; (*irritabile*) hot tempered

**ne'vrite** *nf* neuritis

**ne'vrosi** *nf inv* neurosis

**ne'vrotico** *a* neurotic

'**nibbio** *nm* kite

**Nica'ragua** *nm* Nicaragua

**nicara'guense** *a & nmf* Nicaraguan

'**nicchia** *nf* niche

**nicchi'are** *vi* shilly-shally

'**nichel** *nm* nickel

**nichi'lista** *nmf* nihilist ● *a* nihilistic

**nico'tina** *nf* nicotine

**nidi'ace** *nm* nestling

**nidi'ata** *nf* brood

**nidifi'care** *vi* nest

**nidifi'cato** *a Comput* nested

**nidificazi'one** *nf Zool* nesting

'**nido** *nm* nest; (*giardino d'infanzia*) crèche; **a ~ d'ape** (*tessuto*) honeycomb. **~ di uccello** bird's nest. **~ di vipere** *fig* nest of vipers

**ni'ente** *pron* nothing, not... anything; (*qualcosa*) anything; **non ho fatto ~ di male** I didn't do anything wrong, I did nothing wrong; **nient'altro?** anything else?; **grazie! – di ~!** thank you! – don't mention it!; **non serve a ~** it is no use; **vuoi ~?** do you want anything?; **dal ~** (*venire su*) from nothing; **da ~** (*poco importante*) minor; (*di poco valore*) worthless ● *a inv fam* **~ pesci oggi** no fish today; **non ho ~ fame** I'm not the slightest bit hungry ● *adv* **non fa ~** (*non importa*) it doesn't matter; **per ~** at all; (*litigare*) over nothing; **~ affatto!** no way! ● *nm* **un bel ~** absolutely nothing, damn-all *fam*; **basta un ~ per spaventarlo** it doesn't take much to scare him

**nientedi'meno, niente'meno** *adv* **~ che** no less than ● *int* fancy that!

**night** *nm inv* night club

'**Nilo** *nm* Nile

'**ninfa** *nf* nymph

**nin'fea** *nf* water-lily

**nin'fomane** *nf* nymphomaniac; **da ~** nymphomaniac

**ninna'nanna** *nf* lullaby

'**ninnolo** *nm* plaything; (*fronzolo*) knickknack

**ni'pote** *nm* (*di zii*) nephew; (*di nonni*) grandson, grandchild; **nipoti** *pl* grandchildren, nephews and nieces ● *nf* (*di zii*) niece; (*di nonni*) granddaughter, grandchild

**nip'ponico** *a* Japanese

'**nisba** *pron* (*sl: niente*) zilch

'**nitido** *a* neat; (*chiaro*) clear

'**nitrato** *nm* nitrate

'**nitrico** *a* nitric

**ni'trire** *vi* neigh

**ni'trito** *nm* (*di cavallo*) neigh; *Chem* nitrite

**nitro+** *pref* nitro+

**nitroglice'rina** *nf* nitroglycerine

'**niveo** *a* snow-white

**N.N.** *abbr* (**numeri**) Nos

**NO** *abbr* (**nord-ovest**) NW

**N°** *abbr* (**numero**) No.

**no** *adv* no; **credo di no** I don't think so; **perché no?** why not?; **io no** not me; **sì o no?** yes or no?; **ha detto così, no?** he said so, didn't he?; **fa freddo, no?** it's cold, isn't it?; **se no** otherwise ● *nm* no; (*nelle votazioni*) nay

**nobil'donna** *nf* noblewoman

**'nobile** *a* noble: **metallo ~** noble metal; **di animo ~** noble-minded ● *nm* noble, nobleman ● *nf* noble, noblewoman

**nobili'are** *a* noble

**nobiltà** *nf* nobility

**nobilu'omo** *nm* nobleman

**'nocca** *nf* knuckle

**nocci'ola** *nf* hazelnut

**noccio'line [americane]** *nfpl* peanuts

**nocci'olo** *nm* (*albero*) hazel

**'nocciolo** *nm* stone; *Phys* core; *fig* heart; **il ~ della questione** the heart of the matter

**'noce** *nf* walnut. **~ moscata** nutmeg. **~ pecan** pecan. **~ di vitello** veal with mushrooms ● *nm* (*legno*) walnut; (*albero*) walnut [tree]

**noce'pesca** *nf* nectarine

**no'cino** *nm* walnut liqueur

**no'civo** *a* harmful

**no'dino** *nm* veal chop

**'nodo** *nm* knot; *fig* lump; *Comput* node; **fare il ~ della cravatta** do up one's tie. **~ alla gola** lump in the throat; **~ della questione** crux of the matter. **~ ferroviario** railway junction. **~ piano** reef knot. **~ scorsoio** slipknot

**no'doso** *a* knotty

**'nodulo** *nm* nodule

**Noè** *nm* Noah

**'noi** *pers pron* (*soggetto*) we; (*oggetto, con prep*) us; **chi è? – siamo ~** who is it? – it's us; **noi due** the two of us

**'noia** *nf* boredom; (*fastidio*) bother; (*persona*) bore; **dar ~** annoy

**noi'altri** *pers pron* we

**noi'oso** *a* boring; (*fastidioso*) tiresome

**noleggi'are** *vt* hire; (*dare a noleggio*) hire out; charter ⟨*nave, aereo*⟩

**no'leggio** *nm* hire; (*di nave, aereo*) charter. **~ barche/biciclette/sci** boat/cycle/ski hire

**'nolo** *nm* hire; *Naut* freight; **a ~** for hire

**'nomade** *a* nomadic ● *nmf* nomad

**'nome** *nm* name; *Gram* noun; **a ~ di** (*da parte di*) on behalf of; **di ~** by name; **farsi un ~** make a name for oneself; **nel ~ di...** in the name of.... **~ d'arte** professional name. **~ di battaglia** nom de guerre. **~ di battesimo** first name, Christian name. **~ depositato** trade-name. **~ di famiglia** surname, family name. **~ proprio** proper name, proper noun. **~ da ragazza** maiden name. **~ da sposata** married name

**no'mea** *nf* reputation

**nomencla'tura** *nf* nomenclature

**no'mignolo** *nm* nickname

**'nomina** *nf* appointment; **di prima ~** newly appointed

**nomi'nale** *a* nominal; *Gram* noun *attrib*

**nomi'nare** *vt* name; (*menzionare*) mention; (*eleggere*) appoint

**nomina'tivo** *a* nominative; *Comm* registered ● *nm* nominative; (*nome*) name; **caso ~** nominative case

**non** *adv* not; **~ ti amo** I do not *o* don't love you; **~ c'è di che** not at all; **~ più** no longer

**nonché** *conj* (*tanto meno*) let alone; (*e anche*) as well as

**nonconfor'mista** *a & nmf inv* nonconformist

**nonconformità** *nf* noncompliance

**noncu'rante** *a* nonchalant; (*negligente*) indifferent

**noncu'ranza** *nf* nonchalance; (*negligenza*) indifference

**nondi'meno** *conj* nevertheless

**'nonna** *nf* grandmother, grandma *fam*, gran *fam*

**'nonno** *nm* grandfather, grandpa *fam*; **nonni** *pl* grandparents

**non'nulla** *nm inv* trifle

**'nono** *a & nm* ninth

**nono'stante** *prep* in spite of ● *conj* although

**non stop** *a inv & adv* nonstop

**nontiscordardimé** *nm inv* forget-me-not

**nonvio'lento** *a* nonviolent

**nonvio'lenza** *nf* nonviolence

**nor'cino** *nm* pig butcher

**nord** *nm* north; **del ~** northern

**nord-'est** *nm* northeast; **a ~** northeasterly; **del ~** northeastern; **vento di ~** northeasterly [wind]

**'nordico** *a* northern

**nor'dista** *a & nmf* Yankee

**nordocciden'tale** *a* northwestern

**nordorien'tale** *a* northeastern

**nord-'ovest** *nm* northwest; **a ~** northwesterly; **del ~** northwestern **vento di ~** northwesterly [wind]

**'norma** *nf* norm; (*regola*) rule; (*per l'uso*) instruction; **a ~ di legge** according to law; **è buona ~** it's advisable; **di ~** as a rule, normally

**nor'male** *a* normal ● *nm* **fuori del ~** out of the ordinary; **superiore al ~** above average

**normalità** *nf* normality; **rientrare nella ~** be quite normal

**normaliz'zare** *vt* normalize

**normal'mente** *adv* normally

**Norman'dia** *nf* Normandy

**nor'manno** *a* from Normandy; (*storico*) Norman

**norma'tivo** *a* normative, prescriptive

**nor'mografo** *nm* stencil

**nor'reno** *a* Norse

**norve'gese** *a & nmf* Norwegian

**Nor'vegia** *nf* Norway

**noso'comio** *nm fml* hospital

**nossi'gnore** *adv* (*assolutamente no*) no way

**nostal'gia** *nf* (*di casa, patria*) homesickness; (*del passato*) nostalgia; **aver ~** be homesick; **aver ~ di qcno** miss sb

**no'stalgico, -a** *a* nostalgic ● *nmf* reactionary

**nostra** *vedi* **nostro**

**no'strale** *a* local

**no'strano** *a* local; (*fatto in casa*) home-made

**'nostre** *vedi* **nostro**

**'nostri** *vedi* **nostro**

**'nostro** (**il nostro** *m*, **la nostra** *f*, **i nostri**

*mpl*. **le nostre** *fpl*) *poss a*: our: **quella macchina è nostra** that car is ours; **~ padre** our father; **un ~ amico** a friend of ours ● *poss pron* ours

**no'stromo** *nm* bo's'n, boatswain

**'nota** *nf* (*segno*) sign; (*comunicazione, commento, Mus*) note; (*conto*) bill; (*lista*) list; **degno di ~** noteworthy; **prendere ~** take note; **una ~ di colore** a touch of colour; **mettere in ~ qcsa** add sth to the list. **~ di accredito** *Comm* credit note. **note** *pl* **caratteristiche** distinguishing marks. **~ spese** expense account

**no'tabile** *a & nm* notable

**no'taio** *nm* notary

**no'tare** *vt* (*segnare*) mark; (*annotare*) note down; (*osservare*) notice; **far ~ qcsa** point sth out; **farsi ~** get oneself noticed; **nota bene che...** please note that...

**notazi'one** *nf* marking; (*annotazione*) notation

**'notebook** *nm inv Comput* notebook

**'notes** *nm inv* notepad

**no'tevole** *a* (*degno di nota*) remarkable; (*grande*) considerable

**no'tifica** *nf* notification

**notifi'care** *vt* notify; *Comm* advise; **~ un ordine di comparizione [in giudizio]** subpoena

**notificazi'one** *nf* notification

**no'tizia** *nf* **una ~** a piece of news, some news; (*informazione*) a piece of information, some information; **le notizie** the news *sg*; **per avere ~ di** (*telefonare*) for news of; **non ha più dato notizie di sé** he hasn't been in touch since. **~ di attualità** news item

**notizi'ario** *nm* news *sg*

**'noto** *a* [well-]known; **rendere ~** (*far sapere*) announce

**notorietà** *nf* fame; **raggiungere la ~** become famous

**no'torio** *a* a well-known; *pej* notorious

**not'tambulo** *nm* night-bird

**not'tata** *nf* night; **far ~** stay up all night

**'notte** *nf* night; **di ~** at night; **a ~ fatta** when night had fallen; **la ~** (*durante la notte*) at night; **buona ~** good night; **fermarsi per la ~** stay overnight; **peggio che andar di ~** worse than ever; **prima ~ di nozze** wedding night. **~ bianca** sleepless night

**notte'tempo** *adv* at night[time]

**not'turno** *a* nocturnal; (*servizio ecc*) night *attrib*; **in notturna** (*partita*) under floodlights

**'notula** *nf* (*conto*) fee note

**no'vanta** *a & nm* ninety

**novan'tenne** *a & nmf* ninety year old

**novan'tesimo** *a & nm* ninetieth

**novan'tina** *nf* about ninety

**'nove** *a & nm* nine; **prova del nove** *Math* casting out nines

**nove'cento** *a & nm* nine hundred. **il N~** the twentieth century; **stile ~** twentieth-century

**no'vella** *nf* short story

**novelli'ere** *nm* short-story writer

**novel'lino, -a** *a* inexperienced ● *nmf* novice, beginner

**no'vello** *a* new

**no'vembre** *nm* November

**nove'mila** *a & nm* nine thousand

**no'vena** *nf* novena

**novi'lunio** *nm* new moon

**novità** *nf inv* novelty; (*notizie*) news *sg*; **l'ultima ~** (*moda*) the latest fashion

**novizi'ato** *nm Relig* novitiate; (*tirocinio*) apprenticeship

**nozi'one** *nf* notion; **perdere la ~ del tempo** lose track of time; **non avere la ~ del tempo** have no sense of time; **nozioni** *pl* rudiments; **poche nozioni di inglese** very basic English

**nozio'nismo** *nm* accumulation of facts

**'nozze** *nfpl* marriage *sg*; (*cerimonia*) wedding *sg*; **andare a ~** (*godersela*) have a field day. **~ d'argento** silver wedding [anniversary]. **~ di diamante** diamond wedding [anniversary]. **~ d'oro** golden wedding [anniversary]

**'nube** *nf* cloud. **~ di mistero** shroud of mystery. **~ tossica** toxic cloud

**nubi'fragio** *nm* cloudburst

**'nubile** *a* unmarried ● *nf* unmarried woman

**'nuca** *nf* nape

**nucle'are** *a* nuclear

**'nucleo** *nm* nucleus; (*unità*) unit

**nu'dismo** *nm* nudism

**nu'dista** *nmf* nudist

**nudità** *nf* nudity, nakedness

**'nudo** *a* naked; (*spoglio, terra*) bare; **a occhio ~** to the naked eye; **verità nuda e cruda** naked truth; **a piedi nudi** bare-foot

**'nugolo** *nm* large number

**'nulla** *pron* **= niente**; **da ~** worthless; **per ~** for nothing

**nulla'osta** *nm inv* permit

**nullate'nente** *nm* **i nullatenenti** the have-nots

**nullità** *nf inv* (*persona*) nonentity

**'nullo** *a Jur* null and void

**'nume** *nm* numen

**nume'rabile** *a* countable

**nume'rale** *a & nm* numeral

**nume'rare** *vt* number

**numera'tore** *nm Math* numerator

**numerazi'one** *nf* numbering

**nu'merico** *a* numerical

**'numero** *nm* number; (*romano, arabo*) numeral; (*di scarpe ecc*) size; **fare o comporre il ~** dial [the number]; **dare i numeri** *fam* be off one's head; **avere tutti i numeri per** have what it takes to. **~ arretrato** back issue. **~ cardinale** cardinal [number]. **~ di conto** account number. **~ decimale** decimal. **~ intero** whole number. **~ ordinale** ordinal [number]. **~ d'ordine** *Comm* order number. **~ di previdenza sociale** ≈ National Insurance number. **~ di protocollo** reference number. **~ di scarpa** shoe size. **~ di telefono** phone number. **~ uno** number one. **~ verde** ≈ Freephone number; toll-free number *Am*. **~ di volo** flight number

**nume'roso** *a* numerous

**numi'smatico** *a* numismatic

**'nunzio** *nm* nuncio

**nu'ocere** *vi* **~ a** harm

**nu'ora** *nf* daughter-in-law

**nuo'tare** *vi* swim; *fig* wallow; **~ come un pesce** swim like a fish; **~ nell'oro** be stinking rich, be rolling in it

**nuo'tata** *nf* swim; **fare una ~** have a swim

**nuota|'tore, -'trice** *nmf* swimmer

**nu'oto** *nm* swimming; **stili** *mpl* **del ~** swimming strokes

**nu'ova** *nf* piece of news; **buone nuove** good news; **nessuna ~, buona ~** no news is good news

**Nu'ova Cale'donia** *nf* New Caledonia

**Nu'ova Gui'nea** *nf* New Guinea

**nuova'mente** *adv* again

**Nu'ova Ze'landa** *nf* New Zealand

**nu'ovo** *a* new; **di ~** again; **uscire di nuovo** go/come back out, go/come out again; **mi risulta ~** that's news to me; **~ di pacca** o

**zecca** brand new; **rimettere a ~** give a new lease of life to; **~ del mestiere** new to the job; **il ~ anno** [the] New Year. **nuova linfa** *nf* new blood. **~ stile** *nm* new look. **N~ Testamento** *nm* New Testament

**'nursery** *nf* nursery

**nutri'ente** *a* nourishing

**nutri'mento** *nm* nourishment

**nu'trire** *vt* feed ⟨*animale, malato, pianta*⟩; harbour ⟨*sentimenti*⟩; cherish ⟨*sogno*⟩ ● *vi* (*essere nutriente*) be nourishing

**nu'trirsi** *vr* eat; **~ di** *fig* live on

**nutri'tivo** *a* nourishing, nutritional

**nutrizi'one** *nf* nutrition

**'nuvola** *nf* cloud; **avere la testa fra le nuvole** have one's head in the clouds; **vivere fra le nuvole** live in cloud cuckoo land; **cadere dalle nuvole** be astounded

**nuvo'loso** *a* cloudy

**nuzi'ale** *a* nuptial; ⟨*vestito, anello ecc*⟩ wedding *attrib*; **pranzo ~** wedding breakfast

# Oo

**O** *abbr* (**ovest**) W

**o** *conj* or; **~ l'uno ~ l'altro** one or the other, either; **o... o...** either... or...

**'oasi** *nf inv* oasis

**obbedi'ente** = **ubbidiente**

**obbedi'enza** = **ubbidienza**

**obbe'dire** = **ubbidire**

**obbli'gare** *vt* force, oblige

**obbli'garsi** *vr* **~ a** undertake to

**obbli'gato** *a* obliged

**obbligatoria'mente** *adv* **fare qcsa ~** be obliged to do sth; **bisogna ~ farlo** you absolutely have to do it

**obbliga'torio** *a* compulsory

**obbligazi'one** *nf* obligation; *Comm* bond

**'obbligo** *nm* obligation; (*dovere*) duty; **avere obblighi verso** be under an obligation to; **d'~** obligatory

**ob'brobrio** *nm* disgrace

**obbrobri'oso** *a* disgraceful

**obe'lisco** *nm* obelisk

**obe'rare** *vt* overburden

**obesità** *nf* obesity

**o'beso** *a* obese

**obiet'tare** *vt/i* object; **~ su** object to

**obiettiva'mente** *adv* objectively

**obiettività** *nf* objectivity

**obiet'tivo** *a* objective ● *nm* objective; (*scopo*) object

**obiet'tore** *nm* objector. **~ di coscienza** conscientious objector

**obiezi'one** *nf* objection; **fare ~ di coscienza** be a conscientious objector

**obi'torio** *nm* mortuary

**o'blio** *nm* oblivion

**o'bliquo** *a* oblique; *fig* underhand

**oblite'rare** *vt* obliterate

**oblò** *nm inv* porthole

**ob'lungo** *a* oblong

**'oboe** *nm* oboe

**obsole'scenza** *nf* obsolescence

**obso'leto** *a* obsolete

**'oca** *nf* (*pl* **oche**) goose; (*donna*) silly girl

**occasio'nale** *a* occasional

**occasional'mente** *adv* occasionally

**occasi'one** *nf* occasion; (*buon affare*) bargain; (*motivo*) cause; (*opportunità*) chance; **d'~** secondhand

**occhi'aia** *nf* eye socket; **occhiaie** *pl* shadows under the eyes

**occhi'ali** *nmpl* glasses, spectacles. **~ scuri** dark glasses. **~ da sole** sunglasses. **~ da vista** glasses, spectacles

**occhia'luto** *a* wearing glasses

**occhi'ata** *nf* look; **dare un'~ a** have a look at

**occhieggi'are** *vt* ogle ● *vi* (*far capolino*) peep

**occhi'ello** *nm* buttonhole; (*asola*) eyelet

**'occhio** *nm* eye; **~!** watch out!; **~ ai falsi** beware of imitations; **a quattr'occhi** in private; **abbassare gli occhi** look down, lower one's eyes; **sollevare gli occhi** look up, raise one's eyes; **tenere d'~ qcno** keep an eye on sb; **perdere d'~** lose sight of; **a ~ [e croce]** roughly; **chiudere un'~ (su qcsa)** turn a blind eye (to sth); **dare nell'~** attract attention; **pagare** o **spendere un ~** [**della testa**] pay an arm and a leg; **saltare agli occhi** be blindingly obvious. **~ di falco** eagle eye. **~ nero** (*pesto*) black eye. **~ di pernice** (*callo*) corn

**occhio'lino** *nm* **fare l'~ a qcno** wink at sb, give sb a wink

**occiden'tale** *a* western ● *nmf* westerner

**occi'dente** *nm* west; (*paesi capitalisti*) West

**oc'cludere** *vt* obstruct

**occlusi'one** *nf* occlusion

**occor'rente** *a* necessary ● *nm* the necessary

**occor'renza** *nf* need; **all'~** if need be

**oc'correre** *vi* be necessary; **non occorre farlo** there is no need to do it

**occulta'mento** *nm* **~ di prove** concealment of evidence

**occul'tare** *vt* hide

**occul'tismo** *nm* occult

**oc'culto** *a* hidden; (*magico*) occult

**occu'pante** *nmf* occupier; (*abusivo*) squatter

**occu'pare** *vt* occupy; spend ⟨*tempo*⟩; take up ⟨*spazio*⟩; (*dar lavoro a*) employ

**occu'parsi** *vr* occupy oneself; (*trovare lavoro*) find a job; **~ di** (*badare*) look after; **occupati dei fatti tuoi!** mind your own business!

**occu'pato** *a* engaged; ⟨*persona*⟩ busy; ⟨*posto*⟩ taken; **casa occupata** (*alloggio abusivo*) squat

**occupazi'one** *nf* occupation; *Comm* employment; (*passatempo*) pastime; **trovarsi un'~** (*interesse*) find oneself something to do

**o'ceano** *nm* ocean. **~ Atlantico** Atlantic [Ocean]. **~ Indiano** Indian Ocean. **~ Pacifico** Pacific [Ocean]

**'ocra** *nf* ochre

**OCSE** *nf abbr* (**Organizzazione per la Cooperazione el lo Sviluppo Economico**) OECD

**ocu'lare** *a* ocular; ⟨*testimone, bagno*⟩ eye *attrib*

**ocula'tezza** *nf* care

**ocu'lato** *a* ⟨*scelta, persona*⟩ prudent

**ocu'lista** *nmf* optician; (*per malattie*) ophthalmologist

**od** *conj* (*davanti alla vocale o*) or

**'ode** *nf* ode

**odi'are** *vt* hate; **~ a morte** not be able to stand

**odi'erno** *a* of today; (*attuale*) present

**'odio** *nm* hatred; **avere in ~** hate

**odi'oso** *a* hateful

**odis'sea** *nf* odyssey

**o'dometro** *nm Auto* mileometer, odometer *Am*

**odo'rare** *vt* smell; (*profumare*) perfume ● *vi* **~ di** smell of

**odo'rato** *nm* sense of smell

**o'dore** *nm* smell; (*profumo*) scent; **c'è ~ di...** there's a smell of...; **avere un buon/cattivo ~** smell nice/awful; **sentire ~ di** smell; **odori** *pl Culin* herbs

**odo'roso** *a* fragrant

**of'fendere** *vt* offend; (*ferire*) injure

**of'fendersi** *vr* take offence

**offen'siva** *nf Mil, fig* offensive

**offen'sivo** *a* offensive

**offen'sore** *nm* offender

**offe'rente** *nmf* offerer; (*in aste*) bidder; **il miglior ~** the highest bidder

**of'ferta** *nf* offer; (*donazione*) donation; *Comm* supply; (*nelle aste*) bid; (*di appalto*) tender; **in ~ speciale** on special offer; **"offerte d'impiego"** "situations vacant". **~ pubblica di acquisto** takeover bid

**of'ferto** *pp di* offrire

**offer'torio** *nm* offertory

**of'fesa** *nf* offence

**of'feso** *pp di* **offendere** ● *a* offended

**offi'ciare** *vt* officiate

**offi'cina** *nf* workshop; **~** [**meccanica**] garage; **capo** [**di**] **~** foreman

**of'frire** *vt* offer

**of'frirsi** *vr* offer oneself; ⟨*occasione:*⟩ present itself; **~ di fare qcsa** offer to do sth

**off'set** *nm inv* offset printing

**off'shore** *nm inv* (*motoscafo*) speedboat

**offu'scare** *vt* darken; *fig* dull ⟨*memoria, bellezza*⟩; blur ⟨*vista*⟩

**offu'scarsi** *vr* darken; ⟨*fig: memoria, bellezza:*⟩ fade away; ⟨*vista:*⟩ become blurred

**of'talmico** *a* ophthalmic

**ogget'tistica** *nf* manufacture and selling of household and gift items; (*oggetti*) household and gift items; **negozio di ~** gift shop

**oggettività** *nf* objectivity

**ogget'tivo** *a* objective

**og'getto** *nm* object; (*argomento*) subject; **oggetti** *pl* **smarriti** lost property, lost and found *Am*

**'oggi** *adv & nm* today; (*al giorno d'oggi*) nowadays; **da ~ in poi** from today on; **~** [**a**] **otto** a week today; **dall'~ al domani** overnight; **il giornale di ~** today's paper; **al giorno d'~** these days, nowadays

**oggigi'orno** *adv* nowadays

**o'giva** *nf Mil* warhead

**'ogni** *a inv* every; (*qualsiasi*) any; **~ tre giorni** every three days; **ad ~ costo** at any cost; **ad ~ modo** anyway; **~ ben di Dio** all sorts of good things; **~ cosa** everything; **~ tanto** now and then; **~ volta che** every time, whenever

**o'gnuno** *pron* everyone, everybody; **~ di voi** each of you

**ohibò** *int* oh dear!

**ohimè** *int* oh dear!

**o'kay** *nm* **dare l'~ a qcno/qcsa** give sb/sth the OK

**'ola** *nf inv* Mexican wave

**O'landa** *nf* Holland

**olan'dese** *a* Dutch ● *nm* Dutchman; (*lingua*) Dutch; (*formaggio*) Edam ● *nf* Dutchwoman

**ole'andro** *nm* oleander

**ole'ato** *a* oiled; **carta oleata** grease-proof paper

**oleo'dotto** *nm* oil pipeline

**ole'oso** *a* oily

**ol'fatto** *nm* sense of smell

**oli'are** *vt* oil

**olia'tore** *nm* oilcan

**oli'era** *nf* cruet

**olim'piadi** *nfpl* Olympic games, Olympics

**o'limpico** *a* Olympic

**olim'pionico** *a* ⟨*primato, squadra*⟩ Olympic; **costume ~** Olympic swimming costume

**+olino** *suff* **bestiolina** *nf* (*affettuoso*) little creature; **macchiolina** *nf* spot; **pesciolino** *nm* little fish; **risolino** *nm* giggle; **sassolino** *nm* pebble; **strisciolina** *nf* thin strip; **magrolino** *a* skinny

**'olio** *nm* oil; **sott'~** in oil; **colori a ~** oils; **quadro a ~** oil painting. **~ di fegato di merluzzo** cod-liver oil. **~ di gomito** elbow grease. **~ lubrificante** lubricating oil. **~ di mais** corn oil. **~ minerale** mineral oil. **~ [del] motore** engine oil. **~ d'oliva** olive oil. **~ di semi** vegetable oil. **~ [di semi] di lino** linseed oil. **~ solare** suntan oil

**o'liva** *nf* olive

**oli'vastro** *a* olive

**oli'veto** *nm* olive grove

**oli'vetta** *nf* toggle

**o'livo** *nm* olive tree

**'olmo** *nm* elm

**olo'causto** *nm* holocaust; **l'O~** the Holocaust

**o'lografo** *a* holograph

**olo'gramma** *nm* hologram

**oltraggi'are** *vt* offend

**ol'traggio** *nm* offence. **~ al pudore** *Jur* gross indecency

**oltraggi'oso** *a* offensive

**ol'tranza** *nf* **ad ~** to the bitter end

**'oltre** *adv* (*di luogo*) further; (*di tempo*) longer ● *prep* (*nello spazio*) beyond; (*di tempo*) later than; (*più di*) more than; (*in aggiunta*) besides; **~ a** (*eccetto*) except, apart from; **per ~ due settimane** for more than two weeks; **una settimana e ~** a week and more

**oltrecon'fine** *a* cross-border

**oltre'mare** *adv* overseas

**oltre'modo** *adv* extremely

**oltrepas'sare** *vt* go beyond; (*eccedere*) exceed; **oltrepassi il semaforo** go past the traffic lights; **~ il limite di velocità** break the speed limit; **'non ~'** 'no trespassing'

**OM** *abbr Radio* (**onde medie**) MW

**omacci'one** *nm* bruiser

**o'maggi** *nmpl* (*saluti*) respects

**o'maggio** *nm* homage; (*dono*) gift; **in ~ con** free with

**ombeli'cale** *a* umbilical; **cordone ~** umbilical cord

**ombe'lico** *nm* navel

**'ombra** *nf* (*zona*) shade; (*immagine oscura*) shadow; **all'~** in the shade

**ombreggi'are** *vt* shade

**ombreggia'tura** *nfpl* shading

**om'brello** *nm* umbrella

**ombrel'lone** *nm* beach umbrella

**om'bretto** *nm* eye-shadow

**om'broso** *a* shady; ⟨*cavallo*⟩ skittish; ⟨*persona*⟩ touchy

**ome'lette** *nf inv* omelette

**ome'lia** *nf Relig* sermon

**omeopa'tia** *nf* homoeopathy

**omeo'patico** *a* homoeopathic ● *nm* homoeopath

**omertà** *nf inv* conspiracy of silence

**o'messo** *pp di* omettere

**o'mettere** *vt* omit

**omi'cida** *a* murderous ● *nmf* murderer

**omi'cidio** *nm* murder. **~ colposo** manslaughter. **~ di massa** mass murder. **~ volontario** *Jur* culpable homicide

**omissi'one** *nf* omission

**'omnibus** *nm inv* omnibus

**omofo'bia** *nf* homophobia

**omogeneiz'zare** *vt* homogenize

**omogeneiz'zato** *a* homogenized

**omo'geneo** *a* homogeneous

**o'mografo** *nm* homograph

**omolo'gare** *vt* approve; **fare ~ un testamento** prove a will

**omologazi'one** *nf* probate

**o'monimo, -a** *nmf* namesake ● *nm* (*parola*) homonym ● *a* of the same name

**omosessu'ale** *a* & *nmf* homosexual

**omosessualità** *nf* homosexuality

**On.** *abbr* (**onorevole**) MP

**'oncia** *nf* ounce. **~ fluida** fluid ounce

**'onda** *nf* wave; **andare in ~** *TV, Radio* go on the air; **seguire l'~** go with the crowd. **onde** *pl* **corte** short wave. **onde** *pl* **lunghe** long wave. **~ di maremoto** tidal wave. **onde** *pl* **medie** medium wave. **onde** *pl* **radio** radio waves. **~ d'urto** shock wave

**on'data** *nf* wave; **a ondate** in waves. **~ di freddo** cold snap

**'onde** *conj fml* so that

**ondeggi'are** *vi* wave; ⟨*barca:*⟩ roll

**ondu'lato** *a* wavy

**ondula'torio** *a* undulating

**ondulazi'one** *nf* undulation; (*di capelli*) wave

**+one** *suff* **cucchiaione** *nm* big spoon; **gattone** *nm* fat cat; **bacione** *nm* smacker; **bacioni** *pl* (*in lettera*) love and kisses; **omone** *nm* big guy; **nasone** *nm* big nose; **nebbione** *nm* dense fog, peasouper *fam*; **simpaticone** *nm* very friendly person; **lumacone** *nm* slowcoach; **testone** *nm* mule; **facilone** *nm pej* over-casual sort of person; **grassone** *nm pej* fat slob; **pigrone** *nm* lazybones *sg*; **chiacchierone** *nm* chatterbox; **criticone** *nm* nit-picker; **pasticcione** *nm* bungler

**'onere** *nm* burden

**oner'oso** *a* onerous

**onestà** *nf* honesty; (*rettitudine*) integrity, honesty

190

o'nesto *a* honest; (*giusto*) just

'onice *nf* onyx

o'nirico *a* dream *attrib*

o'nisco *nm* slater

onnipo'tente *a* omnipotent

onnipre'sente *a* ubiquitous; *Rel* omnipresent

onnisci'ente *a* omniscient

ono'mastico *nm* name-day

onomato'pea *nf* onomatopoeia

onomato'peico *a* onomatopoeic

ono'rabile *a* honourable

ono'rare *vt* (*fare onore a*) be a credit to; honour (*promessa*)

ono'rario *a* honorary ● *nm* fee

ono'rarsi *vr* ~ **di** be proud of

ono'rato *a* (*famiglia, professione*) respectable; **considerarsi** ~ **da qcsa** consider oneself honoured by sth. **l'onorata società** *nf* the Mafia

o'nore *nm* honour; **in** ~ **di** (*festa, ricevimento*) in honour of; **fare** ~ **a** do justice to (*pranzo*); **farsi** ~ **in** excel in; **a onor del vero** to tell the truth; **fare gli onori di casa** do the honours

ono'revole *a* honourable ● *nmf* Member of Parliament

onorifi'cenza *nf* honour; (*decorazione*) decoration

ono'rifico *a* honorary

'onta *nf* shame

on'tano *nm* alder

O.N.U. *nf abbr* (**Organizzazione delle Nazioni Unite**) UN

opacità *nf* opaqueness, opacity

o'paco *a* opaque; (*colori ecc*) dull; (*fotografia, rossetto*) matt

o'pale *nf* opal

OPEC *nf inv* Opec, OPEC

'opera *nf* (*lavoro*) work; (*azione*) deed; *Mus* opera; (*teatro*) opera house; (*ente*) institution; **mettere in** ~ put into effect; **mettersi all'**~ get to work. ~ **d'arte** work of art. ~ **lirica** opera. **opere** *pl* **pubbliche** public works

ope'rabile *a* operable

ope'raio, -a *a* working ● *nmf* worker. ~ **edile** building worker. ~ **specializzato** skilled worker

ope'rare *vt Med* operate on; ~ **qcno al cuore** operate on sb's heart; **farsi** ~ have an operation ● *vi* operate; (*agire*) work

opera'tivo, opera'torio *a* operating *attrib*

opera|'tore, -'trice *nmf* operator; *TV* cameraman. ~ **ecologico** refuse collector. ~ **sanitario** health worker. ~ **turistico** tour operator

operazi'one *nf* operation; *Comm* transaction. ~ **antidroga** anti-drug operation. **operazioni** *pl* **di soccorso** rescue operations. ~ **d'urgenza** emergency operation

ope'retta *nf* operetta

ope'roso *a* industrious

opini'one *nf* opinion; **rimanere della propria** ~ still feel the same way. ~ **pubblica** public opinion, vox pop

oplà *int* oops

o'possum *nm inv* possum

'oppio *nm* opium

oppo'nente *a* opposing ● *nmf* opponent

op'porre *vt* oppose; (*obiettare*) object; ~ **resistenza** offer resistance

op'porsi *vr* ~ **a** oppose

opportu'nismo *nm* expediency

opportu'nista *nmf* opportunist

opportunità *nf inv* opportunity; (*l'essere opportuno*) timeliness; **avere il senso dell'**~ have a sense of what is appropriate

oppor'tuno *a* opportune; (*adeguato*) appropriate; **ritenere** ~ **fare qcsa** think it appropriate to do sth; **il momento** ~ the right moment

opposi'tore *nm* opposer

opposizi'one *nf* opposition; **d'**~ (*giornale, partito*) opposition *attrib*; **in** ~ in opposition

op'posto *pp di* **opporre** ● *a* opposite; (*opinioni*) opposing ● *nm* opposite; **all'**~ on the contrary

oppressi'one *nf* oppression

oppres'sivo *a* oppressive

op'presso *pp di* **opprimere** ● *a* oppressed

oppres'sore *nm* oppressor

oppri'mente *a* oppressive

op'primere *vt* oppress; (*gravare*) weigh down

op'pure *conj* otherwise, or [else]; **lunedì** ~ **martedì** Monday or Tuesday

ops *int* oops

op'tare *vi* ~ **per** opt for

'optional *nm inv* optional extra

opu'lento *a* opulent

opu'lenza *nf* opulence

o'puscolo *nm* booklet; (*pubblicitario*) brochure

opzio'nale *a* optional

opzi'one *nf* option

'ora¹ *nf* time; (*unità*) hour; **di buon'**~ early; **che** ~ **è?, che ore sono?** what time is it?; **a che** ~? at what time?; **mezz'**~ half an hour; **a ore** (*lavorare, pagare*) by the hour; **50 km all'**~ 50 km an hour; **è** ~ **di finirla!** that's enough now!; **a un'**~ **di macchina** one hour by car; **non vedo l'**~ **di vederti** I can't wait to see you; **fare le ore piccole** stay up until the small hours. ~ **d'arrivo** arrival time. ~ **di cena** dinnertime. **l'**~ **esatta** *Teleph* speaking clock. ~ **legale** daylight saving time. ~ **locale** local time. ~ **di pranzo** dinnertime. ~ **di punta, ore** *pl* **di punta** peak time; (*per il traffico*) rush hour. ~ **solare** Greenwich Mean Time, GMT. ~ **zero** *Mil, fig* zero hour

'ora² *adv* now; (*tra poco*) presently; ~ **come** ~ just now, at the moment; **d'**~ **in poi** from now on; **per** ~ for the time being, now ● *conj* (*dunque*) now [then]; ~ **che ci penso,...** now that I [come to] think about it...

**o'racolo** *nm* oracle

**'orafo** *nm* goldsmith

**o'rale** *a* & *nm* oral; **per via ~** by mouth

**ora'mai** *adv* = **ormai**

**o'rario** *a* ‹*tariffa*› hourly; ‹*segnale*› time *attrib*; ‹*velocità*› per hour: **in senso ~** clockwise ● *nm* time; ‹*tabella dell'orario*› timetable. schedule *Am*; **essere in ~** be on time; **partire in ~** leave on time; **lavorare fuori ~** work outside normal hours. **~ di apertura** opening hours *pl*. **~ di chiusura** closing time. **~ estivo** summer timetable. **~ ferroviario** railway timetable. railroad schedule *Am*. **~ flessibile** flexitime. **~ invernale** winter timetable. **~ di lavoro** working hours *pl*. **~ degli spettacoli** performance times *pl*. **~ di sportello** banking hours *pl*. **~ d'ufficio** business hours *pl*. **~ di visita** visiting hours *pl*, visiting time; ‹*del medico*› consulting hours *pl*. **~ di volo** flight time

**o'rata** *nf* gilthead

**ora|'tore, -'trice** *nmf* orator; ‹*conferenziere*› speaker

**ora'torio, -a** *a* oratorical ● *nm Mus* oratorio ● *nmf* oratory

**orazi'one** *nf Relig* prayer

**'orbita** *nf* orbit; *Anat* [eye-]socket

**'Orcadi** *nfpl* Orkneys

**or'chestra** *nf* orchestra; ‹*parte del teatro*› pit. **~ da camera** chamber orchestra

**orche'strale** *a* orchestral ● *nmf* member of an/the orchestra

**orche'strare** *vt* orchestrate

**orchi'dea** *nf* orchid

**'orco** *nm* ogre

**'orda** *nf* horde

**or'digno** *nm* device; ‹*arnese*› tool. **~ esplosivo** explosive device. **~ incendiario** incendiary device

**ordi'nale** *a* & *nm* ordinal

**ordina'mento** *nm* order; ‹*leggi*› rules *pl*

**ordi'nanza** *nf* ‹*del sindaco*› bylaw; **d'~** ‹*soldato*› on duty

**ordi'nare** *vt* ‹*sistemare*› arrange; ‹*comandare*› order; ‹*prescrivere*› prescribe; *Relig* ordain

**ordi'nario** *a* ordinary; ‹*grossolano*› common; ‹*professore*› with a permanent position; **di ordinaria amministrazione** routine ● *nm* ordinary; *Univ* professor; **fuori dell'~** out of the ordinary

**ordi'nato** *a* ‹*in ordine*› tidy

**ordinazi'one** *nf* order; **fare un'~** place an order

**'ordine** *nm* order; ‹*di avvocati, medici*› association; **mettere in ~** put in order; tidy up ‹*appartamento ecc*›; **di prim'~** first-class; **di terz'~** ‹*film, albergo*› third-rate; **di pratico/economico** ‹*problema*› of a practical/economic nature; **fino a nuovo ~** until further notice; **parola d'~** password. **~ di acquisto** *Comm* purchase order. **~ del giorno** agenda. **~ di pagamento** banker's order. **~ permanente** *Fin* standing order. **ordini** *pl* **sacri** Holy Orders

**or'dire** *vt* ‹*tramare*› plot

**orecchi'ette** *nfpl* small pasta shells

**orec'chino** *nm* ear-ring. **orecchini** *pl* **con le clip** clip-ons

**o'recchio** *nm* (*pl nf* **orecchie**) ear; **avere ~** have a good ear; **esser duro d'~** be hard of hearing; **mi è giunto all'~ che...** I've heard that...; **parlare all'~ a qcno** whisper in sb's ear; **suonare a ~** play by ear

**orecchi'oni** *nmpl Med* mumps *sg*

**o'refice** *nm* jeweller

**orefice'ria** *nf* ‹*arte*› goldsmith's art; ‹*negozio*› goldsmith's [shop]

**'orfano, -a** *a* orphan ● *nmf* orphan

**orfano'trofio** *nm* orphanage

**orga'netto** *nm* barrel-organ; ‹*a bocca*› mouth-organ; ‹*fisarmonica*› accordion

**or'ganico** *a* organic ● *nm* personnel

**orga'nino** *nm* hurdy-gurdy

**orga'nismo** *nm* organism: ‹*corpo umano*› body

**orga'nista** *nmf* organist

**organiz'zare** *vt* organize

**organiz'zarsi** *vr* get organized

**organizza'tivo** *a* organizational

**organizza|'tore, -'trice** *nmf* organizer

**organizzazi'one** *nf* organization. **~ dei soccorsi** relief organization

**'organo** *nm* organ

**or'gasmo** *nm* orgasm; *fig* agitation

**'orgia** *nf* orgy

**or'goglio** *nm* pride

**orgogli'oso** *a* proud

**orien'tale** *a* eastern; ‹*cinese ecc*› oriental

**orienta'mento** *nm* orientation; **perdere l'~** lose one's bearings; **senso dell'~** sense of direction. **~ professionale** careers guidance. **~ scolastico** educational guidance

**orien'tare** *vt* orientate

**orien'tarsi** *vr* find one's bearings; ‹*tendere*› tend

**ori'ente** *nm* east. **l'Estremo O~** the Far East. **il Medio O~** the Middle East

**orien'teering** *nm inv* orienteering

**o'rigano** *nm* oregano

**origi'nale** *a* original; ‹*eccentrico*› odd ● *nm* original

**originalità** *nf* originality

**origi'nare** *vt/i* originate

**origi'nario** *a* ‹*nativo*› native

**o'rigine** *nf* origin; **in ~** originally; **aver ~ da** originate from; **dare ~ a** give rise to

**origli'are** *vi* eavesdrop

**o'rina** *nf* urine

**ori'nale** *nm* chamber-pot

**ori'nare** *vi* urinate

**ori'undo** *a* native

**orizzon'tale** *a* horizontal

**orizzon'tare** *vt* = **orientare**

**oriz'zonte** *nm* horizon

**or'lare** *vt* hem

**orla'tura** *nf* hem

**'orlo** *nm* edge; ‹*di vestito ecc*› hem

**'orma** *nf* track; ‹*di piede*› footprint; ‹*impronta*› mark

**or'mai** *adv* by now: (*passato*) by then: (*quasi*) almost

**ormegg'iare** *vt* moor

**or'meggio** *nm* mooring

**ormo'nale** *a* hormonal

**or'mone** *nm* hormone

**ornamen'tale** *a* ornamental

**orna'mento** *nm* ornament; **d'~** (*oggetto*) ornamental

**or'nare** *vt* decorate

**or'narsi** *vr* deck oneself

**or'nato** *a* (*stile*) ornate

**ornitolo'gia** *nf* ornithology

**orni'tologo, -a** *nmf* ornithologist

**ornito'rinco** *nm* platypus

**'oro** *nm* gold; **d'~** gold; *fig* golden; **una persona d'~** a wonderful person. **~ nero** black gold

**orologe'ria** *nf* watchmaker

**orologi'aio, -a** *nmf* clockmaker, watchmaker

**oro'logio** *nm* (*portatile*) watch; (*da tavolo, muro ecc*) clock. **~ biologico** biological clock. **~ a carica automatica** self-winding watch. **~ a cucù** cuckoo clock. **~ digitale** digital clock. **~ a pendolo** grandfather clock. **~ da polso** wrist-watch. **~ al quarzo** quartz watch. **~ a sveglia** alarm clock

**o'roscopo** *nm* horoscope

**or'rendo** *a* awful, dreadful

**or'ribile** *a* horrible

**orribil'mente** *adv* horribly

**orripi'lante** *a* horrifying

**or'rore** *nm* horror; **avere qcsa in ~** hate sth; **~!** heck!; **film/romanzo dell'~** horror film/story

**orsacchi'otto** *nm* teddy bear

**or'setto** *nm* **~ lavatore** raccoon

**'orso** *nm* bear; (*persona scontrosa*) hermit. **~ bianco** polar bear. **~ bruno** brown bear

**orsù** *int* come now!

**or'taggio** *nm* vegetable

**or'tensia** *nf* hydrangea

**or'tica** *nf* nettle; **buttare qcsa alle ortiche** *fig fam* chuck in

**orti'caria** *nf* nettle-rash

**orticol'tura** *nf* horticulture

**'orto** *nm* vegetable plot

**orto'dontico** *a* orthodontic

**ortodon'zia** *nf* orthodontics

**ortodos'sia** *nf* conformity

**orto'dosso** *a* orthodox

**ortofrut'ticolo** *a* **mercato ~** fruit and vegetable market

**ortofrutticol'tore** *nm* market gardener, truck farmer *Am*

**ortogo'nale** *a* perpendicular

**ortogra'fia** *nf* spelling

**orto'grafico** *a* spelling *attrib*

**orto'lano** *nm* market gardener, truck farmer *Am;* (*negozio*) greengrocer's

**ortope'dia** *nf* orthopaedics

**orto'pedico** *a* orthopaedic ● *nm* orthopaedic specialist

**orzai'olo** *nm* sty

**or'zata** *nf* barley-water

**'orzo** *nm* barley. **~ perlato** pearl barley

**osan'nato** *a* (*esaltato*) praised to the skies

**o'sare** *vt/i* dare; (*avere audacia*) be daring

**oscenità** *nf inv* obscenity

**o'sceno** *a* obscene

**oscil'lare** *vi* swing; (*prezzi ecc:*) fluctuate; *Tech* oscillate; (*fig: essere indeciso*) vacillate

**oscillazi'one** *nf* swinging; (*di prezzi*) fluctuation; *Tech* oscillation

**oscura'mento** *nm* darkening; (*fig: di vista, mente*) dimming; (*totale*) black-out

**oscu'rare** *vt* darken; *fig* obscure

**oscu'rarsi** *vr* get dark

**oscurità** *nf* darkness; (*incomprensibilità*) obscurity; **uscire dall'~** *fig* emerge from obscurity; **morire nell'~** *fig* die in obscurity

**o'scuro** *a* dark; (*triste*) gloomy; (*incomprensibile*) obscure

**o'smosi** *nf inv* osmosis

**ospe'dale** *nm* hospital

**ospedali'ero** *a* hospital *attrib*

**ospi'tale** *a* hospitable

**ospitalità** *nf* hospitality; **non voglio abusare della tua ~** I don't want to outstay my welcome

**ospi'tare** *vt* give hospitality to

**'ospite** *nm* (*chi ospita*) host; (*chi viene ospitato*) guest ● *nf* hostess; guest

**o'spizio** *nm* (*per vecchi*) [old people's] home

**ossa'tura** *nf* bone structure; (*di romanzo*) structure, framework

**'osseo** *a* bone *attrib*

**osse'quente** *a* deferential; **~ alla legge** law-abiding

**ossequi'are** *vt* pay one's respects to

**os'sequio** *nm* homage; **ossequi** *pl* respects

**ossequi'oso** *a* obsequious

**osser'vabile** *a* observable

**osser'vante** *a* (*cattolico*) practising

**osser'vanza** *nf* observance

**osser'vare** *vt* observe; (*notare*) notice; keep (*ordine, silenzio*)

**osserva|'tore, -'trice** *nmf* observer

**osser'vanza** *nf* observance

**osserva'torio** *nm* *Astr* observatory; *Mil* observation post

**osservazi'one** *nf* observation; (*rimprovero*) reproach

**ossessio'nante** *a* haunting; (*persona*) nagging

**ossessio'nare** *vt* obsess; (*infastidire*) nag

**ossessi'one** *nf* obsession; (*assillo*) pain in the neck

**osses'sivo** *a* obsessive; (*paura*) neurotic

**os'sesso** *a* obsessed

**os'sia** *conj* that is

**ossi'dabile** *a* liable to tarnish

**ossi'dante** *a* tarnishing

**ossi'dare** *vt* oxidize

**ossi'darsi** *vr* oxidize

**'ossido** *nm* oxide. **~ di carbonio** carbon monoxide. **~ di zinco** zinc oxide

**os'sidrico** *a* **fiamma ossidrica** blowlamp

**ossige'nare** *vt* oxygenate; (*decolorare*) bleach

**ossige'narsi** *vr* put back on its feet ⟨*azienda*⟩; ~ **i capelli** dye one's hair blonde

**os'sigeno** *nm* oxygen

**'osso** *nm* (*Anat pl nf* **ossa**) bone; (*di frutto*) stone; **senz'~** boneless. ~ **mascellare** jaw-bone

**osso'buco** *nm* marrowbone

**os'suto** *a* bony

**ostaco'lare** *vt* hinder, obstruct

**ostaco'lista** *nmf* hurdler

**o'stacolo** *nm* obstacle; *Sport* hurdle

**o'staggio** *nm* hostage; **prendere in ~** take hostage

**o'stello** *nm* ~ **della gioventù** youth hostel

**osten'tare** *vt* show off; ~ **indifferenza** pretend to be indifferent

**ostentata'mente** *adv* ostentatiously

**ostentazi'one** *nf* ostentation

**osteopo'rosi** *nf inv* osteoporosis

**oste'ria** *nf* inn

**oste'tricia** *nf* obstetrics

**o'stetrico, -a** *a* obstetric ● *nmf* obstetrician

**'ostia** *nf* host; (*cialda*) wafer

**'ostico** *a* tough

**o'stile** *a* hostile

**ostilità** *nf inv* hostility

**osti'narsi** *vr* ~ **persist** (**a** in)

**osti'nato** *a* obstinate

**ostinazi'one** *nf* obstinacy

**ostra'cismo** *nm* ostracism

**'ostrica** *nf* oyster

**ostro'goto** *nm* **parlare ~** talk double Dutch

**ostru'ire** *vt* obstruct

**ostruzi'one** *nf* obstruction

**ostruzio'nismo** *nm* obstructionism; *Sport* obstruction. ~ **sindacale** work-to-rule

**oto'rino** *nm* ear, nose and throat *attrib*

**otorinolaringoi'atra** *nmf* ear, nose and throat specialist

**'otre** *nm* leather bottle

**ottago'nale** *a* octagonal

**ot'tagono** *nm* octagon

**ot'tanta** *a & nm* eighty

**ottan'tenne** *a & nmf* eighty-year-old

**ottan'tesimo** *a & nm* eightieth

**ottan'tina** *nf* about eighty

**ot'tava** *nf* octave

**ot'tavo** *a & nm* eighth

**otte'nere** *vt* obtain; (*più comune*) get; (*conseguire*) achieve

**ot'tetto** *nm Mus* octet

**'ottico, -a** *a* optic[al] ● *nmf* optician ● *nf* (*scienza*) optics *sg*; (*di lenti ecc*) optics *pl*

**otti'male** *a* optimum

**ottima'mente** *adv* very well

**otti'mismo** *nm* optimism

**otti'mista** *nmf* optimist

**otti'mistico** *a* optimistic

**ottimiz'zare** *vt* optimize

**'ottimo** *a* very good ● *nm* optimum; **essere all'~ della forma** be on top form

**'otto** *a & nm* eight

**+otto** *suff* **bassotto** (*piuttosto basso*) quite short; **contadinotto** *nm pej* (*sempliciotto*) country bumpkin; **paesotto** *nm* hamlet; **leprotto** *nm* leveret; (*affettuoso*) baby hare; **pienotto** *a* ⟨*viso*⟩ chubby

**ot'tobre** *nm* October

**otto'cento** *a & nm* eight hundred; **l'O~** the nineteenth century

**ot'tone** *nm* brass; **gli ottoni** *Mus* the brass

**ottuage'nario, -a** *a & nmf* octogenarian

**ot'tundere** *vt* blunt

**ottu'rare** *vt* block; fill ⟨*dente*⟩

**ottu'rarsi** *vr* clog

**ottura'tore** *nm Phot* shutter

**otturazi'one** *nf* stopping; (*di dente*) filling

**ot'tuso** *pp di* **ottundere** ● *a* obtuse

**ouver'ture** *nf inv* overture

**o'vaia** *nf* ovary

**o'vale** *a & nm* oval

**o'vatta** *nf* cotton wool, absorbent cotton *Am*

**ovat'tato** *a* ⟨*suono, passi*⟩ muffled

**ovazi'one** *nf* ovation

**'ove** *adv liter* where

**over'dose** *nf inv* overdose

**'overdrive** *nm inv Auto* overdrive

**'ovest** *nm* west

**o'vile** *nm* sheep-fold, pen

**o'vino** *a* sheep *attrib*

**ovoi'dale** *a* egg-shaped

**ovo'via** *nf* two-seater cable car

**ovulazi'one** *nf* ovulation

**o'vunque** *adv* = **dovunque**

**ov'vero** *conj* or; (*cioè*) that is

**ovvia'mente** *adv* obviously

**ovvi'are** *vi* ~ **a qcsa** counter sth

**'ovvio** *a* obvious

**ozi'are** *vi* laze around

**'ozio** *nm* idleness; **stare in ~** idle about

**ozi'oso** *a* idle; ⟨*questione*⟩ pointless

**o'zono** *nm* ozone; **buco nell'~** hole in the ozone layer

# Pp

**pa'care** vt calm
**paca'tezza** nf calm[ness]
**pa'cato** a calm
**'pacca** nf slap
**pac'chetto** nm packet; (postale) parcel, package; (di sigarette) pack, packet. **~ integrato** Comput integrated package; **~ software** software package
**'pacchia** nf (fam: situazione) bed of roses
**pacchia'nata** nf è una **~** it's so garish
**pacchi'ano** a garish
**'pacco** nm parcel; (involto) bundle; **disfare un ~** unwrap a parcel; **fare un ~** make up a parcel. **pacchi pl postali** parcels, packages. **~ regalo** gift-wrapped package; **le faccio un ~?** would you like it gift-wrapped?
**paccot'tiglia** nf (roba scadente) junk, rubbish
**'pace** nf peace; **darsi ~** forget it; **fare ~ con qcno** make it up with sb; **lasciare in ~ qcno** leave sb in peace; **mettere ~ fra** pacify. make [the] peace between; **andare in ~** Relig peace be with you; **in tempo di ~** in peacetime; **del tempo di ~** peacetime; **di ~** (milizia) peacekeeping; **firmare la ~** sign a peace treaty; **per amor di ~** for a quiet life
**pace-'maker** nm (apparecchio) pacemaker
**pachi'derma** nm (animale) pachyderm; fig thick-skinned person
**pachi'stano, -a** nmf & a Pakistani
**paci'ere** nm peacemaker
**pacifi'care** vt reconcile; (mettere pace) pacify
**pacificazi'one** nf reconciliation
**pa'cifico** a pacific; (calmo) peaceful; **è che...** (comunemente accettato) it is clear that... ● nm **il P~** the Pacific
**paci'fismo** nm pacifism
**paci'fista** a & nmf pacifist
**pacioc'cone, -a** nmf fam chubby-chops
**paci'ugo** nm (poltiglia) mush
**pa'dano** a **pianura padana** Po Valley
**pa'della** nf frying-pan; (per malati) bedpan; **cuocere in ~** fry; **dalla ~ alla brace** out of the frying pan into the fire
**padel'lata** nf una **~ di** a frying-panful of
**padigli'one** nm pavilion. **~ auricolare** auricle
**'Padova** nf Padua
**'padre** nm father; **padri pl** (antenati) forefathers; **i padri della chiesa** the Church Fathers; **di ~ in figlio** from father to son. **~ adottivo** (marito della madre) stepfather. **~ di famiglia** father, paterfamilias; **sono ~ ~**

**~ I** have a family to look after. **~ spirituale** spiritual father
**padre'nostro** nm **il ~** the Lord's Prayer
**padre'terno** nm God Almighty
**pa'drino** nm godfather; **~ e madrina** godparents
**padro'nale** a principal
**padro'nanza** nf mastery. **~ di sé** self-control
**pa'drone, -a** nmf master; mistress; (datore di lavoro) boss; (proprietario) owner. **~ di casa** (di inquilini) landlord; landlady; (in ricevimento) master of the house; lady of the house
**padroneggi'are** vt master
**padro'nesco** a domineering
**padro'nissimo** a **essere ~ di fare qcsa** be quite at liberty to do sth
**pae'saggio** nm scenery; (pittura) landscape. **~ marino** seascape. **~ montano** mountain landscape
**paesag'gista** nmf landscape architect
**paesag'gistico** a landscape attrib
**pae'sano, -a** a country attrib ● nmf villager
**pa'ese** nm (nazione) country; (territorio) land; (villaggio) village; **il Bel Paese** Italy; **va' a quel ~!** get lost!; **il mio ~ natio** where I was born; **Paesi pl Bassi** Netherlands. **paesi pl dell'est** Eastern Bloc countries
**paf'futo** a plump
**pag.** abbr (pagina) p.
**'paga** nf pay, wages pl
**pa'gabile** a payable
**pa'gaia** nf paddle
**paga'mento** nm payment; **a ~** (parcheggio) which you have to pay to use. **~ anticipato** Comm advance payment. **~ alla consegna** cash on delivery, COD. **~ pedaggio** toll
**paga'nesimo** nm paganism
**pa'gano, -a** a & nmf pagan
**pa'gante** nmf payer
**pa'gare** vt/i pay; **~ da bere a qcno** buy sb a drink; **pagato in anticipo** prepaid, paid in advance; **te la faccio ~** you'll pay for this; **quanto pagherei per poter venire!** what I wouldn't give to be able to come!
**pa'gella** nf [school] report
**pagg.** abbr (pagine) pp.
**'pagina** nf page; **prima ~** Journ front page; **~ economica** financial news, financial pages; **pagine pl gialle** Yellow Pages. **~ mastra** master page. **~ web** Comput web page
**pagi'none** nm centre-fold

**'paglia** *nf* straw: ~ **e fieno** *Culin mixture of ordinary and green tagliatelle*
**pagliac'cesco** *a* farcical
**pagliac'cetto** *nm* (*per bambini*) rompers *pl*; (*da donna*) camiknickers
**pagliac'ciata** *nf* farce
**pagli'accio** *nm* clown; **fare il ~** act *or* play the clown
**pagli'aio** *nm* haystack
**paglie'riccio** *nm* straw mattress
**pagli'etta** *nf* (*cappello*) boater; (*per pentole*) steel wool
**pagli'uzza** *nf* wisp of straw; (*di metallo*) particle
**pa'gnotta** *nf* [round] loaf
**'pago** *a* satisfied
**pa'goda** *nf* pagoda
**pa'guro** *nm* hermit crab
**pail'lard** *nf inv* slice of grilled veal
**pail'lette** *nf inv* sequin
**'paio** *nm* (*pl nf* **paia**) pair; **un ~** (*circa due*) a couple; **un ~ di** (*scarpe, forbici*) a pair of; **è un altro ~ di maniche** *fig* that's a different kettle of fish
**pai'olo** *nm* copper pot
**'Pakistan** *nm* Pakistan
**paki'stano, -a** *a* & *nmf* Pakistani
**'pala** *nf* shovel; (*di remo, elica*) blade; (*di ruota*) paddle; (*di mulino*) blade, vane. **~ d'altare** altar piece. **~ da fornaio** shovel. **~ meccanica** mechanical digger
**pala'dino** *nm* paladin; *fig* champion
**pala'fitta** *nf* pile-dwelling
**palan'drana** *nf* (*abito largo*) big long coat
**pala'sport** *nm inv* indoor sports arena
**pa'late** *nfpl* **a ~** (*fare soldi*) hand over fist
**pa'lato** *nm* palate
**palaz'zetto** *nm* **~ dello sport** indoor sports arena
**palaz'zina** *nf* villa
**pa'lazzo** *nm* palace; (*edificio*) building. **~ comunale** town hall. **P~ Ducale** Doge's Palace. **~ delle esposizioni** exhibition centre. **~ di giustizia** law courts *pl*, courthouse. **~ dello sport** indoor sports arena
**'palco** *nm* (*pedana*) platform; *Theat* box; (*palcoscenico*) stage
**palco'scenico** *nm* stage
**paleogra'fia** *nf* palaeography
**paleo'grafico** *a* palaeographical
**paleo'grafo, -a** *nmf* palaeographer
**paleo'litico** *a* palaeolithic
**pale'sare** *vt* disclose
**pale'sarsi** *vr* reveal oneself
**pa'lese** *a* evident
**Pale'stina** *nf* Palestine
**palesti'nese** *a* & *nmf* Palestinian
**pa'lestra** *nf* gymnasium, gym; (*ginnastica*) gymnastics *pl*
**pa'letta** *nf* spade; (*per focolare*) shovel. **~ [della spazzatura]** dustpan
**palet'tata** *nf* shovelful
**pa'letto** *nm* peg

**palin'sesto** *nm* (*documento*) palimpsest; *TV* programme schedule
**'palio** *nm* (*premio*) prize. **il P~** *horse-race held at Siena*
**palis'sandro** *nm* rosewood
**paliz'zata** *nf* fence
**'palla** *nf* ball; (*proiettile*) bullet; (*fam: bugia*) porkie; **prendere la ~ al balzo** seize an opportunity; **essere una ~** *sl* be a drag; **che palle!** *vulg* this is a pain in the arse!, what a drag!. **~ da biliardo** billiard ball. **~ medica** medicine ball. **~ di neve** snowball. **~ al piede** *fig* millstone round one's neck
**pallaca'nestro** *nf* basketball
**palla'mano** *nf* handball
**pallanu'tista** *nmf* water polo player
**pallanu'oto** *nf* water polo
**palla-'goal** *nf* **hanno avuto molte palle-goal** they had a lot of goal-scoring opportunities
**pallavo'lista** *nmf* volleyball player
**palla'volo** *nf* volleyball
**palleggi'are** *vi* (*calcio*) practise ball control; *Tennis* knock up
**pal'leggio** *nm* *Sport* warm-up
**'pallet** *nm inv* pallet
**pallet'toni** *nmpl* buckshot
**pallia'tivo** *nm* palliative
**'pallido** *a* pale; **non ne ho la più pallida idea** I don't have the faintest *or* foggiest idea
**pal'lina** *nf* (*di vetro*) marble
**pal'lino** *nm* **avere il ~ del calcio** be crazy about football, be football crazy
**pallon'cino** *nm* balloon; (*lanterna*) Chinese lantern; (*fam: etilometro*) Breathalyzer®
**pal'lone** *nm* ball; (*calcio*) football; (*aerostato*) balloon; **essere/andare nel ~** be/become confused. **~ da calcio** football. **~ gonfiato: è un ~ ~** he's so puffed-up. **~ sonda** weather balloon
**pallo'netto** *nm* lob
**pal'lore** *nm* pallor
**pal'loso** *a sl* boring
**pal'lottola** *nf* pellet; (*proiettile*) bullet. **~ dum-dum** dumdum bullet
**pallottoli'ere** *nm* abacus
**'palma** *nf* *Bot* palm. **~ da cocco** coconut palm. **~ da datteri** date palm
**palmarès** *nm inv* (*di festival*) award winners *pl*; (*fig: i migliori*) top names *pl*
**pal'mato** *a* (*piede*) webbed
**pal'mento** *nm* **mangiava a quattro palmenti** he was really tucking in
**pal'meto** *nm* palm grove
**palmi'pede** *nm* web-footed animal
**'palmo** *nm* *Anat* palm; (*misura*) hand's-breadth; **restare con un ~ di naso** feel disappointed
**'palo** *nm* pole; (*di sostegno*) stake; (*in calcio*) goalpost; **fare il ~** (*ladro:*) keep a lookout. **~ d'arrivo** (*in ippica*) finishing post **~ della luce** lamppost. **~ di partenza** (*in ippica*) starting post
**palom'baro** *nm* diver

**pa'lombo** *nm* dogfish

**pal'pare** *vt* feel

**pal'pata** *nf* **dare una ~ a qcsa** give sth a feel

**'palpebra** *nf* eyelid

**palpeggi'are** *vt* feel

**palpi'tare** *vi* throb; (*fremere*) quiver

**palpitazi'one** *nf* palpitation; **avere le palpitazioni** have palpitations

**'palpito** *nm* throb; (*del cuore*) beat

**paltò** *nm inv* overcoat

**pa'lude** *nf* marsh, swamp

**palu'doso** *a* marshy

**pa'lustre** *a* marshy; ⟨*piante, uccelli*⟩ marsh *attrib*

**'pampas** *nfpl* pampas

**'pamphlet** *nm inv* pamphlet

**pamphlet'tista** *nmf* pamphleteer

**'pampino** *nm* vine leaf

**pan** *nm vedi* **pane**

**pana'cea** *nf* panacea

**pa'nache** *nm inv* far ~ (*in ippica*) fall

**'panca** *nf* bench; (*in chiesa*) pew

**pancarré** *nm* sliced bread

**pan'cetta** *nf* Culin bacon; (*di una certa età*) paunch. ~ **affumicata** smoked bacon

**pan'chetto** *nm* [foot]stool

**pan'china** *nf* garden seat; (*in calcio*) bench

**'pancia** *nf* belly, tummy *fam*; (*di bottiglia, vaso*) body; **mal di ~** stomach-ache; **a ~ piena/vuota** on a full/empty stomach; **metter su ~** develop a paunch; **a ~ in giù** lying face down

**panci'ata** *nf* **prendere una ~** (*in tuffo*) do a belly flop

**panci'era** *nf* corset

**panci'olle: stare in ~** lounge about

**panci'one** *nm* (*persona*) pot belly

**panci'otto** *nm* waistcoat

**panci'uto** *a* potbellied

**'pancreas** *nm inv* pancreas

**pancre'atico** *a* pancreatic

**'panda** *a* panda

**pande'monio** *nm* pandemonium

**pan'dolce** *nm Christmas cake similar to panettone*

**pan'doro** *nm kind of sponge cake traditionally eaten at Christmas time*

**'pane** *nm* bread; (*pagnotta*) loaf; (*di burro*) block. ~ **casereccio** home-made bread. ~ **a cassetta** sliced bread. **pan grattato** breadcrumbs *pl*. ~ **integrale** wholemeal bread. ~ **nero** blackbread. ~ **di segale** rye bread. **pan di Spagna** sponge cake. ~ **tostato** toast

**'panel** *nm inv* (*gruppo*) panel

**panette'ria** *nf* bakery; (*negozio*) baker's [shop]

**panetti'ere, -a** *nmf* baker

**panet'tone** *nf* dome-shaped cake with sultanas and candied fruit eaten at Christmas

**'panfilo** *nm* yacht

**pan'forte** *nm nougat-like spicy delicacy from Siena*

**'panico** *nm* panic; **lasciarsi prendere dal ~** panic

**pani'ere** *nm* basket; (*cesta*) hamper

**pani'ficio** *nm* bakery; (*negozio*) baker's [shop]

**pani'naro** *nm sl* preppie

**pa'nino** *nm* [bread] roll. ~ **imbottito** filled roll. ~ **al prosciutto** ham roll

**panino'teca** *nf* sandwich bar

**'panna** *nf* cream. ~ **cotta** *kind of creme caramel*. ~ **da cucina** [single] cream. ~ **montata** whipped cream

**'panne** *nf Mech* **in ~** broken down; **restare in ~** break down

**panneggi'ato** *a* draped

**pan'neggio** *nm* drapery

**pan'nello** *nm* panel. ~ **comandi** control panel. ~ **solare** solar panel

**'panno** *nm* cloth; (*di tavolo da gioco e da biliardo*) baize; **panni** *pl* (*abiti*) clothes; **mettersi nei panni di qcno** *fig* put oneself in sb's shoes

**pan'nocchia** *nf* (*di granoturco*) cob

**panno'lenci** *nm inv* brightly coloured felt

**panno'lino** *nm* (*per bambini*) nappy; (*da donna*) sanitary towel

**pano'rama** *nm* panorama; *fig* overview

**pano'ramica** *nf* (*rassegna*) overview

**pano'ramico** *a* panoramic

**panpe'pato** *nm type of gingerbread*

**pantacol'lant** *nmpl* leggings

**pantagru'elico** *a* ⟨*pranzo*⟩ gargantuan

**pantalon'cini** *nmpl* shorts. ~ **da ciclista** cycling shorts. ~ **corti** shorts

**panta'loni** *nmpl* trousers, pants *Am*. ~ **da sci** ski pants. ~ **a tubo** drain-pipe trousers. ~ **a zampa d'elefante** bell-bottoms

**pan'tano** *nm* bog

**panta'noso** *a* marshy

**pan'tera** *nf* panther; (*auto della polizia*) high-speed police car. ~ **nera** black panther

**pan'tofola** *nf* slipper

**pantofo'laio, -a** *nmf fig* stay-at-home

**panto'mima** *nf* pantomime; *fig* act

**pan'zana** *nf* fib

**'panzer** *nm inv Mil* tank

**pao'nazzo** *a* purple

**'papa** *nm* Pope; **a ogni morte di ~** *fig* once in a blue moon

**papà** *nm inv* dad[dy]

**pa'paia** *nf* papaw, papaya

**pa'pale** *a* papal

**papa'lina** *nf* skull-cap

**papa'razzo** *nm* paparazzo

**pa'pato** *nm* papacy

**pa'pavero** *nm* poppy

**'papera** *nf* (*errore*) slip of the tongue

**'papero** *nm* gosling

**pa'pilla** *nf* **~ gustativa** taste bud

**papil'lon** *nm inv* bow tie

**pa'piro** *nm* papyrus

**'pappa** *nf* (*per bambini*) baby food; **trovare la ~ pronta** *fig* have everything ready and waiting

**pappagal'lino** *nm* budgerigar, budgie

**pappa'gallo** *nm* parrot
**pappa'gorgia** *nf* double chin
**pappa'molle** *nmf* wimp
**pap'parsi** *vr fam* tuck away
**pappar'delle** *nfpl* strips of pasta with a meat sauce
**pap'pone** *nm sl* (*mangione*) pig; (*sfruttatore*) pimp
**'paprica** *nf* paprika
**Pap test** *nm inv* smear test
**'para** *nf* **suole di ~** crêpe soles
**parà** *nm inv* para
**pa'rabola** *nf* parable; (*curva*) parabola
**para'bolico** *a* parabolic
**para'brezza** *nm inv* windscreen, windshield *Am*
**paracadu'tare** *vt* parachute
**paracadu'tarsi** *vr* parachute
**paraca'dute** *nm inv* parachute
**paracadu'tismo** *nm* parachuting. **~ ascensionale** parascending
**paracadu'tista** *nmf* parachutist
**para'carro** *nm* roadside post
**para'digma** *nm Gram* paradigm
**paradi'siaco** *a* heavenly
**para'diso** *nm* paradise. **~ fiscale** tax haven. **~ terrestre** Eden, earthly paradise
**parados'sale** *a* paradoxical
**para'dosso** *nm* paradox
**para'fango** *nm* mudguard
**paraf'fina** *nf* paraffin
**parafra'sare** *vt* paraphrase
**pa'rafrasi** *nf inv* paraphrase
**para'fulmine** *nm* lightning-conductor
**para'fuoco** *nm* fire-screen
**pa'raggi** *nmpl* neighbourhood *sg*
**parago'nabile** *a* comparable (**a** to)
**parago'nare** *vt* compare
**parago'narsi** *vr* compare oneself
**para'gone** *nm* comparison; **a ~ di** in comparison with; **non c'è ~!** there's no comparison!
**paragra'fare** *vt* paragraph
**pa'ragrafo** *nm* paragraph
**paraguai'ano, -a** *a & nmf* Paraguyan
**Paragu'ay** *nm* Paraguay
**pa'ralisi** *nf inv* paralysis
**para'litico, -a** *a & nmf* paralytic
**paraliz'zante** *a* crippling
**paraliz'zare** *vt* paralyse
**paraliz'zato** *a* (*dalla paura*) transfixed
**paral'lela** *nf* parallel line; **è una ~ di...** ⟨*strada:*⟩ it runs parallel to...; **parallele** *pl* parallel bars
**parallela'mente** *adv* in parallel
**paralle'lismo** *nm* parallelism
**paral'lelo** *a & nm* parallel; **fare un ~ tra** draw a parallel between
**parallelo'gramma** *nm* parallelogram
**para'lume** *nm* lampshade
**para'medico** *nm* paramedic
**para'mento** *nm* hangings *pl*
**pa'rametro** *nm* parameter
**paramili'tare** *a* paramilitary
**pa'ranco** *nm* block and tackle

**para'noia** *nf* paranoia
**para'noico, -a** *a & nmf* paranoid
**paranor'male** *a & nm* paranormal
**para'occhi** *nmpl* blinkers
**parao'recchie** *nm* earmuffs
**parapen'dio** *nm* paragliding
**para'petto** *nm* parapet
**para'piglia** *nm* turmoil
**para'plegico, -a** *a & nmf* paraplegic
**pa'rare** *vt* (*addobbare*) adorn; (*riparare*) shield; save ⟨*tiro, pallone*⟩; ward off, parry ⟨*schiaffo, pugno*⟩ ● *vi* (*mirare*) lead up to
**pa'rarsi** *vr* (*abbigliarsi*) dress up; (*da pioggia, pugni*) protect oneself; **~ dinanzi a** qcno appear in front of sb
**parasco'lastico** *a* ⟨*attività*⟩ extracurricular
**para'sole** *nm inv* parasol
**paras'sita** *a* parasitic ● *nm* parasite
**parassi'tario** *a anche fig* parasitic
**parassi'tismo** *nm* parasitism
**parasta'tale** *a* government-controlled
**para'stinchi** *nm inv* shin-guard
**pa'rata** *nf* parade; (*in calcio*) save; (*in scherma, pugilato*) parry. **~ aerea** flypast
**para'tia** *nf* bulkhead
**parauniversi'tario** *a* at university level
**para'urti** *nm inv* Auto bumper, fender *Am*
**para'vento** *nm* screen
**par'boiled** *a* **riso ~** parboiled rice
**par'cella** *nf* bill
**parcheggi'are** *vt anche fig* park; **~ in doppia fila** double-park
**parcheggia|'tore, -'trice** *nmf* parking attendant. **~ abusivo** person who illegally earns money by looking after parked cars
**par'cheggio** *nm* parking; (*posteggio*) carpark, parking lot *Am*. **~ carta** Comput paper park. **~ custodito** car park with attendant. **~ incustodito** unattended car park. **~ a pagamento** paying car-park. **~ sotterraneo** underground car park, underground parking garage *Am*
**par'chimetro** *nm* parking meter
**'parco¹** *a* sparing; (*moderato*) moderate; **essere ~ nel mangiare** eat sparingly
**'parco²** *nm* park. **~ di divertimenti** fun-fair. **~ giochi** playground. **~ macchine** Auto fleet of cars. **~ naturale** wildlife park. **~ nazionale** national park. **~ regionale** [regional] wildlife park
**pa'recchio** *a* quite a lot of; **parecchi** *pl* several, quite a lot of ● *pron* several, quite a lot; **parecchi** *pl* several, quite a lot ● *adv* rather; (*parecchio tempo*) quite a time
**pareggi'are** *vt* level; (*eguagliare*) equal; *Comm* balance; **~ il bilancio** balance the scales ● *vi* draw
**pa'reggio** *nm* Comm balance; Sport draw
**paren'tado** *nm* relatives *pl*; (*vincolo di sangue*) relationship
**pa'rente** *nmf* relative, relation. **~ acquisito** relation by marriage. **~ alla lontana** distant relation. **~ stretto** close relation
**paren'tela** *nf* relatives *pl*; (*vincolo di*

*sangue*) relationship; **grado di ~** degree of kinship

**pa'rentesi** *nf inv* parenthesis: (*segno grafico*) bracket: (*fig: pausa*) break: **aprire una ~** (*fig*) digress. **~** *pl* **graffe** curly brackets. **~ quadre** square brackets. **~ tonde** round brackets; **fra ~,...** (*tra l'altro*) in parenthesis

**pa'reo** *nm* (*copricostume*) sarong; **a ~** (*gonna*) wrap-around

**pa'rere**[1] *nm* opinion; **a mio ~** in my opinion; **essere del ~ che** be of the opinion that

**pa'rere**[2] *vi* seem; (*pensare*) think; **che te ne pare?** what do you think of it?; **pare di sì** it seems so; **mi pare che...** I think that...; **non mi par vero** I can't believe it; **mi pareva bene!** I thought as much!

**pa'rete** *nf* wall; (*in alpinismo*) face. **~ divisoria** partition wall

**'pargolo** *nf liter* child

**'pari** *a inv* equal; (*numero*) even; **andare di ~ passo** keep pace; **essere ~** be even *o* quits; **arrivare ~** draw; **~ ~** (*copiare, ripetere*) word for word; **fare ~ o dispari** toss a coin ● *nmf inv* equal, peer; **ragazza alla ~** au pair [girl]; **lavorare alla ~** work [as an] au pair; **mettersi in ~ con qcsa** catch up with sth ● *nm* (*titolo nobiliare*) peer

**'paria** *nm inv* pariah

**parifi'cato** *a* (*scuola*) state-recognized

**Pa'rigi** *nf* Paris

**pari'gino, -a** *a & nmf* Parisian

**pa'riglia** *nf* pair; **rendere la ~ a qcno** give sb tit for tat

**parità** *nf* equality; *Tennis* deuce; **a ~ di condizioni/voti** if all circumstances/the votes are equal; **finire in ~** (*partita:*) end in a draw. **~ dei diritti** equal rights. **~ monetaria** monetary parity. **~ dei sessi** sexual equality, equality of the sexes

**pari'tario** *a* parity *attrib*

**'parka** *nm inv* parka

**parlamen'tare** *a* parliamentary ● *nmf* Member of Parliament ● *vi* discuss

**parla'mento** *nm* Parliament. **il P~ europeo** the European Parliament

**parlan'tina** *nf* **avere la ~** be a chatterbox

**par'lare** *vt/i* speak, talk; speak (*inglese, italiano*); (*confessare*) talk; **~ bene/male di qcno** speak well/ill of somebody; **~ da solo** speak to oneself; **chi parla?** *Teleph* who's speaking?; **senti chi parla!** look who's talking!; **non parliamone più** let's forget about it; **non se ne parla nemmeno!** don't even mention it!; **~ a braccio** speak off the top of one's head; **far ~ qcno** make sb talk

**par'lato** *a* (*lingua*) spoken

**parla|'tore, -'trice** *nmf* speaker

**parla'torio** *nm* parlour; (*in prigione*) visiting room

**parlot'tare** *vi* mutter

**parlot'tio** *nm* muttering

**parlucchi'are** *vt* speak a little, have a smattering of (*lingua*)

**parmigi'ano** *nm* Parmesan

**paro'dia** *nf* parody: **fare la ~ di** parody

**parodi'are** *vt* parody

**paro'distico** *a* (*tono*) parodying: **programma ~** parody

**pa'rola** *nf* word: (*facoltà*) speech: **è una ~!** it is easier said than done!: **parole** *pl* (*di canzone*) words. lyrics: **rivolgere la ~ a** address; **passare ~** spread the word; **non fare ~ di qcsa con nessuno** not breathe a word of sth to anybody; **ti credo sulla ~** I'll take your word for it; **togliere la ~ di bocca a qcno** take the words [right] out of sb's mouth; **voler sempre l'ultima ~** always want to have the last word; **dire due parole a qcno** have a word *o* chat with sb; **di poche parole** (*persona*) of few words; **dare a qcno la propria ~** give sb one's word; **~ per ~** word-for-word; **in parole povere** crudely speaking. **~ chiave** *inv* keyword. **parole** *pl* **incrociate** crossword [puzzle]. **~ di moda** buzzword. **~ d'onore** word of honour. **~ d'ordine** password

**paro'laccia** *nf* swear-word

**paro'lina** *nf* **dire due paroline a qcno** have a word *o* chat with sb

**paro'loni** *nmpl* mumbo jumbo

**paros'sismo** *nm* paroxysm

**paros'sistico** *a Med* paroxysmal

**par'quet** *nm inv* (*pavimento*) parquet flooring

**parri'cida** *nmf* parricide

**parri'cidio** *nm* parricide

**par'rocchia** *nf* parish

**parrocchi'ale** *a* parish *attrib*

**parrocchi'ano, -a** *nmf* parishioner

**'parroco** *nm* parish priest

**par'rucca** *nf* wig

**parrucchi'ere, -a** *nmf* hairdresser

**parruc'chino** *nm* toupée, hairpiece

**parsi'monia** *nf* thrift

**parsimoni'oso** *a* thrifty

**'parso** *pp di* **parere**

**'parte** *nf* part; (*lato*) side; (*partito*) party; (*porzione*) share; (*fazione*) group; **a ~** apart from; **in ~** in part; **la maggior ~ di** the majority of; **d'altra ~** on the other hand; **da ~** aside; (*in disparte*) to one side; **farsi da ~** stand aside; **da ~ di** from; (*per conto di*) on behalf of; **è gentile da ~ tua** it is kind of you; **fare una brutta ~ a qcno** behave badly towards sb; **da che ~ è...?** whereabouts is...?; **da una parte..., dall'altra...** on the one hand..., on the other hand...; **dall'altra di** on the other side of; **da nessuna ~** nowhere; **da qualche ~** somewhere; **da qualche altra** somewhere else, elsewhere; **da tutte le parti** (*essere*) everywhere; **da questa ~** (*in questa direzione*) this way; **da queste parti** hereabouts; **da un anno a questa** ~ for about a year now; **mettere qcsa da ~** put sth aside; **essere dalla ~ di qcno** be on sb's side; **prendere le parti di qcno** take sb's side; **dalla ~ della ragione/del torto** in the right/the wrong; **essere ~ in causa** be involved; **fare ~ di** (*appartenere* *a)* be a member of; **fare la propria ~** do one's share *o* bit; **far ~ di qcsa a qcno** inform sb of sth; **rendere ~ a** take part in; **prendere ~ a qcsa** take part in sth. ● **civile** plaintiff. **~ del discorso** part of speech

**parteci'pante** *nmf* participant

**parteci'pare** *vi* **~ a** participate in, take part in; (*condividere*) share in

**partecipazi'one** *nf* participation; (*annuncio*) announcement; *Fin* shareholding; (*presenza*) presence; **con la ~ [straordinaria] di...** featuring... **~ statale** (*quota*) state interest

**par'tecipe** *a* participating

**parteggi'are** *vi* **~ per** side with

**par'tenza** *nf* departure; *Sport* start; **in ~** per leaving for; **falsa ~** false start

**parti'cella** *nf* particle

**parti'cina** *nf* bit part

**parti'cipio** *nm* participle. **~ passato** past participle. **~ presente** present participle

**partico'lare** *a* particular; (*privato*) private; (*speciale*) special, particular ● *nm* detail, particular; **fin nei minimi particolari** down to the smallest detail; **in ~** (*particolarmente*) in particular

**particolareggi'ato** *a* detailed

**particolarità** *nf inv* particularity; (*dettaglio*) detail

**particolar'mente** *adv* particularly

**partigi'ano, -a** *a & nmf* partisan

**par'tire** *vi* leave; (*aver inizio*) start; (*fam: rompersi*) break. **a ~ da** [beginning] from; **molto bene** get off to a flying start; **~ in quarta** go off at half cock; **è partito** (*fam: ubriaco*) he's away

**par'tita** *nf* game; (*incontro*) match; *Comm* lot; (*contabilità*) entry; **dare ~ vinta a qcno** *fig* give in to sb. **~ amichevole** friendly [match]. **~ di calcio** football match. **~ a carte** game of cards. **~ doppia** *Comm* double-entry book keeping. **~ di ritorno** *Sport* return match, rematch. **~ semplice** *Comm* single-entry book keeping

**parti'tario** *nm Comm* ledger. **~ vendite** sales ledger

**par'tito** *nm* party; (*scelta*) choice; (*occasione di matrimonio*) match; **per ~ preso** out of sheer pig-headedness. **~ di governo** governing party. **~ di maggioranza** majority party. **~ politico** political party

**partitocra'zia** *nf* concentration of power in the hands of political parties to the detriment of parliamentary democracy

**partizi'one** *nf* (*divisione*) division; (*Comput: di disco*) partition

'**partner** *nmf inv* (*in affari, coppia*) partner

'**parto** *nm* childbirth; **un ~ facile** an easy birth *o* labour; **dolori** *pl* **del ~** labour pains; **morire di ~** die in childbirth. **~ cesareo** Caesarian section. **~ indolore** natural childbirth. **~ indotto** induction, induced labour. **~ prematuro** premature birth

**partori'ente** *nf* woman in labour

**parto'rire** *vt anche fig* give birth to

**part-'time** *a* part-time ● *nm* **chiedere il ~** ask to work part-time

**pa'rure** *nf inv* (*di gioielli*) set of jewellery; (*di biancheria intima*) set of matching lingerie

**par'venza** *nf* appearance

**parzi'ale** *a* partial

**parzialità** *nf* partiality; **fare ~ per qcno** be biased towards sb

**parzial'mente** *adv* partially; (*con parzialità*) with bias; **~ cieco** partially sighted; **~ scremato** semi-skimmed

'**pascere** *vi* ⟨*mucche:*⟩ graze ● *vt* graze on ⟨*erba*⟩

**pasci'uto** *a* **ben ~** plump

**pasco'lare** *vt* graze

'**pascolo** *nm* pasture

'**Pasqua** *nf* Easter

**pa'squale** *a* Easter *attrib*; **l'isola di P~** Easter Island

**pa'squetta** *nf* (*lunedì di Pasqua*) Easter Monday

'**passa: e ~** *adv* (*e oltre*) plus

**pas'sabile** *a* passable

**pas'saggio** *nm* passage; (*traversata*) crossing; *Sport* pass; (*su veicolo*) lift, ride; **essere di ~** be passing through; **è stato un ~ obbligato** *fig* it was something essential, it had to be done. **~ a livello** level crossing, grade crossing *Am*. **~ pedonale** pedestrian crossing, crosswalk *Am*. **~ di proprietà** transfer of ownership

**passamane'ria** *nf* braid

**passamon'tagna** *nm inv* balaclava

**pas'sante** *nmf* passer-by ● *nm* (*di cintura*) loop ● *a Tennis* passing

**passa'porto** *nm anche fig* passport. **~ europeo** European passport, Europassport

**pas'sare** *vi* pass; (*attraversare*) pass through; (*far visita*) call; (*andare*) go; (*essere approvato*) be passed; **~ davanti a qcno** go in front of sb; **~ alla storia** go down in history; **~ di moda** go out of fashion; **mi è passato di mente** it slipped my mind; **~ sopra a qcsa** pass over sth; **~ per un genio/idiota** be taken for a genius/an idiot; **farsi ~ per qcno** pass oneself off as sb; **passo!** (*nelle carte*) pass!; (*per radio*) over! ● *vt* (*far scorrere*) pass over; (*sopportare*) go through; (*al telefono*) put through; *Culin* strain; pass ⟨*esame, visita*⟩; **~ in rivista** review; **~ qcsa a qcno** pass sth to sb; **le passo il signor Rossi** *Teleph* I'll put you through to Mr Rossi; **~ qcsa su qcsa** ⟨*crema, cera ecc*⟩ give sth a coat of sth ; **~ il limite** go over the limit; **passarsela bene** be well off; **come te la passi?** how are you doing? ● *nm* **col ~ del tempo** with the passing *or* passage of time

**pas'sata** *nf* (*di vernice*) coat; (*spolverata*) dusting; (*occhiata*) look

**passa'tempo** *nm* pastime

**pas'sato** *a* past; **l'anno ~** last year; **sono le tre passate** it's past *o* after three o'clock ● *nm* past; *Culin* purée; *Gram* past tense; **in ~** in the past. **~ di moda** old-fashioned. **~**

**prossimo** *Gram* present perfect. **~ remoto** *Gram* [simple] past. **~ di verdure** cream of vegetable soup

**passaver'dure** *nm inv* food mill

**passavi'vande** *nm inv* serving hatch

**passeg'gero, -a** *a* passing ● *nmf* passenger. **~ in transito** transit passenger

**passeggi'are** *vi* walk, stroll

**passeg'giata** *nf* walk, stroll; (*luogo*) public walk; (*in bicicletta*) ride; **fare una ~** go for a walk

**passeggia'trice** *nf* streetwalker

**passeg'gino** *nm* pushchair, stroller *Am*

**pas'seggio** *nm* walk; (*luogo*) promenade; **andare a ~** go for a walk; **scarpe da ~** walking shoes

**passe-par'tout** *nm inv* master-key

**passe'rella** *nf* gangway; *Aeron* boarding bridge; (*per sfilate*) catwalk

**'passero** *nm* sparrow

**passe'rotto** *nm* (*passero*) sparrow

**pas'sibile** *a* **~ di** liable to

**passio'nale** *a* passionate; **delitto ~** crime of passion

**passi'one** *nf* passion; **avere la ~ del gioco** have a passion for gambling

**passiva'mente** *adv* passively

**passività** *nf* (*inerzia*) passiveness, passivity; *Fin* liabilities *pl*. **~ pl correnti** current liabilities

**pas'sivo** *a* passive ● *nm* passive; *Fin* liabilities *pl*; **in ~** ⟨*azienda*⟩ in deficit; ⟨*bilancio*⟩ debit, in deficit

**'passo** *nm* step; (*orma*) footprint; (*andatura*) pace, step; (*di libro*) passage; (*valico*) pass; **a due passi da qui** a stone's throw away; **a ~ d'uomo** at walking pace; **di buon ~** at a spanking pace, at a cracking pace; **a passi felpati** stealthily; **di questo ~** at this rate; **~ ~** step by step; **fare due passi** go for a stroll; **allungare il ~** quicken one's pace, step out; **tornare sui propri passi** retrace one's steps; **fare un ~ avanti** *anche fig* take a step forward; **fare un ~ falso** *fig* make a wrong move; **di pari ~** *fig* hand in hand; **stare al ~ con i tempi** keep up with the times, keep abreast of the times; **tenere il ~** keep up. **~ carrabile, ~ carraio** driveway. **~ dell'oca** goose-step

**'pasta** *nf* (*impasto per pane ecc*) dough; (*per dolci, pasticcino*) pastry; (*pastasciutta*) pasta; (*massa molle*) paste; *fig* nature; **sono fatti della stessa ~** they're birds of a feather. **~ e fagioli** very thick soup with blended borlotti beans and small pasta. **~ al forno** pasta baked in white sauce with grated cheese. **~ frolla** shortcrust pastry. **~ al ragù** pasta with Bolognese sauce

**pastasci'utta** *nf* pasta

**pa'stella** *nf* batter

**pa'stello** *nm* pastel

**pa'sticca** *nf* pastille; (*fam: pastiglia*) pill

**pasticce'ria** *nf* cake shop, patisserie; (*pasticcini*) pastries *pl*; (*arte*) confectionery

**pasticci'are** *vi* make a mess ● *vt* make a mess of

**pasticci'ere, -a** *nmf* confectioner

**pastic'cino** *nm* little cake

**pa'sticcio** *nm* *Culin* pie; (*lavoro disordinato*) mess; **mettersi nei pasticci** get into trouble

**pasticci'one, -a** *nmf* bungler ● *a* bungling

**pasti'ficio** *nm* pasta factory

**pa'stiglia** *nf* *Med* pill, tablet; (*di menta*) sweet. **~ dei freni** brake pad. **~ per la gola** throat pastille. **~ per la tosse** cough sweet

**pa'stina** *nf* small pasta shape. **~ in brodo** noodle soup

**'pasto** *nm* meal; **fuori ~** between meals; **dare qcsa in ~ a** *fig* serve sth up on a platter to ⟨*pubblico, stampa*⟩

**pa'stora** *nf* shepherdess

**pasto'rale** *a* pastoral

**pa'store** *nm* shepherd; *Relig* pastor, vicar. **~ scozzese** collie. **~ tedesco** German shepherd, Alsatian

**pasto'rizio** *a* sheep farming *attrib*

**pastoriz'zare** *vt* pasteurize

**pastoriz'zato** *a* pasteurized

**pastorizzazi'one** *nf* pasteurization

**pa'stoso** *a* doughy; *fig* mellow

**pa'strocchio** *nm* mess

**pa'stura** *nf* pasture; (*per pesci*) bait

**pa'tacca** *nf* (*macchia*) stain; (*fig: oggetto senza valore*) piece of junk

**pa'tata** *nf* potato. **patate** *pl* **arrosto** roast potatoes. **patate** *pl* **al cartoccio** jacket potatoes. **patate** *pl* **fritte** chips *Br*, French fries. **patate** *pl* **in insalata** potato salad. **patate** *pl* **lesse** boiled potatoes

**pata'tine** *nfpl* [potato] crisps, chips *Am*

**pata'trac** *nm inv* (*crollo*) crash

**patch'work** *nm inv* patchwork

**pâté** *nm inv* pâté. **~ di fegato** liver pâté

**pa'tella** *nf* limpet

**pa'tema** *nm* anxiety

**pa'tente** *nf* licence; **prendere la ~** get one's driving licence. **~ di guida** driving licence, driver's license *Am*

**pater'nale** *nf* scolding

**paterna'lismo** *nm* paternalism

**paterna'lista** *nmf* paternalist

**paterna'listico** *a* paternalistic

**paternità** *nf inv* paternity

**pa'terno** *a* paternal; ⟨*affetto ecc*⟩ fatherly

**pa'tetico** *a* pathetic; **cadere nel ~** become over-sentimental

**'pathos** *nm* pathos

**pa'tibolo** *nm* gallows *sg*

**pati'mento** *nm* suffering

**'patina** *nf* patina; (*sulla lingua*) coating

**'patio** *nm* patio garden

**pa'tire** *vt/i* suffer

**pa'tito, -a** *a* suffering ● *nmf* fanatic. **~ della musica** music lover

**patolo'gia** *nf* pathology

**pato'logico** *a* pathological

**pa'tologo, -a** *nmf* pathologist

**'patria** *nf* native land; **amor di ~** love of one's country
**patri'arca** *nm* patriarch
**patriar'cale** *a* patriarchal
**patriar'cato** *nm* patriarchy
**pa'trigno** *nm* stepfather
**patrimoni'ale** *a* property *attrib*
**patri'monio** *nm* estate
**patri'ota** *nmf* patriot
**patri'ottico** *a* patriotic
**patriot'tismo** *nm* patriotism
**pa'trizio, -a** *a & nmf* patrician
**patroci'nante** *a* sponsoring
**patroci'nare** *vt* support
**patro'cinio** *nm* support; **sotto il ~ di** under the sponsorship of; *Jur* defended by. **~ gratuito** legal aid
**patro'nato** *nm* patronage
**pa'trono** *nm Relig* patron saint; *Jur* counsel
**'patta**[1] *nf (di tasca)* flap
**'patta**[2] *nf (pareggio)* draw
**patteggia'mento** *nm* bargaining
**patteggi'are** *vt/i* negotiate
**patti'naggio** *nm* skating. **~ artistico** figure skating. **~ su ghiaccio** ice skating. **~ a rotelle** roller skating
**patti'nare** *vi* skate; *(auto:)* skid
**pattina**|**'tore, -'trice** *nmf* skater
**'pattino** *nm* skate; *Aeron* skid. **~ da ghiaccio** ice skate. **~ a rotelle** roller skate
**'patto** *nm* deal; *Pol* pact; **a ~ che** on condition that; **scendere a patti, venire a patti** reach a compromise
**pat'tuglia** *nf* patrol; **essere di ~** be on patrol. **~ stradale** highway patrol *Am*, ≈ patrol car; police motorbike
**pattu'ire** *vt* negotiate
**pat'tume** *nm* rubbish
**pattumi'era** *nf* dustbin, trashcan *Am*
**pa'ura** *nf* fear; *(spavento)* fright; **aver ~ be** afraid; **mettere ~ a** frighten; **per ~ di** for fear of; **da ~** *(sl: libro, film)* brilliant
**pau'roso** *a (che fa paura)* frightening; *(che ha paura)* fearful; *(fam: enorme)* awesome
**'pausa** *nf* pause; *(nel lavoro)* break; **fare una ~** pause; *(nel lavoro)* have a break. **~ per il caffè** coffee break. **~ del pranzo** lunch break, lunch hour
**pavida'mente** *adv* timidly
**'pavido** *a* cowardly ● *nm* coward
**pavimen'tare** *vt* pave *(strada)*
**pavimentazi'one** *nf* paving
**pavi'mento** *nm* floor
**pa'vone** *nm* peacock
**pavoneggi'arsi** *vr* strut
**pay tv** *nf inv* pay TV
**pazien'tare** *vi* be patient
**pazi'ente** *a & nmf* patient
**paziente'mente** *adv* patiently
**pazi'enza** *nf* patience; **~!** never mind!; **perdere la ~** lose one's patience
**'pazza** *nf* madwoman
**pazza'mente** *adv* madly
**pazzerel'lone, -a** *nmf* madcap
**paz'zesco** *a* foolish; *(esagerato)* crazy

**paz'zia** *nf* madness; *(azione)* [act of] folly
**'pazzo** *a* mad; *fig* crazy; **sei ~?** you must be crazy!, are you crazy? ● *nm* madman; **essere ~ di/per** be crazy about; **~ di gioia** mad with joy; **da pazzi** *fam* crackpot; **darsi alla pazza gioia** live it up
**paz'zoide** *a fam* whacky
**P.C.I.** *nm abbr* (**Partito Comunista Italiano**) Italian Communist Party
**'pecan** *nm inv* pecan
**'pecca** *nf* fault; **senza ~** flawless
**peccami'noso** *a* sinful
**pec'care** *vi* sin; **~ di** be guilty of *(ingratitudine)*
**pec'cato** *nm* sin; **~ che...** it's a pity that...; **[che] ~!** [what a] pity!. **~ di gioventù** youthful folly
**pecca**|**'tore, -'trice** *nmf* sinner
**'pece** *nf* pitch; **nero come la ~** black as pitch
**pechi'nese** *nm* Pekin[g]ese
**Pe'chino** *nf* Peking
**'pecora** *nf* sheep. **~ nera** black sheep
**peco'raio** *nm* shepherd
**peco'rella** *nf* **cielo a pecorelle** sky full of fluffy white clouds. **~ smarrita** lost sheep
**peco'rino** *nm (formaggio)* sheep's milk cheese
**peculi'are** *a* **~ di** peculiar to
**peculiarità** *nf inv* peculiarity
**pecuni'ario** *a* money *attrib*
**pe'daggio** *nm* toll
**pedago'gia** *nf* pedagogy
**peda'gogico** *a* pedagogical
**peda'gogo, -a** *nmf* pedagogue
**peda'lare** *vi* pedal
**peda'lata** *nf* push on the pedals
**pe'dale** *nm* pedal. **~ del freno** brake pedal
**pedalò** *nm inv* pedalo
**pe'dana** *nf* footrest; *Sport* springboard
**pe'dante** *a* pedantic
**pedante'ria** *nf* pedantry
**pedan'tesco** *a* pedantic
**pe'data** *nf (in calcio)* kick; *(impronta)* footprint
**pede'rasta** *nm* pederast
**pe'destre** *a* pedestrian
**pedi'atra** *nmf* paediatrician
**pedia'tria** *nf* paediatrics
**pedi'atrico** *a* paediatric
**pedi'cure** *nmf inv* chiropodist, podiatrist *Am* ● *nm (cura dei piedi)* pedicure
**pedi'gree** *nm inv* pedigree
**pedi'luvio** *nm* footbath
**pe'dina** *nf (alla dama)* piece; *fig* pawn
**pedina'mento** *nm* shadowing
**pedi'nare** *vt* shadow
**pedofi'lia** *nf* paedophilia
**pe'dofilo, -a** *nmf* paedophile
**pedo'nale** *a* pedestrian
**pe'done, -a** *nmf* pedestrian
**'pedula** *nf* desert boot
**'peeling** *nm inv* exfoliation treatment
**'peggio** *adv* worse; **~ per te!** too bad!, tough!; **~ di così** any worse; **la persona ~**

**vestita** the worst dressed person ● *a* worse; **niente di ~** nothing worse; **stare ~ di** be worse off than ● *nm* **il ~ è che...** the worst of it is that...; **pensare al ~** think the worst ● *nf* **alla ~** at worst: **avere la ~** get the worst of it; **alla meno ~** as best I can

**peggiora'mento** *nm* worsening

**peggio'rare** *vt* make worse. worsen ● *vi* get worse, worsen

**peggiora'tivo** *a* pejorative

**peggi'ore** *a* worse; (*superlativo*) worst; **nella ~ delle ipotesi** if the worst comes to the worst; **tanto ~** too bad ● *nmf* **il/la ~** the worst

'**pegno** *nm* pledge; (*nei giochi di società*) forfeit; *fig* token; **dare qcsa in ~** pawn sth; **in ~ d'amicizia** as a token of friendship

**pelan'drone** *nm* slob

**pe'lare** *vt* (*spennare*) pluck; (*spellare*) skin; (*sbucciare*) peel; (*fam: spillare denaro*) fleece

**pe'larsi** *vr fam* lose one's hair

**pe'lati** *nmpl* (*pomodori*) peeled tomatoes

**pe'lato** *a* (*calvo*) bald

**pel'lame** *nm* skins *pl*

'**pelle** *nf* skin; (*cuoio*) leather; (*buccia*) peel; **avere la ~ d'oca** have goose-flesh; **non stare più nella ~** be beside oneself; **salvare la ~** save one's skin; **lasciarci la ~** buy it; **essere ~ e ossa** be all skin and bones; **avere la ~ dura** be tough; **borsa di ~** leather bag. **~ scamosciata** suede

**pellegri'naggio** *nm* pilgrimage

**pelle'grino, -a** *nmf* pilgrim

**pelle'rossa** *nmf* Red Indian, Redskin

**pellette'ria** *nf* leather goods *pl*

**pelli'cano** *nm* pelican

**pellicce'ria** *nf* furrier's [shop]

**pel'liccia** *nf* fur; (*indumento*) fur [coat]

**pellicci'aio, -a** *nmf* furrier

**pel'licola** *nf Phot, Cinema* film. **~ a colori** colour film. **~ trasparente** *Culin* cling film

'**pelo** *nm* hair; (*di animale*) coat; (*di lana*) pile; **per un ~** by the skin of one's teeth; **cavarsela per un ~** have a narrow escape; **cercare il ~ nell'uovo** nitpick

**pe'loso** *a* hairy

'**peltro** *nm* pewter

**pe'luche** *nm inv* **giocattolo di ~** soft toy; **orsetto di ~** teddy bear

**pe'luria** *nf* down

'**pelvico** *a* pelvic

'**pena** *nf* (*punizione*) punishment; (*sofferenza*) pain; (*dispiacere*) sorrow; (*disturbo*) trouble; **a mala ~** hardly; **mi fa ~** I pity him; **vale la ~ andare** it is worth [while] going. **pene** *pl* **dell'inferno** hellfire. **~ di morte** death sentence

**pe'nale** *a* criminal; **diritto ~** criminal law

**pena'lista** *nmf* criminal lawyer

**penalità** *nf inv* penalty

**penaliz'zare** *vt* penalize

**penalizzazi'one** *nf* (*penalità*) penalty

**pe'nare** *vi* suffer; (*faticare*) find it difficult

**pen'daglio** *nm* pendant

**pen'dant** *nm inv* **fare ~ [con]** match

**pen'dente** *a* hanging; *Comm* outstanding ● *nm* (*ciondolo*) pendant; **pendenti** *pl* drop earrings

**pen'denza** *nf* slope; *Comm* outstanding account

'**pendere** *vi* hang; (*superficie:*) slope; (*essere inclinato*) lean

**pen'dio** *nm* slope; **in ~** sloping

'**pendola** *nf* clock

**pendo'lare** *a* pendulum ● *nmf* commuter

**pendo'lino** *nm* (*treno*) special, first class only, fast train

'**pendolo** *nm* pendulum; **orologio a ~** pendulum clock

'**pene** *nm* penis

**pene'trante** *a* penetrating; (*freddo*) biting

**pene'trare** *vt/i* penetrate; (*trafiggere*) pierce ● *vt* (*odore:*) get into ● *vi* (*entrare furtivamente*) steal in

**penetrazi'one** *nf* penetration

**penicil'lina** *nf* penicillin

**pe'nisola** *nf* peninsula

**peni'tente** *a & nmf* penitent

**peni'tenza** *nf* penitence; (*punizione*) penance; (*in gioco*) forfeit

**penitenzi'ario** *nm* penitentiary

'**penna** *nf* (*da scrivere*) pen; (*di uccello*) feather. **~ a feltro** felt-tip[ped pen]. **~ ottica** light pen. **~ a sfera** ball-point [pen]. **~ stilografica** fountain-pen

**pen'nacchio** *nm* plume

**penna'rello** *nm* felt-tip[ped pen]

'**penne** *nfpl* pasta quills

**pennel'lare** *vt* paint

**pennel'lata** *nf* brushstroke

**pen'nello** *nm* brush; **a ~** (*a perfezione*) perfectly. **~ da barba** shaving brush

**pen'nino** *nm* nib

**pen'none** *nm* (*di bandiera*) flagpole

**pen'nuto** *a* feathered

**pe'nombra** *nf* half-light

**pe'noso** *a* (*fam: pessimo*) painful

**pen'sabile** *a* **non è ~** it's unthinkable

**pen'sare** *vi* think; **penso di sì** I think so; **~ a** think of; remember to (*chiudere il gas ecc*); **pensa ai fatti tuoi!** mind your own business!; **ci penso io** I'll take care of it; **~ di fare qcsa** think of doing sth; **a pensarci bene** on second thoughts; **~ tra sé e sé** think to oneself; **pensarci su** think over ● *vt* think

**pen'sata** *nf* idea

**pensa|'tore, -'trice** *nmf* thinker

**pensi'ero** *nm* thought; (*mente*) mind; (*preoccupazione*) worry; **stare in ~ per** be anxious about; **levarsi il ~** to get something out of the way

**pensie'roso** *a* pensive

**pen'sile** *a* hanging; **giardino ~** roof-garden ● *nm* (*mobile*) wall unit

**pensi'lina** *nf* (*di fermata d'autobus*) bus shelter

**pensio'nante** *nmf* boarder; (*ospite pagante*) lodger

**pensio'nato, -a** *nmf* pensioner ● *nm* (*per*

*anziani)* [old folks'] home: (*per studenti*) hostel

**pensi'one** *nf* pension; (*albergo*) boarding-house; (*vitto e alloggio*) board and lodging; **andare in ~** retire; **essere in ~** be retired; **mezza ~** half board. **~ di anzianità** old-age pension. **~ completa** full board. **~ di invalidità** disability pension

**pen'soso** *a* pensive

**pen'tagono** *nm* pentagon; **il P~** the Pentagon

**pen'tathlon** *nm inv* pentathlon

**Pente'coste** *nf* Whitsun

**penti'mento** *nm* repentance

**pen'tirsi** *vr* **~ di** repent of; (*rammaricarsi*) regret

**penti'tismo** *nm* turning informant

**pen'tito** *nm* Mafioso turned informant

**'pentola** *nf* saucepan; (*contenuto*) potful. **~ a pressione** pressure cooker

**pento'lino** *nf* saucepan

**pe'nultimo** *a* last but one, penultimate

**pe'nuria** *nf* shortage

**penzo'lare** *vi* dangle

**penzo'loni** *adv* dangling

**pe'onia** *nf* peony

**pepai'ola** *nf* pepper pot

**pe'pare** *vt* pepper

**pe'pato** *a* peppery

**'pepe** *nm* pepper; **grano di ~** peppercorn. **~ di Caienna** cayenne pepper. **~ in grani** whole peppercorns. **~ macinato** ground pepper. **~ nero** black pepper

**pepero'nata** *nf* dish of green peppers and tomatoes

**peperon'cino** *nm* chilli pepper

**pepe'rone** *nm* [sweet] pepper; **rosso come un ~** red as a beetroot; **peperoni** *pl* **ripieni** stuffed peppers. **~ verde** green pepper

**pepi'era** *nf* pepper pot; (*macinino*) pepper mill

**pe'pita** *nf* nugget

**'peptico** *a* peptic

**'per** *prep* for; (*attraverso*) through; (*stato in luogo*) in, on; (*distributivo*) per; (*mezzo, entro*) by; (*causa*) with; (*in qualità di*) as; **mi è passato per la mente** it crossed my mind; **~ strada** on the street; **~ la fine del mese** by the end of the month; **in fila ~ due** in double file; **l'ho sentito ~ telefono** I spoke to him on the phone; **~ iscritto** in writing; **~ caso** by chance; **~ esempio** for example; **ho aspettato ~ ore** I've been waiting for hours; **~ tutta la durata del viaggio** for the entire journey; **~ tempo** in time; **~ sempre** forever; **~ scherzo** as a joke; **gridare ~ il dolore** scream with pain; **vendere ~ 10 milioni** sell for 10 million; **uno ~ volta** one at a time; **uno ~ uno** one by one; **venti ~ cento** twenty per cent; **~ fare qcsa** [in order to] do sth; **stare ~** be about to; **è troppo bello ~ essere vero** it's too good to be true

**'pera** *nf* pear; **farsi una ~** (*sl: di eroina*) shoot up

**perbe'nismo** *nm* prissiness

**perbe'nista** *a inv* prissy

**per'calle** *nm* gingham

**per'cento** *adv* per cent

**percentu'ale** *nf* percentage

**perce'pibile** *a* perceivable; (*somma*) payable

**perce'pire** *vt* perceive; (*riscuotere*) cash

**percet'tibile** *a* perceptible

**percettibil'mente** *adv* perceptibly

**percezi'one** *nf* perception

**perché** *conj* (*in interrogazioni*) why; (*per il fatto che*) because; (*affinché*) so that; **~ non vieni?** why don't you come?; **dimmi ~** tell me why; **~ no/sì!** because!; **la ragione ~ l'ho fatto** the reason [that] I did it, the reason why I did it; **è troppo difficile ~ lo possa capire** it's too difficult for me to understand ● *nm inv* reason [why]; **senza un ~** without any reason

**perciò** *conj* so

**per'correre** *vt* cover (*distanza*); (*viaggiare*) travel

**percor'ribile** *a* (*strada*) driveable, passable

**percorribilità** *nf* **~ delle strade** road conditions *pl*

**per'corso** *pp di* percorrere ● *nm* (*tragitto*) course, route; (*distanza*) distance; (*viaggio*) journey. **~ ecologico** nature trail. **~ di guerra** assault course. **~ a ostacoli** obstacle course

**per'cossa** *nf* blow; **percosse** *pl* Jur assault and battery

**per'cosso** *pp di* percuotere

**percu'otere** *vt* strike

**percussi'one** *nf* percussion; **strumenti a ~** percussion instruments

**percussio'nista** *nmf* percussionist

**per'dente** *nmf* loser

**'perdere** *vt* lose; (*sprecare*) waste; (*non prendere*) miss; (*fig: vizio:*) ruin; **~ tempo** waste time; **lascia ~!** forget it!; **~ di vista** lose touch [with each other] ● *vi* lose; (*recipiente:*) leak; **a ~** (*vuoto*) nonreturnable; **non avere niente da ~** have nothing to lose

**'perdersi** *vr* get lost; (*reciproco*) lose touch

**perdifi'ato: a ~** *adv* (*gridare*) at the top of one's voice

**perdigi'orno** *nmf inv* idler

**'perdita** *nf* loss; (*spreco*) waste; (*falla*) leak; **a ~ d'occhio** as far as the eye can see; **chiudere in ~** (*azienda:*) show a loss. **~ di gas** gas leak. **~ di sangue** loss of blood, bleeding. **~ di tempo** waste of time

**perdi'tempo** *nm* waste of time

**perdizi'one** *nf* perdition

**perdo'nare** *vt* forgive; (*scusare*) excuse; **mi perdoni se interrompo** sorry to interrupt, excuse me for interrupting; **per farsi ~** as an apology ● *vi* **~ a qcno** forgive sb; **un male che non perdona** an incurable disease

**per'dono** *nm* forgiveness; Jur pardon; **chiedere ~** ask for forgiveness; (*scusarsi*) apologize

**perdu'rare** *vi* last; (*perseverare*) persist

**perduta'mente** *adv* hopelessly

**per'duto** pp di **perdere** ● a lost; (rovinato) ruined

**pe'renne** a everlasting; Bot perennial; **nevi perenni** perpetual snow

**perenne'mente** adv perpetually

**peren'torio** a peremptory

**per'fetto** a perfect ● nm Gram perfect [tense]

**perfezio'nare** vt perfect; (migliorare) improve

**perfezio'narsi** vr improve oneself; (specializzarsi) specialize

**perfezi'one** nf perfection; **alla ~** to perfection

**perfezio'nismo** nm perfectionism

**perfezio'nista** nmf perfectionist

**per'fidia** nf wickedness; (atto) wicked act

**'perfido** a treacherous; (malvagio) perverse

**per'fino** adv even

**perfo'rare** vt pierce; punch ‹schede›; Mech drill

**perfora'tore** nm (apparecchio) punch. **~ di schede** card punch

**perfora|'tore, -'trice** nmf punch-card operator

**perforazi'one** nf perforation; (di schede) punching

**per'formance** nf inv Theat performance

**perga'mena** nf parchment

**'pergola** nf pergola

**pergo'lato** nm bower

**periar'trite** nf rheumatoid arthritis

**perico'lante** a precarious; ‹azienda› shaky

**pe'ricolo** nm danger; (rischio) risk; **mettere in ~** endanger; **essere fuori ~** be out of danger. **~ pubblico** danger to society. **~ di valanghe** danger of avalanches

**pericolosa'mente** adv dangerously

**pericolosità** nf danger

**perico'loso** a dangerous

**peridu'rale** nf epidural

**perife'ria** nf periphery; (di città) outskirts pl; fig fringes pl

**peri'ferica** nf peripheral; (strada) ring road. **~ di input** Comput input device

**peri'ferico** a peripheral; ‹quartiere› outlying

**pe'rifrasi** nf inv circumlocution

**perime'trale** a ‹muro› perimeter attrib

**pe'rimetro** nm perimeter

**peri'odico** nm periodical ● a periodical; ‹vento, mal di testa, Math› recurring

**pe'riodo** nm period; Gram sentence. **~ nero** bad patch. **~ di prova** trial period. **~ di ripensamento** cooling-off period. **~ di riposo** breathing space. **~ di transizione** transitional period, interim. **~ di validità** period of validity

**peripe'zie** nfpl misadventures

**pe'rire** vi perish

**peri'scopio** nm periscope

**pe'rito, -a** a skilled ● nmf expert. **~ agrario** agriculturalist. **~ di assicurazione** Comm loss adjuster. **~ edile** chartered surveyor. **~ elettronico** electronics engineer

**perito'nite** nf peritonitis

**pe'rizia** nf skill; (valutazione) survey

**peri'zoma** nm inv loincloth

**'perla** nf pearl. **~ coltivata** cultured pearl

**per'lina** nf bead

**perli'nato** nm matchboard

**perlo'meno** adv at least

**perlu'strare** vt patrol

**perlustrazi'one** nf patrol; **andare in ~** go on patrol

**perma'loso** a touchy

**perma'nente** a permanent ● nf perm; **farsi [fare] la ~** have a perm

**perma'nenza** nf permanence; (soggiorno) stay; **in ~** permanently. **~ in carica** tenure

**perma'nere** vi remain

**perme'are** vt permeate

**perme'ato a ~ di** fig permeated with

**per'messo** pp di **permettere** ● nm permission; (autorizzazione) permit, licence; Mil leave; **[è] ~?, con ~** (posso entrare?) may I come in?; (posso passare?) excuse me. **~ di lavoro** work permit. **~ di soggiorno** residence permit

**per'mettere** vt allow, permit; **potersi ~ qcsa** (finanziariamente) be able to afford sth

**per'mettersi** vr **~ di fare qcsa** allow oneself to do sth; **come si permette?** how dare you?

**permis'sivo** a permissive

**permutazi'one** nf exchange; Math permutation

**per'nacchia** nf (sl: con la bocca) raspberry sl

**per'nice** nf partridge

**pernici'oso** a pernicious

**'perno** nm pivot

**pernot'tare** vi stay overnight

**'pero** nm pear-tree

**però** conj but; (tuttavia) however

**pe'rone** nm Anat fibula

**pero'rare** vt plead

**perpendico'lare** a & nf perpendicular

**perpe'trare** vt perpetrate

**per'petua** nf (di prete) priest's housekeeper

**perpetu'are** vt perpetuate

**per'petuo** a perpetual

**perplessità** nf inv perplexity; (dubbio) doubt

**per'plesso** a perplexed

**perqui'sire** vt search

**perquisizi'one** nf search. **~ domiciliare** search of the premises

**persecu|'tore, -'trice** nmf persecutor

**persecuzi'one** nf persecution

**persegu'ire** vt pursue

**persegui'tare** vt persecute

**persegui'tato, -a** nmf victim of persecution

**perseve'rante** a persevering

**perseve'ranza** nf perseverance

**perseve'rare** vi persevere

**'Persia** nf Persia

**persi'ana** nf shutter. **~ avvolgibile** roller shutter

**persi'ano, -a** *a & nmf* Persian
**'persico** *a* Persian
**per'sino** *adv* = **perfino**
**persi'stente** *a* persistent; ⟨*dubbio*⟩ nagging
**persi'stenza** *nf* persistence
**per'sistere** *vi* persist; **~ nel fare qcsa** persist in doing sth
**'perso** *pp di* **perdere** ● *a* lost; **a tempo ~** in one's spare time
**per'sona** *nf* person; ⟨*un tale*⟩ somebody; **di ~, in ~** in person, personally; **per ~** per person, a head; **per interposta ~** through an intermediary; **curare la propria ~** look after oneself, look after number one; **persone** *pl* people. **~ a carico** dependant. **~ di colore** nonwhite, coloured person. **~ giuridica** legal person. **~ di servizio** domestic
**perso'naggio** *nm* ⟨*persona di riguardo*⟩ personality; *Theat ecc* character
**perso'nale** *a* personal ● *nm* staff; ⟨*aspetto*⟩ build. **~ di terra** ground crew
**personalità** *nf inv* personality
**personaliz'zare** *vt* customize ⟨*auto ecc*⟩; personalize ⟨*penna ecc*⟩
**personifi'care** *vt* personify
**personificazi'one** *nf* personification
**perspi'cace** *a* shrewd
**perspi'cacia** *nf* shrewdness
**persua'dere** *vt* convince; impress ⟨*critici*⟩; **~ qcno a fare qcsa** persuade sb to do sth
**persuasi'one** *nf* persuasion; **fare opera di ~ su qcno** try to persuade sb
**persuasività** *nf* persuasiveness
**persua'sivo** *a* persuasive
**persu'aso** *pp di* **persuadere**
**persua'sore** *nm* persuader
**per'tanto** *conj* therefore
**'pertica** *nf* pole
**perti'nace** *a* pertinacious
**perti'nente** *a* relevant
**per'tosse** *nf* whooping cough
**per'tugio** *nm* opening
**pertur'bare** *vt* perturb
**perturbazi'one** *nf* disturbance. **~ atmosferica** atmospheric disturbance
**Perù** *nm* Peru
**peruvi'ano, -a** *a & nmf* Peruvian
**per'vadere** *vt* pervade
**perva'sivo** *a* pervasive
**per'vaso** *pp di* **pervadere**
**perven'ire** *vi* reach; **far ~ qcsa a qcno** send sth to sb
**perversa'mente** *adv* perversely
**perversi'one** *nf* perversion
**perversità** *nf* perversity
**per'verso** *a* perverse
**perver'tire** *vt* pervert
**perver'tirsi** *vr* ⟨*gusti, costumi:*⟩ become debased
**perver'tito** *a* perverted ● *nm* pervert
**pervi'cace** *a* obstinate
**pervicace'mente** *adv* obstinately
**pervi'cacia** *nf* obstinacy
**per'vinca** *nm* ⟨*colore*⟩ blue with a touch of purple

**per'vinca** *nf Bot* periwinkle
**p. es.** *abbr* (**per esempio**) e.g.
**'pesa** *nf* weighing; ⟨*bilancia*⟩ weighing machine; ⟨*per veicoli*⟩ weighbridge
**pe'sante** *a* heavy; ⟨*stomaco*⟩ overfull; ⟨*accusa, ingiuria*⟩ serious; ⟨*noioso*⟩ boring; **andarci ~ con qcno** be heavy-handed with sb ● *adv* ⟨*vestirsi*⟩ warmly
**pesante'mente** *adv* ⟨*cadere*⟩ heavily; ⟨*insultare*⟩ seriously
**pesan'tezza** *nf* heaviness
**pesaper'sone** *nm inv* scales
**pe'sare** *vt* weigh; **~ le parole** weigh one's words ● *vi* weigh; ⟨*essere pesante*⟩ be heavy; **~ su** *fig* lie heavy on
**pe'sarsi** *vr* weigh oneself
**'pesca¹** *nf* ⟨*frutto*⟩ peach
**'pesca²** *nf* fishing; **andare a ~** go fishing. **~ di beneficenza** lucky dip. **~ con la lenza** angling. **~ subacquea** underwater fishing
**pe'scare** *vt* ⟨*andare a pesca di*⟩ fish for; ⟨*prendere*⟩ catch; ⟨*fam: trovare*⟩ dig up, find; **guai se ti pesco!** there will be trouble if I catch you!
**pesca'tore** *nm* fisherman. **~ di frodo** poacher. **~ di perle** pearl diver
**'pesce** *nm* fish; **non sapere che pesci pigliare** *fig* not know which way to turn; **prendere qcno a pesci in faccia** *fig* treat sb like dirt; **sentirsi un ~ fuor d'acqua** feel like a fish out of water. **~ d'aprile!** April Fool!. **~ in carpione** soused fish. **~ al cartoccio** fish baked in foil. **~ gatto** catfish. **~ grosso** *fig* big fish. **~ persico** perch. **~ piccolo** *fig* small fry. **~ rosso** goldfish. **~ spada** swordfish
**pesce'cane** *nm* shark
**pesche'reccio** *nm* fishing boat
**pesche'ria** *nf* fishmonger's [shop]
**peschi'era** *nf* fish-pond
**'Pesci** *nmpl Astr* Pisces
**pescio'lino** *nm* **~ d'acqua dolce** minnow
**pesci'vendolo** *nm* fishmonger
**'pesco** *nm* peach tree
**pe'scoso** *a* teeming with fish
**pe'seta** *nf* peseta
**pe'sista** *nm* ⟨*in sollevamento pesi*⟩ weightlifter; ⟨*in lancio del peso*⟩ shotputter
**'peso** *nm* weight; **essere di ~ per qcno** be a burden to sb; **alzare di ~** lift up in one go; **avere un ~ sullo stomaco** have a lead weight on one's stomach; **di poco ~** ⟨*senza importanza*⟩ not very important; **non dare ~ a qcsa** not attach any importance to sth. **~ massimo** ⟨*nel pugilato*⟩ heavy weight. **~ medio** ⟨*nel pugilato*⟩ middleweight. **~ morto** dead weight. **~ netto** net weight. **~ piuma** ⟨*nel pugilato*⟩ featherweight **~ specifico** specific gravity
**pessi'mismo** *nm* pessimism
**pessi'mista** *nmf* pessimist ● *a* pessimistic
**pessimistica'mente** *adv* pessimistically
**'pessimo** *a* very bad
**pe'staggio** *nm* beating-up

**pe'stare** *vt* tread on; (*picchiare*) beat; crush (*aglio, prezzemolo, uva*); **~ i piedi** [**per terra**] stamp one's feet [on the ground]; **~ un piede a qcno** tread on sb's foot

**pe'stata** *nf* bash; **dare una ~ a un piede a qcno** tread on sb's foot

**'peste** *nf* plague; (*persona*) pest; **dire ~ e corna di qcno** tear sb to bits. **~ bubbonica** bubonic plague

**pe'stello** *nm* pestle

**pesti'cida** *nm* pesticide

**pe'stifero** *a* (*fastidioso*) pestilential

**pesti'lenza** *nf* pestilence; (*fetore*) stench, stink

**pestilenzi'ale** *a* (*odore, aria*) noxious

**'pesto** *a* ground; **occhio ~** black eye ● *nm* basil and garlic sauce

**'petalo** *nm* petal

**pe'tardo** *nm* banger

**petizi'one** *nf* petition; **fare una ~** draw up a petition

**petrol'chimico** *a* petrochemical

**petrol'dollaro** *nm* petrodollar

**petroli'era** *nf* [oil] tanker

**petroli'ere** *nm* oilman

**petro'lifero** *a* oil-bearing

**pe'trolio** *nm* oil

**pettego'lare** *vi* gossip

**pettego'lezzo** *nm* piece of gossip; **pettegolezzi** *pl* gossip *sg*; **far pettegolezzi** gossip

**pet'tegolo, -a** *a* gossipy ● *nmf* gossip

**petti'nare** *vt* comb

**petti'narsi** *vr* comb one's hair

**pettina'tura** *nf* combing; (*acconciatura*) hairstyle. **~ a caschetto** bob

**'pettine** *nm* comb

**'petting** *nm* petting

**petti'nino** *nm* (*fermaglio*) comb

**petti'rosso** *nm* robin [redbreast]

**'petto** *nm* chest; (*seno*) breast; **a doppio ~** double-breasted; **prendere qcsa/qcno di ~** face up to sth/sb. **~ pl di pollo** chicken breasts

**petto'rale** *nm* Sport number ● *a* pectoral

**petto'rina** *nf* (*di salopette*) bib

**petto'ruto** *a* (*donna*) full-breasted; (*uomo*) broad-chested

**petu'lante** *a* impertinent

**petu'lanza** *nf* impertinence

**pe'tunia** *nf* petunia

**'pezza** *nf* cloth; (*toppa*) patch; (*rotolo di tessuto*) roll; **trattare qcno come una ~ da piedi** walk all over sb. **~ d'appoggio** voucher. **~ giustificativa** voucher

**pez'zato** *a* (*cavallo, mucca*) piebald

**pez'zente** *nmf* tramp; (*avaro*) miser

**'pezzo** *nm* piece; (*parte*) part; Mus piece. **un bel ~ d'uomo** a fine figure of a man; **un ~** (*di tempo*) some time; (*di spazio*) a long way; **al ~** (*costare*) each; **essere a pezzi** (*stanco*) be shattered; **fare a pezzi** tear to shreds; **andare in mille pezzi** break into a thousand pieces; **cadere a pezzi** fall to pieces, fall to bits. **~ forte** centre-piece. **pezzi** *pl* **grossi**

top brass. **~ grosso** bigwig. big shot. **~ di imbecille** stupid idiot. **~ di ricambio** spare [part]

**pezzu'ola** *nf* scrap of material

**photo'fit**[K] *nm inv* Photofit

**pia'cente** *a* attractive

**pia'cere** *nm* pleasure; (*favore*) favour; **a ~** as much as one likes; **per ~!** please!; **[di conoscerla]!** (*nelle presentazioni*) pleased to meet you!; **con ~** with pleasure; **fare un ~ a qcno** do sb a favour ● **vi la Scozia mi piace** I like Scotland; **mi piacciono i dolci** I like sweets; **mi piacerebbe venire** I'd like to come; **faccio come mi pare e piace** I do as I please; **ti piace?** do you like it?; **lo spettacolo è piaciuto** the show was a success

**pia'cevole** *a* pleasant

**piacevol'mente** *adv* agreeably

**piaci'mento** *nm* **a ~** as much as you like

**pia'dina** *nf* unleavened focaccia bread

**pi'aga** *nf* sore; *fig* scourge; (*fig: persona noiosa*) pain; (*fig: ricordo doloroso*) wound

**pia'gato** *a* covered with sores

**piagni'steo** *nm* whining

**piagnuco'lare** *vi* whimper

**piagnuco'lio** *nm* whimpering

**piagnuco'loso** *a* maudlin

**pi'alla** *nf* plane

**pial'lare** *vt* plane

**pialla'tura** *nf* planing

**pi'ana** *nf* (*pianura*) plane

**pianeggi'ante** *a* level

**piane'rottolo** *nm* landing

**pia'neta** *nm* planet

**pi'angere** *vi* cry; (*disperatamente*) weep; **mi piange il cuore** my heart bleeds; **mettersi a ~ come una fontana** turn the waterworks on; **~ sul latte versato** cry over spilt milk ● *vt* (*lamentare*) lament; (*per un lutto*) mourn; **~ la morte di qcno** mourn sb's death

**pianifi'care** *vt* plan

**pianificazi'one** *nf* planning. **~ aziendale** corporate planning. **~ familiare** family planning

**pia'nista** *nmf Mus* pianist

**pi'ano** *a* flat; (*a livello*) flush; (*regolare*) smooth; (*facile*) easy; **i 400 metri piani** the 400 metres flat race ● *adv* slowly; (*con cautela*) gently; (*sottovoce*) quietly; **andarci ~** go carefully ● *nm* plain; (*di edificio*) floor, storey; (*livello*) plane; (*progetto*) plan; *Mus* piano; **di primo ~** first-rate; **primo ~** *Phot* close-up; **in ~ piano** in the foreground; **essere/mettersi in ~ piano** *fig* take/occupy centre-stage; **secondo ~** middle distance. **~ d'emergenza** contingency plan. **~ di lavoro** work surface; (*programma*) work schedule. **~ di pensionamento** pension plan, pension scheme. **~ regolatore** town plan. **~ di sopra** upstairs. **~ di sotto** downstairs. **~ di studi** syllabus. **~ superiore** upper floor

**piano'forte** *nm* piano. **~ bar** piano bar. **~ a**

**coda** grand [piano]. **~ verticale** upright [piano]

**pia'nola**ᴿ *nf* pianola

**piano'terra** *nm inv* ground floor, first floor *Am*

**pi'anta** *nf* plant; (*del piede*) sole; (*disegno*) plan; (*di città*) map; **di sana ~** (*totalmente*) entirely; **in ~ stabile** permanently. **~ da appartamento** house-plant. **~ stradale** road map

**piantagi'one** *nf* plantation

**pianta'grane** *nmf fam* **è un/una ~** he's/she's bolshy

**pian'tare** *vt* plant; (*conficcare*) drive; pitch ⟨*tenda*⟩; (*fam: abbandonare*) dump; **piantala!** *fam* stop it!; **piantato in** ⟨*spina, chiodo*⟩ embedded in; **~ baracca e burattini** drop everything; (*per sempre*) chuck everything in

**pian'tarsi** *vr* plant oneself; (*fam: lasciarsi*) leave each other

**pianta'|tore, -'trice** *nmf* planter

**pianter'reno** *nm* ground floor, first floor *Am*

**pi'anto** *pp di* **piangere** ● *nm* crying; (*disperato*) weeping; (*lacrime*) tears *pl*

**pianto'nare** *vt* guard

**pian'tone** *nm* guard; **stare di ~** stand guard; **mettere di ~** put on guard. **~ dello sterzo** *Auto* steering column

**pia'nura** *nf* plain. **~ padana** Po valley

**pi'astra** *nf* plate; (*lastra*) slab; *Culin* griddle. **~ elettronica** circuit board. **~ madre** *Comput* motherboard. **~ di registrazione** cassette deck

**pia'strella** *nf* tile

**pia'strina** *nf Mil* identity disc; *Med* platelet; *Comput* chip. **~ di riconoscimento** identity tag. **~ di silicio** silicon chip

**piatta'forma** *nf* platform. **~ di lancio** launch pad. **~ petrolifera** oil platform, offshore rig. **~ rivendicativa** *o* **sindacale** union claims *pl*

**piat'tino** *nm* saucer

**pi'atto** *a* flat; (*monotono*) dull ● *nm* plate; (*da portata, vivanda*) dish; (*portata*) course; (*parte piatta*) flat; (*di giradischi*) turntable; (*di bilancia*) pan. **piatti** *pl Mus* cymbals; **lavare i piatti** do the dishes, do the washing-up. **piatti** *pl* **caldi** hot dishes. **piatti** *pl* **carne** meat dishes. **~ fondo** soup plate. **~ del giorno** dish of the day. **~ piano** [ordinary] plate. **~ di portata** serving dish, server. **~ unico** cold sliced meat with pickles

**pi'azza** *nf* square; *Comm* market; **letto a una ~** single bed; **letto a due piazze** double bed; **far ~ pulita** make a clean sweep; **mettere qcsa in ~** *fig* make sth public; **scendere in ~** *fig* take to the streets. **~ d'armi** parade ground. **~ del mercato** market square. **P~ San Pietro** St Peter's Square

**piazza'forte** *nf* stronghold

**piaz'zale** *nm* large square

**piazza'mento** *nm* (*in classifica*) placing

**piaz'zare** *vt* place

**piaz'zarsi** *vr Sport* be placed; **~ secondo** come second, be placed second

**piaz'zato** *a* ⟨*cavallo*⟩ placed; **ben ~** (*robusto*) well-built

**piaz'zista** *nm* salesman ● *nf* saleswoman

**piaz'z[u]ola** *nf* **~ di partenza** (*nel golf*) tee. **~ di sosta** pull-in

**pic'cante** *a* hot; (*pungente*) sharp; (*salace*) spicy

**pic'carsi** *vr* (*risentirsi*) take offence; **~ di** (*vantarsi di*) claim to

**pic'cata** *nf* veal in sour lemon sauce

**'picche** *nfpl* (*in carte*) spades

**picchet'taggio** *nm* picketing

**picchet'tare** *vt* stake; ⟨*scioperanti:*⟩ picket

**pic'chetto** *nm* picket

**picchi'are** *vt* hit; **~ la testa (contro qcsa)** bang *o* hit one's head (against sth) ● *vi* (*bussare*) knock; *Aeron* nosedive; **~ in testa** ⟨*motore:*⟩ knock

**picchi'arsi** *vr* **~ il petto** beat one's breast

**picchi'ata** *nf* beating; *Aeron* nosedive; **scendere in ~** nosedive

**picchi'ato** *a* (*matto*) touched

**picchia'tore** *nm* goon

**picchiet'tare** *vt* tap; (*punteggiare*) spot

**picchiet'tato** *a* spotted

**picchiet'tio** *nm* tapping

**'picchio** *nm* woodpecker

**pic'cino** *a* tiny; (*gretto*) mean; (*di poca importanza*) petty ● *nm* little one, child

**piccion'cini** *nmpl fam* lovebirds; **fare i ~** get all lovey-dovey

**picci'one** *nm* pigeon; **prendere due piccioni con una fava** kill two birds with one stone. **~ viaggiatore** carrier pigeon

**'picco** *nm* peak; **a ~** vertically; **colare a ~** sink

**picco'lezza** *nf* (*di persona, ambiente*) smallness; (*grettezza*) meanness; (*inezia*) trifle

**'piccolo, -a** *a* small, little; (*vacanza, pausa*) little, short; (*di statura*) short; (*gretto*) petty ● *nmf* child, little one; **da ~** as a child; **in ~** in miniature; **nel mio ~** in my own small way

**pic'cone** *nm* pickaxe. **~ da ghiaccio** ice pick

**pic'cozza** *nf* ice axe

**pic'nic** *nm inv* picnic

**pi'docchio** *nm* louse

**pidocchi'oso** *a* flea-bitten; (*fam: avaro*) stingy ● *nm fam* miser

**piè** *nm inv* **a ~ di pagina** at the foot of the page; **saltare a ~ pari** skip; **ad ogni ~ sospinto** all the time, endlessly

**pi'ede** *nm* foot; (*di armadio, letto*) leg; **a piedi** on foot; **andare a piedi** walk; **a piedi nudi** barefoot; **avere i piedi piatti** have flat feet, be flat-footed; **a ~ libero** free; **in piedi** standing; **alzarsi in piedi** stand up; **in punta di piedi** on tiptoe; **ai piedi di** ⟨*montagna*⟩ at the foot of; **avere qcno ai propri piedi** have sb at one's feet; **essere sul ~ di guerra** be ready for action; ⟨*nazione:*⟩ be on war footing; **prendere ~** *fig* gain ground; ⟨*moda:*⟩ catch on: **partire col ~ sbagliato** get off on the wrong foot; **mettere in piedi** (allestire) set up; **togliti dai piedi!** get out of the way!. **~ di insalata** head of lettuce. **~ di porco** (strumento) jemmy

**pie'dino** nm **fare ~ a qcno** fam play footsie with sb

**piedi'stallo** nm pedestal

**pi'ega** nf (piegatura) fold; (di gonna) pleat; (di pantaloni) crease; (grinza) wrinkle; (andamento) turn; **a pieghe** with pleats, pleated: **non fare una ~** (ragionamento:) be flawless: (persona:) not bat an eyelid; **prendere una brutta ~** get into bad ways

**pie'gare** vt fold; (flettere) bend ● vi bend

**pie'garsi** vr bend; **~ a** fig yield to

**piega'tura** nf folding; (piega) fold

**pieghet'tare** vt pleat

**pieghet'tato** a pleated

**pie'ghevole** a pliable; (tavolo) folding ● nm leaflet

**Pie'monte** nm Piedmont

**piemon'tese** a & nmf Piedmontese

**pi'ena** nf (di fiume) flood; (folla) crowd

**pi'eno** a full; (massiccio) solid; **in piena estate** in the middle of summer; **a pieni voti** (diplomarsi) ≈ with A-grades, with first class honours ● nm (colmo) height; (carico) full load; **in ~** (completamente) fully; **fare il ~** (di benzina) fill up; **nel ~ delle forze** in top physical form

**pie'none** nm **c'era il ~** the place was packed

**pietà** nf pity; (misericordia) mercy; **senza ~** (persona) pitiless; (spietatamente) pitilessly; **avere ~ di qcno** take pity on sb; **far ~** (far pena) be pitiful; (fam: essere orrendo) be useless

**pie'tanza** nf dish

**pie'toso** a pitiful, merciful; (fam: pessimo) terrible

**pi'etra** nf stone. **~ dura** semiprecious stone. **~ preziosa** precious stone. **~ dello scandalo** cause of the scandal

**pie'traia** nf scree

**pie'trame** nm stones pl

**pietrifi'care** vt petrify

**pie'trina** nf (di accendino) flint

**pie'troso** a stony

**'piffero** nm fife

**pigi'ama** nm pyjamas pl, pajamas Am

**'pigia 'pigia** nm inv crowd, crush

**pigi'are** vt press

**pigia'trice** nf winepress

**pigi'one** nf rent; **dare a ~** let, rent out; **prendere a ~** rent

**pigli'are** vt (fam: afferrare) catch

**'piglio** nm air

**pig'mento** nm pigment

**pig'meo, -a** a & nmf pygmy

**'pigna** nf cone. **~ di abete** fir cone

**pi'gnolo** a pedantic

**pignora'mento** nm Jur distraint

**pigno'rare** vt Jur distrain upon

**pigo'lare** vi chirp

**pigo'lio** nm chirping

**pigra'mente** adv lazily

**pi'grizia** nf laziness

**'pigro** a lazy; (intelletto) slow

**PIL** abbr (prodotto interno lordo) GDP

**'pila** nf pile; Electr battery; (fam: lampadina tascabile) torch; (vasca) basin; **a pile** battery operated, battery powered

**pi'lastro** nm pillar

**'pillola** nf pill; **prendere la ~** be on the pill. **~ del giorno dopo** morning-after pill

**pi'lone** nm pylon; (di ponte) pier

**pi'lota** nmf pilot. **~ automatico** automatic pilot. **~ di caccia** fighter pilot ● nm Auto driver ● a inv **progetto ~** pilot project

**pilo'taggio** nm flying; **cabina di ~** flight deck

**pilo'tare** vt pilot; drive (auto)

**pinaco'teca** nf art gallery

**'Pinco Pal'lino** nm so-and-so

**pi'neta** nf pine-wood

**ping-'pong** nm table tennis, ping-pong fam

**'pingue** a fat

**pingu'edine** nf fatness

**pingu'ino** nm penguin; (gelato) choc ice on a stick

**'pinna** nf fin; (per nuotare) flipper

**pin'nacolo** nm pinnacle

**'pino** nm pine[-tree]. **~ marittimo** cluster pine, maritime pine

**pi'nolo** nm pine kernel

**'pinta** nf pint

**pin-'up** nf inv pin-up [girl]

**'pinza** nf pliers pl; Med forceps pl; **prendere qcsa con le pinze** fig treat sth cautiously

**pin'zare** vt (con pinzatrice) staple

**pinza'trice** nf stapler

**pin'zette** nfpl tweezers

**pinzi'monio** nm sauce for crudités

**'pio** a pious; (benefico) charitable

**piogge'rella** nf drizzle

**pi'oggia** nf rain; (fig: di pietre, insulti) hail, shower; **sotto la ~** in the rain. **~ acida** acid rain. **~ radioattiva** radioactive fallout

**piom'bare** vi fall heavily; **~ su** fall upon; **~ all'improvviso nella stanza** suddenly burst into the room ● vt **~ qcno nella disperazione** plunge sb into despair

**piom'bino** nm (sigillo) [lead] seal; (da pesca) sinker; (in gonne) weight

**pi'ombo** nm lead; (sigillo) [lead] seal; **a ~** plumb; **senza ~** (benzina) lead-free; **avere un sonno di ~** be a very heavy sleeper; **andare con i piedi di ~** tread carefully; **anni di ~** years when terrorism was at its height

**pioni'ere, -a** nmf pioneer

**pi'oppo** nm poplar

**pior'rea** nf pyorrhoea

**pio'vano** a **acqua piovana** rainwater

**pi'overe** vi rain; **~** it's raining; **~ addosso a qcno** (guai, debiti:) rain down on sb; **non ci piove [sopra]** fam that's for sure

**pioviggi'nare** vi drizzle

**pio'voso** *a* rainy

**pi'ovra** *nf* octopus

**pio'vuto** *a* ~ **dal cielo** fallen into one's lap

**'pipa** *nf* pipe

**pipe'rito** *a* **menta piperita** peppermint

**pipì** *nf* **fare [la]** ~ pee, piddle; **andare a fare [la]** ~ go for a pee

**pipi'strello** *nm* bat

**piqué** *nm inv* piqué

**'pira** *nf* pyre

**pi'ramide** *nf* pyramid

**pi'ranha** *nm inv* piranha

**pi'rata** *nm* pirate. ~ **della strada** hit-and-run driver; (*prepotente*) road-hog ● *a inv* pirate

**pirate'ria** *nf* piracy. ~ **informatica** hacking

**pi'rite** *nf* pyrite

**piro'etta** *nf* pirouette

**pi'rofila** *nf* (*tegame*) oven-proof dish

**pi'rofilo** *a* heat-resistant

**pi'romane** *nmf* pyromaniac

**piroma'nia** *nf* pyromania

**pi'roscafo** *nm* steamer. ~ **di linea** liner

**'piscia** *nf vulg* piss

**pisci'are** *vi vulg* piss

**pisci'ata** *nf vulg* piss

**pi'scina** *nf* [swimming] pool. ~ **coperta** indoor [swimming] pool. ~ **gonfiabile** [inflatable] paddling pool. ~ **olimpionica** Olympic [swimming] pool. ~ **scoperta** outdoor [swimming] pool, lido

**pi'sello** *nm* pea; (*fam: pene*) willie. **piselli** *pl* **odorosi** sweetpeas

**piso'lino** *nm* nap; **fare un** ~ have a nap

**'pista** *nf* track; *Aeron* runway, tarmac; (*orma*) footprint; (*sci*) slope, piste. ~ **d'atterraggio** runway. ~ **da ballo** dance floor. ~ **ciclabile** cycle track. ~ **da fondo** cross-country ski track. ~ **da pattinaggio** ice rink. ~ **per principianti** nursery slope. ~ **da sci** ski slope, ski run, piste. ~ **per slitte** toboggan run

**pi'stacchio** *nm* pistachio

**pi'stola** *nf* pistol; (*per spruzzare*) spray-gun. ~ **a capsule** cap gun. ~ **a spruzzo** paint spray. ~ **a tamburo** revolver

**pisto'lero** *nm* gunslinger

**pi'stone** *nm* piston

**pi'tocco** *nm* miser

**pi'tone** *nm* python

**pitto'gramma** *nm* pictogram

**pit|'tore, -'trice** *nmf* painter

**pitto'resco** *a* picturesque

**pit'torico** *a* pictorial

**pit'tura** *nf* painting. **pitture** *pl* **di guerra** warpaint. ~ **rupestre** cave painting

**pittu'rare** *vt* paint

**pitui'tario** *a* pituitary

**più** *adv* more; (*superlativo*) most; *Math* plus; ~ **importante** more important; **il** ~ **importante** the most important; ~ **caro/grande** dearer/bigger; **il** ~ **caro/grande** the dearest/biggest; **di** ~ more; **una coperta in** ~ an extra blanket; **non ho** ~ **soldi** I don't have any more money; **non vive** ~ **a Milano** he no longer lives in Milan; ~ **o meno** more or less; **il** ~ **lentamente possibile** as slow as possible; **al** ~ **presto** as soon as possible; **per di** ~ what's more; **mai** ~! never again!; ~ **di** more than; **sempre** ~ more and more ● *a* more; (*superlativo*) most; ~ **tempo** more time; **la classe con** ~ **alunni** the class with most pupils; ~ **volte** several times ● *nm* most; *Math* plus sign; **il** ~ **è fatto** the worst is over; **parlare del** ~ **e del meno** make small talk; **i** ~ the majority

**piuccheper'fetto** *nm* pluperfect

**pi'uma** *nf* feather

**piu'maggio** *nm* plumage

**piu'mato** *a* plumed

**piu'mino** *nm* (*di cigni*) down; (*copriletto*) eiderdown; (*per cipria*) powder-puff; (*per spolverare*) feather duster; (*giacca*) down jacket

**piu'mone**ᴿ *nm* duvet, continental quilt

**piut'tosto** *adv* rather; (*invece*) instead

**'piva** *nf* **con le pive nel sacco** empty-handed

**pi'vello** *nm fam* greenhorn

**'pivot** *nm inv* (*in pallacanestro*) centre

**'pizza** *nf* pizza; *Cinema* reel; (*fam: noia*) bore. ~ **margherita** tomato and mozzarella pizza. ~ **marinara** pizza with tomato, oregano, garlic and anchovies. ~ **napoletana** pizza with tomato, mozzarella and anchovies. ~ **quattro stagioni** pizza with tomato, mozzarella, ham, mushrooms and baby artichokes

**pizzai'ola** *alla* ~ with tomatoes, garlic and oregano

**pizze'ria** *nf* pizza restaurant, pizzeria

**piz'zetta** *nf* small pizza

**pizzi'care** *vt* pinch; (*pungere*) sting; (*di sapore*) taste sharp; (*fam: sorprendere*) catch; *Mus* pluck ● *vi* scratch; ‹*cibo:*› be spicy

**'pizzico, pizzi'cotto** *nm* pinch

**'pizzo** *nm* lace; (*di montagna*) peak

**pla'care** *vt* placate; assuage ‹*fame, dolore*›

**pla'carsi** *vr* calm down

**'placca** *nf* plate; (*commemorativa, dentale*) plaque; *Med* patch. ~ **batterica** plaque

**plac'care** *vt* plate

**plac'cato** *a* ~ **d'argento** silver-plated. ~ **d'oro** gold-plated

**placca'tura** *nf* plating

**pla'cebo** *nm inv* placebo; **effetto** ~ placebo effect

**pla'centa** *nf* placenta, afterbirth

**'placido** *a* placid

**pla'fond** *nm inv* *Comm* ceiling

**plafoni'era** *nf* ceiling light

**plagi'are** *vt* plagiarize; pressure ‹*persona*›

**'plagio** *nm* plagiarism

**plaid** *nm inv* tartan rug

**pla'nare** *vi* glide

**'plancia** *nf Naut* bridge; (*passerella*) gangplank

**'plancton** *nm* plankton

**plane'tario** *a* planetary ● *nm* planetarium

**pla'smare** *vt* mould

**'plastica** *nf* (*materia*) plastic; *Med* plastic

surgery; ⟨*arte*⟩ plastic art; **sacchetto di ~** plastic bag

'**plastico** *a* plastic; ⟨*rappresentazione*⟩ three-dimensional ● *nm* plastic model

'**platano** *nm* plane tree

pla'**tea** *nf* stalls *pl*; ⟨*pubblico*⟩ audience

'**platino** *nm* platinum

pla'**tonico** *a* platonic

plau'**sibile** *a* plausible; **poco ~** implausible

plausibi**lità** *nf* plausibility

'**plauso** *nm* ⟨*consenso*⟩ approval

'**play**back *nm* **cantare in ~** mime

'**play**boy *nm inv* playboy

'**play**maker *nm inv Sport* playmaker

**p.le** *abbr* (**piazzale**) Sq.

ple'**baglia** *nf pej* mob

'**plebe** *nf* common people

ple'**beo, -a** *a & nmf* plebeian

plebi'**scito** *nm* plebiscite

ple'**nario** *a* plenary

pleni'**lunio** *nm* full moon

'**plettro** *nm* plectrum

pleu'**rite** *nf* pleurisy

'**plico** *nm* packet; **in ~ a parte** under separate cover

**plissé** *a inv* plissé; ⟨*gonna*⟩ accordeon pleated

**plop** *nm inv* plop; **fare ~** plop

plo'**tone** *nm* platoon; ⟨*di ciclisti*⟩ group. **~ d'esecuzione** firing squad

'**plotter** *nm inv Comput* plotter. **~ da tavolo** flatbed plotter

'**plumbeo** *a* leaden

**plum-'cake** *nm inv* fruit cake

plu'**rale** *a & nm* plural; **al ~** in the plural

plura**lità** *nf* ⟨*maggioranza*⟩ majority

pluridisci**pli'nare** *a* multidisciplinary

plurien'**nale** *a* **~ esperienza** many years' experience

plurigemel'**lare** *a* ⟨*parto*⟩ multiple

pluripar'**titico** *a Pol* multi-party

plu'**tonio** *nm* plutonium

pluvi'**ale** *a* rain *attrib*

pluvi'**ometro** *nm* rain gauge

pneu'**matico** *a* pneumatic ● *nm* tyre. **~ radiale** radial [tyre]

pneu'**monia** *nf* pneumonia

**PNL** *abbr* (**prodotto nazionale lordo**) GNP

**Po** *nm* Po

**po'** *vedi* **poco**

po'**chette** *nf inv* clutch bag

po'**chino** *nm* **un ~** a little bit

'**poco** *a* little; ⟨*tempo*⟩ short; (*con nomi plurali*) few ● *pron* little; (*poco tempo*) a short time; (*plurale*) few ● *nm* little; **un po'** a little [bit]; **un po' di** a little, some; (*con nomi plurali*) a few; **a ~ a ~** little by little; **fra ~** soon; **per ~** (*a poco prezzo*) cheap; (*quasi*) nearly; **~ fa** a little while ago; **sono arrivato da ~** I have just arrived; **un bel po'** quite a lot; **un bel po' di più/meno** quite a lot more/less; **un ~ di buono** a shady character ● *adv*

(*con verbi*) not much; (*con avverbi, aggettivi*) not very; **parla ~** he doesn't speak much; **lo conosco ~** I don't know him very well; **~ spesso** not very often

po'**dere** *nm* farm

pode'**roso** *a* powerful

'**podio** *nm* dais; *Mus* podium

po'**dismo** *nm* walking

po'**dista** *nmf* walker

po'**ema** *nm* poem. **~ epico** epic [poem]. **~ sinfonico** symphonic poem

poe'**sia** *nf* poetry; ⟨*componimento*⟩ poem

po'**eta** *nm* poet

poe'**tessa** *nf* poetess

po'**etico** *a* poetic

poggiapi'**edi** *nm inv* footrest

poggi'**are** *vt* lean; ⟨*posare*⟩ place ● *vi* **~ su** be based on

poggia'**testa** *nm inv* head-rest

'**poggio** *nm* hillock

poggi'**olo** *nm* balcony

'**poi** *adv* ⟨*dopo*⟩ then; ⟨*più tardi*⟩ later [on]; ⟨*finalmente*⟩ finally. **d'ora in ~** from now on; **questa ~!** well! ● *nm* **pensare al ~** think of the future

poi**ché** *conj* since

**pois** *nm inv* **a ~** polka-dot

'**poker** *nm* poker

po'**lacco, -a** *a* Polish ● *nmf* Pole ● *nm* ⟨*lingua*⟩ Polish

po'**lare** *a* polar

pola**rità** *nf inv* polarity

polariz'**zare** *vt* polarize

'**polca** *nf* polka

po'**lemica** *nf* controversy

polemica'**mente** *adv* controversially

polemiciz'**zare** *vi* engage in controversy

po'**lemico** *a* controversial

po'**lenta** *nf* cornmeal porridge

poli'**clinico** *nm* general hospital

policro'**mia** *nf* polychromy

po'**licromo** *a* polychrome

poli'**estere** *nm* polyester

polieti'**lene** *nm* polyethylene

poliga'**mia** *nf* polygamy

poli'**gamico** *a* polygamous

po'**ligamo** *a* polygamous

poli'**glotta** *nmf* polyglot

po'**ligono** *nm* polygon; ⟨*di tiro*⟩ rifle range

poli'**mero** *nm* polymer

Poli'**nesia** *nf* Polynesia

polinesi'**ano** *a & nmf* Polynesian

'**polio[mie'lite]** *nf* polio[myelitis]

'**polipo** *nm* polyp

polisti'**rolo** *nm* polystyrene

poli'**tecnico** *nm* polytechnic

po'**litica** *nf* politics *sg*; ⟨*linea di condotta*⟩ policy; **fare ~** be in politics; **darsi alla ~** go into politics. **~ estera** foreign policy. **~ monetaria** monetary policy

politica'**mente** *adv* politically; **~ corretto** politically correct, pc

politi'**chese** *nm* political jargon

politiciz'**zare** *vt* politicize

po'**litico, -a** *a* political ● *nmf* politician

**poliva'lente** *a* all-purpose

**poli'zia** *nf* police. ~ **giudiziaria** ≈ Criminal Investigation Department, CID. ~ **stradale** traffic police

**polizi'esco** *a* police *attrib*; ⟨romanzo, film⟩ detective *attrib*

**polizi'otto** *nm* policeman. ~ **in borghese** plain clothes policeman. ~ **privato** private detective ● *a* police *attrib*

**'polizza** *nf* policy. ~ **di assicurazione** insurance policy

**pol'laio** *nm* chicken run; (fam: luogo chiassoso) mad house

**pol'lame** *nm* poultry

**polla'strella** *nf* spring chicken; *fig fam* bird

**polla'strello** *nm* spring chicken

**pol'lastro** *nm* cockerel

**polle'ria** *nf* poultry butcher. poulterer

**'pollice** *nm* thumb; (unità di misura) inch

**'polline** *nm* pollen; **allergia al** ~ hay fever

**polli'vendolo, -a** *nmf* poulterer

**'pollo** *nm* chicken; (fam: semplicione) simpleton; **far ridere i polli** be ridiculous. ~ **arrosto** roast chicken. ~ **alla cacciatora** chicken chasseur

**polmo'nare** *a* pulmonary

**pol'mone** *nm* lung. ~ **d'acciaio** iron lung

**polmo'nite** *nf* pneumonia

**'polo** *nm* pole; *Sport* polo; (maglietta) polo top; *Pol* party; (conservatori) Italian Conservatives. ~ **magnetico** magnetic pole. ~ **nord** North Pole. ~ **sud** South Pole

**Po'lonia** *nf* Poland

**'polpa** *nf* pulp

**pol'paccio** *nm* calf

**polpa'strello** *nm* fingertip

**pol'petta** *nf* meatball. ~ **di carne** meatball

**polpet'tone** *nm* meatloaf. ~ **sentimentale** *fam* hokum

**'polpo** *nm* octopus

**pol'poso** *a* fleshy

**pol'sino** *nm* cuff

**'polso** *nm* pulse; *Anat* wrist; *fig* authority; **avere** ~ be strict; **essere privo di** ~ be soft

**pol'tiglia** *nf* mush

**pol'trire** *vi* lie around

**pol'trona** *nf* armchair; *Theat* seat in the stalls

**pol'trone** *a* lazy

**'polvere** *nf* dust; (sostanza polverizzata) powder; **in** ~ powdered; **sapone in** ~ soap powder. ~ **da sparo** gun powder

**polveri'era** *nf* gunpowder magazine; *fig* tinderbox

**polve'rina** *nf* (medicina) powder

**polveriz'zare** *vt* pulverize; (nebulizzare) atomize; smash, shatter ⟨record⟩; ~ **qcno** pulverize sb

**polve'rone** *nm* cloud of dust

**polve'roso** *a* dusty

**po'mata** *nf* ointment, cream. ~ **cicatrizzante** healing cream for cuts

**pomel'lato** *a* dappled

**po'mello** *nm* knob; (guancia) cheek

**pomeridi'ano** *a* afternoon *attrib*; **alle tre**

**pomeridiane** at three in the afternoon, at three pm

**pome'riggio** *nm* afternoon; **buon** ~! have a good afternoon!; **oggi** ~ this afternoon; **questo** ~ this afternoon

**'pomice** *nf* pumice

**pomici'are** *vi fam* snog, neck

**pomici'ata** *nf fam* snogging, necking

**'pomo** *nm* (oggetto) knob. ~ **d'Adamo** Adam's apple

**pomo'doro** *nm* tomato

**'pompa** *nf* pump; (sfarzo) pomp. ~ **della benzina** petrol pump, gas pump *Am*. **pompe** *pl* **funebri** (funzione) funeral

**pom'pare** *vt* pump; (gonfiare d'aria) pump up; (fig: esagerare) exaggerate; ~ **fuori** pump out

**pompei'ano, -a** *a & nmf* Pompeian

**pom'pelmo** *nm* grapefruit

**pompi'ere** *nm* fireman; **i pompieri** the fire brigade

**pom'pon** *nm inv* pompom

**pom'poso** *a* pompous

**'poncho** *nm inv* poncho

**ponde'rare** *vt* ponder

**ponde'roso** *a* ponderous

**po'nente** *nm* west

**'ponte** *nm* bridge; *Naut* deck; (impalcatura) scaffolding; **fare il** ~ *fig* make a long weekend of it; **legge** ~ interim *or* bridging law; **governo** ~ interim government. ~ **aereo** airlift. ~ **di coperta** main deck. ~ **levatoio** drawbridge. ~ **radio** radio link. ~ **dei Sospiri** Bridge of Sighs. ~ **di volo** flight deck

**pon'tefice** *nm* pontiff

**pontifi'care** *vi* pontificate

**pontifi'cato** *nm* pontificate

**ponti'ficio** *a* papal

**pon'tile** *nm* jetty

**'pony** *nm inv* pony. ~ **express** express delivery service

**pool** *nm inv Comm* consortium; (di giornalisti) team; (di esperti) pool, team. ~ **genico** gene pool

**pop'corn** *nm inv* popcorn

**pope'lin** *nm* poplin

**popò** *nm inv fam* bottie, bum

**popò** *nf inv fam* pooh

**popo'lano** *a* of the [common] people

**popo'lare** *a* popular; (comune) common ● *vt* populate; **essere popolato da** (pieno di) be full by

**popolarità** *nf* popularity

**popo'larsi** *vr* get crowded

**popolazi'one** *nf* population

**'popolo** *nm* people

**popo'loso** *a* populous

**'poppa** *nf Naut* stern; (mammella) breast; **a** ~ astern

**pop'pare** *vt* suck

**pop'pata** *nf* (pasto) feed

**poppa'toio** *nm* [feeding-]bottle

**popu'lista** *nmf* populist

**por'caio** *nf anche fig* pigsty; **fare un** ~ *fam* make a mess

**por'cata** *nf* load of rubbish; **porcate** *pl*
(*fam: cibo*) junk food; **fare una ~ a qcno**
play a dirty trick on sb

**porcel'lana** *nf* porcelain, china. **~ fine**
bone china

**porcel'lino** *nm* piglet. **~ d'India** guinea-pig

**porche'ria** *nf* dirt; (*fig: cosa orrenda*) piece
of filth; (*fam: robaccia*) rubbish

**por'chetta** *nf* roast sucking pig

**por'cile** *nm* pigsty

**por'cino** *a* pig *attrib* ● *nm* (*fungo*) cep (*edible mushroom*)

**'porco** *nm* pig; (*carne*) pork

**porco'spino** *nm* porcupine

**'porfido** *nm* porphyry

**'porgere** *vt* give; (*offrire*) offer; **~ orecchio**
lend an ear; **porgo distinti saluti** (*in lettera*)
I remain, yours sincerely

**'porno** *a inv* porn

**pornogra'fia** *nf* pornography

**porno'grafico** *a* pornographic

**'poro** *nm* pore

**po'roso** *a* porous

**'porpora** *nf* purple

**'porre** *vt* put; (*collocare*) place; (*supporre*)
suppose; ask ⟨*domanda*⟩; present
⟨*candidatura*⟩; **~ una domanda a qcno** ask
sb a question; **poniamo [il caso] che...** let
us suppose that...; **~ fine** *o* **termine a** put an
end to

**'porro** *nm Bot* leek; (*verruca*) wart

**'porsi** *vr* put oneself; **~ a sedere** sit down; **~
in cammino** set out

**'porta** *nf* door; *Sport* goal; (*di città*) gate;
*Comput* port. **~ a ~** door-to-door; **mettere
alla ~** show sb the door; **a porte chiuse**
⟨*riunione, processo*⟩ behind closed doors, in
camera; **essere alle porte** (*vicino*) be on the
doorstep. **~ a due battenti** double door[s]. **~
d'ingresso** front door. **~ parallela** *Comput*
parallel port. **~ seriale** *Comput* serial port.
**~ di servizio** tradesman's entrance. **~ di
sicurezza** emergency exit. **~ per la
stampante** *Comput* printer port. **~ a vento**
swing-door

**portaba'gagli** *nm inv* (*facchino*) porter; (*di
treno ecc*) luggage-rack; *Auto* boot, trunk *Am*;
(*sul tetto di un'auto*) roof-rack

**portabandi'era** *nmf inv* standard-bearer

**portabici'clette** *nm inv* cycle rack

**portabot'tiglie** *nm inv* bottle rack, wine
rack

**porta'burro** *nm inv* butter dish

**porta'cenere** *nm inv* ashtray

**portachi'avi** *nm inv* keyring

**porta'cipria** *nm inv* compact

**portacon'tainers** *nm inv* container truck

**portadocu'menti** *nm inv* document wallet

**porta'erei** *nf inv* aircraft carrier

**portafi'nestra** *nf* French window

**porta'foglio** *nm* wallet; (*per documenti*)
portfolio; (*ministero*) ministry

**portafor'tuna** *nm inv* lucky charm ● *a inv*
lucky

**portagi'oie** *nm inv* jewellery box

**por'tale** *nm* door

**portama'tite** *nm inv* pencil case

**porta'mento** *nm* carriage; (*condotta*) behaviour

**porta'mina** *nm inv* propelling pencil

**portamo'nete** *nm inv* purse

**por'tante** *a* bearing *attrib*

**portan'tina** *nf* sedan-chair

**portaom'brelli** *nm inv* umbrella stand

**porta'pacchi** *nm inv* roof rack; (*su
bicicletta*) luggage rack

**porta'penne** *nm inv* pencil case

**por'tare** *vt* (*verso chi parla*) bring; (*lontano
da chi parla*) take; (*sorreggere, Math*) carry;
(*condurre*) lead; (*indossare*) wear; (*avere*)
bear; **~ a spasso il cane** take the dog for a
walk; **~ a termine** bring to a close; **~ avanti**
carry on; **~ ~ bene/male** bring good/bad
luck; **~ fortuna** be lucky; **~ rancore** bear a
grudge; **~ via** take away

**portari'viste** *nm inv* magazine rack

**por'tarsi** *vr* (*trasferirsi*) move; (*comportarsi*)
behave; **~ bene/male gli anni** look young/
old for one's age

**porta'sci** *nm inv* ski rack

**portasciuga'mano** *nm* towel rail

**portasiga'rette** *nm inv* cigarette-case

**porta'spilli** *nm inv* pin-cushion

**por'tata** *nf* (*di pranzo*) course; *Auto* carrying
capacity; (*di arma*) range; (*fig: abilità*) capability; **a ~ di mano** within reach; **alla ~ di
tutti** accessible to all; (*finanziariamente*)
within everybody's reach; **di grande ~**
⟨*scoperta*⟩ with far-reaching consequences

**por'tatile** *a & nm* portable

**por'tato** *a* ⟨*indumento*⟩ worn; (*dotato*)
gifted; **essere ~ per qcsa** have a gift for sth;
**essere ~ a** (*tendere a*) be inclined to

**porta|'tore, -'trice** *nmf* bearer; **al ~** to the
bearer. **~ di handicap** disabled person

**portatovagli'olo** *nm* napkin ring

**portau'ovo** *nm inv* egg-cup

**porta'voce** *nm inv* spokesman ● *nf inv*
spokeswoman

**por'tello** *nm* hatch. **~ di sicurezza** escape
hatch

**por'tento** *nm* marvel; (*persona dotata*)
prodigy

**porten'toso** *a* wonderful

**port'folio** *nm inv* (*di fotografie ecc*) portfolio

**porti'cato** *nm* portico

**'portico** *nm* portico

**porti'era** *nf* door; (*tendaggio*) door curtain

**porti'ere** *nm* porter, doorman; *Sport* goalkeeper. **~ di notte** night porter

**porti'naio, -a** *nmf* caretaker, concierge

**portine'ria** *nf* concierge's room; (*di
ospedale*) porter's lodge

**'porto** *pp di* **porgere** ● *nm* harbour;
(*complesso*) port; (*vino*) port [wine]; (*spesa di
trasporto*) carriage; **andare in ~** succeed. **~
d'armi** gun licence. **~ container** container
port. **~ fluviale** river port. **~ franco** free
port. **~ marittimo** seaport

**Porto'gallo** *nm* Portugal

**porto'ghese** *a & nmf* Portuguese

**por'tone** *nm* main door

**portori'cano, -a** *a & nmf* Puerto Rican

**Porto'rico** *nf* Puerto Rico

**portu'ale** *nm* dockworker, docker

**porzi'one** *nf* portion

**'posa** *nf* laying; *(riposo)* rest; *Phot* exposure; *(atteggiamento)* pose; **mettersi in ~** pose; **senza ~** without rest

**po'sare** *vt* put; *(giù)* put [down] ● *vi* *(poggiare)* rest; *(per un ritratto)* pose

**po'sarsi** *vr* alight; *(sostare)* rest; *Aeron* land

**po'sata** *nf* piece of cutlery; **posate** *pl* cutlery *sg*, flatware *sg Am*

**po'sato** *a* sedate

**po'scritto** *nm* postscript

**posi'tivo** *a* positive

**posizio'nare** *vt* position

**posizi'one** *nf* position; **farsi una ~** get ahead; **prendere ~** take a stand

**posolo'gia** *nf* dosage

**po'sporre** *vt* place after; *(posticipare)* postpone

**po'sposto** *pp di* posporre

**posse'dere** *vt* possess, own

**possedi'mento** *nm* possession

**posses'sivo** *a* possessive

**pos'sesso** *nm* possession, ownership; *(bene)* possession; **entrare in ~ di** come into possession of; **essere in ~ di** be in possession of; **prendere ~ di** take possession of

**posses'sore** *nm* owner

**pos'sibile** *a* possible; **il più presto ~** as soon as possible ● *nm* **fare [tutto] il ~** do one's best

**possibilità** *nf inv* possibility; *(occasione)* chance; **avere la ~ di fare qcsa** have the chance *o* opportunity to do sth ● *nfpl (mezzi)* means

**possi'dente** *nmf* land-owner

**'posso** *vedi* potere

**'posta** *nf* post, mail; *(ufficio postale)* post office; *(al gioco)* stake; **spese di ~** postage; **per ~** by post, by mail; **la ~ in gioco è...** *fig* what's at stake is...; **a bella ~** on purpose; **Poste e Telecomunicazioni** [Italian] Post Office. **~ aerea** airmail. **~ centrale** main post office, central post office. **~ del cuore** agony column. **~ elettronica** electronic mail, e-mail; **spedire via ~ ~** e-mail. **~ elettronica vocale** voicemail

**posta'giro** *nm* postal giro

**po'stale** *a* postal

**postazi'one** *nf* position; *Mil* emplacement

**post'bellico** *a* postwar

**postda'tare** *vt* postdate *(assegno)*

**posteggi'are** *vt/i* park

**posteggia'tore, -'trice** *nmf* parking attendant

**po'steggio** *nm* car-park, parking lot *Am*; *(di taxi)* taxi-rank

**'posteri** *nmpl* descendants

**posteri'ore** *a* back *attrib*, rear *attrib*; *(nel tempo)* later ● *nm fam* posterior, behind

**posterità** *nf* posterity

**po'sticcio** *a* artificial; *(baffi, barba)* false ● *nm* hair-piece

**postici'pare** *vt* postpone

**po'stilla** *nf* note; *Jur* rider

**po'stino** *nm* postman, mailman *Am*

**'posto** *pp di* porre ● *nm* place; *(spazio)* room; *(impiego)* job; *Mil* post; *(sedile)* seat; **a/fuori ~** in/out of place; **prendere ~** take up room; **sul ~** on-site; **essere a ~** *(casa, libri)* be tidy; **non grazie, sono a ~** no thanks, I'm all right; **mettere a ~** tidy *(stanza)*; **fare ~ a** make room for; **al ~ di** *(invece di)* in place of, instead of. **~ di blocco** checkpoint. **~ di guardia** guard post. **~ di guida** driving seat. **~ di lavoro** job; *Comput* workstation. **posti in piedi** standing room. **~ di polizia** police station. **posti** *pl* **a sedere** seating, seats

**post-'partum** *a* post-natal

**'postumo** *a* posthumous ● *nm* after-effect; **postumi** *pl* **della sbornia** hangover

**po'tabile** *a* drinkable; **acqua ~** drinking water; **non ~** undrinkable

**po'tare** *vt* prune

**po'tassa** *nf* potash

**po'tassio** *nm* potassium

**po'tente** *a* powerful; *(efficace)* potent

**po'tenza** *nf* power; *(efficacia)* potency. **~ nucleare** nuclear power

**potenzi'ale** *a & nm* potential

**po'tere** *nm* power; **al ~** in power. **~ d'acquisto** purchasing power. **il quarto ~** the fourth estate ● *vi* can, be able to; **posso entrare?** can I come in?; *(formale)* may I come in?; **mi spiace, non posso venire alla festa** I'm sorry, I can't come to the party *or* I won't be able to come to the party; **posso fare qualche cosa?** can I do something?; **che tu possa essere felice!** may you be happy!; **non ne posso più** *(sono stanco)* I can't go on; *(sono stufo)* I can't take any more; **può darsi** perhaps; **può darsi che sia vero** perhaps it's true; **potrebbe aver ragione** he could be right, he might be right; **avresti potuto telefonare** you could have phoned, you might have phoned; **spero di poter venire** I hope to be able to come; **senza poter telefonare** without being able to phone; **spero che potremo incontrarci presto** I hope we can meet soon

**potestà** *nf* power

**pot-pour'ri** *nm inv* medley

**'povero, -a** *a* poor; *(semplice)* plain; **~ di** *(paese, terreno)* lacking in; **in parole povere** in a few words ● *nf* poor woman ● *nm* poor man; **i poveri** the poor

**povertà** *nf* poverty

**pozi'one** *nf* potion

**'pozza** *nf* pool

**poz'zanghera** *nf* puddle

**'pozzo** *nm* well; *(minerario)* pit. **~ petrolifero** oil well. **~ di petrolio** oil well. **~ di ventilazione** air shaft

**pp.** *(pagine) abbr* pp

**PP.TT.** *abbr* **(Poste e Telecomunicazioni)** [Italian] Post Office

**PR** *nfpl abbr* PR

'**Praga** *nf* Prague

**prag'matico** *a* pragmatic

**prali'nato** *a* ⟨*mandorla, gelato*⟩ praline-coated

**pram'matica** *nf* **essere di ~** be customary

**pranotera'pia** *nf* laying on of hands

**pran'zare** *vi* dine; ⟨*a mezzogiorno*⟩ lunch

'**pranzo** *nm* dinner; ⟨*a mezzogiorno*⟩ lunch. **~ di lavoro** business lunch, working lunch. **~ di nozze** wedding breakfast

'**prassi** *nf* standard procedure

**prate'ria** *nf* grassland

'**pratica** *nf* practice; ⟨*esperienza*⟩ experience; ⟨*documentazione*⟩ file; **avere ~ di qcsa** be familiar with sth, have experience of sth; **mettere qcsa in ~** put sth into practice; **far ~** gain experience; **fare le pratiche per** gather the necessary papers for

**prati'cabile** *a* practicable; ⟨*strada*⟩ passable

**pratica'mente** *adv* practically

**prati'cante** *nmf* apprentice; *Relig* [regular] church-goer

**prati'care** *vt* practise; ⟨*frequentare*⟩ associate with; ⟨*fare*⟩ make

**praticità** *nf* practicality

'**pratico** *a* practical; ⟨*esperto*⟩ experienced, knowledgeable; ⟨*comodo*⟩ convenient; **essere ~ di qcsa** know about sth; **all'atto ~** in practice

'**prato** *nm* meadow; ⟨*di giardino*⟩ lawn. **~ all'inglese** lawn

**preaccensi'one** *nf* *Auto* pre-ignition

**pre'ambolo** *nm* preamble

**preannunci'are** *vt* give advance notice of

**prean'nuncio** *nm* advance notice

**preavvi'sare** *vt* forewarn

**preav'viso** *nm* warning

**precari'cato** *a* preloaded

**precarietà** *nf inv* frailty

**pre'cario** *a* precarious

**precauzi'one** *nf* precaution; ⟨*cautela*⟩ care

**prece'dente** *a* previous ● *nm* precedent; **avere dei precedenti penali** have a police record; **senza precedenti** ⟨*successo*⟩ unprecedented

**precedente'mente** *adv* previously

**prece'denza** *nf* precedence; ⟨*di veicoli*⟩ right of way; **dare la ~ a** give priority to; *Auto* give way to; **avere la ~** have priority; *Auto* have right of way; **~ assoluta** top priority

**pre'cedere** *vt* precede

**pre'cetto** *nm* precept

**precet'tore, -'trice** *nmf* tutor

**precipi'tare** *vt* **~ le cose** precipitate events; **~ qcno nella disperazione** cast sb into a state of despair ● *vi* fall headlong; ⟨*situazione, eventi:*⟩ come to a head

**precipi'tarsi** *vr* ⟨*gettarsi*⟩ throw oneself; ⟨*affrettarsi*⟩ rush; **~ a fare qcsa** rush to do sth

**precipitazi'one** *nf* ⟨*fretta*⟩ haste; ⟨*atmosferica*⟩ precipitation

**precipi'toso** *a* hasty; ⟨*avventato*⟩ reckless; ⟨*caduta*⟩ headlong

**preci'pizio** *nm* precipice; **a ~** headlong

**preci'sabile** *a* specifiable

**precisa'mente** *adv* precisely

**preci'sare** *vt* specify; ⟨*spiegare*⟩ clarify; **ci tengo a ~ che...** I want to make the point that...

**precisazi'one** *nf* clarification

**precisi'one** *nf* precision

**pre'ciso** *a* precise; ⟨*calcolo, risposta*⟩ accurate; ⟨*ore*⟩ sharp; ⟨*identico*⟩ identical

**pre'cludere** *vt* preclude

**pre'cludersi** *vr* **~ ogni possibilità** preclude every possibility

**pre'cluso** *pp di* **precludere**

**pre'coce** *a* precocious; ⟨*prematuro*⟩ premature

**precocità** *nf* precociousness

**precon'cetto** *a* preconceived ● *nm* prejudice

**preconfezio'nato** *a* pre-packed

**preconfigu'rato** *a* preconfigured

**pre'correre** *vt* ⟨*anticipare*⟩ anticipate; **~ i tempi** be ahead of one's time

**precorri|'tore, -'trice** *nmf* precursor, forerunner

**precur'sore** *nm* forerunner, precursor

'**preda** *nf* prey; ⟨*bottino*⟩ booty; **essere in ~ al panico** be panic-stricken; **in ~ alle fiamme** engulfed in flames

**pre'dare** *vt* plunder

**preda'tore** *nm* predator

**predeces'sore** *nmf* predecessor

**pre'della** *nf* platform

**predel'lino** *nm* step

**predesti'nare** *vt* predestine

**predesti'nato** *a* predestined, preordained

**predestinazi'one** *nf* predestination

**predetermi'nare** *vt* predetermine

**predetermi'nato** *a* predetermined, preordained

**pre'detto** *pp di* **predire**

'**predica** *nf* sermon; *fig* lecture

**predi'care** *vt* preach

**predi'cato** *nm* predicate

**predige'rito** *a* predigested

**predi'letto, -a** *pp di* **prediligere** ● *a* favourite ● *nmf* pet

**predilezi'one** *nf* predilection; **avere una ~ per** have a predilection for, be partial to

**predi'ligere** *vt* prefer

**prediposizi'one** *nf* predisposition; ⟨*al disegno ecc*⟩ bent (**a** for)

**pre'dire** *vt* foretell

**predi'sporre** *vt* arrange; **~ qcno a qcsa** *Med* predispose sb to sth; ⟨*preparare*⟩ prepare sb for sth

**predi'sporsi** *vr* **~ a** prepare oneself for

**predi'sposto** *pp di* **predisporre**

**predizi'one** *nf* prediction

**predomi'nante** *a* predominant

**predomi'nare** *vi* predominate

**predo'minio** *nm* predominance

**pre'done** *nm* robber

**prefabbri'cato** *a* prefabricated ● *nm* prefabricated building

**prefazi'one** *nf* preface

**prefe'renza** *nf* preference; **di ~** preferably

**preferenzi'ale** *a* preferential; **corsia ~** bus and taxi lane

**prefe'ribile** *a* preferable

**preferibil'mente** *adv* preferably

**prefe'rire** *vt* prefer

**prefe'rito, -a** *a & nmf* favourite

**pre'fetto** *nm* prefect

**prefet'tura** *nf* prefecture

**pre'figgere** *vt* decide in advance, pre-arrange ⟨*termine*⟩

**pre'figgersi** *vr* **~ uno scopo** set oneself an objective

**prefigu'rare** *vt* ⟨*anticipare*⟩ foreshadow

**prefinanzia'mento** *nm* bridging loan

**prefis'sare** *vt* pre-arrange ⟨*data, appuntamento*⟩

**pre'fisso** *pp di* **prefiggere** ● *nm* prefix; *Teleph* [dialling] code

**pre'gare** *vi* Relig pray ● *vt* Relig pray to; ⟨*supplicare*⟩ beg; **farsi ~** need persuading; **~ qcno di fare qcsa** ask sb to do sth; **si prega di...** please...; **si prega di non...** please do not...; **si prega di non fumare** please refrain from smoking

**pre'gevole** *a* valuable

**preghi'era** *nf* prayer; ⟨*richiesta*⟩ request

**pregi'arsi** *vr* **si pregia di non essere mai in ritardo** he prides himself on never being late

**pregi'ato** *a* esteemed; ⟨*prezioso*⟩ valuable

**'pregio** *nm* esteem; ⟨*valore*⟩ value; ⟨*di persona*⟩ good point; **di ~** valuable

**pregiudi'care** *vt* prejudice; ⟨*danneggiare*⟩ harm

**pregiudi'cato** *a* prejudiced ● *nm* Jur previous offender

**pregiu'dizio** *nm* prejudice; ⟨*danno*⟩ detriment

**pre'gnante** *a* ⟨*parola*⟩ pregnant, pregnant with meaning

**'pregno** *a* ⟨*parola*⟩ pregnant; ⟨*pieno*⟩ full; **~ di** ⟨*umidità*⟩ saturated with; ⟨*significato*⟩ pregnant with

**'prego** *int* ⟨*non c'è di che*⟩ don't mention it!; ⟨*per favore*⟩ please; **~?** I beg your pardon?; **posso? - ~** may I? - please do

**pregu'stare** *vt* look forward to

**preinstal'lato** *a* preinstalled

**prei'storia** *nf* prehistory

**prei'storico** *a* prehistoric

**pre'lato** *nm* prelate

**prela'vaggio** *nm* prewash

**preleva'mento** *nm* withdrawal

**prele'vare** *vt* withdraw ⟨*denaro*⟩; collect ⟨*merci*⟩; Med take

**preli'evo** *nm* ⟨*di soldi*⟩ withdrawal. **~ di sangue** blood sample

**prelimi'nare** *a* preliminary ● *nm* **preliminari** *pl* preliminaries

**pre'ludere** *vi* **~ a** herald

**pre'ludio** *nm* prelude

**prema'man** *nm inv* maternity dress ● *a* maternity *attrib*

**prematrimoni'ale** *a* premarital

**prematura'mente** *adv* prematurely

**prema'turo, -a** *a* premature ● *nmf* premature baby

**premedi'tare** *vt* premeditate

**premeditazi'one** *nf* premeditation; **con ~** ⟨*omicidio*⟩ premeditated

**'premere** *vt* press; *Comput* hit ⟨*tasto*⟩ ● *vi* **~ a** ⟨*importare*⟩ matter to; **mi preme sapere** I need to know; **~ su** press on; push ⟨*pulsante*⟩; ⟨*fig: fare pressione su*⟩ put pressure on, pressure; **~ per ottenere qcsa** push for sth

**pre'messa** *nf* introduction; **senza tante premesse** without further ado

**pre'messo** *pp di* **premettere**; **~ che** bearing in mind that

**pre'mettere** *vt* ⟨*mettere prima*⟩ put before; **premetto che...** I want to make it clear first that...; **~ un'introduzione a un libro** put an introduction at the beginning of a book

**premi'are** *vt* give a prize to; ⟨*ricompensare*⟩ reward

**premi'ato** *a* award-winning

**premiazi'one** *nf* prize giving

**premi'nente** *a* pre-eminent

**premi'nenza** *nf* pre-eminence

**'premio** *nm* prize; ⟨*ricompensa*⟩ reward; ⟨*di produzione ecc*⟩ bonus; *Fin* premium. **~ di assicurazione** insurance premium. **~ di consolazione** consolation prize; ⟨*ridicolo*⟩ booby prize. **~ di ingaggio** *Sport* signing fee. **~ di produzione** productivity bonus

**premoni'tore** *a* ⟨*sogno, segno*⟩ premonitory

**premonizi'one** *nf* premonition

**premu'nire** *vt* fortify

**premu'nirsi** *vr* take protective measures; **~ di** provide oneself with; **~ contro** protect oneself against

**pre'mura** *nf* ⟨*fretta*⟩ hurry; ⟨*cura*⟩ care; **far ~ a qcno** hurry sb up

**premu'roso** *a* thoughtful

**prena'tale** *a* antenatal

**'prendere** *vt* take; ⟨*afferrare*⟩ seize; catch ⟨*treno, malattia, ladro, pesce*⟩; have ⟨*cibo, bevanda*⟩; ⟨*far pagare*⟩ charge; ⟨*assumere*⟩ take on; ⟨*ottenere*⟩ get; ⟨*occupare*⟩ take up; ⟨*guadagnare*⟩ earn; **~ informazioni** make inquiries; **~ qcno in giro** pull sb's leg; **~ a calci/pugni** kick/punch; **che ti prende?** what's got into you?; **quanto prende?** what do you charge?; **~ una persona per un'altra** mistake a person for somebody else; **passare a ~ qcno** collect sb, pick sb up ● *vi* ⟨*voltare*⟩ turn; ⟨*attecchire*⟩ take root; ⟨*rapprendersi*⟩ set; ⟨*fuoco:*⟩ catch, take; **~ a destra/sinistra** turn right/left; **~ a fare qcsa** start doing sth; **la colla non ha preso** the glue didn't take

**'prendersi** *vr* **~ a pugni** come to blows; **~ cura di** take care of ⟨*ammalato*⟩; **prendersela** take it to heart; **si prende troppo sul serio** he takes himself too seriously

**prendi'sole** *nm* sundress
**preno'tare** *vt* book. reserve
**preno'tarsi** *vr* ~ **per** put one's name down for
**preno'tato** *a* booked, reserved
**prenotazi'one** *nf* booking, reservation
**'prensile** *a* prehensile
**preoccu'pante** *a* alarming
**preoccu'pare** *vt* worry
**preoccu'parsi** *vr* ~ worry (**di** about); ~ **di fare qcsa** take the trouble to do sth
**preoccu'pato** *a* (*ansioso*) worried
**preoccupazi'one** *nf* worry; (*apprensione*) concern
**preopera'torio** *a* preoperative
**prepa'rare** *vt* prepare; study for ‹*esame*›: ~ **da mangiare** prepare a meal
**prepa'rarsi** *vr* get ready
**prepara'tivi** *nmpl* preparations
**prepa'rato** *nm* (*prodotto*) preparation
**prepara'torio** *a* preparatory
**preparazi'one** *nf* preparation; (*competenza*) knowledge
**prepensiona'mento** *nm* early retirement
**preponde'rante** *a* predominant. preponderant
**preponde'ranza** *nf* preponderance, prevalence
**pre'porre** *vt* place before
**preposizi'one** *nf* preposition
**pre'posto** *pp di* **preporre** ● *a* ~ **a** (*addetto a*) in charge of
**prepo'tente** *a* overbearing ● *nmf* bully; **fare il** ~ **con qcno** bully sb
**prepo'tenza** *nf* high-handedness
**preprogram'mato** *a* *Comput* preprogrammed
**pre'puzio** *nm* foreskin, prepuce
**preroga'tiva** *nf* prerogative
**'presa** *nf* taking; (*conquista*) capture; (*stretta*) hold; (*di cemento ecc*) setting; *Electr* socket; (*di gas, acqua*) inlet, connection; (*pizzico*) pinch; **essere alle prese con** be struggling *o* grappling with; **macchina da** ~ cine camera; **a** ~ **rapida** ‹*cemento, colla*› quick-setting; **fare** ~ **su qcno** influence sb. ~ **d'aria** air vent. ~ **in giro** leg-pull. ~ **multipla** adaptor
**pre'sagio** *nm* omen
**presa'gire** *vt* foretell
**presa'lario** *nm* maintenance grant
**'presbite** *a* long-sighted
**presbiteri'ano, -a** *a & nmf* Presbyterian
**presbi'terio** *nm* presbytery
**pre'scelto** *a* selected
**pre'scindere** *vi* ~ **da** leave aside; **a** ~ **da** apart from
**presco'lare** *a* pre-school; **in età** ~ preschool
**pre'scritto** *pp di* **prescrivere**
**pre'scrivere** *vt* prescribe
**prescrizi'one** *nf* prescription; (*norma*) rule; **cadere in** ~ cease to be valid as a result of the statute of limitations
**preselezi'one** *nf* preliminary selection;

(*per il traffico*) advance lane markings: *Sport* [qualifying] heats *pl*
**presen'tare** *vt* present; (*far conoscere*) introduce; show ‹*documento*›; (*inoltrare*) submit
**presen'tarsi** *vr* present oneself; (*farsi conoscere*) introduce oneself; (*a ufficio*) attend; (*alla polizia ecc*) report; (*come candidato*) stand, run (**a** for); ‹*occasione:*› occur; ~ **bene/male** ‹*persona:*› make a good/ bad impression; ‹*situazione:*› look good/bad
**presenta|'tore, -'trice** *nmf* presenter; (*di notizie*) announcer
**presentazi'one** *nf* presentation; (*per conoscersi*) introduction; **fare le presentazioni** do the introductions; **dietro** ~ **di ricetta medica** on doctor's prescription only
**pre'sente** *a* present; (*attuale*) current; (*questo*) this; **aver** ~ remember ● *nm* present; **i presenti** those present ● *nf* **allegato alla** ~ (*in lettera*) enclosed
**presenti'mento** *nm* foreboding
**pre'senza** *nf* presence; (*aspetto*) appearance; **in** ~ **di, alla** ~ **di** in the presence of; **di bella** ~ personable. ~ **di spirito** presence of mind
**presenzi'are** *vi* ~ **a** attend
**pre'sepe** *nm*, **pre'sepio** *nm* crib
**preser'vare** *vt* preserve; (*proteggere*) protect (**da** from)
**preserva'tivo** *nm* condom
**preservazi'one** *nf* preservation
**'preside** *nm* headmaster; *Univ* dean ● *nf* headmistress; *Univ* dean
**presi'dente** *nm* chairman; *Pol* president ● *nf* chairwoman; *Pol* president. ~ **del consiglio [dei ministri]** Prime Minister. ~ **della repubblica** President of the Republic
**presiden'tessa** *nf* chairwoman
**presi'denza** *nf* presidency; (*di assemblea*) chairmanship
**presidenzi'ale** *a* presidential
**presidi'are** *vt* garrison
**pre'sidio** *nm* garrison
**presi'edere** *vt* preside over
**'preso** *pp di* **prendere**
**'pressa** *nf Mech* press
**press-'agent** *mf inv* publicist, press agent
**pres'sante** *a* urgent
**pressap'poco** *adv* about
**pres'sare** *vt* press
**pressi'one** *nf* pressure; **far** ~ **su** put pressure on; **essere sotto** ~ *fig* be under pressure; **esercitare pressioni su qcno** put pressure on sb; **a/di alta** ~ high pressure. ~ **fiscale** tax burden. ~ **gomme** tyre pressure. ~ **del sangue** blood pressure
**'presso** *prep* near; (*a casa di*) with; (*negli indirizzi*) care of, c/o; ‹*lavorare*› for; **richiedere qcsa** ~ **una società** request sth from a company ● *nmpl* **pressi: nei pressi di…** in the neighbourhood *or* vicinity of…
**pressoché** *adv* almost
**pressuriz'zare** *vt* pressurize

**pressuriz'zato** a pressurized

**prestabi'lire** vt arrange in advance

**prestabi'lito** a agreed, predetermined

**prestam'pato** a printed ● nm (modulo) form

**pre'stante** a good-looking

**pre'stanza** nf good looks pl

**pre'stare** vt lend; ~ **attenzione** pay attention; ~ **aiuto** lend a hand; ~ **ascolto** lend an ear; ~ **fede a** give credence to; ~ **giuramento** take the oath; **farsi** ~ borrow (da from)

**pre'starsi** vr (frase:) lend itself; (persona:) offer

**prestazi'one** nf performance; **prestazioni** pl (servizi) services

**prestigia'tore, -'trice** nmf conjurer

**pre'stigio** nm prestige; **gioco di** ~ conjuring trick

**prestigi'oso** nm prestigious

**'prestito** nm loan; **dare in** ~ lend; **prendere in** ~ borrow. ~ **bancario** bank loan. ~ **con garanzia collaterale** collateral loan

**'presto** adv soon; (di buon'ora) early; (in fretta) quickly; **a** ~ see you soon; **al più** ~ as soon as possible; ~ **o tardi** sooner or later; **far** ~ be quick

**pre'sumere** vt presume; (credere) think

**presu'mibile** a è ~ **che...** presumably,...

**pre'sunto** a (colpevole) presumed

**presuntu'oso** a presumptuous ● nmf presumptuous person

**presunzi'one** nf presumption

**presup'porre** vt suppose; (richiedere) presuppose

**presupposizi'one** nf presupposition

**presup'posto** nm essential requirement

**prêt-à-por'ter** nm ready-to-wear clothing

**'prete** nm priest

**preten'dente** nmf pretender ● nm (corteggiatore) suitor

**pre'tendere** vt (sostenere) claim; (esigere) demand ● vi ~ **a** a claim to; ~ **di** (esigere) demand to

**pretensi'one** nf pretension

**pretenzi'oso** a pretentious

**preterintenzio'nale** a **omicidio** ~ manslaughter

**pre'terito** nm preterite

**pre'tesa** nf pretension; (esigenza) claim; **senza pretese** unpretentious

**pre'teso** pp di **pretendere**

**pre'testo** nm pretext

**pre'tore** nm magistrate

**pretta'mente** adv decidedly

**'pretto** a pure

**pre'tura** nf magistrate's court

**preva'lente** a prevalent

**prevalente'mente** adv primarily

**preva'lenza** nf prevalence

**preva'lere** vi prevail

**pre'valso** pp di **prevalere**

**preve'dere** vt foresee; forecast (tempo); (legge ecc:) provide for

**preve'nire** vt precede; (evitare) prevent; (avvertire) forewarn

**preventi'vare** vt estimate; (aspettarsi) budget for

**preven'tivo** a preventive; **bilancio** ~ budget ● nm Comm estimate

**preve'nuto** a forewarned; (mal disposto) prejudiced

**prevenzi'one** nf prevention; (preconcetto) prejudice

**previ'dente** a provident

**previ'denza** nf foresight. ~ **integrativa** supplementary social security, supplementary welfare Am. ~ **sociale** social security, welfare Am

**previdenzi'ale** a provident

**'previo** a ~ **pagamento** on payment

**previsi'one** nf forecast; **in** ~ **di** in anticipation of. **previsioni** pl **del tempo** weather forecast

**pre'visto** pp di **prevedere** ● a foreseen ● nm **più/meno/prima del** ~ more/less/earlier than expected

**prezi'oso** a precious

**prez'zemolo** nm parsley

**'prezzo** nm price; **[a] metà** ~ half price; **a** ~ **ribassato** at a reduced price; **non aver** ~ fig be priceless. ~ **d'acquisto** purchase price. ~ **di costo** cost price. ~ **al dettaglio** retail price. ~ **di fabbrica** factory price. ~ **di favore** special price. ~ **all'ingrosso** wholesale price. ~ **intero** full price. ~ **di mercato** market price. ~ **al minuto** retail price. ~ **d'offerta** offer price. ~ **politico** subsidized price. ~ **di riferimento** benchmark price. ~ **sorvegliato** controlled price. ~ **stracciato** slashed price, drastically reduced price. ~ **trattabile** price negotiable. ~ **unitario** unit price. ~ **di vendita** selling price

**prigi'one** nf prison; (pena) imprisonment; **mettere in** ~ imprison, put in prison

**prigio'nia** nf imprisonment

**prigioni'ero, -a** a imprisoned ● nmf prisoner; **tenere** ~ qcno keep sb prisoner. ~ **di guerra** prisoner of war, POW

**'prima** adv before; (più presto) earlier; (in anticipo) beforehand; (in primo luogo) first; ~, **finiamo questo** let's finish this first; **puoi venire** ~? (di giorni) can't you come any sooner?; (di ore) can't you come any earlier?; ~ **o poi** sooner or later; **quanto** ~ as soon as possible ● prep ~ **di** before; ~ **di mangiare** before eating; ~ **d'ora** before now ● conj ~ **che** before; ~ **che posso** as soon as I can ● nf first class; Theat first night; Auto first [gear]

**pri'mario** a primary; (principale) principal

**pri'mate** nm primate

**pri'mato** nm supremacy; Sport record

**prima'vera** nf spring

**primave'rile** a spring attrib

**primeggi'are** vi excel

**primi'tivo** a primitive; (originario) original

**pri'mizie** nfpl early produce sg

**'primo** a first; (fondamentale) principal; (in

*importanza*) main; (*precedente di due*) former;
(*iniziale*) early; (*migliore*) best ● *nm* first; **il ~
d'aprile** April the first, April Fools' Day;
**primi** *pl* (*i primi giorni*) the beginning; **in un
~ tempo** at first. **prima colazione** *nf* breakfast. **prima copia** *nf* master copy. **prima
linea** *nf* Mil front line. **prima serata** *nf*
prime time; **in ~ ~ trasmetteremo...** in the
early evening slot we're bringing you...

**primo'genito, -a** *a & nmf* first-born

**primogeni'tura** *nf* primogeniture; **vendere la ~** sell one's birthright

**primordi'ale** *a* primordial

**'primula** *nf* primrose

**princi'pale** *a* main ● *nm* head, boss *fam*

**princi'pato** *nm* principality

**'principe** *nm* prince; **da ~** princely. **~
ereditario** crown prince. **~ del foro** famous
lawyer

**princi'pesco** *a* princely

**princi'pessa** *nf* princess

**principi'ante** *nmf* beginner

**principi'are** *vt/i* begin, start

**prin'cipio** *nm* beginning; (*concetto*) principle; (*causa*) cause; **per ~** on principle; **una
questione di ~** a matter of principle. **~
attivo** active ingredient

**pri'ore** *nm* prior

**pri'ori**: **a ~** *adv* (*decidere*) a priori; **farsi ~
un'opinione di** prejudge ● *a* a priori

**priorità** *nf inv* priority

**priori'tario** *a* having priority; (*obiettivo*)
priority *attrib*; **la nostra scelta prioritaria**
our decision, which must take priority

**'prisma** *nm* prism

**'privacy** *nf* privacy

**pri'vare** *vt* deprive

**pri'varsi** *vr* deprive oneself

**privatiz'zare** *vt* privatize

**privatizzazi'one** *nf* privatization

**pri'vato, -a** *a* private ● *nmf* private citizen;
**in ~** in private; **ritirarsi a vita privata** withdraw from public life

**privazi'one** *nf* deprivation

**privilegi'are** *vt* privilege; (*considerare più
importante*) favour

**privi'legio** *nm* privilege; **avere il ~ di** have
the privilege of; **questo dizionario ha il ~
della chiarezza** this dictionary has the
merit of clarity

**'privo** *a* **~ di** devoid of; (*mancante*) lacking in

**pro** *prep* for ● *nm* advantage; **a che ~?**
what's the point?; **il ~ e il contro** the pros
and cons

**pro'babile** *a* probable

**probabilità** *nf inv* probability; **avere
buone ~** have a fighting chance; **~ di
riuscita** chances of success

**probabil'mente** *adv* probably

**pro'bante** *a* convincing

**probità** *nf* probity

**pro'blema** *nm* problem; **non c'è ~** no problem

**proble'matico** *a* problematic

**pro'boscide** *nf* trunk

**procacci'are** *vt* obtain

**procacci'arsi** *vr* obtain

**pro'cace** *a* (*ragazza*) provocative

**pro'cedere** *vi* (*in percorso, discorso*) go on,
proceed *fml*; (*iniziare*) start; **il lavoro
procede bene** the work is going well; **~
contro** *Jur* start legal proceedings against

**procedi'mento** *nm* process; *Jur* proceedings *pl*

**proce'dura** *nf* procedure. **~ civile** civil proceedings *pl*. **~ fallimentare** bankruptcy proceedings *pl*

**procedu'rale** *a* procedural

**proces'sare** *vt Jur* try

**processi'one** *nf* procession

**pro'cesso** *nm* process; *Jur* trial; **essere
sotto ~** be on trial; **mettere sotto ~** put on
trial

**proces'sore** *nm* Comput processor

**processu'ale** *a* trial *attrib*

**pro'cinto** *nm* **essere in ~ di** be about to

**proci'one** *nm* raccoon

**procla'ma** *nm* proclamation

**procla'mare** *vt* proclaim

**proclamazi'one** *nf* proclamation

**procrasti'nare** *vt liter* postpone

**procre'are** *vt* procreate

**procreazi'one** *nf* procreation

**pro'cura** *nf* power of attorney; **per ~** by
proxy. **P~ [della Repubblica]** Public Prosecutor's office

**procu'rare** *vt/i* procure; (*causare*) cause;
(*cercare*) try

**procura'tore** *nm* attorney. **P~ Generale**
Attorney General. **~ legale** ≈ lawyer. **~
della repubblica** public prosecutor

**'prode** *a* brave

**pro'dezza** *nf* bravery

**prodi'gare** *vt* lavish

**prodi'garsi** *vr* do one's best

**pro'digio** *nm* prodigy

**prodigi'oso** *a* prodigious

**'prodigo** *a* prodigal

**prodi'torio** *a* treasonable

**pro'dotto** *pp di* **produrre** ● *nm* product.
**prodotti** *pl* **agricoli** farm produce *sg*. **~
artigianalmente** *a* made by craftsmen.
**prodotti** *pl* **di bellezza** cosmetics. **~
derivato** by-product. **~ di fabbrica** *a* fac-
tory-made. **~ finito** end product, finished
product. **~ interno lordo** gross domestic
product. **~ nazionale lordo** gross national
product

**pro'durre** *vt* produce

**pro'dursi** *vr* (*attore:*) play; (*accadere*) happen, occur

**produttività** *nf* productivity

**produt'tivo** *a* productive

**produt'tore, -'trice** *a* producing; **~ di
petrolio** oil-producing ● *nmf* producer

**produzi'one** *nf* production. **~ in serie**
mass production

**Prof.** *abbr* (**professore**) Prof.

**profa'nare** *vt* desecrate

**profanazi'one** *nf* desecration

219

**profano | promontorio**

**pro'fano** *a* profane ● *nm* **i profani** *pl* the uninitiated
**profe'rire** *vt* utter
**Prof.essa** *abbr* (**Professoressa**) Prof.
**profes'sare** *vt* profess; practise ⟨*professione*⟩
**professio'nale** *a* professional; **istituto ~**
training college
**professionalità** *nf* professionalism
**professi'one** *nf* profession; **libera ~** profession
**professio'nismo** *nm* professionalism
**professio'nista** *nmf* professional
**professo'rale** *a* professorial
**profes'sor|e, -'essa** *nmf Sch* teacher;
*Univ* lecturer; (*titolare di cattedra*) professor
**pro'feta** *nm* prophet
**pro'fetico** *a* prophetic
**profetiz'zare** *vt* prophesy
**profe'zia** *nf* prophecy
**pro'ficuo** *a* profitable
**profi'lare** *vt* outline; (*ornare*) border; *Aeron*
streamline
**profi'larsi** *vr* stand out
**profi'lattico** *a* prophylactic ● *nm* condom
**pro'filo** *nm* profile; (*breve studio*) outline; **di
~** in profile
**profite'roles** *nmpl* profiteroles
**profit'tare** *vi* **~ di** (*avvantaggiarsi*) profit
by; (*approfittare*) take advantage of
**pro'fitto** *nm* profit; (*vantaggio*) advantage;
**mettere qcsa a ~** turn sth to one's advantage; **trarre ~ da** (*vantaggio*) derive benefit
from
**profonda'mente** *adv* deeply, profoundly
**profondità** *nf inv* depth; (*del pensiero ecc*)
depth, profundity; **in ~** in depth; **passaggio
in ~** *Sport* deep pass [down the field]. **~ di
campo** *Phot* depth of field
**pro'fondo** *a* deep; ⟨*pensiero ecc*⟩ profound;
⟨*cultura*⟩ great
**pro 'forma** *a* routine; **fattura ~ ~** pro forma
[invoice] ● *adv* as a formality ● *nm* formality
**'profugo, -a** *nmf* refugee
**profu'mare** *vt* perfume
**profu'marsi** *vr* put on perfume
**profumata'mente** *adv* **pagare ~** pay
through the nose
**profu'mato** *a* ⟨*fiore*⟩ fragrant; ⟨*fazzoletto
ecc*⟩ scented
**profume'ria** *nf* perfumery
**pro'fumo** *nm* perfume, scent
**profusi'one** *nf* profusion; **a ~** in profusion
**pro'fuso** *pp di* **profondere** ● *a* profuse
**pro'genie** *nf* progeny
**progeni|'tore, -'trice** *nmf* ancestor
**proget'tare** *vt* plan; plan, design
⟨*costruzione*⟩
**progettazione** *nf* planning, design. **~
assistita da computer** computer-aided design, CAD
**proget'tista** *nmf* designer
**pro'getto** *nm* plan; (*di lavoro importante*)
project. **~ di legge** bill

**prog'nosi** *nf inv* prognosis: **in ~ riservata**
on the danger list
**pro'gramma** *nm* programme; *Comput* program; **avere qcsa in ~** have sth planned,
have sth on. **~ di antivirus** *Comput* antivirus
program. **~ assemblatore** *Comput* assembler. **~ aziendale** business plan. **~ per la
gestione dei file** *Comput* file manager. **~ di
grafico** *Comput* graphics program. **~ politico** manifesto. **~ scolastico** syllabus. **~
di setup** *Comput* setup program. **~ di utilità**
*Comput* utility
**program'mare** *vt* programme; *Comput* program
**program'mato** *a* ⟨*sviluppo*⟩ planned
**programma|'tore, -'trice** *nmf* [compu-
ter] programmer
**programmazi'one** *nf* programming
**progre'dire** *vi* [make] progress
**progres'sione** *nf* progression
**progres'sista** *nmf* progressive
**progres'sivo** *a* progressive
**pro'gresso** *nm* progress; **fare progressi**
make progress
**proi'bire** *vt* forbid
**proibi'tivo** *a* prohibitive
**proibito** *a* forbidden; **è ~ fumare qui** it's no
smoking here
**proibizi'one** *nf* prohibition
**proibizio'nismo** *nm* prohibition
**proiet'tare** *vt* project; show ⟨*film*⟩
**proi'ettile** *nm* bullet
**proiet'tore** *nm* projector; *Auto* headlight
**proiezi'one** *nf* projection
**'prole** *nf* offspring
**proletari'ato** *nm* proletariat
**prole'tario** *a & nm* proletarian
**prolife'rare** *vi* proliferate
**pro'lifico** *a* prolific
**prolissità** *nf* prolixity, diffuseness
**pro'lisso** *a* verbose, prolix
**pro 'loco** *nf* tourist office (*in small places*)
**'prologo** *nm* prologue
**pro'lunga** *nf Electr* extension
**prolunga'mento** *nm* extension
**prolun'gare** *vt* extend ⟨*contratto, scadenza,
strada*⟩; prolong ⟨*vita*⟩; lengthen ⟨*vita,
strada*⟩
**prolun'garsi** *vr* continue, go on; **~ su**
(*dilungarsi*) dwell upon
**prome'moria** *nm* memo; (*per se stessi*) reminder, note; (*formale*) memorandum
**pro'messa** *nf* promise; **era già una ~
del...** he was already a promising new talent
in...
**pro'messo** *pp di* **promettere** ● *a* ⟨*terra*⟩
promised. **promessa sposa** *nf* betrothed. **~
sposo** *nm* betrothed
**promet'tente** *a* promising
**pro'mettere** *vt/i* promise
**promi'nente** *a* prominent
**promi'nenza** *nf* prominence
**promiscuità** *nf* promiscuity
**pro'miscuo** *a* promiscuous
**promon'torio** *nm* promontory

**pro'mosso** *pp di* **promuovere** ● *a Sch* who has gone up a year; *Univ* who has passed an exam

**promo|'tore, -'trice** *nmf* promoter

**promozio'nale** *a* promotional; **vendita ~** special offer

**promozi'one** *nf* promotion

**promul'gare** *vt* promulgate

**promulgazi'one** *nf* promulgation

**promu'overe** *vt* promote; *Sch* move up a class; **essere promosso** *Sch, Univ* pass one's exams

**proni'pote** *nm* (*di bisnonno*) great-grandson; (*di prozio*) great-nephew; **pronipoti** *pl* great-grandchildren ● *nf* (*di bisnonno*) great-granddaughter; (*di prozio*) great-niece

**pro'nome** *nm* pronoun

**pronomi'nale** *a* pronominal

**pronosti'care** *vt* forecast, predict

**pronostica|'tore, -'trice** *nmf* forecaster

**pro'nostico** *nm* forecast

**pron'tezza** *nf* readiness; (*rapidità*) quickness; **~ di riflessi** quick reflexes *pl*; **con ~ di spirito** quick-wittedly

**'pronto** *a* ready; (*rapido*) quick; **~!** *Teleph* hello!; **tenersi ~ (per qcsa)** be ready (*for* sth); **pronti, via!** (*in gare*) ready! steady! go!; **a pronta cassa** cash on delivery. **~ intervento** *nm* emergency service. **~ soccorso** *nm* first aid; (*in ospedale*) accident and emergency, A&E

**prontu'ario** *nm* handbook

**pro'nuncia** *nf* pronunciation

**pronunci'are** *vt* pronounce; (*dire*) utter; deliver (*discorso*)

**pronunci'arsi** *vr* (*su un argomento*) give one's opinion; **~ a favore/contro qcsa** pronounce oneself in favour of/against sth

**pronunci'ato** *a* pronounced; (*prominente*) prominent

**pro'nunzia** = **pronuncia**

**pronunzi'are** = **pronunciare**

**propa'ganda** *nf* propaganda. **~ elettorale** electioneering. **~ di partito** party political propaganda

**propa'gare** *vt* propagate

**propa'garsi** *vr* spread

**propagazi'one** *nf* propagation

**prope'deutico** *a* introductory

**propel'lente** *nm* propellant

**pro'pendere** *vi* **~ per** be in favour of

**propensi'one** *nf* inclination, propensity

**pro'penso** *pp di* **propendere** ● *a* **essere ~ a fare qcsa** be inclined to do sth

**propi'nare** *vt* administer

**pro'pizio** *a* favourable

**proponi'mento** *nm* resolution

**pro'porre** *vt* propose; (*suggerire*) suggest

**pro'porsi** *vr* set oneself (*obiettivo, meta*); **~ di** intend to

**proporzio'nale** *a* proportional

**proporzio'nare** *vt* proportion

**proporzio'nato** *a* proportioned

**proporzi'one** *nf* proportion

**pro'posito** *nm* intention; **ho fatto il ~ di...** I have made the decision to...; **a ~** by the way; **a ~ di** with regard to; **di ~** (*apposta*) on purpose; **capitare a ~, giungere a ~** come at just the right time. **propositi** *pl* **per l'anno nuovo** New Year's resolutions

**proposizi'one** *nf* clause; (*frase*) sentence

**pro'posta** *nf* proposal, suggestion. **~ di legge** bill. **~ di matrimonio** [marriage] proposal

**pro'posto** *pp di* **proporre**

**propria'mente** *adv* **~ detto** in the strict sense of the word

**proprietà** *nf inv* property; (*diritto*) ownership; (*correttezza*) propriety; **essere di ~ di qcno** be sb's property. **~ collettiva** collective ownership. **~ immobiliare** property. **~ di linguaggio** correct use of language. **~ privata** private property

**proprie'taria** *nf* owner; (*di casa affittata*) landlady

**proprie'tario** *nm* owner; (*di casa affittata*) landlord

**'proprio** *a* one's [own]; (*caratteristico*) typical; (*appropriato*) proper ● *adv* just; (*veramente*) really; **non ~** not really, not exactly; (*affatto*) not... at all ● *pron* one's own ● *nm* one's own; **lavorare in ~** be one's own boss; **mettersi in ~** set up on one's own

**propu'gnare** *vt* support

**propulsi'one** *nf* propulsion; **a ~ atomica** atomic[-powered]. **~ a getto** jet propulsion

**propul'sore** *nm* propeller

**'prora** *nf Naut* prow

**'proroga** *nf* extension

**proro'gabile** *a* extendable

**proro'gare** *vt* extend

**pro'rompere** *vi* burst out

**'prosa** *nf* prose

**pro'saico** *a* prosaic

**pro'sciogliere** *vt* release; *Jur* acquit

**prosciogli'mento** *nm* release

**pro'sciolto** *pp di* **prosciogliere**

**prosciu'gare** *vt* dry up; (*bonificare*) reclaim

**prosciu'garsi** *vr* dry up

**prosci'utto** *nm* ham. **~ cotto** cooked ham. **~ crudo** type of dry-cured ham, Parma ham

**pro'scritto, -a** *pp di* **proscrivere** ● *nmf* exile

**pro'scrivere** *vt* exile, banish

**proscrizi'one** *nf* exile, banishment

**prosecuzi'one** *nf* continuation

**prosegui'mento** *nm* continuation; **buon ~!** (*viaggio*) have a good journey!; (*festa*) enjoy the rest of the party!

**prosegu'ire** *vt* continue ● *vi* go on, continue

**pro'selito** *nm* convert

**prospe'rare** *vi* prosper

**prosperità** *nf* prosperity

**'prospero** *a* prosperous; (*favorevole*) favourable

**prospe'roso** *a* flourishing; (*ragazza*) buxom

**prospet'tare** *vt* show

**prospet'tarsi** *vr* seem

**prospet'tiva** *nf* perspective; (*panorama*) view; *fig* prospect

**pro'spetto** *nm* (*vista*) view; (*facciata*) façade; (*tabella*) table

**prospici'ente** *a* facing

**prossima'mente** *adv* soon

**prossimità** *nf* proximity; **in ~ di** near

**'prossimo, -a** *a* near; (*seguente*) next; (*molto vicino*) close; **l'anno ~** next year; **~ venturo** next; **essere ~ a fare qcsa** be about to do sth ● *nmf* neighbour

**'prostata** *nf* prostate

**prostitu'irsi** *vr* prostitute oneself

**prosti'tuta** *nf* prostitute

**prostituzi'one** *nf* prostitution

**pro'strare** *vt* prostrate

**pro'strarsi** *vr* prostrate oneself

**pro'strato** *a* prostrate

**protago'nista** *nmf* protagonist

**pro'teggere** *vt* protect; (*favorire*) favour

**pro'teico** *a* protein *attrib*; **molto ~** rich in protein

**prote'ina** *nf* protein

**pro'tendere** *vt* stretch out

**pro'tendersi** *vr* (*in avanti*) lean out

**pro'teso** *pp di* **protendere**

**pro'testa** *nf* protest; (*dichiarazione*) protestation

**prote'stante** *a & nmf* Protestant

**prote'stare** *vt/i* protest

**prote'starsi** *vr* **~ innocente** protest one's innocence

**protet'tivo** *a* protective

**pro'tetto** *pp di* **proteggere**

**protetto'rato** *nm* protectorate

**protet'tore, -'trice** *nmf* protector; (*sostenitore*) patron ● *nm* (*di prostituta*) pimp

**protezi'one** *nf* protection. **~ civile** civil defence. **~ della natura** nature conservancy

**protocol'lare** (*visita*) protocol ● *vt* register

**proto'collo** *nm* protocol; (*registro*) register; **carta ~** official stamped paper

**pro'totipo** *nm* prototype

**pro'trarre** *vt* protract; (*differire*) postpone

**pro'trarsi** *vr* go on, continue

**pro'tratto** *pp di* **protrarre**

**protube'rante** *a* protuberant

**protube'ranza** *nf* protuberance

**'prova** *nf* test; (*dimostrazione*) proof; (*tentativo*) try, attempt; (*di abito*) fitting; *Sport* heat; *Theat* rehearsal; (*bozza*) proof; **prove** *pl* evidence; **fino a ~ contraria** until I'm told otherwise; **in ~** (*assumere*) for a trial period; **mettere alla ~** put to the test; **a ~ di bomba** bombproof; **a ~ di ladro** burglar-proof. **~ del fuoco** acid test. **~ generale** dress rehearsal

**pro'vare** *vt* test; (*dimostrare*) prove; (*tentare*) try; try on (*abiti ecc*); (*sentire*) feel; *Theat* rehearse; **prova!** just try!

**pro'varsi** *vr* try

**proveni'enza** *nf* origin

**prove'nire** *vi* **~ da** come from

**pro'vento** *nm* proceeds *pl*

**prove'nuto** *pp di* **provenire**

**pro'verbio** *nm* proverb

**pro'vetta** *nf* test-tube; **bambino in ~** test-tube baby

**pro'vetto** *a* skilled

**pro'vincia** *nf* province; (*strada*) B road, secondary road

**provinci'ale** *a* provincial; **strada ~** B road, secondary road

**pro'vino** *nm* specimen; *Cinema* screen test

**provo'cante** *a* provocative

**provo'care** *vt* provoke; (*causare*) cause

**provoca|'tore, -'trice** *nmf* trouble-maker

**provoca'torio** *a* provocative

**provocazi'one** *nf* provocation

**provo'lone** *nm* type of cheese with a slightly smoked flavour

**provve'dere** *vi* **~ a** provide for

**provvedi'mento** *nm* measure; (*previdenza*) precaution. **~ disciplinare** disciplinary measure

**provvedito'rato** *nm* **~ agli studi** education department

**provvedito're** *nm* **~ agli studi** director of education

**provvi'denza** *nf* providence

**provvidenzi'ale** *a* providential

**provvigi'one** *nf* *Comm* commission; **lavorare a ~** work on commission

**provvi'sorio** *a* provisional; **in via provvisoria** provisionally, for the time being

**prov'vista** *nf* supply

**pro'zia** *nf* great-aunt

**pro'zio** *nm* great-uncle

**'prua** *nf* *Naut* prow

**pru'dente** *a* prudent

**pru'denza** *nf* prudence; **per ~** as a precaution

**prudenzi'ale** *a* prudential

**'prudere** *vi* itch

**'prugna** *nf* plum. **~ secca** prune. **~ selvatica** damson

**'prugno** *nm* plum[-tree]

**'prugnolo** *nm* sloe

**pruri'gnoso** *a* itchy

**pru'rito** *nm* itch

**P.S.** *abbr* (**Pubblica Sicurezza**) police

**pseu'donimo** *nm* pseudonym

**psica'nalisi** *nf* psychoanalysis

**psicana'lista** *nmf* psychoanalyst

**psicanaliz'zare** *vt* psychoanalyse

**'psiche** *nf* psyche

**psiche'delico** *a* psychedelic

**psichi'atra** *nmf* psychiatrist

**psichia'tria** *nf* psychiatry

**psichi'atrico** *a* psychiatric

**'psichico** *a* mental

**psico'farmaco** *nm* drug that affects the mind

**psicolo'gia** *nf* psychology

**psico'logico** *a* psychological

**psi'cologo, -a** *nmf* psychologist

**psico'patico, -a** *a* psychopathic ● *nmf* psychopath

**psicopedago'gia** *nf* educational psychology

**psi'cosi** *nf inv* psychosis

**psicoso'matico** *a* psychosomatic

**psicotera'peuta** *nmf* psychotherapist

**psicotera'pista** *nmf* psychotherapist

**psi'cotico, -a** *a & nmf* psychotic

**PT** *abbr* (**Posta e Telegrafi**) PO

**puàh** *int* yuck!

**pub** *nm* pub

**pubbli'care** *vt* publish

**pubblicazi'one** *nf* publication. **pubblicazioni** *pl* (*di matrimonio*) banns. ~ **periodica** periodical

**pubbli'cista** *nmf Journ* correspondent

**pubblicità** *nf inv* publicity, advertising; (*annuncio*) advertisement, advert; **fare ~ a qcsa** advertise sth; **piccola ~** small advertisements

**pubblici'tario** *a* advertising

**'pubblico** *a* public; **scuola pubblica** state school ● *nm* public; (*spettatori*) audience; **in ~** in public; **grande ~** general public. **Pubblica Sicurezza** police. **~ ministero** public prosecutor. **~ ufficiale** civil servant

**'pube** *nm* pubis

**pubertà** *nf* puberty

**pu'dico** *a* modest

**pu'dore** *nm* modesty

**pue'rile** *a* children's; *pej* childish

**'puerpera** *nf* new mother

**puerpe'rale** *a* of childbirth, puerperal *fml*; (*depressione*) postnatal

**puer'perio** *nm* postnatal period

**pugi'lato** *nm* boxing

**'pugile** *nm* boxer

**'Puglia** *nf* Apulia

**pugli'ese** *a & nmf* Apulian

**pugna'lare** *vt* stab

**pugna'lata** *nf* stab

**pu'gnale** *nm* dagger

**'pugno** *nm* fist; (*colpo*) punch; (*manciata*) fistful; (*fig: numero limitato*) handful; **dare un ~ a** punch; **di proprio ~** (*scrivere*) in one's own hand; **fare a pugni** (*colori:*) clash; **tenere in ~** (*situazione*) have under control; have in the palm of one's hand (*persona*); **un ~ in un occhio** *fig* an eyesore. **~ di ferro** iron fist

**'pula** *nf sl* **la ~** the fuzz

**'pulce** *nf* flea; (*microfono*) bug; **mettere la ~ nell'orecchio a qcno** sow a doubt in sb's mind

**pul'cino** *nm* chick; (*nel calcio*) junior

**pu'ledra** *nf* filly

**pu'ledro** *nm* foal, colt

**pu'leggia** *nf* pulley

**pu'lire** *vt* clean. **~ a secco** dry-clean; **far ~ qcsa** have sth cleaned

**puliscipi'edi** *nm inv* boot scraper

**pu'lito** *a* clean

**puli'tura** *nf* cleaning

**puli'zia** *nf* (*il pulire*) cleaning; (*l'essere pulito*) cleanliness; **pulizie** *pl* housework; **fare le pulizie** do the cleaning. **~ personale** personal hygiene

**'pullman** *nm inv* coach, bus; (*urbano*) bus; **gita in ~** coach trip

**pull'over** *nm* pullover

**pul'mino** *nm* minibus

**'pulpito** *nm* pulpit

**pul'sante** *nm* button; *Electr* [push-]button. **~ di accensione** on/off switch. **~ di alimentazione** power switch

**pul'sare** *vi* pulsate

**pulsazi'one** *nf* pulsation

**pul'viscolo** *nm* dust

**'puma** *nm inv* puma

**pun'gente** *a* prickly; (*insetto*) stinging; (*odore ecc*) sharp

**'pungere** *vt* prick; (*insetto:*) sting; **~ qcno sul vivo** cut sb to the quick

**pungersi** *vr* prick oneself; **~ un dito** prick one's finger

**pungigli'one** *nm* sting

**pungo'lare** *vt* goad

**pu'nire** *vt* punish

**puni'tivo** *a* punitive

**punizi'one** *nf* punishment; *Sport* penalty; (*in calcio*) free kick. **~ corporale** corporal punishment

**'punta** *nf* point; (*estremità*) tip; (*di monte*) peak, top; (*un po'*) pinch; *Sport* forward; **doppie punte** (*di capelli*) split ends; **di ~** (*ore*) peak; (*personaggio*) leading

**pun'tare** *vt* point; (*spingere con forza*) push; (*scommettere*) bet; (*fam: appuntare*) fasten ● *vi* **~ su** rely on; (*scommettere*) bet on; **~ verso** (*dirigersi*) head for; **~ a** aspire to; **punta e clicca** *Comput* point and click

**punta'spilli** *nm inv* pincushion

**pun'tata** *nf* (*di una storia*) instalment; (*televisiva*) episode; (*al gioco*) stake, bet; (*breve visita*) flying visit; **a puntate** serialized, in instalments; **fare una ~ a/in** pop over to (*luogo*)

**punteggia'tura** *nf* punctuation

**pun'teggio** *nm* score

**puntel'lare** *vt* prop

**pun'tello** *nm* prop

**punteru'olo** *nm* awl

**pun'tiglio** *nm* spite; (*ostinazione*) obstinacy

**puntigli'oso** *a* punctilious, pernickety *pej*

**pun'tina** *nf* (*da disegno*) drawing pin, thumb tack *Am*; (*di giradischi*) stylus. **~ da disegno** drawing pin, thumb tack *Am*

**pun'tine** *nfpl* points

**pun'tino** *nm* dot; **a ~** perfectly; (*cotto*) to a T. **puntini** *pl* [**di sospensione**] suspension points

**'punto** *nm* point; (*in cucito, Med*) stitch; (*in punteggiatura*) full stop; **in che ~?** where, exactly?; **di ~ in bianco** all of a sudden; **essere sul ~ di fare qcsa** be on the point of doing sth, be about to do sth; **in ~** sharp; **mettere a ~** put right; *fig* fine-tune; tune up (*motore*); **messa a ~** fine tuning; **due punti** colon. **punti** *pl* **cardinali** points of the compass. **~ cieco** blind spot. **~ di congela-**

**mento** freezing point. ~ **croce** cross-stitch. ~ **debole** blind spot. ~ **di domanda** question mark. ~ **di ebollizione** boiling point. ~ **esclamativo** exclamation mark. ~ **di fuga** vanishing point. ~ **di fusione** melting point. ~ **d'incontro** meeting-point. ~ **di infiammabilità** flashpoint. ~ **interrogativo** question mark. ~ **nero** Med blackhead. ~ **di pareggio** Fin breakeven point. ~ **di partenza** starting point. ~ **di riferimento** landmark; (per la qualità) benchmark. ~ **di rottura** breaking point. ~ **a smerlo** blanket stitch. ~ **di vendita** point of sale, outlet; **pubblicità al** ~ ~ ~ point-of-sale publicity. ~ **e virgola** semicolon. ~ **di vista** point of view

**puntu'ale** a punctual; **essere** ~ be punctual, be on time

**puntualità** nf punctuality

**puntualiz'zare** vt make clear, clarify

**puntual'mente** adv punctually, on time; (come al solito) as usual

**pun'tura** nf (di insetto) sting; (di ago ecc) prick; Med puncture; (iniezione) injection; (fitta) stabbing pain. ~ **d'ape** bee sting. ~ **d'insetto** insect bite. ~ **di spillo** pinprick. ~ **di zanzara** mosquito bite

**punzecchi'are** vt prick; fig tease

**punzo'nare** vt Techn punch, stamp

**pun'zone** nm punch

**può** vedi **potere**; ~ **darsi** maybe, perhaps

'**pupa** nf doll

**pu'pazzo** nm puppet. ~ **di neve** snowman

**pup'illa** nf Anat pupil

**pu'pillo, -a** nmf Jur ward; (di professore) favourite

**purché** conj provided

'**pure** adv too, also; (concessivo) **fate** ~! please do! ● conj (tuttavia) yet; (anche se) even if; **pur di** just to; **io** ~ me too; **è venuto** ~ **lui** he came too, he also came

**purè** nm inv purée. ~ **di patate** mashed potatoes, creamed potatoes

**pu'rezza** nf purity

'**purga** nf purge

**pur'gante** nm laxative

**pur'gare** vt purge

**purga'torio** nm purgatory

**purifi'care** vt purify

**purificazi'one** nf purification

**pu'rista** nmf purist

**puri'tano, -a** a & nmf Puritan

'**puro** a pure; (vino ecc) undiluted; **per** ~ **caso** by sheer chance, purely by chance. ~ **cotone** nm pure cotton, 100% cotton. **pura lana vergine** nf pure new wool. **pura seta** nf pure silk

**puro'sangue** a & nm thoroughbred

**pur'troppo** adv unfortunately

'**pus** nm pus

'**pustola** nf pimple

**puti'ferio** nm uproar

**putre'fare** vi putrefy

**putre'farsi** vr putrefy

**putre'fatto** a rotten

**putrefazi'one** nf putrefaction

'**putrido** a putrid

**putt** nm inv putt

**put'tana** nf vulg whore

'**puzza** nf stink; **avere la** ~ **sotto il naso** be sniffy

**puz'zare** vi anche fig stink; ~ **di bruciato** fig smell fishy; ~ **d'imbroglio** stink; ~ **di corruzione** stink of corruption; **questa storia mi puzza** the story stinks

'**puzzo** nm stink

'**puzzola** nf polecat

**puzzo'lente** a stinking

**puz'zone** nm fam bastard

**p.zza** abbr (piazza) Sq.

# Qq

**QI** abbr (quoziente di intelligenza) IQ

**qua** adv here; **da un anno in** ~ for the last year; **da quando in** ~? since when?; **di** ~ this way; **di** ~ **di** on this side of; ~ **dentro** in here; ~ **sotto** under here; ~ **vicino** near here; ~ **e là** here and there

'**quacchero, -a** nmf Quaker

**qua'derno** nm exercise book; (per appunti) notebook. ~ **a quadretti** maths exercise book. ~ **a righe** lined exercise book

**quadrango'lare** a (forma) quadrangular; **incontro** ~ Sport four-sided tournament

**qua'drangolo** nm quadrangle

**qua'drante** nm quadrant; (di orologio) dial

**qua'drare** vt square; (contabilità) balance ● vi fit in

**qua'drato** a square; (equilibrato) level-headed ● nm square; (nel pugilato) ring; **al** ~ squared

**quadra'tura** nf Math squaring; (di bilancio) balancing

**quadret'tare** vt divide into small squares

**quadret'tato** a squared; (carta) graph attrib; (tessuto) check, checked

**qua'dretto** nm square; (piccolo quadro) small picture; **a quadretti** (tessuto) check

**quadrico'mia** nf four-colour printing

**quadrien'nale** a (che dura quattro anni) four-year; (ogni quattro anni) four-yearly

**quadri'foglio** *nm* four-leaf clover

**qua'driglia** *nf* square dance

**quadri'latero** *nm* quadrilateral

**quadri'mestre** *nm* (*periodo*) four-month period; *Sch* term

**quadrimo'tore** *nm* four-engined plane

**quadri'nomio** *nm* *Math* quadrinomial

**quadripar'tito** *a* four-party ● *nm* (*politica*) four-party government

**quadri'plegico** *a* quadriplegic

**'quadro** *nm* picture, painting; (*quadrato*) square; (*fig: scena*) sight; (*tabella*) table; *Theat* scene; (*dirigente*) executive; **fare il ~ della situazione** outline the situation; **fuori ~** *Cinema, TV* out of shot; **quadri** *pl* (*carte*) diamonds; **a quadri** (*tessuto, giacca, motivo*) check, checked. **~ clinico** case history. **~ di comando** control panel. **quadri** *pl* **direttivi** senior management. **~ di distribuzione** *Electr* switchboard. **quadri** *pl* **intermedi** middle management. **~ degli interruttori** switch panel

**qua'drupede** *nm* quadruped

**quadrupli'care** *vt* quadruple

**quadrupli'carsi** *vr* quadruple

**qua'druplice** *a* quadruple

**'quadruplo** *a & nm* quadruple

**quaggiù** *adv* down here

**'quaglia** *nf* quail

**'qualche** *a* (*alcuni*) a few, some; (*un certo*) some; (*in interrogazioni*) any; **ho ~ problema** I have a few problems, I have some problems; **~ tempo fa** some time ago; **hai ~ libro italiano?** have you any Italian books?; **posso prendere ~ libro?** can I take some books?; **in ~ modo** somehow; **in ~ posto** somewhere; **~ volta** sometimes; **~ cosa = qualcosa**

**qualche'duno** *pron* somebody, someone

**qual'cosa** *pron* something; (*in interrogazioni*) anything; **qualcos'altro** something else; **vuoi qualcos'altro?** would you like anything else?; **~ di strano** something strange; **vuoi ~ da mangiare?** would you like something to eat?; **vuoi ~ da bere?** would you like a drink?, would you like something to drink?

**qual'cuno** *pron* someone, somebody; (*in interrogazioni*) anyone, anybody; (*alcuni*) some; (*in interrogazioni*) any; **c'è ~?** is anybody in?; **qualcun altro** someone else, somebody else; **c'è qualcun altro che aspetta?** is anybody else waiting?; **ho letto ~ dei suoi libri** I've read some of his books; **conosci ~ dei suoi amici?** do you know any of his friends?

**'quale** *a* which; (*indeterminato*) what; (*come*) as, like; **~ macchina è la tua?** which car is yours?; **~ motivo avrà di parlare così?** what reason would he have to speak like that?; **~ onore!** what an honour!; **città quali Venezia** towns like Venice; **~ che sia la tua opinione** whatever you may think ● *pron inter* which [one]; **~ preferisci?** which [one] do you prefer? ● *pron rel* **il/la ~** (*persona*)

who; (*animale, cosa*) that, which; (*oggetto: con prep*) whom; (*oggetto: animale, cosa*) which; **ho incontrato tua madre, la ~ mi ha detto...** I met your mother who told me...; **l'ufficio nel ~ lavoro** the office in which I work; **l'uomo con il ~ parlavo** the man to whom I was speaking ● *adv* (*come*) as

**qua'lifica** *nf* qualification; (*titolo*) title

**qualifi'cabile** *a* qualifiable

**qualifi'care** *vt* qualify; (*definire*) define

**qualifi'carsi** *vr* be placed

**qualifica'tivo** *a* qualifying

**qualifi'cato** *a* (*operaio*) semi-skilled

**qualificazi'one** *nf* qualification

**qualità** *nf inv* quality; (*specie*) kind; **in ~ di** in one's capacity as; **di prima ~** high quality; **di ottima/cattiva ~** top/poor quality

**qualitativa'mente** *adv* qualitatively

**qualita'tivo** *a* qualitative

**qua'lora** *conj* in case

**qual'siasi, qua'lunque** *a* any; (*non importa quale*) whatever; (*ordinario*) ordinary; **dammi una penna ~** give me any pen [whatsoever]; **farei ~ cosa** I would do anything; **~ cosa io faccia** whatever I do; **~ persona** anyone, anybody; **in ~ caso** in any case; **uno ~** any one, whichever; **l'uomo qualunque** the man in the street; **vivo in una casa ~** I live in an ordinary house

**qualun'quismo** *nm* lack of political views

**qualunqu'ista** *nmf* (*menefreghista*) person with no political views

**'quando** *conj & adv* when; **da ~ ti ho visto** since I saw you; **da ~ esci con lui?** how long have you been going out with him?; **da ~ in qua?** since when?; **~... ~...** sometimes..., sometimes...; **continua ad insistere ~ sa di avere torto** he keeps on insisting even when he knows he's wrong

**quantifi'cabile** *a* quantifiable

**quantifi'care** *vt* quantify

**quantità** *nf inv* quantity; **una ~ di** (*gran numero*) a great deal of

**quantitativa'mente** *adv* quantitatively

**quantita'tivo** *nm* amount ● *a* quantitative

**'quanto** *a inter* how much; (*con nomi plurali*) how many; (*in esclamazione*) what a lot of; (*tempo*) how long; **quanti anni hai?** how old are you? ● *a rel* as much... as; (*tempo*) as long as; (*con nomi plurali*) as many... as; **prendi ~ denaro ti serve** take as much money as you need; **prendi quanti libri vuoi** take as many books as you like ● *pron inter* how much; (*quanto tempo*) how long; (*plurale*) how many; **quanti ne abbiamo oggi?** what date is it today? ● *pron rel* as much as; (*quanto tempo*) as long as; (*plurale*) as many as; **prendine ~/ quanti ne vuoi** take as much/as many as you like; **stai ~ vuoi** stay as long as you like; **questo è ~** that's it ● *adv inter* how much; (*quanto tempo*) how long; **~ sei alto?** how tall are you?; **~ hai aspettato?** how long did you wait for?; **~ costa?** how much is it?; **~ mi dispiace!** I'm so sorry!; **~ è bello!** how nice! ● *adv rel* as much as; **lavoro ~ posso** I work as much as I can: **è tanto intelligente ~ bello** he's as intelligent as he's good-looking: **in ~** (*in qualità di*) as; (*poiché*) since; **~ a** as for; **in ~ a me** as far as I'm concerned; **per ~** however; **per ~ ne sappia** as far as I know; **per ~ mi riguarda** as far as I'm concerned; **per ~ mi sia simpatico** much as I like him; **~ prima** (*al più presto*) as soon as possible

**quan'tunque** *conj* although

**qua'ranta** *a & nm* forty

**quaran'tena** *nf* quarantine

**quaran'tenne** *a* forty-year-old; (*sulla quarantina*) in his/her forties ● *nmf* forty-year-old; (*sulla quarantina*) person in his/her forties

**quaran'tennio** *nm* period of forty years

**quaran'tesimo** *a & nm* fortieth

**quaran'tina** *nf* **una ~** about forty

**qua'resima** *nf* Lent

**quar'tetto** *nm* quartet

**quarti'ere** *nm* district, area; *Mil* quarters *pl.* **quartieri** *pl* **alti** smart districts. **quartieri** *pl* **bassi** poor areas. **~ cinese** Chinatown. **~ dormitorio** dormitory town. **~ generale** headquarters. **~ residenziale** residential area

**quar'tino** *nm* (*strumento musicale*) instrument similar to a clarinet; *Typ* quarto; (*di vino*) quarter litre

**'quarto** *a* fourth ● *nm* fourth; (*quarta parte*) quarter; **le sette e un ~** [a] quarter past seven, [a] quarter after seven *Am*; **a tre quarti** (*giacca, maniche*) three-quarter length. **quarti** *pl* **di finale** quarter-finals. **~ d'ora** quarter of an hour ● *nf* (*marcia*) fourth [gear]

**quarto'genito, -a** *nmf* fourth child

**quar'tultimo, -a** *a & nmf* fourth last

**'quarzo** *nm* quartz; **al ~** quartz. **~ rosa** rose quartz

**'quasi** *adv* almost, nearly; **~ mai** hardly ever ● *conj* (*come se*) as if; **~ ~ sto a casa** I'm tempted to stay home

**quassù** *adv* up here

**qua'terna** *nf* (*lotto, tombola*) set of four winning numbers

**quater'nario** *nm* (*era*) Quaternary

**'quatto** *a* crouching; (*silenzioso*) silent; **starsene ~ ~** keep very quiet

**quattordi'cenne** *a & nmf* fourteen-year-old

**quattordi'cesimo** *a & nm* fourteenth

**quat'tordici** *a & nm* fourteen

**quat'trini** *nmpl* money *sg*, dosh *sg fam*

**'quattro** *a & nm* four; **dirne ~ a qcno** give sb a piece of one's mind; **farsi in ~** (*per qcno/per fare qcsa*) go to a lot of trouble (*for* sb/to do sth); **in ~ e quattr'otto** in a flash. **~ per ~** *nm inv Auto* four-wheel drive [vehicle]; **a ~ tempi** *Auto* four-stroke

**quat'trocchi** *adv* **a ~** in private

**quattrocen'tesco** *a* fifteenth-century

**quattro'cento** *a & nm* four hundred; **il Q~** the fifteenth century

**quattro'mila** *a & nm* four thousand

**Qué'bec** *nm* Quebec

**'quello** *a* that (*pl* those): **quell'albero** that tree: **quegli alberi** those trees; **quel cane** that dog; **quei cani** those dogs ● *pron* that [one] (*pl* those [ones]); **~ lì** that one over there; **~ che** the one that; (*ciò che*) what; **quelli che** the ones that, those that; **~ a destra** the one on the right

**'quercia** *nf* oak; **di ~** oak

**que'rela** *nf* [legal] action

**quere'lante** *nmf* plaintiff

**quere'lare** *vt* bring an action against

**quere'lato, -a** *nmf* defendant

**que'sito** *nm* question

**questio'nare** *vi* dispute

**questio'nario** *nm* questionnaire

**quest'ione** *nf* question; (*faccenda*) matter; (*litigio*) quarrel; **in ~** in doubt; **è fuori ~** it's out of the question; **è ~ di vita o di morte** it's a matter of life and death; **mettere qcsa in ~** cast doubt on sth; **una ~ personale** a personal matter

**'questo** *a* this (*pl* these) ● *pron* this [one] (*pl* these [ones]); **~ qui, ~ qua** this one here; **~ è quello che a detto** that's what he said; **per ~** for this *or* that reason; **quest'oggi** today

**que'store** *nm* chief of police

**'questua** *nf* collection

**que'stura** *nf* police headquarters

**qui** *adv* here; **da ~ in poi, da ~ in avanti** from now on; **di ~ a una settimana** in a week's time; **fin ~** (*di tempo*) up till now, until now; **~ dentro** in here; **~ sotto** under here; **qui vicino** *adv* near here ● *nm* **~ pro quo** misunderstanding

**quie'scenza** *nf* (*di vulcano*) dormancy; (*pensione*) retirement; **trattamento di ~** retirement package

**quie'tanza** *nf* receipt

**quie'tare** *vt* calm

**quie'tarsi** *vr* calm down

**qui'ete** *nf* quiet; **disturbo della ~ pubblica** breach of the peace; **stato di ~** *Phys* state of rest

**qui'eto** *a* quiet

**'quindi** *adv* then ● *conj* therefore

**quindi'cenne** *a & nmf* fifteen-year-old

**quindi'cesimo** *a & nm* fifteenth

**'quindici** *a & nm* fifteen; **~ giorni** a fortnight *Br*, two weeks *pl*

**quindi'cina** *nf* **una ~** about fifteen; **una ~ di giorni** a fortnight *Br*, two weeks *pl*

**quindici'nale** *a* fortnightly *Br*, twice-monthly ● *nm* fortnightly magazine *Br*, twice-monthly magazine

**quinquen'nale** *a* (*che dura cinque anni*) five-year; (*ogni cinque anni*) five-yearly

**quin'quennio** *nm* [period of] five years

**'quinta** *nf Auto* fifth [gear], overdrive

**quin'tale** *nm* a hundred kilograms

**'quinte** *nfpl Theat* wings

**quintes'senza** *nf* quintessence

**quin'tetto** *nm* quintet

**'quinto** *a & nm* fifth

**quintupli'care** *vt* quintuple

**quin'tuplo** *a* quintuple

**qui'squiglia** *nf* trifle; **perdersi in quisquiglie** get bogged down in details

**quiz** *nm inv* [**gioco a**] ~ quiz game. ~ **radiofonico** radio quiz

**'quota** *nf* quota; (*rata*) instalment; (*altitudine*) height; *Aeron* altitude, height; (*ippica*) odds *pl*; **perdere/prendere** ~ lose/gain altitude *o* height: **da alta** ~ high-flying. ~ **fissa** fixed amount. ~ **non imponibile** personal allowance. ~ **di iscrizione** entry fee; (*di club*) membership fee. ~ **di mercato** market share. ~ **zero** sea level

**quo'tare** *vt Comm* quote

**quo'tato** *a* quoted; **essere** ~ **in Borsa** be quoted on the Stock Exchange

**quotazi'one** *nf* quotation. ~ **d'acquisto** buying rate. ~ **ufficiale** (*in Borsa*) official quotation. ~ **di vendita** selling rate

**quotidiana'mente** *adv* daily

**quotidi'ano** *a* daily; (*ordinario*) everyday ● *nm* daily [paper]

**'quoto** *nm Math* quotient

**quozi'ente** *nm* quotient. ~ **d'intelligenza** intelligence quotient, IQ. ~ **di purezza** purity

# Rr

**ra'barbaro** *nm* rhubarb

**'rabbia** *nf* rage; (*ira*) anger; *Med* rabies *sg*; **che** ~! what a nuisance!; **mi fa** ~ it makes me angry

**'rabbico** *a* ‹*virus*› rabies *attrib*

**rab'bino** *nm* rabbi

**rabbiosa'mente** *adv* furiously

**rabbi'oso** *a* hot-tempered; *Med* rabid; (*violento*) violent

**rabboc'care** *vt* top up ‹*fiasco*›

**rabbo'nire** *vt* pacify

**rabbo'nirsi** *vr* calm down

**rabbrivi'dire** *vi* shudder; (*di freddo*) shiver

**rabbuf'fare** *vt* reprimand; ruffle ‹*capelli*›

**rab'buffo** *nm* reprimand

**rabbui'arsi** *vr* get dark; ‹*viso:*› darken

**rabdo'mante** *nmf* water diviner

**rabdoman'zia** *nf* water divining

**raccapez'zare** *vt* put together

**raccapez'zarsi** *vr* see one's way ahead

**raccapricci'ante** *a* horrifying

**raccatta'palle** *nm inv* ball boy ● *nf inv* ball girl

**raccat'tare** *vt* pick up

**rac'chetta** *nf* racket. ~ **da neve** snowshoe. ~ **da ping pong** table-tennis bat. ~ **da sci** ski stick, ski pole. ~ **da tennis** tennis racket

**'racchio** *a fam* ugly

**racchi'udere** *vt* contain

**rac'cogliere** *vt* pick; (*da terra*) pick up; (*mietere*) harvest; (*collezionare*) collect; (*radunare*) gather; win ‹*voti ecc*›; (*dare asilo a*) take in

**rac'cogliersi** *vr* gather; (*concentrarsi*) collect one's thoughts

**raccogli'mento** *nm* concentration

**raccogli'|tore, -'trice** *nmf* collector ● *nm* ~ [**a fogli mobili**] ring-binder

**rac'colta** *nf* collection; (*di scritti*) compilation; (*del grano ecc*) harvesting; (*adunata*) gathering; **chiamare a** ~ call *o* gather together. ~ **differenziata** *collection of items for recycling.* ~ **di fondi** fund-raising

**rac'colto, -a** *pp di* **raccogliere** ● *a* (*rannicchiato*) hunched; (*intimo*) cosy; (*concentrato*) engrossed ● *nm* (*mietitura*) harvest

**raccoman'dabile** *a* advisable; **poco** ~ ‹*persona*› shady

**raccoman'dare** *vt* recommend; (*affidare*) entrust

**raccoman'darsi** *vr* (*implorare*) beg

**raccoman'data** *nf* letter sent by recorded delivery; **per** ~ by recorded delivery. ~ **con ricevuta di ritorno** *letter sent by recorded delivery with acknowledgement of receipt*

**raccoman'data-e'spresso** *nf express recorded delivery service*

**raccomandazi'one** *nf* recommendation

**raccomo'dare** *vt* repair

**raccon'tare** *vt* tell

**rac'conto** *nm* story

**raccorci'are** *vt* shorten

**raccorci'arsi** *vr* become shorter; ‹*giorni:*› draw in

**raccor'dare** *vt* join

**rac'cordo** *nm* connection; (*stradale*) feeder. ~ **anulare** ring road. ~ **autostradale** motorway junction *Br*. intersection. ~ **ferroviario** siding. ~ **a gomito** elbow

**ra'chitico** *a* rickety; (*poco sviluppato*) stunted

**racimo'lare** *vt* scrape together

**'racket** *nm inv* racket

**'rada** *nf Naut* roads *pl*

**'radar** *nm* radar; **uomo** ~ air traffic controller

**radden'sare** *vt* thicken

**radden'sarsi** *vr* thicken

**raddob'bare** *vt* refit

**rad'dobbo** *nm* refit

**raddol'cire** *vt* sweeten; *fig* soften

**raddol'cirsi** *vr* become milder; ⟨*carattere:*⟩ mellow

**raddoppia'mento** *nm* doubling

**raddoppi'are** *vt* double

**rad'doppio** *nm* doubling; (*equitazione*) gallop; (*biliardo*) double

**raddriz'zabile** *a* which can be straightened

**raddriz'zare** *vt* straighten

**raddrizza'tore** *nm* (*di corrente*) rectifier

**ra'dente** *a* grazing, shaving; **tiro ~** *Mil* grazing fire; *Sport* low shot just skimming the surface; **volo ~** *Aeron* hedge-hopping

**'radere** *vt* shave; graze ⟨*muro*⟩; **~ al suolo** raze [to the ground]

**'radersi** *vr* shave

**radi'ale** *a* radial

**radi'ante** *a* radiant ● *nm Math* radian

**radi'are** *vt* strike off; **~ dall'albo** strike off ⟨*medico*⟩; debar ⟨*avvocato*⟩

**radia'tore** *nm* radiator

**radiazi'one** *nf* radiation. **~ nucleare** nuclear radiation

**'radica** *nf* briar

**radi'cale** *a* radical ● *nm Gram* root; *Pol* radical

**radical'mente** *adv* radically

**radi'carsi** *vr* **~ in** be rooted in

**radi'cato** *a* deep-seated

**ra'dicchio** *nm* chicory

**ra'dice** *nf* root; **mettere [le] radici** ⟨*pianta:*⟩ take root; *fig* put down roots. **~ quadrata** square root

**'radio** *nf inv* radio; **via ~** by radio; **contatto ~** radio contact; **ponte ~** radio link. **~ pirata** pirate radio. **~ portatile** portable radio. **~ ricevente** receiver. **~ [a] transistor** transistor radio. **~ trasmittente** transmitter ● *nm Chem* radium

**radioama|'tore, -'trice** *nmf* radio ham

**radioascolta|'tore, -'trice** *nmf* listener

**radioassi'stito** *a* radio-assisted

**radioattività** *nf* radioactivity

**radioat'tivo** *a* radioactive

**radiobiolo'gia** *nf* radiobiology

**radio'bussola** *nf* radio compass

**radiocoman'dare** *vt* operate by remote control

**radiocoman'dato** *a* remote-controlled, radio-controlled

**radio'cronaca** *nf* radio commentary; **fare la ~ di** commentate on

**radiocro'nista** *nmf* radio reporter

**radiodiffusi'one** *nf* broadcasting

**radio'faro** *nm* radio beacon

**radio'fonico** *a* radio *attrib*

**radiofre'quenza** *nf* radio frequency

**radiogo'niometro** *nm* direction finder, radiogoniometer

**radiogra'fare** *vt* X-ray

**radiogra'fia** *nf* X-ray [photograph]; (*radiologia*) radiography; **fare una ~** ⟨*paziente:*⟩ have an X-ray; ⟨*dottore:*⟩ take an X-ray

**radio'lina** *nf* transistor

**radiolocaliz'zare** *vt* locate by radar

**radi'ologo, -a** *nmf* radiologist

**radio'onda** *nf* radio wave

**radioregistra'tore** *nm* **~ portatile** portable radio cassette recorder

**radiosco'pia** *nf Med* radioscopy

**radio'scopico** *a* radioscopic

**radi'oso** *a* radiant

**radio'spia** *nf* bug

**radio'sveglia** *nf* radio alarm, clock radio

**radio'taxi** *nm inv* radio taxi

**radiote'lefono** *nm* radio-telephone; (*privato*) cordless [phone]

**radiotelevi'sivo** *a* broadcasting *attrib*

**radiotera'pia** *nf* radiotherapy

**radiotra'smettere** *vt* radio

**radiotrasmetti'tore** *nm* radio

**radiotrasmit'tente** *nf* radio station

**'rado** *a* sparse; (*non frequente*) rare; **di ~** seldom

**radu'nare** *vt* gather [together]

**radu'narsi** *vr* gather [together]

**radu'nata** *nf* gathering. **~ sediziosa** seditious assembly

**ra'duno** *nm* meeting; *Sport* rally

**ra'dura** *nf* clearing

**'rafano** *nm* horseradish

**raffazzo'nato** *a* ⟨*discorso, lavoro*⟩ botched

**raf'fermo** *a* stale

**'raffica** *nf* gust; (*di armi da fuoco*) burst; (*di domande, insulti*) barrage

**raffigu'rare** *vt* represent

**raffigurazi'one** *nf* representation

**raffi'nare** *vt* refine

**raffinata'mente** *adv* elegantly

**raffina'tezza** *nf* refinement

**raffi'nato** *a* refined

**raffine'ria** *nf* refinery. **~ di petrolio** oil refinery

**rafforza'mento** *nm* reinforcement; (*di muscolatura, carattere*) strengthening

**rafforz'are** *vt* reinforce

**rafforza'tivo** *a Gram* intensifying ● *nm Gram* intensifier

**raffredda'mento** *nm* (*processo*) cooling; **di ~** cooling. **~ ad acqua** water-cooling. **~ ad aria** air-cooling

**raffred'dare** *vt* cool

**raffred'darsi** *vr* get cold; (*prendere un raffreddore*) catch a cold; ⟨*sentimento, passione:*⟩ cool [off]

**raffred'dato** *a* **essere ~** ⟨*persona*⟩ have a cold

**raffred'dore** *nm* cold; **avere il ~** have a cold. **~ da fieno** hay fever

**raf'fronto** *nm* comparison

**'rafia** *nf* raffia

**Rag.** *abbr* ragioniere

**ra'gazza** *nf* girl; (*fidanzata*) girlfriend; **nome da ~** maiden name. **~ copertina** cover girl. **~ madre** unmarried mother. **~ alla pari** au pair [girl]. **~ squillo** call girl

**ragaz'zata** *nf* prank

ra'gazzo *nm* boy; (*fidanzato*) boyfriend; da ~ (*da giovane*) as a boy. ~ padre unmarried father. ~ di strada guttersnipe. ~ di vita rent boy

ragge'lare *vt fig* freeze

ragge'larsi *vr fig* turn to ice

raggi'ante *a* radiant; ~ di successo flushed with success

raggi'era *nf* a ~ with a pattern like spokes radiating from a centre

raggi'era *nf* (*di ruota*) spokes *pl*

'raggio *nm* ray; *Math* radius; (*di ruota*) spoke; a raggi infrarossi infrared. ~ d'azione range. ~ laser laser beam. ~ di luna moonbeam. ~ di sole ray of sunshine, sunbeam. ~ di speranza ray of hope. ~ ultravioletto ultraviolet ray. raggi *pl* X X-rays

raggi'rare *vt* trick

rag'giro *nm* trick

raggi'ungere *vt* reach; (*conseguire*) achieve

raggiun'gibile *a* (*luogo*) within reach

raggiungi'mento *nm* attainment

raggomito'lare *vt* wind

raggomito'larsi *vr* curl up

raggranel'lare *vt* scrape together

raggrin'zire *vt* wrinkle

raggrin'zirsi *vr* wrinkle

raggru'mare *vt* curdle (*latte*)

raggru'marsi *vr* (*latte*) curdle

raggruppa'mento *nm* (*gruppo*) group; (*azione*) grouping; *Comm* groupage

raggrup'pare *vt* group together

ragguagli'are *vt* compare; (*informare*) inform

raggu'aglio *nm* comparison; (*informazione*) information

ragguar'devole *a* considerable

'ragia *nf* resin; acqua ~ turpentine

ragià *nm inv* rajah

ragiona'mento *nm* reasoning; (*discussione*) discussion. ~ per assurdo reductio ad absurdum

ragio'nare *vi* reason; (*discutere*) discuss

ragio'nato *a* (*argomento*) reasoned; (*cruciverba*) cryptic

ragi'one *nf* reason; (*ciò che è giusto*) right; a ~ o a torto rightly or wrongly; aver ~ be right; perdere la ~ go out of one's mind; ragion veduta after due consideration; prenderle/darle di santa ~ get/give a good walloping. ragion d'essere raison d'être. ~ di scambio terms of trade. ~ sociale company name. ragion di Stato reasons of State

ragione'ria *nf* accountancy; (*scuola*) *secondary school which provides training in accountancy*

ragio'nevole *a* reasonable

ragionevol'mente *adv* reasonably

ragioni'ere, -a *nmf* accountant

ra'glan *a inv* (*manica*) raglan

ragli'are *vi* bray

'raglio *nm* bray

ragna'tela *nf* cobweb

'ragno *nm* spider

ragù *nm inv* meat sauce

RAI *nf abbr* (Radio Audizioni Italiane) Italian public broadcasting company

'raid *nm inv* raid

'raion[R] *nm* rayon[R]

ra'lenti *nm* al ~ in slow motion

rallegra'menti *nmpl* congratulations

ralle'grare *vt* gladden

ralle'grarsi *vr* rejoice; ~ con qcno congratulate sb

rallenta'mento *nm* slowing down

rallen'tare *vt/i* slow down; (*allentare*) slacken

rallen'tarsi *vr* slow down

rallenta'tore *nm* (*su strada*) speed bump; al ~ in slow motion

'rally *nm inv* rally

RAM *nf inv* RAM

ramai'olo *nm* ladle

raman'zina *nf* reprimand

ra'mare *vt* stake (*pianta*)

ra'marro *nm* (*animale*) type of lizard

ra'mato *a* (*capelli*) copper[-coloured], coppery

'rame *nm* copper; color ~ copper-coloured

ramifi'care *vi* (*pianta:*) put out branches

ramifi'carsi *vr* (*pianta:*) put out branches; (*strada, fiume, matematica ecc:*) branch; (*teoria:*) ramify, branch

ramificazi'one *nf* ramification

ra'mino *nm* rummy

rammari'carsi *vr* ~ di regret; (*lamentarsi*) complain (di about)

ram'marico *nm* regret

rammen'dare *vt* darn

ram'mendo *nm* darning

rammen'tare *vt* remember; ~ qcsa a qcno (*richiamare alla memoria*) remind sb of sth

rammen'tarsi *vr* remember

rammol'lire *vt* soften

rammol'lirsi *vr* go soft

rammol'lito, -a *nmf* wimp

'ramo *nm* branch

ramo'scello *nm* twig

'rampa *nf* (*di scale*) flight. ~ d'accesso slip road. ~ di carico loading ramp. ~ di lancio launch[ing] pad

ram'pante *a* (*leone, cavallo*) rampant; giovane ~ yuppie

rampi'cante *a* climbing ● *nm Bot* creeper

ram'pino *nm* hook; *fig* pretext

ram'pollo *nm hum* brat; (*discendente*) descendant

ram'pone *nm* harpoon; (*per scarpe*) crampon

'rana *nf* frog; (*nel nuoto*) breaststroke; uomo ~ frogman

ranch *nm inv* ranch

'rancido *a* rancid

'rancio *nm* rations *pl*

ran'core *nm* rancour, resentment; serbare ~ verso qcno bear sb a grudge

'randa *nf* mainsail

ran'dagio *a* stray

randel'lata *nf* blow with a club

**ran'dello** *nm* club
**'rango** *nm* rank
**rannicchi'arsi** *vr* huddle up
**rannuvola'mento** *nm* clouding over
**rannuvo'larsi** *vr* cloud over
**ra'nocchio** *nm* frog
**ranto'lare** *vi* wheeze
**'rantolo** *nm* wheeze; (*di moribondo*) death-rattle
**ra'nuncolo** *nm* buttercup
**'rapa** *nf* turnip
**ra'pace** *a* rapacious; ⟨*uccello*⟩ predatory
**rapa'nello** *nm* radish
**ra'pare** *vt* crop
**ra'parsi** *vr fam* have one's head shaved
**'rapida** *nf* rapids *pl*
**rapida'mente** *adv* quickly, rapidly
**rapidità** *nf* speed
**'rapido** *a* fast, quick; ⟨*guarigione, sviluppo*⟩ rapid ● *nm* (*treno*) express [train]
**rapi'mento** *nm* (*crimine*) kidnapping
**ra'pina** *nf* robbery, hold-up *fam;* ~ **a mano armata** armed robbery. ~ **in banca** bank robbery
**rapi'nare** *vt* rob
**rapina'tore** *nm* robber. ~ **di banca** bank robber
**ra'pire** *vt* abduct; (*per riscatto*) kidnap; (*fig: estasiare*) ravish
**ra'pito, -a** *a* abducted; (*per riscatto*) kidnapped; (*estasiato*) rapt ● *nmf* kidnap victim
**rapi'|tore, -'trice** *nmf* kidnapper
**rappacifi'care** *vt* pacify
**rappacifi'carsi** *vr* be reconciled, make it up
**rappacificazi'one** *nf* reconciliation
**'rapper** *nmf inv Mus* rapper
**rappez'zare** *vt* patch up
**rappor'tare** *vt* reproduce ⟨*disegno*⟩; (*confrontare*) compare
**rap'porto** *nm* report; (*connessione*) relation; (*legame*) relationship; *Math, Techn* ratio; **rapporti** *pl* relations, relationship; **essere in buoni rapporti** be on good terms. **rapporti** *pl* **d'affari** business relations. ~ **di amicizia** friendship; **avere un ~ ~ ~ con qcno** be friends with sb. ~ **di lavoro** working relationship. ~ **di parentela** family relationship; **aver un ~ ~ ~ con qcno** be related to sb. **rapporti** *pl* **prematrimoniali** premarital sex. ~ **prezzo-prestazioni** price/performance ratio. ~ **prezzo-qualità** value for money. **rapporti** *pl* **sessuali** sexual intercourse. ~ **di trasmissione** *Auto* gear
**rap'prendersi** *vr* set; ⟨*latte:*⟩ curdle
**rappre'saglia** *nf* reprisal
**rappresen'tante** *nmf* representative. ~ **di classe** class representative. ~ **di commercio** sales representative, [sales] rep *fam.* ~ **sindacale** trade union representative
**rappresen'tanza** *nf* delegation; *Comm* agency; **spese di** ~ entertainment expenses; **di** ~ ⟨*appartamento, macchina*⟩ company

attrib. ~ **esclusiva** sole agency. ~ **legale** legal representation. ~ **proporzionale** proportional representation. PR
**rappresen'tare** *vt* represent; *Theat* perform
**rappresentativa** *nf* representatives *pl*
**rappresenta'tivo** *a* representative
**rappresentazi'one** *nf* representation; (*spettacolo*) performance
**rap'preso** *pp di* **rapprendersi**
**rapso'dia** *nf* rhapsody
**'raptus** *nm inv* fit of madness
**rara'mente** *adv* rarely, seldom
**rare'fare** *vt* rarefy
**rare'farsi** *vr* rarefy
**rare'fatto** *a* rarefied
**rarità** *nf inv* rarity
**'raro** *a* rare
**ra'sare** *vt* shave; trim ⟨*siepe ecc*⟩
**ra'sarsi** *vr* shave
**ra'sato** *a* shaved
**rasa'tura** *nf* shaving
**raschia'mento** *nm Med* curettage
**raschi'are** *vt* scrape; (*togliere*) scrape off
**raschi'arsi** *vr* ~ **la gola** clear one's throat
**rasen'tare** *vt* go close to
**ra'sente** *prep* very close to
**'raso** *pp di* **radere** ● *a* smooth; (*colmo*) full to the brim; ⟨*barba*⟩ close-cropped; ~ **terra** close to the ground; **un cucchiaio** ~ a level spoonful ● *nm* satin
**ra'soio** *nm* razor. ~ **elettrico** electric shaver. ~ **a mano libera** cut-throat razor
**'raspa** *nf* rasp
**'raspo** *nm* (*di uva*) small bunch
**ras'segna** *nf* review; (*mostra*) exhibition; (*musicale, cinematografica*) festival; **passare in** ~ review; *Mil* inspect
**rasse'gnare** *vt* present
**rasse'gnarsi** *vr* resign oneself
**rassegnata'mente** *adv* with resignation
**rasse'gnato** *a* ⟨*persona, aria, tono*⟩ resigned
**rassegnazi'one** *nf* resignation
**rassere'nare** *vt* clear; *fig* cheer up
**rassere'narsi** *vr* become clear; *fig* cheer up
**rasset'tare** *vt* tidy up; (*riparare*) mend
**rassicu'rante** *a* ⟨*persona, parole, presenza*⟩ reassuring
**rassicu'rare** *vt* reassure
**rassicurazi'one** *nf* reassurance
**rasso'dare** *vt* harden; *fig* strengthen
**rassomigli'ante** *a* similar
**rassomigli'anza** *nf* resemblance
**rassomigli'are** *vi* ~ **a** resemble
**rastrella'mento** *nm* (*di fieno*) raking; (*perlustrazione*) combing
**rastrel'lare** *vt* rake; (*perlustrare*) comb
**rastrelli'era** *nf* rack; (*per biciclette*) bicycle rack; (*scolapiatti*) [plate] rack
**ra'strello** *nm* rake
**'rata** *nf* instalment; (*di mutuo*) mortgage repayment; **pagare a rate** pay by instalments; **comprare qcsa a rate** buy sth on hire purchase, buy sth on the installment plan *Am*

**rate'ale** *a* by instalments; **pagamento** ~ payment by instalments; **vendita** ~ hire purchase

**rate'are, rateiz'zare** *vt* divide into instalments

**ra'tifica** *nf Jur* ratification

**ratifi'care** *vt Jur* ratify

**'ratto**[1] *nm (rapimento)* abduction

**'ratto**[2] *nm (roditore)* rat. ~ **comune** black rat

**rattop'pare** *vt* patch

**rat'toppo** *nm* patch

**rattrap'pire** *vt* make stiff

**rattrap'pirsi** *vr* become stiff

**rattri'stare** *vt* sadden

**rattri'starsi** *vr* become sad

**rau'cedine** *nf* hoarseness

**'rauco** *a* hoarse

**rava'nello** *nm* radish

**ravi'oli** *nmpl* ravioli *sg*

**ravve'dersi** *vr* mend one's ways

**ravvi'are** *vt* tidy *(capelli, stanza)*

**ravvicina'mento** *nm (tra persone)* reconciliation; *Pol* rapprochement

**ravvici'nare** *vt* bring closer; *(riconciliare)* reconcile

**ravvici'narsi** *vr* be reconciled

**ravvi'sare** *vt* recognize

**ravvi'vare** *vt* revive; *fig* brighten up

**ravvi'varsi** *vr* revive

**rav'volgere** *vt* roll up

**rav'volgersi** *vr* wrap oneself up

**'rayon** *nm* rayon

**razio'cinio** *nm* rational thought; *(buon senso)* common sense

**razio'nale** *a* rational

**razionalità** *nf (raziocinio)* rationality; *(di ambiente)* functional nature

**razionaliz'zare** *vt* rationalize *(programmi, metodi, spazio)*

**razional'mente** *adv (con raziocinio)* rationally

**raziona'mento** *nm* rationing

**razio'nare** *vt* ration

**razi'one** *nf* ration

**'razza** *nf* race; *(di cani ecc)* breed; *(genere)* kind; **che ~ di idiota!** *fam* what an idiot!

**raz'zia** *nf* raid

**razzi'ale** *a* racial

**raz'zismo** *nm* racism

**raz'zista** *a & nmf* racist

**'razzo** *nm* rocket. ~ **da segnalazione** flare

**razzo'lare** *vi (polli:)* scratch about

**re** *nm inv* king; *(Mus: chiave, nota)* D. **Re** *pl* **Magi** Wise Men

**rea'gente** *a & nm* reactant

**rea'gire** *vi* react

**re'ale** *a* real; *(di re)* royal

**rea'lismo** *nm* realism

**rea'lista** *nmf* realist; *(fautore del re)* royalist

**realistica'mente** *adv* realistically

**rea'listico** *a* realistic

**realiz'zabile** *a* feasible

**realiz'zare** *vt (attuare)* carry out, realize; *Comm* make; score ⟨*gol, canestro*⟩; *(rendersi conto di)* realize

**realiz'zarsi** *vr* come true; *(nel lavoro ecc)* fulfil oneself

**realiz'zato** *a ⟨persona⟩* fulfilled

**realizzazi'one** *nf* realization; *(di sogno, persona)* fulfilment. ~ **scenica** production

**rea'lizzo** *nm (vendita)* proceeds *pl; (riscossione)* yield

**real'mente** *adv* really

**realtà** *nf inv* reality; **in** ~ in reality; *(a dire il vero)* actually. ~ **virtuale** virtual reality

**re'ame** *nm* realm

**re'ato** *nm* crime, criminal offence. ~ **minore** minor offence

**reattività** *nf* reactivity; *(a farmaco)* reaction

**reat'tivo** *a* reactive

**reat'tore** *nm* reactor; *Aeron* jet [aircraft]. ~ **nucleare** atomic reactor

**reazio'nario, -a** *a & nmf* reactionary

**reazi'one** *nf* reaction; **a** ~ *⟨motore, aereo⟩* jet. ~ **a catena** chain reaction. ~ **chimica** chemical reaction

**'rebus** *nm inv* rebus; *(enigma)* puzzle

**recapi'tare** *vt* deliver

**re'capito** *nm* address; *(consegna)* delivery; **in caso di mancato ~...** if undelivered.... ~ **a domicilio** home delivery. ~ **telefonico** contact telephone number

**re'care** *vt* bear; *(produrre)* cause

**re'carsi** *vr* go

**re'cedere** *vi* recede; *fig* give up

**recensi'one** *nf* review

**recen'sire** *vt* review

**recen'sore** *nm* reviewer

**re'cente** *a* recent; **di** ~ recently

**recente'mente** *adv* recently

**re'ception** *nf inv* reception [desk]

**re'ceptionist** *nmf* receptionist

**recessi'one** *nf* recession

**reces'sivo** *a Biol* recessive; *Econ* recessionary

**re'cesso** *nm* recess

**re'cidere** *vt* cut off

**reci'diva** *nf Jur* recidivism; *Med* relapse; **furto con** ~ repeat offence of theft

**recidività** *nf inv* recidivism

**reci'divo, -a** *a Med* recurrent ● *nmf* repeat offender, recidivist *fml*; **è** ~ *fig* he's lapsed back into his old ways

**recin'tare** *vt* close off

**re'cinto** *nm* enclosure; *(per animali)* pen; *(per bambini)* play-pen. ~ **delle grida** *Fin* [trading] floor. ~ **del peso** *(ippica)* weigh-in room

**recinzi'one** *nf (azione)* enclosure; *(muro)* wall; *(rete)* wire fence; *(cancellata)* railings *pl*

**recipi'ente** *nm* container

**re'ciproco** *a* reciprocal

**re'ciso** *pp di recidere* ● *a (risoluto)* definite

**'recita** *nf* performance. ~ **scolastica** school play

**re'cital** *nm inv* recital

**reci'tare** *vt* recite; *Theat* act; play ⟨*ruolo*⟩ ● *vi* act; ~ **a soggetto** improvise

**recitazi'one** *nf* recitation; *Theat* acting; **scuola di** ~ drama school

**recla'mare** *vi* protest ● *vt* claim

**ré'clame** *nf inv* advertising; (*avviso pubblicitario*) advertisement

**reclamiz'zare** *vt* advertise

**re'clamo** *nm* complaint; **ufficio reclami** complaints department

**recli'nabile** *a* reclining; **sedile** ~ reclining seat

**recli'nare** *vt* tilt ⟨*sedile*⟩; lean ⟨*capo*⟩

**reclusi'one** *nf* imprisonment

**re'cluso, -a** *a* secluded ● *nmf* prisoner

**'recluta** *nf* recruit

**recluta'mento** *nm* recruitment

**reclu'tare** *vt* recruit

**re'condito** *a* secluded; (*intimo*) secret

**'record** *nm inv* record; **a tempo di** ~ in record time ● *a inv* ⟨*cifra*⟩ record *attrib*

**recrimi'nare** *vi* recriminate

**recriminazi'one** *nf* recrimination

**recrude'scenza** *nf Med* fresh outbreak; *fig* (*di violenza*) renewed outbreak; (*di criminalità*) upsurge

**recupe'rare** *vt* recover; rehabilitate ⟨*tossicodipendente*⟩; make up ⟨*ore di assenza*⟩; ~ **il tempo perduto** make up for lost time ● *vi* catch up

**re'cupero** *nm* recovery; (*di tossicodipendenti*) rehabilitation; (*salvataggio*) rescue; **corso di** ~ additional classes *pl*; **materiali di** ~ recycled material; (*che possono essere recuperati*) recyclable material; [**minuti di**] ~ *Sport* injury time; **partita di** ~ rematch. ~ **crediti** debt collection. ~ [**dei**] **dati** data recovery

**redargu'ire** *vt* rebuke

**re'datto** *pp di* **redigere**

**redat|'tore, -'trice** *nmf* editor; (*di testo*) writer. ~ **capo** editor in chief

**redazi'one** *nf* (*ufficio*) editorial office; (*di testi*) editing

**redditività** *nf* earning power

**reddi'tizio** *a* profitable

**'reddito** *nm* income; **imposta sul** ~ income tax. ~ **complessivo** gross income. ~ **imponibile** taxable income. ~ **non imponibile** non-taxable income. ~ **da lavoro** earned income. **redditi** *pl* **occasionali** casual earnings. ~ **pubblico** government revenue

**re'dento** *pp di* **redimere**

**reden'tore** *nm* redeemer

**redenzi'one** *nf* redemption

**re'digere** *vt* write; draw up ⟨*documento*⟩

**re'dimere** *vt* redeem

**re'dimersi** *vr* redeem oneself

**redi'mibile** *a* ⟨*titoli*⟩ redeemable

**'redine** *nf* rein

**redin'gote** *nf inv* frock-coat; **abito a** ~ fitted button-through dress

**'redini** *nfpl* reins

**redi'vivo** *a* restored to life

**'reduce** *a* ~ **da** back from ● *nmf* survivor

**refe'rendum** *nm inv* referendum

**refe'renza** *nf* reference

**referenzi'ato** *a* with references

**re'ferto** *nm* report. ~ **medico** medical report

**refet'torio** *nm* refectory

**reflazio'nare** *vt Econ* reflate

**reflazi'one** *nf Econ* reflation

**'reflex** *nm inv* reflex camera

**'refluo** *nm* effluent

**refrat'tario** *a* refractory; **essere** ~ *a fig* be insensitive to ⟨*sentimenti*⟩; **sono** ~ **alla matematica** maths are a closed book to me

**refrige'rante** *a* cooling *attrib*

**refrige'rare** *vt* refrigerate

**refrigerazi'one** *nf* refrigeration

**refur'tiva** *nf* stolen goods *pl*

**re'fuso** *nm Typ* literal, typo

**rega'lare** *vt* give

**re'gale** *a* regal

**re'galo** *nm* present, gift; **articoli da** ~ gifts ● *a* **confezione** ~ gift set

**re'gata** *nf* regatta

**'reggae** *nm inv Mus* reggae

**reg'gente** *nmf* regent

**reg'genza** *nf* regency

**'reggere** *vt* (*sorreggere*) bear; (*tenere in mano*) hold; (*dirigere*) run; (*governare*) govern; *Gram* take ● *vi* (*resistere*) hold out; (*durare*) last; *fig* stand

**'reggersi** *vr* stand

**'reggia** *nf* royal palace

**reggi'calze** *nm inv* suspender belt

**reggi'mento** *nm* regiment; (*fig: molte persone*) army

**reggi'petto, reggi'seno** *nm* bra

**re'gia** *nf Cinema* direction; *Theat* production

**re'gime** *nm* regime; (*dieta*) diet; (*di fiume*) rate of flow; **a** ~ **torrentizio** in spate; **a pieno** ~ ⟨*funzionare*⟩ at full speed. ~ **alimentare** diet. ~ **fiscale** tax system. ~ **di giri** (*di motore*) revs per minute, rpm. ~ **militare** military regime. ~ **monetario aureo** gold standard. ~ **di vita** lifestyle

**re'gina** *nf* queen; **ape** ~ queen bee. ~ **madre** queen mother

**'regio** *a* royal

**regio'nale** *a* regional

**regiona'lismo** *nm* (*parola*) regionalism

**regional'mente** *adv* regionally

**regi'one** *nf* region

**re'gista** *nmf Cinema*, *TV* director; *Theat* producer

**regi'strare** *vt* register; *Comm* enter; (*incidere su nastro*) tape, record; (*su disco*) record

**registra'tore** *nm* recorder; (*magnetofono*) tape-recorder. ~ **di cassa** cash register. ~ **a cassette** tape recorder, cassette recorder. ~ **di volo** flight recorder

**registrazi'one** *nf* registration; *Comm* entry; (*di programma*) recording; **sala di** ~ recording studio. ~ [**dei**] **dati** data capture

**re'gistro** *nm* register; (*ufficio*) registry. ~ **di**

bordo log. ~ **di cassa** ledger. ~ **di classe** class register. ~ **linguistico** register

**re'gnare** *vi* reign

**'regno** *nm* kingdom; (*sovranità*) reign. ~ **animale** animal kingdom. **R~ Unito** United Kingdom. ~ **vegetale** plant kingdom

**'regola** *nf* rule; **essere in ~** be in order; (*persona:*) have one's papers in order; **a ~ d'arte** in a workmanlike fashion

**rego'labile** *a* (*velocità, luminosità*) adjustable

**regola'mento** *nm* regulation; *Comm* settlement. ~ **di conti** settling of scores

**rego'lare** *a* regular ● *vt* regulate; (*ridurre, moderare*) limit; (*sistemare*) settle

**regolarità** *nf inv* regularity

**regolariz'zare** *vt* settle (*debito*); regularize (*situazione*)

**rego'larsi** *vr* (*agire*) act; (*moderarsi*) control oneself

**rego'lata** *nf* **darsi una ~** pull oneself together

**regola'tore, -'trice** *a* **piano ~** urban development plan ● *nmf* regulator

**'regolo** *nm* ruler. ~ **calcolatore** slide-rule

**regre'dire** *vi* *Biol, Psych* regress

**regressi'one** *nf* regression

**regres'sivo** *a* regressive

**re'gresso** *nm* decline

**reincar'narsi** *vr* ~ **in...** be reincarnated as...

**reincarnazi'one** *nf* reincarnation

**reinseri'mento** *nm* (*di persona*) reintegration

**reinser'irsi** *vr* (*in ambiente*) reintegrate

**reinte'grare** *vt* restore

**reinven'tare** *vt* reinvent

**reinvesti'mento** *nm* reinvestment

**reinve'stire** *vt* reinvest (*soldi*)

**reite'rare** *vt* reiterate

**reiterazi'one** *nf* reiteration

**re'lais** *nm inv* relay

**relativa'mente** *adv* relatively; ~ **a** as regards

**relatività** *nf* relativity

**rela'tivo** *a* relative

**rela|'tore, -'trice** *nmf* (*in una conferenza*) speaker; (*di tesi*) supervisor

**re'lax** *nm* relaxation

**relazi'one** *nf* relation; (*di lavoro ecc*) relationship; (*rapporto amoroso*) [love] affair; (*resoconto*) report; **pubbliche relazioni** *pl* public relations. ~ **extraconiugale** extramarital relationship

**rele'gare** *vt* relegate

**relegazi'one** *nf* relegation

**religi'one** *nf* religion

**religi'oso, -a** *a* religious ● *nm* monk ● *nf* nun

**re'liquia** *nf* relic

**reliqui'ario** *nm* reliquary

**re'litto** *nm* wreck

**re'mainder** *nm inv* (*libro*) remainder

**re'make** *nm inv* remake

**re'mare** *vi* row

**rema|'tore, -'trice** *nmf* rower

**remini'scenza** *nf* reminiscence

**remissi'one** *nf* remission; (*sottomissione*) submissiveness. ~ **del debito** remission of debt. ~ **di querela** withdrawal of an action

**remissiva'mente** *adv* submissively

**remis'sivo** *a* submissive

**re'mix** *nm inv* *Mus* remix

**'remo** *nm* oar

**'remora** *nf* **senza remore** without hesitation

**re'moto** *a* remote

**remo'vibile** *a* removeable

**remune'rare** *vt* remunerate

**remune'rativo** *a* remunerative

**remunerazi'one** *nf* remuneration

**re'nale** *a* renal

**'rendere** *vt* (*restituire*) return; (*esprimere*) render; (*fruttare*) yield; (*far diventare*) make

**'rendersi** *vr* become; ~ **conto di qcsa** realize sth; ~ **utile** make oneself useful

**rendi'conto** *nm* report

**rendi'mento** *nm* rendering; (*produzione*) yield

**'rendita** *nf* income; (*dello Stato*) revenue; **vivere di ~** *fig* rest on one's laurels. ~ **vitalizia** life annuity

**'rene** *nm* kidney. ~ **artificiale** kidney machine

**'reni** *nfpl* (*schiena*) back

**reni'tente** *a* **essere ~ a** (*consigli di qcno*) be loth to accept; refuse to obey (*legge*) ● *nm* ~ **alla leva** *person who fails to report for military service after being called up*

**'renna** *nf* reindeer (*pl inv*); (*pelle*) buckskin

**'Reno** *nm* Rhine

**'reo, -a** *a* guilty ● *nmf* criminal. ~ **confesso** self-confessed criminal

**Rep.** *abbr* (*repubblica*) Rep.

**re'parto** *nm* department; *Mil* unit. **reparti** *pl* **d'assalto** Mil assault troops. ~ **d'attacco** *Sport* attack. ~ **difensivo** *Sport* defence. ~ **grandi ustionati** *Med* burns unit. ~ **maternità** obstetrics [department]

**repel'lente** *a* repulsive

**repen'taglio** *nm* **mettere a ~** risk

**repentina'mente** *adv* suddenly

**repen'tino** *a* sudden

**reper'ibile** *a* available; **non è ~** (*perduto*) it's not to be found

**reperibilità** *nf* availability

**repe'rire** *vt* trace (*fondi*)

**re'perto** *nm* ~ **archeologico** find. ~ **giudiziario** exhibit

**reper'torio** *nm* repertory; (*elenco*) index; **immagini** *pl* **di ~** archive footage

**re'play** *nm inv* [instant] replay

**'replica** *nf* reply; (*obiezione*) objection; (*copia*) replica; *Theat* repeat performance

**repli'care** *vt* reply; *Theat* repeat

**repor'tage** *nm inv* report

**repressi'one** *nf* repression

**repres'sivo** *a* repressive

**re'presso** *pp di* **reprimere**

**re'primere** *vt* repress

**re'pubblica** *nf* republic. **R~ Ceca** Czech Republic. **R~ Dominicana** Dominican Republic. **R~ Federale Tedesca** Federal Republic of Germany. **R~ d'Irlanda** Republic of Ireland. **~ parlamenta.re** parliamentary republic. **R~ Popolare cinese** People's Republic of China. **~ presidenziale** presidential-style republic. **R~ Slovacca** Slovakia

**repubbli'cano, -a** *a & nmf* republican

**repu'tare** *vt* consider

**repu'tarsi** *vr* consider oneself

**reputazi'one** *nf* reputation

**'requiem** *nm inv* requiem

**requi'sire** *vt* requisition

**requi'sito** *nm* requirement

**requisi'toria** *nf* (*arringa*) closing speech

**requisizi'one** *nf* requisition

**'resa** *nf* surrender; *Comm* rendering. **~ dei conti** rendering of accounts. **~ incondizionata** unconditional surrender

**re'scindere** *vt* cancel

**'residence** *nm inv* residential hotel

**resi'dente** *a & nmf* resident

**resi'denza** *nf* residence; (*soggiorno*) stay

**residenzi'ale** *a* residential; **zona ~** residential district

**re'siduo** *a* residual ● *nm* remainder. **residui** *pl* **industriali** industrial waste

**'resina** *nf* resin

**resi'stente** *a* resistant; **~ all'acqua** water resistant

**resi'stenza** *nf* resistance; (*fisica*) stamina; *Electr* resistor; **la ~** the Resistance. **~ passiva** passive resistance. **~ a pubblico ufficiale** resisting arrest

**re'sistere** *vi* **~ [a]** resist; (*a colpi, scosse*) stand up to; **~ alla pioggia/al vento** be rain-/wind-resistant

**'reso** *pp di* **rendere**

**reso'conto** *nm* report

**respin'gente** *nm* *Rail* buffer

**re'spingere** *vt* repel; (*rifiutare*) reject; (*bocciare*) fail

**re'spinto** *pp di* **respingere**

**respi'rare** *vt/i* breathe

**respira'tore** *nm* respirator; **~ [a tubo]** snorkel

**respira'torio** *a* respiratory

**respirazi'one** *nf* breathing; *Med* respiration. **~ artificiale** artificial respiration. **~ bocca a bocca** mouth-to-mouth resuscitation, kiss of life

**re'spiro** *nm* breath; (*il respirare*) breathing; *fig* respite. **~ di sollievo** sigh of relief

**respon'sabile** *a* responsible (**di** for); *Jur* liable ● *nmf* person responsible. **~ della produzione** production manager

**responsabilità** *nf inv* responsibility; *Jur* liability. **~ civile** *Jur* civil liability. **~ limitata** limited liability. **~ penale** criminal liability

**responsabiliz'zare** *vt* give responsibity to 〈*dipendente*〉; give a sense of responsibility to 〈*gente*〉

**responsabil'mente** *adv* responsibly

**re'sponso** *nm* response

**'ressa** *nf* crowd

**re'stante** *a* remaining ● *nm* remainder

**re'stare** *vi* = **rimanere**

**restau'rare** *vt* restore

**restaura|'tore, -'trice** *nmf* restorer

**restaurazi'one** *nf* restoration

**re'stauro** *nm* (*riparazione*) repair

**re'stio** *a* restive; **~ a** reluctant to

**restitu'ibile** *a* returnable

**restitu'ire** *vt* return; (*reintegrare*) restore

**restituzi'one** *nf* return; *Jur* restitution

**'resto** *nm* rest, remainder; (*saldo*) balance; (*denaro*) change; **resti** *pl* (*avanzi*) remains; **del ~** besides

**re'stringere** *vt* contract; take in 〈*vestiti*〉; (*limitare*) restrict; shrink 〈*stoffa*〉

**re'stringersi** *vr* contract; (*farsi più vicini*) close up; 〈*stoffa:*〉 shrink

**restringi'mento** *nm* (*di tessuto*) shrinkage

**restrit'tivo** *a* restrictive

**restrizi'one** *nf* restriction

**resurrezi'one** *nf* resurrection

**resusci'tare** *vt* revive; resuscitate 〈*moribondo*〉 ● *vi* 〈*Cristo:*〉 rise again; *fig* revive

**re'taggio** *nm* hangover

**re'tata** *nf* round-up

**'rete** *nf* net; (*sistema*) network; (*televisiva*) channel; (*in calcio, hockey*) goal; *fig* trap; (*la spesa*) string bag. **~ commutata pubblica** *Teleph* switched public network. **~ di distribuzione** *Comm* distribution network. **~ locale** *Comput* local [area] network, LAN. **~ di protezione** (*per acrobata*) safety net. **~ stradale** road network. **~ telematica** communications network. **~ televisiva** television channel

**reti'cente** *a* reticent

**reti'cenza** *nf* reticence

**retico'lato** *nm* grid; (*rete metallica*) wire netting

**re'ticolo** *nm* network. **~ geografico** grid

**re'tina** *nf* (*per capelli*) hair net

**'retina** *nf* *Anat* retina

**re'tino** *nm* net

**retorica'mente** *adv* rhetorically

**re'torico, -a** *a* rhetorical; **domanda retorica** rhetorical question; **figura retorica** figure of speech ● *nf* rhetoric

**re'trattile** *a* 〈*punta:*〉 retractable

**retribu'ire** *vt* remunerate

**retribu'tivo** *a* salary *attrib*

**retribuzi'one** *nf* remuneration

**'retro** *adv* behind; **vedi ~** see over ● *nm inv* back. **~ di copertina** outside back cover

**retroat'tivo** *a* retroactive

**retrobot'tega** *nm inv* back shop

**retro'cedere** *vi* retreat ● *vt* *Mil* demote; *Sport* relegate

**retrocessi'one** *nf* *Sport* relegation

**retroda'tare** *vt* backdate

**retro'fit** *nm inv* *Auto* retrofitted catalytic converter

**re'trogrado** *a* retrograde; *fig* old-fashioned; *Pol* reactionary

**retrogu'ardia** *nf Mil* rearguard

**retro'gusto** *nm* after-taste

**retro'marcia** *nf* reverse [gear]

**retro'scena** *nm inv Theat* backstage; **i ~** *fig* the real story

**retrospettiva'mente** *adv* retrospectively

**retrospet'tivo** *a* retrospective

**retro'stante** *a* **il palazzo ~** the building behind

**retro'via** *nf Mil* area behind the front lines

**retro'virus** *nm inv* retrovirus

**retrovi'sore** *nm* rear-view mirror

**'retta¹** *nf Math* straight line; (*di collegio, pensionato*) fee

**'retta²** *nf* **dar ~ a** qcno take sb's advice

**rettango'lare** *a* rectangular

**ret'tangolo** *a* right-angled ● *nm* rectangle

**ret'tifica** *nf* rectification

**rettifi'care** *vt* rectify

**'rettile** *nm* reptile

**retti'lineo** *a* rectilinear; (*retto*) upright ● *nm Sport* back straight

**retti'tudine** *nf* rectitude

**'retto** *pp di* **reggere** ● *a* straight; *fig* upright; (*giusto*) correct; **angolo ~** right angle

**'retto** *nm* rectum

**ret'tore** *nm Relig* rector; *Univ* chancellor

**reu'matico** *a* rheumatic

**reuma'tismi** *nmpl* rheumatism

**reve'rendo** *a* reverend

**rever'sibile** *a* reversible

**revisio'nare** *vt* revise; *Comm* audit; *Auto* overhaul

**revisi'one** *nf* revision; *Comm* audit; *Auto* overhaul. **~ di bilancio** audit. **~ di bozze** proof-reading. **~ dello stipendio** salary review

**revisio'nismo** *nm Pol* revisionism

**revisio'nista** *a* (*politica*) revisionist

**revi'sore** *nm* (*di conti*) auditor; (*di bozze*) proof-reader; (*di traduzioni*) revisor. **~ di bozze** proof-reader. **~ dei conti** auditor

**re'vival** *nm inv* revival

**'revoca** *nf* repeal

**revo'care** *vt* repeal

**revolve'rata** *nf* revolver shot

**rhythm and blues** *nm* rhythm and blues, R & B

**riabbas'sare** *vt* lower again

**riabbas'sarsi** *vr* (*acque:*) recede; (*temperatura:*) fall again

**riabbotto'nare** *vt* button up again

**riabbracci'are** *vt* (*abbracciare di nuovo*) embrace again; (*fig: rivedere*) see again

**riabili'tare** *vt* rehabilitate

**riabilitazi'one** *nf* rehabilitation; **centro di ~** rehabilitation centre

**riabitu'are** *vt* **~** qcno a qcsa reaccustom sb to sth, get sb used to sth again

**riabitu'arsi** *vr* **~ a qcsa** get used to sth again, reaccustom oneself to sth

**riac'cendere** *vt* switch on again (*luce, tv*);

rekindle, revive (*interesse, passione*); rekindle (*fuoco*)

**riac'cendersi** *vr* (*luce:*) come back on; (*interesse, passione:*) rekindle, revive

**riaccensi'one** *nf* **la continua ~** continual switching on and off

**riaccer'tare** *vt* reassess

**riacqui'stare** *vt* buy back; regain (*libertà, prestigio*); recover (*vista, udito*)

**riacutiz'zarsi** *vr* get worse again

**riadatta'mento** *nm* readjustment

**riadat'tare** *vt* convert (*stanza*); alter (*indumento*)

**riadat'tarsi** *vr* readjust

**riaddormen'tare** *vt* get [back] to sleep again

**riaddormen'tarsi** *vr* fall asleep again

**riadope'rare** *vt* reuse

**riaffacci'arsi** *vr* (*alla finestra*) appear again; (*idea:*) surface again

**riaffer'mare** *vt* reaffirm

**riaffon'dare** *vi* sink again

**riaffron'tare** *vt* deal with again (*situazione*); take up again (*argomento*)

**riagganci'are** *vt* replace (*ricevitore*); **~ la cornetta** hang up ● *vi* hang up

**riaggre'garsi** *vr* regroup

**riallac'ciare** *vt* refasten; reconnect (*corrente*); renew (*amicizia*)

**riallar'gare** *vt* widen again (*tunnel, strada*)

**riallinea'mento** *nm* realignment

**rialline'are** *vt* realign

**rialloggi'are** *vt* rehouse

**rial'zare** *vt* raise ● *vi* rise

**rial'zarsi** *vr* get up again

**rial'zato** *a* **piano ~** mezzanine

**ri'alzo** *nm* rise; **al ~** *Fin* bullish

**ria'mare** *vt* **~** qcno reciprocate sb's love, love sb back

**riamma'larsi** *vr* fall ill again

**riam'mettere** *vt* readmit (*socio, studente*)

**rian'dare** *vi* return

**riani'mare** *vt Med* resuscitate; (*ridare forza a*) revive; (*ridare coraggio a*) cheer up

**riani'marsi** *vr* regain consciousness; (*riprendere forza*) revive; (*riprendere coraggio*) cheer up

**rianimazi'one** *nf* intensive care [unit]; **centro di ~** intensive care unit

**rian'nodare** *vt* retie (*filo*); renew (*rapporti*)

**riaper'tura** *nf* reopening

**riappa'rire** *vi* reappear

**riap'pendere** *vt* replace (*cornetta*); **mi ha riappeso il telefono in faccia** he hung up on me, he slammed the phone down on me

**riappiso'larsi** *vr* doze off again

**riappropri'arsi** *vr* **~ di** take back

**ria'prire** *vt* reopen

**ria'prirsi** *vr* reopen

**ri'armo** *nm* rearmament

**riascol'tare** *vt* listen to again

**riasse'gnare** *vt* reallocate

**riassicu'rare** *vt* reinsure

**riassicurazi'one** *nf* reinsurance

**riassorbi'mento** *nm* reabsorption

**riassor'bire** *vt* reabsorb

**rias'sumere** *vt* re-employ, take on again ⟨*impiegato*⟩; ⟨*ricapitolare*⟩ resume

**riassu'mibile** *a* ⟨*riepilogabile*⟩ which can be summarized, summarizable

**riassun'tivo** *a* summarizing

**rias'sunto** *pp di* **riassumere** ● *nm* summary

**riattac'care** *vt* ~ **il telefono** hang up ● *vi* ⟨*al telefono*⟩ hang up

**riatti'vare** *vt* reactivate ⟨*processo*⟩; reintroduce, bring back ⟨*servizio*⟩; start up again, restart ⟨*congegno*⟩; stimulate ⟨*circolazione sanguigna*⟩

**ria'vere** *vt* get back; regain ⟨*salute, vista*⟩

**ria'versi** *vr* recover

**riavvicina'mento** *nm* ⟨*tra persone*⟩ reconciliation; ⟨*tra paesi*⟩ rapprochement

**riavvici'nare** *vt fig* reconcile ⟨*paesi, persone*⟩

**riavvici'narsi** *vr* ⟨*riconciliarsi*⟩ be reconciled, make it up *fam*

**riav'volgere** *vt* rewind

**riba'dire** *vt* ⟨*confermare*⟩ reaffirm

**ri'balta** *nf* flap; *Theat* footlights *pl; fig* limelight

**ribal'tabile** *a* tip-up

**ribal'tare** *vt/i* tip over; *Naut* capsize

**ribal'tarsi** *vr* tip over; *Naut* capsize

**ribas'sare** *vt* lower ● *vi* fall

**ribas'sato** *a* reduced

**ri'basso** *nm* fall; ⟨*sconto*⟩ discount

**ri'battere** *vt* ⟨*a macchina*⟩ retype; ⟨*controbattere*⟩ deny ● *vi* answer back

**ribattez'zare** *vt* rename

**ribel'larsi** *vr* rebel

**ri'belle** *a* rebellious ● *nmf* rebel

**ribelli'one** *nf* rebellion

**'ribes** *nm inv* ⟨*rosso*⟩ redcurrant; ⟨*nero*⟩ blackcurrant

**ribol'lire** *vi* ⟨*fermentare*⟩ ferment; *fig* seethe

**ri'brezzo** *nm* disgust; **far ~ a** disgust

**ribut'tante** *a* repugnant

**ribut'tare** *vt* ⟨*buttare di nuovo*⟩ throw back

**rica'dere** *vi* fall back; ⟨*nel peccato ecc*⟩ lapse; ⟨*pendere*⟩ hang [down]; ~ **su** ⟨*riversarsi*⟩ fall on

**rica'duta** *nf* relapse; **avere una ~** to have a relapse

**rical'care** *vt* trace

**ricalci'trante** *a* recalcitrant

**ricalco'lare** *vt* recalculate

**rica'mare** *vt* embroider

**rica'mato** *a* embroidered

**ri'cambi** *nmpl* spare parts

**ricambi'are** *vt* return; reciprocate ⟨*sentimento*⟩; ~ **qcsa a qcno** repay sb for sth

**ri'cambio** *nm* replacement; *Biol* metabolism; **pezzo di ~** spare [part]

**ri'camo** *nm* embroidery

**ricandi'dare** *vt* ⟨*a elezioni*⟩ put forward as a candidate again

**ricandi'darsi** *vr* ⟨*a elezioni*⟩ stand again

**ricapito'lare** *vt* sum up; **ricapitoliamo** let's recap

**ricapitolazi'one** *nf* summary, recap *fam*

**ri'carica** *nf* ⟨*di sveglia*⟩ winder; ⟨*di batteria*⟩ recharging; ⟨*di penna*⟩ refill; ⟨*di fucile*⟩ reloading

**ricari'care** *vt* reload ⟨*macchina fotografica, fucile, camion*⟩; recharge ⟨*batteria*⟩; *Comput* reboot; rewind ⟨*orologio*⟩

**ricat'tare** *vt* blackmail

**ricatta|'tore, -'trice** *nmf* blackmailer

**ricatta'torio** *a* blackmail *attrib*

**ri'catto** *nm* blackmail. **~ morale** moral blackmail, emotional blackmail

**rica'vare** *vt* get; ⟨*ottenere*⟩ obtain; ⟨*dedurre*⟩ draw

**rica'vato** *nm* proceeds *pl*

**ri'cavo** *nm* proceeds *pl*

**'ricca** *nf* rich woman

**ricca'mente** *adv* lavishly

**ric'chezza** *nf* wealth; *fig* richness; **ricchezze** *pl* riches

**'riccio** *a* curly ● *nm* curl; ⟨*animale*⟩ hedgehog. **~ di mare** sea-urchin

**'ricciolo** *nm* curl

**riccio'luto** *a* curly

**ricci'uto** *a* ⟨*barba*⟩ curly; ⟨*persona*⟩ curlyhaired

**'ricco** *a* rich. **~ sfondato** *fam* filthy rich ● *nm* rich man

**ri'cerca** *nf* search; ⟨*indagine*⟩ investigation; ⟨*scientifica*⟩ research; *Sch* project. **~ sul campo** field work. **~ di mercato** market research. **~ operativa** operational research. **~ scientifica** scientific research

**ricer'care** *vt* search for; ⟨*fare ricerche su*⟩ research

**ricer'cata** *nf* wanted woman

**ricercata'mente** *adv* ⟨*vestire*⟩ with refinement; ⟨*parlare*⟩ in a refined way

**ricerca'tezza** *nf* refinement

**ricer'cato** *a* sought-after; ⟨*raffinato*⟩ refined ● *nm* ⟨*dalla polizia*⟩ wanted man

**ricerca|'tore, -'trice** *nmf* researcher

**ricetrasmit'tente** *nf* transceiver

**ri'cetta** *nf Culin* recipe; *Med* prescription

**ricet'tacolo** *nm* receptacle

**ricet'tario** *nm* ⟨*di cucina*⟩ recipe book; ⟨*di medico*⟩ prescription pad

**ricetta|'tore, -'trice** *nmf* receiver of stolen goods, fence *fam*

**ricettazi'one** *nf* receiving [stolen goods]

**rice'vente** *a* ⟨*apparecchio, stazione*⟩ receiving ● *nmf* receiver

**ri'cevere** *vt* receive; ⟨*dare il benvenuto*⟩ welcome; ⟨*di albergo*⟩ accommodate

**ricevi'mento** *nm* receiving; ⟨*accoglienza*⟩ welcome; ⟨*trattenimento*⟩ reception

**ricevi'tore** *nm* receiver. **~ delle imposte** tax man. **~ del lotto** lottery ticket agent

**ricevito'ria** *nf* ~ **delle imposte** ≈ Inland Revenue. **~ del lotto** *agency authorized to sell lottery tickets*

**rice'vuta** *nf* receipt. **~ doganale** docket. **~ fiscale** tax receipt. **~ di ritorno** acknowledgement of receipt. **~ di versamento** receipt ⟨*given for bills etc paid at the Post Office*⟩

**rice'vuto** int roger

**ricezi'one** nf Radio. TV reception

**richia'mare** vt (al telefono) call back; (far tornare) recall; (rimproverare) rebuke; (attirare) draw; **~ alla mente** call to mind

**richi'amo** nm recall; (attrazione) call

**richie'dente** nmf applicant

**richi'edere** vt ask for; (di nuovo) ask again for: **~ a qcno di fare qcsa** ask o request sb to do sth

**richi'esta** nf request; Comm demand. **~ di indennizzo** claim for damages

**richi'esto** a sought-after

**ri'chiudere** vt shut again, close again

**ri'chiudersi** vr ⟨ferita:⟩ heal; ⟨porta:⟩ shut again, close again

**rici'clabile** a recyclable

**rici'claggio** nm recycling; (di denaro) laundering

**rici'clare** vt recycle

**rici'clarsi** vr retrain; (cambiare lavoro) change one's line of work

**'ricino** nm olio di **~** castor oil

**ricogni'tore** nm reconnaissance plane

**ricognizi'one** nf Mil reconnaissance

**ricolle'gare** vt (collegare di nuovo) reconnect

**ricolle'garsi** vr **~ a** ⟨evento, fatto:⟩ relate to, tie up with

**ricol'mare** vt fill to the brim

**ri'colmo** a full

**ricominci'are** vt/i start again; **~ da capo** start all over again

**ricompa'rire** vi reappear

**ricom'parsa** nf reappearance

**ricom'pensa** nf reward

**ricompen'sare** vt reward

**ricom'porre** vt (riscrivere) rewrite; (ricostruire) reform; Typ reset

**ricom'porsi** vr regain one's composure

**riconcili'are** vt reconcile

**riconcili'arsi** vr be reconciled

**riconciliazi'one** nf reconciliation

**riconfer'mare** vt reappoint

**ricongi'ungere** vt reunite

**ricongi'ungersi** vr become reunited

**ricono'scente** a grateful

**ricono'scenza** nf gratitude

**rico'noscere** vt recognize; (ammettere) acknowledge

**riconosci'mento** nm recognition; (ammissione) acknowledgement; (per la polizia) identification

**riconosci'uto** a recognized

**ricon'quista** nf reconquest

**riconqui'stare** vt Mil reconquer

**ricon'segna** nf return

**riconse'gnare** vt return

**riconside'rare** vt rethink

**ricontrol'lare** vt double-check

**riconversi'one** nf Econ restructuring

**ricopi'are** vt copy again

**rico'prire** vt re-cover; (rivestire) coat; (di insulti) shower (di with); hold ⟨carica⟩; **~ qcno di attenzioni** lavish attention on sb

**ricor'dare** vt remember; (richiamare alla memoria) recall; (far ricordare) remind; (rassomigliare) look like

**ricor'darsi** vr **~** [di] remember; **~ di fare qcsa** remember to do sth

**ri'cordo** nm memory; (oggetto) memento; (di viaggio) souvenir; **ricordi** pl (memorie) memoirs. **~ di famiglia** family heirloom

**ricor'reggere** vt correct again

**ricor'rente** a recurrent

**ricor'renza** nf recurrence; (anniversario) anniversary

**ri'correre** vi recur; (accadere) occur; ⟨data:⟩ fall; **~ a** have recourse to; (rivolgersi a) turn to

**ri'corso** pp di ricorrere ● nm recourse; Jur appeal

**ricostitu'ente** nm tonic

**ricostitu'ire** vt re-establish

**ricostru'ire** vt reconstruct

**ricostruzi'one** nf reconstruction

**ricove'rare** vt give shelter to; **~ in ospedale** admit to hospital, hospitalize

**ricove'rato, -a** nmf hospital patient

**ri'covero** nm shelter; (ospizio) home

**ricre'are** vt re-create; (ristorare) restore

**ricre'arsi** vr amuse oneself

**ricrea'tivo** a recreational

**ricreazi'one** nf recreation; Sch break

**ri'credersi** vr change one's mind

**ri'crescere** vi grow again

**ricu'cire** vt sew up; stitch up ⟨ferita⟩

**ricupe'rare, ri'cupero** = recuperare, recupero

**ri'curvo** a bent

**ricu'sare** vt refuse

**ridacchi'are** vi giggle

**ri'dare** vt give back, return

**rida'rella** nf giggles pl

**ridefi'nire** vt redefine

**ri'dente** a (piacevole) pleasant

**'ridere** vi laugh; **~ di** (deridere) laugh at

**ride'stare** vt reawaken ⟨ricordo, sentimento⟩

**ri'detto** pp di ridire

**ridicoliz'zare** vt ridicule

**ri'dicolo** a ridiculous

**ridimensiona'mento** nm restructuring

**ridimensio'nare** vt restructure ⟨azienda⟩; fig get into perspective

**ridi'pingere** vt repaint

**ri'dire** vt repeat; **trova sempre da ~** he's always finding fault; **hai qualcosa da ~?** do you have something to say?; **se non hai niente da ~,...** if you've no objection...

**ridi'scendere** vi go back down

**ridistribu'ire** vt redistribute

**ridistribuzi'one** nf redistribution

**ridon'dante** a redundant

**ri'dosso: a ~ di** adv behind

**ri'dotto** pp di ridurre ● a essere **~ a uno straccio** be worn out ● nm Theat foyer ● a reduced

**ri'durre** vt reduce

**ri'dursi** vr diminish: ~ **a fare qcsa** be reduced to doing sth: ~ **a** ⟨problema:⟩ come down to
**ridut'tivo** a reductive
**ridut'tore** nm Electr adaptor
**riduzi'one** nf reduction; (per cinema, teatro) adaptation. ~ **cinematografica** film adaptation. ~ **della pena** reduced sentence. ~ **teatrale** adaptation for the theatre
**riedifi'care** vt rebuild
**rieducazi'one** nf (di malato) rehabilitation
**rie'leggere** vt re-elect
**rielezi'one** nf re-election
**rie'mergere** vi resurface
**riem'pire** vt fill [up]; fill in ⟨moduli ecc⟩
**riem'pirsi** vr fill [up]
**riempi'tivo** a filling ● nm filler
**rien'tranza** nf recess
**rien'trare** vi go/come back in; (tornare) return; (piegare indentro) recede; ~ **in** (far parte) fall within
**ri'entro** nm return; (di astronave) re-entry
**riepilo'gare** vt recapitulate
**rie'pilogo** nm summing-up
**rie'same** nm reassessment
**riesami'nare** vt reappraise
**ri'essere** vi ci risiamo! here we go again!
**riesu'mare** vt exhume
**rievo'care** vt (commemorare) commemorate; recall ⟨passato⟩
**rievocazi'one** nf (commemorazione) commemoration; (ricordo) recollection
**rifaci'mento** nm remake
**ri'fare** vt do again; (creare) make again; (riparare) repair; (imitare) imitate; make ⟨letto⟩
**ri'farsi** vr (rimettersi) recover; (vendicarsi) get even; ~ **una vita/carriera** make a new life/career for oneself; ~ **il trucco** touch up one's makeup; ~ **di** make up for
**ri'fatto** pp di rifare
**riferi'mento** nm reference
**rife'rire** vt report; ~ **a** attribute to ● vi make a report
**rife'rirsi** vr ~ **a** refer to
**rifi'lare** vt (tagliare a filo) trim; (fam: affibbiare) saddle
**rifi'nire** vt finish off
**rifini'tura** nf finish
**rifio'rire** vi blossom again; fig flourish again
**rifiu'tare** vt refuse; ~ **di fare qcsa** refuse to do sth
**rifi'uto** nm refusal; **acque** pl **di** ~ waste water; **rifiuti** pl (immondizie) rubbish. **rifiuti** pl **industriali** industrial waste. **rifiuti** pl **urbani** urban waste
**riflessi'one** nf reflection; (osservazione) remark
**rifles'sivo** a thoughtful; Gram reflexive
**ri'flesso** pp di riflettere ● nm (luce) reflection; Med reflex; **per** ~ indirectly
**ri'flettere** vt reflect ● vi think (**su** about)
**ri'flettersi** vr be reflected
**riflet'tore** nm reflector; (proiettore) searchlight

**ri'flusso** nm ebb
**rifocil'lare** vt restore
**rifocil'larsi** vr liter, hum take some refreshment
**rifondazi'one** nf refounding; **R~ Comunista** diehard Communist party
**ri'fondere** vt (rimborsare) refund
**ri'forma** nf reform; Relig reformation; Mil exemption on medical grounds
**rifor'mare** vt re-form; (migliorare) reform; Mil declare unfit for military service
**rifor'mato** a ⟨chiesa⟩ Reformed; ⟨recluta, soldato⟩ unfit for military service
**riforma|'tore, -'trice** nmf reformer
**riforma'torio** nm reformatory
**riformat'tare** vt Comput reformat
**rifor'mista** a & nmf reformist
**riformu'lare** vt recast
**riforni'mento** nm supply; (scorta) stock; (di combustibile) refuelling; **stazione di** ~ petrol station
**rifor'nire** vt restock; ~ **di** provide with
**rifor'nirsi** vr restock, stock up (**di** with)
**ri'frangere** vt refract
**ri'fratto** pp di rifrangere
**rifrazi'one** nf refraction
**rifug'gire** vt shun ⟨gloria, celebrità⟩ ● vi escape again; ~ **da** fig shun
**rifugi'arsi** vr take refuge
**rifugi'ato, -a** nmf refugee
**ri'fugio** nm shelter; (nascondiglio) hideaway. ~ **antiaereo** bomb shelter. ~ **antiatomico** fallout shelter
**'riga** nf line; (fila) row; (striscia) stripe; (scriminatura) parting; (regolo) rule; **a righe** ⟨stoffa⟩ striped; ⟨quaderno⟩ ruled; **mettersi in** ~ line up
**ri'gaglie** nfpl (interiora) giblets
**ri'gagnolo** nm rivulet
**ri'gare** vt rule ⟨foglio⟩ ● vi ~ **dritto** behave well
**riga'toni** nmpl small ridged pasta tubes
**rigatti'ere** nm junk dealer
**rigene'rante** a regenerative
**rigene'rare** vt regenerate
**riget'tare** vt (gettare indietro) throw back; (respingere) reject; (vomitare) throw up
**ri'getto** nm rejection
**ri'ghello** nm ruler
**rigida'mente** adv rigidly
**rigidità** nf rigidity; (di clima) severity; (severità) strictness. ~ **cadaverica** rigor mortis
**'rigido** a rigid; (freddo) severe; (severo) strict
**rigi'rare** vt turn again; (ripercorrere) go round; fig twist ⟨argomentazione⟩ ● vi walk about
**rigi'rarsi** vr turn round; (nel letto) turn over
**ri'giro** nm (imbroglio) trick
**'rigo** nm line; Mus staff
**ri'goglio** nm bloom
**rigogliosa'mente** adv luxuriantly
**rigogli'oso** a luxuriant
**rigonfia'mento** nm swelling

**rigonfi'are** *vt* reinflate
**ri'gonfio** *a* swollen
**ri'gore** *nm* rigours *pl*: **a rigor di logica**
strictly speaking; **calcio di ~** penalty [kick];
**area di ~** penalty area; **essere di ~** be compulsory .
**rigorosa'mente** *adv* ⟨*giudicare*⟩ severely;
⟨*seguire istruzioni*⟩ exactly; **vestito ~ in
giacca e cravatta** wearing the obligatory
jacket and tie
**rigo'roso** *a* (*severo*) strict; (*scrupoloso*) rigorous
**rigover'nare** *vt* wash up
**riguada'gnare** *vt* regain, win back ⟨*stima*⟩;
win more ⟨*tempo, punti*⟩
**riguar'dare** *vt* look at again; (*considerare*)
regard; (*concernere*) concern; **per quanto
riguarda...** with regard to...
**riguar'darsi** *vr* take care of oneself
**rigu'ardo** *nm* care; (*considerazione*) consideration; **nei riguardi di** towards; **~ a** with
regard to
**rigurgi'tante** *a* **~ di** swarming with
**rigurgi'tare** *vt* regurgitate ● *vi* **~ di** *fig* be
swarming with
**ri'gurgito** *nm* regurgitation; (*di rabbia*) fit;
(*di razzismo*) resurgence
**rilanci'are** *vt* throw back ⟨*palla*⟩; (*di nuovo*)
throw again; increase ⟨*offerta*⟩; revive
⟨*moda*⟩; relaunch ⟨*prodotto*⟩ ● *vi* (*a carte*)
raise the stakes; **rilancio di dieci** I'll raise
you ten
**ri'lancio** *nm* (*di offerta*) increase; (*di
prodotto*) re-launch
**rilasci'are** *vt* (*concedere*) grant; (*liberare*) release; issue ⟨*documento*⟩
**rilasci'arsi** *vr* relax
**ri'lascio** *nm* release; (*di documento*) issue
**rilassa'mento** *nm* relaxation. **~ cutaneo**
sagging of the skin
**rilas'sare** *vt* relax
**rilas'sarsi** *vr* relax
**rilas'sato** *a* relaxed
**rile'gare** *vt* bind ⟨*libro*⟩
**rile'gato** *a* bound
**rilega|'tore, -'trice** *nmf* bookbinder
**rilega'tura** *nf* binding
**ri'leggere** *vt* reread
**ri'lento: a ~** *adv* slowly
**rileva'mento** *nm* survey; *Comm* buyout. **~
dirigenti** management buyout, MBO
**rile'vante** *a* considerable
**rile'vanza** *nf* significance
**rile'vare** *vt* (*trarre*) get; (*mettere in evidenza*)
point out; (*notare*) notice; (*topografia*) survey; *Comm* take over; *Mil* relieve
**rilevazi'one** *nf* (*statistica*) survey
**rili'evo** *nm* relief; *Geog* elevation;
(*topografia*) survey; (*importanza*) importance; (*osservazione*) remark; **mettere in ~
qcsa** point sth out
**rilut'tante** *a* reluctant
**rilut'tanza** *nf* reluctance
**'rima** *nf* rhyme; **far ~ con qcsa** rhyme with
sth; **rispondere a qcno per le rime** give sb

as good as one gets. **~ alternata** alternate
rhyme. **~ baciata** rhyming couplet
**riman'dare** *vt* (*posporre*) postpone; (*mandare indietro*) send back; (*mandare di nuovo*)
send again; (*far ridare un esame*) make resit
an examination
**ri'mando** *nm* return; (*in un libro*) cross-reference
**rimaneggia'mento** *nm* rejig
**rimaneggi'are** *vt* rejig, recast
**rima'nente** *a* remaining ● *nm* remainder
**rima'nenza** *nf* remainder; **rimanenze** *pl*
remnants. **rimanenze** *pl* **di magazzino** unsold stock
**rima'nere** *vi* stay, remain; (*essere d'avanzo*)
be left; (*venirsi a trovare*) be; (*restare stupito*)
be astonished; (*restare d'accordo*) agree; **~
senza parole** be speechless
**rimangi'are** *vt* (*mangiare di nuovo*) have
again, eat again
**rimangi'arsi** *vr* **~ la parola** break one's
promise
**rimar'care** *vt* remark
**rimar'chevole** *a* remarkable
**ri'mare** *vt/i* rhyme
**rimargi'nare** *vt* heal
**rimargi'narsi** *vr* heal
**ri'masto** *pp di* **rimanere**
**rima'sugli** *nmpl* (*di cibo*) leftovers
**rimbal'zare** *vi* rebound; ⟨*proiettile:*⟩ ricochet; **far ~** bounce
**rim'balzo** *nm* rebound; (*di proiettile*) ricochet
**rimbam'bire** *vi* be in one's dotage ● *vt* stun
**rimbam'bito** *a* in one's dotage
**rimbec'care** *vi* retort
**rimbecil'lire** *vt* make brain-dead
**rimbecil'lito** *a* (*stupido*) brain-dead;
(*frastornato*) stunned
**rimboc'care** *vt* turn up; roll up ⟨*maniche*⟩;
tuck in ⟨*coperte*⟩; **~ le coperte a qcno** tuck
sb into bed
**rimboc'carsi** *vr* **~ le maniche** roll up
one's sleeves
**rimbom'bare** *vi* boom, resound
**rim'bombo** *nm* boom
**rimbor'sare** *vt* reimburse, repay
**rim'borso** *nm* reimbursement, repayment.
**~ d'imposta** tax rebate. **~ spese** reimbursement of expenses
**rimboschi'mento** *nm* reafforestation *Br*,
reforestation
**rim'brotto** *nm* reproach
**rimedi'abile** *a* ⟨*errore*⟩ which can be rem-
edied
**rimedi'are** *vi* **~ a** remedy; make up for
⟨*errore*⟩; (*procurare*) scrape up
**ri'medio** *nm* remedy
**rimesco'lare** *vt* mix [up]; shuffle ⟨*carte*⟩;
(*rivangare*) rake up; **mi fa ~ il sangue** it
makes my blood boil
**rimesco'lio** *nm* (*turbamento*) shock
**ri'messa** *nf* (*locale per veicoli*) garage; (*per
aerei*) hangar; (*per autobus*) depot; (*di denaro*)

remittance; (*di merci*) consignment. ~ **laterale** *Sport* throw-in

**ri'messo** *pp di* **rimettere**

**rime'stare** *vt* stir well

**ri'mettere** *vt* (*a posto*) put back; (*restituire*) return; (*affidare*) entrust; (*perdonare*) remit; (*rimandare*) put off; (*vomitare*) bring up; ~ **in gioco** (*nel calcio*) throw in; **rimetterci** (*fam: perdere*) lose [out]

**ri'mettersi** *vr* (*ristabilirsi*) recover; ⟨*tempo:*⟩ clear up; ~ **a** start again

**'rimmel**<sup>R</sup> *nm inv* mascara

**rimoder'nare** *vt* modernize

**ri'monta** *nf Sport* recovery

**rimon'tare** *vt* (*risalire*) go up; *Mech* reassemble ● *vi* remount; ~ **a** (*risalire*) go back to

**rimorchi'are** *vt* tow; *fam* pick up ⟨*ragazza*⟩

**rimorchia'tore** *nm* tug[boat]

**ri'morchio** *nm* tow; (*veicolo*) trailer

**ri'mordere** *vt* **mi rimorde la coscienza** *fig* it's preying on my conscience

**ri'morso** *nm* remorse

**rimo'stranza** *nf* complaint

**rimo'vibile** *a* removable

**rimozi'one** *nf* removal; (*da un incarico*) dismissal. ~ **forzata** *illegally parked vehicles removed at owner's expense*

**rimpagi'nare** *vt* regret

**rim'pallo** *nm* bounce

**rim'pasto** *nm Pol* reshuffle

**rimpatri'are** *vt* repatriate ● *vi* return home

**rimpatri'ata** *nf* reunion

**rim'patrio** *nm* repatriation

**rim'piangere** *vt* regret

**rimpiangi'mento** *pp di* **rimpiangere** ● *nm* regret

**rimpiat'tino** *nm* hide-and-seek

**rimpiaz'zare** *vt* replace

**rimpi'azzo** *nm* replacement

**rimpiccioli'mento** *nm* shrinkage

**rimpiccio'lire** *vt* make smaller ● *vi* become smaller

**rimpinz'are** *vt* ~ **di** stuff with

**rimpin'zarsi** *vr* stuff oneself

**rimpol'pare** *vt* (*ingrassare*) fatten up; *fig* pad out ⟨*scritto*⟩

**rimprove'rare** *vt* reproach; ~ **qcsa a qcno** reproach sb for sth

**rim'provero** *nm* reproach

**rimugi'nare** *vt* rummage; *fig* ~ **su** brood over

**rimune'rare** *vt* remunerate

**rimunera'tivo** *a* remunerative

**rimunerazi'one** *nf* remuneration

**ri'muovere** *vt* remove

**ri'nascere** *vi* be reborn, be born again

**rinascimen'tale** *a* Renaissance

**Rinasci'mento** *nm* Renaissance

**ri'nascita** *nf* rebirth

**rincal'zare** *vt* (*sostenere*) support; (*rimboccare*) tuck in

**rin'calzo** *nm* support; **rincalzi** *pl Mil* reserves

**rincantucci'arsi** *vr* hide oneself away in a corner

**rinca'rare** *vt* increase the price of ● *vi* become more expensive

**rin'caro** *nm* price increase

**rincar'tare** *vt* rewrap

**rinca'sare** *vi* return home

**rinchi'udere** *vt* shut up

**rinchi'udersi** *vr* shut oneself up

**rincon'trare** *vt* meet again

**rincon'trarsi** *vr* meet [each other] again

**rin'correre** *vt* run after

**rin'corsa** *nf* run-up

**rin'corso** *pp di* **rincorrere**

**rin'crescere** *vi* **mi rincresce di non...** I'm sorry *o* I regret that I can't...; **se non ti rincresce** if you don't mind; **rincresce vedere...** it's sad to see...

**rincresci'mento** *nm* regret

**rincresci'uto** *pp di* **rincrescere**

**rincreti'nire** *vt* make brain-dead ● *vi* go brain-dead

**rincu'lare** *vi* ⟨*arma:*⟩ recoil; ⟨*cavallo:*⟩ shy

**rin'culo** *nm* recoil

**rincuo'rare** *vt* encourage

**rincuo'rarsi** *vr* take heart

**rinfacci'are** *vt* ~ **qcsa a qcno** throw sth in sb's face

**rinfode'rare** *vt* sheathe

**rinfor'zare** *vt* strengthen; (*rendere più saldo*) reinforce

**rinfor'zarsi** *vr* become stronger

**rin'forzo** *nm* reinforcement; *fig* support; **rinforzi** *pl Mil* reinforcements

**rinfran'care** *vt* reassure

**rinfre'scante** *a* cooling

**rinfre'scare** *vt* cool; (*rinnovare*) freshen up ● *vi* get cooler

**rinfre'scarsi** *vr* freshen [oneself] up

**rin'fresco** *nm* light refreshment; (*ricevimento*) party

**rin'fusa** *nf* **alla** ~ at random

**ringalluz'zire** *vt* make cocky ● *vi* get cocky

**ringhi'are** *vi* snarl

**ringhi'era** *nf* railing; (*di scala*) banisters *pl*

**ringhi'oso** *a* snarling

**ringiova'nire** *vt* rejuvenate ⟨*pelle, persona*⟩; ⟨*vestito:*⟩ make look younger ● *vi* become young again; (*sembrare*) look young again

**ringrazia'mento** *nm* thanks *pl*

**ringrazi'are** *vt* thank

**rinne'gare** *vt* disown

**rinne'gato, -a** *nmf* renegade

**rinno'vabile** *a* renewable

**rinnova'mento** *nm* renewal; (*di edifici*) renovation

**rinno'vare** *vt* renew; renovate ⟨*edifici*⟩

**rinno'varsi** *vr* be renewed; (*ripetersi*) recur, happen again

**rin'novo** *nm* renewal

**rinoce'ronte** *nm* rhinoceros

**rino'mato** *a* renowned

**rinsal'dare** *vt* consolidate

**rinsa'vire** *vi* come to one's senses

**rinsec'chire** *vi* shrivel up

**rinsec'chito** *a* shrivelled up

**rinta'narsi** *vr* hide oneself away; ⟨*animale:*⟩ retreat into its den

**rintoc'care** *vi* ⟨*campana:*⟩ toll; ⟨*orologio:*⟩ strike

**rin'tocco** *nm* toll; (*di orologio*) stroke

**rinton'tire** *vt anche fig* stun

**rinton'tito** *a* (*stordito*) dazed

**rintracci'are** *vt* trace

**rintro'nare** *vt* stun ● *vi* boom

**rintuz'zare** *vt* blunt; (*ribattere*) retort; (*reprimere*) repress

**ri'nuncia** *nf* renunciation

**rinunci'are** *vi* ~ **a** renounce, give up

**rinuncia'tario** *a* defeatist

**ri'nunzia, rinunzi'are** = **rinuncia, rinunciare**

**rinveni'mento** *nm* (*di reperti*) discovery; (*di refurtiva*) recovery

**rinve'nire** *vt* find ● *vi* (*riprendere i sensi*) come round; (*ridiventare fresco*) revive

**rinvi'are** *vt* put off; (*mandare indietro*) return; (*in libro*) refer; ~ **a giudizio** indict

**rinvigo'rire** *vt* strengthen

**rin'vio** *nm Sport* goal kick; (*in libro*) cross-reference; (*di appuntamento*) postponement; (*di merce*) return. ~ **a giudizio** indictment

**rioccu'pare** *vt* reoccupy

**rio'nale** *a* local

**ri'one** *nm* district

**riordina'mento** *nm* reorganization

**riordi'nare** *vt* tidy [up]; (*ordinare di nuovo*) reorder

**riorganiz'zare** *vt* reorganize

**riorganizzazi'one** *nf* reorganization

**R.I.P.** *abbr* (*riposi in pace*) RIP

**ripa'gare** *vt* repay

**ripa'rare** *vt* (*proteggere*) shelter, protect; (*aggiustare*) repair; (*porre rimedio*) remedy ● *vi* ~ **a** make up for

**ripa'rarsi** *vr* take shelter

**ripa'rato** *a* ⟨*luogo*⟩ sheltered

**riparazi'one** *nf* repair; *fig* reparation

**ripar'lare** *vi* **ne riparliamo stasera** we'll talk about it again tonight

**ri'paro** *nm* shelter; (*rimedio*) remedy

**ripar'tire** *vt* (*dividere*) divide ● *vi* leave again

**ripartizi'one** *nf* division

**ripas'sare** *vt* recross; (*rivedere*) revise ● *vi* pass again

**ripas'sata** *nf* (*spolverata*) quick dust; (*stirata*) quick iron; (*di vernice*) second coat; (*fam: rimprovero*) telling-off; **dar una ~ a** ⟨*lezione*⟩ revise

**ri'passo** *nm* (*di lezione*) revision

**ripensa'mento** *nm* second thoughts *pl*

**ripen'sare** *vi* ~ **a** think back to; **ripensarci** (*cambiare idea*) change one's mind; **ripensaci!** think again!

**riper'correre** *vt* (*con la memoria*) go back over; trace ⟨*storia*⟩; ~ **la strada fatta** go back the way one came

**riper'cosso** *pp di* **ripercuotere**

**ripercu'otere** *vt* strike again

**ripercu'otersi** *vr* ⟨*suono:*⟩ reverberate: ~ **su qcsa** (*fig: avere conseguenze*) impact on sth

**ripercussi'one** *nf* repercussion

**ripe'scare** *vt* (*recuperare*) fish out; (*ritrovare*) find again

**ripe'tente** *nmf* student who is repeating a year

**ri'petere** *vt* repeat

**ri'petersi** *vr* ⟨*evento:*⟩ recur; ⟨*persona:*⟩ repeat oneself

**ripeti'tore** *nm TV* relay

**ripetizi'one** *nf* repetition; (*di lezione*) revision; (*lezione privata*) private lesson

**ripetuta'mente** *adv* repeatedly

**ri'piano** *nm* (*di scaffale*) shelf; (*terreno pianeggiante*) terrace

**ri'picca** *nf* spite; **fare qcsa per** ~ do sth out of spite

**ri'picco** = **ripicca**

**ripida'mente** *adv* steeply

**'ripido** *a* steep

**ripie'gare** *vt* refold; (*abbassare*) lower ● *vi* (*indietreggiare*) retreat

**ripie'garsi** *vr* bend; ⟨*sedile:*⟩ fold

**ripi'ego** *nm* expedient; (*via d'uscita*) way out

**ripi'eno** *a* full; *Culin* stuffed ● *nm* filling; *Culin* stuffing

**ripiom'bare** *vi* (*per terra*) fall down again; (*fig: tornare*) turn up on the doorstep again; (*nello sconforto*) sink back

**ripopo'lare** *vt* repopulate

**ripopo'larsi** *vr* be repopulated

**ri'porre** *vt* put back; (*mettere da parte*) put away; (*collocare*) place; repeat ⟨*domanda*⟩

**ripor'tare** *vt* (*restituire*) bring/take back; (*riferire*) report; (*subire*) suffer; *Math* carry; win ⟨*vittoria*⟩; transfer ⟨*disegno*⟩

**ripor'tarsi** *vr* go back; (*riferirsi*) refer

**ri'porto** *nm* (*su abito, scarpa*) appliqué; ~ **di 4** *Math* carry 4; **cane da** ~ gun dog, retriever; **nascondere la calvizie con un** ~ comb one's hair over a bald spot

**ripo'sante** *a* restful

**ripo'sare** *vi* rest ● *vt* put back

**ripo'sarsi** *vr* rest

**ripo'sato** *a* ⟨*mente*⟩ fresh; ⟨*viso*⟩ rested

**ri'poso** *nm* rest; **andare a** ~ retire; ~**!** *Mil* at ease!; **giorno di** ~ day off

**ripo'stiglio** *nm* cupboard

**ri'posto** *pp di* **riporre**

**ri'prendere** *vt* take again; (*prendere indietro*) take back; (*riconquistare*) recapture; (*ricuperare*) recover; (*ricominciare*) resume; (*rimproverare*) reprimand; take in ⟨*cucitura*⟩; *Cinema* shoot

**ri'prendersi** *vr* recover; (*correggersi*) correct oneself

**ri'presa** *nf* resumption; (*ricupero*) recovery; *Theat* revival; *Cinema* shot; *Auto* acceleration; *Mus* repeat; ~ **aerea** bird's-eye view

**ripresen'tare** *vt* resubmit ⟨*domanda, certificato*⟩; reintroduce ⟨*problema, persona*⟩

**ripresen'tarsi** vr (a ufficio) go/come back again; (come candidato) stand again, run again: ⟨occasione:⟩ arise again; ⟨problema:⟩ come up again, reappear; (a esame) resit

**ri'preso** pp di **riprendere**

**ripristi'nare** vt restore

**ripro'dotto** pp di **riprodurre**

**ripro'durre** vt reproduce

**ripro'dursi** vr Biol reproduce; ⟨fenomeno:⟩ happen again, recur

**riprodut'tivo** a reproductive

**riproduzi'one** nf reproduction. **'~ vietata'** 'copyright'

**ripro'mettersi** vr (intendere) intend

**ripro'porre** vt put forward again

**ripro'porsi** vr ~ di fare qcsa intend to do sth; (come candidato) stand again; ⟨problema:⟩ come up again, reappear

**ri'prova** nf confirmation; **a ~ di** as confirmation of

**ripro'vare** vt/i Comput retry

**riprovazi'one** nf ~ **generale** outcry

**riprove'vole** a reprehensible

**ripubbli'care** vt republish

**ripudi'are** vt repudiate

**ripu'gnante** a repugnant

**ripu'gnanza** nf disgust

**ripu'gnare** vi ~ **a** disgust

**ripu'lire** vt clean [up]; fig polish

**ripu'lita** nf quick clean; **darsi una ~** have a wash and brushup

**ripulsi'one** nf repulsion

**ripul'sivo** a repulsive

**ri'quadro** nm square; (pannello) panel

**ri'sacca** nf undertow

**ri'saia** nf rice field, paddy field

**risa'lire** vt go back up ● vi ~ **a** (nel tempo) go back to; (essere datato a) date back to, go back to

**risa'lita** nf ascent; **impianto di ~** ski lift

**risal'tare** vi (emergere) stand out

**ri'salto** nm prominence; (rilievo) relief

**risana'mento** nm improvement

**risa'nare** vt heal; (bonificare) reclaim

**risa'puto** a well-known

**risar'cibile** a indemnifiable

**risarci'mento** nm compensation

**risar'cire** vt indemnify; **mi hanno risarcito i danni** they compensated me for the damage

**ri'sata** nf laugh

**riscalda'mento** nm heating. **~ autonomo** central heating (for one flat). **~ centralizzato** central heating system for whole block of flats

**riscal'dare** vt heat; warm ⟨persona⟩

**riscal'darsi** vr warm up

**riscat'tabile** a redeemable

**riscat'tare** vt ransom

**riscat'tarsi** vr redeem oneself

**ri'scatto** nm ransom; (morale) redemption

**rischia'rare** vt light up; brighten ⟨colore⟩

**rischia'rarsi** vr light up; ⟨cielo:⟩ clear up

**rischi'are** vt risk ● vi run the risk; ~ **inutilmente** take needless risks

**'rischio** nm risk

**rischi'oso** a risky

**risciac'quare** vt rinse

**risci'acquo** nm rinse

**risciò** nm inv rickshaw

**riscon'trare** vt (confrontare) compare; (verificare) verify; (rilevare) find

**ri'scontro** nm comparison; (verifica) verification; (Comm: risposta) reply

**risco'prire** vt rediscover

**ri'scossa** nf revolt; (riconquista) recovery

**riscossi'one** nf collection

**ri'scosso** pp di **riscuotere**

**ri'scrivere** vt (scrivere di nuovo) rewrite; (rispondere) write back

**riscu'otere** vt shake; (percepire) draw; (ottenere) gain; cash ⟨assegno⟩

**riscu'otersi** vr rouse oneself

**risen'tire** vt hear again; (provare) feel ● vi ~ **di** feel the effect of

**risen'tirsi** vr (offendersi) take offence

**risentita'mente** adv resentfully

**risen'tito** a resentful

**ri'serbo** nm reserve; **mantenere il ~** remain tight-lipped

**ri'serva** nf reserve; (di caccia, pesca) preserve; Sport substitute, reserve; **di ~** spare. **~ di caccia** game reserve. **~ indiana** Indian reservation. **~ naturale** wildlife reserve

**riser'vare** vt reserve; (prenotare) book; (per occasione) keep

**riser'varsi** vr (ripromettersi) plan for oneself ⟨cambiamento⟩; **mi riservo la sorpresa** I want it to be a surprise

**riserva'tezza** nf reserve

**riser'vato** a reserved; **'~ ai clienti dell'albergo'** 'for hotel guests only'; **'~ carico'** 'loading only'

**ri'sguardo** nm endpaper

**ri'siedere** vi ~ **a** reside in

**'risma** nf ream; fig kind

**'riso**[1] pp di **ridere** ● nm (pl nf **risa**) laughter; (singolo) laugh

**'riso**[2] nm (cereale) rice. **~ integrale** brown rice

**riso'lino** nm giggle

**risolle'vare** vt raise again; raise ⟨il morale⟩; raise again, bring up again ⟨problema, questione⟩; increase, improve ⟨le sorti⟩

**risolle'varsi** vr (da terra) rise again; fig pick up

**ri'solto** pp di **risolvere**

**risoluta'mente** adv energetically

**risolu'tezza** nf determination

**risolu'tivo** a (determinante) decisive; **scelta risolutiva** solution

**riso'luto** a resolute, determined

**risoluzi'one** nf resolution

**ri'solvere** vt resolve; Math solve

**ri'solversi** vr (decidersi) decide; ~ **in** turn into

**riso'nanza** nf resonance; **aver ~** fig arouse great interest. **~ magnetica** magnetic resonance

**riso'nare** vi resound; (rimbombare) echo

**ri'sorgere** vi rise again

**risorgi'mento** *nm* revival; **il R~** (*storico*) the Risorgimento

**ri'sorsa** *nf* resource; (*espediente*) resort. **risorse** *pl* **energetiche** energy resources. **risorse** *pl* **naturali** natural resources. **risorse** *pl* **umane** human resources

**ri'sorto** *pp di* **risorgere**

**ri'sotto** *nm* risotto. **~ alla marinara** seafood risotto. **~ alla milanese** risotto with saffron

**ri'sparmi** *nmpl* (*soldi*) savings

**risparmi'are** *vt* save; (*salvare*) spare

**risparmia|'tore, -'trice** *nmf* saver

**ri'sparmio** *nm* saving. **~ energetico** energy saving

**rispecchi'are** *vt* reflect

**rispe'dire** *vr* send back, return

**rispet'tabile** *a* respectable

**rispettabilità** *nf* respectability

**rispet'tare** *vt* respect; **farsi ~** command respect

**rispet'tivo** *a* respective

**ri'spetto** *nm* respect; **~ a** as regards; (*in paragone a*) compared to

**rispettosa'mente** *adv* respectfully

**rispet'toso** *a* respectful

**risplen'dente** *a* shining

**ri'splendere** *vi* shine

**rispon'dente** *a* **~ a** in keeping with

**rispon'denza** *nf* correspondence

**ri'spondere** *vi* answer; (*rimbeccare*) answer back; (*obbedire*) respond; **~ a** reply to; **~ di** (*rendersi responsabile*) answer for

**rispo'sare** *vt* remarry

**rispo'sarsi** *vr* remarry

**ri'sposta** *nf* answer, reply; (*reazione*) response

**ri'sposto** *pp di* **rispondere**

**rispun'tare** *vi* (*persona, sole:*) reappear

**'rissa** *nf* brawl

**ris'soso** *a* pugnacious

**ristabi'lire** *vt* re-establish

**ristabi'lirsi** *vr* (*in salute*) recover

**rista'gnare** *vi* stagnate; (*sangue:*) coagulate

**ri'stagno** *nm* stagnation

**ri'stampa** *nf* reprint; (*azione*) reprinting

**ristam'pare** *vt* reprint

**risto'rante** *nm* restaurant

**risto'rare** *vt* refresh

**risto'rarsi** *vr liter* take some refreshment; (*riposarsi*) take a rest

**ristora|'tore, -'trice** *nmf* (*proprietario di ristorante*) restaurateur; (*fornitore*) caterer ● *a* refreshing

**ri'storo** *nm* refreshment; (*sollievo*) relief; **servizio di ~** refreshments *pl*

**ristret'tezza** *nf* narrowness; (*povertà*) poverty; **vivere in ristrettezze** live in straitened circumstances

**ri'stretto** *pp di* **restringere** ● *a* narrow; (*condensato*) condensed; (*limitato*) restricted; **di idee ristrette** narrow-minded

**ristruttu'rante** *a* (*cosmetico*) conditioning

**ristruttu'rare** *vt Comm* restructure; renovate (*casa*); repair (*capelli*)

**ristrutturazi'one** *nf Comm* restructuring; (*di casa*) renovation

**risucchi'are** *vt* suck in

**ri'succhio** *nm* whirlpool; (*di corrente*) undertow

**risul'tare** *vi* result; (*riuscire*) turn out

**risul'tato** *nm* result. **risultati** *pl* **parziali** (*di elezioni*) preliminary results; (*di partite*) half-time results

**risuo'nare** *vt* play again (*pezzo musicale*); ring again (*campanello*) ● *vi* (*grida, parola:*) echo; *Phys* resonate

**risurrezi'one, risusci'tare** = **resurrezione, resuscitare**

**risvegli'are** *vt* reawaken (*interesse*)

**risvegli'arsi** *vr* wake up; (*natura:*) awake; (*desiderio:*) be aroused

**ri'sveglio** *nm* waking up; (*dell'interesse*) revival; (*del desiderio*) arousal

**ri'svolto** *nm* (*di giacca*) lapel; (*di pantaloni*) turn-up, cuff *Am*; (*di manica*) cuff; (*di tasca*) flap; (*di libro*) inside flap

**ritagli'are** *vt* cut out

**ri'taglio** *nm* cutting; (*di stoffa*) scrap

**ritar'dare** *vi* be late; (*orologio:*) be slow ● *vt* delay; slow down (*progresso*); (*differire*) postpone

**ritarda'tario, -a** *nmf* latecomer

**ritar'dato** *a Psych* retarded

**ri'tardo** *nm* delay; **essere in ~** be late; (*volo:*) be delayed

**ri'tegno** *nm* reserve

**ritem'prare** *vt* restore

**rite'nere** *vt* retain; deduct (*somma*); (*credere*) believe

**riten'tare** *vt* try again

**rite'nuta** *nf* (*sul salario*) deduction. **~ d'acconto** tax deducted in advance from payments made to self-employed people. **~ diretta** taxation at source. **~ alla fonte** taxation at source, deduction at source

**ritenzi'one** *nf Med* retention

**riti'rare** *vt* throw back (*palla*); (*prelevare*) withdraw; (*riscuotere*) draw; collect (*pacco*)

**riti'rarsi** *vr* withdraw; (*stoffa:*) shrink; (*da attività*) retire; (*marea:*) recede

**riti'rata** *nf* retreat; (*WC*) toilet

**ri'tiro** *nm* withdrawal; *Relig* retreat; (*da attività*) retirement; **~ bagagli** baggage reclaim

**'ritmica** *nf* rhythmic gymnastics

**ritmica'mente** *adv* rhythmically

**'ritmico** *a* rhythmic[al]

**'ritmo** *nm* rhythm; **a ~ serrato** at a cracking pace

**'rito** *nm* rite; **di ~** customary. **~ funebre** funeral service

**ritoc'care** *vt* (*correggere*) touch up

**ri'tocco** *nm* alteration; **ritocchi** *pl Phot* retouching

**ri'torcersi** *vr* **~ contro qcno** boomerang on sb

**ritor'nare** *vi* return; (*andare/venire indietro*) go/come back; (*ricorrere*) recur; (*ridiventare*) become again

**ritor'nello** *nm* refrain

**ri'torno** *nm* return

**ritorsi'one** *nf* retaliation

**ritra'durre** *vt* (*tradurre di nuovo*) re-translate

**ri'trarre** *vt* (*ritirare*) withdraw; (*distogliere*) turn away; (*rappresentare*) portray

**ritra'smettere** *vt* TV show again, re-broadcast

**ritrat'tabile** *a* ‹*accuso*› which can be withdrawn

**ritrat'tare** *vt* retract, withdraw ‹*dichiarazione*›

**ritrattazi'one** *nf* withdrawal, retraction

**ritrat'tista** *nmf* portrait painter

**ri'tratto** *pp di* **ritrarre** ● *nm* portrait

**ritrazi'one** *nf* retraction

**ritrosa'mente** *adv* shyly

**ritro'sia** *nf* shyness

**ri'troso** *a* (*timido*) shy; **a ~** backwards; **~ a** reluctant to

**ritrova'mento** *nm* (*azione*) finding; (*cosa*) find

**ritro'vare** *vt* find [again]; regain ‹*salute*›

**ritro'varsi** *vr* meet; (*di nuovo*) meet again; (*capitare*) find oneself; (*raccapezzarsi*) see one's way

**ritro'vato** *nm* discovery

**ri'trovo** *nm* meeting-place. **~ notturno** night club

**'ritto** *a* upright; (*diritto*) straight

**ritu'ale** *a & nm* ritual

**ritual'mente** *adv* ritually

**riunifi'care** *vt* reunify

**riunifi'carsi** *vr* be reunited

**riunificazi'one** *nf* reunification

**riuni'one** *nf* meeting; (*dopo separazione*) reunion

**riu'nire** *vt* (*unire*) join together; (*radunare*) gather

**riu'nirsi** *vr* be reunited; (*adunarsi*) meet

**riu'sare** *vt* reuse

**riusc'ire** *vi* (*aver successo*) succeed; (*in matematica ecc*) be good (**in** at); (*aver esito*) turn out; **le è riuscito simpatico** she found him likeable

**riu'scita** *nf* (*esito*) result; (*successo*) success

**ri'uso** *nm* reuse

**riutiliz'zare** *vt* reuse

**'riva** *nf* (*di mare, lago*) shore; (*di fiume*) bank

**rivacci'nare** *vt* revaccinate

**ri'vale** *nmf* rival

**rivaleggi'are** *vi* compete (**con** with)

**rivalità** *nf inv* rivalry

**ri'valsa** *nf* revenge; **prendersi una ~ su qcno** take revenge on sb

**rivalu'tare** *vt* reappraise

**rivalutazi'one** *nf* revaluation

**rivan'gare** *vt* dig up again

**rive'dere** *vt* see again; revise ‹*lezione*›; review ‹*accordo*›; (*verificare*) check

**rive'dibile** *a* ‹*accordo*› reviewable; ‹*recluta*› temporarily unfit

**rive'lare** *vt* reveal

**rive'larsi** *vr* (*dimostrarsi*) turn out

**rivela'tore** *a* revealing ● *nm Techn* detector. **~ di mine** mine detector

**rivelazi'one** *nf* revelation

**ri'vendere** *vt* resell

**rivendi'care** *vt* claim

**rivendicazi'one** *nf* claim

**ri'vendita** *nf* (*negozio*) shop. **~ autorizzata** authorized retailer

**rivendi'tore, -'trice** *nmf* retailer. **~ autorizzato** authorized retailer

**riverbe'rare** *vt* reflect ‹*luce*›

**ri'verbero** *nm* reverberation; (*bagliore*) glare

**rive'renza** *nf* reverence; (*inchino*) curtsy; (*di uomo*) bow

**rive'rire** *vt* respect; (*ossequiare*) pay one's respects to

**rivernici'are** *vt* repaint; (*con flatting*) revarnish

**river'sare** *vt* pour

**river'sarsi** *vr* (*fiume*) flow

**river'sibile** *a* reversible

**rivesti'mento** *nm* covering

**rive'stire** *vt* (*rifornire di abiti*) clothe; (*ricoprire*) cover; (*internamente*) line; hold ‹*carica*›

**rive'stirsi** *vr* get dressed again; (*per una festa*) dress up

**rive'stito** *a* **~ di** covered with

**rivi'era** *nf* coast; **la ~ ligure** the Italian Riviera

**ri'vincita** *nf Sport* return match; (*vendetta*) revenge

**rivis'suto** *pp di* **rivivere**

**ri'vista** *nf* review; (*pubblicazione*) magazine; *Theat* revue; **passare in ~** review

**rivitaliz'zare** *vt* revitalize

**rivitalizzazi'one** *nf* revitalization

**ri'vivere** *vi* come to life again; (*riprendere le forze*) revive ● *vt* relive

**'rivo** *nm* stream

**rivo'lere** *vt* (*volere di nuovo*) want again; (*volere indietro*) want back

**ri'volgere** *vt* turn; (*indirizzare*) address; **~ da** (*distogliere*) turn away from

**ri'volgersi** *vr* turn round; **~ a** (*indirizzarsi*) turn to

**rivolgi'mento** *nm* upheaval

**ri'volta** *nf* revolt

**rivol'tante** *a* revolting, disgusting

**rivol'tare** *vt* turn [over]; (*mettendo l'interno verso l'esterno*) turn inside out; (*sconvolgere*) upset

**rivol'tarsi** *vr* (*ribellarsi*) revolt

**rivol'tella** *nf* revolver

**ri'volto** *pp di* **rivolgere**

**rivol'toso, -a** *nmf* rebel, insurgent

**rivoluzio'nare** *vt* revolutionize

**rivoluzio'nario, -a** *a & nmf* revolutionary

**rivoluzi'one** *nf* revolution; (*fig: disordine*) chaos. **~ francese** French Revolution. **~ industriale** Industrial Revolution

**riz'zare** *vt* raise; (*innalzare*) erect; prick up ‹*orecchie*›

**riz'zarsi** *vr* stand up; ‹*capelli*› stand on end; ‹*orecchie*› prick up

'**roast-beef** *nm inv* thin slices of roast beef served cold with lemon

'**roba** *nf* stuff; (*personale*) belongings *pl*, stuff; (*faccenda*) thing; (*sl: droga*) drugs *pl*; ~ **da matti**! absolute madness!. ~ **da bere** drink. ~, **da lavare** washing. ~ **da mangiare** food, things to eat. ~ **da stirare** ironing

ro'**baccia** *nf* rubbish

robi'**vecchi** *nm inv* second-hand dealer

ro'**bot** *nm inv* robot; (*da cucina*) food processor

ro'**botica** *nf* robotics

ro'**botico** *a* robotic

robotiz'**zato** *a* robotic, robotized

robu'**stezza** *nf* sturdiness, robustness; (*forza*) strength

ro'**busto** *a* sturdy, robust; (*forte*) strong

rocambo'**lesco** *a* incredible

'**rocca** *nf* fortress

rocca'**forte** *nf* stronghold

rocchetti'**era** *nf* winder

roc'**chetto** *nm* reel

'**roccia** *nf* rock; (*sport*) rock-climbing

**rock** *nm* rock [music]. ~ **acrobatico** rock 'n' roll

'**roco** *a* throaty

ro'**daggio** *nm* running in

'**Rodano** *nm* Rhone

ro'**dare** *vt* run in

ro'**deo** *nm* rodeo

'**rodere** *vt* gnaw; (*corrodere*) corrode

'**rodersi** *vr* ~ **da** (*logorarsi*) be consumed with

rodi'**tore** *nm* rodent

rodo'**dendro** *nm* rhododendron

'**rogito** *nm Jur* deed

'**rogna** *nf* scabies *sg; fig* nuisance

ro'**gnone** *nm Culin* kidney

ro'**gnoso** *a* scabby

'**rogo** *nm* (*supplizio*) stake; (*per cadaveri*) pyre

rol'**lare** *vt* roll (*sigaretta*) ● *vi* (*aereo, nave:*) roll

**ROM** *nf inv Comput* ROM

'**Roma** *nf* Rome

Roma'**nia** *nf* Romania

ro'**manico** *a* Romanesque

ro'**mano, -a** *a & nmf* Roman

romantica'**mente** *adv* romantically

romanti'**cismo** *nm* romanticism

ro'**mantico** *a* romantic

ro'**manza** *nf* romance

roman'**zato** *a* romanticized

roman'**zesco** *a* fictional; (*stravagante*) wild, unrealistic

roman'**zetto** *nm* ~ **rosa** novelette

romanzi'**ere** *nm* novelist

ro'**manzo** *a* Romance ● *nm* novel; (*storia incredibile romantica*) romance. ~ **d'appendice** serial story. ~ **giallo** thriller. ~ **sceneggiato** novel adapted for television/radio

rom'**bare** *vi* rumble

'**rombo** *nm* rumble; *Math* rhombus; (*pesce*) turbot

romboi'**dale** *a* rhomboid, diamond-shaped

'**rompere** *vt* break; break off (*relazione*); **non** ~ **[le scatole]**! (*fam: seccare*) don't be a pain [in the neck]!

'**rompersi** *vr* break; ~ **una gamba** break one's leg

rompi'**capo** *nm* nuisance; (*indovinello*) puzzle

rompi'**collo** *nm* daredevil; **a** ~ at breakneck speed

rompighi'**accio** *nm* ice-breaker

rompi'**mento** *nm fam* pain

rompi'**scatole** *nmf inv fam* pain

'**ronda** *nf* rounds *pl*

ron'**della** *nf Mech* washer

'**rondine** *nf* swallow

ron'**done** *nm* swift

ron'**fare** *vi* (*russare*) snore; (*fare le fusa*) purr

ron'**zare** *vi* buzz; ~ **attorno a qcno** *fig* hang about sb

ron'**zino** *nm* jade

ron'**zio** *nm* buzz

'**rosa** *nf* rose. ~ **rampicante** rambler, rambling rose. ~ **selvatica** wild rose. ~ **dei venti** wind rose ● *a & nm* (*colore*) pink

ro'**saio** *nm* rosebush

ro'**sario** *nm* rosary

ro'**sato** *a* rosy ● *nm* (*vino*) rosé

'**rosbif** = **roast-beef**

**rosé** *nm inv* rosé

'**roseo** *a* pink

ro'**seto** *nm* rose garden

ro'**setta** *nf* (*coccarda*) rosette; *Mech* washer

rosicchi'**are** *vt* nibble; (*rodere*) gnaw

rosma'**rino** *nm* rosemary

'**roso** *pp di* **rodere**

roso'**lare** *vt* brown

roso'**lato** *a* sauté

roso'**lia** *nf* German measles *sg*

ro'**sone** *nm* rosette; (*apertura*) rose window

'**rospo** *nm* toad

ros'**setto** *nm* (*per labbra*) lipstick

'**rosso** *a & nm* red; **diventare** ~ go red; **passare col** ~ go through a red light, jump a red light. ~ **carota** *a* (*capelli*) ginger. ~ **mattone** *a* brick red. ~ **sangue** *a* blood red. ~ **scarlatto** *a* scarlet. ~ **d'uovo** [egg] yolk. ~ **vermiglio** *a* vermilion

ros'**sore** *nm* redness; (*della pelle*) flush

rosticce'**ria** *nf* shop selling cooked meat and other prepared food

'**rostro** *nm* rostrum; (*becco*) bill

ro'**tabile** *a* **strada** ~ carriageway

ro'**taia** *nf* rail; (*solco*) rut

ro'**tante** *a* rotating

ro'**tare** *vt/i* rotate

rota'**tiva** *nf* rotary press

rota'**torio** *a* rotary

rotazi'**one** *nf* rotation; (*di personale*) turnover. ~ **delle colture** crop rotation

rote'**are** *vt/i* roll

ro'**tella** *nf* small wheel; (*di mobile*) castor

**roto'calco** *nm* (*sistema*) rotogravure: (*rivista*) illustrated magazine
**roto'lare** *vt/i* roll
**roto'larsi** *vr* roll [about]
**roto'lio** *nm* rolling
**'rotolo** *nm* roll: **andare a rotoli** go to rack and ruin. **~ di carta igienica** toilet roll
**roto'loni** *adv* **cadere ~** tumble
**ro'tonda** *nf* roundabout. traffic circle *Am*
**rotondità** *nf* (*qualità*) roundness: **~** *pl* (*curve femminili*) curves *pl*, curvaceousness
**ro'tondo, -a** *a* round ● *nf* (*spiazzo*) terrace
**ro'tore** *nm* rotor
**'rotta**[1] *nf Naut. Aeron* course: **far ~ per** set a course for: **fuori ~** off course: **in ~ di collisione** on a collision course
**'rotta**[2] *nf* **a ~ di collo** at breakneck speed: **essere in ~ con** be on bad terms with
**rotta'maio** *nm* junkyard
**rot'tame** *nm* scrap; *fig* wreck
**'rotto** *pp di* **rompere** ● *a* broken; (*stracciato*) torn
**rot'tura** *nf* break; **che ~ di scatole!** *fam* what a pain!
**'rotula** *nf* kneecap
**rou'lette** *nf inv* roulette. **~ russa** Russian roulette
**rou'lotte** *nf inv* caravan. trailer *Am*
**rou'tine** *nf inv* routine: **di ~** (*operazioni. controlli*) routine
**ro'vente** *a* scorching
**'rovere** *nm* (*legno*) oak
**rovescia'mento** *nm* overthrow
**rovesci'are** *vt* (*buttare a terra*) knock over; (*sottosopra*) turn upside down; (*rivoltare*) turn inside out; spill (*liquido*); overthrow (*governo*); reverse (*situazione*)
**rovesci'arsi** *vr* (*capovolgersi*) overturn; (*riversarsi*) pour
**ro'vescio** *a* (*contrario*) reverse; **alla rovescia** (*capovolto*) upside down; (*con l'interno all'esterno*) inside out ● *nm* reverse; (*nella maglia*) purl; (*di pioggia*) downpour; *Tennis* backhand
**ro'vina** *nf* ruin; (*crollo*) collapse: **in ~** in ruins
**rovi'nare** *vt* ruin: (*guastare*) spoil ● *vi* crash
**rovi'narsi** *vr* be ruined; (*persona:*) ruin oneself
**rovi'nato** *a* ruined
**ro'vine** *nfpl* ruins
**rovi'noso** *a* ruinous
**rovi'stare** *vt* ransack
**'rovo** *nm* bramble
**rozza'mente** *adv* crudely
**roz'zezza** *nf* indelicacy
**'rozzo** *a* rough
**R.R.** *abbr* (**ricevuta di ritorno**) acknowledgment of receipt
**R.U.** *abbr* (**Regno Unito**) UK
**'ruba** *nf* **andare a ~** sell like hot cakes
**rubacchi'are** *vt* pilfer
**rubacu'ori** *nm inv* heart-throb
**ru'bare** *vt* steal
**rubi'condo** *a* ruddy

**rubi'netto** *nm* tap. faucet *Am*
**ru'bino** *nm* ruby
**ru'bizzo** *a* spry
**'rublo** *nm* rouble
**ru'brica** *nf* (*in giornale*) column; (*in programma televisivo*) TV report; (*quaderno con indice*) address book. **~ sportiva** sports column. **~ telefonica** telephone and address book
**'rucola** *nf* rocket
**'rude** *a* rough
**'rudere** *nm* ruin
**ru'dezza** *nf* bluntness
**rudimen'tale** *a* rudimentary
**rudi'menti** *nmpl* rudiments
**ruffi'ana** *nf* procuress
**ruffi'ano** *nm* pimp; (*adulatore*) bootlicker
**'ruga** *nf* wrinkle
**'ruggine** *nf* rust; **fare la ~** go rusty
**ruggi'noso** *a* rusty
**rug'gire** *vi* roar
**rug'gito** *nm* roar
**rugi'ada** *nf* dew
**ru'goso** *a* wrinkled
**rul'lare** *vi* roll; *Aeron* taxi
**rul'lino** *nm* film
**rul'lio** *nm* rolling; *Aeron* taxiing
**'rullo** *nm* roll; *Techn* roller
**rum** *nm inv* rum
**ru'meno, -a** *a & nmf* Romanian
**rumi'nante** *nm* ruminant
**rumi'nare** *vt* ruminate
**ru'more** *nm* noise; *fig* rumour
**rumoreggi'are** *vi* rumble
**rumorosa'mente** *adv* noisily
**rumo'roso** *a* noisy; (*sonoro*) loud
**ru'olo** *nm* roll; *Theat* role; **di ~** on the staff. **~ delle imposte** tax notice. **~ primario/ secondario** major/minor role
**ru'ota** *nf* wheel; **andare a ~ libera** free- wheel; **fare la ~** do a cartwheel. **~ dentata** cogwheel. **~ di scorta** spare wheel. **~ di stampa** (*di stampante*) print wheel. **~ del timone** helm
**'rupe** *nf* cliff
**ru'pestre** *a* (*pittura*) rock *attrib*
**ru'pia** *nf* rupee
**ru'rale** *a* rural
**ru'scello** *nm* stream
**'ruspa** *nf* bulldozer
**ru'spante** *a* free-range
**rus'sare** *vi* snore
**'Russia** *nf* Russia
**'russo, -a** *a & nmf* Russian ● *nm* (*lingua*) Russian
**'rustico** *a* rural; (*carattere*) rough
**'ruta** *nf Bot* rue
**rut'tare** *vi* belch. burp
**rut'tino** *nm* (*di bambino*) burp
**'rutto** *nm* belch. burp
**'ruvido** *a* coarse
**ruzzo'lare** *vi* tumble down
**ruzzo'lone** *nm* tumble; **cadere ruzzoloni** tumble down, tumble [helter-skelter]

# Ss

**S.** *abbr* (**santo, santa**) St.; *abbr* (**sud**) south
**'sabato** *nm* Saturday; **di ~** on Saturdays
**sab'batico** *a* sabbatical; **anno ~** sabbatical [year]
**'sabbia** *nf* sand. **sabbie** *pl* **mobili** quicksand
**sabbi'are** *vt* sandblast
**sabbia'tura** *nf* (*di vetro, metallo*) sandblasting; (*terapeutica*) sand-bath
**sabbi'oso** *a* sandy
**sabo'taggio** *nm* sabotage
**sabo'tare** *vt* sabotage
**sabota|'tore, -'trice** *nmf* saboteur
**'sacca** *nf* bag. **~ di resistenza** pocket of resistance. **~ da viaggio** travel[ling]-bag
**sacca'rina** *nf* saccharin
**sac'cente** *a* conceited ● *nmf* know-all, know-it-all *Am*
**saccente'ria** *nf* conceit
**saccheggi'are** *vt* sack; *hum* plunder (*frigo*)
**saccheggia|'tore, -'trice** *nmf* plunderer
**sac'cheggio** *nm* sack
**sac'chetto** *nm* bag. **~ di plastica** plastic bag. **~ per la spazzatura** bin liner
**'sacco** *nm* sack; *Anat* sac; (*sl: biglietto da mille lire*) thousand lire note; (*contenuto*) sack[ful]; **mettere nel ~** *fig* swindle; **un ~** (*moltissimo*) a lot; **un ~ di** (*gran quantità*) lots of. **~ a pelo** sleeping-bag. **~ postale** mail-bag
**saccope'lista** *nmf* backpacker
**sacer'dote** *nm* priest
**sacer'dozio** *nm* priesthood
**sacra'mento** *nm* sacrament
**sacrifi'cale** *a* sacrificial
**sacrifi'care** *vt* sacrifice
**sacrifi'carsi** *vr* sacrifice oneself
**sacrifi'cato** *a* sacrificed; (*non valorizzato*) wasted
**sacri'ficio** *nm* sacrifice
**sacri'legio** *nm* sacrilege
**sa'crilego** *a* sacrilegious
**'sacro** *a* sacred ● *nm Anat* sacrum
**sacro'santo** *a* sacrosanct; (*verità*) gospel; (*diritto*) sacred
**'sadico, -a** *a* sadistic ● *nmf* sadist
**sa'dismo** *nm* sadism
**sa'etta** *nf* arrow; (*fulmine*) thunderbolt; **correre come una ~** run like the wind
**sa'fari** *nm inv* safari
**'saga** *nf* saga
**sa'gace** *a* shrewd
**sa'gacia** *nf* sagacity
**sag'gezza** *nf* wisdom

**saggia'mente** *adv* sagely
**saggi'are** *vt* test
**'saggio¹** *nm* (*scritto*) essay; (*prova*) proof; (*di metallo*) assay; (*campione*) sample; (*esempio*) example
**'saggio²** *a* wise ● *nm* (*persona*) sage
**sag'gista** *nmf* essayist
**sag'gistica** *nf* non-fiction
**Sagit'tario** *nm Astr* Sagittarius
**'sago** = sagù
**'sagoma** *nf* shape; (*profilo*) outline; (*in falegnameria*) template; **che ~!** *fam* what a character!
**sago'mare** *vt* make according to a template
**'sagra** *nf* festival
**sa'grato** *nm* churchyard
**sagre'stano** *nm* sacristan
**sagre'stia** *nf* sacristy
**sagù** *nm inv* sago
**Sa'hara** *nm* Sahara
**'sala** *nf* hall; (*salotto*) living room; (*per riunioni ecc*) room; (*di cinema*) cinema. **~ arrivi** arrivals lounge. **~ d'aspetto** waiting room. **~ d'attesa** waiting room. **~ da ballo** ballroom. **~ di comando** control room. **~ conferenze** conference hall. **~ giochi** amusement arcade. **~ d'imbarco** departure lounge. **~ di lettura** reading room. **~ macchine** engine room. **~ operatoria** operating theatre *Br*, operating room *Am*. **~ parto** delivery room. **~ da pranzo** dining room. **~ professori** staff room, common room. **~ di regia** *Radio, TV* control room. **~ di ricevimento** function room. **~ riunioni** conference room. **~ da tè** tea shop
**sa'lace** *a* salacious
**sa'lame** *nm* salami
**salame'lecchi** *nmpl* **fare ~** bow and scrape; **prendi quello che vuoi senza tanti ~** don't stand on ceremony, take what you want
**sala'moia** *nf* brine
**sa'lare** *vt* salt
**salari'ato** *nm* wage earner
**sa'lario** *nm* wages *pl*
**salas'sare** *vt Med* bleed; *fig* bleed dry
**sa'lasso** *nm* bleeding; **essere un ~** *fig* cost a fortune
**sala'tini** *nmpl* savouries (*eaten with aperitifs*)
**sa'lato** *a* salty; (*costoso*) dear; **acqua salata** salt water
**sal'ciccia** *nf* = salsiccia
**sal'dare** *vt* weld; set (*osso*); pay off (*debito*); settle (*conto*); **~ a stagno** solder

**sal'darsi** *vr* ⟨osso:⟩ knit; ⟨ferita:⟩ heal

**saldat'rice** *nf* soldering iron

**salda'tura** *nf* soldering; (giunzione) join

**'saldo** *a* firm; (resistente) strong; **~ come una roccia** solid as a rock; **essere ~ nei propri principi** stick to one's principles ● *nm* (pagamento) settlement; *Comm* balance; (di conto corrente) bank balance; **saldi** *pl* sale; **i ~ di fine stagione** the end of season sales; **in ~** ⟨essere⟩ on sale; ⟨comprato⟩ in a sale. **~ iniziale** opening balance

**'sale** *nm* salt; **non ha ~ in zucca** *fam* he hasn't got an ounce of common sense; **restare di ~** be struck dumb [with astonishment]; **sali** *pl Med* smelling salts. **sali** *pl* **da bagno** bath salts. **~ da cucina** cooking salt. **~ fino** table salt. **~ grosso** cooking salt. **sali** *pl* **e tabacchi** (negozio) tobacconist's shop

**'salice** *nm* willow. **~ piangente** weeping willow

**sali'ente** *a* outstanding; **i punti salienti** the main points, the highlights

**sali'era** *nf* salt-cellar

**sa'lina** *nf* salt-works *sg*

**salinità** *nf* saltiness

**sa'lino** *a* saline

**sa'lire** *vi* go/come up; (levarsi) rise; (su treno ecc) get on; (in macchina) get in ● *vt* go/come up ⟨scale⟩

**sa'lita** *nf* climb; (aumento) rise; **in ~** uphill

**sa'liva** *nf* saliva

**sali'vare** *vt* salivate ● *a* ⟨ghiandola⟩ salivary

**'salma** *nf* corpse

**sal'mastro** *a* brackish ● *nm* salt air

**salmì** *nm* **in ~** marinated and slowly cooked in the marinade

**salmi'strare** *vt Culin* cure

**'salmo** *nm* psalm

**sal'mone** *nm & a inv* salmon. **~ affumicato** smoked salmon

**salmo'nella** *nf* salmonella

**sa'lone** *nm* (salotto) living room; (di parrucchiere) salon. **~ dell'automobile** motor show. **~ di bellezza** beauty parlour. **~ del libro** book fair

**salo'pette** *nf inv* dungarees *pl*

**salotti'ero** *a pej* mundane; **discorso ~** small talk

**salot'tino** *nm* bower

**sa'lotto** *nm* drawing room; (soggiorno) sitting room; (mobili) [three-piece] suite; **fare ~** chat. **~ letterario** literary salon

**sal'pare** *vi* sail ● *vt* **~ l'ancora** weigh anchor

**'salsa** *nf* sauce; *Mus* salsa. **~ di pomodoro** tomato sauce. **~ di soia** soy sauce. **~ tartara** tartar sauce

**sal'sedine** *nf* saltiness

**sal'siccia** *nf* sausage

**salsi'era** *nf* sauce-boat

**sal'tare** *vi* jump; (venir via) come off; (balzare) leap; (esplodere) blow up; **saltar fuori** spring from nowhere; ⟨oggetto cercato:⟩ turn up; **è saltato fuori che...** it emerged that...; **~ fuori con...** come out with...; **salta agli occhi** (è evidente) it hits you; **~ in aria** blow up; **~ in mente** spring to mind ● *vt* jump [over]; skip ⟨pasti, lezioni⟩; *Culin* sauté

**sal'tato** *a Culin* sautéed

**saltel'lare** *vi* hop; (di gioia) skip

**saltim'banco** *nm* acrobat

**saltim'bocca** *nm inv* slice of veal rolled with ham and sage and fried

**'salto** *nm* jump; (balzo) leap; (dislivello) drop; (fig: omissione, lacuna) gap; **fare un ~ da** (visitare) drop in on; **in un ~** *fig* in a jiffy; **fare i salti mortali** *fig* go to great lengths; **fare quattro salti** *fam* go dancing; **fare un ~ nel buio** *fig* take a leap in the dark. **~ in alto** high jump. **~ con l'asta** pole-vault. **~ della corda** skipping. **~ in lungo** long jump. **~ pagina** *Comput* page down. **~ di qualità** quality leap

**saltuaria'mente** *adv* occasionally, from time to time

**saltu'ario** *a* desultory; **lavoro ~** casual work

**sa'lubre** *a* healthy

**salume'ria** *nf* delicatessen

**sa'lumi** *nmpl* cold cuts

**salumi'ere** *nm* person who sells cold meat

**salu'tare** *vt* greet; (congedandosi) say goodbye to; (portare i saluti a) give one's regards to; *Mil* salute; **ti saluto!** *fam* cheerio! ● *a* healthy

**salu'tarsi** *vr* ⟨all'arrivo⟩ greet each other; (in partenza) say goodbye to each other

**sa'lute** *nf* health; **godere di ottima ~** be in the best of health, enjoy excellent health; **in ~** in good health; **~!** (dopo uno starnuto) bless you!; (a un brindisi) cheers!. **~ di ferro** iron constitution

**salu'tista** *nmf* health fanatic; (dell'Esercito della Salvezza) Salvationist

**sa'luto** *nm* greeting; (di addio) goodbye; *Mil* salute; **saluti** *pl* (ossequi) regards

**'salva** *nf* salvo; **sparare a salve** shoot blanks; **a salve** ⟨pistola⟩ loaded with blank cartridges

**salvacon'dotto** *nm* safe conduct

**salvada'naio** *nm* money box

**salva'gente** *nm* lifebelt; (a giubbotto) lifejacket; (ciambella) rubber ring; (spartitraffico) traffic island

**salvaguar'dare** *vt* protect, safeguard

**salvaguar'darsi** *vr* protect oneself

**salvagu'ardia** *nf* safeguard

**sal'vare** *vt* save; (proteggere) protect; **~ la faccia** save face; **~ la pelle** save one's skin

**sal'varsi** *vr* save oneself

**salva'schermo** *nm Comput* screen saver

**salva'slip** *nm inv* panty-liner

**salva'taggio** *nm* rescue; *Naut* salvage; *Comput* saving; **battello di ~** lifeboat

**salva|'tore, -'trice** *nmf* saviour

**'salve** *vedi* salva

**sal'vezza** *nf* safety; *Relig* salvation; **ancora di ~** *fig* salvation

**'salvia** *nf* sage

**salvi'etta** nf serviette

**'salvo** a safe ● nm **trarre in ~** rescue ● prep except [for] ● conj **~ che** (a meno che) unless; (eccetto che) except that

**samari'tano, -a** a & nmf Samaritan

**'samba** nf samba

**sam'buca** nf sambuca

**sam'buco** nm elder

**san** nm (before proper names starting with a consonant) saint; vedi **santo**

**sa'nabile** a curable

**sa'nare** vt heal; (bonificare) reclaim; **~ il bilancio** balance the books

**sana'toria** nf decree legitimizing a situation which is in principle illegal

**sana'torio** nm sanatorium

**san'cire** vt sanction

**'sandalo** nm sandal; Bot sandalwood

**sandi'nista** a & nmf Sandinista

**'sandwich** nm inv sandwich; **uomo ~** sandwich-man

**san'gallo** nm (tessuto) broderie anglaise

**san'gria** nf sangria

**'sangue** nm blood; **a ~ freddo** in cold blood; **al ~** Culin rare; **appena al ~** Culin medium-rare; **farsi cattivo ~ per** worry about; **iniettato di ~** ⟨occhio⟩ bloodshot; **all'ultimo ~** ⟨lotta⟩ to the death; **di ~ blu** blue-blooded; **sudare ~** sweat blood. **~ freddo** composure. **~ da naso** nose bleed

**sangue'misto** nm half-caste

**sangu'igno** a blood attrib

**sangui'naccio** nm Culin black pudding

**sangui'nante** a bleeding

**sangui'nare** vi bleed

**sangui'nario** a bloodthirsty

**sangui'noso** a bloody

**sangui'suga** nf leech

**sanità** nf soundness; (salute) health; **ministero della ~** Department of Health. **~ di costumi** morality. **~ mentale** sanity, mental health

**sani'tario** a sanitary; **servizio ~** health service ● nm doctor

**San Ma'rino** nm San Marino

**'sano** a sound; (salutare) healthy; **~ di mente** sane; **~ come un pesce** as fit as a fiddle

**'sansa** nf husk

**San Sil'vestro** nm New Year's Eve

**santifi'care** vt sanctify

**santità** nf sainthood

**'santo, -a** a holy; (con nome proprio) saint; **Sant'Antonio** St Anthony; **San Francesco d'Assisi** St Francis of Assisi; **di santa ragione** in no uncertain terms ● nmf saint. **~ patrono, -a** patron saint

**san'tone** nm guru

**santo'reggia** nf Bot savory

**santu'ario** nm sanctuary

**san Valen'tino** nm St Valentine's Day; **giorno di ~** ~ Valentine's Day

**sanzio'nare** vt sanction

**sanzi'one** nf sanction. **~ amministrativa** administrative sanction. **~ penale** legal sanction

**sa'pere** vt know; (essere capace di) be able to; (venire a sapere) hear; **saperla lunga** know a thing or two; **non lo so** I don't know; **non so che farci** there's nothing I can do about it; **~ a memoria** know by heart; **~ il fatto proprio** know what one is talking about; **per quanto ne sappia** insofar as I know ● **vi ~ di** know about; (aver sapore di) taste of; (aver odore di) smell of; **saperci fare** know how to go about it; **saperci fare con i bambini** be good with children ● nm knowledge

**sapi'ente** a wise; (esperto) expert ● nm sage

**sapiente'mente** adv wisely; (abilmente) skilfully

**sapien'tone** nm smart alec[k]

**sapi'enza** nf wisdom

**sa'pone** nm soap; **bolla di ~** soap bubble; **finire in una bolla di ~** fig come to nothing. **~ da barba** shaving soap. **~ da bucato** washing soap

**sapo'netta** nf bar of soap

**sapo'noso** a soapy

**sa'pore** nm taste; **sentire ~ di** detect a hint of

**saporita'mente** adv ⟨condire⟩ skilfully; ⟨mangiare⟩ appreciatively; ⟨dormire⟩ soundly

**sapo'rito** a tasty

**sapu'tello, -a** a & nm sl know-all, know-it-all Am

**sara'banda** nf fig uproar

**sara'ceno, -a** a & nmf Saracen; **grano ~** buckwheat

**saraci'nesca** nf roller shutter; (di chiusa) sluice gate

**'sarago** nm white bream

**sar'casmo** nm sarcasm

**sarcasticamente** adv sarcastically

**sar'castico** a sarcastic

**sar'cofago** nm sarcophagus

**Sar'degna** nf Sardinia

**sar'dina** nf sardine

**'sardo, -a** a & nmf Sardinian

**sar'donico** a sardonic

**sarti'ame** nm rigging

**'sarto, -a** nm tailor ● nf dressmaker

**sarto'ria** nf (da uomo) tailor's; (da donna) dressmaker's; (arte) couture

**s.a.s.** abbr **società in accomandita semplice**

**sas'saia** nf stony ground

**sassai'ola** nf hail of stones

**sas'sata** nf blow with a stone; **una ~ ha rotto il vetro** a stone broke the window; **prendere a sassate** throw stones at, stone

**'sasso** nm stone; (ciottolo) pebble; **sono rimasto di ~** I was struck dumb [with astonishment]

**sassofo'nista** nmf saxophonist

**sas'sofono** nm saxophone

**'sassone** nmf Saxon; **genitivo ~** Saxon genitive

**sas'soso** a stony

'**Satana** *nm* Satan
sa'**tanico** *a* satanic
sa'**tellite** *a inv & nm* satellite; **città ~** satellite town
sati'**nare** *vt* glaze; polish ⟨*metallo*⟩
sati'**nato** *a* glazed; ⟨*metallo*⟩ polished
'**satira** *nf* satire
sa'**tirico** *a* satirical
satol'**lare** *vt hum* stuff
sa'**tollo** *a hum* replete, full
satu'**rare** *vt* saturate
saturazi'**one** *nf* saturation
satur'**nismo** *nm* lead poisoning
Sa'**turno** *nm* Saturn
'**saturo** *a* saturated; (*pieno*) full
**S.A.U.B.** *nf abbr* (**Struttura Amministrativa Unificata di Base**) *Italian national health service*
'**sauna** *nf* sauna
sa'**vana** *nf* savannah
savoi'**ardo** *nm* (*biscotto*) sponge finger
savoir-'**faire** *nm inv* expertise, know-how
sazi'**are** *vt* satiate
sazi'**arsi** *vr* **~ di** *fig* weary of, grow tired of
sazi**età** *nf* **mangiare a ~** eat one's fill
'**sazio** *a* satiated
sbaciucchi'**are** *vt* smother with kisses
sbaciucchi'**arsi** *vr* kiss and cuddle
sbada'**taggine** *nf* carelessness; **è stata una ~** it was careless
sbadata'**mente** *adv* carelessly
sba'**dato** *a* careless
sbadigli'**are** *vi* yawn
sba'**diglio** *nm* yawn
sba'**fare** *vt* sponge
sba'**fata** *nf fam* nosh; **farsi una ~** *fam* have a nosh-up
'**sbaffo** *nm* smear
'**sbafo** *nm* sponging; **a ~** (*gratis*) without paying
sbagli'**are** *vi* make a mistake; (*aver torto*) be wrong ● *vt* make a mistake in; **~ strada** go the wrong way; **~ numero** get the number wrong; *Teleph* dial a wrong number; **sbagliando s'impara** practice makes perfect
sbagli'**arsi** *vr* make a mistake; **ti sbagli** you're mistaken, you're wrong; **~ di grosso** be totally wrong
sbagli'**ato** *a* wrong
'**sbaglio** *nm* mistake; **per ~** by mistake
sbale'**strare** *vt fig* disconcert
sbale'**strato** *a* disconcerted
sbal'**lare** *vt* unpack; *fam* screw up ⟨*conti*⟩ ● *vi fam* go crazy
sbal'**lato** *a* (*squilibrato*) unbalanced
'**sballo** *nm fam* scream; (*per droga*) trip; **da ~** *sl* terrific
sballot'**tare** *vt* toss about
sbalordi'**mento** *nm* amazement
sbalor'**dire** *vt* stun ● *vi* be stunned
sbalordi'**tivo** *a* amazing
sbalor'**dito** *a* stunned; **restare ~** be stunned

sbal'**zare** *vt* throw; (*da una carica*) dismiss ● *vi* bounce; (*saltare*) leap
'**sbalzo** *nm* bounce; (*sussulto*) jolt; (*di temperatura*) sudden change; **a sbalzi** in spurts; **a ~** (*a rilievo*) embossed
sban'**care** *vt* bankrupt; excavate ⟨*terreno*⟩; **~ il banco** break the bank
sbanda'**mento** *nm* Auto skid; *Naut* list; *fig* going off the rails
sban'**dare** *vi* Auto skid; *Naut* list
sban'**darsi** *vr* (*disperdersi*) disperse
sban'**data** *nf* skid; *Naut* list; **prendere una ~ per** get a crush on
sban'**dato, -a** *a* mixed-up ● *nmf* mixed-up person
sbandie'**rare** *vt* wave; *fig* display
sbarac'**care** *vt/i* clear up
sbaragli'**are** *vt* rout
sba'**raglio** *nm* rout; **mettere allo ~** rout
sbaraz'**zare** *vt* clear
sbaraz'**zarsi** *vr* **~ di** get rid of
sbaraz'**zino, -a** *a* mischievous ● *nmf* scamp
sbar'**bare** *vt* shave
sbar'**barsi** *vr* shave
sbarba'**tello, -a** *a & nmf* novice
sbar'**care** *vt/i* disembark; **~ il lunario** make ends meet
'**sbarco** *nm* landing; (*di merci*) unloading
'**sbarra** *nf* bar; (*di passaggio a livello*) barrier. **~ spaziatrice** space bar
sbarra'**mento** *nm* barricade
sbar'**rare** *vt* bar; (*ostruire*) block; cross ⟨*assegno*⟩; (*spalancare*) open wide
sbar'**retta** *nf* oblique
sbatacchi'**are** *vt/i sl* bang, slam
'**sbattere** *vt* bang; slam, bang ⟨*porta*⟩; (*urtare*) knock; *Culin* beat; flap ⟨*ali*⟩; shake ⟨*tappeto*⟩; **~ le palpebre** blink ● *vi* bang; ⟨*porta:*⟩ slam, bang; **~ contro** knock against; **andare a ~ contro** run into
sbat'**tersi** *vr sl* rush around; **sbattersene di qcsa** not give a toss about sth
sbat'**tuto** *a* tossed; *Culin* beaten; *fig* run down
sba'**vare** *vi* dribble; ⟨*colore:*⟩ smear
sbava'**tura** *nf* smear; **senza sbavature** *fig* faultless
sbeccucci'**are** *vt* chip
sbeccucci'**ato** *a* chipped
sbeffeggi'**are** *vt* mock
sbelli'**carsi** *vr* **~ dalle risa** split one's sides [with laughter]
sben'**dare** *vt* unbandage
'**sberla** *nf* slap
sbevaz'**zare** *vi fam* tipple
sbia'**dire** *vt/i* fade
sbia'**dirsi** *vr* fade
sbia'**dito** *a* faded; *fig* colourless
sbian'**cante** *nm* whitener
sbian'**care** *vt/i* whiten
sbian'**carsi** *vr* whiten
sbi'**eco** *a* slanting; **di ~** on the slant;

⟨*guardare*⟩ sidelong; **guardare qcno di ~** look askance at sb; **tagliare di ~** cut on the bias

**sbigot'tire** *vt* dismay ● *vi* be dismayed

**sbigot'tirsi** *vr* be dismayed

**sbigot'tito** *a* dismayed

**sbilanci'are** *vt* unbalance ● *vi* (*perdere l'equilibrio*) overbalance

**sbilanci'arsi** *vr* lose one's balance

**sbi'lancio** *nm* lack of balance; *Comm* deficit

**sbirci'are** *vt* cast sidelong glances at

**sbirci'ata** *nf* furtive glance

**sbircia'tina** *nf* **dare una ~ a** sneak a glance at

**'sbirro** *nm pej* cop

**sbizzar'rirsi** *vr* satisfy one's whims

**sbloc'care** *vt* unblock; *Mech* release; decontrol ⟨*prezzi*⟩

**'sbobba** *nf fam* pigswill

**sboc'care** *vi* **~ in** ⟨*fiume:*⟩ flow into; ⟨*strada:*⟩ lead to; ⟨*folla:*⟩ pour into

**sboc'cato** *a* foul-mouthed

**sbocci'are** *vi* blossom

**'sbocco** *nm* flowing; (*foce*) mouth; *Comm* outlet

**sbolo'gnare** *vt fam* get rid of

**'sbornia** *nf* **prendere una ~** get drunk; **smaltire la ~** sober up

**sbor'sare** *vt* pay out

**sbot'tare** *vi* burst out

**sbotto'nare** *vt* unbutton

**sbotto'narsi** *vr* (*fam: confidarsi*) open up; **~ la camicia** unbutton one's shirt

**sboz'zare** *vt* draft; sketch out ⟨*dipinto*⟩

**sbra'carsi** *vr* put on something more comfortable; **~ dalle risate** *fam* kill oneself laughing

**sbracci'arsi** *vr* wave one's arms

**sbracci'ato** *a* bare-armed; ⟨*abito*⟩ sleeveless

**sbrai'tare** *vi* bawl

**sbra'nare** *vt* tear to shreds *or* pieces

**sbra'narsi** *vr* tear each other to shreds

**sbrat'tare** *vt* clean up

**sbrec'cato** *a* chipped

**sbricio'lare** *vt* crumble

**sbricio'larsi** *vr* crumble

**sbri'gare** *vt* expedite; (*occuparsi di*) attend to

**sbri'garsi** *vr* hurry up, be quick

**sbriga'tivo** *a* hurried, quick

**sbrigli'ato** *a* ⟨*fantasia*⟩ unbridled

**sbri'nare** *vt* defrost; *Auto* de-ice

**sbrina'tore** *nm Auto* de-icer; (*di frigo*) defrost button

**sbrindel'lare** *vt* tear to shreds

**sbrindel'lato** *a* in rags

**sbrodo'lare** *vt* stain

**sbrodo'lone, -a** *nmf* messy eater

**sbrogli'are** *vt* disentangle

**'sbronza** *nf fam* **prendersi una ~** get drunk

**sbron'zarsi** *vr* get drunk

**'sbronzo** *a* (*ubriaco*) drunk

**sbruffo'nata** *nf* boast

**sbruf'fone, -a** *nmf* boaster

**sbu'care** *vi* come out

**sbucci'are** *vt* peel; shell ⟨*piselli*⟩

**sbucci'arsi** *vr* graze oneself

**sbuccia'tore** *nm* parer

**sbuccia'tura** *nf* graze

**sbudel'lare** *vt* gut ⟨*pesce*⟩; draw ⟨*pollo*⟩; disembowel ⟨*persona*⟩

**sbudel'larsi** *vr* **~ dal ridere** die laughing

**sbuf'fare** *vi* snort; (*per impazienza*) fume

**'sbuffo** *nm* puff; **a ~** ⟨*maniche*⟩ puff *attrib*

**sbugiar'dare** *vt* show to be a liar

**sbuz'zare** *vt* gut ⟨*pesce*⟩; draw ⟨*pollo*⟩; disembowel ⟨*persona*⟩

**'scabbia** *nf* scabies *sg*

**'scabro** *a* rough; ⟨*terreno*⟩ uneven; ⟨*stile*⟩ bald

**sca'broso** *a* rough; ⟨*terreno*⟩ uneven; ⟨*fig: questione*⟩ difficult; ⟨*scena*⟩ offensive

**scacchi'era** *nf* chess-board

**scacciapensi'eri** *nm inv Mus* Jew's harp

**scacci'are** *vt* chase away

**'scacco** *nm* check; **scacchi** *pl* (*gioco*) chess; (*pezzi*) chessmen; **dare ~ matto a** checkmate; **a scacchi** ⟨*tessuto*⟩ checked; **subire uno ~** *fig* suffer a humiliating defeat

**sca'dente** *a* shoddy

**sca'denza** *nf* (*di contratto*) expiry; (*di progetto, candidatura*) deadline; *Comm* maturity; **a breve/lunga ~** short-/long-term

**scaden'zario** *nm* schedule

**sca'dere** *vi* expire; ⟨*valore:*⟩ decline; ⟨*debito:*⟩ be due

**sca'duto** *a* ⟨*biglietto*⟩ out-of-date

**sca'fandro** *nm* diving suit; (*di astronauta*) spacesuit

**scaffala'tura** *nf* shelves *pl*, shelving

**scaf'fale** *nm* shelf; (*libreria*) bookshelf

**'scafo** *nm* hull

**scagion'are** *vt* exonerate

**'scaglia** *nf* scale; (*di sapone*) flake; (*scheggia*) chip

**scagli'are** *vt* fling

**scagli'arsi** *vr* fling oneself; **~ contro** *fig* rail against

**scaglio'nare** *vt* space out

**scagli'one** *nm* group; **a scaglioni** in groups. **~ di reddito** tax bracket

**sca'gnozzo** *nm* henchman

**'scala** *nf* staircase; (*portatile*) ladder; (*Mus, misura*) scale; **scale** *pl* stairs; **in ~** to scale; **modello in ~** scale model; **su larga ~** large-scale *attrib*. **~ allungabile** extension ladder. **~ antincendio** fire escape. **~ Beaufort** Beaufort scale. **~ a chiocciola** spiral staircase. **~ mobile** escalator; (*dei salari*) cost of living index. **~ Richter** Richter scale. **~ di servizio** backstairs. **~ di sicurezza** fire escape. **~ di valori** scale of values

**sca'lare** *a* scalar ● *vt* climb; layer ⟨*capelli*⟩; (*detrarre*) deduct

**sca'lata** *nf* climb; (*dell'Everest ecc*) ascent; **fare delle scalate** go climbing

**scala|'tore, -'trice** *nmf* climber

**scalca'gnato** *a* down at heel

**scalci'are** *vi* kick

**scalci'nato** *a* shabby

**scalda'bagno** *nm* water heater

**scalda'muscoli** *nm inv* legwarmer

**scal'dare** *vt* heat

**scal'darsi** *vr* warm up; (*eccitarsi*) get excited

**sca'leno** *a* scalene

**sca'leo** *nm* step-ladder

**scal'fire** *vt* scratch

**scalfit'tura** *nf* scratch

**scali'nata** *nf* flight of steps. ~ **di piazza di Spagna** Spanish Steps

**sca'lino** *nm* step; (*di scala a pioli*) rung

**scalma'narsi** *vr* rush about; (*nel parlare*) get worked up

**scalma'nato** *a* worked up; **è ~** (*vivace*) he can't sit still

**'scalmo** *nm* rowlock

**'scalo** *nm* slipway; *Naut* port of call; **fare ~ a** call at; *Aeron* land at; **senza ~** nonstop. ~ **merci** freight depot, goods yard. ~ **passeggeri** stopover

**sca'logna** *nf fam* bad luck

**scalo'gnato** *a fam* unlucky

**sca'logno** *nm Bot* scallion

**scalop'pina** *nf* escalope

**scal'pare** *vt* scalp

**scalpel'lare** *vt* chisel

**scalpel'lino** *nm* stone-cutter

**scal'pello** *nm* chisel

**scalpi'tare** *vi* paw the ground; *fig* champ at the bit

**scalpi'tio** *nm* pawing of the ground

**'scalpo** *nm* scalp

**scal'pore** *nm* noise; **far ~** *fig* cause a sensation

**scal'trezza** *nf* shrewdness

**scal'trirsi** *vr* get shrewder

**scal'tro** *a* shrewd

**scal'zare** *vt* bare the roots of ⟨*albero*⟩; *fig* undermine; (*da una carica*) oust

**'scalzo** *a & adv* barefoot

**scambi'are** *vt* exchange; ~ **qcno per qualcun altro** mistake sb for somebody else

**scambi'arsi** *vr* exchange; ~ **i saluti** exchange greetings

**scambi'evole** *a* reciprocal

**'scambio** *nm* exchange; *Comm* trade; **libero ~** free trade. ~ **di persona** mistaken identity

**scamici'ato** *nf* pinafore [dress]

**sca'morza** *nf* soft cheese

**scamosci'ato** *a* suede

**scampa'gnata** *nf* trip to the country

**scampa'nato** *a* ⟨*gonna*⟩ flared

**scampanel'lata** *nf* [loud] ring

**scampanel'lio** *nm* ringing

**scampan'io** *nm* peal[ing]

**scam'pare** *vt* save; (*evitare*) escape; **scamparla bella** have a lucky escape

**scam'pato** *a* **lo ~ pericolo** the escape from danger ● *nmf* survivor

**'scampi** *nmpl* (*crostaceo*) scampi

**'scampo** *nm* escape; **non c'è ~** there's no way out

**'scampolo** *nm* remnant

**scanala'tura** *nf* groove

**scandagli'are** *vt* sound

**scanda'lismo** *nm* muckraking

**scanda'listico** *a* sensational; ⟨*giornale*⟩ sensationalist

**scandaliz'zare** *vt* scandalize

**scandaliz'zarsi** *vr* be scandalized

**'scandalo** *nm* scandal

**scanda'loso** *a* scandalous; ⟨*somma ecc*⟩ scandalous; ⟨*fortuna*⟩ outrageous

**Scandi'navia** *nf* Scandinavia

**scan'dinavo, -a** *a & nmf* Scandinavian

**scan'dire** *vt* scan ⟨*verso*⟩; pronounce clearly ⟨*parole*⟩; ~ **il tempo** beat time

**scandi'tore** *nm* ~ **ottico** *Comput* optical scanner

**scan'nare** *vt* slaughter

**scan'nello** *nm* lectern

**'scanner** *nm inv* scanner. ~ **manuale** *Comput* handheld scanner

**scanneriz'zare** *vt Comput* scan

**scansafa'tiche** *nmf inv* lazybones *sg*

**scan'sare** *vt* shift; (*evitare*) avoid

**scan'sarsi** *vr* get out of the way

**scan'sia** *nf* shelves *pl*

**scansi'one** *nf Comput* scanning

**'scanso** *nm* **a ~ di** in order to avoid; **a ~ di equivoci** to avoid any misunderstanding

**scanti'nato** *nm* basement

**scanto'nare** *vi* turn the corner; (*svignarsela*) sneak off

**scanzo'nato** *a* easy-going

**scapacci'one** *nm* smack

**scape'strato** *a* dissolute

**scapigli'ato** *a* dishevelled

**'scapito** *nm* loss; **a ~ di** to the detriment of

**'scapola** *nf* shoulder-blade

**'scapolo** *nm* bachelor

**scappa'mento** *nm Auto* exhaust

**scap'pare** *vi* escape; (*andarsene*) dash [off]; (*sfuggire*) slip; **mi scappa da ridere!** I want to burst out laughing; **mi scappa la pipì** I'm bursting, I need a pee; **mi ha fatto ~ la pazienza** he tried my patience a bit too far; **lasciarsi ~ l'occasione** let the opportunity slip; **scappar via** run off *or* away

**scap'pata** *nf fam* short visit

**scappa'tella** *nf* escapade; (*infedeltà*) fling

**scappa'toia** *nf* way out

**scappel'lotto** *nm* cuff

**scara'beo¹** *nm* scarab beetle

**scara'beo² ᴿ** *nm* Scrabble ᴿ

**scarabocchi'are** *vt* scribble

**scara'bocchio** *nm* scribble

**scara'faggio** *nm* cockroach

**scara'mantico** *a* ⟨*gesto*⟩ to ward off the evil eye

**scaraman'zia** *nf* superstition

**scara'mazzo** *a* ⟨*perla*⟩ baroque

**scara'muccia** *nf* skirmish

**scaraven'tare** *vt* hurl

**scarcas'sato** *a* ⟨*fam: macchina*⟩ beat-up

**scarce'rare** *vt* release [from prison]

**scardi'nare** *vt* unhinge

**'scarica** *nf* discharge; (*di arma da fuoco*) volley; *fig* shower; **una ~ di botte** a hail of blows

**scaricaba'rili** *nm* **fare a ~** blame each other

**scari'care** *vt* discharge; unload ⟨*arma, merci, auto*⟩; *fig* unburden

**scari'carsi** *vr* ⟨*fiume:*⟩ flow; ⟨*orologio, batteria:*⟩ run down; *fig* unwind

**scarica'tore** *nm* loader; (*di porto*) docker

**'scarico** *a* unloaded; (*vuoto*) empty; ⟨*orologio*⟩ run-down; ⟨*batteria*⟩ flat; *fig* untroubled ● *nm* unloading; (*di rifiuti*) dumping; (*di acqua*) draining; (*di sostanze inquinanti*) discharge; (*luogo*) [rubbish] dump; *Auto* exhaust; (*idraulico*) drain; (*tubo*) waste pipe; **'divieto di ~'** 'no dumping'; **tubo di ~** waste pipe

**scarlat'tina** *nf* scarlet fever

**scar'latto** *a* scarlet

**scarmigli'ato** *a* ruffled

**sca'rnire** *vt fig* simplify

**'scarno** *a* thin; ⟨*fig: stile*⟩ bare

**sca'rogna, scaro'gnato** = **scalogna, scalognato**

**sca'rola** *nf* curly endive

**'scarpa** *nf* shoe; (*fam: persona*) dead loss; **fare le scarpe a qcno** *fig* double-cross sb. **scarpe** *pl* **basse** flat shoes, flats. **scarpe** *pl* **da danza** ballet shoes. **scarpe** *pl* **da ginnastica** trainers. **scarpe** *pl* **col tacco** high heels. **scarpe** *pl* **col tacco a spillo** stilettos. **scarpe** *pl* **con la zeppa** platform shoes

**scar'pata** *nf* slope; (*burrone*) escarpment

**scarpi'era** *nf* shoe rack

**scarpi'nare** *vi* hike

**scar'pone** *nm* boot. **~ da alpinismo** climbing boot. **scarponi** *pl* **da sci** ski boots. **scarponi** *pl* **da trekking** walking boots

**scarroz'zare** *vt/i* drive around

**scarroz'zata** *nf fam* trip

**scarruf'fato** *a* ruffled

**scarseggi'are** *vi* be scarce; **~ di** (*mancare*) be short of

**scar'sezza** *nf* scarcity, shortage

**scarsità** *nf* shortage

**'scarso** *a* scarce; (*manchevole*) short

**scartabel'lare** *vt* skim through

**scarta'mento** *nm Rail* gauge. **~ ridotto** narrow gauge

**scar'tare** *vt* discard; unwrap ⟨*pacco*⟩; (*respingere*) reject ● *vi* (*deviare*) swerve

**scartave'trare** *vt* sand

**'scarto** *nm* scrap; (*in carte*) discard; (*deviazione*) swerve; (*distacco*) gap

**scartocci'are** *vt* unwrap

**scar'toffie** *nfpl* bumf, bumph

**scas'sare** *vt* break

**scas'sato** *a fam* clapped out

**scassi'nare** *vt* force open

**scassina|'tore, -'trice** *nmf* burglar

**'scasso** *nm* (*furto*) house-breaking

**scata'fascio** = **catafascio**

**scate'nare** *vt fig* stir up ⟨*folla*⟩; arouse ⟨*sentimenti*⟩

**scate'narsi** *vr* break out; ⟨*fig: temporale:*⟩ break; (*fam: darsi alla pazza gioia*) go crazy, go wild; (*fam: infiammarsi*) get excited

**scate'nato** *a* crazy, wild; **pazzo ~** *fam* off his head

**'scatola** *nf* box; (*di latta*) can, tin *Br*; **in ~** ⟨*cibo*⟩ canned, tinned *Br*; **rompere le scatole a qcno** *fam* get on sb's nerves; **a ~ chiusa** ⟨*comprare*⟩ sight unseen. **~ del cambio** gearbox. **~ nera** *Aeron* black box

**scato'lame** *nm* (*cibo*) canned food

**scato'letta** *nf* small box

**scato'logico** *a* scatological

**scat'tante** *a* zippy

**scat'tare** *vi* go off; (*balzare*) spring up; (*adirarsi*) lose one's temper; take ⟨*foto*⟩

**'scatto** *nm* (*balzo*) spring; (*d'ira*) outburst; (*di telefono*) unit; (*dispositivo*) release; **a scatti** jerkily; **di ~** suddenly

**scatu'rire** *vi* spring

**scaval'care** *vt* jump over ⟨*muretto*⟩; climb over ⟨*muro*⟩; (*fig: superare*) overtake

**sca'vare** *vt* dig ⟨*buca*⟩; dig up ⟨*tesoro*⟩; excavate ⟨*città sepolta*⟩

**scava'trice** *nf* excavator

**scavezza'collo** *nm* daredevil

**'scavo** *nm* excavation

**scazzot'tare** *vt fam* beat up

**scazzot'tata** *nf fam* punch-up; **prendersi una ~** get beaten up

**'scegliere** *vt* choose, select

**sce'icco** *nm* sheikh

**scelle'rato** *a* wicked

**'scelta** *nf* choice; (*di articoli*) range; **...a ~** (*in menù*) choice of...; **prendine uno a ~** take your choice o pick; **di prima ~** top-grade, choice; ⟨*albergo*⟩ first-rate; **di seconda ~** second grade; *pej* second-rate

**'scelto** *pp di* **scegliere** ● *a* select; ⟨*merce ecc*⟩ choice; **tiratore ~** marksman

**sce'mare** *vt/i* diminish

**sce'menza** *nf* silliness; (*azione*) silly thing to do/say; **non diciamo scemenze!** let's not be silly!

**'scemo** *a* idiotic ● *nm* idiot

**scempi'aggine** *nf* foolish thing to do/say

**'scempio** *nm* havoc; (*fig: di paesaggio*) ruination; **fare ~ di** play havoc with

**'scena** *nf* scene; (*palcoscenico*) stage; **entrare in ~** *Theat* go/come on [stage]; *fig* come on the scene; **fare ~** put on an act; **fare una ~** make a scene; **fare scene** make a fuss; **andare in ~** ⟨*Theat: spettacolo:*⟩ be staged, be put on; **fare ~ muta** not open one's mouth; **scomparire dalla ~** *fig* vanish from the scene; **mettere in ~** produce, stage; **messa in ~** production, staging; *fig* set-up

**sce'nario** *nm* scenery

**sce'nata** *nf* row, scene

**'scendere** *vi* go/come down; (*da treno, autobus*) get off; (*da macchina*) get out;

⟨strada:⟩ slope; ⟨notte, prezzi:⟩ fall ● vt go/ come down ⟨scale⟩

**scendi'letto** nm bedside rug

**sceneggi'are** vt dramatize

**sceneggi'ato** nm television serial

**sceneggia'tura** nf screenplay

**'scenico** a scenic

**scenogra'fia** nf set design

**sce'nografo, -a** nmf set designer

**sce'riffo** nm sheriff

**scervel'larsi** vr rack one's brains

**scervel'lato** a brainless

**'sceso** pp di **scendere**

**scetti'cismo** nm scepticism

**'scettico, -a** a sceptical ● nmf sceptic

**'scettro** nm sceptre

**'scheda** nf card. ~ **audio** Comput sound card. ~ **elettorale** ballot-paper. ~ **di espansione** Comput expansion card. ~ **grafica** Comput graphics card. ~ **madre** Comput motherboard. ~ **magnetica** card key. ~ **perforata** punch card. ~ **di rete** Comput network card. ~ **sonora** Comput sound card. ~ **telefonica** phonecard. ~ **video** Comput video card

**sche'dare** vt file

**sche'dario** nm file; ⟨mobile⟩ filing cabinet

**sche'dato, -a** a with a police record ● nmf person with a police record

**sche'dina** nf ≈ pools coupon; **giocare la ~** ≈ do the pools

**'scheggia** nf fragment; ⟨di legno⟩ splinter

**scheggi'are** vt splinter

**scheggi'arsi** vr chip; ⟨legno:⟩ splinter

**sche'letrico** a skeletal

**'scheletro** nm skeleton; **essere ridotto ad uno ~** be all skin and bones

**'schema** nm diagram; ⟨abbozzo⟩ outline; **uscire dagli schemi** break with tradition

**schematica'mente** adv schematically

**sche'matico** a schematic

**schematiz'zare** vt present schematically

**'scherma** nf fencing

**scher'maglia** nf skirmish

**scher'mirsi** vr protect oneself

**'schermo** nm screen; **grande ~** big screen; **farsi ~ con** shield oneself with. ~ **panoramico** wide screen. ~ **a sfioramento** Comput touch-sensitive screen

**scher'nire** vt mock

**'scherno** nm mockery

**scher'zare** vi joke; ⟨giocare⟩ play; **c'è poco da ~!** it's nothing to laugh about!

**'scherzo** nm joke; ⟨trucco⟩ trick; ⟨effetto⟩ play; Mus scherzo; **fare uno ~ a qcno** play a joke on sb; **giocare brutti scherzi (a qcno)** ⟨memoria, vista:⟩ play tricks (on sb); **per ~** for fun; **scherzi a parte** joking apart, seriously; **stare allo ~** take a joke. ~ **di natura** freak of nature

**scher'zoso** a playful

**schiaccia'noci** nm inv nutcrackers pl

**schiacci'ante** a damning; ⟨vittoria⟩ crushing

**schiacci'are** vt crush; (in tennis ecc)

smash; press ⟨pulsante⟩; crack ⟨noce⟩; ~ **un pisolino** grab forty winks

**schiacci'arsi** vr get crushed

**schiaccia'sassi** nf inv steamroller

**schiaf'fare** vt fam shove

**schiaffeggi'are** vt slap

**schi'affo** nm slap; **dare uno ~ a** slap. ~ **morale** slap in the face; **avere una faccia da schiaffi** have the kind of face you'd love to take a swipe at

**schiamaz'zare** vi make a racket; ⟨galline:⟩ cackle

**schia'mazzo** nm din. **schiamazzi** pl **notturni** disturbing the peace

**schian'tare** vt break

**schian'tarsi** vr crash ● vi **schianto dalla fatica** I'm wiped out

**'schianto** nm crash; fam knock-out; ⟨divertente⟩ scream

**schia'rire** vt clear; ⟨sbiadire⟩ fade ● vi brighten up

**schia'rirsi** vr brighten up; ~ **la gola** clear one's throat; ~ **le idee** get things clear in one's head; ⟨dopo aver bevuto⟩ clear one's head

**schia'rita** nf sunny interval

**schiat'tare** vi burst; ~ **di invidia** be green with envy

**schia'vista** nmf slave-driver

**schiavitù** nf slavery

**schi'avo, -a** nmf slave

**schi'ena** nf back; **mal di ~** backache

**schie'nale** nm ⟨di sedia⟩ back

**schi'era** nf Mil rank; ⟨moltitudine⟩ crowd

**schiera'mento** nm lining up; Mil battle line. ~ **di forze** rallying of the troops

**schie'rare** vt draw up; rally ⟨forze⟩

**schie'rarsi** vr draw up; ⟨forze:⟩ rally; ~ **dalla parte di qcno**, ~ **con qcno** rally [in support] to sb; ~ **contro qcno** rally in opposition to sb

**schiet'tezza** nf frankness

**schi'etto** a frank; ⟨puro⟩ pure

**schi'fezza** nf **è una ~** it's disgusting; ⟨film, libro:⟩ it's rubbish

**schifil'toso** a fussy

**'schifo** nm disgust; **fare ~** be disgusting; **è uno ~!** it's disgusting!

**schi'foso** a disgusting; ⟨di cattiva qualità⟩ rubbishy

**schioc'care** vt crack ⟨frusta⟩; snap, click ⟨dita⟩; click ⟨lingua⟩ ● vi crack

**schi'occo** nm ⟨di frusta⟩ crack; ⟨di bacio⟩ smack; ⟨di dita, lingua⟩ click

**schioppet'tata** nf shot

**schi'oppo** nm fam rifle; **a un tiro di ~** fig a stone's throw away

**schiri'bizzo** nm fam fancy; **se mi salta lo ~...** if it takes my fancy...

**schi'udere** vt open

**schi'udersi** vr open

**schi'uma** nf foam; ⟨di sapone⟩ lather; ⟨di bucato⟩ suds; ⟨feccia⟩ scum. ~ **da barba** shaving foam

**schiu'mare** vt skim ● vi foam

**schiuma'rola** nf Culin skimmer
**schiu'mogeno** a foaming
**schiu'moso** a ⟨birra, crema⟩ frothy, foamy; ⟨liquido⟩ scummy
**schi'uso** pp di **schiudere**
**schi'vare** vt avoid
**'schivo** a bashful
**schizofre'nia** nf schizophrenia
**schizo'frenico, -a** a & nmf schizophrenic
**schiz'zare** vt squirt; (inzaccherare) splash; (abbozzare) sketch; ~ **qcno/qcsa di qcsa** splatter sb/sth with sth ● vi spurt ~ **via** fig scurry away
**schiz'zato, -a** a & nmf fam loony
**schizzi'noso** a squeamish
**'schizzo** nm squirt; (di fango) splash; (abbozzo) sketch
**sci** nm inv ski; (sport) skiing. ~ **d'acqua,** ~ **acquatico** water-skiing. ~ **acrobatico** hot dogging. ~ **di fondo** cross-country skiing
**'scia** nf wake; (di fumo ecc) trail; **sulla ~ di qcno** following in sb's footsteps
**sci'abola** nf sabre
**sciabor'dare** vt/i lap
**sciabor'dio** nm lapping
**sciacal'laggio** nm profiteering
**scia'callo** nm jackal; fig profiteer
**sciac'quare** vt rinse
**sciac'quarsi** vr rinse oneself
**sci'acquo** nm mouthwash
**scia'gura** nf disaster
**sciagu'rato** a unfortunate; (scellerato) wicked
**scialac'quare** vt squander
**scialacqua|'tore, -'trice** nmf squanderer
**scia'lare** vi spend money like water
**sci'albo** a pale; fig dull
**sci'alle** nm shawl
**scia'luppa** nf dinghy. ~ **di salvataggio** lifeboat
**sciaman'nato** a good-for-nothing
**scia'mano** n shaman
**scia'mare** vi swarm
**sci'ame** nm swarm; **a sciami** in swarms
**sci'ampo** nm shampoo
**scian'cato** a lame
**sci'are** vi ski; **andare a ~** go skiing
**sci'arpa** nf scarf
**sci'atica** nf Med sciatica
**scia|'tore, -'trice** nmf skier
**sciatte'ria** nf slovenliness
**sci'atto** a slovenly; ⟨stile⟩ careless
**sciat'tone, -a** nmf slovenly person
**'scibile** nm knowledge; **lo ~ umano** the sum of human knowledge
**scic'coso** a fam snazzy
**scienti'fico** a scientific
**sci'enza** nf science; (sapere) knowledge; **avere la ~ infusa** be naturally talented
**scienzi'ato, -a** nmf scientist
**sci'ita** a & nmf Shiite
**scilin'guagnolo** nm fig **avere lo ~** be a chatterbox
**'scimmia** nf monkey

**scimmiot'tare** vt ape
**scimpanzé** nm inv chimpanzee, chimp
**scimu'nito** a idiotic
**'scindere** vt separate; ~ **in** break down into
**'scindersi** vr divide; ~ **in** divide into
**scin'tilla** nf spark
**scintil'lante** a sparkling
**scintil'lare** vi sparkle
**scintil'lio** nm sparkle
**sciò** int shoo!
**scioc'cante** a shocking
**scioc'care** vt shock
**scioc'chezza** nf foolishness; (assurdità) foolish thing; **sciocchezze!** nonsense!
**sci'occo** a foolish
**sci'ogliere** vt untie; undo, untie ⟨nodo⟩; (liberare) release; (liquefare) melt; dissolve ⟨contratto, qcsa nell'acqua⟩; loosen up ⟨muscoli⟩
**sci'ogliersi** vr ⟨nodo:⟩ come undone; (liquefarsi) melt; ⟨contratto:⟩ be dissolved; ⟨pastiglia:⟩ dissolve
**sciogli'lingua** nm inv tongue-twister
**scio'lina** nf ski wax
**sciol'tezza** nf agility; (disinvoltura) ease
**sci'olto** pp di **sciogliere** ● a loose; (agile) agile; (disinvolto) easy; **versi** pl **sciolti** blank verse
**sciope'rante** nmf striker
**sciope'rare** vi go on strike, strike
**sci'opero** nm strike; **in ~** on strike. ~ **bianco** work-to-rule. ~ **generale** general strike. ~ **a singhiozzo** on-off strike
**sciori'nare** vt fig show off
**sciovi'nismo** nm chauvinism
**sciovi'nista** nmf Pol chauvinist
**sciovi'nistico** a Pol chauvinistic
**sci'pito** a insipid
**scip'pare** vt fam snatch; ~ **qcno** snatch sb's bag/bracelet etc
**scippa|'tore, -trice** nmf bag-snatcher
**'scippo** nm bag-snatching
**sci'rocco** nm sirocco
**scirop'pato** a ⟨frutta⟩ in syrup
**sci'roppo** nm syrup
**scirop'poso** a syrupy
**'scisma** nm schism
**scissi'one** nf division
**scissio'nista** a breakaway attrib
**'scisso** pp di **scindere**
**sciupacchi'are** vt spoil
**sciupacchi'ato** a spoilt
**sciu'pare** vt spoil; (sperperare) waste
**sciu'parsi** vr get spoiled; (deperire) wear oneself out
**sciu'pio** nm waste
**scivo'lare** vi slide; (involontariamente) slip
**'scivolo** nm slide; Techn chute
**scivo'lone** nm fall; (fig: errore) blunder
**scivo'loso** a slippery
**scle'rosi** nf sclerosis. ~ **multipla,** ~ **a placche** multiple sclerosis. MS
**scoc'care** vt fire ⟨freccia⟩; strike ⟨ore⟩ ● vi ⟨scintilla:⟩ shoot out; **sono scoccate le cinque** five o'clock has just struck

**scocci'are** *vt fam* (*dare noia a*) bother

**scocci'arsi** *vr fam* be bored; **mi sono scocciato di aspettare** I'm fed up waiting

**scocci'ato** *a fam* fed up

**scoccia|'trice** *nmf* nuisance

**scoccia'tura** *nf fam* nuisance

**sco'della** *nf* bowl

**scodel'lare** *vt* dish out. dish up

**scodinzo'lare** *vi* wag its tail

**scogli'era** *nf* cliff; (*a fior d'acqua*) reef

**'scoglio** *nm* rock; (*fig: ostacolo*) stumbling block

**scoglio'nato** *a vulg* pissed off

**scoi'attolo** *nm* squirrel

**scola'pasta** *nm inv* colander

**scolapi'atti** *nm inv* dish drainer

**sco'lara** *nf* schoolgirl

**sco'lare**[1] *vt* drain; strain (*pasta, verdura*) ● *vi* drip

**sco'lare**[2] *a* school *attrib*; **in età ~** (*bambino*) school-age

**scola'resca** *nf* pupils *pl*

**sco'laro** *nm* schoolboy

**sco'lastico** *a* school *attrib*; **gita scolastica** school trip

**scoli'osi** *nf* curvature of the spine

**scollacci'ato** *a* low-cut

**scol'lare** *vt* cut away the neck of (*abito*); (*staccare*) unstick

**scol'lato** *a* (*abito*) low-necked

**scolla'tura** *nf* neckline; **~ profonda** plunging neckline

**scolle'gare** *vt* disconnect

**'scollo** *nm* neckline

**'scolo** *nm* drainage

**scolo'rare** *vt* fade

**scolori'mento** *nm* fading

**scolo'rire** *vt* fade

**scolo'rirsi** *vr* fade

**scolo'rito** *a* faded

**scol'pire** *vt* carve; (*imprimere*) engrave

**scombi'nare** *vt* upset

**scombusso'lare** *vt* muddle up

**scom'messa** *nf* bet

**scom'messo** *pp di* **scommettere**

**scom'mettere** *vt* bet; **ci puoi ~!** you bet!

**scomo'dare** *vt* trouble

**scomo'darsi** *vr* trouble

**scomodità** *nf inv* discomfort

**'scomodo** *a* uncomfortable ● *nm* **essere di ~ a qcno** be a trouble to sb

**scompagin'are** *vt* mess up

**scompa'gnare** *vt* split

**scompa'gnato** *a* odd

**scompa'rire** *vi* disappear; (*morire*) pass away

**scom'parsa** *nf* disappearance; (*morte*) death, passing

**scom'parso, -a** *pp di* **scomparire** ● *a* departed ● *nmf* departed

**scomparti'mento** *nm* compartment

**scom'parto** *nf* compartment

**scompen'sare** *vt* throw off balance

**scom'penso** *nm* imbalance. **~ cardiaco** cardiac insufficiency

**scompigli'are** *vt* disarrange

**scom'piglio** *nm* confusion

**scompisci'arsi** *vr fam* **~** [**dalle risa**] wet oneself, split one's sides laughing

**scom'porre** *vt* break down; ruffle (*capelli*); (*fig: turbare*) upset

**scom'porsi** *vr* lose one's composure

**scomposizi'one** *nf* breaking down

**scom'posto** *pp di* **scomporre** ● *a* (*sguaiato*) unseemly; (*disordinato*) untidy

**sco'munica** *nf* excommunication

**scomuni'care** *vt* excommunicate

**sconcer'tante** *a* disconcerting; (*che rende perplesso*) bewildering

**sconcer'tare** *vt* disconcert; (*rendere perplesso*) bewilder

**sconcer'tato** *a* disconcerted; (*perplesso*) bewildered

**scon'cezza** *nf* indecency

**'sconcio** *a* indecent ● *nm* **è uno ~ che...** it's a disgrace that...

**sconclusio'nato** *a* incoherent

**scon'dito** *a* unseasoned; (*insalata*) with no dressing

**sconfes'sare** *vt* disown

**scon'figgere** *vt* defeat

**sconfi'nare** *vi* cross the border; (*in proprietà privata*) trespass

**sconfi'nato** *a* unlimited

**scon'fitta** *nf* defeat; **subire una ~** be defeated, suffer defeat

**scon'fitto** *pp di* **sconfiggere**

**sconfor'tante** *a* disheartening, discouraging

**scon'forto** *nm* discouragement; **farsi prendere dallo ~** get discouraged, get disheartened

**sconge'lare** *vt* thaw out (*cibo*); defrost (*frigo*)

**scongiu'rare** *vt* beseech; (*evitare*) avert

**scongi'uro** *nm* **fare gli scongiuri** ≈ touch wood, knock on wood *Am*

**scon'nesso** *pp di* **sconnettere** ● *a fig* incoherent

**scon'nettere** *vt* disconnect

**sconosci'uto, -a** *a* unknown ● *nmf* stranger

**sconquas'sare** *vt* smash; (*sconvolgere*) upset

**sconsa'crare** *vt* deconsecrate

**sconsiderata'mente** *adv* inconsiderately

**sconsidera'tezza** *nf* lack of consideration, thoughtlessness

**sconside'rato** *a* inconsiderate, thoughtless

**sconsigli'abile** *a* not advisable

**sconsigli'are** *vt* advise against

**sconso'lato** *a* disconsolate

**scon'tare** *vt* discount; (*dedurre*) deduct; (*pagare*) pay off; serve (*pena*); **~ la propria colpa** pay for one's sins

**scon'tato** *a* discounted; (*ovvio*) expected; **~ del 10%** with 10% discount; **era ~** it was to be expected; **dare qcsa per ~** take sth for granted

**scon'tento** *a* displeased ● *nm* discontent

**'sconto** *nm* discount; **fare uno ~** give a discount. **~ commerciale** trade discount

**scon'trarsi** *vr* clash; *(urtare)* collide

**scon'trino** *nm* ticket; *(di cassa)* receipt; **'munirsi dello ~ alla cassa'** *sign reminding customers that payment must be made at the cash desk beforehand*

**'scontro** *nm* clash; *(urto)* collision. **~ frontale** head-on collision. **~ a fuoco** shootout

**scontrosità** *nf* blackness

**scon'troso** *a* disagreeable

**sconveni'ente** *a* unprofitable; *(scorretto)* unseemly

**sconvol'gente** *a* mind-blowing

**scon'volgere** *vt* upset; *(mettere in disordine)* disarrange

**sconvolgi'mento** *nm* upheaval

**scon'volto** *pp di* **sconvolgere** ● *a* distraught

**'scooter** *nm inv* scooter

**'scopa** *nf* broom; *(gioco di carte)* type of card game

**sco'pare** *vt* sweep; *vulg* shag

**sco'pata** *nf* sweep; *vulg* shag; **dare una ~ per terra** give the floor a sweep

**scoperchi'are** *vt* take the lid off ⟨*pentola*⟩; take the roof off ⟨*casa*⟩

**sco'perta** *nf* discovery

**sco'perto** *pp di* **scoprire** ● *a* uncovered; *(senza riparo)* exposed; *(conto)* overdrawn; *(spoglio)* bare

**'scopo** *nm* aim; **a ~ di** for the sake of; **allo ~ di** in order to

**sco'pone** *nm* *(gioco di carte)* type of card game

**scoppi'are** *vi* burst; *fig* break out

**scoppiet'tare** *vi* crackle

**'scoppio** *nm* burst; *(di guerra)* outbreak; *(esplosione)* explosion; **a ~ ritardato** ⟨*bomba*⟩ delayed action; **ha reagito a ~ ritardato** he did a double take

**sco'prire** *vt* discover; *(togliere la copertura a)* uncover; unveil ⟨*statua*⟩; **~ gli altarini** *fam* reveal his/her etc guilty secrets

**scoraggia'mento** *nm* discouragement

**scoraggi'ante** *a* discouraging

**scoraggi'are** *vt* discourage

**scoraggi'arsi** *vr* lose heart

**scor'butico** *a* *Med* suffering from scurvy; *(fig: scontroso)* disagreeable

**scor'buto** *nm* *Med* scurvy

**scorci'are** *vt* shorten

**scorcia'toia** *nf* short cut

**'scorcio** *nm* *(di cielo)* patch; *(in arte)* foreshortening; **di ~** ⟨*vedere*⟩ from an angle. **~ panoramico** panoramic view. **~ del secolo** end of the century

**scor'dare** *vt* forget; **~ qcsa a casa** leave sth at home

**scor'darsi** *vr* forget; **~ di qcsa** forget sth

**scor'dato** *a* *Mus* out of tune

**scorda'tura** *nf* *Mus* going out of tune

**sco'reggia** *nf fam* fart

**scoreggi'are** *vi fam* fart

**'scorfano** *nm* scorpion fish

**'scorgere** *vt* make out; *(notare)* notice

**'scoria** *nf* waste; *(di carbone)* slag

**scor'nare** *vt fig* humiliate

**scor'narsi** *vr fig* come a cropper

**scor'nato** *a fig* hangdog

**'scorno** *nm* humiliation

**scorpacci'ata** *nf* bellyful; **fare una ~ di** stuff oneself with

**scorpi'one** *nm* scorpion; *Astr* Scorpio

**scorraz'zare** *vi* run about

**'scorrere** *vt* *(dare un'occhiata)* glance through ● *vi* run; *(scivolare)* slide; *(fluire)* flow; *Comput* scroll; *(attorno a un oggetto)* wrap

**scorre'ria** *nf* raid

**scorret'tezza** *nf* *(mancanza di educazione)* bad manners *pl*

**scor'retto** *a* incorrect; *(sconveniente)* improper

**scor'revole** **a porta ~** sliding door

**scorri'banda** *nf* raid; *fig* excursion

**scorri'mento** *nm* *Comput* scrolling; *(attorno a un oggetto)* wrapping

**'scorsa** *nf* glance; **dare una ~ a** glance through

**'scorso** *pp di* **scorrere** ● *a* last; **l'anno ~** last year

**scor'soio** *a* **nodo ~** noose

**'scorta** *nf* escort; *(provvista)* supply

**scor'tare** *vt* escort

**scortecci'are** *vt* debark ⟨*albero*⟩; strip ⟨*muro*⟩

**scor'tese** *a* rude

**scorte'sia** *nf* rudeness

**scorti'care** *vt* skin

**scortica'tura** *nf* graze

**'scorto** *pp di* **scorgere**

**'scorza** *nf* peel; *(crosta)* crust; *(corteccia)* bark; *fig* exterior. **~ d'arancia** orange peel

**scorzo'nera** *nf* salsify

**sco'sceso** *a* steep

**'scossa** *nf* shake; *Electr, fig* shock; **prendere la ~** get an electric shock. **~ elettrica** electric shock. **~ sismica** earth tremor

**'scosso** *pp di* **scuotere** ● *a* shaken; *(sconvolto)* upset

**scos'sone** *nm* jolt

**sco'stante** *a* off-putting

**sco'stare** *vt* push away

**sco'starsi** *vr* stand aside

**scostu'mato** *a* dissolute; *(maleducato)* ill-mannered

**scoten'nare** *vt* skin ⟨*maiale*⟩; scalp ⟨*persona*⟩

**scot'tante** *a* ⟨*argomento*⟩ burning; *(fig: notizia)* sensational

**scot'tare** *vt* burn; *(con liquido, vapore)* scald; *Culin* blanch ● *vi* ⟨*bevanda, cibo*:⟩ be too hot; ⟨*sole, pentola*:⟩ be very hot

**scot'tarsi** *vr* burn oneself; *(con liquido, vapore)* scald oneself; *(al sole)* get sunburnt; *fig* get one's fingers burnt

**scot'tato** *a* *Culin* blanched

**scotta'tura** nf burn; (da liquido) scald; fig painful experience; ~ **solare** sunburn

**'Scottex**ᴿ nm paper towel

**'scotto**¹ a overcooked

**'scotto**² nm score; **pagare lo ~ di qcsa** pay for sth

**scout** a inv scout attrib ● nmf inv scout

**scou'tismo** nm scout movement

**sco'vare** vt (scoprire) discover

**scovo'lino** nm bottle brush; (per pipa) pipe cleaner

**'Scozia** nf Scotland

**scoz'zese** a Scottish ● nmf Scot

**'scrambler** nm inv Radio, Teleph scrambler

**screan'zato** a rude

**scredi'tare** vt discredit

**scre'mare** vt skim

**screpo'lare** vt chap

**screpo'larsi** vr get chapped; ⟨intonaco:⟩ crack

**screpo'lato** a chapped; ⟨intonaco⟩ cracked

**screpola'tura** nf crack

**screzi'ato** a speckled

**'screzio** nm disagreement

**scribacchi'are** vt scribble

**scribac'chino, -a** nmf scribbler; (impiegato) penpusher

**scricchio'lante** a creaky

**scricchio'lare** vi creak

**scricchio'lio** nm creaking

**'scricciolo** nm wren; fig delicate-looking creature

**'scrigno** nm casket

**scrimina'tura** nf parting

**scriteri'ato** a empty-headed

**'scritta** nf writing; (su muro) graffiti

**'scritto** pp di **scrivere** ● a written; ~ **col computer** word-processed; ~ **a macchina** typed; ~ **a mano** handwritten ● nm writing; (lettera) letter

**scrit'toio** nm writing-desk

**scrit|'tore, -'trice** nmf writer

**scrit'tura** nf writing; Relig scripture; (calligrafia) handwriting. **scritture** pl **contabili** account books. ~ **privata** Jur legal document drawn up by an individual

**scrittu'rare** vt engage

**scriva'nia** nf desk

**scri'vente** nmf writer

**'scrivere** vt write; (descrivere) write about; ~ **a macchina** type

**scroc'care** vt fam ~ **a** sponge off

**scrocchi'are** vi crack

**'scrocco**¹ nm fam **a ~** without paying; **vivere a ~** sponge off other people

**'scrocco**² nm **coltello a ~** pocket knife; **serratura a ~** spring lock

**scroc'cone, -a** nmf fam sponger

**'scrofa** nf sow

**scrol'lare** vt shake; ~ **le spalle** shrug one's shoulders; ~ **la testa** shake one's head

**scrol'larsi** vr shake oneself; ~ **qcsa di dosso** shake sth off

**'scrolling** nm Comput scrolling

**scrosci'ante** a pouring; ⟨applausi⟩ thunderous

**scrosci'are** vi roar; ⟨pioggia:⟩ pelt down

**'scroscio** nm roar; (di pioggia) pelting; **uno ~ di applausi** thunderous applause; **piovere a ~** lash down

**scro'stare** vt scrape

**scro'starsi** vr flake

**scro'stato** a flaky

**'scroto** nm scrotum

**'scrupolo** nm scruple; (diligenza) care; **senza scrupoli** unscrupulous, without scruples; **farsi scrupoli per qcsa** have scruples about sth

**scrupo'loso** a scrupulous

**scru'tare** vt scan; (indagare) search

**scruta'tore** nm (di voti) returning officer

**scruti'nare** vt scrutinize

**scru'tinio** nm (di voti) poll; Sch assessment of progress; **scrutini** pl Sch meeting of teachers to discuss pupils' work and assign marks. ~ **segreto** secret ballot

**scu'cire** vt unstitch; **scuci i soldi!** fig fam cough up [the money]!

**scu'cirsi** vr come unstitched; (fig: parlare) talk; **non si scuce** he won't talk

**scuci'tura** nf unstitching

**scude'ria** nf stable; **scuderie** pl mews

**scu'detto** nm Sport championship shield; (campionato) national championship

**scudi'ero** nm squire

**scudisci'ata** nf whipping

**'scudo** nm shield; **farsi ~ con qcsa** shield oneself with sth

**scuffi'are** vi capsize

**scu'gnizzo** nm street urchin

**sculacci'are** vt spank

**sculacci'ata** nf spanking; **prendere a sculacciate** spank

**sculacci'one** nm spanking

**scule'ttare** vi wiggle one's hips

**scul|'tore, -'trice** nm sculptor ● nf sculptress

**scul'tura** nf sculpture

**scu'ola** nf school. ~ **allievi ufficiali** cadet school. ~ **elementare** primary school. ~ **guida** driving school. ~ **materna** day nursery. ~ **media** secondary school. ~ **media inferiore** secondary school (10-13). ~ **media superiore** secondary school (13-18). ~ **dell'obbligo** compulsory education. ~ **privata** private school, public school Br. ~ **di sci** ski school. ~ **serale** evening school. ~ **statale** state school. ~ **superiore** high school

**scu'otere** vt shake

**scu'otersi** vr (destarsi) rouse oneself; ~ **qcsa di dosso** fig shake sth off

**'scure** nf axe

**scu'rire** vt/i darken

**'scuro** a dark ● nm darkness; (imposta) shutter

**scur'rile** a scurrilous

**'scusa** nf excuse; (giustificazione) apology;

(*pretesto*) pretext: **chiedere** ~ apologize; |**chiedo**| ~**!** [I'm] sorry!

**scu'sare** *vt* excuse

**scu'sarsi** *vr* apologize (**di** for); |**mi**| **scusi!** excuse me!; (*chiedendo perdono*) [I'm] sorry!

**'sdarsi** *vr fam* lose interest

**sdebi'tarsi** *vr* repay the kindness

**sde'gnare** *vt* despise; (*fare arrabbiare*) enrage

**sde'gnarsi** *vr* become angry

**sde'gnato** *a* indignant

**'sdegno** *nm* disdain; (*ira*) indignation

**sde'gnoso** *a* disdainful

**sden'tato** *a* toothless

**sdipa'nare** *vt* wind

**sdogana'mento** *nm* customs clearance

**sdoga'nare** *vt* clear through customs

**sdolci'nato** *a* sentimental, schmaltzy

**sdoppia'mento** *nm* splitting. ~ **della personalità** split personality

**sdoppi'are** *vt* halve

**sdrai'arsi** *vr* lie down

**'sdraio** *nm* [**sedia a**] ~ deckchair

**sdrammatiz'zare** *vt* take the heat out of ● *vi* take the heat out of the situation

**sdruccio'lare** *vi* slither

**sdruccio'levole** *a* slippery

**sdruccio'lone** *nm* slip

**SE** *abbr* (**sud-est**) SE

**se** *conj* if; (*interrogativo*) whether, if; **se mai** (*caso mai*) if need be; **se mai telefonasse,...** should he call,..., if he calls,...; **se no** otherwise, or else; **se non altro** at least, if nothing else; **se pure** (*sebbene*) even though; (*anche se*) even if: **non so se sia vero** I don't know whether it's true, I don't know if it's true; **come se** as if; **se lo avessi saputo prima!** if only I had known before!; **e se andassimo fuori a cena?** how about going out for dinner? ● *nm inv* if; **non voglio né se né ma** I don't want any ifs or buts

**sé** *pers pron* oneself; (*lui*) himself; (*lei*) herself; (*esso, essa*) itself; (*loro*) themselves; **l'ha fatto da sé** he did it himself; **ha preso i soldi con sé** he took the money with him; **si sono tenuti le notizie per sé** they kept the news to themselves

**se'baceo** *a* sebaceous

**seb'bene** *conj* although

**'sebo** *nm* sebum

**sec.** *abbr* (**secolo**) c.

**'secca** *nf* shallows *pl*; **in** ~ (*nave*) grounded

**sec'cante** *a* annoying

**sec'care** *vt* dry; (*importunare*) annoy ● *vi* dry up

**sec'carsi** *vr* dry up; (*irritarsi*) get annoyed

**secca|'tore, -'trice** *nmf* nuisance

**secca'tura** *nf* bother; **dare una** ~ **a qcno** trouble sb, bother sb; **non voglio seccature!** I don't want the bother!

**secchi'ata** *nf* bucketful

**secchi'ello** *nm* bucket. ~ **del ghiaccio** ice bucket

**'secchio** *nm* bucket. ~ **della spazzatura** rubbish bin, trash can *Am*

**'secco, -a** *a* dry; (*disseccato*) dried; (*magro*) thin; (*brusco*) curt; (*preciso*) sharp; **restare a** ~ be left penniless; **restarci** ~ (*fam: morire di colpo*) be killed on the spot; **frutta secca** nuts *pl* ● *nm* (*siccità*) drought; **lavare a** ~ dry-clean

**secessi'one** *nf* secession; **guerra di** ~ War of Secession

**seco'lare** *a* age-old; (*laico*) secular

**'secolo** *nm* century; (*epoca*) age; **è un** ~ **che non lo vedo** *fam* I haven't seen him for ages o yonks

**se'conda** *nf Sch, Rail* second class; *Auto* second [gear] ● *prep* **a** ~ **di** according to

**secon'dario** *a Jur* collateral; **effetto** ~ side effect

**se'condo** *a* second ● *nm* second, sec *fam;* (*secondo piatto*) main course; **un** ~**!** just a sec[ond]! ● *prep* according to; ~ **me** in my opinion

**secondo'genito, -a** *a & nm* second-born

**secrezi'one** *nf* secretion

**'sedano** *nm* celery. ~ **rapa** celeriac

**se'dare** *vt* put down, suppress (*rivolta*); *fig* soothe

**seda'tivo** *a & nm* sedative; **somministrare sedativi a** sedate

**'sede** *nf* seat; (*centro*) centre; *Relig* see; *Comm* head office; **in** ~ **di esami** during the exams; **in separata** ~ in private. ~ **centrale** head office. ~ **sociale** registered office

**seden'tario** *a* sedentary

**se'dere** *vi* sit

**se'dersi** *vr* sit down ● *nm* (*deretano*) bottom

**'sedia** *nf* chair. ~ **a dondolo** rocking chair. ~ **elettrica** electric chair. ~ **da giardino** garden seat. ~ **a rotelle** wheelchair. ~ **a sdraio** deckchair

**sedi'cenne** *a & nmf* sixteen-year-old

**sedi'cente** *a* self-styled

**sedi'cesimo, -a** *a & nm* sixteenth

**'sedici** *a & nm* sixteen

**se'dile** *nm* seat

**sedimen'tare** *vi* leave a sediment

**sedi'mento** *nm* sediment

**sedizi'one** *nf* sedition

**sedizi'oso** *a* seditious

**se'dotto** *pp di* **sedurre**

**sedu'cente** *a* seductive; (*allettante*) enticing

**se'durre** *vt* seduce

**se'duta** *nf* session; (*di posa*) sitting. ~ **stante** *adv* here and now

**se'duto** *a* sitting

**sedut|'tore, -'trice** *nm* charmer ● *nf* temptress

**seduzi'one** *nf* seduction

**seg.** *abbr* (**seguente**) foll.

**'sega** *nf* saw; *vulg* wank; **mezza** ~ *vulg* tosser; **non capire una** ~ understand damn all. ~ **circolare** circular saw. ~ **a mano** handsaw. ~ **a nastro** band saw

**'segale** *nf* rye; **pane di** ~ rye bread

**sega'ligno** *a* wiry

**se'gare** *vt* saw

**sega'trice** *nf* saw. **~ a nastro** band saw

**sega'tura** *nf* sawdust

**'seggio** *nm* seat. **~ elettorale** polling station

**seg'giola** *nf* chair

**seggio'lino** *nm* seat; (*da bambino*) child's seat; **~ regolabile** adjustable seat

**seggio'lone** *nm* (*per bambini*) high chair

**seggio'via** *nf* chair lift

**seghe'ria** *nf* sawmill

**se'ghetto** *nm* hacksaw

**segmen'tare** *vt* segment

**seg'mento** *nm* segment

**segna'carte** *nm* bookmark

**segna'lare** *vt* signal; (*annunciare*) announce; (*indicare*) point out

**segna'larsi** *vr* distinguish oneself

**segnalazi'one** *nf* signals *pl*; (*di candidato*) recommendation. **~ stradale** road signs *pl*

**se'gnale** *nm* signal; (*stradale*) sign. **~ acustico** beep. **~ d'allarme** alarm; (*in treno*) communication cord *Br*, emergency brake; *fig* danger signal. **~ digitale** *Comput* digital signal. **~ di libero** *Teleph* dialling tone. **~ orario** time signal

**segna'letica** *nf* signals *pl*; '**~ in rifacimento**' 'road signs being repainted'. **~ orizzontale** painted road markings *pl*. **~ stradale** road signs *pl*

**segna'letico** *a* **dati segnaletici** description; **foto segnaletica** *photograph used for identification purposes*

**segna'libro** *nm* bookmark

**segna'punti** *nm inv* pegboard

**se'gnare** *vt* mark; (*prendere nota*) note; (*indicare*) indicate; *Sport* score; **~ la fine di qcsa** sound the death knell for sth; **~ il passo** mark time

**se'gnarsi** *vr* cross oneself

**se'gnato** *a* marked

**'segno** *nm* sign; (*traccia, limite*) mark; (*bersaglio*) target; **far ~** (*col capo*) nod; (*con la mano*) beckon; **fare ~ di no** (*con la testa*) shake one's head; **fare ~ di sì** (*con la testa*) nod [one's head]; **lasciare il ~** leave a mark; **non dare segni di vita** give no sign of life; **oltrepassare il ~** *fig* overstep the mark. **~ della croce** sign of the cross. **~ premonitore** early warning. **~ zodiacale** sign of the Zodiac, birth sign

**segre'gare** *vt* segregate

**segre'garsi** *vr* cut oneself off

**segre'gato** *a* in isolation

**segregazi'one** *nf* segregation

**segretari'ato** *nm* secretariat

**segre'tario, -a** *nmf* secretary; **fare da ~ a qcno** be sb's secretary. **~ bilingue** bilingual secretary. **~ comunale** town clerk. **~ di direzione** executive secretary. **~ personale** personal assistant, PA. **S~ di Stato** Secretary of State. **segretaria tuttofare** girl Friday

**segre'teria** *nf* (*ufficio*) administrative office; (*segretariato*) secretariat. **~ telefonica** answering machine, answerphone

**segre'tezza** *nf* secrecy

**se'greto** *a & nm* secret; **in ~** in secret

**segu'ace** *nmf* follower; **avere molti seguaci** have a large following

**segu'ente** *a* following, next

**se'gugio** *nm* bloodhound

**segu'ire** *vt/i* follow; (*continuare*) continue; **~ con lo sguardo** follow with one's eyes; **~ le orme di qcno** follow in sb's footsteps; **~ un corso** take a course

**segui'tare** *vt/i* continue

**'seguito** *nm* retinue; (*sequela*) series; (*continuazione*) continuation; **di ~** in succession; **in ~** later on; **in ~ a** following; **al ~** in his/her wake; (*a causa di*) owing to; **fare ~ a** *Comm* follow up; **di ~** one after the other

**'sei** *a & nm* six

**sei'cento** *a & nm* six hundred; **il S~** the seventeenth century

**sei'mila** *a & nm* six thousand

**'selce** *nf* flint

**sel'ciato** *nm* paving

**se'lenio** *nm* selenium

**selettività** *nf* selectivity

**selet'tivo** *a* selective; **memoria selettiva** selective memory

**selet'tore** *nm* selector

**selezio'nare** *vt* select; '**~ il numero**' 'dial [the number]'

**selezi'one** *nf* selection. **~ naturale** natural selection

**self-con'trol** *nm* self-control

**self-'service** *a & nm inv* self-service

**'sella** *nf* saddle

**sel'lare** *vt* saddle

**seltz** *nm inv* soda water

**'selva** *nf* forest; (*fig: di errori, capelli*) mass; (*di ammiratori*) horde

**selvag'gina** *nf* game

**sel'vaggio, -a** *a* wild; (*primitivo*) savage ● *nmf* savage

**sel'vatico** *a* wild

**selvicol'tura** *nf* forestry

**se'maforo** *nm* traffic lights *pl*

**se'mantica** *nf* semantics

**se'mantico** *a* semantic

**sembi'anza** *nf* semblance; **sembianze** *pl* (*di persona*) appearance

**sem'brare** *vi* seem; (*assomigliare*) look like; **che te ne sembra?** what do you think?; **mi sembra che...** I think...; **sembra che vada bene** it's fine, seemingly *or* apparently

**'seme** *nm* seed; (*di mela*) pip; (*di carte*) suit; (*sperma*) semen. **~ della discordia** seeds *pl* of discord

**se'mente** *nf* seed

**seme'strale** *a* (*corso*) six-month; (*pagamento*) six-monthly, half-yearly

**se'mestre** *nm* six months; *Univ* term, semester *Am*

**semia'perto** *a* half-open

**semi'asse** *nm* axle

**semiauto'matico** *a* semiautomatic

**semi'breve** *nf Mus* semibreve

**semi'cerchio** *nm* semicircle

**semicirco'lare** *a* semicircular
**semiconfe'renza** *nf* semicircle
**semicondut'tore** *a & nm* semiconductor
**semicon'vitto** *nm* **scuola a ~** *school for dayboarders*
**semicosci'ente** *a* semi-conscious, half-conscious
**semi'croma** *nf Mus* semiquaver
**semifi'nale** *nf* semifinal
**semi'freddo** *nm* cold dessert resembling ice cream
**semilavo'rato** *a* semi-finished ● *nm* **semilavorati** *pl* semi-finished goods
**semi'minima** *nf Mus* crotchet
**'semina** *nf* sowing
**semi'nare** *vt* sow; *fam* shake off ⟨inseguitori⟩; **seminar zizzania** cause trouble
**semi'nario** *nm* seminar; *Relig* seminary
**semina'rista** *nm* seminarist
**seminfermità** *nf* partial disability. **~ mentale** diminished responsibility
**seminter'rato** *nm* basement
**semi'nudo** *a* half-naked
**semioscurità** *nf* semi-darkness
**semiprezi'oso** *a* semiprecious
**semi'secco** *a* medium-dry
**semi'serio** *a* semi-serious
**se'mitico** *a* Semitic
**semi'tono** *nm Mus* semitone
**sem'mai** *conj* in case ● *adv* **è lui, ~, che...** if anyone, it's him who...
**'semola** *nf* bran
**semo'lato** *a* ⟨zucchero⟩ caster *attrib*
**semo'lino** *nm* semolina
**'semplice** *a* simple; **in parole semplici** in plain words
**semplice'mente** *adv* simply
**semplici'otto, -a** *nmf* simpleton
**sempli'cistico** *a* simplistic
**semplicità** *nf* simplicity
**semplifi'care** *vt* simplify
**'sempre** *adv* always; ⟨ancora⟩ still; **per ~** for ever; **~ più** more and more; **pur ~** still, nevertheless
**sempre'verde** *a & nm* evergreen
**'senape** *nf* mustard
**se'nato** *nm* senate
**sena|'tore, -'trice** *nmf* senator
**se'nile** *a* senile
**senilità** *nf* senility
**'senior** *a* senior ● *nmf* (*pl* **seniores**) *Sport* senior
**'senno** *nm* sense; **giudicare col ~ del poi** use hindsight
**sennò** *adv* otherwise, or else
**sennonché** *conj* but, except that; ⟨fuorché⟩ but, except
**'seno** *nm* ⟨petto⟩ breast; *Math* sine; **in ~ a** in the bosom of
**sen'sale** *nm* broker
**sen'sato** *a* sensible
**sensazio'nale** *a* sensational
**sensazi'one** *nf* sensation; **fare ~** ⟨notizia, scoperta:⟩ cause a sensation
**sen'sibile** *a* sensitive; ⟨percepibile⟩ percepti-

ble; ⟨notevole⟩ considerable; **mondo ~** tangible world
**sensibilità** *nf* sensitivity
**sensibiliz'zare** *vt* make more aware (**a** of)
**sensibil'mente** *adv* appreciably
**sensi'tivo** *a* sensory ● *nmf* sensitive person; ⟨medium⟩ medium
**'senso** *nm* sense; ⟨significato⟩ meaning; ⟨direzione⟩ direction; **far ~ a qcno** make sb shudder; **in ~ orario/antiorario** clockwise/anticlockwise; **ai sensi della legge** in accordance with the law; **non ha ~** it doesn't make sense; **avere il ~ degli affari** have good business sense; **senza ~** meaningless; **in un certo ~...** in a sense o way...; **perdere i sensi** lose consciousness; **a ~** ⟨ripetere, tradurre⟩ in general terms; **in ~ opposto** in the opposite direction; **a ~ unico** ⟨strada⟩ one-way; **a doppio ~** [**di marcia**] ⟨strada⟩ two-way; **a doppio ~** ⟨parola, espressione⟩ with a double meaning. **~ dell'umorismo** sense of humour. **'~ vietato'** 'no entry'
**sen'sore** *nm* sensor
**sensu'ale** *a* sensual
**sensualità** *nf* sensuality
**sen'tenza** *nf* sentence; ⟨massima⟩ saying; **pronunciare una ~** hand down a sentence; **pronunciare la ~** pronounce sentence
**sentenzi'are** *vi* pass judgment
**senti'ero** *nm* path. **~ luminoso di avvicinamento** *Aeron* approach lights
**sentimen'tale** *a* sentimental
**sentimenta'lista** *nmf* sentimentalist
**sentimental'mente** *adv* sentimentally
**senti'mento** *nm* feeling; **essere fuori di ~** be out of one's mind
**sen'tina** *nf Naut* bilge
**senti'nella** *nf* sentry; **essere di ~** be on guard
**sen'tire** *vt* feel; ⟨udire⟩ hear; ⟨ascoltare⟩ listen to; ⟨gustare⟩ taste; ⟨odorare⟩ smell ● *vi* feel; ⟨udire⟩ hear; **~ caldo/freddo** feel hot/cold
**sen'tirsi** *vr* feel; **~ di fare qcsa** feel like doing sth; **~ bene/male** feel well/ill; **sen'tirsela di fare qcsa** feel up to doing sth
**sen'tito** *a* ⟨sincero⟩ sincere; **per ~ dire** by hearsay
**sen'tore** *nm* inkling
**'senza** *prep* without; **~ ombrello** without an umbrella; **~ correre** without running; **senz'altro** certainly; **~ un soldo** penniless; **'~ conservanti'** 'no preservatives'; **fare ~** do without
**senza'tetto** *nm inv* **i ~** the homeless
**'sepalo** *nm* sepal
**sepa'rare** *vt* separate
**sepa'rarsi** *vr* separate; ⟨prendere commiato⟩ part; **~ da** be separated from
**separata'mente** *adv* separately
**separa'tista** *nmf* separatist
**sepa'rato** *a* separate
**separazi'one** *nf* separation. **~ consensuale** separation by mutual consent. **~ legale** legal separation

**sepol'crale** *a liter* sepulchral
**se'polcro** *nm* sepulchre
**se'polto** *pp di* **seppellire** ● *a* buried; **morto e ~** *fig* dead and buried
**sepol'tura** *nf* burial; **dare ~ a qcno** bury sb
**seppel'lire** *vt* bury
**seppel'lirsi** *vr fig* cut oneself off
**'seppia** *nf* cuttle fish ● *a inv* sepia
**sep'pure** *conj* even if
**se'quela** *nf* series, succession; *(di insulti)* string
**se'quenza** *nf* sequence
**sequenzi'ale** *a* sequential
**seque'strare** *vt (rapire)* kidnap; *(confiscare)* confiscate; *Jur* impound
**sequestra'tore, -'trice** *nmf* kidnapper
**se'questro** *nm Jur* impounding; *(di persona)* kidnap[ping]
**se'quoia** *nf* sequoia
**'sera** *nf* evening, night; **di ~, la ~** in the evening; **da ~** *(abito)* evening *attrib*; **alle 8 di ~** at 8 o'clock in the evening, at 8 o'clock at night; **buona ~!** good evening!; **dalla mattina alla ~** from morning to night; **ieri ~** yesterday evening, last night; **questa ~** this evening, tonight
**se'rale** *a* evening *attrib*
**seral'mente** *adv* every evening, every night
**se'rata** *nf* evening; *(ricevimento)* party. **~ danzante** dance. **~ di gala** gala night
**ser'bare** *vt* keep; harbour *(odio)*; cherish *(speranza)*
**serba'toio** *nm* tank. **~ d'acqua** water tank; *(per una città)* reservoir. **~ della benzina** petrol tank, gas tank *Am*
**'Serbia** *nf* Serbia
**'serbo, -a** *a & nmf* Serbian ● *nm (lingua)* Serbian
**'serbo** *nm* **mettere in ~** put aside
**serbo-cro'ato** *nmf* Serbo-Croat[ian]
**sere'nata** *nf* serenade
**sere'nità** *nf* serenity
**se'reno** *a* serene; *(cielo)* clear; **un fulmine a ciel ~** *fam* bolt from the blue
**ser'gente** *nm* sergeant
**'serial** *nm* **~ [televisivo]** television serial
**seri'ale** *a* serial
**seria'mente** *adv* seriously
**'serico** *a* silk
**'serie** *nf inv* series; *(complesso)* set; *Sport* division; **~ A** *(di calcio)* ≈ Premier League; **~ B** *(di calcio)* ≈ First Division; **di ~ B** *fig* second-rate; **fuori ~** custom-built; **produzione in ~** mass production. **~ numerica** numerical series
**serietà** *nf* seriousness
**'serio** *a* serious; *(degno di fiducia)* reliable; **sul ~** seriously; *(davvero)* really
**ser'mone** *nm* sermon
**'serpe** *nf liter* viper
**serpeggi'ante** *a (strada)* twisting, winding
**serpeggi'are** *vi (strada:)* twist, wind; *(fig: diffondersi)* spread

**ser'pente** *nm* snake. **~ a sonagli** rattlesnake. **~ velenoso** poisonous snake
**serpen'tina** *nf* **a ~** twisting and turning, winding; **fare una ~** weave
**'serra** *nf* greenhouse; **effetto ~** greenhouse effect
**ser'raglio** *nm* harem
**ser'randa** *nf* shutter
**ser'rare** *vt* shut; *(stringere)* tighten; *(incalzare)* press on
**ser'rata** *nf* lockout
**serra'tura** *nf* lock
**ser'vibile** *a* usable
**ser'vile** *a* servile
**servi'lismo** *nm* servility
**ser'vire** *vt* serve; *(al ristorante)* wait on ● *vi* serve; *(essere utile)* be of use; **non serve** it's no good; **'~ freddo'** 'serve chilled'
**ser'virsi** *vr (di cibo)* help oneself; **~ da** buy from; **~ di** use
**servi'tore, -'trice** *nmf* retainer ● *nm Comput* server
**servitù** *nf* servitude; *(personale di servizio)* servants *pl*
**servizi'evole** *a* obliging
**ser'vizio** *nm* service; *(da caffè ecc)* set; *(di cronaca, sportivo)* report; *(in tennis)* serve. **servizi** *pl* bathroom; **donna di ~** maid; **essere di ~** be on duty; **fare ~** *(autobus ecc:)* run; **fuori ~** *(bus)* not in service; *(ascensore)* out of order; **~ compreso** service charge included; **~ escluso** not including service charge; **area di ~** service station; **servizi** *pl (terziario)* services. **~ bancario a domicilio** home banking. **~ in camera** room service. **~ civile** *civilian duties done instead of national service*. **~ filmato** film report. **servizi** *pl* **igienici** toilet block. **~ di linea** passenger service. **~ militare** military service. **servizi** *pl* **di pronto intervento** emergency services. **~ pubblico** utility company. **servizi** *pl* **pubblici** *(bagni)* public toilets. **servizi** *pl* **sociali** welfare services. **~ al tavolo** waiter service. **~ traghetto** passenger ferry
**'servo, -a** *nmf* servant
**servo'freno** *nm* servo brake
**servo'sterzo** *nm* power steering
**'sesamo** *nm* sesame
**ses'santa** *a & nm* sixty
**sessan'tenne** *a & nmf* sixty-year-old
**sessan'tesimo** *a & nm* sixtieth
**sessan'tina** *nf* **una ~ di** about sixty
**Sessan'totto** *nm protest movement of 1968*
**sessi'one** *nf* session
**ses'sista** *a* sexist
**'sesso** *nm* sex; **fare ~** *sl* have sex. **~ forte** stronger sex. **gentil ~** fair sex. **~ sicuro** safe sex
**sessu'ale** *a* sexual
**sessualità** *nf* sexuality
**'sesto¹** *a & nm* sixth
**'sesto²** *nm* **rimettere in ~** put back on its feet *(azienda)*; restore *(vestito)*; recondition *(motore, auto)*

**set** *nm inv* set

**'seta** *nf* silk; **di ~** silk *attrib*

**setacci'are** *vt* sieve

**se'taccio** *nm* sieve; **passare qcsa al ~** *fig* go through sth with a fine-tooth comb

**'sete** *nf* thirst; **avere ~** be thirsty. **~ di sangue** blood lust

**'setola** *nf* bristle

**'setta** *nf* sect

**set'tanta** *a & nm* seventy

**settan'tenne** *a & nmf* seventy-year-old

**settan'tesimo** *a & nm* seventieth

**settan'tina** *nf* **una ~ di** about seventy

**set'tario** *a* sectarian

**'sette** *a & nm* seven

**sette'cento** *a & nm* seven hundred; **il S~** the eighteenth century

**set'tembre** *nm* September

**settentrio'nale** *a* northern ●*nmf* northerner

**settentri'one** *nm* north

**'setter** *nm inv* setter

**'settico** *a* septic

**setti'mana** *nf* week; **alla ~** per week; **a metà ~** midweek, half-way through the week. **~ corta** five-day week. **~ lavorativa** working week

**settima'nale** *a & nm* weekly

**setti'mino, -a** *a born two months premature* ●*nmf* baby born two months premature

**'settimo** *a & nm* seventh

**set'tore** *nm* sector

**settori'ale** *a* sector-based

**severità** *nf* severity

**se'vero** *a* severe; (*rigoroso*) strict

**se'vizia** *nf* torture; **se'vizie** *pl* torture *sg*

**sevizi'are** *vt* torture

**sezio'nare** *vt* divide; *Med* dissect

**sezi'one** *nf* section; (*reparto*) department; *Med* dissection

**sfaccen'dare** *vi* bustle about

**sfaccen'dato** *a* idle

**sfaccet'tare** *vt* cut

**sfaccet'tato** *a* cut; *fig* many-sided, multi-faceted

**sfaccetta'tura** *nf* cutting; *fig* facet

**sfacchi'nare** *vi* toil

**sfacchi'nata** *nf* drudgery

**sfaccia'taggine** *nf* cheek

**sfacciata'mente** *adv* cheekily

**sfacci'ato** *a* cheeky, fresh *Am*

**sfa'celo** *nm* ruin; **in ~** in ruins

**sfagio'lare** *vi fam* **non mi sfagiola** it's/he's/she's not my cup of tea

**sfal'darsi** *vr* flake off

**sfal'sare** *vt* stagger; **~ il tiro** shoot wide

**sfa'mare** *vt* feed

**sfa'marsi** *vr* satisfy one's hunger, eat one's fill

**sfarfal'lio** *nm* (*di schermo, luce*) flicker

**'sfarzo** *nm* pomp

**sfar'zoso** *a* sumptuous

**sfa'sato** *a fam* confused; (*motore*) which needs tuning; **sentirsi ~** *fam* be out of sync[h]

**sfasci'are** *vt* unbandage; (*fracassare*) smash

**sfasci'arsi** *vr* fall to pieces

**sfasci'ato** *a* beat-up

**'sfascio** *nm* ruin: **andare allo ~** go to rack and ruin

**sfa'tare** *vt* explode

**sfati'cato** *a* lazy

**'sfatto** *a* unmade

**sfavil'lante** *a* sparkling

**sfavil'lare** *vi* sparkle

**sfavo'revole** *a* unfavourable

**sfavo'rire** *vt* disadvantage, put at a disadvantage

**sfeb'brare** *vi* **comincia a ~** his temperature is starting to come down

**'sfera** *nf* sphere. **~ affettiva** area of feelings and emotions. **~ celeste** celestial sphere. **~ di cristallo** crystal ball. **~ di influenza** sphere of influence

**'sferico** *a* spherical

**sfer'rare** *vt* unshoe ‹*cavallo*›; give ‹*calcio, pugno*›

**sferruz'zare** *vi* knit

**sfer'zare** *vt* whip

**sfer'zata** *nf* whip; *fig* telling-off

**sfian'cante** *a* wearing

**sfian'care** *vt* wear out

**sfian'carsi** *vr* wear oneself out

**sfiata'toio** *nm* blowhole

**sfi'brare** *vt* exhaust

**sfi'brato** *a* exhausted

**'sfida** *nf* challenge

**sfi'dare** *vt* challenge

**sfi'ducia** *nf* mistrust

**sfiduci'ato** *a* discouraged

**'sfiga** *nf sl* bloody bad luck; **avere ~** be bloody unlucky

**sfi'gato, -a** *sl a* bloody unlucky ●*nmf* unlucky beggar

**sfigu'rare** *vt* disfigure ●*vi* (*far cattiva figura*) look out of place

**sfilacci'are** *vt* fray

**sfilacci'arsi** *vr* fray

**sfi'lare** *vt* unthread; (*togliere di dosso*) take off ●*vi* ‹*truppe:*› march past; (*in parata*) parade

**sfi'larsi** *vr* come unthreaded; ‹*collant:*› ladder; take off ‹*pantaloni*›

**sfi'lata** *nf* parade; (*sfilza*) series. **~ di moda** fashion show

**sfila'tino** *nm* long, thin loaf

**'sfilza** *nf* string

**'sfinge** *nf* sphinx

**sfi'nirsi** *vr* wear oneself out

**sfi'nito** *a* worn out

**sfio'rare** *vt* skim; touch on ‹*argomento*›

**sfio'rire** *vi* wither; ‹*bellezza:*› fade

**sfis'sare** *vt* cancel

**'sfitto** *a* vacant

**'sfizio** *nm* whim, fancy; **togliersi uno ~** satisfy a whim

**sfizi'oso** *a* nifty

**sfo'cato** *a* out of focus

**sfoci'are** *vi* **~ in** flow into

**sfode'rare** vt draw ⟨pistola, spada⟩; fig show off ⟨cultura⟩; **~ un sorriso** smile insincerely

**sfode'rato** a ⟨giacca⟩ unlined

**sfo'gare** vt vent

**sfo'garsi** vr give vent to one's feelings

**sfoggi'are** vt/i show off

**'sfoggio** nm show, display; **fare ~ di** show off

**'sfoglia** nf sheet of pastry; **pasta ~** puff pastry

**sfogli'are** vt leaf through

**sfogli'ata**[1] nf flaky pastry with filling

**sfogli'ata**[2] nf **dare una ~ a** ⟨libro, giornale⟩ flick through

**'sfogo** nm outlet; fig outburst; Med rash; **dare ~ a** give vent to

**sfolgo'rante** a blazing

**sfolgo'rare** vi blaze

**sfolla'gente** nm truncheon, billy Am

**sfol'lare** vt clear ● vi Mil be evacuated

**sfol'lato, -a** nmf evacuee

**sfol'tire** vt thin [out]; **farsi ~ i capelli** have one's hair thinned

**sfon'dare** vt break down ● vi ⟨aver successo⟩ make a name for oneself

**'sfondo** nm background

**sfon'done** nm fam blunder

**sfor'mare** vt pull out of shape ⟨tasche⟩

**sfor'marsi** vi lose its shape; ⟨persona:⟩ lose one's figure

**sfor'mato** nm Culin flan

**sfor'nito** a **~ di** ⟨negozio⟩ out of

**sfor'tuna** nf bad luck

**sfortunata'mente** adv unfortunately

**sfortu'nato** a unlucky

**sfor'zare** vt force

**sfor'zarsi** vr try hard

**sfor'zato** a forced

**'sforzo** nm effort; ⟨tensione⟩ stress

**'sfottere** vt sl tease

**sfracel'larsi** vr smash; **~ al suolo** crash to the ground

**sfrangi'ato** a fringed

**sfrat'tare** vt evict

**'sfratto** nm eviction

**sfrecci'are** vi flash past

**sfrega'mento** nm crackling

**sfre'gare** vt rub

**sfregi'are** vt slash

**sfregi'ato, -a** a scarred ● nmf scarface

**'sfregio** nm slash

**sfre'narsi** vr run wild

**sfre'nato** a wild

**sfrigo'lio** nm crackling

**sfron'dare** vt prune

**sfron'tato** a shameless

**sfrutta'mento** nm exploitation

**sfrut'tare** vt exploit; take advantage of, make the most of ⟨occasione⟩

**sfug'gente** a elusive; ⟨mento⟩ receding

**sfug'gire** vi escape; ⟨da qcno⟩ escape [from]; **mi sfugge** it escapes me; **mi è sfuggito** [di mente] it [completely] slipped my mind; **mi è sfuggito di mano** I lost hold of it;

lasciarsi **~ un'occasione** let an opportunity slip; **mi è sfuggito un rutto** I just came out with a belch; **gli è sfuggito un colpo dal fucile** the rifle just went off in his hands ● vt avoid

**sfug'gita** nf **di ~** in passing

**sfu'mare** vi ⟨svanire⟩ vanish; ⟨colore:⟩ shade off ● vt soften ⟨colore⟩

**sfuma'tura** nf shade

**sfuri'ata** nf outburst [of anger]

**sga'bello** nm stool

**sgabuz'zino** nm cupboard

**sgam'bato** a ⟨costume da bagno⟩ high-cut

**sgambet'tare** vi kick one's legs; ⟨camminare⟩ trot

**sgam'betto** nm **fare lo ~ a qcno** trip sb up

**sganasci'arsi** vr **~ dalle risa** roar with laughter

**sganci'are** vt unhook; Rail uncouple; drop ⟨bombe⟩; fam cough up ⟨denaro⟩

**sganci'arsi** vr become unhooked; fig get away

**sganghe'rato** a ramshackle

**sgar'bato** a rude

**'sgarbo** nm discourtesy; **fare uno ~ a qcno** be rude to sb; **ricevere uno ~** be treated rudely

**sgargi'ante** a garish

**sgar'rare** vi be wrong; ⟨da regola⟩ stray from the straight and narrow

**'sgarro** nm mistake, slip

**sga'sato** a flat

**sgattaio'lare** vi sneak away; **~ via** decamp

**sge'lare** vt/i thaw

**'sghembo** a slanting; **a ~** obliquely

**sghiacci'are** vt defrost; thaw out ⟨carne⟩

**sghignaz'zare** vi laugh scornfully

**sghiri'bizzo** nm whim, fancy

**sgob'bare** vi slog; ⟨fam: studente:⟩ swot

**sgob'bone, -a** nmf slogger; ⟨fam: studente⟩ swot

**sgoccio'lare** vi drip

**'sgocciolo** nm dripping

**sgo'larsi** vr shout oneself hoarse

**sgomb[e]'rare** vt clear [out]

**'sgombro** a clear ● nm ⟨trasloco⟩ removal; ⟨pesce⟩ mackerel

**sgomen'tare** vt dismay

**sgomen'tarsi** vr be dismayed

**sgo'mento** nm dismay

**sgomi'nare** vt defeat

**sgom'mare** vi make the tyres screech

**sgom'mata** nf screech of tyres

**sgonfi'are** vt deflate

**sgonfi'arsi** vr go down

**'sgonfio** a flat

**'sgorbio** nm scrawl; ⟨fig: vista sgradevole⟩ sight

**sgor'gare** vi gush [out] ● vt flush out, unblock ⟨lavandino⟩

**sgoz'zare** vt **~ qcno** cut sb's throat

**sgra'devole** a disagreeable

**sgra'dito** a unwelcome

**sgraffi'are** vt scratch

**'sgraffio** nm scratch

**sgrammaticata'mente** *adv* ungrammatically

**sgrammati'cato** *a* ungrammatical

**sgra'nare** *vt* shell ⟨*piselli*⟩; open wide ⟨*occhi*⟩

**sgra'nato** *a* grainy; ⟨*fagioli*⟩ shelled; ⟨*occhi*⟩ wide-open

**sgran'chire** *vt* stretch

**sgran'chirsi** *vr* stretch

**sgranocchi'are** *vt* munch

**sgras'sare** *vt* remove the grease from

**'sgravio** *nm* relief. **~ fiscale** tax relief

**sgrazi'ato** *a* ungainly

**sgreto'lare** *vt* crumble

**sgreto'larsi** *vr* crumble

**sgri'dare** *vt* scold

**sgri'data** *nf* scolding

**sgron'dare** *vt* drain

**sgros'sare** *vt* rough-hew ⟨*marmo*⟩; *fig* polish

**sguai'ato** *a* coarse

**sgual'cire** *vt* crumple

**sgual'drina** *nf* slut

**sgu'ardo** *nm* look; (*breve*) glance; **dare uno ~ a** a glance at ⟨*giornale, testo*⟩. **~ di insieme** overview

**sguar'nito** *a* unadorned; (*privo di difesa*) undefended

**'sguattero, -a** *nmf* skivvy

**sguaz'zare** *vi* splash; (*nel fango*) wallow

**'sguincio** *nm* sidelong glance

**sguinzagli'are** *vt* unleash

**sgusci'are** *vt* shell ● *vi* (*sfuggire*) slip away; **~ fuori** slip out

**'shaker** *nm inv* shaker

**shake'rare** *vt* shake

**'shampoo** *nm inv* shampoo; **~ e messa in piega** shampoo and set

**'shopper** *nm inv* carrier bag

**'shuttle** *nm inv* [space] shuttle

**si** *pers pron* (*riflessivo*) oneself; (*lui*) himself; (*lei*) herself; (*esso, essa*) itself; (*loro*) themselves; (*reciproco*) each other; (*tra più di due*) one another; (*impersonale*) you, one *fml*; **lavarsi** wash [oneself]; **si è lavata** she washed [herself]; **lavarsi le mani** wash one's hands; **si è lavata le mani** she washed her hands; **si è mangiato un pollo intero** he ate an entire chicken by himself; **incontrarsi** meet each other; **la gente si aiuta a vicenda** people help one another; **si potrebbe pensare che...** you might think that..., one might think that... *fml*; **non si sa mai** you never know, one never knows; **queste cose si dimenticano facilmente** these things are easily forgotten

**si** *nm Mus* (*chiave, nota*) B

**sì** *adv* yes; **credo di sì** I believe so; **penso di sì** I think so; **ha detto di sì** she said yes; **sì?** really?; **sì che mi piace!** yes I do like it!

**'sia¹** *vedi* essere

**'sia²** *conj* **~...~...** (*entrambi*) both...and...; (*o l'uno o l'altro*) either...or...**~ che venga**, **~ che non venga** whether he comes or not; **scegli ~ questo ~ quello** choose either

this one or that one; **voglio ~ questo che quello** I want both this one and that one; **verranno ~ Giuseppe ~ Giacomo** both Giuseppe and Giacomo are coming

**sia'mese** *a* Siamese

**sibi'lare** *vi* hiss

**sibil'lino** *a* sibylline

**'sibilo** *nm* hiss

**si'cario** *nm* hired killer

**sicché** *conj* (*perciò*) so [that]; (*allora*) then

**siccità** *nf* drought

**sic'come** *conj* as

**Si'cilia** *nf* Sicily

**sicili'ano, -a** *a & nmf* Sicilian

**sico'moro** *nm* sycamore

**si'cura** *nf* safety catch; (*di portiera*) child-proof lock

**sicura'mente** *adv* definitely; **~, sarà arrivato** he must have arrived by now

**sicu'rezza** *nf* (*certezza*) certainty; (*salvezza*) safety; **di ~** ⟨*dispositivo*⟩ safety *attrib*; **uscita di ~** emergency exit; **di massima** top security

**si'curo** *a* (*non pericoloso*) safe; (*certo*) sure; ⟨*saldo*⟩ steady; *Comm* sound ● *adv* certainly ● *nm* safety; **al ~** safe; **andare sul ~** play [it] safe; **di ~** definitely; **di ~, sarà arrivato** he must have arrived; **~!** sure!

**'sidecar** *nm inv* sidecar

**siderur'gia** *nf* iron and steel industry

**side'rurgico** *a* iron and steel *attrib*

**'sidro** *nm* cider

**si'epe** *nf* hedge

**si'ero** *nm* serum

**sieroposi'tivo, -a** *a* HIV positive ● *nmf* person who is HIV positive

**Si'erra Le'one** *nf* Sierra Leone

**si'esta** *nf* afternoon nap, siesta; **fare la ~** have an afternoon nap

**si'fone** *nm* siphon

**Sig.** *abbr* (**signore**) Mr

**Sig.a** *abbr* (**signora**) Mrs, Ms

**siga'retta** *nf* cigarette; **pantaloni** *pl* **a ~** drainpipes

**'sigaro** *nm* cigar

**Sigg.** *abbr* (**signori**) Messrs

**sigil'lare** *vt* seal

**si'gillo** *nm* seal

**'sigla** *nf* initials *pl*. **~ musicale** signature tune

**si'glare** *vt* initial

**Sig.na** *abbr* (**signorina**) Miss, Ms

**signifi'care** *vt* mean

**significa'tivo** *a* significant

**signifi'cato** *nm* meaning

**si'gnora** *nf* lady; (*davanti a nome proprio*) Mrs; (*non sposata*) Miss; (*in lettere ufficiali*) Dear Madam; **la ~ Rossi** Mrs Rossi; **il signor Venè e ~** Mr and Mrs Venè

**si'gnore** *nm* gentleman; *Relig* lord; (*davanti a nome proprio*) Mr; **il signor Rossi** Mr Rossi

**signo'rile** *a* gentlemanly; (*di lusso*) luxury

**signo'rina** *nf* young lady; (*seguito da nome proprio*) Miss; **la ~ Rossi** Miss Rossi

**silenzia'tore** *nm* silencer

**si'lenzio** *nm* silence. ~ **di tomba** deathly hush

**silenzi'oso** *a* silent

**'silfide** *nf* sylph

**silhou'ette** *nf inv* silhouette, outline; **che ~!** you're so slim!

**si'licio** *nm* **piastrina di ~** silicon chip

**sili'cone** *nm* silicone

**'sillaba** *nf* syllable

**silla'bario** *nm* primer

**sillaba'tore** *nm Comput* hyphenation program

**sillo'gismo** *nm* syllogism

**silu'rare** *vt* torpedo

**si'luro** *nm* torpedo

**simbi'osi** *nf* symbiosis; **vivere in ~** need each other, have a symbiotic relationship

**simboleggi'are** *vt* symbolize

**sim'bolico** *a* symbolic[al]

**simbo'lismo** *nm* symbolism

**simbo'lista** *nmf* symbolist

**'simbolo** *nm* symbol

**similarità** *nf inv* similarity

**'simile** *a* similar; (*tale*) such; **è ~ a...** it's like..., it's similar to...; **qualcosa di ~** something similar ● *nm* (*il prossimo*) fellow human being, fellow man

**simili'tudine** *nf Gram* simile

**simil'mente** *adv* similarly

**simil'pelle** *nf* Leatherette"

**simme'tria** *nf* symmetry

**sim'metrico** *a* symmetric[al]

**simpa'tia** *nf* liking; (*compenetrazione*) sympathy; **prendere qcno in ~** take a liking to sb; **provare ~ per** like

**sim'patico** *a* nice; **inchiostro ~** invisible ink

**simpatiz'zante** *nmf* well-wisher

**simpatiz'zare** *vt* ~ **con** take a liking to; ~ **per qcsa/qcno** lean towards sth/sb

**sim'posio** *nm* symposium

**simu'lare** *vt* simulate; feign (*amicizia, interesse*)

**simula'tore** *nm* simulator

**simulazi'one** *nf* simulation. ~ **di reato** *Jur* making of false accusations

**simul'tanea** *nf* **in ~** simultaneously

**simul'taneo** *a* simultaneous

**sina'goga** *nf* synagogue

**sincera'mente** *adv* sincerely; (*a dire il vero*) honestly

**since'rarsi** *vr* make sure

**sincerità** *nf* sincerity

**sin'cero** *a* sincere

**'sincope** *nf* syncopation; *Med* fainting fit

**sincron'ia** *nf* sync[h]

**sincro'nismo** *nm* synchronism

**sincroniz'zare** *vt* synchronize

**sincroniz'zato** *a* synchronized; **essere ben ~ con** be in sync[h] with

**sincronizzazi'one** *nf* synchronization

**'sincrono** *a* synchronous

**sinda'cabile** *a* arguable

**sinda'cale** *a* [trade] union *attrib*, [labor] union *Am*

**sindaca'lista** *nmf* trade unionist, labor union member *Am*

**sinda'care** *vt* inspect

**sinda'cato** *nm* [trade] union, [labor] union *Am*; (*associazione*) syndicate. ~ **di categoria** trade union

**'sindaco** *nm* mayor

**'sindrome** *nf* syndrome. ~ **di Down** Down's syndrome. ~ **premestruale** premenstrual syndrome, PMS

**sinfo'nia** *nf* symphony

**sin'fonico** *a* symphonic

**singhioz'zare** *vi* (*di pianto*) sob

**singhi'ozzo** *nm* hiccup; (*di pianto*) sob; **avere il ~** have the hiccups

**'single** *nmf inv* single

**singo'lare** *a* singular; (*strano*) peculiar ● *nm Gram* singular

**singolar'mente** *adv* individually; (*stranamente*) peculiarly

**'singolo** *a* single ● *nm* individual; *Tennis* singles *pl*

**si'nistra** *nf* left; **a ~** on the left; **girare a ~** turn to the left; **la seconda a ~** the second on the left; **con la guida a ~** (*auto*) with left-hand drive; **la ~** *Pol* the left; **di ~** *Pol* left wing

**sini'strare** *vt* injure; damage (*casa*)

**sini'strato** *a* injured; (*casa*) damaged

**si'nistro** *a* left[-hand]; (*avverso*) sinister ● *nm* accident

**sini'strorso, -a** *nmf pej* leftie

**'sino** *prep* = **fino**

**si'nonimo** *a* synonymous ● *nm* synonym

**sin'tassi** *nf* syntax

**sin'tattico** *a* syntactic[al]

**'sintesi** *nf* synthesis; (*riassunto*) summary

**sin'tetico** *a* synthetic; (*conciso*) summary

**sintetiz'zare** *vt* summarize

**sintetizza'tore** *nm* synthesizer

**sinto'matico** *a* symptomatic

**'sintomo** *nm* symptom

**sinto'nia** *nf* tuning; **in ~** on the same wavelength; **in ~ con** in harmony with, in tune with

**sintonizza'tore** *nm* tuner

**sinu'oso** *a* (*strada*) winding

**sinu'site** *nf* sinusitis

**sio'nismo** *nm* Zionism

**sio'nista** *a* & *nmf* Zionist

**si'pario** *nm* curtain

**si'rena** *nf* siren; (*di nave*) hooter

**'Siria** *nf* Syria

**siri'ano, -a** *a* & *nmf* Syrian

**si'ringa** *nf* syringe

**'sismico** *a* seismic

**si'smografo** *nm* seismograph

**sismolo'gia** *nf* seismology

**si'stema** *nm* system; **non è il ~!** that's no way to behave!. ~ **di gestione banca dati** database management system, DBMS. ~ **immunitario** immune system. **S~ Monetario Europeo** European Monetary System. ~

**nervoso** nervous system. **~ operativo** *Comput* operating system. **~ solare** solar system. **~ di vita** way of life

**siste'mare** *vt* (*mettere*) put; tidy up ‹*casa, camera*›: (*risolvere*) sort out; (*procurare lavoro a*) fix up with a job; (*trovare alloggio a*) find accommodation for; (*sposare*) marry off; (*fam: punire*) sort out

**siste'marsi** *vr* settle down; (*trovare un lavoro*) find a job; (*trovare alloggio*) find accommodation; (*sposarsi*) marry

**sistematica'mente** *adv* systematically

**siste'matico** *a* systematic

**sistemazi'one** *nf* arrangement; (*di questione*) settlement; (*lavoro*) job; (*alloggio*) accommodation; (*matrimonio*) marriage

**siste'mista** *nmf Comput* systems engineer

**'sistole** *nf* systole

**'sit-in** *nm inv* sit-in

**'sito** *nm* site. **~ web** *Comput* web site

**situ'are** *vt* place

**situazi'one** *nf* situation; **essere all'altezza della ~** be equal to the situation, be up to the situation

**'skai** *nm* Leatherette[R]

**'skateboard** *nm inv* skateboard

**sketch** *nm inv* sketch

**ski-'lift** *nm* ski tow

**'skipper** *nmf inv* skipper

**slab'brare** *vt* stretch out of shape ‹*maglia, tasca*›

**slab'brato** *a* ‹*maglia, tasca*› shapeless

**slacci'are** *vt* unfasten

**'slalom** *nm inv* slalom; **a ~** slalom *attrib*

**slanci'arsi** *vr* hurl oneself

**slanci'ato** *a* slender

**'slancio** *nm* impetus; (*impulso*) impulse; **agire di ~** act on impulse

**sla'vato** *a* ‹*carnagione, capelli*› fair

**'slavo** *a* Slav[onic]

**sle'ale** *a* disloyal; **concorrenza ~** unfair competition

**slealtà** *nf* disloyalty

**sle'gare** *vt* untie

**sle'garsi** *vr* untie oneself

**slip** *nmpl* underpants

**'slitta** *nf* sledge; (*trainata*) sleigh

**slitta'mento** *nm* (*di macchina*) skid; (*fig: di riunione*) postponement

**slit'tare** *vi Auto* skid; ‹*riunione:*› be put off

**slit'tata** *nf* skid

**slit'tino** *nm* toboggan

**'slogan** *nm inv* slogan

**slo'gare** *vt* dislocate

**slo'garsi** *vr* **~ una caviglia** sprain one's ankle

**slo'gato** *a* sprained

**sloga'tura** *nf* sprain

**sloggi'are** *vt* dislodge ● *vi* move out

**slot** *nm* **~ di espansione** *Comput* expansion slot

**slot-ma'chine** *nf inv* slot-machine, one-armed bandit

**Slo'vacchia** *nf* Slovakia

**slo'vacco, -a** *a & nmf* Slovak

**Slo'venia** *nf* Slovenia

**smacchi'are** *vt* clean

**smacchia'tore** *nm* stain remover

**'smacco** *nm* humiliating defeat

**smache'rarsi** *vr* (*tradirsi*) give oneself away

**smagli'ante** *a* dazzling

**smagli'arsi** *vr* ‹*calza:*› ladder *Br*, run

**smaglia'tura** *nf* ladder *Br*. run

**smagnetiz'zare** *vt* demagnetize

**smagnetiz'zatore** *nm* demagnetizer

**sma'grito** *a* thinner

**smalizi'ato** *a* cunning

**smal'tare** *vt* enamel; glaze ‹*ceramica*›; varnish ‹*unghie*›

**smal'tato** *a* enamelled; ‹*ceramica*› glazed; ‹*unghie*› varnished

**smalta'tura** *nf* enamelling; (*di ceramica*) glazing

**smalti'mento** *nm* disposal; (*di merce*) selling off. **~ rifiuti** waste disposal; (*di grassi*) burning off

**smal'tire** *vt* burn off; (*merce*) sell off; *fig* get through ‹*corrispondenza*›; **~ la sbornia** sober up

**'smalto** *nm* enamel; (*di ceramica*) glaze; (*per le unghie*) nail varnish, nail polish

**smance'ria** *nf* **fare smancerie** be overpolite

**smance'roso** *a* simpering

**'smania** *nf* fidgets *pl*; (*desiderio*) longing; **avere la ~ di** have a craving for

**smani'are** *vi* have the fidgets; **~ per** long for

**smani'oso** *a* restless

**smantella'mento** *nm* dismantling

**smantel'lare** *vt* dismantle

**smarri'mento** *nm* loss; (*psicologico*) bewilderment

**smar'rire** *vt* lose; (*temporaneamente*) mislay

**smar'rirsi** *vr* get lost; (*turbarsi*) be bewildered

**smar'rito** *a* lost; ‹*sguardo*› bewildered, lost

**smasche'rare** *vt* unmask

**smasche'rarsi** *vr fig* reveal oneself

**SME** *nm abbr* **(Sistema Monetario Europeo)** EMS

**smem'brare** *vt* dismember

**smemo'rato, -a** *a* forgetful ● *nmf* scatterbrain

**smen'tire** *vt* deny

**smen'tita** *nf* denial

**sme'raldo** *nm & a* emerald

**smerci'are** *vt* sell off

**'smercio** *nm* sale

**smerigli'ato** *a* emery; **vetro ~** frosted glass

**sme'riglio** *nm* emery

**smer'lare** *vt* scallop

**'smerlo** *nm* scallop

**'smesso** *pp di* **smettere** ● *a* ‹*abiti*› cast-off

**'smettere** *vt* stop; stop wearing ‹*abiti*›; **smettila!** stop it!

**smidol'lato** *a* spineless

**smilitariz'zare** *vt* demilitarize

**'smilzo** *a* thin

**sminu'ire** *vt* diminish

**sminu'irsi** *vr fig* belittle oneself

**sminuz'zare** *vt* crumble: (*fig: analizzare*) analyse in detail

**smista'mento** *nm* clearing; (*postale*) sorting: **stazione di ~** shunting yard, marshalling yard. **~ rifiuti** sorting of waste

**smi'stare** *vt* sort; *Mil* post; *Rail* marshall

**smisu'rato** *a* boundless; (*esorbitante*) excessive

**smitiz'zare** *vt* demythologize

**smobili'tare** *vt* demobilize

**smobilitazi'one** *nf* demobilization

**smo'dato** *a* immoderate

**smog** *nm* smog

**'smoking** *nm inv* dinner jacket, tuxedo *Am*

**smon'tabile** *a* jointed

**smon'taggio** *nm* disassembly

**smon'tare** *vt* take to pieces: (*scoraggiare*) dishearten: take down ⟨*tenda*⟩ ● *vi* (*da veicolo*) get off: (*da cavallo*) dismount; (*dal servizio*) go off duty

**smon'tarsi** *vr* lose heart

**'smorfia** *nf* grimace; (*moina*) simper; **fare smorfie** make faces

**smorfi'oso** *a* affected

**'smorto** *a* pale; ⟨*colore*⟩ dull

**smor'zare** *vt* dim ⟨*luce*⟩; tone down ⟨*colori*⟩: deaden ⟨*suoni*⟩; quench ⟨*sete*⟩

**smor'zata** *nf Sport* drop shot

**'smosso** *pp di* **smuovere**

**smotta'mento** *nm* landslide

**'smunto** *a* emaciated

**smu'overe** *vt* shift; (*commuovere*) move

**smu'oversi** *vr* move; (*commuoversi*) be moved

**smus'sare** *vt* round off; (*fig: attenuare*) tone down

**smus'sarsi** *vr* go blunt

**smussa'tura** *nf* bevel

**snack bar** *nm inv* snack bar

**snatu'rato** *a* inhuman

**snazionaliz'zare** *vt* denationalize

**S.N.C.** *abbr* **società in nome collettivo**

**snel'lire** *vt* slim down

**snel'lirsi** *vr* slim [down]

**'snello** *a* slim

**sner'vante** *a* enervating

**sner'vare** *vt* enervate

**sner'varsi** *vr* get exhausted

**sni'dare** *vt* drive out

**snif'fare** *vt* snort

**snob'bare** *vt* snub

**sno'bismo** *nm* snobbery

**snocciо'lare** *vt* stone: *fig* blurt out

**snoccio'lato** *a* ⟨*olive*⟩ pitted, with the stones removed

**sno'dabile** *a* jointed

**sno'dare** *vt* untie; (*sciogliere*) loosen

**sno'darsi** *vr* come untied; ⟨*strada*:⟩ wind

**sno'dato** *a* ⟨*persona*⟩ double-jointed; ⟨*dita*⟩ flexible

**'snodo** *nm* coupling. **~ ferroviario** coupling

**SO** *abbr* (**sud-ovest**) SW

**soap 'opera** *nf inv* soap [opera]

**so'ave** *a* gentle

**sobbal'zare** *vi* jerk; (*trasalire*) start

**sob'balzo** *nm* jerk; (*trasalimento*) start

**sobbar'carsi** *vr* **~ a** undertake

**sobbol'lire** *vi* simmer

**sob'borgo** *nm* suburb

**sobil'lare** *vt* stir up

**sobilla|'tore, -'trice** *nm* instigator

**sobrietà** *nf inv* sobriety

**'sobrio** *a* sober

**soc'chiudere** *vt* half-close

**socchi'uso** *pp di* **socchiudere** ● *a* ⟨*occhi*⟩ half-closed; ⟨*porta*⟩ ajar

**soc'combere** *vi* succumb

**soc'correre** *vt* assist

**soc'corso** *pp di* **soccorrere** ● *nm* assistance, help; **venire in ~** come to help, come to the rescue; **venire in ~ a qcno** come to sb's rescue; **soccorsi** *pl* help; (*persone*) rescuers; (*dopo disastro*) relief workers. **~ alpino** mountain rescue. **~ stradale** breakdown service, wrecking service *Am*

**socialdemo'cratico, -a** *a* Social Democratic ● *nmf* Social Democrat

**socialdemocra'zia** *nf* Social Democracy

**soci'ale** *a* social

**socia'lismo** *nm* Socialism

**socia'lista** *a & nmf* Socialist

**socializ'zare** *vi* socialize

**società** *nf inv* society; *Comm* company. **~ in accomandita semplice** limited partnership. **~ per azioni** public limited company, plc. **~ dei consumi** consumer society. **~ in nome collettivo** commercial partnership. **~ a responsabilità limitata** limited liability company

**soci'evole** *a* sociable

**'socio, -a** *nmf* member; *Comm* partner

**socioeco'nomico** *a* socio-economic

**soci'ologa** *nf* sociologist

**sociolo'gia** *nf* sociology

**socio'logico** *a* sociological

**soci'ologo** *nm* sociologist

**'soda** *nf* soda. **~ da bucato** washing soda

**soda'lizio** *nf* association, society

**soddisfa'cente** *a* satisfactory

**soddi'sfare** *vt/i* satisfy: meet ⟨*richiesta*⟩: make amends for ⟨*offesa*⟩

**soddi'sfatto** *pp di* **soddisfare** ● *a* satisfied

**soddisfazi'one** *nf* satisfaction

**'sodo** *a* hard; *fig* firm; ⟨*sodo*⟩ hard-boiled ● *adv* hard; **dormire ~** sleep soundly ● *nm* **venire al ~** get to the point

**sofà** *nm inv* sofa

**soffe'rente** *a* (*malato*) ill

**soffe'renza** *nf* suffering

**soffer'marsi** *vr* pause; **~ su** dwell on

**sof'ferto** *pp di* **soffrire**

**soffi'are** *vt* blow; reveal ⟨*segreto*⟩; (*rubare*) pinch *fam* ● *vi* blow

**soffi'ata** *nf* datti una **~** al naso blow your nose; **fare una ~ a qcno** *fig sl* tip sb off, give sb a tip-off

**'soffice** *a* soft

**soffi'etto** *nm* bellows: **a ~** ‹*borsa*› expanding. **~ editoriale** blurb

**'soffio** *nm* puff; *Med* murmur

**sof'fitta** *nf* attic

**sof'fitto** *nm* ceiling

**soffoca'mento** *nm* suffocation

**soffo'cante** *a* suffocating

**soffo'care** *vt/i* choke; *fig* stifle

**sof'friggere** *vt* fry lightly

**sof'frire** *vt/i* suffer; (*sopportare*) bear; **~ di** suffer from; **~ di [mal di] cuore** suffer from *o* have a heart condition

**sof'fritto** *pp di* **soffriggere** ● *nm* fried ingredients *pl*

**sof'fuso** *a* ‹*luce*› soft, suffused

**sofisti'care** *vt* (*adulterare*) adulterate ● *vi* (*sottilizzare*) quibble

**sofisti'cato** *a* sophisticated

**soft** *a* soft

**'softcopy** *nf Comput* soft copy

**'soft-core** *nm* softcore, soft porn ● *a inv* **pornografia ~** soft porn

**'software** *vt/i inv* software; **dei ~** software packages. **~ di accesso** access software. **~ applicativo** application software. **~ di autoapprendimento** tutorial package, tutorial software. **~ di comunicazione** communications software, comms software. **~ didattico** educational software. **~ di gestione errori** error correction software. **~ di OCR** OCR software. **~ di sistema** system software

**softwa'rista** *nm Comput* software engineer

**soggettiva'mente** *adv* subjectively

**sogget'tivo** *a* subjective

**sog'getto** *nm* subject; **cattivo ~** bad sort ● *a* subject; **essere ~ a** be subject to

**soggezi'one** *nf* subjection; (*rispetto*) awe

**sogghi'gnare** *vi* sneer

**sog'ghigno** *nm* sneer

**soggio'gare** *vt* subdue

**soggior'nare** *vi* stay

**soggi'orno** *nm* stay; (*stanza*) living room; **permesso di ~** residence permit

**soggi'ungere** *vt* add

**'soglia** *nf* threshold; **alle soglie di qcsa** on the threshold of sth. **~ del dolore** pain threshold

**'sogliola** *nf* sole. **~ limanda** lemon sole

**so'gnare** *vt/i* dream; **~ a occhi aperti** daydream; **non te lo sogni neppure!** forget it!, don't even think of it!

**so'gnarsi** *vr* dream

**sogna|'tore, -'trice** *nmf* dreamer

**'sogno** *nm* dream; **fare un ~** have a dream; **neanche per ~!** not on your life!; **essere un ~** (*bellissimo*) be a dream; **il mio ~ nel cassetto** my secret dream

**'soia** *nf* soya

**sol** *nm Mus* (*chiave, nota*) G

**so'laio** *nm* attic

**sola'mente** *adv* only

**so'lare** *a* ‹*energia, raggi*› solar; ‹*crema*› sun *attrib*

**so'larium** *nm inv* solarium

**sol'care** *vt* plough

**'solco** *nm* furrow; (*di ruota*) track; (*di nave*) wake; (*di disco*) groove

**sol'dato** *nm* soldier. **~ semplice** private

**'soldo** *nm* **non ha un ~** he hasn't got a penny to his name; **senza un ~** penniless; **al ~ di** in the pay of; **soldi** *pl* (*denaro*) money *sg*; **fare [i] soldi** make money; **prelevare dei soldi** withdraw money; **da quattro soldi** cheapo, nickel-and-dime *Am*

**'sole** *nm* sun; (*luce del sole*) sun[light]; **al ~** in the sun; **prendere il ~** sunbathe

**sole'cismo** *nm* solecism

**soleggi'ato** *a* sunny

**so'lenne** *a* solemn

**solennità** *nf* solemnity

**so'lere** *vi* be in the habit of; **come si suol dire** as they say

**so'letta** *nf* insole

**sol'fato** *nm* sulphate

**sol'feggio** *nm* solfa

**'solfuro** *nm* sulphur

**soli'dale** *a* in agreement

**solidarietà** *nf* solidarity

**solidifi'care** *vt/i* solidify

**solidifi'carsi** *vr* solidify

**solidità** *nf* solidity; (*di colori*) fastness

**'solido** *a* solid; (*robusto*) sturdy; ‹*colore*› fast; **in ~** *Jur* jointly and severally ● *nm* solid

**soli'loquio** *nm* soliloquy

**so'lista** *a* solo ● *nmf* soloist

**solita'mente** *adv* usually

**soli'tario** *a* solitary; (*isolato*) lonely ● *nm* (*brillante*) solitaire; (*gioco di carte*) patience, solitaire

**'solito** *a* usual; **essere ~ fare qcsa** be in the habit of doing sth ● *nm* the usual; **di ~** usually

**soli'tudine** *nf* solitude

**solleci'tare** *vt* speed up; urge ‹*persona*›

**sollecitazi'one** *nf* (*richiesta*) request; (*preghiera*) entreaty

**sol'lecito** *a* prompt ● *nm* reminder

**solleci'tudine** *nf* promptness; (*interessamento*) concern; **con la massima ~** *Comm* as soon as possible

**solle'one** *nm* noonday sun; (*periodo*) dog days of summer

**solleti'care** *vt* tickle

**sol'letico** *nm* tickling; **fare il ~ a qcno** tickle sb; **soffrire il ~** be ticklish

**solleva'mento** *nm* **~ pesi** weightlifting

**solle'vare** *vt* lift; (*elevare*) raise; (*confortare*) comfort; **~ una questione** raise a question; **~ qcno da un incarico** relieve sb of a responsibility

**solle'varsi** *vr* rise; (*riaversi*) recover

**solle'vato** *a* relieved

**solli'evo** *nm* relief; **che ~!** what a relief!

**'solo, -a** *a* alone; (*isolato*) lonely; (*unico*) only; *Mus* solo; **da ~** by myself/yourself/himself etc ● *nmf* **il ~, la sola** the only one ● *nm Mus* solo ● *adv* only; **~ il sabato/la**

**domenica** Saturdays/Sundays only, only on Saturdays/Sundays
**sol'stizio** *nm* solstice
**sol'tanto** *adv* only
**so'lubile** *a* soluble; ⟨*caffè*⟩ instant
**soluzi'one** *nf* solution; *Comm* payment; **senza ~ di continuità** without interruption; **in unica ~** *Comm* as a lump sum. **~ salina per lenti** soaking solution
**sol'vente** *nm* solvent. **~ per lo smalto** nail varnish remover. **~ per unghie** nail polish remover ● *a* solvent; **reparto ~** pay ward
**solvibilità** *nf Fin* solvency
**'soma** *nf* load; **bestia da ~** beast of burden
**'somalo, -a** *a & nmf* Somali
**so'maro** *nm* ass, donkey; *Sch* dunce
**so'matico** *a* somatic; **tratti somatici** physical features
**somatiz'zare** *vt* react psychosomatically to
**som'brero** *nm* sombrero
**somigli'ante** *a* similar
**somigli'anza** *nf* resemblance
**somigli'are** *vi* **~ a** look like, resemble; **chi si somiglia si piglia** birds of a feather flock together
**somigli'arsi** *vr* be alike
**'somma** *nf* sum; *Math* addition
**som'mare** *vt* add; ⟨*totalizzare*⟩ add up
**sommaria'mente** *adv* summarily
**som'mario** *a & nm* summary
**som'mato** *a* **tutto ~** all things considered
**somme'lier** *nm inv* wine waiter
**som'mergere** *vt* submerge
**sommer'gibile** *nm* submarine
**som'merso** *pp di* **sommegere** ● *nm Econ* black economy
**som'messo** *a* soft
**sommini'strare** *vt* administer
**somministrazi'one** *nf* administration; **~ per via orale** to be taken orally
**sommità** *nf inv* summit
**'sommo** *a* highest; *fig* supreme ● *nm* summit
**som'mossa** *nf* rising
**sommozza'tore** *nm* frogman
**so'naglio** *nm* bell
**'sonar** *nm* sonar
**so'nata** *nf* sonata; *fig fam* beating
**'sonda** *nf Mech* drill; ⟨*spaziale, Med*⟩ probe
**son'daggio** *nm* drilling; ⟨*spaziale, Med*⟩ probe; ⟨*indagine*⟩ survey. **~ d'opinioni** opinion poll
**son'dare** *vt* sound; ⟨*investigare*⟩ probe
**so'netto** *nm* sonnet
**sonnambu'lismo** *nm* sleepwalking
**son'nambulo, -a** *nmf* sleepwalker
**sonnecchi'are** *vi* doze
**son'nifero** *nm* sleeping-pill
**'sonno** *nm* sleep; **aver ~** be sleepy; **morire di ~** be dead tired, be dead on one's feet; **morto di ~** ⟨*fam: stupido*⟩ zombie; **perdere il ~** *anche fig* lose sleep. **~ eterno** *Relig* eternal rest
**sonno'lenza** *nf* sleepiness
**'sono** *vedi* **essere**

**sonoriz'zare** *vt* add a soundtrack to
**so'noro** *a* resonant; ⟨*rumoroso*⟩ loud; ⟨*onde, scheda*⟩ sound *attrib* ● *nm* ⟨*Tech: di film*⟩ soundtrack
**sontu'oso** *a* sumptuous
**sopo'rifero** *a* soporific
**sop'palco** *nm* platform
**soppe'rire** *vi* **~ a qcsa** provide for sth
**soppe'sare** *vt* weigh up ⟨*situazione*⟩
**soppi'atto: di ~** *adv* furtively
**soppor'tare** *vt* support; ⟨*tollerare*⟩ stand; bear ⟨*dolore*⟩
**sopportazi'one** *nf* patience
**soppressi'one** *nf* removal; ⟨*di legge*⟩ abolition; ⟨*di diritti, pubblicazione*⟩ suppression; ⟨*annullamento*⟩ cancellation
**sop'presso** *pp di* **sopprimere**
**sop'primere** *vt* get rid of; abolish ⟨*legge*⟩; suppress ⟨*diritti, pubblicazione*⟩; ⟨*annullare*⟩ cancel
**'sopra** *adv* on top; ⟨*più in alto*⟩ higher [up]; ⟨*al piano superiore*⟩ upstairs; ⟨*in testo*⟩ above; **mettilo lì ~** put it up there; **di ~** upstairs; **dormirci ~** *fig* sleep on it; **pensarci ~** think about it; **vedi ~** see above ● *prep* **~ [a]** on; ⟨*senza contatto, oltre*⟩ over; ⟨*riguardo a*⟩ about; **è ~ al tavolo, è ~ il tavolo** it's on the table; **il quadro è appeso ~ al camino** the picture is hanging over the fireplace; **il ponte passa ~ all'autostrada** the bridge crosses over the motorway; **è caduto ~ il tetto** it fell on the roof; **l'uno sopra l'altro** one on top of the other; ⟨*senza contatto*⟩ one above the other; **abita ~ di me** he lives upstairs from me; **i bambini ~ i dieci anni** children over ten; **20° ~ lo zero** 20 above zero; **~ il livello del mare** above sea level; **rifletti ~ quello che è successo** think about what happened; **prendere ~ di sé la responsabilità di qcsa** assume responsibility for sth; **scaricare la colpa ~ qcno** put the blame on sb; **non ha nessuno ~ di sé** he has nobody above him; **al di ~ di** over; **al di ~ di ogni sospetto** beyond suspicion ● *nm* **il [di] ~** the top
**so'prabito** *nm* overcoat
**soprac'ciglio** *nm* (*pl nf* **sopracciglia**) eyebrow
**sopracco'perta** *nf* ⟨*di letto*⟩ bedspread; ⟨*di libro*⟩ [dust-]jacket
**sopraccoper'tina** *nf* book jacket
**soprad'detto** *a* above-mentioned
**sopraele'vare** *vt* raise
**sopraele'vata** *nf* elevated railway
**sopraele'vato** *a* raised
**sopraf'fare** *vt* overwhelm
**sopraf'fatto** *pp di* **sopraffare**
**sopraffazi'one** *nf* abuse of power
**sopraf'fino** *a* excellent; ⟨*gusto, udito*⟩ highly refined
**sopraggi'ungere** *vi* ⟨*persona:*⟩ turn up; ⟨*accadere*⟩ happen; **è sopraggiunta la pioggia** and then it started to rain
**soprallu'ogo** *nm* inspection
**sopram'mobile** *nm* ornament

**soprannatu'rale** *a & nm* supernatural

**sopran'nome** *nm* nickname

**soprannomi'nare** *vt* nickname

**sopran'numero** *adv* **sono in ~** there are too many of them; **ce ne sono 15 in ~** there are 15 too many of them, there are 15 of them too many

**so'prano** *nmf* soprano

**soprappensi'ero** *adv* lost in thought

**sopras'salto** *nm* **di ~** with a start

**soprasse'dere** *vi* **~ a** postpone

**soprat'tassa** *nf* surtax. **~ postale** excess postage

**soprat'tenda** *nm* fly sheet

**soprat'tetto** *nm* fly sheet

**soprat'tutto** *adv* above all

**sopravvalu'tare** *vt* overvalue; overestimate ‹forze›

**sopravvalutazi'one** *nf* overvaluation; (di forze) overestimation

**sopravve'nire** *vi* turn up; (accadere) happen

**soprav'vento** *nm* fig upper hand; **prendere il ~** take the upper hand

**sopravvis'suto, -a** *pp di* **sopravvivere** ● *nmf* survivor

**sopravvi'venza** *nf* survival

**soprav'vivere** *vi* survive; **~ a** outlive ‹persona›

**soprinten'dente** *nmf* supervisor; (di museo ecc) keeper

**soprinten'denza** *nf* supervision; (ente) board

**so'pruso** *nm* abuse of power

**soq'quadro** *nm* **mettere a ~** turn upside down

**sor'betto** *nm* sorbet

**sor'bire** *vt* sip; fig put up with

**'sorcio** *nm* mouse; **far vedere i sorci verdi a qcno** give sb a rough time

**'sordido** *a* sordid; (avaro) stingy

**sor'dina** *nf* mute; **in ~** fig on the quiet

**sordità** *nf* deafness

**'sordo, -a** *a* deaf; ‹rumore, dolore› dull ● *nmf* deaf person

**sordo'muto, -a** *a* deaf-and-dumb ● *nmf* deaf mute

**so'rella** *nf* sister. **~ gemella** twin sister

**sorel'lastra** *nf* stepsister

**sor'gente** *nf* spring; (fonte) source; **programma ~** Comput source program

**'sorgere** *vi* rise; fig arise

**sormon'tare** *vt* surmount

**sorni'one** *a* sly

**sorpas'sare** *vt* surpass; (eccedere) exceed; overtake, pass Am ‹veicolo›

**sorpas'sato** *a* old-fashioned

**sor'passo** *nm* overtaking, passing Am

**sorpren'dente** *a* surprising; (straordinario) remarkable

**sorprendente'mente** *adv* surprisingly

**sor'prendere** *vt* surprise; (cogliere in flagrante) catch

**sor'prendersi** *vr* be surprised; **~ a fare**

**qcsa** catch oneself doing sth: **non c'è da ~** it's hardly surprising

**sor'presa** *nf* surprise; **di ~** by surprise; **provare ~** feel surprised

**sor'preso** *pp di* **sorprendere**

**sor'reggere** *vt* support; (tenere) hold up

**sor'reggersi** *vr* support oneself

**sor'retto** *pp di* **sorreggere**

**sorri'dente** *a* smiling

**sor'ridere** *vi* smile; **la fortuna mi ha sorriso** fortune smiled on me

**sor'riso** *pp di* **sorridere** ● *nm* smile

**sorseggi'are** *vt* sip

**'sorso** *nm* sip; (piccola quantità) drop

**'sorta** *nf* sort; **di ~** whatever; **ogni ~ di** all sorts of

**'sorte** *nf* fate; (caso imprevisto) chance; **tirare a ~** draw lots; **per buona ~** liter by good fortune

**sorteggi'are** *vt* draw lots for

**sor'teggio** *nm* draw

**sorti'legio** *nm* witchcraft

**sor'tire** *vi* come out ● *vt* bring about ‹effetto›

**sor'tita** *nf* Mil sortie; (battuta) witticism

**'sorto** *pp di* **sorgere**

**sorvegli'ante** *nmf* keeper; (controllore) overseer

**sorvegli'anza** *nf* watch; Mil ecc surveillance

**sorvegli'are** *vt* watch over; (controllare) oversee; ‹polizia:› watch, keep under surveillance

**sorvegli'ato, -a** *a* under surveillance ● *nmf* **~ speciale** person kept under special surveillance

**sorvo'lare** *vt* fly over; fig skip

**SOS** *nm* SOS

**'sosia** *nm inv* double

**so'spendere** *vt* hang; (interrompere) stop; (privare di una carica) suspend

**sospensi'one** *nf* suspension

**sospen'sorio** *nm* Sport jockstrap

**so'speso** *pp di* **sospendere** ● *a* ‹impiegato, alunno› suspended; **~ a** hanging from; **~ a un filo** fig hanging by a thread ● *nm* **in ~** pending; (emozionato) in suspense

**sospet'tare** *vt* suspect

**so'spetto** *a* suspicious ● *nm* suspicion; (persona) suspect; **al di sopra di ogni ~** above suspicion

**sospet'toso** *a* suspicious

**so'spingere** *vt* drive

**so'spinto** *pp di* **sospingere**

**sospi'rare** *vi* sigh ● *vt* long for

**so'spiro** *nm* sigh

**'sosta** *nf* stop; (pausa) pause; **senza ~** nonstop; **'divieto di ~'** 'no parking'; **'~ autorizzata...'** 'parking permitted for...'

**sostan'tivo** *nm* noun

**so'stanza** *nf* substance; **sostanze** *pl* (patrimonio) property *sg*; **in ~** to sum up; **la ~ della questione** the nub of the matter

**sostanzi'oso** *a* substantial; ‹cibo› nourishing; **poco ~** insubstantial

**so'stare** *vi* stop; (fare una pausa) pause

**so'stegno** *nm* support. ~ **morale** moral support

**soste'nere** *vt* support; *(sopportare)* bear; *(resistere)* withstand; *(affermare)* maintain; *(nutrire)* sustain; *(esame)*: ~ **le spese** meet the costs; ~ **delle spese** incur expenditure; ~ **una carica** hold a position; ~ **una parte** play a role

**soste'nersi** *vr* support oneself

**sosteni'tore, -'trice** *nmf* supporter

**sostenta'mento** *nm* maintenance

**soste'nuto** *a* ⟨*stile*⟩ formal; ⟨*velocità*⟩ high; ⟨*mercato, prezzi*⟩ steady ● *nm* **fare il** ~ be stand-offish

**sostitu'ire** *vt* substitute (**a** for), replace (**con** with)

**sostitu'irsi** *vr* ~ **a** replace

**sosti'tuto, -a** *nmf* replacement, stand-in ● *nm (surrogato)* substitute

**sostituzi'one** *nf* substitution

**sotta'ceto** *a* pickled; **sottaceti** *pl* pickles

**sot'tacqua** *adv* underwater

**sot'tana** *nf* petticoat; *(di prete)* cassock

**sotter'fugio** *nm* subterfuge; **di** ~ secretly

**sotter'raneo** *a* underground ● *nm* cellar

**sotter'rare** *vt* bury

**sottigli'ezza** *nf* slimness; *fig* subtlety

**sot'tile** *a* thin; ⟨*udito, odorato*⟩ keen; ⟨*osservazione, distinzione*⟩ subtle

**sotti'letta**ᴿ *nf* cheese slice

**sottiliz'zare** *vi* split hairs

**sottin'tendere** *vt* imply

**sottin'teso** *pp di* **sottintendere** ● *nm* allusion; **senza sottintesi** openly ● *a* implied

**'sotto** *adv* below; *(più in basso)* lower [down]; *(al di sotto)* underneath; *(al piano di sotto)* downstairs; **è lì** ~ it's underneath; ~ ~ deep down; *(di nascosto)* on the quiet; **di** ~ downstairs; **mettersi** ~ *fig* get down to it; **mettere** ~ *(fam: investire)* knock down; **fatti** ~! *fam* get stuck in! ● *prep* ~ [**a**] under; *(al di sotto di)* under[neath]; **il fiume passa** ~ **un ponte** the river passes under[neath] a bridge; **è** ~ **il tavolo, è** ~ **al tavolo** it's under[neath] the table; **abita** ~ **di me** he lives downstairs from me; **i bambini** ~ **i dieci anni** children under ten; **20°** ~ **zero** 20° below zero; ~ **il livello del mare** below sea level; ~ **la pioggia** in the rain; ~ **Elisabetta I** under Elizabeth I; ~ **calmante** under sedation; ~ **chiave** under lock and key; ~ **condizione che...** on condition that...; ~ **giuramento** under oath; ~ **sorveglianza** under surveillance; ~ **Natale/gli esami** around Christmas/exam time; **al di** ~ **di** under; **andare** ~ **i 50 all'ora** do less than 50km an hour ● *nm* **il [di]** ~ the bottom

**sotto'banco** *adv* ⟨*vendere, comprare*⟩ under the counter

**sottobicchi'ere** *nm* coaster

**sotto'bosco** *nm* undergrowth

**sotto'braccio** *adv* arm in arm

**sottoccu'pato** *a* underemployed

**sottochi'ave** *adv* under lock and key

**sotto'costo** *a & adv* at less than cost price

**sottodi'rectory** *nf Comput* subdirectory

**sottoe'sporre** *vt* underexpose

**sotto'fondo** *nm* background

**sotto'gamba** *adv* **prendere qcsa** ~ take sth lightly

**sotto'gonna** *nf* underskirt

**sottoindi'cato** *a* undermentioned

**sottoinsi'eme** *nm Math* subset

**sottoline'are** *vt* underline; *fig* underline ⟨*importanza*⟩; emphasize ⟨*forma degli occhi ecc*⟩

**sot'tolio** *adv* in oil

**sotto'mano** *adv* within reach

**sottoma'rino** *a & nm* submarine

**sotto'messo** *pp di* **sottomettere** ● *a (remissivo)* submissive

**sotto'mettere** *vt* submit; subdue ⟨*popolo*⟩

**sotto'mettersi** *vr* submit

**sottomissi'one** *nf* submission

**sottopa'gare** *vt* underpay

**sottopas'saggio** *nm* underpass; *(pedonale)* subway

**sottopi'atto** *nm* place mat

**sotto'porre** *vt* submit; *(costringere)* subject

**sotto'porsi** *vr* submit oneself; ~ **a** undergo

**sotto'posto** *pp di* **sottoporre**

**sottoproletari'ato** *nm* underclass

**sotto'scala** *nm* cupboard under the stairs

**sotto'scritto** *pp di* **sottoscrivere** ● *nm* undersigned

**sotto'scrivere** *vt* sign; *(approvare)* sanction, subscribe to

**sottoscrizi'one** *nf (petizione)* petition; *(approvazione)* sanction; *(raccolta di denaro)* appeal

**sottosegre'tario** *nm* undersecretary

**sotto'sopra** *adv* upside-down

**sotto'stante** *a* **la strada** ~ the road below

**sottosu'olo** *nm* subsoil

**sottosvilup'pato** *a* underdeveloped

**sottosvi'luppo** *nm* underdevelopment

**sottote'nente** *nm* second lieutenant; *Naut* sub-lieutenant

**sotto'terra** *adv* underground

**sotto'titolo** *nm* subtitle

**sottovalu'tare** *vt* underestimate

**sotto'vento** *adv* downwind

**sotto'veste** *nf* slip

**sotto'voce** *adv* in a low voice

**sottovu'oto** *a* vacuum-packed

**sotto'zero** *a inv* subzero

**sot'trarre** *vt* remove; embezzle ⟨*fondi*⟩; *Math* subtract

**sot'trarsi** *vr* ~ **a** escape from; avoid ⟨*responsabilità*⟩

**sot'tratto** *pp di* **sottrarre**

**sottrazi'one** *nf* removal; *(di fondi)* embezzlement; *Math* subtraction

**sottuffici'ale** *nm* non-commissioned officer; *Naut* petty officer

**sou'brette** *nf* showgirl

**souf'flé** *nm inv* soufflé

**souve'nir** *nm inv* souvenir; **negozio di** ~ souvenir shop

**so'vente** *adv liter* often

**soverchie'ria** *nf* bullying: **fare sover- chierie a** bully

**so'vietico, -a** *a & nmf* Soviet

**sovrabbon'danza** *nf* overabundance

**sovraccari'care** *vt* overload

**sovrac'carico** *a* overloaded (**di** with) ● *nm* overload

**sovraffati'carsi** *vr* overexert oneself

**sovraffolla'mento** *nm* overcrowding

**sovralimen'tare** *vt* overfeed

**sovrannatu'rale** *a & nm* = **sopran- naturale**

**sovrannazio'nale** *a* supranational

**so'vrano, -a** *a* sovereign; *fig* supreme ● *nmf* sovereign

**sovrappopo'lato** *a* overpopulated

**sovrap'porre** *vt* superimpose

**sovrap'porsi** *vr* overlap

**sovrapposizi'one** *nf* superimposition

**sovrapro'fitto** *nm* excess profits

**sovra'stare** *vt* dominate; ⟨fig: pericolo:⟩ hang over

**sovrastrut'tura** *nf* superstructure

**sovratensi'one** *nf Electr* overload, over- tension

**sovrecci'tarsi** *vr* get overexcited

**sovrecci'tato** *a* overexcited

**sovresposizi'one** *nf Phot* overexposure

**sovrimpressi'one** *nf Phot* double expo- sure

**sovrinten'dente, sovrinten'denza** = **soprintendente, soprintendenza**

**sovru'mano** *a* superhuman

**sovvenzio'nare** *vt* subsidize

**sovvenzi'one** *nf* subsidy

**sovver'sivo, -a** *a & nmf* subversive

**sovver'tire** *vt* subvert

**'sozzo** *a* filthy

**SP** *nf abbr* (**strada provinciale**) secondary road

**S.p.A.** *abbr* (**società per azioni**) plc

**spac'care** *vt* split; chop ⟨legna⟩; ~ **il minuto** keep perfect time; ~ **il muso a qcno** *sl* smash sb's face in; **o la va o la spacca** it's all or nothing; **un sole che spacca le pietre** a sun hot enough to fry an egg

**spac'carsi** *vr* split

**spacca'tura** *nf* split

**spacci'are** *vt* deal in, push ⟨droga⟩; ~ **qcsa per qcsa** pass sth off as sth; **essere spacciato** be done for, be a goner

**spacci'arsi** *vr* ~ **per** pass oneself off as

**spaccia|'tore, -'trice** *nmf* ⟨di droga⟩ pusher; ⟨di denaro falso⟩ distributor of forged bank notes

**'spaccio** *nm* ⟨di droga⟩ dealer, pusher; ⟨negozio⟩ shop

**'spacco** *nm* split

**spacco'nate** *nfpl* blustering

**spac'cone, -a** *nmf* boaster

**'spada** *nf* sword

**spadac'cino** *nm* swordsman

**spadroneggi'are** *vi* act the boss

**spae'sato** *a* disorientated

**spa'ghetti** *nmpl* spaghetti *sg.* ~ **in bianco**

spaghetti with butter, oil and cheese. ~ **alla carbonara** spaghetti with egg, cheese and diced bacon. ~ **al sugo** spaghetti with a sauce

**spa'ghetto** *nm* ⟨fam: spavento⟩ fright

**'Spagna** *nf* Spain

**spagno'letta** *nf* spool

**spa'gnolo, -a** *a* Spanish ● *nmf* Spaniard ● *nm* ⟨lingua⟩ Spanish

**'spago** *nm* string; ⟨fam: spavento⟩ fright; **dare** ~ **a qcno** encourage sb

**spai'ato** *a* odd

**spalan'care** *vt* open wide

**spalan'carsi** *vr* open wide

**spalan'cato** *a* wide open

**spa'lare** *vt* shovel

**'spalla** *nf* shoulder; ⟨di comico⟩ straight man; **spalle** *pl* ⟨schiena⟩ back; **alzata di spalle** shrug [of the shoulders]; **alle spalle di** be- hind; **alle spalle di qcn** ⟨ridere⟩ behind sb's back; **avere qnco/qcsa alle spalle** have sb/sth behind one; **di** ~ ⟨violino ecc⟩ sec- ond; **vivere alle spalle di qcno** live off sb: **con le spalle al muro** *anche fig* with one's back to the wall; **voltare le spalle** turn one's back

**spal'lata** *nf* push with the shoulder; ⟨alzata di spalle⟩ shrug [of the shoulders]

**spalleggi'are** *vt* back up

**spal'letta** *nf* parapet

**spalli'era** *nf* back; ⟨di letto⟩ headboard; ⟨ginnastica⟩ wall bars *pl*

**spal'lina** *nf* strap; ⟨imbottitura⟩ shoulder pad; **senza spalline** strapless

**spal'mare** *vt* spread

**spal'marsi** *vr* cover oneself

**spa'nato** *a* ⟨vite⟩ threadless

**spanci'ata** *nf* belly flop

**'spandere** *vt* spread; ⟨versare⟩ spill: **spendere e** ~ spend and spend

**'spandersi** *vr* spread

**spandighi'aia** *nm inv* gritter

**'spaniel** *nm inv* spaniel

**spappo'lare** *vt* crush

**spa'rare** *vt/i* shoot; **spararle grosse** talk big; ~ **fandonie** talk nonsense

**spa'rarsi** *vr* shoot oneself; **si è sparato un colpo di pistola alla tempia** he shot him- self in the temple

**spa'rata** *nf fam* tall story

**spa'rato** *nm* ⟨della camicia⟩ dicky

**spara'toria** *nf* shooting

**sparecchi'are** *vt* clear

**spa'reggio** *nm Comm* deficit; *Sport* play-off

**'spargere** *vt* scatter; ⟨diffondere⟩ spread; shed ⟨lacrime, sangue⟩

**'spargersi** *vr* spread

**spargi'mento** *nm* scattering; ⟨di lacrime, sangue⟩ shedding; ~ **di sangue** bloodshed

**spa'rire** *vi* disappear; **sparisci!** get lost!, scram!

**sparizi'one** *nf* disappearance

**spar'lare** *vi* ~ **di** run down

**'sparo** *nm* shot

**sparpagli'are** *vt* scatter

**sparpagli'arsi** *vr* scatter

**sparpagli'ato** *a* far-flung

**'sparso** *pp di* **spargere** ● *a* scattered; ⟨*sciolto*⟩ loose

**sparti'neve** *nm inv* snowplough

**spar'tire** *vt* share out; ⟨*separare*⟩ separate

**spar'tirsi** *vr* share

**spar'tito** *nm Mus* score

**sparti'traffico** *nm inv* traffic island; ⟨*di autostrada*⟩ central reservation, median strip *Am*

**spartizi'one** *nf* division

**spa'ruto** *a* gaunt; ⟨*gruppo*⟩ small; ⟨*peli, capelli*⟩ sparse

**sparvi'ero** *nm* sparrow-hawk

**spasi'mante** *nm hum* admirer

**spasi'mare** *vi* suffer agonies; **~ per** be madly in love with

**'spasimo** *nm* spasm

**spa'smodico** *a* spasmodic

**spas'sarsi** *vr* amuse oneself; **spas'sarsela** have a good time

**spassio'nato** *a* ⟨*osservatore*⟩ dispassionate, impartial

**'spasso** *nm* fun; **essere uno ~** be hilarious; **andare a ~** go for a walk; **essere a ~** be out of work

**spas'soso** *a* hilarious

**'spastico** *a* spastic

**'spatola** *nf* spatula

**spau'racchio** *nm* scarecrow; *fig* bugbear

**spau'rire** *vt* frighten

**spa'valdo** *a* defiant

**spaventa'passeri** *nm inv* scarecrow

**spaven'tare** *vt* frighten, scare

**spaven'tarsi** *vr* be frightened, be scared

**spa'vento** *nm* fright; **brutto da fare ~** incredibly ugly

**spaven'toso** *a* frightening; ⟨*fam: enorme*⟩ incredible

**spazi'ale** *a* spatial; ⟨*cosmico*⟩ space *attrib*

**spazi'are** *vt* space out ● *vi* range

**spazien'tirsi** *vr* lose [one's] patience

**'spazio** *nm* space. **~ aereo** airspace. **~ indietro** *Comput* backspace. **~ di tempo** period of time. **~ vitale** elbowroom

**spazi'oso** *a* spacious

**spazio-tempo'rale** *a* spatiotemporal

**spazzaca'mino** *nm* chimney sweep

**spazza'neve** *nm inv* ⟨*anche sci*⟩ snowplough

**spaz'zare** *vt* sweep; **~ via** sweep away; ⟨*fam: mangiare*⟩ devour

**spazza'trice** *nf* sweeper

**spazza'tura** *nf* ⟨*immondizia*⟩ rubbish

**spaz'zino** *nm* road sweeper; ⟨*netturbino*⟩ dustman

**'spazzola** *nf* brush; ⟨*di tergicristallo*⟩ blade; **capelli a ~** crew cut

**spazzo'lare** *vt* brush

**spazzo'larsi** *vr* **~ i capelli** brush one's hair

**spazzo'lino** *nm* small brush. **~ da denti** toothbrush. **~ per le unghie** nailbrush

**spazzo'lone** *nm* scrubbing brush

**'speaker** *nm inv Radio, TV* announcer

**specchi'arsi** *vr* look at oneself in a/the mirror; ⟨*riflettersi*⟩ be mirrored; **~ in qcno** model oneself on sb

**specchi'ato** *a* **di specchiata onestà** of spotless integrity

**specchi'etto** *nm* small mirror. **~ laterale** wing mirror. **~ retrovisore** driving mirror, rear-view mirror

**'specchio** *nm* mirror

**speci'ale** *a* special ● *nm TV* special [programme]

**specia'lista** *nmf* specialist

**specialità** *nf inv* speciality, specialty

**specializ'zare** *vt* specialize

**specializ'zarsi** *vr* specialize

**specializ'zato** *a* ⟨*operaio*⟩ skilled; **siamo specializzati in...** we specialize in...

**special'mente** *adv* especially

**'specie** *nf* ⟨*scientifico*⟩ species; ⟨*tipo*⟩ kind; **fare ~ a** surprise; **in ~** especially

**specifi'care** *vt* specify

**specificata'mente** *adv* specifically

**spe'cifico** *a* specific

**speci'oso** *a* specious

**specu'lare** *vi* speculate; **~ su** ⟨*indagare*⟩ speculate on; *Fin* speculate in

**specu'lare** *a* mirror *attrib*

**specula'tivo** *a* speculative

**specula'tore** *nm* speculator

**speculazi'one** *nf* speculation

**spe'dire** *vt* send; **~ per posta** mail, post *Br*; **~ qcno all'altro mondo** send sb to meet his/her maker

**spe'dito** *pp di* **spedire** ● *a* quick; ⟨*parlata*⟩ fluent

**spedizi'one** *nf* ⟨*di lettere ecc*⟩ dispatch; *Comm* consignment, shipment; ⟨*scientifica*⟩ expedition

**spedizioni'ere** *nm Comm* freight forwarder

**'spegnere** *vt* put out; turn off, switch off ⟨*motore, luce, televisione*⟩; turn off ⟨*gas*⟩; quench, slake ⟨*sete*⟩

**'spegnersi** *vr* go out; ⟨*morire*⟩ pass away

**spegni'mento** *nm* standby

**spelacchi'ato** *a* ⟨*tappeto*⟩ threadbare; ⟨*cane*⟩ mangy

**spe'lare** *vt* remove the fur of ⟨*coniglio*⟩

**spe'larsi** *vr* ⟨*cane, tappeto:*⟩ moult; ⟨*persona:*⟩ peel

**speleolo'gia** *nf* potholing, speleology

**spel'lare** *vt* skin; *fig* fleece

**spel'larsi** *vr* ⟨*serpente:*⟩ shed its skin; ⟨*per il sole*⟩ peel; **mi sono spellato un ginocchio** I grazed *or* skinned my knee

**spe'lonca** *nf* cave; *fig* dingy hole

**spendacci'one, -a** *nmf* spendthrift

**'spendere** *vt* spend; **~ fiato** waste one's breath

**spen'nare** *vt* pluck; *fam* fleece ⟨*cliente*⟩

**spennel'lare** *vt* brush ● *vi* paint

**spensierata'mente** *adv* blithely

**spensiera'tezza** *nf* lightheartedness

**spensie'rato** *a* lighthearted, carefree

**'spento** *pp di* **spegnere** ● *a* off; ⟨*gas*⟩ out; ⟨*smorto*⟩ dull; ⟨*vulcano*⟩ extinct

**spenzo'lare** vt dangle

**spe'ranza** nf hope; **pieno di ~** hopeful; **senza ~** hopeless

**spe'rare** vt hope for; (aspettarsi) expect ● vi **~ in** trust in; **spero di sì** I hope so

**'sperdersi** vr get lost

**sper'duto** a lost; (isolato) secluded

**spergiu'rare** vi commit perjury

**spergi'uro, -a** nmf perjurer ● nm perjury

**sperico'lato** a swashbuckling

**sperimen'tale** a experimental

**sperimen'tare** vt experiment with; test ⟨resistenza, capacità, teoria⟩

**sperimen'tato** a ⟨metodo⟩ tried and tested

**sperimentazi'one** nf experimentation; **~ sugli animali** animal testing

**'sperma** nm sperm

**spermi'cida** a spermicidal ● nm spermicide

**spero'nare** vt ram

**spe'rone** nm spur

**sperpe'rare** vt squander

**'sperpero** nm waste, squandering

**spersonaliz'zare** vt depersonalize

**spersonaliz'zarsi** vr become depersonalized

**spersonalizzazi'one** nf depersonalization

**'spesa** nf expense; (acquisto) purchase; **andare a far spese** go shopping; **fare la ~** do the shopping; **fare le spese di** pay for; **a proprie spese** at one's own expense. **spese** pl **bancarie** bank charges. **spese** pl **di capitale** capital expenditure. **spese** pl **a carico del destinatario** carriage forward. **spese** pl **di esercizio** business expenses. **spese** pl **extra** out-of-pocket expenses. **spese** pl **di gestione** operating costs. **spese** pl **di spedizione** shipping costs. **spese** pl **di viaggio** travel expenses

**spe'sare** vt pay expenses for; **spesato della ditta** paid for by the company, on the company

**spe'sato** a all-expenses-paid

**'speso** pp di spendere

**'spesso¹** a thick

**'spesso²** adv often

**spes'sore** nm thickness; (fig: consistenza) substance

**spet'tabile** a (Comm abbr **Spett.**) **S~ ditta Rossi** Messrs Rossi

**spettaco'lare** a spectacular

**spet'tacolo** nm spectacle; (rappresentazione) show; **dare ~ di sé** make a spectacle o an exhibition of oneself; **il mondo dello ~** show business. **~ di burattini** Punch-and-Judy show

**spettaco'loso** a spectacular

**spet'tanza** nf concern

**spet'tare** vi **~ a** be up to; ⟨diritto:⟩ be due to

**spetta|'tore, -'trice** nmf spectator; **spettatori** pl (di cinema ecc) audience sg

**spettego'lare** vi gossip

**spetti'nare** vt **~ qcno** ruffle sb's hair

**spetti'narsi** vr ruffle one's hair

**spet'trale** a ghostly

**'spettro** nm ghost; (fig: della fame) spectre; Phys spectrum; **ad ampio ~** ⟨medicina⟩ broad-spectrum

**spezi'are** vt add spices to, spice

**spezi'ato** a spicy

**'spezie** nfpl spices

**spez'zare** vt break

**spez'zarsi** vr break

**spezza'tino** nm stew

**spez'zato** a broken ● nm coordinated jacket and trousers

**spezzet'tare** vt break into small pieces

**spez'zone** nm Cinema clip, footage no pl; (bomba) cluster bomb

**'spia** nf spy; (della polizia) informer; (di porta) peep-hole; **fare la ~** sneak. **~ di accensione** power-on light. **~ di attività dell'hard disk** Comput hard disk activity light. **~ della benzina** petrol gauge. **~ [luminosa]** light. **~ dell'olio** oil [warning] light

**spiacci'care** vt squash

**spia'cente** a sorry

**spia'cevole** a unpleasant

**spi'aggia** nf beach

**spia'nare** vt level; (rendere liscio) smooth; roll out ⟨pasta⟩; raze to the ground ⟨edificio⟩

**spia'nata** nf flat ground

**spi'ano** nm **a tutto ~** flat out

**spian'tato** a fig penniless

**spi'are** vt spy on; wait for ⟨occasione ecc⟩

**spiattel'lare** vt blurt out; shove ⟨oggetto⟩

**spiaz'zare** vt wrong-foot

**spi'azzo** nm (radura) clearing

**spic'care** vt **~ un salto** jump; **~ il volo** take flight ● vi stand out

**spic'cato** a marked

**'spicchio** nm (di agrumi) segment; (di aglio) clove

**spicci'arsi** vr hurry up

**spiccia'tivo** a speedy

**'spiccio** a no-nonsense

**'spiccioli** nmpl change

**'spicciolo** a (comune) banal; ⟨denaro, 10 000 lire⟩ in change

**'spicco** nm relief; **fare ~** stand out; **di ~** high-profile

**'spider** nmf inv open-top sports car

**spie'dino** nm kebab

**spi'edo** nm spit; **allo ~** on a spit, spit-roasted

**spiega'mento** nm deployment

**spie'gare** vt explain; open out ⟨cartina⟩; unfurl ⟨vele⟩

**spie'garsi** vr explain oneself; ⟨vele, bandiere:⟩ unfurl; **non so se mi spiego** need I say more?; **mi sono spiegato?** (minaccia) do I make myself clear?; **non riesco a spiegarmi come...** I can't understand how...

**spie'gato** a ⟨ale⟩ outspread; **a sirene spiegate** with sirens blaring; **a voce spiegata** at the top of one's voice; **a vele spiegate** under full sail, with all sails in the wind

**spiegazi'one** *nf* explanation: **venire a una ~ con qcno** sort things out with sb

**spiegaz'zare** *vt* crumple

**spiegaz'zato** *a* crumpled

**spieta'tezza** *nf* ruthlessness

**spie'tato** *a* ruthless

**spiffe'rare** *vt* blurt out ● *vi* ‹*vento:*› whistle

**'spiffero** *nm* ‹*corrente d'aria*› draught

**'spiga** *nf* spike; *Bot* ear

**spi'gato** *a* herringbone

**spigli'ato** *a* self-possessed

**spigola** *nf* sea bass

**spigo'lare** *vt* glean

**'spigolo** *nm* edge; ‹*angolo*› corner

**spilla** *nf* ‹*gioiello*› brooch. **~ da balia** safety pin. **~ di sicurezza** safety pin

**spil'lare** *vt* tap

**'spillo** *nm* pin. **~ di sicurezza** safety pin; ‹*in arma*› safety catch

**spil'lone** *nm* hatpin

**spilluzzi'care** *vt* pick at

**spi'lorcio, -a** *a* stingy ● *nm* miser, skinflint

**spilun'gone, -a** *nmf* beanpole

**'spina** *nf* thorn; ‹*di pesce*› bone; *Electr* plug; **a ~ di pesce** ‹*tessuto, disegno*› herringbone; ‹*parcheggio*› in two angled rows: **stare sulle spine** be on tenterhooks. **~ dorsale** spine; **essere una ~ nel fianco** thorn in one's side

**spi'naci** *nmpl* spinach

**spi'nale** *a* spinal

**spi'nato** *a* ‹*filo*› barbed; ‹*pianta*› thorny ● *nm* herringbone

**spi'nello** *nm* ‹*fam: droga*› joint

**'spingere** *vt* push; *fig* drive

**'spingersi** *vr* ‹*andare*› proceed

**'spinnaker** *nm* spinnaker

**spi'noso** *a* thorny

**spi'notto** *nm* *Electr* plug

**'spinta** *nf* push; ‹*violenta*› thrust; *fig* spur; **dare una ~ a qcsa/qcno** give sb/sth a push; **farsi largo a spinte** push one's way through

**'spinto** *pp di* **spingere**

**spio'naggio** *nm* espionage, spying

**spi'one, -a** *nmf* tell-tale

**spio'vente** *a* ‹*tetto*› sloping ● *nm* slope

**spi'overe** *vi liter* stop raining; ‹*ricadere*› fall; ‹*scorrere*› flow down

**'spira** *nf* coil

**spi'raglio** *nm* small opening; ‹*soffio d'aria*› breath of air; ‹*raggio di luce*› gleam of light

**spi'rale** *a* spiral ● *nm* spiral; ‹*negli orologi*› hairspring; ‹*anticoncezionale*› coil; **a ~** spiral-shaped

**spi'rare** *vi* ‹*soffiare*› blow; ‹*morire*› pass away

**spiri'tato** *a* possessed; ‹*espressione*› wild

**spiri'tismo** *nm* spiritualism

**spiri'tista** *nmf* spiritualist

**spiri'tistico** *a* spiritualist

**'spirito** *nm* spirit; ‹*arguzia*› wit; ‹*intelletto*› mind; **fare dello ~** be witty; **persona di ~** witty person; **sotto ~** in brandy. **~ civico** community spirit. **~ di contraddizione** contrariness. **S~ Santo** Holy Spirit, Holy Ghost

**spirito'saggine** *nf* witticism

**spiri'toso** *a* witty

**spiritu'ale** *a* spiritual

**spiritual'mente** *adv* spiritually

**splen'dente** *a* shining

**'splendere** *vi* shine

**'splendido** *a* splendid

**splen'dore** *nm* splendour

**'spocchia** *nf* conceit

**spocchi'oso** *a* conceited

**spode'stare** *vt* dispossess; depose ‹*re*›

**spoetiz'zare** *vt* disenchant

**'spoglia** *nf* ‹*di animale*› skin; **spoglie** *pl* ‹*salma*› mortal remains; ‹*bottino*› spoils; **sotto false spoglie** under false pretences

**spogli'are** *vt* strip; ‹*svestire*› undress; ‹*fare lo spoglio di*› go through; **~ qcno di un diritto** divest sb of a right

**spoglia'rello** *nm* strip-tease

**spogliarel'lista** *nf* strip-tease artist, stripper

**spogli'arsi** *vr* strip, undress

**spoglia'toio** *nm* dressing room; *Sport* changing room; ‹*guardaroba*› cloakroom, checkroom *Am*

**'spoglio** *a* undressed; ‹*albero, muro*› bare. **~ di** ‹*privo*› stripped of ● *nm* ‹*scrutinio*› perusal

**'spoiler** *nm inv* *Auto* spoiler

**'spola** *nf* shuttle; **fare la ~** shuttle

**spo'letta** *nf* spool

**spolmo'narsi** *vr* shout oneself hoarse

**spol'pare** *vt* take the flesh off; *fig* fleece

**spolve'rare** *vt* dust; *fam* devour ‹*cibo*›

**'sponda** *nf* ‹*di mare, lago*› shore; ‹*di fiume*› bank; ‹*bordo*› edge

**sponsoriz'zare** *vt* sponsor

**sponsorizzazi'one** *nf* sponsorship

**spontaneità** *nf* spontaneity

**spon'taneo** *a* spontaneous

**'spooling** *nm* *Comput* spooling

**spopo'lare** *vt* depopulate ● *vi* ‹*avere successo*› draw the crowds

**spopo'larsi** *vr* become depopulated

**'spora** *nf* spore

**sporadica'mente** *adv* sporadically

**spo'radico** *a* sporadic

**sporcacci'one, -a** *nmf* dirty pig

**spor'care** *vt* dirty; ‹*macchiare*› soil

**spor'carsi** *vr* get dirty

**spor'cizia** *nf* dirt

**'sporco** *a* dirty; **avere la coscienza sporca** have a guilty conscience ● *nm* dirt

**spor'gente** *a* jutting

**spor'genza** *nf* projection

**'sporgere** *vt* stretch out; **~ querela contro** take legal action against ● *vi* jut out

**'sporgersi** *vr* lean out

**sport** *nm inv* sport; **fare qcsa per ~** do sth for fun. **~ invernali** *pl* winter sports

**'sporta** *nf* shopping basket

**spor'tello** *nm* door; ‹*di banca ecc*› window. **~ automatico** cash dispenser, cash point. **~ pacchi** parcels counter

**spor'tivo, -a** *a* sports *attrib*; ‹*persona*› sporty ● *nm* sportsman ● *nf* sportswoman

**'sporto** *pp di* **sporgere**

'**sposa** *nf* bride; **dare in ~** give in marriage, give away; **prendere in ~** marry

**sposa'lizio** *nm* wedding

**spo'sare** *vt* marry; *fig* espouse

**spo'sarsi** *vr* get married; ⟨*vino:*⟩ go (**con** with)

**spo'sato** *a* married

**spo'sini** *nmpl* newly-weds

'**sposo** *nm* bridegroom; **sposi** *pl* [**novelli**] newlyweds

**spossa'tezza** *nf* exhaustion

**spos'sato** *a* exhausted, worn out

**sposses'sato** *a* dispossessed

**sposta'mento** *nm* displacement. **~ d'aria** airflow

**spo'stare** *vt* move; (*differire*) postpone; (*cambiare*) change

**spo'starsi** *vr* move

**spo'stato, -a** *a* ill-adjusted ● *nmf* (*disadattato*) misfit

**spot** *nm inv* ~ [**pubblicitario**] commercial

'**spranga** *nf* bar

**spran'gare** *vt* bar

'**sprazzo** *nm* (*di colore*) splash; (*di luce*) flash; *fig* glimmer

**spre'care** *vt* waste

'**spreco** *nm* waste

**spre'cone** *a* spendthrift

**spre'gevole** *a* despicable

**spregia'tivo** *a* pejorative

**spregio** *nm* contempt; **fare uno ~ a qcno** offend sb

**spregiudi'cato** *a* unprejudiced; *pej* unscrupulous

'**spremere** *vt* squeeze

'**spremersi** *vr* **~ le meningi** rack one's brains

**spremi'aglio** *nm inv* garlic press

**spremia'grumi** *nm inv* lemon squeezer

**spremili'moni** *nm inv* lemon squeezer

**spre'muta** *nf* juice. **~ d'arancia** fresh orange [juice], freshly squeezed orange juice

**spre'tato** *nm* former priest

**sprez'zante** *a* contemptuous

**sprigio'nare** *vt* emit

**sprigio'narsi** *vr* burst out

**sprint** *nm* sprint; **fare uno ~** put on a spurt

**spriz'zare** *vt/i* spurt; be bursting with ⟨*salute, gioia*⟩

**sprofon'dare** *vi* sink; (*crollare*) collapse

**sprofon'darsi** *vr* **~ in** sink into; *fig* be engrossed in

**spron** *nm vedi* **sprone**

**spro'nare** *vt* spur on

'**sprone** *nm* spur; (*sartoria*) yoke; **a spron battuto** instantly; **andare a spron battuto** go hell-for-leather

**sproporzio'nato** *a* disproportionate

**sproporzi'one** *nf* disproportion

**sproposi'tato** *a* full of blunders; (*enorme*) huge

**spro'posito** *nm* blunder; (*eccesso*) excessive amount; **a ~** inopportunely

**sprovve'duto** *a* unprepared; **~ di** lacking in

**sprov'visto** *a* **~ di** out of; lacking in ⟨*fantasia, pazienza*⟩; **alla sprovvista** unexpectedly

**spruz'zare** *vt* sprinkle; (*vaporizzare*) spray; (*inzaccherare*) spatter

**spruzza'tore** *nm* spray

'**spruzzo** *nm* spray; (*di fango*) splash

**spudorata'mente** *adv* shamelessly

**spudora'tezza** *nf* shamelessness

**spudo'rato** *a* shameless

'**spugna** *nf* sponge; (*tessuto*) towelling

**spu'gnoso** *a* spongy

'**spuma** *nf* foam; (*schiuma*) froth; *Culin* mousse

**spu'mante** *nm* sparkling wine, spumante

**spumeggi'ante** *a* bubbly; (*mare*) foaming

**spumeggi'are** *vi* ⟨*champagne:*⟩ bubble; ⟨*birra:*⟩ foam

**spun'tare** *vt* (*rompere la punta di*) break the point of; trim ⟨*capelli*⟩; **spuntarla** *fig* win ● *vi* ⟨*pianta:*⟩ sprout; ⟨*capelli:*⟩ begin to grow; (*sorgere*) rise; (*apparire*) appear

**spun'tarsi** *vr* get blunt

**spun'tata** *nf* trim

**spun'tino** *nm* snack

'**spunto** *nm* cue; *fig* starting point; **dare ~ a** give rise to

**spur'gare** *vt* purge

**spur'garsi** *vr Med* expectorate

'**spurio** *a* spurious

**spu'tacchio** *nm* spittle

**spu'tare** *vt/i* spit; spit out ⟨*cibo*⟩; **~ sentenze** pass judgment; **~ l'osso** *sl* spit it out

'**sputo** *nm* spit

'**squadra** *nf* (*gruppo*) team, squad; (*di polizia ecc*) squad; (*da disegno*) square; **lavoro di ~** teamwork. **~ del buoncostume** Vice Squad. **~ mobile** Flying Squad. **~ narcotici** Drug Squad. **~ soccorso** rescue team

**squa'drare** *vt* square; (*guardare*) look up and down

**squa'driglia** *nf*, **squadrigli'one** *nm* squadron

**squa'drone** *nm* squadron

**squagli'are** *vt* melt

**squagli'arsi** *vr* melt; **squagliarsela** (*fam: svignarsela*) steal out

**squa'lifica** *nf* disqualification

**squalifi'care** *vt* disqualify

'**squallido** *a* squalid

**squal'lore** *nm* squalor

'**squalo** *nm* shark

'**squama** *nf* scale; (*di pelle*) flake

**squa'mare** *vt* scale

**squa'marsi** *vr* ⟨*pelle:*⟩ flake off

**squa'moso** *a* scaly; ⟨*pelle*⟩ flaky

**squarcia'gola: a ~** *adv* at the top of one's voice

**squarci'are** *vt* rip

'**squarcio** *nm* rip; (*di ferita, in nave*) gash; (*di cielo*) patch

**squar'tare** *vt* quarter; dismember ⟨*animale*⟩

**squarta'tore** *nm* **Jack lo ~** Jack the Ripper

**squash** *nm inv* squash

**squas'sare** *vt* shake

**squattri'nato** *a* penniless

**squaw** *nf inv* squaw

**squilib'rare** *vt* unbalance

**squili'brato, -a** *a* unbalanced ● *nmf* lunatic

**squi'librio** *nm* imbalance

**squil'lante** *a* shrill

**squil'lare** *vi* ⟨campana:⟩ peal; ⟨tromba:⟩ blare; ⟨telefono:⟩ ring

**'squillo** *nm* blare; *Teleph* ring; ⟨ragazza⟩ call girl

**squinter'nato** *a anche fig* crazy

**squisi'tezza** *nf* refinement

**squi'sito** *a* exquisite

**squit'tire** *vi* ⟨pappagallo, fig:⟩ squawk; ⟨topo:⟩ squeak

**sradi'care** *vt* uproot; eradicate ⟨vizio, male⟩

**sragio'nare** *vi* rave

**sregola'tezza** *nf* dissipation

**srego'lato** *a* inordinate; ⟨dissoluto⟩ dissolute

**s.r.l.** *abbr* (**società a responsabilità limitata**) Ltd

**sroto'lare** *vt* uncoil

**SS** *abbr* (**strada statale**) national road; *abbr* (**Santissimo**) Most Holy

**ss** *abbr* (**seguenti**) following

**sst** *int* sh!

**'stabile** *a* stable; ⟨permanente⟩ lasting; ⟨saldo⟩ steady; **compagnia ~** *Theat* repertory company ● *nm* ⟨edificio⟩ building

**stabili'mento** *nm* factory; ⟨industriale⟩ plant; ⟨edificio⟩ establishment. **~ balneare** lido

**stabi'lire** *vt* establish; ⟨decidere⟩ decide

**stabi'lirsi** *vr* settle

**stabilità** *nf* stability

**stabi'lito** *a* established

**stabiliz'zare** *vt* stabilize

**stabiliz'zarsi** *vr* stabilize

**stabilizza'tore** *nm* stabilizer

**stacano'vista** *nmf* workaholic

**stac'care** *vt* detach; pronounce clearly ⟨parole⟩; ⟨separare⟩ separate; turn off ⟨corrente⟩; **~ gli occhi da** take one's eyes off ● *vi* ⟨fam: finire di lavorare⟩ knock off

**stac'carsi** *vr* come off; **~ da** break away from ⟨partito, famiglia⟩; **si stacca alle cinque** knocking off time is five o'clock

**staccata'mente** *adv* staccato

**stac'cato** *a Mus* staccato

**staccio'nata** *nf* fence

**'stacco** *nm* gap

**'stadio** *nm* stadium

**'staffa** *nf* stirrup; **perdere le staffe** *fig* fly off the handle

**staf'fetta** *nf* dispatch rider

**staffet'tista** *nmf Sport* anchorman

**stagio'nale** *a* seasonal

**stagio'nare** *vt* season ⟨legno⟩; mature ⟨formaggio⟩

**stagio'nato** *a* ⟨legno⟩ seasoned; ⟨formaggio⟩ matured

**stagiona'tura** *nf* ⟨di legno⟩ seasoning; ⟨di formaggio⟩ maturation, maturing

**stagi'one** *nf* season; **alta/bassa ~** high/low season; **di ~** in season; **fuori ~** out of season. **~ lirica** opera season

**stagli'arsi** *vr* stand out

**sta'gnante** *a* stagnant

**sta'gnare** *vt* ⟨saldare⟩ solder; ⟨chiudere ermeticamente⟩ seal ● *vi* ⟨acqua:⟩ stagnate

**'stagno** *a* ⟨a tenuta d'acqua⟩ watertight ● *nm* ⟨acqua ferma⟩ pond; ⟨metallo⟩ tin

**sta'gnola** *nf* tinfoil

**stalag'mite** *nf* stalagmite

**stalat'tite** *nf* stalactite

**'stalla** *nf* stable; ⟨per buoi⟩ cowshed

**stalli'ere** *nm* groom

**stal'lone** *nm* stallion

**sta'mani, stamat'tina** *adv* this morning

**stam'becco** *nm* ibex

**stam'berga** *nf* hovel

**'stampa** *nf Typ* printing; ⟨giornali, giornalisti⟩ press; ⟨riproduzione⟩ print. **stampe** ⟨postale⟩ printed matter. **~ fronte retro** two-sided printing, duplex printing. **~ scandalistica** gutter press, tabloid press

**stam'pante** *nf* printer. **~ ad aghi** dot matrix [printer]. **~ a getto d'inchiostro** inkjet [printer]. **~ laser** laser [printer]. **~ a matrice di punti** dot matrix [printer]. **~ seriale** serial printer. **~ termica** thermal printer

**stam'pare** *vt* print

**stampa'tello** *nm* block letters *pl*, block capitals *pl*

**stam'pato** *a* printed ● *nm* leaflet; *Comput* hard copy, printout; ⟨modulo⟩ print; **stampati** ⟨pubblicità⟩ promotional literature

**stam'pella** *nf* crutch

**stampigli'are** *vt* stamp

**stampiglia'tura** *nf* stamping; ⟨dicitura⟩ stamp

**stam'pino** *nm* stencil

**'stampo** *nm* mould; **di vecchio ~** ⟨persona⟩ of the old school

**sta'nare** *vt* drive out

**stan'care** *vt* tire; ⟨annoiare⟩ bore

**stan'carsi** *vr* get tired

**stan'chezza** *nf* tiredness

**'stanco** *a* tired; **~ di** ⟨stufo⟩ fed up with. **~ morto** dead tired, knackered *fam*

**stand** *nm inv* stand

**'standard** *a & nm inv* standard

**standardiz'zare** *vt* standardize

**standardizzazi'one** *nf* standardization

**'stand-by** *a inv* stand-by

**'stanga** *nf* bar; ⟨persona⟩ beanpole

**stan'gare** *vt fam* fail ⟨studente⟩; ⟨con le tasse ecc⟩ clobber

**stan'gata** *nf fig* blow; ⟨fam: nel calcio⟩ big kick; **prendere una ~** ⟨fam: agli esami, economica⟩ come a cropper

**stan'ghetta** *nf* ⟨di occhiali⟩ leg

**sta'notte** *nf* tonight; ⟨la notte scorsa⟩ last night

**'stante** *prep* on account of; **a sé ~** separate

**stan'tio** *a* stale

**stan'tuffo** *nm* piston

**'stanza** *nf* room; (*metrica*) stanza. ~ **dei giochi** games room. ~ **da pranzo** dining room

**stanzia'mento** *nm* appropriation

**stanzi'are** *vt* allocate

**stan'zino** *nm* walk-in

**stap'pare** *vt* uncork

**star** *nf inv Cinema* star

**'stare** *vi* (*rimanere*) stay; (*abitare*) live; (*con gerundio*) be; **sto solo cinque minuti** I'll stay only five minutes; **sto in piazza Peyron** I live in Peyron Square; **sta dormendo** he's sleeping; ~ **a** (*attenersi*) keep to; (*spettare*) be up to; ~ **bene** (*economicamente*) be well off; (*di salute*) be well; (*addirsi*) suit; **sta bene!** that's fine!; ~ **dietro a** (*seguire*) follow; (*sorvegliare*) keep an eye on; (*corteggiare*) run after; ~ **in piedi** stand; ~ **per** be about to; ~ **sempre a fare qcsa** be always doing sth; **ben ti sta!** it serves you right!; **come stai/sta?** how are you?; **lasciar** ~ leave alone; **starci** (*essere contenuto*) go into; (*essere d'accordo*) agree; **il 3 nel 12 ci sta 4 volte** 3 into 12 goes 4; **non sa** ~ **agli scherzi** he can't take a joke; ~ **su** (*con la schiena*) sit up straight; ~ **sulle proprie** keep oneself to oneself

**'starna** *nf* partridge

**starnaz'zare** *vi* quack; *fig* shriek

**starnu'tire** *vi* sneeze

**star'nuto** *nm* sneeze

**'starsene** *vr* (*rimanere*) stay

**'starter** *nm inv* choke

**sta'sera** *adv* this evening, tonight

**'stasi** *nm* stasis

**sta'tale** *a* state *attrib* ● *nmf* state employee, civil servant ● *nf* (*strada*) main road, trunk road

**'statico** *a* static

**sta'tista** *nm* statesman

**sta'tistica** *nf* statistics *sg*

**sta'tistico** *a* statistical

**'Stati 'Uniti [d'America]** *nmpl* gli ~ ~ the United States [of America]

**'stato** *pp di* **essere, stare** ● *nm* state; (*posizione sociale*) position; *Jur* status; **lo S**~ *Pol* the state. ~ **d'animo** frame of mind. ~ **di attesa** *Comput* wait state. ~ **civile** marital status. ~ **cuscinetto** buffer state. **S**~ **Maggiore** *Mil* General Staff. ~ **di salute** state of health

**stato-nazi'one** *nm* nation-state

**'statua** *nf* statue

**statu'ario** *a* statuesque

**statuni'tense** *a* United States *attrib*, US *attrib* ● *nmf* citizen of the United States, US citizen

**sta'tura** *nf* height; **di alta** ~ tall; **di bassa** ~ short; **di media** ~ of average height. ~ **morale** moral stature

**sta'tuto** *nm* statute

**stazio'nario** *a* stationary

**stazi'one** *nf* station; (*città*) resort. ~ **degli autobus** bus station. ~ **balneare** seaside resort. ~ **climatica** health resort. ~ **delle corriere** coach station *Br*, bus station. ~ **ferroviaria** railway station *Br*, train station. ~ **marittima** ferry terminal. ~ **master** *Comput* master station. ~ **multimediale** *Comput* multimedia station. ~ **dei pullman** coach station *Br*, bus station. ~ **di servizio** petrol station *Br*, service station. ~ **slave** *Comput* slave station ~ **termale** spa, health resort

**'stecca** *nf* stick; (*di ombrello*) rib; (*da biliardo*) cue; *Med* splint; (*di sigarette*) carton; (*di reggiseno*) stiffener; **fare una** ~ *Mus* fluff a note

**stec'cato** *nm* fence

**stec'chino** *nm* cocktail stick

**stec'chito** *a* skinny; (*rigido*) stiff; (*morto*) stone cold dead

**'stele** *nf* stele

**'stella** *nf* star; **salire alle stelle** ⟨*prezzi:*⟩ rise sky-high, rocket. ~ **alpina** edelweiss. ~ **cadente** shooting star. ~ **del cinema** movie star. ~ **cometa** comet. ~ **filante** streamer. ~ **di mare** starfish. ~ **polare** Pole Star, North Star

**stel'lare** *a* star *attrib*; ⟨*grandezza*⟩ stellar

**stel'lato** *a* starry

**stel'lina** *nf* starlet

**'stelo** *nm* stem; **lampada a** ~ standard lamp *Br*, floor lamp

**'stemma** *nm* coat of arms

**stempe'rare** *vt* dilute

**stempi'ato** *a* bald at the temples

**'stendere** *vt* spread out; (*appendere*) hang out; (*distendere*) stretch [out]; (*scrivere*) write down

**'stendersi** *vr* stretch out

**stendibianche'ria** *nm inv* clothes horse

**stendi'toio** *nm* clothes horse

**stenodattilogra'fia** *nf* shorthand typing

**stenodatti'lografo, -a** *nmf* shorthand typist

**stenogra'fare** *vt* take down in shorthand

**stenogra'fia** *nf* shorthand

**sten'tare** *vi* ~ **a find it hard to**

**sten'tato** *a* laboured

**'stento** *nm* (*fatica*) effort; **a** ~ with difficulty; **stenti** *pl* hardships, privations

**'steppa** *nf* steppe

**'sterco** *nm* dung

**'stereo['fonico]** *a* stereo[phonic]

**stereo'scopico** *a* stereoscopic

**stereoti'pato** *a* stereotyped; ⟨*sorriso*⟩ insincere

**stere'otipo** *nm* stereotype

**'sterile** *a* sterile; ⟨*terreno*⟩ barren

**sterilità** *nf* sterility

**steriliz'zare** *vt* sterilize

**sterilizzazi'one** *nf* sterilization

**ster'lina** *nf* pound; **lira** ~ [pound] sterling

**stermi'nare** *vt* exterminate

**stermi'nato** *a* immense

**ster'minio** *nm* extermination

**'sterno** *nm* breastbone

**sternu'tire, ster'nuto** = **starnutire, starnuto**

**ste'roide** *nm* steroid

**ster'paglia** *nf* brushwood

**ster'rare** *vt* excavate; dig up ⟨*strada*⟩

**ster'rato** *a* ⟨*strada*⟩ dug up ● *nm* excavation; (*di strada*) digging up

**ster'zare** *vi* steer

**'sterzo** *nm* steering; (*volante*) steering wheel

**'steso** *pp di* **stendere**

**'stesso** *a* same; **io ~** myself; **tu ~** yourself; **me ~** myself; **se ~** himself; **in quel momento ~** at that very moment; **è stato ricevuto dalla stessa regina** (*in persona*) he was received by the Queen herself; **tuo fratello ~ dice che hai torto** even your brother says you're wrong; **l'ho visto coi miei stessi occhi** I saw it with my own eyes; **con le mie stesse mani** with my own hands ● *pron* **lo ~** the same one; (*la stessa cosa*) the same; **fa lo ~** it's all the same; **ci vado io ~** I'll go just the same; **è venuto il giorno ~** he came the same day, he came that very day; **lo farò oggi ~** I'll do it straight away today

**ste'sura** *nf* drawing up; (*documento*) draft

**steto'scopio** *nm* stethoscope

**'steward** *nm inv* steward

**stick** *nm inv* **colla a ~** glue stick; **deodorante a ~** stick deodorant

**stiepi'dire** *vt* warm

**'stigma** *nm* stigma

**'stigmate** *nfpl* stigmata

**sti'lare** *vt* draw up

**'stile** *nm* style; **in grande ~** in style; **essere nello ~ di qcno** be typical of sb, be just like sb. **~ libero** (*nel nuoto*) freestyle, crawl. **~ di vita** life style

**sti'lista** *nmf* [fashion] designer; (*parrucchiere*) stylist

**stiliz'zato** *a* stylized

**'stilla** *nf* drop

**stil'lare** *vi* ooze

**stilo'grafica** *nf* fountain pen

**stilo'grafico** *a* **penna stilografica** fountain pen

**'stima** *nf* esteem; (*valutazione*) estimate

**sti'mare** *vt* esteem; (*valutare*) estimate; (*ritenere*) consider

**sti'marsi** *vr* consider oneself

**sti'mato** *a* well-thought-of

**stimo'lante** *a* stimulating ● *nm* stimulant

**stimo'lare** *vt* stimulate; (*incitare*) incite

**'stimolo** *nm* stimulus; (*fitta*) pang

**'stinco** *nm* shin; **non è uno ~ di santo** *fam* he's no saint

**'stingere** *vt/i* fade

**'stingersi** *vr* fade

**'stinto** *pp di* **stingere**

**sti'pare** *vt* cram

**sti'parsi** *vr* crowd together

**stipendi'are** *vt* pay a salary to

**stipendi'ato** *a* salaried ● *nm* salaried worker

**sti'pendio** *nm* salary. **~ base** basic salary. **~ iniziale** starting salary

**'stipite** *nm* doorpost

**stipu'lare** *vt* stipulate

**stipulazi'one** *nf* stipulation; (*accordo*) agreement

**stira'mento** *nm* sprain

**sti'rare** *vt* iron; (*distendere*) stretch

**sti'rarsi** *vr* (*distendersi*) stretch; pull ⟨*muscolo*⟩

**stira'tura** *nf* ironing

**'stiro** *nm* **ferro da ~** iron

**'stirpe** *nf* stock

**stiti'chezza** *nf* constipation

**'stitico** *a* constipated

**'stiva** *nf Naut* hold

**sti'vale** *nm* boot; **lo S~** (*Italia*) Italy. **stivali pl di gomma** Wellington boots, Wellingtons; **poeta dei miei stivali**! *fam* poet my eye!, poet my foot!

**stiva'letto** *nm* ankle boot

**stiva'lone** *nm* high boot; **stivaloni pl da caccia** hunting boots; **stivaloni pl di gomma** waders

**sti'vare** *vt* load

**'stizza** *nf* anger

**stiz'zire** *vt* irritate

**stiz'zirsi** *vr* become irritated

**stiz'zito** *a* irritated

**stiz'zoso** *a* peevish

**stocca'fisso** *nm* stockfish

**stoc'cata** *nf* stab; (*battuta pungente*) gibe

**stock** *nm Comm* stock

**'stock-car** *nm inv* stock car

**'stoffa** *nf* material; *fig* stuff; **avere ~** have what it takes

**stoi'cismo** *nm* stoicism

**'stoico** *a & nm* stoic

**sto'ino** *nm* doormat

**'stola** *nf* stole

**'stolido** *a* stolid

**'stolto** *a* foolish

**stoma'chevole** *a* revolting

**'stomaco** *nm* stomach; **mal di ~** stomach-ache

**stoma'tite** *nf* stomatitis

**sto'nare** *vt/i* sing/play out of tune ● *vi* (*non intonarsi*) clash

**sto'nato** *a* out of tune; (*discordante*) clashing; (*confuso*) bewildered

**stona'tura** *nf* false note; (*discordanza*) clash

**stop** *nm inv* (*segnale stadale*) stop sign; (*in telegramma*) stop

**stop'pare** *vt* stop

**'stopper** *nm Sport* fullback

**'stoppia** *nf* stubble

**stop'pino** *nm* wick

**stop'poso** *a* tough

**'storcere** *vt* twist

**'storcersi** *vr* twist

**stor'dire** *vt* stun; (*intontire*) daze

**stor'dirsi** *vr* dull one's senses

**stor'dito** *a* stunned; (*intontito*) dazed; (*sventato*) heedless

**'storia** *nf* history; (*racconto, bugia*) story;

(*pretesto*) excuse; **senza storie!** no fuss!; **fare [delle] storie** make a fuss. ~ **d'amore** love story

'**storico** a historical; (*di importanza storica*) historic ● nm historian

stori'**ella** nf fam little story

storiogra'**fia** nf historiography

stori'**ografo** nm historiographer

stori'**one** nm sturgeon

'**stormo** nm flock

stor'**nare** vt avert; transfer (*somma*)

'**storno** nm starling

storpi'**are** vt cripple; mangle (*parole*)

storpia'**tura** nf deformation

'**storpio, -a** a crippled ● nmf cripple

'**storta** nf (*distorsione*) sprain; **prendere una ~ alla caviglia** sprain one's ankle

'**storto** pp di **storcere** ● a crooked; (*ritorto*) twisted; (*gambe*) bandy; *fig* wrong

stor'**tura** nf deformity; ~ **mentale** twisted way of thinking

sto'**viglie** nfpl crockery sg, flatware Am

'**strabico** a cross-eyed; **essere ~** be cross-eyed, [have a] squint

strabili'**ante** a astonishing

strabili'**are** vt astonish

stra'**bismo** nm squint

straboc'**care** vi overflow

strabuz'**zare** vt ~ **gli occhi** goggle; **ha strabuzzato gli occhi** his eyes popped out of his head

straca'**narsi** vr fam work like a slave, slave away

stra'**carico** a overloaded

strac'**chino** nm soft cheese from Lombardy

stracci'**are** vt tear; (*fam: vincere*) thrash

straccia'**tella** nf vanilla ice cream with chocolate chips

stracci'**ato** a torn; (*persona*) in rags; (*prezzi*) slashed; **a un prezzo ~** at a knock-down price, dirt cheap

'**straccio** a torn ● nm rag; (*strofinaccio*) cloth; **essere ridotto ad uno ~** feel like a wet rag

stracci'**one** nm tramp

stracci'**vendolo** nm ragman

stracol'**larsi** vr sprain

stra'**cotto** a overdone; (*fam: innamorato*) head over heels ● nm stew

'**strada** nf road; (*di città*) street; (*fig: cammino*) way; **essere fuori ~** be on the wrong track; **fare ~** lead the way; **tener la macchina in ~** keep the car on the road; (*parcheggiare*) keep the car on the street; **su ~** (*trasportare*) by road; **farsi ~** (*aver successo*) make one's way [in the world]. ~ **d'accesso** approach road. ~ **camionabile** road for heavy vehicles. ~ **maestra** main road. ~ **pedonale** pedestrianized street. ~ **principale** main road. ~ **privata** private road. ~ **secondaria** secondary road. ~ **a senso unico** one-way street. ~ **senza uscita** dead end, cul-de-sac. ~ **di terra battuta** dirt track

stra'**dale** a road *attrib* traffic police ● nm **la S~** fam traffice police

stra'**dina** nf little street; (*in campagna*) little road

strafalci'**one** nm blunder

stra'**fare** vi overdo it, overdo things

stra'**foro: di ~** adv on the sly

strafot'**tente** a arrogant

strafot'**tenza** nf arrogance

'**strage** nf slaughter

stra'**grande** a vast

stralci'**are** vt remove

'**stralcio** nm removal; (*parte*) extract

stralu'**nare** vt ~ **gli occhi** open one's eyes wide

stralu'**nato** a (*occhi*) staring; (*persona*) distraught

stramaz'**zare** vi fall heavily; ~ **al suolo** crash to the ground

strambe'**ria** nf oddity

'**strambo** a strange

strampa'**lato** a odd

stra'**nezza** nf strangeness

strango'**lare** vt strangle

strangugli'**one** nm tonsillitis

strani'**ero, -a** a foreign ● nmf foreigner

'**strano** a strange; ~ **ma vero** surprisingly enough, funnily enough

straordinaria'**mente** adv extraordinarily

straordi'**nario** a extraordinary; (*notevole*) remarkable; (*edizione*) special; **lavoro ~** overtime; **treno ~** special [train]

strapaz'**zare** vt ill-treat; scramble (*uova*)

strapaz'**zarsi** vr tire oneself out

stra'**pazzo** nm strain; **da ~** *fig* worthless

strapi'**eno** a overflowing

strapi'**ombo** nm projection; **a ~** sheer

strapo'**tere** nm overwhelming power

strappa'**lacrime** a inv weepy

strap'**pare** vt tear; (*per distruggere*) tear up; pull out (*dente, capelli*); (*sradicare*) pull up; (*estorcere*) wring

strap'**parsi** vr get torn; (*allontanarsi*) tear oneself away; ~ **i capelli** *fig* be tearing one's hair out

'**strappo** nm tear; (*strattone*) jerk; (*fam: passaggio*) lift; **fare uno ~ alla regola** make an exception to the rule. ~ **muscolare** muscle strain

strapun'**tino** nm folding seat

strari'**pare** vi flood

strasci'**care** vt trail; shuffle (*piedi*); drawl (*parole*)

'**strascico** nm train; *fig* after-effect

strasci'**coni: a ~** adv dragging one's feet

straseco'**lare** vi be amazed

**strass** nm inv rhinestone

strata'**gemma** nm stratagem

stra'**tega** nmf strategist

strate'**gia** nf strategy

stra'**tegico** a strategic; **mossa strategica** strategic move

stratifi'**care** vt stratify

stratigra'**fia** nf *Geol* stratigraphy

'**strato** nm layer; (*di vernice ecc*) coat, layer; (*roccioso, sociale*) stratum. ~ **di nuvole** cloud layer

**strato'sfera** *nf* stratosphere

**strato'sferico** *a* stratospheric: *fig* sky-high

**stravac'carsi** *vr fam* slouch

**stravac'cato** *a fam* slouching

**strava'gante** *a* extravagant; *(eccentrico)* eccentric

**strava'ganza** *nf* extravagance; *(eccentricità)* eccentricity

**stra'vecchio** *a* ancient

**strave'dere** *vt* ~ **per** worship

**stravizi'are** *vi* indulge oneself

**stra'vizio** *nm* excess

**stra'volgere** *vt* twist; *(turbare)* upset

**stravolgi'mento** *nm* twisting

**stra'volto** *a* distraught; *(fam: stanco)* done in

**strazi'ante** *a* heartrending; *(dolore)* agonizing

**strazi'are** *vt* grate on *(orecchie)*; break *(cuore)*

**'strazio** *nm* agony; **essere uno** ~ be agony: **che** ~*! fam* it's awful!; **fare** ~ **di qcsa** *(fam: attore, cantante:)* murder sth

**'streamer** *nm inv Comput* streamer

**'strega** *nf* witch

**stre'gare** *vt* bewitch

**stre'gone** *nm* wizard

**stregone'ria** *nf* witchcraft

**'stregua** *nf* **alla** ~ **di** in the same way as; **alla stessa** ~ *(giudicare)* by the same yardstick; **a questa** ~ at this rate

**stre'mare** *vt* exhaust

**stre'mato** *a* exhausted

**'stremo** *a* extreme ● *nm* **ridotto allo** ~ at the end of one's tether

**'strenna** *nf* present

**'strenuo** *a* strenuous

**strepi'tare** *vi* make a din

**strepi'tio** *nm* din, uproar

**strepi'toso** *a* noisy: *fig* resounding

**strepto'cocco** *nm Med* streptococcus

**streptomi'cina** *nf Med* streptomycin

**stress** *nm* stress

**stres'sante** *a* *(lavoro, situazione)* stressful

**stres'sare** *vt* put under stress, be stressful for

**stres'sarsi** *vr* get stressed

**stres'sato** *a* stressed [out]

**'stretta** *nf* grasp; *(dolore)* pang; **essere alle strette** be in dire straits; **mettere alle strette qcno** have sb's back up against the wall; **provare una** ~ **al cuore** feel a pang. ~ **di mano** handshake

**stret'tezza** *nf* narrowness; **stret'tezze** *pl* *(difficoltà finanziarie)* financial difficulties

**'stretto** *pp di* **stringere** ● *a* narrow; *(serrato)* tight; *(vicino)* close; *(dialetto)* broad; *(rigoroso)* strict; **lo** ~ **necessario** the bare minimum ● *nm Geog* strait. ~ **di Messina** Straits of Messina

**stret'toia** *nf* bottleneck; *(fam: difficoltà)* tight spot

**stri'ato** *a* striped

**stria'tura** *nf* streak

**stri'dente** *a* strident

**'stridere** *vi* squeak: *fig* clash

**stri'dore** *nm* screech

**'stridulo** *a* shrill

**strigli'are** *vt* groom

**strigli'ata** *nf* grooming: *fig* dressing down

**stril'lare** *vi/t* scream

**'strillo** *nm* scream

**stril'lone** *nm* newspaper seller

**strimin'zito** *a* skimpy; *(magro)* skinny

**strimpel'lare** *vt* strum

**stri'nare** *vt* singe, scorch

**'stringa** *nf* lace; *Comput* string

**strin'gato** *a fig* terse

**'stringere** *vt* press; *(serrare)* squeeze; *(tenere stretto)* hold tight; take in *(abito)*; *(comprimere)* be tight; *(restringere)* tighten; ~ **la mano a** shake hands with ● *vi* *(premere)* press

**'stringersi** *vr* *(accostarsi)* draw close **(a** to); *(avvicinarsi)* squeeze up

**strip'pata** *nf fam* nosh-up; **farsi una** ~ have a nosh-up

**strip-'tease** *nm* striptease

**'striscia** *nf* strip; *(riga)* stripe; **a strisce** striped. **strisce** *pl* **di mezzeria** *Auto* lane markings. **strisce** *pl* **[pedonali]** zebra crossing *sg*, crosswalk *Am*

**strisci'are** *vi* crawl; *(sfiorare)* graze ● *vt* drag *(piedi)*

**strisci'arsi** *vr* ~ **a** rub against

**strisci'ata** *nf* scratch

**'striscio** *nm* graze; *Med* smear; **colpire di** ~ graze

**strisci'one** *nm* banner

**strito'lare** *vt* grind

**strizzacer'velli** *nmf sl* shrink

**striz'zare** *vt* squeeze; *(torcere)* wring [out]; ~ **l'occhio** wink

**'strofa** *nf* strophe

**strofi'naccio** *nm* cloth; *(per spolverare)* duster. ~ **da cucina** tea towel

**strofi'nare** *vt* rub

**strofi'nio** *nm* rubbing

**strom'bare** *vt* splay

**strombaz'zare** *vt* boast about ● *vi* hoot

**strombaz'zata** *nf* *(di clacson)* hoot

**stron'care** *vt* cut off; *(reprimere)* crush; *(criticare)* tear to shreds

**stron'zate** *nfpl vulg* crap

**'stronzo** *nm vulg* shit

**stropicci'are** *vt* rub; crumple *(vestito)*

**stropicci'ata** *nf* rub

**stro'piccio** *nm* rubbing

**stroppi'are** *vt* **il troppo stroppia** enough is as good as a feast

**stroz'zare** *vt* strangle

**strozza'tura** *nf* strangling; *(di strada)* narrowing

**strozzi'naggio** *nm* loan-sharking

**stroz'zino** *nm pej* usurer; *(truffatore)* shark

**struc'cante** *nm* make-up remover

**struc'carsi** *vr* remove one's make-up

**strug'gente** *a* all-consuming

**'struggersi** *vr liter* pine [away]; ~ **di invidia/desiderio** be consumed with envy/desire

**struggi'mento** nm yearning
**strumen'tale** a instrumental
**strumentaliz'zare** vt make use of
**strumen'tario** nm instruments pl
**strumentazi'one** nf instrumentation
**strumen'tista** nm instrumentalist
**stru'mento** nm instrument; (arnese) tool. ~ a corda/fiato string/wind instrument. ~ musicale musical instrument. ~ a percussione percussion instrument
**strusci'are** vt rub
**strusci'arsi** vr (gatto:) rub itself; (due innamorati:) caress each other; ~ intorno a qcno fam suck up to sb
**'strutto** nm lard
**strut'tura** nf structure
**struttu'rale** a structural
**struttura'lismo** nm structuralism
**struttural'mente** adv structurally
**struttu'rare** vt structure
**strutturazi'one** nf structuring
**'struzzo** nm ostrich
**stuc'care** vt plaster; (per decorazione) stucco; put putty in (vetri)
**stucca'tore** nm plasterer; (decorativo) stucco worker
**stucca'tura** nf plastering; (decorativo) stucco work
**stuc'chevole** a nauseating
**'stucco** nm plaster; (decorativo) stucco; (per vetro) putty; rimanere di ~ be thunderstruck
**stu'dente, studen'tessa** nmf student; (di scuola) schoolboy; schoolgirl
**studen'tesco** a student; (di scolaro) school attrib
**studi'are** vt study
**studi'arsi** vr ~ di try to
**'studio** nm studying; (stanza, ricerca) study; (di artista, TV ecc) studio; (di professionista) office. ~ dentistico dental surgery
**studi'oso, -a** a studious ● nmf scholar
**'stufa** nf stove. ~ elettrica electric fire. ~ a gas gas fire. ~ a legna wood[-burning] stove
**stu'fare** vt Culin stew; (dare fastidio) bore
**stu'farsi** vr get bored
**stu'fato** nm stew
**'stufo** a bored; essere ~ di be bored with, be fed up with
**stu'oia** nf mat
**stu'olo** nm crowd
**stupefa'cente** a amazing ● nm drug
**stupe'fare** vt stun
**stu'pendo** a stupendous; ~! brilliant!
**stupi'daggine** nf (azione) stupid thing; (cosa da poco) nothing; non dire stupidaggini! don't talk stupid!
**stupi'data** nf stupid thing
**stupidità** nf stupidity
**'stupido** a stupid
**stu'pire** vt astonish ● vi be astonished
**stu'pirsi** vr be astonished
**stu'pore** nm amazement
**stu'prare** vt rape
**stupra'tore** nm rapist

**'stupro** nm rape
**sturabot'tiglie** nm inv corkscrew
**sturalavan'dini** nm inv plunger
**stu'rare** vt uncork; unblock (lavandino)
**stuzzica'denti** nm inv toothpick
**stuzzi'care** vt prod [at]; pick (denti); poke (fuoco); (molestare) tease; whet (appetito)
**stuzzi'chino** nm Culin appetizer
**su** prep on; (senza contatto) over; (riguardo a) about; (circa, intorno a) about, around; le chiavi sono sul tavolo the keys are on the table; il quadro è appeso sul camino the picture is hanging over the fireplace; un libro sull'antico Egitto a book on o about Ancient Egypt; sarò lì sulle cinque I'll be there about five, I'll be there around five; è durato sulle tre ore it lasted for about three hours; costa sulle 50 000 lire it costs about 50,000 lire; decidere sul momento decide at the time; su commissione on commission; su due piedi on the spot; su misura made to measure; uno su dieci one out of ten; stare sulle proprie keep oneself to oneself; sul mare (casa) by the sea ● adv (sopra) up; (al piano di sopra) upstairs; (addosso) on; andare su go up; (al piano di sopra) go upstairs; ho su il cappotto I've got my coat on; in su (guardare) up; dalla vita in su from the waist up; su! come on!
**sua'dente** a persuasive
**sub** nmf inv skin-diver
**sub+** pref sub+
**su'bacqueo, -a** a underwater ● nmf skin-diver
**subaffit'tare** vt sublet
**subaf'fitto** nm sublet; in ~ sublet
**suba'gente** nm subagent
**subal'terno** a & nm subordinate
**subappal'tare** vt subcontract
**subappalta'tore, -'trice** nmf subcontractor
**subap'palto** nm subcontract; in ~ subcontracted; dare in ~ subcontract; prendere in ~ take on a subcontract basis
**sub'buglio** nm turmoil
**sub'conscio** a & nm subconscious
**subconti'nente** nm subcontinent
**subcosci'ente** a & nm subconscious
**subdi'rectory** nf Comput subdirectory
**subdola'mente** adv deviously
**'subdolo** a devious, underhand
**suben'trare** vi (circostanze:) come up; ~ a take the place of
**su'bentro** nm changeover
**subequatori'ale** a subequatorial
**su'bire** vt undergo; (patire) suffer
**subis'sare** vt fig ~ di overwhelm with
**subi'taneo** a sudden
**'subito** adv at once, immediately; ~ dopo straight after; vengo ~ I'll be right there
**subli'mare** vt sublimate
**su'blime** a sublime
**sublimi'nale** a subliminal
**sublingu'ale** a sublingual
**sublo'care** vt sublease

**subloca'tario** *nm* sublessor

**sublocazi'one** *nf* sublease

**subnor'male** *a* subnormal

**subodo'rare** *vt* suspect

**subordi'nare** *vt* subordinate

**subordi'nato, -a** *a & nmf* subordinate

**su'bordine** *nm* in ~ second in order of importance

**subrou'tine** *nf Comput* subroutine

**subsi'denza** *nf Geol* subsidence

**sub'strato** *nm* substratum, substrate

**subto'tale** *nm* subtotal

**subtropi'cale** *a* subtropical

**subu'mano** *a* subhuman

**subur'bano** *a* suburban

**suc'cedere** *vi* (*accadere*) happen; ~ a succeed; (*venire dopo*) follow; ~ al trono succeed to the throne

**suc'cedersi** *vr* happen one after the other; **si sono succeduti molti...** there was a series of...

**successi'one** *nf* succession; in ~ in succession

**successiva'mente** *adv* subsequently

**succes'sivo** *a* successive; (*mese, giorno*) following

**suc'cesso** *pp di succedere* ● *nm* success; (*esito*) outcome; (*disco ecc*) hit

**succes'sone** *nm* huge success

**succes'sore** *nm* successor

**succhi'are** *vt* suck [up]; ~ il sangue a qcno *fig* bleed sb dry

**succhi'ello** *nm* gimlet

**succinta'mente** *adv* succinctly

**suc'cinto** *a* (*conciso*) concise; (*abito*) scanty

**'succo** *nm* juice; *fig* essence. ~ d'arancia orange juice. ~ di frutta fruit juice. ~ di limone lemon juice

**suc'coso** *a* juicy

**'succube** *nm* essere ~ di qcno be totally dominated by sb

**succu'lento** *a* succulent

**succur'sale** *nf* branch [office]

**sud** *nm* south; del ~ southern; a ~ di [to the] south of

**Sud 'Africa** *nm* South Africa

**sudafri'cano** *a & nmf* South African

**Suda'merica** *nf* South America

**sudameri'cano, -a** *a & nmf* South American

**Su'dan** *nm* il ~ the Sudan

**suda'nese** *a & nmf* Sudanese

**su'dare** *vi* sweat, perspire; (*faticare*) sweat blood; ~ freddo be in a cold sweat; ~ sangue sweat blood; mi fa ~ freddo it brings me out in a cold sweat; ~ sette camicie sweat blood

**su'data** *nf anche fig* sweat

**suda'ticcio** *a* sweaty

**su'dato** *a* sweaty; (*vittoria*) hard-won; (*pane*) hard-earned

**sud'detto** *a* above-mentioned

**'suddito, -a** *nmf* subject

**suddi'videre** *vt* subdivide

**suddivisi'one** *nf* subdivision

**su'd-est** *nm* southeast

**'sudicio** *a* dirty, filthy

**sudici'ume** *nm* dirt, filth

**sudocciden'tale** *a* southwestern

**sudorazi'one** *nf* perspiring

**su'dore** *nm* sweat, perspiration; *fig* sweat: in un bagno di ~ bathed in sweat. ~ freddo cold sweat; con il ~ della fronte *fig* by the sweat of one's brow

**sudo'riparo** *a* sweat *attrib*

**su'd-ovest** *nm* southwest

**'sue** *vedi* suo

**suffici'ente** *a* sufficient; (*presuntuoso*) conceited ● *nm* bare essentials *pl*; *Sch* pass mark

**suffici'enza** *nf* sufficiency; (*presunzione*) conceit; *Sch* pass; a ~ enough; prendere la ~ get the pass-mark

**suf'fisso** *nm* suffix

**sufflè** *nm Culin* soufflé

**suffra'getta** *nf* suffragette

**suf'fragio** *nm* (*voto*) vote; in ~ di qcno in homage to. ~ universale universal suffrage

**suffu'migio** *nm* inhalation

**suggel'lare** *vt* seal

**suggeri'mento** *nm* suggestion

**sugge'rire** *vt* suggest; *Theat* prompt

**suggeri'tore, -'trice** *nmf Theat* prompter

**suggestio'nabile** *a* suggestible

**suggestio'nare** *vt* influence

**suggestio'nato** *a* influenced

**suggesti'one** *nf* influence

**sugge'stivo** *a* suggestive; (*musica ecc*) evocative

**'sughero** *nm* cork

**'sugli** = su + gli

**'sugo** *nm* (*di frutta*) juice; (*di carne*) gravy; (*salsa*) sauce; (*sostanza*) substance

**'sui** = su + i

**sui'cida** *a* suicidal ● *nmf* suicide

**suici'darsi** *vr* commit suicide

**sui'cidio** *nm* anche *fig* suicide; commettere ~ commit suicide; tentato ~ attempted suicide

**su'ino** *a* carne suina pork ● *nm* swine

**suite** *nf* suite

**sul** = su + il

**sulfa'midico** *nm* sulphonamide/sulpha drug

**sul'fureo** *a* sulphuric

**'sulla** = su + la

**'sulle** = su + le

**'sullo** = su + lo

**sul'tana** *nf* (*persona*) sultana

**sulta'nina** *a* uva ~ sultana

**sul'tano** *nm* sultan

**'sunto** *nm* summary

**'suo, -a** *poss a* il ~, i suoi his; (*di cosa, animale*) its; (*forma di cortesia*) your; la sua, le sue her; (*di cosa, animale*) its; (*forma di cortesia*) your; questa macchina è sua this car is his/hers; ~ padre his/her/your father; un ~ amico a friend of his/hers/yours ● *poss pron* il ~, i suoi his; (*di cosa, animale*) its;

(*forma di cortesia*) yours; **la sua, le sue** hers; (*di cosa animale*) its; (*forma di cortesia*) yours; **i suoi** his/her folk[s]

**su'ocera** *nf* mother-in-law

**su'ocero** *nm* father-in-law

**su'oi** *vedi* **suo**

**su'ola** *nf* sole. **suole** *pl* **di para** crepe soles

**su'olo** *nm* ground; (*terreno*) soil; **~ pubblico** public land

**suo'nare** *vt Mus* play; ring (*campanello*); sound (*allarme, clacson*); (*orologio:*) strike; **~ il clacson** sound the horn, hoot the horn; (*fam: imbrogliare*) do ● *vi* (*campanello, telefono, sveglia:*) ring; (*clacson:*) hoot; (*sirena:*) go [off]; (*giradischi:*) play

**suo'nato** *a fam* bonkers

**suona|'tore, -'trice** *nmf* player

**suone'ria** *nf* alarm

**su'ono** *nm* sound

**su'ora** *nf* nun; **Suor Maria** Sister Maria

**'super** *nf* 4-star [petrol], premium [gas] *Am*

**super+** *pref* super+

**supe'rabile** *a* surmountable

**superal'colico** *nm* spirit ● *a* **bevande superalcoliche** spirits

**supera'mento** *nm* (*di timidezza*) overcoming; (*di esame*) success (**di** in)

**supe'rare** *vt* surpass; (*eccedere*) exceed; (*vincere*) overcome; overtake, pass *Am* (*veicolo*); pass (*esame*); **~ la barriera del suono** break the sound barrier; **~ se stessi** surpass oneself; **ha superato la trentina** he's over thirty

**su'perbia** *nf* haughtiness

**su'perbo** *a* haughty; (*magnifico*) superb

**super'donna** *nf* superwoman

**superdo'tato** *a* highly gifted, super-talented

**superfici'ale** *a* superficial ● *nmf* superficial person

**superficialità** *nf* superficiality

**super'ficie** *nf* surface; (*area*) area; **in ~** on the surface; (*fig: esaminare*) superficially

**su'perfluo** *a* superfluous

**superi'ora** *nf* superior; *Relig* mother superior

**superi'ore** *a* superior; (*di grado*) senior; (*più elevato*) higher; (*sovrastante*) upper; (*al di sopra*) above ● *nm* superior

**superiorità** *nf* superiority

**Super-'Io** *nm Psych* superego

**superla'tivo** *a & nm* superlative

**supermer'cato** *nm* supermarket

**supermo'della** *nf* supermodel

**super'nova** *nf Astr* supernova

**superpetroli'era** *nf Naut* supertanker

**superpo'tenza** *nf* superpower

**super'sonico** *a* supersonic

**su'perstite** *a* surviving ● *nmf* survivor

**superstizi'one** *nf* superstition

**superstizi'oso** *a* superstitious

**super'strada** *nf* toll-free motorway. **~ dell'informatica** information superhighway

**superu'omo** *nm* superman

**supervalu'tare** *vt* overvalue

**supervalutazi'one** *nf* overvaluation

**supervisi'one** *nf* supervision

**supervi'sore** *nm* supervisor

**su'pino** *a* supine

**suppel'lettili** *nfpl* furnishings

**suppergiù** *adv* about

**supplemen'tare** *a* additional, supplementary

**supple'mento** *nm* supplement. **~ illustrato** colour supplement. **~ rapido** express train supplement

**sup'plente** *a* temporary ● *nmf Sch* supply teacher

**sup'plenza** *nf* temporary post

**'supplica** *nf* plea; (*domanda*) petition

**suppli'care** *vt* beg

**suppli'chevole** *a* imploring

**sup'plire** *vt* replace ● *vi* **~ a** (*compensare*) make up for

**sup'plizio** *nm* torture

**sup'porre** *vt* suppose

**supportare** *vt Comput* support

**sup'porto** *nm* support. **~ di sistema** *Comput* system support

**supposizi'one** *nf* supposition

**sup'posta** *nf* suppository

**sup'posto** *pp di* **supporre**

**suppu'rare** *vi* fester

**suppurazi'one** *nf* suppuration; **andare in ~** fester

**suprema'zia** *nf* supremacy

**su'premo** *a* supreme

**surclas'sare** *vt* outclass

**surf** *nm* surfboard; (*sport*) surfboarding

**sur'fare** *vi* **~ in Internet** surf the Net

**sur'fista** *nmf Sport, Comput* surfer

**surge'lare** *vt* deep-freeze

**surge'lato** *a* frozen ● *nm* **surgelati** *pl* frozen food *sg*

**'surplus** *nm* surplus

**surre'ale** *a* surreal

**surrea'lismo** *nm* surrealism

**surrea'lista** *nmf* surrealist

**surrea'listico** *a* surrealist

**surre'nale** *a* adrenal

**surriscal'dare** *vt* overheat

**surriscal'darsi** *vr* overheat

**surro'gato** *nm* substitute

**suscet'tibile** *a* touchy

**suscettibilità** *nf* touchiness

**susci'tare** *vt* stir up; arouse (*ammirazione ecc*)

**su'sina** *nf* plum. **~ selvatica** damson

**su'sino** *nm* plumtree

**su'spense** *nf* suspense

**sussegu'ente** *a* subsequent

**sussegu'irsi** *vr* follow one after the other

**sussidi'are** *vt* subsidize

**sussidi'ario** *a* subsidiary

**sus'sidio** *nm* subsidy; (*aiuto*) aid. **~ di disoccupazione** unemployment benefit. **~ di malattia** sickness benefit

**sussi'ego** *nm* haughtiness; **con ~** haughtily

**sussi'stenza** *nf* subsistence

**sus'sistere** *vi* subsist; (*essere valido*) hold good

**sussul'tare** *vi* start; **far ~ qcno** give sb a start

**sus'sulto** *nm* start

**sussur'rare** *vt/i* whisper; **si sussurra che...** it is rumoured that...

**sussur'rio** *nm* murmur

**sus'surro** *nm* whisper

**su'tura** *nf* suture

**sutu'rare** *vt* suture

**suv'via** *int* come on!

**sva'gare** *vt* amuse

**sva'garsi** *vr* amuse oneself

**'svago** *nm* relaxation; (*divertimento*) amusement; **prendersi un po' di ~** have a break

**svaligi'are** *vt* rob; burgle ⟨*casa*⟩

**svalu'tare** *vt* devalue; *fig* underestimate

**svalu'tarsi** *vr* lose value

**svalutazi'one** *nf* devaluation

**svam'pito** *a* absent-minded

**sva'nire** *vi* vanish

**sva'nito, -a** *a* ⟨*persona*⟩ absent-minded; ⟨*sapore, sogno*⟩ faded ● *nmf* absent-minded person

**svantaggi'ato** *a* at a disadvantage; ⟨*bambino, paese*⟩ disadvantaged

**svan'taggio** *nm* disadvantage; **essere in ~** *Sport* be losing; **in ~ di tre punti** three points down; **in ~ rispetto a qcno** at a disadvantage compared with sb

**svantaggi'oso** *a* disadvantageous

**svapo'rare** *vi* evaporate

**svari'ato** *a* varied

**svari'one** *nm* blunder

**sva'sare** *vt* splay; flare ⟨*gonna*⟩

**sva'sato** *a* ⟨*gonna*⟩ flared

**svasa'tura** *nf* flare

**'svastica** *nf* swastika

**sve'dese** *a* & *nm* ⟨*lingua*⟩ Swedish ● *nmf* Swede

**'sveglia** *nf* (*orologio*) alarm [clock]; **~!** get up!; **mettere la ~** set the alarm [clock]. **~ automatica** alarm call. **~ telefonica** wake-up call

**svegli'are** *vt* wake up; *fig* awaken; **~ l'appetito a qcno** whet sb's appetite

**svegli'arsi** *vr* wake up

**'sveglio** *a* awake; (*di mente*) alert, sharp

**sve'lare** *vt* reveal

**svel'tezza** *nf* speed; *fig* quick-wittedness

**svel'tire** *vt* quicken

**svel'tirsi** *vr* ⟨*persona:*⟩ liven up

**'svelto** *a* quick; (*slanciato*) svelte; **alla svelta** quickly; **a passo ~** quickly

**sve'narsi** *vr* slash one's wrists; *fig* reduce oneself to poverty

**'svendere** *vt* undersell

**'svendita** *nf* [clearance] sale

**sve'nevole** *a* sentimental

**sveni'mento** *nm* fainting fit

**sve'nire** *vi* faint; **da ~** incredibly

**sven'tare** *vt* foil

**sven'tato** *a* thoughtless ● *nmf* thoughtless person

**'sventola** *nf* slap; **orecchie a ~** protruding ears, jug-handle ears *fam*

**svento'lare** *vt/i* wave

**svento'larsi** *vr* fan oneself

**svento'lio** *nm* flutter

**sventra'mento** *nm* disembowelment; (*di pollo*) gutting; (*fig: di edificio*) demolition ⟨*edificio*⟩

**sven'trare** *vt* disembowel; gut ⟨*pollo*⟩; *fig* demolish ⟨*edificio*⟩

**sven'tura** *nf* misfortune

**sventu'rato** *a* unfortunate

**sve'nuto** *pp di* **svenire**

**svergi'nare** *vt* deflower

**svergo'gnato** *a* shameless

**sver'nare** *vi* winter

**svernici'ante** *nm* paint stripper

**svernici'are** *vt* strip

**sve'stire** *vt* undress

**sve'stirsi** *vr* undress, get undressed

**svet'tare** *vi* ⟨*albero, torre:*⟩ stand out; **~ verso il cielo** stretch skywards

**'Svezia** *nf* Sweden

**svezza'mento** *nm* weaning

**svez'zare** *vt* wean

**svi'are** *vt* divert; (*corrompere*) lead astray

**svi'arsi** *vr* *fig* go astray

**svico'lare** *vi* turn down a side street; (*fig: dalla questione ecc*) evade the issue; (*fig: da una persona*) dodge out of the way

**svi'gnarsela** *vr* slip away

**svigo'rire** *vt* emasculate

**svili'mento** *nm* debasement

**svi'lire** *vt* debase

**svilup'pare** *vt* develop

**svilup'parsi** *vr* develop

**sviluppa|'tore, -'trice** *nmf* developer

**svi'luppo** *nm* development; **paese in via di ~** developing country

**svinco'lare** *vt* release; clear ⟨*merce*⟩; redeem ⟨*deposito*⟩

**svinco'larsi** *vr* free oneself

**'svincolo** *nm* clearance; (*di autostrada*) exit; **~ di un deposito cauzionale** redemption of a deposit

**svioli'nata** *nf* fawning

**svisce'rare** *vt* gut; *fig* dissect

**svisce'rato** *a* ⟨*amore*⟩ passionate; (*ossequioso*) obsequious

**'svista** *nf* oversight

**svi'tare** *vt* unscrew

**svi'tato** *a* (*fam: matto*) cracked, nutty

**'Svizzera** *nf* Switzerland

**'svizzera** *nf* hamburger

**'svizzero, -a** *a* & *nmf* Swiss

**svoglia'taggine** *nf* laziness; (*riluttanza*) unwillingness

**svoglia'tamente** *adv* half-heartedly; (*senza energia*) listlessly

**svoglia'tezza** *nf* half-heartedness; (*mancanza di energia*) listlessness

**svogli'ato** *a* half-hearted; (*senza energia*) listless

**svolaz'zante** *a* ⟨*capelli*⟩ wind-swept

**svolaz'zare** *vi* flutter

**svolaz'zio** *nm* flutter

**'svolgere** *vt* unwind; unwrap ⟨*pacco*⟩; ⟨*risolvere*⟩ solve; ⟨*portare a termine*⟩ carry out; ⟨*sviluppare*⟩ develop

**'svolgersi** *vr* ⟨*accadere*⟩ take place

**svolgi'mento** *nm* course; ⟨*sviluppo*⟩ development

**'svolta** *nf* turning; *fig* turning-point

**svol'tare** *vi* turn

**'svolto** *pp di* **svolgere**

**svuo'tare** *vt* empty [out]; ⟨*fig: di significato*⟩ deprive

**swing** *nm Mus* swing

**switch** *nm Comput* switch

# Tt

**T** *abbr* ⟨**tabaccheria**⟩ tobacconist

**tabac'caio, -a** *nmf* tobacconist

**tabacche'ria** *nf* tobacconist's ⟨*which also sells stamps, postcards etc*⟩

**ta'bacco** *nm* tobacco; **tabacchi** *pl* cigarettes and tobacco

**taba'gismo** *nm* nicotine addiction

**ta'bella** *nf* table; ⟨*lista*⟩ list. ~ **di conversione** conversion table. ~ **di marcia** *fig* schedule. ~ **dei prezzi** price list. ~ **retributiva** salary scale

**tabel'lina** *nf Math* multiplication table

**tabel'lone** *nm* wall chart. ~ **degli arrivi** arrivals board. ~ **del canestro** backboard. ~ **delle partenze** departures board. ~ **segnapunti** scoreboard

**taber'nacolo** *nm* tabernacle

**tabù** *a & nm inv* taboo

**tabu'lare** *vt* tabulate

**tabu'lato** *nm Comput* [data] printout

**tabula'tore** *nm* tabulator

**tabulazi'one** *nf* tabulation

**'tacca** *nf* notch; **di mezza** ~ ⟨*attore, giornalista*⟩ second-rate

**taccagne'ria** *nf* penny-pinching

**tac'cagno** *a fam* stingy

**taccheggia|'tore, -'trice** *nmf* shoplifter

**tac'cheggio** *nm Sport* shoplifting

**tac'chetto** *nm Sport* stud

**tac'chino** *nm* turkey

**tacci'are** *vt* ~ **qcno di qcsa** accuse sb of sth

**'tacco** *nm* heel; **alzare i tacchi** take to one's heels; **scarpe senza** ~ flat shoes, flats; **colpo di** ~ backheel; **tacchi** *pl* **a spillo** stiletto heels, stilettos

**taccu'ino** *nm* notebook

**ta'cere** *vi* be silent ● *vt* say nothing about; **mettere a** ~ **qcsa** ⟨*scandalo*⟩ hush sth up; **mettere a** ~ **qcno** silence sb

**tachicar'dia** *nf* tachycardia

**ta'chigrafo** *nm* tachograph

**ta'chimetro** *nm* speedometer

**tacita'mente** *adv* tacitly; ⟨*in silenzio*⟩ silently

**'tacito** *a* tacit; ⟨*silenzioso*⟩ silent

**taci'turno** *a* taciturn

**ta'fano** *nm* horsefly

**taffe'ruglio** *nm* scuffle

**taffettà** *nm* taffeta

**'taglia** *nf* ⟨*riscatto*⟩ ransom; ⟨*ricompensa*⟩ reward; ⟨*statura*⟩ height; ⟨*di abiti*⟩ size; **per taglie forti** outsize, OS. ~ **unica** one size

**taglia'carte** *nm inv* paperknife

**taglia'erba** *nm inv* lawn-mower

**tagliafu'oco** *a inv* **porta** ~ fire door; **striscia** ~ fire break ● *nm* ⟨*in bosco*⟩ fire break

**tagli'ando** *nm* coupon; **fare il** ~ ≈ put one's car in for its MOT. ~ **di controllo** manufacturer's sticker; ⟨*da raccogliere*⟩ token. ~ **controllo bagaglio** baggage claim sticker. ~ **di garanzia** warranty

**taglia'pasta** *a* **rotella** ~ pastry cutter ● *nm inv* pastry cutter

**tagliapa'tate** *nm inv* potato peeler

**tagli'are** *vt* cut; ⟨*attraversare*⟩ cut across; cut off ⟨*telefono, elettricità*⟩; carve ⟨*carne*⟩; mow ⟨*erba*⟩; **farsi** ~ **i capelli** have a haircut, have one's hair cut; ~ **i viveri a qcno** stop sb's allowance ● *vi* cut

**tagli'arsi** *vr* cut oneself; ~ **i capelli** have a haircut, have one's hair cut

**taglia'sigari** *nm inv* cigar cutter

**tagli'ata** *nf finely-cut beef fillet*; **dare una** ~ **a qcsa** give sth a cut, cut sth

**tagli'ato** *a* ⟨*a pezzi*⟩ jointed; **essere** ~ **per qcsa** *fig* be cut out for sth

**taglia'unghie** *nm inv* nail clippers *pl*

**taglieggi'are** *vt* extort money from

**tagli'ente** *a* sharp ● *nm* cutting edge

**tagli'ere** *nm* chopping board. ~ **per il pane** breadboard

**taglie'rina** *nf* ⟨*per carta*⟩ guillotine; ⟨*foto*⟩ trimmer; ⟨*per metallo, vetro*⟩ cutter

**'taglio** *nm* cut; ⟨*di stoffa*⟩ length; ⟨*di capelli*⟩ [hair-]cut; ⟨*parte tagliente*⟩ cutting edge; **di** ~ edgeways; **a doppio** ~ *fig* double-edged; ~ **e cucito** dressmaking; **dacci un** ~**!** *fam* put a sock in it!. ~ **di carne** cut of meat. ~ **cesareo** Caesarean section. ~ **di personale** personnel cut. ~ **dei prezzi** price cutting

**tagli'ola** *nf* trap

**taglio'lini** *nmpl* thin soup noodles

**tagli'one** *nm* **legge del** ~ an eye for an eye and a tooth for a tooth, law of talion

**tagliuz'zare** *vt* cut into small pieces

**tail'leur** *nm inv* [lady's] suit

**ta'lare** *a* **prendere la veste** ~ take holy orders

**talassotera'pia** *nf therapy based on seawater*

'**talco** *nm* talcum powder, talc

'**tale** *a* such a; (*con nomi plurali*) such; **c'è un** ~ **disordine** there is such a mess; **non accetto tali scuse** I won't accept such excuses; **è un** ~ **bugiardo!** he's such a liar!; **il rumore era** ~ **che non si sentiva nulla** there was so much noise you couldn't hear yourself think; **il** ~ **giorno** on such and such a day; **quel tal signore** that gentleman; ~ **padre** ~ **figlio** like father like son; ~ **quale** just like ● *pron* **un** ~ someone; **quel** ~ that man; **il tal dei tali** such and such a person

**ta'lea** *nf* cutting

**ta'lento** *nm* talent

'**talent scout** *nmf inv* talent scout

**tali'smano** *nm* talisman

**tallo'nare** *vt* be hot on the heels of

**tallon'cino** *nm* coupon. ~ **del prezzo** price tag

**tal'lone** *nm* heel. ~ **di Achille** *fig* Achilles' heel. ~ **aureo** *Econ* gold standard

**tal'mente** *adv* so

**ta'lora** *adv* = talvolta

'**talpa** *nf* mole

**tal'volta** *adv* sometimes

**tamburel'lare** *vi* (*con le dita*) drum; ⟨*pioggia:*⟩ beat, drum

**tambu'rello** *nm* tambourine

**tambu'rino** *nm* drummer

**tam'buro** *nm* drum. ~ **del freno** brake drum

**tame'rice** *nf* tamarisk

'**tamia** *nm inv* chipmunk

**Ta'migi** *nm* Thames

**tampona'mento** *nm Auto* collision; (*di ferita*) dressing; (*di falla*) plugging. ~ **a catena** pile-up

**tampo'nare** *vt* (*urtare*) crash into; plug ⟨*falla*⟩; dress ⟨*ferita*⟩

**tam'pone** *nm* swab; (*per timbri*) pad; (*per mestruazioni*) tampon; (*per treni, Comput*) buffer

**tam'tam** *nm inv* bush telegraph

'**tana** *nf* den

'**tandem** *nm inv* tandem; **in** ~ ⟨*lavorare*⟩ in tandem

'**tanfo** *nm* stench

'**tanga** *nm inv* tanga

**tan'gente** *a* tangent ● *nf* tangent; (*somma*) bribe

**tangen'topoli** *nf widespread corruption in Italy in the early 90s*

**tangenzi'ale** *nf* orbital road

**tan'gibile** *a* tangible

**tangibil'mente** *adv* tangibly

'**tango** *nm inv* tango

'**tanica** *nf* (*contenitore*) jerry can; (*serbatoio di nave*) tank

**tan'nino** *nm* tannin

**tan'tino**: **un** ~ *adv* a little [bit]

'**tanto** *a* [so] much; (*con nomi plurali*) [so] many, [such] a lot of; ~ **tempo** [such] a long time; **non ha tanta pazienza** he doesn't have much patience; ~ **tempo quanto ti serve** as much time as you need; **non è** ~ **intelligente quanto suo padre** he's not as intelligent as his father; **tanti amici quanti parenti** as many friends as relatives ● *pron* much; (*plurale*) many; (*tanto tempo*) much time; **è un uomo come tanti** he's just an ordinary man; **tanti** (*molte persone*) many people; **non ci vuole così** ~ it doesn't take that long; ~ **quanto** as much as; **tanti quanti** as many as ● *conj* (*comunque*) anyway, in any case ● *adv* (*così*) so; (*con verbi*) so much; **è** ~ **debole che non sta in piedi** he's so weak that he can't stand; **è** ~ **ingenuo da crederle** he's naive enough to believe her; **di** ~ **in** ~ every now and then; ~ **l'uno come l'altro** both; ~ **quanto** as much as; **tre volte** ~ three times as much; **una volta** ~ once in a while; ~ **meglio così!** so much the better!; **tant'è** so much so; ~ **vale che andiamo a casa** we might as well go home; ~ **per cambiare** for a change

**tapi'oca** *nf* tapioca

**ta'piro** *nm* tapir

**ta'pis rou'lant** *nm inv* conveyor belt

'**tappa** *nf* (*parte di viaggio*) stage; **fare** ~ a break one's journey in

**tappa'buchi** *nm inv* stopgap

**tap'pare** *vt* plug; cork ⟨*bottiglia*⟩; ~ **la bocca a qcno** *fam* shut sb up

**tappa'rella** *nf fam* roller blind; **tirar su la** ~ pull the blind up

**tap'parsi** *vr* ~ **gli occhi** cover one's eyes; ~ **il naso** hold one's nose; ~ **le orecchie** put one's fingers in one's ears

**tappe'tino** *nm* mat; *Comput* mouse mat. ~ **antiscivolo** [anti-slip] safety bathmat. ~ **da bagno** bathmat

**tap'peto** *nm* carpet; (*piccolo*) rug; **andare al** ~ ⟨*pugilato:*⟩ hit the canvas; **mandare qcno al** ~ knock sb down; **bombardamento a** ~ carpet bombing. ~ **erboso** lawn. ~ **persiano** Persian carpet. ~ **stradale** road surface. ~ **verde** (*tavolo*) card table. ~ **volante** magic carpet

**tappez'zare** *vt* paper ⟨*pareti*⟩; (*con manifesti*) cover

**tappezze'ria** *nf* tapestry; (*di carta*) wallpaper; (*arte*) upholstery; **fare da** ~ *fig* be a wallflower

**tappezzi'ere** *nm* upholsterer; (*imbianchino*) decorator

'**tappo** *nm* plug; (*di sughero*) cork; (*di metallo, per penna*) top; (*fam: persona piccola*) dwarf. ~ **di bottiglia** bottle top. ~ **a corona** crown cap. **tappi** *pl* **per le orecchie** earplugs. ~ **salvagocce** anti-drip top. ~ **di scarico** (*della coppa*) sump drain plug. ~ **a strappo** ring-pull. ~ **di sughero** cork. ~ **a vite** screw top

**'tara** nf (difetto) flaw; (ereditaria) hereditary defect; (peso) tare
**taran'tella** nf tarantella
**ta'rantola** nf tarantula
**ta'rare** vt Techn calibrate; Comm discount
**ta'rato** a Comm discounted; Techn calibrated; Med with a hereditary defect; fam crazy
**tarchi'ato** a stocky
**tar'dare** vi be late ● vt delay
**'tardi** adv late; **al più ~** at the latest; **più ~** later [on]; **sul ~** late in the day; **far ~** (essere in ritardo) be late; (con gli amici) stay up late; **a più ~** see you later; **svegliarsi troppo ~** oversleep
**tardiva'mente** adv late
**tar'divo** a late; ‹bambino› retarded
**'tardo** a slow; ‹pomeriggio, mattinata› late
**'targa** nf plate; Auto numberplate
**tar'gato** a un'auto targata... a car with the registration number...
**targ'hetta** nf (su porta) nameplate; (sulla valigia) name tag. **~ di circolazione** numberplate. **~ commemorativa** memorial plaque. **~ stradale** street sign
**ta'riffa** nf rate, tariff; **a ~ ridotta** Teleph off-peak. **~ doganale** customs tariff. **~ ferroviaria** [rail] fares. **~ interna** inland postage. **~ professionale** [professional] fee. **~ telefonica** telephone charges. **~ unica** flat rate
**tarif'fario** a tariff attrib ● nm price list
**tar'larsi** vr get worm-eaten
**tar'lato** a worm-eaten
**'tarlo** nm woodworm
**'tarma** nf moth
**tar'marsi** vr get moth-eaten
**tarmi'cida** nm ≈ moth-repellent
**ta'rocco** nm tarot; **tarocchi** pl tarot
**tar'pare** vt clip
**tartagli'are** vi stutter
**'tartaro** a & nm tartar; **salsa tartara** tartar[e] sauce
**tarta'ruga** nf tortoise; (di mare) turtle; (per pettine ecc) tortoiseshell
**tartas'sare** vt (angariare) harass
**tar'tina** nf canapé
**tar'tufo** nm truffle
**'tasca** nf pocket; (in borsa) compartment; Culin icing bag; **da ~** pocket attrib; **avere le tasche piene di qcsa** fam have had a bellyful of sth; **se ne è stato con le mani in ~** fig he didn't lift a finger [to help]. **~ a battente** flap pocket. **~ del nero** (di polpo, seppia) ink sac. **~ da pasticciere** icing bag. **~ tagliata** slit pocket. **~ a toppa** patch-pocket
**ta'scabile** a pocket attrib ● nm paperback
**tasca'pane** nm inv haversack
**ta'schino** nm breast pocket
**'tassa** nf tax; (d'iscrizione ecc) fee; (doganale) duty. **~ di circolazione** road tax. **~ di esportazione** export duty. **~ d'iscrizione** registration fee. **~ di soggiorno** tourist tax, visitors' tax

**tas'sabile** a taxable
**tas'sametro** nm meter
**tas'sare** vt tax
**tassativa'mente** adv without fail
**tassa'tivo** a strict
**tassazi'one** nf taxation
**tas'sello** nm wedge; (di stoffa) gusset
**tassi** nm inv taxi
**tas'sista** nmf taxi driver
**'tasso¹** nm Bot yew; (animale) badger
**'tasso²** Comm rate. **~ agevolato** cut rate; **prestito a ~ agevolato** soft loan. **~ base** base rate. **~ base di interesse** base lending rate. **~ di cambio** exchange rate. **~ di crescita** growth rate. **~ inquinamento** pollution level. **~ di interesse** interest rate. **~ di mortalità** death rate. **~ di sconto** discount rate
**ta'stare** vt feel; **~ il terreno** fig test the water or ground
**tasti'era** nf keyboard. **~ numerica** Comput numeric keypad
**tastie'rino** nm **~ numerico** numeric keypad
**tastie'rista** nmf keyboarder
**'tasto** nm key; (tatto) touch. **~ di controllo** Comput control key. **~ cursore** Comput cursor key. **~ delicato** fig touchy subject. **~ funzione** Comput function key. **~ numerico** Comput numeric[al] key. **~ di ritorno a margine** return key. **~ tabulatore** tab [key]
**ta'stoni:** **a ~** adv gropingly; **camminare a ~** grope around; **cercare qcsa a ~** grope for sth
**'tattica** nf tactics pl
**'tattico** a tactical
**'tattile** a tactile
**'tatto** nm (senso) touch; (accortezza) tact; **aver ~** be tactful
**tatu'aggio** nm tattoo
**tatu'are** vt tattoo
**tautolo'gia** nf tautology
**tauto'logico** a tautological
**'tavola** nf table; (illustrazione) plate; (asse) plank; **saper stare a ~** have good table manners; **calmo come una ~** (mare) like a mill pond. **~ calda** snackbar. **~ fredda** salad bar. **~ periodica degli elementi** periodic table. **~ pitagorica** multiplication table. **~ rotonda** fig round table. **~ a vela** sailboard; **fare ~ ~** sailboard, windsurf
**tavo'lato** nm (pavimento) wooden flooring
**tavo'letta** nf bar; (medicinale) tablet; **andare a ~** Auto drive flat out. **~ di cioccolata** chocolate bar. **~ grafica** Comput digitizer
**tavo'lino** nm [small] table; (da salotto) occasional table
**'tavolo** nm table. **~ anatomico** mortuary table, slab fam. **~ da cucina** kitchen table. **~ da gioco** card table. **~ operatorio** Med operating table. **~ da pranzo** dining-table
**tavo'lozza** nf palette
**'tazza** nf cup; (del water) bowl. **~ da caffè/tè** coffee-cup/teacup

**taz'zina** *nf* ~ **da caffè** espresso coffee cup

**TBC** *abbr* (**tubercolosi**) TB

**T.C.I.** *abbr* (**Touring Club Italiano**) *association promoting tourism nationally and internationally*

**te** *pers pron* you; **te l'ho dato** I gave it to you

**tè** *nm inv* tea. **tè al latte** tea with milk. **tè al limone** lemon tea

**tea'trale** *a* theatre *attrib*; (*affettato*) theatrical

**te'atro** *nm* theatre. ~ **all'aperto** open-air theatre. ~ **lirico** opera [house]. ~ **neorealista** kitchen sink drama. ~ **di posa** Cinema set. ~ **tenda** *marquee for theatre performances*

**'tecnico, -a** *a* technical ● *nmf* technician. ~ **elettronico** electronics engineer. ~ **informatico** computer engineer. ~ **delle luci** Cinema, TV gaffer. ~ **del suono** sound technician ● *nf* technique

**tec'nigrafo** *nm* drawing board

**tec'nocrate** *nmf* technocrat

**tecnolo'gia** *nf* technology

**tecno'logico** *a* technological

**te'desco, -a** *a & nmf* German. ~ **dell'est** East German

**'tedio** *nm* tedium

**tedi'oso** *a* tedious

**TEE** *nm abbr* (**treno espresso trans-europeo**) Trans-Europe-Express [train]

**te'game** *nm* saucepan; **uova al** ~ fried eggs

**'teglia** *nf* baking tin

**'tegola** *nf* tile; *fig* blow

**tei'era** *nf* teapot

**te'ina** *nf* theine

**tek** *nm* teak

**tel.** *abbr* (**telefono**) tel.

**'tela** *nf* cloth; (*per quadri, vele*) canvas; *Theat* curtain. ~ **cerata** oilcloth. ~ **indiana** cheesecloth. ~ **di iuta** hessian. ~ **di lino** linen. ~ **rigida** buckram

**te'laio** *nm* (*di bicicletta, finestra*) frame; *Auto* chassis; (*per tessere*) loom

**'tele** *nf fam* telly, TV

**tele'camera** *nf* television camera

**telecoman'dato** *a* remote-controlled, remote control *attrib*

**teleco'mando** *nm* remote control

**'Telecom I'talia** *nf* Italian State telephone company

**telecomunicazi'oni** *nfpl* telecommunications, telecomms

**teleconfe'renza** *nf* teleconference

**tele'cronaca** *nf* [television] commentary; **fare la** ~ **di** commentate on. ~ **diretta** live [television] coverage. ~ **registrata** recording

**telecro'nista** *nmf* television commentator

**tele'ferica** *nf* cableway

**tele'film** *nm inv* film [made] for television; ~ **a episodi** series

**telefo'nare** *vt/i* [tele]phone, ring

**telefo'nata** *nf* call, [tele]phone call; **fare una** ~ make a phone call. ~ **anonima** nuisance call. ~ **a carico del destinatario** reverse charge [phone] call; **fare una** ~ **a carico [del destinatario]** reverse the charges. ~ **interurbana** long-distance call. ~ **di lavoro** business call. ~ **in teleselezione** ≈ STD call. ~ **urbana** local call

**telefonica'mente** *adv* by [tele]phone

**tele'fonico** *a* [tele]phone *attrib*

**telefo'nino** *nm* mobile [phone]

**telefo'nista** *nmf* operator

**te'lefono** *nm* [tele]phone; **numero di** ~ [tele]phone number. ~ **azzurro** children in need help line. ~ **cellulare** cellular [tele]phone, cellular. ~ **senza filo** cordless [phone]. ~ **a gettoni** pay phone. ~ **interno** intercom. ~ **a monete** pay phone. ~ **pubblico** public telephone. ~ **rosso** *Mil, Pol* hotline. ~ **a scatti** *telephone with call charges based on time-units.* ~ **a schede** cardphone. ~ **a tastiera** push-button phone

**tele'genico** *a* telegenic

**telegior'nale** *nm* television news

**telegra'fare** *vt* telegraph

**telegra'fia** *nf* telegraphy

**telegrafica'mente** *adv* (*con telegrafo*) by telegram

**tele'grafico** *a* telegraphic; ⟨*risposta*⟩ monosyllabic; **sii** ~ keep it brief

**te'legrafo** *nm* telegraph

**tele'gramma** *nm* telegram

**tele'matica** *nf* data communications, telematics

**teleno'vela** *nf* soap opera

**teleobiet'tivo** *nm* telephoto lens

**telepa'tia** *nf* telepathy

**tele'patico** *a* telepathic

**tele'quiz** *nm inv* TV quiz programme

**teleradiotra'smettere** *vt* simulcast

**telero'manzo** *nm* television serial

**tele'schermo** *nm* television screen

**tele'scopio** *nm* telescope

**telescri'vente** *nf* telex [machine]

**teleselet'tivo** *a* direct dialling

**teleselezi'one** *nf* subscriber trunk dialling, STD; **chiamare in** ~ call direct, dial direct. ~ **internazionale** international direct dialling

**telespetta|'tore, -'trice** *nmf* viewer; **i telespettatori** the viewing public

**tele'text**ᴿ *nm* Teletext

**'telethon** *nm inv* telethon

**tele'video** *nm* videophone

**televisi'one** *nf* television; **guardare la** ~ watch television; **alla** ~ on television. ~ **in bianco e nero** black and white television. ~ **via cavo** cable TV. ~ **a circuito chiuso** closed-circuit television, CCT. ~ **a colori** colour television

**televi'sivo** *a* television, TV *attrib*; **operatore** ~ television cameraman; **apparecchio** ~ television set

**televi'sore** *nm* television [set], TV [set]. ~ **portatile** portable [TV], portable [television set]

**'telex** *nm inv* telex ● *a inv* telex *attrib*

**tel'lurico** *a* telluric

**'telo** *nm* [piece of] cloth; ~ **da bagno** beach towel. ~ **di salvataggio** rescue blanket

**'tema** *nm* theme; *Sch* essay

**te'matica** *nf* main theme

**teme'rario** *a* reckless

**te'mere** *vt* be afraid of ● *vi* be afraid

**tem'paccio** *nm* filthy weather

**'tempera** *nf* tempera; (*pittura*) painting in tempera

**temperama'tite** *nm inv* pencil-sharpener

**tempera'mento** *nm* temperament

**tempe'rare** *vt* temper; sharpen ⟨*matita*⟩

**tempe'rato** *a* temperate

**tempera'tura** *nf* temperature. ~ **ambiente** room temperature

**tempe'rino** *nm* penknife

**tem'pesta** *nf* storm. ~ **magnetica** magnetic storm. ~ **di neve** snowstorm. ~ **di sabbia** sandstorm

**tempe'stare** *vt* ~ **qcno di colpi** rain blows on sb; ~ **qcno di domande** bombard sb with questions

**tempe'stato** *a* ⟨*anello, diadema*⟩ encrusted (**di** with)

**tempestiva'mente** *adv* quickly, in a short space of time

**tempe'stivo** *a* timely

**tempe'stoso** *a* stormy

**'tempia** *nf Anat* temple

**'tempio** *nm Relig* temple

**tem'pismo** *nm* timing

**'tempo** *nm* time; (*atmosferico*) weather; *Mus* tempo; *Gram* tense; (*di film*) part; (*di partita*) half; **a suo** ~ in due course; ~ **fa** some time ago; **per molto** ~, **per tanto** ~ for a long time; **tanto** ~ **fa** a long time ago; **un** ~ once; **ha fatto il suo** ~ it's out of date; **a** ~ **indeterminato** ⟨*contratto*⟩ permanent; **primo** ~ (*di film, partita*) first half. ~ **di accesso** *Comput* access time. ~ **di cottura** cooking time. ~ **di esposizione** *Phot* exposure time. ~ **libero** free time, leisure time. ~ **limite di accettazione** latest check-in time. ~ **di pace** peacetime. ~ **reale** *Comput* real time; **in** ~ ~ real-time *attrib*. ~ **supplementare** extra time; *Sport* extra time, overtime *Am*; **andare ai tempi supplementari** *Sport* go into extra time

**tempo'rale** *a* temporal ● *nm* [thunder]storm

**temporanea'mente** *adv* temporarily

**tempo'raneo** *a* temporary

**temporeggi'are** *vi* play for time

**tem'prare** *vt* form

**te'nace** *a* tenacious

**tenace'mente** *adv* tenaciously

**te'nacia** *nf* tenacity

**te'naglia** *nf* pincers *pl*

**'tenda** *nf* curtain; (*per campeggio*) tent; (*tendone*) awning; **tirare le tende** draw the curtains. ~ **della doccia** shower curtain. ~ **a ossigeno** oxygen tent

**ten'denza** *nf* tendency. ~ **al rialzo/ribasso** *Fin* bull/bear market

**tendenzial'mente** *adv* by nature

**tendenzi'oso** *a* tendentious

**'tendere** *vt* (*allargare*) stretch [out]; (*tirare*) tighten; (*porgere*) hold out; *fig* lay ⟨*trappola*⟩ ● *vi* ~ **a** aim at; (*essere portato a*) tend to

**'tendersi** *vr* tauten

**'tendine** *nm* tendon. ~ **d'Achille** Achilles tendon. ~ **del garretto** hamstring. ~ **del ginocchio** hamstring

**ten'done** *nm* awning; (*di circo*) tent. ~ **del circo** big top

**ten'dopoli** *nf inv* tent city

**'tenebre** *nfpl* darkness

**tene'broso** *a* gloomy ● *nm* **bel** ~ dark and handsome man

**te'nente** *nm* lieutenant. ~ **colonnello** wing commander

**tenera'mente** *adv* tenderly

**te'nere** *vt* hold; (*mantenere*) keep; (*gestire*) run; (*prendere*) take; (*seguire*) follow; (*considerare*) consider ● *vi* hold; ~ **stretto** hold tight; ~ **a** qcsa (*oggetto*) be fond of sth; **tengo alla sua presenza** I very much want him to be there; ~ **per** ⟨*squadra*⟩ support

**tene'rezza** *nf* tenderness

**'tenero** *a* tender

**tene'rone, -a** *nmf* softie

**te'nersi** *vr* hold on (**a** to); (*in una condizione*) keep oneself; ~ **indietro** stand back

**'tenia** *nf* tapeworm

**'tennis** *nm* tennis. ~ **da tavolo** table tennis

**ten'nista** *nmf* tennis player

**te'nore** *nm* standard; *Mus* tenor; **a** ~ **di legge** by law. ~ **di vita** standard of living

**tensi'one** *nf* tension; *Electr* voltage; **mettere sotto** ~ energize; **in** ~ under stress. **alta** ~ high voltage. ~ **premestruale** premenstrual tension, PMT

**ten'tacolo** *nm* tentacle

**ten'tare** *vt* attempt; (*sperimentare*) try; (*indurre in tentazione*) tempt; ~ **la strada di** make a foray *or* venture into

**tenta'tivo** *nm* attempt

**ten'tato** *a* ~ **suicidio** suicide attempt

**tentazi'one** *nf* temptation

**tenten'namento** *nm* wavering; **ha avuto dei tentennamenti** he wavered a bit

**tenten'nare** *vi* waver

**ten'toni** *adv* **cercare** qcsa **a** ~ grope for sth

**'tenue** *a* fine; (*debole*) weak; (*esiguo*) small; (*leggero*) slight

**te'nuta** *nf* (*capacità*) capacity; (*Sport: resistenza*) stamina; (*possedimento*) estate; (*divisa*) uniform; (*abbigliamento*) clothes *pl*; **a** ~ **d'aria** airtight. ~ **di strada** road holding

**teolo'gia** *nf* theology

**teo'logico** *a* theological

**te'ologo** *nm* theologian

**teo'rema** *nm* theorem

**teo'ria** *nf* theory

**teorica'mente** *adv* theoretically

**te'orico** *a* theoretical

**te'pore** *nm* warmth

**'teppa** nf mob

**tep'pismo** nm hooliganism

**tep'pista** nm hooligan

**te'quila** nf inv tequila

**tera'peutico** a therapeutic

**tera'pia** nf therapy; **in ~** in therapy. **~ di gruppo** group therapy. **~ d'urto** shock treatment

**tergicri'stallo** nm windscreen wiper, windshield wiper Am

**tergilu'notto** nm rear windscreen wiper

**tergiver'sante** a equivocating, pussyfooting fam

**tergiver'sare** vi equivocate, pussyfoot around fam

**'tergo** nm **a ~** behind; **segue a ~** please turn over, PTO

**teri'lene**ᴷ nm Terylene*ᴿ*

**'terital**ᴿ nm Terylene*ᴿ*

**ter'male** a thermal; **stazione ~** spa

**'terme** nfpl thermal baths

**'termico** a thermal; **borsa termica** cool bag

**'terminal** nm inv air terminal

**termi'nale** a & nm terminal; **malato ~** terminally ill person

**termina'lista** nmf computer operator

**termi'nare** vt/i end, finish

**terminazi'one** nf (fine) termination; Gram ending. **~ nervosa** nerve ending

**'termine** nm (limite) limit; (fine) end; (condizione, parola) term; (scadenza) deadline; **ai termini della legge...** under the terms of act...; **contratto a ~** fixed-term contract. **~ di paragone** Gram term of comparison. **~ ultimo** final deadline

**terminolo'gia** nf terminology

**'termite** nf termite

**termoco'perta** nf electric blanket

**ter'mometro** nm thermometer

**'termos** nm inv thermos*ᴿ*

**termosi'fone** nm radiator; (sistema) central heating

**ter'mostato** nm thermostat

**termotera'pia** nf Med heat treatment

**termoventila'tore** nm fan heater

**'terra** nf earth; (regione) land; (terreno) ground; (argilla) clay; (cosmetico) bronzing powder; **a ~** (sulla costa) ashore; (installazioni) onshore; **essere a ~** (gomma:) be flat; fig be at rock bottom; **per ~** on the ground; (su pavimento) on the floor; **sotto ~** underground; **far ~ bruciata** carry out a scorched earth policy. **~ promessa** Promised Land. **~ di Siena** sienna

**terra'cotta** nf terracotta; **vasellame di ~** earthenware

**terra'ferma** nf dry land

**Terra'nova** nf Newfoundland

**terrapi'eno** nm embankment

**ter'razza** nf, **ter'razzo** nm balcony

**terremo'tato, -a** a (zona) affected by an earthquake ● nmf earthquake victim

**terre'moto** nm earthquake

**ter'reno** a earthly ● nm ground; (suolo) soil; (proprietà terriera) land; **perdere/guadagnare ~** lose/gain ground. **~ alluvionale** alluvial soil. **~ di bonifica** reclaimed land. **~ edificabile** building land. **~ di gioco** playing field. **~ di scontro** battlefield

**ter'restre** a terrestrial; (superficie, diametro) of the earth; **esercito ~** land forces pl

**ter'ribile** a terrible

**terribil'mente** adv terribly

**ter'riccio** nm potting compost

**'terrier** nm inv terrier

**terri'ero** a (proprietario) land attrib; (aristocrazia) landed; **proprietà** pl **terriere** landed property

**terrifi'cante** a terrifying

**territori'ale** a territorial; **acque territoriali** territorial waters

**terri'torio** nm territory

**ter'rone, -a** nmf pej bloody Southerner

**ter'rore** nm terror

**terro'rismo** nm terrorism

**terro'rista** nmf terrorist

**terroriz'zare** vt terrorize

**'terso** a clear

**'terza** nf (marcia) third [gear]

**ter'zetto** nm trio

**terzi'ario** a tertiary ● nm service sector, tertiary sector. **~ avanzato** high technology, hitech sector

**'terzo** a third; **di terz'ordine** (locale, servizio) third-rate; **fare il ~ grado a qcno** give sb the third degree; **la terza età** the third age; **il ~ mondo** the Third World ● nm third; **terzi** pl Jur third party

**terzo'genito, -a** nmf third-born

**ter'zultimo, -a** a & n third from last

**'tesa** nf brim

**'teschio** nm skull

**'tesi** nf inv thesis

**'teso** pp di **tendere** ● a taut; fig tense

**tesore'ria** nf treasury

**tesori'ere** nm treasurer

**te'soro** nm treasure; (tesoreria) treasury; **ministro del T~** Finance Minister, ≈ Chancellor of the Exchequer Br

**'tessera** nf card; (abbonamento all'autobus) season ticket; (di club) membership card

**'tessere** vt weave; hatch (complotto); **~ le lodi di qcsa** sing the praises of sth

**tesse'rino** nm travel card

**tes'sile** a textile ● nm **tessili** pl textiles; (operai) textile workers

**tessi|'tore, -'trice** nmf weaver

**tessi'tura** nf weaving

**tes'suto** pp di **tessere** ● a woven; **~ a mano** hand-woven ● nm fabric, material; Anat tissue. **~ sintetico** synthetic material

**'testa** nf head; (cervello) brain; **essere in ~ a** be ahead of; **in ~** Sport in the lead; **~ o croce?** heads or tails?; **fare ~ o croce** spin a coin, toss a coin; **andare a ~ alta** hold one's head up. **~ di rapa** fam pinhead. **~ di sbarco** beachhead. **~ di serie** (squadra) seeded team. **~ del treno** front of the train

**testa-'coda** *nm inv* **fare un** ~ spin right round

**testa'mento** *nm* will. **Antico T~** *Relig* Old Testament. **Nuovo T~** *Relig* New Testament

**testar'daggine** *nf* stubbornness

**testarda'mente** *adv* stubbornly

**te'stardo** *a* stubborn

**te'stata** *nf* head; (*intestazione*) heading; (*colpo*) [head]butt. ~ **nucleare** nuclear warhead

**'teste** *nmf* witness

**'tester** *nm inv* tester

**te'sticolo** *nm* testicle

**testi'mone** *nmf* witness; **essere** ~ **di qcsa** witness sth. ~ **di Geova** Jehovah's Witness. ~ **oculare** eye witness

**testi'monial** *nmf inv celebrity who promotes a brand of cosmetics*

**testimoni'anza** *nf* testimony; **falsa** ~ *Jur* perjury

**testimoni'are** *vt* testify to ● *vi* testify, give evidence

**te'stina** *nf* head; (*di stampante*) printhead. ~ **di cancellazione** *Comput* erase head. ~ **di lettura** *Comput* read head. ~ **rotante** (*di macchina da scrivere*) golf-ball. ~ **di vitello** *Culin* calf's head

**'testo** *nm* text; **far** ~ be authoritative; **con** ~ **a fronte** ‹*traduzione*› with the original text on the opposite page

**te'stone, -a** *nmf* blockhead

**testoste'rone** *nm* testosterone

**testu'ale** *a* textual

**'tetano** *nm* tetanus

**te'traggine** *nf* bleakness

**tetra'pak**ᴿ *nm inv* tetrapak

**'tetro** *a* bleak

**tetta'rella** *nf* teat

**'tetto** *nm* roof; **abbandono del** ~ **coniugale** *Jur* desertion. ~ **apribile** (*di auto*) sun[shine] roof. ~ **a terrazza** flat roof

**tet'toia** *nf* roofing

**tet'tuccio** *nm* ~ **apribile** sun-roof

**teu'tonico** *a* Teutonic

**'Tevere** *nm* Tiber

**ti** *pers pron* you; (*riflessivo*) yourself; **ti ha dato un libro** he gave you a book; **lavati le mani** wash your hands; **eccoti!** here you are!; **sbrigati!** hurry up!

**ti'ara** *nf* tiara

**tic** *nm inv* tic

**ticchet'tare** *vi* tick

**ticchet'tio** *nm* ticking

**'ticchio** *nm* tic; (*ghiribizzo*) whim

**'ticket** *nm inv* (*per farmaco, esame*) *amount paid by National Health patients*

**tie-break** *nm inv* tie break[er]

**tiepida'mente** *adv* half-heartedly

**ti'epido** *a* lukewarm; *fig* half-hearted

**ti'fare** *vi* ~ **per** shout for

**'tifo** *nm* *Med* typhus; **far il** ~ **per** *fig* be a fan of

**tifoi'dea** *nf* typhoid

**ti'fone** *nm* typhoon

**ti'foso, -a** *nmf* fan

**tight** *nm inv* morning dress

**'tiglio** *nm* lime

**'tigna** *nf* ringworm

**ti'grato** *a* **gatto** ~ tabby [cat]

**'tigre** *nf* tiger

**'tilde** *nmf* tilde

**tim'ballo** *nm* *Culin* pie

**tim'brare** *vt* stamp; ~ **il cartellino** (*all'entrata*) clock in; (*all'uscita*) clock out

**'timbro** *nm* stamp; (*di voce*) tone. ~ **a secco** embossing stamp

**time out** *nm inv* *Sport* time-out

**'timer** *nm inv* timer

**timida'mente** *adv* timidly, shyly

**timi'dezza** *nf* timidity, shyness

**'timido** *a* timid, shy

**'timo** *nm* thyme

**ti'mone** *nm* rudder. ~ **di direzione** (*di aereo*) rudder. ~ **di quota** (*di aereo*) elevator

**timoni'ere** *nm* helmsman

**timo'rato** *a* ~ **di Dio** God-fearing

**ti'more** *nm* fear; (*soggezione*) awe

**timo'roso** *a* timorous

**'timpano** *nm* eardrum; *Mus* kettledrum; **timpani** *pl Mus* timpani, kettledrums; **rompere i timpani a qcno** *fig* shatter sb's eardrums

**ti'nello** *nm* dining-room

**'tingere** *vt* dye; (*macchiare*) stain

**'tingersi** *vr* ‹*viso, cielo:*› be tinged (**di** with); ~ **i capelli** have one's hair dyed; (*da solo*) dye one's hair

**'tino** *nm*, **ti'nozza** *nf* tub

**'tinta** *nf* dye; (*colore*) colour; **in** ~ **unita** plain, self-coloured

**tinta'rella** *nf fam* suntan

**tintin'nare** *vi* tinkle

**'tinto** *pp di* **tingere**

**tinto'ria** *nf* (*negozio*) cleaner's

**tin'tura** *nf* dyeing; (*colorante*) dye. ~ **di iodio** iodine

**tipica'mente** *adv* typically

**'tipico** *a* typical

**'tipo** *nm* type; (*fam: individuo*) chap, guy

**tipogra'fia** *nf* printer's; (*arte*) typography

**tipo'grafico** *a* typographic[al]

**ti'pografo** *nm* printer

**tip tap** *nm* tap dancing

**ti'raggio** *nm* draught

**tiranneggi'are** *vt* tyrannize

**tiran'nia** *nf* tyranny

**ti'ranno, -a** *a* tyrannical ● *nmf* tyrant

**tiranno'sauro** *nm* tyrannosaurus

**ti'rante** *nm* rope

**tirapi'edi** *nm inv pej* hanger-on

**tira'pugni** *nm inv* knuckle-duster

**ti'rare** *vt* pull; (*gettare*) throw; (*nel calcio*) kick; (*tracciare*) draw; (*stampare*) print; *fam* land ‹*calci, pugni*› ● *vi* pull; ‹*vento:*› blow; ‹*abito:*› be tight; (*sparare*) fire; ~ **avanti** *fig* get by; ~ **su** bring up ‹*figli*›; (*da terra*) pick up; **tirar su [col naso]** sniffle

**ti'rarsi** *vr* ~ **indietro** *fig* back out, pull out

**tiras'segno** *nm* target shooting; (*alla fiera*) rifle range

**ti'rata** *nf* (*strattone*) pull, tug; **in una ~** in one go; **dare a qcno una ~ d'orecchi** *fig* give sb a telling off

**tira'tore** *nm* shot. **~ scelto** marksman

**tira'tura** *nf* printing; (*di giornali*) circulation; (*di libri*) [print]run

**tirchie'ria** *nf* meanness

**'tirchio** *a* mean

**tiri'tera** *nf* spiel

**'tiro** *nm* (*lancio*) throw; (*azione*) throwing; (*sparo*) shot; (*azione*) shooting; (*scherzo*) trick; **cavallo da ~** draught horse. **~ con l'arco** archery. **~ al bersaglio** target practice. **~ alla fune** tug-of-war. **~ al piattello** clay pigeon shooting. **~ in porta** shot at goal. **~ a segno** rifle-range

**tiroci'nante** *nmf* trainee

**tiro'cinio** *nm* training

**ti'roide** *nf* thyroid

**Tir'reno** *nm* **il** [mar] **~** the Tyrrhenian Sea

**ti'sana** *nf* herb[al] tea

**'tisi** *nf* consumption

**ti'tanio** *nm* titanium

**tito'lare** *a* permanent ● *nmf* (*proprietario*) owner; (*calcio*) regular player; (*Jur: di diritto*) holder

**'titolo** *nm* title; (*accademico*) qualification; *Comm* security; **a ~ di** as; **a ~ di favore** as a favour; **titoli** *pl* (*di giornale, telegiornale*) headlines. **titoli** *pl* **di coda** closing credits. **~ di credito** credit instrument. **~ mondiale** world title. **~ obbligazionario** bond. **titoli** *pl* **delle principali notizie** news headlines. **~ in sovrimpressione** superimposed title. **~ di Stato** government security. **titoli** *pl* **di studio** qualifications. **titoli** *pl* **di testa** *Cinema, TV* opening credits. **~ a tutta pagina** banner headline

**titu'bante** *a* hesitant

**titu'banza** *nf* hesitation

**titu'bare** *vi* hesitate

**tivù** *nf inv fam* TV, telly

**'tizio, -a** *nm* so-and-so; **un ~** some man ● *nf* **una tizia** some woman

**tiz'zone** *nm* brand

**toc'cante** *a* touching

**toc'care** *vt* touch; touch on (*argomento*); (*tastare*) feel; (*riguardare*) concern ● *vi* **~ a** (*capitare*) happen to; **mi tocca aspettare** I'll have to wait; **tocca a te** it's your turn; (*da pagare da bere*) it's your round; **'non ~'** 'please do not touch'

**tocca'sana** *nm inv* panacea

**toc'cato** *a* (*fam: matto*) touched

**'tocco** *nm* touch; (*di pennello, orologio*) stroke; (*di pane ecc*) chunk; **il ~ finale** the finishing touches ● *a fam* crazy, touched

**toc 'toc** *nm inv* knock, knock

**'toga** *nf* toga; (*accademica, di magistrato*) gown

**'togliere** *vt* take off (*coperta*); (*Math, da scuola*) take away; quench (*sete*); take out, remove (*tonsille, dente ecc*); **~ qcsa di mano a qcno** take sth away from sb; **~ qcno dei guai** get sb out of trouble; **ciò non toglie che...** nevertheless..., the fact remains that...; **farsi ~ le tonsille** have one's tonsils [taken] out

**'togliersi** *vr* take off (*abito*); **~ la vita** take one's [own] life; **~ di mezzo** get out of the way; **togliti dai piedi!** get out of the way!

**toi'lette** *nf inv* toilet; (*mobile*) dressing table

**to'letta** *nf* toilet; (*mobile*) dressing table

**tolle'rante** *a* tolerant

**tolle'ranza** *nf* tolerance; **casa di ~** brothel

**tolle'rare** *vt* tolerate

**'tolto** *pp di* **togliere**

**to'maia** *nf* upper

**'tomba** *nf* grave

**tom'bino** *nm* manhole cover

**'tombola** *nf* bingo; (*caduta*) tumble

**to'mino** *nm* goat cheese

**'tomo** *nm* tome

**tomogra'fia** *nf Med* tomography. **~ assiale computerizzata** computerized axial tomography, CAT

**'tonaca** *nf* habit

**to'nale** *a* tonal

**tonalità** *nf inv Mus* tonality

**to'nante** *a* booming

**'tondo** *a* (*cifra*) round ● *nm* circle

**'toner** *nm inv* toner

**'tonfo** *nm* thud; (*in acqua*) splash

**'tonica** *nf Mus* keynote

**'tonico** *a* (*sillaba*) stressed; (*muscoli*) well toned ● *nm* tonic

**tonifi'care** *vt* tone up (*muscoli*)

**ton'nara** *nf* tuna-fishing net

**ton'nato** *a* **vitello ~** veal with a tuna and mayonnaise sauce

**tonnel'laggio** *nm* tonnage

**tonnel'lata** *nf* ton. **~ corta americana** short ton, net ton

**'tonno** *nm* tuna [fish]

**'tono** *nm* tone

**ton'sille** *nfpl* tonsils

**tonsil'lite** *nf* tonsillitis

**'tonto** *a fam* thick

**top** *nm inv* (*indumento*) sun-top

**to'pazio** *nm* topaz

**'topless** *nm inv* **in ~** topless

**top 'model** *nf inv* supermodel, top model

**'topo** *nm* mouse. **~ di albergo/appartamento** thief in a hotel/block of flats. **~ di biblioteca** bookworm. **~ domestico** domestic mouse

**topogra'fia** *nf* topography

**topo'grafico** *a* topographic[al]

**to'ponimo** *nm* place name

**topo'ragno** *nm* shrew

**'toppa** *nf* (*rattoppo*) patch; (*serratura*) keyhole

**to'race** *nm* chest

**to'racico** *a* thoracic; **gabbia toracica** rib cage

**'torba** *nf* peat

**'torbido** *a* cloudy; *fig* troubled

**'torcere** *vt* twist; wring [out] (*biancheria*)

**'torcersi** *vr* twist

**'torchio** *nm* press

'**torcia** *nf* torch. ~ **elettrica** torch

**torci'collo** *nm* stiff neck

'**tordo** *nm* thrush

**to'rero** *nm* bullfighter

**To'rino** *nf* Turin

**tor'menta** *nf* snowstorm

**tormen'tare** *vt* torment

**tormen'tato** *a* tormented

**tor'mento** *nm* torment

**torna'conto** *nm* benefit

**tor'nado** *nm* tornado

**tor'nante** *nm* hairpin bend

**tor'nare** *vi* return, go/come back; (*ridiventare*) become again; ⟨*conto:*⟩ add up; ~ **a sorridere** smile again; ~ **su** go back up

**tor'neo** *nm* tournament

'**tornio** *nm* lathe

'**torno** *nm* **togliersi di** ~ get out of the way

'**toro** *nm* bull; *Astr* Taurus

**tor'pedine** *nf* torpedo

**torpedini'era** *nf* torpedo boat

**tor'pore** *nm* torpor

'**torre** *nf* tower; (*scacchi*) castle. ~ **d'avorio** ivory tower. ~ **di controllo** control tower. ~ **di osservazione** observation tower. ~ **pendente,** ~ **di Pisa** Leaning Tower of Pisa

**torrefazi'one** *nf* roasting; (*negozio*) coffee retailer

**tor'rente** *nm* torrent, mountain stream; (*fig: di lacrime*) flood; (*fig: di parole*) torrent

**torrenzi'ale** *a* torrential; **in regime** ~ **in** spate

**tor'retta** *nf* turret

'**torrido** *a* torrid

**torri'one** *nm* keep

**tor'rone** *nm* nougat

**torsi'one** *nf* twisting; (*in ginnastica*) twist

'**torso** *nm* torso; (*di mela, pera*) core; **a** ~ **nudo** bare-chested

'**torsolo** *nm* core

'**torta** *nf* cake; (*crostata*) tart. ~ **di compleanno** birthday cake. ~ **di mele** apple tart. ~ **nuziale** wedding cake. ~ **pasqualina** spinach pie

**torti'era** *nf* cake tin

**tor'tino** *nm* pie

'**torto** *pp di* **torcere** ● *a* twisted ● *nm* wrong; (*colpa*) fault; **aver** ~ be wrong; **a** ~ wrongly; **far** ~ **a qcno** wrong sb; *fig* not do sb justice; **non hai tutti i torti** you're not altogether wrong

'**tortora** *nf* turtle-dove

**tortuosa'mente** *adv* tortuously

**tortu'oso** *a* winding; (*ambiguo*) tortuous

**tor'tura** *nf* torture

**tortu'rare** *vt* torture

'**torvo** *a* ⟨*sguardo*⟩ menacing

**tosa'erba** *nm inv* lawnmower

**to'sare** *vt* shear

**tosasi'epi** *nm inv* hedge trimmer

**tosa'tura** *nf* shearing

**To'scana** *nf* Tuscany

**to'scano, -a** *a & nmf* Tuscan

'**tosse** *nf* cough

'**tossico** *a* toxic ● *nm* poison

**tossicodipen'denza** *nf* drug addiction

**tossi'comane** *nmf* drug addict, drug user

**tos'sire** *vi* cough

**tosta'pane** *nm inv* toaster. ~ **a espulsione automatica** pop-up toaster

**to'stare** *vt* toast ⟨*pane*⟩; roast ⟨*caffè*⟩

'**tosto** *adv* (*subito*) soon ● *a fam* cool; **faccia tosta** cheek

**tot** *a inv* **una cifra** ~ such and such a figure ● *nm* **un** ~ so much

**to'tale** *a & nm* total. ~ **parziale** subtotal

**totalità** *nf* entirety; **la** ~ **dei presenti** all those present

**totali'tario** *a* totalitarian

**totaliz'zare** *vt* total; score ⟨*punti*⟩

**totalizza'tore** *nm* (*per scommesse*) totalizer, tote

**total'mente** *adv* totally

'**totano** *nm* squid

'**totem** *nm inv* totem pole

**toto'calcio** *nm* ≈ [football] pools *pl*

**touche** *nf inv* touch line

**tou'pet** *nm inv* toupee

**tournée** *nf inv* tour

**to'vaglia** *nf* tablecloth

**tovagli'etta** *nf* ~ **[all'americana]** place mat

**tovagli'olo** *nm* napkin. ~ **di carta** paper napkin

'**tozzo** *a* squat ● *nm* ~ **di pane** stale piece of bread

**tra** = **fra**

**trabal'lante** *a* staggering; ⟨*sedia*⟩ rickety, wonky

**trabal'lare** *vi* stagger; ⟨*veicolo:*⟩ jolt

**tra'biccolo** *nm fam* contraption; (*auto*) jalopy

**traboc'care** *vi* overflow

**traboc'chetto** *nm* trap

**traca'gnotto** *a* dumpy

**tracan'nare** *vt* gulp down

'**traccia** *nf* track; (*orma*) footstep; (*striscia*) trail; (*residuo*) trace; *fig* sign

**tracci'are** *vt* trace; sketch out ⟨*schema*⟩; draw ⟨*linea*⟩

**tracci'ato** *nm* (*schema*) layout. ~ **di gara** circuit

**tra'chea** *nf* windpipe, trachea

**tra'colla** *nf* shoulder-strap; **borsa a** ~ shoulder-bag

**tra'collo** *nm* collapse

**tradi'mento** *nm* betrayal; *Pol* treason; **alto** ~ high treason

**tra'dire** *vt* betray; be unfaithful to ⟨*moglie, marito*⟩

**tradi'|tore, -'trice** *nmf* traitor

**tradizio'nale** *a* traditional

**tradiziona'lista** *nmf* traditionalist

**tradizional'mente** *adv* traditionally

**tradizi'one** *nf* tradition

**tra'dotto** *pp di* **tradurre**

**tra'durre** *vt* translate

**tradut'|tore, -'trice** *nmf* translator. ~ **elettronico** electronic phrasebook

**traduzi'one** *nf* translation. ~ **consecutiva**

consecutive interpreting. **~ simultanea** simultaneous interpreting

**tra'ente** *nmf Comm* drawer

**trafe'lato** *a* breathless

**traffi'cante** *nmf* dealer. **~ d'armi** arms dealer. **~ di droga** drug dealer

**traffi'care** *vi* (*affaccendarsi*) busy oneself; **~ in** *pej* traffic in

**'traffico** *nm* traffic: *Comm* trade. **~ aereo** air traffic. **~ della droga** drug trafficking. **~ ferroviario** rail traffic. **~ di stupefacenti** drug trafficking

**traffi'cone, -a** *nmf fam* wheeler dealer

**tra'figgere** *vt* penetrate, pierce; *fig* pierce

**tra'fila** *nf fig* rigmarole

**trafi'letto** *nm* minor news item

**trafo'rare** *vt* bore, drill

**tra'foro** *nm* boring, drilling; (*galleria*) tunnel; **lavoro di ~** fretwork

**trafu'gare** *vt* steal

**tra'gedia** *nf* tragedy

**traghet'tare** *vt* ferry

**tra'ghetto** *nm* ferrying; (*nave*) ferry

**tragica'mente** *adv* tragically

**'tragico** *a* tragic ● *nm* (*autore*) tragedian

**tra'gitto** *nm* journey; (*per mare*) crossing

**tragu'ardo** *nm* finishing post; (*meta*) goal

**traiet'toria** *nf* trajectory

**trai'nare** *vt* drag; (*rimorchiare*) tow

**tralasci'are** *vt* interrupt; (*omettere*) leave out; **~ di fare qcsa** fail to do sth, omit to do sth

**'tralcio** *nm Bot* shoot

**tra'liccio** *nm* (*tela*) ticking; (*graticcio*) trellis

**tra'lice: in ~** *adv* ‹*tagliare*› on the slant; ‹*guardare*› sideways

**tralu'cente** *a* shining

**tram** *nm inv* tram, streetcar *Am*

**'trama** *nf* weft; (*di film ecc*) plot

**traman'dare** *vt* hand down

**tra'mare** *vt* weave; (*macchinare*) plot

**tram'busto** *nm* turmoil

**trame'stio** *nm* bustle

**tramez'zino** *nm* sandwich

**tra'mezzo** *nm* partition

**'tramite** *prep* through ● *nm* link; **con il ~ di** by means of; **fare da ~** act as go-between

**tramon'tana** *nf* north wind

**tramon'tare** *vi* set; (*declinare*) decline

**tra'monto** *nm* sunset; (*declino*) decline

**tramor'tire** *vt* stun ● *vi* faint

**trampoli'ere** *nm* wader

**trampo'lino** *nm* springboard; (*per lo sci*) ski-jump. **~ di lancio** *fig* launch pad

**'trampolo** *nm* stilt

**tramu'tare** *vt* transform

**trance** *nf inv* trance; **essere in ~** be in a trance

**'trancia** *nf* shears *pl*; (*fetta*) slice

**tra'nello** *nm* trap

**trangugi'are** *vt* gulp down

**'tranne** *prep* except

**tranquilla'mente** *adv* peacefully

**tranquil'lante** *nm* tranquillizer

**tranquillità** *nf* calm; (*di spirito*) tranquillity

**tranquilliz'zare** *vt* reassure

**tran'quillo** *a* quiet; (*pacifico*) peaceful; (*coscienza*) easy; **stai ~!** (*non preoccuparti*) don't worry!

**transa'tlantico** *a* transatlantic ● *nm* ocean liner

**tran'satto** *pp di* **transigere**

**transazi'one** *nf Comm* transaction; *Jur* settlement

**tran'senna** *nf* (*barriera*) barrier

**transessu'ale** *nmf* transsexual

**tran'setto** *nm* transept

**'transfert** *nm inv Psych* transference

**tran'sigere** *vi Jur* reach a settlement; (*cedere*) compromise

**tran'sistor** *nm inv fam* transistor [radio]

**transi'tabile** *a* passable

**transi'tare** *vi* pass

**transi'tivo** *a* transitive

**'transito** *nm* transit; **'divieto di ~'** 'no thoroughfare'; **diritto di ~** right of way; **'~ alterno'** 'temporary one-way system'

**transi'torio** *a* transitory

**transizi'one** *nf* transition; **di ~** transitional

**tran'tran** *nm fam* routine

**tranvi'ere** *nm* tram driver, streetcar driver *Am*

**'trapano** *nm* drill. **~ elettrico** electric drill

**trapas'sare** *vt* pierce, penetrate ● *vi* (*morire*) pass away

**trapas'sato** *nm* pluperfect

**tra'passo** *nm* passage

**trape'lare** *vi anche fig* leak out

**tra'pezio** *nm* trapeze; *Math* trapezium

**trapian'tare** *vt* transplant

**trapi'anto** *nm* transplant. **~ di cuore** heart transplant

**'trappola** *nf* trap

**tra'punta** *nf* quilt

**'trarre** *vt* draw; (*ricavare*) obtain; **~ in inganno** deceive

**trasa'lire** *vi* start

**trasan'dato** *a* shabby

**trasbor'dare** *vt* transfer; *Naut* tran[s]ship ● *vi* change

**tra'sbordo** *nm* trans[s]hipment

**trascenden'tale** *a* transcendental

**tra'scendere** *vt* transcend ● *vi* (*eccedere*) go too far

**trasci'nare** *vt* drag; ‹*fig: entusiasmo:*› carry away

**trasci'narsi** *vr* drag oneself; (*camminare piano*) dawdle

**tra'scorrere** *vt* spend ● *vi* pass

**tra'scritto** *pp di* **trascrivere**

**tra'scrivere** *vt* transcribe

**trascrizi'one** *nf* transcription

**trascu'rabile** *a* negligible

**trascu'rare** *vt* neglect; (*non tenere conto di*) disregard

**trascurata'mente** *adv* carelessly

**trascura'tezza** *nf* negligence

**trascu'rato** *a* negligent; (*curato male*) neglected; (*nel vestire*) slovenly

**traseco'lato** *a* amazed

**trasferi'mento** *nm* transfer; (*trasloco*) move. **~ automatico** direct debit. **~ bancario** bank transfer

**trasfe'rire** *vt* transfer

**trasfe'rirsi** *vr* move

**tra'sferta** *nf* transfer; (*indennità*) subsistence allowance; *Sport* away match; **in ~** (*impiegato*) on secondment; **giocare in ~** play away

**trasfigu'rare** *vt* transfigure

**trasfor'mare** *vt* transform; (*in rugby*) convert

**trasfor'marsi** *vr* be transformed; **~ in** turn into

**trasforma'tore** *nm* transformer

**trasformazi'one** *nf* transformation; (*in rugby*) conversion

**trasfor'mista** *nmf* (*artista*) quick-change artist

**trasfusi'one** *nf* transfusion

**trasgre'dire** *vt* disobey; *Jur* infringe

**trasgredi'trice** *nf* transgressor

**trasgressi'one** *nf* infringement; (*di ordine*) failure to obey

**trasgres'sivo** *a* intended to shock

**trasgres'sore** *nm* transgressor

**tra'slato** *a* metaphorical

**traslitte'rare** *vt* transliterate

**traslo'care** *vt* move ● *vi* move [house]

**traslo'carsi** *vr* move [house]

**tra'sloco** *nm* move; **compagnia di ~** removal company

**tra'smesso** *pp di* trasmettere

**tra'smettere** *vt* pass on; *TV, Radio* broadcast; *Techn, Med* transmit

**trasmetti'tore** *nm* transmitter

**trasmis'sibile** *a* transmissible

**trasmissi'one** *nf* transmission; *TV, Radio* programme. **~ dati** data transmission. **~ via fax** fax transmission. **~ radiofonica** radio programme. **~ remota** remote transmission. **~ televisiva** television programme

**trasmit'tente** *nm* transmitter ● *nf* broadcasting station

**traso'gnare** *vi* day-dream

**traso'gnato** *a* dreamy

**traspa'rente** *a* transparent

**traspa'renza** *nf* transparency; **in ~** against the light

**traspa'rire** *vi* show [through]

**traspi'rare** *vi* perspire; *fig* transpire

**traspirazi'one** *nf* perspiration

**tra'sporre** *vt* transpose

**traspor'tare** *vt* transport; **lasciarsi ~ da** get carried away by; **~ con ponte aereo** airlift

**traspor'tato** *a* transported; **~ dall'aria** airborne

**trasporta'tore** *nm* conveyor; (*società*) transport company, road haulier

**tra'sporto** *nm* transport; (*fig: passione*) passion; **ministro dei trasporti** Ministry of Transport. **~ aereo** air freight. **~ ferroviario** rail transport. **~ pesante** heavy goods transport. **trasporti** *pl* **pubblici** public transport. **~ stradale** road transport, road haulage

**trastul'lare** *vt* amuse

**trastul'larsi** *vr* amuse oneself; (*perdere tempo*) fool around

**trasu'dare** *vt* ooze [with] ● *vi* ooze

**trasver'sale** *a* transverse; **strada ~** cross street

**trasversal'mente** *adv* widthways

**trasvo'lare** *vt* fly over ● *vi* **~ su** *fig* skim over

**trasvo'lata** *nf* crossing [by air]

**'tratta** *nf* (*traffico illegale*) trade; *Comm* draft. **~ bancaria** *Fin* banker's draft. **~ delle bianche** white slave trade. **~ documentaria** documentary bill

**trat'tabile** *a* or nearest offer, o.n.o.

**tratta'mento** *nm* treatment. **~ automatico delle informazioni** electronic data processing, EDP. **~ di bellezza** beauty treatment. **~ di fine rapporto** severance pay. **~ di riguardo** special treatment

**trat'tante** *a* conditioning

**trat'tare** *vt* treat; (*commerciare in*) deal in; (*negoziare*) negotiate ● *vi* **~ di** deal with

**trat'tarsi** *vr* **di che si tratta?** what's it about?; **si tratta di...** it's about...

**tratta'tive** *nfpl* negotiations; **il tavolo delle ~** the negotiating table

**trat'tato** *nm* treaty; (*opera scritta*) treatise. **~ di pace** peace treaty

**tratteggi'are** *vt* outline; (*descrivere*) sketch

**tratte'nere** *vt* (*far restare*) keep; hold (*respiro, in questura*); hold back (*lacrime, riso*); (*frenare*) restrain; (*da paga*) withhold; **sono stato trattenuto** (*ritardato*) I got held up

**tratte'nersi** *vr* restrain oneself; (*fermarsi*) stay; **~ su** (*indugiare*) dwell on

**tratteni'mento** *nm* entertainment; (*ricevimento*) party

**tratte'nuta** *nf* deduction

**trat'tino** *nm* dash; (*in parole composte*) hyphen

**'tratto** *pp di* trarre ● *nm* (*di spazio, tempo*) stretch; (*di penna*) stroke; (*linea*) line; (*brano*) passage; **'tratti** *pl* (*lineamenti*) features; **a tratti** at intervals; **ad un ~** suddenly

**trat'tore** *nm* tractor

**tratto'ria** *nf* restaurant

**'trauma** *nm* trauma

**trau'matico** *a* traumatic

**traumatiz'zante** *a* traumatic

**traumatiz'zare** *vt* traumatize

**tra'vaglio** *nm* labour; (*angoscia*) anguish

**trava'sare** *vt* decant

**tra'vaso** *nm* decanting

**trava'tura** *nf* beams *pl*

**'trave** *nf* beam. **~ a sbalzo** cantilever

**tra'veggole** *nfpl* **avere le ~** be seeing things

**'travellers cheque** *nm inv* traveller's cheque

**tra'versa** *nf* (*nel calcio*) crossbar; **è una ~ di via Roma** it's off via Roma, it crosses via Roma

**traver'sare** *vt* cross

**traver'sata** *nf* crossing

**traver'sie** *nfpl* misfortunes

**traver'sina** *nf Rail* sleeper

**tra'verso** *a* crosswise ● *adv* **di ~** crossways; **andare di ~** ⟨*cibo:*⟩ go down the wrong way; **camminare di ~** not walk in a straight line; **guardare qcno di ~** look askance at sb; **sapere per vie traverse** *fam* find out indirectly

**traver'sone** *nm* (*in calcio*) cross

**travesti'mento** *nm* disguise

**trave'stire** *vt* disguise

**trave'stirsi** *vr* disguise oneself

**travesti'tismo** *nm* transvestism, cross-dressing

**trave'stito** *a* disguised ● *nm* transvestite

**travi'are** *vt* lead astray

**travisa'mento** *nm* distortion

**travi'sare** *vt* distort

**travol'gente** *a* overwhelming

**tra'volgere** *vt* sweep away; (*sopraffare*) overwhelm

**tra'volto** *pp di* **travolgere**

**trazi'one** *nf* traction. **~ anteriore/ posteriore** front-/rear-wheel drive

**tre** *a & nm* three

**tre'alberi** *nm inv* three-masted ship, three-master

**trebbi'are** *vt* thresh

**trebbia'trice** *nf* threshing machine

**'treccia** *nf* plait, braid; (*in maglia*) cable; **a trecce** cable *attrib*

**tre'cento** *a & nm* three hundred; **il T~** the fourteenth century

**tredi'cesima** *nf extra month's salary paid as a Christmas bonus*

**tredi'cesimo, -a** *a & nm* thirteenth

**'tredici** *a & nm* thirteen

**'tregua** *nf* truce; *fig* respite

**'trekking** *nm* trekking

**tre'mante** *a* trembling, quivering; (*per il freddo*) shivering

**tre'mare** *vi* tremble, quiver; (*di freddo*) shiver

**trema'rella** *nf fam* jitters *pl*

**tremenda'mente** *adv* terribly, tremendously

**tre'mendo** *a* terrible, tremendous; **ho una fame tremenda** I'm terribly hungry

**tremen'tina** *nf* turpentine

**tre'mila** *a & nm* three thousand

**'tremito** *nm* tremble, quiver; (*per il freddo*) shiver

**tremo'lare** *vi* shake; ⟨*luce:*⟩ flicker

**tre'more** *nm* trembling

**'tremulo** *a* tremulous

**tre'nino** *nm* miniature railway

**'treno** *nm* train. **~ merci** freight train, goods train. **~ navetta** shuttle. **~ passeggeri** passenger train. **~ postale** mail train. **~ straordinario** special train

**'trenta** *a & nm* thirty; **~ e lode** *Univ* ≈ first-class honours

**trentatré 'giri** *nm inv* LP

**tren'tenne** *a & nmf* thirty-year-old

**tren'tesimo** *a & nm* thirtieth

**tren'tina** *nf* **una ~ di** about thirty

**trepi'dare** *vi* be anxious

**'trepido** *a* anxious

**treppi'ede** *nm* tripod

**'tresca** *nf* intrigue; (*amorosa*) affair

**'trespolo** *nm* perch

**triango'lare** *a* triangular

**tri'angolo** *nm* triangle. **~ delle Bermude** Bermuda Triangle. **~ equilatero** equilateral triangle. **~ isoscele** isosceles triangle. **~ rettangolo** right-angled triangle

**tri'bale** *a* tribal

**tribo'lare** *vi* (*soffrire*) suffer; (*fare fatica*) go to a lot of trouble

**tribolazi'one** *nf* suffering

**tri'bordo** *nm* starboard

**tribù** *nf inv* tribe

**tri'buna** *nf* podium, dais; (*per uditori*) gallery; *Sport* stand. **~ coperta** stand. **~ riservata al pubblico** public gallery. **~ della stampa** press gallery

**tribu'nale** *nm* court. **~ fallimentare** bankruptcy court. **~ minorile** juvenile court

**tribu'tare** *vt* bestow, confer

**tribu'tario** *a* tax *attrib*

**tri'buto** *nm* tribute; (*tassa*) tax

**tri'checo** *nm* walrus

**tri'ciclo** *nm* tricycle

**trico'lore** *a* three-coloured ● *nm* (*bandiera*) Italian flag

**tri'dente** *nm* trident

**tridimensio'nale** *a* three-dimensional

**trien'nale** *a* (*ogni tre anni*) three-yearly; (*lungo tre anni*) three-year

**tri'ennio** *nm* three-year period

**tri'fase** *a* three-phase

**tri'foglio** *nm* clover

**trifo'lato** *a sliced thinly and cooked with olive oil, parsley and garlic*

**tri'gemino** *a* **parto ~** birth of triplets

**'triglia** *nf* mullet

**trigonome'tria** *nf* trigonometry, **trig** *fam*

**tri'lingue** *a* trilingual

**tril'lare** *vi* trill

**'trillo** *nm* trill

**trilo'gia** *nf* trilogy

**trime'strale** *a* quarterly

**tri'mestre** *nm* quarter

**'trina** *nf* lace

**trin'cea** *nf* trench

**trince'rare** *vt* entrench

**trincia'pollo** *nm inv* poultry shears *pl*

**trinci'are** *vt* cut up

**trincia'trice** *nf* **~ di documenti** document shredder

**Trinità** *nf* Trinity

**'trio** *nm* trio

**trion'fale** *a* triumphal

**trionfal'mente** *adv* triumphantly

**trion'fante** *a* triumphant

**trion'fare** vi triumph (**su** over)

**tri'onfo** nm triumph

**tri'pletta** nf Sport hat trick

**tripli'care** vt triple

**tri'plice** a triple; **in ~** [copia] in triplicate

**'triplo** a treble, triple; **una somma tripla del previsto** an amount three times as much as forecast ● nm **il ~** (**di**) three times as much (as)

**'trippa** nf tripe; (fam: pancia) belly

**tripudi'are** vi rejoice

**tri'pudio** nm jubilation

**tris** nm (gioco) noughts and crosses, tick-tack-toe Am

**'triste** a sad; (luogo) gloomy

**tri'stezza** nf sadness; (di luogo) gloominess

**'tristo** a nasty

**trita'carne** nm inv mincer

**tritaghi'accio** nm inv ice-crusher

**tri'tare** vt mince

**trita'tutto** nm inv (elettrico) [food] processor

**'trito** a **~ e ritrito** well-worn, trite

**tri'tolo** nm TNT

**tri'tone** nm (mitologia) Triton; Zool newt

**trittico** nm triptych

**trit'tongo** nm triphthong

**tritu'rare** vt chop finely

**triumvi'rato** nm triumvirate

**tri'vella** nf drill

**trivel'lare** vt drill

**trivi'ale** a vulgar

**tro'feo** nm trophy

**troglo'dita** nmf (preistoria) cave-dweller; fig Neanderthal

**'trogolo** nm (per maiali) trough

**'troia** nf sow; vulg bitch; (sessuale) whore

**'tromba** nf trumpet; Auto horn; (delle scale) well; **partire in ~** dive in head first. **~ d'aria** whirlwind. **~ di Eustachio** Eustachian tube. **~ di Falloppio** Fallopian tube. **~ delle scale** stairwell

**trom'bare** vt vulg bonk; (fam: in esame) fail ● vi vulg bonk

**trom'betta** nm toy trumpet

**trombetti'ere** nm bugler

**trombet'tista** nmf trumpet-player

**trom'bone** nm trombone

**trom'bosi** nf thrombosis. **~ coronarica** coronary thrombosis

**tron'care** vt sever; truncate (parola)

**tron'chese** nm wire cutters pl

**tronche'sino** nm (per le unghie) nail clippers pl

**tron'chetto** nm **~ natalizio** Yule log

**'tronco** a truncated; **licenziare in ~** fire on the spot ● nm trunk; (di strada) section. **~ d'albero** tree trunk. **~ di cono** truncated cone

**tron'cone** nm stump

**troneggi'are** vi **~ su** tower over

**'trono** nm throne

**tropi'cale** a tropical

**'tropici** nmpl Tropics

**'tropico** nm tropic. **~ del Cancro** Tropic of Cancer. **~ del Capricorno** Tropic of Capricorn

**'troppo** a too much; (con nomi plurali) too many ● pron too much; (plurale) too many; (troppo tempo) too long; **troppi** (troppa gente) too many people; **me ne hai dato ~** you gave me too much ● adv too; (con verbi) too much; **~ stanco** too tired; **ho mangiato ~** I ate too much; **hai fame? – non ~** are you hungry? – not very; **sentirsi di ~** feel unwanted

**'trota** nf trout. **~ di mare** sea trout. **~ salmonata** salmon trout

**trot'tare** vi trot

**trotterel'lare** vi trot along; (bambino:) toddle

**'trotto** nm trot; **andare al ~** trot

**'trottola** nf [spinning] top; (movimento) spin

**troupe** nf inv **~ televisiva** camera crew

**trousse** nf inv (per trucco) make-up bag

**tro'vare** vt find; (scoprire) find out; (incontrare) meet; (ritenere) think; **andare a ~** go to see

**trova'robe** nmf (persona) props sg

**tro'varsi** vr find oneself; (luogo:) be; (sentirsi) feel

**tro'vata** nf bright idea. **~ pubblicitaria** advertising gimmick

**trova'tello, -a** nmf foundling

**truc'care** vt make up; cook (libri contabili); soup up (motore); rig (partita, elezioni)

**truc'carsi** vr put one's make-up on

**truc'cato** a made-up; (libri contabili) cooked; (partita, elezioni) rigged; (motore) souped up

**trucca|'tore, -'trice** nmf make-up artist

**'trucco** nm (cosmetici) make-up; (imbroglio) trick; **trucchi** pl **del mestiere** tricks of the trade

**'truce** a fierce; (delitto) savage

**truci'dare** vt slay

**trucio'lato** nm chipboard

**'truciolo** nm shaving

**trucu'lento** a (delitto) savage; (film) violent

**'truffa** nf fraud

**truf'fare** vt defraud

**truffa|'tore, -'trice** nmf fraudster

**'trullo** nm traditional house with a conical roof found in Apulia

**'truppa** nf troops pl; (gruppo) group; **truppe** pl **d'assalto** assault troops

**T-shirt** nf inv tee-shirt, T-shirt

**tu** pers pron you; **sei tu?** is that you?; **l'hai fatto tu?** did you do it yourself?; **a tu per tu** in private; **darsi del tu** use the familiar tu to each other

**'tua** vedi **tuo**

**'tuba** nf Mus tuba; (cappello) top hat

**tu'bare** vi coo; (innamorati:) bill and coo

**tuba'tura** nf piping

**tubazi'one** nf piping; **tubazioni** pl piping sg, pipes

**tuberco'lina** nf tuberculin

**tuberco'losi** nf tuberculosis

**'tubero** nm tuber

**tube'rosa** nf tuberose

**tu'betto** nm tube. **~ di colore** tube of paint

**tu'bino** *nm* (*vestito*) shift; (*cappello*) bowler, derby *Am*

**'tubo** *nm* pipe; *Anat* canal; **non ho capito un ~** *fam* I understood zilch. ~ **digerente** alimentary canal. ~ **a raggi catodici** cathode-ray tube. ~ **di scappamento** exhaust [pipe]. ~ **di scarico** waste pipe

**tubo'lare** *a* tubular

**'tue** *vedi* **tuo**

**tuf'fare** *vt* plunge

**tuf'farsi** *vr* dive; **'vietato ~'** 'no diving'

**tuffa|'tore, -'trice** *nmf* diver

**'tuffo** *nm* dive; (*bagno*) dip; **ho avuto un ~ al cuore** my heart leapt into my mouth. ~ **di testa** dive

**'tufo** *nm* tufa

**tu'gurio** *nm* hovel

**tuli'pano** *nm* tulip

**'tulle** *nm* tulle

**tume'fatto** *a* swollen

**tumefazi'one** *nf* swelling

**'tumido** *a* swollen

**tu'more** *nm* tumour. ~ **benigno** benign tumour. ~ **maligno** malignant tumour

**tumulazi'one** *nf* burial

**'tumulo** *nm* (*di pietre*) cairn

**tu'multo** *nm* turmoil; (*sommossa*) riot

**tumultu'oso** *a* tumultuous

**tung'steno** *nm* tungsten

**'tunica** *nf* tunic

**Tuni'sia** *nf* Tunisia

**tuni'sino** *a & nmf* Tunisian

**'tunnel** *nm inv* tunnel. ~ **sotto la Manica** Channel Tunnel

**'tuo** (**il ~** *m*, **la tua** *f*, **i tuoi** *mpl*, **le tue** *fpl*) *poss a* your; **è tua questa macchina?** is this car yours?; **un ~ amico** a friend of yours; ~ **padre** your father ● *poss pron* yours; **i tuoi** your folk

**tu'oi** *vedi* **tuo**

**tuo'nare** *vi* thunder

**tu'ono** *nm* thunder

**tu'orlo** *nm* yolk

**tu'racciolo** *nm* stopper; (*di sughero*) cork

**tu'rare** *vt* block; cork ⟨*bottiglia*⟩

**tu'rarsi** *vr* become blocked; ~ **le orecchie** stick one's fingers in one's ears; ~ **il naso** hold one's nose

**'turba** *nf* (*folla*) rabble. ~ **psichica** mental illness

**turba'mento** *nm* disturbance; (*sconvolgimento*) upsetting. ~ **della quiete pubblica** breach of the peace

**tur'bante** *nm* turban

**tur'bare** *vt* upset

**tur'barsi** *vr* get upset

**tur'bato** *a* upset

**tur'bina** *nf* turbine

**turbi'nare** *vi* whirl

**'turbine** *nm* whirl. ~ **di polvere** dust storm. ~ **di vento** whirlwind

**'turbo** *nm inv* turbo

**turbocompres'sore** *nm* *Tech* turbocharger

**turbo'lento** *a* turbulent

**turbo'lenza** *nf* turbulence

**turboreat'tore** *nm* turbo-jet

**tur'chese** *a & nmf* turquoise

**Tur'chia** *nf* Turkey

**tur'chino** *a & nm* deep blue

**'turco, -a** *a* Turkish ● *nmf* Turk; **fumare come un ~** smoke like a chimney; **bestemmiare come un ~** swear like a trooper ● *nm* (*lingua*) Turkish; *fig* double Dutch

**'turgido** *a* turgid

**tu'rismo** *nm* tourism

**tu'rista** *nmf* tourist

**tu'ristico** *a* tourist *attrib*

**tur'nista** *nmf* shift-worker

**'turno** *nm* turn; **a ~** in turn; **fare a ~** take turns; **fare i turni** work shifts; **di ~** on duty. ~ **eliminatorio** heat. ~ **di giorno** day shift. ~ **di guardia** guard duty. ~ **di lavoro** shift. ~ **di notte** night shift; **del ~ ~ ~** night shift *attrib*; **fare il ~ ~ ~** be on night shift

**'turpe** *a* base

**turpi'loquio** *nm* foul language

**'tuta** *nf* overalls *pl*; *Sport* tracksuit. ~ **da ginnastica** tracksuit. ~ **da lavoro** overalls *pl*. ~ **mimetica** camouflage. ~ **spaziale** spacesuit. ~ **subacquea** wetsuit

**tu'tela** *nf* *Jur* guardianship; (*protezione*) protection. ~ **dell'ambiente** environmental protection

**tute'lare** *vt* protect

**tu'tina** *nf* sleepsuit; (*da danza*) leotard

**tu|'tore, -'trice** *nmf* guardian

**'tutta** *nf* **mettercela ~ per fare qcsa** go flat out for sth

**tutta'via** *conj* nevertheless, still

**'tutto** *a* whole; (*con nomi plurali*) all; (*ogni*) every; **tutta la classe** the whole class, all the class; **tutti gli alunni** all the pupils; **a tutta velocità** at full speed; **ho aspettato ~ il giorno** I waited all day [long]; **vestito di ~ punto** all kitted out; **in ~ il mondo** all over the world; **noi tutti** all of us; **era tutta contenta** she was delighted; **tutti e due** both; **tutti e tre** all three ● *pron* all; (*tutta la gente*) everybody; (*tutte le cose*) everything; (*qualunque cosa*) anything; **c'è ancora del dolce? – no, l'ho mangiato ~** is there still some cake? – no, I ate it all; **le finestre sono pulite, le ho lavate tutte** the windows are clean, I washed them all; **raccontami ~** tell me everything; **lo sanno tutti** everybody knows; **è capace di ~** he's capable of anything; ~ **compreso** all in; **del ~** quite; **in ~** altogether ● *adv* completely; **tutt'a un tratto** all at once; **tutt'altro** not at all; **tutt'altro che** anything but ● *nm* whole; **tentare il ~ per ~** go for broke; ~ **compreso** all-inclusive. ~ **esaurito** *Theat* full house

**tutto'fare** *a inv & nmf* [**impiegato**] ~ general handyman

**tut'tora** *adv* still

**tutù** *nm inv* tutu; (*lungo*) ballet dress

**tv** *nf inv* TV. **tv interattiva** interactive TV. **tv via cavo** cable TV

**tweed** *nm inv* tweed

# Uu

**ubbidi'ente** *a* obedient

**ubbidiente'mente** *adv* obediently

**ubbidi'enza** *nf* obedience

**ubbi'dire** *vi* ~ **(a)** obey

**ubi'cato** *a* located

**ubicazi'one** *nf* location

**ubiquità** *nf* **non ho il dono dell'**~ I can't be in two places at once

**ubria'care** *vt* get drunk

**ubria'carsi** *vr* get drunk; ~ **di** *fig* become intoxicated with

**ubria'chezza** *nf* drunkenness; **in stato di** ~ inebriated; **in stato di** ~ **molesta** drunk and disorderly

**ubri'aco, -a** *a* drunk; ~ **fradicio** dead *o* blind drunk ● *nmf* drunk

**ubria'cone** *nm* drunkard ● *a* **un marito** ~ a drunkard of a husband

**uccelli'era** *nf* aviary

**uccel'lino** *nm* baby bird

**uc'cello** *nm* bird; (*vulg: pene*) cock. ~ **acquatico** water fowl. ~ **da cacciagione** game bird. ~ **del malaugurio** bird of ill omen. ~ **notturno** night *o* nocturnal bird. ~ **del paradiso** bird of paradise. ~ **di passo** bird of passage. ~ **rapace** bird of prey

**uc'cidere** *vt* kill

**uc'cidersi** *vr* kill oneself; (*morire*) be killed

**+uccio** *suff* **boccuccia** *nf* pretty little mouth; **calduccio** *nm* cosy warmth; **c'è un bel calduccio** it's nice and cosy; **tesoruccio** *nm* sweetie; **avvocatuccio** *nm pej* small town lawyer; **cosuccia** *nf* trifle; **è una cosuccia da niente** it's nothing; **doloruccio** *nm* twinge; **vestituccio** *nm pej* skimpy little dress

**uccisi'one** *nf* killing

**uc'ciso** *pp di* **uccidere**

**ucci'sore** *nm* killer

**U'craina** *nf* **l'**~ the Ukraine

**u'craino, -a** *a & nmf* Ukrainian

**u'dente** *a* **i non udenti** the hearing-impaired

**u'dibile** *a* audible

**udi'enza** *nf* audience; (*colloquio*) interview; *Jur* hearing. ~ **a porte chiuse** hearing in camera

**u'dire** *vt* hear

**udi'tivo** *a* auditory

**u'dito** *nm* hearing

**udi'tore, -'trice** *nmf* listener; *Sch* unregistered student (*allowed to sit in on lectures*)

**udi'torio** *nm* audience

**UE** *abbr* (**Unione Europea**) EU

**'uffa** *int* (*con impazienza*) come on!; (*con tono seccato*) damn!

**uffici'ale** *a* official ● *nm* officer; (*funzionario*) official; **pubblico** ~ public official. ~ **dell'esercito** army officer. ~ **giudiziario** clerk of the court. ~ **sanitario** health officer. ~ **dello Stato civile** registrar

**ufficialità** *nf* official status

**ufficializ'zare** *vt* make official, officialize

**ufficial'mente** *adv* officially

**uf'ficio** *nm* office; (*dovere*) duty; (*reparto*) department; **andare in** ~ go to the office; **grazie a suoi buoni uffici** thanks to his kind offices. ~ **acquisti** purchasing department. ~ **cambi** bureau de change, exchange bureau. ~ **di collocamento** employment office, jobcentre *Br*. **U**~ **Dazi e Dogana** Customs and Excise. ~ **funebre** *Relig* funeral service. ~ **informazioni** information office. ~ **di informazioni turistiche** tourist information office *o* centre. ~ **oggetti smarriti** lost property office, lost and found *Am*. ~ **del personale** personnel department. ~ **postale** post office. ~ **prenotazioni** advance booking office. ~ **della redazione** newspaper office. ~ **del turismo** tourist office. ~ **turistico** tourist office

**ufficiosa'mente** *adv* unofficially

**uffici'oso** *a* unofficial

**uff** *int* phew!

**'ufo**[1] *nm inv* ufo

**'ufo**[2]: **a** ~ *adv* without paying

**ufolo'gia** *nf* ufology

**U'ganda** *nf* Uganda

**ugan'dese** *a & nmf* Ugandan

**uggiosità** *nf* dullness

**uggi'oso** *a* boring

**uguagli'anza** *nf* equality

**uguagli'are** *vt* make equal; (*essere uguale*) equal; (*livellare*) level

**uguagli'arsi** *vr* ~ **a** compare oneself to

**ugu'ale** *a* equal; (*lo stesso*) the same; (*simile*) like; **due più due è** ~ **a quattro** two plus two equals four ● *nm Math* equals sign; **che non ha** ~ unequalled

**ugual'mente** *adv* equally; (*malgrado tutto*) all the same

**'ulcera** *nf* ulcer. ~ **gastrica** gastric ulcer. ~ **peptica** peptic ulcer

**u'liva** *nf vedi* **oliva**

**uli'veto** *nm* olive grove

**u'livo** *nm* olive[-tree]

**'ulna** *nf Anat* ulna

**ulteri'ore** *a* further

**ulterior'mente** *adv* further

**ultima'mente** *adv* lately

**ulti'mare** *vt* complete

**ulti'matum** *nm inv* ultimatum

**ulti'missime** *nfpl Journ* stop press. latest news *sg*

**'ultimo** *a* last; *(notizie ecc)* latest; *(più lontano)* farthest; *fig* ultimate; *(prezzo)* rock-bottom ● *nm* last; **fino all' ~** to the last; **per ~** at the end; **l'~ piano** the top floor

**ultimo'genito, -a** *nmf* last-born

**ultrà** *nmf inv Sport* fanatical supporter

**ultramo'derno** *a* ultra-modern

**ultrapi'atto** *a* ultra-thin

**ultrapo'tente** *a* extra-strong

**ultra'rapido** *a* extra-fast

**ultraresi'stente** *a* extra-strong

**ultrasen'sibile** *a* ultrasensitive

**ultra'sonico** *a* ultrasonic

**ultrasu'ono** *nm* ultrasound

**ultrater'reno** *(vita)* after death

**ultravio'letto** *a* ultraviolet

**ulu'lare** *vi* howl

**ulu'lato** *nm* howling; **gli ululati** the howls, the howling

**umana'mente** *adv (trattare)* humanely; **~ impossibile** not humanly possible

**uma'nesimo** *nm* humanism

**uma'nista** *nmf* humanist

**umanità** *nf* humanity

**umani'tario** *a* humanitarian

**u'mano** *a* human; *(benevolo)* humane

**'Umbria** *nf* Umbria

**'umbro, -a** *a & nmf* Umbrian

**umet'tare** *vt* moisten

**umidifica'tore** *nm* humidifier

**umidità** *nf* dampness; *(di clima)* humidity

**'umido** *a* damp; *(clima)* humid; *(mani, occhi)* moist ● *nm* dampness; **in ~** *Culin* stewed

**'umile** *a* humble

**umili'ante** *a* humiliating

**umili'are** *vt* humiliate

**umili'arsi** *vr* humble oneself

**umiliazi'one** *nf* humiliation

**umil'mente** *adv* humbly

**umiltà** *nf* humility

**u'more** *nm* humour; *(stato d'animo)* mood; **di cattivo/buon ~** in a bad/good mood

**umo'rismo** *nm* humour

**umo'rista** *nmf* humorist

**umoristica'mente** *adv* humorously

**umo'ristico** *a* humorous

**un** *vedi* **uno**

**un'** *vedi* **uno**

**'una** *vedi* **uno**

**u'nanime** *a* unanimous

**unanime'mente** *adv* unanimously

**unanimità** *nf* unanimity; **all'~** unanimously

**unci'nare** *vt* hook

**unci'nato** *a* hooked; *(parentesi)* angle *attrib*

**unci'netto** *nm* crochet hook

**un'cino** *nm* hook

**undi'cenne** *a & nmf* eleven-year-old

**undi'cesimo, -a** *a & nm* eleventh

**'undici** *a & nm* eleven

**'ungere** *vt* grease; *(sporcare)* get greasy; *Relig* anoint; *(blandire)* flatter

**'ungersi** *vr (con olio solare)* oil oneself; **~ le mani** get one's hands greasy

**unghe'rese** *a & nmf* Hungarian ● *nm (lingua)* Hungarian

**Unghe'ria** *nf* Hungary

**'unghia** *nf* nail; *(di animale)* claw; **cadere sotto le unghie di qcno** fall into sb's clutches. **~ fessa** cloven hoof

**unghi'ata** *nf (graffio)* scratch

**ungu'ento** *nm* ointment

**unica'mente** *adv* only

**unicellu'lare** *a* single-cell, unicellular

**unicità** *nf* uniqueness

**'unico** *a* only; *(singolo)* single; *(incomparabile)* unique

**uni'corno** *nm* unicorn

**unidimensio'nale** *a* one-dimensional

**unidirezio'nale** *a* unidirectional

**unifamili'are** *a* one-family

**unifi'care** *vt* unify

**unificazi'one** *nf* unification

**unifor'mare** *vt* level

**unifor'marsi** *vr* conform (**a** to)

**uni'forme** *a* uniform ● *nf* uniform. **~ di gala** *Mil* mess dress

**uniformità** *nf* uniformity

**unilate'rale** *a* unilateral

**unilateral'mente** *adv* unilaterally

**uninomi'nale** *a Pol* single-candidate

**uni'one** *nf* union; *(armonia)* unity. **U~ economica e monetaria** Economic and Monetary Union. **U~ Europea** European Union. **U~ Monetaria Europea** European Monetary Union. **~ sindacale** trade union, labor union *Am*. **U~ Sovietica** Soviet Union

**u'nire** *vt* unite; *(collegare)* join; blend *(colori ecc)*

**u'nirsi** *vr* unite; *(collegarsi)* join

**'unisex** *a inv* unisex

**u'nisono** *nm* all'**~** in unison

**unità** *nf inv* unity; *(Math, Mil, reparto ecc)* unit; *Comput* drive. **~ di backup a nastro** *Comput* tape backup drive. **~ centrale di elaborazione** *Comput* central processing unit, CPU. **~ floppy disk** *Comput* floppy disk drive. **~ di inizializzazione** *Comput* boot drive. **~ di memoria di massa** *Comput* mass storage device. **~ di misura** unit of measurement. **~ a nastro magnetico** *Comput* tapedrive. **~ periferica** *Comput* peripheral. **~ di produzione** factory unit. **~ socio-sanitaria locale** local health centre. **~ di visualizzazione** *Comput* visual display unit, VDU

**uni'tario** *a* unitary; **prezzo ~** unit price

**u'nito** *a* united; *(tinta)* plain; *(comunità)* tight-knit

**univer'sale** *a* universal

**universaliz'zare** *vt* universalize

**universal'mente** *adv* universally

**università** *nf inv* university

**universi'tario, -a** *a* university *attrib* ● *nmf (insegnante)* university lecturer; *(studente)* undergraduate

**uni'verso** *nm* universe

**u'nivoco** *a* unambiguous

**'unto** *pp di* **ungere** ● *a* greasy ● *nm* grease

**untu'oso** *a* greasy

**uno, -a** *art indef* a: *(davanti a vocale o h muta)* an; **un esempio** an example; ● *pron* one: **a ~ 'a** ~ one by one; **~ alla volta** one at a time; **l'~ e l'altro** both [of them]; **né l'~ né l'altro** neither [of them]; **~ di noi** one of us; **~ fa quello che può** you do what you can ● *a* a, one ● *nm (numerale)* one; *(un tale)* some man ● *nf* some woman

**unzi'one** *nf* **l'Estrema U~** Extreme Unction, last rites

**u'omo** *nm (pl* **uomini)** man; **'uomini'** *(bagni)* 'gents', 'men's room'. **~ d'affari** business man. **~ di colore** black man. **~ di fiducia** right-hand man. **~ di mondo** man of the world. **~-oggetto** toy boy. **~ delle pulizie** cleaner. **~ sandwich** sandwich-man. **~ di Stato** statesman. **~ della strada** man on the street

**u'ovo** *nm (pl f* **uova)** egg. **uova** *pl* **al bacon** bacon and eggs. **~ barzotto** *o* **bazzotto** soft-boiled egg. **~ in camicia** poached egg. **~ di Colombo** obvious simple solution. **~ alla coque** boiled egg. **~ all'occhio di bue** fried egg. **~ all'ostrica** raw egg. **~ di Pasqua** Easter egg. **uova** *pl* **al prosciutto** ham and eggs. **~ sodo** hard-boiled egg. **~ strapazzato** scrambled egg. **~ al tegamino** fried egg

**upgra'dabile** *a* upgradeable

**'upupa** *nf* hoopoe

**ura'gano** *nm* hurricane

**u'ranio** *nm* uranium

**urba'nesimo** *nm* urbanization

**urba'nista** *nmf* town planner

**urba'nistica** *nf* town planning

**urba'nistico** *a* urban

**urbaniz'zare** *vt* urbanize

**urbanizzazi'one** *nf* urbanization

**ur'bano** *a* urban; *(cortese)* urbane

**u'rea** *nf* urea

**u'retra** *nf Anat* urethra

**ur'gente** *a* urgent

**urgente'mente** *adv* urgently

**ur'genza** *nf* urgency; **in caso d'~** in an emergency; **d'~** *(misura, chiamata)* emergency *attrib*; **operare d'~** perform an emergency operation on

**'urgere** *vi* be urgent

**u'rina** *nf* urine

**uri'nare** *vi* urinate

**ur'lare** *vi* shout, yell; *(cane, vento:)* howl

**'urlo** *nm (pl m* **urli,** *pl f* **urla)** shout; *(di cane, vento)* howling

**'urna** *nf* urn; *(elettorale)* ballot box; **andare alle urne** go to the polls

**urrà** *int* hurrah!

**URSS** *nf abbr* **(Unione delle Repubbliche Socialiste Sovietiche)** USSR

**ur'tare** *vt* knock against; *(scontrarsi)* bump into; *fig* irritate

**ur'tarsi** *vr* collide; *fig* clash

**'urto** *nm* knock; *(scontro)* crash; *(contrasto)* conflict; *fig* clash; **d'~** *(misure, terapia)* shock

**U.S.A.** *nmpl* US[A] *sg*

**usa e getta** *a inv (rasoio, siringa)* throw-away, disposable

**u'sanza** *nf* custom; *(moda)* fashion

**u'sare** *vt* use; *(impiegare)* employ; *(esercitare)* exercise; **~ fare qcsa** be in the habit of doing sth ● *vi (essere di moda)* be fashionable; **non si usa più** it is out of fashion; *(attrezzatura, espressione:)* it's not used any more

**u'sato** *a* used; *(non nuovo)* second-hand ● *nm* second-hand goods *pl*; **dell'~** second-hand; **fuori dell'~** unusual

**u'sbeco, -a** *a & nmf* Uzbekistani

**u'scente** *a (presidente)* outgoing

**usci'ere** *nm* usher

**'uscio** *nm* door

**u'scire** *vi* come out; *(andare fuori)* go out; *(sfuggire)* get out; *(essere sorteggiato)* come up; *(giornale:)* come out; **~ da** *Comput* exit from, quit; **~ di strada** leave the road

**u'scita** *nf* exit, way out; *(spesa)* outlay; *(di autostrada)* junction; *(battuta)* witty remark; *(in ginnastica artistica)* dismount; **uscite** *pl Fin* outgoings; **essere in libera ~** be off duty. **~ di servizio** back door. **~ di sicurezza** emergency exit

**usi'gnolo** *nm* nightingale

**'uso** *nm* use; *(abitudine)* custom; *(usanza)* usage; **fuori ~** out of use; **per ~ esterno** *(medicina)* for external use only; **~ e dosi** use and dosage

**us'saro** *nm* hussar

**U.S.S.L.** *nf abbr* **(Unità Socio-Sanitaria Locale)** local health centre

**ustio'narsi** *vr* burn oneself

**ustio'nato, -a** *nmf* burns case ● *a* burnt

**usti'one** *nf* burn; **ustioni di primo grado** first-degree burns

**usu'ale** *a* usual

**usual'mente** *adv* usually

**usucapi'one** *nf Jur* usucaption

**usufru'ire** *vi* **~ di** take advantage of, make use of

**usufruttu'ario, -a** *nmf* user, usufructuary *fml*

**usu'frutto** *nm Jur* use, usufruct *fml*

**u'sura** *nf* usury

**usu'raio** *nm* usurer

**usur'pare** *vt* usurp

**usurpa'tore, -'trice** *nmf* usurper

**u'tensile** *nm* tool; *Culin* utensil; **cassetta degli utensili** tool box; **utensili** *pl* **da cucina** kitchen utensils

**u'tente** *nmf* user. **~ finale** end user. **utenti** *pl* **della strada** road users

**u'tenza** *nf* use; *(utenti)* users *pl*; **~ finale** end users *pl*

**ute'rino** *a* uterine

**'utero** *nm* womb

**'utile** *a* useful ● *nm Comm* profit; **unire l'~ al dilettevole** combine business with pleasure. **~ su cambi** foreign exchange gain. **~ sul capitale investito** return on investment

**utilità** *nf* usefulness, utility; *Comput* utility

**utili'tario, -a** *a* utilitarian ● *nf Auto* small car

**utilita'ristico** *a* utilitarian

**u'tility** *nm* utility

**utiliz'zare** *vt* utilize

**utilizzazi'one** *nf* utilization

**uti'lizzo** *nm* use

**util'mente** *adv* usefully

**Uto'pia** *nf* Utopia

**uto'pista** *nmf* Utopian

**uto'pistico** *a* Utopian

**UVA** *nmpl abbr* (**ultravioletto prossimo**) UV

**'uva** *nf* grapes *pl*; **chicco d'~** grape. **~ bianca** white grapes. **~ nera** black grapes. **~ passa** raisins *pl*. **~ sultanina** currants *pl*. **~ da tavola** [eating] grapes. **~ da vino** wine grapes

**u'vetta** *nf* raisins *pl*

**uxori'cida** *nm* wife-killer, uxoricide *fml* ● *nf* husband-killer

**Uzbeki'stan** *nm* Uzbekistan

# Vv

**va'** *vedi* **andare**

**va'cante** *a* vacant

**va'canza** *nf* holiday, vacation *Am*; [**giorno di**] **~** holiday; (*posto vacante*) vacancy; **vacanze** *pl* holidays, vacation *Am*; *Univ* vacation, vac *fam*. **essere in ~** be on holiday/vacation; **prendersi una ~** take a holiday/vacation; **andare in ~** go on holiday/vacation; **è ~** it's a holiday. **vacanze** *pl* **estive** summer holidays/vacation. **vacanze** *pl* **di Natale** Christmas holidays/vacation. **vacanze** *pl* **di Pasqua** Easter holidays/vacation. **vacanze** *pl* **scolastiche** school holidays/vacation

**'vacca** *nf* cow. **~ da latte** dairy cow

**vac'caro** *m*, **-a** *nf* cowherd

**vacci'nare** *vt* vaccinate; **farsi ~** get vaccinated

**vaccinazi'one** *nf* vaccination

**vac'cino** *nm* vaccine

**vacil'lante** *a* tottering; ⟨*oggetto*⟩ wobbly; ⟨*luce*⟩ flickering; *fig* wavering

**vacil'lare** *vi* totter; ⟨*oggetto:*⟩ wobble; ⟨*luce:*⟩ flicker; *fig* waver

**'vacuo** *a* (*vano*) vain; *fig* empty ● *nm* vacuum

**'vado** *vedi* **andare**

**vaffan'culo** *int vulg* fuck off!

**vagabon'daggio** *nm Jur* vagrancy

**vagabon'dare** *vi* wander

**vaga'bondo** *a* ⟨*cane*⟩ stray; **gente** *pl* **vagabonda** tramps ● *nmf* tramp

**vaga'mente** *adv* vaguely

**va'gante** *a* wandering; **mina ~** floating mine; **proiettile ~** stray bullet

**va'gare** *vi* wander

**vagheggi'are** *vt* long for

**va'ghezza** *nf* vagueness

**va'gina** *nf* vagina

**vagi'nale** *a* vaginal

**va'gire** *vi* whimper

**va'gito** *nm* whimper

**'vaglia** *nm inv* money order. **~ bancario** bank draft. **~ cambiario** promissory note. **~ internazionale** international money order. **~ postale** postal order

**vagli'are** *vt* sift; *fig* weigh

**'vaglio** *nm* sieve

**'vago** *a* vague

**vagon'cino** *nm* (*di funivia*) car. **~ a piattaforma** flat[bed] wagon

**va'gone** *nm* (*per passeggeri*) carriage, car; (*per merci*) truck, wagon. **~ bagagliaio** luggage van, baggage car *Am*. **~ frigorifero** refrigerator van. **~ letto** sleeper. **~ postale** mail coach. **~ ristorante** restaurant car, dining car

**vai'olo** *nm* smallpox

**va'langa** *nf* avalanche

**val'chiria** *nf* Valkyrie

**val'dese** *a & nmf* Waldensian

**va'lente** *a* skilful

**va'lenza** *nf Chem* valency; (*fig: valore*) value

**va'lere** *vi* be worth; (*contare*) count; ⟨*regola:*⟩ apply (**per** to); (*essere valido*) be valid; **far ~ i propri diritti** assert one's rights; **farsi ~** assert oneself; **non vale!** that's not fair!; **tanto vale che me ne vada** I might as well go ● *vt* **~ qcsa a qcno** (*procurare*) earn sb sth; **valerne la pena** be worth it; **vale la pena di vederlo** it's worth seeing; **valersi di** avail oneself of

**valeri'ana** *nf* valerian

**va'levole** *a* valid

**'valgo** *a* **alluce ~** hallux valgus; **ginocchia** *pl* **valghe** knock knees

**vali'care** *vt* cross

**'valico** *nm* pass

**valida'mente** *adv* validly; (*efficacemente*) efficiently; ⟨*contribuire*⟩ effectively

**validità** *nf inv* validity; **con ~ illimitata** valid indefinitely

**'valido** *a* valid; (*efficace*) efficient; ⟨*contributo*⟩ valuable

**valige'ria** *nf* (*fabbrica*) leather factory; (*negozio*) leather goods shop

**vali'getta** *nf* small case; (*per attrezzi*) box. ~ **del pronto soccorso** first aid kit. ~ **ventiquattrore** overnight bag

**va'ligia** *nf* suitcase; **fare le valigie** pack; *fig* pack one's bags. ~ **diplomatica** diplomatic bag

**val'lata** *nf* valley

**'valle** *nf* valley; **a** ~ downstream

**val'letta** *nf* TV assistant

**val'letto** *nm* valet; *TV* assistant

**'vallo** *nm* wall; **il ~ Adriano** Hadrian's Wall

**val'lone** *nm* (*valle*) deep valley

**val'lone, -a** *a & nmf* Walloon

**va'lore** *nm* value, worth; (*merito*) merit; (*coraggio*) valour; **valori** *pl Comm* securities; **di ~** (*oggetto*) valuable; **oggetti di ~** valuables; **di grande ~** of great value; (*medico, scienziato*) top *attrib*; **senza ~** worthless; **a ~ aggiunto** value-added. ~ **bollato** revenue stamp. ~ **contabile** book value. ~ **effettivo** real value. ~ **di mercato** market value. ~ **mobiliare** security. ~ **nominale** nominal value. ~ **di realizzo** break-up value. ~ **di riscatto** surrender value

**valoriz'zare** *vt* (*mettere in valore*) use to advantage; (*aumentare di valore*) increase the value of; (*migliorare l'aspetto di*) enhance

**valoriz'zarsi** *vr* **il paese ha bisogno di ~ migliorando...** the country needs to enhance the value of its assets by improving...

**valorosa'mente** *adv* courageously

**valo'roso** *a* courageous

**'valso** *pp di* **valere**

**va'luta** *nf* currency. ~ **a corso legale** legal tender. ~ **estera** foreign currency

**valu'tare** *vt* value; weigh up (*situazione*)

**valu'tario** *a* (*mercato, norme*) currency *attrib*

**valuta'tivo** *a* for evaluation, evaluative

**valutazi'one** *nf* valuation

**'valva** *nf* valve

**'valvola** *nf* valve; *Electr* fuse. ~ **a farfalla** butterfly valve. ~ **pneumatica** air valve. ~ **di sicurezza** *anche fig* safety valve

**'valzer** *nm inv* waltz

**vamp** *nf inv* vamp

**vam'pata** *nf* blaze; (*di calore*) blast; (*al viso*) flush

**vam'piro** *nm* vampire; *fig* blood-sucker

**va'nadio** *nm* vanadium

**vanaglori'oso** *a* vainglorious

**vana'mente** *adv* (*inutilmente*) in vain; (*con vanità*) vainly

**van'dalico** *a* **atto ~** act of vandalism

**vanda'lismo** *nm* vandalism

**vandalizzare** *vt* vandalize

**vandalizzazione** *nf* vandalizing

**'vandalo, -a** *nmf* vandal

**vaneggia'mento** *nm* delirium

**vaneggi'are** *vi* rave

**va'nesio** *a* conceited

**'vanga** *nf* spade

**van'gare** *vt* dig

**van'gata** *nf* (*quantità*) spadeful; (*azione*) blow with a spade

**van'gelo** *nm* Gospel; (*fam: verità*) gospel [truth]

**vanifi'care** *vt* nullify

**va'niglia** *nf* vanilla

**vanigli'ato** *a* (*zucchero*) vanilla

**vanil'lina** *nf* vanillin

**vanità** *nf* vanity

**vanitosa'mente** *adv* vainly

**vani'toso** *a* vain

**'vano** *a* vain ●*nm* (*stanza*) room; (*spazio vuoto*) hollow. ~ **doccia** shower room. ~ **portabagagli** *Auto* boot, trunk *Am*

**van'taggio** *nm* advantage; *Sport* lead; *Tennis* advantage; **trarre ~ da qcsa** derive benefit from sth

**vantaggiosa'mente** *adv* advantageously

**vantaggi'oso** *a* advantageous

**van'tare** *vt* praise; (*possedere*) boast

**van'tarsi** *vr* boast

**vante'ria** *nf* boasting; **vanterie** *pl* boasting

**'vanto** *nm* boast

**'vanvera** *nf* **a ~** at random; **parlare a ~** talk nonsense

**va'pore** *nm* steam; (*di benzina, cascata*) vapour; **a ~** steam *attrib*; **al ~** *Culin* steamed; **battello a ~** steamboat. ~ **acqueo** steam, water vapour

**vapo'retto** *nm* ferry

**vapori'era** *nf* steam engine

**vaporiz'zare** *vt* vaporize

**vaporizza'tore** *nm* spray

**vapo'roso** *a* (*vestito*) filmy; **capelli** *pl* **vaporosi** big hair

**va'rano** *nm* monitor [lizard]

**va'rare** *vt* launch

**var'care** *vt* cross

**'varco** *nm* passage; **aspettare al ~** lie in wait

**vare'china** *nf* bleach

**vari'abile** *a* changeable, variable ●*nf Math* variable

**variabilità** *nf* changeableness, variability

**varia'mente** *adv* variously

**vari'ante** *nf* variant

**vari'are** *vt/i* vary; ~ **di umore** change one's mood

**vari'ato** *a* varied

**variazi'one** *nf* variation

**va'rice** *nf* varicose vein

**vari'cella** *nf* chickenpox

**vari'coso** *a* varicose

**varie'gato** *a* variegated

**varietà** *nf inv* variety ●*nm inv* variety show

**'vario** *a* varied; (*al pl, parecchi*) various; **varie** *pl* (*molti*) several; **varie ed eventuali** any other business

**vario'pinto** *a* multicoloured

**'varo** *nm* launch

**Var'savia** Warsaw

**vas'aio** *nm* potter

**'vasca** *nf* tub; (*piscina*) pool; (*lunghezza*)

length. **~ da bagno** bath. **~ di sviluppo** *Phot* developing tank

**va'scello** *nm* vessel: **capitano di ~** captain

**va'schetta** *nf* tub; *Phot* tray. **~ per il ghiaccio** ice-tray

**vasco'lare** *a Anat, Bot* vascular

**vasecto'mia** *nf* vasectomy

**vase'lina** *nf* Vaseline[R]

**vasel'lame** *nm* china. **~ d'oro/d'argento** gold/silver plate

**va'setto** *nm* small pot; (*per marmellata*) jam jar

**'vaso** *nm* pot; (*da fiori*) vase; *Anat* vessel; (*per cibi*) jar. **~ da notte** chamberpot. **~ sanguigno** blood vessel

**vasocostrit'tore** *a* vasoconstrictor

**vasodilata'tore** *a* vasodilator

**vas'sallo** *nm* vassal

**vas'soio** *nm* tray

**vastità** *nf* vastness

**'vasto** *a* vast; **di vaste vedute** broadminded

**Vati'cano** *nm* Vatican

**vati'cinio** *nm* prophecy

**vattela'pesca** *adv fam* God knows

**'vattene!** go away!; *vedi* **andarsene**

**VCR** *abbr* (**videoregistratore**) VCR

**ve** *pers pron* you; **ve l'ho dato** I gave it to you

**'vecchia** *nf* old woman

**vecchi'aia** *nf* old age

**'vecchio, -a** *a* old ● *nmf* old man; old woman; **i vecchi** old people; **~ mio** old man

**'veccia** *nf* vetch

**'vece** *nf* **in ~ di** in place of; **fare le veci di qcno** take sb's place

**ve'dente** *a* **i non ~** the visually handicapped

**ve'dere** *vt* see; see, watch (*film, partita*); **far ~** show; **farsi ~** show one's face; **non si vede** (*macchia, imperfezione:*) it doesn't show; **non veder l'ora di fare qcsa** be raring to go; **non poter ~ qcno** not be able to stand the sight of sb; **vederci doppio** have double vision; **ne ho viste di tutti i colori** *fig* I've really seen life; **da ~** (*film, spettacolo*) not to be missed; **questo è da ~!** that remains to be seen!; **chi si vede!** *fam* look who it is! ● *vi* see

**ve'dersi** *vr* see oneself; (*reciproco*) see each other; **vedersela brutta** have a narrow escape

**ve'detta** *nf* (*luogo*) lookout; *Naut* patrol vessel

**'vedova** *nf* widow. **~ nera** *Zool* black widow [spider]

**'vedovo** *nm* widower

**ve'duta** *nf* view

**vee'mente** *a* vehement

**vege'tale** *a & nm* vegetable

**vegetali'ano** *a & nmf* vegan

**vege'tare** *vi* vegetate

**vegetari'ano, -a** *a & nmf* vegetarian

**vegeta'tivo** *a* vegetative

**vegetazi'one** *nf* vegetation

**'vegeto** *a vedi* **vivo**

**veg'gente** *nmf* clairvoyant

**'veglia** *nf* watch: **fare la ~** keep watch. **~ funebre** vigil

**vegli'are** *vi* be awake; **~ su** watch over

**vegli'one** *nm* **~ di capodanno** New Year's Eve celebration

**veico'lare** *vt* carry (*malattia*) ● *a* (*traffico*) vehicular

**ve'icolo** *nm* vehicle. **~ pesante** heavy goods vehicle, HGV. **~ spaziale** spacecraft

**'vela** *nf* sail; *Sport* sailing; **andare a gonfie vele** *fig* go beautifully; (*affari:*) be booming; **far ~** set sail. **~ di taglio** mainsail

**ve'lare** *vt* veil; (*fig: nascondere*) hide

**ve'larsi** *vr* (*vista:*) mist over; (*voce:*) go husky

**velata'mente** *adv* indirectly

**ve'lato** *a* veiled; (*occhi*) misty; (*collant*) sheer

**vela'tura** *nf* sails *pl*

**'velcro**[R] *nm* velcro

**veleggi'are** *vi* sail

**ve'leno** *nm* poison

**velenosa'mente** *adv* (*rispondere*) venomously

**vele'noso** *a* poisonous; (*frase*) venomous

**ve'letta** *nf* (*di cappello*) veil

**'velico** *a* (*circolo*) sailing *attrib*; **superficie velica** sail area

**veli'ero** *nm* sailing ship

**ve'lina** *nf* (*carta*) **~ tissue paper**; (*copia*) carbon copy

**ve'lista** *nm* yachtsman ● *nf* yachtswoman

**ve'livolo** *nm* aircraft

**velleità** *nf inv* foolish ambition

**vellei'tario** *a* unrealistic

**'vello** *nm* fleece

**vellu'tato** *a* velvety

**vel'luto** *nm* velvet. **~ a coste** corduroy

**'velo** *nm* veil; (*di zucchero, cipria*) dusting; (*tessuto*) voile

**ve'loce** *a* fast

**veloce'mente** *adv* quickly

**velo'cipede** *nm* penny-farthing

**velo'cista** *nmf Sport* sprinter

**velocità** *nf inv* speed; (*Auto: marcia*) gear. **~ di clock** *Comput* clock speed. **~ di crociera** cruising speed. **~ di stampa** print speed

**velociz'zare** *vt* speed up

**ve'lodromo** *nm* cycle track

**'vena** *nf* vein; **essere in ~ di** be in the mood for. **~ poetica** poetic mood

**ve'nale** *a* venal; (*persona*) mercenary, venal

**ve'nato** *a* grainy

**vena'torio** *a* hunting *attrib*

**vena'tura** *nf* (*di legno*) grain; (*di foglia, marmo*) vein

**ven'demmia** *nf* grape harvest

**vendemmi'are** *vt* harvest

**vendemmia|'tore, -'trice** *nmf* grape-picker

**'vendere** *vt* sell

**'vendersi** *vr* sell oneself; **vendesi** for sale

**ven'detta** *nf* revenge. **~ trasversale** vendetta

**vendi'care** *vt* avenge

**vendi'carsi** *vr* take revenge, get one's revenge; ~ **di qcno** take one's vengeance on sb; ~ **di qcsa** take revenge for sth

**vendicativa'mente** *adv* vindictively

**vendica'tivo** *a* vindictive

**vendica|'tore, -'trice** *nmf* avenger

**'vendita** *nf* sale; **in** ~ on sale. ~ **all'asta** sale by auction. ~ **di beneficenza** bring and buy sale. ~ **per corrispondenza** mail-order; **azienda di** ~ ~ ~ mail-order company; **catalogo di** ~ ~ ~ mail-order catalogue. ~ **al dettaglio** retailing. ~ **all'ingrosso** wholesaling. ~ **al minuto** retailing. ~ **porta a porta** door-to-door selling. ~ **a rate** hire purchase, installment plan *Am*

**vendi|'tore, -'trice** *nmf* seller. ~ **ambulante** hawker, pedlar. ~ **al dettaglio** retailer. ~ **all'ingrosso** wholesaler. ~ **al mercato** market trader. ~ **al minuto** retailer

**ven'duto** *a* ⟨merce⟩ sold; ⟨fig: arbitro⟩ bent; **arbitro ~!** whose side are you on, ref!

**vene'rabile, vene'rando** *a* venerable

**vene'rare** *vt* revere

**venerazi'one** *nf* reverence

**venerdì** *nm inv* Friday; **di ~** on Fridays. **V~ Santo** Good Friday

**'Venere** *nf* Venus

**ve'nereo** *a* venereal

**'Veneto** *nm* Veneto

**'veneto** *a* from the Veneto

**Ve'nezia** *nf* Venice

**venezi'ano, -a** *a & nmf* Venetian ● *nf* ⟨persiana⟩ Venetian blind; *Culin* sweet bun

**Vene'zuela** *nm* Venezuela

**venezue'lano, -a** *a & nmf* Venezuelan

**'vengo** *vedi* **venire**

**veni'ale** *a* venial

**ve'nire** *vi* come; ⟨riuscire⟩ turn out; ⟨costare⟩ cost; ⟨in passivi⟩ be; **quanto viene?** how much is it?; **viene prodotto in serie** it's mass-produced; ⟨a sapere⟩ learn; ~ **in mente** occur; **mi è venuto un dubbio** I've just had a doubt; **gli è venuta la febbre** he's got a temperature; ~ **meno** ⟨svenire⟩ faint; ~ **meno a un contratto** go back on a contract, renege on a contract; ~ **via** come away; ⟨staccarsi⟩ come off; **mi viene da piangere** I feel like crying; **vieni a prendermi** come and pick me up; **vieni a trovarmi** come and see me; **nei giorni a ~** in [the] days to come

**ve'noso** *a* venous

**ven'taglio** *nm* fan

**ven'tata** *nf* gust [of wind]; *fig* breath

**ven'tenne** *a & nmf* twenty-year-old

**ven'tesimo** *a & nm* twentieth

**'venti** *a & nm* twenty

**venti'lare** *vt* ventilate, air; ~ **un'idea** give an idea an airing; **poco ventilato** ⟨stanza⟩ airless

**ventila'tore** *nm* fan

**ventilazi'one** *nf* ventilation

**ven'tina** *nf* **una ~** ⟨circa venti⟩ about twenty

**ventiquat'trore** *nf inv* ⟨valigia⟩ overnight case ● *adv* ~ **su ventiquattro** ⟨lavorare⟩ round-the-clock; ⟨aperto⟩ 24 hours

**'vento** *nm* wind; **c'è molto ~** it's very windy; **farsi ~** fan oneself. ~ **contrario** headwind. ~ **di prua** headwind. ~ **di traverso** crosswind

**'ventola** *nf* fan

**vento'lina** *nf* fan. ~ **di raffeddamento** *Comput* cooling fan

**ven'tosa** *nf* sucker

**ven'toso** *a* windy

**'ventre** *nm* stomach; ⟨fig: di terra⟩ bowels *pl*; **basso** ~ lower abdomen

**ventrico'lare** *a Med* ventricular

**ven'tricolo** *nm* ventricle

**ven'triloquo** *nm* ventriloquist

**ventu'nesimo** *a & nm* twenty-first

**ven'tuno** *a & nm* twenty-one

**ven'tura** *nf* fortune; **andare alla ~** trust to luck

**ven'turo** *a* next

**ve'nuta** *nf* coming. ~ **meno a** breaking

**'vera** *nf* ⟨anello⟩ wedding ring

**vera'mente** *adv* really

**ve'randa** *nf* veranda

**ver'bale** *a* verbal ● *nm* ⟨di riunione⟩ minutes *pl*. ~ **di contravvenzione** fine

**verbal'mente** *adv* verbally

**ver'bena** *nf* verbena

**'verbo** *nm* verb; **il V~** *Relig* the Word. ~ **ausiliare** auxiliary [verb]. ~ **modale** modal auxiliary

**ver'boso** *a* verbose

**ver'dastro** *a* greenish

**'verde** *a* green; ~ **d'invidia** green with envy ● *nm* green; ⟨vegetazione⟩ greenery; ⟨semaforo⟩ green light; **essere al ~** be broke. ~ **bottiglia** bottle green. ~ **oliva** olive green. ~ **pisello** pea green. ~ **pubblico** public parks *pl*

**verdeggi'ante** *a liter* verdant

**verde'mare** *a & nm inv* sea-green

**verde'rame** *nm* verdigris

**ver'detto** *nm* verdict. ~ **di assoluzione** not guilty verdict. ~ **di condanna** guilty verdict

**ver'done** *nm* greenfinch

**ver'dura** *nf* vegetables *pl*; **una ~** a vegetable; **verdure** *pl* **miste** mixed vegetables

**'verga** *nf* rod

**ver'gato** *a* lined

**vergi'nale** *a* virginal

**'vergine** *nf* virgin; *Astr* Virgo ● *a* virgin; ⟨cassetta⟩ blank

**verginità** *nf* virginity

**ver'gogna** *nf* shame; ⟨timidezza⟩ shyness

**vergo'gnarsi** *vr* feel ashamed; ⟨essere timido⟩ feel shy

**vergognosa'mente** *adv* shamefully

**vergo'gnoso** *a* ashamed; ⟨timido⟩ shy; ⟨disonorevole⟩ shameful

**veridicità** *nf* veracity

**ve'rifica** *nf* check. ~ **dei bilanci** audit. ~ **di cassa** cash check

**verifi'cabile** *a* verifiable

**verifi'care** *vt* check; verify ⟨teoria⟩

**verifi'carsi** *vr* come true

**verifica|'tore, -'trice** *nmf* checker

**ve'rismo** *nm* realism
**verità** *nf inv* truth
**veriti'ero** *a* truthful
**'verme** *nm* worm. **~ solitario** tapeworm
**vermi'celli** *nmpl* vermicelli *sg* (*pasta thinner than spaghetti*)
**ver'mifugo** *a* vermifugal ● *nm* vermifuge
**ver'miglio** *a* & *nm* vermilion
**'vermut** *nm inv* vermouth
**ver'nacolo** *nm* vernacular
**ver'nice** *nf* paint; (*trasparente*) varnish; (*pelle*) patent leather; *fig* veneer; **'~ fresca'** wet paint. **~ a spirito** spirit varnish
**vernici'are** *vt* paint; (*con vernice trasparente*) varnish
**vernicia'tura** *nf* painting; (*con vernice trasparente*) varnishing; (*strato*) paintwork; *fig* veneer
**vernis'sage** *nm inv* vernissage
**'vero** *a* true; (*autentico*) real; (*perfetto*) perfect; **è ~?** is that so?; **~ e proprio** full-blown; **sei stanca, ~?** you're tired, aren't you; **non ti piace, ~?** you don't like it, do you?. **~ cuoio** real leather ● *nm* truth; (*realtà*) life
**verosimigli'anza** *nf* plausibility
**vero'simile** *a* probable, likely
**verosimil'mente** *adv* probably
**ver'ruca** *nf* wart; (*sotto la pianta del piede*) verruca
**versa'mento** *nm* (*pagamento*) payment; (*in banca*) deposit
**ver'sante** *nm* slope
**ver'sare** *vt* pour; (*spargere*) shed; (*rovesciare*) spill; pay (*denaro*); (*in banca*) pay in ● *vi* (*trovarsi*) be
**ver'sarsi** *vr* spill; (*sfociare*) flow
**ver'satile** *a* versatile
**versatilità** *nf* versatility
**ver'sato** *a* (*pratico*) versed
**ver'setto** *nm* verse
**versifica'|tore, -'trice** *nmf* versifier
**versi'one** *nf* version; (*traduzione*) translation; **'~ integrale'** 'unabridged version'; **~ originale** original version. **'~ ridotta'** 'abridged version'. **~ teatrale** dramatization
**'verso**[1] *nm* verse; (*grido*) cry; (*gesto*) gesture; (*senso*) direction; (*modo*) manner; **fare il ~ a qcno** ape sb; **non c'è ~ di** there is no way of. **versi** *pl* **sciolti** blank verse
**'verso**[2] *prep* towards; (*nei pressi di*) round about; **~ dove?** which way?
**'vertebra** *nf* vertebra
**verte'brale** *a* vertebral
**verte'brato** *nm* vertebrate
**ver'tenza** *nf* dispute. **~ sindacale** industrial dispute
**'vertere** *vi* **~ su** focus on
**verti'cale** *a* vertical; (*in parole crociate*) down ● *nm* vertical ● *nf* handstand; **fare la ~** do a handstand
**vertical'mente** *adv* vertically
**'vertice** *nm* summit; *Math* vertex; **conferenza al ~** summit conference; **incontro al ~** summit meeting
**ver'tigine** *nf* dizziness; *Med* vertigo; **ver-**

**tigini** *pl* giddy spells; **aver le vertigini** feel dizzy
**vertiginosa'mente** *adv* dizzily
**vertigi'noso** *a* dizzy; (*velocità*) breakneck; (*prezzi*) sky-high; (*scollatura*) plunging
**'vescia** *nf* puffball
**ve'scica** *nf* bladder; (*sulla pelle*) blister
**'vescovo** *nm* bishop
**'vespa** *nf* wasp
**vespasi'ano** *nm* urinal
**'vespro** *nm* vespers *pl*
**ves'sare** *vt fml* oppress
**ves'sillo** *nm* standard
**ve'staglia** *nf* dressing gown, robe *Am*
**'veste** *nf* dress; (*rivestimento*) covering; **in ~ di** in the capacity of; **in ~ ufficiale** in an official capacity. **~ da camera** dressing gown, robe *Am*. **~ editoriale** layout. **~ tipografica** typographical design
**vesti'ario** *nm* clothing
**ve'stibolo** *nm* hall
**ve'stigio** *nm* (*pl m* vestigi, *pl f* vestigia) trace
**ve'stire** *vt* dress
**ve'stirsi** *vr* get dressed; **~ da** dress up as a
**ve'stito** *a* dressed ● *nm* (*da uomo*) suit; (*da donna*) dress; **vestiti** *pl* clothes. **~ da sposa** wedding dress. **~ da uomo** suit
**vete'rano, -a** *a* & *nmf* veteran
**veteri'nario, -a** *a* veterinary ● *nm* veterinary surgeon ● *nf* veterinary science
**'veto** *nm inv* veto
**ve'traio** *nm* glazier
**ve'trato, -a** *a* glazed ● *nf* big window; (*in chiesa*) stained-glass window; (*porta*) glass door
**vetre'ria** *nf* glass works
**ve'trina** *nf* [shop-]window; (*mobile*) display cabinet
**vetri'nista** *nmf* window dresser
**ve'trino** *nm* (*di microscopio*) slide
**vetri'olo** *nm* vitriol
**'vetro** *nm* glass; (*di finestra, porta*) pane. **~ di sicurezza** safety glass
**vetro'resina** *nf* fibreglass
**ve'troso** *a* vitreous
**'vetta** *nf* peak
**vet'tore** *nm* vector
**vetto'vaglie** *nfpl* provisions
**vet'tura** *nf* coach; (*ferroviaria*) coach, carriage; *Auto* car. **~ d'epoca** vintage car
**vettu'rino** *nm* coachman
**vezzeggi'are** *vt* fondle
**vezzeggia'tivo** *nm* pet name
**'vezzo** *nm* habit; (*attrattiva*) charm; **vezzi** *pl* (*moine*) affectation
**vez'zoso** *a* charming; *pej* affected
**VF** *abbr* (*Vigili del Fuoco*) fire brigade, fire department *Am*
**vi** *pers pron* you; (*riflessivo*) yourselves; (*reciproco*) each other; (*tra più persone*) one another; **vi ho dato un libro** I gave you a book; **lavatevi le mani** wash your hands; **eccovi!** here you are! ● *adv* = **ci**
**'via**[1] *nf* street, road; *fig* way; *Anat* tract; **in ~**

**di** in the course of; **per ~ di** on account of; **per ~ aerea** by airmail. **V~ Lattea** *Astr* Milky Way. **~ di mezzo** halfway house. **~ respiratoria** *Anat* airway. **~ d'uscita** let-out

**'via²** *adv* away; (*fuori*) out; **andar ~** go away; (*macchia:*) come off. come out; **e così ~** and so on; **e ~ dicendo** and whatnot; **~ ~ che** as ● *int* **~!** go away!; *Sport* go!; (*andiamo*) come on!; **~,** **non ci credo** come off it *or* come on, I don't believe it ● *nm* starting signal

**viabilità** *nf* road conditions *pl*; (*rete*) road network; (*norme*) road and traffic laws *pl*

**via'card** *nf inv* motorway card

**vi'ado** *nm* (*pl* **viados**) rent boy

**via'dotto** *nm* viaduct

**viaggi'are** *vi* travel; **il treno viaggia con 20 minuti di ritardo** the train is 20 minutes late

**viaggia'|tore, -'trice** *nmf* traveller

**vi'aggio** *nm* journey; (*breve*) trip; **buon ~!** safe journey!, have a good trip!; **fare un ~** go on a journey; **essere in ~** be underway; **mettersi in ~** get underway. **~ d'affari** business trip. **~ di lavoro** working trip **~ di nozze** honeymoon. **~ organizzato** package tour

**vi'ale** *nm* avenue; (*privato*) drive

**via'letto** *nm* path

**via'vai** *nm* coming and going

**vi'brante** *a* vibrant

**vi'brare** *vi* vibrate; (*fremere*) quiver

**vibra'tore** *nm* vibrator

**vibra'torio** *a* vibratory

**vibrazi'one** *nf* vibration

**vi'cario** *nm* vicar

**'vice** *nmf* deputy

**vice+** *pref* vice+

**vicecoman'dante** *nm* *Mil* second in command

**vicediret|'tore, -'trice** *nm* assistant manager ● *nf* assistant manageress

**vi'cenda** *nf* event; **a ~** (*fra due*) each other; (*a turno*) in turn[s]

**vicendevol'mente** *adv* each other

**vice'preside** *nmf* vice-principal

**vicepresi'dente** *nm* vice-president; *Comm* vice-chairman, vice-president *Am*

**vicepresi'denza** *nf* vice-presidency; *Sch* deputy head's office

**vicerè** *nm inv* viceroy

**viceret'tore** *nm* vice-chancellor

**vice'versa** *adv* vice versa

**vi'chingo, -a** *a & nmf* Viking

**vi'cina** *nf* neighbour

**vici'nanza** *nf* nearness; **vicinanze** (*pl: paraggi*) neighbourhood

**vici'nato** *nm* neighbourhood; (*vicini*) neighbours *pl*

**vi'cino, -a** *a* near; (*accanto*) next ● *adv* near, close ● *prep* **~ a** near [to] ● *nmf* neighbour. **~ di casa** nextdoor neighbour

**vicissi'tudine** *nf* vicissitude

**'vicolo** *nm* alley. **~ cieco** *anche fig* blind alley

**'video** *nm* (*musicale*) video; (*schermo*) screen. **~ interattivo** interactive video

**video'camera** *nf* camcorder

**videocas'setta** *nf* video, video cassette

**videoci'tofono** *nm* video entry phone

**video'clip** *nm inv* video clip

**videoconfe'renza** *nf* videoconference

**videogi'oco** *nm* video game

**video'leso, -a** *a* visually handicapped ● *nmf* visually handicapped person

**videoregistra'tore** *nm* videorecorder

**videoscrit'tura** *nf* word processing

**videosorvegli'anza** *nf* video surveillance

**video'teca** *nf* video library

**video'tel**ᴿ *nm* ≈ Videotex ᴿ

**videote'lefono** *nm* view phone

**videotermi'nale** *nm* visual display unit, VDU

**vidi'mare** *vt* authenticate

**vi'eni** *vedi* **venire**

**Vi'enna** *nf* Vienna

**vien'nese** *a & nmf* Viennese

**vie'tare** *vt* forbid; **~ qcsa a qcno** forbid sb sth

**vie'tato** *a* forbidden; **sosta vietata** no parking; **~ fumare** no smoking; **~ ai minori di 18 anni** prohibited to children under the age of 18

**Vi'etnam** *nm* Vietnam

**vietna'mita** *a & nmf* Vietnamese

**vi'gente** *a* in force

**'vigere** *vi* be in force

**vigi'lante** *a* vigilant

**vigi'lanza** *nf* vigilance; (*sorveglianza*) (*a scuola*) supervision; (*di polizia*) surveillance. **~ notturna** night security guards *pl*. **~ urbana** traffic police (*in towns*)

**vigi'lare** *vt* keep an eye on ● *vi* keep watch

**vigi'lato, -a** *a* under surveillance ● *nmf* person under police surveillance. **~ speciale** person under special police surveillance

**'vigile** *a* watchful ● *nm* **~ [urbano]** traffic policeman. **~ del fuoco** fireman. **vigili** *pl* **del fuoco** firemen, fire brigade. **vigili** *pl* **urbani** traffic police (*in towns*)

**vi'gilia** *nf* eve; *Relig* fast. **~ di Natale** Christmas Eve

**vigliacca'mente** *adv* in a cowardly way

**vigliacche'ria** *nf* cowardice

**vigli'acco, -a** *a* cowardly ● *nmf* coward

**'vigna** *nf*, **vi'gneto** *nm* vineyard

**vi'gnetta** *nf* cartoon

**vignet'tista** *nm* cartoonist

**vi'gogna** *nf* (*tessuto*) vicuña

**vi'gore** *nm* vigour; **entrare in ~** come into force; **essere in ~** be in force

**vigorosa'mente** *adv* energetically

**vigo'roso** *a* vigorous

**'vile** *a* cowardly; (*abietto*) vile

**vili'pendio** *nm* scorn, contempt

**'villa** *nf* villa

**vil'laggio** *nm* village. **~ olimpico** Olympic village. **~ residenziale** commuter town. **~ satellite** satellite village. **~ turistico** holiday village

**villa'nia** *nf* rudeness

**vil'lano** *a* rude ● *nm* boor; (*contadino*) peasant

**villeggi'ante** *nmf* holiday-maker

**villeggi'are** *vi* spend one's holidays

**villeggia'tura** *nf* holiday[s] [*pl*]. vacation *Am*

**vil'letta** *nf* small detached house. **~ bifamiliare** semi-detached house. **villette** *pl* **a schiera** terraced houses

**vil'lino** *nm* detached house

**vil'loso** *a* hairy

**vil'mente** *adv* in a cowardly way; (*in modo spreggevole*) contemptibly

**viltà** *nf* cowardice

**'vimine** *nm* wicker; **sedia di vimini** wicker chair

**vi'naio, -a** *nmf* wine merchant

**'vincere** *vt* win; (*sconfiggere*) beat; (*superare*) overcome

**'vincita** *nf* win; (*somma vinta*) winnings *pl*

**vinci|'tore, -'trice** *nmf* winner; (*di battaglia*) victor, winner ● *a* winning, victorious

**vinco'lante** *a* binding

**vinco'lare** *vt* bind; *Comm* tie up

**vinco'lato** *a* *Fin* nonredeemable; **deposito ~** fixed deposit, term deposit

**'vincolo** *nm* bond

**vi'nicolo** *a* wine *attrib*

**vi'nile** *nm* vinyl

**vi'nilico** *a* vinyl

**vinil'pelle**[R] *nm* Leatherette[R]

**'vino** *nm* wine. **~ d'annata** vintage wine. **~ bianco** white wine. **~ brûlé** mulled wine. **~ della casa** house wine. **~ da dessert** dessert wine. **~ nuovo** new wine. **~ rosato** rosé [wine]. **~ rosé** rosé [wine]. **~ rosso** red wine. **~ spumante** sparkling wine. **~ da taglio** blending wine. **~ da tavola** table wine

**vin'santo** *nm* dessert wine from Tuscany

**'vinto** *pp di* vincere

**vi'ola** *nf* *Bot* violet; *Mus* viola. **~ del pensiero** *Bot* pansy

**vio'laceo** *a* purplish; (*labbra*) blue

**vio'lare** *vt* violate

**violazi'one** *nf* violation. **~ di contratto** breach of contract. **~ di domicilio** breaking and entering

**violen'tare** *vt* rape

**violente'mente** *adv* violently

**vio'lento** *a* violent

**vio'lenza** *nf* violence. **~ carnale** rape

**vio'letto, -a** *a & nm* (*colore*) violet ● *nf* violet

**violi'nista** *nmf* violinist

**vio'lino** *nm* violin

**violon'cello** *nm* cello

**vi'ottolo** *nm* path

**'vipera** *nf* viper

**vi'raggio** *nm* *Phot* toning; *Naut, Aeron* turn

**vi'rale** *a* viral

**vi'rare** *vi* turn; (*nave:*) put about; **~ di bordo** change course

**vi'rata** *nf* (*di aereo*) turning; (*di nave*) coming about; (*nel nuoto*) turn; *fig* change of direction

**'virgola** *nf* comma; *Math* [decimal] point; **punto e ~** semicolon; **quattro ~ due (4,2)** (*decimali*) four point two (4.2)

**virgo'lette** *nfpl* inverted commas, quotation marks

**vi'rile** *a* virile; (*da uomo*) manly

**virilità** *nf* virility; manliness

**viril'mente** *adv* in a manly way

**vi'rologo** *nm* virologist

**virtù** *nf inv* virtue; **in ~ di** ⟨legge⟩ under

**virtu'ale** *a* virtual

**virtual'mente** *adv* virtually

**virtuo'sismo** *nm* bravura

**virtu'oso** *a* virtuous ● *nm* virtuoso

**viru'lento** *a* virulent

**'virus** *nm* virus

**visa'gista** *nmf* beautician

**visce'rale** *a* visceral; ⟨odio⟩ deep-seated; ⟨reazione⟩ gut

**'viscere** *nm* internal organ ● *nfpl* guts

**'vischio** *nm* mistletoe

**vischi'oso** *a* viscous; (*appiccicoso*) sticky

**'viscido** *a* slimy

**vi'sconte** *nm* viscount

**viscon'tessa** *nf* viscountess

**vi'scoso** *a* viscous

**vi'sibile** *a* visible

**visi'bilio** *nm* profusion; **andare in ~** go into ecstasies

**visibilità** *nf* visibility; **scarsa ~** poor visibility

**visi'era** *nf* (*di elmo*) visor; (*di berretto*) peak

**visio'nare** *vt* examine; *Cinema* screen

**visio'nario, -a** *a & nmf* visionary

**visi'one** *nf* vision; **prima ~** *Cinema* first showing; **seconda ~** re-release, second showing. **~ notturna** night vision

**'visita** *nf* visit; (*breve*) call; *Med* examination; **fare ~ a qcno** pay sb a visit. **~ di controllo** *Med* checkup. **~ di convenienza** courtesy visit. **~ doganale** customs inspection. **~ a domicilio** home visit, call-out. **~ fiscale** tax inspection. **~ guidata** guided tour. **~ lampo** flying visit. **~ di leva** medical examination

**visi'tare** *vt* visit; (*brevemente*) call on; *Med* examine

**visita|'tore, -'trice** *nmf* visitor

**visiva'mente** *adv* visually

**vi'sivo** *a* visual

**'viso** *nm* face. **~ pallido** paleface

**vi'sone** *nm* mink

**'vispo** *a* lively

**vis'suto** *pp di* vivere ● *a* experienced

**'vista** *nf* sight; (*veduta*) view; **a ~ d'occhio** ⟨crescere⟩ visibly; ⟨estendersi⟩ as far as the eye can see; **in ~ di** in view of; **perdere di ~ qcno** lose sight of sb; *fig* lose touch with sb; **a prima ~** at first sight

**'visto** *pp di* vedere ● *nm* visa. **~ di entrata o di ingresso** entry visa, entry permit. **~ d'uscita** exit visa ● *conj* **~ che...** seeing that...

**vistosa'mente** *adv* conspicuously

**vi'stoso** *a* showy; (*notevole*) considerable

**visu'ale** *a* visual

**visualiz'zare** *vt* visualize; *Comput* display

**visualizza'tore** *nm Comput* display, VDU. ~ **a cristalli liquidi** *Comput* liquid crystal display

**visualizzazi'one** *nf Comput* display

**'vita** *nf* life; (*durata della vita*) lifetime; *Anat* waist; **a ~** for life; **essere in fin di ~** be at death's door; **essere in ~** be alive; **fare la bella ~** lead the good life; **costo della ~** cost of living. **~ eterna** eternal life. **~ media** *Biol* life expectancy. **~ mondana** high life; **fare ~ ~** lead the high life. **~ notturna** night life. **~ terrena** *Relig* life on earth

**vi'taccia** *nf* slog

**vi'tale** *a* vital

**vitalità** *nf* vitality

**vita'lizio** *a* life *attrib* ● *nm* [life] annuity

**vita'mina** *nf* vitamin

**vita'minico** *a* vitamin-enriched

**vitaminiz'zato** *a* vitamin-enriched

**'vite** *nf Mech* screw; *Bot* vine; **giro di ~** *fig* turn of the screw. **~ canadese** Virginia creeper. **~ di coda** *Aeron* tailspin. **~ perpetua** endless screw

**vi'tella** *nf* (*animale*) calf; (*carne*) veal

**vi'tello** *nm* calf; (*carne*) veal; (*pelle*) calfskin. **~ di latte** milk-fed veal. **~ tonnato** *sliced veal with tuna, anchovy, oil and lemon sauce*

**vi'ticcio** *nm* tendril

**viticol'tore** *nm* wine grower

**viticol'tura** *nf* wine growing

**vi'tino** *nm* narrow waist; **~ di vespa** slender little waist

**'vitreo** *a* vitreous; (*sguardo*) glassy

**'vittima** *nf* victim

**'vitto** *nm* food; (*pasti*) board. **~ e alloggio** board and lodging

**vit'toria** *nf* victory

**vittori'ano** *a* Victorian

**vittoriosa'mente** *adv* victoriously, triumphantly

**vittori'oso** *a* victorious

**vitupe'rare** *vt* vituperate

**vitu'perio** *nm* insult

**vi'uzza** *nf* narrow lane

**'viva** *int* hurrah!; **~ la Regina!** long live the Queen!

**vi'vace** *a* vivacious; (*mente*) lively; (*colore*) bright

**vivace'mente** *adv* vivaciously

**vivacità** *nf* vivacity; (*di mente*) liveliness; (*di colore*) brightness

**vivaciz'zare** *vt* liven up

**vi'vaio** *nm* nursery; (*per pesci*) pond; *fig* breeding ground

**viva'mente** *adv* (*ringraziare*) warmly

**vi'vanda** *nf* food; (*piatto*) dish

**vi'vente** *a* living ● *nmpl* **i viventi** the living

**'vivere** *vi* live; **~ di** live on; **vive** *Typ* stet ● *vt* (*passare*) go through ● *nm* life; **modo di ~** way of life

**'viveri** *nmpl* provisions

**vivida'mente** *adv* vividly

**'vivido** *a* vivid

**vivi'paro** *a* viviparous

**vivise'zionare** *vt* vivisect

**vivisezi'one** *nf* vivisection

**'vivo** *a* alive; (*vivente*) living; (*vivace*) lively; (*colore*) bright; **~ e vegeto** alive and kicking; **farsi ~** keep in touch; (*arrivare*) turn up ● *nm* **colpire qcno sul ~** cut sb to the quick; **dal ~** (*trasmissione*) live; (*disegnare*) from life; **i vivi** the living

**vizi'are** *vt* spoil (*bambino ecc*); (*guastare*) vitiate

**vizi'ato** *a* spoilt; (*aria*) stale

**'vizio** *nm* vice; (*cattiva abitudine*) bad habit; (*difetto*) flaw. **~ capitale** deadly sin. **~ di forma** legal technicality. **~ procedurale** procedural error

**vizi'oso** *a* dissolute; (*difettoso*) faulty; **circolo ~** vicious circle

**'vizzo** *a* (*pelle*) wrinked; (*pianta*) withered

**V.le** *abbr* (**viale**) Ave

**vocabo'lario** *nm* dictionary; (*lessico*) vocabulary

**vo'cabolo** *nm* word

**vo'cale** *a* vocal ● *nf* vowel

**vo'calico** *a* (*corde*) vocal; (*suono*) vowel *attrib*

**vocazi'one** *nf* vocation

**'voce** *nf* voice; (*diceria*) rumour; (*di bilancio, dizionario*) entry. **~ bianca** *Mus* treble voice. **~ fuori campo** voiceover

**voci'are** *vi* (*spettegolare*) gossip ● *nm* buzz of conversation

**vocife'rare** *vi* shout; **si vocifera che...** it is rumoured that...

**'vodka** *nf inv* vodka

**'voga** *nf* rowing; (*lena*) enthusiasm; (*moda*) vogue; **essere in ~** be in vogue

**vo'gare** *vi* row. **~ a bratto** scull. **~ di coppia** scull

**voga'tore** *nm* oarsman; (*attrezzo*) rowing machine

**'voglia** *nf* desire; (*volontà*) will; (*della pelle*) birthmark; **aver ~ di fare qcsa** feel like doing sth; **morire dalla ~ di qcsa** be dying for sth; **di buona ~** willingly

**'voglio** *vedi* **volere**

**vogli'oso** *a* (*occhi, persona*) covetous; **essere ~ di qcsa** want sth

**'voi** *pers pron* you; **siete ~?** is that you?; **l'avete fatto ~?** did you do it yourself?

**voia'ltri** *pers pron* you

**vo'lano** *nm* shuttlecock; *Mech* flywheel

**vo'lant** *nm inv* valance

**vo'lante** *a* flying; (*foglio*) loose ● *nm* steering-wheel

**volanti'nare** *vi* hand out leaflets

**volan'tino** *nm* leaflet

**vo'lare** *vi* fly

**vo'lata** *nf Sport* final sprint; **di ~** in a rush

**vo'latile** *a* (*liquido*) volatile ● *nm* bird

**volatiliz'zarsi** *vr* vanish

**vol-au-'vent** *nm inv* vol-au-vent

**vo'lée** *nf inv Tennis* volley

**vo'lente** *a* ~ **o nolente** whether you like it or not

**volente'roso** *a* willing

**volenti'eri** *adv* willingly: ~**!** with pleasure!

**vo'lere** *vt* want; (*chiedere di*) ask for; (*aver bisogno di*) need: **non voglio** I don't want to; **vuole che lo faccia** he wants me to do it; **fai come vuoi** do as you like; **se tuo padre vuole, ti porto al cinema** if your father agrees, I'll take you to the cinema; **questa pianta vuole molte cure** this plant needs a lot of care; **vorrei un caffè** I'd like a coffee; **la leggenda vuole che...** legend has it that...; **la vuoi smettere?** will you stop that!; **senza** ~ without meaning to; **voler bene/ male a qcno** love/have something against sb; **voler dire** mean; **ci vuole il latte** we need milk; **ci vuole tempo/pazienza** it takes time/patience; **volerne a** have a grudge against; **vuoi... vuoi...** either... or... ● *nm* will; **voleri** *pl* wishes

**vol'gare** *a* vulgar; (*popolare*) common

**volgarità** *nf* vulgarity; **dire** ~ use vulgar language, be vulgar

**volgariz'zare** *vt* popularize

**volgarizzazi'one** *nf* popularization

**volgar'mente** *adv* (*grossolanamente*) vulgarly; (*comunemente*) commonly, popularly

**'volgere** *vt/i* turn

**'volgersi** *vr* turn [round]; ~ **a** (*dedicarsi*) take up

**'volgo** *nm* common people

**voli'era** *nf* aviary

**voli'tivo** *a* strong-minded

**'volo** *nm* flight; **al** ~ ⟨*fare qcsa*⟩ quickly; ⟨*prendere qcsa*⟩ in mid-air; **alzarsi in** ~ ⟨*uccello:*⟩ take off; **in** ~ airborne. ~ **di anda-ta** outward flight. ~ **charter** charter flight. ~ **diretto** direct flight. ~ **di linea** scheduled flight. ~ **nazionale** domestic flight. ~ **di ritorno** return flight. ~ **strumentale** flying on instruments. ~ **a vela** gliding

**volontà** *nf inv* will; (*desiderio*) wish; **a** ~ ⟨*mangiare*⟩ as much as you like

**volontaria'mente** *adv* voluntarily

**volon'tario** *a* voluntary ● *nm* volunteer

**volonte'roso** *a* willing

**'volpe** *nf* fox

**vol'pino** *a* ⟨*astuzia*⟩ fox-like ● *nm* ⟨*cane*⟩ Pomeranian

**volt** *nm inv* volt

**'volta** *nf* time; (*turno*) turn; (*curva*) bend; *Archit* vault; **4 volte 4** 4 times 4; **a volte, qualche** ~ sometimes; **c'era una** ~**...** once upon a time, there was...; **una** ~ once; **due volte** twice; **tre/quattro volte** three/four times; **una** ~ **per tutte** once and for all; **una** ~ **ogni tanto** every so often; **uno alla** ~ one at a time; **alla** ~ **di** in the direction of. ~ **a botte** barrel vault. ~ **celeste** vault of heaven. ~ **cranica** cranial vault. ~ **a crociera** groin vault. ~ **a vela** ribbed vault. ~ **a ventaglio** fan vault

**volta'faccia** *nm inv* volte-face

**voltagab'bana** *mf inv* turncoat

**vol'taggio** *nm* voltage

**vol'tare** *vt/i* turn; (*rigirare*) turn round; (*rivoltare*) turn over; ~ **pagina** *fig* start with a clean sheet

**vol'tarsi** *vr* turn [round]

**volta'stomaco** *nm* nausea; *fig* disgust

**volteggi'are** *vi* circle; (*ginnastica*) vault

**'volto** *pp di* **volgere** ● *nm* face; **mi ha mostrato il suo vero** ~ he revealed his true colours

**vol'tura** *nf* (*catastale*) transfer of property. ~ **di contratto** transfer of contract

**vo'lubile** *a* fickle

**volubil'mente** *adv* in a fickle way, inconstantly

**vo'lume** *nm* volume. ~ **di gioco** *Sport* possession

**volumi'noso** *a* voluminous

**vo'luta** *nf* (*spirale*) spiral; (*di capitello*) volute

**voluta'mente** *adv* deliberately

**vo'luto** *a* deliberate, intended

**voluttà** *nf* voluptuousness

**volutt'ario** *a* non-essential; **beni** *pl* **voluttuari** non-essentials

**voluttu'oso** *a* voluptuous

**vomi'tare** *vt* vomit, be sick

**vomi'tevole** *a* nauseating

**'vomito** *nm* vomit

**'vongola** *nf* clam

**vo'race** *a* voracious

**vorace'mente** *adv* voraciously

**vo'ragine** *nf* abyss

**vor'rei** *vedi* **volere**

**'vortice** *nm* whirl; (*gorgo*) whirlpool; (*di vento*) whirlwind

**vorticosa'mente** *adv* in whirls

**'vostro** (**il** ~ *m*, **la vostra** *f*, **i vostri** *mpl*, **le vostre** *fpl*) *poss a* your; **è vostra questa macchina?** is this car yours?; **un** ~ **amico** a friend of yours; ~ **padre** your father ● *poss pron* yours; **i vostri** your folk

**vo'tante** *nmf* voter

**vo'tare** *vi* vote

**votazi'one** *nf* voting; *Sch* marks *pl.* ~ **di fiducia** *Pol. fig* vote of confidence. ~ **a scrutinio segreto** secret ballot

**'voto** *nm* vote; *Sch* mark; *Relig* vow. ~ **decisivo** casting vote

**vs.** *abbr Comm* (**vostro**) yours

**'vudu** *nm inv* voodoo

**vul'canico** *a* volcanic

**vul'cano** *nm* volcano. ~ **intermittente** dormant volcano. ~ **spento** extinct volcano

**vulne'rabile** *a* vulnerable

**vulnerabilità** *nf* vulnerability

**'vulva** *nf* vulva

**vuo'tare** *vt* empty

**vuo'tarsi** *vr* empty

**vu'oto** *a* empty; (*non occupato*) vacant; ~ **di** (*sprovvisto*) devoid of ● *nm* empty space; *Phys* vacuum; *fig* void; **assegno a** ~ dud cheque; **sotto** ~ ⟨*prodotto*⟩ vacuum-packed. ~ **d'aria** air pocket. ~ **a perdere** no deposit. ~ **a rendere** ⟨*bottiglia*⟩ returnable

**W** *abbr* (**viva**) long live
**'wafer** *nm inv* (*biscotto*) wafer
**wagon-'lit** *nm inv* sleeping car
**walkie-'talkie** *nm inv* walkie-talkie
**'water** *nm inv* toilet, loo *fam*
**watt** *nm inv* watt
**wat'tora** *nm inv* Phys watt-hour

**WC** *nm* WC
**week'end** *nm inv* weekend
**'welter** *a & nm inv* (*in pugilato*) welterweight
**'western** *a inv* cowboy *attrib* ● *nm inv* Cinema western
**'whisky** *nm inv* whisky. ~ **di malto** malt [whisky]

**xenofo'bia** *nf* xenophobia
**xe'nofobo, -a** *a* xenophobic ● *nmf* xenophobe
**xe'res** *nm inv* sherry
**xero'copia** *nf* xerox

**xerocopi'are** *vt* photocopy
**xerocopia'trice** *nf* photocopier
**xilofo'nista** *nmf* xylophone player
**xi'lofono** *nm* xylophone

# Yy

**yacht** *nm inv* yacht
**yak** *nm inv* Zool yak
**'yankee** *nmf inv* Yank
**'Yemen** *nm* Yemen
**yeme'nita** *nmf* Yemeni
**yen** *nm inv* yen
**'yeti** *nm* yeti

**'yiddish** *a inv & nm* Yiddish
**'yoga** *nm* yoga ● *a inv* yoga *attrib*
**yogurt** *nm inv* yoghurt
**yogurti'era** *nf* yoghurt-maker
**'yorkshire** *nm inv* (*cane*) Yorkshire terrier
**yo-'yo** [R] *nm inv* yoyo
**yup'pismo** *nm* yuppiedom

# Zz

**zaba[gl]i'one** *nm* zabaglione (*dessert made from eggs, wine or marsala and sugar*)

**'zacchera** *nf* (*schizzo*) splash of mud

**zaf'fata** *nf* whiff; (*di fumo*) cloud

**zaffe'rano** *nm* saffron

**zaf'firo** *nm* sapphire

**'zagara** *nf* orange-blossom

**'zaino** *nm* rucksack

**'zampa** *nf* leg; **a quattro zampe** (*animale*) four-legged; (*carponi*) on all fours. **zampe pl di gallina** *fig* crow's feet

**zam'pata** *nf* paw; **dare una ~ a** hit with its paw

**zampet'tare** *vi* scamper

**zam'petto** *nm* Culin knuckle

**zampil'lante** *a* spurting

**zampil'lare** *vi* spurt

**zam'pillo** *nm* spurt

**zam'pino** *nm* paw; **mettere lo ~ in** *fig* have a hand in

**zam'pogna** *nf* bagpipe

**zampo'gnaro** *nm* piper

**zam'pone** *nfpl* stuffed pig's trotter with lentils

**'zanna** *nf* fang; (*di elefante*) tusk

**zan'zara** *nf* mosquito

**zanzari'era** *nf* (*velo*) mosquito net; (*su finestra*) insect screen

**'zappa** *nf* hoe; **darsi la ~ sui piedi** *fig* shoot oneself in the foot

**zap'pare** *vt* hoe

**zap'pata** *nf* **dare una ~ a** hit with a hoe

**zappet'tare** *vt* hoe

**zar** *nm inv* tzar

**za'rina** *nf* tzarina

**za'rista** *a & nmf* tzarist

**'zattera** *nf* raft

**zatte'roni** *nmpl* (*scarpe*) wedge shoes

**za'vorra** *nf* ballast; *fig* dead wood

**zavor'rare** *vt* load with ballast

**'zazzera** *nf* mop of hair

**'zebra** *nf* zebra; **zebre** *pl* (*passaggio pedonale*) zebra crossing, crosswalk *Am*

**ze'brato** *a* (*tessuto*) with black and white stripes

**'zecca¹** *nf* mint; **nuovo di ~** brand-new

**'zecca²** *nf* (*parassita*) tick

**zec'chino** *nm* sequin; **oro ~** pure gold

**ze'lante** *a* zealous

**'zelo** *nm* zeal

**'zenit** *nm* zenith

**'zenzero** *nm* ginger

**'zeppa** *nf* wedge

**'zeppo** *a* packed full; **pieno ~ di** crammed *o* packed with

**zer'bino** *nm* doormat

**'zero** *nm* zero, nought; (*in calcio*) nil; *Tennis* love; **due a ~** (*in partite*) two nil; **rico-minciare da ~** *fig* start again from scratch; **sparare a ~ su qcno** *fig* lay into sb; **avere il morale sotto ~** *fig* be down in the dumps

**'zeta** *nf* zed. zee *Am*

**'zia** *nf* aunt

**zibel'lino** *nm* sable

**zi'gano, -a** *a & nmf* gypsy

**'zigolo** *nm* Zool bunting

**'zigomo** *nm* cheek-bone

**zigri'nato** *a* (*pelle*) grained; (*metallo*) milled

**zig'zag** *nm inv* zigzag; **andare a ~** zigzag

**Zim'babwe** *nm* Zimbabwe

**zim'bello** *nm* decoy; (*oggetto di scherno*) laughing-stock

**'zinco** *nm* zinc

**zinga'resco** *a* gypsy *attrib*

**'zingaro, -a** *nmf* gypsy

**'zio** *nm* uncle

**'zippo** *nm sl* lighter

**zi'tella** *nf* spinster; *pej* old maid

**zitel'lona** *nf pej* old maid

**zit'tire** *vi* fall silent ● *vt* silence

**'zitto** *a* silent; **sta' ~!** keep quiet!

**ziz'zania** *nf* (*discordia*) discord; **seminare ~** cause trouble

**'zoccola** *nf vulg* whore

**'zoccolo** *nm* clog; (*di cavallo*) hoof; (*di terra*) clump; (*di parete*) skirting board, baseboard *Am*; (*di colonna*) base. **~ duro** *Pol* hard core. **~ fesso** cloven foot, cloven hoof

**zodia'cale** *a* of the zodiac; **segno ~** sign of the zodiac, birth sign

**zo'diaco** *nm* zodiac

**zolfa'nello** *nm* match

**'zolfo** *nm* sulphur

**'zolla** *nf* clod; (*di zucchero*) lump

**zol'letta** *nf* sugar cube, sugar lump

**'zombi** *nmf inv fig* zombi

**zom'pare** *vi sl* bonk

**'zona** *nf* zone; (*area*) area. **~ denuclea-rizzata** nuclear-free zone. **~ di depressione** area of low pressure. **~ disastrata** disaster area. **~ disco** area for parking discs only. **~ erogena** erogenous zone. **~ giorno** living area. **~ industriale** industrial estate. **~ notte** sleeping area. **~ pedonale** pedestrian precinct. **~ a traffico limitato** restricted traffic area. **~ verde** green belt

**zonizzazi'one** *nf* zoning

**'zonzo: andare a ~** stroll about

**zoo** *nm inv* zoo

**zoolo'gia** *nf* zoology

**zoo'logico** *a* zoological

**zo'ologo, -a** *nmf* zoologist

**zoosa'fari** *nm inv* safari park

**zootec'nia** *nf* animal husbandry

**zoo'tecnico** *a* ⟨*progresso*⟩ in animal husbandry; **patrimonio ~** livestock

**zoppi'cante** *a* limping; *fig* shaky

**zoppi'care** *vi* limp; (*essere debole*) be shaky

**'zoppo,.-a** *a* lame ● *nmf* cripple

**'zotico** *a* uncouth

**zoti'cone** *nm* boor

**zu'ava** *nf* **calzoni** *pl* **alla ~** plus-fours

**'zucca** *nf* marrow; (*fam: testa*) head; (*fam: persona*) thickie; **cos'hai in quella ~?** haven't you got anything between your ears?

**zuc'cata** *nf* **prendere una ~** *fam* hit one's head

**zucche'rare** *vt* sugar

**zuccherato** *a* sugared; **non ~** ⟨*succo d'arancia ecc*⟩ unsweetened

**zuccheri'era** *nf* sugar bowl

**zuccheri'ficio** *nm* sugar refinery

**zucche'rino** *a* sugary ● *nm* sugar cube, sugar lump; *fig* sweetener; **essere uno ~** *fig* ⟨*persona:*⟩ be a softy; ⟨*cosa:*⟩ be a cinch

**'zucchero** *nm* sugar. **~ di canna** cane sugar. **~ greggio** brown sugar. **~ vanigliato** vanilla sugar. **~ a velo** icing sugar, confectioners' sugar *Am*

**zucche'roso** *a fig* honeyed

**zuc'china** *nf* courgette, zucchini *Am*

**zuc'chino** *nm* courgette, zucchini *Am*

**zuc'cone** *nm fam* blockhead

**zuc'cotto** *nm dessert made with sponge, cream, chocolate and candied fruit*

**'zuffa** *nf* scuffle

**zufo'lare** *vt/i* whistle

**'zufolo** *nm* penny whistle

**zu'mare** *vi* zoom

**zu'mata** *nf* zoom

**'zuppa** *nf* soup. **~ inglese** trifle

**zup'petta** *nf* **fare ~ [con]** dunk

**zuppi'era** *nf* soup tureen

**'zuppo** *a* soaked

# Aa

**a, A** /eɪ/ (*letter*) a, A *f inv*; *Mus* la *m inv*
**a** /ə/, accentato /eɪ/ (*davanti a una vocale* **an**) *indef art* un *m*, una *f*; (*before s + consonant, gn, ps, z*) uno; (*before nf starting with vowel*) un'; (*each*) a; **I am a lawyer** sono avvocato: **a tiger is a feline** la tigre è un felino; **a knife and fork** un coltello e una forchetta: **a Mr Smith is looking for you** un certo signor Smith ti sta cercando; **£2 a kilo/a head** due sterline al chilo/a testa ● *n Mus* la *m inv*
**A4** *a* A4
**AA** *n Br abbr* (**Automobile Association**) ≈ A.C.I. *f*; *abbr* **Alcoholics Anonymous**
**aback** /ə'bæk/ *adv* **be taken ~** essere preso in contropiede
**abacus** /'æbəkəs/ *n* (*pl* **-cuses**) abaco *m*
**abandon** /ə'bændən/ *vt* abbandonare; (*give up*) rinunciare a ● *n* abbandono *m*
**abandoned** /ə'bændnd/ *a* abbandonato; ‹*behaviour*› dissoluto
**abandonment** /ə'bændnmənt/ *n* (*of strike, plan etc*) rinuncia *f*
**abashed** /ə'bæʃt/ *a* imbarazzato
**abate** /ə'beɪt/ *vi* calmarsi
**abattoir** /'æbətwɑː(r)/ *n* mattatoio *m*
**abbess** /'æbes/ *n* badessa *f*
**abbey** /'æbɪ/ *n* abazia *f*
**abbot** /'æbət/ *n* abate *m*
**abbreviate** /ə'briːvɪeɪt/ *vt* abbreviare
**abbreviation** /əbriːvɪ'eɪʃn/ *n* abbreviazione *f*
**ABC** *n* (*alphabet*) alfabeto *m*; **the ~ of** (*basics*) l'ABC *m inv* di ● *n abbr* (**American Broadcasting Company**) rete *f* televisiva americana
**abdicate** /'æbdɪkeɪt/ *vi* abdicare ● *vt* rinunciare a
**abdication** /æbdɪ'keɪʃn/ *n* abdicazione *f*
**abdomen** /'æbdəmən/ *n* addome *m*
**abdominal** /əb'dɒmɪnl/ *a* addominale
**abduct** /əb'dʌkt/ *vt* rapire
**abduction** /əb'dʌkʃn/ *n* rapimento *m*
**abductor** /əb'dʌktə(r)/ *n* rapitore, -trice *mf*
**aberrant** /ə'berənt/ *a* ‹*behaviour, nature*› aberrante
**aberration** /æbə'reɪʃn/ *n* aberrazione *f*
**abet** /ə'bet/ *vt* (*pt/pp* **abetted**) **aid and ~** *Jur* essere complice di
**abeyance** /ə'beɪəns/ *n* **in ~** in sospeso; **fall into ~** cadere in disuso
**abhor** /əb'hɔː(r)/ *vt* (*pt/pp* **abhorred**) aborrire
**abhorrence** /əb'hɒrəns/ *n* orrore *m*
**abhorrent** /əb'hɒrənt/ *a* ripugnante
**abide** /ə'baɪd/ *vt* (*pt/pp* **abided**) (*tolerate*) sopportare. ● **abide by** *vi* rispettare

**abiding** /ə'baɪdɪŋ/ *a* perpetuo
**ability** /ə'bɪlətɪ/ *n* capacità *f inv*
**abject** /'æbdʒekt/ *a* ‹*poverty*› degradante; ‹*apology*› umile; ‹*coward*› abietto
**ablative** /'æblətɪv/ *n* ablativo *m*
**ablaze** /ə'bleɪz/ *a* in fiamme; **be ~ with light** risplendere di luci
**able** /'eɪbl/ *a* capace, abile; **be ~ to do sth** poter fare qcsa; **were you ~ to...?** sei riuscito a...?
**able-bodied** /-'bɒdɪd/ *a* robusto; *Mil* abile
**able seaman** *n* marinaio *m* scelto
**ably** /'eɪblɪ/ *adv* abilmente
**abnegation** /æbnɪ'geɪʃn/ *n* (*of rights, privileges*) rinuncia *f*; (*self-abnegation*) abnegazione *f*
**abnormal** /æb'nɔːml/ *a* anormale
**abnormality** /æbnɔː'mælətɪ/ *n* anormalità *f inv*
**abnormally** /æb'nɔːməlɪ/ *adv* in modo anormale
**aboard** /ə'bɔːd/ *adv & prep* a bordo
**abode** /ə'bəʊd/ *n* dimora *f*
**abolish** /ə'bɒlɪʃ/ *vt* abolire
**abolition** /æbə'lɪʃn/ *n* abolizione *f*
**abominable** /ə'bɒmɪnəbl/ *a* abominevole
**abominably** /ə'bɒmɪnəblɪ/ *adv* disgustosamente
**abominate** /ə'bɒmɪneɪt/ *vt* abominare
**aboriginal** /æbə'rɪdʒɪnl/ *a & n* (*native*) aborigeno, -a *mf*, indigeno, -a *mf*
**Aborigine** /æbə'rɪdʒəniː/ *n* aborigeno, -a *mf* d'Australia
**abort** /ə'bɔːt/ *vt* fare abortire; *fig* annullare
**abortion** /ə'bɔːʃn/ *n* aborto *m*; **have an ~** abortire
**abortionist** /ə'bɔːʃnɪst/ *n* persona *f* che pratica aborti, specialmente clandestini
**abortive** /ə'bɔːtɪv/ *a* ‹*attempt*› infruttuoso
**abound** /ə'baʊnd/ *vi* abbondare (**in** di)
**about** /ə'baʊt/ *adv* (*here and there*) [di] qua e [di] là; (*approximately*) circa; **be** ~ ‹*illness, tourists:*› essere in giro; **be up and** ~ essere alzato; **leave sth lying** ~ lasciare in giro qcsa ● *prep* (*concerning*) su; (*in the region of*) intorno a; (*here and there in*) per; **what is the book/the film** ~? di cosa parla il libro/il film?; **he wants to see you – what** ~? ti vuole vedere – a che proposito?; **talk/know** ~ parlare/sapere di; **I know nothing** ~ **it** non ne so niente; ~ **5 o'clock** intorno alle 5; **travel** ~ **the world** viaggiare per il mondo; **be** ~ **to do sth** stare per fare qcsa; **how** ~ **going to the cinema?** e se andassimo al cinema?
**about-face** *n*, **about-turn** *n* dietro front *m inv*

**above** /əˈbʌv/ adv & prep sopra; ~ **all** soprattutto

**above: above-board** a onesto. **aboveground** adv in superficie. **above-mentioned** /-menˈʃnd/ a suddetto. **above-named** /-neɪmd/ a suddetto

**abrasion** /əˈbreɪʒn/ n (injury) abrasione f

**abrasive** /əˈbreɪsɪv/ a abrasivo; ⟨remark⟩ caustico ● n abrasivo m

**abreast** /əˈbrest/ adv fianco a fianco; **come ~ of** allinearsi con; **keep ~ of** tenersi al corrente di

**abridged** /əˈbrɪdʒd/ a ridotto

**abridg[e]ment** /əˈbrɪdʒmnt/ n (version) edizione f ridotta

**abroad** /əˈbrɔːd/ adv all'estero

**abrupt** /əˈbrʌpt/ a brusco

**abruptly** /əˈbrʌptlɪ/ adv bruscamente

**ABS** n abbr (**anti-lock braking system**) ABS m inv

**abscess** /ˈæbsɪs/ n ascesso m

**abscond** /əbˈskɒnd/ vi fuggire

**absence** /ˈæbsəns/ n assenza f; (lack) mancanza f

**absent**[1] /ˈæbsənt/ a assente

**absent**[2] /æbˈsent/ vt ~ **oneself** essere assente

**absentee** /æbsənˈtiː/ n assente mf

**absenteeism** /æbsənˈtiːɪzm/ n assenteismo m

**absentee landlord** n proprietario m che affitta una casa in cui non abita

**absently** /ˈæbsəntlɪ/ adv ⟨say, look⟩ distrattamente

**absent-minded** /-ˈmaɪndɪd/ a distratto

**absent-mindedly** /-ˈmaɪndɪdlɪ/ adv distrattamente

**absent-mindedness** /-ˈmaɪndɪdnɪs/ n distrazione f

**absolute** /ˈæbsəluːt/ a assoluto; **an ~ idiot** un perfetto idiota

**absolutely** /ˈæbsəluːtlɪ/ adv assolutamente; (fam: indicating agreement) esattamente; ~ **not** assolutamente no

**absolution** /æbsəˈluːʃn/ n assoluzione f

**absolve** /əbˈzɒlv/ vt assolvere

**absorb** /əbˈsɔːb/ vt assorbire; ~**ed in** assorto in

**absorbency** /əbˈsɔːbənsɪ/ n capacità f d'assorbimento

**absorbent** /əbˈsɔːbənt/ a assorbente

**absorbent cotton** n Am cotone m idrofilo, ovatta f

**absorbing** /əbˈsɔːbɪŋ/ a avvincente

**absorption** /əbˈsɔːpʃn/ n assorbimento m; (in activity) concentrazione f

**abstain** /əbˈsteɪn/ vi astenersi (**from** da)

**abstemious** /əbˈstiːmɪəs/ a moderato

**abstention** /əbˈstenʃn/ n Pol astensione f

**abstinence** /ˈæbstɪnəns/ n astinenza f

**abstract** /ˈæbstrækt/ a astratto ● n astratto m; (summary) estratto m

**abstraction** /əbˈstrækʃn/ n **an air of ~** un'aria distratta

**absurd** /əbˈsɜːd/ a assurdo

**absurdity** /əbˈsɜːdətɪ/ n assurdità f inv

**absurdly** /əbˈsɜːdlɪ/ adv assurdamente

**abundance** /əˈbʌndəns/ n abbondanza f

**abundant** /əˈbʌndənt/ a abbondante

**abundantly** /əˈbʌndəntlɪ/ adv ~ **clear** più che chiaro

**abuse**[1] /əˈbjuːz/ vt (misuse) abusare di; (insult) insultare; (ill-treat) maltrattare

**abuse**[2] /əˈbjuːs/ n abuso m; (verbal) insulti mpl; (ill-treatment) maltrattamento m; ~ **of power** sopraffazione f

**abusive** /əˈbjuːsɪv/ a offensivo

**abut** /əˈbʌt/ vi (pt/pp **abutted**) confinare (**onto** con)

**abysmal** /əˈbɪzml/ a fam pessimo; ⟨ignorance⟩ abissale

**abyss** /əˈbɪs/ n abisso m

**a/c** abbr (**account**) c/c

**academia** /ækəˈdiːmɪə/ n mondo m accademico

**academic** /ækəˈdemɪk/ a teorico; ⟨qualifications, system⟩ scolastico; **be ~** ⟨person:⟩ avere predisposizione allo studio ● n docente mf universitario, -a

**academically** /ækəˈdemɪklɪ/ adv ⟨gifted⟩ accademicamente

**academician** /əkædəˈmɪʃn/ n accademico, -a mf

**academy** /əˈkædəmɪ/ n accademia f; (of music) conservatorio m

**ACAS** /ˈeɪkæs/ n Br abbr (**Advisory Conciliation and Arbitration Service**) organismo m pubblico di mediazione tra i lavoratori e i datori di lavoro

**accede** /əkˈsiːd/ vi ~ **to** accedere a ⟨request⟩; salire a ⟨throne⟩

**accelerate** /əkˈseləreɪt/ vt/i accelerare

**acceleration** /əkseləˈreɪʃn/ n accelerazione f

**accelerator** /əkˈseləreɪtə(r)/ n Auto, Comput acceleratore m

**accent**[1] /ˈæksənt/ n accento m

**accent**[2] /ækˈsent/ vt accentare

**accented** /ˈæksəntɪd/ a ⟨speech⟩ con accento marcato

**accentuate** /əkˈsentjʊeɪt/ vt accentuare

**accept** /əkˈsept/ vt accettare

**acceptability** /ækseptəˈbɪlɪtɪ/ n ammissibilità f

**acceptable** /əkˈseptəbl/ a accettabile

**acceptance** /əkˈseptəns/ n accettazione f

**access** /ˈækses/ n accesso m ● vt Comput accedere a

**accessible** /əkˈsesəbl/ a accessibile

**accession** /əkˈseʃn/ n (to throne) ascesa f al trono

**accessory** /əkˈsesərɪ/ n accessorio m; Jur complice mf

**accident** /ˈæksɪdənt/ n incidente m; (chance) caso m; **by ~** per caso; (unintentionally) senza volere; **I'm sorry, it was an ~** mi dispiace, non l'ho fatto apposta

**accidental** /æksɪˈdentl/ a ⟨meeting⟩ casuale; ⟨death⟩ incidentale; (unintentional) involontario

**accidentally** /æksɪ'dentəlɪ/ adv per caso: (unintentionally) inavvertitamente

**acclaim** /ə'kleɪm/ n acclamazione f ● vt acclamare (as come)

**acclimatization** /əklaɪmətaɪ'zeɪʃn/ n acclimatazione f

**acclimatize** /ə'klaɪmətaɪz/ vt become ~d acclimatarsi

**accolade** /'ækəleɪd/ n riconoscimento m

**accommodate** /ə'kɒmədeɪt/ vt ospitare: (oblige) favorire

**accommodating** /ə'kɒmədeɪtɪŋ/ a accomodante

**accommodation** /əkɒmə'deɪʃn/ n (place to stay) sistemazione f; **look for ~** cercare una sistemazione

**accompaniment** /ə'kʌmpənɪmənt/ n accompagnamento m

**accompanist** /ə'kʌmpənɪst/ n Mus accompagnatore, -trice mf

**accompany** /ə'kʌmpənɪ/ vt (pt/pp -ied) accompagnare

**accomplice** /ə'kʌmplɪs/ n complice mf

**accomplish** /ə'kʌmplɪʃ/ vt (achieve) concludere; realizzare (aim)

**accomplished** /ə'kʌmplɪʃt/ a dotato: (fact) compiuto

**accomplishment** /ə'kʌmplɪʃmənt/ n realizzazione f; (achievement) risultato m: (talent) talento m

**accord** /ə'kɔːd/ n (treaty) accordo m; **with one ~** tutti d'accordo; **of his own ~** di sua spontanea volontà ● vt accordare

**accordance** /ə'kɔːdəns/ n **in ~ with** in conformità di o a

**according** /ə'kɔːdɪŋ/ adv **~ to** secondo

**accordingly** /ə'kɔːdɪŋlɪ/ adv di conseguenza

**accordion** /ə'kɔːdɪən/ n fisarmonica f

**accost** /ə'kɒst/ vt abbordare

**account** /ə'kaʊnt/ n conto m; (report) descrizione f; (of eyewitness) resoconto m; **~s** pl Comm nessun conti mpl; **on ~ of** a causa di; **on no ~** per nessun motivo; **on this ~** per questo motivo; **on my ~** per causa mia; **of no ~** di nessuna importanza; **take into ~** tener conto di ■ **account for** vt (explain) spiegare; (person:) render conto di; (constitute) costituire; (destroy) distruggere

**accountability** /əkaʊntə'bɪlətɪ/ n responsabilità f

**accountable** /ə'kaʊntəbl/ a responsabile (for di)

**accountant** /ə'kaʊntənt/ n (book-keeper) contabile mf: (consultant) commercialista mf

**account:** account book n libro m contabile. **account director** n account director mf inv. **account holder** /ə'kaʊnthəʊldə(r)/ n (with bank, credit company) titolare mf del conto

**accounting** /ə'kaʊntɪŋ/ n (field) ragioneria f; (auditing) contabilità f

**accounting period** n periodo m contabile

**account number** n numero m di conto

**accounts:** accounts department n [ufficio m] contabilità f. **accounts payable** npl conto m creditori diversi. **accounts receivable** npl conto m debitori diversi

**accoutrements** /ə'kuːtrəmənts/ npl equipaggiamento msg

**accredited** /ə'kredɪtɪd/ a accreditato

**accretion** /ə'kriːʃn/ n accrescimento m

**accrue** /ə'kruː/ vi (interest:) maturare

**accumulate** /ə'kjuːmjʊleɪt/ vt accumulare ● vi accumularsi

**accumulation** /əkjuːmjʊ'leɪʃn/ n accumulazione f

**accumulator** /ə'kjuːmjʊleɪtə(r)/ n Electr accumulatore m

**accuracy** /'ækjʊrəsɪ/ n precisione f

**accurate** /'ækjʊrət/ a preciso

**accurately** /'ækjʊrətlɪ/ adv con precisione

**accusation** /ækjʊ'zeɪʃn/ n accusa f

**accusative** /ə'kjuːzətɪv/ a & n ~ [case] Gram accusativo m

**accuse** /ə'kjuːz/ vt accusare; **~ sb of doing sth** accusare qcno di fare qcsa

**accused** /ə'kjuːzd/ n **the ~** l'accusato m, l'accusata f

**accuser** /ə'kjuːzə(r)/ n accusatore, -trice mf

**accusing** /ə'kjuːzɪŋ/ a accusatore

**accusingly** /ə'kjuːzɪŋlɪ/ adv (say, point) in modo accusatorio

**accustom** /ə'kʌstəm/ vt abituare (to a)

**accustomed** /ə'kʌstəmd/ a abituato; **grow or get ~ to** abituarsi a

**ace** /eɪs/ n (in cards) asso m; Tennis ace m inv

**acerbic** /ə'sɜːbɪk/ a acido

**acetate** /'æsɪteɪt/ n acetato m

**ache** /eɪk/ n dolore m ● vi dolere, far male; **~ all over** essere tutto indolenzito

**achieve** /ə'tʃiːv/ vt ottenere (success); realizzare (goal, ambition)

**achievement** /ə'tʃiːvmənt/ n (feat) successo m

**achiever** /ə'tʃiːvə(r)/ n persona f di successo

**Achilles' heel** /əkɪliːz'hiːl/ n tallone m di Achille

**aching** /'eɪkɪŋ/ a (body, limbs) dolorante; **an ~ void** un vuoto incolmabile

**acid** /'æsɪd/ a acido ● n acido m

**acid drop** n caramella f agli agrumi

**acidic** /ə'sɪdɪk/ a acido

**acidity** /ə'sɪdətɪ/ n acidità f

**acid:** acid rain n pioggia f acida. **acid stomach** n Med acidità f di stomaco. **acid test** n fig prova f del fuoco

**acknowledge** /ək'nɒlɪdʒ/ vt riconoscere; rispondere a (greeting); far cenno di aver notato (sb's presence); **~ receipt of** accusare ricevuta di; **~ defeat** dichiararsi vinto

**acknowledgement** /ək'nɒlɪdʒmənt/ n riconoscimento m; **send an ~ of a letter** confermare il ricevimento di una lettera

**acme** /'ækmɪ/ n **the ~ of** l'apice m di

**acne** /'æknɪ/ n acne f

**acorn** /'eɪkɔːn/ n ghianda f

**acoustic** /ə'kuːstɪk/ a acustico

**acoustically** /ə'kuːstɪklɪ/ adv acusticamente

**acoustic guitar** n chitarra f acustica
**acoustics** /ə'ku:stɪks/ npl acustica fsg
**acquaint** /ə'kweɪnt/ vt ~ **sb with** metter qcno al corrente di; **be ~ed with** conoscere ⟨person⟩; essere a conoscenza di ⟨fact⟩
**acquaintance** /ə'kweɪntəns/ n ⟨person⟩ conoscente mf; **make sb's ~** fare la conoscenza di qcno
**acquiesce** /ækwr'es/ vi acconsentire (**to, in** a)
**acquiescence** /ækwr'esəns/ n acquiescenza f
**acquiescent** /ækwr'esənt/ a arrendevole
**acquire** /ə'kwaɪə(r)/ vt acquisire
**acquired** /ə'kwaɪəd/ a ⟨characteristic⟩ acquisito; **it's an ~ taste** è una cosa che si impara ad apprezzare
**acquisition** /ækwr'zɪʃn/ n acquisizione f
**acquisitive** /ə'kwɪzətɪv/ a avido
**acquit** /ə'kwɪt/ vt ⟨pt/pp acquitted⟩ assolvere; **~ oneself well** cavarsela bene
**acquittal** /ə'kwɪtəl/ n assoluzione f
**acre** /'eɪkə(r)/ n acro m (= 4 047 m²)
**acreage** /'eɪkərɪdʒ/ n superficie f in acri
**acrid** /'ækrɪd/ a acre
**acrimonious** /ækrɪ'məʊnɪəs/ a aspro
**acrimony** /'ækrɪmənɪ/ n asprezza f
**acrobat** /'ækrəbæt/ n acrobata mf
**acrobatic** /ækrə'bætɪk/ a acrobatico
**acrobatics** /ækrə'bætɪks/ npl acrobazie fpl
**acronym** /'ækrənɪm/ n acronimo m
**across** /ə'krɒs/ adv dall'altra parte; ⟨wide⟩ in larghezza; ⟨not lengthwise⟩ attraverso; ⟨in crossword⟩ orizzontale; **come ~ sth** imbattersi in qcsa; **go ~** attraversare ● prep ⟨crosswise⟩ di traverso su; ⟨on the other side of⟩ dall'altra parte di
**across-the-board** a generale ● adv in generale
**acrylic** /ə'krɪlɪk/ n acrilico m ● attrib ⟨garment⟩ acrilico
**act** /ækt/ n atto m; ⟨in variety show⟩ numero m; **put on an ~** fam fare scena ● vi agire; ⟨behave⟩ comportarsi; Theat recitare; ⟨pretend⟩ fingere; **~ as** fare da ● vt recitare ⟨role⟩
■ **act for** vi agire per conto di
■ **act up** vi ⟨child, photocopier:⟩ fare i capricci
**acting** /'æktɪŋ/ a ⟨deputy⟩ provvisorio ● n Theat recitazione f; ⟨profession⟩ teatro m; **~ profession** professione f dell'attore
**action** /'ækʃn/ n azione f; Mil combattimento m; Jur azione f legale; **out of ~** ⟨machine:⟩ fuori uso; **take ~** agire; **~ !** Cinema ciac si gira!
**action: action-packed** a ⟨film⟩ d'azione. **action painting** n pittura f d'azione. **action replay** n replay m inv
**activate** /'æktɪveɪt/ vt attivare; (Chem, Phys) rendere attivo
**active** /'æktɪv/ a attivo
**active duty, active service** n Mil **be on ~ ~** prestare servizio in zona di operazioni
**actively** /'æktɪvlɪ/ adv attivamente

**activist** /'æktɪvɪst/ n attivista mf
**activity** /æk'tɪvətɪ/ n attività f inv
**activity holiday** n Br vacanza f con attività ricreative
**act of God** n causa f di forza maggiore
**actor** /'æktə(r)/ n attore m
**actress** /'æktrəs/ n attrice f
**actual** /'æktʃʊəl/ a ⟨real⟩ reale
**actually** /'æktʃʊəlɪ/ adv in realtà
**actuary** /'æktʃʊərɪ/ n attuario, -a mf
**acumen** /'ækjʊmən/ n acume m
**acupuncture** /'ækjʊpʌŋktʃə(r)/ n agopuntura f
**acupuncturist** /ækjʊ'pʌŋktʃərɪst/ n agopuntore, -trice mf
**acute** /ə'kju:t/ a acuto; ⟨shortage, hardship⟩ estremo
**acute accent** n accento m acuto
**acute angle** n angolo m acuto
**acutely** /ə'kju:tlɪ/ adv acutamente; ⟨embarrassed, aware⟩ estremamente
**AD** abbr (**Anno Domini**) d.C.
**ad** /æd/ n pubblicità f inv; ⟨in paper⟩ inserzione f, annuncio m
**adage** /'ædɪdʒ/ n detto m, adagio m
**adamant** /'ædəmənt/ a categorico (**that** sul fatto che)
**Adam's apple** /'ædəmz/ n pomo m di Adamo
**adapt** /ə'dæpt/ vt adattare ⟨play⟩ ● vi adattarsi
**adaptability** /ədæptə'bɪlətɪ/ n adattabilità f
**adaptable** /ə'dæptəbl/ a adattabile
**adaptation** /ædæp'teɪʃn/ n Theat adattamento m
**adapter, adaptor** /ə'dæptə(r)/ n adattatore m; ⟨two-way⟩ presa f multipla
**add** /æd/ vt aggiungere; Math addizionare ● vi addizionare. **~ to** vi ⟨fig: increase⟩ aggravare
■ **add in** vt ⟨include⟩ includere
■ **add on** vt aggiungere
■ **add up** vt addizionare ⟨figures⟩ ● vi addizionare; **it doesn't ~ up** fig non quadra; **~ up to** ammontare a
**added** /'ædɪd/ a maggiore
**adder** /'ædə(r)/ n vipera f
**addict** /'ædɪkt/ n tossicodipendente mf; fig fanatico, -a mf
**addicted** /ə'dɪktɪd/ a assuefatto (**to** a); **~ to drugs** tossicodipendente; **he's ~ to television** è videodipendente
**addiction** /ə'dɪkʃn/ n dipendenza f; ⟨to drugs⟩ tossicodipendenza f
**addictive** /ə'dɪktɪv/ a **be ~** dare assuefazione
**addition** /ə'dɪʃn/ n Math addizione f; ⟨thing added⟩ aggiunta f; **in ~** in aggiunta
**additional** /ə'dɪʃnəl/ a supplementare
**additionally** /ə'dɪʃnəlɪ/ adv in più
**additive** /'ædɪtɪv/ n additivo m
**addled** /'ædld/ a ⟨thinking⟩ confuso
**add-on** a accessorio
**address** /ə'dres/ n indirizzo m; ⟨speech⟩ discorso m; **form of ~** formula f di cortesia

● *vt* indirizzare: (*speak to*) rivolgersi a ⟨*person*⟩: tenere un discorso a ⟨*meeting*⟩

**address book** *n* rubrica *f*

**addressee** /ædre'si:/ *n* destinatario, -a *mf*

**adenoids** /'ædənɔɪdz/ *npl* adenoidi *fpl*

**adept** /'ædept/ *a* esperto, -a *mf* (**at** in)

**adequate** /'ædɪkwət/ *a* adeguato

**adequately** /'ædɪkwətlɪ/ *adv* adeguatamente

**adhere** /əd'hɪə(r)/ *vi* aderire; **~ to** attenersi a ⟨*principles, rules*⟩

**adherence** /əd'hɪərəns/ *n* fedeltà *f*

**adherent** /əd'hɪərənt/ *n* (*of doctrine*) adepto, -a *mf*; (*of policy*) sostenitore, -trice *mf*; (*of cult*) seguace *mf*

**adhesion** /əd'hi:ʒn/ *n* adesione *f*

**adhesive** /əd'hi:sɪv/ *a* adesivo ● *n* adesivo *m*

**ad hoc** /æd'hɒk/ *a* ⟨*alliance, arrangement*⟩ ad hoc; ⟨*committee, legislation*⟩ apposito; **on an ~ ~ basis** secondo le esigenze del momento

**adieu** /ə'dju:/ *n* **bid sb ~** dire addio a qcno

**ad infinitum** /ædɪnfɪ'naɪtəm/ *adv* (*continue*) all'infinito

**adjacent** /ə'dʒeɪsənt/ *a* adiacente

**adjective** /'ædʒɪktɪv/ *n* aggettivo *m*

**adjoin** /ə'dʒɔɪn/ *vt* essere adiacente a

**adjoining** /ə'dʒɔɪnɪŋ/ *a* adiacente

**adjourn** /ə'dʒɜ:n/ *vt/i* aggiornare (**until** a)

**adjournment** /ə'dʒɜ:nmənt/ *n* aggiornamento *m*

**adjudge** /ə'dʒʌdʒ/ *vt* *Jur* (*decree*) giudicare; aggiudicare ⟨*costs, damages*⟩

**adjudicate** /ə'dʒu:dɪkeɪt/ *vi* decidere; (*in competition*) giudicare

**adjudicator** /ə'dʒu:dɪkeɪtə(r)/ *n* giudice *m*, arbitro *m*

**adjunct** /'ædʒʌŋkt/ *n* aggiunta *f*; (*hum: person*) appendice *f*

**adjust** /ə'dʒʌst/ *vt* modificare; regolare ⟨*focus, sound etc*⟩ ● *vi* adattarsi

**adjustable** /ə'dʒʌstəbl/ *a* regolabile

**adjustable spanner** *n* chiave *f* [inglese] a rullino

**adjustment** /ə'dʒʌstmənt/ *n* adattamento *m*; *Techn* regolamento *m*

**adjutant** /'ædʒʊtənt/ *n* *Mil* aiutante *mf*

**ad lib** /æd'lɪb/ *a* improvvisato ● *adv* a piacere ● *vi* (*pt/pp* **ad libbed**) *fam* improvvisare

**adman** /'ædmæn/ *n* *fam* pubblicitario *m*

**admin** /'ædmɪn/ *n* *Br fam* amministrazione *f*

**administer** /əd'mɪnɪstə(r)/ *vt* amministrare; somministrare ⟨*medicine*⟩

**administration** /ədmɪnɪ'streɪʃn/ *n* amministrazione *f*; *Pol* governo *m*

**administration costs** *n* costi *mpl* di gestione

**administrative** /əd'mɪnɪstrətɪv/ *a* amministrativo

**administrator** /əd'mɪnɪstreɪtə(r)/ *n* amministratore, -trice *mf*

**admirable** /'ædmərəbl/ *a* ammirevole

**admiral** /'ædmərəl/ *n* ammiraglio *m*

**admiralty** /'ædmərəltɪ/ *n* *Br* ministero *m* della marina militare britannica

**admiration** /ædmə'reɪʃn/ *n* ammirazione *f*

**admire** /əd'maɪə(r)/ *vt* ammirare

**admirer** /əd'maɪrə(r)/ *n* ammiratore, -trice *mf*

**admiring** /əd'maɪrɪŋ/ *a* ⟨*person*⟩ pieno d'ammirazione: ⟨*look*⟩ ammirativo

**admiringly** /əd'maɪrɪŋlɪ/ *adv* ⟨*look, say*⟩ con ammirazione

**admissible** /əd'mɪsəbl/ *a* ammissibile

**admission** /əd'mɪʃn/ *n* ammissione *f*; (*to hospital*) ricovero *m*; (*entry*) ingresso *m*

**admit** /əd'mɪt/ *vt* (*pt/pp* **admitted**) (*let in*) far entrare; (*to hospital*) ricoverare; (*acknowledge*) ammettere ● *vi* **~ to sth** ammettere qcsa

**admittance** /əd'mɪtəns/ *n* ammissione *f*; '**no ~**' 'vietato l'ingresso'

**admittedly** /əd'mɪtɪdlɪ/ *adv* bisogna riconoscerlo

**admonish** /əd'mɒnɪʃ/ *vt* ammonire

**admonition** /ædmə'nɪʃn/ *n* ammonimento *m*

**ad nauseam** /æd'nɔ:zɪæm/ *adv* ⟨*discuss, repeat*⟩ fino alla nausea

**ado** /ə'du:/ *n* **without more ~** senza ulteriori indugi

**adolescence** /ædə'lesns/ *n* adolescenza *f*

**adolescent** /ædə'lesnt/ *a* & *n* adolescente *mf*

**adopt** /ə'dɒpt/ *vt* adottare; *Pol* scegliere ⟨*candidate*⟩

**adopted** /ə'dɒptɪd/ *a* ⟨*son, daughter*⟩ adottivo

**adoption** /ə'dɒpʃn/ *n* adozione *f*

**adoption agency** *n* agenzia *f* di adozioni

**adoptive** /ə'dɒptɪv/ *a* adottivo

**adorable** /ə'dɔ:rəbl/ *a* adorabile

**adoration** /ædə'reɪʃn/ *n* adorazione *f*

**adore** /ə'dɔ:(r)/ *vt* adorare

**adoring** /ə'dɔ:rɪŋ/ *a* ⟨*fan*⟩ in adorazione; **she has an ~ husband** ha un marito che la adora

**adoringly** /ə'dɔ:rɪŋlɪ/ *adv* con adorazione

**adorn** /ə'dɔ:n/ *vt* adornare

**adornment** /ə'dɔ:nmənt/ *n* ornamento *m*

**adrenalin** /ə'drenəlɪn/ *n* adrenalina *f*

**Adriatic** /eɪdrɪ'ætɪk/ *a* & *n* **the ~ [Sea]** il mare Adriatico, l'Adriatico *m*

**adrift** /ə'drɪft/ *a* alla deriva; **be ~** andare alla deriva; **come ~** staccarsi

**adroit** /ə'drɔɪt/ *a* abile

**adroitly** /ə'drɔɪtlɪ/ *adv* abilmente

**adulation** /ædjʊ'leɪʃn/ *n* adulazione *f*

**adult** /'ædʌlt/ *n* adulto, -a *mf*

**Adult Education** *n Br* ≈ corsi *mpl* serali

**adulterate** /ə'dʌltəreɪt/ *vt* adulterare ⟨*wine*⟩

**adulterated** /ə'dʌltəreɪtɪd/ *a* ⟨*wine*⟩ adulterato

**adulterous** /ə'dʌltərəs/ *a* ⟨*relationship*⟩ adulterino; ⟨*person*⟩ adultero

**adultery** /ə'dʌltərɪ/ *n* adulterio *m*

**adulthood** /'ædʌlthʊd/ *n* età *f* adulta

**adult literacy classes** *n Br* lezioni *fpl* di alfabetizzazione per adulti

**advance** /əd'vɑ:ns/ *n* avanzamento *m*; *Mil*

avanzata *f*. (*payment*) anticipo *m*; **in ~** in anticipo ● *vi* avanzare; (*make progress*) fare progressi ● *vt* promuovere ‹*cause*›; avanzare ‹*theory*›; anticipare ‹*money*›

**advance booking** *n* prenotazione *f* [in anticipo]

**advance booking office** *n* ufficio *m* prenotazioni

**advanced** /əd'vɑ:nst/ *a* avanzato

**Advanced Level** *n Br Sch* = **A-Level**

**advancement** /əd'vɑ:nsmənt/ *n* promozione *f*

**advance: advance notice** *n* preannuncio *m*. **advance party** *n Mil* avanguardia *f*. **advance payment** *n Comm* pagamento *m* anticipato. **advance warning** *n* preavviso *m*

**advantage** /əd'vɑ:ntɪdʒ/ *n* vantaggio *m*; **take ~ of** approfittare di

**advantageous** /ædvən'teɪdʒəs/ *a* vantaggioso

**advent** /'ædvent/ *n* avvento *m*; **A~** *Relig* Avvento *m*

**adventure** /əd'ventʃə(r)/ *n* avventura *f*

**adventure playground** *n Br* parco *m* giochi

**adventurer** /əd'ventʃərə(r)/ *n* avventuriero, -a *mf*

**adventuress** /əd'ventʃərɪs/ *n* avventuriera *f*

**adventurous** /əd'ventʃərəs/ *a* avventuroso

**adverb** /'ædvɜ:b/ *n* avverbio *m*

**adversary** /'ædvəsərɪ/ *n* avversario, -a *mf*

**adverse** /'ædvɜ:s/ *a* avverso

**adversity** /əd'vɜ:sətɪ/ *n* avversità *f*

**advert** /'ædvɜ:t/ *n fam* = **advertisement**

**advertise** /'ædvətaɪz/ *vt* reclamizzare; mettere un annuncio per ‹*job, flat*› ● *vi* fare pubblicità; (*for job, flat*) mettere un annuncio

**advertisement** /əd'vɜ:tɪsmənt/ *n* pubblicità *f inv*; (*in paper*) inserzione *f*, annuncio *m*

**advertiser** /'ædvətaɪzə(r)/ *n* (*in newspaper*) inserzionista *mf*

**advertising** /'ædvətaɪzɪŋ/ *n* pubblicità *f* ● *attrib* pubblicitario

**advertising: advertising agency** *n* agenzia *f* di pubblicità. **advertising campaign** *n* campagna *f* pubblicitaria. **advertising executive** *n* dirigente *mf* pubblicitario, -a. **advertising industry** *n* settore *m* pubblicitario. **Advertising Standards Authority** *n Br* organo *m* di controllo sulla pubblicità

**advice** /əd'vaɪs/ *n* consigli *mpl*; **piece of ~** consiglio *m*

**advice note** *n* avviso *m*

**advisability** /ədvaɪzə'bɪlətɪ/ *n* opportunità *f*

**advisable** /əd'vaɪzəbl/ *a* consigliabile

**advise** /əd'vaɪz/ *vt* consigliare; (*inform*) avvisare; **~ sb to do sth** consigliare a qcno di fare qcsa; **~ sb against sth** sconsigliare qcsa a qcno

**advisedly** /əd'vaɪzɪdlɪ/ *adv* ‹*say*› deliberatamente

**adviser** /əd'vaɪzə(r)/ *n* consulente *mf*

**advisory** /əd'vaɪzərɪ/ *a* consultivo

**advisory committee** *n* comitato *m* consultivo

**advocacy** /'ædvəkəsɪ/ *n* appoggio *m*

**advocate¹** /'ædvəkət/ *n* (*supporter*) fautore, -trice *mf*

**advocate²** /'ædvəkeɪt/ *vt* propugnare

**Aegean** /ɪ'dʒɪən/ *n* **the ~** l'Egeo *m*

**aegis** /'i:dʒɪs/ *n* **under the ~ of** sotto l'egida di

**aeon** /'i:ən/ *n* **~s ago** milioni *mpl* e milioni di anni fa

**aerate** /'eəreɪt/ *vt* aerare; addizionare anidride carbonica a ‹*water*›

**aerial** /'eərɪəl/ *a* aereo ● *n* antenna *f*

**aerial camera** *n* macchina *f* fotografica per fotografie aeree

**aerial warfare** *n* guerra *f* aerea

**aerie** /'eərɪ/ *n Am* (*eyrie*) nido *m* [d'aquila]

**aerobatics** /eərə'bætɪks/ *npl* (*manoeuvres*) acrobazie *fpl* aeree

**aerobics** /eə'rəʊbɪks/ *n* aerobica *fsg*

**aerodrome** /'eərədrəʊm/ *n* aerodromo *m*

**aerodynamic** /eərəʊdar'næmɪk/ *a* aerodinamico

**aerodynamics** /eərəʊdar'næmɪks/ *n* aerodinamica *f*

**aerogram[me]** /'eərəʊgræm/ *n* aerogramma *m*

**aeronautic[al]** /eərə'nɔ:tɪk[əl]/ *a* aeronautico

**aeronautic[al] engineer** *n* ingegnere *m* aeronautico

**aeronautic[al] engineering** *n* ingegneria *f* aeronautica

**aeronautics** /eərə'nɔ:tɪks/ *n* aeronautica *f*

**aeroplane** /'eərəpleɪn/ *n* aeroplano *m*

**aerosol** /'eərəsɒl/ *n* bomboletta *f* spray

**aerospace** /'eərəspeɪs/ *n* (*industry*) industria *f* aerospaziale ● *attrib* ‹*engineer, company*› aerospaziale

**aesthete** /'i:sθi:t/ *n* esteta *mf*

**aesthetic** /i:s'θetɪk/ *a* estetico

**aesthetically** /i:s'θetɪklɪ/ *adv* ‹*restore*› con gusto; ‹*satisfying*› esteticamente

**aestheticism** /i:s'θetɪsɪzm/ *n* (*taste*) esteticità *f*; (*doctrine, quality*) estetismo *m*

**aesthetics** /i:s'θetɪks/ *n* estetica *f*

**afar** /ə'fɑ:(r)/ *adv* **from ~** da lontano

**affable** /'æfəbl/ *a* affabile

**affably** /'æfəblɪ/ *adv* affabilmente

**affair** /ə'feə(r)/ *n* affare *m*; (*scandal*) caso *m*; (*sexual*) relazione *f*

**affect** /ə'fekt/ *vt* influire su; (*emotionally*) colpire; (*concern*) riguardare; (*pretend*) affettare

**affectation** /æfek'teɪʃn/ *n* affettazione *f*

**affected** /ə'fektɪd/ *a* affettato

**affectedly** /ə'fektɪdlɪ/ *adv* ‹*talk*› con affettazione

**affection** /ə'fekʃn/ *n* affetto *m*

**affectionate** /ə'fekʃnət/ *a* affettuoso

**affectionately** /ə'fekʃnətlɪ/ *adv* affettuosamente

**affidavit** /æfr'deɪvɪt/ *n* affidavit *m inv* (di-

*chiarazione scritta e giurata davanti a un pubblico ufficiale*)

**affiliated** /ə'fɪlɪeɪtɪd/ *a* affiliato

**affiliation** /əfɪlɪ'eɪʃn/ *n* (*process, state*) affiliazione *f*; (*link*) legame *m*

**affinity** /ə'fɪnətɪ/ *n* affinità *f inv*

**affirm** /ə'fɜ:m/ *vt* affermare; *Jur* dichiarare solennemente

**affirmative** /ə'fɜ:mətɪv/ *a* affermativo ● *n* **in the ~** affermativamente

**affix** /ə'fɪks/ *vt* affiggere; apporre (*signature*)

**afflict** /ə'flɪkt/ *vt* affliggere

**affliction** /ə'flɪkʃn/ *n* afflizione *f*

**affluence** /'æfluəns/ *n* agiatezza *f*

**affluent** /'æfluənt/ *a* agiato

**afford** /ə'fɔ:d/ *vt* (*provide*) fornire; **be able to ~ sth** potersi permettere qcsa

**affordable** /ə'fɔ:dəbl/ *a* abbordabile

**affray** /ə'freɪ/ *n* rissa *f*

**affront** /ə'frʌnt/ *n* affronto *m* ● *vt* fare un affronto a

**Afghan** /'æfgæn/ *n* (*person*) afgano, -a *mf*; (*language*) afgano *m*; (*coat*) pellicciotto *m* afgano

**Afghan hound** *n* levriero *m* afgano

**Afghanistan** /æf'gænɪstæn/ *n* Afganistan *m*

**aficionado** /æfɪsjə'na:dəʊ/ *n* aficionado, -a *mf*

**afield** /ə'fi:ld/ *adv* **further ~** più lontano

**aflame** /ə'fleɪm/ *a* & *adv liter* in fiamme, sfolgorante; **be ~** (*cheek:*) essere in fiamme; **be ~ with desire** ardere dal desiderio

**afloat** /ə'fləʊt/ *a* a galla

**afoot** /ə'fʊt/ *a* **there's something ~** si sta preparando qualcosa

**aforesaid** /ə'fɔ:sed/ *a Jur* suddetto

**afraid** /ə'freɪd/ *a* **be ~** aver paura; **I'm ~ not** purtroppo no; **I'm ~ so** temo di sì; **I'm ~ I can't help you** mi dispiace, ma non posso esserle d'aiuto

**afresh** /ə'freʃ/ *adv* da capo

**Africa** /'æfrɪkə/ *n* Africa *f*

**African** /'æfrɪkən/ *a* & *n* africano, -a *mf*

**Afrikaans** /æfrɪ'ka:ns/ *n* afrikaans *m*

**Afrikaner** /æfrɪ'ka:nə(r)/ *n* boero, -a *mf*

**Afro-American** /æfrəʊə'merɪkən/ *a* & *n* afroamericano, -a *mf*

**Afro-Caribbean** /æfrəʊkærə'bɪən/ *a* & *n* afrocaraibico, -a *mf*

**aft** /a:ft/ *adv Naut* a poppa; (*towards the stern*) verso poppa

**after** /'a:ftə(r)/ *adv* dopo; **the day ~** il giorno dopo; **be ~** cercare ● *prep* dopo; **~ all** dopotutto; **the day ~ tomorrow** dopodomani ● *conj* dopo che

**after: after-birth** *n* residui *mpl* di placenta. **after-care** *n Med* ospedalizzazione *f* domiciliare. **after-dinner speaker** *n* persona *f* invitata a tenere un discorso dopo una cena o un ricevimento. **after-effect** *n* conseguenza *f*. **after-life** *n* vita *f* nell'aldilà

**aftermath** /'a:ftəma:θ/ *n* conseguenze *fpl*; **the ~ of war** il dopoguerra; **in the ~ of** nel periodo successivo a

**after: afternoon** *n* pomeriggio *m*; **good ~!** buon giorno!. **afternoon tea** *n* merenda *f*. **after-pains** *npl* dolori *mpl* post-partum. **after-sales service** *n* servizio *m* assistenza clienti. **aftershave** *n* [lozione *f*] dopobarba *m inv*. **after-shock** *n fig* effetti *mpl*. **aftersun** *n* & *a* doposole *m inv*. **after-taste** *n* retrogusto *m*. **after-tax** *a* (*profits, earnings*) al netto. **afterthought** *n* **added as an ~** aggiunto in un secondo momento; **as an ~, why not...?** ripensandoci bene, perché non...?

**afterwards** /'a:ftəwədz/ *adv* in seguito

**again** /ə'gen/ *adv* di nuovo; [**then**] ~ (*besides*) inoltre; (*on the other hand*) d'altra parte; **~ and ~** continuamente

**against** /ə'genst/ *prep* contro

**age** /eɪdʒ/ *n* età *f inv*; (*era*) era *f*; **~s** *fam* secoli; **~s ago** *fam* secoli fa; **what ~ are you?** quanti anni hai?; **be under ~** non avere l'età richiesta; **he's two years of ~** ha due anni ● *vt/i* (*pres p ageing*) invecchiare

**age bracket, age group** *n* fascia *f* d'età

**aged**[1] /eɪdʒd/ *a* **~ two** di due anni

**aged**[2] /'eɪdʒɪd/ *a* anziano ● *n* **the ~** *pl* gli anziani

**aged debt** *n Fin* somma *f* in scadenza

**ageing** /'eɪdʒɪŋ/ *n* invecchiamento *m* ● *a* (*person, population*) che sta invecchiando

**ageism** /'eɪdʒɪzm/ *n* discriminazione *f* contro chi non è più giovane

**ageless** /'eɪdʒlɪs/ *a* senza età

**agency** /'eɪdʒənsɪ/ *n* agenzia *f*; **have the ~ for** essere un concessionario di

**agency-fee** *n* commissione *f*

**agency-nurse** *n* infermiere, -a *mf* privato, -a

**agenda** /ə'dʒendə/ *n* ordine *m* del giorno; **on the ~** all'ordine del giorno; *fig* in programma

**agent** /'eɪdʒənt/ *n* agente *mf*

**age-old** *a* secolare

**age range** *n* fascia *f* d'età

**aggravate** /'ægrəveɪt/ *vt* aggravare; (*annoy*) esasperare

**aggravating** /'ægrəveɪtɪŋ/ *a Jur* aggravante; (*fam: irritating*) irritante

**aggravation** /ægrə'veɪʃn/ *n* aggravamento *m*; (*annoyance*) esasperazione *f*

**aggregate** /'ægrɪgət/ *a* totale ● *n* totale *m*; **on ~** nel complesso

**aggression** /ə'greʃn/ *n* aggressione *f*

**aggressive** /ə'gresɪv/ *a* aggressivo

**aggressively** /ə'gresɪvlɪ/ *adv* aggressivamente

**aggressiveness** /ə'gresɪvnɪs/ *n* aggressività *f*

**aggressor** /ə'gresə(r)/ *n* aggressore *m*

**aggrieved** /ə'gri:vd/ *a* risentito

**aggro** /'ægrəʊ/ *n fam* aggressività *f*; (*problems*) grane *fpl*

**aghast** /ə'ga:st/ *a* inorridito

**agile** /'ædʒaɪl/ *a* agile

**agility** /ə'dʒɪlətɪ/ *n* agilità *f*

**agitate** /'ædʒɪteɪt/ *vt* mettere in agitazione;

(*shake*) agitare ● *vi fig* ~ **for** creare delle agitazioni per

**agitated** /'adʒɪteɪtɪd/ *a* agitato

**agitation** /adʒɪ'teɪʃn/ *n* agitazione *f*

**agitator** /'adʒɪteɪtə(r)/ *n* agitatore. -trice *mf*

**AGM** *n abbr* (**annual general meeting**) assemblea *f* generale annuale

**agnostic** /æg'nɒstɪk/ *a & n* agnostico, -a *mf*

**ago** /ə'gəʊ/ *adv* fa; **a long time/a month** ~ molto tempo/un mese fa; **how long** ~ **was it?** quanto tempo fa è successo?

**agog** /ə'gɒg/ *a* eccitato

**agonize** /'ægənaɪz/ *vi* angosciarsi (**over** per)

**agonized** /'ægənaɪzd/ *a* ⟨*expression, cry*⟩ angosciato

**agonizing** /'ægənaɪzɪŋ/ *a* angosciante

**agony** /'ægənɪ/ *n* agonia *f*; (*mental*) angoscia *f*; **be in** ~ avere dei dolori atroci

**agony aunt** *n persona f chi tiene la posta del cuore in una rivista*

**agoraphobia** /ægərə'fəʊbɪə/ *n* agorafobia *f*

**agoraphobic** /ægərə'fəʊbɪk/ *a* agorafobo, -a *mf*

**agree** /ə'griː/ *vt* accordarsi su; ~ **to do sth** accettare di fare qcsa; ~ **that** essere d'accordo [sul fatto] che ● *vi* essere d'accordo; ⟨*figures*⟩ concordare; (*reach agreement*) mettersi d'accordo; (*get on*) andare d'accordo; (*consent*) acconsentire (**to** a); **it doesn't** ~ **with me** mi fa male; ~ **with sth** (*approve of*) approvare qcsa

**agreeable** /ə'griːəbl/ *a* gradevole; (*willing*) d'accordo

**agreeably** /ə'griːəblɪ/ *adv* (*pleasantly*) piacevolmente; (*amicably*) in modo amichevole

**agreed** /ə'griːd/ *a* convenuto

**agreement** /ə'griːmənt/ *n* accordo *m*; **in** ~ d'accordo; **reach** ~ arrivare a un accordo

**agricultural** /ægrɪ'kʌltʃərəl/ *a* agricolo

**agriculturalist** /ægrɪ'kʌltʃərəlɪst/ *n* agronomo, -a *mf*

**agricultural show** *n* fiera *f* agricola

**agriculture** /'ægrɪkʌltʃə(r)/ *n* agricoltura *f*

**agronomy** /ə'grɒnəmɪ/ *n* agronomia *f*

**aground** /ə'graʊnd/ *adv* **run** ~ ⟨*ship:*⟩ arenarsi

**ah** /ɑː/ *int* ~ **well!** (*resignedly*) va be'!

**ahead** /ə'hed/ *adv* avanti; **be** ~ **of** essere davanti a; *fig* essere avanti rispetto a; **draw** ~ passare davanti (**of** a); **go on** ~ cominciare ad andare; **get** ~ (*in life*) riuscire; **go** ~! fai pure!; **look** ~ pensare all'avvenire; **plan** ~ fare progetti per l'avvenire

**AI** *n abbr* (**artificial intelligence**) I.A. *f*

**aid** /eɪd/ *n* aiuto *m*; **in** ~ **of** a favore di ● *vt* aiutare

**aide** /eɪd/ *n* assistente *mf*

**Aids** /eɪdz/ *n* AIDS *m*

**ailing** /'eɪlɪŋ/ *a* malato

**ailment** /'eɪlmənt/ *n* disturbo *m*

**aim** /eɪm/ *n* mira *f*; *fig* scopo *m*; **take** ~ prendere la mira ● *vt* puntare ⟨*gun*⟩ (**at** su) ● *vi* mirare; ~ **to do sth** aspirare a fare qcsa

**aimless** /'eɪmlɪs/ *a* senza scopo

**aimlessly** /'eɪmlɪslɪ/ *adv* senza scopo

**ain't** /eɪnt/ *fam* = **am not; is not; are not; have not; has not**

**air** /eə(r)/ *n* aria *f*: **be on the** ~ ⟨*programme:*⟩ essere in onda; **put on** ~**s** darsi delle arie; **by** ~ in aereo; (*airmail*) per via aerea ● *vt* arieggiare; far conoscere ⟨*views*⟩; *pej* sfoggiare ⟨*knowledge*⟩

**air: air ambulance** *n* aereo *m* ambulanza; (*helicopter*) eliambulanza *f*. **air bag** *n* Auto air bag *m inv*. **air-bed** *n* materassino *m* [gonfiabile]

**airborne** /'eəbɔːn/ *a* ⟨*plane*⟩ in volo; ⟨*troops*⟩ aerotrasportato

**air: airbrush** *n* aerografo *m*. **airbubble** *n* (*in liquid, plastic, wallpaper*) bolla *f* d'aria. **air-conditioned** *a* con aria condizionata. **air conditioner** *n* condizionatore *m*. **air-conditioning** *n* aria *f* condizionata. **air-cooled** *a* ⟨*engine*⟩ raffreddato ad aria. **aircraft** *n* aereo *m*. **aircraft carrier** *n* portaerei *f inv*. **aircraft[s]man** *n Br* aviere *m*. **aircrew** *n* equipaggio *m* di volo. **air cushion** *n* (*inflatable cushion*) cuscino *m* gonfiabile; (*of hovercraft*) cuscino *m* d'aria. **air disaster** *n* disastro *m* aereo. **airdrop** *n* lancio *m* con paracadute. **air duct** *n* condotto *m* dell'aria. **airfare** *n* tariffa *f* aerea. **airfield** *n* campo *m* d'aviazione. **airflow** *n* spostamento *m* d'aria. **air force** *n* aviazione *f*. **airfreight** *n* (*goods*) merce *f* spedita via aerea; (*method of transport*) trasporto *m* aereo; (*charge*) costo *m* per trasporto aereo. **air freshener** *n* deodorante *m* per l'ambiente. **airgun** *n* fucile *m* pneumatico. **airhead** *n pej fam* idiota *mf*. **air hole** *n* sfiatatoio *m*. **air hostess** *n* hostess *f inv*

**airing** /'eərɪŋ/ *n* **give a room an** ~ arieggiare una stanza; **give an idea an** ~ *fig* ventilare un'idea

**airing cupboard** *n Br sgabuzzino m del boiler dove viene riposta la biancheria ad asciugare*

**airless** /'eəlɪs/ *a* ⟨*evening*⟩ senza vento; ⟨*room*⟩ poco ventilato

**air: air letter** *n* aerogramma *m*. **airlift** *vt* trasportare con ponte aereo ● *n* ponte *m* aereo. **airline** *n* compagnia *f* aerea. **airliner** *n* aereo *m* di linea. **airlock** *n* bolla *f* d'aria. **airmail** *n* posta *f* aerea. **air marshal** *n Br* maresciallo *m* d'aviazione. **airplane** *n Am* aereo *m*. **air pocket** *n* vuoto *m* d'aria. **airport** *n* aeroporto *m*. **air power** *n* potenza *f* aerea. **air-raid** *n* incursione *f* aerea. **air-raid shelter** *n* rifugio *m* antiaereo. **air-raid siren** *n* allarme *m* aereo. **air-raid warning** *n* allarme *m* aereo. **air rifle** *n* fucile *m* ad aria compressa. **air-sea rescue** *n salvataggio m dal mare con impiego di mezzi aerei*. **air shaft** *n* (*in mine*) pozzo *m* di ventilazione. **airship** *n* dirigibile *m*. **air show** *n* (*trade exhibition*) salone *m* dell'aviazione; (*flying show*) manifestazione *f* aerea. **airsickness** *n* mal *m* d'aereo. **air sock** *n* manica *f* a vento. **airspeed** *n* velocità *f* relativa all'aria. **airspeed indicator** *n* indicatore *m* di velocità (*su un aereo*). **airstream** *n* corrente *f* d'aria. **airstrip** *n* pista *f* d'atterraggio. **air terminal** *n* (*in town, terminus*) [air-]terminal *m inv*. **airtight** *a* ermetico. **airtime** *n* Radio, TV spazio *m* radiofonico/televisivo. **air-to-air** *a* ⟨*missile*⟩ aria-aria; ⟨*refuelling*⟩ in volo. **air traffic** *n* traffico *m* aereo. **air-traffic controller** *n* controllore *m* di volo. **air valve** *n* valvola *f* pneumatica. **air vent** *n* presa *f* d'aria. **air vice-marshal** *n* Br vice-maresciallo *m* dell'aviazione. **airwaves** *npl* Radio, TV ondo *fpl* radio. **airway** *n* (*route*) rotta *f* aerea; ⟨*airline*⟩ compagnia *f* aerea; Anat via *f* respiratoria; ⟨*ventilating passage*⟩ pozzo *m* di ventilazione. **air waybill** *n* polizza *f* di carico aerea. **airworthiness** *n* idoneità *f* di volo. **airworthy** *a* idoneo al volo

**airy** /'eərɪ/ *a* (-ier, -iest) arieggiato; ⟨*manner*⟩ noncurante

**airy-fairy** /ˌeərɪ'feərɪ/ *a* Br fam ⟨*plan, person*⟩ fuori dalla realtà

**aisle** /aɪl/ *n* corridoio *m*; (*in supermarket*) corsia *f*; (*in church*) navata *f*

**ajar** /ə'dʒɑː(r)/ *a* socchiuso

**aka** *abbr* (**also known as**) alias

**akin** /ə'kɪn/ *a* ~ **to** simile a

**alabaster** /'æləbɑːstə(r)/ *n* alabastro *m*

**alacrity** /ə'lækrətɪ/ *n* alacrità *f inv*

**alarm** /ə'lɑːm/ *n* allarme *m*; **set the** ~ (*of alarm clock*) mettere la sveglia; **in** ~ in stato di allarme ● *vt* allarmare; **don't be ~ed!** non si allarmi!

**alarm: alarm bell** *n* campanello *m* d'allarme; **set the** ~ **~s ringing** *n* Br *fig* far scattare il campanello d'allarme. **alarm call** *n* Teleph sveglia *f* automatica. **alarm clock** *n* sveglia *f*

**alarming** /ə'lɑːmɪŋ/ *a* allarmante, preoccupante

**alarmist** /ə'lɑːmɪst/ *a & n* allarmista *mf*

**alas** /ə'læs/ *int* ahimè

**Albania** /æl'beɪnɪə/ *n* Albania *f*

**Albanian** /æl'beɪnɪən/ *n* (*person*) albanese *mf*; (*language*) albanese *m* ● *a* albanese

**albatross** /'ælbətrɒs/ *n* (*also in golf*) albatro *m*

**albeit** /ɔːl'biːɪt/ *adv & conj* benché

**albino** /æl'biːnəʊ/ *a & n* albino, -a *mf*

**album** /'ælbəm/ *n* album *m inv*

**albumen** /'ælbjʊmɪn/ *n* Biol, Bot albume *m*

**alchemist** /'ælkɪmɪst/ *n* alchimista *m*

**alchemy** /'ælkɪmɪ/ *n* Chem, fig alchimia *f*

**alcohol** /'ælkəhɒl/ *n* alcool *m*

**alcoholic** /ælkə'hɒlɪk/ *a* alcolico ● *n* alcolizzato, -a *mf*

**Alcoholics Anonymous** *n* Anonima *f* Alcolisti

**alcoholism** /'ælkəhɒlɪzm/ *n* alcolismo *m*

**alcove** /'ælkəʊv/ *n* alcova *f*

**alder** /ɔːldə(r)/ *n* (*tree, wood*) ontano *m*

**ale** /eɪl/ *n* birra *f*

**alert** /ə'lɜːt/ *a* attento; (*watchful*) vigile ● *n* segnale *m* d'allarme; **be on the** ~ stare allerta ● *vt* allertare

**alertness** /ə'lɜːtnɪs/ *n* (*attentiveness*) attenzione *f*; (*liveliness*) vivacità *f*

**A-level** *n* Br Sch ~**s** ≈ esami *mpl* di maturità; **he got an** ~ **in history** ha portato storia alla maturità

**Alexandria** /ælɪg'zændrɪə/ *n* Alessandria *f* [d'Egitto]

**alfalfa** /æl'fælfə/ *n* erba *f* medicinale

**alfresco** /æl'freskəʊ/ *a & adv* all'aperto

**algae** /'ældʒiː/ *npl* alghe *fpl*

**algebra** /'ældʒɪbrə/ *n* algebra *f*

**Algeria** /æl'dʒɪərɪə/ *n* Algeria *f*

**Algerian** /æl'dʒɪərɪən/ *a & n* algerino, -a *mf*

**Algiers** /æl'dʒɪəz/ *n* Algeri *f*

**algorithm** /'ælgərɪðm/ *n* algoritmo *m*

**alias** /'eɪlɪəs/ *n* pseudonimo *m* ● *adv* alias

**alibi** /'ælɪbaɪ/ *n* alibi *m inv*

**alien** /'eɪlɪən/ *a* straniero; *fig* estraneo ● *n* straniero, -a *mf*; (*from space*) alieno, -a *mf*

**alienate** /'eɪlɪəneɪt/ *vt* alienare

**alienation** /eɪlɪə'neɪʃn/ *n* alienazione *f*

**alight¹** /ə'laɪt/ *vi* scendere; ⟨*bird:*⟩ posarsi

**alight²** *a* **be** ~ essere in fiamme; **set** ~ dar fuoco a

**align** /ə'laɪn/ *vt* allineare

**alignment** /ə'laɪnmənt/ *n* allineamento *m*; **out of** ~ non allineato

**alike** /ə'laɪk/ *a* simile; **be** ~ rassomigliarsi ● *adv* in modo simile; **look** ~ rassomigliarsi; **summer and winter** ~ sia d'estate che d'inverno

**alimentary** /ælɪ'mentərɪ/ *a* ⟨*system*⟩ digerente; ⟨*process*⟩ digestivo

**alimentary canal** *n* tubo *m* digerente

**alimony** /'ælɪmənɪ/ *n* alimenti *mpl*

**alive** /ə'laɪv/ *a* vivo; ~ **with** brulicante di; ~ **to** sensibile a; ~ **and kicking** vivo e vegeto

**alkali** /'ælkəlaɪ/ *n* alcali *m*

**alkaline** /'ælkəlaɪn/ *a* alcalino

**all** /ɔːl/ *a* tutto; ~ **the children**, ~ **children** tutti i bambini; ~ **day** tutto il giorno; **he refused** ● **help** ha rifiutato qualsiasi aiuto; **for** ~ **that** (*nevertheless*) perciò; **in** ~ **sincerity** in tutta sincerità; **be** ~ **for** essere favorevole a ● *pron* tutto; ~ **of you/them** tutti voi/loro; ~ **of it** tutto; ~ **of the town** tutta la città; ~ **but one** tutti tranne uno; **in** ~ in tutto; ~ **in** ~ tutto sommato; **most of** ~ più di ogni altra cosa; **once and for** ~ una volta per tutte; ~ **being well** salvo complicazioni ● *adv* completamente; ~ **but** quasi; ~ **at once** (*at the same time*) tutto in una volta; ~ **at once**, ~ **of a sudden** all'improvviso; ~ **too soon** troppo presto; ~ **the same** (*nevertheless*) ciononostante; ~ **the better** meglio ancora; **she's not** ~ **that good an actress** non è poi così brava come attrice; ~ **in** in tutto; *fam* esausto; **thirty/three** ~ (*in sport*) trenta/tre pari; ~ **over** (*finished*) tutto finito; (*everywhere*) dappertutto; **it's** ~ **right** (*I don't mind*) non fa niente; **I'm** ~ **right** (*not hurt*) non ho niente; ~ **right!** va bene!

**all-American** *a* ⟨*record, champion*⟩ americano; ⟨*girl, boy, hero*⟩ tipicamente americano

**all-around** *a* ⟨*improvement*⟩ generale

**allay** /ə'leɪ/ *vt* placare ⟨*suspicions, anger*⟩

**all-clear** *n* Mil cessato *m* allarme/pericolo;

(*from doctor*) autorizzazione *f*; **give sb the ~ ~** *fig* dare il via libera a qcno

**all-consuming** *a* ⟨*passion*⟩ sfrenato; ⟨*ambition*⟩ smisurato

**all-day** *a* ⟨*event*⟩ che dura tutto il giorno

**allegation** /ælɪˈɡeɪʃn/ *n* accusa *f*

**allege** /əˈledʒ/ *vt* dichiarare

**alleged** /əˈledʒd/ *a* presunto

**allegedly** /əˈledʒɪdlɪ/ *adv* a quanto si dice

**allegiance** /əˈliːdʒəns/ *n* fedeltà *f*

**allegorical** /ælɪˈɡɒrɪkl/ *a* allegorico

**allegory** /ˈælɪɡərɪ/ *n* allegoria *f*

**all-embracing** /-əmˈbreɪsɪŋ/ *a* globale

**allergic** /əˈlɜːdʒɪk/ *a* allergico

**allergist** /ˈælədʒɪst/ *n* allergologo, -a *mf*

**allergy** /ˈælədʒɪ/ *n* allergia *f*

**alleviate** /əˈliːvɪeɪt/ *vt* alleviare

**alleviation** /əliːvɪˈeɪʃn/ *n* alleviamento *m*, alleggerimento *m*

**alley** /ˈælɪ/ *n* vicolo *m*; (*for bowling*) corsia *f*

**alley-way** /ˈælɪweɪ/ *n* vicolo *m*

**all-found** *a* £200 ~ 200 sterline inclusi vitto e alloggio

**alliance** /əˈlaɪəns/ *n* alleanza *f*

**allied** /ˈælaɪd/ *a* alleato; (*fig: related*) connesso (**to** a)

**alligator** /ˈælɪɡeɪtə(r)/ *n* alligatore *m*

**all-important** *a* essenziale

**all in** *a* (*Br fam: exhausted*) distrutto; ⟨*fee, price*⟩ tutto compreso

**all-inclusive** *a* ⟨*fee, price*⟩ tutto compreso

**all-in-one** *a* ⟨*garment*⟩ in un pezzo solo

**all-in wrestling** *n* Sport catch *m*

**all-night** *a* ⟨*party, meeting*⟩ che dura tutta la notte; ⟨*radio station*⟩ che trasmette tutta la notte; ⟨*service*⟩ notturno

**allocate** /ˈæləkeɪt/ *vt* assegnare; distribuire ⟨*resources*⟩

**allocation** /æləˈkeɪʃn/ *n* assegnazione *f*; (*of resources*) distribuzione *f*

**all-or-nothing** *a* ⟨*approach, policy*⟩ senza vie di mezzo

**allot** /əˈlɒt/ *vt* (*pt/pp* **allotted**) distribuire

**allotment** /əˈlɒtmənt/ *n* distribuzione *f*; (*share*) parte *f*; (*land*) piccolo lotto *m* di terreno

**all-out** *a* ⟨*effort*⟩ estremo; ⟨*attack*⟩ senza esclusione di colpi ● *adv* **go all out to do sth/for sth** mettercela tutta per fare qcsa/per qcsa

**all-over** *a* ⟨*tan*⟩ integrale

**all over** *prep* ~ ~ **China** in/per tutta la Cina; **the news is ~ ~ the village** lo sanno tutti in paese; **be ~ ~ sb** (*fawning over*) stare appiccicato a qcno ● *adv* **be trembling ~ ~** tremare tutto; **that's Mary ~ ~!** è proprio da Mary! ● *a* **when it's ~ ~** (*finished*) quando è tutto finito

**allow** /əˈlaʊ/ *vt* permettere; (*grant*) accordare; (*reckon on*) contare; (*agree*) ammettere; ~ **for** tener conto di; ~ **sb to do sth** permettere a qcno di fare qcsa; **you are not ~ed to...** è vietato...; **how much are you ~ed?** qual è il limite?

**allowable** /əˈlaʊəbl/ *a* permissibile; *Jur* lecito; ⟨*tax*⟩ deducibile

**allowance** /əˈlaʊəns/ *n* sussidio *m*; (*Am: pocket money*) paghetta *f*; (*for petrol etc*) indennità *f inv*; (*of luggage, duty free*) limite *m*; (*for tax purposes*) deduzione *f*; **make ~s for** essere indulgente verso ⟨*sb*⟩; tener conto di ⟨*sth*⟩

**alloy** /ˈælɔɪ/ *n* lega *f*

**alloy steel** *n* lega *f* d'acciaio

**alloy wheel** *n* cerchione *m* in lega d'acciaio

**all points bulletin** *n Am* allarme *m* generale

**all-powerful** *a* onnipotente

**all-purpose** *a* ⟨*building*⟩ polivalente; ⟨*utensil*⟩ multiuso

**all right** *a* **is it ~ ~ if...?** va bene se...?; **is that ~ ~ with you?** ti va bene?; **sounds ~ ~ to me** per me va bene; **that's [quite] ~ ~** (*it doesn't matter*) non c'è problema; **is my hair ~ ~?** sono a posto i miei capelli?; **it's ~ ~ for you!** è facile per te!; **she's ~ ~** (*competent*) è abbastanza brava; (*attractive*) non è niente male; (*pleasant*) è piuttosto simpatica; **will you be ~ ~?** (*able to manage*) te la caverai?; **feel ~ ~** (*well*) sentirsi bene ● *adv* ⟨*function, see*⟩ bene; (*not brilliantly*) così così; **can I? – ~ ~** posso? – d'accordo; **she's doing ~ ~** (*in life*) le cose le vanno bene; (*in health*) sta bene; (*in activity*) se la cava bene; **she knows ~ ~!** (*without doubt*) lei lo sa di sicuro!; ~ ~, ~ ~! va bene, va bene!

**all-risk** *a* ⟨*policy, cover*⟩ multirischi

**all-round** *a* ⟨*improvement*⟩ generale; ⟨*athlete*⟩ completo

**all-rounder** /-ˈraʊndə(r)/ *n* **be a good ~** essere versatile

**allspice** /ˈɔːlspaɪs/ *n* pepe *m* della Giamaica

**all square** *a* **be ~ ~** ⟨*people:*⟩ essere pari; ⟨*accounts:*⟩ quadrare

**all-time** *a* ⟨*record*⟩ assoluto, senza precedenti; **the ~ greats** (*people*) i grandi; ~ **high** massimo *m* storico; **be at an ~ low** ⟨*person, morale:*⟩ essere a terra; ⟨*figures, shares:*⟩ toccare il minimo storico

**all told** *adv* tutto sommato

**allude** /əˈluːd/ *vi* alludere

**allure** /æˈljʊə(r)/ *n* attrattiva *f*

**alluring** /əˈljʊrɪŋ/ *a* allettante, affascinante

**allusion** /əˈluːʒn/ *n* allusione *f*

**ally[1]** /ˈælaɪ/ *n* alleato, -a *mf*

**ally[2]** /əˈlaɪ/ *vt* (*pt/pp* **-ied**) alleare; ~ **oneself with** allearsi con

**almighty** /ɔːlˈmaɪtɪ/ *a* (*fam: big*) mega *inv* ● *n* **the A ~** l'Onnipotente *m*

**almond** /ˈɑːmənd/ *n* mandorla *f*; (*tree*) mandorlo *m*

**almost** /ˈɔːlməʊst/ *adv* quasi

**alms** /ɑːmz/ *npl* (*liter*) elemosina *fsg*

**aloft** /əˈlɒft/ *adv* in alto; *Naut* sull'alberatura; **from ~** dall'alto

**alone** /əˈləʊn/ *a* solo; **leave me ~!** lasciami in pace!; **let ~** (*not to mention*) figurarsi ● *adv* da solo ~

**along** /ə'lɒŋ/ *prep* lungo ● *adv* ~ **with** assieme a; **all** ~ tutto il tempo; **come** ~! (*hurry up*) vieni qui!; **I'll bring it** ~ lo porto lì; **I'll be** ~ **in a minute** arrivo tra un attimo; **move** ~ spostarsi; **move** ~! circolare!

**alongside** /əlɒŋ'saɪd/ *adv* lungo bordo ● *prep* lungo; **work** ~ **sb** lavorare fianco a fianco con qcno

**aloof** /ə'luːf/ *a* distante

**aloud** /ə'laʊd/ *adv* ad alta voce

**alpaca** /æl'pækə/ *n* alpaca *m inv*

**alpha** /'ælfə/ *n* (*letter*) alfa *f inv*; *Br Univ* ≈ trenta *m inv* e lode

**alphabet** /'ælfəbet/ *n* alfabeto *m*

**alphabetical** /ælfə'betɪkl/ *a* alfabetico

**alphabetically** /ælfə'betɪklɪ/ *adv* in ordine alfabetico

**alpine** /'ælpaɪn/ *a* alpino

**Alps** /ælps/ *npl* Alpi *fpl*

**already** /ɔːl'redɪ/ *adv* già

**alright** /ɔːl'raɪt/ = **all right**

**Alsace** /æl'zæs/ *n* Alsazia *f*

**Alsatian** /æl'seɪʃn/ *n* (*dog*) pastore *m* tedesco

**also** /'ɔːlsəʊ/ *adv* anche; ~, **I need…** inoltre, ho bisogno di…

**altar** /'ɔːltə(r)/ *n* altare *m*

**altar: altar boy** *n* chierichetto *m*. **altar cloth** *n* tovaglia *f* da altare. **altar piece** *n* pala *f* d'altare

**alter** /'ɔːltə(r)/ *vt* cambiare; aggiustare ⟨*clothes*⟩ ● *vi* cambiare

**alteration** /ɔːltə'reɪʃn/ *n* modifica *f*

**altercation** /ɔːltə'keɪʃn/ *n* alterco *m*

**alternate¹** /'ɔːltəneɪt/ *vi* alternarsi ● *vt* alternare

**alternate²** /ɔːl'tɜːnət/ *a* alterno; **on** ~ **days** a giorni alterni

**alternately** /ɔːl'tɜːnətlɪ/ *adv* in modo alterno; (*Am: alternatively*) alternativamente

**alternating current** /'ɔːltəneɪtɪŋ/ *n* corrente *f* alternata

**alternation** /ɔːltə'reɪʃn/ *n* alternanza *f*

**alternative** /ɔːl'tɜːnətɪv/ *a* alternativo ● *n* alternativa *f*

**alternatively** /ɔːl'tɜːnətɪvlɪ/ *adv* alternativamente

**alternative medicine** *n* medicina *f* alternativa

**alternative technology** *n* tecnologia *f* alternativa

**alternator** /'ɔːltəneɪtə(r)/ *n Electr* alternatore *m*

**although** /ɔːl'ðəʊ/ *conj* benché, sebbene

**altimeter** /'æltɪmiːtə(r)/ *n* altimetro *m*

**altitude** /'æltɪtjuːd/ *n* altitudine *f*

**alto** /'æltəʊ/ *n* contralto *m*

**altogether** /ɔːltə'geðə(r)/ *adv* (*in all*) in tutto; (*completely*) completamente; **I'm not** ~ **sure** non sono del tutto sicuro

**altruism** /'æltrʊɪzm/ *n* altruismo *m*

**altruistic** /æltrʊ'ɪstɪk/ *a* altruistico

**aluminium** /æljʊ'mɪnɪəm/ *n*, *Am* **aluminum** /ə'luːmɪnəm/ *n* alluminio *m*

**aluminium foil** *n* carta *f* stagnola

**alumna** /ə'lʌmnə/ *n Am Sch*, *Univ* ex allieva *f*

**alumnus** /ə'lʌmnəs/ *n Am Sch*, *Univ* ex allievo *m*

**always** /'ɔːlweɪz/ *adv* sempre

**am** /æm/ *see* **be**

**a.m.** *abbr* (**ante meridiem**) del mattino

**amalgam** /ə'mælgəm/ *n* amalgama *m*

**amalgamate** /ə'mælgəmeɪt/ *vt* fondere ● *vi* fondersi

**amalgamation** /əmælgə'meɪʃn/ *n* fusione *f*; (*of styles*) amalgama *m*

**amass** /ə'mæs/ *vt* accumulare

**amateur** /'æmətə(r)/ *n* non professionista *mf*; *pej* dilettante *mf* ● *attrib* dilettante; ~ **dramatics** filodrammatica *f*

**amateurish** /'æmətərɪʃ/ *a* dilettantesco

**amaze** /ə'meɪz/ *vt* stupire

**amazed** /ə'meɪzd/ *a* stupito

**amazement** /ə'meɪzmənt/ *n* stupore *m*; **to her** ~ con suo grande stupore; **in** ~ stupito

**amazing** /ə'meɪzɪŋ/ *a* incredibile

**amazingly** /ə'meɪzɪŋlɪ/ *adv* incredibilmente

**Amazon** /'æməzən/ *n* (*in myths*) Amazzone *f*; (*fig: strong woman*) amazzone *f*; (*river*) Rio *m* delle Amazzoni ● *attrib* ⟨*basin, forest, tribe*⟩ amazzonico

**ambassador** /æm'bæsədə(r)/ *n* ambasciatore, -trice *mf*

**ambassador-at-large** *n Am* ambasciatore, -trice *mf* a disposizione

**amber** /'æmbə(r)/ *n* ambra *f* ● *a* (*colour*) ambra *inv*

**ambidextrous** /æmbɪ'dekstrəs/ *a* ambidestro

**ambience** /'æmbɪəns/ *n* atmosfera *f*

**ambient** /'æmbɪənt/ *a* ⟨*temperature*⟩ ambiente *inv*; ⟨*noise*⟩ circostante

**ambiguity** /æmbɪ'gjuːətɪ/ *n* ambiguità *f inv*

**ambiguous** /æm'bɪgjʊəs/ *a* ambiguo

**ambiguously** /æm'bɪgjʊəslɪ/ *adv* in modo ambiguo

**ambition** /æm'bɪʃn/ *n* ambizione *f*; (*aim*) aspirazione *f*

**ambitious** /æm'bɪʃəs/ *a* ambizioso

**ambivalence** /æm'bɪvələns/ *n* ambivalenza *f*

**ambivalent** /æm'bɪvələnt/ *a* ambivalente

**amble** /'æmb(ə)l/ *vi* camminare senza fretta

**ambulance** /'æmbjʊləns/ *n* ambulanza *f*

**ambulance man** *n* guidatore *m* di ambulanze

**ambush** /'æmbʊʃ/ *n* imboscata *f* ● *vt* tendere un'imboscata a

**ameba** /ə'miːbə/ *n Am* ameba *f*

**amen** /ɑː'men/ *int* amen

**amenability** /əmiːnə'bɪlɪtɪ/ *n* arrendevolezza *f*

**amenable** /ə'miːnəbl/ *a* conciliante; ~ **to** sensibile a

**amend** /ə'mend/ *vt* modificare ● *npl* **make** ~**s** fare ammenda (**for** di, per)

**amendment** /ə'mendmənt/ *n* modifica *f*

**amenities** /ə'miːnətɪz/ *npl* comodità *fpl*

**America** /ə'merɪkə/ n America f
**American** /ə'merɪkən/ a & n americano, -a mf
**American: American Civil War** n guerra f di secessione [americana]. **American English** n inglese m americano. **American Indian** n indiano, -a mf d'America
**Americanism** /ə'merɪkənɪzm/ n americanismo m
**amethyst** /'æməθɪst/ n (gem) ametista f
**Amex** /'æmeks/ n abbr (**American Stock Exchange**) Borsa f valori americana; abbr **American Express**
**amiable** /'eɪmɪəbl/ a amabile
**amicable** /'æmɪkəbl/ a amichevole
**amicably** /'æmɪkəblɪ/ adv amichevolmente
**amid[st]** /ə'mɪd[st]/ prep in mezzo a
**amino acid** /ə'mi:nəʊ/ n amminoacido m
**amiss** /ə'mɪs/ a **there's something** ~ c'è qualcosa che non va ● adv **take sth** ~ prendersela [a male]; **it won't come** ~ non sarebbe sgradito
**ammo** /'æməʊ/ n abbr (**ammunition**) munizioni fpl
**ammonia** /ə'məʊnɪə/ n ammoniaca f
**ammunition** /æmjʊ'nɪʃn/ n munizioni fpl
**amnesia** /æm'ni:zɪə/ n amnesia f
**amnesty** /'æmnəstɪ/ n amnistia f
**amoeba** /ə'mi:bə/ n ameba f
**amoebic** /ə'mi:bɪk/ a (dysentry etc) amebico
**amok** /ə'mɒk/ adv **run** ~ essere in preda a furore; (imagination:) scatenarsi
**among[st]** /ə'mʌŋ[st]/ prep tra, fra; **talk** ~ **yourselves** parlate tra [di] voi
**amoral** /eɪ'mɒrəl/ a amorale
**amorality** /eɪmə'rælətɪ/ n amoralità f
**amorous** /'æmərəs/ a amoroso
**amorphous** /ə'mɔ:fəs/ a Chem amorfo; (ideas, plans) confuso; (shape, collection) informe
**amount** /ə'maʊnt/ n quantità f inv; (sum of money) montante m ● vi ~ **to** ammontare a; fig equivalere a
**amp** /æmp/ n ampère m inv
**ampere** /'æmpeə(r)/ n ampere m inv
**ampersand** /'æmpəsænd/ n e f inv commerciale
**amphetamine** /æm'fetəmi:n/ n anfetamina f
**amphibian** /æm'fɪbɪən/ n anfibio m
**amphibious** /æm'fɪbɪəs/ a anfibio
**amphitheatre** /'æmfɪθɪətə(r)/ n anfiteatro m
**ample** /'æmpl/ a (large) grande; (proportions) ampio; (enough) largamente sufficiente
**amplifier** /'æmplɪfaɪə(r)/ n amplificatore m
**amplify** /'æmplɪfaɪ/ vt (pt/pp -ied) amplificare (sound)
**amply** /'æmplɪ/ adv largamente
**amputate** /'æmpjʊteɪt/ vt amputare
**amputation** /æmpjʊ'teɪʃn/ n amputazione f
**amputee** /æmpjʊ'ti:/ n mutilato, -a mf (in seguito ad amputazione)
**amuse** /ə'mju:z/ vt divertire

**amused** /ə'mju:zd/ a divertito
**amusement** /ə'mju:zmənt/ n divertimento m
**amusement arcade** n sala f giochi
**amusement park** n luna park m inv
**amusing** /ə'mju:zɪŋ/ a divertente
**an** /ən/, accentato /æn/ see **a**
**anabolic steroid** /ænə'bɒlɪk/ n anabolizzante m
**anachronism** /ə'nækrənɪzm/ n **be an** ~ (object, custom etc:) essere anacronistico
**anaemia** /ə'ni:mɪə/ n anemia f
**anaemic** /ə'ni:mɪk/ a anemico
**anaerobic** /æneə'rəʊbɪk/ a anaerobico
**anaesthesia** /ænəs'θi:zɪə/ n anestesia f
**anaesthetic** /ænəs'θetɪk/ n anestesia f; **give sb an** ~ somministrare a qcno l'anestesia
**anaesthetist** /ə'ni:sθətɪst/ n anestesista mf
**anaesthetize** /ə'ni:sθətaɪz/ vt anestetizzare
**anagram** /'ænəgræm/ n anagramma m
**analgesic** /ænəl'dʒi:zɪk/ a & n analgesico m
**analogous** /ə'næləgəs/ a analogo
**analog[ue]** /'ænəlɒg/ a analogico
**analogy** /ə'nælədʒɪ/ n analogia f
**analyse** /'ænəlaɪz/ vt analizzare
**analysis** /ə'næləsɪs/ n analisi f inv
**analyst** /'ænəlɪst/ n analista mf
**analytical** /ænə'lɪtɪkl/ a analitico
**anarchic[al]** /ə'nɑ:kɪk[l]/ a anarchico
**anarchist** /'ænəkɪst/ n anarchico, -a mf
**anarchy** /'ænəkɪ/ n anarchia f
**anathema** /ə'næθəmə/ n eresia f
**anatomical** /ænə'tɒmɪkl/ a anatomico
**anatomically** /ænə'tɒmɪklɪ/ adv anatomicamente
**anatomy** /ə'nætəmɪ/ n anatomia f
**ANC** n abbr (**African National Congress**) Congresso m Nazionale Africano
**ancestor** /'ænsestə(r)/ n antenato, -a mf
**ancestral** /æn'sestrəl/ a ancestrale; (home) avito
**ancestry** /'ænsestrɪ/ n antenati mpl
**anchor** /'æŋkə(r)/ n ancora f ● vi gettar l'ancora ● vt ancorare
**anchorage** /'æŋkərɪdʒ/ n ancoraggio m
**anchorman** /'æŋkəmæn/ n Radio, TV anchor man m inv; Sport staffettista m dell'ultima frazione
**anchorwoman** /'æŋkəwʊmən/ n Radio TV anchor woman f inv
**anchovy** /'æntʃəvɪ/ n acciuga f
**ancient** /'eɪnʃənt/ a antico; fam vecchio; ~ **Rome** l'antica Roma f
**ancillary** /æn'sɪlərɪ/ a ausiliario
**and** /ənd/, accentato /ænd/ conj e; ~ **so on** e così via; **two** ~ **two** due più due; **six hundred** ~ **two** seicentodue; **more** ~ **more** sempre più; **nice** ~ **warm** bello caldo; **try** ~ **come** cerca di venire; **go** ~ **get** vai a prendere
**Andean** /'ændɪən/ a andino
**Andes** /'ændi:z/ npl **the** ~ le Ande
**Andorra** /æn'dɔ:rə/ n Andorra f
**anecdote** /'ænɪkdəʊt/ n aneddoto m

**anemone** /ə'nemənɪ/ *n Bot* anemone *m*

**anew** /ə'nju:/ *adv* di nuovo

**angel** /'eɪndʒl/ *n* angelo *m*

**angel cake** *n* dolce *m* di pan di Spagna

**angelfish** /'eɪnʒlfɪʃ/ *n* angelo *m* di mare

**angelic** /æn'dʒelɪk/ *a* angelico

**anger** /'æŋgə(r)/ *n* rabbia *f* ● *vt* far arrabbiare

**angina (pectoris)** /æn'dʒaɪnə('pektərɪs)/ *n* angina *f* pectoris

**angle[1]** /'æŋgl/ *n* angolo *m*; *fig* angolazione *f*: **at an ~** storto

**angle[2]** *vi* pescare con la lenza; **~ for** *fig* cercare di ottenere

**angle bracket** *n Techn* parentesi *f inv* uncinata

**Anglepoise [lamp]** /'æŋglpɔɪz/ *n* lampada *f* a braccio estensibile

**angler** /'æŋglə(r)/ *n* pescatore, -trice *mf*

**Anglican** /'æŋglɪkən/ *a & n* anglicano, -a *mf*

**anglicism** /'æŋglɪsɪzm/ *n* anglicismo *m*

**anglicize** /'æŋglɪsaɪz/ *vt* anglicizzare

**angling** /'æŋglɪŋ/ *n* pesca *f* con la lenza

**Anglo+** /'æŋgləʊ/ *pref* anglo+

**Anglo-American** *a & n* angloamericano, -a *mf*

**Anglophone** /'æŋgləfəʊn/ *a & n* anglofono, -a *mf*

**Anglo-Saxon** /æŋgləʊ'sæksn/ *a & n* anglo-sassone *mf*

**Angola** /æŋ'gəʊlə/ *n* Angola *f*

**angora** /æn'gɔ:rə/ *n* lana *f* d'angora

**angrily** /'æŋgrɪlɪ/ *adv* rabbiosamente

**angry** /'æŋgrɪ/ *a* (**-ier, -iest**) arrabbiato; **get ~** arrabbiarsi; **~ with** *or* **at sb** arrabbiato con qcno; **~ at** *or* **about sth** arrabbiato per qcsa

**anguish** /'æŋgwɪʃ/ *n* angoscia *f*; **in ~** in preda all'angoscia

**anguished** /'æŋgwɪʃt/ *a* (*suffering*) straziante; ⟨*person*⟩ angosciato

**angular** /'æŋgjʊlə(r)/ *a* angolare

**animal** /'ænɪm(ə)l/ *a & n* animale *m*

**animal: animal activist** *n* animalista *mf*. **animal experiment** *n* esperimento *m* sugli animali. **animal husbandry** *n* allevamento *m*. **animal kingdom** *n* regno *m* animale. **animal lover** *n* amante *mf* degli animali. **animal product** *n* prodotto *m* di origine animale. **animal sanctuary** *n* rifugio *m* per animali. **animal testing** *n* sperimentazione *f* sugli animali

**animate[1]** /'ænɪmət/ *a* animato

**animate[2]** /'ænɪmeɪt/ *vt* animare

**animated** /'ænɪmeɪtɪd/ *a* animato; ⟨*person*⟩ vivace

**animation** /ænɪ'meɪʃn/ *n* animazione *f*

**animator** /'ænɪmeɪtə(r)/ *n* (*film cartoonist*) animatore, -trice *mf*; (*director*) regista *mf* di film d'animazione

**animosity** /ænɪ'mɒsətɪ/ *n* animosità *f inv*

**aniseed** /'ænɪsi:d/ *n* anice *f*

**ankle** /'æŋk(ə)l/ *n* caviglia *f*

**ankle: anklebone** *n* astragalo *m*. **ankle-deep** *a* **be ~ in mud** *a* essere nel fan-

go fino alle caviglie. **ankle-length** *a* ⟨*dress*⟩ alla caviglia. **ankle sock** *n* calzino *m*

**annals** /'ænəlz/ *npl* **go down in the ~** [**of history**] passare agli annali

**annex** /ə'neks/ *vt* annettere

**annexation** /ænek'seɪʃn/ *n* (*action*) annessione *f*; (*land annexed*) territorio *m* annesso

**annex[e]** /'æneks/ *n* annesso *m*

**annihilate** /ə'naɪəleɪt/ *vt* annientare

**annihilation** /ənaɪə'leɪʃn/ *n* annientamento *m*

**anniversary** /ænɪ'vɜ:sərɪ/ *n* anniversario *m*

**Anno Domini** /ænəʊ'dɒmɪnaɪ/ *adv* dopo Cristo

**annotate** /'ænəteɪt/ *vt* annotare

**announce** /ə'naʊns/ *vt* annunciare

**announcement** /ə'naʊnsmənt/ *n* annuncio *m*

**announcer** /ə'naʊnsə(r)/ *n* annunciatore, -trice *mf*

**annoy** /ə'nɔɪ/ *vt* dare fastidio a; **get ~ed** essere infastidito

**annoyance** /ə'nɔɪəns/ *n* seccatura *f*; (*anger*) irritazione *f*

**annoying** /ə'nɔɪɪŋ/ *a* fastidioso

**annual** /'ænjʊəl/ *a* annuale; ⟨*income*⟩ annuo ● *n Bot* pianta *f* annua; (*children's book*) almanacco *m*

**Annual General Meeting** *n* assemblea *f* generale annuale

**annually** /'ænjʊəlɪ/ *adv* annualmente; **she earns £50,000 ~** guadagna 50 000 sterline all'anno

**annuity** /ə'nju:ətɪ/ *n* annualità *f inv*

**annul** /ə'nʌl/ *vt* (*pt/pp* **annulled**) annullare

**Annunciation** /ənʌnsɪ'eɪʃn/ *n* Annunciazione *f*

**anode** /'ænəʊd/ *n* anodo *m*

**anodyne** /'ænədaɪn/ *a liter* (*bland*) anodino; (*inoffensive*) innocuo

**anoint** /ə'nɔɪnt/ *vt* ungere

**anomalous** /ə'nɒmələs/ *a* anomalo

**anomaly** /ə'nɒməlɪ/ *n* anomalia *f*

**anon** /ə'nɒn/ *abbr* (**anonymous**) anonimo

**anonymity** /ænə'nɪmətɪ/ *n* anonimità *f*

**anonymous** /ə'nɒnɪməs/ *a* anonimo; **remain ~** mantenere l'anonimato

**anonymously** /ə'nɒnɪməslɪ/ *adv* anonimamente

**anorak** /'ænəræk/ *n* giacca *f* a vento

**anorexia** /ænə'reksɪə/ *n* anoressia *f*

**anorexic** /ænə'reksɪk/ *a & n* anoressico, -a *mf*

**another** /ə'nʌðə(r)/ *a & pron*: **~ [one]** un altro, un'altra; **~ day** un altro giorno; **in ~ way** diversamente; **~ time** un'altra volta; **one ~** l'un l'altro

**answer** /'ɑ:nsə(r)/ *n* risposta *f*; (*solution*) soluzione *f* ● *vt* rispondere a ⟨*person, question, letter*⟩; esaudire ⟨*prayer*⟩; **~ the door** aprire la porta; **~ the telephone** rispondere al telefono ● *vi* rispondere

■ **answer back** *vi* ribattere

■ **answer for** *vt* rispondere di

**answerable** /'ɑ:nsərəbl/ a responsabile; **be ~ to sb** rispondere a qcno

**answering machine** n Teleph segreteria f telefonica

**answering service** n servizio m di segreteria telefonica

**answerphone** /'ɑ:nsəfəʊn/ n segreteria f telefonica

**ant** /ænt/ n formica f

**antacid** /ænt'æsɪd/ a & n antiacido m

**antagonism** /æn'tægənɪzm/ n antagonismo m

**antagonistic** /æntægə'nɪstɪk/ a antagonistico

**antagonize** /æn'tægənaɪz/ vt provocare l'ostilità di

**Antarctic** /æn'tɑ:ktɪk/ n Antartico m ●a antartico

**Antarctica** /æn'tɑ:ktɪkə/ n Antartide f

**Antarctic Circle** n Circolo m polare antartico

**Antarctic Ocean** n mare m antartico

**anteater** /'ænti:tə(r)/ n formichiere m

**antecedent** /æntɪ'si:dənt/ n (precedent) antecedente m; (ancestor) antenato, -a mf

**antedate** /æntɪ'deɪt/ vt (put earlier date on) retrodatare; (predate) precedere

**antediluvian** /æntɪdɪ'lu:vɪən/ a antidiluviano

**antelope** /'æntɪləʊp/ n antilope m

**antenatal** /æntɪ'neɪtl/ a prenatale

**antenatal class** n corso m di preparazione al parto

**antenatal clinic** n Br assistenza f medica prenatale

**antenna** /æn'tenə/ n antenna f

**anterior** /æn'tɪərɪə/ a anteriore

**ante-room** /'æntɪ-/ n anticamera f

**antheap** /'ænθi:p/ = **anthill**

**anthem** /'ænθəm/ n inno m

**anthill** /'ænθɪl/ n formicaio m

**anthology** /æn'θɒlədʒɪ/ n antologia f

**anthracite** /'ænθrəsaɪt/ n antracite f

**anthrax** /'ænθræks/ n (disease) carbonchio m; (pustule) pustola f di carbonchio

**anthropological** /ænθrəpə'lɒdʒɪkl/ a antropologico

**anthropologist** /ænθrə'pɒlədʒɪst/ n antropologo, -a mf

**anthropology** /ænθrə'pɒlədʒɪ/ n antropologia f

**anti** /'ænti/ pref anti- ● prep be ~ essere contro

**anti-abortion** a antiabortista

**anti-abortionist** n antiabortista mf

**anti-aircraft** a antiaereo

**anti-apartheid** a antiapartheid inv

**antibacterial** /æntɪbæk'tɪərɪəl/ a antibatterico

**antiballistic missile** /æntɪbəlɪstɪk-'mɪsaɪl/ n missile m antimissile

**antibiotic** /æntɪbaɪ'ɒtɪk/ n antibiotico m

**antibody** /'æntɪbɒdɪ/ n anticorpo m

**anticipate** /æn'tɪsɪpeɪt/ vt prevedere; (forestall) anticipare

**anticipation** /æntɪsɪ'peɪʃn/ n anticipo m; (excitement) attesa f; **in ~ of** in previsione di

**anticlimax** /æntɪ'klaɪmæks/ n delusione f

**anticlockwise** /æntɪ'klɒkwaɪz/ a & adv in senso antiorario

**antics** /'æntɪks/ npl gesti mpl buffi

**anticyclone** /æntɪ'saɪkləʊn/ n anticiclone m

**antidepressant** /æntɪdɪ'pres(ə)nt/ a & n antidepressivo m

**antidote** /'æntɪdəʊt/ n antidoto m

**anti-establishment** a contestatario

**antifreeze** /'æntɪfri:z/ n antigelo m

**antiglare** /æntɪ'gleə(r)/ a (screen) antirifles-so inv

**antihistamine** /æntɪ'hɪstəmi:n/ n antistaminico m

**anti-inflammatory** /-ɪn'flæmətrɪ/ a & n antinfiammatorio m

**anti-inflation** a anti-inflazione inv

**anti-inflationary** /-ɪn'fleɪʃnərɪ/ a antinflazionistico

**anti-lock** a antibloccaggio inv

**antipathy** /æn'tɪpəθɪ/ n antipatia f

**antiperspirant** /æntɪ'pɜ:spɪrənt/ n deodorante m antitraspirante

**antipodean** /æntɪpə'di:ən/ a & n australiano, -a e/o neozelandese mf

**Antipodes** /æn'tɪpədi:z/ npl Br the ~ gli antipodi

**antiquarian** /æntɪ'kweərɪən/ a antiquario; ~ **bookshop** negozio m di libri antichi

**antiquated** /'æntɪkweɪtɪd/ a antiquato

**antique** /æn'ti:k/ a antico ● n antichità f inv

**antique: antiques fair** n fiera f dell'antiquariato. **antique dealer** n antiquario, -a mf. **antique shop** n negozio m d'antiquariato. **antiques trade** n antiquariato m

**antiquity** /æn'tɪkwətɪ/ n antichità f

**anti-racism** n antirazzismo m

**anti-riot** a (police) antisommossa inv

**anti-rust** a antiruggine inv

**anti-Semitic** /æntɪsɪ'mɪtɪk/ a antisemita

**anti-Semitism** /æntɪ'semɪtɪzm/ n antisemitismo m

**antiseptic** /æntɪ'septɪk/ a & n antisettico m

**anti-skid** a antiscivolo inv

**anti-smoking** a contro il fumo, antifumo

**antisocial** /æntɪ'səʊʃəl/ a (behaviour) antisociale; (person) asociale

**anti-terrorist** a antiterrorista

**anti-theft** a (lock, device) antifurto inv; (camera) di sorveglianza; ~ **steering lock** bloccasterzo m

**antithesis** /æn'tɪθəsɪs/ n antitesi f

**antitrust** /æntɪ'trʌst/ a antitrust inv

**antivirus** /æntɪ'vaɪrəs/ **program** n Comput programma m antivirus

**antivivisectionist** /æntɪvɪvɪ'sekʃənɪst/ n antivivisezionista mf ● a antivivisezionistico

**antlers** /'æntləz/ npl corna fpl

**antonym** /'æntənɪm/ n antonimo m

**Antwerp** /'æntwɜ:p/ n Anversa f

**anus** /'eɪnəs/ n ano m

**anvil** /'ænvɪl/ n incudine f

15

**anxiety** /æŋ'zaɪətɪ/ *n* ansia *f*
**anxious** /'æŋkʃəs/ *a* ansioso
**anxiously** /'æŋkʃəslɪ/ *adv* con ansia
**any** /'enɪ/ *a* (*no matter which*) qualsiasi, qualunque; **have we ~ wine/biscuits?** abbiamo del vino/dei biscotti?; **have we ~ jam/apples?** abbiamo della marmellata/delle mele?; **~ colour/number you like** qualsiasi colore/numero ti piaccia; **we don't have ~ wine/biscuits** non abbiamo vino/biscotti; **I don't have ~ reason to lie** non ho nessun motivo per mentire; **for ~ reason** per qualsiasi ragione ● *pron* (*some*) ne; (*no matter which*) uno qualsiasi; **I don't want ~** [of it] non ne voglio [nessuno]; **there aren't ~** non ce ne sono; **have we ~?** ne abbiamo?; **have you read ~ of her books?** hai letto qualcuno dei suoi libri? ● *adv* **I can't go ~ quicker** non posso andare più in fretta; **is it ~ better?** va un po' meglio?; **would you like ~ more?** ne vuoi ancora?; **I can't eat ~ more** non posso mangiare più niente
**anybody** /'enɪbʌdɪ/ *pron* chiunque; (*after negative*) nessuno; **~ can do that** chiunque può farlo; **I haven't seen ~** non ho visto nessuno
**anyhow** /'enɪhaʊ/ *adv* ad ogni modo, comunque; (*badly*) non importa come
**anyone** /'enɪwʌn/ *pron* = **anybody**
**anyplace** /'enɪpleɪs/ *adv Am* = **anywhere**
**anything** /'enɪθɪŋ/ *pron* qualche cosa, qualcosa; (*no matter what*) qualsiasi cosa; (*after negative*) niente; **take/buy ~ you like** prendi/compra quello che vuoi; **I don't remember ~** non mi ricordo niente; **he's ~ but stupid** è tutto, ma non stupido; **I'll do ~ but that** farò qualsiasi cosa, tranne quello
**anytime** /'enɪtaɪm/ *adv* **if at ~ you feel lonely…** se mai ti dovessi sentire solo…; **he could arrive ~ now** potrebbe arrivare da un momento all'altro; **~ after 2 pm** a qualsiasi ora dopo le due; **at ~ of the day or night** a qualsiasi ora del giorno o della notte; **~ you like** quando vuoi
**anyway** /'enɪweɪ/ *adv* ad ogni modo, comunque
**anywhere** /'enɪweə(r)/ *adv* dovunque; (*after negative*) da nessuna parte; **put it ~** mettilo dove vuoi; **I can't find it ~** non lo trovo da nessuna parte; **~ else** da qualch'altra parte; (*after negative*) da nessun'altra parte; **I don't want to go ~ else** non voglio andare da nessun'altra parte
**aorta** /eɪ'ɔːtə/ *n* aorta *f*
**Aosta** /æ'ɒstə/ *n* Aosta *f*
**apace** /ə'peɪs/ *adv liter* rapidamente
**apart** /ə'pɑːt/ *adv* lontano; **live ~** vivere separati; **100 miles ~** lontani 100 miglia; **born 20 minutes ~** nati a distanza di 20 minuti; **~ from** a parte; **you can't tell them ~** non si possono distinguere; **joking ~** scherzi a parte
**apartheid** /ə'pɑːthaɪt/ *n* apartheid *f*
**apartment** /ə'pɑːtmənt/ *n* (*Am: flat*) appartamento *m*; **in my ~** a casa mia

**apartment block** *n* stabile *m*
**apartment house** *n* stabile *m*
**apathetic** /æpə'θetɪk/ *a* (*by nature*) apatico; **~ about sth/towards sb** (*from illness, depression*) indifferente a qcsa/nei confronti di qcno
**apathy** /'æpəθɪ/ *n* apatia *f*
**ape** /eɪp/ *n* scimmia *f* ● *vt* scimmiottare
**Apennines** /'æpənaɪnz/ *npl* **the ~** gli Appennini
**aperitif** /ə'perətiːf/ *n* aperitivo *m*
**aperture** /'æpətʃə(r)/ *n* apertura *f*
**apex** /'eɪpeks/ *n* vertice *m*
**aphid** /'eɪfɪd/ *n* afide *m*
**aphrodisiac** /æfrə'dɪzɪæk/ *a & n* afrodisiaco *m*
**apiary** /'eɪpɪərɪ/ *n* apiario *m*
**apiece** /ə'piːs/ *adv* ciascuno
**aplenty** /ə'plentɪ/ *adv* **there were goals ~** c'è stata una valanga di gol
**apocalypse** /ə'pɒkəlɪps/ *n* Apocalisse *f*; (*disaster, destruction*) apocalisse *f*
**apocalyptic** /əpɒkə'lɪptɪk/ *a* apocalittico
**apocryphal** /ə'pɒkrɪfəl/ *a* apocrifo
**apogee** /'æpədʒiː/ *n* apogeo *m*
**apolitical** /eɪpə'lɪtɪkl/ *a* apolitico
**Apollo** /ə'pɒləʊ/ *n also fig* Apollo *m*
**apologetic** /əpɒlə'dʒetɪk/ *a* (*air, remark*) di scusa; **be ~** essere spiacente
**apologetically** /əpɒlə'dʒetɪklɪ/ *adv* per scusarsi
**apologist** /ə'pɒlədʒɪst/ *n* apologeta *mf* (**for** di)
**apologize** /ə'pɒlədʒaɪz/ *vi* scusarsi (**for** per)
**apology** /ə'pɒlədʒɪ/ *n* scusa *f*; *fig* **an ~ for a dinner** una sottospecie di cena
**apoplectic** /æpə'plektɪk/ *a* (*furious*) furibondo; (*fit, attack*) apoplettico
**apoplexy** /'æpəpleksɪ/ *n Med* apoplessia *f*; (*rage*) rabbia *f*
**apostle** /ə'pɒsl/ *n* apostolo *m*
**apostrophe** /ə'pɒstrəfɪ/ *n* apostrofo *m*
**apotheosis** /əpɒθɪ'əʊsɪs/ *n* apoteosi *f inv*
**appal** /ə'pɔːl/ *vt* (*pt/pp* **appalled**) sconvolgere
**Appalachians** /æpə'leɪtʃnz/ *npl* **the ~** gli Appalachi
**appalling** /ə'pɔːlɪŋ/ *a* sconvolgente; **he's an ~ teacher** *fig* è un disastro come professore
**appallingly** /ə'pɔːlɪŋlɪ/ *adv* (*behave, treat*) orribilmente; **unemployment figures are ~ high** il tasso di disoccupazione è spaventosamente alto; **furnished in ~ bad taste** arredato con pessimo gusto
**apparatus** /æpə'reɪtəs/ *n* apparato *m*
**apparel** /ə'pærəl/ *n* abbigliamento *m*
**apparent** /ə'pærənt/ *a* evidente; (*seeming*) apparente
**apparently** /ə'pærəntlɪ/ *adv* apparentemente
**apparition** /æpə'rɪʃn/ *n* apparizione *f*
**appeal** /ə'piːl/ *n* appello *m*; (*attraction*) attrattiva *f* ● *vi* fare appello; **~ to** (*be attractive to*) attrarre
**appeal[s] court** *n* corte *f* d'appello

**appeal fund** n raccolta f di fondi
**appealing** /ə'pi:lɪŋ/ a attraente
**appealingly** /ə'pi:lɪŋlɪ/ adv (beseechingly) in modo supplichevole; (attractively) in modo attraente
**appear** /ə'pɪə(r)/ vi apparire; (seem) sembrare; ⟨publication:⟩ uscire; Theat esibirsi; **he finally ~ed at...** fam si è fatto finalmente vedere alle...; ~ **in court** comparire in giudizio
**appearance** /ə'pɪərəns/ n apparizione f; (look) aspetto m; **to all ~s** a giudicare dalle apparenze; **keep up ~s** salvare le apparenze
**appease** /ə'pi:z/ vt placare
**appeasement** /ə'pi:zmənt/ n **a policy of ~** una politica troppo conciliante
**append** /ə'pend/ vt apporre ⟨signature⟩ (**to** a)
**appendage** /ə'pendɪdʒ/ n appendice f
**appendicitis** /əpendɪ'saɪtɪs/ n appendicite f
**Appenine** /'æpənaɪn/ a appenninico
**Appenines** /'æpənaɪnz/ npl Appennini mpl
**appendix** /ə'pendɪks/ n (pl **-ices** /-ɪsi:z/) (of book) appendice f; (pl **-es**) Anat appendice f
**appertain** /æpə'teɪn/ vi ~ **to** essere pertinente a
**appetite** /'æpɪtaɪt/ n appetito m
**appetite suppressant** n pillola f antifame
**appetizer** /'æpɪtaɪzə(r)/ n (drink) aperitivo m; (starter) antipasto m; (biscuit, olive etc) stuzzichino m
**appetizing** /'æpɪtaɪzɪŋ/ a appetitoso
**applaud** /ə'plɔ:d/ vt/i applaudire
**applause** /ə'plɔ:z/ n applauso m
**apple** /'æpl/ n mela f; **she's the ~ of his eye** è la luce dei suoi occhi
**apple: apple core** n torsolo m di mela. **apple orchard** n meleto m. **apple tree** n melo m
**appliance** /ə'plaɪəns/ n attrezzo m; [electrical] ~ elettrodomestico m
**applicable** /'æplɪkəbl/ a **be ~ to** essere valido per; **not ~** (on form) non applicabile
**applicant** /'æplɪkənt/ n candidato, -a mf
**application** /æplɪ'keɪʃn/ n applicazione f; (request) domanda f; (for job) candidatura f; **on ~** su richiesta
**application form** n modulo m di domanda
**applicator** /'æplɪkeɪtə(r)/ n applicatore m
**applied** /ə'plaɪd/ a applicato
**appliqué** /æ'pli:keɪ/ n applicazione f ● attrib ⟨motif, decoration⟩ applicato
**apply** /ə'plaɪ/ vt (pt/pp **-ied**) applicare; ~ **oneself** applicarsi; ~ **the brakes** frenare ● vi applicarsi; ⟨law:⟩ essere applicabile; ~ **to** (ask) rivolgersi a; ~ **for** fare domanda per ⟨job etc⟩
**appoint** /ə'pɔɪnt/ vt nominare; fissare ⟨time⟩; **well ~ed** ben equipaggiato
**appointee** /əpɔɪn'ti:/ n incaricato, -a mf
**appointment** /ə'pɔɪntmənt/ n appuntamento m; (to job) nomina f; (job) posto m
**apportion** /ə'pɔ:ʃn/ vt ripartire, attribuire
**apposite** /'æpəzɪt/ a appropriato
**apposition** /æpə'zɪʃn/ n apposizione f

**appraisal** /ə'preɪzəl/ n valutazione f; **make an ~ of sth** valutare qcsa
**appraise** /ə'preɪz/ vt valutare
**appreciable** /ə'pri:ʃəbl/ a sensibile
**appreciably** /ə'pri:ʃəblɪ/ adv sensibilmente
**appreciate** /ə'pri:ʃeɪt/ vt apprezzare; (understand) comprendere ● vi (increase in value) aumentare di valore
**appreciation** /əpri:sɪ'eɪʃn/ n (gratitude) riconoscenza f; (enjoyment) apprezzamento m; (understanding) comprensione f; (in value) aumento m; **in ~** come segno di riconoscenza (**of** per)
**appreciative** /ə'pri:ʃətɪv/ a riconoscente
**apprehend** /æprɪ'hend/ vt arrestare
**apprehension** /æprɪ'henʃn/ n arresto m; (fear) apprensione f
**apprehensive** /æprɪ'hensɪv/ a apprensivo
**apprehensively** /æprɪ'hensɪvlɪ/ adv con apprensione
**apprentice** /ə'prentɪs/ n apprendista mf
**apprenticeship** /ə'prentɪsʃɪp/ n apprendistato m
**apprise** /ə'praɪz/ vt fml informare (**of** di)
**approach** /ə'prəʊtʃ/ n avvicinamento m; (to problem) approccio m; (access) accesso m; **make ~es to** fare degli approcci con ● vi avvicinarsi ● vt avvicinarsi a; (with request) rivolgersi a; affrontare ⟨problem⟩
**approachable** /ə'prəʊtʃəbl/ a accessibile
**approach: approach lights** npl Aeron sentiero m luminoso di avvicinamento. **approach path** n Aeron rotta f di avvicinamento. **approach road** n strada f d'accesso
**approbation** /æprə'beɪʃn/ n approvazione f
**appropriate¹** /ə'prəʊprɪət/ a appropriato
**appropriate²** /ə'prəʊprɪeɪt/ vt appropriarsi di
**appropriately** /ə'prəʊprɪətlɪ/ adv (suitably) in modo appropriato; (sited) convenientemente; (designed, chosen, behave) adeguatamente
**appropriation** /əprəʊprɪ'eɪʃn/ n Am Comm stanziamento m; (Jur: removal) appropriazione f
**approval** /ə'pru:vl/ n approvazione f; **on ~** in prova
**approve** /ə'pru:v/ vt approvare ● vi ~ **of** approvare ⟨sth⟩; avere una buona opinione di ⟨sb⟩
**approving** /ə'pru:vɪŋ/ a ⟨smile, nod⟩ d'approvazione
**approvingly** /ə'pru:vɪŋlɪ/ adv con approvazione
**approximate¹** /ə'prɒksɪmeɪt/ vi ~ **to** avvicinarsi a
**approximate²** /ə'prɒksɪmət/ a approssimativo
**approximately** /ə'prɒksɪmətlɪ/ adv approssimativamente
**approximation** /əprɒksɪ'meɪʃn/ n approssimazione f
**APR** n abbr (annual percentage rate) tasso m percentuale annuo

**apricot** /'eɪprɪkɒt/ *n* albicocca *f*; ~ **tree** albicocco *m*

**April** /'eɪprəl/ *n* aprile *m*; **make an ~ Fool of sb** fare un pesce d'aprile a qcno; ~ **Fool's Day** il primo d'aprile

**apron** /'eɪprən/ *n* grembiule *m*

**apropos** /'æprəpəʊ/ *adv* ~ [**of**] a proposito [di]

**apse** /æps/ *n* abside *f*

**apt** /æpt/ *a* appropriato; ⟨*pupil*⟩ dotato; **be ~ to do sth** avere tendenza a fare qcsa

**aptitude** /'æptɪtjuːd/ *n* disposizione *f*

**aptitude test** *n* test *m inv* attitudinale

**aptly** /'æptlɪ/ *adv* appropriatamente

**Apulia** /ə'pjuːlɪə/ *n* Puglia *f*

**aqualung** /'ækwəlʌŋ/ *n* autorespiratore *m*

**aquamarine** /ˌækwəmə'riːn/ *a & n* acquamarina *f*

**aquaplane** /'ækwəpleɪn/ *vi Sport* praticare l'acquaplano; *Br Auto* andare in aquaplaning

**aquarium** /ə'kweərɪəm/ *n* acquario *m*

**Aquarius** /ə'kweərɪəs/ *n Astr* Acquario *m*; **be ~** essere dell'Acquario

**aquatic** /ə'kwætɪk/ *a* acquatico

**aqueduct** /'ækwədʌkt/ *n* acquedotto *m*

**aquiline** /'ækwɪlaɪn/ *a* ⟨*nose, features*⟩ aquilino

**Arab** /'ærəb/ *a & n* arabo, -a *mf*

**Arabia** /ə'reɪbɪə/ *n* Arabia *f*

**Arabian** /ə'reɪbɪən/ *a* arabo

**Arabic** /'ærəbɪk/ *a* arabo; ~ **numerals** numeri *mpl* arabici ● *n* arabo *m*

**Arab-Israeli** *a* arabo-israeliano

**arable** /'ærəbl/ *a* coltivabile

**arbiter** /'ɑːbɪtə(r)/ *n* arbitro *m*

**arbitrarily** /ɑːbɪ'trerɪlɪ/ *adv* arbitrariamente

**arbitrary** /'ɑːbɪtrərɪ/ *a* arbitrario

**arbitrate** /'ɑːbɪtreɪt/ *vi* arbitrare

**arbitration** /ɑːbɪ'treɪʃn/ *n* arbitraggio *m*

**arbitrator** /'ɑːbɪtreɪtə(r)/ *n* arbitro *m*

**arbour** /'ɑːbə(r)/ *n* pergolato *m*

**arc** /ɑːk/ *n* arco *m*

**arcade** /ɑː'keɪd/ *n* portico *m*; (*shops*) galleria *f*

**arcane** /ɑː'keɪn/ *a* arcano

**arch** /ɑːtʃ/ *n* arco *m*; (*of foot*) dorso *m* del piede ● *vt* **the cat ~ed its back** il gatto ha arcuato la schiena

**archaeological** /ɑːkɪə'lɒdʒɪkl/ *a* archeologico

**archaeologist** /ɑːkɪ'ɒlədʒɪst/ *n* archeologo, -a *mf*

**archaeology** /ɑːkɪ'ɒlədʒɪ/ *n* archeologia *f*

**archaic** /ɑː'keɪɪk/ *a* arcaico

**archbishop** /ɑːtʃ'bɪʃəp/ *n* arcivescovo *m*

**arched** /ɑːtʃt/ *a* ⟨*eyebrows*⟩ arcuato

**arch-enemy** *n* acerrimo nemico *m*

**archer** /'ɑːtʃə(r)/ *n* arciere *m*

**archery** /'ɑːtʃərɪ/ *n* tiro *m* con l'arco

**archetypal** /ɑːkɪ'taɪpl/ *a* **the ~ hero** il prototipo dell'eroe

**archetype** /'ɑːkɪtaɪp/ *n* archetipo *m*

**archipelago** /ɑːkɪ'pelǝgəʊ/ *n* arcipelago *m*

**architect** /'ɑːkɪtekt/ *n* architetto *m*

**architectural** /ɑːkɪ'tektʃərəl/ *a* architettonico

**architecturally** /ɑːkɪ'tektʃərəlɪ/ *adv* architettonicamente

**architecture** /'ɑːkɪtektʃə(r)/ *n* architettura *f*

**archives** /'ɑːkaɪvz/ *npl* archivi *mpl*

**archiving** /'ɑːkaɪvɪŋ/ *n Comput* archiviazione *f*

**archway** /'ɑːtʃweɪ/ *n* arco *m*

**Arctic** /'ɑːktɪk/ *a* artico ● *n* **the ~** l'Artico

**Arctic Circle** *n* Circolo *m* polare artico

**Arctic Ocean** *n* mare *m* artico

**ardent** /'ɑːdənt/ *a* ardente

**ardently** /'ɑːdəntlɪ/ *adv* ardentemente

**ardour** /'ɑːdə(r)/ *n* ardore *m*

**arduous** /'ɑːdjʊəs/ *a* arduo

**arduously** /'ɑːdjʊəslɪ/ *adv* con fatica, con difficoltà

**are** /ɑː(r)/ *see* **be**

**area** /'eərɪə/ *n* area *f*; (*region*) zona *f*; (*fig: field*) campo *m*

**area code** *n* prefisso *m* [telefonico]

**area manager** *n* direttore, -trice *mf* di zona

**aren't** /ɑːnt/ = **are not** *see* **be**

**arena** /ə'riːnə/ *n* arena *f*

**Argentina** /ɑːdʒən'tiːnə/ *n* Argentina *f*

**Argentine** /'ɑːdʒəntaɪn/ *a* argentino

**Argentinian** /ɑːdʒən'tɪnɪən/ *a & n* argentino, -a *mf*

**arguable** /'ɑːgjʊəbl/ *a* **it's ~ that...** si può sostenere che...

**arguably** /'ɑːgjʊəblɪ/ *adv* **he is ~...** è probabilmente...

**argue** /'ɑːgjuː/ *vi* litigare (**about** su); (*debate*) dibattere; **don't ~!** non discutere! ● *vt* (*debate*) dibattere; (*reason*) ~ **that** sostenere che

**argument** /'ɑːgjʊmənt/ *n* argomento *m*; (*reasoning*) ragionamento *m*; **have an ~** litigare

**argumentative** /ɑːgjʊ'mentətɪv/ *a* polemico

**aria** /'ɑːrɪə/ *n* aria *f*

**arid** /'ærɪd/ *a* arido

**aridity** /ə'rɪdətɪ/ *n also fig* aridità *f*

**Aries** /'eəriːz/ *n Astr* Ariete *m*; **be ~** essere dell'Ariete

**arise** /ə'raɪz/ *vi* (*pt* **arose**, *pp* **arisen**) ⟨*opportunity, need, problem:*⟩ presentarsi; (*result*) derivare

**aristocracy** /ærɪ'stɒkrəsɪ/ *n* aristocrazia *f*

**aristocrat** /'ærɪstəkræt/ *n* aristocratico, -a *mf*

**aristocratic** /ærɪstə'krætɪk/ *a* aristocratico

**arithmetic** /ə'rɪθmətɪk/ *n* aritmetica *f*

**arithmetical** /ærɪθ'metɪkl/ *a* aritmetico

**ark** /ɑːk/ *n* **Noah's A ~** l'Arca *f* di Noè

**arm** /ɑːm/ *n* braccio *m*; (*of chair*) bracciolo *m*; ~**s** *pl* (*weapons*) armi *fpl*; ~ **in ~** a braccetto; **up in ~s** *fam* furioso (**about** per); *fig* **with open ~s** a braccia aperte ● *vt* armàre

**armadillo** /ɑːmə'dɪləʊ/ *n* armadillo *m*

**armaments** /'ɑːməmənts/ *npl* armamenti *mpl*

**armband** /'ɑːmbænd/ *n* (*for swimmer*) bracciolo m (*per nuotare*): (*for mourner*) fascia f al braccio

**armchair** /'ɑ:mtʃeə(r)/ n poltrona f

**armchair traveller** n *persona f che si interessa di viaggi senza viaggiare*

**armed** /ɑ:md/ a armato

**armed forces** /'fɔ:sɪz/ npl forze fpl armate

**armed robbery** n rapina f a mano armata

**Armenia** /ɑ:'mi:nɪə/ n Armenia f

**Armenian** /ɑ:'mi:nɪən/ a & n (*person*) armeno, -a mf; (*language*) armeno m

**armful** /'ɑ:mfʊl/ n bracciata f

**armhole** /'ɑ:mhəʊl/ n giro m manica inv

**armistice** /'ɑ:mɪstɪs/ n armistizio m

**Armistice Day** n l'Anniversario m dell'Armistizio (*1 nov. 1918*)

**armour** /'ɑ:mə(r)/ n armatura f

**armour-clad** /-'klæd/ a ⟨vehicle⟩ blindato; ⟨ship⟩ corazzato

**armoured** /'ɑ:məd/ a ⟨vehicle⟩ blindato

**armoured car** n autoblinda[ta] f

**armour plate, armour plating** /'pleɪtɪŋ/ n corazzatura f

**armour-plated** /-'pleɪtɪd/ a corazzato

**armoury** /'ɑ:mərɪ/ n (*factory*) fabbrica f d'armi; (*store*) arsenale m, armeria f

**armpit** /'ɑ:mpɪt/ n ascella f

**armrest** /'ɑ:mrest/ n bracciolo m (*di sedia*)

**arms: arms control** n controllo m degli armamenti. **arms dealer** n trafficante mf d'armi. **arms dump** n deposito m d'armi. **arms factory** n fabbrica f d'armi. **arms limitation** n controllo m degli armamenti. **arms manufacturer** n fabbricante mf d'armi. **arms race** n corsa f agli armamenti. **arms treaty** n trattato m sul controllo degli armamenti

**arm-twisting** /'ɑ:mtwɪstɪŋ/ n pressioni fpl

**arm-wrestling** n braccio m di ferro

**army** /'ɑ:mɪ/ n esercito m; **join the ~** arruolarsi

**A road** n *Br* [strada f] statale f

**aroma** /ə'rəʊmə/ n aroma f

**aromatherapy** /ərəʊmə'θerəpɪ/ n aromaterapia f

**aromatic** /ærə'mætɪk/ a aromatico

**arose** /ə'rəʊz/ see **arise**

**around** /ə'raʊnd/ adv intorno; **all ~** tutt'intorno; **I'm not from ~ here** non sono di qui; **he's not ~** non c'è ● prep intorno a; in giro per ⟨room, shops, world⟩

**arousal** /ə'raʊzl/ n eccitazione f

**arouse** /ə'raʊz/ vt svegliare; (*sexually*) eccitare

**arpeggio** /ɑ:'pedʒɪəʊ/ n arpeggio m

**arrange** /ə'reɪndʒ/ vt sistemare ⟨furniture, books⟩; organizzare ⟨meeting⟩; fissare ⟨date, time⟩; **~ to do sth** combinare di fare qcsa

**arrangement** /ə'reɪndʒmənt/ n (*of furniture*) sistemazione f; *Mus* arrangiamento m; (*agreement*) accordo; (*of flowers*) composizione f; **make ~s** prendere disposizioni; **I've made other ~s** ho preso altri impegni

**array** /ə'reɪ/ n (*clothes*) abbigliamento m; (*of troops, people*) schieramento m; (*of numbers*)

tabella f; (*of weaponry*) apparato m; (*of goods, products*) assortimento m; *Comput* matrice f ● vt **~ed in ceremonial robes** abbigliato da gran cerimonia

**arrears** /ə'rɪəz/ npl arretrati mpl; **be in ~** essere in arretrato; **paid in ~** pagato a lavoro eseguito

**arrest** /ə'rest/ n arresto m; **under ~** in stato d'arresto ● vt arrestare

**arresting** /ə'restɪŋ/ a (*striking*) che colpisce

**arrival** /ə'raɪvl/ n arrivo m; **new ~s** pl nuovi arrivati mpl

**arrival: arrival lounge** n sala f arrivi. **arrivals board** n tabellone m degli arrivi. **arrival time** n ora f d'arrivo

**arrive** /ə'raɪv/ vi arrivare; **~ at** fig raggiungere

**arrogance** /'ærəg(ə)ns/ n arroganza f

**arrogant** /'ærəg(ə)nt/ a arrogante

**arrogantly** /'ærəg(ə)ntlɪ/ adv con arroganza

**arrow** /'ærəʊ/ n freccia f

**arrowhead** /'ærəʊhed/ n punta f di freccia

**arse** /ɑ:s/ n vulg culo m

■ **arse about, arse around** vi vulg coglioneggiare

**arsenal** /'ɑ:sən(ə)l/ n arsenale m

**arsenic** /'ɑ:sənɪk/ n arsenico m

**arson** /'ɑ:sən/ n incendio m doloso

**arsonist** /'ɑ:sənɪst/ n incendiario, -a mf

**art** /ɑ:t/ n arte f; **work of ~** opera f d'arte; **~s and crafts** pl artigianato m; **the A~s** pl l'arte f; **A~s degree** *Univ* laurea f in Lettere

**art: art collection** n collezione f d'arte. **art collector** n collezionista d'arte. **art college** n ≈ accademia f di belle arti. **art dealer** n commerciante mf di oggetti d'arte. **art deco** n art déco f

**artefact** /'ɑ:tɪfækt/ n manufatto m

**arterial** /ɑ:'tɪərɪəl/ a *Anat* arterioso

**arterial road** n arteria f [stradale]

**artery** /'ɑ:tərɪ/ n arteria f

**art exhibition** n mostra f d'arte. **art form** n forma f d'arte

**artful** /'ɑ:tfl/ a scaltro

**artfully** /'ɑ:tfʊlɪ/ adv astutamente

**art gallery** n galleria f d'arte

**arthritic** /ɑ:'θrɪtɪk/ a & n artritico, -a mf

**arthritis** /ɑ:'θraɪtɪs/ n artrite f

**artichoke** /'ɑ:tɪtʃəʊk/ n carciofo m

**article** /'ɑ:tɪkl/ n articolo m; **~ of clothing** capo m d'abbigliamento

**articulate¹** /ɑ:'tɪkjʊlət/ a ⟨speech⟩ chiaro; **be ~** esprimersi bene

**articulate²** /ɑ:'tɪkjʊleɪt/ vt scandire ⟨words⟩

**articulated lorry** /ɑ:'tɪkjʊleɪtɪd/ n autotreno m

**articulately** /ɑ:'tɪkjʊlətlɪ/ adv chiaramente

**articulation** /ɑ:tɪkjʊ'leɪʃn/ n (*pronunciation, Anat*) articolazione f; (*expression*) espressione f

**artifice** /'ɑ:tɪfɪs/ n artificio m

**artificial** /ɑ:tɪ'fɪʃl/ a artificiale

**artificial insemination** n inseminazione f artificiale

**artificial intelligence** *n* intelligenza *f* artificiale

**artificiality** /ɑːtɪfɪʃɪ'ælətɪ/ *n* artificiosità *f*

**artificial limb** *n* arto *m* artificiale

**artificially** /ɑːtɪ'fɪʃəlɪ/ *adv* artificialmente; ⟨*smile*⟩ artificiosamente

**artificial respiration** *n* respirazione *f* artificiale

**artillery** /ɑː'tɪlərɪ/ *n* artiglieria *f*

**artisan** /ɑːtɪ'zæn/ *n* artigiano, -a *mf*

**artist** /ɑː'tɪst/ *n* artista *mf*

**artiste** /ɑː'tiːst/ *n* Theat artista *mf*

**artistic** /ɑː'tɪstɪk/ *a* artistico

**artistically** /ɑː'tɪstɪklɪ/ *adv* artisticamente

**artistry** /'ɑːtɪstrɪ/ *n* arte *f*, talento *m*

**artless** /'ɑːtlɪs/ *a* spontaneo

**artlessly** /'ɑːtlɪslɪ/ *adv* ⟨*smile*⟩ ingenuamente

**art nouveau** /ɑːnuː'vəʊ/ *a* & *n* liberty *m*

**art school** *n* ≈ accademia *f* di belle arti

**arts: arts degree** *n* laurea *f* in Lettere. **arts funding** *n* sovvenzioni *fpl* alle belle arti. **arts student** *n* studente, -essa *mf* di Lettere

**art student** *n* studente, -essa *mf* di belle arti

**artwork** /'ɑːtwɜːk/ *n* illustrazioni *fpl*

**arty** /'ɑːtɪ/ *a fam* ⟨*person*⟩ intellettualoide; ⟨*district*⟩ degli intellettuali

**Aryan** /'eərɪən/ *a* & *n* ariano, -a *mf*

**as** /æz/ *conj* come; ⟨*since*⟩ siccome; ⟨*while*⟩ mentre; **as he grew older** diventando vecchio; **as you get to know her** conoscendola meglio; **young as she is** per quanto sia giovane ● *prep* come; **as a friend** come amico; **as a child** da bambino; **as a foreigner** in quanto straniero; **disguised as** travestito da ● *adv* **as well** ⟨*also*⟩ anche; **as soon as I get home** [non] appena arrivo a casa; **as quick as you** veloce quanto te; **as quick as you can** più veloce che puoi; **as far as** ⟨*distance*⟩ fino a; **as far as I'm concerned** per quanto mi riguarda; **as long as** finché; ⟨*provided that*⟩ purché

**asbestos** /æz'bestɒs/ *n* amianto *m*

**ascend** /ə'send/ *vi* salire ● *vt* salire a ⟨*throne*⟩

**ascendancy** /ə'send(ə)nsɪ/ *n* **gain the ~ over sb** acquisire una posizione dominante su qcno

**ascendant** /ə'send(ə)nt/ *n* **be in the ~** Astr essere in ascendente; ⟨*fig: person*⟩ essere in auge

**Ascension** /ə'senʃn/ *n* Relig Ascensione *f*

**ascent** /ə'sent/ *n* ascesa *f*

**ascertain** /æsə'teɪn/ *vt* accertare

**ascetic** /ə'setɪk/ *a* & *n* ascetico, -a *mf*

**asceticism** /ə'setɪsɪzm/ *n* ascesi *f*

**ascribable** /ə'skraɪbəbl/ *a* attribuibile

**ascribe** /ə'skraɪb/ *vt* attribuire

**aseptic** /eɪ'septɪk/ *a* asettico

**asexual** /eɪ'seksjʊəl/ *a* asessuale, asessuato

**ash**[1] /æʃ/ *n* ⟨*tree*⟩ frassino *m*

**ash**[2] *n* cenere *f*

**ashamed** /ə'ʃeɪmd/ *a* **be/feel ~** vergognarsi

**ash blond** *a* biondo cenere

**ashen** /'æʃ(ə)n/ *a* ⟨*complexion*⟩ cinereo

**ashore** /ə'ʃɔː(r)/ *adv* a terra; **go ~** sbarcare

**ash: ashtray** *n* portacenere *m*. **ash tree** *n* frassino *m*. **Ash Wednesday** *n* mercoledì *m inv* delle Ceneri

**Asia** /'eɪʒə/ *n* Asia *f*

**Asia Minor** *n* Asia *f* Minore

**Asian** /'eɪʒ(ə)n/ *a* & *n* asiatico, -a *mf*; (Br: Indian, Pakistani) indiano, -a *mf*

**Asiatic** /eɪʒɪ'ætɪk/ *a* asiatico

**aside** /ə'saɪd/ *adv* **take sb ~** prendere qcno a parte; **put sth ~** mettere qcsa da parte; **~ from you** Am a parte te; **~ from his injuries** Am a parte le sue ferite ● *n* **in an ~** tra parentesi

**asinine** /'æsɪnaɪn/ *a* sciocco

**ask** /ɑːsk/ *vt* fare ⟨*question*⟩; ⟨*invite*⟩ invitare; **~ sb sth** domandare *or* chiedere qcsa a qcno; **~ sb to do sth** domandare *or* chiedere a qcno di fare qcsa ● *vi* **~ about sth** informarsi su qcsa; **~ after** chiedere [notizie] di; **~ for** chiedere ⟨*sths*⟩; chiedere di ⟨*sb*⟩; **~ for trouble** *fam* andare in cerca di guai

∎ **ask in** *vt* **~ sb in** invitare qcno ad entrare

∎ **ask out** *vt* **~ sb out** chiedere a qcno di uscire

**askance** /ə'skɑːns/ *adv* **look ~ at sb/sth** guardare qcno/qcsa di traverso

**askew** /ə'skjuː/ *a* & *adv* di traverso

**asking price** /'ɑːskɪŋ/ *n* prezzo *m* trattabile

**asleep** /ə'sliːp/ *a* **be ~** dormire; **fall ~** addormentarsi

**asparagus** /ə'spærəgəs/ *n* asparagi *mpl*

**aspect** /'æspekt/ *n* aspetto *m*

**aspen** /'æspən/ *n* pioppo *m* tremulo

**aspersions** /ə'spɜːʃnz/ *npl* **cast ~ on** diffamare

**asphalt** /'æsfælt/ *n* asfalto *m*

**asphyxia** /əs'fɪksɪə/ *n* asfissia *f*

**asphyxiate** /əs'fɪksɪeɪt/ *vt* asfissiare

**asphyxiation** /əsfɪksɪ'eɪʃn/ *n* asfissia *f*

**aspirate**[1] /'æspəreɪt/ *vt* aspirare

**aspirate**[2] /'æspɪrət/ *a* aspirato

**aspirations** /æspə'reɪʃnz/ *npl* aspirazioni *fpl*

**aspire** /ə'spaɪə(r)/ *vi* **~ to** aspirare a

**aspiring** /ə'spaɪərɪŋ/ *a* **~ authors/ journalists** aspiranti scrittori/giornalisti

**ass** /æs/ *n* asino *m*

**assailant** /ə'seɪlənt/ *n* assalitore, -trice *mf*

**assassin** /ə'sæsɪn/ *n* assassino, -a *mf*

**assassinate** /ə'sæsɪneɪt/ *vt* assassinare

**assassination** /əsæsɪ'neɪʃn/ *n* assassinio *m*

**assault** /ə'sɔːlt/ *n* Mil assalto *m*; Jur aggressione *f* ● *vt* aggredire

**assault and battery** *n* Jur lesioni *fpl* personali

**assault course** *n* Mil percorso *m* di guerra

**assemblage** /ə'semblɪdʒ/ *n* assemblaggio *m*

**assemble** /ə'sembl/ *vi* radunarsi ● *vt* radunare; Techn montare

**assembler** /ə'semblə(r)/ *n* (in factory)

montatore, -trice *mf*; *Comput* [programma *m*] assemblatore *m*

**assembly** /ə'semblı/ *n* assemblea *f*; *Sch assemblea f giornaliera di alunni e professori di una scuola*; *Techn* montaggio *m*

**assembly line** *n* catena *f* di montaggio

**assent** /ə'sent/ *n* assenso *m* ● *vi* acconsentire

**assert** /ə'sɜːt/ *vt* asserire; far valere ⟨*one's rights*⟩; ~ **oneself** farsi valere

**assertion** /ə'sɜːʃn/ *n* asserzione *f*

**assertive** /ə'sɜːtɪv/ *a* **be ~** farsi valere

**assertiveness** /ə'sɜːtɪvnɪs/ *n* capacità *f* di farsi valere; **lack of ~** scarsa sicurezza *f* di sé

**assess** /ə'ses/ *vt* valutare; (*for tax purposes*) stabilire l'imponibile di

**assessment** /ə'sesmənt/ *n* valutazione *f*; (*of tax*) accertamento *m*

**assessor** /ə'sesə(r)/ *n* (*Jur, in insurance*) perito *m*; (*tax*) agente *m* del fisco

**asset** /'æset/ *n* (*advantage*) vantaggio *m*; (*person*) elemento *m* prezioso. **~s** *pl* beni *mpl*; (*on balance sheet*) attivo *msg*

**asset stripping** /'æsetstrɪpɪŋ/ *n* rilevamento *m* di un'azienda per rivenderne le singole attività fisse

**assiduity** /æsɪ'djuːətɪ/ *n* assiduità *f*

**assiduous** /ə'sɪdjuəs/ *a* assiduo

**assign** /ə'saɪn/ *vt* assegnare

**assignation** /æsɪg'neɪʃn/ *n* *hum* appuntamento *m* galante

**assignment** /ə'saɪnmənt/ *n* (*task*) incarico *m*

**assimilate** /ə'sɪmɪleɪt/ *vt* assimilare; integrare ⟨*person*⟩

**assimilation** /əsɪmɪ'leɪʃn/ *n* assimilazione *f*

**assist** /ə'sɪst/ *vt/i* assistere; ~ **sb to do sth** assistere qcno nel fare qcsa

**assistance** /ə'sɪstəns/ *n* assistenza *f*

**assistant** /ə'sɪstənt/ *n* assistente *mf*; (*in shop*) commesso, -a *mf*

**assistant manager** *n* vicedirettore, -trice *mf*

**assistant professor** *n* *Am Univ* docente *mf* universitario, -a del grado più basso

**associate¹** /ə'səʊʃɪeɪt/ *vt* associare (**with** a); **be ~d with sth** (*involved in*) essere coinvolto in qcsa ● *vi* ~ **with** frequentare

**associate²** /ə'səʊʃɪət/ *a* associato ● *n* collega *mf*; (*member*) socio, -a *mf*

**associate: associate company** *n* consociata *f*. **associate director** *n* *Comm* amministratore *m* aggiunto. **associate editor** *n* coredattore, -trice *mf*. **associate member** *n* membro *m* associato

**association** /əsəʊsɪ'eɪʃn/ *n* associazione *f*

**Association Football** *n* [gioco *m* del] calcio *m*

**assorted** /ə'sɔːtɪd/ *a* assortito

**assortment** /ə'sɔːtmənt/ *n* assortimento *m*

**assuage** /ə'sweɪdʒ/ *vt* *liter* alleviare

**assume** /ə'sjuːm/ *vt* presumere; assumere ⟨*control*⟩; ~ **office** entrare in carica; **assuming that you're right,…** ammettendo che tu abbia ragione,…

**assumption** /ə'sʌmpʃn/ *n* supposizione *f*; **on the ~ that** partendo dal presupposto che; **the A~** *Relig* l'Assunzione *f*

**assurance** /ə'ʃʊərəns/ *n* assicurazione *f*; (*confidence*) sicurezza *f*

**assure** /ə'ʃʊə(r)/ *vt* assicurare; **he ~d me of his innocence** mi ha assicurato di essere innocente

**assured** /ə'ʃʊəd/ *a* sicuro

**Assyria** /ə'sɪrɪə/ *n* Assiria *f*

**asterisk** /'æstərɪsk/ *n* asterisco *m*

**astern** /ə'stɜːn/ *adv* a poppa

**asteroid** /'æstərɔɪd/ *n* asteroide *m*

**asthma** /'æsmə/ *n* asma *f*

**asthmatic** /æs'mætɪk/ *a* asmatico

**astigmatism** /ə'stɪgmətɪzm/ *n* astigmatismo *m*

**astonish** /ə'stɒnɪʃ/ *vt* stupire

**astonished** /ə'stɒnɪʃt/ *a* sorpreso

**astonishing** /ə'stɒnɪʃɪŋ/ *a* stupefacente

**astonishingly** /ə'stɒnɪʃɪŋlɪ/ *adv* sorprendentemente

**astonishment** /ə'stɒnɪʃmənt/ *n* stupore *m*

**astound** /ə'staʊnd/ *vt* stupire

**astounding** /ə'staʊndɪŋ/ *a* incredibile

**astrakhan** /æstrə'kæn/ *n* astrakan *m*

**astray** /ə'streɪ/ *adv* **go ~** smarrirsi; (*morally*) uscire dalla retta via; **lead ~** traviare

**astride** /ə'straɪd/ *adv* [a] cavalcioni ● *prep* a cavalcioni di

**astringent** /ə'strɪndʒənt/ *a* astringente; *fig* austero ● *n* astringente *m*

**astrologer** /ə'strɒlədʒə(r)/ *n* astrologo, -a *mf*

**astrological** /æstrə'lɒdʒɪkl/ *a* astrologico

**astrology** /ə'strɒlədʒɪ/ *n* astrologia *f*

**astronaut** /'æstrənɔːt/ *n* astronauta *mf*

**astronomer** /ə'strɒnəmə(r)/ *n* astronomo, -a *mf*

**astronomic** /æstrə'nɒmɪk/ *a* *fig* astronomico

**astronomical** /æstrə'nɒmɪkl/ *a* *also* *fig* astronomico

**astronomically** /æstrə'nɒmɪklɪ/ *adv* ~ **expensive** dal prezzo astronomico; **prices are ~ high** i prezzi sono astronomici

**astronomy** /ə'strɒnəmɪ/ *n* astronomia *f*

**astrophysicist** /æstrəʊ'fɪzɪsɪst/ *n* astrofisico, -a *mf*

**astrophysics** /æstrəʊ'fɪzɪks/ *n* astrofisica *f*

**astute** /ə'stjuːt/ *a* astuto

**astutely** /ə'stjuːtlɪ/ *adv* con astuzia

**astuteness** /ə'stjuːtnɪs/ *n* astuzia *f*

**asylum** /ə'saɪləm/ *n* [**political**] ~ asilo *m* politico; [**lunatic**] ~ manicomio *m*

**asylum-seeker** /ə'saɪləmsiːkə(r)/ *n* persona *f* che chiede asilo politico

**asymmetric[al]** /æsɪ'metrɪk, æsɪ'metrɪkl/ *a* asimmetrico

**at** /ət/, *accentato* /æt/ *prep* a; **at the station/the market** alla stazione/al mercato; **at the office/the bank** in ufficio/banca; **at the beginning** all'inizio; **at John's** da John; **at the hairdresser's** dal parrucchiere; **at home** a casa; **at work** al lavoro; **at**

**school** a scuola; **at a party/wedding** a una festa/un matrimonio; **at one o'clock** all'una; **at 50 km an hour** ai 50 all'ora; **at Christmas/Easter** a Natale/Pasqua; **at times** talvolta; **two at a time** due alla volta; **good at languages** bravo nelle lingue; **at sb's request** su richiesta di qcno; **are you at all worried?** sei preoccupato?

**atavistic** /ætə'vɪstɪk/ a atavico

**ate** /et/ see **eat**

**atheism** /'eɪθɪɪzm/ n ateismo m

**atheist** /'eɪθɪɪst/ n ateo, -a mf

**atheistic** /eɪθɪ'ɪstɪk/ a ‹principle› ateistico; ‹person› ateo

**Athenian** /ə'θi:nɪən/ a & n ateniese mf

**Athens** /'æθənz/ n Atene f

**athlete** /'æθli:t/ n atleta mf

**athlete's foot** n micosi f

**athletic** /æθ'letɪk/ a atletico

**athletics** /æθ'letɪks/ n atletica fsg

**Atlantic** /ət'læntɪk/ a & n **the ~ [Ocean]** l'[Oceano m] Atlantico m

**atlas** /'ætləs/ n atlante m

**Atlas Mountains** npl Monti mpl dell'Atlante

**ATM** n abbr (**automatic teller machine**) cassa f continua di prelevamento

**atmosphere** /'ætməsfɪə(r)/ n atmosfera f

**atmospheric** /ætməs'ferɪk/ a atmosferico

**atom** /'ætəm/ n atomo m

**atom bomb** n bomba f atomica

**atomic** /ə'tɒmɪk/ a atomico

**atomic: atomic power station** n centrale f atomica. **atomic reactor** n reattore m nucleare. **atomic scientist** n fisico, -a mf nucleare

**atomize** /'ætəmaɪz/ vt atomizzare

**atomizer** /'ætəmaɪzə(r)/ n atomizzatore m

**atone** /ə'təʊn/ vi **~ for** pagare per

**atonement** /ə'təʊnmənt/ n espiazione f

**atrocious** /ə'trəʊʃəs/ a atroce; ‹fam: meal, weather› abominevole

**atrociously** /ə'trəʊʃəslɪ/ adv atrocemente; ‹rude etc› terribilmente

**atrocity** /ə'trɒsətɪ/ n atrocità f inv

**atrophy** /'ætrəfɪ/ n Med atrofia f ● vi Med, fig atrofizzarsi

**attach** /ə'tætʃ/ vt attaccare; attribuire ‹importance›; **be ~ed to** fig essere attaccato a

**attaché** /ə'tæʃeɪ/ n addetto m

**attaché case** n ventiquattrore f inv

**attachment** /ə'tætʃmənt/ n (affection) attaccamento m; (accessory) accessorio m

**attack** /ə'tæk/ n attacco m; (physical) aggressione f ● vt attaccare; (physically) aggredire

**attacker** /ə'tækə(r)/ n assalitore, -trice mf; ‹critic› detrattore, -trice mf

**attain** /ə'teɪn/ vt raggiungere ‹ambition›; raggiungere ‹success, age, goal›

**attainable** /ə'teɪnəbl/ a ‹ambition› realizzabile; ‹success› raggiungibile

**attainment** /ə'teɪnmənt/ n (of knowledge) acquisizione f; (of goal) realizzazione f, raggiungimento m; (success) risultato m

**attempt** /ə'tempt/ n tentativo m ● vt tentare

**attend** /ə'tend/ vt essere presente a; (go regularly to) frequentare; (accompany) accompagnare; ‹doctor:› avere in cura ● vi essere presente; (pay attention) prestare attenzione

■ **attend to** vt occuparsi di; (in shop) servire

**attendance** /ə'tendəns/ n presenza f

**attendance record** n (of MP, committee member, schoolchild) tasso m di presenza

**attendance register** n Sch registro m

**attendant** /ə'tendənt/ n guardiano, -a mf

**attention** /ə'tenʃn/ n attenzione f; **~!** Mil attenti!; **pay ~** prestare attenzione; **need ~** aver bisogno di attenzioni; ‹skin, hair, plant:› dover essere curato; ‹car, tyres:› dover essere riparato; **for the ~ of** all'attenzione di

**attention-seeking** /ə'tenʃnsi:kɪŋ/ n bisogno m di attirare l'attenzione ● a ‹person› che cerca di attirare l'attenzione.

**attention span** n **he has a very short ~** non è capace di mantenere a lungo la concentrazione

**attentive** /ə'tentɪv/ a ‹pupil, audience› attento; ‹son› premuroso

**attentively** /ə'tentɪvlɪ/ adv attentamente

**attentiveness** /ə'tentɪvnɪs/ n (concentration) attenzione f; (solicitude) sollecitudine f

**attenuate** /ə'tenjʊeɪt/ vt attenuare

**attest** /ə'test/ vt/i attestare

**attic** /'ætɪk/ n soffitta f

**attic room** n mansarda f

**attic window** n lucernario m

**attire** /ə'taɪə(r)/ n abiti mpl ● vt vestire (**in** con)

**attitude** /'ætɪtju:d/ n atteggiamento m

**attorney** /ə'tɜ:nɪ/ n (Am: lawyer) avvocato m; **power of ~** delega f

**Attorney General** n Br ≈ Procuratore m Generale; Am ≈ Ministro m di Grazia e Giustizia

**attract** /ə'trækt/ vt attirare

**attraction** /ə'trækʃn/ n attrazione f; (feature) attrattiva f

**attractive** /ə'træktɪv/ a ‹person› attraente; ‹proposal, price› allettante

**attractiveness** /ə'træktɪvnɪs/ n (of person, place) fascino m; (of proposal) carattere m allettante; (of investment) convenienza f

**attributable** /ə'trɪbjʊtəbl/ a ‹error, fall, loss etc› attribuibile; **be ~ to** ‹change, profit, success etc:› essere dovuto a

**attribute**[1] /'ætrɪbju:t/ n attributo m

**attribute**[2] /ə'trɪbju:t/ vt attribuire

**attribution** /ætrɪ'bju:ʃn/ n attribuzione f

**attributive** /ə'trɪbjʊtɪv/ a attributivo

**attrition** /ə'trɪʃn/ n **war of ~** guerra f di logoramento

**attune** /ə'tju:n/ vt **be ~d to** (in harmony with) essere sintonizzato con; (accustomed to) essere abituato a

**aubergine** /'əʊbəʒi:n/ n melanzana f

**auburn** /'ɔ:bən/ a castano ramato

**auction** /'ɔ:kʃn/ n asta f ● vt vendere all'asta

**auctioneer** /ɔ:kʃə'nɪə(r)/ n banditore m

**auction rooms** npl sala f d'aste

**auction sale** n vendita f all'asta
**audacious** /ɔːˈdeɪʃəs/ a sfacciato; (*daring*) audace
**audaciously** /ɔːˈdeɪʃəslɪ/ adv sfacciatamente; (*daringly*) con audacia
**audacity** /ɔːˈdæsətɪ/ n sfacciataggine f; (*daring*) audacia f
**audible** /ˈɔːdəbl/ a udibile
**audience** /ˈɔːdɪəns/ n Theat pubblico m; TV telespettatori mpl; (*Radio*) ascoltatori mpl; (*meeting*) udienza f
**audience:** **audience participation** n partecipazione f del pubblico. **audience ratings** npl indici mpl di ascolto. **audience research** n sondaggio m tra il pubblico
**audio** /ˈɔːdɪəʊ/: **audiobook** n audiolibro m. **audio cassette** n audiocassetta f. **audio system** n impianto m stereo. **audiotape** n audiocassetta f. **audiotyping** n trascrizione f da audiocassetta. **audio typist** n dattilografo, -a mf (*che trascrive registrazioni*). **audiovisual** a audiovisivo
**audit** /ˈɔːdɪt/ n verifica f del bilancio ● vt verificare
**auditing** /ˈɔːdɪtɪŋ/ n auditing m inv
**audition** /ɔːˈdɪʃn/ n audizione f ● vi fare un'audizione
**auditor** /ˈɔːdɪtə(r)/ n revisore m di conti
**auditorium** /ɔːdɪˈtɔːrɪəm/ n sala f
**auditory** /ˈɔːdɪt(ə)rɪ/ a acustico, uditivo
**augment** /ɔːgˈment/ vt aumentare
**augur** /ˈɔːgə(r)/ vi ~ **well/ill** essere di buon/cattivo augurio
**August** /ˈɔːgəst/ n agosto m
**august** /ɔːˈgʌst/ a augusto
**Augustinian** /ɔːgəˈstɪnɪən/ a agostiniano
**aunt** /ɑːnt/ n zia f
**auntie, aunty** /ˈɑːntɪ/ n fam zietta f
**au pair** /əʊˈpeə(r)/ n ~ **[girl]** ragazza f alla pari
**aura** /ˈɔːrə/ n aura f
**aural** /ˈɔːrəl/ a uditivo; (*Sch: comprehension, test*) orale; (*Med: test*) audiometrico ● n Sch esercizio m di comprensione ed espressione orale; *Mus* ~ dettato m musicale
**aurora australis/borealis** /ɔːˈrɔːrəʊˈstrɑːlɪs/bɔːrɪˈɑːlɪs/ n aurora f australe/boreale
**auspices** /ˈɔːspɪsɪz/ npl under the ~ of sotto l'egida di
**auspicious** /ɔːˈspɪʃəs/ a di buon augurio
**Aussie** /ˈɒzɪ/ a & n fam australiano, -a mf
**austere** /ɒˈstɪə(r)/ a austero
**austerity** /ɒˈsterətɪ/ n austerità f
**Australasia** /ɒstrəˈleɪʒə/ n Australasia f
**Australia** /ɒˈstreɪlɪə/ n Australia f
**Australian** /ɒˈstreɪlɪən/ a & n australiano, -a mf
**Austria** /ˈɒstrɪə/ n Austria f
**Austrian** /ˈɒstrɪən/ a & n austriaco, -a mf
**Austro-Hungarian** /ɒstrəʊhʌŋˈgeərɪən/ a austroungarico
**autarchy** /ˈɔːtɑːkɪ/ n autarchia f
**authentic** /ɔːˈθentɪk/ a autentico
**authenticate** /ɔːˈθentɪkeɪt/ vt autenticare

**authenticity** /ɔːθenˈtɪsətɪ/ n autenticità f
**author** /ˈɔːθə(r)/ n autore m
**authoritarian** /ɔːθɒrɪˈteərɪən/ a autoritario
**authoritative** /ɔːˈθɒrɪtətɪv/ a autorevole; (*manner*) autoritario
**authority** /ɔːˈθɒrətɪ/ n autorità f; (*permission*) autorizzazione f; **who's in ~ here?** chi è il responsabile qui?; **be in ~ over** avere autorità su; **be an ~ on** essere un'autorità in materia di
**authorization** /ɔːθəraɪˈzeɪʃn/ n autorizzazione f
**authorize** /ˈɔːθəraɪz/ vt autorizzare
**authorized dealer** /ˈɔːθəraɪzd/ rivenditore m autorizzato
**autism** /ˈɔːtɪzm/ n autismo m
**autistic** /ɔːˈtɪstɪk/ a autistico
**auto** /ˈɔːtəʊ/ n Am fam auto f ● attrib (*industry*) automobilistico; (*workers*) dell'industria automobilistica
**autobiographical** /ɔːtəbaɪəˈgræfɪkl/ a autobiografico
**autobiography** /ɔːtəbaɪˈɒgrəfɪ/ n autobiografia f
**autocrat** /ˈɔːtəkræt/ n autocrate m
**autocratic** /ɔːtəˈkrætɪk/ a autocratico
**autocue** /ˈɔːtəkjuː/ n TV gobbo m
**autograph** /ˈɔːtəgrɑːf/ n autografo m ● vt autografare
**autoimmune** /ɔːtəʊɪˈmjuːn/ a (*disease, system*) autoimmune
**automate** /ˈɔːtəmeɪt/ vt automatizzare
**automatic** /ɔːtəˈmætɪk/ a automatico ● n (*car*) macchina f col cambio automatico; (*washing machine*) lavatrice f automatica
**automatically** /ɔːtəˈmætɪklɪ/ adv automaticamente
**automatic pilot** n (*device*) pilota m automatico; **be on ~ ~** also fig viaggiare con il pilota automatico inserito
**automatic teller machine** /ˈtelə/ n cassa f continua di prelevamento
**automation** /ɔːtəˈmeɪʃn/ n automazione f
**automaton** /ɔːˈtɒmətən/ n automa m
**automobile** /ˈɔːtəməbiːl/ n automobile f
**automotive** /ɔːtəˈməʊtɪv/ a (*self-propelling*) autopropulso; (*design, industry*) automobilistico
**autonomous** /ɔːˈtɒnəməs/ a autonomo
**autonomously** /ɔːˈtɒnəməslɪ/ adv autonomamente
**autonomy** /ɔːˈtɒnəmɪ/ n autonomia f
**autopilot** /ˈɔːtəʊpaɪlət/ n Aeron, fig pilota m automatico
**autopsy** /ˈɔːtɒpsɪ/ n autopsia f
**auto-suggestion** /ɔːtəʊsəˈdʒestʃən/ n autosuggestione f
**autumn** /ˈɔːtəm/ n autunno m
**autumnal** /ɔːˈtʌmnl/ a autunnale
**auxiliary** /ɔːgˈzɪlɪərɪ/ a ausiliario ● n ausiliare m
**auxiliary nurse** n infermiere, -a mf ausiliario, -a
**auxiliary verb** n ausiliare m

**avail** /ə'veɪl/ *n* **to no ~** invano ● *vi* **~ oneself of** approfittare di

**availability** /əveɪlə'bɪlətɪ/ *n* (*of option, service*) disponibilità *f*; (*of drugs*) reperibilità *f*. disponibilità *f*; **subject to ~** fino ad esaurimento

**available** /ə'veɪləbl/ *a* disponibile; ⟨*book, record etc*⟩ in vendita

**avalanche** /'ævəlɑːnʃ/ *n* valanga *f*

**avant-garde** /ævɒ̃'gɑːd/ *n* avanguardia *f* ● *a* d'avanguardia

**avarice** /'ævərɪs/ *n* avidità *f*

**avaricious** /ævə'rɪʃəs/ *a* avido

**Ave** *abbr* (**Avenue**) V.le

**avenge** /ə'vendʒ/ *vt* vendicare

**avenger** /ə'vendʒə(r)/ *n* vendicatore, -trice *mf*

**avenging** /ə'vendʒɪŋ/ *a* vendicatore

**avenue** /'ævənjuː/ *n* viale *m*; *fig* strada *f*

**average** /'ævərɪdʒ/ *a* medio; (*mediocre*) mediocre ● *n* media *f*; **on ~** in media; **above ~** superiore al normale ● *vt* ⟨*sales, attendance etc*⟩ raggiungere una media di

**average out at** *vt* risultare in media

**averse** /ə'vɜːs/ *a* **not be ~ to sth** non essere contro qcsa

**aversion** /ə'vɜːʃn/ *n* avversione *f* (**to** per)

**avert** /ə'vɜːt/ *vt* evitare ⟨*crisis*⟩; distogliere ⟨*eyes*⟩

**aviary** /'eɪvɪərɪ/ *n* uccelliera *f*

**aviation** /eɪvɪ'eɪʃn/ *n* aviazione *f*

**aviation fuel** *n* benzina *f* avio

**aviation industry** *n* industria *f* aeronautica

**aviator** /'eɪvɪeɪtə(r)/ *n* aviatore, -trice *mf*

**avid** /'ævɪd/ *a* avido (**for** di); ⟨*reader*⟩ appassionato

**avidity** /ə'vɪdətɪ/ *n* avidità

**avidly** /'ævɪdlɪ/ *adv* ⟨*read, collect*⟩ avidamente; ⟨*support*⟩ con entusiasmo

**avocado** /ævə'kɑːdəʊ/ *n* avocado *m*

**avoid** /ə'vɔɪd/ *vt* evitare

**avoidable** /ə'vɔɪdəbl/ *a* evitabile

**avoidance** /ə'vɔɪdəns/ *n* **~ of one's duty** astensione *f* dal proprio dovere

**avowed** /ə'vaʊd/ *a* dichiarato

**avuncular** /ə'vʌŋkʊlə(r)/ *a* benevolo

**await** /ə'weɪt/ *vt* attendere

**awake** /ə'weɪk/ *a* sveglio; **wide ~** completamente sveglio ● *vi* (*pt* **awoke**, *pp* **awoken**) svegliarsi

**awaken** /ə'weɪkn/ *vt* svegliare ● *vi* svegliarsi

**awakening** /ə'weɪknɪŋ/ *n* risveglio *m*

**award** /ə'wɔːd/ *n* premio *m*; (*medal*) riconoscimento *m*; (*of prize*) assegnazione *f* ● *vt* assegnare; (*hand over*) consegnare

**award: award ceremony** *n* cerimonia *f* di premiazione. **award winner** *n* vincitore, -trice *mf* di un premio. **award-winning** *a* ⟨*book, film, design*⟩ premiato

**aware** /ə'weə(r)/ *a* **be ~ of** (*sense*) percepire; (*know*) essere conscio di; **become ~ of** accorgersi di; (*learn*) venire a sapere di; **be ~ that** rendersi conto che

**awareness** /ə'weənɪs/ *n* percezione *f*; (*knowledge*) consapevolezza *f*

**awash** /ə'wɒʃ/ *a* inondato (**with** di)

**away** /ə'weɪ/ *adv* via; **go/stay ~** andare/stare via; **he's ~ from his desk/the office** non è alla sua scrivania/in ufficio; **far ~** lontano; **four kilometres ~** a quattro chilometri; **play ~** *Sport* giocare fuori casa

**away game** *n* partita *f* fuori casa

**awe** /ɔː/ *n* soggezione *f*; **stand in ~ of sb** avere soggezione di qcno

**awe-inspiring** *a* maestoso

**awesome** /'ɔːsəm/ *a* imponente

**awful** /'ɔːf(ə)l/ *a* terribile; **that's an ~ pity** è un gran peccato ● *adv fam* estremamente

**awfully** /'ɔːf(ʊ)lɪ/ *adv* terribilmente; ⟨*pretty*⟩ estremamente; **that's ~ nice of you** è veramente gentile da parte tua; **thanks ~** grazie mille

**awhile** /ə'waɪl/ *adv* per un po'

**awkward** /'ɔːkwəd/ *a* ⟨*movement*⟩ goffo; ⟨*moment, situation*⟩ imbarazzante; ⟨*time*⟩ scomodo

**awkwardly** /'ɔːkwədlɪ/ *adv* ⟨*move*⟩ goffamente; ⟨*say*⟩ con imbarazzo; **the meeting is ~ timed** la riunione è ad un orario scomodo

**awkwardness** /'ɔːkwədnɪs/ *n* (*clumsiness*) goffaggine *f*; (*inconvenience*) scomodità *f*; (*embarrassment*) imbarazzo *m*; (*delicacy of situation*) delicatezza *f*

**awl** /ɔːl/ *n* (*for wood etc*) punteruolo *m*

**awning** /'ɔːnɪŋ/ *n* tendone *m*

**awoke(n)** /ə'wəʊk(ən)/ *see* **awake**

**AWOL** /'eɪwɒl/ *a* & *adv abbr* (**absent without leave**) **be/go ~** *Mil* assentarsi senza permesso; *hum* volatilizzarsi

**awry** /ə'raɪ/ *adv* storto

**axe** /æks/ *n* scure *f*; **have an ~ to grind** *fig* avere il proprio tornaconto ● *vt* (*pres p* **axing**) fare dei tagli a ⟨*budget*⟩; sopprimere ⟨*jobs*⟩; annullare ⟨*project*⟩

**axiom** /'æksɪəm/ *n* assioma *m*

**axiomatic** /æksɪə'mætɪk/ *a* **it is ~ that...** è indiscutibile che...

**axis** /'æksɪs/ *n* (*pl* **axes** /-siːz/) asse *m*

**axle** /'æksl/ *n Techn* asse *m*

**ay[e]** /aɪ/ *adv* sì ● *n* sì *m invar*

**Azerbaijan** /æzəbaɪ'dʒɑːn/ *n* Azerbaigian *m*

**Azerbaijani** /æzəbaɪ'dʒɑːnɪ/ *a* & *n* (*person*) azerbaigiano, -a *mf*; (*language*) azerbaigiano *m*

**Azores** /ə'zɔːz/ *npl* **the ~** le Azzorre

**Aztec** /'æztek/ *a* & *n* (*person*) azteco, -a *mf*; (*language*) azteco *m*

**azure** /'eɪʒə(r)/ *a* & *n* azzurro *m*

# Bb

**b, B** /biː/ n (letter) b, B f inv; Mus si m inv
**b** abbr **born**
**BA** abbr **Bachelor of Arts**
**BAA** n abbr (**British Airports Authority**)
ente m che gestisce gli aeroporti britannici
**baa** /baː/ vi belare ● int bee
**b. & b.** abbr **bed and breakfast**
**babble** /'bæbl/ vi farfugliare; ⟨stream:⟩ gorgogliare
**babe** /beɪb/ n liter bimbo, -a mf; (fam: woman) ragazza f; (fam: form of address) bella f; **a ~ in arms** un bimbo in fasce; fig uno sprovveduto
**baboon** /bə'buːn/ n babbuino m
**baby** /'beɪbɪ/ n bambino, -a mf; (fam: darling) tesoro m
**baby: baby bird** n uccellino m. **baby boom** n baby boom m inv. **baby boomer** n persona f nata durante il baby boom. **baby buggy** n Br carrozzina f. **baby carriage** n Am carrozzina f. **baby carrier** n zaino m portabimbo inv. **baby-faced** a ⟨person⟩ con la faccia da bambino
**babyish** /'beɪbɪɪʃ/ a bambinesco
**baby: baby-sit** vi fare da baby-sitter. **baby-sitter** n baby-sitter mf. **baby-sitting** n do ~ fare il/la baby-sitter. **baby talk** n linguaggio m infantile. **baby tooth** n dente m di latte. **baby walker** n girello m. **babywear** n abbigliamento m per bambini
**bachelor** /'bætʃələ(r)/ n scapolo m; **B~ of Arts/Science** laureato, -a mf in lettere/in scienze
**bachelor apartment, bachelor flat** Br n appartamento m da scapolo
**bachelorhood** /'bætʃələhʊd/ n celibato m
**bacillus** /bə'sɪləs/ n (pl **-lli**) bacillo m
**back** /bæk/ n schiena f; (of horse, hand) dorso m; (of chair) schienale m; (of house, cheque, page) retro m; (in football) difesa f; **at the ~** in fondo; **in the ~** Auto dietro; **stand ~ to** stare in piedi schiena contro schiena. **~ to front** ⟨sweater⟩ il davanti di dietro; **you've got it all ~ to front** fig hai capito tutto all'incontrario; **at the ~ of beyond** in un posto sperduto ● a posteriore; ⟨taxes, payments⟩ arretrato ● adv indietro; (returned) di ritorno; **turn/move ~** tornare/spostarsi indietro; **put it ~ here/there** rimettilo qui/là; **~ at home** di ritorno a casa; **I'll be ~ in five minutes** torno fra cinque minuti; **I'm just ~** sono appena tornato; **when do you want the book ~?** quando rivuoi il libro?; **pay ~** ripagare ⟨sb⟩; restituire ⟨money⟩; **~ in power** di nuovo al potere ● vt (support) sostenere; (with money) finanziare; puntare su ⟨horse⟩;

(cover the back of) rivestire il retro di ● vi Auto fare retromarcia
■ **back away** vi tirarsi indietro
■ **back down** vi battere in ritirata
■ **back in** vi Auto entrare in retromarcia; ⟨person:⟩ entrare camminando all'indietro
■ **back out** vi Auto uscire in retromarcia; ⟨person:⟩ uscire camminando all'indietro; fig tirarsi indietro (**of** da)
■ **back up** vt sostenere; confermare ⟨person's alibi⟩; Comput fare una copia di salvataggio di; **be ~ed up** ⟨traffic:⟩ essere congestionato ● vi Auto fare retromarcia
**back: backache** n mal m di schiena. **backbench** n Br Pol scanni mpl del Parlamento dove siedono i parlamentari ordinari. **backbencher** n Br Pol parlamentare mf ordinario, -a. **backbiting** n maldicenza f. **backboard** n (in basketball) tabellone m. **back boiler** n caldaia f (posta dietro un caminetto). **backbone** n spina f dorsale. **back-breaking** a massacrante. **back burner** n put sth on the ~ rimandare qcsa. **backchat** n risposta f impertinente. **backcloth** n Theat fondale m; fig sfondo m. **back comb** vt cotonare. **back copy** n numero m arretrato. **back cover** n retro m di copertina. **backdate** vt retrodatare ⟨cheque⟩; **~d to** valido a partire da. **back door** n porta f di servizio. **backdrop** n Theat fondale m; fig sfondo m. **back-end** n (rear) fondo m
**backer** /'bækə(r)/ n sostenitore, -trice mf; (with money) finanziatore, -trice mf
**back: backfire** vi Auto avere un ritorno di fiamma; ⟨fig: plan⟩ fallire; **the joke ~d on him** lo scherzo si è ritorto contro di lui. **backgammon** n backgammon m. **background** n sfondo m; (environment) ambiente m. **background noise** n rumore m di sottofondo. **background reading** n letture fpl generali. **backhand** n Tennis rovescio m. **backhanded** a ⟨compliment⟩ implicito. **backhander** n (fam: bribe) bustarella f
**backing** /'bækɪŋ/ n (support) supporto m; (material used) fondo m; Mus accompagnamento m
**backing group** n gruppo m d'accompagnamento
**back issue** n numero m arretrato
**backlash** /'bæklæʃ/ n fig reazione f opposta
**backless** /'bæklɪs/ a ⟨dress⟩ scollato dietro
**back: backlist** n opere fpl pubblicate. **backlog** n ~ **of work** lavoro m arretrato. **back marker** n Sport ultimo, -a mf. **back number** n numero m arretrato. **backpack** n zaino m. **backpacker** n saccopelista mf.

**backpacking** *n* **go** ~ viaggiare con zaino e sacco a pelo. **back passage** *n Anat* retto *m*. **back pay** *n* arretrato *m* di stipendio. **backpedal** *vi* pedalare all'indietro; *fig* fare marcia indietro. **back pocket** *n* tasca *f* di dietro. **backrest** *n* schienale *m*. **back room** *n* stanza *f* sul retro. **back room boys** *npl* esperti *mpl* che lavorano dietro le quinte. **backscratcher** *n* manina *f* grattaschiena *inv*. **back seat** *n* sedile *m* posteriore. **back-seat driver** *n* persona *f* che dà consigli non richiesti. **backside** *n fam* fondoschiena *m inv*. **backslash** *n Typ* barra *f* retroversa. **backspace** *n Comput* spazio *m* indietro. **backstage** *a & adv* dietro le quinte. **backstairs** *npl* scala *f* di servizio. **backstitch** *n* impuntura *f* ● *vi* impunturare. **backstop** *n Sport* ricevitore *m*. **back straight** *n Sport* rettilineo *m*. **backstreet** *n* vicolo *m* ● *attrib* ⟨abortionist⟩ clandestino. **backstroke** *n* dorso *m*. **backtalk** *n Am* = **backchat**. **backtrack** *vi* tornare indietro; *fig* fare marcia indietro. **back translation** *n* traduzione *f* di una traduzione. **backup** *n* rinforzi *mpl*; *Comput* riserva *f*, backup *m inv*; **do a** ~ realizzare un backup. **backup copy** *n* copia *f* di riserva. **backup light** *n Am* luce *f* della retromarcia

**backward** /'bækwəd/ *a* ⟨step⟩ indietro; ⟨child⟩ lento nell'apprendimento; ⟨country⟩ arretrato

**backward-looking** /'bækwədlukıŋ/ *a* retrogrado

**backwards** /'bækwədz/ *adv* (*also Am:* **backward**) indietro; ⟨fall, walk⟩ all'indietro; ~ **and forwards** avanti e indietro

**backwater** /'bækwɔːtə(r)/ *n fig* luogo *m* allo scarto

**backyard** /bæk'jɑːd/ *n* cortile *m*; **not in my** ~ **yard** *fam* non a casa propria

**bacon** /'beɪk(ə)n/ *n* ≈ pancetta *f*

**bacon-slicer** /'beɪkənslaɪsə(r)/ *n* affettatrice *f*

**bacteria** /bæk'tɪərɪə/ *npl* batteri *mpl*

**bacterial** /bæk'tɪərɪəl/ *a* batterico

**bacteriology** /bæktɪərɪ'ɒlədʒɪ/ *n* batteriologia *f*

**bad** /bæd/ *a* (**worse, worst**) cattivo; ⟨weather, habit, news, accident⟩ brutto; ⟨apple etc⟩ marcio; **the light is** ~ non c'è una buona luce; **my eyesight is** ~ non ho una buona vista; **use** ~ **language** dire delle parolacce; **she's going through a** ~ **patch** sta attraversando un brutto periodo; **feel** ~ sentirsi male; (*feel guilty*) sentirsi in colpa; **have a** ~ **back** avere dei problemi alla schiena; **smoking is** ~ **for you** fumare fa male; **go** ~ andare a male; **that's just too** ~! pazienza!; **not** ~ niente male; **things have gone from** ~ **to worse** le cose sono andate di male in peggio

**bad: bad blood** *n* **there is** ~ ~ **between them** tra loro non corre buon sangue. **bad boy** *n* ragazzaccio *m*. **bad breath** *n* alito *m* cattivo. **bad cheque** *n* assegno *m* a vuoto

**bad debt** *n* credito *m* inesigibile

**baddie, baddy** /'bædɪ/ *n fam* cattivo, -a *mf*

**bade** /bæd/ *see* bid

**bad faith** *n* malafede *f*

**badge** /bædʒ/ *n* distintivo *m*

**badger** /'bædʒə(r)/ *n* tasso *m* ● *vt* tormentare

**badly** /'bædlɪ/ *adv* male; ⟨hurt⟩ gravemente; ~ **off** povero; ~ **behaved** maleducato; **need** ~ aver estremamente bisogno di

**bad-mannered** /-'mænəd/ *a* maleducato

**badminton** /'bædmɪntən/ *n* badminton *m*

**bad-tempered** /-'tempəd/ *a* irascibile

**baffle** /'bæfl/ *vt* confondere

**baffling** /'bæflɪŋ/ *a* sconcertante

**bag** /bæg/ *n* borsa *f*; (*of paper*) sacchetto *m*; **old** ~ *sl* megera *f*; ~**s under the eyes** occhiaie *fpl*; ~**s of** *fam* un sacco di; **it's in the** ~ *fig* è fatta ● *vt* (*pt/pp* **bagged**) (*fam: take*) accaparrarsi; ~ **sb a seat** tenere un posto a qcno

**bagel** /'beɪgəl/ *n* panino *m* a forma di ciambella

**baggage** /'bægɪdʒ/ *n* bagagli *mpl*

**baggage: baggage allowance** *n* franchigia *f* bagaglio. **baggage car** *n Rail* bagagliaio *m*. **baggage carousel** *n* nastro *m* trasportatore per ritiro bagagli. **baggage check** *n* controllo *m* bagagli. **baggage handler** *n* addetto, -a *mf* ai bagagli. **baggage locker** *n* armadietto *m* per deposito bagagli. **baggage reclaim** *n* ritiro *m* bagagli

**baggy** /'bægɪ/ *a* ⟨clothes⟩ ampio

**Baghdad** /bæg'dæd/ *n* Baghdad *f*

**bag: bag lady** *n fam* barbona *f*. **bag person** *n fam* barbone, -a *mf*. **bagpipes** *npl* cornamusa *fsg*. **bag snatcher** *n* scippatore, -trice *mf*

**Bahamas** /bə'hɑːməz/ *npl* **the** ~ le Bahamas

**Bahrain, Bahrein** /bɑː'reɪn/ *n* Bahrein *m*

**bail** /beɪl/ *n* cauzione *f*; **on** ~ su cauzione

■ **bail out** *vt Naut* aggottare; ~ **sb out** *Jur* pagare la cauzione per qcno; *fig* trarre qcno d'impaccio ● *vi Aeron* paracadutarsi

**bail bond** *n Am Jur* cauzione *f*

**bailiff** /'beɪlɪf/ *n* ufficiale *m* giudiziario; (*of estate*) fattore *m*

**bait** /beɪt/ *n* esca *f*; **rise to the** ~ abboccare [all'amo] ● *vt* innescare; (*fig: torment*) tormentare

**baize** /beɪz/ *n* panno *m* (*di tavolo da gioco e da biliardo*)

**bake** /beɪk/ *vt* cuocere al forno; (*make*) fare ● *vi* cuocersi al forno

**baked beans** /beɪkt'biːnz/ *n Culin* fagioli *mpl* al pomodoro

**baked potato** *n* patata *f* cotta al forno (*con la buccia*)

**baker** /'beɪkə(r)/ *n* fornaio, -a *mf*, panettiere, -a *mf*

**baker's [shop]** /'beɪkəz/ *n* panetteria *f*

**bakery** /'beɪkərɪ/ *n* panificio *m*, forno *m*

**baking** /'beɪkɪŋ/ *n* cottura *f* al forno

**baking: baking powder** *n* lievito *m* in polvere. **baking soda** *n Culin* bicarbonato *m* di sodio. **baking tin** *n* teglia *f*

**balaclava** /bælə'klɑ:və/ *n* passamontagna *m inv*

**balance** /'bæləns/ *n* (*equilibrium*) equilibrio *m*; *Comm* bilancio *m*; (*outstanding sum*) saldo *m*; [**bank**] ~ saldo *m*; **be** *or* **hang in the** ~ *fig* essere in sospeso; **on** ~ tutto sommato ● *vt* bilanciare; equilibrare ⟨*budget*⟩; *Comm* fare il bilancio di ⟨*books*⟩ ● *vi* bilanciarsi; *Comm* essere in pareggio

**balanced:** /'bælənst/ *a* equilibrato

**balance: balance of payments** *n* bilancia *f* dei pagamenti. **balance of power** *n Pol* equilibrio *m* delle forze. **balance sheet** *n* bilancio *m* [d'esercizio]. **balance of trade** *n* bilancia *f* commerciale

**balancing act** /'bælənsɪŋ/ *n fig* **do a** ~ ~ fare equilibrismo

**balcony** /'bælkənɪ/ *n* balcone *m*

**bald** /bɔ:ld/ *a* ⟨*person*⟩ calvo; ⟨*tyre*⟩ liscio; ⟨*statement*⟩ nudo e crudo; **go** ~ perdere i capelli

**balderdash** /'bɔ:ldədæʃ/ *n* sciocchezze *fpl*

**balding** /'bɔ:ldɪŋ/ *a* **be** ~ stare perdendo i capelli

**baldly** /'bɔ:ldlɪ/ *adv* ⟨*state*⟩ in modo nudo e crudo

**baldness** /'bɔ:ldnɪs/ *n* calvizie *f*

**bale** /beɪl/ *n* balla *f*

**Balearic Islands** /bælɪ'ærɪk/ *npl* isole *fpl* Baleari

**baleful** /'beɪlfl/ *a* malvagio; (*sad*) triste

**balefully** /'beɪlfʊlɪ/ *adv* con malvagità

**balk** /bɔ:lk/ *vt* ostacolare ● *vi* ~ **at** ⟨*horse:*⟩ impennarsi davanti a; *fig* tirarsi indietro davanti a

**Balkans** /'bɔ:lknz/ *npl* Balcani *mpl*

**ball**[1] /bɔ:l/ *n* palla *f*; (*football*) pallone *m*; (*of yarn*) gomitolo *m*; **on the** ~ *fam* sveglio

**ball**[2] *n* (*dance*) ballo *m*

**ballad** /'bæləd/ *n* ballata *f*

**ball and chain** *n* palla *f* al piede

**ball-and-socket joint** *n* giunto *m* sferico

**ballast** /'bæləst/ *n* zavorra *f*

**ball: ball-bearing** *n* cuscinetto *m* a sfera. **ballboy** *n Tennis* raccattapalle *m inv.* **ballcock** *n Techn* galleggiante *m* (*in serbatoio*). **ball control** *n* controllo *m* della palla. **ball dress** *n* abito *m* da sera

**ballerina** /bælə'ri:nə/ *n* ballerina *f* [classica]

**ballet** /'bæleɪ/ *n* balletto *m*; (*art form*) danza *f*

**ballet: ballet dancer** *n* ballerino, -a *mf* [classico, -a]. **ballet dress** *n* tutù *m inv.* **ballet shoes** scarpe *fpl* da danza

**ball: ballgame** *n* gioco *m* con la palla; *Am* partita *f* di baseball; **that's a whole different** ~ *fig* è tutto un altro paio di maniche. **ballgirl** *n Tennis* raccattapalle *f inv.* **ball gown** *n* abito *m* da sera

**ballistic** /bə'lɪstɪk/ *a* balistico

**ballistics** *n* balistica *fsg*

**balloon** /bə'lu:n/ *n* pallone *m*; *Aeron* mongolfiera *f*

**balloonist** /bə'lu:nɪst/ *n* aeronauta *mf*

**ballot** /'bælət/ *n* votazione *f*

**ballot box** *n* urna *f*

**ballot paper** *n* scheda *f* di votazione

**ball: ballpark** *n Am* stadio *m* di baseba[l]. **ballpark figure** *n fam* cifra *f* approssimativ[a]. **ball-point [pen]** *n* penna *f* a sfera. **ballroo**[m] *n* sala *f* da ballo. **ballroom dancing** *n* ballo [?] liscio

■ **balls up** *vulg vi* incasinarsi ● [?] incasinare

**ballyhoo** /bælɪ'hu:/ *n* (*publicity*) battage [?] *inv* pubblicitario; (*uproar*) baccano *m*

**balm** /bɑ:m/ *n* balsamo *m*

**balmy** /'bɑ:mɪ/ *a* (**-ier, -iest**) mite; (*fam*[?] *crazy*) strampalato

**balsam** /'bɒlsəm/ *n* (*oily*) balsamo *m*

**Baltic** /'bɔ:ltɪk/ *a & n* **the** ~ [*Sea*] il [ma]r Baltico

**balustrade** /bælə'streɪd/ *n* balaustra *f*

**bamboo** /bæm'bu:/ *n* bambù *m*

**bamboozle** /bæm'bu:zl/ *vt* (*fam: mystif*[y]) confondere

**ban** /bæn/ *n* proibizione *f* ● *vt* (*pt/p*[p] **banned**) proibire; ~ **from** espellere d[a] ⟨*club*⟩; **she was** ~**ned from driving** le ha[nno] no ritirato la patente

**banal** /bə'nɑ:l/ *a* banale

**banality** /bə'nælətɪ/ *n* banalità *f inv*

**banana** /bə'nɑ:nə/ *n* banana *f*

**banana republic** *n pej* repubblica *f* del[le] banane

**banana skin** *n* buccia *f* di banana

**band** /bænd/ *n* banda *f*; (*stripe*) nastro *m*[?] (*Mus: pop group*) complesso *m*; (*Mus: brass* ~) banda *f*; *Mil* fanfara *f*

■ **band together** *vi* riunirsi

**bandage** /'bændɪdʒ/ *n* benda *f* ● *vt* fasciare

■ **bandage up** *vt* fasciare

**Band-Aid** *n Med* cerotto *m*

**bandit** /'bændɪt/ *n* bandito *m*

**band: band leader** *n* leader *mf* di un com[?] plesso. **bandmaster** *n* capobanda *m* (*di ban*[da] *da musicale*). **band saw** *n* segatrice *f* a na[?] stro. **bandsman** *n* bandista *m*. **bandstand** *n* palco *m* coperto [dell'orchestra]. **band[?] wagon** *n* **jump on the** ~ *fig* seguire la cor[?] rente

**bandy**[1] /'bændɪ/ *vt* (*pt/pp* **-ied**) scambiars[i] ⟨*words*⟩

■ **bandy about** *vt* far circolare

**bandy**[2] *a* (**-ier, -iest**) **be** ~ avere le gamb[e] storte

**bandy-legged** /-'legd/ *a* con le gambe stor[?] te

**bane** /beɪn/ *n* **she/it is the** ~ **of my life!** è l[a] mia rovina!

**bang** /bæŋ/ *n* (*noise*) fragore *m*; (*of gun*[?] *firework*) scoppio *m*; (*blow*) colpo *m*; **go wit[h]** **a** ~ *fam* essere una cannonata ● *adv* ~ **in th[e]** **middle of** *fam* proprio nel mezzo di; **go** ~ ⟨*gun:*⟩ sparare; ⟨*balloon:*⟩ esplodere ● *in*[?] bum! ● *vt* battere ⟨*fist*⟩; battere su ⟨*table*[?] sbattere ⟨*door, head*⟩ ● *vi* scoppiare; ⟨*door:*⟩ sbattere

**bang about, bang around** *vi* far rumore

**bang into** *vt* sbattere contro

**anger** /'bæŋə(r)/ *n* (*firework*) petardo *m*; (*fam: sausage*) salsiccia *f*; **old ~** (*fam: car*) macinino *m*

**angladesh** /bæŋglə'deʃ/ *n* Bangladesh *m*

**angle** /'bæŋgl/ *n* braccialetto *m*

**anish** /'bænɪʃ/ *vt* bandire

**anishment** /'bænɪʃmənt/ *n* bando *m*

**anisters** /'bænɪstəz/ *npl* ringhiera *fsg*

**anjo** /'bændʒəʊ/ *n* banjo *m inv*

**ank¹** /bæŋk/ *n* (*of river*) sponda *f*; (*slope*) carpata *f* ● *vi* Aeron inclinarsi in virata

**ank²** *n* banca *f* ● *vt* depositare in banca ● *vi* **~ with** avere un conto [bancario] presso

**bank on** *vt* contare su

**ank: bank account** *n* conto *m* in banca. **~ank balance** *n* saldo *m*. **bank-book** *n* libretto *m* di risparmio. **bank borrowings** *npl* restiti *mpl* bancari. **bank card** *n* carta *f* assegni. **bank charges** *npl* spese *fpl* bancarie, ommissioni *fpl*. **bank clerk** *n* bancario, -a *f*

**anker** /'bæŋkə(r)/ *n* banchiere *m*

**anker's draft** *n* tratta *f* bancaria

**anker's order** *n* ordine *m* di pagamento

**ank Giro Credit** *n* Br accreditamento *m* ramite bancogiro

**ank holiday** *n* giorno *m* festivo

**anking** /'bæŋkɪŋ/ *n* bancario *m*

**anking hours** *npl* orario *m* di sportello [n banca]

**ank: bank manager** *n* direttore, -trice *mf* i banca. **banknote** *n* banconota *f*. **bank raid** rapina *f* in banca. **bank robber** *n* rapinato-e, -trice *mf* di banca. **bank robbery** *n* rapina in banca. **bankroll** *n* finanziamento *m* ● *vt* nanziare (*person, party*)

**ankrupt** /'bæŋkrʌpt/ *a* fallito; **go ~** fallire *n* persona *f* che ha fatto fallimento ● *vt* far allire

**ankruptcy** /'bæŋkrʌptsɪ/ *n* bancarotta *f*

**ankruptcy court** *n* tribunale *m* fallimentare

**ankruptcy proceedings** *npl* procedura *f* fallimentare

**ank statement** *n* estratto *m* conto

**ank transfer** *n* bonifico *m* bancario

**anner** /'bænə(r)/ *n* stendardo *m*; (*of emonstrators*) striscione *m*

**anner headline** *n* titolo *m* a tutta pagina

**anns** /bænz/ *npl* Relig pubblicazioni *fpl* [di atrimonio]

**anquet** /'bæŋkwɪt/ *n* banchetto *m*

**antam** /'bæntəm/ *n* gallo *m* bantam

**anter** /'bæntə(r)/ *n* battute *fpl* di spirito

**aptism** /'bæptɪzm/ *n* battesimo *m*; **~ of** re *fig* battesimo *m* del fuoco

**aptist** /'bæptɪst/ *n* battista *mf*

**aptize** /bæp'taɪz/ *vt* battezzare

**ar** /bɑ:(r)/ *n* sbarra *f*; Jur ordine *m* degli avcati; (*of chocolate*) tavoletta *f*; (*café*) bar *m* v; (*counter*) banco *m*; Mus battuta *f*; (*fig: bstacle*) ostacolo *m*; **~ of soap/gold** sapo-

netta *f*/lingotto *m*; **be called to the ~** Jur entrare a far parte dell'ordine degli avvocati; **behind ~s** *fam* dietro le sbarre ● *vt* (*pt/pp* **barred**) sbarrare (*way*); sprangare (*door*); escludere (*person*) ● *prep* tranne; **~ none** in assoluto

**barb** /bɑ:b/ *n* barbiglio *m*; (*fig: remark*) frecciata *f*

**Barbados** /bɑ:'beɪdɒs/ *n* Barbados *fsg*

**barbarian** /bɑ:'beərɪən/ *n* barbaro, -a *mf*

**barbaric** /bɑ:'bærɪk/ *a* barbarico

**barbarism** /bɑ:'bærɪzm/ *n* (*brutality, primitiveness*) barbarie *f inv*; (*error of style*) barbarismo *m*

**barbarity** /bɑ:'bærəti/ *n* barbarie *f inv*

**barbarous** /bɑ:'bərəs/ *a* barbaro

**barbecue** /'bɑ:bɪkju:/ *n* barbecue *m inv*; (*party*) grigliata *f*, barbecue *m inv* ● *vt* arrostire sul barbecue

**barbed** /bɑ:bd/ *a* **~ wire** filo *m* spinato

**barber** /'bɑ:bə(r)/ *n* barbiere *m*

**barber's shop** *n* barbiere *m*

**barbiturate** /bɑ:'bɪtjʊrət/ *n* barbiturico *m*

**bar: bar chart** *n* istogramma *m*. **bar code** *n* codice *m* a barre. **bar-coded** *a* con codice a barre. **bar code reader** *n* lettore *m* di codice a barre

**bard** /bɑ:d/ *n liter* bardo *m*

**bare** /beə(r)/ *a* nudo; (*tree, room*) spoglio; (*floor*) senza moquette; **the ~ bones** l'essenziale *m* ● *vt* scoprire; mostrare (*teeth*)

**bare: bareback** *adv* senza sella. **barefaced** *a* sfacciato. **barefoot** *adv* scalzo. **bareheaded** *a* a capo scoperto

**barely** /'beəlɪ/ *adv* appena

**bareness** /'beənɪs/ *n* nudità *f*

**bargain** /'bɑ:gɪn/ *n* (*agreement*) patto *m*; (*good buy*) affare *m*; **into the ~** per di più ● *vi* contrattare; (*haggle*) trattare

**■ bargain for** *vt* (*expect*) aspettarsi

**bargain basement** *n* reparto *m* occasioni

**bargaining** /'bɑ:gɪnɪŋ/ *n* (*over pay*) contrattazione *f* ● *attrib* (*power, rights*) contrattuale; (*position*) di negoziato

**barge** /bɑ:dʒ/ *n* barcone *m*

**■ barge in** *vi fam* (*to room*) piombare dentro; (*into conversation*) interrompere bruscamente; **~ into** piombare dentro a (*room*); venire addosso a (*person*)

**bargepole** /'bɑ:dʒpəʊl/ *n* **I wouldn't touch him/it with a ~** non lo toccherei nemmeno con un dito

**baritone** /'bærɪtəʊn/ *n* baritono *m*

**bark¹** /bɑ:k/ *n* (*of tree*) corteccia *f*

**bark²** *n* abbaiamento *m* ● *vi* abbaiare

**barking** /'bɑ:kɪŋ/ *n* abbaiamento *m* ● *a* (*dog*) che abbaia; (*cough, laugh*) convulso ● *adv* **be ~ mad** Br *fam* essere matto da legare

**barley** /'bɑ:lɪ/ *n* orzo *m*

**barley: barleycorn** *n* orzo *m*; (*grain*) chicco *m* d'orzo. **barley sugar** *n* caramella *f* d'orzo. **barley water** *n* Br orzata *f*. **barley wine** *n* Br birra *f* molto forte

**barmaid** /'bɑ:meɪd/ *n* barista *f*

**barman** /'bɑ:mən/ *n* barista *m*

**barmy** /'bɑːmɪ/ *a fam* strampalato

**barn** /bɑːn/ *n* granaio *m*

**barnacle** /'bɑːnəkl/ *n* cirripede *m*

**barn: barn dance** *n* ballo *m* tradizionale statunitense; (*social gathering*) festa *f* negli USA in cui si fanno balli tradizionali. **barn owl** *n* barbagianni *m inv*. **barnstorming** *a* sensazionale. **barnyard** *n* aia *f*

**barometer** /bə'rɒmɪtə(r)/ *n* barometro *m*

**baron** /'bærn/ *n* barone *m*

**baroness** /'bærənɪs/ *n* baronessa *f*

**baronial** /bə'rəʊnɪəl/ *a* baronale

**baroque** /bə'rɒk/ *a & n* barocco *m*

**barracking** /'bærəkɪŋ/ *n* fischi *mpl* e insulti *mpl*

**barrack room** *n* camerata *f* ● *attrib pej* ⟨language⟩ da caserma

**barracks** /'bærəks/ *npl* caserma *fsg*

**barrage** /'bærɑːʒ/ *n* (*in river*) [opera *f* di] sbarramento *m*; *Mil* sbarramento *m*; (*fig: of criticism, abuse*) sfilza *f*

**barrage balloon** *n* pallone *m* di sbarramento

**barrel** /'bærəl/ *n* barile *m*, botte *f*; (*of gun*) canna *f*

**barrel organ** *n* organetto *m* [a cilindro]

**barren** /'bærən/ *a* sterile; ⟨landscape⟩ brullo

**barrette** /bæ'ret/ *n Am* (*for hair*) molletta *f*

**barricade** /'bærɪkeɪd/ *n* barricata *f* ● *vt* barricare

**barrier** /'bærɪə(r)/ *n* barriera *f*; *Rail* cancello *m*; *fig* ostacolo *m*

**barrier: barrier cream** *n* crema *f* protettiva. **barrier method** *n Med* metodo *m* anticoncezionale meccanico. **barrier reef** *n* barriera *f* corallina

**barring** /'bɑːrɪŋ/ *prep* ~ **accidents** tranne imprevisti

**barrister** /'bærɪstə(r)/ *n* avvocato *m*

**barrow** /'bærəʊ/ *n* carretto *m*; (*wheel~*) carriola *f*

**bar stool** *n* sgabello *m* da bar

**bartender** /'bɑːtendə(r)/ *n* barista *mf*

**barter** /'bɑːtə(r)/ *vi* barattare (**for** con)

**base** /beɪs/ *n* base *f* ● *a* vile ● *vt* basare; **be ~d on** basarsi su

**baseball** /'beɪsbɔːl/ *n* baseball *m*

**baseball cap** *n* berretto *m* da baseball

**base: base camp** *n* campo *m* base *inv*. **base form** *n* (*of verb*) forma *f* non coniugata di un verbo. **base lending rate** *n* tasso *m* base *inv* di interesse

**baseless** /'beɪslɪs/ *a* infondato

**baseline** /'beɪslaɪn/ *n Tennis* linea *f* di fondo; *fig* riferimento *m*

**basement** /'beɪsmənt/ *n* seminterrato *m*

**basement flat** *n* appartamento *m* nel seminterrato

**base metal** *n* metallo *m* vile *inv*

**base rate** *n* tasso *m* base *inv*

**bash** /bæʃ/ *n* colpo *m* violento; **have a ~!** *fam* provaci! ● *vt* colpire [violentemente]; (*dent*) ammaccare; **~ed in** ammaccato ■ **bash down** *vt* sfondare ⟨door⟩

**bashful** /'bæʃfl/ *a* timido

**bashfully** /'bæʃfʊlɪ/ *adv* timidamente

**bashing** /'bæʃɪŋ/ *n fam* (*beating*) pestaggio *m*; (*criticism*) critica *f* feroce; (*defeat*) batosta *f*; **take a ~** prendere una batosta

**basic** /'beɪsɪk/ *a* di base; ⟨condition requirement⟩ basilare; ⟨living conditions⟩ povero; **my Italian is pretty ~** il mio italiano è abbastanza rudimentale; **the ~s** (*of language, science*) i rudimenti; (*essentials*) l'essenziale *m*

**basically** /'beɪsɪklɪ/ *adv* fondamentalmente

**basic rate** *n* tariffa *f* minima; (*in tax*) aliquota *f* minima

**basil** /'bæzɪl/ *n* basilico *m*

**basilica** /bə'zɪlɪkə/ *n* basilica *f*

**basin** /'beɪsn/ *n* bacinella *f*; (*wash-hand* ~) lavabo *m*; (*for food*) recipiente *m*; *Geog* bacino *m*

**basinful** /'beɪsɪnfʊl/ *n* bacinella *f* (*contenuto*)

**basis** /'beɪsɪs/ *n* (*pl* **-ses** /'beɪsiːz/) base *f*

**bask** /bɑːsk/ *vi* crogiolarsi

**basket** /'bɑːskɪt/ *n* cestino *m*

**basket: basketball** *n* pallacanestro *f*. **basket chair** *n* sedia *f* di vimini. **basketwork** *n* (*objects*) oggetti *mpl* in vimini; (*craft*) lavoro *m* artigianale di oggetti in vimini

**Basle** /bɑːl/ *n* Basilea *f*

**Basque** /bæsk/ *a & n* (*person*) basco, -a *mf*; (*language*) basco *m*

**bass** /beɪs/ *a* basso; **~ voice** voce *f* di basso ● *n* basso *m*

**bass: bass-baritone** *n* baritono *m* basso. **bass clef** *n* chiave *f* di basso. **bass drum** *n* grancassa *f*

**basset hound** /'bæsɪt/ *n* basset hound *m inv*

**bassist** /'beɪsɪst/ *n* bassista *mf*

**bassoon** /bə'suːn/ *n* fagotto *m*

**bastard** /'bɑːstəd/ *n* (*illegitimate child*) bastardo, -a *mf*; *sl* figlio *m* di puttana

**baste**[1] /beɪst/ *vt* (*sew*) imbastire

**baste**[2] *vt Culin* ungere con grasso

**bastion** /'bæstɪən/ *n* bastione *m*

**bat**[1] /bæt/ *n* mazza *f*; (*for table tennis*) racchetta *f*; **off one's own ~** *fam* tutto da solo ● *vt* (*pt/pp* **batted**) battere; **she didn't ~ an eyelid** *fig* non ha battuto ciglio

**bat**[2] *n Zool* pipistrello *m*

**batch** /bætʃ/ *n* gruppo *m*; (*of goods*) partita *f*; (*of bread*) infornata *f*

**batch file** *n Comput* batch file *m inv*

**batch processing** /'prəʊsesɪŋ/ *n Comput* elaborazione *f* a gruppi

**bated** /'beɪtɪd/ *a* **with ~ breath** col fiato sospeso

**bath** /bɑːθ/ *n* (*pl* **~s** /bɑːðz/) bagno *m*; (*tub*) vasca *f* da bagno; **~s** *pl* piscina *f*; **have a ~** fare un bagno ● *vt* fare il bagno a ● *vi* fare il bagno

**bathe** /beɪð/ *n* bagno *m* ● *vi* fare il bagno ● *vt* lavare ⟨wound⟩

**bather** /'beɪðə(r)/ *n* bagnante *mf*

**bathing** /'beɪðɪŋ/ *n* bagni *mpl*

**bathing: bathing cap** *n* cuffia *f*. **bathing**

**costume** *n* costume *m* da bagno. **bathing hut** *n* cabina *f* (*al mare*). **bathing suit** *n* costume *m* da bagno. **bathing trunks** *n* calzoncini *mpl* da bagno

**bath mat** *n* tappetino *m* da bagno

**bathrobe** /'bæθrəʊb/ *n* accappatoio *m*

**bathroom** /'bæθru:m/ *n* (*also: toilet*) bagno *m*

**bathroom: bathroom cabinet** *n* armadietto *m* del bagno. **bathroom fittings** *npl* accessori *mpl* per il bagno. **bathroom scales** *npl* bilancia *f* pesapersone

**bath: bath salts** *npl* sali *mpl* da bagno. **bath-towel** *n* asciugamano *m* da bagno. **bathtub** *n* vasca *f* da bagno

**baton** /'bæt(ə)n/ *n Mus* bacchetta *f*

**baton charge** *n Br* carica *f* con lo sfollagente

**baton round** *n Br* proiettile *m* di gomma

**batsman** /'bætsmən/ *n Sport* battitore *m*

**battalion** /bə'tælɪən/ *n* battaglione *m*

**batten** /'bætn/ *n* assicella *f*

**batter** /'bætə(r)/ *n Culin* pastella *f*

**battered** /'bætəd/ *a* ‹*car*› malandato; ‹*wife, baby*› maltrattato

**battering** /'bæt(ə)rɪŋ/ *n* **take a ~** (*from bombs, storm, waves*) essere colpito; (*from other team*) prendersi una batosta; (*from other boxer*) prendersele

**battering ram** *n* ariete *m*

**battery** /'bætərɪ/ *n* batteria *f*; (*of torch, radio*) pila *f*

**battery: battery charger** *n* caricabatterie *m inv*. **battery chicken** *n* pollo *m* di allevamento in batteria. **battery controlled** *a* a pile. **battery farming** *n* allevamento *m* in batteria. **battery hen** *n* gallina *f* d'allevamento in batteria. **battery life** *n* autonomia *f*. **battery operated, battery powered** *a* a pile

**battle** /'bæt(ə)l/ *n* battaglia *f*; *fig* lotta *f* ● *vi fig* lottare

**battle: battleaxe** *n fam* virago *f inv*. **battle cry** *n also fig* grido *m* di battaglia. **battle dress** *n* uniforme *f* da combattimento. **battlefield** *n*, **battleground** *n* campo *m* di battaglia; *fig* terreno *m* di scontro. **battle lines** *npl Mil* schieramenti *mpl*

**battlements** /'bætlmənts/ *npl* bordo *m* merlato; (*crenellations*) merlatura *f*

**battle: battle order** *n also fig* ordine *m* di battaglia. **battle-scarred** *a* agguerrito; *fig* segnato dalla vita. **battleship** *n* corazzata *f*

**batty** /'bætɪ/ *a fam* strampalato

**bauble** /'bɔ:b(ə)l/ *n* (*ornament*) gingillo *m*; (*jewellery*) ninnolo *m*

**bawdiness** /'bɔ:dɪnɪs/ *n* oscenità *f*

**bawdy** /'bɔ:dɪ/ *a* (-**ier**, -**iest**) piccante

**bawl** /bɔ:l/ *vt/i* urlare

**■ bawl out** *vt fam* urlare ‹*name, order*›; fare una sfuriata a ‹*sb*›

**bay**¹ /beɪ/ *n Geog* baia *f*

**bay**² *n* **keep at ~** tenere a bada

**bay**³ *n Bot* alloro *m*

**bay**⁴ *n* (*horse*) baio *m*

**bay leaf** *n* foglia *f* d'alloro

**bayonet** /'beɪənet/ *n* baionetta *f*

**bay window** *n* bay window *f inv* (*grande finestra sporgente*)

**bazaar** /bə'zɑ:(r)/ *n* bazar *m inv*

**bazooka** /bə'zu:kə/ *n* bazooka *m inv*

**BBC** *n abbr* (**British Broadcasting Corporation**) BBC *f*

**BC** *abbr* (**before Christ**) a.C.

**BE** *abbr* (**bill of exchange**) cambiale *f*

**be** /bi:/ *vi* (*pres* **am, are, is, are**; *pt* **was, were**; *pp* **been**) essere; **he is a teacher** è insegnante, fa l'insegnante; **what do you want to be?** cosa vuoi fare?; **be quiet!** sta' zitto!; **I am cold/hot** ho freddo/caldo; **it's cold/hot, isn't it?** fa freddo/caldo, vero?; **how are you?** come stai?; **I am well** sto bene; **there is c'è; there are** ci sono; **I have been to Venice** sono stato a Venezia; **has the postman been?** è passato il postino?; **you're coming too, aren't you?** vieni anche tu, no?; **it's yours, is it?** è tuo, vero?; **was John there? – yes, he was** c'era John? – sì; **John wasn't there – yes he was!** John non c'era – sì che c'era!; **three and three are six** tre più tre fanno sei; **he is five** ha cinque anni; **that will be £10, please** fanno 10 sterline, per favore; **how much is it?** quanto costa?; **that's £5 you owe me** mi devi 5 sterline ● *v aux* **I am coming/reading** sto venendo/leggendo; **I'm staying** (*not leaving*) resto; **I am being lazy** sono pigro; **I was thinking of you** stavo pensando a te; **you are not to tell him** non devi dirgielo; **you are to do that immediately** devi farlo subito ● *passive* essere; **I have been robbed** sono stato derubato

**beach** /bi:tʃ/ *n* spiaggia *f*

**beach: beach ball** *n* pallone *m* da spiaggia. **beach buggy** *n* dune buggy *f inv*. **beachcomber** *n* persona *f* che vive rivendendo gli oggetti trovati sulla spiaggia. **beachhead** *n* testa *f* di sbarco. **beach hut** *n* cabina *f* [da spiaggia]. **beachrobe** *n* accappatoio *m*. **beachwear** *n* abbigliamento *m* da spiaggia

**beacon** /'bi:k(ə)n/ *n* faro *m*; *Naut, Aeron* fanale *m*

**bead** /bi:d/ *n* perlina *f*

**beady-eyed** /bi:dɪ'aɪd/ *a* (*sharp-eyed*) a cui non sfugge niente

**beagle** /'bi:g(ə)l/ *n* beagle *m inv*, bracchetto *m*

**beak** /bi:k/ *n* becco *m*

**beaker** /'bi:kə(r)/ *n* coppa *f*; (*in laboratory*) becher *m inv*

**beam** /bi:m/ *n* trave *f*; (*of light*) raggio *m* ● *vi* irradiare; ‹*person:*› essere raggiante; **~ at sb** fare un gran sorriso a qcno

**beaming** /'bi:mɪŋ/ *a* raggiante

**bean** /bi:n/ *n* fagiolo *m*; (*of coffee*) chicco *m*; **spill the ~s** *fam* spiattellare tutto

**bean: bean bag** *n* (*seat*) poltrona *f* imbottita di pallini di polistirolo. **beanfeast** *n fam* festa *f*. **beanpole** *n* (*fig fam: tall thin person*) spilungone, -a *mf*. **beansprout** *n* germoglio *m* di soia

**bear¹** /beə(r)/ *n* orso *m*

**bear²** *v* (*pt* **bore**, *pp* **borne**) ● *vt* (*endure*) sopportare; mettere al mondo ⟨*child*⟩; (*carry*) portare; **~ in mind** tenere presente; **~ fruit** ⟨*tree:*⟩ produrre; *fig* dare frutto ● *vi* **~ left/right** andare a sinistra/a destra

■ **bear out** *vt* confermare ⟨*story, statement*⟩

■ **bear with** *vt* aver pazienza con

**bearable** /'beərəbl/ *a* sopportabile

**bear cub** *n* cucciolo *m* di orso

**beard** /bɪəd/ *n* barba *f*; **have a ~** avere la barba

**bearded** /'bɪədɪd/ *a* barbuto

**bearer** /'beərə(r)/ *n* portatore, -trice *mf*; (*of passport*) titolare *mf*

**bearing** /'beərɪŋ/ *n* portamento *m*; *Techn* cuscinetto *m* [a sfera]; **have a ~ on** avere attinenza con; **get one's ~s** orientarsi; **lose one's ~s** perdere l'orientamento

**bear market** *n Fin* mercato *m* al ribasso

**bearskin** *n* (*pelt*) pelle *f* d'orso; (*hat*) colbacco *m* militare

**beast** /bi:st/ *n* bestia *f*; (*fam: person*) animale *m*

**beastly** /'bi:stlɪ/ *a* (**-ier, -iest**) *fam* orribile

**beat** /bi:t/ *n* battito *m*; (*rhythm*) battuta *f*; (*of policeman*) giro *m* d'ispezione ● *v* (*pt* **beat**, *pp* **beaten**) ● *vt* battere; picchiare ⟨*person*⟩; **~ a retreat** *Mil* battere in ritirata; **~ it!** *fam* darsela a gambe!; **it ~s me why...** *fam* non capisco proprio perché...

■ **beat down** *vt* buttare giù ⟨*door*⟩ ● *vi* ⟨*sun:*⟩ battere a picco

■ **beat off** *vt* respingere ⟨*attacker*⟩

■ **beat out** *vt* domare ⟨*flames*⟩

■ **beat up** *vt* picchiare

**beaten** /'bi:tn/ *a* **off the ~ track** fuori mano

**beatify** /bɪ'ætɪfaɪ/ *vt* beatificare

**beating** /'bi:tɪŋ/ *n* bastonata *f*; **get a ~** (*with fists*) essere preso a pugni; ⟨*team, player:*⟩ prendere una batosta

**beating-up** *vt fam* pestaggio *m*

**beat-up** *a* ⟨*fam: car*⟩ sfasciato

**beau** /bəʊ/ *n liter, hum* spasimante *m*

**Beaufort scale** /'bəʊfət/ *n* scala *f* Beaufort

**beautician** /bju:'tɪʃn/ *n* estetista *mf*

**beautiful** /'bju:tɪfl/ *a* bello; **the ~ people** il bel mondo

**beautifully** /'bju:tɪfʊlɪ/ *adv* splendidamente

**beautify** /'bju:tɪfaɪ/ *vt* (*pt/pp* **-ied**) abbellire

**beauty** /'bju:tɪ/ *n* bellezza *f*

**beauty: beauty contest** *n* concorso *m* di bellezza. **beauty editor** *n* redattore, -trice *mf* di articoli di bellezza. **beauty parlour** *n* istituto *m* di bellezza. **beauty queen** *n* reginetta *f* di bellezza. **beauty salon** *n* istituto *m* di bellezza. **beauty sleep** *n hum* **need one's ~ ~** aver bisogno delle proprie ore di sonno. **beauty spot** *n* neo *m*; (*place*) luogo *m* pittoresco

**beaver** /'bi:və(r)/ *n* castoro *m*

■ **beaver away** *vi* (*fam: work hard*) sgobbare

**becalmed** /bɪ'kɑ:md/ *a* in bonaccia

**became** /bɪ'keɪm/ *see* **become**

**because** /bɪ'kɒz/ *conj* perché; (*at start of sentence*) poiché ● *adv* **~ of** a causa di

**beck** /bek/ *n* **be at sb's ~ and call** dover essere a completa disposizione di qcno

**beckon** /'bekn/ *vt/i* **~ [to]** chiamare con un cenno

**become** /bɪ'kʌm/ *v* (*pt* **became**, *pp* **become**) ● *vt* diventare ● *vi* diventare; **what has ~ of her?** che ne è di lei?

**becoming** /bɪ'kʌmɪŋ/ *a* ⟨*clothes*⟩ bello

**bed** /bed/ *n* letto *m*; (*of sea, lake*) fondo *m*; (*layer*) strato *m*; (*of flowers*) aiuola *f*; **in ~** a letto; **go to ~** andare a letto; **~ and breakfast** *pensione f familiare in cui il prezzo della camera comprende anche la prima colazione*

■ **bed down** *vi* coricarsi

**BEd** *n abbr* (**Bachelor of Education**) ≈ laurea *f* in magistero

**bed: bed and board** *n* vitto e alloggio *m*. **bed base** *n* fondo *m* del letto. **bed bath** *n* **give sb a ~ ~** lavare qcno a letto. **bedbug** *n* cimice *f*. **bedchamber** *n* camera *f* da letto. **bedclothes** *npl* lenzuola e coperte *fpl*

**bedding** /'bedɪŋ/ *n* biancheria *f* per il letto, materasso e guanciali

**bedeck** /bɪ'dek/ *vt* ornare

**bedevil** /bɪ'devəl/ *vt* tormentare ⟨*person*⟩; intralciare ⟨*plans*⟩

**bed: bedfellow** *n* **make strange ~s** *fig* fare una strana coppia. **bedhead** *n* testata *f* del letto. **bed jacket** *n* liseuse *f inv*

**bedlam** /'bedləm/ *n* baraonda *f*

**bed linen** *n* biancheria *f* per il letto

**bedpan** /'bedpæn/ *n* padella *f*

**bedraggled** /bɪ'drægld/ *a* inzaccherato

**bedridden** /'bedrɪdən/ *a* costretto a letto

**bedrock** /'bedrɒk/ *n* basamento *m*; *fig* fondamento *m*

**bedroom** /'bedru:m/ *n* camera *f* da letto

**bedroom: bedroom farce** *n Theat* pochade *f inv*. **bedroom slipper** *n* pantofola *f*. **bedroom suburb** *n Am* città *f inv* dormitorio

**bed-settee** *n* divano *m* letto

**bedside** /'bedsaɪd/ *n* **at his ~** al suo capezzale

**bedside: bedside lamp** *n* abat-jour *m inv*. **bedside manner** *n* modo *m* di trattare i pazienti; **have a good ~ ~** saperci fare con i pazienti. **bedside rug** *n* scendiletto *m*. **bedside table** *n* comodino *m*

**bed: bed-sit** *n*, **bed-sitter** *n*, **bed-sitting-room** *n* camera *f* ammobiliata [fornita di cucina]. **bedsock** *n* calzino *m* da notte. **bedsore** *n* piaga *f* da decubito. **bedspread** *n* copriletto *m*. **bedstead** *n* fusto *m* del letto. **bedtime** *n* l'ora *f* di andare a letto. **bedwetting** *n* il bagnare il letto

**bee** /bi:/ *n* ape *f*

**beech** /bi:tʃ/ *n* faggio *m*

**beef** /bi:f/ n manzo m

**beef: beefburger** n hamburger m inv. **beefeater** n guardia f della Torre di Londra. **beefsteak** n bistecca f. **beefsteak tomato** n grosso pomodoro m. **beef stew** n stufato m di manzo. **beef tea** n brodo m di manzo

**beefy** /bi:fi/ a ⟨flavour⟩ di manzo; ⟨fam: man⟩ grande e grosso

**beehive** /bi:haɪv/ n alveare m

**bee: bee-keeper** n apicoltore, -trice mf. **bee-keeping** n apicoltura f. **bee-line** n **make a ~ for** fam precipitarsi verso

**been** /bi:n/ see be

**beep** /bi:p/ n ⟨of car⟩ suono m di clacson; ⟨of telephone⟩ segnale m acustico; ⟨of electronic device, radio⟩ bip m inv ● vi ⟨car, driver:⟩ clacsonare; ⟨device:⟩ fare bip ● vt ⟨with beeper⟩ chiamare con il cercapersone; **~ the horn** clacsonare

**beeper** /bi:pə(r)/ n cercapersone m inv

**beer** /bɪə(r)/ n birra f

**beer: beer belly** n pancia f da beone. **beer bottle** n bottiglia f da birra. **beer garden** n giardino m di un pub. **beer mat** n sottobicchiere m. **beerswilling** a pej ubriacone

**bee sting** n puntura f d'ape

**beeswax** /bi:zwæks/ n cera f d'api

**beet** /bi:t/ n (Am: beetroot) barbabietola f; [**sugar**] ~ barbabietola f da zucchero

**beetle** /bi:tl/ n scarafaggio m

■ **beetle off** vi ⟨fam: hurry away⟩ scappare

**beetroot** /bi:tru:t/ n barbabietola f

**befall** /bɪfɔ:l/ vt liter accadere a

**befit** /bɪfɪt/ vt liter addirsi a

**befitting** /bɪfɪtɪŋ/ a ⟨modesty, honesty⟩ opportuno

**before** /bɪfɔ:(r)/ prep prima di; **the day ~ yesterday** ieri l'altro; **~ long** fra poco ● adv prima; **never ~ have I seen...** non ho mai visto prima...; **~ that** prima; **~ going** prima di andare ● conj ⟨time⟩ prima che; **~ you go** prima che tu vada

**beforehand** /bɪfɔ:hænd/ adv in anticipo

**before tax** a ⟨profit, income⟩ lordo, al lordo di imposte

**befriend** /bɪfrend/ vt trattare da amico

**befuddle** /bɪfʌdl/ vt confondere ⟨mind⟩

**beg** /beg/ v (pt/pp begged) ● vi mendicare ● vt pregare; chiedere ⟨favour, forgiveness⟩

**began** /bɪgæn/ see begin

**beggar** /begə(r)/ n mendicante mf; **you lucky ~!** che fortuna sfacciata!; **poor ~!** povero cristo!; **you little ~!** monellaccio!

**beggarly** /begəlɪ/ a ⟨existence, meal⟩ miserabile; ⟨wage⟩ da fame

**begging bowl** /begɪŋ/ n ciotola f del mendicante

**begging letter** n lettera f che sollecita offerte in denaro

**begin** /bɪgɪn/ vt/i (pt began, pp begun, pres p beginning) cominciare; **well, to ~ with** dunque, per cominciare

**beginner** /bɪgɪnə(r)/ n principiante mf

**beginning** /bɪgɪnɪŋ/ n principio m

**begonia** /bɪgəʊnɪə/ n begonia f

**begrudge** /bɪgrʌdʒ/ vt ⟨envy⟩ essere invidioso di; dare malvolentieri ⟨money⟩

**beguile** /bɪgaɪl/ vt ⟨charm⟩ affascinare; ⟨cheat⟩ ingannare

**beguiling** /bɪgaɪlɪŋ/ a accattivante

**begun** /bɪgʌn/ see begin

**behalf** /bɪhɑ:f/ n **on ~ of** a nome di; **on my ~** a nome mio; **say hello on my ~** salutato da parte mia

**behave** /bɪheɪv/ vi comportarsi; **~ [oneself]** comportarsi bene

**behaviour** /bɪheɪvjə(r)/ n comportamento m; ⟨of prisoner, soldier⟩ condotta f

**behavioural** /bɪheɪvjərəl/ a comportamentale

**behaviourist** /bɪheɪvjərɪst/ a & n comportamentista mf

**behaviour pattern** n modello m comportamentale

**behead** /bɪhed/ vt decapitare

**beheld** /bɪheld/ see behold

**behind** /bɪhaɪnd/ prep dietro; ⟨with pronoun⟩ dietro di; **be ~ sth** fig stare dietro qcsa ● adv dietro, indietro; ⟨late⟩ in ritardo; **a long way ~** molto indietro; **in the car ~** nella macchina dietro ● n fam didietro m

**behindhand** /bɪhaɪndhænd/ adv indietro

**behold** /bɪhəʊld/ vt (pt/pp beheld) liter vedere

**beholden** /bɪhəʊldn/ a obbligato (**to** verso)

**beholder** /bɪhəʊldə(r)/ n **beauty is in the eye of the ~** è bello ciò che piace

**beige** /beɪʒ/ a & n beige m inv

**Beijing** /beɪdʒɪŋ/ n Pechino f

**being** /bi:ɪŋ/ n essere m; **come into ~** nascere

**Beirut** /beɪru:t/ n Beirut f

**bejewelled** /bɪdʒu:əld/ a ingioiellato

**belated** /bɪleɪtɪd/ a tardivo

**belatedly** /bɪleɪtɪdlɪ/ adv tardi

**belch** /beltʃ/ vi ruttare ● vt **~ [out]** eruttare ⟨smoke⟩

**beleaguered** /bɪli:gəd/ a ⟨city⟩ assediato; ⟨troops⟩ accerchiato; ⟨fig: person⟩ tormentato; ⟨fig: company⟩ in difficoltà

**Belfast** /belfɑ:st/ n Belfast f

**belfry** /belfrɪ/ n campanile m

**Belgian** /beldʒən/ a & n belga mf

**Belgium** /beldʒəm/ n Belgio m

**Belgrade** /belgreɪd/ n Belgrado f

**belie** /bɪlaɪ/ vt ⟨give false impression of⟩ dissimulare; ⟨disprove⟩ smentire

**belief** /bɪli:f/ n fede f; ⟨opinion⟩ convinzione f

**believable** /bɪli:vəbl/ a credibile

**believe** /bɪli:v/ vt/i credere

■ **believe in** vt avere fiducia in ⟨person⟩; credere a ⟨ghosts⟩

**believer** /bɪli:və(r)/ n Relig credente mf; **be a great ~ in** credere fermamente in

**belittle** /bɪlɪtl/ vt sminuire ⟨person, achievements⟩

**belittling** /bɪlɪtlɪŋ/ a ⟨comment⟩ che sminuisce

**Belize** /beli:z/ n Belize m

**bell** /bel/ *n* campana *f*; *(on door)* campanello *m*; **that rings a ~** *fig* mi dice qualcosa
**bell-bottoms** *npl* pantaloni *mpl* a zampa d'elefante
**bellboy** /'belbɔɪ/ *n Am* fattorino *m* d'albergo
**belle** /bel/ *n* bella *f*
**bellhop** /'belhɒp/ *n Am* fattorino *m* d'albergo
**belligerence** /bɪ'lɪdʒərəns/ *n* bellicosità *f*; *Pol* belligeranza *f*
**belligerent** /bɪ'lɪdʒərənt/ *a* belligerante; *(aggressive)* bellicoso
**bell-jar** *n* campana *f* di vetro
**bellow** /'beləʊ/ *vi* gridare a squarciagola; *⟨animal:⟩* muggire
■ **bellow out** *vt* urlare *⟨name, order⟩*
**bellows** /'beləʊz/ *npl (for fire)* soffietto *m*
**bell:** **bell-pull** *n (rope)* cordone *m* di campanello. **bell-push** *n* pulsante *m* di campanello. **bell-ringer** *n* campanaro *m*. **bell-shaped** *a* a campana. **bell tower** *n* campanile *m*
**belly** /'belɪ/ *n* pancia *f*
**belly:** **bellyache** *n fam* mal *m* di pancia ● *vi fam* lamentarsi. **belly button** *n fam* ombelico *m*. **belly dancer** *n* danzatrice *f* del ventre. **belly flop** *n (in swimming)* spanciata *f*
**bellyful** /'belɪfʊl/ *n fam* **have had a ~ of sth** avere le tasche piene di qcsa
**belong** /bɪ'lɒŋ/ *vi* appartenere **(to** a); *(be member)* essere socio **(to** di)
**belongings** /bɪ'lɒŋɪŋz/ *npl* cose *fpl*
**beloved** /bɪ'lʌvɪd/ *a & n* amato, -a *mf*
**below** /bɪ'ləʊ/ *prep* sotto; *(with numbers)* al di sotto di ● *adv* sotto, di sotto; *Naut* sotto coperta; **see ~** guarda qui di seguito
**belt** /belt/ *n* cintura *f*; *(area)* zona *f*; *Techn* cinghia *f* ● *vi (fam: rush)* **~ along** filare velocemente ● *vt (fam: hit)* picchiare
■ **belt up** *vi (in car)* mettersi la cintura [di sicurezza]; **~ up!** *(sl: be quiet)* stai zitto!
**bemoan** /bɪ'məʊn/ *vt* lamentare
**bemused** /bɪ'mjuːzd/ *a* confuso
**bench** /bentʃ/ *n* panchina *f*; *(work~)* piano *m* da lavoro; **the B~** *Jur* la magistratura
**benchmark** /'bentʃmɑːk/ *n* punto *m* di riferimento; *Comput* paragone *m* con un campione; *(fin: price)* prezzo *m* di riferimento
**bend** /bend/ *n* curva *f*; *(of river)* ansa *f*; **round the ~** *fam* fuori di testa ● *v (pt/pp bent)* ● *vt* piegare ● *vi* piegarsi; *⟨road:⟩* curvare; **~ [down]** chinarsi
■ **bend over** *vi* inchinarsi
**beneath** /bɪ'niːθ/ *prep* sotto, al di sotto di; **he thinks it's ~ him** *fig* pensa che sia sotto al suo livello; **~ contempt** indegno ● *adv* giù
**Benedictine** /benɪ'dɪktiːn/ *n & n Relig* benedettino *m*
**benediction** /benɪ'dɪkʃn/ *n Relig* benedizione *f*
**benefactor** /'benɪfæktə(r)/ *n* benefattore, -trice *mf*
**beneficial** /benɪ'fɪʃl/ *a* benefico
**beneficiary** /benɪ'fɪʃərɪ/ *n* beneficiario, -a *mf*
**benefit** /'benɪfɪt/ *n* vantaggio *m*; *(allowance)*

indennità *f inv* ● *v (pt/pp* **-fited,** *pres p* **-fiting)** ● *vt* giovare a ● *vi* trarre vantaggio **(from** da)
**Benelux** /'benɪlʌks/ *n* Benelux *m* ● *attrib ⟨countries, organization⟩* del Benelux
**benevolence** /bɪ'nevələns/ *n* benevolenza *f*
**benevolent** /bɪ'nevələnt/ *a* benevolo
**benevolently** /bɪ'nevələntlɪ/ *adv* con benevolenza
**Bengal** /beŋ'gɔːl/ *n* Bengala *m*
**benign** /bɪ'naɪn/ *a* benevolo; *Med* benigno
**benignly** /bɪ'naɪnlɪ/ *adv* con benevolenza
**Benin** /be'niːn/ *n* Benin *m*
**bent** /bent/ *see* **bend** ● *a ⟨person⟩* ricurvo; *(distorted)* curvato; *(fam: dishonest)* corrotto; **be ~ on doing sth** essere ben deciso a fare qcsa ● *n* predisposizione *f*
**benzene** /'benziːn/ *n* benzene *m*
**benzine** /'benziːn/ *n* benzina *f*
**bequeath** /bɪ'kwiːð/ *vt* lasciare in eredità
**bequest** /bɪ'kwest/ *n* lascito *m*
**berate** /bɪ'reɪt/ *vt fml* redarguire
**bereaved** /bɪ'riːvd/ *n* **the ~** *pl* i familiari del defunto
**bereavement** /bɪ'riːvmənt/ *n* lutto *m*
**bereft** /bɪ'reft/ *a* **~ of** privo di
**beret** /'bereɪ/ *n* berretto *m*
**Berlin** /bɜː'lɪn/ *n* Berlino *f*
**Berliner** /bɜː'lɪnə(r)/ *n* berlinese *mf*
**Bermuda** /bə'mjuːdə/ *n* le Bermuda.
**Bermuda shorts** *npl* bermuda *m inv*
**Berne** /bɜːn/ *n* Berna *f*
**berry** /'berɪ/ *n* bacca *f*
**berserk** /bə'sɜːk/ *a* **go ~** diventare una belva
**berth** /bɜːθ/ *n (bed)* cuccetta *f*; *(anchorage)* ormeggio *m*; **give a wide ~ to** *fam* stare alla larga da ● *vi* ormeggiare
**beseech** /bɪ'siːtʃ/ *vt (pt/pp* **beseeched** *or* **besought)** supplicare
**beseeching** /bɪ'siːtʃɪŋ/ *a* implorante
**beset** /bɪ'set/ *a* **a country ~ by strikes** un paese vessato dagli scioperi
**beside** /bɪ'saɪd/ *prep* accanto a; **~ oneself** fuori di sé
**besides** /bɪ'saɪdz/ *prep* oltre a ● *adv* inoltre
**besiege** /bɪ'siːdʒ/ *vt* assediare
**besotted** /bɪ'sɒtɪd/ *a* infatuato **(with** di)
**besought** /bɪ'sɔːt/ *see* **beseech**
**bespatter** /bɪ'spætə(r)/ *vt* schizzare
**bespectacled** /bɪ'spektək(ə)ld/ *a* con gli occhiali
**bespoke** /bɪ'spəʊk/ *a ⟨suit⟩* su misura; *⟨tailor⟩* che lavora su ordinazione
**best** /best/ *a* migliore; **the ~ part of a year** la maggior parte dell'anno; **~ before** *Comm* preferibilmente prima di; **~ wishes** migliori auguri ● *n* **the ~** il meglio; *(person)* il/la migliore; **at ~** tutt'al più; **all the ~!** tanti auguri!; **do one's ~** fare del proprio meglio; **to the ~ of my knowledge** per quel che ne so; **make the ~ of it** cogliere il lato buono della cosa ● *adv* meglio, nel modo migliore; **as ~ I could** meglio che potevo; **like ~** preferire
**best before date** *n* data *f* di scadenza

**best friend** n migliore amico, -a mf

**bestial** /'bestɪəl/ a also fig bestiale

**bestiality** /bestɪ'ælətɪ/ n bestialità f

**best man** n testimone m

**bestow** /bɪ'stəʊ/ vt conferire (**on** a)

**best-seller** /-'selə(r)/ n bestseller m inv

**best-selling** /-'selɪŋ/ a ‹novelist› più venduto

**bet** /bet/ n scommessa f ● vt/i (pt/pp **bet** or **betted**) scommettere

**beta blocker** /'bi:təblɒkə(r)/ n betabloccante m

**Bethlehem** /'beθlɪhem/ n Betlemme f

**betray** /bɪ'treɪ/ vt tradire

**betrayal** /bɪ'treɪəl/ n tradimento m

**betrothal** /bɪ'trəʊðəl/ n fidanzamento m

**betrothed** /bɪ'trəʊðd/ n liter, hum promesso sposo m; promessa sposa f; **be ~** essere fidanzato

**better** /'betə(r)/ a migliore, meglio; **get ~** migliorare; (after illness) rimettersi; **I waited the ~ part of a week** ho aspettato buona parte della settimana ● adv meglio; **~ off** meglio; (wealthier) più ricco; **all the ~** tanto meglio; **the sooner the ~** prima è, meglio è; **I've thought ~ of it** ci ho ripensato; **you'd ~ stay** faresti meglio a restare; **I'd ~ not** è meglio che non lo faccia ● vt migliorare; **~ oneself** migliorare le proprie condizioni

**betting** /'betɪŋ/ n (activity) scommesse fpl; **what's the ~ that...?** quanto scommettiamo che...?

**betting shop** n ricevitoria f (dell'allibratore)

**between** /bɪ'twi:n/ prep fra, tra; **~ you and me** detto fra di noi; **~ us** (together) tra me e te ● adv [**in**] **~** in mezzo; (time) frattempo

**betwixt** /bɪ'twɪkst/ adv **be ~ and between** essere una via di mezzo

**bevel** /'bevl/ n (edge) spigolo m smussato; (tool) squadra f falsa ● vt smussare ‹mirror, edge›

**beverage** /'bevərɪdʒ/ n bevanda f

**bevy** /'bevɪ/ n frotta f

**beware** /bɪ'weə(r)/ vi guardarsi (**of** da); **~ of the dog!** attenti al cane!

**bewilder** /bɪ'wɪldə(r)/ vt disorientare

**bewildered** /bɪ'wɪldəd/ a ‹look, person› perplesso, sconcertato

**bewildering** /bɪ'wɪldərɪŋ/ a sconcertante

**bewilderment** /bɪ'wɪldəmənt/ n perplessità f

**bewitch** /bɪ'wɪtʃ/ vt stregare; fig affascinare completamente

**beyond** /bɪ'jɒnd/ prep oltre; **~ reach** irraggiungibile; **~ doubt** senza alcun dubbio; **~ belief** da non credere; **it's ~ me** fam non riesco proprio a capire ● adv più in là

**B film** n film m inv di serie B

**bias** /'baɪəs/ n (preference) preferenza f; pej pregiudizio m ● vt (pt/pp **biased**) (influence) influenzare

**bias binding, bias tape** /'baɪndɪŋ/ n (in sewing) fettuccia f in sbieco

**biased** /'baɪəst/ a parziale

**bib** /bɪb/ n bavaglino m

**Bible** /'baɪbl/ n Bibbia f

**Bible Belt** n zona f del sud degli USA, dove predomina il fondamentalismo protestante

**biblical** /'bɪblɪkl/ a biblico

**bibliographic[al]** /bɪblɪə'græfɪk[ɪ]/ a bibliografico

**bibliography** /bɪblɪ'ɒɡrəfɪ/ n bibliografia f

**bicarbonate** /baɪ'kɑ:bənɪt/ n **~ of soda** bicarbonato m di sodio

**bicentenary** /baɪsen'ti:nərɪ/ n bicentenario m ● attrib ‹celebration, year› bicentenario

**biceps** /'baɪseps/ n bicipite m

**bicker** /'bɪkə(r)/ vi litigare

**bickering** /'bɪkərɪŋ/ n bisticci mpl

**bicycle** /'baɪsɪkl/ n bicicletta f ● vi andare in bicicletta

**bicycle: bicycle clip** n molletta f (per pantaloni). **bicycle lane** n pista f ciclabile. **bicycle rack** n (in yard) rastrelliera f per biciclette; (on car) portabiciclette m inv

**bid¹** /bɪd/ n offerta f; (attempt) tentativo m ● vt/i (pt/pp **bid**, pres p **bidding**) offrire; (in cards) dichiarare

**bid²** vt (pt **bade** or **bid**, pp **bidden** or **bid**, pres p **bidding**) liter (command) comandare; **~ sb welcome** dare il benvenuto a qcno

**bidder** /'bɪdə(r)/ n offerente mf

**bide** /baɪd/ vt **~ one's time** aspettare il momento buono

**bidet** /'bi:deɪ/ n bidè m inv

**biennial** /baɪ'enɪəl/ a biennale

**bier** /bɪə(r)/ n catafalco m

**bifocals** /baɪ'fəʊklz/ npl occhiali mpl bifocali

**big** /bɪɡ/ a (**bigger, biggest**) grande; ‹brother, sister› più grande; (fam: generous) generoso; **make ~ money** fare i soldi ● adv **talk ~** fam spararle grosse

**bigamist** /'bɪɡəmɪst/ n bigamo, -a mf

**bigamous** /'bɪɡəməs/ a bigamo

**bigamy** /'bɪɡəmɪ/ n bigamia f

**big: big bang** n (in astronomy) big bang m. **big business** n le grandi imprese; **be ~ ~** essere un grosso affare. **big cat** n grosso felino m. **big deal** n fam **~ ~!** bella forza!. **big dipper** n (Br: at fair) montagne fpl russe. **big game hunting** n caccia f grossa. **bighead** n fam montato, -a mf, gasato, -a mf. **big-headed** a fam montato, gasato. **big-hearted** a generoso. **bigmouth** n fam pej chiacchierone, -a mf; **he's such a ~!** (indiscreet) ha una lingua lunga!. **big name** n (in film, art) grosso nome m. **big noise** n fam pezzo m grosso

**bigot** /'bɪɡət/ n fanatico, -a mf

**bigoted** /'bɪɡətɪd/ a di mentalità ristretta

**big: big screen** n grande schermo m. **big shot** n fam pezzo m grosso. **Big Smoke** n Br hum Londra f. **big time** n **make** or **hit the ~ ~** n fam raggiungere il successo ● attrib **big-time** ‹crook› di alto livello. **big toe** n alluce m. **big top** n (tent) tendone m del circo; (fig: circus) circo m. **bigwig** n fam pezzo m grosso

**bike** /baɪk/ *n fam* bici *f inv*

**biker['s] jacket** /'baɪkə(z)dʒækɪt/ *n fam* giubbotto *m* di pelle

**bikini** /bɪ'kiːnɪ/ *n* bikini *m inv*

**bilateral** /baɪ'lætrəl/ *a* bilaterale

**bilberry** /'bɪlbərɪ/ *n* mirtillo *m*

**bile** /baɪl/ *n* bile *f*

**bilge** /bɪldʒ/ *n Naut* (*place*) carena *f*; (*substance*) sentina *f*: (*fam: nonsense*) idiozie *fpl*

**bilingual** /baɪ'lɪŋgwəl/ *a* bilingue

**bilingual secretary** *n* segretario, -a *mf* bilingue

**bilious** /'bɪljəs/ *a Med* ~ **attack** attacco *m* di bile

**bill¹** /bɪl/ *n* fattura *f*; (*in restaurant etc*) conto *m*; (*poster*) manifesto *m*; *Pol* progetto *m* di legge; (*Am: note*) biglietto *m* di banca; *Theat* **be top of the** ~ essere in testa al cartellone ● *vt* fatturare

**bill²** *n* (*beak*) becco *m*

**billboard** /'bɪlbɔːd/ *n* cartellone *m* pubblicitario

**billet** /'bɪlɪt/ *n Mil* alloggio *m* ● *vt* (*pt/pp* **billeted**) alloggiare (**on** presso)

**bill: bill of exchange** *n* cambiale *f*. **bill of fare** *n* menù *m inv*. **billfold** *n Am* portafoglio *m*. **bill of rights** *n* dichiarazione *f* dei diritti. **bill of sale** *n* atto *m* di vendita

**billiard ball** *n* palla *f* da biliardo

**billiards** /'bɪljədz/ *n* biliardo *m*

**billiard table** /'bɪljəd/ tavolo *m* da biliardo

**billing** /'bɪlɪŋ/ *n Comm* fatturazione *f*; **get top** ~ *Theat* comparire in testa al cartellone

**billion** /'bɪljən/ *n* (*thousand million*) miliardo *m*; (*old-fashioned Br: million million*) mille miliardi *pl*

**billionaire** /bɪljə'neə(r)/ *n* miliardario, -a *mf*

**billow** /'bɪləʊ/ *n* (*of smoke*) nube *f* ● *vi* alzarsi in volute

**billposter** /'bɪlpəʊstə(r)/ *n* attacchino *m*

**billy** /'bɪlɪ/ *n* (*Am: truncheon*) sfollagente *m inv*

**billycan** /'bɪlɪkæn/ *n* gamella *f*

**billy goat** *n* caprone *m*

**bimbo** /'bɪmbəʊ/ *n pej fam* bambolona *f*; **his latest** ~ la sua ultima amichetta

**bin** /bɪn/ *n* bidone *m*

**binary** /'baɪnərɪ/ *a* binario

**bind** /baɪnd/ *vt* (*pt/pp* **bound**) legare (**to** a); (*bandage*) fasciare; *Jur* obbligare

**binder** /'baɪndə(r)/ *n* (*for papers*) raccoglitore *m*; (*for cement, paint*) agglomerante *m*

**binding** /'baɪndɪŋ/ *a* (*promise, contract*) vincolante ● *n* (*of book*) rilegatura *f*; (*on ski*) attacco *m*

**binge** /bɪndʒ/ *n fam* **have a** ~ fare baldoria; (*eat a lot*) abbuffarsi ● *vi* abbuffarsi (**on** di)

**bingo** /'bɪŋgəʊ/ *n* ≈ tombola *f*

**bin liner** *n Br* sacchetto *m* per la spazzatura

**binoculars** /bɪ'nɒkjʊləz/ *npl* [**pair of**] ~ binocolo *msg*

**biochemist** /baɪəʊ'kemɪst/ *n* biochimico, -a *mf*

**biochemistry** /baɪəʊ'kemɪstrɪ/ *n* biochimica *f*

**biodegradable** /baɪəʊdɪ'greɪdəbl/ *a* biodegradabile

**biodiversity** /baɪəʊdaɪ'vɜːsətɪ/ *n* biodiversità *f*

**bioengineering** /baɪəʊendʒɪ'nɪərɪŋ/ *n* bioingegneria *f*

**biographer** /baɪ'ɒgrəfə(r)/ *n* biografo, -a *mf*

**biographical** /baɪə'græfɪkl/ *a* biografico

**biography** /baɪ'ɒgrəfɪ/ *n* biografia *f*

**biological** /baɪə'lɒdʒɪkl/ *a* biologico

**biological clock** *n* orologio *m* biologico

**biologically** /baɪə'lɒdʒɪklɪ/ *adv* biologicamente

**biological powder** *n* detersivo *m* biologico

**biological warfare** *n* guerra *f* biologica

**biologist** /baɪ'ɒlədʒɪst/ *n* biologo, -a *mf*

**biology** /baɪ'ɒlədʒɪ/ *n* biologia *f*

**bionic** /baɪ'ɒnɪk/ *a* bionico

**biopic** /'baɪəʊpɪk/ *n Cin film m* basato su una biografia

**biopsy** /'baɪɒpsɪ/ *n* biopsia *f*

**biorhythm** /'baɪəʊrɪðəm/ *n* bioritmo *m*

**biotechnology** /baɪəʊtek'nɒlədʒɪ/ *n* biotecnologia *f*

**bipartisan** /baɪpɑː'tɪzæn/ *a Pol* bipartitico

**bipartite** /baɪ'pɑːtaɪt/ *a* bipartito

**birch** /bɜːtʃ/ *n* (*tree*) betulla *f*

**bird** /bɜːd/ *n* uccello *m*; (*fam: girl*) ragazza *f*; **kill two** ~**s with one stone** prendere due piccioni con una fava

**birdbrain** /'bɜːdbreɪn/ *n fam* **he's such a** ~ ha un cervello da gallina

**bird call** *n* cinguettio *m*

**birdie** /'bɜːdɪ/ *n* (*in golf*) birdie *m*

**birdlike** /'bɜːdlaɪk/ *a* come un uccello

**bird: bird of paradise** *n* uccello *m* del paradiso. **bird of prey** *n* [uccello *m*] rapace *m*. **bird sanctuary** *n* riserva *f* per uccelli. **birdseed** *n* becchime *m*. **bird's eye view** *n* veduta *f* panoramica dall'alto. **bird's nest** *n* nido *m* di uccello. **bird's nest soup** *n* zuppa *f* di nidi di rondine. **birdsong** *n* canto *m* degli uccelli. **birdwatcher** *n* persona *f* che pratica il bird-watching. **bird-watching** *n* **go** ~ fare del bird-watching

**Biro®** /'baɪrəʊ/ *n* biro® *f inv*

**birth** /bɜːθ/ *n* nascita *f*; **give** ~ partorire; **give** ~ **to** partorire

**birth: birth certificate** *n* certificato *m* di nascita. **birth-control** *n* controllo *m* delle nascite. **birthday** *n* compleanno *m*. **birthday party** *n* festa *f* di compleanno. **birthmark** *n* voglia *f*. **birthplace** *n* luogo *m* di nascita. **birth-rate** *n* natalità *f*. **birthright** *n* diritto *m* di nascita. **births column** *n* annunci *mpl* delle nascite (*nel giornale*). **birth sign** *n* segno *m* zodiacale. **births, marriages, and deaths** *npl* annunci *mpl* di nascite, di matrimonio, mortuari (*nel giornale*)

**biscuit** /'bɪskɪt/ *n* biscotto *m*

**biscuit barrel, biscuit tin** *n* biscottiera *f*

**bisect** /baɪˈsekt/ vt dividere in due [parti]

**bisexual** /baɪˈseksjʊəl/ a & n bisessuale mf

**bishop** /ˈbɪʃəp/ n vescovo m; Chess alfiere m

**bistro** /ˈbiːstrəʊ/ n bistrò m inv

**bit¹** /bɪt/ n pezzo m; (smaller) pezzetto m; (for horse) morso m; Comput bit m inv; **a ~ of** un pezzo di ‹cheese, paper›; un po' di ‹time, rain, silence›; **~ by ~** poco a poco; **do one's ~** fare la propria parte

**bit²** see bite

**bitch** /bɪtʃ/ n cagna f; sl arpia f

**bitchy** /ˈbɪtʃɪ/ a velenoso

**bite** /baɪt/ n morso m; (insect ~) puntura f; (mouthful) boccone m ● vt (pt bit, pp bitten) mordere; ‹insect:› pungere; **~ one's nails** mangiarsi le unghie ● vi mordere; ‹insect:› pungere

■ **bite off** vt staccare (con un morso)

**biting** /ˈbaɪtɪŋ/ a ‹wind, criticism› pungente; ‹remark› mordace

**bit part** n Theat particina f

**bitter** /ˈbɪtə(r)/ a amaro ● n Br birra f amara

**bitter almond** n mandorla f amara

**bitter lemon** n limonata f amara

**bitterly** /ˈbɪtəlɪ/ adv amaramente; **it's ~ cold** c'è un freddo pungente

**bitterness** /ˈbɪtənɪs/ n amarezza f

**bittersweet** /bɪtəˈswiːt/ a liter agrodolce

**bitty** /ˈbɪtɪ/ a Br fam frammentario

**bitumen** /ˈbɪtjʊmɪn/ n bitume m

**bivouac** /ˈbɪvʊæk/ n bivacco m ● vi bivaccare

**bizarre** /bɪˈzɑː(r)/ a bizzarro

**blab** /blæb/ vi (pt/pp blabbed) cianciare

**black** /blæk/ a nero; **be ~ and blue** essere coperto di lividi ● n nero m ● vt boicottare ‹goods›

■ **black out** vt cancellare ● vi (lose consciousness) perdere coscienza

**black:** **Black Africa** n Africa f nera. **Black American** n negro, -a americano, -a mf. **black and white** n bianco e nero. **blackball** vt dare voto contrario a. **black belt** n cintura f nera. **blackberry** n mora f. **blackberry bush** n rovo m. **blackbird** n merlo m. **blackboard** n Sch lavagna f. **black box** n Aeron scatola f nera. **black bread** n pane m nero. **blackcurrant** n ribes m inv nero

**blacken** /ˈblækən/ vt annerire

**black:** **black eye** n occhio m nero. **Black Forest gateau** n dolce m a base di cioccolato, panna e ciliegie. **black gold** n fam oro m nero

**blackguard** /ˈblægəd/ n hum brigante m

**black:** **blackhead** n Med punto m nero. **black-headed gull** n gabbiano m comune. **black humour** n umorismo m nero. **black ice** n ghiaccio m (sulla strada)

**blacking** /ˈblækɪŋ/ (Br: boycotting) boicottaggio m; (polish) lucido m nero (per scarpe)

**blackish** /ˈblækɪʃ/ a nerastro

**black:** **blackjack** n blackjack m. **blackleg** n Br crumiro m. **blacklist** vt mettere sulla lista nera. **blackmail** n ricatto m ● vt ricattare. **blackmailer** n ricattatore, -trice mf. **black mark** n fig neo m. **black market** n borsa f

nera. **black marketeer** n borsanerista mf.

**black mass** n messa f nera

**blackness** /ˈblæknɪs/ n nero m; (evilness) cattiveria f; (of moods) scontrosità f

**black:** **black-out** n blackout m inv; **have a ~** Med perdere coscienza. **black pepper** n pepe m nero. **black pudding** n ≈ sanguinaccio m. **Black Sea** n Mar m Nero. **Blackshirt** n camicia f nera. **blacksmith** n fabbro m. **black sheep** n fig pecora f nera. **black spot** n fig luogo m conosciuto per gli incidenti stradali. **black swan** n cigno m nero. **black tie** (on invitation) abito scuro. **black widow [spider]** n vedova f nera

**bladder** /ˈblædə(r)/ n Anat vescica f

**blade** /bleɪd/ n lama f; (of grass) filo m

**blame** /bleɪm/ n colpa f ● vt dare la colpa a; **~ sb for doing sth** dare la colpa a qcno per aver fatto qcsa; **no one is to ~** non è colpa di nessuno

**blameless** /ˈbleɪmlɪs/ a innocente

**blameworthy** /ˈbleɪmwɜːðɪ/ a biasimevole

**blanch** /blɑːntʃ/ vi sbiancare ● vt Culin sbollentare

**blancmange** /bləˈmɒnʒ/ n biancomangiare m

**bland** /blænd/ a ‹food› insipido; ‹person› insulso

**blandly** /ˈblændlɪ/ adv ‹say› in modo piatto

**blank** /blæŋk/ a bianco; ‹look› vuoto ● n spazio m vuoto; (cartridge) cartuccia f a salve

**blank cheque** n assegno m in bianco

**blanket** /ˈblæŋkɪt/ n coperta f; **wet ~** fam guastafeste mf inv

**blanket:** **blanket box, blanket chest** n Br cassapanca f. **blanket cover** n (in insurance) assicurazione f che copre tutti i rischi. **blanket stitch** n punto m di rinforzo

**blankly** /ˈblæŋklɪ/ adv (uncomprehendingly) con espressione attonita; (without expression) senza espressione

**blank verse** n versi mpl sciolti

**blare** /bleə(r)/ vi suonare a tutto volume

■ **blare out** vt strombazzare rumorosamente

**blarney** /ˈblɑːnɪ/ n fam lusinga f

**blasé** /ˈblɑːzeɪ/ a blasé inv

**blaspheme** /blæsˈfiːm/ vi bestemmiare

**blasphemous** /ˈblæsfəməs/ a blasfemo

**blasphemy** /ˈblæsfəmɪ/ n bestemmia f

**blast** /blɑːst/ n (gust) raffica f; (sound) scoppio m ● vt (with explosive) far saltare ● int sl maledizione!

**blasted** /ˈblɑːstɪd/ a sl maledetto

**blast furnace** n altoforno m

**blasting** /ˈblɑːstɪŋ/ n brillamento m

**blast-off** n (of missile) lancio m

**blatant** /ˈbleɪtənt/ a sfacciato

**blatantly** /ˈbleɪtəntlɪ/ adv ‹copy, disregard› sfacciatamente; **it's ~ obvious** è lampante

**blather** /ˈblæðə(r)/ vi fam blaterare

**blaze** /bleɪz/ n incendio m; **a ~ of colour** un'esplosione f di colori ● vi ardere

■ **blaze down** vi (sun:) essere cocente

**blazer** /ˈbleɪzə(r)/ n blazer m inv

**bleach** /bli:tʃ/ n decolorante m; (for cleaning) candeggina f, varechina f ● vt sbiancare; ossigenare ⟨hair⟩

**bleak** /bli:k/ a desolato; ⟨fig: prospects, future⟩ tetro

**bleakly** /'bli:klɪ/ adv ⟨stare, say⟩ in modo tetro

**bleakness** /'bli:knɪs/ n (of weather) tetraggine f; (of surroundings, future) desolazione f

**bleary-eyed** /blɪərɪ'aɪd/ a **be** ~ avere gli occhi gonfi

**bleat** /bli:t/ vi belare ● n belato m

**bleed** /bli:d/ v (pt/pp **bled**) ● vi sanguinare ● vt spurgare ⟨brakes, radiator⟩

**bleeding** /'bli:dɪŋ/ n perdita di sangue f; (heavy) emorragia f; (deliberate) salasso m ● a ⟨wound, hand⟩ sanguinante; sl = **bloody**

**bleeding heart** n fig pej cuore m troppo tenero

**bleep** /bli:p/ n bip m ● vi suonare ● vt chiamare col cercapersone

**bleeper** /'bli:pə(r)/ n cercapersone m inv

**blemish** /'blemɪʃ/ n macchia f

**blend** /blend/ n (of tea, coffee, whisky) miscela f; (of colours) insieme m ● vt mescolare ● vi ⟨colours, sounds:⟩ fondersi (**with** con)

**blender** /'blendə(r)/ n Culin frullatore m

**blending** /'blendɪŋ/ n (of coffees, whiskies) miscela f

**bless** /bles/ vt benedire

**blessed** /'blesɪd/ a also sl benedetto

**blessing** /'blesɪŋ/ n benedizione f

**blew** /blu:/ see **blow**[2]

**blight** /blaɪt/ n Bot ruggine f ● vt far avvizzire ⟨plants⟩

**blighter** /'blaɪtə(r)/ (Br fam: annoying person) idiota mf; **you lucky** ~ hai una fortuna sfacciata!; **poor** ~ povero diavolo m

**blimey** /'blaɪmɪ/ int Br fam accidenti!

**blind** /blaɪnd/ a cieco; ~ **man/woman** cieco/cieca ● npl **the** ~ i ciechi ● vt accecare ● n [**roller**] ~ avvolgibile m; [**Venetian**] ~ veneziana f

**blind: blind alley** n vicolo m cieco. **blind date** n appuntamento m galante con una persona sconosciuta. **blind drunk** a ubriaco fradicio. **blindfold** adv con gli occhi bendati ● a **be** ~ avere gli occhi bendati ● n benda f ● vt bendare gli occhi a

**blinding** /'blaɪndɪŋ/ a ⟨light⟩ accecante; ⟨headache⟩ da impazzire, tremendo

**blindingly** /'blaɪndɪŋlɪ/ adv ⟨shine⟩ in modo accecante; **be** ~ **obvious** essere così lampante

**blindly** /'blaɪndlɪ/ adv ciecamente

**blind-man's buff** n moscacieca f

**blindness** /'blaɪndnɪs/ n cecità f

**blind spot** n (in car, on hill) punto m privo di visibilità; (in eye) punto m cieco; (fig: point of ignorance) punto m debole

**blink** /blɪŋk/ vi sbattere le palpebre; ⟨light:⟩ tremolare

**blinkered** /'blɪŋkəd/ a ⟨fig: attitude, approach⟩ ottuso; **be** ~ avere i paraocchi

**blinkers** /'blɪŋkəz/ npl paraocchi mpl

**blinking** /'blɪŋkɪŋ/ n (of light) intermittenza f; (of eye) battere m

**blip** /blɪp/ n (on screen) segnale m luminoso a intermittenza; (on graph, line) piccola irregolarità f; (sound) ticchettio m; (hitch) intoppo m

**bliss** /blɪs/ n Rel beatitudine f; (happiness) felicità f

**blissful** /'blɪsfʊl/ a beato; (happy) meraviglioso

**blissfully** /'blɪsfəlɪ/ adv beatamente; ~ **ignorant** beatamente ignaro

**blister** /'blɪstə(r)/ n Med vescica f; (in paint) bolla f ● vi ⟨paint:⟩ formare una bolla/delle bolle

**blistering** /'blɪst(ə)rɪŋ/ n (of skin) vescica f; (of paint) bolle fpl ● a ⟨sun⟩ scottante; ⟨heat⟩ soffocante; ⟨attack, criticism⟩ feroce

**blister pack** n blister m inv

**blithe** /blaɪð/ a (cheerful) gioioso; (nonchalant) spensierato

**blithely** /'blaɪðlɪ/ adv (nonchalantly) spensieratamente

**blitz** /blɪts/ n bombardamento m aereo; **have a** ~ **on sth** fig darci sotto con qcsa

**blitzkrieg** /'blɪtskri:g/ n guerra f lampo

**blizzard** /'blɪzəd/ n tormenta f

**bloated** /'bləʊtɪd/ a gonfio

**blob** /blɒb/ n goccia f

**bloc** /blɒk/ n Pol blocco m

**block** /blɒk/ n blocco m; (building) isolato m; (building ~) cubo m (per giochi di costruzione); ~ **of flats** palazzo m ● vt bloccare

■ **block up** vt bloccare

**blockade** /blɒ'keɪd/ n blocco m ● vt bloccare

**blockage** /'blɒkɪdʒ/ n ostruzione f

**block: block and tackle** n paranco m. **block book** vt prenotare in blocco. **block booking** n prenotazione f in blocco. **blockbuster** n (fam: book, film) successore m; Mil bomba f potente. **block capital** n in ~ ~s in stampatello. **blockhead** n fam testone, -a mf. **blockhouse** n Mil fortino m. **block letters** npl stampatello m. **block vote** n voto m per delega. **block voting** n votazione f per delega

**bloke** /bləʊk/ n fam tizio m

**blonde** /blɒnd/ a biondo ● n bionda f

**blood** /blʌd/ n sangue m

**blood: blood-and-thunder** a ⟨novel, film⟩ pieno di sangue. **blood bank** n banca f del sangue. **blood bath** n bagno m di sangue. **blood blister** n vescica f di sangue. **blood brother** n fratello m di sangue. **blood cell**, **blood corpuscle** n globulo m. **blood count** n esame m emocromocitometrico. **blood-curdling** a raccapricciante. **blood donor** n donatore, -trice mf di sangue. **blood group** n gruppo m sanguigno. **bloodhound** n segugio m

**bloodless** /'blʌdlɪs/ a (pale) esangue; ⟨revolution, coup⟩ senza spargimento di sangue

**blood: blood-letting** n Med salasso m; ⟨killing⟩ spargimento m di sangue. **blood lust** n sete f di sangue. **blood money** n compenso versato ad un killer o delatore. **blood**

**orange** *n* arancia *f* sanguigna. **blood poisoning** *n* setticemia *f*. **blood pressure** *n* pressione *f* del sangue. **blood-red** *a* rosso sangue *inv*. **blood relative** *n* parente *mf* consanguineo, -a. **bloodshed** *n* spargimento *m* di sangue. **bloodshot** *a* iniettato di sangue. **blood sports** *npl* sport *mpl* cruenti. **bloodstained** *a* macchiato di sangue. **bloodstream** *n* sangue *m*. **bloodsucker** *n* *also fig* sanguisuga *f*. **blood test** *n* analisi *f* del sangue. **bloodthirsty** *a* assetato di sangue. **blood transfusion** *n* trasfusione *f* del sangue. **blood type** *n* gruppo *m* sanguigno. **blood vessel** *n* vaso *m* sanguigno

**bloody** /'blʌdɪ/ *a* (-ier, -iest) insanguinato; *sl* maledetto ● *adv sl* ~ **easy/difficult** facile/difficile da matti; ~ **tired/funny** stanco/divertente da morire; **you ~ well will!** e, accidenti, lo farai!

**bloody-minded** /blʌdɪ'maɪndɪd/ *a* scorbutico

**bloom** /blu:m/ *n* fiore *m*; **in ~** (*of flower*) sbocciato; (*of tree*) in fiore ● *vi* fiorire; *fig* essere in forma smagliante

**bloomer** /'blu:mə(r)/ *n fam* papera *f*

**bloomers** /'blu:məz/ *npl* mutandoni *mpl* da donna

**blooming** /'blu:mɪŋ/ *a fam* maledetto

**blossom** /'blɒsəm/ *n* fiori *mpl* (*d'albero*); (*single one*) fiore *m* ● *vi* sbocciare
■ **blossom out** *vi fig* trasformarsi

**blot** /blɒt/ *n also fig* macchia *f*
■ **blot out** *vt* (*pt/pp* **blotted**) *fig* cancellare

**blotch** /blɒtʃ/ *n* macchia *f*

**blotchy** /'blɒtʃɪ/ *a* chiazzato

**blotter** /'blɒtə(r)/ *n* tampone *m* di carta assorbente; (*Am: police*) registro *m* di polizia

**blotting paper** /'blɒtɪŋ/ *n* carta *f* assorbente

**blotto** /'blɒtəʊ/ *a fam* ubriaco fradicio

**blouse** /blaʊz/ *n* camicetta *f*

**blow¹** /bləʊ/ *n* colpo *m*

**blow²** *v* (*pt* **blew**, *pp* **blown**) ● *vi* (*wind:*) soffiare; (*fuse:*) saltare ● *vt* (*fam: squander*) sperperare; ~ **one's nose** soffiarsi il naso; ~ **one's top** *fam* andare in bestia
■ **blow away** *vt* far volar via (*papers*) ● *vi* (*papers:*) volare via
■ **blow down** *vt* abbattere ● *vi* abbattersi al suolo
■ **blow off** *vt* (*wind:*) portar via ● *vi* (*hat, roof:*) volare via
■ **blow out** *vt* (*extinguish*) soffiare ● *vi* (*candle:*) spegnersi
■ **blow over** *vt* (*wind:*) buttare giù ● *vi* (*storm:*) passare; (*fig: fuss, trouble:*) dissiparsi
■ **blow up** *vt* (*inflate*) gonfiare; (*enlarge*) ingrandire (*photograph*); (*shatter by explosion*) far esplodere ● *vi* esplodere

**blow: blow-by-blow** *a* (*account*) particolareggiato. **blow-dry** *vt* asciugare con l'asciugacapelli. **blowfly** *n* moscone *m* (*della carne*). **blowhole** *n* (*of whale*) sfiatatoio *m*. **blowlamp** *n* fiamma *f* ossidrica

**blown** /bləʊn/ *see* **blow²**

**blow: blowout** *n* *Elec* corto circuito *m*; (*in oil or gas well*) fuga *f*; (*of tyre*) scoppio *m*; (*fam: meal*) abbuffata *f*. **blowpipe** *n* cerbottana *f*. **blowtorch** *n* cannello *m* ossidrico. **blow-up** *n* *Phot* ingrandimento *m* ● *a* (*doll, toy, dinghy*) gonfiabile

**blowy** /'bləʊɪ/ *a* ventoso

**blowzy** /'blaʊzɪ/ *a pej* (*woman*) volgarmente appariscente

**blubber** /'blʌbə(r)/ *n* (*of whale*) grasso *m* di balena; (*fam: of person*) ciccia *f* ● *vi fam* piagnucolare

**bludgeon** /'blʌdʒən/ *vt* manganellare

**blue** /blu:/ *a* (*pale*) celeste; (*navy*) blu *inv*; (*royal*) azzurro; **feel ~** essere giù di corda; ~ **with cold** livido per il freddo; **once in a ~ moon** una volta ogni morte di papa ● *n* blu *m inv*; **have the ~s** essere giù di corda; **out of the ~** inaspettatamente; **a bolt from the ~** un fulmine a ciel sereno

**blue: bluebell** *n* giacinto *m* di bosco. **Blue Berets** *npl Mil* Caschi blu *mpl*. **blueberry** *n* mirtillo *m*. **blue blood** *n* sangue *m* blu. **blue-blooded** *a* di sangue blu. **bluebottle** *n* moscone *m*. **blue chip** *a* (*company*) di altissimo livello; (*investment*) sicuro. **blue-collar job** *n* lavoro *m* manuale. **blue-collar worker** *n* operaio *m*. **blue-eyed** *a* con gli occhi azzurri. **blue-eyed boy** *n Br fig fam* prediletto *m*. **blue film** *n* film *m* a luci rosse. **blue jeans** *npl* bluejeans *mpl inv*. **blue light** *n* (*on emergency vehicles*) luce *f* della sirena della macchina della polizia

**blueness** /'blu:nɪs/ *n* azzurro *m*

**blue: blue pencil** *n* **go through sth with the ~ ~** (*censure*) censurare qcsa; (*edit*) fare una revisione di qcsa. **blueprint** *n fig* progetto *m*. **blue rinse** *n* **she's had a ~** si è tinta i capelli color grigio argentato. **bluestocking** *n pej* [donna] intellettualoide *f*. **blue tit** *n* cinciarella *f*. **blue whale** *n* balenottera *f* azzurra

**bluff** /blʌf/ *n* bluff *m inv* ● *vi* bluffare

**bluish** /'blu:ɪʃ/ *a* bluastro, azzurrognolo

**blunder** /'blʌndə(r)/ *n* gaffe *f inv* ● *vi* fare una/delle gaffe

**blundering** /'blʌnd(ə)rɪŋ/ *a* ~ **idiot** rimbecillito *m*

**blunt** /blʌnt/ *a* spuntato; (*person*) reciso

**bluntly** /'blʌntlɪ/ *adv* schiettamente

**bluntness** /'blʌntnɪs/ *n* (*of manner*) rudezza *f*; (*of person*) brutale schiettezza *f*

**blur** /blɜ:(r)/ *n* **it's all a ~** *fig* è tutto confuso ● *vt* (*pt/pp* **blurred**) rendere confuso

**blurb** /blɜ:b/ *n* soffietto *m* editoriale

**blurred** /blɜ:d/ *a* (*vision, photo*) sfocato

■ **blurt out** /blɜ:t/ *vt* spifferare

**blush** /blʌʃ/ *n* rossore *m* ● *vi* arrossire

**blusher** /'blʌʃə(r)/ *n* fard *m inv*

**bluster** /'blʌstə(r)/ *n* (*showing off*) sbruffonata *f*

**blustering** /'blʌst(ə)rɪŋ/ *n* (*rage*) sfuriata *f*; (*boasting*) spacconata *f* ● *a* (*angry*) infuriato; (*boastful*) sbruffone

**blustery** /'blʌst(ə)rɪ/ a ⟨wind⟩ furioso; ⟨day, weather⟩ molto ventoso

**B movie** n film m inv di serie B

**BO** n fam puzza f di sudore

**boa** /'bəʊə/ n boa m inv

**boa constrictor** /kən'strɪktə(r)/ boa m inv

**boar** /bɔː(r)/ n cinghiale m

**board** /bɔːd/ n tavola f; (for notices) tabellone m; (committee) assemblea f; (of directors) consiglio m; **~ of directors** consiglio m di amministrazione; **full ~** Br pensione f completa; **half ~** Br mezza pensione f; **~ and lodging** vitto e alloggio m; **go by the ~** fam andare a monte ● vt Naut, Aeron salire a bordo di ● vi ⟨passengers:⟩ salire a bordo; **~ with** stare a pensione da

■ **board up** vt sbarrare con delle assi

**boarder** /'bɔːdə(r)/ n pensionante mf; Sch convittore, -trice mf

**board game** n gioco m da tavolo

**boarding** /'bɔːdɪŋ/ n Aeron, Naut imbarco m; (by customs officer) ispezione f; Mil abbordaggio m

**boarding: boarding card** n carta f di imbarco. **boarding house** n pensione f. **boarding party** n squadra f d'ispezione. **boarding school** n collegio m.

**board: board meeting** n riunione f del consiglio di amministrazione. **boardroom** n sala f consiglio, sala f riunioni del consiglio di amministrazione. **boardwalk** n Am (by sea) lungomare m

**boast** /bəʊst/ vi vantarsi (**about** di) ● vt vantare

**boaster** /'bəʊstɪə(r)/ n sbruffone, -a mf

**boastful** /'bəʊstfʊl/ a vanaglorioso

**boat** /bəʊt/ n barca f; (ship) nave f

**boater** /'bəʊtə(r)/ n (hat) paglietta f

**boat-hook** n gaffa f

**boathouse** /'bəʊthaʊs/ n rimessa f [per imbarcazioni]

**boating** /'bəʊtɪŋ/ n canottaggio m ● a ⟨accident⟩ di navigazione

**boating trip** n traversata f per mare

**boat: boatload** n carico m; **~s of tourists** navi fpl cariche di turisti. **boatswain** /'bəʊs(ə)n/ n nostromo m. **boatyard** n cantiere m per imbarcazioni

**bob** /bɒb/ n (hairstyle) caschetto m ● vi (pt/pp **bobbed**) (also **~ up and down**) andare su e giù

**bobbin** /'bɒbɪn/ n bobina f

**bobble hat** /'bɒblhæt/ n berretto m a pompon

**bobby** /'bɒbɪ/ n Br fam poliziotto m

**bobcat** /'bɒbkæt/ n lince f

**bobsleigh** /'bɒbsleɪ/ n bob m inv ● vi andare sul bob

**bode** /bəʊd/ vi **~ well/ill** essere di buono/cattivo augurio

**bodge** /bɒdʒ/ Br = **botch**

**bodice** /'bɒdɪs/ n corpetto m

**bodily** /'bɒdɪlɪ/ a fisico ● adv (forcibly) fisicamente

**body** /'bɒdɪ/ n corpo m; (organization) ente m; (amount: of poems etc) quantità f; **over my dead ~!** fam devi passare prima sul mio corpo!

**body: body blow** n deal a **~ to** fig assestare un duro colpo a. **bodybuilder** n culturista mf. **body-building** n culturismo m. **bodyguard** n guardia f del corpo. **body heat** n calore m del corpo. **body language** n linguaggio m del corpo. **body odour** n fam puzza f di sudore. **body politic** n corpo m sociale. **body shop** n autocarrozzeria f. **body snatching** n furto m dei cadaveri. **body stocking, body suit** n body m inv. **body warmer** n gilet m inv imbottito. **bodywork** n Auto auto-carrozzeria f

**boffin** /'bɒfɪn/ n Br fam scienziato m

**bog** /bɒg/ n palude f

■ **bog down** vt (pt/pp **bogged**) **get ~ged down** impantanarsi

**bogey** /'bəʊgɪ/ n (evil spirit) spirito m malvagio; (to frighten people) spauracchio m

**boggle** /'bɒg(ə)l/ vi **the mind ~s** non posso neanche immaginarlo

**boggy** /'bɒgɪ/ a (swampy) paludoso; (muddy) fangoso

**bogus** /'bəʊgəs/ a falso

**bohemian** /bəʊ'hiːmɪən/ a ⟨lifestyle, person⟩ bohémien

**boil¹** /bɔɪl/ n Med foruncolo m

**boil²** n **bring/come to the ~** portare/arrivare ad ebollizione ● vt [far] bollire ● vi bollire; (fig: with anger) ribollire; **the water** or **kettle's ~ing** l'acqua bolle

■ **boil away** vi ⟨water:⟩ evaporare

■ **boil down to** vi fig ridursi a

■ **boil over** vi straboccare (bollendo)

■ **boil up** vt far bollire

**boiler** /'bɔɪlə(r)/ n caldaia f

**boiler: boiler house** n caldaia f. **boiler room** n locale m per la caldaia. **boiler suit** n tuta f

**boiling** /'bɔɪlɪŋ/ a ⟨water⟩ bollente; **it's ~ in here!** qui si bolle!

**boiling hot** a fam ⟨liquid⟩ bollente; ⟨day⟩ torrido

**boiling point** n punto m di ebollizione

**boisterous** /'bɔɪstərəs/ a chiassoso

**bold** /bəʊld/ a audace ● n Typ neretto m

**boldly** /'bəʊldlɪ/ adv audacemente

**boldness** /'bəʊldnɪs/ n audacia f

**Bolivia** /bə'lɪvɪə/ n Bolivia f

**bollard** /'bɒlɑːd/ n colonnina m di sbarramento al traffico

**Bolognese** /bɒlə'neɪz/ n sugo m al ragù

**boloney** /bə'ləʊnɪ/ n fam idiozie fpl

**bolshy** /'bɒlʃɪ/ a Br fam (on one occasion) brontolone; **he's/she's ~** (by temperament) è un/una piantagrane; **get ~** fare [delle] storie

**bolster** /'bəʊlstə(r)/ n cuscino m (lungo e rotondo) ● vt **~ [up]** sostenere

**bolt** /bəʊlt/ n (for door) catenaccio m; (for fixing) bullone m ● vt fissare [con bulloni] (**to** a); chiudere col chiavistello ⟨door⟩; ingurgitare ⟨food⟩ ● vi svignarsela; ⟨horse:⟩ scappar via ● adv **~ upright** diritto come un fuso

**bolt-hole** *n Br* rifugio *m*
**bomb** /bɒm/ *n* bomba *f* ● *vt* bombardare
■ **bomb along** *vi* (*fam: move quickly*) sfrecciare
**bombard** /bɒm'bɑːd/ *vt also fig* bombardare
**bombardment** /bɒm'bɑːdmənt/ *n* bombardamento *m*
**bombastic** /bɒm'bæstɪk/ *a* ampolloso
**bomb: bomb attack** *n* bombardamento *m*. **bomb blast** *n* esplosione *f*. **bomb disposal** *n* disinnesco *m*. **bomb disposal expert** *n* artificiere *m*. **bomb disposal squad** *n* squadra *f* artificieri
**bomber** /'bɒmə(r)/ *n Aviat* bombardiere *m*; (*person*) dinamitardo *m*
**bomber jacket** *n* bomber *m inv*
**bombing** /'bɒmɪŋ/ *n Mil* bombardamento *m*; (*by terrorists*) attentato *m* dinamitardo
**bomb: bombproof** *a* a prova di bomba. **bombscare** *n* stato *m* di allarme per la presunta presenza di una bomba. **bombshell** *n* (*fig: news*) bomba *f*; **blonde ~** bionda *f* esplosiva. **bomb shelter** *n* rifugio *m* antiaereo. **bombsite** *n* zona *f* bombardata; (*fig: mess*) campo *m* di battaglia. **Bomb Squad** *n* squadra *f* artificieri
**bona fide** /bəʊnə'faɪdɪ/ *a* (*member, refugee*) autentico; (*attempt*) genuino; (*offer*) serio
**bonanza** /bə'nænzə/ *n* (*windfall*) momento *m* di prosperità; (*in mining*) filone *m* d'oro/d'argento
**bond** /bɒnd/ *n fig* legame *m*; *Comm* obbligazione *f* ● *vt* (*glue:*) attaccare
**bondage** /'bɒndɪdʒ/ *n* schiavitù *f*
**bonded warehouse** /'bɒndɪd/ *n* magazzino *m* doganale
**bonding** /'bɒndɪŋ/ *n* (*between mother and baby*) legame *m* madre-figlio; **male ~** solidarietà *f* maschile
**bone** /bəʊn/ *n* osso *m*; (*of fish*) spina *f* ● *vt* disossare (*meat*); togliere le spine da (*fish*)
**bone china** *n* porcellana *f* fine
**boned** /bəʊnd/ *a* (*joint, leg, chicken*) disossato; (*fish*) senza lische; (*corset, bodice*) con le stecche
**bone: bone-dry** *a* secco. **bonehead** *n fam* cretino, -a *mf*. **bone idle** *a fam* fannullone
**boneless** /'bəʊnlɪs/ *a* (*chicken*) disossato; (*chicken breast*) senz'osso; (*fish*) senza lische
**bone: bone marrow** *n* midollo *m* osseo. **bone-marrow transplant** *n* trapianto *m* di midollo osseo. **bonemeal** *n* farina *f* d'ossa
**bonfire** /'bɒnfaɪə(r)/ *n* falò *m inv*
**Bonfire Night** *n Br* sera *f* del 5 novembre festeggiata con falò e fuochi d'artificio
**bonk** /bɒŋk/ *vt sl* zompare
**bonkers** /'bɒŋkəz/ *a fam* suonato
**bonnet** /'bɒnɪt/ *n* cuffia *f*; (*of car*) cofano *m*
**bonus** /'bəʊnəs/ *n* (*individual*) gratifica *f*; (*production ~*) premio *m*; (*life insurance*) dividendo *m*; **a ~** *fig* qualcosa in più
**bonus point** *n* **five ~ ~s** un bonus di cinque punti
**bony** /'bəʊnɪ/ *a* (**-ier, -iest**) ossuto; (*fish*) pieno di spine

**boo** /buː/ *interj* (*to surprise or frighten*) bu! ● *vt/i* fischiare
**boob** /buːb/ *n* (*fam: mistake*) gaffe *f inv*; (*breast*) tetta *f* ● *vi fam* fare una gaffe
**booboo** /'buːbuː/ *n fam* gaffe *f inv*
**booby prize** /'buːbɪ/ *n* premio *m* di consolazione per il peggior contendente
**booby trap** *n Mil* ordigno *m* che esplode al contatto; (*joke*) trabocchetto *m* ● *vt Mil* mettere un ordigno esplosivo in
**boogie** /'buːgɪ/ *n fam* boogie *m*
**booing** /'buːɪŋ/ *n* fischi *mpl*
**book** /bʊk/ *n* libro *m*; (*of tickets*) blocchetto *m*; **keep the ~s** *Comm* tenere la contabilità; **be in sb's bad/good ~s** essere nel libro nero/nelle grazie di qcno; **do sth by the ~** seguire strettamente le regole ● *vt* (*reserve*) prenotare; (*for offence*) multare ● *vi* (*reserve*) prenotare
**bookable** /'bʊkəbl/ *a* (*event, ticket*) che si può prenotare; (*offence*) che può essere multato
**book: bookbinder** *n* rilegatore, -trice *mf*. **bookbinding** *n* rilegatura *f*. **bookcase** *n* libreria *f*. **book club** *n* club *m inv* del libro. **book-ends** *npl* reggilibri *mpl*. **book fair** *n* fiera *f* del libro
**bookie** /'bʊkɪ/ *n fam* bookmaker *m inv*, allibratore *m*
**booking** /'bʊkɪŋ/ *n* (*Br: reservation*) prenotazione *f*; **make a ~** fare una prenotazione; **get a ~** (*Br: from referee*) ricevere un'ammonizione
**booking: booking clerk** *n Br* impiegato, -a *mf* in un ufficio prenotazioni. **booking form** *n Br* modulo *m* di prenotazione. **booking office** *n* biglietteria *f*
**bookish** /'bʊkɪʃ/ *a* (*person*) secchione
**book: book jacket** *n* sopraccoperta *f*. **bookkeeper** *n* contabile *mf*. **bookkeeping** *n* contabilità *f*
**booklet** /'bʊklɪt/ *n* opuscolo *m*
**book: book lover** *n* amante *mf* della lettura. **bookmaker** *n* allibratore *m*. **bookmark** *n* segnalibro *m*. **bookplate** *n* ex libris *m inv*. **bookrest** *n* leggio *m*. **bookseller** *n* libraio, -a *mf*. **bookshelf** *n* (*single*) scaffale *f*; (*bookcase*) libreria *f*. **bookshop** *n* libreria *f*. **bookstall** *n* edicola *f*. **bookstore** *n Am* libreria *f*. **book token** *n Br* buono *m* acquisto per libri. **bookworm** *n* topo *m* di biblioteca
**boom** /buːm/ *n Comm* boom *m inv*; (*upturn*) impennata *f*; (*of thunder, gun*) rimbombo *m* ● *vi* (*thunder, gun:*) rimbombare; *fig* prosperare
**boomerang** /'buːməræŋ/ *n* boomerang *m inv* ● *vi* **~ on sb** (*plan:*) ritorcersi contro qcno
**boomerang effect** *n* effetto *m* boomerang
**booming** /'buːmɪŋ/ *a* (*sound*) sonoro; (*voice*) tonante; (*economy*) fiorente; (*demand, exports, sales*) in crescita
**boom microphone** *n* microfono *m* a stelo
**boon** /buːn/ *n* benedizione *f*
**boor** /bʊə(r)/ *n* zoticone *m*

**boorish** /'bʊərɪʃ/ a maleducato

**boost** /buːst/ n spinta f ● vt stimolare ⟨sales⟩; sollevare ⟨morale⟩; far crescere ⟨hopes⟩

**booster** /'buːstə(r)/ n Med dose f supplementare

**boot** /buːt/ n stivale m; (up to ankle) stivaletto m; (football) scarpetta f; (climbing) scarpone m; Auto portabagagli m inv ● vt Comput mettere in funzione

■ **boot out** vt fam cacciare

■ **boot up** Comput vi caricarsi ● vt caricare

**boot black** n lustrascarpe mf inv

**boot drive** n Comput unità f inv di inizializzazione

**bootee** /buːˈtiː/ n (knitted) babbuccia f di lana; (leather) stivaletto m

**booth** /buːð/ n (for phoning, voting) cabina f; (at market) bancarella f

**boot: bootlace** n laccio m, stringa f. **bootlegger** n Am contrabbandiere m di alcolici. **bootlicker** n leccapiedi mf inv. **bootmaker** n calzolaio m. **boot polish** n lucido m da scarpe. **boot scraper** n pulisicipiedi m inv. **bootstrap** n (on boot) linguetta f calzastivali; Comput lancio m; **pull oneself up by one's ~s** riuscire con le proprie forze. **boot-up** n Comput boot m inv

**booty** /'buːtɪ/ n bottino m

**booze** /buːz/ n fam alcolici mpl

**boozer** /'buːzə(r)/ n fam (person) beone, -a mf; (Br: pub) bar m inv

**booze-up** n bella bevuta f

**boozy** /'buːzɪ/ a fam ⟨laughter⟩ da ubriaco; ⟨meal⟩ in cui si beve molto

**bop** /bɒp/ fam n (blow) colpo m ● vt dare un colpo a ● vi Br (dance) ballare

**border** /'bɔːdə(r)/ n bordo m; (frontier) frontiera f; (in garden) bordura f ● vi ~ **on** confinare con; fig essere ai confini di

**border: border dispute** n (fight) conflitto m al confine; (disagreement) contesa f sul confine. **border guard** n guardia f di frontiera. **borderline** n linea f di demarcazione; ~ **case** caso m dubbio. **border raid** n incursione f

**bore[1]** /bɔː(r)/ see **bear[2]**

**bore[2]** vt Techn forare

**bore[3]** n (of gun) calibro m; (person) seccatore, -trice mf; (thing) seccatura f ● vt annoiare

**bored** /bɔːd/ a annoiato, stufo; **be ~** (**to tears** or **to death**) annoiarsi (da morire)

**boredom** /'bɔːdəm/ n noia f

**boring** /'bɔːrɪŋ/ a noioso

**born** /bɔːn/ pp **be ~** nascere; **I was ~ in 1963** sono nato nel 1963 ● a nato; **a ~ liar/actor** un bugiardo/un attore nato

**born-again** a convertito alla chiesa evangelica

**borne** /bɔːn/ see **bear[2]**

**Borneo** /'bɔːnɪəʊ/ n Borneo m

**borough** /'bʌrə/ n municipalità f inv

**borough council** n Br ≈ comune m

**borrow** /'bɒrəʊ/ vt prendere a prestito (**from** da); **can I ~ your pen?** mi presti la tua penna?

**borrower** /'bɒrəʊə(r)/ n debitore, -trice mf

**borrowing** /'bɒrəʊɪŋ/ n prestito m; **increase in ~** Fin aumento m dell'indebitamento

**borrowing costs** n Fin costo m del denaro

**borstal** /'bɔːstəl/ n Br riformatorio m

**Bosnia** /'bɒznɪə/ n Bosnia f

**Bosnia-Herzegovina** /-hɜːtsəgəʊ'viːnə/ n Bosnia-Erzegovina f

**Bosnian** /'bɒznɪən/ a & n bosniaco, -a mf

**bosom** /'bʊzm/ n seno m

**bosom buddy, bosom friend** n fam amico, -a mf del cuore

**boss** /bɒs/ n direttore, -trice mf ● vt (also ~ **about**) comandare a bacchetta

**bossy** /'bɒsɪ/ a autoritario

**bosun** /'bəʊsən/ n nostromo m

**botanical** /bə'tænɪkl/ a botanico

**botanist** /'bɒtənɪst/ n botanico, -a mf

**botany** /'bɒtənɪ/ n botanica f

**botch** /bɒtʃ/ vt fare un pasticcio con

**both** /bəʊθ/ a & pron tutti e due, entrambi ● adv ~ **men and women** entrambi uomini e donne; ~ [**of**] **the children** tutti e due i bambini; **they are ~ dead** sono morti entrambi; ~ **of them** tutti e due

**bother** /'bɒðə(r)/ n preoccupazione f; (minor trouble) fastidio m; **it's no ~** non c'è problema ● int fam che seccatura! ● vt (annoy) dare fastidio a; (disturb) disturbare ● vi preoccuparsi (**about** di); **don't ~** lascia perdere

**Botswana** /bɒt'swɑːnə/ n Botswana m

**bottle** /'bɒt(ə)l/ n bottiglia f; (baby's) biberon m inv ● vt imbottigliare

■ **bottle up** vt fig reprimere

**bottle: bottle bank** n contenitore m per la raccolta del vetro. **bottle-feed** vt allattare col biberon. **bottle-feeding** n allattamento m col biberon. **bottle green** a & n verde m bottiglia inv. **bottleneck** n fig ingorgo m. **bottle-opener** n apribottiglie m inv. **bottle top** n tappo m di bottiglia. **bottle-washer** n hum **chief cook and ~** tuttofare mf inv

**bottom** /'bɒtm/ a ultimo; **the ~ shelf** l'ultimo scaffale in basso ● n (of container) fondo m; (of river) fondale m; (of hill) piedi mpl; (buttocks) sedere m; **at the ~** in fondo; **at the ~ of the page** in fondo alla pagina; **get to the ~ of** fig vedere cosa c'è sotto

■ **bottom out** vi ⟨inflation, unemployment etc.⟩ assestarsi

**bottom drawer** n fig corredo m

**bottom gear** n Br Auto prima f

**bottomless** /'bɒtəmlɪs/ a senza fondo

**bottom line** n Fin utile m; **that's the ~ ~** (decisive factor) la questione è tutta qui

**botulism** /'bɒtjʊlɪzm/ n botulismo m

**bouffant** /'buːfɒ̃/ a ⟨hair, hairstyle⟩ cotonato; ⟨sleeve⟩ a sbuffo

**bough** /baʊ/ n ramoscello m

**bought** /bɔːt/ see **buy**

**boulder** /'bəʊldə(r)/ n masso m

**bounce** /baʊns/ vi rimbalzare; ⟨fam: cheque:⟩ essere respinto ● vt far rimbalzare ⟨ball⟩

■ **bounce back** *vi fig* riprendersi

**bouncer** /'baʊnsə(r)/ *n fam* buttafuori *m inv*

**bouncy** /'baʊnsɪ/ *a* ‹*ball*› che rimbalza bene; ‹*mattress, walk*› molleggiato; ‹*fig: person*› esuberante

**bound¹** /baʊnd/ *n* balzo *m* ● *vi* balzare

**bound²** *see* bind ● *a* ~ **for** ‹*ship*› diretto a; **be ~ to do** ‹*likely*› dovere fare per forza; ‹*obliged*› essere costretto a fare

**boundary** /'baʊndərɪ/ *n* limite *m*

**boundless** /'baʊndlɪs/ *a* illimitato

**bounds** /baʊndz/ *npl fig* limiti *mpl*; **out of ~** fuori dai limiti

**bounty** /'baʊntɪ/ *n* ‹*gift*› dono *m*; ‹*generosity*› munificenza *f*

**bounty hunter** *n* cacciatore *m* di taglie

**bouquet** /bʊ'keɪ/ *n* mazzo *m* di fiori; ‹*of wine*› bouquet *m*

**bourbon** /'bʊəbən/ *n* bourbon *m inv*

**bourgeois** /'bʊəʒwɑː/ *a pej* borghese

**bourgeoisie** /bʊəʒwɑː'ziː/ *n* borghesia *f*

**bout** /baʊt/ *n Med* attacco *m*; *Sport* incontro *m*

**boutique** /buː'tiːk/ *n* negozio *m*; **fashion ~** negozio *m* di abbigliamento

**bovine** /'bəʊvaɪn/ *a* bovino

**bow¹** /bəʊ/ *n* ‹*weapon*› arco *m*; *Mus* archetto *m*; ‹*knot*› nodo *m*

**bow²** /baʊ/ *n* inchino *m* ● *vi* inchinarsi ● *vt* piegare ‹*head*›

**bow³** /baʊ/ *n Naut* prua *f*

■ **bow out** *vi* ‹*withdraw*› ritirarsi (**of** da)

**bowel** /'baʊəl/ *n* intestino *m*; **have a ~ movement** andare di corpo; **~s** *pl* intestini *mpl*

**bower** /'baʊə(r)/ *n* ‹*in garden*› pergolato *m*; ‹*liter: chamber*› salottino *m*

**bowl¹** /bəʊl/ *n* ‹*for soup, cereal*› scodella *f*; ‹*of pipe*› fornello *m*

**bowl²** *n* ‹*ball*› boccia *f* ● *vt* lanciare ● *vi* *Cricket* servire; ‹*in bowls*› lanciare

■ **bowl along** *vi* ‹*in car etc*› andare spedito

■ **bowl over** *vt* buttar giù; ‹*fig: leave speechless*› lasciar senza parole

**bow-legged** /bəʊ'legd/ *a* dalle gambe storte

**bowler¹** /'bəʊlə(r)/ *n Cricket* lanciatore *m*; *Bowls* giocatore *m* di bocce

**bowler²** *n* ~ [**hat**] bombetta *f*

**bowling** /'bəʊlɪŋ/ *n* gioco *m* delle bocce

**bowling alley** /'bəʊlŋælɪ/ *n* pista *f* da bowling

**bowling green** *n* prato *m* da bocce

**bowls** /bəʊlz/ *n* gioco *m* delle bocce

**bow** /bəʊ/: **bowstring** *n* corda *f* d'arco. **bow tie** *n* cravatta *f* a farfalla. **bow window** *n* bow window *f inv*

**box¹** /bɒks/ *n* scatola *f*; *Theat* palco *m*

**box²** *vi Sport* fare il pugile ● *vt* ~ **sb's ears** dare uno scapaccione a qcno

**boxer** /'bɒksə(r)/ *n* pugile *m*

**boxer shorts** *npl* boxer *mpl*

**boxing** /'bɒksɪŋ/ *n* pugilato *m*

**Boxing Day** *n Br* [giorno *m* di] Santo Stefano *m*

**box: box number** *n* casella *f*. **box office** *n*

*Theat* botteghino *m*. **boxroom** *n Br* sgabuzzino *m*. **boxwood** *n* bosso *m*

**boy** /bɔɪ/ *n* ragazzo *m*; ‹*younger*› bambino *m*

**boycott** /'bɔɪkɒt/ *n* boicottaggio *m* ● *vt* boicottare

**boyfriend** /'bɔɪfrend/ *n* ragazzo *m*

**boyhood** /'bɔɪhʊd/ *n* ‹*childhood*› infanzia *f*; ‹*adolescence*› adolescenza *f*

**boyish** /'bɔɪʃ/ *a* da ragazzino

**boy scout** *n* boy scout *m inv*

**BR** *abbr* (**British Rail**) ente *m* ferroviario britannico, ≈ FS

**bra** /brɑː/ *n* reggiseno *m*

**brace** /breɪs/ *n* sostegno *m*; ‹*dental*› apparecchio *m* ● *vt* ~ **oneself** *fig* farsi forza (**for** per affrontare)

**bracelet** /'breɪslɪt/ *n* braccialetto *m*

**braces** /'breɪsɪz/ *npl* bretelle *fpl*

**bracing** /'breɪsɪŋ/ *a* tonificante

**bracken** /'brækn/ *n* felce *f*

**bracket** /'brækɪt/ *n* mensola *f*; ‹*group*› categoria *f*; *Typ* parentesi *f inv* ● *vt* mettere fra parentesi

**brackish** /'brækɪʃ/ *a* salmastro

**bradawl** /'brædɔːl/ *n* punteruolo *m*

**brag** /bræg/ *vi* (*pt/pp* **bragged**) vantarsi (**about** di)

**bragging** /'brægɪŋ/ *n* vanterie *fpl*

**Brahmin** /'brɑːmɪn/ *n Relig* bramino *m*

**braid** /breɪd/ *n* ‹*edging*› passamano *m*

**braille** /breɪl/ *n* braille *m*

**brain** /breɪn/ *n* cervello *m*; **~s** *pl fig* testa *fsg*

**brain: brainbox** *n fam* capoccione *m*. **brainchild** *n* invenzione *f* personale. **brain damage** *n* lesione *f* cerebrale. **brain-dead** *a Med* cerebralmente morto; *fig* senza cervello. **brain death** *n* morte *f* cerebrale. **brain drain** *n* fuga *f* di cervelli

**brainless** /'breɪnlɪs/ *a* senza cervello

**brain: brain scan** *n* scan *m inv* del cervello. **brain scanner** *n* scanner *m inv* (*per il cervello*). **brainstorm** *n Med, fig* accesso *m* di pazzia; (*Am: brainwave*) lampo *m* di genio. **brainstorming session** *n* brain-storming *m inv*. **brains trust** *n* brains-trust *m inv*, gruppo *m* di esperti. **brain surgeon** *n* neurochirurgo *m*. **brain surgery** *n* chirurgia *f* cerebrale. **brain teaser** *n fam* rompicapo *m*. **brainwash** *vt* fare il lavaggio del cervello a. **brainwashing** *n* lavaggio *m* del cervello. **brainwave** *n* lampo *m* di genio

**brainy** /'breɪnɪ/ *a* (**-ier, -iest**) intelligente

**braise** /breɪz/ *vt* brasare

**brake** /breɪk/ *n* freno *m* ● *vi* frenare

**brake: brake block** *n* pastiglia *f*. **brake disc** *n* disco *m* dei freni. **brake drum** *n* tamburo *m* del freno. **brake fluid** *n* liquido *m* dei freni. **brake-light** *n* stop *m inv*. **brake lining** *n* guarnizione *f* del freno. **brake pad** *n* ganascia *f* del freno. **brake pedal** *n* pedale *m* del freno

**bramble** /'bræmb(ə)l/ *n* rovo *m*; ‹*fruit*› mora *f*

**bran** /bræn/ *n* crusca *f*

**branch** /brɑːntʃ/ *n also fig* ramo *m*; *Comm*

succursale *f*, filiale *f*; (*of bank*) agenzia *f*; **our Oxford St ~** (*of store*) il negozio di Oxford St ● *vi* ⟨*road*⟩ biforcarsi
■ **branch off** *vi* biforcarsi
■ **branch out** *vi* **~ out into** allargare le proprie attività nel ramo di

**branch: branch line** *n* linea *f* secondaria. **branch manager** *n* (*of bank*) direttore, -trice *mf* di agenzia; (*of company*) direttore, -trice *mf* di filiale; (*of shop*) direttore, -trice *mf* di succursale. **branch office** *n* filiale *f*; (*of bank*) agenzia *f*

**brand** /brænd/ *n* marca *f*; (*on animal*) marchio *m* ● *vt* marcare ⟨*animal*⟩; *fig* tacciare (**as** di)

**brand image** *n* immagine *f* della marca
**brandish** /'brændɪʃ/ *vt* brandire
**brand: brand leader** *n* marca *f* leader *inv*. **brand name** *n* marca *f*. **brand-new** *a* nuovo fiammante

**brandy** /'brændɪ/ *n* brandy *m inv*
**brash** /bræʃ/ *a* sfrontato
**brass** /brɑːs/ *n* ottone *m*; **the ~** *Mus* gli ottoni *mpl*; **top ~** *fam* pezzi *mpl* grossi
**brass band** *n* banda *f* (*di soli ottoni*)
**brassiere** /'bræzɪə(r)/ *n fml, Am* reggipetto *m*
**brass: brass instrument** *n Mus* ottone *m*. **brass neck** *n Br fam* faccia *f* tosta. **brass rubbing** *n* ricalco *m* di iscrizione tombale o commemorativa

**brassy** /'brɑːsɪ/ *a* (-**ier**, -**iest**) *fam* volgare
**brat** /bræt/ *n pej* marmocchio, -a *mf*
**bravado** /brə'vɑːdəʊ/ *n* bravata *f*
**brave** /breɪv/ *a* coraggioso ● *vt* affrontare
**bravely** /'breɪvlɪ/ *adv* con coraggio
**bravery** /'breɪvərɪ/ *n* coraggio *m*
**bravo** /brɑː'vəʊ/ *int* bravo!
**bravura** /brə'vjʊərə/ *n* virtuosismo *m*
**brawl** /brɔːl/ *n* rissa ● *vi* azzuffarsi
**brawn** /brɔːn/ *n Culin* ≈ soppressata *f*
**brawny** /'brɔːnɪ/ *a* muscoloso
**brazen** /'breɪzn/ *a* sfrontato
**brazier** /'breɪzɪə(r)/ *n* braciere *m*
**Brazil** /brə'zɪl/ *n* Brasile *m*
**Brazilian** /brə'zɪlɪən/ *a & n* brasiliano, -a *mf*
**Brazil [nut]** *n* noce *f* del Brasile
**breach** /briːtʃ/ *n* (*of law*) violazione *f*; (*gap*) breccia *f*; (*fig: in party*) frattura *f* ● *vt* recedere ⟨*contract*⟩
**breach: breach of contract** *n Jur* inadempienza *f* contrattuale. **breach of promise** *n Jur* inadempienza *f* a una promessa di matrimonio. **breach of the peace** *n Jur* violazione *f* dell'ordine pubblico. **breach of trust** *n Jur* abuso *m* di fiducia

**bread** /bred/ *n* pane *m*; **a slice of ~ and butter** una fetta di pane imburrato
**bread: breadbasket** *n* cestino *m* per il pane; *fig* granaio *m*. **breadbin** *n Br* cassetta *f* portapane *inv*. **breadboard** *n* tagliere *m* per il pane. **breadcrumbs** *npl* briciole *fpl*; *Culin* pangrattato *m*. **breadfruit** *n* frutto *m* dell'albero del pane. **breadknife** *n* coltello *m* per il pane. **breadline** *n* **be on the ~** essere povero

in canna. **bread roll** *n* panino *m*. **breadstick** *n* filoncino *m*
**breadth** /bredθ/ *n* larghezza *f*
**breadwinner** /'bredwɪnə(r)/ *n* quello, -a *mf* che porta il soldi a casa
**break** /breɪk/ *n* rottura *f*; (*interval*) intervallo *m*; (*interruption*) interruzione *f*; (*fam: chance*) opportunità *f inv* ● *v* (*pt* **broke**, *pp* **broken**) ● *vt* rompere; (*interrupt*) interrompere; **~ one's arm** rompersi un braccio ● *vi* rompersi; (*day:*) spuntare; (*storm:*) scoppiare; (*news:*) diffondersi; (*boy's voice:*) cambiare
■ **break away** *vi* scappare; *fig* chiudere (**from** con)
■ **break down** *vi* (*machine, car:*) guastarsi; (*negotiations:*) interrompersi; (*in tears*) scoppiare in lacrime ● *vt* sfondare ⟨*door*⟩; ripartire ⟨*figures*⟩
■ **break in** *vi* ⟨*burglar:*⟩ introdursi
■ **break into** *vt* introdursi con la forza in; forzare ⟨*car*⟩
■ **break off** *vt* rompere ⟨*engagement*⟩ ● *vi* (*part of whole:*) rompersi; (*when speaking:*) interrompersi
■ **break out** *vi* ⟨*argument, war:*⟩ scoppiare
■ **break through** *vi* ⟨*sun:*⟩ spuntare
■ **break up** *vt* far cessare ⟨*fight*⟩; disperdere ⟨*crowd*⟩ ● *vi* ⟨*crowd:*⟩ disperdersi; (*marriage:*) naufragare; (*couple:*) separarsi; *Sch* iniziare le vacanze
**breakable** /'breɪkəbl/ *a* fragile
**breakage** /'breɪkɪdʒ/ *n* rottura *f*
**breakaway** /'breɪkəweɪ/ *n* (*from person*) separazione *f*, allontanamento *m*; (*from organization*) scissione *f*; *Sport* contropiede *m* ● *attrib* ⟨*faction, group, state*⟩ separatista
**breakdown** /'breɪkdaʊn/ *n* (*of car, machine*) guasto *m*; *Med* esaurimento *m* nervoso; (*of figures*) analisi *f inv*
**breaker** /'breɪkə(r)/ *n* (*wave*) frangente *m*
**breaker's yard** *n Auto* cimitero *m* delle macchine
**break-even** *n* pareggio *m*
**break-even point** *n* punto *m* di pareggio, punto *m* di equilibrio
**breakfast** /'brekfəst/ *n* [prima] colazione *f*
**breakfast: breakfast bar** *n* tavolo *m* a penisola. **breakfast bowl** *n* scodella *f* per i cereali. **breakfast cereals** *npl* cereali *mpl* per la colazione. **breakfast television** *n* programmi *mpl* televisivi del mattino
**break-in** *n* irruzione *f*
**breaking** /'breɪkɪŋ/ *n* (*of glass, seal, contract*) rottura *f*; (*of bone*) frattura *f*; (*of law, treaty*) violazione *f*; (*of voice*) cambiamento *m*; (*of promise*) venuta *f* meno; (*of horse*) domatura *f*; (*of link, sequence, tie*) interruzione *f*
**breaking and entering** /breɪkɪŋənd 'entərɪŋ/ *n Jur* effrazione *f* con scasso
**breaking point** *n Techn* punto *m* di rottura; *fig* limite *m* di sopportazione
**break: breakneck** *a* ⟨*pace, speed*⟩ a rotta di collo. **break-out** *n* (*from prison*) evasione *f*.
**breakpoint** *n Tennis* breakpoint *m inv*.

**breakthrough** *n* (*discovery*) scoperta *f*; (*in negotiations*) passo *m* avanti. **break-up** *n* (*of family, company*) disgregazione *f*; (*of alliance, relationship*) rottura *f*; (*of marriage*) dissoluzione *f*. **breakwater** *n* frangiflutti *m inv*

**breast** /brest/ *n* seno *m*

**breast: breastbone** *n* sterno *m*. **breastfeed** *vt* allattare al seno. **breast pocket** *n* taschino *m*. **breast-stroke** *n* nuoto *m* a rana

**breath** /breθ/ *n* respiro *m*, fiato *m*; **out of ~** senza fiato; **under one's ~** sottovoce; **a ~ of air** un filo d'aria

**breathalyse** /'breθəlaɪz/ *vt* sottoporre alla prova del palloncino

**breathalyser®** /'breθəlaɪzə(r)/ *n Br* alcoltest *m inv*

**breathe** /briːð/ *vt/i* respirare; **~ a sigh of relief** tirare un sospiro di sollievo

■ **breathe in** *vi* inspirare ● *vt* respirare ⟨*scent, air*⟩

■ **breathe out** *vt/i* espirare

**breather** /'briːðə(r)/ *n* pausa *f*

**breathing** /'briːðɪŋ/ *n* respirazione *f*

**breathing apparatus** *n* respiratore *m*

**breathing space** *n* (*respite*) tregua *f*; **give oneself a ~ ~** riprendere fiato

**breathless** /'breθlɪs/ *a* senza fiato

**breathlessly** /'breθlɪslɪ/ *adv* senza fiato

**breathtaking** /'breθteɪkɪŋ/ *a* mozzafiato

**breathtakingly** /'breθteɪkɪŋlɪ/ *adv* ~ **audacious** di un'audacia stupefacente; ~ **beautiful** di una bellezza mozzafiato

**breath test** *n* prova *f* del palloncino

**bred** /bred/ *see* **breed**

**breech** /briːtʃ/ *n Med* natiche *fpl*; (*of gun*) culatta *f*

**breed** /briːd/ *n* razza *f* ● *v* (*pt/pp* **bred**) ● *vt* allevare; (*give rise to*) generare ● *vi* riprodursi

**breeder** /'briːdə(r)/ *n* allevatore, -trice *mf*

**breeding** /'briːdɪŋ/ *n* allevamento *m*; *fig* educazione *f*

**breeding ground** *n* zona *f* di riproduzione; *fig* terreno *m* fertile

**breeding period, breeding season** *n* stagione *f* di riproduzione

**breeze** /briːz/ *n* brezza *f*

**breeze block** *n Br* mattone *m* fatto con scorie di coke

**breezily** /'briːzɪlɪ/ *adv* (*confidently*) con sicurezza; (*casually*) con disinvoltura; (*cheerfully*) allegramente

**breezy** /'briːzɪ/ *a* ventoso

**brevity** /'brevətɪ/ *n* brevità *f*

**brew** /bruː/ *n* infuso *m* ● *vt* mettere in infusione ⟨*tea*⟩; produrre ⟨*beer*⟩ ● *vi fig* ⟨*trouble:*⟩ essere nell'aria

**brewer** /'bruːə(r)/ *n* birraio *m*

**brewery** /'bruːərɪ/ *n* fabbrica *f* di birra

**brew-up** *n Br fam* tè *m inv*

**briar** /'braɪə(r)/ *n* rosa *f* selvatica; (*heather*) erica *f*; (*thorns*) rovo *m*; (*pipe*) *n* pipa *f* in radica

**bribe** /braɪb/ *n* (*money*) bustarella *f*; (*large sum of money*) tangente *f* ● *vt* corrompere

**bribery** /'braɪbərɪ/ *n* corruzione *f*

**brick** /brɪk/ *n* mattone *m*

■ **brick up** *vt* murare

**brick: brickbat** *n fig* critica *f* spietata. **brick-built** *a* di mattoni. **bricklayer** *n* muratore *m*. **bricklaying** *n* muratura *f*. **brick red** *a* rosso mattone *inv*. **brickwork** *n* muratura *f* di mattoni. **brickworks** *n* fabbrica *f* di mattoni

**bridal** /'braɪdl/ *a* nuziale

**bridal: bridal party** *n* corteo *m* nuziale. **bridal suite** *n* camera *f* nuziale. **bridal wear** *n* confezioni *fpl* da sposa

**bride** /braɪd/ *n* sposa *f*

**bridegroom** /'braɪdgruːm/ *n* sposo *m*

**bridesmaid** /'braɪdzmeɪd/ *n* damigella *f* d'onore

**bridge¹** /brɪdʒ/ *n* ponte *m*; (*of nose*) setto *m* nasale; (*of spectacles*) ponticello *m* ● *vt fig* colmare ⟨*gap*⟩

**bridge²** *n Cards* bridge *m*

**bridge-building** *n* costruzione *f* di ponti provvisori; *fig* mediazione *f*

**bridging loan** *n Br Fin* prefinanziamento *m*, credito *m* provvisorio

**bridle** /'braɪd(ə)l/ *n* briglia *f*

**bridle track, bridleway** /'braɪd(ə)lweɪ/ *n* sentiero *m* per cavalli

**brief¹** /briːf/ *a* breve; **in ~** in breve

**brief²** *n* istruzioni *fpl*; (*Jur: case*) causa *f* ● *vt* dare istruzioni a; *Jur* affidare la causa a

**briefcase** /'briːfkeɪs/ *n* cartella *f*

**briefing** /'briːfɪŋ/ *n* briefing *m inv*

**briefly** /'briːflɪ/ *adv* brevemente; **briefly,...** in breve,...

**briefness** /'briːfnɪs/ *n* brevità *f*

**briefs** /briːfs/ *npl* slip *m inv*

**brigade** /brɪ'geɪd/ *n* brigata *f*

**brigadier** /brɪgə'dɪə(r)/ *n* generale *m* di brigata

**bright** /braɪt/ *a* ⟨*metal, idea*⟩ brillante; ⟨*day, room, future*⟩ luminoso; (*clever*) intelligente; ~ **red** rosso *m* acceso

**brighten** /'braɪt(ə)n/ *v* ~ [**up**] ● *vt* ravvivare; rallegrare ⟨*person*⟩ ● *vi* ⟨*weather:*⟩ schiarirsi; ⟨*face:*⟩ illuminarsi; ⟨*person:*⟩ rallegrarsi

**brightly** /'braɪtlɪ/ *adv* ⟨*shine*⟩ intensamente; ⟨*smile*⟩ allegramente

**brightness** /'braɪtnɪs/ *n* luminosità *f*; (*intelligence*) intelligenza *f*

**bright spark** *n Br fam* genio *m*

**bright young things** *npl Br* i giovani di belle speranze

**brill** /brɪl/ *n Zool* rombo *m* liscio ● *a Br fam* fantastico

**brilliance** /'brɪljəns/ *n* luminosità *f*; (*of person*) genialità *f*

**brilliant** /'brɪljənt/ *a* (*very good*) eccezionale; (*very intelligent*) brillante; ⟨*sunshine*⟩ splendente

**brilliantly** /'brɪljəntlɪ/ *adv* ⟨*shine*⟩ intensamente; ⟨*perform*⟩ in modo eccezionale

**Brillo pad®** /'brɪləʊ/ *n* paglietta *f* d'acciaio

**brim** /brɪm/ *n* bordo *m*; (*of hat*) tesa *f*

■ **brim over** *vi* (*pt/pp* **brimmed**) traboccare

**brine** /braɪn/ n salamoia f
**bring** /brɪŋ/ vt (pt/pp **brought**) portare ⟨person, object⟩
■ **bring about** vt causare
■ **bring along** vt portare [con sé]
■ **bring back** vt restituire ⟨sth borrowed⟩; reintrodurre ⟨hanging⟩; fare ritornare in mente ⟨memories⟩
■ **bring down** vt portare giù; fare cadere ⟨government⟩; fare abbassare ⟨price⟩
■ **bring in** vt introdurre ⟨legislation⟩; **his job ~s in £30,000 a year** guadagna 30 000 sterline all'anno
■ **bring off** vt ~ **sth off** riuscire a fare qcsa
■ **bring on** vt (cause) provocare
■ **bring out** vt (emphasize) mettere in evidenza; pubblicare ⟨book⟩
■ **bring round** vt (persuade) convincere; far rinvenire ⟨unconscious person⟩
■ **bring up** vt (vomit) rimettere; allevare ⟨children⟩; tirare fuori ⟨question, subject⟩
**bring and buy sale** n Br vendita f di beneficenza
**brink** /brɪŋk/ n orlo m; **on the ~ of disaster** sull'orlo del disastro
**brinkmanship** /ˈbrɪŋkmənʃɪp/ n strategia f del rischio calcolato
**brisk** /brɪsk/ a svelto; ⟨person⟩ sbrigativo; ⟨trade, business⟩ redditizio; ⟨walk⟩ a passo spedito
**brisket** /ˈbrɪskɪt/ n Culin punta f di petto
**briskly** /ˈbrɪsklɪ/ adv velocemente; ⟨say⟩ frettolosamente; ⟨walk⟩ di buon passo
**bristle** /ˈbrɪsl/ n setola f ● vi **bristling with** pieno di
**bristly** /ˈbrɪslɪ/ a ⟨chin⟩ ispido
**Britain** /ˈbrɪtn/ n Gran Bretagna f
**British** /ˈbrɪtɪʃ/ a britannico; ⟨ambassador⟩ della Gran Bretagna ● npl **the ~** il popolo britannico
**British: British Airports Authority** n ente m che gestisce gli aeroporti britannici. **British Broadcasting Corporation** n ente m radiotelevisivo nazionale britannico. **British Columbia** n Columbia f Britannica
**Britisher** /ˈbrɪtɪʃə(r)/ n Am britannico, -a mf
**British: British Gas** n Br società f del gas britannica. **British Isles** npl Isole fpl Britanniche. **British Rail** n ente m ferroviario britannico. **British Telecom** n Br società f britannica di telecomunicazioni
**Briton** /ˈbrɪtən/ n cittadino, -a britannico, -a mf
**Brittany** /ˈbrɪtənɪ/ n Bretagna f
**brittle** /ˈbrɪtl/ a fragile
**brittle-bone disease** n decalcificazione f ossea, osteoporosi f
**broach** /brəʊtʃ/ vt toccare ⟨subject⟩
**B road** n Br ≈ strada f provinciale
**broad** /brɔːd/ a ampio; ⟨hint⟩ chiaro; ⟨accent⟩ marcato. **two metres ~** largo due metri; **in ~ daylight** in pieno giorno
**broad-based** /-ˈbeɪst/ a ⟨coalition, education⟩ diversificato; ⟨approach, campaign⟩ su larga scala; ⟨consensus⟩ generale

**broad bean** n fava f
**broadcast** /ˈbrɔːdkæst/ n trasmissione f ● vt/i (pt/pp **-cast**) trasmettere
**broadcaster** /ˈbrɔːdkæstə(r)/ n giornalista mf radiotelevisivo, -a
**broadcasting** /ˈbrɔːdkæstɪŋ/ n diffusione f radiotelevisiva; **be in ~** lavorare per la televisione/radio
**broad-chested** a con il torace robusto
**broaden** /ˈbrɔːdn/ vt allargare; **~ one's horizons** allargare i propri orizzonti ● vi allargarsi
**broadly** /ˈbrɔːdlɪ/ adv largamente; **~ [speaking]** generalmente
**broad-minded** /-ˈmaɪndɪd/ a di larghe vedute
**broadness** /ˈbrɔːdnɪs/ n larghezza f
**broad: broadsheet** n quotidiano m di grande formato. **broad-shouldered** a con le spalle larghe. **broadside** n (Naut: of ship) fiancata f; (enemy fire) bordata f; n (criticism) attacco m; **deliver a ~** lanciare un attacco ● adv di fianco
**brocade** /brəˈkeɪd/ n broccato m
**broccoli** /ˈbrɒkəlɪ/ n inv broccoli mpl
**brochure** /ˈbrəʊʃə(r)/ n opuscolo m; (travel ~) dépliant m inv
**brogue** /brəʊg/ n (shoe) scarpa m da passeggio; (accent) cadenza f dialettale
**broil** /brɔɪl/ vt Culin cuocere alla griglia ⟨meat⟩ ● vi cuocere alla griglia; fig arrostire
**broiler** /ˈbrɔɪlə(r)/ n (chicken) pollastro m; (Am: grill) griglia f
**broke** /brəʊk/ see **break** ● a fam al verde
**broken** /ˈbrəʊk(ə)n/ see **break** ● a rotto; **~ English** inglese m stentato
**broken: broken-down** a ⟨machine⟩ guasto; ⟨wall⟩ pericolante. **broken heart** n cuore m infranto; **die of a ~** ~ essere distrutto da una delusione amorosa. **broken-hearted** /-ˈhɑːtɪd/ a affranto. **broken home** n **he comes from a ~** ~ i suoi sono divisi. **broken marriage** n matrimonio m fallito
**broker** /ˈbrəʊkə(r)/ n broker m inv
**brokerage** /ˈbrəʊkərɪdʒ/ n (fee, business) intermediazione f
**broking** /ˈbrəʊkɪŋ/ n attività f di intermediazione
**brolly** /ˈbrɒlɪ/ n fam ombrello m
**bromide** /ˈbrəʊmaɪd/ n (in pharmacy, printing) bromuro m; (fig: comment) banalità f inv
**bronchial** /ˈbrɒŋkɪəl/ a ⟨infection⟩ bronchiale; ⟨wheeze, cough⟩ di petto
**bronchitis** /brɒŋˈkaɪtɪs/ n bronchite f
**bronze** /brɒnz/ n bronzo m ● attrib di bronzo
**Bronze Age** n età f del Bronzo
**brooch** /brəʊtʃ/ n spilla f
**brood** /bruːd/ n covata f; (hum: children) prole f ● vi covare; fig rimuginare
**brooding** /ˈbruːdɪŋ/ a ⟨person, face⟩ pensieroso; ⟨landscape⟩ sinistro
**broody** /ˈbruːdɪ/ a ⟨depressed⟩ pensieroso; **feel ~** ⟨Br fam: woman:⟩ desiderare un figlio
**broody hen** n chioccia f

**brook**[1] /brʊk/ n ruscello m

**brook**[2] vt sopportare

**broom** /bru:m/ n scopa f; Bot ginestra f

**broom:** broom cupboard n ripostiglio m. broom handle n Br manico m di scopa. broomstick n manico m di scopa

**Bros.** abbr (brothers) F.lli

**broth** /brɒθ/ n brodo m

**brothel** /ˈbrɒθ(ə)l/ n bordello m

**brother** /ˈbrʌðə(r)/ n fratello m

**brotherhood** /ˈbrʌðəhʊd/ n (bond) fratellanza f; (of monks) confraternita f

**brother-in-law** n (pl -s-in-law) cognato m

**brotherly** /ˈbrʌðəlɪ/ a fraterno

**brought** /brɔ:t/ see bring

**brow** /braʊ/ n fronte f; (eye~) sopracciglio m; (of hill) cima f

**browbeat** /ˈbraʊbi:t/ vt (pt -beat, pp -beaten) intimidire

**brown** /braʊn/ a marrone; castano (hair) ● n marrone m ● vt rosolare (meat) ● vi (meat:) rosolarsi

**brown:** brown ale n Br birra f scura. brown bear n orso m bruno. brown bread n pane m integrale

**browned-off** /braʊndˈɒf/ a Br fam stufo (with di)

**brown envelope** n busta f di carta da pacchi

**Brownie** /ˈbraʊnɪ/ n coccinella f (negli scout)

**brownie point** n fam punto m di merito

**brownish** /ˈbraʊnɪʃ/ a sul marrone

**brown:** brownout n Am oscuramento m parziale. brown owl n allocco m. brown paper n carta f da pacchi. brown rice n riso m integrale. brown-skinned /-ˈskɪnd/ a scuro di pelle. brownstone n (Am: house) palazzo m in arenaria. brown sugar n Culin zucchero m greggio

**browse** /braʊz/ vi (read) leggicchiare; (in shop) curiosare

**bruise** /bru:z/ n livido m; (on fruit) ammaccatura f ● vt ammaccare (fruit); ~ one's arm farsi un livido sul braccio

**bruised** /bru:zd/ a (physically) contuso; (eye) pesto; (fruit) ammaccato; (ego, spirit) ferito

**bruiser** /ˈbru:zə(r)/ n fam omaccione m

**bruising** /ˈbru:zɪŋ/ n livido m, contusione f ● a (game) violento; (emotionally) (remark) pesante; (campaign, encounter) traumatizzante; (defeat) cocente

**brunch** /brʌntʃ/ n brunch m inv

**Brunei** /bru:ˈnaɪ/ n Brunei m

**brunette** /bru:ˈnet/ n bruna f

**brunt** /brʌnt/ n bear the ~ of sth subire maggiormente qcsa

**brush** /brʌʃ/ n spazzola f; (with long handle) spazzolone m; (for paint) pennello m; (bushes) boscaglia f; (fig: conflict) breve scontro m ● vt spazzolare (hair); lavarsi (teeth); scopare (stairs, floor)

▪ **brush against** vt sfiorare

▪ **brush aside** vt fig ignorare

▪ **brush off** vt spazzolare; (with hands) togliere; ignorare (criticism)

▪ **brush up** vt/i fig ~ up [on] rinfrescare

**brush:** brush-off n fam give sb the ~ mandare qcno a quel paese. brushstroke n pennellata f. brushup n Br have a [wash and] brushup darsi una ripulita. brushwork n tocco m

**brusque** /brʊsk/ a brusco

**brusquely** /ˈbrʊsklɪ/ adv bruscamente

**Brussels** /ˈbrʌs(ə)lz/ n Bruxelles f

**Brussels sprouts** npl cavoletti mpl di Bruxelles

**brutal** /ˈbru:t(ə)l/ a brutale

**brutality** /bru:ˈtælətɪ/ n brutalità f inv

**brutalize** /ˈbru:təlaɪz/ vt brutalizzare

**brutally** /ˈbru:təlɪ/ adv brutalmente

**brute** /bru:t/ n bruto m; ~ force n forza f bruta

**brutish** /ˈbru:tɪʃ/ a da bruto

**BSc** abbr Bachelor of Science

**BSE** n abbr (bovine spongiform encephalitis) encefalite f bovina spongiforme

**B side** n (of record) lato m B

**BST** abbr (British Summer Time) ora f legale in Gran Bretagna

**bubble** /ˈbʌbl/ n bolla f; (in drink) bollicina f

**bubble:** bubble bath n bagnoschiuma m inv. bubble car n Br fam auto f monoposto a tre ruote. bubblegum n gomma f da masticare. bubble pack n Br (for pills) blister m inv; (for small item) involucro m di plastica. bubble wrap n plastica f a bolle

**bubbling** /ˈbʌblɪŋ/ n (sound) gorgoglio m ● a che ribolle

**bubbly** /ˈbʌblɪ/ n fam champagne m inv, spumante m ● a (liquid) effervescente; (personality) spumeggiante

**bubonic plague** /bju:bɒnɪkˈpleɪg/ n peste f bubbonica

**buccaneer** /bʌkəˈnɪə(r)/ n bucaniere m

**Bucharest** /bju:kəˈrest/ n Bucarest f

**buck**[1] /bʌk/ n maschio m del cervo; (rabbit) maschio m del coniglio ● vi (horse:) saltare a quattro zampe

**buck**[2] n Am fam dollaro m

**buck**[3] n pass the ~ scaricare la responsabilità

▪ **buck up** vi fam tirarsi su; (hurry) sbrigarsi ● vt you'll have to ~ your ideas up fam dovresti darti una regolata

**bucket** /ˈbʌkɪt/ n secchio m; kick the ~ (fam: die) crepare ● vi it's ~ing down fam piove a catinelle

**bucketful** /ˈbʌkɪtfʊl/ n secchio m

**bucket seat** n Auto, Aeron sedile m anatomico

**bucket shop** n Br fam agenzia f di viaggi che vende biglietti a prezzi scontati

**bucking bronco** /bʌkɪŋˈbrɒŋkəʊ/ n cavallo m da rodeo

**buckle** /ˈbʌkl/ n fibbia f ● vt allacciare ● vi (shelf:) piegarsi; (wheel:) storcersi

▪ **buckle down** vi (to work) mettersi sotto

▪ **buckle in** vt legare

**buck: buckram** *n* tela *f* rigida. **buckshot** *n* pallettoni *mpl*. **buckskin** *n* pelle *f* di daino. **buck teeth** *npl* denti *mpl* da coniglio.
**buckwheat** *n* grano *m* saraceno
**bucolic** /bjʊ'kɒlɪk/ *a* & *n* bucolico *m*
**bud** /bʌd/ *n* bocciolo *m*
**Buddha** /'bʊdə/ *n* Budda *m* *inv*
**Buddhism** /'bʊdɪzm/ *n* buddismo *m*
**Buddhist** /'bʊdɪst/ *a* & *n* buddista *mf*
**budding** /'bʌdɪŋ/ *a* Bot (*into leaf*) in germoglio; (*into flower*) in boccio; ‹*athlete, champion, artist*› in erba; ‹*talent, romance*› nascente; ‹*career*› promettente
**buddy** /'bʌdɪ/ *n fam* amico, -a *mf*
**budge** /bʌdʒ/ *vt* spostare ● *vi* spostarsi
**budgerigar** /'bʌdʒərɪgɑː(r)/ *n* cocorita *f*
**budget** /'bʌdʒɪt/ *n* bilancio *m*; (*allotted to specific activity*) budget *m inv*; **I'm on a ~** cerco di limitare le spese ● *vi* (*pt/pp* **budgeted**) prevedere le spese; **~ for sth** includere qcsa nelle spese previste
**budgetary** /'bʌdʒɪt(ə)rɪ/ *a* budgetario; **~ year** esercizio *m* finanziario
**budget day** *n Br Pol* giorno *m* della presentazione del bilancio dello Stato
**budgie** /'bʌdʒɪ/ *n fam* = **budgerigar**
**buff** /bʌf/ *a* (*colour*) [color] camoscio ● *n* [color *m*] camoscio *m*; *fam* fanatico, -a *mf* ● *vt* lucidare
**buffalo** /'bʌfələʊ/ *n* (*inv or pl* -**es**) bufalo *m*
**buffer** /'bʌfə(r)/ *n Rail* respingente *m*; *Comput* buffer *m inv*; **old ~** *fam* vecchio bacucco *m*
**buffer state** *n* stato *m* cuscinetto *inv*
**buffer zone** *n* zona *f* cuscinetto *inv*
**buffet**[1] /'bʊfeɪ/ *n* (*meal, in station*) buffet *m inv*
**buffet**[2] /'bʌfɪt/ *vt* (*pt/pp* **buffeted**) sferzare
**buffet car** *n Br Rail* carrozza *f* ristorante
**buffoon** /bə'fuːn/ *n* buffone, -a *mf*
**bug** /bʌg/ *n* (*insect*) insetto *m*; *Comput* bug *m inv*; (*fam: device*) cimice ● *vt* (*pt/pp* **bugged**) *fam* installare delle microspie in ‹*room*›; mettere sotto controllo ‹*telephone*›; (*fam: annoy*) scocciare
**bugbear** /'bʌgbeə(r)/ *n* (*problem, annoyance*) spauracchio *m*
■ **bugger** /'bʌgə(r)/ *fam n* bastardo *m* ● *int* merda!
■ **bugger about, bugger around** *fam vi* (*behave stupidly*) fare il cretino ● *vt* **~ sb about** creare problemi a qcno
■ **bugger off** *vi* (*fam: go away*) andarsene; **~ off!** vai a farti friggere!
**bugging device** /'bʌgɪŋ/ *n* microfono *m* spia
**buggy** /'bʌgɪ/ *n* [**baby**] **~** passeggino *m*
**bugle** /'bjuːg(ə)l/ *n* tromba *f*
**bugler** /'bjuːglə(r)/ *n* trombettiere *m*
**build** /bɪld/ *n* (*of person*) corporatura *f* ● *vt/i* (*pt/pp* **built**) costruire
■ **build on** *vt* aggiungere ‹*extra storey*›; sviluppare ‹*previous work*›
■ **build up** *vt* **~ up one's strength** rimettersi in forza ● *vi* ‹*pressure, traffic:*› aumentare; ‹*excitement, tension:*› crescere

**builder** /'bɪldə(r)/ *n* (*company*) costruttore *m*; (*worker*) muratore *m*
**builder's labourer** *n* muratore *m*
**builder's merchant** *n* fornitore *m* di materiale da costruzione
**building** /'bɪldɪŋ/ *n* edificio *m*
**building: building block** *n* (*child's toy*) pezzo *m* delle costruzioni; (*basic element*) componente *m*. **building contractor** *n* imprenditore *m* edile. **building land** *n* terreno *m* edificabile. **building materials** *npl* materiali *mpl* da costruzione. **building permit** *n* permesso *m* per edificare. **building plot** *n* terreno *m* edificabile. **building site** *n* cantiere *m* [di costruzione]. **building society** *n* istituto *m* di credito immobiliare. **building trade** *n* edilizia *f*. **building worker** *n Br* muratore *m*
**build-up** *n* (*increase*) aumento *m*; (*in tension, of gas, in weapons*) accumulo *m*; (*publicity*) battage *m inv* pubblicitario; **give sth a good ~** (*publicity*) fare buona pubblicità a qcsa
**built** /bɪlt/ *see* **build**
**built-in** *a* ‹*unit*› a muro; ‹*fig: feature*› incorporato
**built-up area** *n Auto* centro *m* abitato
**bulb** /bʌlb/ *n* bulbo *m*; *Electr* lampadina *f*
**bulbous** /'bʌlbəs/ *a* grassoccio
**Bulgaria** /bʌl'geərɪə/ *n* Bulgaria *f*
**bulge** /bʌldʒ/ *n* rigonfiamento *m*; **it shows all my ~s** mette in evidenza tutti i miei cuscinetti [di grasso] ● *vi* esser gonfio (**with** di); ‹*stomach, wall:*› sporgere; ‹*eyes, with surprise:*› uscire dalle orbite
**bulging** /'bʌldʒɪŋ/ *a* gonfio; ‹*eyes*› sporgente
**bulimia (nervosa)** /bʊ'lɪmɪə(nɜː'vəʊsə)/ *n* bulimia *f*
**bulimic** /bʊ'lɪmɪk/ *a* & *n* bulimico, -a *mf*
**bulk** /bʌlk/ *n* volume *m*; (*greater part*) grosso *m*; **in ~** in grande quantità; (*loose*) sfuso
**bulk: bulk-buy** *vt/i* comprare in grandi quantità. **bulk-buying** *n* acquisto *m* in grande quantità. **bulk carrier** *n* mezzo *m* per il trasporto di rinfuse. **bulkhead** *n Naut, Aeron* paratia *f*
**bulky** /'bʌlkɪ/ *a* voluminoso
**bull** /bʊl/ *n* toro *m*; **take the ~ by the horns** *fig* prendere il toro per le corna
**bull: bulldog** *n* bulldog *m inv*. **bulldog clip** *n* fermafogli *m inv*. **bulldoze** *vt* (*knock down*) demolire [con bulldozer]; (*clear*) spianare [con bulldozer]; (*fig: force*) costringere. **bulldozer** /'bʊldəʊzə(r)/ *n* bulldozer *m inv*
**bullet** /'bʊlɪt/ *n* pallottola *f*
**bulletin** /'bʊlɪtɪn/ *n* bollettino *m*
**bulletin board** *n Comput* bacheca *f* elettronica
**bulletproof** /'bʊlɪtpruːf/ *a* antiproiettile *inv*; ‹*vehicle*› blindato
**bulletproof vest** giubbotto *m* antiproiettile
**bullfight** /'bʊlfaɪt/ *n* corrida *f*
**bullfighter** /'bʊlfaɪtə(r)/ *n* torero *m*
**bullion** /'bʊlɪən/ *n* **gold ~** oro *m* in lingotti
**bullish** /'bʊlɪʃ/ *a* (*optimistic*) ottimistico; ‹*market, shares, stocks*› al rialzo

**bull market** n Fin mercato m al rialzo

**bullock** /'bʊlək/ n manzo m

**bullring** /'bʊlrɪŋ/ n arena f

**bull's-eye** /'bʊlzaɪ/ n centro m del bersaglio; **score a ~** fare centro

**bully** /'bʊlɪ/ n prepotente mf ● vt fare il/la prepotente con

**bullying** /'bʊlɪŋ/ n prepotenze fpl

**bulrush** /'bʊlrʌʃ/ n giunco m di palude

**bulwark** /'bʊlwək/ n Mil, fig baluardo m; Naut parapetto m; (breakwater) frangiflutti m inv

**bum**[1] /bʌm/ n sl sedere m

**bum**[2] n Am fam vagabondo, -a mf

■ **bum around** vi fam vagabondare

**bumbag** /'bʌmbæg/ n Br fam marsupio m

**bumble-bee** /'bʌmblbi:/ n calabrone m

**bumbling** /'bʌmblɪŋ/ a (attempt) maldestro; (person) inconcludente

**bumf** /bʌmf/ n (Br: toilet paper) carta f igienica; (fam: documents) scartoffie f pl

**bump** /bʌmp/ n botta f; (swelling) bozzo m, gonfiore m; (in road) protuberanza f ● vt sbattere

■ **bump into** vt sbattere contro; (meet) imbattersi in

■ **bump off** vt fam far fuori

■ **bump up** vt fam [far] aumentare (prices, salaries)

**bumper** /'bʌmpə(r)/ n Auto paraurti m inv ● a abbondante

**bumper car** n autoscontro m

**bumph** /bʌmf/ n = **bumf**

**bumpkin** /'bʌmpkɪn/ n country ~ zoticone, -a mf

**bumptious** /'bʌmpʃəs/ a presuntuoso

**bumpy** /'bʌmpɪ/ a (road) accidentato; (flight) turbolento

**bun** /bʌn/ n focaccina f (dolce); (hair) chignon m inv

**bunch** /bʌntʃ/ n (of flowers, keys) mazzo m; (of bananas) casco m; (of people) gruppo m; ~ **of grapes** grappolo m d'uva

**bundle** /'bʌndl/ n fascio m; (of money) mazzetta f; **a ~ of nerves** fam un fascio di nervi ● vt ~ **[up]** affastellare

**bung** /bʌŋ/ vt fam (throw) buttare

■ **bung up** vt (block) otturare

**bungalow** /'bʌŋgələʊ/ n bungalow m inv

**bungee jumping** /'bʌndʒɪdʒʌmpɪŋ/ n salto m da ponti, grattacieli, ecc. con un cavo elastico attaccato alla caviglia

**bungle** /'bʌŋgl/ vt fare un pasticcio di

**bunion** /'bʌnjən/ n Med callo m all'alluce

**bunk** /bʌŋk/ n cuccetta f; **do a ~** fam svignarsela ● vi ~ **off school** fam marinare la scuola

**bunk beds** npl letti mpl a castello

**bunker** /'bʌŋkə(r)/ n (for coal) carbonaia f; (golf) ostacolo m; Mil bunker m inv

**bunkum** /'bʌŋkəm/ n fandonie fpl

**bunny** /'bʌnɪ/ n fam coniglietto m

**Bunsen** [**burner**] /'bʌnsən[bɜ:nə(r)]/ n becco m Bunsen

**bunting** /'bʌntɪŋ/ n (flags on ship) gran pavese m; Zool zigolo m

**buoy** /bɔɪ/ n boa f

■ **buoy up** vt fig sostenere (prices); tirare su (person)

**buoyancy** /'bɔɪənsɪ/ n galleggiabilità f

**buoyancy aid** n salvagente m

**buoyant** /'bɔɪənt/ a (boat) galleggiante; (water) che aiuta a galleggiare; (fig: person) allegro; (prices) in aumento

**burble** /'bɜ:b(ə)l/ n (of stream) gorgoglio m; (of voices) borbottio m ● vi (stream:) gorgogliare; ~ **on about sth** (person:) blaterare di qcsa

**burbling** /'bɜ:blɪŋ/ n (of stream) gorgoglio m; (rambling talk) borbottio m ● a (stream) gorgogliante; (voice) che borbotta

**burden** /'bɜ:dn/ n carico m ● vt caricare

**burdensome** /'bɜ:dnsəm/ a gravoso

**bureau** /'bjʊərəʊ/ n (pl **-x** /'bjʊərəʊz/ or **~s**) (desk) scrivania f; (office) ufficio m

**bureaucracy** /bjʊə'rɒkrəsɪ/ n burocrazia f

**bureaucrat** /'bjʊərəkræt/ n burocrate mf

**bureaucratic** /bjʊərə'krætɪk/ a burocratico

**burgeon** /'bɜ:dʒən/ vi (plant:) germogliare; (fig: flourish) fiorire; (fig: multiply) moltiplicarsi rapidamente, crescere rapidamente

**burger** /'bɜ:gə(r)/ n hamburger m inv

**burger bar** n fast-food m inv

**burglar** /'bɜ:glə(r)/ n svaligiatore, -trice mf

**burglar alarm** n antifurto m inv

**burglarize** /'bɜ:gləraɪz/ vt Am svaligiare

**burglar-proof** a a prova di ladro

**burglary** /'bɜ:glərɪ/ n furto m con scasso

**burgle** /'bɜ:gl/ vt svaligiare; **they have been ~d** sono stati svaligiati

**Burgundy** /'bɜ:gəndɪ/ n Borgogna f; **b~** (wine) borgogna m inv ● a (colour) rosso scuro

**burial** /'berɪəl/ n sepoltura f

**burial ground** n cimitero m

**burlesque** /bɜ:'lesk/ n parodia f

**burly** /'bɜ:lɪ/ a (-**ier**, -**iest**) corpulento

**Burma** /'bɜ:mə/ n Birmania f

**Burmese** /bɜ:'mi:z/ a & n birmano, -a mf

**burn** /bɜ:n/ n bruciatura f ● v (pt/pp **burnt** or **burned**) ● vt bruciare; ~ **one's boats** or **bridges** fig tagliarsi i ponti alle spalle ● vi bruciare

■ **burn down** vt/i bruciare

■ **burn out** vi fig esaurirsi

**burned-out** a = **burnt-out**

**burner** /'bɜ:nə(r)/ n (on stove) bruciatore m ● a (ember, coal) acceso; (on fire) in fiamme; (fig: fever, desire) bruciante; **a ~ sensation** una sensazione di bruciore; **a ~ question** una questione scottante

**burnish** /'bɜ:nɪʃ/ vt lucidare

**burns unit** n Med reparto m grandi ustionati

**burnt** /bɜ:nt/ see **burn**

**burnt-out** a (building, car) distrutto dalle fiamme; (fig: person) sfinito

**burp** /bɜːp/ n fam rutto m ● vi fam ruttare
**burr** /bɜː(r)/ n Bot lappa f; (in language) erre f moscia
**burrow** /ˈbʌrəʊ/ n tana f ● vt scavare ⟨hole⟩
**bursar** /ˈbɜːsə(r)/ n economo, -a mf
**bursary** /ˈbɜːsərɪ/ n borsa f di studio
**burst** /bɜːst/ n (of gunfire, energy, laughter) scoppio m; (of speed) scatto m ● v (pt/pp burst) ● vt far scoppiare; ~ its banks ⟨river:⟩ rompere gli argini ● vi scoppiare; ~ into tears scoppiare in lacrime; ~ into flames andare in fiamme; she ~ into the room ha fatto irruzione nella stanza; be ~ing at the seams ⟨room:⟩ scoppiare
■ **burst in** vi (enter suddenly) fare irruzione
■ **burst out** vi ~ out laughing/crying scoppiare a ridere/piangere
**Burundi** /bʊˈrʊndɪ/ n Burundi m
**bury** /ˈberɪ/ vt (pt/pp -ied) seppellire; (hide) nascondere
**bus** /bʌs/ n autobus m inv, pullman m inv; (long distance) pullman m inv, corriera f ● vt (pt/pp bussed) trasportare in autobus
**busby** /ˈbʌzbɪ/ n colbacco m militare
**bus:** bus conductor n ≈ bigliettaio m. **bus conductress** n ≈ bigliettaia f. **bus driver** n conducente mf di autobus
**bush** /bʊʃ/ n cespuglio m; (land) boscaglia f
**bushed** /bʊʃt/ a (fam: tired) distrutto
**bushel** /ˈbʊʃ(ə)l/ n hide one's light under a ~ essere troppo modesto; Am fam ~s of un sacco di
**bush:** bushfighting n Mil guerriglia f. **bushfire** n incendio m in aperta campagna. **bush telegraph** n fig hum tamtam m inv
**bushy** /ˈbʊʃɪ/ a (-ier, -iest) folto
**busily** /ˈbɪzɪlɪ/ adv con grande impegno
**business** /ˈbɪznɪs/ n affare m; Comm affari mpl; (establishment) attività f di commercio; on ~ per affari; he has no ~ to non ha alcun diritto di; mind one's own ~ farsi gli affari propri; that's none of your ~ non sono affari tuoi
**business:** business activity n attività f inv economica; (of single company) attività f inv aziendale. **business analyst** n analista mf finanziario, -a. **business associate** n socio, -a mf. **business call** n (phone call) telefonata f di lavoro; (visit) appuntamento m di lavoro. **business card** n biglietto m da visita. **business centre** n centro m affari. **business class** n Aeron business class f inv. **business college** n scuola f di amministrazione aziendale. **business contact** n contatto m di lavoro. **business cycle** n ciclo m economico. **business deal** n operazione f commerciale. **business expenses** npl spese fpl di lavoro. **business failures** npl chiusura f di aziende. **business hours** npl (in office) orario m d'ufficio; (of shop) orario m d'apertura. **business-like** a efficiente. **business lunch** n pranzo m di lavoro or d'affari
**businessman** /ˈbɪznɪsmən/ n uomo m d'affari
**business:** business management n am-
ministrazione f aziendale. **business park** n centro m affari. **business plan** n piano m economico; (of single company) programma m aziendale. **business premises** npl sede f di un'azienda. **business proposition** n proposta f d'affari. **business reply envelope** n busta f affrancata. **business school** n scuola f di amministrazione aziendale. **business software** n software m per l'ufficio. **business studies** npl economia f e commercio. **business suit** n (for man) abito m scuro. **business trip** n viaggio m di lavoro
**businesswoman** /ˈbɪznɪswʊmən/ n donna f d'affari
**busk** /bʌsk/ vi Br ⟨singer:⟩ cantare per strada; ⟨musician:⟩ suonare per strada
**busker** /ˈbʌskə(r)/ n suonatore, -trice mf ambulante
**bus lane** n corsia f autobus
**busload** /ˈbʌsləʊd/ n a ~ of tourists una comitiva di turisti; by the ~ in massa
**busman's holiday** /ˈbʌsmənzˈhɒlɪdeɪ/ n Br vacanze fpl passate a fare quello che si fa normalmente
**bus:** bus pass n abbonamento m all'autobus. **bus route** n percorso m dell'autobus. **bus shelter** n pensilina f alla fermata dell'autobus. **bus station** n stazione f degli autobus. **bus stop** n fermata f d'autobus
**bust¹** /bʌst/ n busto m; (chest) petto m
**bust²** a fam rotto; go ~ fallire ● v (pt/pp busted or bust) fam ● vt far scoppiare ● vi scoppiare
**bustle** /ˈbʌsl/ n (activity) trambusto m
■ **bustle about** vi affannarsi
**bustling** /ˈbʌslɪŋ/ a animato
**bust size** n circonferenza f del torace
**bust-up** n fam lite f
**busy** /ˈbɪzɪ/ a (-ier, -iest) occupato; (day, time) intenso; (street) affollato; (with traffic) pieno di traffico; be ~ doing essere occupato a fare ● vt ~ oneself darsi da fare
**busybody** /ˈbɪzɪbɒdɪ/ n ficcanaso mf inv
**but** /bʌt/, /bət/ conj ma ● prep eccetto, tranne; nobody ~ you nessuno tranne te; ~ for (without) se non fosse stato per; the last ~ one il penultimo; the next ~ one il secondo ● adv soltanto; there were ~ two ce n'erano soltanto due
**butane** /ˈbjuːteɪn/ n butano m
**butch** /bʊtʃ/ a fam ⟨man⟩ macho inv; ⟨woman⟩ mascolino
**butcher** /ˈbʊtʃə(r)/ n macellaio m ● vt macellare; fig massacrare
**butcher's [shop]** /ˈbʊtʃəz[ʃɒp]/ n macelleria f
**butchery** /ˈbʊtʃərɪ/ n (trade) macelleria f; (slaughter) massacro m
**butler** /ˈbʌtlə(r)/ n maggiordomo m
**butt** /bʌt/ n (of gun) calcio m; (of cigarette) mozzicone m; (for water) barile m; (fig: target) bersaglio m ● vt dare una testata a; ⟨goat:⟩ dare una cornata a
■ **butt in** vi interrompere
**butter** /ˈbʌtə(r)/ n burro m ● vt imburrare

■ **butter up** *vt fam* arruffianarsi
**butter: butter-bean** *n* fagiolo *m* bianco.
**buttercup** *n* ranuncolo *m*. **butter dish** *n* portaburro *m inv*. **butter-fingered** *a* con le mani di pasta frolla. **butter-fingers** *n fam* mani *fpl* di pasta frolla
**butterfly** /'bʌtəflaɪ/ *n* farfalla *f*
**butterfly: butterfly net** *n* retino *m* per farfalle. **butterfly nut** *n* dado *m* ad alette. **butterfly stroke** *n* nuoto *m* a farfalla
**buttermilk** /'bʌtəmɪlk/ *n* latticello *m*
**butterscotch** /'bʌtəskɒtʃ/ *n* caramella *f* dura a base di burro e zucchero
**buttocks** /'bʌtəks/ *npl* natiche *fpl*
**button** /'bʌtn/ *n* bottone *m*; (*on mouse, of status bar*) pulsante *m* ● *vt* ~ [**up**] abbottonare ● *vi* ~ [**up**] abbottonarsi
**button: button-down** *a* (*collar*) button down, coi bottoni; (*shirt*) con il colletto coi bottoni, button down. **buttonhole** *n* occhiello *m*, asola *f*. **buttonhook** *n* asola *f*, occhiello *m*. **button mushroom** *n* piccolo champignon *m inv*
**buttress** /'bʌtrɪs/ *n* contrafforte *m* ● *vt fig* sostenere
**buxom** /'bʌksəm/ *a* formosa
**buy** /baɪ/ *n* good/bad ~ buon/cattivo acquisto *m* ● *vt* (*pt/pp* bought) comprare; ~ **sb a drink** pagare da bere a qcno; **I'll ~ this one** (*drink*) questo, lo offro io
■ **buy off** *vt* (*bribe*) comprare
■ **buy out** *vt* rilevare la quota di (*one's partner*)
■ **buy up** *vt* (*buy all of*) accaparrarsi
**buyer** /'baɪə(r)/ *n* compratore, -trice *mf*
**buyout** /'baɪaʊt/ *n Comm* rilevamento *m*
**buzz** /bʌz/ *n* ronzio *m*; **give sb a ~** *fam* (*on phone*) dare un colpo di telefono a qcno; (*excite*) mettere in fermento qcno ● *vi* ronzare ● *vt* ~ **sb** chiamare qcno col cicalino
■ **buzz off** *vi fam* levarsi di torno
**buzzard** /'bʌzəd/ *n* poiana *f*
**buzzer** /'bʌzə(r)/ *n* cicalino *m*

**buzzing** /'bʌzɪŋ/ *n* (*of buzzer*) trillo *m*; (*of insects*) ronzio *m* ● *a* (*party, atmosphere, town*) molto animato
**buzzword** /'bʌzwɜːd/ *n fam* parola *f* di moda
**by** /baɪ/ *prep* (*near, next to*) vicino a; (*at the latest*) per; **by Mozart** di Mozart; **he was run over by a bus** è stato investito da un autobus; **by oneself** da solo; **by the sea** al mare; **by sea** via mare; **by car/bus** in macchina/autobus; **by day/night** di giorno/notte; **by the hour/metre** a ore/metri; **six metres by four** sei metri per quattro; **he won by six metres** ha vinto di sei metri; **I missed the train by a minute** ho perso il treno per un minuto; **I'll be home by six** sarò a casa per le sei; **by this time next week** a quest'ora tra una settimana; **he rushed by me** mi è passato accanto di corsa ● *adv* **she'll be here by and by** sarà qui fra poco; **by and by the police arrived** poco dopo, la polizia è arrivata; **by and large** in complesso; **put by** mettere da parte; **go/pass by** passare
**bye-bye** /baɪ'baɪ/ *int fam* ciao, arrivederci; **go ~s** *Br* (*baby talk*) andare a fare la nanna
**by-election** *n* elezione *f* straordinaria indetta per coprire una carica rimasta vacante in Parlamento
**Byelorussia** /bjeləʊ'rʌʃə/ *n* Bielorussia *f*
**Byelorussian** /bjeləʊ'rʌʃn/ *a & n* bielorusso
**by: bygone** *a* passato. **by-law** *n* legge *f* locale. **by-line** *n* (*in newspaper*) nome *m* dell'autore; *Sport* linea *f* laterale. **bypass** *n* circonvallazione *f*; *Med* by-pass *m inv* ● *vt* evitare. **by-product** *n* sottoprodotto *m*. **by-road** *n* strada *f* secondaria. **bystander** *n* spettatore, -trice *mf*
**byte** /baɪt/ *n Comput* byte *m inv*
**by: byway** *n* strada *f* secondaria. **byword** *n* **be a ~ for** essere sinonimo di. **by-your-leave** *n* **without so much as a ~** senza neanche chiedere il permesso
**Byzantine** /bɪ'zæntaɪn/ *a* bizantino

# Cc

**c, C** /siː/ *n* (*letter*) c, C *f inv*; (*Br Sch: grade*) voto *m* scolastico corrispondente alla sufficienza; *Mus* do *m inv*
**c, C** *abbr* (**Celsius, centigrade**) C; *abbr* (**cent(s)**) c; *abbr* (**circa**) ca
**CA** *Br abbr* (**Chartered Accountant**) [dottore *m*] commercialista *m*; *Am abbr* (**California**) Cal; *abbr* (**Central America**) America *f* centrale
**CAA** *n Br abbr* (**Civil Aviation Authority**) organismo *m* di controllo dell'aviazione civile
**CAB** *n Br abbr* (**Citizens' Advice Bureau**)

ufficio *m* di consulenza legale gratuita per i cittadini
**cab** /kæb/ *n* taxi *m inv*; (*of lorry, train*) cabina *f*
**cabana** /kə'bɑːnə/ *n* (*Am: hut*) cabina *f* da spiaggia
**cabaret** /'kæbəreɪ/ *n* cabaret *m inv*
**cabbage** /'kæbɪdʒ/ *n* cavolo *m*
**cabby** /'kæbɪ/ *n fam* tassista *mf*
**cab driver** *n* tassista *mf*
**cabin** /'kæbɪn/ *n* (*of plane, ship*) cabina *f*; (*hut*) capanna *f*

**cabin: cabin boy** n mozzo m. **cabin crew** n Aeron equipaggio m. **cabin cruiser** n cabinato m

**cabinet** /'kæbɪnɪt/ n armadietto m; [**display**] ~ vetrina f; **C~** Pol consiglio m dei ministri

**cabinet: cabinet-maker** n ebanista mf. **cabinet meeting** n Br riunione f del governo. **cabinet minister** n Br ministro m. **cabinet reshuffle** n Br rimpasto m del governo

**cable** /'keɪb(ə)l/ n cavo m

**cable: cable car** n cabina f (della funivia). **cablegram** n cablogramma m. **cable-knit** (sweater) a trecce. **cable railway** n funicolare f. **cable television** n televisione f via cavo. **cable TV** n TV f inv via cavo. **cableway** n (for people) funivia f

**caboodle** /kə'buːdl/ n fam **the whole ~** baracca e burattini

**cab rank, cab stand** n posteggio m dei taxi

**cache** /kæʃ/ n nascondiglio m; **~ of arms** deposito m segreto di armi

**cache memory** n Comput memoria f cache

**cachet** /'kæʃeɪ/ n prestigio m

**cackle** /'kækl/ vi ridacchiare

**cacophony** /kə'kɒfənɪ/ n cacofonia f

**cactus** /'kæktəs/ n (pl -ti /'kæktaɪ/ or -tuses) cactus m inv

**CAD** /kæd/ n abbr (**computer-aided design**) CAD m inv

**cadaver** /kə'dɑːvə(r)/ n cadavere m

**cadaverous** /kə'dævərəs/ a cadaverico

**CADCAM** /'kædkæm/ n abbr (**computer-aided design and computer-aided manufacture**) CADCAM m inv

**caddie** /'kædɪ/ n portabastoni m inv

**caddy** /'kædɪ/ n [**tea-**]~ barattolo m del tè

**cadence** /'keɪdəns/ n cadenza f

**cadet** /kə'det/ n cadetto m

**cadet corps** n Mil corpo m dei cadetti

**cadet school** n scuola f allievi ufficiali

**cadge** /kædʒ/ vt/i fam scroccare

**cadre** /'kɑːdr(ə)/ n Admin, Pol quadri mpl

**CAE** n abbr (**computer-aided engineering**) CAE m inv

**Caesarean** /sɪ'zeərɪən/ n parto m cesareo

**café** /'kæfeɪ/ n caffè m inv

**cafeteria** /kæfə'tɪərɪə/ n tavola f calda

**caffeine** /'kæfiːn/ n caffeina f

**cage** /keɪdʒ/ n gabbia f

**cage bird** n uccello m da gabbia

**cagey** /'keɪdʒɪ/ a fam riservato (**about** su)

**cagoule** /kə'guːl/ n Br K-way® m inv

**cahoots** /kə'huːts/ npl fam **be in ~** essere in combutta

**cairn** /keən/ n (of stones) tumulo m di pietre

**Cairo** /'kaɪrəʊ/ n il Cairo

**cajole** /kə'dʒəʊl/ vt persuadere con le lusinghe

**cake** /keɪk/ n torta f; (small) pasticcino m; ~ **of soap** saponetta f; **it was a piece of ~** fam è stato un gioco da ragazzi; **you can't have your ~ and eat it** fig non si può avere

la botte piena e la moglie ubriaca; **sell like hot ~s** andare a ruba

**caked** /keɪkt/ a incrostato (**with** di)

**cake: cake mix** n miscela f per torte. **cake shop** n pasticceria f. **cake tin** n (for baking) tortiera f; (for storing) scatola f di latta (per torte)

**Calabria** /kə'læbrɪə/ n Calabria f

**Calabrian** /kə'læbrɪən/ a & n calabrese

**calamine lotion** /'kæləmaɪn/ n lozione f alla calamina

**calamitous** /kə'læmɪtəs/ a disastroso

**calamity** /kə'læmətɪ/ n calamità f inv

**calcify** /'kælsɪfaɪ/ vi calcificarsi

**calcium** /'kælsɪəm/ n calcio m

**calculate** /'kælkjʊleɪt/ vt calcolare

**calculated** /'kælkjʊleɪtɪd/ a (risk, insult, decision) calcolato; (crime) premeditato

**calculating** /'kælkjʊleɪtɪŋ/ a fig calcolatore

**calculating machine** n calcolatrice f

**calculation** /kælkjʊ'leɪʃn/ n calcolo m

**calculator** /'kælkjʊleɪtə(r)/ n calcolatrice f

**calculus** /'kælkjʊləs/ n Math, Med calcolo m

**calendar** /'kælɪndə(r)/ n calendario m

**calendar month** n mese m civile

**calendar year** n anno m civile

**calf¹** /kɑːf/ n (pl calves) vitello m

**calf²** n (pl calves) Anat polpaccio m

**calfskin** /'kɑːfskɪn/ n [pelle f di] vitello m

**calibrate** /'kælɪbreɪt/ vt calibrare (instrument); tarare (scales)

**calibre** /'kælɪbə(r)/ n calibro m

**calico** /'kælɪkəʊ/ n cotone m grezzo

**California** /kælɪ'fɔːnɪə/ n California f

**Californian** /kælɪ'fɔːnɪən/ a & n californiano, -a mf

**CALL** n abbr (**computer-assisted language learning**) CALL m inv

**call** /kɔːl/ n grido m; Teleph telefonata f; (visit) visita f; **be on ~** (doctor:) essere di guardia ●vt chiamare; indire (strike); **be ~ed** chiamarsi ●vi chiamare; ~ [**in** or **round**] passare

■ **call back** vt/i richiamare

■ **call by** vi (make brief visit) passare

■ **call for** vt (ask for) chiedere; (require) richiedere; (fetch) passare a prendere

■ **call off** vt richiamare (dog); disdire (meeting); revocare (strike)

■ **call on** vt chiamare; (appeal to) fare un appello a; (visit) visitare

■ **call out** vt chiamare ad alta voce (names) ●vi chiamare ad alta voce

■ **call together** vt riunire

■ **call up** vt Mil chiamare alle armi; Teleph chiamare

**callback facility** /'kɔːlbæk/ n Teleph servizio m telefonico che permette di individuare il numero che ha chiamato

**call box** n cabina f telefonica

**caller** /'kɔːlə(r)/ n visitatore, -trice mf; Teleph persona f che telefona

**call-girl** n call-girl f inv, [ragazza f] squillo f inv

**calligrapher** /kə'lɪɡrəfə(r)/ n calligrafo, -a mf

**calligraphy** /kə'lɪɡrəfɪ/ n calligrafia f

**calling** /'kɔ:lɪŋ/ n vocazione f

**calliper** /'kælɪpə(r)/ n (for measuring) calibro m; (leg support) tutore m

**callisthenics** /kælɪs'θenɪks/ n ginnastica f

**callous** /'kæləs/ a insensibile

**callousness** /'kæləsnɪs/ n insensibilità f

**call-out** n (doctor) visita f a domicilio; (plumber, electrician) chiamata f

**call-out charge** n costo m della chiamata

**callow** /'kæleʊ/ a immaturo

**call: call sign** n Radio segnale m di chiamata. **call-up** n Mil chiamata f alle armi. **call-up papers** npl cartolina f precetto

**calm** /kɑ:m/ a calmo ● n calma f
  ■ **calm down** vt calmare ● vi calmarsi

**calmly** /'kɑ:mlɪ/ adv con calma

**calmness** /'kɑ:mnɪs/ n calma f

**Calor gas**® /'kælə/ n Br liquigas⋆ m inv

**calorie** /'kælərɪ/ n caloria f

**calorific** /kælə'rɪfɪk/ a calorico

**calve** /kɑ:v/ vi figliare

**calves** /kɑ:vz/ npl see **calf**¹ & ²

**cam** /kæm/ n Techn camma f

**camaraderie** /kæmə'rædərɪ/ n cameratismo m

**camber** /'kæmbə(r)/ n curvatura f

**Cambodia** /kæm'bəʊdɪə/ n Cambogia f

**Cambodian** /kæm'bəʊdɪən/ a & n cambogiano, -a mf

**camcorder** /'kæmkɔ:də(r)/ n videocamera f

**came** /keɪm/ see **come**

**camel** /'kæml/ n cammello m

**camel hair** n cammello m

**camellia** /kə'mi:lɪə/ n camelia f

**cameo** /'kæmɪəʊ/ n cammeo m

**cameo role** n Theat, Cinema breve apparizione f

**camera** /'kæmərə/ n macchina f fotografica; TV telecamera f

**camera crew** n troupe f inv televisiva

**cameraman** /'kæmərəmæn/ n operatore m [televisivo], cameraman m inv

**Cameroon** /kæmə'ru:n/ n il Camerun

**camisole** /'kæmɪsəʊl/ n canottiera f

**camomile** /'kæməmaɪl/ n camomilla f

**camouflage** /'kæməflɑ:ʒ/ n mimetizzazione f ● vt mimetizzare

**camp**¹ /kæmp/ n campeggio f; Mil campo m ● vi campeggiare; Mil accamparsi

**camp**² a (affected) affettato

**campaign** /kæm'peɪn/ n campagna f ● vi fare una campagna

**campaign trail** n be on the ~ ~ fare la campagna elettorale

**campaign worker** n Br Pol membro m dello staff di una campagna elettorale

**camp bed** n letto m da campo

**camper** /'kæmpə(r)/ n campeggiatore, -trice mf; Auto camper m inv

**campfire** /'kæmpfaɪə(r)/ n fuoco m di bivacco

**camphor** /'kæmfə(r)/ n canfora f

**camping** /'kæmpɪŋ/ n campeggio m

**camping: camping equipment** n attrezzatura f da campeggio. **camping gas** n gas m inv da campeggio. **camping holiday** n vacanza f in tenda. **camping site** n campeggio m. **camping stool** n Br sgabello m pieghevole. **camping stove** n fornello m da campeggio

**campsite** /'kæmpsaɪt/ n campeggio m

**campus** /'kæmpəs/ n (pl -puses) Univ città f universitaria, campus m inv

**camshaft** /'kæmʃɑ:ft/ n albero m a camme

**can**¹ /kæn/ n (for petrol) latta f; (tin) scatola f; ~ **of beer** lattina f di birra ● vt mettere in scatola

**can**² /kæn/, atono /kən/ v aux (pres **can**; pt **could**) (be able to) potere; (know how to) sapere; **I cannot** or **can't go** non posso andare; **he could not** or **couldn't go** non poteva andare; **she can't swim** non sa nuotare; **I ~ smell something burning** sento odor di bruciato

**Canada** /'kænədə/ n Canada m

**Canadian** /kə'neɪdɪən/ a & n canadese mf

**canal** /kə'næl/ n canale m

**canal boat, canal barge** n chiatta f

**canapé** /'kænəpeɪ/ n canapè m inv

**Canaries** /kə'neərɪz/ npl Canarie fpl

**canary** /kə'neərɪ/ n canarino m

**cancel** /'kænsl/ v (pt/pp **cancelled**) ● vt disdire ⟨meeting, newspaper⟩; revocare ⟨contract, order⟩; annullare ⟨reservation, appointment, stamp⟩ ● vi ⟨guest, host:⟩ annullare

**cancellation** /kænsə'leɪʃn/ n (of meeting, contract) revoca f; (in hotel, restaurant, for flight) cancellazione f

**cancer** /'kænsə(r)/ n cancro m; **C~** Astr Cancro m

**cancerous** /'kænsərəs/ a canceroso

**cancer research** n ricerca f sul cancro

**candelabra** /kændə'lɑ:brə/ n candelabro m

**candid** /'kændɪd/ a franco

**candidacy** /'kændɪdəsɪ/ n Pol candidatura f

**candidate** /'kændɪdət/ n candidato, -a mf

**candidly** /'kændɪdlɪ/ adv francamente

**candied** /'kændɪd/ a candito

**candle** /'kænd(ə)l/ n candela f

**candlelight** /'kænd(ə)llaɪt/ n by ~ a lume di candela

**candlelit dinner** /'kænd(ə)llɪt/ n cena f a lume di candela

**candlestick** /'kænd(ə)lstɪk/ n portacandele m inv

**candlewick bedspread** /'kænd(ə)lwɪk/ n copriletto m inv di ciniglia

**candour** /'kændə(r)/ n franchezza f

**candy** /'kændɪ/ n Am caramella f; **a [piece of] ~** una caramella

**candyfloss** /'kændɪflɒs/ n zucchero m filato

**candy-striped** /straɪpt/ a (blue) a righe bianche e celesti; (pink) a righe bianche e rosa

**cane** /keɪn/ n (stick) bastone m; Sch bacchetta f ● vt prendere a bacchettate ⟨pupil⟩

**cane sugar** n zucchero m di canna

**canine** /ˈkeɪnaɪn/ a canino
**canine tooth** n canino m
**canister** /ˈkænɪstə(r)/ n barattolo m
**cannabis** /ˈkænəbɪs/ n cannabis f
**canned** /kænd/ a in scatola; ~ **music** fam musica f registrata
**cannibal** /ˈkænɪbl/ n cannibale mf
**cannibalism** /ˈkænɪbəlɪzm/ n cannibalismo m
**cannibalize** /ˈkænɪbəlaɪz/ vt riciclare parti di
**cannon** /ˈkænən/ n inv cannone m
**cannon ball** n palla f di cannone
**cannon fodder** n carne f da cannone, carne f da macello
**cannot** /ˈkænɒt/ see **can²**
**canny** /ˈkænɪ/ a astuto
**canoe** /kəˈnuː/ n canoa f ● vi andare in canoa
**canon** /ˈkænən/ n (rule) canone m; (person) canonico m
**canonization** /kænənaɪˈzeɪʃn/ n canonizzazione f
**canonize** /ˈkænənaɪz/ vt canonizzare
**canoodle** /kəˈnuːdl/ vi fam sbaciucchiarsi
**can-opener** n apriscatole m inv
**canopy** /ˈkænəpɪ/ n baldacchino f; (of parachute) calotta f
**cant** /kænt/ n (hypocrisy) ipocrisia f; (jargon) gergo m
**can't** /kɑːnt/ = **cannot** see **can²**
**cantankerous** /kænˈtæŋkərəs/ a stizzoso
**cantata** /kænˈtɑːtə/ n Mus cantata f
**canteen** /kænˈtiːn/ n mensa f; ~ **of cutlery** servizio m di posate
**canter** /ˈkæntə(r)/ n piccolo galoppo m ● vi andare a piccolo galoppo
**cantilever** /ˈkæntɪliːvə(r)/ n cantilever m inv, trave f a sbalzo
**cantonal** /ˈkæntənəl/ a cantonale
**canvas** /ˈkænvəs/ n tela f; (painting) dipinto m su tela
**canvass** /ˈkænvəs/ vi Pol fare propaganda elettorale
**canvassing** /ˈkænvəsɪŋ/ n (door to door for votes) propaganda f porta a porta; (door to door for sales) vendita f porta a porta
**canyon** /ˈkænjən/ n canyon m inv
**cap** /kæp/ n berretto m; (nurse's) cuffia f; (top, lid) tappo m ● vt (pt/pp capped) (fig: do better than) superare
**capability** /keɪpəˈbɪlətɪ/ n capacità f
**capable** /ˈkeɪpəbl/ a capace; (skilful) abile; **be ~ of doing sth** essere capace di fare qcsa
**capably** /ˈkeɪpəblɪ/ adv con abilità
**capacious** /kəˈpeɪʃəs/ a (pocket, car boot) capace
**capacity** /kəˈpæsətɪ/ n capacità f; (function) qualità f; **in my ~ as** in qualità di
**cape¹** /keɪp/ n (cloak) cappa f
**cape²** n Geog capo m
**Cape of Good Hope** n Capo m di Buona Speranza
**caper¹** /ˈkeɪpə(r)/ vi saltellare ● n fam birichinata f
**caper²** n Culin cappero m

**Cape Town** n Città f del Capo
**capful** /ˈkæpfʊl/ n tappo m
**cap gun** n pistola f a capsule
**capillary** /kəˈpɪlərɪ/ a & n capillare m
**capital** /ˈkæpɪtl/ n (town) capitale f; (money) capitale m; (letter) lettera f maiuscola
**capital: capital allowances** npl detrazioni mpl per ammortamento. **capital city** n capitale f. **capital expenditure** n spese fpl in conto capitale; (personal) spese fpl di capitale. **capital gains tax** n imposta f sui redditi di capitale. **capital goods** npl beni mpl strumentali. **capital-intensive** a ad uso intensivo di capitale. **capital investment** n investimento m di capitale
**capitalism** /ˈkæpɪtəlɪzm/ n capitalismo m
**capitalist** /ˈkæpɪtəlɪst/ a & n capitalista mf
**capitalize** /ˈkæpɪtəlaɪz/ vi ~ **on** fig trarre vantaggio da
**capital: capital letter** n lettera f maiuscola. **capital punishment** n pena f capitale. **capital spending** n spese fpl in conto capitale. **capital transfer tax** n imposta f sui trasferimenti di capitale
**capitulate** /kəˈpɪtjʊleɪt/ vi capitolare
**capitulation** /kəpɪtjʊˈleɪʃn/ n capitolazione f
**capon** /ˈkeɪpɒn/ n cappone m
**caprice** /kəˈpriːs/ n (whim) capriccio m
**capricious** /kəˈprɪʃəs/ a capriccioso
**Capricorn** /ˈkæprɪkɔːn/ n Astr Capricorno m
**capsicum** /ˈkæpsɪkəm/ n peperone m
**capsize** /kæpˈsaɪz/ vi capovolgersi ● vt capovolgere
**caps lock** n Comput bloccamaiuscole m inv
**capstan** /ˈkæpstən/ n argano m
**capsule** /ˈkæpsjuːl/ n capsula f
**captain** /ˈkæptɪn/ n capitano m ● vt comandare (team)
**caption** /ˈkæpʃn/ n intestazione f; (of illustration) didascalia f
**captious** /ˈkæpʃəs/ a (remark) ipercritico
**captivate** /ˈkæptɪveɪt/ vt incantare
**captive** /ˈkæptɪv/ a prigioniero; **hold/take ~** tenere/fare prigioniero ● n prigioniero, -a mf
**captivity** /kæpˈtɪvətɪ/ n prigionia f; (animals) cattività f
**captor** /ˈkæptə(r)/ n (of person) persona f che tiene prigioniero qcno; (of person for ransom) rapitore, -trice mf
**capture** /ˈkæptʃə(r)/ n cattura f ● vt catturare; attirare (attention)
**car** /kɑː(r)/ n macchina f; **by ~** in macchina
**carafe** /kəˈræf/ n caraffa f
**caramel** /ˈkærəməl/ n (sweet) caramella f al mou; Culin caramello m
**carat** /ˈkærət/ n carato m
**caravan** /ˈkærəvæn/ n roulotte f inv; (horse-drawn) carovana f
**caraway** /ˈkærəweɪ/ n (plant) cumino m dei prati
**carbohydrate** /kɑːbəˈhaɪdreɪt/ n carboidrato m
**carbolic** /kɑːˈbɒlɪk/ a (soap) al fenolo

**car bomb** n autobomba f
**carbon** /'kɑːbən/ n carbonio m: (paper) carta f carbone; (copy) copia f in carta carbone
**carbon: carbon copy** n copia f in carta carbone; (fig: person) ritratto m. **carbon-date** vt datare con il carbonio 14. **carbon dating** n datazione f con il carbonio 14. **carbon dioxide** n anidride f carbonica. **carbon filter** n filtro m al carbone. **carbon monoxide** n monossido m di carbonio. **carbon paper** n carta f carbone
**car boot sale** n Br mercatino m di oggetti usati, esposti nei bagagliai delle macchine
**carbuncle** /'kɑːbʌŋk(ə)l/ n Med foruncolo m
**carburettor** /kɑːbjʊ'retə(r)/ n carburatore m
**carcass** /'kɑːkəs/ n carcassa f
**carcinogen** /kɑː'sɪnədʒən/ n cancerogeno m
**carcinogenic** /kɑːsɪnə'dʒenɪk/ a cancerogeno
**card** /kɑːd/ n (for birthday, Christmas etc) biglietto m di auguri; (playing ~) carta f [da gioco]; (membership ~) tessera f; (business ~) biglietto m da visita; (credit ~) carta f di credito; Comput scheda f
**cardboard** /'kɑːdbɔːd/ n cartone m
**cardboard box** n scatola f di cartone; (large) scatolone m
**card game** n gioco m di carte
**cardiac** /'kɑːdɪæk/ a cardiaco
**cardigan** /'kɑːdɪgən/ n cardigan m inv
**cardinal** /'kɑːdɪml/ a cardinale; ~ **number** numero m cardinale ● n Relig cardinale m
**card index** n schedario m
**cardiologist** /kɑːdɪ'ɒlədʒɪst/ n cardiologo, -a mf
**cardiology** /kɑːdɪ'ɒlədʒɪ/ n cardiologia f
**cardiovascular** /kɑːdɪə'væskjʊlə(r)/ a cardiovascolare
**card: card key** n scheda f magnetica. **card table** n tappeto m verde. **card trick** n trucco m con le carte
**care** /keə(r)/ n cura f; (caution) attenzione f; (worry) preoccupazione f; ~ **of** (on letter abbr c/o) presso; **take** ~ (be cautious) fare attenzione; **bye, take** ~ ciao, stammi bene; **take** ~ **of** occuparsi di; **be taken into** ~ essere preso in custodia da un ente assistenziale; '[handle] **with** ~' 'fragile' ● vi ~ **about** interessarsi di; ~ **for** (feel affection for) volere bene a; (look after) aver cura di; **I don't** ~ **for chocolate** non mi piace il cioccolato; **I don't** ~ non me ne importa; **who** ~**s?** chi se ne frega?; **for all I** ~ per quello che me ne importa
**care assistant** n Br Med assistente mf a domicilio
**career** /kə'rɪə(r)/ n carriera f; (profession) professione f. ~ **woman** n donna in carriera ● vi andare a tutta velocità
**career: career break** n pausa f nella carriera. **career move** n passo m utile per un avanzamento di carriera. **careers adviser** n consulente mf di orientamento professionale. **careers office** n centro m di orientamento

professionale. **careers service** n servizio m di orientamento professionale
**carefree** /'keəfriː/ a spensierato
**careful** /'keəfʊl/ a attento; (driver) prudente
**carefully** /'keəfʊlɪ/ adv con attenzione
**careless** /'keəlɪs/ a irresponsabile; (in work) trascurato; (work) fatto con poca cura; (driver) distratto
**carelessly** /'keəlɪslɪ/ adv negligentemente
**carelessness** /'keəlɪsnɪs/ n trascuratezza f
**carer** /'keərə(r)/ n Br (relative) familiare m che assiste un anziano o un handicappato; (professional) assistente mf a domicilio
**caress** /kə'res/ n carezza f ● vt accarezzare
**caretaker** /'keəteɪkə(r)/ n custode mf; (in school) bidello m
**careworn** /'keəwɔːn/ a (face) segnato dalle preoccupazioni
**car ferry** n traghetto m (per il trasporto di auto)
**cargo** /'kɑːgəʊ/ n (pl -es) carico m
**cargo plane** n aereo m da carico
**cargo ship** n nave f da carico
**car hire** n autonoleggio m
**Caribbean** /kærɪ'biːən/ n **the** ~ (sea) il Mar m dei Caraibi ● a caraibico
**caricature** /'kærɪkətjʊə(r)/ n caricatura f ● vt fare una caricatura di
**caricaturist** /'kærɪkətjʊərɪst/ n caricaturista mf
**caring** /'keərɪŋ/ a (parent) premuroso; (attitude) altruista; **the** ~ **professions** le attività assistenziali
**carjacking** /'kɑːdʒækɪŋ/ n furto m d'auto con aggressione al conducente
**carload** /'kɑːləʊd/ n **a** ~ **of people** un'automobile f piena di persone
**carnage** /'kɑːnɪdʒ/ n carneficina f
**carnal** /'kɑːn(ə)l/ a carnale
**carnation** /kɑː'neɪʃn/ n garofano m
**carnival** /'kɑːnɪvl/ n carnevale m
**carnivore** /'kɑːnɪvɔː(r)/ n carnivoro m
**carnivorous** /kɑː'nɪvərəs/ a carnivoro
**carob** /'kærəb/ n (pod) carruba f; (tree) carrubo m
**carol** /'kærəl/ n [**Christmas**] ~ canzone f natalizia; ~ **concert** concerto m natalizio; **go** ~ **singing** andare a cantare le canzoni natalizie per le strade
**carousel** /kærʊ'sel/ n (merry-go-round) giostra f; (for luggage) nastro m trasportatore; (for slides) caricatore m circolare
**carp**[1] /kɑːp/ n inv carpa f
**carp**[2] vi lamentarsi; ~ **at** trovare da ridire su
**car park** n parcheggio m
**carpenter** /'kɑːpəntə(r)/ n falegname m
**carpentry** /'kɑːpəntrɪ/ n falegnameria f
**carpet** /'kɑːpɪt/ n tappeto m; (wall-to-wall) moquette f inv; **be on the** ~ fig essere ammonito ● vt mettere la moquette in (room)
**carpet: carpet fitter** n artigiano m che mette in opera la moquette. **carpet slipper** n pantofola f. **carpet sweeper** n battitappeto m inv. **carpet tile** n riquadro m di moquette
**car phone** n telefono m in macchina

**car radio** n autoradio f inv

**carriage** /'kærɪdʒ/ n carrozza f; (of typewriter) carrello m; (of goods) trasporto m; (cost) spese fpl di trasporto; (bearing) portamento m; ~ **paid** Comm franco di porto

**carriage clock** n orologio m da tavolo

**carriageway** /'kærɪdʒweɪ/ n strada f carrozzabile; **north-bound** ~ carreggiata f nord

**carrier** /'kærɪə(r)/ n (company) impresa f di trasporti; Aeron compagnia f di trasporto aereo; (of disease) portatore, -trice mf

**carrier [bag]** n borsa f [per la spesa]

**carrier pigeon** n piccione m viaggiatore

**carrot** /'kærət/ n carota f

**carry** /'kærɪ/ v (pt/pp -ied) ● vt portare; (transport) trasportare; Math riportare; **get carried away** fam lasciarsi prender la mano ● vi ⟨sound:⟩ trasmettersi

■ **carry off** vt portare via; vincere ⟨prize⟩

■ **carry on** vi continuare; (fam: make scene) fare delle storie; ~ **on with sth** continuare qcsa; ~ **on with sb** fam intendersela con qcno ● vt mantenere ⟨business⟩; ~ **on doing sth** continuare a fare qcsa

■ **carry out** vt portare fuori; eseguire ⟨instructions, task⟩; mettere in atto ⟨threat⟩; effettuare ⟨experiment, survey⟩

**carrycot** /'kærɪkɒt/ n porte-enfant m inv

**carry-on** n fam (complicated procedure) impresa f; (bad behaviour) storie fpl

**carsick** /'kɑːsɪk/ a **be** ~ avere il mal d'auto

**cart** /kɑːt/ n carretto m; **put the** ~ **before the horse** fig mettere il carro davanti ai buoi ● vt (fam: carry) portare

**cartel** /kɑː'tel/ n cartello m

**carthorse** /'kɑːθɔːs/ n cavallo m da tiro

**cartilage** /'kɑːtɪlɪdʒ/ n Anat cartilagine f

**cartographer** /kɑː'tɒɡrəfə(r)/ n cartografo, -a mf

**cartography** /kɑː'tɒɡrəfɪ/ n cartografia f

**carton** /'kɑːt(ə)n/ n scatola f di cartone; (for drink) cartone m; (of cream, yoghurt) vasetto m; (of cigarettes) stecca f

**cartoon** /kɑː'tuːn/ n vignetta f; (strip) vignette fpl; (film) cartone m animato; (in art) bozzetto m

**cartoonist** /kɑː'tuːnɪst/ n vignettista mf; (for films) disegnatore, -trice mf di cartoni animati

**cartridge** /'kɑːtrɪdʒ/ n cartuccia f; (for film) bobina f; (of record player) testina f

**cartwheel** /'kɑːtwiːl/ n (of cart) ruota f di carro; (in gymnastics) ruota f; **do a** ~ (in gymnastics) fare la ruota

**carve** /kɑːv/ vt scolpire; tagliare ⟨meat⟩

**carving** /'kɑːvɪŋ/ n scultura f

**carving knife** n trinciante m

**car wash** n autolavaggio m inv

**car worker** n operaio, -a mf dell'industria automobilistica

**Casanova** /kæsənəʊvə/ n casanova m inv

**cascade** /kæs'keɪd/ vi scendere a cascata ● n cascata f

**case¹** /keɪs/ n caso m; **in any** ~ in ogni caso;

**in that** ~ in questo caso; **just in** ~ per sicurezza; **in** ~ **he comes** nel caso in cui venisse; **in** ~ **of emergency** nel caso d'emergenza

**case²** n (container) scatola f; (crate) cassa f; (for spectacles) astuccio m; (suitcase) valigia f; (for display) vetrina f

**case history** n Med cartella f clinica

**casement window** /'keɪsmənt/ n finestra f a battenti

**case: casenotes** npl pratica f. **case study** n analisi f inv. **casework** n **do** ~ occuparsi di assistenza sociale

**cash** /kæʃ/ n denaro m contante; (fam: money) contanti mpl; **pay [in]** ~ pagare in contanti; ~ **on delivery** pagamento alla consegna ● vt incassare ⟨cheque⟩

■ **cash in on** vt fam approfittarsi di

**cash: cash-and-carry** n cash and carry m inv. **cash box** n cassetta f portavalori. **cash card** n bancomat® m inv. **cash desk** n cassa f. **cash dispenser** n sportello m automatico, cassa f automatica

**cashew** /kə'ʃuː/ n anacardio m

**cash flow** n flusso m di cassa; ~ **difficulties** difficoltà fpl di flusso di cassa; ~ **management** gestione f del flusso di cassa

**cashier** /kæ'ʃɪə(r)/ n cassiere, -a mf

**cashmere** /'kæʃmɪə(r)/ n cachemire m inv

**cash: cash on delivery** n pagamento alla consegna. **cashpoint** n sportello m automatico. **cash register** n registratore m di cassa

**casing** /'keɪsɪŋ/ n (of machinery) rivestimento m; (of gearbox) scatola f; (of tyre) copertone m

**casino** /kə'siːnəʊ/ n casinò m inv

**cask** /kɑːsk/ n barile m

**casket** /'kɑːskɪt/ n scrigno m; (Am: coffin) bara f

**casserole** /'kæsərəʊl/ n casseruola f; (stew) stufato m

**cassette** /kə'set/ n cassetta f

**cassette: cassette deck** n piastra f di registrazione. **cassette player** n mangiacassette m inv. **cassette recorder** n registratore m ⟨a cassette⟩. **cassette tape** n cassetta f

**cassock** /'kæsək/ n tonaca f

**cast** /kɑːst/ n (throw) lancio m; (mould) forma f; Theat cast m inv; [plaster] ~ Med ingessatura f ● vt (pt/pp cast) dare ⟨vote⟩; Theat assegnare le parti di ⟨play⟩; fondere ⟨metal⟩; (throw) gettare; (shed) sbarazzarsi di; ~ **an actor as** dare ad un attore il ruolo di; ~ **a glance at** lanciare uno sguardo a

■ **cast off** vi Naut sganciare gli ormeggi ● vt (in knitting) diminuire

■ **cast on** vt (in knitting) avviare

**castanets** /kæstə'nets/ npl nacchere fpl

**castaway** /'kɑːstəweɪ/ n naufrago, -a mf

**caste** /kɑːst/ n casta f

**caster** /'kɑːstə(r)/ n (wheel) rotella f

**caster sugar** n zucchero m raffinato

**casting director** /'kɑːstɪŋ/ n direttore m del casting

**casting vote** n voto m decisivo

**cast iron** *n* ghisa *f* ● *a* **cast-iron** di ghisa; *fig* solido

**castle** /'kɑːsl/ *n* castello *m*; (*in chess*) torre *f*

**cast-offs** *npl* abiti *mpl* smessi

**castor** /'kɑːstə(r)/ *n* (*wheel*) rotella *f*

**castor oil** *n* olio *m* di ricino

**castor sugar** *n* zucchero *m* raffinato

**castrate** /kæ'streɪt/ *vt* castrare

**castration** /kæ'streɪʃn/ *n* castrazione *f*

**castrato** /kæs'trɑːtəʊ/ *n* castrato *m*

**casual** /'kæʒʊəl/ *a* (*chance*) casuale; (*remark*) senza importanza; (*glance*) di sfuggita; (*attitude, approach*) disinvolto; (*chat*) informale; (*clothes*) casual *inv*; (*work*) saltuario; ~ **wear** abbigliamento *m* casual

**casually** /'kæʒʊəlɪ/ *adv* (*dress*) casual; (*meet*) casualmente

**casualty** /'kæʒʊəltɪ/ *n* (*injured person*) ferito *m*; (*killed*) vittima *f*

**casualty** [**department**] *n* pronto soccorso *m*

**cat** /kæt/ *n* gatto *m*; *pej* arpia *f*

**catacombs** /'kætəkuːmz/ *npl* catacombe *fpl*

**catalogue** /'kætəlɒg/ *n* catalogo *m* ● *vt* catalogare

**catalyst** /'kætəlɪst/ *n* *Chem & fig* catalizzatore *m*

**catalytic converter** /kætə'lɪtɪk/ *n* *Auto* marmitta *f* catalitica

**catamaran** /kætəmə'ræn/ *n* catamarano *m*

**catapult** /'kætəpʌlt/ *n* catapulta *f*; (*child's*) fionda *f* ● *vt fig* catapultare

**cataract** /'kætərækt/ *n* *Med* cataratta *f*

**catarrh** /kə'tɑː(r)/ *n* catarro *m*

**catastrophe** /kə'tæstrəfɪ/ *n* catastrofe *f*

**catastrophic** /kætə'strɒfɪk/ *a* catastrofico

**cat burglar** *n* *Br* scassinatore, -trice *mf* acrobata

**catch** /kætʃ/ *n* (*of fish*) pesca *f*; (*fastener*) fermaglio *m*; (*on door*) fermo *m*; (*on window*) gancio *m*; (*fam: snag*) tranello *m* ● *v* (*pt/pp* **caught**) ● *vt* acchiappare (*ball*); (*grab*) afferrare; prendere (*illness, fugitive, train*); ~ **a cold** prendersi un raffreddore; ~ **sight of** scorgere; **I caught him stealing** l'ho sorpreso mentre rubava; ~ **one's finger in the door** chiudersi il dito nella porta; ~ **sb's eye** *or* **attention** attirare l'attenzione di qcno ● *vi* (*fire:*) prendere; (*get stuck*) impigliarsi

■ **catch on** *vi fam* (*understand*) afferrare; (*become popular*) diventare popolare

■ **catch out** *vt* (*show to be wrong*) prendere in castagna

■ **catch up** *vt* raggiungere ● *vi* recuperare; (*runner:*) riguadagnare terreno; ~ **up with** raggiungere (*sb*); mettersi in pari con (*work*)

**catch-22 situation** *n* situazione *f* senza uscita

**catch-all** *a* (*term*) polivalente; (*clause*) che comprende tutte le possibilità

**catching** /'kætʃɪŋ/ *a* contagioso

**catchment area** /'kætʃmənt/ *n* bacino *m* d'utenza

**catchphrase** /'kætʃfreɪz/ *n* tormentone *m*

**catchword** /'kætʃwɜːd/ *n* slogan *m inv*

**catchy** /'kætʃɪ/ *a* (**-ier, -iest**) orecchiabile

**catechism** /'kætɪkɪzm/ *n* catechismo *m*

**categorical** /kætɪ'gɒrɪkl/ *a* categorico

**categorically** /kætə'gɒrɪlkɪ/ *adv* categoricamente

**category** /'kætɪgərɪ/ *n* categoria *f*

**cater** /'keɪtə(r)/ *vi* ~ **for** provvedere a (*needs*); *fig* venire incontro alle esigenze di ● *vt* occuparsi del rinfresco di (*party*)

**caterer** /'keɪtərə(r)/ *n* persona *f* che si occupa di ristorazione

**catering** /'keɪtərɪŋ/ *n* (*trade*) ristorazione *f*; (*food*) rinfresco *m*

**caterpillar** /'kætəpɪlə(r)/ *n* bruco *m*

**caterwaul** /'kætəwɔːl/ *vi* miagolare

**cat: catfish** *n* pesce *m* gatto. **catflap** *n* gattaiola *f*. **catgut** *n* catgut *m inv*

**cathedral** /kə'θiːdrl/ *n* cattedrale *f*

**Catherine wheel** /'kæθ(ə)rɪn/ *n* girandola *f*

**catheter** /'kæθɪtə(r)/ *n* catetere *m*

**cathode-ray tube** /kæθəʊd'reɪ/ *n* tubo *m* a raggi catodici

**Catholic** /'kæθəlɪk/ *a & n* cattolico, -a *mf*

**Catholicism** /kə'θɒlɪsɪzm/ *n* cattolicesimo *m*

**catkin** /'kætkɪn/ *n* *Bot* amento *m*

**cat: cat litter** *n* lettiera *f* del gatto. **catnap** *vi* fare un pisolino ● *n* pisolino *m*. **cat-o'-nine-tails** *n* gatto *m* a nove code. **cat's-eye** *n* *Br* catarifrangente *m* (*inserito nell'asfalto*). **catsuit** *n* tuta *f*

**cattery** /'kætərɪ/ *n* pensione *f* per gatti

**cattle** /'kæt(ə)l/ *npl* bestiame *msg*

**cattle: cattle grid** *n* recinto *m* metallico che impedisce al bestiame di accedere a una strada. **cattle market** *n* mercato *m* del bestiame; (*fig fam: for sexual encounters*) locale *m* dove la gente va per rimorchiare. **cattle shed** *n* stalla *f*

**catty** /'kætɪ/ *a* (**-ier, -iest**) dispettoso

**catwalk** /'kætwɔːk/ *n* passerella *f*

**Caucasian** /kɔː'keɪz(ə)n/ *n* (*Geog: inhabitant*) caucasico, -a *mf*; (*white person*) bianco, -a *mf* ● *a* *Geog* caucasico; (*race, man*) bianco

**caught** /kɔːt/ *see* **catch**

**cauldron** /'kɔːldrən/ *n* calderone *m*

**cauliflower** /'kɒlɪflaʊə(r)/ *n* cavolfiore *m*

**cauliflower cheese** *n* cavolfiori *mpl* gratinati

**causal** /'kɔːzəl/ *a* causale

**cause** /kɔːz/ *n* causa *f*; (*reason*) motivo *m*; **good** ~ buona causa ● *vt* causare; ~ **sb to do sth** far fare qcsa a qcno

**causeway** /'kɔːzweɪ/ *n* strada *f* sopraelevata

**caustic** /'kɔːstɪk/ *a* caustico

**cauterize** /'kɔːtəraɪz/ *vt* cauterizzare

**caution** /'kɔːʃn/ *n* cautela *f*; (*warning*) ammonizione *f* ● *vt* mettere in guardia; *Jur* ammonire

**cautious** /'kɔːʃəs/ *a* cauto

**cautiously** /'kɔːʃəslɪ/ *adv* cautamente

**cavalcade** /kævəl'keɪd/ *n* sfilata *f*

**cavalier** /kævə'lɪə(r)/ *a* noncurante ● *n* C~

*sostenitore, -trice mf di Carlo I durante la guerra civile inglese*

**cavalry** /'kævəlrı/ n cavalleria f

**cave** /keıv/ n caverna f

■ **cave in** vi ⟨roof:⟩ crollare; (fig: give in) capitolare

**caveat** /'kævıæt/ n avvertimento m

**cave: cave dweller** n cavernicolo, -a mf. **caveman** n cavernicolo m. **cave painting** n pittura f rupestre

**caver** /'keıvə(r)/ n speleologo, -a mf

**cavern** /'kævən/ n caverna f

**caviare** /'kævıɑː(r)/ n caviale m

**caving** /'keıvıŋ/ n speleologia f

**cavity** /'kævətı/ n cavità f inv; (in tooth) carie f inv

**cavity wall insulation** n isolamento m per muri a intercapedine

**cavort** /kə'vɔːt/ vi saltellare

**caw** /kɔː/ n (noise) gracchio m ● vi gracchiare

**cayenne pepper** /'kaıen/ n pepe m di Caienna

**cayman** /'keımən/ n caimano m

**CB** n abbr (**Citizens' Band**) CB f inv ● attrib ⟨equipment, radio, wavelength⟩ CB

**cc** n abbr (**cubic centimetres**) cc m inv

**CCTV** abbr (**closed-circuit television**) televisione f a circuito chiuso

**CD** n abbr (**Civil Defence**) difesa f civile; abbr (**compact disc**) CD m inv; Am abbr (**Congressional District**) circoscrizione f del Congresso; abbr (**corps diplomatique**) CD m inv

**CD player** n lettore m [di] compact, lettore m di CD

**CD-Rom** /siː'diː'rɒm/ n CD-Rom m inv

**CD-Rom drive** n lettore m CD-Rom

**cease** /siːs/ n **without ~** incessantemente ● vt/i cessare

**ceasefire** /'siːsfaıə(r)/ n cessate il fuoco m inv

**ceaseless** /'siːslıs/ a incessante

**ceaselessly** /'siːslıslı/ adv incessantemente

**cedar** /'siːdə(r)/ n cedro m

**cede** /siːd/ vt cedere

**ceiling** /'siːlıŋ/ n soffitto m; fig tetto m [massimo]

**celebrate** /'selıbreıt/ vt festeggiare ⟨birthday, victory⟩ ● vi far festa

**celebrated** /'selıbreıtıd/ a celebre (**for** per)

**celebration** /selı'breıʃn/ n celebrazione f

**celebrity** /sı'lebrıtı/ n celebrità f inv

**celeriac** /sı'lerıæk/ n sedano m rapa

**celery** /'selərı/ n sedano m

**celestial** /sı'lestıəl/ a celestiale

**celibacy** /'selıbəsı/ n celibato m

**celibate** /'selıbət/ a ⟨man⟩ celibe; ⟨woman⟩ nubile

**cell** /sel/ n cella f; Biol cellula f

**cellar** /'selə(r)/ n scantinato m; (for wine) cantina f

**cellist** /'tʃelıst/ n violoncellista mf

**cello** /'tʃeləʊ/ n violoncello m

**Cellophane®** /'seləfeın/ n cellofan® m inv

**cellphone** /'selfəʊn/ n [telefono m] cellulare m

**cellular phone** /seljʊlə'fəʊn/ n [telefono m] cellulare m

**cellulite** /'seljʊlaıt/ n cellulite f

**celluloid** /'seljʊlɔıd/ n celluloide f

**Celsius** /'selsıəs/ a Celsius

**Celt** /kelt/ n celta mf

**Celtic** /'keltık/ a celtico

**cement** /sı'ment/ n cemento m; (adhesive) mastice m ● vt cementare; (stick) attaccare col mastice; fig consolidare

**cement mixer** n betoniera f

**cemetery** /'semətrı/ n cimitero m

**cenotaph** /'senətɑːf/ n cenotafio m

**censor** /'sensə(r)/ n censore m ● vt censurare

**censorship** /'sensəʃıp/ n censura f

**censure** /'senʃə(r)/ n biasimo m ● vt biasimare

**census** /'sensəs/ n censimento m

**cent** /sent/ n (coin) centesimo m

**centenary** /sen'tiːnərı/ n, Am **centennial** /sen'tenıəl/ n centenario m

**center** /'sentə(r)/ n Am = **centre**

**centigrade** /'sentıgreıd/ a centigrado

**centilitre** /'sentılıːtə(r)/ n centilitro m

**centimetre** /'sentımıːtə(r)/ n centimetro m

**centipede** /'sentıpiːd/ n centopiedi m inv

**central** /'sentrəl/ a centrale

**central heating** n riscaldamento m autonomo

**centralize** /'sentrəlaız/ vt centralizzare

**central locking** n Auto chiusura f centralizzata

**centrally** /'sentrəlı/ adv al centro; **~ heated** con riscaldamento autonomo

**central: central nervous system** n sistema m nervoso centrale. **central processing unit** n Comput unità f inv centrale di elaborazione. **central reservation** n Auto banchina f spartitraffico inv

**centre** /'sentə(r)/ n centro m ● v (pt/pp **centred**) ● vt centrare ● vi **~ on** fig incentrarsi su

**centre: centrefold** n (pin-up picture) paginone m; (model) pin-up f inv. **centre forward** n centravanti m inv. **centre half** n Sport centromediano m. **centre of gravity** n centro m di gravità. **centrepiece** n (of table) centrotavola m; (fig: of exhibition) pezzo m forte. **centre spread** n paginone m. **centre stage** n Theat centro m della scena; **stand ~ ~** tenersi al centro della scena; **take/occupy ~ ~** fig essere/mettersi in primo piano

**centrifugal** /sentrı'fjʊgl/ a **~ force** forza f centrifuga

**century** /'sentʃərı/ n secolo m

**CEO** n abbr (**Chief Executive Officer**) n direttore, -trice mf generale

**ceramic** /sı'ræmık/ a ceramico

**ceramics** /sı'ræmıks/ n (art) ceramica f sg; (objects) ceramiche f pl

**cereal** /'sıərıəl/ n cereale m

**cerebral** /'serɪbrl/ a cerebrale
**cerebral palsy** /'pɔːlzɪ/ n paralisi f cerebrale
**ceremonial** /serɪ'məʊnɪəl/ a da cerimonia ● n cerimoniale m
**ceremonially** /serɪ'məʊnɪəlɪ/ adv secondo il rituale
**ceremonious** /serɪ'məʊnɪəs/ a cerimonioso
**ceremoniously** /serɪ'məʊnɪəslɪ/ adv in modo cerimonioso
**ceremony** /'serɪmənɪ/ n cerimonia f; **without** ~ senza cerimonie
**cert** /sɜːt/ n Br fam **it's a [dead] ~!** ci puoi scommettere!
**certain** /'sɜːtn/ a certo; **for** ~ di sicuro; **make** ~ accertarsi; **he is** ~ **to win** è certo di vincere; **it's not** ~ **whether he'll come** non è sicuro che venga
**certainly** /'sɜːtnlɪ/ adv certamente; ~ **not!** no di certo!
**certainty** /'sɜːtntɪ/ n certezza f; **it's a** ~ è una cosa certa
**certifiable** /'sɜːtɪfaɪəbl/ a ⟨verifiable statement, evidence⟩ dimostrabile; ⟨mad⟩ pazzo
**certificate** /sə'tɪfɪkət/ n certificato m
**certify** /'sɜːtɪfaɪ/ vt (pt/pp -**ied**) certificare; ⟨declare insane⟩ dichiarare malato di mente
**certitude** /'sɜːtɪtjuːd/ n certezza f
**cervical** /'sɜːvɪkl/ a cervicale
**cervix** /'sɜːvɪks/ n cervice f uterina, collo m dell'utero
**cessation** /se'seɪʃn/ n cessazione f
**cesspool** /'sespuːl/ n pozzo m nero
**cf.** abbr (**compare**) cf, cfr
**CFC** n abbr (**chlorofluorocarbon**) CFC m inv
**CFE** abbr **College of Further Education**
**chafe** /tʃeɪf/ vt irritare
**chaff** /tʃɑːf/ n pula f
**chaffinch** /'tʃæfɪntʃ/ n fringuello m
**chagrin** /'ʃægrɪn/ n **much to his** ~ con suo grande dispiacere
**chain** /tʃeɪn/ n catena f ● vt incatenare ⟨prisoner⟩; attaccare con la catena ⟨dog⟩ (**to** a)
■ **chain up** vt legare alla catena ⟨dog⟩
**chain: chain gang** n gruppo m di prigionieri incatenati. **chain letter** n lettera f della catena di Sant'Antonio. **chain mail** n cotta f di maglia. **chain reaction** n reazione f a catena. **chain saw** n motosega f. **chain-smoke** vi fumare una sigaretta dopo l'altra. **chain-smoker** n fumatore, -trice mf accanito, -a. **chain store** n negozio m appartenente a una catena
**chair** /tʃeə(r)/ n sedia f; Univ cattedra f ● vt presiedere
**chairlift** /'tʃeəlɪft/ n seggiovia f
**chairman** /'tʃeəmən/ n presidente m; ~ **and managing director** presidente m direttore generale
**chairperson** /'tʃeəpɜːs(ə)n/ n presidente m, -essa f
**chairwoman** /'tʃeəwʊmən/ n presidentessa f

**chalet** /'ʃæleɪ/ n chalet m inv; (in holiday camp) bungalow m inv
**chalice** /'tʃælɪs/ n Relig calice m
**chalk** /tʃɔːk/ n gesso m
**chalky** /'tʃɔːkɪ/ a gessoso
**challenge** /'tʃælɪndʒ/ n sfida f; Mil intimazione f ● vt sfidare; Mil intimare il chi va là a; fig mettere in dubbio ⟨statement⟩
**challenger** /'tʃælɪndʒə(r)/ n sfidante mf
**challenging** /'tʃælɪndʒɪŋ/ a ⟨job⟩ impegnativo
**chamber** /'tʃeɪmbə(r)/ n **C~ of Commerce** camera f di commercio
**chamber: chambermaid** n cameriera f [d'albergo]. **chamber music** n musica f da camera. **Chamber of Commerce** n Camera f di Commercio. **chamber orchestra** n orchestra f da camera. **chamber pot** n vaso m da notte
**chambers** /'tʃeɪmbəz/ n pl Jur studio m [legale]
**chameleon** /kə'miːlɪən/ n also fig camaleonte m
**chamois**[1] /'ʃæmwɑː/ n inv (animal) camoscio m
**chamois**[2] /'ʃæmɪ/ n ~[-**leather**] [pelle f di] camoscio m
**champagne** /ʃæm'peɪn/ n champagne m inv
**champion** /'tʃæmpɪən/ n Sport campione m; (of cause) difensore m, difenditrice f ● vt (defend) difendere; (fight for) lottare per
**championship** /'tʃæmpɪənʃɪp/ n Sport campionato m
**chance** /tʃɑːns/ n caso m; (possibility) possibilità f inv; (opportunity) occasione f; **by** ~ per caso; **take a** ~ provarci; **give sb a second** ~ dare un'altra possibilità a qcno ● attrib fortuito ● vt **if you** ~ **to see him** se ti capita di vederlo; **I'll** ~ **it** fam corro il rischio
**chancel** /'tʃɑːnsəl/ n Archit coro m
**chancellor** /'tʃɑːnsələ(r)/ n cancelliere m; Univ rettore m; **C~ of the Exchequer** ≈ ministro m del tesoro
**chancy** /'tʃɑːnsɪ/ a rischioso
**chandelier** /ʃændə'lɪə(r)/ n lampadario m
**chandler** /'tʃɑːndlə(r)/ n fornitore m navale
**change** /tʃeɪndʒ/ n cambiamento m; (money) resto m; (small coins) spiccioli mpl; **for a** ~ tanto per cambiare; **have a** ~ **of heart** cambiare idea; **a** ~ **of clothes** un cambio di vestiti; ~ **of address** cambiamento m d'indirizzo; **a** ~ **of scene** also fig un cambiamento di scena; **the** ~ [**of life**] la menopausa ● vt cambiare; (substitute) scambiare (**for** con); ~ **one's clothes** cambiarsi [i vestiti]; ~ **trains** cambiare treno ● vi cambiare; ⟨clothes⟩ cambiarsi; **all** ~! stazione terminale!
■ **change down** vi Auto passare alla marcia inferiore
■ **change up** vi Auto passare alla marcia superiore
**changeability** /tʃeɪndʒə'bɪlɪtɪ/ n (of weather) instabilità f

**changeable** /'tʃeɪndʒəbl/ a mutevole; ⟨weather⟩ variabile

**changeless** /'tʃeɪndʒlɪs/ a ⟨appearance⟩ inalterabile; ⟨character⟩ costante; ⟨law, routine⟩ immutabile

**change machine** n distributore m di monete

**changeover** /'tʃeɪndʒəʊvə(r)/ n (time period) periodo m di transizione; (transition) passaggio m; (of leaders) subentro m; (of employees, guards) cambio m; (Sport: in relay) passaggio m del testimone; (Sport: of ends) cambiamento m

**changing-room** n camerino m; (for sports) spogliatoio m

**channel** /'tʃænl/ n canale m; **the [English] C~** la Manica ● vt (pt/pp **channelled**) ~ **one's energies into sth** convogliare le proprie energie in qcsa

**channel: channel ferry** n traghetto m attraverso la Manica. **Channel Islands** npl Isole fpl del Canale. **Channel Tunnel** n tunnel m inv sotto la Manica

**chant** /tʃɑːnt/ n cantilena f; (of demonstrators) slogan m inv di protesta ● vt cantare; ⟨demonstrators⟩ gridare ● vi ⟨demonstrators⟩ gridare slogan di protesta

**chaos** /'keɪɒs/ n caos m

**chaotic** /keɪ'ɒtɪk/ a caotico

**chap** /tʃæp/ n fam tipo m

**chapel** /'tʃæpl/ n cappella f

**chaperon** /'ʃæpərəʊn/ n chaperon f inv ● vt fare da chaperon a ⟨sb⟩

**chaplain** /'tʃæplɪn/ n cappellano m

**chapped** /tʃæpt/ a ⟨skin, lips⟩ screpolato

**chapter** /'tʃæptə(r)/ n capitolo m

**char¹** /tʃɑː(r)/ n fam donna f delle pulizie

**char²** vt (pt/pp **charred**) (burn) carbonizzare

**character** /'kærɪktə(r)/ n carattere m; (in novel, play) personaggio m; **that's out of ~** non è da te/lui; **quite a ~** fam un tipo particolare

**character actor** n caratterista mf

**character assassination** n denigrazione f

**characteristic** /kærəktə'rɪstɪk/ a caratteristico ● n caratteristica f

**characteristically** /kærəktə'rɪstɪlkɪ/ adv tipicamente

**characterization** /kærɪktərar'zeɪʃn/ n caratterizzazione f

**characterize** /'kærɪktəraɪz/ vt caratterizzare

**character reference** n referenze fpl (relative al carattere)

**charade** /ʃə'rɑːd/ n farsa f; ~s sciarada fsg

**charcoal** /'tʃɑːkəʊl/ n carbonella f

**charge** /tʃɑːdʒ/ n (cost) prezzo m; Electr, Mil carica f; Jur accusa f; **free of ~** gratuito; **be in ~** essere responsabile (**of** di); **take ~** assumersi la responsabilità; **take ~ of** occuparsi di ● vt far pagare (fee); far pagare a (person); Electr, Mil caricare; Jur accusare (**with** di); ~ **sb for sth** far pagare qcsa a qcno; **what do you ~?** quanto prende?; ~ **it to my account**

lo addebiti sul mio conto ● vi (attack) caricare

**charge card** n (credit card) carta f di addebito; (store card) carta f di credito [di un negozio]

**charged** /tʃɑːdʒd/ a Phys carico; **emotionally ~** (atmosphere) carico di emozione

**chargé d'affaires** /ʃaːʒeɪdæ'feə(r)/ n incaricato m d'affari

**charge hand** n caposquadra mf

**charge nurse** n caposala mf

**char-grilled** /-'grɪld/ a alla brace

**chariot** /'tʃærɪət/ n cocchio m

**charisma** /kə'rɪzmə/ n carisma m

**charismatic** /kærɪz'mætɪk/ a carismatico

**charitable** /'tʃærɪtəbl/ a caritatevole; (kind) indulgente

**charity** /'tʃærətɪ/ n carità f; (organization) associazione f di beneficenza; **concert given for ~** concerto m di beneficenza; **live on ~** vivere di elemosina

**charity: charity box** n (in church) cassetta f delle offerte. **charity shop** n negozio m dell'usato a scopo di beneficenza. **charity work** n lavoro m volontario (per beneficenza)

**charlady** /'tʃɑːleɪdɪ/ n Br donna f delle pulizie

**charlatan** /'ʃɑːlətən/ n ciarlatano, -a mf

**charm** /tʃɑːm/ n fascino m; (object) ciondolo m ● vt affascinare

**charmer** /'tʃɑːmə(r)/ n **he's a real ~** è un vero seduttore

**charming** /'tʃɑːmɪŋ/ a affascinante

**charmingly** /'tʃɑːmɪŋlɪ/ adv in modo affascinante

**chart** /tʃɑːt/ n carta f nautica; (table) tabella f

**charter** /'tʃɑːtə(r)/ n ~ **[flight]** [volo m] charter m inv ● vt noleggiare

**chartered: chartered accountant** n commercialista mf. **chartered flight** n Br volo m charter inv. **chartered surveyor** n Br perito m edile

**charter plane** n Br charter m inv

**charwoman** /'tʃɑːwʊmən/ n donna f delle pulizie

**chase** /tʃeɪs/ n inseguimento m; **give ~** mettersi all'inseguimento ● vt inseguire

■ **chase away, chase off** vt cacciare via

■ **chase up** vt fam cercare

**chaser** /'tʃeɪsə(r)/ n (fam: drink) liquore m bevuto dopo la birra

**chasm** /'kæz(ə)m/ n abisso m

**chassis** /'ʃæsɪ/ n (pl chassis /'ʃæsɪz/) telaio m

**chaste** /tʃeɪst/ a casto

**chasten** /'tʃeɪs(ə)n/ vt castigare; **they looked suitably ~ed** avevano l'aria mortificata

**chastise** /tʃæ'staɪz/ vt castigare

**chastity** /'tʃæstətɪ/ n castità f

**chat** /tʃæt/ n chiacchierata f; **have a ~ with** fare quattro chiacchere con ● vi (pt/pp **chatted**) chiacchierare

■ **chat up** vt abbordare

**chat show** n talk show m inv

**chattel** /'tʃæt(ə)l/ *n Jur* **goods and ~s** beni *mpl* mobili

**chatter** /'tʃætə(r)/ *n* chiacchiere *fpl* ● *vi* chiacchierare; ‹*teeth:*› battere

**chatterbox** /'tʃætəbɒks/ *n fam* chiacchierone, -a *mf*

**chatty** /'tʃætɪ/ *a* (**-ier, -iest**) chiacchierone; ‹*style*› familiare

**chauffeur** /'ʃəʊfə(r)/ *n* autista *mf*

**chauvinism** /'ʃəʊvɪnɪzm/ *n* sciovinismo *m*

**chauvinist** /'ʃəʊvɪnɪst/ *n* sciovinista *mf*. **male ~** *fam* maschilista *m*

**cheap** /tʃi:p/ *a* a buon mercato; ‹*rate*› economico; ‹*vulgar*› grossolano; (*of poor quality*) scadente ● *adv* a buon mercato

**cheapen** /'tʃi:p(ə)n/ *vt* **~ oneself** screditarsi

**cheaply** /'tʃi:plɪ/ *adv* a buon mercato

**cheap rate** *a* & *adv Teleph* a tariffa ridotta

**cheat** /tʃi:t/ *n* imbroglione, -a *mf*; (*at cards*) baro *m* ● *vt* imbrogliare; **~ sb out of sth** sottrarre qcsa a qcno con l'inganno ● *vi* imbrogliare; (*at cards*) barare

■ **cheat on** *vt fam* tradire ‹*wife*›

**check**[1] /tʃek/ *a* ‹*pattern*› a quadri ● *n* disegno *m* a quadri

**check**[2] *n* verifica *f*; (*of tickets*) controllo *m*; (*in chess*) scacco *m*; (*Am: bill*) conto *m*; (*Am: cheque*) assegno *m*; (*Am: tick*) segnetto *m*; **keep a ~ on** controllare; **keep in ~** tenere sotto controllo ● *vt* verificare; controllare ‹*tickets*›; (*restrain*) contenere; (*stop*) bloccare ● *vi* controllare; **~ on sth** controllare qcsa

■ **check in** *vi* registrarsi all'arrivo (*in albergo*); *Aeron* fare il check-in ● *vt* registrare all'arrivo (*in albergo*)

■ **check out** *vi* (*of hotel*) saldare il conto ● *vt* (*fam: investigate*) controllare

■ **check up** *vi* accertarsi

■ **check up on** *vt* prendere informazioni su

**checked** /tʃekt/ *a* a quadri

**checkers** /'tʃekəz/ *n Am* dama *f*

**check-in** *n* accettazione *f*, check-in *m inv*

**check-in desk** *n* banco *m* dell'accettazione, banco *m* del check-in

**check-in time** *n* check-in *m inv*

**checking account** /'tʃekɪŋ/ *n Am* conto *m* corrente

**check: checklist** *n* lista *f* di controllo. **check mark** *n Am* segnetto *m*. **checkmate** *int* scacco matto!. **checkout** *n* (*in supermarket*) cassa *f*. **checkout assistant, checkout operator** *n Br* cassiere, -a *mf*. **checkpoint** *n* posto *m* di blocco. **checkroom** *n Am* deposito *m* bagagli. **check-up** *n Med* visita *f* di controllo, check-up *m inv*

**cheddar** /'tʃedə(r)/ *n formaggio m semistagionato*

**cheek** /tʃi:k/ *n* guancia *f*; (*impudence*) sfacciataggine *f*

**cheekbone** /'tʃi:kbəʊn/ *n* zigomo *m*

**cheekily** /'tʃi:kɪlɪ/ *adv* sfacciatamente

**cheeky** /'tʃi:kɪ/ *a* sfacciato

**cheep** /tʃi:p/ *vi* pigolare

**cheer** /tʃɪə(r)/ *n* evviva *m inv*; **three ~s** tre

urrà; **~s!** salute!; (*goodbye*) arrivederci!; (*thanks*) grazie! ● *vt/i* acclamare

■ **cheer up** *vt* tirare su [di morale] ● *vi* tirarsi su [di morale]; **~ up!** su con la vita!

**cheerful** /'tʃɪəfʊl/ *a* allegro

**cheerfully** /'tʃɪəfʊlɪ/ *adv* allegramente; **I could ~ strangle him!** lo strangolerei volentieri!

**cheerfulness** /'tʃɪəfʊlnɪs/ *n* allegria *f*

**cheerily** /'tʃɪərɪlɪ/ *adv* allegramente

**cheering** /'tʃɪərɪŋ/ *n* acclamazione *f*

**cheerio** /tʃɪərɪ'əʊ/ *int fam* arrivederci

**cheerleader** /'tʃɪəli:də(r)/ *n* leader *mf* dei tifosi

**cheerless** /'tʃɪəlɪs/ *a* triste, tetro

**cheery** /'tʃɪərɪ/ *a* allegro

**cheese** /tʃi:z/ *n* formaggio *m*

■ **cheese off** *vt fam* **be ~d off with one's job** essere stufo del proprio lavoro; **I'm really ~d off about it** ne ho le scatole piene

**cheese: cheeseboard** *n* (*object*) vassoio *m* dei formaggi; (*selection*) piatto *m* di formaggi. **cheeseburger** *n* cheeseburger *m inv*. **cheesecake** *n* dolce *m* al formaggio. **cheesecloth** *n* mussola *f*, tela *f* indiana. **cheese counter** *n* banco *m* dei formaggi

**cheesy** /'tʃi:zɪ/ *a* ‹*smell*› di formaggio; ‹*grin*› smagliante

**cheetah** /'tʃi:tə/ *n* ghepardo *m*

**chef** /ʃef/ *n* cuoco, -a *mf*, chef *mf inv*

**chemical** /'kemɪk/ *a* chimico ● *n* prodotto *m* chimico

**chemically** /'kemɪklɪ/ *adv* chimicamente

**chemise** /ʃə'mi:z/ *n* (*undergarment*) sottoveste *f inv*; (*dress*) chemisier *m inv*

**chemist** /'kemɪst/ *n* (*pharmacist*) farmacista *mf*; (*scientist*) chimico, -a *mf*

**chemistry** /'kemɪstrɪ/ *n* chimica *f*

**chemist's** [**shop**] *n* farmacia *f*

**chemotherapy** /ki:məʊ'θerəpɪ/ *n* chemioterapia *f*

**cheque** /tʃek/ *n* assegno *m*

**chequebook** /'tʃekbʊk/ *n* libretto *m* degli assegni

**cheque card** *n* carta *f* assegni

**chequer** /'tʃekə(r)/ *n* (*square*) scacco *m*; (*pattern*) motivo *m* a scacchi; (*in game*) pedina *f*

**chequered** /'tʃekəd/ *a* (*patterned*) a scacchi; ‹*fig: career, history*› movimentato

**chequers** /'tʃekəz/ *n* dama *f*

**cherish** /'tʃerɪʃ/ *vt* curare teneramente; (*love*) avere caro; nutrire ‹*hope*›

**cherry** /'tʃerɪ/ *n* ciliegia *f*; (*tree*) ciliegio *m*

**cherry brandy** *n* cherry-brandy *m inv*

**cherry tree** *n* ciliegio *m*

**cherub** /'tʃerəb/ *n* cherubino *m*

**chervil** /'tʃɜ:vɪl/ *n* cerfoglio *m*

**chess** /tʃes/ *n* scacchi *mpl*

**chess: chessboard** *n* scacchiera *f*. **chessman** *n* pezzo *m* degli scacchi. **chessplayer** *n* scacchista *mf*. **chess set** *n* scacchi *mpl*

**chest** /tʃest/ *n* petto *m*; (*box*) cassapanca *f*; **get sth off one's ~** *fig* levarsi un peso [dallo stomaco]

**chest freezer** n freezer m inv orizzontale. congelatore m orizzontale

**chestnut** /'tʃesnʌt/ n castagna f; (tree) castagno m

**chest of drawers** n cassettone m, comò m inv

**chesty** /'tʃestɪ/ a ‹person› che soffre di bronchite; ‹cough› bronchitico

**chew** /tʃuː/ vt masticare

■ **chew over** vt (fam: think about carefully) rimuginare su

**chewing gum** /'tʃuːɪŋ/ n gomma f da masticare

**chewy** /'tʃuːɪ/ a ‹meat› legnoso; ‹toffee› gommoso

**chic** /ʃiːk/ a chic inv

**chick** /tʃɪk/ n pulcino m; (fam: girl) ragazza f

**chicken** /'tʃɪkn/ n pollo m ● attrib ‹soup, casserole› di pollo ● a fam fifone

■ **chicken out** vi fam he ~ed out gli è venuta fifa

**chicken: chicken breast** n petto m di pollo. **chicken curry** n pollo m al curry. **chicken feed** n mangime m per i polli; (fam: paltry sum) miseria f. **chicken livers** npl fegatini mpl di pollo. **chicken noodle soup** n vermicelli mpl in brodo di pollo. **chickenpox** n varicella f. **chicken wire** n rete f metallica (a maglia esagonale)

**chickpea** /'tʃɪkpiː/ n cece m

**chicory** /'tʃɪkərɪ/ n cicoria f

**chief** /tʃiːf/ a principale ● n capo m

**chief executive officer** n direttore, -trice mf generale

**chief inspector** n (Br: of police) ispettore m capo

**chiefly** /'tʃiːflɪ/ adv principalmente

**chief superintendent** n (Br: of police) commissario m capo

**chiffon** /'ʃɪfon/ n chiffon m ● a ‹dress, scarf› di chiffon

**chilblain** /'tʃɪlbleɪn/ n gelone m

**child** /tʃaɪld/ n (pl ~ren) bambino, -a mf; (son/daughter) figlio, -a mf

**child: child abuse** n violenza f sui minori; (sexual) violenza f sessuale sui minori. **childbearing** n gravidanza f; of ~ age in età feconda. **child benefit** n Br assegni mpl familiari. **childbirth** n parto m. **childcare** n (bringing up children) educazione f dei bambini; (nurseries etc) strutture fpl di assistenza ai bambini

**childhood** /'tʃaɪldhʊd/ n infanzia f

**childish** /'tʃaɪldɪʃ/ a infantile

**childishness** /'tʃaɪldɪʃnɪs/ n puerilità f

**childless** /'tʃaɪldlɪs/ a senza figli

**childlike** /'tʃaɪldlaɪk/ a ingenuo

**child: child-minder** n baby-sitter mf inv. **child molester** n molestatore, -trice mf di bambini. **child prodigy** n bambino prodigio. **child-proof** a ‹container› a prova di bambino; ~ **lock** sicura f a prova di bambino

**children** /'tʃɪldrən/ npl see **child**

**children's home** n istituto m per l'infanzia

**Chile** /'tʃɪlɪ/ n Cile m

**Chilean** /'tʃɪlɪən/ a & n cileno, -a mf

**chill** /tʃɪl/ n freddo m; (illness) infreddatura ● vt raffreddare

**chilli** /'tʃɪlɪ/ n (pl -es) ~ [pepper] peperoncino m

**chilly** /'tʃɪlɪ/ a freddo

**chime** /tʃaɪm/ vi suonare

**chimera** /kɪ'mɪərə/ n (beast, idea) chimera f

**chimney** /'tʃɪmnɪ/ n camino m

**chimney: chimneybreast** n bocca f del camino. **chimney-pot** n comignolo m. **chimney-sweep** n spazzacamino m

**chimp** /tʃɪmp/ n fam scimpanzé m

**chimpanzee** /tʃɪmpæn'ziː/ n scimpanzé m inv

**chin** /tʃɪn/ n mento m

**China** /'tʃaɪnə/ n Cina f

**china** n porcellana f

**China: China Sea** n Mar m Cinese. **China tea** n tè m inv cinese. **Chinatown** n quartiere m cinese

**Chinese** /tʃaɪ'niːz/ a & n cinese mf; (language) cinese m; **the** ~ pl i cinesi

**Chinese lantern** n lanterna f cinese

**chink¹** /tʃɪŋk/ n (slit) fessura f

**chink²** n (noise) tintinnio m ● vi tintinnare

**chinos** /'tʃiːnəʊz/ npl pantaloni mpl cachi di cotone

**chintz** /tʃɪnts/ n chintz m inv

**chip** /tʃɪp/ n (fragment) scheggia f; (in china, paintwork) scheggiatura f; Comput chip m inv; (in gambling) fiche f inv: ~s pl Br Culin patatine fpl fritte; Am Culin patatine fpl; **have a** ~ **on one's shoulder** avere un complesso di inferiorità ● vt (pt/pp **chipped**) (damage) scheggiare

■ **chip in** fam vi intromettersi; (with money) contribuire

**chipboard** /'tʃɪpbɔːd/ n truciolato m

**chipmunk** /'tʃɪpmʌŋk/ n tamia m inv

**chip pan** n friggitrice f

**chipped** /tʃɪpt/ a (damaged) scheggiato

**chippings** /'tʃɪpɪŋz/ npl (on road) breccia f; 'loose ~' 'attenzione: breccia'

**chippy** /'tʃɪpɪ/ n (Br fam: chip shop) negozio m di fish and chips

**chip shop** n Br negozio m di fish and chips

**chiropodist** /kɪ'rɒpədɪst/ n podiatra mf inv

**chiropody** /kɪ'rɒpədɪ/ n podiatria f

**chirp** /tʃɜːp/ vi cinguettare; ‹cricket:› fare cri cri

**chirpy** /'tʃɜːpɪ/ a fam pimpante

**chisel** /'tʃɪzl/ n scalpello m ● vt (pt/pp **chiselled**) scalpellare

**chit** /tʃɪt/ n bigliettino m

**chitchat** /'tʃɪ(t)tʃæt/ n fam chiacchiere fpl; **spend one's time in idle** ~ fam perdere tempo in chiacchiere

**chivalrous** /'ʃɪvlrəs/ a cavalleresco

**chivalrously** /'ʃɪvlrəslɪ/ adv con cavalleria

**chivalry** /'ʃɪvlrɪ/ n cavalleria f

**chives** /tʃaɪvz/ npl erba f cipollina

**chlorine** /'klɔːriːn/ n cloro m

**chlorofluorocarbon** /klɔːrəʊˈfluərəʊˈkɑː-b(ə)n/ n clorofluorocarburo m

**chloroform** /ˈklɒrəfɔːm/ n cloroformio m

**chlorophyll** /ˈklɒrəfɪl/ n clorofilla f

**choc ice** n Br gelato m ricoperto di cioccolato

**chock** /tʃɒk/ n zeppa f

**chock-a-block** /tʃɒkəˈblɒk/, **chock-full** /tʃɒkˈfʊl/ a pieno zeppo

**chocolate** /ˈtʃɒkələt/ n cioccolato m; (drink) cioccolata f; **a ~** un cioccolatino

**choice** /tʃɔɪs/ n scelta f ● a scelto

**choir** /ˈkwaɪə(r)/ n coro m

**choirboy** /ˈkwaɪəbɔɪ/ n corista m

**choirgirl** /ˈkwaɪəɡɜːl/ n corista m

**choke** /tʃəʊk/ n Auto aria f ● vt/i soffocare; **I ~d on a fishbone** mi è rimasta in gola una lisca

**choker** /ˈtʃəʊkə(r)/ n girocollo m

**cholera** /ˈkɒlərə/ n colera m

**cholesterol** /kəˈlestərɒl/ n colesterolo m

■ **chomp on** /tʃɒmp/ vi fam masticare rumorosamente

**choose** /tʃuːz/ vt/i (pt **chose**, pp **chosen**) scegliere; **~ to do sth** scegliere di fare qcsa; **as you ~y** come vuoi

**choos[e]y** /ˈtʃuːzɪ/ a fam difficile

**chop** /tʃɒp/ n (blow) colpo m (d'ascia); Culin costata f; **get the ~** ⟨fam: employee⟩ essere licenziato; ⟨project:⟩ essere bocciato ● vt (pt/pp **chopped**) tagliare

■ **chop down** vt abbattere ⟨tree⟩

■ **chop off** vt spaccare

**chopper** /ˈtʃɒpə(r)/ n accetta f; fam elicottero m

**chopping: chopping block** n ceppo m; **put one's head on the ~ ~** fig esporsi a rischi. **chopping board** n tagliere m. **chopping knife** n coltello m

**choppy** /ˈtʃɒpɪ/ a increspato

**chopsticks** /ˈtʃɒpstɪks/ npl bastoncini mpl cinesi

**choral** /ˈkɔːrəl/ a corale; **~ society** coro m

**chord** /kɔːd/ n Mus corda f

**chore** /tʃɔː(r)/ n corvé f inv; [household] **~s** faccende fpl domestiche

**choreographer** /kɒrɪˈɒɡrəfə(r)/ n coreografo, -a mf

**choreography** /kɒrɪˈɒɡrəfɪ/ n coreografia f

**chorister** /ˈkɒrɪstə(r)/ n corista mf

**chortle** /ˈtʃɔːtl/ vi ridacchiare

**chorus** /ˈkɔːrəs/ n coro m; (of song) ritornello m

**chorus girl** n ballerina f di varietà

**chose, chosen** /tʃəʊz, ˈtʃəʊzn/ see **choose**

**chowder** /ˈtʃaʊdə/n/ n zuppa m di pesce

**chow mein** /tʃaʊˈmeɪn/ n piatto m cinese di spaghetti fritti con gamberetti, ecc. e verdure

**Christ** /kraɪst/ n Cristo m; **~ Almighty!** fam porca miseria!

**christen** /ˈkrɪs(ə)n/ vt battezzare

**christening** /ˈkrɪsnɪŋ/ n battesimo m

**Christian** /ˈkrɪstʃən/ a & n cristiano, -a mf

**Christianity** /krɪstɪˈænətɪ/ n cristianesimo m

**Christian name** n nome m di battesimo

**Christmas** /ˈkrɪsməs/ n Natale m ● attrib di Natale

**Christmas: Christmas box** n Br mancia f natalizia. **Christmas card** n biglietto m d'auguri di Natale. **Christmas carol** n canto m natalizio, canto m di Natale. **Christmas cracker** n tubo m di cartone colorato contente una sorpresa. **Christmas Day** n il giorno di Natale. **Christmas Eve** n la vigilia di Natale. **Christmas present** n regalo m di Natale. **Christmas stocking** n calza f (per i doni di Babbo Natale). **Christmas tree** n albero m di Natale

**chrome** /krəʊm/ n, **chromium** /ˈkrəʊmɪəm/ n cromo m

**chromium-plated** /-ˈpleɪtɪd/ a cromato

**chromosome** /ˈkrəʊməsəʊm/ n cromosoma m

**chronic** /ˈkrɒnɪk/ a cronico

**chronicle** /ˈkrɒnɪkl/ n cronaca f

**chronological** /krɒnəˈlɒdʒɪkl/ a cronologico

**chronologically** /krɒnəˈlɒdʒɪklɪ/ adv ⟨ordered⟩ in ordine cronologico

**chrysalis** /ˈkrɪsəlɪs/ n crisalide f

**chrysanthemum** /krɪˈsænθəməm/ n crisantemo m

**chubby** /ˈtʃʌbɪ/ a (-ier, -iest) paffuto

**chuck** /tʃʌk/ vt fam buttare

■ **chuck in** vt fam mollare ⟨job, boyfriend⟩

■ **chuck out** vt fam buttare via ⟨object⟩; buttare fuori ⟨person⟩

■ **chuck up** vt fam = **chuck in**

**chuckle** /ˈtʃʌk(ə)l/ vi ridacchiare

**chuffed** /tʃʌft/ a fam felice come una Pasqua

**chug** /tʃʌɡ/ vi **the train ~ged into/out of the station** il treno è entrato nella/uscito dalla stazione sbuffando

**chum** /tʃʌm/ n fam amico, -a mf

**chummy** /ˈtʃʌmɪ/ a fam **be ~ with** essere amico di

**chump** /tʃʌmp/ n fam zuccone m, -a f; Culin braciola f

**chunk** /tʃʌŋk/ n grosso pezzo m

**chunky** /ˈtʃʌŋkɪ/ a ⟨sweater⟩ di lana grossa; ⟨jewellery⟩ massiccio; ⟨fam: person⟩ tarchiato

**Chunnel** /ˈtʃʌnl/ n Br fam tunnel m inv sotto la Manica

**church** /tʃɜːtʃ/ n chiesa f

**church hall** n sala f parrocchiale

**churchyard** /ˈtʃɜːtʃjɑːd/ n cimitero m

**churlish** /ˈtʃɜːlɪʃ/ a sgarbato

**churn** /tʃɜːn/ n zangola f; (for milk) bidone m ● vt churn out sfornare

**chute** /ʃuːt/ n scivolo m; (for rubbish) canale m di scarico

**chutney** /ˈtʃʌtnɪ/ n salsa f piccante a base di frutti e spezie

**CID** abbr **Criminal Investigation Department**

**cider** /ˈsaɪdə(r)/ n sidro m

**cigar** /sɪˈɡɑː(r)/ n sigaro m

**cigarette** /sɪɡəˈret/ n sigaretta f

**cigarette: cigarette butt, cigarette end**

*n* cicca *f*, mozzicone *m* di sigaretta. **cigarette lighter** *n* accendino *m*

**cinch** /sɪntʃ/ *n fam* **it's a ~** è un gioco da ragazzi

**cinder** /'sɪndə(r)/ *n* (*glowing*) brace *f*; **burn sth to a**.~ carbonizzare qcsa

**Cinderella** /sɪndə'relə/ *n* cenerentola *f*

**cinder track** *n* pista *f* di cenere

**cine-camera** /'sɪnɪ-/ *n* cinepresa *f*

**cine-film** *n* filmino *m* a passo ridotto

**cinema** /'sɪnɪmə/ *n* cinema *m inv*

**cinema complex** *n* cinema *m inv* multisale

**cinemagoer** /'sɪnɪməgəʊə(r)/ *n* (*spectator*) spettatore, -trice *mf*; (*regular*) cinefilo, -a *mf*

**cinematography** /sɪnəmə'tɒgrəfɪ/ *n* cinematografia *f*

**cinnamon** /'sɪnəmən/ *n* cannella *f*

**cipher** /'saɪfə(r)/ *n* (*code*) cifre *fpl*; *fig* nullità *f inv*

**circa** /'sɜːkə/ *prep* circa

**circle** /'sɜːkl/ *n* cerchio *m*; *Theat* galleria *f*; **in a ~** in cerchio ● *vt* girare intorno a; cerchiare (*mistake*) ● *vi* descrivere dei cerchi

**circuit** /'sɜːkɪt/ *n* circuito *m*; (*lap*) giro *m*

**circuit board** *n* circuito *m* stampato

**circuitous** /sə'kju:ɪtəs/ *a* **~ route** percorso *m* lungo e indiretto

**circular** /'sɜːkjʊlə(r)/ *a* & *n* circolare *f*

**circular letter** *n* circolare *f*

**circular saw** *n* sega *f* circolare

**circulate** /'sɜːkjʊleɪt/ *vt* far circolare ● *vi* circolare

**circulation** /sɜːkjʊ'leɪʃn/ *n* circolazione *f*; (*of newspaper*) tiratura *f*

**circulatory** /sɜːkjʊ'leɪtərɪ/ *a Med* circolatorio

**circumcise** /'sɜːkəmsaɪz/ *vt* circoncidere

**circumcision** /sɜːkəm'sɪʒn/ *n* circoncisione *f*

**circumference** /ʃə'kʌmfərəns/ *n* conconferenza *f*

**circumflex** /'sɜːkəmfleks/ *n* accento *m* circonflesso

**circumnavigate** /sɜːkəm'nævɪgeɪt/ *vt* doppiare (*cape*); circumnavigare (*world*)

**circumnavigation** /sɜːkəmnævɪ'geɪʃn/ *n* circumnavigazione *f*

**circumspect** /'sɜːkəmspekt/ *a* circospetto

**circumspectly** /'sɜːkəmspektlɪ/ *adv* in modo circospetto

**circumstance** /'sɜːkəmstəns/ *n* circostanza *f*; **~s** *pl* (*financial*) condizioni *fpl* finanziarie

**circumstantial** /sɜːkəm'stænʃl/ *a* (*Jur: evidence*) indiziario; (*detailed*) circostanziato

**circus** /'sɜːkəs/ *n* circo *m*

**cirrhosis** /sɪ'rəʊsɪs/ *n* cirrosi *f inv*

**CIS** *abbr* (**Commonwealth of Independent States**) CSI *f*

**cistern** /'sɪstən/ *n* (*tank*) cisterna *f*; (*of WC*) serbatoio *m*

**citadel** /'sɪtədel/ *n* cittadella *f*

**cite** /saɪt/ *vt* citare

**citizen** /'sɪtɪzn/ *n* cittadino, -a *mf*; (*of town*) abitante *mf*

**citizen: Citizens' Advice Bureau** *n* ufficio *m* di consulenza legale gratuita per i cittadini. **citizen's arrest** *n* arresto *m* effettuato da un privato cittadino. **citizens' band** *n Radio* banda *f* cittadina

**citizenship** /'sɪtɪznʃɪp/ *n* cittadinanza *f*

**citric acid** /sɪtrɪk'æsɪd/ acido *m* citrico

**citrus** /'sɪtrəs/ *n* ~ [**fruit**] agrume *m*

**city** /'sɪtɪ/ *n* città *f inv*; **the C~** la City [di Londra]

**city centre** *n Br* centro *m* [della città]

**city slicker** *n fam* cittadino *m* sofisticato

**civic** /'sɪvɪk/ *a* civico ● **~s** *npl* educazione *fsg* civica

**civic centre** *n* centro *m* municipale

**civil** /'ʃɪvl/ *a* civile

**civil engineer** *n* ingeniere *m* civile

**civil engineering** *n* ingegneria *f* civile

**civilian** /sɪ'vɪljən/ *a* civile; **in ~ clothes** in borghese ● *n* civile *mf*

**civility** /sɪ'vɪlətɪ/ *n* cortesia *f*

**civilization** /sɪvɪlaɪ'zeɪʃn/ *n* civiltà *f inv*

**civilize** /'sɪvɪlaɪz/ *vt* civilizzare

**civilized** /'sɪvɪlaɪzd/ *a* (*country*) civilizzato; (*person, behaviour*) civile; **become ~** civilizzarsi

**civil: civil law** *n* diritto *m* civile. **civil liability** *n Jur* responsabilità *f inv* civile. **civil liberty** *n* libertà *f inv* civile

**civilly** /'sɪvɪlɪ/ *adv* civilmente

**civil: civil rights** *npl* diritti *mpl* civili ● *attrib* (*march, activist*) per i diritti civili. **civil servant** *n* impiegato, -a *mf* statale. **Civil Service** *n* pubblica amministrazione *f*. **civil war** *n* guerra *f* civile. **civil wedding** *n* matrimonio *m* civile

**civvies** /'sɪvɪz/ *npl fam* **in ~** in borghese

**cl** *abbr* (**centilitre(s)**) cl

**clad** /klæd/ *a* vestito (**in** di)

**cladding** /'klædɪŋ/ *n* rivestimento *m*

**claim** /kleɪm/ *n* richiesta *f*; (*right*) diritto *m*; (*assertion*) dichiarazione *f*; **lay ~ to sth** rivendicare qcsa ● *vt* richiedere; reclamare (*lost property*); rivendicare (*ownership*); **~ that** sostenere che

■ **claim back** *vt* reclamare (*money*)

**claimant** /'kleɪmənt/ *n* richiedente *mf*; (*to throne*) pretendente *mf*

**clairvoyant** /kleə'vɔɪənt/ *n* chiaroveggente *mf*

**clam** /klæm/ *n Culin* vongola *f*

■ **clam up** *vi* zittirsi

**clamber** /'klæmbə(r)/ *vi* arrampicarsi

**clammy** /'klæmɪ/ *a* (**-ier, -iest**) appiccicaticcio

**clamour** /'klæmə(r)/ *n* (*noise*) clamore *m*; (*protest*) rimostranza *f* ● *vi* ~ **for** chiedere a gran voce

**clamp** /klæmp/ *n* morsa *f* ● *vt* ammorsare; *Auto* mettere i ceppi bloccaruote a

■ **clamp down** *vi fam* essere duro

■ **clamp down on** *vt* reprimere

**clan** /klæn/ *n* clan *m inv*

**clandestine** /klæn'destɪn/ a clandestino

**clang** /klæŋ/ n suono m metallico

**clanger** /'klæŋə(r)/ n fam gaffe f inv

**clank** /klæŋk/ n rumore m metallico ● vi fare un rumore metallico

**clannish** /'klænɪʃ/ a ⟨pej: family, profession⟩ chiuso

**clap** /klæp/ n **give sb a ~** applaudire qcno; **~ of thunder** tuono m ● vt/i (pt/pp **clapped**) applaudire; **~ one's hands** applaudire

**clapboard** /'klæpbɔːd/ n Am rivestimento m di legno ● attrib Am rivestito di legno

**clapped out** /klæpt/ a fam ⟨past it⟩ sfinito; ⟨exhausted⟩ stanco morto; ⟨car, machine⟩ scassato

**clapping** /'klæpɪŋ/ n applausi mpl

**claptrap** /'klæptræp/ n fam sciocchezze fpl

**claret** /'klærət/ n claret m inv

**clarification** /klærɪfɪ'keɪʃn/ n chiarimento m

**clarify** /'klærɪfaɪ/ vt/i (pt/pp -ied) chiarire

**clarinet** /klærɪ'net/ n clarinetto m

**clarinettist** /klærɪ'netɪst/ n clarinettista mf

**clarity** /'klærətɪ/ n chiarezza f

**clash** /klæʃ/ n scontro m; ⟨noise⟩ fragore m ● vi scontrarsi; ⟨colours:⟩ stonare; ⟨events:⟩ coincidere

**clasp** /klɑːsp/ n chiusura f ● vt agganciare; ⟨hold⟩ stringere

**class** /klɑːs/ n classe f; ⟨lesson⟩ corso m ● vt classificare

**class-conscious** a classista

**class-consciousness** n classismo m

**classic** /'klæsɪk/ a classico ● n classico m; **~s** pl Univ lettere fpl classiche

**classical** /'klæsɪk(ə)l/ a classico

**classification** /klæsɪfɪ'keɪʃn/ n classificazione f

**classified ad** /klæsɪfaɪd'æd/ n annuncio m

**classified section** n pagina f degli annunci

**classify** /'klæsɪfaɪ/ vt (pt/pp -ied) classificare

**class: classmate** n compagno, -a mf di classe. **classroom** n aula f. **class system** n sistema m classista

**classy** /'klɑːsɪ/ a (-ier, -iest) fam d'alta classe

**clatter** /'klætə(r)/ n fracasso m ● vi far fracasso

**clause** /klɔːz/ n clausola f; Gram proposizione f

**claustrophobia** /klɒstrə'fəʊbɪə/ n claustrofobia f

**claustrophobic** /klɒstrə'fəʊbɪk/ a claustrofobico

**clavichord** /'klævɪkɔːd/ n clavicordo m

**clavicle** /'klævɪkl/ n clavicola f

**claw** /klɔː/ n artiglio m; ⟨of crab, lobster & Techn⟩ tenaglia f ● vt ⟨cat:⟩ graffiare

**clay** /kleɪ/ n argilla f

**clayey** /'kleɪɪ/ a ⟨soil⟩ argilloso

**clay pigeon shooting** n tiro m al piattello

**clean** /kliːn/ a pulito, lindo ● adv completa-

mente ● vt pulire ⟨shoes, windows⟩; **~ one's teeth** lavarsi i denti; **have a coat ~ed** portare un cappotto in lavanderia

■ **clean out** vt ripulire ⟨room⟩; **be ~ed out** ⟨fig: have no money⟩ essere senza un soldo

■ **clean up** vt pulire ● vi far pulizia

**clean-cut** a ⟨image, person⟩ rispettabile

**cleaner** /'kliːnə(r)/ n uomo m/donna f delle pulizie; ⟨substance⟩ detersivo m; [dry] **~'s** lavanderia f, tintoria f

**cleaning** /'kliːnɪŋ/ n pulizia f; **do the ~** fare le pulizie

**cleaning lady** n donna f delle pulizie

**cleaning product** n detergente m

**cleanliness** /'klenlɪnɪs/ n pulizia f

**clean-living** /-'lɪvɪŋ/ n vita f integra ● a ⟨person⟩ integro

**cleanse** /klenz/ vt pulire

**cleanser** /'klenzə(r)/ n detergente m

**clean-shaven** /-'ʃeɪvən/ a sbarbato

**clean sheet** n **start with a ~** fig voltare pagina

**cleansing cream** /'klenzɪŋ/ n latte m detergente

**clear** /klɪə(r)/ a chiaro; ⟨conscience⟩ pulito; ⟨road⟩ libero; ⟨profit, advantage, majority⟩ netto; ⟨sky⟩ sereno; ⟨water⟩ limpido; ⟨glass⟩ trasparente; **make sth ~** mettere qcsa in chiaro; **have I made myself ~?** mi sono fatto capire?; **I'm not ~ about what I have to do** non mi è ben chiaro quello che devo fare; **five ~ days** cinque giorni buoni; **be in the ~** essere a posto ● adv **stand ~ of** allontanarsi da; **keep ~ of** tenersi alla larga da ● vt sgombrare ⟨room, street⟩; sparecchiare ⟨table⟩; ⟨acquit⟩ scagionare; ⟨authorize⟩ autorizzare; scavalcare senza toccare ⟨fence, wall⟩; guadagnare ⟨sum of money⟩; passare ⟨Customs⟩; **~ one's throat** schiarirsi la gola ● vi ⟨face, sky:⟩ rasserenarsi; ⟨fog:⟩ dissiparsi

■ **clear away** vt metter via

■ **clear off** vi fam filar via

■ **clear out** vt sgombrare ● vi fam filar via

■ **clear up** vt ⟨tidy⟩ mettere a posto; chiarire ⟨mystery⟩ ● vi ⟨weather:⟩ schiarirsi

**clearance** /'klɪərəns/ n ⟨space⟩ spazio m libero; ⟨authorization⟩ autorizzazione f; ⟨Customs⟩ sdoganamento m

**clearance sale** n liquidazione f

**clear-cut** a ⟨plan, division⟩ ben definito; ⟨problem, rule⟩ chiaro; ⟨difference, outline⟩ netto; **the matter is not so ~** la faccenda non è così semplice

**clear-headed** /-'hedɪd/ a lucido

**clearing** /'klɪərɪŋ/ n radura f

**clearly** /'klɪəlɪ/ adv chiaramente

**clear-sighted** /-'saɪtɪd/ a perspicace

**clearway** /'klɪəweɪ/ n Auto strada f con divieto di sosta

**cleavage** /'kliːvɪdʒ/ n ⟨woman's⟩ décolleté m inv

**cleave** /kliːv/ vt spaccare

**cleaver** /'kliːvə(r)/ n mannaia f

**clef** /klef/ n Mus chiave f

**cleft** /kleft/ n fenditura f

**clemency** /'klemənsɪ/ n clemenza f

**clement** /'klemənt/ a clemente

**clench** /klentʃ/ vt serrare

**clergy** /'klɜ:dʒɪ/ npl clero m

**clergyman** /'klɜ:dʒɪmən/ n ecclesiastico m

**cleric** /'klerɪk/ n ecclesiastico m

**clerical** /'klerɪlk/ a impiegatizio; Relig clericale

**clerical assistant** n impiegato, -a mf

**clerk** /klɑ:k/, Am /klɜ:k/ n impiegato, -a mf; (Am: shop assistant) commesso, -a mf

**clever** /'klevə(r)/ a intelligente; (skilful) abile

**cleverly** /'klevəlɪ/ adv intelligentemente; (skilfully) abilmente

**cliché** /'kli:ʃeɪ/ n cliché m inv

**clichéd** /'kli:ʃeɪd/ a ⟨idea, technique⟩ convenzionale; ⟨art, music⟩ stereotipato; ~ **expression** frase f fatta

**click** /klɪk/ vi scattare; (Comput: with mouse) cliccare ● n (Comput: with mouse) click m inv ■ **click on** vt Comput cliccare su

**client** /'klaɪənt/ n cliente mf

**clientele** /kli:ɒn'tel/ n clientela f

**cliff** /klɪf/ n scogliera f

**cliffhanger** /'klɪfhæŋə(r)/ n **it was a real ~** ci ha lasciato in sospeso

**climate** /'klaɪmət/ n clima f

**climatic** /klaɪ'mætɪk/ a climatico

**climax** /'klaɪmæks/ n punto m culminante

**climb** /klaɪm/ n salita f ● vt scalare ⟨mountain⟩; arrampicarsi su ⟨ladder, tree⟩ ● vi arrampicarsi; (rise) salire; ⟨road:⟩ salire ■ **climb down** vi scendere; (from ladder, tree) scendere; fig tornare sui propri passi ■ **climb over** vt scavalcare ⟨fence, wall⟩ ■ **climb up** vt salire su ⟨hill⟩

**climber** /'klaɪmə(r)/ n alpinista mf; (plant) rampicante m

**climbing: climbing boot** n scarpone m da alpinismo. **climbing expedition** n scalata f. **climbing frame** n struttura f su cui possono arrampicarsi i bambini

**clinch** /klɪntʃ/ vt fam concludere ⟨deal⟩ ● n (in boxing) clinch m inv

**clincher** /'klɪntʃə(r)/ n (fam: act, remark) fattore m decisivo; (argument) argomento m decisivo

**cling** /klɪŋ/ vi (pt/pp clung) aggrapparsi; (stick) aderire

**cling film** n pellicola f trasparente

**clingy** /'klɪŋɪ/ a ⟨dress⟩ attillato; ⟨person⟩ appiccicoso

**clinic** /'klɪnɪk/ n ambulatorio m

**clinical** /'klɪnɪkl/ a clinico

**clinically** /'klɪnɪklɪ/ adv clinicamente

**clink** /klɪŋk/ n tintinnio m; (fam: prison) galera f ● vi tintinnare

**clip¹** /klɪp/ n fermaglio m; (jewellery) spilla f ● vt (pt/pp clipped) attaccare

**clip²** n (extract) taglio m ● vt obliterare ⟨ticket⟩

**clip: clipboard** n fermablocco m. **clip-clop** n rumore m fatto dagli zoccoli dei cavalli. **clip-on** a ⟨bow tie⟩ con la clip. **clip-on**

**microphone** n microfono m con la clip.

**clip-ons** npl (earrings) orecchini mpl con le clip

**clippers** /'klɪpəz/ npl (for hair) rasoio m; (for hedge) tosasiepi m inv; (for nails) tronchesina f

**clipping** /'klɪpɪŋ/ n (from newspaper) ritaglio m

**clique** /kli:k/ n cricca f

**cliquey, cliquish** /'kli:kɪ, 'kli:kɪʃ/ a ⟨atmosphere⟩ esclusivo; ⟨profession, group⟩ chiuso

**cloak** /kləʊk/ n mantello m

**cloak: cloak-and-dagger** a ⟨film⟩ d'avventura; (surreptitious) clandestino. **cloakroom** n guardaroba m inv; (toilet) bagno m. **cloakroom attendant** n (Br: at toilets) addetto, -a mf ai bagni; (in hotel) guardarobiere, -a mf. **cloakroom ticket** n scontrino m del guardaroba

**clobber** /'klɒbə(r)/ n fam armamentario m ● vt (fam: hit) colpire; (defeat) stracciare

**cloche** /klɒʃ/ n (in garden) campana f di vetro

**cloche hat** n cloche f inv

**clock** /klɒk/ n orologio m; (fam: speedometer) tachimetro m ■ **clock in** vi attaccare ■ **clock out** vi staccare

**clock: clock face** n quadrante m. **clockmaker** n orologiaio, -a mf. **clock radio** n radiosveglia f. **clock speed** n Comput velocità f di clock. **clock tower** n torre f dell'orologio. **clock-watch** vi guardare continuamente l'orologio. **clockwise** a & adv in senso orario. **clockwork** n meccanismo m; **like ~** fam alla perfezione ● attrib a molla

**clod** /klɒd/ n zolla f

**clog** /klɒg/ n zoccolo m ● vt (pt/pp clogged) **~ [up]** intasare ⟨drain⟩; inceppare ⟨mechanism⟩ ● vi ⟨drain:⟩ intasarsi

**cloister** /'klɔɪstə(r)/ n chiostro m

**clone** /kləʊn/ n Biol, Comput, fig clone m ● vt clonare

**close¹** /kləʊs/ a vicino; ⟨friend⟩ intimo; ⟨weather⟩ afoso; **have a ~ shave** fam scamparla bella; **be ~ to sb** essere unito a qcno ● adv vicino; **~ by** vicino; **it's ~ on five o'clock** sono quasi le cinque

**close²** /kləʊz/ n fine f; **draw to a ~** concludere ● vt chiudere ● vi chiudersi; ⟨shop:⟩ chiudere ■ **close down** vt chiudere ● vi ⟨TV station:⟩ interrompere la trasmissione; ⟨factory:⟩ chiudere ■ **close in** vi ⟨mist:⟩ calare; ⟨enemy:⟩ avvicinarsi da ogni lato ■ **close up** vi (come closer together) stringersi; ⟨shop:⟩ chiudere ● vt (bring closer together) avvicinare; chiudere ⟨shop⟩

**close combat** n corpo a corpo m inv

**close-cropped** /-'krɒpt/ a ⟨hair⟩ rasato

**closed-circuit television** /kləʊzdsɜ:kɪttelɪ'vɪʒən/ n televisione f a circuito chiuso

**closed shop** /kləʊzd'ʃɒp/ n azienda f che as-

*sume solo personale aderente ad un dato sindacato*

**close-fitting** /kləʊsˈfɪtɪŋ/ *a ⟨garment⟩* attillato

**close-knit** /kləʊsˈnɪt/ *a fig ⟨family, group⟩* affiatato

**closely** /ˈkləʊslɪ/ *adv* da vicino; *⟨watch, listen⟩* attentamente

**close season** /kləʊs/ *n* stagione *f* di chiusura della caccia e della pesca

**closet** /ˈklɒzɪt/ *n Am* armadio *m*

**close-up** /ˈkləʊs-/ *n* primo piano *m*

**closing: closing date** *n* data *f* di scadenza. **closing-down sale** *n* liquidazione *f* totale [per cessata attività]. **closing time** *n* orario *m* di chiusura

**closure** /ˈkləʊʒə(r)/ *n* chiusura *f*

**clot** /klɒt/ *n* grumo *m*; *(fam: idiot)* tonto, -a *mf* ● *vi (pt/pp* **clotted***) ⟨blood:⟩* coagularsi

**cloth** /klɒθ/ *n (fabric)* tessuto *m*; *(duster etc)* straccio *m*

**clothe** /kləʊð/ *vt* vestire

**clothes** /kləʊðz/ *npl* vestiti *mpl*, abiti *mpl*

**clothes: clothes-brush** *n* spazzola *f* per abiti. **clothes horse** *n* stendibiancheria *m inv*. **clothes-line** *n* corda *f* stendibiancheria

**clothing** /ˈkləʊðɪŋ/ *n* abbigliamento *m*

**clotted cream** *n Br* panna *f* rappresa (ottenuta scaldando il latte)

**cloud** /klaʊd/ *n* nuvola *f*

■ **cloud over** *vi* rannuvolarsi

**cloudburst** /ˈklaʊdbɜːst/ *n* acquazzone *m*

**cloudy** /ˈklaʊdɪ/ *a* (**-ier, -iest**) nuvoloso; *⟨liquid⟩* torbido

**clout** /klaʊt/ *n fam* colpo *m*; *(influence)* impatto *m* (**with** su) ● *vt fam* colpire

**clove** /kləʊv/ *n* chiodo *m* di garofano; ~ **of garlic** spicchio *m* d'aglio

**cloven foot, cloven hoof** /ˈkləʊvən/ *n (of animal)* zoccolo *m* fesso; *(of devil)* piede *m* biforcuto

**clover** /ˈkləʊvə(r)/ *n* trifoglio *m*

**clover leaf** *n* raccordo *m* di due autostrade

**clown** /klaʊn/ *n* pagliaccio *m* ● *vi* ~ [**about**] fare il pagliaccio

**club** /klʌb/ *n* club *m inv*; *(weapon)* clava *f*; *Sport* mazza *f*; ~**s** *pl (Cards)* fiori *mpl* ● *v (pt/pp* **clubbed***)* ● *vt* bastonare

■ **club together** *vi* unirsi

**club: club foot** *n* piede *m* deformato. **clubhouse** *n (for socializing)* circolo *m*; *(Am: for changing)* spogliatoio *m*. **club sandwich** *n* club-sandwich *m inv*

**cluck** /klʌk/ *vi* chiocciare

**clue** /kluː/ *n* indizio *m*; *(in crossword)* definizione *f*; **I haven't a ~** *fam* non ne ho idea

**clued-up** /kluːˈdʌp/ *a Br fam* beninformato

**clueless** /ˈkluːlɪs/ *a Br fam* incapace

**clump** /klʌmp/ *n* gruppo *m*

**clump about, clump around** *vi (walk noisily)* camminare con passo pesante

**clumsily** /ˈklʌmzɪlɪ/ *adv* in modo maldestro; *⟨remark⟩* senza tatto

**clumsiness** /ˈklʌmzɪnɪs/ *n* goffaggine *f*

**clumsy** /ˈklʌmzɪ/ *a* (**-ier, -iest**) maldestro; *⟨tool⟩* scomodo; *⟨remark⟩* senza tatto

**clung** /klʌŋ/ *see* **cling**

**cluster** /ˈklʌstə(r)/ *n* gruppo *m* ● *vi* raggrupparsi (**round** intorno a)

**clutch** /klʌtʃ/ *n* stretta *f*; *Auto* frizione *f*; **be in sb's ~** essere in balia di qcno ● *vt* stringere; *(grab)* afferrare ● *vi* ~ **at** afferrare

**clutch bag** *n* pochette *f inv*

**clutch cable** *n* cavo *m* della frizione

**clutter** /ˈklʌtə(r)/ *n* caos *m* ● *vt* ~ [**up**] ingombrare

**cm** *abbr (**centimetre**)* cm

**CND** *n abbr (**Campaign for Nuclear Disarmament**)* campagna *f* per il disarmo nucleare

**Co.** *abbr (**company**)* C., C.ia; **and ~** *hum* e compagnia; *abbr (**county**)* contea *f*

**c/o** *abbr (**care of**)* c/o, presso

**coach** /kəʊtʃ/ *n* pullman *m inv*; *Rail* vagone *m*; *(horse-drawn)* carrozza *f*; *Sport* allenatore, -trice *mf* ● *vt* fare esercitare; *Sport* allenare

**coach: coach party** *n Br* gruppo *m* di gitanti *(in pullman)*. **coach station** *n Br* stazione *f* dei pullman. **coach trip** *n* viaggio *m* in pullman. **coachwork** *n Br* carrozzeria *f*

**coagulate** /kəʊˈægjʊleɪt/ *vi* coagularsi

**coagulation** /kəʊəgjʊˈleɪʃn/ *n* coagulazione *f*

**coal** /kəʊl/ *n* carbone *m*

**coalition** /kəʊəˈlɪʃn/ *n* coalizione *f*

**coal: coal-mine** *n* miniera *f* di carbone. **coal scuttle** *n* secchio *m* del carbone. **coal seam** *n* giacimento *m* di carbone

**coarse** /kɔːs/ *a* grossolano; *⟨joke⟩* spinto

**coarse-grained** /-ˈgreɪnd/ *a ⟨texture⟩* a grana grossa

**coarsely** /ˈkɔːslɪ/ *adv ⟨ground⟩* grossolanamente; *⟨joke⟩* in modo spinto

**coast** /kəʊst/ *n* costa *f* ● *vi (freewheel)* scendere a ruota libera; *Auto* scendere in folle

**coastal** /ˈkəʊstəl/ *a* costiero

**coastguard** /ˈkəʊs(t)gɑːd/ *n* guardia *f* costiera

**coaster** /ˈkəʊstə(r)/ *n (mat)* sottobicchiere *m inv*

**coastline** /ˈkəʊstlaɪn/ *n* litorale *m*

**coat** /kəʊt/ *n* cappotto *m*; *(of animal)* manto *m*; *(of paint)* mano *f*; ~ **of arms** stemma *f* ● *vt* coprire; *(with paint)* ricoprire

**coat-hanger** *n* gruccia *f*

**coat-hook** *n* gancio *m* [appendiabiti]

**coating** /ˈkəʊtɪŋ/ *n* rivestimento *m*; *(of paint)* stato *m*

**coat-tails** *npl* falde *fpl*; **be always hanging on sb's ~** attaccarsi sempre alle falde di qcno

**coax** /kəʊks/ *vt* convincere con le moine

**cob** /kɒb/ *n (of corn)* pannocchia *f*

**cobble** /ˈkɒbl/ *vt* ~ **together** raffazzonare

**cobbler** /ˈkɒblə(r)/ *n* ciabattino *m*

**cobblestones** /ˈkɒbəlstəʊnz/ *npl* ciottolato *msg*

**cobra** /ˈkəʊbrə/ *n* cobra *m inv*

**cobweb** /ˈkɒbweb/ *n* ragnatela *f*

**cocaine** /kə'keɪn/ n cocaina f

**coccyx** /'kɒksɪks/ n coccige m

**cock** /kɒk/ n gallo m; (any male bird) maschio m; vulg cazzo m ● vt sollevare il grilletto di (gun); ~ **its ears** (animal:) drizzare le orecchie

■ **cock up** fam vt incasinare ● vi incasinarsi

**cock-a-doodle-doo** /kɒkədu:d(ə)l'du:/ int chicchirichì

**cock-a-hoop** a fam al settimo cielo

**cock-and-bull story** n fam panzana f

**cockatoo** /kɒkə'tu:/ n cacatoa m inv

**cockcrow** /'kɒkkrəʊ/ n at ~ al primo canto del gallo

**cocked hat** /kɒk'hæt/ n fam **knock sb/sth into a ~** ~ schiacciare qcno/qcsa

**cockerel** /'kɒkərəl/ n galletto m

**cocker spaniel** /'kɒkə(r)/ n cocker m inv [spaniel]

**cock-eyed** /-'aɪd/ a fam storto; (absurd) assurdo

**cockfighting** /'kɒkfaɪtɪŋ/ n combattimenti mpl di galli

**cockle** /'kɒkl/ n cardio m

**cockney** /'kɒknɪ/ n (dialect) dialetto m londinese; (person) abitante mf dell'est di Londra

**cockpit** /'kɒkpɪt/ n Aeron cabina f

**cockroach** /'kɒkrəʊtʃ/ n scarafaggio m

**cocksure** /kɒk'ʃʊə(r)/ a (person, manner, attitude) presuntuoso

**cocktail** /'kɒkteɪl/ n cocktail m inv

**cocktail:** **cocktail bar** n [cocktail] bar m inv. **cocktail dress** n abito m da cocktail. cocktail-party m inv. **cocktail party** n cocktail m inv. **cocktail shaker** n shaker m inv. **cocktail stick** n stecchino m

**cock-up** n sl **make a ~** fare un casino (of con)

**cocky** /'kɒkɪ/ a (-ier, -iest) fam presuntuoso

**cocoa** /'kəʊkəʊ/ n cacao m

**coconut** /'kəʊkənʌt/ n noce f di cocco

**coconut palm** n palma f di cocco

**coconut shy** n Br tiro m al bersaglio in cui si devono abbattere noci di cocco

**cocoon** /kə'ku:n/ n bozzolo m

**COD** abbr (cash on delivery) pagamento m alla consegna

**cod** /kɒd/ n inv merluzzo m

**coddle** /'kɒd(ə)l/ vt coccolare

**code** /kəʊd/ n codice m

**coded** /'kəʊdɪd/ a codificato

**codeine** /'kəʊdi:n/ n codeina f

**coding** /'kəʊdɪŋ/ n Comput codifica f

**cod-liver oil** n olio m di fegato di merluzzo

**coeducational** /kəʊedjʊ'keɪʃənəl/ a misto

**coefficient** /kəʊɪ'fɪʃənt/ n coefficiente m

**coerce** /kəʊ'ɜ:s/ vt costringere

**coercion** /kəʊ'ɜ:ʃn/ n coercizione f

**coexist** /kəʊɪg'zɪst/ vi coesistere

**coexistence** /kəʊɪg'zɪstəns/ n coesistenza f

**coffee** /'kɒfɪ/ n caffè m inv

**coffee:** **coffee bar** n caffè m inv, bar m inv. **coffee bean** n chicco m di caffè. **coffee bre-**

ak n pausa f per il caffè. **coffee grinder** n macinacaffè m inv. **coffee machine** n (in café) macchina f per l'espresso. **coffeemaker** n (on stove) caffettiera f; (electric) macchina f per il caffè (con il filtro). **coffee morning** n Br riunione m mattutina in cui viene servito il caffè. **coffee percolator** n (on stove) caffettiera f; (electric) macchina f per il caffè (con il filtro). **coffee-pot** n caffettiera f. **coffee shop** n torrefazione f; (café) caffè m inv, bar m inv. **coffee table** n tavolino m

**coffer** /'kɒfə(r)/ n forziere m

**coffin** /'kɒfɪn/ n bara f

**cog** /kɒg/ n Techn dente m

**cogent** /'kəʊdʒənt/ a convincente

**cogitate** /'kɒdʒɪteɪt/ vi cogitare

**cognac** /'kɒnjæk/ n Cognac m

**cognoscenti** /kɒnə'ʃentɪ/ npl intenditori mpl

**cogwheel** /'kɒgwi:l/ n ruota f dentata

**cohabit** /kəʊ'hæbɪt/ vi Jur convivere

**coherent** /kəʊ'hɪərənt/ a coerente; (when speaking) logico

**cohesion** /kəʊ'hi:ʒən/ n coesione f

**cohort** /'kəʊhɔ:t/ n fig seguito m

**coil** /kɔɪl/ n rotolo m; Electr bobina f; ~s pl spire fpl ● vt ~[up] avvolgere

**coin** /kɔɪn/ n moneta f ● vt coniare (word)

**coinage** /'kɔɪnɪdʒ/ n (of coins, currency) coniatura f; (word, phrase) neologismo m

**coin box** n (pay phone) telefono m a monete; (on pay phone, in laundromat) gettoniera f

**coincide** /kəʊɪn'saɪd/ vi coincidere

**coincidence** /kəʊ'ɪnsɪdəns/ n coincidenza f

**coincidental** /kəʊɪnsɪ'dentl/ a casuale

**coincidentally** /kəʊɪnsɪ'dentlɪ/ adv casualmente

**Coke®** /kəʊk/ n Coca® f

**coke** n [carbone m] coke m

**colander** /'kʌləndə(r)/ n Culin colapasta m inv

**cold** /kəʊld/ a freddo; **I'm ~** ho freddo; **get ~ feet** farsi prendere dalla fifa; **give sb the ~ shoulder** trattare qcno freddamente ● n freddo m; Med raffreddore m

**cold:** **cold-blooded** /-'blʌdɪd/ a spietato. **cold calling** n Comm visita f senza preavviso. **cold comfort** n magra consolazione f. **cold frame** n telaio m coperto di vetro per proteggere le piante dal gelo. **cold-hearted** /-'hɑ:tɪd/ a insensibile

**coldly** /'kəʊldlɪ/ adv fig freddamente

**cold meat** n salumi mpl

**coldness** /'kəʊldnɪs/ n freddezza f

**cold:** **cold shoulder** n **give sb the ~ ~** snobbare qcno ● **cold-shoulder** vt trattare freddamente. **cold snap** n ondata f di freddo. **cold sore** n herpes m inv. **cold store** n cella f frigorifera. **cold sweat** n sudore m freddo; **bring sb out in a ~ ~** far sudare freddo qcno. **cold turkey** n (reaction) crisi f inv di astinenza; **be ~ ~** avere una crisi di astinenza; **quit ~ ~** smettere di colpo di drogarsi.

**Cold War** n guerra f fredda

**coleslaw** /'kəʊlslɔ:/ n insalata f di cavolo crudo, cipolle e carote in maionese

**colic** /'kɒlɪk/ n colica f

**collaborate** /kə'læbəreɪt/ vi collaborare; ~ **on sth** collaborare in qcsa

**collaboration** /kəlæbə'reɪʃn/ n collaborazione f; (with enemy) collaborazionismo m

**collaborator** /kə'læbəreɪtə(r)/ n collaboratore, -trice mf; (with enemy) collaborazionista mf

**collage** /kɒ'lɑ:ʒ/ n collage m inv; (film) montaggio m

**collapse** /kə'læps/ n crollo m ● vi ⟨person:⟩ svenire; ⟨roof, building:⟩ crollare

**collapsible** /kə'læpsəbl/ a pieghevole

**collar** /'kɒlə(r)/ n colletto m; (for animal) collare m

**collarbone** /'kɒləbəʊn/ n clavicola f

**collar size** n taglia f di camicia

**collate** /kə'leɪt/ vt collazionare

**collateral** /kɒ'lætərəl/ n garanzia f collaterale; **put up ~** offrire una garanzia collaterale

**collateral loan** a Fin prestito m con garanzia collaterale

**colleague** /'kɒli:g/ n collega mf

**collect** /kə'lekt/ vt andare a prendere ⟨person⟩; ritirare ⟨parcel, tickets⟩; riscuotere ⟨taxes⟩; raccogliere ⟨rubbish⟩; (as hobby) collezionare ● vi riunirsi ● adv **call ~** Am telefonare a carico del destinatario

**collected** /kə'lektɪd/ a controllato

**collection** /kə'lekʃn/ n collezione f; (in church) questua f; (of rubbish) raccolta f; (of post) levata f

**collective** /kə'lektɪv/ a collettivo

**collective: collective bargaining** n contrattazione f collettiva. **collective farm** n comune f. **collective noun** n nome m collettivo. **collective ownership** n comproprietà f

**collector** /kə'lektə(r)/ n (of stamps etc) collezionista mf

**collector's item** n pezzo m da collezionista

**college** /'kɒlɪdʒ/ n istituto m parauniversitario; **C~ of...** Scuola f di...

**college of education** n Br ≈ facoltà f inv di magistero

**college of further education** n Br istituto m parauniversitario

**collide** /kə'laɪd/ vi scontrarsi

**collie** /'kɒlɪ/ n pastore m scozzese, collie m inv

**colliery** /'kɒlɪərɪ/ n miniera f di carbone

**collision** /kə'lɪʒn/ n scontro m; **be on a ~ course** essere in rotta di collisione

**colloquial** /kə'ləʊkwɪəl/ a colloquiale

**colloquialism** /kə'ləʊkwɪəlɪzm/ n espressione f colloquiale

**colloquially** /kə'ləʊkwɪəlɪ/ adv colloquialmente

**colloquium** /kə'ləʊkwɪəm/ n colloquio m

**collude** /kə'l(j)u:d/ vi complottare

**collusion** /kə'l(j)u:ʒn/ n collusione f; **in ~ with** in accordo con

**cologne** /kə'ləʊn/ n colonia f

**Colombia** /kə'lɒmbɪə/ n Colombia f

**Colombian** /kə'lɒmbɪən/ a & n colombiano, -a mf

**colon** /'kəʊlən/ n due punti mpl; Anat colon m inv

**colonel** /'kɜ:nl/ n colonnello m

**colonial** /kə'ləʊnɪəl/ a coloniale

**colonize** /'kɒlənaɪz/ vt colonizzare

**colonnade** /kɒlə'neɪd/ n colonnato m

**colony** /'kɒlənɪ/ n colonia f

**Colorado beetle** /kɒlə'rɑ:dəʊ/ n dorifora f

**colossal** /kə'lɒsl/ a colossale

**colour** /'kʌlə(r)/ n colore m; (complexion) colorito m; **~s** pl (flag) bandiera fsg; **show one's true ~s** fig buttare giù la maschera; **in ~** a colori; **off ~** fam giù di tono ● vt colorare; **~ [in]** colorare ● vi (blush) arrossire

**colour: colour bar** n discriminazione f razziale. **colour-blind** a daltonico. **colour code** vt distinguere per mezzo di colori diversi

**coloured** /'kʌləd/ a colorato; (person) di colore ● n (person) persona f di colore

**colour fast** a dai colori resistenti

**colour film** n film m inv a colori

**colourful** /'kʌləfʊl/ a pieno di colore

**colouring** /'kʌlərɪŋ/ n (of plant, animal) colorazione f; (complexion) colorito m; (dye: for hair) tinta f; (for food) colorante m

**colouring book** n album m inv da colorare

**colourless** /'kʌlələs/ a incolore

**colour: colour photo[graph]** n fotografia f a colori. **colour scheme** n [combinazione f di] colori mpl. **colour sense** n senso m del colore. **colour supplement** n supplemento m illustrato a colori. **colour television** n televisione f a colori

**colt** /kəʊlt/ n puledro m

**column** /'kɒləm/ n colonna f

**columnist** /'kɒləmnɪst/ n giornalista mf che cura una rubrica

**coma** /'kəʊmə/ n coma m inv

**comatose** /'kəʊmətəʊz/ a Med in stato comatoso

**comb** /kəʊm/ n pettine m; (for wearing) pettinino m ● vt pettinare; (fig: search) setacciare; **~ one's hair** pettinarsi i capelli ■ **comb through** vt setacciare ⟨files, desk⟩

**combat** /'kɒmbæt/ n combattimento m ● vt (pt/pp **combated**) combattere

**combat jacket** n giubba f da combattimento

**combination** /kɒmbɪ'neɪʃn/ n combinazione f

**combine¹** /kəm'baɪn/ vt unire; **~ a job with being a mother** conciliare il lavoro con il ruolo di madre ● vi ⟨chemical elements:⟩ combinarsi

**combine²** /'kɒmbaɪn/ n Comm associazione f

**combine [harvester]** n mietitrebbia f

**combustible** /kəm'bʌstəbl/ a combustibile

**combustion** /kəm'bʌstʃn/ n combustione f

**come** /kʌm/ vi (pt **came**, pp **come**) venire; **after coming all this way** dopo tutta questa strada; **where do you ~ from?** da dove vieni?; **~ to** (*reach*) arrivare a; **that ~s to £10** fanno 10 sterline; **I've ~ to appreciate her** ho finito per apprezzarla; **I don't know what the world is coming to** mi chiedo dove andremo a finire; **~ into money** ricevere dei soldi; **that's what comes of being ...** ecco cosa significa essere ...; **~ true/open** verificarsi/aprirsi; **~ first** arrivare primo; *fig* venire prima di tutto; **~ in two sizes** esistere in due misure; **the years to ~** gli anni a venire; **how ~?** *fam* come mai?

■ **come about** *vi* succedere

■ **come across** *vi* **~ across as being** *fam* dare l'impressione di essere ● *vt* (*find*) imbattersi in

■ **come after** *vt* (*follow*) venire dopo; (*chase, pursue*) inseguire

■ **come along** *vi* venire; ⟨*job, opportunity:*⟩ presentarsi; (*progress*) andare bene

■ **come apart** *vi* smontarsi; (*break*) rompersi

■ **come at** *vt* (*attack*) avventarsi su

■ **come away** *vi* venir via; ⟨*button, fastener:*⟩ staccarsi

■ **come back** *vi* ritornare

■ **come before** *vt* (*precede*) precedere; (*be more important than*) venire prima di

■ **come by** *vi* passare ● *vt* (*obtain*) avere

■ **come down** *vi* scendere; **~ down to** (*reach*) arrivare a; **the situation comes down to...** la situazione si riduce a...; **don't ~ down too hard on her** vacci piano con lei; **~ down with flu** prendersi l'influenza

■ **come forward** *vi* farsi avanti

■ **come in** *vi* entrare; (*in race*) arrivare; ⟨*tide:*⟩ salire; **~ in with sb** (*in an undertaking*) associarsi a qcno

■ **come in for** *vt* **~ in for criticism** essere criticato

■ **come off** *vi* staccarsi; (*take place*) esserci; (*succeed*) riuscire; **~ off it!** non farmi ridere!

■ **come on** *vi* (*make progress*) migliorare; **~ on!** (*hurry*) dai!; (*indicating disbelief*) ma va là!

■ **come out** *vi* venir fuori; ⟨*book, sun:*⟩ uscire; ⟨*stain:*⟩ andar via; ⟨*homosexual:*⟩ rivelare la propria omosessualità; **~ out [on strike]** scioperare

■ **come out with** *vt* venir fuori con ⟨*joke, suggestion*⟩

■ **come over** *vi* venire; **what's ~ over you?** cosa ti prende?

■ **come round** *vi* venire; (*after fainting*) riaversi; (*change one's mind*) farsi convincere

■ **come through** *vi* ⟨*news:*⟩ arrivare ● *vt* attraversare ⟨*operation*⟩

■ **come to** *vi* (*after fainting*) riaversi.

■ **come under** *vi* trovarsi sotto

■ **come up** *vi* salire; ⟨*sun:*⟩ sorgere; ⟨*plant:*⟩ crescere; ⟨*name, subject:*⟩ venir fuori; ⟨*job, opportunity:*⟩ presentarsi; **something came up** (*I was prevented*) ho avuto un imprevisto

■ **come up against** *vt* incontrare

■ **come up to** *vt* (*reach*) arrivare a; essere all'altezza di ⟨*expectations*⟩

■ **come up with** *vt* tirar fuori

**come-back** *n* ritorno *m*

**comedian** /kə'mi:dɪən/ *n* [attore *m*] comico *m*

**comedienne** /kəmi:dɪ'en/ *n* attrice *f* comica

**come-down** *n* passo *m* indietro

**comedy** /'kɒmədɪ/ *n* commedia *f*

**comer** /'kʌmə(r)/ *n* **open to all ~s** aperto a tutti; **take on all ~s** battersi contro tutti gli sfidanti

**comet** /'kɒmɪt/ *n* cometa *f*

**come-uppance** /kʌm'ʌpəns/ *n* **get one's ~** *fam* avere quel che si merita

**comfort** /'kʌmfət/ *n* benessere *m*; (*consolation*) conforto *m*; **all the ~s** tutti i comfort ● *vt* confortare

**comfortable** /'kʌmfətəbl/ *a* comodo; **be ~** ⟨*person:*⟩ stare comodo; (*fig: in situation*) essere a proprio agio; (*financially*) star bene

**comfortably** /'kʌmfətəblɪ/ *adv* comodamente

**comforting** /'kʌmfətɪŋ/ *a* confortante

**comfort station** *n* *Am* bagno *m* pubblico

**comfy** /'kʌmfɪ/ *a* *fam* comodo

**comic** /'kɒmɪk/ *a* comico ● *n* comico, -a *mf*; (*periodical*) fumetto *m*

**comical** /'kɒmɪk(ə)l/ *a* comico

**comically** /'kɒmɪk(ə)lɪ/ *adv* comicamente

**comic: comic book** *n* giornalino *m* [a fumetti]. **comic relief** *n* *Theat* **provide some ~** fare una parentesi comica; *fig* sdrammatizzare. **comic strip** *n* striscia *f* di fumetti

**coming** /'kʌmɪŋ/ *a* promettente ● *n* venuta *f*; **~s and goings** viavai *m*

**comma** /'kɒmə/ *n* virgola *f*

**command** /kə'mɑ:nd/ *n* *also Comput* comando *m*; (*order*) ordine *m*; (*mastery*) padronanza *f*; **in ~** al comando ● *vt* ordinare; comandare ⟨*army*⟩

**commandant** /'kɒməndænt/ *n* *Mil* comandante *m*

**commandeer** /kɒmən'dɪə(r)/ *vt* requisire

**commander** /kə'mɑ:ndə(r)/ *n* comandante *m*

**commanding** /kə'mɑ:ndɪŋ/ *a* ⟨*view*⟩ imponente; ⟨*lead*⟩ dominante

**commanding officer** *n* comandante *m*

**commandment** /kə'mɑ:ndmənt/ *n* comandamento *m*

**commando** /kə'mɑ:ndəʊ/ *n* commando *m* *inv*

**command performance** *n* *Br Theat* serata *f* di gala (su richiesta del capo di stato)

**commemorate** /kə'meməreɪt/ *vt* commemorare

**commemoration** /kəmemə'reɪʃn/ *n* commemorazione *f*

**commemorative** /kə'memərətɪv/ *a* commemorativo

**commence** /kə'mens/ *vt/i* cominciare

**commencement** /kə'mensmənt/ n inizio m

**commend** /kə'mend/ vt complimentarsi con (**on** per); (*recommend*) raccomandare (**to** a)

**commendable** /kə'mendəbl/ a lodevole

**commendation** /kɒmen'deɪʃn/ n elogio m; (*for bravery*) riconoscimento m

**commensurate** /kə'menʃərət/ a proporzionato (**with** a)

**comment** /'kɒment/ n commento m; **no ~!** no comment! ● vi fare commenti (**on** su)

**commentary** /'kɒməntrɪ/ n commento m; [**running**] ~ (*on radio, TV*) cronaca f diretta

**commentate** /'kɒmənteɪt/ vt ~ **on** TV, Radio fare la cronaca di

■ **commentate on** vt fare la radiocronaca/telecronaca di ‹*sporting event*›

**commentator** /'kɒmənteɪtə(r)/ n cronista mf

**commerce** /'kɒmɜːs/ n commercio m

**commercial** /kə'mɜːʃl/ a commerciale ● n TV pubblicità f inv

**commercial break** n spot m inv [pubblicitario], interruzione f pubblicitaria

**commercialism** /kə'mɜːʃ(ə)lɪzm/ n pej affarismo m

**commercialize** /kə'mɜːʃ(ə)laɪz/ vt commercializzare

**commercial law** n diritto m commerciale

**commercially** /kə'mɜːʃ(ə)lɪ/ adv commercialmente

**commiserate** /kə'mɪzəreɪt/ vi esprimere il proprio rincrescimento (**with** a)

**commissar** /kɒmɪ'sɑː(r)/ n commissario m

**commission** /kə'mɪʃn/ n commissione f; **receive one's** ~ Mil essere promosso ufficiale; **out of** ~ fuori uso ● vt commissionare; Mil promuovere ufficiale; ~ **a painting from sb**, ~ **sb to do a painting** commissionare un dipinto a qcno

**commissionaire** /kəmɪʃə'neə(r)/ n portiere m

**commissioner** /kə'mɪʃənə(r)/ n commissario m; **C~ for Oaths** ≈ notaio m

**commit** /kə'mɪt/ vt (pt/pp **committed**) commettere; (*to prison, hospital*) affidare (**to** a); impegnare ‹*funds*›; ~ **oneself** impegnarsi; ~ **sth to memory** imparare qcsa a memoria

**commitment** /kə'mɪtmənt/ n impegno m; (*involvement*) compromissione f

**committed** /kə'mɪtɪd/ a impegnato

**committee** /kə'mɪtɪ/ n comitato m

**commodity** /kə'mɒdətɪ/ n prodotto m

**commodore** /'kɒmədɔː(r)/ n commodoro m

**common** /'kɒmən/ a comune; (*vulgar*) volgare ● n prato m pubblico; **have in** ~ avere in comune; **House of C~s** Camera f dei Comuni

**common cold** n raffreddore m

**commoner** /'kɒmənə(r)/ n persona f non nobile

**common: common ground** n fig terreno m d'intesa. **common law** n diritto m consuetudinario. **common-law husband** n conviven-

te m (*more uxorio*). **common-law wife** n convivente f (*more uxorio*)

**commonly** /'kɒmənlɪ/ adv comunemente

**common: Common Market** n Mercato m Comune. **common-or-garden** a ordinario. **commonplace** a banale. **common-room** n sala f dei professori/degli studenti. **common sense** n buon senso m. **Commonwealth** n Br Commonwealth m inv ● attrib ‹*country, Games*› del Commonwealth

**commotion** /kə'məʊʃn/ n confusione f

**communal** /'kɒmjʊnəl/ a comune

**commune** /'kɒmjuːn/ n comune f ● /kə'mjuːn/ vi ~ **with** essere in comunione con ‹*nature*›; comunicare con ‹*person*›

**communicable** /kə'mjuːnɪkəbl/ a ‹*disease*› trasmissibile

**communicate** /kə'mjuːnɪkeɪt/ vt/i comunicare

**communication** /kəmjuːnɪ'keɪʃn/ n comunicazione f; (*of disease*) trasmissione f; **be in** ~ **with sb** essere in contatto con qcno; ~**s** pl (*technology*) telecomunicazioni fpl

**communication cord** n fermata f d'emergenza

**communications satellite** n satellite m per telecomunicazioni

**communications software** n software m di comunicazione

**communication studies** /'stʌdɪz/ n studi mpl di comunicazione

**communicative** /kə'mjuːnɪkətɪv/ a comunicativo

**Communion** /kə'mjuːnɪən/ n [**Holy**] ~ comunione f

**communiqué** /kə'mjuːnɪkeɪ/ n comunicato m stampa

**Communism** /'kɒmjʊnɪzm/ n comunismo m

**Communist** /'kɒmjʊnɪst/ a & n comunista mf

**Communist Party** n partito m communista

**community** /kə'mjuːnətɪ/ n comunità f

**community: community care** n cura f fuori dell'ambito ospedaliero. **community centre** n centro m sociale. **community policing** n polizia f di quartiere. **community service** n servizio m civile (*in sostituzione di pene per reati minori*). **community spirit** n spirito m civico

**commute** /kə'mjuːt/ vi fare il pendolare ● vt Jur commutare

**commuter** /kə'mjuːtə(r)/ n pendolare mf

**commuter belt** n zona f suburbana abitata dai pendolari

**commuter train** n treno m dei pendolari

**compact**[1] /kəm'pækt/ a compatto

**compact**[2] /'kɒmpækt/ n portacipria m inv

**compact disc** n compact disc m inv

**compact disc player** n lettore m di compact disc

**companion** /kəm'pænjən/ n compagno, -a mf

**companionable** /kəm'pænjənəbl/ *a* ⟨*person*⟩ socievole; ⟨*silence*⟩ non pesante

**companionship** /kəm'pænjənʃɪp/ *n* compagnia *f*

**company** /'kʌmpənɪ/ *n* compagnia *f*; (*guests*) ospiti *mpl*; **I didn't know you had ~** pensavo che fossi solo

**company: company brochure** *n* opuscolo *m* dell'azienda. **company car** *n* macchina *f* della ditta. **company letterhead** *n* carta *f* intestata dell'azienda. **company pension scheme** *n* piano *m* di pensionamento aziendale. **company policy** *n* politica *f* aziendale. **company secretary** *n* direttore, -trice *mf* amministrativo, -a

**comparable** /'kɒmpərəbl/ *a* paragonabile

**comparative** /kəm'pærətɪv/ *a* comparativo; (*relative*) relativo ● *n* *Gram* comparativo *m*

**comparatively** /kəm'pærətɪvlɪ/ *adv* relativamente

**compare** /kəm'peə(r)/ *vt* paragonare (**with/** to a) ● *vi* **it can't ~** non ha paragoni

**comparison** /kəm'pærɪsn/ *n* paragone *m*

**compartment** /kəm'pɑːtmənt/ *n* compartimento *m*; *Rail* scompartimento *m*

**compass** /'kʌmpəs/ *n* bussola *f*

**compasses** /'kʌmpəsɪz/ *npl* pair of ~ compasso *msg*

**compassion** /kəm'pæʃn/ *n* compassione *f*

**compassionate** /kəm'pæʃənət/ *a* compassionevole

**compatible** /kəm'pætəbl/ *a* compatibile; **be ~** ⟨*people:*⟩ avere caratteri compatibili

**compatriot** /kəm'pætrɪət/ *n* compatriota *mf*

**compel** /kəm'pel/ *vt* (*pt/pp* **compelled**) costringere

**compelling** /kəm'pelɪŋ/ *a* ⟨*reason, argument*⟩ convincente; ⟨*performance, film, speaker*⟩ avvincente

**compendium** /kəm'pendɪəm/ *n* (*handbook*) compendio *m*; (*Br: box of games*) scatola *f* di giochi

**compensate** /'kɒmpənseɪt/ *vt* risarcire ● *vi* **~ for** *fig* compensare *f*

**compensation** /kɒmpən'seɪʃn/ *n* risarcimento *m*; (*fig: comfort*) consolazione *f*

**compère** /'kɒmpeə(r)/ *n* presentatore, -trice *mf*

**compete** /kəm'piːt/ *vi* competere; (*take part*) gareggiare

**competence** /'kɒmpɪtəns/ *n* competenza *f*

**competent** /'kɒmpɪtənt/ *a* competente

**competition** /kɒmpə'tɪʃn/ *n* concorrenza *f*; (*contest*) gara *f*

**competitive** /kəm'petɪtɪv/ *a* competitivo; **~ prices** prezzi *mpl* concorrenziali

**competitor** /kəm'petɪtə(r)/ *n* concorrente *mf*

**compilation** /kɒmpɪ'leɪʃn/ *n* compilazione *f*; (*collection*) raccolta *f*

**compile** /kəm'paɪl/ *vt* compilare

**complacency** /kəm'pleɪsənsɪ/ *n* compiacimento *m*

**complacent** /kəm'pleɪsənt/ *a* compiaciuto

**complacently** /kəm'pleɪsəntlɪ/ *adv* con compiacimento

**complain** /kəm'pleɪn/ *vi* lamentarsi (**about** di); (*formally*) reclamare; **~ of** *Med* accusare

**complaint** /kəm'pleɪnt/ *n* lamentela *f*; (*formal*) reclamo *m*; *Med* disturbo *m*

**complement¹** /'kɒmplɪmənt/ *n* complemento *m*; **with a full ~ of 25** con un effettivo al completo di 25

**complement²** /'kɒmplɪment/ *vt* complementare; **~ each other** complementarsi a vicenda

**complementary** /kɒmplɪ'mentərɪ/ *a* complementare

**complete** /kəm'pliːt/ *a* completo; (*utter*) finito ● *vt* completare; compilare ⟨*form*⟩

**completely** /kəm'pliːtlɪ/ *adv* completamente

**completion** /kəm'pliːʃn/ *n* fine *f*

**complex** /'kɒmpleks/ *a* & *n* complesso *m*

**complexion** /kəm'plekʃn/ *n* carnagione *f*; **that puts a different ~ on the matter** questo mette la questione in una luce nuova

**complexity** /kəm'pleksətɪ/ *n* complessità *f inv*

**compliance** /kəm'plaɪəns/ *n* accettazione *f*; (*with rules*) osservanza *f*; **in ~ with** in osservanza a ⟨*law*⟩; conformemente a ⟨*request*⟩

**complicate** /'kɒmplɪkeɪt/ *vt* complicare

**complicated** /'kɒmplɪkeɪtɪd/ *a* complicato

**complication** /kɒmplɪ'keɪʃn/ *n* complicazione *f*

**complicity** /kəm'plɪsətɪ/ *n* complicità *f*

**compliment** /'kɒmplɪmənt/ *n* complimento *m*; **~s** *pl* omaggi *mpl* ● *vt* complimentare

**complimentary** /kɒmplɪ'mentərɪ/ *a* complimentoso; (*given free*) in omaggio

**comply** /kəm'plaɪ/ *vi* (*pt/pp* **-ied**) **~ with** conformarsi a

**component** /kəm'pəʊnənt/ *a* & *n* **~ [part]** componente *m*

**compose** /kəm'pəʊz/ *vt* comporre; **~ oneself** ricomporsi; **be ~d of** essere composto da

**composed** /kəm'pəʊzd/ *a* (*calm*) composto

**composer** /kəm'pəʊzə(r)/ *n* compositore, -trice *mf*

**composite** /'kɒmpəzɪt/ *a* composto; ⟨*style*⟩ composito

**composition** /kɒmpə'zɪʃn/ *n* composizione *f*; (*essay*) tema *m*

**compos mentis** /kɒmpɒs'mentɪs/ *a* nel pieno possesso delle proprie facoltà

**compost** /'kɒmpɒst/ *n* composta *f*

**composure** /kəm'pəʊʒə(r)/ *n* calma *f*

**compound¹** /kəm'paʊnd/ *vt* (*make worse*) aggravare

**compound²** /'kɒmpaʊnd/ *a* composto ● *n* *Chem* composto *m*; *Gram* parola *f* composta; (*enclosure*) recinto *m*

**compound fracture** *n* frattura *f* esposta

**compound interest** *n* interesse *m* composto

**comprehend** /kɒmprɪ'hend/ *vt* comprendere

**comprehensible** /kɒmprɪ'hensəbl/ a comprensibile

**comprehensibly** /kɒmprɪ'hensəblɪ/ adv comprensibilmente

**comprehension** /kɒmprɪ'henʃn/ n comprensione f

**comprehensive** /kɒmprɪ'hensɪv/ a & n comprensivo; ~ [**school**] scuola f media in cui gli allievi hanno capacità d'apprendimento diverse

**comprehensive insurance** n Auto polizza f casco

**compress¹** /'kɒmpres/ n compressa f

**compress²** /kəm'pres/ vt comprimere

**compressed air** /kəm'prest/ n aria f compressa

**compression** /kəm'preʃn/ n compressione f

**comprise** /kəm'praɪz/ vt comprendere; (form) costituire

**compromise** /'kɒmprəmaɪz/ n compromesso m ● vt compromettere ● vi fare un compromesso

**compulsion** /kəm'pʌlʃn/ n desiderio m irresistibile

**compulsive** /kəm'pʌlsɪv/ a Psych patologico; ~ **eating** voglia f ossessiva di mangiare

**compulsory** /kəm'pʌlsərɪ/ a obbligatorio; ~ **subject** materia f obbligatoria

**compulsory purchase** n Br espropriazione f (per pubblica utilità)

**compunction** /kəm'pʌŋkʃn/ n liter scrupolo m

**computation** /kɒmpjʊ'teɪʃn/ n calcolo m

**computer** /kəm'pjuːtə(r)/ n computer m inv

**computer: computer-aided** a assistito da computer. **computer-aided design** n progettazione f assistita da computer. **computer-assisted language learning** n apprendimento m della lingua assistito da computer. **computer dating service** n agenzia f matrimoniale computerizzata. **computer engineer** n tecnico m informatico. **computer error** n errore m informatico. **computer game** n gioco m su computer; ~ **s** intelligiochi mpl. **computer graphics** n grafica f su computer. **computer hacker** n pirata m informatico

**computerization** /kəmpjuːtəraɪ'zeɪʃn/ n computerizzazione f

**computerize** /kəm'pjuːtəraɪz/ vt computerizzare

**computer: computer-literate** a che sa usare il computer. **computer operator** n terminalista mf. **computer program** n programma m [di computer]. **computer programmer** n programmatore, -trice mf di computer. **computer virus** n virus m inv [su computer]

**computing** /kəm'pjuːtɪŋ/ n informatica f

**comrade** /'kɒmreɪd/ n camerata m; Pol compagno, -a mf

**comradeship** /'kɒmreɪdʃɪp/ n cameratismo m

**con¹** /kɒn/ see **pro**

**con²** n fam fregatura f ● vt (pt/pp **conned**) fam fregare

**concave** /'kɒnkeɪv/ a concavo

**conceal** /kən'siːl/ vt nascondere

**concealment** /kən'siːlmənt/ n dissimulazione f

**concede** /kən'siːd/ vt (admit) ammettere; (give up) rinunciare a; lasciar fare (goal)

**conceit** /kən'siːt/ n presunzione f

**conceited** /kən'siːtɪd/ a presuntuoso

**conceivable** /kən'siːvəbl/ a concepibile

**conceive** /kən'siːv/ vt Biol concepire ● vi aver figli; ~ **of** fig concepire

**concentrate** /'kɒnsəntreɪt/ vt concentrare ● vi concentrarsi ● n concentrato m

**concentration** /kɒnsən'treɪʃn/ n concentrazione f

**concentration camp** n campo m di concentramento

**concentric** /kən'sentrɪk/ a concentrico

**concept** /'kɒnsept/ n concetto m

**conception** /kən'sepʃn/ n concezione f; (idea) idea f

**conceptual** /kən'septjʊəl/ a concettuale

**concern** /kən'sɜːn/ n preoccupazione f; Comm attività f inv ● vt (be about, affect) riguardare; (worry) preoccupare; **be ~ed about** essere preoccupato per; ~ **oneself with** preoccuparsi di; **as far as I am ~ed** per quanto mi riguarda

**concerning** /kən'sɜːnɪŋ/ prep riguardo a

**concert** /'kɒnsət/ n concerto m

**concerted** /kən'sɜːtɪd/ a collettivo

**concert hall** n sala f da concerti

**concertina** /kɒnsə'tiːnə/ n piccola fisarmonica f

**concert master** n Am primo violino m

**concerto** /kən'tʃeətəʊ/ n concerto m

**concession** /kən'seʃn/ n concessione f; (reduction) sconto m

**concessionary** /kən'seʃənrɪ/ a (reduced) scontato

**conciliate** /kən'sɪlɪeɪt/ vt blandire

**conciliation** /kənsɪlɪ'eɪʃn/ n conciliazione f

**conciliator** /kən'sɪlɪeɪtə(r)/ n mediatore, -trice f

**concise** /kən'saɪs/ a conciso

**concisely** /kən'saɪslɪ/ adv in modo conciso

**conciseness** /kən'saɪsnɪs/ n concisione f

**conclude** /kən'kluːd/ vt concludere ● vi concludersi

**concluding** /kən'kluːdɪŋ/ a finale, conclusivo

**conclusion** /kən'kluːʒn/ n conclusione f; **in ~** per concludere

**conclusive** /kən'kluːsɪv/ a definitivo

**conclusively** /kən'kluːsɪvlɪ/ adv in modo definitivo

**concoct** /kən'kɒkt/ vt confezionare; fig inventare

**concoction** /kən'kɒkʃn/ n mistura f; (drink) intruglio m

**concord** /'kɒnkɔːd/ n concordia f

**concordance** /kən'kɔːdəns/ n accordo m;

*(index)* concordanze *fpl*; **be in ~ with** essere in accordo con

**concourse** /'kɒŋkɔːs/ *n* atrio *m*

**concrete** /'kɒŋkriːt/ *a* concreto ● *n* calcestruzzo *m* ● *vt* ricoprire di calcestruzzo

**concrete jungle** *n* giungla *f* d'asfalto

**concrete mixer** *n* betoniera *f*

**concur** /kənˈkɜː(r)/ *vi* (*pt/pp* **concurred**) essere d'accordo

**concurrently** /kənˈkʌrəntlɪ/ *adv* contemporaneamente

**concussion** /kənˈkʌʃn/ *n* commozione *f* cerebrale

**condemn** /kənˈdem/ *vt* condannare; dichiarare inagibile ‹*building*›

**condemnation** /kɒndemˈneɪʃn/ *n* condanna *f*

**condensation** /kɒndenˈseɪʃn/ *n* condensazione *f*

**condense** /kənˈdens/ *vt* condensare; *Phys* condensare ● *vi* condensarsi

**condensed milk** /kəndenstˈmɪlk/ *n* latte *m* condensato

**condescend** /kɒndɪˈsend/ *vi* degnarsi

**condescending** /kɒndɪˈsendɪŋ/ *a* condiscendente

**condescendingly** /kɒndɪˈsendɪŋlɪ/ *adv* in modo condiscendente

**condiment** /'kɒndɪmənt/ *n* condimento *m*

**condition** /kənˈdɪʃn/ *n* condizione *f*; **on ~ that** a condizione che ● *vt Psych* condizionare

**conditional** /kənˈdɪʃənəl/ *a* ‹*acceptance*› condizionato; *Gram* condizionale; **be ~ on** essere condizionato da ● *n Gram* condizionale

**conditionally** /kənˈdɪʃənəlɪ/ *adv* condizionatamente

**conditioner** /kənˈdɪʃənə(r)/ *n* balsamo *m*; (*for fabrics*) ammorbidente *m*

**conditioning** /kənˈdɪʃənɪŋ/ *n* (*of hair*) balsamo *m*; *Psych* condizionamento *m* ● *a* ‹*shampoo, lotion etc*› trattante

**condole** /kənˈdəʊl/ *vi* fare le condoglianze (**with** a)

**condolences** /kənˈdəʊlənsɪz/ *npl* condoglianze *fpl*

**condom** /'kɒndəm/ *n* preservativo *m*

**condo[minium]** /'kɒndəʊ, kɒndəˈmɪnɪəm/ *n Am* condominio *m*

**condone** /kənˈdəʊn/ *vt* passare sopra a

**conducive** /kənˈdjuːsɪv/ *a* **be ~ to** contribuire a

**conduct¹** /'kɒndʌkt/ *n* condotta *f*

**conduct²** /kənˈdʌkt/ *vt* condurre; dirigere ‹*orchestra*›

**conduction** /kənˈdʌkʃn/ *n* conduzione *f*

**conductor** /kənˈdʌktə(r)/ *n* direttore *m* d'orchestra; (*of bus*) bigliettaio *m*; *Phys* conduttore *m*

**conductress** /kənˈdʌktrɪs/ *n* bigliettaia *f*

**cone** /kəʊn/ *n* cono *m*; *Bot* pigna *f*; *Auto* birillo *m*

■ **cone off** *vt* **be ~d off** *Auto* essere chiuso da birilli

**confection** /kənˈfekʃn/ *n* (*cake, dessert*) dolce *m*; **a ~ of** (*combination*) una combinazione di

**confectioner** /kənˈfekʃənə(r)/ *n* pasticciere, -a *mf*

**confectionery** /kənˈfekʃənərɪ/ *n* pasticceria *f*

**confederation** /kənfedəˈreɪʃn/ *n* confederazione *f*

**confer** /kənˈfɜː(r)/ *v* (*pt/pp* **conferred**) ● *vt* conferire (**on** a) ● *vi* (*discuss*) conferire

**conference** /'kɒnfərəns/ *n* conferenza *f*

**conference room** *n* sala *f* riunioni

**confess** /kənˈfes/ *vt* confessare ● *vi* confessare; *Relig* confessarsi

**confession** /kənˈfeʃn/ *n* confessione *f*

**confessional** /kənˈfeʃənəl/ *n* confessionale *m*

**confessor** /kənˈfesə(r)/ *n* confessore *m*

**confetti** /kənˈfetɪ/ *n* coriandoli *mpl*

**confide** /kənˈfaɪd/ *vt* confidare

■ **confide in** *vt* **~ in sb** fidarsi di

**confidence** /'kɒnfɪdəns/ *n* (*trust*) fiducia *f*; (*self-assurance*) sicurezza *f* di sé; (*secret*) confidenza *f*; **in ~** in confidenza

**confidence trick** *n* truffa *f*

**confidence trickster** /'kɒnfɪdəns-trɪkstə(r)/ *n* imbroglione, -a *mf*

**confident** /'kɒnfɪdənt/ *a* fiducioso; (*self-assured*) sicuro di sé

**confidential** /kɒnfɪˈdenʃl/ *a* confidenziale

**confidentiality** /kɒnfɪdenʃɪˈælətɪ/ *n* riservatezza *f*

**confidentially** /kɒnfɪˈdenʃəlɪ/ *adv* confidenzialmente

**confidently** /'kɒnfɪdəntlɪ/ *adv* con aria fiduciosa; **we ~ expect to win** siamo fiduciosi nella vittoria

**confine** /kənˈfaɪn/ *vt* rinchiudere; (*limit*) limitare; **be ~d to bed** essere confinato a letto

**confined** /kənˈfaɪnd/ *a* ‹*space*› limitato

**confinement** /kənˈfaɪnmənt/ *n* detenzione *f*; *Med* parto *m*

**confines** /'kɒnfaɪnz/ *npl* confini *mpl*

**confirm** /kənˈfɜːm/ *vt* confermare; *Relig* cresimare

**confirmation** /kɒnfəˈmeɪʃn/ *n* conferma *f*; *Relig* cresima *f*

**confirmed** /kənˈfɜːmd/ *a* incallito; **~ bachelor** scapolo *m* impenitente

**confiscate** /'kɒnfɪskeɪt/ *vt* confiscare

**confiscation** /kɒnfɪsˈkeɪʃn/ *n* confisca *f*

**conflagration** /kɒnfləˈgreɪʃn/ *n* conflagrazione *f*

**conflate** /kənˈfleɪt/ *vt* fondere

**conflict¹** /'kɒnflɪkt/ *n* conflitto *m*

**conflict²** /kənˈflɪkt/ *vi* essere in contraddizione

**conflicting** /kənˈflɪktɪŋ/ *a* contraddittorio

**confluence** /'kɒnfluəns/ *n* (*of rivers*) confluenza *f*; *fig* convergenza *f*

**conform** /kənˈfɔːm/ *vi* ‹*person:*› conformarsi; ‹*thing:*› essere conforme (**to** a)

**conformist** /kənˈfɔːmɪst/ *n* conformista *mf*

**conformity** /kən'fɔ:mətɪ/ n conformità f; *Relig* ortodossia f; **in ~ with** in conformità a

**confound** /kən'faʊnd/ vt (perplex) confondere; (show to be wrong) confutare

**confounded** /kən'faʊndɪd/ a fam maledetto

**confront** /kən'frʌnt/ vt affrontare; **the problems ~ing us** i problemi che dobbiamo affrontare

**confrontation** /kɒnfrʌn'teɪʃn/ n confronto m

**confuse** /kən'fju:z/ vt confondere

**confused** /kən'fju:zd/ a (presentation, idea) ingarbugliato

**confusing** /kən'fju:zɪŋ/ a che confonde

**confusion** /kən'fju:ʒn/ n confusione f

**congeal** /kən'dʒi:l/ vi (blood:) coagularsi

**congenial** /kən'dʒi:nɪəl/ a congeniale

**congenital** /kən'dʒenɪtl/ a congenito

**congested** /kən'dʒestɪd/ a congestionato

**congestion** /kən'dʒestʃn/ n congestione f

**conglomerate** /kən'glɒmərət/ n conglomerato m

**Congo** /'kɒŋgəʊ/ n Congo m

**Congolese** /kɒŋgəli:z/ a & n congolese mf

**congratulate** /kən'grætjʊleɪt/ vt congratularsi con (**on** per)

**congratulations** /kəngrætjʊ'leɪʃnz/ npl congratulazioni fpl

**congregate** /'kɒŋgrɪgeɪt/ vi radunarsi

**congregation** /kɒŋgrɪ'geɪʃn/ n Relig assemblea f

**congress** /'kɒŋgres/ n congresso m

**congressman** /'kɒŋgresmən/ n Am Pol membro m del congresso

**conical** /'kɒnɪkl/ a conico

**conifer** /'kɒnɪfə(r)/ n conifera f

**conjecture** /kən'dʒektʃə(r)/ n congettura f ● vt congetturare ● vi fare congetture

**conjugal** /'kɒndʒʊgl/ a coniugale

**conjugate** /'kɒndʒʊgeɪt/ vt coniugare

**conjugation** /kɒndʒʊ'geɪʃn/ n coniugazione f

**conjunction** /kən'dʒʌŋkʃn/ n congiunzione f; **in ~ with** insieme a

**conjunctivitis** /kəndʒʌŋktɪ'vaɪtɪs/ n congiuntivite f

■ **conjure up** /'kʌndʒə(r)/ vt evocare (image); tirar fuori dal nulla (meal)

**conjuring** /'kʌndʒərɪŋ/ n giochi mpl di prestigio

**conjuring trick** /'kʌndʒərɪŋ/ n gioco m di prestigio

**conjuror** /'kʌndʒərə(r)/ n prestigiatore, -trice mf

**conk** /kɒŋk/ vi ~ **out** fam (machine:) guastarsi; (person:) crollare

**conker** /'kɒŋkə(r)/ n fam castagna f (d'ippocastano)

**conman** /'kɒnmæn/ n fam truffatore m

**connect** /kə'nekt/ vt collegare; **be ~ed with** avere legami con; (be related to) essere imparentato con; **be well ~ed** aver conoscenze influenti ● vi essere collegato (**with** a); (train:) fare coincidenza

**connecting** /kə'nektɪŋ/ a (room) di comunicazione

**connecting flight** n coincidenza f

**connection** /kə'nekʃn/ n (between ideas) nesso m; (in travel) coincidenza f; Electr, Comput collegamento m; **in ~ with** con riferimento a; **~s** pl (people) conoscenze fpl

**connector** /kə'nektə(r)/ n Comput connettore m

**connivance** /kə'naɪvəns/ n connivenza f

**connive** /kə'naɪv/ vi ~ **at** essere connivente a

**connoisseur** /kɒnə'sɜ:(r)/ n intenditore, -trice mf

**connotation** /kɒnə'teɪʃn/ n connotazione f

**connote** /kə'nəʊt/ vt evocare; (in linguistics) connotare

**conquer** /'kɒŋkə(r)/ vt conquistare; fig superare (fear)

**conqueror** /'kɒŋkərə(r)/ n conquistatore m

**conquest** /'kɒŋkwest/ n conquista f

**conscience** /'kɒnʃəns/ n coscienza f

**conscientious** /kɒnʃɪ'enʃəs/ a coscienzioso

**conscientiously** /kɒnsɪ'enʃəslɪ/ adv coscienziosamente

**conscientious objector** /əb'dʒektə(r)/ n obiettore m di coscienza

**conscious** /'kɒnʃəs/ a conscio; (decision) meditato; [fully] ~ cosciente; **be/become ~ of sth** rendersi conto di qcsa

**consciously** /'kɒnʃəslɪ/ adv consapevolmente

**consciousness** /'kɒnʃəsnɪs/ n consapevolezza f; Med conoscenza f

**conscript[1]** /'kɒnskrɪpt/ n coscritto m

**conscript[2]** /kən'skrɪpt/ vt Mil chiamare alle armi; ~ **sb to do sth** fig reclutare qcno per fare qcsa

**conscription** /kən'skrɪpʃn/ n coscrizione f, leva f

**consecrate** /'kɒnsɪkreɪt/ vt consacrare

**consecration** /kɒnsɪ'kreɪʃn/ n consacrazione f

**consecutive** /kən'sekjʊtɪv/ a consecutivo

**consecutively** /kən'sekjʊtɪvlɪ/ adv consecutivamente

**consensus** /kən'sensəs/ n consenso m

**consent** /kən'sent/ n consenso m ● vi acconsentire

**consequence** /'kɒnsɪkwəns/ n conseguenza f; (importance) importanza f

**consequent** /'kɒnsɪkwənt/ a conseguente

**consequently** /'kɒnsɪkwəntlɪ/ adv di conseguenza

**conservation** /kɒnsə'veɪʃn/ n conservazione f

**conservationist** /kɒnsə'veɪʃənɪst/ n fautore, -trice mf della tutela ambientale

**conservatism** /kən'sɜ:vətɪzm/ n conservatorismo m

**conservative** /kən'sɜ:vətɪv/ a conservativo; (estimate) ottimistico; **C~** Pol conservatore ● n conservatore, -trice mf

**conservatory** /kən'sɜ:vətrɪ/ n spazio m chiuso da vetrate adiacente alla casa

**conserve** /kən'sɜ:v/ vt conservare

**consider** /kən'sɪdə(r)/ vt considerare; **~ doing sth** considerare la possibilità di fare qcsa

**considerable** /kən'sɪdərəbl/ a considerevole

**considerably** /kən'sɪdərəblɪ/ adv considerevolmente

**considerate** /kən'sɪdərət/ a pieno di riguardo

**considerately** /kən'sɪdərətlɪ/ adv con riguardo

**consideration** /kənsɪdə'reɪʃn/ n considerazione f; (thoughtfulness) attenzione f; (respect) riguardo m; (payment) compenso m; **take into ~** prendere in considerazione

**considering** /kən'sɪdərɪŋ/ prep considerando; **~ that** considerando che

**consign** /kən'saɪn/ vt affidare

**consignment** /kən'saɪnmənt/ n consegna f

**consist** /kən'sɪst/ vi **~ of** consistere di

**consistency** /kən'sɪstənsɪ/ n coerenza f; (density) consistenza f

**consistent** /kən'sɪstənt/ a coerente; (loyalty) costante; **be ~ with** far pensare a

**consistently** /kən'sɪstəntlɪ/ adv coerentemente; (late, loyal) costantemente

**consolation** /kɒnsə'leɪʃn/ n consolazione f

**consolation prize** n premio m di consolazione

**console** /kən'səʊl/ vt consolare

**consolidate** /kən'sɒlɪdeɪt/ vt consolidare

**consolidation** /kənsɒlɪ'deɪʃn/ n (of knowledge, position) consolidamento m

**consoling** /kən'səʊlɪŋ/ a consolante

**consonant** /'kɒnsənənt/ n consonante f

**consort¹** /'kɒnsɔ:t/ n consorte mf

**consort²** /kən'sɔ:t/ vi **~ with** frequentare

**consortium** /kən'sɔ:tɪəm/ n consorzio m

**conspicuous** /kən'spɪkjʊəs/ a facilmente distinguibile; **be ~ by one's absence** brillare per la propria assenza

**conspicuously** /kən'spɪkjʊəslɪ/ adv (dressed) vistosamente; (placed) in evidenza; (silent, empty) in modo evidente

**conspiracy** /kən'spɪrəsɪ/ n cospirazione f

**conspirator** /kən'spɪrətə(r)/ n cospiratore, -trice mf

**conspire** /kən'spaɪə(r)/ vi cospirare

**constable** /'kʌnstəbl/ n agente m [di polizia]

**constabulary** /kən'stæbjʊlərɪ/ n Br polizia f

**constancy** /'kɒnstənsɪ/ n costanza f

**constant** /'kɒnstənt/ a costante

**constantly** /'kɒnstəntlɪ/ adv costantemente

**constellation** /kɒnstə'leɪʃn/ n costellazione f

**consternation** /kɒnstə'neɪʃn/ n costernazione f

**constipated** /'kɒnstɪpeɪtɪd/ a stitico

**constipation** /kɒnstɪ'peɪʃn/ n stitichezza f

**constituency** /kən'stɪtjʊənsɪ/ n area f elettorale di un deputato nel Regno Unito

**constituent** /kən'stɪtjʊənt/ n costituente m; Pol elettore, -trice mf

**constitute** /'kɒnstɪtju:t/ vt costituire

**constitution** /kɒnstɪ'tju:ʃn/ n costituzione f

**constitutional** /kɒnstɪ'tju:ʃənl/ a costituzionale ● n passeggiata f salutare

**constitutionally** /kɒnstɪ'tju:ʃənəlɪ/ adv Pol costituzionalmente; (innately) di costituzione

**constrain** /kən'streɪn/ vt costringere

**constraint** /kən'streɪnt/ n costrizione f; (restriction) restrizione f; (strained manner) disagio m

**constrict** /kən'strɪkt/ vt (tight jacket:) stringere

**constriction** /kən'strɪkʃn/ n (of chest, throat) senso m di oppressione; (constraint) costrizione f; (of blood vessel) restrizione f

**construct** /kən'strʌkt/ vt costruire

**construction** /kən'strʌkʃn/ n costruzione f; (interpretation) interpretazione f; **under ~** in costruzione

**construction: construction engineer** n ingegnere m edile. **construction site** n cantiere m. **construction worker** n [operaio m] edile m

**constructive** /kən'strʌktɪv/ a costruttivo

**constructively** /kən'strʌktɪvlɪ/ adv in modo costruttivo

**construe** /kən'stru:/ vt interpretare

**consul** /'kɒnsl/ n console m

**consular** /'kɒnsjʊlə(r)/ a consolare

**consulate** /'kɒnsjʊlət/ n consolato m

**consult** /kən'sʌlt/ vt consultare

**consultancy** /kən'sʌltənsɪ/ n (advice) consulenza f; (firm) ufficio m di consulenza; Br Med posto m di specialista; **do ~** fare il/la consulente ● attrib (fees, service, work) di consulenza

**consultant** /kən'sʌltənt/ n consulente mf; Med specialista mf

**consultation** /kɒnsl'teɪʃn/ n consultazione f; Med consulto m

**consultative** /kən'sʌltətɪv/ a di consulenza

**consulting hours** /kən'sʌltɪŋ/ npl Med orario m di visita

**consulting room** n Med ambulatorio m

**consumable** /kən'sju:məbl/ n bene m di consumo

**consume** /kən'sju:m/ vt consumare

**consumer** /kən'sju:mə(r)/ n consumatore, -trice mf

**consumer: consumer advice** n consigli mpl ai consumatori. **consumer confidence** n fiducia f del consumatore. **consumer goods** npl beni mpl di consumo

**consumerism** /kən'sju:mərɪzm/ n consumismo m

**consumer: consumer organization** n organizzazione f per la tutela dei consumatori. **consumer products** npl beni mpl di consumo. **consumer protection** n tutela f dei consumatori. **consumer society** *n* società *f inv* consumista, società *f inv* dei consumi

**consuming** /kən'sju:mɪŋ/ *a* ⟨*passion*⟩ struggente; ⟨*urge*⟩ pressante; ⟨*hatred*⟩ insaziabile

**consummate** /'kɒnsjʊmeɪt/ *vt* consumare

**consummation** /kɒnsjʊ'meɪʃn/ *n* consumazione *f*

**consumption** /kən'sʌmpʃn/ *n* consumo *m*

**contact** /'kɒntækt/ *n* contatto *m*; ⟨*person*⟩ conoscenza *f* ● *vt* mettersi in contatto con

**contactable** /'kɒntæktəbl/ *a* ⟨*person*⟩ reperibile

**contact lenses** *npl* lenti *fpl* a contatto

**contagious** /kən'teɪdʒəs/ *a* contagioso

**contain** /kən'teɪn/ *vt* contenere; ~ **oneself** controllarsi

**container** /kən'teɪnə(r)/ *n* recipiente *m*; ⟨*for transport*⟩ container *m inv*

**container: container port** *n* porto *m* container. **container ship** *n* [nave *f*] portacontainers *f inv*. **container truck** *n* [autocarro *m*] portacontainers *m inv*

**contaminate** /kən'tæmɪneɪt/ *vt* contaminare

**contamination** /kəntæmɪ'neɪʃn/ *n* contaminazione *f*

**contd** *abbr* **(continued)** segue

**contemplate** /'kɒntəmpleɪt/ *vt* contemplare; ⟨*consider*⟩ considerare; ~ **doing sth** considerare di fare qcsa

**contemplation** /kɒntəm'pleɪʃn/ *n* contemplazione *f*

**contemplative** /kən'templətɪv/ *a* contemplativo

**contemporaneous** /kəntempə'reɪnɪəs/ *a* contemporaneo **(with** a)

**contemporaneously** /kəntempə'reɪnɪəslɪ/ *adv* contemporaneamente **(with** a)

**contemporary** /kən'tempərərɪ/ *a* & *n* contemporaneo, -a *mf*

**contempt** /kən'tempt/ *n* disprezzo *m*; **beneath** ~ più che vergognoso; ~ **of court** oltraggio *m* alla Corte

**contemptible** /kən'tem(p)təbl/ *a* spregevole

**contemptuous** /kən'tem(p)tjʊəs/ *a* sprezzante

**contemptuously** /kən'tem(p)tjʊəslɪ/ *adv* sprezzantemente

**contend** /kən'tend/ *vi* ~ **with** occuparsi di ● *vt* ⟨*assert*⟩ sostenere

**contender** /kən'tendə(r)/ *n* concorrente *mf*

**content**[1] /'kɒntent/ *n* contenuto *m*

**content**[2] /kən'tent/ *a* soddisfatto ● *n* **to one's heart's** ~ finché se ne ha voglia ● *vt* ~ **oneself** accontentarsi **(with** di)

**contented** /kən'tentɪd/ *a* soddisfatto

**contentedly** /kən'tentɪdlɪ/ *adv* con aria soddisfatta

**contention** /kən'tenʃn/ *n* ⟨*assertion*⟩ opinione *f*

**contentious** /kən'tenʃəs/ *a* ⟨*subject*⟩ controverso; ⟨*view*⟩ discutibile; ⟨*person, group*⟩ polemico

**contentment** /kən'tentmənt/ *n* soddisfazione *f*

**contents** /'kɒntents/ *npl* contenuto *m*

**contest**[1] /'kɒntest/ *n* gara *f*

**contest**[2] /kən'test/ *vt* contestare ⟨*statement*⟩; impugnare ⟨*will*⟩; *Pol* ⟨*candidates:*⟩ contendersi; ⟨*one candidate:*⟩ aspirare a

**contestant** /kən'testənt/ *n* concorrente *mf*

**context** /'kɒntekst/ *n* contesto *m*

**continent** /'kɒntɪnənt/ *n* continente *m*; **the C~** l'Europa *f* continentale

**continental** /kɒntɪ'nentl/ *a* continentale

**continental breakfast** *n* prima colazione *f* a base di pane, burro, marmellata, croissant ecc

**continental quilt** *n* piumone *m*

**contingency** /kən'tɪndʒənsɪ/ *n* eventualità *f inv*

**contingency fund** *n* fondo *m* sopravvenienze passive

**contingency plan** *n* piano *m* d'emergenza

**contingent** /kən'tɪndʒənt/ *a* **be** ~ **on** dipendere da ● *n* *Mil* contingente *m*

**continual** /kən'tɪnjʊəl/ *a* continuo

**continually** /kən'tɪnjʊəlɪ/ *adv* continuamente

**continuation** /kəntɪnjʊ'eɪʃn/ *n* continuazione *f*

**continue** /kən'tɪnju:/ *vt* continuare; ~ **doing** *or* **to do sth** continuare a fare qcsa; **to be** ~**d** continua ● *vi* continuare

**continued** /kən'tɪnju:d/ *a* continuo

**continuity** /kɒntɪ'nju:ətɪ/ *n* continuità *f*

**continuity announcer** *n* annunciatore, -trice *mf*

**continuity girl** *n* segretaria *f* di produzione

**continuous** /kən'tɪnjʊəs/ *a* continuo

**continuously** /kən'tɪnjʊəslɪ/ *adv* continuamente

**continuum** /kən'tɪnjʊəm/ *n* continuum *m inv*

**contort** /kən'tɔ:t/ *vt* contorcere

**contortion** /kən'tɔ:ʃn/ *n* contorsione *f*

**contortionist** /kən'tɔ:ʃənɪst/ *n* contorsionista *mf*

**contour** /'kɒntʊə(r)/ *n* contorno *m*; ⟨*line*⟩ curva *f* di livello

**contraband** /'kɒntrəbænd/ *n* contrabbando *m*

**contraception** /kɒntrə'sepʃn/ *n* contraccezione *f*; **use** ~ ricorrere alla contraccezione

**contraceptive** /kɒntrə'septɪv/ *a* & *n* contraccettivo *m*

**contract**[1] /'kɒntrækt/ *n* contratto *m*

**contract**[2] /kən'trækt/ *vi* (*get smaller*) contrarsi ● *vt* contrarre ⟨*illness*⟩

**contraction** /kən'trækʃn/ *n* contrazione *f*

**contract killer** *n* sicario *m*

**contractor** /kən'træktə(r)/ *n* imprenditore, -trice *mf*

**contractual** /kən'træktjʊəl/ *a* contrattuale

**contract work** *n* lavoro *m* su commissione

**contract worker** *n* lavoratore, -trice *mf* con contratto a termine

**contradict** /kɒntrə'dɪkt/ *vt* contraddire

**contradiction** /kɒntrə'dɪkʃn/ n contraddizione f

**contradictory** /kɒntrə'dɪktərɪ/ a contraddittorio

**contraflow** /'kɒntrəfləʊ/ n utilizzazione f di una corsia nei due sensi di marcia durante lavori stradali

**contraindication** /kɒntrəɪndr'keɪʃn/ n controindicazione f

**contralto** /kən'træltəʊ/ n contralto m

**contraption** /kən'træpʃn/ n fam aggeggio m

**contrariness** /kən'treərɪnɪs/ n spirito m di contraddizione

**contrariwise** /kən'treərɪwaɪz/ adv (conversely) d'altra parte, d'altro canto; (in the opposite direction) in direzione opposta

**contrary**[1] /'kɒntrərɪ/ a contrario ● adv ~ **to** contrariamente a ● n contrario m; **on the ~** al contrario

**contrary**[2] /kən'treərɪ/ a disobbediente

**contrast**[1] /'kɒntrɑːst/ n contrasto m

**contrast**[2] /kən'trɑːst/ vt confrontare ● vi contrastare

**contrasting** /kən'trɑːstɪŋ/ a contrastante

**contravene** /kɒntrə'viːn/ vt trasgredire

**contravention** /kɒntrə'venʃn/ n trasgressione f

**contribute** /kən'trɪbjuːt/ vt/i contribuire

**contribution** /kɒntrɪ'bjuːʃn/ n contribuzione f; (what is contributed) contributo m

**contributor** /kən'trɪbjʊtə(r)/ n contributore, -trice mf

**contributory** /kən'trɪbjʊtərɪ/ a ⟨factor⟩ concomitante; **be ~ to** contribuire a

**contrite** /kən'traɪt/ a contrito

**contrive** /kən'traɪv/ vt escogitare; ~ **to do sth** riuscire a fare qcsa

**contrived** /kən'traɪvd/ a ⟨style, effect⟩ artificioso; ⟨plot, ending⟩ forzato; ⟨incident, meeting⟩ non fortuito

**control** /kən'trəʊl/ n controllo m; **~s** pl (of car, plane) comandi mpl; **get out of ~** sfuggire al controllo ● vt (pt/pp **controlled**) controllare; **~ oneself** controllarsi

**control column** n Aeron cloche f inv

**control key** n Comput tasto m di controllo

**controlled** /kən'trəʊld/ a ⟨explosion, performance, person⟩ controllato; **Labour-~** dominato dai laburisti

**controller** /kən'trəʊlə(r)/ n controllore m; Fin controllore m [della gestione]; Radio, TV direttore, -trice mf

**control: control panel** n (on machine) quadro m dei comandi; (for plane) quadro m di comando. **control room** n sala f di comando; Radio, TV sala f di regia. **control tower** n torre f di controllo

**controversial** /kɒntrə'vɜːʃl/ a controverso

**controversy** /'kɒntrəvɜːsɪ/ n controversia f

**conundrum** /kə'nʌndrəm/ n enigma m

**conurbation** /kɒnɜː'beɪʃn/ n conurbazione f

**convalesce** /kɒnvə'les/ vi essere in convalescenza

**convalescence** /kɒnvə'lesəns/ n convalescenza f

**convalescent** /kɒnvə'lesənt/ a convalescente

**convalescent home** n convalescenziario m

**convection** /kən'vekʃn/ n convezione f

**convector** /kən'vektə(r)/ n ~ **[heater]** convettore m

**convene** /kən'viːn/ vt convocare ● vi riunirsi

**convener** /kən'viːnə(r)/ n (organizer) organizzatore, -trice mf; (chair) presidente m

**convenience** /kən'viːnɪəns/ n convenienza f; [**public**] ~ gabinetti mpl pubblici; **with all modern ~s** con tutti i comfort

**convenience foods** npl cibi mpl precotti

**convenience store** n negozio m aperto fino a tardi

**convenient** /kən'viːnɪənt/ a comodo; **be ~ for sb** andar bene per qcno; **if it is ~ [for you]** se ti va bene

**conveniently** /kən'viːnɪəntlɪ/ adv comodamente; ~ **located** in una posizione comoda

**convent** /'kɒnvənt/ n convento m

**convention** /kən'venʃn/ n convenzione f; (assembly) convegno m

**conventional** /kən'venʃnəl/ a convenzionale

**conventionally** /kən'venʃnəlɪ/ adv convenzionalmente

**convention centre** n palazzo m dei congressi

**convent school** n scuola f retta da religiose

**converge** /kən'vɜːdʒ/ vi convergere

**conversant** /kən'vɜːsənt/ a ~ **with** pratico di

**conversation** /kɒnvə'seɪʃn/ n conversazione f

**conversational** /kɒnvə'seɪʃnəl/ a di conversazione

**conversationalist** /kɒnvə'seɪʃnəlɪst/ n conversatore, -trice mf

**converse**[1] /kən'vɜːs/ vi conversare

**converse**[2] /'kɒnvɜːs/ n inverso m

**conversely** /'kɒnvɜːslɪ/ adv viceversa

**conversion** /kən'vɜːʃn/ n conversione f

**conversion rate** n [tasso m di] cambio m

**conversion table** n tabella f di conversione

**convert**[1] /'kɒnvɜːt/ n convertito, -a mf

**convert**[2] /kən'vɜːt/ vt convertire (**into** in); sconsacrare ⟨church⟩

**converter** /kən'vɜːtə(r)/ n Electr convertitore m

**convertible** /kən'vɜːtəbl/ a convertibile ● n Auto macchina f decappottabile

**convex** /'kɒnveks/ a convesso

**convey** /kən'veɪ/ vt portare; trasmettere ⟨idea, message⟩

**conveyance** /kən'veɪəns/ n trasporto m; (vehicle) mezzo m di trasporto

**conveyor** /kən'veɪə(r)/ n (of goods, persons) trasportatore m

**conveyor belt** n nastro m trasportatore

**convict**[1] /'kɒnvɪkt/ n condannato, -a mf

**convict²** /kən'vɪkt/ vt giudicare colpevole

**conviction** /kən'vɪkʃn/ n condanna f; (belief) convinzione f; **previous ~** precedente m penale

**convince** /kən'vɪns/ vt convincere

**convincing** /kən'vɪnsɪŋ/ a convincente

**convincingly** /kən'vɪnsɪŋlɪ/ adv in modo convincente

**convivial** /kən'vɪvɪəl/ a conviviale

**convoluted** /'kɒnvəluːtɪd/ a contorto

**convoy** /'kɒnvɔɪ/ n convoglio m

**convulse** /kən'vʌls/ vt sconvolgere; **be ~d with laughter** contorcersi dalle risa

**convulsion** /kən'vʌlʃn/ n convulsione f

**convulsive** /kən'vʌlsɪv/ a convulso; Med convulsivo

**convulsively** /kən'vʌlsɪvlɪ/ adv convulsamente

**coo** /kuː/ vi tubare

**cooing** /'kuːɪŋ/ n (of bird, lovers) tubare m inv

**cook** /kʊk/ n cuoco, -a mf ● vt cucinare; **is it ~ed?** è cotto? ~ **the books** fam truccare i libri contabili ● vi ⟨food:⟩ cuocere; ⟨person:⟩ cucinare

■ **cook up** vt (fam) inventare ⟨excuse, story etc⟩

**cookbook** /'kʊkbʊk/ n libro m di cucina

**cooked meats** /kʊkt'miːts/ npl salumi mpl

**cooker** /'kʊkə(r)/ n cucina f; (apple) mela f da cuocere

**cookery** /'kʊkərɪ/ n cucina f

**cookery book** n libro m di cucina

**cookie** /'kʊkɪ/ n Am biscotto m

**cooking** /'kʊkɪŋ/ n cucina f; **be good at ~** saper cucinare bene; **do the ~** cucinare

**cooking: cooking apple** n mela f da cuocere. **cooking chocolate** n cioccolato m da pasticceria. **cooking foil** n carta f stagnola. **cooking salt** n sale m da cucina. **cooking time** n tempo m di cottura

**cool** /kuːl/ a fresco; (calm) calmo; (unfriendly) freddo ● n fresco m; **keep/lose one's ~** mantenere/perdere la calma ● vt rinfrescare ● vi rinfrescarsi

■ **cool down** vi ⟨soup, tea etc:⟩ raffreddarsi; (fig: become calm) calmarsi ● vt raffreddare ⟨soup, tea etc⟩; (fig) calmare

**cool: cool bag** n Br borsa f frigo. **cool-box** n borsa f termica. **cool-headed** a equilibrato

**cooling** /'kuːlɪŋ/ n raffreddamento m ● a ⟨agent⟩ refrigerante; ⟨system, tower⟩ di raffreddamento; ⟨drink, swim⟩ rinfrescante

**cooling-off period** n (in industrial relations) periodo m di tregua [sindacale]; Comm fase f di riflessione

**coolly** /'kuːllɪ/ adv freddamente

**coolness** /'kuːlnɪs/ n freddezza f

**coop** /kuːp/ n stia f ● vt ~ **up** rinchiudere

**co-op** /'kəʊɒp/ n abbr (**cooperative**) cooperativa f

**cooperate** /kəʊ'ɒpəreɪt/ vi cooperare

**cooperation** /kəʊɒpə'reɪʃn/ n cooperazione f

**cooperative** /kəʊ'ɒpərətɪv/ a & n cooperativa f

**co-opt** /kəʊ'ɒpt/ vt eleggere

**coordinate** /kəʊ'ɔːdɪneɪt/ vt coordinare

**coordinated** /kəʊ'ɔːdɪneɪtɪd/ a coordinato

**coordination** /kəʊɔː'dɪneɪʃn/ n coordinazione f

**coordinator** /kəʊ'ɔːdɪneɪtə(r)/ n coordinatore, -trice mf

**co-owner** /kəʊ'əʊnə(r)/ n comproprietario, -a mf

**cop** /kɒp/ n fam poliziotto m

**cope** /kəʊp/ vi fam farcela; **can she ~ by herself?** ce la fa da sola?; ~ **with** farcela con; **I couldn't ~ with five kids** non ce la farei con cinque bambini

**Copenhagen** /kəʊpən'heɪgən/ n Copenhagen f

**copier** /'kɒpɪə(r)/ n fotocopiatrice f

**co-pilot** /'kəʊpaɪlət/ n copilota m

**copious** /'kəʊpɪəs/ a abbondante

**copiously** /'kəʊpɪəslɪ/ adv abbondantemente

**cop-out** n fam (evasive act) bidone m; (excuse) scappatoia f

**copper¹** /'kɒpə(r)/ n rame m; ~**s** pl monete fpl da uno o due pence ● attrib di rame

**copper²** n fam poliziotto m

**copper: copper beech** n faggio m rosso. **copper-coloured** a (color) rame inv; ⟨hair⟩ ramato. **copperplate** n calligrafia f ornata

**coppice** /'kɒpɪs/ n, **copse** /kɒps/ n boschetto m

**co-property** /'kəʊprɒpətɪ/ n comproprietà f inv

**copulate** /'kɒpjʊleɪt/ vi accoppiarsi

**copulation** /kɒpjʊ'leɪʃn/ n copulazione f

**copy** /'kɒpɪ/ n copia f ● vt (pt/pp -ied) copiare

■ **copy down** vt = copy

■ **copy out** vt = copy

**copy: copybook** n blot one's ~ rovinarsi la reputazione. **copycat** n pej fam copione, -a mf ● a ⟨crime, murder⟩ ispirato da un altro. **copy editor** n segretario, -a mf di redazione. **copyright** n diritti mpl d'autore. **copytypist** n dattilografo, -a mf. **copywriter** n copywriter mf inv

**coquetry** /'kɒkɪtrɪ/ n civetteria f

**coquettish** /kɒ'ketɪʃ/ a civettuolo

**coral** /'kɒrəl/ n corallo m

**coral: coral island** n isola f di corallo. **coral pink** a & n rosa m inv corallo. **coral reef** n barriera f corallina

**cord** /kɔːd/ n corda f; (thinner) cordoncino m; (fabric) velluto m a coste; ~**s** pl pantaloni mpl di velluto a coste

**cordial** /'kɔːdɪəl/ a cordiale ● n analcolico m

**cordially** /'kɔːdɪəlɪ/ adv con tutto il cuore

**cordless telephone** /'kɔːdlɪs/ a telefono m senza fili

**cordon** /'kɔːdn/ n cordone m (di persone)

■ **cordon off** vt bloccare

**corduroy** /'kɔːdərɔɪ/ n velluto m a coste

**core** /kɔː(r)/ n (of apple, pear) torsolo m; (fig:

*of organization*) cuore *m*; (*of problem, theory*) nocciolo *m*

**co-respondent** /kəʊrɪ'spɒndənt/ *n Jur* correo, -a *mf* in adulterio

**Corfu** /kɔː'fuː/ *n* Corfù *f*

**coriander** /kɒrɪ'ændə(r)/ *n* coriandolo *m*

**cork** /kɔːk/ *n* sughero *m*; (*for bottle*) turacciolo *m*

**corkage** /'kɔːkɪdʒ/ *n* somma *f* pagata a un ristorante per servire una bottiglia di vino portata da fuori

**corker** /'kɔːkə(r)/ *n Br fam* (*story*) storia *f* strabiliante; (*stroke, shot*) tiro *m* da maestro

**corkscrew** /'kɔːkskruː/ *n* cavatappi *m inv*

**corkscrew curls** *npl* boccoli *mpl*

**corn¹** /kɔːn/ *n* grano *m*; (*Am: maize*) granturco *m*

**corn²** *n Med* callo *m*

**corncob** /'kɔːnkɒb/ *n* pannocchia *f* [di mais]

**cornea** /'kɔːnɪə/ *n* cornea *f*

**corned beef** /kɔːnd'biːf/ *n* manzo *m* sotto sale

**corner** /'kɔːnə(r)/ *n* angolo *m*; (*football*) calcio *m* d'angolo, corner *m inv* ● *vt fig* bloccare; *Comm* accaparrarsi ‹*market*›

**corner shop** *n* negozio *m* di quartiere

**cornerstone** /'kɔːnəstəʊn/ *n* pietra *f* angolare

**cornet** /'kɔːnɪt/ *n Mus* cornetta *f*; (*for ice-cream*) cono *m*

**cornfield** /'kɔːnfiːld/ *n* campo *m* di grano; (*sweetcorn*) campo *m* di mais

**cornflour** /'kɔːnflaʊə(r)/ *n* farina *f* finissima di mais

**cornflower** /'kɔːnflaʊə(r)/ *n* fiordaliso *m*

**cornice** /'kɔːnɪs/ *n* (*inside*) cornice *f*; (*outside*) cornicione *m*

**Cornish pasty** /kɔːnɪʃ'pæstɪ/ *n* fagottino *m* di pasta sfoglia ripieno di carne e verdura

**corn: corn oil** *n* olio *m* di mais. **corn on the cob** *n* pannocchia *f* cotta. **corn plaster** *n* [cerotto *m*] callifugo *m*. **cornstarch** *n Am* farina *f* di granturco

**cornucopia** /kɔːnjʊ'kəʊpɪə/ *n* cornucopia *f*; *fig* abbondanza *f*

**Cornwall** /'kɔːnwɔːl/ *n* Cornovaglia *f*

**corny** /'kɔːnɪ/ *a* (**-ier, -iest**) ‹*fam: joke, film*› scontato; ‹*person*› banale; (*sentimental*) sdolcinato

**corollary** /kə'rɒlərɪ/ *n* corollario *m*

**coronary** /'kɒrənərɪ/ *a* coronario ● *n* ~ **[thrombosis]** trombosi *f* coronarica

**coronation** /kɒrə'neɪʃn/ *n* incoronazione *f*

**coroner** /'kɒrənə(r)/ *n* coroner *m inv* (*nel diritto britannico, ufficiale incaricato delle indagini su morti sospette*)

**coronet** /'kɒrənet/ *n* coroncina *f*

**corporal¹** /'kɔːpərəl/ *n Mil* caporale *m*

**corporal²** *a* corporale; ~ **punishment** punizione *f* corporale

**corporate** /'kɔːpərət/ *a* ‹*decision, policy, image*› aziendale; ~ **life** la vita in un'azienda

**corporate: corporate image** *n* immagine *f* aziendale. **corporate lawyer** *n* legale *mf* specializzato, -a in diritto aziendale.

**corporate planning** *n* pianificazione *f* aziendale

**corporation** /kɔːpə'reɪʃn/ *n* ente *m*; (*of town*) ≃ consiglio *m* comunale

**corporation tax** *n Br* imposta *f* sul reddito delle aziende

**corps** /kɔː(r)/ *n* (*pl* **corps** /kɔːz/) corpo *m*

**corps de ballet** /kɔːdə'bæleɪ/ *n* corpo *m* di ballo

**corpse** /kɔːps/ *n* cadavere *m*

**corpulent** /'kɔːpjʊlənt/ *a* corpulento

**corpus** /'kɔːpəs/ *n* (*of words*) corpus *m inv*

**corpuscle** /'kɔːpʌsl/ *n* globulo *m*

**correct** /kə'rekt/ *a* corretto; **be** ~ ‹*person:*› aver ragione; ~! esatto! ● *vt* correggere

**correcting fluid** *n* bianchetto *m*

**correction** /kə'rekʃn/ *n* correzione *f*

**corrective** /kə'rektɪv/ *n* correttivo *m*

**correctly** /kə'rektlɪ/ *adv* correttamente

**correlate** /'kɒrəleɪt/ *vt* correlare ● *vi* essere correlato

**correlation** /kɒrə'leɪʃn/ *n* correlazione *f*

**correspond** /kɒrɪ'spɒnd/ *vi* corrispondere (**to** a); ‹*two things:*› corrispondere; (*write*) scriversi

**correspondence** /kɒrɪ'spɒndəns/ *n* corrispondenza *f*

**correspondence course** *n* corso *m* per corrispondenza

**correspondent** /kɒrɪ'spɒndənt/ *n* corrispondente *mf*

**corresponding** /kɒrɪ'spɒndɪŋ/ *a* corrispondente

**correspondingly** /kɒrɪ'spɒndɪŋlɪ/ *adv* in modo corrispondente

**corridor** /'kɒrɪdɔː(r)/ *n* corridoio *m*

**corroborate** /kə'rɒbəreɪt/ *vt* corroborare

**corrode** /kə'rəʊd/ *vt* corrodere ● *vi* corrodersi

**corrosion** /kə'rəʊʒn/ *n* corrosione *f*

**corrugated** /'kɒrəgeɪtɪd/ *a* ondulato

**corrugated iron** *n* lamiera *f* ondulata

**corrupt** /kə'rʌpt/ *a* corrotto ● *vt* corrompere

**corruption** /kə'rʌpʃn/ *n* corruzione *f*

**corset** /'kɔːsɪt/ *n & -s pl* busto *m*

**Corsica** /'kɔːsɪkə/ *n* Corsica *f*

**Corsican** /'kɔːsɪkən/ *a & n* corso, -a *mf*

**cortège** /kɔː'teɪʒ/ *n* [**funeral**] ~ corteo *m* funebre

**cosh** /kɒʃ/ *n* randello *m*

**co-signatory** /kəʊ'sɪgnətrɪ/ *n* cofirmatario, -a *mf*

**cosily** /'kəʊzɪlɪ/ *adv* ‹*sit, lie*› in modo confortevole

**cosiness** /'kəʊzɪnɪs/ *n* (*of room*) comodità *f*; (*intimacy*) intimità *f*

**cos lettuce** /kɒs/ *n* lattuga *f* romana

**cosmetic** /kɒz'metɪk/ *a* cosmetico ● *n* ~**s** *pl* cosmetici *mpl*

**cosmetic surgery** *n* chirurgia *f* estetica

**cosmic** /'kɒzmɪk/ *a* cosmico

**cosmonaut** /'kɒzmənɔːt/ *n* cosmonauta *mf*

**cosmopolitan** /kɒzmə'pɒlɪtən/ *a* cosmopolita

**cosmos** /'kɒzmɒs/ *n* cosmo *m*

**Cossack** /ˈkɒsæk/ a & n cosacco, -a mf
**cosset** /ˈkɒsɪt/ vt coccolare
**cost** /kɒst/ n costo m; ~s pl Jur spese fpl processuali; **at all** ~s a tutti i costi; **I learnt to my** ~ ho imparato a mie spese ● vt (pt/pp **cost**) costare; **it** ~ **me £20** mi è costato 20 sterline ● vt (pt/pp **costed**) ~ **[out]** stabilire il prezzo di
**co-star** /ˈkəʊstɑː/ n Cinema, Theat co-protagonista mf ● **film** ~**ring X and Y** un film con X e Y come protagonisti
**cost: cost centre** n centro m di costi. **cost-cutting** n tagli mpl sulle spese; **as a** ~ **exercise** [come misura] per ridurre le spese. **cost-effective** a conveniente. **cost-effectiveness** n convenienza f
**costing** /ˈkɒstɪŋ/ n (process) determinazione f dei costi; (discipline) costing m inv
**costly** /ˈkɒstlɪ/ a (-ier, -iest) costoso
**cost of living** n costo m della vita
**cost-of-living index** n indice m del costo della vita
**cost price** n prezzo m di costo
**costume** /ˈkɒstjuːm/ n costume m
**costume drama** n dramma m storico
**costume jewellery** n bigiotteria f
**cosy** /ˈkəʊzɪ/ a (-ier, -iest) (pub, chat) intimo; **it's nice and** ~ **in here** si sta bene qui ● n **tea** ~ copriteiera m inv
**cot** /kɒt/ n lettino m; (Am: camp bed) branda f
**cot death** n Br morte f inspiegabile di un neonato nel sonno
**Côte d'Azur** /kəʊtdæˈzʊə(r)/ n Costa f Azzurra
**cottage** /ˈkɒtɪdʒ/ n casetta f
**cottage: cottage cheese** n fiocchi mpl di latte. **cottage hospital** n Br piccolo ospedale m (in zona rurale). **cottage industry** n attività f inv artigianale basata sul lavoro a domicilio. **cottage loaf** n pagnotta f casereccia. **cottage pie** n Br pasticcio m di patate e carne macinata
**cotton** /ˈkɒtn/ n cotone m ● attrib di cotone
■ **cotton on** vi fam capire
**cotton: cotton bud** n cotton fiocᴿ m inv. **cotton mill** n cotonificio m. **cotton reel** n rocchetto m, spagnoletta f. **cotton wool** n Br cotone m idrofilo
**couch** /kaʊtʃ/ n divano m
**couchette** /kuːˈʃet/ n cuccetta f
**couch potato** n pantofolaio, -a mf
**cougar** /ˈkuːgə(r)/ n coguaro m
**cough** /kɒf/ n tosse f ● vi tossire
■ **cough up** vt/i sputare; (fam: pay) sborsare
**cough mixture** n sciroppo m per la tosse
**could** /kʊd/, atono /kəd/ v aux (see also can²) ~ **I have a glass of water?** potrei avere un bicchier d'acqua?; **I** ~**n't do it even if I wanted to** non potrei farlo nemmeno se lo volessi; **I** ~**n't care less** non potrebbe importarmene di meno; **he** ~**n't have done it without help** non avrebbe potuto farlo senza aiuto; **you** ~ **have phoned** avresti potuto telefonare

**council** /ˈkaʊnsl/ n consiglio m
**council: council estate** n Br complesso m di case popolari. **council house** n casa f popolare. **council housing** n Br case fpl popolari
**councillor** /ˈkaʊnsələ(r)/ n consigliere, -a mf
**council tax** n imposta f locale sugli immobili
**counsel** /ˈkaʊnsl/ n consigli mpl; Jur avvocato m ● vt (pt/pp **counselled**) consigliare a (person)
**counselling**, Am **counseling** /ˈkaʊnsəlɪŋ/ n (psychological) terapia f [psichiatrica]; Sch orientamento m scolastico; **careers** ~ orientamento m professionale ● attrib (group, centre, service) di assistenza
**counsellor** /ˈkaʊnsələ(r)/ n consigliere, -a mf
**count¹** /kaʊnt/ n (nobleman) conte m
**count²** n conto m; **keep** ~ tenere il conto ● vt/i contare
■ **count against** vt (inexperience, police record:) deporre a sfavore di
■ **count among** vt ~ **sb among one's friends** annoverare qcno tra i propri amici
■ **count in** vt (include) includere; ~ **me in!** io ci sto!
■ **count on** vt contare su
■ **count out** vt contare (money); ~ **me out!** fate senza di me!
■ **count up** vt contare ● vi ~ **to ten** contare fino a dieci
**countable** /ˈkaʊntəbl/ a (noun) numerabile
**countdown** /ˈkaʊntdaʊn/ n conto m alla rovescia
**countenance** /ˈkaʊntənəns/ n espressione f ● vt approvare
**counter¹** /ˈkaʊntə(r)/ n banco m; (in games) gettone m
**counter²** adv ~ **to** contro, in contrasto a; **go** ~ **to sth** andare contro qcsa ● vt/i opporre (measure, effect); parare (blow)
**counteract** /kaʊntərˈækt/ vt neutralizzare
**counter-attack** n contrattacco m
**counterbalance** /ˈkaʊntəbæləns/ n contrappeso m ● vt controbilanciare
**counter-claim** n replica f
**counter-culture** /ˈkaʊntəkʌltʃə(r)/ n controcultura f
**counter-espionage** n controspionaggio m
**counterfeit** /ˈkaʊntəfɪt/ a contraffatto ● n contraffazione f ● vt contraffare
**counterfoil** /ˈkaʊntəfɔɪl/ n matrice f
**counter-inflationary** /-ɪnˈfleɪʃənərɪ/ a antinflazionistico
**counter-insurgency** /-ɪnˈsɜːdʒənsɪ/ attrib per reprimere un'insurrezione
**counter-intelligence** n controspionaggio m
**countermeasure** /ˈkaʊntəmeʒə(r)/ n contromisura f
**counter-offensive** n controffensiva f
**counterpane** /ˈkaʊntəpeɪn/ n copriletto m
**counterpart** /ˈkaʊntəpɑːt/ n equivalente mf

**counterpoint** /ˈkaʊntəpɔɪnt/ n contrappunto mf

**counter-productive** a controproduttivo

**countersign** /ˈkaʊntəsaɪn/ vt controfirmare

**counter. staff** n commessi mpl

**counter-terrorism** n antiterrorismo m

**countess** /ˈkaʊntɪs/ n contessa f

**countless** /ˈkaʊntlɪs/ a innumerevole

**countrified** /ˈkʌntrɪfaɪd/ a ⟨person⟩ campagnolo

**country** /ˈkʌntrɪ/ n nazione f, paese m; (native land) patria f; (countryside) campagna f; **in the ~** in campagna; **go to the ~** andare in campagna; Pol indire le elezioni politiche

**country: country and western** n country m inv. **country bumpkin** n pej buzzurro , -a mf. **country club** n club m inv sportivo e ricreativo in campagna. **country cousin** n pej provinciale mf. **country dancing** n danza f folcloristica. **country house** n villa f di campagna. **countryman** n uomo m di campagna; (fellow ~man) compatriota m. **country music** n country m inv. **countryside** n campagna f. **countrywide** a & adv in tutto il paese

**county** /ˈkaʊntɪ/ n contea f (unità amministrativa britannica)

**county council** n Br Pol consiglio m di contea

**county court** n Br Jur tribunale m di contea

**coup** /kuː/ n Pol colpo m di stato

**couple** /ˈkʌpl/ n coppia f; **a ~ of** un paio di

**coupon** /ˈkuːpɒn/ n tagliando m; (for discount) buono m sconto

**courage** /ˈkʌrɪdʒ/ n coraggio m

**courageous** /kəˈreɪdʒəs/ a coraggioso

**courageously** /kəˈreɪdʒəslɪ/ adv coraggiosamente

**courgette** /kʊəˈʒet/ n zucchino m

**courier** /ˈkʊrɪə(r)/ n corriere m; (for tourists) guida f

**course** /kɔːs/ n Sch corso m; Naut rotta f; Culin portata f; (for golf) campo m; **~ of treatment** Med serie f inv di cure; **of ~** naturalmente; **in the ~ of** durante; **in due ~** a tempo debito; **~ of action** linea f d'azione

**course book** n libro m di testo

**coursework** /ˈkɔːswɜːk/ n Sch, Univ esercitazioni fpl scritte che contano per la media

**court** /kɔːt/ n tribunale m; Sport campo m; **take sb to ~** citare qcno in giudizio ● vt fare la corte a ⟨woman⟩; sfidare ⟨danger⟩; **~ing couples** coppiette fpl

**court circular** n bollettino quotidiano f di corte

**courteous** /ˈkɜːtɪəs/ a cortese

**courteously** /ˈkɜːtɪəslɪ/ adv cortesemente

**courtesy** /ˈkɜːtəsɪ/ n cortesia f

**courthouse** /ˈkɔːthaʊs/ n Jur palazzo m di giustizia, tribunale m

**courtier** /ˈkɔːtɪə(r)/ n cortigiano, -a mf

**court: court martial** n (pl ~s martial) corte f marziale ● **court-martial** vt (pt ~-martialled) portare davanti alla corte marziale. **court of inquiry** n commissione f d'inchiesta. **court of law** n Jur corte f di giustizia. **court order** n Jur ingiunzione f. **courtroom** n Jur aula f [di tribunale]

**courtship** /ˈkɔːtʃɪp/ n corteggiamento m

**courtyard** /ˈkɔːtjɑːd/ n cortile m

**cousin** /ˈkʌzn/ n cugino, -a mf

**cove** /kəʊv/ n insenatura f

**covenant** /ˈkʌvənənt/ n (agreement) accordo m; (payment agreement) impegno m scritto a pagare

**cover** /ˈkʌvə(r)/ n copertura f; (of cushion, to protect sth) fodera f; (of book, magazine) copertina f; **take ~** mettersi al riparo; **under separate ~** a parte ● vt coprire; foderare ⟨cushion⟩; Journ fare un servizio su
■ **cover for** vt (replace) sostituire ⟨sb⟩
■ **cover up** vt coprire; fig soffocare ⟨scandal⟩
■ **cover up for** vt fare da copertura a ⟨sb⟩

**coverage** /ˈkʌvərɪdʒ/ n Journ **it got a lot of ~** i media gli hanno dedicato molto spazio

**cover charge** n coperto m

**covered market** n mercato m coperto

**covered wagon** n carro m coperto

**cover girl** n ragazza f copertina

**covering** /ˈkʌv(ə)rɪŋ/ n copertura f; (for floor) rivestimento m; **~ of snow** strato m di neve

**covering fire** n fuoco m di copertura

**covering letter** n lettera f d'accompagnamento

**cover note** n (from insurance company) polizza f provvisoria

**cover story** n (in paper) articolo m di prima pagina

**covert** /ˈkəʊvɜːt/ a ⟨threat⟩ velato; ⟨operation⟩ segreto; ⟨glance⟩ furtivo

**covertly** /ˈkəʊvɜːtlɪ/ adv furtivamente; ⟨operate⟩ in segreto

**cover-up** n messa f a tacere

**cover version** n Mus versione f non originale

**covet** /ˈkʌvɪt/ vt bramare

**covetous** /ˈkʌvətəs/ a avido

**covetously** /ˈkʌvətəslɪ/ adv avidamente

**cow** /kaʊ/ n vacca f, mucca f

**coward** /ˈkaʊəd/ n vigliacco, -a mf

**cowardice** /ˈkaʊədɪs/ n vigliaccheria f

**cowardly** /ˈkaʊədlɪ/ a da vigliacco

**cowbell** /ˈkaʊbel/ n campanaccio m

**cowboy** /ˈkaʊbɔɪ/ n cowboy m inv; fig fam buffone m

**cower** /ˈkaʊə(r)/ vi acquattarsi

**cowherd** /ˈkaʊhɜːd/ n vaccaro m

**cowhide** /ˈkaʊhaɪd/ n (leather) pelle f di mucca

**cowl** /kaʊl/ n cappuccio m

**cowlick** /ˈkaʊlɪk/ n fam ciocca f ribelle

**cowl neck** n collo m a anello

**cowpat** /ˈkaʊpæt/ n sterco m di vacca

**cowshed** /ˈkaʊʃed/ n stalla f

**cox** /kɒks/ n, **coxswain** /ˈkɒks(ə)n/ n timoniere, -a mf

**coy** /kɔɪ/ a falsamente timido; ⟨flirtatiously⟩ civettuolo; **be ~ about sth** essere evasivo su qcsa

**coyly** /'kɔɪlɪ/ adv con falsa modestia; ⟨flirtatiously⟩ con civetteria

**CPU** n abbr (**central processing unit**) CPU f inv

**crab** /kræb/ n granchio m

**crab apple** n mela f selvatica

**crack** /kræk/ n (in wall) crepa f; (in china, glass, bone) incrinatura f; (noise) scoppio m; (fam: joke) battuta f; **have a ~** (try) fare un tentativo ● a (fam: best) di prim'ordine ● vt incrinare ⟨china, glass⟩; schiacciare ⟨nut⟩; decifrare ⟨code⟩; fam risolvere ⟨problem⟩; **~ a joke** fam fare una battuta ● vi ⟨china, glass:⟩ incrinarsi; ⟨whip:⟩ schioccare

■ **crack down** vi fam prendere seri provvedimenti

■ **crack down on** vt fam prendere seri provvedimenti contro

■ **crack up** vi crollare

**crackdown** /'krækdaʊn/ n misure fpl (**on** contro)

**cracked** /krækt/ a ⟨plaster⟩ crepato; ⟨skin⟩ screpolato; ⟨rib⟩ incrinato; (fam: crazy) svitato

**cracker** /'krækə(r)/ n (biscuit) cracker m inv; (firework) petardo m; [**Christmas**] **~** cilindro m di cartone contenente una sorpresa che produce una piccola esplosione quando viene aperto

**crackers** /'krækəz/ a fam matto

**cracking** /'krækɪŋ/ a Br fam eccellente; **at a ~ pace** a ritmo incalzante

**crackle** /'krækl/ vi crepitare

**crackling** /'kræklɪŋ/ n (on radio) disturbo m; (of foil, cellophane) sfregamento m; (of fire) crepitio m; (crisp pork) cotenna f arrostita

**crackpot** /'krækpɒt/ fam n pazzo, -a mf ● a da pazzi

**cradle** /'kreɪdl/ n culla f

**cradle-snatcher** n fam he's/she's a **~** se la intende con i ragazzini/le ragazzine

**craft**[1] /krɑːft/ n inv (boat) imbarcazione f

**craft**[2] n mestiere m; (technique) arte f

**craftily** /'krɑːftɪlɪ/ adv con astuzia

**craftsman** /'krɑːftsmən/ n artigiano m

**craftsmanship** /'krɑːftsmənʃɪp/ n maestria f

**crafty** /'krɑːftɪ/ a (-ier, -iest) astuto

**crag** /kræg/ n rupe f

**craggy** /'krægɪ/ a scosceso; ⟨face⟩ dai lineamenti marcati

**cram** /kræm/ v (pt/pp **crammed**) ● vt stipare (**into** in) ● vi (for exams) sgobbare

**crammer** /'kræmə(r)/ n (Br fam: school) ≈ istituto m di recupero

**cramp** /kræmp/ n crampo m

**cramped** /kræmpt/ a ⟨room⟩ stretto; ⟨handwriting⟩ appiccicato; **it's a bit ~ed in here** si sta un po' stretti qui

**crampon** /'kræmpən/ n rampone m

**cranberry** /'krænbərɪ/ n Culin mirtillo m rosso

**crane** /kreɪn/ n (at docks, bird) gru f inv ● vt **~ one's neck** allungare il collo

**cranium** /'kreɪnɪəm/ n cranio m

**crank**[1] /kræŋk/ n tipo, -a mf strampalato, -a

**crank**[2] n Techn manovella f

**crankshaft** /'kræŋkʃɑːft/ n albero m a gomiti

**cranky** /'kræŋkɪ/ a strampalato; (Am: irritable) irritabile

**cranny** /'krænɪ/ n fessura f

**crap** /kræp/ n sl (faeces) merda f; (film, book etc) schifezza f; (nonsense) stronzate fpl; **have a ~** cacare

**crappy** /'kræpɪ/ a sl di merda

**crash** /kræʃ/ n (noise) fragore m; Auto, Aeron incidente m; Comm crollo m; Comput crash m inv ● vi schiantarsi (**into** contro); ⟨plane:⟩ precipitare ● vt schiantare ⟨car⟩

■ **crash out** vi (sl: go to sleep) crollare; (on sofa etc) dormire

**crash: crash barrier** n guardrail m inv. **crash course** n corso m intensivo. **crash diet** n dieta f drastica. **crash-helmet** n casco m. **crash-land** vi fare un atterraggio di fortuna. **crash-landing** n atterraggio m di fortuna

**crass** /kræs/ a ⟨ignorance⟩ crasso

**crate** /kreɪt/ n (for packing) cassa f

**crater** /'kreɪtə(r)/ n cratere m

**cravat** /krə'væt/ n foulard m inv

**crave** /kreɪv/ vt morire dalla voglia di

**craving** /'kreɪvɪŋ/ n voglia f smodata

**crawl** /krɔːl/ n (swimming) stile m libero; **do the ~** nuotare a stile libero; **at a ~** a passo di lumaca ● vi andare carponi; **~ with** brulicare di

**crawler lane** /'krɔːlə/ n Auto corsia f riservata al traffico lento

**crayfish** /'kreɪfɪʃ/ n gambero m d'acqua dolce

**crayon** /'kreɪən/ n pastello m a cera; (pencil) matita f colorata

**craze** /kreɪz/ n mania f

**crazed** /kreɪzd/ a ⟨china, glaze⟩ screpolato; ⟨animal, person⟩ impazzito; **power-~** ubriaco di potere

**crazy** /'kreɪzɪ/ a (-ier, -iest) matto; **be ~ about** andar matto per

**crazy golf** n Br minigolf m inv

**crazy paving** n Br pavimentazione f a mosaico irregolare

**creak** /kriːk/ n scricchiolio m ● vi scricchiolare

**creaky** /'kriːkɪ/ a ⟨leather⟩ che cigola; ⟨door, hinge⟩ cigolante; ⟨joint, bone, floorboard⟩ scricchiolante; ⟨fig fam: alibi, policy⟩ traballante

**cream** /kriːm/ n crema f; (fresh) panna f ● a (colour) [bianco] panna inv ● vt Culin sbattere

■ **cream off** vt accaparrarsi ⟨top pupils, scientists etc⟩

**cream: cream cheese** n formaggio m cremoso. **cream cracker** n Br cracker m inv. **cream puff** n sfogliatina f alla panna inv. **cream soda** n soda f aromatizzata alla vaniglia. **cream tea** n Br tè m inv servito con pasticcini da mangiare con marmellata e panna

**creamy** /'kri:mɪ/ a ( -ier, iest) cremoso

**crease** /kri:s/ n piega f ● vt stropicciare ● vi stropicciarsi

**crease-resistant** a che non si stropiccia

**create** /kri:'eɪt/ vt creare

**creation** /kri:'eɪʃn/ n creazione f

**creative** /kri:'eɪtɪv/ a creativo

**creative director** n direttore, -trice mf creativo, -a

**creative writing** n (school subject) composizione f

**creativity** /kri:eɪ'tɪvətɪ/ n creatività f

**creator** /kri:'eɪtə(r)/ n creatore, -trice mf

**creature** /kri:tʃə(r)/ n creatura f

**creature comforts** npl comodità fpl; **like one's ~ ~** amare le proprie comodità

**crèche** /kreʃ/ n asilo m nido inv

**credence** /'kri:dəns/ n credito m; **give ~ to sth** (believe) dare credito a qcsa

**credentials** /krɪ'denʃlz/ npl credenziali fpl

**credibility** /kredə'bɪlətɪ/ n credibilità f

**credible** /'kredəbl/ a credibile

**credit** /'kredɪt/ n credito m; (honour) merito m; **take the ~ for** prendersi il merito di ● vt accreditare; **~ sb with sth** Comm accreditare qcsa a qcno; fig attribuire qcsa a qcno

**creditable** /'kredɪtəbl/ a lodevole

**credit: credit balance** n saldo m attivo. **credit card** n carta f di credito. **credit control** n controllo m del credito. **credit limit** n limite m di credito. **credit note** n Comm nota f di accredito

**creditor** /'kredɪtə(r)/ n creditore, -trice mf

**credit: credit side** n on the **~ ~** tra i lati positivi. **credit squeeze** n stretta f creditizia. **credit terms** npl condizioni fpl di credito. **credit transfer** n bonifico m

**creditworthiness** /'kredɪ(t)wɜ:ðmɪs/ n capacità f di credito

**creditworthy** /'kredɪ(t)wɜ:ðɪ/ a meritevole di credito

**credulity** /krɪ'dju:lətɪ/ n credulità f; **strain sb's ~** essere ai limiti della credibilità

**credulous** /'kredjʊləs/ a credulo

**creed** /kri:d/ n credo m inv

**creek** /kri:k/ n insenatura f; (Am: stream) torrente m; **up the ~** (fam: in trouble) nei guai

**creep** /kri:p/ vi (pt/pp crept) muoversi furtivamente ● n fam tipo m viscido; **it gives me the ~s** mi fa venire i brividi

**creeper** /'kri:pə(r)/ n pianta f rampicante

**creepy** /'kri:pɪ/ a che fa venire i brividi

**creepy-crawly** /-'krɔ:lɪ/ n fam insetto

**cremate** /krɪ'meɪt/ vt cremare

**cremation** /krɪ'meɪʃn/ n cremazione f

**crematorium** /kremə'tɔ:rɪəm/ n crematorio m

**crepe** /kreɪp/ n (fabric) crespo m

**crepe: crepe bandage** n fascia f elastica. **crepe paper** n carta f crespata. **crepe soles** npl suole fpl di para

**crept** /krept/ see creep

**crescendo** /krɪ'ʃendəʊ/ n Mus crescendo m; **reach a ~** fig (noise, protests:) raggiungere il picco; (campaign:) raggiungere il culmine

**crescent** /'kresənt/ n mezzaluna f

**crescent moon** n mezzaluna f

**cress** /kres/ n crescione m

**crest** /krest/ n cresta f; (coat of arms) cimiero m; **be on the ~ of a wave** essere sulla cresta dell'onda

**crestfallen** /'krestfɔ:lən/ a mogio

**Crete** /kri:t/ n Creta f

**crevasse** /krɪ'væs/ n crepaccio m

**crevice** /'krevɪs/ n crepa f

**crew** /kru:/ n equipaggio m; (gang) équipe f inv

**crew cut** n capelli mpl a spazzola

**crew neck** n girocollo m

**crew neck sweater** n maglione m a girocollo

**crib¹** /krɪb/ n (for baby) culla f

**crib²** vt/i (pt/pp cribbed) fam copiare

**cribbage** /'krɪbɪdʒ/ n gioco m di carte

**crick** /krɪk/ n **~ in the neck** torcicollo m

**cricket¹** /'krɪkɪt/ n (insect) grillo m

**cricket²** n cricket m

**cricketer** /'krɪkɪtə(r)/ n giocatore m di cricket

**crime** /kraɪm/ n crimine m; (criminality) criminalità f; **it's a ~** fig è un delitto

**crime of passion** n delitto m passionale

**crime prevention** n prevenzione f della criminalità

**criminal** /'krɪmɪnl/ a criminale; (law, court) penale ● n criminale mf

**criminal: criminal charges** npl **face ~ ~** essere imputato. **criminal investigation** n inchiesta f giudiziaria. **Criminal Investigation Department** n Br ≈ polizia f giudiziaria. **criminal justice** n sistema m penale. **criminal law** n diritto m penale.

**criminally insane** /'krɪmɪnəlɪ/ a pazzo criminale

**criminal offence** n reato m

**criminal record** n **have a/no ~ ~** avere la fedina penale sporca/pulita

**criminology** /krɪmɪ'nɒlədʒɪ/ n criminologia f

**crimp** /krɪmp/ vt pieghettare (fabric); increspare (pastry); arricciare (hair)

**crimson** /'krɪmz(ə)n/ a cremisi inv

**cringe** /krɪndʒ/ vi (cower) acquattarsi; (at bad joke etc) fare una smorfia

**crinkle** /'krɪŋk(ə)l/ vt spiegazzare ● vi spiegazzarsi

**crinkly** /'krɪŋklɪ/ a (paper, material) crespato; (hair) crespo

**cripple** /'krɪpl/ n storpio, -a mf ● vt storpiare; fig danneggiare

**crippled** /'krɪpld/ a (person) storpio; (ship) danneggiato

**crippling** /'krɪplɪŋ/ a (taxes, debts) esorbitante; (disease) devastante; (strike, effect) paralizzante

**crisis** /'kraɪsɪs/ n (pl -ses /'kraɪsiːz/) crisi f inv

**crisp** /krɪsp/ a croccante; ⟨air⟩ frizzante; ⟨style⟩ incisivo

**crispbread** /'krɪs(p)bred/ n crostini mpl di pane

**crisps** /krɪsps/ npl patatine fpl

**crispy** /'krɪspɪ/ a croccante

**criss-cross** /'krɪs-/ a a linee incrociate

**criterion** /kraɪ'tɪərɪən/ n (pl -ria /kraɪ'tɪərɪə/) criterio m

**critic** /'krɪtɪk/ n critico, -a mf

**critical** /'krɪtɪkl/ a critico

**critically** /'krɪtɪklɪ/ adv in modo critico; ~ ill gravemente malato

**critical path analysis** n analisi f inv del percorso critico

**criticism** /'krɪtɪsɪzm/ n critica f; he doesn't like ~ non ama le critiche

**criticize** /'krɪtɪsaɪz/ vt criticare

**croak** /krəʊk/ vi gracchiare; ⟨frog:⟩ gracidare

**Croatia** /krəʊ'eɪʃə/ n Croazia f

**crochet** /'krəʊʃeɪ/ n lavoro m all'uncinetto ● vt fare all'uncinetto

**crochet-hook** n uncinetto m

**crock** /krɒk/ n fam old ~ ⟨person⟩ rudere m; ⟨car⟩ macinino m

**crockery** /'krɒkərɪ/ n terrecotte fpl

**crocodile** /'krɒkədaɪl/ n coccodrillo m

**crocodile tears** npl lacrime fpl di coccodrillo

**crocus** /'krəʊkəs/ n (pl -es) croco m

**croft** /krɒft/ n piccola fattoria f

**crone** /krəʊn/ n pej vecchiaccia f

**crony** /'krəʊnɪ/ n compare m

**crook** /krʊk/ n ⟨fam: criminal⟩ truffatore, -trice mf

**crooked** /'krʊkɪd/ a storto; ⟨limb⟩ storpiato; ⟨fam: dishonest⟩ disonesto; ~ deal fregatura f

**croon** /kruːn/ vt/i canticchiare

**crop** /krɒp/ n raccolto m; fig quantità f inv ● v (pt/pp cropped) ● vt coltivare

■ **crop up** vi fam presentarsi

**crop rotation** n rotazione f delle colture

**crop spraying** /'krɒpspreɪɪŋ/ n irrorazione f

**croquet** /'krəʊkeɪ/ n croquet m

**croquette** /krəʊ'ket/ n crocchetta f

**cross** /krɒs/ a ⟨annoyed⟩ arrabbiato; talk at ~ purposes fraintendersi ● n croce f; Bot, Zool incrocio m ● vt sbarrare ⟨cheque⟩; incrociare ⟨road, animals⟩; ~ oneself farsi il segno della croce; ~ one's arms incrociare le braccia; ~ one's legs accavallare le gambe; keep one's fingers ~ed for sb tenere le dita incrociate per qcno; it ~ed my mind mi è venuto in mente ● vi ⟨go across⟩ attraversare; ⟨lines:⟩ incrociarsi

■ **cross off** vt ⟨from list⟩ depennare

■ **cross out** vt sbarrare; ⟨from list⟩ depennare

**cross: crossbar** n ⟨of goal⟩ traversa f; ⟨on bicycle⟩ canna f. **cross-border** a oltreconfine. **crossbow** n balestra f. **crossbred** a ibrido. **crossbreed** vt ibridare, incrociare ⟨animals, plants⟩ ● n ⟨animal⟩ incrocio m, ibrido m. **cross-Channel** a attraverso la Manica; ⟨ferry⟩ che attraversa la Manica. **cross-check** n controprova f ● vt fare la controprova di. **cross-country** n Sport corsa f campestre. **cross-country skiing** n sci m di fondo. **cross-court** a ⟨shot, volley⟩ diagonale. **cross-cultural** a multiculturale. **crosscurrent** n corrente f trasversale. **cross-dressing** n travestitismo m. **cross-examination** n controinterrogatorio m. **cross-examine** vt sottoporre a controinterrogatorio. **cross-eyed** /'krɒsaɪd/ a strabico. **crossfire** n fuoco m incrociato

**crossing** /'krɒsɪŋ/ n ⟨for pedestrians⟩ passaggio m pedonale; ⟨sea journey⟩ traversata f

**cross-legged** /krɒs'legd/ a & adv con le gambe incrociate

**crossly** /'krɒslɪ/ adv con rabbia

**cross: crossover** a ⟨straps⟩ incrociato. **cross-purposes** npl we are at ~ non ci siamo capiti. **cross-question** vt interrogare ⟨person⟩. **cross-reference** n rimando m. **crossroads** n incrocio m; reach a ~ fig arrivare a un bivio. **cross-section** n sezione f; ⟨of community⟩ campione m. **cross-stitch** n punto m croce. **crosswalk** n Am attraversamento m pedonale. **crosswind** n vento m di traverso. **crosswise** adv in diagonale. **crossword** n ~ [puzzle] parole fpl crociate

**crotch** /krɒtʃ/ n Anat inforcatura f; ⟨in trousers⟩ cavallo m

**crotchet** /'krɒtʃɪt/ n Mus semiminima f

**crotchety** /'krɒtʃɪtɪ/ a irritabile

**crouch** /kraʊtʃ/ vi accovacciarsi

**croupier** /'kruːpɪə(r)/ n croupier m inv

**crouton** /'kruːtɒn/ n crostino m

**crow** /krəʊ/ n corvo m; as the ~ flies in linea d'aria ● vi cantare

**crowbar** /'krəʊbɑː/ n piede m di porco

**crowd** /kraʊd/ n folla f ● vt affollare ● vi affollarsi

**crowd control** n controllo m della folla

**crowded** /'kraʊdɪd/ a affollato

**crowd-puller** /'kraʊdpʊlə(r)/ n ⟨event⟩ grande attrazione f

**crowd scene** n Cinema, Theat scena f di massa

**crown** /kraʊn/ n corona f ● vt incoronare; incapsulare ⟨tooth⟩

**Crown court** n Br Jur ≈ corte f d'assise

**crowning glory** /'kraʊnɪŋ/ n culmine m; her hair is her ~ ~ i capelli sono il suo punto forte

**crown jewels** npl gioielli mpl della corona

**crown prince** n principe m ereditario

**crow's feet** /krəʊz'fiːt/ npl ⟨on face⟩ zampe fpl di gallina

**crow's nest** /krəʊz'nest/ n coffa f

**crucial** /'kruːʃl/ a cruciale

**crucially** /'kruːʃəlɪ/ adv ~ important di vitale importanza

**crucifix** /'kruːsɪfɪks/ n crocifisso m

**crucifixion** /kruːˈsɪfɪkʃn/ n crocifissione f
**crucify** /ˈkruːsɪfaɪ/ vt (pt/pp -ied) crocifiggere
**crude** /kruːd/ a ⟨oil⟩ greggio; ⟨language⟩ crudo; ⟨person⟩ rozzo
**crudely** /ˈkruːdlɪ/ adv ⟨vulgarly⟩ in modo crudo; ⟨simply⟩ schematicamente; ⟨roughly: assembled⟩ sommariamente; ⟨painted, made⟩ rozzamente; ~ **speaking** in parole povere
**crudity** /ˈkruːdətɪ/ n ⟨vulgarity⟩ volgarità f
**cruel** /ˈkruːəl/ a (-ler, -lest) crudele (**to** ver-so)
**cruelly** /ˈkruːəlɪ/ adv con crudeltà
**cruelty** /ˈkruːəltɪ/ n crudeltà f
**cruise** /kruːz/ n crociera f ● vi fare una crociera; ⟨car:⟩ andare a velocità di crociera
**cruise liner** n nave f da crociera
**cruise missile** n missile m cruise inv
**cruiser** /ˈkruːzə(r)/ n Mil incrociatore m; (motor boat) motoscafo m
**cruising speed** /ˈkruːzɪŋ/ n velocità m inv di crociera
**crumb** /krʌm/ n briciola f
**crumble** /ˈkrʌmbl/ vt sbriciolare ● vi sbriciolarsi; ⟨building, society:⟩ sgretolarsi
**crumbling** /ˈkrʌmblɪŋ/ a fatiscente
**crumbly** /ˈkrʌmblɪ/ a friabile
**crummy** /ˈkrʌmɪ/ a fam (substandard) scadente; (Am: unwell) malato
**crumpet** /ˈkrʌmpɪt/ n Culin focaccina f da tostare e mangiare con burro e marmellata
**crumple** /ˈkrʌmpl/ vt spiegazzare ● vi spiegazzarsi
**crunch** /krʌntʃ/ n fam **when it comes to the** ~ quando si viene al dunque ● vt sgranocchiare ● vi ⟨snow:⟩ scricchiolare
**crunchy** /ˈkrʌntʃɪ/ a ⟨vegetables, biscuits⟩ croccante
**crusade** /kruːˈseɪd/ n crociata f
**crusader** /kruːˈseɪdə(r)/ n crociato m
**crush** /krʌʃ/ n ⟨crowd⟩ calca f; **have a** ~ **on sb** essersi preso una cotta per qcno ● vt schiacciare; sgualcire ⟨clothes⟩
**crushed ice** /krʌʃt'aɪs/ n ghiaccio m frantumato
**crushed velvet** n velluto m stazzonato
**crust** /krʌst/ n crosta f
**crustacean** /krʌˈsteɪʃn/ n crostaceo m
**crusty** /ˈkrʌstɪ/ a ⟨bread⟩ croccante; (irritable) scontroso
**crutch** /krʌtʃ/ n gruccia f; Anat inforcatura f
**crux** /krʌks/ n fig punto m cruciale; ~ **of the matter** nodo m della questione
**cry** /kraɪ/ n grido m; ~ **for help** grido d'aiuto; **have a** ~ farsi un pianto; **a far** ~ **from** fig tutta un'altra cosa rispetto a ● vi (pt/pp cried) (weep) piangere; (call) gridare
■ **cry out** vi (shout) urlare
**crypt** /krɪpt/ n cripta f
**cryptic** /ˈkrɪptɪk/ a criptico
**cryptically** /ˈkrɪptɪklɪ/ adv ⟨say, speak⟩ in modo enigmatico; ~ **worded** espresso in maniera sibillina
**crystal** /ˈkrɪstl/ n cristallo m; (glassware) cristalli mpl

**crystal ball** n sfera f di cristallo
**crystal clear** a ⟨water, sound⟩ cristallino; **let me make it** ~ ~ lasciatemelo spiegare chiaramente
**crystal-gazing** /ˈkrɪstlgeɪzɪŋ/ n predizione f del futuro (con la sfera di cristallo)
**crystallize** /ˈkrɪstəlaɪz/ vi (become clear) concretizzarsi
**CS gas** n Br gas m inv lacrimogeno
**cub** /kʌb/ n (animal) cucciolo m; **C~** [Scout] lupetto m
**Cuba** /ˈkjuːbə/ n Cuba f
**Cuban** /ˈkjuːbən/ a & n cubano -a, mf
**cubby-hole** /ˈkʌbɪ-/ n (compartment) scomparto m; (room) ripostiglio m
**cube** /kjuːb/ n cubo m
**cubic** /ˈkjuːbɪk/ a cubico
**cubicle** /ˈkjuːbɪkl/ n cabina f
**cubism** /ˈkjuːbɪzm/ n cubismo m
**cubist** /ˈkjuːbɪst/ a & n cubista mf
**cub reporter** n cronista mf alle prime armi
**cuckoo** /ˈkʊkuː/ n cuculo m
**cuckoo clock** n orologio m a cucù
**cucumber** /ˈkjuːkʌmbə(r)/ n cetriolo m
**cud** /kʌd/ n also fig **chew the** ~ ruminare
**cuddle** /ˈkʌd(ə)l/ vt coccolare ● vi ~ **up to** starsene accoccolato insieme a ● n **have a** ~ ⟨child:⟩ farsi coccolare; ⟨lovers:⟩ abbracciarsi
**cuddly** /ˈkʌd(ə)lɪ/ a tenerone; (wanting cuddles) coccolone
**cuddly toy** n peluche m inv
**cudgel** /ˈkʌdʒl/ n randello m
**cue¹** /kjuː/ n segnale m; Theat battuta f d'entrata
**cue²** n (in billiards) stecca f
**cue ball** n pallino m
**cuff** /kʌf/ n polsino m; (Am: turn-up) orlo m; (blow) scapaccione m; **off the** ~ improvvisando ● vt dare una pacca a
**cuff link** n gemello m
**cuisine** /kwɪˈziːn/ n cucina f; **haute** ~ /əʊt/ haute cuisine f
**cul-de-sac** /ˈkʌldəsæk/ n vicolo m cieco
**culinary** /ˈkʌlɪnərɪ/ a culinario
**cull** /kʌl/ vt scegliere ⟨flowers⟩; (kill) selezionare e uccidere
**culminate** /ˈkʌlmɪneɪt/ vi culminare
**culmination** /kʌlmɪˈneɪʃn/ n culmine m
**culottes** /kjuːˈlɒts/ npl gonna f sg pantalone
**culpable** /ˈkʌlpəbl/ a colpevole
**culpable homicide** n Jur omicidio m colposo
**culprit** /ˈkʌlprɪt/ n colpevole mf
**cult** /kʌlt/ n culto m
**cultivate** /ˈkʌltɪveɪt/ vt coltivare; fig coltivarsi ⟨person⟩
**cultivated** /ˈkʌltɪveɪtɪd/ a ⟨soil⟩ lavorato; ⟨person⟩ colto
**cultural** /ˈkʌltʃərəl/ a culturale
**cultural attaché** n addetto m culturale
**culture** /ˈkʌltʃə(r)/ n cultura f
**cultured** /ˈkʌltʃəd/ a colto
**cultured pearl** n perla f coltivata
**culture shock** n shock m inv culturale

**culture vulture** n fam fanatico, -a mf di cultura

**culvert** /'kʌlvət/ n condotto m sotterraneo

**cumbersome** /'kʌmbəsəm/ a ingombrante

**cumin** /'kju:mɪn/ n cumino m nero

**cummerbund** /'kʌməbʌnd/ n fascia f (dello smoking)

**cumulative** /'kju:mjʊlətɪv/ a cumulativo

**cunning** /'kʌnɪŋ/ a astuto ● n astuzia f

**cup** /kʌp/ n tazza f; (prize, of bra) coppa f

**cupboard** /'kʌbəd/ n armadio m

**cupboard love** n Br hum amore m interessato

**cupboard space** n spazio m negli armadi

**Cup Final** n finale f di coppa

**cupful** /'kʌpfʊl/ n tazza f (contenuto)

**Cupid** /'kju:pɪd/ n Cupido m

**cupola** /'kju:pələ/ n Archit cupola f

**cup tie** n Br partita f eliminatoria

**cur** /kɜ:(r)/ n (pej: dog) cagnaccio m

**curable** /'kjʊərəbl/ a curabile

**curate** /'kjʊərət/ n curato m

**curator** /kjʊə'reɪtə(r)/ n direttore, -trice mf (di museo)

**curb** /kɜ:b/ vt tenere a freno

**curd cheese** /kɜ:d/ n cagliata f

**curdle** /'kɜ:dl/ vi coagularsi

**cure** /kjʊə(r)/ n cura f ● vt curare; (salt) mettere sotto sale; (smoke) affumicare

**cure-all** n toccasana m inv, panacea f

**curfew** /'kɜ:fju:/ n coprifuoco m

**curio** /'kjʊərɪəʊ/ n curiosità f inv

**curiosity** /kjʊərɪ'ɒsətɪ/ n curiosità f

**curious** /'kjʊərɪəs/ a curioso

**curiously** /'kjʊərɪəslɪ/ adv curiosamente

**curl** /kɜ:l/ n ricciolo m ● vt arricciare ● vi arricciarsi

■ **curl up** vi raggomitolarsi

**curler** /'kɜ:lə(r)/ n bigodino m

**curling** /'kɜ:lɪŋ/ n Sport curling m

**curly** /'kɜ:lɪ/ a (-ier, -iest) riccio

**curly-haired, curly-headed** /-'heəd, -'hedɪd/ a (tight curls) dai capelli crespi; (loose curls) riccio

**currant** /'kʌrənt/ n (dried) uvetta f

**currency** /'kʌrənsɪ/ n valuta f; (of word) ricorrenza f; **foreign ~** valuta f estera

**current** /'kʌrənt/ a corrente ● n corrente f. **~ affairs** or **events** npl attualità fsg

**current: current account** n Br conto m corrente. **current assets** n Fin disponibilità fpl correnti. **current liabilities** npl Fin passività fpl correnti

**currently** /'kʌrəntlɪ/ adv attualmente

**curriculum** /kə'rɪkjʊləm/ n programma m di studi

**curriculum vitae** /-'vi:taɪ/ n curriculum vitae m inv

**curry** /'kʌrɪ/ n curry m inv; (meal) piatto m cucinato nel curry ● vt (pt/pp -ied) **~ favour with sb** cercare d'ingraziarsi qcno

**curry powder** n curry m in polvere

**curse** /kɜ:s/ n maledizione f; (oath) imprecazione f ● vt maledire ● vi imprecare

**cursor** /'kɜ:sə(r)/ n cursore m

**cursor keys** npl tasti mpl cursore

**cursory** /'kɜ:sərɪ/ a sbrigativo

**curt** /kɜ:t/ a brusco

**curtail** /kə'teɪl/ vt ridurre

**curtailment** /kə'teɪlmənt/ n (of rights, freedom) limitazione f; (of expenditure, service) riduzione f; (of holiday) interruzione f

**curtain** /'kɜ:tn/ n tenda f; Theat sipario m

■ **curtain off** vt separare con una tenda

**curtain call** n Theat chiamata f alla ribalta

**curtly** /'kɜ:tlɪ/ adv bruscamente

**curtsy** /'kɜ:tsɪ/ n inchino m ● vi (pt/pp -ied) fare l'inchino

**curvaceous** /kɜ:'veɪʃəs/ a formoso

**curve** /kɜ:v/ n curva f ● vi curvare; **~ to the right/left** curvare a destra/sinistra

**curved** /kɜ:vd/ a curvo

**curvy** /'kɜ:vɪ/ a (-ier, iest) (woman) formoso

**cushion** /'kʊʃn/ n cuscino m ● vt attutire; (protect) proteggere

**cushy** /'kʊʃɪ/ a (-ier, -iest) fam facile

**custard** /'kʌstəd/ n (liquid) crema f pasticciera

**custard: custard cream** n Br biscotto m farcito alla crema. **custard pie** n torta f alla crema (nei film comici). **custard tart** n torta f alla crema

**custodial sentence** /kʌ'stəʊdɪəl/ n condanna f a una pena detentiva

**custodian** /kʌ'stəʊdɪən/ n custode mf

**custody** /'kʌstədɪ/ n (of child) custodia f; (imprisonment) detenzione f preventiva

**custom** /'kʌstəm/ n usanza f; Jur consuetudine f; Comm clientela f

**customary** /'kʌstəmərɪ/ a (habitual) abituale; **it's ~ to...** è consuetudine...

**custom-built** /-'bɪlt/ a (house) ad hoc

**custom car** n vettura f personalizzata

**customer** /'kʌstəmə(r)/ n cliente mf

**customer: customer feedback** n feedback m inv dai clienti. **customer relations** npl rapporto m con i clienti. **customer service** n assistenza f ai clienti

**customize** /'kʌstəmaɪz/ vt personalizzare

**custom-made** /-'meɪd/ a su misura

**customs** /'kʌstəmz/ npl dogana f

**customs: Customs and Excise** n Br Ufficio m Dazi e Dogana. **customs clearance** n sdoganamento m. **customs declaration** n dichiarazione f doganale. **customs duties** npl dazi mpl doganali. **customs hall** n dogana f. **customs officer** n doganiere m, guardia f di finanza

**cut** /kʌt/ n (with knife etc, of clothes) taglio m; (reduction) riduzione f; (in public spending) taglio m ● vt/i (pt/pp cut, pres p cutting) tagliare; (reduce) ridurre; **~ one's finger** tagliarsi il dito; **~ sb's hair** tagliare i capelli a qcno ● vi (with cards) alzare

■ **cut away** vt tagliar via

■ **cut back** vt tagliare (hair); potare (hedge); (reduce) ridurre

■ **cut back on** vt (reduce) ridurre

■ **cut down** vt abbattere ‹tree›; (reduce) ridurre

■ **cut in** vi Auto tagliare la strada; (into conversation) interrompere ● vt ~ **sb in on a deal** dare una percentuale a qcno

■ **cut off** vt tagliar via; (disconnect) interrompere; fig isolare; **I was ~ off** Teleph la linea è caduta

■ **cut out** vt ritagliare; (delete) eliminare; **be ~ out for** fam essere tagliato per; ~ **it out!** fam dacci un taglio!

■ **cut up** vt (slice) tagliare a pezzi

**cut-and-dried** a ‹answer, solution› ovvio; **I like everything to be ~** mi piace che tutto sia ben chiaro e definito

**cut and thrust** n **the ~ ~ ~ of debate** gli scambi mpl animati del dibattito

**cutback** /ˈkʌtbæk/ n riduzione f; (in government spending) taglio m

**cute** /kjuːt/ a fam (in appearance) carino; (clever) acuto

**cut glass** n vetro m intagliato

**cuticle** /ˈkjuːtɪkl/ n cuticola f

**cutlery** /ˈkʌtlərɪ/ n posate fpl

**cutlet** /ˈkʌtlɪt/ n cotoletta f

**cut-off** n (upper limit) limite m [massimo]

**cut-off date** n data f di scadenza

**cut-off point** n limite m; Comm data f di scadenza

**cut-offs** npl (jeans) jeans mpl tagliati

**cut-out** n (outline) ritaglio m

**cut-price** a a prezzo ridotto; ‹shop› che fa prezzi ridotti

**cutter** /ˈkʌtə(r)/ n (ship) cutter m inv; (on ship) lancia f; (for metal, glass) taglierina f

**cut-throat** n assassino, -a mf ● a ‹competition› spietato

**cut-throat razor** n Br rasoio m da barbiere

**cutting** /ˈkʌtɪŋ/ a ‹remark› tagliente ● n (from newspaper) ritaglio m; (of plant) talea f

**cutting edge** n (blade) filo m; **be at the ~ ~** fig essere all'avanguardia

**cuttingly** /ˈkʌtɪŋlɪ/ adv ‹speak› in maniera tagliente

**cutting room** n Cinema **end up on the ~ ~ floor** essere tagliato in fase di montaggio

**CV** abbr of **curriculum vitae**

**cwt** abbr (**hundredweight**) ≈ 50 kg, Am ≈ 45 kg

**cyanide** /ˈsaɪənaɪd/ n cianuro m

**cybernetics** /saɪbəˈnetɪks/ n cibernetica f

**cyberspace** /ˈsaɪbəspeɪs/ n ciberspazio m

**cyclamen** /ˈsɪkləmən/ n ciclamino m

**cycle** /ˈsaɪk(ə)l/ n ciclo m; (bicycle) bicicletta f, fam bici f inv ● vi andare in bicicletta

**cycle: cycle clip** n fermacalzoni m inv. **cycle lane** n pista f ciclabile. **cycle race** n corsa f ciclistica. **cycle rack** n portabiciclette m inv. **cycle track** n pista f ciclabile

**cyclical** /ˈsaɪklɪkl/ a ciclico

**cycling** /ˈsaɪklɪŋ/ n ciclismo m

**cycling holiday** n Br vacanza f in bicicletta; **go on a ~ ~** fare una vacanza in bicicletta

**cycling shorts** npl pantaloncini mpl da ciclista

**cyclist** /ˈsaɪklɪst/ n ciclista mf

**cyclo-cross** /ˈsaɪkləʊ-/ n ciclocross m inv

**cyclone** /ˈsaɪkləʊn/ n ciclone m

**cygnet** /ˈsɪgnɪt/ n cigno m giovane

**cylinder** /ˈsɪlɪndə(r)/ n cilindro m

**cylindrical** /sɪˈlɪndrɪkl/ a cilindrico

**cymbals** /ˈsɪmblz/ npl Mus piatti mpl

**cynic** /ˈsɪnɪk/ n cinico, -a mf

**cynical** /ˈsɪnɪk(ə)l/ a cinico

**cynically** /ˈsɪnɪklɪ/ adv cinicamente

**cynicism** /ˈsɪnɪsɪzm/ n cinismo m

**cypress** /ˈsaɪprəs/ n cipresso m

**Cypriot** /ˈsɪprɪət/ a & n cipriota mf

**Cyprus** /ˈsaɪprəs/ n Cipro m

**Cyrillic** /sɪˈrɪlɪk/ a cirillico

**cyst** /sɪst/ n ciste f

**cystitis** /sɪˈstaɪtɪs/ n cistite f

**Czar, czar** /zɑː(r)/ n zar m inv

**Czech** /tʃek/ a & n ceco, -a mf

**Czechoslovak** /tʃekəˈsləʊvæk/ a cecoslovacco

**Czechoslovakia** /tʃekəsləˈvækɪə/ n Cecoslovacchia f

**Czech Republic** n Repubblica f Ceca

# Dd

**d, D** /di:/ *n* (*letter*) d, D *f inv*; *Mus* re *m inv*

**d** *abbr* (**died**) morto

**dab** /dæb/ *n* colpetto *m*; **a ~ of** un pochino di ● *vt* (*pt/pp* **dabbed**) toccare leggermente ⟨*eyes*⟩

■ **dab on** *vt* mettere un po' di ⟨*paint etc*⟩

**dabble** /'dæbl/ *vi* ~ **in sth** *fig* occuparsi di qcsa a tempo perso

**dachshund** /'dækshʊnd/ *n* bassotto *m*

**dad[dy]** /'dæd[ɪ]/ *n fam* papà *m inv*, babbo *m*

**daddy-long-legs** *n* zanzarone *m* [dei boschi]; ⟨*Am: spider*⟩ ragno *m*

**daffodil** /'dæfədɪl/ *n* giunchiglia *f*

**daft** /dɑ:ft/ *a* sciocco

**dagger** /'dægə(r)/ *n* stiletto *m*; *Typ* croce *f*; **be at ~s drawn** *fam* essere ai ferri corti

**dahlia** /'deɪlɪə/ *n* dalia *f*

**daily** /'deɪlɪ/ *a* giornaliero ● *adv* giornalmente ● *n* (*newspaper*) quotidiano *m*; (*fam: cleaner*) donna *f* delle pulizie

**daintily** /'deɪntɪlɪ/ *adv* delicatamente

**dainty** /'deɪntɪ/ *a* (**-ier, -iest**) grazioso; ⟨*movement*⟩ delicato

**dairy** /'deərɪ/ *n* caseificio *m*; (*shop*) latteria *f*

**dairy cow** *n* mucca *f* da latte

**dairyman** /'deərɪmən/ *n* (*on farm*) operaio *m* addetto all'allevamento di mucche [da latte]; (*Am: farmer*) allevatore *m*

**dairy products** *npl* latticini *mpl*

**dais** /'deɪɪs/ *n* pedana *f*

**daisy** /'deɪzɪ/ *n* margheritina *f*; (*larger*) margherita *f*

**dale** /deɪl/ *n liter* valle *f*

**dally** /'dælɪ/ *vi* (*pt/pp* **-ied**) stare a gingillarsi

**dam** /dæm/ *n* diga *f* ● *vt* (*pt/pp* **dammed**) costruire una diga su

**damage** /'dæmɪdʒ/ *n* danno *m* (**to** a); **~s** *pl Jur* risarcimento *msg* ● *vt* danneggiare; *fig* nuocere a

**damaging** /'dæmɪdʒɪŋ/ *a* dannoso

**damask** /'dæməsk/ *n* damasco *m*

**dame** /deɪm/ *n liter* dama *f*; *Am sl* donna *f*

**dammit** /'dæmɪt/ *int Br fam* accidenti

**damn** /dæm/ *c fam* maledetto ● *adv* ⟨*lucky, late*⟩ maledettamente ● *n* **I don't care** *or* **give a ~** *fam* non me ne frega un accidente ● *vt* dannare

**damnation** /dæm'neɪʃn/ *n* dannazione *f* ● *int fam* accidenti!

**damnedest** /'dæmdɪst/ *n* **do one's ~** (**to do**) (*fam: hardest*) fare del proprio meglio (per fare) ● *a* **it was the ~ thing** (*surprising*) era la cosa più straordinaria

**damning** /'dæmɪŋ/ *a* schiacciante

**damp** /dæmp/ *a* umido ● *n* umidità *f* ● *vt* = **dampen**

**dampen** /'dæmpən/ *vt* inumidire; *fig* raffreddare ⟨*enthusiasm*⟩

**damper** /'dæmpə(r)/ *n* **the news put a ~ on the evening** *fam* la notizia ha raggelato l'atmosfera della serata

**dampness** /'dæmpnɪs/ *n* umidità *f*

**damson** /'dæmzən/ *n* (*fruit*) susina *f* selvatica, prugna *f* selvatica

**dance** /dɑ:ns/ *n* ballo *m* ● *vt/i* ballare

**dance hall** *n* sala *f* da ballo

**dance music** *n* musica *f* da ballo

**dancer** /'dɑ:nsə(r)/ *n* ballerino, -a *mf*

**dandelion** /'dændɪlaɪən/ *n* dente *m* di leone

**dandruff** /'dændrʌf/ *n* forfora *f*

**Dane** /deɪn/ *n* danese *mf*; **Great ~** danese *m*

**danger** /'deɪndʒə(r)/ *n* pericolo *m*; **in/out of ~** in/fuori pericolo

**danger level** *n* livello *m* di guardia

**danger list** *n* **on the ~ ~** in prognosi riservata; **off the ~ ~** fuori pericolo

**danger money** *n* indennità *f* di rischio

**dangerous** /'deɪndʒərəs/ *a* pericoloso

**dangerously** /'deɪndʒərəslɪ/ *adv* pericolosamente; **~ ill** in pericolo di vita

**danger signal** *n also fig* segnale *m* di pericolo

**dangle** /'dæŋgl/ *vi* penzolare; *fig* **leave sb dangling** lasciare qcno in sospeso ● *vt* far penzolare

**Danish** /'deɪnɪʃ/ *a* danese ● *n* (*language*) danese *m*

**Danish pastry** *n* dolce *m* di pasta sfoglia contenente pasta di mandorle, mele ecc.

**dank** /dæŋk/ *a* umido e freddo

**Danube** /'dænjuːb/ *n* Danubio *m*

**dapper** /'dæpə(r)/ *a* azzimato

**dappled** /'dæp(ə)ld/ *a* ⟨*grey, horse*⟩ pomellato; ⟨*sky*⟩ screziato; ⟨*shade, surface*⟩ chiazzato

**dare** /deə(r)/ *vt/i* osare; (*challenge*) sfidare (**to** a); **~** [**to**] **do sth** osare fare qcsa; **I ~ say!** molto probabilmente! ● *n* sfida *f*

**daredevil** /'deədevl/ *n* spericolato, -a *mf*

**daring** /'deərɪŋ/ *a* audace ● *n* audacia *f*

**dark** /dɑ:k/ *a* buio; **~ blue/brown** blu/marrone scuro; **it's getting ~** sta cominciando a fare buio; **~ horse** *fig* (*in race, contest*) vincitore *m* imprevisto; (*not much known about*) misterioso *m*; **keep sth ~** *fig* tenere qcsa nascosto ● *n* **after ~** col buio; **in the ~** al buio; **keep sb in the ~** *fig* tenere qcno all'oscuro

**Dark Ages** *n* alto Medioevo *m*

**dark chocolate** *n* cioccolato *m* fondente

**darken** /'dɑ:kn/ *vt* oscurare ● *vi* oscurarsi

**dark-eyed** /-'aɪd/ *a* ⟨*person*⟩ dagli occhi scuri

**dark glasses** *npl* occhiali *mpl* scuri
**darkly** /'dɑːklɪ/ *adv* ‹mutter, hint› cupamente
**darkness** /'dɑːknɪs/ *n* buio *m*
**darkroom** /'dɑːkruːm/ *n* camera *f* oscura
**dark-skinned** *a* ‹person› dalla pelle scura
**darling** /'dɑːlɪŋ/ *a* adorabile; **my ~ Joan** carissima Joan ● *n* tesoro *m*; **be a ~ and...** sii gentile e...
**darn** /dɑːn/ *vt* rammendare
**darning needle** /'dɑːnɪŋ/ *n* ago *m* da rammendo
**dart** /dɑːt/ *n* dardo *m*; ‹in sewing› pince *f inv*; **~s** *sg* ‹game› freccette *fpl* ● *vi* lanciarsi
**dartboard** /'dɑːtbɔːd/ *n* bersaglio *m* [per freccette]
**dash** /dæʃ/ *n* Typ trattino *m*; ‹in Morse› linea *f*; **a ~ of milk** un goccio di latte; **make a ~ for** lanciarsi verso ● *vi* **I must ~** devo scappare ● *vt* far svanire ‹hopes›; ‹hurl› gettare
■ **dash off** *vi* scappar via ● *vt* ‹write quickly› buttare giù
■ **dash out** *vi* uscire di corsa
**dashboard** /'dæʃbɔːd/ *n* cruscotto *m*
**dashing** /'dæʃɪŋ/ *a* ‹bold› ardito; ‹in appearance› affascinante
**DAT** *abbr* (digital audio tape) DAT *f inv*
**data** /'deɪtə/ *npl & sg* dati *mpl*
**data:** **databank** *n* banca *f* di dati. **database** *n* banca *f* dati, database *m inv*. **database management system** *n* sistema *m* di gestione di data base
**data:** **data capture** *n* registrazione *f* di dati. **data communications** *npl* comunicazione *f* dati, telematica *f*. **data compression** *n* compressione *f* dati. **data disk** *n* dischetto *m* di dati. **data entry** *n* immissione *f* [di dati]. **data file** *n* file *m inv* dati. **data handling** *n* manipolazione *f* [di] dati. **data input** *n* input *m* dati. **data link** *n* collegamento *m* dati. **data processing** *n* elaborazione *f* [di] dati. **data protection** *n* protezione *f* dati. **data protection act** *n* Jur legge *f* britannica per la salvaguardia delle informazioni personali. **data retrieval** *n* recupero *m* dati. **data security** *n* sicurezza *f* dei dati. **data storage** *n* archiviazione *f* dati. **data transmission** *n* trasmissione *f* dati
**date¹** /deɪt/ *n* ‹fruit› dattero *m*
**date²** *n* data *f*; ‹meeting› appuntamento *m*; **to ~** fino ad oggi; **out of ~** ‹not fashionable› fuori moda; ‹expired› scaduto; ‹information› non aggiornato; **make a ~ with sb** dare un appuntamento a qcno; **be up to ~** essere aggiornato ● *vt/i* datare; ‹go out with› uscire con
■ **date back to** *vi* risalire a
**dated** /'deɪtɪd/ *a* fuori moda; ‹language› antiquato
**date line** *n* linea *f* [del cambiamento] di data
**date of issue** *n* data *f* di emissione
**date stamp** *n* ‹mark› timbro *m* con la data
**dating agency** /'deɪtɪŋ/ *n* agenzia *f* matrimoniale
**dative** /'deɪtɪv/ *n* dativo *m*
**daub** /dɔːb/ *vt* imbrattare ‹walls›

**daughter** /'dɔːtə(r)/ *n* figlia *f*
**daughter-in-law** *n* (*pl* **~s-in-law**) nuora *f*
**daunt** /dɔːnt/ *vt* scoraggiare; **nothing ~ed** per niente scoraggiato
**daunting** /'dɔːntɪŋ/ *a* ‹task, prospect› poco allettante; **I'm faced with a ~ amount of work** mi aspetta una quantità di lavoro preoccupante; **it can be (quite) ~** può essere (piuttosto) allarmante
**dauntless** /'dɔːntlɪs/ *a* intrepido
**dawdle** /'dɔːdl/ *vi* bighellonare; ‹over work› cincischiarsi
**dawn** /dɔːn/ *n* alba *f*; **at ~** all'alba ● *vi* albeggiare; **it ~ed on me** *fig* mi è apparso chiaro
**dawn raid** *n* ‹police› raid *m* della polizia all'alba; ‹stock market› dawn raid *m inv*
**day** /deɪ/ *n* giorno *m*; ‹whole day› giornata *f*; ‹period› epoca *f*; **~ by ~** giorno per giorno; **~ after ~** giorno dopo giorno; **these ~s** oggigiorno; **in those ~s** a quei tempi; **it's had its ~** *fam* ha fatto il suo tempo
**day:** **day-boy** *n* Br Sch alunno *m* esterno.
**daybreak** *n* **at ~** allo spuntar del giorno.
**day-care** *n* ‹for young children› scuola *f* materna. **day centre** *n* centro *m* di accoglienza.
**day-dream** *n* sogno *m* ad occhi aperti ● *vi* sognare ad occhi aperti. **day-girl** *n* Sch alunna *f* esterna. **daylight** *n* luce del giorno *f*.
**daylight robbery** *n fam* **it's ~ ~** è un furto!.
**daylight saving time** *n* ora *f* legale. **day nursery** *n* (0-3 years) asilo *m* nido; (3-6 years) scuola *f* materna. **day off** *n* giorno *m* di riposo
**day pass** *n* biglietto *m* giornaliero. **day release** *n* giorno *m* di congedo settimanale dal lavoro da dedicare a corsi di formazione.
**day return** *n* (ticket) biglietto *m* di andata e ritorno con validità giornaliera. **day school** *n* scuola *f* che non fornisce alloggio. **daytime** *n* giorno *m*; **in the ~** di giorno. **day-to-day** *a* quotidiano; **on a ~ basis** giorno per giorno.
**day trip** *n* gita *f* ‹di un giorno›. **day tripper** *n* gitante *mf*
**daze** /deɪz/ *n* **in a ~** stordito; *fig* sbalordito
**dazed** /deɪzd/ *a* stordito; *fig* sbalordito
**dazzle** /'dæzl/ *vt* abbagliare
**DBMS** *n abbr* (database management system) DBMS *m*
**D-day** *n* Mil D-day *m inv*; ‹important day› giorno *m* fatidico
**deacon** /'diːkən/ *n* diacono *m*
**dead** /ded/ *a* morto; ‹numb› intorpidito; **~ and buried** morto e sepolto **~ body** morto *m*; **~ centre** pieno centro *m* ● *adv* **~ tired** stanco morto; **~ slow/easy** lentissimo/facilissimo; **you're ~ right** hai perfettamente ragione; **stop ~** fermarsi di colpo; **be ~ on time** essere in perfetto orario ● *n* **the ~** *pl* i morti ; **in the ~ of night** nel cuore della notte
**deaden** /'dedən/ *vt* attutire ‹sound›; calmare ‹pain›
**dead:** **dead end** *n* vicolo *m* cieco ● *attrib* **dead-end** ‹job› senza prospettive. **dead heat** *n* **it was a ~ ~** è finita a pari merito.

**deadline** n scadenza f. **deadlock** n **reach ~** fig giungere a un punto morto. **dead loss** n fam (person) buono, -a mf a nulla; (thing) oggetto m inutile

**deadly** /'dedli/ a (**-ier, -iest**) mortale; (fam: dreary) barboso; **~ sins** peccati mpl capitali

**dead: dead on arrival** a Med deceduto durante il trasporto. **deadpan** a impassibile; (humour) all'inglese. **dead ringer** n fam **be a ~ ~ for sb** essere la copia spiccicata di qualcuno. **Dead Sea** n Mar m Morto. **dead weight** n (fig: burden) peso m morto. **dead wood** n Br fig zavorra f

**deaf** /def/ a sordo; **~ and dumb** sordomuto

**deaf aid** n apparecchio m acustico

**deafen** /'def(ə)n/ vt assordare; (permanently) render sordo

**deafening** /'defənɪŋ/ a assordante

**deaf mute** a & n sordomuto, -a mf

**deafness** /'defnɪs/ n sordità f

**deal** /di:l/ n (agreement) patto m; (in business) accordo m; **who's ~?** (Cards) a chi tocca dare le carte?; **a good** or **great ~** molto; **get a raw ~** fam ricevere un trattamento ingiusto ● v (pt/pp **dealt** /delt/) ● vt (in cards) dare; **~ sb a blow** dare un colpo a qcno

■ **deal in** vt trattare in

■ **deal out** vt (hand out) distribuire

■ **deal with** vt (handle) occuparsi di; trattare con (company); (be about) trattare di; **that's been ~t with** è stato risolto

**dealer** /'di:lə(r)/ n commerciante mf; (in drugs) spacciatore, -trice mf

**dealership** /'di:ləʃɪp/ n Comm concessione f

**dealing room** /'di:lɪŋ/ n Fin borsino m

**dealings** /'di:lɪŋz/ npl **have ~ with** avere a che fare con

**dean** /di:n/ n decano m; Univ preside mf di facoltà

**dear** /dɪə(r)/ a caro; (in letter) Caro; (formal) Gentile ● n caro, -a mf ● int **oh ~!** Dio mio!

**dearly** /'dɪəlɪ/ adv (love) profondamente; (pay) profumatamente

**dearth** /dɜ:θ/ n penuria f

**death** /deθ/ n morte f

**death: deathbed** n letto m di morte. **death camp** n campo m di sterminio. **death certificate** n certificato m di morte. **death duty** n tassa f di successione. **death knell** n campane fpl a morto; fig tramonto m. **death list** n lista f dei bersagli (di un assassino)

**deathly** /'deθlɪ/ a **~ silence** silenzio m di tomba ● adv **~ pale** di un pallore cadaverico

**death: death mask** n maschera f mortuaria. **death penalty** n pena f di morte. **death rate** n tasso m di mortalità. **death ray** n raggio m mortale. **death row** n Am braccio m della morte. **death sentence** n also fig condanna f a morte. **death's head** n teschio m. **death threat** n minaccia f di morte. **death throes** npl also fig agonia f. **death toll** n bilancio m delle vittime. **death trap** n trappola f mortale. **death warrant** n ordine m di esecuzione di una condanna a morte. **death wish** n desiderio m di morire

**debacle** /deɪ'bɑ:k(ə)l/ n sfacelo m

**debar** /dɪ'bɑ:(r)/ vt (pt/pp **debarred**) escludere

**debase** /dɪ'beɪs/ vt degradare

**debatable** /dɪ'beɪtəbl/ a discutibile

**debate** /dɪ'beɪt/ n dibattito m ● vt discutere; (in formal debate) dibattere ● vi **~ whether to...** considerare se

**debauchery** /dɪ'bɔ:tʃərɪ/ n dissolutezza f

**debenture bond** /dɪ'bentʃə(r)/ n obbligazione f non garantita

**debilitating** /dɪ'bɪlɪteɪtɪŋ/ a (disease) debilitante

**debility** /dɪ'bɪlətɪ/ n debilitazione f

**debit** /'debɪt/ n debito m ● vt (pt/pp **debited**) Comm addebitare (sum, account)

**debonair** /debə'neə(r)/ a (person) elegante e cortese

**debrief** /di:'bri:f/ vt chiamare a rapporto; **be ~ed** (defector, freed hostage:) essere interrogato; (diplomat, agent:) essere chiamato a rapporto

**debriefing** /di:'bri:fɪŋ/ n (of hostage, defector) interrogatorio m

**debris** /'debri:/ n macerie fpl

**debt** /det/ n debito m; **be in ~** avere dei debiti

**debt collection** n esazione f crediti

**debt collection agency** n agenzia f di recupero crediti

**debt collector** n esattore m dei crediti

**debtor** /'detə(r)/ n debitore, -trice mf

**debug** /di:'bʌg/ vt (pt/pp **debugged**) Comput correggere gli errori di; togliere i microfoni spia da (room)

**debunk** /di:'bʌŋk/ vt ridicolizzare (theory, myth)

**début** /'deɪbu:/ n debutto m

**decade** /'dekeɪd/ n decennio m

**decadence** /'dekədəns/ n decadenza f

**decadent** /'dekədənt/ a decadente

**decaffeinated** /di:'kæfɪneɪtɪd/ a decaffeinato

**decalitre** /'dekəli:tə(r)/ n decalitro m

**decametre** /'dekəmi:tə(r)/ n decametro m

**decamp** /dɪ'kæmp/ vi sgattaiolare via; **~ with sth** (steal) squagliarsela con qcsa

**decant** /dɪ'kænt/ vt travasare

**decanter** /dɪ'kæntə(r)/ n caraffa f (di cristallo)

**decapitate** /dɪ'kæpɪteɪt/ vt decapitare

**decathlon** /dɪ'kæθlɒn/ n decathlon m inv

**decay** /dɪ'keɪ/ n (also fig) decadenza f; (rot) decomposizione f; (of tooth) carie f inv ● vi imputridire; (rot) decomporsi; (tooth:) cariarsi

**deceased** /dɪ'si:st/ a defunto ● n **the ~** il defunto; la defunta

**deceit** /dɪ'si:t/ n inganno m

**deceitful** /dɪ'si:tful/ a falso

**deceitfully** /dɪ'si:tfulɪ/ adv falsamente

**deceive** /dɪ'si:v/ vt ingannare

**decelerate** /di:'seləreɪt/ vi decelerare

**deceleration** /di:selə'reɪʃn/ n decelerazione f

**December** /dɪˈsembə(r)/ n dicembre m

**decency** /ˈdiːsənsɪ/ n decenza f

**decent** /ˈdiːsənt/ a decente; (respectable) rispettabile; **very ~ of you** molto gentile da parte tua

**decently** /ˈdiːsəntlɪ/ adv decentemente; (kindly) gentilmente

**decentralization** /diːˌsentrəlaɪˈzeɪʃn/ n decentramento m

**decentralize** /diːˈsentrəlaɪz/ vt decentrare

**deception** /dɪˈsepʃn/ n inganno m

**deceptive** /dɪˈseptɪv/ a ingannevole

**deceptively** /dɪˈseptɪvlɪ/ adv ingannevolmente; **it looks ~ easy** sembra facile, ma non lo è

**decibel** /ˈdesɪbel/ n decibel m inv

**decide** /dɪˈsaɪd/ vt decidere; **that's ~d then** siamo d'accordo, allora ● vi decidere (**on** di)

**decided** /dɪˈsaɪdɪd/ a risoluto

**decidedly** /dɪˈsaɪdɪdlɪ/ adv risolutamente; (without doubt) senza dubbio

**decider** /dɪˈsaɪdə(r)/ n (point) punto m decisivo; (goal) goal m inv decisivo; (game) spareggio m

**deciduous** /dɪˈsɪdjʊəs/ a a foglie decidue

**decigram[me]** /ˈdesɪgræm/ n decigrammo m

**decilitre** /ˈdesɪliːtə(r)/ n decilitro m

**decimal** /ˈdesɪml/ a decimale ● n numero m decimale

**decimal point** n virgola f

**decimal system** n sistema m decimale

**decimate** /ˈdesɪmeɪt/ vt decimare

**decimetre** /ˈdesɪmiːtə(r)/ n decimetro m

**decipher** /dɪˈsaɪfə(r)/ vt decifrare

**decision** /dɪˈsɪʒn/ n decisione f

**decision-maker** /dɪˈsɪʒnmeɪkə(r)/ n persona f che ama o ha il potere di prendere decisioni

**decision-making** /dɪˈsɪʒnmeɪkɪŋ/ n **be good/bad at ~** saper/non saper prendere decisioni; **~ process** n processo m decisionale

**decisive** /dɪˈsaɪsɪv/ a decisivo

**decisively** /dɪˈsaɪsɪvlɪ/ adv con decisione

**deck¹** /dek/ vt abbigliare

**deck²** n Naut ponte m; **on ~** in coperta; **top ~** (of bus) piano m di sopra; **~ of cards** mazzo m

**deckchair** /ˈdektʃeə(r)/ n [sedia f a] sdraio f inv

**declaration** /dekləˈreɪʃn/ n dichiarazione f

**declare** /dɪˈkleə(r)/ vt dichiarare; **anything to ~?** niente da dichiarare?; **~ one's love** dichiararsi

**declassify** /diːˈklæsɪfaɪ/ vt rimuovere dai vincoli di segretezza (document, information)

**declension** /dɪˈklenʃn/ n declinazione f

**decline** /dɪˈklaɪn/ n declino m ● vt also Gram declinare ● vi (decrease) diminuire; (health:) deperire; (say no) rifiutare

**declutch** /diːˈklʌtʃ/ vi Br lasciare la frizione

**decode** /diːˈkəʊd/ vt decifrare; Comput decodificare

**decoding** /diːˈkəʊdɪŋ/ n decodifica f, decodificazione f

**décolleté** /deɪˈkɒlteɪ/ a décolleté inv, scollato

**decompose** /diːkəmˈpəʊz/ vi decomporsi

**decomposition** /diːkɒmpəˈzɪʃn/ n scomposizione f

**decompression** /diːkəmˈpreʃn/ n decompressione f

**decontaminate** /diːkənˈtæmɪneɪt/ vt decontaminare

**décor** /ˈdeɪkɔː(r)/ n decorazione f; (including furniture) arredamento m

**decorate** /ˈdekəreɪt/ vt decorare; (paint) pitturare; (wallpaper) tappezzare

**decoration** /dekəˈreɪʃn/ n decorazione f

**decorative** /ˈdekərətɪv/ a decorativo

**decorator** /ˈdekəreɪtə(r)/ n **painter and ~** imbianchino m

**decorous** /ˈdekərəs/ a decoroso

**decorously** /ˈdekərəslɪ/ adv decorosamente

**decorum** /dɪˈkɔːrəm/ n decoro m

**decoy¹** /ˈdiːkɔɪ/ n esca f

**decoy²** /dɪˈkɔɪ/ vt adescare

**decrease¹** /ˈdiːkriːs/ n diminuzione f; **be on the ~** essere in diminuzione

**decrease²** /dɪˈkriːs/ vt/i diminuire

**decreasingly** /dɪˈkriːsɪŋlɪ/ adv sempre meno

**decree** /dɪˈkriː/ n decreto m ● vt decretare

**decrepit** /dɪˈkrepɪt/ a decrepito

**decriminalization** /diːkrɪmɪnəlaɪˈzeɪʃn/ n depenalizzazione f

**decriminalize** /diːˈkrɪmɪnəlaɪz/ vt depenalizzare

**dedicate** /ˈdedɪkeɪt/ vt dedicare

**dedicated** /ˈdedɪkeɪtɪd/ a (person) scrupoloso

**dedication** /dedɪˈkeɪʃn/ n dedizione f; (in book) dedica f

**deduce** /dɪˈdjuːs/ vt dedurre (**from** da)

**deduct** /dɪˈdʌkt/ vt dedurre

**deduction** /dɪˈdʌkʃn/ n deduzione f

**deed** /diːd/ n azione f; Jur atto m di proprietà

**deed of covenant** n Jur accordo m accessorio ad un contratto immobiliare

**deed poll** n **change one's name by ~** cambiare nome con un atto unilaterale

**deem** /diːm/ vt ritenere

**deep** /diːp/ a profondo; **go off the ~ end** fam arrabbiarsi

**deepen** /ˈdiːpn/ vt approfondire; scavare più profondamente (trench) ● vi approfondirsi; (fig: mystery:) infittirsi

**deep: deep-fat-fryer** n friggitrice f. **deep-felt** a profondo. **deep-freeze** n congelatore m. **deep-fried** a fritto (in molto olio). **deep-frozen** a surgelato. **deep-fry** vt friggere (in molto olio)

**deeply** adv profondamente

**deep: deep-rooted** a (habit, prejudice) radicato. **deep-sea** a (exploration, diving) in profondità; (fisherman, fishing) d'alto mare. **deep-sea diver** n palombaro m. **deep-seated** a radicato. **deep-set** a (eyes) infossato. **deep South** n Am il profondo Sud

**deer** /dɪə(r)/ n inv cervo m

91

**deface** | **deliberate**

**deface** /dɪ'feɪs/ vt sfigurare ⟨picture⟩; deturpare ⟨monument⟩
**defamation** /defə'meɪʃn/ n diffamazione f
**defamatory** /dɪ'fæmətərɪ/ a diffamatorio
**default** /dɪ'fɔːlt/ n ⟨Jur: non-payment⟩ morosità f; ⟨failure to appear⟩ contumacia f; **win by** ~ Sport vincere per abbandono dell'avversario; **in** ~ **of** per mancanza di ●a ~ **drive** Comput lettore m di default ● vi ⟨not pay⟩ venir meno a un pagamento
**defeat** /dɪ'fiːt/ n sconfitta f ● vt sconfiggere; ⟨frustrate⟩ vanificare ⟨attempts⟩; **that** ~**s the object** questo fa fallire l'obiettivo
**defeatist** /dɪ'fiːtɪst/ a & n disfattista mf
**defecate** /'defəkeɪt/ vi defecare
**defect¹** /dɪ'fekt/ vi Pol fare defezione
**defect²** /'diːfekt/ n difetto m
**defective** /dɪ'fektɪv/ a difettoso
**defector** /dɪ'fektə(r)/ n ⟨from party⟩ defezionista mf; ⟨from country⟩ fuor[i]uscito, -a mf
**defence** /dɪ'fens/ n difesa f
**defenceless** /dɪ'fenslɪs/ a indifeso
**Defence Minister** n ministro m della difesa
**defend** /dɪ'fend/ vt difendere; ⟨justify⟩ giustificare
**defendant** /dɪ'fendənt/ n Jur imputato, -a mf
**defender** /dɪ'fendə(r)/ n difensore m, -ditrice f
**defensive** /dɪ'fensɪv/ a difensivo ● n difensiva f; **on the** ~ sulla difensiva
**defer** /dɪ'fɜː(r)/ vt ⟨pt/pp deferred⟩ ⟨postpone⟩ rinviare ● vi ~ **to sb** rimettersi a qcno
**deference** /'defərəns/ n deferenza f
**deferential** /defə'renʃl/ a deferente
**deferentially** /defə'renʃəlɪ/ adv con deferenza
**deferment, deferral** /dɪ'fɜːmənt, dɪ'fɜːrəl/ n ⟨postponement⟩ rinvio m
**defiance** /dɪ'faɪəns/ n sfida f; **in** ~ **of** sfidando
**defiant** /dɪ'faɪənt/ a ⟨person⟩ ribelle; ⟨gesture, attitude⟩ di sfida
**defiantly** /dɪ'faɪəntlɪ/ adv con aria di sfida
**deficiency** /dɪ'fɪʃənsɪ/ n insufficienza f
**deficient** /dɪ'fɪʃənt/ a insufficiente; **be** ~ **in** mancare di
**deficit** /'defɪsɪt/ n deficit m inv
**defile** /dɪ'faɪl/ vt fig contaminare
**define** /dɪ'faɪn/ vt definire
**defined** a ⟨role⟩ definito
**definite** /'defɪnɪt/ a definito; ⟨certain⟩ ⟨answer, yes⟩ definitivo; ⟨improvement, difference⟩ netto; **he was** ~ **about it** è stato chiaro in proposito
**definite article** n ⟨grammatical⟩ articolo m determinativo
**definitely** /'defɪnɪtlɪ/ adv sicuramente
**definition** /defɪ'nɪʃn/ n definizione f
**definitive** /dɪ'fɪnɪtɪv/ a definitivo
**deflate** /dɪ'fleɪt/ vt sgonfiare
**deflation** /dɪfl'eɪʃn/ n Comm deflazione f
**deflationary** /dɪ'fleɪʃənrɪ/ a deflazionistico

**deflect** /dɪ'flekt/ vt deflettere
**deformed** /dɪ'fɔːmd/ a deforme
**deformity** /dɪ'fɔːmətɪ/ n deformità f inv
**defraud** /dɪ'frɔːd/ vt defraudare
**defray** /dɪ'freɪ/ vt fml sostenere
**defrost** /diː'frɒst/ vt sbrinare ⟨fridge⟩; scongelare ⟨food⟩
**deft** /deft/ a abile
**deftly** /'deftlɪ/ adv con destrezza
**deftness** /'deftnɪs/ n destrezza f
**defunct** /dɪ'fʌŋkt/ a morto e sepolto; ⟨law⟩ caduto in disuso
**defuse** /diː'fjuːz/ vt disinnescare; calmare ⟨situation⟩
**defy** /dɪ'faɪ/ vt ⟨pt/pp -ied⟩ ⟨challenge⟩ sfidare; resistere a ⟨attempt⟩; ⟨not obey⟩ disobbedire a
**degenerate¹** /dɪ'dʒenəreɪt/ vi degenerare; ~ **into** fig degenerare in
**degenerate²** /dɪ'dʒenərət/ a degenerato
**degeneration** /dɪdʒenə'reɪʃn/ n degenerazione f
**degenerative** /dɪ'dʒenərətɪv/ a degenerativo
**degradation** /degrə'deɪʃn/ n ⟨debasement⟩ degradazione f; ⟨of culture⟩ deterioramento m; ⟨squalor⟩ desolazione f
**degrade** /dɪ'greɪd/ vt ⟨humiliate⟩ degradare ⟨person⟩; ⟨damage⟩ deteriorare ⟨environment⟩
**degrading** /dɪ'greɪdɪŋ/ a degradante
**degree** /dɪ'griː/ n grado m; Univ laurea f; **20** ~**s** 20 gradi; **not to the same** ~ non allo stesso livello
**degree ceremony** n Br Univ cerimonia f di consegna delle lauree
**degree course** n Br Univ corso m di laurea
**dehydrate** /diːhaɪ'dreɪt/ vt disidratare
**dehydrated** /diːhaɪ'dreɪtɪd/ a disidratato
**dehydration** /diːhaɪ'dreɪʃn/ n disidratazione f
**de-ice** /diː'aɪs/ vt togliere il ghiaccio da
**de-icer** /diː'aɪsə(r)/ n ⟨mechanical⟩ sbrinatore m; ⟨chemical⟩ liquido m scongelante
**deign** /deɪn/ vi ~ **to do sth** degnarsi di fare qcsa
**deity** /'diːətɪ/ n divinità f inv
**déjà vu** /deɪʒɑː'vuː/ n déjà vu m inv
**dejected** /dɪ'dʒektɪd/ a demoralizzato
**dejectedly** /dɪ'dʒektɪdlɪ/ adv con aria demoralizzata
**dejection** /dɪ'dʒekʃn/ n abbacchiamento m
**delay** /dɪ'leɪ/ n ritardo m **without** ~ senza indugio ● vt ritardare **be** ~**ed** ⟨person:⟩ essere trattenuto; ⟨train, aircraft:⟩ essere in ritardo ● vi indugiare
**delayed action** /dɪ'leɪd/ a ad azione ritardata; ⟨bomb⟩ a scoppio ritardato
**delegate¹** /'delɪgət/ n delegato, -a mf
**delegate²** /'delɪgeɪt/ vt delegare
**delegation** /delɪ'geɪʃn/ n delegazione f
**delete** /dɪ'liːt/ vt cancellare
**deletion** /dɪ'liːʃn/ n cancellatura f
**deliberate¹** /dɪ'lɪbərət/ a deliberato; ⟨slow⟩ posato

**deliberate | denounce**

**deliberate²** /dɪˈlɪbəreɪt/ vt/i deliberare
**deliberately** /dɪˈlɪbərətlɪ/ adv deliberatamente; ⟨slowly⟩ in modo posato
**deliberation** /dɪlɪbəˈreɪʃn/ n deliberazione f; **with ~** in modo posato
**delicacy** /ˈdelɪkəsɪ/ n delicatezza f; ⟨food⟩ prelibatezza f
**delicate** /ˈdelɪkət/ a delicato
**delicately** /ˈdelɪkətlɪ/ adv ⟨handle, phrase⟩ con delicatezza; ⟨crafted, flavoured⟩ con raffinatezza
**delicatessen** /delɪkəˈtesn/ n negozio m di specialità gastronomiche
**delicious** /dɪˈlɪʃəs/ a delizioso
**delight** /dɪˈlaɪt/ n piacere m ● vt deliziare ● vi ~ **in** dilettarsi con
**delighted** /dɪˈlaɪtɪd/ a lieto
**delightful** /dɪˈlaɪtfʊl/ a delizioso
**delineate** /dɪˈlɪnɪeɪt/ vt also fig delineare
**delineation** /dɪlɪnɪˈeɪʃn/ n delineazione f
**delinquency** /dɪˈlɪŋkwənsɪ/ n delinquenza f
**delinquent** /dɪˈlɪŋkwənt/ a delinquente ● n delinquente mf
**delirious** /dɪˈlɪrɪəs/ a **be ~** delirare; ⟨fig: very happy⟩ essere pazzo di gioia
**delirium** /dɪˈlɪrɪəm/ n delirio m
**deliver** /dɪˈlɪvə(r)/ vt consegnare; recapitare ⟨post, newspaper⟩; tenere ⟨speech⟩; dare ⟨message⟩; tirare ⟨blow⟩; ⟨set free⟩ liberare; ~ **a baby** far nascere un bambino
**deliverance** /dɪˈlɪv(ə)rəns/ n liberazione f
**delivery** /dɪˈlɪvərɪ/ n consegna f; ⟨of post⟩ distribuzione f; Med parto m; **cash on ~** pagamento m alla consegna
**delivery: delivery address** n indirizzo m del destinatario. **delivery man** n fattorino m. **delivery room** n Med sala f parto
**delta** /ˈdeltə/ n delta m inv
**delude** /dɪˈluːd/ vt ingannare; ~ **oneself** illudersi
**deluge** /ˈdeljuːdʒ/ n diluvio m ● vt ⟨fig: with requests etc⟩ inondare
**delusion** /dɪˈluːʒn/ n illusione; **~s of grandeur** mania f di grandezza
**de luxe** /dəˈlʌks/ a di lusso
**delve** /delv/ vi ~ **into** ⟨into pocket etc⟩ frugare in; ⟨into notes, the past⟩ fare ricerche in
**demagnetize** /diːˈmægnətaɪz/ vt smagnetizzare
**demand** /dɪˈmɑːnd/ n richiesta f; Comm domanda f; **in ~** richiesto; **on ~** a richiesta ● vt esigere (**of/from** da)
**demanding** /dɪˈmɑːndɪŋ/ a esigente
**demanning** /diːˈmænɪŋ/ n Br taglio m di personale
**demarcation** /diːmɑːˈkeɪʃn/ n demarcazione f
**demean** /dɪˈmiːn/ vt ~ **oneself** abbassarsi (**to** a)
**demeaning** /dɪˈmiːnɪŋ/ a degradante
**demeanour** /dɪˈmiːnə(r)/ n comportamento m
**demented** /dɪˈmentɪd/ a demente
**dementia** /dɪˈmenʃə/ n demenza f

**demerara** [**sugar**] /deməˈreərə/ n zucchero m grezzo di canna
**demilitarization** /diːmɪlɪtəraɪˈzeɪʃn/ n demilitarizzazione f
**demilitarize** /diːˈmɪlɪtəraɪz/ vt smilitarizzare
**demise** /dɪˈmaɪz/ n decesso m
**demister** /diːˈmɪstə(r)/ n Auto sbrinatore m
**demo** /ˈdeməʊ/ n (pl **~s**) fam manifestazione f
**demobilize** /diːˈməʊbəlaɪz/ vt Mil smobilitare
**democracy** /dɪˈmɒkrəsɪ/ n democrazia f
**democrat** /ˈdeməkræt/ n democratico, -a mf
**democratic** /deməˈkrætɪk/ a democratico
**democratically** /deməˈkrætɪklɪ/ adv democraticamente
**demo disk** n Comput demodisk m inv
**demographic** /deməˈgræfɪk/ a demografico
**demolish** /dɪˈmɒlɪʃ/ vt demolire
**demolition** /deməˈlɪʃn/ n demolizione f
**demon** /ˈdiːmən/ n demonio m
**demonic** /dɪˈmɒnɪk/ a ⟨aspect, power⟩ demoniaco
**demonize** /ˈdiːmənaɪz/ vt demonizzare
**demonstrable** /ˈdemənstrəbl/ a dimostrabile
**demonstrably** /ˈdemənstrəblɪ/ adv ⟨false, untrue⟩ manifestamente
**demonstrate** /ˈdemənstreɪt/ vt dimostrare; fare una dimostrazione sull'uso di ⟨appliance⟩ ● vi Pol manifestare
**demonstration** /demənˈstreɪʃn/ n dimostrazione f; Pol manifestazione f
**demonstrative** /dɪˈmɒnstrətɪv/ a Gram dimostrativo; **be ~** essere espansivo
**demonstrator** /ˈdemənstreɪtə(r)/ n Pol manifestante mf; ⟨for product⟩ dimostratore, -trice mf
**demoralize** /dɪˈmɒrəlaɪz/ vt demoralizzare
**demoralizing** /dɪˈmɒrəlaɪzɪŋ/ a demoralizzante, avvilente
**demote** /dɪˈməʊt/ vt retrocedere di grado; Mil degradare
**demur** /dɪˈmɜː/ vi (pt/pp **demurred**) ⟨complain⟩ protestare; ⟨disagree⟩ obiettare ● n **without ~** senza obiezioni
**demure** /dɪˈmjʊə(r)/ a schivo
**demurely** /dɪˈmjʊəlɪ/ adv in modo schivo
**den** /den/ n tana f; ⟨room⟩ rifugio m
**denationalize** /diːˈnæʃ(ə)nəlaɪz/ vt denazionalizzare
**denial** /dɪˈnaɪəl/ n smentita f
**denier** /ˈdenɪə(r)/ n denaro m
**denigrate** /ˈdenɪgreɪt/ vt denigrare
**denigrating** /ˈdenɪgreɪtɪŋ/ a denigratore
**denim** /ˈdenɪm/ n [tessuto m] jeans m; **~s** pl [blue]jeans mpl
**Denmark** /ˈdenmɑːk/ n Danimarca f
**denomination** /dɪnɒmɪˈneɪʃn/ n Relig confessione f; ⟨money⟩ valore f
**denote** /dɪˈnəʊt/ vt denotare
**denounce** /dɪˈnaʊns/ vt denunciare

**dense** /dens/ a denso; ⟨crowd, forest⟩ fitto; ⟨stupid⟩ ottuso

**densely** /'densli/ adv ⟨populated⟩ densamente; ~ **wooded** fittamente ricoperto di alberi

**density** /'densətɪ/ n densità f inv; ⟨of forest⟩ fittezza f

**dent** /dent/ n ammaccatura f ● vt ammaccare

**dental** /'dentl/ a dei denti; ⟨treatment⟩ dentistico; ⟨hygiene⟩ dentale

**dental: dental appointment** n appuntamento m dal dentista. **dental clinic** n ⟨hospital⟩ clinica f odontoiatrica; ⟨part of hospital⟩ reparto m odontoiatrico. **dental floss** n filo m interdentale. **dental plate** n dentiera f. **dental surgeon** n odontoiatra mf, medico m dentista. **dental surgery** n Br ⟨premises⟩ studio m dentistico; ⟨treatment⟩ visita f dentistica

**dented** /'dentɪd/ a ammaccato; ~ **pride** orgoglio m ferito

**dentist** /'dentɪst/ n dentista mf

**dentistry** /'dentɪstrɪ/ n odontoiatria f

**dentures** /'dentʃəz/ npl dentiera fsg

**denude** /dɪ'njuːd/ vt denudare

**denunciation** /dɪnʌnsɪ'eɪʃn/ n denuncia f

**deny** /dɪ'naɪ/ vt (pt/pp -ied) negare; ⟨officially⟩ smentire; ~ **sb sth** negare qcsa a qcno; **I can't ~ it** non posso negarlo

**deodorant** /diː'əʊdərənt/ n deodorante m

**deodorize** /diː'əʊdəraɪz/ vt deodorare

**depart** /dɪ'paːt/ vi ⟨plane, train:⟩ partire; ⟨liter: person⟩ andare via; ⟨deviate⟩ allontanarsi (**from** da)

**departed** /dɪ'paːtɪd/ a ⟨euph: dead⟩ scomparso

**department** /dɪ'paːtmənt/ n reparto m; Pol ministero m; ⟨of company⟩ sezione f; Univ dipartimento m

**departmental** /diːpaːt'mentl/ a ⟨Pol: colleague, meeting⟩ di sezione; ⟨in business⟩ di reparto

**department: Department of Defense** n Am ministero m della difesa. **Department of Energy** n Am ≈ Ministero m dell'Industria. **Department of the Environment** n Br Ministero m dell'Ambiente. **department head** n caporeparto mf; Univ direttore, -trice mf d'istituto. **Department of Health** n ministero m della sanità. **department manager** n ⟨of business⟩ direttore, -trice mf di reparto; ⟨of store⟩ caporeparto mf. **Department of Social Security** n Br ≈ Istituto m Nazionale della Previdenza Sociale. **department store** n grande magazzino m. **Department of Trade and Industry** n Br Ministero m del Commercio e dell'Industria

**departure** /dɪ'paːtʃə(r)/ n partenza f; ⟨from rule⟩ allontanamento m; **new ~** svolta f

**departure: departure gate** n ⟨at airport⟩ uscita f. **departure lounge** n ⟨at airport⟩ sala f d'attesa. **departure platform** n Rail binario m. **departures board** n tabellone m delle partenze

**depend** /dɪ'pend/ vi dipendere (**on** da); ⟨rely⟩

contare (**on** su); **it all ~s** dipende; ~**ing on what he says** a seconda di quello che dice

**dependability** /dɪpendə'bɪlətɪ/ n affidabilità f

**dependable** /dɪ'pendəbl/ a fidato

**dependant** /dɪ'pendənt/ n persona f a carico

**dependence** /dɪ'pendəns/ n dipendenza f

**dependent** /dɪ'pendənt/ a dipendente (**on** da)

**depict** /dɪ'pɪkt/ vt ⟨in writing⟩ dipingere; ⟨with picture⟩ rappresentare

**depiction** /dɪ'pɪkʃn/ n rappresentazione f

**depilatory** /dɪ'pɪlətərɪ/ n ⟨cream⟩ crema f depilatoria

**deplete** /dɪ'pliːt/ vt ridurre; **totally ~d** completamente esaurito

**depletion** /dɪ'pliːʃn/ n ⟨of resources, funds⟩ impoverimento m

**deplorable** /dɪ'plɔːrəbl/ a deplorevole

**deplore** /dɪ'plɔː(r)/ vt deplorare

**deploy** /dɪ'plɔɪ/ vt Mil spiegare ● vi schierarsi

**deployment** /dɪ'plɔɪmənt/ n schieramento m

**depoliticize** /diːpə'lɪtɪsaɪz/ vt depoliticizzare

**depopulate** /diː'pɒpjʊleɪt/ vt spopolare

**deport** /dɪ'pɔːt/ vt deportare

**deportation** /diːpɔː'teɪʃn/ n deportazione f

**deportee** /diːpɔː'tiː/ n deportato, -a mf

**deportment** /dɪ'pɔːtmənt/ n portamento m

**depose** /dɪ'pəʊz/ vt deporre

**deposit** /dɪ'pɒzɪt/ n deposito m; ⟨against damage⟩ cauzione f; ⟨first instalment⟩ acconto m ● vt depositare

**deposit account** n libretto m di risparmio; ⟨without instant access⟩ conto m vincolato

**depositor** /dɪ'pɒzɪtə(r)/ n Fin depositante mf

**deposit slip** n ⟨in bank⟩ distinta f di versamento

**depot** /'depəʊ/ n deposito m; Am Rail stazione f ferroviaria

**deprave** /dɪ'preɪv/ vt depravare

**depraved** /dɪ'preɪvd/ a depravato

**depravity** /dɪ'prævətɪ/ n depravazione f

**deprecate** /'deprəkeɪt/ vt disapprovare

**deprecatory** /deprɪ'keɪtərɪ/ a ⟨disapproving⟩ di disapprovazione; ⟨apologetic⟩ di scusa

**depreciate** /dɪ'priːʃɪeɪt/ vi deprezzarsi

**depreciation** /dɪpriːsɪ'eɪʃn/ n deprezzamento m

**depress** /dɪ'pres/ vt deprimere; ⟨press down⟩ premere

**depressed** /dɪ'prest/ a depresso; ~ **area** zona f depressa

**depressing** /dɪ'presɪŋ/ a deprimente

**depression** /dɪ'preʃn/ n depressione f

**depressive** /dɪ'presɪv/ a depressivo ● n depresso, -a mf

**depressurize** /diː'preʃəraɪz/ vi depressurizzare

**deprivation** /deprɪ'veɪʃn/ n privazione f

**deprive** /dɪˈpraɪv/ vt ~ **sb of sth** privare qcno di qcsa

**deprived** /dɪˈpraɪvd/ a ⟨area, childhood⟩ disagiato

**dept** abbr **department**

**depth** /depθ/ n profondità f inv: **in ~** ⟨study, analyse⟩ in modo approfondito; **in the ~s of winter** in pieno inverno; **in the ~s of despair** nella più profonda disperazione; **be out of one's ~** (in water) non toccare il fondo: fig sentirsi in alto mare

**deputation** /depjʊˈteɪʃn/ n deputazione f

**deputize** /ˈdepjʊtaɪz/ vi ~ **for** fare le veci di

**deputy** /ˈdepjʊtɪ/ n vice mf; (temporary) sostituto, -a mf ● attrib ~ **leader** ≈ vicesegretario, -a mf; ~ **chairman** vicepresidente mf

**deputy: deputy chairman** n vicepresidente m. **deputy leader** n Br Pol sottosegretario m. **deputy premier, deputy prime minister** n Pol vice primo ministro m. **deputy president** n vicepresidente mf

**derail** /dɪˈreɪl/ vt be ~**ed** ⟨train:⟩ essere deragliato

**derailleur gears** /dɪˈreɪljə/ npl deragliatore msg

**derailment** /dɪˈreɪlmənt/ n deragliamento m

**deranged** /dɪˈreɪndʒd/ a squilibrato

**deregulate** /diːˈreɡjʊleɪt/ vt deregolamentare ⟨market⟩

**deregulation** /diːreɡjʊˈleɪʃn/ n deregolamentazione f

**derelict** /ˈderəlɪkt/ a abbandonato

**deride** /dɪˈraɪd/ vt deridere

**derision** /dɪˈrɪʒn/ n derisione f

**derisive** /dɪˈraɪsɪv/ a derisorio

**derisory** /dɪˈraɪsərɪ/ a ⟨laughter⟩ derisorio; ⟨offer⟩ irrisorio

**derivation** /derɪˈveɪʃn/ n derivazione f

**derivative** /dɪˈrɪvətɪv/ a derivato ● n derivato m

**derive** /dɪˈraɪv/ vt (obtain) derivare; be ~**d from** ⟨word:⟩ derivare da ● vi ~ **from** derivare da

**dermatitis** /dɜːməˈtaɪtɪs/ n dermatite f

**dermatologist** /dɜːməˈtɒlədʒɪst/ n dermatologo, -a mf

**derogatory** /dɪˈrɒɡətrɪ/ a ⟨comments⟩ peggiorativo

**derrick** /ˈderɪk/ n derrick m inv

**derv** /dɜːv/ n Br gasolio m

**descaler** /diːˈskeɪlə(r)/ n Br disincrostante m

**descend** /dɪˈsend/ vi scendere; be ~**ed from** discendere da ● vt scendere da
∎ **descend on** vt (attack) piombare su; (visit) capitare [all'improvviso]

**descendant** /dɪˈsendənt/ n discendente mf

**descent** /dɪˈsent/ n discesa f; (lineage) origine f

**descrambler** /diːˈskræmblə(r)/ n Teleph, TV decodificatore m

**describe** /dɪˈskraɪb/ vt descrivere

**description** /dɪˈskrɪpʃn/ n descrizione f;

they had no help of any ~ non hanno avuto proprio nessun aiuto

**descriptive** /dɪˈskrɪptɪv/ a descrittivo; (vivid) vivido

**desecrate** /ˈdesɪkreɪt/ vt profanare

**desecration** /desɪˈkreɪʃn/ n profanazione f

**desegregate** /diːˈseɡrɪɡeɪt/ vt abolire la segregazione razziale in ⟨school⟩

**deselect** /diːsɪˈlekt/ vt Br be ~**ed** non avere riconferma della candidatura alle elezioni da parte del proprio partito

**desensitize** /diːˈsensɪtaɪz/ vt desensibilizzare

**desert¹** /ˈdezət/ n deserto m ● a deserto; ~ **island** isola f deserta

**desert²** /dɪˈzɜːt/ vt abbandonare ● vi disertare

**deserted** /dɪˈzɜːtɪd/ a deserto

**deserter** /dɪˈzɜːtə(r)/ n Mil disertore m

**desertion** /dɪˈzɜːʃn/ n Mil diserzione f; (of family) abbandono m

**deserts** /dɪˈzɜːts/ npl **get one's just ~** ottenere ciò che ci si merita

**deserve** /dɪˈzɜːv/ vt meritare

**deservedly** /dɪˈzɜːvədlɪ/ adv meritatamente

**deserving** /dɪˈzɜːvɪŋ/ a meritevole; ~ **cause** opera f meritoria

**design** /dɪˈzaɪn/ n progettazione f; (fashion ~, appearance) design m inv; (pattern) modello m; (aim) proposito m; **have ~s on** aver mire su ● vt progettare; disegnare ⟨clothes, furniture, model⟩; be ~**ed for** essere fatto per

**designate** /ˈdezɪɡneɪt/ vt designare

**designation** /dezɪɡˈneɪʃn/ n designazione f

**design consultant** n progettista mf

**designer** /dɪˈzaɪnə(r)/ n progettista mf; (of clothes) stilista mf; (Theat: of set) scenografo, -a mf

**design fault** n difetto m di concezione

**design feature** n prestazione f

**designing** /dɪˈzaɪnɪŋ/ a pej calcolatore

**desirable** /dɪˈzaɪərəbl/ a desiderabile

**desire** /dɪˈzaɪə(r)/ n desiderio m ● vt desiderare

**desist** /dɪˈzɪst/ vi desistere (**from** da)

**desk** /desk/ n scrivania f; (in school) banco m; (in hotel) reception f inv; (cash ~) cassa f; (check-in ~) check-in m inv

**desk: deskbound** a ⟨job⟩ sedentario. **desk diary** n agenda da tavolo. **desk pad** n (blotter) tampone m; (notebook) block-notes m inv. **desktop** n piano m della scrivania; (computer) [computer m inv] desktop m inv. **desktop publishing** n desktop publishing m inv, editoria f da tavolo

**desolate** /ˈdesələt/ a desolato

**desolation** /desəˈleɪʃn/ n desolazione f

**despair** /dɪˈspeə(r)/ n disperazione f; **in ~** disperato; ⟨say⟩ per disperazione ● vi I ~ **of that boy** quel ragazzo mi fa disperare

**desperate** /ˈdespərət/ a disperato; **be ~** ⟨criminal:⟩ essere un disperato; **be ~ for sth** morire dalla voglia di

**desperately** /'despərətlɪ/ adv disperatamente; **he said ~** ha detto, disperato

**desperation** /despə'reɪʃn/ n disperazione f; **in ~** per disperazione

**despicable** /dɪ'spɪkəbl/ a disprezzevole

**despise** /dɪ'spaɪz/ vt disprezzare

**despite** /dɪ'spaɪt/ prep malgrado

**despondency** /dɪ'spɒndənsɪ/ n abbattimento m

**despondent** /dɪ'spɒndənt/ a abbattuto

**despot** /'despɒt/ n despota m

**despotism** /'despətɪzm/ n dispotismo m

**des res** /dez'rez/ n abbr fam (**desirable residence**) abitazione f desiderabile

**dessert** /dɪ'zɜːt/ n dolce m

**dessert spoon** n cucchiaio m da dolce

**dessert wine** n vino m da dessert

**destabilize** /diː'steɪbɪlaɪz/ vt destabilizzare

**destination** /destɪ'neɪʃn/ n destinazione f

**destine** /'destɪn/ vt destinare; **be ~d for sth** essere destinato a qcsa; **~d for each other** fatti l'uno per l'altra

**destined** /'destɪnd/ a ~ **for Paris** ⟨train, package⟩ a destinazione di Parigi; **it was ~ to happen** era destino che succedesse

**destiny** /'destɪnɪ/ n destino m

**destitute** /'destɪtjuːt/ a bisognoso

**destitution** /destɪ'tjuːʃn/ n indigenza f

**destroy** /dɪ'strɔɪ/ vt distruggere

**destroyer** /dɪ'strɔɪə(r)/ n Naut cacciatorpediniere m

**destruct** /dɪ'strʌkt/ vi distruggersi

**destruction** /dɪ'strʌkʃn/ n distruzione f

**destructive** /dɪ'strʌktɪv/ a distruttivo; ⟨fig: criticism⟩ negativo

**destructiveness** /dɪ'strʌktɪvnɪs/ n distruttività f

**desultory** /'desəltrɪ/ a ⟨conversation⟩ sconnesso; ⟨friendship⟩ incostante; ⟨attempt⟩ poco convinto

**detach** /dɪ'tætʃ/ vt staccare

**detachable** /dɪ'tætʃəbl/ a separabile

**detached** /dɪ'tætʃt/ a fig distaccato; ~ **house** villetta f

**detached retina** n Med retina f distaccata

**detachment** /dɪ'tætʃmənt/ n distacco m; Mil distaccamento m

**detail** /'diːteɪl/ n particolare m, dettaglio m; **in ~** particolareggiatamente ● vt esporre con tutti i particolari; Mil assegnare

**detail drawing** n disegno m dettagliato

**detailed** /'diːteɪld/ a particolareggiato, dettagliato

**detain** /dɪ'teɪn/ vt ⟨police:⟩ trattenere; ⟨delay⟩ far ritardare

**detainee** /diːteɪ'niː/ n detenuto, -a mf

**detect** /dɪ'tekt/ vt individuare; ⟨perceive⟩ percepire

**detectable** /dɪ'tektəbl/ a individuabile

**detection** /dɪ'tekʃn/ n scoperta f

**detective** /dɪ'tektɪv/ n investigatore, -trice mf

**detective: detective constable** n Br agente mf della polizia giudiziaria. **detective inspector** n Br ispettore, -trice mf della polizia giudiziaria. **detective story** n racconto m poliziesco. **detective work** n indagini fpl

**detector** /dɪ'tektə(r)/ n ⟨for metal⟩ cercametalli m inv, metal detector m inv

**detention** /dɪ'tenʃn/ n detenzione f; Sch punizione f

**deter** /dɪ'tɜː(r)/ vt (pt/pp deterred) impedire; **~ sb from doing sth** impedire a qcno di fare qcsa

**detergent** /dɪ'tɜːdʒənt/ n detersivo m

**deteriorate** /dɪ'tɪərɪəreɪt/ vi deteriorarsi

**deterioration** /dɪtɪərɪə'reɪʃn/ n deterioramento m

**determination** /dɪtɜːmɪ'neɪʃn/ n determinazione f

**determine** /dɪ'tɜːmɪn/ vt ⟨ascertain⟩ determinare; ~ **to** ⟨resolve⟩ decidere di

**determined** /dɪ'tɜːmɪnd/ a deciso

**determining** /dɪ'tɜːmɪnɪŋ/ a determinante

**deterrent** /dɪ'terənt/ n deterrente m

**detest** /dɪ'test/ vt detestare

**detestable** /dɪ'testəbl/ a detestabile

**detonate** /'detəneɪt/ vt far detonare ● vi detonare

**detonation** /detə'neɪʃn/ n detonazione f

**detonator** /'detəneɪtə(r)/ n detonatore m

**detour** /'diːtʊə(r)/ n deviazione f

**detoxify** /diː'tɒksɪfaɪ/ vt disintossicare

**detract** /dɪ'trækt/ vi ~ **from** sminuire ⟨merit⟩; rovinare ⟨pleasure, beauty⟩

**detractor** /dɪ'træktə(r)/ n detrattore, -trice mf

**detriment** /'detrɪmənt/ n **to the ~ of** a danno di

**detrimental** /detrɪ'mentl/ a dannoso

**detritus** /dɪ'traɪtəs/ n detriti mpl

**deuce** /djuːs/ n Tennis deuce m inv

**devaluation** /diːvæljʊ'eɪʃn/ n svalutazione f

**devalue** /diː'væljuː/ vt svalutare ⟨currency⟩

**devastate** /'devəsteɪt/ vt devastare

**devastated** /'devəsteɪtɪd/ a fam sconvolto

**devastating** /'devəsteɪtɪŋ/ a devastante; ⟨news⟩ sconvolgente

**devastation** /devə'steɪʃn/ n devastazione f

**develop** /dɪ'veləp/ vt sviluppare; contrarre ⟨illness⟩; ⟨add to value of⟩ valorizzare ⟨area⟩ ● vi svilupparsi; ~ **into** divenire

**developer** /dɪ'veləpə(r)/ n [property] ~ imprenditore, -trice mf edile

**developing** /dɪ'veləpɪŋ/: **developing bath** n Phot bagno m di sviluppo, bagno m rivelatore. **developing country** n paese m in via di sviluppo. **developing tank** n Phot vasca f di sviluppo

**development** /dɪ'veləpmənt/ n sviluppo m; ⟨of vaccine etc⟩ messa f a punto

**development company** n ⟨for property⟩ impresa f edile

**deviant** /'diːvɪənt/ a deviato

**deviate** /'diːvɪeɪt/ vi deviare

**deviation** /diːvɪ'eɪʃn/ n deviazione f

**device** /dɪ'vaɪs/ n dispositivo m; **leave sb to his own ~s** lasciare qcno per conto suo

**devil** /'devl/ n diavolo m

**devilish** /'dev(ə)lıʃ/ *a* diabolico

**devilishly** /'dev(ə)lıʃlı/ *adv fig fam* terribilmente

**devil-may-care** *a* menefreghista

**deviliment** /'dev(ə)lmənt/ *n Br* cattiveria *f*

**devil's advocate** *n* avvocato *m* del diavolo

**devil worship** *n* culto *m* demoniaco

**devious** /'di:vıəs/ *a* ⟨person⟩ subdolo; ⟨route⟩ tortuoso

**deviously** /'di:vıəslı/ *adv* subdolamente

**devise** /dɪ'vaɪz/ *vt* escogitare

**devoid** /dɪ'vɔɪd/ *a* ~ **of** privo di

**devolution** /di:və'lu:ʃn/ *n* (*of power*) decentramento *m*

**devote** /dɪ'vəʊt/ *vt* dedicare

**devoted** /dɪ'vəʊtɪd/ *a* ⟨daughter etc⟩ affezionato; **be** ~ **to sth** consacrarsi a qcsa

**devotedly** /dɪ'vəʊtɪdlı/ *adv* con dedizione

**devotee** /devə'ti:/ *n* appassionato, -a *mf*

**devotion** /dɪ'vəʊʃn/ *n* dedizione *f*; ~**s** *pl Relig* devozione *fsg*

**devour** /dɪ'vaʊə(r)/ *vt* divorare

**devout** /dɪ'vaʊt/ *a* devoto

**devoutly** /dɪ'vaʊtlı/ *adv Relig* devotamente; ⟨sincerely⟩ fervidamente

**dew** /dju:/ *n* rugiada *f*

**dewy** /'dju:ɪ/ *a* rugiadoso

**dewy-eyed** /-'aɪd/ *a* ⟨moved⟩ con gli occhi lucidi; ⟨naive⟩ ingenuo

**dexterity** /dek'sterətı/ *n* destrezza *f*

**dexterous** /'dekstrəs/ *a* ⟨person, movement⟩ agile, destro; ⟨hand⟩ abile; ⟨mind⟩ acuto

**dexterously** /'dekstrəslı/ *adv* ⟨move⟩ agilmente; ⟨manage⟩ abilmente

**dg** *abbr* (**decigram**) dg *m*

**diabetes** /daɪə'bi:ti:z/ *n* diabete *m*

**diabetic** /daɪə'betɪk/ *a & n* diabetico, -a *mf*

**diabolical** /daɪə'bɒlɪkl/ *a* diabolico

**diabolically** /daɪə'bɒlɪklı/ *adv* ⟨wickedly⟩ diabolicamente; ⟨fam: badly⟩ orribilmente

**diacritic** /daɪə'krɪtɪk/ *a* ⟨accent, mark⟩ diacritico

**diaeresis** /daɪ'erɪsɪs/ *n* dieresi *f inv*

**diagnose** /daɪəg'nəʊz/ *vt* diagnosticare

**diagnosis** /daɪəg'nəʊsɪs/ *n* (*pl* -**oses** /daɪəg'nəʊsi:z/) diagnosi *f inv*

**diagnostic** /daɪəg'nɒstɪk/ *a* diagnostico

**diagnostics** /daɪəg'nɒstɪks/ *n Med* diagnostica *f*

**diagonal** /daɪ'ægənl/ *a & n* diagonale *f*

**diagonally** /daɪ'ægənlı/ *adv* diagonalmente

**diagram** /'daɪəgræm/ *n* diagramma *m*

**dial** /'daɪəl/ *n* ⟨of clock, machine⟩ quadrante *m*; *Teleph* disco *m* combinatore ● *v* (*pt/pp* **dialled**) ● *vi Teleph* fare il numero; ~ **direct** chiamare in teleselezione ● *vt* fare ⟨number⟩

**dialect** /'daɪəlekt/ *n* dialetto *m*

**dialectic** /daɪə'lektɪk/ *n* dialettica *f* ● *a* dialettico

**dialectics** /daɪə'lektɪks/ *n* dialettica *f*

**dialling code** /'daɪəlɪŋ/ *n* prefisso *m*

**dialling tone** *n* segnale *m* di linea libera

**dialogue** /'daɪəlɒg/ *n* dialogo *m*

**dial tone** *n Am Teleph* segnale *m* di linea libera

**dial-up** *a* ⟨network⟩ collegato telefonicamente

**dialysis** /daɪ'ælɪsɪs/ *n* dialisi *f*

**dialysis machine** *n* rene *m* artificiale

**diameter** /daɪ'æmɪtə(r)/ *n* diametro *m*

**diametrically** /daɪə'metrɪklı/ *adv* ~ **opposed** diametralmente opposto

**diamond** /'daɪəmənd/ *n* diamante *m*, brillante *m*; ⟨shape⟩ losanga *f*; ~**s** *pl* ⟨in cards⟩ quadri *mpl*

**diamond: diamond jubilee** *n* sessantesimo anniversario *m*. **diamond-shaped** *a* romboidale. **diamond wedding** [**anniversary**] *n* nozze *fpl* di diamante

**diaper** /'daɪəpə(r)/ *n Am* pannolino *m*

**diaphanous** /daɪ'æfənəs/ *a* diafano

**diaphragm** /'daɪəfræm/ *n* diaframma *m*

**diarist** /'daɪərɪst/ *n* ⟨author⟩ diarista *mf*; ⟨journalist⟩ giornalista *mf* di piccola cronaca

**diarrhoea** /daɪə'ri:ə/ *n* diarrea *f*

**diary** /'daɪərɪ/ *n* ⟨for appointments⟩ agenda *f*; ⟨for writing in⟩ diario *m*

**diatribe** /'daɪətraɪb/ *n* diatriba *f*

**dice** /daɪs/ *n inv* dadi *mpl* ● *vt Culin* tagliare a dadini

**dicey** /'daɪsɪ/ *a fam* rischioso

**dichotomy** /daɪ'kɒtəmɪ/ *n* dicotomia *f*

**dicky** /'dɪkɪ/ *n* ⟨shirtfront⟩ pettino *m*, sparato *m* ● *a* ⟨Br fam: heart⟩ malandato

**dictate** /dɪk'teɪt/ *vt/i* dettare

**dictation** /dɪk'teɪʃn/ *n* dettato *m*

**dictator** /dɪk'teɪtə(r)/ *n* dittatore *m*

**dictatorial** /dɪktə'tɔ:rɪəl/ *a* dittatoriale

**dictatorship** /dɪk'teɪtəʃɪp/ *n* dittatura *f*

**diction** /'dɪkʃn/ *n* dizione *f*

**dictionary** /'dɪkʃənrɪ/ *n* dizionario *m*

**dictum** /'dɪktəm/ *n* ⟨maxim⟩ massima *f*; ⟨statement⟩ affermazione *f*

**did** /dɪd/ *see* **do**

**didactic** /dɪ'dæktɪk/ *a* didattico

**diddle** /'dɪdl/ *vt fam* gabbare

**didn't** /'dɪdnt/ = **did not**

**die¹** /daɪ/ *n Techn* ⟨metal mould⟩ stampo *m*; ⟨for cutting⟩ matrice *f*

**die²** *vi* (*pres p* **dying**) morire (**of** di); **be dying to do sth** *fam* morire dalla voglia di fare qcsa; **be dying for a drink** *fam* morire dalla voglia di bere qualcosa

■ **die away** *vi* ⟨noise, applause:⟩ smorzarsi

■ **die down** *vi* calmarsi; ⟨fire, flames:⟩ spegnersi

■ **die off** *vi* morire uno dopo l'altro

■ **die out** *vi* estinguersi; ⟨custom:⟩ morire

**diehard** /'daɪhɑ:d/ *n* ⟨pol: in party⟩ fanatico, -a *mf*; ⟨stubborn person⟩ ultraconservatore *mf*

**diesel** /'di:zl/ *n* diesel *m*. ~ **engine** *n* motore *m* diesel

**diesel train** *n* treno *m* con locomotiva diesel

**diet** /'daɪət/ *n* regime *m* alimentare; ⟨restricted⟩ dieta *f*; **be on a** ~ essere a dieta ● *vi* essere a dieta

**dietary** /'daɪətrɪ/ *a* ⟨habit⟩ alimentare

**dietary fibre** *n* fibre *fpl* alimentari

**dietary supplement** *n* integratore *m* dietetico

**dietician** /daɪə'tɪʃn/ *n* dietologo, -a *mf*

**differ** /'dɪfə(r)/ *vi* differire; (*disagree*) non essere d'accordo

**difference** /'dɪfrəns/ *n* differenza *f*; (*disagreement*) divergenza *f*

**different** /'dɪfrənt/ *a* diverso, differente; (*various*) diversi; **be ~ from** essere diverso da

**differential** /dɪfə'renʃl/ *a* differenziale ● *n* differenziale *m*

**differentiate** /dɪfə'renʃɪeɪt/ *vt* distinguere (**between** fra); (*discriminate*) discriminare (**between** fra); (*make different*) differenziare

**differentiation** /dɪfərenʃɪ'eɪʃn/ *n* differenziazione *f*

**differently** /'dɪfrəntlɪ/ *adv* in modo diverso; **~ from** diversamente da

**difficult** /'dɪfɪkəlt/ *a* difficile

**difficulty** /'dɪfɪkəltɪ/ *n* difficoltà *f inv*; **with ~** con difficoltà

**diffidence** /'dɪfɪdəns/ *n* mancanza *f* di sicurezza

**diffident** /'dɪfɪdənt/ *a* senza fiducia in se stesso

**diffidently** /'dɪfɪdəntlɪ/ *adv* senza fiducia in se stesso

**diffuse**[1] /dɪ'fjuːs/ *a* diffuso; (*wordy*) prolisso

**diffuse**[2] /dɪ'fjuːz/ *vt Phys* diffondere

**diffuseness** /dɪ'fjuːsnɪs/ *n* (*of organization*) estensione *f*; (*of argument*) prolissità *f*

**dig** /dɪg/ *n* (*poke*) spinta *f*; (*remark*) frecciata *f*; *Archaeol* scavo *m*; **~s** *pl fam* camera *fsg* ammobiliata ● *vt/i* (*pt/pp* **dug**, *pres p* **digging**) scavare (*hole*); vangare (*garden*); (*thrust*) conficcare; **~ sb in the ribs** dare una gomitata a qcno

■ **dig out** *vt fig* tirar fuori

■ **dig up** *vt* scavare (*garden, street, object*); sradicare (*tree, plant*); (*fig: find*) scovare

**digest**[1] /'daɪdʒest/ *n* compendio *m*

**digest**[2] /daɪ'dʒest/ *vt* digerire

**digestible** /daɪ'dʒestəbl/ *a* digeribile

**digestion** /daɪ'dʒestʃn/ *n* digestione *f*

**digestive** /daɪ'dʒestɪv/ *a* digestivo

**digestive: digestive [biscuit]** *n Br* biscotto *m* di farina integrale. **digestive system** *n* apparato *m* digerente. **digestive tract** *n* apparato *m* digerente

**digger** /'dɪgə(r)/ *n Techn* scavatrice *f*

**diggings** /'dɪgɪŋz/ *npl* (*in archaeology*) scavi *mpl*

**digit** /'dɪdʒɪt/ *n* cifra *f*; (*finger*) dito *m*

**digital** /'dɪdʒɪtl/ *a* digitale

**digital: digital audio tape** *n* audiocassetta *f* digitale. **digital clock** *n* orologio *m* digitale. **digital computer** *n* computer *m* digitale

**digitizer** /'dɪdʒɪtaɪzə(r)/ *n Comput* tavoletta *f* grafica

**dignified** /'dɪgnɪfaɪd/ *a* dignitoso

**dignify** /'dɪgnɪfaɪ/ *vt* nobilitare (*occasion, building*)

**dignitary** /'dɪgnɪtərɪ/ *n* dignitario *m*

**dignity** /'dɪgnətɪ/ *n* dignità *f*

**digress** /daɪ'gres/ *vi* divagare

**digression** /daɪ'greʃn/ *n* digressione *f*

**dike** /daɪk/ *n* diga *f*

**dilapidated** /dɪ'læpɪdeɪtɪd/ *a* cadente

**dilapidation** /dɪlæpɪ'deɪʃn/ *n* rovina *f*

**dilate** /daɪ'leɪt/ *vt* dilatare ● *vi* dilatarsi

**dilation** /daɪ'leɪʃn/ *n* dilatazione *f*

**dilatory** /'dɪlətərɪ/ *a* dilatorio

**dilemma** /dɪ'lemə/ *n* dilemma *m*

**dilettante** /dɪlɪ'tæntɪ/ *n* dilettante *mf*

**diligence** /'dɪlɪdʒəns/ *n* diligenza *f*

**diligent** /'dɪlɪdʒənt/ *a* diligente

**dill** /dɪl/ *n* aneto *m*

**dilly-dally** /'dɪlɪdælɪ/ *vi* (*pt/pp* **-ied**) *fam* tentennare

**dilute** /daɪ'ljuːt/ *vt* diluire

**dilution** /daɪ'ljuːʃn/ *n also fig* diluizione *f*

**dim** /dɪm/ *a* (**dimmer, dimmest**) debole (*light*); (*dark*) scuro; (*prospect, chance*) scarso; (*indistinct*) impreciso; (*fam: stupid*) tonto ● *vt/i* (*pt/pp* **dimmed**) affievolire

**dime** /daɪm/ *n Am* moneta *f* da dieci centesimi

**dimension** /daɪ'menʃn/ *n* dimensione *f*

**dime store** *n Am grande magazzino m con prezzi molto bassi*

**diminish** /dɪ'mɪnɪʃ/ *vt/i* diminuire

**diminished** /dɪ'mɪnɪʃt/ *a* ridotto; *Mus* diminuito; **on grounds of ~ responsibility** *Jur* per seminfermità mentale

**diminutive** /dɪ'mɪnjʊtɪv/ *a & n* diminutivo *m*

**dimly** /'dɪmlɪ/ *adv* (*see, remember*) indistintamente; (*shine*) debolmente

**dimmer** /'dɪmə(r)/ *n* interruttore *m* a reostato

**dimple** /'dɪmpl/ *n* fossetta *f*

**dimwit** /'dɪmwɪt/ *n fam* stupido *m*

**dim-witted** /-'wɪtɪd/ *a fam* stupido

**din** /dɪn/ *n* baccano *m*

■ **din into** *vt* **~ sth into sb** ficcare qcsa in testa a qcno

**dine** /daɪn/ *vi* pranzare

**diner** /'daɪnə(r)/ *n* (*Am: restaurant*) tavola *f* calda; **the last ~ in the restaurant** l'ultimo cliente nel ristorante

**dingdong** /'dɪŋdɒŋ/ *n* dindon *m*

**dingdong battle** *n Br* battibecco *m*

**dinghy** /'dɪŋgɪ/ *n* dinghy *m*; (*inflatable*) canotto *m* pneumatico

**dingy** /'dɪndʒɪ/ *a* (**-ier, -iest**) squallido e tetro

**dining** /'daɪnɪŋ/: **dining car** *n* carrozza *f* ristorante. **dining hall** *n* refettorio *m*. **dining room** *n* sala *f* da pranzo. **dining table** *n* tavolo *m* da pranzo

**dinky** /'dɪŋkɪ/ *a Br fam* carino

**dinner** /'dɪnə(r)/ *n* cena *f*; (*at midday*) pranzo *m*

**dinner: dinner dance** *n* cena *f* danzante. **dinner fork** *n* forchetta *f*. **dinner hour** *n Br Sch* pausa *f* del pranzo. **dinner jacket** *n* smoking *m inv*. **dinner knife** *n* coltello *m*. **dinner money** *n Br Sch* soldi *mpl* dati dai genitori agli scolari per il pranzo. **dinner party** *n* cena *f* (*con invitati*). **dinner plate** *n* piatto *m* piano. **dinner service, dinner set** *n* servizio *m* da tavola. **dinner time** *n* (*evening*) ora *f* di cena; (*midday*) ora *f* di pranzo

**dinnerware** /ˈdɪnəweə(r)/ *n* servizio *m* da tavola

**dinosaur** /ˈdaɪnəsɔː(r)/ *n* dinosauro *m*

**dint** /dɪnt/ *n* **by ~ of** a forza di

**diocese** /ˈdaɪəsɪs/ *n* diocesi *f inv*

**diode** /ˈdaɪəʊd/ *n* diodo *m*

**dioxide** /daɪˈɒksaɪd/ *n* biossido *m*

**dip** /dɪp/ *n* (*in ground*) inclinazione *f*; *Culin* salsina *f*; **go for a ~** andare a fare una nuotata ● *v* (*pt/pp* **dipped**) ● *vt* (*in liquid*) immergere; abbassare ⟨*head, headlights*⟩ ● *vi* ⟨*land:*⟩ formare un avvallamento

■ **dip into** *vt* scorrere ⟨*book*⟩

**diphtheria** /dɪfˈθɪərɪə/ *n* difterite *f*

**diphthong** /ˈdɪfθɒŋ/ *n* dittongo *m*

**diploma** /dɪˈpləʊmə/ *n* diploma *m*

**diplomacy** /dɪˈpləʊməsɪ/ *n* diplomazia *f*

**diplomat** /ˈdɪpləmæt/ *n* diplomatico, -a *mf*

**diplomatic** /dɪpləˈmætɪk/ *a* diplomatico

**diplomatically** /dɪpləˈmætɪklɪ/ *adv* con diplomazia

**diplomatic bag** *n* valigia *f* diplomatica

**diplomatic immunity** *n* immunità *f* diplomatica

**dippy** /ˈdɪpɪ/ *a* (*fam: crazy, weird*) pazzo

**dipstick** /ˈdɪpstɪk/ *n Auto* astina *f* dell'olio

**dire** /ˈdaɪə(r)/ *a* ⟨*situation, consequences*⟩ terribile

**direct** /daɪˈrekt/ *a* diretto ● *adv* direttamente ● *vt* (*aim*) rivolgere ⟨*attention, criticism*⟩; (*control*) dirigere; fare la regia di ⟨*film, play*⟩; **~ sb** (*show the way*) indicare la strada a qcno; **~ sb to do sth** ordinare a qcno di fare qcsa

**direct: direct access** *n Comput* accesso *m* diretto. **direct current** *n* corrente *m* continua. **direct debit** *n* addebitamento *m* diretto. **direct dialling** *n* teleselezione *f*. **direct hit** *n Mil* colpo *m* diretto

**direction** /daɪˈrekʃn/ *n* direzione *f*; (*of play, film*) regia *f*; **~s** *pl* indicazioni *fpl*; **~s for use** istruzioni *fpl* per l'uso

**directional** /daɪˈrekʃənəl/ *a* direzionale

**directive** /daɪˈrektɪv/ *n* direttiva *f*

**directly** /daɪˈrektlɪ/ *adv* direttamente; (*at once*) immediatamente ● *conj* [non] appena

**directness** /daɪˈrektnɪs/ *n* (*of person, attitude*) franchezza *f*; (*of play, work, writing*) chiarezza *f*

**direct object** *n* complemento *m* oggetto

**director** /dɪˈrektə(r)/ *n Comm* direttore, -trice *mf*; (*of play, film*) regista *mf*

**directorate** /daɪˈrektərət/ *n* (*board*) consiglio *m* d'amministrazione

**director general** *n* presidente *mf*

**Director of Public Prosecutions** *n Br* ≈ Procuratore *m* della Repubblica

**directorship** /dɪˈrektəʃɪp/ *n* posto *m* di direttore

**directory** /dɪˈrektərɪ/ *n* elenco *m*; *Teleph* elenco *m* [telefonico]; (*of streets*) stradario *m*

**directory assistance** *n Am* servizio *m* informazioni abbonati

**directory enquiries** *npl Br* servizio *m* informazioni abbonati

**direct: direct rule** *n Pol* sottomissione *f* al governo centrale. **direct speech** *n* discorso *m* diretto. **direct transfer** *n* trasferimento *m* automatico

**dirt** /dɜːt/ *n* sporco *m*; **~ cheap** *fam* a [un] prezzo stracciato

**dirtiness** /ˈdɜːtɪnɪs/ *n* (*of person etc*) sporcizia *f*

**dirt track** *n* (*road*) strada *f* sterrata; *Sport* pista *f* sterrata

**dirty** /ˈdɜːtɪ/ *a* (**-ier, -iest**) sporco ● *vt* sporcare

**dirty: dirty-minded** /-ˈmaɪndɪd/ *a* fissato sul sesso. **dirty trick** *n* brutto scherzo *m*. **dirty tricks** *npl Pol* faccende *fpl* sporche. **dirty weekend** *n fam* weekend *m inv* clandestino con l'amante. **dirty word** *n* parolaccia *f*

**disability** /dɪsəˈbɪlətɪ/ *n* infermità *f inv*

**disable** /dɪsˈeɪbl/ *vt* (*make useless*) mettere fuori uso ⟨*machine*⟩; (*in accident*) rendere invalido; *Comput* disabilitare; **be ~d by arthritis** essere menomato dall'artrite

**disabled** /dɪsˈeɪbld/ *a* invalido

**disabled: disabled access** *n* (*to public building etc*) accesso *m* per gli invalidi. **disabled driver** *n* guidatore, -trice *mf* invalido, -a. **disabled person** *n* invalido, -a *mf*

**disabuse** /dɪsəˈbjuːz/ *vt* disingannare

**disadvantage** /dɪsədˈvɑːntɪdʒ/ *n* svantaggio *m*; **at a ~** in una posizione di svantaggio

**disadvantaged** /dɪsədˈvɑːntɪdʒd/ *a* svantaggiato

**disadvantageous** /dɪsædvənˈteɪdʒəs/ *a* svantaggioso

**disaffected** /dɪsəˈfektɪd/ *a* disilluso

**disagree** /dɪsəˈɡriː/ *vi* non essere d'accordo; **~ with** ⟨*food:*⟩ far male a

**disagreeable** /dɪsəˈɡriːəbl/ *a* sgradevole

**disagreement** /dɪsəˈɡriːmənt/ *n* disaccordo *m*; (*quarrel*) dissidio *m*

**disallow** /dɪsəˈlaʊ/ *vt* respingere; *Sport* annullare

**disappear** /dɪsəˈpɪə(r)/ *vi* scomparire

**disappearance** /dɪsəˈpɪərəns/ *n* scomparsa *f*

**disappoint** /dɪsəˈpɔɪnt/ *vt* deludere

**disappointed** /dɪsəˈpɔɪntɪd/ *a* deluso; **I am ~ in you** mi hai deluso

**disappointing** /dɪsəˈpɔɪntɪŋ/ *a* deludente

**disappointment** /dɪsəˈpɔɪntmənt/ *n* delusione *f*

**disapproval** /dɪsəˈpruːvəl/ *n* disapprovazione *f*

**disapprove** /dɪsəˈpruːv/ *vi* disapprovare; **~ of sb/sth** disapprovare qcno/qcsa

**disapproving** /dɪsəˈpruːvɪŋ/ *a* ⟨*look, gesture*⟩ di disapprovazione

**disarm** /dɪsˈɑːm/ *vt* disarmare ● *vi Mil* disarmarsi

**disarmament** /dɪsˈɑːməmənt/ *n* disarmo *m*

**disarming** /dɪsˈɑːmɪŋ/ *a* ⟨*frankness etc*⟩ disarmante

**disarrange** /dɪsəˈreɪndʒ/ *vt* scompigliare

**disarray** /dɪsə'reɪ/ n **in ~** in disordine

**disaster** /dɪ'zɑːstə(r)/ n disastro m

**disaster: disaster area** n zona f disastrata; (fig: person) disastro m. **disaster fund** n fondi mpl a favore dei disastrati. **disaster victim** n disastrato, -a mf

**disastrous** /dɪ'zɑːstrəs/ a disastroso

**disastrously** /dɪ'zɑːstrəslɪ/ adv (fail) disastrosamente; (end, turn out) in modo catastrofico: **go ~ wrong** essere un disastro

**disband** /dɪs'bænd/ vt scogliere; smobilitare (troops) ● vi scogliersi; (regiment:) essere smobilitato

**disbelief** /dɪsbɪ'liːf/ n incredulità f; **in ~** con incredulità

**disbelieve** /dɪsbɪ'liːv/ vt non credere

**disc** /dɪsk/ n disco m; (CD) compact disc m inv

**discard** /dɪ'skɑːd/ vt scartare; (throw away) eliminare; scaricare (boyfriend)

**disc brakes** npl Auto freni mpl a disco

**discern** /dɪ'sɜːn/ vt discernere

**discernible** /dɪ'sɜːnəbl/ a discernibile

**discerning** /dɪ'sɜːnɪŋ/ a perspicace

**discharge¹** /'dɪstʃɑːdʒ/ n Electr scarica f; (dismissal) licenziamento m; Mil congedo m; (Med: of blood) emissione f; (of cargo) scarico m

**discharge²** /dɪs'tʃɑːdʒ/ vt scaricare (battery, cargo); (dismiss) licenziare; Mil congedare; Jur assolvere (accused); dimettere (patient); **~ one's duty** esaurire il proprio compito ● vi Electr scaricarsi

**disciple** /dɪ'saɪpl/ n discepolo m

**disciplinarian** /dɪsɪplɪ'neərɪən/ n persona f autoritaria

**disciplinary** /'dɪsɪplɪnərɪ/ a disciplinare

**discipline** /'dɪsɪplɪn/ n disciplina f ● vt disciplinare; (punish) punire

**disciplined** /'dɪsɪplɪnd/ a (person, approach) sistematico

**disc jockey** n disc jockey m inv

**disclaim** /dɪs'kleɪm/ vt negare

**disclaimer** /dɪs'kleɪmə(r)/ n rifiuto m

**disclose** /dɪs'kləʊz/ vt svelare

**disclosure** /dɪs'kləʊʒə(r)/ n rivelazione f

**disco** /'dɪskəʊ/ n discoteca f

**discoloration** /dɪskʌlə'reɪʃn/ n (process) scolorimento m; (spot) macchia f scolorita

**discolour** /dɪs'kʌlə(r)/ vt scolorire ● vi scolorirsi

**discomfort** /dɪs'kʌmfət/ n scomodità f; fig disagio m

**disconcert** /dɪskən'sɜːt/ vt sconcertare

**disconcerting** /dɪskən'sɜːtɪŋ/ a sconcertante

**disconnect** /dɪskə'nekt/ vt disconnettere

**disconsolate** /dɪs'kɒnsələt/ a sconsolato

**discontent** /dɪskən'tent/ n scontentezza f

**discontented** /dɪskən'tentɪd/ a scontento

**discontinue** /dɪskən'tɪnjuː/ vt cessare, smettere; Comm sospendere la produzione di; **~d line** fine f serie

**discontinuity** /dɪskɒntɪ'njuːtɪ/ n discontinuità f

**discord** /'dɪskɔːd/ n discordia f; Mus dissonanza f

**discordant** /dɪ'skɔːdənt/ a **~ note** nota f discordante

**discothèque** /'dɪskətek/ n discoteca f

**discount¹** /'dɪskaʊnt/ n sconto m

**discount²** /dɪs'kaʊnt/ vt (not believe) non credere a; (leave out of consideration) non tener conto di

**discount flight** n volo m a prezzo ridotto

**discount store** n discount m inv

**discourage** /dɪs'kʌrɪdʒ/ vt scoraggiare; (dissuade) dissuadere

**discouragement** /dɪs'kʌrɪdʒmənt/ n (despondency) scoraggiamento m; (disincentive) disincentivo m

**discourse** /'dɪskɔːs/ n discorso m

**discourteous** /dɪs'kɜːtɪəs/ a scortese

**discourteously** /dɪs'kɜːtɪəslɪ/ adv scortesemente

**discover** /dɪ'skʌvə(r)/ vt scoprire

**discovery** /dɪ'skʌvərɪ/ n scoperta f

**discredit** /dɪs'kredɪt/ n discredito m ● vt screditare

**discreet** /dɪ'skriːt/ a discreto

**discreetly** /dɪ'skriːtlɪ/ adv discretamente

**discrepancy** /dɪ'skrepənsɪ/ n discrepanza f

**discretion** /dɪ'skreʃn/ n discrezione f

**discriminate** /dɪ'skrɪmɪneɪt/ vi discriminare (**against** contro); **~ between** distinguere tra

**discriminating** /dɪ'skrɪmɪneɪtɪŋ/ a esigente

**discrimination** /dɪskrɪmɪ'neɪʃn/ n discriminazione f; (quality) discernimento m

**discriminatory** /dɪs'krɪmɪnətərɪ/ a discriminatorio, discriminativo

**discus** /'dɪskəs/ n disco m

**discuss** /dɪ'skʌs/ vt discutere; (examine critically) esaminare

**discussion** /dɪ'skʌʃn/ n discussione f

**discussion document, discussion paper** n documento m in abbozzo

**disdain** /dɪs'deɪn/ n sdegno f ● vt sdegnare

**disdainful** /dɪs'deɪnful/ a sdegnoso

**disease** /dɪ'ziːz/ n malattia f

**diseased** /dɪ'ziːzd/ a malato

**disembark** /dɪsem'bɑːk/ vi sbarcare

**disembodied** /dɪsem'bɒdɪd/ a (voices) evanescente; (head) senza corpo; (soul) disincarnato

**disenchant** /dɪsen'tʃɑːnt/ vt disincantare

**disenchantment** /dɪsen'tʃɑːntmənt/ n disincanto m

**disenfranchise** /dɪsen'fræntʃaɪz/ vt privare del diritto di voto

**disengage** /dɪsen'geɪdʒ/ vt disimpegnare; disinnestare (clutch)

**disentangle** /dɪsen'tæŋgəl/ vt districare

**disfavour** /dɪs'feɪvə(r)/ n sfavore m; **fall into ~** perdere il favore

**disfigure** /dɪs'fɪgə(r)/ vt deformare

**disgorge** /dɪs'gɔːdʒ/ vt rigettare

**disgrace** /dɪz'greɪs/ n vergogna f; **fall into ~** cadere in disgrazia; **I am in ~** sono caduto in disgrazia: **it's a ~** è una vergogna ● *vt* disonorare

**disgraceful** /dɪz'greɪsfʊl/ *a* vergognoso

**disgruntled** /dɪs'grʌntld/ *a* malcontento

**disguise** /dɪs'gaɪz/ *n* travestimento *m*; **in ~** travestito ● *vt* contraffare ⟨*voice*⟩; dissimulare ⟨*emotions*⟩: **~d as** travestito da

**disgust** /dɪs'gʌst/ *n* disgusto *m*: **in ~** con aria disgustata ● *vt* disgustare

**disgusting** /dɪs'gʌstɪŋ/ *a* disgustoso

**dish** /dɪʃ/ *n* piatto *m*; **do the ~es** lavare i piatti

■ **dish out** *vt* (*serve*) servire; (*distribute*) distribuire

■ **dish up** *vt* servire

**dishcloth** /'dɪʃklɒθ/ *n* strofinaccio *m*

**dishearten** /dɪs'hɑ:t(ə)n/ *vt* scoraggiare

**disheartening** /dɪs'hɑ:t(ə)nɪŋ/ *a* scoraggiante

**dishevelled** /dɪ'ʃevld/ *a* scompigliato

**dishonest** /dɪs'ɒnɪst/ *a* disonesto

**dishonestly** /dɪs'ɒnɪstlɪ/ *adv* disonestamente

**dishonesty** /dɪs'ɒnɪstɪ/ *n* disonestà *f*

**dishonour** /dɪs'ɒnə(r)/ *n* disonore *m* ● *vt* disonorare ⟨*family*⟩; non onorare ⟨*cheque*⟩

**dishonourable** /dɪs'ɒnərəbl/ *a* disonorevole

**dishonourably** /dɪs'ɒnərəblɪ/ *adv* in modo disonorevole

**dishwasher** /'dɪʃwɒʃə(r)/ *n* lavapiatti *f inv*

**dishy** /'dɪʃɪ/ *a* (**-ier, est**) ⟨*Br fam: man, woman*⟩ fico, figo

**disillusion** /dɪsɪ'lu:ʒn/ *vt* disilludere

**disillusioned** /dɪsɪ'lu:ʒnd/ *a* deluso (**with** di)

**disillusionment** /dɪsɪ'lu:ʒnmənt/ *n* disillusione *f*

**disincentive** /dɪsɪn'sentɪv/ *n* disincentivo *m*

**disinclined** /dɪsɪn'klaɪnd/ *a* riluttante

**disinfect** /dɪsɪn'fekt/ *vt* disinfettare

**disinfectant** /dɪsɪn'fektənt/ *n* disinfettante *m*

**disingenuous** /dɪsɪn'dʒenjʊəs/ *a* ⟨*comment*⟩ insincero; ⟨*smile*⟩ falso

**disinherit** /dɪsɪn'herɪt/ *vt* diseredare

**disintegrate** /dɪs'ɪntɪgreɪt/ *vi* disintegrarsi

**disintegration** /dɪsɪntɪ'greɪʃn/ *n* disgregazione *f*

**disinterested** /dɪs'ɪntərestɪd/ *a* disinteressato

**disjointed** /dɪs'dʒɔɪntɪd/ *a* sconnesso

**disk** /dɪsk/ *n* *Comput* disco *m*; (*diskette*) dischetto *m*

**disk drive** *n* lettore *m* [di disco]

**disk operating system** /'dɪskɒpəreɪtɪŋ/ *n* sistema *m* operativo su disco

**dislike** /dɪs'laɪk/ *n* avversione *f*; **your likes and ~s** i tuoi gusti ● *vt* **I ~ him/it** non mi piace; **I don't ~ him/it** non mi dispiace

**dislocate** /'dɪsləkeɪt/ *vt* slogare; **~ one's shoulder** slogarsi una spalla

**dislocation** /dɪslə'keɪʃn/ *n* (*of hip, knee*) lussazione *f*

**dislodge** /dɪs'lɒdʒ/ *vt* sloggiare

**disloyal** /dɪs'lɔɪəl/ *a* sleale

**disloyally** /dɪs'lɔɪəlɪ/ *adv* slealmente

**disloyalty** /dɪs'lɔɪəltɪ/ *n* slealtà *f*

**dismal** /'dɪzməl/ *a* ⟨*person*⟩ abbacchiato; ⟨*news, weather*⟩ deprimente; ⟨*performance*⟩ mediocre

**dismantle** /dɪs'mæntl/ *vt* smontare ⟨*tent, machine*⟩; *fig* smantellare

**dismay** /dɪs'meɪ/ *n* sgomento *m*; **much to my ~** con mio grande sgomento

**dismayed** /dɪs'meɪd/ *a* sgomento

**dismember** /dɪs'membə(r)/ *vt also fig* smembrare

**dismiss** /dɪs'mɪs/ *vt* licenziare ⟨*employee*⟩; (*reject*) scartare ⟨*idea, suggestion*⟩

**dismissal** /dɪs'mɪsəl/ *n* licenziamento *m*

**dismissive** /dɪs'mɪsɪv/ *a* ⟨*person, attitude*⟩ sprezzante: **be ~ of** essere sprezzante verso

**dismount** /dɪs'maʊnt/ *vi* smontare

**disobedience** /dɪsə'bi:dɪəns/ *n* disubbidienza *f*

**disobedient** /dɪsə'bi:dɪənt/ *a* disubbidiente

**disobey** /dɪsə'beɪ/ *vt* disubbidire a ⟨*rule*⟩ ● *vi* disubbidire

**disorder** /dɪs'ɔ:də(r)/ *n* disordine *m*; *Med* disturbo *m*

**disordered** /dɪs'ɔ:dəd/ *a* ⟨*life*⟩ disordinato: ⟨*mind*⟩ disturbato

**disorderly** /dɪs'ɔ:dəlɪ/ *a* disordinato; ⟨*crowd*⟩ turbolento: **~ conduct** turbamento *m* della quiete pubblica

**disorganization** /dɪsɔ:gənaɪ'zeɪʃn/ *n* disorganizzazione *f*

**disorganized** /dɪs'ɔ:gənaɪzd/ *a* disorganizzato

**disorientate** /dɪs'ɔ:rɪənteɪt/ *vt* disorientare

**disorientation** /dɪsɔ:rɪən'teɪʃn/ *n* disorientamento *m*

**disown** /dɪs'əʊn/ *vt* disconoscere; **I'll ~ you** *fam* faccio finta di non conoscerti

**disparaging** /dɪ'spærɪdʒɪŋ/ *a* sprezzante

**disparagingly** /dɪ'spærɪdʒɪŋlɪ/ *adv* sprezzantemente

**disparate** /'dɪspərət/ *a* (*different*) eterogeneo; (*incompatible*) disparato

**disparity** /dɪ'spærətɪ/ *n* disparità *f inv*

**dispassionate** /dɪ'spæʃənət/ *a* spassionato

**dispassionately** /dɪs'pæʃənətlɪ/ *adv* spassionatamente

**dispatch** /dɪ'spætʃ/ *n* *Comm* spedizione *f*; (*Mil, report*) dispaccio *m*; **with ~** con prontezza ● *vt* spedire; (*kill*) spedire al creatore

**dipatch: Dispatch Box** *n Br Pol* postazione *f* da cui parlano i ministri nel Parlamento britannico. **dispatch box** *n* valigia *f* diplomatica. **dispatch rider** *n* staffetta *f*

**dispel** /dɪ'spel/ *vt* (*pt/pp* **dispelled**) dissipare

**dispensable** /dɪ'spensəbl/ *a* dispensabile

**dispensary** /dɪ'spensərɪ/ *n* farmacia *f*

**dispense** /dɪ'spens/ *vt* distribuire; **~ with** fare a meno di

**dispenser** /dɪ'spensə(r)/ *n* (*device*) distributore *m*

**dispensing chemist** /dɪ'spensɪŋ/ n farmacista mf; (shop) farmacia f

**dispensing optician** n Br ottico m

**dispersal** /dɪ'spɜːsl/ n disperzione f

**disperse** /dɪ'spɜːs/ vt disperdere ● vi dispersi

**dispersion** /dɪ'spɜːʃn/ n dispersione f

**dispirited** /dɪ'spɪrɪtɪd/ a scoraggiato

**displace** /dɪs'pleɪs/ vt spostare

**displaced person** n profugo, -a mf

**displacement** /dɪs'pleɪsmənt/ n spostamento m

**display** /dɪ'spleɪ/ n mostra f; Comm esposizione f; (of feelings) manifestazione f; pej ostentazione f; Comput display m inv ● vt mostrare; esporre (goods); manifestare (feelings); Comput visualizzare

**display: display advertisement** n annuncio m pubblicitario di grande formato. **display cabinet, display case** n vetrina f. **display rack** n espositore m. **display window** n vetrina f

**displease** /dɪs'pliːz/ vt non piacere a; **be ~d with** essere scontento di

**displeasure** /dɪs'pleʒə(r)/ n malcontento m; **incur sb's ~** scontentare qcno

**disposable** /dɪ'spəʊzəbl/ a (throwaway) usa e getta; (income) disponibile

**disposal** /dɪ'spəʊzl/ n (getting rid of) eliminazione f; **be at sb's ~** essere a disposizione di qcno

**dispose** /dɪ'spəʊz/ vi ~ **of** (get rid of) disfarsi di; **be well ~d** essere ben disposto (**to** verso)

**disposition** /dɪspə'zɪʃn/ n disposizione f; (nature) indole f

**dispossessed** /dɪspə'zest/ a (family) spossessato; (son) diseredato

**disproportionate** /dɪsprə'pɔːʃənət/ a sproporzionato

**disproportionately** /dɪsprə'pɔːʃəntlɪ/ adv in modo sproporzionato

**disprove** /dɪs'pruːv/ vt confutare

**dispute** /dɪ'spjuːt/ n disputa f; (industrial) contestazione f ● vt contestare (statement)

**disqualification** /dɪskwɒlɪfɪ'keɪʃn/ n squalifica f; (from driving) ritiro m della patente

**disqualify** /dɪs'kwɒlɪfaɪ/ vt escludere; Sport squalificare; ~ **sb from driving** ritirare la patente a qcno

**disquiet** /dɪs'kwaɪət/ n inquietudine f

**disquieting** /dɪs'kwaɪətɪŋ/ a allarmante

**disregard** /dɪsrɪ'gɑːd/ n mancanza f di considerazione ● vt ignorare

**disrepair** /dɪsrɪ'peə(r)/ n **fall into ~** deteriorarsi; **in a state of ~** in cattivo stato

**disreputable** /dɪs'repjʊtəbl/ a malfamato

**disrepute** /dɪsrɪ'pjuːt/ n discredito m; **bring sb into ~** rovinare la reputazione a qcno

**disrespect** /dɪsrɪ'spekt/ n mancanza f di rispetto

**disrespectful** /dɪsrɪ'spektfʊl/ a irrispettoso

**disrespectfully** /dɪsrɪ'spektfʊlɪ/ adv irrispettosamente

**disrupt** /dɪs'rʌpt/ vt creare scompiglio in; sconvolgere (plans)

**disruption** /dɪs'rʌpʃn/ n scompiglio m; (of plans) sconvolgimento m

**disruptive** /dɪs'rʌptɪv/ a (person, behaviour) indisciplinato

**dissatisfaction** /dɪ(s)sætɪs'fækʃn/ n malcontento m

**dissatisfied** /dɪ(s)'sætɪsfaɪd/ a scontento

**dissect** /dɪ'sekt/ vt sezionare

**dissection** /dɪ'sekʃn/ n dissezione f

**disseminate** /dɪ'semɪneɪt/ vt divulgare

**dissemination** /dɪsemɪ'neɪʃn/ n divulgazione f

**dissension** /dɪ'senʃn/ n (discord) dissenso m

**dissent** /dɪ'sent/ n dissenso m ● vi dissentire

**dissertation** /dɪsə'teɪʃn/ n tesi f inv

**disservice** /dɪ(s)'sɜːvɪs/ n **do sb/oneself a ~** rendere un cattivo servizio a qcno/se stesso

**dissidence** /'dɪsɪdəns/ n dissidenza f

**dissident** /'dɪsɪdənt/ n dissidente mf

**dissimilar** /dɪ(s)'sɪmɪlə(r)/ a dissimile (**to** da)

**dissimilarity** /dɪs(s)ɪmɪ'lærətɪ/ n diversità f inv

**dissipate** /'dɪsɪpeɪt/ vt dissipare (hope, enthusiasm)

**dissipated** /'dɪsɪpeɪtɪd/ a dissipato

**dissipation** n dissipatezza f, sregolatezza f

**dissociate** /dɪ'səʊʃɪeɪt/ vt dissociare; ~ **oneself from** dissociarsi da

**dissolute** /'dɪsəluːt/ a dissoluto

**dissolution** /dɪsə'luːʃn/ n scioglimento m

**dissolve** /dɪ'zɒlv/ vt dissolvere ● vi dissolversi

**dissonance** /'dɪsənəns/ n dissonanza f

**dissonant** /'dɪsənənt/ a Mus dissonante

**dissuade** /dɪ'sweɪd/ vt dissuadere

**distance** /'dɪstəns/ n distanza f; **it's a short ~ from here to the station** la stazione non è lontana da qui; **in the ~** in lontananza; **from a ~** da lontano

**distant** /'dɪstənt/ a distante; (relative) lontano

**distantly** /'dɪstəntlɪ/ adv (reply) con distacco

**distaste** /dɪs'teɪst/ n avversione f

**distasteful** /dɪs'teɪstfʊl/ a spiacevole

**distemper** /dɪ'stempə(r)/ n (paint) tempera f; (in horses, dogs) cimurro m

**distend** /dɪ'stend/ vi dilatarsi

**distil** /dɪ'stɪl/ vt (pt/pp **distilled**) distillare

**distillation** /dɪstɪ'leɪʃn/ n distillazione f

**distillery** /dɪ'stɪlərɪ/ n distilleria f

**distinct** /dɪ'stɪŋkt/ a chiaro; (different) distinto

**distinction** /dɪ'stɪŋkʃn/ n distinzione f; Sch massimo m dei voti

**distinctive** /dɪ'stɪŋktɪv/ a caratteristico

**distinctly** /dɪ'stɪŋktlɪ/ adv chiaramente

**distinguish** /dɪ'stɪŋgwɪʃ/ vt/i distinguere; ~ **oneself** distinguersi

**distinguishable** /dɪˈstɪŋgwɪʃəbl/ a distin-guibile

**distinguished** /dɪˈstɪŋgwɪʃt/ a rinomato; ⟨appearance⟩ distinto; ⟨career⟩ brillante

**distort** /dɪˈstɔːt/ vt distorcere

**distortion** /dɪˈstɔːʃn/ n distorsione f

**distract** /dɪˈstrækt/ vt distrarre

**distracted** /dɪˈstræktɪd/ a assente; ⟨fam: worried⟩ preoccupato

**distracting** /dɪˈstræktɪŋ/ a che distrae; **I found the noise too ~** il rumore mi disturbava troppo

**distraction** /dɪˈstrækʃn/ n distrazione f; ⟨despair⟩ disperazione f; **drive sb to ~** portare qcno alla disperazione

**distraught** /dɪˈstrɔːt/ a sconvolto

**distress** /dɪˈstres/ n angoscia f; ⟨pain⟩ sofferenza f; ⟨danger⟩ difficoltà f ● vt sconvolgere; ⟨sadden⟩ affliggere

**distressed** /dɪˈstrest/ a ⟨upset⟩ turbato; ⟨stronger⟩ afflitto

**distressing** /dɪˈstresɪŋ/ a penoso; ⟨shocking⟩ sconvolgente

**distress signal** n segnale m di richiesta di soccorso

**distribute** /dɪˈstrɪbjuːt/ vt distribuire

**distribution** /ˌdɪstrɪˈbjuːʃn/ n distribuzione f

**distribution network** n rete f di distribuzione

**distributor** /dɪˈstrɪbjʊtə(r)/ n distributore m

**district** /ˈdɪstrɪkt/ n regione f; Admin distretto m

**district: district council** n Br consiglio m distrettuale. **district court** n Am corte f distrettuale federale. **district manager** n direttore, -trice mf di zona. **district nurse** n infermiere, -a mf che fa visite a domicilio

**distrust** /dɪsˈtrʌst/ n sfiducia f ● vt non fidarsi di

**distrustful** /dɪsˈtrʌstfʊl/ a diffidente

**disturb** /dɪˈstɜːb/ vt disturbare; ⟨emotionally⟩ turbare; spostare ⟨papers⟩

**disturbance** /dɪˈstɜːbəns/ n disturbo m; **~s** pl ⟨rioting etc⟩ disordini mpl

**disturbed** /dɪˈstɜːbd/ a turbato; [**mentally**] **~** malato di mente

**disturbing** /dɪˈstɜːbɪŋ/ a inquietante

**disuse** /dɪsˈjuːs/ n **fall into ~** cadere in disuso

**disused** /dɪsˈjuːzd/ a non utilizzato

**ditch** /dɪtʃ/ n fosso m ● vt ⟨fam: abandon⟩ abbandonare ⟨plan, car⟩; piantare ⟨lover⟩

**ditchwater** /ˈdɪtʃwɔːtə(r)/ n **as dull as ~** una barba

**dither** /ˈdɪðə(r)/ vi titubare

**ditto** /ˈdɪtəʊ/ adv idem; ⟨in list⟩ idem come sopra

**ditto marks** npl virgolette fpl

**divan** /dɪˈvæn/ n divano m

**dive** /daɪv/ n tuffo m; Aeron picchiata f; ⟨fam: place⟩ bettola f ● vi tuffarsi; ⟨when in water⟩ immergersi; Aeron scendere in picchiata; ⟨fam: rush⟩ precipitarsi

**dive-bomb** vt Mil bombardare in picchiata

**diver** /ˈdaɪvə(r)/ n ⟨from board⟩ tuffatore,

-trice mf; ⟨scuba⟩ sommozzatore, -trice mf; ⟨deep sea⟩ palombaro m

**diverge** /daɪˈvɜːdʒ/ vi divergere

**divergent** /daɪˈvɜːdʒənt/ a divergente

**diverse** /daɪˈvɜːs/ a vario

**diversify** /daɪˈvɜːsɪfaɪ/ vt/i ⟨pt/pp **-ied**⟩ diversificare; Comm diversificare

**diversion** /daɪˈvɜːʃn/ n deviazione f; ⟨distraction⟩ diversivo m

**diversionary** /daɪˈvɜːʃənərɪ/ a ⟨tactic, attack⟩ diversivo

**diversity** /daɪˈvɜːsətɪ/ n varietà f

**divert** /daɪˈvɜːt/ vt deviare ⟨traffic⟩; distogliere ⟨attention⟩

**divest** /daɪˈvest/ vt privare (**of** di)

**divide** /dɪˈvaɪd/ vt dividere (**by** per); **six ~d by two** sei diviso due ● vi dividersi

■ **divide out** vt = **divide**

■ **divide up** vt = **divide**

**dividend** /ˈdɪvɪdend/ n dividendo m; **pay ~s** fig ripagare

**divider** /dɪˈvaɪdə(r)/ n ⟨in room⟩ divisorio m; ⟨in file⟩ cartoncino m separatore

**dividers** /dɪˈvaɪdəz/ npl compasso m a punte fisse

**dividing** /dɪˈvaɪdɪŋ/ a ⟨wall, fence⟩ divisorio

**dividing line** n linea f di demarcazione

**divine** /dɪˈvaɪn/ a divino

**divinely** /dɪˈvaɪnlɪ/ adv also fam divinamente

**diving** /ˈdaɪvɪŋ/ n ⟨from board⟩ tuffi mpl; ⟨scuba⟩ immersione f

**diving: diving board** n trampolino m. **diving mask** n maschera f [subacquea]. **diving suit** n muta f; ⟨deep sea⟩ scafandro m

**divinity** /dɪˈvɪnətɪ/ n divinità f inv; ⟨subject⟩ teologia f; ⟨at school⟩ religione f

**divisible** /dɪˈvɪzəbl/ a divisibile (**by** per)

**division** /dɪˈvɪʒn/ n divisione f; ⟨in sports league⟩ serie f

**divisional** /dɪˈvɪʒənl/ a ⟨commander, officer⟩ di divisione

**divisive** /dɪˈvaɪsɪv/ a ⟨policy⟩ che crea discordia; **be socially ~** creare delle divisioni sociali

**divorce** /dɪˈvɔːs/ n divorzio m ● vt divorziare da

**divorced** /dɪˈvɔːst/ a divorziato; **get ~** divorziare

**divorcee** /dɪvɔːˈsiː/ n divorziato, -a mf

**divulge** /daɪˈvʌldʒ/ vt rendere pubblico

■ **divvy up** vt fam = **divide up**

**DIY** abbr **do-it-yourself**

**dizziness** /ˈdɪzɪnɪs/ n giramenti mpl di testa

**dizzy** /ˈdɪzɪ/ a (**-ier, -iest**) vertiginoso; **I feel ~** mi gira la testa

**DJ** n abbr ⟨**disc jockey**⟩ DJ m inv; Br abbr ⟨**dinner jacket**⟩ smoking m inv

**DNA** n abbr ⟨**deoxyribonucleic acid**⟩ DNA m inv ● attrib ⟨testing⟩ del DNA

**do** /duː/ n ⟨pl **dos** or **do's**⟩ fam festa f ● v (3 sg pres tense **does**; pt **did**; pp **done**) ● vt fare; ⟨fam: cheat⟩ fregare; **do sb out of sth** ⟨money⟩ fregare qcsa a qcno; ⟨opportunity⟩ defraudare qcno di qcsa; **be done** Culin essere cotto; **well done** bravo; *Culin* ben cotto; **do the flowers** sistemare i fiori; **do the washing up** lavare i piatti; **do one's hair** farsi i capelli ● *vi* (*be suitable*) andare; (*be enough*) bastare; **this will do** questo va bene; **that will do!** basta così!; **do well/badly** cavarsela bene/male; **how is he doing?** come sta? ● *v aux* **do you speak Italian?** parli italiano?; **you don't like him, do you?** non ti piace, vero?; (*expressing astonishment*) non dirmi che ti piace!; **yes, I do** sì; (*emphatic*) invece sì; **no, I don't** no; **I don't smoke** non fumo; **don't you/doesn't he?** vero?; **so do I** anch'io; **do come in, John** entra, John; **how do you do?** piacere

■ **do away with** *vt* abolire ⟨rule⟩
■ **do for** *vt* (*ruin*) rovinare
■ **do in** *vt* (*fam: kill*) uccidere; farsi male a ⟨back⟩; **done in** *fam* esausto
■ **do up** *vt* (*fasten*) abbottonare; (*renovate*) rimettere a nuovo; (*wrap*) avvolgere
■ **do with** *vt* **I could do with a spanner** mi ci vorrebbe una chiave inglese
■ **do without** *vt* fare a meno di

**d.o.b.** *abbr* (**date of birth**) data *f* di nascita
**docile** /ˈdəʊsaɪl/ *a* docile
**dock**[1] /dɒk/ *n Jur* banco *m* degli imputati
**dock**[2] *n Naut* bacino *m* ● *vi* entrare in porto; ⟨spaceship:⟩ congiungersi
**docker** /ˈdɒkə(r)/ *n* portuale *m*
**docket** /ˈdɒkɪt/ *n* (*Comm: label*) etichetta *f*; (*customs certificate*) ricevuta *f* doganale ● *vt Comm* etichettare ⟨parcel, package⟩
**docking** /ˈdɒkɪŋ/ *n Naut* ormeggio *m*; (*of spaceshuttle*) aggancio *m*
**docks** /dɒks/ *npl* porto *m*
**dockworker** /ˈdɒkwɜːkə(r)/ *n* portuale *m*
**dockyard** /ˈdɒkjɑːd/ *n* cantiere *m* navale
**doctor** /ˈdɒktə(r)/ *n* dottore *m*, dottoressa *f* ● *vt* alterare ⟨drink⟩; castrare ⟨cat⟩
**doctorate** /ˈdɒktərət/ *n* dottorato *m*
**Doctor of Philosophy** *n* titolare *mf* di un dottorato di ricerca
**doctor's note** /ˈdɒktəz/ *n* certificato *m* medico
**doctrine** /ˈdɒktrɪn/ *n* dottrina *f*
**document** /ˈdɒkjʊmənt/ *n* documento *m*
**documentary** /dɒkjʊˈmentərɪ/ *a & n* documentario *m*
**documentation** /dɒkjʊmenˈteɪʃn/ *n* documentazione *f*
**document holder** *n* (*for keyboarder*) leggio *m*
**document wallet** *n* (*folder*) cartellina *f*
**doddery** /ˈdɒdərɪ/ *a fam* barcollante
**doddle** /ˈdɒd(ə)l/ *n Br fam* **it's a ~** è un gioco da ragazzi
**dodge** /dɒdʒ/ *n fam* trucco *m* ● *vt* schivare ⟨blow⟩; evitare ⟨person⟩ ● *vi* scansarsi; **~ out of the way** scansarsi
**dodgems** /ˈdɒdʒəmz/ *npl* autoscontro *msg*
**dodgy** /ˈdɒdʒɪ/ *a* (**-ier, -iest**) (*fam: dubious*) sospetto
**DOE** *n Br abbr* (**Department of the Environment**) ministero *m* dell'ambiente; *Am*

*abbr* (**Department of Energy**) ≈ ministero *m* dell'industria
**doe** /dəʊ/ *n* femmina *f* (*di daino, renna, lepre*); (*rabbit*) coniglia *f*
**does** /dʌz/ *see* **do**
**doesn't** /ˈdʌznt/ = **does not**
**dog** /dɒɡ/ *n* cane *m* ● *vt* (*pt/pp* **dogged**) ⟨illness, bad luck:⟩ perseguitare
**dog: dog biscuit** *n* biscotto *m* per cani. **dog breeder** *n* allevatore, -trice *mf* di cani. **dog collar** *n* collare *m* (*per cani*); *Relig fam* collare *m* del prete. **dog-eared** /-ɪəd/ *a* con le orrechie. **dog-end** *n fam* cicca *f*. **dogfight** *n* combattimento *m* di cani; *Aeron* combattimento *m* aereo
**dogged** /ˈdɒɡɪd/ *a* ostinato
**doggedly** /ˈdɒɡɪdlɪ/ *adv* ostinatamente
**doggy bag** /ˈdɒɡɪ/ *n* sacchetto *m* per portarsi a casa gli avanzi di un pasto al ristorante
**doggy-paddle** *n fam* nuoto *m* a cagnolino
**dog handler** *n* addestratore, -trice *mf* di cani
**doghouse** /ˈdɒɡhaʊs/ *n Am* canile *m*; **in the ~** *Br & Am fam* in disgrazia
**dogma** /ˈdɒɡmə/ *n* dogma *m*
**dogmatic** /dɒɡˈmætɪk/ *a* dogmatico
**do-gooder** /duːˈɡʊdə(r)/ *n pej* pseudo benefattore, -trice *mf*
**dog: dog-paddle** *n* nuoto *m* a cagnolino. **dogsbody** *n fam* tirapiedi *mf inv*. **dog tag** *n Am Mil fam* piastrina *f* di riconoscimento
**doh** /dəʊ/ *n Mus* do *m*
**doily** /ˈdɔɪlɪ/ *n* centrino *m*
**doing** /ˈduːɪŋ/ *n* **it's none of my ~** non sono stato io; **this is her ~** questa è opera sua; **it takes some ~!** ce ne vuole!
**do-it-yourself** /duːɪtjəˈself/ *n* fai da te *m*, bricolage *m*
**do-it-yourself shop** *n* negozio *m* di bricolage
**doldrums** /ˈdɒldrəmz/ *npl* **be in the ~** essere giù di corda; ⟨business:⟩ essere in fase di stasi
**dole** /dəʊl/ *n* sussidio *m* di disoccupazione; **be on the ~** essere disoccupato
■ **dole out** *vt* distribuire
**doleful** /ˈdəʊlfl/ *a* triste
**dolefully** /ˈdəʊlfʊlɪ/ *adv* tristemente
**dole queue** *n Br* coda *f* per riscuotere il sussidio di disoccupazione; (*fig: number of unemployed*) numero *m* dei disoccupati
**doll** /dɒl/ *n* bambola *f*
■ **doll up** *vt fam* **~ oneself up** mettersi in ghingheri
**dollar** /ˈdɒlə(r)/ *n* dollaro *m*
**dollar: dollar bill** *n* banconota *f* da un dollaro. **dollar diplomacy** *n* politica *f* di investimenti all'estero. **dollar sign** *n* simbolo *m* del dollaro
**dollop** /ˈdɒləp/ *n fam* cucchiaiata *f*
**dolly** /ˈdɒlɪ/ *n* (*fam: doll*) bambola *f*; *Cinema, TV* dolly *m inv*
**Dolomites** /ˈdɒləmaɪts/ *npl* Dolomiti *mpl*
**dolphin** /ˈdɒlfɪn/ *n* delfino *m*
**domain** /dəˈmeɪn/ *n* dominio *m*

**dome** /dəʊm/ *n* cupola *f*

**domed** /dəʊmd/ *a* ‹skyline, city› ricco di cupole; ‹roof, ceiling› a cupola; ‹forehead, helmet› bombato

**domestic** /də'mestɪk/ *a* domestico; *Pol* interno; *Comm* nazionale.

**domestic animal** *n* animale *m* domestico

**domestic appliance** *n* elettrodomestico *m*

**domesticated** /də'mestɪkeɪtɪd/ *a* ‹animal› addomesticato

**domestic flight** *n* volo *m* nazionale

**domestic help** *n* collaboratore, -trice *mf* familiare

**domesticity** /dɒme'stɪsətɪ/ *n* ‹home life› vita *f* di famiglia; ‹household duties› faccende *fpl* domestiche

**domestic servant** *n* domestico, -a *mf*

**domiciliary** /dɒmɪ'sɪliərɪ/ *a* ‹visit, care› a domicilio

**dominance** /'dɒmɪnəns/ *n* *Biol*, *Zool* dominanza *f*; ‹domination› predominio *m*; ‹numerical strength› preponderanza *f*

**dominant** /'dɒmɪnənt/ *a* dominante

**dominate** /'dɒmɪneɪt/ *vt/i* dominare

**domination** /dɒmɪ'neɪʃn/ *n* dominio *m*

**domineering** /dɒmɪ'nɪərɪŋ/ *a* autoritario

**Dominican Republic** /də'mɪnɪkən/ *n* Repubblica *f* Dominicana

**dominion** /də'mɪnjən/ *n* *Br Pol* dominion *m* *inv*

**domino** /'dɒmɪnəʊ/ *n* (*pl* -es) tessera *f* del domino; **~es** *sg* (*game*) domino *m*

**don**[1] /dɒn/ *vt* (*pt/pp* **donned**) *liter* indossare

**don**[2] *n* docente *mf* universitario, -a

**donate** /dəʊ'neɪt/ *vt* donare

**donation** /dəʊ'neɪʃn/ *n* donazione *f*

**done** /dʌn/ *see* **do**

**donkey** /'dɒŋkɪ/ *n* asino *m*

**donkey: donkey jacket** *n* giacca *f* pesante. **donkey's years** *fam* **not for ~** non da secoli. **donkey-work** *n* sgobbata *f*

**donor** /'dəʊnə(r)/ *n* donatore, -trice *mf*

**donor card** *n* tessera *f* del donatore di organi

**don't** /dəʊnt/ = **do not**

**doodle** /'du:dl/ *vi* scarabocchiare

**doom** /du:m/ *n* fato *m*; (*ruin*) rovina *f* ● *vt* **be ~ed to failure** essere destinato al fallimento

**doomed** /du:md/ *a* ‹vessel› destinato ad affondare

**doomsday** /'du:mzdeɪ/ *n* giorno *m* del giudizio

**doomwatch** /'du:mwɒtʃ/ *n* catastrofismo *m*

**door** /dɔ:(r)/ *n* porta *f*; (*of car*) portiera *f*; **out of ~s** all'aperto

**door: door bell** *n* campanello *m*. **doorman** *n* portiere *m*. **doormat** *n* zerbino *m*. **door plate** *n* (*of doctor etc*) targa *f*. **doorstep** *n* gradino *m* della porta. **doorstop** *n* fermaporta *m* *inv*. **door-to-door** *a* ‹canvassing, selling› porta a porta ● *adv* ‹sell› porta a porta. **doorway** *n* vano *m* della porta

**dope** /dəʊp/ *n* *fam* (*drug*) droga *f* leggera;

(*information*) indiscrezioni *fpl*; (*idiot*) idiota *mf* ● *vt* drogare; *Sport* dopare

**dope test** *n* *Sport* antidoping *m* *inv*

**dopey** /'dəʊpɪ/ *a* *fam* addormentato

**dormant** /'dɔ:mənt/ *a* latente; ‹volcano› inattivo

**dormer** /'dɔ:mə(r)/ *n* **~** [**window**] abbaino *m*

**dormitory** /'dɔ:mɪtərɪ/ *n* dormitorio *m*

**dormouse** /'dɔ:maʊs/ *n* (*pl* **dormice** /'dɔ:maɪs/) ghiro *m*

**dosage** /'dəʊsɪdʒ/ *n* dosaggio *m*

**dose** /dəʊs/ *n* dose *f*

**doss** /dɒs/ *vi* *sl* accamparsi

■ **doss down** *vi* sistemarsi [a dormire]

**dosser** /'dɒsə(r)/ *n* barbone, -a *mf*

**doss-house** *n* dormitorio *m* pubblico

**dot** /dɒt/ *n* punto *m*; **at 8 o'clock on the ~** alle 8 in punto

**dotage** /'dəʊtɪdʒ/ *n* **be in one's ~** essere un vecchio rimbambito

**dote** /dəʊt/ *vi* **~ on** stravedere per

**dot matrix** [**printer**] *n* stampante *f* a matrice di punti

**dotted** /'dɒtɪd/ *a* **~ line** linea *f* punteggiata; **sign on the ~ line** firmare nell'apposito spazio; **be ~ with** essere punteggiato di

**dotty** /'dɒtɪ/ *a* (**-ier, -iest**) *fam* tocco; ‹idea› folle

**double** /'dʌbl/ *a* doppio ● *adv* **cost ~** costare il doppio; **see ~** vedere doppio; **~ the amount** la quantità doppia ● *n* doppio *m*; (*person*) sosia *m* *inv*; **~s** *pl* *Tennis* doppio *m*; **at the ~** di corsa ● *vt* raddoppiare; (*fold*) piegare in due ● *vi* raddoppiare

■ **double back** *vi* (*go back*) fare dietro front

■ **double up** *vi* (*bend over*) piegarsi in due. (**with** per); (*share*) dividere una stanza

**double: double act** *n* *Theat*, *fig* numero *m* eseguito da due attori. **double-barrelled** /-'bærəld/ *a* ‹gun› a doppia canna. **double-barrelled surname** *n* cognome *m* doppio. **double-bass** *n* contrabbasso *m*. **double bed** *n* letto *m* matrimoniale. **double bend** *n* *Auto* doppia curva *f*. **double bill** *n* *Theat* rappresentazione *f* di due spettacoli. **double bluff** *n* atto *m* del dire la verità facendola sembrare una menzogna. **double-book** *vi* ‹hotel, airline, company:› fare prenotazioni doppie ● *vt* **~ a room/seat etc** riservare la stessa camera/lo stesso posto a due persone. **double-breasted** *a* a doppio petto. **double-check** *vt/i* ricontrollare ● *n* **double check** ulteriore controllo *m*. **double chin** *n* doppio mento *m*. **double cream** *n* *Br* ≈ panna *f* densa. **double-cross** *vt* ingannare. **double cuff** *n* polsino *m* con risvolto. **double-dealing** *n* doppio gioco *m* ● *a* doppio. **double-decker** *n* autobus *m* *inv* a due piani. **double door[s]** *n*[*pl*] porta *f* a due battenti. **double Dutch** *n* *fam* ostrogoto *m*. **double-edged** /-'edʒd/ *a* *also fig* a doppio taglio. **double entendre** /du:blɒ'tɒdr(ə)/ *n* doppio senso *m*. **double entry book-keeping** *n* contabilità *f* in partita doppia. **double exposure** *n* *Phot* sovrimpressione *f*. **double fault** *n* *Tennis* doppio fallo m. **double feature** n Cinema proiezione f di due film con biglietto unico. **double-fronted** /-'frʌntɪd/ a ⟨house⟩ con due finestre ai lati della porta principale. **double glazing** n doppiovetro m. **double-jointed** a ⟨person, limb⟩ snodato. **double knitting** [**wool**] n lana f grossa. **double lock** vt chiudere a doppia mandata. **double-park** vt/i parcheggiare in doppia fila. **double-quick** adv rapidissimamente ● a **in ~ time** in un baleno. **double room** n camera f doppia. **double saucepan** n Br bagnomaria m inv. **double spacing** n Typ interlinea f doppia. **double spread** n Journ articolo m/pubblicità f su due pagine. **double standard** n **have ~ ~s** usare metri diversi. **double take** n **do a ~ ~** reagire a scoppio ritardato. **double talk** n pej discorso m ambiguo. **double time** n Am Mil marcia f forzata; **be paid ~ ~** ricevere doppia paga per lo straordinario. **double vision** n **have ~ ~** vederci doppio. **double whammy** n ( fam: two bits of bad luck) sfortuna f doppia. **double yellow line[s]** n[pl] Br Aut due linee fpl gialle continue indicanti divieto di fermata e di sosta

**doubly** /'dʌblɪ/ adv doppiamente

**doubt** /daʊt/ n dubbio m ● vt dubitare di

**doubtful** /'daʊtfʊl/ a dubbio; ⟨having doubts⟩ in dubbio

**doubtfully** /'daʊtfʊlɪ/ adv con aria dubbiosa

**doubtless** /'daʊtlɪs/ adv indubbiamente

**douche** /duːʃ/ n (Med: vaginal) irrigazione f

**dough** /dəʊ/ n pasta f; ( for bread) impasto m; ( fam: money) quattrini mpl

**doughnut** /'dəʊnʌt/ n bomboloni m, krapfen m inv

**dour** /'dʊə(r)/ a ⟨mood, landscape⟩ cupo; ⟨person, expression⟩ arcigno; ⟨building⟩ austero

**douse** /daʊs/ vt spegnere

**dove** /dʌv/ n colomba f

**dovecot[e]** /'dʌvkɒt/ n colombaia f

**dovetail** /'dʌvteɪl/ n Techn incastro m a coda di rondine

**dowdy** /'daʊdɪ/ a (-ier, -iest) trasandato

**down**[1] /daʊn/ n ( feathers) piumino m

**down**[2] /daʊn/ adv giù; **go**/**come ~** scendere; **~ there** laggiù; **sales are ~** le vendite sono diminuite; **£50 ~** 50 sterline d'acconto; **~ 10%** ridotto del 10%; **~ with...!** abbasso...! ● prep **walk ~ the road** camminare per strada; **~ the stairs** giù per le scale; **fall ~ the stairs** cadere giù dalle scale; **get that ~ you!** fam butta giù!; **be ~ the pub** fam essere al pub ● vt bere tutto d'un fiato ⟨drink⟩; **~ tools** staccare; (in protest) interrompere il lavoro per protestare

**down: down-and-out** n spiantato, -a mf. **downbeat** a ( pessimistic) pessimistico; (laidback) distaccato. **downcast** a abbattuto. **downfall** n caduta f; (of person) rovina f. **downgrade** vt (in seniority) degradare. **down-hearted** /-'hɑːtɪd/ a scoraggiato. **downhill** adv in discesa; **go ~** fig essere in declino. **downhill skiing** n sci m di fondo.

**down-in-the-mouth** a fam abbattuto. **download** vt Comput scaricare. **down-market** a ⟨newspaper, programme⟩ rivolto al pubblico delle fasce basse; ⟨products⟩ dozzinale; ⟨area⟩ popolare; ⟨hotel, restaurant⟩ economico. **down payment** n deposito m. **downpipe** n Br tubo m di scolo. **downpour** n acquazzone m. **downright** a ⟨absolute⟩ totale; ⟨lie⟩ bell'e buono; ⟨idiot⟩ perfetto ● adv ⟨completely⟩ completamente

**downs** /daʊnz/ npl Br ⟨hills⟩ colline fpl di gesso nell'Inghilterra meridionale

**downside** /'daʊnsaɪd/ n svantaggio m

**downside up** a & adv Am sottosopra

**Down's syndrome** /'daʊnz/ n sindrome f di Down

**down: downstairs** adv al piano di sotto ● a del piano di sotto. **downstream** adv a valle. **down-to-earth** a ⟨person⟩ con i piedi per terra. **downtown** adv Am in centro. **downtrodden** /'daʊntrɒd(ə)n/ a oppresso. **downturn** n (in economy) fase f discendente; (in career) svolta f negativa. **down under** adv fam in Australia e/o Nuova Zelanda

**downward[s]** /'daʊnwəd[z]/ a verso il basso; ⟨slope⟩ in discesa ● adv verso il basso

**downwind** /daʊn'wɪnd/ adv sottovento

**downy** /'daʊnɪ/ a (-ier, -iest) coperto di peluria

**dowry** /'daʊrɪ/ n dote f

**doz** abbr (**dozen**) dozzina f

**doze** /dəʊz/ n sonnellino m ● vi sonnecchiare ■ **doze off** vi assopirsi

**dozen** /'dʌzn/ n dozzina f; **~s of books** libri a dozzine

**DPhil** n abbr (**Doctor of Philosophy**) titolare mf di un dottorato di ricerca

**DPP** n Br abbr (**Director of Public Prosecutions**) ≈ Procuratore m della Repubblica

**Dr** abbr (**doctor**) Dott. m, Dott.essa f; abbr (**drive**) ≈ via f

**drab** /dræb/ a ⟨colour⟩ spento; ⟨building⟩ tetro; ⟨life⟩ scialbo

**draft**[1] /drɑːft/ n abbozzo m; Comm cambiale f; Am Mil leva f ● vt abbozzare; Am Mil arruolare

**draft**[2] n Am = **draught**

**drag** /dræg/ n fam scocciatura f; **in ~** fam ⟨man⟩ travestito da donna ● vt ( pt/pp **dragged**) trascinare; dragare ⟨river⟩
■ **drag on** vi ⟨time, meeting:⟩ trascinarsi
■ **drag out** vt tirare per le lunghe ⟨discussion⟩; **~ sth out of sb** tirar fuori qcsa a qcno con le pinze
■ **drag up** vt (mention unnecessarily) tirare in ballo

**dragon** /'drægən/ n drago m

**dragonfly** /'drægənflaɪ/ n libellula f

**drag show** n spettacolo m di travestiti

**drain** /dreɪn/ n tubo m di scarico; (grid) tombino m; **the ~s** le fognature (pl); **be a ~ on sb's finances** prosciugare le finanze di qcno ● vt drenare ⟨land, wound⟩; scolare ⟨liquid, vegetables⟩; svuotare ⟨tank, glass, person⟩

● *vi* ~ [**away**] andar via; **leave sth to** ~ lasciare qcsa a scolare

**drainage** /'dreɪnɪdʒ/ *n* (*system*) drenaggio *m*; (*of land*) scolo *m*

**draining board** /'dreɪnɪŋ/ *n* scolapiatti *m inv*

**drainpipe** /'dreɪnpaɪp/ *n* tubo *m* di scarico

**drainpipe trousers** *npl* pantaloni *mpl* a tubo

**drake** /dreɪk/ *n* maschio *m* dell'anatra

**drama** /'drɑːmə/ *n* arte *f* drammatica; (*play*) opera *f* teatrale; (*event*) dramma *m*

**dramatic** /drə'mætɪk/ *a* drammatico

**dramatically** /drə'mætɪklɪ/ *adv* in modo drammatico

**dramatics** /drə'mætɪks/ *npl* arte *f* drammatica; *pej* atteggiamento *m* teatrale

**dramatist** /'dræmətɪst/ *n* drammaturgo, -a *mf*

**dramatization** /dræmətaɪ'zeɪʃn/ *n* (*for cinema*) adattamento *m* cinematografico; (*for stage*) adattamento *m* teatrale; (*for TV*) adattamento *m* televisivo; (*exaggeration*) drammatizzazione *f*

**dramatize** /'dræmətaɪz/ *vt* adattare per il teatro; *fig* drammatizzare

**drank** /dræŋk/ *see* **drink**

**drape** /dreɪp/ *n Am* tenda *f* ● *vt* appoggiare (**over** su)

**drastic** /'dræstɪk/ *a* drastico

**drastically** /'dræstɪklɪ/ *adv* drasticamente

**draught** /drɑːft/ *n* corrente *f* [d'aria]

**draught beer** *n* birra *f* alla spina

**draught-proof** *a* a tenuta d'aria ● *vt* tappare le fessure di

**draughts** /drɑːfts/ *n sg* (*game*) [gioco *m* della] dama *fsg*

**draughtsman** /'drɑːftsmən/ *n* disegnatore, -trice *mf*

**draughty** /'drɑːftɪ/ *a* pieno di correnti d'aria; **it's** ~ c'è corrente

**draw** /drɔː/ *n* (*attraction*) attrazione *f*; *Sport* pareggio *m*; (*in lottery*) sorteggio *m* ● *vi* (*pt* **drew**, *pp* **drawn**) ● *vt* tirare; (*attract*) attirare; disegnare (*picture*); tracciare (*line*); ritirare (*money*); attingere (*water*); ~ **lots** tirare a sorte ● *vi* (*tea*:) essere in infusione; *Sport* pareggiare; ~ **near** avvicinarsi

■ **draw back** *vt* tirare indietro; ritirare (*hand*); tirare (*curtains*) ● *vi* (*recoil*) tirarsi indietro

■ **draw in** *vt* ritrarre (*claws etc*) ● *vi* (*train:*) arrivare; (*days:*) accorciarsi

■ **draw on** *vt* attingere a (*savings, sb's experience*)

■ **draw out** *vt* (*pull out*) tirar fuori; ritirare (*money*) ● *vi* (*train:*) partire; (*days:*) allungarsi

■ **draw up** *vt* redigere (*document*); accostare (*chair*); ~ **oneself up** [**to one's full height**] drizzarsi ● *vi* (*stop*) fermarsi

**drawback** /'drɔːbæk/ *n* inconveniente *m*

**drawbridge** /'drɔːbrɪdʒ/ *n* ponte *m* levatoio

**drawee** *n* trattario *m*

**drawer** /drɔː(r)/ *n* cassetto *m*; *Fin* traente *mf*

**drawing** /'drɔːɪŋ/ *n* disegno *m*

**drawing: drawing board** *n* tavolo *m* da disegno: *fig* **go back to the** ~ ~ ricominciare da capo. **drawing pin** *n* puntina *f*. **drawing rights** *npl Fin* diritti *mf* di prelievo. **drawing room** *n* salotto *m*

**drawl** /drɔːl/ *n* pronuncia *f* strascicata

**drawn** /drɔːn/ *see* **draw**

**dread** /dred/ *n* terrore *m* ● *vt* aver il terrore di

**dreadful** /'dredfʊl/ *a* terribile

**dreadfully** /'dredfʊlɪ/ *adv* terribilmente

**dream** /driːm/ *n* sogno *m* ● *attrib* di sogno ● *vt/i* (*pt/pp* **dreamt** /dremt/ *or* **dreamed**) sognare (**about/of** di)

**dreamer** /'driːmə(r)/ *n* (*idealist*) sognatore, -trice *mf*; (*inattentive*) persona *f* con la testa fra le nuvole

**dream-world** *n* **live in a** ~ vivere tra le nuvole

**dreamy** /'driːmɪ/ *a fam* (*house etc*) di sogno; (*person*) che è un sogno; (*distracted*) distratto; (*sound, music*) dolce

**dreary** /'drɪərɪ/ *a* (-**ier**, -**iest**) tetro; (*boring*) monotono

**dredge** /dredʒ/ *vt/i* dragare

■ **dredge up** *vt* riesumare (*the past*)

**dredger** /'dredʒə(r)/ *n* draga *f*

**dregs** /dregz/ *npl* feccia *fsg*

**drench** /drentʃ/ *vt* **get** ~**ed** inzupparsi

**drenched** /drentʃt/ *a* zuppo

**dress** /dres/ *n* (*woman's*) vestito *m*; (*clothing*) abbigliamento *m* ● *vt* vestire; (*decorate*) adornare; *Culin* condire; *Med* fasciare; ~ **oneself**, **get** ~**ed** vestirsi

■ **dress up** *vi* mettersi elegante; (*in disguise*) travestirsi (**as** da)

**dress: dress circle** *n Theat* prima galleria *f*. **dress designer** *n* stilista *mf*

**dresser** /'dresə(r)/ *n* (*furniture*) credenza *f*; (*Am: dressing table*) toilette *f inv*

**dressing** /'dresɪŋ/ *n Culin* condimento *m*; *Med* fasciatura *f*

**dressing: dressing down** *n fam* sgridata *f*. **dressing gown** *n* vestaglia *f*. **dressing room** *n* (*in gym*) spogliatoio *m*; *Theat* camerino *m*. **dressing table** *n* toilette *f inv*

**dress: dressmaker** *n* sarta *f*. **dressmaking** *n* confezioni *fpl* (*per donna*). **dress rehearsal** *n* prova *f* generale. **dress sense** *n* **have** ~ ~ saper abbinare i capi d'abbigliamento

**dressy** /'dresɪ/ *a* (-**ier**, -**iest**) elegante

**drew** /druː/ *see* **draw**

**dribble** /'drɪbl/ *vi* gocciolare; (*baby*:) sbavare; *Sport* dribblare

**dribs and drabs** /'drɪbzən'dræbz/ *npl* **in** ~ alla spicciolata

**dried** /draɪd/ *a* (*food*) essiccato

**drier** /'draɪə(r)/ *n* asciugabiancheria *m inv*

**drift** /drɪft/ *n* movimento *m* lento; (*of snow*) cumulo *m*; (*meaning*) senso *m* ● *vi* (*off course*) andare alla deriva; (*snow*:) accumularsi; (*fig: person*:) procedere senza meta

■ **drift apart** *vi* ⟨*people:*⟩ allontanarsi l'uno dall'altro

**drifter** /'drɪftə(r)/ *n* persona *f* senza meta

**driftwood** /'drɪftwʊd/ *n* pezzi *mpl* di legno galleggianti

**drill** /drɪl/ *n* trapano *m*; *Mil* esercitazione *f* ● *vt* trapanare; *Mil* fare esercitare ● *vi Mil* esercitarsi; ~ **for oil** trivellare in cerca di petrolio

**drily** /'draɪlɪ/ *adv* seccamente

**drink** /drɪŋk/ *n* bevanda *f*; (*alcoholic*) bicchierino *m*; **have a** ~ bere qualcosa; **a** ~ **of water** un po' d'acqua ● *vt/i* (*pt* **drank**, *pp* **drunk**) bere

■ **drink to** *vt* (*toast*) brindare a

■ **drink up** *vt* finire ● *vi* finire il bicchiere

**drinkable** /'drɪŋkəbl/ *a* potabile

**drink-driving** *n Br* guida *f* in stato di ebbrezza

**drinker** /'drɪŋkə(r)/ *n* bevitore, -trice *mf*

**drinking chocolate** /'drɪŋkɪŋ/ *n Br* cioccolata *f* in polvere

**drinking water** *n* acqua *f* potabile

**drink: drink problem** *n Br* **he has a** ~ ~ beve. **drinks cupboard** *n Br* mobile *m* bar. **drinks dispenser** *n Br* distributore *m* di bevande. **drinks machine** *n Br* distributore *m* di bevande. **drinks party** *n Br* cocktail *m inv*

**drip** /drɪp/ *n* gocciolamento *m*; (*drop*) goccia *f*; *Med* flebo *f inv*; (*fam: person*) mollaccione, -a *mf* ● *vi* (*pt/pp* **dripped**) gocciolare

**drip-dry** *a* che non si stira

**drip-feed** *n* flebo[clisi] *f inv*

**dripping** /'drɪpɪŋ/ *n* (*from meat*) grasso *m* d'arrosto ● *a* ~ [**wet**] fradicio

**drive** /draɪv/ *n* (*in car*) giro *m*; (*entrance*) viale *m*; (*energy*) grinta *f*; *Psych* pulsione *f*; (*organized effort*) operazione *f*; *Techn* motore *m*; *Comput* lettore *m*, unità *f inv* ● *v* (*pt* **drove** *pp* **driven**) ● *vt* portare ⟨*person by car*⟩; guidare ⟨*car*⟩; (*Sport: hit*) mandare; *Techn* far funzionare; ~ **sb mad** far diventare matto qcno ● *vi* guidare

■ **drive at** *vt* **what are you driving at?** dove vuoi arrivare?

■ **drive away** *vt* portare via in macchina; (*chase*) cacciare ● *vi* andare via in macchina

■ **drive in** *vt* piantare ⟨*nail*⟩ ● *vi* arrivare [in macchina]

■ **drive off** *vt* portare via in macchina; (*chase*) cacciare ● *vi* andare via in macchina

■ **drive on** *vi* proseguire; ~ **on!** avanti!

■ **drive up** *vi* arrivare (*in macchina*)

**drive-in** *a* ~ **cinema** cinema *m inv* drive-in

**drivel** /'drɪvl/ *n fam* sciocchezze *fpl*

**driven** /'drɪvn/ *see* **drive**

**driver** /'draɪvə(r)/ *n* guidatore, -trice *mf*; (*of train*) conducente *mf*

**drive-through** *n Am* drive-in *m inv*

**driveway** /'draɪvweɪ/ *n* strada *f* d'accesso

**driving** /'draɪvɪŋ/ *a* ⟨*rain*⟩ violento; ⟨*force*⟩ motore ● *n* guida *f*

**driving: driving force** *n* spinta *f*; (*person behind*) forza *f* trainante. **driving instructor** *n* istruttore, -trice *mf* di guida. **driving**

**lesson** *n* lezione *f* di guida. **driving licence** *n* patente *f* di guida. **driving mirror** *n* (*rearview*) specchietto *m* retrovisore. **driving school** *n* scuola *f* guida. **driving seat** *n* **be in the** ~ ~ essere alla guida. **driving test** *n* esame *m* di guida; **take one's** ~ ~ fare l'esame di guida

**drizzle** /'drɪzl/ *n* pioggerella *f* ● *vi* piovigginare

**droll** /drəʊl/ *a* divertente

**drone** /drəʊn/ *n* (*bee*) fuco *m*; (*sound*) ronzio *m*

■ **drone on** *vi* (*talk boringly*) tirarla per le lunghe

**drool** /druːl/ *vi* sbavare; ~ **over sth/sb** *fig fam* sbavare per qcsa/qcno

**droop** /druːp/ *vi* abbassarsi; ⟨*flowers:*⟩ afflosciarsi

**drop** /drɒp/ *n* (*of liquid*) goccia *f*; (*fall*) caduta *f*; (*in price, temperature*) calo *m* ● *v* (*pt/pp* **dropped**) ● *vt* far cadere; sganciare ⟨*bomb*⟩; (*omit*) omettere; (*give up*) abbandonare; ~ **the subject** cambiare discorso ● *vi* cadere; ⟨*price, temperature, wind:*⟩ calare; ⟨*ground:*⟩ essere in pendenza

■ **drop behind** *vi* rimanere indietro

■ **drop by** *vi* = **drop in**

■ **drop in** *vi* passare

■ **drop off** *vt* depositare ⟨*person*⟩ ● *vi* cadere; (*fall asleep*) assopirsi

■ **drop out** *vi* cadere; (*from race, society*) ritirarsi; ~ **out of school** lasciare la scuola

**drop handlebars** *npl* manubrio *m* ricurvo

**drop-out** *n* persona *f* contro il sistema sociale

**droppings** /'drɒpɪŋz/ *npl* sterco *m*

**drop shot** *n Sport* drop shot *m inv*, smorzata *f*

**drop zone** *n* (*for supplies etc*) zona *f* di lancio

**drought** /draʊt/ *n* siccità *f*

**drove** /drəʊv/ *see* **drive**

**droves** /drəʊvz/ *npl* **in** ~ in massa

**drown** /draʊn/ *vi* annegare ● *vt* annegare; coprire ⟨*noise*⟩; **he was** ~**ed** è annegato

**drowse** /draʊz/ *vi* sonnecchiare; (*be very sleepy*) essere sonnolento

**drowsiness** /'draʊzɪnɪs/ *n* sonnolenza *f*

**drowsy** /'draʊzɪ/ *a* sonnolento

**drudgery** /'drʌdʒərɪ/ *n* lavoro *m* pesante e noioso

**drug** /drʌg/ *n* droga *f*; *Med* farmaco *m*; **take** ~**s** drogarsi ● *vt* (*pt/pp* **drugged**) drogare

**drug: drug abuse** *n* abuso *m* di stupefacenti. **drug addict** *n* tossicomane, -a *mf*. **drug addiction** *n* tossicodipendenza *f*. **drug dealer** *n* spacciatore, -trice *mf* [di droga]

**druggist** /'drʌgɪst/ *n Am* farmacista *mf*

**drug: Drug Squad** *n Br* [squadra *f*] narcotici *f*. **drugs raid** *n* operazione *f* antidroga. **drugs ring** *n* rete *f* di narcotrafficanti. **drugstore** /'drʌgstɔː(r)/ *n Am* negozio *m* di generi vari, inclusi medicinali, che funge anche da bar; (*dispensing*) farmacia *f*. **drug-taking** *n* consumo *m* di stupefacenti; *Sport* doping *m inv*.

**drug test** n Sport antidoping m inv. **drug user** n tossicomane -a mf

**drum** /drʌm/ n tamburo m; (for oil) bidone m; **~s** pl (in pop group) batteria f ● v (pt/pp **drummed**) ● vi suonare il tamburo; (in pop group) suonare la batteria ● vt ~ sth into sb fam ripetere qcsa a qcno cento volte; ~ one's **fingers on the table** taburellare con le dita sul tavolo

**drum kit** n batteria f

**drummer** /ˈdrʌmə(r)/ n percussionista mf; (in pop group) batterista mf

**drumstick** /ˈdrʌmstɪk/ n bacchetta f; (of chicken, turkey) coscia f

**drunk** /drʌŋk/ see **drink** ● a ubriaco; **get ~** urbiacarsi ● n ubriaco, -a mf

**drunkard** /ˈdrʌŋkəd/ n ubriacone, -a mf

**drunken** /ˈdrʌŋkən/ a ubriaco

**drunken driving** n guida f in stato di ebbrezza

**dry** /draɪ/ a (**drier**, **driest**) asciutto; (climate, country) secco ● vt/i asciugare; ~ one's **eyes** asciugarsi le lacrime

■ **dry out** vi (clothes:) asciugarsi; (alcoholic:) disintossicarsi

■ **dry up** vi seccarsi; (fig: source:) prosciugarsi; (fam: be quiet) stare zitto; (do dishes) asciugare i piatti

**dry**: **dry cell** n cella f a secco. **dry-clean** vt pulire a secco. **dry-cleaner's** n (shop) tintoria f

**dryer** /ˈdraɪə/ n = **drier**

**dry ice** n ghiaccio m secco

**drying-up** /draɪɪŋ-ʹ/ n Br **do the ~** asciugare i piatti

**dryness** /ˈdraɪnɪs/ n secchezza f

**dry rot** n carie f del legno

**DSS** n Br abbr (**Department of Social Security**) (local office) ≈ Ufficio m della Previdenza Sociale; (ministry) ≈ Istituto m Nazionale della Previdenza Sociale

**DTI** n Br abbr (**Department of Trade and Industry**) ≈ Ministero m del Commercio e dell'Industria

**DTP** n abbr (**desktop publishing**) desktop publishing m inv

**dual** /ˈdjuːəl/ a doppio

**dual carriageway** n strada f a due carreggiate

**dual-purpose** a a doppio uso

**dub** /dʌb/ vt (pt/pp **dubbed**) doppiare (film); (name) soprannominare

**dubbing** /ˈdʌbɪŋ/ n doppiaggio m

**dubious** /ˈdjuːbɪəs/ a dubbio; **be ~ about** avere dei dubbi riguardo

**dubiously** /ˈdjuːbɪəslɪ/ adv (look at) con aria dubbiosa; (say) con esitazione

**Dublin** /ˈdʌblɪn/ n Dublino f

**duchess** /ˈdʌtʃɪs/ n duchessa f

**duck** /dʌk/ n anatra f ● vt (in water) immergere; ~ one's **head** abbassare la testa ● vi abbassarsi

■ **duck out of** vt sottrarsi a (task)

**duckling** /ˈdʌklɪŋ/ n anatroccolo m

**duct** /dʌkt/ n condotto m; Anat dotto m

**dud** /dʌd/ a Mil fam disattivato; (coin) falso; (cheque) a vuoto ● n fam (banknote) banconota f falsa; (Mil: shell) granata f disattivata

**due** /djuː/ a dovuto; **be ~** (train:) essere previsto; **the baby is ~ next week** il bambino dovrebbe nascere la settimana prossima; ~ **to** (owing to) a causa di; **be ~ to** (causally) essere dovuto a; **I'm ~ to...** dovrei...; **in ~ course** a tempo debito ● adv ~ **north** direttamente a nord

**duel** /ˈdjuːəl/ n duello m

**dues** /djuːz/ npl quota f [di iscrizione]

**duet** /djuːˈet/ n duetto m

**duffle coat** /ˈdʌf(ə)l/ n montgomery m inv

**dug** /dʌg/ see **dig**

**duke** /djuːk/ n duca m

**dull** /dʌl/ a (overcast, not bright) cupo; (not shiny) opaco; (sound) soffocato; (boring) monotono; (stupid) ottuso ● vt intorpidire (mind); attenuare (pain)

**dullness** /ˈdʌlnɪs/ n (of life) monotonia f; (of company, conversation) noia f; (no shine) opacità f

**dully** /ˈdʌllɪ/ adv (say, repeat) monotonamente

**duly** /ˈdjuːlɪ/ adv debitamente

**dumb** /dʌm/ a muto; (fam: stupid) ottuso

**dumbfounded** /dʌmˈfaʊndɪd/ a sbigottito

**dummy** /ˈdʌmɪ/ n (tailor's) manichino m; (for baby) succhiotto m; (model) riproduzione f

**dummy run** n (trial) prova f

**dump** /dʌmp/ n (for refuse) scarico m; (fam: town) mortorio m; **be down in the ~s** fam essere depresso ● vt scaricare; (fam: put down) lasciare; (fam: get rid of) liberarsi di

**dumping** /ˈdʌmpɪŋ/ n Fin dumping m inv, esportazione f sottocosto; **no ~** divieto m di scarico

**dumpling** /ˈdʌmplɪŋ/ n gnocco m

**dumpy** /ˈdʌmpɪ/ a (plump) tracagnotto

**dunce** /dʌns/ n zuccone, -a mf

**dune** /djuːn/ n duna f

**dung** /dʌŋ/ n sterco m

**dungarees** /dʌŋgəˈriːz/ npl tuta fsg

**dungeon** /ˈdʌndʒən/ n prigione f sotterranea

**dunk** /dʌŋk/ vt inzuppare

**dunno** /dəˈnəʊ/ fam (I don't know) boh

**duo** /ˈdjuːəʊ/ n duo m inv; Mus duetto m

**dupe** /djuːp/ n zimbello m ● vt gabbare

**duplicate¹** /ˈdjuːplɪkət/ a doppio ● n duplicato m; (document) copia f; **in ~** in duplicato

**duplicate²** /ˈdjuːplɪkeɪt/ vt fare un duplicato di; (research:) essere una ripetizione di (work)

**duplicator** /ˈdjuːplɪkeɪtə(r)/ n duplicatore m

**duplicity** /djuːˈplɪsətɪ/ n duplicità f, doppiezza f

**durable** /ˈdjʊərəbl/ a resistente; durevole (basis, institution)

**duration** /djʊəˈreɪʃn/ n durata f

**duress** /djʊˈres/ n costrizione f; **under ~** sotto minaccia

**during** /ˈdjʊərɪŋ/ prep durante

**dusk** /dʌsk/ n crepuscolo m
**dusky** /'dʌskɪ/ a ‹complexion› scuro
**dust** /dʌst/ n polvere f ● vt spolverare; (sprinkle) cospargere ‹cake› (**with** di) ● vi spolverare
**dust: dustbin** n pattumiera f. **dustbin man** n Br netturbino m. **dust-cart** n camion m della nettezza urbana. **dust cover** n (on book) sopraccoperta f; (on furniture) telo m di protezione
**duster** /'dʌstə(r)/ n strofinaccio m
**dust: dust-jacket** n sopraccoperta f. **dustman** n spazzino m. **dustpan** n paletta f per la spazzatura. **dust sheet** n (on furniture) telo m di protezione
**dusty** /'dʌstɪ/ a (-ier, -iest) polveroso
**Dutch** /dʌtʃ/ a olandese: **go ~** fam fare alla romana ● n ‹language› olandese m; **the ~** pl gli olandesi
**Dutch courage** n spavalderia f ispirata dall'alcool
**Dutchman** /'dʌtʃmən/ n olandese m
**dutiable** /'dju:tɪəbl/ a soggetto a imposta
**dutiful** /'dju:tɪfl/ a rispettoso
**dutifully** /'dju:tɪfʊlɪ/ adv a dovere
**duty** /'dju:tɪ/ n dovere m; (task) compito m; (tax) dogana f; **be on ~** essere di servizio
**duty: duty chemist** n farmacia f di turno. **duty-free** a esente da dogana ● n duty-free m inv. **duty-free allowance** n limite m d'acquisto di merci esenti da dogana. **duty roster, duty rota** n tabella f dei turni

**duvet** /'du:veɪ/ n piumone m
**duvet cover** n Br copripiumone m
**dwarf** /dwɔːf/ n (pl **-s** or **dwarves**) nano, -a mf ● vt rimpicciolire
**dwell** /dwel/ vi (pt/pp **dwelt**) liter dimorare
■ **dwell on** vt fig soffermarsi su
**dweller** /'dwelə(r)/ n **city/town ~** cittadino, -a mf
**dwelling** /'dwelɪŋ/ n abitazione f
**dwindle** /'dwɪndl/ vi diminuire
**dwindling** /'dwɪndlɪŋ/ a ‹strength, health› in calo; ‹resources, audience, interest› in diminuzione
**dye** /daɪ/ n tintura f ● vt (pres p **dyeing**) tingere
**dyed-in-the-wool** /daɪdɪnðə'wʊl/ a inveterato
**dying** /'daɪɪŋ/ see **die**[2]
**dyke** /daɪk/ n (to prevent flooding) diga f; (beside ditch) argine m; (Br: ditch) canale m di scolo
**dynamic** /daɪ'næmɪk/ a dinamico
**dynamics** /daɪ'næmɪks/ n dinamica fsg
**dynamism** /daɪnə'mɪzm/ n dinamismo m
**dynamite** /'daɪnəmaɪt/ n dinamite f
**dynamo** /'daɪnəməʊ/ n dinamo f inv
**dynasty** /'dɪnəstɪ/ n dinastia f
**dysentery** /'dɪsəntrɪ/ n dissenteria f
**dyslexia** /dɪs'leksɪə/ n dislessia f
**dyslexic** /dɪs'leksɪk/ a dislessico

# Ee

**e, E** /iː/ n (letter) e, E f inv; Mus mi m
**E** abbr (east) E
**each** /iːtʃ/ a ogni ● pron ognuno; **£1 ~** una sterlina ciascuno; **they love/hate ~ other** si amano/odiano; **we lend ~ other money** ci prestiamo i soldi; **bet on a horse ~ way** puntare su un cavallo piazzato e vincente
**eager** /'iːgə(r)/ a ansioso (**to do** di fare); ‹pupil› avido di sapere
**eager beaver** n fam **be an ~ ~** essere pieno di zelo
**eagerly** /'iːgəlɪ/ adv ‹wait› ansiosamente; ‹offer› premurosamente
**eagerness** /'iːgənɪs/ n premura f
**eagle** /'iːgl/ n aquila f
**eagle-eyed** /'-aɪd/ a (sharp-eyed) che ha un occhio di falco
**ear** /ɪə(r)/ n orecchio m; (of corn) spiga f
**earache** /'ɪəreɪk/ n mal m d'orecchi
**eardrum** /'ɪədrʌm/ n timpano m
**earl** /ɜːl/ n conte m
**ear lobe** n lobo m dell'orecchio
**early** /'ɜːlɪ/ a (-ier, -iest) (before expected time) in anticipo; ‹spring› prematuro; ‹reply› pronto; ‹works, writings› primo; **be here ~!** sii puntuale!; **you're ~!** sei in anticipo!; **~ morning walk** passeggiata f mattutina; **in the ~ morning** la mattina presto; **in the ~ spring** all'inizio della primavera; **~ retirement** prepensionamento m ● adv presto; (ahead of time) in anticipo; **~ in the morning** la mattina presto
**early warning** n **come as an ~ ~ of sth** essere il segno premonitore di qcsa
**early warning system** n Mil sistema m d'allarme avanzato
**earmark** /'ɪəmɑːk/ vt riservare (**for** a)
**earmuffs** /'ɪəmʌfs/ npl paraorecchie m inv
**earn** /ɜːn/ vt guadagnare; (deserve) meritare
**earned income** /ɜːnd/ n reddito m da lavoro
**earner** /'ɜːnə(r)/ n (person) persona f che guadagna; **the main [revenue] ~** la principale fonte di sostentamento; **a nice little ~** fam un'ottima fonte di guadagno
**earnest** /'ɜːnɪst/ a serio ● n **in ~** sul serio

**earnestly** /'ɜ:nɪstlɪ/ adv con aria seria
**earning power** /'ɜ:nɪŋ/ n (of person) capacità f di guadagno; (of company) redditività f inv
**earnings** /'ɜ:nɪŋz/ npl guadagni mpl; (salary) stipendio m
**ear nose and throat department** n reparto m otorinolaringoiatrico
**ear: earphones** npl cuffia fsg. **earplug** n (for noise) tappo m per le orecchie. **ear-ring** n orecchino m. **earshot** n **within ~** a portata d'orecchio; **he is out of ~** non può sentire. **ear-splitting** /'ɪəsplɪtɪŋ/ a ‹scream, shout› lacerante
**earth** /ɜ:θ/ n terra f; (of fox) tana f; **where/what on ~?** dove/che diavolo? ● vt Electr mettere a terra
**earthenware** /'ɜ:θnweə/ n terraglia f
**earthly** /'ɜ:θlɪ/ a terrestre; **be no ~ use** fam essere perfettamente inutile
**earth: earthquake** n terremoto m. **earth sciences** npl scienze fpl della terra. **earthshaking** a fam ‹news› sconvolgente; ‹experience› travolgente. **earth tremor** n scossa f sismica. **earthwork** n (embankment) terrapieno m; (excavation work) lavori mpl di scavo. **earthworm** n lombrico m
**earthy** /'ɜ:θɪ/ a terroso; (coarse) grossolano
**earwax** /'ɪəwæks/ n cerume m
**earwig** /'ɪəwɪg/ n forbicina f
**ease** /i:z/ n **at ~** a proprio agio; **at ~!** Mil riposo!; **ill at ~** a disagio; **with ~** con facilità ● vt calmare ‹pain›; alleviare ‹tension, shortage›; (slow down) rallentare; (loosen) allentare ● vi ‹pain, situation, wind:› calmarsi
■ **ease off** vi ‹pain, pressure, tension:› attenuarsi ● vt (remove gently) togliere con delicatezza
■ **ease up** vi = ease off
**easel** /'i:zl/ n cavalletto m
**easily** /'i:zɪlɪ/ adv con facilità; **~ the best** certamente il meglio
**east** /i:st/ n est m; **to the ~ of** a est di ● a dell'est ● adv verso est
**east: East Africa** n Africa f orientale. **East Berlin** n Berlino f Est. **eastbound** a ‹carriageway, traffic› diretto a est. **East End** n quartiere m nella zona est di Londra
**Easter** /'i:stə(r)/ n Pasqua f
**Easter: Easter egg** n uovo m di Pasqua; **Easter Monday** n lunedì m dell'Angelo, Pasquetta f. **Easter Sunday** n [domenica f di] Pasqua f
**easterly** /'i:stəlɪ/ a da levante
**eastern** /'i:stən/ a orientale
**Eastern block** n paesi mpl dell'est
**east: East German** n Pol tedesco, -a mf dell'est. **East Germany** n Pol Germania f est. **East Indies** npl Indie fpl orientali
**eastward[s]** /'i:stwəd[z]/ adv verso est
**easy** /'i:zɪ/ a (-ier, -iest) facile; **take it or things ~** prendersela con calma; **take it ~!** (don't get excited) calma!; **go ~ with** andarci piano con
**easy: easy-care** a facilmente lavabile. **easy**

**chair** n poltrona f. **easy-going** a conciliante; **too ~** troppo accomodante. **easy money** n facili guadagni mpl. **easy terms** npl facilitazioni fpl di pagamento
**eat** /i:t/ vt/i (pt **ate**, pp **eaten**) mangiare
■ **eat into** vt intaccare
■ **eat out** vi mangiar fuori
■ **eat up** vt mangiare tutto ‹food›; fig inghiottire ‹profits›
**eatable** /'i:təbl/ a mangiabile
**eater** /'i:tə(r)/ n (apple) mela f da tavola; **be a big ~** ‹person:› essere una buona forchetta; **he's a fast ~** mangia sempre in fretta
**eatery** /'i:tərɪ/ n fam tavola f calda
**eating** /'i:tɪŋ/: **eating apple** n mela f non da cuocere. **eating disorder** n disoressia f. **eating habits** npl abitudini fpl alimentari
**eau-de-Cologne** /əʊdəkə'ləʊn/ n acqua f di Colonia
**eaves** /i:vz/ npl cornicione msg
**eavesdrop** /'i:vzdrɒp/ vi (pt/pp **~dropped**) origliare; **~ on** ascoltare di nascosto
**ebb** /eb/ n (tide) riflusso m; **at a low ~** fig a terra ● vi rifluire; fig declinare
**ebony** /'ebənɪ/ n ebano m
**EBRD** n abbr (**European Bank for Reconstruction and Development**) BERS f
**ebullient** /ɪ'bʌlɪənt/ a esuberante
**EC** n abbr (**European Community**) CE f
**eccentric** /ek'sentrɪk/ a & n eccentrico, -a mf
**eccentricity** /eksen'trɪsətɪ/ n eccentricità f inv
**ecclesiastical** /ɪkli:zɪ'æstɪkl/ a ecclesiastico
**ECG** n abbr (**electrocardiogram; electrocardiograph**) ECG
**echo** /'ekəʊ/ n (pl **-es**) eco f or m ● v (pt/pp **echoed**, pres p **echoing**) ● vt echeggiare; ripetere ‹words› ● vi risuonare (**with** di)
**eclectic** /ɪ'klektɪk/ n eclettico
**eclipse** /ɪ'klɪps/ n Astr eclissi f inv ● vt fig eclissare
**eco+** /'i:kəʊ/ pref eco+
**eco-friendly** a che rispetta l'ambiente
**ecological** /i:kə'lɒdʒɪkl/ a ecologico
**ecologist** /ɪ'kɒlədʒɪst/ n ecologo, -a mf ● a ecologico
**ecology** /ɪ'kɒlədʒɪ/ n ecologia f
**economic** /i:kə'nɒmɪk/ a economico
**economical** /i:kə'nɒmɪkl/ a economico
**economically** /i:kə'nɒmɪklɪ/ adv economicamente; (thriftily) in economia; **~ priced** a prezzo economico
**economic analyst** n analista mf economico, -a
**economics** /i:kə'nɒmɪks/ n economia f
**economist** /ɪ'kɒnəmɪst/ n economista mf
**economize** /ɪ'kɒnəmaɪz/ vi economizzare (**on** su)
**economy** /ɪ'kɒnəmɪ/ n economia f
**economy: economy class** n Aeron classe f turistica. **economy drive** n campagna f di risparmio. **economy pack, economy size** n confezione f economica inv

111

**ecosystem** /'i:kəʊsɪstəm/ n ecosistema m
**ecstasy** /'ekstəsɪ/ n estasi f inv; (drug) ecstasy f
**ecstatic** /ɪk'stætɪk/ a estatico
**ecstatically** /ɪk'stætɪklɪ/ adv estaticamente
**ectopic pregnancy** /ek'tɒpɪk/ n gravidanza f extrauterina
**ecu** /'eɪkju:/ n ecu m inv
**Ecuador** /'ekwədɔ:(r)/ n Ecuador m
**ecumenical** /i:kjʊ'menɪkl/ a ecumenico
**eczema** /'eksɪmə/ n eczema m
**eddy** /'edɪ/ n vortice m
**Eden** /'i:d(ə)n/ n eden m, paradiso m terrestre
**edge** /edʒ/ n bordo m; (of knife) filo m; (of road) ciglio m; **on** ~ con i nervi tesi; **have the** ~ **on** fam avere un vantaggio su ● vt bordare
▪ **edge forward** vi avanzare lentamente
**edgeways** /'edʒweɪz/ adv di fianco; **I couldn't get a word in** ~ non ho potuto infilare neanche mezza parola nel discorso
**edging** /'edʒɪŋ/ n bordo m
**edgy** /'edʒɪ/ a nervoso
**edible** /'edəbl/ a commestibile; **this pizza's not** ~ questa pizza è immangiabile
**edict** /'i:dɪkt/ n editto m
**edifice** /'edɪfɪs/ n edificio m
**edify** /'edɪfaɪ/ vt (pt/pp -ied) edificare
**edifying** /'edɪfaɪɪŋ/ a edificante
**Edinburgh** /'edɪmb(ə)rə/ n Edimburgo f
**edit** /'edɪt/ vt (pt/pp edited) far la revisione di (text); curare l'edizione di (anthology, dictionary); dirigere (newspaper); montare (film); editare (tape); ~ed by (book) a cura di
▪ **edit out** vt tagliare
**edition** /ɪ'dɪʃn/ n edizione f
**editor** /'edɪtə(r)/ n (of anthology, dictionary) curatore, -trice mf; (of newspaper) redattore, -trice mf; (of film) responsabile mf del montaggio
**editorial** /edɪ'tɔ:rɪəl/ a redazionale ● n Journ editoriale m
**educate** /'edjʊkeɪt/ vt istruire; educare (public, mind); **be** ~**d at Eton** essere educato a Eton
**educated** /'edjʊkeɪtɪd/ a istruito
**education** /edjʊ'keɪʃn/ n istruzione f; (culture) cultura f, educazione f
**educational** /edjʊ'keɪʃnəl/ a istruttivo; (visit) educativo; (publishing) didattico
**educationalist** /edjʊ'keɪʃnəlɪst/ n studioso, -a mf di pedagogia
**educationally** /edjʊ'keɪʃnəlɪ/ adv (disadvantaged, privileged) dal punto di vista degli studi; (useless, useful) dal punto di vista didattico
**educational: educational psychology** n psicopedagogia f, psicologia f dell'educazione. **educational television** n televisione f scolastica
**education: education authority** n Br autorità fpl scolastiche. **education committee** n Br consiglio m scolastico. **education de-**

**partment** n Br ministero m della pubblica istruzione; (in local government) provveditorato m agli studi; (in university) istituto m di pedagogia
**educative** /'edjʊkətɪv/ a educativo, istruttivo
**educator** /'edjʊkeɪtə(r)/ n educatore, -trice mf
**Edwardian** /ed'wɔ:dɪən/ n del regno di Edoardo VII
**EEC** n abbr (**European Economic Community**) CEE f ● attrib (policy, directive) della CEE
**eel** /i:l/ n anguilla f
**eerie** /'ɪərɪ/ a (-ier, -iest) inquietante
**efface** /ɪ'feɪs/ vt cancellare
**effect** /ɪ'fekt/ n effetto m; **in** ~ in effetti; **take** ~ (law:) entrare in vigore; (medicine:) fare effetto ● vt effettuare
**effective** /ɪ'fektɪv/ a efficace; (striking) che colpisce; (actual) di fatto; ~ **from** in vigore a partire da
**effectively** /ɪ'fektɪvlɪ/ adv efficacemente; (actually) di fatto
**effectiveness** /ɪ'fektɪvnɪs/ n efficacia f
**effeminate** /ɪ'femɪnət/ a effeminato
**effervescent** /efə'vesnt/ a effervescente
**effete** /ɪ'fi:t/ a (person) senza nerbo; (civilization) che ha fatto il suo tempo
**efficacious** /efɪ'keɪʃəs/ a efficace
**efficacy** /'efɪkəsɪ/ n efficacia f
**efficiency** /ɪ'fɪʃənsɪ/ n efficienza f; (of machine) rendimento m
**efficient** /ɪ'fɪʃənt/ a efficiente
**efficiently** /ɪ'fɪʃəntlɪ/ adv efficientemente
**effigy** /'efɪdʒɪ/ n effigie f
**effluent** /'efluənt/ n (waste) refluo m; (river) emissario m ● attrib (treatment, management) dei reflui
**effort** /'efət/ n sforzo m; **make an** ~ sforzarsi
**effortless** /'efətlɪs/ a facile
**effortlessly** /'efətlɪslɪ/ adv con facilità
**effrontery** /ɪ'frʌntərɪ/ n sfrontatezza f
**effusion** /ɪ'fju:ʒn/ n (emotional) effusione f
**effusive** /ɪ'fju:sɪv/ a espansivo; (speech) caloroso
**EFL** n abbr (**English as a Foreign Language**) EFL m ● attrib (teacher, course) di inglese come lingua straniera
**EFT** n abbr **electronic funds transfer**
**EFTA** /'eftə/ n abbr (**European Free Trade Association**) EFTA f
**e.g.** abbr (**exempli gratia**) per es.
**egalitarian** /ɪgælɪ'teərɪən/ a egalitario
**egg** /eg/ n uovo m
▪ **egg on** vt fam incitare
**egg: egg box** n cartone m di uova. **eggcup** n portauovo m inv. **egg custard** n crema f pasticciera. **egghead** n pej fam intellettuale mf. **eggplant** n Am melanzana f. **eggshaped** /'egʃeɪpt/ a ovale. **eggshell** n guscio m d'uovo. **egg-timer** n clessidra f per misurare il tempo di cottura delle uova. **egg whisk** n

frusta *f*. **egg white** *n* albume *m*, bianco *m* d'uovo. **egg yolk** *n* tuorlo *m*, rosso *m* d'uovo
**ego** /'i:gəʊ/ *n* ego *m*
**egocentric** /i:gəʊ'sentrɪk/ *a* egocentrico
**egoism** /'egəʊɪzm/ *n* egoismo *m*
**egoist** /'egəʊɪst/ *n* egoista *mf*
**egotism** /'egəʊtɪzm/ *n* egotismo *m*
**egotist** /'egəʊtɪst/ *n* egotista *mf*
**Egypt** /'i:dʒɪpt/ *n* Egitto *m*
**Egyptian** /ɪ'dʒɪpʃn/ *a & n* egiziano, -a *mf*
**eiderdown** /'aɪdədaʊn/ *n* (*quilt*) piumino *m*
**eight** /eɪt/ *a & n* otto *m*
**eighteen** /eɪ'ti:n/ *a & n* diciotto *m*
**eighteenth** /eɪ'ti:nθ/ *a & n* diciottesimo, -a *mf*
**eighth** /eɪtθ/ *a & n* ottavo, -a *mf*
**eightieth** /'eɪtɪθ/ *a & n* ottantesimo, -a *mf*
**eighty** /'eɪtɪ/ *a & n* ottanta *m*
**Eire** /'eərə/ *n* Repubblica *f* d'Irlanda
**either** /'aɪðə(r)/ *a & pron* ~ [**of them**] l'uno o l'altro; **I don't like** ~ [**of them**] non mi piace né l'uno né l'altro; **on** ~ **side** da tutte e due le parti ● *adv* **I don't** ~ nemmeno io; **I don't like John or his brother** ~ non mi piace John e nemmeno suo fratello ● *conj* ~ **John or his brother will be there** ci saranno o John o suo fratello; **I don't like** ~ **John or his brother** non mi piacciono né John né suo fratello; ~ **you go to bed or** [**else**]... o vai a letto o [altrimenti]...
**ejaculate** /ɪ'dʒækjʊleɪt/ *vi* eiaculare ● *vt* (*exclaim*) prorompere
**ejaculation** /ɪdʒækjʊleɪʃn/ *n* eiaculazione *f*; (*exclamation*) esclamazione *f*
**eject** /ɪ'dʒekt/ *vt* eiettare (*pilot*); espellere (*tape, drunk*)
**ejection** /ɪ'dʒekʃn/ *n* (*of gases, waste, troublemaker*) espulsione *f*; (*of lava*) emissione *f*; Aeron eiezione *f*
**eke** /i:k/ *vt* ~ **out** far bastare; (*increase*) arrotondare; ~ **out a living** arrangiarsi
**elaborate**[1] /ɪ'læbərət/ *a* elaborato
**elaborate**[2] /ɪ'læbəreɪt/ *vi* entrare nei particolari (**on** di)
**elaborately** /ɪ'læbərətlɪ/ *adv* in modo elaborato
**elaboration** /ɪlæbə'reɪʃn/ *n* (*of plan, theory*) elaborazione *f*
**elapse** /ɪ'læps/ *vi* trascorrere
**elastic** /ɪ'læstɪk/ *a* elastico ● *n* elastico *m*
**elasticated** /ɪ'læstɪkeɪtɪd/ *a* (*waistband, bandage*) elastico; (*material*) elasticizzato
**elastic band** *n* elastico *m*
**elasticity** /ɪlæs'tɪsətɪ/ *n* elasticità *f*
**elated** /ɪ'leɪtɪd/ *a* esultante
**elation** /ɪ'leɪʃn/ *n* euforia *f*
**elbow** /'elbəʊ/ *n* gomito *m*
**elbow grease** *n fam* olio *m* di gomito
**elbow room** *n* (*room to move*) spazio *m* vitale; **there isn't much** ~~ **in this kitchen** si è un po' allo stretto in questa cucina
**elder**[1] /'eldə(r)/ *n* (*tree*) sambuco *m*
**elder**[2] *a* maggiore ● *n* **the** ~ il/la maggiore
**elderberry** /'eldəberɪ/ *n* baca *f* di sambuco
**elderly** /'eldəlɪ/ *a* anziano
**elder statesman** *n* decano *m* della politica

**eldest** /'eldɪst/ *a* maggiore ● *n* **the** ~ il/la maggiore
**elect** /ɪ'lekt/ *a* **the president** ~ il futuro presidente ● *vt* eleggere; ~ **to do sth** decidere di fare qcsa
**election** /ɪ'lekʃn/ *n* elezione *f*
**electioneering** /ɪ'lekʃənɪərɪŋ/ *n* (*campaigning*) propaganda *f* elettorale; *pej* elettoralismo *m*
**elective** /ɪ'lektɪv/ *a* (*office, official*) elettivo, eletto; (*empowered to elect*) elettorale; *Sch, Univ* facoltativo; ~ **surgery** interventi *mpl* chirurgici facoltativi
**elector** /ɪ'lektə(r)/ *n* elettore, -trice *mf*
**electoral** /ɪ'lektərəl/ *a* elettorale
**electoral roll** *n* liste *fpl* elettorali
**electorate** /ɪ'lektərət/ *n* elettorato *m*
**electric** /ɪ'lektrɪk/ *a* elettrico
**electrical** /ɪ'lektrɪkl/ *a* elettrico
**electrical engineer** *n* elettrotecnico *m*
**electrical engineering** *n* elettrotecnica *f*
**electrically** /ɪ'lektrɪk(ə)lɪ/ *adv* ~ **driven** [a motore] elettrico
**electric blanket** *n* termocoperta *f*
**electric fire** *n* stufa *f* elettrica
**electrician** /ɪlek'trɪʃn/ *n* elettricista *m*
**electricity** /ɪlek'trɪsətɪ/ *n* elettricità *f*
**electricity board** *n Br* azienda *f* elettrica
**electricity supply** *n* alimentazione *f* elettrica
**electric shock** *n* **get an** ~ ~ prendere la scossa
**electric storm** *n* temporale *m*
**electrify** /ɪ'lektrɪfaɪ/ *vt* (*pt/pp* **-ied**) elettrificare; *fig* elettrizzare
**electrifying** /ɪ'lektrɪfaɪɪŋ/ *a fig* elettrizzante
**electrocute** /ɪ'lektrəkju:t/ *vt* fulminare; (*execute*) giustiziare sulla sedia elettrica
**electrocution** /ɪlektrə'kju:ʃn/ *n* elettrocuzione *f*
**electrode** /ɪ'lektrəʊd/ *n* elettrodo *m*
**electrolysis** /ɪlek'trɒlɪsɪs/ *n* Chem elettrolisi *f*; (*hair removal*) depilazione *f* diatermica
**electron** /ɪ'lektrɒn/ *n* elettrone *m*
**electronic** /ɪlek'trɒnɪk/ *a* elettronico
**electronic: electronic banking** *n* servizi *mpl* bancari telematici. **electronic engineer** *n* tecnico *m* elettronico; (*with diploma*) perito *m* elettronico; (*with degree*) ingegnere *m* elettronico. **electronic engineering** *n* ingegneria *f* elettronica. **electronic eye** *n* cellula *f* fotoelettrica. **electronic funds transfer** *n* sistemi *mpl* telematici di trasferimento fondi. **electronic mail** *n* posta *f* elettronica
**electronics** /ɪlek'trɒnɪks/ *n* elettronica *f*
**electro-shock therapy, electro-shock treatment** /ɪ'lektrəʊ-/ *n* terapia *f* elettroshock
**elegance** /'elɪgəns/ *n* eleganza *f*
**elegant** /'elɪgənt/ *a* elegante
**elegantly** /'elɪgəntlɪ/ *adv* elegantemente
**elegy** /'elɪdʒɪ/ *n* elegia *f*

**element** /'elɪmənt/ n elemento m

**elementary** /elɪ'mentərɪ/ a elementare

**elephant** /'elɪfənt/ n elefante m

**elephantine** /elɪ'fæntaɪn/ a ‹person› mastodontico

**elevate** /'elɪveɪt/ vt elevare

**elevation** /elɪ'veɪʃn/ n elevazione f; (height) altitudine f; (angle) alzo m

**elevator** /'elɪveɪtə(r)/ n Am ascensore m

**eleven** /ɪ'levn/ a & n undici m

**eleven plus** n (formerly) esame m di ammissione alla scuola secondaria inglese

**elevenses** /ɪ'levənzɪz/ n Br fam pausa f per il caffè (a metà mattina)

**eleventh** /ɪ'levənθ/ a & n undicesimo, -a mf; **at the ~ hour** fam all'ultimo momento

**elf** /elf/ n (pl **elves**) elfo m

**elicit** /ɪ'lɪsɪt/ vt ottenere

**eligible** /'elɪdʒəbl/ a eleggibile; **~ young man** buon partito; **be ~ for** aver diritto a

**eliminate** /ɪ'lɪmɪneɪt/ vt eliminare

**elimination** /ɪlɪmɪ'neɪʃn/ n eliminazione f; **by a process of ~** procedendo per eliminazione

**élite** /er'li:t/ n fior fiore m

**élitist** /ɪ'li:tɪst/ a elitista

**ellipse** /ɪ'lɪps/ n ellisse f

**elliptical** /ɪ'lɪptɪk(ə)l/ a also fig ellittico

**elm** /elm/ n olmo m

**elocution** /elə'kju:ʃn/ n elocuzione f

**elongate** /'i:lɒŋgeɪt/ vt allungare

**elope** /ɪ'ləup/ vi fuggire [per sposarsi]

**elopement** /ɪ'ləupmənt/ n fuga f romantica

**eloquence** /'eləkwəns/ n eloquenza f

**eloquent** /'eləkwənt/ a eloquente

**eloquently** /'eləkwəntlɪ/ adv con eloquenza

**El Salvador** /el'sælvədɔ:(r)/ n El Salvador m; **in ~ ~** nel Salvador

**else** /els/ adv altro; **who ~?** e chi altro?; **he did of course, who ~?** l'ha fatto lui e chi, se no?; **nothing ~** nient'altro; **or ~** altrimenti; **someone ~** qualcun altro; **somewhere ~** da qualche altra parte; **anyone ~** chiunque altro; (as question) nessun'altro?; **anything ~** qualunque altra cosa; (as question) altro?

**elsewhere** /els'weə(r)/ adv altrove

**elucidate** /ɪ'lu:sɪdeɪt/ vt delucidare

**elude** /ɪ'lu:d/ vt eludere; (avoid) evitare; **the name ~s me** il nome mi sfugge

**elusive** /ɪ'lu:sɪv/ a elusivo

**emaciated** /ɪ'meɪsɪeɪtɪd/ a emaciato

**e-mail** n e-mail f, posta f elettronica ● vt spedire per e-mail

**e-mail address** n indirizzo m di posta elettronica

**emanate** /'eməneɪt/ vi emanare

**emancipated** /ɪ'mænsɪpeɪtɪd/ a emancipato

**emancipation** /ɪmænsɪ'peɪʃn/ n emancipazione f; (of slaves) liberazione f

**emasculate** /ɪ'mæskjʊleɪt/ vt evirare; fig svigorire

**embalm** /ɪm'bɑ:m/ vt imbalsamare

**embankment** /ɪm'bæŋkmənt/ n argine m; Rail massicciata f

**embargo** /em'bɑ:gəʊ/ n (pl **-es**) embargo m

**embark** /ɪm'bɑ:k/ vi imbarcarsi; **~ on** intraprendere

**embarkation** /embɑ:'keɪʃn/ n imbarco m

**embarrass** /em'bærəs/ vt imbarazzare

**embarrassed** /em'bærəst/ a imbarazzato

**embarrassing** /em'bærəsɪŋ/ a imbarazzante

**embarrassment** /em'bærəsmənt/ n imbarazzo m

**embassy** /'embəsɪ/ n ambasciata f

**embed** /ɪm'bedɪd/ vt Comput integrare ‹command›; **~ded in** ‹gem› incastonato in; ‹plant› piantato in; ‹sharp object› conficcato in; ‹rock› incluso in; **~ded** ‹traditions, feelings› radicato; **be ~ded in** fig radicarsi in

**embellish** /ɪm'belɪʃ/ vt abbellire

**embers** /'embəz/ npl braci fpl

**embezzle** /ɪm'bezl/ vt appropriarsi indebitamente di

**embezzlement** /ɪm'bez(ə)lmənt/ n appropriazione f indebita

**embitter** /ɪm'bɪtə(r)/ vt amareggiare

**emblem** /'embləm/ n emblema m

**emblematic** /emblə'mætɪk/ a emblematico

**embodiment** /ɪm'bɒdɪmənt/ n incarnazione f

**embody** /ɪm'bɒdɪ/ vt (pt/pp **-ied**) incorporare; **~ what is best in...** rappresentare quanto c'è di meglio di...

**embolism** /'embəlɪzm/ n Med embolia f

**emboss** /ɪm'bɒs/ vt sbalzare ‹metal›; stampare in rilievo ‹paper›

**embossed** /ɪm'bɒst/ a in rilievo

**embrace** /ɪm'breɪs/ n abbraccio m ● vt abbracciare ● vi abbracciarsi

**embroider** /ɪm'brɔɪdə(r)/ vt ricamare ‹design›; fig abbellire

**embroidery** /ɪm'brɔɪdərɪ/ n ricamo m

**embroil** /ɪm'brɔɪl/ vt **become ~ed in sth** rimanere invischiato in qcsa

**embryo** /'embrɪəʊ/ n embrione m

**embryonic** /embrɪ'ɒnɪk/ a Biol, fig embrionale

**emend** /ɪ'mend/ vt emendare

**emerald** /'emərəld/ n smeraldo m

**emerge** /ɪ'mɜ:dʒ/ vi emergere; (come into being: nation) nascere; (sun, flowers) spuntare fuori

**emergence** /ɪ'mɜ:dʒəns/ n emergere m; (of new country) nascita f

**emergency** /ɪ'mɜ:dʒənsɪ/ n emergenza f; **in an ~** in caso di emergenza

**emergency: emergency ambulance service** n pronto soccorso m autoambulanze. **emergency case** n Med caso m di emergenza. **emergency centre** n (for refugees etc) centro m di accoglienza; Med centro m di soccorso mobile. **emergency exit** n uscita f di sicurezza. **emergency landing** n Aeron atterraggio m di fortuna. **emergency laws** npl Pol leggi fpl straordinarie. **emergency number** n numero m di emergenza. **emergency powers** npl Pol poteri mpl straordinari. **emergency rations** npl viveri *mpl* di sopravvivenza. **emergency service** *n Med* servizio *m* di pronto soccorso. **emergency services** *npl* servizi *mpl* di pronto intervento. **emergency surgery** *n* **undergo** ~ ~ essere operato d'urgenza. **emergency ward** *n* [reparto *m* di] pronto soccorso *m*. **emergency worker** *n* addetto *m* a operazioni di soccorso

**emergent** /ɪ'mɜːdʒənt/ *a* ⟨*industry, nation*⟩ emergente

**emery board** /'emərɪ/ *n* limetta *f* per le unghie ⟨*di carta*⟩.

**emery paper** *n* carta *f* vetrata

**emigrant** /'emɪɡrənt/ *n* emigrante *mf*

**emigrate** /'emɪɡreɪt/ *vi* emigrare

**emigration** /emɪ'ɡreɪʃn/ *n* emigrazione *f*

**eminence** /'emɪnəns/ *n* ⟨*fame*⟩ eminenza *f*, gloria *f*; ⟨*honour*⟩ distinzione *f*; ⟨*hill*⟩ altura *f*

**eminent** /'emɪnənt/ *a* eminente

**eminently** /'emɪnəntlɪ/ *adv* eminentemente

**emirate** /'emɪərət/ *n* emirato *m*

**emissary** /'emɪsərɪ/ *n* emissario *m* (**to** di)

**emission** /ɪ'mɪʃn/ *n* emissione *f*; ⟨*of fumes*⟩ esalazione *f*

**emit** /ɪ'mɪt/ *vt* (*pt/pp* **emitted**) emettere; esalare ⟨*fumes*⟩

**Emmy** /'emɪ/ *n* Emmy *m* Oscar *m inv* televisivo americano

**emotion** /ɪ'məʊʃn/ *n* emozione *f*

**emotional** /ɪ'məʊʃənəl/ *a* denso di emozione; ⟨*person, reaction*⟩ emotivo; **become** ~ avere una reazione emotiva; **don't get so** ~ non lasciarci prendere dalle emozioni

**emotionless** /ɪ'məʊʃənlɪs/ *a* impassibile

**emotive** /ɪ'məʊtɪv/ *a* emotivo

**empathize** /'empəθaɪz/ *vi* ~ **with sb** immedesimarsi nei problemi di qcno

**empathy** /'empəθɪ/ *n* comprensione *f*

**emperor** /'empərə(r)/ *n* imperatore *m*

**emphasis** /'emfəsɪs/ *n* enfasi *f*; **put the** ~ **on sth** accentuare qcsa

**emphasize** /'emfəsaɪz/ *vt* accentuare ⟨*word, syllable*⟩; sottolineare ⟨*need*⟩

**emphatic** /ɪm'fætɪk/ *a* categorico

**emphatically** /ɪm'fætɪklɪ/ *adv* categoricamente

**empire** /'empaɪə(r)/ *n* impero *m*

**empirical** /em'pɪrɪkl/ *a* empirico

**empiricism** /em'pɪrɪsɪzm/ *n* empirismo *m*

**employ** /em'plɔɪ/ *vt* impiegare; *fig* usare ⟨*tact*⟩

**employable** /em'plɔɪəbl/ *a* ⟨*person*⟩ che ha i requisiti per svolgere un lavoro

**employee** /emplɔɪ'iː/ *n* impiegato, -a *mf*

**employee buyout** *n* rilevamento *m* dipendenti

**employer** /em'plɔɪə(r)/ *n* datore *m* di lavoro

**employment** /em'plɔɪmənt/ *n* occupazione *f*; ⟨*work*⟩ lavoro *m*

**employment: employment agency** *n* ufficio *m* di collocamento. **employment contract** *n* contratto *m* di lavoro. **employment exchange** *n* agenzia *f* di collocamento. **employment figures** *npl* dati *mpl* su l'occupazione. **Employment Minister, Em-**

**ployment Secretary** *n* ministro *m* del lavoro

**emporium** /em'pɔːrɪəm/ *n hum* emporio *m*

**empower** /ɪm'paʊə(r)/ *vt* autorizzare; ⟨*enable*⟩ mettere in grado

**empress** /'emprɪs/ *n* imperatrice *f*

**empties** /'emptɪz/ *npl* vuoti *mpl*

**emptiness** /'emptɪnɪs/ *n* vuoto *m*

**empty** /'emptɪ/ *a* vuoto; ⟨*promise, threat*⟩ vano ● *v* (*pt/pp* **-ied**) ● *vt* vuotare ⟨*container*⟩ ● *vi* vuotarsi

**■ empty out** *vt/i* = **empty**

**empty-handed** /-'hændɪd/ *a* ⟨*arrive, leave*⟩ a mani vuote

**empty-headed** /-'hedɪd/ *a* scriteriato

**EMS** *n abbr* (**European Monetary System**) SME *m*

**emulate** /'emjʊleɪt/ *vt* emulare

**emulsify** /ɪ'mʌlsɪfaɪ/ *v* (*pt/pp* **-ied**) ● *vt* emulsionare ● *vi* emulsionarsi

**emulsion** /ɪ'mʌlʃn/ *n* emulsione *f*

**enable** /ɪ'neɪbl/ *vt* ~ **sb to** mettere qcno in grado di

**enact** /ɪ'nækt/ *vt Theat* rappresentare; decretare ⟨*law*⟩

**enamel** /ɪ'næml/ *n* smalto *m* ● *vt* (*pt/pp* **enamelled**) smaltare

**enamelling** /ɪ'næməlɪŋ/ *n* ⟨*process*⟩ smaltatura *f*; ⟨*art*⟩ decorazione *f* a smalto

**enamoured** /ɪ'næməd/ *a* **be** ~ **of** essere innamorato di

**enc.** *abbr* (**enclosures**) alleg.

**encampment** /ɪn'kæmpmənt/ *n* accampamento *m*

**encapsulate** /en'kæpsjʊleɪt/ *vt* ⟨*include*⟩ incapsulare; ⟨*summarize*⟩ sintetizzare

**encase** /en'keɪs/ *vt* rivestire (**in** di)

**encash** /en'kæʃ/ *vt Br* incassare

**encephalogram** /en'kefələɡræm/ *n* encefalogramma *m*

**enchant** /ɪn'tʃɑːnt/ *vt* incantare

**enchanting** /ɪn'tʃɑːntɪŋ/ *a* incantevole

**enchantment** /ɪn'tʃɑːntmənt/ *n* incanto *m*

**encircle** /ɪn'sɜːkl/ *vt* circondare

**encl** *abbr* (**enclosed; enclosure**) all.

**enclave** /'enkleɪv/ *n* enclave *f inv*; *fig* territorio *m*

**enclose** /ɪn'kləʊz/ *vt* circondare ⟨*land*⟩; ⟨*in letter*⟩ allegare (**with** a)

**enclosed** /ɪn'kləʊzd/ *a* ⟨*space*⟩ chiuso; ⟨*in letter*⟩ allegato

**enclosure** /ɪn'kləʊʒə(r)/ *n* ⟨*at zoo*⟩ recinto *m*; ⟨*in letter*⟩ allegato *m*

**encode** /ɪn'kəʊd/ *vt* codificare

**encoder** /ɪn'kəʊdə(r)/ *n* codificatore, -trice *mf*

**encompass** /ɪn'kʌmpəs/ *vt* ⟨*include*⟩ comprendere

**encore** /'ɒŋkɔː(r)/ *n & int* bis *m inv*

**encounter** /ɪn'kaʊntə(r)/ *n* incontro *m*; ⟨*battle*⟩ scontro *m* ● *vt* incontrare

**encourage** /ɪn'kʌrɪdʒ/ *vt* incoraggiare; promuovere ⟨*the arts, independence*⟩

**encouragement** /ɪn'kʌrɪdʒmənt/ *n* incoraggiamento *m*; ⟨*of the arts*⟩ promozione *f*

**encouraging** /ɪnˈkʌrɪdʒɪŋ/ *a* incoraggiante; ‹*smile*› di incoraggiamento

**encroach** /ɪnˈkrəʊtʃ/ *vt* ~ **on** invadere ‹*land, privacy*›; abusare di ‹*time*›; interferire con ‹*rights*›

**encrust** /enˈkrʌst/ *vt* **be ~ed with** ‹*ice*› essere incrostato di; ‹*jewels*› essere tempestato di

**encumber** /ɪnˈkʌmbə(r)/ *vt* ~**ed with** essere carico di ‹*children, suitcases*›; ingombro di ‹*furniture*›

**encumbrance** /ɪnˈkʌmbrəns/ *n* peso *m*

**encyclop[a]edia** /ɪnsaɪklə'piːdɪə/ *n* enciclopedia *f*

**encyclop[a]edic** /ɪnsaɪklə'piːdɪk/ *a* enciclopedico

**end** /end/ *n* fine *f*; ‹*of box, table, piece of string*› estremità *f*; ‹*of town, room*› parte *f*; ‹*purpose*› fine *m*; **in the ~** alla fine; **at the ~ of May** alla fine di maggio; **at the ~ of the street/garden** in fondo alla strada/al giardino; **on ~** ‹*upright*› in piedi; **for days on ~** per giorni e giorni; **for six days on ~** per sei giorni di fila; **put an ~ to sth** mettere fine a qcsa; **make ~s meet** *fam* sbarcare il lunario; **no ~ of** *fam* un sacco di ● *vt/i* finire
▪ **end in** *vt* ‹*word:*› terminare in; finire in ‹*failure, argument*›
▪ **end off** *vt* concludere ‹*meal, speech*›
▪ **end up** *vi* finire; ~ **up doing sth** finire col fare qcsa

**endanger** /ɪnˈdeɪndʒə(r)/ *vt* rischiare ‹*one's life*›; mettere a repentaglio ‹*sb else, success of sth*›

**endear** /ɪnˈdɪə(r)/ *vt* ~ **oneself to sb** conquistarsi la simpatia di qcno; ~ **sb to** conquistare a qcno la simpatia di

**endearing** /ɪnˈdɪərɪŋ/ *a* accattivante

**endearingly** /ɪnˈɪərɪŋlɪ/ *adv* ‹*smile*› in modo accattivante; ~ **honest** di un'onestà disarmante

**endearment** /ɪnˈdɪəmənt/ *n* **term of ~** vezzeggiativo *m*

**endeavour** /ɪnˈdevə(r)/ *n* tentativo *m* ● *vi* sforzarsi (**to** di)

**endemic** /enˈdemɪk/ *a* endemico ● *n* ‹*situation*› endemia *f*

**ending** /ˈendɪŋ/ *n* fine *f*; *Gram* desinenza *f*

**endive** /ˈendaɪv/ *n* indivia *f*

**endless** /ˈendlɪs/ *a* interminabile; ‹*patience*› infinito

**endlessly** /ˈendlɪslɪ/ *adv* continuamente; ‹*patient*› infinitamente

**endocrinology** /endəʊkrɪˈnɒlədʒɪ/ *n* endocrinologia *f*

**endorse** /ɪnˈdɔːs/ *vt* girare ‹*cheque*›; ‹*sports personality:*› fare pubblicità a ‹*product*›; approvare ‹*plan*›

**endorsement** /enˈdɔːsmənt/ *n* ‹*of cheque*› girata *f*; ‹*of plan*› conferma *f*; ‹*on driving licence*› registrazione *f* su patente di un'infrazione

**endow** /ɪnˈdaʊ/ *vt* dotare

**endowment insurance** /ɪnˈdaʊmənt/ *n* assicurazione *f* sulla vita che fornisce un reddito in caso di sopravvivenza

**end: endpaper** *n* risguardo *m*. **end product** *n* prodotto *m* finito. **end result** *n* risultato *m* finale

**endurable** /ɪnˈdjʊərəbl/ *a* sopportabile

**endurance** /ɪnˈdjʊərəns/ *n* resistenza *f*; **it is beyond ~** è insopportabile

**endurance test** *n* prova *f* di resistenza

**endure** /ɪnˈdjʊə(r)/ *vt* sopportare ● *vi* durare

**enduring** /ɪnˈdjʊərɪŋ/ *a* duraturo

**end user** *n* utente *m* finale

**enema** /ˈenɪmə/ *n* *Med* clistere *m*

**enemy** /ˈenəmɪ/ *n* nemico, -a *mf* ● *attrib* nemico

**energetic** /enəˈdʒetɪk/ *a* energico

**energetically** /enəˈdʒetɪklɪ/ *adv* ‹*speak, promote, publicize*› vigorosamente; ‹*work, exercise*› con energia; ‹*deny*› risolutamente

**energize** /ˈenədʒaɪz/ *vt* stimolare; *Electr* alimentare [elettricamente]

**energizing** /ˈenədʒaɪzɪŋ/ *a* ‹*influence*› stimolante

**energy** /ˈenədʒɪ/ *n* energia *f*

**energy: energy efficiency** *n* razionalizzazione *f* del consumo energetico. **energy resources** *npl* risorse *fpl* energetiche. **energy saving** *n* risparmio *m* energetico ● *a* **energy-saving** ‹*device*› che fa risparmiare energia; ‹*measure*› per risparmiare energia

**enervate** /ˈenəveɪt/ *vt* snervare

**enfold** /enˈfəʊld/ *vt* avvolgere

**enforce** /ɪnˈfɔːs/ *vt* far rispettare ‹*law*›

**enforced** /ɪnˈfɔːst/ *a* forzato

**enforcement** /ɪnˈfɔːsmənt/ *n* applicazione *f*; ‹*of discipline*› imposizione *f*

**engage** /ɪnˈgeɪdʒ/ *vt* assumere ‹*staff*›; *Theat* ingaggiare; *Auto* ingranare ‹*gear*›; ~ **sb in conversation** fare conversazione con qcno ● *vi* *Techn* ingranare; ~ **in** impegnarsi in

**engaged** /ɪnˈgeɪdʒd/ *a* ‹*a in use, busy*› occupato; ‹*person*› impegnato; ‹*to be married*› fidanzato; **get ~** fidanzarsi (**to** con)

**engaged tone** *n* *Br* segnale *m* di occupato

**engagement** /ɪnˈgeɪdʒmənt/ *n* fidanzamento *m*; ‹*appointment*› appuntamento *m*; *Mil* combattimento *m*

**engagement ring** *n* anello *m* di fidanzamento

**engagements book** *n* agenda *f*

**engaging** /ɪnˈgeɪdʒɪŋ/ *a* attraente

**engender** /ɪnˈdʒendə(r)/ *vt fig* generare

**engine** /ˈendʒɪn/ *n* motore *m*; *Rail* locomotrice *f*

**engine driver** *n* macchinista *m*

**engineer** /endʒɪˈnɪə(r)/ *n* ingegnere *m*; ‹*service, installation*› tecnico *m*; *Naut, Am Rail* macchinista *m* ● *vt fig* architettare

**engineering** /endʒɪˈnɪərɪ/ *n* ingegneria *f*

**engine: engine failure** *n* guasto *m* [al motore]; ‹*in jet*› avaria *f*. **engine oil** *n* olio *m* [del] motore. **engine room** *n* sala *f* macchine. **engine shed** *n* *Rail* deposito *m*

**England** /ˈɪŋglənd/ *n* Inghilterra *f*

**English** /ˈɪŋglɪʃ/ *a* inglese; **the ~ Channel**

la Manica ● *n* (*language*) inglese *m*; **the ~** *pl* gli inglesi

**English: English as a Foreign Language** *n* inglese *m* come lingua straniera. **English as a Second Language** *n* inglese *m* come seconda .lingua. **Englishman** *n* inglese *m*. **English rose** *n* donna *f* dalla bellezza tipicamente inglese. **English speaker** *n* anglofono, -a *mf*. **English-speaking** *a* anglofono. **Englishwoman** *n* inglese *f*

**engrave** /ɪn'greɪv/ *vt* incidere

**engraving** /ɪn'greɪvɪŋ/ *n* incisione *f*

**engross** /ɪn'grəʊs/ *vt* **~ed in** assorto in

**engrossing** /ɪn'grəʊsɪŋ/ *a* avvincente

**engulf** /ɪn'ɡʌlf/ *vt* (*fire, waves:*) inghiottire

**enhance** /ɪn'hɑːns/ *vt* accrescere (*beauty, reputation*); migliorare (*performance*)

**enigma** /ɪ'nɪgmə/ *n* enigma *m*

**enigmatic** /enɪg'mætɪk/ *a* enigmatico

**enjoy** /ɪn'dʒɔɪ/ *vt* godere di (*good health*); **~ oneself** divertirsi; **I ~ cooking/painting** mi piace cucinare/dipingere; **I ~ed the meal/film** mi è piaciuto il pranzo/il film; **~ your meal** buon appetito

**enjoyable** /ɪn'dʒɔɪəbl/ *a* piacevole

**enjoyment** /ɪn'dʒɔɪmənt/ *n* piacere *m*

**enlarge** /ɪn'lɑːdʒ/ *vt* ingrandire ● *vi* **~ upon** dilungarsi su

**enlargement** /ɪn'lɑːdʒmənt/ *n* ingrandimento *m*

**enlarger** /ɪn'lɑːdʒə(r)/ *n* Phot ingranditore *m*

**enlighten** /ɪn'laɪtn/ *vt* illuminare

**enlightened** /ɪn'laɪtənd/ *a* progressista

**enlightenment** /ɪn'laɪtənmənt/ *n* **The E~** l'Illuminismo *m*

**enlist** /ɪn'lɪst/ *vt* Mil reclutare; **~ sb's help** farsi aiutare da qcno ● *vi* Mil arruolarsi

**enliven** /ɪn'laɪvn/ *vt* animare

**enmesh** /en'meʃ/ *vt* **become ~ed in** *fig* impegolarsi in

**enmity** /'enmətɪ/ *n* inimicizia *f*

**ennoble** /en'nəʊbl/ *vt* nobilitare

**enormity** /ɪ'nɔːmətɪ/ *n* enormità *f*

**enormous** /ɪ'nɔːməs/ *a* enorme

**enormously** /ɪ'nɔːməslɪ/ *adv* estremamente; (*grateful*) infinitamente

**enough** /ɪ'nʌf/ *a & n* abbastanza; **I didn't bring ~ clothes** non ho portato abbastanza vestiti; **have you had ~?** (*to eat/drink*) hai mangiato/bevuto abbastanza?; **I've had ~!** *fam* ne ho abbastanza!; **is that ~?** basta?; **that's ~!** basta così!; **£50 isn't ~** 50 sterline non sono sufficienti ● *adv* abbastanza; **you're not working fast ~** non lavori abbastanza in fretta; **funnily ~** stranamente

**enquire** /ɪn'kwaɪə(r)/ *vi* domandare; **~ about** chiedere informazioni su

**enquiry** /ɪn'kwaɪərɪ/ *n* domanda *f*; (*investigation*) inchiesta *f*

**enrage** /ɪn'reɪdʒ/ *vt* fare arrabbiare

**enrich** /ɪn'rɪtʃ/ *vt* arricchire; (*improve*) migliorare (*vocabulary*)

**enrol** /ɪn'rəʊl/ *vi* (*pt/pp* -**rolled**) (*for exam, in club*) iscriversi (**for, in** a)

**enrolment** /ɪn'rəʊlmənt/ *n* iscrizione *f*

**ensconced** /ɪn'skɒnst/ *a* comodamente sistemato (**in** in)

**ensemble** /ɒn'sɒmbl/ *n* (*clothing & Mus*) complesso *m*

**ensign** /'ensaɪn/ *n* insegna *f*

**enslave** /ɪn'sleɪv/ *vt* render schiavo

**ensue** /ɪn'sjuː/ *vi* seguire; **~ from** sorgere da; **the ensuing discussion** la discussione che ne è seguita

**en suite** /ɒ'swiːt/ *n* (*bathroom*) camera *f* con bagno annesso ● *a* (*bathroom*) annesso; (*room*) con bagno

**ensure** /ɪn'ʃʊə(r)/ *vt* assicurare; **~ that** (*person:*) assicurarsi che; (*measure:*) garantire che

**ENT** *n abbr* (**Ear Nose and Throat**) otorino *m*

**entail** /ɪn'teɪl/ *vt* comportare; **what does it ~?** in che cosa consiste?

**entangle** /ɪn'tæŋgl/ *vt* **get ~d in** rimanere impigliato in; *fig* rimanere coinvolto in

**entanglement** /ɪn'tæŋg(ə)lmənt/ *n* (*emotional*) legame *m* sentimentale; (*complicated situation*) pasticcio *m*

**enter** /'entə(r)/ *vt* entrare in; iscrivere (*horse, runner in race*); cominciare (*university*); partecipare a (*competition*); Comput immettere (*data*); (*write down*) scrivere ● *vi* entrare; Theat entrare in scena; (*register as competitor*) iscriversi; (*take part*) partecipare (**in** a) ● *n* Comput invio *m*

**■ enter into** *vt* (*begin*) intavolare (*negotiations, an argument*)

**enteritis** /entə'raɪtɪs/ *n* enterite *f*

**enterprise** /'entəpraɪz/ *n* impresa *f*; (*quality*) iniziativa *f*

**enterprising** /'entəpraɪzɪŋ/ *a* intraprendente

**entertain** /entə'teɪn/ *vt* intrattenere; (*invite*) ricevere; nutrire (*ideas, hopes*); prendere in considerazione (*possibility*) ● *vi* intrattenersi; (*have guests*) ricevere

**entertainer** /entə'teɪnə(r)/ *n* artista *mf*

**entertaining** /entə'teɪnɪŋ/ *a* (*person*) di gradevole compagnia; (*evening, film, play*) divertente

**entertainment** /entə'teɪnmənt/ *n* (*amusement*) intrattenimento *m*

**enthral** /ɪn'θrɔːl/ *vt* (*pt/pp* **enthralled**) **be ~led** essere affascinato (**by** da)

**enthralling** /ɪn'θrɔːlɪŋ/ *a* (*novel, performance*) affascinante

**enthuse** /ɪn'θjuːz/ *vi* **~ over** entusiasmarsi per

**enthusiasm** /ɪn'θjuːzɪæzm/ *n* entusiasmo *m*

**enthusiast** /ɪn'θjuːzɪæst/ *n* entusiasta *mf*

**enthusiastic** /ɪnθjuːzɪ'æstɪk/ *a* entusiastico

**enthusiastically** /ɪnθjuːzɪ'æstɪklɪ/ *adv* entusiasticamente

**entice** /ɪn'taɪs/ *vt* attirare

**enticement** /ɪn'taɪsmənt/ *n* (*incentive*) incentivo *m*

**enticing** /ɪn'taɪsɪŋ/ *a* (*prospect, offer*) allettante; ⟨person⟩ seducente; ⟨food, smell⟩ invitante

**entire** /ɪnˈtaɪə(r)/ a intero

**entirely** /ɪnˈtaɪəlɪ/ adv del tutto; **I'm not ~ satisfied** non sono completamente soddisfatto

**entirety** /ɪnˈtaɪərətɪ/ n **in its ~** nell'insieme

**entitled** /ɪnˈtaɪtld/ a ⟨book⟩ intitolato; **be ~ to sth** aver diritto a qcsa

**entitlement** /ɪnˈtaɪtlmənt/ n diritto m

**entity** /ˈentətɪ/ n entità f

**entomology** /entəˈmɒlədʒɪ/ n entomologia f

**entourage** /ˈɒntʊrɑːʒ/ n entourage m inv

**entrails** /ˈentreɪlz/ npl intestini mpl

**entrance**[1] /ˈentrəns/ n entrata f; Theat entrata f in scena; ⟨right to enter⟩ ammissione f; **'no ~'** 'ingresso vietato'

**entrance**[2] /ɪnˈtrɑːns/ vt estasiare

**entrance: entrance examination** n esame m di ammissione. **entrance fee** n **how much is the ~ ~?** quanto costa il biglietto di ingresso? **entrance hall** n ⟨in house⟩ ingresso m. **entrance requirements** npl requisiti mpl di ammissione. **entrance ticket** n biglietto m d'ingresso

**entrancing** /ɪnˈtrɑːnsɪŋ/ a incantevole

**entrant** /ˈentrənt/ n concorrente mf

**entreat** /ɪnˈtriːt/ vt supplicare

**entreatingly** /ɪnˈtriːtɪŋlɪ/ adv ⟨beg, ask⟩ in tono implorante

**entreaty** /ɪnˈtriːtɪ/ n supplica f

**entrée** /ˈɒtreɪ/ n Br ⟨starter⟩ primo m; ⟨Am: main course⟩ secondo m; **her wealth gave her an ~ into high society** il denaro le ha aperto le porte dell'alta società

**entrenched** /ɪnˈtrentʃt/ a ⟨ideas, views⟩ radicato

**entrepreneur** /ɒntrəprəˈnɜː(r)/ n imprenditore, -trice mf

**entrepreneurial** /ɒntrəprəˈnɜːrɪəl/ a imprenditoriale; **have ~ skills** avere il senso degli affari

**entrust** /ɪnˈtrʌst/ vt **~ sb with sth, ~ sth to sb** affidare qcsa a qcno

**entry** /ˈentrɪ/ n ingresso m; ⟨way in⟩ entrata f; ⟨in directory etc⟩ voce f; ⟨in appointment diary⟩ appuntamento m; **no ~** ingresso vietato; Auto accesso vietato

**entry: entry fee** n quota f di iscrizione. **entry form** n modulo m di ammissione. **entry permit** n visto m di entrata. **entryphone** n citofono m. **entry requirements** npl requisiti mpl di ammissione. **entry visa** n visto m di ingresso

**entwine** /ɪnˈtwaɪn/ vt also fig intrecciare

**E-number** n Br sigla f degli additivi

**enumerate** /ɪˈnjuːməreɪt/ vt enumerare

**enumeration** /ɪnjuːməˈreɪʃn/ n ⟨list⟩ enumerazione f; ⟨counting⟩ conto m

**enunciate** /ɪˈnʌnsɪeɪt/ vt enunciare

**enunciation** /ɪnʌnsɪˈeɪʃn/ n ⟨of principle, facts⟩ enunciazione f; ⟨of word⟩ articolazione f

**envelop** /ɪnˈveləp/ vt ⟨pt/pp **enveloped**⟩ avviluppare

**envelope** /ˈenvələʊp/ n busta f

**enviable** /ˈenvɪəbl/ a invidiabile

**envious** /ˈenvɪəs/ a invidioso

**enviously** /ˈenvɪəslɪ/ adv con invidia

**environment** /ɪnˈvaɪrənmənt/ n ambiente m

**environmental** /ɪnvaɪrənˈmentl/ a ambientale

**environmental health** n salute f pubblica

**environmentalist** /ɪnvaɪrənˈmentəlɪst/ n ambientalista mf

**environmentally** /ɪnvaɪrənˈmentəlɪ/ adv **~ friendly** che rispetta l'ambiente

**environmental scientist** n studioso, -a mf di ecologia applicata

**Environmental Studies** npl Br Sch ecogeografia f e ecobiologia f

**envisage** /ɪnˈvɪzɪdʒ/ vt prevedere

**envoy** /ˈenvɔɪ/ n inviato, -a mf

**envy** /ˈenvɪ/ n invidia f ● vt ⟨pt/pp **-ied**⟩ **~ sb sth** invidiare qcno per qcsa

**enzyme** /ˈenzaɪm/ n enzima m

**ephemeral** /ɪˈfemərəl/ a effimero

**epic** /ˈepɪk/ a epico ● n epopea f

**epicentre** /ˈepɪsentə(r)/ n epicentro m

**epidemic** /epɪˈdemɪk/ n epidemia f

**epidermis** /epɪˈdɜːmɪs/ n epidermide f

**epidural** /epɪˈdjʊərəl/ n Med anestesia f epidurale

**epigram** /ˈepɪgræm/ n epigramma m

**epilepsy** /ˈepɪlepsɪ/ n epilessia f

**epileptic** /epɪˈleptɪk/ a & n epilettico, -a mf

**epilogue** /ˈepɪlɒg/ n epilogo m

**Epiphany** /ɪˈpɪfənɪ/ n Epifania f

**episode** /ˈepɪsəʊd/ n episodio m

**episodic** /epɪˈsɒdɪk/ a episodico

**epistle** /ɪˈpɪsl/ n liter epistola f

**epitaph** /ˈepɪtɑːf/ n epitaffio m

**epithet** /ˈepɪθet/ n epiteto m

**epitome** /ɪˈpɪtəmɪ/ n epitome f

**epitomize** /ɪˈpɪtəmaɪz/ vt essere il classico esempio di

**epoch** /ˈiːpɒk/ n epoca f

**epoch-making** a che fa epoca

**eponymous** /ɪˈpɒnɪməs/ a eponimo

**equable** /ˈekwəbl/ a ⟨climate⟩ temperato; ⟨temperament⟩ equilibrato

**equably** /ˈekwəblɪ/ adv con serenità

**equal** /ˈiːkwl/ a ⟨parts, amounts⟩ uguale; **of ~ height** della stessa altezza; **be ~ to the task** essere a l'altezza del compito ● n pari m inv; **treat sb as an ~** trattare qcno da pari a pari ● vt ⟨pt/pp **equalled**⟩ ⟨be same in quantity as⟩ essere pari a; ⟨rival⟩ uguagliare; **5 plus 5 ~s 10** 5 più 5 [è] uguale a 10

**equality** /ɪˈkwɒlətɪ/ n uguaglianza f

**equalize** /ˈiːkwəlaɪz/ vi Sport pareggiare

**equalizer** /ˈiːkwəlaɪzə(r)/ n Sport pareggio m; **get the ~** pareggiare

**equally** /ˈiːkwəlɪ/ adv ⟨divide⟩ in parti uguali; **~ intelligent** della stessa intelligenza; **~,...** allo stesso tempo...

**equal: equal opportunities** npl uguaglianza f dei diritti. **Equal Opportunities Commission** n Br commissione f per l'ugua-

*glianza dei diritti nei rapporti di lavoro.*
**equal opportunity** *attrib ⟨legislation⟩* per l'uguaglianza dei diritti nei rapporti di lavoro; *⟨employer⟩* che applica l'uguaglianza dei diritti. **equal rights** *npl* parità *f* dei diritti.
**equals sign** *n* segno *m* uguale
**equanimity** /ekwə'nımətı/ *n* equanimità *f*
**equate** /ı'kweıt/ *vt* ~ **sth with sth** equiparare qcsa a qcsa
**equation** /ı'kweıʒn/ *n Math* equazione *f*
**equator** /ı'kweıtə(r)/ *n* equatore *m*
**equatorial** /ekwə'tɔ:rıəl/ *a* equatoriale
**equestrian** /ı'kwestrıən/ *a* equestre
**equidistant** /i:kwı'dıstənt/ *a* equidistante
**equilateral** /i:kwı'lætərəl/ *a* equilatero
**equilibrium** /i:kwı'lıbrıəm/ *n* equilibrio *m*
**equine** /'ekwaın/ *a ⟨disease, species⟩* equino; *⟨features⟩* cavallino
**equinox** /'i:kwınɒks/ *n* equinozio *m*
**equip** /ı'kwıp/ *vt (pt/pp* **equipped)** equipaggiare; attrezzare *⟨kitchen, office⟩*
**equipment** /ı'kwıpmənt/ *n* attrezzatura *f*
**equitable** /'ekwıtəbl/ *a* giusto
**equity** /'ekwətı/ *n (justness)* equità *f; Comm* azioni *fpl*
**equity: equity capital** *n Fin* capitale *m* azionario. **equity financing** *n Fin* finanziamento *m* attraverso l'emissione di azioni
**equity market** *n Fin* mercato *m* azionario
**equivalent** /ı'kwıvələnt/ *a* equivalente; **be** ~ **to** equivalere a ● *n* equivalente *m*
**equivocal** /ı'kwıvəkl/ *a* equivoco
**equivocate** /ı'kwıvəkeıt/ *vi* parlare in modo equivoco, giocare sull'equivoco
**equivocation** /ıkwıvə'keıʃn/ *n* affermazione *f* equivoca; **too much** ~ troppi equivoci
**era** /'ıərə/ *n* età *f; (geological)* era *f*
**eradicate** /ı'rædıkeıt/ *vt* eradicare
**erase** /ı'reız/ *vt* cancellare
**erase head** *n Comput* testina *f* di cancellazione
**eraser** /ı'reızə(r)/ *n* gomma *f* [da cancellare]; *(for blackboard)* cancellino *m*
**erasure** /ı'reıʒə(r)/ *n (act)* cancellazione *f; (on paper)* cancellatura *f*
**erect** /ı'rekt/ *a* eretto ● *vt* erigere
**erection** /ı'rekʃn/ *n* erezione *f*
**ergonomic** /ɜ:gə'nɒmık/ *a* ergonomico; *⟨seat⟩* anatomico
**ergonomics** /ɜ:gə'nɒmıks/ *n* ergonomia *f*
**Erie** /'ıərı/ *n* **Lake** ~ il lago Erie
**ERM** *n abbr* **Exchange Rate Mechanism**
**ermine** /'ɜ:mın/ *n* ermellino *m*
**erode** /ı'rəud/ *vt ⟨water:⟩* erodere; *⟨acid:⟩* corrodere
**erogenous** /ı'rɒdʒınəs/ *a* erogeno
**erosion** /ı'rəuʒn/ *n* erosione *f; (by acid)* corrosione *f*
**erotic** /ı'rɒtık/ *a* erotico
**erotica** /ı'rɒtıkə/ *npl (art)* arte *f* erotica; *(literature)* letteratura *f* erotica; *Cinema* film *mpl* erotici
**eroticism** /ı'rɒtısızm/ *n* erotismo *m*
**err** /ɜ:(r)/ *vi* errare; *(sin)* peccare
**errand** /'erənd/ *n* commissione *f*

**errant** /'erənt/ *a ⟨husband, wife⟩* infedele
**erratic** /ı'rætık/ *a* irregolare; *⟨person, moods⟩* imprevedibile; *⟨exchange rate⟩* incostante
**erroneous** /ı'rəunıəs/ *a* erroneo
**erroneously** /ı'rəunıəslı/ *adv* erroneamente
**error** /'erə(r)/ *n* errore *m*; **in** ~ per errore
**error message** *n Comput* messaggio *m* di errore
**ersatz** /'ɜ:sæts/ *n* surrogato *m*; ~ **tobacco** surrogato del tabacco
**erudite** /'eruːdaıt/ *a* erudito
**erudition** /eru'dıʃn/ *n* erudizione *f*
**erupt** /ı'rʌpt/ *vi* eruttare; *⟨spots:⟩* spuntare; *(fig: in anger)* dare in escandescenze
**eruption** /ı'rʌpʃn/ *n* eruzione *f; fig* scoppio *m*
**escalate** /'eskəleıt/ *vi* intensificarsi ● *vt* intensificare
**escalation** /eskə'leıʃn/ *n* escalation *f inv*
**escalator** /'eskəleıtə(r)/ *n* scala *f* mobile
**escapade** /'eskəpeıd/ *n* scappatella *f*
**escape** /ı'skeıp/ *n* fuga *f; (from prison)* evasione *f;* **have a narrow** ~ cavarsela per un pelo ● *vi ⟨prisoner:⟩* evadere **(from** da); sfuggire **(from sb** alla sorveglianza di qcno); *⟨animal:⟩* scappare; *⟨gas:⟩* fuoriuscire ● *vt* ~ **notice** passare inosservato; **the name** ~**s me** mi sfugge il nome
**escape chute** *n Aeron* scivolo *m*
**escape clause** *n* clausola *f* di recesso
**escapee** /ıskeı'pi:/ *n* evaso *m*
**escape hatch** *n Naut* portello *m* di sicurezza
**escape route** *n (for fugitives)* itinerario *m* di fuga; *(in case of fire etc)* percorso *m* di emergenza
**escapism** /ı'skeıpızm/ *n* evasione *f* dalla realtà
**escapologist** /eskə'pɒlədʒıst/ *n illusionista mf capace di liberarsi dalle catene*
**escarpment** /es'kɑ:pmənt/ *n* scarpata *f*
**eschew** /ıs'tʃu:/ *vt* evitare *⟨discussion⟩*; rifuggire *⟨temptation⟩*; rifuggire da *⟨violence ecc⟩*
**escort¹** /'eskɔ:t/ *n (of person)* accompagnatore, -trice *mf; Mil etc* scorta *f*
**escort²** /ı'skɔ:t/ *vt* accompagnare; *Mil etc* scortare
**Eskimo** /'eskıməu/ *n* esquimese *mf*
**esophagus** /ı'sɒfəgəs/ *n Am* esofago *m*
**esoteric** /esə'terık/ *a* esoterico
**ESP** *n abbr* **(extrasensory perception)** ESP *f, n abbr* **English for Special Purposes**
**esp** *abbr* **especially**
**especial** /ı'speʃl/ *a* speciale
**especially** /ı'speʃlı/ *adv* specialmente; *⟨kind⟩* particolarmente
**espionage** /'espıənɑ:ʒ/ *n* spionaggio *m*
**espouse** /ı'spauz/ *vt* abbracciare *⟨cause⟩*
**espresso** /ı'spresəu/ *n (coffee)* espresso *m*
**Esq** *Br abbr* **(esquire) James McBride,** ~ Egr. Sig. James McBride
**essay** /'eseı/ *n* saggio *m; Sch* tema *f*

**essence** /'esns/ n essenza f; **in ~** in sostanza

**essential** /ɪˈsenʃl/ a essenziale ● n **the ~s** pl l'essenziale m

**essentially** /ɪˈsenʃəlɪ/ adv essenzialmente

**est** abbr (**established**) fondato nel

**establish** /ɪˈstæblɪʃ/ vt stabilire ⟨contact, lead⟩; fondare ⟨firm⟩; (prove) accertare; **~ oneself as** affermarsi come

**established** /ɪˈstæblɪʃt/ a ⟨way of doing sth, view⟩ generalmente accettato; ⟨company⟩ affidabile; ⟨brand⟩ riconosciuto; **a well ~ fact** un dato di fatto; **the ~ church** la religione di Stato

**establishment** /ɪˈstæblɪʃmənt/ n (firm) azienda f; **the E~** l'establishment m

**estate** /ɪˈsteɪt/ n tenuta f; (possessions) patrimonio m; (housing) quartiere m residenziale

**estate: estate agent** n agente m immobiliare. **estate car** n giardiniera f. **estate duty** n Br imposta f di successione

**esteem** /ɪˈstiːm/ n stima f ● vt stimare; (consider) giudicare

**ester** /'estə(r)/ n estere m

**estimate¹** /'estmət/ n valutazione f; Comm preventivo m; **at a rough ~** a occhio e croce

**estimate²** /'estmeɪt/ vt stimare

**estimated time of arrival** /'estɪmeɪtɪd/ n ora f prevista di arrivo

**estimation** /estɪˈmeɪʃn/ n (esteem) stima f; **in my ~** (judgement) a mio giudizio

**Estonia** /ɪˈstəʊnɪə/ n Estonia f

**estrange** /ɪˈstreɪndʒ/ vt estraniare; **~d from sb** separato da qcno; **her ~d husband** il marito da cui è separata

**estrangement** /ɪˈstreɪndʒmənt/ n disamoramento m

**estuary** /'estjʊərɪ/ n estuario m

**ETA** n abbr **estimated time of arrival**

**et al** /et'æl/ abbr (**et alii**) e altri

**etc** /et'setərə/ abbr (**et cetera**) ecc

**et cetera, etcetera** /et'setərə/ adv eccetera

**etch** /etʃ/ vt incidere all'acquaforte; **~ed on her memory** fig impresso nella sua memoria

**etching** /'etʃɪŋ/ n acquaforte f

**eternal** /ɪˈtɜːnl/ a eterno

**eternal life** n vita f eterna

**eternally** /ɪˈtɜːnəlɪ/ adv eternamente

**eternal triangle** n eterno triangolo m

**eternity** /ɪˈtɜːnətɪ/ n eternità f

**ether** /'iːθə(r)/ n etere m

**ethereal** /ɪˈθɪərɪəl/ a etereo

**ethic** /'eθɪk/ n etica f

**ethical** /'eθɪkl/ a etico

**ethics** /'eθɪks/ n etica f

**Ethiopia** /iːθɪˈəʊpɪə/ n Etiopia f

**ethnic** /'eθnɪk/ a etnico

**ethnically** /'eθnɪklɪ/ adv etnicamente

**ethnic cleansing** n epurazione f etnica

**ethnology** /eθ'nɒlədʒɪ/ n etnologia f

**ethos** /'iːθɒs/ n **company ~** filosofia f dell'azienda

**etiquette** /'etɪket/ n etichetta f

**etymology** /etɪˈmɒlədʒɪ/ n etimologia f

**EU** n abbr (**European Union**) UE f

**eucalyptus** /juːkəˈlɪptəs/ n eucalipto m

**eugenics** /juːˈdʒenɪks/ n eugenetica f

**eulogize** /'juːlədʒaɪz/ vt fare il panegirico di ● vi **~ over sth** tessere le lodi di qcsa

**eulogy** /'juːlədʒɪ/ n elogio m

**eunuch** /'juːnək/ n eunuco m

**euphemism** /'juːfəmɪzm/ n eufemismo m

**euphemistic** /juːfəˈmɪstɪk/ a eufemistico

**euphemistically** /juːfəˈmɪstɪklɪ/ adv eufemisticamente

**euphoria** /juːˈfɔːrɪə/ n euforia f

**euphoric** /juːˈfɒrɪk/ a euforico

**Eurasian** /jʊˈreɪʒ(ə)n/ a ⟨people, region⟩ eurasiatico

**EURATOM** /jʊˈrætəm/ n abbr (**European Atomic Energy Community**) EURATOM f

**eurhythmics** /jʊˈrɪðmɪks/ n ginnastica f ritmica

**Euro-** /'jʊərəʊ-/: **eurobond** n eurobbligazione f. **Eurocheque** n eurochèque m inv. **eurocurrency** n eurovaluta f. **Eurodollar** n eurodollaro m. **euromarket** n euromercato m. **Euro-MP** n eurodeputato, -a mf

**Europe** /'jʊərəp/ n Europa f

**European** /jʊərəˈpɪən/ a & n europeo, -a mf

**European: European Bank for Reconstruction and Development** n Banca f Europea per la Ricostruzione e lo Sviluppo. **European Commission** n Commissione f Europea. **European Community** n Comunità f Europea. **European Court of Human Rights** n Corte f europea per i diritti dell'uomo. **European Court of Justice** n Corte f europea di giustizia. **European Economic Community** n Comunità f Economica Europea. **European Free Trade Association** n Associazione f Europea di Libero Scambio. **European Monetary System** n Sistema m Monetario Europeo. **European Monetary Union** n Unione f Monetaria Europea. **European Parliament** n Parlamento m Europeo. **European Union** n Unione f Europea

**Euro-sceptic** n Br euroscettico, -a mf

**euthanasia** /juːθəˈneɪzɪə/ n eutanasia f

**evacuate** /ɪˈvækjʊeɪt/ vt evacuare ⟨building, area⟩

**evacuation** /ɪvækjʊˈeɪʃn/ n evacuazione f

**evacuee** /ɪvækjʊˈiː/ n sfollato m

**evade** /ɪˈveɪd/ vt evadere ⟨taxes⟩; evitare ⟨the enemy, authorities⟩; **~ the issue** evitare l'argomento

**evaluate** /ɪˈvæljʊeɪt/ vt valutare

**evaluation** /ɪvæljʊˈeɪʃn/ n valutazione f, stima f

**evangelical** /iːvænˈdʒelɪkl/ a evangelico

**evangelist** /ɪˈvændʒəlɪst/ n evangelista m

**evaporate** /ɪˈvæpəreɪt/ vi evaporare; fig svanire

**evaporation** /ɪvæpəˈreɪʃn/ n evaporazione f

**evasion** /ɪˈveɪʒn/ n evasione f

**evasive** /ɪˈveɪsɪv/ a evasivo

**evasively** /ɪˈveɪsɪvlɪ/ adv in modo evasivo

**eve** /iːv/ n liter vigilia f

**even** /'iːvn/ a (level) piatto; (same, equal) uguale; (regular) regolare; ⟨number⟩ pari;

get ~ with vendicarsi di; now we're ~ adesso siamo pari ● *adv* anche, ancora; ~ if anche se; ~ so con tutto ciò; not ~ nemmeno; ~ bigger/hotter ancora più grande/caldo ● *vt* ~ the score *Sport* pareggiare

■ **even out** *vi* livellarsi

■ **even up** *vt* livellare

**even-handed** /-'hændɪd/ *a* imparziale

**evening** /'i:vnɪŋ/ *n* sera *f*; (*whole evening*) serata *f*; this ~ stasera; in the ~ la sera

**evening: evening class** *n* corso *m* serale. **evening dress** *n* (*man's*) abito *m* scuro; (*woman's*) abito *m* da sera. **evening performance** *n* spettacolo *m* serale. **evening primrose** *n* enotera *f*. **evening star** *n* Venere *f*

**evenly** /'i:vnlɪ/ *adv* (*distributed*) uniformemente; (*breathe*) regolarmente; (*divided*) in uguali parti

**event** /ɪ'vent/ *n* avvenimento *m*; (*function*) manifestazione *f*; *Sport* gara *f*; in the ~ of nell'eventualità di; in the ~ alla fine

**even-tempered** /-'tempəd/ *a* pacato

**eventful** /ɪ'ventful/ *a* movimentato

**eventing** /ɪ'ventɪŋ/ *n* *Br* concorso *m* ippico completo

**eventual** /ɪ'ventjʊəl/ *a* the ~ winner was... alla fine il vincitore è stato...

**eventuality** /ɪventjʊ'ælətɪ/ *n* eventualità *f*

**eventually** /ɪ'ventjʊəlɪ/ *adv* alla fine; ~! finalmente!

**ever** /'evə(r)/ *adv* mai; I haven't ~... non ho mai...; for ~ per sempre; hardly ~ quasi mai; ~ since da quando; (*since that time*) da allora; ~ so *fam* veramente

**evergreen** /'evəgri:n/ *n* sempreverde *m*

**everlasting** /evə'læstɪŋ/ *a* eterno

**every** /'evrɪ/ *a* ogni; ~ one ciascuno; ~ other day un giorno sì un giorno no

**everybody** /'evrɪbɒdɪ/ *pron* tutti *pl*

**everyday** /'evrɪdeɪ/ *a* quotidiano, di ogni giorno

**everyone** /'evrɪwʌn/ *pron* tutti *pl*; ~ else tutti gli altri

**everyplace** /'evrɪpleɪs/ *adv* *Am fam* = everywhere

**everything** /'evrɪθɪŋ/ *pron* tutto; ~ else tutto il resto

**everywhere** /'evrɪweə(r)/ *adv* dappertutto; (*wherever*) dovunque

**evict** /ɪ'vɪkt/ *vt* sfrattare

**eviction** /ɪ'vɪkʃn/ *n* sfratto *m*

**evidence** /'evɪdəns/ *n* evidenza *f*; *Jur* testimonianza *f*; give ~ testimoniare

**evident** /'evɪdənt/ *a* evidente

**evidently** /'evɪdəntlɪ/ *adv* evidentemente

**evil** /'i:vl/ *a* cattivo ● *n* male *m*

**evil-smelling** /-'smelɪŋ/ *a* puzzolente

**evocative** /ɪ'vɒkətɪv/ *a* evocativo; be ~ of evocare

**evoke** /ɪ'vəʊk/ *vt* evocare

**evolution** /i:və'lu:ʃn/ *n* evoluzione *f*

**evolutionary** /i:və'lu:ʃn(ə)rɪ/ *a* evolutivo

**evolve** /ɪ'vɒlv/ *vt* evolvere ● *vi* evolversi

**ewe** /ju:/ *n* pecora *f*

**ex** /eks/ *n* (*fam: former partner*) ex *mf*

**ex+** *pref* ex+

**exacerbate** /ɪg'sæsəbeɪt/ *vt* esacerbare (*situation*)

**exact** /ɪg'zækt/ *a* esatto ● *vt* esigere

**exacting** /ɪg'zæktɪŋ/ *a* esigente

**exactitude** /ɪg'zæktɪtju:d/ *n* esattezza *f*

**exactly** /ɪg'zæktlɪ/ *adv* esattamente; not ~ non proprio

**exactness** /ɪg'zæktnɪs/ *n* precisione *f*

**exaggerate** /ɪg'zædʒəreɪt/ *vt/i* esagerare

**exaggerated** /ɪg'zædʒəreɪtɪd/ *a* esagerato; he has an ~ sense of his own importance si crede chissà chi

**exaggeration** /ɪgzædʒə'reɪʃn/ *n* esagerazione *f*

**exalt** /ɪg'zɔ:lt/ *vt* elevare; (*praise*) vantare

**exam** /ɪg'zæm/ *n* esame *m*

**examination** /ɪgzæmɪ'neɪʃn/ *n* esame *m*; (*of patient*) visita *f*; (*of wreckage*) ispezione *f*

**examination paper** *n* testo *m* d'esame

**examine** /ɪg'zæmɪn/ *vt* esaminare; visitare (*patient*)

**examinee** /ɪgzæmɪ'ni:/ *n* esaminando *m*

**examiner** /ɪg'zæmɪnə(r)/ *n* *Sch* esaminatore, -trice *mf*

**example** /ɪg'zɑ:mpl/ *n* esempio *m*; for ~ esempio; make an ~ of sb punire qcno per dare un esempio; be an ~ to sb dare il buon esempio a qcno

**exasperate** /ɪg'zæspəreɪt/ *vt* esasperare

**exasperation** /ɪgzæspə'reɪʃn/ *n* esasperazione *f*

**excavate** /'ekskəveɪt/ *vt* scavare; *Archaeol* fare gli scavi di

**excavation** /ekskə'veɪʃn/ *n* scavo *m*

**excavator** /'ekskəveɪtə(r)/ *n* (*machine*) escavatrice *f*, escavatore *m*

**exceed** /ɪk'si:d/ *vt* eccedere

**exceedingly** /ɪk'si:dɪŋlɪ/ *adv* estremamente

**excel** /ɪk'sel/ *v* (*pt/pp* excelled) ● *vi* eccellere ● *vt* ~ oneself superare se stessi

**excellence** /'eksələns/ *n* eccellenza *f*

**Excellency** /'eksələnsɪ/ *n* (*title*) Eccellenza *f*

**excellent** /'eksələnt/ *a* eccellente

**excellently** /'eksələntlɪ/ *adv* in modo eccellente

**except** /ɪk'sept/ *prep* eccetto, tranne; ~ for eccetto, tranne; ~ that... eccetto che... ● *vt* eccettuare

**excepting** /ɪk'septɪŋ/ *prep* eccetto, tranne

**exception** /ɪk'sepʃn/ *n* eccezione *f*; take ~ to fare obiezioni a

**exceptional** /ɪk'sepʃənəl/ *a* eccezionale

**exceptionally** /ɪk'sepʃənəlɪ/ *adv* eccezionalmente

**excerpt** /'eksɜ:pt/ *n* estratto *m*

**excess** /ɪk'ses/ *n* eccesso *m*; in ~ of oltre

**excess baggage** *n* bagaglio *m* eccedente

**excess fare** *n* supplemento *m*

**excessive** /ɪk'sesɪv/ *a* eccessivo

**excessively** /ɪk'sesɪvlɪ/ *adv* eccessivamente

**excess postage** *n* soprattassa *f* postale

**excess profits** *npl* sovraprofitto *m*

**exchange** /ɪks'tʃeɪndʒ/ n scambio m; Teleph centrale f; Comm cambio m; **[stock]** ~ borsa f valori; **in** ~ in cambio **(for** di) ● vt scambiare **(for** con); cambiare ⟨money⟩; ~ **views** scambiarsi i punti di vista; ~ **contracts** fare il rogito

**exchange: exchange control** n controllo m dei cambi. **exchange controls** npl misure fpl di controllo dei cambi. **exchange rate** n tasso m di cambio. **Exchange Rate Mechanism** n meccanismo m di cambio dello Sme.

**exchequer** /ɪks'tʃekə(r)/ n Pol tesoro m

**excise¹** /'eksaɪz/ n dazio m

**excise²** /ek'saɪz/ vt recidere

**excise duty** n dazio m

**excitable** /ɪk'saɪtəbl/ a eccitabile

**excite** /ɪk'saɪt/ vt eccitare

**excited** /ɪk'saɪtɪd/ a eccitato; **get** ~ eccitarsi

**excitedly** /ɪk'saɪtɪdlɪ/ adv tutto eccitato

**excitement** /ɪk'saɪtmənt/ n eccitazione f

**exciting** /ɪk'saɪtɪŋ/ a eccitante; ⟨story, film⟩ appassionante; ⟨holiday⟩ entusiasmante

**excl** abbr **excluding**

**exclaim** /ɪk'skleɪm/ vt/i esclamare

**exclamation** /eksklə'meɪʃn/ n esclamazione f

**exclamation mark** n, Am **exclamation point** n punto m esclamativo

**exclude** /ɪk'sklu:d/ vt escludere

**excluding** /ɪk'sklu:dɪŋ/ pron escluso

**exclusion** /ɪk'sklu:ʒn/ n esclusione f

**exclusion zone** n zona f proibita

**exclusive** /ɪk'sklu:sɪv/ a ⟨rights, club⟩ esclusivo; ⟨interview⟩ in esclusiva; ~ **of...** ...escluso

**exclusively** /ɪk'sklu:sɪvlɪ/ adv esclusivamente

**excommunicate** /ekskə'mju:nɪkeɪt/ vt scomunicare

**excrement** /'ekskrɪmənt/ n escremento m

**excreta** /ɪk'skri:tə/ npl escrementi mpl

**excrete** /ɪk'skri:t/ vt espellere; secernere ⟨liquid⟩

**excretion** /ɪk'skri:ʃn/ n ⟨of animal, human⟩ escremento m

**excruciating** /ɪk'skru:ʃɪeɪtɪŋ/ a atroce ⟨pain⟩; ⟨fam: very bad⟩ spaventoso

**excursion** /ɪk'skɜ:ʃn/ n escursione f

**excusable** /ɪk'skju:zəbl/ a perdonabile

**excuse¹** /ɪk'skju:s/ n scusa f

**excuse²** /ɪk'skju:z/ vt scusare; ~ **from** esonerare da; ~ **me!** (to get attention) scusi!; (to get past) permesso!, scusi!; (indignant) come ha detto?

**ex-directory** a be ~ non figurare sull'elenco telefonico

**exec** /ɪg'zek/ n Am abbr fam **executive**

**execrable** /'eksɪkrəbl/ a esecrabile

**executable file** /'eksɪkju:təbl/ n Comput eseguibile m

**execute** /'eksɪkju:t/ vt eseguire; (put to death) giustiziare; attuare ⟨plan⟩

**execution** /eksɪ'kju:ʃn/ n esecuzione f; (of plan) attuazione f

**executioner** /eksɪ'kju:ʃənə(r)/ n boia m inv

**executive** /ɪg'zekjʊtɪv/ a esecutivo ● n dirigente mf; Pol esecutivo m

**executive: executive committee** n comitato m esecutivo. **executive director** n direttore, -trice mf [esecutivo, -a]. **executive jet** n jet m inv privato. **executive producer** n Cinema direttore, -trice mf di produzione. **executive secretary** n segretario, -a mf di direzione

**executor** /ɪg'zekjʊtə(r)/ n Jur esecutore, -trice mf

**exemplary** /ɪg'zemplərɪ/ a esemplare

**exemplify** /ɪg'zemplɪfaɪ/ vt (pt/pp -ied) esemplificare

**exempt** /ɪg'zempt/ a esente ● vt esentare **(from** da)

**exemption** /ɪg'zempʃn/ n esenzione f

**exercise** /'eksəsaɪz/ n esercizio m; Mil esercitazione f; **physical** ~s ginnastica f; **take** ~ fare del moto; **you need more** ~ devi muoverti di più ● vt esercitare ⟨muscles, horse⟩; portare a spasso ⟨dog⟩; usare ⟨patience⟩; mettere in pratica ⟨skills⟩ ● vi esercitarsi; ~ **more** fare più moto

**exercise bike** n cyclette″ f inv

**exercise book** n quaderno m

**exert** /ɪg'zɜ:t/ vt esercitare; ~ **oneself** sforzarsi

**exertion** /ɪg'zɜ:ʃn/ n sforzo m

**ex gratia** /eks'greɪʃə/ a ⟨award, payment⟩ a titolo di favore

**exhale** /eks'heɪl/ vt/i esalare

**exhaust** /ɪg'zɔ:st/ n Auto scappamento m; (pipe) tubo m di scappamento

**exhausted** /ɪg'zɔ:stɪd/ a esausto

**exhaust fumes** npl fumi mpl di scarico m ● vt esaurire

**exhausting** /ɪg'zɔ:stɪŋ/ a estenuante; ⟨climate, person⟩ sfibrante

**exhaustion** /ɪg'zɔ:stʃn/ n esaurimento m

**exhaustive** /ɪg'zɔ:stɪv/ a fig esauriente

**exhibit** /ɪg'zɪbɪt/ n oggetto m esposto; Jur reperto m ● vt esporre; fig dimostrare

**exhibition** /eksɪ'bɪʃn/ n mostra f; (of strength, skill) dimostrazione f

**exhibition centre** n palazzo m delle esposizioni

**exhibitionist** /eksɪ'bɪʃənɪst/ n esibizionista mf

**exhibitor** /ɪg'zɪbɪtə(r)/ n espositore, -trice mf

**exhilarated** /ɪg'zɪləreɪtɪd/ a rallegrato

**exhilarating** /ɪg'zɪləreɪtɪŋ/ a stimolante; ⟨mountain air⟩ tonificante

**exhilaration** /ɪgzɪlə'reɪʃn/ n allegria f

**exhort** /ɪg'zɔ:t/ vt esortare

**exhume** /ɪg'zju:m/ vt esumare

**exile** /'eksaɪl/ n esilio m; (person) esule mf ● vt esiliare

**exist** /ɪg'zɪst/ vi esistere

**existence** /ɪg'zɪstəns/ n esistenza f; **in** ~ esistente; **be in** ~ esistere

**existential** /egzɪ'stenʃ(ə)l/ a esistenziale

**existentialism** /egzɪ'stenʃəlɪzm/ n esistenzialismo m

**existing** /ɪɡ'zɪstɪŋ/ a ⟨policy, management, leadership⟩ attuale: ⟨laws, order⟩ vigente

**exit** /'eksɪt/ n uscita f; Theat uscita f di scena ● vi Theat uscire di scena; Comput uscire (**from** da)

**exit sign** n cartello m di uscita

**exodus** /'eksədəs/ n esodo m

**ex officio** /eksə'fɪʃɪəʊ/ a ⟨member⟩ di diritto

**exonerate** /ɪɡ'zɒnəreɪt/ vt esonerare

**exorbitant** /ɪɡ'zɔ:bɪtənt/ a esorbitante

**exorcism** /'eksɔ:sɪzm/ n esorcismo m

**exorcist** /'eksɔ:sɪst/ n esorcista mf

**exorcize** /'eksɔ:saɪz/ vt esorcizzare

**exotic** /ɪɡ'zɒtɪk/ a esotico

**exotica** /ɪɡ'zɒtɪkə/ npl oggetti mpl esotici

**expand** /ɪk'spænd/ vt espandere; sviluppare ⟨economy⟩ ● vi espandersi; Comm svilupparsi; ⟨metal:⟩ dilatarsi

■ **expand on** vt (explain better) approfondire

**expandable** /ɪk'spændəbl/ a ⟨Comput: memory⟩ espandibile

**expanding** /ɪk'spændɪŋ/ a ⟨file⟩ a soffietto inv; ⟨population, sector⟩ in espansione; ⟨bracelet⟩ allungabile

**expanse** /ɪk'spæns/ n estensione f

**expansion** /ɪk'spænʃn/ n espansione f; Comm sviluppo m; (of metal) dilatazione f

**expansion board, expansion card** n Comput scheda f di espansione

**expansionist** /ɪk'spænʃənɪst/ n & a espansionista mf

**expansion slot** n Comput fessura f [per la scheda] di espansione, slot m di espansione

**expansive** /ɪk'spænsɪv/ a espansivo

**expatriate** /eks'pætrɪət/ n espatriato, -a mf

**expect** /ɪk'spekt/ vt aspettare ⟨letter, baby⟩; (suppose) pensare; (demand) esigere; **I ~ so** penso di sì; **we ~ to arrive on Monday** contiamo di arrivare lunedì; **I didn't ~ that** questo non me lo aspettavo; **she ~s too much from him** pretende troppo da lui; **be ~ing** essere in stato interessante

**expectancy** /ɪk'spektənsɪ/ n aspettativa f

**expectant** /ɪk'spektənt/ a in attesa; **~ mother** donna f incinta

**expectantly** /ɪk'spektəntlɪ/ adv con impazienza

**expectation** /ekspek'teɪʃn/ n aspettativa f, speranza f

**expediency** /ɪk'spi:dɪənsɪ/ n (appropriateness) opportunità f; (self-interest) opportunismo m

**expedient** /ɪk'spi:dɪənt/ a conveniente ● n espediente m

**expedite** /'ekspɪdaɪt/ vt fml accelerare

**expedition** /ekspɪ'dɪʃn/ n spedizione f

**expeditionary** /ekspɪ'dɪʃənərɪ/ a Mil di spedizione

**expeditionary force** n corpo m di spedizione

**expel** /ɪk'spel/ vt (pt/pp **expelled**) espellere

**expend** /ɪk'spend/ vt consumare

**expendable** /ɪk'spendəbl/ a sacrificabile

**expenditure** /ɪk'spendɪtʃə(r)/ n spesa f

**expense** /ɪk'spens/ n spesa f; **business ~** pl spese fpl; **at my ~** a mie spese; **at the ~ c** fig a spese di

**expense account** n conto m spese

**expensive** /ɪk'spensɪv/ a caro, costoso

**expensively** /ɪk'spensɪvlɪ/ adv costosa mente

**experience** /ɪk'spɪərɪəns/ n esperienza ● vt provare ⟨sensation⟩; avere ⟨problem⟩

**experienced** /ɪk'spɪərɪənst/ a esperto

**experiment** n esperiment ● /ɪk'sperɪment/ vi sperimentare

**experimental** /ɪksperɪ'mentl/ a sperimen tale

**experimentation** /ɪksperɪmen'teɪʃn/ sperimentazione f; **~ with drugs** esperienz f della droga

**expert** /'eksps:t/ a & n esperto, -a mf

**expertise** /eksps:'ti:z/ n competenza f

**expertly** /'eksps:tlɪ/ adv abilmente

**expiate** /'ekspɪeɪt/ vt espiare ⟨crime, sin⟩ fare ammenda per ⟨guilt⟩

**expiration** /ekspɪ'reɪʃn/ n (end, exhalation espirazione f

**expire** /ɪk'spaɪə(r)/ vi scadere

**expiry** /ɪk'spaɪərɪ/ n scadenza f

**expiry date** n data f di scadenza

**explain** /ɪk'spleɪn/ vt spiegare

■ **explain away** vt (give reasons for) trova re delle giustificazioni per

**explanation** /eksplə'neɪʃn/ n spiegazione f

**explanatory** /ɪk'splænətərɪ/ a esplicativo

**expletive** /ɪk'spli:tɪv/ n imprecazione f

**explicit** /ɪk'splɪsɪt/ a esplicito

**explicitly** /ɪk'splɪsɪtlɪ/ adv esplicitamente

**explode** /ɪk'spləʊd/ vi esplodere ● vt far esplodere

**exploit¹** /'eksplɔɪt/ n impresa f

**exploit²** /ɪk'splɔɪt/ vt sfruttare

**exploitation** /eksplɔɪ'teɪʃn/ n sfruttamen to m

**exploitative** /ɪk'splɔɪtətɪv/ a inteso a sfrut tare gli individui; ⟨attitude, system⟩ a caratte re di sfruttamento

**exploration** /eksplə'reɪʃn/ n esplorazio ne f

**exploratory** /ɪk'splɒrətərɪ/ a esplorativo

**explore** /ɪk'splɔ:(r)/ vt esplorare; fig studiare ⟨implications⟩

**explorer** /ɪk'splɔ:rə(r)/ n esploratore, -trice mf

**explosion** /ɪk'spləʊʒn/ n esplosione f

**explosive** /ɪk'spləʊsɪv/ a & n esplosivo m

**exponent** /ɪk'spəʊnənt/ n esponente mf

**exponential** /ekspə'nenʃəl/ a esponenziale

**export¹** /'ekspɔ:t/ n esportazione f

**export²** /ek'spɔ:t/ vt esportare

**export: export agent** n esportatore, -trice mf. **export control** n controllo m delle esportazioni. **export credit** n credito m all'esportazione. **export drive** n campagna f di esportazione. **export duty** n tassa f di esportazione. **export earnings** npl ricavato m delle esportazioni

**exporter** /ek'spɔːtə(r)/ n esportatore, -trice mf

**export: export finance** n finanziamento m delle esportazioni. **export-import company** n azienda di import-export. **export licence** n licenza f di esportazione. **export market** n mercato m delle esportazioni. **export trade** n commercio m di esportazione

**expose** /ɪk'spəʊz/ vt esporre; (reveal) svelare; smascherare (traitor etc)

**exposé** /ɪk'spəʊzeɪ/ n (of scandal) rivelazioni fpl

**exposition** /ekspə'zɪʃn/ n (of facts) esposizione f

**exposure** /ɪk'spəʊʒə(r)/ n esposizione f; Med espozione f prolungata al freddo/caldo; (of crimes) smascheramento m; **24 ~s** Phot 24 pose

**exposure meter** n Phot esposimetro m

**exposure time** n Phot tempo m di esposizione

**expound** /ɪk'spaʊnd/ vt esporre

**express** /ɪk'spres/ a espresso ● adv (send) per espresso ● n (train) espresso m ● vt esprimere; **~ oneself** esprimersi

**expression** /ɪk'spreʃn/ n espressione f

**expressionless** /ɪk'spreʃənlɪs/ a (tone, voice) distaccato; (playing) piatto; (eyes, face) inespressivo

**expressive** /ɪk'spresɪv/ a espressivo

**expressively** /ɪk'spresɪvlɪ/ adv espressamente

**expulsion** /ɪk'spʌlʃn/ n espulsione f

**expurgate** /'ekspəgeɪt/ vt espurgare

**exquisite** /ek'skwɪzɪt/ a squisito

**exquisitely** /ek'skwɪzɪtlɪ/ adv (dressed, written) in modo elegante e raffinato; **~ beautiful** di una bellezza fine

**ex-serviceman** /'sɜːvɪsmən/ n ex-combattente m

**ex-servicewoman** /'sɜːvɪswʊmən/ n ex-combattente f

**extant** /ɪk'stænt/ a ancora esistente

**extempore** /ɪk'stempərɪ/ adv (speak) senza preparazione

**extend** /ɪk'stend/ vt prolungare (visit, road); prorogare (visa, contract); ampliare (building, knowledge); (stretch out) allungare; tendere (hand) ● vi (garden, knowledge:) estendersi

**extendable** /ɪk'stendəbl/ a (cable) allungabile; (contract) prorogabile

**extension** /ɪk'stenʃn/ n) prolungamento m; (of visa, contract) proroga f; (of treaty) ampliamento m; (part of building) annesso m; (length of cable) prolunga f; Teleph interno m; **~ 226** interno 226

**extension ladder** n scala f allungabile

**extension lead** n Electr prolunga f

**extensive** /ɪk'stensɪv/ a ampio, vasto

**extensively** /ɪk'stensɪvlɪ/ adv ampiamente

**extent** /ɪk'stent/ n (scope) portata f; **to a certain ~** fino a un certo punto; **to such an ~ that...** fino al punto che...

**extenuating** /ɪk'stenjʊeɪtɪŋ/ a **~ circumstances** attenuanti fpl

**exterior** /ɪk'stɪərɪə(r)/ a & n esterno m

**exterminate** /ɪk'stɜːmɪneɪt/ vt sterminare

**extermination** /ɪkstɜː'mɪ'neɪʃn/ n sterminio m

**external** /ɪk'stɜːnl/ a esterno; **for ~ use only** Med per uso esterno

**externalize** /ɪk'stɜːnəlaɪz/ vt esteriorizzare

**externally** /ɪk'stɜːnəlɪ/ adv esternamente

**externals** /ɪk'stɜːn(ə)lz/ npl apparenze fpl

**extinct** /ɪk'stɪŋkt/ a estinto

**extinction** /ɪk'stɪŋkʃn/ n estinzione f

**extinguish** /ɪk'stɪŋwɪʃ/ vt estinguere

**extinguisher** /ɪk'stɪŋwɪʃə(r)/ n estintore m

**extol** /ɪk'stəʊl/ vt (pt/pp extolled) lodare

**extort** /ɪk'stɔːt/ vt estorcere

**extortion** /ɪk'stɔːʃn/ n estorsione f

**extortionate** /ɪk'stɔːʃənət/ a esorbitante

**extra** /'ekstrə/ a in più; (train) straordinario; **an ~ £10** 10 sterline extra, 10 sterline in più ● adv in più; (especially) più; **pay ~** pagare in più, pagare extra; **~ strong/busy** fortissimo/occupatissimo ● n Theat comparsa f; **~s** pl extra mpl

**extra charge** n supplemento m; **at no ~** senza ulteriori spese

**extract¹** /'ekstrækt/ n estratto m

**extract²** /ɪk'strækt/ vt estrarre (tooth, oil); strappare (secret); ricavare (truth)

**extraction** /ɪk'strækʃn/ n (process) estrazione f; **of French ~** di origine francese

**extractor** [**fan**] /ɪk'stræktə(r)/ n aspiratore m

**extra-curricular** /-kə'rɪkjʊlə(r)/ a extra-scolastico

**extradite** /'ekstrədaɪt/ vt Jur estradare

**extradition** /ekstrə'dɪʃn/ n estradizione f

**extra-dry** a (sherry, wine) extra dry inv

**extra-fast** a ultrarapido

**extra-large** a (pullover, shirt) extra large inv

**extramarital** /ekstrə'mærɪtəl/ a extraconiugale

**extramural** /ekstrə'mjʊərəl/ a Br Univ (course, lecture) organizzato dall'università e aperto a tutti

**extraneous** /ɪk'streɪnɪəs/ a (not essential) inessenziale; (issue, detail) superfluo

**extraordinarily** /ɪk'strɔːdɪnərɪlɪ/ adv straordinariamente

**extraordinary** /ɪk'strɔːdɪnərɪ/ a straordinario

**extrapolate** /ɪk'stræpəleɪt/ vt arguire; Math estrapolare

**extrasensory perception** /ekstrə'sensərɪ/ n percezione f extrasensoriale

**extra-special** a eccezionale

**extra-strong** a (thread) robustissimo; (coffee) fortissimo; (disinfectant, weed killer) potentissimo; (paper) ultraresistente inv

**extraterrestrial** /ekstrətɪ'restrɪəl/ n & a extraterrestre mf

**extra time** n tempo m supplementare; **play ~ ~** giocare i tempi supplementari

**extravagance** /ɪk'strævəgəns/ n (with money) prodigalità f; (of behaviour) stravaganza f

**extravagant** /ɪk'strævəgənt/ a spendaccione; (bizarre) stravagante; ⟨claim⟩ esagerato

**extravagantly** /ɪk'strævəgəntlɪ/ adv dispendiosamente

**extravaganza** /ɪkstrævə'gænzə/ n rappresentazione f spettacolare

**extreme** /ɪk'striːm/ a estremo ● n estremo m; **in the ~** al massimo

**extremely** /ɪk'striːmlɪ/ adv estremamente

**extremism** /ɪk'striːmɪzm/ n estremismo m

**extremist** /ɪk'striːmɪst/ n estremista mf

**extremity** /ɪk'stremətɪ/ n (end) estremità f inv

**extricate** /'ekstrɪkeɪt/ vt districare

**extrovert** /'ekstrəvəːt/ n estroverso, -a mf

**exuberance** /ɪg'zjuːbərəns/ n esuberanza f

**exuberant** /ɪg'zjuːbərənt/ a esuberante

**exude** /ɪg'zjuːd/ vt also fig trasudare

**exult** /ɪg'zʌlt/ vi esultare

**exultant** /ɪg'zʌltənt/ a esultante; ⟨cry⟩ di esultanza

**exultantly** /ɪg'zʌltəntlɪ/ adv con esultanza

**ex-works** a ⟨price, value⟩ franco fabbrica

**eye** /aɪ/ n occhio m; (of needle) cruna f; **keep an ~ on** tener d'occhio; **see ~ to ~** aver le stesse idee ● vt (pt/pp **eyed**, pres p **ey[e]ing**) guardare

■ **eye up** vt adocchiare ⟨sb⟩

**eye: eyeball** n bulbo m oculare. **eyebath** n bagno m oculare. **eyebrow** n sopracciglio m (pl sopracciglia f). **eyebrow pencil** n matita f per le sopracciglia. **eye-catching** /'aɪkætʃɪŋ/ a che attira l'attenzione. **eye contact** n **avoid ~ ~ with sb** evitare di incrociare lo sguardo di qcno; **try to make ~ ~ with sb** tentare di incrociare lo sguardo di qcno. **eyedrops** npl collirio m

**eyeful** /'aɪfʊl/ n **get an ~ (of sth)** avere gli occhi pieni (di qcsa); (fam: good look) lustrarsi la vista

**eye: eyeglass** n (monocle) monocolo m. **eyeglasses** npl Am occhiali mpl [da vista]. **eyelash** n ciglio m (pl ciglia f)

**eyelet** /'aɪlɪt/ n occhiello m

**eye: eye-level** a ⟨grill, shelf⟩ all'altezza degli occhi. **eyelid** n palpebra f. **eye make-up** n trucco m per gli occhi. **eye-opener** n rivelazione f. **eyepatch** n benda f per gli occhi. **eye-shade** n visiera f. **eyeshadow** n ombretto m. **eyesight** n vista f. **eyesore** n fam pugno m nell'occhio. **eye strain** n affaticamento m degli occhi. **eye test** n esame m della vista. **eyewash** n bagno m oculare; (fig: nonsense) fumo m negli occhi. **eyewitness** n testimone mf oculare

**eyrie** /'ɪərɪ/ n nido m d'aquila

# Ff

**f, F** /ef/ n (letter) f, F f inv; Mus fa m inv

**FA** n Br abbr (**Football Association**) associazione f calcistica britannica, ≈ FIGC f

**fable** /'feɪbl/ n favola f

**fabric** /'fæbrɪk/ n also fig tessuto m

**fabricate** /'fæbrɪkeɪt/ vt fabbricare; inventare ⟨story⟩

**fabrication** /fæbrɪ'keɪʃn/ n invenzione f; (manufacture) fabbricazione f

**fabric softener** /sɒfnə(r)/ n ammorbidente m

**fabulous** /'fæbjʊləs/ a fam favoloso

**façade** /fə'sɑːd/ n (of building, person) facciata f

**face** /feɪs/ n faccia f, viso m; (grimace) smorfia f; (surface) faccia f; (of clock) quadrante m; **pull ~s** far boccacce; **in the ~ of** di fronte a; **on the ~ of it** in apparenza ● vt essere di fronta a; (confront) affrontare; **~ north** ⟨house:⟩ dare a nord; **~ the fact that** arrendersi al fatto che

■ **face up to** vt accettare ⟨facts⟩; affrontare ⟨person⟩

**face flannel** n ≈ guanto m di spugna

**faceless** /'feɪslɪs/ a anonimo

**facelift** /'feɪslɪft/ n plastica f facciale

**face powder** n cipria f

**facet** /'fæsɪt/ n sfaccettatura f; fig aspetto m

**facetious** /fə'siːʃəs/ a spiritoso. **~ remarks** spiritosaggini mpl

**face: face pack** n maschera f di bellezza. **face saving** a ⟨plan, solution⟩ per salvare la faccia. **face to face** a ⟨meeting⟩ a quattr'occhi ● adv ⟨be seated⟩ faccia a faccia; **meet sb ~ to ~** avere un incontro a quattr'occhi con qcno; **come ~ to ~ with** trovarsi di fronte a. **face value** n (of money) valore m nominale; **take sb/sth at ~ ~** fermarsi alle apparenze

**facial** /'feɪʃl/ a facciale ● n trattamento m di bellezza al viso

**facile** /'fæsaɪl/ a semplicistico

**facilitate** /fə'sɪlɪteɪt/ vt rendere possibile; (make easier) facilitare

**facility** /fə'sɪlətɪ/ n facilità f; **facilities** pl (of area, in hotel etc) attrezzature fpl; **credit facilities** pl facilitazioni fpl di pagamento

**facing** /'feɪsɪŋ/ prep **~ the sea** ⟨house⟩ che

dà sul mare; **the person ~ me** la persona di fronte a me

**facsimile** /fæk'sɪməlɪ/ n facsimile m

**fact** /fækt/ n fatto m; **in ~** infatti

**fact finding** a ⟨mission, tour, trip⟩ di inchiesta

**faction** /'fækʃn/ n fazione f

**factional** /'fækʃnəl/ a ⟨leader, activity⟩ di una fazione; ⟨fighting, arguments⟩ tra fazioni

**factor** /'fæktə(r)/ n fattore m

**factory** /'fæktərɪ/ n fabbrica f

**factory: factory farming** n allevamento m su scala industriale. **factory floor** n ⟨place⟩ reparto m produzione; ⟨workers⟩ operai mpl. **factory inspector** n verificatore, -trice mf. **factory made** a prodotto in fabbrica. **factory unit** n unità f inv di produzione. **factory worker** n operaio, -a mf

**fact sheet** n ⟨one issue⟩ prospetto m illustrativo; ⟨periodical⟩ bollettino m d'informazione

**factual** /'fæktʃʊəl/ a **be ~** attenersi ai fatti

**factually** /'fæktʃʊəlɪ/ adv ⟨inaccurate⟩ dal punto di vista dei fatti

**faculty** /'fækəltɪ/ n facoltà f inv

**fad** /fæd/ n capriccio m

**faddish** /'fædɪʃ/ a ⟨person⟩ sempre in preda a una nuova mania

**fade** /feɪd/ vi sbiadire; ⟨sound, light:⟩ affievolirsi; ⟨flower:⟩ appassire

■ **fade in** vt cominciare in dissolvenza ⟨picture⟩

■ **fade out** vt finire in dissolvenza ⟨picture⟩

**faded** /'feɪdɪd/ a ⟨clothing, carpet, colour⟩ sbiadito; ⟨flower, beauty⟩ appassito; ⟨glory⟩ svanito

**faeces** /'fiːsiːz/ npl feci fpl

**fag** /fæg/ n ⟨chore⟩ fatica f; ⟨fam: cigarette⟩ sigaretta f; ⟨Am sl: homosexual⟩ frocio m

**fag end** n fam mozzicone m di sigaretta, cicca f; ⟨of day, decade, conversation⟩ fine f; ⟨of material⟩ scampolo m

**fagged** /fægd/ a **~ out** fam stanco morto

**faggot** /'fægət/ n ⟨meatball⟩ polpetta f di carne; ⟨firewood⟩ fascina f

**Fahrenheit** /'færənhaɪt/ a Fahrenheit

**fail** /feɪl/ n **without ~** senz'altro ● vi ⟨attempt:⟩ fallire; ⟨eyesight, memory:⟩ indebolirsi; ⟨engine, machine:⟩ guastarsi; ⟨marriage:⟩ andare a rotoli; ⟨in exam⟩ essere bocciato; **~ to do sth** non fare qcsa; **I tried but I ~ed** ho provato ma non ci sono riuscito; **a ~ed politician** un politico fallito ● vt non superare ⟨exam⟩; bocciare ⟨candidate⟩; ⟨disappoint⟩ deludere; **words ~ me** mi mancano le parole; **unless my memory ~s me** se la memoria non mi tradisce

**failing** /'feɪlɪŋ/ n difetto m ● prep **~ that** altrimenti

**fail-safe** a ⟨device, system⟩ di sicurezza

**failure** /'feɪljə(r)/ n fallimento m; ⟨mechanical⟩ guasto m; ⟨person⟩ incapace mf

**faint** /feɪnt/ a leggero; ⟨memory⟩ vago; **feel ~** sentirsi mancare ● n svenimento m ● vi svenire

**faint-hearted** /-'hɑːtɪd/ a timido

**fainting fit** /'feɪntɪŋ/ n svenimento m

**faintly** /'feɪntlɪ/ adv ⟨slightly⟩ leggermente

**faintness** /'feɪntnɪs/ n ⟨physical⟩ debolezza f

**fair**[1] /feə(r)/ n fiera f

**fair**[2] a ⟨hair, person⟩ biondo; ⟨skin⟩ chiaro; ⟨weather⟩ bello; ⟨just⟩ giusto; ⟨quite good⟩ discreto; Sch abbastanza bene; **a ~ amount** abbastanza ● adv **play ~** fare un gioco pulito

**fair copy** n bella copia f

**fairground** /'feəgraʊnd/ n luna park m inv

**fairly** /'feəlɪ/ adv con giustizia; ⟨rather⟩ discretamente, abbastanza

**fair-minded** /feə'maɪndɪd/ a equo

**fairness** /'feənɪs/ n giustizia f

**fair: fair play** n fair play m inv. **fair skinned** /-'skɪnd/ a di carnagione chiara. **fairway** n Naut via f d'acqua navigabile; ⟨in golf⟩ fairway m inv. **fair weather friend** n pej amico m finché tutto va bene

**fairy** /'feərɪ/ n fata f; **good ~** fata [buona]; **wicked ~** strega f

**fairy: fairy godmother** n fata f buona. **fairy lights** npl Br lampadine fpl colorate. **fairy story, fairy-tale** n fiaba f

**faith** /feɪθ/ n fede f; ⟨trust⟩ fiducia f; **in good/bad ~** in buona/mala fede

**faithful** /'feɪθfl/ a fedele

**faithfully** /'feɪθfʊlɪ/ adv fedelmente; **yours ~** distinti saluti

**faithfulness** /'feɪθfʊlnɪs/ n fedeltà f

**faith-healer** /hɪ:lə(r)/ n guaritore, -trice mf

**faithless** /'feɪθlɪs/ a ⟨friend, servant⟩ sleale; ⟨husband⟩ infedele

**fake** /feɪk/ a falso ● n falsificazione f; ⟨person⟩ impostore m ● vt falsificare; ⟨pretend⟩ fingere

**falcon** /'fɔːlkən/ n falcone m

**Falklands** /'fɔːlkləndz/ npl le isole Falkland, le isole Malvine

**fall** /fɔːl/ n caduta f; ⟨in prices⟩ ribasso m; ⟨Am: autumn⟩ autunno m; **have a ~** fare una caduta ● vi ⟨pt fell, pp fallen⟩ cadere; ⟨night:⟩ scendere; **~ in love** innamorarsi

■ **fall about** vi ⟨with laughter⟩ morire dal ridere

■ **fall back on** vt ritornare su

■ **fall down** vi cadere; ⟨building:⟩ crollare

■ **fall for** vt fam innamorarsi di ⟨person⟩; cascarci ⟨sth, trick⟩

■ **fall in** vi caderci dentro; ⟨collapse⟩ crollare; Mil mettersi in riga; **~ in with** concordare con ⟨suggestion, plan⟩

■ **fall off** vi cadere; ⟨diminish⟩ diminuire

■ **fall out** vi ⟨quarrel⟩ litigare; **his hair is ~ing out** perde i capelli

■ **fall over** vi cadere

■ **fall through** vi ⟨plan:⟩ andare a monte

**fallacious** /fə'leɪʃəs/ a fallace

**fallacy** /'fæləsɪ/ n errore m

**fallible** /'fæləbl/ a fallibile

**Fallopian tube** /fə'ləʊpɪən/ n tromba f di Falloppio

**fallout** /'fɔːlaʊt/ n pioggia f radioattiva

**fallout shelter** n rifugio m antiatomico

**fallow** /'fæləʊ/ a lie ~ essere a maggese

**false** /fɔːls/ a falso

**false bottom** n doppio fondo m

**falsehood** /'fɔːlshʊd/ n menzogna f

**falsely** /'fɔːlslɪ/ adv falsamente

**falseness** /'fɔːlsnɪs/ n falsità f

**false: false pretences** npl under ~ ~ sotto false spoglie; Jur con la frode. **false start** n Sport falsa partenza f. **false teeth** npl dentiera f

**falsetto** /fɔːl'setəʊ/ n (voice) falsetto m inv ● a in falsetto

**falsification** /fɔːlsɪfɪ'keɪʃn/ n (of document, figures) falsificazione f; (of truth, facts) deformazione f

**falsify** /'fɔːlsɪfaɪ/ vt (pt/pp -ied) falsificare

**falsity** /'fɔːlsətɪ/ n falsità f

**falter** /'fɔːltə(r)/ vi vacillare; (making speech) esitare

**fame** /feɪm/ n fama f

**famed** /feɪmd/ a rinomato

**familiar** /fə'mɪljə(r)/ a familiare; **be ~ with** (know) conoscere; **become too ~** prendersi troppe confidenze

**familiarity** /fəmɪlɪ'ærətɪ/ n familiarità f

**familiarize** /fə'mɪlɪəraɪz/ vt familiarizzare; **~ oneself with sth** familiarizzarsi con qcsa

**family** /'fæməlɪ/ n famiglia f

**family: family allowance** n assegni mpl familiari. **family circle** n (group) cerchia f familiare; Am Theat seconda galleria f. **family doctor** n medico m di famiglia. **family life** n vita f familiare. **family name** n cognome m. **family planning** n pianificazione f familiare. **family tree** n albero m genealogico

**famine** /'fæmɪn/ n carestia f

**famished** /'fæmɪʃt/ a **be ~** fam avere una fame da lupo

**famous** /'feɪməs/ a famoso

**fan¹** /fæn/ n ventilatore m; (handheld) ventaglio m ● v (pt/pp **fanned**) ● vt far vento a; **~ oneself** sventagliarsi; fig **~ the flames** soffiare sul fuoco

■ **fan out** vi spiegarsi a ventaglio

**fan²** n (admirer) ammiratore, -trice mf, fan mf; Sport tifoso m; (of Verdi etc) appassionato, -a mf

**fanatic** /fə'nætɪk/ n fanatico, -a mf

**fanatical** /fə'nætɪkl/ a fanatico

**fanatically** /fə'nætɪklɪ/ adv con fanatismo

**fanaticism** /fə'nætɪsɪzm/ n fanatismo m

**fan belt** n cinghia f per ventilatore

**fanciful** /'fænsɪfl/ a fantasioso

**fancy** /'fænsɪ/ n fantasia f; **I've taken a real ~ to him** mi è molto simpatico; **as the ~ takes you** come ti pare ● a fantasia inv ● vt (believe) credere; (fam: want) aver voglia di; **he fancies you** fam gli piaci; **~ that!** ma guarda un po'!

**fancy dress** n costume m

**fanfare** /'fænfeə(r)/ n fanfara f

**fang** /fæŋ/ n zanna f; (of snake) dente m

**fan: fan heater** n termoventilatore m.

**fanlight** n lunetta f. **fan mail** n posta f dei fans

**fantasize** /'fæntəsaɪz/ vi fantasticare

**fantastic** /fæn'tæstɪk/ a fantastico

**fantasy** /'fæntəsɪ/ n fantasia f

**far** /fɑː(r)/ adv lontano; (much) molto; **by ~** di gran lunga; **~ away** lontano; **as ~ as the church** fino alla chiesa; **how ~ is it from here?** quanto dista da qui? **as ~ as I know** per quanto io sappia ● a (end, side) altro; **the F~ East** l'Estremo Oriente m; **in the ~ distance** in lontananza

**farce** /fɑːs/ n farsa f

**farcical** /'fɑːsɪkl/ a ridicolo

**fare** /feə(r)/ n tariffa f; (food) vitto m

**fare-dodger** /-dɒdʒə(r)/ n passeggero, -a mf senza biglietto

**farewell** /feə'wel/ int liter addio! ● n addio m; **~ dinner** cena f d'addio

**far-fetched** /-'fetʃt/ a improbabile

**far flung** /-'flʌŋ/ a (remote) remoto; (widely distributed) sparpagliato; (network) esteso

**farm** /fɑːm/ n fattoria f ● vi fare l'agricoltore ● vt coltivare (land)

**farmer** /'fɑːmə(r)/ n agricoltore m

**farmhand** /'fɑːmhænd/ n bracciante m

**farmhouse** /'fɑːmhaʊs/ n casa f colonica

**farming** /'fɑːmɪŋ/ n agricoltura f

**farm produce** n prodotto m agricolo

**farmyard** /'fɑːmjɑːd/ n aia f

**far-reaching** /-'riːtʃɪŋ/ a (programme, plan, proposal) di larga portata; (effect, implication, change) notevole

**far-sighted** /-'saɪtɪd/ a (policy) lungimirante; (Am: long-sighted) presbite

**fart** /fɑːt/fam n scoreggia f ● vi scoreggiare

**farther** /'fɑːðə(r)/ adv più lontano ● a **at the ~ end of** all'altra estremità di

**fascia** /'feɪʃɪə/ n Br (dashboard) cruscotto m

**fascinate** /'fæsɪneɪt/ vt affascinare

**fascinating** /'fæsɪneɪtɪŋ/ a affascinante

**fascination** /fæsɪ'neɪʃn/ n fascino m

**fascism** /'fæʃɪzm/ n fascismo m

**fascist** /'fæʃɪst/ a & n fascista mf

**fashion** /'fæʃn/ n moda f; (manner) maniera f; **in ~** di moda; **out of ~** non più di moda ● vt modellare

**fashionable** /'fæʃ(ə)nəbl/ a di moda; **be ~** essere alla moda

**fashionably** /'fæʃ(ə)nəblɪ/ adv alla moda

**fashion: fashion designer** n stilista mf. **fashion house** n casa f di moda. **fashion model** n indossatore, -trice mf, modello, -a m f

**fast¹** /fɑːst/ a veloce; (colour) indelebile; **be ~** (clock:) andare avanti ● adv velocemente; (firmly) saldamente; **~er!** più in fretta!; **be ~ asleep** dormire profondamente

**fast²** n digiuno m ● vi digiunare

**fasten** /'fɑːsn/ vt allacciare; chiudere (window); (stop flapping) mettere un fermo a ● vi allacciarsi

**fastener** /'fɑːsnə(r)/ n, **fastening** /'fɑːsnɪŋ/ n chiusura f

**fast: fast food** n fast food m inv ● attrib (chain) di fast food; **~ ~ restaurant** n fast

food *m inv*. **fast forward** *n* avanzamento *m*
veloce ● *vt* far avanzare velocemente ⟨*tape*⟩
● *attrib* ⟨*key, button*⟩ di avanzamento veloce.
**fast growing** *a* in rapida espansione.

**fastidious** /fə'stɪdɪəs/ *a* esigente

**fast: fast lane** *n Auto* corsia *f* di sorpasso;
**life in the ~ ~** *fig* vita *f* frenetica. **fast-talking** *a* ⟨*salesperson*⟩ che raggira con la sua
parlantina

**fat** /fæt/ *a* (**fatter, fattest**) ⟨*person, cheque*⟩
grasso; *fam* **that's a ~ a lot of use** non serve a
un accidente ● *n* grasso *m*

**fatal** /'feɪtl/ *a* mortale; ⟨*error*⟩ fatale

**fatalism** /'feɪtəlɪzm/ *n* fatalismo *m*

**fatalist** /'feɪtəlɪst/ *n* fatalista *mf*

**fatality** /fə'tælətɪ/ *n* morte *f*

**fatally** /'feɪtəlɪ/ *adv* mortalmente

**fate** /feɪt/ *n* destino *m*

**fated** /'feɪtɪd/ *a* destinato; **it was ~** era destino

**fateful** /'feɪtfʊl/ *a* fatidico

**fat free** *a* magro

**fat-head** *n fam* zuccone, -a *mf*

**father** /'fɑːðə(r)/ *n* padre *m* ● *vt* generare
⟨*child*⟩

**father: Father Christmas** Babbo *m* Natale.
**father confessor** *n Relig* confessore *m*. **father figure** *n* figura *f* paterna. **fatherhood** *n*
paternità *f*. **father-in-law** *n* (*pl* ~**s-in-law**)
suocero *m*. **fatherland** *n* patria *f*

**fatherly** /'fɑːðəlɪ/ *a* paterno

**Father's Day** /'fɑːðəz/ *n* la festa del papà

**fathom** /'fæðəm/ *n Naut* braccio *m* ● *vt* ~
[**out**] comprendere

**fatigue** /fə'tiːg/ *n* fatica *f* ● *vt* affaticare

**fatness** /'fætnɪs/ *n* grassezza *f*

**fatten** /'fætn/ *vt* ingrassare ⟨*animal*⟩

**fattening** /'fætnɪŋ/ *a* **a cream is ~** la panna
fa ingrassare

**fatty** /'fætɪ/ *a* grasso ● *n fam* ciccione, -a *mf*

**fatuous** /'fætjʊəs/ *a* fatuo

**faucet** /'fɔːsɪt/ *n Am* rubinetto *m*

**fault** /fɔːlt/ *n* difetto *m*; *Geol* faglia *f*; *Tennis*
fallo *m*; **be at ~** avere torto; **find ~ with** trovare da ridire su; **it's your ~** è colpa tua ● *vt*
criticare

**fault-finding** /'fɔːltfaɪndɪŋ/ *n* ⟨*of person*⟩ atteggiamento *m* ipercritico; *Techn* localizzazione *f* del guasto ● *a* ⟨*attitude*⟩ da criticone;
⟨*person*⟩ ipercritico

**faultless** /'fɔːltlɪs/ *a* impeccabile

**faultlessly** /'fɔːltlɪslɪ/ *adv* impeccabilmente

**faulty** /'fɔːltɪ/ *a* difettoso

**fauna** /'fɔːnə/ *n* fauna *f*

**faux pas** /fəʊ'pɑː/ *n* gaffe *f inv*

**favour** /'feɪvə(r)/ *n* favore *m*; **be in ~ of sth**
essere a favore di qcsa; **do sb a ~** fare un piacere a qcno ● *vt* (*prefer*) preferire

**favourable** /'feɪv(ə)rəbl/ *a* favorevole

**favourably** /'feɪv(ə)rəblɪ/ *adv* favorevolmente

**favourite** /'feɪv(ə)rɪt/ *a* preferito ● *n* preferito, -a *mf*; *Sport* favorito, -a *mf*

**favouritism** /'feɪv(ə)rɪtɪzm/ *n* favoritismo *m*

**fawn** /fɔːn/ *a* fulvo ● *n* ⟨*animal*⟩ cerbiatto *m*

**fax** /fæks/ *n* (*document, machine*) fax *m inv*;
**by ~** per fax ● *vt* faxare

**fax machine** *n* fax *m inv*

**fax-modem** *n* fax-modem *m inv*

**faze** /feɪz/ *vt fam* scompaginare

**fear** /fɪə(r)/ *n* paura *f*; **no ~!** *fam* vai tranquillo! ● *vt* temere ● *vi* ~ **for sth** temere per qcsa

**fearful** /'fɪəfl/ *a* pauroso; ⟨*awful*⟩ terribile

**fearless** /'fɪəlɪs/ *a* impavido

**fearlessly** /'fɪəlɪslɪ/ *adv* senza paura

**fearsome** /'fɪəsəm/ *a* spaventoso

**feasibility** /fiːzɪ'bɪlətɪ/ *n* praticabilità *f*

**feasible** /'fiːzəbl/ *a* fattibile; (*possible*) probabile

**feast** /fiːst/ *n* festa *f*; (*banquet*) banchetto *m*
● *vi* banchettare
■ **feast on** *vt* godersi

**feat** /fiːt/ *n* impresa *f*

**feather** /'feðə(r)/ *n* piuma *f*; **you could have
knocked me down with a ~** sono rimasto
di sasso

**feather: feather-brained** /-breɪnd/ *a* che
non ha un briciolo di cervello. **feather
duster** *n* piumino *m* (*per spolverare*). **featherweight** *n* peso *m* piuma *inv*

**feature** /'fiːtʃə(r)/ *n* (*quality*) caratteristica *f*;
*Journ* articolo *m*; ~**s** *pl* (*of face*) lineamenti
*mpl* ● *vt* ⟨*film:*⟩ avere come protagonista ● *vi*
(*on a list etc*) comparire

**feature film** *n* lungometraggio *m*

**feature length film** *n* lungometraggio *m*

**February** /'februərɪ/ *n* febbraio *m*

**feces** /'fiːsiːz/ *npl* feci *fpl*

**feckless** /'feklɪs/ *a* inetto

**fecund** /'fekənd/ *a* fecondo

**fed** /fed/ *see* **feed** ● *a* **be ~ up** *fam* essere stufo (**with** di)

**federal** /'fed(ə)rəl/ *a* federale

**federalist** /'fed(ə)rəlɪst/ *n & a* federalista *mf*

**Federal Republic of Germany** *n* Repubblica *f* Federale Tedesca

**federate** /'fed(ə)rət/ *a* federato

**federation** /fedə'reɪʃn/ *n* federazione *f*

**fee** /fiː/ *n* tariffa *f*; (*lawyer's, doctor's*) onorario *m*; (*for membership, school*) quota *f*

**feeble** /'fiːbl/ *a* debole; ⟨*excuse*⟩ fiacco

**feeble minded** /-'maɪndɪd/ *a* deficiente

**feebleness** /'fiːblnɪs/ *n* debolezza *f*

**feed** /fiːd/ *n* mangiare *m*; (*for baby*) pappa *f*;
**five ~s a day** cinque pasti al giorno ● *v* (*pt/pp* **fed**) ● *vt* dar da mangiare a ⟨*animal*⟩;
(*support*) nutrire; ~ **sth into sth** inserire
qcsa in qcsa; ~ **paper into the printer** alimentare la stampante con fogli ● *vi* mangiare
■ **feed up** *vt* ingrassare ⟨*sb*⟩

**feedback** /'fiːdbæk/ *n* controreazione *f*; (*of
information*) reazione *f*, feedback *m*

**feeder** /'fiːdə(r)/ *n* (*for printer, photocopier*)
mettifoglio *m inv*; (*Br: bib*) bavaglino *m*;
(*road*) raccordo *m*

**feeding bottle** /'fiːdɪŋ/ *n Br* biberon *m inv*

**feeding time** *n* (*in zoo*) l'ora *f* del pasto degli animali

**feel** /fiːl/ *v* (*pt/pp* **felt**) ● *vt* sentire;
(*experience*) provare; (*think*) pensare; (*touch:*

*searching*) tastare; (*touch: for texture*) toccare ● *vi* ~ **soft/hard** essere duro/morbido al tatto; ~ **hot/hungry** aver caldo/fame; ~ **ill** sentirsi male; **I don't** ~ **like it** non ne ho voglia; **how do you** ~ **about it?** (*opinion*) che te ne pare?; **it doesn't** ~ **right** non mi sembra giusto
■ **feel for** *vt* (*feel sympathy for*) dispiacersi per
■ **feel up to** *vt* ~ **up to doing sth** sentirsi in grado di fare qcsa; **I don't** ~ **up to it** non me la sento
**feeler** /'fi:lə(r)/ *n* (*of animal*) antenna *f*; **put out** ~**s** *fig* tastare il terreno
**feel-good factor** *n* sensazione *f* di benessere
**feeling** /'fi:lɪŋ/ *n* sentimento *m*; (*awareness*) sensazione *f*
**fee paying** *a* (*school*) a pagamento, privato; (*parent, pupil*) che paga l'iscrizione (*a una scuola privata*)
**feet** /fi:t/ *see* **foot**
**feign** /feɪn/ *vt* simulare
**feint** /feɪnt/ *n* finta *f*
**feisty** /'faɪstɪ/ *a Am* (*quarrelsome*) stizzoso; (*fam: lively*) esuberante
**felicitous** /fə'lɪsɪtəs/ *a* felice
**feline** /'fi:laɪn/ *a* felino
**fell¹** /fel/ *vt* (*knock down*) abbattere
**fell²** *see* **fall**
**fellow** /'feləʊ/ *n* (*of society*) socio *m*; (*fam: man*) tipo *m*
**fellow: fellow citizen** *n* concittadino, -a *mf*. **fellow countryman** *n* compatriota *m*. **fellow men** *npl* prossimi *mpl*
**fellowship** /'feləʊʃɪp/ *n* cameratismo *m*; (*group*) associazione *f*; *Univ* incarico *m* di ricercatore, -trice *mf*
**fellow traveller** *n* compagno, -a *mf* di viaggio; *Pol, fig* compagno, -a *mf* di strada
**felon** /'felən/ *n Jur* criminale *mf*
**felony** /'felənɪ/ *n* delitto *m*
**felt¹** /felt/ *see* **feel**
**felt²** *n* feltro *m*. ~**[-tipped] pen** /-tɪpt'pen/ pennarello *m*
**female** /'fi:meɪl/ *a* femminile; **the** ~ **antelope** l'antilope femmina ● *n* femmina *f*
**feminine** /'femɪnɪn/ *a* femminile ● *n Gram* femminile *m*
**femininity** /femɪ'nɪnətɪ/ *n* femminilità *f*
**feminist** /'femɪnɪst/ *a & n* femminista *mf*
**fen** /fen/ *n* zona *f* paludosa
**fence** /fens/ *n* recinto *m*; (*fam: person*) ricettatore *m* ● *vi Sport* tirar di scherma
■ **fence in** *vt* chiudere in un recinto
**fencer** /'fensə(r)/ *n* schermidore *m*
**fencing** /'fensɪŋ/ *n* steccato *m*; *Sport* scherma *f*
**fend** /fend/ *vi* ~ **for oneself** badare a se stesso
■ **fend off** *vt* parare; difendersi da (*criticisms*)
**fender** /'fendə(r)/ *n* parafuoco *m inv*; *Naut* parabordo *m*; (*Am: on car*) parafango *m*
**fennel** /'fenl/ *n* finocchio *m*

**ferment¹** /'fɜ:ment/ *n* fermento *m*
**ferment²** /fə'ment/ *vi* fermentare ● *vt* far fermentare
**fermentation** /fɜ:men'teɪʃn/ *n* fermentazione *f*
**fern** /fɜ:n/ *n* felce *f*
**ferocious** /fə'rəʊʃəs/ *a* feroce
**ferocity** /fə'rɒsətɪ/ *n* ferocia *f*
**ferret** /'ferɪt/ *n* furetto *m*
■ **ferret out** *vt* scovare
**ferrous** /'ferəs/ *a* ferroso
**ferry** /'ferɪ/ *n* traghetto *m* ● *vt* (*pt/pp* -**ied**) traghettare
**ferryman** /'ferɪmən/ *n* traghettatore *m*
**fertile** /'fɜ:taɪl/ *a* fertile
**fertility** /fɜ:'tɪlətɪ/ *n* fertilità *f*
**fertility drug** *n* farmaco *m* contro la sterilità
**fertilize** /'fɜ:tɪlaɪz/ *vt* fertilizzare (*land, ovum*)
**fertilizer** /'fɜ:tɪlaɪzə(r)/ *n* fertilizzante *m*
**fervent** /'fɜ:vənt/ *a* fervente
**fervour** /'fɜ:və(r)/ *n* fervore *m*
**fester** /'festə(r)/ *vi* suppurare
**festival** /'festɪvl/ *n Mus, Theat* festival *m*; *Relig* festa *f*
**festive** /'festɪv/ *a* festivo; ~ **season** periodo *m* delle feste natalizie
**festivities** /fe'stɪvətɪz/ *npl* festeggiamenti *mpl*
**festoon** /fe'stu:n/ *vt* ~ **with** ornare di
**fetch** /fetʃ/ *vt* andare/venire a prendere; (*be sold for*) raggiungere [il prezzo di]
**fetching** /'fetʃɪŋ/ *a* attraente
**fête** /feɪt/ *n* festa *f* ● *vt* festeggiare
**fetid** /'fetɪd/ *a* fetido
**fetish** /'fetɪʃ/ *n* feticcio *m*
**fetter** /'fetə(r)/ *vt* incatenare
**fettle** /'fetl/ *n* **in fine** ~ in buona forma
**fetus** /'fi:təs/ *n* (*pl* -**tuses**) feto *m*
**feud** /fju:d/ *n* faida *f*
**feudal** /'fju:dl/ *a* feudale
**fever** /'fi:və(r)/ *n* febbre *f*
**fevered** /'fi:vəd/ *a* (*brow*) febbricitante; (*imagination*) febbrile
**feverish** /'fi:vərɪʃ/ *a* febbricitante; *fig* febbrile
**fever pitch** *n* **bring a crowd to** ~ ~ esaltare la folla
**few** /fju:/ *a* pochi; **every** ~ **days** ogni due o tre giorni; **a** ~ **people** alcuni; ~ **people know that** poche persone lo sanno; ~**er reservations** meno prenotazioni; **the** ~**est number** il numero più basso ● *pron* pochi; ~ **of us** pochi di noi; **a** ~ alcuni; **quite a** ~ parecchi; ~**er than last year** meno dell'anno scorso
**fez** /fez/ *n* fez *m inv*
**fiancé** /fɪ'ɒnseɪ/ *n* fidanzato *m*
**fiancée** /fɪ'ɒnseɪ/ *n* fidanzata *f*
**fiasco** /fɪ'æskəʊ/ *n* fiasco *m*
**fib** /fɪb/ *n* storia *f*; **tell a** ~ raccontare una storia
**fibber** /'fɪbə(r)/ *n fam* contaballe *mf inv*
**fibre** /'faɪbə(r)/ *n* fibra *f*

**fibre: fibreglass** *n* fibra *f* di vetro ● *attrib* in fibra di vetro. **fibre optic** *a* ⟨*cable*⟩ a fibre ottiche. **fibre optics** *n* fibra *f* ottica

**fibroid** /'faɪbrɔɪd/ *n* fibroma *m* ● *a* fibroso

**fibula** /'fɪbjʊlə/ *n Anat* perone *m*

**fiche** /fiːʃ/ *n* microscheda *f*

**fickle** /'fɪkl/ *a* incostante

**fiction** /'fɪkʃn/ *n* [**works of**] ~ narrativa *f*; (*fabrication*) finzione *f*

**fictional** /'fɪkʃənəl/ *a* immaginario

**fictitious** /fɪk'tɪʃəs/ *a* fittizio

**fiddle** /'fɪdl/ *n fam* violino *m*; (*cheating*) imbroglio *m* ● *vi* gingillarsi (**with** con) ● *vt fam* truccare ⟨*accounts*⟩

**fiddly** /'fɪdlɪ/ *a* intricato

**fidelity** /fɪ'delətɪ/ *n* fedeltà *f*

**fidget** /'fɪdʒɪt/ *vi* agitarsi

**fidgety** /'fɪdʒətɪ/ *a* agitato

**field** /fiːld/ *n* campo *m*

**field day** *n* have a ~ ~ ⟨*press, critics:*⟩ godersela; (*make money*) fare affari d'oro

**fielder** /'fiːldə(r)/ *n Sport* esterno *m*

**field: field events** *npl* atletica *fsg* leggera. **field glasses** *npl* binocolo *msg*. **Field Marshal** *n* feldmaresciallo *m*. **field mouse** *n* topo *m* campagnolo. **fieldwork** *n* ricerche *fpl* sul terreno

**fiend** /fiːnd/ *n* demonio *m*

**fiendish** /'fiːndɪʃ/ *a* diabolico

**fierce** /fɪəs/ *a* feroce

**fiercely** /'fɪəslɪ/ *adv* ferocemente

**fierceness** /'fɪəsnɪs/ *n* ferocia *f*

**fiery** /'faɪərɪ/ *a* (**-ier, -iest**) focoso

**fiesta** /fɪ'estə/ *n* sagra *f*

**fife** /faɪf/ *n* piffero *m*

**fifteen** /fɪf'tiːn/ *a & n* quindici *m*

**fifteenth** /fɪf'tiːnθ/ *a & n* quindicesimo, -a *mf*

**fifth** /fɪfθ/ *a & n* quinto, -a *mf*

**fiftieth** /'fɪftɪɪθ/ *a & n* cinquantesimo, -a *mf*

**fifty** /'fɪftɪ/ *a & n* cinquanta *m*

**fifty-fifty** *a* have a ~ **chance** avere una probabilità su due ● *adv* go ~ fare [a] metà e metà; **split sth** ~ dividersi qcsa a metà

**fig** /fɪg/ *n* fico *m*

**fight** /faɪt/ *n* lotta *f*; (*brawl*) zuffa *f*; (*argument*) litigio *m*; (*boxing*) incontro *m* ● *v* (*pt/pp* **fought**) ● *vt also fig* combattere ● *vi* combattere; (*brawl*) azzuffarsi; (*argue*) litigare

■ **fight back** *vi* reagire ● *vt* frenare ⟨*tears*⟩

■ **fight for** *vt* lottare per ⟨*freedom, independence*⟩

■ **fight off** *vt* combattere ⟨*cold*⟩

**fighter** /'faɪtə(r)/ *n* combattente *mf*; *Aeron* caccia *m inv*; **he's a** ~ ha uno spirito combattivo

**fighter-bomber** *n* cacciabombardiere *m*

**fighter pilot** *n* pilota *m* di cacciabombardiere

**fighting** /'faɪtɪŋ/ *n* combattimento *m*

**fighting chance** *n* have a ~ ~ avere buone probabilità

**fighting fit** *a* in piena forma

**figment** /'fɪgmənt/ *n* **it's a** ~ **of your**

**imagination** questo è tutta una tua invenzione

**fig tree** *n* fico *m*

**figurative** /'fɪɡərətɪv/ *a* ⟨*sense*⟩ figurato; ⟨*art*⟩ figurativo

**figuratively** /'fɪɡərətɪvlɪ/ *adv* ⟨*use*⟩ in senso figurato

**figure** /'fɪɡə(r)/ *n* (*digit*) cifra *f*; (*carving, sculpture, illustration, form*) figura *f*; (*body shape*) linea *f*; ~ **of speech** modo *m* di dire ● *vi* (*appear*) figurare ● *vt* (*Am: think*) pensare

■ **figure out** *vt* dedurre; capire ⟨*person*⟩

**figure: figurehead** *n* figura *f* simbolica. **figure of speech** *n* modo *m* di dire; (*literary device*) figura *f* retorica. **figure skating** *n* pattinaggio *m* artistico

**figurine** /'fɪɡəriːn/ *n* statuetta *f*

**filament** /'fɪləmənt/ *n* filamento *m*

**filch** /fɪltʃ/ *vt fam* rubacchiare

**file**[1] /faɪl/ *n* scheda *f*; (*set of documents*) incartamento *m*; (*folder*) cartellina *f*; *Comput* file *m inv* ● *vt* archiviare ⟨*documents*⟩

**file**[2] *n* (*line*) fila *f*; **in single** ~ in fila

**file**[3] *n Techn* lima *f* ● *vt* limare

**file manager** *n Comput* file manager *m inv*

**filial** /'fɪlɪəl/ *a* filiale

**filibuster** /'fɪlɪbʌstə(r)/ *n* ostruzionismo *m* parlamentare

**filigree** /'fɪlɪgriː/ *n* filigrana *f*

**filing** /'faɪlɪŋ/ *n* archiviazione *f*

**filing: filing cabinet** *n* schedario *m*, classificatore *m*. **filing card** *n* scheda *f*. **filing clerk** *n* archivista *mf*

**filings** /'faɪlɪŋz/ *npl* limatura *fsg*

**filing system** *n* sistema *m* di classificazione, sistema *m* di archivio

**fill** /fɪl/ *n* eat one's ~ mangiare a sazietà ● *vt* riempire; otturare ⟨*tooth*⟩ ● *vi* riempirsi

■ **fill in** *vt* compilare ⟨*form*⟩

■ **fill in for** *vt* rimpiazzare ⟨*sb*⟩

■ **fill in on** *vt* ~ sb in on sth mettere qcno al corrente di qcsa

■ **fill out** *vt* compilare ⟨*form*⟩

■ **fill up** *vi* ⟨*room, tank:*⟩ riempirsi; *Auto* far il pieno ● *vt* riempire

**fillet** /'fɪlɪt/ *n* filetto *m* ● *vt* (*pt/pp* **filleted**) disossare

**fillet steak** *n* bistecca *f* di filetto

**fill in** *n* (*fam: replacement*) rimpiazzo *m*

**filling** /'fɪlɪŋ/ *n Culin* ripieno *m*; (*of tooth*) piombatura *f*

**filling station** *n* stazione *f* di rifornimento

**filly** /'fɪlɪ/ *n* puledra *f*

**film** /fɪlm/ *n Cinema* film *m inv*; *Phot* pellicola *f*; [**cling**] ~ pellicola *f* per alimenti ● *vt/i* filmare

**film: film-goer** /'fɪlmɡəʊə(r)/ *n* frequentatore, -trice *mf* di cinema. **film industry** *n* industria *f* cinematografica. **filmset** *n* allestimento *m* scenico. **film star** *n* star *f inv*, divo, -a *mf*

**filmy** /'fɪlmɪ/ *a* (*thin: fabric, screen*) trasparente; (*thin*) sottilissimo

**filter** /'fɪltə(r)/ *n* filtro *m* ● *vt* filtrare

■ **filter through** *vi* ⟨*news:*⟩ trapelare

**filter: filter cigarette** *n* sigaretta *f* con filtro. **filter coffee** *n* (*ground coffee*) caffè *m* macinato per filtro; (*cup of coffee*) caffè *m inv* fatto con il filtro. **filter-paper** *n* carta *f* da filtro. **filter tip** *n* filtro *m*; (*cigarette*) sigaretta *f* col filtro

**filth** /fɪlθ/ *n* sudiciume *m*

**filthy** /'fɪlθɪ/ *a* (-ier, -iest) sudicio; (*language*) sconcio

**filthy rich** *a fam* ricco sfondato

**fin** /fɪn/ *n* pinna *f*

**final** /'faɪnl/ *a* finale; (*conclusive*) decisivo ● *n Sport* finale *f*; ~s *pl Univ* esami *mpl* finali

**finale** /fɪ'nɑːlɪ/ *n* finale *m*

**finalist** /'faɪnəlɪst/ *n* finalista *mf*

**finality** /faɪ'nælətɪ/ *n* finalità *f*

**finalize** /'faɪnəlaɪz/ *vt* mettere a punto (*text*); definire (*agreement*)

**finally** /'faɪnəlɪ/ *adv* (*at last*) finalmente; (*at the end*) alla fine; (*to conclude*) per finire

**finance** /'faɪnæns/ *n* finanza *f* ● *vt* finanziare

**finance director** *n* direttore, -trice *mf* finanziario, -a

**finance company, finance house** *n* società *f* finanziaria

**financial** /faɪ'nænʃl/ *a* finanziario

**financially** /faɪ'nænʃəlɪ/ *adv* finanziariamente

**financial year** *n Br* esercizio *m* [finanziario]

**finch** /fɪntʃ/ *n* fringuello *m*

**find** /faɪnd/ *n* scoperta *f* ● *vt* (*pt/pp* found) trovare; (*establish*) scoprire; ~ **sb guilty** *Jur* dichiarare qcno colpevole

■ **find out** *vt* scoprire ● *vi* (*enquire*) informarsi

**findings** /'faɪndɪŋz/ *npl* conclusioni *fpl*

**fine¹** /faɪn/ *n* (*penalty*) multa *f* ● *vt* multare

**fine²** *a* bello; (*slender*) fine; **he's ~** (*in health*) sta bene ● *adv* bene; **that's cutting it ~** non ci lascia molto tempo. ● *int* [va] bene

**fine arts** *npl* belle arti *fpl*

**finely** /'faɪnlɪ/ *adv* (*cut*) finemente

**finery** /'faɪnərɪ/ *n* splendore *m*

**finesse** /fɪ'nes/ *n* finezza *f*

**fine-tooth[ed] comb** /-tuː'θ[t]/ *n* **go over sth with a ~ ~** passare qcsa al setaccio

**fine-tune** *vt* mettere a punto

**fine tuning** *n* messa *f* a punto

**finger** /'fɪŋgə(r)/ *n* dito *m* (*pl* dita *f*) ● *vt* tastare

**finger: finger bowl** *n* lavadita *m inv*. **finger hole** *n Mus* foro *m*. **fingermark** *n* ditata *f*. **fingernail** *n* unghia *f*. **finger-paint** *vi* dipingere con le dita. **fingerprint** *n* impronta *f* digitale. **fingertip** *n* punta *f* del dito; **have sth at one's ~s** sapere qcsa a menadito; (*close at hand*) avere qcsa a portata di mano

**finicky** /'fɪnɪkɪ/ *a* (*person*) pignolo; (*task*) intricato

**finish** /'fɪnɪʃ/ *n* fine *f*; (*finishing line*) traguardo *m*; (*of product*) finitura *f*; **have a good ~** (*runner:*) avere un buon finale ● *vt* finire; ~ **reading** finire di leggere ● *vi* finire

■ **finish off** *vt* finire (*sth*); (*fam: exhaust*) sfinire

■ **finish with** *vt* (*no longer be using*) finire (*di adoperare*); (*end relationship with*) lasciare

■ **finish up** *vt* finire (*drink, meal*)

**finishing line** /'fɪnɪʃɪŋlaɪn/ *n* traguardo *m*

**finishing touches** /'tʌtʃɪz/ *npl* ritocchi *mpl*

**finite** /'faɪnaɪt/ *a* limitato

**Finland** /'fɪnlənd/ *n* Finlandia *f*

**Finn** /fɪn/ *n* finlandese *mf*

**Finnish** /'fɪnɪʃ/ *a* finlandese ● *n* (*language*) finnico *m*

**fiord** /fjɔːd/ *n* fiordo *m*

**fir** /fɜː(r)/ *n* abete *m*

**fir cone** *n* pigna *f* (*di abete*)

**fire** /'faɪə(r)/ *n* fuoco *m*; (*forest, house*) incendio *m*; **be on ~** bruciare; **catch ~** prendere fuoco; **set ~ to** dar fuoco a; **under ~** sotto il fuoco ● *vt* cuocere (*pottery*); sparare (*shot*); tirare (*gun*); (*fam: dismiss*) buttar fuori ● *vi* sparare (**at** a)

**fire: fire alarm** *n* allarme *m* antincendio *inv*. **firearm** *n* arma *f* da fuoco. **fire brigade** *n* vigili *mpl* del fuoco. **fire door** *n* porta *f* antincendio. **fire drill** *n* esercitazione *f* per l'evacuazione in caso di incendio. **fire engine** *n* autopompa *f*. **fire escape** *n* uscita *f* di sicurezza. **fire extinguisher** *n* estintore *m*. **fireman** *n* pompiere *m*, vigile *m* del fuoco. **fireplace** *n* caminetto *m*. **fireside** *n* **by** or **at the ~** accanto al fuoco. **fire station** *n* caserma *f* dei pompieri. **firewood** *n* legna *f* (*da ardere*). **firework** *n* fuoco *m* d'artificio; ~s *pl* (*display*) fuochi *mpl* d'artificio

**firing squad** /'faɪərɪŋ/ *n* plotone *m* d'esecuzione

**firm¹** /fɜːm/ *n* ditta *f*, azienda *f*

**firm²** *a* fermo; (*soil*) compatto; (*stable, properly fixed*) solido; (*resolute*) risoluto

**firmly** /'fɜːmlɪ/ *adv* (*hold*) stretto; (*say*) con fermezza

**first** /fɜːst/ *a & n* primo, -a *mf*; **at ~** all'inizio; **who's ~?** chi è il primo?; **from the ~** [fin] dall'inizio ● *adv* (*arrive, leave*) per primo; (*beforehand*) prima; (*in listing*) prima di tutto, innanzitutto

**first: first aid** *n* pronto soccorso *m*. **first-aid kit** *n* cassetta *f* di pronto soccorso. **first-class** *a* di prim'ordine; *Rail* di prima classe ● *adv* (*travel*) in prima classe. **first edition** *n* prima edizione *f*. **first floor** *n* primo piano *m*; (*Am: ground floor*) pianterreno *m*

**firstly** /'fɜːstlɪ/ *adv* in primo luogo

**first: first name** *n* nome *m* di battesimo. **first night** *n Theat* prima *f*. **first-rate** *a* ottimo. **first time buyer** *n* acquirente *mf* della prima casa

**firth** /fɜːθ/ *n* foce *f*

**fiscal** /'fɪskəl/ *a* fiscale

**fiscal year** *n Am* esercizio *m* finanziario

**fish** /fɪʃ/ *n* pesce *m* ● *vt/i* pescare

■ **fish out** *vt* tirar fuori

**fishbone** /'fɪʃbəʊn/ *n* lisca *f*

**fishmonger** /'fɪʃmʌŋgə(r)/ n pescivendolo m

**fisherman** /'fɪʃəmən/ n pescatore m

**fish farm** n vivaio m

**fish finger** n bastoncino m di pesce

**fishing** /'fɪʃɪŋ/ n pesca f

**fishing boat** n peschereccio m

**fishing rod** n canna f da pesca

**fishnet** /'fɪʃnet/ a ‹stockings› a rete

**fish slice** n paletta f per fritti

**fishy** /'fɪʃɪ/ a (fam: suspicious) sospetto

**fission** /'fɪʃn/ n Phys fissione f

**fist** /fɪst/ n pugno m

**fistful** /'fɪstfʊl/ n manciata f, pugno m

**fit¹** /fɪt/ n (attack) attacco m; (of rage) accesso m; (of generosity) slancio m

**fit²** a (**fitter**, **fittest**) (suitable) adatto; (healthy) in buona salute; Sport in forma; **be ~ to do sth** essere in grado di fare qcsa; **~ to eat** buono da mangiare; **keep ~** tenersi in forma; **do as you see ~** fai come ritieni meglio

**fit³** n (of clothes) taglio m; **it's a good ~** ‹coat etc:› ti/le sta bene ● v (pt/pp **fitted**) ● vi (be the right size) andare bene; **it won't ~** (no room) non ci sta ● vt (fix) applicare (**to** a); (install) installare; **it doesn't ~ me** ‹coat etc:› non mi va bene; **~ with** fornire di

■ **fit in** vi ‹person:› adattarsi; **it won't ~ in** (no room) non ci sta ● vt (in schedule, vehicle) trovare un buco per

**fitful** /'fɪtfl/ a irregolare

**fitfully** /'fɪtfʊlɪ/ adv ‹sleep› a sprazzi

**fitment** /'fɪtmənt/ n ~s (in house) impianti mpl fissi

**fitness** /'fɪtnɪs/ n (suitability) capacità f; [physical] ~ forma f, fitness m

**fitted: fitted carpet** n moquette f inv. **fitted cupboard** n armadio m a muro; (smaller) armadietto m a muro. **fitted kitchen** n cucina f componibile. **fitted sheet** n lenzuolo m con angoli

**fitter** /'fɪtə(r)/ n installatore, -trice mf

**fitting** /'fɪtɪŋ/ a appropriato ● n (of clothes) prova f; Techn montaggio m; ~s pl accessori mpl

**fitting room** n camerino m

**five** /faɪv/ a & n cinque m

**five-a-side** n Br (football) partita f di calcio con cinque giocatori per squadra

**fiver** /'faɪvə(r)/ n fam biglietto m da cinque sterline

**fix** /fɪks/ n (sl: drugs) pera f; **be in a ~** fam essere nei guai ● vt fissare; (repair) aggiustare; preparare ‹meal›

■ **fix up** vt fissare ‹meeting›

**fixation** /fɪk'seɪʃn/ n fissazione f

**fixative** /'fɪksətɪv/ n fissativo m

**fixed** /'fɪkst/ a fisso

**fixed assets** npl attività fpl fisse, immobilizzazioni fpl

**fixed price** n prezzo m a forfait

**fixer** /'fɪksə(r)/ n Phot fissatore m; (fam: person) trafficone, -a mf

**fixture** /'fɪkstʃə(r)/ n Sport incontro m; ~**s and fittings** impianti mpl fissi

**fizz** /fɪz/ vi frizzare

**fizzle** /'fɪzl/ vi ~ **out** finire in nulla

**fizzy** /'fɪzɪ/ a gassoso

**fizzy drink** n bibita f gassata

**fjord** /fjɔːd/ n fiordo m

**flab** /flæb/ n fam ciccia f cascante

**flabbergasted** /'flæbəgɑːstɪd/ a **be ~** rimanere a bocca aperta

**flabby** /'flæbɪ/ a floscio

**flag¹** /flæg/ n bandiera f

**flag²** vi (pt/pp **flagged**) cedere

■ **flag down** vt (pt/pp **flagged**) far segno di fermarsi a ‹taxi›

**flagellation** /flædʒəˈleɪʃn/ n flagellazione f

**flagon** /'flægən/ n bottiglione m

**flagpole** /'flægpəʊl/ n asta f della bandiera

**flagrant** /'fleɪgrənt/ a flagrante

**flagship** /'flægʃɪp/ n Naut nave f ammiraglia; fig fiore m all'occhiello

**flagstone** /'flægstəʊn/ n pietra f da lastricare

**flail** /fleɪl/ n (for threshing corn etc) correggiato m ● vt battere ‹corn›

■ **flail about, flail around** vi ‹arms, legs:› agitare

**flair** /fleə(r)/ n (skill) talento m; (style) stile m

**flak** /flæk/ n Mil artiglieria f antiaerea; (fig fam: criticism) valanga f di critiche; **take a lot of ~** subire molte critiche

**flake** /fleɪk/ n fiocco m ● vi ~ [off] cadere in fiocchi

**flaky** /'fleɪkɪ/ a a scaglie

**flaky pastry** n pasta f sfoglia

**flamboyant** /flæm'bɔɪənt/ a ‹personality› brillante; ‹tie› sgargiante

**flame** /fleɪm/ n fiamma f

**flamenco** /flə'meŋkəʊ/ n flamenco m

**flame retardant** /rɪtɑːdənt/ a ‹substance, chemical› ignifugo; ‹furniture, fabric› ignifugato

**flame-thrower** /-θrəʊə(r)/ n Mil lanciafiamme m inv

**flamingo** /flə'mɪŋgəʊ/ n fenicottero m

**flammable** /'flæməbl/ a infiammabile

**flan** /flæn/ n [fruit] ~ crostata f

**flange** /flændʒ/ n (on pipe etc) flangia f

**flank** /flæŋk/ n fianco m ● vt fiancheggiare

**flannel** /'flæn(ə)l/ n flanella f; (for washing) ≈ guanto m di spugna

**flannelette** /flænə'let/ n flanella f di cotone

**flannels** /'flæn(ə)lz/ npl (trousers) pantaloni mpl di flanella

**flap** /flæp/ n (of pocket, envelope) risvolto m; (of table) ribalta f; **in a ~** fam in grande agitazione ● v (pt/pp **flapped**) ● vi sbattere; fam agitarsi ● vt ~ **its wings** battere le ali

**flapjack** /'flæpdʒæk/ n Br dolcetto m di fiocchi d'avena; Am frittella f

**flare** /fleə(r)/ n fiammata f; (device) razzo m

■ **flare up** vi ‹rash:› venire fuori; ‹fire:› fare una fiammata; ‹person, situation:› esplodere

**flared** /fleəd/ a ‹garment› svasato

**flash** /flæʃ/ n lampo m; **in a ~** fam in un attimo ● *vi* lampeggiare; ~ **past** passare come un bolide ● *vt* lanciare ‹*smile*›; ~ **one's headlights** lampeggiare; ~ **a torch at** puntare una torcia su

**flash: flashback** *n* scena *f* retrospettiva.
**flashbulb** *n Phot* flash *m inv*. **flashcard** *n Sch* scheda *f* didattica

**flasher** /'flæʃə(r)/ *n Auto* lampeggiatore *m*

**flash: flash flood** *n* alluvione *f* improvvisa. **flashgun** *n Phot* flash *m inv*. **flashlight** *n Phot* flash *m inv*; (*Am: torch*) torcia *f* [elettrica]. **flashpoint** *n* (*trouble spot*) punto *m* caldo; *Chem* punto *m* di infiammabilità

**flashy** /'flæʃɪ/ *a* vistoso

**flask** /flɑːsk/ *n* fiasco *m*; (*vacuum ~*) termos *m inv*

**flat** /flæt/ *a* (**flatter**, **flattest**) piatto; ‹*refusal*› reciso; ‹*beer*› sgassato; ‹*battery*› scarico; ‹*tyre*› a terra; **A ~** *Mus* la bemolle ● *n* appartamento *m*; *Mus* bemolle *m*; (*puncture*) gomma *f* a terra

**flat: flat broke** *a fam* completamente al verde. **flat feet** *npl* piedi *mpl* piatti. **flatfish** *n* pesce *m* piatto. **flat-footed** *a* **be ~** avere i piedi piatti. **flat hunting** *n Br* **go ~ ~** andare in cerca di un appartamento

**flatly** /'flætlɪ/ *adv* ‹*refuse*› categoricamente

**flat: flatmate** *n Br* persona *f* con cui si divide *un appartamento*. **flat out** *adv* ‹*drive, work*› a tutto gas; **it only does 120 kph ~ ~** arriva a 120 km all'ora andando a tutta manetta; **go ~ ~ for sth** mettercela tutta per fare qcsa. **flat racing** *n* corse *fpl* piane. **flat rate** *n* forfait *m inv*; (*unitary rate*) tariffa *f* unica ● *attrib* ‹*fee, tax*› forfettario. **flat spin** *n Aeron* virata *f* piatta; **be in a ~ ~** *fam* essere in fibrillazione

**flatten** /'flætn/ *vt* appiattire

**flatter** /'flætə(r)/ *vt* adulare

**flattering** /'flætərɪŋ/ *a* ‹*comments*› lusinghiero; ‹*colour, dress*› che fa sembrare più bello

**flattery** /'flætərɪ/ *n* adulazione *f*

**flat tyre** *n* gomma *f* a terra

**flatulence** /'flætjʊləns/ *n* flatulenza *f*

**flaunt** /flɔːnt/ *vt* ostentare

**flautist** /'flɔːtɪst/ *n* flautista *mf*

**flavour** /'fleɪvə(r)/ *n* sapore *m* ● *vt* condire; **chocolate ~ed** al sapore di cioccolato

**flavour-enhancer** /-ɪnhɑːnsə(r)/ *n* esaltatore *m* dell'aroma

**flavouring** /'fleɪvərɪŋ/ *n* condimento *m*

**flavourless** /'fleɪvəlɪs/ *a* insipido

**flaw** /flɔː/ *n* difetto *m*

**flawless** /'flɔːlɪs/ *a* perfetto

**flax** /flæks/ *n* lino *m*

**flaxen** /'flæksən/ *a* ‹*hair*› biondo platino

**flea** /fliː/ *n* pulce *f*

**flea: flea-bitten** /'fliːbɪtən/ *a* infestato dalle pulci; *fig* pidocchioso. **flea market** *n* mercato *m* delle pulci. **fleapit** *n Br fam pej* pidocchietto *m*

**fleck** /flek/ *n* macchiolina *f*

**fled** /fled/ *see* **flee**

**fledg[e]ling** /'fledʒlɪŋ/ *n* uccellino *m* (*che ha*

appena messo le ali) ● *attrib fig* ‹*democracy, enterprise*› giovane; ‹*party, group*› alle prime armi

**flee** /fliː/ *vt/i* (*pt/pp* **fled**) fuggire (**from** da)

**fleece** /fliːs/ *n* pelliccia *f* ● *vt fam* spennare

**fleecy** /'fliːsɪ/ *a* ‹*lining*› felpato

**fleet** /fliːt/ *n* flotta *f*; (*of cars*) parco *m*

**fleeting** /'fliːtɪŋ/ *a* **catch a ~ glance of sth** intravedere qcsa; **for a ~ moment** per un attimo

**Flemish** /'flemɪʃ/ *a* fiammingo

**flesh** /fleʃ/ *n* carne *f*; **in the ~** in persona; **one's own ~ and blood** il proprio sangue ■ **flesh out** *vt* dare più consistenza a ‹*essay etc*›

**flesh eating** /-iːtɪŋ/ *a* carnivoro

**flesh wound** *n* ferita *f* superficiale

**fleshy** /'fleʃɪ/ *a* carnoso

**flew** /fluː/ *see* **fly**[2]

**flex**[1] /fleks/ *vt* flettere ‹*muscle*›

**flex**[2] *n Electr* filo *m*

**flexibility** /fleksə'bɪlətɪ/ *n* flessibilità *f*

**flexible** /'fleksəbl/ *a* flessibile

**flexitime** /'fleksɪtaɪm/ *n* orario *m* flessibile

**flick** /flɪk/ *vt* dare un buffetto a; ~ **sth off sth** togliere qcsa da qcsa con un colpetto ■ **flick through** *vt* sfogliare

**flicker** /'flɪkə(r)/ *vi* tremolare

**flick knife** *n Br* coltello *m* a scatto

**flier** /'flaɪə(r)/ *n* = **flyer**

**flight**[1] /flaɪt/ *n* ‹*fleeing*› fuga *f*; **take ~** darsi alla fuga

**flight**[2] *n* ‹*flying*› volo *m*; ~ **of stairs** rampa *f*

**flight: flight attendant** *n* assistente *mf* di volo. **flight bag** *n* bagaglio *m* a mano. **flight deck** *n Aeron* cabina *f* di pilotaggio; *Naut* ponte *m* di volo. **flight engineer** *n* motorista *mf* di bordo. **flight lieutenant** *n Mil* capitano *m*. **flight path** *n* traiettoria *f* di volo. **flight recorder** *n* registratore *m* di volo

**flighty** /'flaɪtɪ/ *a* (**-ier, -iest**) frivolo

**flimsy** /'flɪmzɪ/ *a* (**-ier, -iest**) ‹*material*› leggero; ‹*shelves*› poco robusto; ‹*excuse*› debole

**flinch** /flɪntʃ/ *vi* (*wince*) sussultare; (*draw back*) ritirarsi; ~ **from a task** *fig* sottrarsi a un compito

**fling** /flɪŋ/ *n* **have a ~** (*fam: affair*) aver un'avventura ● *vt* (*pt/pp* **flung**) gettare

**flint** /flɪnt/ *n* pietra *f* focaia; (*for lighter*) pietrina *f*

**flip** /flɪp/ *v* (*pt/pp* **flipped**) *vt* dare un colpetto a; buttare in aria ‹*coin*›. ● *vi fam* uscire dai gangheri; (*go mad*) impazzire ■ **flip through** *vt* sfogliare

**flip chart** *n* lavagna *f* a fogli mobili

**flip-flop** *n* (*sandal*) infradito *m inv*; (*Comput: device*) flip-flop *m inv*, multivibratore *m* bistabile; (*Am: about face*) voltafaccia *m inv*

**flippant** /'flɪpənt/ *a* irriverente

**flipper** /'flɪpə(r)/ *n* pinna *f*

**flipping** /'flɪpɪŋ/ *Br fam a* maledetto ● *adv* ‹*stupid, painful, cold*› maledettamente

**flip side** *n* (*of record*) retro *m*; (*fig: other side*) rovescio *m*

**flirt** /flɜːt/ *n* civetta *f* ● *vi* flirtare

**flirtation** /fləːˈteɪʃn/ n flirt m inv

**flirtatious** /fləːˈteɪʃəs/ a civettuolo

**flit** /flɪt/ vi (pt/pp **flitted**) volteggiare

**float** /fləʊt/ n galleggiante m; (in procession) carro m; (money) riserva f di cassa ● vi galleggiare; Fin fluttuare

**floating rate interest** /ˈfləʊtɪŋ/ n Fin interesse m a tasso variabile

**floating voter** n Pol elettore. -trice mf indeciso.-a

**flock** /flɒk/ n gregge m; (of birds) stormo m ● vi affollarsi

**floe** /fləʊ/ n banchisa f

**flog** /flɒg/ vt (pt/pp **flogged**) bastonare; (fam: sell) vendere

**flood** /flʌd/ n alluvione f; (of river) straripamento m; (fig: of replies, letters, tears) diluvio m; **be in ~** ⟨river:⟩ essere straripato ● vt allagare ● vi ⟨river:⟩ straripare

**flood: flood control** n prevenzione f delle inondazioni. **flood damage** n danno m provocato da un'inondazione. **floodgate** n chiusa f; **open the ~s** fig spalancare le porte. **floodlight** n riflettore m ● vt (pt/pp **floodlit**) illuminare con riflettori. **floodplain** n pianura f alluvionale. **flood tide** n marea f montante. **flood waters** npl acque fpl alluvionali

**floor** /flɔː(r)/ n pavimento m; (storey) piano m; (for dancing) pista f ● vt (baffle) confondere; (knock down) stendere ⟨person⟩

**floor: floorboard** n asse f del pavimento. **floorcloth** n straccio m per lavare il pavimento. **floor exercises** npl esercizi mpl a terra. **floor manager** n TV direttore, -trice mf di studio; Comm gerente mf di un negozio. **floor polish** n cera f per il pavimento. **floor show** n spettacolo m di varietà. **floor space** n superficie f; **we don't have the ~ ~** non abbiamo lo spazio

**flop** /flɒp/ n fam (failure) tonfo m; Theat fiasco m ● vi (pt/pp **flopped**) (fam: fail) far fiasco

■ **flop down** vi accasciarsi

**floppy** /ˈflɒpɪ/ a floscio

**floppy disk** n floppy disk m inv

**floppy [disk] drive** n lettore m di floppy

**flora** /ˈflɔːrə/ n flora f

**floral** /ˈflɔːrəl/ a floreale

**Florence** /ˈflɒrəns/ n Firenze f

**Florentine** /ˈflɒrəntaɪn/ a fiorentino

**florid** /ˈflɒrɪd/ a ⟨complexion⟩ florido; ⟨style⟩ troppo ricercato

**florist** /ˈflɒrɪst/ n fioriao, -a mf

**flotsam** /ˈflɒtsəm/ n relitti mpl alla deriva

**flounce** /flaʊns/ n balza f ● vi **~ out** uscire con aria melodrammatica

**flounder**[1] /ˈflaʊndə(r)/ vi dibattersi; ⟨speaker:⟩ impappinarsi

**flounder**[2] n (fish) passera f di mare

**flour** /ˈflaʊə(r)/ n farina f

**flourish** /ˈflʌrɪʃ/ n gesto m drammatico; ⟨scroll⟩ ghirigoro m ● vi prosperare ● vt brandire

**floury** /ˈflaʊərɪ/ a farinoso

**flout** /flaʊt/ vt fregarsene di ⟨rules⟩

**flow** /fləʊ/ n flusso m ● vi scorrere; (hang loosely) ricadere

**flow chart** n diagramma m di flusso

**flower** /ˈflaʊə(r)/ n fiore m ● vi fiorire

**flower arrangement** n composizione f floreale

**flower bed** n aiuola f

**flowered** /ˈflaʊəd/ a a fiori

**flower garden** n giardino m fiorito

**flowering** /ˈflaʊərɪŋ/ n Bot fioritura f; (fig: development) espansione f ● a ⟨shrub, tree⟩ in fiore; **early/late ~** a fioritura precoce/tardiva

**flower: flowerpot** n vaso m [per i fiori]. **flower shop** n fiorista m. **flower show** n mostra f floreale

**flowery** /ˈflaʊərɪ/ a fiorito

**flown** /fləʊn/ see **fly**[2]

**fl oz** abbr **fluid ounces**

**flu** /fluː/ n influenza f

**fluctuate** /ˈflʌktjʊeɪt/ vi fluttuare

**fluctuation** /flʌktjʊˈeɪʃn/ n fluttuazione f

**flue** /fluː/ n (of chimney, stove) canna f fumaria

**fluent** /ˈfluːənt/ a spedito; **speak ~ Italian** parlare correntemente l'italiano

**fluently** /ˈfluːəntlɪ/ adv speditamente

**fluff** /flʌf/ n peluria f

**fluffy** /ˈflʌfɪ/ a (**-ier, -iest**) vaporoso; ⟨toy⟩ di peluche

**fluid** /ˈfluːɪd/ a fluido ● n fluido m

**fluid ounce** n oncia f fluida

**fluke** /fluːk/ n colpo m di fortuna

**flummox** /ˈflʌməks/ vt fam sbalestrare

**flung** /flʌŋ/ see **fling**

**flunk** /flʌŋk/ vt Am fam essere bocciato in

**fluorescent** /flʊəˈresnt/ a fluorescente

**fluorescent lighting** n luce f fluorescente

**fluoride** /ˈflʊəraɪd/ n fluoruro m

**flurry** /ˈflʌrɪ/ n (snow) raffica f; fig agitazione f

**flush** /flʌʃ/ n (blush) [vampata f di] rossore m ● vi arrossire ● vt lavare con un getto d'acqua; **~ the toilet** tirare l'acqua ● a a livello (**with** di); (fam: affluent) a soldi

**flushed** /flʌʃt/ a ⟨cheeks⟩ rosso; **~ with** eccitato da ⟨success⟩; raggiante di ⟨pride⟩

**flustered** /ˈflʌstəd/ a in agitazione; **get ~** mettersi in agitazione

**flute** /fluːt/ n flauto m

**flutter** /ˈflʌtə(r)/ n battito m ● vi svolazzare

**flux** /flʌks/ n **in a state of ~** in uno stato di flusso

**fly**[1] /flaɪ/ n (pl **flies**) mosca f

**fly**[2] v (pt **flew**, pp **flown**) ● vi volare; (go by plane) andare in aereo; ⟨flag:⟩ sventolare; (rush) precipitarsi; **~ open** spalancarsi ● vt pilotare ⟨plane⟩; trasportare [in aereo] ⟨troops, supplies⟩; volare con ⟨Alitalia etc⟩

**fly**[3] n & **flies** pl (on trousers) patta f

**flyaway** /ˈflaɪəweɪ/ a ⟨hair⟩ che non stanno a posto

**fly: fly-by-night** a ⟨person⟩ irresponsabile; ⟨company⟩ non affidabile. **flycatcher**

/'flaɪkætʃə(r)/ *n* pigliamosche *m inv.* **fly-drive** *a* con la formula aereo più auto

**flyer** /'flaɪə(r)/ *n* aviatore *m*; (*leaflet*) volantino *m*

**fly-fishing** *n* pesca *f* con la mosca

**flying** /'flaɪɪŋ/ *n* aviazione *f*

**flying: flying buttress** *n* arco *m* rampante. **flying colours: with ~ ~** a pieni voti. **flying saucer** *n* disco *m* volante. **flying start** *n* ottima partenza *f*; **get off to a ~ ~** partire benissimo. **flying visit** *n* visita *f* lampo *inv*

**fly: flyleaf** *n* risguardo *m*. **fly on the wall** *a* ⟨*documentary*⟩ con telecamera nascosta. **flyover** *n* cavalcavia *m inv*. **fly-past** *n Br Aeron* parata *f* aerea. **flysheet** *n* ⟨*handbill*⟩ volantino *m*; ⟨*of tent*⟩ soprattenda *m inv*

**foal** /fəʊl/ *n* puledro *m*

**foam** /fəʊm/ *n* schiuma *f*; (*synthetic*) gommapiuma[ᴿ] *f* ● *vi* spumare; **~ at the mouth** far la bava alla bocca

**foam rubber** *n* gommapiuma[ᴿ] *f*

**fob** /fɒb/ *vt* (*pt/pp* **fobbed**) **~ sth off** affibbiare qcsa (**on sb** a qcno); **~ sb off** liquidare qcno

**focal** /'fəʊkl/ *a* focale

**focal point** *n* (*of village, building*) centro *m* di attrazione; (*main concern*) punto *m* centrale; (*in optics*) fuoco *m*; **the room lacks a ~ ~** nella stanza manca un punto che focalizzi l'attenzione

**focus** /'fəʊkəs/ *n* fuoco *m*; **in ~** a fuoco; **out of ~** sfocato ● *v* (*pt/pp* **focused** *or* **focussed**) ● *vt fig* concentrare (**on** su) ● *vi* **~ on sth** *Phot* mettere a fuoco qcsa; *fig* concentrarsi su qcsa

**fodder** /'fɒdə(r)/ *n* foraggio *m*

**foe** /fəʊ/ *n* nemico, -a *mf*

**foetal** /'fiːtl/ *a* fetale

**foetid** /'fetɪd/ *a* fetido

**foetus** /'fiːtəs/ *n* (*pl* **-tuses**) feto *m*

**fog** /fɒg/ *n* nebbia *f*

**fog bank** *n* banco *m* di nebbia

**fogey** /'fəʊgɪ/ *n* **old ~** persona *f* antiquata

**foggy** /'fɒgɪ/ *a* (**foggier, foggiest**) nebbioso; **it's ~** c'è nebbia; **I haven't got the foggiest [idea]** *fam* hon ne ho la più pallida idea

**foghorn** /'fɒghɔːn/ *n* sirena *f* da nebbia

**fog lamp, foglight** /'fɒglaɪt/ *n Auto* [faro *m*] antinebbia *m inv*

**foible** /'fɔɪbl/ *n* punto *m* debole

**foil**[1] /fɔɪl/ *n* lamina *f* di metallo

**foil**[2] *vt* (*thwart*) frustrare

**foil**[3] *n* (*sword*) fioretto *m*

**foist** /fɔɪst/ *vt* appioppare (**on sb** a qcno)

**fold**[1] /fəʊld/ *n* (*for sheep*) ovile *m*

**fold**[2] *n* piega *f* ● *vt* piegare; **~ one's arms** incrociare le braccia ● *vi* piegarsi; (*fail*) crollare

■ **fold up** *vt* ripiegare ⟨*chair*⟩ ● *vi* essere pieghevole; ⟨*fam: business:*⟩ collassare

**foldaway** /'fəʊldəweɪ/ *a* ⟨*bed*⟩ pieghevole; ⟨*table*⟩ estraibile

**folder** /'fəʊldə(r)/ *n* cartella *f*

**folding** /'fəʊldɪŋ/ *a* pieghevole

**folding seat** *n* strapuntino *m*, sedile *m* pieghevole

**folding stool** *n* sgabello *m* pieghevole

**fold-out** *n* (*in magazine*) pieghevole *m*

**foliage** /'fəʊlɪdʒ/ *n* fogliame *m*

**folk** /fəʊk/ *npl* gente *f*; **my ~s** (*family*) i miei; **hello there ~s** ciao a tutti

**folk: folk dance** *n* danza *f* popolare. **folklore** *n* folclore *m*. **folk medicine** *n* rimedio *m* della nonna. **folk memory** *n* memoria *f* collettiva. **folk music** *n* musica *f* folk. **folk song** *n* canto *m* popolare. **folk wisdom** *n* saggezza *f* popolare

**follow** /'fɒləʊ/ *vt/i* seguire; **it doesn't ~** non è necessariamente così; **~ suit** *fig* fare lo stesso; **as ~s** come segue

■ **follow up** *vt* fare seguito a ⟨*letter*⟩

**follower** /'fɒləʊə(r)/ *n* seguace *mf*

**following** /'fɒləʊɪŋ/ *a* seguente ● *n* seguito *m*; (*supporters*) seguaci *mpl* ● *prep* in seguito a

**follow-on** *n* seguito *m*

**follow-up** *n* (*of socialwork case*) controllo *m*; (*of patient, ex inmate*) visita *f* di controllo; (*film, record, single, programme*) seguito *m* ● *attrib* ⟨*survey, visit, interview*⟩ successivo; **~ letter** lettera *f* che fa seguito

**folly** /'fɒlɪ/ *n* follia *f*

**foment** /fə'ment/ *vt fig* fomentare

**fond** /fɒnd/ *a* affezionato; ⟨*hope*⟩ vivo; **be ~ of** essere appassionato di ⟨*music*⟩; **I'm ~ of...** ⟨*food, person*⟩ mi piace moltissimo...

**fondle** /'fɒndl/ *vt* coccolare

**fondly** /'fɒndlɪ/ *adv* ⟨*hope*⟩ ingenuamente

**fondness** /'fɒndnɪs/ *n* affetto *m*; (*for things*) amore *m*

**font** /fɒnt/ *n* fonte *f* battesimale; *Typ* carattere *m* di stampa

**food** /fuːd/ *n* cibo *m*; (*for animals, groceries*) mangiare *m*; **let's buy some ~** compriamo qualcosa da mangiare

**food: food mixer** *n* frullatore *m*. **food poisoning** *n* intossicazione *f* alimentare. **food processor** *n* tritatutto *m inv* elettrico. **foodstuffs** *npl* generi *mpl* alimentari

**fool**[1] /fuːl/ *n* sciocco, -a *mf*; **she's no ~** non è una stupida; **make a ~ of oneself** rendersi ridicolo ● *vt* prendere in giro ● *vi* **~ around** giocare; ⟨*husband, wife:*⟩ avere l'amante

**fool**[2] *n Culin* crema *f*

**foolhardy** /'fuːlhɑːdɪ/ *a* temerario

**foolish** /'fuːlɪʃ/ *a* stolto

**foolishly** /'fuːlɪʃlɪ/ *adv* scioccamente

**foolishness** /'fuːlɪʃnɪs/ *n* sciocchezza *f*

**foolproof** /'fuːlpruːf/ *a* facilissimo

**foolscap** /'fuːlskæp/ *n* (*Br: paper*) carta *f* protocollo

**foot** /fʊt/ *n* (*pl* **feet**) piede *m*; (*of animal*) zampa *f*; (*measure*) piede (=30,48 cm); **on ~** a piedi; **on one's feet** in piedi; **put one's ~ in it** *fam* fare una gaffe

**footage** /'fʊtɪdʒ/ *n* (*piece of film*) spezzone *m*; **news ~** servizio *m* [filmato]

**foot: foot-and-mouth disease** *n* afta *f*

epizootica. **football** n calcio m; (ball) pallone m. **footballer** n giocatore m di calcio. **football pools** npl totocalcio m. **footbrake** n freno m a pedale. **footbridge** n passerella f. **foothills** npl colline fpl pedemontane. **foothold** n punto m d'appoggio. **footing** n **lose one's ~** perdere l'appiglio; **on an equal ~** in condizioni di parità. **footlights** npl luci npl della ribalta. **footloose and fancy-free** a libero come l'aria. **footman** n valletto m. **footnote** n nota f a piè di pagina. **footpath** n sentiero m. **footprint** n orma f; (of machine) ingombro m. **footrest** n poggiapiedi m inv. **footsore** a **be ~** avere male ai piedi. **footstep** n passo m; **follow in sb's ~s** fig seguire l'esempio di qcno. **footstool** n sgabellino m. **footwear** n calzature fpl

**for** /fə(r)/, accentato /fɔː(r)/ prep per; **~ this reason** per questa ragione; **I have lived here ~ ten years** vivo qui da dieci anni; **~ supper** per cena; **~ all that** nonostante questo; **what ~?** a che scopo?; **send ~ a doctor** chiamare un dottore; **fight ~ a cause** lottare per una causa; **go ~ a walk** andare a fare una passeggiata; **there's no need ~ you to go** non c'è bisogno che tu vada; **it's not ~ me to say** no sta a me dirlo; **now you're ~ it** ora sei nei pasticci ● conj poiché, perché

**forage** /'fɒrɪdʒ/ n foraggio m ● vi **~ for** cercare

**foray** /'fɒreɪ/ n Mil incursione f; **make a ~ into** (politics, acting) tentare la strada di

**forbade** /fə'bæd/ see **forbid**

**forbearance** /fɔː'beərəns/ n pazienza f

**forbearing** /fɔː'beərɪŋ/ a tollerante

**forbid** /fə'bɪd/ vt (pt forbade, pp forbidden) proibire

**forbidding** /fə'bɪdɪŋ/ a (prospect) che spaventa; (stern) severo

**force** /fɔːs/ n forza f; **in ~** in vigore; (in large numbers) in massa; **come into ~** entrare in vigore; **the** (armed) **~s** pl le forze armate ● vt forzare; **~ sth on sb** (decision) imporre qcsa a qcno; (drink) costringere qcno a fare qcsa

■ **force back** vt trattenere (tears)

■ **force down** vt buttar giù (controvoglia) (food, drink)

**forced** /fɔːst/ a forzato

**forced landing** n atterraggio m forzato

**force-feed** vt (pt/pp -fed) nutrire a forza

**forceful** /'fɔːsfʊl/ a energico

**forcefully** /'fɔːsfʊlɪ/ adv (say, argue) con forza

**forceps** /'fɔːseps/ npl forcipe m

**forcible** /'fɔːsəbl/ a forzato

**forcibly** /'fɔːsəblɪ/ adv forzatamente

**ford** /fɔːd/ n guado m ● vt guadare

**fore** /fɔː(r)/ n **to the ~** in vista; **come to the ~** salire alla ribalta

**forearm** /'fɔːrɑːm/ n avambraccio m

**forebears** /'fɔːbeəz/ npl antenati mpl

**foreboding** /fɔː'bəʊdɪŋ/ n presentimento m

**forecast** /'fɔːkɑːst/ n previsione f ● vt (pt/pp forecast) prevedere

**forecaster** /'fɔːkɑːstə(r)/ n pronosticatore, -trice mf; (economic) analista mf della congiuntura; (of weather) meteorologo, -a mf

**fore: forecourt** n (of garage) spiazzo m [antistante]. **forefathers** npl antenati mpl. **forefinger** n [dito m] indice m. **forefront** n **be in the ~** essere all'avanguardia. **foregone** a **be a ~ conclusion** essere una cosa scontata. **foreground** n primo piano m. **forehand** n Tennis diritto m

**forehead** /'fɒrɪd, 'fɔːd/ n fronte f

**foreign** /'fɒrən/ a straniero; (trade) estero; (not belonging) estraneo; **he is ~** è uno straniero

**foreign currency** n valuta f estera

**foreigner** /'fɒrənə(r)/ n straniero, -a mf

**foreign: foreign exchange** n (currency) valuta f estera. **foreign language** n lingua f straniera. **Foreign Office** n ministero m degli [affari] Esteri. **Foreign Secretary** n Ministro m degli Esteri

**foreleg** /'fɔːleg/ n zampa f anteriore

**foreman** /'fɔːmən/ n caporeparto m

**foremost** /'fɔːməʊst/ a principale ● adv **first and ~** in primo luogo

**forename** /'fɔːneɪm/ n nome m di battesimo

**forensic** /fə'rensɪk/ a **~ medicine** medicina legale

**forensic scientist** n medico m legale

**forerunner** /'fɔːrʌnə(r)/ n precursore m

**foresee** /fɔː'siː/ vt (pt -saw, pp -seen) prevedere

**foresight** /'fɔːsaɪt/ n previdenza f

**foreskin** /'fɔːskɪn/ n Anat prepuzio m

**forest** /'fɒrɪst/ n foresta f

**forestall** /fɔː'stɔːl/ vt prevenire

**forester** /'fɒrɪstə(r)/ n guardia f forestale

**forest fire** n incendio m del bosco

**forest ranger** /'reɪndʒə(r)/ n Am guardia f forestale

**forestry** /'fɒrɪstrɪ/ n silvicoltura f

**foretaste** /'fɔːteɪst/ n pregustazione f

**foretell** /fɔː'tel/ vt (pt/pp -told) predire

**forethought** /'fɔːθɔːt/ n accortezza f, previdenza f

**forever** /fə'revə(r)/ adv per sempre; **he's ~ complaining** si lamenta sempre

**forewarn** /fɔː'wɔːn/ vt avvertire

**foreword** /'fɔːwɜːd/ n prefazione f

**forfeit** /'fɔːfɪt/ n (in game) pegno m; Jur penalità f ● vt perdere

**forfeiture** /'fɔːfɪtʃə(r)/ n (of right) perdita f; (of property) confisca f

**forgave** /fə'geɪv/ see **forgive**

**forge**[1] /fɔːdʒ/ vi **~ ahead** (runner:) lasciarsi indietro gli altri; fig farsi strada

**forge**[2] n fucina f ● vt fucinare; (counterfeit) contraffare

**forger** /'fɔːdʒə(r)/ n contraffattore m

**forgery** /'fɔːdʒərɪ/ n contraffazione f

**forget** /fə'get/ vt/i (pt -got, pp -gotten) dimenticare; dimenticarsi di (language, skill); **~ oneself** perdere la padronanza di sé

**forgetful** /fə'getfʊl/ a smemorato

**forgetfulness** /fə'getfʊlnɪs/ n smemoratezza f

**forget-me-not** n non-ti-scordar-di-mé m inv

**forgettable** /fə'getəbl/ a ⟨day, fact, film⟩ da dimenticare

**forgive** /fə'gɪv/ vt (pt **-gave**, pp **-given**) ~ **sb for sth** perdonare qcno per qcsa

**forgiveness** /fə'gɪvnɪs/ n perdono m

**forgiving** /fə'gɪvɪŋ/ a ⟨person⟩ indulgente

**forgo** /fɔː'gəʊ/ vt (pt **-went**, pp **-gone**) rinunciare a

**forgot(ten)** /fə'gɒt(n)/ see **forget**

**fork** /fɔːk/ n forchetta f; ⟨for digging⟩ forca f; ⟨in road⟩ bivio m ● vi ⟨road:⟩ biforcarsi; ~ **right** prendere a destra
  ■ **fork out** vt fam sborsare ● vi sborsare soldi

**forked lightning** /fɔːkt/ n fulmine m ramificato

**fork-lift truck** n elevatore m

**forlorn** /fə'lɔːn/ a ⟨look⟩ perduto; ⟨place⟩ derelitto; ~ **hope** speranza f vana

**form** /fɔːm/ n forma f; ⟨document⟩ modulo m; Sch classe f ● vt formare; formulare ⟨opinion⟩ ● vi formarsi

**formal** /'fɔːml/ a formale

**formalin** /'fɔːməlɪn/ n formalina f

**formality** /fɔː'mælətɪ/ n formalità f inv

**formally** /'fɔːməlɪ/ adv in modo formale; ⟨officially⟩ ufficialmente

**format** /'fɔːmæt/ n formato m ● vt formattare ⟨disk, page⟩

**formation** /fɔː'meɪʃn/ n formazione f

**formative** /'fɔːmətɪv/ a ~ **years** anni formativi

**former** /'fɔːmə(r)/ a precedente; ⟨PM, colleague⟩ ex; **the ~, the latter** il primo, l'ultimo

**formerly** /'fɔːməlɪ/ adv precedentemente; ⟨in olden times⟩ in altri tempi

**formidable** /'fɔːmɪdəbl/ a formidabile

**formless** /'fɔːmlɪs/ a ⟨mass⟩ informe; ⟨novel⟩ che manca di struttura

**form teacher** n Br Sch ≈ coordinatore, -trice mf del consiglio di classe

**formula** /'fɔːmjʊlə/ n (pl **-ae** /'fɔːmjʊliː/ or **-s**) formula f

**formulate** /'fɔːmjʊleɪt/ vt formulare

**formulation** /fɔːmjʊ'leɪʃn/ n formulazione f

**fornication** /fɔːnɪ'keɪʃn/ n fornicazione f

**forsake** /fə'seɪk/ vt (pt **-sook** /fə'sʊk/, pp **-saken**) abbandonare

**forseeable** /fə'siːəbl/ a **in the ~ future** in futuro per quanto si possa prevedere

**forswear** /fɔː'sweə(r)/ vt ⟨renounce⟩ abiurare

**fort** /fɔːt/ n Mil forte m

**forte** /'fɔːteɪ/ n [pezzo m] forte m

**forth** /fɔːθ/ adv **back and ~** avanti e indietro; **and so ~** e così via

**forthcoming** /fɔː'θkʌmɪŋ/ a prossimo; ⟨communicative⟩ comunicativo; **no re-**

**sponse was ~** non arrivava nessuna risposta

**forthright** /'fɔːθraɪt/ a schietto

**forthwith** /fɔː'θwɪθ/ adv immediatamente

**fortieth** /'fɔːtɪɪθ/ a & n quarantesimo, -a mf

**fortification** /fɔːtɪfɪ'keɪʃn/ n fortificazione f

**fortify** /'fɔːtɪfaɪ/ vt (pt/pp **-ied**) fortificare; fig rendere forte

**fortitude** /'fɔːtɪtjuːd/ n coraggio m

**fortnight** /'fɔːtnaɪt/ n Br quindicina f

**fortnightly** /'fɔːtnaɪtlɪ/ a bimensile ● adv ogni due settimane

**fortress** /'fɔːtrɪs/ n fortezza f

**fortuitous** /fɔː'tjuːɪtəs/ a fortuito

**fortunate** /'fɔːtʃənət/ a fortunato; **that's ~!** meno male!

**fortunately** /'fɔːtʃənətlɪ/ adv fortunatamente

**fortune** /'fɔːtʃuːn/ n fortuna f

**fortune cookie** n Am biscottino m che racchiude un foglietto con una predizione

**fortune-teller** n indovino, -a mf

**forty** /'fɔːtɪ/ a & n quaranta m; **have ~ winks** fam fare un pisolino

**forum** /'fɔːrəm/ n foro m

**forward** /'fɔːwəd/ adv avanti; ⟨towards the front⟩ in avanti; **move ~** andare avanti ● a in avanti; ⟨presumptuous⟩ sfacciato ● n Sport attaccante m ● vt inoltrare ⟨letter⟩; spedire ⟨goods⟩

**forward buying** n Fin acquisto m a termine

**forwarding address** n indirizzo m a cui inoltrare la corrispondenza

**forward planning** n pianificazione f a lungo termine

**forwards** /'fɔːwədz/ adv avanti

**fossil** /'fɒs(ə)l/ n fossile m

**fossil fuel** n combustibile m fossile

**fossilized** /'fɒsɪlaɪzd/ a fossile; ⟨ideas⟩ fossilizzato

**foster** /'fɒstə(r)/ vt allevare ⟨child⟩

**foster child** n figlio, -a mf inaffidamento

**foster mother** n madre f affidatoria

**fought** /fɔːt/ see **fight**

**foul** /faʊl/ a ⟨smell, taste⟩ cattivo; ⟨air⟩ viziato; ⟨language⟩ osceno; ⟨mood, weather⟩ orrendo ● vt inquinare ⟨water⟩; Sport commettere un fallo contro; ⟨nets, rope:⟩ impigliarsi in
  ■ **foul up** vt ⟨fam: spoil⟩ mandare in malora

**foul-mouthed** /-'maʊðd/ a sboccato

**foul play** n Jur delitto m ● n Sport fallo m

**foul-smelling** /-'smelɪŋ/ a puzzo. **foul up** n fam intoppo m

**found¹** /faʊnd/ see **find**

**found²** vt fondare

**foundation** /faʊn'deɪʃn/ n ⟨basis⟩ fondamento m; ⟨charitable⟩ fondazione f; **~s** pl ⟨of building⟩ fondamenta fpl; **lay the ~-stone** porre la prima pietra

**foundation course** n Br Univ corso m propedeutico

**founder¹** /'faʊndə(r)/ n fondatore, -trice mf

**founder²** vi ⟨ship:⟩ affondare

**foundry** /ˈfaʊndrɪ/ n fonderia f

**fount** /faʊnt/ n Typ carattere m [stampa]

**fountain** /ˈfaʊntɪn/ n fontana f

**fountain pen** n penna f stilografica

**four** /fɔː(r)/ a & n quattro m

**four: four four time** n Mus quattro quarti.
**four-letter word** n parolaccia f. **four-poster**
[**bed**] n letto m a baldacchino

**foursome** /ˈfɔːsəm/ n quartetto m

**four-stroke** a ⟨engine⟩ a quattro tempi

**fourteen** /fɔːˈtiːn/ a & n quattordici m

**fourteenth** /fɔːˈtiːnθ/ a & n quattordicesi-
mo, -a mf

**fourth** /fɔːθ/ a & n quarto, -a mf

**fourthly** /ˈfɔːθlɪ/ adv in quarto luogo

**fourth rate** a ⟨job, hotel, film⟩ di terz'ordine

**four-wheel drive** [**vehicle**] n quattro per
quattro m inv

**fowl** /faʊl/ n pollame m

**fox** /fɒks/ n volpe f ● vt (puzzle) ingannare

**fox: fox cub** n volpacchiotto m. **fox fur** n
pelliccia f di volpe. **foxglove** n digitale f.
**foxhound** n foxhound m inv. **fox-hunt** n caccia f alla volpe. **fox terrier** n fox-terrier m inv.
**foxtrot** n fox-trot m inv

**foxy** /ˈfɒksɪ/ a (-ier, -iest) (fam: sexy) sexy
inv; (crafty) scaltro

**foyer** /ˈfɔɪeɪ/ n Theat ridotto m; (in hotel) salone m d'ingresso

**fracas** /ˈfrækɑː/ n baruffa f

**fraction** /ˈfrækʃn/ n frazione f

**fractionally** /ˈfrækʃənəlɪ/ adv (slightly) leggermente

**fracture** /ˈfræktʃə(r)/ n frattura f ● vt
fratturare ● vi fratturarsi

**fragile** /ˈfrædʒaɪl/ a fragile

**fragment** /ˈfrægmənt/ n frammento m

**fragmentary** /ˈfrægm(ə)ntərɪ/ a frammentario

**fragrance** /ˈfreɪɡrəns/ n fragranza f

**fragrant** /ˈfreɪɡrənt/ a fragrante

**frail** /freɪl/ a gracile

**frailty** /ˈfreɪltɪ/ n (imperfection) debolezza f;
(of person: moral) fragilità f inv; (of person:
physical) gracilità f; (of health, state)
precarietà f inv

**frame** /freɪm/ n (of picture, door, window) cornice f; (of spectacles) montatura f; Anat ossatura f; (structure, of bike) telaio m; ~ **of mind**
stato m d'animo ● vt incorniciare ⟨picture⟩;
fig formulare; (sl: incriminate) montare

**framework** /ˈfreɪmwɜːk/ n struttura f;
**within the** ~ **of the law** nell'ambito della
legge

**franc** /fræŋk/ n franco m

**France** /frɑːns/ n Francia f

**franchise** /ˈfræntʃaɪz/ n Pol diritto m di
voto; Comm franchigia f

**Franciscan** /frænˈsɪskən/ n francescano m

**frank**[1] /fræŋk/ vt affrancare ⟨letter⟩

**frank**[2] a franco

**Frankfurt** /ˈfræŋkfɜːt/ n Francoforte f

**frankfurter** /ˈfræŋkfɜːtə(r)/ n würstel m inv

**frankincense** /ˈfræŋkɪnsens/ n incenso m

**franking machine** /ˈfræŋkɪŋ/ n affranca-
trice f

**frankly** /ˈfræŋklɪ/ adv francamente

**frantic** /ˈfræntɪk/ a frenetico; **be** ~ **with
worry** essere agitatissimo

**frantically** /ˈfræntɪklɪ/ adv freneticamente

**fraternal** /frəˈtɜːnl/ a fraterno

**fraternity** /frəˈtɜːnətɪ/ n (club) associazione
f; (spirit, brotherhood) fratellanza f

**fraud** /frɔːd/ n frode f; (person) impostore m

**fraudulent** /ˈfrɔːdjʊlənt/ a fraudolento

**fraught** /frɔːt/ a ~ **with** pieno di

**fray**[1] /freɪ/ n mischia f

**fray**[2] vi sfilacciarsi

**frayed** /freɪd/ a (cuffs) sfilacciato; (nerves) a
pezzi

**frazzle** /ˈfræz(ə)l/ n **be worn to a** ~ essere
ridotto uno straccio; **burn sth to a** ~
carbonizzare qcsa

**freak** /friːk/ n fenomeno m; (person) scherzo
m di natura; (fam: weird person) tipo m
strambo ● a anormale

■ **freak out** vi (fam: lose control, go crazy)
andar fuori di testa

**freakish** /ˈfriːkɪʃ/ a strambo

**freckle** /ˈfrekl/ n lentiggine f

**freckled** /ˈfrekld/ a lentigginoso

**free** /friː/ a (**freer, freest**) libero; ⟨ticket,
copy⟩ gratuito; (lavish) generoso; ~ **of
charge** gratuito; **set** ~ liberare; ~ **with...**
Comm in ommagio per... ● vt (pt/pp freed) liberare

**free agent** n persona f libera di agire come
vuole

**free and easy** a disinvolto

**freebee, freebie** /ˈfriːbɪ/ n fam (free gift)
omaggio m; (trip) viaggio m gratuito;
(newspaper) giornale m gratuito

**freedom** /ˈfriːdəm/ n libertà f

**free: free enterprise** n liberalismo m economico. **free fall** n caduta f libera. **free-for-
all** n (disorganized situation, fight) baraonda
f. **freehand** adv a mano libera. **freehold** n
proprietà f [fondiaria] assoluta. **free house** n
Br pub m inv che non è legato a nessun produttore di birra. **free-kick** n calcio m di punizione. **freelance** a & adv indipendente.
**freeloader** n fam scroccone m

**freely** /ˈfriːlɪ/ adv liberamente; (generously)
generosamente; **I** ~ **admit that...** devo ammettere che...

**free: Freemason** n massone m. **Freemasonry** n massoneria f. **freephone
number** n numero m verde. **free-range egg**
n uovo m di gallina ruspante. **free sample** n
campione m gratuito. **free spirit** n persona f
che ama la sua indipendenza. **free-standing**
a ⟨heater⟩ non incassato; ⟨statue⟩ a tutto tondo; ⟨lamp⟩ a stelo. **freestyle** n stile m libero.
**free trade** n libero scambio m. **free trial
period** n periodo m di prova gratuito.
**freeway** n Am autostrada f. **freewheel** vi
⟨car:⟩ (in neutral) andare in folle; (with engine
switched off) andare a motore spento;
⟨bicycle:⟩ andare a ruota libera

**freeze** /fri:z/ vt (pt **froze**, pp **frozen**) gelare; bloccare ‹wages› ● vi ‹water:› gelare; **it's freezing** si gela; **my hands are freezing** ho le mani congelate

**freeze-dried** a liofilizzato

**freeze-frame** n (video) fermo m immagine

**freezer** /'fri:zə(r)/ n freezer m inv, congelatore m

**freezing** /'fri:zɪŋ/ a gelido ● n **below ~** sotto zero

**freezing fog** n nebbia f ghiacciata

**freezing point** n punto m di congelamento

**freight** /freɪt/ n carico m

**freight charges** npl costi mpl di spedizione

**freighter** /'freɪtə(r)/ n nave f da carico

**freight forwarder** n spedizioniere m

**freight train** n Am treno m merci

**French** /frentʃ/ a francese ● n (language) francese m; **the ~** pl i francesi

**French: French beans** npl fagiolini mpl [verdi]. **French bread** n filone m (di pane). **French Canadian** n canadese mf francofono, -a ● a del Canada francofono. **French doors** npl porta-finestra f inv. **French dressing** n Br vinaigrette f inv. **French fries** npl patate fpl fritte. **French horn** n corno m da caccia. **French kiss** n bacio m profondo. **French knickers** npl culottes fpl. **Frenchman** n francese m. **French polish** n vernice f a olio e gommalacca. **French toast** n pane m immerso nell'uovo sbattuto e fritto. **French window** n porta-finestra f. **Frenchwoman** n francese f

**frenetic** /frə'netɪk/ a ‹activity› frenetico

**frenzied** /'frenzɪd/ a frenetico

**frenzy** /'frenzɪ/ n frenesia f

**frequency** /'fri:kwənsɪ/ n frequenza f

**frequent**[1] /'fri:kwənt/ a frequente

**frequent**[2] /frɪ'kwent/ vt frequentare

**frequently** /'fri:kwəntlɪ/ adv frequentemente

**fresco** /'freskəʊ/ n affresco m

**fresh** /freʃ/ a fresco; (new) nuovo; (Am: cheeky) sfacciato

**freshen** /'freʃn/ vi ‹wind:› rinfrescare

■ **freshen up** vt dare una rinfrescata a ● vi rinfrescarsi

**fresh-faced** /-'feɪst/ a dalla faccia giovanile

**freshly** /'freʃlɪ/ adv di recente

**freshman** /'freʃmən/ n Am matricola f; (fig: in congress, in firm) nuovo arrivato m

**freshness** /'freʃnɪs/ n freschezza f

**freshwater** /'freʃwɔ:tə(r)/ a di acqua dolce

**fret** /fret/ vi (pt/pp **fretted**) inquietarsi

**fretful** /'fretfʊl/ a irritabile

**fretsaw** /'fretsɔ:/ n seghetto m da traforo

**fretwork** /'fretwɜ:k/ n [lavoro m di] traforo m

**Freudian slip** /'frɔɪdɪən/ n lapsus m inv freudiano

**friar** /'fraɪə(r)/ n frate m

**friction** /'frɪkʃn/ n frizione f

**Friday** /'fraɪdeɪ/ n venerdì m inv

**fridge** /frɪdʒ/ n frigo m

**fried** /fraɪd/ see **fry** ● a fritto; **~ egg** uovo m fritto

**friend** /frend/ n amico, -a mf

**friendly** /'frendlɪ/ a (**-ier**, **-iest**) ‹relations, meeting, match› amichevole; ‹neighbourhood, smile› piacevole; ‹software› di facile uso; **be ~ with** essere amico di

**friendship** /'frendʃɪp/ n amicizia f

**frieze** /fri:z/ n fregio m

**frigate** /'frɪɡət/ n fregata f

**fright** /fraɪt/ n paura f; **take ~** spaventarsi

**frighten** /'fraɪt(ə)n/ vt spaventare

■ **frighten away** vt far scappare ‹bird, intruder›

**frightened** /'fraɪtənd/ a spaventato; **be ~** aver paura (**of** di)

**frightening** /'fraɪt(ə)nɪŋ/ a spaventoso

**frightful** /'fraɪtfl/ a terribile

**frightfully** /'fraɪtfʊlɪ/ adv terribilmente

**frigid** /'frɪdʒɪd/ a frigido

**frigidity** /frɪ'dʒɪdətɪ/ n freddezza f; Psych frigidità f

**frill** /frɪl/ n volant m inv

**frilly** /'frɪlɪ/ a ‹dress› con tanti volant

**fringe** /frɪndʒ/ n frangia f; (of hair) frangetta f; (fig: edge) margine m

**fringe benefits** npl benefici mpl supplementari

**frisk** /frɪsk/ vt (search) perquisire

**frisky** /'frɪskɪ/ a (**-ier**, **-iest**) vispo

**fritter** /'frɪtə(r)/ n frittella f

■ **fritter away** vt sprecare

**frivolity** /frɪ'vɒlətɪ/ n frivolezza f

**frivolous** /'frɪvələs/ a frivolo

**frizzy** /'frɪzɪ/ a (**-ier**, **-iest**) crespo

**fro** /frəʊ/ see **to**

**frock** /frɒk/ n abito m

**frog** /frɒɡ/ n rana f

**frog: frogman** n uomo m rana inv. **frogmarch** vt Br portare via a forza. **frogs' legs** npl cosce fpl di rana. **frogspawn** n uova fpl di rana

**frolic** /'frɒlɪk/ vi (pt/pp **frolicked**) ‹lambs:› sgambettare; ‹fam: people› folleggiare

**from** /frɒm/ prep da; **~ Monday** da lunedì; **~ that day** da quel giorno; **he's ~ London** è di Londra; **this is a letter ~ my brother** questa è una lettera di mio fratello; **documents ~ the 16th century** documenti del XVI secolo; **made ~** fatto con; **she felt ill ~ fatigue** si sentiva male dalla stanchezza; **~ now on** d'ora in poi

**front** /frʌnt/ n parte f anteriore; (fig: organization etc) facciata f; (of garment) davanti m; (sea~) lungomare m; Mil, Pol, Meteorol fronte m; **in ~ of** davanti a; **in** or **at the ~** davanti; **to the ~** avanti ● a davanti; ‹page, row, wheel› anteriore

**frontage** /'frʌntɪdʒ/ n (of house) facciata f; **with ocean/river ~** (access) prospiciente l'oceano/il fiume

**frontal** /'frʌntl/ a frontale

**front: front bench** n Br Pol parlamentari mpl di maggiore importanza. **front door** n porta *f* d'entrata. **front garden** *n* giardino *m* d'avanti

**frontier** /'frʌntɪə(r)/ *n* frontiera *f*

**front: front line** *n Mil* prima linea *f*; **be in the ~** *~ fig* essere in prima linea. **front of house** *n Br Theat* foyer *m inv*. **front runner** *n Sport* concorrente *mf* in testa; (*favourite*) favorito, -a *mf*. **front-wheel drive** *n* trazione *f* anteriore

**frost** /frɒst/ *n* gelo *m*; (*hoar~*) brina *f*

**frostbite** /'frɒs(t)baɪt/ *n* congelamento *m*

**frostbitten** /'frɒs(t)bɪtən/ *a* congelato

**frosted** /'frɒstɪd/ *a* **~ glass** vetro *m* smerigliato

**frostily** /'frɒstɪlɪ/ *adv* gelidamente

**frosting** /'frɒstɪŋ/ *n Am Culin* glassa *f*

**frosty** /'frɒstɪ/ *a* (**-ier, iest**) *also fig* gelido

**froth** /frɒθ/ *n* schiuma *f* ● *vi* far schiuma

**frothy** /'frɒθɪ/ *a* (**-ier, iest**) schiumoso

**frown** /fraʊn/ *n* cipiglio *m* ● *vi* aggrottare le sopraciglia

■ **frown on** *vt* disapprovare

**froze** /frəʊz/ *see* **freeze**

**frozen** /'frəʊzn/ *see* **freeze** ● *a* (*corpse, hand*) congelato; (*wastes*) gelido; *Culin* surgelato; **I'm ~** sono gelato

**frozen food** *n* surgelati *mpl*

**frugal** /'fru:gl/ *a* frugale

**frugally** /'fru:gəlɪ/ *adv* frugalmente

**fruit** /fru:t/ *n* frutto *m*; (*collectively*) frutta *f*; **eat more ~** mangia più frutta

**fruit: fruit bowl** *n* fruttiera *f*. **fruit cake** *n* dolce *m* con frutta candita. **fruit cocktail** *n* macedonia *f* [di frutta]. **fruit drop** *n* drop *m inv* alla frutta

**fruiterer** /'fru:tərə(r)/ *n* fruttivendolo, -a *mf*

**fruit farmer** *n* frutticoltore *m*

**fruit fly** *n* moscerino *m* della frutta

**fruitful** /'fru:tfʊl/ *a fig* fruttuoso

**fruit gum** *n* caramella *f* alla frutta

**fruition** /fru:'ɪʃn/ *n* **come to ~** dare dei frutti

**fruit juice** *n* succo *m* di frutta

**fruitless** /'fru:tlɪs/ *a* infruttuoso

**fruitlessly** /'fru:tlɪslɪ/ *adv* senza risultato

**fruit machine** *n* macchinetta *f* mangiasoldi

**fruit salad** *n* macedonia *f* [di frutta]

**fruity** /'fru:tɪ/ *a* (*wine*) fruttato

**frump** /frʌmp/ *n* donna *f* scialba

**frumpy** /'frʌmpɪ/ *a* scialbo

**frustrate** /frʌ'streɪt/ *vt* frustrare; rovinare (*plans*)

**frustrating** /frʌ'streɪtɪŋ/ *a* frustrante

**frustration** /frʌ'streɪʃn/ *n* frustrazione *f*

**fry**[1] /fraɪ/ *n inv* **small ~** *fig* pesce *m* piccolo

**fry**[2] *vt/i* (*pt/pp* **fried**) friggere

**frying pan** *n* padella *f*

**fuchsia** /'fju:ʃə/ *n* fucsia *f*

**fuck** /fʌk/ *vulg vt/i* scopare ● *n* **I don't give a ~** me ne sbatto; **what the ~ are you doing?** che cazzo fai? ● *int* cazzo!

■ **fuck off** *vi* (*vulg*) **~ off!** vaffanculo!

■ **fuck up** *vt* (*vulg: ruin*) mandare a puttane

**fucking** /'fʌkɪŋ/ *a vulg* del cazzo

**fuddled** /'fʌd(ə)ld/ *a* (*confused*) confuso; (*slightly drunk*) brillo

**fuddy-duddy** /'fʌdɪdʌdɪ/ *n fam* matusa *mf inv*

**fudge** /fʌdʒ/ *n* caramella *f* a base di zucchero, burro e latte

**fuel** /'fju:əl/ *n* carburante *m*; *fig* nutrimento *m* ● *vt fig* alimentare

**fuel: fuel consumption** *n* consumo *m* di carburante. **fuel efficient** *a* economico. **fuel injection** *n* iniezione *f*. **fuel injection engine** *n* motore *m* a iniezione. **fuel oil** *n* nafta *f*. **fuel pump** *n* pompa *f* della benzina. **fuel tank** *n* serbatoio *m*

**fuggy** /'fʌgɪ/ *a* (*Br: smoky*) fumoso

**fugitive** /'fju:dʒɪtɪv/ *n* fuggiasco, -a *mf*

**fugue** /fju:g/ *n Mus* fuga *f*

**fulcrum** /'fʊlkrəm/ *n* fulcro *m*

**fulfil** /fʊl'fɪl/ *vt* (*pt/pp* **-filled**) soddisfare (*conditions, need*); adempiere a (*promise*); realizzare (*dream, desire*); **~ oneself** realizzarsi

**fulfilling** /fʊl'fɪlɪŋ/ *a* soddisfacente

**fulfilment** /fʊl'fɪlmənt/ *n* **sense of ~** senso *m* di appagamento

**full** /fʊl/ *a* pieno (**of** di); (*detailed*) esauriente; (*bus, hotel*) completo; (*skirt*) ampio; **at ~ speed** a tutta velocità; **in ~ swing** in pieno fervore ● *adv* in pieno; **you know ~ well that** sai benissimo che ● *n* **in ~** per intero

**full: full-back** *n* difensore *m*. **full beam** *n Auto* [fari *mpl*] abbaglianti *mpl*. **full-blown** /-'bləʊn/ *a* (*epidemic*) vero e proprio; (*disease*) conclamato. **full board** *n* pensione *f* completa. **full-bodied** /-'bɒdɪd/ *a* (*wine*) corposo. **full-frontal** *a* (*photograph*) di nudo frontale. **full house** *n Theat* tutto esaurito *m inv*; (*in poker*) full *m inv*. **full-length** *a* (*dress*) lungo; (*curtain*) lungo fino a terra; (*portrait*) intero; **~ ~ film** lungometraggio *m*. **full moon** *n* luna *f* piena. **full-scale** *a* (*model*) in scala reale; (*alert*) di massima gravità. **full stop** *n* punto *m*. **full-time** *a & adv* a tempo pieno

**fully** /'fʊlɪ/ *adv* completamente; (*in detail*) dettagliatamente; **~ booked** (*hotel, restaurant*) tutto prenotato

**fully fledged** /-'fledʒd/ *a* (*bird*) che ha messo tutte le penne; (*lawyer*) con tutte le qualifiche; (*member*) a tutti gli effetti

**fulsome** /'fʊlsəm/ *a* esagerato

**fumble** /'fʌmbl/ *vi* **~ in** rovistare in; **~ with** armeggiare con; **~ for one's keys** rovistare alla ricerca delle chiavi

**fume** /fju:m/ *vi* (*be angry*) essere furioso

**fumes** /fju:mz/ *npl* fumi *mpl*; (*from car*) gas *mpl* di scarico

**fumigate** /'fju:mɪgeɪt/ *vt* suffumicare

**fun** /fʌn/ *n* divertimento *m*; **for ~** per ridere; **make ~ of** prendere in giro; **have ~** divertirsi

**function** /'fʌŋkʃn/ *n* funzione *f*; (*event*) cerimonia *f* ● *vi* funzionare; **~ as** (*serve as*) funzionare da

**functional** /'fʌŋkʃ(ə)nəl/ *a* funzionale

**function key** n Comput tasto m [di] funzioni

**function room** n sala f di ricevimento

**fund** /fʌnd/ n fondo m; fig pozzo m; ~s pl fondi mpl ● vt finanziare

**fundamental** /fʌndə'mentl/ a fondamentale

**fundamentalist** /fʌndə'mentəlist/ n fondamentalista mf

**funding** /'fʌndɪŋ/ n (financial aid) finanziamento m; (of debt) consolidamento m

**fund-raiser** /-reɪzə(r)/ n (person) promotore, -trice mf di raccolte di fondi; (event) manifestazione f per la raccolta di fondi

**fund-raising** /-reɪzɪŋ/ n raccolta f di fondi

**funeral** /'fju:nərəl/ n funerale m

**funeral: funeral directors** n impresa f di pompe funebri. **funeral home, funeral parlour** Am n camera f ardente. **funeral march** n marcia f funebre. **funeral service** n rito m funebre

**funereal** /fju:'nɪərɪəl/ a lugubre

**funfair** /'fʌnfeə(r)/ n luna park m inv

**fungal** /'fʌŋgəl/ a (infection) micotico

**fungus** /'fʌŋgəs/ n (pl -gi /'fʌŋgaɪ/) fungo m

**funicular** /fju:'nɪkjʊlə(r)/ n funicolare f

**fun loving** /'fʌnlʌvɪŋ/ a (person) amante del divertimento

**funnel** /'fʌnl/ n imbuto m; (on ship) ciminiera f

**funnily** /'fʌnɪlɪ/ adv comicamente; (oddly) stranamente; ~ enough strano a dirsi

**funny** /'fʌnɪ/ a (-ier, -iest) buffo; (odd) strano

**funny bone** n osso m del gomito

**funny business** n fam affare m losco

**fur** /fɜ:(r)/ n pelo m; (for clothing) pelliccia f; (in kettle) deposito m

**fur coat** n pelliccia f

**furious** /'fjʊərɪəs/ a furioso

**furiously** /'fjʊərɪəslɪ/ adv furiosamente

**furl** /fɜ:l/ vt serrare (sail)

**furnace** /'fɜ:nɪs/ n fornace f

**furnish** /'fɜ:nɪʃ/ vt ammobiliare (flat); fornire (supplies)

**furnished** /'fɜ:nɪʃt/ a ~ room stanza f ammobiliata

**furnishings** /'fɜ:nɪʃɪŋz/ npl mobili mpl

**furniture** /'fɜ:nɪtʃə(r)/ n mobili mpl

**furniture remover** /rɪmu:və(r)/ n Br impresa f di traslochi

**furniture van** n furgone m per i traslochi

**furore** /fjʊ'rɔ:rɪ/ n (outrage, criticism) scalpore m; (acclaim) entusiasmo m

**furred** /fɜ:d/ a (tongue) impastato

**furrow** /'fʌrəʊ/ n solco m

**furry** /'fɜ:rɪ/ a (animal) peloso; (toy) di peluche

**further** /'fɜ:ðə(r)/ a (additional) ulteriore; **at the ~ end** all'altra estremità; **until ~ notice** fino a nuovo avviso ● adv più lontano; ~,... inoltre,...; ~ off più lontano ● vt promuovere

**further education** n istruzione f parauniversitaria

**furthermore** /fɜ:ðə'mɔ:(r)/ adv per di più

**furthest** /'fɜ:ðɪst/ a più lontano ● adv più lontano; **the ~ advanced of the students** lo studente più avanti

**furtive** /'fɜ:tɪv/ a furtivo

**furtively** /'fɜ:tɪvlɪ/ adv furtivamente

**fury** /'fjʊərɪ/ n furore m

**fuse¹** /fju:z/ n (of bomb) detonatore m; (cord) miccia f

**fuse²** n Electr fusibile m ● vt fondere; Electr far saltare ● vi fondersi; Electr saltare; **the lights have ~d** sono saltate le luci

**fuse box** n scatola f dei fusibili

**fuselage** /'fju:zəlɑ:ʒ/ n Aeron fusoliera f

**fuse wire** n (filo m di) fusibile m

**fusillade** /fju:zɪl'ɑ:d/ n Mil scarica f; fig raffica f

**fusion** /'fju:ʒn/ n fusione f

**fuss** /fʌs/ n storie fpl; **make a ~** fare storie; **make a ~ of** colmare di attenzioni ● vi fare storie

**fussy** /'fʌsɪ/ a (-ier, -iest) (person) difficile da accontentare; (clothes etc) pieno di fronzoli

**fusty** /'fʌstɪ/ a che odora di stantio; (smell) di stantio

**futile** /'fju:taɪl/ a inutile

**futility** /fju:'tɪlətɪ/ n futilità f

**future** /'fju:tʃə(r)/ a & n futuro; **in ~** in futuro

**future perfect** n futuro m anteriore

**futures** npl Fin contratti mpl a termine

**futuristic** /fju:tʃə'rɪstɪk/ a futuristico

**fuzz** /fʌz/ n **the ~** (sl: police) la pula

**fuzzy** /'fʌzɪ/ a (-ier, -iest) (hair) crespo; (photo) sfuocato

# Gg

**g, G** /dʒi:/ n (letter) g, G f inv; Mus sol m inv
**g** abbr (**gram(s)**) g
**gab** /gæb/ n fam **have the gift of the ~** avere la parlantina
**gabardine** /ˈgæbəˈdi:n/ n gabardine f
**gabble** /ˈgæb(ə)l/ vi parlare troppo in fretta
**gable** /ˈgeɪb(ə)l/ n frontone m
**gad** /gæd/ vi (pt/pp **gadded**) **~ about** andarsene in giro
**gadget** /ˈgædʒɪt/ n aggeggio m
**Gaelic** /ˈgeɪlɪk/ a & n gaelico m
**gaff** /gæf/ n Br fam **blow the ~** spifferare un segreto; **blow the ~ on sth** svelare la verità su qcsa
**gaffe** /gæf/ n gaffe f inv
**gaffer** /ˈgæfə(r)/ n (Br: foreman) caposquadra m; (Br: boss) capo m; Cinema, TV tecnico m delle luci
**gag** /gæg/ n bavaglio m; (joke) battuta f ● vt (pt/pp **gagged**) imbavagliare
**gaga** /ˈgɑ:gɑ:/ a fam rimbambito
**gage** /geɪdʒ/ n & vt Am = **gauge**
**gaiety** /ˈgeɪətɪ/ n allegria f
**gaily** /ˈgeɪlɪ/ adv allegramente
**gain** /geɪn/ n guadagno m; (increase) aumento m ● vt acquisire; **~ weight** aumentare di peso; **~ access** accedere ● vi ⟨clock:⟩ andare avanti
**gainful** /ˈgeɪnful/ a **~ employment** lavoro m remunerativo
**gainsay** /geɪnˈseɪ/ vt contraddire ⟨person⟩; contestare ⟨argument⟩
**gait** /geɪt/ n andatura f
**gala** /ˈgɑ:lə/ n gala f; **swimming ~** manifestazione f di nuoto ● attrib di gala
**galaxy** /ˈgæləksɪ/ n galassia f
**gale** /geɪl/ n bufera f
**gale warning** n avvertimento m di imminente bufera
**gall** /gɔ:l/ n (impudence) impudenza f
**gallant** /ˈgælənt/ a coraggioso; (chivalrous) galante
**gallantly** /ˈgæləntlɪ/ adv galantemente
**gallantry** /ˈgæləntrɪ/ n coraggio m
**gall bladder** n cistifellea f
**gallery** /ˈgælərɪ/ n galleria f
**galley** /ˈgælɪ/ n (ship's kitchen) cambusa f
**galley** [**proof**] n bozza f in colonna
**Gallic** /ˈgælɪk/ a francese
**gallivant** /ˈgælɪvænt/ vi fam andare in giro
**gallon** /ˈgælən/ n gallone m (= 4,5 l; Am = 3,7 l)
**gallop** /ˈgæləp/ n galoppo m ● vi galoppare
**gallows** /ˈgæləʊz/ n forca f
**gallstone** /ˈgɔ:lstəʊn/ n calcolo m biliare
**galore** /gəˈlɔ:(r)/ adv a bizzeffe

**galvanize** /ˈgælvənaɪz/ vt Techn galvanizzare; fig stimolare (**into** a)
**Gambia** /ˈgæmbɪə/ n Gambia f
**gambit** /ˈgæmbɪt/ n prima mossa f
**gamble** /ˈgæmbl/ n (risk) azzardo m ● vi giocare; (on Stock Exchange) speculare; **~ on** (rely) contare su
**gambler** /ˈgæmblə(r)/ n giocatore, -trice mf [d'azzardo]
**gambling** /ˈgæmblɪŋ/ n gioco m [d'azzardo]
**gambol** /ˈgæmb(ə)l/ vi saltellare
**game** /geɪm/ n gioco m; (match) partita f; (animals, birds) selvaggina f; **~s** pl Sch ≈ ginnastica f ● a (brave) coraggioso; **are you ~?** ti va?; **be ~ for** essere pronto per
**game: game bird** n uccello m da cacciagione. **gamekeeper** n guardacaccia m inv. **game park** n = **game reserve**. **game point** n Tennis game point m inv. **game reserve** n (for hunting) riserva f di caccia; (for preservation) parco m naturale [faunistico]. **game show** n ≈ quiz m inv televisivo
**gamesmanship** /ˈgeɪmzmənʃɪp/ n stratagemmi mpl
**game warden** n guardacaccia m inv
**gaming laws** /ˈgeɪmɪŋ/ npl leggi fpl che regolano il gioco d'azzardo
**gaming machine** n slot machine f inv
**gammon** /ˈgæmən/ n coscia f di maiale affumicata
**gamut** /ˈgæmət/ n fig gamma f
**gander** /ˈgændə(r)/ n oca f maschio; **take a ~ at sth** fam dare un'occhiata a qcsa
**gang** /gæŋ/ n banda f; (of workmen) squadra f ■ **gang up** vi far comunella (**on** contro)
**gangland** /ˈgæŋlænd/ n malavita f
**gangleader** /ˈgæŋli:də(r)/ n capobanda mf inv
**gangling** /ˈgæŋglɪŋ/ a spilungone
**gangplank** /ˈgæŋplæŋk/ n passerella f
**gang rape** n stupro m collettivo
**gangrene** /ˈgæŋgri:n/ n cancrena f
**gangrenous** /ˈgæŋgrɪnəs/ a cancrenoso
**gangster** /ˈgæŋstə(r)/ n gangster m inv
**gangway** /ˈgæŋweɪ/ n passaggio m; Naut, Aeron passerella f
**gaol** /dʒeɪl/ n carcere m ● vt incarcerare
**gaoler** /ˈdʒeɪlə(r)/ n carceriere m
**gap** /gæp/ n spazio m; (in ages, between teeth) scarto m; (in memory) vuoto m; (in story) punto m oscuro
**gape** /geɪp/ vi stare a bocca aperta; (be wide open) spalancarsi; **~ at** guardare a bocca aperta
**gaping** /ˈgeɪpɪŋ/ a aperto
**garage** /ˈgærɑ:ʒ/ n garage m inv; (for

*repairs)* meccanico *m*; *(for petrol)* stazione *f* di servizio

**garage mechanic** *n* meccanico *m*

**garage sale** *n* vendita *f* di articoli usati a casa propria

**garb** /gɑːb/ *n* tenuta *f*

**garbage** /'gɑːbɪdʒ/ *n* immondizia *f*; *(nonsense)* idiozie *fpl*

**garbage can** *n Am* bidone *m* dell'immondizia

**garbled** /'gɑːbld/ *a* confuso

**garden** /'gɑːdn/ *n* giardino *m*; [**public**] ~**s** *pl* giardini *mpl* pubblici ● *vi* fare giardinaggio

**garden centre** *n Br* vivaio *m* *(che vende anche articoli da giardinaggio)*

**garden city** *n* città *f inv* giardino

**gardener** /'gɑːdnə(r)/ *n* giardiniere, -a *mf*

**garden flat** *n* appartamento *m* al pianterreno o seminterrato che dà sul giardino

**gardening** /'gɑːdnɪŋ/ *n* giardinaggio *m*

**garden: garden shears** *npl* cesoie *fpl*. **garden suburb** *n* periferia *f* verde. **garden-variety** *a* ⟨*Am: writer, book*⟩ insignificante

**gargle** /'gɑːgl/ *n* gargarismo *m* ● *vi* fare gargarismi

**gargoyle** /'gɑːgɔɪl/ *n* gargouille *f inv*

**garish** /'geərɪʃ/ *a* sgargiante

**garland** /'gɑːlənd/ *n* ghirlanda *f*

**garlic** /'gɑːlɪk/ *n* aglio *m*

**garlic bread** *n* pane *m* condito con aglio

**garlic press** *n* spremiaglio *m inv*

**garment** /'gɑːmənt/ *n* indumento *m*

**garnet** /'gɑːnɪt/ *n* granato *m*

**garnish** /'gɑːnɪʃ/ *n* guarnizione *f* ● *vt* guarnire

**garret** /'gærɪt/ *n* soffitta *f*

**garrison** /'gærɪsn/ *n* guarnigione *f*

**garrotte** /gə'rɒt/ *n Br* garrotta *f* ● *vt* *(strangle)* strangolare

**garrulous** /'gærʊləs/ *a* chiacchierone

**garter** /'gɑːtə(r)/ *n* giarrettiera *f*; *(Am: for man's socks)* reggicalze *m inv* da uomo

**gas** /gæs/ *n* gas *m inv*; *(Am fam: petrol)* benzina *f* ● *v* *(pt/pp* **gassed**) ● *vt* asfissiare ● *vi fam* blaterare

**gas: gas burner** *n* becco *m* a gas. **gas chamber** *n* camera *f* a gas. **gas cooker** *n* cucina *f* a gas

**gaseous** /'gæsɪəs/ *a* gassoso

**gas fire** *n* stufa *f* a gas

**gas-fired** /-faɪəd/ *a* ⟨*boiler, water heater*⟩ a gas

**gash** /gæʃ/ *n* taglio *m* ● *vt* tagliare; ~ **one's arm** farsi un taglio nel braccio

**gasket** /'gæskɪt/ *n Techn* guarnizione *f*

**gas: gas main** *n* conduttura *f* del gas. **gas mask** *n* maschera *f* antigas. **gas meter** *n* contatore *m* del gas

**gasoline** /'gæsəliːn/ *n Am* benzina *f*

**gasp** /gɑːsp/ *vi* avere il fiato mozzato

**gas ring** *n Br* *(fixed)* bruciatore *m*; *(portable)* fornelletto *m* [portatile]

**gas station** *n Am* distributore *m* di benzina

**gassy** /'gæsɪ/ *a* ⟨*drink*⟩ gassato

**gastric** /'gæstrɪk/ *a* gastrico

**gastric flu** *n* influenza *f* gastro-intestinale

**gastric ulcer** *n* ulcera *f* gastrica

**gastritis** /gæ'straɪtɪs/ *n* gastrite *f*

**gastroenteritis** /gæstrəʊentə'raɪtɪs/ *n* gastroenterite *f*

**gastronomy** /gæ'strɒnəmɪ/ *n* gastronomia *f*

**gate** /geɪt/ *n* cancello *m*; *(at airport)* uscita *f*

**gâteau** /'gætəʊ/ *n* torta *f*

**gate: gatecrash** *vt* entrare senza invito a ● *vi* entrare senza invito. **gatecrasher** *n* intruso, -a *mf*. **gatehouse** *n* ⟨*to castle*⟩ corpo *m* di guardia; *(to park)* casa *f* del custode. **gatekeeper** *n* custode *mf*. **gatepost** *n* palo *m* del cancello. **gateway** *n* ingresso *m*

**gather** /'gæðə(r)/ *vt* raccogliere; *(conclude)* dedurre; *(in sewing)* arricciare; ~ **speed** acquistare velocità; ~ **together** radunare ⟨*people, belongings*⟩; *(obtain gradually)* acquistare ● *vi* ⟨*people:*⟩ radunarsi; **a storm is** ~**ing** si sta preparando un acquazzone

**gathering** /'gæðərɪŋ/ *n* **family** ~ ritrovo *m* di famiglia

**gauche** /gəʊʃ/ *a* ⟨*person, attitude*⟩ impacciato; ⟨*remark*⟩ inopportuno

**gaudy** /'gɔːdɪ/ *a* (**-ier, -iest**) pacchiano

**gauge** /geɪdʒ/ *n* calibro *m*; *Rail* scartamento *m*; *(device)* indicatore *m* ● *vt* misurare; *fig* stimare

**gaunt** /gɔːnt/ *a* *(thin)* smunto

**gauntlet** /'gɔːntlɪt/ *n* **throw down the** ~ lanciare il guanto della sfida

**gauze** /gɔːz/ *n* garza *f*

**gave** /geɪv/ *see* give

**gawky** /'gɔːkɪ/ *a* (**-ier, -iest**) sgraziato

**gawp** /gɔːp/ *vi* ~ (**at**) *fam* guardare con aria da ebete

**gay** /geɪ/ *a* gaio; *(homosexual)* omosessuale ⟨*bar, club*⟩ gay

**gaze** /geɪz/ *n* sguardo *m* fisso ● *vi* guardare; ~ **at** fissare; ~ **into space** avere lo sguardo perso nel vuoto

**gazelle** /gə'zel/ *n* gazzella *f*

**gazette** /gə'zet/ *n* *(official journal)* bollettino *m* ufficiale; *(newspaper title)* gazzetta *f*

**gazetteer** /gæzɪ'tɪə(r)/ *n* *(book)* dizionario *m* geografico; *(part of book)* indice *m* dei nomi geografici

**gazump** /gə'zʌmp/ *vt Comm sl* **we've been** ~**ed** il proprietario della casa ha optato per un'offerta migliore dopo avere accettato la nostra

**GB** *abbr* (**Great Britain**) GB

**GBH** *n abbr* (**grievous bodily harm**) lesioni *fpl* personali grave

**GCSE** *n Br abbr* (**General Certificate of Secondary Education**) *esami mpl conclusivi della scuola dell'obbligo*

**GDP** *n abbr* (**gross domestic product**) PIL *m*

**gear** /gɪə(r)/ *n* equipaggiamento *m*; *Techn* ingranaggio *m*; *Auto* marcia *f*; **in** ~ con la marcia innestata; **change** ~ cambiare marcia ● *vt* finalizzare (**to** a) ● *vi* ~ **up for** prepararsi per ⟨*election*⟩

**gearbox** /'gɪəbɒks/ n Auto scatola f del cambio

**gear lever**, Am **gear shift** n leva f del cambio

**geese** /giːs/ see **goose**

**geezer** /'giːzə(r)/ n sl tipo m

**gel** /dʒel/ n gel m inv

**gelatine** /'dʒelatɪn/ n gelatina f

**gelatinous** /dʒɪ'lætɪnəs/ a gelatinoso

**gelding** /'geldɪŋ/ n (horse) castrone m; (castration) castrazione f

**gelignite** /'dʒelɪgnaɪt/ n gelatina f esplosiva

**gem** /dʒem/ n gemma f

**Gemini** /'dʒemɪnaɪ/ n Astr Gemelli mpl

**gen** /dʒen/ n Br fam informazioni fpl; **what's the ~ on this?** cosa c'è da sapere su questo?

**gender** /'dʒendə(r)/ n Gram genere m

**gene** /dʒiːn/ n gene m

**genealogy** /dʒiːnɪ'ælədʒɪ/ n genealogia f

**gene pool** n pool m genetico

**general** /'dʒenrəl/ a generale ● n generale m; **in ~** in generale

**general election** n elezioni fpl politiche

**generalization** /dʒenrəlaɪ'zeɪʃn/ n generalizzazione f

**generalize** /'dʒenrəlaɪz/ vi generalizzare

**general knowledge** n cultura f generale

**generally** /'dʒenrəlɪ/ adv generalmente

**general: general practitioner** n medico m generico. **general public** n [grande] pubblico m. **general-purpose** a multiuso inv

**generate** /'dʒenəreɪt/ vt generare

**generation** /dʒenə'reɪʃn/ n generazione f

**generation gap** n gap m inv generazionale

**generator** /'dʒenəreɪtə(r)/ n generatore m

**generic** /dʒɪ'nerɪk/ a **~ term** termine m generico

**generosity** /dʒenə'rɒsətɪ/ n generosità f

**generous** /'dʒenərəs/ a generoso

**generously** /'dʒenərəslɪ/ adv generosamente

**genesis** /'dʒenəsɪs/ n fig genesi f inv

**genetic** /dʒɪ'netɪk/ a genetico

**genetic engineering** n ingegneria f genetica

**genetic fingerprinting** /'fɪŋɡəprɪntɪŋ/ n impronte fpl genetiche

**geneticist** /dʒɪ'netɪsɪst/ n genetista mf

**genetics** /dʒɪ'netɪks/ n genetica f

**Geneva** /dʒɪ'niːvə/ n Ginevra f

**genial** /'dʒiːnɪəl/ a gioviale

**genially** /'dʒiːnɪəlɪ/ adv con giovialità

**genie** /'dʒiːnɪ/ n genio m

**genitals** /'dʒenɪtlz/ npl genitali mpl

**genitive** /'dʒenɪtɪv/ a & n **~ [case]** genitivo m

**genius** /'dʒiːnɪəs/ n (pl **-uses**) genio m

**Genoa** /'dʒenəʊə/ n Genova f

**genocide** /'dʒenəsaɪd/ n genocidio m

**genre** /'ʒɒrə/ n genere m [letterario]

**gent** /dʒent/ n fam signore m; **the ~s** sg il bagno per uomini

**genteel** /dʒen'tiːl/ a raffinato

**gentle** /'dʒentl/ a delicato; (breeze, tap, slope) leggero

**gentleman** /'dʒentlmən/ n signore m; (well-mannered) gentiluomo m

**gentleness** /'dʒentlnɪs/ n delicatezza f

**gently** /'dʒentlɪ/ adv delicatamente

**gentry** /'dʒentrɪ/ n alta borghesia f

**genuine** /'dʒenjʊɪn/ a genuino

**genuinely** /'dʒenjʊɪnlɪ/ adv (sorry) sinceramente

**genus** /'dʒiːnəs/ n Biol genere m

**geographer** /dʒɪ'ɒɡrəfə(r)/ n geografo m

**geographical** /dʒɪə'ɡræfɪkl/ a geografico

**geographically** /dʒɪə'ɡræfɪklɪ/ adv geographicamente

**geography** /dʒɪ'ɒɡrəfɪ/ n geografia f

**geological** /dʒɪə'lɒdʒɪkl/ a geologico

**geologist** /dʒɪ'ɒlədʒɪst/ n geologo. -a mf

**geology** /dʒɪ'ɒlədʒɪ/ n geologia f

**geometric[al]** /dʒɪə'metrɪk[l]/ a geometrico

**geometry** /dʒɪ'ɒmətrɪ/ n geometria f

**geophysics** /dʒɪəʊ'fɪzɪks/ n geofisica f

**geopolitical** /dʒiː'əʊpə'lɪtɪkl/ a geopolitico

**Georgian** /'dʒɔːdʒən/ n & a georgiano, -a mf; (language) georgiano m

**geranium** /dʒə'reɪnɪəm/ n geranio m

**gerbil** /'dʒɜːbəl/ n gerbillo m

**geriatric** /dʒerɪ'ætrɪk/ a geriatrico

**geriatrics** /dʒerɪ'ætrɪks/ n geriatria f

**geriatric ward** n reparto m geriatria

**germ** /dʒɜːm/ n germe m; **~s** pl microbi mpl

**German** /'dʒɜːmən/ n & a tedesco, -a mf; (language) tedesco m

**germane** /dʒə'meɪn/ a (point, remark) pertinente

**Germanic** /dʒə'mænɪk/ a germanico

**German measles** n rosolia f

**German shepherd** n pastore m tedesco

**Germany** /'dʒɜːmənɪ/ n Germania f

**germinate** /'dʒɜːmɪneɪt/ vi germogliare

**germ warfare** n guerra f batteriologica

**gerrymandering** /'dʒerɪmænd(ə)rɪŋ/ n manipolazione f dei confini di una circoscrizione elettorale

**gerund** /'dʒerənd/ n gerundio m

**gestate** /dʒe'steɪt/ vi Biol essere incinta; fig maturare

**gestation** /dʒe'steɪʃən/ n gestazione f

**gesticulate** /dʒe'stɪkjʊleɪt/ vi gesticolare

**gesture** /'dʒestʃə(r)/ n gesto m

**get** /get/ v (pt/pp **got**, pp Am also **gotten**, pres p **getting**) ● vt (receive) ricevere; (obtain) ottenere; trovare (job); (buy, catch, fetch) prendere; (transport, deliver to airport etc) portare; (reach on telephone) trovare; (fam: understand) comprendere; preparare (meal); **~ sb to do sth** far fare qcsa a qcno ● vi (become) **~ tired/bored/angry** stancarsi/annoiarsi/arrabbiarsi; **I'm ~ting hungry** mi sta venendo fame; **~ real!** fatti furbo!; **~ dressed/married** vestirsi/sposarsi; **~ sth ready** preparare qcsa; **~ nowhere** non concludere nulla; **this is ~ting us nowhere** questo non ci è di nessun aiuto; **~ to** (reach) arrivare a

■ **get about** vi ⟨person:⟩ muoversi; ⟨rumour:⟩ circolare

■ **get along** vi = get on

■ **get along with** vt andare d'accordo con ⟨sb⟩

■ **get around** vi = get about

■ **get at** vt ⟨criticize⟩ criticare; **I see what you're ~ting at** ho capito cosa vuoi dire; **what are you ~ting at?** dove vuoi andare a parare?

■ **get away** vi ⟨leave⟩ andarsene; ⟨escape⟩ scappare

■ **get back** vi tornare; **I'll ~ back to you** ci faccio sapere ● vt ⟨recover⟩ riavere; **~ one's own back** rifarsi

■ **get behind with** vt rimanere indietro con

■ **get by** vi passare; ⟨manage⟩ cavarsela

■ **get down** vi scendere; **~ down to work** mettersi al lavoro ● vt ⟨depress⟩ buttare giù

■ **get in** vi entrare ● vt mettere dentro ⟨washing⟩; far venire ⟨plumber⟩

■ **get off** vi scendere; ⟨from work⟩ andarsene; Jur essere assolto; **~ off the bus/one's bike** scendere dal pullman/dalla bici ● vt ⟨remove⟩ togliere

■ **get on** vi salire; ⟨be on good terms⟩ andare d'accordo; ⟨make progress⟩ andare avanti; ⟨in life⟩ riuscire; **~ on the bus/one's bike** salire sul pullman/sulla bici; **how are you ~ting on?** come va?

■ **get out** vi uscire; ⟨of car⟩ scendere; **~ out!** fuori! ● vt togliere ⟨cork, stain⟩

■ **get out of** vt ⟨avoid doing⟩ evitare

■ **get over** vi andare al di là ● vt fig riprendersi da ⟨illness⟩

■ **get round** vt aggirare ⟨rule⟩; rigirare ⟨person⟩ ● vi **I never ~ round to it** non mi sono mai deciso a farlo

■ **get through** vi ⟨on telephone⟩ prendere la linea

■ **get up** vi alzarsi; ⟨climb⟩ salire; **~ up a hill** salire su una collina

**get: getaway** n fuga f. **get-together** n incontro m fra amici. **get-up** n tenuta f. **get-up-and-go** n dinamismo m

**geyser** /'giːzə(r)/ n scaldabagno m; Geol geyser m inv

**G-force** n forza f di gravità

**ghastly** /'gɑːstlɪ/ a (-ier, -iest) terribile; **feel ~** sentirsi da cani

**gherkin** /'gɜːkɪn/ n cetriolino m

**ghetto** /'getəʊ/ n ghetto m

**ghetto blaster** /blɑːstə(r)/ n fam radioregistratore m stereo portatile

**ghost** /gəʊst/ n fantasma m

**ghostly** /'gəʊstlɪ/ a spettrale

**ghost town** n città f inv fantasma

**ghost writer** n negro m

**ghoulish** /'guːlɪʃ/ a macabro

**giant** /'dʒaɪənt/ n gigante m ● a gigante

**gibberish** /'dʒɪbərɪʃ/ n stupidaggini fpl

**gibe** /dʒaɪb/ n malignità f inv ● vi beffarsi (at di)

**giblets** /'dʒɪblɪts/ npl frattaglie fpl

**giddiness** /'gɪdɪnɪs/ n vertigini fpl

**giddy** /'gɪdɪ/ a (-ier, -iest) vertiginoso; **feel ~** avere le vertigini

**giddy spell** n giramento m di testa

**gift** /gɪft/ n dono m; ⟨made to charity⟩ donazione f

**gifted** /'gɪftɪd/ a dotato

**gift: gift token** n Br buono m acquisto. **gift voucher** n Br buono m acquisto. **gift-wrap** vt impacchettare in carta da regalo

**gig** /gɪg/ n Mus fam concerto m

**gigantic** /dʒaɪˈgæntɪk/ a gigantesco

**giggle** /'gɪg(ə)l/ n risatina f ● vi ridacchiare

**giggly** /'gɪglɪ/ a ⟨person⟩ che ha la ridarella

**gild** /gɪld/ vt dorare

**gilding** /'gɪldɪŋ/ n doratura f

**gill** /dʒɪl/ n ⟨measure⟩ quarto m di pinta

**gills** /gɪlz/ npl branchia fsg

**gilt** /gɪlt/ a dorato ● n doratura f

**gilt-edged stock** /-edʒd/ n Fin investimento m sicuro

**gimlet** /'gɪmlɪt/ n succhiello m

**gimmick** /'gɪmɪk/ n trovata f

**gimmicky** /'gɪmɪkɪ/ a ⟨production⟩ pieno di trovate a effetto

**gin** /dʒɪn/ n gin m inv

**ginger** /'dʒɪndʒə(r)/ a rosso fuoco inv; ⟨cat⟩ rosso ● n zenzero m

**ginger: ginger ale** n bibita f gassata allo zenzero. **ginger beer** n bibita f allo zenzero. **gingerbread** n panpepato m. **ginger-haired** /-'heəd/ a con i capelli rossi

**gingerly** /'dʒɪndʒəlɪ/ adv con precauzione

**ginger nut, ginger snap** n biscotto m allo zenzero

**gingham** /'gɪŋəm/ n tessuto m vichy

**gin rummy** n variante f del gioco del ramino

**gipsy** /'dʒɪpsɪ/ n = gypsy

**giraffe** /dʒɪˈrɑːf/ n giraffa f

**girder** /'gɜːdə(r)/ n Techn trave f

**girdle** /'gɜːdl/ n cintura f; ⟨corset⟩ busto m

**girl** /gɜːl/ n ragazza f; ⟨female child⟩ femmina f

**girl: girl Friday** n segretaria f tuttofare inv. **girlfriend** n amica f; ⟨of boy⟩ ragazza f. **girl guide** n Br giovane esploratrice f

**girlish** /'gɜːlɪʃ/ a da ragazza

**giro** /'dʒaɪərəʊ/ n bancogiro m; ⟨cheque⟩ sussidio m di disoccupazione

**girth** /gɜːθ/ n circonferenza f

**gist** /dʒɪst/ n **the ~** la sostanza

**give** /gɪv/ n elasticità f ● v (pt gave, pp given) ● vt dare; ⟨as present⟩ regalare (to a); fare ⟨lecture, present, shriek⟩; donare ⟨blood⟩; **~ birth** partorire ● vi ⟨to charity⟩ fare delle donazioni; ⟨yield⟩ cedere

■ **give away** vt dar via; ⟨betray⟩ tradire; ⟨distribute⟩ assegnare; **~ away the bride** portare la sposa all'altare

■ **give back** vt restituire

■ **give in** vt consegnare ● vi ⟨yield⟩ arrendersi

■ **give off** vt emanare

■ **give out** vi ⟨supplies, patience:⟩ esaurirsi;

⟨engine, heart:⟩ fermarsi ● vt (distribute) distribuire; diffondere ⟨heat⟩

■ **give over** vi ~ over! piantala!

■ **give up** vt rinunciare a; ~ **oneself up** arrendersi ● vi rinunciare

■ **give way** vi cedere; Auto dare la precedenza; (collapse) crollare

**give-and-take** n concessioni fpl reciproche

**given** /'gɪvn/ see give ● a ~ **name** nome m di battesimo

**glacier** /'glæsɪə(r)/ n ghiacciaio m

**glad** /glæd/ a contento (of di)

**gladden** /'glædn/ vt rallegrare

**glade** /gleɪd/ n radura f

**gladiator** /'glædɪeɪtə(r)/ n gladiatore m

**gladiolus** /glædɪ'əʊləs/ n gladiolo m

**gladly** /'glædlɪ/ adv volentieri

**glamorize** /'glæməraɪz/vt rendere affascinante

**glamorous** /'glæmərəs/ a affascinante

**glamour** /'glæmə(r)/ n fascino m

**glance** /glɑːns/ n sguardo m ● vi ~ **at** dare un'occhiata a

■ **glance up** vi alzare gli occhi

**gland** /glænd/ n glandola f

**glandular** /'glændjʊlə(r)/ a ghiandolare

**glandular fever** n mononucleosi f

**glare** /gleə(r)/ n bagliore m; (look) occhiataccia f ● vi ~ **at** dare un'occhiataccia a

**glaring** /'gleərɪŋ/ a sfolgorante; ⟨mistake⟩ madornale

**glass** /glɑːs/ n vetro m; (for drinking) bicchiere m

**glasses** /'glɑːsɪz/ npl (spectacles) occhiali mpl

**glasshouse** /'glɑːshaʊs/ n serra f

**glassy** /'glɑːsɪ/ a vitreo

**glassy-eyed** /-'aɪd/ a (from drink, illness) che ha gli occhi vitrei

**glaucoma** /glɔː'kəʊmə/ n glaucoma m

**glaze** /gleɪz/ n smalto m ● vt mettere i vetri a ⟨door, window⟩; smaltare ⟨pottery⟩; Culin spennellare

**glazed** /gleɪzd/ a ⟨eyes⟩ vitreo

**glazier** /'gleɪzɪə(r)/ n vetraio m

**gleam** /gliːm/ n luccichio m ● vi luccicare

**glean** /gliːn/ vt racimolare ⟨information⟩

**glee** /gliː/ n gioia f

**gleeful** /'gliːfʊl/ a gioioso

**gleefully** /'gliːfʊlɪ/ adv giosamente

**glen** /glen/ n vallone m

**glib** /glɪb/ a pej insincero

**glibly** /'glɪblɪ/ adv pej senza sincerità

**glide** /glaɪd/ vi scorrere; (through the air) planare

**glider** /'glaɪdə(r)/ n aliante m

**gliding** /'glaɪdɪŋ/ n volo m a vela

**glimmer** /'glɪmə(r)/ n barlume m ● vi emettere un barlume

**glimpse** /glɪmps/ n occhiata f; **catch a ~ of** intravedere ● vt intravedere

**glint** /glɪnt/ n luccichio m ● vi luccicare

**glisten** /'glɪsn/ vi luccicare

**glitch** /glɪtʃ/ n Comput problema m tecnico

**glitter** /'glɪtə(r)/ vi brillare

**gloat** /gləʊt/ vi gongolare (**over** su)

**global** /'gləʊbl/ a mondiale

**global warming** n riscaldamento m dell'atmosfera terrestre

**globe** /gləʊb/ n globo m; (as a map) mappamondo m

**globe-trotting** /-trɒtɪŋ/ n viaggi mpl intorno al mondo ● a ⟨life⟩ da giramondo; ⟨person⟩ giramondo

**globule** /'glɒbjuːl/ n globulo m

**gloom** /gluːm/ n oscurità f; (sadness) tristezza f

**gloomily** /'gluːmɪlɪ/ adv (sadly) con aria cupa

**gloomy** /'gluːmɪ/ a (-ier, -iest) cupo

**glorify** /'glɔːrɪfaɪ/ vt (pt/pp -ied) glorificare; **a glorified waitress** niente più che una cameriera

**glorious** /'glɔːrɪəs/ a splendido; ⟨deed, hero⟩ glorioso

**glory** /'glɔːrɪ/ n gloria f; (splendour) splendore m; (cause for pride) vanto m ● vi ~ **in** vantarsi di

**glory-hole** n fam ripostiglio m

**gloss** /glɒs/ n lucentezza f

■ **gloss over** vt sorvolare su

**glossary** /'glɒsərɪ/ n glossario m

**gloss paint** n vernice f lucida

**glossy** /'glɒsɪ/ a (-ier, -iest) lucido; ⟨paper⟩ patinato; ~ [**magazine**] rivista f femminile

**glottal stop** /'glɒt(ə)l/ n occlusiva f glottale

**glove** /glʌv/ n guanto m

**glove compartment** n Auto cruscotto m

**glove puppet** n burattino m

**glow** /gləʊ/ n splendore m; (in cheeks) rossore m; (of candle) luce f soffusa ● vi risplendere; ⟨candle:⟩ brillare; ⟨person:⟩ avvampare

**glower** /'glaʊə(r)/ vi ~ (**at**) guardare in cagnesco

**glowing** /'gləʊɪŋ/ a ardente; ⟨account⟩ entusiastico

**glow-worm** n lucciola f

**glucose** /'gluːkəʊs/ n glucosio m

**glue** /gluː/ n colla f ● vt (pres p **gluing**) incollare

**glue-sniffing** /-snɪfɪŋ/ n sniffare m la colla

**glum** /glʌm/ a (**glummer, glummest**) tetro

**glumly** /'glʌmlɪ/ adv con aria tetra

**glut** /glʌt/ n eccesso m

**glutinous** /'gluːtɪnəs/ a colloso

**glutton** /'glʌtən/ n ghiottone, -a mf

**gluttonous** /'glʌtənəs/ a ghiotto

**gluttony** /'glʌtənɪ/ n ghiottoneria f

**glycerine** /'glɪsəriːn/ n glicerina f

**gm** abbr (**gram**) g

**gnarled** /nɑːld/ a nodoso

**gnash** /næʃ/ vt ~ **one's teeth** digrignare i denti

**gnat** /næt/ n moscerino m

**gnaw** /nɔː/ vt rosicchiare

**gnome** /nəʊm/ n gnomo m

**GNP** n abbr (**gross national product**) PNL m

**go** /gəʊ/ n (pl **goes**) energia f; (attempt) tentativo *m*; **on the go** in movimento; **at one go** in una sola volta; **it's your go** tocca a te; **make a go of it** riuscire ● *vi* (*pt* went, *pp* gone) andare; (*leave*) andar via; (*vanish*) sparire; (*become*) diventare; (*be sold*) vendersi; **go and see** andare a vedere; **go swimming/ shopping** andare a nuotare/fare spese; **where's the time gone?** come ha fatto il tempo a volare così?; **it's all gone** è finito; **be going to do** stare per fare; **I'm not going to** non ne ho nessuna intenzione; **to go** ⟨*Am: hamburgers etc*⟩ da asporto: **a coffee to go** un caffè da portar via

■ **go about** *vi* andare in giro
■ **go about** *vt* affrontare ⟨*task*⟩
■ **go after** *vt* (*chase, pursue*) correr dietro a
■ **go ahead** *vi* (*event*) aver luogo; **go ahead with** mandare avanti ⟨*plans, wedding*⟩
■ **go away** *vi* andarsene
■ **go back** *vi* ritornare
■ **go by** *vi* passare
■ **go down** *vi* scendere; ⟨*sun:*⟩ tramontare; ⟨*ship:*⟩ affondare; ⟨*swelling:*⟩ diminuire
■ **go for** *vt* andare a prendere; andare a cercare ⟨*doctor*⟩; (*choose*) optare per; (*fam: attack*) aggredire; **he's not the kind I go for** non è il genere che mi attira
■ **go in** *vi* entrare
■ **go in for** *vt* partecipare a ⟨*competition*⟩; darsi a ⟨*tennis*⟩
■ **go off** *vi* andarsene; ⟨*alarm:*⟩ scattare; ⟨*gun, bomb:*⟩ esplodere; ⟨*food, milk:*⟩ andare a male; **go off well** riuscire
■ **go on** *vi* andare avanti; **what's going on?** cosa succede?
■ **go on at** *vt fam* scocciare
■ **go on with** *vt* (*continue*) andare avanti con
■ **go out** *vi* uscire; ⟨*light, fire:*⟩ spegnersi
■ **go out with** *vt* uscire con ⟨*sb*⟩
■ **go over** *vi* andare ● *vt* (*check*) controllare
■ **go round** *vi* andare in giro; (*visit*) andare; (*turn*) girare; **is there enough to go round?** ce n'è abbastanza per tutti?
■ **go through** *vi* ⟨*bill, proposal:*⟩ passare ● *vt* (*suffer*) subire; (*check*) controllare; (*read*) leggere
■ **go under** *vi* passare sotto; ⟨*ship, swimmer:*⟩ andare sott'acqua; (*fail*) fallire
■ **go up** *vi* salire; ⟨*Theat: curtain:*⟩ aprirsi
■ **go with** *vt* accompagnare
■ **go without** *vt* fare a meno di ⟨*supper, sleep*⟩ ● *vi* fare senza

**goad** /gəʊd/ *vt* spingere (**into** a); (*taunt*) spronare

**go-ahead** *a* ⟨*person, company*⟩ intraprendente ● *n* okay *m*

**goal** /gəʊl/ *n* porta *f*; (*point scored*) gol *m inv*; (*in life*) obiettivo *m*; **score a ~** segnare

**goalie** /'gəʊlɪ/ *fam*, **goalkeeper** /'gəʊlki:pə(r)/ *n* portiere *m*

**goalpost** /'gəʊlpəʊst/ *n* palo *m*

**goat** /gəʊt/ *n* capra *f*

**goatee** /gəʊ'ti:/ *n* pizzo *m*

■ **gobble up** /'gɒbl/ *vt* tranguigiare

**gobbledygook** /'gɒb(ə)ldɪgu:k/ *n* ostrogoto *m*

**go-between** *n* intermediario. -a *mf*

**goblet** /'gɒblɪt/ *n* calice *m*

**goblin** /'gɒblɪn/ *n* folletto *m*

**gobsmacked** /'gɒbsmækt/ *a Br fam* **I was ~** sono rimasto a bocca aperta

**God, god** /gɒd/ *n* Dio *m*, dio *m*

**god: godchild** *n* figlioccio, -a *mf*. **goddamn** *a* maledetto. **god-daughter** *n* figlioccia *f*

**goddess** /'gɒdes/ *n* dea *f*

**god: godfather** *n* padrino *m*. **god-fearing** /-fɪərɪŋ/ *a* timorato di Dio. **god-forsaken** /-fəseɪkən/ *a* dimenticato da Dio

**godless** /'gɒdlɪs/ *a* empio

**godlike** /'gɒdlaɪk/ *a* divino

**godly** /'gɒdlɪ/ *a* (**-ier, iest**) pio

**god: godmother** *n* madrina *f*. **godparents** *npl* padrino *m* e madrina *f*. **godsend** *n* manna *f*. **godson** *n* figlioccio *m*

**goer** /'gəʊə(r)/ *n Br* **be a ~** ⟨*car:*⟩ essere una bomba

**go-getter** *n* ambizioso, -a *mf*

**go-getter** /'gəʊgetə(r)/ *n* persona *f* intraprendente

**go-getting** /-getɪŋ/ *a* intraprendente

**goggle** /'gɒgl/ *vi fam* **~ at** fissare con gli occhi sgranati ·

**goggles** *npl* occhiali *mpl*; (*of swimmer*) occhialini *mpl* [da piscina]; (*of worker*) occhiali *mpl* protettivi

**going** /'gəʊɪŋ/ *a* ⟨*price, rate*⟩ corrente; **~ concern** azienda *f* florida ● *n* **it's hard ~** è una faticaccia; **while the ~ is good** finché si può

**going-over** *n* (*cleaning*) pulizia *f* da cima a fondo; (*examination*) revisione *f*; **the doctor gave me a thorough ~** il dottore mi ha fatto una visita completa; **give sb a ~** (*beat up*) dare una manica di botte a qcno

**goings-on** *npl* avvenimenti *mpl*

**go-kart** /-kɑ:t/ *n* go-kart *m inv*

**go-karting** /-kɑ:tɪŋ/ *n* kartismo *m*; **go ~** fare del kartismo

**gold** /gəʊld/ *n* oro *m* ● *a* d'oro

**gold-digger** *n fig* cacciatore, -trice *mf* di dote

**gold dust** *n* polvere *f* d'oro; *fig* cosa *f* rara

**golden** /'gəʊldn/ *a* dorato

**golden handshake** *n Br* buonuscita *f* (*al termine di un rapporto di lavoro*)

**golden wedding** *n* nozze *fpl* d'oro

**gold: goldfish** *n inv* pesce *m* rosso. **gold mine** *n* miniera *f* d'oro. **gold-plated** /'pleɪtɪd/ *a* placcato d'oro. **goldsmith** *n* orefice *m*

**golf** /gɒlf/ *n* golf *m*

**golf club** *n* circolo *m* di golf; (*implement*) mazza *f* da golf

**golf course** *n* campo *m* di golf

**golfer** /'gɒlfə(r)/ *n* giocatore, -trice *mf* di golf

**golliwog** /'gɒlɪwɒg/ *n* bambolotto *m* negro

**gondola** /'gɒndələ/ *n* gondola *f*

**gondolier** /gɒndə'lɪə(r)/ *n* gondoliere *m*

**gone** /gɒn/ *see* go

**goner** /'gɒnə(r)/ n fam **be a ~** essere spacciato

**gong** /gɒŋ/ n gong m inv

**gonorrh[o]ea** /gɒnə'rɪə/ n gonorrea f

**good** /gʊd/ a (**better, best**) buono; ⟨child, footballer, singer⟩ bravo; ⟨holiday, film⟩ bello; **~ at** bravo in; **a ~ deal of anger** molta rabbia; **as ~ as** (almost) quasi; **~ morning, ~ afternoon** buon giorno; **~ evening** buona sera; **~ night** buonanotte; **have a ~ time** divertirsi ● **n** bene m; **for ~** per sempre; **do ~** far del bene; **do sb ~** far bene a qcno; **it's no ~** è inutile; **be up to no ~** combinare qualcosa

**goodbye** /gʊd'baɪ/ int arrivederci

**good: good-for-nothing** n buono, -a mf a nulla ● a her **~ son** quel buono a nulla di suo figlio. **Good Friday** n Venerdì m Santo. **good-humoured** /-'hju:məd/ a amichevole; ⟨remark, smile⟩ bonario

**goodies** /'gʊdɪz/ npl (fam: to eat) bontà fpl

**good-looking** /-'lʊkɪŋ/ a bello

**good-natured** /-'neɪtʃəd/ a **be ~** avere un buon carattere

**goodness** /'gʊdnɪs/ n bontà f; **my ~!** santo cielo!; **thank ~!** grazie al cielo!

**goods** /gʊdz/ npl prodotti mpl

**goods train** n treno m merci

**good-time girl** n (fun-loving) ragazza f allegra; (euph: prostitute) donnina f allegra

**goodwill** /gʊd'wɪl/ n buona f volontà; Comm avviamento m

**goody** /'gʊdɪ/ n (fam: person) buono m

**goody-goody** n santarellino, -a mf

**gooey** /'gu:ɪ/ a fam appiccicaticcio; fig sdolcinato

**goof** /gu:f/ vi fam cannare

**goofy** /'gu:fɪ/ a fam sciocco

**goon** /gu:n/ n (clown) svitato m; (thug) picchiatore m

**goose** /gu:s/ n (pl geese) oca f

**goose: gooseberry** /'gʊzbərɪ/ n uva f spina. **goose-flesh** n, **goose-pimples** npl pelle f sg d'oca. **goose-step** n passo m dell'oca

**gore¹** /gɔ:(r)/ n sangue m

**gore²** vt incornare

**gorge** /gɔ:dʒ/ n Geog gola f ● vt **~ oneself** ingozzarsi

**gorgeous** /'gɔ:dʒəs/ a stupendo

**gorilla** /gə'rɪlə/ n gorilla m inv

**gormless** /'gɔ:mlɪs/ a fam stupido

**gorse** /gɔ:s/ n ginestrone m

**gory** /'gɔ:rɪ/ a (-ier, -iest) cruento

**gosh** /gɒʃ/ int fam caspita

**gosling** /'gɒzlɪŋ/ n ochetta f

**go-slow** n forma f di protesta che consiste in un rallentamento del ritmo di lavoro

**gospel** /'gɒspl/ n vangelo m

**gospel truth** n sacrosanta verità f

**gossamer** /'gɒsəmə(r)/ n (fabric) mussola f; (cobweb) fili mpl di ragnatela

**gossip** /'gɒsɪp/ n pettegolezzi mpl; (person) pettegolo, -a mf ● vi pettegolare

**gossip column** n cronaca f mondana

**gossipy** /'gɒsɪpɪ/ a pettegolo

**got** /gɒt/ see **get**; **have ~** avere; **have ~ to do sth** dover fare qcsa

**Gothic** /'gɒθɪk/ a gotico

**gotten** /'gɒtn/ Am see **get**

**gouge** /gaʊdʒ/ vt **~ out** cavare

**goulash** /'gu:læʃ/ n gulash m inv

**gourd** /gʊəd/ n (fruit) zucca f

**gourmet** /'gʊəmeɪ/ n buongustaio, -a mf

**gout** /gaʊt/ n gotta f

**govern** /'gʌv(ə)n/ vt/i governare; (determine) determinare

**governess** /'gʌvənɪs/ n istitutrice f

**government** /'gʌvnmənt/ n governo m

**governmental** /gʌvn'mentl/ a governativo

**government stocks** npl titoli mpl di stato

**governor** /'gʌvənə(r)/ n governatore m; (of school) amministratore, -trice mf; (of prison) direttore, -trice mf; (fam: boss) capo m

**gown** /gaʊn/ n vestito m; Univ, Jur toga f

**GP** abbr **general practitioner**

**grab** /græb/ vt (pt/pp **grabbed**) **~ [hold of]** afferrare

**Grace** n his/your **~** (duke) il signor duca; (archbishop) Sua Eccellenza; her/your **~** (duchess) la signora duchessa

**grace** /greɪs/ n grazia f; (before meal) benedicite m inv; **with good ~** volentieri; **say ~** dire il benedicite; **three days' ~** tre giorni di proroga

**graceful** /'greɪsfʊl/ a aggraziato

**gracefully** /'greɪsfʊlɪ/ adv con grazia

**gracious** /'greɪʃəs/ a cortese; (elegant) lussuoso

**gradation** /grə'deɪʃn/ n gradazione f

**grade** /greɪd/ n livello m; Comm qualità f; Sch voto m; (Am Sch: class) classe f; Am = **gradient** ● vt Comm classificare; Sch dare il voto a

**grade crossing** n Am passaggio m a livello

**gradient** /'greɪdɪənt/ n pendenza f

**gradual** /'grædʒʊəl/ a graduale

**gradually** /'grædʒʊəlɪ/ adv gradualmente

**graduate¹** /'grædʒʊət/ n laureato, -a mf

**graduate²** /'grædʒʊeɪt/ vi Univ laurearsi

**graduated** /'grædʒʊeɪtɪd/ a (container) graduato

**graduation** /grædʒʊ'eɪʃn/ n laurea f; (calibration) graduazione f

**graduation ceremony** n cerimonia f di consegna dei diplomi di laurea

**graffiti** /grə'fi:tɪ/ npl graffiti mpl

**graffiti artist** n pittore, -trice mf di graffiti

**graft** /grɑ:ft/ n Bot, Med innesto m; (Med: organ) trapianto m; (fam: hard work) duro lavoro m; (fam: corruption) corruzione f ● vt innestare; trapiantare (organ)

**grain** /greɪn/ n (of sand, salt) granello m; (of rice) chicco m; (cereals) cereali mpl; (in wood) venatura f; **it goes against the ~** fig è contro la mia/sua natura

**grainy** /'greɪnɪ/ a (photograph) sgranato; (paintwork) granulato

**gram** /græm/ n grammo m

**grammar** /'græmə(r)/ n grammatica f

**grammarian** /grə'meərɪən/ n grammatico, -a mf

**grammar school** n ≈ liceo m

**grammatical** /grə'mætɪkl/ a grammaticale

**grammatically** /grə'mætɪklɪ/ adv grammaticalmente

**gran** /græn/ n fam nonna f

**granary** /'grænərɪ/ n granaio m

**grand** /grænd/ a grandioso; fam eccellente

**grand: grandad** /'grændæd/ n fam nonno m. **grandchild** n nipote mf. **granddaughter** n nipote f

**grandeur** /'grændʒə(r)/ n grandiosità f

**grand: grandfather** n nonno m. **grandfather clock** n pendolo m (che poggia a terra)

**grandiose** /'grændɪəʊs/ a grandioso

**grand: grandmother** n nonna f. **grandparents** npl nonni mpl. **grand piano** n pianoforte m a coda. **grand slam** n vittoria f di tutte le fasi di una gara. **grandson** n nipote m. **grandstand** n tribuna f

**granite** /'grænɪt/ n granito m

**granny** /'grænɪ/ n fam nonna f

**granny flat** n Br appartamentino m indipendente per genitori anziani annesso all'abitazione principale

**grant** /grɑ:nt/ n (money) sussidio m; Univ borsa f di studio ● vt accordare; (admit) ammettere; **take sth for ~ed** dare per scontato qcsa; **take sb for ~ed** considerare quello che qcno fa come dovuto

**granular** /'grænjʊlə(r)/ a granulare

**granulated** /'grænjʊleɪtɪd/ a ~ **sugar** zucchero m semolato

**granule** /'grænjuːl/ n granello m

**grape** /greɪp/ n acino m; ~s pl uva fsg

**grapefruit** /'greɪpfruːt/ n inv pompelmo m

**grapevine** /'greɪpvaɪn/ n vite f; **hear sth on the ~** sentir dire in giro qcsa

**graph** /grɑːf/ n grafico m

**graphic** /'græfɪk/ a grafico; (vivid) vivido

**graphically** /'græfɪklɪ/ adv graficamente; (vividly) vividamente

**graphic design** n grafica f

**graphic designer** n grafico, -a mf

**graphics** /'græfɪks/ n grafica f

**graphics card** n Comput scheda f grafica

**graphite** /'græfaɪt/ n grafite f

**graphologist** /græ'fɒlədʒɪst/ n grafologo, -a mf

**graph paper** n carta f millimetrata

**grapple** /'græpl/ vi ~ **with** also fig essere alle prese con

**grasp** /grɑːsp/ n stretta f; (understanding) comprensione f ● vt afferrare

**grasping** /'grɑːspɪŋ/ a avido

**grass** /grɑːs/ n erba f;

**grass: grasshopper** n cavalletta f. **grassland** n prateria f. **grassroots** npl base f; **at the ~** alla base. **grass snake** n biscia f

**grassy** /'grɑːsɪ/ a erboso

**grate¹** /greɪt/ n grata f

**grate²** vt Culin grattugiare; ~ **one's teeth** far stridere i denti ● vi stridere

**grateful** /'greɪtfl/ a grato

**gratefully** /'greɪtfʊlɪ/ adv con gratitudine

**grater** /'greɪtə(r)/ n Culin grattugia f

**gratification** /grætɪfɪ'keɪʃn/ n soddisfazione f

**gratified** /'grætɪfaɪd/ a appagato

**gratify** /'grætɪfaɪ/ vt (pt/pp -ied) appagare

**gratifying** /'grætɪfaɪɪŋ/ a appagante

**grating** /'greɪtɪŋ/ n grata f

**gratis** /'grɑːtɪs/ adv gratis

**gratitude** /'grætɪtjuːd/ n gratitudine f

**gratuitous** /grə'tjuːɪtəs/ a gratuito

**gratuity** /grə'tjuːətɪ/ n gratifica f

**grave¹** /greɪv/ a grave

**grave²** n tomba f

**gravedigger** /'greɪvdɪgə(r)/ n becchino m

**gravel** /'grævl/ n ghiaia f

**gravelly** /'grævəlɪ/ a (voice) rauco

**gravely** /'greɪvlɪ/ adv gravemente

**graven image** /'greɪvən/ n idolo m

**gravestone** /'greɪvstəʊn/ n lapide f

**graveyard** /'greɪvjɑːd/ n cimitero m

**gravitate** /'grævɪteɪt/ vi gravitare

**gravity** /'grævɪtɪ/ n gravità f

**gravy** /'greɪvɪ/ n sugo m della carne

**gray** /greɪ/ a Am = **grey**

**graze¹** /greɪz/ vi (animal:) pascolare

**graze²** n escoriazione f ● vt (touch lightly) sfiorare; (scrape) escoriare; sbucciarsi (knee)

**grease** /griːs/ n grasso m ● vt ungere

**greasepaint** /'griːspeɪnt/ n cerone m

**greaseproof paper** /griːspruːf'peɪpə(r)/ n carta f oleata

**greaser** /'griːsə(r)/ n (motorcyclist) componente m di una banda giovanile di motociclisti

**greasy** /'griːsɪ/ a (-ier, -iest) untuoso; (hair, skin) grasso

**great** /greɪt/ a grande; (fam: marvellous) eccezionale

**great: great-aunt** n prozia f. **Great Britain** n Gran Bretagna f. **Great Dane** n danese m. **great-grandchildren** npl pronipoti mpl. **great-grandfather** n bisnonno m. **great-grandmother** n bisnonna f

**greatly** /'greɪtlɪ/ adv enormemente

**greatness** /'greɪtnɪs/ n grandezza f

**great-uncle** n prozio m

**Grecian** /'griːʃ(ə)n/ a greco

**Greece** /griːs/ n Grecia f

**greed** /griːd/ n avidità f; (for food) ingordigia f

**greedily** /'griːdɪlɪ/ adv avidamente; (eat) con ingordigia

**greedy** /'griːdɪ/ a (-ier, -iest) avido; (for food) ingordo

**Greek** /griːk/ a & n greco, -a mf; (language) greco m

**green** /griːn/ a verde; (fig: inexperienced) immaturo ● n verde m; (grass) prato m; (in golf) green m inv; ~s pl verdura f; **the G~s** pl Pol i verdi

**green: green beans** n fagiolini mpl. **green belt** n zona f verde intorno a una città. **green card** n carta f verde; Am permesso m di soggiorno

**greenery** /'gri:nərı/ n verde m

**green: green-eyed monster** /-aɪd-'mɒnstə(r)/ n gelosia f. **greenfinch** n verdone m. **green fingers** npl **have ~ ~** avere il police verde. **greenfly** n afide m. **greengage** n susina f verde. **greengrocer** n fruttivendolo, -a mf. **greenhorn** n (new) novellino m; (gullible) pivello m. **greenhouse** n serra f. **greenhouse effect** n effetto m serra. **Greenland** n Groenlandia f. **green light** n fam verde m. **green salad** n insalata f verde

**greet** /gri:t/ vt salutare; (welcome) accogliere

**greeting** /'gri:tɪŋ/ n saluto m; (welcome) accoglienza f

**greetings card** /'gri:tɪŋz/ n biglietto m d'auguri

**gregarious** /grɪ'geərɪəs/ a gregario; (person) socievole

**gremlin** /'gremlɪn/ n hum spirito m maligno

**grenade** /grɪ'neɪd/ n granata f

**grenadier** /grenə'dɪə(r)/ n Mil guardia f reale inglese

**grew** /gru:/ see **grow**

**grey** /greɪ/ a grigio; (hair) bianco ● n grigio m ● vi diventare bianco

**grey: greyhound** n levriero m. **grey matter** n (brain) materia f grigia. **grey squirrel** n scoiattolo m grigio

**grid** /grɪd/ n griglia f; (on map) reticolato m; Electr rete f

**griddle** /'grɪd(ə)l/ n (for meat) piastra f

**grid: gridiron** n griglia f; Am campo m di football americano. **gridlock** n (fig: deadlock) situazione f di stallo; (in traffic) imbottigliamento m. **grid reference** n coordinate fpl

**grief** /gri:f/ n dolore m; **come to ~** (plans:) naufragare

**grief-stricken** /-strɪkən/ a affranto dal dolore

**grievance** /'gri:vəns/ n lamentela f

**grieve** /gri:v/ vt addolorare ● vi essere addolorato

**grievous** /'gri:vəs/ a doloroso

**grievously** /'gri:vəslɪ/ adv tristemente

**grill** /grɪl/ n graticola f; (for grilling) griglia f; **mixed ~** grigliata f mista ● vt/i cuocere alla griglia; (interrogate) sottoporre al terzo grado

**grille** /grɪl/ n grata f

**grim** /grɪm/ a (**grimmer**, **grimmest**) arcigno; (determination) accanito

**grimace** /'grɪməs/ n smorfia f ● vi fare una smorfia

**grime** /graɪm/ n sudiciume m

**grimly** /'grɪmlɪ/ adv accanitamente

**Grim Reaper** n Morte f

**grimy** /'graɪmɪ/ a (**-ier, -iest**) sudicio

**grin** /grɪn/ n sorriso m ● vi (pt/pp **grinned**) fare un gran sorriso

**grind** /graɪnd/ n (fam: hard work) sfacchinata f ● vt (pt/pp **ground**) macinare; affilare (knife); (Am: mince) tritare; **~ one's teeth** digrignare i denti

**grindstone** /'graɪndstəʊn/ n mola f; **keep**

**one's nose to the ~** lavorare indefessamente

**grip** /grɪp/ n presa f; fig controllo m; (bag) borsone m; **be in the ~ of** essere in preda a; **get a ~ of oneself** controllarsi ● vt (pt/pp **gripped**) afferrare; (tyres:) far presa su; tenere avvinto (attention)

**gripe** /graɪp/ vi (fam: grumble) lagnarsi

**gripping** /'grɪpɪŋ/ a avvincente

**grisly** /'grɪzlɪ/ a (**-ier, -iest**) raccapricciante

**gristle** /'grɪsl/ n cartilagine f

**grit** /grɪt/ n graniglia f; (for roads) sabbia f; (courage) coraggio m ● vt (pt/pp **gritted**) spargere sabbia su (road); **~ one's teeth** serrare i denti

**gritter** /'grɪtə(r)/ n Br Aut spandighiaia m inv

**gritty** /'grɪtɪ/ a (sandy) pieno di terra; (gravelly) ghiaioso; (hard, determined) grintoso; (novel, film) crudo

**grizzle** /'grɪzl/ vi piagnucolare

**grizzly** /'grɪzlɪ/ n (bear) grizzly m inv

**groan** /grəʊn/ n gemito m ● vi gemere

**grocer** /'grəʊsə(r)/ n droghiere, -a mf

**groceries** /'grəʊsərɪz/ npl generi mpl alimentari

**grocer's [shop]** n drogheria f

**groggy** /'grɒgɪ/ a (**-ier, -iest**) stordito; (unsteady) barcollante

**groin** /grɔɪn/ n Anat inguine m

**groom** /gru:m/ n sposo m; (for horse) stalliere m ● vt strigliare (horse); fig preparare; **well-~ed** ben curato

**groove** /gru:v/ n scanalatura f

**grope** /grəʊp/ vi brancolare; **~ for** cercare a tastoni

**gross** /grəʊs/ a obeso; (coarse) volgare; (glaring) grossolano; (salary, weight) lordo ● n inv grossa f

**gross domestic product** n prodotto m interno lordo

**gross indecency** n Jur oltraggio m al pudore

**grossly** /'grəʊslɪ/ adv (very) enormemente

**gross national product** n prodotto m nazionale lordo

**grotesque** /grəʊ'tesk/ a grottesco

**grotesquely** /grəʊ'tesklɪ/ adv in modo grottesco

**grotto** /'grɒtəʊ/ n (pl **-es**) grotta f

**grotty** /'grɒtɪ/ a (**-ier, -iest**) (fam: flat, street) squallido

**grouch** /graʊtʃ/ vi brontolare (**about** contro)

**grouchy** /'graʊtʃɪ/ a brontolone

**ground**[1] /graʊnd/ see **grind**

**ground**[2] n terra f; Sport terreno m; (reason) ragione f; **~s** pl (park) giardini mpl; (of coffee) fondi mpl ● vi (ship:) arenarsi ● vt bloccare a terra (aircraft); Am Electr mettere a terra

**ground: ground control** n base f di controllo. **ground crew** n personale m di terra. **ground floor** n pianterreno m

**grounding** /'graʊndɪŋ/ n base f

**groundless** /'graʊndlɪs/ a infondato
**ground: ground rules** npl principi mpl fondamentali. **groundsheet** n telone m impermeabile. **groundwork** n lavoro m di preparazione
**group**·/gru:p/ n gruppo m ● vt raggruppare ● vi raggrupparsi
**groupage** /'gru:pɪdʒ/ n Comm raggruppamento m
**group leader** n capogruppo m
**grouse**[1] /graʊs/ n inv gallo m cedrone
**grouse**[2] vi fam brontolare
**grove** /grʊːv/ n boschetto m
**grovel** /'grɒvl/ vi (pt/pp **grovelled**) strisciare
**grovelling** /'grɒv(ə)lɪŋ/ a leccapiedi inv
**grow** /grəʊ/ v (pt **grew**, pp **grown**) ● vi crescere; (become) diventare; ⟨unemployment, fear:⟩ aumentare; ⟨town:⟩ ingrandirsi ● vt coltivare; ~ **one's hair** farsi crescere i capelli
■ **grow on** vt (fam: become pleasing to) **it'll ~ on you** finirà a per piacerti
■ **grow out** of vt he's ~**n out of his jumper** il golf gli è diventato troppo piccolo
■ **grow up** vi crescere; ⟨town:⟩ svilupparsi
**growbag** /'grəʊbæg/ n sacco m di terriccio entro cui si coltivano piante
**grower** /'grəʊə(r)/ n coltivatore, -trice mf
**growing pains** /'grəʊɪŋ/ npl (of child) dolori mpl della crescita; (fig: of firm, project) difficoltà fpl iniziali nello sviluppo
**growl** /graʊl/ n grugnito m ● vi ringhiare
**grown** /grəʊn/ see **grow** ● a adulto
**grown-up** a & n adulto, -a mf
**growth** /grəʊθ/ n crescita f; (increase) aumento m; Med tumore m
**growth rate** n tasso m di crescita
**groyne** /grɔɪn/ n Br pennello m (per difendere le spiagge dall'erosione)
**grub** /grʌb/ n larva f; (fam: food) mangiare m
**grubby** /'grʌbɪ/ a (-ier, -iest) sporco
**grudge** /grʌdʒ/ n rancore m; **bear sb a ~** portare rancore a qcno ● vt dare a malincuore
**grudging** /'grʌdʒɪŋ/ a reluttante
**grudgingly** /'grʌdʒɪŋlɪ/ adv a malincuore
**gruelling** /'gru:əlɪŋ/ a estenuante
**gruesome** /'gru:səm/ a macabro
**gruff** /grʌf/ a burbero
**gruffly** /'grʌflɪ/ adv in modo burbero
**grumble** /'grʌmbl/ vi brontolare (**at** contro)
**grumpy** /'grʌmpɪ/ a (-ier, -iest) scorbutico
**grunge** /grʌndʒ/ n (dirt) lerciume m; (style) grunge m inv
**grunt** /grʌnt/ n grugnito m ● vi fare un grugnito
**G-string** n (garment) tanga m inv
**guarantee** /gærən'ti:/ n garanzia f ● vt garantire
**guarantor** /gærən'tɔ:(r)/ n garante mf
**guard** /gɑ:d/ n guardia f; (security) guardiano m; (on train) capotreno m; Techn schermo m protettivo; **be on ~** essere di guardia; **on one's ~** in guardia ● vt sorvegliare; (protect) proteggere
■ **guard against** vt guardarsi da

**guard-dog** n cane m da guardia
**guarded** /'gɑ:dɪd/ a guardingo
**guardian** /'gɑ:dɪən/ n (of minor) tutore, -trice mf
**guardian angel** n also fig angelo m custode
**guard: guard of honour** n guardia f d'onore. **guardroom** n corpo m di guardia. **guard's van** n Br Rail carrozza f bagagliaio
**guava** /'gwɑ:və/ n (fruit) guava f; (tree) albero m di guava
**guerrilla** /gə'rɪlə/ n guerrigliero, -a mf
**guerrilla warfare** n guerriglia f
**guess** /ges/ n supposizione f ● vt indovinare ● vi indovinare; (Am: suppose) supporre
**guesstimate** /'gestɪmət/ n calcolo m approssimativo
**guesswork** /'gesw3:k/ n supposizione f
**guest** /gest/ n ospite mf; (in hotel) cliente mf
**guest: guest house** n pensione f. **guest room** n camera f degli ospiti. **guest worker** n lavoratore m immigrato; lavoratrice f immigrata
**guff** /gʌf/ n (nonsense) stupidaggini fpl
**guffaw** /gʌ'fɔ:/ n sghignazzata f ● vi sghignazzare
**guidance** /'gaɪdəns/ n guida f; (advice) consigli mpl
**guide** /gaɪd/ n guida f; [**Girl**] **G~** giovane esploratrice f ● vt guidare
**guidebook** /'gaɪdbʊk/ n guida f turistica
**guided missile** /'gaɪdɪd/ n missile m teleguidato
**guide dog** n cane m per ciechi
**guided tour** n giro m guidato
**guidelines** /'gaɪdlaɪnz/ npl direttive fpl
**guiding principle** /gaɪdɪŋ'prɪnsɪp(ə)l/ n direttrice f
**guild** /gɪld/ n corporazione f
**guile** /gaɪl/ n astuzia f
**guileless** /'gaɪllɪs/ a senza malizia
**guillotine** /'gɪləti:n/ n ghigliottina f; (for paper) taglierina f
**guilt** /gɪlt/ n colpa f
**guiltily** /'gɪltɪlɪ/ adv con aria colpevole
**guilty** /'gɪltɪ/ a (-ier, -iest) colpevole; **have a ~ conscience** avere la coscienza sporca
**guinea** /'gɪnɪ/ n ghinea f
**guinea fowl** faraona f
**guinea pig** n porcellino m d'India; (in experiments) cavia f
**guise** /gaɪz/ n **in the ~ of** sotto le spoglie di
**guitar** /gɪ'tɑ:(r)/ n chitarra f
**guitarist** /gɪ'tɑ:rɪst/ n chitarrista mf
**Gulag** /'gu:læg/ n gulag m inv
**gulf** /gʌlf/ n Geog golfo m; fig abisso m
**gull** /gʌl/ n gabbiano m
**gullet** /'gʌlɪt/ n esofago m; (throat) gola f
**gullible** /'gʌləbl/ a credulone
**gully** /'gʌlɪ/ n burrone m; (drain) canale m di scolo
**gulp** /gʌlp/ n azione f di deglutire; (of food) boccone m; (of liquid) sorso m ● vt deglutire
■ **gulp down** vt trangugiare ⟨food⟩; scolarsi ⟨liquid⟩

**gum¹** /gʌm/ n Anat gengiva f
**gum²** n gomma f; (chewing-gum) gomma f da masticare, chewing-gum m inv ● vt ⟨pt/pp gummed⟩ ingommare (**to** a)
**gumboot** /'gʌmbuːt/ n stivale m di gomma
**gummed** /gʌmd/ see **gum²** ● a ⟨label⟩ adesivo
**gumption** /'gʌmpʃn/ n fam buon senso m
**gumshoe** /'gʌmʃuː/ n (fam: private investigator) investigatore m privato
**gum tree** n fam **be up a ~ ~** essere in difficoltà
**gun** /gʌn/ n pistola f; (rifle) fucile m; (cannon) cannone m; **he had a ~** era armato
■ **gun down** vt ⟨pt/pp gunned⟩ freddare
**gun: gun barrel** n canna f di fucile. **gunboat** n cannoniera f. **gun dog** n cane m da caccia.
**gunfire** n spari mpl; (of cannon) colpi mpl [di cannone]
**gunge** /gʌndʒ/ n Br poltiglia f [disgustosa]
**gung-ho** /gʌŋ'həʊ/ a hum (eager for war) guerrafondaio; (overzealous) esaltato
**gunman** /'gʌnmən/ n uomo m armato
**gunner** /'gʌnə(r)/ n artigliere m
**gun: gunpoint** n **hold sb up at ~** assalire qcno a mano armata. **gunpowder** n polvere f da sparo. **gunshot** n colpo m [di pistola].
**gunslinger** n pistolero m
**gurgle** /'gɜːgl/ vi gorgogliare; ⟨baby:⟩ fare degli urletti
**guru** /'gʊruː/ n guru m inv
**gush** /gʌʃ/ vi sgorgare; (enthuse) parlare con troppo entusiasmo (**over** di)
■ **gush out** vi sgorgare
**gushing** /'gʌʃɪŋ/ a eccessivamente entusiastico
**gusset** /'gʌsɪt/ n gherone m
**gust** /gʌst/ n (of wind) raffica f
**gusto** /'gʌstəʊ/ n **with ~** con trasporto
**gusty** /'gʌstɪ/ a ventoso

**gut** /gʌt/ n intestino m; **~s** pl pancia f; (fam: courage) fegato m ● vt ⟨pt/pp gutted⟩ Culin svuotare delle interiora; **~ted by fire** sventrato da un incendio
**gutsy** /'gʌtsɪ/ a (brave) coraggioso; (spirited) gagliardo
**gutter** /'gʌtə(r)/ n canale m di scolo; (on roof) grondaia f, fig bassifondi mpl
**guttering** /'gʌtərɪŋ/ n grondaie fpl
**gutter press** n stampa f scandalistica
**guttersnipe** /'gʌtəsnaɪp/ n ragazzo, -a mf di strada
**guttural** /'gʌtərəl/ a gutturale
**guv, guvnor** /gʌv, 'gʌvnə(r)/ n (Br fam: boss) capo m
**guy** /gaɪ/ n fam tipo m, tizio m
**Guy Fawkes Day** /fɔːks/ n Br anniversario m del fallimento della Congiura delle Polveri (5 novembre)
**guzzle** /'gʌzl/ vt ingozzarsi con ⟨food⟩; **he's ~d the lot** si è sbafato tutto
**gym** /dʒɪm/ n fam palestra f; (gymnastics) ginnastica f
**gymkhana** /dʒɪm'kɑːnə/ n manifestazione f equestre
**gymnasium** /dʒɪm'neɪzɪəm/ n palestra f
**gymnast** /'dʒɪmnæst/ n ginnasta mf
**gymnastics** /dʒɪm'næstɪks/ n ginnastica f
**gym shoes** npl scarpe fpl da ginnastica
**gym-slip** n Sch ≈ grembiule m (da bambina)
**gynaecologist** /gaɪnɪ'kɒlədʒɪst/ n ginecologo, -a mf
**gynaecology** /gaɪnɪ'kɒlədʒɪ/ n ginecologia f
**gyp** /dʒɪp/ n Br **my back is giving me ~** ho un terribile mal di schiena
**gypsum** /'dʒɪpsəm/ n gesso m
**gypsy** /'dʒɪpsɪ/ n zingaro, -a mf
**gyrate** /dʒaɪ'reɪt/ vi roteare

# Hh

**h, H** /eɪtʃ/ n h, H f inv
**haberdashery** /hæbə'dæʃərɪ/ n merceria f; Am negozio m d'abbigliamento da uomo
**habit** /'hæbɪt/ n abitudine f; (Relig: costume) tonaca f; **be in the ~ of doing sth** avere l'abitudine di fare qcsa
**habitable** /'hæbɪtəbl/ a abitabile
**habitat** /'hæbɪtæt/ n habitat m inv
**habitation** /hæbɪ'teɪʃn/ n **unfit for human ~** inagibile
**habit-forming** /-fɔːmɪŋ/ a **be ~** creare assuefazione
**habitual** /hə'bɪtjʊəl/ a abituale; ⟨smoker, liar⟩ inveterato
**habitually** /hə'bɪtjʊəlɪ/ adv regolarmente

**hack¹** /hæk/ n (writer) scribacchino, -a mf
**hack²** vt tagliare; **~ to pieces** tagliare a pezzi
**hacker** /'hækə(r)/ n Comput pirata m informatico
**hacking** /'hækɪŋ/ n Comput pirateria f informatica
**hacking cough** n brutta tosse f
**hackles** /'hæk(ə)lz/ npl (on animal) pelo m del collo; (on bird) piumaggio m del collo; **make sb's ~ rise** fig far imbestialire qcno
**hackney cab** /'hæknɪ/ n fml taxi m inv
**hackneyed** /'hæknɪd/ a trito [e ritrito]
**hacksaw** /'hæksɔː/ n seghetto m
**had** /hæd/ see **have**

**haddock** /'hædək/ n inv eglefino m

**haematoma** /hi:mə'təʊmə/ n ematoma m

**haemoglobin** /hi:mə'gləʊbɪn/ n emoglobina f

**haemophilia** /hi:mə'fɪliə/ n emofilia f

**haemophiliac** /hi:mə'fɪliæk/ n emofiliaco, -a mf

**haemorrhage** /'hemərɪdʒ/ n emorragia f

**haemorrhoids** /'hemərɔɪdz/ npl emorroidi fpl

**hag** /hæg/ n old ~ vecchia befana f

**haggard** /'hægəd/ a sfatto

**haggis** /'hægɪs/ n piatto m scozzese a base di frattaglie di pecora e avena

**haggle** /'hægl/ vi contrattare (**over** per)

**ha! ha!** /hɑː'hɑː/ int ah! ah!

**hail**[1] /heɪl/ vt salutare; far segno a ‹taxi› ● vi ~ **from** provenire da

**hail**[2] n grandine f ● vi grandinare

**hailstone** /'heɪlstəʊn/ n chicco m di grandine

**hailstorm** /'heɪlstɔːm/ n grandinata f

**hair** /heə(r)/ n capelli mpl; (on body, of animal) pelo m; **wash one's** ~ lavarsi i capelli

**hair: hairband** n (rigid) cerchietto m; (elastic) fascia f [per capelli]. **hairbrush** n spazzola f per capelli. **hair curler** n arricciacapelli m inv. **haircut** n taglio m di capelli; **have a** ~ farsi tagliare i capelli. **hairdo** n fam pettinatura f. **hairdresser** n parrucchiere, -a mf. **hairdryer** n fon m inv; (with hood) casco m [asciugacapelli]. **hair gel** n gel m inv [per capelli]. **hairgrip** n molletta f

**hairless** /'heəlɪs/ a ‹animal› senza peli; ‹body, chin› glabro

**hair: hairline** n (on head) attaccatura f dei capelli. **hairline crack** n incrinatura f sottilissima. **hairline fracture** n Med frattura f capillare. **hairnet** n retina f per capelli. **hairpiece** n toupet m inv. **hairpin** n forcina f. **hairpin bend** n tornante m, curva f a gomito. **hair-raising** /'heəreɪzɪŋ/ a terrificante. **hair remover** n crema f depilatoria. **hairslide** n Br fermacapelli m inv. **hair-splitting** /'heəsplɪtɪŋ/ n pedanteria f. **hairspray** n lacca f [per capelli]. **hairstyle** n acconciatura f. **hairstylist** n parrucchiere, -a mf. **hair transplant** n trapianto m di capelli

**hairy** /'heərɪ/ a (-ier, -iest) peloso; (fam: frightening) spaventoso

**Haiti** /'heɪtɪ/ n Haiti m

**Haitian** /'heɪʃ(ə)n/ n & a haitiano, -a mf; (language) haitiano m

**hake** /heɪk/ n inv nasello m

**halcyon days** /'hælsɪən/ npl bei tempi mpl andati

**hale** /heɪl/ a ~ **and hearty** in piena forma

**half** /hɑːf/ n (pl **halves**) metà f inv; **cut in** ~ tagliare a metà; **one and a** ~ uno e mezzo; ~ **a dozen** mezza dozzina; ~ **an hour** mezz'ora ● a mezzo; [at] ~ **price** [a] metà prezzo ● adv a metà; ~ **past two** le due e mezza

**half: half-and-half** a mezzo e mezzo ● adv a metà; **go** ~ fare a metà. **half-back** n mediano

m. **half-baked** a fam che non sta in piedi. **half board** n mezza pensione f. **half-breed** n & a mezzosangue mf inv. **half-brother** n fratellastro m. **half-caste** n meticcio, -a mf. **half-century** n mezzo secolo m. **half cock** n **go off at** ~ ~ partire col piede sbagliato. **half-conscious** a semicosciente. **half-crown, half a crown** n Br mezza corona f. **half-cut** a (fam: drunk) ciucco. **half day** n mezza giornata f. **half-dead** a also fig mezzo morto. **half-dozen** n mezza dozzina f. **half fare** n metà tariffa f. **half-hearted** /-'hɑːtɪd/ a esitante. **half hour** n mezz'ora f. **half-hourly** a & adv ogni mezz'ora. **half-length** a ‹portrait› a mezzo busto. **half-light** n penombra f. **half mast** n at ~ ~ a mezz'asta. **half measures** npl mezze misure fpl. **half-moon** n mezzaluna f; (of fingernail) lunula f ● attrib ‹spectacles› a mezzaluna. **half pay** n metà stipendio m. **halfpenny** /'heɪpnɪ/ n Br mezzo penny m inv. **half-pint** n mezza pinta f (Br = 0, 28 l, Am = 0, 24 l); (beer) piccola f; fig mezza calzetta f. **half price** a a metà prezzo ● adv [a] metà prezzo. **half size** n (of shoe) mezzo numero m ● a ‹copy› ridotto della metà. **half smile** n mezzo sorriso m. **half-starved** a mezzo morto di fame. **half-term** n vacanza f di metà trimestre. **half-time** n Sport intervallo m. **half-truth** n mezza verità f inv. **halfway** a **the** ~ **mark/stage** il livello intermedio ● adv a metà strada; **get** ~ fig arrivare a metà. **halfway house** n (compromise) via f di mezzo; (rehabilitation centre) centro m di riabilitazione per ex detenuti. **halfway line** n Sport linea f mediana. **halfwit** n idiota mf. **half-year** n Fin, Comm semestre m ● attrib ‹profit, results› semestrale. **half-yearly** a ‹meeting, payment› semestrale

**halibut** /'hælɪbət/ n inv ippoglosso m

**halitosis** /hælɪ'təʊsɪs/ n alitosi f inv

**hall** /hɔːl/ n (entrance) ingresso m; (room) sala f; (mansion) residenza f di campagna; ~ **of residence** Univ casa f dello studente

**hallelujah** /(h)ælɪ'luːjə/ int alleluia!

**hallmark** /'hɔːlmɑːk/ n marchio m di garanzia; fig marchio m

**hallo** /hə'ləʊ/ int ciao!; (on telephone) pronto!; **say** ~ **to** salutare

**hall of residence** n residenza f universitaria

**hallowed** /'hæləʊd/ a ‹ground› consacrato; ‹tradition› sacro

**Halloween** /hæləʊ'iːn/ n vigilia f d'Ognissanti e notte delle streghe, celebrata soprattutto dai bambini

**hallucinate** /hə'luːsɪneɪt/ vi avere le allucinazioni

**hallucination** /həluːsɪ'neɪʃn/ n allucinazione f

**hallucinatory** /hə'luːsɪnət(ə)rɪ/ a ‹drug› allucinogeno

**hallucinogen** /hə'luːsɪnədʒən/ n sostanza f allucinante

**hallucinogenic** /həluːsɪnə'dʒenɪk/ a allucinogeno

# 153         **hallway | hanger**

**hallway** /ˈhɔːlweɪ/ *n* ingresso *m*

**halo** /ˈheɪləʊ/ *n* (*pl* **-es**) aureola *f*; *Astr* alone *m*

**halogen** /ˈhælədʒən/ *n* alogeno *m*

**halt** /hɔːlt/ *n* alt *m inv*; **come to a ~** fermarsi; ⟨*traffic:*⟩ bloccarsi ● *vi* fermarsi; **~!** alt! ● *vt* fermare

**halter** /ˈhɔːltə(r)/ *n* (*for horse*) cavezza *f*

**halter-neck** *n* modello *m* con allacciatura dietro il collo che lascia la schiena scoperta

**halting** /ˈhɔːltɪŋ/ *a* esitante

**haltingly** /ˈhɔːltɪŋlɪ/ *adv* con esitazione

**halve** /hɑːv/ *vt* dividere a metà; (*reduce*) dimezzare

**ham** /hæm/ *n* prosciutto *m*; *Theat* attore, -trice *mf* da strapazzo

**hamburger** /ˈhæmbɜːgə(r)/ *n* hamburger *m inv*

**ham-fisted** /-ˈfɪstɪd/ *a Br fam* maldestro

**hamlet** /ˈhæmlɪt/ *n* paesino *m*

**hammer** /ˈhæmə(r)/ *n* martello *m* ● *vt* martellare ● *vi* **~ at/on** picchiare a

■ **hammer in** *vt* piantare ⟨*nail*⟩

**hammer and sickle** *n* falce *f* e martello *m*

**hammock** /ˈhæmək/ *n* amaca *f*

**hamper**[1] /ˈhæmpə(r)/ *n* cesto *m*; [*gift*] ~ cestino *m*

**hamper**[2] *vt* ostacolare

**hamster** /ˈhæmstə(r)/ *n* criceto *m*

**hamstring** /ˈhæmstrɪŋ/ *n* (*of horse*) tendine *m* del garretto; (*of human*) tendine *m* del ginocchio ● *vt fig* rendere impotente

**hand** /hænd/ *n* mano *f*; (*of clock*) lancetta *f*; (*writing*) scrittura *f*; (*worker*) manovale *m*; **all ~s** *Naut* l'equipaggio al completo; **at ~**, **to ~** a portata di mano; **by ~** a mano; **on the one ~** da un lato; **on the other ~** d'altra parte; **out of ~** incontrollabile; (*summarily*) su due piedi; **in ~** in corso; ⟨*situation*⟩ sotto controllo; (*available*) disponibile; **give sb a ~** dare una mano a qcno; **~ in ~** ⟨*run, walk*⟩ mano nella mano; **go ~ in ~** *fig* andare di pari passo (**with** con) ● *vt* porgere

■ **hand back** *vt* restituire ⟨*sth*⟩

■ **hand down** *vt* tramandare

■ **hand in** *vt* consegnare

■ **hand on** *vt* passare

■ **hand out** *vt* distribuire

■ **hand over** *vt* passare; (*to police*) consegnare

**hand:** **handbag** *n* borsa *f* (*da signora*). **hand baggage** *n* bagaglio *m* a mano. **handball** *n* pallamano *f*; (*fault in football*) fallo *m* di mano; **~!** mano! **handbasin** *n* lavandino *m*. **handbook** *n* manuale *m*. **handbrake** *n* freno *m* a mano. **handcart** *n* carretto *m*. **hand cream** *n* crema *f* per le mani. **handcuffs** *npl* manette *fpl*. **hand-dryer**, **hand-drier** *n* asciugamani *m inv* ad aria

**handful** /ˈhændfʊl/ *n* manciata *f*; **be [quite] a ~** *fam* essere difficile da tenere a freno

**hand:** **hand grenade** *n* bomba *f* a mano. **handgun** *n* pistola *f*. **hand-held** *a* a mano **handicap** /ˈhændɪkæp/ *n* handicap *m inv*

**handicapped** /ˈhændɪkæpt/ *a* **mentally/ physically** ~ mentalmente/fisicamente handicappato

**handicraft** /ˈhændɪkrɑːft/ *n* artigianato *m*

**handiwork** /ˈhændɪwɜːk/ *n* opera *f*

**handkerchief** /ˈhæŋkətʃɪf/ *n* (*pl* **~s &** **-chieves**) fazzoletto *m*

**handle** /ˈhændl/ *n* manico *m*; (*of door*) maniglia *f*; **fly off the ~** *fam* perdere le staffe ● *vt* maneggiare; occuparsi di ⟨*problem, customer*⟩; prendere ⟨*difficult person*⟩; trattare ⟨*subject*⟩; **be good at handling sb** saperci fare con qcno

**handlebar moustache** /hændlbɑːməˈstɑːʃ/ *n* baffi *mpl* a manubrio

**handlebars** /ˈhændlbɑːz/ *npl* manubrio *m*

**handler** /ˈhændlə(r)/ *n* (*of dog*) addestratore, -trice *mf*

**hand:** **hand lotion** *n* lozione *f* per le mani. **hand-luggage** *n* bagaglio *m* a mano. **handmade** *a* fatto a mano. **handout** *n* (*at lecture*) foglio *m* informativo; (*fam: money*) elemosina *f*. **handover** *n* (*of prisoner, ransom*) consegna *f*; (*of property, territory*) cessione *f*; **~ of power** passaggio *m* delle consegne. **hand-pick** *vt* scegliere ⟨*produce*⟩; selezionare con cura ⟨*staff*⟩. **handrail** *n* corrimano *m*. **hand-reared** *a* ⟨*animal*⟩ allattato con il biberon. **handset** *n* *Teleph* ricevitore *m*. **handshake** *n* stretta *f* di mano. **hand signal** *n* *Auto* segnalazione *f* con la mano. **hands-off** *a* ⟨*policy*⟩ di non intervento; ⟨*manager*⟩ che delega le responsabilità

**handsome** /ˈhænsəm/ *a* bello; (*fig: generous*) generoso; ⟨*salary*⟩ considerevole

**hand:** **hands-on** *a* ⟨*experience*⟩ pratico; ⟨*approach*⟩ pragmatico; ⟨*control*⟩ diretto; ⟨*manager*⟩ che segue direttamente le varie attività. **handspring** *n* salto *m* sulle mani. **handstand** *n* verticale *f*. **hand-to-hand** *a* & *adv* ⟨*fight*⟩ corpo a corpo. **hand-to-mouth** *a* ⟨*existence*⟩ precario. **hand towel** *n* asciugamano *m*. **hand-woven** /ˈwəʊvən/ *a* tessuto a mano. **handwriting** *n* calligrafia *f*. **handwritten** *a* scritto a mano

**handy** /ˈhændɪ/ *a* (**-ier**, **-iest**) pratico; ⟨*person*⟩ abile; **have/keep ~** avere/tenere a portata di mano

**handyman** /ˈhændɪmæn/ *n* tuttofare *m inv*

**hang** /hæŋ/ *vt* (*pt/pp* **hung**) appendere ⟨*picture*⟩; (*pt/pp* **hanged**) impiccare ⟨*criminal*⟩; **~ oneself** impiccarsi; **~ wallpaper** tappezzare ● *vi* (*pt/pp* **hung**) pendere; ⟨*hair:*⟩ scendere ● *n* **get the ~ of it** *fam* afferrare

■ **hang about** *vi* gironzolare

■ **hang on** *vi* tenersi stretto; (*fam: wait*) aspettare; *Teleph* restare in linea

■ **hang on to** *vt* tenersi stretto a; (*keep*) tenere

■ **hang out** *vi* spuntare; **where does he usually ~ out?** *fam* dove bazzica di solito? ● *vt* stendere ⟨*washing*⟩

■ **hang up** *vt* appendere; *Teleph* riattaccare ● *vi* essere appeso; *Teleph* riattaccare

**hangar** /ˈhæŋə(r)/ *n* hangar *m inv*

**hanger** /ˈhæŋə(r)/ *n* gruccia *f*

**hanger-on** n leccapiedi mf inv
**hang-glider** n deltaplano m
**hang-gliding** n deltaplano m
**hang: hangman** n boia m. **hangover** n postumi mpl della sbornia. **hang-up** n fam complesso m
**hank** /hæŋk/ n (of hair) ciocca f; (of wool etc) matassa f
**hanker** /'hæŋkə(r)/ vi ~ **after sth** smaniare per qcsa
**hanky** /'hæŋkɪ/ n fam fazzoletto m
**hanky-panky** /hæŋkɪ'pæŋkɪ/ n fam qualcosa m di losco
**ha'penny** /'heɪpnɪ/ n Br abbr (**halfpenny**) mezzo penny m inv
**haphazard** /hæp'hæzəd/ a a casaccio; **in a ~ fashion** a casaccio
**haphazardly** /hæp'hæzədlɪ/ adv a casaccio
**hapless** /'hæplɪs/ a sventurato
**happen** /'hæpn/ vi capitare, succedere; **as it ~s** per caso; **I ~ed to meet him** mi è capitato di incontrarlo; **what has ~ed to him?** cosa gli è capitato?; (become of) che fine ha fatto?
**happening** /'hæp(ə)nɪŋ/ n avvenimento m
**happily** /'hæpɪlɪ/ adv felicemente; (fortunately) fortunatamente
**happiness** /'hæpɪnɪs/ n felicità f
**happy** /'hæpɪ/ a (-ier, -iest) contento, felice
**happy: happy-go-lucky** a spensierato. **happy hour** n ora f in cui nei pub le bevande vengono vendute a prezzi scontati. **happy medium** n giusto mezzo m
**harangue** /hə'ræŋ/ vt (morally) fare un sermone a; (politically) arringare
**harass** /'hærəs/ vt perseguitare
**harassed** /'hærəst/ a stressato
**harassment** /'hærəsmənt/ n persecuzione f; **sexual ~** molestie fpl sessuali
**harbinger** /'hɑ:bɪndʒə(r)/ n liter segnale m; (person) precursore m; precorritrice f
**harbour** /'hɑ:bə(r)/ n porto m ● vt dare asilo a; nutrire (grudge)
**hard** /hɑ:d/ a duro; (question, problem) difficile; **~ of hearing** duro d'orecchi; **be ~ on sb** (person:) essere duro con qcno ● adv (work) duramente; (pull, hit, rain, snow) forte; **~ hit by unemployment** duramente colpito dalla disoccupazione; **take sth ~** non accettare qcsa; **think ~!** pensaci bene!; **try ~** mettercela tutta; **try ~er** metterci più impegno; **~ done by** fam trattato ingiustamente
**hard: hard and fast** a (rule, distinction) preciso. **hardback** n edizione f rilegata. **hardboard** n truciolato m. **hard-boiled** /-'bɔɪld/ a (egg) sodo. **hard cash** n contante m. **hard copy** n copia f stampata. **hard core** n (in construction) massicciata f; (of group, demonstrators) zoccolo m duro ● a (pornography, video) hard-core; (supporter, opponent) irriducibile. **hard disk** n hard disk m inv, disco m rigido. **hard drug** n droga f pesante. **hard-earned** /-'ɜ:nd/ a (cash) sudato
**harden** /'hɑ:dn/ vi indurirsi
**hard: hard-faced** /-'feɪst/ a (person) dai tratti duri. **hard-fought** a (battle) accanito. **hard hat** n casco m. **hard-headed** /-'hedɪd/ a pratico; (businessman) dal sangue freddo. **hard-hearted** /-'hɑ:tɪd/ a dal cuore duro. **hard labour** n Br lavori mpl forzati. **hard lens** n lente f a contatto rigida. **hardline** a (policy, regime) duro ● n linea f dura; **~ lines!** che sfortuna!. **hardliner** n Pol fautore, -trice mf della linea dura. **hard luck** n sfortuna f. **hard-luck story** n **give sb a ~ ~** raccontare a qcno le proprie disgrazie
**hardly** /'hɑ:dlɪ/ adv appena; **~ ever** quasi mai
**hardness** /'hɑ:dnɪs/ n durezza f
**hard: hard-nosed** /-'nəʊzd/ a (attitude, businessman, government) duro. **hard-on** n fam erezione f. **hard porn** n pornografia f hard-core. **hard-pressed** /-'prest/ a in difficoltà; (for time) a corto di tempo. **hard rock** n Mus hard rock m. **hard sell** n tecnica f di vendita aggressiva
**hardship** /'hɑ:dʃɪp/ n avversità f inv
**hard: hard shoulder** n Auto corsia f d'emergenza. **hard up** a fam a corto di soldi; **~ up for sth** a corto di qcsa. **hardware** n ferramenta fpl; Comput hardware m inv. **hard-wearing** /-'weərɪŋ/ a resistente. **hardwood** n legno m duro. **hard-working** /-'wɜ:kɪŋ/ a **be ~** essere un gran lavoratore
**hardy** /'hɑ:dɪ/ a (-ier, -iest) dal fisico resistente; (plant) che sopporta il gelo
**hare** /heə(r)/ n lepre f
**hare-brained** /'heəbreɪnd/ a (scheme) da scervellati; (person) scervellato
**harelip** /heə'lɪp/ n labbro m leporino
**harem** /hɑ:'ri:m/ n serraglio m
**■ hark back** /hɑ:k/ vt fig **~ ~ to** ritornare su
**harm** /hɑ:m/ n male m; (damage) danni mpl; **out of ~'s way** in un posto sicuro; **it won't do any ~** non farà certo male ● vt far male a; (damage) danneggiare
**harmful** /'hɑ:mful/ a dannoso
**harmless** /'hɑ:mlɪs/ a innocuo
**harmonica** /hɑ:'mɒnɪkə/ n armonica f [a bocca]
**harmonious** /hɑ:'məʊnɪəs/ a armonioso
**harmoniously** /hɑ:'məʊnɪəslɪ/ adv in armonia
**harmonize** /'hɑ:mənaɪz/ vi fig armonizzare
**harmony** /'hɑ:mənɪ/ n armonia f
**harness** /'hɑ:nɪs/ n finimenti mpl; (of parachute) imbracatura f ● vt bardare (horse); sfruttare (resources)
**harp** /hɑ:p/ n arpa f
**■ harp on** vi fam insistere (**about** su)
**harpist** /'hɑ:pɪst/ n arpista mf
**harpoon** /hɑ:'pu:n/ n arpione m
**harpsichord** /'hɑ:psɪkɔ:d/ n clavicembalo m
**harrow** /'hærəʊ/ n erpice m
**harrowing** /'hærəʊɪŋ/ a straziante
**harry** /'hærɪ/ vt (pursue, harass) assillare
**harsh** /hɑ:ʃ/ a duro; (light) abbagliante
**harshly** /'hɑ:ʃlɪ/ adv duramente

**harshness** /'hɑːʃnɪs/ n durezza f

**harvest** /'hɑːvɪst/ n raccolta f; (of grapes) vendemmia f; (crop) raccolto m ● vt raccogliere

**harvester** /'hɑːvɪstə(r)/ n (person) mietitore, -trice mf; (machine) mietitrice f

**harvest festival** n festa f del raccolto

**has** /hæz/ see **have**

**has-been** /-biːn/ n fam (person) persona f che ha fatto il suo tempo; (thing) anticaglia f

**hash** /hæʃ/ n **make a ~ of** fam fare un casino con

**hashish** /'hæʃɪʃ/ n hascish m

**hassle** /'hæsl/ n fam rottura f ● vt rompere le scatole a

**hassock** /'hæsək/ n cuscino m di inginocchiatoio

**haste** /heɪst/ n fretta f; **make ~** affrettarsi

**hasten** /'heɪsn/ vi affrettarsi ● vt affrettare

**hastily** /'heɪstɪlɪ/ adv frettolosamente

**hasty** /'heɪstɪ/ a (-ier, -iest) frettoloso; (decision) affrettato

**hat** /hæt/ n cappello m

**hatbox** /'hætbɒks/ n cappelliera f

**hatch**[1] /hætʃ/ n (for food) sportello m passavivande inv; Naut boccaporto m

**hatch**[2] vi ~ [out] rompere il guscio; (egg:) schiudersi ● vt covare; tramare (plot)

■ **hatch up** vt tramare (plot)

**hatchback** /'hætʃbæk/ n Auto tre/cinque porte m inv; (door) porta f del bagagliaio

**hatchet** /'hætʃɪt/ n ascia f

**hate** /heɪt/ n odio m ● vt odiare

**hateful** /'heɪtfʊl/ a odioso

**hate mail** n lettere fpl offensive o minatorie

**hatpin** /'hætpɪn/ n spillone m

**hatred** /'heɪtrɪd/ n odio m

**hat-trick** n tripletta f

**haughtily** /'hɔːtɪlɪ/ adv altezzosamente

**haughty** /'hɔːtɪ/ a (-ier, -iest) altezzoso

**haul** /hɔːl/ n (fish) pescata f; (loot) bottino m; (pull) tirata f ● vt tirare; trasportare (goods) ● vi ~ **on** tirare

**haulage** /'hɔːlɪdʒ/ n trasporto m

**haulier** /'hɔːlɪə(r)/ n autotrasportatore m

**haunch** /hɔːntʃ/ n anca f

**haunt** /hɔːnt/ n ritrovo m ● vt frequentare; (linger in the mind) perseguitare; **this house is ~ed** questa casa è abitata da fantasmi

**have** /hæv/ vt (3 sg pres tense **has**; pt/pp **had**) avere; fare (breakfast, bath, walk etc); ~ **a drink** bere qualcosa; ~ **lunch/dinner** pranzare/cenare; ; ~ **a rest** riposarsi; **I had my hair cut** mi sono tagliata i capelli; **we had the flat painted** abbiamo fatto tinteggiare la casa; **I had it made** l'ho fatto fare; ~ **to do sth** dover fare qcsa; ~ **him telephone me tomorrow** digli di telefonarmi domani; **he has** or **he's got two houses** ha due case; **you've got the money, ~n't you?** hai i soldi, no? ● v aux avere; (with verbs of motion & some others) essere; **I ~ seen him** l'ho visto; **he has never been there** non ci è mai stato ● npl **the ~s and the ~-nots** i ricchi e i poveri

■ **have in** vt avere in casa/ufficio etc (builders etc)

■ **have off** vt fam **he's having it off with his secretary** si fa la segretaria

■ **have on** vt (be wearing) portare; (dupe) prendere in giro; **I've got something on tonight** ho un impegno stasera; **you're having me on!** tu mi stai prendendo in giro!

■ **have out** vt ~ **it out with sb** chiarire le cose con qcno; ~ **a tooth out** farsi togliere un dente

**haven** /'heɪvn/ n fig rifugio m

**haver** /'heɪvə(r)/ vi (dither) titubare

**haversack** /'hævəsæk/ n zaino m

**havoc** /'hævək/ n strage f; **play ~ with** fig scombussolare

**haw** /hɔː/ see **hum**

**Hawaii** /hə'waɪɪ/ n le Hawaii

**Hawaiian** /hə'waɪən/ n & a hawaiano, -a mf; (language) hawaiano m

**hawk**[1] /hɔːk/ n falco m

**hawk**[2] vt vendere in giro

**hawker** /'hɔːkə(r)/ n venditore, -trice mf ambulante

**hawkish** /'hɔːkɪʃ/ a Pol intransigente

**hawthorn** /'hɔːθɔːn/ n biancospino m

**hay** /heɪ/ n fieno m

**hay: hay fever** n raffreddore m da fieno. **hayloft** n fienile m. **haymaking** n fienagione f. **haystack** n pagliaio m. **haywire** a fam **go ~** dare i numeri; (plans:) andare all'aria

**hazard** /'hæzəd/ n (risk) rischio m ● vt rischiare; ~ **a guess** azzardare un'ipotesi

**hazardous** /'hæzədəs/ a rischioso

**hazard [warning] lights** npl Auto luci fpl d'emergenza

**haze** /heɪz/ n foschia f

**hazel** /'heɪz(ə)l/ n nocciolo m; (colour) [color m] nocciola m

**hazelnut** /'heɪz(ə)lnʌt/ n nocciola f

**hazy** /'heɪzɪ/ a (-ier, -iest) nebbioso; (fig: person) confuso; (memories) vago

**he** /hiː/ pron lui; **he's tired** è stanco; **I'm going but he's not** io vengo, ma lui no

**head** /hed/ n testa f; (of firm) capo m; (of primary school) direttore, -trice mf; (of secondary school) preside mf; (on beer) schiuma f; **use your ~!** usa la testa!; **be off one's ~** essere fuori di testa; **have a good ~ for business** avere il senso degli affari; **have a good ~ for heights** non soffrire di vertigini; **10 pounds a ~** 10 sterline a testa; **20 ~ of cattle** 20 capi di bestiame; ~ **first** a capofitto; ~ **over heels in love** innamorato pazzo; ~**s or tails?** testa o croce? ● vt essere a capo di; essere in testa a (list); colpire di testa (ball) ● vi ~ **for** dirigersi verso

**head: headache** n mal m di testa. **headband** n fascia f per capelli. **head boy** n Br Sch alunno m che rappresenta la scuola nelle manifestazioni ufficiali e che ha responsabilità speciali. **head-butt** vt dare una testata a. **head case** n fam **be a ~ ~** essere matto da legare. **head cold** n raffreddore m di testa. **headcount** n **do a ~** contare i presenti.

**head of department** n capo mf reparto.
**headdress** n acconciatura f
**header** /'hedə(r)/ n colpo m di testa; (dive) tuffo m di testa; (on document) intestazione f
**head: headgear** n copricapo m. **head girl** n Br Sch alunna f che rappresenta la scuola nelle manifestazioni ufficiali e che ha responsabilità speciali. **headhunter** n also Comm cacciatore, -trice mf di teste. **headhunting** n Comm ricerca f ad hoc di personale. **heading** n (in list etc) titolo m. **headlamp** n Auto fanale m. **headland** n promontorio m. **headlight** n Auto fanale m. **headline** n titolo m. **headlong** a & adv a capofitto. **head louse** n pidocchio m. **headmaster** n (of primary school) direttore m; (of secondary school) preside m. **headmistress** n (of primary school) direttrice f; (of secondary school) preside f. **head office** n sede f centrale. **head-on** a ‹collision› frontale ● adv frontalmente. **headphones** npl cuffie fpl. **headquarters** npl sede fsg; Mil quartier msg generale. **headrest** n poggiatesta m inv. **headroom** n sottotetto m; (of bridge) altezza f libera di passaggio. **headscarf** n foulard m inv, fazzoletto m. **headstand** n do a ~ fare la verticale. **head start** n have a ~ ~ partire avvantaggiato. **headstone** n (of grave) lapide f. **headstrong** a testardo. **head teacher** n (of primary school) direttore, -trice mf; (of secondary school) preside mf. **head-to-head** n confronto m diretto ● a diretto. **head waiter** n capocameriere m. **headway** n progresso m. **headwind** n vento m di prua
**heady** /'hedɪ/ a che dà alla testa
**heal** /hiːl/ vt/i guarire
**healer** /'hiːlə(r)/ n guaritore, -trice mf; **time is a great ~** il tempo guarisce tutti i mali
**health** /helθ/ n salute f
**health: health care** n assistenza f sanitaria. **health centre** n Br ambulatorio m. **health check** n controllo m medico. **health club** n club m ginnico. **health farm** n centro m di rimessa in forma. **health foods** npl alimenti mpl macrobiotici. **health-food shop** n negozio m di macrobiotica. **health hazard** n pericolo m per la salute
**healthily** /'helθɪlɪ/ adv in modo sano
**health: health insurance** n assicurazione f contro malattie. **health officer** n ufficiale m sanitario. **health resort** n (in mountains, by sea) stazione f climatica; (spa town) stazione f termale. **health visitor** n Br infermiere, -a mf che fa visite a domicilio. **health warning** n avviso m del ministero della sanità
**healthy** /'helθɪ/ a (-ier, -iest) sano
**heap** /hiːp/ n mucchio m; **~s of** fam un sacco di ● vt ~ [up] ammucchiare; **~ed teaspoon** un cucchiaino abbondante
**hear** /hɪə(r)/ vt/i (pt/pp heard) sentire; ~, ~! bravo!
■ **hear about** vt (learn of) sentir parlare di
■ **hear from** vi aver notizie di
■ **hear of** vi sentir parlare di; **he would not ~ of it** non ne ha voluto sentir parlare

**hearing** /'hɪərɪŋ/ n udito m; Jur udienza f
**hearing aid** n apparecchio m acustico
**hearing-impaired** /-ɪm'peəd/ a audioleso
**hearsay** /'hɪəseɪ/ n **from ~** per sentito dire
**hearse** /hɜːs/ n carro m funebre
**heart** /hɑːt/ n cuore m; **~s** pl (Cards) cuori mpl; **at ~** di natura; **by ~** a memoria
**heart: heartache** n pena f. **heart attack** n infarto m. **heartbeat** n battito m cardiaco. **heartbreak** n afflizione f. **heartbreaking** a straziante. **heart-broken** a **be ~** avere il cuore spezzato. **heartburn** n mal m di stomaco. **heart disease** n malattia f cardiaca
**hearten** /'hɑːt(ə)n/ vt rincuorare
**heart failure** n arresto m cardiaco
**heartfelt** /'hɑːtfelt/ a di cuore
**hearth** /hɑːθ/ n focolare m
**hearthrug** /'hɑːθrʌg/ n tappeto m davanti al camino
**heartily** /'hɑːtɪlɪ/ adv di cuore; ‹eat› con appetito; **be ~ sick of sth** non poterne più di qcsa
**heartland** /'hɑːtlænd/ n (industrial, rural) cuore m; Pol roccaforte f
**heartless** /'hɑːtlɪs/ a spietato
**heartlessly** /'hɑːtlɪslɪ/ adv in modo spietato
**heart: heart-lung machine** n polmone m artificiale. **heart rate** n battito m cardiaco. **heart-rending** /-rendɪŋ/ a ‹sigh, story› straziante. **heart-searching** n esame m di coscienza. **heart surgeon** n cardiochirurgo, -a mf. **heartthrob** n fam rubacuori m inv. **heart-to-heart** n conversazione f a cuore aperto ● a a cuore aperto. **heart transplant** n trapianto m di cuore. **heart-warming** a toccante
**hearty** /'hɑːtɪ/ a caloroso; ‹meal› copioso; ‹person› gioviale
**heat** /hiːt/ n calore m; Sport prova f eliminatoria ● vt scaldare ● vi scaldarsi
■ **heat up** vt scaldare ‹food, drink›; riscaldare ‹room›
**heated** /'hiːtɪd/ a ‹swimming pool› riscaldato; ‹discussion› animato
**heater** /'hiːtə(r)/ n (for room) stufa f; (for water) boiler m inv; Auto riscaldamento m
**heath** /hiːθ/ n brughiera f
**heat haze** n foschia f (dovuta all'afa)
**heathen** /'hiːðn/ a & n pagano, -a mf
**heather** /'heðə(r)/ n erica f
**heating** /'hiːtɪŋ/ n riscaldamento m
**heat: heat loss** n perdita f di calore. **heat-resistant** a resistente al calore. **heat sink** n dissipatore m termico. **heatstroke** n colpo m di sole. **heat treatment** n Med termoterapia f. **heatwave** n ondata f di calore
**heave** /hiːv/ vt tirare; (lift) tirare su; (fam: throw) gettare; emettere ‹sigh› ● vi tirare; **my stomach ~d** avevo la nausea
**heaven** /'hev(ə)n/ n paradiso m; **~ help you if...** Dio ti scampi se...; **raise one's eyes to ~** alzare gli occhi al cielo; **H~s!** santo cielo!
**heavenly** /'hev(ə)nlɪ/ a celeste; fam delizioso

**heaven-sent** /-'sent/ *a* ⟨*opportunity*⟩ provvidenziale

**heavily** /'hevɪlɪ/ *adv* pesantemente; ⟨*smoke, drink etc*⟩ molto

**heaviness** /'hevɪnɪs/ *n* pesantezza *f*

**heavy** /'hevɪ/ *a* (**-ier, -iest**) pesante; ⟨*traffic*⟩ intenso; ⟨*rain, cold*⟩ forte; **be a ~ smoker/ drinker** essere un gran fumatore/bevitore

**heavy: heavy-duty** *a* ⟨*equipment, shoes*⟩ molto resistente. **heavy goods vehicle** *n* veicolo *m* pesante da trasporto. **heavy-handed** /-'hændɪd/ *a* ⟨*severe*⟩ severo; ⟨*clumsy*⟩ maldestro. **heavy industry** *n* industria *f* pesante. **heavy metal** *n Mus* heavy metal *m*. **heavyweight** *n* peso *m* massimo

**Hebrew** /'hi:bru:/ *a & nm* ebreo

**heck** /hek/ *fam int* cavolo • **a ~ of a lot of** un sacco di; **what the ~ !** chi se ne frega!; **what the ~ is going on?** che cavolo succede?

**heckle** /'hekl/ *vt* interrompere di continuo

**heckler** /'heklə(r)/ *n* disturbatore, -trice *mf*

**hectare** /'hektɛə(r)/ *n* ettaro *m*

**hectic** /'hektɪk/ *a* frenetico

**hectoring** /'hektərɪŋ/ *a* prepotente

**hedge** /hedʒ/ *n* siepe *f* • *vi fig* essere evasivo

**hedge: hedge-clippers** *npl* cesoie *fpl*. **hedgehog** *n* riccio *m*. **hedgerow** *n* siepe *f*

**hedonism** /'hi:dənɪzm/ *n* edonismo *m*

**hedonistic** /'hi:də'nɪstɪk/ *a* edonistico

**heebie-jeebies** /hi:bɪ'dʒi:bɪz/ *npl fam* **give sb the ~** far venire i brividi a qcno

**heed** /hi:d/ *n* **pay ~ to** prestare ascolto a • *vt* prestare ascolto a

**heedless** /'hi:dlɪs/ *a* noncurante

**heel**[1] /hi:l/ *n* tallone *m*; ⟨*of shoe*⟩ tacco *m*; **down at ~** *fig* trasandato; **take to one's ~s** *fam* darsela a gambe

**heel**[2] *vi* **~ over** *Naut* inclinarsi

**heel bar** *n* calzolaio *m*

**hefty** /'heftɪ/ *a* (**-ier, -iest**) massiccio

**heifer** /'hefə(r)/ *n* giovenca *f*

**height** /haɪt/ *n* altezza *f*; ⟨*of plane*⟩ altitudine *f*; ⟨*of season, fame*⟩ culmine *m*

**heighten** /'haɪt(ə)n/ *vt fig* accrescere

**heinous** /'hi:nəs/ *a* abominevole

**heir** /eə(r)/ *n* erede *mf*

**heiress** /'eə'res/ *n* ereditiera *f*

**heirloom** /'eəlu:m/ *n* cimelio *m* di famiglia

**heist** /haɪst/ *n Am fam* furto *m*; ⟨*armed*⟩ rapina *f*

**held** /held/ *see* **hold**[2]

**helicopter** /'helɪkɒptə(r)/ *n* elicottero *m*

**heliport** /'helɪpɔ:t/ *n* eliporto *m*

**helium** /'hi:lɪəm/ *n* elio *m*

**helix** /'hi:lɪks/ *n* elica *f*

**hell** /hel/ *n* inferno *m*; **go to ~!** *sl* va' al diavolo!; **make sb's life ~** rendere la vita infernale a qcno • *int* porca miseria!

**hell-bent** *a* **~ on doing sth** deciso a tutti i costi a fare qcsa

**Hellenic** /hɪ'lenɪk/ *a* ellenico

**hellfire** /'helfaɪə(r)/ *n* pene *fpl* dell'inferno

**hell-for-leather** *adv fam* **go ~** andare a spron battuto

**hello** /hə'ləʊ/ *int & n* = **hallo**

**Hell's angel** *n* Hell's angel *m inv*

**helm** /helm/ *n* timone *m*; **at the ~** *fig* al timone

**helmet** /'helmɪt/ *n* casco *m*

**help** /help/ *n* aiuto *m*; ⟨*employee*⟩ aiuto *m* domestico; **that's no ~** non è d'aiuto • *vt* aiutare; **~ oneself to sth** servirsi di qcsa; **~ yourself** (*at table*) serviti pure; **I could not ~ laughing** non ho potuto trattenermi dal ridere; **it cannot be ~ed** non c'è niente da fare; **I can't ~ it** non ci posso far niente • *vi* aiutare

■ **help out** *vt* dare una mano a • *vi* dare una mano

**helper** /'helpə(r)/ *n* aiutante *mf*

**helpful** /'helpfʊl/ *a* ⟨*person*⟩ di aiuto; ⟨*advice*⟩ utile

**helping** /'helpɪŋ/ *n* porzione *f*

**helping hand** *n* **give sb a ~ ~** dare una mano a qcno

**helpless** /'helplɪs/ *a* ⟨*unable to manage*⟩ incapace; ⟨*powerless*⟩ impotente

**helplessly** /'helplɪslɪ/ *adv* con impotenza; ⟨*laugh*⟩ incontrollatamente

**help window** *n Comput* finestrella *f* di aiuto

**helter-skelter** /heltə'skeltə(r)/ *adv* in fretta e furia • *n* scivolo *m* a spirale nei luna park

**hem** /hem/ *n* orlo *m* • *vt* (*pt/pp* **hemmed**) orlare

■ **hem in** *vt* intrappolare

**hemisphere** /'hemɪsfɪə(r)/ *n* emisfero *m*

**hemline** /'hemlaɪn/ *n* orlo *m*

**hemlock** /'hemlɒk/ *n* cicuta *f*

**hemp** /hemp/ *n* canapa *f*

**hen** /hen/ *n* gallina *f*; ⟨*any female bird*⟩ femmina *f*

**hence** /hens/ *adv* ⟨*for this reason*⟩ quindi; ⟨*from now on*⟩ a partire da ora; ⟨*from here*⟩ da qui

**henceforth** /hens'fɔ:θ/ *adv fml* ⟨*from that time on*⟩ da allora in poi; ⟨*from now on*⟩ d'ora in poi

**henchman** /'hentʃmən/ *n pej* tirapiedi *m inv*

**hen-coop** *n* stia *f*

**hen house** *n* pollaio *m*

**henna** /'henə/ *n* henné *m*

**hen-party** *n fam* festa *f* di addio al celibato per sole donne

**henpecked** /'henpekt/ *a* tiranneggiato dalla moglie

**hepatitis** /hepə'taɪtɪs/ *n* epatite *f*

**her** /hɜ:(r)/ *poss a* suo *m*, sua *f*, suoi *mpl*, sue *fpl*; **~ job/house** il suo lavoro/la sua casa; **her mother/father** sua madre/suo padre • *pers pron* (*direct object*) la; (*indirect object*) le; (*after prep*) lei; **I know ~** la conosco; **give ~ the money** dalle i soldi; **give it to ~** daglielo; **I came with ~** sono venuto con lei; **it's ~** è lei; **I've seen ~** l'ho vista; **I've seen ~, but not him** ho visto lei, ma non lui

**herald** /'herəld/ *vt* annunciare

**heraldic** /he'rældɪk/ *a* araldico

**heraldry** /ˈherəldrɪ/ n araldica f

**herb** /hɜːb/ n erba f

**herbaceous** /hɜːˈbeɪʃəs/ a erbaceo; ~ **border** aiuola f

**herbal** /ˈhɜːb(ə)l/ a alle erbe

**herbalist** /ˈhɜːbəlɪst/ n erborista mf

**herbal tea** n tisana f

**herb garden** n aromatario m

**herbs** /hɜːbz/ npl (for cooking) aromi mpl [da cucina]; (medicinal) erbe fpl

**herb tea** n tisana f

**herculean** /hɜːkjʊˈliːən/ a (task) erculeo

**herd** /hɜːd/ n gregge m ● vt (tend) sorvegliare; (drive) far muovere; fig ammassare ■ **herd together** vi raggrupparsi ● vt raggruppare

**here** /hɪə(r)/ adv qui, qua; **in** ~ qui dentro; **come/bring** ~ vieni/porta qui; ~ **is...,** ~ **are...** ecco...; ~ **you are!** ecco qua!

**here: hereabouts** /hɪərəˈbaʊts/ adv Br da queste parti. **hereafter** adv in futuro. **here and now** adv seduta stante ● n the ~ ~ ~ il presente. **hereby** adv con la presente

**hereditary** /hɪˈredɪtərɪ/ a ereditario

**heredity** /hɪˈredɪtɪ/ n ereditarietà f

**heresy** /ˈherəsɪ/ n eresia f

**heretic** /ˈherətɪk/ n eretico, -a mf

**herewith** /hɪəˈwɪð/ adv Comm con la presente

**heritage** /ˈherɪtɪdʒ/ n eredità f

**hermetic** /hɜːˈmetɪk/ a ermetico

**hermetically** /hɜːˈmetɪklɪ/ adv ermeticamente

**hermit** /ˈhɜːmɪt/ n eremita mf

**hernia** /ˈhɜːnɪə/ n ernia f

**hero** /ˈhɪərəʊ/ n (pl -es) eroe m

**heroic** /hɪˈrəʊɪk/ a eroico

**heroically** /hɪˈrəʊɪklɪ/ adv eroicamente

**heroin** /ˈherəʊɪn/ n eroina f (droga)

**heroine** /ˈherəʊɪn/ n eroina f

**heroism** /ˈherəʊɪzm/ n eroismo m

**heron** /ˈherən/ n airone m

**hero-worship** n culto m degli eroi ● vt venerare

**herpes** /ˈhɜːpiːz/ n herpes m

**herring** /ˈherɪŋ/ n aringa f

**herringbone** /ˈherɪŋbəʊn/ a (pattern) spigato

**hers** /hɜːz/ poss pron il suo m, la sua f, i suoi mpl, le sue fpl; **a friend of** ~ un suo amico; **friends of** ~ dei suoi amici; **that is** ~ quello è suo; (as opposed to mine) quello è il suo

**herself** /həˈself/ pers pron (reflexive) si; (emphatic) lei stessa; (after prep) sé, se stessa; **she poured** ~ **a drink** si è versata da bere; **she told me so** ~ me lo ha detto lei stessa; **she's proud of** ~ è fiera di sé; **by** ~ da sola

**hesitant** /ˈhezɪtənt/ a esitante

**hesitantly** /ˈhezɪtəntlɪ/ adv con esitazione

**hesitate** /ˈhezɪteɪt/ vi esitare

**hesitation** /hezɪˈteɪʃn/ n esitazione f

**hessian** /ˈhesɪən/ n tela f di iuta

**heterogeneous** /hetərəˈdʒiːnɪəs/ a eterogeneo

**heterosexual** /hetərəʊˈsekʃʊəl/ a eterosessuale

**het up** /het/ a fam agitato

**hew** /hjuː/ vt (pt hewed, pp hewed or hewn) spaccare

**hexagon** /ˈheksəgən/ n esagono m

**hexagonal** /hekˈsægənl/ a esagonale

**hey** /heɪ/ int ehi!

**heyday** /ˈheɪdeɪ/ n tempi mpl d'oro

**hey presto** /heɪˈprestəʊ/ int (magic) e voilà!

**HGV** abbr **heavy goods vehicle**

**hi** /haɪ/ int ciao!

**hiatus** /haɪˈeɪtəs/ n (pl -tuses) iato m

**hibernate** /ˈhaɪbəneɪt/ vi andare in letargo

**hibernation** /haɪbəˈneɪʃn/ n letargo m

**hiccup** /ˈhɪkʌp/ n singhiozzo m; (fam: hitch) intoppo m; **have the ~s** avere il singhiozzo ● vi fare un singhiozzo

**hick** /hɪk/ n Am fam buzzurro, -a mf

**hick town** n Am fam città f inv provinciale

**hid** /hɪd/, **hidden** /ˈhɪdn/ see **hide²**

**hide¹** /haɪd/ n (leather) pelle f (di animale)

**hide²** vt (pt hid, pp hidden) nascondere ● vi nascondersi

**hide-and-seek** n play ~ giocare a nascondino

**hideaway** /ˈhaɪdəweɪ/ n (secluded place) rifugio m; (hiding place) nascondiglio m

**hidebound** /ˈhaɪdbaʊnd/ a (conventional) limitato

**hideous** /ˈhɪdɪəs/ a orribile

**hideously** /ˈhɪdɪəslɪ/ adv orribilmente

**hideout** /ˈhaɪdaʊt/ n nascondiglio m

**hiding¹** /ˈhaɪdɪŋ/ n (fam: beating) bastonata; (defeat) batosta f

**hiding²** n go into ~ sparire dalla circolazione

**hierarchic[al]** /haɪəˈrɑːkɪk[l]/ a gerarchico

**hierarchy** /ˈhaɪərɑːkɪ/ n gerarchia f

**hieroglyphics** /haɪərəˈglɪfɪks/ npl geroglifici mpl

**hi-fi** /ˈhaɪfaɪ/ n abbr (**high fidelity**) hi-fi m inv; (set of equipment) impianto m hi-fi, stereo m inv

**higgledy-piggledy** /hɪɡldɪˈpɪɡldɪ/ adv alla rinfusa

**high** /haɪ/ a alto; (meat) che comincia ad andare a male; (wind) forte; (on drugs) fatto; **it's** ~ **time we did something about it** è ora di fare qualcosa in proposito ● adv in alto; ~ **and low** in lungo e in largo ● n massimo m; (temperature) massima f; **from** ~ **on** dall'alto; **be on a** ~ fam essere fatto

**high: high and dry** a fig **leave sb** ~ ~ ~ piantare in asso qcno. **high beam** n Am abbagliante m. **high-born** a nobile. **highbrow** a & n intellettuale mf. **high chair** n seggiolone m. **high-class** a (hotel, shop, car) d'alta classe; (prostitute) di alto bordo. **high command** n stato m maggiore. **High Commission** n alto commissariato m. **High Commissioner** n alto commissario m. **High Court** n ≈ Corte f Suprema. **high-definition** a ad alta definizione. **high diving** n tuffo m

**higher education** /haɪərˈedjʊˈkeɪʃn/ n istruzione f universitaria

**higher mathematics** n matematica f avanzata

**high: highfaluting** /haɪfəˈluːtɪŋ/ a fam ⟨ideas⟩ pretenzioso: ⟨language⟩ pomposo. **high fashion** n alta moda f. **high-fibre** a ⟨diet⟩ ricco di fibre. **high-fidelity** n alta fedeltà f ● a ad alta fedeltà. **high finance** n alta finanza f. **high-flier** n ⟨person⟩ persona f che mira alto. **high-flown** a ⟨phrases⟩ ampolloso. **high-flying** a ⟨aircraft⟩ da alta quota; ⟨career⟩ ambizioso; ⟨person⟩ che mira alto. **high-frequency** a alta frequenza f. **High German** n alto tedesco m. **high-grade** a ⟨oil, mineral, product⟩ di prima qualità. **high ground** n collina f; **take the moral ~ ~** assumere un atteggiamento moralistico. **high-handed** /-ˈhændɪd/ a dispotico. **high-handedly** /-ˈhændɪdlɪ/ adv dispoticamente. **high-heeled** /-hi:ld/ a coi tacchi alti. **high heels** npl tacchi mpl alti. **high jinks** /dʒɪŋks/ npl baldoria f. **high jump** n salto m in alto

**Highland games** /haɪlənd/ n manifestazione f tradizionale scozzese con gare sportive e musicali

**Highlands** /ˈhaɪləndz/ npl Highlands fpl (regione della Scozia del nord)

**high-level** a ⟨talks⟩ ad alto livello; ⟨official⟩ di alto livello

**high life** n bella vita f

**highlight** /ˈhaɪlaɪt/ vt (emphasize, with pen) evidenziare ● n (in art) luce f; (in hair) riflesso m, colpo m di sole; (of exhibition) parte f saliente; (of week, year) avvenimento m saliente; (of match, show) momento m clou

**highlighter** /ˈhaɪlaɪtə(r)/ n (marker) evidenziatore m

**highly** /ˈhaɪlɪ/ adv molto; **speak ~ of** lodare; **think ~ of** avere un'alta opinione di

**highly-paid** /-ˈpeɪd/ a ben pagato

**highlystrung** /-ˈstrʌn/ a nervoso

**high: High Mass** n messa f solenne. **high-minded** /-ˈmaɪndɪd/ a ⟨person⟩ di animo nobile. **high-necked** /-ˈnekt/ a a collo alto

**Highness** /ˈhaɪnɪs/ n altezza f; **Your ~** Sua Altezza

**high: high noon** n mezzogiorno m in punto. **high-performance** a ad alta prestazione. **high-pitched** /-ˈpɪtʃt/ a ⟨voice, sound⟩ acuto. **high point** n momento m culminante. **high-powered** a ⟨car, engine⟩ molto potente; ⟨job⟩ di alta responsabilità; ⟨person⟩ dinamico. **high pressure** n Meteorol alta pressione f ● attrib Techn ad alta pressione; ⟨job⟩ stressante. **high priest** n Relig gran sacerdote m; fig guru m inv. **high priestess** n Relig, fig gran sacerdotessa f. **high-principled** a ⟨person⟩ di alti principi. **high-profile** a ⟨politician, group⟩ di spicco; ⟨visit⟩ di grande risonanza. **high-ranking** a di alto rango. **high-rise** a ⟨building⟩ molto alto ● n edificio m molto alto. **high road** n strada f principale. **high school** n Am ≈ scuola f superiore; Br ≈ scuola f media e superiore. **high sea** n on

the **~ ~s** in alto mare. **high season** n alta stagione f. **high society** n alta società f. **high-sounding** /-ˈsaʊndɪŋ/ a ⟨title⟩ altisonante. **high-speed** a ⟨train, film⟩ rapido. **high-spirited** a pieno di brio. **high spirits** npl brio m. **high spot** n momento m culminante. **high street** n strada f principale. **high-street shop** n negozio m popolare. **high tea** n pasto m pomeridiano servito insieme al tè. **high tech** /ˈtek/ n high tech f. **high tide** n alta marea f. **high treason** n alto tradimento m. **high voltage** n alta tensione f

**highway** /ˈhaɪweɪ/ n **public ~** strada f pubblica

**highway: Highway Code** n Br Codice m stradale. **highwayman** n brigante m. **highway robbery** n brigantaggio m

**high wire** n filo m (per acrobati)

**hijack** /ˈhaɪdʒæk/ vt dirottare ● n dirottamento m

**hijacker** /ˈhaɪdʒækə(r)/ n dirottatore, -trice mf

**hijacking** /ˈhaɪdʒækɪŋ/ n dirottamento m

**hike** /haɪk/ n escursione f a piedi; (in price) aumento m ● vi fare un'escursione a piedi

**hiker** /ˈhaɪkə(r)/ n escursionista mf

**hilarious** /hɪˈleərɪəs/ a da morir dal ridere

**hilarity** /hɪˈlærətɪ/ n ilarità f

**hill** /hɪl/ n collina f; (mound) collinetta f; (slope) altura f

**hill-billy** /-bɪlɪ/ n Am montanaro m degli Stati Uniti sudorientali

**hillock** /ˈhɪlək/ n poggio m

**hillside** /ˈhɪlsaɪd/ n pendio m

**hilltop** /ˈhɪltɒp/ n sommità f inv di una collina

**hilly** /ˈhɪlɪ/ a collinoso

**hilt** /hɪlt/ n impugnatura f; **to the ~** ⟨fam: support⟩ fino in fondo; ⟨mortgaged⟩ fino al collo

**him** /hɪm/ pers pron (direct object) lo; (indirect object) gli; (with prep) lui; **I know ~** lo conosco; **give ~ the money** dagli i soldi; **give it to ~** daglielo; **I spoke to ~** gli ho parlato; **it's ~** è lui; **she loves ~** lo ama;a **she loves ~, not you** ama lui, non te

**Himalayas** /hɪməˈleɪəz/ npl Himalaia msg

**himself** /hɪmˈself/ pers pron (reflexive) si; (emphatic) lui stesso; (after prep) sé, se stesso; **he poured ~ out a drink** si è versato da bere; **he told me so ~** me lo ha detto lui stesso; **he's proud of ~** è fiero di sé; **by ~** da solo

**hind** /haɪnd/ a posteriore

**hinder** /ˈhɪndə(r)/ vt intralciare

**hindquarters** /ˈhaɪn(d)kwɔːtəz/ npl didietro m

**hindrance** /ˈhɪndrəns/ n intralcio m

**hindsight** /ˈhaɪndsaɪt/ n **with ~** con il senno del poi

**Hindu** /ˈhɪnduː/ a & n indù mf inv

**Hinduism** /ˈhɪndʊɪzm/ n induismo m

**hinge** /hɪndʒ/ n cardine m ● vi **~ on** fig dipendere da

**hint** /hɪnt/ n (clue) accenno m; (advice) sugge-

rimento *m*; (*indirect suggestion*) allusione *f*;
(*trace*) tocco *m* ● *vt* ~ **that...** far capire che...
● *vi* ~ **at** alludere a

**hinterland** /'hɪntəlænd/ *n* entroterra *m inv*,
hinterland *m inv*

**hip** /hɪp/ *n* fianco *m*

**hip bone** *n* ileo *m*

**hip flask** *n* fiaschetta *f*

**hippie** /'hɪpɪ/ *n* hippy *mf inv*

**hippo** /'hɪpəʊ/ *n fam* ippopotamo *m*

**hip pocket** *n* tasca *f* posteriore

**Hippocratic oath** /hɪpə'krætɪk/ *a* giuramento *m* d'Ippocrate

**hippopotamus** /hɪpə'pɒtəməs/ *n* (*pl*
-**muses** *or* -**mi** /hɪpə'pɒtəmaɪ/) ippopotamo *m*

**hip replacement** *n* protesi *f inv* all'anca

**hire** /haɪə(r)/ *vt* affittare; assumere (*person*);
~ [**out**] affittare ● *n* noleggio *m*; '**for ~**'
'affittasi'

**hire car** *n* macchina *f* a noleggio

**hire purchase** *n* Br acquisto *m* rateale; **on**
~ ~ a rate

**his** /hɪz/ *poss a* suo *m*, sua *f*, suoi *mpl*, sue *fpl*;
~ **job/house** il suo lavoro/la sua casa; ~
**mother/father** sua madre/suo padre ● *poss
pron* il suo *m*, la sua *f*, i suoi *mpl*, le sue *fpl*; **a
friend of** ~ un suo amico; **friends of** ~ dei
suoi amici; **that is** ~ questo è suo; (*as
opposed to mine*) questo è il suo

**Hispanic** /hɪ'spænɪk/ *a* ispanico

**hiss** /hɪs/ *n* sibilo *m*; (*of disapproval*) fischio
*m* ● *vt* fischiare ● *vi* sibilare; (*in disapproval*)
fischiare

**historian** /hɪ'stɔːrɪən/ *n* storico, -a *mf*

**historic** /hɪ'stɒrɪk/ *a* storico

**historical** /hɪ'stɒrɪkl/ *a* storico

**historically** /hɪ'stɒrɪklɪ/ *adv* storicamente

**history** /'hɪstərɪ/ *n* storia *f*; **make** ~ passare
alla storia

**histrionic** /hɪstrɪ'ɒnɪk/ *a* istrionico

**histrionics** /hɪstrɪ'ɒnɪks/ *npl* scene *fpl*

**hit** /hɪt/ *n* (*blow*) colpo *m*; (*fam: success*) successo *m*; **score a direct** ~ (*missile:*) colpire
in pieno ● *vt/i* (*pt/pp* **hit**, *pres p* **hitting**) colpire; ~ **one's head on the table** battere la
testa contro il tavolo; **the car** ~ **the wall** la
macchina ha sbattuto contro il muro; ~ **the
target** colpire il bersaglio; ~ **the nail on
the head** fare centro; ~ **the roof** *fam* perdere le staffe

■ **hit back** *vi* (*retaliate*) ribattere

■ **hit off** *vt* ~ **it off** andare d'accordo

■ **hit on** *vt fig* trovare

**hit:** **hit-and-miss** *a* (*affair, undertaking*) imprevedibile; (*method*) a casaccio. **hit-and-run**
*a* (*raid, attack*) lampo *inv*; (*accident*) causato
da un pirata della strada. **hit-and-run driver**
*a* pirata *m* della strada

**hitch** /hɪtʃ/ *n* intoppo *m*; **technical** ~ problema *m* tecnico ● *vt* attaccare; ~ **a lift** chiedere
un passaggio

■ **hitch up** *vt* tirarsi su (*trousers*)

**hitch:** **hitch-hike** *vi* fare l'autostop. **hitch-
hiker** *n* autostoppista *mf*. **hitch-hiking** *n* autostop *m*

**hi-tech** *a see* **high tech**

**hither** /'hɪðə(r)/ *adv* ~ **and thither** di qua e
di là

**hitherto** /hɪðə'tuː/ *adv* finora

**hit:** **hit list** *n* lista *f* degli obiettivi. **hit man** *n*
sicario *m*. **hit-or-miss** *a* on a very ~ **basis**
all'improvvisata. **hit parade** *n* hit parade *f
inv*, classifica *f*

**HIV** *n abbr* (**human immunodeficiency virus**) HIV *m*

**hive** /haɪv/ *n* alveare *m*; ~ **of industry** fucina
*f* di lavoro

■ **hive off** *vt Comm* separare

**HIV positive** *a* sieropositivo

**HMS** *abbr* **His/Her Majesty's Ship**

**hoard** /hɔːd/ *n* provvista *f*; (*of money*)
gruzzolo *m* ● *vt* accumulare

**hoarding** /'hɔːdɪŋ/ *n* palizzata *f*; (*with
advertisements*) tabellone *m* per manifesti
pubblicitari

**hoar frost** /'hɔː(r)/ *n* brina *f*

**hoarse** /hɔːs/ *a* rauco

**hoarsely** /'hɔːslɪ/ *adv* con voce rauca

**hoarseness** /'hɔːsnɪs/ *n* raucedine *f*

**hoary** /'hɔːrɪ/ *a* (*person*) con i capelli bian-
chi; ~ **old joke** barzelletta *f* vecchia

**hoax** /həʊks/ *n* scherzo *m*; (*false alarm*) falso
allarme *m*

**hoaxer** /'həʊksə(r)/ *n* burlone, -a *mf*

**hob** /hɒb/ *n* piano *m* di cottura

**hobble** /'hɒbl/ *vi* zoppicare

**hobby** /'hɒbɪ/ *n* hobby *m inv*

**hobby horse** *n fig* fissazione *f*

**hobnailed** /'hɒbneɪld/ *a* ~ **boots** *pl* scarponi *mpl* chiodati

■ **hobnob with** /'hɒbnɒb/ *vt* (*pt/pp*
**hobnobbed**) frequentare

**hobo** /'həʊbəʊ/ *n Am* vagabondo, -a *mf*

**hock** /hɒk/ *n* vino *m* bianco del Reno

**hockey** /'hɒkɪ/ *n* hockey *m*

**hocus-pocus** /həʊkəs'pəʊkəs/ *n* (*trickery*)
trucco *m*

**hod** /hɒd/ *n* (*for coal*) secchio *m* del carbone;
(*for bricks*) cassetta *f* (*per trasportare mattoni*)

**hoe** /həʊ/ *n* zappa *f* ● *vt* (*pres p* **hoeing**) zap-
pare

**hog** /hɒg/ *n* maiale *m* ● *vt* (*pt/pp* **hogged**)
*fam* monopolizzare

**hog-tie** /'hɒgtaɪ/ *vt* legare le quattro zampe
di (*pig, cow*); *Am fig* ostacolare (*person*)

**hogwash** /'hɒgwɒʃ/ *n fam* cretinate *fpl*

**hoi polloi** /hɔɪpɒ'lɔɪ/ *npl* plebaglia *fsg*

**hoist** /hɔɪst/ *n* montacarichi *m inv*; (*fam:
push*) spinta *f* in su ● *vt* sollevare; innalzare
(*flag*); levare (*anchor*)

**hoity-toity** /hɔɪtɪ'tɔɪtɪ/ *a fam* altezzoso

**hokum** /'həʊkəm/ *n Am fam* (*sentimentality*)
polpettone *m* sentimentale; (*nonsense*)
cretinate *fpl*

**hold¹** /həʊld/ *n Naut*, Aeron stiva *f*

**hold²** *n* presa *f*; (*fig: influence*) ascendente *m*;
**get** ~ **of** trovare; procurarsi (*information*)
● *v* (*pt/pp* **held**) ● *vt* tenere; (*container:*) contenere; essere titolare di (*licence, passport*);

trattenere ⟨breath, suspect⟩; mantenere vivo ⟨interest⟩; ⟨civil servant etc:⟩ occupare ⟨position⟩; (retain) mantenere; **~ sb's hand** tenere qcno per mano; **~ one's tongue** tenere la bocca chiusa; **~ sb responsible** considerare qcno responsabile; **~ that** (believe) ritenere che ● vi tenere; ⟨weather, luck:⟩ durare; ⟨offer:⟩ essere valido; Teleph restare in linea; **I don't ~ with the idea that...** fam non sono d'accordo sul fatto che...

■ **hold against** vt **~ sth against sb** avercela con qcno per qcsa

■ **hold back** vt rallentare ● vi esitare

■ **hold down** vt tenere a bada ⟨sb⟩

■ **hold on** vi (wait) attendere; Teleph restare in linea

■ **hold on to** vt aggrapparsi a; (keep) tenersi

■ **hold out** vt porgere ⟨hand⟩; fig offrire ⟨possibility⟩ ● vi (resist) resistere

■ **hold up** vt tenere su; (delay) rallentare; (rob) assalire; **~ one's head up** fig tenere la testa alta

**holdall** /'hɔʊldɔːl/ n borsone m

**holder** /'hɔʊldə(r)/ n titolare mf; (of record) detentore, -trice mf; (container) astuccio m

**holding** /'hɔʊldɪŋ/ n (land) terreno m in affitto; Comm azioni fpl

**holding company** n società f inv finanziaria

**hold-up** n ritardo m; (attack) rapina f a mano armata

**hole** /hɔʊl/ n buco m

**holiday** /'hɒlɪdeɪ/ n vacanza f; (public) giorno m festivo; (day off) giorno m di ferie; **go on ~** andare in vacanza ● vi andare in vacanza

**holiday: holiday home** n casa f per le vacanze. **holiday job** n (Br: in summer) lavoretto m estivo. **holiday-maker** n vacanziere mf. **holiday resort** n luogo m di villeggiatura

**holier-than-thou** /hɔʊlɪəðən'ðaʊ/ a ⟨attitude⟩ da santerellino

**holiness** /'hɔʊlɪnɪs/ n santità f; **Your H~** Sua Santità

**Holland** /'hɒlənd/ n Olanda f

**holler** /'hɒlə(r)/ vi urlare (at contro)

**hollow** /'hɒlɔʊ/ a cavo; ⟨promise⟩ a vuoto; ⟨voice⟩ assente; ⟨cheeks⟩ infossato ● n cavità f inv; (in ground) affossamento m

■ **hollow out** vt scavare

**holly** /'hɒlɪ/ n agrifoglio m

**hollyhock** /'hɒlɪhɒk/ n malvone m

**holocaust** /'hɒləkɔːst/ n olocausto m

**hologram** /'hɒləgræm/ n ologramma m

**holograph** /'hɒləgrɑːf/ n documento m olografo

**hols** /hɒlz/ n Br fam abbr (holidays) vacanze fpl

**holster** /'hɔʊlstə(r)/ n fondina f

**holy** /'hɔʊlɪ/ a (-ier, -est) santo; ⟨water⟩ benedetto

**holy: Holy Ghost** or **Spirit** n Spirito m Santo. **Holy Scriptures** sacre scritture fpl. **Holy Week** n settimana f santa

**homage** /'hɒmɪdʒ/ n omaggio m; **pay ~ to** rendere omaggio a

**homburg** /'hɒmbɜːg/ n cappello m di feltro

**home** /hɔʊm/ n casa f; (for children) istituto m; (for old people) casa f di riposo; (native land) patria f ● adv **at ~** a casa; (football) in casa; **feel at ~** sentirsi a casa propria; **come/go ~** venire/andare a casa; **drive a nail ~** piantare un chiodo a fondo. ● a domestico; ⟨movie, video⟩ casalingo; ⟨team⟩ ospitante; Pol nazionale

**home: home address** n indirizzo m di casa. **home brew** n (beer) birra f fatta in casa. **homecoming** n (return home) ritorno m a casa. **home computer** n computer m inv da casa. **Home Counties** npl contee fpl intorno a Londra. **home economics** n Sch economia f domestica. **home front** n (during war) fronte m interno; (in politics) politica f interna. **home game** n gioco m in casa. **home ground** n **play on one's ~** ~ giocare in casa. **home-grown** /-'grəʊn/ a ⟨produce⟩ del proprio orto; fig nostrano. **home help** n aiuto m domestico (per persone non autosufficienti). **homeland** n patria f

**homeless** /'hɔʊmlɪs/ a senza tetto

**home loan** n mutuo m per la casa

**homeloving** /'hɔʊmlʌvɪŋ/ a casalingo

**homely** /'hɔʊmlɪ/ a (-ier, -iest) a semplice; ⟨atmosphere⟩ familiare; (Am: ugly) bruttino

**home-made** a fatto in casa

**home market** n mercato m interno

**Home Office** n Br ministero m degli interni

**homeopathic** /hɔʊmɪə'pæθɪk/ a omeopatico

**homeopathy** /hɔʊmɪ'ɒpəθɪ/ n omeopatia f

**home: Home Secretary** n Br ≈ ministro m degli interni. **homesick be ~** avere nostalgia (**for** di). **homesickness** n nostalgia f di casa. **homestead** n fattoria f. **home town** n città f inv natia. **home truth** n **tell sb a few ~s** dirne quattro a qcno. **home video** n filmato m di videoamatore

**homeward** /'hɔʊmwəd/ a di ritorno ● adv **~[s]** verso casa; **~ bound** sulla strada del ritorno; **travel ~[s]** tornare a casa

**homework** /'hɔʊmwɜːk/ n Sch compiti mpl

**homey** /'hɔʊmɪ/ a (home-loving) casalingo; (cosy) accogliente

**homicide** /'hɒmɪsaɪd/ n (crime) omicidio m

**homily** /'hɒmɪlɪ/ n omelia f

**homing** /'hɔʊmɪŋ/ a ⟨missile, device⟩ autoguidato

**homing pigeon** piccione f homing

**homoeopathic** /hɔʊmɪə'pæθɪk/ a omeopatico

**homoeopathy** /hɔʊmɪ'ɒpəθɪ/ n omeopatia f

**homogeneous** /hɒmə'dʒiːnɪəs/ a omogeneo

**homogenize** /hə'mɒdʒənaɪz/ vt omogeneizzare

**homogenous** /hə'mɒdʒənəs/ a omogeneo

**homograph** /'hɒməgrɑːf/ n omografo m

**homonym** /'hɒmənɪm/ n omonimo m

**homophobia** /ˌhəʊməˈfəʊbɪə/ n omofobia f

**homosexual** /ˌhəʊməˈsekʃʊəl/ a & n omosessuale mf

**hone** /həʊn/ vt (sharpen) affilare; (perfect) affinare

**honest** /ˈɒnɪst/ a onesto; (frank) sincero

**honestly** /ˈɒnɪstlɪ/ adv onestamente; (frankly) sinceramente; ~! ma insomma!

**honesty** /ˈɒnɪstɪ/ n onestà f; (frankness) sincerità f

**honey** /ˈhʌnɪ/ n miele m; (fam: darling) tesoro m

**honeycomb** /ˈhʌnɪkəʊm/ n favo m

**honeydew melon** /ˈhʌnɪdjuː/ n melone m (dalla buccia gialla)

**honeymoon** /ˈhʌnɪmuːn/ n luna f di miele

**honeysuckle** /ˈhʌnɪsʌkl/ n caprifoglio m

**Hong Kong** /hɒŋˈkɒŋ/ n Hong Kong f

**honk** /hɒŋk/ vi Aut clacsonare

**honky-tonk** /ˈhɒŋkɪtɒŋk/ a (piano) honkytonky inv

**honorary** /ˈɒnərərɪ/ a onorario

**honorific** /ɒnəˈrɪfɪk/ a onorifico

**honour** /ˈɒnə(r)/ n onore m ● vt onorare

**honourable** /ˈɒnərəbl/ a onorevole

**honourably** /ˈɒnərəblɪ/ adv con onore

**honours degree** /ˈɒnəz/ n ≈ diploma m di laurea

**hood** /hʊd/ n cappuccio m; (of pram) tettuccio m; (over cooker) cappa f; Am Auto cofano m

**hoodlum** /ˈhuːdləm/ n teppista m

**hoodwink** /ˈhʊdwɪŋk/ vt fam infinocchiare

**hoof** /huːf/ n (pl ~s or hooves) zoccolo m

**hoo-ha** /ˈhuːhɑː/ n fam cause a ~ fare scalpore

**hook** /hʊk/ n gancio m; (for crochet) uncinetto m; (for fishing) amo m; off the ~ Teleph staccato; fig fuori pericolo; by ~ or by crook in un modo o nell'altro ● vt agganciare ● vi agganciarsi

**hookah** /ˈhʊkə/ n narghilè m inv

**hook and eye** n gancino m

**hooked** /hʊkt/ a (nose) adunco; ~ on (fam: drugs) dedito a; be ~ on skiing essere un fanatico dello sci

**hooker** /ˈhʊkə(r)/ n Am sl battona f

**hookey** /ˈhʊkɪ/ n play ~ Am fam marinare la scuola

**hooligan** /ˈhuːlɪgən/ n teppista f

**hooliganism** /ˈhuːlɪgənɪzm/ n teppismo m

**hoop** /huːp/ n cerchio m

**hoopla** /ˈhuːplɑː/ n (Br: at fair) lancio m degli anelli (nei luna park); (Am: fuss) trambusto m

**hooray** /hʊˈreɪ/ int & n = hurrah

**hoot** /huːt/ n colpo m di clacson; (of siren) ululato m; (of owl) grido m; ~s of laughter risate fpl ● vi (owl:) gridare; (car:) clacsonare; (siren:) ululare; (jeer) fischiare

**hooter** /ˈhuːtə(r)/ n (of siren) sirena f; Auto clacson m inv; (Br fam: nose) nasone f

**hoover®** /ˈhuːvə(r)/ n aspirapolvere m inv ● vt passare l'aspirapolvere su (carpet); pas-

sare l'aspirapolvere in (room) ● vi passare l'aspirapolvere

**hop**[1] /hɒp/ n luppolo m

**hop**[2] n saltello m; catch sb on the ~ fam prendere qcno alla sprovvista ● vi (pt/pp **hopped**) saltellare; ~ it! fam tela!

■ **hop in** vi fam saltar su

■ **hop out** vi fam saltar giù; ~ ~ to the shops fare un salto ai negozi

**hope** /həʊp/ n speranza f; there's no ~ of that happening non c'è nessuna speranza che succeda ● vi sperare (for in); I ~ so/not spero di sì/no ● vt ~ that sperare che

**hopeful** /ˈhəʊpfʊl/ a pieno di speranza; (promising) promettente; be ~ that avere buone speranze che

**hopefully** /ˈhəʊpfʊlɪ/ adv con speranza; (it is hoped) se tutto va bene

**hopeless** /ˈhəʊplɪs/ a senza speranza; (useless) impossibile; (incompetent) incapace

**hopelessly** /ˈhəʊplɪslɪ/ adv disperatamente; (inefficient, lost) completamente

**hopelessness** /ˈhəʊplɪsnɪs/ n disperazione f

**hopscotch** /ˈhɒpskɒtʃ/ n campana f (gioco)

**horde** /hɔːd/ n orda f

**horizon** /həˈraɪzn/ n orizzonte m; on the ~ all'orizzonte

**horizontal** /hɒrɪˈzɒntl/ a orizzontale

**horizontal bar** n sbarra f orizzontale

**horizontally** /hɒrɪˈzɒntəlɪ/ adv orizzontalmente

**hormonal** /hɔːˈməʊnəl/ a ormonale

**hormone** /ˈhɔːməʊn/ n ormone m

**hormone replacement therapy** n terapia f ormonale sostitutiva

**horn** /hɔːn/ n corno m; Auto clacson m inv

**hornet** /ˈhɔːnɪt/ n calabrone m

**horn-rimmed** /-rɪmd/ a (spectacles) con la montatura di tartaruga

**horny** /ˈhɔːnɪ/ a calloso; (fam: sexually) arrapato

**horoscope** /ˈhɒrəskəʊp/ n oroscopo m

**horrendous** /həˈrendəs/ a spaventoso

**horrible** /ˈhɒrəbl/ a orribile

**horribly** /ˈhɒrəblɪ/ adv orribilmente

**horrid** /ˈhɒrɪd/ a orrendo

**horrific** /həˈrɪfɪk/ a raccapricciante; (fam: accident, prices, story) terrificante

**horrify** /ˈhɒrɪfaɪ/ vt (pt/pp -ied) far inorridire; I was horrified ero inorridito

**horrifying** /ˈhɒrɪfaɪɪŋ/ a terrificante

**horror** /ˈhɒrə(r)/ n orrore m

**horror film** n film m dell'orrore

**hors-d'œuvre** /ɔːˈdɜːvr/ n antipasto m

**horse** /hɔːs/ n cavallo m

**horse: horseback** n on ~ a cavallo. **horsebox** n furgone m per il trasporto dei cavalli. **horse chestnut** n ippocastano m. **horsefly** n tafano m. **horsehair** n crine m di cavallo. **horseman** n cavaliere m. **horse manure** n concime m. **horseplay** n gioco m pesante. **horsepower** n cavallo m [vapore]. **horse racing** n corse fpl di cavalli.

**horseradish** *n* rafano *m*. **horseshoe** *n* ferro *m* di cavallo

**hors[e]y** /'hɔːsɪ/ *a* ⟨person⟩ che adora i cavalli; ⟨face⟩ cavallino

**horticultural** /hɔːtɪ'kʌltʃʊrəl/ *a* di orticoltura

**horticulture** /'hɔːtɪkʌltʃə(r)/ *n* orticoltura *f*

**hose** /həʊz/ *n* ⟨pipe⟩ manichetta *f*

■ **hose down** *vt* lavare con la manichetta

**hosepipe** /'həʊzpaɪp/ *n* manichetta *f*

**hosiery** /'həʊzərɪ/ *n* maglieria *f*

**hospice** /'hɒspɪs/ *n* (*for the terminally ill*) ospedale *m* per i malati in fase terminale

**hospitable** /hɒ'spɪtəbl/ *a* ospitale

**hospitably** /hɒ'spɪtəblɪ/ *adv* con ospitalità

**hospital** /'hɒspɪtl/ *n* ospedale *m*

**hospitality** /hɒsprɪ'tælətɪ/ *n* ospitalità *f*

**hospitalize** /'hɒspɪtəlaɪz/ *vt* ricoverare [in ospedale]

**host¹** /həʊst/ *n* **a ~ of** una moltitudine di

**host²** *n* ospite *m*

**host³** *n* Relig ostia *f*

**hostage** /'hɒstɪdʒ/ *n* ostaggio *m*; **hold sb ~** tenere qcno in ostaggio

**hostel** /'hɒstl/ *n* ostello *m*

**hostess** /'həʊstɪs/ *n* padrona *f* di casa; Aeron hostess *f inv*

**hostile** /'hɒstaɪl/ *a* ostile

**hostility** /hɒ'stɪlətɪ/ *n* ostilità *f*; **hostilities** *pl* ostilità *fpl*

**hot** /hɒt/ *a* (**hotter, hottest**) caldo; (*spicy*) piccante; **I am** *or* **feel ~** ho caldo; **it is ~** fa caldo; **in ~ water** *fig* nei guai

**hot: hot-air balloon** *n* mongolfiera *f*. **hotbed** *n* *fig* focolaio *m*. **hot-blooded** /-'blʌdɪd/ *a* ⟨person⟩ focoso; ⟨reaction⟩ passionale. **hot cake** *n* **sell like ~ ~s** andare a ruba

**hotchpotch** /'hɒtʃpɒtʃ/ *n* miscuglio *m*

**hot: hot cross bun** *n* panino *m* dolce con spezie e uvette, tipicamente pasquale. **hot dog** *n* hot dog *m inv*. **hotdogging** *n* sci *m* acrobatico

**hotel** /həʊ'tel/ *n* hotel *m inv*, albergo *m*

**hotelier** /həʊ'telɪə(r)/ *n* albergatore, -trice *mf*

**hot: hotfoot** *adv* hum ⟨go⟩ di gran carriera. **hothead** *n* persona *f* impetuosa. **hot-headed** /-'hedɪd/ *a* impetuoso. **hothouse** *n* serra *f*. **hotline** *n* linea *f* diretta; Mil, Pol telefono *m* rosso

**hotly** /'hɒtlɪ/ *adv* *fig* accanitamente

**hot: hotplate** *n* piastra *f* riscaldante. **hotshot** *n* *fam* persona *f* di successo; *pej* carrierista *mf*. **hot tap** *n* rubinetto *m* dell'acqua calda. **hot-tempered** /-'tempəd/ *a* irascibile. **hot-water bottle** *n* borsa *f* dell'acqua calda

**hound** /haʊnd/ *n* cane da caccia *m* ● *vt fig* perseguire

**hour** /'aʊə(r)/ *n* ora *f*

**hourglass** /'aʊəglɑːs/ *n* clessidra *f*

**hourly** /'aʊəlɪ/ *a* ad ogni ora; ⟨pay, rate⟩ a ora. ● *adv* ogni ora

**house¹** /haʊs/ *n* casa *f*; Pol Camera *f*; Theat sala *f*; **at my ~** a casa mia, da me

**house²** /haʊz/ *vt* alloggiare ⟨person⟩; incastrare ⟨machine⟩

**house: houseboat** *n* casa *f* galleggiante. **housebreaking** *n* furto *m* con scasso. **household** *n* casa *f*, famiglia *f*. **householder** *n* capo *m* di famiglia. **housekeeper** *n* governante *f* di casa. **housekeeping** *n* governo *m* della casa; (*money*) soldi *mpl* per le spese di casa. **house plant** *n* pianta *f* da appartamento. **house-proud** *a* orgoglioso della propria casa. **house-trained** /-treɪnd/ *a* che non sporca in casa. **house-warming [party]** *n* festa *f* di inaugurazione della nuova casa. **housewife** *n* casalinga *f*. **housework** *n* lavori *mpl* domestici

**housing** /'haʊzɪŋ/ *n* alloggio *m*; Techn alloggiamento *m*

**housing estate** *n* zona *f* residenziale

**hovel** /'hɒvl/ *n* tugurio *m*

**hover** /'hɒvə(r)/ *vi* librarsi; (*linger*) indugiare; **~ on the brink of doing sth** essere sul punto di fare qcsa

**hovercraft** /'hɒvəkrɑːft/ *n* hovercraft *m inv*

**how** /haʊ/ *adv* come; **~ are you?** come stai?; **~ about a coffee/going on holiday?** che ne diresti di un caffè/di andare in vacanza?; **~ do you do?** molto lieto!; **~ old are you?** quanti anni hai?; **~ long** quanto tempo; **~ many** quanti; **~ much** quanto; **~ often** ogni quanto; **and ~!** eccome!; **~ odd!** che strano!

**however** /haʊ'evə(r)/ *adv* (*nevertheless*) comunque; **~ small** per quanto piccolo

**howl** /haʊl/ *n* ululato *m* ● *vi* ululare; (*cry with laughter*) singhiozzare

**howler** /'haʊlə(r)/ *n fam* strafalcione *m*

**HP** *abbr* hire purchase; *abbr* (**horse power**) C.V.

**HQ** *n* Mil *abbr* (**headquarters**) Q.G.

**HRT** *n* *abbr* (**hormone replacement therapy**) terapia *f* ormonale sostitutiva

**hub** /hʌb/ *n* mozzo *m*; *fig* centro *m*

**hubbub** /'hʌbʌb/ *n* baccano *m*

**hubcap** /'hʌbkæp/ *n* coprimozzo *m*

**huckleberry** /'hʌklbərɪ/ *n* Am mirtillo *m* americano

**huddle** /'hʌdl/ *vi* **~ together** rannicchiarsi l'uno contro l'altro

**hue¹** /hjuː/ *n* colore *m*

**hue²** *n* **~ and cry** clamore *m*

**huff** /hʌf/ *n* **be in a/go into a ~** fare il broncio

**hug** /hʌg/ *n* abbraccio *m*; **give sb a ~** abbracciare qcno ● *vt* (*pt/pp* **hugged**) abbracciare; (*keep close to*) tenersi vicino a; aggrapparsi a ⟨wall⟩

**huge** /hjuːdʒ/ *a* enorme

**hugely** /'hjuːdʒlɪ/ *adv* enormemente

**huh** /hʌ/ *int* (*inquiry*) eh?; (*in surprise*) oh!

**hulk** /hʌlk/ *n* (*of ship, tank etc*) carcassa *f*

**hulking** /'hʌlkɪŋ/ *a fam* grosso

**hull** /hʌl/ *n* Naut scafo *m*

**hullabaloo** /hʌləbə'luː/ *n fam* (*noise*) trambusto *m*; (*outcry*) fracasso *m*

**hullo** /hə'ləʊ/ int = **hallo**

**hum** /hʌm/ n ronzio m ● vt (pt/pp **hummed**) canticchiare ● vi ⟨motor:⟩ ronzare; fig fervere di attività: **~ and haw** esitare

**human** /'hju:mən/ a umano ● n essere m umano

**human being** n essere m umano

**human resources** npl risorse fpl umane

**humane** /hju:'meɪn/ a umano

**humanely** /hju:'meɪnlɪ/ adv umanamente

**humanitarian** /hju:mænɪ'teərɪən/ a & n umanitario, -a mf

**humanities** /hju:'mænɪtɪz/ pl Univ dottrine fpl umanistiche

**humanity** /hju:'mænətɪ/ n umanità f

**humble** /'hʌmbl/ a umile ● vt umiliare

**humbly** /'hʌmblɪ/ adv umilmente

**humbug** /'hʌmbʌg/ n ⟨nonsense⟩ sciocchezze fpl; ⟨dishonesty⟩ falsità f; ⟨Br: sweet⟩ caramella f alla menta

**humdrum** /'hʌmdrʌm/ a noioso

**humid** /'hju:mɪd/ a umido

**humidifier** /hju:'mɪdɪfaɪə(r)/ n umidificatore m

**humidity** /hju:'mɪdətɪ/ n umidità f

**humiliate** /hju:'mɪlɪeɪt/ vt umiliare

**humiliating** /hju:'mɪlɪeɪtɪŋ/ a avvilente

**humiliation** /hju:mɪlɪ'eɪʃn/ n umiliazione f

**humility** /hju:'mɪlətɪ/ n umiltà f

**hummingbird** /'hʌmɪŋbɜːd/ n colibrì m inv

**hummock** /'hʌmək/ n ⟨of earth⟩ poggio m

**humorist** /'hju:mərɪst/ n umorista mf

**humorous** /'hju:mərəs/ a umoristico

**humorously** /'hju:mərəslɪ/ adv con spirito

**humour** /'hju:mə(r)/ n umorismo m; ⟨mood⟩ umore m; **have a sense of ~** avere il senso dell'umorismo ● vt compiacere

**hump** /hʌmp/ n protuberanza f; ⟨of camel, hunchback⟩ gobba f; **he's got the ~** sl è di malumore

**humpback[ed] bridge** /'hʌm(p)bæk[t]/ n ponte m a schiena d'asino

**humus** /'hju:məs/ n humus m

**hunch** /hʌntʃ/ n ⟨idea⟩ intuizione f

**hunchback** /'hʌntʃbæk/ n gobbo, -a mf

**hunched** /hʌntʃt/ a **~ up** incurvato

**hundred** /'hʌndrəd/ a **one/a ~** cento ● n cento m inv; **~s of** centinaia di

**hundredfold** /'hʌndrədfəʊld/ adv **increase a ~** centuplicare

**hundredth** /'hʌndrədθ/ a & n centesimo m

**hundredweight** /'hʌndrədweɪt/ n cinquanta chili m

**hung** /hʌŋ/ see **hang**

**Hungarian** /hʌŋ'geərɪən/ n & a ungherese mf; ⟨language⟩ ungherese m

**Hungary** /'hʌŋgərɪ/ n Ungheria f

**hunger** /'hʌŋgə(r)/ n fame f

■ **hunger for** vt aver fame di

**hunger strike** n sciopero m della fame

**hung-over** a be **~** avere i postumi della sbornia

**hungrily** /'hʌŋgrɪlɪ/ adv con appetito

**hungry** /'hʌŋgrɪ/ a (-ier, -iest) affamato; **be ~** aver fame

**hung-up** a fam ⟨tense⟩ complessato; **be ~ on sb/sth** ⟨obsessed⟩ essere fissato con qcsa

**hunk** /hʌŋk/ n grosso pezzo m; ⟨fam: man⟩ figo m

**hunky-dory** /hʌŋkɪ'dɔ:rɪ/ a fam perfetto

**hunt** /hʌnt/ n caccia f ● vt andare a caccia di ⟨animal⟩; dare la caccia a ⟨criminal⟩ ● vi andare a caccia; **~ for** cercare

**hunter** /'hʌntə(r)/ n cacciatore m

**hunting** /'hʌntɪŋ/ n caccia f

**hunt saboteur** n Br sabotatore, -trice mf della caccia

**huntsman** /'hʌntsmən/ n ⟨hunter⟩ cacciatore m; ⟨fox-hunter⟩ cacciatore m di volpe

**hurdle** /'hɜːdl/ n Sport & fig ostacolo m

**hurdler** /'hɜːdlə(r)/ n ostacolista mf

**hurdy-gurdy** /hɜːdɪ'gɜːdɪ/ n organino m

**hurl** /hɜːl/ vt scagliare

**hurly-burly** /hɜːlɪ'bɜːlɪ/ n chiasso m

**hurrah** /hʊ'rɑː/, **hurray** /hʊ'reɪ/ int urrà! ● n urrà m

**hurricane** /'hʌrɪkən/ n uragano m

**hurried** /'hʌrɪd/ a affrettato; ⟨job⟩ fatto in fretta

**hurriedly** /'hʌrɪdlɪ/ adv in fretta

**hurry** /'hʌrɪ/ n fretta f; **be in a ~** aver fretta ● vi (pt/pp -ied) affrettarsi

■ **hurry up** vi sbrigarsi ● vt mettere fretta a ⟨person⟩; accelerare ⟨things⟩

**hurt** /hɜːt/ n male m ● v (pt/pp hurt) ● vt far male a; ⟨offend⟩ ferire ● vi far male; **my leg ~s** mi fa male la gamba

**hurtful** /'hɜːtfʊl/ a fig offensivo

**hurtle** /'hɜːtl/ vi **~ along** andare a tutta velocità

**husband** /'hʌzbənd/ n marito m

**hush** /hʌʃ/ n silenzio m

■ **hush up** vt mettere a tacere

**hushed** /hʌʃt/ a ⟨voice⟩ sommesso

**hush-hush** a fam segretissimo

**husky** /'hʌskɪ/ a (-ier, -iest) ⟨voice⟩ rauco

**hussar** /hʊ'zɑː(r)/ n ussaro m

**hustings** /'hʌstɪŋz/ n **on the ~** in campagna elettorale

**hustle** /'hʌsl/ vt affrettare ● n attività f incessante; **~ and bustle** trambusto m

**hut** /hʌt/ n capanna f

**hutch** /hʌtʃ/ n conigliera f

**hyacinth** /'haɪəsɪnθ/ n giacinto m

**hybrid** /'haɪbrɪd/ a ibrido ● n ibrido m

**hydrangea** /haɪ'dreɪndʒə/ n ortensia f

**hydrant** /'haɪdrənt/ n [fire] **~** idrante m

**hydraulic** /haɪ'drɔ:lɪk/ a idraulico

**hydrocarbon** /haɪdrəʊ'kɑ:bən/ n idrocarburo m

**hydrochloric** /haɪdrə'klɒrɪk/ a **~ acid** acido m cloridrico

**hydroelectric** /haɪdrəʊɪ'lektrɪk/ a idroelettrico

**hydroelectric power station** n centrale f idroelettrica

**hydrofoil** /'haɪdrəfɔɪl/ n aliscafo m

**hydrogen** /'haɪdrədʒən/ n idrogeno m

**hydrolysis** /haɪ'drɒləsɪs/ n idrolisi f

**hydrophobia** /haɪdrə'fəʊbɪə/ n idrofobia f

**hydroplane** /'haɪdrəpleɪn/ n (boat) aliscafo m; (Am: seaplane) idrovolante m
**hydrotherapy** /haɪdrəʊ'θerəpɪ/ n idroterapia f
**hyena** /haɪ'iːnə/ n iena f
**hygiene** /'haɪdʒiːn/ n igiene m
**hygienic** /haɪ'dʒiːnɪk/ a igienico
**hygienically** /haɪ'dʒiːnɪklɪ/ adv igienicamente
**hymn** /hɪm/ n inno m
**hymn book** n libro m dei canti
**hype** /haɪp/ n fam grande pubblicità f; **media** ~ battage m pubblicitario
■ **hype up** vt fam fare grande pubblicità a ‹film, star, book›; (exaggerate) gonfiare
**hyper** /'haɪpə(r)/ a fam eccitato
**hyperactive** /haɪpər'æktɪv/ a iperattivo
**hyperactivity** /haɪpəræk'tɪvɪtɪ/ n iperattività f
**hyperbole** /haɪ'pɜːbəlɪ/ n iperbole f
**hypercritical** /haɪpə'krɪtɪkl/ a ipercritico
**hypermarket** /'haɪpəmɑːkɪt/ n ipermercato m
**hypersensitive** /haɪpə'sensɪtɪv/ a pej permaloso; (physically) ipersensibile
**hypertension** /haɪpə'tenʃn/ n ipertensione f
**hypertext** /'haɪpətekst/ n Comput ipertesto m
**hyperventilate** /haɪpə'ventɪleɪt/ vi iperventilare
**hyphen** /'haɪfn/ n trattino m
**hyphenate** /'haɪfəneɪt/ vt unire con trattino
**hypnosis** /hɪp'nəʊsɪs/ n ipnosi f

**hypnotherapy** /hɪpnəʊ'θerəpɪ/ n ipnoterapia f
**hypnotic** /hɪp'nɒtɪk/ a ipnotico
**hypnotism** /'hɪpnətɪzm/ n ipnotismo m
**hypnotist** /'hɪpnətɪst/ n ipnotizzatore, -trice mf
**hypnotize** /'hɪpnətaɪz/ vt ipnotizzare
**hypoallergenic** /haɪpəʊælə'dʒenɪk/ a anallergico
**hypochondria** /haɪpə'kɒndrɪə/ n ipocondria f
**hypochondriac** /haɪpə'kɒndrɪæk/ a & n ipocondriaco, -a mf
**hypocrisy** /hɪ'pɒkrəsɪ/ n ipocrisia f
**hypocrite** /'hɪpəkrɪt/ n ipocrita mf
**hypocritical** /hɪpə'krɪtɪkl/ a ipocrita
**hypocritically** /hɪpə'krɪtɪklɪ/ adv ipocriticamente
**hypodermic** /haɪpə'dɜːmɪk/ a & n ~ [**syringe**] siringa f ipodermica
**hypotenuse** /haɪ'pɒtənjuːz/ n ipotenusa f
**hypothermia** /haɪpəʊ'θɜːmɪə/ n ipotermia f
**hypothesis** /haɪ'pɒθəsɪs/ n ipotesi f inv
**hypothetical** /haɪpə'θetɪkl/ a ipotetico
**hypothetically** /haɪpə'θetɪklɪ/ adv in teoria; ‹speak› per ipotesi
**hysterectomy** /hɪstə'rektəmɪ/ n isterectomia f
**hysteria** /hɪ'stɪərɪə/ n isterismo m
**hysterical** /hɪ'sterɪkl/ a isterico
**hysterically** /hɪ'sterɪklɪ/ adv istericamente; ~ **funny** da morir dal ridere
**hysterics** /hɪ'sterɪks/ npl attacco m isterico

# Ii

**i, I** /aɪ/ n (letter) i, I f inv
**I** /aɪ/ pron io; **I'm tired** sono stanco; **he's going, but I'm not** lui va, ma io no
**ibex** /'aɪbeks/ n stambecco m
**ice** /aɪs/ n ghiaccio m ● vt glassare ‹cake›
■ **ice over, ice up** vi ghiacciarsi
**ice:** **ice age** n era f glaciale. **ice axe** n piccozza f per il ghiaccio. **iceberg** n iceberg m inv. **icebox** n Am frigorifero m. **ice-breaker** n Naut rompighiaccio m inv. **ice bucket** n secchiello m del ghiaccio. **ice cap** n calotta f glaciale. **ice-cold** a ghiacciato. **ice cream** n gelato m. **ice-cream parlour** n gelateria f. **ice-cream sundae** n coppa f [di] gelato guarnita. **ice cube** n cubetto m di ghiaccio. **ice dancer** n ballerino, -a mf sul ghiaccio. **ice floe** n banco m di ghiaccio. **ice hockey** hockey m su ghiaccio
**Iceland** /'aɪslənd/ n Islanda f
**Icelander** /'aɪsləndə(r)/ n islandese mf
**Icelandic** /aɪs'lændɪk/ a & n islandese m

**ice:** **ice lolly** n ghiacciolo m. **ice pack** n impacco m di ghiaccio. **ice pick** n piccone m da ghiaccio. **ice rink** n pista f di pattinaggio. **ice-skate** n pattino m da ghiaccio. **ice-skater** pattinatore, -trice mf sul ghiaccio. **ice-skating** pattinaggio m sul ghiaccio. **ice-tray** n vaschetta f per il ghiaccio
**icicle** /'aɪsɪkl/ n ghiacciolo m
**icily** /'aɪsɪlɪ/ adv gelidamente
**icing** /'aɪsɪŋ/ n glassa f
**icing sugar** n zucchero m a velo
**icon** /'aɪkɒn/ n icona f
**icy** /'aɪsɪ/ a (-ier, -iest) ghiacciato; fig gelido
**id** /ɪd/ n the ~ l'Es m
**ID** n abbr (**identification, identity**) documento m d'identità; **ID card** n carta f d'identità
**idea** /aɪ'dɪə/ n idea f; **I've no ~!** non ne ho idea!
**ideal** /aɪ'dɪəl/ a ideale ● n ideale m
**idealism** /aɪ'dɪəlɪzm/ n idealismo m

**idealist** /aɪˈdɪəlɪst/ n idealista mf
**idealistic** /aɪdɪəˈlɪstɪk/ a idealistico
**idealize** /aɪˈdɪəlaɪz/ vt idealizzare
**ideally** /aɪˈdɪəlɪ/ adv idealmente
**identical** /aɪˈdentɪkl/ a identico
**identifiable** /aɪdentɪˈfaɪəbl/ a identificabile
**identification** /aɪdentɪfɪˈkeɪʃn/ n identificazione f; (proof of identity) documento m di riconoscimento
**identify** /aɪˈdentɪfaɪ/ vt (pt/pp -ied) identificare ● vi ~ with identificarsi con
**identikit®** /aɪˈdentɪkɪt/ n identikit m inv
**identikit® picture** n identikit m inv
**identity** /aɪˈdentətɪ/ n identità f inv
**identity card** n carta f d'identità
**identity parade** n confronto m all'americana
**ideological** /aɪdɪəˈlɒdʒɪkl/ a ideologico
**ideology** /aɪdɪˈɒlədʒɪ/ n ideologia f
**idiocy** /ˈɪdɪəsɪ/ n idiozia f
**idiom** /ˈɪdɪəm/ n idioma f
**idiomatic** /ɪdɪəˈmætɪk/ a idiomatico
**idiomatically** /ɪdɪəˈmætɪklɪ/ adv in modo idiomatico
**idiosyncrasy** /ɪdɪəˈsɪŋkrəsɪ/ n idiosincrasia f
**idiot** /ˈɪdɪət/ n idiota mf
**idiotic** /ɪdɪˈɒtɪk/ a idiota
**idle** /ˈaɪd(ə)l/ a (lazy) pigro, ozioso; (empty) vano; (machine) fermo ● vi oziare; (engine:) girare a vuoto
**idleness** /ˈaɪd(ə)lnɪs/ n ozio m
**idly** /ˈaɪdlɪ/ adv oziosamente
**idol** /ˈaɪd(ə)l/ n idolo m
**idolize** /ˈaɪdəlaɪz/ vt idolatrare
**idyll** /ˈɪdɪl/ n idillio m
**idyllic** /ɪˈdɪlɪk/ a idillico
**i.e.** abbr (id est) cioè
**if** /ɪf/ conj se; **as if** come se
**iffy** /ˈɪfɪ/ a incerto
**igloo** /ˈɪɡluː/ n igloo m inv
**ignite** /ɪɡˈnaɪt/ vt dar fuoco a ● vi prender fuoco
**ignition** /ɪɡˈnɪʃn/ n Auto accensione f
**ignition key** n chiave f d'accensione
**ignoramus** /ɪɡnəˈreɪməs/ n ignorante mf
**ignorance** /ˈɪɡnərəns/ n ignoranza f
**ignorant** /ˈɪɡnərənt/ a (lacking knowledge) ignaro; (rude) ignorante
**ignore** /ɪɡˈnɔː(r)/ vt ignorare
**ill** /ɪl/ a ammalato; **feel ~ at ease** sentirsi a disagio ● adv male ● n male m
**ill: ill-advised** /-ədˈvaɪzd/ a avventato. **ill-bred** /-ˈbred/ a maleducato. **ill-considered** /-kənˈsɪdəd/ a (measure, remark) avventato. **ill effect** n effetto m negativo
**illegal** /ɪˈliːɡl/ a illegale
**illegality** /ɪlɪˈɡælətɪ/ n illegalità f
**illegally** /ɪˈliːɡəlɪ/ adv illegalmente
**illegible** /ɪˈledʒəbl/ a illeggibile
**illegibly** /ɪˈledʒəblɪ/ adv in modo illeggibile
**illegitimacy** /ɪlɪˈdʒɪtɪməsɪ/ n illegittimità f
**illegitimate** /ɪlɪˈdʒɪtɪmət/ a illegittimo
**ill: ill-equipped** /-ɪˈkwɪpt/ a non equipaggiato. **ill-fated** /-ˈfeɪtɪd/ a sfortunato. **ill feeling**

n rancore m. **ill-fitting** a (garment, shoe) che non va bene. **ill-founded** /-ˈfaʊndɪd/ a (argument, gossip) infondato. **ill-gotten gains** /ɪlɡɒ(t)nˈɡeɪnz/ a guadagni mpl illeciti.
**ill health** n problemi mpl di salute
**illicit** /ɪˈlɪsɪt/ a illecito
**illicitly** /ɪˈlɪsɪtlɪ/ adv illecitamente
**ill-informed** /-ɪnˈfɔːmd/ a (person) male informato
**illiteracy** /ɪˈlɪtərəsɪ/ n analfabetismo m
**illiterate** /ɪˈlɪtərət/ a & n analfabeta mf
**ill-mannered** /-ˈmænəd/ a maleducato
**illness** /ˈɪlnɪs/ n malattia f
**illogical** /ɪˈlɒdʒɪkl/ a illogico
**illogically** /ɪˈlɒdʒɪklɪ/ adv illogicamente
**ill: ill-prepared** /-prɪˈpeəd/ a impreparato. **ill-timed** /-ˈtaɪmd/ a (arrival) inopportuno; (campaign) fatto al momento sbagliato. **ill-treat** vt maltrattare. **ill-treatment** n maltrattamento m
**illuminate** /ɪˈluːmɪneɪt/ vt illuminare
**illuminating** /ɪˈluːmɪneɪtɪŋ/ a chiarificatore
**illumination** /ɪluːmɪˈneɪʃn/ n illuminazione f
**illusion** /ɪˈluːʒn/ n illusione f; **be under the ~ that** avere l'illusione che
**illusory** /ɪˈluːsərɪ/ a illusorio
**illustrate** /ˈɪləstreɪt/ vt illustrare
**illustration** /ɪləˈstreɪʃn/ n illustrazione f
**illustrative** /ˈɪləstrətɪv/ a illustrativo
**illustrator** /ˈɪləstreɪtə(r)/ n illustratore, -trice mf
**illustrious** /ɪˈlʌstrɪəs/ a illustre
**ill will** n malanimo m
**image** /ˈɪmɪdʒ/ n immagine f; (exact likeness) ritratto m
**image-conscious** a attento all'immagine
**imagery** /ˈɪmɪdʒərɪ/ n immagini fpl
**imaginable** /ɪˈmædʒɪnəbl/ a immaginabile
**imaginary** /ɪˈmædʒɪnərɪ/ a immaginario
**imagination** /ɪmædʒɪˈneɪʃn/ n immaginazione f, fantasia f; **it's your ~** è solo una tua idea
**imaginative** /ɪˈmædʒɪnətɪv/ a fantasioso
**imaginatively** /ɪˈmædʒɪnətɪvlɪ/ adv con fantasia or immaginazione
**imagine** /ɪˈmædʒɪn/ vt immaginare; (wrongly) inventare
**imbalance** /ɪmˈbæləns/ n squilibrio m
**imbecile** /ˈɪmbəsiːl/ n imbecille mf
**imbibe** /ɪmˈbaɪb/ vt ingerire; fig assorbire ● vi hum bere
**imbue** /ɪmˈbjuː/ vt ~d with impregnato di
**imitate** /ˈɪmɪteɪt/ vt imitare
**imitation** /ɪmɪˈteɪʃn/ n imitazione f
**imitative** /ˈɪmɪtətɪv/ a imitativo
**imitator** /ˈɪmɪteɪtə(r)/ n imitatore, -trice mf
**immaculate** /ɪˈmækjʊlət/ a immacolato
**immaculately** /ɪˈmækjʊlətlɪ/ adv immacolatamente
**immaterial** /ɪməˈtɪərɪəl/ a (unimportant) irrilevante
**immature** /ɪməˈtʃʊə(r)/ a immaturo
**immeasurable** /ɪˈmeʒərəbl/ a incommensurabile

**immediacy** /ɪˈmiːdɪəsɪ/ n immediatezza f
**immediate** /ɪˈmiːdɪət/ a immediato; ⟨relative⟩ stretto; **in the ~ vicinity** nelle immediate vicinanze
**immediately** /ɪˈmiːdɪətlɪ/ adv immediatamente; **~ next to** subito accanto a ● conj [non] appena
**immemorial** /ɪmɪˈmɔːrɪəl/ a **from time ~** da tempo immemorabile
**immense** /ɪˈmens/ a immenso
**immensely** /ɪˈmenslɪ/ adv immensamente
**immensity** /ɪˈmensətɪ/ n immensità f
**immerse** /ɪˈmɜːs/ vt immergere; **be ~d in** fig essere immerso in
**immersion** /ɪˈmɜːʃn/ n immersione f
**immersion heater** n scaldabagno m inv elettrico
**immigrant** /ˈɪmɪɡrənt/ n immigrante mf
**immigrate** /ˈɪmɪɡreɪt/ vi immigrare
**immigration** /ɪmɪˈɡreɪʃn/ n immigrazione f
**imminence** /ˈɪmɪnəns/ n imminenza f
**imminent** /ˈɪmɪnənt/ a imminente
**immobile** /ɪˈməʊbaɪl/ a immobile
**immobilize** /ɪˈməʊbɪlaɪz/ vt immobilizzare
**immoderate** /ɪˈmɒdərət/ a smodato
**immodest** /ɪˈmɒdɪst/ a immodesto
**immoral** /ɪˈmɒrəl/ a immorale
**immorality** /ɪməˈrælətɪ/ n immoralità f
**immortal** /ɪˈmɔːtl/ a immortale
**immortality** /ɪmɔːˈtælətɪ/ n immortalità f
**immortalize** /ɪˈmɔːtəlaɪz/ vt immortalare
**immovable** /ɪˈmuːvəbl/ a fig irremovibile
**immune** /ɪˈmjuːn/ a immune (**to/from** da)
**immune system** n sistema m immunitario
**immunity** /ɪˈmjuːnətɪ/ n immunità f
**immunization** /ɪmjʊnarˈzeɪʃn/ n immunizzazione f
**immunize** /ˈɪmjʊnaɪz/ vt immunizzare
**immunodeficiency** /ɪmjʊnəʊdɪˈfɪʃənsɪ/ n immunodeficienza f
**immunology** /ɪmjʊˈnɒlədʒɪ/ n immunologia f
**immutable** /ɪˈmjuːtəbl/ a immutabile
**imp** /ɪmp/ n diavoletto m
**impact** /ˈɪmpækt/ n impatto m
**impacted** /ɪmˈpæktɪd/ a ⟨tooth⟩ incluso; ⟨fracture⟩ incuneato
**impair** /ɪmˈpeə(r)/ vt danneggiare
**impale** /ɪmˈpeɪl/ vt impalare
**impalpable** /ɪmˈpælpəbl/ a (intangible) impalpabile
**impart** /ɪmˈpɑːt/ vt impartire
**impartial** /ɪmˈpɑːʃəl/ a imparziale
**impartiality** /ɪmpɑːʃɪˈælətɪ/ n imparzialità f
**impassable** /ɪmˈpɑːsəbl/ a impraticabile
**impasse** /æmˈpɑːs/ n fig impasse f inv
**impassioned** /ɪmˈpæʃnd/ a appassionato
**impassive** /ɪmˈpæsɪv/ a impassibile
**impassively** /ɪmˈpæsɪvlɪ/ adv impassibilmente
**impatience** /ɪmˈpeɪʃns/ n impazienza f
**impatient** /ɪmˈpeɪʃnt/ a impaziente
**impatiently** /ɪmˈpeɪʃntlɪ/ adv impazientemente
**impeach** /ɪmˈpiːtʃ/ vt accusare

**impeccable** /ɪmˈpekəbl/ a impeccabile
**impeccably** /ɪmˈpekəblɪ/ adv in modo impeccabile
**impede** /ɪmˈpiːd/ vt impedire
**impediment** /ɪmˈpedɪmənt/ n impedimento m; (in speech) difetto m
**impel** /ɪmˈpel/ vt (pt/pp **impelled**) costringere; **feel ~led to** sentire l'obbligo di
**impending** /ɪmˈpendɪŋ/ a imminente
**impenetrable** /ɪmˈpenɪtrəbl/ a impenetrabile
**imperative** /ɪmˈperətɪv/ a imperativo; ● n Gram imperativo m
**imperceptible** /ɪmpəˈseptəbl/ a impercettibile
**imperfect** /ɪmˈpɜːfɪkt/ a imperfetto; (faulty) difettoso ● n Gram imperfetto m
**imperfection** /ɪmpəˈfekʃn/ n imperfezione f
**imperial** /ɪmˈpɪərɪəl/ a imperiale
**imperialism** /ɪmˈpɪərɪəlɪzm/ n imperialismo m
**imperialist** /ɪmˈpɪərɪəlɪst/ n imperialista mf
**imperil** /ɪmˈperəl/ vt (pt/pp **imperilled**) mettere in pericolo
**imperious** /ɪmˈpɪərɪəs/ a imperioso
**imperiously** /ɪmˈpɪərɪəslɪ/ adv di modo imperioso
**impermeable** /ɪmˈpɜːmɪəbl/ a impermeabile
**impersonal** /ɪmˈpɜːsənəl/ a impersonale
**impersonate** /ɪmˈpɜːsəneɪt/ vt impersonare
**impersonation** /ɪmpɜːsəˈneɪʃn/ n imitazione f
**impersonator** /ɪmˈpɜːsəneɪtə(r)/ n imitatore, -trice mf
**impertinence** /ɪmˈpɜːtɪnəns/ n impertinenza f
**impertinent** /ɪmˈpɜːtɪnənt/ a impertinente
**imperturbable** /ɪmpəˈtɜːbəbl/ a imperturbabile
**impervious** /ɪmˈpɜːvɪəs/ a **~ to** fig indifferente a
**impetuous** /ɪmˈpetjʊəs/ a impetuoso
**impetuously** /ɪmˈpetjʊəslɪ/ adv impetuosamente
**impetus** /ˈɪmpɪtəs/ n impeto m
**impiety** /ɪmˈpaɪətɪ/ n Relig empietà f
■ **impinge on** /ɪmˈpɪndʒ/ vt (affect) influire su; (restrict) condizionare
**impious** /ˈɪmpɪəs/ a Relig empio
**impish** /ˈɪmpɪʃ/ a birichino
**implacable** /ɪmˈplækəbl/ a implacabile
**implant**[1] /ɪmˈplɑːnt/ vt trapiantare; fig inculcare
**implant**[2] /ˈɪmplɑːnt/ n trapianto m
**implausible** /ɪmˈplɔːzəbl/ a poco plausibile
**implement**[1] /ˈɪmplɪmənt/ n attrezzo m
**implement**[2] /ˈɪmplɪment/ vt mettere in atto
**implicate** /ˈɪmplɪkeɪt/ vt implicare
**implication** /ɪmplɪˈkeɪʃn/ n implicazione f; **by ~** implicitamente
**implicit** /ɪmˈplɪsɪt/ a implicito; (absolute) assoluto

**implicitly** /ɪmˈplɪsɪtlɪ/ *adv* implicitamente; ⟨*absolutely*⟩ completamente

**implied** /ɪmˈplaɪd/ *a* implicito, sottinteso

**implore** /ɪmˈplɔː(r)/ *vt* implorare

**imploring** /ɪmˈplɔːrɪŋ/ *a* implorante

**implosion** /ɪmˈpləʊʒn/ *n* implosione *f*

**imply** /ɪmˈplaɪ/ *vt* (*pt/pp* **-ied**) implicare; **what are you ~ing?** che cosa vorresti insinuare?

**impolite** /ɪmpəˈlaɪt/ *a* sgarbato

**impolitely** /ɪmpəˈlaɪtlɪ/ *adv* sgarbatamente

**import¹** /ˈɪmpɔːt/ *n Comm* importazione *f*; (*importance*) importanza *f*; (*meaning*) rilevanza *f*

**import²** /ɪmˈpɔːt/ *vt* importare

**importance** /ɪmˈpɔːtəns/ *n* importanza *f*

**important** /ɪmˈpɔːtənt/ *a* importante

**importation** /ɪmpɔːˈteɪʃn/ *n Comm* importazione *f*

**import duty** /ˈɪmpɔːt/ *n* dazio *m* d'importazione

**importer** /ɪmˈpɔːtə(r)/ *n* importatore, -trice *mf*

**import-export** /ˈɪmpɔːtˈekspɔːt/ *n* import-export *m*

**importing country** /ɪmˈpɔːtɪŋ/ *n* paese *m* di importazione

**impose** /ɪmˈpəʊz/ *vt* imporre (**on** a) ● *vi* imporsi; **~ on** abusare di

**imposing** /ɪmˈpəʊzɪŋ/ *a* imponente

**imposition** /ɪmpəˈzɪʃn/ *n* imposizione *f*

**impossibility** /ɪmˌpɒsɪbɪlətɪ/ *n* impossibilità *f*

**impossible** /ɪmˈpɒsəbl/ *a* impossibile

**impossibly** /ɪmˈpɒsəblɪ/ *adv* impossibilmente

**impostor** /ɪmˈpɒstə(r)/ *n* impostore, -trice *mf*

**impotence** /ˈɪmpətəns/ *n* impotenza *f*

**impotent** /ˈɪmpətənt/ *a* impotente

**impound** /ɪmˈpaʊnd/ *vt* confiscare

**impoverished** /ɪmˈpɒvərɪʃt/ *a* impoverito

**impracticable** /ɪmˈpræktɪkəbl/ *a* impraticabile

**impractical** /ɪmˈpræktɪkl/ *a* non pratico

**imprecise** /ɪmprɪˈsaɪs/ *a* impreciso

**impregnable** /ɪmˈpregnəbl/ *a* imprendibile

**impregnate** /ˈɪmpregneɪt/ *vt* impregnare (**with** di); *Biol* fecondare

**impresario** /ɪmprɪˈsɑːrɪəʊ/ *n* (*pl* **-os**) impresario *m* (*di spettacoli*)

**impress** /ɪmˈpres/ *vt* imprimere; *fig* colpire ⟨*positivamente*⟩; **~ sth [up]on sb** fare capire qcsa a qcno

**impression** /ɪmˈpreʃn/ *n* impressione *f*; (*imitation*) imitazione *f*

**impressionable** /ɪmˈpreʃənəbl/ *a* ⟨*child, mind*⟩ influenzabile

**impressionism** /ɪmˈpreʃənɪzm/ *n* impressionismo *m*

**impressionist** /ɪmˈpreʃənɪst/ *n* imitatore, -trice *mf*; (*artist*) impressionista *mf*

**impressionistic** /ɪmpreʃəˈnɪstɪk/ *a* impressionista; ⟨*account*⟩ approssimativo

**impressive** /ɪmˈpresɪv/ *a* imponente

**imprint¹** /ˈɪmprɪnt/ *n* impressione *f*

**imprint²** /ɪmˈprɪnt/ *vt* imprimere; **~ed on my mind** impresso nella mia memoria

**imprison** /ɪmˈprɪzən/ *vt* incarcerare

**imprisonment** /ɪmˈprɪzənmənt/ *n* reclusione *f*

**improbable** /ɪmˈprɒbəbl/ *a* improbabile

**impromptu** /ɪmˈprɒmptjuː/ *a* improvvisato ● *adv* in modo improvvisato

**improper** /ɪmˈprɒpə(r)/ *a* ⟨*use*⟩ improprio; ⟨*behaviour*⟩ scorretto

**improperly** /ɪmˈprɒpəlɪ/ *adv* scorrettamente

**impropriety** /ɪmprəˈpraɪətɪ/ *n* scorrettezza *f*

**improve** /ɪmˈpruːv/ *vt/i* migliorare ■ **improve [up]on** *vt* perfezionare

**improvement** /ɪmˈpruːvmənt/ *n* miglioramento *m*

**improvident** /ɪmˈprɒvɪdənt/ *a* ⟨*heedless of the future*⟩ imprevidente

**improvisation** /ɪmprəvaɪˈzeɪʃn/ *n* improvvisazione *f*

**improvise** /ˈɪmprəvaɪz/ *vt/i* improvvisare

**imprudent** /ɪmˈpruːdənt/ *a* imprudente

**impudence** /ˈɪmpjʊdəns/ *n* sfrontatezza *f*

**impudent** /ˈɪmpjʊdənt/ *a* sfrontato

**impudently** /ˈɪmpjʊdəntlɪ/ *adv* sfrontatamente

**impulse** /ˈɪmpʌls/ *n* impulso *m*; **on [an] ~** impulsivamente

**impulse buying** *n* acquisti *mpl* fatti d'impulso

**impulsive** /ɪmˈpʌlsɪv/ *a* impulsivo

**impulsively** /ɪmˈpʌlsɪvlɪ/ *adv* impulsivamente

**impunity** /ɪmˈpjuːnətɪ/ *n* **with ~** impunemente

**impure** /ɪmˈpjʊə(r)/ *a* impuro

**impurity** /ɪmˈpjʊərətɪ/ *n* impurità *f inv*; **impurities** *pl* impurità *fpl*

**impute** /ɪmˈpjuːt/ *vt* imputare (**to** a)

**in** /ɪn/ *prep* in; (*with names of towns*) a; **in the garden** in giardino; **in the street** in *or* per strada; **in bed/hospital** a letto/all'ospedale; **in the world** nel mondo; **in the rain** sotto la pioggia; **in the sun** al sole; **in this heat** con questo caldo; **in summer/winter** in estate/inverno; **in 1995** nel 1995; **in the evening** la sera; **he's arriving in two hours' time** arriva fra due ore; **deaf in one ear** sordo da un orecchio; **in the army** nell'esercito; **in English/Italian** in inglese/italiano; **in ink/pencil** a penna/matita; **in red** ⟨*dressed, circled*⟩ di rosso; **the man in the raincoat** l'uomo con l'impermeabile; **in a soft/loud voice** a voce bassa/alta; **one in ten people** una persona su dieci; **in doing this, he...** nel far questo,...; **in itself** in sé; **in that** in quanto ● *adv* (*at home*) a casa; (*indoors*) dentro; **he's not in yet** non è ancora arrivato; **in there/here** lì/qui dentro; **ten in all** dieci in tutto; **day in, day out** giorno dopo giorno; **have it in for sb** *fam* avercela con qcno; **send him in** fallo entrare; **come in** entrare; **bring in the washing** portare dentro i panni ● *a* (*fam: in* _fashion_) di moda ● _n_ **the ins and outs** i dettagli

**inability** /ɪnəˈbɪlətɪ/ _n_ incapacità _f_

**inaccessible** /ɪnækˈsesəbl/ _a_ inaccessibile

**inaccuracy** /ɪnˈækjʊrəsɪ/ _n_ inesattezza _f_

**inaccurate** /ɪnˈækjʊrət/ _a_ inesatto

**inaccurately** /ɪnˈækjʊrətlɪ/ _adv_ in modo inesatto

**inaction** /ɪnˈækʃn/ _n_ (_not being active_) inazione _f_; (_failure to act_) inerzia _f_

**inactive** /ɪnˈæktɪv/ _a_ inattivo

**inactivity** /ɪnækˈtɪvətɪ/ _n_ inattività _f_

**inadequacy** /ɪnˈædɪkwəsɪ/ _n_ inadeguatezza _f_

**inadequate** /ɪnˈædɪkwət/ _a_ inadeguato

**inadequately** /ɪnˈædɪkwətlɪ/ _adv_ inadeguatamente

**inadmissible** /ɪnædˈmɪsəbl/ _a_ inammissibile

**inadvertent** /ɪnədˈvɜːtənt/ _a_ involontario

**inadvertently** /ɪnədˈvɜːtəntlɪ/ _adv_ inavvertitamente

**inadvisable** /ɪnædˈvaɪzəbl/ _a_ sconsigliabile

**inalienable** /ɪnˈeɪlɪənəbl/ _a_ inalienabile

**inane** /ɪˈneɪn/ _a_ futile

**inanely** /ɪˈneɪnlɪ/ _adv_ in modo vacuo

**inanimate** /ɪnˈænɪmət/ _a_ esanime

**inanity** /ɪˈnænətɪ/ _n_ stupidità _f inv_

**inapplicable** /ɪnəˈplɪkəbl/ _a_ inapplicabile

**inappropriate** /ɪnəˈprəʊprɪət/ _a_ inadatto

**inapt** /ɪnˈæpt/ _a_ (_inappropriate_) inappropriato

**inarticulate** /ɪnɑːˈtɪkjʊlət/ _a_ inarticolato

**inasmuch** /ɪnəzˈmʌtʃ/ _conj_ ~ **as** (_insofar as_) in quanto; (_seeing that_) poiché

**inattention** /ɪnəˈtenʃn/ _n_ disattenzione _f_

**inattentive** /ɪnəˈtentɪv/ _a_ disattento

**inaudible** /ɪnˈɔːdəbl/ _a_ impercettibile

**inaudibly** /ɪnˈɔːdəblɪ/ _adv_ in modo impercettibile

**inaugural** /ɪˈnɔːgjʊrəl/ _a_ inaugurale

**inaugurate** /ɪˈnɔːgjʊreɪt/ _vt_ inaugurare

**inauguration** /ɪnɔːgjʊˈreɪʃn/ _n_ inaugurazione _f_

**inauspicious** /ɪnɔːˈspɪʃəs/ _a_ infausto

**in-between** _a_ intermedio

**inborn** /ˈɪnbɔːn/ _a_ innato

**inbred** /ɪnˈbred/ _a_ congenito

**inbreeding** /ɪnˈbriːdɪŋ/ _n_ (_in animals_) inbreeding _m_; (_in humans_) unioni _mpl_ fra consanguinei

**inbuilt** /ɪnˈbɪlt/ _a_ (_feeling_) innato

**incalculable** /ɪnˈkælkjʊləbl/ _a_ incalcolabile

**incandescence** /ɪnkænˈdesəns/ _n liter_ incandescenza _f_

**incandescent** /ɪnkænˈdesənt/ _a liter_ incandescente

**incapable** /ɪnˈkeɪpəbl/ _a_ incapace

**incapacitate** /ɪnkəˈpæsɪteɪt/ _vt_ rendere incapace

**incapacity** /ɪnkəˈpæsətɪ/ _n also Jur_ incapacità _f_

**incarcerate** /ɪnˈkɑːsəreɪt/ _vt_ incarcerare

**incarnate** /ɪnˈkɑːnət/ _a_ **the devil** ~ il diavolo in carne e ossa

**incarnation** /ɪnkɑːˈneɪʃn/ _n_ incarnazione _f_

**incendiary** /ɪnˈsendɪərɪ/ _a_ incendiario ● _n_ ~ [**bomb**] bomba _f_ incendiaria

**incendiary device** _n_ ordigno _m_ incendiario

**incense**[1] /ˈɪnsens/ _n_ incenso _m_

**incense**[2] /ɪnˈsens/ _vt_ esasperare

**incentive** /ɪnˈsentɪv/ _n_ incentivo _m_

**inception** /ɪnˈsepʃn/ _n_ inizio _m_

**incessant** /ɪnˈsesənt/ _a_ incessante

**incessantly** /ɪnˈsesəntlɪ/ _adv_ incessantemente

**incest** /ˈɪnsest/ _n_ incesto _m_

**incestuous** /ɪnˈsestjʊəs/ _a_ incestuoso

**inch** /ɪntʃ/ _n_ pollice _m_ (= _2.54 cm_) ● _vi_ ~ **forward** avanzare gradatamente

**incidence** /ˈɪnsɪdəns/ _n_ incidenza _f_

**incident** /ˈɪnsɪdənt/ _n_ incidente _m_

**incidental** /ɪnsɪˈdentl/ _a_ incidentale; ~ **expenses** spese _fpl_ accessorie

**incidentally** /ɪnsɪˈdent(ə)lɪ/ _adv_ incidentalmente; (_by the way_) a proposito

**incident room** _n_ (_for criminal investigation_) centrale _f_ operativa

**incinerate** /ɪnˈsɪnəreɪt/ _vt_ incenerire

**incinerator** /ɪnˈsɪnəreɪtə(r)/ _n_ inceneritore _m_

**incipient** /ɪnˈsɪpɪənt/ _a_ incipiente

**incision** /ɪnˈsɪʒn/ _n_ incisione _f_

**incisive** /ɪnˈsaɪsɪv/ _a_ incisivo

**incisor** /ɪnˈsaɪzə(r)/ _n_ incisivo _m_

**incite** /ɪnˈsaɪt/ _vt_ incitare

**incitement** /ɪnˈsaɪtmənt/ _n_ incitamento _m_

**incivility** /ɪnsɪˈvɪlətɪ/ _n_ scortesia _f_

**incl** _abbr_ **inclusive**; _abbr_ **including**

**inclement** /ɪnˈklemənt/ _a_ inclemente

**inclination** /ɪnklɪˈneɪʃn/ _n_ inclinazione _f_

**incline**[1] /ɪnˈklaɪn/ _vt_ inclinare; **be** ~**d to do sth** essere propenso a fare qcsa ● _vi_ inclinarsi

**incline**[2] /ˈɪnklaɪn/ _n_ pendio _m_

**include** /ɪnˈkluːd/ _vt_ includere

**including** /ɪnˈkluːdɪŋ/ _prep_ incluso

**inclusion** /ɪnˈkluːʒn/ _n_ inclusione _f_

**inclusive** /ɪnˈkluːsɪv/ _a_ incluso; ~ **of** comprendente; **be** ~ **of** comprendere. ● _adv_ incluso

**incognito** /ɪnkɒgˈniːtəʊ/ _adv_ incognito

**incoherent** /ɪnkəˈhɪərənt/ _a_ incoerente; (_because drunk etc_) incomprensibile

**incoherently** /ɪnkəˈhɪərəntlɪ/ _adv_ incoerentemente; (_because drunk etc_) incomprensibilmente

**income** /ˈɪnkəm/ _n_ reddito _m_

**income bracket** _n_ fascia _f_ di reddito

**income tax** _n_ imposta _f_ sul reddito

**income tax return** _n_ dichiarazione _f_ dei redditi

**incoming** /ˈɪnkʌmɪŋ/ _a_ in arrivo; ~ **tide** marea _f_ montante

**incommunicado** /ɪnkəmjuːnɪˈkɑːdəʊ/ _a_ (_involuntarily_) segregato; **he's** ~ (_in meeting_) non vuole essere disturbato

**incomparable** /ɪnˈkɒmp(ə)rəbl/ a incomparabile

**incompatibility** /ɪnkəmpætɪˈbɪlətɪ/ n incompatibilità f

**incompatible** /ɪnkəmˈpætəbl/ a incompatibile

**incompetence** /ɪnˈkɒmpɪtəns/ n incompetenza f

**incompetent** /ɪnˈkɒmpɪtənt/ a incompetente

**incomplete** /ɪnkəmˈpliːt/ a incompleto

**incomprehensible** /ɪnkɒmprɪˈhensəbl/ a incomprensibile

**inconceivable** /ɪnkənˈsiːvəbl/ a inconcepibile

**inconclusive** /ɪnkənˈkluːsɪv/ a inconcludente

**incongruity** /ɪnkɒŋˈgruːətɪ/ n (of appearance) contrasto m; (of situation) assurdità f inv

**incongruous** /ɪnˈkɒŋgrʊəs/ a contrastante

**inconsequential** /ɪnkɒnsɪˈkwenʃl/ a senza importanza

**inconsiderate** /ɪnkənˈsɪdərət/ a trascurabile

**inconsistency** /ɪnkənˈsɪstənsɪ/ n incoerenza f

**inconsistent** /ɪnkənˈsɪstənt/ a incoerente; **be ~ with** non essere coerente con

**inconsistently** /ɪnkənˈsɪstəntlɪ/ adv in modo incoerente

**inconsolable** /ɪnkənˈsəʊləbl/ a inconsolabile

**inconspicuous** /ɪnkənˈspɪkjʊəs/ a non appariscente

**inconspicuously** /ɪnkənˈspɪkjʊəslɪ/ adv modestamente

**inconstancy** /ɪnˈkɒnstənsɪ/ n incostanza f

**inconstant** /ɪnˈkɒnstənt/ a (conditions) variabile; (lover) volubile

**incontestable** /ɪnkənˈtestəbl/ a incontestabile

**incontinence** /ɪnˈkɒntɪnəns/ n incontinenza f

**incontinent** /ɪnˈkɒntɪnənt/ a incontinente

**inconvenience** /ɪnkənˈviːnɪəns/ n scomodità f; (drawback) inconveniente m; **put sb to ~** dare disturbo a qcno

**inconvenient** /ɪnkənˈviːnɪənt/ a scomodo; (time, place) inopportuno

**inconveniently** /ɪnkənˈviːnɪəntlɪ/ adv in modo inopportuno

**incorporate** /ɪnˈkɔːpəreɪt/ vt incorporare; (contain) comprendere

**incorrect** /ɪnkəˈrekt/ a incorretto

**incorrectly** /ɪnkəˈrektlɪ/ adv scorrettamente

**incorrigible** /ɪnˈkɒrɪdʒəbl/ a incorreggibile

**incorruptible** /ɪnkəˈrʌptəbl/ a incorruttibile

**increase**[1] /ˈɪnkriːs/ n aumento m; **on the ~** in aumento

**increase**[2] /ɪnˈkriːs/ vt/i aumentare

**increasing** /ɪnˈkriːsɪŋ/ a (impatience etc) crescente; (numbers) in aumento

**increasingly** /ɪnˈkriːsɪŋlɪ/ adv sempre più

**incredible** /ɪnˈkredəbl/ a incredibile

**incredibly** /ɪnˈkredəblɪ/ adv incredibilmente

**incredulity** /ɪnkrəˈdjuːlətɪ/ n incredulità f

**incredulous** /ɪnˈkredjʊləs/ a incredulo

**increment** /ˈɪnkrɪmənt/ n incremento m

**incremental** /ɪnkrɪˈmentl/ a Comput Math incrementale; (effect, measures) progressivo

**incriminate** /ɪnˈkrɪmɪneɪt/ vt Jur incriminare

**in-crowd** n **be in with the ~** frequentare gente alla moda

**incubate** /ˈɪnkjʊbeɪt/ vt incubare

**incubation** /ɪnkjʊˈbeɪʃn/ n incubazione f

**incubation period** n Med periodo m di incubazione

**incubator** /ˈɪnkjʊbeɪtə(r)/ n (for baby) incubatrice f

**inculcate** /ˈɪnkʌlkeɪt/ vt inculcare

**incumbent** /ɪnˈkʌmbənt/ a **be ~ on sb** incombere a qcno

**incur** /ɪnˈkɜː(r)/ vt (pt/pp incurred) incorrere; contrarre (debts)

**incurable** /ɪnˈkjʊərəbl/ a incurabile

**incurably** /ɪnˈkjʊərəblɪ/ adv incurabilmente

**incursion** /ɪnˈkɜːʃn/ n incursione f

**indebted** /ɪnˈdetɪd/ a obbligato (to verso)

**indecency** /ɪnˈdiːsənsɪ/ n oscenità f; (offence) atti mpl osceni; **gross ~** atti mpl osceni

**indecent** /ɪnˈdiːsənt/ a indecente

**indecent assault** n atti mpl di libidine violenta

**indecent exposure** n esibizionismo m (dei genitali)

**indecipherable** /ɪndɪˈsaɪfərəbl/ a indecifrabile

**indecision** /ɪndɪˈsɪʒn/ n indecisione f

**indecisive** /ɪndɪˈsaɪsɪv/ a indeciso

**indecisiveness** /ɪndɪˈsaɪsɪvnɪs/ n indecisione f

**indeed** /ɪnˈdiːd/ adv (in fact) difatti; **yes ~!** sì, certamente!; **~ I am/do** veramente!; **very much ~** moltissimo; **thank you very much ~** grazie infinite; **~?** davvero?

**indefatigable** /ɪndɪˈfætɪgəbl/ a instancabile

**indefensible** /ɪndɪˈfensəbl/ a Mil indifendibile; (morally) ingiustificabile; (logically) insostenibile

**indefinable** /ɪndɪˈfaɪnəbl/ a indefinibile

**indefinite** /ɪnˈdefɪnɪt/ a indefinito

**indefinitely** /ɪnˈdefɪnɪtlɪ/ adv indefinitamente; (postpone) a tempo indeterminato

**indelible** /ɪnˈdeləbl/ a indelebile

**indelibly** /ɪnˈdeləblɪ/ adv in modo indelebile

**indelicacy** /ɪnˈdelɪkəsɪ/ n (tactlessness) mancanza f di tatto; (coarseness) rozzezza f

**indelicate** /ɪnˈdelɪkət/ a (tactless) privo di tatto; (coarse) rozzo

**indemnity** /ɪnˈdemnətɪ/ n indennità f inv

**indent**[1] /ˈɪndent/ n Typ rientranza f dal margine

**indent²** /ɪn'dent/ *vt Typ* fare rientrare dal margine

**indentation** /ɪnden'teɪʃn/ *n* (*notch*) intaccatura *f*

**independence** /ɪndɪ'pendəns/ *n* indipendenza *f*

**Independence Day** *n Am* = *anniversario m dell'Indipendenza degli USA (4 luglio)*

**independent** /ɪndɪ'pendənt/ *a* indipendente

**independently** /ɪndɪ'pendəntlɪ/ *adv* indipendentemente

**in-depth** *a* ⟨*analysis, study, knowledge*⟩ approfondito

**indescribable** /ɪndɪ'skraɪbəbl/ *a* indescrivibile

**indescribably** /ɪndɪ'skraɪbəblɪ/ *adv* indescrivibilmente

**indestructible** /ɪndɪ'strʌktəbl/ *a* indistruttibile

**indeterminate** /ɪndɪ'tɜːmmət/ *a* indeterminato

**index** /'ɪndeks/ *n* indice *m*

**indexation** /ɪndek'seɪʃn/ *n* indicizzazione *f*

**index**: **index card** *n* scheda *f*. **index finger** *n* dito *m* indice. **index-linked** *a* ⟨*pension*⟩ legato al costo della vita

**India** /'ɪndɪə/ *n* India *f*

**Indian** /'ɪndɪən/ *a* indiano; (*American*) indiano [d'America] ● *n* indiano, -a *mf*; (*American*) indiano [d'America], pellerossa *mf inv*

**Indian**: **Indian elephant** *n* elefante *m* indiano. **Indian ink** *n* inchiostro *m* di China. **Indian Ocean** *n* oceano *m* Indiano. **Indian summer** *n* estate *f* di San Martino

**indicate** /'ɪndɪkeɪt/ *vt* indicare; (*register*) segnare ● *vi Auto* mettere la freccia; ~ **left** mettere la freccia a sinistra

**indication** /ɪndɪ'keɪʃn/ *n* indicazione *f*

**indicative** /ɪn'dɪkətɪv/ *a* **be** ~ **of** essere indicativo di ● *n Gram* indicativo *m*

**indicator** /'ɪndɪkeɪtə(r)/ *n Auto* freccia *f*

**indict** /ɪn'daɪt/ *vt* accusare

**indictment** /ɪn'daɪtmənt/ *n Jur* imputazione *f*

**indie** /'ɪndɪ/ *a fam Cinema, Mus* indipendente; ● *n* (*band*) complesso *m* musicale legato a un'etichetta indipendente; (*film*) film *m* prodotto da una casa di produzione indipendente

**indifference** /ɪn'dɪf(ə)rəns/ *n* indifferenza *f*

**indifferent** /ɪn'dɪf(ə)rənt/ *a* indifferente; (*not good*) mediocre

**indifferently** /ɪn'dɪf(ə)rəntlɪ/ *adv* in modo indifferente; (*not well*) in modo mediocre

**indigenous** /ɪn'dɪdʒɪnəs/ *a* indigeno

**indigestible** /ɪndɪ'dʒestəbl/ *a* indigesto

**indigestion** /ɪndɪ'dʒestʃn/ *n* indigestione *f*

**indignant** /ɪn'dɪgnənt/ *a* indignato

**indignantly** /ɪn'dɪgnəntlɪ/ *adv* con indignazione

**indignation** /ɪndɪg'neɪʃn/ *n* indignazione *f*

**indignity** /ɪn'dɪgnətɪ/ *n* umiliazione *f*

**indigo** /'ɪndɪgəʊ/ *n* indaco *m*

**indirect** /ɪndaɪ'rekt/ *a* indiretto

**indirectly** /ɪndaɪ'rektlɪ/ *adv* indirettamente

**indiscernible** /ɪndɪ'sɜːnəbl/ *a* indistinguibile

**indiscreet** /ɪndɪ'skriːt/ *a* indiscreto

**indiscretion** /ɪndɪ'skreʃn/ *n* indiscrezione *f*

**indiscriminate** /ɪndɪ'skrɪmɪnət/ *a* indiscriminato

**indiscriminately** /ɪndɪ'skrɪmɪnətlɪ/ *adv* senza distinzione

**indispensable** /ɪndɪ'spensəbl/ *a* indispensabile

**indisposed** /ɪndɪ'spəʊzd/ *a* indisposto

**indisputable** /ɪndɪ'spjuːtəbl/ *a* indisputabile

**indisputably** /ɪndɪ'spjuːtəblɪ/ *adv* indisputabilmente

**indistinct** /ɪndɪ'stɪnkt/ *a* indistinto

**indistinctly** /ɪndɪ'stɪŋktlɪ/ *adv* indistintamente

**indistinguishable** /ɪndɪ'stɪŋgwɪʃəbl/ *a* indistinguibile

**individual** /ɪndɪ'vɪdjʊəl/ *a* individuale ● *n* individuo *m*

**individualist** /ɪndɪ'vɪdjʊəlɪst/ *n* individualista *mf*

**individualistic** /ɪndɪvɪdjʊə'lɪstɪk/ *a* individualistico

**individuality** /ɪndɪvɪdjʊ'ælətɪ/ *n* individualità *f*

**individually** /ɪndɪ'vɪdjʊəlɪ/ *adv* individualmente

**indivisible** /ɪndɪ'vɪzəbl/ *a* indivisibile

**Indochina** /ɪndəʊ'tʃaɪnə/ *n* Indocina *f*

**indoctrinate** /ɪn'dɒktrɪneɪt/ *vt* indottrinare

**Indo-European** /ɪndəʊ-jʊərə'pɪən/ *a* indo-europeo

**indolence** /'ɪndələns/ *n* indolenza

**indolent** /'ɪndələnt/ *a* indolente

**indomitable** /ɪn'dɒmɪtəbl/ *a* indomito

**Indonesia** /ɪndə'niːzjə/ *n* Indonesia *f*

**Indonesian** /ɪndə'niːzjən/ *a & n* (*person*) indonesiano, -a *mf*; (*language*) indonesiano *m*

**indoor** /'ɪndɔː(r)/ *a* interno; ⟨*shoes*⟩ per casa; ⟨*plant*⟩ da appartamento; ⟨*swimming pool etc*⟩ coperto

**indoors** /ɪn'dɔːz/ *adv* dentro; **go** ~ andare dentro

**indubitable** /ɪn'djuːbɪtəbl/ *a* indubitabile

**indubitably** /ɪn'djuːbɪtəblɪ/ *adv* indubitabilmente

**induce** /ɪn'djuːs/ *vt* indurre (**to** a); (*produce*) causare

**inducement** /ɪn'djuːsmənt/ *n* (*incentive*) incentivo *m*

**induction** /ɪn'dʌkʃn/ *n* (*inauguration*) introduzione *f*; (*of labour*) parto *m* indotto; *Electr* induzione *f*

**induction ceremony** *n* cerimonia *f* inaugurale

**induction course** *n* corso *m* introduttivo

**indulge** /ɪn'dʌldʒ/ *vt* soddisfare; viziare ⟨*child*⟩ ● *vi* ~ **in** concedersi

**indulgence** /ɪn'dʌldʒəns/ *n* lusso *m*; (*leniency*) indulgenza *f*

**indulgent** /ɪn'dʌldʒənt/ *a* indulgente

**industrial** /ɪnˈdʌstrɪəl/ a industriale; **take ~ action** scioperare

**industrial: industrial accident** n infortunio m sul lavoro. **industrial dispute** n vertenza f sindacale. **industrial espionage** n spionaggio m industriale. **industrial estate** n zona f industriale. **industrial tribunal** n tribunale m del lavoro

**industrialist** /ɪnˈdʌstrɪəlɪst/ n industriale mf

**industrialized** /ɪnˈdʌstrɪəlaɪzd/ a industrializzato

**industrial tribunal** n tribunale m competente per i conflitti di lavoro

**industrial waste** n rifiuti mpl industriali

**industrious** /ɪnˈdʌstrɪəs/ a industrioso

**industriously** /ɪnˈdʌstrɪəslɪ/ adv in modo industrioso

**industry** /ˈɪndəstrɪ/ n industria f; (zeal) operosità f

**inebriated** /ɪˈniːbrɪeɪtɪd/ a ebbro

**inedible** /ɪnˈedəbl/ a immangiabile

**ineffective** /ɪnɪˈfektɪv/ a inefficace

**ineffectively** /ɪnɪˈfektɪvlɪ/ adv inutilmente, invano

**ineffectual** /ɪnɪˈfektʃʊəl/ a inutile; (person) inconcludente

**inefficiency** /ɪnɪˈfɪʃənsɪ/ n inefficienza f

**inefficient** /ɪnɪˈfɪʃnt/ a inefficiente

**ineligible** /ɪnˈelɪdʒəbl/ a inadatto

**inept** /ɪˈnept/ a inetto

**ineptitude** /ɪˈneptɪtjuːd/ n inettitudine f

**inequality** /ɪnɪˈkwɒlətɪ/ n ineguaglianza f

**inert** /ɪˈnɜːt/ a inerte

**inertia** /ɪˈnɜːʃə/ n inerzia f

**inescapable** /ɪnɪˈskeɪpəbl/ a inevitabile

**inestimable** /ɪnˈestɪməbl/ a inestimabile

**inevitable** /ɪnˈevɪtəbl/ a inevitabile

**inevitably** /ɪnˈevɪtəblɪ/ adv inevitabilmente

**inexact** /ɪnɪɡˈzækt/ a inesatto

**inexcusable** /ɪnɪkˈskjuːzəbl/ a imperdonabile

**inexhaustible** /ɪnɪɡˈzɔːstəbl/ a inesauribile

**inexorable** /ɪnˈeksərəbl/ a inesorabile

**inexorably** /ɪnˈeɡzərəblɪ/ adv inesorabilmente

**inexpensive** /ɪnɪkˈspensɪv/ a poco costoso

**inexpensively** /ɪnɪkˈspensɪvlɪ/ adv a buon mercato

**inexperience** /ɪnɪkˈspɪərɪəns/ n inesperienza f

**inexperienced** /ɪnɪkˈspɪərɪənst/ a inesperto

**inexplicable** /ɪnɪkˈsplɪkəbl/ a inesplicabile

**inexplicably** /ɪnɪkˈsplɪkəblɪ/ adv inesplicabilmente, inspiegabilmente

**inextricable** /ɪnɪkˈstrɪkəbl/ a inestricabile

**inextricably** /ɪnɪkˈstrɪkəblɪ/ adv inestricabilmente

**infallibility** /ɪnfælɪˈbɪlətɪ/ n infallibilità f

**infallible** /ɪnˈfæləbl/ a infallibile

**infamous** /ˈɪnfəməs/ a infame; (person) famigerato

**infamy** /ˈɪnfəmɪ/ n infamia f

**infancy** /ˈɪnfənsɪ/ n infanzia f; **in its ~** fig agli inizi

**infant** /ˈɪnfənt/ n bambino, -a mf piccolo, -a

**infanticide** /ɪnˈfæntɪsaɪd/ n infanticidio m

**infantile** /ˈɪnfəntaɪl/ a infantile

**infantry** /ˈɪnfəntrɪ/ n fanteria f

**infant school** n scuola f elementare per bambini dai 5 ai 7 anni

**infatuated** /ɪnˈfætʃʊeɪtɪd/ a infatuato (**with** di)

**infatuation** /ɪnfætʃʊˈeɪʃn/ n infatuazione f

**infect** /ɪnˈfekt/ vt infettare; **become ~ed** (wound:) infettarsi

**infection** /ɪnˈfekʃn/ n infezione f

**infectious** /ɪnˈfekʃəs/ a infettivo

**infer** /ɪnˈfɜː(r)/ vt (pt/pp **inferred**) dedurre (**from** da); (imply) implicare

**inference** /ˈɪnfərəns/ n deduzione f

**inferior** /ɪnˈfɪərɪə(r)/ a inferiore; (goods) scadente; (in rank) subalterno ● n inferiore mf; (in rank) subalterno, -a mf

**inferiority** /ɪnfɪərɪˈɒrətɪ/ n inferiorità f

**inferiority complex** n complesso m di inferiorità

**infernal** /ɪnˈfɜːnl/ a infernale

**inferno** /ɪnˈfɜːnəʊ/ n inferno m

**infertile** /ɪnˈfɜːtaɪl/ a sterile

**infertility** /ɪnfəˈtɪlətɪ/ n sterilità f

**infest** /ɪnˈfest/ vt be **~ed with** essere infestato di

**infestation** /ɪnfeˈsteɪʃn/ n infestazione f

**infidelity** /ɪnfɪˈdelətɪ/ n infedeltà f inv

**infighting** /ˈɪnfaɪtɪŋ/ n fig lotta f per il potere

**infiltrate** /ˈɪnfɪltreɪt/ vt infiltrare; Pol infiltrarsi in

**infiltration** /ɪnfɪlˈtreɪʃn/ n infiltrazione f

**infinite** /ˈɪnfɪnɪt/ a infinito

**infinitely** /ˈɪnfɪnɪtlɪ/ adv infinitamente

**infinitesimal** /ɪnfɪnɪˈtesɪml/ a infinitesimo

**infinitive** /ɪnˈfɪnɪtɪv/ n Gram infinito m

**infinity** /ɪnˈfɪnətɪ/ n infinità f

**infirm** /ɪnˈfɜːm/ a debole

**infirmary** /ɪnˈfɜːm(ə)rɪ/ n infermeria f

**infirmity** /ɪnˈfɜːmətɪ/ n debolezza f

**in flagrante delicto** /ɪnfləɡræntɪdɪˈlɪktəʊ/ adv in flagrante

**inflame** /ɪnˈfleɪm/ vt infiammare

**inflamed** /ɪnˈfleɪmd/ a infiammato; **become ~** infiammarsi

**inflammable** /ɪnˈflæməbl/ a infiammabile

**inflammation** /ɪnfləˈmeɪʃn/ n infiammazione f

**inflammatory** /ɪnˈflæmətrɪ/ a incendiario

**inflatable** /ɪnˈfleɪtəbl/ a gonfiabile

**inflate** /ɪnˈfleɪt/ vt gonfiare

**inflated** /ɪnˈfleɪtɪd/ a (price, fee, claim) eccessivo; (style) ampolloso; (tyre) gonfio; **an ~ ego** un'alta opinione di sé

**inflation** /ɪnˈfleɪʃn/ n inflazione f

**inflationary** /ɪnˈfleɪʃənərɪ/ a inflazionario

**inflect** /ɪnˈflekt/ vt flettere (noun, adjective); modulare (voice)

**inflected** /ɪnˈflektɪd/ a (language) flessivo; (form) flesso

**inflection** /ɪnˈflekʃn/ n (of voice) modulazione f

**inflexible** /ɪnˈfleksəbl/ a inflessibile

**inflexion** /ɪnˈflekʃn/ n inflessione f

**inflict** /ɪnˈflɪkt/ vt infliggere (**on** a)

**in-flight** a a bordo

**influence** /ˈɪnflʊəns/ n influenza f; **use one's ~** esercitare la propria influenza ● vt influenzare

**influential** /ɪnflʊˈenʃl/ a influente

**influenza** /ɪnflʊˈenzə/ n influenza f

**influx** /ˈɪnflʌks/ n affluenza f

**info** /ˈɪnfəʊ/ n fam informazione f

**inform** /ɪnˈfɔːm/ vt informare; **keep sb ~ed** tenere qcno al corrente ● vi ~ **against** denunziare

**informal** /ɪnˈfɔːməl/ a informale; ⟨agreement⟩ ufficioso

**informality** /ɪnfəˈmælətɪ/ n informalità f inv

**informally** /ɪnˈfɔːməlɪ/ adv in modo informale

**informant** /ɪnˈfɔːmənt/ n informatore, -trice mf

**information** /ɪnfəˈmeɪʃn/ n informazioni fpl; **a piece of ~** un'informazione

**information: information desk** n banco m informazioni. **information highway** n autostrada f telematica. **information officer** n addetto, -a mf stampa. **information processing** n elaborazione f dati. **information system** n sistema m informativo. **information technology** n informatica f

**informative** /ɪnˈfɔːmətɪv/ a informativo; ⟨film, book⟩ istruttivo

**informer** /ɪnˈfɔːmə(r)/ n informatore, -trice mf; Pol delatore, -trice mf

**infra-red** /ɪnfrəˈred/ a infrarosso

**infrastructure** /ˈɪnfrəstrʌktʃə(r)/ n infrastruttura f

**infrequent** /ɪnˈfriːkwənt/ a infrequente

**infrequently** /ɪnˈfriːkwəntlɪ/ adv raramente

**infringe** /ɪnˈfrɪndʒ/ vt ~ **on** usurpare

**infringement** /ɪnˈfrɪndʒmənt/ n violazione f

**infuriate** /ɪnˈfjʊərɪeɪt/ vt infuriare

**infuriating** /ɪnˈfjʊərɪeɪtɪŋ/ a esasperante

**infuse** /ɪnˈfjuːz/ vi ⟨tea:⟩ restare in infusione

**infusion** /ɪnˈfjuːʒn/ n ⟨drink⟩ infusione f; ⟨of capital, new blood⟩ afflusso m

**ingenious** /ɪnˈdʒiːnɪəs/ a ingegnoso

**ingenuity** /ɪndʒɪˈnjuːətɪ/ n ingegnosità f

**ingenuous** /ɪnˈdʒenjʊəs/ a ingenuo

**ingest** /ɪnˈdʒest/ vt ingerire ⟨food⟩; assimilare ⟨fact⟩

**ingot** /ˈɪŋgət/ n lingotto m

**ingrained** /ɪnˈgreɪnd/ a (in person) radicato; ⟨dirt⟩ incrostato

**ingratiate** /ɪnˈgreɪʃɪeɪt/ vt ~ **oneself with sb** ingraziarsi qcno

**ingratitude** /ɪnˈgrætɪtjuːd/ n ingratitudine f

**ingredient** /ɪnˈgriːdɪənt/ n ingrediente m

**ingrowing** /ˈɪngrəʊɪŋ/ a ⟨nail⟩ incarnito

**inhabit** /ɪnˈhæbɪt/ vt abitare

**inhabitable** /ɪnˈhæbɪtəbl/ a abitabile

**inhabitant** /ɪnˈhæbɪtənt/ n abitante mf

**inhale** /ɪnˈheɪl/ vt aspirare; Med inalare ● vi inspirare; (when smoking) aspirare

**inhaler** /ɪnˈheɪlə(r)/ n (device) inalatore m

**inherent** /ɪnˈhɪərənt/ a inerente

**inherit** /ɪnˈherɪt/ vt ereditare

**inheritance** /ɪnˈherɪtəns/ n eredità f inv

**inhibit** /ɪnˈhɪbɪt/ vt inibire

**inhibited** /ɪnˈhɪbɪtɪd/ a inibito

**inhibition** /ɪnhɪˈbɪʃn/ n inibizione f

**inhospitable** /ɪnhɒˈspɪtəbl/ a inospitale

**in-house** a ⟨training⟩ interno all'azienda; ⟨magazine⟩ aziendale

**inhuman** /ɪnˈhjuːmən/ a disumano

**inimitable** /ɪˈnɪmɪtəbl/ a inimitabile

**iniquitous** /ɪˈnɪkwɪtəs/ a iniquo

**initial** /ɪˈnɪʃl/ a iniziale ● n iniziale f ● vt (pt/pp initialled) siglare

**initially** /ɪˈnɪʃəlɪ/ adv all'inizio

**initiate** /ɪˈnɪʃɪeɪt/ vt iniziare

**initiation** /ɪnɪʃɪˈeɪʃn/ n iniziazione f

**initiative** /ɪˈnɪʃətɪv/ n iniziativa f; **take the ~** prendere l'iniziativa

**inject** /ɪnˈdʒekt/ vt iniettare

**injection** /ɪnˈdʒekʃn/ n iniezione f

**in-joke** n **it's an ~** è una battuta tra di noi/loro

**injunction** /ɪnˈdʒʌŋkʃn/ n ingiunzione f

**injure** /ˈɪndʒə(r)/ vt ferire; (wrong) nuocere; **the ~d party** la parte lesa

**injury** /ˈɪndʒərɪ/ n ferita f; (wrong) torto m

**injury time** n Sport recupero m

**injustice** /ɪnˈdʒʌstɪs/ n ingiustizia f; **do sb an ~** giudicare qcno in modo sbagliato

**ink** /ɪŋk/ n inchiostro m

**ink-jet printer** n stampante f a getto d'inchiostro

**inkling** /ˈɪŋklɪŋ/ n sentore m

**inky** /ˈɪŋkɪ/ a macchiato d'inchiostro

**inlaid** /ɪnˈleɪd/ a intarsiato

**inland** /ˈɪnlənd/ a interno ● adv all'interno

**Inland Revenue** n fisco m

**in-laws** /ˈɪnlɔːz/ npl fam parenti mpl acquisiti

**inlay** /ˈɪnleɪ/ n intarsio m

**inlet** /ˈɪnlet/ n insenatura f; Techn entrata f

**inmate** /ˈɪnmeɪt/ n (of hospital) degente mf; (of prison) carcerato, -a mf

**inn** /ɪn/ n locanda f

**innards** /ˈɪnədz/ npl fam frattaglie fpl

**innate** /ɪˈneɪt/ a innato

**inner** /ˈɪnə(r)/ a interno

**inner city** n quartieri mpl nel centro di una città caratterizzati da problemi sociali ● attrib ⟨problems⟩ dell'area urbana con problemi sociali

**inner ear** n orecchio m interno

**innermost** /ˈɪnəməʊst/ a il più profondo

**inner tube** n camera f d'aria

**innings** /ˈɪnɪŋz/ nsg (in cricket) turno m di battuta; **have had a good ~** (Br fig: when leaving job etc) aver avuto una carriera lunga e gratificante; (when dead) aver avuto una vita lunga e piena di soddisfazioni

**innkeeper** /'ɪnkiːpə(r)/ *n* locandiere, -a *mf*
**innocence** /'ɪnəsəns/ *n* innocenza *f*
**innocent** /'ɪnəsənt/ *a* innocente
**innocently** /'ɪnəsəntlɪ/ *adv* innocentemente
**innocuous** /ɪ'nɒkjʊəs/ *a* innocuo
**innovate** /'ɪnəveɪt/ *vi* innovare
**innovation** /ɪnə'veɪʃn/ *n* innovazione *f*
**innovative** /'ɪnəvətɪv/ *a* innovativo
**innovator** /'ɪnəveɪtə(r)/ *n* innovatore, -trice *mf*
**innuendo** /ɪnjʊ'endəʊ/ *n* (*pl* **-es**) insinuazione *f*
**innumerable** /ɪ'njuːmərəbl/ *a* innumerevole
**inoculate** /ɪ'nɒkjʊleɪt/ *vt* vaccinare
**inoculation** /ɪnɒkjʊ'leɪʃn/ *n* vaccinazione *f*
**inoffensive** /ɪnə'fensɪv/ *a* inoffensivo
**inoperable** /ɪn'ɒpərəbl/ *a* inoperabile
**inopportune** /ɪn'ɒpətjuːn/ *a* inopportuno
**inordinate** /ɪ'nɔːdɪnət/ *a* smodato
**inordinately** /ɪ'nɔːdɪnətlɪ/ *adv* smodatamente
**inorganic** /ɪnɔː'ɡænɪk/ *a* inorganico
**in-patient** *n* degente *mf*
**input** /'ɪnpʊt/ *n* input *m inv*, ingresso *m*
**inquest** /'ɪnkwest/ *n* inchiesta *f*
**inquire** /ɪn'kwaɪə(r)/ *vi* informarsi (**about** su); ~ **into** far indagini su ● *vt* domandare
**inquiring** /ɪn'kwaɪərɪŋ/ *a* ⟨*mind*⟩ curioso; ⟨*look, voice*⟩ interrogativo
**inquiry** /ɪn'kwaɪərɪ/ *n* domanda *f*; (*investigation*) inchiesta *f*
**inquisitive** /ɪn'kwɪzətɪv/ *a* curioso
**inquisitively** /ɪn'kwɪzɪtɪvlɪ/ *adv* con molta curiosità
**inroad** /'ɪnrəʊd/ *n* **make ~s into** intaccare ⟨*savings*⟩; cominciare a risolvere ⟨*problem*⟩
**insalubrious** /ɪnsə'luːbrɪəs/ *a* (*dirty*) insalubre; (*sleazy*) sordido
**insane** /ɪn'seɪn/ *a* pazzo; *fig* insensato
**insanitary** /ɪn'sænɪt(ə)rɪ/ *a* malsano
**insanity** /ɪn'sænətɪ/ *n* pazzia *f*
**insatiable** /ɪn'seɪʃəbl/ *a* insaziabile
**inscribe** /ɪn'skraɪb/ *vt* iscrivere
**inscription** /ɪn'skrɪpʃn/ *n* iscrizione *f*
**inscrutable** /ɪn'skruːtəbl/ *a* impenetrabile
**insect** /'ɪnsekt/ *n* insetto *m*
**insecticide** /ɪn'sektɪsaɪd/ *n* insetticida *m*
**insect repellent** *n* insettifugo *m*
**insecure** /ɪnsɪ'kjʊə(r)/ *a* malsicuro; ⟨*fig: person*⟩ insicuro
**insecurity** /ɪnsɪ'kjʊərətɪ/ *n* mancanza *f* di sicurezza
**insemination** /ɪnsemɪ'neɪʃn/ *n* inseminazione *f*
**insensitive** /ɪn'sensɪtɪv/ *a* insensibile
**inseparable** /ɪn'sep(ə)rəbl/ *a* inseparabile
**insert**[1] /'ɪnsɜːt/ *n* inserto *m*
**insert**[2] /ɪn'sɜːt/ *vt* inserire
**insertion** /ɪn'sɜːʃn/ *n* inserzione *f*
**inset** /'ɪnset/ *n* (*map, photo*) dettaglio *m* ● *a* ~ **with** ⟨*necklace*⟩ incastonato di; ⟨*table*⟩ intarsiato di
**inshore** /'ɪnʃɔː(r)/ *a* ⟨*current*⟩ diretta a riva; ⟨*fishing, waters, current*⟩ costiero; ⟨*wind*⟩ dal mare ● *adv* ⟨*fish*⟩ sotto costa

**inside** /ɪn'saɪd/ *n* interno *m*; ~**s** *pl fam* pancia *f* ● *adv* dentro; ~ **out** a rovescio; (*thoroughly*) a fondo ● *prep* dentro; (*of time*) entro
**inside lane** *n Auto* corsia *f* interna
**inside leg** *n* interno *m* della gamba
**insider** /ɪn'saɪdə(r)/ *n* persona *f* all'interno
**insider dealer**, **insider trader** *n Fin* persona *f* che pratica l'insider trading
**insider dealing**, **insider trading** /'diːlɪŋ, 'treɪdɪŋ/ *n Fin* insider trading *m*
**insidious** /ɪn'sɪdɪəs/ *a* insidioso
**insidiously** /ɪn'sɪdɪəslɪ/ *adv* insidiosamente
**insight** /'ɪnsaɪt/ *n* intuito *m* (**into** per); **an ~ into** un quadro di
**insignia** /ɪn'sɪɡnɪə/ *npl* insegne *fpl*
**insignificant** /ɪnsɪɡ'nɪfɪkənt/ *a* insignificante
**insincere** /ɪnsɪn'sɪə(r)/ *a* poco sincero
**insincerity** /ɪnsɪn'serətɪ/ *n* mancanza *f* di sincerità
**insinuate** /ɪn'sɪnjʊeɪt/ *vt* insinuare
**insinuation** /ɪnsɪnjʊ'eɪʃn/ *n* insinuazione *f*
**insipid** /ɪn'sɪpɪd/ *a* insipido
**insist** /ɪn'sɪst/ *vi* insistere (**on** per) ● *vt* ~ **that** insistere che
**insistence** /ɪn'sɪstəns/ *n* insistenza *f*
**insistent** /ɪn'sɪstənt/ *a* insistente
**insistently** /ɪn'sɪstəntlɪ/ *adv* insistentemente
**insofar** /ɪnsə'fɑː(r)/ *conj* ~ **as** (*to the extent that*) nella misura in cui; (*seeing that*) in quanto; ~ **as I know** per quanto ne sappia
**insole** /'ɪnsəʊl/ *n* soletta *f*
**insolence** /'ɪnsələns/ *n* insolenza *f*
**insolent** /'ɪnsələnt/ *a* insolente
**insolently** /'ɪnsələntlɪ/ *adv* con insolenza
**insoluble** /ɪn'sɒljʊbl/ *a* insolubile
**insolvency** /ɪn'sɒlvənsɪ/ *n* insolvenza *f*
**insolvent** /ɪn'sɒlvənt/ *a* insolvente
**insomnia** /ɪn'sɒmnɪə/ *n* insonnia *f*
**insomniac** /ɪn'sɒmɪæk/ *n* persona *f* che soffre di insonnia
**insomuch** /ɪnsə'mʌtʃ/ *conj* ~ **as** (*to the extent that*) nella misura in cui; (*seeing that*) in quanto
**inspect** /ɪn'spekt/ *vt* ispezionare; controllare ⟨*ticket*⟩
**inspection** /ɪn'spekʃn/ *n* ispezione *f*; (*of ticket*) controllo *m*
**inspector** /ɪn'spektə(r)/ *n* ispettore, -trice *mf*; (*of tickets*) controllore *m*
**inspiration** /ɪnspə'reɪʃn/ *n* ispirazione *f*
**inspire** /ɪn'spaɪə(r)/ *vt* ispirare
**inspired** /ɪn'spaɪəd/ *a* ⟨*person, performance*⟩ ispirato; ⟨*idea*⟩ luminosa
**instability** /ɪnstə'bɪlətɪ/ *n* instabilità *f*
**install** /ɪn'stɔːl/ *vt* installare; insediare ⟨*person*⟩
**installation** /ɪnstə'leɪʃn/ *n* installazione *f*
**instalment** /ɪn'stɔːlmənt/ *n Comm* rata *f*; (*of serial*) puntata *f*; (*of publication*) fascicolo *m*
**instance** /'ɪnstəns/ *n* (*case*) caso *m*;

(*example*) esempio *m*; **in the first** ~ in primo luogo; **for** ~ per esempio

**instant** /'ɪnstənt/ *a* immediato; *Culin* espresso ● *n* istante *m*

**instantaneous** /ɪnstən'teɪnɪəs/ *a* istantaneo

**instant coffee** *n* caffè *m inv* solubile

**instantly** /'ɪnstəntlɪ/ *adv* immediatamente

**instant replay** *n Sport* replay *m inv*

**instead** /ɪn'sted/ *adv* invece; ~ **of doing** anziché fare; ~ **of me** al mio posto; ~ **of going** invece di andare

**instep** /'ɪnstep/ *n* collo *m* del piede

**instigate** /'ɪnstɪget/ *vt* istigare

**instigation** /ɪnstɪ'geɪʃn/ *n* istigazione *f*; **at his** ~ dietro suo suggerimento

**instigator** /'ɪnstɪgeɪtə(r)/ *n* istigatore, -trice *mf*

**instil** /ɪn'stɪl/ *vt* (*pt/pp* **instilled**) inculcare (**into** in)

**instinct** /'ɪnstɪŋkt/ *n* istinto *m*

**instinctive** /ɪn'stɪŋktɪv/ *a* istintivo

**instinctively** /ɪn'stɪŋktɪvlɪ/ *adv* istintivamente

**institute** /'ɪnstɪtjuːt/ *n* istituto *m* ● *vt* istituire ⟨*scheme*⟩; iniziare ⟨*search*⟩; intentare ⟨*legal action*⟩

**institution** /ɪnstɪ'tjuːʃn/ *n* istituzione *f*; (*home for elderly*) istituto *m* per anziani; (*for mentally ill*) istituto *m* per malati di mente

**institutionalize** /ɪnstɪ'tjuːʃənəlaɪz/ *vt* istituzionalizzare

**institutionalized** /ɪnstɪ'tjuːʃənəlaɪzd/ *a* ⟨*racism, violence*⟩ istituzionalizzato; **become** ~ (*officially established*) essere istituzionalizzato; **be ~d** ⟨*person:*⟩ non essere autonomo a causa di un lungo soggiorno in ospedale psichiatrico

**instruct** /ɪn'strʌkt/ *vt* istruire; (*order*) ordinare

**instruction** /ɪn'strʌkʃn/ *n* istruzione *f*; ~**s** *pl* (*orders*) ordini *mpl*

**instructive** /ɪn'strʌktɪv/ *a* istruttivo

**instructor** /ɪn'strʌktə(r)/ *n* istruttore, -trice *mf*

**instrument** /'ɪnstrʊmənt/ *n* strumento *m*

**instrumental** /ɪnstrʊ'ment(ə)l/ *a* strumentale; **be** ~ **in** contribuire a

**instrumentalist** /ɪnstrʊ'mentəlɪst/ *n* strumentista *mf*

**insubordinate** /ɪnsə'bɔːdɪnət/ *a* insubordinato

**insubordination** /ɪnsəbɔːdɪ'neɪʃn/ *n* insubordinazione *f*

**insubstantial** /ɪnsəb'stænʃəl/ *a* (*unreal*) irreale; ⟨*evidence*⟩ inconsistente; ⟨*flimsy, building*⟩ poco solido; ⟨*meal*⟩ poco sostanzioso

**insufferable** /ɪn'sʌf(ə)rəbl/ *a* insopportabile

**insufficient** /ɪnsə'fɪʃənt/ *a* insufficiente

**insufficiently** /ɪnsə'fɪʃəntlɪ/ *adv* insufficientemente

**insular** /'ɪnsjʊlə(r)/ *a fig* gretto

**insulate** /'ɪnsjʊleɪt/ *vt* isolare

**insulating tape** /'ɪnsjʊleɪtɪŋ/ *n* nastro *m* isolante

**insulation** /ɪnsjʊ'leɪʃn/ *n* isolamento *m*

**insulator** /'ɪnsjʊleɪtə(r)/ *n* isolante *m*

**insulin** /'ɪnsjʊlɪn/ *n* insulina *f*

**insult**[1] /'ɪnsʌlt/ *n* insulto *m*

**insult**[2] /ɪn'sʌlt/ *vt* insultare

**insuperable** /ɪn'suːpərəbl/ *a* insuperabile

**insurable value** /ɪn'ʃʊərəbl/ *n* valore *m* assicurabile

**insurance** /ɪn'ʃʊərəns/ *n* assicurazione *f*

**insurance: insurance broker** *n* broker *mf inv* d'assicurazioni. **insurance claim** *n* richiesta *f* di indennizzo (*ad assicurazione*). **insurance policy** *n* polizza *f* d'assicurazione. **insurance premium** *n* premio *m* assicurativo

**insure** /ɪn'ʃʊə(r)/ *vt* assicurare

**insurgent** /ɪn'sɜːdʒənt/ *n* rivoltoso, -a *mf*

**insurmountable** /ɪnsə'maʊntəbl/ *a* insormontabile

**insurrection** /ɪnsə'rekʃn/ *n* insurrezione *f*

**intact** /ɪn'tækt/ *a* intatto

**intake** /'ɪnteɪk/ *n* immissione *f*; (*of food*) consumo *m*

**intangible** /ɪn'tændʒəbl/ *a* intangibile

**integral** /'ɪntɪgrəl/ *a* integrale

**integrate** /'ɪntɪgreɪt/ *vt* integrare ● *vi* integrarsi

**integration** /ɪntɪ'greɪʃn/ *n* integrazione *f*

**integrity** /ɪn'tegrətɪ/ *n* integrità *f*

**intellect** /'ɪntəlekt/ *n* intelletto *m*

**intellectual** /ɪntə'lektjʊəl/ *a & n* intellettuale *mf*

**intelligence** /ɪn'telɪdʒəns/ *n* intelligenza *f*; *Mil* informazioni *fpl*

**intelligent** /ɪn'telɪdʒənt/ *a* intelligente

**intelligently** /ɪn'telɪdʒəntlɪ/ *adv* intelligentemente

**intelligentsia** /ɪntelɪ'dʒentsɪə/ *n* intellighenzia *f*

**intelligible** /ɪn'telɪdʒəbl/ *a* intelligibile

**intemperate** /ɪn'temp(ə)rət/ *a* ⟨*language, person*⟩ intemperante; ⟨*weather*⟩ rigido; ⟨*attack*⟩ violento

**intend** /ɪn'tend/ *vt* destinare; (*have in mind*) aver intenzione di; **be ~ed for** essere destinato a

**intended** /ɪn'tendɪd/ *a* ⟨*visit, purchase*⟩ programmato; ⟨*result*⟩ voluto, desiderato ● *n* **her** ~ *hum* il suo fidanzato; **his** ~ *hum* la sua fidanzata

**intense** /ɪn'tens/ *a* intenso; ⟨*person*⟩ dai sentimenti intensi

**intensely** /ɪn'tenslɪ/ *adv* intensamente; (*very*) estremamente

**intensification** /ɪntensɪfɪ'keɪʃn/ *n* intensificazione *f*

**intensify** /ɪn'tensɪfaɪ/ *v* (*pt/pp* -**ied**) ● *vt* intensificare ● *vi* intensificarsi

**intensity** /ɪn'tensətɪ/ *n* intensità *f*

**intensive** /ɪn'tensɪv/ *a* intensivo; ~ **care** [**unit**] terapia *f* intensiva; (*for people in coma*) rianimazione *f*

**intensive care [unit]** n [reparto m] rianimazione f

**intensively** /ɪn'tensɪvlɪ/ adv intensivamente

**intent** /ɪn'tent/ a intento; **~ on** (absorbed in) preso da; **be ~ on doing sth** essere intento a fare qcsa • n intenzione f; **to all ~s and purposes** a tutti gli effetti

**intention** /ɪn'tenʃn/ n intenzione f

**intentional** /ɪn'tenʃənəl/ a intenzionale

**intentionally** /ɪn'tenʃənəlɪ/ adv intenzionalmente

**intently** /ɪn'tentlɪ/ adv attentamente

**inter** /ɪn'tɜː(r)/ vt (pt/pp **interred**) fml interrare

**interaction** /ɪntər'ækʃn/ n cooperazione f

**interactive** /ɪntər'æktɪv/ a interattivo

**interactive video** n video m interattivo

**interbreed** /ɪntə'briːd/ vt ibridare • vi incrociarsi

**interbreeding** /ɪntə'briːdɪŋ/ n ibridazione f

**intercede** /ɪntə'siːd/ vi intercedere (**on behalf of** a favore di)

**intercept** /ɪntə'sept/ vt intercettare

**interchange** /'ɪntətʃeɪndʒ/ n scambio m; Auto raccordo m [autostradale]

**interchangeable** /ɪntə'tʃeɪndʒəbl/ a interscambiabile

**intercity** /ɪntə'sɪtɪ/ n (Br: train) intercity m inv • a intercity

**intercom** /'ɪntəkɒm/ n citofono m

**interconnecting** /ɪntəkə'nektɪŋ/ a ⟨rooms⟩ comunicante

**intercontinental** /ɪntəkɒntɪ'nentəl/ a intercontinentale

**intercourse** /'ɪntəkɔːs/ n (sexual) rapporti mpl [sessuali]

**interdepartmental** /ɪntədiːpɑːt'ment(ə)l/ a Univ, Comm interdipartimentale; Pol interministeriale

**interdependent** /ɪntədɪ'pendənt/ a interdipendente

**interdisciplinary** /ɪntədɪsɪ'plɪnərɪ/ a interdisciplinare

**interest** /'ɪntrəst/ n interesse m; **have an ~ in** Comm essere cointeressato in; **be of ~** essere interessante • vt interessare • a interessato

**interest-bearing** a fruttifero

**interest-free loan** n prestito m senza interessi

**interesting** /'ɪnt(ə)rəstɪŋ/ a interessante

**interest rate** n tasso m di interesse

**interface** /'ɪntəfeɪs/ n Comput, fig interfaccia f • vi interfacciarsi • vt interfacciare

**interfere** /ɪntə'fɪə(r)/ vi interferire; **~ with** interferire con

**interference** /ɪntə'fɪərəns/ n interferenza f

**interim** /'ɪntərɪm/ a temporaneo; **~ payment** acconto m • n **in the ~** nel frattempo

**interior** /ɪn'tɪərɪə(r)/ a interiore • n interno m

**interior decorator** n arredatore, -trice mf

**interior designer** n (of colours, fabrics etc)

arredatore, -trice mf; (of walls, space) architetto m d'interni

**interject** /ɪntə'dʒekt/ vt intervenire

**interjection** /ɪntə'dʒekʃn/ n Gram interiezione f; (remark) intervento m

**interlink** /ɪntə'lɪŋk/ vt connettere; **be ~ed with** essere connesso con

**interlocking** /'ɪntəlɒkɪŋ/ a a incastro

**interloper** /'ɪntələʊpə(r)/ n intruso, -a mf

**interlude** /'ɪntəluːd/ n intervallo m

**intermarry** /ɪntə'mærɪ/ vi sposarsi tra parenti; ⟨different groups:⟩ contrarre matrimoni misti

**intermediary** /ɪntə'miːdɪərɪ/ n intermediario, -a mf

**intermediate** /ɪntə'miːdɪət/ a intermedio

**interminable** /ɪn'tɜːmɪnəbl/ a interminabile

**intermission** /ɪntə'mɪʃn/ n intervallo m

**intermittent** /ɪntə'mɪtənt/ a intermittente

**intermittently** /ɪntə'mɪtəntlɪ/ adv a intermittenza

**intern** /ɪn'tɜːn/ vt internare

**internal** /ɪn'tɜːnl/ a interno

**internal combustion engine** n motore m a scoppio

**internally** /ɪn'tɜːnəlɪ/ adv internamente; ⟨deal with⟩ all'interno

**international** /ɪntə'næʃ(ə)nəl/ a internazionale • n (game) incontro m internazionale; (player) competitore, -trice mf in gare internazionali

**internationally** /ɪntə'næʃ(ə)nəlɪ/ adv internazionalmente; **it applies ~** ha validità internazionale

**international: international money order** n vaglia m inv postale internazionale. **International Phonetic Alphabet** n Alfabeto m Fonetico Internazionale. **international reply coupon** n tagliando m di risposta internazionale

**Internet** /'ɪntənet/ n Internet m

**internist** /ɪn'tɜːnɪst/ n Am internista mf

**internment** /ɪn'tɜːnmənt/ n internamento m

**interplay** /'ɪntəpleɪ/ n azione f reciproca

**interpolate** /ɪn'tɜːpəleɪt/ vt interpolare

**interpose** /ɪntə'pəʊz/ vt (insert) frapporre; interrompere con ⟨comment, remark⟩

**interpret** /ɪn'tɜːprɪt/ vt interpretare • vi fare l'interprete.

**interpretation** /ɪntɜːprɪ'teɪʃn/ n interpretazione f

**interpreter** /ɪn'tɜːprɪtə(r)/ n interprete mf

**interpreting** /ɪn'tɜːprɪtɪŋ/ n interpretariato m

**interrelated** /ɪntərɪ'leɪtɪd/ a ⟨facts⟩ in correlazione

**interrogate** /ɪn'terəgeɪt/ vt interrogare

**interrogation** /ɪnterə'geɪʃn/ n interrogazione f; (by police) interrogatorio m

**interrogative** /ɪntə'rɒgətɪv/ a & n ~ [**pronoun**] interrogativo m

**interrupt** /ɪntə'rʌpt/ vt/i interrompere

**interruption** /ɪntə'rʌpʃn/ n interruzione f

**intersect** /ɪntə'sekt/ *vi* intersecarsi ● *vt* intersecare

**intersection** /ɪntə'sekʃn/ *n* intersezione *f*; (*of street*) incrocio *m*

**interspersed** /ɪntə'spɜ:st/ *a* ~ **with** inframmezzato di

**interstate** /'ɪntəsteɪt/ *Am n* superstrada *f* fra stati ● *a* ⟨commerce, links⟩ fra stati

**intertwine** /ɪntə'twaɪn/ *vi* attorcigliarsi

**interval** /'ɪntəvl/ *n* intervallo *m*; **bright ~s** *pl* schiarite *fpl*

**intervene** /ɪntə'vi:n/ *vi* intervenire

**intervention** /ɪntə'venʃn/ *n* intervento *m*

**interview** /'ɪntəvju:/ *n Journ* intervista *f*; (*for job*) colloquio *m* [di lavoro] ● *vt* intervistare

**interviewee** /ɪntəvju:'i:/ *n* (*on TV, radio, in survey*) intervistato, -a *mf*; (*for job*) persona *f* sottoposta a un colloquio di lavoro

**interviewer** /'ɪntəvju:ə(r)/ *n* intervistatore, -trice *mf*

**interweave** /ɪntə'wi:v/ *vt* intrecciare ⟨themes, threads⟩; mischiare ⟨rhythms⟩

**intestinal** /ɪnte'staɪnəl/ *a* intestinale

**intestine** /ɪn'testɪn/ *n* intestino *m*

**intimacy** /'ɪntɪməsɪ/ *n* intimità *f*

**intimate¹** /'ɪntɪmət/ *a* intimo; **be ~ with** (*sexually*) avere relazioni intime con

**intimate²** /'ɪntɪmeɪt/ *vt* far capire; (*imply*) suggerire

**intimately** /'ɪntɪmətlɪ/ *adv* intimamente

**intimidate** /ɪn'tɪmɪdeɪt/ *vt* intimidire

**intimidation** /ɪntɪmɪ'deɪʃn/ *n* intimidazione *f*

**into** /'ɪntə/, *di fronte a una vocale* /'ɪntʊ/ *prep* dentro, in; **go ~ the house** andare dentro [casa] *o* in casa; **be ~** (*fam: like*) essere appassionato di; **I'm not ~ that** questo non mi piace; **7 ~ 21 goes 3** il 7 nel 21 ci sta 3 volte; **translate ~ French** tradurre in francese; **get ~ trouble** mettersi nei guai

**intolerable** /ɪn'tɒlərəbl/ *a* intollerabile

**intolerance** /ɪn'tɒlərəns/ *n* intolleranza *f*

**intolerant** /ɪn'tɒlərənt/ *a* intollerante

**intonation** /ɪntə'neɪʃn/ *n* intonazione *f*

**intone** /ɪn'təʊn/ *vt* recitare ⟨prayer⟩

**intoxicated** /ɪn'tɒksɪkeɪtɪd/ *a* inebriato

**intoxication** /ɪntɒksɪ'keɪʃn/ *n* ebbrezza *f*

**intractable** /ɪn'træktəbl/ *a* intrattabile; ⟨problem⟩ insolubile

**intramural** /ɪntrə'mjʊərəl/ *a* ⟨studies⟩ tenuto in sede

**intransigence** /ɪn'trænzɪdʒəns/ *n* intransigenza *f*

**intransigent** /ɪn'trænzɪdʒənt/ *a* intransigente

**intransitive** /ɪn'trænzɪtɪv/ *a* intransitivo

**intransitively** /ɪn'trænzɪtɪvlɪ/ *adv* intransitivamente

**intrauterine device** /ɪntrəju:təraɪmdɪ'vaɪs/ *n Med* spirale *f*, dispositivo *m* anticoncezionale intrauterino

**intravenous** /ɪntrə'vi:nəs/ *a* endovenoso

**intravenous drip** *n* flebo[clisi] *f inv*

**intravenously** /ɪntrə'vi:nəslɪ/ *adv* per via endovenosa

**in-tray** *n* vassoio *m* per pratiche e corrispondenza da evadere

**intrepid** /ɪn'trepɪd/ *a* intrepido

**intricacy** /'ɪntrɪkəsɪ/ *n* complessità *f*

**intricate** /'ɪntrɪkət/ *a* complesso

**intrigue** /ɪn'tri:g/ *n* intrigo *m* ● *vt* intrigare ● *vi* tramare

**intriguing** /ɪn'tri:gɪŋ/ *a* intrigante

**intrinsic** /ɪn'trɪnsɪk/ *a* intrinseco

**introduce** /ɪntrə'dju:s/ *vt* presentare; (*bring in, insert*) introdurre

**introduction** /ɪntrə'dʌkʃn/ *n* introduzione *f*; (*to person*) presentazione *f*; (*to book*) prefazione *f*

**introductory** /ɪntrə'dʌktərɪ/ *a* introduttivo

**introspective** /ɪntrə'spektɪv/ *a* introspettivo

**introvert** /'ɪntrəvɜ:t/ *n* introverso, -a *mf*

**introverted** /'ɪntrəvɜ:tɪd/ *a* introverso

**intrude** /ɪn'tru:d/ *vi* intromettersi

**intruder** /ɪn'tru:də(r)/ *n* intruso, -a *mf*

**intrusion** /ɪn'tru:ʒn/ *n* intrusione *f*

**intuition** /ɪntjʊ'ɪʃn/ *n* intuito *m*

**intuitive** /ɪn'tju:ɪtɪv/ *a* intuitivo

**intuitively** /ɪn'tju:ɪtɪvlɪ/ *adv* intuitivamente

**inundate** /'ɪnəndeɪt/ *vt fig* inondare (**with** di)

**inure** /ɪn'jʊə(r)/ *vt* **become ~d to sth** assuefarsi a qcsa

**invade** /ɪn'veɪd/ *vt* invadere

**invader** /ɪn'veɪdə(r)/ *n* invasore *m*

**invalid¹** /'ɪnvəlɪd/ *n* invalido, -a *mf*

**invalid²** /ɪn'vælɪd/ *a* non valido

**invalidate** /ɪn'vælɪdeɪt/ *vt* invalidare

**invaluable** /ɪn'væljʊ(ə)bl/ *a* prezioso; (*priceless*) inestimabile

**invariable** /ɪn'veərɪəbl/ *a* invariabile

**invariably** /ɪn'veərɪəblɪ/ *adv* invariabilmente

**invasion** /ɪn'veɪʒn/ *n* invasione *f*

**invective** /ɪn'vektɪv/ *n* invettiva *f*

**invent** /ɪn'vent/ *vt* inventare

**invention** /ɪn'venʃn/ *n* invenzione *f*

**inventive** /ɪn'ventɪv/ *a* inventivo

**inventor** /ɪn'ventə(r)/ *n* inventore, -trice *mf*

**inventory** /'ɪnvəntrɪ/ *n* inventario *m*

**inverse** /ɪn'vɜ:s/ *a* inverso ● *n* inverso *m*

**inversely** /ɪn'vɜ:slɪ/ *adv* inversamente

**invert** /ɪn'vɜ:t/ *vt* invertire; **in ~ed commas** tra virgolette

**invertebrate** /ɪn'vɜ:tɪbrət/ *a & n* invertebrato *m*

**invest** /ɪn'vest/ *vt* investire ● *vi* fare investimenti; **~ in** (*fam: buy*) comprarsi

**investigate** /ɪn'vestɪgeɪt/ *vt* investigare

**investigation** /ɪnvestɪ'geɪʃn/ *n* investigazione *f*

**investigative journalism** /ɪn'vestɪgətɪv/ *n* dietrologia *f*

**investiture** /ɪn'vestɪtjə(r)/ *n* investitura *f*

**investment** /ɪn'vestmənt/ *n* investimento *m*

**investment: investment capital** *n* capitale *m* di investimento. **investment income** *n* reddito *m* da investimenti. **investment trust** *n* fondo *m* comune di investimento

**investor** /ɪn'vestə(r)/ *n* investitore, -trice *mf*

**inveterate** /ɪn'vetərət/ *a* inveterato

**invidious** /ɪn'vɪdɪəs/ *a* ingiusto; ‹*position*› antipatico

**invigilate** /ɪn'vɪdʒɪleɪt/ *vi* Sch sorvegliare lo svolgimento di un esame

**invigilator** /ɪn'vɪdʒɪleɪtə(r)/ *n* persona *f che sorveglia lo svolgimento di un esame*

**invigorate** /ɪn'vɪɡəreɪt/ *vt* rinvigorire

**invigorating** /ɪn'vɪɡəreɪtɪŋ/ *a* tonificante

**invincible** /ɪn'vɪnsəbl/ *a* invincibile

**inviolable** /ɪn'vaɪələbl/ *a* inviolabile

**invisible** /ɪn'vɪzəbl/ *a* invisibile

**invisible ink** *n* inchiostro *m* simpatico

**invitation** /ɪnvɪ'teɪʃn/ *n* invito *m*

**invite** /ɪn'vaɪt/ *vt* invitare; ‹*attract*› attirare
■ **invite in** *vt* invitare a entrare
■ **invite round** *vt* invitare a casa

**inviting** /ɪn'vaɪtɪŋ/ *a* invitante

**in vitro fertilization** /ɪnvi:trəʊfɜ:tɪlaɪ'zeɪʃn/ *n* fecondazione *f* in vitro

**invoice** /'ɪnvɔɪs/ *n* fattura *f* ● *vt* ~ **sb** emettere una fattura a qcno

**invoke** /ɪn'vəʊk/ *vt* invocare

**involuntarily** /ɪn'vɒləntərɪlɪ/ *adv* involontariamente

**involuntary** /ɪn'vɒləntrɪ/ *a* involontario

**involve** /ɪn'vɒlv/ *vt* comportare; ‹*affect, include*› coinvolgere; ‹*entail*› implicare; **get ~d with sb** legarsi a qcno; ‹*romantically*› legarsi sentimentalmente a qcno

**involved** /ɪn'vɒlvd/ *a* complesso

**involvement** /ɪn'vɒlvmənt/ *n* coinvolgimento *m*

**invulnerable** /ɪn'vʌln(ə)rəbl/ *a* invulnerabile; ‹*position*› inattaccabile

**inward** /'ɪnwəd/ *a* interno; ‹*thoughts etc*› interiore

**inward investment** *n* Comm investimento *m* di capitali stranieri

**inward-looking** /'ɪnwədlʊkɪŋ/ *a* ‹*person*› egocentrico; ‹*society, policy*› chiuso

**inwardly** /'ɪnwədlɪ/ *adv* interiormente

**inward[s]** /'ɪnwəd[z]/ *adv* verso l'interno

**iodine** /'aɪədi:n/ *n* iodio *m*

**Ionian Sea** /aɪəʊnɪən/ *n* mar *m* Ionio

**iota** /aɪ'əʊtə/ *n* briciolo *m*

**IOU** *abbr* (**I owe you**) pagherò *m inv*

**IPA** *n abbr* (**International Phonetic Alphabet**) AFI *m*

**IQ** *abbr* (**intelligence quotient**) Q.I. *m*

**IRA** *abbr* (**Irish Republican Army**) I.R.A. *f*

**Iran** /ɪ'rɑ:n/ *n* Iran *m*

**Iranian** /ɪ'reɪnɪən/ *a & n* iraniano, -a *mf*

**Iraq** /ɪ'rɑ:k/ *n* Iraq *m*

**Iraqi** /ɪ'rɑ:kɪ/ *a & n* iracheno, -a *mf*

**irascible** /ɪ'ræsəbl/ *a* irascibile

**irate** /aɪ'reɪt/ *a* adirato

**Ireland** /'aɪələnd/ *n* Irlanda *f*

**iris** /'aɪrɪs/ *n* Anat iride *f*; Bot iris *f inv*

**Irish** /'aɪrɪʃ/ *a* irlandese ● *n* **the ~** *pl* gli irlandesi

**Irishman** /'aɪrɪʃmən/ *n* irlandese *m*

**Irishwoman** /'aɪrɪʃwʊmən/ *n* irlandese *f*

**irk** /ɜ:k/ *vt* infastidire

**irksome** /'ɜ:ksəm/ *a* fastidioso

**iron** /'aɪən/ *a* di ferro ● *n* ferro *m*; ‹*appliance*› ferro *m* [da stiro] ● *vt/i* stirare
■ **iron out** *vt* eliminare stirando; *fig* appianare

**Iron Curtain** *n* cortina *f* di ferro

**iron fist** *n fig* pugno *m* di ferro

**ironic[al]** /aɪ'rɒnɪk[l]/ *a* ironico

**ironing** /'aɪənɪŋ/ *n* stirare *m*; ‹*articles*› roba *f* da stirare; **do the ~** stirare

**ironing board** *n* asse *f* da stiro

**iron lung** *n* polmone *m* d'acciaio

**ironmonger** /'aɪənmʌŋɡə(r)/ *n* **~'s [shop]** negozio *m* di ferramenta

**irony** /'aɪərənɪ/ *n* ironia *f*

**irradiate** /ɪ'reɪdɪeɪt/ *vt* irradiare

**irrational** /ɪ'ræʃənl/ *a* irrazionale

**irreconcilable** /ɪ'rekənsaɪləbl/ *a* irreconciliabile

**irrecoverable** /ɪrɪ'kʌv(ə)rəbl/ *a* ‹*debt, object*› irrecuperabile; ‹*loss*› irreparabile

**irredeemable** /ɪrɪ'di:məbl/ *a* ‹*Fin: shares, loan*› irredimibile; ‹*loss*› irreparabile; ‹*Relig: sinner*› che non è redimibile

**irrefutable** /ɪrɪ'fju:təbl/ *a* irrefutabile

**irregular** /ɪ'reɡʊlə(r)/ *a* irregolare

**irregularity** /ɪreɡʊ'lærətɪ/ *n* irregolarità *f inv*

**irregularly** /ɪ'reɡʊləlɪ/ *adv* in modo irregolare

**irrelevant** /ɪ'reləvənt/ *a* non pertinente

**irreparable** /ɪ'repərəbl/ *a* irreparabile

**irreparably** /ɪ'rep(ə)rəblɪ/ *adv* irreparabilmente

**irreplaceable** /ɪrɪ'pleɪsəbl/ *a* insostituibile

**irrepressible** /ɪrɪ'presəbl/ *a* irrefrenabile; ‹*person*› incontenibile

**irreproachable** /ɪrɪ'prəʊtʃəbl/ *a* irreprensibile

**irresistible** /ɪrɪ'zɪstəbl/ *a* irresistibile

**irresolute** /ɪ'rezəlu:t/ *a* irresoluto

**irrespective** /ɪrɪ'spektɪv/ *a* **~ of** senza riguardo per

**irresponsible** /ɪrɪ'spɒnsəbl/ *a* irresponsabile

**irresponsibly** /ɪrɪ'spɒnsəblɪ/ *adv* irresponsabilmente

**irretrievable** /ɪrɪ'tri:vəbl/ *a* ‹*loss, harm*› irreparabile

**irreverence** /ɪ'revərəns/ *n* irriverenza *f*

**irreverent** /ɪ'revərənt/ *a* irriverente

**irreverently** /ɪ'revərəntlɪ/ *adv* in modo irreverente

**irreversible** /ɪrɪ'vɜ:səbl/ *a* irreversibile

**irreversibly** /ɪrɪ'vɜ:sɪblɪ/ *adv* irreversibilmente

**irrevocable** /ɪ'revəkəbl/ *a* irrevocabile

**irrevocably** /ɪ'revəkəblɪ/ *adv* irrevocabilmente

**irrigate** /'ɪrɪɡeɪt/ *vt* irrigare

**irrigation** /ɪrɪ'ɡeɪʃn/ *n* irrigazione *f*

**irritability** /ɪrɪtə'bɪlətɪ/ *n* irritabilità *f*

**irritable** /'ɪrɪtəbl/ *a* irritabile

**irritant** /'ɪrɪtənt/ n sostanza f irritante: (*fig: person*) persona f irritante
**irritate** /'ɪrɪteɪt/ vt irritare
**irritated** /'ɪrɪteɪtɪd/ a irritato, stizzito
**irritating** /'ɪrɪteɪtɪŋ/ a irritante
**irritation** /ɪrɪ'teɪʃn/ n irritazione f
**is** /ɪz/ see **be**
**Islam** /'ɪzlɑ:m/ n Islam m
**Islamic** /ɪz'læmɪk/ a islamico
**island** /'aɪlənd/ n isola f; (*in road*) isola f spartitraffico
**islander** /'aɪləndə(r)/ n isolano, -a mf
**island hopping** /'aɪləndhɒpɪŋ/ n **go ~ ~** andare di isola in isola
**isle** /aɪl/ n liter isola f
**isms** /'ɪz(ə)mz/ npl pej ismi mpl
**isobar** /'aɪsəbɑ:(r)/ n isobara f
**isolate** /'aɪsəleɪt/ vt isolare
**isolated** /'aɪsəleɪtɪd/ a isolato
**isolation** /aɪsə'leɪʃn/ n isolamento m
**isosceles** /aɪ'sɒsəli:z/ a isoscele
**Israel** /'ɪzreɪl/ n Israele m
**Israeli** /ɪz'reɪlɪ/ a & n israeliano, -a mf
**issue** /'ɪʃu:/ n (*outcome*) risultato m; (*of magazine*) numero m; (*of stamps etc*) emissione f; (*offspring*) figli mpl; (*matter, question*) questione f; **at ~** in questione; **take ~ with sb** prendere posizione contro qcno ● vt distribuire ⟨*supplies*⟩; rilasciare ⟨*passport*⟩; emettere ⟨*stamps, order*⟩; pubblicare ⟨*book*⟩; **be ~d with sth** ricevere qcsa ● vi **~ from** uscire da
**isthmus** /'ɪsməs/ n (*pl* **-muses**) istmo m
**it** /ɪt/ pron (*direct object*) lo m, la f; (*indirect object*) gli m, le f; (*subject*) esso; **will it be enough?** basterà?; **it's hot** fa caldo; **it's raining** piove; **it's me** sono io; **who is it?** chi è?; **it's two o'clock** sono le due; **I doubt it** ne dubito; **take it with you** prendilo con te; **give it a wipe** dagli una pulita

**IT** n abbr (**information technology**) informatica f
**Italian** /ɪ'tæljən/ a & n italiano, -a mf; (*language*) italiano m
**italic** /ɪ'tælɪk/ a in corsivo
**italics** /ɪ'tælɪks/ npl corsivo msg; **in ~** in corsivo
**Italy** /'ɪtəlɪ/ n Italia f
**itch** /ɪtʃ/ n prurito m ● vi avere prurito, prudere; **be ~ing to** fam avere una voglia matta di
**itching powder** /'ɪtʃɪŋ/ n polverina f che dà prurito
**itchy** /'ɪtʃɪ/ a che prude; **my foot is ~** ho prurito al piede; **have ~ feet** fig avere la terra che scotta sotto i piedi
**item** /'aɪtəm/ n articolo m; (*on agenda, programme*) punto m; (*on invoice*) voce f; **~ [of news]** notizia f
**itemize** /'aɪtəmaɪz/ vt dettagliare ⟨*bill*⟩
**itinerant** /aɪ'tɪnərənt/ a itinerante
**itinerary** /aɪ'tɪnərərɪ/ n itinerario m
**its** /ɪts/ poss pron suo m, sua f, suoi mpl, sue fpl; **~ mother/cage** sua madre/la sua gabbia
**it's** = **it is, it has**
**itself** /ɪt'self/ pron (*reflexive*) si; (*emphatic*) essa stessa; **the baby looked at ~ in the mirror** il bambino si è guardato nello specchio; **by ~** da solo; **the machine in ~ is simple** la macchina di per sé è semplice
**ITV** abbr (**Independent Television**) stazione f televisiva privata
**IUD** n abbr (**intrauterine device**) spirale f
**IVF** n abbr **in vitro fertilization**
**ivory** /'aɪvərɪ/ n avorio m ● attrib d'avorio
**Ivory Coast** n Costa f d'Avorio
**ivory tower** n fig torre f d'avorio
**ivy** /'aɪvɪ/ n edera f

**j, J** /dʒeɪ/ n (*letter*)j, J f inv
**jab** /dʒæb/ n colpo m secco; (*fam: injection*) puntura f ● vt (*pt/pp* **jabbed**) punzecchiare
**jabber** /'dʒæbə(r)/ vi borbottare
**jack** /dʒæk/ n Auto cric m inv; Teleph jack m inv; (*in cards*) fante m, jack m inv
  ■ **jack in** vt sl piantare ⟨*job*⟩
  ■ **jack up** vt Auto sollevare [con il cric]; fam aumentare di molto ⟨*salary etc*⟩
**jackal** /'dʒæk(ə)l/ n sciacallo m
**jackboot** /'dʒækbu:t/ n stivale m militare
**jackdaw** /'dʒækdɔ:/ n taccola f
**jacket** /'dʒækɪt/ n giacca f; (*of book*) sopraccoperta f

**jacket potato** n patata f cotta al forno con la buccia
**jack-in-the-box** n scatola f a sorpresa contenente un pupazzo a molla
**jackknife** /'dʒæknaɪf/ n coltello m a serramanico ● vi sbandare finendo di traverso rispetto al rimorchio
**jackpot** /'dʒækpɒt/ n premio m (*di una lotteria*); **win the ~** vincere alla lotteria; **hit the ~** fig fare un colpo grosso
**jackrabbit** /'dʒækræbɪt/ n lepre f americana
**jade** /dʒeɪd/ n giada f ● attrib di giada
**jaded** /'dʒeɪdɪd/ a spossato
**jagged** /'dʒægɪd/ a dentellato

**jail** /dʒeɪl/ = **gaol**

**jail:** **jailbird** n avanzo m di galera. **jailbreak** n evasione f. **jail sentence** n condanna f al carcere

**jalopy** /dʒə'lɒpɪ/ n fam vecchia carretta f

**jam¹** /dʒæm/ n marmellata f

**jam²** n Auto ingorgo m; (fam: difficulty) guaio m ● v (pt/pp **jammed**) ● vt (cram) pigiare; disturbare (broadcast); inceppare (mechanism, drawer etc); **be** ~**med** (roads:) essere congestionato ● vi (mechanism:) incepparsi; (window, drawer:) incastrarsi

■ **jam on** vt ~ **on the brakes** inchiodare

**Jamaica** /dʒə'meɪkə/ n Giamaica f

**Jamaican** /dʒə'meɪkən/ a & n giamaicano, -a mf

**jam:** **jam jar** n barattolo m per la marmellata. **jam-packed** a fam pieno zeppo. **jampot** n vasetto m per la marmellata

**jangle** /'dʒæŋgl/ vt far squillare ● vi squillare

**janitor** /'dʒænɪtə(r)/ n (caretaker) custode m; (in school) bidello, -a mf

**January** /'dʒænjʊərɪ/ n gennaio m

**Japan** /dʒə'pæn/ n Giappone m

**Japanese** /dʒæpə'niːz/ a & n giapponese mf; (language) giapponese m

**jar¹** /dʒɑː(r)/ n (glass) barattolo m

**jar²** vi (pt/pp **jarred**) (sound:) stridere

**jargon** /'dʒɑːgən/ n gergo m

**jarring** /'dʒɑːrɪŋ/ a stridente

**jasmine** /'dʒæsmɪn/ n gelsomino m

**jaundice** /'dʒɔːndɪs/ n itterizia f

**jaundiced** /'dʒɔːndɪst/ a fig inacidito

**jaunt** /dʒɔːnt/ n gita f

**jaunty** /'dʒɔːntɪ/ a (-ier, -iest) sbarazzino

**javelin** /'dʒævlɪn/ n giavellotto m

**jaw** /dʒɔː/ n mascella f; (bone) mandibola f ● vi fam ciarlare

**jawbone** /'dʒɔːbəʊn/ n Anat osso m mascellare

**jaywalker** /'dʒeɪwɔːkə(r)/ n pedone m indisciplinato

**jazz** /dʒæz/ n jazz m

■ **jazz up** vt ravvivare

**jazz band** n complesso m di jazz

**jazzy** /'dʒæzɪ/ a vistoso

**jealous** /'dʒeləs/ a geloso

**jealously** /'dʒeləslɪ/ adv gelosamente

**jealousy** /'dʒeləsɪ/ n gelosia f

**jeans** /dʒiːnz/ npl [blue] jeans mpl

**jeep** /dʒiːp/ n jeep f inv

**jeer** /dʒɪə(r)/ n scherno m ● vi schernire; ~ **at** prendersi gioco di ● vt (boo) fischiare

**jell** /dʒel/ vi concretarsi

**jellied** /'dʒelɪd/ a (eels) in gelatina

**jelly** /'dʒelɪ/ n gelatina f

**jelly:** **jelly baby** n caramella f gommosa a forma di pupazzetto. **jelly bean** n caramella f di gelatina di frutta. **jellyfish** n medusa f

**jemmy** /'dʒemɪ/ n piede m di porco

**jeopardize** /'dʒepədaɪz/ vt mettere in pericolo

**jeopardy** /'dʒepədɪ/ n **in** ~ in pericolo

**jerk** /dʒɜːk/ n scatto m, scossa f ● vt scattare

● vi sobbalzare; (limb, muscle:) muoversi a scatti

**jerkily** /'dʒɜːkɪlɪ/ adv a scatti

**jerkin** /'dʒɜːkɪn/ n gilè m inv

**jerky** /'dʒɜːkɪ/ a traballante

**jerry-built** /'dʒerɪbɪlt/ a pej costruito alla bell'e meglio

**jersey** /'dʒɜːzɪ/ n maglia f; Sport maglietta f; (fabric) jersey m

**Jerusalem** /dʒə'ruːsələm/ n Gerusalemme f

**jest** /dʒest/ n scherzo m; **in** ~ per scherzo ● vi scherzare

**jester** /'dʒestə(r)/ n buffone m

**Jesuit** /'dʒezjʊɪt/ n gesuita m ● a gesuitico

**Jesus** /'dʒiːzəs/ n Gesù m

**jet¹** /dʒet/ n (stone) giaietto m

**jet²** n (of water) getto m; (nozzle) becco m; (plane) aviogetto m, jet m inv

**jet:** **jet-black** a nero ebano. **jet engine** n motore m a reazione. **jet fighter** n caccia m inv a reazione. **jetfoil** n aliscafo m. **jet lag** n scombussolamento m da fuso orario. **jet-propelled** /-prə'peld/ a a reazione. **jet propulsion** n propulsione f a getto

**jettison** /'dʒetɪsn/ vt gettare a mare; fig abbandonare

**jetty** /'dʒetɪ/ n molo m

**Jew** /dʒuː/ n ebreo m

**jewel** /'dʒuːəl/ n gioiello m

**jewelled** /'dʒuːəld/ a ornato di pietre preziose

**jeweller** /'dʒuːələ(r)/ n gioielliere m; ~**'s** [shop] gioielleria f

**jewellery** /'dʒuːəlrɪ/ n gioielli mpl

**Jewess** /'dʒuːɪs/ n ebrea f

**Jewish** /'dʒuːɪʃ/ a ebreo

**Jew's harp** n Mus scacciapensieri m inv

**jib** /dʒɪb/ vi (pt/pp **jibbed**) fig mostrarsi riluttante (**at** a)

**jibe** /dʒaɪb/ n see **gibe**

**jiffy** /'dʒɪfɪ/ n fam **in a** ~ in un batter d'occhio

**Jiffy bag®** n busta f imbottita

**jig** /dʒɪg/ n Mus giga f (danza popolare)

**jiggle** /'dʒɪg(ə)l/ vt scuotere

**jigsaw** /'dʒɪgsɔː/ n ~ [**puzzle**] puzzle m inv

**jilt** /dʒɪlt/ vt piantare

**jingle** /'dʒɪŋgl/ n (rhyme) canzoncina f pubblicitaria ● vi tintinnare ● vt far tintinnare

**jingoist** /'dʒɪŋgəʊɪst/ n Pol sciovinista mf

**jingoistic** /dʒɪŋgəʊ'ɪstɪk/ a Pol sciovinistico

**jinx** /dʒɪŋks/ n fam (person) iettatore, -trice mf; **it's got a** ~ **on it** è iellato

**jinxed** /dʒɪŋkst/ a **be** ~ essere iellato

**jitters** /'dʒɪtəz/ npl fam **have the** ~ aver una gran fifa

**jittery** /'dʒɪtərɪ/ a fam in preda alla fifa

**jive** /dʒaɪv/ n (Am fam: talk) storie fpl

**Jnr** abbr **junior**

**job** /dʒɒb/ n lavoro m; **this is going to be quite a** ~ fam [questa] non sarà un'impresa facile; **it's a good** ~ **that ...** meno male che...

**job:** **jobcentre** n ufficio m statale di collocamento. **job description** n mansionario m. **job-hunting** n ricerca f impiego

**jobless** /'dʒɒblɪs/ a senza lavoro

**job: job lot** n (*at auction*) insieme m di oggetti disparati. **job satisfaction** n soddisfazione f nel lavoro. **job security** n sicurezza f di impiego. **job-share** n (*position*) posto m condiviso ● attrib (*scheme*) di condivisione del posto di lavoro. **job-sharing** /-'ʃeərɪŋ/ n job sharing m inv

**jockey** /'dʒɒkɪ/ n fantino m

**jocular** /'dʒɒkjʊlə(r)/ a scherzoso

**jocularly** /'dʒɒkjʊləlɪ/ adv scherzosamente

**jodhpurs** /'dʒɒdpəz/ npl calzoni mpl alla cavallerizza

**Joe Bloggs** /dʒəʊ'blɒgz/ n l'uomo qualunque

**jog** /'dʒɒg/ n colpetto m; **at a ~** in un balzo: Sport **go for a ~** andare a fare jogging ● v (pt/pp **jogged**) ● vt (hit) urtare; **~ sb's memory** farlo ritornare in mente a qcno ● vi Sport fare jogging

■ **jog along** vi fig tirare avanti

**jogging** /'dʒɒgɪŋ/ n jogging m

**john** /dʒɒn/ n (Am fam: toilet) gabinetto m

**John Bull** n il tipico inglese

**John Doe** n Am uomo m non identificato

**join** /dʒɔɪn/ n giuntura f ● vt raggiungere, unire; raggiungere ⟨person⟩; (become member of) iscriversi a; entrare in ⟨firm⟩ ● vi ⟨roads:⟩ congiungersi

■ **join in** vi partecipare

■ **join up** vi Mil arruolarsi ● vt unire

■ **join up with** vt (meet) raggiungere ⟨friends⟩; congiungersi a ⟨road, river⟩

**joiner** /'dʒɔɪnə(r)/ n falegname m

**joint** /dʒɔɪnt/ a comune ● n articolazione f; (in wood, brickwork) giuntura f; Culin arrosto m; (fam: bar) bettola f; (sl: drug) spinello m

**joint account** n conto m [corrente] comune

**joint agreement** n accordo m collettivo

**jointed** /'dʒɔɪntɪd/ a ⟨Culin, chicken⟩ tagliato a pezzi; ⟨doll, puppet⟩ snodabile; ⟨rod, pole⟩ smontabile

**joint effort** n collaborazione f

**joint honours** npl Br Univ laurea f in due discipline

**jointly** /'dʒɔɪntlɪ/ adv unitamente

**joint owner** n comproprietario, -a mf

**joint venture** n joint venture f inv

**joist** /dʒɔɪst/ n travetto m

**joke** /dʒəʊk/ n (trick) scherzo m; (funny story) barzelletta f ● vi scherzare

**joker** /'dʒəʊkə(r)/ n burlone, -a mf; (in cards) jolly m inv

**joking** /'dʒəʊkɪŋ/ n **~ apart** scherzi a parte

**jokingly** /'dʒəʊkɪŋlɪ/ adv per scherzo

**jollity** /'dʒɒlətɪ/ n allegria f

**jolly** /'dʒɒlɪ/ a (**-ier, -iest**) allegro ● adv fam molto

**Jolly Roger** /'rɒdʒə(r)/ n bandiera f dei pirati

**jolt** /dʒəʊlt/ n scossa f, sobbalzo m ● vt far sobbalzare ● vi sobbalzare

**Jordan** /'dʒɔ:dn/ n Giordania f; (river) Giordano m

**Jordanian** /dʒɔ:'deɪnɪən/ a & n giordano, -a mf

**joss stick** /'dʒɒs/ n bastoncino m d'incenso

**jostle** /'dʒɒsl/ vt spingere

**jot** /dʒɒt/ n nulla f

■ **jot down** vt (pt/pp **jotted**) annotare

**jotter** /'dʒɒtə(r)/ n taccuino m; (with a spine) quaderno m

**jottings** /'dʒɒtɪŋz/ npl annotazioni fpl

**journal** /'dʒɜ:nl/ n giornale m; (diary) diario m

**journalese** /dʒɜ:nə'li:z/ n gergo m giornalistico

**journalism** /'dʒɜ:nəlɪzm/ n giornalismo m

**journalist** /'dʒɜ:nəlɪst/ n giornalista mf

**journey** /'dʒɜ:nɪ/ n viaggio m ● vi viaggiare

**jovial** /'dʒəʊvɪəl/ a gioviale

**jowl** /dʒaʊl/ n (jaw) mascella f; (fleshy fold) guancia f; **cheek by ~ with sb** fianco a fianco con qcno

**joy** /dʒɔɪ/ n gioia f

**joyful** /'dʒɔɪfʊl/ a gioioso

**joyfully** /'dʒɔɪfʊlɪ/ adv con gioia

**joyless** /'dʒɔɪlɪs/ a ⟨occasion⟩ triste; ⟨marriage⟩ infelice

**joy: joyride** n fam giro m con una macchina rubata. **joyrider** n fam persona f che ruba una macchina per andare a fare un giro. **joystick** n Comput joystick m inv

**Jr** abbr **junior**

**jubilant** /'dʒu:bɪlənt/ a giubilante

**jubilation** /dʒu:br'leɪʃn/ n giubilo m

**jubilee** /'dʒu:bɪli:/ n giubileo m

**Judaism** /'dʒu:deɪɪzm/ n giudaismo m

**judder** /'dʒʌdə(r)/ vi vibrare violentemente

**judge** /dʒʌdʒ/ n giudice m ● vt giudicare; (estimate) valutare; (consider) ritenere ● vi giudicare (**by** da)

**judgement** /'dʒʌdʒmənt/ n giudizio m; Jur sentenza f

**judicial** /dʒu:'dɪʃl/ a giudiziario

**judiciary** /dʒu:'dɪʃərɪ/ n magistratura f

**judicious** /dʒu:'dɪʃəs/ a giudizioso

**judo** /'dʒu:dəʊ/ n judo m

**jug** /dʒʌg/ n brocca f; (small) bricco m

**juggernaut** /'dʒʌgənɔ:t/ n fam grosso autotreno m

**juggle** /'dʒʌgl/ vi fare giochi di destrezza

**juggler** /'dʒʌglə(r)/ n giocoliere, -a mf

**jugular** /'dʒʌgjʊlə(r)/ n giugulare f; **go straight for the ~** fig colpire nel punto debole

**juice** /dʒu:s/ n succo m; **~ extractor** n spremiagrumi m inv elettrico

**juicy** /'dʒu:sɪ/ a (**-ier, -iest**) succoso; (fam: story) piccante

**jukebox** /'dʒu:kbɒks/ n juke-box m inv

**July** /dʒu'laɪ/ n luglio m

**jumble** /'dʒʌmbl/ n accozzaglia f ● vt **~ [up]** mischiare

**jumble sale** n vendita f di beneficenza

**jumbo** /'dʒʌmbəʊ/ n **~ [jet]** jumbo jet m inv

**jump** /dʒʌmp/ n salto m; (in prices) balzo m; (in horse racing) ostacolo m ● vi saltare; (with fright) sussultare; ⟨prices:⟩ salire rapidamente; **~ to conclusions** saltare alle conclusioni ● *vt* saltare; **~ the gun** *fig* precipitarsi; **~ the queue** non rispettare la fila

■ **jump at** *vt fig* accettare con entusiasmo ⟨*offer*⟩

■ **jump down** *vt* **~ down sb's throat** saltare addosso a qcno

■ **jump in** *vi* (*to vehicle*) saltar su

■ **jump up** *vi* rizzarsi in piedi

**jumped-up** /dʒʌmpt'ʌp/ *a* montato

**jumper** /'dʒʌmpə(r)/ *n* (*sweater*) golf *m inv*

**jump: jump jet** *n* aeroplano *m* a decollo e atterraggio verticali. **jump leads** *npl* cavi *mpl* per batteria. **jump-start** *vt far partire con i cavi da batteria*. **jumpsuit** *n* tuta *f*

**jumpy** /'dʒʌmpɪ/ *a* nervoso

**junction** /'dʒʌŋkʃn/ *n* (*of roads*) incrocio *m*; *Rail* nodo *m* ferroviario

**juncture** /'dʒʌŋktʃə(r)/ *n* **at this ~** a questo punto

**June** /dʒuːn/ *n* giugno *m*

**Jungian** /'jʊŋɪən/ *a* junghiano

**jungle** /'dʒʌŋgl/ *n* giungla *f*

**junior** /'dʒuːnɪə(r)/ *a* giovane; (*in rank*) subalterno; *Sport* junior *inv* ● *n* **the ~s** *pl Sch* i più giovani

**junior doctor** *n* assistente *mf* ospedaliero, -a

**junior school** *n* scuola *f* elementare

**juniper** /'dʒuːnɪpə(r)/ *n* ginepro *m*

**junk** /dʒʌŋk/ *n* cianfrusaglie *fpl*

**junk food** *n fam* cibo *m* poco sano, porcherie *fpl*

**junkie** /'dʒʌŋkɪ/ *n sl* tossico, -a *mf*

**junk: junk mail** *n* posta *f* spazzatura. **junk shop** *n* negozio *m* di rigattiere. **junkyard** *n* (*for scrap*) rottamaio *m*; (*for old cars*) cimitero *m* delle macchine

**junta** /'dʒʌntə/ *n* giunta *f* militare

**jurisdiction** /dʒʊərɪs'dɪkʃn/ *n* giurisdizione *f*

**jurisprudence** /dʒʊrɪs'pruːdəns/ *n* giurisprudenza *f*

**jurist** /'dʒʊərɪst/ *n* giurista *mf*

**juror** /'dʒʊərə(r)/ *n* giurato. -a *mf*

**jury** /'dʒʊərɪ/ *n* giuria *f*

**jury box** *n* banco *m* dei giurati

**jury service** *n* do **~ ~** far parte di una giuria popolare

**just** /dʒʌst/ *a* giusto ● *adv* (*barely*) appena; (*simply*) solo; (*exactly*) esattamente; **~ as tall** altrettanto alto; **~ as I was leaving** proprio quando stavo andando via; **I've ~ seen her** l'ho appena vista; **it's ~ as well** meno male; **~ at that moment** proprio in quel momento; **~ listen!** almeno ascolta!; **I'm ~ going** sto andando proprio ora

**justice** /'dʒʌstɪs/ *n* giustizia *f*; do **~** to rendere giustizia a; **J~ of the Peace** giudice *m* conciliatore

**justifiable** /dʒʌstɪ'faɪəbl/ *a* giustificabile

**justifiably** /dʒʌstɪ'faɪəblɪ/ *adv* in modo giustificato

**justification** /dʒʌstɪfɪ'keɪʃn/ *n* giustificazione *f*

**justified** /'dʒʌstɪfaɪd/ *a* ⟨*action*⟩ motivato

**justify** /'dʒʌstɪfaɪ/ *vt* (*pt/pp* -ied) giustificare

**justly** /'dʒʌstlɪ/ *adv* giustamente

**justness** /'dʒʌstnɪs/ *n* (*of decision*) giustezza *f*; (*of claim, request*) legittimità *f*

**jut** /dʒʌt/ *vi* (*pt/pp* jutted) **~ out** sporgere

**jute** /dʒuːt/ *n* iuta *f*

**juvenile** /'dʒuːvənaɪl/ *a* giovanile; (*childish*) infantile; (*for the young*) per i giovani ● *n* giovane *mf*

**juvenile: juvenile crime** *n* criminalità *f* presso i giovani . **juvenile delinquency** *n* delinquenza *f* giovanile. **juvenile delinquent** *n* delinquente *mf* minorile. **juvenile offender** *n Jur* imputato, -a *mf* minorenne

**juxtapose** /dʒʌkstə'pəʊz/ *vt* giustapporre

# Kk

**k, K** /keɪ/ *n* (*letter*) k, K *f inv*

**K** *abbr* (**kilo**) k; *abbr* (**kilobyte**) KB, Kbyte *m inv*; *abbr* **thousand pounds**; **he earns £50 K** guadagna 50 mila sterline

**kaleidoscope** /kə'laɪdəskəʊp/ *n* caleidoscopio *m*

**kangaroo** /kæŋgə'ruː/ *n* canguro *m*

**kaput** /kə'pʊt/ *a fam* kaput *inv*

**karaoke** /kærɪ'əʊkɪ/ *n* karaoke *m inv*

**karate** /kə'rɑːtɪ/ *n* karatè *m*

**kart** /kɑːt/ *n* kart *m inv*

**Kashmir** /kæʃ'mɪə(r)/ *n* Kashmir *m*

**Kashmiri** /kæʃ'mɪərɪ/ *a* del Kashmir ● *n* nativo, -a *mf* del Kashmir

**kayak** /'kaɪæk/ *n* kayak *m inv*

**KB** *n abbr* (**kilobyte**) KB, Kbyte *m inv*

**kebab** /kɪ'bæb/ *n Culin* spiedino *m* di carne

**kedgeree** /'kedʒərɪ/ *n Br piatto m indiano a base di pesce, riso e uova*

**keel** /kiːl/ *n* chiglia *f*

■ **keel over** *vi* capovolgersi

**keen** /kiːn/ *a* (*intense*) acuto; ⟨*interest*⟩ vivo; (*eager*) entusiastico; ⟨*competition*⟩ feroce; ⟨*wind, knife*⟩ tagliente; **~ on** entusiasta di; **she's ~ on him** le piace molto; **be ~ to do sth** avere voglia di fare qcsa

**keenly** /'kiːnlɪ/ *adv* intensamente

**keenness** /'kiːnnɪs/ *n* entusiasmo *m*

**keep** /ki:p/ *n* (*maintenance*) mantenimento *m*; (*of castle*) maschio *m*; **for ~s** per sempre ● *v* (*pt/pp* **kept**) ● *vt* tenere; (*not throw away*) conservare; (*detain*) trattenere; mantenere (*family, promise*); tenere (*shop*); allevare (*animals*); rispettare (*law, rules*); **~ sth hot** tenere qcsa in caldo; **~ sb waiting** far aspettare qcno; **~ sth to oneself** tenere qcsa per sé; ● *vi* (*remain*) rimanere; (*food:*) conservarsi; **~ calm** rimanere calmo; **~ left/right** tenere la sinistra/la destra; **~ [on] doing sth** continuare a fare qcsa

■ **keep at** *vt* (*persevere with*) **~ at it!** non mollare!

■ **keep away** *vi* non avvicinarsi, stare alla larga ● *vt* tenere lontano

■ **keep away from** *vt* non avvicinarsi a (*fire*); stare alla larga da (*sb*); **~ sb away from sth** tener qcno lontano da qcsa

■ **keep back** *vt* trattenere (*person*); **~ sth back from sb** tenere nascosto qcsa a qcno ● *vi* tenersi indietro

■ **keep down** *vi* star giù ● *vt* mandar giù (*food*); mantenere basso (*prices, inflation etc*); **~ one's voice down** non alzare la voce

■ **keep from** *vt* **~ sb from doing sth** prevenire qcno dal fare qcsa; **~ sb from** impedire a qcno di (*falling*); distogliere qcno dal lavoro; **~ sth from sb** tenere nascosto qcsa a qcno; **~ the truth from sb** nascondere la verità a qcno

■ **keep in** *vt* (*in school*) trattenere oltre l'orario per punizione; reprimere (*indignation, anger etc*)

■ **keep in with** *vt* mantenersi in buoni rapporti con

■ **keep off** *vt* (*avoid*) astenersi da (*cigarettes, chocolate etc*); evitare (*delicate subject*)

■ **keep on** *vi* (*continue one's journey*) proseguire; *fam* assillare (**at sb** qcno) ● *vt* non togliersi (*coat, hat*); tenere (*employee*)

■ **keep out of** *vt* (*person:*) non entrare in (*place*); tenersi fuori da (*argument*); **~ sb out of** tenere qcno alla larga da (*place*); **~ me out of this!** lasciamene fuori!

■ **keep to** *vt* non deviare da (*path, subject*); **~ sth to oneself** tenere qcsa per sé

■ **keep up** *vi* (*remain level*) stare al passo; (*rain, good weather:*) mantenersi ● *vt* (*continue*) continuare; (*prevent from going to bed*) tenere alzato; mantenere alto (*prices*); tener su (*trousers*)

**keeper** /'ki:pə(r)/ *n* custode *mf*

**keep-fit** *n* ginnastica *f*

**keeping** /'ki:pɪŋ/ *n* custodia *f*; **be in ~ with** essere in armonia con

**keepsake** /'ki:pseɪk/ *n* ricordo *m*

**keg** /keg/ *n* barilotto *m*

**kelp** /kelp/ *n* laminaria *f*, fuco *m*

**kennel** /'kenl/ *n* canile *m*; **~s** *pl* (*boarding*) canile *m*; (*breeding*) allevamento *m* di cani

**Kenya** /'kenjə/ *n* Kenia *m*

**Kenyan** /'kenjən/ *a* & *n* keniota *mf*

**kept** /kept/ *see* **keep**

**kerb** /kɜ:b/ *n* bordo *m* del marciapiede

**kernel** /'kɜ:nl/ *n* nocciolo *m*

**kerosene** /'kerəsi:n/ *n Am* cherosene *m*

**kestrel** /'kestrəl/ *n* gheppio *m*

**ketchup** /'ketʃʌp/ *n* ketchup *m*

**kettle** /'ket(ə)l/ *n* bollitore *m*; **put the ~ on** mettere l'acqua a bollire

**kettledrum** /'ket(ə)ldrʌm/ *n* timpano *m*

**key** /ki:/ *n also Mus* chiave *f*; (*of piano, typewriter*) tasto *m* ● *vt* **~ [in]** digitare (*character*); **could you ~ this?** puoi battere questo?

**key: keyboard** *n Comput, Mus* tastiera *f*. **keyboarder** *n* tastierista *mf*. **keyboard player** *n* tastierista *mf*

**keyed-up** /ki:d'ʌp/ *a* (*excited*) teso; (*anxious*) estremamente agitato; (*ready to act*) psicologicamente preparato

**key: keyhole** *n* buco *m* della serratura. **key money** *n* (*for apartment*) somma *f* richiesta ad un affittuario quando si trasferisce nell'abitazione. **keynote** *n Mus* tonica *f*; (*main theme*) tema *m* principale. **keynote speech** *n* discorso *m* programmatico. **keypad** *n Comput* tastiera *f* numerica. **keyring** *n* portachiavi *m inv*. **key signature** *n Mus* armatura *f* di chiave. **keystroke** *n Comput* keystroke *m inv*. **keyword** *n* parola *f* chiave

**kg** *abbr* (**kilogram**) kg

**khaki** /'kɑ:kɪ/ *a* cachi *inv* ● *n* cachi *m*

**kibbutz** /kɪ'bʊts/ *n* (*pl* **-es** *or* **-im**) kibbutz *m inv*

**kibosh** /'kaɪbɒʃ/ *n fam* **put the ~ on sth** mandare all'aria qcsa

**kick** /kɪk/ *n* calcio *m*; (*fam: thrill*) piacere *m*; **for ~s** *fam* per spasso; **get a ~ out of sth** trovare un piacere incredibile in qcsa ● *vt* dar calci a; **~ the bucket** *fam* crepare ● *vi* (*animal:*) scalciare; (*person:*) dare calci

■ **kick around** *vi fam* essere in giro ● *vt* buttar giù (*idea*)

■ **kick in** *vt* sfondare a calci (*door*)

■ **kick off** *vi Sport* dare il calcio d'inizio; *fam* iniziare

■ **kick out** *vt* (*fam: of school, club etc*) sbatter fuori

■ **kick up** *vt* **~ up a row** fare une scenata

**kickback** /'kɪkbæk/ *n fam* tangente *f*

**kick-off** *n Sport* calcio *m* d'inizio; **for a ~** *fam* tanto per cominciare

**kid** /kɪd/ *n* capretto *m*; (*fam: child*) ragazzino, -a *mf* ● *v* (*pt/pp* **kidded**) ● *vt fam* prendere in giro. ● *vi fam* scherzare

**kid gloves** *npl* guanti *mpl* di capretto; **handle sb with ~ ~** trattare qcno con i guanti

**kidnap** /'kɪdnæp/ *vt* (*pt/pp* **-napped**) rapire, sequestrare

**kidnapper** /'kɪdnæpə(r)/ *n* sequestratore, -trice *mf*, rapitore, -trice *mf*

**kidnapping** /'kɪdnæpɪŋ/ *n* rapimento *m*, sequestro *m* [di persona]

**kidney** /'kɪdnɪ/ *n* rene *m*; *Culin* rognone *m*

**kidney: kidney bean** *n* fagiolo *m* comune. **kidney dialysis** *n* dialisi *f*. **kidney failure** *n* collasso *m* renale. **kidney machine** *n* rene *m* artificiale. **kidney-shaped** /'kɪdnɪʃeɪpt/ a a forma di fagiolo. **kidney stone** n calcolo m renale

**kill** /kɪl/ vt uccidere; fig metter fine a; ammazzare ⟨time⟩

■ **kill off** vt eliminare ⟨people⟩; distruggere ⟨plants, insects⟩

**killer** /'kɪlə(r)/ n assassino, -a mf; **it was a real ~** fig è stato micidiale

**killer instinct** n istinto m di uccidere; fig spietatezza f

**killer whale** n orca f

**killing** /'kɪlɪŋ/ n uccisione f; ⟨murder⟩ omicidio m

**killjoy** /'kɪldʒɔɪ/ n guastafeste mf inv

**kiln** /kɪln/ n fornace f

**kilo** /'ki:ləʊ/ n chilo m

**kilo** /'kɪlə/: **~byte** kilobyte m inv. **kilogram** n chilogrammo m. **kilohertz** /'kɪləhɜ:ts/ n chilohertz m inv. **kilometre** n chilometro m. **kilowatt** n chilowatt m inv

**kilt** /kɪlt/ n kilt m inv ⟨gonnellino degli scozzesi⟩

**kimono** /kɪ'məʊnəʊ/ n kimono m inv, chimono m inv

**kin** /kɪn/ n congiunti mpl; **next of ~** parente m stretto

**kind¹** /kaɪnd/ n genere m, specie f; ⟨brand, type⟩ tipo m; **what ~ of car?** che tipo di macchina?; **~ of** fam alquanto; **two of a ~** due della stessa specie

**kind²** a gentile, buono; **~ to animals** amante degli animali; **~ regards** cordiali saluti

**kindergarten** /'kɪndəɡɑ:tn/ n asilo m infantile

**kind-hearted** /-'hɑ:tɪd/ a ⟨person⟩ di [buon] cuore

**kindle** /'kɪndl/ vt accendere

**kindly** /'kaɪndlɪ/ a (-**ier**, -**iest**) benevolo ● adv gentilmente; ⟨if you please⟩ per favore

**kindness** /'kaɪndnɪs/ n gentilezza f

**kindred** /'kɪndrɪd/ a **she's a ~ spirit** è la mia/sua/tua anima gemella

**kinetic** /kɪ'netɪk/ a cinetico

**king** /kɪŋ/ n re m inv

**kingdom** /'kɪŋdəm/ n regno m

**kingfisher** /'kɪŋfɪʃə(r)/ n martin m inv pescatore

**kingly** /'kɪŋlɪ/ a also fig regale

**king-sized** /'kɪŋsaɪzd/ a ⟨cigarette⟩ king-size inv, lungo; ⟨bed⟩ matrimoniale grande

**kink** /kɪŋk/ n attorcigliamento m

**kinky** /'kɪŋkɪ/ a fam bizzarro

**kinship** /'kɪnʃɪp/ n ⟨blood relationship⟩ parentela f; ⟨empathy⟩ affinità f

**kiosk** /'ki:ɒsk/ n chiosco m; Teleph cabina f telefonica

**kip** /kɪp/ n fam pisolino m; **have a ~** schiacciare un pisolino ● vi ⟨pt/pp **kipped**⟩ fam dormire

**kipper** /'kɪpə(r)/ n aringa f affumicata

**kirk** /kɜ:k/ n ⟨Scottish⟩ chiesa f

**kiss** /kɪs/ n bacio m ● vt baciare ● vi baciarsi

**kiss of death** n colpo m di grazia

**kiss of life** n respirazione f bocca a bocca;

**give sb the ~ ~ ~** fare la respirazione bocca a bocca a qcno

**kissogram** /'kɪsəɡræm/ n servizio m commerciale in cui un messaggio di auguri viene scherzosamente recapitato con un bacio da una ragazza in abiti succinti

**kit** /kɪt/ n equipaggiamento m, kit m inv; ⟨tools⟩ attrezzi mpl; ⟨construction ~⟩ pezzi mpl da montare, kit m inv ● vt ⟨pt/pp **kitted**⟩ **~ out** equipaggiare

**kitbag** /'kɪtbæɡ/ n sacco m a spalla

**kitchen** /'kɪtʃɪn/ n cucina f ● attrib di cucina

**kitchenette** /kɪtʃɪ'net/ n cucinino m

**kitchen: kitchen foil** n carta f di alluminio. **kitchen garden** n orto m. **kitchen paper** n carta f da cucina. **kitchen roll** n Scottex® m inv. **kitchen scales** npl bilancia f da cucina. **kitchensink** n lavello m; **everything bar the ~** fig proprio tutto quanto. **kitchen-sink drama** n teatro m neorealista. **kitchen towel** n Scottex® m inv. **kitchen unit** n elemento m componibile da cucina. **kitchenware** n ⟨crockery⟩ stoviglie fpl; ⟨implements⟩ utensili mpl da cucina

**kite** /kaɪt/ n aquilone m

**kitemark** /'kaɪtmɑ:k/ n Br marchio m di conformità alle norme britanniche

**kith** /kɪθ/ n **~ and kin** amici e parenti mpl

**kitsch** /kɪtʃ/ n kitsch m inv

**kitten** /'kɪtn/ n gattino m

**kitty** /'kɪtɪ/ n ⟨money⟩ cassa f comune

**kiwi** /'ki:wi:/ n Zool kiwi m inv

**kiwi fruit** n kiwi m inv

**kleptomania** /kleptə'meɪnɪə/ n cleptomania f

**kleptomaniac** /kleptə'meɪnɪæk/ n cleptomane mf

**km** abbr (**kilometre**) km

**kmh** abbr (**kilometres per hour**) km/h

**knack** /næk/ n tecnica f; **have the ~ for doing sth** avere la capacità di fare qcsa

**knapsack** /'næpsæk/ n sacco m da montagna

**knave** /neɪv/ m ⟨in cards⟩ fante m; ⟨rogue⟩ furfante m

**knead** /ni:d/ vt impastare

**knee** /ni:/ n ginocchio m; **go down on one's ~s to sb** inginocchiarsi davanti qcno

**kneecap** /'ni:kæp/ n rotula f

**kneel** /ni:l/ vi ⟨pt/pp **knelt**⟩ **~ [down]** inginocchiarsi; **be ~ing** essere inginocchiato

**knee-length** a ⟨boots⟩ alto; ⟨skirt⟩ al ginocchio; ⟨socks⟩ lungo

**knee-pad** n ginocchiera f

**knees-up** /'ni:zʌp/ n Br fam festa f

**knell** /nel/ n campana f a morto; **sound the death ~ for sth** segnare la fine di qcsa

**knelt** /nelt/ see **kneel**

**knew** /nju:/ see **know**

**knickerbocker glory** /nɪkəbɒkə'ɡlɔ:rɪ/ n coppa f [gelato] gigante

**knickers** /'nɪkəz/ npl mutandine fpl

**knick-knacks** /'nɪknæks/ npl ninnoli mpl

**knife** /naɪf/ n ⟨pl **knives**⟩ coltello m ● vt fam accoltellare

**knife: knife-edge** n **be on a ~** ‹person:› trovarsi sul filo del rasoio; ‹negotiations:› essere appeso a un filo. **knifepoint** n **at ~** sotto la minaccia di un coltello. **knife sharpener** n affilacoltelli m inv

**knight** /naɪt/ n cavaliere m; (in chess) cavallo m ● vt nominare cavaliere

**knighthood** /'naɪthʊd/ n **receive a ~** ricevere il titolo di cavaliere

**knit** /nɪt/ vt/i (pt/pp **knitted**) lavorare a maglia; **~ one, purl one** un diritto, un rovescio; **~ one's brow** aggrottare le sopracciglia

**knitted** /'nɪtɪd/ a lavorato a maglia

**knitting** /'nɪtɪŋ/ n lavorare m a maglia; (product) lavoro m a maglia

**knitting needle** n ferro m da calza

**knitwear** /'nɪtweə(r)/ n maglieria f

**knives** /naɪvz/ npl see **knife**

**knob** /nɒb/ n pomello m; (of stick) pomo m; (of butter) noce f

**knobbly** /'nɒblɪ/ a nodoso; (bony) spigoloso

**knock** /nɒk/ n colpo m; **there was a ~ at the door** hanno bussato alla porta ● vt bussare a ‹door›; (fam: criticize) denigrare; **~ a hole in sth** fare un buco in qcsa; **~ one's head** battere la testa (**on** contro) ● vi (at door) bussare

■ **knock about** vt malmenare ● vi fam girovagare

■ **knock back** vt (fam: drink quickly) buttar giù tutto d'un fiato

■ **knock down** vt far cadere; (with fist) stendere con un pugno; (in car) investire; (demolish) abbattere; (fam: reduce) ribassare ‹price›

■ **knock off** vt (fam: steal) fregare; (fam: complete quickly) fare alla bell'e meglio ● vi (fam: cease work) staccare

■ **knock out** vt eliminare; (make unconscious) mettere K.O.; (fam: anaesthetize) addormentare

■ **knock over** vt rovesciare; (in car) investire

■ **knock up** vt fam (prepare quickly) buttare giù; (sl: make pregnant) mettere incinta

**knock: knockabout** n Sport **have a ~** palleggiare. **knock-down furniture** n mobili mpl scomponibili. **knock-down price** n prezzo m stracciato

**knocker** /'nɒkə(r)/ n battente m; (critic) denigratore, -trice mf

**knocking-off time** /nɒkɪŋ'ɒf/ n **~ ~ is five o'clock** si stacca alle cinque

**knock: knock-kneed** /-'niːd/ a con gambe storte. **knock-on effect** n implicazioni fpl. **knock-out** n knock-out m inv; **be a ~** fig essere uno schianto

**knoll** /nəʊl/ n collinetta f

**knot** /nɒt/ n nodo m; **to tie the ~** fam convolare a giuste nozze ● vt (pt/pp **knotted**) annodare; Br fam **get ~ted!** vai a farti friggere!

**knotty** /'nɒtɪ/ a (**-ier, -iest**) fam spinoso

**know** /nəʊ/ v (pt **knew**, pp **known**) ● vt sapere; conoscere ‹person, place›; (recognize) riconoscere; **get to ~ sb** conoscere qcno; **~ how to swim** sapere nuotare; **~ right from wrong** saper distinguere il bene dal male ● vi sapere; **did you ~ about this?** lo sapevi? ● n **in the ~** fam al corrente

■ **know of** vt conoscere; **not that I ~ of** non che io sappia

**know-all** n fam sapientone, -a mf

**know-how** n abilità f

**knowing** /'nəʊɪŋ/ a d'intesa

**knowingly** /'nəʊɪŋlɪ/ adv (intentionally) consapevolmente; ‹smile etc› con un aria d'intesa

**knowledgable** /'nɒlɪdʒəbl/ a ben informato

**knowledge** /'nɒlɪdʒ/ n conoscenza f

**known** /nəʊn/ see **know** ● a noto

**knuckle** /'nʌkl/ n nocca f

■ **knuckle down** vi darci sotto (**to** con)

■ **knuckle under** vi sottomettersi

**koala** [**bear**] /kəʊ'ɑːlə/ n koala m inv

**Koran** /kə'rɑːn/ n Corano m

**Korea** /kə'rɪə/ n Corea f

**Korean** /kə'rɪən/ a & n coreano, -a mf; (language) coreano m

**Korean** // a & n coreano, -a mf

**kosher** /'kəʊʃə(r)/ a kasher inv

**kowtow** /kaʊ'taʊ/ vi piegarsi

**kph** abbr (**kilometres per hour**) km/h

**kudos** /'kjuːdɒs/ n fam gloria f

**Kurd** /kɜːd/ n curdo, -a mf ● a curdo

**Kurdish** /'kɜːdɪʃ/ a & n (language) curdo m

**Kurdistan** /kɜːdɪr'stɑːn/ n Kurdistan m

**Kuwait** /kʊ'weɪt/ n Kuwait m

**Kuwaiti** /kʊ'weɪtɪ/ a & n kuwaitiano, -a mf

**kW** abbr (**kilowatt**) kW

**kWh** abbr (**kilowatt-hour**) kWh

**I, L** /el/ *n* (*letter*) l, L *f inv*
**L** *abbr* (**lake**) L; *abbr* (**large**) L; *abbr* (**learner**) P; *abbr* (**left**) sinistra *f*; *abbr* (**line**) v; *abbr* (**litre(s)**) l
**lab** /læb/ *n fam* laboratorio *m*
**lab assistant** *n* assistente *mf* di laboratorio
**lab coat** *n* camice *m*
**label** /'leibl/ *n* etichetta *f* ● *vt* (*pt/pp* **labelled**) mettere un'etichetta a; *fig* etichettare ⟨*person*⟩
**labelling** /'leibəlɪŋ/ *n* (*act*) etichettatura *f*
**laboratory** /lə'bɒrətrɪ/ *n* laboratorio *m*
**laborious** /lə'bɔːrɪəs/ *a* laborioso
**laboriously** /lə'bɔːrɪəslɪ/ *adv* in modo laborioso
**labor union** /'leibə/ *n Am* sindacato *m*
**labour** /'leibə(r)/ *n* lavoro *m*; (*workers*) manodopera *f*; *Med* doglie *fpl*; **be in ~** avere le doglie; **L~** *Pol* partito *m* laburista ● *vi* lavorare ● *vt* **~ the point** *fig* ribadire il concetto
**labour camp** *n* campo *m* di lavoro
**laboured** /'leibəd/ *a* ⟨*breathing*⟩ affannoso
**labourer** /'leibərə(r)/ *n* manovale *m*
**labour exchange** *n old* ufficio *m* di collocamento
**labour force** *n* manodopera *f*
**labouring** /'leibərɪŋ/ *n* lavoro *m* manuale
**labour: labour-intensive** *a* ad uso intensivo di lavoro; **be ~** richiedere molta manodopera. **labour market** *n* mercato *m* del lavoro. **Labour Party** *n* Partito *m* laburista. **labour relations** *npl* relazioni *fpl* industriali. **labour-saving** /'leibəseivɪŋ/ *a* che fa risparmiare lavoro e fatica. **labour ward** *n* reparto *m* maternità
**labrador** /'læbrədɔː(r)/ *n* (*dog*) labrador *m inv*
**lab technician** *n* technico, -a *mf* di laboratorio
**laburnum** /lə'bɜːnəm/ *n* maggiociondolo *m*
**labyrinth** /'læbərɪnθ/ *n* labirinto *m*
**lace** /leis/ *n* pizzo *m*; (*of shoe*) laccio *m* ● *attrib* di pizzo ● *vt* allacciare ⟨*shoes*⟩; correggere ⟨*drink*⟩
**lacerate** /'læsəreit/ *vt* lacerare
**laceration** /læsə'reiʃn/ *n* lacerazione *f*
**lace-up [shoe]** *n* scarpa *f* stringata
**lack** /læk/ *n* mancanza *f*; **~ of interest** disinteressamento *m*; **~ of evidence** insufficienza *f* di prove ● *vt* **the programme ~s originality** il programma manca di originalità; **I ~ the time** mi manca il tempo ● *vi* **be ~ing** mancare; **be ~ing in sth** mancare di qcsa
**lackadaisical** /lækə'deizikl/ *a* senza entu-

siasmo
**lackey** /'lækɪ/ *n* lacchè *m inv*
**lacklustre** /'læklʌstə(r)/ *a* scialbo
**laconic** /lə'kɒnɪk/ *a* laconico
**laconically** /lə'kɒnɪklɪ/ *adv* laconicamente
**lacquer** /'lækə(r)/ *n* lacca *f*
**lactate** /læk'teit/ *vi* produrre latte
**lactation** /læk'teiʃn/ *n* lattazione *f*
**lacy** /'leisɪ/ *a* di pizzo
**lad** /læd/ *n* ragazzo *m*
**ladder** /'lædə(r)/ *n* scala *f*; (*in tights*) sfilatura *f* ● *vi* sfilarsi
**ladderproof** /'lædəpruːf/ *a* ⟨*stockings*⟩ indemagliabile
**laddish** /'lædɪʃ/ *a fam* da ragazzacci
**laden** /'leidn/ *a* carico (**with** di)
**la-di-da** /lɑːdɪ'dɑː/ *a* affettato
**ladle** /'leidl/ *n* mestolo *m* ● *vt* **~** [**out**] versare ⟨*col mestolo*⟩
**lady** /'leidɪ/ *n* signora *f*; (*title*) Lady *f*; **ladies** [**room**] *n* bagno *m* per donne
**lady: ladybird** *n*, *Am* **ladybug** *n* coccinella *f*. **lady-in-waiting** /-'weitɪŋ/ *n* dama *f* di corte. **ladykiller** *n fam* dongiovanni *m inv*
**ladylike** /'leidɪlaɪk/ *a* signorile
**lady: lady mayoress** *n* moglie *f* del Lord Mayor. **Ladyship** *n* **her/your ~** (*to aristocrat*) ≈ Signora Contessa. **lady's maid** *n* cameriera *f* personale
**lag**[1] /læg/ *vi* (*pt/pp* **lagged**) **~ behind** restare indietro
**lag**[2] *vt* (*pt/pp* **lagged**) isolare ⟨*pipes*⟩
**lager** /'lɑːgə(r)/ *n* birra *f* chiara
**lager lout** *n Br pej* giovinastro *m* ubriaco
**lagging** /'lægɪŋ/ *n* (*for pipes*) materiale *m* isolante
**lagoon** /lə'guːn/ *n* laguna *f*
**laid** /leid/ *see* **lay**[3]; *sl* **get ~** scopare
**laid-back** *a fam* rilassato
**lain** /lein/ *see* **lie**[2]
**lair** /leə(r)/ *n* tana *f*
**laird** /leəd/ *n* (*in Scotland*) proprietario *m* terriero
**laity** /'leiətɪ/ *n* laicato *m*
**lake** /leik/ *n* lago *m*. **~ Garda** lago di Garda
**lakeside** /'leiksaid/ *n* riva *f* del lago ● *attrib* ⟨*café, scenery*⟩ della/sulla riva del lago
**lama** /'læmə/ *n* lama *m inv*
**lamb** /læm/ *n* agnello *m*
**lambast[e]** /læm'beist/ *vt* biasimare ⟨*person, organization*⟩
**lamb: lamb chop** *n* cotoletta *f* d'agnello. **lambskin** *n* pelle *f* d'agnello. **lambswool** *n* lana *f* d'agnello, lambswool *m inv*
**lame** /leim/ *a* zoppo; *fig* ⟨*argument*⟩ zoppicante; ⟨*excuse*⟩ traballante

# 187

**lamé** /'lɑ:meɪ/ *n* lamé *m*

**lame duck** *n* (*person*) inetto. -a *mf*; (*firm*) azienda *f* in cattive acque

**lament** /lə'ment/ *n* lamento *m* ● *vt* lamentare ● *vi* lamentarsi

**lamentable** /'læməntəbl/ *a* deplorevole

**laminated** /'læmɪneɪtɪd/ *a* laminato

**lamp** /læmp/ *n* lampada *f*; (*in street*) lampione *m*

**lampoon** /læm'pu:n/ *n* satira *f* ● *vt* fare oggetto di satira

**lamp-post** *n* lampione *m*

**lampshade** /'læmpʃeɪd/ *n* paralume *m*

**lance** /lɑ:ns/ *n* lancia *f* ● *vt* Med incidere

**lance corporal** *n* appuntato *m*

**lancet** /'lɑ:nsɪt/ *n* Med bisturi *m inv*

**land** /lænd/ *n* terreno *m*; (*country*) paese *m*; (*as opposed to sea*) terra *f*; plot of ~ pezzo *m* di terreno ● *vt* Naut sbarcare; (*fam: obtain*) assicurarsi; **be ~ed with sth** *fam* ritrovarsi fra capo e collo qcsa ● *vi* Aeron atterrare; (*fall*) cadere; ~ **on one's feet** *fig* cadere in piedi

■ **land up** *vi fam* finire

**land: land agent** *n* (*on estate*) fattore *m*. **land army** *n* gruppo *m* di lavoratrici agricole durante la seconda guerra mondiale. **landfall** *n* Naut approdo *m*; **make ~** (*reach*) approdare; (*sight*) avvistare terra. **landfill site** *n* discarica *f* in cui i rifiuti vengono interrati

**landing** /'lændɪŋ/ *n* Naut sbarco *m*; Aeron atterraggio *m*; (*top of stairs*) pianerottolo *m*

**landing: landing card** *n* Aeron, Naut carta *f* di sbarco. **landing craft** *n* mezzo *m* da sbarco. **landing gear** *n* Aeron carrello *m* d'atterraggio. **landing lights** *npl* luci *fpl* d'atterraggio. **landing party** *n* Mil reparto *m* da sbarco. **landing-stage** *n* pontile *m* da sbarco. **landing strip** *n* pista *f* d'atterraggio

**land: landlady** *n* proprietaria *f*; (*of flat*) padrona *f* di casa. **landlocked** *a* privo di sbocco sul mare. **landlord** *n* proprietario *m*; (*of flat*) padrone *m* di casa. **landlubber** *n* marinaio *m* d'acqua dolce. **landmark** *n* punto *m* di riferimento; *fig* pietra *f* miliare. **land mass** *n* continente *m*. **landmine** *n* Mil mina *f* terrestre. **landowner** *n* proprietario, -a *mf* terriero, -a. **landscape** *n* paesaggio *m*. **landscape architect** *n* paesaggista *mf*. **landscape gardener** *n* paesaggista *mf*. **landslide** *n* frana *f*; Pol valanga *f* di voti. **landslip** *n* smottamento *m*

**lane** /leɪn/ *n* sentiero *m*; Auto, Sport corsia *f*

**lane closure** *n* (*on motorway*) chiusura *f* di corsia

**lane markings** *n* (*on road*) [strisce *fpl* di] mezzeria *f*

**langoustine** /'lɒŋgʊsti:n/ *n* scampo *m*

**language** /'læŋgwɪdʒ/ *n* lingua *f*; (*speech, style, Comput*) linguaggio *m*

**language barrier** *n* barriera *f* linguistica

**language laboratory** *n* laboratorio *m* linguistico

**languid** /'læŋgwɪd/ *a* languido

**languidly** /'læŋgwɪdlɪ/ *adv* languidamente

**languish** /'læŋgwɪʃ/ *vi* languire

**languor** /'læŋgə(r)/ *n* languore *m*

**lank** /læŋk/ *a* (*hair*) liscio

**lanky** /'læŋkɪ/ *a* (-ier, -iest) allampanato

**lanolin** /'lænəlɪn/ *n* lanolina *f*

**lantern** /'læntən/ *n* lanterna *f*

**lanyard** /'lænjəd/ *n* (*Naut: rope*) cima *f*

**lap**[1] /læp/ *n* grembo *m*

**lap**[2] *n* (*Sport, of journey*) tappa *f*; ~ **of honour** giro *m* d'onore ● *v* (*pt/pp* lapped) ● *vi* (*water:*) ~ **against** lambire ● *vt* Sport doppiare

**lap**[3] *vt* (*pt/pp* lapped) ~ **up** bere avidamente; bersi completamente (*lies*); credere ciecamente a (*praise*)

**lap and shoulder belt** *n* Auto, Aeron cintura *f* di sicurezza

**laparoscope** /'læpərəʃkəʊp/ *n* laparoscopio *m*

**laparoscopy** /læpə'rɒskəpɪ/ *n* laparoscopia *f*

**lap belt** *n* Auto, Aeron cintura *f* di sicurezza addominale

**lapdog** /'læpdɒg/ *n* cane *m* da salotto; **he's her ~** è il suo cagnolino

**lapel** /lə'pel/ *n* bavero *m*

**Lapland** /'læplænd/ *n* Lapponia *f*

**lapse** /læps/ *n* sbaglio *m*; (*moral*) sbandamento *m* [morale]; (*of time*) intervallo *m* ● *vi* (*expire*) scadere; (*morally*) scivolare; ~ **into** cadere in

**laptop** /'læptɒp/ *n* ~ **[computer]** computer *m inv* portabile, laptop *m inv*

**larceny** /'lɑ:sənɪ/ *n* furto *m*

**larch** /lɑ:tʃ/ *n* larice *m*

**lard** /lɑ:d/ *n* strutto *m*

**larder** /'lɑ:də(r)/ *n* dispensa *f*

**large** /lɑ:dʒ/ *a & adv* grande; (*number, amount*) grande, grosso; **by and ~** in complesso; **at ~** in libertà; (*in general*) ampiamente

**large intestine** *n* intestino *m* crasso

**largely** /'lɑ:dʒlɪ/ *adv* ~ **because of** in gran parte a causa di

**largeness** /'lɑ:dʒnɪs/ *n* grandezza *f*

**large-scale** *a* (*map*) a grande scala; (*operation*) su larga scala

**largesse** /lɑ:'ʒes/ *n* generosità *f*

**lark**[1] /lɑ:k/ *n* (*bird*) allodola *f*

**lark**[2] *n* (*joke*) burla *f*

■ **lark about** *vi* giocherellare

**larva** /'lɑ:və/ *n* (*pl* -**vae** /'lɑ:vi:/) larva *f*

**laryngitis** /lærɪn'dʒaɪtɪs/ *n* laringite *f*

**larynx** /'lærɪŋks/ *n* laringe *f*

**lasagne** /lə'zænjə/ *n* lasagne *fpl*

**lascivious** /lə'sɪvɪəs/ *a* lascivo

**laser** /'leɪzə(r)/ *n* laser *m inv*

**laser disc** *n* disco *m* laser

**laser printer** *n* stampante *f* laser

**lash** /læʃ/ *n* frustata *f*; (*eyelash*) ciglio *m* ● *vt* (*whip*) frustare; (*tie*) legare fermamente

■ **lash out** *vi* attaccare; (*spend*) sperperare (**on** in)

**lashings** /'læʃɪŋz/ *npl* ~ **of** *fam* una marea di

**lass** /læs/ n ragazzina f

**lasso** /ləˈsuː/ n lazo m

**last** /lɑːst/ a ⟨final⟩ ultimo; ⟨recent⟩ scorso; ~ **year** l'anno scorso; ~ **night** ieri sera; **at** ~ alla fine; **at** ~! finalmente!; **that's the** ~ **straw** fam questa è l'ultima goccia ● n ultimo, -a mf; **the** ~ **but one** il penultimo ● adv per ultimo; ⟨last time⟩ l'ultima volta; ~ **but not least** per ultimo ma non il meno importante ● vi durare

**lasting** /ˈlɑːstɪŋ/ a durevole

**lastly** /ˈlɑːstlɪ/ adv infine

**last: last name** n ⟨surname⟩ cognome m. **last rites** npl Relig estrema unzione f. **Last Supper** n Ultima Cena f

**latch** /lætʃ/ n chiavistello m; ⟨on gate⟩ saliscendi m inv; **leave the door on the** ~ chiudere la porta senza far scattare la serratura

■ **latch on to** vt fissarsi con ⟨person, idea⟩

**latchkey** /ˈlætʃkiː/ n chiave f di casa

**latchkey child** n bambino m che ha le chiavi di casa in quanto i genitori lavorano

**late** /leɪt/ a ⟨delayed⟩ in ritardo; ⟨at a late hour⟩ tardo; ⟨deceased⟩ defunto; **it's** ~ ⟨at night⟩ è tardi; **in** ~ **November** alla fine di Novembre; **of** ~ recentemente; **be a** ~ **developer** ⟨child:⟩ essere lento nell'apprendimento ● adv tardi; **stay up** ~ stare alzati fino a tardi

**latecomer** /ˈleɪtkʌmə(r)/ n ritardatario, -a mf; ⟨to political party etc⟩ nuovo, -a arrivato, -a mf

**lately** /ˈleɪtlɪ/ adv recentemente

**lateness** /ˈleɪtnɪs/ n ora f tarda; ⟨delay⟩ ritardo m

**latent** /ˈleɪtnt/ a latente

**later** /ˈleɪtə(r)/ a ⟨train⟩ che parte più tardi; ⟨edition⟩ più recente ● adv più tardi; ~ **on** più tardi, dopo

**lateral** /ˈlætərəl/ a laterale

**late riser** /ˈraɪzə(r)/ n dormiglione, -a mf

**latest** /ˈleɪtɪst/ a ultimo; ⟨most recent⟩ più recente; **the** ~ ⟨news⟩ le ultime notizie ● n **six o'clock at the** ~ alle sei al più tardi

**latex** /ˈleɪteks/ n la[t]tice m

**lath** /læθ/ n assicella f

**lathe** /leɪð/ n tornio m

**lather** /ˈlɑːðə(r)/ n schiuma f ● vt insaponare ● vi far schiuma

**Latin** /ˈlætɪn/ a latino ● n latino m

**Latin America** n America f Latina

**Latin American** n & a latino-americano mf

**Latino** /ləˈtiːnəʊ/ n Am latino-americano, -a mf

**latitude** /ˈlætɪtjuːd/ n Geog latitudine f; fig libertà f d'azione

**latrine** /ləˈtriːn/ n latrina f

**latter** /ˈlætə(r)/ a ultimo ● n **the** ~ quest'ultimo

**latter-day** a moderno

**latterly** /ˈlætəlɪ/ adv ultimamente

**lattice** /ˈlætɪs/ n traliccio m

**lattice window** n finestra f con vetri a losanghe

**lattice-work** n intelaiatura f a traliccio

**Latvia** /ˈlætvɪə/ n Lettonia f

**Latvian** /ˈlætvɪən/ a & n lettone mf; ⟨language⟩ lettone m

**laudable** /ˈlɔːdəbl/ a lodevole

**laudatory** /ˈlɔːdətrɪ/ a elogiativo

**laugh** /lɑːf/ n risata f ● vi ridere ⟨at/about di⟩; ~ **at sb** ⟨mock⟩ prendere in giro qcno

**laughable** /ˈlɑːfəbl/ a ridicolo

**laughing gas** /ˈlɑːfɪŋ/ n gas m inv esilarante

**laughing stock** n zimbello m

**laughter** /ˈlɑːftə(r)/ n risata f

**launch**[1] /lɔːntʃ/ n ⟨boat⟩ lancia f

**launch**[2] n lancio m; ⟨of ship⟩ varo m ● vt lanciare ⟨rocket, product⟩; varare ⟨ship⟩; sferrare ⟨attack⟩

■ **launch into** vt intraprendere ⟨career⟩; imbarcarsi in ⟨speech⟩

**launcher** /ˈlɔːntʃə(r)/ n lanciamissili m inv

**launch[ing] pad** /ˈlɔːntʃ[ɪŋ]/ n piattaforma f di lancio; fig trampolino m di lancio

**launder** /ˈlɔːndə(r)/ vt lavare e stirare; ~ **money** fig riciclare denaro sporco

**launderette** /lɔːndəˈret/ n lavanderia f automatica

**laundry** /ˈlɔːndrɪ/ n lavanderia f; ⟨clothes⟩ bucato m

**laureate** /ˈlɒrɪət/ a **poet** ~ poeta m di corte; **Nobel** ~ vincitore, -trice mf del Nobel

**laurel** /ˈlɒrəl/ n lauro m; **rest on one's** ~s fig dormire sugli allori

**lav** /læv/ n Br fam gabinetto m

**lava** /ˈlɑːvə/ n lava f

**lavatorial** /lævəˈtɔːrɪəl/ a ⟨humour⟩ scatologico

**lavatory** /ˈlævətrɪ/ n gabinetto m

**lavender** /ˈlævəndə(r)/ n lavanda f

**lavender blue** a color lavanda

**lavish** /ˈlævɪʃ/ a copioso; ⟨wasteful⟩ prodigo; **on a** ~ **scale** su vasta scala ● vt ~ **sth on sb** ricoprire qcno di qcsa

**lavishly** /ˈlævɪʃlɪ/ adv copiosamente

**law** /lɔː/ n legge f; **study** ~ studiare giurisprudenza, studiare legge; ~ **and order** ordine m pubblico; **take the** ~ **into one's own hands** farsi giustizia da sé; ~ **of the jungle** legge della giungla

**law-abiding** /ˈlɔːəbaɪdɪŋ/ a che rispetta la legge

**lawbreaker** /ˈlɔːbreɪkə(r)/ n persona f che infrange la legge

**law court** n tribunale m

**lawful** /ˈlɔːfʊl/ a legittimo

**lawfully** /ˈlɔːfʊlɪ/ adv legittimamente

**lawfulness** /ˈlɔːfʊlnɪs/ n legalità f

**lawless** /ˈlɔːlɪs/ a senza legge

**lawmaker** /ˈlɔːmeɪkə(r)/ n legislatore m

**lawn** /lɔːn/ n prato m [all'inglese]

**lawnmower** /ˈlɔːnməʊə(r)/ n tosaerba m inv

**law school** n facoltà f di giurisprudenza

**lawsuit** /ˈlɔːsuːt/ n causa f

**lawyer** /ˈlɔːjə(r)/ n avvocato m

**lax** /læks/ a negligente; ⟨morals etc⟩ lassista

**laxative** /ˈlæksətɪv/ n lassativo m

**laxity** /'læksətɪ/ n lassismo m
**lay¹** /leɪ/ a laico: fig profano
**lay²** see **lie²**
**lay³** vt (pt/pp **laid**) porre, mettere: apparecchiare ‹table› ● vi ‹hen.› fare le uova
■ **lay aside** vt mettere da parte
■ **lay down** vt posare; stabilire ‹rules, conditions›
■ **lay in** vt farsi una scorta di ‹coal, supplies etc›
■ **lay into** vt sl picchiare
■ **lay off** vt licenziare ‹workers› ● vi (fam: stop) ~ off! smettila!
■ **lay on** vt (organize) organizzare
■ **lay out** vt (display, set forth) esporre; (plan) pianificare ‹garden›; (spend) sborsare; Typ impaginare
■ **lay up** vt I was laid up in bed for a week sono stato costretto a letto per una settimana
**layabout** /'leɪəbaʊt/ n fannullone, -a mf
**lay-by** n piazzola f di sosta
**layer** /'leɪə(r)/ n strato m
**layette** /leɪ'et/ n corredino m
**layman** /'leɪmən/ n profano m
**layout** /'leɪaʊt/ n disposizione f; Typ impaginazione f, layout m inv
**lay preacher** n predicatore m laico
**laze** /leɪz/ vi ~ [about] oziare
**lazily** /'leɪzɪlɪ/ adv (move, wander etc) pigramente
**laziness** /'leɪzɪnɪs/ n pigrizia f
**lazy** /'leɪzɪ/ a (-ier, -iest) pigro
**lazybones** /'leɪzɪbəʊnz/ n poltrone, -a mf
**lazy eye** n ambliopia f
**lb** abbr (**pound**) libbra
**LCD** n abbr (**liquid crystal display**) LCD m
**lead¹** /led/ n piombo m; (of pencil) mina f
**lead²** /liːd/ n guida f; (leash) giunzaglio m; (flex) filo m; (clue) indizio m; Theat parte f principale; (distance ahead) distanza f (over su); in the ~ in testa; follow sb's ~ seguire l'esempio di qcno ● vt (pt/pp **led**) condurre; dirigere ‹expedition, party etc›; (induce) indurre; ~ the way mettersi in testa; ~ into temptation indurre in tentazione ● vi (be in front) condurre; (in race, competition) essere in testa
■ **lead astray** vt sviare
■ **lead away** vt portar via
■ **lead on** vt ingannare
■ **lead off** vi (begin) cominciare ● vt (take away) portare via
■ **lead to** vt portare a
■ **lead up to** vt preludere; the period ~ing up to the election il periodo precedente le elezioni; what's this ~ing up to? dove porta questo?
**leaded** /'ledɪd/ a con piombo
**leaden** /'ledən/ a di piombo
**leader** /'liːdə(r)/ n capo m; (of orchestra) primo violino m; (in newspaper) articolo m di fondo
**leadership** /'liːdəʃɪp/ n direzione f, leadership f inv; show ~ mostrare capacità di comando

**lead-free** /'ledfriː/ a senza piombo
**lead-in** /'liːdɪn/ n presentazione f
**leading¹** /'liːdɪŋ/ a principale
**leading²** /'ledɪŋ/ n Typ interlinea m
**leading** /'liːdɪŋ/: **leading article** n articolo m di fondo. **leading edge** n Aeron bordo m d'attacco; **at the ~ of** (technology) all'avanguardia in. **leading lady** attrice f principale. **leading light** n personaggio m di spicco. **leading man** attore m principale. **leading question** n domanda f che influenza la risposta
**lead poisoning** n saturnismo m
**leaf** /liːf/ n (pl **leaves**) foglia f; (of table) asse f; fig **take a ~ out of sb's book** imparare la lezione di qcno; **turn over a new ~** voltare pagina
■ **leaf through** vt sfogliare
**leaflet** /'liːflɪt/ n déplant m inv; (advertising) dépliant m inv pubblicitario; (political) manifestino m
**leafy** /'liːfɪ/ a (tree) ricco di foglie; (wood) molto verde; (suburb, area) ricco di verde
**league** /liːg/ n lega f; Sport campionato m; **be in ~ with** essere in combutta con
**league table** n classifica f del campionato
**leak** /liːk/ n (hole) fessura f; Naut falla f; (of gas & fig) fuga f ● vi colare; (ship:) fare acqua; (liquid, gas:) fuoriuscire ● vt ~ **sth to sb** fig far trapelare qcsa a qcno
**leakage** /'liːkɪdʒ/ n perdita f; (of gas & fig) fuga f
**leaky** /'liːkɪ/ a che perde; Naut che fa acqua
**lean¹** /liːn/ a magro
**lean²** v (pt/pp **leaned** or **leant** /lent/) ● vt appoggiare (against/on contro/su); ~ **one's elbows on the table** appoggiare i gomiti sul tavolo ● vi appoggiarsi (against/on contro/su); (not be straight) pendere; **be ~ing against** essere appoggiato contro; ~ **on sb** (depend on) appoggiarsi a qcno; (fam: exert pressure on) stare alle calcagna di qcno
■ **lean back** vi sporgersi indietro
■ **lean forward** vi piegarsi in avanti
■ **lean out** vi sporgersi
■ **lean over** vi piegarsi
■ **lean towards** vt (favour) propendere per
**leaning** /'liːnɪŋ/ a pendente; **the L~ Tower of Pisa** la torre di Pisa, la torre pendente ● n tendenza f
**leanness** /'liːnnɪs/ n magrezza f
**lean-to** n garage m inv adiacente alla casa
**leap** /liːp/ n salto m ● vi (pt/pp **leapt** /lept/ or **leaped**) saltare; **he leapt at it** fam l'ha preso al volo
**leapfrog** /'liːpfrɒg/ n cavallina f
**leap year** n anno m bisestile
**learn** /lɜːn/ v (pt/pp **learnt** or **learned**) ● vt imparare; ~ **to swim** imparare a nuotare; **I have ~ed that...** (heard) sono venuto a sapere che...; fig **he's ~t his lesson** ha imparato la lezione ● vi imparare; **as I've ~t to my cost** come ho imparato a mie spese
**learned** /'lɜːnɪd/ a colto

**learner** /ˈlɜːnə(r)/ n also Auto principiante mf

**learning** /ˈlɜːnɪŋ/ n cultura f

**learning: learning curve** n curva f di apprendimento. **learning difficulties** npl (of schoolchildren) difficoltà fpl d'apprendimento. **learning disability** n difficoltà fpl d'apprendimento

**lease** /liːs/ n contratto m d'affitto; (rental) affitto m: **the job has given him a new ~ of life** grazie al lavoro ha ripreso gusto alla vita ● vt affittare

**leasehold** /ˈliːshəʊld/ n proprietà f in affitto

**leaseholder** /ˈliːshəʊldə(r)/ n titolare mf di un contratto d'affitto

**leash** /liːʃ/ n guinzaglio m

**least** /liːst/ a più piccolo; (smallest amount) meno; **you've got ~ luggage** hai meno bagagli di tutti ● n **the ~** il meno; **that's the ~ of my worries** questa è la cosa che mi preoccupa di meno; **at ~** almeno; **not in the ~** niente affatto ● adv meno; **the ~ expensive wine** il vino meno caro

**leather** /ˈleðə(r)/ n pelle f; (of soles) cuoio m ● attrib di pelle/cuoio; **~ jacket** giubbotto m di pelle

**leathery** /ˈleðəri/ a (meat, skin) duro

**leave** /liːv/ n (holiday) congedo m; Mil licenza f; **on ~** in congedo/licenza; **take one's ~** accomiatarsi; **~ of absence** aspettativa f ● v (pt/pp **left**) ● vt lasciare; uscire da (house, office); (forget) dimenticare; **there is nothing left** non è rimasto niente; **~ sb in peace** lasciare in pace qcno ● vi andare via; (train, bus:) partire

■ **leave aside** vt (disregard) lasciare da parte

■ **leave behind** vt lasciare; (forget) dimenticare

■ **leave out** vt omettere; (not put away) lasciare fuori

**leaves** /liːvz/ see leaf

**Lebanese** /lebəˈniːz/ a & n libanese mf

**Lebanon** /ˈlebənən/ n Libano m

**lecher** /ˈletʃə(r)/ n libertino m

**lecherous** /ˈletʃərəs/ a lascivo

**lechery** /ˈletʃəri/ n lascivia f

**lectern** /ˈlektɜːn/ n leggio m, scannello m

**lecture** /ˈlektʃə(r)/ n conferenza f; Univ lezione f; (reproof) ramanzina f ● vi fare una conferenza (**on** su): Univ insegnare (**on sth** qcsa) ● vt ~ **sb** rimproverare qcno

**lecturer** /ˈlektʃərə(r)/ n conferenziere, -a mf; Univ docente mf universitario, -a

**lecture room** n Br Univ aula f magna

**lectureship** /ˈlektʃəʃɪp/ n Br Univ docenza f universitaria

**lecture theatre** n Br Univ aula f magna

**LED** n abbr (**light-emitting diode**) LED m inv

**led** /led/ see lead²

**ledge** /ledʒ/ n cornice f; (of window) davanzale m

**ledger** /ˈledʒə(r)/ n libro m mastro

**leech** /liːtʃ/ n sanguisuga f

**leek** /liːk/ n porro m

**leer** /lɪə(r)/ n sguardo m libidinoso ● vi ~ (**at**) guardare in modo libidinoso

**lees** /liːz/ npl (wine sediment) fondi mpl

**leeway** /ˈliːweɪ/ n fig libertà f di azione

**left¹** /left/ see leave

**left²** a sinistro ● adv a sinistra ● n also Pol sinistra f; **on the ~** a sinistra

**left-hand drive** a (car) con la guida a sinistra

**left-handed** /-ˈhændɪd/ a mancino; (scissors etc) per mancini

**leftie** /ˈlefti/ n sinistrorso, -a mf

**leftist** /ˈleftɪst/ a & n sinistrorso, -a mf

**left: left luggage [office]** n deposito m bagagli. **leftovers** npl rimasugli mpl. **left wing** n Pol sinistra f; Sport ala f sinistra. **left-wing** a Pol di sinistra. **left-winger** n Pol persona f di sinistra; Sport ala f sinistra

**leg** /leg/ n gamba f; (of animal) zampa f; (of journey) tappa f; Culin (of chicken) coscia f; (of lamb) cosciotto m; **be on one's last ~s** (machine:) funzionare per miracolo; **not have a ~ to stand on** non avere una ragione che regga ● vi ~ **it** fam darsela a gambe

**legacy** /ˈlegəsi/ n lascito m

**legal** /ˈliːgl/ a legale; **take ~ action** intentare un'azione legale

**legal: legal adviser** n consulente mf legale. **legal aid** n gratuito patrocinio m. **legal eagle** n hum principe m del foro

**legality** /lɪˈgæləti/ n legalità f

**legalization** /liːgəlarˈzeɪʃn/ n legalizzazione f

**legalize** /ˈliːgəlaɪz/ vt legalizzare

**legally** /ˈliːgəli/ adv legalmente

**legal tender** n valuta f a corso legale

**legend** /ˈledʒənd/ n leggenda f

**legendary** /ˈledʒəndəri/ a leggendario

**leggings** /ˈlegɪŋz/ npl (for baby) ghette fpl; (for woman) pantacollant mpl; (for man) gambali mpl

**leggy** /ˈlegi/ a (person) con le gambe lunghe

**Leghorn** /ˈleghɔːn/ n Livorno f

**legibility** /ledʒəˈbɪləti/ n leggibilità f

**legible** /ˈledʒəbl/ a leggibile

**legibly** /ˈledʒəbli/ adv in modo leggibile

**legion** /ˈliːdʒn/ n legione f

**legionnaire** /liːdʒəˈneə(r)/ n Mil legionario m

**legionnaire's disease** n legionellosi f

**legislate** /ˈledʒɪsleɪt/ vi legiferare

**legislation** /ledʒɪsˈleɪʃn/ n legislazione f

**legislative** /ˈledʒɪslətɪv/ a legislativo

**legislator** /ˈledʒɪsleɪtə(r)/ n legislatore m

**legislature** /ˈledʒɪsleɪtʃə(r)/ n legislatura f

**legitimacy** /lɪˈdʒɪtɪməsi/ n (lawfulness) legittimità f; (of argument) validità f

**legitimate** /lɪˈdʒɪtɪmət/ a legittimo; (excuse) valido

**legitimately** /lɪˈdʒɪtɪmətli/ adv legittimamente

**legitimize** /lɪdʒɪtɪˈmaɪz/ vt rendere legittimo

**legless** /ˈleglɪs/ a senza gambe; (Br: drunk) ubriaco fradicio

**leg: leg-pulling** n presa f in giro. **legroom** n spazio m per le gambe. **leg warmer** n scaldamuscoli m inv. **legwork** n fatica f: **do the ~** fare da galoppino

**leisure** /'leʒə(r)/ n tempo m libero; **at your ~** con comodo

**leisure centre** n centro m sportivo e ricreativo

**leisurely** /'leʒəlɪ/ a senza fretta

**leisure time** n tempo m libero

**leisurewear** /'leʒəweə(r)/ n abbigliamento m per il tempo libero

**lemming** /'lemɪŋ/ n lemming m inv

**lemon** /'lemən/ n limone m

**lemonade** /lemə'neɪd/ n limonata f

**lemon: lemon curd** n crema f al limone. **lemon juice** n (drink) succo m di limone. **lemon sole** n sogliola f limanda. **lemon squash** n sciroppo m di limone. **lemon tea** n tè m inv al limone. **lemon yellow** n giallo m limone ● a giallo limone

**lend** /lend/ vt (pt/pp lent) prestare; **~ a hand** fig dare una mano; **~ an ear** prestare ascolto; **~ itself to** prestarsi a

**lender** /'lendə(r)/ n prestatore, -trice mf

**lending library** /'lendɪŋ/ n biblioteca f per il prestito

**length** /leŋθ/ n lunghezza f; (piece) pezzo m; (of wallpaper) parte f, (of visit) durata f; **at ~** a lungo; (at last) alla fine

**lengthen** /'leŋθən/ vt allungare ● vi allungarsi

**lengthways** /'leŋθweɪz/ adv per lungo

**lengthwise** /'leŋθwaɪz/ adv longitudinale

**lengthy** /'leŋθɪ/ a (-ier, -iest) lungo

**lenience** /'li:nɪəns/ n indulgenza f

**lenient** /'li:nɪənt/ a indulgente

**leniently** /'li:nɪəntlɪ/ adv con indulgenza

**lens** /lenz/ n lente f; Phot obiettivo m; (of eye) cristallino m

**Lent** /lent/ n Quaresima f

**lent** see **lend**

**lentil** /'lentl/ n Bot lenticchia f

**Leo** /'li:əʊ/ n Astr Leone m

**leopard** /'lepəd/ n leopardo m

**leopardskin** /'lepədskɪn/ n pelle f di leopardo ● attrib di [pelle di] leopardo

**leotard** /'li:əta:d/ n body m inv

**leper** /'lepə(r)/ n lebbroso, -a mf; fig appestato, -a mf

**leprosy** /'leprəsɪ/ n lebbra f

**lesbian** /'lezbɪən/ a lesbico ● n lesbica f

**lesbianism** /'lezbɪənɪzm/ n lesbismo m

**lesion** /'li:ʒn/ n lesione f

**less** /les/ a meno di; **~ and ~** sempre meno; ● adv & prep meno ● n meno m

**lessee** /le'si:/ n Jur affittuario, -a mf

**lessen** /'lesn/ vt/i diminuire

**lesser** /'lesə(r)/ a minore; **the ~ of two evils** il minore fra i due mali

**lesson** /'lesn/ n lezione f; **teach sb a ~** fig dare una lezione a qcno

**lessor** /le'sɔ:/ n Jur locatore, -trice mf

**lest** /lest/ conj liter per timore che

**let** /let/ vt (pt/pp let, pres p letting) lasciare,

permettere; (rent) affittare: **~ alone** (not to mention) tanto meno; **'to ~'** 'affittasi'; **~ us go** andiamo; **~ sb do sth** lasciare fare qcsa a qcno, permettere a qcno di fare qcsa; **~ me know** fammi sapere; **just ~ him try!** che ci provi solamente!; **~ oneself go** lasciarsi andare; **~ oneself in for sth** fam impelagarsi in qcsa ● n Tennis colpo m nullo; (Br: lease) contratto m d'affitto ● vi **~ fly at sb** aggredire qcno

■ **let down** vt sciogliersi ‹hair›; abbassare ‹blinds›; (lengthen) allungare; (disappoint) deludere; **don't ~ me down** conto su di te

■ **let in** vt far entrare

■ **let off** vt far partire; (not punish) perdonare; **~ sb off doing sth** abbonare qcsa a qcno; **~ off steam** fig scaricarsi

■ **let on** vi sl **don't ~ on** non spifferare niente

■ **let out** vt far uscire; (make larger) allargare; emettere ‹scream, groan›

■ **let through** vt far passare

■ **let up** vi fam diminuire

**let-down** n delusione f

**lethal** /'li:θl/ a letale; **~ dose** n dose f letale

**lethargic** /lɪ'θɑ:dʒɪk/ a apatico

**lethargy** /'leθədʒɪ/ n apatia f

**let-out** n fam via f d'uscita

**letter** /'letə(r)/ n lettera f

**letter: letter of apology** n lettera f di scuse. **letter bomb** n lettera f esplosiva. **letter box** n buca f per le lettere. **letter of credit** n Comm lettera f di credito. **letterhead** n (heading) intestazione f; (paper) carta f intestata

**lettering** /'letərɪŋ/ n caratteri mpl

**letter of introduction** n lettera f di presentazione

**lettuce** /'letɪs/ n lattuga f

**let-up** n fam pausa f

**leukaemia** /lu:'ki:mɪə/ n leucemia f

**level** /'levl/ a piano; (in height, competition) allo stesso livello; ‹spoonful› raso; **draw ~ with sb** affiancare qcno; **do one's ~ best** fare del proprio meglio ● n livello m; **on the ~** fam giusto ● vt (pt/pp levelled) livellare; (aim) puntare (**at** su)

■ **level off** vi ‹inflation, unemployment:› stabilizzarsi

■ **level out** vi ‹surface:› diventare pianeggiante; ‹aircraft:› mettersi in orizzontale

■ **level with** vt (fam: be honest with) essere franco con

**level: level crossing** n passaggio m a livello. **level-headed** /-'hedɪd/ a posato. **level pegging** n **it's ~ ~ so far** finora sono alla pari

**lever** /'li:və(r)/ n leva f

■ **lever off, lever up** vt sollevare (con una leva)

**leverage** /'li:vərɪdʒ/ n azione f di una leva; fig influenza f

**leveret** /'levərət/ n leprotto m

**levitate** /'levɪteɪt/ vi levitare

**levity** /'levətɪ/ n leggerezza f

**levy** /'levɪ/ *vt* (*pt/pp* **levied**) imporre ‹*tax*›
**lewd** /lju:d/ *a* osceno
**lexical** /'leksɪkəl/ *a* lessicale
**lexicographer** /leksɪ'kɒɡrəfə(r)/ *n* lessicografo. -a *mf*
**lexicographic** /leksɪkə'græfɪk/ *a* lessicografico
**lexicography** /leksɪ'kɒɡrəfɪ/ *n* lessicografia *f*
**lexicon** /'leksɪkən/ *n* lessico *m*
**liability** /laɪə'bɪlətɪ/ *n* responsabilità *f*; (*fam: burden*) peso *m*; **liabilities** *pl* passività *fpl*
**liable** /'laɪəbl/ *a* responsabile (**for** di); **be ~ to** ‹*rain, break etc*› rischiare di; (*tend to*) tendere a
**liaise** /lɪ'eɪz/ *vi fam* essere in contatto
**liaison** /lɪ'eɪzɒn/ *n* contatti *mpl*; *Mil* collegamento *m*; (*affair*) relazione *f*
**liar** /'laɪə(r)/ *n* bugiardo, -a *mf*
**Lib Dem** /lɪb'dem/ *Br Pol abbr* **Liberal Democrat**
**libel** /'laɪbl/ *n* diffamazione *f* ● *vt* (*pt/pp* **libelled**) diffamare
**libellous** /'laɪbələs/ *a* diffamatorio
**liberal** /'lɪb(ə)rəl/ *a* (*tolerant*) di larghe vedute; (*generous*) generoso. **L~** *a Pol* liberale ● *n* liberale *mf*
**Liberal Democrat** *n Br Pol* liberal-democratico, -a *mf*
**liberalization** /lɪbərəlaɪ'zeɪʃn/ *n* (*of trade*) liberalizzazione *f*
**liberalize** /'lɪbərəlaɪz/ *vt* liberalizzare
**liberally** /'lɪbrəlɪ/ *adv* liberalmente
**liberate** /'lɪbəreɪt/ *vt* liberare
**liberated** /'lɪbəreɪtɪd/ *a* ‹*woman*› emancipata
**liberating** /'lɪbəretɪŋ/ *a* liberatorio
**liberation** /lɪbə'reɪʃn/ *n* liberazione *f*; (*of women*) emancipazione *f*
**liberator** /'lɪbəreɪtə(r)/ *n* liberatore, -trice *mf*
**libertarian** /lɪbə'teərɪən/ *a & n* liberale *nmf*
**libertarianism** /lɪbə'teərɪənɪzm/ *n* liberalismo *m*
**liberty** /'lɪbətɪ/ *n* libertà *f*; **take the ~ of doing sth** prendersi la libertà di fare qcsa; **take liberties** prendersi delle libertà; **be at ~ to do sth** essere libero di fare qcsa
**libido** /lɪ'bi:dəʊ/ *n* libido *f inv*
**Libra** /'li:brə/ *n Astr* Bilancia *f*
**librarian** /laɪ'breərɪən/ *n* bibliotecario, -a *mf*
**library** /'laɪbrərɪ/ *n* biblioteca *f*
**libretto** /lɪ'bretəʊ/ *n* (*pl* **-tti** *or* **-ttos**) libretto *m* di opera
**Libya** /'lɪbɪə/ *n* Libia *f*
**Libyan** /'lɪbɪən/ *a & n* libico, -a *mf*
**lice** /laɪs/ *see* **louse**
**licence** /'laɪsns/ *n* licenza *f*; (*for TV*) canone *m* televisivo; (*for driving*) patente *f*; (*freedom*) sregolatezza *f*
**licence number** *n* numero *m* di targa
**licence plate** *n* targa *f*
**license** /'laɪsns/ *vt* autorizzare; **be ~d** ‹*car*:› avere il bollo; ‹*restaurant*:› essere autorizzato alla vendita di alcolici

**licensee** /laɪsən'si:/ *n* titolare *mf* di licenza (*per la vendita di alcolici*)
**licensing hours** /'laɪsənsɪŋ/ *npl Br* orario *m in cui è permessa la vendita di alcolici*
**licentious** /laɪ'senʃəs/ *a* licenzioso
**licentiousness** /laɪ'senʃəsnɪs/ *n* licenziosità *f*
**lichen** /'laɪkən/ *n Bot* lichene *m*
**lick** /lɪk/ *n* leccata *f*; **a ~ of paint** una passata leggera di pittura ● *vt* leccare; (*fam: defeat*) battere; leccarsi ‹*lips*›; *fam* **~ sb into shape** rendere qcno efficiente
**lid** /lɪd/ *n* coperchio *m*; (*of eye*) palpebra *f*; **keep the ~ on sth** *fam* non lasciare trapelare qcsa
**lido** /'li:dəʊ/ *n* (*beach*) lido *m*; (*Br: pool*) piscina *f* scoperta
**lie¹** /laɪ/ *n* bugia *f*; **tell a ~** mentire ● *vi* (*pt/pp* **lied**, *pres p* **lying**) mentire
**lie²** *vi* (*pt* **lay**, *pp* **lain**, *pres p* **lying**) ‹*person*:› sdraiarsi; ‹*object*:› stare; (*remain*) rimanere; **leave sth lying about** *or* **around** lasciare qcsa in giro; **here ~s...** qui giace...; **~ low** tenersi nascosto
■ **lie back** *vi* (*relax*) rilassarsi
■ **lie down** *vi* sdraiarsi
■ **lie in** *vi* (*stay in bed*) rimanere a letto
**Liechtenstein** /'lɪktənstaɪn/ *n* Liechtenstein *m*
**lie detector** *n* macchina *f* della verità
**lie-down** *n* **have a ~** fare un riposino
**lie-in** *n fam* **have a ~** restare a letto fino a tardi
**lieu** /lju:/ *n* **in ~ of** in luogo di
**lieutenant** /lef'tenənt/ *n* tenente *m*
**life** /laɪf/ *n* (*pl* **lives**) vita *f*; **give one's ~ for sb/one's country** dare la vita per qcno/la patria; **give one's ~ to** (*devote oneself to*) dedicare la propria vita a; **lose one's ~** perdere la vita; **for dear ~** per salvare la pelle; **not on your ~!** *fam* neanche morto!
**life:** **life-and-death** *a* ‹*struggle*› disperato. **lifebelt** *n* salvagente *m*. **lifeblood** *n fig* linfa *f* vitale. **lifeboat** *n* lancia *f* di salvataggio; (*on ship*) scialuppa *f* di salvataggio. **lifebuoy** *n* salvagente *m*. **life expectancy** *n* vita *f* media. **life form** *n* forma *f* di vita. **lifeguard** *n* (*on beach etc*) bagnino, -a *mf*. **life-imprisonment** *n* ergastolo *m*. **life insurance** *n* assicurazione *f* sulla vita. **life jacket** *n* giubbotto *m* di salvataggio
**lifeless** /'laɪflɪs/ *a* inanimato
**life:** **lifelike** *a* realistico. **lifeline** *n* sagola *f* di salvataggio. **lifelong** *a* di tutta la vita
**lifer** /'laɪfə(r)/ *n fam* ergastolano, -a *mf*
**life:** **life sentence** *n* condanna *f* all'ergastolo. **life-size[d]** /'laɪfsaɪz[d]/ *a* in grandezza naturale. **lifespan** *n* durata *f* della vita. **life story** *n* biografia *f*. **lifestyle** *n* stile *m* di vita. **lifetime** *n* vita *f*; **the chance of a ~** un'occasione unica; **~ guarantee** garanzia *f* a vita
**lift** /lɪft/ *n* ascensore *m*; *Auto* passaggio *m*; **give sb a ~** dare un passaggio a qcno; **I got a ~** mi hanno dato un passaggio ● *vt* sollevare;

revocare ⟨*restrictions*⟩; ⟨*fam: steal*⟩ rubare ● *vi* ⟨*fog:*⟩ alzarsi
■ **lift off** *vi* ⟨*rocket:*⟩ partire
■ **lift up** *vt* sollevare
**liftboy** *n* Br lift *m inv*
**lift-off** *n* decollo *m* (*di razzo*)
**ligament** /'lɪgəmənt/ *n* Anat legamento *m*
**light¹** /laɪt/ *a* (*not dark*) luminoso; ~ **green** verde chiaro ● *n* luce *f*; (*lamp*) lampada *f*; **in the ~ of** *fig* alla luce di; **have you got a ~?** ha da accendere?; **come to ~** essere rivelato ● *vt* (*pt/pp* **lit** *or* **lighted**) accendere; (*illuminate*) illuminare
■ **light up** *vt* accendere ⟨*pipe, cigarette*⟩; illuminare ⟨*face*⟩; rischiarare ⟨*sky*⟩ ● *vi* ⟨*face:*⟩ illuminarsi
**light²** *a* (*not heavy*) leggero; **make ~ of** non dare peso a ● *adv* **travel ~** viaggiare con poco bagaglio
**light bulb** *n* lampadina *f*
**lighten¹** /'laɪtn/ *vt* illuminare
**lighten²** *vt* alleggerire ⟨*load*⟩
**light entertainment** *n* varietà *m inv*
**lighter** /'laɪtə(r)/ *n* accendino *m*
**lighter fuel** *n* (*liquid*) gas *m inv* da accendino
**light: light-fingered** /-'fɪŋgəd/ *a* svelto di mano. **light-headed** /-'hedɪd/ *a* sventato. **light-hearted** /-'hɑ:tɪd/ *a* spensierato. **lighthouse** *n* faro *m*. **light industry** *n* industria *f* leggera
**lighting** /'laɪtɪŋ/ *n* illuminazione *f*
**lightly** /'laɪtlɪ/ *adv* leggermente; ⟨*accuse*⟩ con leggerezza; ⟨*take sth*⟩ alla leggera; (*without concern*) senza dare importanza alla cosa; **get off ~** cavarsela a buon mercato
**lightness** /'laɪtnɪs/ *n* leggerezza *f*
**lightning** /'laɪtnɪŋ/ *n* lampo *m*, fulmine *m*
**lightning conductor** *n* parafulmine *m*
**lightning strike** *n* sciopero *m* a sorpresa
**light: light-pen** *n* (*for computer screen*) penna *f* ottica. **lightweight** *a* leggero ● *n* (*in boxing*) peso *m* leggero. **light year** *n* anno *m* luce; **it was ~ ~s ago** è stato secoli fa
**like¹** /laɪk/ *a* simile ● *prep* come; ~ **this/that** così; **what's he ~?** com'è? ● *conj* (*fam: as*) come; (*Am: as if*) come se
**like²** *vt* piacere, gradire; **I should** *or* **would ~** vorrei, gradirei; **I ~ him** mi piace; **I ~ this car** mi piace questa macchina; **I ~ dancing** mi piace ballare; **I ~ that!** *fam* questa mi è piaciuta!; ~ **it or lump it!** abbozzala! ● *n* ~s **and dislikes** *pl* gusti *mpl*
**likeable** /'laɪkəbl/ *a* simpatico
**likelihood** /'laɪklɪhʊd/ *n* probabilità *f*
**likely** /'laɪklɪ/ *a* (**-ier, -iest**) probabile ● *adv* probabilmente; **not ~!** *fam* neanche per sogno!
**like-minded** /laɪk'maɪndɪd/ *a* con gusti affini
**liken** /'laɪkən/ *vt* paragonare (**to** a)
**likeness** /'laɪknɪs/ *n* somiglianza *f*
**likewise** /'laɪkwaɪz/ *adv* lo stesso
**liking** /'laɪkɪŋ/ *n* gusto *m*; **is it to your ~?** è di suo gusto?; **take a ~ to sb** prendere qcno in simpatia

**lilac** /'laɪlək/ *n* lillà *m* ● *a* color lillà
**Lilo®** /'laɪləʊ/ *n* materassino *m* gonfiabile
**lilting** /'lɪltɪŋ/ *a* cadenzato
**lily** /'lɪlɪ/ *n* giglio *m*
**lily of the valley** *n* mughetto *m*
**lily pond** *n* stagno *m* con ninfee
**limb** /lɪm/ *n* arto *m*
**limber** /'lɪmbə(r)/ *vi* ~ **up** sciogliersi i muscoli
**limbo** /'lɪmbəʊ/ *n* (*Relig, fig, dance*) limbo *m*; **be in ~** ⟨*person:*⟩ essere nel limbo del dubbio; ⟨*future of sth:*⟩ essere in sospeso
**lime¹** /laɪm/ *n* (*fruit*) cedro *m*; (*tree*) tiglio *m*
**lime²** *n* calce *f*
**lime: lime-green** *a* & *n* verde *m* limone.
**limelight** /'laɪmlaɪt/ *n* **be in the ~** essere molto in vista. **limestone** /'laɪmstəʊn/ *n* calcare *m*
**limit** /'lɪmɪt/ *n* limite *m*; **be the ~** essere il colmo; **that's the ~!** *fam* questo è troppo! ● *vt* limitare (**to** a)
**limitation** /lɪmɪ'teɪʃn/ *n* limite *m*
**limited** /'lɪmɪtɪd/ *a* ristretto
**limited: limited company** *n* società *f inv* a responsabilità limitata. **limited edition** *n* (*book, lithograph*) edizione *f* limitata. **limited liability** *n* responsabilità *f* limitata
**limitless** /'lɪmɪtlɪs/ *a* infinito
**limousine** /'lɪməzi:n/ *n* limousine *f inv*
**limp¹** /lɪmp/ *n* andatura *f* zoppicante; **have a ~** zoppicare ● *vi* zoppicare
**limp²** *a* floscio
**limpet** /'lɪmpɪt/ *n* **be like a ~** *fig* essere attaccaticcio
**limpid** /'lɪmpɪd/ *a* limpido
**limp-wristed** /-'rɪstɪd/ *a pej* effeminato
**linchpin** /'lɪntʃpɪn/ *n* (*fig: essential element*) perno *m*
**line¹** /laɪn/ *n* linea *f*; (*length of rope, cord*) filo *m*; (*of writing*) riga *f*; (*of poem*) verso *m*; (*row*) fila *f*; (*wrinkle*) ruga *f*; (*of business*) settore *m*; (*Am: queue*) coda *f*; **in ~ with** in conformità con; **bring into ~** mettere al passo ⟨*structure, law*⟩; **in the ~ of duty** (*of policeman*) nell'esercizio delle proprie funzioni; ~ **of fire** linea *f* di tiro; **stand in ~** (*Am: queue*) fare la coda; **in ~ for** (*promotion etc*) in lista per; **on the ~** ⟨*job, career*⟩ in serio pericolo; **read between the ~s** *fig* leggere tra le righe ● *vt* segnare; fiancheggiare ⟨*street*⟩; foderare ⟨*garment*⟩
■ **line up** *vi* allinearsi ● *vt* allineare
**lineage** /'lɪnɪɪdʒ/ *n* lignaggio *m*
**linear** /'lɪnɪə(r)/ *a* lineare
**lined¹** /laɪnd/ *a* ⟨*face*⟩ rugoso; ⟨*paper*⟩ a righe
**lined²** *a* ⟨*garment*⟩ foderato
**line manager** *n* line manager *m inv*
**linen** /'lɪnɪn/ *n* lino *m*; (*articles*) biancheria *f* ● *attrib* di lino
**linen basket** *n* cesto *m* della biancheria
**liner** /'laɪnə(r)/ *n* nave *f* di linea
**linesman** /'laɪnzmən/ *n* Sport guardalinee *m inv*
**line-up** *n* (*personnel, Sport*) formazione *f*; (*identification*) confronto *m* all'americana

**linger** /'lɪŋgə(r)/ *vi* indugiare
**lingerie** /'lɒʒərɪ/ *n* biancheria *f* intima (*da donna*)
**lingering** /'lɪŋgərɪŋ/ *a* ⟨*illness*⟩ lento; ⟨*look*⟩ prolungato; ⟨*doubt*⟩ persistente
**linguist** /'lɪŋgwɪst/ *n* linguista *mf*
**linguistic** /lɪŋ'gwɪstɪk/ *a* linguistico
**linguistically** /lɪŋ'gwɪstɪklɪ/ *adv* linguisticamente
**linguistics** /lɪŋ'gwɪstɪks/ *n* linguistica *fsg*
**lining** /'laɪnɪŋ/ *n* (*of garment*) fodera *f*; (*of brakes*) guarnizione *f*
**link** /lɪŋk/ *n* (*of chain*) anello *m*; *fig* legame *m* ● *vt* collegare; **~ arms** prendersi sotto braccio
■ **link up** *vi* unirsi (**with** a); *TV* collegarsi
**linkage** /'lɪŋkɪdʒ/ *n* (*connection*) connessione *f*; (*in genetics*) associazione *f*
**links** /lɪŋks/ *n or npl* campo *msg* da golf
**link-up** *n* collegamento *m*
**lino** /'laɪnəʊ/ *n*, **linoleum** /lɪ'nəʊlɪəm/ *n* linoleum *m*
**linseed oil** /'lɪnsi:dɔɪl/ *n* olio *m* [di semi] di lino
**lint** /lɪnt/ *n* garza *f*
**lintel** /'lɪntəl/ *n* architrave *m*
**lion** /'laɪən/ *n* leone *m*; **get the ~'s share** *fig* prendersi la fetta più grossa
**lion cub** *n* leoncino *m*
**lioness** /'laɪənɪs/ *n* leonessa *f*
**lip** /lɪp/ *n* labbro *m* (*pl* labbra *f*); (*edge*) bordo *m*
**lip gloss** *n* lucidalabbra *m inv*
**liposuction** /'laɪpəʊsʌkʃn/ *n* liposuzione *f*
**lip: lip-read** *vi* leggere le labbra. **lip-reading** *n* lettura *f* delle labbra. **lip-salve** *n* burro *m* [di] cacao. **lip-service** *n* pay **~ to** approvare soltanto a parole. **lipstick** *n* rossetto *m*
**liquefy** /'lɪkwɪfaɪ/ *v* (*pt/pp* **-ied**) ● *vt* liquefare ● *vi* liquefarsi
**liqueur** /lɪ'kjʊə(r)/ *n* liquore *m*
**liquid** /'lɪkwɪd/ *n* liquido *m* ● *a* liquido
**liquidate** /'lɪkwɪdeɪt/ *vt* liquidare
**liquidation** /lɪkwɪ'deɪʃn/ *n* liquidazione *f*; **go into ~** *Comm* andare in liquidazione
**liquidator** /'lɪkwɪdeɪtə(r)/ *n* liquidatore, -trice *mf*
**liquid crystal display** *n* visualizzatore *m* a cristalli liquidi
**liquidize** /'lɪkwɪdaɪz/ *vt* rendere liquido
**liquidizer** /'lɪkwɪdaɪzə(r)/ *n* Culin frullatore *m*
**liquor** /'lɪkə(r)/ *n* bevanda *f* alcoolica
**liquorice** /'lɪkərɪs/ *n* liquirizia *f*
**liquor store** *n Am* negozio *m* di alcolici
**lira** /'lɪərə/ *n* lira *f*; **50,000 lire** 50.000 lire
**lisp** /lɪsp/ *n* pronuncia *f* con la lisca; **have a ~** parlare con la lisca ● *vi* parlare con la lisca
**list¹** /lɪst/ *n* lista *f* ● *vt* elencare
**list²** *vi* ⟨*ship:*⟩ inclinarsi
**listen** /'lɪsn/ *vi* ascoltare; **~ to** ascoltare
**listener** /'lɪs(ə)nə(r)/ *n* ascoltatore, -trice *mf*
**listeria** /lɪ'stɪərɪə/ *n* (*illness*) listeriosi *f*; (*bacteria*) listeria *f*
**listings** /'lɪstɪŋz/ *npl* TV programma *m* tv
**listless** /'lɪstlɪs/ *a* svogliato
**listlessly** /'lɪstlɪslɪ/ *adv* in modo svogliato

**lit** /lɪt/ *see* **light¹**
**litany** /'lɪtənɪ/ *n* litania *f*
**literacy** /'lɪtərəsɪ/ *n* alfabetizzazione *f*
**literal** /'lɪtərəl/ *a* letterale
**literally** /'lɪt(ə)rəlɪ/ *adv* letteralmente
**literary** /'lɪtərərɪ/ *a* letterario
**literary critic** *n* critico, -a *mf* letterario, -a
**literate** /'lɪtərət/ *a* **be ~** saper leggere e scrivere
**literati** /lɪtə'rɑːtɪ/ *npl* letterati *mpl*
**literature** /'lɪtrətʃə(r)/ *n* letteratura *f*
**lithe** /laɪð/ *a* flessuoso
**lithographer** /lɪ'θɒgrəfə(r)/ *n* litografo, -a *mf*
**lithography** /lɪ'θɒgrəfɪ/ *n* litografia *f*
**Lithuania** /lɪθjʊ'eɪnɪə/ *n* Lituania *f*
**Lithuanian** /lɪθjʊ'eɪnɪən/ *a & n* lituano, -a *mf*; (*language*) lituano *m*
**litigation** /lɪtɪ'geɪʃn/ *n* causa *f* [giudiziaria]
**litmus paper** /'lɪtməs/ *n* cartina *f* di tornasole
**litmus test** *n Chem* test *m inv* con cartina di tornasole; *fig* prova *f* del nove
**litre** /'liːtə(r)/ *n* litro *m*
**litter** /'lɪtə(r)/ *n* immondizie *fpl*; *Zool* figliata *f* ● *vt* **be ~ed with sth** essere ingombrato di qcsa
**litter-bin** *n* bidone *m* della spazzatura
**litterbug** /'lɪtəbʌg/ *n persona f che butta per terra cartacce e rifiuti*
**little** /'lɪtl/ *a* piccolo; (*not much*) poco ● *adv* & *n* poco *m*; **a ~** un po'; **a ~ water** un po' d'acqua; **a ~ better** un po' meglio; **~ by ~** a poco a poco
**little finger** *n* mignolo *m* (*della mano*)
**little-known** *a* poco noto
**liturgical** /lɪ'tɜːdʒɪkl/ *a* liturgico
**liturgy** /'lɪtədʒɪ/ *n* liturgia *f*
**live¹** /laɪv/ *a* vivo; ⟨*ammunition*⟩ carico; **~ broadcast** trasmissione *f* in diretta; **be ~** *Electr* essere sotto tensione; **~ wire** *n fig* persona *f* dinamica ● *adv* ⟨*broadcast*⟩ in diretta
**live²** /lɪv/ *vi* vivere; (*reside*) abitare; **~ with** convivere con
■ **live down** *vt* far dimenticare
■ **live for** *vt* vivere solo per ⟨*one's work, family*⟩
■ **live off** *vt* vivere alle spalle di
■ **live on** *vt* vivere di ● *vi* sopravvivere
■ **live through** *vt* vivere
■ **live together** *vi* ⟨*friends:*⟩ vivere insieme; ⟨*lovers:*⟩ convivere
■ **live up** *vt* **~ it up** far la bella vita
■ **live up to** *vt* essere all'altezza di
■ **live with** *vt* convivere con ⟨*lover, situation*⟩; vivere con ⟨*mother etc*⟩
**lived-in** /'lɪvdɪn/ *a* **have that ~ look** ⟨*room, flat:*⟩ avere un'aria vissuta
**live-in** *a* ⟨*maid, nanny*⟩ che vive in casa
**livelihood** /'laɪvlɪhʊd/ *n* mezzi *mpl* di sostentamento
**liveliness** /'laɪvlɪnɪs/ *n* vivacità *f*
**lively** /'laɪvlɪ/ *a* (**-ier, -iest**) vivace
■ **liven up** /'laɪvn/ *vt* vivacizzare ● *vi* vivacizzarsi

**liver** /'lɪvə(r)/ *n* fegato *m*

**liver pâté** *n* pâté *m inv* di fegato

**Liverpudlian** /lɪvə'pʌdlɪən/ *n* (*born there*) originario, -a *mf* di Liverpool; (*living there*) abitante *mf* di Liverpool

**lives** /laɪvz/ *see* **life**

**livestock** /'laɪvstɒk/ *n* bestiame *m*

**livid** /'lɪvɪd/ *a fam* livido

**living** /'lɪvɪŋ/ *a* vivo ● *n* **earn one's ~** guadagnarsi da vivere; **the ~** *pl* i vivi

**living room** *n* soggiorno *m*

**lizard** /'lɪzəd/ *n* lucertola *f*

**load** /ləʊd/ *n* carico *m*; **~s of** *fam* un sacco di; **that's a ~ off my mind** mi sono tolto un peso [dallo stomaco] ● *vt* **~** [**up**] caricare

**loaded** /'ləʊdɪd/ *a* carico; (*fam: rich*) ricchissimo; **~ question** domanda *f* esplosiva *f*

**loading bay** /'ləʊdɪŋ/ *n* piazzola *f* di carico e scarico

**loaf¹** /ləʊf/ *n* (*pl* **loaves**) pane *m*; (*round*) pagnotta *f*; **use one's ~** (*fam*) pensare con il proprio cervello

**loaf²** *vi* oziare

**loafer** /'ləʊfə(r)/ *n* (*idler*) scansafatiche *mf inv*; (*shoe*) mocassino *m*

**loan** /ləʊn/ *n* prestito *m*; **on ~** in prestito ● *vt* prestare

**loan shark** *n fam* strozzino, -a *mf*

**loath** /ləʊθ/ *a* **be ~ to do sth** essere restio a fare qcsa

**loathe** /ləʊð/ *vt* detestare

**loathing** /'ləʊðɪŋ/ *n* disgusto *m*

**loathsome** /'ləʊðsəm/ *a* disgustoso

**loaves** /ləʊvz/ *see* **loaf**

**lob** /lɒb/ *vt* (*pres p etc* **-bb-**) lanciare in alto; *Sport* respingere a pallonetto ● *n Sport* pallonetto *m*

**lobby** /'lɒbɪ/ *n* atrio *m*; *Pol* gruppo *m* di pressione, lobby *m inv*

**lobbyist** /'lɒbɪɪst/ *n* lobbista *mf*

**lobe** /ləʊb/ *n* (*of ear*) lobo *m*

**lobelia** /lə'bi:lɪə/ *n* lobelia *f*

**lobster** /'lɒbstə(r)/ *n* aragosta *f*

**lobster pot** *n* nassa *f* per aragoste

**local** /'ləʊkl/ *a* locale; **under ~ anaesthetic** sotto anestesia locale; **I'm not ~** non sono del posto ● *n* abitante *mf* del luogo; (*fam: public house*) pub *m inv* locale

**local: local authority** *n* autorità *f* locale. **local bus** *n* bus *m* locale. **local call** *n Teleph* telefonata *f* urbana. **local government** *n* autorità *f inv* locale. **local network** *n Comput* rete *f* locale

**locality** /ləʊ'kælətɪ/ *n* zona *f*

**localized** /'ləʊkəlaɪzd/ *a* localizzato

**locally** /'ləʊkəlɪ/ *adv* localmente; ⟨*live, work*⟩ nei paraggi

**locate** /ləʊ'keɪt/ *vt* situare; trovare ⟨*person*⟩; **be ~d** essere situato

**location** /ləʊ'keɪʃn/ *n* posizione *f*; **filmed on ~** girato in esterni

**loch** /lɒx/ *n* lago *m*

**lock¹** /lɒk/ *n* (*of hair*) ciocca *f*

**lock²** *n* (*on door*) serratura *f*; (*on canal*) chiu-sa *f* ● *vt* chiudere a chiave; bloccare ⟨*wheels*⟩ ● *vi* chiudersi

■ **lock in** *vt* chiudere dentro

■ **lock out** *vt* chiudere fuori

■ **lock up** *vt* (*in prison*) mettere dentro ● *vi* chiudere

**locker** /'lɒkə(r)/ *n* armadietto *m*

**locket** /'lɒkɪt/ *n* medaglione *m*

**lock: lockout** *n* serrata *f*. **locksmith** *n* fabbro *m*. **lock-up** *n* (*prison*) guardina *f*

**loco** /'ləʊkəʊ/ *a* (*Br: crazy*) toccato

**locomotion** /ləʊkə'məʊʃn/ *n* locomozione *f*

**locomotive** /ləʊkə'məʊtɪv/ *n* locomotiva *f*

**locum** /'ləʊkəm/ *n* sostituto, -a *mf*

**locust** /'ləʊkəst/ *n* locusta *f*

**lodge** /lɒdʒ/ *n* (*porter's*) portineria *f*; (*masonic*) loggia *f* ● *vt* presentare ⟨*claim, complaint*⟩; (*with bank, solicitor*) depositare; **be ~d** essersi conficcato ● *vi* essere a pensione (**with** da); (*become fixed*) conficcarsi

**lodger** /'lɒdʒə(r)/ *n* inquilino, -a *mf*

**lodgings** /'lɒdʒɪŋ/ *npl* camere *fpl* in affitto

**loft** /lɒft/ *n* soffitta *f*

**lofty** /'lɒftɪ/ *a* (**-ier, -iest**) alto; (*haughty*) altezzoso

**log** /lɒg/ *n* ceppo *m*; *Auto* libretto *m* di circolazione; *Naut* giornale *m* di bordo; **sleep like a ~** *fam* dormire come un ghiro ● *vt* (*pt/pp* **logged**) registrare

■ **log in** *vi* aprire una sessione

■ **log off** *vi* disconnettersi

■ **log on** *vi* connettersi (**to** a)

■ **log out** *vi* chiudere una sessione

**logarithm** /'lɒgərɪðm/ *n* logaritmo *m*

**logbook** /'lɒgbʊk/ *n Naut* giornale *m* di bordo; *Auto* libretto *m* di circolazione

**logger** /'lɒgə(r)/ *n* boscaiolo *m*

**loggerheads** /'lɒgəhedz/ *npl* **be at ~** *fam* essere in totale disaccordo

**logic** /'lɒdʒɪk/ *n* logica *f*

**logical** /'lɒdʒɪkl/ *a* logico

**logically** /'lɒdʒɪklɪ/ *adv* logicamente

**logistics** /lə'dʒɪstɪks/ *npl* logistica *f*

**logo** /'ləʊgəʊ/ *n* logo *m inv*

**loin** /lɔɪn/ *n Culin* lombata *f*

**loin chop** *n* lombatina *f*

**loincloth** /'lɔɪnklɒθ/ *n* perizoma *m*

**loiter** /'lɔɪtə(r)/ *vi* gironzolare

**loll** /lɒl/ *vi* **~ about** (*posture*) stravaccarsi; (*do nothing*) starsene in panciolle

**lollipop** /'lɒlɪpɒp/ *n* lecca-lecca *m inv*

**lollop** /'lɒləp/ *vi* ⟨*rabbit, person:*⟩ avanzare a balzi

**lolly** /'lɒlɪ/ *n* lecca-lecca *m inv*; (*fam: money*) quattrini *mpl*

**Lombardy** /'lɒmbədɪ/ *n* Lombardia *f*

**London** /'lʌndən/ *n* Londra *f* ● *attrib* londinese, di Londra

**Londoner** /'lʌndənə(r)/ *n* londinese *mf*

**lone** /ləʊn/ *a* solitario

**loneliness** /'ləʊnlɪnɪs/ *n* solitudine *f*

**lonely** /'ləʊnlɪ/ *a* (**-ier, -iest**) solitario; ⟨*person*⟩ solo

**loner** /'ləʊnə(r)/ *n* persona *f* solitaria

**lonesome** /'ləʊnsəm/ *a* solo

**long¹** /lɒŋ/ a (**-er** /'lɒŋgə(r)/, **-est** /'lɒŋgɪst/) lungo; **a ~ time** molto tempo; **a ~ way** distante: **in the ~ run** a lungo andare; (*in the end*) alla fin fine ● adv a lungo, lungamente: **how ~ is it?** quanto è lungo?: (*in time*) quanto dura?; **all day ~** tutto il giorno; **not ~ ago** non molto tempo fa; **before ~** fra breve; **he's no ~er here** non è più qui; **as** or **so ~ as** finché; (*provided that*) purché; **so ~!** fam ciao!; **will you be ~?** ti ci vuole molto?

**long²** vi **~ for** desiderare ardentemente

**long: long-awaited** a tanto atteso. **long-distance** a a grande distanza; *Sport* di fondo; (*call*) interurbano. **long division** n divisione f

**longevity** /lɒn'dʒevətɪ/ n longevità f

**long: long face** n muso m lungo. **longhand** /'lɒŋhænd/ n in **~** in scrittura ordinaria. **long-haul** attrib su lunga distanza; (*plane*) per lunghi tragitti

**longing** /'lɒŋɪŋ/ a desideroso ● n brama f

**longingly** /'lɒŋɪŋlɪ/ adv con desiderio

**longitude** /'lɒŋgɪtjuːd/ n Geog longitudine f

**long: long-life milk** n latte m a lunga conservazione. **long-lived** /-'lɪvd/ a longevo. **long jump** n salto m in lungo. **long-playing record** n 33 giri m inv. **long-range** a Mil, Aeron a lunga portata; (*forecast*) a lungo termine. **long-sighted** /-'saɪtɪd/ a presbite. **long-sleeved** /-'sliːvd/ a a maniche lunghe. **long-standing** a di vecchia data. **long-suffering** a infinitamente paziente. **long-term** a a lunga scadenza. **long wave** n onde fpl lunghe. **long-winded** /-'wɪndɪd/ a prolisso

**loo** /luː/ n fam gabinetto m

**look** /lʊk/ n occhiata f; (*appearance*) aspetto m; [**good**] **~s** pl bellezza f; **have a ~ at** dare un'occhiata a ● vi guardare; (*seem*) sembrare; **~ here!** mi ascolti bene!; **~ at** guardare; **~ for** cercare; **~ sb in the eye** guardare negli occhi qcno; **~ sb up and down** guardare qcno dall'alto in basso; **~ a fool** fare la figura del cretino; **~ young/old for one's age** portarsi bene/male gli anni; **~ like** (*resemble*) assomigliare a; **it ~s as if it's going to rain** sembra che stia per piovere; **~ sharp** (*fam: hurry up*) darsi una mossa

■ **look after** vt badare a

■ **look ahead** vi (*think of the future*) guardare al futuro

■ **look back** vi girarsi; (*think of the past*) guardare indietro

■ **look down** vi guardare in basso; **~ down on sb** guardare dall'alto in basso qcno

■ **look forward to** vt essere impaziente di

■ **look in on** vt passare da

■ **look into** vt (*examine*) esaminare

■ **look on** vi (*watch*) guardare ● vt **~ sb/sth as** (*consider to be*) considerare qcno/qcsa come

■ **look on to** vt (*room*) dare su

■ **look out** vi guardare fuori; (*take care*) fare attenzione; **~ out!** attento! ● vt cercare (*sth for sb*)

■ **look out for** vt cercare

■ **look over** vt riguardare (*notes*); ispezionare (*house*)

■ **look round** vi girarsi; (*in shop, town etc*) dare un'occhiata

■ **look through** vt dare un'occhiata a (*script, notes*)

■ **look to** vt (*rely on*) contare su

■ **look up** vi guardare in alto ● vt cercare [nel dizionario] (*word*); (*visit*) andare a trovare

■ **look up to** vt fig rispettare

**look-alike** n sosia mf inv

**looker-on** /lʊkər'ɒn/ n (pl **lookers-on**) spettatore, -trice mf

**look-in** n Br fam **give sb a ~** dare una chance a qcno; **get a ~** avere una chance

**lookout** /'lʊkaʊt/ n guardia f; (*prospect*) prospettiva f; **be on the ~ for** tenere gli occhi aperti per

**loom¹** /luːm/ n telaio m

**loom²** vi apparire; fig profilarsi

**loony** /'luːnɪ/ a & n fam matto, -a mf; **~ bin** manicomio m

**loop** /luːp/ n cappio m; (*on garment*) passante m

**loophole** /'luːphəʊl/ n (*in the law*) scappatoia f

**loopy** /'luːpɪ/ a fam matto

**loose** /luːs/ a libero; (*knot*) allentato; (*page*) staccato; (*clothes*) largo; (*morals*) dissoluto; (*inexact*) vago; **be at a ~ end** non sapere cosa fare; **come ~** (*knot:*) sciogliersi; **set ~** liberare

**loose: loose change** n spiccioli mpl. **loose chippings** npl ghiaino m. **loose-leaf notebook** n raccoglitore m di fogli

**loosely** /'luːslɪ/ adv scorrevolmente; (*defined*) vagamente

**loosen** /'luːsn/ vt sciogliere

■ **loosen up** vt sciogliere (*muscles*) ● vi (*fam: relax*) rilassarsi

**loot** /luːt/ n bottino m ● vt/i depredare

**looter** /'luːtə(r)/ n predatore, -trice mf

**looting** /'luːtɪŋ/ n saccheggio m

■ **lop off** /lɒp/ vt (pt/pp **lopped**) potare

**lop-eared** /'lɒpɪəd/ a con le orecchie [a] penzoloni

■ **lope off** /ləʊp'ɒf/ vi andarsene a passi lunghi

**lopsided** /lɒp'saɪdɪd/ a sbilenco

**loquacious** /lə'kweɪʃəs/ a loquace

**lord** /lɔːd/ n signore m; (*title*) Lord m; **House of L~s** Camera f dei Lords; **the L~'s Prayer** il Padrenostro; **good L~!** Dio mio!

**Lordship** /'lɔːdʃɪp/ n **your/his ~** (*of noble*) Sua Signoria; **your ~** (*to judge*) Signor Giudice

**lore** /lɔː(r)/ n tradizioni fpl

**lorry** /'lɒrɪ/ n camion m inv

**lorry driver** n camionista mf

**lose** /luːz/ v (pt/pp **lost**) ● vt perdere; **~ heart** perdersi d'animo; **~ one's inhibitions** disinibirsi; **~ one's nerve** farsi prendere dalla paura; **~ sight of** perdere di vista, perdere d'occhio; **~ touch with** perdere di vista; **~ track of time** perdere la nozio-

ne del tempo; ~ **weight** calare di peso ● *vi*
perdere; ‹*clock*:› essere indietro
■ **lose out** *vi* rimetterci
**loser** /'luːzə(r)/ *n* perdente *mf*
**losing battle** /'luːzɪŋ/ *n* battaglia *f* persa
**loss** /lɒs/ *n* perdita *f*; **~es** *pl Comm* perdite
*fpl*; **be at a ~** essere perplesso; **be at a ~ for**
**words** non trovare le parole; **make a ~**
*Comm* subire una perdita
**loss: loss adjuster** /'lɒsədʒʌstə(r)/ *n Comm*
perito *m* di assicurazione. **loss-leader** *n* articolo *m* civetta. **loss-making** /'lɒsmeɪkɪŋ/ *a*
‹*company*› in passivo; ‹*product*› che non vende
**lost** /lɒst/ *see* **lose** ● *a* perduto; **get ~** perdersi; **get ~!** *fam* va a quel paese!
**lost and found** *n Am* oggetti *mpl* smarriti
**lost property office** *n* ufficio *m* oggetti
smarriti
**lot¹** /lɒt/ (*at auction*) lotto *m*; (*piece of land*)
lotto *m*; **draw ~s** tirare a sorte
**lot²** *n* **the ~** il tutto; **a ~ of, ~s of** molti; **the**
**~ of you** tutti voi; **it has changed a ~** è
cambiato molto
**lotion** /'ləʊʃn/ *n* lozione *f*
**lottery** /'lɒtərɪ/ *n* lotteria *f*
**lottery ticket** *n* biglietto *m* della lotteria
**loud** /laʊd/ *a* sonoro, alto; ‹*colours*› sgargiante ● *adv* forte; **out ~** ad alta voce
**loud hailer** /'heɪlə(r)/ *n* megafono *m*
**loudly** /'laʊdlɪ/ *adv* forte
**loudspeaker** /laʊd'spiːkə(r)/ *n* altoparlan-
te *m*
**lounge** /laʊndʒ/ *n* salotto *m*; (*in hotel*) salone
*m* ● *vi* poltrire
■ **lounge about** *vi* stare in panciolle
**lounge suit** *n* vestito *m* da uomo (*formale*)
**louse** /laʊs/, *n* (*pl* **lice**) pidocchio *m*
■ **louse up** *vt* (*fam: ruin*) guastare
**lousy** /'laʊzɪ/ *a* (**-ier, -iest**) *fam* schifoso
**lout** /laʊt/ *n* zoticone *m*
**loutish** /'laʊtɪʃ/ *a* rozzo
**louvred** /'luːvəd/ *a* ‹*door, blinds*› con le gelo-
sie
**lovable** /'lʌvəbl/ *a* adorabile
**love** /lʌv/ *n* amore *m*; (*Tennis*) zero *m*; **in ~**
innamorato (**with** di) ● *vt* amare ‹*person,*
*country*›; **I ~ watching tennis** mi piace molto guardare il tennis
**love: love affair** *n* relazione *f* [sentimentale].
**lovebite** *n* succhiotto *m*. **love letter** *n* lettera
*f* d'amore. **love life** *n* vita *f* sentimentale.
**lovemaking** *n* il fare l'amore
**lovely** /'lʌvlɪ/ *a* (**-ier, -iest**) bello; (*in looks*)
bello, attraente; (*in character*) piacevole;
‹*meal*› delizioso; **have a ~ time** divertirsi
molto
**lover** /'lʌvə(r)/ *n* amante *mf*
**love song** *n* canzone *f* d'amore
**love story** *n* storia *f* d'amore
**lovey-dovey** /lʌvɪ'dʌvɪ/ *a Br fam* **get all ~**
fare i piccioncini
**loving** /'lʌvɪŋ/ *a* affettuoso
**lovingly** /'lʌvɪŋlɪ/ *adv* affettuosamente
**low** /ləʊ/ *a* basso; (*depressed*) giù *inv* ● *adv*

basso: **feel ~** sentirsi giù ● *n* minimo *m*;
*Meteorol* depressione *f*; **at an all-time ~**
‹*prices etc*› al livello minimo
**low:** **lowbrow** /'ləʊbraʊ/ *a* di scarsa cultura.
**low-calorie** *a* ipocalorico. **low-cut** *a* ‹*dress*›
scollato. **low gear** *n Auto* marcia *f* bassa
**lower** /'ləʊə(r)/ *a* & *adv see* **low** ● *vt* abbassare; **~ oneself** abbassarsi
**lowest common denominator** /'ləʊɪst
...dɪ'nɒmɪneɪtə(r)/ *n* minimo denominatore *m*
comune
**low: low-fat** *a* ‹*diet*› a basso contenuto di
grassi; ‹*cheese, milk*› magro. **low-grade** *a* di
qualità inferiore. **low-key** *a fig* moderato.
**lowlands** *npl* pianure *fpl*
**lowly** /'ləʊlɪ/ *a* (**-ier, -iest**) umile
**low tide** *n* bassa marea *f*
**loyal** /'lɔɪəl/ *a* leale
**loyally** /'lɔɪəlɪ/ *adv* lealmente
**loyalty** /'lɔɪəltɪ/ *n* lealtà *f*
**lozenge** /'lɒzɪndʒ/ *n* losanga *f*; (*tablet*) pastiglia
**LP** *n abbr* (**long-playing record**) LP *m inv*
**L-plate** *n Br Auto* cartello *m* che indica che il
conducente non ha ancora preso la patente
**LSD** *n* LSD *m*
**Ltd** *abbr* (**Limited**) s.r.l.
**lubricant** /'luːbrɪkənt/ *n* lubrificante *m*
**lubricate** /'luːbrɪkeɪt/ *vt* lubrificare
**lubrication** /luːbrɪ'keɪʃn/ *n* lubrificazione *f*
**lucid** /'luːsɪd/ *a* ‹*explanation*› chiaro; (*sane*)
lucido
**lucidity** /luː'sɪdətɪ/ *n* lucidità *f*; (*of*
*explanation*) chiarezza *f*
**luck** /lʌk/ *n* fortuna *f*; **bad ~** sfortuna *f*; **good**
**~!** buona fortuna!
**luckily** /'lʌkɪlɪ/ *adv* fortunatamente
**lucky** /'lʌkɪ/ *a* (**-ier, -iest**) fortunato; **be ~** essere fortunato; ‹*thing*:› portare fortuna
**lucky charm** *n* portafortuna *m inv*
**lucky dip** *n* pesca *f* di beneficenza
**lucrative** /'luːkrətɪv/ *a* lucrativo
**lucre** /'luːkə(r)/ *n* (*fam: money*) soldi *mpl*
**ludicrous** /'luːdɪkrəs/ *a* ridicolo
**ludicrously** /'luːdɪkrəslɪ/ *adv* ‹*expensive,*
*complex*› eccessivamente
**ludo** /'luːdəʊ/ *n Br* gioco *m* da tavola
**lug** /lʌg/ *vt* (*pt/pp* **lugged**) *fam* trascinare
**luggage** /'lʌgɪdʒ/ *n* bagaglio *m*
**luggage: luggage-rack** *n* portabagagli *m*
*inv*. **luggage trolley** *n* carrello *m* portabagagli. **luggage van** *n* bagagliaio *m*
**lughole** /'lʌghəʊl/ *n* (*Br fam: ear*) orecchio *m*
**lugubrious** /lʊ'guːbrɪəs/ *a* lugubre
**lukewarm** /'luːkwɔːm/ *a* tiepido; *fig* poco
entusiasta
**lull** /lʌl/ *n* pausa *f* ● *vt* **~ to sleep** cullare
**lullaby** /'lʌləbaɪ/ *n* ninnananna *f*
**lumbago** /lʌm'beɪgəʊ/ *n* lombaggine *f*
**lumbar** /'lʌmbə(r)/ *a* lombare
**lumber** /'lʌmbə(r)/ *n* cianfrusaglie *fpl*; (*Am:*
*timber*) legname *m* ● *vt fam* **~ sb with sth**
affibbiare qcsa a qcno
**lumberjack** /'lʌmbədʒæk/ *n* tagliaboschi *m*
*inv*

**luminary** /'lu:mɪnərɪ/ n (fig: person) luminare mf

**luminous** /'lu:mɪnəs/ a luminoso

**lump**[1] /lʌmp/ n (of sugar) zolletta f; (swelling) gonfiore m; (in breast) nodulo m; (in sauce) grumo m; a ~ in one's throat un groppo alla gola ● vt ~ together ammucchiare

**lump**[2] vt ~ it fam you'll just have to ~ it che ti piaccia o no è così

**lump sugar** n zucchero m in zollette

**lump sum** n somma f globale

**lumpy** /'lʌmpɪ/ a (-ier, -iest) grumoso

**lunacy** /'lu:nəsɪ/ n follia f

**lunar** /'lu:nə(r)/ a lunare

**lunatic** /'lu:nətɪk/ n pazzo, -a mf

**lunch** /lʌntʃ/ n pranzo m; she's gone to ~ è andata a pranzo; let's have ~ together sometime pranziamo qualche volta insieme ● vi pranzare

**lunch box** n cestino m del pranzo

**luncheon** /'lʌntʃn/ n (formal) pranzo m

**luncheon meat** n carne f in scatola

**luncheon voucher** n buono m pasto

**lunch hour** n intervallo m per il pranzo

**lunchtime** /'lʌntʃtaɪm/ n ora f di pranzo

**lung** /lʌŋ/ n polmone m

**lung cancer** n cancro m al polmone

**lunge** /lʌndʒ/ vi lanciarsi (at su)

**lurch**[1] /lɜ:tʃ/ n leave in the ~ fam lasciare nei guai

**lurch**[2] vi barcollare

**lure** /lʊə(r)/ n esca f; fig lusinga f ● vt adescare

**lurid** /'lʊərɪd/ a (gaudy) sgargiante; (sensational) sensazionalistico

**lurk** /lɜ:k/ vi appostarsi

**luscious** /'lʌʃəs/ a saporito; fig sexy inv

**lush** /lʌʃ/ a lussureggiante

**lust** /lʌst/ n lussuria f ● vi ~ after desiderare [fortemente]

**lustful** /'lʌstfʊl/ a lussurioso

**lustre** /'lʌstə(r)/ n lustro m

**lusty** /'lʌstɪ/ a (-ier, -iest) vigoroso

**lute** /lu:t/ n liuto m

**Luxembourg** /'lʌksəmbɜ:g/ n (city) Lussemburgo f; (state) Lussemburgo m

**luxuriant** /lʌg'ʒʊərɪənt/ a lussureggiante, rigoglioso

**luxuriantly** /lʌg'ʒʊərɪəntlɪ/ adv rigogliosamente

**luxurious** /lʌg'ʒʊərɪəs/ a lussuoso

**luxuriously** /lʌg'ʒʊərɪəslɪ/ adv lussuosamente

**luxury** /'lʌkʃərɪ/ n lusso m; live in ~ vivere nel lusso ● attrib di lusso

**LV** abbr **luncheon voucher**

**LW** abbr (**long wave**) OL

**lychee** /'laɪtʃi:/ n litchi m inv

**lych-gate** /'lɪtʃ-/ n entrata f coperta di un cimitero

**lycra**® /'laɪkrə/ n lycra f

**lying** /'laɪɪŋ/ see **lie**[1], **lie**[2] ● n mentire m

**lymph gland** /'lɪmf/ n linfoghiandola f

**lymph node** n linfonodo m

**lynch** /lɪntʃ/ vt linciare

**lynchpin** /'lɪntʃpɪn/ n fig pilastro m

**lynx** /lɪŋks/ n lince f

**lyric** /'lɪrɪk/ a lirico

**lyrical** /'lɪrɪkl/ a lirico; (fam: enthusiastic) entusiasta. ~ **poetry** n poesia f lirica

**lyricism** /'lɪrɪsɪzm/ n lirismo m

**lyrics** /'lɪrɪks/ npl parole fpl

# Mm

**m, M** /em/ n (letter) m, M f inv

**m** abbr (**metre(s)**) m; abbr (**million**) milione m; abbr (**mile(s)**) miglio

**MA** n abbr (**Master of Arts**) (diploma) laurea f in lettere; (person) laureato, -a mf in lettere; Am abbr **Massachusetts**

**ma'am** /mɑ:m/ int signora; (to queen) Sua Altezza

**mac** /mæk/ n fam impermeabile m

**macabre** /mə'kɑ:br/ a macabro

**macaroni** /mækə'rəʊnɪ/ n maccheroni mpl

**macaroni cheese** n maccheroni mpl gratinati al formaggio

**macaroon** /mækə'ru:n/ n ≈ amaretto m

**mace**[1] /meɪs/ n (staff) mazza f

**mace**[2] n (spice) macis mf

**Macedonia** /mæsə'dəʊnɪə/ n Macedonia f

**machete** /mə'ʃetɪ/ n machete m inv

**Machiavellian** /mækɪə'velɪən/ a machiavellico

**machinations** /mækɪ'neɪʃnz/ macchinazioni fpl

**machine** /mə'ʃi:n/ n macchina f ● vt (sew) cucire a macchina; Techn lavorare a macchina

**machine: machine-gun** n mitragliatrice f. **machine operator** n addetto, -a mf alle macchine. **machine-readable** a ‹data, text› leggibile dalla macchina

**machinery** /mə'ʃi:nərɪ/ n macchinario m; fig meccanismo m

**machine: machine-stitch** vt cucire a macchina. **machine tool** n macchina f utensile. **machine translation** n traduzione f elettronica

**machinist** /mə'ʃi:nɪst/ n macchinista mf;

199

**machismo | maintain**

(on sewing machine) lavorante mf adetto, -a alla macchina da cucire

**machismo** /məˈkɪzməʊ/ n machismo m
**macho** /ˈmætʃəʊ/ a macho inv
**mackerel** /ˈmækr(ə)l/ n inv sgombro m
**mackintosh** /ˈmækɪntɒʃ/ n impermeabile m
**macro** /ˈmækrəʊ/ n Comput macro f inv
**macrocosm** /ˈmækrəʊkɒzm/ n macrocosmo m
**mad** /mæd/ a (madder, maddest) pazzo, matto; (fam: angry) furioso (at con); like ~ fam come un pazzo; be ~ about sb/sth (fam: keen on) andare matto per qcno/qcsa
**Madagascar** /mædəˈgæskə(r)/ n Madagascar m
**madam** /ˈmædəm/ n signora f
**mad cow disease** n morbo m della mucca pazza
**madden** /ˈmædən/ vt (make angry) far diventare matto
**maddening** /ˈmæd(ə)nɪŋ/ a ⟨delay, person⟩ esasperante
**made** /meɪd/ see make
**Madeira cake** /məˈdɪərə/ n pan m di Spagna
**made to measure** a [fatto] su misura
**made-up** a (wearing make-up) truccato; ⟨road⟩ asfaltata; ⟨story⟩ inventato
**madhouse** /ˈmædhaʊs/ n fam manicomio m; it's like a ~ in here! sembra di essere in un manicomio
**madly** /ˈmædlɪ/ adv fam follemente; ~ in love innamorato follemente
**madman** /ˈmædmən/ n pazzo m
**madness** /ˈmædnɪs/ n pazzia f
**madonna** /məˈdɒnə/ n madonna f
**madwoman** /ˈmædwʊmən/ n pazza f
**mafia** /ˈmæfɪə/ n also fig mafia f
**mag** /mæg/ n abbr magazine
**magazine** /mægəˈziːn/ n rivista f; Mil, Phot magazzino m
**maggot** /ˈmægət/ n verme m
**maggoty** /ˈmægətɪ/ a coi vermi
**Magi** /ˈmeɪdʒaɪ/ npl the ~ i Re Magi
**magic** /ˈmædʒɪk/ n magia f; ⟨tricks⟩ giochi mpl di prestigio ● a magico; ⟨trick⟩ di prestigio
**magical** /ˈmædʒɪkl/ a magico
**magic carpet** n tappeto m volante
**magician** /məˈdʒɪʃn/ n mago, -a mf; (entertainer) prestigiatore, -trice mf
**magistrate** /ˈmædʒɪstreɪt/ n magistrato m
**magistrate's court** n ≈ pretura f
**magnanimity** /mægnəˈnɪmətɪ/ n magnanimità f
**magnanimous** /mægˈnænɪməs/ a magnanimo
**magnesia** /mægˈniːʃə/ n magnesia f
**magnet** /ˈmægnɪt/ n magnete m, calamita f
**magnetic** /mægˈnetɪk/ a magnetico
**magnetic tape** n nastro m magnetico
**magnetism** /ˈmægnətɪzm/ n magnetismo m
**magnetize** /ˈmægnətaɪz/ vt magnetizzare
**magnification** /mægnɪfɪˈkeɪʃn/ n ingrandimento m

**magnificence** /mægˈnɪfɪsəns/ n magnificenza f
**magnificent** /mægˈnɪfɪsənt/ a magnifico
**magnificently** /mægˈnɪfɪsəntlɪ/ adv magnificamente
**magnify** /ˈmægnɪfaɪ/ vt (pt/pp -ied) ingrandire; (exaggerate) ingigantire
**magnifying glass** /ˈmægnɪfaɪɪŋ/ n lente f d'ingrandimento
**magnitude** /ˈmægnɪtjuːd/ n grandezza f; (importance) importanza f; a project of this ~ un progetto di tale portata
**magnum opus** /mægnəmˈɒpəs/ n opera f principale
**magpie** /ˈmægpaɪ/ n gazza f
**mahogany** /məˈhɒgənɪ/ n mogano m ● attrib di mogano
**maid** /meɪd/ n cameriera f; old ~ pej zitella f
**maiden** /ˈmeɪdn/ n liter fanciulla f ● a ⟨speech, voyage⟩ inaugurale
**maiden aunt** n zia f zitella
**maiden name** n nome m da ragazza
**mail** /meɪl/ n posta f ● vt impostare
**mail: mailbag** n sacco m postale. **mail bomb** n pacco m esplosivo (arrivato per posta). **mailbox** n Am cassetta f delle lettere; (e-mail) casella f postale. **mail coach** n Rail vagone m postale. **mail delivery** n consegna f della posta
**mailing address** /ˈmeɪlɪŋ/ n recapito m postale
**mailing list** n elenco m d'indirizzi per un mailing
**mail: mailman** /ˈmeɪlmən/ n Am postino m. **mail order** n vendita f per corrispondenza ● attrib ⟨business⟩ di vendita per corrispondenza; ⟨goods⟩ comprati per corrispondenza. **mail-order catalogue** catalogo m di vendita per corrispondenza. **mail-order firm** n ditta f di vendita per corrispondenza. **mail room** n reparto m spedizioni. **mailshot** n mailing m inv. **mail train** n treno m postale. **mail van** n (delivery vehicle) furgone m postale; (in train) vagone m postale
**maim** /meɪm/ vt menomare
**main**[1] /meɪn/ n (water, gas, electricity) conduttura f principale
**main**[2] a principale; the ~ thing is to... la cosa essenziale è di... ● n in the ~ in complesso
**main: main course** n secondo m. **main deck** n ponte m di coperta. **mainframe** n Comput mainframe m inv. **mainland** n continente m. **main line** n Rail linea f principale ● attrib ⟨station, terminus, train⟩ della linea principale
**mainly** /ˈmeɪnlɪ/ adv principalmente
**main: main memory** n Comput memoria f principale. **main office** n (of company) sede f centrale. **main road** n strada f principale. **mainsail** n randa f, vela f di taglio. **mainstay** n fig pilastro m. **main street** n via f principale
**maintain** /meɪnˈteɪn/ vt mantenere; (keep in repair) curare la manutenzione di; (claim) sostenere

**maintenance** /'meɪntənəns/ n mantenimento m; (care) manutenzione f; (allowance) alimenti mpl

**maintenance grant** n (for student) presalario m

**maintenance order** n Br obbligo m degli alimenti

**maisonette** /meɪzə'net/ n appartamento m a due piani

**maize** /meɪz/ n granoturco m

**Maj** abbr (**Major**) Mag

**majestic** /mə'dʒestɪk/ a maestoso

**majestically** /mə'dʒestɪklɪ/ adv maestosamente

**majesty** /'mædʒəstɪ/ n maestà f inv; **His/Her M~** Sua Maestà

**major** /'meɪdʒə(r)/ a maggiore; **~ road** strada f con diritto di precedenza ● n Mil, Mus maggiore m ● vi Am **~ in** specializzarsi in

**Majorca** /mə'jɔ:kə/ n Maiorca f

**major general** n generale m di divisione

**majority** /mə'dʒɒrətɪ/ n maggioranza f; **be in the ~** avere la maggioranza

**make** /meɪk/ n (brand) marca f ● v (pt/pp made) ● vt fare; (earn) guadagnare; rendere ⟨happy, clear⟩; prendere ⟨decision⟩; **~ sb laugh** far ridere qcno; **~ sb do sth** far fare qcsa a qcno; **~ it** (to party, top of hill etc) farcela; **what time do you ~ it?** che ore fai? ● vi **~ as if to** fare per

■ **make after** vt (chase) inseguire

■ **make do** vi arrangiarsi

■ **make for** vt dirigersi verso

■ **make good** vi riuscire ● vt compensare ⟨loss⟩; risarcire ⟨damage⟩

■ **make off** vi fuggire

■ **make off with** vt (steal) sgraffignare

■ **make out** vt (distinguish) distinguere; (write out) rilasciare ⟨cheque⟩; compilare ⟨list⟩; (claim) far credere

■ **make over** vt cedere

■ **make up** vt (constitute) comporre; (complete) completare; (invent) inventare; (apply cosmetics to) truccare; fare ⟨parcel⟩; **~ up one's mind** decidersi; **~ it up** (after quarrel) riconciliarsi ● vi (after quarrel) fare la pace

■ **make up for** vt compensare; **~ up for lost time** recuperare il tempo perso

■ **make up to** vt arruffianarsi

**make: make-believe** a finto ● n finzione f. **make-do-and-mend** vi arrangiarsi col poco che si ha. **make-over** n trasformazione f

**maker** /'meɪkə(r)/ n fabbricante mf; **M~** Relig Creatore m; **send sb to meet his/her ~** spedire qcno all'altro mondo

**make: makeshift** a di fortuna ● n espediente m. **make-up** n trucco m; (character) natura f. **make-up artist** n truccatore, -trice mf. **make-up bag** n astuccio m per il trucco. **make-up remover** n struccante m

**making** /'meɪkɪŋ/ n (manufacture) fabbricazione f; **be the ~ of** essere la causa del successo di; **have the ~s of** aver la stoffa di; **in the ~** in formazione

**maladjusted** /mælə'dʒʌstɪd/ a disadattato

**maladjustment** /mælə'dʒʌstmənt/ n disadattamento m

**Malagasy** /mælə'gæzɪ/ n (native of Madagascar) malgascio, -a mf; (language) malgascio m

**malaise** /mə'leɪz/ n fig malessere m

**malaria** /mə'leərɪə/ n malaria f

**Malaysia** /mə'leɪzə/ n Malesia f

**Malaysian** /mə'leɪzən/ n & a malese mf

**male** /meɪl/ a maschile ● n maschio m

**male: male chauvinist [pig]** n [sporco m] maschilista m. **male menopause** n andropausa f. **male model** n indossatore m. **male nurse** n infermiere m. **male voice choir** n coro m maschile

**malevolence** /mə'levələns/ n malevolenza f

**malevolent** /mə'levələnt/ a malevolo

**malformation** /mælfɔ:'meɪʃn/ n malformazione f

**malformed** /mæl'fɔ:md/ a malformato

**malfunction** /mæl'fʌŋkʃn/ n funzionamento m imperfetto ● vi funzionare male

**Mali** /'mɑ:lɪ/ n Mali m

**malice** /'mælɪs/ n malignità f; **bear sb ~** voler del male a qcno

**malicious** /mə'lɪʃəs/ a maligno

**maliciously** /mə'lɪʃəslɪ/ adv con malignità

**malign** /mə'laɪn/ vt malignare su

**malignancy** /mə'lɪgnənsɪ/ n malignità f

**malignant** /mə'lɪgnənt/ a maligno

**malinger** /mə'lɪŋgə(r)/ vi fingersi malato

**malingerer** /mə'lɪŋgərə(r)/ n scansafatiche mf inv

**mall** /mæl/ n (shopping arcade, in suburb) centro m commerciale; (Am: street) strada f pedonale

**mallard** /'mælɑ:d/ n germano m reale

**malleable** /'mælɪəbl/ a malleabile

**mallet** /'mælɪt/ n martello m di legno

**malnourished** /mæl'nʌrɪʃt/ a malnutrito

**malnutrition** /mælnju:'trɪʃn/ n malnutrizione f

**malpractice** /mæl'præktɪs/ n negligenza f

**malt** /mɔ:lt/ n malto m

**Malta** /'mɔ:ltə/ n Malta f

**Maltese** /mɔ:l'ti:z/ a & n maltese mf

**maltreat** /mæl'tri:t/ vt maltrattare

**maltreatment** /mæl'tri:tmənt/ n maltrattamento m

**malt whisky** n whisky m inv di malto

**mammal** /'mæml/ n mammifero m

**mammary** /'mæmərɪ/ a mammario

**mammograph** /'mæməgrɑ:f/ n mammografia f

**mammoth** /'mæməθ/ a mastodontico ● n mammut m inv

**man** /mæn/ n (pl men) uomo m; (chess, draughts) pedina f; **the ~ in the street** l'uomo della strada; **~ to ~** da uomo a uomo ● vt (pt/pp manned) equipaggiare; far funzionare ⟨pump⟩; essere di servizio a ⟨counter, telephones⟩

**manacle** /'mænəkl/ vt ammanettare

**manage** /'mænɪdʒ/ vt dirigere; gestire ⟨shop, affairs⟩; (cope with) farcela; **~ to do sth** riuscire a fare qcsa ● *vi* riuscire; (*cope*) farcela (*on* con)

**manageable** /'mænɪdʒəbl/ *a* ⟨*hair*⟩ docile; ⟨*size*⟩ maneggevole

**management** /'mænɪdʒmənt/ *n* gestione *f*; **the ~** la direzione

**management: management accounting** *n* contabilità *f* di gestione. **management buyout** *n* buyout *m inv* da parte dei manager, rilevamento *m* dirigenti. **management consultancy** *n* (*firm*) consulente *m* aziendale; (*activity*) consulenza *f* aziendale. **management consultant** *n* consulente *mf* aziendale

**manager** /'mænɪdʒə(r)/ *n* direttore *m*; (*of shop, bar*) gestore *m*; *Sport* manager *m inv*

**manageress** /mænɪdʒə'res/ *n* direttrice *f*

**managerial** /mænɪ'dʒɪərɪəl/ *a* **~ staff** personale *m* direttivo

**managing** /'mænɪdʒɪŋ/ *a* **~ director** direttore, -trice *mf* generale

**mandarin** /'mændərɪn/ *n* **~ [orange]** mandarino *m*

**mandate** /'mændeɪt/ *n* mandato *m*

**mandatory** /'mændətrɪ/ *a* obbligatorio

**mandolin** /'mændəlɪn/ *n* mandolino *m*

**mandrake** /'mændreɪk/ *n* mandragola *f*

**mane** /meɪn/ *n* criniera *f*

**manful** /'mænfl/ *a* coraggioso

**manfully** /'mænfʊlɪ/ *adv* coraggiosamente

**mangle** /'mæŋgl/ *vt* (*damage*) maciullare

**mango** /'mæŋgəʊ/ *n* (*pl* **-es**) mango *m*

**mangrove** /'mæŋgrəʊv/ *n* mangrovia *f*

**mangy** /'meɪndʒɪ/ *a* ⟨*dog*⟩ rognoso

**manhandle** /'mænhændl/ *vt* malmenare

**manhole** /'mænhəʊl/ *n* botola *f*

**manhole cover** *n* tombino *m*

**manhood** /'mænhʊd/ *n* età *f* adulta; (*quality*) virilità *f*

**man-hour** *n* ora *f* lavorativa

**manhunt** /'mænhʌnt/ *n* caccia *f* all'uomo

**mania** /'meɪnɪə/ *n* mania *f*

**maniac** /'meɪnɪæk/ *n* maniaco, -a *mf*

**manic** /'mænɪk/ *a* (*obsessive*) maniacale; (*frenetic*) frenetico

**manic depression** *n* psicosi *f inv* maniaco-depressiva

**manic-depressive** *a* maniaco-depressivo

**manicure** /'mænɪkjʊə(r)/ *n* manicure *f inv* ● *vt* fare la manicure a

**manicurist** /'mænɪkjʊərɪst/ *n* manicure *f inv*

**manifest** /'mænɪfest/ *a* manifesto ● *n Comm* manifesto *m* ● *vt* manifestare; **~ itself** manifestarsi

**manifestation** /mænɪfe'steɪʃn/ *n* manifestazione *f*

**manifestly** /'mænɪfestlɪ/ *adv* palesemente

**manifesto** /mænɪ'festəʊ/ *n* manifesto *m*

**manifold** /'mænɪfəʊld/ *a* molteplice

**manipulate** /mə'nɪpjuleɪt/ *vt* manipolare

**manipulation** /mənɪpjʊ'leɪʃn/ *n* manipolazione *f*

**mankind** /mæn'kaɪnd/ *n* genere *m* umano

**manly** /'mænlɪ/ *a* virile

**man-made** *a* artificiale; **~ fibre** *n* fibra *f* sintetica

**manna** /'mænə/ *n* manna *f*; **~ from heaven** *fig* manna *f* dal cielo

**mannequin** /'mænɪkɪn/ *n* manichino *m*

**manner** /'mænə(r)/ *n* maniera *f*; **in this ~** in questo modo; maniera *f*; **have no ~s** avere dei pessimi modi; **good/bad ~s** buone/cattive maniere

**mannered** /'mænəd/ *pej* manierato

**mannerism** /'mænərɪzm/ *n* affettazione *f*

**mannish** /'mænɪʃ/ *a* mascolino

**manoeuvrable** /mə'nu:vrəbl/ *a* manovrabile

**manoeuvre** /mə'nu:və(r)/ *n* manovra *f* ● *vt* fare manovra con ⟨*vehicle*⟩; manovrare ⟨*person*⟩

**manor** /'mænə(r)/ *n* maniero *m*

**manpower** /'mænpaʊə(r)/ *n* manodopera *f*

**manse** /mæns/ *n* canonica *f*

**mansion** /'mænʃn/ *n* palazzo *m*

**manslaughter** /'mænslɔ:tə(r)/ *n* omicidio *m* colposo

**mantelpiece** /'mæntlpi:s/ *n* mensola *f* di caminetto

**mantis** /'mæntɪs/ *n* mantide *f*

**Mantua** /'mæntjʊə/ *n* Mantova *f*

**manual** /'mænjʊəl/ *a* manuale ● *n* manuale *m*

**manufacture** /mænjʊ'fæktʃə(r)/ *vt* fabbricare ● *n* manifattura *f*

**manufacturer** /mænjʊ'fæktʃərə(r)/ *n* fabbricante *m*

**manure** /mə'njʊə(r)/ *n* concime *m*

**manuscript** /'mænjʊskrɪpt/ *n* manoscritto *m*

**Manx** /mæŋks/ *n* (*language*) lingua *f* parlata nell'isola di Man; **the ~** *pl* (*people*) gli abitanti dell'isola di Man

**many** /'menɪ/ *a & pron* molti; **there are as ~ boys as girls** ci sono tanti ragazzi quante ragazze; **as ~ as 500** ben 500; **as ~ as that** così tanti; **as ~** altrettanti; **very ~**, **a good/great ~** moltissimi; **~ a time** molte volte

**many-sided** /-'saɪdɪd/ *a* ⟨*personality, phenomenon*⟩ sfaccettato

**map** /mæp/ *n* carta *f* geografica; (*of town*) mappa *f*

■ **map out** *vt* (*pt/pp* **mapped**) *fig* programmare

**maple** /'meɪpl/ *n* acero *m*

**mar** /mɑ:(r)/ *vt* (*pt/pp* **marred**) rovinare

**marathon** /'mærəθən/ *n* maratona *f*

**marauder** /mə'rɔ:də(r)/ *n* predone *m*

**marble** /'mɑ:bl/ *n* marmo *m*; (*for game*) pallina *f* ● *attrib* di marmo

**March** /mɑ:tʃ/ *n* marzo *m*

**march** *n* marcia *f*; (*protest*) dimostrazione *f* ● *vi* marciare ● *vt* far marciare; **~ sb off** scortare qcno fuori

**marcher** /'mɑ:tʃə(r)/ *n* (*in procession, band*) persona *f* che marcia in una processione, in un corteo ecc; (*in demonstration*) dimostrante *mf*

**marchioness** /mɑ:ʃə'nes/ *n* marchesa *f*

**march past** *n* sfilata *f*

**mare** /'meə(r)/ *n* giumenta *f*

**margarine** /mɑːdʒəˈriːn/ n margarina f

**marge** /mɑːdʒ/ n (Br fam: margarine) margarina f

**margin** /ˈmɑːdʒɪn/ n margine m

**marginal** /ˈmɑːdʒɪnəl/ a marginale

**marginally** /ˈmɑːdʒɪnəlɪ/ adv marginalmente

**marigold** /ˈmærɪɡəʊld/ n calendula f

**marijuana** /mærʊˈwɑːnə/ n marijuana f

**marina** /məˈriːnə/ n porticciolo m

**marinade** /mærɪˈneɪd/ n marinata f ● vt marinare

**marine** /məˈriːn/ a marino ● n (sailor) soldato m di fanteria marina

**Marine Corps** n i Marine

**marine engineer** n ingegnere m navale; (works in engine room) macchinista m

**marionette** /mærɪəˈnet/ n marionetta f

**marital** /ˈmærɪtl/ a coniugale; ~ **status** stato m civile

**maritime** /ˈmærɪtaɪm/ a marittimo

**marjoram** /ˈmɑːdʒərəm/ n maggiorana f

**mark**¹ /mɑːk/ n (currency) marco m

**mark**² n (stain) macchia f; (sign, indication) segno m; Sch voto m; **be the ~ of** designare ● vt segnare; (stain) macchiare; Sch correggere; Sport marcare; ~ **time** Mil segnare il passo; fig non far progressi; ~ **my words** ricordati quello che dico

■ **mark down** vt (reduce the price of) ribassare

■ **mark out** vt delimitare; fig designare

■ **mark up** vt (increase the price of) aumentare

**marked** /mɑːkt/ a marcato

**markedly** /ˈmɑːkɪdlɪ/ adv notevolmente

**marker** /ˈmɑːkə(r)/ n (for highlighting) evidenziatore m; Sport marcatore m; (of exam) esaminatore, -trice mf

**marker pen** n evidenziatore m

**market** /ˈmɑːkɪt/ n mercato m ● vt vendere al mercato; (launch) commercializzare; **on the ~** sul mercato

**market: market analyst** n analista mf di mercato. **market day** n giorno m di mercato. **market economy** n economia f di mercato. **market forces** npl forze fpl di mercato. **market garden** n orto m. **market gardener** n ortofrutticoltore, -trice mf

**marketing** /ˈmɑːkɪtɪŋ/ n marketing m

**marketing: marketing campaign** n campagna f promozionale or pubblicitaria. **marketing department** n ufficio m marketing. **marketing man** n addetto, -a mf al marketing. **marketing mix** n mix m inv del marketing. **marketing strategy** n strategia f di marketing

**market: market leader** n (company, product) leader m inv del mercato. **market place** n (square, Fin) mercato m. **market price** n prezzo m di mercato. **market research** n ricerca f di mercato. **market square** n piazza f del mercato. **market stall** n banco m del mercato. **market survey** n indagine f di mercato. **market town** n cittadina f dove si tiene il mercato. **market trader** n venditore, -trice mf al mercato. **market value** n valore m di mercato

**markings** /ˈmɑːkɪŋz/ npl (on animal) colori mpl

**marksman** /ˈmɑːksmən/ n tiratore m scelto

**marksmanship** /ˈmɑːksmənʃɪp/ n abilità f nel tiro

**mark-up** n (margin) margine m di vendita; (price increase) aumento m

**marmalade** /ˈmɑːməleɪd/ n marmellata f d'arance

**maroon** /məˈruːn/ a marrone rossastro

**marooned** /məˈruːnd/ a abbandonato

**marquee** /mɑːˈkiː/ n tendone m; (Am: awning) pensilina f con pubblicità

**marquess** /ˈmɑːkwɪs/ n marchese m

**marquetry** /ˈmɑːkɪtrɪ/ n intarsio m

**marquis** /ˈmɑːkwɪs/ n marchese m

**marriage** /ˈmærɪdʒ/ n matrimonio m

**marriage: marriage ceremony** n cerimonia f nuziale. **marriage certificate** n certificato m di matrimonio. **marriage guidance counsellor** n consulente mf matrimoniale. **marriage of convenience** n matrimonio m di convenienza

**married** /ˈmærɪd/ a sposato; (life) coniugale

**marrow** /ˈmærəʊ/ n Anat midollo m; (vegetable) zucca f

**marrowbone** /ˈmærəʊbəʊn/ n midollo m osseo

**marry** /ˈmærɪ/ vt (pt/pp -ied) sposare; **get married** sposarsi ● vi sposarsi

**marsh** /mɑːʃ/ n palude f

**marshal** /ˈmɑːʃl/ n (steward) cerimoniere m ● vt (pt/pp **marshalled**) fig organizzare (arguments)

**marshmallow** /mɑːʃˈmæləʊ/ n caramella f gommosa e pastosa

**marshy** /ˈmɑːʃɪ/ a paludoso

**marsupial** /mɑːˈsuːpɪəl/ n marsupiale m

**marten** /ˈmɑːtɪn/ n martora f

**martial** /ˈmɑːʃl/ a marziale

**Martian** /ˈmɑːʃn/ a & n marziano, -a mf

**martinet** /mɑːtɪˈnet/ n fanatico, -a mf della disciplina

**martyr** /ˈmɑːtə(r)/ n martire mf ● vt martirizzare

**martyrdom** /ˈmɑːtədəm/ n martirio m

**martyred** /ˈmɑːtəd/ a fam da martire

**marvel** /ˈmɑːvl/ n meraviglia f ● vi (pt/pp **marvelled**) meravigliarsi (**at** di)

**marvellous** /ˈmɑːvələs/ a meraviglioso

**marvellously** /ˈmɑːvələslɪ/ adv meravigliosamente

**Marxism** /ˈmɑːksɪzm/ n marxismo m

**Marxist** /ˈmɑːksɪst/ a & n marxista mf

**marzipan** /ˈmɑːzɪpæn/ n marzapane m

**mascara** /mæˈskɑːrə/ n mascara m inv

**mascot** /ˈmæskət/ n mascotte f inv

**masculine** /ˈmæskjʊlɪn/ a maschile ● n Gram maschile m

**masculinity** /mæskjʊˈlɪnətɪ/ n mascolinità f

**mash** /mæʃ/ n Culin fam purè m inv ● vt pastare

203 mashed potatoes | matrimonial

**mashed potatoes** /mæʃt/ *npl* purè *m inv* di patate
**mask** /mɑːsk/ *n* maschera *f* ● *vt* mascherare
**masked ball** /mɑːskt'bɔːl/ *n* ballo *m* in maschera
**masking tape** /'mɑːskɪŋ/ *n* nastro *m* di carta adesiva
**masochism** /'mæsəkɪzm/ *n* masochismo *m*
**masochist** /'mæsəkɪst/ *n* masochista *mf*
**Mason** /'meɪsn/ *n* massone *m*
**mason** *n* muratore *m*
**Masonic** /mə'sɒnɪk/ *a* massonico
**masonry** /'meɪsnrɪ/ *n* muratura *f*; **two tons of** ~ due tonnellate di pietre
**masquerade** /mæskə'reɪd/ *n fig* maschera-ta *f* ● *vi* ~ **as** (*pose*) farsi passare per
**mass**[1] /mæs/ *n Relig* messa *f*
**mass**[2] *n* massa *f*; ~**es of** *fam* un sacco di ● *vi* ammassarsi
**massacre** /'mæsəkə(r)/ *n* massacro *m* ● *vt* massacrare
**massage** /'mæsɑːʒ/ *n* massaggio *m* ● *vt* massaggiare; *fig* manipolare ‹*statistics*›
**masseur** /mæ'sɜː(r)/ *n* massaggiatore *m*
**masseuse** /mæ'sɜːz/ *n* massaggiatrice *f*
**mass grave** *n* fossa *f* comune
**mass hysteria** *n* isterismo *m* di massa
**massive** /'mæsɪv/ *a* enorme
**massively** /'mæsɪvlɪ/ *adv* estremamente
**mass: mass market** *n* mercato *m* di massa ● *attrib* del mercato di massa. **mass media** *npl* mezzi *mpl* di comunicazione di massa, mass media *mpl*. **mass murder** *n* omicidio *m* di massa. **mass murderer** *n* omicida *mf* di massa. **mass-produce** *vt* produrre in serie. **mass production** *n* produzione *f* in serie. **mass screening** *n Med* controllo *m* su larga scala
**mast** /mɑːst/ *n Naut* albero *m*; (*for radio*) antenna *f*
**master** /'mɑːstə(r)/ *n* maestro *m*, padrone *m*; (*teacher*) professore *m*; (*of ship*) capitano *m*; **M**~ (*boy*) signorino *m* ● *vt* imparare perfettamente; avere padronanza di ‹*language*›
**master: master bedroom** *n* camera *f* da letto principale. **master builder** *n* capomastro *m*. **master copy** *n* originale *m*. **master disk** *n Comput* disco *m* master. **master key** *n* passe-partout *m inv*
**masterly** /'mɑːstəlɪ/ *a* magistrale
**master: mastermind** *n* cervello *m* ● *vt* ideare e dirigere. **Master of Arts** *n* (*diploma*) laurea *f* in lettere; (*person*) laureato, -a *mf* in lettere. **master of ceremonies** *n* (*presenting entertainment*) presentatore *m*; (*of formal occasion*) maestro *m* delle cerimonie. **Master of Science** *n* (*diploma*) laurea *f* in discipline scientifiche; (*person*) laureato, -a *mf* in discipline scientifiche. **masterpiece** *n* capolavoro *m*. **master plan** *n* piano *m* generale. **master race** *n* razza *f* superiore. **master stroke** *n* colpo *m* da maestro. **master tape** *n* nastro *m* matrice
**mastery** /'mæstərɪ/ *n* (*of subject*) padronan-za *f*

**masticate** /'mæstɪkeɪt/ *vi* masticare
**masturbate** /'mæstəbeɪt/ *vi* masturbarsi
**masturbation** /mæstə'beɪʃn/ *n* masturba-zione *f*
**mat** /mæt/ *n* stuoia *f*: (*on table*) sottopiatto *m*
**match**[1] /mætʃ/ *n Sport* partita *f*; (*equal*) uguale *mf*; (*marriage*) matrimonio *m*; (*person to marry*) partito *m*; **be a good** ~ ‹*colours:*› intonarsi bene; **be no** ~ **for** non essere dello stesso livello di ● *vt* (*equal*) uguagliare; (*be like*) andare bene con ● *vi* intonarsi
**match**[2] *n* fiammifero *m*
**matchbox** /'mætʃbɒks/ *n* scatola *f* di fiammiferi
**matching** /'mætʃɪŋ/ *a* intonato
**match: matchmaker** *n* **he's a successful** ~ (*for couples*) è stato l'artefice di molti matrimoni. **match point** *n Tennis* match point *m inv*. **matchstick** *n* fiammifero *m*
**mate**[1] /meɪt/ *n* compagno, -a *mf*; (*assistant*) aiuto *m*; *Naut* secondo *m*; (*fam: friend*) amico, -a *mf* ● *vi* accoppiarsi ● *vt* accoppiare
**mate**[2] *n* (*in chess*) scacco *m* matto
**material** /mə'tɪərɪəl/ *n* materiale *m*; (*fabric*) stoffa *f*; **raw** ~**s** *pl* materie *fpl* prime ● *a* materiale
**materialism** /mə'tɪərɪəlɪzm/ *n* materiali-smo *m*
**materialistic** /mətɪərɪə'lɪstɪk/ *a* materiali-stico
**materialize** /mə'tɪərɪəlaɪz/ *vi* materializzar-si
**maternal** /mə'tɜːnl/ *a* materno
**maternity** /mə'tɜːnətɪ/ *n* maternità *f*
**maternity: maternity clothes** *npl* abiti *mpl* pre-maman. **maternity department** *n* (*in store*) reparto *m* pre-maman. **maternity hospital** *n* maternità *f inv*. **maternity leave** *n* congedo *m* per maternità. **maternity unit** *n* reparto *m* maternità. **maternity ward** *n* maternità *f inv*
**matey** /'meɪtɪ/ *a fam* amichevole
**math** /mæθ/ *n Am* matematica *f*
**mathematical** /mæθə'mætɪkl/ *a* matematico
**mathematically** /mæθə'mætɪklɪ/ *adv* matematicamente
**mathematician** /mæθəmə'tɪʃn/ *n* matematico, -a *mf*
**mathematics** /mæθ'mætɪks/ *n* matematica *fsg*
**maths** /mæθs/ *n fam* matematica *fsg*
**matinée** /'mætɪneɪ/ *n Theat* matinée *f inv*
**mating** /'meɪtɪŋ/ *n* accoppiamento *m*
**mating call** *n* richiamo *m* [per l'accoppia-mento]
**mating season** *n* stagione *f* degli amori
**matriarchal** /meɪtrɪ'ɑːkl/ *a* matriarcale
**matriarchy** /'meɪtrɪɑːkɪ/ *n* matriarchia *f*
**matrices** /'meɪtrɪsiːz/ *see* **matrix**
**matriculate** /mə'trɪkjʊleɪt/ *vi* immatrico-larsi
**matriculation** /mətrɪkjʊ'leɪʃn/ *n* immatri-colazione *f*
**matrimonial** /mætrɪ'məʊnɪəl/ *a* matrimo-niale

**matrimony** /'mætrɪmənɪ/ n matrimonio m
**matrix** /'meɪtrɪks/ n (pl **matrices** /'meɪtrɪsiːz/) matrice f
**matron** /'meɪtrən/ n (of hospital) capo-infermiera f; (of school) governante f
**matronly** /'meɪtrənlɪ/ a matronale
**matron of honour** n Br damigella f d'onore (sposata)
**matt** /mæt/ a opaco
**matted** /'mætɪd/ a ~ **hair** capelli mpl tutti appiccicati tra loro
**matter** /'mætə(r)/ n (affair) faccenda f; (question) questione f; (pus) pus m; (Phys: substance) materia f; **money** ~s questioni fpl di soldi; **as a** ~ **of fact** a dire la verità; **what is the** ~? che cosa c'è? ● vi importare; ~ **to sb** essere importante per qcno; **it doesn't** ~ non importa
**matter-of-fact** a pratico
**matting** /'mætɪŋ/ n materiale m per stuoie
**mattress** /'mætrɪs/ n materasso m
**maturation** /mætʃʊ'reɪʃn/ n (of tree, body) sviluppo m; (of whisky, wine) invecchiamento m; (of cheese) stagionatura f
**mature** /mə'tʃʊə(r)/ a maturo; Comm in scadenza ● vi maturare ● vt far maturare
**mature student** n Br persona f che riprende gli studi universitari dopo i 25 anni
**maturity** /mə'tʃʊərətɪ/ n maturità f; Comm maturazione f
**maudlin** /'mɔːdlɪn/ a (song) sdolcinato; (person) piagnucoloso
**maul** /mɔːl/ vt malmenare
**Maundy** /'mɔːndɪ/ n ~ **Thursday** giovedì m santo
**Mauritius** /mə'rɪʃəs/ n (isola f di) Maurizio f
**mausoleum** /mɔːsə'liːəm/ n mausoleo m
**mauve** /məʊv/ a malva
**maverick** /'mævərɪk/ n, a anticonformista mf
**mawkish** /'mɔːkɪʃ/ a sdolcinato
**maxi** /'mæksɪ/ n (dress) vestito m alla caviglia; (skirt) gonna f alla caviglia
**maxim** /'mæksɪm/ n massima f
**maximization** /mæksɪmaɪ'zeɪʃn/ n massimizzazione f
**maximum** /'mæksɪməm/ a massimo; **ten minutes** ~ dieci minuti al massimo ● n (pl-ima) massimo m
**maximum security prison** n carcere m di massima sicurezza
**May** /meɪ/ n maggio m
**may** v aux (solo al presente) potere; ~ **I come in?** posso entrare?; **if I** ~ **say so** se mi posso permettere; ~ **you both be very happy** siate felici; **I** ~ **as well stay** potrei anche rimanere; **it** ~ **be true** potrebbe esser vero; **she** ~ **be old, but...** sarà anche vecchia, ma...
**maybe** /'meɪbɪ/ adv forse, può darsi
**may:** May-bug n maggiolino m. **Mayday** n Radio mayday m inv. **May Day** n il primo maggio
**mayhem** /'meɪhem/ n create ~ creare scompiglio
**mayonnaise** /meɪə'neɪz/ n maionese f

**mayor** /'meə(r)/ n sindaco m
**mayoress** /meə'res/ n sindaco m; (wife of mayor) moglie f del sindaco
**maypole** /'meɪpəʊl/ n palo m intorno al quale si balla durante la celebrazione del primo maggio
**May queen** n reginetta f di calendimaggio
**maze** /meɪz/ n labirinto m
**Mb** abbr (**megabyte**) Mb m inv
**MBA** n abbr (**Master of Business Administration**) laurea f inv in economia e commercio
**MBE** n Br abbr (**Member of the Order of the British Empire**) onorificenza f britannica
**MBO** n abbr **management buyout**
**MC** n abbr (**Master of Ceremonies**) (in cabaret) presentatore m; (at banquet) maestro m delle cerimonie; Am abbr (**Member of Congress**) membro m del Congresso
**McCoy** /mə'kɔɪ/ n this whisky is the real ~ questo è un vero whisky
**MD** abbr (**Managing Director**) direttore, -trice mf generale; abbr (**Doctor of Medicine**) dottore m in medicina; Am abbr **Maryland**
**ME** n abbr (**myalgic encephalomyelitis**) encefalomielite f mialgica; Am abbr **Maine**
**me** /miː/ pers pron (object) mi; (with preposition) me; **he knows me** mi conosce; **she called me, not you** ha chiamato me, non te; **give me the money** dammi i soldi; **give it to me** dammelo; **he explained it to me** me lo ha spiegato; **it's me** sono io
**mead** /miːd/ n idromele m
**meadow** /'medəʊ/ n prato m
**meagre** /'miːgə(r)/ a scarso
**meal¹** /miːl/ n pasto m; **did you enjoy your** ~? ha mangiato bene?
**meal²** n (grain) farina f
**meal ticket** n (fig: quality, qualification) fonte f di guadagno; **he's only a** ~ ~ **to her** le interessano solo i suoi soldi
**mealy-mouthed** /miːlɪ'maʊðd/ a ambiguo
**mean¹** /miːn/ a avaro; (unkind) meschino; (low in rank) basso; (accommodation) misero
**mean²** a medio ● n (average) media f; **Greenwich** ~ **time** ora f media di Greenwich
**mean³** vt (pt/pp meant) voler dire; (signify) significare; (intend) intendere; **I** ~ **it** lo dico seriamente; ~ **well** avere buone intenzioni; **be** ~**t for** (present:) essere destinato a; (remark:) essere riferito a
**meander** /mɪ'ændə(r)/ vi vagare
**meaning** /'miːnɪŋ/ n significato m
**meaningful** /'miːnɪŋfʊl/ a significativo
**meaningless** /'miːnɪŋlɪs/ a senza senso
**meanness** /'miːnnɪs/ n (with money) avarizia f; (unkindness) meschinità f
**means** /miːnz/ n mezzo m; ~ **of transport** mezzo m di trasporto; **by** ~ **of** per mezzo di; **by all** ~! certamente!; **by no** ~ niente affatto ● npl (resources) mezzi mpl; ~ **test** n accertamento m patrimoniale

**meant** /ment/ *see* **mean³**
**meantime** /'miːntaɪm/ *n* **in the ~** nel frattempo ● *adv* intanto
**meanwhile** /'miːnwaɪl/ *adv* intanto
**measles** /'miːzlz/ *nsg* morbillo *m*
**measly** /'miːzlɪ/ *a fam* misero
**measurable** /'meʒərəbl/ *a* misurabile
**measure** /'meʒə(r)/ *n* misura *f* ● *vt/i* misurare
■ **measure out** *vt* dosare ⟨*amount*⟩
■ **measure up to** *vt fig* essere all'altezza di
**measured** /'meʒed/ *a* misurato
**measurement** /'meʒəmənt/ *n* misura *f*
**measuring jug** /'meʒərɪŋ/ *n* dosatore *m*
**measuring spoon** *n* misurino *m*
**meat** /miːt/ *n* carne *f*
**meat: meatball** *n Culin* polpetta *f* di carne.
**meat-eater** *n* ⟨*animal*⟩ carnivoro *m*; **I'm not a ~** non mangio carne. **meat hook** *n* gancio *m* da macellaio. **meat loaf** *n* polpettone *m*. **meat pie** *n* tortino *m* di carne
**meaty** /'miːtɪ/ *a* (**-ier, -iest**) di carne; *fig* sostanzioso
**Mecca** /'mekə/ *n* La Mecca
**mechanic** /mɪ'kænɪk/ *n* meccanico *m*
**mechanical** /mɪ'kænɪkl/ *a* meccanico
**mechanical engineering** *n* ingegneria *f* meccanica
**mechanically** /mɪ'kænɪklɪ/ *adv* meccanicamente
**mechanics** /mɪ'kænɪks/ *n* meccanica *f* ● *npl* meccanismo *msg*
**mechanism** /'mekənɪzm/ *n* meccanismo *m*
**mechanize** /'mekənaɪz/ *vt* meccanizzare
**medal** /'medl/ *n* medaglia *f*
**medallion** /mɪ'dælɪən/ *n* medaglione *m*
**medallist** /'medəlɪst/ *n* vincitore, -trice *mf* di una medaglia
**meddle** /'medl/ *vi* immischiarsi (**in** di); ⟨*tinker*⟩ armeggiare (**with** con)
**media** /'miːdɪə/ *n see* **medium** ● *npl* **the ~** i mass media
**median** /'miːdɪən/ *a* **~ strip** *Am* banchina *f* spartitraffico
**media studies** *npl* scienze *fpl* delle comunicazioni
**mediate** /'miːdɪeɪt/ *vi* fare da mediatore
**mediation** /miːdɪ'eɪʃn/ *n* mediazione *f*
**mediator** /'miːdɪeɪtə(r)/ *n* mediatore, -trice *mf*
**medic** /'medɪk/ *n* ⟨*fam: doctor*⟩ medico *m*; ⟨*fam: student*⟩ studente, -essa *mf* di medicina; *Mil fam* infermiere, -a *mf* militare
**medical** /'medɪkl/ *a* medico ● *n* visita *f* medica
**medical: medical care** *n* assistenza *f* medica. **medical check-up** *n* controllo *m* medico. **medical history** *n* anamnesi *f inv*. **medical insurance** *n* assicurazione *f* sanitaria
**medically** /'medɪklɪ/ *adv* **~ qualified** con qualifiche di medico; **~ fit** in buona salute
**medical: medical officer** *n Mil* ufficiale *m* medico. **medical profession** *n* ⟨*occupation*⟩ professione *f* del medico; ⟨*doctors collectively*⟩

categoria *f* medica. **medical student** *n* studente, -essa *mf* di medicina
**medicated** /'medɪkeɪtɪd/ *a* medicato
**medication** /medɪ'keɪʃn/ *n* ⟨*drugs*⟩ medicinali *mpl*; **are you on any ~?** sta prendendo delle medicine?
**medicinal** /mɪ'dɪsɪnl/ *a* medicinale
**medicine** /'medsən/ *n* medicina *f*
**medicine: medicine ball** *n* palla *f* medica. **medicine bottle** *n* flacone *m*. **medicine cabinet** *n* armadietto *m* dei medicinali. **medicine man** *n* stregone *m*
**medieval** /medɪ'iːvl/ *a* medievale
**mediocre** /miːdɪ'əʊkə(r)/ *a* mediocre
**mediocrity** /miːdɪ'ɒkrəti/ *n* mediocrità *f*
**meditate** /'medɪteɪt/ *vi* meditare (**on** su)
**meditative** /'medɪtətɪv/ *a* ⟨*music, person*⟩ meditativo; ⟨*mood, expression*⟩ meditabondo
**Mediterranean** /medɪtə'reɪnɪən/ *n* **the ~ [Sea]** il [mare] Mediterraneo ● *a* mediterraneo
**medium** /'miːdɪəm/ *a* medio; *Culin* di media cottura ● *n* (*pl* **media**) mezzo *m*; (*pl* **-s**) ⟨*person*⟩ medium *mf inv*
**medium: medium dry** *a* ⟨*drink*⟩ semisecco. **medium-length** *a* ⟨*book, film, hair*⟩ di media lunghezza. **medium-range** *a* ⟨*missile*⟩ di media portata. **medium-rare** *a* ⟨*meat*⟩ appena al sangue. **medium-sized** /'miːdɪəmsaɪzd/ *a* di taglia media. **medium wave** *n* onde *fpl* medie
**medley** /'medlɪ/ *n* miscuglio *m*; *Mus* miscellanea *f*
**meek** /miːk/ *a* mite, mansueto
**meekly** /'miːklɪ/ *adv* docilmente
**meet** /miːt/ *v* (*pt/pp* **met**) ● *vt* incontrare; ⟨*at station, airport*⟩ andare incontro a; ⟨*for first time*⟩ far la conoscenza di; pagare ⟨*bill*⟩; soddisfare ⟨*requirements*⟩ ● *vi* incontrarsi; ⟨*committee:*⟩ riunirsi; **~ with** incontrare ⟨*problem*⟩; incontrarsi con ⟨*person*⟩ ● *n* raduno *m* [sportivo]
■ **meet up** *vi* ⟨*people:*⟩ incontrarsi; **~ up with sb** incontrarsi con qcno
**meeting** /'miːtɪŋ/ *n* riunione *f*, meeting *m inv*; ⟨*large*⟩ assemblea *f*; ⟨*by chance*⟩ incontro *m*; **be in a ~** essere in riunione
**meeting-place** *n* luogo *m* d'incontro
**meeting-point** *n* punto *m* d'incontro
**mega+** /'megə/ *pref* mega+
**megabyte** /'megəbaɪt/ *n Comput* megabyte *m inv*
**megalith** /'megəlɪθ/ *n* megalite *m*
**megalomania** /megələ'meɪnɪə/ *n* megalomania *f*
**megaphone** /'megəfəʊn/ *n* megafono *m*
**melancholy** /'melənkəlɪ/ *a* malinconico ● *n* malinconia *f*
**mellow** /'meləʊ/ *a* ⟨*wine*⟩ generoso; ⟨*sound, colour*⟩ caldo; ⟨*person*⟩ dolce ● *vi* ⟨*person:*⟩ addolcirsi
**melodic** /mɪ'lɒdɪk/ *a* melodico
**melodious** /mɪ'ləʊdɪəs/ *a* melodioso
**melodrama** /'melədrɑːmə/ *n* melodramma *m*

**melodramatic** /melədrə'mætɪk/ a melo-drammatico

**melodramatically** /melədrə'mætɪklɪ/ adv in modo melodrammatico

**melody** /'melədɪ/ n melodia f

**melon** /'melən/ n melone m

**melt** /melt/ vt sciogliere ● vi sciogliersi

■ **melt away** vi ⟨snow:⟩ sciogliersi; ⟨crowd:⟩ disperdersi; ⟨support:⟩ venir meno

■ **melt down** vt fondere

**meltdown** /'meltdaʊn/ n (in nuclear reactor) fusione f del nocciolo

**melting point** /'meltɪŋ/ n punto m di fusione

**melting pot** n fig crogiuolo m

**member** /'membə(r)/ n membro m; **be a ~ of the family** far parte della famiglia

**member: member countries** paesi mpl membri. **Member of Parliament** deputato, -a mf. **Member of the European Parliament** n eurodeputato, -a mf

**membership** /'membəʃɪp/ n iscrizione f; (members) soci mpl

**membrane** /'membreɪn/ n membrana f

**memento** /mɪ'mentəʊ/ n ricordo m

**memo** /'meməʊ/ n promemoria m inv

**memoirs** /'memwɑːz/ npl ricordi mpl

**memo pad** n blocchetto m

**memorabilia** /memərə'bɪlɪə/ npl cimeli mpl

**memorable** /'memərəbl/ a memorabile

**memorandum** /memə'rændəm/ n promemoria m inv

**memorial** /mɪ'mɔːrɪəl/ n monumento m

**memorial service** n funzione f commemorativa

**memorize** /'meməraɪz/ vt memorizzare

**memory** /'memərɪ/ n also Comput memoria f; (thing remembered) ricordo m; **from ~** a memoria; **in ~ of** in ricordo di

**men** /men/ see **man**

**menace** /'menəs/ n minaccia f; (nuisance) piaga f ● vt minacciare

**menacing** /'menəsɪŋ/ a minaccioso

**menacingly** /'menəsɪŋlɪ/ adv minacciosamente

**mend** /mend/ vt riparare; (darn) rammendare ● n **on the ~** in via di guarigione

**menfolk** /'menfəʊk/ n uomini mpl

**menial** /'miːnɪəl/ a umile

**meningitis** /menɪn'dʒaɪtɪs/ n meningite f

**menopause** /'menəpɔːz/ n menopausa f

**Menorca** /mɪ'nɔːkə/ n Minorca f

**men's room** n toilette f inv degli uomini

**menstruate** /'menstrʊeɪt/ vi mestruare

**menstruation** /menstrʊ'eɪʃn/ n mestruazione f

**menswear** /'menzweə(r)/ n abbigliamento m per uomo

**mental** /'mentl/ a mentale; (fam: mad) pazzo

**mental: mental arithmetic** n calcolo m mentale. **mental block** n blocco m psicologico. **mental health** n (of person) salute f mentale. **mental health care** n assistenza f psi-chiatrica. **mental home** n clinica f psichiatrica. **mental illness** n malattia f mentale

**mentality** /men'tælətɪ/ n mentalità f inv

**mentally** /'mentəlɪ/ adv mentalmente; **~ ill** malato di mente

**mentholated** /'menθəleɪtɪd/ a al mentolo

**mention** /'menʃn/ n menzione f ● vt menzionare; **don't ~ it** non c'è di che

**mentor** /'mentɔː(r)/ n mentore m

**menu** /'menjuː/ n menu m inv

**MEP** n abbr (**Member of the European Parliament**) eurodeputato, -a mf

**mercantile** /'mɜːkəntaɪl/ a mercantile

**mercenary** /'mɜːsɪnərɪ/ a mercenario ● n mercenario m

**merchandise** /'mɜːtʃəndaɪz/ n merce f

**merchant** /'mɜːtʃənt/ n commerciante mf

**merchant: merchant bank** n Br banca f d'affari. **merchant banker** n (owner) proprietario, -a mf di una banca d'affari; (executive) dirigente mf di banca d'affari. **merchant navy** n marina f mercantile

**merciful** /'mɜːsɪfl/ a misericordioso

**mercifully** /'mɜːsɪfʊlɪ/ adv fam grazie a Dio

**merciless** /'mɜːsɪlɪs/ a spietato

**mercilessly** /'mɜːsɪlɪslɪ/ adv senza pietà

**mercurial** /mɜː'kjʊərɪəl/ a fig volubile

**mercury** /'mɜːkjʊrɪ/ n mercurio m

**mercy** /'mɜːsɪ/ n misericordia f; **be at sb's ~** essere alla mercé o in balia di qcno

**mercy killing** n eutanasia f

**mere** /mɪə(r)/ a solo

**merely** /'mɪəlɪ/ adv solamente

**merest** /'mɪərɪst/ a minimo

**merge** /mɜːdʒ/ vi fondersi ● vt Comm fondere

**merger** /'mɜːdʒə(r)/ n fusione f

**meridian** /mə'rɪdɪən/ n meridiano m

**meringue** /mə'ræŋ/ n meringa f

**merit** /'merɪt/ n merito m; (advantage) qualità f inv ● vt meritare

**mermaid** /'mɜːmeɪd/ n sirena f

**merrily** /'merɪlɪ/ adv allegramente

**merriment** /'merɪmənt/ n baldoria f

**merry** /'merɪ/ a (-ier, -iest) allegro; **~ Christmas!** Buon Natale!; **make ~** far festa

**merry-go-round** n giostra f

**merry-making** /'merɪmeɪkɪŋ/ n festa f

**mesh** /meʃ/ n maglia f

**mesmerize** /'mezməraɪz/ vt ipnotizzare

**mesmerized** /'mezməraɪzd/ a fig ipnotizzato

**mess** /mes/ n disordine m, casino m fam; (trouble) guaio m; (something spilt) sporco m; Mil mensa f; **make a ~ of** (botch) fare un pasticcio di

■ **mess about** vi perder tempo; **~ about with** armeggiare con ● vt prendere in giro ⟨person⟩

■ **mess up** vt mettere in disordine, incasinare fam; (botch) mandare all'aria

■ **mess with** vt (fam: interfere with) trafficare con ⟨computer, radio etc⟩; contrariare ⟨person⟩

**message** /'mesɪdʒ/ n messaggio m

**mess dress** *n Mil* uniforme *f* di gala
**messenger** /'mesɪndʒə(r)/ *n* messaggero *m*
**messenger boy** *n* fattorino *m*
**Messiah** /mɪ'saɪə/ *n* Messia *m*
**Messrs** /'mesəz/ *npl (on letter)* ~ **Smith** Spett. ditta Smith
**messy** /'mesɪ/ *a* (**-ier, -iest**) disordinato; (*in dress*) sciatto
**met** /met/ *see* **meet**
**metabolism** /mɪ'tæbəlɪzm/ *n* metabolismo *m*
**metal** /'metl/ *n* metallo *m* ● *a* di metallo
**metal detector** *n* metal detector *m inv*
**metal fatigue** *n* fatica *f* del metallo
**metallic** /mɪ'tælɪk/ *a* metallico
**metallurgy** /mɪ'tælədʒɪ/ *n* metallurgia *f*
**metal polish** *n* lucido *m* per metalli
**metalwork** /'metlwɜ:k/ *n* lavorazione *f* del metallo
**metamorphose** /metə'mɔ:fəʊz/ *vt* trasformare ● *vi* trasformarsi (**into** in)
**metamorphosis** /metə'mɔ:fəsɪs/ *n* (*pl* **-phoses** /metə'mɔ:fəsi:z/) metamorfosi *f inv*
**metaphor** /'metəfə(r)/ *n* metafora *f*
**metaphorical** /metə'fɒrɪkl/ *a* metaforico
**metaphorically** /metə'fɒrɪklɪ/ *adv* metaforicamente
**metaphysical** /metə'fɪzɪkl/ *a* metafisico; (*abstract*) astruso
**meteor** /'mi:tɪə(r)/ *n* meteora *f*
**meteoric** /mi:tɪ'ɒrɪk/ *a fig* fulmineo
**meteorite** /'mi:tɪəraɪt/ *n* meteorite *m*
**meteorological** /mi:tɪərə'lɒdʒɪkl/ *a* meteorologico
**Meteorological Office** *n* Ufficio *m* meteorologico
**meteorologist** /mi:tɪə'rɒlədʒɪst/ *n* meteorologo, -a *mf*
**meteorology** /mi:tɪə'rɒlədʒɪ/ *n* meteorologia *f*
**meter¹** /'mi:tə(r)/ *n* contatore *m*
**meter²** *n Am* = **metre**
**meter reader** *n* persona *f* incaricata di leggere il contatore (*di gas, elettricità*)
**methane** /'mi:θeɪn/ *n* metano *m*
**method** /'meθəd/ *n* metodo *m*
**method acting** *n* metodo *m* dell'Actors' Studio
**method actor** *n* attore *m* che segue il metodo dell'Actors' Studio
**methodical** /mɪ'θɒdɪkl/ *a* metodico
**methodically** /mɪ'θɒdɪklɪ/ *adv* metodicamente
**Methodist** /'meθədɪst/ *n* metodista *mf*
**methodology** /meθə'dɒlədʒɪ/ *n* metodologia *f*
**meths** /meθs/ *n fam* alcol *m* denaturato
**methyl** /'mi:θaɪl/ *n* metile *m*
**methylated** /'meθɪleɪtɪd/ *a* ~ **spirit[s]** alcol *m* denaturato
**meticulous** /mɪ'tɪkjʊləs/ *a* meticoloso
**meticulously** /mɪ'tɪkjʊləslɪ/ *adv* meticolosamente
**metre** /'mi:tə(r)/ *n* metro *m*
**metric** /'metrɪk/ *a* metrico

**metrication** /metrɪ'keɪʃn/ *n* conversione *f* al sistema metrico
**metronome** /'metrənəʊm/ *n* metronomo *m*
**metropolis** /mɪ'trɒpəlɪs/ *n* metropoli *f inv*
**metropolitan** /metrə'pɒlɪtən/ *a* metropolitano
**metropolitan district** *n Br* circoscrizione *f* amministrativa urbana
**Metropolitan police** *n Br* polizia *f* di Londra
**mew** /mju:/ *n* miao *m* ● *vi* miagolare
**mews** /mju:z/ *n Br* (*stables*) scuderie *fpl*; (*street*) stradina *f*; (*yard*) cortile *m*
**mews flat** *n Br* piccolo appartamento *m* ricavato da vecchie scuderie
**Mexican** /'meksɪkən/ *a & n* messicano, -a *mf*
**Mexican wave** *n* ola *f inv*
**Mexico** /'meksɪkəʊ/ *n* Messico *m*
**mezzanine** /'metsəni:n/ *n* mezzanino *m*
**miaow** /mɪ'aʊ/ *n* miao *m* ● *vi* miagolare
**mice** /maɪs/ *see* **mouse**
**Michaelmas** /'mɪkəlməs/ *n* festa *f* di San Michele (*29 settembre*)
**Michaelmas daisy** *n Br* margherita *f* settembrina
**Michaelmas Term** *n Br Univ* primo trimestre *m*
**mickey** /'mɪkɪ/ *n* **take the ~ out of** prendere in giro
**Mickey Mouse** *n* Topolino *m*
**microbe** /'maɪkrəʊb/ *n* microbo *m*
**microchip** /'maɪkrəʊtʃɪp/ *n* microchip *m inv*
**microcomputer** /'maɪkrəʊkəmpju:tə(r)/ *n* microcomputer *m inv*
**microcosm** /'maɪkrəkɒzm/ *n* microcosmo *m*
**micro: microfilm** *n* microfilm *m* *inv*. **micromesh tights** *npl* collant *mpl* velati. **microphone** *n* microfono *m*. **microphysics** *n* microfisica *f*. **microprocessor** *n* microprocessore *m*. **microscope** *n* microscopio *m*. **microscopic** *a* microscopico. **microsurgery** *n* microchirurgia *f*. **microwave** *n* microonda *f*; (*oven*) forno *m* a microonde
**mid** /mɪd/ *a* ~ **May** metà maggio; **in ~ air** a mezz'aria
**midday** /mɪd'deɪ/ *n* mezzogiorno *m*
**middle** /'mɪdl/ *a* di centro; **the M~ Ages** il medioevo; **the ~ class[es]** la classe media; **the M~ East** il Medio Oriente ● *n* mezzo *m*; **in the ~ of** ⟨*room, floor etc*⟩ in mezzo a; **in the ~ of the night** nel pieno della notte, a notte piena
**middle: middle-aged** /-'eɪdʒd/ *a* di mezza età. **middle-age spread** *n* pancetta *f* di mezza età. **Middle America** *n* (*social group*) ceto *m* medio americano a tendenza conservatrice. **middlebrow** *a* ⟨*book*⟩ per il lettore medio; ⟨*person*⟩ con interessi culturali convenzionali. **middle-class** *a* borghese. **middle distance** *n Phot, Cinema* secondo piano *m*; **gaze into the ~ ~** avere lo sguardo perso nel vuoto. **Middle English** *n* medio inglese *m*. **middle finger** *n* dito *m* medio. **middle ground** *m Pol* centro *m*; **occupy the ~ ~**

adottare una posizione intermedia. **middle-income** *a* ⟨*person, family, country*⟩ dal reddito medio

**middleman** /'mɪdlmæn/ *n Comm* intermediario *m*

**middle: middle manager** *n* quadro *m* intermedio. **middle-of-the-road** *a* ⟨*ordinary*⟩ ordinario; ⟨*policy*⟩ moderato. **middle-size[d]** /-saɪz[d]/ *a* di misura media. **middleweight** *n* peso *m* medio

**middling** /'mɪdlɪŋ/ *a* discreto

**midfield** /mɪd'fiːld/ *n* centrocampo *m*

**midfield player** *n* centrocampista *m*

**midge** /mɪdʒ/ *n* moscerino *m*

**midget** /'mɪdʒɪt/ *n* nano. -a *mf*

**Midlands** /'mɪdləndz/ *npl* the ~ l'Inghilterra *fsg* centrale

**mid-life** *n* mezza età *f*

**mid-life crisis** *n* crisi *f inv* di mezza età

**midnight** /'mɪdnaɪt/ *n* mezzanotte *f*

**mid-range** *attrib* ⟨*car*⟩ ⟨*in price*⟩ di prezzo medio; ⟨*in power*⟩ di media cilindrata; ⟨*hotel*⟩ intermedio; **be in the ~** ⟨*product, hotel:*⟩ essere nella media

**midriff** /'mɪdrɪf/ *n* diaframma *m*

**mid-season** *a* di metà stagione

**midshipman** /'mɪdʃɪpmən/ *n Br* cadetto *m* di marina; *Am* allievo *m* dell'Accademia Navale

**midst** /mɪdst/ *n* **in the ~ of** in mezzo a; **in our ~** fra di noi, in mezzo a noi

**midstream** /mɪd'striːm/ *adv* **in ~** ⟨*in river*⟩ nel mezzo della corrente; ⟨*fig: in speech*⟩ nel mezzo del discorso

**midsummer** /'mɪdsʌmə(r)/ *n* mezza estate *f*

**Midsummer's Day** *n* festa *f* di San Giovanni (*24 giugno*)

**mid-term** *attrib Sch* di metà trimestre; *Pol* a metà del mandato del governo

**midway** /'mɪdweɪ/ *adv* a metà strada

**midweek** /mɪd'wiːk/ *a* di metà settimana ● *adv* a metà settimana

**midwife** /'mɪdwaɪf/ *n* ostetrica *f*

**midwifery** /'mɪdwɪfrɪ/ *n* ostetricia *f*

**midwinter** /mɪd'wɪntə(r)/ *n* pieno inverno *m*

**miffed** /mɪft/ *a fam* seccato

**might**[1] /maɪt/ *v aux* **I ~** potrei; **will you come? – I ~** vieni? – può darsi; **it ~ be true** potrebbe essere vero; **I ~ as well stay** potrei anche restare; **he asked if he ~ go** ha chiesto se poteva andare; **you ~ have drowned** avresti potuto affogare; **you ~ have said so!** avresti potuto dirlo!

**might**[2] *n* potere *m*

**mighty** /'maɪtɪ/ *a* (**-ier, -iest**) potente ● *adv fam* molto

**migraine** /'miːgreɪn/ *n* emicrania *f*

**migrant** /'maɪgrənt/ *a* migratore ● *n* ⟨*bird*⟩ migratore, -trice *mf*; ⟨*person: for work*⟩ emigrante *mf*

**migrate** /maɪ'greɪt/ *vi* migrare

**migration** /maɪ'greɪʃn/ *n* migrazione *f*

**migratory** /'maɪgreɪtərɪ/ *a* ⟨*animal*⟩ migratore

**mike** /maɪk/ *n fam* microfono *f*

**Milan** /mɪ'læn/ *n* Milano *f*

**Milanese** /mɪlə'niːz/ *a* milanese

**mild** /maɪld/ *a* ⟨*weather*⟩ mite; ⟨*person*⟩ dolce; ⟨*flavour*⟩ delicato; ⟨*illness*⟩ leggero

**mildew** /'mɪldjuː/ *n* muffa *f*

**mildly** /'maɪldlɪ/ *adv* moderatamente; ⟨*say*⟩ dolcemente; **to put it ~** a dir poco, senza esagerazione

**mildness** /'maɪldnɪs/ *n* ⟨*of person, words*⟩ dolcezza *f*; ⟨*of weather*⟩ mitezza *f*

**mile** /maɪl/ *n* miglio *m* (= *1,6 km*); **~s nicer** *fam* molto più bello; **~s too big** *fam* eccessivamente grande

**mileage** /'maɪldʒ/ *n* chilometraggio *m*

**mileage allowance** *n* indennità *f inv* di trasferta per chilometro

**milestone** /'maɪlstəʊn/ *n* pietra *f* miliare

**milieu** /mɪ'ljɜː/ *n* ambiente *m*

**militant** /'mɪlɪtənt/ *a* & *n* militante *mf*

**militarism** /'mɪlɪtərɪzm/ *n* militarismo *m*

**militarize** /'mɪlɪtəraɪz/ *vt* militarizzare

**military** /'mɪlɪtrɪ/ *a* militare

**military: military academy** *n* accademia *f* militare. **military policeman** *n* agente *m* di polizia militare. **military service** *n* servizio *m* militare

**militate** /'mɪlɪteɪt/ *vi* **~ against** opporsi a

**militia** /mɪ'lɪʃə/ *n* milizia *f*

**milk** /mɪlk/ *n* latte *m* ● *vt* mungere

**milk: milk chocolate** *n* cioccolato *m* al latte. **milk float** *n Br* furgone *m* del lattaio. **milk jug** *n* bricco *m* del latte. **milkman** *n* lattaio *m*. **milk pudding** *n* budino *m* a base di latte. **milk shake** *n* frappé *m inv*. **milk train** *n* primo treno *m* del mattino

**milky** /'mɪlkɪ/ *a* (**-ier, -iest**) latteo; ⟨*tea etc*⟩ con molto latte. **Milky Way** *n Astr* Via *f* Lattea

**mill** /mɪl/ *n* mulino *m*; ⟨*factory*⟩ fabbrica *f*; ⟨*for coffee etc*⟩ macinino *m* ● *vt* macinare ⟨*grain*⟩

■ **mill about, mill around** *vi* brulicare

**millennium** /mɪ'lenɪəm/ *n* millennio *m*

**miller** /'mɪlə(r)/ *n* mugnaio *m*

**millet** /'mɪlɪt/ *n* miglio *m*

**milligram** /'mɪlɪgræm/ *n* milligrammo *m*

**millimetre** /'mɪlɪmiːtə(r)/ *n* millimetro *m*

**million** /'mɪljən/ *a* & *n* milione *m*; **a ~ pounds** un milione di sterline

**millionaire** /mɪljə'neə(r)/ *n* miliardario, -a *mf*

**millipede** /'mɪlɪpiːd/ *n* millepiedi *m inv*

**mill: millpond** *n* **like a ~** calmo come una tavola. **millstone** *n* **a ~ round one's neck** *fig* un peso; **mill-wheel** *n* ruota *f* di mulino

**milometer** /maɪ'lɒmɪtə(r)/ *n Br* ≈ contachilometri *m inv*

**mime** /maɪm/ *n* mimo *m* ● *vt* mimare

**mime artist** *n* mimo, -a *mf*

**mimic** /'mɪmɪk/ *n* imitatore, -trice *mf* ● *vt* (*pt/pp* **mimicked**) imitare

**mimicry** /'mɪmɪkrɪ/ *n* mimetismo *m*

**mimosa** /mɪ'məʊzə/ *n* mimosa *f*

**minaret** /mɪnə'ret/ *n* minareto *m*

**mince** /mɪns/ *n* carne *f* tritata ● *vt Culin* tritare; **not ~ words** parlare senza mezzi termini

**mincemeat** /'mɪnsmiːt/ n miscuglio m di frutta secca; **make ~ of** fig demolire

**mince pie** n pasticcino m a base di frutta secca

**mincer** /'mɪnsə(r)/ n tritacarne m inv

**mind** /maɪnd/ n mente f; (sanity) ragione f; **to my ~** a mio parere; **give sb a piece of one's ~** dire chiaro e tondo a qcno quello che si pensa; **make up one's ~** decidersi; **have sth in ~** avere qcsa in mente; **bear sth in ~** tenere presente qcsa; **have something on one's ~** essere preoccupato; **have a good ~ to** avere una grande voglia di; **I have changed my ~** ho cambiato idea; **be out of one's ~** essere fuori di sé ● vt (look after) occuparsi di; **I don't ~ the noise** il rumore non mi dà fastidio; **I don't ~ what we do** non mi importa quello che facciamo; **~ the step!** attenzione al gradino! ● vi **I don't ~** non mi importa; **never ~!** non importa!; **do you ~ if...?** ti dispiace se...?
■ **mind out** vi **~ out!** [fai] attenzione!

**mind:** **mind-bending** /-bendɪŋ/ a ⟨problem⟩ complicatissimo; **~ drugs** psicofarmaci mpl. **mind-blowing** /-bləʊɪŋ/ a fam sconvolgente. **mind-boggling** /-bɒglɪŋ/ a fam incredibile

**minded** /'maɪndɪd/ a **if you're so ~** se vuole

**minder** /'maɪndə(r)/ n (Br: bodyguard) gorilla m inv; (for child) baby-sitter mf inv

**mindful** /'maɪndfʊl/ a **~ of** attento a

**mindless** /'maɪndlɪs/ a noncurante

**mind-reader** n persona f che legge nel pensiero; **I'm not a ~** non leggo nel pensiero

**mine**[1] /maɪn/ poss pron il mio m, la mia f, i miei mpl, le mie fpl; **a friend of ~** un mio amico; **friends of ~** dei miei amici; **that is ~** questo è mio; (as opposed to yours) questo è il mio

**mine**[2] n miniera f; (explosive) mina f ● vt estrarre; Mil minare

**mine-detector** n rivelatore m di mine

**minefield** /'maɪnfiːld/ n also fig campo m minato

**miner** /'maɪnə(r)/ n minatore m

**mineral** /'mɪnərəl/ n minerale m ● a minerale

**mineral: mineral oil** n (Am: paraffin) olio m minerale. **mineral rights** npl concessioni fpl minerarie. **mineral water** n acqua f minerale

**minesweeper** /'maɪnswiːpə(r)/ n dragamine m inv

**mingle** /'mɪŋgl/ vi **~ with** mescolarsi a

**mini** /'mɪnɪ/ n see **miniskirt**

**mini+** pref mini+

**miniature** /'mɪnɪtʃə(r)/ a in miniatura ● n miniatura f

**miniature golf** n minigolf m inv

**miniature railway** n trenino m

**mini: mini-budget** n Br Pol budget m inv provvisorio. **minibus** n minibus m inv, pulmino m. **minicab** n taxi m inv

**minim** /'mɪnɪm/ n Mus minima f

**minimal** /'mɪnɪməl/ a minimo

**minimally** /'mɪnɪməlɪ/ adv (very slightly) minimamente

**minimarket** /'mɪnɪmɑːkɪt/ n minimarket m inv

**minimize** /'mɪnɪmaɪz/ vt minimizzare

**minimum** /'mɪnɪməm/ n (pl -ima) minimo m ● a minimo; **ten minutes ~** minimo dieci minuti

**mining** /'maɪnɪŋ/ n estrazione f ● attrib estrattivo

**mining engineer** n ingegnere m minerario

**miniskirt** /'mɪnɪskɜːt/ n minigonna f

**minister** /'mɪnɪstə(r)/ n ministro m; Relig pastore m

**ministerial** /mɪnɪ'stɪərɪəl/ a ministeriale

**minister of state** n Br Pol titolo m di un parlamentare con competenze specifiche in seno a un ministero

**ministry** /'mɪnɪstrɪ/ n Pol ministero m; **the ~** Relig il ministero sacerdotale

**mink** /mɪŋk/ n visone m

**minnow** /'mɪnəʊ/ n (fish) pesciolino m d'acqua dolce

**minor** /'maɪnə(r)/ a minore ● n minorenne mf

**Minorca** /mɪ'nɔːkə/ n Minorca f

**minority** /maɪ'nɒrətɪ/ n minoranza f; (age) minore età f

**minority leader** n Am Pol leader mf inv dell'opposizione

**minority rule** n governo m di minoranza

**minor offence** n Br reato m minore

**minor road** n strada f secondaria

**minster** /'mɪnstə(r)/ n (cathedral) cattedrale f

**mint**[1] /mɪnt/ n zecca f; fam patrimonio m ● a **in ~ condition** in condizione perfetta ● vt coniare

**mint**[2] n (herb) menta f

**mint-flavoured** /-fleɪvəd/ a al gusto di menta

**minuet** /mɪnjʊ'et/ n minuetto m

**minus** /'maɪnəs/ prep meno; (fam: without) senza ● n [sign] meno m

**minute**[1] /'mɪnɪt/ n minuto m; **in a ~** (shortly) in un minuto; **~s** pl (of meeting) verbale msg

**minute**[2] /maɪ'njuːt/ a minuto; (precise) minuzioso

**minute hand** /'mɪnɪt/ n lancetta f dei minuti

**minutely** /maɪ'njuːtlɪ/ adv ⟨vary, differ⟩ di poco; ⟨describe, examine⟩ minuziosamente

**minutiae** /maɪ'njuːʃɪaɪ/ npl minuzie fpl

**miracle** /'mɪrəkl/ n miracolo m

**miraculous** /mɪ'rækjʊləs/ a miracoloso

**mirage** /'mɪrɑːʒ/ n miraggio m

**mire** /'maɪə(r)/ n pantano m

**mirror** /'mɪrə(r)/ n specchio m ● vt rispecchiare

**mirror image** n (exact replica) copia f esatta; (inverse) immagine f speculare

**mirth** /mɜːθ/ n ilarità f

**misadventure** /mɪsæd'ventʃə(r)/ n disavventura f

**misanthropist** /mɪˈzænθrəpɪst/ n misantropo, -a mf

**misapprehension** /mɪsæprɪˈhenʃn/ n malinteso m; **be under a ~** avere frainteso

**misappropriate** /mɪsəˈprəʊprɪeɪt/ vt appropriarsi indebitamente di ‹funds›

**misbehave** /mɪsbɪˈheɪv/ vi comportarsi male

**misbehaviour** /mɪsbɪˈheɪvjə(r)/ n comportamento m scorretto

**miscalculate** /mɪsˈkælkjʊleɪt/ vt/i calcolare male

**miscalculation** /mɪskælkjʊˈleɪʃn/ n calcolo m sbagliato

**miscarriage** /ˈmɪskærɪdʒ/ n aborto m spontaneo; **~ of justice** errore m giudiziario

**miscarry** /mɪsˈkærɪ/ vi abortire

**miscellaneous** /mɪsəˈleɪnɪəs/ a assortito

**miscellany** /mɪˈselənɪ/ n ‹of people, things› misto m; ‹anthology› miscellanea f

**mischief** /ˈmɪstʃɪf/ n malefatta f; ‹harm› danno m

**mischievous** /ˈmɪstʃɪvəs/ a ‹naughty› birichino; ‹malicious› dannoso

**mischievously** /ˈmɪstʃɪvəslɪ/ adv in modo birichino

**misconceived** /mɪskənˈsiːvd/ a ‹argument, project› sbagliato

**misconception** /mɪskənˈsepʃn/ n concetto m erroneo

**misconduct** /mɪsˈkɒndʌkt/ n cattiva condotta f

**misconstrue** /mɪskənˈstruː/ vt fraintendere

**miscount** /mɪsˈkaʊnt/ vt/i contare male

**misdeed** /mɪsˈdiːd/ n misfatto m

**misdemeanour** /mɪsdɪˈmiːnə(r)/ n reato m

**misdirect** /mɪsdaɪˈrekt/ vt mettere l'indirizzo sbagliato su ‹letter, parcel›; dare istruzioni sbagliate a ‹jury›; **the letter was ~ed to our old address** la lettera ci è stata erroneamente spedita al vecchio indirizzo

**miser** /ˈmaɪzə(r)/ n avaro m

**miserable** /ˈmɪzrəbl/ a ‹unhappy› infelice; ‹wretched› miserabile; ‹fig: weather› deprimente

**miserably** /ˈmɪzrəblɪ/ adv ‹live, fail› miseramente; ‹say› tristemente

**miserly** /ˈmaɪzəlɪ/ a avaro; ‹amount› ridicolo

**misery** /ˈmɪzərɪ/ n miseria f; ‹fam: person› piagnone, -a mf

**misfire** /mɪsˈfaɪə(r)/ vi ‹gun:› far cilecca; ‹plan etc:› non riuscire

**misfit** /ˈmɪsfɪt/ n disadattato, -a mf

**misfortune** /mɪsˈfɔːtʃuːn/ n sfortuna f

**misgivings** /mɪsˈɡɪvɪŋz/ npl dubbi mpl

**misguided** /mɪsˈɡaɪdɪd/ a fuorviato

**mishandle** /mɪsˈhændl/ vt gestire male ‹operation, meeting›; non prendere per il verso giusto ‹person›; ‹roughly› maneggiare senza precauzioni ‹object›; maltrattare ‹person, animal›

**mishap** /ˈmɪshæp/ n disavventura f

**mishear** /mɪsˈhɪə(r)/ vt sentire male

**mishmash** /ˈmɪʃmæʃ/ n fam guazzabuglio m

**misinform** /mɪsɪnˈfɔːm/ vt informar male

**misinformation** /mɪsɪnfəˈmeɪʃn/ n informazioni fpl sbagliate

**misinterpret** /mɪsɪnˈtɜːprɪt/ vt fraintendere

**misinterpretation** /mɪsɪntɜːprɪˈteɪʃn/ n interpretazione f sbagliata

**misjudge** /mɪsˈdʒʌdʒ/ vt giudicar male; ‹estimate wrongly› valutare male

**mislay** /mɪsˈleɪ/ vt (pt/pp -laid) smarrire

**mislead** /mɪsˈliːd/ vt (pt/pp -led) fuorviare

**misleading** /mɪsˈliːdɪŋ/ a fuorviante

**mismanage** /mɪsˈmænɪdʒ/ vt amministrare male

**mismanagement** /mɪsˈmænɪdʒmənt/ n cattiva amministrazione f

**mismatch** /ˈmɪsmætʃ/ n discordanza f

**misname** /mɪsˈneɪm/ vt dare il nome sbagliato a

**misnomer** /mɪsˈnəʊmə(r)/ n termine m improprio

**misogynist** /mɪˈsɒdʒənɪst/ n misogino m

**misplace** /mɪsˈpleɪs/ vt mettere in un posto sbagliato; **~ one's trust** riporre male la propria fiducia

**misprint** /ˈmɪsprɪnt/ n errore m di stampa

**mispronounce** /mɪsprəˈnaʊns/ vt pronunciare male

**mispronunciation** /mɪsprənʌnsɪˈeɪʃn/ n ‹act› pronuncia f sbagliata; ‹instance› errore m di pronuncia

**misquote** /mɪsˈkwəʊt/ vt citare erroneamente

**misread** /mɪsˈriːd/ vt leggere male ‹sentence, meter›; ‹misinterpret› fraintendere ‹actions›

**misrepresent** /mɪsreprɪˈzent/ vt rappresentare male

**misrepresentation** /mɪsreprɪzenˈteɪʃn/ n ‹of facts, opinions› travisamento m

**Miss** /mɪs/ n (pl -es) signorina f

**miss** n colpo m mancato ● vt ‹fail to hit or find› mancare; perdere ‹train, bus, class›; ‹feel the loss of› sentire la mancanza di; **I ~ed that part** ‹failed to notice› mi è sfuggita quella parte; **~ the point** non afferrare il punto ● vi but **he ~ed** ‹failed to hit› ma l'ha mancato

▪ **miss out** vt saltare, omettere

**misshapen** /mɪsˈʃeɪpən/ a malformato

**missile** /ˈmɪsaɪl/ n missile m

**missing** /ˈmɪsɪŋ/ a mancante; ‹person› scomparso; Mil disperso; **be ~** essere introvabile; **~ in action** Mil disperso

**mission** /ˈmɪʃn/ n missione f

**missionary** /ˈmɪʃənrɪ/ n missionario, -a mf

**missive** /ˈmɪsɪv/ n missiva f

**misspell** /mɪsˈspel/ vt (pt/pp -spelt, -spelled) sbagliare l'ortografia di

**misspent** /mɪsˈspent/ a **a ~ youth** una gioventù sprecata

**mist** /mɪst/ n ‹fog› foschia f; **because of the ~ on the windows** a causa dei vetri appannati

▪ **mist up** vi appannarsi, annebbiarsi

**mistake** /mɪˈsteɪk/ n sbaglio m; **by ~** per sbaglio ● vt (pt mistook, pp mistaken) sbagliare ⟨*road, house*⟩; fraintendere ⟨*meaning, words*⟩; ~ **for** prendere per

**mistaken** /mɪ'steɪkən/ *a* sbagliato; **be ~** sbagliarsi; ~ **identity** errore *m* di persona

**mistakenly** /mɪ'steɪkənlɪ/ *adv* erroneamente

**mister** /'mɪstə(r)/ *n* signore *m*

**mistletoe** /'mɪsltəʊ/ *n* vischio *m*

**mistranslate** /mɪstrænz'leɪt/ *vt* tradurre in modo sbagliato

**mistranslation** /mɪstrænz'leɪʃn/ *n* traduzione *f* sbagliata

**mistreat** /mɪs'tri:t/ maltrattare

**mistreatment** /mɪs'tri:tmənt/ *n* maltrattamento *m*

**mistress** /'mɪstrɪs/ *n* padrona *f*; ⟨*teacher*⟩ maestra *f*; ⟨*lover*⟩ amante *f*

**mistrust** /mɪs'trʌst/ *n* sfiducia *f* ● *vt* non aver fiducia in

**misty** /'mɪstɪ/ *a* (**-ier, -iest**) nebbioso; *fig* indistinto

**misty-eyed** /-'aɪd/ *a* ⟨*look*⟩ commosso; **he goes all ~ about it** a parlarne si commuove

**misunderstand** /mɪsʌndə'stænd/ *vt* (*pt/pp* **-stood**) fraintendere

**misunderstanding** /mɪsʌndə'stændɪŋ/ *n* malinteso *m*

**misuse¹** /mɪs'ju:z/ *vt* usare male

**misuse²** /mɪs'ju:s/ *n* cattivo uso *m*

**mite** /maɪt/ *n* *Zool* acaro *m*; ⟨*child*⟩ piccino, -a *mf*

**mitigate** /'mɪtɪgeɪt/ *vt* attenuare

**mitigating** /'mɪtɪgeɪtɪŋ/ *a* attenuante

**mitt** /mɪt/ *n* ⟨*no separate fingers*⟩ muffola *f*; ⟨*cut-off fingers*⟩ mezzo guanto *m*; ⟨*in baseball*⟩ guantone *m*; ⟨*fam: hand*⟩ mano *f*

**mitten** /'mɪtn/ *n* manopola *f*, muffola *f*

**mix** /mɪks/ *n* ⟨*combination*⟩ mescolanza *f*; *Culin* miscuglio *m*; ⟨*ready-made*⟩ preparato *m* ● *vt* mischiare ● *vi* mischiarsi; ⟨*person:*⟩ inserirsi; ~ **with** ⟨*associate with*⟩ frequentare

■ **mix in** *vt* incorporare ⟨*eggs, flour etc*⟩

■ **mix up** *vt* mescolare ⟨*papers*⟩; ⟨*confuse, mistake for*⟩ confondere

**mixed** /mɪkst/ *a* misto; ~ **up** ⟨*person*⟩ confuso

**mixed: mixed ability** *a* ⟨*class, teaching*⟩ per alunni di capacità diverse. **mixed bag: it was a very ~ ~** *n fig* c'era un po' di tutto. **mixed blessing: be a ~ ~** *n* avere vantaggi e svantaggi. **mixed doubles** *npl Tennis* doppio *m* misto. **mixed economy** *n* economia *f* mista. **mixed grill** *n* grigliata *f* di carne mista. **mixed marriage** *n* matrimonio *m* misto. **mixed-media** *a* multimediale. **mixed metaphor** *n* abbinamento *m* di parte di due o più metafore diverse con effetto comico

**mixed-up** *a* ⟨*person, emotions*⟩ confuso

**mixed vegetables** *npl* verdure *fpl* miste

**mixer** /'mɪksə(r)/ *n Culin* frullatore *m*, mixer *m inv*; **he's a good ~** è un tipo socievole

**mixing** /'mɪksɪŋ/ *n* ⟨*of people, objects, ingredients*⟩ mescolamento *m*, *Mus* mixaggio *m*

**mixture** /'mɪkstʃə(r)/ *n* mescolanza *f*; ⟨*medicine*⟩ sciroppo *m*; *Culin* miscela *f*

**mix-up** *n* ⟨*confusion*⟩ confusione *f*; ⟨*mistake*⟩ pasticcio *m*

**mm** *abbr* (**millimetre(s)**) mm

**MO** *abbr* (**medical officer**) ufficiale *m* medico; *abbr* (**money order**) vaglia *m inv* postale; *Am abbr* **Missouri**

**moan** /məʊn/ *n* lamento *m* ● *vi* lamentarsi; ⟨*complain*⟩ lagnarsi

**moat** /məʊt/ *n* fossato *m*

**mob** /mɒb/ *n* folla *f*; ⟨*rabble*⟩ gentaglia *f*; ⟨*fam: gang*⟩ banda *f* ● *vt* (*pt/pp* **mobbed**) assalire

**mobile** /'məʊbaɪl/ *a* mobile ● *n* composizione *f* mobile; ⟨*phone*⟩ [telefono *m*] cellulare *m*

**mobile: mobile home** *n* casa *f* roulotte. **mobile library** *n Br* biblioteca *f* itinerante. **mobile phone** *n* [telefono *m*] cellulare *m*. **mobile shop** *n* furgone *m* attrezzato per la vendita

**mobility** /mə'bɪlətɪ/ *n* mobilità *f*

**mobility allowance** *n Br* indennità *f inv* di accompagnamento

**mobilization** /məʊbɪlaɪ'zeɪʃn/ *n* mobilitazione *f*

**mobilize** /'məʊbɪlaɪz/ *vt* mobilitare

**mocha** /'mɒkə/ *n* moca *m inv*

**mock** /mɒk/ *a* finto ● *vt* canzonare

**mockery** /'mɒkərɪ/ *n* derisione *f*; **a ~ of** una parodia di

**mock-up** *n* modello *m* in scala

**MoD** *n Br abbr* (**Ministry of Defence**) Ministero *m* della Difesa

**modal** /'məʊdl/ *a* ~ **auxiliary** verbo *m* modale

**mod con** /mɒd'kɒn/ *Br abbr* (**modern convenience**) **all ~ ~s** tutti i confort

**mode** /məʊd/ *n* modo *m*; *Comput* modalità *f*

**model** /'mɒdl/ *n* modello *m*; [**fashion**] ~ indossatore, -trice *mf*, modello, -a *mf* ● *a* ⟨*yacht, plane*⟩ in miniatura; ⟨*pupil, husband*⟩ esemplare, modello ● *v* (*pt/pp* **modelled**) ● *vt* indossare ⟨*clothes*⟩ ● *vi* fare l'indossatore, -trice *mf*; ⟨*for artist*⟩ posare

**modelling** /'mɒd(ə)lɪŋ/ *n* ⟨*with clay etc*⟩ modellare *m* con la creta; ⟨*of clothes*⟩ professione *f* di indossatore; **do some ~** ⟨*for artist*⟩ fare il modello

**modelling clay** *n* creta *f* per modellare

**modem** /'məʊdem/ *n* modem *m inv* ● *vt* mandare per modem

**moderate¹** /'mɒdəreɪt/ *vt* moderare ● *vi* moderarsi

**moderate²** /'mɒdərət/ *a* moderato ● *n Pol* moderato, -a *mf*

**moderately** /'mɒdərətlɪ/ *adv* ⟨*drink, speak etc*⟩ moderatamente; ⟨*good, bad etc*⟩ relativamente

**moderation** /mɒdə'reɪʃn/ *n* moderazione *f*; **in ~** con moderazione

**modern** /'mɒdn/ *a* moderno

**modern-day** *a* attuale

**modernism** /'mɒdənɪzm/ *n* modernismo *m*

**modernity** /mə'dɜ:nətɪ/ *n* modernità *f*

**modernization** /mɒdənaɪ'zeɪʃn/ *n* modernizzazione *f*

**modernize** /'mɒdənaɪz/ *vt* modernizzare

**modern languages** *npl* lingue *fpl* moderne

**modest** /'mɒdɪst/ *a* modesto

**modesty** /'mɒdɪstɪ/ *n* modestia *f*

**modicum** /'mɒdɪkəm/ *n* **a ~ of** un po' di

**modification** /mɒdɪfɪ'keɪʃn/ *n* modificazione *f*

**modifier** /'mɒdɪfaɪə(r)/ *n* (*in linguistics*) modificatore *m*

**modify** /'mɒdɪfaɪ/ *vt* (*pt/pp* **-fied**) modificare

**modular** /'mɒdjʊlə(r)/ *a* ‹*course*› a moduli; ‹*construction, furniture*› modulare

**modulate** /'mɒdjʊleɪt/ *vt/i* modulare

**module** /'mɒdjuːl/ *n* modulo *m*

**modus operandi** /məʊdəsɒpə'rændiː/ *n* modus operandi *m inv*

**mohican** /məʊ'hiːkən/ *n* (*hairstyle*) taglio *m* [di capelli] alla moicana

**moist** /mɔɪst/ *a* umido

**moisten** /'mɔɪsn/ *vt* inumidire

**moisture** /'mɔɪstʃə(r)/ *n* umidità *f*

**moisturizer** /'mɔɪstʃəraɪzə(r)/ *n* [crema *f*] idratante *m*

**molar** /'məʊlə(r)/ *n* molare *m*

**molasses** /mə'læsɪz/ *n Am* melassa *f*

**mole[1]** /məʊl/ *n* (*on face etc*) neo *m*

**mole[2]** *n Zool* talpa *f*

**mole[3]** *n* (*breakwater*) molo *m*

**molecular** /mə'lekjʊlə(r)/ *a* molecolare

**molecule** /'mɒlɪkjuːl/ *n* molecola *f*

**molehill** /'məʊlhɪl/ *n* monticello *m*

**moleskin** /'məʊlskɪn/ *n* (*fur*) pelliccia *f* di talpa

**molest** /mə'lest/ *vt* molestare

**mollify** /'mɒlɪfaɪ/ *vt* (*pt/pp* **-ied**) placare

**mollusc** /'mɒləsk/ *n* mollusco *m*

**mollycoddle** /'mɒlɪkɒdl/ *vt* tenere nella bambagia

**molten** /'məʊltən/ *a* fuso

**mom** /mɒm/ *n Am fam* mamma *f*

**moment** /'məʊmənt/ *n* momento *m*: **at the ~** in questo momento

**momentarily** /məʊmən'terɪlɪ/ *adv* (*for an instant*) per un momento; (*Am: at any moment*) da un momento all'altro: (*Am: very soon*) tra un momento

**momentary** /'məʊməntrɪ/ *a* momentaneo

**momentous** /mə'mentəs/ *a* molto importante

**momentum** /mə'mentəm/ *n* impeto *m*

**monarch** /'mɒnək/ *n* monarca *m*

**monarchist** /'mɒnəkɪst/ *n* monarchico, -a *mf*

**monarchy** /'mɒnəkɪ/ *n* monarchia *f*

**monastery** /'mɒnəstrɪ/ *n* monastero *m*

**monastic** /mə'næstɪk/ *a* monastico

**Monday** /'mʌndeɪ/ *n* lunedì *m inv*

**monetary** /'mʌnɪtrɪ/ *a* monetario

**money** /'mʌnɪ/ *n* denaro *m*

**money: money box** *n* salvadanaio *m*. **moneylender** *n* usuraio *m*. **money order** *n* vaglia *m inv* postale

**mongrel** /'mʌŋgrəl/ *n* bastardo *m*

**monitor** /'mɒnɪtə(r)/ *n Techn* monitor *m inv* ● *vt* controllare

**monk** /mʌŋk/ *n* monaco *m*

**monkey** /'mʌŋkɪ/ *n* scimmia *f*

■ **monkey about with** *vt* (*fam: interfere with*) armeggiare con

**monkey: monkey business** *n fam* (*fooling*) scherzi *mpl*: (*cheating*) imbrogli *mpl*. **monkey-nut** *n* nocciolina *f* americana. **monkey wrench** *n* chiave *f* inglese a rullino

**monkfish** /'mʌŋkfɪʃ/ *n* bottatrice *f*

**mono** /'mɒnəʊ/ *n* mono *m*

**monochrome** /'mɒnəkrəʊm/ *a* monocromatico; *Cinema, TV* in bianco e nero

**monocle** /'mɒnəkl/ *n* monocolo *m*

**monogamy** /mə'nɒgəmɪ/ *n* monogamia *f*

**monogram** /'mɒnəgræm/ *n* monogramma *m*

**monograph** /'mɒnəgrɑːf/ *n* monografia *f*

**monolith** /'mɒnəlɪθ/ *n* monolito *m*

**monologue** /'mɒnəlɒg/ *n* monologo *m*

**monomania** /mɒnə'meɪnɪə/ *n* monomania *f*

**monoplane** /'mɒnəpleɪn/ *n* monoplano *m*

**monopolize** /mə'nɒpəlaɪz/ *vt* monopolizzare

**monopoly** /mə'nɒpəlɪ/ *n* monopolio *m*

**monoski** /'mɒnəʊski:/ *n* monosci *m inv* ● *vi* praticare il monosci

**monosodium glutamate** /mɒnəsəʊdɪəm'gluːtəmeɪt/ *n* glutammato *m* di sodio

**monosyllabic** /mɒnəsɪ'læbɪk/ *a* monosillabico

**monosyllable** /'mɒnəsɪləbl/ *n* monosillabo *m*

**monotone** /'mɒnətəʊn/ *n* **speak in a ~** parlare con tono monotono

**monotonous** /mə'nɒtənəs/ *a* monotono

**monotonously** /mə'nɒtənəslɪ/ *adv* di modo monotono

**monotony** /mə'nɒtənɪ/ *n* monotonia *f*

**monsoon** /mɒn'suːn/ *n* monsone *m*

**monster** /'mɒnstə(r)/ *n* mostro *m*

**monstrosity** /mɒn'strɒsətɪ/ *n* mostruosità *f*

**monstrous** /'mɒnstrəs/ *a* mostruoso

**montage** /mɒn'tɑːʒ/ *n* montaggio *m*

**Mont Blanc** /mɒn'blɒ̃/ *n* Monte *m* Bianco

**month** /mʌnθ/ *n* mese *m*

**monthly** /'mʌnθlɪ/ *a* mensile ● *adv* mensilmente ● *n* (*periodical*) mensile *m*

**monument** /'mɒnjʊmənt/ *n* monumento *m*

**monumental** /mɒnjʊ'mentl/ *a fig* monumentale

**monumentally** /mɒnjʊ'mentlɪ/ *adv* ‹*boring, ignorant*› enormemente

**moo** /muː/ *n* muggito *m* ● *vi* (*pt/pp* **mooed**) muggire

**mooch** /muːtʃ/ *vi* **~ about** *fam* gironzolare; **~ about the house** gironzolare per casa

**mood** /muːd/ *n* umore *m*; **be in a good/bad ~** essere di buon/cattivo umore; **be in the ~ for** essere in vena di

**moody** /'muːdɪ/ *a* (**-ier, -iest**) (*variable*) lunatico: (*bad-tempered*) di malumore

**moon** /muːn/ *n* luna *f*: **over the ~** *fam* al settimo cielo

■ **moon about, moon around** *vi* (*fam: wander aimlessly*) gironzolare

■ **moon over** vt fam sospirare d'amore per ⟨sb⟩

**moon: moonbeam** n raggio m di luna. **moon buggy** n veicolo m lunare. **moonlight** n chiaro m di luna ● vi fam lavorare in nero. **moonlighting** n fam lavoro m nero. **moonlit** a illuminato dalla luna. **moonshine** n (nonsense) fantasie fpl; (Am: liquor) liquore m di contrabbando

**moor**¹ /muə(r)/ n brughiera f

**moor**² vt Naut ormeggiare

**moorhen** /'muəhen/ n gallinella f d'acqua

**mooring** /'muərɪŋ/ n (place) ormeggio m; **~s** pl (chains) ormeggi mpl

**Moorish** /'muərɪʃ/ a moresco

**moorland** /'muələnd/ n brughiera f

**moose** /mu:s/ n (pl **moose**) alce m

**moot** /mu:t/ a **it's a ~ point** è un punto controverso

**mop** /mɒp/ n mocio ʀ m inv; **~ of hair** zazzera f ● vt (pt/pp **mopped**) lavare con il mocio

■ **mop up** vt (dry) asciugare con il mocio ʀ; (clean) pulire con il mocio

**mope** /məup/ vi essere depresso

■ **mope about, mope around** vi trascinarsi

**moped** /'məuped/ n ciclomotore m

**moral** /'mɒrəl/ a morale ● n morale f

**morale** /mə'rɑ:l/ n morale m; **be a ~- booster** tirare su di morale

**moral fibre** n forza f morale

**moralistic** /mɒrə'lɪstɪk/ a moralistico

**morality** /mə'ræləti/ n moralità f

**moralize** /'mɒrəlaɪz/ vi moraleggiare

**morally** /'mɒrəli/ adv moralmente

**morals** /'mɒrəlz/ npl moralità f

**moratorium** /mɒrə'tɔ:riəm/ n moratoria f

**morbid** /'mɔ:bɪd/ a morboso

**more** /mɔ:(r)/ a più; **a few ~ books** un po' più di libri; **some ~ tea?** ancora un po' di tè?; **there's no ~ bread** non c'è più pane; **there are no ~ apples** non ci sono più mele; **one ~ word and...** ancora una parola e... ● pron di più; **would you like some ~?** ne vuoi ancora?; **no ~, thank you** non ne voglio più, grazie ● adv più; **~ interesting** più interessante; **~ (and ~) quickly** (sempre) più veloce; **~ than** più di; **I don't love him any ~** no lo amo più; **once ~** ancora una volta; **~ or less** più o meno; **the ~ I see him, the ~ I like him** più lo vedo, più mi piace

**moreish** /'mɔ:rɪʃ/ a fam **be ~** tirare per la gola

**moreover** /mɔ:r'əuvə(r)/ adv inoltre

**morgue** /mɔ:g/ n obitorio m

**MORI** /'mɔ:rɪ/ n abbr (**Market Opinion Research Institute**) istituto m di sondaggio e ricerche di mercato

**moribund** /'mɒrɪbʌnd/ a moribondo

**morning** /'mɔ:nɪŋ/ n mattino m, mattina f; **spend the ~ doing sth** passare la mattinata facendo qcsa; **in the ~** del mattino; (tomorrow) domani mattina

**morning: morning-after pill** n pillola f del giorno dopo. **morning coffee** n caffè m inv del mattino. **morning dress** n tight m inv. **morning sickness** n nausea f mattutina

**Moroccan** /mə'rɒk(ə)n/ a & n marocchino, -a mf

**Morocco** /mə'rɒkəu/ n Marocco m

**morocco leather** n marocchino m

**moron** /'mɔ:rɒn/ n fam deficiente mf

**morose** /mə'rəus/ a scontroso

**morosely** /mə'rəusli/ adv in modo scontroso

**morphine** /'mɔ:fi:n/ n morfina f

**morris dance** /'mɒrɪs/ n danza f tradizionale inglese

**Morse** /mɔ:s/ n **~ [code]** [codice m] Morse m

**morsel** /'mɔ:sl/ n (food) boccone m

**mortal** /'mɔ:tl/ a & n mortale mf

**mortal combat** n duello m mortale

**mortality** /mɔ:'tæləti/ n mortalità f

**mortally** /'mɔ:təli/ adv ⟨wounded, offended⟩ a morte; ⟨afraid⟩ da morire

**mortar** /'mɔ:tə(r)/ n mortaio m

**mortgage** /'mɔ:gɪdʒ/ n mutuo m; (money raised on collateral of property) ipoteca f ● vt ipotecare

**mortgage: mortgage rate** n tasso m d'interesse sui mutui. **mortgage relief** n sgravio m fiscale sul mutuo. **mortgage repayment** n rata f del mutuo

**mortician** /mɔ:'tɪʃn/ n Am impresario, -a mf di pompe funebri

**mortification** /mɔ:tɪfɪ'keɪʃn/ n (of the flesh, embarrassment) mortificazione f

**mortify** /'mɔ:tɪfaɪ/ vt (pt/pp **-ied**) mortificare

**mortuary** /'mɔ:tjuəri/ n camera f mortuaria

**mosaic** /məu'zeɪɪk/ n mosaico m

**Moscow** /'mɒskəu/ n Mosca f

**Moselle** /məu'zel/ n (wine) vino m della Mosella

**Moses** /'məuzɪz/ n Mosè

**Moslem** /'mʊzlɪm/ a & n musulmano, -a mf

**mosque** /mɒsk/ n moschea f

**mosquito** /mɒs'ki:təu/ n (pl **-es**) zanzara f

**mosquito: mosquito bite** n puntura m di zanzara. **mosquito net** n zanzariera f. **mosquito repellent** n antizanzare m inv

**moss** /mɒs/ n muschio m

**mossy** /'mɒsi/ a muschioso

**most** /məust/ a (majority) la maggior parte di; **for the ~ part** per lo più ● adv più, maggiormente; (very) estremamente, molto; **the ~ interesting day** la giornata più interessante; **a ~ interesting day** una giornata estremamente interessante; **the ~ beautiful woman in the world** la donna più bella del mondo; **~ unlikely** veramente improbabile ● pron **~ of them** la maggior parte di loro; **at [the] ~** al massimo; **make the ~ of** sfruttare al massimo; **~ of the time** la maggior parte del tempo

**mostly** /'məus(t)li/ adv per lo più

**MOT** n Br revisione f obbligatoria di autoveicoli

**motel** /məu'tel/ n motel m inv

**moth** /mɒθ/ n falena f; **[clothes-]~** tarma f

**mothball** /'mɒθbɔ:l/ n pallina f di naftalina

**moth-eaten** /-i:tən/ a tarmato
**mother** /'mʌðə(r)/ n madre f; **Mother's Day**
la festa della mamma ● vt fare da madre a
**motherboard** /'mʌðəbɔ:d/ n scheda f madre
**motherhood** /'mʌðəhʊd/ n maternità f
**Mothering Sunday** /mʌðərɪŋ'sʌndeɪ/ n la
festa della mamma
**mother-in-law** n (pl **mothers-in-law**) suo-
cera f
**motherland** /'mʌðəlænd/ n patria f
**motherless** /'mʌðəlɪs/ a orfano, -a mf di
madre
**motherly** /'mʌðəlɪ/ a materno
**mother: mother-of-pearl** n madreperla f.
**mother's boy** n mammone m. **Mother's Day**
n la festa della mamma. **mother's help** n Br
aiuto m domestico. **mother-to-be** n futura
mamma f. **mother tongue** n madrelingua f
**mothproof** /'mɒθpru:f/ a antitarmico
**motif** /məʊ'ti:f/ n motivo m
**motion** /'məʊʃn/ n moto m; (proposal) mozione f; (gesture) gesto m ● vt/i ~ **[to] sb to
come in** fare segno a qcno di entrare
**motionless** /'məʊʃ(ə)nlɪs/ a immobile
**motionlessly** /'məʊʃənlɪslɪ/ adv senza alcun movimento
**motion picture** n film m inv [per il cine-
ma] ● attrib (industry) cinematografico
**motivate** /'məʊtɪveɪt/ vt motivare
**motivation** /məʊtɪ'veɪʃn/ n motivazione f
**motive** /'məʊtɪv/ n motivo m
**motley** /'mɒtlɪ/ a disparato
**motor** /'məʊtə(r)/ n motore m; (car) macchina f ● a a motore; Anat motore ● vi andare in
macchina
**Motorail** /'məʊtəreɪl/ n treno m per trasporto auto
**motorbike** /'məʊtəbaɪk/ n fam moto f inv
**motor boat** n motoscafo m
**motorcade** /'məʊtəkeɪd/ n Am corteo m di
auto
**motor: motor car** n automobile f. **motorcycle** n motocicletta f. **motorcycle escort** n
scorta f di motociclette. **motorcycle
messenger** n corriere m in moto. **motorcyclist** n motociclista mf. **motorhome** n
camper m inv; (towed) roulotte f inv
**motoring** /'məʊtərɪŋ/ n automobilismo m
**motorist** /'məʊtərɪst/ n automobilista mf
**motor: motor launch** n motolancia f.
**motor mechanic** n meccanico m.
**motormouth** n fam chiacchierone, -a mf.
**motor oil** n olio m lubrificante. **motor
racing** n corse fpl automobilistiche. **motor
scooter** n vespa f. **motor vehicle** n autovei-
colo m. **motorway** n autostrada f
**mottled** /'mɒtld/ a chiazzato
**motto** /'mɒtəʊ/ n (pl -es) motto m
**mould¹** /məʊld/ n (fungus) muffa f
**mould²** n stampo m ● vt foggiare; fig formare
**moulder** /'məʊldə(r)/ vi (corpse, refuse:) andare in decomposizione
**moulding** /'məʊldɪŋ/ n Archit cornice f
**mouldy** /'məʊldɪ/ a ammuffito; (fam:
worthless) ridicolo

**moult** /məʊlt/ vi (bird:) fare la muta;
(animal:) perdere il pelo
**mound** /maʊnd/ n mucchio m; (hill)
collinetta f
**mount** /maʊnt/ n (horse) cavalcatura f; (of
jewel, photo, picture) montatura f ● vt montare a (horse); salire su (bicycle); incastonare
(jewel); incorniciare (photo, picture) ● vi aumentare
■ **mount up** vi aumentare
**mountain** /'maʊntɪn/ n montagna f; **make a
~ out of a molehill** fare di una mosca un
elefante
**mountain bike** n mountain bike f inv
**mountain climbing** n alpinismo m
**mountaineer** /maʊntɪ'nɪə(r)/ n alpinista mf
**mountaineering** /maʊntɪ'nɪərɪŋ/ n alpinismo m
**mountainous** /'maʊntɪnəs/ a montagnoso
**mountain range** n catena f montuosa
**mountain top** n cima f di montagna
**mounted police** /maʊntɪdpə'li:s/ n polizia
f a cavallo
**mourn** /mɔ:n/ vt lamentare ● vi ~ **for** piangere la morte di
**mourner** /'mɔ:nə(r)/ n persona f che
participa a un funerale
**mournful** /'mɔ:nfʊl/ a triste
**mournfully** /'mɔ:nfʊlɪ/ adv tristemente
**mourning** /'mɔ:nɪŋ/ n **in ~** in lutto
**mouse** /maʊs/ n (pl **mice**) topo m; Comput
mouse m inv
**mouse: mousehole** n tana f di topi/di un
topo. **mouse mat** n Comput tappetino m.
**mousetrap** n trappola f [per topi]
**mousse** /mu:s/ n Culin mousse f inv
**moustache** /mə'stɑ:ʃ/ n baffi mpl
**mousy** /'maʊsɪ/ a (colour) grigio topo
**mouth¹** /maʊð/ vt ~ sth dire qcsa silenziosamente muovendo solamente le labbra
**mouth²** /maʊθ/ n bocca f; (of river) foce f
**mouthful** /'maʊθfʊl/ n boccone m
**mouth: mouth organ** n armonica f [a boc-
ca]. **mouthpiece** n imboccatura f; (fig:
person) portavoce m inv. **mouth-to-mouth
resuscitation** n respirazione f bocca-bocca.
**mouthwash** n acqua f dentifricia. **mouth-
watering** /-wɔ:tərɪŋ/ a che fa venire l'acquolina in bocca
**movable** /'mu:vəbl/ a movibile
**move** /mu:v/ n mossa f; (moving house) trasloco m; **on the ~** in movimento; **get a ~ on**
fam darsi una mossa ● vt muovere;
(emotionally) commuovere; spostare (car,
furniture); (transfer) trasferire; (propose) proporre; ~ **house** traslocare ● vi muoversi;
(move house) traslocare; **don't ~!** non muoverti!
■ **move about, move around** vi (in
house) muoversi; (in country) spostarsi
■ **move along** vi andare avanti ● vt muovere in avanti
■ **move away** vi allontanarsi; (move house)
trasferirsi ● vt allontanare

■ **move forward** *vi* avanzare ● *vt* spostare avanti

■ **move in** *vi* (*to a house*) trasferirsi

■ **move off** *vi* (*vehicle:*) muoversi

■ **move on** *vi* (*move to another place*) muoversi ● *vt* (*police:*) far circolare

■ **move on to** *vt* passare a (*new topic, next question*)

■ **move out** *vi* (*of house*) andare via

■ **move over** *vi* spostarsi ● *vt* spostare

■ **move up** *vi* muoversi; (*advance, increase*) avanzare

**movement** /'mu:vmənt/ *n* movimento *m*; (*of clock*) meccanismo *m*

**movie** /'mu:vɪ/ *n* film *m inv*; **go to the ~s** andare al cinema

**movie: movie camera** *n* cinepresa *f*. **movie director** *n* regista *mf* cinematografico, -a. **movie-goer** *n* persona *f* che va al cinema. **movie star** *n* stella *f* del cinema, star *f inv* del cinema

**moving** /'mu:vɪŋ/ *a* mobile; (*touching*) commovente

**mow** /məʊ/ *vt* (*pt* mowed, *pp* mown *or* mowed) tagliare (*lawn*)

■ **mow down** *vt* (*destroy*) sterminare

**mower** /'məʊə(r)/ *n* tosaerba *m inv*

**MP** *abbr* (**Member of Parliament**) deputato, -a *mf*

**mpg** *abbr* (**miles per gallon**) miglia al gallone

**mph** *abbr* (**miles per hour**) miglia all'ora

**Mr** /'mɪstə(r)/ *n* (*pl* **Messrs**) Signor *m*

**Mrs** /'mɪsɪz/ *n* Signora *f*

**Ms** /mɪz/ *n* Signora *f* (*modo m formale di rivolgersi ad una donna quando non si vuole connotarla come sposata o nubile*)

**MS** *n abbr* (**multiple sclerosis**) sclerosi *f* a placche *or* multipla; *abbr* (**manuscript**) ms; *Am abbr* **Mississippi**

**MSc** *n abbr* (**Master of Science**) (*diploma*) laurea *f* in discipline scientifiche; (*person*) laureato, -a *mf* in discipline scientifiche

**much** /mʌtʃ/ *a, adv & pron* molto; **~ as** per quanto; **I love you just as ~ as before/him** ti amo quanto prima/lui; **as ~ as £5 million** ben cinque milioni di sterline; **as ~ as that** così tanto; **very ~** tantissimo, moltissimo; **~ the same** quasi uguale

**muck** /mʌk/ *n* (*dirt*) sporcizia *f*; (*farming*) letame *m*; (*fam: filth*) porcheria *f*

■ **muck about** *vi fam* perder tempo; **~ about with** trafficare con

■ **muck in** *vi fam* dare una mano

■ **muck up** *vt fam* rovinare; (*make dirty*) sporcare

**muckraking** /'mʌkreɪkɪŋ/ *n* scandalismo *m*

**mucky** /'mʌkɪ/ *a* (**-ier, -iest**) sudicio

**mucus** /'mju:kəs/ *n* muco *m*

**mud** /mʌd/ *n* fango *m*

**muddle** /'mʌdl/ *n* disordine *m*; (*mix-up*) confusione *f* ● *vt* **~** [**up**] confondere (*dates*)

■ **muddle through** *vi* farcela alla bell'e meglio

**muddle-headed** /-'hedɪd/ *a* (*plan*) confuso; (*person*) confusionario

**muddy** /'mʌdɪ/ *a* (**-ier, -iest**) (*path*) fangoso; (*shoes*) infangato

**mud: mudflat** *n* distesa *f* di fango. **mudguard** *n* parafango *m*. **mud hut** *n* capanna *f* di fango. **mudpack** *n* (*for beauty treatment*) maschera *f* di fango. **mud pie** *n* formina *f* di fango. **mudslide** *n* colata *f* di fango. **mud-slinging** /-slɪŋɪŋ/ *n* diffamazione *f*

**muesli** /'mju:zlɪ/ *n* muesli *m inv*

**muffle** /'mʌfl/ *vt* smorzare (*sound*)

■ **muffle up** *vi* (*for warmth*) imbacuccarsi

**muffler** /'mʌflə(r)/ *n* sciarpa *f*; *Am Auto* marmitta *f*

**mug¹** /mʌg/ *n* tazza *f*; (*for beer*) boccale *m*; (*fam: face*) muso *m*; (*fam: simpleton*) pollo *m*

**mug²** *vt* (*pt/pp* **mugged**) aggredire e derubare

■ **mug up** *vt* (*fam: learn*) imparare alla bell'e meglio

**mugger** /'mʌgə(r)/ *n* assalitore, -trice *mf*

**mugging** /'mʌgɪŋ/ *n* aggressione *f* per furto

**muggy** /'mʌgɪ/ *a* (**-ier, -iest**) afoso

**mulatto** /mju:'lætəʊ/ *a & n Am* mulatto, -a *mf*

**mulberry** /'mʌlb(ə)rɪ/ *n Am* (*fruit*) mora *f* di gelso; (*tree*) gelso *m*

**mule¹** /mju:l/ *n* mulo *m*

**mule²** *n* (*slipper*) ciabatta *f*

**mulish** /'mju:lɪʃ/ *a* testardo

**mull** /mʌl/ *vt* **~ over** rimuginare su

**mulled** /mʌld/ *a* **~ wine** vin brûlé *m inv*

**multi-access** *n Comput* accesso *m* multiplo

**multichannel** /mʌltɪ'tʃænəl/ *a* (*television*) con molti canali

**multicoloured** /'mʌltɪkʌləd/ *a* variopinto

**multicultural** /mʌltɪ'kʌltʃərəl/ *a* multiculturale

**multidisciplinary** /mʌltɪdɪsɪ'plɪnərɪ/ *a Sch, Univ* pluridisciplinare

**multifaceted** /mʌltɪ'fæsɪtɪd/ *a* (*gemstone*) sfaccettato; (*career*) variegato; (*personality*) sfaccettato

**multifunction** /mʌltɪ'fʌŋkʃn/ *a* multifunzionale

**multigym** /'mʌltɪdʒɪm/ *n* attrezzo *m* multiuso

**multilateral** /mʌltɪ'læt(ə)rəl/ *a Pol* multilaterale

**multilevel** /'mʌltɪlevəl/ *a* (*parking, access*) a più piani; (*analysis*) a più livelli

**multilingual** /mʌltɪ'lɪŋgwəl/ *a* multilingue *inv*

**multimedia** /mʌltɪ'mi:dɪə/ *n* multimedia *mpl* ● *a* multimediale

**multinational** /mʌltɪ'næʃnəl/ *a* multinazionale ● *n* multinazionale *f*

**multi-party** /'mʌltɪpɑ:tɪ/ *a* (*government, system*) pluripartitico

**multiple** /'mʌltɪpl/ *a & n* multiplo *m*

**multiple: multiple choice question** *n Sch* test *m inv* a scelta multipla. **multiple**

**ownership** n comproprietà f. **multiple pile-up** n tamponamento m a catena. **multiple sclerosis** n sclerosi f a placche or multipla. **multiple store** n Br negozio m appartenente a una catena

**multiplex** /ˈmʌltɪpleks/ n Teleph multiplex m inv; Cinema cinema m inv multisale ● a Teleph in multiplex

**multiplication** /mʌltɪplɪˈkeɪʃn/ n moltiplicazione f

**multiply** /ˈmʌltɪplaɪ/ v (pt/pp -ied) ● vt moltiplicare (by per) ● vi moltiplicarsi

**multi-purpose** a ⟨tool, gadget⟩ multiuso inv; ⟨organization⟩ con più scopi

**multi-storey** a ~ car park parcheggio m a più piani

**multi-track** a ⟨sound system⟩ a più piste

**multitude** /ˈmʌltɪtjuːd/ n moltitudine f; hide a ~ of sins ⟨rug etc.⟩ nascondere un sacco di magagne

**multi-user** a ⟨system, installation⟩ multiutente

**mum¹** /mʌm/ a keep ~ fam non aprire bocca

**mum²** n fam mamma f

**mumble** /ˈmʌmbl/ vt/i borbottare

**mumbo-jumbo** /mʌmbəʊˈdʒʌmbəʊ/ n ⟨fam: speech, writing⟩ paroloni mpl

**mummy¹** /ˈmʌmɪ/ n fam mamma f

**mummy²** n Archaeol mummia f

**mummy's boy** n Br pej mammone m

**mumps** /mʌmps/ n orecchioni mpl

**munch** /mʌntʃ/ vt/i sgranocchiare

**mundane** /mʌnˈdeɪn/ a ⟨everyday⟩ banale

**municipal** /mjʊˈnɪsɪpl/ a municipale

**munitions** /mjʊˈnɪʃnz/ npl munizioni fpl

**mural** /ˈmjʊərəl/ n dipinto m murale

**murder** /ˈmɜːdə(r)/ n assassinio m ● vt assassinare; ⟨fam: ruin⟩ massacrare

**murder case** n caso m di omicidio

**murder charge** n imputazione f di omicidio

**murderer** /ˈmɜːdərə(r)/ n assassino, -a mf

**murderous** /ˈmɜːdərəs/ a omicida

**murky** /ˈmɜːkɪ/ a (-ier, -iest) oscuro

**murmur** /ˈmɜːmə(r)/ n mormorio m ● vt/i mormorare

**murmuring** /ˈmɜːmərɪŋ/ n mormorio m; ~s pl ⟨of discontent⟩ segnali mpl di malcontento

**muscle** /ˈmʌsl/ n muscolo m

■ **muscle in** vi sl intromettersi (**to** in)

**muscle strain** n strappo m muscolare

**muscular** /ˈmʌskjʊlə(r)/ a muscolare; ⟨strong⟩ muscoloso

**muscular dystrophy** /ˈdɪstrəfɪ/ n distrofia f muscolare

**muse** /mjuːz/ vi meditare (**on** su)

**museum** /mjuːˈzɪəm/ n museo m

**mushroom** /ˈmʌʃrʊm/ n fungo m ● vi fig spuntare come funghi

**mushroom cloud** n fungo m atomico

**mushy** /ˈmʌʃɪ/ a fig sdolcinato

**music** /ˈmjuːzɪk/ n musica f; ⟨written⟩ spartito m; **set to** ~ musicare

**musical** /ˈmjuːzɪkl/ a musicale; ⟨person⟩ dotato di senso musicale ● n commedia f musicale

**musical box** n carillon m inv

**musical instrument** n strumento m musicale

**music: music box** n carillon m inv. **music centre** n impianto m stereo. **music hall** n teatro m di varietà

**musician** /mjuːˈzɪʃn/ n musicista mf

**music lover** n amante mf della musica

**musicology** /mjuːzɪˈkɒlədʒɪ/ n musicologia f

**music: music stand** n leggio m. **music stool** n sgabello m per pianoforte. **music video** n video clip m inv

**musings** /ˈmjuːzɪŋz/ npl riflessioni fpl

**musket** /ˈmʌskɪt/ n moschetto m

**musketeer** /mʌskɪˈtɪə(r)/ n moschettiere m

**musky** /ˈmʌskɪ/ a muschiato

**Muslim** /ˈmʊzlɪm/ a & n musulmano, -a mf

**mussel** /ˈmʌsl/ n cozza f

**must** /mʌst/ v aux (solo al presente) dovere; **you ~ not be late** non devi essere in ritardo; **she ~ have finished by now** ⟨probability⟩ deve aver finito ormai ● n a ~ fam una cosa da non perdere

**mustard** /ˈmʌstəd/ n senape f

**muster** /ˈmʌstə(r)/ vt radunare ⟨troops⟩; fare appello a ⟨strength⟩

**musty** /ˈmʌstɪ/ a (-ier, -iest) stantio

**mutant** /ˈmjuːtənt/ n & a mutante mf

**mutate** /mjuːˈteɪt/ vi ⟨cell, organism⟩ subire una mutazione; ~ **into** ⟨alien, monster⟩ trasformarsi in ● vt far subire una mutazione

**mutation** /mjuːˈteɪʃn/ n Biol mutazione f

**mute** /mjuːt/ a muto

**muted** /ˈmjuːtɪd/ a smorzato

**mutilate** /ˈmjuːtɪleɪt/ vt mutilare

**mutilation** /mjuːtɪˈleɪʃn/ n mutilazione f

**mutinous** /ˈmjuːtɪnəs/ a ammutinato

**mutiny** /ˈmjuːtɪnɪ/ n ammutinamento m ● vi (pt/pp -ied) ammutinarsi

**mutter** /ˈmʌtə(r)/ n borbottio m ● vt/i borbottare

**mutton** /ˈmʌtn/ n carne f di montone

**mutual** /ˈmjuːtjʊəl/ a reciproco; ⟨fam: common⟩ comune

**mutually** /ˈmjuːtjʊəlɪ/ adv reciprocamente

**Muzak®** /ˈmjuːzæk/ n musica f di sottofondo

**muzzle** /ˈmʌzl/ n ⟨of animal⟩ muso m; ⟨of firearm⟩ bocca f; ⟨for dog⟩ museruola f ● vt fig mettere il bavaglio a

**MW** abbr (medium wave) OM

**my** /maɪ/ poss a mio m, mia f, miei mpl, mie fpl; **my job/house** il mio lavoro/la mia casa; **my mother/father** mia madre/mio padre

**myalgic encephalomyelitis** /maɪˌældʒɪkensefələʊmaɪˈlaɪtɪs/ n encefalomielite f mialgica

**myopic** /maɪˈɒpɪk/ a miope

**myself** /maɪˈself/ pers pron ⟨reflexive⟩ mi; ⟨emphatic⟩ me stesso; ⟨after prep⟩ me; **I've seen it** ~ l'ho visto io stesso; **by** ~ da solo; **I thought to** ~ ho pensato tra me e me; **I'm proud of** ~ sono fiero di me

**mysterious** /mɪˈstɪərɪəs/ a misterioso

**mysteriously** /mɪˈstɪərəslɪ/ adv misteriosamente

**mystery** /ˈmɪstərɪ/ n mistero m; ~ [story] racconto m del mistero

**mystery play** n mistero m (teatrale)

**mystery tour** n viaggio m con destinazione a sorpresa

**mystic[al]** /ˈmɪstɪk[l]/ a mistico

**mysticism** /ˈmɪstɪsɪzm/ n misticismo m

**mystification** /mɪstɪfɪˈkeɪʃn/ n disorientamento m

**mystified** /ˈmɪstɪfaɪd/ a disorientato

**mystify** /ˈmɪstɪfaɪ/ vt disorientare

**mystique** /mɪˈstiːk/ n mistica f

**myth** /mɪθ/ n mito m

**mythical** /ˈmɪθɪkl/ a mitico

**mythological** /mɪθəˈlɒdʒɪkl/ a mitologico

**mythology** /mɪˈθɒlədʒɪ/ n mitologia f

# Nn

**n, N** /en/ n (letter) n, N f inv

**N** abbr (north) N

**n/a, N/A** abbr (not applicable) non pertinente

**nab** /næb/ vt (pt/pp nabbed) fam beccare

**nadir** /ˈneɪdɪə/ n nadir m; fig punto m più basso, fondo m

**naff** /næf/ a Br fam banale

**nag**[1] /næg/ n (horse) ronzino m

**nag**[2] /næg/ v (pt/pp nagged) • vt assillare • vi essere insistente • n (person) brontolone, -a mf

**nagging** /ˈnægɪŋ/ a (pain) persistente

**nail** /neɪl/ n chiodo m; (of finger, toe) unghia f; **on the ~** fam sull'unghia

■ **nail down** vt inchiodare; ~ **sb down to a time/price** far fissare a qcno un'ora/un prezzo

**nail: nail-biting** /-baɪtɪŋ/ n abitudine f di mangiarsi le unghie • a (match, finish) mozzafiato inv; (wait) esasperante. **nail brush** n spazzolino m da unghie. **nail clippers** npl tronchesina m. **nail file** n limetta f da unghie. **nail polish** n smalto m [per unghie]. **nail polish remover** n acetone m, solvente m per unghie. **nail scissors** npl forbicine fpl da unghie. **nail varnish** n smalto m [per unghie]

**naïve** /naɪˈiːv/ a ingenuo

**naïvely** /naɪˈiːvlɪ/ adv ingenuamente

**naïvety** /naɪˈiːvətɪ/ n ingenuità f

**naked** /ˈneɪkɪd/ a nudo; **with the ~ eye** a occhio nudo

**nakedness** /ˈneɪkɪdnɪs/ n nudità f

**name** /neɪm/ n nome m; **what's your ~?** come ti chiami?; **my ~ is Matthew** mi chiamo Matthew; **I know her by ~** la conosco di nome; **by the ~ of Bates** di nome Bates; **make a ~ for oneself** farsi un nome; **call sb ~s** fam insultare qcno • vt (to position) nominare; chiamare (baby); (identify) citare; **be ~d after** essere chiamato col nome di

**name day** n Relig onomastico m

**name-drop** vi **he's always ~ping** si vanta sempre di conoscere persone famose

**nameless** /ˈneɪmlɪs/ a senza nome

**namely** /ˈneɪmlɪ/ adv cioè

**name: nameplate** n targhetta f. **namesake** n omonimo, -a mf. **name tag** n targhetta f attaccata a un oggetto con il nome del proprietario. **name tape** n fettuccia f attaccata a un oggetto con il nome del proprietario

**Namibia** /nəˈmɪbɪə/ n Namibia f

**nanny** /ˈnænɪ/ n bambinaia f

**nanny goat** n capra f

**nap** /næp/ n pisolino m; **have a ~** fare un pisolino • vi **catch sb ~ping** cogliere qcno alla sprovvista

**napalm** /ˈneɪpɑːm/ n napalm m

**nape** /neɪp/ n ~ **[of the neck]** nuca f

**napkin** /ˈnæpkɪn/ n tovagliolo m

**Naples** /ˈneɪp(ə)lz/ n Napoli f

**nappy** /ˈnæpɪ/ n pannolino m

**nappy liner** n filtrante m

**nappy rash** n Br eritema m da pannolini

**narcotic** /nɑːˈkɒtɪk/ a & n narcotico m

**narcotics agent** n Am agente m della squadra antidroga

**narked** /nɑːkt/ a fam scocciato

**narrate** /nəˈreɪt/ vt narrare

**narration** /nəˈreɪʃn/ n narrazione f

**narrative** /ˈnærətɪv/ a narrativo • n narrazione f

**narrator** /nəˈreɪtə(r)/ n narratore, -trice mf

**narrow** /ˈnærəʊ/ a stretto; (fig: views) ristretto; (margin, majority) scarso; **have a ~ escape** scamparla per un pelo • vi restringersi

■ **narrow down** vt (reduce) restringere

**narrowly** /ˈnærəʊlɪ/ adv ~ **escape death** evitare la morte per un pelo

**narrow-minded** /-ˈmaɪndɪd/ a di idee ristrette

**nasal** /ˈneɪzl/ a nasale

**nasal spray** n spray m inv nasale

**nastily** /ˈnɑːstɪlɪ/ adv (spitefully) con cattiveria

**nasty** /ˈnɑːstɪ/ a (-ier, -iest) (smell, person, remark) cattivo; (injury, situation, weather) brutto; **turn ~** (person:) diventare cattivo; (situation:) mettersi male; (weather:) volgere al brutto

**nation** /ˈneɪʃn/ n nazione f

**national** /'næʃən(ə)l/ *a* nazionale ● *n* cittadino, -a *mf*
**national: national anthem** *n* inno *m* nazionale. **National Curriculum** *n* *Br* programma *m* scolastico ministeriale per il Galles e l'Inghilterra. **national debt** *n* debito *m* pubblico. **National Front** *n* *Br* partito *m* britannico di estrema destra. **national grid** *n* *Electr* rete *f* elettrica nazionale. **National Health** *n* *Br* servizio *m* nazionale di assistenza sanitaria. **National Health Service** *n* servizio *m* sanitario britannico. **National Insurance** *n* ≈ Previdenza *f* sociale. **National Insurance number** *n* numero *m* di Previdenza sociale
**nationalism** /'næʃənəlɪzm/ *n* nazionalismo *m*
**nationality** /næʃə'nælətɪ/ *n* nazionalità *f inv*
**nationalization** /næʃənəlaɪ'zeɪʃn/ *n* nazionalizzazione
**nationalize** /'næʃənəlaɪz/ *vt* nazionalizzare
**nationally** /'næʃənəlɪ/ *adv* a livello nazionale
**national: national monument** *n* monumento *m* nazionale. **National Savings Bank** *n* *Br* Cassa *f* di risparmio. **national service** *n* *Br* servizio *m* militare. **National Trust** *n* *Br* associazione *f* per la tutela del patrimonio culturale e ambientale in Gran Bretagna
**nation state** *n* stato-nazione *m*
**nationwide** /'neɪʃnwaɪd/ *a* su scala nazionale
**native** /'neɪtɪv/ *a* nativo; (*innate*) innato ● *n* nativo, -a *mf*; (*local inhabitant*) abitante *mf* del posto; (*outside Europe*) indigeno, -a *mf*; **she's a ~ of Venice** è originaria di Venezia
**native: Native American** *a* & *n* amerindio, -a *mf*. **native land** *n* paese *m* nativo. **native language** *n* lingua *f* madre. **native speaker** *n* persona *f* di madrelingua; **Italian ~ ~s** Italiani madrelingua
**Nativity** /nə'tɪvətɪ/ *n* **the ~** la Natività
**Nativity play** *n* rappresentazione *f* sulla nascita di Gesù
**Nato, NATO** /'neɪtəʊ/ *n* *abbr* (**North Atlantic Treaty Organization**) NATO *f*
**natter** /'nætə(r)/ *n* **have a ~** *fam* fare quattro chiacchiere ● *vi* *fam* chiacchierare
**natty** /'nætɪ/ *a* *fam* (*smart*) chic *inv*; (*clever*) geniale
**natural** /'nætʃ(ə)rəl/ *a* naturale
**natural: natural childbirth** *n* parto *m* indolore. **natural gas** *n* metano *m*. **natural history** *n* storia *f* naturale
**naturalist** /'nætʃ(ə)rəlɪst/ *n* naturalista *mf*
**naturalization** /nætʃ(ə)rəlaɪ'zeɪʃn/ *n* naturalizzazione *f*
**naturalize** /'nætʃ(ə)rəlaɪz/ *vt* naturalizzare
**naturally** /'nætʃ(ə)rəlɪ/ *adv* (*of course*) naturalmente; (*by nature*) per natura
**nature** /'neɪtʃə(r)/ *n* natura *f*; **by ~** per natura
**nature: nature conservancy** *n* protezione *f* della natura. **nature reserve** *n* riserva *f* naturale. **nature trail** *n* percorso *m* ecologico
**naturism** /'neɪtʃərɪzm/ *n* nudismo *m*

**naturist** /'neɪtʃərɪst/ *n* naturista *mf* ● *a* naturistico
**naught** /nɔːt/ *n* = **nought**
**naughtily** /'nɔːtɪlɪ/ *adv* male
**naughtiness** /'nɔːtɪnɪs/ *n* (*of child, pet*) birbanteria *f*; (*of joke, suggestion*) maliziosità *f inv*
**naughty** /'nɔːtɪ/ *a* (**-ier, -iest**) monello; (*slightly indecent*) spinto
**nausea** /'nɔːzɪə/ *n* nausea *f*
**nauseate** /'nɔːzɪeɪt/ *vt* nauseare
**nauseating** /'nɔːzɪeɪtɪŋ/ *a* nauseante
**nauseatingly** /'nɔːzɪeɪtɪŋlɪ/ *adv* (*rich, sweet*) disgustosamente
**nauseous** /'nɔːzɪəs/ *a* **I feel ~** ho la nausea
**nautical** /'nɔːtɪkl/ *a* nautico
**nautical mile** *n* miglio *m* marino
**naval** /'neɪvl/ *a* navale
**naval: naval base** *n* base *f* navale. **naval dockyard** *n* cantiere *m* navale militare. **naval officer** *n* ufficiale *m* di marina. **naval station** *n* base *f* navale. **naval stores** *npl* (*depot*) magazzini *mpl* della marina militare
**nave** /neɪv/ *n* navata *f* centrale
**navel** /'neɪvl/ *n* ombelico *m*
**navigable** /'nævɪgəbl/ *a* navigabile
**navigate** /'nævɪgeɪt/ *vi* navigare; *Auto* fare da navigatore ● *vt* navigare su (*river*)
**navigation** /nævɪ'geɪʃn/ *n* navigazione *f*
**navigational** /nævɪ'geɪʃənəl/ *a* (*instruments*) di navigazione; (*science*) della navigazione
**navigator** /'nævɪgeɪtə(r)/ *n* navigatore *m*
**navvy** /'nævɪ/ *n* manovale *m*
**navy** /'neɪvɪ/ *n* marina *f* ● **~ [blue]** *a* blu scuro *inv* ● *n* blu *m inv* scuro
**nay** /neɪ/ *adv* anzi ● *n* (*negative vote*) no *m*
**Nazi** /'nɑːtsɪ/ *n* & *a* nazista *mf*
**NBC** *n* *abbr* (**National Broadcasting Company**) NBC *f* (*rete nazionale televisiva statunitense*)
**NC** *Am abbr* **North Carolina**
**NCO** *n* *abbr* (**non-commissioned officer**) sottufficiale *m*
**ND** *Am abbr* **North Dakota**
**NE** *abbr* (**north-east**) NE
**Ne** *Am abbr* **Nebraska**
**Neapolitan** /nɪə'pɒlɪtən/ *a* & *n* napoletano, -a *mf*
**near** /nɪə(r)/ *a* vicino; (*future*) prossimo; **the ~est bank** la banca più vicina ● *adv* vicino; **draw ~** avvicinarsi; **~ at hand** a portata di mano ● *prep* vicino a; **he was ~ to tears** aveva le lacrime agli occhi ● *vt* avvicinarsi a
**nearby** /nɪə'baɪ/ *a* & *adv* vicino
**Near East** *n* Medio Oriente *m*
**nearly** /'nɪəlɪ/ *adv* quasi; **it's not ~ enough** non è per niente sufficiente
**near miss** *n* **have a ~ ~** (*planes, cars:*) evitare per poco uno scontro
**nearness** /'nɪənɪs/ *n* vicinanza *f*
**near: nearside** *n* *Auto* (*in Britain*) lato *m* sinistro; (*in America, rest of Europe*) lato *m* de-

stro. **near-sighted** /-'saɪtɪd/ a Am miope.
**near-sightedness** n miopia f

**neat** /niːt/ a (tidy) ordinato; (clever) efficace;
(undiluted) liscio

**neaten** /'niːtən/ vt riordinare ⟨pile of paper⟩;
dare un'aggiustatina a ⟨tie, skirt⟩

**neatly** /'niːtlɪ/ adv ordinatamente; (cleverly)
efficacemente

**neatness** /'niːtnɪs/ n (tidiness) ordine m

**necessarily** /nesə'serɪlɪ/ adv necessariamente

**necessary** /'nesəsərɪ/ a necessario

**necessitate** /nɪ'sesɪteɪt/ vt rendere necessario

**necessity** /nɪ'sesətɪ/ n necessità f inv

**neck** /nek/ n collo m; (of dress) colletto m; ~
**and** ~ testa a testa

**necking** /'nekɪŋ/ n fam pomiciate fpl

**neck: necklace** /'neklɪs/ n collana f.
**neckline** n scollatura f. **necktie** n cravatta f

**nectar** /'nektə(r)/ n nettare m

**neé** /neɪ/ a ~ **Brett** nata Brett

**need** /niːd/ n bisogno m; **be in** ~ essere bisognoso; **be in** ~ **of** avere bisogno di; **if** ~ **be** se
ce ne fosse bisogno; **there is a** ~ **for** c'è
bisogno di; **there is no** ~ **for that** non ce n'è
bisogno; **there is no** ~ **for you to go** non c'è
bisogno che tu vada ● vt aver bisogno di; **I** ~
**to know** devo saperlo; **it** ~**s to be done**
bisogna farlo ● v aux **you** ~ **not go** non c'è
bisogno che tu vada; ~ **I come?** devo venire?

**needful** /'niːdfʊl/ a necessario ● n **do the** ~
fare il necessario

**needle** /'niːdl/ n ago m; (for knitting) uncinetto m; (of record player) puntina f ● vt (fam:
annoy) punzecchiare

**needless** /'niːdlɪs/ a inutile

**needlessly** /'niːdlɪslɪ/ adv inutilmente

**needlework** /'niːdlwɜːk/ n cucito m

**needs** /niːdz/ adv ~ **must** il dovere chiama

**need-to-know** a **we have a** ~ **policy** la
nostra politica consiste nel tenere informati
solo i diretti interessati

**needy** /'niːdɪ/ a (-ier, -iest) bisognoso

**negate** /nɪ'geɪt/ vt (cancel out) annullare;
mettere in forma negativa ⟨sentence⟩;
(contradict) contraddire; (deny) negare

**negation** /nɪ'geɪʃn/ n negazione f

**negative** /'negətɪv/ a negativo ● n negazione f; Phot negativo m; **in the** ~ Gram alla forma negativa

**neglect** /nɪ'glekt/ n trascuratezza f; **state of**
~ stato di abbandono ● vt trascurare; **he**
~**ed to write** non si è curato di scrivere

**neglected** /nɪ'glektɪd/ a trascurato

**neglectful** /nɪ'glektfʊl/ a negligente; **be** ~
**of** trascurare

**negligée** /'neglɪʒeɪ/ n négligé m inv

**negligence** /'neglɪdʒəns/ n negligenza f

**negligent** /'neglɪdʒənt/ a negligente

**negligently** /'neglɪdʒəntlɪ/ adv con negligenza

**negligible** /'neglɪdʒəbl/ a trascurabile

**negotiable** /nɪ'gəʊʃəbl/ a ⟨road⟩ transitabi-

le; Comm negoziabile: **not** ~ ⟨cheque⟩ non
trasferibile

**negotiate** /nɪ'gəʊʃɪeɪt/ vt negoziare; Auto
prendere ⟨bend⟩ ● vi negoziare

**negotiating** /nɪ'gəʊʃɪeɪtɪŋ/ a ⟨rights⟩ al negoziato; ⟨team, committee⟩ che conduce le
trattative; ⟨ploy, position⟩ di negoziato; **the** ~
**table** il tavolo delle trattative

**negotiation** /nɪgəʊʃɪ'eɪʃn/ n negoziato m

**negotiator** /nɪ'gəʊʃɪeɪtə(r)/ n negoziatore,
-trice mf

**Negro** /'niːgrəʊ/ a & n (pl -es) negro, -a mf

**neigh** /neɪ/ vi nitrire

**neighbour** /'neɪbə(r)/ n vicino, -a mf

**neighbourhood** /'neɪbəhʊd/ n vicinato m;
**in the** ~ **of** nei dintorni di; fig circa

**neighbourhood watch scheme** n vigilanza f da parte della gente del quartiere

**neighbouring** /'neɪbərɪŋ/ a vicino

**neighbourly** /'neɪbəlɪ/ a amichevole

**neither** /'naɪðə(r)/ a & pron nessuno dei due,
né l'uno né l'altro ● adv ~**... nor** né... né
● conj nemmeno, neanche; ~ **do/did I** nemmeno io

**neo+** /'niːəʊ/ pref neo+

**neologism** /nɪ'vlədʒɪzm/ n neologismo m

**neon** /'niːɒn/ n neon m

**neon light** n luce f al neon

**nephew** /'nevjuː/ n nipote m

**nephritis** /nɪ'fraɪtɪs/ n nefrite f

**nepotism** /'nepətɪzm/ n nepotismo m

**nerve** /nɜːv/ n nervo m; (fam: courage) coraggio m; (fam: impudence) faccia f tosta!; **lose
one's** ~ perdersi d'animo; **you've got a** ~!
hai una bella faccia tosta!; **live on one's** ~**s**
vivere con i nervi a fior di pelle; **be a bag of**
~**s** avere i nervi a fior di pelle

**nerve-racking** /'nɜːvrækɪŋ/ a logorante

**nerviness** /'nɜːvɪnɪs/ n Br nervosismo m;
Am grinta f

**nervous** /'nɜːvəs/ a nervoso; **he makes me**
~ mi mette in agitazione

**nervous breakdown** n esaurimento m
nervoso

**nervous energy** n energia f in eccesso

**nervously** /'nɜːvəslɪ/ adv nervosamente

**nervousness** /'nɜːvəsnɪs/ n nervosismo m;
(before important event) tensione f

**nervous system** n sistema m nervoso

**nervous wreck** n fascio m di nervi

**nervy** /'nɜːvɪ/ a (-ier, -iest) nervoso; (Am:
impudent) sfacciato

**nest** /nest/ n nido m ● vi fare il nido

**nested** /'nestɪd/ a Comput nidificato

**nest egg** n gruzzolo m

**nesting** /'nestɪŋ/ n Zool nidificazione f;
Comput nesting m inv, nidificazione f ● attrib
⟨habit⟩ di nidificare; ⟨place⟩ per nidificare;
⟨season⟩ della nidificazione

**nestle** /'nesl/ vi accoccolarsi

■ **nestle up to** vt accoccolarsi accanto a
⟨sb⟩

**nestling** /'neslɪŋ/ n nidiace m

**net**[1] /net/ n rete f ● vt (pt/pp netted) (catch)
prendere (con la rete)

**net²** *a* netto; ~ **of VAT** al netto dell'IVA ● *vt* (*pt/pp* **netted**) incassare un utile netto di

**netball** /'netbɔ:l/ *n* sport *m inv* femminile, simile a pallacanestro

**net cord** *n* corda *f* di rete; *Tennis* (*shot*) net *m inv*

**Netherlands** /'neðələndz/ *npl* **the** ~ i Paesi Bassi

**netting** /'netɪŋ/ *n* [**wire**] ~ reticolato *m*

**nettle** /'netl/ *n* ortica *f*

**net ton** *n Am* tonnellata *f* corta americana

**network** /'netwɜ:k/ *n* rete *f*

**network card** *n Comput* scheda *f* di rete

**networked** /'netwɜ:kt/ *a Comput* collegato in rete

**networking** /'netwɜ:kɪŋ/ *n* (*establishing contacts*) stabilimento *m* di una rete di contatti; *Comput* collegamento *m* in rete

**neuralgia** /njʊə'rældʒə/ *n* nevralgia *f*

**neuritis** /njʊə'raɪtɪs/ *n* nevrite *f*

**neurologist** /njʊə'rɒlədʒɪst/ *n* neurologo, -a *mf*

**neurology** /njʊə'rɒlədʒɪ/ *n* neurologia *f*

**neurosis** /njʊə'rəʊsɪs/ *n* (*pl* **-oses** /njʊə-'rəʊsi:z/) nevrosi *f inv*

**neurosurgeon** /'njʊərəsɜ:dʒən/ *n* neurochirurgo *m*

**neurotic** /njʊə'rɒtɪk/ *a* nevrotico

**neurotically** /njʊə'rɒtɪklɪ/ *adv* in modo ossessivo

**neuter** /'nju:tə(r)/ *a Gram* neutro ● *n Gram* neutro *m* ● *vt* sterilizzare

**neutral** /'nju:trəl/ *a* neutro; (*country, person*) neutrale ● *n* **in** ~ *Auto* in folle

**neutrality** /nju:'trælətɪ/ *n* neutralità *f*

**neutralize** /'nju:trəlaɪz/ *vt* neutralizzare

**never** /'nevə(r)/ *adv* [non...] mai; (*fam: expressing disbelief*) ma va; ~ **again** mai più; **well I** ~! chi l'avrebbe detto!

**never-ending** *a* interminabile

**nevermore** /nevə'mɔ:(r)/ *adv* mai più

**never-never** *n fam* **buy sth on the** ~ comprare qcsa a rate

**never-never land** *n* mondo *m* dei sogni

**nevertheless** /nevəðə'les/ *adv* tuttavia

**new** /nju:/ *a* nuovo

**new: New Age** *n* New Age *f inv* ● *attrib* (*music, ideas, sect*) New Age *inv*. **new blood** *n* nuove leve *fpl*. **newborn** *a* neonato. **New Caledonia** *n* Nuova Caledonia *f*. **newcomer** *n* nuovo, -a arrivato, -a *mf*. **newfangled** *a pej* modernizzante. **newfound** *a* nuovo

**Newfoundland** /'nju:fən(d)lənd/ *n* Terranova *f*

**New Guinea** *n* Nuova Guinea *f*

**newish** /'nju:ɪʃ/ *a* abbastanza nuovo

**new: new-laid** /'nju:leɪd/ *a* fresco. **new look** *a* (*car, team*) nuovo; (*edition, show*) rinnovato; (*product*) dall'aspetto nuovo ● *n* **they have given the shop a completely** ~ ~ hanno completamente rinnovato il negozio

**newly** /'nju:lɪ/ *adv* (*recently*) di recente

**newly-built** *a* costruito di recente

**newly-weds** /'nju:lɪwedz/ *npl* sposini *mpl*

**new moon** *n* luna *f* nuova

**newness** /'nju:nɪs/ *n* novità *f*

**news** /nju:z/ *n* notizie *fpl*; *TV* telegiornale *m*; *Radio* giornale *m* radio; **piece of** ~ notizia *f*

**news: news agency** *n* agenzia *f* di stampa. **newsagent's** *n Br* giornalaio *m* (*che vende anche tabacchi, caramelle ecc*). **news bulletin** *n* notiziario *m*. **newscast** *n Am* notiziario *m*. **newscaster** *n* giornalista *mf* televisivo, -a/radiofonico, -a. **news conference** *n* conferenza *f* stampa *inv*. **newsdealer** *n Am* giornalaio, -a *mf*. **news desk** *n* (*at newspaper*) redazione *f*. **news editor** *n* caporedattore, -trice *mf* di servizi di cronaca. **newsflash** *n* notizia *f* flash. **news headlines** *npl TV* titoli *mpl* delle principali notizie. **news item** *n* notizia *f* di attualità. **newsletter** *n* bollettino *m* d'informazione

**newspaper** /'nju:zpeɪpə(r)/ *n* giornale *m*; (*material*) carta *f* di giornale

**newspaper: newspaperman** *n* giornalista *m*. **newspaper office** *n* ufficio *m* della redazione. **newspaperwoman** *n* giornalista *f*

**newspeak** /'nju:spi:k/ *n Am* politichese *m*

**news: newsprint** *n* (*paper*) carta *f* da giornale; (*ink*) inchiostro *m* di stampa. **newsreader** *n* giornalista *mf* televisivo, -a/radiofonico, -a. **newsroom** *n* redazione *f*. **news sheet** *n* bollettino *m*. **newsstand** *n* edicola *f*. **news value** *n* interesse *m* mediatico. **newsworthy** *a* che merita di essere pubblicato

**newsy** /'nju:zɪ/ *a* (*letter*) pieno di notizie

**newt** /nju:t/ *n* tritone *m*

**new: new technology** *n* nuova technologia *f*. **New Testament** *n* Nuovo Testamento *m*. **new wave** *n & a* new wave *f inv*. **New Year** *n* (*January 1st*) capodanno *m*; (*next year*) l'anno *m* nuovo; **Happy** ~ ~ ! buon anno!; **closed for** ~ ~ chiuso per le feste di capodanno; **see in the** ~ ~ festeggiare il capodanno. **New Year Honours list** *n Br* lista *f* delle persone che ricevono decorazioni il 1 gennaio. **New Year's Day** *n* Capodanno *m*. **New Year's Eve** *n* vigilia *f* di Capodanno. **New Year's resolution** *n* proposito *m* per l'anno nuovo. **New Zealand** *n* Nuova Zelanda *f*. **New Zealander** *n* neozelandese *mf*

**next** /nekst/ *a* prossimo; (*adjoining*) vicino; **who's** ~? a chi tocca?; **the** ~ **best thing would be to** alternativamente la cosa migliore sarebbe di; ~ **door** accanto; ~ **to nothing** quasi niente; **the** ~ **day** il giorno dopo; ~ **week** la settimana prossima; **the week after** ~ fra due settimane; **the** ~ **thing I knew** la sola cosa che ho saputo dopo ● *adv* dopo; **when will you see him** ~? quando lo rivedi la prossima volta?; ~ **to** accanto a ● *n* seguente *mf*; ~ **of kin** parente *m* prossimo

**next door** *a* (*dog, bell*) dei vicini; (*office*) accanto *inv*; **the girl** ~ *also fig* la ragazza della porta accanto ● *adv* (*live, move in*) nella casa accanto

**next-door neighbour** *n* vicino *m* di casa

**nexus** /'neksəs/ *n* (*network*) rete *f*

**NF** *n Br Pol abbr* **National Front**

**NH** *Am abbr* **New Hampshire**
**NHS** *n abbr* **National Health Service**
**NI** *n Br abbr* (**National Insurance**) previdenza *f* sociale; *abbr* (**Northern Ireland**) Irlanda *f* del Nord
**nib** /nɪb/ *n* pennino *m*
**nibble** /'nɪbl/ *vt/i* mordicchiare
**a nibble at, nibble on** *vt* = **nibble**
**Nicaragua** /nɪkə'ræɡjʊə/ *n* Nicaragua *m*
**nice** /naɪs/ *a* ⟨day, weather, holiday⟩ bello; ⟨person⟩ gentile, simpatico; ⟨food⟩ buono; **it was ~ meeting you** è stato un piacere conoscerla
**nicely** /'naɪslɪ/ *adv* gentilmente; (well) bene
**niceties** /'naɪsətɪz/ *npl* finezze *fpl*
**niche** /niːʃ/ *n* nicchia *f*
**niche market** *n* mercato *m* specializzato
**nick** /nɪk/ *n* tacca *f*; (on chin etc) taglietto *m*; (fam: prison) galera *f*; (fam: police station) centrale *f* [di polizia]; **in the ~ of time** *fam* appena in tempo; **in good ~** *fam* in buono stato ● *vt* intaccare; (fam: steal) fregare; (fam: arrest) beccare; **~ one's chin** farsi un taglietto nel mento
**nickel** /'nɪkl/ *n* nichel *m*; *Am* moneta *f* da cinque centesimi
**nickel-and-dime** *a Am fam* da quattro soldi
**nickelodeon** /nɪkəl'əʊdɪən/ *n* (*Am: juke box*) juke box *m inv*
**nickname** /'nɪkneɪm/ *n* soprannome *m* ● *vt* soprannominare
**nicotine** /'nɪkətiːn/ *n* nicotina *f*
**niece** /niːs/ *n* nipote *f*
**nifty** /'nɪftɪ/ *a fam* (skilful) geniale; (attractive) sfizioso
**Nigeria** /naɪ'dʒɪərɪə/ *n* Nigeria *f*
**Nigerian** /naɪ'dʒɪərɪən/ *a & n* nigeriano, -a *mf*
**niggardly** /'nɪɡədlɪ/ *a* ⟨person⟩ tirchio; ⟨salary⟩ misero
**niggle** /'nɪɡl/ *fam n* (complaint) cosetta *f* da ridire ● *vi* (complain) lamentarsi in continuazione ● *vt* (irritate) dar fastidio a
**niggling** /'nɪɡlɪŋ/ *a* ⟨detail⟩ insignificante; ⟨pain⟩ fastidioso; ⟨doubt⟩ persistente
**night** /naɪt/ *n* notte *f*; (evening) sera *f*; **at ~** la notte, di notte; (in the evening) la sera, di sera; **Monday ~** lunedì notte/sera; **work ~s** lavorare la notte ● *a* di notte
**night:** **nightcap** *n* papalina *f*; (drink) bicchierino *m* bevuto prima di andare a letto. **nightclub** *n* locale *m* notturno, night[-club] *m inv*. **nightclubbing** *n* **go ~** andare nei night [club]. **nightdress** *n* camicia *f* da notte. **nightfall** *n* crepuscolo *m*. **nightgown**, *fam* **nightie** *n* camicia *f* da notte. **nightlife** *n* vita *f* notturna. **night light** *n* lumino *m* da notte
**nightly** /'naɪtlɪ/ *a* di notte, di sera ● *adv* ogni notte, ogni sera
**nightmare** /'naɪtmeə(r)/ *n* also fig incubo *m*
**nightmarish** /'naɪtmeərɪʃ/ *a* da incubo
**night:** **night owl** nottambulo, -a *mf*. **night porter** *n* portiere *m* di notte. **night school** scuola *f* serale. **nightshade** *n Bot* **deadly ~**

belladonna *f*. **night shelter** *n* dormitorio *m* pubblico. **nightshift** *n* (workers) turno *m* di notte; **be on the ~** fare il turno di notte. **nightshirt** *n* camicia *f* da notte (da uomo). **nightspot** *n* night club *m inv*. **nightstand** *n Am* comodino *m*. **nightstick** *n* (Am: truncheon) manganello *m*. **night-time** *n* **at ~** di notte, la notte. **night vision** *n* visione *f* notturna. **nightwatchman** *n* guardiano *m* notturno. **nightwear** *n* indumenti *mpl* da notte
**nil** /nɪl/ *n* nulla *m*; *Sport* zero *m*
**Nile** /naɪl/ *n* Nilo *m*
**nimble** /'nɪmbl/ *a* agile
**nimbly** /'nɪmblɪ/ *adv* agilmente
**nincompoop** /'nɪŋkəmpuːp/ *n fam* scemo *m*
**nine** /naɪn/ *a & n* nove *m*
**ninepin** /'naɪnpɪn/ *n* birillo *m*; **be falling like ~s** ⟨troops, guards, candidates:⟩ cadere come le mosche
**nineteen** /naɪn'tiːn/ *a & n* diciannove *m*
**nineteenth** /naɪn'tiːnθ/ *a & n* diciannovesimo, -a *mf*
**ninetieth** /'naɪntɪɪθ/ *a & n* novantesimo, -a *mf*
**nine-to-five** *a* ⟨job⟩ in un ufficio; ⟨routine⟩ dell'ufficio ● *adv* ⟨work⟩ dalle nove alle cinque
**ninety** /'naɪntɪ/ *a & n* novanta *m*
**ninth** /naɪnθ/ *a & n* nono, -a *mf*
**nip** /nɪp/ *n* pizzicotto *m*; (bite) morso *m* ● *vt* pizzicare; (bite) mordere; **~ in the bud** fig stroncare sul nascere ● *vi* (fam: run) fare un salto
**nipper** /'nɪpə(r)/ *n fam* ragazzino, -a *mf*
**nipple** /'nɪpl/ *n* capezzolo *m*; (Am: on bottle) tettarella *f*
**nippy** /'nɪpɪ/ *a* (-ier, -iest) *fam* (cold) pungente; (quick) svelto
**nit** /nɪt/ *n* (egg) lendine *m*; (larva) larva *f* di pidocchio
**nit-pick** *vi* cercare il pelo nell'uovo
**nitrate** /'naɪtreɪt/ *n* nitrato *m*
**nitric** /'naɪtrɪk/ *a* nitrico
**nitrogen** /'naɪtrədʒn/ *n* azoto *m*
**nitty-gritty** /nɪtɪ'ɡrɪtɪ/ *n fam* **the ~** il nocciolo [della questione]; **get down to the ~** arrivare al dunque
**nitwit** /'nɪtwɪt/ *n fam* imbecille *mf*
**NJ** *Am abbr* **New Jersey**
**NM** *Am abbr* **New Mexico**
**no** /nəʊ/ *adv* no ● *n* (pl **noes**) no *m invar* ● *a* nessuno; **I have no time** non ho tempo; **in no time** in un baleno; **'no parking'** 'sosta vietata'; **'no smoking'** 'vietato fumare'; **it's no go** è inutile; **no one** = **nobody**
**no., No.** *abbr* (**number**) No.
**Noah** /'nəʊə/ *n* Noè *m*; **~'s Ark** l'arca *f* di Noè
**nobility** /nəʊ'bɪlətɪ/ *n* nobiltà *f*
**noble** /'nəʊbl/ *a* nobile
**nobleman** /'nəʊblmən/ *n* nobile *m*
**noble-minded** /-'maɪndɪd/ *a* di animo nobile
**noble savage** *n* buon selvaggio *m*
**nobly** /'nəʊblɪ/ *adv* (selflessly) generosamente; **~ born** di nobili natali

**nobody** /'nəʊbədɪ/ *pron* nessuno: **he knows ~** non conosce nessuno; **he's ~ important** non è nessuno d'importante ● *n* **he's a ~** non è nessuno

**no claims bonus** *n* abbuono *m* in assenza di sinistri

**nocturnal** /nɒk'tɜ:nl/ *a* notturno

**nod** /nɒd/ *n* cenno *m* del capo; **give a ~** fare un cenno col capo ● *v* (*pt/pp* **nodded**) ● *vi* fare un cenno col capo; (*in agreement*) fare di sì col capo ● *vt* **~ one's head** fare di sì col capo

■ **nod off** *vi* assopirsi

**node** /nəʊd/ *n* nodo *m*

**nodule** /'nɒdju:l/ *n* nodulo *m*

**no-go** *a fam* **it's ~** non è possibile

**no-go area** *n* quartiere *m* caldo in cui la polizia può accedere solo con la forza

**no-hoper** /nəʊ'həʊpə(r)/ *n* persona *f* senza prospettive

**noise** /nɔɪz/ *n* rumore *m*; (*loud*) rumore *m*, chiasso *m*

**noiseless** /'nɔɪzlɪs/ *a* silenzioso

**noiselessly** /'nɔɪzlɪslɪ/ *adv* silenziosamente

**noise level** *n* intensità *f inv* del rumore

**noise pollution** *n* inquinamento *m* da rumore

**noisily** /'nɔɪzɪlɪ/ *adv* rumorosamente

**noisy** /'nɔɪzɪ/ *a* (**-ier**, **-iest**) rumoroso

**nomad** /'nəʊmæd/ *n* nomade *mf*

**nomadic** /nəʊ'mædɪk/ *a* nomade

**nominal** /'nɒmɪnl/ *a* nominale

**nominally** /'nɒmɪnəlɪ/ *adv* nominalmente

**nominate** /'nɒmɪneɪt/ *vt* proporre come candidato; (*appoint*) designare

**nomination** /nɒmɪ'neɪʃn/ *n* nomina *f*; (*person nominated*) candidato, -a *mf*

**nominative** /'nɒmɪnətɪv/ *a* & *n Gram* **~ [case]** nominativo *m*

**nominee** /nɒmɪ'ni:/ *n* persona *f* nominata

**non+** /nɒn/ *pref* non+, in+

**non-academic** *a* (*course*) pratico; (*staff*) non insegnante

**non-addictive** *a* che non dà assuefazione

**non-alcoholic** *a* analcolico

**non-attendance** *n* mancata presenza *f*

**non-believer** *n* non credente *mf*

**nonchalant** /'nɒnʃələnt/ *a* disinvolto

**nonchalantly** /'nɒnʃələntlɪ/ *adv* in modo disinvolto

**non-classified** *a* (*information*) non confidenziale

**non-combustible** *a* incombustibile

**non-commercial** *a* (*event, activity*) senza fini di lucro

**non-commissioned** /-kə'mɪʃnd/ *a* **~ officer** sottufficiale *m*

**non-committal** /-kə'mɪtəl/ *a* che non si sbilancia

**non-compliance** *n* (*with standards*) non conformità *f* (**with** a); (*with orders*) inadempienza *f* (**with** a)

**nonconformist** /nɒnkən'fɔ:mɪst/ *a* & *n* anticonformista *mf*

**non-cooperation** *n* non cooperazione *f*

**non-denominational** /-dɪnɒmɪ'neɪʃənəl/ *a* (*church*) ecumenico; (*school*) laico

**nondescript** /'nɒndɪskrɪpt/ *a* qualunque

**none** /nʌn/ *pron* (*person*) nessuno; (*thing*) niente; **~ of us** nessuno di noi; **~ of this** niente di questo; **there's ~ left** non ce n'è più ● *adv* **she's ~ too pleased** non è per niente soddisfatta; **I'm ~ the wiser** non ne so più di prima

**non-EC** *a* (*national*) extracomunitario; (*country*) che non appartiene alla Comunità Europea

**nonentity** /nɒ'nentətɪ/ *n* nullità *f inv*

**non-essentials** /-ɪ'senʃɪz/ *npl* (*details*) dettagli *mpl*; (*objects*) cose *fpl* accessorie

**nonetheless** /nʌnðə'les/ *adv* = **nevertheless**

**non-event** *n* delusione *f*

**non-existent** *a* inesistente

**non-family** *a* al di fuori della famiglia

**non-fat** *a* magro; (*diet*) senza grassi

**non-fiction** *n* saggistica *f*

**non-flammable** *a* non infiammabile

**non-fulfilment** *n* (*of contract, obligation*) inadempienza *f* (**of** a); (*of desire*) inappagamento *m*

**non-infectious** *a* non infettivo

**non-iron** *a* che non si stira

**non-judgmental** *a* imparziale

**non-league** *a Sport* fuori campionato

**no-no** *n fam* cosa *f* proibita; **that's a ~** è un argomento tabù

**no-nonsense** *a* (*manner, attitude*) diretto; (*tone*) spiccio; (*look, policy*) pratico; (*person*) franco

**non-partisan** *a* imparziale

**non-party** *a* (*issue, decision*) apartitico; (*person*) indipendente

**non-person** *n* (*insignificant person*) nullità *f inv*; **officially, he is a ~** *Pol* ufficialmente non è mai esistito

**nonplussed** /nɒn'plʌst/ *a* perplesso

**non-professional** *a* dilettante

**non-profit-making** /-'prɒfɪtmeɪkɪŋ/ *a* (*organization*) senza fini di lucro

**non-redeemable** *a Fin* vincolato

**non-refillable** *a* (*lighter, pen*) non ricaricabile; (*can, bottle*) non riutilizzabile

**non-religious** *a* laico

**non-resident** *a* (*job, course*) non residenziale; *Comput* che non risiede in permanenza nella memoria centrale ● *n* non residente *mf*

**non-residential** *a* (*guest*) di passaggio; (*student, visitor*) non residente; (*caretaker*) che non alloggia sul posto; (*area*) non residenziale

**non-returnable** *a* (*bottle*) a perdere

**non-segregated** *a* (*area*) non segregato; (*society*) non segregazionista

**nonsense** /'nɒnsəns/ *n* sciocchezze *fpl*

**nonsensical** /nɒn'sensɪkl/ *a* assurdo

**non sequitur** /nɒn'sekwɪtə(r)/ *n* affermazione *f* senza legame con quanto detto prima

**non-skid** *a* antiscivolo *inv*

**non-smoker** *n* non fumatore, -trice *mf*;

*(compartment)* scompartimento *m* non fumatori

**non-specialized** *a* non specializzato

**non-starter** *n* be a ~ *(person:)* non avere nessuna probabilità di riuscita; *(plan, idea:)* essere destinato al fallimento

**non-stick** *a* antiaderente

**non-stop** *a (talk, work, pressure, noise)* continuo; *(train)* diretto; *(journey)* senza fermate; *(flight)* senza scalo ● *adv (work, talk)* senza sosta; *(travel, fly)* senza scalo

**non-swimmer** *n* persona *f* che non sa nuotare

**non-taxable** *a* non imponibile

**non-union** *a (person)* non iscritto a un sindacato; *(company)* non sindacalizzato

**non-violent** *a* non violento

**non-white, non-White** *n* persona *f* di colore

**noodles** /'nuːdlz/ *npl* taglierini *mpl*

**nook** /nʊk/ *n* cantuccio *m*

**noon** /nuːn/ *n* mezzogiorno *m*; at ~ a mezzogiorno

**no one** *pron* nessuno

**noose** /nuːs/ *n* nodo *m* scorsoio

**nor** /nɔː(r)/ *adv & conj* né; ~ **do I** neppure io

**Nordic** /'nɔːdɪk/ *a* nordico

**norm** /nɔːm/ *n* norma *f*

**normal** /'nɔːml/ *a* normale

**normality** /nɔː'mælətɪ/ *n* normalità *f*

**normally** /'nɔːməlɪ/ *adv (usually)* normalmente

**Norman** /'nɔːmən/ *a* normanno; *(landscape, village)* della Normandia ● *n* normanno *m*

**Norse** /nɔːs/ *a (mythology, saga)* norreno

**north** /nɔːθ/ *n* nord *m*; to the ~ of a nord di ● *a* del nord, settentrionale ● *adv* a nord

**North Africa** *n* Africa *f* del Nord

**North African** *a & n* nordafricano, -a *mf*

**North America** *n* America *f* del Nord

**North American** *a & n* nordamericano, -a *mf*

**Northants** /nɔː'θænts/ *Br abbr* **Northamptonshire**

**northbound** /'nɔːθbaʊnd/ *a (traffic, carriageway)* in direzione nord

**Northd** *Br abbr* **Northumberland**

**north:** **north-east** *a* di nord-est, nord-orientale ● *n* nord-est *m* ● *adv* a nord-est; *(travel)* verso nord-est. **north-easterly** *a (point)* a nord-est; *(wind)* di nord-est ● *n* vento *m* di nord-est. **northeastern** /nɔː'θiːstən/ *a* nordorientale

**northerly** /'nɔːðəlɪ/ *a (direction)* nord; *(wind)* del nord

**northern** /'nɔːðən/ *a* del nord, settentrionale

**Northern Ireland** *n* Irlanda *f* del Nord

**Northern Lights** *npl* aurora *f* boreale

**north: North Pole** *n* polo *m* nord. **North Sea** *n* Mare *m* del Nord. **North Star** *n* stella *f* polare

**northward[s]** /'nɔːθwəd(z)/ *adv* verso nord

**north:** **north-west** *a* di nord-ovest, nordoccidentale ● *n* nord-ovest *m* ● *adv* a nord-ovest; *(travel)* verso nord-ovest. **north-**

**westerly** *a (point)* a nord-ovest; *(wind)* di nord-ovest ● *n* vento *m* di nord-ovest. **northwestern** *a* nordoccidentale

**Norway** /'nɔːweɪ/ *n* Norvegia *f*

**Norwegian** /nɔː'wiːdʒn/ *a & n* norvegese *mf*

**nose** /nəʊz/ *n* naso *m*

■ **nose about** *vi* curiosare

**nosebleed** /'nəʊzbliːd/ *n* emorragia *f* nasale

**nosedive** /'nəʊzdaɪv/ *n* Aeron picchiata *f*; **take a ~** *(fig: prices:)* scendere vertiginosamente

**nosey** /'nəʊzɪ/ *a* = **nosy**

**no-show** *n* persona *f* che non si è presentata

**nosily** /'nəʊzɪlɪ/ *adv* in modo indiscreto

**nostalgia** /nɒ'stældʒɪə/ *n* nostalgia *f*

**nostalgic** /nɒ'stældʒɪk/ *a* nostalgico

**nostril** /'nɒstrəl/ *n* narice *f*

**nosy** /'nəʊzɪ/ *a* (-ier, -iest) *fam* ficcanaso *inv*

**not** /nɒt/ *adv* non; **he is ~ Italian** non è italiano; **I hope ~** spero di no; **~ all of us have been invited** non siamo stati tutti invitati; **if ~** se no; **~ at all** niente affatto; **~ a bit** per niente; **~ even** neanche; **~ yet** non ancora; **in the ~ too distant future** in un futuro non troppo lontano; **~ only... but also...** non solo... ma anche...

**notable** /'nəʊtəbl/ *a (remarkable)* notevole

**notably** /'nəʊtəblɪ/ *adv (in particular)* in particolare

**notary** /'nəʊtərɪ/ *n* notaio *m*; **~ public** notaio *m*

**notation** /nəʊ'teɪʃn/ *n* notazione *f*

**notch** /nɒtʃ/ *n* tacca *f*

■ **notch up** *vt (score)* segnare

**note** /nəʊt/ *n* nota *f*; *(short letter, banknote)* biglietto *m*; *(memo, written comment etc)* appunto *m*; **of ~** *(person)* di spicco; *(comments, event)* degno di nota; **make a ~ of** prendere nota di; **take ~ of** *(notice)* prendere nota di ● *vt (notice)* notare; *(write)* annotare

■ **note down** *vt* annotare

**notebook** /'nəʊtbʊk/ *n* taccuino *m*; Comput notebook *m inv*

**noted** /'nəʊtɪd/ *a* noto, celebre **(for** per)

**note: notepad** *n* blocco *m* per appunti. **notepaper** *n* carta *f* da lettere. **noteworthy** *a* degno di nota

**nothing** /'nʌθɪŋ/ *pron* niente, nulla ● *adv* niente affatto; **for ~** *(free, in vain)* per niente; *(with no reason)* senza motivo; **~ but** nient'altro che; **~ much** poco o nulla; **~ interesting** niente di interessante; **it's ~ to do with you** non ti riguarda

**notice** /'nəʊtɪs/ *n (on board)* avviso *m*; *(review)* recensione *f*; *(termination of employment)* licenziamento *m*; **[advance] ~** preavviso *m*; **two months' ~** due mesi di preavviso; **at short ~** con breve preavviso; **until further ~** fino nuovo avviso; **give [in one's] ~** *(employee:)* dare le dimissioni; **give an employee ~** dare il preavviso a un impiegato; **take no ~ of** non fare caso a; **take no ~!** non farci caso! ● *vt* notare

**noticeable** /'nəʊtɪsəbl/ *a* evidente

**noticeably** /'nəʊtɪsəblɪ/ *adv* sensibilmente

**noticeboard** /'nəʊtɪsbɔːd/ *n* bacheca *f*
**notification** /nəʊtɪfɪ'keɪʃn/ *n* notifica *f*
**notify** /'nəʊtɪfaɪ/ *vt* (*pt/pp* **-ied**) notificare
**notion** /'nəʊʃn/ *n* idea *f*, nozione *f*; **he hasn't the slightest ~ of time** gli manca completamente la nozione del tempo; **~s** *pl* (*Am: haberdashery*) merceria *f*
**notoriety** /nəʊtə'raɪətɪ/ *n* notorietà *f*
**notorious** /nəʊ'tɔːrɪəs/ *a* famigerato; **be ~ for** essere tristemente famoso per
**notoriously** /nəʊ'tɔːrɪəslɪ/ *adv* **they're ~ unreliable** tutti sanno che su di loro non si può mai fare affidamento
**Notts** /nɒts/ *Br abbr* **Nottinghamshire**
**notwithstanding** /nɒtwɪð'stændɪŋ/ *prep* malgrado ● *adv* ciononostante
**nougat** /'nuːgət/ *n* torrone *m*
**nought** /nɔːt/ *n* zero *m*
**noughts and crosses** *n* tris *m*
**noun** /naʊn/ *n* nome *m*, sostantivo *m*
**nourish** /'nʌrɪʃ/ *vt* nutrire
**nourishing** /'nʌrɪʃɪŋ/ *a* nutriente
**nourishment** /'nʌrɪʃmənt/ *n* nutrimento *m*
**novel** /'nɒvl/ *a* insolito ● *n* romanzo *m*
**novelette** /nɒvə'let/ *n* (*oversentimental*) romanzetto *m* rosa
**novelist** /'nɒvəlɪst/ *n* romanziere, -a *mf*
**novelty** /'nɒvltɪ/ *n* novità *f*; **novelties** *pl* (*objects*) oggettini *mpl*
**November** /nəʊ'vembə(r)/ *n* novembre *m*
**novice** /'nɒvɪs/ *n* novizio, -a *mf*
**now** /naʊ/ *adv* ora, adesso; **by ~** ormai; **just ~** proprio ora; **right ~** subito; **~ and again, ~ and then** ogni tanto; **~, ~!** su! ● *conj* **~ [that]** ora che, adesso che
**nowadays** /'naʊədeɪz/ *adv* oggigiorno
**nowhere** /'nəʊweə(r)/ *adv* in nessun posto, da nessuna parte
**noxious** /'nɒkʃəs/ *a* nocivo
**nozzle** /'nɒzl/ *n* bocchetta *f*
**nr** *abbr* **near**
**NSPCC** *n Br abbr* (**National Society for the Prevention of Cruelty to Children**) Società *f* nazionale per la protezione dell'infanzia
**NT** *abbr* **New Testament**
**nth** /enθ/ *a Math, fig* **to the ~ power/ degree** all'ennesima potenza; **for the ~ time** per l'ennesima volta
**nuance** /'njuːɒ̃s/ *n* sfumatura *f*
**nub** /nʌb/ *n* **the ~ of the matter** il nocciolo della questione
**nubile** /'njuːbaɪl/ *a* ‹*attractive*› desiderabile
**nuclear** /'njuːklɪə(r)/ *a* nucleare
**nuclear: nuclear bomb** *n* bomba *f* atomica. **nuclear deterrent** *n* deterrente *m* nucleare. **nuclear energy** *n* energia *f* nucleare. **nuclear-free zone** *n Br* zona *f* denuclearizzata. **nuclear physics** *n* fisica *f* nucleare. **nuclear power** *n* (*energy*) energia *f* nucleare; (*country*) potenza *f* nucleare. **nuclear power station** *n* centrale *f* nucleare. **nuclear shelter** *n* rifugio *m* antiatomico
**nucleus** /'njuːklɪəs/ *n* (*pl* **-lei** /'njuːklɪaɪ/) nucleo *m*

**nude** /njuːd/ *a* nudo ● *n* nudo *m*; **in the ~** nudo
**nudge** /nʌdʒ/ *n* colpetto *m* di gomito ● *vt* dare un colpetto col gomito a
**nudism** /'njuːdɪzm/ *n* nudismo *m*
**nudist** /'njuːdɪst/ *n* nudista *mf*
**nudity** /'njuːdətɪ/ *n* nudità *f*
**nugget** /'nʌgɪt/ *n* pepita *f*
**nuisance** /'njuːsəns/ *n* seccatura *f*; (*person*) piaga *f*; **what a ~!** che seccatura!
**nuisance call** *n Teleph* telefonata *f* anonima
**null** /nʌl/ *a* **~ and void** nullo
**nullify** /'nʌlɪfaɪ/ *vt* (*pt/pp* **-ied**) annullare
**numb** /nʌm/ *a* intorpidito; **~ with cold** intirizzito dal freddo ● *vt* intorpidire
**number** /'nʌmbə(r)/ *n* numero *m*; **a ~ of people** un certo numero di persone ● *vt* numerare; (*include*) annoverare
**numbering** /'nʌmbərɪŋ/ *n* numerazione *f*
**number one** *n* (*most important*) numero uno *m*; **look after ~ ~** (*oneself*) pensare prima di tutto a se stessi
**number plate** *n* targa *f*
**numeracy** /'njuːmərəsɪ/ *n* **improve standards of ~** migliorare il livello nel calcolo
**numeral** /'njuːmərəl/ *n* numero *m*, cifra *f*
**numerate** /'njuːmərət/ *a* **be ~** saper fare i calcoli
**numerical** /njuː'merɪkl/ *a* numerico; **in ~ order** in ordine numerico
**numerically** /njuː'merɪklɪ/ *adv* numericamente
**numeric keypad** /njuː'merɪk/ *n Comput* tastierino *m* numerico
**numerous** /'njuːmərəs/ *a* numeroso
**nun** /nʌn/ *n* suora *f*
**nuptial** /'nʌpʃl/ *a* nuziale ● **~s** *npl* nozze *fpl*
**nurse** /nɜːs/ *n* infermiere, -a *mf*; **children's ~** bambinaia *f* ● *vt* curare
**nursery** /'nɜːsərɪ/ *n* stanza *f* dei bambini; (*for plants*) vivaio *m*; [**day**] **~** asilo *m*
**nursery: nursery rhyme** *n* filastrocca *f*. **nursery school** *n* scuola *f* materna. **nursery slope** *n Br* pista *f* per principianti
**nurse's aid** *n Am* aiuto infermiere, -a *mf*
**nursing** /'nɜːsɪŋ/ *n* professione *f* d'infermiere
**nursing auxiliary** *n Br* aiuto infermiere, -a *mf*
**nursing home** *n* casa *f* di cura per anziani
**nurture** /'nɜːtʃə(r)/ *vt* allevare; *fig* coltivare
**nut** /nʌt/ *n* noce *f*; *Techn* dado *m*; (*fam: head*) zucca *f*
**nutcrackers** /'nʌtkrækəz/ *npl* schiaccianoci *m inv*
**nutmeg** /'nʌtmeg/ *n* noce *f* moscata
**nutrient** /'njuːtrɪənt/ *n* sostanza *f* nutritiva
**nutrition** /njuː'trɪʃn/ *n* nutrizione *f*
**nutritionist** /njuː'trɪʃənɪst/ *n* nutrizionista *mf*
**nutritious** /njuː'trɪʃəs/ *a* nutriente
**nuts** /nʌts/ *npl* frutta *f* secca; **be ~** *fam* essere svitato

**nutshell** /'nʌtʃel/ n guscio m di noce; **in a ~** *fig* in parole povere

**nuzzle** /'nʌzl/ vt ⟨*horse, dog:*⟩ strofinare il muso contro

**NV** *Am abbr* **Nevada**

**NW** *abbr* (**north-west**) NO

**NY** *Am abbr* **New York**

**NYC** *Am abbr* **New York City**

**nylon** /'naɪlɒn/ n nailon m; **~s** *pl* calze *fpl* di nailon ● *attrib* di nailon

**nymph** /nɪmf/ n ninfa f

**nymphomaniac** /nɪmfə'meɪnɪæk/ n ninfomane f ● a da ninfomane

**NZ** *abbr* **New Zealand**

# Oo

**o, O** /əʊ/ n (*letter*) o, O f inv

**O** /əʊ/ n *Teleph* zero m

**oaf** /əʊf/ n (*pl* **oafs**) zoticone, -a mf

**oak** /əʊk/ n quercia f ● *attrib* di quercia

**OAP** *abbr* (**old-age pensioner**) pensionato, -a mf

**oar** /ɔː(r)/ n remo m

**oarsman** /'ɔːzmən/ n vogatore m

**oasis** /əʊ'eɪsɪs/ n (*pl* **oases** /əʊ'eɪsiː z/) oasi f inv

**oatcake** /'əʊtkeɪk/ n galletta f di avena

**oath** /əʊθ/ n giuramento m; (*swear-word*) bestemmia f

**oatmeal** /'əʊtmiːl/ n farina f d'avena

**oats** /əʊts/ npl avena fsg; *Culin* [**rolled**] **~** fiocchi mpl di avena

**obdurate** /'ɒbdjʊrət/ a (*stubborn*) irremovibile; (*hardhearted*) insensibile

**OBE** n Br abbr (**Officer of the (Order of the) British Empire**) onorificenza f britannica

**obedience** /ə'biːdɪəns/ n ubbidienza f

**obedient** /ə'biːdɪənt/ a ubbidiente

**obediently** /ə'biːdɪəntlɪ/ adv ubbidientemente

**obelisk** /'ɒbəlɪsk/ n obelisco m

**obese** /ə'biːs/ a obeso

**obesity** /ə'biːsətɪ/ n obesità f

**obey** /ə'beɪ/ vt ubbidire a; osservare ⟨*instructions, rules*⟩ ● vi ubbidire

**obituary** /ə'bɪtjʊərɪ/ n necrologio m

**object¹** /'ɒbdʒɪkt/ n oggetto m; *Gram* complemento m oggetto; **money is no ~** i soldi non sono un problema

**object²** /əb'dʒekt/ vi (*be against*) opporsi (**to** a); **~ that...** obiettare che...

**objection** /əb'dʒekʃn/ n obiezione f; **have no ~** non avere niente in contrario

**objectionable** /əb'dʒekʃ(ə)nəbl/ a discutibile; ⟨*person*⟩ sgradevole

**objective** /əb'dʒektɪv/ a oggettivo ● n obiettivo m

**objectively** /əb'dʒektɪvlɪ/ adv obiettivamente

**objectivity** /ɒbdʒek'tɪvətɪ/ n oggettività f

**objector** /əb'dʒektə(r)/ n oppositore, -trice mf

**obligation** /ɒblɪ'geɪʃn/ n obbligo m; **be**

**under an ~** avere un obbligo; **without ~** senza impegno

**obligatory** /ə'blɪɡətrɪ/ a obbligatorio

**oblige** /ə'blaɪdʒ/ vt (*compel*) obbligare; ⟨*do a small service for*⟩ fare una cortesia a; **much ~d** grazie mille

**obliging** /ə'blaɪdʒɪŋ/ a disponibile

**oblique** /ə'bliːk/ a obliquo; *fig* indiretto. **~ [stroke]** n barra f

**obliterate** /ə'blɪtəreɪt/ vt obliterare

**obliteration** /əblɪtə'reɪʃn/ n (*of mark, memory*) rimozione f; (*of city*) annientamento m

**oblivion** /ə'blɪvɪən/ n oblio m

**oblivious** /ə'blɪvɪəs/ a **be ~** essere dimentico (**of, to** di)

**oblong** /'ɒblɒŋ/ a oblungo ● n rettangolo m

**obnoxious** /əb'nɒkʃəs/ a detestabile

**oboe** /'əʊbəʊ/ n oboe m inv

**obscene** /əb'siːn/ a osceno; ⟨*profits, wealth*⟩ vergognoso

**obscenity** /əb'senətɪ/ n oscenità f inv

**obscure** /əb'skjʊə(r)/ a oscuro ● vt oscurare; (*confuse*) mettere in ombra

**obscurity** /əb'skjʊərətɪ/ n oscurità f

**obsequious** /əb'siːkwɪəs/ a ossequioso

**observable** /əb'zɜːvəbl/ a (*discernible*) percettibile

**observance** /əb'zɜːvəns/ n (*of custom*) osservanza f

**observant** /əb'zɜːvənt/ a attento

**observation** /ɒbzə'veɪʃn/ n osservazione f

**observation car** n carrozza f belvedere

**observation tower** n torre f di osservazione

**observatory** /əb'zɜːvətrɪ/ n osservatorio m

**observe** /əb'zɜːv/ vt osservare; (*notice*) notare; (*keep, celebrate*) celebrare

**observer** /əb'zɜːvə(r)/ n osservatore, -trice mf

**obsess** /əb'ses/ vt **be ~ed by** essere fissato con

**obsession** /əb'seʃn/ n fissazione f

**obsessive** /əb'sesɪv/ a ossessivo

**obsessively** /əb'sesɪvlɪ/ adv ossessivamente

**obsolescence** /ɒbsə'lesəns/ n obsolescenza f; **built-in ~** obsolescenza f programmata

**obsolete** /'ɒbsəliːt/ a obsoleto; ⟨*word*⟩ desueto; ⟨*idea*⟩ sorpassato

**obstacle** /'ɒbstəkl/ *n* ostacolo *m*
**obstacle course** *n* Mil. *fig* percorso *m* a ostacoli
**obstacle race** *n* corsa *f* a ostacoli
**obstetrician** /ɒbstə'trɪʃn/ *n* ostetrico, -a *mf*
**obstetrics** /əb'stetrɪks/ *n* ostetricia *f*
**obstinacy** /'ɒbstɪnəsɪ/ *n* ostinazione *f*
**obstinate** /'ɒbstɪnət/ *a* ostinato
**obstinately** /'ɒbstɪnətlɪ/ *adv* ostinatamente
**obstreperous** /əb'strepərəs/ *a* turbolento
**obstruct** /əb'strʌkt/ *vt* ostruire; (*hinder*) ostacolare
**obstruction** /əb'strʌkʃn/ *n* ostruzione *f*; (*obstacle*) ostacolo *m*
**obstructive** /əb'strʌktɪv/ *a* be ~ ⟨person:⟩ creare dei problemi
**obtain** /əb'teɪn/ *vt* ottenere ● *vi* prevalere
**obtainable** /əb'teɪnəbl/ *a* ottenibile
**obtrusive** /əb'truːsɪv/ *a* ⟨object⟩ stonato
**obtuse** /əb'tjuːs/ *a* ottuso
**obverse** /'ɒbvɜːs/ *a* the ~ side/face (*of coin*) l'altra faccia *f*
**obviate** /'ɒbvɪeɪt/ *vt fml* ovviare a
**obvious** /'ɒbvɪəs/ *a* ovvio
**obviously** /'ɒbvɪəslɪ/ *adv* ovviamente
**occasion** /ə'keɪʒn/ *n* occasione *f*; (*event*) evento *m*; on ~ talvolta; on the ~ of in occasione di ● *vt* cagionare
**occasional** /ə'keɪʒənl/ *a* saltuario; he has the ~ glass of wine ogni tanto beve un bicchiere di vino
**occasionally** /ə'keɪʒənlɪ/ *adv* ogni tanto
**occult** /ɒ'kʌlt/ *a* occulto
**occupancy** /'ɒkjʊpənsɪ/ *n* available for immediate ~ libero immediatamente; change of ~ cambio *m* di inquilino
**occupant** /'ɒkjʊpənt/ *n* occupante *mf*; (*of vehicle*) persona *f* a bordo
**occupation** /ɒkjʊ'peɪʃn/ *n* occupazione *f*; (*job*) professione *f*
**occupational** /ɒkjʊ'peɪʃənl/ *a* professionale
**occupational:** occupational hazard *n* rischio *m* professionale. occupational health *n* medicina *f* del lavoro. occupational pension *n* Br pensione *f* di lavoro. occupational psychologist *n* psicologo, -a *mf* del lavoro. occupational therapist *n* ergoterapista *mf*. occupational therapy *n* ergoterapia *f*
**occupier** /'ɒkjʊpaɪə(r)/ *n* residente *mf*
**occupy** /'ɒkjʊpaɪ/ *vt* (*pt/pp* occupied) occupare; (*keep busy*) tenere occupato
**occur** /ə'kɜː(r)/ *vi* (*pt/pp* occurred) accadere; (*exist*) trovarsi; it ~red to me that mi è venuto in mente che
**occurrence** /ə'kʌrəns/ *n* (*event*) fatto *m*
**ocean** /'əʊʃn/ *n* oceano *m*
**ocean-going** /'əʊʃəngəʊɪŋ/ *a* ⟨ship⟩ d'alto mare
**ochre** /'əʊkə(r)/ *n & a* (*colour*) ocra *f*
**o'clock** /ə'klɒk/ *adv* it's 7 ~ sono le sette; at 7 ~ alle sette
**octagon** /'ɒktəgən/ *n* ottagono *m*
**octagonal** /ɒk'tægənl/ *a* ottagonale

**octave** /'ɒktɪv/ *n* Mus ottava *f*
**octet** /ɒk'tet/ *n* Mus ottetto *m*
**October** /ɒk'təʊbə(r)/ *n* ottobre *m*
**octogenarian** /ɒktədʒɪ'neərɪən/ *n & a* ottantenne *mf*
**octopus** /'ɒktəpəs/ *n* (*pl* -puses) polpo *m*
**oculist** /'ɒkjʊlɪst/oculista *mf*
**OD** *n abbr* (overdose) overdose *f inv*
**odd** /ɒd/ *a* ⟨number⟩ dispari; (*not of set*) scompagnato; (*strange*) strano; forty ~ quaranta e rotti; ~ jobs lavoretti *mpl*; the ~ one out l'eccezione *f*; at ~ moments a tempo perso; have the ~ glass of wine avere un bicchiere di vino ogni tanto
**oddball** /'ɒdbɔːl/ *n fam* eccentrico, -a *mf*
**odd bod** /'ɒdbɒd/ *n* Br fam tipo, -a *mf* strano, -a
**oddity** /'ɒdɪtɪ/ *n* stranezza *f*
**odd-job man** *n* tuttofare *m inv*
**oddly** /'ɒdlɪ/ *adv* stranamente; ~ enough stranamente
**oddment** /'ɒdmənt/ *n* (*of fabric*) scampolo *m*
**odds** /ɒdz/ *npl* (*chances*) probabilità *fpl*; at ~ in disaccordo; ~ and ends cianfrusaglie *fpl*; it makes no ~ non fa alcuna differenza
**odds-on** *a* be the ~ favourite (*in betting*) essere il gran favorito; she has an ~ chance of... ha molte probabilità di...; it is ~ that è molto probabile che
**ode** /əʊd/ *n* ode *f*
**odious** /'əʊdɪəs/ *a* odioso
**odium** /'əʊdɪəm/ *n* odio *m*
**odometer** /əʊ'dɒmɪtə(r)/ *n* Am contachilometri *m inv*, odometro *m*
**odour** /'əʊdə(r)/ *n* odore *m*
**odourless** /'əʊdəlɪs/ *a* inodore
**odyssey** /'ɒdɪsɪ/ *n* odissea *f*
**OECD** *n abbr* (Organization for Economic Cooperation and Development) OCSE *f*
**oedema** /ɪ'diːmə/ *n* edema *m*
**oesophagus** /ɪ'sɒfəgəs/ *n* esofago *m*
**oestrogen** /'iːstrədʒən/ *n* estrogeno *m*
**of** /ɒv/ *prep* di; a cup of tea/coffee una tazza di tè/caffè; the hem of my skirt l'orlo della mia gonna; the summer of 1989 l'estate del 1989; the two of us noi due; made of di; that's very kind of you è molto gentile da parte tua; a friend of mine un mio amico; a child of three un bambino di tre anni; the fourth of January il quattro gennaio; within a year of their divorce a circa un anno dal loro divorzio; half of it la metà; the whole of the room tutta la stanza
**off** /ɒf/ *prep* da; (*distant from*) lontano da; take £10 ~ the price ridurre il prezzo di 10 sterline; ~ the coast presso la costa; a street ~ the main road una traversa della via principale; (*near*) una strada vicina alla via principale; get ~ the ladder scendere dalla scala; get ~ the bus uscire dall'autobus; leave the lid ~ the saucepan lasciare la pentola senza il coperchio ● *adv* ⟨button, handle⟩ staccato; ⟨light, machine⟩ spento; ⟨brake⟩ tolto; ⟨tap⟩ chiuso; 'off' (*on appliance*) 'off'; 2 kilometres ~ a due chilo-

metri di distanza; **a long way** ~ molto distante; (*time*) lontano; ~ **and on** di tanto in tanto; **with his hat/coat** ~ senza il cappotto/ cappello; **with the light** ~ a luce spenta; **20%** ~ 20% di sconto; **be** ~ (*leave*) andar via; *Sport* essere partito; (*food:*) essere andato a male; (*all gone*) essere finito; (*wedding, engagement:*) essere cancellato; **I'm** ~ **drugs/ alcohol** ho smesso di drogarmi/bere; **be** ~ **one's food** non avere appetito; **she's** ~ **today** (*on holiday*) è in ferie oggi; (*ill*) è malata oggi; **I'm** ~ **home** vado a casa; **you'd be better** ~ **doing...** faresti meglio a fare...; **have a day** ~ avere un giorno di vacanza; **drive/sail** ~ andare via

**offal** /'ɒfl/ *n Culin* frattaglie *fpl*

**offbeat** /'ɒfbiːt/ *a* insolito

**off-centre** *a Br* fuori centro

**off chance** *n* **there's an** ~ ~ **that** c'è una remota possibilità che; **just on the** ~ ~ **that** nella remota possibilità che

**off colour** *a* (*not well*) giù di forma; (*joke, story*) sporco

**offence** /ə'fens/ *n* (*illegal act*) reato *m*; **give** ~ offendere; **take** ~ offendersi (**at** per)

**offend** /ə'fend/ *vt* offendere

**offender** /ə'fendə(r)/ *n Jur* colpevole *mf*

**offensive** /ə'fensɪv/ *a* offensivo ● *n* offensiva *f*; **go on the** ~ passare all'offensiva

**offer** /'ɒfə(r)/ *n* offerta *f*; **on special** ~ in offerta speciale ● *vt* offrire; opporre (*resistance*); ~ **sb sth** offrire qcsa a qcno; ~ **to do sth** offrirsi di fare qcsa

**offering** /'ɒfərɪŋ/ *n* offerta *f*

**offer price** *n Comm* prezzo *m* d'offerta

**offertory** /'ɒfətrɪ/ *n Relig* offertorio *m*

**offhand** /ɒf'hænd/ *a* (*casual*) spiccio ● *adv* su due piedi

**office** /'ɒfɪs/ *n* ufficio *m*; (*post, job*) carica *f*

**office: office automation** *n* burotica *f*. **office block** *n Br* complesso *m* di uffici. **office building** *n Br* complesso *m* di uffici. **office hours** *npl* orario *m* di ufficio. **office junior** *n* fattorino, -a *mf*. **office politics** *n* intrighi *mpl* di ufficio

**officer** /'ɒfɪsə(r)/ *n* ufficiale *m*; (*police*) agente *m* [di polizia]

**office worker** *n* impiegato, -a *mf*

**official** /ə'fɪʃl/ *a* ufficiale ● *n* funzionario, -a *mf*; *Sport* dirigente *m*

**officialdom** /ə'fɪʃldəm/ *n* burocrazia *f*

**officially** /ə'fɪʃəlɪ/ *adv* ufficialmente

**officiate** /ə'fɪʃɪeɪt/ *vi* officiare

**officious** /ə'fɪʃəs/ *a* autoritario

**officiously** /ə'fɪʃəslɪ/ *adv* in modo autoritario

**offing** /'ɒfɪŋ/ *n* **in the** ~ in vista

**off-key** *a Mus* stonato

**off-licence** *n* negozio *m* per la vendita di alcolici

**off-limits** *a* off-limits *inv*

**off-line** *a Comput* fuori linea *inv*, off-line *inv*

**offload** /ɒf'ləʊd/ *vt* scaricare

**off-peak** *a* (*travel*) fuori dagli orari di pun-

ta; (*electricity*) a tariffa notturna ridotta; ~ **call** *Teleph* telefonata *f* a tariffa ridotta

**offprint** /'ɒfprɪnt/ *n* estratto *m*

**off-putting** /-pʊtɪŋ/ *a fam* scoraggiante

**off-screen** *a* (*voice, action*) fuoricampo *inv*; (*relationship*) nella vita privata ● *adv* nella vita privata

**off-season** *a* (*losses*) di bassa stagione; (*cruise*) in bassa stagione

**offset** /'ɒfset/ *vt* (*pt/pp* **-set**, *pres p* **-setting**) controbilanciare

**offset printing** *n* offset *m inv*

**offshoot** /'ɒfʃuːt/ *n* ramo *m*; *fig* diramazione *f*

**offshore** /'ɒfʃɔː(r)/ *a* (*wind*) di terra; (*company, investment*) offshore *inv*

**offside** /ɒf'saɪd/ *a Sport* [in] fuori gioco; (*wheel etc*) (*left*) sinistro; (*right*) destro

**offspring** /'ɒfsprɪŋ/ *n* prole *m*

**off-stage** *adv* dietro le quinte

**off-the-cuff** *a* (*remark*) spontaneo; (*speech*) improvvisato

**off-the-peg** *a* (*garment*) prêt-à-porter *inv*, confezionato

**off-the-shelf** *a Comm* standard *inv*

**off-the-shoulder** *a* (*dress*) senza bretelle

**off-the-wall** *a* (*fam: sense of humour*) strano

**off-white** *a* bianco sporco

**often** /'ɒfn/ *adv* spesso; **how** ~ ogni quanto; **every so** ~ una volta ogni tanto

**ogle** /'əʊgl/ *vt* mangiarsi con gli occhi

**ogre** /'əʊgə(r)/ *n* orco *m*

**oh** /əʊ/ *int* oh!; **oh dear** oh Dio!

**OHMS** *Br abbr* (**On Her/His Majesty's Service**) abbreviazione *f* apposta su corrispondenza ufficiale del governo

**oil** /ɔɪl/ *n* olio *m*; (*petroleum*) petrolio *m*; (*for heating*) nafta *f* ● *vt* oliare

**oil: oil-burning** *a* (*stove, boiler*) a nafta. **oil can** *n* (*applicator*) oliatore *m*. **oil change** *n* cambio *m* dell'olio. **oilcloth** *n* tela *f* cerata. **oilfield** *n* giacimento *m* di petrolio. **oil filter** *n* filtro *m* dell'olio. **oil-fired** /-faɪəd/ *a* (*furnace, heating*) a nafta. **oil gauge** *n* indicatore *m* [del livello] dell'olio. **oil heater** *n* stufa *f* a nafta. **oil lamp** *n* lampada *f* a olio. **oil paint** *n* colore *m* a olio. **oil painting** *n* pittura *f* a olio. **oil pipeline** *n* oleodotto *m*. **oil pressure** *n* pressione *f* dell'olio. **oil-producing** /-prədjuː-sɪŋ/ *a* (*country*) produttore di petrolio. **oil refinery** *n* raffineria *f* di petrolio. **oil rig** *n* piattaforma *f* petrolifera, offshore *m inv*. **oilskins** *npl* vestiti *mpl* di tela cerata. **oil slick** *n* chiazza *f* di petrolio. **oil spill** *n* fuoriuscita *f* di petrolio. **oil stove** *n* stufa *f* a nafta. **oil tank** *n* (*domestic*) serbatoio *m* della nafta; (*industrial*) cisterna *f* della nafta. **oil tanker** *n* petroliera *f*. **oil well** *n* pozzo *m* petrolifero

**oily** /'ɔɪlɪ/ *a* (**-ier, -iest**) unto; *fig* untuoso

**ointment** /'ɔɪntmənt/ *n* pomata *f*

**OK** /əʊ'keɪ/ *int* va bene, o.k. ● *a* **if that's OK with you** se ti va bene; **she's OK** (*well*) sta bene; **is the milk still OK?** il latte è ancora

buono? ● *adv* (*well*) bene ● *vt* (*anche* okay)
(*pt/pp* OK'd, okayed) dare l'o.k. a

**old** /əʊld/ *a* vecchio; ‹*girlfriend*› ex; **how ~ is
she?** quanti anni ha?; **she is ten years ~** ha
dieci anni

**old:** **old·age** *n* vecchiaia *f*. **old-age pension**
*n Br* pensione *f* di vecchiaia. **old-age
pensioner** *n* pensionato, -a *mf*. **old boy** *n Sch*
ex-allievo *m*. **old country** *n* paese *m* d'origine

**olden** /'əʊldən/ *a* **the ~ days** i tempi andati

**old-established** /-ɪ'stæblɪʃt/ *a* di lunga
data

**olde-worlde** /əʊldɪ'wɜːldɪ/ *a hum* dall'aria
falsamente antica

**old:** **old-fashioned** /-'fæʃ(ə)nd/ *a* antiquato.
**old favourite** *n* (*book, play*) classico *m*; (*song,
film*) vecchio successo *m*. **old flame** *n fam*
vecchia fiamma *f*. **old girl** *n* ex-allieva *f*. **Old
Glory** *n* bandiera *f* statunitense. **old hand** *n*
**be an ~ ~ at sth/at doing sth** saperci fare
con qcsa/a fare qcsa. **old hat** *a fam* **be ~ ~**
essere roba vecchia

**oldie** /'əʊldɪ/ *n* (*person*) vecchio, -a *mf*; (*film,
song*) vecchio successo *m*

**old:** **old lady** *n* (*elderly woman*) signora *f* anziana; **my ~ ~** (*mother*) la mia vecchia; (*wife*)
la mia signora. **old maid** *n* zitella *f*. **old man**
*n* (*elderly man*) uomo *m* anziano; (*old: dear
chap*) vecchio *m* mio; **my ~ ~** (*father*) il mio
vecchio; (*husband*) mio marito *m*; **the ~ ~**
(*boss*) il capo. **old master** *n* (*work*) dipinto *m*
antico (*specialmente di un pittore europeo del
XIII-XVII secolo*). **old people's home** *n* casa
*f* di riposo. **old soldier** *n* (*former soldier*) veterano *m*. **Old Testament** *n* Antico Testamento *m*. **old-time** *a* di un tempo; **~
dancing** ballo *m* liscio. **old-timer** *n* veterano, -a *mf*. **old wives' tale** *n* superstizione *f*.
**old woman** *n* (*elderly lady*) donna *f* anziana;
**my ~ ~** (*mother*) mia madre *f*; (*wife*) la mia
signora; **be an ~ ~** ‹*pej: man*:› essere una
donnicciola

**olive** /'ɒlɪv/ *n* (*fruit, colour*) oliva *f*; (*tree*) oli-
vo *m* ● *a* d'oliva; (*colour*) olivastro

**olive:** **olive branch** *n fig* ramoscello *m* d'oli-
vo. **olive grove** *n* oliveto *m*. **olive oil** *n* olio *m*
di oliva. **olive-skinned** /-'skɪnd/ *a* olivastro

**Olympic** /ə'lɪmpɪk/ *a* olimpico

**Olympic Games, Olympics** *npl* Olimpi-
adi *fpl*

**ombudsman** /'ɒmbʊdzmən/ *n* difensore *m*
civico

**omelette** /'ɒmlɪt/ *n* omelette *f inv*

**omen** /'əʊmən/ *n* presagio *m*

**ominous** /'ɒmɪnəs/ *a* sinistro

**omission** /ə'mɪʃn/ *n* omissione *f*

**omit** /ə'mɪt/ *vt* (*pt/pp* omitted) omettere; **~
to do sth** tralasciare di fare qcsa

**omnibus** /'ɒmnɪbəs/ *n* (*bus*) omnibus *m inv*

**omnibus edition** *n Br TV* replica *f* delle
puntate precedenti

**omnipotent** /ɒm'nɪpətənt/ *a* onnipotente

**on** /ɒn/ *prep* su; (*on horizontal surface*) su, sopra; **on Monday** lunedì; **on Mondays** di lu-

nedì; **on the first of May** il primo di maggio;
**on arriving** all'arrivo; **on one's finger** nel
dito; **on foot** a piedi; **on the right/left** a de-
stra/sinistra; **on the Rhine/Thames** sul
Reno/Tamigi; **on the radio/television** alla
radio/televisione; **on the bus/train** in autobus/treno; **go on the bus/train** andare in
autobus/treno; **get on the bus/train** salire
sull'autobus/sul treno; **on me** (*with me*) con
me; **it's on me** *fam* tocca a me ● *adv* (*further
on*) dopo; (*switched on*) acceso; ‹*brake*› inserito; (*in operation*) in funzione; **'on'** (*on
machine*) 'on'; **he had his hat/coat on** porta-
va il cappello/cappotto; **without his hat/
coat on** senza cappello/capotto; **with/
without the lid on** con/senza coperchio; **be
on** ‹*film, programme, event*:› esserci; **it's not
on** *fam* non è giusto; **be on at** *fam* tormentare (**to** per); **on and on** senza sosta; **on and off**
a intervalli; **and so on** e così via; **go on** continuare; **stick on** attaccare; **sew on** cucire

**once** /wʌns/ *adv* una volta; (*formerly*) un
tempo; **~ upon a time there was** c'era una
volta; **at ~** subito; (*at the same time*) contemporaneamente; **~ and for all** una volta per
tutte ● *conj* [non] appena

**once-over** *n fam* **give sb/sth the ~**
(*look, check*) dare un'occhiata veloce a qcno/
qcsa

**oncoming** /'ɒnkʌmɪŋ/ *a* che si avvicina dalla direzione opposta

**one** /wʌn/ *a* uno, una; **not ~ person** nemmeno una persona ● *n* uno *m* ● *pron* uno;
(*impersonal*) si; **~ another** l'un l'altro; **~ by
~** [a] uno a uno; **~ never knows** non si sa
mai

**one-armed bandit** /wʌnɑːmd'bændɪt/ *n*
slot-machine *f inv*

**one-dimensional** /-daɪ'menʃənəl/ *a* uni-
dimensionale; **be ~** ‹*fig: character*:› mancare
di spessore

**one-eyed** /-'aɪd/ *a* con un occhio solo

**one-for-one** *a* = one-to-one

**one-handed** /-'hændɪd/ *adv* ‹*catch, hold*›
con una sola mano

**one-horse town** *n fam* cittadina *f* di provincia

**one-legged** /-'legɪd/ *a* con una sola gamba

**one-liner** *n* battuta *f* d'effetto

**one-man** *a* ‹*bobsled*› monoposto *inv*; ‹*for
one person*› per una sola persona; **she's a ~
woman** è una donna fedele; **it's a ~ outfit/
operation** manda avanti tutto da solo

**one-man band** *n* musicista *m* che suona più
strumenti contemporaneamente; **be a ~ ~** *fig*
mandare avanti tutto da solo

**one-off** *a Br* ‹*experiment, order, deal*› unico e
irripetibile; ‹*event, decision, offer, payment*›
eccezionale; ‹*example, design*› unico; ‹*issue,
magazine*› speciale

**one-parent family** *n* famiglia *f* con un
solo genitore

**one-room flat, one-room apartment**
*n* monolocale *m*

**one's** /wʌnz/ *poss a* **one has to look after**

**~ health** ci si deve preoccupare della propria salute

**oneself** /wʌn'self/ *pron* (*reflexive*) si; (*emphatic*) sé, se stesso; **by ~** da solo; **be proud of ~** essere fieri di sé

**one-shot** *a Am* = **one-off**

**one-sided** /-'saɪdɪd/ *a* unilaterale

**one-time** *a* ex *inv*

**one-to-one** *a* ⟨*personal relationship*⟩ tra due persone; ⟨*private lesson*⟩ individuale; ⟨*correspondence*⟩ di uno a uno

**one-upmanship** /-'ʌpmənʃɪp/ *n* arte *f* di primeggiare

**one-way** *a* ⟨*street*⟩ a senso unico; ⟨*ticket*⟩ di sola andata

**one-woman** *a* **it's a ~ outfit** manda avanti tutto da sola; **he's a ~ man** è un uomo fedele

**ongoing** /'ɒŋgəʊɪŋ/ *a* ⟨*process*⟩ continuo; ⟨*battle, saga*⟩ in corso

**onion** /'ʌnjən/ *n* cipolla *f*

**on-line** *a Comput* in linea, on-line *inv*; **go ~ to...** connettersi a...; **~ time** durata *f* del collegamento

**onlooker** /'ɒnlʊkə(r)/ *n* spettatore, -trice *mf*

**only** /'əʊnlɪ/ *a* solo; **~ child** figlio, -a *mf* unico, -a ● *adv* & *conj* solo, solamente; **~ just** appena

**o.n.o.** *Br abbr* (**or nearest offer**) trattabile

**on-off** *a* ⟨*button, control*⟩ di accensione

**onrush** /'ɒnrʌʃ/ *n* (*of people, water*) ondata *f*

**on-screen** *a* sullo schermo

**onset** /'ɒnset/ *n* (*beginning*) inizio *m*

**onshore** /'ɒnʃɔː(r)/ *a* ⟨*wind*⟩ di mare; ⟨*work*⟩ a terra

**onside** /ɒn'saɪd/ *a* & *adv Sport* non in fuorigioco

**on-site** *a* sul posto

**onslaught** /'ɒnslɔːt/ *n* attacco *m*

**on-stage** *a* & *adv* in scena

**on-the-job** *a* ⟨*training*⟩ in sede

**on-the-spot** *a* ⟨*advice, quotation*⟩ immediato

**onto** /'ɒntuː/ *prep* (*also* **on to**) su

**onus** /'əʊnəs/ *n* **the ~ is on me** spetta a me la responsabilità (**to** di)

**onward[s]** /'ɒnwəd[z]/ *adv* in avanti; **from then ~** da allora [in poi]

**oodles** /'uːdlz/ *n fam* un sacco

**ooh** /uː/ *int* oh!

**oomph** /uːmf/ *n fam* verve *f inv*

**oops** /uːps/ *int* ops!

**ooze** /uːz/ *vi* fluire

**op** /ɒp/ *n* = **operation**

**opal** /'əʊpl/ *n* opale *f*

**opaque** /əʊ'peɪk/ *a* opaco

**Opec, OPEC** /'əʊpek/ *n abbr* (**Organization of Petroleum Exporting Countries**) OPEC *f*

**open** /'əʊpən/ *a* aperto; (*free to all*) pubblico; ⟨*job*⟩ vacante; **in the ~ air** all'aperto ● *n* **in the ~** all'aperto; *fig* alla luce del sole ● *vt* aprire ● *vi* aprirsi; ⟨*shop:*⟩ aprire; ⟨*flower:*⟩ sbocciare

■ **open onto** *vt* ⟨*door, window:*⟩ dare su

■ **open out** *vi* ⟨*road:*⟩ allargarsi; ⟨*flower:*⟩ aprirsi ● *vt* aprire ⟨*map, newspaper*⟩

■ **open up** *vt* aprire ● *vi* aprirsi

■ **open with** *vi* (*start with*) iniziare con

**open: open-air** *a* ⟨*pool, market, stage*⟩ all'aperto. **opencast mining** *n Br* miniera *f* a cielo aperto. **open competition** *n* concorso *m*. **open day** *n* giorno *m* di apertura al pubblico. **open-ended** /-'endɪd/ *a* ⟨*relationship, question, contract*⟩ aperto; ⟨*stay*⟩ a tempo indeterminato; ⟨*period*⟩ indeterminato; ⟨*strategy*⟩ flessibile

**opener** /'əʊpənə(r)/ *n* (*for tins*) apriscatole *m inv*; (*for bottles*) apribottiglie *m inv*

**open: open government** *n* politica *f* di trasparenza. **open-handed** /-'hændɪd/ *a* generoso. **open-heart surgery** *n* intervento *m* a cuore aperto. **open house** *n* (*Am: open day*) giornata *f* di apertura al pubblico; **it's always ~ ~ at the Batemans'** i Bateman sono sempre molto ospitali

**opening** /'əʊpənɪŋ/ *n* apertura *f*; (*beginning*) inizio *m*; (*job*) posto *m* libero

**opening: opening balance** *n Fin* saldo *m* iniziale. **opening ceremony** *n* cerimonia *f* inaugurale. **opening hours** *npl* orario *m* d'apertura

**openly** /'əʊpənlɪ/ *adv* apertamente

**open: open market** *n Econ* mercato *m* aperto. **open-minded** /-'maɪndɪd/ *a* aperto; (*broad-minded*) di vedute larghe. **open-mouthed** /-'maʊðd/ *a* a bocca aperta. **open-necked** /-'nekt/ *a* ⟨*shirt*⟩ col colletto sbottonato

**openness** /'əʊpənnɪs/ *n* (*of government, atmosphere*) trasparenza *f*; (*candour*) franchezza *f*; (*receptiveness*) apertura *f* mentale

**open: open-plan** *a* a pianta aperta. **open sandwich** *n* tartina *f*. **open scholarship** *n Univ* borsa *f* di studio assegnata per concorso. **open season** *n* (*in hunting*) stagione *f* della caccia. **open secret** *n* segreto *m* di Pulcinella. **open ticket** *n* biglietto *m* aperto. **Open University** *n Br Univ* corsi *mpl* universitari per corrispondenza. **open verdict** *n Jur* verdetto *m* che dichiara non accertabili le cause della morte

**opera** /'ɒpərə/ *n* opera *f*

**operable** /'ɒpərəbl/ *a* operabile

**opera: opera glasses** *npl* binocolo *msg* da teatro. **opera house** *n* teatro *m* lirico. **opera-singer** *n* cantante *mf* lirico, -a

**operate** /'ɒpəreɪt/ *vt* far funzionare ⟨*machine, lift*⟩; azionare ⟨*lever, brake*⟩; mandare avanti ⟨*business*⟩ ● *vi Techn* funzionare; (*be in action*) essere in funzione; *Mil, fig* operare

■ **operate on** *vt Med* operare

**operatic** /ɒpə'rætɪk/ *a* lirico, operistico

**operating** /'ɒpəreɪtɪŋ/: **operating costs** *npl* spese *fpl* di esercizio. **operating instructions** *npl* istruzioni *fpl* per l'uso. **operating room** *n Am* sala *f* operatoria. **operating system** *n Comput* sistema *m* operativo. **operating table** *n Med* tavolo *m* operatorio. **operating theatre** *n Br* sala *f* operatoria

**operation** /ɒpəˈreɪʃn/ n operazione f; Tech funzionamento m; **in ~** Techn in funzione; **come into ~** fig entrare in funzione; ⟨law:⟩ entrare in vigore; **have an ~** Med subire un'operazione

**operational** /ɒpəˈreɪʃənəl/ a operativo; ⟨law etc⟩ in vigore

**operations room** n Mil centro m operativo; (police) centrale f operativa

**operative** /ˈɒpərətɪv/ a operativo

**operator** /ˈɒpəreɪtə(r)/ n (user) operatore, -trice mf; Teleph centralinista mf

**operetta** /ɒpəˈretə/ n operetta f

**ophthalmic** /ɒfˈθælmɪk/ a oftalmico

**opinion** /əˈpɪnjən/ n opinione f; **in my ~** secondo me

**opinionated** /əˈpɪnjəneɪtɪd/ a dogmatico

**opinion poll** n sondaggio m di opinione

**opium** /ˈəʊpɪəm/ n oppio m

**opponent** /əˈpəʊnənt/ n avversario, -a mf

**opportune** /ˈɒpətjuːn/ a opportuno

**opportunist** /ɒpəˈtjuːnɪst/ n opportunista mf

**opportunistic** /ɒpətjʊˈnɪstɪk/ a opportunistico

**opportunity** /ɒpəˈtjuːnəti/ n opportunità f inv

**oppose** /əˈpəʊz/ vt opporsi a; **be ~d to sth** essere contrario a qcsa; **as ~d to** al contrario di

**opposing** /əˈpəʊzɪŋ/ a avversario; (opposite) opposto

**opposite** /ˈɒpəzɪt/ a opposto; ⟨house⟩ di fronte; **~ number** fig controparte f; **the ~ sex** l'altro sesso ● n contrario m ● adv di fronte ● prep di fronte a

**opposition** /ɒpəˈzɪʃn/ n opposizione f

**oppress** /əˈpres/ vt opprimere

**oppression** /əˈpreʃn/ n oppressione f

**oppressive** /əˈpresɪv/ a oppressivo; ⟨heat⟩ opprimente

**oppressor** /əˈpresə(r)/ n oppressore m

■ **opt for** /ɒpt/ vt optare per

■ **opt out** vi dissociarsi (**of** da)

**optic** /ˈɒptɪk/ a ⟨nerve, disc, fibre⟩ ottico

**optical** /ˈɒptɪkl/ a ottico; **~ illusion** illusione f ottica

**optician** /ɒpˈtɪʃn/ n ottico, -a mf

**optics** /ˈɒptɪks/ n ottica f

**optimism** /ˈɒptɪmɪzm/ n ottimismo m

**optimist** /ˈɒptɪmɪst/ n ottimista mf

**optimistic** /ɒptɪˈmɪstɪk/ a ottimistico

**optimistically** /ɒptɪˈmɪstɪkli/ adv ottimisticamente

**optimize** /ˈɒptɪmaɪz/ vt ottimizzare

**optimum** /ˈɒptɪməm/ a ottimale ● n (pl -ima) optimum m

**option** /ˈɒpʃn/ n scelta f; Comm opzione f

**optional** /ˈɒpʃənəl/ a facoltativo; **~ extras** optional m inv

**opulence** /ˈɒpjʊləns/ n opulenza f

**opulent** /ˈɒpjʊlənt/ a opulento

**opus** /ˈəʊpəs/ n (pl opuses or opera) opera f

**or** /ɔː(r)/ conj o, oppure; (after negative) né; **or**

[else] se no; **in a year or two** fra un anno o due

**oracle** /ˈɒrəkl/ n oracolo m

**oral** /ˈɔːrəl/ a orale ● n fam esame m orale

**orally** /ˈɔːrəli/ adv oralmente

**orange** /ˈɒrɪndʒ/ n arancia f; (colour) arancione m ● a arancione

**orangeade** /ɒrɪndʒˈeɪd/ n aranciata f

**orange: orange blossom** n fiori mpl d'arancio. **orange juice** n succo m d'arancia. **orange peel** n scorza f d'arancia. **orange squash** n Br succo m d'arancia (diluito in acqua). **orange tree** n arancio m

**oration** /əˈreɪʃn/ n orazione f

**orator** /ˈɒrətə(r)/ n oratore, -trice mf

**oratorio** /ɒrəˈtɔːrɪəʊ/ n oratorio m

**oratory** /ˈɒrətri/ n oratorio m

**orbit** /ˈɔːbɪt/ n orbita f ● vt orbitare

**orbital** /ˈɔːbɪtl/ a **~ road** tangenziale f

**orchard** /ˈɔːtʃəd/ n frutteto m

**orchestra** /ˈɔːkɪstrə/ n orchestra f

**orchestral** /ɔːˈkestrəl/ a orchestrale

**orchestra pit** n [fossa f dell']orchestra f

**orchestrate** /ˈɔːkɪstreɪt/ vt orchestrare

**orchid** /ˈɔːkɪd/ n orchidea f

**ordain** /ɔːˈdeɪn/ vt decretare; Relig ordinare

**ordeal** /ɔːˈdiːl/ n fig terribile esperienza f

**order** /ˈɔːdə(r)/ n ordine m; Comm ordinazione f; **out of ~** ⟨machine⟩ fuori servizio; **in ~ that** affinché; **in ~ to** per; **take holy ~s** prendere i voti ● vt ordinare

■ **order about, order around** vt (give orders to) impartire ordini a

**order book** n registro m degli ordini

**order form** n modulo m di ordinazione

**orderly** /ˈɔːdəli/ a ordinato ● n Mil attendente m; Med inserviente m

**orderly officer** n Mil attendente m

**order number** n numero m d'ordine

**ordinal** /ˈɔːdɪnəl/ n & a ordinale m

**ordinarily** /ɔːdɪˈnerɪli/ adv (normally) normalmente

**ordinary** /ˈɔːdɪnəri/ a ordinario

**ordination** /ɔːdɪˈneɪʃn/ n Relig ordinazione f

**ordnance** /ˈɔːdnəns/ n Mil materiale m militare

**Ordnance Survey** n Br istituto m cartografico; **Ordnance Survey Map** carta f topografica dell'istituto cartografico

**ore** /ɔː(r)/ n minerale m grezzo

**oregano** /ɒrɪˈgɑːnəʊ/ n origano m

**organ** /ˈɔːɡən/ n Anat, Mus organo m

**organ donor** n Med donatore, -trice mf di organi

**organic** /ɔːˈɡænɪk/ a organico; (without chemicals) biologico

**organically** /ɔːˈɡænɪkli/ adv organicamente; **~ grown** coltivato biologicamente

**organic: organic chemistry** n chimica f organica. **organic farm** n azienda f agricola specializzata in prodotti biologici. **organic farming** n agricoltura f biologica

**organism** /ˈɔːɡənɪzm/ n organismo m

**organist** /ˈɔːɡənɪst/ n organista mf

**organization** /ɔːgənaɪˈzeɪʃn/ n organizzazione f

**organizational** /ɔːgənaɪˈzeɪʃənəl/ a ‹ability, role› organizzativo

**organize** /ˈɔːgənaɪz/ vt organizzare

**organized crime** /ɔːgənaɪzdˈkraɪm/ n criminalità f organizzata

**organized labour** n manodopera f organizzata

**organizer** /ˈɔːgənaɪzə(r)/ n organizzatore, -trice mf

**organ transplant** n Med trapianto m di organi

**orgasm** /ˈɔːgæzm/ n orgasmo m

**orgy** /ˈɔːdʒɪ/ n orgia f

**Orient** /ˈɔːrɪənt/ n Oriente m

**oriental** /ɔːrɪˈentl/ a orientale; **~ carpet** tappeto m persiano ● n orientale mf

**orientate** /ˈɔːrɪenteɪt/ vt **~ oneself** orientarsi

**orientation** /ɔːrɪənˈteɪʃn/ n orientamento m

**orienteering** /ɔːrɪənˈtɪərɪŋ/ n orientamento m

**orifice** /ˈɒrɪfɪs/ n orifizio m

**origin** /ˈɒrɪdʒɪn/ n origine f

**original** /əˈrɪdʒɪnl/ a originario; (not copied, new) originale; ● n originale m; **in the ~** in versione originale

**originality** /ərɪdʒɪˈnælətɪ/ n originalità f

**originally** /əˈrɪdʒɪnəlɪ/ adv originariamente

**originate** /əˈrɪdʒɪneɪt/ vi **~ in** avere origine in

**originator** /əˈrɪdʒɪneɪtə(r)/ n ideatore, -trice mf

**Orkney** /ˈɔːknɪ/ n (also **Orkney Islands**) Orcadi fpl

**ornament** /ˈɔːnəmənt/ n ornamento m; (on mantelpiece etc) soprammobile m

**ornamental** /ɔːnəˈmentl/ a ornamentale

**ornamentation** /ɔːnəmenˈteɪʃn/ n decorazione f

**ornate** /ɔːˈneɪt/ a ornato

**ornithologist** /ɔːnɪˈθɒlədʒɪst/ n ornitologo, -a mf

**ornithology** /ɔːnɪˈθɒlədʒɪ/ n ornitologia f

**orphan** /ˈɔːfn/ n orfano, -a mf ● vt rendere orfano; **be ~ed** rimanere orfano; **be ~ed by...** essere reso orfano da...

**orphanage** /ˈɔːfənɪdʒ/ n orfanotrofio m

**orphaned** /ˈɔːfənd/ a reso orfano

**orthodox** /ˈɔːθədɒks/ a ortodosso

**orthopaedic** /ɔːθəˈpiːdɪk/ a ortopedico

**orthopaedics** /ɔːθəˈpiːdɪks/ n ortopedia f

**OS** abbr ‹outsize› per taglie forti

**oscillate** /ˈɒsɪleɪt/ vi oscillare

**osmosis** /ɒzˈməʊsɪs/ n osmosi f inv; **by ~** per osmosi

**ostensible** /ɒˈstensəbl/ a apparente

**ostensibly** /ɒˈstensəblɪ/ adv apparentemente

**ostentation** /ɒstenˈteɪʃn/ n ostentazione f

**ostentatious** /ɒstenˈteɪʃəs/ a ostentato

**ostentatiously** /ɒstenˈteɪʃəslɪ/ adv ostentatamente

**osteopath** /ˈɒstɪəpæθ/ n osteopata mf

**osteoporosis** /ɒstɪəʊpəˈrəʊsɪs/ n osteoporosi f

**ostracism** /ˈɒstrəsɪzm/ n ostracismo m

**ostracize** /ˈɒstrəsaɪz/ vt ostracizzare

**ostrich** /ˈɒstrɪtʃ/ n struzzo m

**other** /ˈʌðə(r)/ a, pron & n altro, -a mf: **the ~ [one]** l'altro, -a mf; **the ~ two** gli altri due; **two ~s** altri due: **~ people** gli altri; **any ~ questions?** altre domande?: **every ~ day** (alternate days) a giorni alterni; **the ~ day** l'altro giorno; **the ~ evening** l'altra sera; **someone/something or ~** qualcuno/qualcosa ● adv **~ than him** tranne lui; **somehow or ~** in qualche modo; **somewhere or ~** da qualche parte

**otherwise** /ˈʌðəwaɪz/ adv altrimenti; (differently) diversamente

**other-worldly** /ʌðəˈwɜːldlɪ/ a disinteressato alle cose materiali

**OTT** abbr fam (over-the-top) esagerato

**otter** /ˈɒtə(r)/ n lontra f

**OU** n Br abbr (**Open University**) corsi mpl universitari per corrispondenza

**ouch** /aʊtʃ/ int ahi!

**ought** /ɔːt/ v aux I/we **~ to stay** dovrei/dovremmo rimanere; **he ~ not to have done it** non avrebbe dovuto farlo; **that ~ to be enough** questo dovrebbe bastare

**ounce** /aʊns/ n oncia f (= 28,35 g)

**our** /ˈaʊə(r)/ poss a il nostro m, la nostra f, i nostri mpl, le nostre fpl; **~ mother/father** nostra madre/nostro padre

**ours** /ˈaʊəz/ poss pron il nostro m, la nostra f, i nostri mpl, le nostre fpl; **a friend of ~** un nostro amico; **friends of ~** dei nostri amici; **that is ~** quello è nostro; (as opposed to yours) quello è il nostro

**ourselves** /aʊəˈselvz/ pers pron (reflexive) ci; (emphatic) noi, noi stessi; **we poured ~ a drink** ci siamo versati da bere; **we heard it ~** l'abbiamo sentito noi stessi; **we are proud of ~** siamo fieri di noi; **by ~** da soli

**oust** /aʊst/ vt rimuovere

**out** /aʊt/ adv fuori; (not alight) spento; **be ~** ‹flower:› essere sbocciato; ‹workers:› essere in sciopero; ‹calculation:› essere sbagliato; Sport essere fuori; (unconscious) aver perso i sensi; (fig: not feasible) fuori questione; **the sun is ~** è uscito il sole; **~ and about** in piedi; **get ~!** fam fuori!; **you should get ~ more** dovresti uscire più spesso; **~ with it!** fam sputa il rospo!; **be ~ to** avere l'intenzione di; ● prep **~ of** fuori da; **~ of date** non aggiornato; ‹passaporto› scaduto; **~ of order** guasto; **~ of print/stock** esaurito; **~ of sorts** indisposto; **~ of tune** (singer) stonato; (instrument) scordato; **be ~ of bed/ the room** fuori dal letto/dalla stanza; **~ of breath** senza fiato; **~ of danger** fuori pericolo; **~ of work** disoccupato; **nine ~ of ten** nove su dieci; **be ~ of sugar/bread** rimanere senza zucchero/pane; **go ~ of the room** uscire dalla stanza

**out-and-out** a ‹success, failure› totale; ‹villain, liar› vero e proprio

**outback** /ˈaʊtbæk/ n entroterra m inv australiano

**outbid** /aʊtˈbɪd/ vt (pt/pp **-bid**, pres p **-bidding**) ~ **sb** rilanciare l'offerta di qcno

**outboard** /ˈaʊtbɔːd/ a ~ **motor** fuoribordo m inv

**outbreak** /ˈaʊtbreɪk/ n (of war) scoppio m; (of disease) insorgenza f

**outbuilding** /ˈaʊtbɪldɪŋ/ n costruzione f annessa

**outburst** /ˈaʊtbɜːst/ n esplosione f

**outcast** /ˈaʊtkɑːst/ n esule mf; (social) escluso m

**outclass** /aʊtˈklɑːs/ vt surclassare

**outcome** /ˈaʊtkʌm/ n risultato m

**outcrop** /ˈaʊtkrɒp/ n affioramento m

**outcry** /ˈaʊtkraɪ/ n protesta f

**outdated** /aʊtˈdeɪtɪd/ a sorpassato

**outdo** /aʊtˈduː/ vt (pt **-did**, pp **-done**) superare

**outdoor** /ˈaʊtdɔː(r)/ a (life, sports) all'aperto; ~ **swimming pool** piscina f scoperta

**outdoors** /aʊtˈdɔːz/ adv all'aria aperta; **go** ~ uscire all'aria aperta

**outer** /ˈaʊtə(r)/ a esterno

**outer space** n spazio m cosmico

**outfit** /ˈaʊtfɪt/ n equipaggiamento m; (clothes) completo m; (fam: organization) organizzazione f

**outfitter** /ˈaʊtfɪtə(r)/ n men's ~'s negozio m di abbigliamento maschile

**outflow** /ˈaʊtfləʊ/ n (of money) uscite fpl

**outgoing** /ˈaʊtgəʊɪŋ/ a (president) uscente; (mail) in partenza; (sociable) estroverso ● npl ~**s** uscite fpl

**outgrow** /aʊtˈgrəʊ/ vi (pt **-grew**, pp **-grown**) diventare troppo grande per

**outhouse** /ˈaʊthaʊs/ n costruzione f annessa

**outing** /ˈaʊtɪŋ/ n gita f

**outlandish** /aʊtˈlændɪʃ/ a stravagante

**outlast** /aʊtˈlɑːst/ vt durare più a lungo di

**outlaw** /ˈaʊtlɔː/ n fuorilegge mf inv ● vt dichiarare illegale

**outlay** /ˈaʊtleɪ/ n spesa f

**outlet** /ˈaʊtlet/ n sbocco m; fig sfogo m; Comm punto m [di] vendita

**outline** /ˈaʊtlaɪn/ n contorno m; (summary) sommario m ● vt tracciare il contorno di; (describe) descrivere

**outline agreement** n abbozzo m di accordo

**outlive** /aʊtˈlɪv/ vt sopravvivere a

**outlook** /ˈaʊtlʊk/ n vista f; (future prospect) prospettiva f; (attitude) visione f

**outlying** /ˈaʊtlaɪɪŋ/ a ~ **areas** zone fpl periferiche

**outmanoeuvre** /aʊtməˈnuːvə(r)/ vt ~ **sb** passare in vantaggio su qcno con un'abile manovra

**outmoded** /aʊtˈməʊdɪd/ a fuori moda

**outnumber** /aʊtˈnʌmbə(r)/ vt superare in numero

**out of bounds** a & adv (area) vietato all'accesso

**out-of-date** a (theory, concept) sorpassato; (ticket, passport) scaduto

**out-of-pocket** a **be a out of pocket** essere in perdita; ~ **expenses** spese fpl extra

**out-of-the-way** a (places) fuori mano

**outpatient** /ˈaʊtpeɪʃnt/ n paziente mf esterno, -a; ~**s' department** ambulatorio m

**outpost** /ˈaʊtpəʊst/ n avamposto m

**output** /ˈaʊtpʊt/ n produzione f

**outrage** /ˈaʊtreɪdʒ/ n oltraggio m ● vt oltraggiare

**outrageous** /aʊtˈreɪdʒəs/ a oltraggioso; (price) scandaloso

**outrider** /ˈaʊtraɪdə(r)/ n battistrada m inv

**outright**[1] /ˈaʊtraɪt/ a completo; (refusal) netto

**outright**[2] /aʊtˈraɪt/ adv completamente; (at once) immediatamente; (frankly) francamente

**outrun** /aʊtˈrʌn/ vt superare

**outsell** /aʊtˈsel/ vt vendere meglio di (product)

**outset** /ˈaʊtset/ n inizio m; **from the** ~ fin dall'inizio

**outside**[1] /ˈaʊtsaɪd/ a esterno ● n esterno m; **from the** ~ dall'esterno; **at the** ~ al massimo

**outside**[2] /aʊtˈsaɪd/ adv all'esterno, fuori; (out of doors) fuori; **go** ~ andare fuori ● prep fuori da; (in front of) davanti a

**outsider** /aʊtˈsaɪdə(r)/ n estraneo, -a mf

**outsize** /ˈaʊtsaɪz/ a smisurato; (clothes) per taglie forti

**outskirts** /ˈaʊtskɜːts/ npl sobborghi mpl

**outsmart** /aʊtˈsmɑːt/ vt essere più furbo di

**outspoken** /aʊtˈspəʊkn/ a schietto

**outspread** /ˈaʊtspred/ a (wings) spiegato; (arms, fingers) disteso

**outstanding** /aʊtˈstændɪŋ/ a eccezionale; (landmark) prominente; (not settled) in sospeso

**outstandingly** /aʊtˈstændɪŋlɪ/ adv eccezionalmente; ~ **good** eccezionale

**outstay** /aʊtˈsteɪ/ vt ~ **one's welcome** abusare dell'ospitalità di qcno

**outstretched** /ˈaʊtstretʃt/ a allungato

**outstrip** /aʊtˈstrɪp/ vt (pt/pp **-stripped**) superare

**out-tray** n vassoio m per corrispondenza e pratiche evase

**outvote** /aʊtˈvəʊt/ vt mettere in minoranza

**outward** /ˈaʊtwəd/ a esterno; (journey) di andata ● adv verso l'esterno

**outwardly** /ˈaʊtwədlɪ/ adv esternamente

**outwards** /ˈaʊtwədz/ adv verso l'esterno

**outweigh** /aʊtˈweɪ/ vt aver maggior peso di

**outwit** /aʊtˈwɪt/ vt (pt/pp **-witted**) battere in astuzia

**outworker** /ˈaʊtwɜːkə(r)/ n Br lavoratore, -trice mf a domicilio

**outworn** /aʊtˈwɔːn/ a (outmoded) sorpassato

**oval** /ˈəʊvl/ a ovale ● n ovale m

**ovary** /ˈəʊvərɪ/ n Anat ovaia f

**ovation** /əʊˈveɪʃn/ n ovazione f

**oven** /ˈʌvn/ n forno m

**oven: oven cleaner** n detergente m per il forno. **oven glove** n guanto m da forno. **ovenproof** a da forno. **oven-ready** a pronto da mettere in forno

**over** /'əʊvə(r)/ prep sopra: (across) al di là di; (during) durante; (more than) più di; ~ **the phone** al telefono; ~ **the page** alla pagina seguente; **all** ~ **Italy** in tutta (l')Italia; (travel) per l'Italia ● adv Math col resto di; (ended) finito; ~ **again** un'altra volta; ~ **and** ~ più volte; ~ **and above** oltre a; ~ **here/ there** qui/là; **all** ~ (everywhere) dappertutto; **it's all** ~ è tutto finito; **I ache all** ~ ho male dappertutto; **come/bring** ~ venire/portare; **turn** ~ girare

**over+** pref (too) troppo

**overact** /əʊvər'ækt/ vi strafare

**overactive** /əʊvər'æktɪv/ a (imagination) sbrigliato

**overall**[1] /'əʊvərɔ:l/ n grembiule m

**overall**[2] /əʊvər'ɔ:l/ a complessivo; (general) generale ● adv complessivamente

**overalls** /'əʊvərɔ:lz/ npl tuta fsg [da lavoro]

**overarm** /'əʊvərɑ:m/ a & adv (throw) col braccio al di sopra della spalla

**overawe** /əʊvər'ɔ:/ vt fig intimidire

**overbalance** /əʊvə'bæləns/ vi perdere l'equilibrio

**overbearing** /əʊvə'beərɪŋ/ a prepotente

**overblown** /əʊvə'bləʊn/ a (style) ampolloso

**overboard** /'əʊvəbɔ:d/ adv Naut in mare

**overbook** /əʊvə'bʊk/ vt accettare un numero di prenotazioni superiore ai posti disponibili

**overburden** /əʊvə'bɜ:dən/ vt sovraccaricare (**with** di)

**overcapacity** /əʊvəkə'pæsətɪ/ n eccesso m di capacità produttiva

**overcast** /'əʊvəkɑ:st/ a coperto

**overcharge** /əʊvə'tʃɑ:dʒ/ vt ~ **sb** far pagare più del dovuto a ● vi far pagare più del dovuto

**overcoat** /'əʊvəkəʊt/ n cappotto m

**overcome** /əʊvə'kʌm/ vt (pt -came, pp -come) vincere; **be** ~ **by** essere sopraffatto da

**overcompensate** /əʊvə'kɒmpənseɪt/ vi compensare eccessivamente

**overconfident** /əʊvə'kɒnfɪdənt/ a troppo sicuro di sé

**overcook** /əʊvə'kʊk/ vt cuocere troppo

**overcrowded** /əʊvə'kraʊdɪd/ a sovraffollato

**overcrowding** /əʊvə'kraʊdɪŋ/ n (in transport) calca f; (in city, institution) sovraffollamento m

**overdo** /əʊvə'du:/ vt (pt -did, pp -done) esagerare; (cook too long) stracuocere; ~ **it** (fam: do too much) strafare

**overdose** /'əʊvədəʊs/ n overdose f inv

**overdraft** /'əʊvədrɑ:ft/ n scoperto m; **have an** ~ avere il conto scoperto

**overdraw** /əʊvə'drɔ:/ vt (pt -drew, pp -drawn) ~ **one's account** andare allo scoperto; **be** ~**n by...** (account:) essere scoperto di...

**overdressed** /əʊvə'drest/ a troppo elegante

**overdrive** /'əʊvədraɪv/ n Auto overdrive m inv

**overdue** /əʊvə'dju:/ a in ritardo

**overeat** /əʊvər'i:t/ vi mangiare troppo

**overemphasize** /əʊvər'emfəsaɪz/ vt esagerare (importance); dare troppo rilievo a (aspect, fact)

**overenthusiastic** /əʊvərɪnθju:zɪ'æstɪk/ a troppo entusiasta

**overestimate** /əʊvər'estɪmeɪt/ vt sopravvalutare

**overexcited** /əʊvərɪk'saɪtɪd/ a sovreccitato; **get** ~ sovreccitarsi

**overexert** /əʊvərɪg'zɜ:t/ vt ~ **oneself** sovraffaticarsi

**overexposure** /əʊvərek'spəʊʒə(r)/ n Phot sovresposizione f; (in the media) attenzione f eccessiva da parte dei media

**overfeed** /əʊvə'fi:d/ vt sovralimentare (child, pet); concimare troppo (plant)

**overflow**[1] /'əʊvəfləʊ/ n (water) acqua f che deborda; (people) pubblico m in eccesso; (outlet) scarico m

**overflow**[2] /əʊvə'fləʊ/ vi debordare

**overgenerous** /əʊvə'dʒenərəs/ a (amount) troppo generoso

**overgrown** /əʊvə'grəʊn/ a (garden) coperto di erbacce

**overhang**[1] /'əʊvəhæŋ/ n sporgenza f

**overhang**[2] /əʊvə'hæŋ/ v (pt/pp -hung) ● vi sporgere ● vt sovrastare

**overhanging** /əʊvə'hæŋɪŋ/ a (ledge, cliff) sporgente

**overhaul**[1] /'əʊvəhɔ:l/ n revisione f

**overhaul**[2] /əʊvə'hɔ:l/ vt Techn revisionare

**overhead**[1] /əʊvə'hed/ adv in alto

**overhead**[2] /'əʊvəhed/ a aereo; (railway) sopraelevato; (lights) da soffitto ● npl ~**s** spese fpl generali

**overhead: overhead light** n lampada f da soffitto. **overhead locker** n Aeron armadietto m [per il bagaglio a mano]. **overhead projector** n lavagna f luminosa

**overhear** /əʊvə'hɪə(r)/ vt (pt/pp -heard) sentire per caso (conversation); **I** ~**d him saying it** l'ho sentito per caso mentre lo diceva

**overheat** /əʊvə'hi:t/ vi Auto surriscaldarsi ● vt surriscaldare

**over-indulge** vi eccedere ● vt viziare (child)

**over-indulgence** n (excess) eccesso m; (laxity towards) indulgenza f eccessiva

**overjoyed** /əʊvə'dʒɔɪd/ a felicissimo

**overkill** /'əʊvəkɪl/ n (exaggerated treatment) esagerazione f

**overland** /'əʊvəlænd/ a & adv via terra; ~ **route** via f terrestre

**overlap** /əʊvə'læp/ v (pt/pp -lapped) ● vi sovrapporsi ● vt sovrapporre

**overlay** /əʊvə'leɪ/ vt ricoprire

**overleaf** /əʊvə'li:f/ adv sul retro

**overload**[1] /əʊvə'ləʊd/ vt sovraccaricare

**overload**[2] /'əʊvələʊd/ n Electr sovratensioni pl

**overlook** /əʊvə'lʊk/ vt dominare; (fail to see, ignore) lasciarsi sfuggire

**overly** /'əʊvəlɪ/ adv eccessivamente

**overmanned** /əʊvə'mænd/ a con un'eccedenza di personale

**overmanning** /əʊvə'mænɪŋ/ n eccesso m di personale

**overmuch** /əʊvə'mʌtʃ/ adv troppo

**overnight**[1] /əʊvə'naɪt/ adv per la notte; **stay** ~ fermarsi a dormire

**overnight**[2] /'əʊvənaɪt/ a notturno

**overnight bag** n piccola borsa f da viaggio

**overnight stay** n sosta f per la notte

**overpass** /'əʊvəpɑːs/ n cavalcavia m inv

**overpay** /əʊvə'peɪ/ vt (pt/pp **-paid**) strapagare

**overplay** /əʊvə'pleɪ/ vt (exaggerate) esagerare

**overpopulated** /əʊvə'pɒpjʊleɪtɪd/ a sovrappopolato

**overpower** /əʊvə'paʊə(r)/ vt sopraffare

**overpowering** /əʊvə'paʊərɪŋ/ a insostenibile

**overpriced** /əʊvə'praɪst/ a troppo caro

**overproduce** /əʊvəprə'djuːs/ vt produrre in eccesso

**overqualified** /əʊvə'kwɒlɪfaɪd/ a troppo qualificato

**overrate** /əʊvə'reɪt/ vt sopravvalutare

**overrated** /əʊvə'reɪtɪd/ a sopravvalutato

**overreach** /əʊvə'riːtʃ/ vt ~ **oneself** puntare troppo in alto

**overreact** /əʊvərɪ'ækt/ vi avere una reazione eccessiva

**overreaction** /əʊvərɪ'ækʃn/ n reazione f eccessiva

**override** /əʊvə'raɪd/ vt (pt **-rode**, pp **-ridden**) passare sopra a

**overriding** /əʊvə'raɪdɪŋ/ a prevalente

**overrule** /əʊvə'ruːl/ vt annullare (decision); **we were ~d by the chairman** il direttore ha prevalso su di noi

**overrun** /əʊvə'rʌn/ vt (pt **-ran**, pp **-run**, pres p **-running**) invadere; oltrepassare (time); **be** ~ **with** essere invaso da

**overseas**[1] /əʊvə'siːz/ adv oltremare

**overseas**[2] /'əʊvəsiːz/ a d'oltremare

**oversee** /əʊvə'siː/ vt (pt **-saw**, pp **-seen**) sorvegliare

**oversell** /əʊvə'sel/ vt lodare esageratamente (idea, plan)

**oversensitive** /əʊvə'sensɪtɪv/ a (person) ipersensibile

**oversexed** /əʊvə'sekst/ a fam be ~ essere un maniaco/una maniaca del sesso

**overshadow** /əʊvə'ʃædəʊ/ vt adombrare

**overshoot** /əʊvə'ʃuːt/ vt (pt/pp **-shot**) oltrepassare

**oversight** /'əʊvəsaɪt/ n disattenzione f; **an** ~ una svista

**oversimplification** /əʊvəsɪmplɪfɪ'keɪʃn/ n semplificazione f eccessiva

**oversimplified** /əʊvə'sɪmplɪfaɪd/ a semplicistico

**oversimplify** /əʊvə'sɪmplɪfaɪ/ vt semplificare eccessivamente

**oversize[d]** /əʊvə'saɪz[d]/ a più grande del normale

**oversleep** /əʊvə'sliːp/ vi (pt/pp **-slept**) svegliarsi troppo tardi

**overspend** /əʊvə'spend/ vi spendere troppo

**overspending** /əʊvə'spendɪŋ/ n spese fpl eccessive; Fin spese fpl superiori al bilancio di previsione

**overspill** /'əʊvəspɪl/ n (excess amount) eccedenza f ● attrib ~ **housing development** ≈ città f inv satellite; ~ **population** popolazione f in eccesso

**overstaffed** /əʊvə'stɑːft/ a **be** ~ avere personale in eccedenza

**overstaffing** /əʊvə'stɑːfɪŋ/ n eccedenza f di personale

**overstate** /əʊvə'steɪt/ vt esagerare; **its importance cannot be ~d** la sua importanza non sarà mai sottolineata a sufficienza; ~ **the case** esagerare le cose

**overstatement** /əʊvə'steɪtmənt/ n esagerazione f

**overstay** /əʊvə'steɪ/ vt ~ **one's time** trattenersi troppo a lungo; ~ **one's visa** trattenersi oltre la scadenza del visto

**overstep** /əʊvə'step/ vt (pt/pp **-stepped**) ~ **the mark** oltrepassare ogni limite

**overstretched** /əʊvə'stretʃt/ a (person) sovraccarico [di lavoro]; (budget, resources) sfruttato fino al limite

**oversubscribed** /əʊvəsəb'skraɪbd/ a (share issue) sottoscritto in eccesso; (offer, tickets) richiesto oltre la disponibilità

**overt** /əʊ'vɜːt/ a palese

**overtake** /əʊvə'teɪk/ vt/i (pt **-took**, pp **-taken**) sorpassare

**overtaking** /əʊvə'teɪkɪŋ/ n sorpasso m; **no** ~ divieto di sorpasso

**overtax** /əʊvə'tæks/ vt fig abusare di

**over-the-counter** a (medicines) venduto senza ricetta

**over-the-top** a fam esagerato; **go over the top** esagerare

**overthrow**[1] /'əʊvəθrəʊ/ n Pol rovesciamento m

**overthrow**[2] /əʊvə'θrəʊ/ vt (pt **-threw**, pp **-thrown**) Pol rovesciare

**overtime** /'əʊvətaɪm/ n lavoro straordinario m ● adv **work** ~ fare lo straordinario

**overtired** /əʊvə'taɪəd/ a sovraffaticato

**overtly** /əʊ'vɜːtlɪ/ adv apertamente

**overtone** /'əʊvətəʊn/ n fig sfumatura f

**overture** /'əʊvətjʊə(r)/ n Mus preludio m; ~s pl fig approccio msg; **make ~s to** mostrare un atteggiamento di apertura verso

**overturn** /əʊvə'tɜːn/ vt ribaltare ● vi ribaltarsi

**overvalue** /əʊvə'væljuː/ vt sopravvalutare (currency, property)

**overview** /'əʊvəvjuː/ n visione f d'insieme

**overweight** /əʊvə'weɪt/ a sovrappeso

**overwhelm** /əʊvə'welm/ vt sommergere (with di); (with emotion) confondere

**overwhelming** /əʊvə'welmɪŋ/ a travolgen-te; ‹victory, majority› schiacciante

**overwhelmingly** /əʊvə'welmɪŋlɪ/ adv ‹vote, accept, reject› con una maggioranza schiacciante; ‹generous› straordinariamente

**overwork** /əʊvə'wɜːk/ n lavoro m eccessivo ● vt far lavorare eccessivamente ● vi lavorare eccessivamente

**overwrite** /əʊvə'raɪt/ vt Comput registare sopra a

**overwrought** /əʊvə'rɔːt/ a in stato di agita-zione

**ovulation** /ɒvjʊ'leɪʃn/ n ovulazione f

**ow** /aʊ/ int ahi!

**owe** /əʊ/ vt also fig dovere ([to] sb a qcno): ~ sb sth dovere qcsa a qcno

**owing** /'əʊɪŋ/ a be ~ ‹money:› essere da pa-gare ● prep ~ to a causa di

**owl** /aʊl/ n gufo m

**own¹** /əʊn/ a proprio ● pron a car of my ~ una macchina per conto mio; **on one's ~** da solo; **hold one's ~ with** tener testa a; **get one's ~ back** fam prendersi una rivincita

**own²** vt possedere; ‹confess› ammettere; I don't ~ it non mi appartiene

■ **own up** vi confessare (**to sth** qcsa)

**owner** /'əʊnə(r)/ n proprietario, -a mf

**owner: owner-driver** n persona f che guida un'auto di sua proprietà. **owner-occupied** /-'ɒkjʊpaɪd/ a abitato dal proprietario. **owner-occupier** n persona f chi abita in una casa di sua proprietà

**ownership** /'əʊnəʃɪp/ n proprietà f

**ox** /ɒks/ n (pl **oxen**) bue m (pl buoi)

**Oxbridge** /'ɒksbrɪdʒ/ n le università di Oxford e Cambridge

**oxide** /'ɒksaɪd/ n ossido m

**oxidize** /'ɒksɪdaɪz/ vt ossidare ● vi ossidarsi

**oxygen** /'ɒksɪdʒən/ n ossigeno m

**oxygen mask** n maschera f a ossigeno

**oyster** /'ɔɪstə(r)/ n ostrica f

**oz** abbr (**ounce(s)**) oncia f

**ozone** /'əʊzəʊn/ n ozono m

**ozone: ozone depletion** n distruzione f dell'ozonosfera. **ozone-friendly** a che non danneggia l'ozono. **ozone layer** n fascia f d'ozono

# Pp

**p, P** /piː/ n (letter) p, P f inv; Br abbr **penny, pence**

**PA** abbr (**personal assistant**) segretario, -a mf personale; Am abbr (**Pennsylvania**) Pennsylvania f

**p.a.** abbr (**per annum**) all'anno

**pace** /peɪs/ n passo m; ‹speed› ritmo m; **keep ~ with** camminare di pari passo con ● vi ~ **up and down** camminare avanti e indietro

**pacemaker** /'peɪsmeɪkə(r)/ n Med pace-maker m inv; ‹runner› battistrada m inv

**pace-setter** n ‹athlete› battistrada m inv

**Pacific** /pə'sɪfɪk/ a & n the ~ [Ocean] l'oce-ano m Pacifico, il Pacifico

**pacifier** /'pæsɪfaɪə(r)/ n Am ciuccio m, succhiotto m

**pacifism** /'pæsɪfɪzm/ n pacifismo m

**pacifist** /'pæsɪfɪst/ n pacifista mf

**pacify** /'pæsɪfaɪ/ vt (pt/pp **-ied**) placare ‹person›; pacificare ‹country›

**pack** /pæk/ n ‹of cards› mazzo m; ‹of hounds› muta f; ‹of wolves, thieves› branco m; ‹of cigarettes etc› pacchetto m; **a ~ of lies** un mucchio di bugie ● vt impacchettare ‹article›; fare ‹suitcase›; mettere in valigia ‹swimsuit etc›; ‹press down› comprimere; ~**ed** ‹crowded› strapieno, pieno zeppo ● vi fare i bagagli; **send sb ~ing** fam mandare qcno a quel paese

■ **pack in** vt fam mollare ‹job›; ~ **it in!** ‹stop it› piantala!

■ **pack off** vt ‹send› spedire

■ **pack out** vt be ~**ed out** ‹cinema, shops:› essere strapieno, essere pieno zeppo

■ **pack up** vt impacchettare ● vi fam ‹machine:› guastarsi

**package** /'pækɪdʒ/ n pacco m ● vt impac-chettare

**package: package deal** n offerta f tutto compreso. **package holiday** n vacanza f or-ganizzata. **package tour** n viaggio m orga-nizzato

**packaging** /'pækɪdʒɪŋ/ n ‹materials› confe-zione f; ‹promotion: of product› presentazione f pubblicitaria

**packed lunch** /pækt/ n pranzo m al sacco

**packer** /'pækə(r)/ n ‹in factory› imballatore, -trice mf

**packet** /'pækɪt/ n pacchetto m; **cost a ~** fam costare un sacco

**pack ice** n banchisa f

**packing** /'pækɪŋ/ n imballaggio m

**pact** /pækt/ n patto m

**pad¹** /pæd/ n imbottitura f; ‹for writing› bloc-notes m inv, taccuino m; ‹fam: home› casa f ● vt (pt/pp **padded**) imbottire

**pad²** vi (pt/pp **padded**) camminare con passo felpato

■ **pad out** vt gonfiare

**padded** /'pædɪd/: **padded bra** n reggiseno m imbottito. **padded cell** n cella f con le pa-reti imbottite. **padded envelope** n busta f imbottita. **padded shoulders** npl spalline fpl imbottite

**padding** /'pædɪŋ/ n imbottitura f; (in written work) fronzoli mpl

**paddle** /'pædl/ n pagaia f; **go for a ~** sguazzare ● vt (row) spingere remando ● vi (wade) sguazzare

**paddling pool** n (public) piscina f per bambini; (inflatable) piscina f gonfiabile

**paddock** /'pædək/ n recinto m

**padlock** /'pædlɒk/ n lucchetto m ● vt chiudere con lucchetto

**padre** /'pɑːdreɪ/ n padre m

**Padua** /'pædjʊə/ n Padova f

**paediatric** /piːdɪˈætrɪk/ a pediatrico

**paediatrician** /piːdɪəˈtrɪʃn/ n pediatra mf

**paediatrics** /piːdɪˈætrɪks/ n pediatria f

**paedophile** /'piːdəʊfaɪl/ n pedofilo, -a mf

**paedophilia** /piːdəʊˈfɪlɪə/ n pedofilia f

**pagan** /'peɪgən/ a & n pagano, -a mf

**paganism** /'peɪgənɪzm/ n paganesimo m

**page²** /peɪdʒ/ n pagina f

**page²** n (boy) paggetto m; (in hotel) fattorino m ● vt far chiamare ⟨person⟩

**pageant** /'pædʒənt/ n parata f

**pageantry** /'pædʒəntrɪ/ n cerimoniale m

**page proof** n bozza f definitiva

**pager** /'peɪdʒə(r)/ n cercapersone m inv

**page three** n Br terza pagina f di quotidiano scandalistico inglese con una pin-up

**page three girl** n Br pin-up f inv

**paid** /peɪd/ see pay ● a ~ **employment** lavoro m remunerato; **put ~ to** mettere fine a

**paid-up** a Br ⟨member⟩ che ha pagato la sua quota; ⟨instalment⟩ versato

**pail** /peɪl/ n secchio m

**pain** /peɪn/ n dolore m; **be in ~** soffrire; **take ~s to do sth** fare il possibile per fare qcsa; **~ in the neck** fam rottura f di scatole; ⟨person⟩ rompiscatole mf inv ● vt fig addolorare

**pained** /peɪnd/ a addolorato

**painful** /'peɪnfʊl/ a doloroso; (laborious) penoso

**painfully** /'peɪnfʊlɪ/ adv ~ **shy** incredibilmente timido

**painkiller** /'peɪnkɪlə(r)/ n calmante m

**painkilling** /'peɪnkɪlɪŋ/ a antinevralgico

**painless** /'peɪnlɪs/ a indolore

**painlessly** /'peɪnlɪslɪ/ adv in modo indolore

**painstaking** /'peɪnzteɪkɪŋ/ a minuzioso

**paint** /peɪnt/ n pittura f; **~s** pl colori mpl ● vt/i pitturare; ⟨artist:⟩ dipingere; **~ the town red** folleggiare

■ **paint over** vt (cover with paint) coprire di vernice

**paintbox** /'peɪntbɒks/ n scatola f di colori

**paintbrush** /'peɪntbrʌʃ/ n pennello m

**painter** /'peɪntə(r)/ n pittore, -trice mf; (decorator) imbianchino m

**pain threshold** n soglia f del dolore

**painting** /'peɪntɪŋ/ n pittura f; (picture) dipinto m

**paint: paintpot** n latta f di pittura. **paint remover** n sverniciante m. **paint roller** n rullo m. **paint spray** n pistola f a spruzzo.

**paint stripper** n (tool) macchina f sverniciante; (chemical) sverniciante m. **paintwork** n pittura f

**pair** /peə(r)/ n paio m; (of people) coppia f; **a ~ of trousers/scissors** un paio di pantaloni/forbici

■ **pair off** vi mettersi in coppia

**pajamas** /pəˈdʒɑːməz/ npl Am pigiama msg

**Pakistan** /pɑːkɪˈstɑːn/ n Pakistan m

**Pakistani** /pɑːkɪˈstɑːnɪ/ a & n pakistano, -a mf

**pal** /pæl/ n fam amico, -a mf

■ **pal up** vi (fam: become friends) fare amicizia (with con)

**palace** /'pælɪs/ n palazzo m

**palaeontologist** /pælɪənˈtɒlədʒɪst/ n paleontologo, -a mf

**palaentology** /pælɪənˈtɒlədʒɪ/ n paleontologia f

**palatable** /'pælətəbl/ a gradevole al gusto

**palate** /'pælət/ n palato m

**palatial** /pəˈleɪʃl/ a sontuoso

**palaver** /pəˈlɑːvə(r)/ n (fam: fuss) storie fpl

**pale¹** /peɪl/ n (stake) palo m; **beyond the ~** fig inaccettabile

**pale²** a pallido ● vi impallidire; **~ into insignificance** diventare insignificante

**paleness** /'peɪlnɪs/ n pallore m

**Palestine** /'pælɪstaɪn/ n Palestina f

**Palestinian** /pæləˈstɪnɪən/ a & n palestinese mf

**palette** /'pælɪt/ n tavolozza f

**palette knife** n spatola f

**paling** /'peɪlɪŋ/ n (stake) palo m; (fence) palizzata f

**palisade** /pælɪˈseɪd/ n (fence) palizzata f

**pall** /pɔːl/ n drappo m funebre; fig velo m di tristezza; (of smoke) cappa f ● vi stufare

**pallet** /'pælɪt/ n pallet m inv

**palliative** /'pælɪətɪv/ n palliativo m

**pallid** /'pælɪd/ a pallido

**pallor** /'pælə(r)/ n pallore m

**palm** /pɑːm/ n palmo m; (tree) palma f

■ **palm off** vt **~ sth off on sb** rifilare qcsa a qcno

**palmist** /'pɑːmɪst/ n chiromante mf

**palmistry** /'pɑːmɪstrɪ/ n chiromanzia f

**Palm Sunday** n domenica f delle palme

**palpable** /'pælpəbl/ a palpabile; (perceptible) tangibile

**palpate** /pæl'peɪt/ vi palpare

**palpitate** /'pælpɪteɪt/ vi palpitare

**palpitations** /pælpɪ'teɪʃnz/ npl palpitazioni fpl

**paltry** /'pɔːltrɪ/ a (-ier, -iest) insignificante

**pampas** /'pæmpəs/ n pampas fpl

**pamper** /'pæmpə(r)/ vt viziare

**pamphlet** /'pæmflɪt/ n opuscolo m

**pan** /pæn/ n tegame m, pentola f; (for frying) padella f; (of scales) piatto m ● vt (pt/pp panned) (fam: criticize) stroncare

■ **pan out** vi (fam: develop) mettersi

**panacea** /pænə'siːə/ n panacea f

**panache** /pə'næʃ/ n stile m

**pancake** /'pænkeɪk/ n crêpe f inv, frittella f

**Pancake Day** *n* martedì *m inv* grasso

**pancreas** /'pæŋkrɪəs/ *n* pancreas *m inv*

**panda** /'pændə/ *n* panda *m inv*

**panda car** *n* macchina *f* della polizia

**pandemonium** /pændɪ'məʊnɪəm/ *n* pandemonio *m*

**pander** /'pændə(r)/ *vi* ~ **to sb** compiacere qcno

**p & p** *n abbr* (**postage and packing**) spese *fpl* di spedizione

**pane** /peɪn/ *n* ~ **[of glass]** vetro *m*

**panel** /'pænl/ *n* pannello *m*; (*group of people*) giuria *f*; ~ **of experts** gruppo *m* di esperti; ~ **of judges** giuria *f*

**panelling** /'pænəlɪŋ/ *n* pannelli *mpl*

**panellist** /'pænəlɪst/ *n* Radio, TV partecipante *mf*

**pan-fry** *vt* friggere

**pang** /pæŋ/ *n* ~**s of hunger** morsi *mpl* della fame; ~**s of conscience** rimorsi *mpl* di coscienza

**panic** /'pænɪk/ *n* panico *m* ● *vi* (*pt/pp* **panicked**) lasciarsi prendere dal panico

**panic: panic button** *n fam* **hit the** ~ ~ farsi prendere dal panico. **panic buying** *n* accaparramento *m*. **panic-stricken** /'pænɪkstrɪkən/ *a* in preda al panico

**panicky** /'pænɪkɪ/ *a* che si lascia prendere dal panico facilmente

**pannier** /'pænɪə(r)/ *n* (*on bike*) borsa *f*; (*on mule*) bisaccia *f*

**panorama** /pænə'rɑ:mə/ *n* panorama *m*

**panoramic** /pænə'ræmɪk/ *a* panoramico

**pan scourer** *n* paglietta *f*

**pansy** /'pænzɪ/ *n* viola *f* del pensiero; (*fam: effeminate man*) finocchio *m*

**pant** /pænt/ *vi* ansimare

**pantechnicon** /pæn'teknɪkən/ *n* furgone *m* per traslochi

**panther** /'pænθə(r)/ *n* pantera *f*

**panties** /'pæntɪz/ *npl* mutandine *fpl*

**panting** /'pæntɪŋ/ *a* ansante

**pantomime** /'pæntəmaɪm/ *n* pantomima *f*

**pantry** /'pæntrɪ/ *n* dispensa *f*

**pants** /pænts/ *npl* (*underwear*) mutande *fpl*; (*woman's*) mutandine *fpl*; (*trousers*) pantaloni *mpl*

**panty** /'pæntɪ/: **panty girdle** *n* guaina *f*. **pantyhose** *n Am* collant *m inv*. **panty-liner** *n* salvaslip *m inv*

**paparazzi** /pæpə'rætzɪ/ *npl* paparazzi *mpl*

**papal** /'peɪpl/ *a* papale

**paper** /'peɪpə(r)/ *n* carta *f*; (*wallpaper*) carta *f* da parati; (*newspaper*) giornale *m*; (*exam*) esame *m* scritto; (*treatise*) saggio *m*; ~**s** *pl* (*documents*) documenti *mpl*; (*for identification*) documento *msg* [d'identità]; **on** ~ in teoria; **put down on** ~ mettere per iscritto ● *attrib* di carta; (*version*) su carta ● *vt* tappezzare

■ **paper over** *vt* ~ **over the cracks** dissimulare le divergenze

**paper: paperback** *n* edizione *f* economica. **paper bank** *n* cassonetto *m* per la raccolta della carta. **paper boy** *n* ragazzo *m* che reca-

pita i giornali a domicilio. **paper chain** *n* festone *m* di carta. **paper chase** *n corsa f* campestre in cui i partecipanti seguono una scia di pezzetti di carta. **paper clip** *n* graffetta *f*. **paper currency** *n* banconote *fpl*. **paper feed tray** *n* Comput vassoio *m* della carta. **paperknife** *n* tagliacarte *m inv*. **paper mill** *n* cartiera *f*. **paper money** *n* cartamoneta *f*. **paper napkin** *n* tovagliolo *m* di carta. **paper round** *n* **he does a** ~ ~ recapita i giornali a domicilio. **paper shredder** *n* distruttore *m* di documenti. **paper-thin** *a* sottilissimo. **paper towel** *n* (*toilet*) asciugamano *m* di carta; (*kitchen*) carta *f* asciugatutto. **paperweight** *n* fermacarte *m inv*. **paperwork** *n* lavoro *m* d'ufficio

**papery** /'peɪpərɪ/ *a* (*texture, leaves*) cartaceo

**paprika** /pə'pri:kə/ *n* paprica *f*

**par** /pɑ:(r)/ *n* (*in golf*) par *m inv*; **on a** ~ **with** alla pari con; **feel below** ~ essere un po' giù di tono

**para¹** /'pærə/ *n* (*paragraph*) paragrafo *m*

**para²** *n Br Mil* parà *m inv*

**parable** /'pærəbl/ *n* parabola *f*

**parachute** /'pærəʃu:t/ *n* paracadute *m inv* ● *vi* lanciarsi col paracadute

**parachutist** /'pærəʃu:tɪst/ *n* paracadutista *mf*

**parade** /pə'reɪd/ *n* (*military*) parata *f* militare; (*display*) sfoggio *m* ● *vi* sfilare ● *vt* (*show off*) far sfoggio di

**parade ground** *n* piazza *f* d'armi

**paradigm** /'pærədaɪm/ *n* paradigma *m*

**paradise** /'pærədaɪs/ *n* paradiso *m*

**paradox** /'pærədɒks/ *n* paradosso *m*

**paradoxical** /pærə'dɒksɪkl/ *a* paradossale

**paradoxically** /pærə'dɒksɪklɪ/ *adv* paradossalmente

**paraffin** /'pærəfɪn/ *n* paraffina *f*; (*oil*) cherosene *m*

**paragliding** /'pærəglaɪdɪŋ/ *n* parapendio *m*

**paragon** /'pærəgən/ *n* ~ **of virtue** modello *m* di virtù

**paragraph** /'pærəgrɑ:f/ *n* paragrafo *m*

**parallel** /'pærəlel/ *a* & *adv* parallelo ● *n* Geog, fig parallelo *m*; (*line*) parallela *f* ● *vt* essere paragonabile a

**parallel bars** *npl* parallele *fpl*

**parallelogram** /pærə'leləʊgræm/ *n* Math parallelogramma *m*

**parallel port** *n* Comput porta *f* parallela

**paralyse** /'pærəlaɪz/ *vt* paralizzare

**paralysis** /pə'ræləsɪs/ *n* (*pl* **-ses**) /pə'ræləsi:z/ paralisi *f inv*

**paralytic** /pærə'lɪtɪk/ *a* (*person*) paralitico; (*arm, leg*) paralizzato; (*Br fam: drunk*) ubriaco fradicio

**paramedic** /pærə'medɪk/ *n* paramedico *m*

**parameter** /pə'ræmɪtə(r)/ *n* parametro *m*

**paramilitary** /pærə'mɪlɪtrɪ/ *n* appartenente *mf* a un gruppo paramilitare ● *a* paramilitare

**paramount** /'pærəmaʊnt/ *a* supremo; **be** ~ essere essenziale

**paranoia** /pærə'nɔɪə/ *n* paranoia *f*

**paranoid** /'pærənɔɪd/ *a* paranoico

**paranormal** /ˌpærəˈnɔːməl/ a & n paranormale m

**parapet** /ˈpærəpɪt/ n parapetto m

**paraphernalia** /ˌpærəfəˈneɪlɪə/ n armamentario m

**paraphrase** /ˈpærəfreɪz/ n parafrasi f inv ● vt parafrasare

**paraplegic** /ˌpærəˈpliːdʒɪk/ a & n paraplegico, -a mf

**parascending** /ˈpærəsendɪŋ/ n Br paracadutismo m ascensionale

**parasite** /ˈpærəsaɪt/ n parassita mf

**parasitic** /ˌpærəˈsɪtɪk/ a parassitario

**parasol** /ˈpærəsɒl/ n parasole m

**paratrooper** /ˈpærətruːpə(r)/ n paracadutista m

**parboil** /ˈpɑːbɔɪl/ vt scottare

**parcel** /ˈpɑːsl/ n pacco m
■ **parcel up** vt impacchettare ‹clothes etc›

**parch** /pɑːtʃ/ vt disseccare; **be ~ed** ‹person.› morire dalla sete

**parchment** /ˈpɑːtʃmənt/ n pergamena f

**pardon** /ˈpɑːdn/ n perdono m; Jur grazia f; **~?** prego?; **I beg your ~?** fml chiedo scusa?; **I do beg your ~** (sorry) chiedo scusa! ● vt perdonare; Jur graziare

**pare** /peə(r)/ vt (peel) pelare

**parent** /ˈpeərənt/ n genitore m

**parentage** /ˈpeərəntɪdʒ/ n natali mpl

**parental** /pəˈrentl/ a dei genitori

**parent company** n casa f madre

**parenthesis** /pəˈrenθəsɪs/ n (pl -ses /pəˈrenθəsiːz/) parentesi f inv

**parer** /ˈpeərə(r)/ n sbucciatore m

**pariah** /pəˈraɪə/ n paria m

**parings** /ˈpeərɪŋz/ npl (of fruit) bucce fpl; (of nails) ritagli mpl di unghie

**Paris** /ˈpærɪs/ n Parigi f

**parish** /ˈpærɪʃ/ n parrocchia f

**parishioner** /pəˈrɪʃənə(r)/ n parrocchiano, -a mf

**parish priest** n (Catholic) parroco m; (Protestant) pastore m

**Parisian** /pəˈrɪzɪən/ a & n parigino, -a mf

**parity** /ˈpærətɪ/ n parità f

**park** /pɑːk/ n parco m ● vt Auto posteggiare, parcheggiare; **~ oneself** fam installarsi ● vi posteggiare, parcheggiare

**parka** /ˈpɑːkə/ n parka m inv

**park-and-ride** n parcheggio m collegato al centro di una città da mezzi pubblici

**parking** /ˈpɑːkɪŋ/ n parcheggio m, posteggio m; **'no ~'** 'divieto di sosta'

**parking: parking attendant** n parcheggiatore, -trice mf, posteggiatore, -trice mf. **parking lot** n Am posteggio m, parcheggio m. **parking meter** n parchimetro m. **parking space** n posteggio m, parcheggio m

**park: parkland** n parco m. **park ranger, park warden** n guardaparco m inv

**parliament** /ˈpɑːləmənt/ n parlamento m

**parliamentary** /ˌpɑːləˈmentərɪ/ a parlamentare

**parlour** /ˈpɑːlə(r)/ n salotto m

**parochial** /pəˈrəʊkɪəl/ a parrocchiale; fig ristretto

**parochialism** /pəˈrəʊkɪəlɪzm/ n campanilismo m

**parody** /ˈpærədɪ/ n parodia f ● vt (pt/pp -ied) parodiare

**parole** /pəˈrəʊl/ n **on ~** sulla parola; **eligible for ~** suscettibile di essere liberato sulla parola ● vt mettere in libertà sulla parola

**paroxysm** /ˈpærəksɪzm/ n accesso m

**parquet floor** /ˈpɑːkeɪ/ n parquet m

**parquet flooring** /ˈflɔːrɪŋ/ n parquet m inv

**parrot** /ˈpærət/ n pappagallo m

**parry** /ˈpærɪ/ vt (pt/pp -ied) parare ‹blow›; (in fencing) eludere

**parse** /pɑːz/ vt fare l'analisi grammaticale di ‹sentence›; Comput analizzare la sintassi di

**parsimonious** /ˌpɑːsɪˈməʊnɪəs/ a parsimonioso

**parsing** /ˈpɑːzɪŋ/ n analisi f grammaticale; Comput analisi f sintattica

**parsley** /ˈpɑːslɪ/ n prezzemolo m

**parsnip** /ˈpɑːsnɪp/ n pastinaca f

**parson** /ˈpɑːsn/ n pastore m

**part** /pɑːt/ n parte f; (of machine) pezzo m; **for my ~** per quanto mi riguarda; **on the ~ of** da parte di; **take sb's ~** prendere le parti di qcno; **take ~ in** prendere parte a ● adv in parte ● vt ~ **one's hair** farsi la riga ● vi ‹people.› separarsi; **~ with** separarsi da

**part exchange** n **take in ~ ~** prendere indietro come pagamento parziale

**partial** /ˈpɑːʃl/ a parziale; **be ~ to** aver un debole per

**partiality** /ˌpɑːʃɪˈælətɪ/ n (liking) predilezione f

**partially** /ˈpɑːʃəlɪ/ adv parzialmente; **~-sighted** parzialmente cieco

**participant** /pɑːˈtɪsɪpənt/ n partecipante mf

**participate** /pɑːˈtɪsɪpeɪt/ vi partecipare (**in** a)

**participation** /pɑːˌtɪsɪˈpeɪʃn/ n partecipazione f

**participatory** /pɑːˌtɪsɪˈpeɪtərɪ/ a partecipativo

**participle** /ˈpɑːtɪsɪpl/ n participio m; **present/past ~** participio presente/passato

**particle** /ˈpɑːtɪkl/ n Phys, Gram particella f

**particular** /pəˈtɪkjʊlə(r)/ a particolare; (precise) meticoloso; pej difficile; **in ~** in particolare

**particularly** /pəˈtɪkjʊləlɪ/ adv particolarmente

**particulars** /pəˈtɪkjʊləz/ npl particolari mpl

**parting** /ˈpɑːtɪŋ/ n separazione f; (in hair) scriminatura f ● attrib di commiato

**partisan** /ˌpɑːtɪˈzæn/ n partigiano, -a mf

**partition** /pɑːˈtɪʃn/ n (wall) parete f divisoria; Pol divisione f ● vt dividere
■ **partition off** vt separare

**partly** /ˈpɑːtlɪ/ adv in parte

**partner** /ˈpɑːtnə(r)/ n Comm socio, -a mf; (sport, in relationship) compagno, -a mf

**partnership** /'pɑːtnəʃɪp/ *n Comm* società *f inv*

**part: part of speech** *n* categoria *f* grammaticale. **part owner** *n* comproprietario, -a *mf*. **part payment** *n* acconto *m*

**partridge** /'pɑːtrɪdʒ/ *n* pernice *f*

**part-time** *a & adv* part time; **be** *or* **work ~** lavorare part time

**part-way** *adv* **~ through the evening** a metà serata

**party** /'pɑːtɪ/ *n* ricevimento *m*, festa *f*; (*group*) gruppo *m*; *Pol* partito *m*; *Jur* parte *f*: **be ~ to** essere parte attiva in

**party: party dress** *n* abito *m* da sera. **party-goer** *n* festaiolo, -a *mf*. **party hat** *n* cappellino *m* di carta. **party leader** *n* dirigente *m* di partito. **party line** *n Teleph* duplex *m inv*; *Pol* linea *f* del partito. **party piece** *n* pezzo *m* forte; **do one's ~** esibirsi nel proprio pezzo forte. **party political broadcast** *n* comunicato *m* di partito (*trasmesso per radio o per televisione*). **party politics** *n* politica *f* di partito. **party wall** *n* muro *m* divisorio

**pass** /pɑːs/ *n* lasciapassare *m inv*; (*in mountains*) passo *m*; *Sport* passaggio *m*; (*Sch: mark*) [voto *m*] sufficiente *m*; **get a ~** *Sch* ottenere la sufficienza; **make a ~ at** *fam* fare delle avances a ● *vt* passare; (*overtake*) sorpassare; (*approve*) far passare; (*exceed*) oltrepassare;   fare   ⟨*remark*⟩;   esprimere ⟨*judgement*⟩; *Jur* pronunciare ⟨*sentence*⟩; **~ water** orinare; **~ the time** passare il tempo ● *vi* passare; (*in exam*) essere promosso; **let sth ~** *fig* lasciar correre qcsa; **~!** (*in game*) passo!

■ **pass as** *vt* = pass for
■ **pass away** *vi* mancare
■ **pass by** *vi* (*go past*) passare
■ **pass down** *vt* passare; *fig* trasmettere
■ **pass for** *vt* (*be accepted as*) passare per
■ **pass off** *vi* (*disappear*) passare; (*take place*) svolgersi ● *vt* **~ sb/sth off as** far passare qcno/qcsa per
■ **pass on** *vt* passare ⟨*message, information*⟩
■ **pass on to** *vt* passare a ⟨*new subject, next question*⟩
■ **pass out** *vi fam* svenire
■ **pass over** *vt* (*not mention*) passare sopra a; **~ sb over for promotion** non prendere in considerazione qcno per una promozione ● *vi* (*die*) spirare
■ **pass round** *vt* far passare
■ **pass through** *vt* attraversare
■ **pass up** *vt* passare; (*fam: miss*) lasciarsi scappare

**passable** /'pɑːsəbl/ *a* ⟨*road*⟩ praticabile; (*satisfactory*) passabile

**passage** /'pæsɪdʒ/ *n* passaggio *m*; (*corridor*) corridoio *m*; (*voyage*) traversata *f*

**pass book** *n Fin* libretto *m* di risparmio

**passé** /'pæseɪ/ *a pej* sorpassato

**passenger** /'pæsɪndʒə(r)/ *n* passeggero, -a *mf*

**passenger: passenger compartment** *n Br Auto* abitacolo *m*. **passenger ferry** *n* tra-

ghetto *m*. **passenger plane** *n* aereo *m* passeggeri. **passenger seat** *n* posto *m* accanto al guidatore. **passenger train** *n* treno *m* passeggeri

**passepartout** /pæspɑː'tuː/ *n* (*key, frame*) passe-partout *m inv*

**passer-by** /pɑːsə'baɪ/ *n* (*pl* **-s-by**) passante *mf*

**passing place** /'pɑːsɪŋ/ *n* piazzola *f* di sosta per consentire il transito dei veicoli nei due sensi

**passing shot** *n Tennis* passante *m*

**passion** /'pæʃn/ *n* passione *f*

**passionate** /'pæʃənət/ *a* appassionato

**passionately** /'pæʃənətlɪ/ *adv* appassionatamente

**passion fruit** *n* frutto *m* della passione

**passive** /'pæsɪv/ *a & n* passivo *m*

**passively** /'pæsɪvlɪ/ *adv* passivamente

**passiveness** /'pæsɪvnɪs/ *n* passività *f*

**passive resistance** *n* resistenza *f* passiva

**passive smoking** *n* fumo *m* passivo

**pass: pass-key** *n* (*master-key*) passe-partout *m inv*; (*for access*) chiave *f*. **pass-mark** *n Sch* [voto *m*] sufficiente *m*. **Passover** *n* Pasqua *f* ebraica. **passport** *n* passaporto *m*. **password** *n* parola *f* d'ordine

**past** /pɑːst/ *a* passato; (*former*) ex; **that's all ~** tutto questo è passato; **in the ~ few days** nei giorni scorsi; **the ~ week** la settimana scorsa ● *n* passato *m* ● *prep* oltre; **at ten ~ two** alle due e dieci ● *adv* oltre; **go/come ~** passare

**pasta** /'pæstə/ *n* pasta[sciutta] *f*

**paste** /peɪst/ *n* pasta *f*; (*dough*) impasto *m*; (*adhesive*) colla *f* ● *vt* incollare
■ **paste down** *vt* incollare
■ **paste in** *vt* incollare
■ **paste up** *vt* affiggere ⟨*notice, poster*⟩

**paste jewellery** *n* bigiotteria *f*

**pastel** /'pæstl/ *n* pastello *m* ● *attrib* pastello

**pasteurization** /pɑːstʃərar'zeɪʃn/ *n* pastorizzazione *f*

**pasteurize** /'pɑːstʃəraɪz/ *vt* pastorizzare

**pasteurized** /'pɑːstʃəraɪzd/ *a* pastorizzato

**pastille** /'pæstɪl/ *n* pastiglia *f*

**pastime** /'pɑːstaɪm/ *n* passatempo *m*

**pasting** /'peɪstɪŋ/ *n* (*fam: defeat, criticism*) batosta *f*

**past master** *n* esperto, -a *mf*

**pastor** /'pɑːstə(r)/ *n* pastore *m*

**pastoral** /'pɑːstərəl/ *a* pastorale

**past participle** *n* participio *m* passato

**pastrami** /pæ'strɑːmɪ/ *n* carne *f* di manzo affumicata

**pastry** /'peɪstrɪ/ *n* pasta *f*; **pastries** *pl* pasticcini *mpl*

**past tense** *n* passato *m*

**pasture** /'pɑːstʃə(r)/ *n* pascolo *m*

**pasty**[1] /'pæstɪ/ *n* ≈ pasticcio *m*

**pasty**[2] /'peɪstɪ/ *a* smorto

**pat** /pæt/ *n* buffetto *m*; (*of butter*) pezzetto *m* ● *adv* **have sth off ~** conoscere qcsa a menadito ● *vt* (*pt/pp* **patted**) dare un buffetto a; **~ sb on the back** *fig* congratularsi con qcno

**patch** /pætʃ/ *n* toppa *f*; (*spot*) chiazza *f*; (*period*) periodo *m*; **not a ~ on** *fam* molto inferiore a ● *vt* mettere una toppa su

■ **patch up** *vt* riparare alla bell'e meglio; appianare ⟨*quarrel*⟩

**patchwork** /ˈpætʃwɜːk/ *n* patchwork *m inv*; *fig* mosaico *m*

**patchy** /ˈpætʃɪ/ *a* incostante

**pâté** /ˈpæteɪ/ *n* pâté *m inv*

**patent** /ˈpeɪtnt/ *a* palese ● *n* brevetto *m* ● *vt* brevettare

**patent leather** *n* vernice *m*

**patently** /ˈpeɪtntlɪ/ *adv* in modo palese

**paternal** /pəˈtɜːnl/ *a* paterno

**paternalism** /pəˈtɜːnəlɪzm/ *n* paternalismo *m*

**paternalistic** /pətɜːnəˈlɪstɪk/ *a* paternalistico

**paternity** /pəˈtɜːnətɪ/ *n* paternità *f*

**paternity leave** *n* congedo *m* di paternità

**paternity suit** *n* causa *f* per il riconoscimento di paternità

**path** /pɑːθ/ *n* (*pl* ~**s** /pɑːðz/) sentiero *m*; (*orbit*) traiettoria *f*; *fig* strada *f*

**pathetic** /pəˈθetɪk/ *a* patetico; (*fam: very bad*) penoso

**pathological** /pæθəˈlɒdʒɪkl/ *a* patologico

**pathologist** /pəˈθɒlədʒɪst/ *n* patologo, -a *mf*

**pathology** /pəˈθɒlədʒɪ/ *n* patologia *f*

**pathos** /ˈpeɪθɒs/ *n* pathos *m*

**patience** /ˈpeɪʃns/ *n* pazienza *f*; (*game*) solitario *m*

**patient** /ˈpeɪʃnt/ *a* & *n* paziente *mf*

**patiently** /ˈpeɪʃntlɪ/ *adv* pazientemente

**patio** /ˈpætɪəʊ/ *n* terrazza *f*

**patio doors** *npl* portafinestra *f*

**patio garden** *n* cortile *m*

**patriarch** /ˈpeɪtrɪɑːk/ *n* patriarca *m*

**patriarchal** /peɪtrɪˈɑːkəl/ *a* patriarcale

**patriarchy** /ˈpeɪtrɪɑːkɪ/ *n* patriarcato *m*

**patriot** /ˈpætrɪət/ *n* patriota *mf*

**patriotic** /pætrɪˈɒtɪk/ *a* patriottico

**patriotism** /ˈpætrɪətɪzm/ *n* patriottismo *m*

**patrol** /pəˈtrəʊl/ *n* pattuglia *f* ● *vt/i* pattugliare

**patrol car** *n* autopattuglia *f*

**patron** /ˈpeɪtrən/ *n* patrono *m*; (*of charity*) benefattore, -trice *mf*; (*of the arts*) mecenate *mf*; (*customer*) cliente *mf*

**patronage** /ˈpætrənɪdʒ/ *n* patrocinio *m*; (*of shop etc*) frequentazione *f*

**patronize** /ˈpætrənaɪz/ *vt* frequentare abitualmente; *fig* trattare con condiscendenza

**patronizing** /ˈpætrənaɪzɪŋ/ *a* condiscendente

**patronizingly** /ˈpætrənaɪzɪŋlɪ/ *adv* con condiscendenza

**patron saint** *n* [santo, -a *mf*] patrono, -a *mf*

**patter**[1] /ˈpætə(r)/ *n* picchiettio *m* ● *vi* picchiettare

**patter**[2] *n* (*of salesman*) chiacchiere *fpl*

**pattern** /ˈpætn/ *n* motivo *m*; (*for knitting, sewing, in behaviour*) modello *m*

**patterned** /ˈpætənd/ *a* ⟨*material*⟩ fantasia

**paunch** /pɔːntʃ/ *n* pancia *f*

**pauper** /ˈpɔːpə(r)/ *n* povero, -a *mf*

**pause** /pɔːz/ *n* pausa *f* ● *vi* fare una pausa

**pave** /peɪv/ *vt* pavimentare; ~ **the way** preparare la strada (**for** a)

**pavement** /ˈpeɪvmənt/ *n* marciapiede *m*

**pavilion** /pəˈvɪljən/ *n* padiglione *m*; (*Cricket*) costruzione *f* annessa al campo da gioco con gli spogliatoi

**paving** /ˈpeɪvɪŋ/ *n* lastricato *m*

**paving slab, paving stone** *n* lastra *f* di pietra

**paw** /pɔː/ *n* zampa *f* ● *vt fam* mettere le zampe addosso a

**pawn**[1] /pɔːn/ *n* (*in chess*) pedone *m*; *fig* pedina *f*

**pawn**[2] *vt* impegnare ● *n* **in ~** in pegno

**pawnbroker** /ˈpɔːnbrəʊkə(r)/ *n* prestatore, -trice *mf* su pegno

**pawnshop** /ˈpɔːnʃɒp/ *n* monte *m* di pietà

**pawpaw** /ˈpɔːpɔː/ *n* papaia *f*

**pay** /peɪ/ *n* paga *f*; **in the ~ of** al soldo di ● *v* (*pt/pp paid*) ● *vt* pagare; prestare ⟨*attention*⟩; fare ⟨*compliment, visit*⟩; ~ **cash** pagare in contanti ● *vi* pagare; (*be profitable*) rendere; **it doesn't ~ to...** *fig* è fatica sprecata...; ~ **in instalments** pagare a rate; ~ **through the nose** *fam* pagare profumatamente

■ **pay back** *vt* ripagare

■ **pay for** *vt* pagare per

■ **pay in** *vt* versare

■ **pay off** *vt* saldare ⟨*debt*⟩ ● *vi fig* dare dei frutti

■ **pay out** *vt* (*spend*) pagare

■ **pay up** *vi* pagare

**payable** /ˈpeɪəbl/ *a* pagabile; **make ~ to** intestare a

**PAYE** *Br abbr* (**pay-as-you-earn**) trattenute *fpl* fiscali alla fonte

**payee** /peɪˈiː/ *n* beneficiario *m*

**payer** /ˈpeɪə(r)/ *n* pagante *mf*

**paying-in slip** /peɪɪŋˈɪn/ *n* distinta *f* di versamento

**payload** /ˈpeɪləʊd/ *n* (*of bomb*) carica *f* esplosiva; (*of aircraft, ship*) carico *m* utile

**payment** /ˈpeɪmənt/ *n* pagamento *m*; ~ **by instalments** pagamento *m* rateale

**pay: pay packet** *n* busta *f* paga. **payphone** *n* telefono *m* pubblico. **payroll** *n* (*list*) libro *m* paga; (*sum of money*) paga *f* del personale; (*employees collectively*) personale *m*. **payslip** *n* busta *f* paga *inv*

**PC** *abbr* (**personal computer**) PC *m inv*; *abbr* (**police constable**) agente *m* di polizia

**pc** *abbr* (**per cent**) per cento; *abbr* (**politically correct**) politicamente corretto; *abbr* (**postcard**) cartolina *f* postale

**pd** *Am abbr* (**police department**) reparto *m* di polizia

**PE** *n abbr* (**physical education**) educazione *f* fisica

**pea** /piː/ *n* pisello *m*

**peace** /piːs/ *n* pace *f*; ~ **of mind** tranquillità *f*

**peaceable** /ˈpiːsəbl/ *a* pacifico

**peace envoy** *n* mediatore, -trice *mf*

**peaceful** /ˈpiːsfʊl/ *a* calmo, sereno

**peacefully** /'piːsfʊlɪ/ adv in pace
**peace: peacekeeping** n Mil, Pol mantenimento m della pace ● attrib ⟨force, troops⟩ di mantenimento della pace. **peacemaker** n mediatore, -trice mf. **peacetime** n tempo m di pace ● attrib ⟨planning, government⟩ del tempo di pace; ⟨army, alliance, training⟩ in tempo di pace. **peace treaty** n trattato m di pace
**peach** /piːtʃ/ n pesca f; ⟨tree⟩ pesco m
**peacock** /'piːkɒk/ n pavone m
**pea green** a verde pisello
**peak** /piːk/ n picco m; fig culmine m
**peaked cap** /piːkt/ n berretto m a punta
**peak hours** npl ore fpl di punta
**peak season** n alta stagione f
**peaky** /'piːkɪ/ a malaticcio
**peal** /piːl/ n ⟨of bells⟩ scampanio m; ~s of laughter fragore msg di risate
**peanut** /'piːnʌt/ n nocciolina f [americana]; ~s pl fam miseria fsg
**peanut butter** n burro m di arachidi
**pear** /peə(r)/ n pera f; ⟨tree⟩ pero m
**pearl** /pɜːl/ n perla f
**pearl: pearl barley** n orzo m perlato. **pearl-diver** n pescatore, -trice mf di perle. **pearl grey** n grigio m perla inv ● a grigio perla inv
**Pearly Gates** /'pɜːlɪ/ npl hum porte fpl del paradiso
**peasant** /'peznt/ n contadino, -a mf
**peat** /piːt/ n torba f
**pebble** /'pebl/ n ciottolo m
**pebble-dash** n intonaco m a pinocchino
**pecan** /'piːkən/ n ⟨tree⟩ pecan m inv; ⟨nut⟩ noce f pecan inv
**peck** /pek/ n beccata f; ⟨kiss⟩ bacetto m ● vt beccare; ⟨kiss⟩ dare un bacetto a
■ **peck at** vi beccare
**pecking order** /'pekɪŋ/ n gerarchia f
**peckish** /'pekɪʃ/ a be ~ fam avere un languorino allo stomaco
**pectoral** /'pektərəl/ a & n pettorale m
**peculiar** /pɪ'kjuːlɪə(r)/ a strano; ⟨special⟩ particolare; ~ to tipico di
**peculiarity** /pɪkjuːlɪ'ærətɪ/ n stranezza f; ⟨feature⟩ particolarità f inv
**peculiarly** /pɪ'kjuːlɪəlɪ/ adv singolarmente
**pecuniary** /pə'kjuːnɪərɪ/ a pecuniario
**pedagogical** /pedə'gɒdʒɪkl/ a pedagogico
**pedagogy** /'pedəgɒdʒɪ/ n pedagogia f
**pedal** /'pedl/ n pedale m ● vi pedalare
**pedal bin** n pattumiera f a pedale
**pedant** /'pedənt/ n pedante m
**pedantic** /pɪ'dæntɪk/ a pedante
**pedantically** /pɪ'dæntɪklɪ/ adv in modo pedante
**pedantry** /'pedəntrɪ/ n pedanteria f
**peddle** /'pedl/ vt vendere porta a porta
**pedestal** /'pedɪstl/ n piedistallo m
**pedestrian** /pɪ'destrɪən/ n pedone m ● a fig scadente
**pedestrian crossing** n passaggio m pedonale
**pedestrian precinct** n zona f pedonale
**pedicure** /'pedɪkjʊə(r)/ n pedicure f inv

**pedigree** /'pedɪgriː/ n pedigree m inv; ⟨of person⟩ lignaggio m ● attrib ⟨animal⟩ di razza, con pedigree
**pedlar** /'pedlə(r)/ n venditore, -trice mf ambulante
**pee** /piː/ fam vi ⟨pt/pp peed⟩ fare la pipì ● n go for a ~ andare a fare la pipì
**peek** /piːk/ fam vi sbirciare ● n take a ~ at sth dare una sbirciata a qcsa
**peekaboo** /piːkə'buː/ int cucù
**peel** /piːl/ n buccia f ● vt sbucciare ● vi ⟨nose etc.⟩ spellarsi; ⟨paint.⟩ staccarsi
■ **peel off** vt togliersi ⟨item of clothing⟩ ● vi ⟨wallpaper.⟩ staccarsi; ⟨skin.⟩ squamarsi
**peeler** /'piːlə(r)/ n sbucciatore m
**peelings** /'piːlɪŋz/ npl bucce fpl
**peep** /piːp/ n sbirciata f ● vi sbirciare
**peephole** /'piːphəʊl/ n spioncino m
**Peeping Tom** /'piːpɪŋ/ n fam guardone m
**peer¹** /pɪə(r)/ vi ~ at scrutare
**peer²** n nobile m; his ~s pl ⟨in rank⟩ i suoi pari; ⟨in age⟩ i suoi coetanei
**peerage** /'pɪərɪdʒ/ n Br Pol nobiltà f; ⟨book⟩ almanacco m nobiliare; **be given a ~** essere elevato al rango di pari
**peer group** n ⟨of same status⟩ pari mpl; ⟨of same age⟩ coetanei mpl; **~ ~ pressure** pressione f esercitata dal gruppo cui si appartiene
**peerless** /'pɪəlɪs/ a impareggiabile
**peeved** /piːvd/ a fam irritato
**peevish** /'piːvɪʃ/ a fam irritabile
**peg** /peg/ n ⟨hook⟩ piolo m; ⟨for tent⟩ picchetto m; ⟨for clothes⟩ molletta f; **off the ~** fam prêt-à-porter ● vt ⟨pt/pp pegged⟩ fissare ⟨prices⟩; stendere con le mollette ⟨washing⟩
**pegboard** /'pegbɔːd/ n segnapunti m inv
**pejorative** /pɪ'dʒɒrətɪv/ a peggiorativo
**pejoratively** /pɪ'dʒɒrətɪvlɪ/ adv in modo peggiorativo
**Peke** /piːk/ n fam ⟨dog⟩ pechinese m
**Peking** /piː'kɪŋ/ n Pechino f
**Pekin[g]ese** /piːkɪ'niːz/ n pechinese m
**pelican** /'pelɪkən/ n pellicano m
**pelican crossing** n passaggio m pedonale con semaforo
**pellet** /'pelɪt/ n pallottola f
**pell-mell** /pel'mel/ adv alla rinfusa
**pelmet** /'pelmɪt/ n mantovana f
**pelt¹** /pelt/ n ⟨skin⟩ pelliccia f
**pelt²** vt bombardare ● vi ⟨fam: run fast⟩ catapultarsi; ⟨rain heavily⟩ venir giù a fiotti
■ **pelt along** vi⟨move quickly⟩ precipitarsi lungo
■ **pelt down** vi ⟨rain:⟩ venir giù a fiotti
**pelvis** /'pelvɪs/ n Anat bacino m
**pen¹** /pen/ n ⟨for animals⟩ recinto m
**pen²** n penna f; ⟨ball-point⟩ penna f a sfera
**penal** /'piːnl/ a penale
**penal code** n codice m penale
**penalize** /'piːnəlaɪz/ vt penalizzare
**penalty** /'penltɪ/ n sanzione f; ⟨fine⟩ multa f; ⟨in football⟩ [calcio m di] rigore m
**penalty: penalty area, penalty box** n area f di rigore. **penalty clause** n Comm, Jur

clausola *f* penale. **penalty kick** *n* [calcio *m* di] rigore *m*. **penalty shootout** *n* rigori *mpl*

**penance** /'penəns/ *n* penitenza *f*

**pence** /pens/ *see* **penny**

**penchant** /'pɒʃõ/ *n* debole *m*

**pencil** /'pensl/ *n* matita *f* ● *vt* (*pt/pp* **pencilled**) segnare a matita

■ **pencil in** *vt* annotare provvisoriamente ⟨*date*⟩

**pencil case** *n* [astuccio *m*] portamatite *m inv*

**pencil sharpener** *n* temperamatite *m inv*

**pendant** /'pendənt/ *n* ciondolo *m*

**pending** /'pendɪŋ/ *a* in sospeso ● *prep* in attesa di

**pendulum** /'pendjʊləm/ *n* pendolo *m*

**penetrate** /'penɪtreɪt/ *vt/i* penetrare

**penetrating** /'penɪtreɪtɪŋ/ *a* ⟨*sound, stare*⟩ penetrante; ⟨*remark*⟩ acuto

**penetration** /penɪ'treɪʃn/ *n* penetrazione *f*

**penfriend** /'penfrend/ *n* amico, -a *mf* di penna

**penguin** /'peŋgwɪn/ *n* pinguino *m*

**penicillin** /penɪ'sɪlɪn/ *n* penicillina *f*

**peninsula** /pɪ'nɪnsjʊlə/ *n* penisola *f*

**penis** /'piːnɪs/ *n* pene *m*

**penitence** /'penɪtəns/ *n* penitenza *f*

**penitent** /'penɪtənt/ *a & n* penitente *mf*

**penitentiary** /penɪ'tenʃərɪ/ *n Am* penitenziario *m*

**penknife** /'pennaɪf/ *n* temperino *m*

**pen-name** *n* pseudonimo *m*

**pennant** /'penənt/ *n* bandiera *f*

**penniless** /'penɪlɪs/ *a* senza un soldo

**penny** /'penɪ/ *n* (*pl* **pence**; *single coins* **pennies**) penny *m*; *Am* centesimo *m*; **spend a ~** *fam* andare in bagno; **the ~'s dropped!** *fam* ci è arrivato!

**penny: penny-farthing** *n* velocipede *m*. **penny-pinching** /'penɪpɪntʃɪŋ/ *a* taccagno ● *n* taccagneria *f*. **penny whistle** *n* zufolo *m*

**pen-pusher** *n fam* scribacchino, -a *mf*

**pension** /'penʃn/ *n* pensione *f*

■ **pension off** *vt* ⟨*force to retire*⟩ mandare in pensione

**pensioner** /'penʃənə(r)/ *n* pensionato, -a *mf*

**pension fund** *n* fondo *m* pensioni; ⟨*of an individual*⟩ fondo *m* pensione

**pension scheme** *n* piano *m* di pensionamento

**pensive** /'pensɪv/ *a* pensoso

**pentagon** /'pentəgən/ *n* pentagono *m*; *Am Pol* **the P~** il Pentagono

**pentagonal** /pen'tægənl/ *a* pentagonale

**pentathlete** /pen'tæθliːt/ *n* pentatleta *mf*

**pentathlon** /pen'tæθlɒn/ *n* pentathlon *m inv*

**Pentecost** /'pentɪkɒst/ *n* Pentecoste *f*

**pent-up** /'pentʌp/ *a* represso

**penultimate** /pɪ'nʌltɪmət/ *a* penultimo

**penury** /'penjʊrɪ/ *n* miseria *f*

**peony** /'pɪənɪ/ *n* peonia *f*

**people** /'piːpl/ *npl* persone *fpl*, gente *fsg*; ⟨*citizens*⟩ popolo *msg*; **a lot of ~** una marea di gente; **the ~** la gente; **English ~** gli inglesi;

**~ say** si dice; **for four ~** per quattro ● *vt* popolare

**PEP** /pep/ *Br abbr* (**personal equity plan**) piano *m* di investimento azionario personale

■ **pep up** *vt* vivacizzare ⟨*party, conversation*⟩; tirare su ⟨*person*⟩

**pepper** /'pepə(r)/ *n* pepe *m*; ⟨*vegetable*⟩ peperone *m* ● *vt* ⟨*season*⟩ pepare

**pepper: peppercorn** *n* grano *m* di pepe. **peppercorn rent** affitto *m* nominale. **pepper mill** *n* macinapepe *m inv*. **peppermint** *n* menta *f* peperita; ⟨*sweet*⟩ caramella *f* alla menta. **pepper pot** *n* pepiera *f*

**pep pill** /'peppɪl/ *n fam* stimolante *m*

**pep talk** *n* discorso *m* d'incoraggiamento

**peptic** /'peptɪk/ *a* peptico

**peptic ulcer** *n* ulcera *f* peptica

**per** /pɜː(r)/ *prep* per

**per annum** /pər'ænəm/ *adv* all'anno

**per capita** /pə'kæpɪtə/ *a & adv* pro capite

**perceive** /pə'siːv/ *vt* percepire; ⟨*interpret*⟩ interpretare

**per cent** *adv* percento

**percentage** /pə'sentɪdʒ/ *n* percentuale *f*

**perceptible** /pə'septəbl/ *a* percettibile; *fig* sensibile

**perceptibly** /pə'septɪblɪ/ *adv* percettibilmente; *fig* sensibilmente

**perception** /pə'sepʃn/ *n* percezione *f*

**perceptive** /pə'septɪv/ *a* perspicace

**perch**[1] /pɜːtʃ/ *n* pertica *f* ● *vi* ⟨*bird:*⟩ appollaiarsi

**perch**[2] *n inv* ⟨*fish*⟩ pesce *m* persico

**percolate** /'pɜːkəleɪt/ *vi* infiltrarsi; ⟨*coffee:*⟩ passare

**percolator** /'pɜːkəleɪtə(r)/ *n* caffettiera *f* a filtro

**percussion** /pə'kʌʃn/ *n* percussione *f*

**percussion instrument** *n* strumento *m* a percussione

**percussionist** /pə'kʌʃ(ə)nɪst/ *n* percussionista *mf*

**peremptory** /pə'remptərɪ/ *a* perentorio

**perennial** /pə'renɪəl/ *a* perenne ● *n* pianta *f* perenne

**perfect**[1] /'pɜːfɪkt/ *a* perfetto ● *n Gram* passato *m* prossimo

**perfect**[2] /pə'fekt/ *vt* perfezionare

**perfection** /pə'fekʃn/ *n* perfezione *f*; **to ~** alla perfezione

**perfectionism** /pə'fekʃənɪzm/ *n* perfezionismo *m*

**perfectionist** /pə'fekʃ(ə)nɪst/ *a & n* perfezionista *mf*

**perfectly** /'pɜːfɪktlɪ/ *adv* perfettamente

**perfidious** /pə'fɪdɪəs/ *a* perfido

**perforate** /'pɜːfəreɪt/ *vt* perforare

**perforated** /'pɜːfəreɪtɪd/ *a* perforato; ⟨*ulcer*⟩ perforante

**perforation** /pɜːfə'reɪʃn/ *n* perforazione *f*

**perform** /pə'fɔːm/ *vt* compiere, fare; eseguire ⟨*operation, sonata*⟩; recitare ⟨*role*⟩; mettere in scena ⟨*play*⟩ ● *vi Theat* recitare; *Techn* funzionare

**performance** /pə'fɔːməns/ *n* esecuzione *f*;

(*at theatre, cinema*) rappresentazione *f*; Techn rendimento *m*

**performance bonus** *n* premio *m* di produttività

**performance-related** *a* commensurato alla produttività

**performer** /pə'fɔːmə(r)/ *n* artista *mf*

**performing arts** /pə'fɔːmɪŋ/ *npl* arti *fpl* dello spettacolo

**perfume** /'pɜːfjuːm/ *n* profumo *m*

**perfumed** /'pɜːfjuːmd/ *a* profumato

**perfunctory** /pə'fʌŋktərɪ/ *a* superficiale

**perhaps** /pə'hæps/ *adv* forse

**peril** /'perɪl/ *n* pericolo *m*

**perilous** /'perɪləs/ *a* pericoloso

**perilously** /'perɪləslɪ/ *adv* pericolosamente

**perimeter** /pə'rɪmɪtə(r)/ *n* perimetro *m*

**period** /'pɪərɪəd/ *n* periodo *m*; (*menstruation*) mestruazioni *fpl*; Sch ora *f* di lezione; (*full stop*) punto *m* fermo ● *attrib* ⟨costume⟩ d'epoca; ⟨furniture⟩ in stile

**periodic** /pɪərɪ'ɒdɪk/ *a* periodico

**periodical** /pɪərɪ'ɒdɪkl/ *n* periodico *m*, rivista *f*

**periodically** /pɪərɪ'ɒdɪklɪ/ *adv* periodicamente

**period of notice** *n* periodo *m* di preavviso

**peripheral** /pə'rɪfərəl/ *a* periferico ● *n* Comput periferica *f*

**periphery** /pə'rɪfərɪ/ *n* periferia *f*

**periscope** /'perɪskəʊp/ *n* periscopio *m*

**perish** /'perɪʃ/ *vi* (*rot*) deteriorarsi; (*die*) perire

**perishable** /'perɪʃəbl/ *a* deteriorabile ● ~s *npl* merce *f* deperibile

**perished** /'perɪʃt/ *a* (*fam: freezing cold*) be ~ essere intirizzito

**perishing** /'perɪʃɪŋ/ *a fam* it's ~ fa freddo da morire

**peritonitis** /perɪtə'naɪtɪs/ *n* peritonite *f*

**perjure** /'pɜːdʒə(r)/ *vt* ~ oneself spergiurare

**perjury** /'pɜːdʒərɪ/ *n* spergiuro *m*

**perk**[1] /pɜːk/ *n fam* vantaggio *m*

**perk**[2] *vi Am* ⟨coffee:⟩ passare

■ **perk up** *vt* tirare su ● *vi* tirarsi su

**perky** /'pɜːkɪ/ *a* allegro

**perm** /pɜːm/ *n* permanente *f* ● *vt* ~ sb's hair fare la permanente a qno

**permanent** /'pɜːmənənt/ *a* permanente; ⟨job, address⟩ stabile

**permanently** /'pɜːmənəntlɪ/ *adv* stabilmente

**permeable** /'pɜːmɪəbl/ *a* permeabile

**permeate** /'pɜːmɪeɪt/ *vt* impregnare

**permissible** /pə'mɪsəbl/ *a* ammissibile

**permission** /pə'mɪʃn/ *n* permesso *m*

**permissive** /pə'mɪsɪv/ *a* permissivo

**permit**[1] /pə'mɪt/ *vt* (*pt/pp* -mitted) permettere; ~ sb to do sth permettere a qcno di fare qcsa

**permit**[2] /'pɜːmɪt/ *n* autorizzazione *f*

**pernicious** /pə'nɪʃəs/ *a* pernicioso

**pernickety** /pə'nɪkətɪ/ *a Br fam* puntiglioso, pignolo; (*about food*) difficile

**peroxide blonde** /pə'rɒksaɪd/ *n* bionda *f* ossigenata

**perpendicular** /pɜːpən'dɪkjʊlə(r)/ *a & n* perpendicolare *f*

**perpetrate** /'pɜːpɪtreɪt/ *vt* perpetrare

**perpetrator** /'pɜːpɪtreɪtə(r)/ *n* autore, -trice *mf*

**perpetual** /pə'petjʊəl/ *a* perenne

**perpetually** /pə'petjʊəlɪ/ *adv* perennemente

**perpetuate** /pə'petjʊeɪt/ *vt* perpetuare

**perplex** /pə'pleks/ *vt* lasciare perplesso

**perplexed** /pə'plekst/ *a* perplesso

**perplexity** /pə'pleksətɪ/ *n* perplessità *f inv*

**perquisite** /'pɜːkwɪzɪt/ *n* fringe benefit *m inv*, beneficio *m* accessorio

**per se** /pɜː'seɪ/ *adv* in sé

**persecute** /'pɜːsɪkjuːt/ *vt* perseguitare

**persecution** /pɜːsɪ'kjuːʃn/ *n* persecuzione *f*

**persecutor** /'pɜːsɪkjuːtə(r)/ *n* persecutore, -trice *mf*

**perseverance** /pɜːsɪ'vɪərəns/ *n* perseveranza *f*

**persevere** /pɜːsɪ'vɪə(r)/ *vi* perseverare

**persevering** /pɜːsɪ'vɪərɪŋ/ *a* assiduo

**Persian** /'pɜːʃn/ *a* persiano

**persist** /pə'sɪst/ *vi* persistere; ~ in doing sth persistere nel fare qcsa

**persistence** /pə'sɪstəns/ *n* persistenza *f*

**persistent** /pə'sɪstənt/ *a* persistente

**persistently** /pə'sɪstəntlɪ/ *adv* persistentemente

**person** /'pɜːsn/ *n* persona *f*; in ~ di persona

**persona** /pə'səʊnə/ *n* Psych individuo *m*; Theat personaggio *m*

**personable** /'pɜːsənəbl/ *a* di bella presenza

**personage** /'pɜːsənɪdʒ/ *n* personaggio *m*

**personal** /'pɜːsənl/ *a* personale

**personal: personal allowance** *n* (*in taxation*) quota *f* non imponibile. **personal assistant** *n* segretario, -a *mf* personale. **personal belongings** *npl* effetti *mpl* personali. **personal computer** *n* personal computer *m inv*. **personal hygiene** *n* igiene *f* personale

**personality** /pɜːsə'nælətɪ/ *n* personalità *f inv*; (*on TV*) personaggio *m*

**personalize** /'pɜːsənəlaɪz/ *vt* personalizzare ⟨stationery, clothing⟩; mettere sul piano personale ⟨issue, dispute⟩

**personal loan** *n* prestito *m* a privato

**personally** /'pɜːsənəlɪ/ *adv* personalmente

**personal organizer** *n* Comput agenda *f* elettronica

**personal stereo** *n* walkman® *m inv*

**personification** /pəsɒnɪfɪ'keɪʃn/ *n* the ~ of la personificazione di

**personify** /pə'sɒnɪfaɪ/ *vt* (*pt/pp* -ied) personificare

**personnel** /pɜːsə'nel/ *n* personale *m*

**personnel director** *n* direttore, -trice *mf* del personale

**personnel management** *n* gestione *f* del personale

**perspective** /pə'spektɪv/ *n* prospettiva *f*

**perspex®** /'pɜːspeks/ *n* plexiglas® *m*

**perspicacious** /pɜːspɪˈkeɪʃəs/ *a* perspicace
**perspiration** /pɜːspɪˈreɪʃn/ *n* sudore *m*
**perspire** /pəˈspaɪə(r)/ *vi* sudare
**persuade** /pəˈsweɪd/ *vt* persuadere
**persuasion** /pəˈsweɪʒn/ *n* persuasione *f*; (*belief*) convinzione *f*
**persuasive** /pəˈsweɪsɪv/ *a* persuasivo
**persuasively** /pəˈsweɪsɪvlɪ/ *adv* in modo persuasivo
**pert** /pɜːt/ *a* (*lively*) esuberante
**pertinent** /ˈpɜːtɪnənt/ *a* pertinente (**to** a)
**perturb** /pəˈtɜːb/ *vt* perturbare
**perturbing** /pəˈtɜːbɪŋ/ *a* conturbante
**Peru** /pəˈruː/ *n* Perù *m*
**peruse** /pəˈruːz/ *vt* leggere
**Peruvian** /pəˈruːvɪən/ *a & n* peruviano, -a *mf*
**pervade** /pəˈveɪd/ *vt* pervadere
**pervasive** /pəˈveɪsɪv/ *a* pervasivo
**perverse** /pəˈvɜːs/ *a* perverso; (*illogical*) irragionevole
**perversely** /pəˈvɜːslɪ/ *adv* in modo perverso
**perversion** /pəˈvɜːʃn/ *n* perversione *f*
**perversity** /pəˈvɜːsɪtɪ/ *n* perversità *f*
**pervert**[1] /pəˈvɜːt/ *vt* deviare ⟨*course of justice*⟩
**pervert**[2] /ˈpɜːvɜːt/ *n* pervertito, -a *mf*
**perverted** /pəˈvɜːtɪd/ *a* perverso
**pessary** /ˈpesərɪ/ *n* candeletta *f*
**pessimism** /ˈpesɪmɪzm/ *n* pessimismo *m*
**pessimist** /ˈpesɪmɪst/ *n* pessimista *mf*
**pessimistic** /pesɪˈmɪstɪk/ *a* pessimistico
**pessimistically** /pesɪˈmɪstɪklɪ/ *adv* in modo pessimistico
**pest** /pest/ *n* piaga *f*; (*fam: person*) peste *f*
**pester** /ˈpestə(r)/ *vt* molestare
**pesticide** /ˈpestɪsaɪd/ *n* pesticida *m*
**pestilential** /pestɪˈlenʃəl/ *a* (*hum: annoying*) fastidiosissimo
**pestle** /ˈpesl/ *n* pestello *m*
**pet** /pet/ *n* animale *m* domestico; (*favourite*) cocco, -a *mf* ● *a* (*favourite*) prediletto ● *v* (*pt/pp* **petted**) ● *vt* coccolare ● *vi* ⟨*couple:*⟩ praticare il petting
**petal** /ˈpetl/ *n* petalo *m*
**peter** /ˈpiːtə(r)/ *vi* ~ **out** finire
**petite** /pəˈtiːt/ *a* minuto
**petition** /pəˈtɪʃn/ *n* petizione *f*
**pet name** *n* vezzeggiativo *m*
**petrified** /ˈpetrɪfaɪd/ *a* (*frightened*) pietrificato
**petrify** /ˈpetrɪfaɪ/ *vt* (*pt/pp* **-ied**) pietrificare
**petrochemical** /petrəʊˈkemɪkl/ *n* petrolchimico *m*
**petrodollar** /ˈpetrəʊdɒlə(r)/ *n* petroldollaro *m*
**petrol** /ˈpetrəl/ *n Br* benzina *f*
**petrol bomb** *n Br* [bomba *f*] molotov *f inv*
**petroleum** /pɪˈtrəʊlɪəm/ *n* petrolio *m*
**petroleum jelly** *n* vaselina *f*
**petrol: petrol-pump** *n Br* pompa *f* di benzina. **petrol station** *n Br* stazione *f* di servizio. **petrol tank** *n Br* serbatoio *m* della benzina
**pet shop** *n* negozio *m* di animali
**petticoat** /ˈpetɪkəʊt/ *n* sottoveste *f*
**pettifogging** /ˈpetɪfɒgɪŋ/ *a pej* cavilloso

**petty** /ˈpetɪ/ *a* (**-ier, -iest**) insignificante; (*mean*) meschino
**petty cash** *n* cassa *f* per piccole spese
**petty-minded** /-ˈmaɪndɪd/ *a* meschino
**petulance** /ˈpetjʊləns/ *n* petulanza *f*
**petulant** /ˈpetjʊlənt/ *a* petulante
**pew** /pjuː/ *n* banco *m* (*di chiesa*)
**pewter** /ˈpjuːtə(r)/ *n* peltro *m*
**phallic** /ˈfælɪk/ *a* fallico
**phallic symbol** *n* simbolo *m* fallico
**phallus** /ˈfæləs/ *n* fallo *m*
**phantom** /ˈfæntəm/ *n* fantasma *m*
**Pharaoh** /ˈfeərəʊ/ *n* faraone *m*
**pharmaceutical** /fɑːməˈsjuːtɪkl/ *a* farmaceutico
**pharmacist** /ˈfɑːməsɪst/ *n* farmacista *mf*
**pharmacy** /ˈfɑːməsɪ/ *n* farmacia *f*
**phase** /feɪz/ *n* fase *f* ● *vt* **phase in/out** introdurre/eliminare gradualmente
**Ph.D.** *abbr* (**Doctor of Philosophy**) ≈ dottorato *m* di ricerca
**pheasant** /ˈfeznt/ *n* fagiano *m*
**phenomenal** /fɪˈnɒmɪnl/ *a* fenomenale; (*incredible*) incredibile
**phenomenally** /fɪˈnɒmɪnəlɪ/ *adv* incredibilmente
**phenomenon** /fɪˈnɒmɪnən/ *n* (*pl* **-na**) fenomeno *m*
**phew** /fjuː/ *int* (*when too hot, in relief*) uff!; (*in surprise*) oh!
**philanderer** /fɪˈlændərə(r)/ *n* donnaiolo *m*
**philanthropic** /fɪlənˈθrɒpɪk/ *a* filantropico
**philanthropist** /fɪˈlænθrəpɪst/ *n* filantropo, -a *mf*
**philatelist** /fɪˈlætəlɪst/ *n* filatelico, -a *mf*
**philately** /fɪˈlætəlɪ/ *n* filatelia *f*
**philharmonic** /fɪlhɑːˈmɒnɪk/ *n* (*orchestra*) orchestra *f* filarmonica ● *a* filarmonico
**Philippines** /ˈfɪlɪpiːnz/ *npl* Filippine *fpl*
**philistine** /ˈfɪlɪstaɪn/ *a & n* filisteo, -a *mf*
**philology** /fɪˈlɒlədʒɪ/ *n* filologia *f*
**philosopher** /fɪˈlɒsəfə(r)/ *n* filosofo, -a *mf*
**philosophical** /fɪləˈsɒfɪkl/ *a* filosofico
**philosophically** /fɪləˈsɒfɪklɪ/ *adv* con filosofia
**philosophy** /fɪˈlɒsəfɪ/ *n* filosofia *f*
**phlebitis** /flɪˈbaɪtɪs/ *n* flebite *f*
**phlegm** /flem/ *n Med* flemma *f*
**phlegmatic** /flegˈmætɪk/ *a* flemmatico
**phobia** /ˈfəʊbɪə/ *n* fobia *f*
**phobic** /ˈfəʊbɪk/ *a* fobico
**phoenix** /ˈfiːnɪks/ *n* fenice *f*
**phone** /fəʊn/ *n* telefono *m*; **be on the** ~ avere il telefono; (*be phoning*) essere al telefono ● *vt* telefonare a ● *vi* telefonare
■ **phone back** *vt/i* richiamare
■ **phone in** *vi* telefonare al lavoro; **he** ~**d in sick** ha telefonato [al lavoro] per dire che è ammalato
■ **phone up** *vi* telefonare ● *vt* dare un colpo di telefono a
**phone: phone book** *n* guida *f* del telefono. **phone box** *n* cabina *f* telefonica. **phone call** telefonata *f*. **phonecard** *n* scheda *f* telefonica.

**phone-in** *n* trasmissione *f* con chiamate in diretta

**phoneme** /'fəʊniːm/ *n* fonema *m*

**phone number** *n* numero *m* telefonico

**phonetic** /fə'netɪk/ *a* fonetico

**phonetics** /fə'netɪks/ *n* fonetica *f*

**phoney** /'fəʊni/ *a* (**-ier, -iest**) fasullo ● *n* ciarlatano, -a *mf*

**phonology** /fə'nɒlədʒi/ *n* fonologia *f*

**phosphate** /'fɒsfeɪt/ *n* fosfato *m*

**phosphorus** /'fɒsfərəs/ *n* fosforo *m*

**photo** /'fəʊtəʊ/ *n* foto *f*

**photo: photo album** *n* album *m inv* di fotografie. **photocell** *n* fotocellula *f*. **photocopier** *n* fotocopiatrice *f*. **photocopy** *n* fotocopia *f* ● *vt* fotocopiare. **photoengraving** *n* fotoincisione *f*. **photo finish** *n* fotofinish *m*. **Photofit**® *n* Br photofit *m inv*

**photogenic** /fəʊtəʊ'dʒenɪk/ *a* fotogenico

**photograph** /'fəʊtəɡrɑːf/ *n* fotografia *f* ● *vt* fotografare

**photographer** /fə'tɒɡrəfə(r)/ *n* fotografo, -a *mf*

**photographic** /fəʊtə'ɡræfɪk/ *a* fotografico

**photography** /fə'tɒɡrəfi/ *n* fotografia *f*

**photo: photojournalism** *n* fotoreportage *m*. **photojournalist** *n* fotogiornalista *mf*. **photomontage** /fəʊtəʊmɒn'tɑːʒ/ *n* fotomontaggio *m*. **photosynthesis** *n* fotosintesi *f*

**phrase** /freɪz/ *n* espressione *f* ● *vt* esprimere

**phrase book** *n* libro *m* di fraseologia

**phut** /fʌt/ *adv* fam go ~ ⟨car, washing machine etc.⟩ scassarsi; ⟨plan:⟩ andare in fumo

**physical** /'fɪzɪkl/ *a* fisico

**physical education** *n* educazione *f* fisica

**physically** /'fɪzɪklɪ/ *adv* fisicamente

**physician** /fɪ'zɪʃn/ *n* medico *m*

**physicist** /'fɪzɪsɪst/ *n* fisico, -a *mf*

**physics** /'fɪzɪks/ *n* fisica *f*

**physio** /'fɪzɪəʊ/ *n* Br fam (physiotherapist) fisioterapista *mf*; (physiotherapy) fisioterapia *f*

**physiology** /fɪzɪ'ɒlədʒi/ *n* fisiologia *f*

**physiotherapist** /fɪzɪəʊ'θerəpɪst/ *n* fisioterapista *mf*

**physiotherapy** /fɪzɪəʊ'θerəpɪ/ *n* fisioterapia *f*

**physique** /fɪ'ziːk/ *n* fisico *m*

**pianist** /'pɪənɪst/ *n* pianista *mf*

**piano** /pɪ'ænəʊ/ *n* piano *m*

**pianola**® /pɪə'nəʊlə/ *n* pianola ʀ *f*

**piazza** /pɪ'ætsə/ *n* (public square) piazza *f*; (Am: veranda) veranda *f*

**pick**[1] /pɪk/ *n* (tool) piccone *m*

**pick**[2] *n* scelta *f*; **take your** ~ prendi quello che vuoi ● *vt* (select) scegliere; cogliere ⟨flowers⟩; scassinare ⟨lock⟩; borseggiare ⟨pockets⟩; ~ **one's nose** mettersi le dita nel naso; ~ **a quarrel** attaccar briga; ~ **holes in sth** (fam: criticize) criticare qcsa ● *vi* ~ **and choose** fare il difficile; ~ **at one's food** spilluzzicare

■ **pick off** *vt* (remove) togliere

■ **pick on** *vt* (fam: nag) assillare; **he always** ~**s on me** ce l'ha con me

■ **pick out** *vt* (identify) individuare

■ **pick up** *vt* sollevare; raccogliere ⟨fallen object, information⟩; prendere in braccio ⟨baby⟩; prendere ⟨passengers, habit⟩; ⟨police:⟩ arrestare ⟨criminal⟩; fam rimorchiare ⟨girl⟩; prendersi ⟨illness⟩; captare ⟨signal⟩; ⟨buy⟩ comprare; ⟨learn⟩ imparare; ⟨collect⟩ andare/venire a prendere; ~ **oneself up** riprendersi ● *vi* (improve) recuperare; ⟨weather:⟩ rimettersi

**pickaxe** /'pɪkæks/ *n* piccone *m*

**picker** /'pɪkə(r)/ *n* raccoglitore, -trice *mf*

**picket** /'pɪkɪt/ *n* picchettista *mf* ● *vt* picchettare

**picket line** *n* picchetto *m*

**pickle** /'pɪkl/ *n* ~**s** *pl* sottaceti *mpl*; **in a** ~ *fig* nei pasticci ● *vt* mettere sottaceto

**pick-me-up** *n* (alcohol) cicchetto *m*; (medicine) tonico *m*

**pickpocket** /'pɪkpɒkɪt/ *n* borsaiolo *m*

**pick-up** *n* (truck) furgone *m*; (on record-player) pickup *m inv*

**picky** /'pɪkɪ/ *a* (fam: choosy, fussy) difficile

**picnic** /'pɪknɪk/ *n* picnic *m* ● *vi* (pt/pp -**nicked**) fare un picnic

**pictogram** /'pɪktəɡræm/ *n* (symbol) pittogramma *m*; (chart) tabella *f*

**pictorial** /pɪk'tɔːrɪəl/ *a* illustrato

**picture** /'pɪktʃə(r)/ *n* (painting) quadro *m*; (photo) fotografia *f*; (drawing) disegno *m*; (film) film *m inv*; **as pretty as a** ~ ⟨girl⟩ bella come una Madonna; **put sb in the** ~ *fig* mettere qcno al corrente; **the** ~**s** Br fam il cinema ● *vt* (imagine) immaginare

**picturesque** /pɪktʃə'resk/ *a* pittoresco

**piddle** /'pɪdl/ *vi fam* fare pipì

**pie** /paɪ/ *n* torta *f*

**piece** /piːs/ *n* pezzo *m*; (in game) pedina *f*; **a** ~ **of bread /paper** un pezzo di pane /carta; **a** ~ **of news /advice/junk** una notizia /un consiglio/una patacca; **take to** ~**s** smontare

■ **piece together** *vt* montare; *fig* ricostruire

**piecemeal** /'piːsmiːl/ *adv* un po' alla volta

**piecework** /'piːswɜːk/ *n* lavoro *m* a cottimo

**pie chart** *n* grafico *f* a torta

**Piedmont** /'piːdmɒnt/ *n* Piemonte *m*

**pier** /pɪə(r)/ *n* molo *m*; (pillar) pilastro *m*

**pierce** /pɪəs/ *vt* perforare; ~ **a hole in sth** fare un buco in qcsa

**piercing** /'pɪəsɪŋ/ *a* penetrante

**pig** /pɪɡ/ *n* maiale *m*

**pigeon** /'pɪdʒɪn/ *n* piccione *m*

**pigeon-hole** *n* casella *f* ● *vt* incasellare

**pigeon-toed** /-təʊd/ *a* **be** ~ camminare con i piedi in dentro

**piggery** /'pɪɡərɪ/ *n* (pigsty) porcile *m*; (fam: overeating) ingordigia *f*

**piggyback** /'pɪɡɪbæk/ *n* **give sb a** ~ portare qcno sulle spalle

**piggy bank** /'pɪɡɪ/ *n* salvadanaio *m*

**pig-headed** /-'hedɪd/ *a fam* cocciuto

**piglet** /'pɪglət/ n maialino m, porcellino m
**pigment** /'pɪgmənt/ n pigmento m
**pigmentation** /pɪgmən'teɪʃn/ n pigmentazione f
**pigskin** /'pɪgskɪn/ n pelle f di cinghiale
**pigtail** /'pɪgteɪl/ n (plait) treccina f
**pike** /paɪk/ n inv (fish) luccio m
**pilchard** /'pɪltʃəd/ n sardina f
**pile** /paɪl/ n (heap) pila f ● vt ~ sth on to sth appilare qcsa su qcsa
■ **pile in** vi (enter, get on) entrare disordinatamente
■ **pile up** vt accatastare ● vi ammucchiarsi
**piles** /paɪlz/ npl emorroidi fpl
**pile-up** n tamponamento m a catena
**pilfering** /'pɪlfərɪŋ/ n piccoli furti mpl
**pilgrim** /'pɪlgrɪm/ n pellegrino, -a mf
**pilgrimage** /'pɪlgrɪmɪdʒ/ n pellegrinaggio m
**pill** /pɪl/ n pillola f
**pillage** /'pɪlɪdʒ/ vt saccheggiare
**pillar** /'pɪlə(r)/ n pilastro m
**pillar box** n buca f delle lettere
**pillion** /'pɪljən/ n sellino m posteriore; **ride ~** viaggiare dietro
**pillory** /'pɪlərɪ/ vt (pt/pp -ied) fig mettere alla berlina
**pillow** /'pɪləʊ/ n guanciale m
**pillowcase** /'pɪləʊkeɪs/ n federa f
**pilot** /'paɪlət/ n pilota mf ● vt pilotare
**pilot light** n fiamma f di sicurezza
**pimp** /pɪmp/ n protettore m
**pimple** /'pɪmpl/ n foruncolo m
**PIN** /pɪn/ n abbr (**personal identification number**) [numero m di] codice m segreto
**pin** /pɪn/ n spillo m; Electr spinotto m; Med chiodo m; **I have ~s and needles in my leg** fam mi formicola una gamba ● vt (pt/pp **pinned**) appuntare (**to/on** su); (sewing) fissare con gli spilli; (hold down) immobilizzare; **~ sb down to a date** ottenere un appuntamento da qcno; **~ sth on sb** fam addossare a qcno la colpa di qcsa
■ **pin up** vt appuntare; (on wall) affiggere
**pinafore** /'pɪnəfɔː(r)/ n grembiule m
**pinafore dress** n scamiciato m
**pinball** /'pɪnbɔːl/ n flipper m inv
**pinball machine** n flipper m inv
**pincers** /'pɪnsəz/ npl tenaglie fpl
**pinch** /pɪntʃ/ n pizzicotto m; (of salt) presa f; **at a ~** fam in caso di bisogno ● vt pizzicare; (fam: steal) fregare ● vi (shoe:) stringere
**pincushion** /'pɪnkʊʃən/ n puntaspilli m inv
**pine¹** /paɪn/ n (tree) pino m
**pine²** vi **she is pining for you** le manchi molto
■ **pine away** vi deperire
**pine: pineapple** n ananas m inv. **pine cone** n pigna f. **pine-needle** n ago m di pino. **pine nut** n pinolo m
**ping** /pɪŋ/ n rumore m metallico
**ping-pong** n ping-pong m
**pinhead** /'pɪnhed/ n capocchia f di spillo; fam, pej testa f di rapa
**pink** /pɪŋk/ a rosa inv

**pinking shears, pinking scissors** /'pɪŋkɪŋ/ npl forbici fpl a zigzag
**pinnacle** /'pɪnəkl/ n guglia f
**PIN number** n codice m segreto
**pinpoint** /'pɪnpɔɪnt/ vt definire con precisione
**pinprick** /'pɪnprɪk/ n puntura f di spillo: (fig: of jealousy, remorse) punta f
**pinstripe** /'pɪnstraɪp/ a gessato
**pint** /paɪnt/ n pinta f (= 0,571, Am: 0,47 l); **a ~** fam una birra media
**pin-up** n ragazza f da copertina, pin-up f inv
**pioneer** /paɪə'nɪə(r)/ n pioniere, -a mf ● vt essere un pioniere di
**pious** /'paɪəs/ a pio
**pip¹** /pɪp/ n (seed) seme m
**pip²** n **the ~s** il segnale orario; (telephone) il segnale telefonico
**pip³** vt (pt/pp **pipped**) **be ~ped at the post** essere battuto all'ultimo minuto
**pipe** /paɪp/ n tubo m; (for smoking) pipa f; **the ~s** pl Mus la cornamusa ● vt far arrivare con tubature (water, gas etc); Culin mettere
■ **pipe down** vi fam abbassare la voce; (shut up) stare zitto
■ **pipe up** vi **~ with a suggestion** venir fuori con una proposta
**pipe-cleaner** n scovolino m
**piped music** /paɪpt/ n musichetta f di sottofondo
**pipe dream** n illusione f
**pipeline** /'paɪplaɪn/ n conduttura f: **in the ~** fam in cantiere
**piper** /'paɪpə(r)/ n suonatore m di cornamusa
**piping** /'paɪpɪŋ/ a **~ hot** bollente
**pique** /piːk/ n **in a fit of ~** risentito
**piracy** /'paɪrəsɪ/ n pirateria f
**piranha** /pɪ'rɑːnə/ n piranha m
**pirate** /'paɪrət/ n pirata m ● vt pirateggiare
**pirate copy** n copia f pirata
**pirated** a /'paɪrətɪd/ pirateggiato
**pirate radio** n radio f pirata
**pirouette** /pɪrʊ'et/ n piroetta f ● vi piroettare
**Pisces** /'paɪsiːz/ n Astr Pesci mpl
**piss** /pɪs/ sl n piscia f ● vi pisciare
■ **piss about, piss around** sl vi (waste time, play the fool) cazzeggiare ● vt **~ sb about** rompere le palle a qcno
■ **piss down** vi sl **it's ~ing down** (raining heavily) piove a dirotto
■ **piss off** sl vt fare incacchiare; **that type of behaviour ~es me off** questi comportamenti mi stanno sulle palle ● vi (leave) filarsela; **~ off!** levati dalle palle!, va' a cagare!
**pissed** /pɪst/ a sl sbronzo; **~ as a newt** sbronzo come una cucuzza
**pissed off** a sl scoglionato
**pistachio [nut]** /pɪ'stæʃɪəʊ/ n pistacchio m
**pistol** /'pɪstl/ n pistola f
**piston** /'pɪstn/ n Techn pistone m
**pit** /pɪt/ n fossa f; (mine) miniera f; (for orchestra) orchestra f; (of stomach) bocca f ● vt (pt/pp **pitted**) fig opporre (**against** a)
**pit-a-pat** /'pɪtəpæt/ n **go ~** (heart:) palpitare

**pitch¹** /pɪtʃ/ n (tone) tono m; (level) altezza f; (in sport) campo m; (fig: degree) grado m ● vt montare (tent)
**pitch²** n (substance) pece f
■ **pitch in** vi fam mettersi sotto
**pitch-black** a nero come la pece; (night) buio pesto
**pitch-dark** a buio pesto
**pitcher** /'pɪtʃə(r)/ n brocca f
**pitchfork** /'pɪtʃfɔ:k/ n forca f
**piteous** /'pɪtɪəs/ a pietoso
**pitfall** /'pɪtfɔ:l/ n fig trabocchetto m
**pith** /pɪθ/ n (of lemon, orange) interno m della buccia; fig essenza f
**pithy** /'pɪθɪ/ a (-ier, -iest) fig conciso
**pitiable** /'pɪtɪəbl/ a pietoso
**pitiful** /'pɪtɪfl/ a pietoso
**pitifully** /'pɪtɪfʊlɪ/ adv da far pietà
**pitiless** /'pɪtɪlɪs/ a spietato
**pitilessly** /'pɪtɪlɪslɪ/ adv senza pietà
**pittance** /'pɪtns/ n miseria f
**pitted** /'pɪtɪd/ a (surface) bucherellato; (face, skin) butterato; (olive) snocciolato
**pituitary** /pɪ'tju:ɪt(ə)rɪ/ a pituitario
**pituitary gland** n ghiandola f pituitaria, ipofisi f
**pity** /'pɪtɪ/ n pietà f; [what a] ~! che peccato!; **take ~ on** avere compassione di ● vt aver pietà di
**pivot** /'pɪvət/ n perno m; fig fulcro m ● vi imperniarsi (on su)
**pivotal** /'pɪvətl/ a (role) centrale; (decision) cruciale
**pixel** /'pɪksəl/ n pixel m inv
**pixie** /'pɪksɪ/ n folletto m
**pizza** /'pi:tsə/ n pizza f
**placard** /'plækɑ:d/ n cartellone m
**placate** /plə'keɪt/ vt placare
**place** /pleɪs/ n posto m (fam: house) casa f; (in book) segno m; **feel out of ~** sentirsi fuori posto; **take ~** aver luogo; **all over the ~** dappertutto ● vt collocare; (remember) identificare; **~ an order** fare un'ordinazione; **be ~d** (in race) piazzarsi
**placebo** /plə'si:bəʊ/ n Med placebo m inv; fig contentino m
**place mat** n sottopiatto m
**placement** /'pleɪsmənt/ n (act: in accommodation) collocamento m; (Br: job) stage m inv
**place name** n toponimo m
**placenta** /plə'sentə/ n placenta f
**placid** /'plæsɪd/ a placido
**plagiarist** /'pleɪdɪərɪst/ n plagiario, -a mf
**plagiarism** /'pleɪdʒərɪzm/ n plagio m
**plagiarize** /'pleɪdʒəraɪz/ vt plagiare
**plague** /pleɪg/ n peste f
**plaice** /pleɪs/ n inv platessa f
**plaid** /plæd/ n (fabric) plaid m inv; (pattern) motivo m scozzese ● attrib (scarf, shirt) scozzese
**plain** /pleɪn/ a chiaro; (simple) semplice; (not pretty) scialbo; (not patterned) normale; (chocolate) fondente; **in ~ clothes** in borghese ● adv (simply) semplicemente ● n pianura f

**plain-clothes** a (policeman etc) in borghese
**plainly** /'pleɪnlɪ/ adv francamente; (simply) semplicemente; (obviously) chiaramente
**plain paper fax** n fax m inv a carta comune
**plain-spoken** a franco
**plaintiff** /'pleɪntɪf/ n Jur parte f lesa
**plaintive** /'pleɪntɪv/ a lamentoso
**plaintively** /'pleɪntɪvlɪ/ adv con aria lamentosa
**plait** /plæt/ n treccia f ● vt intrecciare
**plan** /plæn/ n progetto m, piano m ● vt (pt/pp **planned**) progettare; (intend) prevedere
**plane¹** /pleɪn/ n (tree) platano m
**plane²** n aeroplano m; (in geometry) piano m
**plane³** n (tool) pialla f ● vt piallare
**plane crash** n incidente m aereo
**planet** /'plænɪt/ n pianeta m
**plank** /plæŋk/ n asse f
■ **plank down** vt (fam: put down) mollare
**plankton** /'plæŋktən/ n plancton m
**planning** /'plænɪŋ/ n pianificazione f
**planning permission** n licenza f edilizia
**plant** /plɑ:nt/ n pianta f; (machinery) impianto m; (factory) stabilimento m ● vt piantare; **~ oneself in front of sb** piantarsi davanti a qcno
**plantation** /plæn'teɪʃn/ n piantagione f
**planter** /'plɑ:ntə(r)/ n (person) piantatore, -trice mf; (machine) piantatrice f
**plant life** n flora f
**plaque** /plɑ:k/ n placca f
**plasma** /'plæzmə/ n plasma m
**plaster** /'plɑ:stə(r)/ n intonaco m; Med gesso m; (sticking ~) cerotto m; **in ~** ingessato ● vt intonacare (wall); (cover) ricoprire
**plastered** /'plɑ:stəd/ a (sl: drunk) sbronzo
**plasterer** /'plɑ:stərə(r)/ n intonacatore m
**plaster of Paris** n gesso m
**plastic** /'plæstɪk/ n plastica f ● a plastico
**Plasticine®** /'plæstɪsi:n/ n Plastilina ᴿ f
**plastic surgeon** n chirurgo m plastico
**plastic surgery** n chirurgia f plastica
**plate** /pleɪt/ n piatto m; (flat sheet) placca f; (gold and silverware) argenteria f; (in book) tavola f fuori testo ● vt (cover with metal) placcare
**plateau** /'plætəʊ/ n (pl ~x /'plætəʊz/) altopiano m ● vi fig livellarsi
**platform** /'plætfɔ:m/ n (stage) palco m; Rail marciapiede m; Pol piattaforma f; **~ 5** binario 5
**platform shoes** npl scarpe fpl con la zeppa
**platinum** /'plætɪnəm/ n platino m ● attrib di platino
**platitude** /'plætɪtju:d/ n luogo m comune
**platonic** /plə'tɒnɪk/ a platonico
**platoon** /plə'tu:n/ n Mil plotone m
**platter** /'plætə(r)/ n piatto m da portata
**platypus** /'plætɪpəs/ n ornitorinco m
**plausibility** /plɔ:zɪ'bɪlɪtɪ/ n plausibilità f
**plausible** /'plɔ:zəbl/ a plausibile
**play** /pleɪ/ n gioco m; Theat, TV dramma m, opera f teatrale; (performance) rappresentazione f; Radio sceneggiato m radiofonico; ~

**on words** gioco *m* di parole ● *vt* giocare a; (*act*) recitare; suonare ⟨*instrument*⟩; giocare ⟨*card*⟩ ● *vi* giocare; *Mus* suonare; **~ by the rules** stare alle regole; **~ with fire** scherzare con il fuoco; **~ dumb** fare lo gnorri; **~ safe** non prendere rischi

■ **play along** *vi* **~ along with sb** (*fam: cooperate*) fare il gioco di qcno

■ **play around with** *vt* (*meddle with*) cincischiarsi con

■ **play back** *vt* riascoltare ⟨*recording*⟩

■ **play down** *vt* minimizzare

■ **play on** *vi* (*continue to play*) continuare a giocare ● *vt* (*exploit*) giocare su

■ **play up** *vi fam* fare i capricci

**play-acting** *n* commedia *f*

**playboy** /'pleɪbɔɪ/ *n* playboy *m inv*

**player** /'pleɪə(r)/ *n* giocatore, -trice *mf*

**playful** /'pleɪfʊl/ *a* scherzoso

**playfully** /'pleɪfʊlɪ/ *adv* in modo scherzoso

**playground** /'pleɪgraʊnd/ *n Sch* cortile *m* (*per la ricreazione*)

**playgroup** /'pleɪgruːp/ *n* asilo *m*

**playing card** /'pleɪɪŋ/ *n* carta *f* da gioco

**playing field** *n* campo *m* da gioco

**play: playmate** *n* compagno, -a *mf* di gioco. **playpen** *n* box *m inv*. **playroom** /'pleɪruːm/ *n* ludoteca *f*. **plaything** *n* giocattolo *m*. **playwright** /'pleɪraɪt/ *n* drammaturgo, -a *mf*

**plaza** /'plɑːzə/ *n* (*public square*) piazza *f*; (*shopping ~*) centro *m* commerciale; (*Am: services point*) area *f* di servizio; (*Am: toll point*) casello *m*

**plc** *abbr* (**public limited company**) s.r.l.

**plea** /pliː/ *n* richiesta *f*; **enter a ~ of not guilty** *Jur* dichiararsi non colpevole; **make a ~ for** fare un appello a

**plead** /pliːd/ *vi* fare appello (**for** a); **~ guilty** dichiararsi colpevole; **~ with sb** implorare qcno ● *vt Jur* perorare ⟨*case*⟩

**pleasant** /'pleznt/ *a* piacevole

**pleasantly** /'plezntlɪ/ *adv* piacevolmente; ⟨*say, smile*⟩ cordialmente

**pleasantry** /'plezntrɪ/ *n* (*joke*) battuta *f*; **pleasantries** (*pl: polite remarks*) convenevoli *mpl*

**please** /pliːz/ *adv* per favore; **~ do** prego ● *vt* far contento; **~ oneself** fare il proprio comodo; **~ yourself!** come vuoi!; *pej* fai come ti pare!

**pleased** /pliːzd/ *a* lieto; **~ with/about** contento di

**pleasing** /'pliːzɪŋ/ *a* gradevole

**pleasurable** /'pleʒərəbl/ *a* gradevole

**pleasure** /'pleʒə(r)/ *n* piacere *m*; **with ~** con piacere, volentieri

**pleat** /pliːt/ *n* piega *f* ● *vt* pieghettare

**pleated** /'pliːtɪd/ *a* a pieghe

**pleb** /pleb/ *n fam* plebeo, -a *mf*

**plebby** /'plebɪ/ *a fam* plebeo

**plebeian** /plɪ'biːən/ *pej n* plebeo, -a *mf* ● *a* plebeo

**plebiscite** /'plebɪsɪt/ *n* plebiscito *m*

**pledge** /pledʒ/ *n* pegno *m*; (*promise*) promes-

sa *f* ● *vt* (*pawn*) impegnare; **~ to do sth** impegnarsi a fare qcsa

**plenary** /'pliːnərɪ/ *a* ⟨*session*⟩ plenario; ⟨*powers*⟩ pieno; ⟨*authority*⟩ assoluto

**plentiful** /'plentɪfl/ *a* abbondante

**plenty** /'plentɪ/ *n* abbondanza *f*; **~ of money** molti soldi; **~ of people** molta gente; **I've got ~** ne ho in abbondanza

**pleurisy** /'plʊərəsɪ/ *n* pleurite *f*

**pliability** /plaɪə'bɪlɪtɪ/ *n* flessibilità *f*

**pliable** /'plaɪəbl/ *a* flessibile

**pliers** /'plaɪəz/ *npl* pinze *fpl*

**plight** /plaɪt/ *n* triste condizione *f*

**plimsolls** /'plɪmsəlz/ *npl* scarpe *fpl* da ginnastica

**plinth** /plɪnθ/ *n* plinto *m*

**plod** /plɒd/ *vi* (*pt/pp* **plodded**) trascinarsi; (*work hard*) sgobbare

**plodder** /'plɒdə(r)/ *n* sgobbone, -a *mf*

**plonk¹** /plɒŋk/ *n fam* vino *m*; (*poor wine*) vinaccio *m*

**plonk²** *vt* (*fam: put*) sbattere

**plop** /plɒp/ *n* plop *m inv* ● *vi* (*pt/pp* **plopped**) fare plop

**plot** /plɒt/ *n* complotto *m*; (*of novel*) trama *f*; **~ of land** appezzamento *m* [di terreno] ● *vt/i* (*pt/pp* **plotted**) complottare

**plotter** /'plɒtə(r)/ *n* (*schemer*) cospiratore, -trice *mf*; *Comput* plotter *m inv*, tracciatore *m*

**plough** /plaʊ/ *n* aratro *m* ● *vt/i* arare

■ **plough back** *vt Comm* reinvestire

■ **plough into** *vt* (*crash into*) schiantarsi contro

■ **plough through** *vt* procedere a fatica in

**ploughman** /'plaʊmən/ *n* aratore *m*

**ploughman's lunch** *n Br* piatto *m* freddo *a base di pane formaggio e sottaceti*

**plow** /plaʊ/ *Am n* aratro *m* ● *vt/i* arare

**ploy** /plɔɪ/ *n fam* manovra *f*

**pluck** /plʌk/ *n* fegato *m* ● *vt* strappare; depilare ⟨*eyebrows*⟩; spennare ⟨*bird*⟩; cogliere ⟨*flower*⟩

■ **pluck up** *vt* **~ up courage** farsi coraggio

**plucky** /'plʌkɪ/ *a* (-**ier**, -**iest**) coraggioso

**plug** /plʌg/ *n* tappo *m*; *Electr* spina *f*; *Auto* candela *f*; (*fam: advertisement*) pubblicità *f inv* ● *vt* (*pt/pp* **plugged**) tappare; (*fam: advertise*) pubblicizzare

■ **plug away** *vi* (*work hard*) lavorare sodo

■ **plug in** *vt Electr* inserire la spina di

**plughole** /'plʌghəʊl/ *n Br* scarico *m*

**plug-in** *a* con la spina

**plum** /plʌm/ *n* prugna *f*; (*tree*) prugno *m*

**plumage** /'pluːmɪdʒ/ *n* piumaggio *m*

**plumb** /plʌm/ *a* verticale ● *adv* esattamente

■ **plumb in** *vt* collegare

**plumber** /'plʌmə(r)/ *n* idraulico *m*

**plumbing** /'plʌmɪŋ/ *n* impianto *m* idraulico

**plumb line** *n* filo *m* a piombo

**plume** /pluːm/ *n* piuma *f*

**plummet** /'plʌmɪt/ *vi* precipitare; ⟨*prices*⟩ crollare

**plump** /plʌmp/ *a* paffuto

■ **plump down** *vt* (*put down*) lasciare cadere

■ **plump for** *vt* scegliere

**plumpness** /'plʌmpnɪs/ *n* rotondità *f*

**plunder** /'plʌndə(r)/ *n* (*booty*) bottino *m* ● *vt* saccheggiare

**plunge** /plʌndʒ/ *n* tuffo *m*; **take the ~** *fam* buttarsi ● *vt* tuffare; *fig* sprofondare; **~ sb into despair** piombare qcno nella disperazione ● *vi* tuffarsi

**plunger** /'plʌndʒə(r)/ *n* (*tool*) sturalavandini *m inv*; (*handle*) stantuffo *m*

**plunging** /'plʌndʒɪŋ/ *a* **~ neckline** scollatura *f* profonda

**pluperfect** /plu:'pɜ:fɪkt/ *n* trapassato *m* prossimo

**plural** /'plʊərəl/ *a & n* plurale *m*

**plus** /plʌs/ *prep* più ● *a* in più; **500 ~** più di 500 ● *n* più *m*; (*advantage*) extra *m inv*

**plush** /plʌʃ/ *a* (*hotel etc*) lussuoso

**plutonium** /plu:'təʊnɪəm/ *n* plutonio *m*

**ply** /plaɪ/ *vt* (*pt/pp* **plied**) esercitare (*trade*); **~ sb with drink** continuare a offrire da bere a qcno

**plywood** /'plaɪwʊd/ *n* compensato *m*

**PM** *abbr* **Prime Minister**

**p.m.** *abbr* (**post meridiem**) del pomeriggio

**PMS** *n abbr* (**premenstrual syndrome**) sindrome *f* premestruale

**PMT** *n abbr* (**premenstrual tension**) tensione *f* premestruale

**pneumatic** /nju:'mætɪk/ *a* pneumatico

**pneumatic drill** *n* martello *m* pneumatico

**pneumonia** /nju:'məʊnɪə/ *n* polmonite *f*

**PO** *abbr* (**Post Office**) ≈ P.T.; *abbr* (**postal order**) vaglia *m inv* postale

**poach** /pəʊtʃ/ *vt Culin* bollire; cacciare di frodo (*deer*); pescare di frodo (*salmon*); **~ed egg** uovo *m* in camicia

**poacher** /'pəʊtʃə(r)/ *n* bracconiere *m*

**PO Box** *n abbr* (**Post Office Box**) C.P. *f*

**pocket** /'pɒkɪt/ *n* tasca *f*; **~ of resistance** sacca *f* di resistenza; **be out of ~** rimetterci ● *vt* intascare

**pocket-book** *n* taccuino *m*; (*wallet*) portafoglio *m*

**pocket-money** *n* denaro *m* per le piccole spese

**pock-marked** /'pɒkmɑ:kt/ *a* butterato

**pod** /pɒd/ *n* baccello *m*

**podgy** /'pɒdʒɪ/ *a* (**-ier, -iest**) grassoccio

**podiatrist** /pə'daɪətrɪst/ *n Am* pedicure *mf inv*

**podium** /'pəʊdɪəm/ *n* podio *m*

**poem** /'pəʊɪm/ *n* poesia *f*

**poet** /'pəʊɪt/ *n* poeta *m*

**poetic** /pəʊ'etɪk/ *a* poetico

**poetic licence** *n* licenza *f* poetica

**Poet Laureate** /'lɔ:rɪət/ *n* poeta *m* laureato

**poetry** /'pəʊɪtrɪ/ *n* poesia *f*

**po-faced** /pəʊ'feɪst/ *a Br fam* **look/be ~** avere un'aria di disapprovazione

**poignancy** /'pɔɪnjənsɪ/ *n* pregnanza *f*

**poignant** /'pɔɪnjənt/ *a* pregnante

**point** /pɔɪnt/ *n* punto *m*; (*sharp end*) punta *f*; (*meaning, purpose*) senso *m*; *Electr* presa *f*; **what is the ~?** a che scopo?; **the ~ is** il fatto

è; **I don't see the ~** non vedo il senso; **up to a ~** fino a un certo punto; **be on the ~ of doing sth** essere sul punto di fare qcsa; **~s** *pl Rail* scambio *m*; **good/bad ~s** aspetti *mpl* positivi/negativi ● *vt* puntare (**at** verso) ● *vi* (*with finger*) puntare il dito; **~ at/to** (*person:*) mostrare col dito; (*indicator:*) indicare; **~ and click** *Comput* punta e clicca

■ **point out** *vt* far notare (*fact*); **~ sth out to sb** far notare qcsa a qcno

**point-blank** *a* a bruciapelo

**pointed** /'pɔɪntɪd/ *a* appuntito; (*question*) diretto

**pointer** /'pɔɪntə(r)/ *n* (*piece of advice*) consiglio *m*

**pointillism** /'pwæntɪlɪzm/ *n* divisionismo *m*

**pointillist** /'pwæntɪlɪst/ *n* divisionista *mf*

**pointing** /'pɔɪntɪŋ/ *n Constr* rifinitura *f* con la malta

**pointing device** *n Comput* dispositivo *m* di puntamento

**pointless** /'pɔɪntlɪs/ *a* inutile

**point:** **point of order** *n* mozione *f* d'ordine. **point of sale** *n* (*place*) punto *m* di vendita; (*promotional material*) materiale *m* pubblicitario. **point-of-sale promotion** *n* promozione *f* punto vendita. **point of view** *n* punto *m* di vista

**poise** /pɔɪz/ *n* padronanza *f*

**poised** /pɔɪzd/ *a* in equilibrio; (*composed*) padrone di sé; **~ to** sul punto di

**poison** /'pɔɪzn/ *n* veleno *m* ● *vt* avvelenare

**poisoned** /'pɔɪz(ə)nd/ *a* avvelenato

**poisoner** /'pɔɪzənə(r)/ *n* avvelenatore, -trice *mf*

**poisonous** /'pɔɪzənəs/ *a* velenoso

**poison-pen letter** *n* lettera *f* anonima diffamatoria

**poke** /pəʊk/ *n* spintarella *f* ● *vt* spingere; (*fire*) attizzare; (*put*) ficcare; **~ fun at** prendere in giro

■ **poke about** *vi* frugare

■ **poke out** *vi* (*protrude*) spuntare

**poker¹** /'pəʊkə(r)/ *n* attizzatoio *m*

**poker²** *n* (*Cards*) poker *m*

**poker-faced** /-'feɪst/ *a* (*person*) impassibile

**poky** /'pəʊkɪ/ *a* (**-ier, -iest**) angusto

**Poland** /'pəʊlənd/ *n* Polonia *f*

**polar** /'pəʊlə(r)/ *a* polare

**polar bear** *n* orso *m* bianco

**polarity** /pə'lærətɪ/ *n Electr, Phys, fig* polarità *f inv*

**polarize** /'pəʊləraɪz/ *vt* polarizzare

**polarized** *a* polarizzato

**Pole** /pəʊl/ *n* polacco, -a *mf*

**pole¹** *n* palo *m*

**pole²** *n Geog, Electr* polo *m*

**polemic** /pə'lemɪk/ *n* polemica *f*

**polemical** /pə'lemɪkl/ *a* polemico

**pole star** *n* stella *f* polare

**pole vault** *n* salto *m* con l'asta

**police** /pə'li:s/ *npl* polizia *f* ● *vt* pattugliare (*area*); sorvegliare (*behaviour*)

**police: police car** *n* gazzella *f*. **policeman** *n* poliziotto *m*. **police state** *n* stato *m*

militarista. **police station** n commissariato m. **policewoman** n donna f poliziotto
**policy¹** /'pɒlɪsɪ/ n politica f
**policy²** n (insurance) polizza f
**polio** /'pəʊlɪəʊ/ n polio f
**Polish** /'pəʊlɪʃ/ a & n polacco m
**polish** /'pɒlɪʃ/ n (shine) lucentezza f; (substance) lucido m; (for nails) smalto m; fig raffinatezza f ● vt lucidare; fig smussare
■ **polish off** vt fam finire; far fuori (food)
■ **polish up** vt rispolverare (Italian)
**polished** /'pɒlɪʃt/ a (manner) raffinato; (performance) senza sbavature
**polisher** /'pɒlɪʃə(r)/ n (machine) lucidatrice f
**polite** /pə'laɪt/ a cortese
**politely** /pə'laɪtlɪ/ adv cortesemente
**politeness** /pə'laɪtnɪs/ n cortesia f
**politic** /'pɒlɪtɪk/ a prudente
**political** /pə'lɪtɪkl/ a politico
**politically** /pə'lɪtɪklɪ/ adv dal punto di vista politico; ~ **correct** politicamente corretto
**politician** /pɒlɪ'tɪʃn/ n politico m
**politicize** /pə'lɪtɪsaɪz/ vt politicizzare
**politics** /'pɒlɪtɪks/ n politica f
**polka** /'pɒlkə/ n polka f
**polka dot** n pois nm inv, pallino m ● attrib a pois
**poll** /pəʊl/ n votazione f; (election) elezioni fpl; [opinion] ~ sondaggio m d'opinione; **go to the** ~s andare alle urne ● vt ottenere (votes)
**pollen** /'pɒlən/ n polline m
**polling booth** /'pəʊlɪŋ/ n cabina f elettorale
**polling station** n seggio m elettorale
**pollster** /'pəʊlstə(r)/ n (person) persona f che esegue un sondaggio d'opinione
**poll tax** n imposta f locale sulle persone fisiche
**pollutant** /pə'lu:tənt/ n sostanza f inquinante
**pollute** /pə'lu:t/ vt inquinare
**polluted** /pə'lu:tɪd/ a inquinato
**polluter** /pə'lu:tə(r)/ n inquinatore, -trice mf
**pollution** /pə'lu:ʃn/ n inquinamento m
**polo** /'pəʊləʊ/ n polo m
**polo neck** n collo m alto
**polo shirt** n dolcevita f
**poly** /'pɒlɪ/ n (Br fam: polytechnic) politecnico m
**poly bag** n sacchetto m di plastica
**polyester** /pɒlɪ'estə(r)/ n poliestere m
**polygamous** /pə'lɪgəməs/ a poligamico
**polygamy** /pə'lɪgəmɪ/ n poligamia f
**polymath** /'pɒlɪmæθ/ n erudito, -a mf
**polymer** /'pɒlɪmə(r)/ n polimero m
**polystyrene®** /pɒlɪ'staɪri:n/ n polistirolo m
**polytechnic** /pɒlɪ'teknɪk/ n politecnico m
**polythene** /'pɒlɪθi:n/ n politene m
**polythene bag** n sacchetto m di plastica
**polyunsaturates** /pɒlɪʌn'sætjʊreɪts/ npl grassi mpl polinsaturi
**pomade** /pə'meɪd/ n pomata f
**pomegranate** /'pɒmɪgrænɪt/ n melagrana f
**pomp** /pɒmp/ n pompa f
**pompon** /'pɒmpɒn/ n pompon m

**pomposity** /pɒm'pɒsətɪ/ n pomposità f
**pompous** /'pɒmpəs/ a pomposo
**pompously** /'pɒmpəslɪ/ adv pomposamente
**poncy** /'pɒnsɪ/ a fam da finocchio; (person) finocchio
**pond** /pɒnd/ n stagno m
**ponder** /'pɒndə(r)/ vt/i ponderare
**ponderous** /'pɒndərəs/ a ponderoso; fig pesante
**pong** /pɒŋ/ n fam puzza f ● vi puzzare
**pontiff** /'pɒntɪf/ n pontefice m
**pontificate** /pɒn'tɪfɪkeɪt/ vi pontificare
**pontoon** /pɒn'tu:n/ n (float) galleggiante m; (pier) pontile m; (Br: game) ventuno m
**pony** /'pəʊnɪ/ n pony m inv
**ponytail** /'pəʊnɪteɪl/ n coda f di cavallo
**pony-trekking** /'pəʊnɪtrekɪŋ/ n escursioni fpl col pony
**pooch** /pu:tʃ/ n (fam: dog) cagnetto m
**poodle** /'pu:dl/ n barboncino m
**poof** /pʊf/, **poofter** /'pʊftə(r)/ n (Br fam: homosexual) finocchio m
**pooh** /pu:/ int (scorn, disgust) puah! ● n (Br: baby talk) popò f inv
**pooh-pooh** /pu:'pu:/ vt fam ridere di (suggestion)
**pool¹** /pu:l/ n (of water, blood) pozza f; [swimming] ~ piscina f
**pool²** n (common fund) cassa f comune; (in cards) piatto m; (game) biliardo m a buca; ~s pl ≈ totocalcio msg ● vt mettere insieme
**pooped** /pu:pt/ a fam be ~ [out] essere stanco morto
**poor** /pʊə(r)/ a povero; (not good) scadente; **in** ~ **health** in cattiva salute ● npl the ~ i poveri
**poorly** /'pʊəlɪ/ a be ~ non stare bene ● adv male
**pop¹** /pɒp/ n botto m; (drink) bibita f gasata ● v (pt/pp popped) ● vt (fam: put) mettere; (burst) far scoppiare ● vi (burst) scoppiare
■ **pop in** vi fam fare un salto
■ **pop out** vi fam fare un salto fuori; ~ **out to the shop** fare un salto al negozio
■ **pop up** vi (fam: appear unexpectedly) saltare fuori
**pop²** n fam musica f pop ● attrib pop inv
**popcorn** /'pɒpkɔ:n/ n popcorn m inv
**pope** /pəʊp/ n papa m
**poplar** /'pɒplə(r)/ n pioppo m
**poppy** /'pɒpɪ/ n papavero m
**pop sock** n gambaletto m
**populace** /'pɒpjʊləs/ n popolo m
**popular** /'pɒpjʊlə(r)/ a popolare; (belief) diffuso
**popularity** /pɒpjʊ'lærətɪ/ n popolarità f
**popularize** /'pɒpjʊləraɪz/ vt divulgare
**populate** /'pɒpjʊleɪt/ vt popolare
**population** /pɒpjʊ'leɪʃn/ n popolazione f
**populist** /'pɒpjʊlɪst/ a & n populista mf
**populous** /'pɒpjʊləs/ a popoloso
**pop-up book** n libro m con immagini tridimensionali
**pop-up toaster** n tostapane m inv a espulsione automatica

**porcelain** /'pɔːsəlɪn/ n porcellana f
**porch** /pɔːtʃ/ n portico m; Am veranda f
**porcupine** /'pɔːkjʊpaɪn/ n porcospino m
**pore¹** /pɔː(r)/ n poro m
**pore²** vi ~ **over** immergersi in
**pork** /pɔːk/ n carne f di maiale
**porn** /pɔːn/ n fam porno m
**porno** /'pɔːnəʊ/ a fam porno inv
**pornographic** /pɔːnə'græfɪk/ a pornografico
**pornography** /pɔː'nɒgrəfɪ/ n pornografia f
**porous** /'pɔːrəs/ a poroso
**porpoise** /'pɔːpəs/ n focena f
**porridge** /'pɒrɪdʒ/ n farinata f di fiocchi d'avena
**port¹** /pɔːt/ n porto m
**port²** n (Naut: side) babordo m
**port³** n (wine) porto m
**portable** /'pɔːtəbl/ a & n portatile m
**Portakabin®** /'pɔːtəkæbɪn/ n baracca f prefabbricata
**portcullis** /pɔː'tkʌlɪs/ n saracinesca f
**portentous** /pɔː'tentəs/ a (significant) solenne; (ominous) infausto
**porter** /'pɔːtə(r)/ n portiere m; (for luggage) facchino m
**portfolio** /pɔː'fəʊlɪəʊ/ n cartella f; Comm portafoglio m
**porthole** /'pɔːthəʊl/ n oblò m inv
**portion** /'pɔːʃn/ n parte f; (of food) porzione f
**portly** /'pɔːtlɪ/ a (-ier, -iest) corpulento
**portrait** /'pɔːtrɪt/ n ritratto m
**portrait painter** n ritrattista mf
**portray** /pɔː'treɪ/ vt ritrarre; (represent) descrivere; (actor:) impersonare
**portrayal** /pɔː'treɪəl/ n ritratto m; (by actor) impersonazione f
**Portugal** /'pɔːtjʊgl/ n Portogallo m
**Portuguese** /pɔːtjʊ'giːz/ a & n portoghese mf; (language) portoghese m
**pose** /pəʊz/ n posa f ● vt porre ⟨problem, question⟩ ● vi (for painter) posare; ~ **as** atteggiarsi a
**poser** /'pəʊzə(r)/ n fam (puzzle) rompicapo m inv; (person) montato, -a mf
**posh** /pɒʃ/ a fam lussuoso; ⟨people⟩ danaroso
**position** /pə'zɪʃn/ n posizione f; (job) posto m; (status) ceto m [sociale] ● vt posizionare
**positive** /'pɒzɪtɪv/ a positivo; (certain) sicuro; (progress) concreto ● n positivo m
**positively** /'pɒzɪtɪvlɪ/ adv positivamente; (decidedly) decisamente
**posse** /'pɒsɪ/ n gruppo m di volontari armati
**possess** /pə'zes/ vt possedere
**possession** /pə'zeʃn/ n possesso m; ~s pl beni mpl
**possessive** /pə'zesɪv/ a possessivo
**possessiveness** /pə'zesɪvnɪs/ n carattere m possessivo
**possessor** /pə'zesə(r)/ n possessore, -ditrice mf
**possibility** /pɒsə'bɪlətɪ/ n possibilità f inv
**possible** /'pɒsəbl/ a possibile
**possibly** /'pɒsəblɪ/ adv possibilmente; **I couldn't ~ accept** non mi è possibile accet-

tare; **he can't ~ be right** non è possibile che abbia ragione; **could you ~...?** potrebbe per favore...?
**possum** /'pɒsəm/ n fam opossum m inv; **play ~** far finta di dormire; (pretend to be dead) fare il morto
**post¹** /pəʊst/ n (pole) palo m ● vt affiggere ⟨notice⟩
**post²** n (place of duty) posto m ● vt appostare; (transfer) assegnare
**post³** n (mail) posta f; **by ~** per posta ● vt spedire; (put in letter box) imbucare; (as opposed to fax) mandare per posta; **keep sb ~ed** tenere qcno al corrente
**post+** pref post+
**postage** /'pəʊstɪdʒ/ n affrancatura f; ~ **and packaging** spese fpl di posta
**postage stamp** n francobollo m
**postal** /'pəʊstl/ a postale
**postal order** n vaglia m inv postale
**post: postbox** n cassetta f delle lettere.
**postcard** n cartolina f. **postcode** n codice m postale. **post-date** vt postdatare
**poster** /'pəʊstə(r)/ n poster m inv; (advertising, election) cartellone m
**posterior** /pɒ'stɪərɪə(r)/ n fam posteriore m
**posterity** /pɒ'sterətɪ/ n posterità f
**postgraduate** /pəʊs(t)'grædjʊət/ n laureato, -a mf che continua gli studi ● a successivo alla laurea
**posthumous** /'pɒstjʊməs/ a postumo
**posthumously** /'pɒstjʊməslɪ/ adv dopo la morte
**posting** /'pəʊstɪŋ/ n (job) incarico m; (Br: in mail) spedizione f
**postman** /'pəʊstmən/ n-postino m
**postmark** /'pəʊstmɑːk/ n timbro m postale
**post-mortem** /-'mɔːtəm/ n autopsia f
**post-natal** /-'neɪtl/ a post-partum
**post office** n ufficio m postale
**post office box** n casella f postale
**postpone** /pəʊs(t)'pəʊn/ vt rimandare
**postponement** /pəʊs(t)'pəʊnmənt/ n rinvio m
**postscript** /'pəʊs(t)skrɪpt/ n poscritto m
**posture** /'pɒstʃə(r)/ n posizione f
**post-war** a del dopoguerra
**pot** /pɒt/ n vaso m; (for tea) teiera f; (for coffee) caffettiera f; (for cooking) pentola f; (sl: marijuana) erba f; ~**s of money** fam un sacco di soldi; **go to ~** fam andare in malora
**potash** /'pɒtæʃ/ n potassa f
**potassium** /pə'tæsɪəm/ n potassio m
**potato** /pə'teɪtəʊ/ n (pl -es) patata f
**potato-peeler** /-'piːlə(r)/ n tagliapatate m inv
**pot-bellied** /'pɒtbelɪd/ a panciuto
**pot-belly** /'pɒtbelɪ/ n fam pancione m
**potent** /'pəʊtənt/ a potente
**potentate** /'pəʊtənteɪt/ n potentato m
**potential** /pə'tenʃl/ a potenziale ● n potenziale m
**potentially** /pə'tenʃəlɪ/ adv potenzialmente
**pot: pothole** n cavità f inv; (in road) buca f.
**potholer** n speleologo, -a mf. **pot-luck** n take

~ affidarsi alla sorte. **pot plant** *n* pianta *f* da appartamento. **pot-shot** *n* take a ~ at sparare a casaccio a

**potted** /'pɒtɪd/ *a* conservato; (*shortened*) condensato

**potted plant** *n* pianta *f* da appartamento

**potter¹** /'pɒtə(r)/ *vi* ~ [**about**] gingillarsi

**potter²** *n* vasaio, -a *mf*

**pottery** /'pɒtərɪ/ *n* lavorazione *f* della ceramica; (*articles*) ceramiche *fpl*; (*workshop*) laboratorio *m* di ceramiche

**potting compost** /'pɒtɪŋ/ *n* terriccio *m*

**potty** /'pɒtɪ/ *a* (**-ier, -iest**) *fam* matto ● *n* vasino *m*

**pouch** /paʊtʃ/ *n* marsupio *m*

**pouffe** /puːf/ *n* pouf *m inv*

**poultry** /'pəʊltrɪ/ *n* pollame *m*

**pounce** /paʊns/ *vi* balzare; ~ **on** saltare su

**pound¹** /paʊnd/ *n* libbra *f* (= *0,454 kg*); (*money*) sterlina *f*

**pound²** *vt* battere ● *vi* ⟨*heart:*⟩ battere forte; (*run heavily*) correre pesantemente

**pound³** *n* (*for cars*) deposito *m* auto

**pounding** /'paʊndɪŋ/ *n* martellio *m* ● *a* martellante

**pour** /pɔː(r)/ *vt* versare ● *vi* riversarsi; (*with rain*) piovere a dirotto

■ **pour out** *vi* riversarsi fuori ● *vt* versare ⟨*drink*⟩; sfogare ⟨*troubles*⟩

**pout** /paʊt/ *vi* fare il broncio ● *n* broncio

**poverty** /'pɒvətɪ/ *n* povertà *f*

**POW** *n abbr* (**prisoner of war**) prigioniero, -a *mf* di guerra

**powder** /'paʊdə(r)/ *n* polvere *f*; (*cosmetic*) cipria *f* ● *vt* polverizzare; (*face*) incipriare

**powder room** *n euph* toilette *f inv* per signore

**powdery** /'paʊdərɪ/ *a* polveroso

**power** /'paʊə(r)/ *n* potere *m*; *Electr* corrente *f* [elettrica]; *Math* potenza *f*

**power cut** *n* interruzione *f* di corrente

**powered** /'paʊəd/ *a* ~ **by electricity** alimentato da corrente elettrica

**powerful** /'paʊəful/ *a* potente

**powerhouse** /'paʊəhaʊs/ *n* (*fig: person*) persona *f* dinamica e energica; **a ~ of ideas** un vulcano di idee

**powerless** /'paʊəlɪs/ *a* impotente

**power: power-on light** *n* spia *f* di accensione. **power station** *n* centrale *f* elettrica. **power steering** *n Auto* servosterzo *m*. **power switch** *n* pulsante *m* di alimentazione. **power unit** (*of computer etc*) alimentatore *m*

**pow-wow** /'paʊwaʊ/ *n* (*of American Indians*) raduno *m* tribale; (*fam: discussion*) discussione *f*

**pp** *abbr* (**pages**) pp.; *abbr* (**per procurationem**) pp.

**PR** *n abbr* (**proportional representation**) proporzionale *f*; *abbr* (**public relations**) pubbliche relazioni *fpl*

**practicable** /'præktɪkəbl/ *a* praticabile

**practical** /'præktɪkl/ *a* pratico

**practicality** /præktɪ'kælɪtɪ/ *n* praticità *f*

**practical joke** *n* scherzo *m* pratico

**practically** /'præktɪklɪ/ *adv* praticamente

**practice** /'præktɪs/ *n* pratica *f*; (*custom*) usanza *f*; (*habit*) abitudine *f*; (*exercise*) esercizio *m*; *Sport* allenamento *m*; **in ~** (*in reality*) in pratica; **out of ~** fuori esercizio; **put into ~** mettere in pratica

**practise** /'præktɪs/ *vt* fare pratica in; (*carry out*) mettere in pratica; esercitare ⟨*profession*⟩ ● *vi* esercitarsi; ⟨*doctor:*⟩ praticare

**practised** /'præktɪst/ *a* esperto

**pragmatic** /præg'mætɪk/ *a* pragmatico

**pragmatism** /'prægmətɪzm/ *n* pragmatismo *m*

**pragmatist** /'prægmətɪst/ *n* pragmatico, -a *mf*

**praise** /preɪz/ *n* lode *f* ● *vt* lodare

**praiseworthy** /'preɪzwɜːðɪ/ *a* lodevole

**pram** /præm/ *n* carrozzella *f*

**prance** /prɑːns/ *vi* saltellare

**prank** /præŋk/ *n* tiro *m*

**prattle** /'prætl/ *vi* parlottare

**prawn** /prɔːn/ *n* gambero *m*

**prawn cocktail** *n* cocktail *m inv* di gamberetti

**pray** /preɪ/ *vi* pregare

**prayer** /preə(r)/ *n* preghiera *f*

**preach** /priːtʃ/ *vt/i* predicare

**preacher** /'priːtʃə(r)/ *n* predicatore, -trice *mf*

**preamble** /priː'æmbl/ *n* preambolo *m*

**pre-arrange** /priː-/ *vt* predisporre

**precarious** /prɪ'keərɪəs/ *a* precario

**precariously** /prɪ'keərɪəslɪ/ *adv* in modo precario

**precast** /'priːkɑːst/ *a* ⟨*concrete*⟩ prefabbricato

**precaution** /prɪ'kɔːʃn/ *n* precauzione *f*; **as a ~** per precauzione

**precautionary** /prɪ'kɔːʃnərɪ/ *a* preventivo

**precede** /prɪ'siːd/ *vt* precedere

**precedence** /'presɪdəns/ *n* precedenza *f*

**precedent** /'presɪdənt/ *n* precedente *m*

**preceding** /prɪ'siːdɪŋ/ *a* precedente

**preceptor** /prɪ'septə(r)/ *n Am Univ* precettore *m*

**precinct** /'priːsɪŋkt/ *n* (*traffic-free*) zona *f* pedonale; (*Am: district*) circoscrizione *f*

**precious** /'preʃəs/ *a* prezioso; ⟨*style*⟩ ricercato ● *adv fam* ~ **little** ben poco

**precipice** /'presɪpɪs/ *n* precipizio *m*

**precipitate¹** /prɪ'sɪpɪtət/ *a* precipitoso

**precipitate²** /prɪ'sɪpɪteɪt/ *vt* precipitare

**precipitation** /prɪsɪpɪ'teɪʃn/ *n* precipitazione *f*

**précis** /'preɪsiː/ *n* (*pl précis* /'preɪsiːz/) sunto *m*

**precise** /prɪ'saɪs/ *a* preciso

**precisely** /prɪ'saɪslɪ/ *adv* precisamente

**precision** /prɪ'sɪʒn/ *n* precisione *f*

**preclude** /prɪ'kluːd/ *vt* precludere

**precocious** /prɪ'kəʊʃəs/ *a* precoce

**precociousness** /prɪ'kəʊʃəsnɪs/ *n* precocità *f*

**preconceived** /pri:kən'si:vd/ *a* preconcetto

**preconception** /pri:kən'sepʃn/ *n* preconcetto *m*

**precondition** /pri:kən'dɪʃn/ *n* presupposto *m* ● *vt Psych* condizionare

**precook** /pri:'kʊk/ *vt* cuocere in anticipo

**precursor** /pri:'kɜ:sə(r)/ *n* precursore *m*

**predator** /'predətə(r)/ *n* predatore. -trice *mf*

**predatory** /'predət(ə)rɪ/ *a* rapace

**predecessor** /'pri:dɪsesə(r)/ *n* predecessore, -a *mf*

**predetermine** /pri:dɪ'tɜ:mɪn/ *vt* predeterminare

**predicament** /prɪ'dɪkəmənt/ *n* situazione *f* difficile

**predicate** /'predɪkət/ *n Gram* predicato *m*

**predicative** /prɪ'dɪkətɪv/ *a* predicativo

**predict** /prɪ'dɪkt/ *vt* predire

**predictable** /prɪ'dɪktəbl/ *a* prevedibile

**prediction** /prɪ'dɪkʃn/ *n* previsione *f*

**predigested** /pri:daɪ'dʒestɪd/ *a* predigerito

**predisposition** /pri:dɪspə'zɪʃn/ *n* predisposizione *f*

**predominant** /prɪ'dɒmɪnənt/ *a* predominante

**predominate** /prɪ'dɒmɪneɪt/ *vi* predominare

**pre-eminent** /pri:'emɪnənt/ *a* preminente

**pre-empt** /pri:'empt/ *vt* (*prevent*) prevenire

**pre-emptive** /pri:'emptɪv/ *a* preventivo

**preen** /pri:n/ *vt* lisciarsi; ~ **oneself** *fig* farsi bello

**prefab** /'pri:fæb/ *n fam* casa *f* prefabbricata

**prefabricated** /pri:'fæbrɪkeɪtɪd/ *a* prefabbricato

**preface** /'prefɪs/ *n* prefazione *f*

**prefatory** /'prefət(ə)rɪ/ *a* (*comments*) preliminare; (*pages, notes*) introduttivo

**prefect** /'pri:fekt/ *n Sch* studente, -tessa *mf della scuola superiore con responsabilità disciplinari ecc*

**prefer** /prɪ'fɜ:(r)/ *vt* (*pt/pp* **preferred**) preferire; **I ~ to walk** preferisco camminare

**preferable** /'pref(ə)rəbl/ *a* preferibile (**to** a)

**preferably** /'pref(ə)rəblɪ/ *adv* preferibilmente

**preference** /'prefərəns/ *n* preferenza *f*

**preferential** /prefə'renʃl/ *a* preferenziale

**prefix** /'pri:fɪks/ *n* prefisso *m*

**pregnancy** /'pregnənsɪ/ *n* gravidanza *f*

**pregnant** /'pregnənt/ *a* incinta

**preheat** /pri:'hi:t/ *vt* preriscaldare (*oven*)

**prehensile** /pri:'hensaɪl/ *a* prensile

**prehistoric** /pri:hɪs'tɒrɪk/ *a* preistorico

**pre-ignition** /pri:ɪg'nɪʃn/ *n* preaccensione *f*

**pre-installed** /pri:ɪn'stɔ:ld/ *a* preinstallato

**prejudge** /pri:'dʒʌdʒ/ *vt* giudicare prematuramente (*issue*)

**prejudice** /'predʒʊdɪs/ *n* pregiudizio *m* ● *vt* influenzare (**against** contro); (*harm*) danneggiare

**prejudiced** /'predʒʊdɪst/ *a* prevenuto

**preliminary** /prɪ'lɪmɪnərɪ/ *a* preliminare

**preloaded** /pri:'ləʊdɪd/ *a* precaricato

**prelude** /'prelju:d/ *n* preludio *m*

**premarital** /pri:'mærɪtl/ *a* prematrimoniale

**premarital sex** *n* rapporti *mpl* prematrimoniali

**premature** /'premətjʊə(r)/ *a* prematuro

**premature birth** *n* parto *m* prematuro

**prematurely** /'premətjʊəlɪ/ *adv* prematuramente

**premeditated** /pri:'medɪteɪtɪd/ *a* premeditato

**premenstrual syndrome** /pri:'menstrʊəl/ *n* sindrome *f* premestruale

**premenstrual tension** *n* tensione *f* premestruale

**premier** /'premɪə(r)/ *a* primario ● *n Pol* primo ministro *m*, premier *m inv*

**première** /'premɪeə(r)/ *n* prima *f*

**premiership** /'premɪəʃɪp/ *n Pol* carica *f* di primo ministro nel Regno Unito; ≈ presidenza *f* del consiglio

**premises** /'premɪsɪz/ *npl* locali *mpl*; **on the ~** sul posto

**premium** /'pri:mɪəm/ *n* premio *m*; **be at a ~** essere una cosa rara

**premonition** /premə'nɪʃn/ *n* presentimento *m*

**prenatal** /pri:'neɪtl/ *a esp Am* prenatale

**preoccupied** /pri:'ɒkjʊpaɪd/ *a* preoccupato

**preoperative** /pri:'ɒp(ə)rətɪv/ *a* preoperatorio

**preordained** /pri:ɔ:'deɪnd/ *a* prestabilito; (*outcome*) predestinato

**prep** /prep/ *n Sch* compiti *mpl*

**pre-packed** /pri:'pækt/ *a* preconfezionato

**prepaid** /pri:'peɪd/ *a* pagato in anticipo; (*envelope*) già affrancato

**preparation** /prepə'reɪʃn/ *n* preparazione *f*; **~s** *pl* preparativi *mpl*

**preparatory** /prɪ'pærətrɪ/ *a* preparatorio; **~ to** come preparazione per

**prepare** /prɪ'peə(r)/ *vt* preparare ● *vi* prepararsi (**for** per); **~d to** disposto a

**prepay** /pri:'peɪ/ *vt* (*pt/pp* **-paid**) pagare in anticipo

**preponderance** /prɪ'pɒndərəns/ *n* preponderanza *f*

**preponderantly** /prɪ'pɒndərəntlɪ/ *adv* in modo preponderante

**preponderate** /prɪ'pɒndəreɪt/ *vi* predominare

**preposition** /prepə'zɪʃn/ *n* preposizione *f*

**prepossessing** /pri:pə'zesɪŋ/ *a* attraente

**preposterous** /prɪ'pɒstərəs/ *a* assurdo

**pre-programmed** /pri:'prəʊgræmd/ *a* programmato; *Comput* preprogrammato

**prep school** *n* scuola *f* elementare privata

**pre-recorded** /-rɪ'kɔ:dɪd/ *a* in differita

**prerequisite** /pri:'rekwɪzɪt/ *n* condizione *f* sine qua non

**prerogative** /prɪ'rɒgətɪv/ *n* prerogativa *f*

**Presbyterian** /prezbɪ'tɪərɪən/ *a & n* presbiteriano, -a *mf*

**pre-school** /'pri:sku:l/ *n Am* scuola *f* materna, asilo *m* ● *a* (*child*) in età prescolastica; (*years*) prescolastico

**prescribe** /prɪ'skraɪb/ vt prescrivere
**prescription** /prɪ'skrɪpʃn/ n Med ricetta f
**prescriptive** /prɪ'skrɪptɪv/ a normativo
**presence** /'prezns/ n presenza f; ~ **of mind** presenza f di spirito
**present¹** /'preznt/ a presente ● n presente m; **at** ~ attualmente
**present²** n (gift) regalo m; **give sb sth as a** ~ regalare qcsa a qcno
**present³** /prɪ'zent/ vt presentare; ~ **sb with an award** consegnare un premio a qcno
**presentable** /prɪ'zentəbl/ a **be** ~ essere presentabile
**presentation** /prezn'teɪʃn/ n presentazione f
**present-day** a attuale
**presenter** /prɪ'zentə(r)/ n TV, Radio presentatore, -trice mf
**presently** /'prezntlɪ/ adv fra poco; (Am: now) attualmente
**preservation** /prezə'veɪʃn/ n conservazione f
**preservative** /prɪ'zɜ:vətɪv/ n conservante m
**preserve** /prɪ'zɜ:v/ vt preservare; (maintain, Culin) conservare ● n (in hunting & fig) riserva f; (jam) marmellata f
**pre-set** /pri:'set/ vt programmare
**pre-shrunk** /pri:'ʃrʌŋk/ a (fabric) irrestringibile
**preside** /prɪ'zaɪd/ vi presiedere (**over** a)
**presidency** /'prezɪdənsɪ/ n presidenza f
**president** /'prezɪdənt/ n presidente m
**presidential** /prezɪ'denʃl/ a presidenziale
**pre-soak** /pri:'səʊk/ vt mettere in ammollo
**press** /pres/ n (machine) pressa f; (newspapers) stampa f ● vt premere; pressare (flower); (iron) stirare; (squeeze) stringere ● vi (urge) incalzare
■ **press ahead** vi (continue) proseguire
■ **press for** vi fare pressione per; **be ~ed for** (short of) essere a corto di
■ **press on** vi andare avanti
**press: press conference** n conferenza f stampa. **press cutting** n ritaglio m di giornale. **press-gang** vt forzare
**pressing** /'presɪŋ/ a urgente
**press: press release** n comunicato m stampa. **press stud** n [bottone m] automatico m. **press-up** n flessione f
**pressure** /'preʃə(r)/ n pressione f ● vt = **pressurize**
**pressure-cooker** n pentola f a pressione
**pressure group** n gruppo m di pressione
**pressurize** /'preʃəraɪz/ vt far pressione su
**pressurized** /'preʃəraɪzd/ a (cabin) pressurizzato
**prestige** /pre'sti:ʒ/ n prestigio m
**prestigious** /pre'stɪdʒəs/ a prestigioso
**presumably** /prɪ'zju:məblɪ/ adv presumibilmente
**presume** /prɪ'zju:m/ vt presumere; ~ **to do sth** permettersi di fare qcsa ● vi ~ **on** approfittare di
**presumption** /prɪ'zʌmpʃn/ n presunzione f; (boldness) impertinenza f

**presumptuous** /prɪ'zʌmptjʊəs/ a impertinente
**presuppose** /pri:sə'pəʊz/ vt presupporre
**presupposition** /pri:sʌpə'zɪʃn/ n presupposizione f
**pre-tax** /pri:'tæks/ a al lordo d'imposta
**pretence** /prɪ'tens/ n finzione f; (pretext) pretesto m; **it's all** ~ è tutta una scena
**pretend** /prɪ'tend/ vt fingere; (claim) pretendere ● vi fare finta
**pretender** /prɪ'tendə(r)/ n pretendente mf
**pretentious** /prɪ'tenʃəs/ a pretenzioso
**preterite** /'pretərɪt/ n preterito m
**pretext** /'pri:tekst/ n pretesto m
**pretty** /'prɪtɪ/ a (-ier, -iest) carino ● adv (fam: fairly) abbastanza
**prevail** /prɪ'veɪl/ vi prevalere; ~ **on sb to do sth** convincere qcno a fare qc
**prevailing** /prɪ'veɪlɪŋ/ a prevalente
**prevalence** /'prevələns/ n diffusione f
**prevalent** /'prevələnt/ a diffuso
**prevaricate** /prɪ'værɪkeɪt/ vi tergiversare
**prevent** /prɪ'vent/ vt impedire; ~ **sb [from] doing sth** impedire a qcno di fare qcsa
**preventable** /prɪ'ventəbl/ a evitabile
**prevention** /prɪ'venʃn/ n prevenzione f
**preventive** /prɪ'ventɪv/ a preventivo
**preview** /'pri:vju:/ n anteprima f
**previous** /'pri:vɪəs/ a precedente
**previously** /'pri:vɪəslɪ/ adv precedentemente
**pre-war** /pri:'wɔ:/ a anteguerra
**pre-wash** /pri:'wɒʃ/ n prelavaggio m
**prey** /preɪ/ n preda f; **bird of** ~ uccello m rapace ● vi ~ **on** far preda di; ~ **on sb's mind** attanagliare qcno
**price** /praɪs/ n prezzo m ● vt Comm fissare il prezzo di
**price: price-conscious** adj consapevole dell'andamento dei prezzi. **price cutting** n taglio m dei prezzi. **price increase** n aumento m di prezzo
**priceless** /'praɪslɪs/ a inestimabile; (fam: amusing) spassosissimo
**price: price list** n listino m prezzi. **price/ performance ratio** n rapporto m prezzo/prestazioni. **price range** n gamma f di prezzi. **price tag** n tallocino m del prezzo. **price war** n guerra f dei prezzi
**pricey** /'praɪsɪ/ a fam caro
**pricing policy** /'praɪsɪŋ/ n politica f di determinazione dei prezzi
**prick** /prɪk/ n puntura f; vulg (penis) cazzo m; (person) stronzo m ● vt pungere
■ **prick up** vt ~ **up one's ears** rizzare le orecchie
**prickle** /'prɪkl/ n spina f; (sensation) formicolio m
**prickly** /'prɪklɪ/ a pungente; (person) irritabile
**pride** /praɪd/ n orgoglio m; (of lions) branco m; ~ **of place** posizione f d'onore ● vt ~ **oneself on** vantarsi di
**priest** /pri:st/ n prete m
**priesthood** /'pri:sthʊd/ n (clergy) clero m;

(calling) sacerdozio m; **enter the** ~ farsi prete

**prig** /prɪg/ n presuntuoso m

**priggish** /'prɪgɪʃ/ a presuntuoso

**prim** /prɪm/ a (**primmer, primmest**) perbenino

**primacy** /'praɪməsɪ/ n primato m; (of party, power) supremazia f; Relig carica f di primate

**prima facie** /praɪmə'feɪʃiː/ adv (at first) a prima vista ● a a prima vista legittimo

**primal** /'praɪməl/ a (quality, myth, feeling) primitivo

**primarily** /'praɪmərɪlɪ/ adv in primo luogo

**primary** /'praɪmərɪ/ a primario; (chief) principale

**primary school** n scuola f elementare

**primate** /'praɪmeɪt/ n Zool, Relig primate m

**prime¹** /praɪm/ a principale, primo; (firstrate) eccellente ● n **be in one's** ~ essere nel fiore degli anni

**prime²** vt preparare (surface, person)

**Prime Minister** n Primo Ministro m

**primer** /'praɪmə(r)/ n (paint) base f; (for detonating) innesco m

**prime time** n prime time m inv, fascia f di massimo ascolto ● attrib (advertising, programme) nella fascia di massimo ascolto

**primeval** /praɪ'miːvl/ a primitivo

**primitive** /'prɪmɪtɪv/ a primitivo

**primordial** /praɪ'mɔːdɪəl/ a primordiale

**primrose** /'prɪmrəʊz/ n primula f

**prince** /prɪns/ n principe m

**princely** /'prɪnslɪ/ a (life, rôle) da principe; (amount, style) principesco

**princess** /prɪn'ses/ n principessa f

**principal** /'prɪnsəpl/ a principale ● n Sch preside m

**principality** /prɪnsɪ'pælɪtɪ/ n principato m

**principally** /'prɪnsəplɪ/ adv principalmente

**principle** /'prɪnsəpl/ n principio m; **in** ~ in teoria; **on** ~ per principio; ~**s** pl (fundamentals) fondamenti mpl

**print** /prɪnt/ n (mark, trace) impronta f; Phot copia f; (letters) stampatello m; (picture) stampa f; **in** ~ (printed out) stampato; (book) in commercio; **out of** ~ esaurito ● vt/i stampare; (write in capitals) scrivere in stampatello

■ **print out** vt/i Comput stampare

**printed matter** /'prɪntɪd/ n stampe fpl

**printer** /'prɪntə(r)/ n stampante f; (person) tipografo, -a mf

**printer port** n porta f per la stampante

**printing** /'prɪntɪŋ/ n tipografia f

**printout** /'prɪntaʊt/ n Comput stampa f

**print speed** n velocità f di stampa

**prior** /'praɪə(r)/ a precedente ● prep ~ **to** prima di

**priority** /praɪ'ɒrətɪ/ n precedenza f; (matter) priorità f inv

**prise** /praɪz/ vt ~ open/up forzare

**prism** /'prɪzm/ n prisma m

**prison** /'prɪzn/ n prigione f

**prisoner** /'prɪz(ə)nə(r)/ n prigioniero, -a mf

**prison sentence** n pena f detentiva

**prissy** /'prɪsɪ/ a (person) perbenista

**pristine** /'prɪstiːn/ a originario; (unspoilt) intatto

**privacy** /'prɪvəsɪ/ n privacy f

**private** /'praɪvət/ a privato; (car, secretary, letter) personale ● n Mil soldato m semplice; **in** ~ in privato

**private enterprise** n iniziativa f privata

**private property** n proprietà f privata

**privately** /'praɪvətlɪ/ adv (funded, educated etc) privatamente; (in secret) in segreto; (confidentially) in privato; (inwardly) interiormente

**privation** /praɪ'veɪʃn/ n privazione f; ~**s** pl stenti mpl

**privatization** /praɪvətaɪ'zeɪʃn/ n privatizzazione f

**privatize** /'praɪvətaɪz/ vt privatizzare

**privilege** /'prɪvəlɪdʒ/ n privilegio m

**privileged** /'prɪvəlɪdʒd/ a privilegiato

**privy** /'prɪvɪ/ a **be** ~ **to** essere al corrente di

**prize** /praɪz/ n premio m ● a (idiot etc) perfetto ● vt apprezzare

**prize: prize-giving** /'praɪzgɪvɪŋ/ n premiazione f. **prizewinner** n vincitore, -trice mf. **prize-winning** a vincente

**pro** /prəʊ/ n (fam: professional) professionista mf; **the** ~**s and cons** il pro e il contro

**probability** /prɒbə'bɪlətɪ/ n probabilità f inv

**probable** /'prɒbəbl/ a probabile

**probably** /'prɒbəblɪ/ adv probabilmente

**probate** /'prəʊbeɪt/ n Jur omologazione f

**probation** /prə'beɪʃn/ n prova f; Jur libertà f vigilata

**probationary** /prə'beɪʃnərɪ/ a in prova; ~ **period** periodo m di prova

**probationer** /prə'beɪʃnə(r)/ n (employee on trial) impiegato, -a mf in prova; (trainee) apprendista mf

**probe** /prəʊb/ n sonda f; (fig: investigation) indagine f ● vt sondare; (investigate) esaminare a fondo

**probing** /'prəʊbɪŋ/ a (question) penetrante

**problem** /'prɒbləm/ n problema m ● attrib difficile

**problematic** /prɒblə'mætɪk/ a problematico

**problem page** n posta f del cuore

**procedural** /prə'siːdʒərəl/ a (detail, error) procedurale

**procedure** /prə'siːdʒə(r)/ n procedimento m

**proceed** /prə'siːd/ vi procedere ● vt ~ **to do sth** proseguire facendo qcsa

**proceedings** /prə'siːdɪŋz/ npl (report) atti mpl; Jur azione fsg legale

**proceeds** /'prəʊsiːdz/ npl ricavato msg

**process** /'prəʊses/ n processo m; (procedure) procedimento m; **in the** ~ nel far ciò ● vt trattare; Admin occuparsi di; Phot sviluppare

**procession** /prə'seʃn/ n processione f

**processor** /'prəʊsesə(r)/ n Comput processore m; (for food) tritatutto m inv

**pro-choice** /prəʊ'tʃɔɪs/ a abortista

**proclaim** /prə'kleɪm/ vt proclamare

**proclamation** /prɒklə'meɪʃn/ n proclamazione f

**proclivity** /prə'klɪvətɪ/ n tendenza f
**procrastinate** /prə'kræstɪneɪt/ vi procrastinare
**procrastination** /prəkræstɪ'neɪʃn/ n procrastinazione f
**procreate** /'prəʊkrɪeɪt/ vi procreare
**procreation** /prəʊkrɪ'eɪʃn/ n procreazione f
**procure** /prə'kjʊə(r)/ vt ottenere
**prod** /prɒd/ n colpetto m ● vt (pt/pp **prodded**) punzecchiare; fig incitare
**prodigal** /'prɒdɪgl/ a prodigo
**prodigal son** n figliol m prodigo
**prodigious** /prə'dɪdʒəs/ a prodigioso
**prodigy** /'prɒdɪdʒɪ/ n [**infant**] ~ bambino m prodigio
**produce**[1] /'prɒdjuːs/ n prodotti mpl; ~ **of Italy** prodotto in Italia
**produce**[2] /prə'djuːs/ vt produrre; (bring out) tirar fuori; (cause) causare; (fam: give birth to) fare
**producer** /prə'djuːsə(r)/ n produttore m
**product** /'prɒdʌkt/ n prodotto m
**product range** n gamma f di prodotti
**production** /prə'dʌkʃn/ n produzione f; Theat spettacolo m
**production: production control** n controllo m della produzione. **production director** n direttore, -trice mf della produzione. **production line** n catena f di montaggio. **production management** n gestione f della produzione. **production manager** n direttore, -trice mf della produzione
**productive** /prə'dʌktɪv/ a produttivo
**productivity** /prɒdʌk'tɪvətɪ/ n produttività f
**product range** n gamma f di prodotti
**profane** /prə'feɪn/ a profano; (blasphemous) blasfemo
**profanity** /prə'fænətɪ/ n (oath) bestemmia f
**profess** /prə'fes/ vt (claim) dichiarare
**professed** /prə'fest/ a (claiming to be) sedicente
**profession** /prə'feʃn/ n professione f
**professional** /prə'feʃnəl/ a professionale; (not amateur) professionista; ⟨piece of work⟩ da professionista; ⟨man⟩ di professione ● n professionista mf
**professionalism** /prə'feʃnəlɪzm/ n (of person, organization, work) professionalità f; Sport professionismo m
**professionally** /prə'feʃnəlɪ/ adv professionalmente
**professor** /prə'fesə(r)/ n professore m [universitario]
**professorial** /prɒfə'sɔːrɪəl/ a ⟨duties, post, salary⟩ professorale
**proffer** /'prɒfə(r)/ vt (hold out) porgere; (fig: offer) offrire
**proficiency** /prə'fɪʃnsɪ/ n competenza f
**proficient** /prə'fɪʃnt/ a competente (**in** in)
**profile** /'prəʊfaɪl/ n profilo m
**profit** /'prɒfɪt/ n profitto m ● vi ~ **from** trarre profitto da
**profitable** /'prɒfɪtəbl/ a proficuo
**profitably** /'prɒfɪtəblɪ/ adv in modo proficuo

**profit and loss account** n conto m profitti e perdite
**profiteer** /prɒfɪ'tɪə(r)/ n profittatore, -trice mf
**profiterole** /prə'fɪtərəʊl/ n profiterole m inv
**profit margin** n margine m di profitto
**profit-sharing** n partecipazione f agli utili
**profligate** /'prɒflɪgət/ a (extravagant) spendaccione; (dissolute) dissoluto; ⟨spending⟩ eccessivo
**pro forma invoice** /fɔːmə/ n fattura f proforma
**profound** /prə'faʊnd/ a profondo
**profoundly** /prə'faʊndlɪ/ adv profondamente
**profuse** /prə'fjuːs/ a ~ **apologies** una profusione di scuse
**profusely** /prə'fjuːslɪ/ adv profusamente
**profusion** /prə'fjuːʒn/ n profusione f; **in** ~ in abbondanza
**progeny** /'prɒdʒənɪ/ n progenie f inv
**prognosis** /prɒg'nəʊsɪs/ n (pl **-oses**) (prediction) previsione f; Med prognosi f inv
**prognosticate** /prɒg'nɒstɪkeɪt/ vt pronosticare
**program** /'prəʊgræm/ n Comput programma m ● vt (pt/pp **programmed**) programmare
**programme** /'prəʊgræm/ n Br programma m
**programmer** /'prəʊgræmə(r)/ n Comput programmatore, -trice mf
**programming** /'prəʊgræmɪŋ/ n programmazione f
**progress**[1] /'prəʊgres/ n progresso m; **in** ~ in corso; **make** ~ fig fare progressi
**progress**[2] /prə'gres/ vi progredire; fig fare progressi
**progressive** /prə'gresɪv/ a progressivo; (reforming) progressista
**progressively** /prə'gresɪvlɪ/ adv progressivamente
**prohibit** /prə'hɪbɪt/ vt proibire
**prohibition** /prəʊhɪ'bɪʃn/ n proibizione; **P~** Am proibizionismo m
**prohibitive** /prə'hɪbɪtɪv/ a proibitivo
**prohibitively** /prə'hɪbɪtɪvlɪ/ adv ⟨expensive⟩ in modo proibitivo
**project**[1] /'prɒdʒekt/ n progetto m; Sch ricerca f
**project**[2] /prə'dʒekt/ vt proiettare ⟨film, image⟩ ● vi (jut out) sporgere
**projectile** /prə'dʒektaɪl/ n proiettile m
**projection** /prə'dʒekʃn/ n (of figures) proiezione f
**projector** /prə'dʒektə(r)/ n proiettore m
**proletarian** /prəʊlə'teərɪən/ a & n proletario, -a mf
**proletariat** /prəʊlɪ'teərɪət/ n proletariato m
**pro-life** /prəʊ'laɪf/ a antiabortista
**proliferate** /prə'lɪfəreɪt/ vi proliferare
**proliferation** /prəlɪfə'reɪʃn/ n proliferazione f
**prolific** /prə'lɪfɪk/ a prolifico
**prologue** /'prəʊlɒg/ n prologo m
**prolong** /prə'lɒŋ/ vt prolungare

**prom** /prɒm/ n (*Br fam: at seaside*) lungomare m inv; (*Am fam: at high school*) ballo m studentesco

**promenade** /prɒmə'nɑːd/ n lungomare m inv

**prominence** /'prɒmɪnəns/ n (*of person, issue*) importanza f; (*of object*) sporgenza f; (*hill*) rilievo m

**prominent** /'prɒmɪnənt/ a prominente; (*conspicuous*) di rilievo

**promiscuity** /prɒmɪ'skjuːəti/ n promiscuità f

**promiscuous** /prə'mɪskjʊəs/ a promiscuo

**promise** /'prɒmɪs/ n promessa f ● vt promettere; **~ sb that** promettere a qcno che; **I ~d to** l'ho promesso

**Promised Land** /prɒmɪst'lænd/ n Terra f Promessa

**promising** /'prɒmɪsɪŋ/ a promettente

**promo** /'prəʊməʊ/ n (*fam: of product*) campagna f promozionale; (*video*) video m inv promozionale

**promontory** /'prɒmənt(ə)rɪ/ n promontorio m

**promote** /prə'məʊt/ vt promuovere; **be ~d** essere promosso

**promoter** /prə'məʊtə(r)/ n promotore, -trice mf

**promotion** /prə'məʊʃn/ n promozione f

**promotional** /prə'məʊʃnəl/ a Comm promozionale

**prompt** /prɒmpt/ a immediato; (*punctual*) puntuale ● adv in punto ● vt incitare (**to** a); Theat suggerire a ● vi suggerire ● n Comput prompt m inv

**prompter** /'prɒmptə(r)/ n suggeritore, -trice mf

**promptly** /'prɒmptlɪ/ adv puntualmente

**Proms** /prɒmz/ npl rassegna f di concerti estivi di musica classica presso l'Albert Hall a Londra

**prone** /prəʊn/ a prono; **be ~ to do sth** essere incline a fare qcsa

**prong** /prɒŋ/ n dente m

**pronoun** /'prəʊnaʊn/ n pronome m

**pronounce** /prə'naʊns/ vt pronunciare; (*declare*) dichiarare

**pronounced** /prə'naʊnst/ a (*noticeable*) pronunciato

**pronouncement** /prə'naʊnsmənt/ n dichiarazione f

**pronunciation** /prənʌnsɪ'eɪʃn/ n pronuncia f

**proof** /pruːf/ n prova f; Typ bozza f, prova f; **12% ~ 12°** ● a **~ against** a prova di

**proof-reader** n correttore, -trice mf di bozze

**proof-reading** n revisione f di bozze

**prop¹** /prɒp/ n puntello m ● vt (*pt/pp* propped) **~ open** tenere aperto; **~ against** (*lean*) appoggiare a
■ **prop up** vt sostenere

**prop²** n Theat, fam accessorio m di scena

**propaganda** /prɒpə'gændə/ n propaganda f

**propagate** /'prɒpəgeɪt/ vt propagare

**propagator** /'prɒpəgeɪtə(r)/ n propagatore m

**propane** /'prəʊpeɪn/ n propano m

**propel** /prə'pel/ vt (*pt/pp* propelled) spingere

**propellant** /prə'pelənt/ n (*in aerosol*) gas m inv propellente; (*in rocket*) propellente m

**propeller** /prə'pelə(r)/ n elica f

**propelling pencil** /prə'pelɪŋ/ n portamina m inv

**propensity** /prə'pensəti/ n tendenza f

**proper** /'prɒpə(r)/ a corretto; (*suitable*) adatto; (*fam: real*) vero [e proprio]

**properly** /'prɒpəlɪ/ adv correttamente

**proper name, proper noun** n nome m proprio

**property** /'prɒpəti/ n proprietà f inv

**property developer** n impresa f edile; (*person*) impresario m edile

**property market** n mercato m immobiliare

**prophecy** /'prɒfəsɪ/ n profezia f

**prophesy** /'prɒfɪsaɪ/ vt (*pt/pp* -ied) profetizzare

**prophet** /'prɒfɪt/ n profeta m

**prophetic** /prə'fetɪk/ a profetico

**prophylactic** /prɒfɪ'læktɪk/ n (*condom*) profilattico m, preservativo m; (*Med: treatment*) misura f profilattica ● a profilattico

**proponent** /prə'pəʊnənt/ n fautore, -trice mf

**proportion** /prə'pɔːʃn/ n proporzione f; (*share*) parte f; **be in ~** essere proporzionato (**to** a); **be out of ~** essere sproporzionato; **~s** pl (*dimensions*) proporzioni fpl

**proportional** /prə'pɔːʃnəl/ a proporzionale

**proportionally** /prə'pɔːʃnəlɪ/ adv in proporzione

**proportional representation** n rappresentanza f proporzionale

**proposal** /prə'pəʊzl/ n proposta f; (*of marriage*) proposta f di matrimonio

**propose** /prə'pəʊz/ vt proporre; (*intend*) proporsi ● vi fare una proposta di matrimonio

**proposition** /prɒpə'zɪʃn/ n proposta f; (*fam: task*) impresa f

**proprietor** /prə'praɪətə(r)/ n proprietario, -a mf

**propriety** /prə'praɪətɪ/ n correttezza f; **the proprieties** pl l'etichetta f

**propulsion** /prə'pʌlʃn/ n propulsione f

**pro rata** /'rɑːtə/ a **on a ~ ~ basis** in proporzione

**prosaic** /prə'zeɪɪk/ a prosaico

**proscribe** /prə'skraɪb/ vt (*exile*) esiliare; (*ban*) bandire

**prose** /prəʊz/ n prosa f

**prosecute** /'prɒsɪkjuːt/ vt intentare azione contro

**prosecution** /prɒsɪ'kjuːʃn/ n azione f giudiziaria; **the ~** l'accusa f

**prosecutor** /'prɒsɪkjuːtə(r)/ n [Public] P~ Pubblico Ministero m

**prospect¹** /'prɒspekt/ n (*expectation*) prospettiva f; (*view*) vista f

**prospect²** /prə'spekt/ vi **~ for** cercare

**prospective** /prə'spektɪv/ a (*future*) futuro; (*possible*) potenziale

**prospector** /prə'spektə(r)/ n cercatore m

**prospectus** /prə'spektəs/ n prospetto m
**prosper** /'prɒspə(r)/ vi prosperare; ⟨person:⟩ stare bene finanziariamente
**prosperity** /prɒ'sperəti/ n prosperità f
**prosperous** /'prɒspərəs/ a prospero
**prostate** /'prɒsteɪt/ n prostata f
**prosthesis** /prɒs'θi:sɪs/ n protesi f
**prostitute** /'prɒstɪtju:t/ n prostituta f ● vt fig prostituire
**prostitution** /prɒstɪ'tju:ʃn/ n prostituzione f
**prostrate** /'prɒstreɪt/ a prostrato; ~ **with grief** fig prostrato dal dolore
**protagonist** /prə'tægənɪst/ n protagonista mf
**protect** /prə'tekt/ vt proteggere (**from** da)
**protection** /prə'tekʃn/ n protezione f
**protective** /prə'tektɪv/ a protettivo
**protector** /prə'tektə(r)/ n protettore, -trice mf
**protégé** /'prɒtɪʒeɪ/ n protetto m
**protein** /'prəʊti:n/ n proteina f
**protest¹** /'prəʊtest/ n protesta f
**protest²** /prə'test/ vt/i protestare
**Protestant** /'prɒtɪstənt/ a & n protestante mf
**Protestantism** /'prɒtɪstəntɪzm/ n protestantesimo m
**protestation** /prɒtɪ'steɪʃn/ n protesta f
**protester** /prə'testə(r)/ n contestatore, -trice mf; ⟨at demonstration⟩ dimostrante mf
**protocol** /'prəʊtəkɒl/ n protocollo m
**prototype** /'prəʊtətaɪp/ n prototipo m
**protract** /prə'trækt/ vt protrarre
**protracted** /prə'træktɪd/ a prolungato
**protractor** /prə'træktə(r)/ n goniometro m
**protrude** /prə'tru:d/ vi sporgere
**protuberance** /prə'tu:bərəns/ n protuberanza f
**proud** /praʊd/ a fiero (**of** di)
**proudly** /'praʊdlɪ/ adv fieramente
**prove** /pru:v/ vt provare ● vi ~ **to be a lie** rivelarsi una bugia
**proven** /'pru:vən/ a dimostrato
**proverb** /'prɒvɜ:b/ n proverbio m
**proverbial** /prə'vɜ:bɪəl/ a proverbiale
**provide** /prə'vaɪd/ vt fornire; ~ **sb with sth** fornire qcsa a qcno ● vi ~ **for** ⟨allow for⟩ tenere conto di; ⟨law:⟩ prevedere
**provided** /prə'vaɪdɪd/ conj ~ **[that]** purché
**providence** /'prɒvɪdəns/ n provvidenza f
**provident** /'prɒvɪdənt/ a previdenza
**providential** /prɒvɪ'denʃl/ a provvidenziale
**provider** /prə'vaɪdə(r)/ n ⟨in family⟩ persona f che mantiene la famiglia
**providing** /prə'vaɪdɪŋ/ conj = **provided**
**province** /'prɒvɪns/ n provincia f; fig campo m
**provincial** /prə'vɪnʃl/ a provinciale
**provincialism** /prə'vɪnʃəlɪzm/ n provincialismo m
**provision** /prə'vɪʒn/ n ⟨of food, water⟩ approvvigionamento m (**of** di); ⟨of law⟩ disposizione f; **make ~ for** ⟨law:⟩ prevedere; **~s** pl provviste f pl
**provisional** /prə'vɪʒ(ə)nəl/ a provvisorio

**provisionally** /prə'vɪʒ(ə)nəlɪ/ adv provvisoriamente
**proviso** /prə'vaɪzəʊ/ n condizione f
**provocation** /prɒvə'keɪʃn/ n provocazione f
**provocative** /prə'vɒkətɪv/ a provocatorio; ⟨sexually⟩ provocante
**provocatively** /prə'vɒkətɪvlɪ/ adv in modo provocatorio; ⟨smile, be dressed⟩ in modo provocante
**provoke** /prə'vəʊk/ vt provocare
**provost** /'prɒvəst/ n Am Univ decano m; Br Univ, Sch rettore m; ⟨in Scotland⟩ sindaco m
**prow** /praʊ/ n prua f
**prowess** /'praʊɪs/ n abilità f inv
**prowl** /praʊl/ vi aggirarsi ● n **on the ~** in cerca di preda
**prowler** /'praʊlə(r)/ n tipo m sospetto
**proximity** /prɒk'sɪmətɪ/ n prossimità f
**proxy** /'prɒksɪ/ n procura f; ⟨person⟩ persona f che agisce per procura
**prude** /pru:d/ n **be a ~** essere eccessivamente pudico
**prudence** /'pru:dəns/ n prudenza f
**prudent** /'pru:dənt/ a prudente; ⟨wise⟩ oculatezza f
**prudently** /'pru:dəntlɪ/ adv con prudenza
**prudish** /'pru:dɪʃ/ a eccessivamente pudico
**prudishness** /'pru:dɪʃnɪs/ n eccessivo pudore m
**prune¹** /pru:n/ n prugna f secca
**prune²** vt potare
**pry** /praɪ/ vi ⟨pt/pp **pried**⟩ ficcare il naso
**prying** /'praɪɪŋ/ a curioso
**PS** n abbr (**postscriptum**) PS m inv
**psalm** /sɑ:m/ n salmo m
**pseud** /sju:d/ n fam intellettualoide mf
**pseudonym** /'sju:dənɪm/ n pseudonimo m
■ **psych out** /saɪk/ vt ⟨fam: unnerve⟩ snervare
■ **psych up** vt ⟨fam: prepare mentally⟩ preparare psicologicamente
**psychedelic** /saɪkə'delɪk/ a psichedelico
**psychiatric** /saɪkɪ'ætrɪk/ a psichiatrico
**psychiatrist** /saɪ'kaɪətrɪst/ n psichiatra mf
**psychic** /'saɪkɪk/ a sensitivo, -a mf ● a psichico; **I'm not ~** non sono un indovino
**psychoanalyse** /saɪkəʊ'ænəlaɪz/ vt psicanalizzare
**psychoanalysis** /saɪkəʊə'nælɪsɪs/ n psicanalisi f
**psychoanalyst** /saɪkəʊ'ænəlɪst/ n psicanalista mf
**psychological** /saɪkə'lɒdʒɪkl/ a psicologico
**psychologically** /saɪkə'lɒdʒɪklɪ/ adv psicologicamente
**psychologist** /saɪ'kɒlədʒɪst/ n psicologo, -a mf
**psychology** /saɪ'kɒlədʒɪ/ n psicologia f
**psychopath** /'saɪkəpæθ/ n psicopatico, -a mf
**psychopathic** /saɪkə'pæθɪk/ a psicopatico
**psychosis** /saɪ'kəʊsɪs/ n psicosi f inv
**psychosomatic** /saɪkəʊsə'mætɪk/ a psicosomatico

**psychotherapist** /saɪkəʊ'θerəpɪst/ n psicoterapista mf, psicoterapeuta mf

**psychotic** /saɪ'kɒtɪk/ a & n psicotico, -a mf

**PT** n abbr (**physical training**) educazione f fisica

**PTA** n abbr (**Parent-Teacher Association**) ≈ consiglio m d'istituto

**PTO** abbr (**please turn over**) vedi retro

**pub** /pʌb/ n fam pub m inv

**puberty** /'pju:bətɪ/ n pubertà f

**pubic hair** /'pju:bɪk/ n peli mpl del pube

**public** /'pʌblɪk/ a pubblico; **make ~** rendere pubblico ● n **the ~** il pubblico; **in ~** in pubblico

**public address system** n impianto m di amplificazione

**publican** /'pʌblɪkən/ n gestore, -trice mf/proprietario, -a mf di un pub

**publication** /pʌblɪ'keɪʃn/ n pubblicazione f

**public: public convenience** n gabinetti mpl pubblici. **public holiday** n festa f nazionale. **public house** n pub m inv

**publicist** /'pʌblɪsɪst/ n (press agent) pressagent mf inv, addetto, -a mf stampa

**publicity** /pʌb'lɪsətɪ/ n pubblicità f

**publicity department** n settore m pubblicità

**publicity director** n direttore, -trice mf della pubblicità

**publicize** /'pʌblɪsaɪz/ vt pubblicizzare

**public library** n biblioteca f pubblica

**public limited company** /'lɪmɪtɪd/ n società f inv per azioni

**publicly** /'pʌblɪklɪ/ adv pubblicamente

**public: public opinion** n opinione f pubblica. **public relations** npl pubbliche relazioni fpl. **public relations department** n ufficio m pubbliche relazioni. **public relations officer** n addetto, -a mf alle pubbliche relazioni. **public school** n scuola f privata; Am scuola f pubblica. **public sector** n settore m pubblico. **public-spirited** a be ~ essere dotato di senso civico. **public transport** n mezzi mpl pubblici

**publish** /'pʌblɪʃ/ vt pubblicare

**publisher** /'pʌblɪʃə(r)/ n editore m; (firm) editore m, casa f editrice

**publishing** /'pʌblɪʃɪŋ/ n editoria f

**puce** /pju:s/ a color bruno rossastro

**puck** /pʌk/ n (in ice-hockey) disco m; (sprite) folletto m

**pucker** /'pʌkə(r)/ vi ⟨material:⟩ arricciarsi

**pudding** /'pʊdɪŋ/ n dolce m cotto al vapore; (course) dolce m

**puddle** /'pʌdl/ n pozzanghera f

**pudgy** /'pʌdʒɪ/ a (-ier, -iest) grassoccio

**puerile** /'pjʊəraɪl/ a puerile

**puff** /pʌf/ n (of wind) soffio m; (of smoke) tirata f; (for powder) piumino m ● vt sbuffare

■ **puff at** vt tirare boccate da ⟨pipe⟩

■ **puff out** vt lasciare senza fiato ⟨person⟩; spegnere ⟨candle⟩

**puffed** /pʌft/ a (out of breath) senza fiato

**puff pastry** n pasta f sfoglia

**puff sleeve** n manica f a palloncino

**puffy** /'pʌfɪ/ a gonfio

**pug** /pʌg/ n (dog) carlino m

**pugnacious** /pʌg'neɪʃəs/ a aggressivo

**pull** /pʊl/ n trazione f; (fig: attraction) attrazione f; (fam: influence) influenza f ● vt tirare; estrarre ⟨tooth⟩; stirarsi ⟨muscle⟩; **~ a fast one** fam giocare un brutto tiro; **~ faces** far boccacce; **~ oneself together** ricomporsi; **~ one's weight** mettercela tutta; **~ sb's leg** fam prendere in giro qcno

■ **pull ahead** vi (move in front) passare davanti

■ **pull away** vi (increase one's lead) distanziarsi

■ **pull down** vt (demolish) demolire

■ **pull in** vi Auto accostare

■ **pull off** vt togliere; fam azzeccare

■ **pull out** vt tirar fuori ● vi Auto spostarsi; (of competition) ritirarsi

■ **pull over** vi Aut accostare

■ **pull through** vi (recover) farcela

■ **pull together** vi (co-operate) sommare le forze

■ **pull up** vt sradicare ⟨plant⟩; (reprimand) rimproverare ● vi Auto fermarsi

**pull-down menu** n Comput menu m inv a discesa

**pulley** /'pʊlɪ/ n Techn puleggia f

**pull-in** n Br (lay-by) piazzuola f di sosta; (café) bar m inv sul bordo della strada

**pullover** /'pʊləʊvə(r)/ n pullover m inv

**pulmonary** /'pʌlmənərɪ/ a polmonare

**pulp** /pʌlp/ n poltiglia f; (of fruit) polpa f; (for paper) pasta f

**pulpit** /'pʊlpɪt/ n pulpito m

**pulsar** /'pʌlsɑ:(r)/ n pulsar m inv

**pulsate** /pʌl'seɪt/ vi pulsare

**pulse** /pʌls/ n polso m

**pulses²** /'pʌlsɪz/ npl legumi mpl secchi

**pulverize** /'pʌlvəraɪz/ vt polverizzare

**puma** /'pju:mə/ n puma m inv

**pumice** /'pʌmɪs/ n pomice f

**pummel** /'pʌml/ vt (pt/pp **pummelled**) prendere a pugni

**pump** /pʌmp/ n pompa f ● vt pompare; fam cercare di estorcere informazioni da

■ **pump up** vt (inflate) gonfiare

**pumpkin** /'pʌmpkɪn/ n zucca f

**pun** /pʌn/ n gioco m di parole

**punch¹** /pʌntʃ/ n pugno m; (device) pinza f per forare ● vt dare un pugno a; forare ⟨ticket⟩; perforare ⟨hole⟩

**punch²** n (drink) punch m inv

**punch: Punch-and-Judy show** n spettacolo m di burattini. **punch-drunk** a (in boxing) groggy inv; fig stordito. **punchline** n battuta f finale. **punch-up** n rissa f

**punctual** /'pʌŋktjʊəl/ a puntuale

**punctuality** /pʌŋktjʊ'ælətɪ/ n puntualità f

**punctually** /'pʌŋktjʊəlɪ/ adv puntualmente

**punctuate** /'pʌŋktjʊeɪt/ vt punteggiàre

**punctuation** /pʌŋktjʊ'eɪʃn/ n punteggiatura f

**punctuation mark** n segno m di interpunzione

**puncture** /'pʌŋktʃə(r)/ n foro m: (tyre) foratura f ● vt forare
**pundit** /'pʌndɪt/ n esperto m
**pungency** /'pʌndʒənsɪ/ n asprezza f
**pungent** /'pʌndʒənt/ a acre
**punish** /'pʌnɪʃ/ vt punire
**punishable** /'pʌnɪʃəbl/ a punibile
**punishment** /'pʌnɪʃmənt/ n punizione f
**punitive** /'pjuːnɪtɪv/ a punitivo
**punk** /pʌŋk/ n punk m inv
**punk rock** n punk rock m inv
**punk rocker** /'rɒkə(r)/ n punk mf inv
**punnet** /'pʌnɪt/ n cestello m
**punt** /pʌnt/ n (boat) barchino m
**punter** /'pʌntə(r)/ n (gambler) scommettitore, -trice mf; (fam: client) consumatore, -trice mf
**puny** /'pjuːnɪ/ a (-ier, -iest) striminzito
**pup** /pʌp/ n = puppy
**pupil** /'pjuːpl/ n alluno, -a mf; (of eye) pupilla f
**puppet** /'pʌpɪt/ n marionetta f; (glove ~, fig) burattino m
**puppy** /'pʌpɪ/ n cucciolo m
**purchase** /'pɜːtʃəs/ n acquisto m; (leverage) presa f ● vt acquistare
**purchase: purchase invoice** n fattura f di acquisto. **purchase ledger** n libro m mastro degli acquisti. **purchase order** n ordine m di acquisto. **purchase price** n prezzo m di acquisto
**purchaser** /'pɜːtʃəsə(r)/ n acquirente mf
**purchasing [department]** /'pɜːtʃəsɪŋ/ n ufficio m acquisti
**purdah** /'pɜːdə/ n reclusione f delle donne in alcune società musulmane e indù
**pure** /pjʊə(r)/ a puro
**pure-bred** /-bred/ n (horse) purosangue m inv ● a purosangue inv
**purée** /'pjʊəreɪ/ n purè m inv ● vt passare
**purely** /'pjʊəlɪ/ adv puramente
**purgatory** /'pɜːgətrɪ/ n purgatorio m
**purge** /pɜːdʒ/ Pol n epurazione f ● vt epurare
**purification** /pjʊərɪfɪ'keɪʃn/ n purificazione f
**purify** /'pjʊərɪfaɪ/ vt (pt/pp -ied) purificare
**purist** /'pjʊərɪst/ a & n purista mf
**puritan** /'pjʊərɪtən/ n puritano, -a mf ● a fig puritano
**puritanical** /pjʊərɪ'tænɪkl/ a puritano
**purity** /'pjʊərɪtɪ/ n purità f
**purl** /pɜːl/ n (Knitting) maglia f rovescia ● vt/i lavorare a rovescio
**purple** /'pɜːpl/ a viola inv
**purport** /pə'pɔːt/ vt ~ to be farsi passare per
**purpose** /'pɜːpəs/ n scopo m; (determination) fermezza f; on ~ apposta
**purpose-built** /-'bɪlt/ a costruito ad hoc
**purposeful** /'pɜːpəsfʊl/ a deciso
**purposefully** /'pɜːpəsfʊlɪ/ adv con decisione
**purposely** /'pɜːpəslɪ/ adv apposta
**purpose-made** a Br fatto appositamente
**purr** /pɜː(r)/ vi (cat:) fare le fusa
**purse** /pɜːs/ n borsellino m; (Am: handbag) borsa f ● vt increspare (lips)

**purser** /'pɜːsə(r)/ n commissario m di bordo
**pursue** /pə'sjuː/ vt inseguire; fig proseguire
**pursuer** /pə'sjuːə(r)/ n inseguitore, -trice mf
**pursuit** /pə'sjuːt/ n inseguimento m; (fig: of happiness) ricerca f; (pastime) attività f inv; in ~ all'inseguimento
**pus** /pʌs/ n pus m
**push** /pʊʃ/ n spinta f, (fig: effort) sforzo m; (drive) iniziativa f; at a ~ in caso di bisogno; get the ~ fam essere licenziato ● vt spingere; premere (button); (pressurize) far pressione su; be ~ed for time fam non avere tempo ● vi spingere
■ **push around** vt (bully) fare il prepotente con
■ **push aside** vt scostare
■ **push back** vt respingere
■ **push for** vt fare pressione per ottenere (reform)
■ **push off** vt togliere ● vi (fam: leave) levarsi dai piedi
■ **push on** vi (continue) continuare
■ **push over** vt (cause to fall) far cadere
■ **push through** vt (have accepted quickly) fare accettare
■ **push up** vt alzare (price)
**push-button** n pulsante m
**pushchair** /'pʊʃtʃeə(r)/ n passeggino m
**pusher** /'pʊʃə(r)/ n (fam: of drugs) spacciatore, -trice mf [di droga]
**push: pushover** n fam bazzecola f. **pushstart** vt spingere (per far partire) (vehicle) ● n give sth a ~ dare una spinta a qcsa. **push-up** n flessione f
**pushy** /'pʊʃɪ/ a fam troppo intraprendente
**puss** /pʊs/ n, **pussy** /'pʊsɪ/ n micio m
■ **pussyfoot around** /'pʊsɪfʊt/ vi fam tergiversare
**pussyfooting** /'pʊsɪfʊtɪŋ/ n fam tentennamento m ● a (fam: attitude, behaviour) tergiversante
**put** /pʊt/ vt (pt/pp put, pres p putting) mettere; ~ the cost of sth at £50 valutare il costo di qcsa 50 sterline; ~ an end to porre fine o termine a; ~ in writing mettere per iscritto; ~ into effect mettere in opera ● vi ~ to sea salpare ● a stay ~! rimani lì!
■ **put about** vt mettere in giro (rumour)
■ **put across** vt raccontare (joke); esprimere (message)
■ **put aside** vt mettere da parte
■ **put away** vt mettere via
■ **put back** vt rimettere; mettere indietro (clock)
■ **put by** vt mettere da parte
■ **put down** vt mettere giù; (suppress) reprimere; (kill) sopprimere; (write) annotare; (criticize unfairly) sminuire; ~ one's foot down fam essere fermo; Auto dare un'accelerata; ~ down to (attribute) attribuire
■ **put forward** vt avanzare; mettere avanti (clock)
■ **put in** vt (insert) introdurre; (submit) presentare ● vi ~ in for far domanda di
■ **put off** vt spegnere (light); (postpone) ri-

mandare; **~ sb off** tenere a bada qcno; (*deter*) smontare qcno; (*disconcert*) distrarre qcno; **~ sb off sth** (*disgust*) disgustare qcno di qcsa

■ **put on** *vt* mettersi ⟨*clothes*⟩; mettere ⟨*brake*⟩; *Culin* mettere su; accendere ⟨*light*⟩; mettere in scena ⟨*play*⟩; prendere ⟨*accent*⟩; **~ on weight** mettere su qualche chilo; **he's just ~ting it on** è solo una messa in scena

■ **put on to** *vt* ⟨*help find*⟩ indicare ⟨*doctor, restaurant etc*⟩

■ **put out** *vt* spegnere ⟨*fire, light*⟩; tendere ⟨*hand*⟩; (*inconvenience*) creare degli inconvenienti a

■ **put through** *vt* far passare; *Teleph* **I'll ~ you through to him** glielo passo

■ **put to** *vt* **~ sb to trouble** scomodare qcno; **I ~ it to you that...** ritengo che...

■ **put together** *vt* montare ⟨*machine*⟩; fare ⟨*model, jigsaw*⟩

■ **put up** *vt* alzare; erigere ⟨*building*⟩; montare ⟨*tent*⟩; aprire ⟨*umbrella*⟩; affiggere ⟨*notice*⟩; aumentare ⟨*price*⟩; ospitare ⟨*guest*⟩; **~ sb up to sth** mettere qcsa in testa a qcno ● *vi* (*at hotel*) stare; **~ up with** sopportare

**putrefaction** /pjuː'trɪfækʃn/ *n* putrefazione *f*
**putrefy** /'pjuːtrɪfaɪ/ *vi* (*pt/pp* -**ied**) putrefarsi
**putrid** /'pjuːtrɪd/ *a* putrido
**putt** /pʌt/ *n* putt *m inv* ● *vi* colpire leggermente
**putty** /'pʌtɪ/ *n* mastice *m*
**put-up job** *n fam* truffa *f*
**puzzle** /'pʌzl/ *n* enigma *m*; (*jigsaw*) puzzle *m inv* ● *vt* lasciare perplesso ● *vi* **~ over** scervellarsi su

■ **puzzle out** *vt* trovare ⟨*solution*⟩
**puzzling** /'pʌzlɪŋ/ *a* inspiegabile
**pvc** *n* PVC *m* ● *attrib* di PVC
**pygmy** /'pɪgmɪ/ *n* pigmeo, -a *mf*
**pyjamas** /pə'dʒɑːməz/ *npl* pigiama *msg*
**pylon** /'paɪlən/ *n* pilone *m*
**pyramid** /'pɪrəmɪd/ *n* piramide *f*
**pyre** /paɪə(r)/ *n* pira *f*
**pyrex®** /'paɪreks/ *n* Pyrex *m*
**pyromaniac** /paɪrə'meɪnɪæk/ *n* piromane *mf*
**pyrotechnics** /paɪrə'teknɪks/ *n* (*display*) fuochi *mpl* pirotecnici
**python** /'paɪθn/ *n* pitone *m*

# Qq

**q, Q** /kjuː/ *n* (*letter*) q, Q *f inv*
**QC** *n Br Jur* avvocato *m* di rango superiore
**QED** *abbr* (**quod erat demonstrandum**) qed
**quack¹** /kwæk/ *n* qua qua *m inv* ● *vi* fare qua qua
**quack²** *n* (*doctor*) ciarlatano *m*
**quad** /kwɒd/ *n* (*fam: court*) = **quadrangle**; **~s** *pl fam* = **quadruplets**
**quadrangle** /'kwɒdræŋgl/ *n* quadrangolo *m*; (*court*) cortile *m* quadrangolare
**quadratic equation** /kwɒ'drætɪk/ *n* equazione *f* di secondo grado
**quadriplegic** /kwɒdrɪ'pliːdʒɪk/ *a* quadriplegico
**quadruped** /'kwɒdruped/ *n* quadrupede *m*
**quadruple** /'kwɒdrupl/ *a* quadruplo ● *vt* quadruplicare ● *vi* quadruplicarsi
**quadruplets** /kwɒd'ruːplɪts/ *npl* quattro gemelli *mpl*
**quadruplicate** /kwɒd'ruːplɪkət/ *n* **in ~** in quattro copie
**quagmire** /'kwɒgmaɪə(r)/ *n* pantano *m*
**quail** /kweɪl/ *vi* farsi prendere dalla paura
**quaint** /kweɪnt/ *a* pittoresco; (*odd*) bizzarro
**quake** /kweɪk/ *n fam* terremoto *m* ● *vi* tremare
**Quaker** /'kweɪkə(r)/ *n* quacchero, -a *mf*
**qualification** /kwɒlɪfɪ'keɪʃn/ *n* qualifica *f*; (*reservation*) riserva *f*

**qualified** /'kwɒlɪfaɪd/ *a* qualificato; (*limited*) con riserva
**qualifier** /'kwɒlɪfaɪə(r)/ *n Sport* concorrente *mf* qualificato, -a
**qualify** /'kwɒlɪfaɪ/ *v* (*pt/pp* -**ied**) ● *vt* ⟨*course:*⟩ dare la qualifica a (**as** di); (*entitle*) dare diritto a; (*limit*) precisare ● *vi* ottenere la qualifica; *Sport* qualificarsi
**qualitative** /'kwɒlɪtətɪv/ *a* qualitativo
**quality** /'kwɒlətɪ/ *n* qualità *f inv*
**quality: quality assurance** *n* verifica *f* qualità. **quality control** *n* controllo *m* [di] qualità. **quality controller** *n* addetto, -a *mf* al controllo di qualità
**qualm** /kwɑːm/ *n* scrupolo *m*
**quandary** /'kwɒndərɪ/ *n* dilemma *m*
**quango** /'kwæŋgəʊ/ *n Br* organismo *m* autonomo, ma finanziato dal governo
**quantifiable** /'kwɒntɪfaɪəbl/ *a* quantificabile
**quantitative** /'kwɒntɪtətɪv/ *a* quantitativo
**quantity** /'kwɒntətɪ/ *n* quantità *f inv*; **in ~** in grande quantità
**quantity surveyor** *n* geometra *mf* che calcola quantità e costo di materiali da costruzione
**quantum leap** /kwɒntəm'liːp/ *n fig* balzo *m* in avanti
**quantum mechanics** *n* meccanica *f* quantistica
**quarantine** /'kwɒrəntiːn/ *n* quarantena *f*

**quarrel** /'kwɒrəl/ n lite f ● vi (pt/pp **quarrelled**) litigare

**quarrelsome** /'kwɒrəlsəm/ a litigioso

**quarry¹** /'kwɒrɪ/ n (prey) preda f

**quarry²** n cava f

**quart** /kwɔːt/ n = 1.14 litro

**quarter** /'kwɔːtə(r)/ n quarto m; (of year) trimestre m; Am 25 centesimi mpl; **~s** pl Mil quartiere msg; **at [a] ~ to six** alle sei meno un quarto; **from all ~s** da tutti i lati ● vt dividere in quattro

**quarterdeck** /'kwɔːtədek/ n Naut cassero m

**quarter-final** n quarto m di finale

**quarterly** /'kwɔːtəlɪ/ a trimestrale ● adv trimestralmente

**quartermaster** /'kwɔːtəmɑːstə(r)/ n (in navy) timoniere m; (in army) furiere m

**quartet** /kwɔːˈtet/ n quartetto m

**quartz** /kwɔːts/ n quarzo m; **~ watch** orologio m al quarzo

**quash** /kwɒʃ/ vt annullare; soffocare ⟨rebellion⟩

**quasi+** /'kweizai/ pref semi+

**quaver** /'kweivə(r)/ n Mus croma f ● vi tremolare

**quay** /kiː/ n banchina f

**queasiness** /'kwiːzɪnɪs/ n nausea f

**queasy** /'kwiːzɪ/ a **I feel ~** ho la nausea

**Quebec** /kwɪˈbek/ n (province) Quebec m; (town) Quebec f

**queen** /kwiːn/ n regina f

**queen bee** n ape f regina; **she thinks she's the ~ ~** fig si crede chissà chi

**queenly** /'kwiːnlɪ/ a da regina

**queen mother** n regina f madre

**Queen:** Queen's Counsel n Br Jur avvocato m di rango superiore. **Queen's English** n Br **speak the ~ ~** parlare un inglese corretto e senza accento. **Queen's evidence** n Br Jur **turn ~ ~** deporre contro i propri complici. **Queen's Regulations** npl Br Mil codice m militare

**queer** /kwɪə(r)/ a strano; (dubious) sospetto; (fam: homosexual) finocchio ● n fam finocchio m

**quell** /kwel/ vt reprimere

**quench** /kwentʃ/ vt **~ one's thirst** dissetarsi

**query** /'kwɪərɪ/ n domanda f; (question mark) punto m interrogativo ● vt (pt/pp -ied) interrogare; (doubt) mettere in dubbio

**quest** /kwest/ n ricerca f (**for** di)

**question** /'kwestʃən/ n domanda f; (for discussion) questione f; **out of the ~** fuori discussione; **without ~** senza dubbio; **in ~** in questione ● vt interrogare; (doubt) mettere in dubbio

**questionable** /'kwestʃ(ə)nəbl/ a discutibile

**questioner** /'kwestʃ(ə)nə(r)/ n interrogante mf

**questioning** /'kwestʃ(ə)nɪŋ/ n (of person) interrogatorio m; (of criteria) messa f in discussione ● a ⟨look, tone⟩ inquisitorio

**question mark** n punto m interrogativo

**question master** n presentatore, -trice mf di quiz

**questionnaire** /kwestʃəˈneə(r)/ n questionario m

**question tag** n domanda f di conferma

**queue** /kjuː/ n coda f, fila f ● vi **~** [**up**] mettersi in coda (**for** per)

**queue-jump** vi Br passare davanti alle altre persone in coda

**quibble** /'kwɪbl/ vi cavillare

**quick** /kwɪk/ a veloce; **be ~!** sbrigati!; **have a ~ meal** fare uno spuntino ● adv in fretta ● n **be cut to the ~** fig essere punto sul vivo

**quick: quick-assembly** a facile da montare. **quick-fire** a ⟨questions⟩ a mitraglia. **quick-freeze** vt surgelare

**quickie** /'kwɪkɪ/ n fam (question) domanda f rapida; (drink) bicchierino m rapido; (film) cortometraggio m

**quicklime** /'kwɪklaɪm/ n calce f viva

**quickly** /'kwɪklɪ/ adv in fretta

**quick: quicksand** n sabbie fpl mobili. **quick-setting** /-'setɪŋ/ a a presa rapida. **quicksilver** n Chem argento m vivo, mercurio m. **quick-tempered** /-'tempəd/ a collerico. **quick-witted** /-'wɪtɪd/ a ⟨reaction⟩ pronto; ⟨person⟩ sveglio

**quid** /kwɪd/ n inv fam sterlina f

**quid pro quo** /kwɪdprəʊˈkwəʊ/ n contraccambio m

**quiet** /'kwaɪət/ a (calm) tranquillo; (silent) silenzioso; (voice, music) basso; **keep ~ about** fam non raccontare a nessuno ● n quiete f; **on the ~** di nascosto

**quieten** /'kwaɪətn/ vt calmare

■ **quieten down** vt calmare ● vi calmarsi

**quietly** /'kwaɪətlɪ/ adv (peacefully) tranquillamente; ⟨say⟩ a bassa voce

**quietness** /'kwaɪətnɪs/ n quiete f

**quiff** /kwɪf/ n (Br: hair) ciocca f

**quill** /kwɪl/ n penna f d'uccello; (spine) spina f

**quilt** /kwɪlt/ n piumino m

**quilted** /'kwɪltɪd/ a trapuntato

**quilting** /'kwɪltɪŋ/ n (fabric) matelassé m inv

**quince** /kwɪns/ n cotogna f; (tree) melo m cotogno

**quinine** /'kwɪniːn/ n chinino m

**quins** /kwɪnz/ npl fam = **quintuplets**

**quintessential** /kwɪntɪˈsenʃl/ a ⟨quality⟩ fondamentale

**quintet** /kwɪnˈtet/ n quintetto m

**quintuple** /'kwɪntjʊpl/ vt quintuplicare ● a quintuplo

**quintuplets** /'kwɪntjʊplɪts/ npl cinque gemelli mpl

**quip** /kwɪp/ n battuta f ● vt (pt/pp **quipped**) dire scherzando

**quirk** /kwɜːk/ n stranezza f

**quisling** /'kwɪzlɪŋ/ n pej collaborazionista mf

**quit** /kwɪt/ v (pt/pp **quitted** or **quit**) ● vt lasciare; (give up) smettere (**doing** di fare); Comput uscire da ● vi (fam: resign) andarsene; *Comput* uscire: **give sb notice to ~** dare a qcno preavviso di sfratto

**quite** /kwaɪt/ *adv* (*fairly*) abbastanza; (*completely*) completamente; (*really*) veramente; **~ [so]!** proprio così!; **~ a few** parecchi

**quits** /kwɪts/ *a* pari

**quiver** /'kwɪvə(r)/ *vi* tremare

**quiz** /kwɪz/ *n* (*game*) quiz *m inv* ● *vt* (*pt/pp* **quizzed**) interrogare

**quiz game, quiz show** *n* quiz *m inv*

**quizzical** /'kwɪzɪkl/ *a* sardonico

**quoit** /kwɔɪt/ *n* anello *m* (*del gioco*)

**quoits** *n* (*game*) gioco *m* degli anelli

**quorum** /'kwɔːrəm/ *n* quorum *m inv*; **have a ~** avere il quorum

**quota** /'kwəʊtə/ *n* quota *f*

**quotation** /kwəʊ'teɪʃn/ *n* citazione *f*; (*price*) preventivo *m*; (*of shares*) quota *f*

**quotation marks** *npl* virgolette *fpl*

**quote** /kwəʊt/ *n* *fam* = **quotation;** **in ~s** tra virgolette ● *vt* citare; quotare ‹*price*›; **~d on the Stock Exchange** quotato in Borsa

# Rr

**r, R** /ɑː(r)/ *n a* (*letter*) r, R *f inv*; **the three Rs** leggere, scrivere e contare

**R** *n Br abbr* (**regina**) regina *f*

**rabbi** /'ræbaɪ/ *n* rabbino *m*; (*title*) rabbi

**rabbit** /'ræbɪt/ *n* coniglio *m*

■ **rabbit on** *vi fam* **what's he ~ting on about now?** cosa sta blaterando?

**rabbit hutch** *n* conigliera *f*

**rabble** /'ræbl/ *n* **the ~** la plebaglia

**rabble rouser** /raʊzə(r)/ *n* agitatore, -trice *nmf*

**rabble rousing** *n* incitazione *f* alla violenza

**rabid** /'ræbɪd/ *a fig* rabbioso

**rabies** /'reɪbiːz/ *n* rabbia *f*

**raccoon** /rə'kuːn/ *n* procione *m*, orsetto *m* lavatore

**race¹** /reɪs/ *n* (*people*) razza *f*

**race²** *n* corsa *f* ● *vi* correre ● *vt* gareggiare con; fare correre ‹*horse*›

**racecourse** /'reɪskɔːs/ *n* ippodromo *m*

**racehorse** /'reɪshɔːs/ *n* cavallo *m* da corsa

**racer** /'reɪsə(r)/ *n* (*bike*) bicicletta *f* da corsa; (*motorbike*) motocicletta *f* da corsa; (*car*) automobile *f* da corsa; (*runner, cyclist etc*) corridore, -trice *mf*

**race relations** *npl* rapporti *mpl* tra le razze

**race riots** *npl* scontri *mpl* razziali

**racetrack** /'reɪstræk/ *n* pista *f*

**racial** /'reɪʃl/ *a* razziale

**racialism** /'reɪʃəlɪzm/ *n* razzismo *m*

**racially** /'reɪʃ(ə)lɪ/ *adv* razzialmente

**racing** /'reɪsɪŋ/ *n* corse *fpl*; (*horse-~*) corse *fpl* dei cavalli

**racing car** *n* macchina *f* da corsa

**racing driver** *n* corridore *m* automobilistico

**racism** /'reɪsɪzm/ *n* razzismo *m*

**racist** /'reɪsɪst/ *a & n* razzista *mf*

**rack¹** /ræk/ *n* (*for bikes*) rastrelliera *f*; (*for luggage*) portabagagli *m inv*; (*for plates*)

scolapiatti *m inv* ● *vt* **~ one's brains** scervellarsi

**rack²** *n* **go to ~ and ruin** andare in rovina

**racket¹** /'rækɪt/ *n Sport* racchetta *f*

**racket²** *n* (*din*) chiasso *m*; (*swindle*) truffa *f*; (*crime*) racket *m inv*, giro *m*

**racketeer** /rækɪ'tɪə(r)/ *n* trafficante *m*

**racketeering** /rækɪ'tɪərɪŋ/ *n* traffici *mpl* illeciti

**racking** /'rækɪŋ/ *a* ‹*pain*› atroce

**raconteur** /'rækɪt/ *n* bravo narratore *m*, brava narratrice *f*

**racy** /'reɪsɪ/ *a* (**-ier, -lest**) vivace; (*risqué*) osé *inv*, spinto

**radar** /'reɪdɑː(r)/ *n* radar *m*

**radar trap** *n Auto* tratto *m* di strada sul quale la polizia controlla la velocità dei veicoli

**radial** /'reɪdɪəl/ *n* (*tyre*) [pneumatico *m*] radiale *m* ● *a* ‹*lines, roads*› radiale

**radiance** /'reɪdɪəns/ *n* radiosità *f*

**radiant** /'reɪdɪənt/ *a* raggiante

**radiate** /'reɪdɪeɪt/ *vt* irradiare ● *vi* ‹*heat:*› irradiarsi; ‹*roads:*› partire

**radiation** /reɪdɪ'eɪʃn/ *n* radiazione *f*

**radiator** /'reɪdɪeɪtə(r)/ *n* radiatore *m*

**radical** /'rædɪkl/ *a & n* radicale *mf*

**radicalism** /'rædɪkəlɪzm/ *n* radicalismo *m*

**radically** /'rædɪklɪ/ *adv* radicalmente

**radio** /'reɪdɪəʊ/ *n* radio *f inv* ● *vt* mandare via radio ‹*message*›

**radioactive** /reɪdɪəʊ'æktɪv/ *a* radioattivo

**radioactive waste** *n* scorie *fpl* radioattive

**radioactivity** /reɪdɪəʊæk'tɪvətɪ/ *n* radioattività *f*

**radio cassette player** *n* radioregistratore *m*

**radio-controlled** *a* radiocomandato

**radiographer** /reɪdɪ'ɒɡrəfə(r)/ *n* radiologo, -a *mf*

**radiography** /reɪdɪ'ɒɡrəfɪ/ *n* radiografia *f*

**radio ham** *n* radioamatore, -trice *mf*

**radiologist** /reɪdɪˈɒlədʒɪst/ n radiologo, -a mf

**radiotherapy** /reɪdɪəʊˈθerəpɪ/ n radioterapia f

**radish** /ˈrædɪʃ/ n ravanello m

**radius** /ˈreɪdɪəs/ n (pl -dii /ˈreɪdɪaɪ/) raggio m

**raffle** /ˈræfl/ n lotteria f ● vt mettere in palio

**raft** /rɑːft/ n zattera f

**rafter** /ˈrɑːftə(r)/ n trave f

**rag¹** /ræg/ n straccio m; (pej: newspaper) giornalaccio m; **in ~s** stracciato

**rag²** vt (pt/pp ragged) fam fare scherzi a ● n Univ festa f di beneficenza organizzata da studenti universitari

**ragamuffin** /ˈrægəmʌfɪn/ n monellaccio m

**rag-and-bone man** n Br rigattiere m, straccivendolo m

**ragbag** /ˈrægbæg/ n fig accozzaglia f

**rage** /reɪdʒ/ n rabbia f; **all the ~** fam all'ultima moda ● vi infuriarsi; (storm:) infuriare; (epidemic:) imperversare

**ragged** /ˈrægɪd/ a logoro; (edge) frastagliato

**raging** /ˈreɪdʒɪŋ/ a (blizzard, sea) furioso; (thirst, pain) atroce; (passion, argument) acceso

**raglan** /ˈræglən/ a raglan inv ● n manica f raglan

**rag trade** n fam settore m dell'abbigliamento

**rag week** n Br Univ settimana f di manifestazioni a scopo benefico organizzate dagli studenti

**raid** /reɪd/ n (by thieves) rapina f; Mil incursione f, raid m inv; (by police) irruzione f ● vt Mil fare un'incursione in; (police, thieves:) fare irruzione in

**raider** /ˈreɪdə(r)/ n (of bank) rapinatore, -trice mf

**rail¹** /reɪl/ n ringhiera f; Rail rotaia f; Naut parapetto m; **by ~** per ferrovia

**rail²** vi **~ against** or **at** inveire contro

**railcard** /ˈreɪlkɑːd/ n tessera f di riduzione ferroviaria

**railings** /ˈreɪlɪŋz/ npl ringhiera f

**railroad** /ˈreɪlrəʊd/ n Am = **railway** ● vt **~ sb into doing sth** spingere qcno a fare qcsa

**railroad schedule** n Am orario m ferroviario

**rail traffic** n traffico m ferroviario

**railway** /ˈreɪlweɪ/ n ferrovia f

**railwayman** /ˈreɪlweɪmən/ n ferroviere m

**railway station** n stazione f ferroviaria

**rain** /reɪn/ n pioggia f ● vi piovere; **~ down on sb** fig piovere addosso a qcno ● vt **~ blows on sb** tempestare qcno di colpi

■ **rain off** vt be **~ed off** essere annullato a causa della pioggia

**rain: rainbow** n arcobaleno m. **raincheck** n Am **can I take a ~?** facciamo un'altra volta. **raincoat** n impermeabile m. **raindrop** n goccia f di pioggia. **rainfall** n precipitazione f [atmosferica]. **rainforest** n foresta f pluviale, foresta f equatoriale. **rainstorm** n temporale m. **rain water** n acqua f piovana

**rainy** /ˈreɪnɪ/ a (-ier, -iest) piovoso

**rainy day** n save sth for a **~ ~** fig mettere qcsa in serbo per i tempi di magra

**raise** /reɪz/ n Am aumento m ● vt alzare; levarsi (hat); allevare (children, animals); sollevare (question); ottenere (money); **~ hell** indiavolarsi; **~ a laugh** (joke, remark:) far ridere; **~ the stakes** rilanciare; **~ one's voice** alzare la voce

**raisin** /ˈreɪzn/ n uvetta f; **~s** pl uvetta f, uva f passa

**Raj** /rɑːʒ/ n governo m britannico in India

**rake** /reɪk/ n rastrello m ● vt rastrellare

■ **rake in** vt fam farsi (profits, money); **he's raking it in** sta facendo un sacco di soldi

■ **rake together** vt fig racimolare (money)

■ **rake up** vt raccogliere col rastrello; fam rivangare

**rake-off** n fam parte f

**rakish** /ˈreɪkɪʃ/ a (dissolute) dissoluto; (jaunty) disinvolto

**rally** /ˈrælɪ/ n raduno m; Auto rally m inv; (Tennis) scambio m; (recovery) ripresa f ● v (pt/pp -ied) ● vt radunare ● vi radunarsi; (recover strength) riprendersi

**RAM** /ræm/ n memoria f RAM

**ram** /ræm/ n montone m; Astr Ariete m ● vt (pt/pp rammed) cozzare contro

**ramble** /ˈræmbl/ n escursione f ● vi gironzolare; (in speech) divagare

■ **ramble on** vi fam parlare/scrivere a ruota libera

**rambler** /ˈræmblə(r)/ n escursionista mf; (rose) rosa f rampicante

**rambling** /ˈræmblɪŋ/ a (in speech) sconnesso; (club) escursionistico

**ramification** /ræmɪfɪˈkeɪʃən/ n ramificazione f

**ramify** /ˈræmɪfaɪ/ vi (pt/pp -ied) ramificarsi

**ramp** /ræmp/ n rampa f; Auto dosso m

**rampage** /ˈræmpeɪdʒ/ n **be/go on the ~** scatenarsi ● vi **~ through the streets** scatenarsi per le strade

**rampant** /ˈræmpənt/ a dilagante; (in heraldry) rampante

**rampart** /ˈræmpɑːt/ n bastione f

**ramshackle** /ˈræmʃækl/ a sgangherato

**ran** /ræn/ see **run**

**ranch** /rɑːntʃ/ n ranch m inv

**rancher** /ˈrɑːntʃə(r)/ n (worker) cow-boy m inv; (owner) proprietario m di ranch

**rancid** /ˈrænsɪd/ a rancido

**rancour** /ˈræŋkə(r)/ n rancore m

**R&B** n rhythm and blues m

**R&D** n ricerca f e sviluppo m

**random** /ˈrændəm/ a casuale; **~ sample** campione m a caso ● n **at ~** a casaccio

**random-access** a ad accesso casuale

**random-access memory** n memoria f viva

**randy** /ˈrændɪ/ a (-ier, -iest) fam eccitato

**rang** /ræŋ/ see **ring²**

**range** /reɪndʒ/ n serie f; Comm, Mus gamma f; (of mountains) catena f; (distance) raggio m;

(*for shooting*) portata *f*; (*stove*) cucina *f* economica; **at a ~ of** a una distanza di ● *vi* estendersi; **~ from... to...** andare da... a...

**ranger** /'reɪndʒə(r)/ *n* guardia *f* forestale

**rank¹** /ræŋk/ *n* (*row*) riga *f*; *Mil* grado *m*; (*social position*) rango *m*; **the ~ and file** la base; **the ~s** *pl Mil* i soldati *mpl* semplici ● *vt* (*place*) annoverare (**among** tra) ● *vi* (*be placed*) collocarsi

**rank²** ⟨*smell*⟩ puzzolente; ⟨*plants*⟩ rigoglioso; *fig* vero e proprio

**rankle** /'ræŋkl/ *vi fig* bruciare; **it still ~s with him** gli brucia ancora

**ransack** /'rænsæk/ *vt* rovistare; (*pillage*) saccheggiare

**ransom** /'rænsəm/ *n* riscatto *m*; **hold sb to ~** tenere qcno in ostaggio per il riscatto

**rant** /rænt/ *vi* **~ [and rave]** inveire; **what's he ~ing on about?** cosa sta blaterando?

**rap** /ræp/ *n* colpo *m* secco; *Mus* rap *m* ● *v* (*pt/pp* **rapped**) ● *vt* dare colpetti a; **~ sb over the knuckles** *fig* dare una tirata d'orecchie a qcno ● *vi* **~ at** bussare a

**rape¹** /reɪp/ *n Bot* colza *f*

**rape²** *n* (*sexual*) stupro *m* ● *vt* violentare, stuprare

**rape[seed] oil** /'reɪp[si:d]/ *n* olio *m* [di semi] di colza

**rapid** /'ræpɪd/ *a* rapido

**rapidity** /rə'pɪdətɪ/ *n* rapidità *f*

**rapidly** /'ræpɪdlɪ/ *adv* rapidamente

**rapids** /'ræpɪdz/ *npl* rapida *fsg*

**rapist** /'reɪpɪst/ *n* violentatore *m*

**rapper** /'ræpə(r)/ *n* (*Br: door-knocker*) battiporta *m inv*; *Mus* rapper *mf inv*

**rapport** /ræ'pɔ:(r)/ *n* rapporto *m* di intesa

**rapt** /ræpt/ *a* ⟨*look*⟩ rapito; **~ in** assorto in

**rapturous** /'ræptʃərəs/ *a* entusiastico

**rapturously** /'ræptʃərəslɪ/ *adv* entusiasticamente

**rapture** /'ræptʃə(r)/ *n* estasi *f*

**rare¹** /reə(r)/ *a* raro

**rare²** *a Culin* al sangue

**rarefied** /'reərɪfaɪd/ *a* rarefatto

**rarely** /'reəlɪ/ *adv* raramente

**raring** /'reərɪŋ/ *a fam* **be ~ to** non vedere l'ora di

**rarity** /'reərətɪ/ *n* rarità *f inv*

**rascal** /'rɑːskl/ *n* mascalzone *m*

**rash¹** /ræʃ/ *n Med* eruzione *f*

**rash²** *a* avventato

**rasher** /'ræʃə(r)/ *n* fetta *f* di pancetta

**rashly** /'ræʃlɪ/ *adv* avventatamente

**rashness** /'ræʃnɪs/ *n* avventatezza *f*

**rasp** /rɑːsp/ *n* (*noise*) stridio *m*

**raspberry** /'rɑːzbərɪ/ *n* lampone *m*

**rasping** /'rɑːspɪŋ/ *a* stridente

**rat** /ræt/ *n* topo *m*; (*fam: person*) carogna *f*; **smell a ~** *fam* sentire puzzo di bruciato ● *vi* (*pt/pp* **ratted**) *fam* **~ on** far la spia a

**rat-a-tat-tat** /rætətæt(t)'tæt/ *n* toc toc *m inv*

**rat-catcher** *n* addetto, -a *mf* alla derattizzazione

**ratchet** /'rætʃɪt/ *n* (*toothed rack*) cremagliera *f*

**rate** /reɪt/ *n* (*speed*) velocità *f inv*; (*of payment*) tariffa *f*; (*of exchange*) tasso *m*; **~s** *pl* (*taxes*) imposte *fpl* comunali sui beni immobili; **at any ~** in ogni caso; **at this ~** di questo passo ● *vt* stimare; **~ among** annoverare tra ● *vi* **~ as** essere considerato

**ratepayer** /'reɪtpeɪə(r)/ *n* contribuente *mf*

**rather** /'rɑːðə(r)/ *adv* piuttosto; **~!** eccome!; **~ too...** un po' troppo...

**ratification** /rætɪfɪ'keɪʃn/ *n* ratifica *f*

**ratify** /'rætɪfaɪ/ *vt* (*pt/pp* **-ied**) ratificare

**rating** /'reɪtɪŋ/ *n* valutazione *f*; (*class*) livello *m*; (*sailor*) marinaio *m* semplice; **~s** *pl Radio, TV* indice *m* d'ascolto, audience *f inv*

**ratio** /'reɪʃɪəʊ/ *n* rapporto *m*; **in a ~ of two to one** in [un] rapporto di due a uno

**ration** /'ræʃn/ *n* razione *f* ● *vt* razionare

**rational** /'ræʃənl/ *a* razionale

**rationale** /ræʃə'nɑːl/ *n* (*logic*) base *f* logica; (*reasons*) ragioni *fpl*

**rationalize** /'ræʃ(ə)nəlaɪz/ *vt/i* razionalizzare

**rationally** /'ræʃ(ə)nəlɪ/ *adv* razionalmente

**rationing** /'ræʃ(ə)nɪŋ/ *n* razionamento *m*

**rat race** *n fam* corsa *f* al successo

**rattan** /rə'tæn/ *n* (*tree, material*) malacca *f*

**rattle** /'rætl/ *n* tintinnio *m*; (*toy*) sonaglio *m* ● *vi* tintinnare ● *vt* (*shake*) scuotere; *fam* innervosire

■ **rattle off** *vt fam* sciorinare

■ **rattle on** *vi* (*talk at length*) parlare ininterrottamente

■ **rattle through** *vt* (*say quickly*) dire velocemente; (*do quickly*) fare velocemente

**rattlesnake** /'rætlsneɪk/ *n* serpente *m* a sonagli

**ratty** /'rætɪ/ *a* (*Br fam: grumpy*) irascibile; ⟨*Am: hair*⟩ sudicio

**raucous** /'rɔːkəs/ *a* rauco

**raunchy** /'rɔːntʃɪ/ *a fam* ⟨*performer, voice, song*⟩ sexy *inv*; (*bawdy*) spinto

**ravage** /'rævɪdʒ/ *vt* devastare

**ravages** /'rævɪdʒɪz/ *npl* danni *mpl*

**rave** /reɪv/ *vi* vaneggiare; **~ about** andare in estasi per

**raven** /'reɪvn/ *n* corvo *m* imperiale

**ravenous** /'rævənəs/ *a* ⟨*person*⟩ affamato

**rave-up** *n Br fam* festa *f* animata

**ravine** /rə'vi:n/ *n* gola *f*

**raving** /'reɪvɪŋ/ *a* **~ mad** *fam* matto da legare

**ravings** /'reɪvɪŋz/ *npl* vaneggiamenti *mpl*

**ravioli** /rævɪ'əʊlɪ/ *n* ravioli *mpl*

**ravishing** /'rævɪʃɪŋ/ *a* incantevole

**raw** /rɔː/ *a* crudo; (*not processed*) grezzo; ⟨*weather*⟩ gelido; (*inexperienced*) inesperto

**raw deal** *n* **get a ~** *fam* farsi fregare

**rawhide** *n* (*leather*) cuoio *m* grezzo

**Rawlplug®** /'rɔːlplʌg/ *n* tassello *m*

**raw materials** *npl* materie *fpl* prime

**ray** /reɪ/ *n* raggio *m*; **~ of hope** barlume *m* di speranza

**rayon®** /'reɪɒn/ *n* raion* *m*

**raze** /reɪz/ *vt* **~ to the ground** radere al suolo

**razor** /'reɪzə(r)/ *n* rasoio *m*

**razor blade** *n* lametta *f* da barba
**razor-sharp** *a* affilatissimo
**razzle** /'ræzl/ *n Br fam* **go on the ~** andare a fare baldoria
**razzle-dazzle** *n fam* baldoria *f*
**razzmatazz** /ræzmə'tæz/ *n fam* clamore *m*
**RC** *n* (**Roman Catholic**) cattolico, -a *mf* ● *a* cattolico
**re** /ri:/ *prep* con riferimento a
**reach** /ri:tʃ/ *n* portata *f*; (*of river*) tratto *m*; **within ~** a portata di mano; **out of ~ of** fuori dalla portata di; **within easy ~** facilmente raggiungibile ● *vt* arrivare a ⟨*place, decision*⟩; ⟨*contact*⟩ contattare; ⟨*pass*⟩ passare; **I can't ~ it** non ci arrivo ● *vi* arrivare (**to** a); **I can't ~** non ci arrivo; **~ for** allungare la mano per prendere
**react** /rɪ'ækt/ *vi* reagire
**reaction** /rɪ'ækʃn/ *n* reazione *f*
**reactionary** /rɪ'ækʃ(ə)nərɪ/ *a & n* reazionario, -a *mf*
**reactor** /rɪ'æktə(r)/ *n* reattore *m*
**read** /ri:d/ *vt* (*pt/pp* read /red/) leggere; *Univ* studiare ● *vi* leggere; ⟨*instrument:*⟩ indicare
■ **read back** *vt* (*say aloud*) rileggere
■ **read on** *vi* (*continue reading*) continuare a leggere
■ **read out** *vt* leggere ad alta voce
■ **read up on** *vt* studiare a fondo
**readable** /'ri:dəbl/ *a* piacevole a leggersi; (*legible*) leggibile
**reader** /'ri:də(r)/ *n* lettore, -trice *mf*; (*book*) antologia *f*
**readership** /'ri:dəʃɪp/ *n* numero *m* di lettori
**read head** *n Comput* testina *f* di lettura
**readily** /'redɪlɪ/ *adv* volentieri; (*easily*) facilmente
**readiness** /'redmɪs/ *n* disponibilità *f*; **in ~** pronto
**reading** /'ri:dɪŋ/ *n* lettura *f*
**readjust** /ri:ə'dʒʌst/ *vt* regolare di nuovo ● *vi* riabituarsi (**to** a)
**readjustment** /ri:ə'dʒʌstmənt/ *n* riadattamento *m*
**read-only memory** *n Comput* memoria *f* di sola lettura
**ready** /'redɪ/ *a* (**-ier, -iest**) pronto; (*quick*) veloce; **get ~** prepararsi
**ready: ready-made** *a* confezionato. **ready-mixed** *a* già miscelato. **ready money** *n* contanti *mpl*. **ready-to-wear** *a* prêt-à-porter
**reaffirm** /ri:ə'fɜ:m/ *vt* riaffermare
**reafforestation** /ri:əfɒrɪ'steɪʃn/ *n* rimboschimento *m*
**real** /ri:l/ *a* vero; ⟨*increase*⟩ reale ● *adv Am fam* veramente
**real estate** *n* beni *mpl* immobili
**realign** /ri:ə'laɪn/ *vt* riallineare ● *vi fig* formare nuove alleanze
**realignment** /ri:ə'laɪnmənt/ *n Pol* formazione *f* di nuove alleanze; *Fin* riallineamento *m*
**realism** /'rɪəlɪzm/ *n* realismo *m*
**realist** /'rɪəlɪst/ *n* realista *mf*

**realistic** /rɪə'lɪstɪk/ *a* realistico
**realistically** /rɪə'lɪstɪklɪ/ *adv* realisticamente
**reality** /rɪ'ælətɪ/ *n* realtà *f inv*
**realization** /rɪəlaɪ'zeɪʃn/ *n* realizzazione *f*
**realize** /'rɪəlaɪz/ *vt* realizzare
**real life** *n* realtà *f*; **in ~ life** nella realtà
**real-life** *attrib* autentico
**reallocate** /ri:'æləkeɪt/ *vt* riassegnare
**reallocation** /ri:ælə'keɪʃn/ *n* riassegnazione *f*
**really** /'rɪəlɪ/ *adv* davvero
**realm** /relm/ *n* regno *m*
**real time** *n* tempo *m* reale; **in ~ ~** in tempo reale ● *a* in tempo reale
**realtor** /'rɪəltə(r)/ *n Am* agente *mf* immobiliare
**realty** /'rɪəltɪ/ *n Am* beni *mpl* immobili
**reanimate** /ri:'ænɪmeɪt/ *vt* rianimare
**reap** /ri:p/ *vt* mietere
**reappear** /ri:ə'pɪə(r)/ *vi* riapparire
**reappearance** /ri:ə'pi:ərəns/ *n* ricomparsa *f*
**reapply** /ri:ə'plaɪ/ *vi* (*pt/pp* **-ied**) ripresentare domanda
**reappoint** /ri:ə'pɔɪnt/ *vt* riconfermare
**reappraisal** /ri:ə'preɪzl/ *n* riconsiderazione *f*
**reappraise** /ri:ə'preɪz/ *vt* riesaminare ⟨*question, policy*⟩; rivalutare ⟨*writer, work*⟩
**rear**[1] /rɪə(r)/ *a* posteriore; *Auto* di dietro
**rear**[2] *vt* allevare ● *vi* ~ [**up**] ⟨*horse:*⟩ impennarsi ● *n* **the ~** (*of building*) il retro; (*of bus, plane*) la parte posteriore; **from the ~** da dietro
**rear end** *n fam* didietro *m*
**rearguard** /'rɪəgɑ:d/ *n Mil, fig* retroguardia *f*
**rear light** *n* luce *f* posteriore
**rearm** /ri:'ɑ:m/ *vt* riarmare ● *vi* riarmarsi
**rearmament** /ri:'ɑ:məmənt/ *n* riarmo *m*
**rearmost** /'rɪəməʊst/ *a* ultimo; ⟨*carriage*⟩ di coda
**rearrange** /ri:ə'reɪndʒ/ *vt* cambiare la disposizione di
**rear-view mirror** *n Auto* specchietto *m* retrovisore
**reason** /'ri:zn/ *n* ragione *f*; **within ~** nei limiti del ragionevole; **listen to ~** ascoltare la ragione ● *vi* ragionare; **~ with** cercare di far ragionare
**reasonable** /'ri:znəbl/ *a* ragionevole
**reasonably** /'ri:znəblɪ/ *adv* (*in reasonable way, fairly*) ragionevolmente
**reasoning** /'ri:znɪŋ/ *n* ragionamento *m*
**reassemble** /ri:ə'semb(ə)l/ *vt* riassemblare
**reassembly** /ri:ə'semblɪ/ *n* riassemblaggio *m*
**reassess** /ri:ə'ses/ *vt* riesaminare ⟨*problem, situation*⟩; riaccertare ⟨*tax liability*⟩
**reassessment** /ri:ə'sesmənt/ *n* (*of situation*) riesame *m*; (*of tax*) nuovo accertamento *m*
**reassurance** /ri:ə'ʃʊərəns/ *n* rassicurazione *f*

**reassure** /riːəˈʃʊə(r)/ vt rassicurare; ~ **sb of sth** rassicurare qcno su qcsa

**reassuring** /riːəˈʃʊərɪŋ/ a rassicurante

**reawaken** /riːəˈweɪkn/ vt fig risvegliare ⟨interest⟩

**rebate** /ˈriːbeɪt/ n rimborso m; ⟨discount⟩ deduzione f

**rebel¹** /ˈrebl/ n ribelle mf

**rebel²** /rɪˈbel/ vi (pt/pp **rebelled**) ribellarsi

**rebellion** /rɪˈbeljən/ n ribellione f

**rebellious** /rɪˈbeljəs/ a ribelle

**rebelliousness** /rɪˈbeliːəsnɪs/ n spirito m di ribellione

**rebirth** /riːˈbɜːθ/ n rinascita f

**reboot** /riːˈbuːt/ vt Comput reinizializzare

**reborn** /riːˈbɔːn/ a Relig be ~ rinascere; **be ~ as sth** rinascere come qcsa

**rebound¹** /rɪˈbaʊnd/ vi rimbalzare; fig ricadere

**rebound²** /ˈriːbaʊnd/ n rimbalzo m

**rebuff** /rɪˈbʌf/ n rifiuto m ● vt respingere

**rebuild** /riːˈbɪld/ vt (pt/pp **-built**) ricostruire

**rebuke** /rɪˈbjuːk/ n rimprovero m ● vt rimproverare

**rebut** /rɪˈbʌt/ vt confutare

**rebuttal** /rɪˈbʌtl/ n rifiuto m

**recalcitrant** /rɪˈkælsɪtrənt/ a fml ricalcitrante

**recalculate** /riːˈkælkjʊleɪt/ vt ricalcolare

**recall** /rɪˈkɔːl/ n richiamo m; **beyond ~** irrevocabile ● vt richiamare; riconvocare ⟨diplomat, parliament⟩; ⟨remember⟩ rievocare

**recant** /rɪˈkænt/ vi abiurare

**recap** /ˈriːkæp/ vt/i fam = **recapitulate** ● n ricapitolazione f

**recapitulate** /riːkəˈpɪtjʊleɪt/ vt/i ricapitolare

**recapture** /riːˈkæptʃə(r)/ vt riconquistare; ricatturare ⟨person, animal⟩

**recast** /riːˈkɑːst/ vt rimaneggiare ⟨text, plan⟩; riformulare ⟨sentence⟩

**recede** /rɪˈsiːd/ vi allontanarsi

**receding** /rɪˈsiːdɪŋ/ a ⟨forehead, chin⟩ sfuggente; **have ~ hair** essere stempiato

**receipt** /rɪˈsiːt/ n ricevuta f; ⟨receiving⟩ ricezione f; ~**s** pl Comm entrate fpl

**receive** /rɪˈsiːv/ vt ricevere

**receiver** /rɪˈsiːvə(r)/ n Teleph ricevitore m; Radio, TV apparecchio m ricevente; ⟨of stolen goods⟩ ricettatore, -trice mf

**receivership** /rɪˈsiːvəʃɪp/ n Br **go into ~** essere sottomesso all'amministrazione controllata

**receiving end** /rɪˈsiːvɪŋ/ n **be on the ~** essere dall'altro lato della barricata

**recent** /ˈriːsnt/ a recente

**recently** /ˈriːsntlɪ/ adv recentemente

**receptacle** /rɪˈseptəkl/ n recipiente m

**reception** /rɪˈsepʃn/ n ricevimento m; ⟨welcome⟩ accoglienza f; Radio ricezione f; ~ **[desk]** ⟨in hotel⟩ reception f inv

**receptionist** /rɪˈsepʃənɪst/ n persona f alla reception

**receptive** /rɪˈseptɪv/ a ricettivo

**recess** /rɪˈses/ n rientranza f; ⟨holiday⟩ vacanza f; Am Sch intervallo m

**recession** /rɪˈseʃn/ n recessione f

**recharge** /riːˈtʃɑːdʒ/ vt ricaricare

**recidivism** /rɪˈsɪdɪvɪzm/ n recidività f

**recidivist** /rɪˈsɪdɪvɪst/ n recidivo, -a mf

**recipe** /ˈresəpɪ/ n ricetta f

**recipe book** n libro m di ricette

**recipient** /rɪˈsɪpɪənt/ n ⟨of letter, parcel⟩ destinatario, -a mf; ⟨of money⟩ beneficiario, -a mf

**reciprocal** /rɪˈsɪprəkl/ a reciproco

**reciprocate** /rɪˈsɪprəkeɪt/ vt ricambiare

**recital** /rɪˈsaɪtl/ n recital m inv

**recitation** /resɪˈteɪʃn/ n recitazione f

**recite** /rɪˈsaɪt/ vt recitare; ⟨list⟩ elencare

**reckless** /ˈreklɪs/ a ⟨action, decision⟩ sconsiderato; **be a ~ driver** guidare in modo spericolato

**recklessly** /ˈreklɪslɪ/ adv in modo sconsiderato

**recklessness** /ˈreklɪsnɪs/ n sconsideratezza f

**reckon** /ˈrekən/ vt calcolare; ⟨consider⟩ pensare; **be ~ed** essere considerato

■ **reckon on, reckon with** vt fare i conti con

■ **reckon without** vt fare i conti senza

**reclaim** /rɪˈkleɪm/ vt reclamare; bonificare ⟨land⟩

**recline** /rɪˈklaɪn/ vi sdraiarsi

**reclining** /rɪˈklaɪnɪŋ/ a ⟨seat⟩ reclinabile

**recluse** /rɪˈkluːs/ n recluso, -a mf

**reclusive** /rɪˈkluːsɪv/ a solitario

**recognition** /rekəgˈnɪʃn/ n riconoscimento m; **in ~** come riconoscimento ⟨of per⟩; **beyond ~** irriconoscibile

**recognize** /ˈrekəgnaɪz/ vt riconoscere

**recoil¹** /ˈriːkɔɪl/ n ⟨of gun⟩ rinculo m

**recoil²** /rɪˈkɔɪl/ vi ⟨in fear⟩ indietreggiare

**recollect** /rekəˈlekt/ vt ricordare

**recollection** /rekəˈlekʃn/ n ricordo m

**recommence** /riːkəˈmens/ vt/i ricominciare

**recommend** /rekəˈmend/ vt raccomandare

**recommendation** /rekəmenˈdeɪʃn/ n raccomandazione f

**recommended retail price** /rekəˈmendɪd/ n Comm prezzo m di vendita raccomandato

**recompense** /ˈrekəmpens/ n ricompensa f ● vt ricompensare

**reconcile** /ˈrekənsaɪl/ vt riconciliare; conciliare ⟨facts⟩; far quadrare ⟨bank statement⟩; ~ **oneself to** rassegnarsi a

**reconciliation** /rekənsɪlɪˈeɪʃn/ n riconciliazione f

**recondition** /riːkənˈdɪʃn/ vt ripristinare; ~**ed engine** motore m che ha subito riparazioni

**reconnaissance** /rɪˈkɒnɪsns/ n Mil ricognizione f; **on ~** in ricognizione

**reconnoitre** /rekəˈnɔɪtə(r)/ vi (pres p **-tring**) fare una recognizione ● vt fare una recognizione di

**reconsider** /ri:kən'sɪdə(r)/ *vt* riconsiderare

**reconstruct** /ri:kən'strʌkt/ *vt* ricostruire

**reconstruction** /ri:kən'strʌkʃn/ *n* ricostruzione *f*

**reconvene** /ri:kən'vi:n/ *vi* riunirsi nuovamente

**record¹** /rɪ'kɔ:d/ *vt* registrare; (*make a note of*) annotare

**record²** /'rekɔ:d/ *n* (*file*) documentazione *f*; *Mus* disco *m*; *Sport* record *m inv*; **~s** *pl* (*files*) schedario *msg*; **keep a ~ of** tener nota di; **off the ~** in via ufficiosa; **have a [criminal] ~** avere la fedina penale sporca

**record-breaker** /'rekɔ:dbreɪkə(r)/ *n* **be a ~** battere un record

**recorded delivery** /rɪ'kɔ:dɪd/ *n* raccomandata *f*

**recorder** /rɪ'kɔ:də(r)/ *n Mus* flauto *m* dolce

**recording** /rɪ'kɔ:dɪŋ/ *n* registrazione *f*

**recording studio** *n* sala *f* di registrazione

**record player** *n* giradischi *m inv*

**recount** /rɪ'kaʊnt/ *vt* raccontare

**re-count¹** /ri:'kaʊnt/ *vt* ricontare

**re-count²** /'ri:kaʊnt/ *n Pol* nuovo conteggio *m*

**recoup** /rɪ'ku:p/ *vt* rifarsi di (*losses*)

**recourse** /rɪ'kɔ:s/ *n* **have ~ to** ricorrere a

**recover** /rɪ'kʌvə(r)/ *vt/i* recuperare

**re-cover** /ri:'kʌvə(r)/ *vt* rifoderare

**recovery** /rɪ'kʌvərɪ/ *n* recupero *m*; (*of health*) guarigione *f*

**recreation** /rekrɪ'eɪʃn/ *n* ricreazione *f*

**recreational** /rekrɪ'eɪʃənəl/ *a* ricreativo

**recrimination** /rɪkrɪmɪ'neɪʃn/ *n* recriminazione *f*

**recruit** /rɪ'kru:t/ *n Mil* recluta *f*; **new ~** (*member*) nuovo, -a adepto, -a *mf*; (*worker*) neoassunto, -a *mf* ● *vt* assumere (*staff*)

**recruitment** /rɪ'kru:tmənt/ *n* assunzione *f*

**rectangle** /'rektæŋgl/ *n* rettangolo *m*

**rectangular** /rek'tæŋgjʊlə(r)/ *a* rettangolare

**rectify** /'rektɪfaɪ/ *vt* (*pt/pp -ied*) rettificare

**rector** /'rektə(r)/ *n Univ* rettore *m*

**rectory** /'rektərɪ/ *n* presbiterio *m*

**rectum** /'rektəm/ *n* retto *m*

**recuperate** /rɪ'kju:pəreɪt/ *vi* ristabilirsi

**recur** /rɪ'kɜ:(r)/ *vi* (*pt/pp* **recurred**) ricorrere; (*illness:*) ripresentarsi

**recurrence** /rɪ'kʌrəns/ *n* ricorrenza *f*; (*of illness*) ricomparsa *f*

**recurrent** /rɪ'kʌrənt/ *a* ricorrente

**recyclable** /ri:'saɪkləbl/ *a* riciclabile

**recycle** /ri:'saɪkl/ *vt* riciclare; **~d paper** carta *f* riciclata

**recycling** /ri:'saɪklɪŋ/ *n* riciclaggio *m*

**red** /red/ *a* (**redder, reddest**) rosso ● *n* rosso *m*; **be in the ~** (*account:*) essere scoperto; (*person:*) avere il conto scoperto

**red: redbrick** *a Univ* di recente fondazione. **Red Cross** *n* Croce *f* rossa. **redcurrant** *n* ribes *m* rosso

**redden** /'redn/ *vt* arrossare ● *vi* arrossire

**reddish** /'redɪʃ/ *a* rossastro

**redecorate** /ri:'dekəreɪt/ *vt* (*paint*) ridipingere; (*wallpaper*) ritappezzare

**redeem** /rɪ'di:m/ *vt* (*Relig, from pawnshop*) riscattare; **~ing quality** unico aspetto *m* positivo

**redefine** /ri:dɪ'faɪn/ *vt* ridefinire

**redemption** /rɪ'dempʃn/ *n* riscatto *m*

**redeploy** /ri:dɪ'plɔɪ/ *vt* ridistribuire

**red: red-faced** *a also fig* paonazzo. **red-haired** /-'heəd/ *a* con i capelli rossi. **red-handed** /-'hændɪd/ *a* **catch sb ~** cogliere qcno con le mani nel sacco. **red herring** *n* diversione *f*. **red-hot** *a* rovente

**redial** /ri:'daɪəl/ *Teleph vt* ricomporre ● *vi* ricomporre il numero

**redirect** /ri:daɪ'rekt/ *vt* mandare al nuovo indirizzo (*letter*)

**rediscover** /ri:dɪ'skʌvə(r)/ *vt* riscoprire

**redistribute** /ri:dɪs'trɪbju:t/ *vt* ridistribuire

**redistribution** /ri:dɪstrɪ'bju:ʃn/ *n* ridistribuzione *f*

**red: red-letter day** *n* giorno *m* memorabile. **red light** *n Auto* semaforo *m* rosso; **go through a ~ ~** passare col rosso. **red light district** *n* quartiere *m* a luci rosse. **red meat** *n* carne *f* rossa

**redness** /'rednɪs/ *n* rossore *m*

**redo** /ri:'du:/ *vt* (*pt* **-did**, *pp* **-done**) rifare

**redolent** /'redələnt/ *a* profumato (**of** di)

**redouble** /ri:'dʌbl/ *vt* raddoppiare

**redraft** /ri:'drɑ:ft/ *vt* stendere nuovamente

**redress** /rɪ'dres/ *n* riparazione *f* ● *vt* ristabilire (*balance*)

**red tape** *n fam* burocrazia *f*

**reduce** /rɪ'dju:s/ *vt* ridurre; *Culin* far consumare

**reductio ad absurdum** /rɪdʌktɪəʊædæb'sɜ:dəm/ *n* ragionamento *m* per assurdo

**reduction** /rɪ'dʌkʃn/ *n* riduzione *f*

**redundancy** /rɪ'dʌndənsɪ/ *n* licenziamento *m*; (*payment*) cassa *f* integrazione

**redundant** /rɪ'dʌndənt/ *a* superfluo: **make ~** licenziare; **be made ~** essere licenziato

**reed** /ri:d/ *n Bot* canna *f*

**reedy** /'ri:dɪ/ *a* (*voice, tone*) acuto

**reef** /ri:f/ *n* scogliera *f*

**reefer** /'ri:fə(r)/ *n* (*jacket*) giubbotto *m* a doppio petto; (*fam: dope*) spinello *m*

**reef knot** *n* nodo *m* piano

**reek** /ri:k/ *vi* puzzare (**of** di)

**reel** /ri:l/ *n* bobina *f* ● *vi* (*stagger*) vacillare ■ **reel off** *vt fig* snocciolare

**re-elect** *vt* rieleggere

**re-election** *n* rielezione *f*

**re-emerge** *vi* riemergere

**re-emergence** *n* ricomparsa *f*

**re-enact** /ri:ɪ'nækt/ *vt* ricostruire (*crime*); *Jur* rimettere in vigore; recitare nuovamente (*role*)

**re-enter** /ri:'entə(r)/ *vt* rientrare in

**re-entry** *n* (*of spacecraft*) rientro *m*

**re-establish** *vt* ristabilire, ripristinare

**re-establishment** *n* ripristino *m*

**re-examination** *n* riesame *m*

**re-examine** *vt* riesaminare

**refectory** /rɪ'fektərɪ/ *n* refettorio *m*; *Univ* mensa *f* universitaria

**refer** /rɪˈfɜː(r)/ v (pt/pp **referred**) ● vt rinviare ⟨matter⟩; indirizzare ⟨person⟩ ● vi ~ **to** fare allusione a; (consult) rivolgersi a ⟨book⟩; **are you ~ring to me?** alludi a me?

**referee** /refəˈriː/ n arbitro m; (for job) garante mf ● vt/i (pt/pp **refereed**) arbitrare

**reference** /ˈref(ə)rəns/ n riferimento m; (in book) nota f bibliografica; (for job) referenza f; Comm **'your ~'** 'riferimento'; **with ~ to** con riferimento a; **make [a] ~ to** fare riferimento a

**reference: reference book** n libro m di consultazione. **reference library** n biblioteca f per la consultazione. **reference number** n numero m di riferimento

**referendum** /refəˈrendəm/ n referendum m inv

**referral** /rɪˈfɜːrəl/ n (of matter, problem) deferimento m; Med (act) invio m di un paziente a un altro medico; (person) paziente mf mandato da un medico a un altro

**refill**[1] /ˈriːfɪl/ vt riempire di nuovo; ricaricare ⟨pen, lighter⟩

**refill**[2] /ˈriːfɪl/ n (for pen) ricambio m

**refine** /rɪˈfaɪn/ vt raffinare

**refined** /rɪˈfaɪnd/ a raffinato

**refinement** /rɪˈfaɪnmənt/ n raffinatezza f

**refinery** /rɪˈfaɪnərɪ/ n raffineria f

**refining** /rɪˈfaɪnɪŋ/ n Techn raffinazione f

**refit**[1] /ˈriːfɪt/ n Naut raddobbo m; (of shop, factory etc) rinnovo m

**refit**[2] /riːˈfɪt/ vt raddobbare ⟨ship⟩; rinnovare ⟨shop, factory etc⟩

**reflate** /riːˈfleɪt/ vt reflazionare ⟨economy⟩

**reflect** /rɪˈflekt/ vt riflettere; **be ~ed in** essere riflesso in ● vi (think) riflettere (**on** su); **~ badly on sb** fig mettere in cattiva luce qcno

**reflection** /rɪˈflekʃn/ n riflessione f; (image) riflesso m; **on ~** dopo riflessione

**reflective** /rɪˈflektɪv/ a riflessivo

**reflectively** /rɪˈflektɪvlɪ/ adv in modo riflessivo

**reflector** /rɪˈflektə(r)/ n riflettore m

**reflex** /ˈriːfleks/ n riflesso m ● attrib di riflesso

**reflexive** /rɪˈfleksɪv/ a riflessivo

**refloat** /riːˈfləʊt/ vt Naut, Comm rimettere a galla

**reforestation** /riːfɒrɪˈsteɪʃn/ n rimboschimento m

**reform** /rɪˈfɔːm/ n riforma f ● vt riformare ● vi correggersi.

**reformat** /riːˈfɔːmæt/ vt riformattare

**Reformation** /refəˈmeɪʃn/ n Relig Riforma f

**reformer** /rɪˈfɔːmə(r)/ n riformatore, -trice mf

**refrain**[1] /rɪˈfreɪn/ n ritornello m

**refrain**[2] vi astenersi (**from** da)

**refresh** /rɪˈfreʃ/ vt rinfrescare

**refresher course** /rɪˈfreʃə(r)/ n corso m d'aggiornamento

**refreshing** /rɪˈfreʃɪŋ/ a rinfrescante

**refreshments** /rɪˈfreʃmənts/ npl rinfreschi mpl

**refrigerate** /rɪˈfrɪdʒəreɪt/ vt conservare in frigo; Ind refrigerare

**refrigerated lorry** /rɪˈfrɪdʒəreɪtɪd/ n camion m inv frigorifero

**refrigeration** /rɪfrɪdʒəˈreɪʃn/ n Ind refrigerazione f

**refrigerator** /rɪˈfrɪdʒəreɪtə(r)/ n frigorifero m

**refuel** /riːˈfjʊəl/ v (pt/pp **-fuelled**) ● vt rifornire di carburante ● vi fare rifornimento

**refuge** /ˈrefjuːdʒ/ n rifugio m; **take ~** rifugiarsi

**refugee** /refjuːˈdʒiː/ n rifugiato, -a mf

**refund**[1] /ˈriːfʌnd/ n rimborso m

**refund**[2] /rɪˈfʌnd/ vt rimborsare

**refurbish** /riːˈfɜːbɪʃ/ vt rimettere a nuovo

**refurbishment** /riːˈfɜːbɪʃmənt/ n rinnovo m

**refusal** /rɪˈfjuːzl/ n rifiuto m

**refuse**[1] /rɪˈfjuːz/ vt/i rifiutare; **~ to do sth** rifiutare di fare qcsa

**refuse**[2] /ˈrefjuːs/ n rifiuti mpl

**refuse collection** n raccolta f dei rifiuti

**refute** /rɪˈfjuːt/ vt confutare

**regain** /rɪˈgeɪn/ vt riconquistare

**regal** /ˈriːgl/ a regale

**regalia** /rɪˈgeɪlɪə/ npl insegne fpl reali

**regard** /rɪˈgɑːd/ n (heed) riguardo m; (respect) considerazione f; **~s** pl saluti mpl; **send/give my ~s to your brother** salutami tuo fratello; **with ~ to** riguardo a ● vt (consider) considerare (**as** come); **as ~s** riguardo a

**regarding** /rɪˈgɑːdɪŋ/ prep riguardo a

**regardless** /rɪˈgɑːdlɪs/ adv lo stesso; **~ of** senza badare a

**regatta** /rɪˈgætə/ n regata f

**regency** /ˈriːdʒənsɪ/ n reggenza f

**regenerate** /rɪˈdʒenəreɪt/ vt rigenerare ● vi rigenerarsi

**regent** /ˈriːdʒənt/ n reggente mf

**reggae** /ˈregeɪ/ n reggae m

**regime** /reɪˈʒiːm/ n regime m

**regiment**[1] /ˈredʒɪmənt/ n reggimento m

**regiment**[2] /ˈredʒɪment/ vt irreggimentare

**regimental** /redʒɪˈmentl/ a reggimentale

**regimentation** /redʒɪmənˈteɪʃn/ n irreggimentazione f

**regimented** /ˈredʒɪmentɪd/ a irreggimentato

**region** /ˈriːdʒən/ n regione f; **in the ~ of** fig approssimativamente

**regional** /ˈriːdʒənl/ a regionale

**register** /ˈredʒɪstə(r)/ n registro m ● vt registrare; mandare tramite assicurata ⟨letter, package⟩; assicurare ⟨luggage⟩; immatricolare ⟨motor vehicle⟩; mostrare ⟨feeling⟩ ● vi ⟨instrument:⟩ funzionare; ⟨student:⟩ iscriversi (**for** a); **it didn't ~ with me** fig non ci ho fatto attenzione; **~ with** iscriversi nella lista di ⟨doctor⟩

**registered letter** /ˈredʒɪstəd/ n lettera f assicurata

**registered trademark** n marchio m depositato

**registrar** /redʒɪˈstrɑː(r)/ n ufficiale m di stato civile

**registration** /redʒɪ'streɪʃn/ n (of vehicle) immatricolazione f; (of letter, luggage) assicurazione f; (for course) iscrizione f

**registration fee** n tassa f d'iscrizione

**registration number** n Auto [numero m di] targa f

**registry office** /'redʒɪstrɪ/ n anagrafe f

**regress** /rɪ'gres/ vi Biol, Psych, fig regredire

**regression** /rɪ'greʃən/ n regressione f

**regressive** /rɪ'gresɪv/ a Biol, Psych regressivo

**regret** /rɪ'gret/ n rammarico m ● vt (pt/pp **regretted**) rimpiangere; **I ~ that** mi rincresce che

**regretfully** /rɪ'gretfʊlɪ/ adv con rammarico

**regrettable** /rɪ'gretəbl/ a spiacevole

**regrettably** /rɪ'gretəblɪ/ adv spiacevolmente; (before adjective) deplorevolmente

**regroup** /riː'gruːp/ vi riorganizzarsi

**regular** /'regjʊlə(r)/ a regolare; (usual) abituale ● n cliente mf abituale

**regularity** /regjʊ'lærətɪ/ n regolarità f

**regularly** /'regjʊləlɪ/ adv regolarmente

**regulate** /'regʊleɪt/ vt regolare

**regulation** /regjʊ'leɪʃn/ n (rule) regolamento m

**regulator** /'regjʊleɪtə(r)/ n (person) regolatore, -trice mf; (device) regolatore m

**regurgitate** /rɪ'gɜːdʒɪteɪt/ vt rigurgitare; fig pej ripetere meccanicamente

**rehabilitate** /riːhə'bɪlɪteɪt/ vt riabilitare

**rehabilitation** /riːhəbɪlɪ'teɪʃn/ n riabilitazione f

**rehash¹** /riː'hæʃ/ vt rimaneggiare

**rehash²** /'riːhæʃ/ n rimaneggiamento m

**rehearsal** /rɪ'hɜːsl/ n Theat prova f

**rehearse** /rɪ'hɜːs/ vt/i provare

**reheat** /riː'hiːt/ vt scaldare di nuovo

**rehouse** /riː'haʊz/ vt rialloggiare

**reign** /reɪn/ n regno m ● vi regnare

**reimburse** /riːɪm'bɜːs/ vt ~ **sb for sth** rimborsare qcsa a qcno

**reimbursement** /riːɪm'bɜːsmənt/ n rimborso m

**rein** /reɪn/ n redine f

**reincarnate** /riːɪn'kɑːneɪt/ vt **be ~d** reincarnarsi

**reincarnation** /riːɪnkɑː'neɪʃn/ n reincarnazione f

**reindeer** /'reɪndɪə(r)/ n inv renna f

**reinforce** /riːɪn'fɔːs/ vt rinforzare

**reinforced concrete** n cemento m armato

**reinforcement** /riːɪn'fɔːsmənt/ n rinforzo m; ~s pl Mil rinforzi mpl

**reinstate** /riːɪn'steɪt/ vt reintegrare

**reinstatement** /riːɪn'steɪtmənt/ n reintegrazione f

**reinterpret** /riːɪn'tɜːprɪt/ vt reinterpretare

**reinterpretation** /riːɪntɜːprɪ'teɪʃn/ n reinterpretazione f

**reintroduce** /riːɪntrə'djuːs/ vt reintrodurre

**reintroduction** /riːɪntrə'dʌkʃn/ n reintroduzione f

**reiterate** /riː'ɪtəreɪt/ vt reiterare

**reiteration** /riːɪtə'reɪʃn/ n reiterazione f

**reject** /rɪ'dʒekt/ vt rifiutare

**rejection** /rɪ'dʒekʃn/ n rifiuto m; Med rigetto m

**rejects** /'riːdʒekts/ npl Comm scarti mpl

**rejig** /riː'dʒɪg/ vt (pt/pp **rejigged**) Br riorganizzare

**rejoice** /rɪ'dʒɔɪs/ vi liter rallegrarsi

**rejoicing** /rɪ'dʒɔɪsɪŋ/ n gioia f

**rejoin** /rɪ'dʒɔɪn/ vt riassociarsi a ‹club, party›; Mil reintegrarsi in ‹regiment›; (answer) replicare

**rejuvenate** /rɪ'dʒuːvəneɪt/ vt rinnovare; ringiovanire ‹person›

**rejuvenation** /rɪdʒuːvə'neɪʃn/ n rinnovamento m; (of person) ringiovanimento m

**rekindle** /riː'kɪndl/ vt riattizzare

**relapse** /rɪ'læps/ n ricaduta f ● vi ricadere

**relate** /rɪ'leɪt/ vt (tell) riportare; (connect) collegare

■ **relate to** vt riferirsi a; identificarsi con ‹person›

**related** /rɪ'leɪtɪd/ a imparentato (**to** a); ‹ideas etc› affine

**relation** /rɪ'leɪʃn/ n rapporto m; (person) parente mf

**relationship** /rɪ'leɪʃnʃɪp/ n rapporto m; (blood tie) parentela f; (affair) relazione f

**relative** /'relətɪv/ n parente mf ● a relativo

**relatively** /'relətɪvlɪ/ adv relativamente

**relativity** /relə'tɪvətɪ/ n relatività f

**relativity theory** n Phys teoria f della relatività

**relaunch¹** /'riːlɔːntʃ/ n rilancio m

**relaunch²** /riː'lɔːntʃ/ vt rilanciare

**relax** /rɪ'læks/ vt rilassare; allentare ‹pace, grip› ● vi rilassarsi

**relaxation** /riːlæk'seɪʃn/ n rilassamento m, relax m; (recreation) svago m

**relaxed** /rɪ'lækst/ a rilassato

**relaxing** /rɪ'læksɪŋ/ a rilassante

**relay¹** /rɪ'leɪ/ vt (pt/pp **-layed**) trasmettere

**relay²** /'riːleɪ/ n Electr relais m inv; **work in ~s** fare i turni

**relay [race]** /'riːleɪ/ n [corsa f a] staffetta f

**release** /rɪ'liːs/ n rilascio m; (of film) distribuzione f ● vt liberare; lasciare ‹hand›; togliere ‹brake›; distribuire ‹film›; rilasciare ‹information etc›

**relegate** /'relɪgeɪt/ vt relegare; **be ~d** Br Sport essere retrocesso

**relegation** /relɪ'geɪʃn/ n relegazione f; Br Sport retrocessione f

**relent** /rɪ'lent/ vi cedere

**relentless** /rɪ'lentlɪs/ a inflessibile; (unceasing) incessante

**relentlessly** /rɪ'lentlɪslɪ/ adv incessantemente

**relevance** /'reləvəns/ n pertinenza f

**relevant** /'reləvənt/ a pertinente (**to** a)

**reliability** /rɪlaɪə'bɪlətɪ/ n affidabilità f

**reliable** /rɪ'laɪəbl/ a affidabile

**reliably** /rɪ'laɪəblɪ/ adv in modo affidabile; **be ~ informed** sapere da fonte certa

**reliance** /rɪ'laɪəns/ n fiducia f (**on** in)

**reliant** /rɪ'laɪənt/ a fiducioso (**on** in)
**relic** /'relɪk/ n Relig reliquia f; **~s** pl resti mpl
**relief** /rɪ'li:f/ n sollievo m; (assistance) soccorso m; (distraction) diversivo m; (replacement) cambio m; (in art) rilievo m: **in ~** in rilievo
**relief map** n carta f in rilievo
**relief train** n treno m supplementare
**relieve** /rɪ'li:v/ vt alleviare; (take over from) dare il cambio a; **~ of** liberare da ⟨burden⟩
**religion** /rɪ'lɪdʒən/ n religione f
**religious** /rɪ'lɪdʒəs/ a religioso
**religiously** /rɪ'lɪdʒəslɪ/ adv (conscientiously) scrupolosamente
**relinquish** /rɪ'lɪŋkwɪʃ/ vt abbandonare; **~ sth to sb** rinunciare a qcsa in favore di qcno
**relish** /'relɪʃ/ n gusto m; Culin salsa f ● vt fig apprezzare
**relive** /ri:'lɪv/ vt rivivere
**reload** /ri:'ləʊd/ vt ricaricare
**relocate** /ri:lə'keɪt/ vt trasferire ● vi trasferirsi
**relocation** /ri:lə'keɪʃn/ n (of employee, company) trasferimento m
**relocation allowance** n indennità f inv di trasferimento
**reluctance** /rɪ'lʌktəns/ n riluttanza f
**reluctant** /rɪ'lʌktənt/ a riluttante
**reluctantly** /rɪ'lʌktəntlɪ/ adv con riluttanza, a malincuore
**rely** /rɪ'laɪ/ vi (pt/pp **-ied**) **~ on** dipendere da; (trust) contare su
**remain** /rɪ'meɪn/ vi restare
**remainder** /rɪ'meɪndə(r)/ n resto m; Comm rimanenza f ● vt Comm svendere
**remaining** /rɪ'meɪnɪŋ/ a restante
**remains** /rɪ'meɪnz/ npl resti mpl; (dead body) spoglie fpl
**remake** /'ri:meɪk/ n (of film, recording) remake m inv
**remand** /rɪ'mɑ:nd/ n **on ~** in custodia cautelare ● vt **~ in custody** rinviare con detenzione provvisoria
**remark** /rɪ'mɑ:k/ n osservazione f ● vt osservare
**remarkable** /rɪ'mɑ:kəbl/ a notevole
**remarkably** /rɪ'mɑ:kəblɪ/ adv notevolmente
**remarry** /ri:'mærɪ/ vi (pt/pp **-ied**) risposarsi
**remaster** /ri:'mɑ:stə(r)/ vt incidere di nuovo ⟨recording⟩
**rematch** /'ri:mætʃ/ n Sport partita f di ritorno; (in boxing) secondo incontro m
**remedial** /rɪ'mi:dɪəl/ a correttivo; Med curativo
**remedy** /'remədɪ/ n rimedio m (**for** contro) ● vt (pt/pp **-ied**) rimediare a
**remember** /rɪ'membə(r)/ vt ricordare, ricordarsi; **~ to do sth** ricordarsi di fare qcsa; **~ me to him** salutamelo ● vi ricordarsi
**Remembrance Day** /rɪ'membrəns/ n commemorazione f dei caduti (11 novembre)
**remind** /rɪ'maɪnd/ vt **~ sb of sth** ricordare qcsa a qcno
**reminder** /rɪ'maɪndə(r)/ n ricordo m; (memo)

promemoria m inv; (letter) lettera f di sollecito; (to pay) sollecitazione f di pagamento
**reminisce** /remɪ'nɪs/ vi rievocare il passato
**reminiscences** /remɪ'nɪsənsɪz/ npl reminiscenze fpl
**reminiscent** /remɪ'nɪsənt/ a **be ~ of** richiamare alla memoria
**remiss** /rɪ'mɪs/ a negligente
**remission** /rɪ'mɪʃn/ n remissione f; (of sentence) condono m
**remit** /rɪ'mɪt/ vt (pt/pp **remitted**) rimettere ⟨money⟩
**remittance** /rɪ'mɪtəns/ n rimessa f
**remix**[1] /ri:'mɪks/ vt Mus rimixare
**remix**[2] /'ri:mɪks/ n Mus rimixaggio m
**remnant** /'remnənt/ n resto m; (of material) scampolo m; (trace) traccia f
**remonstrate** /'remənstreɪt/ vi fare rimostranze (**with sb** a qcno)
**remorse** /rɪ'mɔ:s/ n rimorso m
**remorseful** /rɪ'mɔ:sfʊl/ a pieno di rimorso
**remorsefully** /rɪ'mɔ:sfʊlɪ/ adv con rimorso
**remorseless** /rɪ'mɔ:slɪs/ a spietato
**remorselessly** /rɪ'mɔ:slɪslɪ/ adv senza pietà
**remote** /rɪ'məʊt/ a remoto; (slight) minimo
**remote: remote access** n Comput accesso m remoto. **remote control** n telecomando m. **remote-controlled** a telecomandato
**remotely** /rɪ'məʊtlɪ/ adv lontanamente; **be not ~...** non essere lontanamente...
**remoteness** /rɪ'məʊtnɪs/ n lontananza f
**remould** /'ri:məʊld/ n pneumatico m ricostruito
**remount** /ri:'maʊnt/ vt rimontare in sella a ⟨bike, horse⟩
**remov[e]able** /rɪ'mu:vəbl/ a rimovibile
**removal** /rɪ'mu:vl/ n rimozione f; (from house) trasloco m
**removal man** n addetto m ai traslochi
**removal van** n camion m inv da trasloco
**remove** /rɪ'mu:v/ vt togliere; togliersi ⟨clothes⟩; eliminare ⟨stain, doubts⟩
**remuneration** /rɪmju:nə'reɪʃn/ n rimunerazione f
**remunerative** /rɪ'mju:nərətɪv/ a rimunerativo
**renaissance** /rə'neɪsõs/ n rinascita f; **R~** Rinascimento m
**renal** /'ri:nəl/ a renale
**render** /'rendə(r)/ vt rendere ⟨service⟩
**rendering** /'rend(ə)rɪŋ/ n Mus interpretazione f
**rendezvous** /'rɒndeɪvu:/ vi esp Mil incontrarsi
**rendition** /ren'dɪʃn/ n interpretazione f
**renegade** /'renɪgeɪd/ n rinnegato, -a mf
**renege** /rɪ'neɪg/ vi venire meno (**on** a)
**renegotiate** /ri:nɪ'gəʊʃɪeɪt/ vt rinegoziare
**renegotiation** /ri:nɪgəʊʃɪ'eɪʃn/ n rinegoziato m
**renew** /rɪ'nju:/ vt rinnovare ⟨contract⟩
**renewable** /rɪ'nju:əbl/ a rinnovabile
**renewal** /rɪ'nju:əl/ n rinnovo m
**renounce** /rɪ'naʊns/ vt rinunciare a

**renovate** /'renəveɪt/ vt rinnovare

**renovation** /renə'veɪʃn/ n rinnovo m

**renown** /rɪ'naʊn/ n fama f

**renowned** /rɪ'naʊnd/ a rinomato

**rent** /rent/ n affitto m ● vt affittare; ~ **[out]** dare in affitto

**rental** /'rentl/ n affitto m

**rent boy** n ragazzo m di vita

**rent-free** a ‹accommodation› gratuito ● adv ‹live, use› senza pagare l'affitto

**renunciation** /rɪnʌnsɪ'eɪʃn/ n rinuncia f

**reopen** /ri:'əʊpən/ vt/i riaprire

**reorganization** /ri:ɔ:gənaɪ'zeɪʃn/ n riorganizzazione f

**reorganize** /ri:'ɔ:gənaɪz/ vt riorganizzare

**rep** /rep/ n Comm fam rappresentante mf; Theat ≈ teatro m stabile

**repackage** /ri:'pækɪdʒ/ vt Comm cambiare la confezione di; (fig: change public image of) cambiare l'immagine pubblica di; cambiare i termini di ‹proposal›

**repaint** /ri:'peɪnt/ vt ridipingere

**repair** /rɪ'peə(r)/ n riparazione f; **in good/bad ~** in buone/cattive condizioni ● vt riparare

**reparation** /repə'reɪʃn/ n **make ~s for sth** risarcire qcsa

**repartee** /repa:'ti:/ n botta e risposta m inv; **piece of ~** f; risposta f pronta

**repatriate** /ri:'pætrɪeɪt/ vt rimpatriare

**repatriation** /ri:pætrɪ'eɪʃn/ n rimpatrio m

**repay** /ri:'peɪ/ vt (pt/pp **-paid**) ripagare

**repayment** /ri:'peɪmənt/ n rimborso m

**repeal** /rɪ'pi:l/ n abrogazione f ● vt abrogare

**repeat** /rɪ'pi:t/ n TV replica f ● vt/i ripetere; **~ oneself** ripetersi

**repeated** /rɪ'pi:tɪd/ a ripetuto

**repeatedly** /rɪ'pi:tɪdlɪ/ adv ripetutamente

**repel** /rɪ'pel/ vt (pt/pp **repelled**) respingere; fig ripugnare

**repellent** /rɪ'pelənt/ a ripulsivo

**repent** /rɪ'pent/ vi pentirsi

**repentance** /rɪ'pentəns/ n pentimento m

**repentant** /rɪ'pentənt/ a pentito

**repercussions** /ri:pə'kʌʃnz/ npl ripercussioni fpl

**repertoire** /'repətwa:(r)/ n repertorio m

**repertory** /'repətrɪ/ n ≈ teatro m stabile

**repertory company** n compagnia f di un teatro stabile

**repetition** /repɪ'tɪʃn/ n ripetizione f

**repetitious** /repɪ'tɪʃəs/, **repetitive** /rɪ'petɪtɪv/ a ripetitivo

**replace** /rɪ'pleɪs/ vt (put back) rimettere a posto; (take the place of) sostituire; **~ sth with sth** sostituire qcsa con qcsa

**replacement** /rɪ'pleɪsmənt/ n sostituzione f; (person) sostituto, -a mf

**replacement part** n pezzo m di ricambio

**replant** /ri:'pla:nt/ vt ripiantare

**replay** /'ri:pleɪ/ n Sport partita f ripetuta; **[action] ~** replay m inv

**replenish** /rɪ'plenɪʃ/ vt rifornire ‹stocks›; (refill) riempire di nuovo

**replete** /rɪ'pli:t/ a **~ with** riempito di

**replica** /'replɪkə/ n copia f

**replicate** /'replɪkeɪt/ vt ripetere ‹experiment›

**reply** /rɪ'plaɪ/ n risposta f (**to** a) ● vt/i (pt/pp **replied**) rispondere

**reply-paid envelope** n busta f affrancata per rispondere

**report** /rɪ'pɔ:t/ n rapporto m; TV, Radio servizio m; Journ cronaca f; Sch pagella f; (rumour) diceria f ● vt riportare; **~ sb to the police** denunciare qcno alla polizia ● vi riportare; (present oneself) presentarsi (**to** a)

**reportedly** /rɪ'pɔ:tɪdlɪ/ adv secondo quanto si dice

**reporter** /rɪ'pɔ:tə(r)/ n cronista mf, reporter mf inv

**repose** /rɪ'pəʊz/ n riposo m

**repository** /rɪ'pɒzɪt(ə)rɪ/ n (place) deposito m; (of secret, authority) depositario, -a mf

**repossess** /ri:pə'zes/ vt riprendere possesso di

**repossession** /ri:pə'zeʃn/ n esproprio m

**repot** /ri:'pɒt/ vt rinvasare ‹plant›

**reprehensible** /reprɪ'hensəbl/ a riprovevole

**represent** /reprɪ'zent/ vt rappresentare

**representation** /reprɪzen'teɪʃn/ n rappresentazione f; **make ~s to** fare delle rimostranze a

**representative** /reprɪ'zentətɪv/ a rappresentativo ● n rappresentante mf

**repress** /rɪ'pres/ vt reprimere

**repression** /rɪ'preʃn/ n repressione f

**repressive** /rɪ'presɪv/ a repressivo

**reprieve** /rɪ'pri:v/ n commutazione f della pena capitale; (postponement) sospensione f della pena capitale; fig tregua f ● vt sospendere la sentenza a; fig risparmiare

**reprimand** /'reprɪma:nd/ n rimprovero m ● vt rimproverare

**reprint**[1] /'ri:prɪnt/ n ristampa f

**reprint**[2] /ri:'prɪnt/ vt ristampare

**reprisal** /rɪ'praɪzl/ n rappresaglia f; **in ~ for** per rappresaglia contro

**reproach** /rɪ'prəʊtʃ/ n rimprovero m ● vt rimproverare a (**for doing sth** di fare qcsa)

**reproachful** /rɪ'prəʊtʃfʊl/ a riprovevole

**reproachfully** /rɪ'prəʊtʃfʊlɪ/ adv con aria di rimprovero

**reprocess** /ri:'prəʊses/ vt trattare di nuovo

**reproduce** /ri:prə'dju:s/ vt riprodurre ● vi riprodursi

**reproduction** /ri:prə'dʌkʃn/ n riproduzione f

**reproduction furniture** n riproduzioni fpl di mobili antichi

**reproductive** /ri:prə'dʌktɪv/ a riproduttivo

**reproof** /rɪ'pru:f/ n rimprovero m

**reprove** /rɪ'pru:v/ vt rimproverare

**reptile** /'reptaɪl/ n rettile m

**republic** /rɪ'pʌblɪk/ n repubblica f

**republican** /rɪ'pʌblɪkn/ a & n repubblicano, -a mf

**republish** /ri:'pʌblɪʃ/ vt ripubblicare

**repudiate** /rɪ'pju:dɪeɪt/ *vt* ripudiare; respingere ⟨*view, suggestion*⟩

**repugnance** /rɪ'pʌgnəns/ *n* ripugnanza *f*

**repugnant** /rɪ'pʌgnənt/ *a* ripugnante

**repulse** /rɪ'pʌls/ *vt fml* respingere ⟨*attack*⟩; rifiutare ⟨*assistance*⟩

**repulsion** /rɪ'pʌlʃn/ *n* repulsione *f*

**repulsive** /rɪ'pʌlsɪv/ *a* ripugnante

**reputable** /'repjʊtəbl/ *a* affidabile

**reputation** /repjʊ'teɪʃn/ *n* reputazione *f*

**repute** /rɪ'pju:t/ *n* reputazione *f*

**reputed** /rɪ'pju:tɪd/ *a* presunto; **he is ~ to be** si presume che sia

**reputedly** /rɪ'pju:tɪdlɪ/ *adv* presumibilmente

**request** /rɪ'kwest/ *n* richiesta *f* ● *vt* richiedere

**request stop** *n* fermata *f* a richiesta

**requiem** /'rekwɪəm/ *n* requiem *m inv*

**require** /rɪ'kwaɪə(r)/ *vt* (*need*) necessitare di; (*demand*) esigere

**required** /rɪ'kwaɪəd/ *a* richiesto

**requirement** /rɪ'kwaɪəmənt/ *n* esigenza *f*; (*condition*) requisito *m*

**requisite** /'rekwɪzɪt/ *a* necessario ● *n* **toilet/travel ~s** *pl* articoli *mpl* da toilette/viaggio

**requisition** /rekwɪ'zɪʃn/ *n* ~ **[order]** [domanda *f* di] requisizione *f* ● *vt* requisire

**reread** /ri:'ri:d/ *vt* rileggere

**re-release** /ri:rɪ'li:s/ *n* (*of film*) nuova distribuzione *f* ● *vt* ridistribuire ⟨*film*⟩

**reroof** /ri:'ru:f/ *vt* rifare il tetto di ⟨*building*⟩

**reroute** /ri:'ru:t/ *vt* dirottare ⟨*flight, traffic*⟩

**rerun** /ri:'rʌn/ *n* (*of film, play*) replica *f*; (*fig: repeat*) ripetizione *f*

**resale** /ri:'seɪl/ *n* rivendita *f*

**reschedule** /ri:'ʃedju:l/ *vt* (*change date of*) cambiare la data di; (*change time of*) cambiare l'orario di; rinegoziare ⟨*debt*⟩

**rescind** /rɪ'sɪnd/ *vt* rescindere

**rescue** /'reskju:/ *n* salvataggio *m* ● *vt* salvare

**rescuer** /'reskjʊə(r)/ *n* salvatore, -trice *mf*

**research** /rɪ's3:tʃ/ *n* ricerca *f* ● *vt* fare ricerche su; *Journ* fare un'inchiesta su ● *vi* ~ **into** fare ricerche su

**research and development** *n* ricerca *f* e sviluppo *m*

**researcher** /rɪ's3:tʃə(r)/ *n* ricercatore, -trice *mf*

**research fellow** *n Br Univ* ricercatore, -trice *mf*

**resell** /ri:'sel/ *vt* (*pt/pp* **resold**) rivendere

**resemblance** /rɪ'zembləns/ *n* rassomiglianza *f*

**resemble** /rɪ'zembl/ *vt* rassomigliare a

**resent** /rɪ'zent/ *vt* risentirsi per

**resentful** /rɪ'zentfʊl/ *a* pieno di risentimento

**resentfully** /rɪ'zentfʊlɪ/ *adv* con risentimento

**resentment** /rɪ'zentmənt/ *n* risentimento *m*

**reservation** /rezə'veɪʃn/ *n* (*booking*) prenotazione *f*; (*doubt, enclosure*) riserva *f*

**reserve** /rɪ'z3:v/ *n* riserva *f*; (*shyness*) riserbo *m* ● *vt* riservare; riservarsi ⟨*right*⟩

**reserved** /rɪ'z3:vd/ *a* riservato

**reservoir** /'rezəvwɑ:(r)/ *n* bacino *m* idrico

**reset** /ri:'set/ *vt* riprogrammare ⟨*clock*⟩; (*zero*) azzerare

**reshape** /ri:'ʃeɪp/ *vt* ristrutturare

**reshuffle** /ri:'ʃʌfl/ *Pol n* rimpasto *m* ● *vt* rimpastare

**reside** /rɪ'zaɪd/ *vi* risiedere

**residence** /'rezɪdəns/ *n* residenza *f*; (*stay*) soggiorno *m*

**residence permit** *n* permesso *m* di soggiorno

**resident** /'rezɪdənt/ *a & n* residente *mf*

**residential** /rezɪ'denʃl/ *a* residenziale

**residential area** *n* quartiere *m* residenziale

**residual** /rɪ'zɪdjʊəl/ *a* residuo

**residue** /'rezɪdju:/ *n* residuo *m*

**resign** /rɪ'zaɪn/ *vt* dimettersi da; ~ **oneself to** rassegnarsi a ● *vi* dare le dimissioni

**resignation** /rezɪg'neɪʃn/ *n* rassegnazione *f*; (*from job*) dimissioni *fpl*

**resigned** /rɪ'zaɪnd/ *a* rassegnato

**resignedly** /rɪ'zaɪnɪdlɪ/ *adv* con rassegnazione

**resilient** /rɪ'zɪlɪənt/ *a* elastico; *fig* con buone capacità di ripresa

**resin** /'rezɪn/ *n* resina *f*

**resist** /rɪ'zɪst/ *vt* resistere a ● *vi* resistere

**resistance** /rɪ'zɪstəns/ *n* resistenza *f*

**resistant** /rɪ'zɪstənt/ *a* resistente

**resit** /ri:'sɪt/ *Br vt* (*pt/pp* **resat**) ridare ⟨*exam*⟩ ● *n* esame *m* di recupero

**resize** /ri:'saɪz/ *vt* ridimensionare

**resolute** /'rezəlu:t/ *a* risoluto

**resolutely** /'rezəlu:tlɪ/ *adv* con risolutezza

**resolution** /rezə'lu:ʃn/ *n* risolutezza *f*

**resolve** /rɪ'zɒlv/ *n* risolutezza *f*; (*decision*) risoluzione *f* ● *vt* (*solve*) risolvere; ~ **to do** decidere di fare

**resolved** /rɪ'zɒlvd/ *a* risoluto

**resonance** /'rezənəns/ *n* risonanza *f*

**resonant** /'rezənənt/ *a* risonante

**resonate** /'rezəneɪt/ *vi* risuonare

**resort** /rɪ'zɔ:t/ *n* (*place*) luogo *m* di villeggiatura; **as a last ~** come ultima risorsa ● *vi* ~ **to** ricorrere a

**resound** /rɪ'zaʊnd/ *vi* risonare (**with** di)

**resounding** /rɪ'zaʊndɪŋ/ *a* ⟨*success*⟩ risonante

**resoundingly** /rɪ'zaʊndɪŋlɪ/ *adv* in modo risonante

**resource** /rɪ'sɔ:s/ *n* ~**s** *pl* risorse *fpl*

**resourceful** /rɪ'sɔ:sfʊl/ *a* pieno di risorse; ⟨*solution*⟩ ingegnoso

**resourcefulness** /rɪ'sɔ:sfʊlnɪs/ *n* ingegnosità *f*

**respect** /rɪ'spekt/ *n* rispetto *m*; (*aspect*) aspetto *m*; **with ~ to** per quanto riguarda ● *vt* rispettare

**respectability** /rɪspektə'bɪlətɪ/ *n* rispettabilità *f*

**respectable** /rɪ'spektəbl/ *a* rispettabile

**respectably** /rɪ'spektəblɪ/ adv rispettabilmente

**respectful** /rɪ'spektfʊl/ a rispettoso

**respectfully** /rɪ'spektfʊlɪ/ adv rispettosamente

**respective** /rɪ'spektɪv/ a rispettivo

**respectively** /rɪ'spektɪvlɪ/ adv rispettivamente

**respiration** /respɪ'reɪʃn/ n respirazione f

**respirator** /'respɪreɪtə(r)/ n (apparatus) respiratore m

**respite** /'respaɪt/ n respiro m

**resplendent** /rɪ'splendənt/ a risplendente

**respond** /rɪ'spɒnd/ vi rispondere; (react) reagire (to a); ⟨patient:⟩ rispondere (to a)

**respondent** /rɪ'spɒndənt/ n Jur convenuto, -a mf; (to questionnaire) interrogato, -a mf

**response** /rɪ'spɒns/ n risposta f; (reaction) reazione f

**responsibility** /rɪspɒnsɪ'bɪlətɪ/ n responsabilità f inv

**responsible** /rɪ'spɒnsəbl/ a responsabile; (trustworthy) responsabile; (job) impegnativo

**responsibly** /rɪ'spɒnsəblɪ/ adv in modo responsabile

**responsive** /rɪ'spɒnsɪv/ a be ~ ⟨audience etc:⟩ reagire; ⟨brakes:⟩ essere sensibile; **she wasn't very ~** non era molto cooperativa

**respray**[1] /ri:'spreɪ/ vt riverniciare ⟨vehicle⟩

**respray**[2] /'ri:spreɪ/ n riverniciatura f; **it's had a ~** è stato riverniciato

**rest**[1] /rest/ n riposo m; Mus pausa f; **have a ~** riposarsi ● vt riposare; (lean, place) appoggiare (**on** su) ● vi riposarsi; ⟨elbows:⟩ appoggiarsi; ⟨hopes:⟩ riposare; **it ~s with you** sta a te

∎ **rest up** vi riposarsi

**rest**[2] n **the ~** il resto; (people) gli altri

**restart** /ri:'stɑ:t/ vt rimettere in moto ⟨engine⟩; riprendere ⟨talks⟩

**restate** /ri:'steɪt/ vt (say differently) riformulare; (say again) ribadire

**restaurant** /'restərɒnt/ n ristorante m

**restaurant car** n vagone m ristorante

**restful** /'restfl/ a riposante

**rest home** n casa f di riposo

**restitution** /restɪ'tju:ʃn/ n restituzione f

**restive** /'restɪv/ a irrequieto

**restless** /'restlɪs/ a nervoso

**restlessly** /'restlɪslɪ/ adv nervosamente

**restlessness** /'restlɪsnɪs/ n agitazione f

**restock** /ri:'stɒk/ vt rifornire ⟨shelf, shop⟩ ● vi rifornirsi

**restoration** /restə'reɪʃn/ n ristabilimento m; (of building) restauro m; (of stolen property etc) restituzione f

**restore** /rɪ'stɔ:(r)/ vt ristabilire; restaurare ⟨building⟩; (give back) restituire

**restorer** /rɪ'stɔ:rə(r)/ n (person) restauratore, -trice mf

**restrain** /rɪ'streɪn/ vt trattenere; **~ oneself** controllarsi

**restrained** /rɪ'streɪnd/ a controllato

**restraint** /rɪ'streɪnt/ n restrizione f; (moderation) ritegno m

**restrict** /rɪ'strɪkt/ vt limitare (**to** a)

**restriction** /rɪ'strɪkʃn/ n limite m; (restraint) restrizione f

**restrictive** /rɪ'strɪktɪv/ a limitativo

**restring** /ri:'strɪŋ/ vt rinfilare ⟨necklace, beads⟩; sostituire le corde di ⟨instrument, racket⟩

**restroom** /'restru:m/ n Am toilette f inv

**restructure** /ri:'strʌktʃə(r)/ vt ristrutturare

**restructuring** /ri:'strʌktʃərɪŋ/ n ristrutturazione f

**resubmit** /ri:sʌb'mɪt/ vt ripresentare

**restyle** /ri:'staɪl/ vt cambiare il taglio di ⟨hair⟩; cambiare la linea di ⟨car⟩; rimodernare ⟨shop⟩

**result** /rɪ'zʌlt/ n risultato m; **as a ~** di conseguenza; **as a ~ of** a causa di ● vi ~ **from** risultare da; ~ **in** portare a

**resume** /rɪ'zju:m/ vt/i riprendere

**résumé** /'rezjʊmeɪ/ n riassunto m; Am curriculum m inv vitae

**resumption** /rɪ'zʌmpʃn/ n ripresa f

**resurface** /ri:'sɜ:fɪs/ vi ⟨sub, person, rumour:⟩ riemergere ● vt rifare la copertura di ⟨road⟩

**resurgence** /rɪ'sɜ:dʒəns/ n rinascita f

**resurrect** /rezə'rekt/ vt fig risuscitare

**resurrection** /rezə'rekʃn/ n **the R~** Relig la Risurrezione

**resuscitate** /rɪ'sʌsɪteɪt/ vt rianimare

**resuscitation** /rɪsʌsɪ'teɪʃn/ n rianimazione f

**retail** /'ri:teɪl/ n vendita f al minuto o al dettaglio ● a & adv al minuto ● vt vendere al minuto ● vi ~ **at** essere venduto al pubblico al prezzo di

**retailer** /'ri:teɪlə(r)/ n dettagliante mf

**retail price** n prezzo m al minuto

**retain** /rɪ'teɪn/ vt conservare; (hold back) trattenere

**retainer** /rɪ'teɪnə(r)/ n (fee) anticipo m; (old: servant) servitore, -trice mf

**retake**[1] /ri:'teɪk/ vt Cinema girare di nuovo; Sch, Univ ridare; Mil riconquistare

**retake**[2] /'ri:teɪk/ n Cinema ulteriore ripresa f

**retaliate** /rɪ'tælɪeɪt/ vi vendicarsi

**retaliation** /rɪtælɪ'eɪʃn/ n rappresaglia f; **in ~ for** per rappresaglia contro

**retarded** /rɪ'tɑ:dɪd/ a ritardato

**retch** /retʃ/ vi avere conati di vomito

**retention** /rɪ'tenʃn/ n conservazione f; (of information) memorizzazione f; (of fluid) ritenzione f

**retentive** /rɪ'tentɪv/ a ⟨memory⟩ buono

**retentiveness** /rɪ'tentɪvnɪs/ n capacità f di memorizzazione

**rethink** /ri:'θɪŋk/ vt (pt/pp **rethought**) riconsiderare ● n **have a ~** riconsiderare la cosa

**reticence** /'retɪsəns/ n reticenza f

**reticent** /'retɪsənt/ a reticente

**retina** /'retɪnə/ n retina f

**retinue** /'retɪnju:/ n seguito m

**retire** /rɪ'taɪə(r)/ vi andare in pensione;

(*withdraw*) ritirarsi ● *vt* mandare in pensione ‹*employee*›

**retired** /rɪ'taɪəd/ *a* in pensione

**retirement** /rɪ'taɪəmənt/ *n* pensione *f*; **since my ~** da quando sono andato in pensione

**retirement age** *n* età *f* della pensione

**retiring** /rɪ'taɪərɪŋ/ *a* riservato

**retort** /rɪ'tɔːt/ *n* replica *f*; *Chem* storta *f* ● *vt* ribattere

**retouch** /riː'tʌtʃ/ *vt Phot* ritoccare

**retouching** /riː'tʌtʃɪŋ/ *n Phot* ritocco *m*

**retrace** /rɪ'treɪs/ *vt* ripercorrere; **~ one's steps** ritornare sui propri passi

**retract** /rɪ'trækt/ *vt* ritirare; ritrattare ‹*statement, accusation*› ● *vi* ritrarsi

**retractable** /rɪ'træktəbl/ *a* ‹*landing gear*› retrattile; ‹*pen*› con la punta retrattile

**retraction** /rɪ'trækʃn/ *n* ritiro *m*; (*of statement, accusation*) ritrattazione *f*

**retrain** /riː'treɪn/ *vt* riqualificare ● *vi* riqualificarsi

**retread** /'riː'tred/ *n* pneumatico *m* ricostruito

**retreat** /rɪ'triːt/ *n* ritirata *f*; (*place*) ritiro *m* ● *vi* ritirarsi; *Mil* battere in ritirata

**retrench** /rɪ'trentʃ/ *vi* ridurre le spese

**retrenchment** /rɪ'trentʃmənt/ *n* riduzione *f* delle spese

**retrial** /riː'traɪəl/ *n* nuovo processo *m*

**retribution** /retrɪ'bjuːʃn/ *n* castigo *m*

**retrievable** /rɪ'triːvəbl/ *a* recuperabile

**retrieval** /rɪ'triːvəl/ *n* recupero *m*

**retrieve** /rɪ'triːv/ *vt* recuperare

**retroactive** /retrəʊ'æktɪv/ *a* retroattivo

**retroactively** /retrəʊ'æktɪvlɪ/ *adv* retroattivamente

**retrograde** /'retrəgreɪd/ *a* retrogrado

**retrospect** /'retrəspekt/ *n* **in ~** guardando indietro

**retrospective** /retrə'spektɪv/ *a* ‹*exhibit*› retrospettivo; ‹*legislation*› retroattivo ● *n* retrospettiva *f*

**retrospectively** /retrə'spektɪvlɪ/ *adv* retrospettivamente

**retrovirus** /'retrəʊvaɪrəs/ *n* retrovirus *m* inv

**retry** /riː'traɪ/ *vt Jur* riprocessare; *Comput* riprovare

**return** /rɪ'tɜːn/ *n* ritorno *m*; (*giving back*) restituzione *f*; *Comm* profitto *m*; (*ticket*) biglietto *m* di andata e ritorno; **by ~ [of post]** a stretto giro di posta; **in ~** in cambio (**for** di); **many happy ~s!** cento di questi giorni!; **~ on investment** utile *m* sul capitale investito ● *vi* ritornare ● *vt* (*give back*) restituire; ricambiare ‹*affection, invitation*›; (*put back*) rimettere; (*send back*) mandare indietro; (*elect*) eleggere

**returnable** /rɪ'tɜːnəbl/ *a* restituibile

**return:** **return flight** *n* volo *m* di andata e ritorno. **return match** *n* rivincita *f*. **return ticket** *n* biglietto *m* di andata e ritorno

**reunification** /riːjuːnɪfɪ'keɪʃn/ *n* riunificazione *f*

**reunify** /riː'juːnɪfaɪ/ *vt* riunificare

**reunion** /riː'juːnjən/ *n* riunione *f*

**reunite** /riːjʊ'naɪt/ *vt* riunire

**reusable** /riː'juːzəbl/ *a* riutilizzabile

**reuse** /riː'juːz/ *vt* riutilizzare

**rev** /rev/ *n Auto* giro; **~s per minute** regime *m* di giri ● *vt* **~ [up]** far andare su di giri ● *vi* andare su di giri

**revaluation** /riːvæljʊ'eɪʃn/ *n* rivalutazione *f*

**revalue** /riː'væljuː/ *vt Comm* rivalutare

**revamp** /riː'væmp/ *vt* riorganizzare ‹*company*›; rimodernare ‹*building, clothing*›

**rev counter** *n* contagiri *m*

**Rev[d]** *abbr* (**Reverend**) Reverendo

**reveal** /rɪ'viːl/ *vt* rivelare; ‹*dress:*› scoprire

**revealing** /rɪ'viːlɪŋ/ *a* rivelatore; ‹*dress*› osé inv

**revel** /'revl/ *vi* (*pt/pp* **revelled**) **~ in sth** godere di qcsa

**revelation** /revə'leɪʃn/ *n* rivelazione *f*

**reveller** /'rev(ə)lə(r)/ *n* festaiolo, -a *mf*

**revelry** /'rev(ə)lrɪ/ *n* baldoria *f*

**revenge** /rɪ'vendʒ/ *n* vendetta *f*; *Sport* rivincita *f*; **take ~** vendicarsi (**on sb for sth** di qcno per qcsa) ● *vt* vendicare

**revenue** /'revənjuː/ *n* reddito *m*

**reverberate** /rɪ'vɜːbəreɪt/ *vi* riverberare

**reverberations** /rɪvɜːbə'reɪʃnz/ *npl fig* ripercussione *f*

**revere** /rɪ'vɪə(r)/ *vt* riverire

**reverence** /'revərəns/ *n* riverenza *f*

**Reverend** /'revərənd/ *a* reverendo

**reverent** /'revərənt/ *a* riverente

**reverential** /revə'renʃ(ə)l/ *a* riverente

**reverently** /'revərəntlɪ/ *adv* rispettosamente

**reverie** /'revərɪ/ *n* sogno *m* ad occhi aperti

**reversal** /rɪ'vɜːsl/ *n* inversione *f*

**reverse** /rɪ'vɜːs/ *a* opposto; **in ~ order** in ordine inverso ● *n* contrario *m*; (*back*) rovescio *m*; *Auto* marcia *m* indietro ● *vt* invertire; **~ the car into the garage** entrare in garage a marcia indietro; **~ the charges** *Teleph* fare una telefonata a carico del destinatario ● *vi Auto* fare marcia indietro

**reverse charge [phone-]call** *n* telefonata *f* a carico del destinatario

**reversing lights** /rɪ'vɜːsɪŋ/ *npl* luci *fpl* di retromarcia

**revert** /rɪ'vɜːt/ *vi* **~ to** tornare a

**review** /rɪ'vjuː/ *n* (*survey*) rassegna *f*; (*re-examination*) riconsiderazione *f*; *Mil* rivista *f*; (*of book, play*) recensione *f* ● *vt* riesaminare ‹*situation*›; *Mil* passare in rivista; recensire ‹*book, play*›

**reviewer** /rɪ'vjuːə(r)/ *n* critico, -a *mf*

**revile** /rɪ'vaɪl/ *vt* ingiuriare

**revise** /rɪ'vaɪz/ *vt* rivedere; (*for exam*) ripassare

**revision** /rɪ'vɪʒn/ *n* revisione *f*; (*for exam*) ripasso *m*

**revisionism** /rɪ'vɪʒənɪzm/ *n* revisionismo *m*

**revisionist** /rɪ'vɪʒənɪst/ *a* & *n* revisionista *mf*

**revisit** /ri:'vɪzɪt/ vt rivisitare ⟨person, museum etc⟩

**revitalization** /ri:vaɪtəlaɪ'zeɪʃn/ n rivitalizzazione f

**revitalize** /ri:'vaɪtəlaɪz/ vt rivitalizzare

**revival** /rɪ'vaɪvl/ n ritorno m; (of patient) recupero m; (from coma) risveglio m

**revivalist** /rɪ'vaɪvəlɪst/ a Relig revivalista

**revive** /rɪ'vaɪv/ vt resuscitare; rianimare ⟨person⟩ ● vi riprendersi; ⟨person:⟩ rianimarsi

**revocation** /revə'keɪʃn/ n (of decision, order) revoca f; (of law) abrogazione f; (of will) annullamento m

**revoke** /rɪ'vəʊk/ vt revocare ⟨decision, order⟩; abrogare ⟨law⟩; annullare ⟨will⟩

**revolt** /rɪ'vəʊlt/ n rivolta f ● vi ribellarsi ● vt rivoltare

**revolting** /rɪ'vəʊltɪŋ/ a rivoltante

**revolution** /revə'lu:ʃn/ n rivoluzione f; ~s per minute Auto giri mpl al minuto

**revolutionary** /revə'lu:ʃənərɪ/ a & n rivoluzionario, -a mf

**revolutionize** /revə'lu:ʃənaɪz/ vt rivoluzionare

**revolve** /rɪ'vɒlv/ vi ruotare; ~ around girare intorno a

**revolver** /rɪ'vɒlvə(r)/ n rivoltella f, revolver m inv

**revolving** /rɪ'vɒlvɪŋ/ a ruotante

**revolving doors** npl porta f girevole

**revue** /rɪ'vju:/ n rivista f

**revulsion** /rɪ'vʌlʃn/ n ripulsione f

**reward** /rɪ'wɔːd/ n ricompensa f ● vt ricompensare

**rewarding** /rɪ'wɔːdɪŋ/ a gratificante

**rewind** /ri:'waɪnd/ vt riavvolgere ⟨tape, film⟩

**rewind button** /'ri:waɪnd/ n tasto m di riavvolgimento

**rewire** /ri:'waɪə(r)/ vt rifare l'impianto elettrico di

**reword** /ri:'wɜːd/ vt esprimere con parole diverse

**rework** /ri:'wɜːk/ vt modificare

**rewrite** /ri:'raɪt/ vt (pt rewrote, pp rewritten) riscrivere

**rhapsody** /'ræpsədɪ/ n rapsodia f

**rhesus** /'ri:səs/ n reso m

**rhesus-negative** a Rh-negativo

**rhesus-positive** a Rh-positivo

**rhetoric** /'retərɪk/ n retorica f

**rhetorical** /rɪ'tɒrɪkl/ a retorico

**rhetorically** /rɪ'tɒrɪklɪ/ adv retoricamente

**rhetorical question** n domanda f retorica

**rheumatic** /ru:'mætɪk/ a reumatico

**rheumatism** /'ru:mətɪzm/ n reumatismo m

**rheumatoid arthritis** /'ru:mətɔɪd/ n periartrite f

**Rhine** /raɪn/ n Reno m

**rhino** /'raɪnəʊ/ n fam rinoceronte m

**rhinoceros** /raɪ'nɒsərəs/ n rinoceronte m

**rhombus** /'rɒmbəs/ n rombo m

**rhubarb** /'ru:bɑːb/ n rabarbaro m

**rhyme** /raɪm/ n rima f; (poem) filastrocca f ● vi rimare; ~ with sth far rima con qcsa

**rhythm** /'rɪðm/ n ritmo m

**rhythmic[al]** /'rɪðmɪk[l]/ a ritmico

**rhythmically** /'rɪðmɪklɪ/ adv con ritmo

**rhythm method** n (of contraception) metodo m Ogino-Knauss

**rib** /rɪb/ n costola f; ~s pl Culin costata f ● vt (pt/pp ribbed) fam punzecchiare

**ribald** /'rɪbld/ a spinto

**ribbon** /'rɪbən/ n nastro m; in ~s a brandelli

**ribcage** /'rɪbkeɪdʒ/ n gabbia f toracica, cassa f toracica

**rice** /raɪs/ n riso m

**ricefield** /'raɪsfiːld/ n risaia f

**rice-paper** n Culin carta f di riso

**rich** /rɪtʃ/ a ricco; ⟨food⟩ pesante ● n the ~ pl i ricchi; ~es pl ricchezze fpl

**richly** /'rɪtʃlɪ/ adv riccamente; ⟨deserve⟩ largamente

**Richter scale** /'rɪktə(r)/ n scala f Richter

**rick** /rɪk/ vt Br ~ one's ankle prendere una storta alla caviglia

**rickets** /'rɪkɪts/ n rachitismo m

**rickety** /'rɪkətɪ/ a malfermo

**rickshaw** /'rɪkʃɔː/ n risciò m inv

**ricochet** /'rɪkəʃeɪ/ vi rimbalzare ● n rimbalzo m

**rid** /rɪd/ vt (pt/pp rid, pres p ridding) sbarazzare (of di); get ~ of sbarazzarsi di

**riddance** /'rɪdns/ n good ~! che liberazione!

**ridden** /'rɪdn/ see ride

**riddle** /'rɪdl/ n enigma m

**riddled** /'rɪdld/ a ~ with crivellato di

**ride** /raɪd/ n (on horse) cavalcata f; (in vehicle) giro m; (journey) viaggio m; take sb for a ~ fam prendere qcno in giro ● v (pt rode, pp ridden) ● vt montare ⟨horse⟩; andare su ⟨bicycle⟩ ● vi andare a cavallo; ⟨jockey, showjumper:⟩ cavalcare; ⟨cyclist:⟩ andare in bicicletta; (in vehicle) viaggiare

**rider** /'raɪdə(r)/ n cavallerizzo, -a mf; (in race) fantino m; (on bicycle) ciclista mf; (in document) postilla f

**ridge** /rɪdʒ/ n spigolo m; (on roof) punta f; (of mountain) cresta f; (of high pressure) zona f a alta pressione [atmosferica]

**ridicule** /'rɪdɪkjuːl/ n ridicolo m ● vt mettere in ridicolo

**ridiculous** /rɪ'dɪkjʊləs/ a ridicolo

**ridiculously** /rɪ'dɪkjʊləslɪ/ adv in modo ridicolo; ~ expensive/easy carissimo/facilissimo

**riding** /'raɪdɪŋ/ n equitazione f ● attrib d'equitazione

**rife** /raɪf/ a be ~ essere diffuso; ~ with pieno di

**riff-raff** /'rɪfræf/ n marmaglia f

**rifle** /'raɪfl/ n fucile m ● vt ~ [through] mettere a soqquadro

**rifle-range** n tiro m al bersaglio

**rift** /rɪft/ n fessura f; fig frattura f

**rig[1]** /rɪg/ n equipaggiamento m; (at sea) piattaforma f per trivellazioni subacquee

**rig[2]** vt (pt/pp rigged) manovrare ⟨election⟩

■ **rig out** vt equipaggiare; (with clothes) parare

■ **rig up** *vt* allestire

**rigging** /ˈrɪgɪŋ/ *n Naut* sartiame *m*; (*of election, competition*) broglio *m*

**right** /raɪt/ *a* giusto; (*not left*) destro; **be ~** ⟨*person:*⟩ aver ragione; ⟨*clock:*⟩ essere giusto; **put ~** mettere all'ora ⟨*clock*⟩; correggere ⟨*person*⟩; rimediare a ⟨*situation*⟩; **that's ~!** proprio così!; **do you have the ~ time?** ha l'ora esatta? ● *adv* (*correctly*) bene; (*not left*) a destra; (*directly*) proprio; (*completely*) completamente; **~ away** immediatamente; **too ~!** altroché! ● *n* giusto *m*; (*not left*) destra *f*; (*what is due*) diritto *m*; **the R~** *Pol* la destra; **on/to the ~** a destra; **be in the ~** essere nel giusto; **by ~s** secondo giustizia; **be within one's ~s** avere tutti i diritti (**in doing sth to** fare qcsa) ● *vt* raddrizzare; **~ a wrong** *fig* riparare a un torto

**right angle** *n* angolo *m* retto

**righteous** /ˈraɪtʃəs/ *a* virtuoso; (*cause*) giusto

**rightful** /ˈraɪtfʊl/ *a* legittimo

**rightfully** /ˈraɪtfʊlɪ/ *adv* legittimamente

**right-handed** /-ˈhændɪd/ *a* che usa la mano destra

**right-hand man** *n fig* braccio *m* destro

**rightly** /ˈraɪtlɪ/ *adv* giustamente

**right-minded** /-ˈmaɪndɪd/ *a* sensato

**right of way** *n* diritto *m* di transito; (*path*) passaggio *m*; *Auto* precedenza *f*

**right-on** *int fam* bene! ● *a fam* **they're very ~** sono molto impegnati

**rights issue** *n* emissione *f* riservata agli azionisti

**right: right-thinking** *a* sensato. **right turn** *n* svolta *f* a destra. **right wing** *n Pol* destra; *Sport* ala *f* destra. **right-wing** *a Pol* di destra. **right-winger** *n Pol* persona *f* di destra; *Sport* ala *f* destra

**rigid** /ˈrɪdʒɪd/ *a* rigido

**rigidity** /rɪˈdʒɪdətɪ/ *n* rigidità *f*

**rigmarole** /ˈrɪgmərəʊl/ *n* trafila *f*; (*story*) tiritera *f*

**rigor mortis** /rɪgəˈmɔːtɪs/ *n* rigidità *f* cadaverica

**rigorous** /ˈrɪgərəs/ *a* rigoroso

**rigorously** /ˈrɪgərəslɪ/ *adv* rigorosamente

**rigour** /ˈrɪgə(r)/ *n* rigore *m*

**rig-out** *n* (*fam: clothes*) tenuta *f*

**rile** /raɪl/ *vt fam* irritare

**rim** /rɪm/ *n* bordo *m*; (*of wheel*) cerchione *m*

**rind** /raɪnd/ *n* (*on cheese*) crosta *f*; (*on bacon*) cotenna *f*

**ring**[1] /rɪŋ/ *n* (*circle*) cerchio *m*; (*on finger*) anello *m*; (*boxing*) ring *m inv*; (*for circus*) pista *f*; **stand in a ~** essere in cerchio ● *vt* accerchiare; **~ in red** fare un cerchio rosso intorno a

**ring**[2] *n* suono *m*; **give sb a ~** *Teleph* dare un colpo di telefono a qcno ● *v* (*pt* **rang**, *pp* **rung**) ● *vt* suonare; *Teleph* telefonare a; **it ~s a bell** *fig* mi dice qualcosa; **~ the changes** *fig* cambiare ● *vi* suonare; *Teleph* telefonare; **~ true** aver l'aria di essere vero

■ **ring back** *vt/i Teleph* richiamare

■ **ring off** *vi Teleph* riattaccare

■ **ring out** *vi* (*voice, shot etc:*) risuonare chiaramente

■ **ring round** *vi Teleph* fare un giro di telefonate

■ **ring up** *Teleph vt* telefonare a ● *vi* telefonare

**ring-binder** /ˈrɪŋbaɪndə(r)/ *n* raccoglitore *m* ad anelli

**ring finger** *n* anulare *m*

**ringing** /ˈrɪŋɪŋ/ *n* (*noise of bell, alarm*) suono *m*; (*in ears*) fischio *m*

**ringleader** /ˈrɪŋliːdə(r)/ *n* capobanda *m*

**ringlet** /ˈrɪŋlɪt/ *n* boccolo *m*

**ring: ringmaster** *n* direttore *m* di circo. **ring-pull** *n* linguetta *f*. **ring-pull can** *n* lattina *f* con linguetta. **ring road** *n* circonvallazione *f*. **ringside** *n* **at the ~** in prima fila; **have a ~ seat** *fig* essere in prima fila

**rink** /rɪŋk/ *n* pista *f* di pattinaggio

**rinse** /rɪns/ *n* risciacquo *m*; (*hair colour*) cachet *m inv* ● *vt* sciacquare

■ **rinse off** *vt* sciacquare via

■ **rinse out** *vt* sciacquare ⟨*cup, glass*⟩; sciacquare via ⟨*shampoo, soap*⟩

**riot** /ˈraɪət/ *n* rissa *f*; (*of colour*) accozzaglia *f*; **~s** *pl* disordini *mpl*; **run ~** impazzare ● *vi* creare disordini

**riot act** *n* **read the ~ ~ to sb** *fig* dare una lavata di capo a qcno

**rioter** /ˈraɪətə(r)/ *n* dimostrante *mf*

**riot gear** *n* tenuta *f* antisommossa

**riotous** /ˈraɪətəs/ *a* sfrenato

**riotously** /ˈraɪətəslɪ/ *adv* **~ funny** divertente da morire

**riot police** *n* DIGOS *f*, Divisione *f* Investigazioni Generali e Operazioni Speciali

**RIP** *abbr* (**rest in peace**) R.I.P.

**rip** /rɪp/ *n* strappo *m* ● *v* (*pt/pp* **ripped**) ● *vt* strappare; **~ open** aprire con uno strappo ● *vi* strapparsi; **let ~** scatenarsi

■ **rip off** *vt* (*remove*) togliere; (*fam: cheat*) fregare

■ **rip up** *vt* stracciare ⟨*letter*⟩

**ripcord** /ˈrɪpkɔːd/ *n* cavo *m* di spiegamento

**ripe** /raɪp/ *a* maturo; ⟨*cheese*⟩ stagionato

**ripen** /ˈraɪpn/ *vi* maturare; ⟨*cheese:*⟩ stagionarsi ● *vt* far maturare; stagionare ⟨*cheese*⟩

**ripeness** /ˈraɪpnɪs/ *n* maturazione *f*

**rip-off** *n fam* frode *f*; **these prices are a ~!** questi prezzi sono un furto!

**riposte** /rɪˈpɒst/ *n* replica *f*

**ripple** /ˈrɪpl/ *n* increspatura *f*; (*sound*) mormorio *m* ● *vt* increspare ● *vi* incresparsi

**rip-roaring** /ˈrɪprɔːrɪŋ/ *a* (*fam: success*) travolgente

**rise** /raɪz/ *n* (*of sun*) levata *f*; (*fig: to fame, power*) ascesa *f*; (*increase*) aumento *m*; **give ~ to** dare adito a ● *vi* (*pt* **rose**, *pp* **risen**) alzarsi; ⟨*sun:*⟩ sorgere; ⟨*dough:*⟩ lievitare; ⟨*prices, water level:*⟩ aumentare; ⟨*to power, position*⟩ arrivare (**to** a); ⟨*rebel*⟩ sollevarsi; ⟨*Parliament, court:*⟩ aggiornare la seduta; (*for holidays*) sospendere i lavori

■ **rise above** *vt* superare ⟨*difficulty*⟩

**riser** /'raɪzə(r)/ n **early ~** persona f mattiniera

**rising** /'raɪzɪŋ/ a ⟨sun⟩ levante; **~ generation** nuova generazione f ● n ⟨revolt⟩ sollevazione f

**risk** /rɪsk/ n rischio m; **run the ~ of** correre il rischio di; **at ~** in pericolo; **at one's own ~** a proprio rischio e pericolo; **at the ~ of doing sth** a costo di fare qcsa ● vt rischiare

**risky** /'rɪskɪ/ a (-ier, -iest) rischioso

**risotto** /rɪ'zɒtəʊ/ n risotto m

**risqué** /'rɪskeɪ/ a spinto

**rissole** /'rɪsəʊl/ n crocchetta f

**rite** /raɪt/ n rito m; **last ~s** pl estrema unzione fsg

**ritual** /'rɪtjʊəl/ a & n rituale m

**ritzy** /'rɪtsɪ/ a ⟨fam: hotel, style, decoration⟩ lussuoso

**rival** /'raɪvl/ a rivale ● n rivale mf; **~s** pl Comm concorrenti mpl ● vt (pt/pp **rivalled**) rivaleggiare con

**rivalry** /'raɪv(ə)lrɪ/ n rivalità f inv; Comm concorrenza f

**river** /'rɪvə(r)/ n fiume m

**river: riverbank** n riva f di fiume. **river-bed** n letto m del fiume. **riverside** n lungofiume m ● attrib sul fiume

**rivet** /'rɪvɪt/ n rivetto m ● vt rivettare; **be ~ed by** fig essere avvinto da

**riveting** /'rɪvɪtɪŋ/ a fig avvincente

**Riviera** /rɪvɪ'eərə/ n **the French ~** la Costa Azzurra; **the Italian ~** la riviera ligure

**roach** /rəʊtʃ/ n ⟨fish⟩ lasca f; ⟨Am fam: insect⟩ scarafaggio m

**road** /rəʊd/ n strada f, via f; **be on the ~** viaggiare

**road: roadblock** n blocco m stradale. **road haulage** n trasporto m su strada. **road hog** n fam pirata m della strada

**roadie** /'rəʊdɪ/ n roadie m inv

**road: road map** n carta f stradale. **road safety** n sicurezza f sulle strade. **road sense** n prudenza f ⟨per strada⟩. **roadshow** n ⟨play, show⟩ spettacolo m di tournée; ⟨publicity tour⟩ giro m promozionale. **roadside** n bordo m della strada. **road sign** cartello m stradale. **road surface** n fondo m stradale. **road sweeper** n ⟨person⟩ spazzino, -a nmf; ⟨machine⟩ autospazzatrice f. **road tax** n tassa f di circolazione. **roadway** n carreggiata f, corsia f. **roadworks** npl lavori mpl stradali.

**roadworthy** a sicuro

**roam** /rəʊm/ vi girovagare

**roar** /rɔ:(r)/ n ruggito m; **~s of laughter** scroscio msg di risa ● vi ruggire; ⟨lorry, thunder:⟩ rombare; **~ with laughter** ridere fragorosamente

■ **roar out** vt gridare

■ **roar past** vi ⟨move noisily⟩ passare rombando

**roaring** /'rɔ:rɪŋ/ a **do a ~ trade** fam fare affari d'oro ● adv **~ drunk** fam ubriaco fradicio

**roast** /rəʊst/ a arrosto; **~ pork** arrosto m di maiale ● n arrosto m ● vt arrostire ⟨meat⟩ ● vi arrostirsi

**roasting** [**hot**] /'rəʊstɪŋ/ a fam caldissimo

**roasting pan** n teglia f per arrosti

**rob** /rɒb/ vt (pt/pp **robbed**) derubare ⟨**of** di⟩; svaligiare ⟨bank⟩

**robber** /'rɒbə(r)/ n rapinatore m

**robbery** /'rɒbərɪ/ n rapina f

**robe** /rəʊb/ n tunica f; ⟨Am: bathrobe⟩ accappatoio m

**robin** /'rɒbɪn/ n pettirosso m

**robot** /'rəʊbɒt/ n robot m inv

**robotic** /rəʊ'bɒtɪk/ a ⟨movement, voice⟩ robotico; ⟨tool, device, machine⟩ robotizzato

**robotics** n robotica f

**robust** /rəʊ'bʌst/ a robusto

**rock**[1] /rɒk/ n roccia f; ⟨in sea⟩ scoglio m; ⟨sweet⟩ zucchero m candito; **on the ~s** ⟨ship⟩ incagliato; ⟨marriage⟩ finito; ⟨drink⟩ con ghiaccio

**rock**[2] vt cullare ⟨baby⟩; ⟨shake⟩ far traballare; ⟨shock⟩ scuotere ● vi dondolarsi

**rock**[3] n Mus rock m

**rock: rock and roll** n rock and roll m. **rock-bottom** a bassissimo ● n livello m più basso; **hit ~** toccare il fondo. **rock-climber** n scalatore, -trice nmf. **rock-climbing** n roccia f

**rockery** /'rɒkərɪ/ n giardino m roccioso

**rocket** /'rɒkɪt/ n razzo m; **give sb a ~** fam fare un cicchetto a qcno ● vi salire alle stelle

**rocket launcher** /'lɔ:ntʃə(r)/ n lanciarazzi m inv

**rock face** n parete f rocciosa

**rocking chair** /'rɒkɪŋ/ n sedia f a dondolo

**rocking horse** n cavallo m a dondolo

**rocky** /'rɒkɪ/ a (-ier, -iest) roccioso; fig traballante

**rod** /rɒd/ n bacchetta f; ⟨for fishing⟩ canna f

**rode** /rəʊd/ see **ride**

**rodent** /'rəʊdnt/ n roditore m

**roe**[1] /rəʊ/ n uova fpl di pesce; ⟨soft⟩ latte m di pesce

**roe**[2] n (pl **roe** or **roes**) **~[-deer]** capriolo m

**roebuck** /'rəʊbʌk/ n capriolo m maschio

**roger** /'rɒdʒə(r)/ int Teleph ricevuto

**rogue** /rəʊg/ n farabutto m

**role** /rəʊl/ n ruolo m

**role model** n Psych modello m comportamentale

**role-play, role-playing** /'rəʊlpleɪɪŋ/ n Psych role playing m inv

**roll** /rəʊl/ n rotolo m; ⟨bread⟩ panino m; ⟨list⟩ lista f; ⟨of ship, drum⟩ rullio m ● vi rotolare; **be ~ing in money** fam nuotare nell'oro ● vt spianare ⟨lawn, pastry⟩; **~ed into one** allo stesso tempo

■ **roll back** vt ridurre ⟨prices⟩

■ **roll by** vi ⟨time:⟩ passare

■ **roll in** vi ⟨fam: arrive in large quantities⟩ arrivare a valanghe; ⟨arrive⟩ arrivare

■ **roll on** vi **~ on Friday!** non vedo l'ora che sia venerdì!

■ **roll over** vi rigirarsi; ⟨fam: capitulate⟩ arrendersi

■ **roll up** vt arrotolare; rimboccarsi ⟨sleeves⟩ ● vi fam arrivare

**roll-call** n appello m

**roller** /ˈrəʊlə(r)/ n rullo m; (for hair) bigodino m

**roller: rollerblade** n pattino m a rotelle in linea ● vi pattinare (con pattini in linea). **roller blind** n tapparella f. **roller coaster** n montagne fpl russe. **roller skate** n pattino m a rotelle

**rollicking** /ˈrɒlɪkɪŋ/ a **have a ~ time** divertirsi da pazzi

**rolling** /ˈrəʊlɪŋ/: **rolling pin** n mattarello m. **rolling stock** n materiale m rotabile. **rolling stone** n fig vagabondo, -a mf

**roll: rollneck** n collo m alto; (whole sweater) dolcevita f. **roll-on** n (deodorant) deodorante m a sfera. **roll-on roll-off ferry** n traghetto m roll-on roll-off

**ROM** /rɒm/ n Comput ROM f inv

**Roman** /ˈrəʊmən/ a (also print) romano ● n romano, -a mf

**Roman Catholic** a & n cattolico, -a mf

**romance** /rəʊˈmæns/ n (love-affair) storia f d'amore; (book) romanzo m rosa

**Romania** /rəʊˈmeɪnɪə/ n Romania f

**Romanian** /rəʊˈmeɪnɪən/ a & n rumeno, -a mf; (language) rumeno m

**roman numeral** n numero m romano

**romantic** /rəʊˈmæntɪk/ a romantico

**romantically** /rəʊˈmæntɪklɪ/ adv romanticamente

**romanticism** /rəʊˈmæntɪsɪzm/ n romanticismo m

**romanticize** /rəʊˈmæntɪsaɪz/ vt romanticizzare

**romanticized** /rəʊˈmæntɪsaɪzd/ a romanzato

**Rome** /rəʊm/ n Roma f

**Romeo** /ˈrəʊmɪəʊ/ n (fam: ladykiller) dongiovanni m inv

**romp** /rɒmp/ n gioco m rumoroso ● vi giocare rumorosamente

■ **romp home** vi (win easily) vincere senza difficoltà

■ **romp through** vt fam passare senza difficoltà (exam) ● vi riuscire senza difficoltà

**rompers** /ˈrɒmpəz/ npl pagliaccetto msg

**roof** /ruːf/ n tetto m; (of mouth) palato m; **live under one ~** vivere sotto lo stesso tetto; **go through the ~** (fam: increase) andare alle stelle; (be very angry) andare su tutte le furie ● vt mettere un tetto su

**roof-rack** n portabagagli m inv

**rooftop** /ˈruːftɒp/ n tetto m; **shout it from the ~s** fig gridarlo ai quattro venti

**rook** /rʊk/ n corvo m; (in chess) torre f ● vt (fam: swindle) fregare

**rookie** /ˈrʊkɪ/ n Am fam novellino, -a mf

**room** /ruːm/ n stanza f; (bedroom) camera f; (for functions) sala f; (space) spazio m

**room: room-mate** n (Am: flatmate) compagno, -a mf di appartamento; (in same room) compagno, -a mf di stanza. **room service** n servizio m in camera. **room temperature** n temperatura f ambiente

**roomy** /ˈruːmɪ/ a spazioso; (clothes) ampio

**roost** /ruːst/ n posatoio m ● vi appollaiarsi

**rooster** /ˈruːstə(r)/ n gallo m

**root¹** /ruːt/ n radice f; **take ~** metter radici; **put down ~s** fig metter radici ● vi metter radici

**root²** vi **~ about** grufolare; **~ for sb** Am fam fare il tifo per qcno

■ **root out** vt fig scovare

**rope** /rəʊp/ n corda f; **know the ~s** fam conoscere i trucchi del mestiere

■ **rope in** vt fam coinvolgere

**rope ladder** n scala f di corda

**ropey** /ˈrəʊpɪ/ a Br fam scadente; **feel ~** sentirsi poco bene

**rosary** /ˈrəʊzərɪ/ n rosario m

**rose¹** /rəʊz/ n rosa f; (of watering-can) bocchetta f

**rose²** see **rise**

**rosé** /ˈrəʊzeɪ/ n (vino m) rosé m inv

**rosebud** /ˈrəʊzbʌd/ n bocciolo m di rosa

**rosehip** /ˈrəʊzhɪp/ n frutto m della rosa canina

**rosemary** /ˈrəʊzmərɪ/ n rosmarino m

**rose-tinted spectacles** /ˈrəʊztɪntɪd/ npl **wear ~** vedere tutto rosa

**rosette** /rəʊˈzet/ n coccarda f

**roster** /ˈrɒstə(r)/ n tabella f dei turni

**rostrum** /ˈrɒstrəm/ n podio m

**rosy** /ˈrəʊzɪ/ a (-ier, -iest) roseo

**rot** /rɒt/ n marciume m; (fam: nonsense) sciocchezze fpl ● vi (pt/pp rotted) marcire

**rota** /ˈrəʊtə/ n tabella f dei turni

**rotary** /ˈrəʊtərɪ/ a rotante

**rotate** /rəʊˈteɪt/ vt far ruotare; avvicendare (crops) ● vi ruotare

**rotation** /rəʊˈteɪʃn/ n rotazione f; **in ~** a turno

**rote** /rəʊt/ n **by ~** meccanicamente

**rotten** /ˈrɒtn/ a marcio; fam schifoso; (person) penoso

**rotund** /rəʊˈtʌnd/ a paffuto

**rotunda** /rəʊˈtʌndə/ n rotonda f

**rouble** /ˈruːbl/ n rublo m

**rough** /rʌf/ a (not smooth) ruvido; (ground) accidentato; (behaviour) rozzo; (sport) violento; (area) malfamato; (crossing, time) brutto; (estimate) approssimativo ● adv (play) grossolanamente; **sleep ~** dormire sotto i ponti ● n **do sth in ~** far qcsa alla bell'e meglio ● vt **~ it** vivere senza confort

■ **rough out** vt abbozzare

■ **rough up** vt fam malmenare (person)

**roughage** /ˈrʌfɪdʒ/ n fibre fpl

**rough: rough-and-ready** a (person, manner) sbrigativo; (conditions, method) rudimentale. **rough-and-tumble** n (rough play) zuffa f. **rough copy** n brutta copia f. **rough draft** n abbozzo m

**roughen** /ˈrʌfən/ vt rendere ruvido (surface)

**roughly** /ˈrʌflɪ/ adv rozzamente; (more or less) pressappoco

**roughness** /ˈrʌfnɪs/ n ruvidità f; (of behaviour) rozzezza f

**rough paper** n carta f da brutta

**roughshod** /ˈrʌfʃɒd/ adv **ride ~ over** infischiarsi di ⟨*person, objection*⟩; calpestare ⟨*feelings*⟩

**roulette** /ru:'let/ *n* roulette *f*

**round** /raʊnd/ *a* rotondo ● *n* tondo *m*; (*slice*) fetta *f*; (*of visits, drinks*) giro *m*; (*of competition*) partita *f*; (*boxing*) ripresa *f*, round *m inv*; **do one's ~s** ⟨*doctor:*⟩ fare il giro delle visite ● *prep* intorno a; **open ~ the clock** aperto ventiquattr'ore ● *adv* **all ~** tutt'intorno; **ask sb ~** invitare qcno; **go/come ~ to** (*a friend etc*) andare da; **turn/look ~** girarsi; **~ about** (*approximately*) intorno a ● *vt* arrotondare; girare ⟨*corner*⟩

■ **round down** *vt* arrotondare (*per difetto*)
■ **round off** *vt* (*end*) terminare
■ **round on** *vt* aggredire
■ **round up** *vt* radunare; arrotondare ⟨*prices*⟩

**roundabout** /'raʊndəbaʊt/ *a* indiretto ● *n* giostra *f*; (*for traffic*) rotonda *f*

**round: round bracket** *n* parentesi *f* tonda. **round figure** *n* cifra *f* tonda. **round robin** *n* petizione *f*

**rounders** /'raʊndəz/ *n Br Sport* gioco *m* simile al baseball

**round: round-shouldered** /-'ʃəʊldəd/ *a* con le spalle curve. **round table** *n* tavola *f* rotonda. **round the clock** *adv* 24 ore su 24. **round-the-clock** *a* ⟨*Br: care, surveillance*⟩ ventiquattr'ore su ventiquattro. **round trip** *n* viaggio *m* di andata e ritorno. **round-up** *n* (*of suspects*) retata *f*; (*of cattle*) raduno *m*; (*summary*) riepilogo *m*

**rouse** /raʊz/ *vt* svegliare; risvegliare ⟨*suspicion, interest*⟩

**rousing** /'raʊzɪŋ/ *a* ⟨*speech*⟩ che solleva il morale; ⟨*music*⟩ trionfale

**rout** /raʊt/ *vt Mil, fig* sbaragliare ● *n* disfatta *f*

**route** /ru:t/ *n* itinerario *m*; *Naut, Aeron* rotta *f*; (*of bus*) percorso *m*

**routine** /ru:'ti:n/ *a* di routine ● *n* routine *f inv*; *Theat* numero *m*

**routinely** /ru:'ti:nlɪ/ *adv* d'ufficio

**rove** /rəʊv/ *vi* girovagare

**roving** /'rəʊvɪŋ/ *a* ⟨*reporter, ambassador*⟩ itinerante

**roving eye** *n* **have a ~** essere sempre in cerca di avventure amorose

**row**[1] /rəʊ/ *n* (*line*) fila *f*; **three years in a ~** tre anni di fila

**row**[2] *vi* (*in boat*) remare ● *vt* **~ a boat** remare

**row**[3] /raʊ/ *n fam* (*quarrel*) litigata *f*; (*noise*) baccano *m*; **we've had a ~** abbiamo litigato ● *vi fam* litigare

**rowboat** /'rəʊbəʊt/ *n Am* barca *f* a remi

**rowdy** /'raʊdɪ/ *a* (**-ier, -iest**) chiassoso ● *n* attaccabrighe *m inv*

**rower** /'rəʊə(r)/ *n* rematore, -trice *mf*

**rowing boat** /'rəʊɪŋ/ *n* barca *f* a remi

**rowing machine** *n* vogatore *m*

**rowlock** /'rɒlək/ *n Br* scalmo *m*

**royal** /'rɔɪəl/ *a* reale ● *n* membro *m* della famiglia reale

**royally** /'rɔɪlɪ/ *adv* regalmente

**royalties** /'rɔɪltɪz/ *npl* (*payments*) diritti *mpl* d'autore

**royalty** /'rɔɪltɪ/ *n* appartenenza *f* alla famiglia reale; (*persons*) i membri della famiglia reale

**rpm** *abbr* (**revolutions per minute**) giri *mpl* al minuto

**rub** /rʌb/ *n* sfregata *f* ● *vt* (*pt/pp* **rubbed**) sfregare; **~ one's hands** fregarsi le mani

■ **rub along** *vi* sopportarsi [a vicenda]
■ **rub down** *vt* frizionare ⟨*person, body*⟩; levigare ⟨*wood*⟩
■ **rub in** *vt* far assorbire (massaggiando) ⟨*cream*⟩; **don't ~ it in** *fam* non rigirare il coltello nella piaga
■ **rub off** *vt* mandar via sfregando ⟨*stain*⟩; (*from blackboard*) cancellare ● *vi* andar via; **~ off on** essere trasmesso a
■ **rub out** *vt* cancellare
■ **rub up** *vt* **~ sb up the wrong way** prendere qcno per il verso sbagliato

**rubber** /'rʌbə(r)/ *n* gomma *f*; (*eraser*) gomma *f* [da cancellare]

**rubber: rubber band** *n* elastico *m*. **rubber bullet** *n* proiettile *m* di gomma. **rubberneck** *n fam* (*onlooker*) curioso, -a *mf*; (*tourist*) turista *mf*. **rubber plant** *n* ficus *m inv*. **rubber-stamp** *vt fig* approvare senza discutere

**rubbery** /'rʌbərɪ/ *a* gommoso

**rubbish** /'rʌbɪʃ/ *n* immondizie *fpl*; (*fam: nonsense*) idiozie *fpl*; (*fam: junk*) robaccia *f* ● *vt fam* fare a pezzi

**rubbish bin** *n* pattumiera *f*

**rubbish dump** *n* discarica *f*; (*official*) discarica *f* comunale

**rubbishy** /'rʌbɪʃɪ/ *a fam* schifoso

**rubble** /'rʌbl/ *n* macerie *fpl*

**rub-down** *n* strofinata *f*

**rubella** /ru'belə/ *n* rosolia *f*

**rubric** /'ru:brɪk/ *n* rubrica *f*

**ruby** /'ru:bɪ/ *n* rubino *m* ● *attrib* di rubini; ⟨*lips*⟩ scarlatta

**rucksack** /'rʌksæk/ *n* zaino *m*

**ructions** /'rʌkʃ(ə)nz/ *npl fam* finimondo *msg*; **there'll be ~ if he finds out** se lo scopre, succede il finimondo

**rudder** /'rʌdə(r)/ *n* timone *m*

**ruddy** /'rʌdɪ/ *a* (**-ier, -iest**) rubicondo; *fam* maledetto

**rude** /ru:d/ *a* scortese; (*improper*) spinto

**rudely** /'ru:dlɪ/ *adv* scortesemente

**rudeness** /'ru:dnɪs/ *n* scortesia *f*

**rudimentary** /ru:dɪ'mentərɪ/ *a* rudimentale

**rudiments** /'ru:dɪmənts/ *npl* rudimenti *mpl*

**rue**[1] /ru:/ *vt* pentirsi di ⟨*decision*⟩; **~ the day** maledire il giorno

**rue**[2] *n Bot* ruta *f*

**rueful** /'ru:fl/ *a* rassegnato

**ruefully** /'ru:fʊlɪ/ *adv* con rassegnazione

**ruffian** /'rʌfɪən/ *n* farabutto *m*

**ruffle** /'rʌfl/ *n* gala *f* ● *vt* scompigliare ⟨*hair*⟩

**rug** /rʌg/ *n* tappeto *m*; (*blanket*) coperta *f*

**rugby** /'rʌgbɪ/ *n* ~ [**football**] rugby *m*

**rugby league** *n* rugby *m* a tredici

**rugby union** *n* rugby *m* a quindici

**rugged** /'rʌgɪd/ *a* ⟨*coastline*⟩ roccioso; ⟨*face, personality*⟩ duro

**ruin** /'ruːɪn/ *n* rovina *f*; **in ~s** in rovina ● *vt* rovinare

**ruined** /'ruːɪnd/ *a* ⟨*building, clothes*⟩ rovinato

**ruinous** /'ruːɪnəs/ *a* estremamente costoso

**rule** /ruːl/ *n* regola *f*; ⟨*control*⟩ ordinamento *m*; ⟨*for measuring*⟩ metro *m*; **~s** *pl* regolamento *msg*; **as a ~** generalmente; **make it a ~ to do sth** fare qcsa sistematicamente ● *vt* governare; dominare ⟨*colony, behaviour*⟩; **~ that** stabilire che ● *vi* governare

■ **rule out** *vt* escludere

**ruled** /ruːld/ *a* ⟨*paper*⟩ a righe

**rule of thumb** *n* principio *m* empirico

**ruler** /'ruːlə(r)/ *n* capo *m* di Stato; ⟨*sovereign*⟩ sovrano, -a *mf*; ⟨*measure*⟩ righello *m*, regolo *m*

**ruling** /'ruːlɪŋ/ *a* ⟨*class*⟩ dirigente; ⟨*party*⟩ di governo ● *n* decisione *f*

**rum**[1] /rʌm/ *n* rum *m inv*

**rum**[2] *a* ⟨*fam: peculiar*⟩ curioso

**rumble** /'rʌmbl/ *n* rombo *m*; ⟨*of stomach*⟩ brontolio *m* ● *vi* rombare; ⟨*stomach:*⟩ brontolare

**rumble strip** *n* banda *f* rumorosa

**rumbustious** /rʌm'bʌstʃəs/ *a* ⟨*noisy, very lively*⟩ chiassoso

**ruminant** /'ruːmɪnənt/ *n* ruminante *m*

**ruminate** /'ruːmɪneɪt/ *vi* ⟨*animals:*⟩ ruminare; ⟨*think*⟩ rimuginare

**rummage** /'rʌmɪdʒ/ *vi* rovistare (**in/ through** in)

**rummy** /'rʌmɪ/ *n* ramino *m*

**rumour** /'ruːmə(r)/ *n* diceria *f* ● *vt* **it is ~ed that** si dice che

**rumour-monger** /'ruːməmʌŋgə(r)/ *n* persona *f* che sparge pettegolezzi

**rump** /rʌmp/ *n* natiche *fpl*

**rumple** /'rʌmpl/ *vt* sgualcire ⟨*clothes, sheets, papers*⟩; scompigliare ⟨*hair*⟩

**rump steak** *n* bistecca *f* di girello

**rumpus** /'rʌmpəs/ *n fam* baccano *m*

**run** /rʌn/ *n* ⟨*on foot*⟩ corsa *f*; ⟨*distance to be covered*⟩ tragitto *m*; ⟨*outing*⟩ giro *m*; *Theat* rappresentazioni *fpl*; ⟨*in skiing*⟩ pista *f*; ⟨*Am: ladder*⟩ smagliatura *f* ⟨*in calze*⟩; **at a ~** di corsa; **~ of bad luck** periodo *m* sfortunato; **on the ~** in fuga; **have the ~ of** avere a disposizione; **in the long ~** a lungo termine ● *v* ⟨*pt* **ran**, *pp* **run**, *pres p* **running**⟩ ● *vi* correre; ⟨*river:*⟩ scorrere; ⟨*nose, makeup:*⟩ colare; ⟨*bus:*⟩ fare servizio; ⟨*play:*⟩ essere in cartellone; ⟨*colours:*⟩ sbiadire; ⟨*in election*⟩ presentarsi [come candidato]; ⟨*software:*⟩ girare; **~ aground** insabbiarsi; **~ low on, ~ short of** essere a corto di ● *vt* ⟨*manage*⟩ dirigere; tenere ⟨*house*⟩; ⟨*drive*⟩ dare un passaggio a; correre ⟨*risk*⟩; *Comput* lanciare; *Journ* pubblicare ⟨*article*⟩; ⟨*pass*⟩ far scorrere ⟨*eyes, hand*⟩; **~ a temperature** avere la febbre; **~ a bath** far scorrere l'acqua per il bagno

■ **run about** *vi* ⟨*children:*⟩ correre di qua e di là; ⟨*be busy*⟩ correre

■ **run across** *vt* imbattersi in

■ **run after** *vt* ⟨*chase*⟩ rincorrere; ⟨*romantically*⟩ andare dietro a

■ **run along** *vi* ⟨*go away*⟩ andare via

■ **run away** *vi* scappare [via], andare via di corsa; ⟨*from home*⟩ scappare di casa

■ **run away with** *vt* scappare con ⟨*lover, money*⟩; **she let her enthusiasm ~ away with her** si è lasciata trasportare dall'entusiasmo

■ **run back** *vi* correre indietro ● *vt* ⟨*transport by car*⟩ riaccompagnare

■ **run back over** *vt* ⟨*review*⟩ rivedere

■ **run down** *vi* ⟨*clock:*⟩ scaricarsi; ⟨*stocks:*⟩ esaurirsi ● *vt Auto* investire; ⟨*reduce*⟩ esaurire; ⟨*fam: criticize*⟩ denigrare

■ **run in** *vi* entrare di corsa

■ **run into** *vi* ⟨*meet*⟩ imbattersi in; ⟨*knock against*⟩ urtare

■ **run off** *vi* scappare [via], andare via di corsa; ⟨*from home*⟩ scappare di casa ● *vt* stampare ⟨*copies*⟩

■ **run off with** *vt* = **run away with**

■ **run on** *vi* ⟨*meeting:*⟩ protrarsi; ⟨*person:*⟩ chiacchierare senza sosta

■ **run out** *vi* uscire di corsa; ⟨*supplies, money:*⟩ esaurirsi; **~ out of** rimanere senza

■ **run over** *vi* correre; ⟨*overflow*⟩ traboccare ● *vt* ⟨*review*⟩ dare una scorsa a; *Auto* investire

■ **run through** *vt* ⟨*use up*⟩ fare fuori; ⟨*be present in*⟩ pervadere; ⟨*review*⟩ dare una scorsa a

■ **run to** *vt* ⟨*be enough for*⟩ essere sufficiente per; ⟨*have enough money for*⟩ potersi permettere

■ **run up** *vi* salire di corsa; ⟨*towards*⟩ arrivare di corsa ● *vt* accumulare ⟨*debts, bill*⟩; ⟨*sew*⟩ cucire

■ **run up against** *vt* incontrare ⟨*difficulties*⟩

**run:** **runabout** *n* ⟨*vehicle*⟩ utilitaria *f*. **runaround** *n* **he's giving me/her the ~** mi/la sta menando per il naso. **runaway** *n* fuggitivo, -a *mf*, fuggiasco, -a *mf*; ⟨*child*⟩ ragazzo, -a *mf* scappato, -a di casa ● *a* ⟨*person*⟩ in fuga; ⟨*child*⟩ scappato di casa; ⟨*inflation*⟩ galoppante; ⟨*success*⟩ eclatante. **run-down** *a* ⟨*area*⟩ in abbandono; ⟨*person*⟩ esaurito ● *n* analisi *f*

**rung**[1] /rʌŋ/ *n* ⟨*of ladder*⟩ piolo *m*

**rung**[2] *see* **ring**[2]

**run-in** *n* ⟨*fam: argument*⟩ lite *f*

**runner** /'rʌnə(r)/ *n* podista *mf*; ⟨*in race*⟩ corridore, -trice *mf*; ⟨*on sledge*⟩ pattino *f*; ⟨*carpet*⟩ guida *f*

**runner bean** *n* fagiolino *m*

**runner-up** *n* secondo, -a classificato, -a *mf*

**running** /'rʌnɪŋ/ *a* in corsa; ⟨*water*⟩ corrente; **four times ~** quattro volte di seguito ● *n* corsa *f*; ⟨*management*⟩ direzione *f*; **be in the ~** essere in lizza

**running commentary** *n* cronaca *f*

**runny** /'rʌnɪ/ *a* semiliquido; **~ nose** naso *m* che cola

**run-of-the-mill** *a* ordinario

**runs** /rʌnz/ *npl* **the ~** ⟨*fam: diarrhoea*⟩ la sciolta

**runt** /rʌnt/ *n* ⟨*of litter*⟩ animale *m* più piccolo

_e debole di una figliata_: (_pej: weakling_) mezza cartuccia _f_
**run-through** _n_ prova _f_ generale
**run-up** _n Sport_ rincorsa _f;_ **the ~ to** il periodo precedente
**runway** /'rʌnweɪ/ _n_ pista _f_
**rupee** /ru:'pi:/ _n_ rupia _f_
**rupture** /'rʌptʃə(r)/ _n_ rottura _f; Med_ ernia _f_ ● _vt_ rompere; **~ oneself** farsi venire l'ernia ● _vi_ rompersi
**rural** /'rʊərəl/ _a_ rurale
**ruse** /ru:z/ _n_ astuzia _f_
**rush¹** /rʌʃ/ _n Bot_ giunco _m_
**rush²** _n_ fretta _f;_ **in a ~** di fretta ● _vi_ precipitarsi ● _vt_ far premura a; **~ sb to hospital** trasportare qcno all'ospedale
■ **rush away, rush off** _vi_ andar via in fretta
**rush hour** _n_ ora _f_ di punta ● _attrib_ delle ore di punta
**rusk** /rʌsk/ _n_ biscotto _m_

**Russia** /'rʌʃə/ _n_ Russia _f_
**Russian** /'rʌʃən/ _a_ & _n_ russo, -a _mf;_ (_language_) russo _m_
**Russian roulette** _n_ roulette _f_ russa
**rust** /rʌst/ _n_ ruggine _f_ ● _vi_ arruggininirsi ● _vt_ arruginire
**rustic** /'rʌstɪk/ _a_ rustico
**rustle** /'rʌsl/ _vi_ frusciare ● _vt_ far frusciare; _Am_ rubare ⟨_cattle_⟩
■ **rustle up** _vt fam_ fare ⟨_meal, cup of coffee_⟩
**rustler** /'rʌslə(r)/ _n_ ladro _m_ di bestiame
**rustproof** /'rʌstpru:f/ _a_ a prova di ruggine
**rusty** /'rʌstɪ/ _a_ (-**ier, -iest**) arrugginito
**rut** /rʌt/ _n_ solco _m;_ **in a ~** _fam_ nella routine
**ruthless** /'ru:θlɪs/ _a_ spietato
**ruthlessly** /'ru:θlɪslɪ/ _adv_ spietatamente
**ruthlessness** /'ru:θlɪsnɪs/ _n_ spietatezza _f_
**rutting** /'rʌtɪŋ/ _n_ accoppiamento _m_
**rutting season** _n_ stagione _f_ degli amori
**rye** /raɪ/ _n_ segale _f_

# Ss

**s, S** /es/ _n_ (_letter_) s, S _f inv_
**S** _abbr_ **small**; _abbr_ (**south**) S
**sabbath** /'sæbəθ/ _n_ domenica _f,_ (_Jewish_) sabato _m_
**sabbatical** /sə'bætɪkl/ _n Univ_ anno _m_ sabbatico
**sable** /'seɪbl/ _n_ (_animal, fur_) zibellino _m_
**sabotage** /'sæbəta:ʒ/ _n_ sabotaggio _m_ ● _vt_ sabotare
**saboteur** /sæbə'tɜ:(r)/ _n_ sabotatore, -trice _mf_
**sabre** /'seɪbə(r)/ _n_ sciabola _f_
**sac** /sæk/ _n Anat, Zool_ sacco _m; Bot_ sacca _f;_ **honey ~** cestella _f_
**saccharin** /'sækərɪn/ _n_ saccarina _f_
**sachet** /'sæʃeɪ/ _n_ bustina _f,_ (_scented_) sacchetto _m_ profumato
**sack¹** /sæk/ _vt_ (_plunder_) saccheggiare
**sack²** _n_ sacco _m;_ **get the ~** _fam_ essere licenziato; **give sb the ~** licenziare qcno ● _vt fam_ licenziare
**sackcloth** /'sækklɒθ/ _n_ tela _f_ di sacco; **wear ~ and ashes** cospargersi il capo di cenere
**sackful** /'sækfʊl/ _n_ sacco _m_ (_contenuto_)
**sacking** /'sækɪŋ/ _n_ tela _f_ per sacchi; (_fam: dismissal_) licenziamento _m_
**sackload** /'sækləʊd/ _n_ sacco _m_ (_contenuto_)
**sacrament** /'sækrəmənt/ _n_ sacramento _m_
**sacred** /'seɪkrɪd/ _a_ sacro
**sacred cow** /kaʊ/ _n_ (_institution_) istituzione _f_ intoccabile; (_principle_) principio _m_ inderogabile; (_person_) mostro _m_ sacro
**sacrifice** /'sækrɪfaɪs/ _n_ sacrificio _m_ ● _vt_ sacrificare; **~ oneself** immolarsi
**sacrificial** /sækrɪ'fɪʃl/ _a_ ⟨_victim_⟩ sacrificale

**sacrilege** /'sækrɪlɪdʒ/ _n_ sacrilegio _m_
**sacrilegious** /sækrɪ'lɪdʒəs/ _a_ sacrilego
**sacristy** /'sækrɪstɪ/ _n_ sagrestia _f_
**sacrosanct** /'sækrəʊsæŋkt/ _a_ sacrosanto
**sacrum** /'sækrʌm/ _n Anat_ osso _m_ sacro
**sad** /sæd/ _a_ (**sadder, saddest**) triste
**sadden** /'sædn/ _vt_ rattristare
**saddle** /'sædl/ _n_ sella _f;_ **be in the ~** _fig_ tenere le redini ● _vt_ sellare; **I've been ~d with...** _fig_ mi hanno affibbiato...
**sadism** /'seɪdɪzm/ _n_ sadismo _m_
**sadist** /'seɪdɪst/ _n_ sadico, -a _mf_
**sadistic** /sə'dɪstɪk/ _a_ sadico
**sadistically** /sə'dɪstɪklɪ/ _adv_ sadicamente
**sadly** /'sædlɪ/ _adv_ tristemente; (_unfortunately_) sfortunatamente
**sadness** /'sædnɪs/ _n_ tristezza _f_
**sadomasochism** /seɪdəʊ'mæsəkɪzm/ _n_ sadomasochismo _m_
**sadomasochist** /seɪdəʊ'mæsəkɪst/ _n_ sadomasochismo _m_
**sadomasochistic** /seɪdəʊ'mæsəkɪstɪk/ _a_ sadomasochistico
**sae** _abbr_ **stamped addressed envelope**
**safari** /sə'fɑ:rɪ/ _n_ safari _m inv_
**safari park** _n_ zoosafari _m inv_
**safe** /seɪf/ _a_ sicuro; (_out of danger_) salvo; ⟨_object_⟩ al sicuro; **~ and sound** sano e salvo ● _n_ cassaforte _f_
**safe: safe-breaker** _n_ scassinatore, -trice _mf._ **safeguard** _n_ protezione _f_ ● _vt_ proteggere. **safe keeping** _n_ custodia _f;_ **for ~ ~** in custodia
**safely** /'seɪflɪ/ _adv_ in modo sicuro; ⟨_arrive_⟩ senza incidenti; ⟨_assume_⟩ con certezza

**safe sex** *n* sesso *m* sicuro
**safety** /'seɪftɪ/ *n* sicurezza *f*
**safety: safety belt** *n* cintura *f* di sicurezza.
**safety catch** *n* sicura *f*. **safety curtain** *n*
tagliafuoco *m*. **safety-deposit box** *n* cassetta *f* di sicurezza. **safety glass** *n* vetro *m* di
sicurezza. **safety net** *n* (*for acrobat*) rete *f* di
protezione; *fig* protezione. **safety pin** *n* spilla
*f* di sicurezza o da balia. **safety razor** *n* rasoio *m* di sicurezza. **safety valve** *n* valvola *f* di
sicurezza; *fig* valvola *f* di sfogo
**saffron** /'sæfrən/ *n* zafferano *m*
**sag** /sæg/ *vi* (*pt/pp* **sagged**) abbassarsi
**saga** /'sɑːgə/ *n* saga *f*
**sagacity** /sə'gæsətɪ/ *n* sagacia *f*
**sage**[1] /seɪdʒ/ *n* (*herb*) salvia *f*
**sage**[2] *a* & *n* saggio, -a *mf*
**sagely** /'seɪdʒlɪ/ *adv* (*reply, nod*) saggiamente
**Sagittarius** /sædʒɪ'teərɪəs/ *n* Sagittario *m*
**sago** /'seɪɡəʊ/ *n* sagù *m*
**Sahara** /sə'hɑːrə/ *n* Sahara *m*
**said** /sed/ *see* **say**
**sail** /seɪl/ *n* vela *f*; (*trip*) giro *m* in barca a vela
● *vi* navigare; *Sport* praticare la vela; (*leave*)
salpare ● *vt* pilotare
■ **sail through** *vt* superare senza problemi
(*exam*)
**sailboard** /'seɪlbɔːd/ *n* tavola *f* del windsurf
**sailboarding** /'seɪlbɔːdɪŋ/ *n* windsurf *m inv*
**sailboat** /'seɪlbəʊt/ *n Am* barca *f* a vela
**sailing** /'seɪlɪŋ/ *n* vela *f*
**sailing boat** *n* barca *f* a vela
**sailing ship** *n* veliero *m*
**sailor** /'seɪlə(r)/ *n* marinaio *m*
**saint** /seɪnt/ *n* santo, -a *mf*
**sainthood** /'seɪnthʊd/ *n* santità *f*
**saintly** /'seɪntlɪ/ *a* da santo
**sake** /seɪk/ *n* **for the ~ of** (*person*) per il
bene di; (*peace*) per amor di; **for the ~ of it**
per il gusto di farlo
**salacious** /sə'leɪʃəs/ *a* (*joke*) salace; (*book*)
licenzioso; (*look*) lascivo
**salad** /'sæləd/ *n* insalata *f*
**salad: salad bar** *n* tavola *f* fredda. **salad
bowl** *n* insalatiera *f*. **salad cream** *n* salsa *f*
per condire l'insalata. **salad days** *npl* anni
*mpl* verdi. **salad dressing** *n* condimento *m*
per insalata
**salami** /sə'lɑːmɪ/ *n* salame *m*
**salaried** /'sælərɪd/ *a* stipendiato
**salary** /'sælərɪ/ *n* stipendio *m*
**salary review** *n* revisione *f* dello stipendio
**salary scale** *n* tabella *f* retributiva
**sale** /seɪl/ *n* vendita *f*; (*at reduced prices*)
svendita *f*; **for/on ~** in vendita; **'for ~'**
'vendesi'
**sales: sales and marketing** *n* vendite *fpl* e
marketing. **sales and marketing department** *n* ufficio *m* vendite e marketing. **sales
assistant** *n* commesso, -a *mf*. **sales director** *n* capo *mf* dell'ufficio vendite. **sales engineer** *n* tecnico *m* commerciale. **sales figures** *npl* volumi *mpl* d'affari. **sales force** *n*
rappresentanti *mpl*. **sales invoice** *n* fattura *f*
di vendita. **sales ledger** *n* partitario *m*

**vendite. salesman** *n* venditore *m*; (*traveller*)
rappresentante *m*. **salesroom** *n* (*for auctions*) sala *f* d'aste. **sales team** *n* team *m inv*
vendite. **saleswoman** *n* venditrice *f*
**salient** /'seɪlɪənt/ *a* saliente
**saline** /'seɪlaɪn/ *a* salino
**saliva** /sə'laɪvə/ *n* saliva *f*
**salivary glands** /sə'laɪvərɪ/ *npl* ghiandole
*fpl* salivari
**salivate** /'sælɪveɪt/ *vi* salivare; **the smell of
chicken roasting makes me ~** l'odore di
pollo arrosto mi fa venire l'acquolina in bocca
**sallow** /'sæləʊ/ *a* giallastro
**sally** /'sælɪ/ *n* (*witty remark*) battuta *f*; *Mil*
sortita *f* ● *vi* saltar fuori
**salmon** /'sæmən/ *n* salmone *m*
**salmonella** /sælmə'nelə/ *n* salmonella *f*
**salmon-pink** *a* [rosa *inv*] salmone *inv*
**salmon trout** *n* trota *f* salmonata
**salon** /'sælɒn/ *n* salone *m*
**saloon** /sə'luːn/ *n Auto* berlina *f*; (*Am: bar*)
bar *m*
**salsa** /'sælsə/ *n* salsa *f*
**salt** /sɔːlt/ *n* sale *m* ● *a* salato; (*fish, meat*)
sotto sale ● *vt* salare; (*cure*) mettere sotto
sale
**salt cellar** *n* saliera *f*
**saltiness** /'sɔːltɪnɪs/ *n* salinità *f*
**salt water** *n* acqua *f* di mare
**salt-water fish** *n* pesce *m* d'acqua salata
**salty** /'sɔːltɪ/ *a* salato
**salubrious** /sə'luːbrɪəs/ *a* (*neighbourhood*)
raccomandabile; **it's not a very ~ area** è
una zona poco raccomandabile
**salutary** /'sæljʊtərɪ/ *a* salutare
**salute** /sə'luːt/ *Mil n* saluto *m* ● *vt* salutare
● *vi* fare il saluto
**salvage** /'sælvɪdʒ/ *n Naut* recupero *m* ● *vt*
recuperare
**salvation** /sæl'veɪʃn/ *n* salvezza *f*
**Salvation Army** *n* Esercito *m* della Salvezza
**salve** /sælv/ *vt* **~ one's conscience** mettersi la coscienza a posto
**salver** /'sælvə(r)/ *n* vassoio *m* (*di metallo*)
**salvo** /'sælvəʊ/ *n* salva *f*
**samba** /'sæmbə/ *n* samba *f*
**same** /seɪm/ *a* stesso (**as** di) ● *pron* **the ~** lo
stesso; **be all the ~** essere tutti uguali ● *adv*
**the ~** nello stesso modo; **all the ~** (*however*)
lo stesso; **the ~ to you** altrettanto
**same-day delivery** *n* consegna *f* in giornata
**sample** /'sɑːmpl/ *n* campione *m* ● *vt* testare
**sanatorium** /sænə'tɔːrɪəm/ *n* casa *f* di cura
**sanctify** /'sæŋktɪfaɪ/ *vt* (*pt/pp* **-fied**) santificare
**sanctimonious** /sæŋktɪ'məʊnɪəs/ *a* moraleggiante
**sanction** /'sæŋkʃn/ *n* (*approval*) autorizzazione *f*; (*penalty*) sanzione *f* ● *vt* autorizzare
**sanctity** /'sæŋktɪtɪ/ *n* santità *f*
**sanctuary** /'sæŋktjʊərɪ/ *n Relig* santuario
*m*; (*refuge*) asilo *m*; (*for wildlife*) riserva *f*
**sanctum** /'sæŋktəm/ *n* (*holy place*) santua-

rio *m*; (*private place*) rifugio *m*; **the inner ~**
*Relig* il Sancta Sanctorum
**sand** /sænd/ *n* sabbia *f* ● *vt* ~ **[down]** carteggiare
**sandal** /ˈsændl/ *n* sandalo *m*
**sand:** **sandbag** *n* sacchetto *m* di sabbia.
**sandbank** *n* banco *m* di sabbia. **sand dune** *n*
duna *f*. **sandblast** *vt* sabbiare. **sandblasting**
*n* sabbiatura *f*. **sandcastle** *n* castello *m* di
sabbia
**sander** /ˈsændə(r)/ *n* (*machine*) levigatrice *f*
**Sandinista** /sændrˈniːstə/ *a* & *n* sandinista
**sand:** **sandpaper** *n* carta *f* vetrata ● *vt*
cartavetrare. **sandpit** *n* recinto *m* contenente
sabbia dove giocano i bambini. **sandstone** *n*
arenaria *f*. **sandstorm** *n* tempesta *f* di sabbia
**sandwich** /ˈsænwɪdʒ/ *n* tramezzino *m* ● *vt*
**~ed between** schiacciato tra
**sandwich course** *n* corso *m* che comprende dei periodi di tirocinio
**sandwich-man** *n* uomo *m* sandwich
**sandy** /ˈsændɪ/ *a* (**-ier, -iest**) (*beach, soil*)
sabbioso; (*hair*) biondiccio
**sane** /seɪn/ *a* (*not mad*) sano di mente;
(*sensible*) sensato
**sang** /sæŋ/ *see* **sing**
**sangria** /ˈsæŋˈgrɪə/ *n* sangria *f*
**sanguine** /ˈsæŋgwɪn/ *a* ottimistico
**sanitary** /ˈsænɪtərɪ/ *a* igienico; (*system*) sanitario
**sanitary napkin** *n Am*, **sanitary towel**
*n* assorbente *m* igienico
**sanitation** /sænɪˈteɪʃn/ *n* impianti *mpl* igienici
**sanity** /ˈsænətɪ/ *n* sanità *f* di mente;
(*sensibleness*) buon senso *m*
**sank** /sæŋk/ *see* **sink**
**Santa [Claus]** /ˈsæntə[klɔːz]/ *n* Babbo *m*
Natale
**sap** /sæp/ *n Bot* linfa *f* ● *vt* (*pt/pp* **sapped**) indebolire
**sapling** /ˈsæplɪŋ/ *n* alberello *m*
**sapper** /ˈsæpə(r)/ *n Br Mil* geniere *m*
**sapphire** /ˈsæfaɪə(r)/ *n* zaffiro *m* ● *attrib* blu
zaffiro *inv*
**sarcasm** /ˈsɑːkæzm/ *n* sarcasmo *m*
**sarcastic** /sɑːˈkæstɪk/ *a* sarcastico
**sarcastically** /sɑːˈkæstɪklɪ/ *adv* sarcasticamente
**sarcophagus** /sɑːˈkɒfəgəs/ *n* sarcofago *m*
**sardine** /sɑːˈdiːn/ *n* sardina *f*
**Sardinia** /sɑːˈdɪnɪə/ *n* Sardegna *f*
**Sardinian** /sɑːˈdɪnɪən/ *a* & *n* sardo, -a *mf*
**sardonic** /sɑːˈdɒnɪk/ *a* sardonico
**sardonically** /sɑːˈdɒnɪklɪ/ *adv* sardonicamente
**sari** /ˈsɑːrɪ/ *n* sari *m inv*
**sarong** /səˈrɒŋ/ *n* pareo *m*
**SAS** *n Br abbr* (**Special Air Service**) commando *mpl* britannici per operazioni speciali
**sash** /sæʃ/ *n* fascia *f*; (*for dress*) fusciacca *f*
**sashay** /ˈsæʃeɪ/ *vi fam* (*casually*) camminare
in modo disinvolto; (*seductively*) camminare
in modo provocante

**sassy** /ˈsæsɪ/ *a Am fam* (*cheeky*) sfacciato;
(*smart*) chic *inv*
**sat** /sæt/ *see* **sit**
**Satan** /ˈseɪtən/ *n* Satana *m*
**satanic** /səˈtænɪk/ *a* satanico
**satchel** /ˈsætʃl/ *n* cartella *f*
**sated** /ˈseɪtɪd/ *a* (*person*) sazio; (*desire*) appagato; (*appetite*) soddisfatto
**satellite** /ˈsætəlaɪt/ *n* satellite *m*
**satellite dish** *n* antenna *f* parabolica
**satellite television** *n* televisione *f* via satellite
**satiate** /ˈseɪʃɪeɪt/ *vt* saziare (*person*); appagare (*desire*); soddisfare (*appetite*)
**satin** /ˈsætɪn/ *n* raso *m* ● *attrib* di raso
**satire** /ˈsætaɪə(r)/ *n* satira *f*
**satirical** /səˈtɪrɪkl/ *a* satirico
**satirically** /səˈtɪrɪklɪ/ *adv* satiricamente
**satirist** /ˈsætərɪst/ *n* scrittore, -trice *mf* satirico, -a; (*comedian*) comico, -a *mf* satirico, -a
**satirize** /ˈsætɪraɪz/ *vt* satireggiare
**satisfaction** /sætɪsˈfækʃn/ *n* soddisfazione
*f*; **be to sb's ~** soddisfare qcno
**satisfactorily** /sætɪsˈfækt(ə)rɪlɪ/ *adv* in
modo soddisfacente
**satisfactory** /sætɪsˈfæktərɪ/ *a* soddisfacente
**satisfy** /ˈsætɪsfaɪ/ *vt* (*pt/pp* **-ied**) soddisfare;
(*convince*) convincere; **be satisfied** essere
soddisfatto
**satisfying** /ˈsætɪsfaɪɪŋ/ *a* soddisfacente
**saturate** /ˈsætʃəreɪt/ *vt* inzuppare (**with** di);
*Chem, fig* saturare (**with** di)
**saturated** /ˈsætʃəreɪtɪd/ *a* saturo
**saturation** /sætʃəˈreɪʃn/ *n* **reach ~ point**
raggiungere il punto di saturazione
**Saturday** /ˈsætədeɪ/ *n* sabato *m*
**Saturn** /ˈsætən/ *n* Saturno *m*
**sauce** /sɔːs/ *n* salsa *f*; (*cheek*) impertinenza *f*
**saucepan** /ˈsɔːspən/ *n* pentola *f*
**saucer** /ˈsɔːsə(r)/ *n* piattino *m*
**saucy** /ˈsɔːsɪ/ *a* (**-ier, -iest**) impertinente
**Saudi** /ˈsaʊdɪ/ *a* saudita ● *n* (*person*) saudita
*mf*; (*country*) Arabia *f* Saudita
**Saudi Arabia** /əˈreɪbɪə/ *n* Arabia *f* Saudita
**Saudi Arabian** *a* & *n* saudita *mf*
**sauerkraut** /ˈsaʊəkraʊt/ *n* crauti *mpl*
**sauna** /ˈsɔːnə/ *n* sauna *f*
**saunter** /ˈsɔːntə(r)/ *vi* andare a spasso
**sausage** /ˈsɒsɪdʒ/ *n* salsiccia *f*; (*dried*) salame *m*
**sausage dog** /ˈsɒsɪdʒdɒg/ *n fam* bassotto *m*
**sausage roll** *n* involtino *m* di pasta sfoglia
con salsiccia
**sauté** /ˈsəʊteɪ/ *vt* rosolare ● *a* rosolato
**savage** /ˈsævɪdʒ/ *a* feroce; (*tribe, custom*)
selvaggio ● *n* selvaggio, -a *mf* ● *vt* fare a pezzi
**savagely** /ˈsævɪdʒlɪ/ *adv* (*attack*) selvaggiamente; (*criticize*) ferocemente
**savagery** /ˈsævɪdʒrɪ/ *n* ferocia *f*
**save** /seɪv/ *n Sport* parata *f* ● *vt* salvare
(**from** da); (*keep, collect*) tenere; risparmiare
(*time, money*); (*avoid*) evitare; *Sport* parare
(*goal*); *Comput* salvare, memorizzare; **~ face**
salvar la faccia ● *vi* ~ **[up]** risparmiare
● *prep* salvo

**saver** /'seɪvə(r)/ *n* risparmiatore, -trice *mf*

**saving grace** /seɪvɪŋ'greɪs/ *n* **that's his one ~** ~ si salva grazie a questo

**savings** /'seɪvɪŋz/ *npl* (*money*) risparmi *mpl*

**savings: savings account** *n* libretto *m* di risparmio. **savings and loan association** *n* *Am* associazione *f* mutua di risparmi e prestiti. **savings bank** *n* cassa *f* di risparmio

**saviour** /'seɪvjə(r)/ *n* salvatore *m*

**savoir faire** /sævwɑː'feə(r)/ *n* (*social*) savoir-faire *m*

**savory** /'seɪvərɪ/ *n* Bot santoreggia *f*

**savour** /'seɪvə(r)/ *n* sapore *m* ● *vt* assaporare

**savoury** /'seɪvərɪ/ *a* salato; *fig* rispettabile

**saw¹** /sɔː/ *see* **see¹**

**saw²** *n* sega *f* ● *vt* (*pt* **sawed**, *pp* **sawn** or **sawed**) segare

**sawdust** /'sɔːdʌst/ *n* segatura *f*

**sawmill** /'sɔːmɪl/ *n* segheria *f*

**Saxon** /'sæksən/ *a* & *n* sassone *mf*; (*language*) sassone *m*

**saxophone** /'sæksəfəʊn/ *n* sassofono *m*

**saxophonist** /sæk'sɒfənɪst/ *n* sassofonista *mf*

**say** /seɪ/ *n* **have one's ~** dire la propria; **have a ~** avere voce in capitolo ● *vt/i* (*pt/pp* **said**) dire; **that is to ~** cioè; **that goes without ~ing** questo è ovvio; **when all is said and done** alla fine dei conti; **~ yes/no** dire di sì/no; **just ~ the word and I'll come** tu chiama e io vengo. **what more can I ~?** che altro dire?. **some time next week ~?** la prossima settimana, diciamo?; **the clock ~s ten to six** la sveglia fa le sei meno dieci; **you can ~ that again!** puoi dirlo forte!; **the tree is said to be very old** a quanto pare l'albero è vecchissimo; **he said you were to bring the car** ha detto che dovevi portare la macchina; **it ~s a lot for him that...** il fatto che...la dice lunga sul suo conto; **what have you got to ~ for yourself?** che scusa hai?; **to ~ nothing of...** per non parlare di...; **what would you ~ to a new car?** cosa ne diresti di una macchina nuova?

**saying** /'seɪɪŋ/ *n* proverbio *m*

**scab** /skæb/ *n* crosta *f*; *pej* crumiro *m*

**scabby** /'skæbɪ/ *a* (*plant*) coperto di galle; (*skin*) coperto di croste; (*animal*) rognoso; (*fam: nasty*) schifoso

**scaffold** /'skæfəld/ *n* patibolo *m*

**scaffolding** /'skæfəldɪŋ/ *n* impalcatura *f*

**scalar** /'skeɪlə(r)/ *a* scalare

**scald** /skɔːld/ *vt* scottare; (*milk*) scaldare ● *n* scottatura *f*

**scalding** /'skɔːldɪŋ/ *a* bollente

**scale¹** /skeɪl/ *n* (*of fish*) scaglia *f*

**scale²** *n* scala *f*; **on a grand ~** su vasta scala; **to ~** in scala; **~ of values** scala *f* di valori ● *vt* (*climb*) scalare

**▪ scale down** *vt* diminuire

**scale model** *n* modello *m* in scala

**scales** /skeɪlz/ *npl* (*for weighing*) bilancia *fsg*

**scallop** /'skɒləp/ *n* (*in sewing*) smerlo *m*, festone *m*; *Zool* pettine *m*; *Culin* cappasanta *f*

● *vt* (*in sewing*) smerlare; **~ed potatoes** patate *fpl* gratinate

**scalp** /skælp/ *n* cuoio *m* capelluto ● *vt* scalpare

**scalpel** /'skælpl/ *n* bisturi *m inv*

**scaly** /'skeɪlɪ/ *a* (*wing, fish*) squamoso; (*plaster, wall*) scrostato

**scam** /skæm/ *n fam* fregatura *f*

**scamper** /'skæmpə(r)/ *vi* **~ away** sgattaiolare via

**scampi** /'skæmpɪ/ *npl* scampi *mpl*

**scan** /skæn/ *n* *Med* scanning *m inv*, scansioscintigrafia *f* ● *v* (*pt/pp* **scanned**) ● *vt* scrutare; (*quickly*) dare una scorsa a; *Med* fare uno scanning di; *Comput* scannerizzare ● *vi* (*poetry:*) scandire

**scandal** /'skændl/ *n* scandalo *m*; (*gossip*) pettegolezzi *mpl*

**scandalize** /'skændəlaɪz/ *vt* scandalizzare

**scandalmonger** /'skænd(ə)lmʌŋgə(r)/ *n* malalingua *f*

**scandalous** /'skændələs/ *a* scandaloso

**Scandinavia** /skændɪ'neɪvɪə/ *n* Scandinavia *f*

**Scandinavian** /skændɪ'neɪvɪən/ *a* & *n* scandinavo, -a *mf*

**scanner** /'skænə(r)/ *n* *Med*, *Comput* scanner *m inv*; (*radar*) antenna *f* radar; (*for bar codes*) lettore *m* di codice a barre

**scanning** /'skænɪŋ/ *n* *Comput* scannerizzazione *f*

**scant** /skænt/ *a* scarso

**scantily** /'skæntɪlɪ/ *adv* scarsamente; (*clothed*) succintamente

**scanty** /'skæntɪ/ *a* (**-ier**, **-iest**) scarso; (*clothing*) succinto

**scapegoat** /'skeɪpgəʊt/ *n* capro *m* espiatorio

**scar** /skɑː(r)/ *n* cicatrice *f* ● *vt* (*pt/pp* **scarred**) lasciare una cicatrice a

**scar tissue** *n* tessuto *m* di cicatrizzazione

**scarce** /skeəs/ *a* scarso; *fig* raro; **make oneself ~** *fam* svignarsela

**scarcely** /'skeəslɪ/ *adv* appena; **~ anything** quasi niente

**scarcity** /'skeəsətɪ/ *n* scarsezza *f*

**scare** /skeə(r)/ *n* spavento *m*; (*panic*) panico *m* ● *vt* spaventare; **be ~d** aver paura (**of** di)

**▪ scare away** *vt* far scappare

**scarecrow** /'skeəkrəʊ/ *n* spaventapasseri *m inv*

**scaremonger** /'skeəmʌŋgə(r)/ *n* allarmista *mf*

**scaremongering** /'skeəmʌŋgərɪŋ/ *n* allarmismo *m*

**scarf** /skɑːf/ *n* (*pl* **scarves**) sciarpa *f*; (*square*) foulard *m inv*

**scarlet** /'skɑːlət/ *a* scarlatto

**scarlet fever** *n* scarlattina *f*

**scarper** /'skɑːpə(r)/ *vi* Br fam squagliarsela

**scary** /'skeərɪ/ *a* **be a ~** far paura

**scathing** /'skeɪðɪŋ/ *a* mordace

**scatter** /'skætə(r)/ *vt* spargere; (*disperse*) disperdere ● *vi* disperdersi

**scatterbrained** /'skætəbremd/ *a fam*
scervellato

**scattered** /'skætəd/ *a* sparso

**scatty** /'skæti/ *a* (**-ier, -iest**) *fam* svitato

**scavenge** /'skævɪndʒ/ *vi* frugare nella spazzatura

**scavenger** /'skævɪndʒə(r)/ *n* persona *f* che
fruga nella spazzatura

**scenario** /sɪ'nɑːrɪəʊ/ *n* scenario *m*

**scene** /siːn/ *n* scena *f*; (*quarrel*) scenata *f*;
**behind the ~s** dietro le quinte

**scenery** /'siːnərɪ/ *n* scenario *m*

**scenic** /'siːnɪk/ *a* panoramico

**scent** /sent/ *n* odore *m*; (*trail*) scia *f*;
(*perfume*) profumo *m*

**scented** /'sentɪd/ *a* profumato (**with** di)

**sceptic** /'skeptɪk/ *n* scettico, -a *mf*

**sceptical** /'skeptɪkl/ *a* scettico

**sceptically** /'skeptɪklɪ/ *adv* in modo scettico

**scepticism** /'skeptɪsɪzm/ *n* scetticismo *m*

**schedule** /'ʃedjuːl/ *n* piano *m*, programma
*m*; (*of work*) programma *m*; (*Am: timetable*)
orario *m*; **behind ~** indietro; **on ~** nei tempi
previsti; **according to ~** secondo i tempi
previsti ● *vt* prevedere

**scheduled flight** /ʃedjuːld'flaɪt/ *n* volo *m*
di linea

**schematic** /skɪ'mætɪk/ *a* schematico

**scheme** /skiːm/ *n* (*plan*) piano *m*; (*plot*) mac-
chinazione *f* ● *vi pej* macchinare

**scheming** /'skiːmɪŋ/ *n pej* macchinazioni
*fpl*, intrighi *mpl* ● *a* (*person*) intrigante

**schism** /'skɪzm/ *n* scisma *m*

**schizophrenia** /skɪtsə'friːnɪə/ *n* schizofre-
nia *f*

**schizoprenic** /skɪtsə'frenɪk/ *a* schizofreni-
co

**schmaltzy** /'ʃmɒltsɪ/ *a* sdolcinato

**scholar** /'skɒlə(r)/ *n* studioso, -a *mf*

**scholarly** /'skɒləlɪ/ *a* erudito

**scholarship** /'skɒləʃɪp/ *n* erudizione *f*;
(*grant*) borsa *f* di studio

**scholastic** /skə'læstɪk/ *a* scolastico

**school** /skuːl/ *n* scuola *f*; (*in university*) facoltà *f*; (*of fish*) branco *m* ● *vt* addestrare
⟨*animal*⟩

**school: school age** *n* of **~ ~** in età scolare.
**schoolboy** *n* scolaro *m*. **schoolchild** *n* scolaro, -a *mf*. **schooldays** *npl* tempi *mpl* della
scuola. **schoolgirl** *n* scolara *f*. **school leaver**
*n* ≈ neo-diplomato, *a mf*. **school-leaving
age** *n* età *f* della scuola dell'obbligo

**schooling** /'skuːlɪŋ/ *n* istruzione *f*

**school: schoolmaster** *n* maestro *m*;
(*secondary*) insegnante *m*. **schoolmistress**
*n* maestra *f*; (*secondary*) insegnante *f*.
**schoolteacher** *n* insegnante *mf*

**schooner** /'skuːnə(r)/ *n* (*Am: glass*) boccale
*m* da birra; (*Br: glass*) grande bicchiere *m* da
sherry; (*boat*) goletta *f*

**sciatica** /saɪ'ætɪkə/ *n* sciatica *f*

**science** /'saɪəns/ *n* scienza *f*

**science fiction** *n* fantascienza *f*

**scientific** /saɪən'tɪfɪk/ *a* scientifico

**scientifically** /saɪən'tɪfɪklɪ/ *adv* scientifica-
mente

**scientist** /'saɪəntɪst/ *n* scienziato, -a *mf*

**sci-fi** /'saɪfaɪ/ *n fam* fantascienza *f*

**scintillate** /'sɪntɪleɪt/ *vi fig* brillare

**scintillating** /'sɪntɪleɪtɪŋ/ *a* brillante

**scissors** /'sɪzəz/ *npl* forbici *fpl*

**scoff¹** /skɒf/ *vi* **~ at** schernire

**scoff²** *vt fam* divorare

**scold** /skəʊld/ *vt* sgridare

**scolding** /'skəʊldɪŋ/ *n* sgridata *f*

**scollop** /'skɒləp/ = **scallop**

**scone** /skɒn/ *n* pasticcino *m* da tè

**scoop** /skuːp/ *n* paletta *f*; *Journ* scoop *m inv*

■ **scoop out** *vt* svuotare

■ **scoop up** *vt* tirar su

**scoot** /skuːt/ *vi fam* filare

**scooter** /'skuːtə(r)/ *n* motoretta *f*

**scope** /skəʊp/ *n* portata *f*; (*opportunity*) opportunità *f inv*

**scorch** /skɔːtʃ/ *vt* bruciare

**scorcher** /'skɔːtʃə(r)/ *n fam* giornata *f* torri-
da

**scorching** /'skɔːtʃɪŋ/ *a* caldissimo

**score** /skɔː(r)/ *n* punteggio *m*; *Mus* partitura
*f*; (*for film, play*) musica *f*; **a ~** [**of**] (*twenty*)
una ventina [di]; **keep** [**the**] **~** tenere il punteggio; **on that ~** a questo proposito ● *vt* segnare ⟨*goal*⟩; (*cut*) incidere ● *vi* far punti; (*in
football etc*) segnare; (*keep score*) tenere il
punteggio

■ **score out** *vt* cancellare

**scoreboard** *n* /'skɔːbɔːd/ tabellone *m* segnapunti

**scorer** /'skɔːrə(r)/ *n* segnapunti *m inv*; (*of
goals*) giocatore, -trice *mf* che segna; **top ~**
cannoniere *m*

**scorn** /skɔːn/ *n* disprezzo *m* ● *vt* disprezzare

**scornful** /'skɔːnfʊl/ *a* sprezzante

**scornfully** /'skɔːnfʊlɪ/ *adv* sdegnosamente

**Scorpio** /'skɔːpɪəʊ/ *n Astr* Scorpione *m*

**scorpion** /'skɔːpɪən/ *n* scorpione *m*

**Scot** /skɒt/ *n* scozzese *mf*

**Scotch** *a* scozzese ● *n* (*whisky*) whisky *m*
[scozzese]

**scotch** /skɒtʃ/ *vt* far cessare

**Scotch egg** *n Br* polpetta *f* di salsiccia che
racchiude un uovo sodo

**scot-free** *a* **get off ~** cavarsela impunemente

**Scotland** /'skɒtlənd/ *n* Scozia *f*

**Scots, Scottish** /skɒts, 'skɒtɪʃ/ *a* scozzese

**scoundrel** /'skaʊndrəl/ *n* mascalzone *m*

**scour¹** /'skaʊə(r)/ *vt* (*search*) perlustrare

**scour²** *vt* (*clean*) strofinare

**scourer** /'skaʊərə(r)/ *n* (*pad*) paglietta *f*

**scouring pad** /'skaʊərɪŋ/ *n* paglietta *f* in
lana d'acciaio

**scourge** /skɜːdʒ/ *n* flagello *m*

**Scout** *n* [**Boy**] **~** [boy]scout *m inv*

**scout** /skaʊt/ *n Mil* esploratore *m* ● *vi* **~ for**
andare in cerca di

**scowl** /skaʊl/ *n* sguardo *m* torvo ● *vi* guardare [di] storto

**Scrabble®** /'skræbl/ *n* Scarabeo ᴿ *m*

■ **scrabble around** vi (search) cercare a tastoni

**scraggy** /'skrægɪ/ a (-ier, -iest) pej scarno

**scram** /skræm/ vi fam levarsi dai piedi

**scramble** /'skræmbl/ n (climb) arrampicata f ● vi (clamber) arrampicarsi; ~ **for** azzuffarsi per ● vt Teleph creare delle interferenze in: (eggs) strapazzare

**scrambled eggs** /'skræmbəld/ npl uova fpl strapazzate

**scrambler** /'skræmblə(r)/ n (Br: motorcyclist) [moto]crossista mf

**scrap**[1] /skræp/ n (fam: fight) litigio m

**scrap**[2] n pezzetto m; (metal) ferraglia f; ~**s** pl (of food) avanzi mpl ● vt (pt/pp **scrapped**) buttare via

**scrapbook** /'skræpbʊk/ n album m inv

**scrape** /skreɪp/ vt raschiare; (damage) graffiare

■ **scrape through** vi passare per un pelo

■ **scrape together** vt racimolare

**scraper** /'skreɪpə(r)/ n raschietto m

**scrap:** scrap heap n be on the ~ ~ fig essere inutile. **scrap iron** n ferraglia f. **scrap merchant** n ferrovecchio m. **scrap paper** n carta f qualsiasi

**scrappy** /'skræpɪ/ a frammentario

**scrapyard** /'skræpjɑːd/ n deposito m di ferraglia; (for cars) cimitero m delle macchine

**scratch** /skrætʃ/ n graffio m; (to relieve itch) grattata f; **start from** ~ partire da zero; **up to** ~ (work) all'altezza ● vt graffiare; (to relieve itch) grattare ● vi grattarsi

**scratchy** /'skrætʃɪ/ a (recording) pieno di fruscii

**scrawl** /skrɔːl/ n scarabocchio m ● vt/i scarabocchiare

**scrawny** /'skrɔːnɪ/ a (-ier, -iest) pej magro

**scream** /skriːm/ n strillo m; **be a** ~ (fam: situation, film, person:) essere uno spasso ● vt/i strillare

**scree** /skriː/ n ghiaione m

**screech** /skriːtʃ/ n stridore m; ~ **of tyres** sgommata f ● vi stridere ● vi (tyres:) strillare

**screen** /skriːn/ n paravento m; Cinema, TV, Comput schermo m ● vt proteggere; (conceal) riparare; proiettare (film); (candidates) passare al setaccio; Med sottoporre a visita medica

**screening** /'skriːnɪŋ/ n Med visita f medica; (of film) proiezione f

**screen: screenplay** n sceneggiatura f. **screen saver** n Comput salvaschermo m. **screen test** n Cinema provino m. **screen-writer** n Cinema sceneggiatore, -trice mf

**screw** /skruː/ n vite f ● vt avvitare; vulg trombare; ~ **sth to sth** avvitare qcsa a qcsa

■ **screw up** vt (crumple) accartocciare; strizzare (eyes); storcere (face); (sl: bungle) mandare all'aria; ~ **up one's courage** prendere il coraggio a due mani

**screwdriver** /'skruːdraɪvə(r)/ n cacciavite m inv

**screwed up** /skruːd/ a fam incasinato

**screw top** n tappo m a vite

**screwy** /'skruːɪ/ a (-ier, -iest) fam svitato

**scribble** /'skrɪbl/ n scarabocchio m ● vt/i scarabocchiare

**scrimmage** /'skrɪmɪdʒ/ n (struggle) zuffa f; (Am: in football) mischia f

**scrimp** /skrɪmp/ vi risparmiare; ~ **and save** risparmiare fino all'osso; ~ **on sth** risparmiare su qcsa

**script** /skrɪpt/ n scrittura f; (of film etc) sceneggiatura f

**Scriptures** /'skrɪptʃəz/ npl Sacre Scritture fpl

**scriptwriter** /'skrɪptraɪtə(r)/ n sceneggiatore, -trice mf

**scroll** /skrəʊl/ n rotolo m (di pergamena); (decoration) voluta f ● vi Comput far scorrere

**Scrooge** /skruːdʒ/ n fam tirchio, -a mf

**scrotum** /'skrəʊtəm/ n scroto m

**scrounge** /skraʊndʒ/ vt/i scroccare

**scrounger** /'skraʊndʒə(r)/ n scroccone, -a mf

**scrub**[1] /skrʌb/ n (land) boscaglia f

**scrub**[2] vt/i (pt/pp **scrubbed**) strofinare; (fam: cancel) cancellare (plan)

**scrubbing brush** /'skrʌbɪŋ/ n spazzolone m

**scruff** /skrʌf/ n **by the** ~ **of the neck** per la collottola

**scruffy** /'skrʌfɪ/ a (-ier, -iest) trasandato

**scrum** /skrʌm/ n (in rugby) mischia f

**scrum half** n mediano m di mischia

**scrunch** /skrʌntʃ/ vi (footsteps in snow, tyres:) scricchiolare ● n scricchiolio m

■ **scrunch up** vt accartocciare

**scruple** /'skruːpl/ n scrupolo m; **have no** ~**s** essere senza scrupoli

**scrupulous** /'skruːpjʊləs/ a scrupoloso

**scrupulously** /'skruːpjʊləslɪ/ adv scrupolosamente

**scrutinize** /'skruːtɪnaɪz/ vt scrutinare

**scrutiny** /'skruːtɪnɪ/ n (look) esame m minuzioso

**scuba diver** /'skuːbə/ n sommozzatore, -trice mf

**scuba diving** n immersione f subacquea

**scud** /skʌd/ vi (pt/pp **scudded**) (clouds:) muoversi velocemente

**scuff** /skʌf/ vt strascicare (one's feet)

**scuffle** /'skʌfl/ n tafferuglio m

**scull** /skʌl/ vi (with two oars) vogare di coppia; (with one oar) vogare a bratto ● n (boat) imbarcazione f da regata con un vogatore

**scullery** /'skʌlərɪ/ n retrocucina f

**sculpt** /skʌlpt/ vt/i scolpire

**sculptor** /'skʌlptə(r)/ n scultore m

**sculpture** /'skʌlptʃə(r)/ n scultura f

**scum** /skʌm/ n schiuma f; (people) feccia f

**scurrilous** /'skʌrɪləs/ a scurrile

**scurry** /'skʌrɪ/ vi (pt/pp **-ied**) affrettare il passo

**scuttle**[1] /'skʌtl/ n secchio m per il carbone

**scuttle**[2] vt affondare (ship)

**scuttle**[3] vi (hurry) ~ **away** correre via

**scythe** /saɪð/ n falce f

**SE** *abbr* (**south-east**) SE
**sea** /siː/ *n* mare *m*; **at ~** in mare; *fig* confuso;
**by ~** via mare; **by the ~** sul mare
**sea: seabed** *n* fondale *m* marino. **seabird** *n*
uccello *m* marino. **seaboard** *n* costiera *f*.
**seafaring** *a* ‹*nation*› marinaro. **seafood** *n*
frutti *mpl* di mare. **seagull** *n* gabbiano *m*.
**sea horse** *n* cavalluccio *m* marino
**seal**[1] /siːl/ *n* *Zool* foca *f*
**seal**[2] *n* sigillo *m*; *Techn* chiusura *f* ermetica
● *vt* sigillare; *Techn* chiudere ermeticamente
■ **seal off** *vt* bloccare ‹*area*›
**sea level** *n* livello *m* del mare; **above ~ ~**
sopra il livello del mare
**sealing wax** /ˈsiːlɪŋ/ *n* ceralacca *f*
**sea lion** *n* leone *m* marino
**seam** /siːm/ *n* cucitura *f*; (*of coal*) strato *m*
**seaman** /ˈsiːmən/ *n* marinaio *m*
**seamless** /ˈsiːmlɪs/ *a* senza cucitura
**seamy** /ˈsiːmɪ/ *a* ‹*scandal*› sordido; ‹*area*›
malfamato
**seance** /ˈseɪɑːns/ *n* seduta *f* spiritica
**seaplane** /ˈsiːpleɪn/ *n* idrovolante *m*
**seaport** /ˈsiːpɔːt/ *n* porto *m* di mare
**sear** /sɪə(r)/ *vt* cauterizzare ‹*wound*›; rosolare [a fuoco vivo] ‹*meat*›; ‹*scorch*› disseccare
**search** /sɜːtʃ/ *n* ricerca *f*; (*official*) perquisizione *f*; **in ~ of** alla ricerca di ● *vt* frugare
(**for** alla ricerca di); perlustrare ‹*area*›;
(*officially*) perquisire ● *vi* **~ for** cercare
**search and replace** *n* *Comput* ricerca *f* e
sostituzione
**searching** /ˈsɜːtʃɪŋ/ *a* penetrante
**search: searchlight** *n* riflettore *m*. **search
party** *n* squadra *f* di ricerca. **search
warrant** *n* mandato *m* di perquisizione
**searing** /ˈsɪərɪŋ/ *a* bruciante; ‹*pace*› travolgente; ‹*pain*› lancinante
**sea: seascape** *n* paesaggio *m* marino.
**seasick** *a* **be/get ~** avere il mal di mare.
**seaside** *n* **at/to the ~** al mare. **seaside
resort** *n* stazione *f* balneare. **seaside town**
*n* città *f* di mare
**season** /ˈsiːzn/ *n* stagione *f* ● *vt* (*flavour*)
condire; **in ~** ‹*fruit*› di stagione; ‹*animal*› in
calore
**seasonal** /ˈsiːzənəl/ *a* stagionale
**seasoned** /ˈsiːznd/ *a* ‹*Culin: dish*› condito;
‹*timber*› stagionato; ‹*actor, politician*› consumato; ‹*leader*› di provata capacità; **~
traveller** persona *f* che ha viaggiato molto; **~
soldier** veterano *m*
**seasoning** /ˈsiːzə(ə)nɪŋ/ *n* condimento *m*
**season ticket** *n* abbonamento *m*
**seat** /siːt/ *n* (*chair*) sedia *f*; (*in car*) sedile *m*;
(*place to sit*) posto *m* [a sedere]; (*bottom*)
didietro *m*; (*of government*) sede *f*; **take a ~**
sedersi ● *vt* mettere a sedere; (*have seats for*)
aver posti [a sedere] per; **remain ~ed** mantenere il proprio posto
**seat belt** *n* cintura *f* di sicurezza; **fasten
one's ~ ~** allacciare la cintura di sicurezza
**seating** /ˈsiːtɪŋ/ *n* (*places*) posti *mpl* a sedere;
(*arrangement*) disposizione *f* dei posti a sedere

**seating capacity** *n* numero *m* dei posti a
sedere
**sea: sea urchin** *n* riccio *m* di mare.
**seaweed** *n* alga *f* marina. **seaworthy** *a* in
stato di navigare
**sec** /sek/ *n* (*fam: short instant*) attimo *m*, secondo *m*; *abbr* (**second**) s
**secateurs** /sekəˈtɜːz/ *npl* cesoie *fpl*
**secede** /sɪˈsiːd/ *vi* staccarsi
**secession** /sɪˈseʃn/ *n* secessione *f*
**secluded** /sɪˈkluːdɪd/ *a* appartato
**seclusion** /sɪˈkluːʒn/ *n* isolamento *m*
**second**[1] /ˈsekənd/ *vt* (*transfer*) distaccare
**second**[2] /ˈsekənd/ *a* secondo; **in ~ gear**
*Auto* in seconda; **on ~ thoughts** ripensandoci meglio; **be having ~ thoughts** ripensar-
ci; ● *n* secondo *m*; **~s** *pl* (*goods*) merce *f* sg di
seconda scelta; **have ~s** (*at meal*) fare il bis;
**John the S~** Giovanni Secondo ● *adv* (*in
race*) al secondo posto ● *vt* assistere; appoggiare ‹*proposal*›
**secondary** /ˈsekəndrɪ/ *a* secondario
**secondary school** *n* ≈ scuola *f* media
(*inferiore e superiore*)
**second: second-best** *a* secondo dopo il migliore; **be ~** pej essere un ripiego. **second-
class** *a* di seconda classe. **second class** *adv*
‹*travel, send*› in seconda classe
**seconder** /ˈsekəndə(r)/ *n* (*of motion*) persona *f* che appoggia una mozione
**second-guess** *vt* anticipare
**second hand** *n* (*on watch, clock*) lancetta *f*
dei secondi
**second-hand** *a* ‹*car, goods, news,
information*› di seconda mano; ‹*clothes*› usato; ‹*market*› dell'usato; ‹*opinion*› preso a prestito ● *adv* ‹*sell*› di seconda mano
**second in command** *n* vice *mf inv*; *Mil*
vicecomandante *m*
**secondly** /ˈsekəndlɪ/ *adv* in secondo luogo
**secondment** /sɪˈkɒndmənt/ *n* **on ~** in trasferta
**second-rate** *a* di second'ordine
**secrecy** /ˈsiːkrəsɪ/ *n* segretezza *f*; **in ~** in segreto
**secret** /ˈsiːkrɪt/ *a* segreto ● *n* segreto *m*;
**make no ~ of sth** non fare mistero di qcsa
**secret agent** *n* agente *m* segreto
**secretarial** /sekrəˈteərɪəl/ *a* ‹*work, staff*› di
segreteria
**secretariat** /sekrəˈteərɪət/ *n* segretariato *m*
**secretary** /ˈsekrətərɪ/ *n* segretario, -a *mf*
**Secretary of State** *n* Segretario *m* di Stato; *Am Pol* ministro *m* degli Esteri
**secret ballot** *n* scrutinio *m* segreto, votazione *f* a scrutinio segreto
**secrete** /sɪˈkriːt/ *vt* secernere ‹*poison*›
**secretion** /sɪˈkriːʃn/ *n* secrezione *f*
**secretive** /ˈsiːkrətɪv/ *a* riservato
**secretly** /ˈsiːkrɪtlɪ/ *adv* segretamente
**secretness** /ˈsiːkrɪtnɪs/ *n* riserbo *m*
**secret: secret police** *n* polizia *f* segreta.
**secret service** *n* servizi *mpl* segreti.
**secret society** *n* società *f* segreta
**sect** /sekt/ *n* setta *f*

**sectarian** /sek'teərɪən/ n & a settario, -a mf
**section** /'sekʃn/ n sezione f
**sector** /'sektə(r)/ n settore m
**secular** /'sekjʊlə(r)/ a secolare; ‹education› laico
**secure** /sɪ'kjʊə(r)/ a sicuro ● vt proteggere; chiudere bene ‹door›; rendere stabile ‹ladder›; (obtain) assicurarsi
**securely** /sɪ'kjʊəlɪ/ adv saldamente
**security** /sɪ'kjʊərətɪ/ n sicurezza f; (for loan) garanzia f; **securities** pl titoli mpl
**security: Security Council** n (of the UN) Consiglio m di Sicurezza. **security guard** n guardia f giurata. **security risk** n be a ~ ~ costituire un pericolo per la sicurezza
**sedan** /sɪ'dæn/ n Am berlina f
**sedate¹** /sɪ'deɪt/ a posato
**sedate²** vt somministrare sedativi a
**sedately** /sɪ'deɪtlɪ/ adv in modo posato
**sedation** /sɪ'deɪʃn/ n somministrazione f di sedativi; **be under** ~ essere sotto l'effetto di sedativi
**sedative** /'sedətɪv/ a sedativo ● n sedativo m
**sedentary** /'sedəntərɪ/ a sedentario
**sediment** /'sedɪmənt/ n sedimento m
**seduce** /sɪ'dju:s/ vt sedurre
**seduction** /sɪ'dʌkʃn/ n seduzione f
**seductive** /sɪ'dʌktɪv/ a seducente
**seductively** /sɪ'dʌktɪvlɪ/ adv con aria seducente
**see¹** /si:/ v (pt saw, pp seen) ● vt vedere; (understand) capire; (escort) accompagnare; **go and** ~ andare a vedere; (visit) andare a trovare; ~ **you!** ci vediamo!; ~ **you later!** a più tardi!; ~**ing that** visto che; ~ **sb out,** **sb to the door** accompagnare qcno alla porta; **I can't** ~ **myself doing this forever** non mi ci vedo a farlo per sempre; **I can't think** **what she** ~**s in him** non capisco cosa trovi in lui; ~ **reason** ragionare; **you're** ~**ing** **things** hai le traveggole ● vi vedere; (understand) vedere; ~ **that** (make sure) assicurarsi che; **let me** ~ (think) fammi pensare; **I** ~ (understand) ho capito
▪ **see about** vt occuparsi di
▪ **see off** vt veder partire; (chase away) mandar via
▪ **see through** vi vedere attraverso; fig non farsi ingannare da ● vt portare a buon fine
▪ **see to** vi occuparsi di
**see²** n Relig diocesi f inv
**seed** /si:d/ n seme m; Tennis testa f di serie; **go to** ~ fare seme; fig lasciarsi andare
**seeded player** /'si:dɪd/ n Tennis testa f di serie
**seedless** /'si:dlɪs/ a senza semi
**seedling** /'si:dlɪŋ/ n pianticella f
**seedy** /'si:dɪ/ a (-ier, -iest) squallido; **feel** ~ fam sentirsi poco bene
**seek** /si:k/ vt (pt/pp sought) cercare
▪ **seek out** vt scovare
**seeker** /'si:kə(r)/ n ~ **after** or **for sth** persona f che è alla ricerca di qcsa; **gold** ~ cercatore, -trice mf d'oro
**seem** /si:m/ vi sembrare

**seeming** /'si:mɪŋ/ a apparente
**seemingly** /'si:mɪŋlɪ/ adv apparentemente
**seemly** /'si:mlɪ/ a decoroso
**seen** /si:n/ see **see¹**
**seep** /si:p/ vi filtrare
**seepage** /'si:pɪdʒ/ n (leak: from container) perdita f; Geol trasudamento m superficiale; (trickle) lenta fuoriuscita f; (into structure, soil) infiltrazione f
**see-saw** /'si:sɔ:/ n altalena f
**seethe** /si:ð/ vi ~ **with anger** ribollire di rabbia
**see-through** a trasparente
**segment** /'segmənt/ n segmento m; (of orange) spicchio m
**segregate** /'segrɪgeɪt/ vt segregare
**segregation** /segrɪ'geɪʃn/ n segregazione f
**seismic** /'saɪzmɪk/ a sismico
**seismograph** /'saɪzməgrɑ:f/ n sismografo m
**seismology** /saɪz'mɒlədʒɪ/ n sismologia f
**seize** /si:z/ vt afferrare; Jur confiscare; ~ **the opportunity** prendere la palla al balzo
▪ **seize up** vi Techn bloccarsi
**seizure** /'si:ʒə(r)/ n Jur confisca f; Med colpo m [apoplettico]
**seldom** /'seldəm/ adv raramente
**select** /sɪ'lekt/ a scelto; (exclusive) esclusivo ● vt scegliere; selezionare ‹team›
**selection** /sɪ'lekʃn/ n selezione f
**selective** /sɪ'lektɪv/ a selettivo
**selectively** /sɪ'lektɪvlɪ/ adv con criterio
**selector** /sɪ'lektə(r)/ n Sport selezionatore, -trice mf
**self** /self/ n io m
**self: self-addressed** a con il proprio indirizzo. **self-addressed envelope** n busta f affrancata con il proprio indirizzo. **self-adhesive** a autoadesivo. **self-analysis** n autoanalisi f. **self-assembly** a da montare. **self-assurance** n sicurezza f di sé. **self-assured** a sicuro di sé. **self-catering** a in appartamento attrezzato di cucina. **self-centred** a egocentrico. **self-cleaning** a ‹oven› autopulente. **self-confessed** a dichiarato. **self-confidence** n fiducia f in se stesso. **self-confident** a sicuro di sé. **self-conscious** a impacciato. **self-contained** a ‹flat› con ingresso indipendente. **self-control** n autocontrollo m. **self-defence** n autodifesa f; Jur legittima difesa f. **self-denial** n abnegazione f. **self-destruct** vi ‹missile, spacecraft:› autodistruggersi. **self-destruction** n autodistruzione f; fig autolesionismo m. **self-determination** n autodeterminazione f. **self-discipline** n autodisciplina f. **self-employed** a che lavora in proprio; **the** ~ i lavoratori autonomi. **self-esteem** n stima f di sé. **self-evident** a ovvio. **self-explanatory** a be ~ parlare da sé. **self-financing** /-faɪ'nænsɪŋ/ n autofinanziamento m. **self-governing** /-'gʌvənɪŋ/ a autonomo. **self-government** n autogoverno m. **self-help** n iniziativa f personale. **self-important** a borioso. **self-imposed** /-ɪm'pəʊzd/ a autoimposto. **self-improvement** n crescita f

personale. **self-indulgent** a indulgente con se stesso. **self-inflicted** a **Anna's problems are ~** sono problemi che Anna si è creata da sé; **~ wound** autolesione f. **self-interest** n interesse m personale

**selfish** /'selfɪʃ/ a egoista

**selfishly** /'selfɪʃlɪ/ adv egoisticamente

**selfishness** /'selfɪʃnɪs/ n egoismo m

**selfless** /'selflɪs/ a disinteressato

**selflessly** /'selflɪslɪ/ adv disinteressatamente

**selflessness** /'selflɪsnɪs/ n disinteresse m

**self:** **self-locking** a ⟨door⟩ a chiusura automatica. **self-made** a che si è fatto da sé. **self-pity** n autocommiserazione f. **self-portrait** n autoritratto m. **self-possessed** /-pə'zest/ a padrone di sé. **self-preservation** n istinto m di conservazione. **self-raising flour** Br, **self-rising flour** Am /-'reɪzɪŋ, -'raɪzɪŋ/ n farina f contenente lievito. **self-respect** n amor m proprio. **self-righteous** a presuntuoso. **self-sacrifice** n abnegazione f. **selfsame** a stesso. **self-satisfied** a compiaciuto di sé. **self-service** n self-service m inv ● attrib self-service. **self-styled** a sedicente. **self-sufficiency** n autosufficienza f. **self-sufficient** a autosufficiente. **self-supporting** a ⟨person⟩ indipendente (economicamente). **self-tan** n autoabbronzante m. **self-tanning** /-'tænɪŋ/ a autoabbronzante. **self-taught** /-'tɔːt/ a ⟨person⟩ autodidatta. **self-willed** /-'wɪld/ a ostinato

**sell** /sel/ v (pt/pp **sold**) ● vt vendere; **be sold out** essere esaurito; **~ sb on the idea of...** fam convincere qcno di... ● vi vendersi

■ **sell off** vt liquidare

■ **sell up** vi liquidare i propri beni

**sell-by date** n data f di scadenza per la vendita

**seller** /'selə(r)/ n venditore, -trice mf

**sellers' market** /'seləzmɑːkɪt/ n mercato m al rialzo

**selling price** /'selɪŋ/ n prezzo m di vendita

**Sellotape®** /'seləʊteɪp/ n nastro m adesivo, scotch® m

**sell-out** n (fam: betrayal) tradimento m; **be a ~** ⟨concert:⟩ fare il tutto esaurito

**selvage, selvedge** /'selvɪdʒ/ n cimosa f

**selves** /selvz/ pl of **self**

**semantic** /sɪ'mæntɪk/ a semantico

**semantics** /sɪ'mæntɪks/ n (subject) semantica f; **that's just ~** sono solo sfumature di significato

**semblance** /'sembləns/ n parvenza f

**semen** /'siːmən/ n Anat liquido m seminale

**semester** /sɪ'mestə(r)/ n Am semestre m

**semi** /'semɪ/ n (Br: house) villetta f bifamiliare; Am Auto autoarticolato m

**semi+** pref semi+

**semi:** **semi-automatic** a semiautomatico. **semibreve** n Mus semibreve f. **semicircle** n semicerchio m. **semicircular** a semicircolare. **semicolon** n punto e virgola m. **semi-darkness** n semioscurità f. **semi-**

**detached** a gemella ● n casa f gemella. **semi-final** n semifinale f

**seminal** /'semɪnəl/ a (major) determinante

**seminar** /'semɪnɑː(r)/ n seminario m

**seminary** /'semɪnərɪ/ n seminario m

**semi:** **semi-precious** a semiprezioso; **~ stone** pietra f dura. **semi-skilled** a qualificato. **semi-skimmed** /-'skɪld/ a parzialmente scremato. **semitone** n Mus semitono m

**semolina** /semə'liːnə/ n semolino m

**senate** /'senət/ n senato m

**senator** /'senətə(r)/ n senatore m

**send** /send/ vt/i (pt/pp **sent**) mandare; (by mail) spedire

■ **send away for** vt farsi spedire ⟨information etc⟩

■ **send down** vt (send to prison) mandare in galera

■ **send for** vt mandare a chiamare ⟨person⟩; far venire ⟨thing⟩

■ **send in** vt presentare ⟨application⟩; far entrare ⟨person⟩

■ **send off** vt spedire ⟨letter, parcel⟩; espellere ⟨footballer⟩

■ **send up** vt fam parodiare

**sender** /'sendə(r)/ n mittente mf; **return to ~** (on letter) rispedire al mittente

**send-off** n commiato m

**senile** /'siːnaɪl/ a arteriosclerotico

**senile dementia** /dɪ'menʃə/ n demenza f senile

**senility** /sɪ'nɪlətɪ/ n senilismo m

**senior** /'siːnɪə(r)/ a più vecchio; (in rank) superiore ● n (in rank) superiore mf; (in sport) senior mf; **she's two years my ~** è più vecchia di me di due anni

**senior citizen** n anziano, -a mf

**seniority** /siːnɪ'ɒrətɪ/ n anzianità f di servizio

**senior management** n alta dirigenza f

**sensation** /sen'seɪʃn/ n sensazione f; **cause a ~** fare scalpore

**sensational** /sen'seɪʃənəl/ a sensazionale

**sensationalize** /sen'seɪʃənəlaɪz/ vt pej dare un tono scandalistico a

**sensationally** /sen'seɪʃənəlɪ/ adv in modo sensazionale

**sense** /sens/ n senso m; (common ~) buon senso m; **in a ~** in un certo senso; **make ~** aver senso ● vt sentire

**senseless** /'senslɪs/ a insensato; (unconscious) privo di sensi

**senselessly** /'senslɪslɪ/ adv insensatamente

**sensible** /'sensəbl/ a sensato; (suitable) appropriato

**sensibly** /'sensəblɪ/ adv in modo appropriato

**sensitive** /'sensətɪv/ a sensibile; (touchy) suscettibile

**sensitively** /'sensətɪvlɪ/ adv con sensibilità

**sensitivity** /sensə'tɪvətɪ/ n sensibilità f inv

**sensitize** /'sensɪtaɪz/ vt **become ~d to** (allergic to) diventare ipersensibile a

**sensor** /'sensə(r)/ n sensore m

**sensory** /'sensəri/ a sensoriale

**sensual** /'sensjʊəl/ a sensuale

**sensuality** /sensjʊ'æləti/ n sensualità f inv

**sensuous** /'sensjʊəs/ a voluttuoso

**sent** /sent/ see send

**sentence** /'sentəns/ n frase f; Jur sentenza f; (punishment) condanna f ● vt ~ **to** condannare a

**sentiment** /'sentimənt/ n sentimento m; (opinion) opinione f; (sentimentality) sentimentalismo m

**sentimental** /senti'mentl/ a sentimentale; pej sentimentalista

**sentimentality** /sentimen'tæləti/ n sentimentalità f inv

**sentinel** /'sentinəl/ n sentinella f

**sentry** /'sentri/ n sentinella f

**separable** /'sepərəbl/ a separabile

**separate¹** /'sepərət/ a separato

**separate²** /'sepəreit/ vt separare ● vi separarsi

**separately** /'sepərətli/ adv separatamente

**separates** /'sepərəts/ npl [indumenti npl] coordinati npl

**separation** /sepə'reiʃn/ n separazione f

**separatist** /'sepərətist/ n & a separatista mf

**sepia** /'si:piə/ n (colour) seppia m

**September** /sep'tembə(r)/ n settembre m

**septic** /'septik/ a settico; **go** ~ infettarsi

**septicaemia** /septi'si:miə/ n setticemia f

**septic tank** n fossa f biologica

**sequel** /'si:kwəl/ n seguito m

**sequence** /'si:kwəns/ n sequenza f; **in** ~ nell'ordine giusto

**sequential** /si'kwenʃəl/ a sequenziale

**sequin** /'si:kwin/ n lustrino m, paillette f inv

**Serb** /sɜ:b/ a & n serbo, -a mf

**Serbia** /'sɜ:biə/ n Serbia f

**Serbian** /'sɜ:biən/ n serba, -a mf; (language) serbo m ● a serbo

**Serbo-Croat[ian]** /sɜ:bəʊ'krəʊæt, sɜ:bəʊkrəʊ'eiʃən/ n (language) serbo-croato m ● a serbo-croato

**serenade** /serə'neid/ n serenata f ● vt fare una serenata a

**serene** /si'ri:n/ a sereno

**serenely** /si'ri:nli/ adv serenamente

**serenity** /si'renəti/ n serenità f inv

**sergeant** /'sɑ:dʒənt/ n sergente m

**sergeant major** n sergente m maggiore

**serial** /'siəriəl/ n racconto a puntate; TV sceneggiato m a puntate; Radio commedia f radiofonica a puntate ● a Comput seriale

**serialize** /'siəriəlaiz/ vt pubblicare a puntate; Radio, TV trasmettere a puntate

**serial killer** n serial killer mf inv

**serial number** n numero m di serie

**serial port** n Comput porta f seriale

**series** /'siəri:z/ n serie f inv

**serious** /'siəriəs/ a serio; (illness, error) grave

**seriously** /'siəriəsli/ adv seriamente; (ill) gravemente; **take** ~ prendere sul serio

**seriousness** /'siəriəsnis/ n serietà f; (of situation) gravità f

**sermon** /'sɜ:mən/ n predica f

**seropositive** /siərəʊ'pɒzitiv/ a sieropositivo

**serpent** /'sɜ:pənt/ n serpente m

**serrated** /se'reitid/ a dentellato

**serum** /'siərəm/ n siero m

**servant** /'sɜ:vənt/ n domestico, -a mf

**serve** /sɜ:v/ n Tennis servizio m ● vt servire; Jur notificare (writ) (**on sb** a qcno); scontare (sentence); ~ **its purpose** servire al proprio scopo; **it** ~**s you right!** ben ti sta!; ~**s two** per due persone ● vi prestare servizio; Tennis servire; ~ **as** servire da

**server** /'sɜ:və(r)/ n (piece of cutlery) posata f di portata, (plate) piatto m di portata; (tray) vassoio m di portata; Sport giocatore, -trice mf che effettua il servizio; Comput server m inv, servitore m

**service** /'sɜ:vis/ n servizio m; Relig funzione f; (maintenance) revisione f; ~**s** pl forze fpl armate; (on motorway) area f di servizio; **in the** ~**s** sotto le armi; **of** ~ **to** utile a; **out of** ~ (machine:) guasto ● vt Techn revisionare

**serviceable** /'sɜ:visəbl/ a utilizzabile; (hard-wearing) resistente; (practical) pratico

**service:** **service area** n area f di servizio. **service charge** n servizio m. **service company** n compagnia f del settore terziario. **service industry** n industria f terziaria. **serviceman** n militare m. **service provider** n fornitore m di servizi. **service road** n strada f d'accesso. **service station** n stazione f di servizio

**serviette** /sɜ:vi'et/ n tovagliolo m

**servile** /'sɜ:vail/ a servile

**servility** /sə'viliti/ n servilismo m

**serving** /'sɜ:viŋ/ a (officer) di carriera ● n (helping) porzione f

**session** /'seʃn/ n seduta f; Jur sessione f; Univ anno m accademico

**set** /set/ n serie f inv, set m inv; (of crockery, cutlery) servizio m; TV, Radio apparecchio m; Math insieme m; Theat scenario m; Cinema, Tennis set m inv; (of people) circolo m; (of hair) messa f in piega ● a (ready) pronto; (rigid) fisso; (book) in programma; **be** ~ **on doing sth** essere risoluto a fare qcsa; **be** ~ **in one's ways** essere abitudinario ● v (pt/pp set, pres p setting) ● vt mettere, porre; mettere (alarm clock); assegnare (task, homework); fissare (date, limit); chiedere (questions); montare (gem); assestare (bone); apparecchiare (table); Typ comporre; ~ **fire to** dare fuoco a; ~ **free** liberare; ~ **a good example** dare il buon esempio; ~ **sail for** far vela per; ~ **in motion** dare inizio a; ~ **to music** musicare; **the film is in Rome/the 18th century** il film è ambientato a Roma/ nel XVIII secolo; ~ **to music** musicare; ~ **about doing sth** mettersi a fare qcsa ● vi (sun:) tramontare; (jelly, concrete:) solidificarsi; ~ **to work (on sth)** mettersi al lavoro (su qcsa)

■ **set back** vt mettere indietro: (*hold up*) ritardare; (*fam: cost*) costare a

■ **set off** vi partire ● vt avviare; mettere ⟨*alarm*⟩; fare esplodere ⟨*bomb*⟩

■ **set out** vi partire; ~ **out to do sth** proporsi di fare qcsa ● vt disporre; (*state*) esporre

■ **set to** vi mettersi all'opera

■ **set up** vt fondare ⟨*company*⟩; istituire ⟨*committee*⟩

**setback** /'setbæk/ n (*hitch*) contrattempo m; *Mil* sconfitta f, scacco m; *Fin* tracollo m; (*in health*) ricaduta f

**set design** n scenografia f

**set designer** n scenografo, -a mf

**set meal** n menù m inv fisso

**settee** /se'ti:/ n divano m

**setter** /'setə(r)/ n (*dog*) setter m inv

**setting** /'setɪŋ/ n scenario m; (*position*) posizione f; (*of sun*) tramonto m; (*of jewel*) montatura f

**settle** /'setl/ vt (*decide*) definire; risolvere ⟨*argument*⟩; fissare ⟨*date*⟩; calmare ⟨*nerves*⟩; saldare ⟨*bill*⟩; **that's ~d then** allora è deciso ● vi (*live*) stabilirsi; ⟨*snow, dust, bird:*⟩ posarsi; (*subside*) assestarsi; ⟨*sediment:*⟩ depositarsi

■ **settle down** vi sistemarsi; (*stop making noise*) calmarsi

■ **settle for** vt accontentarsi di

■ **settle up** vi regolare i conti

**settlement** /'setlmənt/ n (*agreement*) accordo m; (*of bill*) saldo m; *Comm* liquidazione f; (*colony*) insediamento m

**settler** /'setlə(r)/ n colonizzatore, -trice mf

**set-to** n fam zuffa f; (*verbal*) battibecco m

**set-up** n situazione f

**seven** /'sevn/ a & n sette m

**seventeen** /sevn'ti:n/ a & n diciassette m

**seventeenth** /sevn'ti:nθ/ a & n diciassettesimo, -a mf

**seventh** /'sevnθ/ a & n settimo, -a mf

**seventieth** /'sevntɪɪθ/ a & n settantesimo, -a mf

**seventy** /'sevntɪ/ a & n settanta m

**seven-year itch** n fam crisi f inv del settimo anno

**sever** /'sevə(r)/ vt troncare ⟨*relations*⟩

**several** /'sevrəl/ a & pron parecchi

**severance** /'sev(ə)rəns/ n ~ **pay** trattamento m di fine rapporto

**severe** /sɪ'vɪə(r)/ a severo; ⟨*pain*⟩ violento; ⟨*illness*⟩ grave; ⟨*winter*⟩ rigido

**severely** /sɪ'vɪəlɪ/ adv severamente; ⟨*ill*⟩ gravemente

**severity** /sɪ'verətɪ/ n severità f; (*of pain*) violenza f; (*of illness*) gravità f; (*of winter*) rigore m

**sew** /səʊ/ vt/i (*pt* **sewed**, *pp* **sewn** or **sewed**) cucire

■ **sew up** vt ricucire

**sewage** /'su:ɪdʒ/ n acque fpl di scolo

**sewer** /'su:ə(r)/ n fogna f

**sewing** /'səʊɪŋ/ n cucito m; (*work*) lavoro m di cucito

**sewing machine** n macchina f da cucire

**sewn** /səʊn/ *see* **sew**

**sex** /seks/ n sesso m; **have ~** avere rapporti sessuali, fare l'amore

**sex appeal** n sex appeal m

**sex change operation** n intervento m per il cambiamento di sesso

**sexism** /'seksɪzm/ n sessismo m

**sexist** /'seksɪst/ a sessista mf

**sex: sex life** n vita f sessuale. **sex maniac** n maniaco m sessuale. **sex offender** n colpevole mf di delitti a sfondo sessuale

**sextet** /seks'tet/ n sestetto m

**sex tourism** n turismo m a scopo sessuale

**sexual** /'seksjʊəl/ a sessuale

**sexual: sexual assault** n atti mpl di libidine violenta. **sexual equality** n parità f dei sessi. **sexual harassment** n molestie fpl sessuali. **sexual intercourse** n rapporti mpl sessuali

**sexuality** /seksjʊ'ælətɪ/ n sessualità f

**sexually** /'seksjʊəlɪ/ adv sessualmente; **be ~ assaulted** subire atti di libidine violenta

**sexually transmitted disease** /trænz'mɪtɪd/ n malattia f trasmissibile per via sessuale

**sexy** /'seksɪ/ a (**-ier, -iest**) sexy inv

**sh** /ʃ/ int silenzio!, sst!

**shabbily** /'ʃæbɪlɪ/ adv in modo scialbo; ⟨*treat*⟩ in modo meschino

**shabbiness** /'ʃæbnɪs/ n trasandatezza f; (*of treatment*) meschinità f

**shabby** /'ʃæbɪ/ a (**-ier, -iest**) scialbo; ⟨*treatment*⟩ meschino

**shack** /ʃæk/ n catapecchia f

**shackles** /'ʃæklz/ npl catene fpl

**shade** /ʃeɪd/ n ombra f; (*of colour*) sfumatura f; (*for lamp*) paralume m; (*Am: for window*) tapparella f; **a ~ better** un tantino meglio ● vt riparare dalla luce; (*draw lines on*) ombreggiare

**shades** /ʃeɪdz/ npl fam occhiali mpl da sole

**shading** /'ʃeɪdɪŋ/ n (*slight variation in colour*) tonalità f inv; (*to give effect of darkness*) ombreggiature fpl

**shadow** /'ʃædəʊ/ n ombra f ● vt (*follow*) pedinare

**shadow boxing** n allenamento m di boxe con l'ombra

**Shadow Cabinet** n governo m ombra

**shadowy** /'ʃædəʊɪ/ a (*indistinct*) confuso

**shady** /'ʃeɪdɪ/ a (**-ier, -iest**) ombroso; (*fam: disreputable*) losco

**shaft** /ʃɑ:ft/ n *Techn* albero m; (*of light*) raggio m; (*of lift, mine*) pozzo m; ~s pl (*of cart*) stanghe fpl

**shaggy** /'ʃægɪ/ a (**-ier, -iest**) irsuto; ⟨*animal*⟩ dal pelo arruffato

**shaggy dog story** n fam barzelletta f interminabile dal finale deludente

**shake** /ʃeɪk/ n scrollata f ● v (*pt* **shook**, *pp* **shaken**) ● vt scuotere; agitare ⟨*bottle*⟩; far tremare ⟨*building*⟩; ~ **hands with** stringere la mano a; ~ **one's head** scuotere la testa ● vi tremare

■ **shake off** vt scrollarsi di dosso

**shaken [up]** /ˈʃeɪkən/ a ⟨after accident etc⟩ scosso

**shaker** /ˈʃeɪkə(r)/ n ⟨for salad⟩ centrifuga f [asciugaverdure]; ⟨for dice⟩ bicchiere m; ⟨for cocktails⟩ shaker m inv; ⟨for pepper⟩ pepaiola f; ⟨for salt⟩ saliera f

**shake-up** n Pol rimpasto m; Comm ristrutturazione f

**shakily** /ˈʃeɪkɪlɪ/ adv ⟨say sth⟩ con voce tremante; ⟨walk⟩ con passo esitante

**shaky** /ˈʃeɪkɪ/ a (-ier, -iest) tremante; ⟨table etc⟩ traballante; ⟨unreliable⟩ vacillante

**shall** /ʃæl/ v aux I ~ go andrò; we ~ see vedremo; what ~ I do? cosa faccio?; I'll come too, ~ I? vengo anch'io, no?; thou shalt not kill liter non uccidere; passengers ~ remain seated i passeggeri devono rimanere seduti

**shallot** /ʃəˈlɒt/ n scalogno m

**shallow** /ˈʃæləʊ/ a basso, poco profondo; ⟨dish⟩ poco profondo; fig superficiale

**sham** /ʃæm/ a falso ● n finzione f; ⟨person⟩ spaccone, -a mf ● vt (pt/pp shammed) simulare

**shambles** /ˈʃæmblz/ n baraonda fsg

**shame** /ʃeɪm/ n vergogna f; it's a ~ that è un peccato che; what a ~! che peccato!; ~ on you! vergognati!; put sb/sth to ~ far sfigurare qcno/qcsa

**shamefaced** /ʃeɪmˈfeɪst/ a vergognoso

**shameful** /ˈʃeɪmfl/ a vergognoso

**shamefully** /ˈʃeɪmfʊlɪ/ adv vergognosamente

**shameless** /ˈʃeɪmlɪs/ a spudorato

**shamelessly** /ˈʃeɪmlɪslɪ/ adv spudoratamente

**shampoo** /ʃæmˈpuː/ n shampoo m inv; ~ and set shampoo m inv e messa in piega ● vt fare uno shampoo a ⟨carpet, person's hair etc⟩

**shamrock** /ˈʃæmrɒk/ n trifoglio m (simbolo dell'Irlanda)

**shandy** /ˈʃændɪ/ n bevanda f a base di birra e gassosa

**shank** /ʃæŋk/ n garretto m; ⟨of knife⟩ manico m; ⟨of golf club⟩ impugnatura f; ⟨of screw⟩ gambo m; ⟨of anchor⟩ fuso m; ⟨of person⟩ gamba f (dal ginocchio in giù)

**shan't** /ʃɑːnt/ = shall not

**shanty** /ˈʃæntɪ/ n (hut) baracca f; (song) marinaro

**shanty town** /ˈʃæntɪtaʊn/ n bidonville f inv, baraccopoli f inv

**shape** /ʃeɪp/ n forma f; ⟨figure⟩ ombra f; take ~ prendere forma; get back in ~ ritornare in forma; be out of ~ non essere in forma ● vt dare forma a (into di) ● vi ~ [up] mettere la testa a posto; ~ up nicely mettersi bene

**shapeless** /ˈʃeɪplɪs/ a informe

**shapely** /ˈʃeɪplɪ/ a (-ier, -iest) ben fatto

**shard** /ʃɑːd/ n frammento m; ⟨of clay⟩ coccio m

**share** /ʃeə(r)/ n porzione f; Comm azione f ● vt dividere; condividere ⟨views⟩ ● vi dividere; ~ in partecipare a

■ **share out** vt spartire; ⟨including oneself⟩ spartirsi

**share: share capital** n capitale m azionario. **share dealing** n contrattazione f di azioni. **shareholder** n azionista mf. **shareholding** n titoli mpl azionari. **share index** n indice m azionario

**shark** /ʃɑːk/ n squalo m, pescecane m; fig truffatore, -trice mf

**sharp** /ʃɑːp/ a ⟨knife etc⟩ tagliente; ⟨pencil⟩ appuntito; ⟨drop⟩ a picco; ⟨reprimand⟩ severo; ⟨outline⟩ marcato; ⟨alert⟩ acuto; ⟨unscrupulous⟩ senza scrupoli; ~ pain fitta f ● adv at three o'clock ~ alle tre in punto; look ~! sbrigati! ● n Mus diesis m inv

**sharpen** /ˈʃɑːpn/ vt affilare ⟨knife⟩; appuntire ⟨pencil⟩

**sharpener** /ˈʃɑːpnə(r)/ n ⟨for pencils⟩ temperamatite m inv; ⟨for knife⟩ affilacoltelli m inv

**shatter** /ˈʃætə(r)/ vt frantumare; fig mandare in frantumi

**shattered** /ˈʃætəd/ a ⟨fam: exhausted⟩ a pezzi ● vi frantumarsi

**shave** /ʃeɪv/ n rasatura f; have a ~ farsi la barba ● vt radere ● vi radersi

**shaver** /ˈʃeɪvə(r)/ n rasoio m elettrico

**shaving** /ˈʃeɪvɪŋ/: **shaving-brush** n pennello m da barba. **shaving foam** n schiuma f da barba. **shaving soap** n sapone m da barba

**shawl** /ʃɔːl/ n scialle m

**she** /ʃiː/ pers pron lei; ~ is tired è stanca; I'm going, but ~ is not io vado, ma lei no

**sheaf** /ʃiːf/ n (pl sheaves) fascio m

**shear** /ʃɪə(r)/ vt (pt sheared, pp shorn or sheared) tosare

**shears** /ʃɪəz/ npl ⟨for hedge⟩ cesoie fpl

**sheath** /ʃiːθ/ n (pl ~s /ʃiːðz/) guaina f

**sheathe** /ʃiːð/ vt rinfoderare; rivestire ⟨cable⟩

**sheaves** /ʃiːvz/ see sheaf

**shed**[1] /ʃed/ n baracca f; ⟨for cattle⟩ stalla f

**shed**[2] vt (pt/pp shed, pres p shedding) perdere; versare ⟨blood, tears⟩; ~ light on far luce su

**sheen** /ʃiːn/ n lucentezza f

**sheep** /ʃiːp/ n inv pecora f

**sheepdog** /ˈʃiːpdɒg/ n cane m da pastore

**sheepish** /ˈʃiːpɪʃ/ a imbarazzato

**sheepishly** /ˈʃiːpɪʃlɪ/ adv con aria imbarazzata

**sheepskin** /ˈʃiːpskɪn/ n [pelle f di] montone m

**sheer** /ʃɪə(r)/ a puro; ⟨steep⟩ a picco; ⟨transparent⟩ trasparente ● adv a picco

**sheet** /ʃiːt/ n lenzuolo m; ⟨of paper⟩ foglio m; ⟨of glass, metal⟩ lastra f

**sheet lightning** n bagliore m diffuso dei lampi; ⟨without a storm⟩ lampi mpl di calore

**sheet music** n spartiti mpl

**sheikh** /ʃeɪk/ n sceicco m

**shelf** /ʃelf/ n (pl shelves) ripiano m; ⟨set of shelves⟩ scaffale m

**shelf-life** n ⟨of product⟩ durata f di conservazione; ⟨fig: of technology, pop music⟩ durata f di vita; (*fig: of politician, star*) periodo *m* di gloria

**shell** /ʃel/ *n* conchiglia *f*; (*of egg, snail, tortoise*) guscio *m*; (*of crab*) corazza *f*; (*of unfinished building*) ossatura *f*; *Mil* granata *f* • *vt* sgusciare (*peas*); *Mil* bombardare
■ **shell out** *vi fam* sborsare
**shell: shellfish** *n inv* mollusco *m*; *Culin* frutti *mpl* di mare. **shell-shocked** /ʃelʃɒkt/ *a* (*soldier*) traumatizzato da un bombardamento; *fig* in stato di shock. **shell suit** *n* tuta *f* di acetato

**shelter** /ʃeltə(r)/ *n* rifugio *m*; (*air raid ~*) rifugio *m* antiaereo; **take** ~ rifugiarsi • *vt* riparare (**from** da); *fig* mettere al riparo; (*give lodging to*) dare asilo a • *vi* rifugiarsi
**sheltered** /ʃeltəd/ *a* (*spot*) riparato; (*life*) ritirato

**shelve** /ʃelv/ *vt* accantonare (*project*) • *vi* (*slope:*) scendere
**shelves** /ʃelvz/ *see* **shelf**
**shelving** /ʃelvɪŋ/ *n* (*shelves*) ripiani *mpl*
**shepherd** /ʃepəd/ *n* pastore *m* • *vt* guidare
**shepherdess** /ʃepədes/ *n* pastora *f*
**shepherd's pie** /ʃepədzˈpaɪ/ *n* pasticcio *m* di carne tritata e patate
**sherbet** /ˈsɜːbət/ *n* (*Br: powder*) polverina *f* effervescente al gusto di frutta; (*Am: sorbet*) sorbetto *m*
**sheriff** /ʃerɪf/ *n* sceriffo *m*
**Sherpa** /ˈʃɜːpə/ *n* scerpa *m*
**sherry** /ˈʃerɪ/ *n* sherry *m inv*
**shield** /ʃiːld/ *n* scudo *m*; (*for eyes*) maschera *f*; *Techn* schermo *m* • *vt* proteggere (**from** da)
**shift** /ʃɪft/ *n* cambiamento *m*; (*in position*) spostamento *m*; (*at work*) turno *m* • *vt* spostare; (*take away*) togliere; riversare (*blame*) • *vi* spostarsi; (*wind:*) cambiare; (*fam: move quickly*) darsi una mossa
**shift key** *n* tasto *m* delle maiuscole
**shiftless** /ʃɪftlɪs/ *a* privo di risorse
**shift work** *n* turni *mpl*
**shift worker** *n* turnista *mf*
**shifty** /ʃɪftɪ/ *a* (**-ier, -iest**) *pej* losco; (*eyes*) sfuggente
**Shiite** /ˈʃiːaɪt/ *a & n* sciita *mf*
**shilling** /ˈʃɪlɪŋ/ *n* scellino *m*
**shilly-shally** /ˈʃɪlɪʃælɪ/ *vi* titubare
**shimmer** /ˈʃɪmə(r)/ *n* luccichio *m* • *vi* luccicare
**shin** /ʃɪn/ *n* stinco *m* • *vi* ~ **up/down sth** (*climb*) arrampicarsi su/scendere giù da qcsa
**shin-guard** *n* parastinchi *m inv*
**shindig** /ˈʃɪndɪg/ *n fam* (*party*) baldoria *f*; (*disturbance*) pandemonio *m*
**shindy** /ˈʃɪndɪ/ *n fam* (*disturbance*) pandemonio *m*; (*party*) baldoria *f*
**shine** /ʃaɪn/ *n* lucentezza *f*; **give sth a** ~ dare una lucidata a qcsa • *v* (*pt/pp* **shone**) • *vi* splendere; (*reflect light*) brillare; (*hair, shoes:*) essere lucido • *vt* ~ **a light on** puntare una luce su
**shingle** /ˈʃɪŋgl/ *n* (*pebbles*) ghiaia *f*
**shingles** /ˈʃɪŋglz/ *n Med* fuochi *mpl* di Sant'Antonio

**shiny** /ʃaɪnɪ/ *a* (**-ier, -iest**) lucido
**ship** /ʃɪp/ *n* nave *f* • *vt* (*pt/pp* **shipped**) spedire; (*by sea*) spedire via mare
**shipbuilder** /ˈʃɪpbɪldə(r)/ *n* costruttore *m* navale
**shipbuilding** /ˈʃɪpbɪldɪŋ/ *n* costruzione *f* di navi
**shipment** /ˈʃɪpmənt/ *n* spedizione *f*; (*consignment*) carico *m*
**shipowner** /ˈʃɪpəʊnə(r)/ *n* armatore *m*
**shipper** /ˈʃɪpə(r)/ *n* spedizioniere *m*
**shipping** /ˈʃɪpɪŋ/ *n* trasporto *m*; (*traffic*) imbarcazioni *fpl*
**shipping agent** *n* spedizioniere *m*
**shipping company** *n* compagnia *f* di spedizione
**ship: shipshape** *a & adv* in perfetto ordine. **shipwreck** *n* naufragio *m*. **shipwrecked** *a* naufragato. **shipyard** *n* cantiere *m* navale
**shire** /ʃaɪə(r)/ *n Br* contea *f*
**shire-horse** *n* cavallo *m* da tiro
**shirk** /ʃɜːk/ *vt* scansare
**shirker** /ʃɜːkə(r)/ *n* scansafatiche *mf inv*
**shirt** /ʃɜːt/ *n* camicia *f*; **in ~-sleeves** in maniche di camicia
**shirty** /ʃɜːtɪ/ *a Br fam* incavolato; **get** ~ **with sb** incavolarsi per qcno
**shish kebab** /ʃɪʃkɪˈbæb/ *n* spiedino *m* di carne e verdure
**shit** /ʃɪt/ *vulg n & int* merda *f* • *vi* (*pt/pp* **shit**) cagare
**shit-scared** *a vulg* **be** ~ farsela sotto
**shiver** /ʃɪvə(r)/ *n* brivido *m* • *vi* rabbrividire
**shoal** /ʃəʊl/ *n* (*of fish*) banco *m*
**shock** /ʃɒk/ *n* (*impact*) urto *m*; *Electr* scossa *f* [elettrica]; *fig* colpo *m*, shock *m inv*; *Med* shock *m inv*; **get a** ~ *Electr* prendere la scossa; **in** ~ *Med* in stato di shock • *vt* scioccare
**shock absorber** *n Auto* ammortizzatore *m*
**shocking** /ʃɒkɪŋ/ *a* scioccante; (*fam: weather, handwriting etc*) tremendo
**shockingly** /ʃɒkɪŋlɪ/ *adv* (*behave*) in modo pessimo; (*expensive*) eccessivamente
**shocking pink** *n* rosa *m* shocking
**shock: shockproof** *a* antiurto. **shock treatment** *n* terapia *f* d'urto. **shock wave** *n* onda *f* d'urto
**shod** /ʃɒd/ *see* **shoe**
**shoddily** /ʃɒdɪlɪ/ *adv* in modo scadente
**shoddy** /ʃɒdɪ/ *a* (**-ier, -iest**) scadente
**shoe** /ʃuː/ *n* scarpa *f*; (*of horse*) ferro *m* • *vt* (*pt/pp* **shod**, *pres p* **shoeing**) ferrare (*horse*)
**shoe: shoehorn** *n* calzante *m*. **shoelace** *n* laccio *m* da scarpa. **shoemaker** *n* calzolaio *m*. **shoe rack** *n* scarpiera *f*. **shoe-shop** *n* calzoleria *f*. **shoestring** *n* **on a** ~ *fam* con una miseria. **shoe-tree** *n* forma *f* da scarpa
**shone** /ʃɒn/ *see* **shine**
**shoo** /ʃuː/ *vt* ~ **away** cacciar via • *int* sciò!
**shook** /ʃʊk/ *see* **shake**
**shoot** /ʃuːt/ *n Bot* germoglio *m*; (*hunt*) battuta *f* di caccia • *v* (*pt/pp* **shot**) • *vt* sparare; girare (*film*); ~ **oneself in the foot** *fig* darsi la zappa sui piedi • *vi* (*hunt*) andare a caccia
■ **shoot down** *vt* abbattere

■ **shoot out** vi (rush) precipitarsi fuori

■ **shoot up** vi (grow) crescere in fretta; ⟨prices:⟩ salire di colpo

**shooting** /'ʃuːtɪŋ/ n (pastime) caccia f; (killing) uccisione f ● a (pain) lancinante

**shooting range** n poligono m di tiro

**shoot-out** n fam sparatoria f

**shop** /ʃɒp/ n negozio m; (workshop) officina f; **talk ~** fam parlare di lavoro ● vi (pt/pp shopped, pres p shopping) far compere; **go ~ping** andare a fare compere

■ **shop around** vi confrontare i prezzi

**shop: shop assistant** n commesso, -a mf. **shop floor n problems on the ~ ~** problemi tra gli operai. **shopkeeper** n negoziante mf. **shoplifter** n taccheggiatore, -trice mf. **shoplifting** n taccheggio m

**shopper** /'ʃɒpə(r)/ n compratore, -trice mf

**shopping** /'ʃɒpɪŋ/ n compere fpl; (articles) acquisti mpl; **do the ~** fare la spesa

**shopping: shopping bag** n borsa f per la spesa. **shopping centre** n centro m commerciale. **shopping list** n lista f della spesa. **shopping mall** n centro m commerciale. **shopping trolley** n carrello m

**shop steward** n rappresentante mf sindacale

**shop window** n vetrina f

**shore** /ʃɔː(r)/ n riva f

■ **shore up** vt puntellare ⟨building, wall⟩

**shorn** /ʃɔːn/ see **shear**

**short** /ʃɔːt/ a corto; (not lasting) breve; ⟨person⟩ basso; (curt) brusco; **a ~ time ago** poco tempo fa; **be ~ of** essere a corto di; **be in ~ supply** essere scarso; fig essere raro; **Mick is ~ for Michael** Mick è il diminutivo di Michael; **cut ~** interrompere ⟨holiday⟩; **to cut a long story ~...** per farla breve...; **in the ~ term** nell'immediato futuro, a breve termine ● adv bruscamente; **in ~** in breve; **~ of doing** a meno di fare; **go ~** essere privato (of di); **stop ~ of doing sth** non arrivare fino a fare qcsa; **you're 10p ~** mancano 10 pence ● n (Cinema) cortometraggio m

**shortage** /'ʃɔːtɪdʒ/ n scarsità f inv

**short: shortbread** n biscotto m di pasta frolla. **short-change** vt dare meno resto del dovuto a; (deliberately) imbrogliare sul resto; fig imbrogliare. **short circuit** n corto m circuito ● vt mandare in cortocircuito ● vi causare un cortocircuito. **shortcoming** n difetto m. **shortcrust pastry** n pasta f frolla. **short cut** n scorciatoia f

**shorten** /'ʃɔːtn/ vt abbreviare; accorciare ⟨garment⟩

**short: shortfall** n (in budget, accounts) deficit m inv. **shorthand** n stenografia f. **short-handed** /-'hændɪd/ a a corto di personale. **shorthand typist** n stenodattilografo, -a mf. **short list** n lista f dei candidati selezionati per un lavoro. **short-lived** /-'lɪvd/ a di breve durata

**shortly** /'ʃɔːtlɪ/ adv presto; **~ before/after** poco prima/dopo

**shortness** /'ʃɔːtnɪs/ n brevità f inv; (of person) bassa statura f

**short notice** n at **~ ~** con poco preavviso

**short-range** a di breve portata

**shorts** /ʃɔːts/ npl calzoncini mpl corti

**short: short-sighted** /-'saɪtɪd/ a miope. **short-sleeved** /-'sliːvd/ a a maniche corte. **short-staffed** /-'stɑːft/ a a corto di personale. **short story** n racconto m, novella f. **short-tempered** /-'tempəd/ a irascibile. **short-term** a a breve termine. **short time** n be on **~ ~** ⟨worker:⟩ fare orario ridotto. **short wave** n onde fpl corte. **short wave radio** n radio f inv a onde corte

**shot** /ʃɒt/ see **shoot** ● n colpo m; (pellets) piombini mpl; (person) tiratore m; Phot foto f inv; (injection) puntura f; (fam: attempt) prova f; **like a ~** fam come un razzo

**shot: shotgun** n fucile m da caccia. **shot-putter** n pesista mf. **shot-putting** n Sport lancio m del peso

**should** /ʃʊd/ v aux **I ~ go** dovrei andare; **I ~ have seen him** avrei dovuto vederlo; **you ~n't have said that** non avresti dovuto dire questo; **I ~ like** mi piacerebbe; **this ~ be enough** questo dovrebbe bastare; **if he ~ come** se dovesse venire, se venisse

**shoulder** /'ʃəʊldə(r)/ n spalla f; **~ to ~** gomito a gomito ● vt mettersi in spalla; fig accollarsi

**shoulder: shoulder bag** n borsa f a tracolla. **shoulder blade** n scapola f. **shoulder pad** n spallina f. **shoulder strap** n spallina f; (of bag) tracolla f

**shout** /ʃaʊt/ n grido m ● vt/i gridare

■ **shout at** vi alzar la voce con

■ **shout down** vt azzittire gridando

**shouting** /'ʃaʊtɪŋ/ n grida fpl

**shove** /ʃʌv/ n spintone m ● vt spingere; (fam: put) ficcare ● vi spingere

■ **shove off** vi fam togliersi di torno

**shovel** /'ʃʌvl/ n pala f ● vt (pt/pp shovelled) spalare

**show** /ʃəʊ/ n (display) manifestazione f; (exhibition) mostra f; (ostentation) ostentazione f; Theat, TV spettacolo m; (programme) programma m; **on ~** esposto ● v (pt showed, pp shown) ● vt mostrare; (put on display) esporre; proiettare ⟨film⟩; **~ sb to the door** accompagnare qcno alla porta; **~ sb the door** mettere alla porta qcno ● vi ⟨film:⟩ essere proiettato; **your slip is ~ing** ti si vede la sottoveste

■ **show in** vt fare accomodare

■ **show off** vi fam mettersi in mostra ● vt mettere in mostra

■ **show out** vt **~ sb out** fare uscire qcno

■ **show up** vi risaltare; (fam: arrive) farsi vedere ● vt (fam: embarrass) far fare una brutta figura a

**show: showbiz** /'ʃəʊbɪz/ n fam mondo m dello spettacolo. **show business** n mondo m dello spettacolo. **showcase** n also fig vetrina f ● attrib ⟨village, prison⟩ modello. **showdown** n regolamento m dei conti

**shower** /'ʃaʊə(r)/ n doccia f; (of rain) acquazzone m; **have a ~** fare la doccia ● vt **~ with** coprire di ● vi fare la doccia

**shower:** **shower-cap** n cuffia f da doccia. **shower-curtain** tenda f della doccia. **shower-head** n bocchetta f. **showerproof** a impermeabile

**showery** /'ʃaʊərɪ/ a **it was ~** ci sono stati diversi acquazzoni

**showjumper** /'ʃəʊdʒʌmpə(r)/ n cavaliere m/cavallerizza f di salto ad ostacoli

**showjumping** /'ʃəʊdʒʌmpɪŋ/ n concorso m ippico

**shown** /ʃəʊn/ see show

**show:** **show-off** n esibizionista mf. **showpiece** n pezzo m forte. **showplace** n attrazione f. **showroom** n salone m [per] esposizioni

**showy** /'ʃəʊɪ/ a appariscente

**shrank** /ʃræŋk/ see shrink

**shrapnel** /'ʃræpnl/ n schegge fpl di granata, shrapnel m

**shred** /ʃred/ n brandello m; fig briciolo m ● vt (pt/pp **shredded**) fare a brandelli; Culin tagliuzzare

**shredder** /'ʃredə(r)/ n distruttore m di documenti

**shrew** /ʃru:/ n Zool toporagno m; (pej: woman) bisbetica f

**shrewd** /ʃru:d/ a accorto

**shrewdly** /'ʃru:dlɪ/ adv con accortezza

**shrewdness** /'ʃru:dnɪs/ n accortezza f

**shriek** /ʃri:k/ n strillo m ● vt/i strillare

**shrift** /ʃrɪft/ n **give sb short ~** liquidare qcno rapidamente

**shrill** /ʃrɪl/ a penetrante

**shrillness** /'ʃrɪlnɪs/ n acutezza f

**shrilly** /'ʃrɪlɪ/ adv in modo penetrante

**shrimp** /ʃrɪmp/ n gamberetto m

**shrine** /ʃraɪn/ n (place) santuario m

**shrink** /ʃrɪŋk/ vi (pt **shrank**, pp **shrunk**) restringersi; (draw back) ritrarsi (**from** da) ● n fam strizzacervelli mf inv

**shrinkage** /'ʃrɪŋkɪdʒ/ n (of fabric) restringimento m; (of area, company) rimpicciolimento m; (in a shop) perdite fpl; (of resources) diminuzione f

**shrinking violet** /ʃrɪŋkɪŋ'vaɪələt/ n hum mammoletta f

**shrink:** **shrink-proof** a irrestringibile. **shrink-resistant** a irrestringibile. **shrink-wrap** vt avvolgere nella pellicola trasparente ● n pellicola f trasparente

**shrivel** /'ʃrɪvl/ vi (pt/pp **shrivelled**) raggrinzare

**shroud** /ʃraʊd/ n sudario m; fig manto m; **~ed in** fig avvolto in

**Shrove** /ʃrəʊv/ n **~ Tuesday** martedì m grasso

**shrub** /ʃrʌb/ n arbusto m

**shrubbery** /'ʃrʌbərɪ/ n (in garden) zona f piantata ad arbusti

**shrug** /ʃrʌg/ n scrollata f di spalle ● vt/i (pt pp **shrugged**) **~ [one's shoulders]** scrollare le spalle

■ **shrug off** vt ignorare

**shrunk** /ʃrʌŋk/ see shrink. **~en** a rimpicciolito

**shudder** /'ʃʌdə(r)/ n fremito m ● vi fremere

**shuffle** /'ʃʌfl/ vi strascicare i piedi ● vt mescolare ⟨cards⟩ ● n strascicamento m; (at cards) mescolata f

**shufty** /'ʃʊftɪ/ n Br fam **have a ~ at sth** dare un'occhiata a qcsa

**shun** /ʃʌn/ vt (pt/pp **shunned**) rifuggire

**shunt** /ʃʌnt/ vt smistare

**shush** /ʃʊʃ/ int zitto!

**shut** /ʃʌt/ v (pt/pp **shut**, pres p **shutting**) ● vt chiudere ● vi chiudersi; ⟨shop:⟩ chiudere

■ **shut down** vt/i chiudere

■ **shut off** vt chiudere ⟨water, gas⟩

■ **shut out** vt bloccare ⟨light⟩; impedire ⟨view⟩; scacciare ⟨memory⟩

■ **shut up** vt chiudere; fam far tacere ● vi fam stare zitto; **~ up!** stai zitto!

**shutdown** /'ʃʌtdaʊn/ n chiusura f

**shut-eye** n (fam: short sleep) **get some ~** fare un pisolino

**shutter** /'ʃʌtə(r)/ n serranda f; Phot otturatore m

**shuttle** /'ʃʌtl/ n navetta f ● vi far la spola

**shuttlecock** /'ʃʌtlkɒk/ n volano m

**shuttle service** n servizio m pendolare

**shy** /ʃaɪ/ a (timid) timido ● vi (pt/pp **shied**) ⟨horse:⟩ fare uno scarto

■ **shy away from** vt rifuggire da

**shyly** /'ʃaɪlɪ/ adv timidamente

**shyness** /'ʃaɪnɪs/ n timidezza f

**sibylline** /'sɪbɪlaɪn/ a sibillino

**Siamese** /saɪə'mi:z/ a siamese

**Siamese twins** npl fratelli mpl/sorelle fpl siamesi

**sibling** /'sɪblɪŋ/ n (brother) fratello m; (sister) sorella f; **~s** pl fratelli mpl

**sibling rivalry** n rivalità f tra fratelli

**Sicilian** /sɪ'sɪlɪən/ a & n siciliano, -a mf

**Sicily** /'sɪsɪlɪ/ n Sicilia f

**sick** /sɪk/ a ammalato; ⟨humour⟩ macabro; **be ~** (vomit) vomitare; **be ~ of sth** fam essere stufo di qcsa; **feel ~** aver la nausea

**sicken** /'sɪkn/ vt disgustare ● vi **be ~ing for something** covare qualche malanno

**sickening** /'sɪkənɪŋ/ a disgustoso

**sick leave** n congedo m per malattia

**sickly** /'sɪklɪ/ a (-ier, -iest) malaticcio

**sickness** /'sɪknɪs/ n malattia f; (vomiting) nausea f

**sickness benefit** n sussidio m di malattia

**sickroom** /'sɪkru:m/ n camera f dell'ammalato

**side** /saɪd/ n lato m; (of person, mountain) fianco m; (of road) bordo m; **on the ~** (as sideline) come attività secondaria; **~ by ~** fianco a fianco; **take ~s** immischiarsi; **take sb's ~** prendere le parti di qcno; **be on the safe ~** andare sul sicuro ● attrib laterale ● vi **~ with** parteggiare per

**side:** **sideboard** n credenza f. **sideburns** npl

basette *fpl*. **side effect** *n* effetto *m* collaterale. **sidekick** *n fam (companion)* compare *mf*; *(assistant)* braccio *m* destro. **sidelights** *npl* luci *fpl* di posizione. **sideline** *n* attività *f inv* complementare. **sidelong** *a* ~ **glance** sguincio *m*. **side road** *n* strada *f* secondaria. **side-saddle** *adv* all'amazzone. **sideshow** *n* attrazione *f*. **sidestep** *vt* schivare. **side street** *n* strada *f* laterale. **sidetrack** *vt* sviare. **sidewalk** *n Am* marciapiede *m*. **sideways** *adv* obliquamente

**siding** /'saɪdɪŋ/ *n* binario *m* di raccordo

**sidle** /'saɪdl/ *vi* camminare furtivamente (**up to** verso)

**siege** /si:dʒ/ *n* assedio *m*

**Sierra Leone** /sɪeərəlɪ'əʊn/ *n* Sierra Leone *f*

**siesta** /sɪ'estə/ *n* siesta *f*; **take a** ~ fare una siesta

**sieve** /sɪv/ *n* setaccio *m* • *vt* setacciare

**sift** /sɪft/ *vt* setacciare; ~ **[through]** *fig* passare al setaccio

**sigh** /saɪ/ *n* sospiro *m*; **give a** ~ sospirare • *vi* sospirare

**sight** /saɪt/ *n* vista *f*; *(on gun)* mirino *m*; **the ~s** *pl* le cose da vedere; **at first** ~ a prima vista; **be within/out of** ~ essere/non essere in vista; **within** ~ **of** vicino a; **lose** ~ **of** perdere di vista; **know by** ~ conoscere di vista; **have bad** ~ vederci male • *vt* avvistare

**sightseeing** /'saɪtsi:ɪŋ/ *n* **go** ~ andare a visitare posti

**sightseer** /'saɪtsi:ə(r)/ *n* turista *mf*

**sign** /saɪn/ *n* segno *m*; *(notice)* insegna *f* • *vt/i* firmare

■ **sign for** *vt* firmare la ricevuta di *(letter, parcel)*; firmare un contratto con *(football club)*

■ **sign in** *vi* *(hotel guest:)* firmare il registro

■ **sign on** *vi (as unemployed)* presentarsi all'ufficio di collocamento; *Mil* arruolarsi

■ **sign up** *vi Mil* arruolarsi; ~ **up for a course** iscriversi a un corso

**signal** /'sɪgnl/ *n* segnale *m* • *v (pt/pp* **signalled)** • *vt* segnalare • *vi* fare segnali; ~ **to sb** far segno a qcno (**to di**)

**signal box** *n* cabina *f* di segnalazione

**signalman** /'sɪgnəlmən/ *n* casellante *m*

**signatory** /'sɪgnət(ə)rɪ/ *n* firmatario, -a *mf*

**signature** /'sɪgnətʃə(r)/ *n* firma *f*

**signature tune** *n* sigla *f* [musicale]

**signet ring** /'sɪgnɪt/ *n* anello *m* con sigillo

**significance** /sɪg'nɪfɪkəns/ *n* significato *m*

**significant** /sɪg'nɪfɪkənt/ *a* significativo

**significantly** /sɪg'nɪfɪkəntlɪ/ *adv* in modo significativo

**signify** /'sɪgnɪfaɪ/ *vt (pt/pp* **-ied)** indicare

**signing** /'saɪnɪŋ/ *n (of treaty)* firma *f*; *(of footballer)* ingaggio *m*; *(footballer)* nuovo acquisto *m*; *(sign language)* linguaggio *m* dei segni

**sign language** *n* linguaggio *m* dei segni

**signpost** /'saɪnpəʊst/ *n* segnalazione *f* stradale

**Sikh** /si:k/ *n* sikh *mf inv* • *a* sikh *inv*

**silage** /'saɪlɪdʒ/ *n* foraggio *m* conservato in silo

**silence** /'saɪləns/ *n* silenzio *m*; **in** ~ in silenzio • *vt* far tacere

**silencer** /'saɪlənsə(r)/ *n (on gun)* silenziatore *m*; *Auto* marmitta *f*

**silent** /'saɪlənt/ *a* silenzioso; *(film)* muto; **remain** ~ rimanere in silenzio; **the** ~ **majority** la maggioranza silenziosa

**silently** /'saɪləntlɪ/ *adv* silenziosamente

**silhouette** /sɪlʊ'et/ *n* sagoma *f*, silhouette *f inv* • *vt* **be ~d** profilarsi

**silica gel** /'sɪlɪkə/ *n* gel *m inv* di silice

**silicon** /'sɪlɪkən/ *n* silicio *m*

**silicon chip** *n Comput* chip *m inv* di silicio, piastrina *f* di silicio

**silicone** /'sɪlɪkəʊn/ *n Chem* silicone *m*

**silicone varnish** *n* vernice *f* siliconica

**silk** /sɪlk/ *n* seta *f* • *attrib* di seta

**silkworm** /'sɪlkwɜ:m/ *n* baco *m* da seta

**silky** /'sɪlkɪ/ *a* (**-ier, -iest)** come la seta

**sill** /sɪl/ *n* davanzale *m*

**silly** /'sɪlɪ/ *a* (**-ier, -iest)** sciocco

**silo** /'saɪləʊ/ *n* silo *m*

**silt** /sɪlt/ *n* melma *f*

**silver** /'sɪlvə(r)/ *a* d'argento; *(paper)* argentato • *n* argento *m*; *(silverware)* argenteria *f*

**silver: silver-plated** *a* placcato d'argento. **silver service** *n* servizio *m* a tavola in cui il cameriere fa il giro dei commensali. **silversmith** *n* argentiere *m*. **silverware** *n* argenteria *f*. **silver wedding** *n* nozze *fpl* d'argento

**silvery** /'sɪlvərɪ/ *a* argentino

**similar** /'sɪmɪlə(r)/ *a* simile

**similarity** /sɪmɪ'lærətɪ/ *n* somiglianza *f*

**similarly** /'sɪmɪləlɪ/ *adv* in modo simile

**simile** /'sɪmɪlɪ/ *n* similitudine *f*

**simmer** /'sɪmə(r)/ *vi* bollire lentamente • *vt* far bollire lentamente

■ **simmer down** *vi* calmarsi

**simper** /'sɪmpə(r)/ *vi* ostentare un sorriso

**simpering** /'sɪmp(ə)rɪŋ/ *a (smile)* affettato; *(person)* smanceroso

**simple** /'sɪmpl/ *a* semplice; *(person)* sempliciotto

**simple-minded** /-'maɪndɪd/ *a* sempliciotto

**simpleton** /'sɪmpltən/ *n* sempliciotto, -a *mf*

**simplicity** /sɪm'plɪsətɪ/ *n* semplicità *f*

**simplification** /sɪmplɪfɪ'keɪʃn/ *n* semplificazione *f*

**simplify** /'sɪmplɪfaɪ/ *vt (pt/pp* **-ied)** semplificare

**simplistic** /sɪm'plɪstɪk/ *a* semplicistico

**simply** /'sɪmplɪ/ *adv* semplicemente

**simulate** /'sɪmjʊleɪt/ *vt* simulare

**simulation** /sɪmjʊ'leɪʃn/ *n* simulazione *f*

**simulcast** /'sɪmʌlkɑ:st/ *vt* teleradiotrasmettere

**simultaneous** /sɪml'teɪnɪəs/ *a* simultaneo

**simultaneously** /sɪməl'teɪnɪəslɪ/ *adv* simultaneamente

**sin** /sɪn/ *n* peccato *m* • *vi (pt/pp* **sinned)** peccare

**since** /sɪns/ *prep* da; ~ **when?** da quando in qua? ●*adv* da allora ●*conj* da quando; (*because*) siccome

**sincere** /sɪn'sɪə(r)/ *a* sincero

**sincerely** /sɪn'sɪəlɪ/ *adv* sinceramente; **Yours** ~ Distinti saluti

**sincerity** /sɪn'serətɪ/ *n* sincerità *f*

**sine** /saɪn/ *n* Math seno *m*

**sinew** /'sɪnjuː/ *n* tendine *m*

**sinful** /'sɪnfl/ *a* peccaminoso

**sing** /sɪŋ/ *vt/i* (*pt* **sang**, *pp* **sung**) cantare

**singalong** /'sɪŋəlɒŋ/ *n* **have a** ~ cantare [tutti] insieme

**singe** /sɪndʒ/ *vt* (*pres p* **singeing**) bruciacchiare

**singer** /'sɪŋə(r)/ *n* cantante *mf*

**singer-songwriter** /-'sɒŋraɪtə(r)/ *n* cantautore, -trice *mf*

**singing** /'sɪŋɪŋ/ *n* canto *m*

**single** /'sɪŋgl/ *a* solo; (*not double*) semplice; (*unmarried*) celibe; ‹*woman*› nubile; ‹*room*› singolo; ‹*bed*› a una piazza; **I haven't spoken to a** ~ **person** non ho parlato con nessuno ●*n* (*ticket*) biglietto *m* di sola andata; (*record*) singolo *m*

■ **single out** *vt* scegliere; (*distinguish*) distinguere

**single: single-breasted** /-'brestɪd/ *a* a un petto. **single cream** *n* panna *f* da cucina fluida. **single currency** *n* (*in Europe*) moneta *f* unica. **single-decker** /-'dekə(r)/ *n* autobus *m inv* (*a un piano solo*). **single file** *adv* in fila indiana. **single-handed** /-'hændɪd/ *a & adv* da solo. **single-handedly** /-'hændɪdlɪ/ *adv* da solo. **single market** *n* mercato *m* unico. **single-minded** /-'maɪndɪd/ *a* risoluto. **single parent** *n* genitore *m* che alleva il figlio da solo

**singles** /'sɪŋglz/ *npl* Tennis singolo *m*; (*people*) single *mpl*; **the women's** ~ il singolo femminile

**singles bar** *n* bar ritrovo *m inv* per single

**single-sex** *a* (*for boys*) maschile; (*for girls*) femminile

**single-storey** *a* ‹*house*› a un piano

**singly** /'sɪŋglɪ/ *adv* singolarmente

**sing-song** Br *a* ‹*voice, dialect*› che ha una sua particolare cadenza ●*n* **have a** ~ cantare [tutti] insieme

**singular** /'sɪŋgjʊlə(r)/ *a* Gram singolare; (*uncommon*) eccezionale ●*n* singolare *m*

**singularly** /'sɪŋgjʊləlɪ/ *adv* singolarmente

**sinister** /'sɪnɪstə(r)/ *a* sinistro

**sink** /sɪŋk/ *n* lavandino *m* ●*v* (*pt* **sank**, *pp* **sunk**) ●*vi* affondare ●*vt* affondare ‹*ship*›; scavare ‹*shaft*›; investire ‹*money*›

■ **sink in** *vi* penetrare; **it took a while to** ~ **in** (*fam: be understood*) c'è voluto un po' a capirlo

**sinker** /'sɪŋkə(r)/ *n* (*in fishing*) piombo *m*; *Am Culin* ≈ bombolone *m*

**sinking** /'sɪŋkɪŋ/ *n* affondamento *m*

**sink unit** *n* mobile *m* di cucina comprendente il lavandino

**sinner** /'sɪnə(r)/ *n* peccatore, -trice *mf*

**sinuous** /'sɪnjʊəs/ *a* sinuoso

**sinus** /'saɪnəs/ *n* seno *m* paranasale

**sinusitis** /saɪnə'saɪtɪs/ *n* sinusite *f*

**sip** /sɪp/ *n* sorso *m* ●*vt* (*pt/pp* **sipped**) sorseggiare

**siphon** /'saɪfn/ *n* (*bottle*) sifone *m*

■ **siphon off** *vt* travasare (*con sifone*)

**sir** /sɜː(r)/ *n* signore *m*; **S**~ (*title*) Sir *m*; **Dear S**~ Egregio Signore; **Dear S**~**s** Spettabile ditta

**sire** /saɪə(r)/ *vt* generare

**siren** /'saɪrən/ *n* sirena *f*

**sirloin** /'sɜːlɔɪn/ *n* (*of beef*) controfiletto *m*

**sirloin steak** *n* bistecca *f* di controfiletto

**sissy** /'sɪsɪ/ *n* feminuccia *f*

**sister** /'sɪstə(r)/ *n* sorella *f*; (*nurse*) [infermiera *f*] caposala *f*

**sisterhood** /'sɪstəhʊd/ *n* Relig congregazione *f* religiosa femminile; (*in feminism*) solidarietà *f inv* femminile

**sister-in-law** *n* (*pl* ~**s-in-law**) cognata *f*

**sisterly** /'sɪstəlɪ/ *a* da sorella

**Sistine Chapel** /'sɪstiːn/ *n* Cappella *f* Sistina

**sit** /sɪt/ *v* (*pt/pp* **sat**, *pres p* **sitting**) ●*vi* essere seduto; (*sit down*) sedersi; ‹*committee:*› riunirsi ●*vt* sostenere ‹*exam*›

■ **sit back** *vi fig* starsene con le mani in mano

■ **sit by** *vi* starsene a guardare

■ **sit down** *vi* mettersi a sedere; **please** ~ **down** si accomodi; ~ **down!** siediti!

■ **sit for** *vi* posare per ‹*portrait*›

■ **sit on** *vt* far parte di ‹*committee*›

■ **sit up** *vi* mettersi seduto; (*not slouch*) star seduto diritto; (*stay up*) stare alzato

**sitcom** /'sɪtkɒm/ *n fam* situation comedy *f inv*

**sit-down** *n Br* **have a** ~ sedersi un momento

**site** /saɪt/ *n* posto *m*; *Archaeol* sito *m*; (*building* ~) cantiere *m* ●*vt* collocare

**sit-in** /'sɪtɪn/ *n* occupazione *f* (*di fabbrica ecc*), sit-in *m inv*

**sitter** /'sɪtə(r)/ *n* (*babysitter*) baby-sitter *mf inv*; (*for artist*) modello *m*

**sitting** /'sɪtɪŋ/ *n* seduta *f*; (*for meals*) turno *m*

**sitting: sitting duck** *n fam* facile bersaglio *m*. **sitting room** *n* salotto *m*. **sitting tenant** *n* locatario *m* residente

**situate** /'sɪtjʊeɪt/ *vt* situare

**situated** /'sɪtjʊeɪtɪd/ *a* situato

**situation** /sɪtjʊ'eɪʃn/ *n* situazione *f*; (*location*) posizione *f*; (*job*) posto *m*; **'**~**s vacant'** 'offerte di lavoro'

**situation report** *n* quadro *m* della situazione

**sit-ups** *npl* addominali *mpl*

**six** /sɪks/ *a & n* sei *m*

**six-pack** *n* confezione *f* da sei (*di bottiglie o lattine*)

**sixteen** /sɪks'tiːn/ *a & n* sedici *m*

**sixteenth** /sɪks'tiːnθ/ *a & n* sedicesimo, -a *mf*

**sixteenth-century** *a* cinquecentesco

**sixth** /sɪksθ/ *a & n* sesto, -a *mf*

**sixth form** n Sch ultimo biennio m facoltativo della scuola superiore

**sixth sense** n sesto senso m

**sixtieth** /ˈsɪkstɪɪθ/ a & n sessantesimo, -a mf

**sixty** /ˈsɪkstɪ/ a & n sessanta m

**size** /saɪz/ n dimensioni fpl; (of clothes) taglia f, misura f; (of shoes) numero m; **what ~ is the room?** che dimensioni ha la stanza?

■ **size up** vt fam valutare

**sizeable** /ˈsaɪzəbl/ a piuttosto grande

**sizzle** /ˈsɪzl/ vi sfrigolare

**skate**[1] /skeɪt/ n inv (fish) razza f

**skate**[2] n pattino m ● vi pattinare

■ **skate over** vt fig glissare su

**skateboard** /ˈskeɪtbɔːd/ n skate-board m inv

**skateboarder** /ˈskeɪtbɔːdə(r)/ n persona f che va in skate-board

**skateboarding** /ˈskeɪtbɔːdɪŋ/ n skate-board m

**skater** /skeɪt/ n pattinatore, -trice mf

**skating** /ˈskeɪtɪŋ/ n pattinaggio m

**skating rink** n pista f di pattinaggio

**skeletal** /ˈskelɪtl/ a also fig scheletrico; (disease) dello scheletro

**skeleton** /ˈskelɪtn/ n scheletro m

**skeleton key** n passe-partout m inv

**skeleton staff** n personale m ridotto

**sketch** /sketʃ/ n schizzo m; Theat sketch m inv ● vt fare uno schizzo di

■ **sketch out** vt delineare

**sketchbook** /ˈsketʃbʊk/ n (for sketching) album m inv per schizzi; (book of sketches) album m inv di schizzi

**sketchily** /ˈsketʃɪlɪ/ adv in modo abbozzato

**sketchpad** /ˈsketʃpæd/ n blocco m per schizzi

**sketchy** /ˈsketʃɪ/ a (-ier, -iest) abbozzato

**skew** /skjuː/ vt alterare (figures)

**skewer** /ˈskjʊə(r)/ n spiedo m

**ski** /skiː/ n sci m inv ● vi (pt/pp skied, pres p skiing) sciare; **go ~ing** andare a sciare

**skid** /skɪd/ n slittata f; **go into a ~** slittare ● vi (pt/pp skidded) slittare

**skid mark** n segno m di frenata

**skier** /ˈskiːə(r)/ n sciatore, -trice mf

**skiing** /ˈskiːɪŋ/ n sci m

**ski instructor** n maestro, -a mf di sci

**ski jump** n (competition) salto m con gli sci; (slope) trampolino m

**skilful** /ˈskɪlfl/ a abile

**skilfully** /ˈskɪlfʊlɪ/ adv abilmente

**ski lift** n impianto m di risalita

**skill** /skɪl/ n abilità f inv

**skilled** /skɪld/ a dotato; (worker) specializzato

**skillet** /ˈskɪlət/ n Am padella f

**skim** /skɪm/ vt (pt/pp skimmed) schiumare; scremare (milk)

■ **skim off** vt togliere

■ **skim over** vt sfiorare (surface, subject)

■ **skim through** vt scorrere

**skimmed milk** /skɪmd/ n latte m scremato

**skimp** /skɪmp/ vi ~ **on** lesinare su

**skimpy** /ˈskɪmpɪ/ a (-ier, -iest) succinto

**skin** /skɪn/ n pelle f; (on fruit) buccia f;

**soaked to the ~** fradicio fino all'osso ● vt (pt/pp **skinned**) spellare

**skin: skin cancer** n cancro m alla pelle. **skincare** n cura f della pella. **skin cream** n crema f per la pelle. **skin-deep** a superficiale. **skin diver** n sub mf inv. **skin diving** n nuoto m subacqueo

**skinflint** /ˈskɪnflɪnt/ n miserabile mf

**skin graft** n innesto m epidermico

**skinhead** /ˈskɪnhed/ n skinhead m

**skinny** /ˈskɪnɪ/ a (-ier, -iest) molto magro

**skint** /skɪnt/ a fam al verde

**skintight** /skɪnˈtaɪt/ a aderente

**skip**[1] /skɪp/ n (container) benna f

**skip**[2] n salto m ● v (pt/pp **skipped**) ● vi saltellare; (with rope) saltare la corda ● vt omettere

**ski: ski pants** npl pantaloni mpl da sci. **ski pass** n ski-pass m inv. **ski pole** n racchetta f da sci

**skipper** /ˈskɪpə(r)/ n skipper m inv

**skipping** /ˈskɪpɪŋ/ n salto m della corda

**skipping rope** n corda f per saltare

**ski rack** n portasci m inv

**ski resort** n stazione f sciistica

**skirmish** /ˈskɜːmɪʃ/ n scaramuccia f

**skirt** /skɜːt/ n gonna f ● vt costeggiare

**skirting board** /ˈskɜːtɪŋ/ n battiscopa m inv, zoccolo m

**ski: ski run** n pista f da sci. **ski slope** n pista f da sci. **ski stick** n racchetta f da sci

**skit** /skɪt/ n bozzetto m comico

**skittish** /ˈskɪtɪʃ/ a (difficult to handle) ombroso; (playful) giocherellone

**skittle** /ˈskɪtl/ n birillo m

**skive** /skaɪv/ vi fam fare lo scansafatiche

**skivvy** /ˈskɪvɪ/ n Br fam sguattera f

**ski wax** n sciolina f

**skulduggery** /skʌlˈdʌgərɪ/ n fam imbrogli mpl

**skulk** /skʌlk/ vi aggirarsi furtivamente

**skull** /skʌl/ n cranio m

**skunk** /skʌŋk/ n moffetta f; (person) farabutto m

**sky** /skaɪ/ n cielo m

**sky: skydiving** n paracadutismo m in caduta libera. **sky-high** a (prices) alle stelle; (rates) esorbitante ● adv **rise ~** salire alle stelle. **skylight** n lucernario m. **skyline** n (of city) profilo m. **skyrocket** vi (prices:) andare alle stelle. **skyscraper** n grattacielo m

**slab** /slæb/ n lastra f; (slice) fetta f; (of chocolate) tavoletta f

**slack** /slæk/ a lento; (person) fiacco ● vi fare lo scansafatiche

■ **slack off** vi rilassarsi

**slacken** /ˈslækn/ vi allentare; ~ **[off]** (trade:) rallentare; (speed, rain:) diminuire ● vt allentare; diminuire (speed)

**slacker** /ˈslækə(r)/ n lazzarone m

**slacks** /slæks/ npl pantaloni mpl sportivi

**slag** /slæg/ n scorie fpl

■ **slag off** vt (pt/pp **slagged**) Br fam sparlare di

**slain** /sleɪn/ see **slay**

**slalom** /'slɑ:ləm/ n slalom m inv
**slam** /slæm/ v (pt/pp **slammed**) ● vt sbattere; (fam: criticize) stroncare ● vi sbattere
**slammer** /'slæmə(r)/ n (fam: prison) galera f
**slander** /'slɑ:ndə(r)/ n diffamazione f ● vt diffamare
**slanderer** /'slɑ:ndərə(r)/ n diffamatore, -trice mf
**slanderous** /'slɑ:nd(ə)rəs/ a diffamatorio
**slang** /slæŋ/ n gergo m
**slangy** /'slæŋɪ/ a gergale
**slant** /slɑ:nt/ n pendenza f; (point of view) angolazione f; **on the ~** in pendenza ● vt pendere; fig distorcere (report) ● vi pendere
**slap** /slæp/ n schiaffo m ● vt (pt/pp **slapped**) schiaffeggiare; (put) schiaffare ● adv in pieno
**slap: slap bang** adv fam **he went ~ ~ into the wall** è andato a sbattere in pieno contro il muro. **slapdash** a fam frettoloso. **slapstick** n farsa f da torte in faccia. **slap-up** a fam di prim'ordine
**slash** /slæʃ/ n taglio m; Typ barra f obliqua ● vt tagliare; ridurre drasticamente (prices); **~ one's wrists** svenarsi
**slat** /slæt/ n stecca f
**slate** /sleɪt/ n ardesia f ● vt fam fare a pezzi
**slater** /'sleɪtə(r)/ n (roofer) addetto m alla ricopertura dei tetti con tegole di ardesia; Zool onisco m
**slatted** /'slætɪd/ a (shutter) a stecche
**slaughter** /'slɔ:tə(r)/ n macello m; (of people) massacro m ● vt macellare; massacrare (people)
**slaughterhouse** /'slɔ:təhaʊs/ n macello m
**Slav** /slɑ:v/ a slavo ● n slavo, -a mf
**slave** /sleɪv/ n schiavo, -a mf ● vi ~ [away] lavorare come un negro
**slave-driver** n schiavista mf
**slavery** /'sleɪvərɪ/ n schiavitù f
**Slavic** /'slɑ:vɪk/ a slavo
**slavish** /'sleɪvɪʃ/ a servile
**slavishly** /'sleɪvɪʃlɪ/ adv in modo servile
**Slavonic** /slə'vɒnɪk/ a slavo
**slay** /sleɪ/ vt (pt **slew**, pp **slain**) ammazzare
**sleaze** /sli:z/ n fam (pornography) pornografia f; (corruption) corruzione f
**sleazy** /'sli:zɪ/ a (-ier, -iest) sordido
**sled** /sled/ n slitta f ● vi andare in slitta
**sledge** /sledʒ/ n slitta f
**sledgehammer** /'sledʒhæmə(r)/ n martello m
**sleek** /sli:k/ a liscio, lucente; (well-fed) pasciuto
**sleep** /sli:p/ n sonno m; **go to ~** addormentarsi; **put to ~** far addormentare; **in my ~** nel sonno; **a good night's ~** una bella dormita ● v (pt/pp **slept**) ● vi dormire; **~ like a log** dormire come un ghiro; **~ on it** dormirci sopra; **~ with sb** andare a letto con qcno ● vt **~s six** ha sei posti letto
■ **sleep around** vi andare a letto con tutti
■ **sleep in** vi dormire più a lungo
**sleeper** /'sli:pə(r)/ n Rail treno m con vagoni

letto; (compartment) vagone m letto; (on track) traversina f; **be a light/heavy ~** avere il sonno leggero/pesante
**sleepily** /'sli:pɪlɪ/ adv con aria assonnata
**sleeping** /'sli:pɪŋ/: **sleeping bag** n sacco m a pelo. **sleeping car** n vagone m letto. **sleeping partner** n Br Comm socio m accomodante. **sleeping pill** n sonnifero m. **sleeping policeman** n dosso m di rallentamento
**sleepless** /'sli:plɪs/ a insonne; **have a ~ night** passare una notte insonne
**sleeplessness** /'sli:plɪsnɪs/ n insonnia f
**sleep: sleepsuit** n tutina f. **sleepwalk** vi essere sonnambulo. **sleepwalker** n sonnambulo, -a mf. **sleepwalking** n sonnambulismo m
**sleepy** /'sli:pɪ/ a (-ier, -iest) assonnato; **be ~** aver sonno
**sleet** /sli:t/ n nevischio m ● vi **it is ~ing** nevischia
**sleeve** /sli:v/ n manica f; (for record) copertina f
**sleeveless** /'sli:vlɪs/ a senza maniche
**sleigh** /sleɪ/ n slitta f
**sleight** /slaɪt/ n **~ of hand** gioco m di prestigio
**slender** /'slendə(r)/ a snello; (fingers, stem) affusolato; fig scarso; (chance) magro
**slept** /slept/ see **sleep**
**sleuth** /slu:θ/ n investigatore m, detective m inv
**slew¹** /slu:/ vi girare
**slew²** see **slay**
**slice** /slaɪs/ n fetta f ● vt affettare; **~d bread** pane m a cassetta
**slick** /slɪk/ a liscio; (cunning) astuto ● n (of oil) chiazza f di petrolio
**slide** /slaɪd/ n scivolata f; (in playground) scivolo m; (for hair) fermaglio m [per capelli]; Phot diapositiva f ● v (pt/pp **slid**) ● vi scivolare ● vt far scivolare
**slide rule** n regolo m calcolatore
**sliding** /'slaɪdɪŋ/ a (door, seat) scorrevole
**sliding scale** n scala f mobile
**slight** /slaɪt/ a leggero; (importance) poco; (slender) esile; **~est** minimo; **not in the ~est** niente affatto ● vt offendere ● n offesa f
**slightly** /'slaɪtlɪ/ adv leggermente
**slim** /slɪm/ a (**slimmer, slimmest**) snello; fig scarso; (chance) magro ● vi dimagrire
**slime** /slaɪm/ n melma f
**slimy** /'slaɪmɪ/ a melmoso; fig viscido
**sling** /slɪŋ/ n Med benda f al collo ● vt (pt/pp **slung**) fam lanciare
**sling-back** n sandalo m (chiuso davanti)
**slingshot** /'slɪŋʃɒt/ n fionda f
■ **slink in** /slɪŋk/ vi (pt/pp **slunk**) entrare furtivamente
**slinky** /'slɪŋkɪ/ a (fam: dress) sexy inv, attillato
**slip** /slɪp/ n scivolata f; (mistake) lieve errore m; (petticoat) sottoveste f; (for pillow) federa f; (paper) scontrino m; **give sb the ~** fam sbarazzarsi di qcno; **~ of the tongue** lapsus

*m inv* ● *v* (*pt/pp* **slipped**) ● *vi* scivolare: (*go quickly*) sgattaiolare; (*decline*) retrocedere; **let sth ~** (*reveal*) lasciarsi sfuggire qcsa ● *vt* **he ~ped it into his pocket** se l'è infilato in tasca; **~ sb's mind** sfuggire di mente a qcno
■ **slip away** *vi* sguscir via; (*time:*) sfuggire
■ **slip into** *vi* infilarsi (*clothes*)
■ **slip on** *vt* infilarsi (*jacket etc*)
■ **slip up** *vi fam* sbagliare
**slip-knot** *n* nodo *m* scorsoio
**slip-on** [**shoe**] *n* mocassino *m*
**slipped disc** /slɪpt'dɪsk/ *n Med* ernia *f* del disco
**slipper** /'slɪpə(r)/ *n* pantofola *f*
**slippery** /'slɪpərɪ/ *a* scivoloso
**slip road** *n* bretella *f*
**slipshod** /'slɪpʃɒd/ *a* trascurato
**slip-up** *n fam* sbaglio *m*
**slit** /slɪt/ *n* spacco *m*; (*tear*) strappo *m*; (*hole*) fessura *f* ● *vt* (*pt/pp* **slit**) tagliare
**slither** /'slɪðə(r)/ *vi* scivolare
**sliver** /'slɪvə(r)/ *n* scheggia *f*
**slob** /slɒb/ *n fam* (*messy*) maiale *m*; (*lazy*) pelandrone *m*
**slobber** /'slɒbə(r)/ *vi* sbavare
**sloe** /sləʊ/ *n* (*fruit*) prugnola *f*; (*bush*) prugnolo *m*
**slog** /slɒg/ *n* [**hard**] **~** sgobbata *f* ● *vi* (*pt/pp* **slogged**) (*work*) sgobbare
**slogan** /'sləʊgən/ *n* slogan *m inv*
**slop** /slɒp/ *vt* (*pt/pp* **slopped**) versare
■ **slop over** *vi* versarsi
**slope** /sləʊp/ *n* pendenza *f*; (*ski ~*) pista *f* ● *vi* essere inclinato, inclinarsi
■ **slope off** *vi* scantonare
**sloping** /'sləʊpɪŋ/ *a* in pendenza
**sloppiness** /'slɒpɪnɪs/ *n* (*of work*) sciatteria *f*
**sloppy** /'slɒpɪ/ *a* (**-ier, -iest**) (*work*) trascurato; (*worker*) negligente; (*in dress*) sciatto; (*sentimental*) sdolcinato
**slosh** /slɒʃ/ *vi fam* (*person, feet:*) sguazzare; (*water:*) scrosciare ● *vt* (*fam: hit*) colpire
**sloshed** /slɒʃt/ *a fam* sbronzo
**slot** /slɒt/ *n* fessura *f*; (*time-~*) spazio *m* ● *vt* (*pt/pp* **slotted**) infilare
■ **slot in** *vi* incastrarsi
**sloth** /sləʊθ/ *n* accidia *f*
**slot machine** *n* distributore *m* automatico; (*for gambling*) slot-machine *f inv*
**slouch** /slaʊtʃ/ *vi* (*in chair*) stare scomposto
**Slovak** /'sləʊvæk/ *a & n* slovacco, -a *mf*
**Slovakia** /sləʊ'vækɪə/ *n* Slovacchia *f*
**Slovene** /'sləʊviːn/ *a & n* sloveno, -a *mf*
**Slovenia** /sləʊə'viːnɪə/ *n* Slovenia *f*
**slovenliness** /'slʌvənlɪnɪs/ *n* sciatteria *f*
**slovenly** /'slʌvnlɪ/ *a* sciatto
**slow** /sləʊ/ *a* lento; **be ~** (*clock:*) essere indietro; **in ~ motion** al rallentatore ● *adv* lentamente
■ **slow down** *vt/i* rallentare
■ **slow up** *vt/i* rallentare
**slowcoach** /'sləʊkəʊtʃ/ *n fam* tartaruga *f*
**slowly** /'sləʊlɪ/ *adv* lentamente
**slowness** /'sləʊnɪs/ *n* lentezza *f*

**slow puncture** *n* foratura *f*
**sludge** /slʌdʒ/ *n* fanghiglia *f*
**slug** /slʌg/ *n* lumacone *m*; (*bullet*) pallottola *f*
**sluggish** /'slʌgɪʃ/ *a* lento
**sluggishly** /'slʌgɪʃnɪs/ *adv* lentamente
**sluice** /sluːs/ *n* chiusa *f*
**sluice gate** *n* saracinesca *f* (*di chiusa*)
**slum** /slʌm/ *n* (*house*) tugurio *m*; **~s** *pl* bassifondi *mpl*
**slumber** /'slʌmbə(r)/ *n* sonno *m* ● *vi* dormire
**slump** /slʌmp/ *n* crollo *m*; (*economic*) depressione *f* ● *vi* crollare
**slung** /slʌŋ/ *see* **sling**
**slunk** /slʌŋk/ *see* **slink**
**slur** /slɜː(r)/ *n* (*discredit*) calunnia *f* ● *vt* (*pt/pp* **slurred**) biascicare
**slurp** /slɜːp/ *vt/i* bere rumorosamente
**slurry** /'slʌrɪ/ *n* (*waste from animals*) liquame *m*; (*waste from factory*) fanghiglia *f* semiliquida; (*of cement*) impasto *m* semiliquido
**slush** /slʌʃ/ *n* pantano *m* nevoso; *fig* sdolcinatezza *f*
**slush fund** *n* fondi *mpl* neri
**slushy** /'slʌʃɪ/ *a* fangoso; (*sentimental*) sdolcinato
**slut** /slʌt/ *n* sgualdrina *f*
**sly** /slaɪ/ *a* (**-er, -est**) scaltro ● *n* **on the ~** di nascosto
**slyly** /'slaɪlɪ/ *adv* scaltramente
**SM** *n abbr* **sadomasochism**
**smacker** /'smækə(r)/ *n* (*fam: kiss*) bacio *m*; **500 ~s** (*£500*) 500 sterline
**smack**[1] /smæk/ *n* (*on face*) schiaffo *m*; (*on bottom*) sculaccione *m* ● *vt* (*on face*) schiaffeggiare; (*on bottom*) sculacciare; **~ one's lips** far schioccare le labbra ● *adv fam* in pieno
**smack**[2] *vi* **~ of** *fig* sapere di
**small** /smɔːl/ *a* piccolo; **be out/work until the ~ hours** fare le ore piccole ● *adv* **chop up ~** fare a pezzettini ● *n* **the ~ of the back** le reni
**small: small ads** *npl* annunci *mpl* [commerciali]. **small business** *n* piccola impresa *f*. **small change** *n* spiccioli *mpl*. **smallholding** *n* piccola tenuta *f*. **small hours** *npl* ore *fpl* piccole. **small letter** *n* lettera *f* minuscola. **small-minded** /-'maɪndɪd/ *a* meschino. **smallpox** *n* vaiolo *m*. **small print** *n* caratteri *mpl* piccoli; **read the ~ ~** *fig* leggere tutto fin nei minimi particolari. **small talk** *n* chiacchiere *fpl*; **make ~** fare conversazione
**smarmy** /'smɑːmɪ/ *a* (**-ier, -iest**) *fam* untuoso
**smart** /smɑːt/ *a* elegante; (*clever*) intelligente; (*brisk*) svelto; **be ~** (*fam: cheeky*) fare il furbo ● *vi* (*hurt*) bruciare
**smart alec**[k] /'smɑːtælɪk/ *n fam* sapientone *m*
**smart card** *n* carta *f* intelligente
**smarten** /'smɑːt(ə)n/ *vt* **~ oneself up** farsi bello
**smartly** /'smɑːtlɪ/ *adv* elegantemente;

(*cleverly*) intelligentemente; (*briskly*) velocemente; (*cheekily*) sfacciatamente

**smart money** *n fam* **the ~ ~ was on Desert Orchid** gli esperti hanno puntato su Desert Orchid

**smash** /smæʃ/ *n* fragore *m*; (*collision*) scontro *m*; *Tennis* schiacciata *f* ● *vt* spaccare; *Tennis* schiacciare ● *vi* spaccarsi; (*crash*) schiantarsi (**into** contro)

■ **smash up** *vt* distruggere ⟨*car, bar*⟩

**smash-and-grab** *n Br* rapina *f* a un negozio (*con sfascio di vetrina*)

**smashed** /smæʃt/ *a* ⟨*window*⟩ in frantumi; ⟨*vehicle*⟩ sfasciato; ⟨*limb*⟩ fracassato; (*fam: on drugs*) fatto; (*fam: on alcohol*) ubriaco fradicio

**smash [hit]** *n* successo *m*

**smashing** /ˈsmæʃɪŋ/ *a fam* fantastico

**smattering** /ˈsmætərɪŋ/ *n* infarinatura *f*

**smear** /smɪə(r)/ *n* macchia *f*; *Med* striscio *m* ● *vt* imbrattare; (*coat*) spalmare (**with** di); *fig* calunniare ● *vi* sbavare

**smear campaign** *n* campagna *f* diffamatoria

**smear test** *n Med* striscio *m*, Pap test *m inv*

**smell** /smel/ *n* odore *m*; (*sense*) odorato *m* ● *v* (*pt/pp* **smelt** *or* **smelled**) ● *vt* odorare; (*sniff*) annusare ● *vi* odorare (**of** di); **that ~s good** ha un buon odore

**smelling salts** /ˈsmelɪŋ/ *npl Med* sali *mpl*

**smelly** /ˈsmelɪ/ *a* (**-ier, -iest**) puzzolente

**smelt**[1] /smelt/ *see* **smell**

**smelt**[2] *vt* fondere

**smidgeon** /ˈsmɪdʒɪn/ *n* (*of something to eat*) pizzico *m*; (*of something to drink*) goccio *m*

**smile** /smaɪl/ *n* sorriso *m* ● *vi* sorridere; **~ at** sorridere a ⟨*sb*⟩; sorridere di ⟨*sth*⟩

**smirk** /smɜːk/ *n* sorriso *m* compiaciuto ● *vi* sorridere con aria compiaciuta

**smithereens** /smɪðəˈriːnz/ *npl* **to/in ~** in mille pezzi

**smithy** /ˈsmɪðɪ/ *n* fucina *f*

**smitten** /ˈsmɪtn/ *a* **~ with** tutto preso da

**smock** /smɒk/ *n* grembiule *m*

**smog** /smɒg/ *n* smog *m inv*

**smoke** /sməʊk/ *n* fumo *m* ● *vt/i* fumare

**smoked** /sməʊkt/ *a* affumicato

**smoke-free zone** *n* zona *f* non-fumatori; '**~**' 'vietato fumare'

**smokeless** /ˈsməʊklɪs/ *a* senza fumo; ⟨*fuel*⟩ che non fa fumo

**smoker** /ˈsməʊkə(r)/ *n* fumatore, -trice *mf*; *Rail* vagone *m* fumatori

**smokescreen** /ˈsməʊkskriːn/ *n* *also fig* cortina *f* di fumo

**smoking** /ˈsməʊkɪŋ/ *n* fumo *m*; '**no ~**' 'vietato fumare'; '**~ or non-~?**' 'fumatori o non fumatori?'

**smoky** /ˈsməʊkɪ/ *a* (**-ier, -iest**) fumoso; ⟨*taste*⟩ di fumo

**smooch** /smuːtʃ/ *vi fam* pomiciare

**smooth** /smuːð/ *a* liscio; ⟨*movement*⟩ scorrevole; ⟨*sea*⟩ calmo; ⟨*manners*⟩ mellifluo ● *vt* lisciare; **~ things over** sistemare le cose

■ **smooth out** *vt* lisciare

**smoothly** /ˈsmuːðlɪ/ *adv* in modo scorrevole; **go ~** andare liscio

**smooth-tongued** /-ˈtʌŋd/ *a pej* mellifluo

**smother** /ˈsmʌðə(r)/ *vt* soffocare

**smoulder** /ˈsməʊldə(r)/ *vi* fumare; (*with rage*) consumarsi

**smudge** /smʌdʒ/ *n* macchia *f* ● *vt/i* imbrattare

**smug** /smʌg/ *a* (**smugger, smuggest**) compiaciuto

**smuggle** /ˈsmʌgl/ *vt* contrabbandare

**smuggler** /ˈsmʌglə(r)/ *n* contrabbandiere, -a *mf*

**smuggling** /ˈsmʌglɪŋ/ *n* contrabbando *m*

**smugly** /ˈsmʌglɪ/ *adv* con aria compiaciuta

**smugness** /ˈsmʌgnɪs/ *n* compiacimento *m*

**smut** /smʌt/ *n* macchia *f* di fuliggine; *fig* sconcezza *f*

**smutty** /ˈsmʌtɪ/ *a* (**-ier, -iest**) fuligginoso; *fig* sconcio

**snack** /snæk/ *n* spuntino *m*

**snack-bar** *n* snack bar *m inv*

**snag**[1] /snæg/ *n* (*problem*) intoppo *m*

**snag**[2] *vt* smagliarsi ⟨*tights*⟩ (**on** con)

**snail** /sneɪl/ *n* lumaca *f*; **at a ~'s pace** a passo di lumaca

**snake** /sneɪk/ *n* serpente *m*

**snake: snakebite** *n* morso *m* di serpente. **snake charmer** *n* incantatore, -trice *mf* di serpenti. **snakes and ladders** *n Br* gioco *m* dell'oca

**snap** /snæp/ *n* colpo *m* secco; (*photo*) istantanea *f* ● *attrib* ⟨*decision*⟩ istantaneo ● *v* (*pt/pp* **snapped**) ● *vi* (*break*) spezzarsi ● *vt* (*break*) spezzare; (*say*) dire seccamente; *Phot* fare un'istantanea di; schioccare ⟨*fingers*⟩

■ **snap at** ⟨*dog*⟩ cercare di azzannare; ⟨*person*⟩ parlare seccamente a

■ **snap off** *vt* **~ sb's head off** *fam* aggredire qcno

■ **snap out** *vi* **~ out of it** venirne fuori

■ **snap up** *vt* afferrare

**snappy** /ˈsnæpɪ/ *a* (**-ier, -iest**) scorbutico; (*smart*) elegante; **make it ~!** sbrigati!

**snapshot** /ˈsnæpʃɒt/ *n* istantanea *f*

**snare** /sneə(r)/ *n* trappola *f*

**snarl** /snɑːl/ *n* ringhio *m* ● *vi* ringhiare

**snarled-up** /snɑːldˈʌp/ *a* ⟨*traffic*⟩ bloccato

**snarl-up** *n* (*in traffic, network*) ingorgo *m*

**snatch** /snætʃ/ *n* strappo *m*; (*fragment*) brano *m*; (*theft*) scippo *m*; **make a ~ at sth** cercare di afferrare qcsa ● *vt* strappare [di mano] (**from** a); (*steal*) scippare; rapire ⟨*child*⟩

**snazzy** /ˈsnæzɪ/ *a fam* sciccoso

**sneak** /sniːk/ *n* (*fam: devious person*) tipo, -a *mf* subdolo, -a; (*Br fam: telltale*) spia *f* ● *vt* (*fam: steal*) fregare; rubare ⟨*kiss*⟩ ● *vi* **~ a glance at** dare una sbirciatina a ● *vi* (*Br fam: tell tales*) fare la spia ● *attrib* ⟨*visit*⟩ furtivo; **have a ~ preview of sth** vedere qcsa in anteprima

■ **sneak away** *vi* sgattaiolare via

■ **sneak in** *vi* sgattaiolare dentro

■ **sneak out** *vi* sgattaiolare fuori

**sneakers** /'sni:kəz/ *npl Am* scarpe *fpl* da ginnastica

**sneaking** /'sni:kɪŋ/ *a* furtivo; ⟨*suspicion*⟩ vago

**sneaky** /'sni:kɪ/ *a* sornione

**sneer** /snɪə(r)/ *n* ghigno *m* ● *vi* sogghignare; ~ **at** ⟨*mock*⟩ ridere di

**sneeze** /sni:z/ *n* starnuto *m* ● *vi* starnutire; **it's not to be ~d at** non ci sputerei sopra

**snide** /snaɪd/ *a fam* insinuante

**sniff** /snɪf/ *n* (*of dog*) annusata *f*; **give a ~** ⟨*person:*⟩ tirare su col naso ● *vi* tirare su col naso ● *vt* odorare ⟨*flower*⟩; sniffare ⟨*glue*⟩; ⟨*dog:*⟩ annusare

**sniffer dog** /'snɪfə/ *n* cane *m* poliziotto (*antidroga, antiterrorismo*)

**sniffle** /'snɪfl/ *n* **have a ~** *or* **the ~s** (*slight cold*) avere un po' di raffreddore; **give a ~** tirar su col naso ● *vi* tirar su col naso

**sniffy** /'snɪfɪ/ *a* (*fam: haughty*) con la puzza sotto il naso

**snigger** /'snɪgə(r)/ *n* risatina *f* soffocata ● *vi* ridacchiare

**snip** /snɪp/ *n* taglio *m*; (*fam: bargain*) affare *m* ● *vt/i* ~ [**at**] tagliare

**snipe** /snaɪp/ *vi* ~ **at** tirare su; *fig* sparare a zero su

**sniper** /'snaɪpə(r)/ *n* cecchino *m*

**snippet** /'snɪpɪt/ *n* **a ~ of information/ news** una breve notizia/informazione

**snivel** /'snɪvl/ *vi* (*pt/pp* **snivelled**) piagnucolare

**snivelling** /'snɪv(ə)lɪŋ/ *a* piagnucoloso

**snob** /snɒb/ *n* snob *mf inv*

**snobbery** /'snɒbərɪ/ *n* snobismo *m*

**snobbish** /'snɒbɪʃ/ *a* da snob; **be ~** ⟨*person:*⟩ essere uno/una snob; ⟨*club etc:*⟩ essere molto snob

**snobbishness** /'snɒbɪʃnɪs/ *n* snobismo *m*

**snog** /snɒg/ *vi Br sl* pomiciare

**snooker** /'snu:kə(r)/ *n* (*game*) snooker *m*; (*shot*) impallatura *f* ● *vt Sport* impallare; *fig* mettere in difficoltà

**snoop** /snu:p/ *n* spia *f* ● *vi fam* curiosare

**snooper** /'snu:pə(r)/ *n* ficcanaso *mf*

**snooty** /'snu:tɪ/ *a fam* sdegnoso

**snooze** /snu:z/ *n* sonnellino *m* ● *vi* fare un sonnellino

**snore** /snɔ:(r)/ *vi* russare

**snoring** /'snɔ:rɪŋ/ *n* il russare

**snorkel** /'snɔ:kl/ *n* respiratore *m*

**snort** /snɔ:t/ *n* sbuffo *n* ● *vi* sbuffare ● *vt* fiutare ⟨*cocaine*⟩

**snot** /snɒt/ *n* (*fam: mucus*) moccolo *m*

**snotty** /'snɒtɪ/ *a fam* ⟨*nose*⟩ moccicoso; (*disagreeable*) sgradevole

**snotty-nosed kid** /-nəʊzd/ *n* mocciosa, -a *mf*

**snout** /snaʊt/ *n* grugno *m*

**snow** /snəʊ/ *n* neve *f* ● *vi* nevicare; **~ed under with** *fig* sommerso di

**snow: snowball** *n* palla *f* di neve ● *vi fig* fare a palle di neve. **snowdrift** *n* cumulo *m* di neve. **snowdrop** *n* bucaneve *m inv*. **snowfall**

*n* nevicata *f*. **snowflake** *n* fiocco *m* di neve.

**snowman** *n* pupazzo *m* di neve.

**snowmobile** /'snəʊməbi:l/ *n* gatto *m* delle nevi. **snowplough** *n* spazzaneve *m inv*.

**snowstorm** *n* tormenta *f*. **snow tyres** *npl* pneumatici *mpl* chiodati

**snowy** /'snəʊɪ/ *a* nevoso

**Snr** *abbr* **Senior**

**snub** /snʌb/ *n* sgarbo *m* ● *vt* (*pt/pp* **snubbed**) snobbare

**snub-nosed** /'snʌbnəʊzd/ *a* dal naso all'insù

**snuff**[1] /snʌf/ *n* tabacco *m* da fiuto

**snuff**[2] *vt* ~ [**out**] spegnere ⟨*candle*⟩; ~ **it** *fam* tirare le cuoia

**snug** /snʌg/ *a* (**snugger, snuggest**) comodo; (*tight*) aderente

**snuggle** /'snʌgl/ *vi* rannicchiarsi (**up to** accanto a)

**so** /səʊ/ *adv* così; **so far** finora; **so am I** anch'io; **so I see** così pare; **you've left the door open – so I have!** hai lasciato la porta aperta – è vero!; **that is so** è così; **so much** così tanto; **so much the better** tanto meglio; **so it is** proprio così; **if so** se è così; **so as to** in modo da; **so long!** *fam* a presto! ● *pron* **I hope/think/am afraid so** spero/penso/temo di sì; **I told you so** te l'ho detto; **because I say so** perché lo dico io; **I did so!** l'ho fatto!; **so saying/doing,...** così dicendo/facendo,...; **or so** circa; **very much so** sì, molto; **and so forth** *or* **on** e così via ● *conj* (*therefore*) perciò; (*in order that*) così; **so that** affinché; **so there!** ecco!; **so what?** e allora?; **so where have you been?** allora, dove sei stato?

**soak** /səʊk/ *vt* mettere a bagno ● *vi* stare a bagno

■ **soak in** *vi* penetrare

■ **soak into** *vt* ⟨*liquid:*⟩ penetrare

■ **soak up** *vt* assorbire

**soaked** /səʊkt/ *a* fradicio; ~ **in sth** impregnato di qcsa

**soaking** /'səʊkɪŋ/ *n* ammollo *m* ● *a & adv* ~ [**wet**] *fam* inzuppato

**so-and-so** *n* Tal dei Tali *mf*; (*euphemism*) specie *f* di imbecille

**soap** /səʊp/ *n* sapone *m*

**soap opera** *n* telenovella *f*, soap opera *f inv*

**soap powder** *n* detersivo *m* in polvere

**soapy** /'səʊpɪ/ *a* (**-ier, -iest**) insaponato

**soar** /sɔ:(r)/ *vi* elevarsi; ⟨*prices:*⟩ salire alle stelle

**S.O.B.** *n Am abbr* **son of a bitch**

**sob** /sɒb/ *n* singhiozzo *m* ● *vi* (*pt/pp* **sobbed**) singhiozzare

**sobbing** /'sɒbɪŋ/ *n* singhiozzi *mpl*

**sober** /'səʊbə(r)/ *a* sobrio; (*serious*) serio

■ **sober up** *vi* ritornare sobrio

**soberly** /'səʊbəlɪ/ *adv* sobriamente; (*seriously*) con aria seria

**sobriety** /sə'braɪətɪ/ *n* (*not drinking*) sobrietà *f*; (*seriousness*) serietà *f*

**sob story** *n* storia *f* lacrimevole

**so-called** /'səʊkɔ:ld/ *a* cosiddetto

**soccer** /'sɒkə(r)/ *n* calcio *m*

**soccer pitch** n campo m di calcio
**soccer player** n giocatore m di calcio
**sociable** /'səʊʃəbl/ a socievole
**social** /'səʊʃl/ a sociale; ⟨sociable⟩ socievole
**social climber** n arrampicatore, -trice mf sociale
**social climbing** n arrivismo m sociale
**socialism** /'səʊʃəlɪzm/ n socialismo m
**socialist** /'səʊʃəlɪst/ a socialista ● n socialista mf
**socialite** /'səʊʃəlaɪt/ n persona f che fa vita mondana
**socialize** /'səʊʃəlaɪz/ vi socializzare
**socially** /'səʊʃəlɪ/ adv socialmente; **know sb ~** frequentare qcno
**social: social security** n previdenza f sociale. **social services** npl servizi mpl sociali. **social work** n assistenza f sociale. **social worker** n assistente mf sociale
**society** /sə'saɪətɪ/ n società f inv
**socio-economic** /səʊsɪəʊi:kə'nɒmɪk/ a socioeconomico
**sociological** /səʊsɪə'lɒdʒɪkl/ a sociologico
**sociologist** /səʊsɪ'ɒlədʒɪst/ n sociologo, -a mf
**sociology** /səʊsɪ'ɒlədʒɪ/ n sociologia f
**sock¹** /sɒk/ n calzino m; ⟨kneelength⟩ calza f
**sock²** fam n pugno m ● vt dare un pugno a
**socket** /'sɒkɪt/ n ⟨of eye⟩ orbita f; ⟨wall plug⟩ presa f [di corrente]; ⟨for bulb⟩ portalampada m inv
**sod** /sɒd/ n fam stronzo m; **you lucky ~!** che fortuna sfacciata!
■ **sod off** vi fam togliersi dai piedi
**soda** /'səʊdə/ n soda f; Am gazzosa f
**soda water** n seltz m inv
**sodden** /'sɒdn/ a inzuppato
**sodium** /'səʊdɪəm/ n sodio m
**sodium bicarbonate** n bicarbonato di sodio
**Sod's Law** /sɒdz/ n fam hum regola f per cui, se qualcosa può andare storto, va storto
**sofa** /'səʊfə/ n divano m
**sofa bed** n divano m letto
**soft** /sɒft/ a morbido, soffice; ⟨voice⟩ sommesso; ⟨light, colour⟩ tenue; ⟨not strict⟩ indulgente; ⟨fam: silly⟩ stupido
**soft: soft-boiled** /-'bɔɪld/ a ⟨egg⟩ bazzotto. **soft contact lenses** npl lenti fpl a contatto morbide. **soft drink** n bibita f analcolica. **soft drug** n droga f leggera
**soften** /'sɒfn/ vt ammorbidire; fig attenuare ● vi ammorbidirsi
**softener** /'sɒf(ə)nə(r)/ n ⟨for water⟩ dolcificatore m; ⟨substance⟩ anti-calcare m inv; ⟨for fabrics⟩ ammorbidente m
**soft: soft furnishings** npl tappeti mpl e tessuti mpl da arredamento. **soft-hearted** a dal cuore tenero. **soft ice-cream** n mantecato m
**softie** /'sɒftɪ/ n fam = **softy**
**softly** /'sɒftlɪ/ adv ⟨say⟩ sottovoce; ⟨treat⟩ con indulgenza; ⟨play music⟩ in sottofondo
**soft: soft-pedal** vt fig minimizzare. **soft porn** n fam pornografia f soft[-core]. **soft sell** n metodo m di vendita basato sulla per-

suasione. **soft soap** n fig lusinghe fpl. **soft-soap** vt fig lusingare. **soft-spoken** a dalla voce dolce. **soft spot** n **have a ~ ~ for sb** avere un debole per qcno. **soft-top** n Auto decappottabile f. **soft touch** n **be a ~ ~** lasciarsi spremere. **soft toy** n pupazzo m di peluche
**software** /'sɒftweə(r)/ n software m
**software: software engineer** n softwarista mf. **software house** n software house f. **software package** n pacchetto m software. **software writer** n scrittore, -trice mf di programmi
**softy** /'sɒftɪ/ n fam ⟨weak person⟩ pappamolle mf inv; ⟨indulgent person⟩ bonaccione, -a mf
**soggy** /'sɒgɪ/ a (-ier, -iest) zuppo
**soil¹** /sɔɪl/ n suolo m
**soil²** vt sporcare
**solace** /'sɒləs/ n sollievo m
**solar** /'səʊlə(r)/ a solare
**solar: solar energy** n energia f solare. **solar panel** n pannello m solare. **solar power** n energia f solare. **solar system** n sistema m solare
**sold** /səʊld/ see **sell**
**solder** /'səʊldə(r)/ n lega f da saldatura ● vt saldare
**soldier** /'səʊldʒə(r)/ n soldato m
■ **soldier on** vi perseverare
**sole¹** /səʊl/ n ⟨of foot⟩ pianta f; ⟨of shoe⟩ suola f
**sole²** n ⟨fish⟩ sogliola f
**sole³** a unico, solo
**sole agency** n rappresentanza f esclusiva
**solecism** /'sɒlɪsɪzm/ n ⟨social⟩ scorrettezza f; ⟨linguistic⟩ solecismo m
**solely** /'səʊllɪ/ adv unicamente
**solemn** /'sɒləm/ a solenne
**solemnity** /sə'lemnətɪ/ n solennità f inv
**solemnly** /'sɒləmlɪ/ adv solennemente
**sol-fa** /'sɒlfɑ:/ n solfeggio m
**solicit** /sə'lɪsɪt/ vt sollecitare ● vi ⟨prostitute:⟩ adescare
**soliciting** /sə'lɪsɪtɪŋ/ n Jur adescamento m
**solicitor** /sə'lɪsɪtə(r)/ n avvocato m
**solicitous** /sə'lɪsɪtəs/ a premuroso
**solicitously** /sə'lɪsɪtəslɪ/ adv premurosamente
**solid** /'sɒlɪd/ a solido; ⟨oak, gold⟩ massiccio; **it took a ~ hour** ci è voluta ben un'ora ● n ⟨figure⟩ solido m; **~s** pl ⟨food⟩ cibi mpl solidi
**solidarity** /sɒlɪ'dærətɪ/ n solidarietà f inv
**solidify** /sə'lɪdɪfaɪ/ vi (pt/pp **-ied**) solidificarsi
**soliloquy** /sə'lɪləkwɪ/ n soliloquio m
**solitaire** /sɒlɪ'teə(r)/ n solitario m
**solitary** /'sɒlɪtərɪ/ a solitario; ⟨sole⟩ solo
**solitary confinement** n cella f di isolamento
**solitude** /'sɒlɪtju:d/ n solitudine f
**solo** /'səʊləʊ/ n Mus assolo m ● a ⟨flight⟩ in solitario ● adv in solitario
**soloist** /'səʊləʊɪst/ n solista mf
**solstice** /'sɒlstɪs/ n solstizio m
**soluble** /'sɒljʊbl/ a solubile

**solution** /sə'luːʃn/ n soluzione f
**solvable** /'sɒlvəbl/ a risolvibile
**solve** /sɒlv/ vt risolvere
**solvency** /'sɒlvənsɪ/ n Fin solvibilità f
**solvent** /'sɒlvənt/ a & n solvente m
**solvent abuse** n uso m di solventi come stupefacenti
**Somali** /səʊ'mɑːlɪ/ a & n somalo, -a mf
**Somalia** /səʊ'mɑːlɪə/ n Somalia f
**sombre** /'sɒmbə(r)/ a tetro; ⟨clothes⟩ scuro
**some** /sʌm/ a (a certain amount of) del; (a certain number of) alcuni, dei; ~ **bread/water** del pane/dell'acqua; ~ **books/oranges** dei libri/delle arance; **I need** ~ **money/books** ho bisogno di soldi/libri; **do** ~ **shopping** fare qualche acquisto; ~ **day** un giorno o l'altro ● pron (a certain amount) un po'; (a certain number) alcuni; **I want** ~ ne voglio; **would you like** ~? ne vuoi?; ~ **of the butter** una parte del burro; ~ **of the apples/women** alcune delle mele/donne
**somebody** /'sʌmbədɪ/ pron qualcuno m; ~ **else will bring it** la porterà un altro ● n **he thinks he's** ~ si crede chissà chi
**somehow** /'sʌmhaʊ/ adv in qualche modo; ~ **or other** in un modo o nell'altro
**someone** /'sʌmwʌn/ pron & n = **somebody**
**somersault** /'sʌməsɔːlt/ n capriola f; **turn a** ~ fare una capriola ● vi fare una capriola
**something** /'sʌmθɪŋ/ pron qualche cosa, qualcosa; ~ **different** qualcosa di diverso; ~ **like** un po' come; (approximately) qualcosa come; **see** ~ **of sb** vedere qcno ogni tanto; **she is** ~ **of an expert** è un'esperta
**sometime** /'sʌmtaɪm/ adv un giorno o l'altro; ~ **last summer** durante l'estate scorsa ● a ex
**sometimes** /'sʌmtaɪmz/ adv qualche volta
**somewhat** /'sʌmwɒt/ adv piuttosto
**somewhere** /'sʌmweə(r)/ adv da qualche parte ● pron ~ **to eat** un posto in cui mangiare
**son** /sʌn/ n figlio m
**sonar** /'səʊnɑː(r)/ n sonar m
**sonata** /sə'nɑːtə/ n sonata f
**song** /sɒŋ/ n canzone f
**song: song and dance** n **make a** ~ ~ **about sth** (fuss) far tante storie per qcsa. **songbird** n uccello m canoro. **songwriter** n compositore, -trice mf di canzoni
**sonic** /'sɒnɪk/ a sonico
**sonic boom** n bang m inv sonico
**son-in-law** n (pl ~**s-in-law**) genero m
**sonnet** /'sɒnɪt/ n sonetto m
**son of a bitch** n fam figlio m di un cane
**sonorous** /'sɒnərəs/ a sonoro; ⟨name⟩ altisonante
**soon** /suːn/ adv presto; (in a short time) tra poco; **as** ~ **as** [non] appena; **as** ~ **as possible** il più presto possibile; ~**er or later** prima o poi; **the** ~**er the better** prima è, meglio è; **no** ~**er had I arrived than...** ero appena arrivato quando...; **I would** ~**er go** preferirei andare; ~ **after** subito dopo
**soot** /sʊt/ n fuliggine f

**soothe** /suːð/ vt calmare
**soothing** /'suːðɪŋ/ a calmante
**sooty** /'sʊtɪ/ a fuligginoso
**sop** /sɒp/ n **throw a** ~ **to** dare un contentino a
**sophisticated** /sə'fɪstɪkeɪtɪd/ a sofisticato; (complex) complesso
**sophistication** /səfɪstɪ'keɪʃn/ n (elegance) sofisticatezza f, raffinatezza f; (complexity) complessità f
**soporific** /sɒpə'rɪfɪk/ a soporifero
**soppiness** /'sɒpɪnɪs/ n fam svenevolezza f
**sopping** /'sɒpɪŋ/ a & adv **be** ~ [**wet**] essere bagnato fradicio
**soppy** /'sɒpɪ/ a (-ier, -iest) fam svenevole
**soprano** /sə'prɑːnəʊ/ n soprano m
**sorcerer** /'sɔːsərə(r)/ n stregone m
**sorceress** /'sɔːsərɪs/ n strega f, maga f
**sorcery** /'sɔːsərɪ/ n (witchcraft) stregoneria f
**sordid** /'sɔːdɪd/ a sordido
**sordidness** /'sɔːdɪdnɪs/ n sordidezza f
**sore** /sɔː(r)/ a dolorante; (Am: vexed) arrabiato; **it's** ~ **fa male**; **have a** ~ **throat** avere mal di gola; **it's a** ~ **point with her** è un punto delicato per lei ● n piaga f
**sorely** /'sɔːlɪ/ adv (tempted) seriamente
**soreness** /'sɔːnɪs/ n dolore m
**sorrel** /'sɒrəl/ n Bot acetosa f
**sorrow** /'sɒrəʊ/ n tristezza f
**sorrowful** /'sɒrəʊfʊl/ a triste
**sorrowfully** /'sɒrəʊfʊlɪ/ adv tristemente
**sorry** /'sɒrɪ/ a (-ier, -iest) (sad) spiacente; (wretched) pietoso; **you'll be** ~! te ne pentirai!; **I am** ~ mi dispiace; **be** or **feel** ~ **for** provare compassione per; ~! scusa!; (more polite) scusi!
**sort** /sɔːt/ n tipo m; **it's a** ~ **of fish** è un tipo di pesce; **be out of** ~**s** (fam: unwell) stare poco bene ● vt classificare; fam sistemare ⟨problem, person⟩
■ **sort out** vt selezionare ⟨papers⟩; fig risolvere ⟨problem⟩; occuparsi di ⟨person⟩
**sort code** n Fin coordinate fpl bancarie
**sorter** /'sɔːtə(r)/ n (on photocopier) fascicolatrice f, fascicolatore m
**SOS** n SOS m; fig segnale m di soccorso
**so-so** a & adv così così
**sotto voce** /sɒtəʊ'vəʊtʃeɪ/ adv ⟨say, add⟩ sottovoce
**soufflé** /'suːfleɪ/ n sufflè m
**sought** /sɔːt/ see **seek**
**sought-after** a ⟨job, brand, person⟩ richiesto
**soul** /səʊl/ n anima f; **poor** ~ poveretto; **there was not a** ~ **in sight** non c'era anima viva
**soul-destroying** /-dɪstrɔɪɪŋ/ a ⟨job⟩ che abbrutisce
**soulful** /'səʊlfʊl/ a sentimentale
**soul: soulmate** n anima f gemella. **soul-searching** /-sɜːtʃɪŋ/ n esame m di coscienza. **soul-stirring** /-stɜːrɪŋ/ a molto commovente
**sound¹** /saʊnd/ a sano; (sensible) saggio;

(*secure*) solido; ⟨*thrashing*⟩ clamoroso ● *adv*
~ **asleep** profondamente addormentato
**sound²** *n* suono *m*; (*noise*) rumore *m*; **I don't**
**like the ~ of it** *fam* non mi suona bene ● *vi*
suonare; (*seem*) aver l'aria; **it ~s to me as**
**if...** mi sa che... ● *vt* (*pronounce*) pronunciare;
*Med* auscoltare ⟨*chest*⟩
■ **sound off** *vi* fare grandi discorsi
■ **sound out** *vt fig* sondare
**sound: sound barrier** *n* muro *m* del suono.
**sound bite** *n* breve frase *f* dal forte impatto
*mediatico*. **sound card** *n Comput* scheda *f* sonora. **sound effect** *n* effetto *m* sonoro.
**sound engineer** *n* tecnico *m* del suono
**soundless** /'saʊndlɪs/ *a* silenzioso
**soundlessly** /'saʊndlɪslɪ/ *adv* silenziosamente
**soundly** /'saʊndlɪ/ *adv* ⟨*sleep*⟩ profondamente; ⟨*defeat*⟩ clamorosamente
**sound: soundproof** *a* impenetrabile al suono ● *vt* insonorizzare. **sound system** *n* (*hifi*)
stereo *m*; (*for disco etc*) impianto *m* audio.
**soundtrack** *n* colonna *f* sonora
**soup** /su:p/ *n* minestra *f*; **in the ~** *fam* nei
pasticci
**souped-up** /su:pt'ʌp/ *a fam* ⟨*engine*⟩ truccato
**soup: soup kitchen** *n* mensa *f* dei poveri.
**soup plate** *n* piatto *m* fondo. **soup spoon** *n*
cucchiaio *m* da minestra
**sour** /'saʊə(r)/ *a* agro; (*not fresh & fig*) acido
**source** /sɔ:s/ *n* fonte *f*; **at ~** ⟨*deducted*⟩ alla
fonte
**sour: sour cream** *n* panna *f* acida. **sour-**
**faced** /saʊə'feɪst/ *a* ⟨*person*⟩ dall'espressione
dura. **sour grapes** *npl pl* **it's just ~ ~** [**on**
**his part**] fa come la volpe con l'uva
**south** /saʊθ/ *n* sud *m*; **to the ~ of** a sud di
● *a* del sud, meridionale ● *adv* a sud
**south: South Africa** *n* Sudafrica *f*. **South**
**African** *a & n* sudafricano, -a *mf*. **South**
**America** *n* America *f* del Sud. **South**
**American** *a & n* sud-americano, -a *mf*.
**southbound** *a* ⟨*traffic*⟩ diretto a sud;
⟨*carriageway*⟩ sud. **south-east** *n* sud-est *m*
**southerly** /'sʌðəlɪ/ *a del sud*
**southern** /'sʌðən/ *a* del sud, meridionale; ~
**Italy** il Mezzogiorno
**southerner** /'sʌðənə(r)/ *n* meridionale *mf*
**southpaw** /'saʊθpɔ:/ *n* (*in boxing*) pugile *m*
mancino
**South Pole** *n* polo *m* Sud
**southward[s]** /'saʊθwəd[z]/ *adv* verso sud
**south-west** /saʊθ'west/ *n* sud-ovest *m*
**south-western** /saʊθ'westən/ *a* sudocci-
dentale
**souvenir** /su:və'nɪə(r)/ *n* ricordo *m*,
souvenir *m inv*
**sovereign** /'sɒvrɪn/ *a & n* sovrano, -a *mf*
**sovereignty** /'sɒvrɪntɪ/ *n* sovranità *f inv*
**Soviet** /'səʊvɪət/ *a* sovietico
**Soviet Union** *n* Unione *f* Sovietica
**sow¹** /saʊ/ *n* scrofa *f*
**sow²** /səʊ/ *vt* (*pt* sowed, *pp* sown *or* sowed)
seminare

**soya bean** /'sɔɪə/ *n* soia *f*
**soy sauce** /sɔɪ/ *n* salsa *f* di soia
**sozzled** /'sɒzld/ *a fam* sbronzo
**spa** /spa:/ *n* stazione *f* termale
**space** /speɪs/ *n* spazio *m* ● *a* ⟨*research etc*⟩
spaziale ● *vt* ~ [**out**] distanziare
**space: space age** *n* era *f* spaziale ● *attrib*
dell'era spaziale. **space bar** *n* barra *f* spazio.
**spacecraft** *n* navetta *f* spaziale. **space**
**cadet** *n fig fam* allucinato, -a *mf*. **space cap-**
**sule** *n* capsula *f* spaziale. **spaced out**
/speɪst'aʊt/ *a fam* **he's completely ~ ~** è
completamente fuori di testa. **space-saving**
*a* poco ingombrante. **spaceship** *n* astronave
*f*. **space shuttle** *n* shuttle *m*. **space travel** *n*
viaggi *mpl* nello spazio. **space walk** *n* passeggiata *f* nello spazio
**spacing** /'speɪsɪŋ/ *n* distanziamento *m*;
**single/double ~** interlinea *m* semplice/dop-
pio
**spacious** /'speɪʃəs/ *a* spazioso
**spade** /speɪd/ *n* vanga *f*; (*for child*) paletta *f*;
**~s** *pl* (*Cards*) picche *fpl*; **call a ~ a ~** dire
pane al pane e vino al vino
**spadework** /'speɪdwɜ:k/ *n fig* lavoro *m* preparatorio
**spaghetti** /spə'getɪ/ *n* spaghetti *mpl*
**spaghetti bolognese** /bɒlə'neɪz/ *n* spaghetti *mpl* al ragù
**spaghetti junction** *n fam* intricato raccordo *m* autostradale
**Spain** /speɪn/ *n* Spagna *f*
**span¹** /spæn/ *n* spanna *f*; (*of arch*) luce *f*; (*of*
*time*) arco *m*; (*of wings*) apertura *f* ● *vt* (*pt/pp*
spanned) estendersi su
**span²** *see* spick
**Spaniard** /'spænjəd/ *n* Spagnolo, -a *mf*
**spaniel** /'spænjəl/ *n* spaniel *m inv*
**Spanish** /'spænɪʃ/ *a* spagnolo ● *n* (*language*)
spagnolo *m*; **the ~** *pl* gli Spagnoli
**spank** /spæŋk/ *vt* sculacciare
**spanking** /'spæŋkɪŋ/ *n* sculacciata *f* ● *a fam*
**at a ~ pace** con passo spedito ● *adv fam* **a ~**
**new car** una macchina nuova di zecca
**spanner** /'spænə(r)/ *n* chiave *f* inglese
**spar** /spa:(r)/ *vi* (*pt/pp* sparred) (*boxing*) allenarsi; (*argue*) litigare
**spare** /speə(r)/ *a* (*surplus*) in più;
(*additional*) di riserva; **go ~** (*fam: be very*
*angry*) andare su tutte le furie ● *n* (*part*) ricambio *m* ● *vt* risparmiare; (*do without*)
fare a meno di; **can you ~ five minutes?**
avresti cinque minuti?; **no expense was**
**~d** non si è badato a spese; **to ~** (*surplus*)
in eccedenza
**spare: spare part** *n* pezzo *m* di ricambio.
**spare ribs** *npl* costine *fpl*. **spare room** *n*
stanza *f* degli ospiti. **spare time** *n* tempo *m*
libero. **spare tyre** *n Br Auto* gomma *f* di scorta; (*fam: fat*) trippa *f*. **spare wheel** *n* ruota *f*
di scorta
**sparing** /'speərɪŋ/ *a* parco (**with** di)
**sparingly** /'speərɪŋlɪ/ *adv* con parsimonia
**spark** /spa:k/ *n* scintilla *f*
■ **spark off** *vt* far scoppiare

**sparkle** /'spɑ:kl/ n scintillio m ● vi scintillare

**sparkling** /'spɑ:klɪŋ/ a frizzante; ⟨wine⟩ spumante

**spark-plug** n Auto candela f

**sparrow** /'spærəʊ/ n passero m

**sparse** /spɑ:s/ a rado

**sparsely** /'spɑ:slɪ/ adv scarsamente; **~ populated** ⟨area⟩ a bassa densità di popolazione

**sparseness** /'spɑ:snɪs/ n (of vegetation) radezza f

**spartan** /'spɑ:tn/ a spartano

**spasm** /'spæzm/ n spasmo m

**spasmodic** /spæz'mɒdɪk/ a spasmodico

**spasmodically** /spæz'mɒdɪklɪ/ adv spasmodicamente

**spastic** /'spæstɪk/ a spastico ● n spastico, -a mf

**spat** /spæt/ see **spit¹**

**spate** /speɪt/ n (series) successione f; **be in full ~** essere in piena

**spatial** /'speɪʃl/ a spaziale

**spatio-temporal** /speɪʃɪəʊ'tempərəl/ a spazio-temporale

**spatter** /'spætə(r)/ vt/i schizzare

**spatula** /'spætjʊlə/ n spatola f

**spawn** /spɔ:n/ n uova fpl (di pesci, rane ecc) ● vi deporre le uova ● vt fig generare

**spay** /speɪ/ vt sterilizzare

**speak** /spi:k/ v (pt spoke, pp spoken) ● vi parlare (**to** a); **~ing!** Teleph sono io! ● vt dire; **~ one's mind** dire quello che si pensa

■ **speak for** vt parlare a nome di; **~ for yourself!** parla per te!

■ **speak of** vt **~ well/ill of sb** parlare bene/male di qcno; **nothing to ~ of** niente di speciale; (quantity) non un granché; **~ing of holidays...** a proposito di vacanze...

■ **speak out** vi (protest) parlare

■ **speak up** vi parlare più forte; **~ up for oneself** farsi valere

**speaker** /'spi:kə(r)/ n parlante mf; (in public) oratore, -trice mf; (of stereo) cassa f

**speaking terms** /'spi:kɪŋ/ npl **we are not on ~** non ci parliamo

**spear** /'spɪə(r)/ n lancia f ● vt trafiggere

**spearhead** /'spɪəhed/ vt fig essere l'iniziatore di

**spearmint** /'spɪəmɪnt/ n menta f verde

**spec** /spek/ n **on ~** fam ⟨take, use⟩ in prova; ⟨go somewhere⟩ per ispezione

**special** /'speʃl/ a speciale

**special: special correspondent** n inviato, -a mf speciale. **special delivery** n espresso m. **special effect** n Cinema, TV effetto m speciale ● attrib **~s** ⟨specialist, team⟩ degli effetti speciali. **special envoy** n inviato, -a mf speciale

**specialist** /'speʃəlɪst/ n specialista mf

**speciality** /speʃɪ'ælətɪ/ n specialità f inv

**specialize** /'speʃəlaɪz/ vi specializzarsi

**specially** /'speʃəlɪ/ adv specialmente; (particularly) particolarmente

**special offer** n vendita f promozionale

**special treatment** n trattamento m di riguardo

**species** /'spi:ʃi:z/ n specie f inv

**specific** /spə'sɪfɪk/ a specifico

**specifically** /spə'sɪfɪklɪ/ adv in modo specifico

**specifications** /spesɪfɪ'keɪʃnz/ npl descrizione f

**specify** /'spesɪfaɪ/ vt (pt/pp **-ied**) specificare

**specimen** /'spesɪmən/ n campione m

**specious** /'spi:ʃəs/ a ⟨argument, reasoning⟩ specioso

**speck** /spek/ n macchiolina f; (particle) granello m

**speckled** /'spekld/ a picchiettato

**specs** /speks/ npl fam occhiali mpl

**spectacle** /'spektəkl/ n (show) spettacolo m

**spectacles** /'spektəklz/ npl occhiali mpl

**spectacular** /spek'tækjʊlə(r)/ a spettacolare

**spectacularly** /spek'tækjʊləlɪ/ adv in modo spettacolare

**spectator** /spek'teɪtə(r)/ n spettatore, -trice mf

**spectator sport** n sport m inv di intrattenimento

**spectre** /'spektə(r)/ n spettro m

**spectrum** /'spektrəm/ n (pl **-tra**) spettro m; fig gamma f

**speculate** /'spekjʊleɪt/ vi speculare

**speculation** /spekjʊ'leɪʃn/ n speculazione f

**speculative** /'spekjʊlətɪv/ a speculativo

**speculator** /'spekjʊleɪtə(r)/ n speculatore, -trice mf

**sped** /sped/ see **speed**

**speech** /spi:tʃ/ n linguaggio m; (address) discorso m; **make a ~, give a ~** fare un discorso

**speech day** n Sch giorno m della premiazione

**speechless** /'spi:tʃlɪs/ a senza parole

**speech: speech therapist** n logoterapista mf. **speech therapy** n logoterapia f. **speech-writer** n persona f che scrive i discorsi di personaggi pubblici

**speed** /spi:d/ n velocità f inv; (gear) marcia f; **at ~** a tutta velocità ● vi (pt/pp **sped**) andare veloce ● (pt/pp **speeded**) (go too fast) andare a velocità eccessiva

■ **speed up** (pt/pp **speeded up**) vt/i accelerare

**speed: speedboat** n motoscafo m. **speed bump** n rallentatore m. **speed camera** n autovelox® m inv

**speedily** /'spi:dɪlɪ/ adv rapidamente

**speeding** /'spi:dɪŋ/ n eccesso m di velocità

**speeding fine** n multa f per eccesso di velocità

**speed limit** n limite m di velocità

**speed merchant** n fam fanatico, -a mf della velocità

**speedometer** /spi:'dɒmɪtə(r)/ n tachimetro m

**speed skating** n pattinaggio m di velocità

**speed trap** n Auto tratto m di strada sul

*quale la polizia controlla la velocità dei veicoli*

**speedy** /'spi:dɪ/ *a* (**-ier, -iest**) rapido

**speleologist** /spi:lɪ'ɒlədʒɪst/ *n* speleologo, -a *mf*

**speleology** /spi:lɪ'ɒlədʒɪ/ *n* speleologia *f*

**spell**[1] /spel/ *n* (*turn*) turno *m*; (*of weather*) periodo *m*

**spell**[2] *v* (*pt/pp* **spelled** *or* **spelt**) ● *vt* **how do you ~...?** come si scrive...?; **could you ~ that for me?** me lo può compitare?; **~ disaster** *fig* essere disastroso ● *vi* **he can't ~** fa molti errori d'ortografia

**spell**[3] *n* (*magic*) incantesimo *m*

■ **spell out** *vt* compitare; *fig* spiegare

**spellbound** /'spelbaʊnd/ *a* affascinato

**spellchecker** /'speltʃekə(r)/ *n Comput* correttore *m* ortografico

**spelling** /'spelɪŋ/ *n* ortografia *f*

**spelt** /spelt/ *see* **spell**[2]

**spend** /spend/ *vt/i* (*pt/pp* **spent**) spendere; passare (*time*)

**spending money** /'spendɪŋ/ *n* soldi *mpl* per le piccole spese

**spendthrift** /'spendθrɪft/ *a* spendaccione; (*habit, policy*) dispendioso ● *n* spendaccione, -a *mf*

**spent** /spent/ *see* **spend**

**sperm** /spɜ:m/ *n* spermatozoo *m*; (*semen*) sperma *m*

**sperm bank** *n* banca *f* dello sperma

**sperm count** *n* conteggio *m* di spermatozoi

**spermicidal** /spɜ:mɪ'saɪdl/ *a* spermicida *inv*

**spermicide** /'spɜ:mɪsaɪd/ *n* spermicida *m*

**spew** /spju:/ *vt/i* vomitare

**sphere** /sfɪə(r)/ *n* sfera *f*

**sphere of influence** *n* sfera *f* di influenza

**spherical** /'sferɪkl/ *a* sferico

**spice** /spaɪs/ *n* spezia *f*; *fig* pepe *m*

**spick** /spɪk/ *a* **~ and span** lindo

**spicy** /'spaɪsɪ/ *a* piccante

**spider** /'spaɪdə(r)/ *n* ragno *m*

**spiel** /ʃpiːl/ *n fam* (*sales pitch*) imbonimento *m*; (*long repetitive speech*) tiritera *f*; **he gave me some ~ about...** mi ha raccontato un sacco di storie su...

**spike** /spaɪk/ *n* punta *f*; *Bot, Zool* spina *f*; (*on shoe*) chiodo *m*

**spikes** *npl* (*shoes*) scarpe *fpl* chiodate

**spiky** /'spaɪkɪ/ *a* (*plant*) spinoso

**spill** /spɪl/ *v* (*pt/pp* **spilt** *or* **spilled**) ● *vt* versare (*blood*); **~ the beans** *fam* vuotare il sacco ● *vi* rovesciarsi

**spillage** /'spɪlɪdʒ/ *n* (*of oil, chemical*) perdita *f*

**spin** /spɪn/ *v* (*pt/pp* **spun**, *pres p* **spinning**) ● *vt* far girare; filare (*wool*); centrifugare (*washing*) ● *vi* girare; (*washing machine:*) centrifugare ● *n* rotazione *f*; (*short drive*) giretto *m*

■ **spin out** *vt* far durare

**spinach** /'spɪnɪdʒ/ *n* spinaci *mpl*

**spinal** /'spaɪnl/ *a* spinale

**spinal column** *n* colonna *f* vertebrale

**spinal cord** *n* midollo *m* spinale

**spindle** /'spɪndl/ *n* fuso *m*

**spindly** /'spɪndlɪ/ *a* affusolato

**spin doctor** *n* persona *f* incaricata di presentare le scelte di un partito politico sotto una luce favorevole

**spin-drier** *n* centrifuga *f*

**spine** /spaɪn/ *n* spina *f* dorsale; (*of book*) dorso *m*; *Bot, Zool* spina *f*

**spineless** /'spaɪnlɪs/ *a fig* smidollato

**spinning** /'spɪnɪŋ/ *n* filatura *f*

**spinning wheel** *n* filatoio *m*

**spin-off** *n* ricaduta *f*

**spinster** /'spɪnstə(r)/ *n* donna *f* nubile; (*old maid, fam*) zitella *f*

**spiny** /'spaɪnɪ/ *a* (*plant, animal*) spinoso

**spiral** /'spaɪrəl/ *a* a spirale ● *n* spirale *f* ● *vi* (*pt/pp* **spiralled**) formare una spirale

**spiral staircase** *n* scala *f* a chiocciola

**spire** /spaɪə(r)/ *n* guglia *f*

**spirit** /'spɪrɪt/ *n* spirito *m*; (*courage*) ardore *m*; **~s** *pl* (*alcohol*) liquori *mpl*; **in good ~s** di buon umore; **in low ~s** abbattuto

■ **spirit away** *vt* far sparire

**spirited** /'spɪrɪtɪd/ *a* vivace; (*courageous*) pieno d'ardore

**spirit level** *n* livella *f* a bolla d'aria

**spirit stove** *n* fornellino *m* [da campeggio]

**spiritual** /'spɪrɪtjʊəl/ *a* spirituale ● *n* spiritual *m*

**spiritualism** /'spɪrɪtjʊəlɪzm/ *n* spiritismo *m*

**spiritualist** /'spɪrɪtjʊəlɪst/ *n* spiritista *mf*

**spit**[1] /spɪt/ *n* (*for roasting*) spiedo *m*

**spit**[2] *n* sputo *m* ● *vt/i* (*pt/pp* **spat**, *pres p* **spitting**) sputare; (*cat:*) soffiare; (*fat:*) sfrigolare; **it's ~ting [with rain]** pioviggina; **the ~ting image of** il ritratto spiccicato di

**spit out** *vt* sputare (*food*); **~ it out!** *fam* sputa l'osso!

**spite** /spaɪt/ *n* dispetto *m*; **in ~ of** malgrado ● *vt* far dispetto a

**spiteful** /'spaɪtfʊl/ *a* indispettito

**spitefully** /'spaɪtfʊlɪ/ *adv* con aria indispettita

**spittle** /'spɪtl/ *n* saliva *f*

**splash** /splæʃ/ *n* schizzo *m*; (*of colour*) macchia *f*; (*fam: drop*) goccio *m* ● *vt* schizzare; **~ sb with sth** schizzare qcno di qcsa ● *vi* schizzare

■ **splash about** *vi* schizzarsi

■ **splash down** *vi* (*spacecraft:*) ammarare

■ **splash out** *vi* (*spend freely*) darsi alle spese folli

**splashdown** /'splæʃdaʊn/ *n* ammaraggio *m*

**splatter** /'splætə(r)/ *vt* schizzare; **~ sb/sth with sth** schizzare qcno/qcsa di qcsa ● *vi* **~ onto/over sth** (*ink, paint:*) schizzare su qcsa

**splay** /spleɪ/ *vt* divaricare (*legs, feet, fingers*); svasare (*end of pipe etc*); strombare (*side of window, door*); **~ed** (*feet, fingers, legs*) scartato

**spleen** /spli:n/ *n Anat* milza *f*

**splendid** /'splendɪd/ *a* splendido

**splendidly** /'splendɪdlɪ/ adv splendidamente

**splendour** /'splendə(r)/ n splendore m

**splint** /splɪnt/ n Med stecca f

**splinter** /'splɪntə(r)/ n scheggia f ●vi scheggiarsi

**splinter group** n gruppo m scissionista

**split** /splɪt/ n fessura f; (quarrel) rottura f; (division) scissione f; (tear) strappo m ● v (pt/pp **split**, pres p **splitting**) ●vt spaccare; (share, divide) dividere; (tear) strappare; ~ **hairs** spaccare il capello in quattro; ~ **one's sides** sbellicarsi dalle risa ●vi spaccarsi; (tear) strapparsi; (divide) dividersi; ~ **on sb** fam denunciare qcno ● a a ~ **second** una frazione di secondo

■ **split up** vt dividersi ● vi ⟨couple:⟩ separarsi

**split: split ends** npl (in hair) doppie punte fpl. **split personality** n sdoppiamento m della personalità. **split screen** n schermo m diviso

**splitting** /'splɪtɪŋ/ a have a ~ **headache** avere un tremendo mal di testa

**splutter** /'splʌtə(r)/ vi farfugliare

**spoil** /spɔɪl/ n ~**s** pl bottino msg ● v (pt/pp **spoilt** or **spoiled**) ●vt rovinare; viziare ⟨person⟩ ●vi andare a male

**spoiler** /'spɔɪlə(r)/ n Auto, Aeron spoiler m inv

**spoilsport** /'spɔɪlspɔːt/ n guastafeste mf inv

**spoilt** /spɔɪlt/ a ⟨child⟩ viziato; **be ~ for choice** non avere che l'imbarazzo della scelta

**spoke¹** /spəʊk/ n raggio m

**spoke²** see speak

**spoken** /'spəʊkən/ see speak ● a ⟨language⟩ parlato; **be ~ for** essere messo da parte per qualcuno

**spokesman** /'spəʊksmən/ n portavoce m inv

**spokesperson** /'spəʊkspɜːsn/ n portavoce mf

**spokeswoman** /'spəʊkswʊmən/ n portavoce f

**sponge** /spʌndʒ/ n spugna f ● vt pulire con la spugna ● vi ~ **on** fam scroccare da

**sponge bag** n nécessaire m inv

**sponge cake** n pan m di Spagna

**sponger** /'spʌndʒə(r)/ n scroccone, -a mf

**spongy** /'spʌndʒɪ/ a spugnoso

**sponsor** /'spɒnsə(r)/ n garante mf; Radio, TV sponsor m inv; (god-parent) padrino m, madrina f; (for membership) socio, -a mf garante ● vt sponsorizzare

**sponsorship** /'spɒnsəʃɪp/ n sponsorizzazione f

**sponsorship deal** n accordo m con uno sponsor

**spontaneity** /spɒntə'neɪɪtɪ/ n spontaneità f

**spontaneous** /spɒn'teɪnɪəs/ a spontaneo

**spontaneously** /spɒn'teɪnɪəslɪ/ adv spontaneamente

**spoof** /spuːf/ n fam parodia f

**spook** /spuːk/ fam vt (haunt) perseguitare; (frighten) spaventare ● n (ghost) fantasma m; (Am: spy) spia f

**spooky** /'spuːkɪ/ a (-ier, -iest) fam sinistro

**spool** /spuːl/ n bobina f

**spooling** /'spuːlɪŋ/ n Comput spooling m

**spoon** /spuːn/ n cucchiaio m ● vt mettere col cucchiaio

**spoonerism** /'spuːnərɪzm/ n scambio m delle iniziali di due parole con effetto umoristico

**spoon-feed** vt (pt/pp **-fed**) fig imboccare

**spoonful** /'spuːnfʊl/ n cucchiaiata f

**sporadic** /spə'rædɪk/ a sporadico

**sporadically** /spə'rædɪklɪ/ adv sporadicamente

**spore** /spɔː(r)/ n spora f

**sporran** /'spɒrən/ n borsa f di cuoio o pelo portata alla cintura dagli scozzesi insieme al kilt

**sport** /spɔːt/ n sport m inv; **be a [good] ~!** sii sportivo! ● vt sfoggiare

**sporting** /'spɔːtɪŋ/ a sportivo

**sporting calendar** n calendario m sportivo

**sporting chance** n possibilità f inv

**sports: sports car** n automobile f sportiva. **sports coat** n, **sports jacket** n giacca f sportiva. **sportsman** n sportivo m. **sportswoman** n sportiva f. **sports writer** n giornalista mf sportivo, -a

**sporty** /'spɔːtɪ/ a (-ier, -iest) sportivo

**spot** /spɒt/ n macchia f; (pimple) brufolo m; (place) posto m; (in pattern) pois m inv; (of rain) goccia f; (of water) goccio m; ~**s** pl (rash) sfogo msg; a ~ **of** fam un po' di; a ~ **of bother** qualche problema; **on the** ~ sul luogo; (immediately) immediatamente; **in a [tight]** ~ fam in difficoltà ● vt (pt/pp **spotted**) macchiare; (fam: notice) individuare

**spot check** n (without warning) controllo m a sorpresa; **do a ~ ~ on sth** dare una controllata a qcsa

**spotless** /'spɒtlɪs/ a immacolato

**spot: spotlight** n riflettore m; fig riflettori mpl. **spot-on** a Br esatto. **spot rate** n Fin tasso m di cambio a vista

**spotted** /'spɒtɪd/ a ⟨material⟩ a pois

**spotty** /'spɒtɪ/ a (-ier, -iest) (pimply) brufoloso

**spot-weld** vt saldare a punti

**spouse** /spaʊz/ n consorte mf

**spout** /spaʊt/ n becco m; **up the** ~ (fam: ruined) all'aria ● vi zampillare (**from** da)

**sprain** /spreɪn/ n slogatura f ● vt slogare; ~ **one's ankle** slogarsi la caviglia

**sprang** /spræŋ/ see spring²

**sprat** /spræt/ n spratto m

**sprawl** /sprɔːl/ vi (in chair) stravaccarsi; ⟨city etc:⟩ estendersi; **go ~ing** (fall) cadere disteso

**sprawling** /'sprɔːlɪŋ/ a ⟨suburb, city⟩ che si propaga disordinatamente; ⟨handwriting⟩ che occupa tutta la pagina

**spray¹** /spreɪ/ n (of flowers) rametto m; (bouquet) mazzolino m

**spray²** n spruzzo m; (from sea) spruzzo m; (preparation) spray m inv; (container) spruzzatore m ● vt spruzzare

**spray-gun** *n* pistola *f* a spruzzo

**spray-on** *a* ⟨*conditioner, glitter*⟩ spray *inv*

**spread** /spred/ *n* estensione *f*; (*of disease*) diffusione *f*; (*paste*) crema *f*; (*fam: feast*) banchetto *m* ● *v* (*pt*/*pp* **spread**) *vt* spargere; spalmare ⟨*butter, jam*⟩; stendere ⟨*cloth, arms*⟩; diffondere ⟨*news, disease*⟩; dilazionare ⟨*payments*⟩; ~ **sth with** spalmare qcsa di ● *vi* spargersi; ⟨*butter:*⟩ spalmarsi; ⟨*disease:*⟩ diffondersi

■ **spread out** *vt* sparpagliare ● *vi* sparpagliarsi

**spread-eagled** /-'i:gld/ *a* a gambe e braccia aperte

**spreadsheet** /'spredʃi:t/ *n Comput* foglio *m* elettronico

**spree** /spri:/ *n fam* **go on a** ~ far baldoria; **go on a shopping** ~ fare spese folli

**sprig** /sprig/ *n* rametto *m*

**sprightly** /'spraitli/ *a* (**-ier, -iest**) vivace

**spring¹** /sprin/ *n* primavera *f*; **in** ~, **in the** ~ in primavera ● *attrib* primaverile

**spring²** *n* (*jump*) balzo *m*; (*water*) sorgente *f*; (*device*) molla *f*; (*elasticity*) elasticità *f* ● *v* (*pt* **sprang**, *pp* **sprung**) ● *vi* balzare; (*arise*) provenire (**from** da); ~ **to mind** saltare in mente ● *vt* **he just sprang it on me** me l'ha detto a cose fatte compiuto

■ **spring up** *vi* balzare; *fig* spuntare

**spring: springboard** *n* trampolino *m*. **spring chicken** *n Culin* pollastrello *m*, pollastrella *f*; **she's no** ~ ~ *fam* non è una giovincella. **spring-clean** *vt* pulire a fondo. **spring-cleaning** *n* pulizie *fpl* di Pasqua. **spring onion** *n* cipollina *f*. **springtime** *n* primavera *f*

**sprinkle** /'sprinkl/ *vt* (*scatter*) spruzzare ⟨*liquid*⟩; spargere ⟨*flour, cocoa*⟩; ~ **sth with** spruzzare qcsa di ⟨*liquid*⟩; cospargere qcsa di ⟨*flour, cocoa*⟩

**sprinkler** /'sprinklɪə(r)/ *n* sprinkler *m inv*; (*for garden*) irrigatore *m*

**sprinkling** /'sprinklin/ *n* (*of liquid*) spruzzatina *f*; (*of pepper, salt*) pizzico *m*; (*of flour, sugar*) spolveratina *f*; (*of knowledge*) infarinatura *f*; (*of people*) pugno *m*

**sprint** /sprint/ *n* sprint *m inv* ● *vi* fare uno sprint; *Sport* sprintare

**sprinter** /'sprintə(r)/ *n* sprinter *mf inv*

**sprite** /sprait/ *n* folletto *m*

**spritzer** /'spritsə(r)/ *n* spriz *m inv*, spritzer *m inv*

**sprout** /spraut/ *n* germoglio *m*; [**Brussels**] ~**s** *pl* cavolini *mpl* di Bruxelles ● *vi* germogliare

**spruce** /spru:s/ *a* elegante ● *n* abete *m*

■ **spruce up** *vt* dare una ripulita a

**sprung** /sprʌŋ/ *see* **spring²** ● *a* molleggiato

**spry** /sprai/ *a* (**-er, -est**) arzillo

**spud** /spʌd/ *n fam* patata *f*

**spun** /spʌn/ *see* **spin**

**spur** /spɜ:(r)/ *n* sperone *m*; (*stimulus*) stimolo *m*; (*road*) svincolo *m*; **on the** ~ **of the moment** su due piedi ● *vt* (*pt*/*pp* **spurred**) ~ [**on**] *fig* spronare

**spurious** /'spjʊərɪəs/ *a* falso

**spuriously** /'spjʊərɪəslɪ/ *adv* falsamente

**spurn** /spɜ:n/ *vt* sdegnare

**spurt** /spɜ:t/ *n* getto *m*; *Sport* scatto *m*; **put on a** ~ fare uno scatto ● *vi* sprizzare; (*increase speed*) scattare

**sputter** /'spʌtə(r)/ *vi* ⟨*engine:*⟩ scoppiettare ● *n* colpi *mpl* irregolari del motore

**spy** /spai/ *n* spia *f* ● *vi* spiare ● *vt* (*fam: see*) spiare

■ **spy on** *vt* spiare

■ **spy out** *vt* esplorare

**spying** /'spaiɪŋ/ *n* spionaggio *m*

**squabble** /'skwɒbl/ *n* bisticcio *m* ● *vi* bisticciare

**squabbling** /'skwɒblɪŋ/ *n* bisticci *mpl*

**squad** /skwɒd/ *n* squadra *f*

**squaddie** /'skwɒdɪ/ *n Br fam* soldato *m* semplice

**squadron** /'skwɒdrən/ *n Mil* squadrone *m*; *Aeron, Naut* squadriglia *f*

**squalid** /'skwɒlɪd/ *a* squallido

**squalidly** /'skwɒlɪdlɪ/ *adv* squallidamente

**squall** /skwɔ:l/ *n* (*howl*) strillo *m*; (*storm*) bufera *f* ● *vi* strillare

**squally** /'skwɔ:lɪ/ *a* burrascoso

**squalor** /'skwɒlə(r)/ *n* squallore *m*

**squander** /'skwɒndə(r)/ *vt* sprecare

**square** /skweə/ *a* quadrato; (*meal*) sostanzioso; (*fam: old-fashioned*) vecchio stampo; **all** ~ *fam* pari ● *n* quadrato *m*; (*in city*) piazza *f*; (*on chessboard*) riquadro *m*; **be back to** ~ **one** riessere al punto di partenza ● *vt* (*settle*) far quadrare; *Math* elevare al quadrato ● *vi* (*agree*) armonizzare

■ **square up** *vi* (*settle accounts*) saldare

■ **square up to** *vt* affrontare

**square dance** *n* quadriglia *f*

**squarely** /'skweəlɪ/ *adv* direttamente

**square root** *n* radice *f* quadrata

**squash** /skwɒʃ/ *n* calca *f*; (*drink*) spremuta *f*; (*sport*) squash *m*; (*vegetable*) zucca *f* ● *vt* schiacciare; soffocare ⟨*rebellion*⟩

**squashy** /'skwɒʃɪ/ *a* floscio

**squat** /skwɒt/ *a* tarchiato ● *n fam* edificio *m* occupato abusivamente ● *vi* (*pt*/*pp* **squatted**) accovacciarsi; ~ **in** occupare abusivamente

**squatter** /'skwɒtə(r)/ *n* occupante *mf* abusivo, -a

**squaw** /skwɔ:/ *n* squaw *f inv*

**squawk** /skwɔ:k/ *n* gracchio *m* ● *vi* gracchiare

**squeak** /skwi:k/ *n* squittio *m*; (*of hinge, brakes*) cigolio *m* ● *vi* squittire; ⟨*hinge, brakes:*⟩ cigolare

**squeaking** /'skwi:kɪŋ/ *n* (*of door, hinge*) cigolio *m*

**squeaky** /'skwi:kɪ/ *a* ⟨*door, hinge*⟩ cigolante

**squeaky-clean** *a fam* ⟨*glass, hair*⟩ lucente; ⟨*floor*⟩ tirato a specchio; *fig* ⟨*person*⟩ senza vizi; ⟨*company*⟩ al di sopra di ogni sospetto

**squeal** /skwi:l/ *n* strillo *m*; (*of brakes*) cigolio *m* ● *vi* strillare; *sl* spifferare

311

**squeamish** /'skwi:mɪʃ/ *a* dallo stomaco delicato; (*scrupulous*) troppo scrupoloso

**squeegee** /'skwi:dʒi:/ *n Phot* rullo *m* asciugatore; (*for glasses*) lavavetri *m inv*

**squeeze** /skwi:z/ *n* stretta *f*; (*crush*) pigia pigia *m inv*; **give sb's hand a ~** dare a qcno una stretta di mano ● *vt* premere; (*to get juice*) spremere; stringere ‹*hand*›; (*force*) spingere a forza; (*fam: extort*) estorcere (**out of** da)

■ **squeeze in/out** *vi* sgusciare dentro/fuori

■ **squeeze up** *vi* stringersi

**squelch** /skwelʧ/ *vi* sguazzare

**squib** /skwɪb/ *n* petardo *m*

**squid** /skwɪd/ *n* calamaro *m*

**squidgy** /'skwɪdʒɪ/ *a* (*Br fam: squashy*) molliccio

**squiggle** /'skwɪgl/ *n* scarabocchio *m*

**squint** /skwɪnt/ *n* strabismo *m* ● *vi* essere strabico

**squire** /'skwaɪə(r)/ *n* signorotto *m* di campagna

**squirm** /skwɜ:m/ *vi* contorcersi; (*feel embarrassed*) sentirsi imbarazzato

**squirrel** /'skwɪrəl/ *n* scoiattolo *m*

**squirt** /skwɜ:t/ *n* spruzzo *m*; (*fam: person*) presuntuoso *m* ● *vt/i* spruzzare

**St** *abbr* (**Saint**) S; *abbr* **Street**

**stab** /stæb/ *n* pugnalata *f*, coltellata *f*; (*sensation*) fitta *f*; (*fam: attempt*) tentativo *m* ● *vt* (*pt/pp* **stabbed**) pugnalare, accoltellare

**stability** /stə'bɪlətɪ/ *n* stabilità *f inv*

**stabilization** /steɪbɪlaɪ'zeɪʃn/ *n* stabilizzazione *f*

**stabilize** /'steɪbɪlaɪz/ *vt* stabilizzare ● *vi* stabilizzarsi

**stabilizer** /'steɪbɪlaɪzə(r)/ *n* stabilizzatore *m*; (*on bike*) rotella *f*; (*in food*) stabilizzante *m*

**stable**[1] /'steɪbl/ *a* stabile

**stable**[2] *n* stalla *f*; (*establishment*) scuderia *f*

**staccato** /stə'kɑ:təʊ/ *a Mus* staccato; ‹*gasps, shots*› intermittente ● *adv* ‹*play*› staccatamente

**stack** /stæk/ *n* catasta *f*; (*of chimney*) comignolo *m*; (*chimney*) ciminiera *f*; (*fam: large quantity*) montagna *f*; **~s of** ‹*money, time, work*› un sacco di ● *vt* accatastare

**stadium** /'steɪdɪəm/ *n* stadio *m*

**staff** /stɑ:f/ *n* (*stick*) bastone *m*; (*employees*) personale *m*; (*teachers*) corpo *m* insegnante; *Mil* Stato *m* Maggiore ● *vt* fornire di personale

**staffroom** /'stɑ:fru:m/ *n Sch* sala *f* insegnanti

**stag** /stæg/ *n* cervo *m*

**stage** /steɪdʒ/ *n* palcoscenico *m*; (*profession*) teatro *m*; (*in journey*) tappa *f*; (*in process*) stadio *m*; **go on the ~** darsi al teatro; **by** *or* **in ~s** a tappe ● *vt* mettere in scena; (*arrange*) organizzare

**stage: stagecoach** *n* diligenza *f*. **stage door** *n* ingresso *m* degli artisti. **stage fright** *n* panico *m* da palcoscenico. **stage-manage** *vt fig* orchestrare. **stage manager** *n* diretto-

re, -trice *mf* di scena. **stage-struck** /-strʌk/ *a* appassionatissimo di teatro

**stagger** /'stægə(r)/ *vi* barcollare ● *vt* sbalordire; scaglionare ‹*holidays, payments etc*›; **I was ~ed** sono rimasto sbalordito ● *n* vacillamento *m*

**staggering** /'stægərɪŋ/ *a* sbalorditivo

**stagnant** /'stægnənt/ *a* stagnante

**stagnate** /stæg'neɪt/ *vi fig* [ri]stagnare

**stagnation** /stæg'neɪʃn/ *n fig* inattività *f*

**stag night, stag party** *n* addio *m* al celibato

**staid** /steɪd/ *a* posato

**stain** /steɪn/ *n* macchia *f*; (*for wood*) mordente *m* ● *vt* macchiare; ‹*wood*› dare il mordente a

**stained glass** /steɪnd'glɑ:s/ *n* vetro *m* colorato

**stained-glass window** *n* vetrata *f* colorata

**stainless** /'steɪnlɪs/ *a* senza macchia

**stainless steel** *n* acciaio *m* inossidabile

**stain remover** *n* smacchiatore *m*

**stair** /steə(r)/ *n* gradino *m*; **~s** *pl* scale *fpl*

**staircase** /'steəkeɪs/ *n* scale *fpl*

**stake** /steɪk/ *n* palo *m*; (*wager*) posta *f*; *Comm* partecipazione *f*; **at ~** in gioco ● *vt* puntellare; (*wager*) scommettere; **~ a claim to sth** rivendicare qcsa

**stake-out** *n fam* sorveglianza *f*

**stalactite** /'stæləktaɪt/ *n* stalattite *f*

**stalagmite** /'stæləgmaɪt/ *n* stalagmite *f*

**stale** /steɪl/ *a* stantio; ‹*air*› viziato; (*uninteresting*) trito [e ritrito]

**stalemate** /'steɪlmeɪt/ *n* (*in chess*) stallo *m*; (*deadlock*) situazione *f* di stallo

**stalk**[1] /stɔ:k/ *n* gambo *m*

**stalk**[2] *vt* inseguire ● *vi* camminare impettito

**stalker** /'stɔ:kə(r)/ *n* (*of person*) persona *f* che perseguita qcno per cui ha una fissazione maniacale

**stalking** /'stɔ:kɪŋ/ *n* (*of person*) persecuzione *f* di una persona per cui si ha una fissazione maniacale

**stall** /stɔ:l/ *n* box *m inv*; (*in market*) bancarella *f*; **~s** *pl Theat* platea *f* ● *vi* ‹*engine:*› spegnersi; *fig* temporeggiare ● *vt* far spegnere ‹*engine*›; tenere a bada ‹*person*›

**stallholder** /'stɔ:lhəʊldə(r)/ *n* bancarellista *mf*

**stallion** /'stæljən/ *n* stallone *m*

**stalwart** /'stɔ:lwət/ *a* fedele ● *n* sostenitore *m* fedele

**stamina** /'stæmɪnə/ *n* [capacità *f* di] resistenza *f*

**stammer** /'stæmə(r)/ *n* balbettio *m* ● *vt/i* balbettare

**stamp** /stæmp/ *n* (*postage ~*) francobollo *m*; (*instrument*) timbro *m*; *fig* impronta *f* ● *vt* affrancare ‹*letter*›; timbrare ‹*bill*›; battere ‹*feet*›

■ **stamp out** *vt* spegnere; *fig* soffocare

**stamp collecting** *n* filatelia *f*

**stamp collector** *n* collezionista *mf* di francobolli

**stamped addressed envelope** busta *f* affrancata per la risposta

**stampede** /stæm'pi:d/ *n* fuga *f* precipitosa; *fam* fuggifuggi *m inv* ● *vi* fuggire precipitosamente

**stance** /sta:ns/ *n* posizione *f*

**stand** /stænd/ *n* (*for bikes*) rastrelliera *f*; (*at exhibition*) stand *m inv*; (*in market*) bancarella *f*; (*in stadium*) gradinata *f*; *fig* posizione *f* ● *v* (*pt/pp* **stood**) ● *vi* stare in piedi; (*rise*) alzarsi [in piedi]; (*be*) trovarsi; (*be candidate*) essere candidato (**for** a); (*stay valid*) rimanere valido; **I don't know where I ~** non so qual'è la mia posizione; **~ still** non muoversi; **~ firm** *fig* tener duro; **~ on ceremony** formalizzarsi; **~ together** essere solidali; **~ to lose/gain** rischiare di perdere/vincere; **~ to reason** essere logico ● *vt* (*withstand*) resistere a; (*endure*) sopportare; (*place*) mettere; **~ a chance** avere una possibilità; **~ one's ground** tener duro; **~ the test of time** superare la prova del tempo; **~ sb a beer** offrire una birra a qcno

■ **stand back** *vi* (*withdraw*) farsi da parte

■ **stand by** *vi* stare a guardare; (*be ready*) essere pronto ● *vt* (*support*) appoggiare

■ **stand down** *vi* (*retire*) ritirarsi

■ **stand for** *vt* (*mean*) significare; (*tolerate*) tollerare

■ **stand in for** *vt* sostituire

■ **stand out** *vi* spiccare

■ **stand up** *vi* alzarsi [in piedi]

■ **stand up for** *vt* prendere le difese di; **~ up for oneself** farsi valere

■ **stand up to** *vt* affrontare

**stand-alone** *a Comput* indipendente

**standard** /'stændəd/ *a* standard; **be ~ practice** essere pratica corrente ● *n* standard *m inv*; *Techn* norma *f*; (*level*) livello *m*; (*quality*) qualità *f inv*; (*flag*) stendardo *m*; **~s** *pl* (*morals*) valori *mpl*

**standardization** /stændədər'zeɪʃn/ *n* standardizzazione *f*

**standardize** /'stændədaɪz/ *vt* standardizzare

**standard lamp** *n* lampada *f* a stelo

**standard of living** *n* tenore *m* di vita

**standby** /'stændbaɪ/ *n* (*person*) riserva *f* ● *attrib* (*circuit, battery*) di emergenza; (*passenger*) in lista di attesa; (*ticket*) stand-by *inv* ● *adv* (*fly*) con biglietto stand-by

**stand-in** *n* controfigura *f*

**standing** /'stændɪŋ/ *a* (*erect*) in piedi; (*permanent*) permanente ● *n* posizione *f*; (*duration*) durata *f*

**standing: standing order** *n* ordine *m* permanente. **standing ovation** *n* give sb a ~ ~ alzarsi per applaudire qcno. **standing room** *n* posti *mpl* in piedi

**stand-offish** /stænd'ɒfɪʃ/ *a* scostante

**stand: standpoint** *n* punto *m* di vista. **standstill** *n* **come to a ~** fermarsi; **at a ~** in un periodo di stasi. **stand-up** *a* (*buffet*) in piedi; (*argument*) accanito ● *n* (*comedy*) recital *m inv* di un comico. **stand-up comedian**

comico *m* che intrattiene il pubblico con barzellette

**stank** /stæŋk/ *see* **stink**

**stanza** /'stænzə/ *n* strofa *f*

**staple**[1] /'steɪpl/ *n* (*product*) prodotto *m* principale

**staple**[2] /'steɪpl/ *n* graffa *f*, pinzatrice *f* ● *vt* pinzare

**staple diet** *n* a ~ ~ **of** una dieta basata principalmente su

**staple gun** *n* pistola *f* sparachiodi

**stapler** /'steɪplə(r)/ *n* pinzatrice *f*, cucitrice *f*

**staple remover** *n* levapunti *m inv*

**star** /sta:(r)/ *n* stella *f*; (*asterisk*) asterisco *m*; *Theat, Cinema, Sport* divo, -a *mf*, stella *f* ● *vi* (*pt/pp* **starred**) essere l'interprete principale (**in** di)

**starboard** /'sta:bəd/ *n* tribordo *m*

**starch** /sta:tʃ/ *n* amido *m* ● *vt* inamidare

**starchy** /'sta:tʃɪ/ *a* ricco di amido; *fig* compito

**stardom** /'sta:dəm/ *n* celebrità *f*

**stare** /steə(r)/ *n* sguardo *m* fisso ● *vi* **it's rude to ~** è da maleducati fissare la gente; **~ at** fissare; **~ into space** guardare nel vuoto

**starfish** /'sta:fɪʃ/ *n* stella *f* di mare

**stark** /sta:k/ *a* austero; (*contrast*) forte ● *adv* completamente; **~ naked** completamente nudo

**starlet** /'sta:lɪt/ *n* stellina *f*

**starling** /'sta:lɪŋ/ *n* storno *m*

**starlit** /'sta:lɪt/ *a* stellato

**starry** /'sta:rɪ/ *a* stellato

**starry-eyed** /-'aɪd/ *a fam* ingenuo

**star-struck** /-strʌk/ *a* ossessionato dalle celebrità

**star-studded** /-stʌdɪd/ *a* (*cast, line-up*) con molti interpreti famosi; (*sky*) stellato

**start** /sta:t/ *n* inizio *m*; (*departure*) partenza *f*; (*jump*) sobbalzo *m*; **from the ~** [fin] dall'inizio; **for a ~** tanto per cominciare; **give sb a ~** *Sport* dare un vantaggio a qcno ● *vi* [in]cominciare; (*set out*) avviarsi; (*engine, car:*) partire; (*jump*) trasalire; **to ~ with,...** tanto per cominciare,... ● *vt* [in]cominciare; (*cause*) dare inizio a; (*found*) mettere su; mettere in moto (*car*); mettere in giro (*rumour*)

■ **start off** *vi* (*begin*) cominciare

■ **start on** *vt fam* (*attack*) criticare; (*nag*) punzecchiare

■ **start out** *vi* (*on journey*) partire

■ **start up** *vt* mettere in funzione (*engine*); intentare (*business*)

**starter** /'sta:tə(r)/ *n Culin* primo *m* [piatto *m*]; (*in race: giving signal*) starter *m inv*; (*participant*) concorrente *mf*; *Auto* motorino *m* d'avviamento

**starting point** /'sta:tɪŋ/ *n* punto *m* di partenza

**starting salary** *n* stipendio *m* iniziale

**startle** /'sta:tl/ *vt* far trasalire; (*news:*) sconvolgere

**startling** /'sta:tlɪŋ/ *a* sconvolgente

**start-up capital** *n* capitale *m* di avviamento

**starvation** /sta:'veɪʃn/ *n* fame *f*

**starve** /stɑ:v/ vi morire di fame ● vt far morire di fame

**stash** /stæʃ/ vt fam ~ [away] nascondere

**state** /steɪt/ n stato m; Pol Stato m; (grand style) pompa f; ; **be in a ~** ⟨person:⟩ essere agitato; **lie in ~** essere esposto ● attrib di Stato; Sch pubblico; (with ceremony) di gala ● vt dichiarare; (specify) precisare

**state-aided** /-'eɪdɪd/ a sovvenzionato dallo Stato

**State Department** n Am Pol ministero m degli [affari] esteri

**stateless** /'steɪtlɪs/ a apolide

**stately** /'steɪtlɪ/ a (-ier, -iest) maestoso

**stately home** n dimora f signorile

**statement** /'steɪtmənt/ n dichiarazione f; Jur deposizione f; (from bank) estratto m conto; (account) rapporto m

**state: state of the art** a ⟨technology⟩ il più avanzato. **state of emergency** n stato m di emergenza. **state of play** punteggio m

**stateside** /'steɪtsaɪd/ a degli Stati Uniti ● adv negli Stati Uniti

**statesman** /'steɪtsmən/ n statista m

**static** /'stætɪk/ a statico

**static electricity** n elettricità f statica

**station** /'steɪʃn/ n stazione f; (police) commissariato m ● vt appostare ⟨guard⟩; **be ~ed in Germany** essere di stanza in Germania

**stationary** /'steɪʃənərɪ/ a immobile

**stationer** /'steɪʃənə(r)/ n ~'s [shop] cartoleria f

**stationery** /'steɪʃənərɪ/ n cartoleria f

**station wagon** n Am familiare f

**statistical** /stə'tɪstɪkl/ a statistico

**statistically** /stə'tɪstɪklɪ/ adv statisticamente

**statistician** /stætɪs'tɪʃn/ n esperto m di statistica

**statistics** /stə'tɪstɪks/ n (subject) statistica f; (pl: figures) statistiche fpl

**statue** /'stætju:/ n statua f

**statuesque** /stætju'esk/ a statuario

**stature** /'stætʃə(r)/ n statura f

**status** /'steɪtəs/ n condizione f; (high rank) alto rango m

**status bar** n Comput barra f di stato

**status symbol** n status symbol m inv

**statute** /'stætju:t/ n statuto m

**statutory** /'stætjʊtərɪ/ a statutario

**staunch** /stɔ:ntʃ/ a fedele

**staunchly** /'stɔ:ntʃlɪ/ adv fedelmente

**stave** /steɪv/ vt ~ **off** tenere lontano

**stay** /steɪ/ n soggiorno m ● vi restare, rimanere; (reside) alloggiare; ~ **the night** passare la notte; ~ **put** non muoversi ● vt ~ **the course** resistere fino alla fine

■ **stay away** vi stare lontano

■ **stay behind** vi non andare con gli altri

■ **stay in** vi (at home) stare in casa; Sch restare a scuola dopo le lezioni

■ **stay on** vi (remain) rimanere; ~ **on at school** continuare gli studi

■ **stay up** vi stare su; ⟨person:⟩ stare alzato

**staying power** /'steɪɪŋ/ n capacità f di resistenza

**STD** abbr **sexually transmitted disease**

**STD [area] code** n Br prefisso m [di teleselezione]

**stead** /sted/ n **in his ~** in sua vece; **stand sb in good ~** tornare utile a qcno

**steadfast** /'stedfɑ:st/ a fedele; ⟨refusal⟩ fermo

**steadily** /'stedɪlɪ/ adv (continually) continuamente

**steady** /'stedɪ/ a (-ier, -iest) saldo, fermo; ⟨breathing⟩ regolare; ⟨job, boyfriend⟩ fisso; (dependable) serio ● adv **be going ~** ⟨couple:⟩ fare coppia fissa

**steak** /steɪk/ n (for stew) spezzatino m; (for grilling, frying) bistecca f

**steal** /sti:l/ vt (pt stole, pp stolen) rubare (from da); ~ **the show** essere al centro d'attenzione

■ **steal in/out** vi entrare/uscire furtivamente

**stealth** /stelθ/ n **by ~** di nascosto

**stealthily** /'stelθɪlɪ/ adv furtivamente

**stealthy** /'stelθɪ/ a furtivo

**steam** /sti:m/ n vapore m; **under one's own ~** fam da solo; **let off ~** fig sfogarsi ● vt Culin cucinare a vapore ● vi fumare

■ **steam up** vi ⟨window:⟩ appannarsi

**steamed up** /sti:md'ʌp/ a **get ~ up** (angry) andare su tutte le furie

**steam engine** n locomotiva f

**steam iron** n ferro m [da stiro] a vapore

**steamer** /'sti:mə(r)/ n piroscafo m; (saucepan) pentola f a vapore

**steamroller** /'sti:mrəʊlə(r)/ n rullo m compressore

**steamy** /'sti:mɪ/ a appannato; ⟨fig: scene⟩ spinto

**steel** /sti:l/ n acciaio m ● vt ~ **oneself** temprarsi

**steel wool** n lana f d'acciaio

**steely** /'sti:lɪ/ a d'acciaio

**steep¹** /sti:p/ vt (soak) lasciare a bagno; ~**ed in** fig immerso in

**steep²** a ripido; ⟨fam: price⟩ esorbitante

**steeple** /'sti:pl/ n campanile m

**steeplechase** /'sti:plˌtʃeɪs/ n corsa f ippica a ostacoli

**steeplejack** /'sti:plˌdʒæk/ n persona f che ripara campanili e ciminiere

**steeply** /'sti:plɪ/ adv ripidamente

**steer** /stɪə(r)/ vt/i guidare; ~ **clear of** stare alla larga da

**steering** /'stɪərɪŋ/ n Auto sterzo m

**steering: steering column** n Auto piantone m dello sterzo. **steering committee** n comitato m direttivo. **steering lock** n Auto bloccasterzo m; (turning circle) angolo m di massima sterzata. **steering wheel** n volante m

**stem¹** /stem/ n stelo m; (of glass) gambo m; (of word) radice f ● vi (pt/pp stemmed) ~ **from** derivare da

**stem²** vt (pt/pp stemmed) contenere

**stem ginger** n zenzero m sciroppato

**stench** /stentʃ/ n fetore m
**stencil** /'stensl/ n stampino m; (decoration) stampo m ● vt (pt/pp **stencilled**) stampinare
**stenographer** /stɪ'nɒgrəfə(r)/ n stenografo, -a mf
**stenography** /stɪ'nɒgrəfɪ/ n stenografia f
**step** /step/ n passo m; (stair) gradino m; ~s pl (ladder) scaleo m; **in** ~ al passo; **be out of** ~ non stare al passo; ~ **by** ~ un passo alla volta; ~ **into** (pt/pp **stepped**) ~ **into** entrare in; ~ **into sb's shoes** succedere a qcno; ~ **out of** uscire da; ~ **out of line** sgarrare
**step down** vi fig dimettersi
**step forward** vi farsi avanti
**step in** vi fig intervenire
**step up** vt (increase) aumentare
**step:** **stepbrother** n fratellastro m. **stepchild** n figliastro, -a mf. **stepdaughter** n figliastra f. **stepfather** n patrigno m. **stepladder** n scaleo m. **stepmother** n matrigna f
**stepping stone** /'stepɪŋ/ n pietra f per guadare; fig trampolino m
**stepsister** /'stepsɪstə(r)/ n sorellastra f
**stepson** /'stepsʌn/ n figliastro m
**stereo** /'sterɪəʊ/ n stereo m; **in** ~ in stereofonia
**stereophonic** /sterɪəʊ'fɒnɪk/ a stereofonico
**stereoscopic** /sterɪəʊ'skɒpɪk/ a stereoscopico
**stereotype** /'sterɪətaɪp/ n stereotipo m
**stereotyped** /'sterɪətaɪpt/ a stereotipato
**sterile** /'steraɪl/ a sterile
**sterility** /stə'rɪlətɪ/ n sterilità f
**sterilization** /sterəlaɪ'zeɪʃn/ n sterilizzazione f
**sterilize** /'sterɪlaɪz/ vt sterilizzare
**sterling** /'stɜːlɪŋ/ a fig apprezzabile ● n sterlina f
**sterling silver** n argento m pregiato
**stern¹** /stɜːn/ a severo
**stern²** n (of boat) poppa f
**sternly** /'stɜːnlɪ/ adv severamente
**steroid** /'sterɔɪd/ n steroide m
**stet** /stet/ (in proofreading) vive
**stethoscope** /'steθəskəʊp/ n stetoscopio m
**stetson** /'stetsən/ n cappello m da cow boy
**stew** /stjuː/ n stufato m; **in a** ~ fam agitato ● vt/i cuocere in umido; **~ed fruit** frutta f cotta
**steward** /'stjuːəd/ n (at meeting) organizzatore, -trice mf; (on ship, aircraft) steward m inv
**stewardess** /stjuːə'des/ n hostess f inv
**stick¹** /stɪk/ n bastone m; (of celery, rhubarb) gambo m; Sport mazza f
**stick²** v (pt/pp **stuck**) ● vt (stab) conficcare; (glue) attaccare; (fam: put) mettere; (fam: endure) sopportare; **be stuck** ⟨vehicle, person:⟩ essere bloccato; ⟨drawer:⟩ essere incastrato; **stuck in a traffic jam** bloccato nel traffico; **be stuck for an answer** non saper cosa rispondere; **stuck on** fam attratto da; **be stuck with sth** fam farsi incastrare con qcsa ● vi (adhere) attaccarsi (**to** a); (jam) bloccarsi

**stick around** vi (fam: stay) rimanere
**stick at** vt ~ **at it** fam tener duro; ~ **at nothing** fam non fermarsi di fronte a niente
**stick by** vt (be faithful to) rimanere al fianco di ⟨sb⟩
**stick down** vt incollare ⟨flap⟩; (fam: write down, put down) mettere
**stick out** vi (project) sporgere; (fam: catch the eye) risaltare ● vt fam fare ⟨tongue⟩; ~ **it out** (endure) tener duro; ~ **one's neck out** sbilanciarsi
**stick to** vt (keep to) attenersi a ⟨rules, facts⟩; mantenere ⟨story⟩; perseverare in ⟨task⟩; **I'll** ~ **to beer** continuo con la birra
**stick up** vi (project) sporgere
**stick up for** vt fam difendere
**stick with** vt (remain with) rimanere con ⟨sb⟩
**sticker** /'stɪkə(r)/ n autoadesivo m
**sticking plaster** /'stɪkɪŋ/ n cerotto m
**stick insect** n stecco m
**stick-in-the-mud** n retrogrado m
**stickler** /'stɪklə(r)/ n **be a** ~ **for** tenere molto a
**stick-up** n fam rapina f a mano armata
**sticky** /'stɪkɪ/ a (-ier, -iest) appiccicoso; (adhesive) adesivo; (fig: difficult) difficile
**stiff** /stɪf/ a rigido; ⟨brush, task⟩ duro; ⟨person⟩ controllato; ⟨drink⟩ forte; ⟨penalty⟩ severo; ⟨price⟩ alto; **bored** ~ fam annoiato a morte; ~ **neck** torcicollo m
**stiffen** /'stɪfn/ vt irrigidire ● vi irrigidirsi
**stiffly** /'stɪflɪ/ adv rigidamente; ⟨smile, answer⟩ in modo controllato
**stiffness** /'stɪfnɪs/ n rigidità f
**stifle** /'staɪfl/ vt soffocare
**stifling** /'staɪflɪŋ/ a soffocante
**stigma** /'stɪgmə/ n marchio m
**stile** /staɪl/ n scaletta f
**stiletto** /stɪ'letəʊ/ n stiletto m; ~ **heels** tacchi mpl a spillo; ~**s** (pl: shoes) scarpe fpl coi tacchi a spillo
**still¹** /stɪl/ n distilleria f
**still²** a fermo; ⟨drink⟩ non gasato; **keep/stand** ~ stare fermo ● n quiete f; (photo) posa f ● adv ancora; (nevertheless) nondimeno, comunque; **I'm** ~ **not sure** non sono ancora sicuro
**stillborn** /'stɪlbɔːn/ a nato morto
**still life** n natura f morta
**stilted** /'stɪltɪd/ a artificioso
**stilts** /stɪlts/ npl trampoli mpl
**stimulant** /'stɪmjʊlənt/ n eccitante m
**stimulate** /'stɪmjʊleɪt/ vt stimolare
**stimulating** /'stɪmjʊleɪtɪŋ/ a stimolante
**stimulation** /stɪmjʊ'leɪʃn/ n stimolo m
**stimulus** /'stɪmjʊləs/ n (pl -li /'stɪmjʊlaɪ/) stimolo m
**sting** /stɪŋ/ n puntura f; (organ) pungiglione m ● v (pt/pp **stung**) ● vt pungere; ⟨jellyfish:⟩ pizzicare ● vi (insect:) pungere
**stinging nettle** /'stɪŋɪŋ/ n ortica f
**stingy** /'stɪndʒɪ/ a (-ier, -iest) tirchio

**stink** /stɪŋk/ n puzza f ● vi (pt **stank**, pp **stunk**) puzzare

**stink bomb** n fialetta f puzzolente

**stinker** /'stɪŋkə(r)/ n (fam: difficult problem etc) rompicapo m

**stinking** /'stɪŋkɪŋ/ adv be ~ **rich** fam essere ricco sfondato

**stint** /stɪnt/ n lavoro m; **do one's** ~ fare la propria parte ● vt ~ **on** lesinare su

**stipend** /'staɪpend/ n congrua f

**stipulate** /'stɪpjʊleɪt/ vt porre come condizione

**stipulation** /stɪpjʊ'leɪʃn/ n condizione f

**stir** /stɜː(r)/ n mescolata f; (commotion) trambusto m ● v (pt/pp **stirred**) ● vt muovere; (mix) mescolare ● vi muoversi

■ **stir up** vt fomentare (hatred)

**stir-fry** vt saltare in padella ● n pietanza f saltata in padella

**stirrup** /'stɪrəp/ n staffa f

**stitch** /stɪtʃ/ n punto m; (Knitting) maglia f; (pain) fitta f; **have sb in ~es** fam far ridere qcno a crepapelle ● vt cucire

■ **stitch up** vt ricucire (wound); **the deal's ~ed up** l'affare è concluso

**stoat** /stəʊt/ n ermellino m

**stock** /stɒk/ n (for use or selling) scorta f, stock m inv; (livestock) bestiame m; (lineage) stirpe f; Fin titoli mpl; Culin brodo m; **in ~** disponibile; **out of** ~ esaurito; **take** ~ fig fare il punto ● a solito ● vt (shop:) vendere; approvvigionare (shelves)

■ **stock up** vi far scorta (**with** di)

**stock: stockbroker** n agente m di cambio. **stock car** n (for racing) stock-car m inv. **stock-car racing** n corsa f di stock-car. **stock cube** n dado m [da brodo]. **Stock Exchange** n Borsa f Valori

**stocking** /'stɒkɪŋ/ n calza f

**stockist** /'stɒkɪst/ n rivenditore m

**stock: stockmarket** n mercato m azionario. **stockpile** vt fare scorta di ● n riserva f. **stock-still** a immobile. **stocktaking** n Comm inventario m

**stocky** /'stɒkɪ/ a (**-ier, -iest**) tarchiato

**stodge** /stɒdʒ/ n (Br fam: food) ammazzafame m inv

**stodgy** /'stɒdʒɪ/ a indigesto

**stoic** /'stəʊɪk/ n stoico, -a mf

**stoical** /'stəʊɪkl/ a stoico

**stoically** /'stəʊɪklɪ/ adv stoicamente

**stoicism** /'stəʊɪsɪzm/ n stoicismo m

**stoke** /stəʊk/ vt alimentare

**stole**[1] /stəʊl/ n stola f

**stole**[2], **stolen** /'stəʊln/ see **steal**

**stolid** /'stɒlɪd/ a apatico

**stolidly** /'stɒlɪdlɪ/ adv apaticamente

**stomach** /'stʌmək/ n pancia f; Anat stomaco m ● vt fam reggere

**stomach-ache** n mal m di pancia

**stomp** /stɒmp/ vi (walk heavily) camminare con passo pesante

**stone** /stəʊn/ n pietra f; (in fruit) nocciolo m; Med calcolo m; (weight) 6,348 kg; **within a**

**~'s throw of** a un tiro di schioppo da ● a di pietra ● vt snocciolare (fruit)

**Stone Age** n età f della pietra

**stone-cold** a gelido

**stone-cold sober** a perfettamente sobrio

**stoned** /stəʊnd/ a (fam: on drugs, drink) fatto

**stone: stone-deaf** a fam sordo come una campana. **stonemason** n scalpellino m. **stonework** n lavoro m in muratura

**stony** /'stəʊnɪ/ a pietroso; (glare) glaciale

**stony-broke** a Br fam al verde

**stood** /stʊd/ see **stand**

**stooge** /stuːdʒ/ n Theat spalla f; (underling) tirapiedi mf inv

**stool** /stuːl/ n sgabello m

**stool-pigeon** n fam informatore, -trice mf

**stoop** /stuːp/ n curvatura f; **walk with a** ~ camminare con la schiena curva ● vi stare curvo; (bend down) chinarsi; fig abbassarsi

**stop** /stɒp/ n (break) sosta f; (for bus, train) fermata f; Gram punto m; **come to a** ~ fermarsi; **put a** ~ **to sth** mettere fine a qcsa ● v (pt/pp **stopped**) ● vt fermare; arrestare (machine); (prevent) impedire; ~ **sb doing sth** impedire a qcno di fare qcsa; ~ **doing sth** smettere di fare qcsa; ~ **that!** smettila!; ~ **a cheque** bloccare un assegno ● vi fermarsi; (rain:) smettere ● int fermo!

■ **stop by** vi (make a brief visit) passare

■ **stop off** vi fare una sosta

■ **stop up** vt otturare (sink); tappare (hole)

■ **stop with** vi (fam: stay with) fermarsi da

**stop: stopcock** n rubinetto m di arresto. **stopgap** n palliativo m; (person) tappabuchi m inv. **stop lights** npl luci fpl di arresto. **stopover** n sosta f; Aeron scalo m

**stoppage** /'stɒpɪdʒ/ n ostruzione f; (strike) interruzione f; (deduction) trattenute fpl

**stopper** /'stɒpə(r)/ n tappo m

**stop press** n ultimissime fpl

**stopwatch** /'stɒpwɒtʃ/ n cronometro m

**storage** /'stɔːrɪdʒ/ n deposito m; (in warehouse) immagazzinaggio m; Comput memoria f

**store** /stɔː(r)/ n (stock) riserva f; (shop) grande magazzino m; (depot) deposito m; **in** ~ in deposito; **there's trouble in** ~ **for him** ci sono guai in vista per lui; **what the future has in** ~ **for me** cosa mi riserva il futuro; **set great** ~ **by** tenere in gran conto ● vt tenere; (in warehouse, Comput) immagazzinare

■ **store up** vt (accumulate) far scorte di

**store card** n carta f di credito di grandi magazzini

**storeroom** /'stɔːruːm/ n magazzino m

**storey** /'stɔːrɪ/ n piano m

**stork** /stɔːk/ n cicogna f

**storm** /stɔːm/ n temporale m; (with thunder) tempesta f ● vt prendere d'assalto

**stormy** /'stɔːmɪ/ a tempestoso

**story** /'stɔːrɪ/ n storia f; (in newspaper) articolo m

**storybook** /'stɔːrɪbʊk/ n libro m di racconti

**storyteller** /'stɔːrɪtelə(r)/ *n* (*writer*) narratore, -trice *mf*; (*liar*) contaballe *mf inv*

**stout** /staʊt/ *a* (*shoes*) resistente; (*fat*) robusto; (*defence*) strenuo ● *n* birra *f* scura

**stoutly** /'staʊtlɪ/ *adv* strenuamente

**stove** /stəʊv/ *n* cucina *f* [economica]; (*for heating*) stufa *f*

**stow** /stəʊ/ *vt* metter via

■ **stow away** *vi Naut* imbarcarsi clandestinamente

**stowaway** /'stəʊəweɪ/ *n* passeggero, -a *mf* clandestino, -a

**straddle** /'strædl/ *vt* stare a cavalcioni su; (*standing*) essere a cavallo su

**strafe** /streɪf/ *vt* mitragliare da bassa quota

**straggle** /'strægl/ *vi* crescere disordinatamente; (*dawdle*) rimanere indietro

**straggler** /'stræglə(r)/ *n* persona *f* che rimane indietro

**straggly** /'stræglɪ/ *a* have ~ hair avere pochi capelli sottili

**straight** /streɪt/ *a* diritto, dritto; (*answer, question, person*) diretto; (*tidy*) in ordine; (*drink, hair*) liscio; **three ~ wins** tre vittorie di seguito ● *adv* diritto, dritto; (*directly*) direttamente; ~ **away** immediatamente; ~ **on** *or* **ahead** diritto; ~ **out** *fig* apertamente; **go** ~ *fam* rigare diritto; **put sth** ~ mettere qcsa in ordine; **sit/stand up** ~ stare diritto; **let's get something** ~ mettiamo una cosa in chiaro

**straighten** /'streɪtn/ *vt* raddrizzare ● *vi* raddrizzarsi; ~ [up] (*person:*) raddrizzarsi

■ **straighten out** *vt fig* chiarire (*situation*)

**straight: straight face** *n* keep a ~ ~ restare serio. **straight-faced** /-'feɪst/ *a* con l'aria seria. **straightforward** *a* franco; (*simple*) semplice. **straight man** *n Theat* spalla *f*

**strain**[1] /streɪn/ *n* (*streak*) vena *f*; *Bot* varietà *f inv*; (*of virus*) forma *f*

**strain**[2] *n* tensione *f*; (*injury*) stiramento *m*; ~s *pl* (*of music*) note *fpl*; **put a ~ on** *fig* introdurre delle tensioni in; **under a lot of** ~ estremamente sotto pressione ● *vt* tirare; sforzare (*eyes, voice*); stirarsi (*muscle*); *Culin* scolare ● *vi* sforzarsi

**strained** /streɪnd/ *a* (*relations*) teso

**strainer** /'streɪnə(r)/ *n* colino *m*

**strait** /streɪt/ *n* stretto *m*; **in dire** ~s in serie difficoltà

**straitjacket** /'streɪtdʒækɪt/ *n* camicia *f* di forza

**strait-laced** /-'leɪst/ *a* puritano

**strand**[1] /strænd/ *n* (*of thread*) gugliata *f*; (*of beads*) filo *m*; (*of hair*) capello *m*

**strand**[2] *vt* be ~ed rimanere bloccato

**strange** /streɪndʒ/ *a* strano; (*not known*) sconosciuto; (*unaccustomed*) estraneo

**strangely** /'streɪndʒlɪ/ *adv* stranamente; ~ **enough** curiosamente

**strangeness** /'streɪndʒnɪs/ *n* stranezza *f*

**stranger** /'streɪndʒə(r)/ *n* estraneo, -a *mf*

**strangle** /'stræŋgl/ *vt* strangolare; *fig* reprimere

**stranglehold** /'stræŋglhəʊld/ *n* (*physical grip*) presa *f* alla gola; (*fig: powerful control*) stretta *f* mortale; **have a ~ on sth** *fig* avere in pugno qcsa

**strangulation** /stræŋgjʊ'leɪʃn/ *n* strangolamento *m*

**strap** /stræp/ *n* cinghia *f*; (*to grasp in vehicle*) maniglia *f*; (*of watch*) cinturino *m*; (*shoulder* ~) bretella *f*, spallina *f* ● *vt* (*pt/pp* **strapped**) legare; ~ **in/down** assicurare

**strapless** /'stræplɪs/ *a* (*bra, dress*) senza spalline

**strapped** /stræpt/ *a fam* be ~ **for** essere a corto di

**strapping** /'stræpɪŋ/ *a* robusto

**strata** /'strɑːtə/ *see* **stratum**

**stratagem** /'strætədʒəm/ *n* stratagemma *m*

**strategic** /strə'tiːdʒɪk/ *a* strategico

**strategically** /strə'tiːdʒɪklɪ/ *adv* strategicamente

**strategist** /'strætədʒɪst/ *n* stratega *mf*

**strategy** /'strætədʒɪ/ *n* strategia *f*

**stratosphere** /'strɑːtəsfɪə(r)/ *n* stratosfera *f*

**stratum** /'strɑːtəm/ *n* (*pl* **strata**) strato *m*

**straw** /strɔː/ *n* paglia *f*; (*single piece*) fuscello *m*; (*for drinking*) cannuccia *f*; **the last** ~ l'ultima goccia

**strawberry** /'strɔːbərɪ/ *n* fragola *f*

**straw poll** *n Pol* sondaggio *m* d'opinione non ufficiale

**stray** /streɪ/ *a* (*animal*) randagio ● *n* randagio *m* ● *vi* andarsene per conto proprio; (*deviate*) deviare (**from** da)

**streak** /striːk/ *n* striatura *f*; (*fig: trait*) vena *f*; ~s (*pl: in hair*) mèches *fpl* ● *vi* (*move fast*) sfrecciare

**streaky** /'striːkɪ/ *a* striato; (*bacon*) grasso

**stream** /striːm/ *n* ruscello *m*; (*current*) corrente *f*; (*of blood, people*) flusso *m*; *Sch* classe *f*; **come on** ~ (*start operating*) entrare in attività; (*oil:*) cominciare a scorrere ● *vi* scorrere

■ **stream in** *vi* entrare a fiotti

■ **stream out** *vi* uscire a fiotti

**streamer** /'striːmə(r)/ *n* (*paper*) stella *f* filante; (*flag*) pennone *m*

**streamline** /'striːmlaɪn/ *vt* rendere aerodinamico; (*simplify*) snellire

**streamlined** /'striːmlaɪnd/ *a* aerodinamico; (*simplified*) snellito

**street** /striːt/ *n* strada *f*

**street: streetcar** *n Am* tram *m inv*. **street cred** *n fam* immagine *f* pubblica. **street lamp** *n* lampione *m*. **streetwalker** *n* passeggiatrice *f*. **streetwise** *a* (*fam: person*) che conosce tutti i trucchi per sopravvivere in una metropoli

**strength** /streŋθ/ *n* forza *f*; (*of wall, bridge etc*) solidità *f*; ~s *pl* punti *mpl* forti; **on the** ~ **of** grazie a

**strengthen** /'streŋθən/ *vt* rinforzare

**strenuous** /'strenjʊəs/ *a* faticoso; (*attempt, denial*) energico

**strenuously** /'strenjʊəslɪ/ adv energica-
mente

**stress** /stres/ n (emphasis) insistenza f;
Gram accento m tonico; (mental) stress m inv;
Mech spinta f ● vt (emphasize) insistere su;
Gram mettere l'accento [tonico] su

**stressed** /strest/ a (mentally) ~ [out]
stressato

**stressful** /'stresfʊl/ a stressante

**stretch** /stretʃ/ n stiramento m; (period) periodo m di tempo; (of road) tratto m;
(elasticity) elasticità f; **at a ~** di fila; **have a
~** stirarsi ● vt tirare; allargare (shoes,
sweater, etc); **~ one's legs** stendere le gambe;
**~ a point** fare uno strappo alla regola ● vi
(become wider) allargarsi; (extend) estendersi;
(person:) stirarsi

■ **stretch out** vt allungare (one's hand,
legs); allargare (arms) ● vi (person:) sdraiarsi; (land:) estendersi

**stretcher** /'stretʃə(r)/ n barella f

**stretchy** /'stretʃɪ/ a elastico

**strew** /struː/ vt (pt/pp strewn or strewed)
sparpagliare; **~n with** coperto di

**stricken** /'strɪkn/ a prostrato; **~ with** affetto
da (illness)

**strict** /strɪkt/ a severo; (precise) preciso

**strictly** /'strɪktlɪ/ adv severamente; **~
speaking** in senso stretto

**strictness** /'strɪktnɪs/ n severità f

**stricture** /'strɪktʃə(r)/ n critica f; (constriction) restringimento m

**stride** /straɪd/ n [lungo] passo m; **make
great ~s** fig fare passi da gigante; **take sth
in one's ~** accettare qcsa con facilità ● vi (pt
strode, pp stridden) andare a gran passi

**strident** /'straɪdənt/ a stridente; (colour) vistoso

**stridently** /'straɪdəntlɪ/ adv con voce stridente

**strife** /straɪf/ n conflitto m

**strike** /straɪk/ n sciopero m; Mil attacco m;
**on ~** in sciopero ● v (pt/pp struck) ● vt colpire; accendere (match); trovare (oil, gold);
(delete) depennare; (occur to) venire in mente
a; Mil attaccare; **~ sb a blow** colpire qcno
● vi (lightning:) cadere; (clock:) suonare; Mil
attaccare; (workers:) scioperare; **~ lucky**
azzeccarla

■ **strike back** vi fare rappresaglia; (at
critics) reagire

■ **strike off** vt eliminare; **be struck off
[the register]** (doctor:) essere radiato [dal-
l'albo]

■ **strike out** vt eliminare

■ **strike up** vt fare (friendship); attaccare
(conversation)

**strike-breaker** n persona f che non aderisce
a uno sciopero

**striker** /'straɪkə(r)/ n scioperante mf

**striking** /'straɪkɪŋ/ a impressionante;
(attractive) affascinante

**string** /strɪŋ/ n spago m; (of musical
instrument, racket) corda f; (of pearls) filo m;
(of lies) serie f; **the ~s** pl Mus gli archi; **pull**

**~s** fam usare le proprie conoscenze ● vt (pt/
pp strung) (thread) infilare (beads)

■ **string along** vt (fam: deceive) prendere in
giro ● vi **I'll ~ along** (come too) vengo anch'io; **~ along with sb** andare/venire con
qcno

■ **string out** vi (spread out) allinearsi ● vt
disporre in fila; **be strung out** (sl: on drugs)
essere fatto

■ **string together** vt mettere insieme
(words, remarks)

**string bean** n fagiolino m

**stringed** /strɪŋd/ a (instrument) a corda

**stringent** /'strɪndʒnt/ a rigido

**stringy** /'strɪŋɪ/ a (person, build) asciutto;
(hair) come spaghetti; Culin filaccioso

**strip** /strɪp/ n striscia f ● v (pt/pp stripped)
● vt spogliare; togliere le lenzuola da (bed);
scrostare (wood, furniture); smontare
(machine); (deprive) privare (of di) ● vi
(undress) spogliarsi

■ **strip down** vt smontare (engine)

**strip cartoon** n striscia f

**strip club** n locale m di strip-tease

**stripe** /straɪp/ n striscia f; Mil gallone m

**striped** /straɪpt/ a a strisce

**stripey** /'straɪpɪ/ a a strisce, a righe

**strip light** n tubo m al neon

**stripper** /'strɪpə(r)/ n spogliarellista mf;
(solvent) sverniciatore m

**strip-search** n perquisizione f (facendo
spogliare qcno) ● vt perquisire (facendo spogliare)

**striptease** /'strɪptiːz/ n spogliarello m,
strip-tease m inv

**strive** /straɪv/ vi (pt strove, pp striven) sforzarsi (to di); **~ for** sforzarsi di ottenere

**strobe** /strəʊb/ n luce f stroboscopica

**strode** /strəʊd/ see stride

**stroke**[1] /strəʊk/ n colpo m; (of pen) tratto m;
(in swimming) bracciata f; Med ictus m inv; **~
of luck** colpo m di fortuna; **put sb off his ~**
far perdere il filo a qcno

**stroke**[2] vt accarezzare ● n carezza f

**stroll** /strəʊl/ n passeggiata f; **go for a ~** andare a far due passi ● vi passeggiare

**stroller** /'strəʊlə(r)/ n (Am: push-chair) passeggino m

**strong** /strɒŋ/ a (-er /'strɒŋgə(r)/, -est /'strɒŋ-
gɪst/) forte; (argument) valido

**strong: strongbox** /'strɒŋbɒks/ n cassaforte
f. **stronghold** /'strɒŋhəʊld/ n roccaforte f.
**strong language** n (forceful terms) linguaggio m incisivo; (swearing) linguaggio m offensivo

**strongly** /'strɒŋlɪ/ adv fortemente; **feel ~
about sth** avere molto a cuore qcsa

**strong: strong-minded** /-'maɪndɪd/ a risoluto. **strong point** n punto m di forza.
**strongroom** n camera f blindata. **strong
stomach** n stomaco m di ferro

**stroppiness** /'strɒpɪnɪs/ n scontrosità f

**stroppy** /'strɒpɪ/ a fam scorbutico, scontroso

**strove** /strəʊv/ see strive

**struck** /strʌk/ *see* **strike**; ~ **on** *a fam* entusiasta di

**structural** /'strʌktʃərəl/ *a* strutturale

**structurally** /'strʌktʃərəlɪ/ *adv* strutturalmente

**structure** /'strʌktʃə(r)/ *n* struttura *f* ● *vt* strutturare

**struggle** /'strʌgl/ *n* lotta *f*; **with a** ~ con difficoltà ● *vi* lottare; ~ **for breath** respirare con fatica; ~ **to do sth** fare fatica a fare qcsa; ~ **to one's feet** alzarsi con fatica

**strum** /strʌm/ *vt/i* (*pt/pp* **strummed**) strimpellare

**strung** /strʌŋ/ *see* **string**

**strut**[1] /strʌt/ *n* (*component*) puntello *m*

**strut**[2] *vi* (*pt/pp* **strutted**) camminare impettito

**stub** /stʌb/ *n* mozzicone *m*; (*counterfoil*) matrice *f* ● *vt* (*pt/pp* **stubbed**) ~ **one's toe** sbattere il dito del piede (**on** contro)

■ **stub out** *vt* spegnere ⟨*cigarette*⟩

**stubble** /'stʌbl/ *n* (*on face*) barba *f* ispida

**stubbly** /'stʌblɪ/ *a* ispido

**stubborn** /'stʌbən/ *a* testardo; ⟨*refusal*⟩ ostinato

**stubbornly** /'stʌbənlɪ/ *adv* testardamente; ⟨*refuse*⟩ ostinatamente

**stubbornness** /'stʌbənnɪs/ *n* (*of person*) testardaggine *f*

**stubby** /'stʌbɪ/ *a* (**-ier, -iest**) tozzo

**stucco** /'stʌkəʊ/ *n* stucco *m*

**stuck** /stʌk/ *see* **stick**[2]

**stuck-up** *a fam* snob *inv*

**stud**[1] /stʌd/ *n* (*on boot*) tacchetto *m*; (*on jacket*) borchia *f*; (*for ear*) orecchino *m* [a bottone]

**stud**[2] *n* (*of horses*) scuderia *f*

**studded with** /'stʌdɪd/ *a fig* tempestato di

**student** /'stju:dənt/ *n* studente *m*, studentessa *f*; (*school child*) scolaro, -a *mf*

**student nurse** *n* studente, -tessa *mf* infermiere, -a

**stud-horse** *n* stallone *m* [da monta]

**studied** /'stʌdɪd/ *a* intenzionale; ⟨*politeness*⟩ studiato

**studio** /'stju:dɪəʊ/ *n* studio *m*

**studio apartment** *n Am* monolocale *m*

**studio flat** *n* monolocale *m*

**studious** /'stju:dɪəs/ *a* studioso; ⟨*attention*⟩ studiato

**studiously** /'stju:dɪəslɪ/ *adv* studiosamente; (*carefully*) attentamente

**stud mare** *n* giumenta *f* fattrice

**study** /'stʌdɪ/ *n* studio *m* ● *vt/i* (*pt/pp* **-ied**) studiare; ~ **for an exam** preparare un esame

**stuff** /stʌf/ *n* materiale *m*; (*fam: things*) roba *f* ● *vt* riempire; (*with padding*) imbottire; *Culin* farcire; ~ **sth into a drawer/one's pocket** ficcare qcsa alla rinfusa in un cassetto/in tasca; ~ **oneself** ingozzarsi (**with** di); **get** ~**ed!** *fam* va' a quel paese!

**stuffing** /'stʌfɪŋ/ *n* (*padding*) imbottitura *f*; *Culin* ripieno *m*

**stuffy** /'stʌfɪ/ *a* (**-ier, -iest**) che sa di chiuso; (*old-fashioned*) antiquato

**stultifying** /'stʌltɪfaɪɪŋ/ *a* che abbrutisce

**stumble** /'stʌmbl/ *vi* inciampare; ~ **across** *or* **on** imbattersi in

**stumbling block** /'stʌmblɪŋ/ *n* ostacolo *m*

**stump** /stʌmp/ *n* ceppo *m*; (*of limb*) moncone *m*

■ **stump up** *vt/i fam* sganciare

**stumped** /stʌmpt/ *a fam* perplesso

**stumpy** /'stʌmpɪ/ *a* (**-ier, -iest**) ⟨*person, legs*⟩ tozzo

**stun** /stʌn/ *vt* (*pt/pp* **stunned**) stordire; (*astonish*) sbalordire

**stung** /stʌŋ/ *see* **sting**

**stunk** /stʌŋk/ *see* **stink**

**stunned** /stʌnd/ *a* ⟨*expression*⟩ sbalordito

**stunning** /'stʌnɪŋ/ *a fam* favoloso; ⟨*blow, victory*⟩ sbalorditivo

**stunt**[1] /stʌnt/ *n fam* trovata *f* pubblicitaria

**stunt**[2] *vt* arrestare lo sviluppo di

**stunted** /'stʌntɪd/ *a* stentato

**stuntman** /'stʌntmən/ *n* stuntman *m inv*, cascatore *m*

**stuntwoman** /'stʌntwʊmən/ *n* stuntwoman *f inv*

**stupefaction** /stju:pɪ'fækʃn/ *n* stupore *m*

**stupefy** /'stju:pɪfaɪ/ *vt* (*pt/pp* **-ied**) (*astonish*) stupire

**stupefying** /'stju:pɪfaɪɪŋ/ *a* stupefacente

**stupendous** /stju:'pendəs/ *a* stupendo

**stupendously** /stju:'pendəslɪ/ *adv* stupendamente

**stupid** /'stju:pɪd/ *a* stupido

**stupidity** /stju:'pɪdətɪ/ *n* stupidità *f*

**stupidly** /'stju:pɪdlɪ/ *adv* stupidamente

**stupor** /'stju:pə(r)/ *n* torpore *m*

**sturdy** /'stɜ:dɪ/ *a* (**-ier, -iest**) robusto; ⟨*furniture*⟩ solido

**stutter** /'stʌtə(r)/ *n* balbuzie *f*; **have a** ~ balbettare ● *vt/i* balbettare

**sty**[1] /staɪ/ *n* (*pl* **sties**) porcile *m*

**sty**[2], **stye** *n* (*pl* **styes**) *Med* orzaiolo *m*

**style** /staɪl/ *n* stile *m*; (*fashion*) moda *f*; (*sort*) tipo *m*; (*hair*~) pettinatura *f*; **in** ~ in grande stile

**stylish** /'staɪlɪʃ/ *a* elegante

**stylishly** /'staɪlɪʃlɪ/ *adv* con eleganza

**stylist** /'staɪlɪst/ *n* stilista *mf*; (*hair*-~) *n* parrucchiere, -a *mf*

**stylistic** /staɪ'lɪstɪk/ *a* stilistico

**stylistically** /staɪ'lɪstɪklɪ/ *adv* stilisticamente

**stylized** /'staɪlaɪzd/ *a* stilizzato

**stylus** /'staɪləs/ *n* (*on record player*) puntina *f*

**styptic pencil** /'stɪptɪk/ *n* matita *f* emostatica

**suave** /swɑ:v/ *a* dai modi garbati

**sub-aqua** /sʌb'ækwə/ *a* ⟨*club*⟩ di sport subacquei

**subcommittee** /'sʌbkəmɪtɪ/ *n* sottocommissione *f*

**subconscious** /sʌb'kɒnʃəs/ *a* subcosciente ● *n* subcosciente *m*

**subconsciously** /sʌb'kɒnʃəslɪ/ *adv* in modo inconscio

319

**subcontinent** /sʌb'kɒntɪnənt/ n subcontinente m

**subcontract** /sʌbkən'trækt/ vt subappaltare (**to** a)

**subcontractor** /'sʌbkəntræktə(r)/ n subappaltatore, -trice mf

**subdirectory** /'sʌbdaɪrektərɪ/ n Comput sottodirectory f inv

**subdivide** /sʌbdɪ'vaɪd/ vt suddividere

**subdivision** /'sʌbdɪvɪʒn/ n suddivisione f

**subdue** /səb'dju:/ vt sottomettere; (make quieter) attenuare

**subdued** /səb'dju:d/ a ⟨light⟩ attenuato; ⟨person, voice⟩ pacato

**subhuman** /sʌb'hju:mən/ a ⟨cruel, not fit for humans⟩ disumano; ⟨fam: appearance⟩ da paleolitico

**subject¹** /'sʌbdʒɪkt/ a ~ **to** soggetto a; (depending on) subordinato a; ~ **to availability** nei limiti della disponibilità ● n soggetto m; (of ruler) suddito, -a mf; Sch materia f; **change the** ~ parlare di qualcos'altro

**subject²** /səb'dʒekt/ vt (to attack, abuse) sottoporre; assoggettare ⟨country⟩

**subjective** /səb'dʒektɪv/ a soggettivo

**subjectively** /səb'dʒektɪvlɪ/ adv soggettivamente

**subjectiveness** /səb'dʒektɪvnɪs/ n soggettività f

**subjugate** /'sʌbdʒʊgeɪt/ vt soggiogare, sottomettere

**subjugation** /sʌbdʒə'geɪʃn/ n sottomissione f

**subjunctive** /səb'dʒʌŋktɪv/ a & n congiuntivo m

**sub-let** /sʌb'let/ vt (pt/pp -let, pres p -letting) subaffittare

**sublime** /sə'blaɪm/ a sublime

**sublimely** /sə'blaɪmlɪ/ adv sublimamente

**subliminal** /sə'blɪmɪnl/ a subliminale

**sub-machine gun** n mitraglietta f

**submarine** /'sʌbməri:n/ n sommergibile m

**submerge** /səb'mɜ:dʒ/ vt immergere; **be ~d** essere sommerso ● vi immergersi

**submission** /səb'mɪʃn/ n sottomissione f

**submissive** /səb'mɪsɪv/ a sottomesso

**submissively** /səb'mɪsɪvlɪ/ adv remissivamente

**submissiveness** /səb'mɪsɪvnɪs/ n remissività f

**submit** /səb'mɪt/ v (pt/pp -mitted, pres p -mitting) ● vt sottoporre ● vi sottomettersi

**subnormal** /sʌb'nɔ:ml/ a ⟨temperature⟩ al di sotto della norma; ⟨person⟩ subnormale

**subordinate¹** /sə'bɔ:dɪnət/ a & n subordinato, -a mf

**subordinate²** /sə'bɔ:dɪneɪt/ vt subordinare (**to** a)

**subpoena** /səb'pi:nə/ n mandato m di comparizione ● vt citare

**subroutine** /'sʌbru:ti:n/ n Comput subroutine f

**subscribe** /səb'skraɪb/ vi contribuire; ~ **to** abbonarsi a ⟨newspaper⟩; sottoscrivere ⟨fund⟩; fig aderire a ⟨theory⟩

**subscriber** /səb'skraɪbə(r)/ n abbonato, -a mf

**subscription** /səb'skrɪpʃn/ n (to club) sottoscrizione f; (to newspaper) abbonamento m

**subsequent** /'sʌbsɪkwənt/ a susseguente

**subsequently** /'sʌbsɪkwəntlɪ/ adv in seguito

**subservience** /səb'sɜ:vɪəns/ n asservimento m

**subservient** /səb'sɜ:vɪənt/ a subordinato; (servile) servile

**subserviently** /səb'sɜ:vɪəntlɪ/ adv servilmente

**subset** /'sʌbset/ n Math sottoinsieme m

**subside** /səb'saɪd/ vi sprofondare; ⟨ground:⟩ avvallarsi; ⟨storm:⟩ placarsi

**subsidence** /'sʌbsɪdəns/ n (of land) cedimento m

**subsidiary** /səb'sɪdɪərɪ/ a secondario ● n ~ [**company**] filiale f

**subsidize** /'sʌbsɪdaɪz/ vt sovvenzionare

**subsidy** /'sʌbsɪdɪ/ n sovvenzione f

**subsist** /səb'sɪst/ vi vivere (**on** di)

**subsistence** /səb'sɪstəns/ n sussistenza f

**substance** /'sʌbstəns/ n sostanza f

**sub-standard** /sʌb'stændəd/ a di qualità inferiore

**substantial** /səb'stænʃl/ a sostanziale; ⟨meal⟩ sostanzioso; (strong) solido

**substantially** /səb'stænʃəlɪ/ adv sostanzialmente; ⟨built⟩ solidamente

**substantiate** /səb'stænʃɪeɪt/ vt comprovare

**substitute** /'sʌbstɪtju:t/ n sostituto m ● vt ~ **A for B** sostituire B con A ● vi ~ **for sb** sostituire qcno

**substitution** /sʌbstɪ'tju:ʃn/ n sostituzione f

**subterfuge** /'sʌbtəfju:dʒ/ n sotterfugio m

**subterranean** /sʌbtə'reɪnɪən/ a sotterraneo

**subtext** /'sʌbtekst/ n storia f secondaria; fig messaggio m implicito

**subtitle** /'sʌbtaɪtl/ n sottotitolo m ● vt sottotitolare

**subtle** /'sʌtl/ a sottile; ⟨taste, perfume⟩ delicato

**subtlety** /'sʌtltɪ/ n sottigliezza f

**subtly** /'sʌtlɪ/ adv sottilmente

**subtotal** /'sʌbtəʊtl/ n totale m parziale

**subtract** /səb'trækt/ vt sottrarre

**subtraction** /səb'trækʃn/ n sottrazione f

**suburb** /'sʌbɜ:b/ n sobborgo m; **in the ~s** in periferia

**suburban** /sə'bɜ:bən/ a suburbano

**suburbia** /sə'bɜ:bɪə/ n sobborghi mpl

**subversive** /səb'vɜ:sɪv/ a sovversivo

**subway** /'sʌbweɪ/ n sottopassaggio m; ⟨Am: railway⟩ metropolitana f, metrò m inv

**sub-zero** /sʌb'zɪərəʊ/ a sottozero inv

**succeed** /sək'si:d/ vi riuscire (**in doing sth** a fare qcsa); (follow) succedere (**to** a) ● vt succedere a ⟨king⟩

**succeeding** /sək'si:dɪŋ/ a successivo

**success** /sək'ses/ n successo m; **be a ~** (in life) aver successo

**successful** /sək'sesfʊl/ a riuscito; ⟨businessman, artist etc⟩ di successo

**successfully** /sək'sesfʊlɪ/ adv con successo

**succession** /sək'seʃn/ n successione f; **in ~** di seguito

**successive** /sək'sesɪv/ a successivo

**successively** /sə'sesɪvlɪ/ adv successivamente

**successor** /sək'sesə(r)/ n successore m

**succinct** /sək'sɪŋkt/ a succinto

**succinctly** /sək'sɪŋktlɪ/ adv succintamente

**succour** /'sʌkə(r)/ vt soccorrere ● n soccorso m

**succulence** /'sʌkjʊləns/ n succuluenza f

**succulent** /'ʃʌkjʊlənt/ a succulento

**succumb** /sə'kʌm/ vi soccombere (**to** a)

**such** /sʌtʃ/ a tale; **~ a book** un libro così; **~ a thing** una cosa del genere; **~ a long time ago** talmente tanto tempo fa; **there is no ~ thing/person** non c'è una cosa/persona così ● pron **as ~** in quanto tale; **~ as** come; **and ~** e simili; **~ as it is** per quel che vale; **if ~ is the case** se questo è il caso

**suchlike** /'sʌtʃlaɪk/ pron fam di tal genere

**suck** /sʌk/ vt succhiare

■ **suck up** vt assorbire

■ **suck up to** vt fam fare il lecchino con

**sucker** /'ʃʌkə(r)/ n Bot pollone m; (fam: person) credulone, -a mf

**suckle** /'ʃʌkl/ vt allattare

**suction** /'sʌkʃn/ n aspirazione f

**Sudan** /su'dæn/ n Sudan m

**Sudanese** /sudən'i:z/ a & n sudanese mf

**sudden** /'sʌdn/ a improvviso ● n **all of a ~** all'improvviso

**suddenly** /'sʌdənlɪ/ adv improvvisamente

**suds** /sʌdz/ npl (foam) schiuma f; (soapy water) acqua f saponata

**sue** /su:/ v (pres p suing) ● vt fare causa a (**for** per) ● vi fare causa

**suede** /sweɪd/ n pelle f scamosciata

**suet** /'su:ɪt/ n grasso m di rognone

**suffer** /'sʌfə(r)/ vi soffrire (**from** per) ● vt soffrire di ⟨pain⟩; subire ⟨loss etc⟩

**sufferance** /'sʌf(ə)rəns/ n **you're here on ~** qui tu sei appena tollerato

**suffering** /'sʌf(ə)rɪŋ/ n sofferenza f

**suffice** /sə'faɪs/ vi bastare

**sufficient** /sə'fɪʃənt/ a sufficiente

**sufficiently** /sə'fɪʃəntlɪ/ adv sufficientemente

**suffix** /'sʌfɪks/ n suffisso m

**suffocate** /'sʌfəkeɪt/ vt/i soffocare

**suffocation** /sʌfə'keɪʃn/ n soffocamento n

**suffrage** /'sʌfrɪdʒ/ n (right) diritto m di voto; (system) suffragio m

**suffragette** /sʌfrə'dʒet/ n suffragetta f

**sugar** /'ʃʊgə(r)/ n zucchero m ● vt zuccherare; **~ the pill** fig addolcire la pillola

**sugar: sugar basin, sugar bowl** n zuccheriera f. **sugar-coated** /-'kəʊtɪd/ a ricoperto di zucchero. **sugar cube** n zolletta f. **sugar daddy** n fam vecchio amante m danaroso. **sugar lump** n zolletta f

**sugary** /'ʃʊgərɪ/ a zuccheroso; fig sdolcinato

**suggest** /sə'dʒest/ vt suggerire; (indicate, insinuate) fare pensare a

**suggestible** /sə'dʒestəbl/ a suggestionabile

**suggestion** /sə'dʒestʃən/ n suggerimento m; (trace) traccia f

**suggestive** /sə'dʒestɪv/ a allusivo; **be ~ of** fare pensare a

**suggestively** /sə'dʒestɪvlɪ/ adv in modo allusivo

**suicidal** /su:ɪ'saɪdl/ a suicida

**suicide** /'su:ɪsaɪd/ n suicidio m; (person) suicida mf; **commit ~** suicidarsi

**suicide attempt** n tentato suicidio m

**suicide pact** n patto m suicida

**suit** /su:t/ n vestito m; (woman's) tailleur m inv; (Cards) seme m; Jur causa f; **follow ~** fig fare lo stesso ● vt andar bene a; (adapt) adattare (**to** a); (be convenient for) andare bene per; **be ~ed to** or **for** essere adatto a; **~ yourself!** fa' come vuoi!

**suitability** /su:tə'bɪlɪtɪ/ n adeguatezza f

**suitable** /'su:təbl/ a adatto

**suitably** /'su:təblɪ/ adv convenientemente

**suitcase** /'su:tkeɪs/ n valigia f

**suite** /swi:t/ n suite f inv; (of furniture) divano m e poltrone fpl assortiti

**sulk** /sʌlk/ vi fare il broncio

**sulkily** /'sʌlkɪlɪ/ adv con aria imbronciata

**sulky** /'sʌlkɪ/ a imbronciato

**sullen** /'sʌlən/ a svogliato

**sullenly** /'sʌlənlɪ/ adv svogliatamente

**sulphur** /'sʌlfə(r)/ n zolfo m

**sulphur dioxide** /daɪ'ɒksaɪd/ n anidride f solforosa

**sulphuric acid** /sʌl'fjʊərɪk/ n acido m solforico

**sultana** /sʌl'tɑːnə/ n uva f sultanina

**sultry** /'sʌltrɪ/ a (-ier, -iest) ⟨weather⟩ afoso; fig sensuale

**sum** /sʌm/ n somma f; Sch addizione f

■ **sum up** v (pt/pp summed) ● vi riassumere ● vt valutare

**summarily** /sʌ'merɪlɪ/ adv sommariamente; ⟨dismissed⟩ sbrigativamente

**summarize** /'sʌməraɪz/ vt riassumere

**summary** /'sʌmərɪ/ n sommario m ● a sommario; ⟨dismissal⟩ sbrigativo

**summer** /'sʌmə(r)/ n estate f; **in ~, in the ~** in estate

**summer: summer house** n padiglione m. **summertime** n (season) estate f. **summer time** n (clock change) ora f legale

**summery** /'sʌmərɪ/ a estivo

**summing-up** /sʌmɪŋ'ʌp/ n riepilogo m; Jur ricapitolazione f del processo

**summit** /'sʌmɪt/ n cima f

**summit conference** n vertice m

**summon** /'sʌmən/ vt convocare; Jur citare

■ **summon up** vt raccogliere ⟨strength⟩; rievocare ⟨memory⟩

**summons** /'sʌmənz/ n Jur citazione f ● vt citare in giudizio

**sump** /sʌmp/ n Auto coppa f dell'olio

**sumptuous** /'sʌmptjʊəs/ a sontuoso

**sumptuously** /'sʌmptjʊəslɪ/ *adv* sontuosamente

**sum total** *n* totale *m*

**sun** /sʌn/ *n* sole *m* ● *vt* (*pt/pp* **sunned**) ~ **oneself** prendere il sole

**sun: sunbathe** *vi* prendere il sole. **sunbed** *n* lettino *m* solare. **sunblock** *n* prodotto *m* solare a protezione totale. **sunburn** *n* scottatura *f* (*solare*). **sunburnt** *a* scottato (*dal sole*). **sun cream** *n* crema *f* solare

**sundae** /'sʌndeɪ/ *n* gelato *m* guarnito

**Sunday** /'sʌndeɪ/ *n* domenica *f*

**sundial** /'sʌndaɪəl/ *n* meridiana *f*

**sun-dried tomatoes** /'sʌndraɪd/ *npl* pomodori *mpl* secchi

**sundry** /'sʌndrɪ/ *a* svariati; **all and** ~ tutti quanti

**sunflower** /'sʌnflaʊə(r)/ *n* girasole *m*

**sung** /sʌŋ/ *see* **sing**

**sunglasses** /'sʌnglɑːsɪz/ *npl* occhiali *mpl* da sole

**sunk** /sʌŋk/ *see* **sink**

**sunken** /'sʌŋkn/ *a* incavato

**sunlamp** /'sʌnlæmp/ *n* lampada *f* abbronzante

**sunlight** /'sʌnlaɪt/ *n* [luce *f* del] sole *m*

**sunny** /'sʌnɪ/ *a* (**-ier, -iest**) assolato

**sun: sunrise** *n* alba *f*. **sunroof** *n* Auto tettuccio *m* apribile. **sunscreen** *n* (*to prevent sunburn*) crema *f* solare protettiva. **sunset** *n* tramonto *m*. **sunshade** *n* parasole *m*. **sunshine** *n* [luce *f* del] sole *m*. **sunshine roof** *n* tettuccio *m* apribile. **sunstroke** *n* insolazione *f*. **suntan** *n* abbronzatura *f*. **suntan lotion** *n* antisolare *m*. **sun-tanned** *a* abbronzato. **suntan oil** *n* olio *m* solare

**super** /'suːpə(r)/ *a fam* fantastico

**superannuated** /suːpər'ænjʊeɪtɪd/ *a fig* che ha fatto il suo tempo

**superannuation** /suːpərænjʊ'eɪʃn/ *n* (*contributions*) contributi *mpl* pensionistici; (*pension*) pensione *f*

**superannuation fund** *n* fondo *m* pensione

**superb** /sʊ'pɜːb/ *a* splendido

**superbly** /sʊ'pɜːblɪ/ *adv* splendidamente

**supercilious** /suːpə'sɪlɪəs/ *a* altezzoso

**superciliously** /suːpə'sɪlɪəslɪ/ *adv* in modo altezzoso

**superficial** /suːpə'fɪʃl/ *a* superficiale

**superficiality** /suːpəfɪʃɪ'ælɪtɪ/ *n* superficialità *f*

**superficially** /suːpə'fɪʃəlɪ/ *adv* superficialmente

**superfluous** /sʊ'pɜːflʊəs/ *a* superfluo

**superhighway** /'suːpəhaɪweɪ/ *n* [**information**] ~ Comput autostrada *f* telematica

**superhuman** /suːpə'hjuːmən/ *a* sovrumano

**superimpose** /suːpərɪm'pəʊz/ *vt* sovrapporre (*picture, soundtrack*) (**on** a); **~d title** titolo *m* in sovrimpressione

**superintendent** /suːpərɪn'tendənt/ *n* (*of police*) commissario *m* di polizia

**superior** /suː'pɪərɪə(r)/ *a & n* superiore, -a *mf*

**superiority** /suːpɪərɪ'ɒrətɪ/ *n* superiorità *f*

**superlative** /suː'pɜːlətɪv/ *a* eccellente ● *n* superlativo *m*

**superlatively** /suː'pɜːlətɪvlɪ/ *adv* ⟨*perform*⟩ in modo eccezionale; ⟨*good*⟩ estremamente

**superman** /'suːpəmæn/ *n* superuomo *m*

**supermarket** /'suːpəmɑːkɪt/ *n* supermercato *m*

**supermodel** /'suːpəmɒdl/ *n* top model *f*, supermodella *f*

**supernatural** /suːpə'nætʃrəl/ *a* soprannaturale

**superpower** /'suːpəpaʊə(r)/ *n* superpotenza *f*

**superscript** /'suːpəskrɪpt/ *a* ⟨*number, letter*⟩ all'esponente

**supersede** /suːpə'siːd/ *vt* rimpiazzare

**supersonic** /suːpə'sɒnɪk/ *a* supersonico

**superstition** /suːpə'stɪʃn/ *n* superstizione *f*

**superstitious** /suːpə'stɪʃəs/ *a* superstizioso

**superstitiously** /suːpə'stɪʃəslɪ/ *adv* in modo superstizioso

**superstore** /'suːpəstɔː(r)/ *n* ipermercato *m*

**superstructure** /'suːpəstrʌktʃə(r)/ *n* sovrastruttura *f*

**supertax** /'suːpətæks/ *n* Fin soprattassa *f*

**supervise** /'suːpəvaɪz/ *vt* supervisionare

**supervision** /suːpə'vɪʒn/ *n* supervisione *f*

**supervisor** /'suːpəvaɪzə(r)/ *n* supervisore *m*

**supervisory** /suːpə'vaɪzərɪ/ *a* di supervisione

**superwoman** /'suːpəwʊmən/ *n* superdonna *f*

**supper** /'sʌpə(r)/ *n* cena *f*; **have** ~ cenare

**supple** /'sʌpl/ *a* slogato

**supplement** /'sʌplɪmənt/ *n* supplemento *m* ● *vt* integrare

**supplementary** /sʌplɪ'mentərɪ/ *a* supplementare

**supplier** /sə'plaɪə(r)/ *n* fornitore, -trice *mf*

**supply** /sə'plaɪ/ *n* fornitura *f*; Econ offerta *f*; **be in short** ~ scarseggiare; ~ **and demand** domanda *f* e offerta *f*; **supplies** *pl Mil* approvvigionamenti *mpl* ● *vt* (*pt/pp* **-ied**) fornire; ~ **sb with sth** fornire qcsa a qcno

**supply teacher** *n* supplente *mf*

**support** /sə'pɔːt/ *n* sostegno *m*; (*base*) supporto *m*; (*keep*) sostentamento *m* ● *vt* sostenere; mantenere ⟨*family*⟩; (*give money to*) mantenere finanziariamente; Sport fare il tifo per; Comput supportare

**supporter** /sə'pɔːtə(r)/ *n* sostenitore, -trice *mf*; Sport tifoso, -a *mf*

**supporting actor** /sə'pɔːtɪŋ/ *n* attore *m* non protagonista

**supporting actress** *n* attrice *f* non protagonista

**supportive** /sə'pɔːtɪv/ *a* incoraggiante; **be** ~ **of sb** dare tutto il proprio appoggio a qcno

**support stockings** *npl* calze *fpl* elastiche

**suppose** /sə'pəʊz/ *vt* (*presume*) supporre; (*imagine*) pensare; **be** ~**d to do** dover fare; **not be** ~**d to** non avere il permesso di; **I** ~ **so** suppongo di sì

**supposedly** /sə'pəʊzɪdlɪ/ *adv* presumibilmente

**supposition** /sʌpə'zɪʃn/ n supposizione f
**suppository** /sʌ'pɒzɪtrɪ/ n supposta f
**suppress** /sə'pres/ vt sopprimere
**suppressant** /sə'presənt/ n Med inibitore m
**suppression** /sə'preʃn/ n soppressione f
**suppurate** /'sʌpjʊreɪt/ vi suppurare
**supremacy** /su:'preməsɪ/ n supremazia f
**supreme** /su:'pri:m/ a supremo
**supremo** /su:'pri:məʊ/ n massima autorità f inv
**surcharge** /'sɜ:tʃɑ:dʒ/ n supplemento m
**sure** /ʃʊə(r)/ a sicuro, certo; **make ~** accertarsi; **be ~ to do it** accertati di farlo ● adv Am fam certamente; **~ enough** infatti
**sure-fire** a fam garantito
**sure-footed** /-'fʊtɪd/ a agile
**surely** /'ʃʊəlɪ/ adv certamente; (Am: gladly) volentieri
**surety** /'ʃʊərətɪ/ n garanzia f; **stand ~ for sb/sth** fare da garante a qcno/per qcsa
**surf** /'sɜ:f/ n schiuma f ● vt **~ the Net** surfare in Internet
**surface** /'sɜ:fɪs/ n superficie f; **on the ~** fig in apparenza ● vi (emerge) emergere
**surface mail** n by **~ ~** per posta ordinaria
**surface-to-air missile** n missile m terraaria
**surfboard** /'sɜ:fbɔ:d/ n tavola f da surf
**surfeit** /'sɜ:fɪt/ n eccesso m
**surfer** /'sɜ:fə(r)/ n surfista mf
**surfing** /'sɜ:fɪŋ/ n surf m
**surge** /sɜ:dʒ/ n (of sea) ondata f; (of interest) aumento m; (in demand) impennata f; (of anger, pity) impeto m ● vi riversarsi; **~ forward** buttarsi in avanti
**surgeon** /'sɜ:dʒən/ n chirurgo m
**surgery** /'sɜ:dʒərɪ/ n chirurgia f; (place, consulting room) ambulatorio m; (hours) ore fpl di visita; **have ~** subire un'intervento [chirurgico]
**surgical** /'sɜ:dʒɪkl/ a chirurgico
**surgically** /'sɜ:dʒɪklɪ/ adv chirurgicamente
**surliness** /'sɜ:lɪnɪs/ n scontrosità f
**surly** /'sɜ:lɪ/ a (-ier, -iest) scontroso
**surmise** /sə'maɪz/ vt supporre
**surmount** /sə'maʊnt/ vt sormontare
**surname** /'sɜ:neɪm/ n cognome m
**surpass** /sə'pɑ:s/ vt superare
**surplus** /'sɜ:pləs/ a d'avanzo; **be ~ to requirements** essere in eccedenza rispetto alle necessità ● n sovrappiù m
**surprise** /sə'praɪz/ n sorpresa f ● vt sorprendere; **be ~d** essere sorpreso (at da)
**surprising** /sə'praɪzɪŋ/ a sorprendente
**surprisingly** /sə'praɪzɪŋlɪ/ adv sorprendentemente; **~ enough** stranamente
**surreal** /sə'rɪəl/ a surreale
**surrealism** /sə'rɪəlɪzm/ n surrealismo m
**surrealist** /sə'rɪəlɪst/ n surrealista mf ● a surrealistico
**surrender** /sə'rendə(r)/ n resa f ● vi arrendersi ● vt cedere
**surreptitious** /sʌrəp'tɪʃəs/ a furtivo
**surreptitiously** /sʌrəp'tɪʃəslɪ/ adv furtivamente

**surrogate** /'sʌrəgət/ n surrogato m
**surrogate mother** n madre f surrogata o in prestito
**surround** /sə'raʊnd/ vt circondare; **~ed by** circondato da
**surrounding** /sə'raʊndɪŋ/ a circostante
**surroundings** /sə'raʊndɪŋz/ npl dintorni mpl
**surtax** /'sɜ:tæks/ n soprattassa f; (on income) imposta f supplementare
**surveillance** /sə'veɪləns/ n sorveglianza f; **under ~** sotto sorveglianza
**survey**[1] /'sɜ:veɪ/ n sguardo m; (poll) sondaggio m; (investigation) indagine f; (of land) rilevamento m; (of house) perizia f
**survey**[2] /sə'veɪ/ vt esaminare; fare un rilevamento di ⟨land⟩; fare una perizia di ⟨building⟩
**surveyor** /sə'veɪə(r)/ n perito m; (of land) topografo, -a mf
**survival** /sə'vaɪvl/ n sopravvivenza f; (relic) resto m
**survive** /sə'vaɪv/ vt sopravvivere a ● vi sopravvivere
**survivor** /sə'vaɪvə(r)/ n superstite mf; **be a ~** fam riuscire sempre a cavarsela
**susceptible** /sə'septəbl/ a influenzabile; **~ to** sensibile a
**suspect**[1] /sə'spekt/ vt sospettare; (assume) supporre
**suspect**[2] /'sʌspekt/ a & n sospetto, -a mf
**suspend** /sə'spend/ vt appendere; (stop, from duty) sospendere
**suspender belt** /sə'spendə/ n reggicalze m inv
**suspenders** /sə'spendəz/ npl giarrettiere fpl; (Am: braces) bretelle fpl
**suspense** /sə'spens/ n tensione f; (in book etc) suspense f
**suspension** /sə'spenʃn/ n Auto sospensione f
**suspension bridge** n ponte m sospeso
**suspicion** /sə'spɪʃn/ n sospetto m; (trace) pizzico m; **under ~** sospettato
**suspicious** /sə'spɪʃəs/ a sospettoso; (arousing suspicion) sospetto
**suspiciously** /sə'spɪʃəslɪ/ adv sospettosamente; (arousing suspicion) in modo sospetto
**■ suss out** /sʌs/ vt Br fam intuire ⟨person⟩; capire ⟨software, technique⟩; **I've got you ~ed [out]** ho scoperto il tuo piano
**sustain** /sə'steɪn/ vt sostenere; mantenere ⟨life⟩; subire ⟨injury⟩
**sustained** /sə'steɪnd/ a (effort) prolungato
**sustenance** /'sʌstɪnəns/ n nutrimento m
**suture** n /'su:tʃə(r)/ sutura f
**SW** abbr (south-west) SO
**swab** /swɒb/ n Med tampone m
**swagger** /'swægə(r)/ vi pavoneggiarsi
**swallow**[1] /'swɒləʊ/ vt/i inghiottire
**■ swallow up** vt divorare; ⟨earth, crowd:⟩ inghiottire
**swallow**[2] n (bird) rondine f
**swam** /swæm/ see **swim**

**swamp** /swɒmp/ *n* palude *f* ● *vt fig* sommergere

**swampy** /'swɒmpɪ/ *a* paludoso

**swan** /swɒn/ *n* cigno *m*

**swank** /swæŋk/ *vi fam* darsi delle arie

**swanky** /'swæŋkɪ/ *a* (*fam: posh*) snob *inv*

**swap** /swɒp/ *n fam* scambio *m* ● *vt* (*pt/pp* **swapped**) *fam* scambiare (**for** con) ● *vi* fare cambio

**swarm** /swɔːm/ *n* sciame *m* ● *vi* sciamare; **be ~ing with** *fig* brulicare di

**swarthy** /'swɔːðɪ/ *a* (**-ier, -iest**) di carnagione scura

**swashbuckling** /'swɒʃbʌklɪŋ/ *a* ⟨*hero, appearance*⟩ spericolato; ⟨*adventure, tale*⟩ di cappa e spada

**swastika** /'swɒstɪkə/ *n* svastica *f*

**swat** /swɒt/ *vt* (*pt/pp* **swatted**) schiacciare

**swathe** /sweɪð/ *n* (*of grass, corn*) falciata *f*; (*land*) larga striscia *f* ● *vt* (*in bandages, silk*) avvolgere

**sway** /sweɪ/ *n fig* influenza *f* ● *vi* oscillare; (*person:*) ondeggiare ● *vt* (*influence*) influenzare

**swear** /sweə(r)/ *v* (*pt* **swore**, *pp* **sworn**) ● *vt* giurare; **I could have sworn that ...** avrei giurato che ... ● *vi* giurare; (*curse*) dire parolacce; **I'd ~ to it!** ci potrei giurare!; **~ at sb** imprecare contro qcno; **~ by** (*believe in*) credere ciecamente in
▪ **swear off** *vt* (*fam: give up*) smettere di

**swear word** *n* parolaccia *f*

**sweat** /swet/ *n* sudore *m* ● *vi* sudare ● *vt* **~ blood** sudare sangue
▪ **sweat out** *vt* **~ it out** (*endure to the end*) tener duro fino alla fine

**sweatband** /'swetbænd/ *n* fascia *f* per il sudore; (*for wrist*) polsino *m*

**sweater** /'swetə(r)/ *n* golf *m inv*

**sweatshirt** /'swetʃɜːt/ *n* felpa *f*

**sweaty** /'swetɪ/ *a* sudato

**Swede** /swiːd/ *n* svedese *mf*

**swede** *n* rapa *f* svedese

**Sweden** /'swiːdn/ *n* Svezia *f*

**Swedish** /'swiːdɪʃ/ *a* & *n* svedese *m*

**sweep** /swiːp/ *n* scopata *f*, spazzata *f*; (*curve*) curva *f*; (*movement*) movimento *m* ampio; **make a clean ~** *fig* fare piazza pulita ● *v* (*pt/pp* **swept**) ● *vt* scopare, spazzare; (*wind:*) spazzare; **~ the board** fare piazza pulita ● *vi* (*go swiftly*) andare rapidamente; (*wind:*) soffiare
▪ **sweep away** *vt fig* spazzare via
▪ **sweep up** *vt* spazzare

**sweeper** /'swiːpə(r)/ *n* (*machine*) spazzatrice *f*; (*person*) spazzino *m*; (*in football*) libero *m*

**sweeping** /'swiːpɪŋ/ *a* (*gesture*) ampio; ⟨*statement*⟩ generico; ⟨*changes*⟩ radicale

**sweet** /swiːt/ *a* dolce; **have a ~ tooth** essere goloso ● *n* caramella *f*; (*dessert*) dolce *m*

**sweet: sweet and sour** *a* agrodolce. **sweetbread** *n* (*veal*) animella *f* di vitello; (*lamb*) animella di agnello. **sweetcorn** *n* mais *m*, granturco *m*

**sweeten** /'swiːtn/ *vt* addolcire

**sweetener** /'swiːtnə(r)/ *n* dolcificante *m*; (*fam: incentive*) incentivo *m*; (*fam: bribe*) bustarella *f*

**sweetheart** /'swiːthɑːt/ *n* innamorato, -a *mf*; **hi, ~** ciao, tesoro

**sweetly** /'swiːtlɪ/ *adv* dolcemente

**sweetness** /'swiːtnɪs/ *n* dolcezza *f*

**sweet: sweet pea** *n* pisello *m* odoroso. **sweetshop** *n* negozio *m* di dolciumi. **sweet-talk** *vt* **~ sb into doing sth** convincere qcno a fare qcsa con tante belle parole

**swell** /swel/ *n* (*of sea*) mare *m* lungo ● *v* (*pt* **swelled**, *pp* **swollen** *or* **swelled**) ● *vi* gonfiarsi; (*increase*) aumentare ● *vt* gonfiare; (*increase*) far salire ● *a fam* eccellente

**swelling** /'swelɪŋ/ *n* gonfiore *m*

**swelter** /'sweltə(r)/ *vi* soffocare [dal caldo]

**sweltering [hot]** /'sweltərɪŋ/ *a* ⟨*day*⟩ afoso

**swept** /swept/ *see* **sweep**

**swerve** /swɜːv/ *vi* deviare bruscamente

**swift** /swɪft/ *a* rapido

**swiftly** /'swɪftlɪ/ *adv* rapidamente

**swiftness** /'swɪftnɪs/ *n* rapidità *f*

**swig** /swɪg/ *fam n* sorso *m* ● *vt* (*pt/pp* **swigged**) scolarsi

**swill** /swɪl/ *n* (*for pigs*) brodaglia *f* ● *vt* **~ [out]** risciacquare

**swim** /swɪm/ *n* **have a ~** fare una nuotata ● *vi* (*pt* **swam**, *pp* **swum**) nuotare; ⟨*room:*⟩ girare; **go ~ming** andare a nuotare; **my head is ~ming** mi gira la testa ● *vt* percorrere a nuoto ⟨*distance*⟩

**swimmer** /'swɪmə(r)/ *n* nuotatore, -trice *mf*

**swimming** /'swɪmɪŋ/ *n* nuoto *m*

**swimming baths** *npl* piscina *fsg*

**swimming costume** *n* costume *m* da bagno

**swimmingly** /'swɪmɪŋlɪ/ *adv* **go ~** andar liscio

**swimming pool** *n* piscina *f*

**swimming trunks** *npl* calzoncini *mpl* da bagno

**swimsuit** /'swɪmsuːt/ *n* costume *m* da bagno

**swindle** /'swɪndl/ *n* truffa *f* ● *vt* truffare

**swindler** /'swɪndlə(r)/ *n* truffatore, -trice *mf*

**swine** /swaɪn/ *n fam* porco *m*

**swing** /swɪŋ/ *n* oscillazione *f*; (*shift*) cambiamento *m*; (*seat*) altalena *f*; *Mus* swing *m*; **in full ~** in piena attività ● *v* (*pt/pp* **swung**) ● *vi* oscillare; (*on swing, sway*) dondolare; (*dangle*) penzolare; (*turn*) girare ● *vt* oscillare; far deviare ⟨*vote*⟩

**swing-door** *n* porta *f* a vento

**swingeing** /'swɪndʒɪŋ/ *a* ⟨*increase*⟩ drastico

**swingometer** /swɪŋ'ɒmɪtə(r)/ *n* strumento *m* che permette di seguire l'andamento delle votazioni

**swipe** /swaɪp/ *n fam* botta *f* ● *vt fam* colpire; (*fam: steal*) rubare; far passare nella macchinetta ⟨*credit card*⟩

**swirl** /swɜːl/ *n* (*of smoke, dust*) turbine *m* ● *vt* far girare ● *vi* ⟨*water:*⟩ fare mulinello

**swish¹** /swɪʃ/ *a fam* chic

**swish²** *vi* schioccare

**Swiss** /swɪs/ *a & n* svizzero, -a *mf*; **the ~** *pl* gli svizzeri

**Swiss roll** *n* rotolo *m* di pan di Spagna ripieno di marmellata

**switch** /swɪtʃ/ *n* interruttore *m*; (*change*) mutamento *m* ●*vt* cambiare; (*exchange*) scambiare ● *vi* cambiare; **~ to** passare a
■ **switch off** *vt* spegnere
■ **switch on** *vt* accendere
■ **switch over** *vi* TV cambiare [canale]; **~ over to** passare a
■ **switch round** *vt* (*change one for the other*) scambiare

**switch: switchback** *n* montagne *fpl* russe. **switchblade** *n* coltello *m* a scatto. **switchboard** *n* centralino *m*

**switched line** /swɪtʃt/ *n* Teleph linea *f* commutata

**swither** /'swɪðə(r)/ *vi* (*fam: hesitate*) tentennare

**Switzerland** /'swɪtsələnd/ *n* Svizzera *f*

**swivel** /'swɪvl/ *v* (*pt/pp* **swivelled**) ● *vt* girare ● *vi* girarsi

**swizz** /swɪz/ *n* (*fam: swindle*) fregatura *f*

**swollen** /'swəʊlən/ *see* **swell** ● *a* gonfio

**swollen-headed** /-'hedɪd/ *a* presuntuoso

**swoon** /swu:n/ *vi* svenire

**swoop** /swu:p/ *n* (*by police*) incursione *f* ● *vi* **~ [down]** ⟨*bird:*⟩ piombare; *fig* fare un'incursione

**sword** /sɔ:d/ *n* spada *f*

**swordfish** /'sɔ:dfɪʃ/ *n* pesce *m* spada *inv*

**swore** /swɔ:(r)/ *see* **swear**

**sworn** /swɔ:n/ *see* **swear**

**sworn enemy** *n* nemico *m* giurato

**swot** /swɒt/ *n fam* sgobbone, -a *mf* ● *vt* (*pt/pp* **swotted**) *fam* sgobbare (**for an exam** per un esame

**swum** /swʌm/ *see* **swim**

**swung** /swʌŋ/ *see* **swing**

**sycamore** /'sɪkəmɔ:(r)/ *n* sicomoro *m*

**sycophant** /'sɪkəfænt/ *n* adulatore, -trice *mf*

**sycophantic** /sɪkə'fæntɪk/ *a* adulatorio

**syllable** /'sɪləbl/ *n* sillaba *f*

**syllabus** /'sɪləbəs/ *n* programma *m* [dei corsi]

**syllogism** /'sɪlədʒɪzm/ *n* sillogismo *m*

**sylph** /sɪlf/ *n* silfide *f*

**symbiosis** /sɪmbar'əʊsɪs/ *n* simbiosi *f inv*

**symbiotic** /sɪmbar'ɒtɪk/ *a* simbiotico

**symbol** /'sɪmbl/ *n* simbolo *m* (**of** di)

**symbolic** /sɪm'bɒlɪk/ *a* simbolico

**symbolically** /sɪm'bɒlɪklɪ/ *adv* simbolicamente

**symbolism** /'sɪmbəlɪzm/ *n* simbolismo *m*

**symbolist** /'sɪmbəlɪst/ *n* simbolista *mf*

**symbolize** /'sɪmbəlaɪz/ *vt* simboleggiare

**symmetrical** /sɪ'metrɪkl/ *a* simmetrico

**symmetrically** /sɪ'metrɪklɪ/ *adv* simmetricamente

**symmetry** /'sɪmətrɪ/ *n* simmetria *f*

**sympathetic** /sɪmpə'θetɪk/ *a* (*understanding*) comprensivo; (*showing pity*) compassionevole

**sympathetically** /sɪmpə'θetɪklɪ/ *adv* con comprensione/compassione

**sympathize** /'sɪmpəθaɪz/ *vi* capire; (*in grief*) solidarizzare; **~ with sb** capire qcno/solidarizzare con qcno

**sympathizer** /'sɪmpəθaɪzə(r)/ *n* Pol simpatizzante *mf*

**sympathy** /'sɪmpəθɪ/ *n* comprensione *f*; (*pity*) compassione *f*; (*condolences*) condoglianze *fpl*; **in ~ with** ⟨*strike*⟩ per solidarietà con

**symphonic** /sɪm'fɒnɪk/ *a* sinfonico

**symphony** /'sɪmfənɪ/ *n* sinfonia *f*

**symptom** /'sɪmptəm/ *n* sintomo *m*

**symptomatic** /sɪmptə'mætɪk/ *a* sintomatico (**of** di)

**synagogue** /'sɪnəgɒg/ *n* sinagoga *f*

**sync[h]** /sɪŋk/ *n* sincronia *f*; **be out of ~** essere sfasato; **be in ~** essere in sincronia; **be in ~ with/out of ~ with** essere sincronizzato/sfasato rispetto a

**synchronize** /'sɪŋkrənaɪz/ *vt* sincronizzare

**synchronous** /'sɪŋkrənəs/ *a* sincrono

**syndicate** /'sɪndɪkət/ *n* gruppo *m*

**syndrome** /'sɪndrəʊm/ *n* sindrome *f*

**synonym** /'sɪnənɪm/ *n* sinonimo *m*

**synonymous** /sɪ'nɒnɪməs/ *a* sinonimo

**synopsis** /sɪ'nɒpsɪs/ *n* (*pl* **-opses** /sɪn'ɒpsi:z/) (*of opera, ballet*) trama *f*; (*of book*) riassunto *m*

**syntactic[al]** /sɪn'tæktɪk[l]/ *a* sintattico

**syntax** /'sɪntæks/ *n* sintassi *f inv*

**synthesis** /'sɪnθəsɪs/ *n* (*pl* **-theses** /'sɪnθəsi:z/) sintesi *f inv*

**synthesize** /'sɪnθəsaɪz/ *vt* sintetizzare

**synthesizer** /'sɪnθəsaɪzə(r)/ *n* Mus sintetizzatore *m*

**synthetic** /sɪn'θetɪk/ *a* sintetico ● *n* fibra *f* sintetica

**syphilis** /'sɪfɪlɪs/ *n* sifilide *f*

**Syria** /'sɪrɪə/ *n* Siria *f*

**Syrian** /'sɪrɪən/ *a & n* siriano, -a *mf*

**syringe** /sɪ'rɪndʒ/ *n* siringa *f* ● *vt* siringare

**syrup** /'sɪrəp/ *n* sciroppo *m*; Br tipo *m* di melassa

**syrupy** /'sɪrəpɪ/ *a* sciropposo

**system** /'sɪstəm/ *n* sistema *m*

**systematic** /sɪstə'mætɪk/ *a* sistematico

**systematically** /sɪstə'mætɪklɪ/ *adv* sistematicamente

**systems:** /sɪstəmz/ **systems analysis** *n* analisi *f* dei sistemi. **systems analyst** *n* analista *mf* programmatore, -trice *mf*. **systems design** *n* progettazione *f* di sistemi. **systems engineer** *n* sistemista *mf*

# Tt

**t, T** /tiː/ *n* (*letter*) t, T *f inv*

**tab** /tæb/ *n* linguetta *f*; (*with name*) etichetta *f*; **keep ~s on** *fam* sorvegliare; **pick up the ~** *fam* pagare il conto

**tabby** /'tæbɪ/ *n* gatto *m* tigrato

**tab key** *n* tasto *m* tabulatore

**table** /'teɪbl/ *n* tavolo *m*; (*list*) tavola *f*; **at [the] ~** a tavola

**table: ~ of contents** tavola *f* delle materie ● *vt* proporre. **table-cloth** *n* tovaglia *f*. **table lamp** *n* lampada *f* da tavolo. **table salt** *n* sale *m* fine. **tablespoon** *n* cucchiaio *m* da tavola. **tablespoonful** *n* cucchiaiata *f*

**tablet** /'tæblɪt/ *n* pastiglia *f*; (*slab*) lastra *f*; **~ of soap** saponetta *f*

**table tennis** *n* tennis *m* da tavolo; (*everyday level*) ping pong *m*

**tabloid** /'tæblɔɪd/ *n* tabloid *m inv*; *pej* giornale *m* scandalistico

**taboo** /tə'buː/ *a* tabù *inv* ● *n* tabù *m inv*

**tabulate** /'tæbjʊleɪt/ *vt* tabulare

**tabulation** /tæbjʊ'leɪʃn/ *n* (*of data, results*) tabulazione *f*

**tabulator** /'tæbjʊleɪtə(r)/ *n* tabulatore *m*

**tachometer** /tæ'kɒmɪtə(r)/ *n* tachimetro *m*

**tachograph** /'tækəɡrɑːf/ *n* tachigrafo *m*

**tacit** /'tæsɪt/ *a* tacito

**tacitly** /'tæsɪtlɪ/ *adv* tacitamente

**taciturn** /'tæsɪtɜːn/ *a* taciturno

**tack** /tæk/ *n* (*nail*) chiodino *m*; (*stitch*) imbastitura *f*; *Naut* virata *f*; *fig* linea *f* di condotta ● *vt* inchiodare; (*sew*) imbastire ● *vi Naut* virare

**tackle** /'tækl/ *n* (*equipment*) attrezzatura *f*; (*football etc*) contrasto *m*, tackle *m inv* ● *vt* affrontare

**tacky** /'tækɪ/ *a* ⟨paint⟩ non ancora asciutto; ⟨glue⟩ appiccicoso; *fig* pacchiano

**tact** /tækt/ *n* tatto *m*

**tactful** /'tæktfʊl/ *a* pieno di tatto; ⟨remark⟩ delicato

**tactfully** /'tæktfʊlɪ/ *adv* con tatto

**tactical** /'tæktɪkl/ *a* tattico

**tactically** /'tæktɪklɪ/ *adv* tatticamente

**tactician** /tæk'tɪʃn/ *n* strategа *mf*

**tactics** /'tæktɪks/ *npl* tattica *fsg*

**tactile** /'tæktaɪl/ *a* tattile

**tactless** /'tæktlɪs/ *a* privo di tatto

**tactlessly** /'tæktlɪslɪ/ *adv* senza tatto

**tactlessness** /'tæktlɪsnɪs/ *n* mancanza *f* di tatto; (*of remark*) indelicatezza *f*

**tadpole** /'tædpəʊl/ *n* girino *m*

**taffeta** /'tæfɪtə/ *n* taffettà *m*

**tag¹** /tæɡ/ *n* (*label*) etichetta *f* ● *vt* (*pt/pp* **tagged**) attaccare l'etichetta a

**tag²** *n* (*game*) acchiapparello *m*

■ **tag along** *vi* seguire passo passo

■ **tag on** *vt* (*attach*) aggiungere

**tail** /teɪl/ *n* coda *f*; **~s** *pl* (*tailcoat*) frac *m inv* ● *vt* (*fam: follow*) pedinare

■ **tail off** *vi* diminuire

**tail: tailback** *n* coda *f*. **tail-end** *n* parte *f* finale; (*of train*) coda *f*. **tail light** *n* fanalino *m* di coda

**tailor** /'teɪlə(r)/ *n* sarto *m* ● *vt* **~ sth to sb's needs** adattare qcsa alle esigenze di qcno

**tailor-made** *a* fatto su misura

**tailspin** /'teɪlspɪn/ *n Aeron* vite *f* di coda

**tailwind** /'teɪlwɪnd/ *n* vento *m* di coda

**taint** /teɪnt/ *vt* contaminare

**take** /teɪk/ *n* (*Cinema*) ripresa *f* ● *v* (*pt* **took**, *pp* **taken**) ● *vt* prendere; (*to a place*) portare ⟨person, object⟩; (*contain*) contenere ⟨passengers etc⟩; (*endure*) sopportare; (*require*) occorrere; (*teach*) insegnare; (*study*) studiare ⟨subject⟩; fare ⟨exam, holiday, photograph, walk, bath⟩; sentire ⟨pulse⟩; misurare ⟨sb's temperature⟩; **~ sth to the cleaner's** portare qcsa in lavanderia; **~ sb home** (*by car*) portare qcno a casa; **~ sb prisoner** fare prigioniero qcno; **be ~n ill** ammalarsi; **~ sth calmly** prendere con calma qcsa; **~ the dog for a walk** portare a spasso il cane; **~ one's time doing sth** fare qcsa con calma; **this will only ~ a minute** ci vuole solo un minuto; **I ~ it that...** (*assume*) presumo che...; **~ it from me!** (*believe me*) dai retta a me! ● *vi* ⟨plant:⟩ attecchire

■ **take aback** *vt* (*surprise*) cogliere di sorpresa

■ **take after** *vt* assomigliare a

■ **take against** *vt* (*turn against*) prendere in antipatia

■ **take apart** *vt* (*dismantle*) smontare

■ **take away** *vt* (*with one*) portare via; (*remove*) togliere; (*subtract*) sottrarre; **'to ~ away'** 'da asporto'

■ **take back** *vt* riprendere; ritirare ⟨statement⟩; (*return*) riportare [indietro]; **she took him back** (*as husband, boyfriend*) lo ha perdonato

■ **take down** *vt* portare giù; (*remove*) tirare giù; (*write down*) prendere nota di

■ **take in** *vt* (*bring indoors*) portare dentro; (*to one's home*) ospitare; (*understand*) capire; (*deceive*) ingannare; riprendere ⟨garment⟩; (*include*) includere; vedere ⟨film etc⟩

■ **take off** *vt* togliersi ⟨clothes⟩; (*deduct*) togliere; (*mimic*) imitare; **~ time off** prendere delle vacanze; **~ oneself off** andarsene ● *vi*

Aeron decollare; (*fam: leave*) andarsene; (*become successful*) decollare

■ **take on** *vt* farsi carico di; assumere ⟨*employee*⟩; (*as opponent*) prendersela con; ~ **it on oneself to do sth** arrogarsi il diritto di fare qcsa

■ **take out** *vt* portare fuori; togliere ⟨*word, stain*⟩; (*withdraw*) ritirare ⟨*money, books*⟩; ~ **out a subscription to sth** abbonarsi a qcsa; **she took a pen out of her pocket** ha preso una penna dalla tasca; **I'm taking my wife out tonight** esco con mia moglie stasera; ~ **sb out to dinner** portare a cena fuori qcno; **it'll ~ you out of yourself** (*take your mind off things*) servirà a distrarti; ~ **it out on sb** *fam* prendersela con qcno

■ **take over** *vt* assumere il controllo di ⟨*firm*⟩ ● *vi* ~ **over from sb** sostituire qcno; (*permanently*) succedere a qcno

■ **take to** *vt* (*as a habit*) darsi a; **I took to her** (*liked*) mi è piaciuta

■ **take up** *vt* portare su; accettare ⟨*offer*⟩; intraprendere ⟨*profession*⟩; dedicarsi a ⟨*hobby*⟩; prendere ⟨*time*⟩; occupare ⟨*space*⟩; tirare su ⟨*floor-boards*⟩; accorciare ⟨*dress*⟩; ~ **sth up with sb** discutere qcsa con qcno; ~ **sb up on sth** (*question further*) chiedere ulteriori chiarimenti a qcno su qcsa; **I'll ~ you up on your offer** (*accept*) accetto la tua offerta ● *vi* ~ **up with sb** legarsi a qcno

**takeaway** /'teɪkəweɪ/ *n* (*meal*) piatto *m* da asporto; (*restaurant*) *ristorante m che prepara piatti da asporto*

**take-home pay** *n* stipendio *m* netto

**taken** /'teɪkən/ *a* ⟨*room etc*⟩ occupato; **be very ~ with sb/sth** essere conquistato da qcno/qcsa

**take: take-off** *n* Aeron decollo *m*. **takeover** *n* rilevamento *m*. **takeover bid** *n* offerta *f* pubblica di acquisto

**takings** /'teɪkɪŋz/ *npl* incassi *mpl*

**talcum** /'tælkəm/ *n* ~ **[powder]** talco *m*

**tale** /teɪl/ *n* storia *f*; *pej* fandonia *f*; **tell ~s** fare la spia

**talent** /'tælənt/ *n* talento *m*

**talent scout** *n* talent scout *mf inv*

**talented** /'tæləntɪd/ *a* [ricco] di talento

**talisman** /'tælɪzmən/ *n* talismano *m*

**talk** /tɔːk/ *n* conversazione *f*; (*lecture*) conferenza *f*; (*gossip*) chiacchere *fpl*; **make small ~** parlare del più e del meno ● *vi* parlare ● *vt* parlare di ⟨*politics etc*⟩; ~ **sb into sth** convincere qcno di qcsa

■ **talk about** *vt* parlare di; ~ **about bad luck!** e quando si dice la sfortuna!

■ **talk back** *vi* (*reply defiantly*) rispondere

■ **talk down to** *vt* (*patronize*) parlare con condiscendenza a

■ **talk of** *vt* parlare di; ~**ing of food…** a proposito di mangiare…

■ **talk over** *vt* discutere

■ **talk to** *vt* parlare con; (*reprimand*) fare un discorsetto a; ~ **to oneself** parlare da solo

**talkative** /'tɔːkətɪv/ *a* loquace

**talking head** /'tɔːkɪŋ/ *n* mezzobusto *m*

**talking-to** *n* sgridata *f*

**talk show** *n* talk show *m inv*

**tall** /tɔːl/ *a* alto; **how ~ are you?** quanto sei alto?

**tall: tallboy** *n* cassettone *m*. ~ **order** *n* impresa *f* difficile. **tall story** *n* frottola *f*

**tally** /'tælɪ/ *n* conteggio *m*; **keep a ~ of** tenere il conto di ● *vi* coincidere

**talon** /'tælən/ *n* artiglio *m*

**tambourine** /tæmbə'riːn/ *n* tamburello *m*

**tame** /teɪm/ *a* ⟨*animal*⟩ domestico; (*dull*) insulso ● *vt* domare

**tamely** /'teɪmlɪ/ *adv* docilmente

**tamer** /'teɪmə(r)/ *n* domatore, -trice *mf*

**tamper** /'tæmpə(r)/ *vi* ~ **with** manomettere

**tampon** /'tæmpɒn/ *n* tampone *m*

**tan** /tæn/ *a* marrone rossiccio *inv* ● *n* marrone *m* rossiccio; (*from sun*) abbronzatura *f* ● *v* (*pt/pp* **tanned**) ● *vt* conciare ⟨*hide*⟩ ● *vi* abbronzarsi

**tandem** /'tændəm/ *n* tandem *m inv*; **in ~** in tandem

**tang** /tæŋ/ *n* sapore *m* forte; (*smell*) odore *m* penetrante

**tanga** /'tæŋgə/ *n* tanga *m inv*

**tangent** /'tændʒənt/ *n* tangente *f*; **go off at a ~** *fam* partire per la tangente

**tangerine** /tændʒə'riːn/ *n* (*fruit*) tipo *m* di mandarino; (*colour*) arancione *m* ● *a* arancione

**tangible** /'tændʒəbl/ *a* tangibile

**tangibly** /'tændʒəblɪ/ *adv* tangibilmente

**tangle** /'tæŋgl/ *n* groviglio *m*; (*in hair*) nodo *m* ● *vt* ~ **[up]** aggrovigliare ● *vi* aggrovigliarsi

**tango** /'tæŋgəʊ/ *n* tango *m*

**tangy** /'tæŋɪ/ *a* forte; (*smell*) penetrante

**tank** /tæŋk/ *n* contenitore *m*; (*for petrol*) serbatoio *m*; (*fish ~*) acquario *m*; *Mil* carro *m* armato

**tankard** /'tæŋkəd/ *n* boccale *m*

**tanker** /'tæŋkə(r)/ *n* nave *f* cisterna; (*lorry*) autobotte *f*

**tank top** *n* canottiera *f*

**tanned** /tænd/ *a* abbronzato

**tannin** /'tænɪn/ *n* tannino *m*

**Tannoy®** /'tænɔɪ/ *n* Br sistema *m* di altoparlanti

**tantalize** /'tæntəlaɪz/ *vt* tormentare

**tantalizing** /'tæntəlaɪzɪŋ/ *a* allettante; ⟨*smell*⟩ stuzziccante

**tantamount** /'tæntəmaʊnt/ *a* ~ **to** equivalente a

**tantrum** /'tæntrəm/ *n* scoppio *m* d'ira; **throw a ~** fare i capricci

**tap** /tæp/ *n* rubinetto *m*; (*knock*) colpo *m*; **on ~** a disposizione ● *v* (*pt/pp* **tapped**) ● *vt* dare un colpetto a; sfruttare ⟨*resources*⟩; mettere sotto controllo ⟨*telephone*⟩ ● *vi* picchiettare

**tap-dance** *n* tip tap *m* ● *vi* ballare il tip tap

**tap-dancer** *n* ballerino, -a *mf* di tip tap

**tape** /teɪp/ *n* nastro *m*; (*recording*) cassetta *f* ● *vt* legare con nastro; (*record*) registrare

**tape: tape backup drive** *n* Comput unità *f*

di backup a nastro. **tape deck** *n* piastra *f*.
**tape-measure** *n* metro *m* [a nastro]
**taper** /'teɪpə(r)/ *n* candela *f* sottile ● *vi* assottigliarsi
■ **taper off** *vi* assottigliarsi
**tapered** /'teɪpəd/ *a* ‹trousers› affusolato
**tape: tape-record** *vt* registrare su nastro.
  **tape recorder** *n* registratore *m*. **tape
recording** *n* registrazione *f*. **tape streamer**
*n* Comput unità *f* a nastro magnetico
**tapestry** /'tæpɪstrɪ/ *n* arazzo *m*
**tapeworm** /'teɪpwɜ:m/ *n* verme *m* solitario,
tenia *f*
**tapping** /'tæpɪŋ/ *n* (noise) picchiettio *m*
**tap water** *n* acqua *f* del rubinetto
**tar** /tɑ:(r)/ *n* catrame *m* ● *vt* (pt/pp **tarred**) incatramare
**tardy** /'tɑ:dɪ/ *a* (**-ier, -iest**) tardivo
**target** /'tɑ:gɪt/ *n* bersaglio *m*; *fig* obiettivo *m*
  ● *vt* stabilire come obiettivo ‹market›
**target market** *n* mercato *m* obiettivo
**target practice** *n* tiro *m* al bersaglio
**tariff** /'tærɪf/ *n* (price) tariffa *f*; (duty) dazio *m*
  ● *a* tariffario
**Tarmac®** /'tɑ:mæk/ *n* macadam *m* al catrame
**tarmac** *n* asfalto *m*; (Br: of airfield) pista *f*
  ● *attrib* ‹road, footpath› asfaltato ● *vt*
asfaltare
**tarnish** /'tɑ:nɪʃ/ *vi* ossidarsi ● *vt* ossidare;
*fig* macchiare
**tarpaulin** /tɑ:'pɔ:lɪn/ *n* telone *m* impermeabile
**tarragon** /'tærəgən/ *n* dragoncello *m*
**tart¹** /tɑ:t/ *a* aspro; *fig* acido
**tart²** *n* crostata *f*; (individual) crostatina *f*;
  (sl: prostitute) donnaccia *f*
■ **tart up** *vt fam* ~ **oneself up** agghindarsi
**tartan** /'tɑ:tn/ *n* tessuto *m* scozzese, tartan *m*
*inv* ● *attrib* di tessuto scozzese
**tartar** /'tɑ:tə(r)/ *n* (on teeth) tartaro *m*
**tartar sauce** *n* salsa *f* tartara
**task** /tɑ:sk/ *n* compito *m*; **take sb to** ~ riprendere qcno
**task force** *n* Pol commissione *f*; Mil taskforce *f* *inv*
**tassel** /'tæsl/ *n* nappa *f*
**taste** /teɪst/ *n* gusto *m*; (sample) assaggio *m*;
**get a** ~ **of sth** *fig* assaporare il gusto di qcsa;
**in good/bad** ~ di buongusto/di cattivo gusto
  ● *vt* sentire il sapore di; (sample) assaggiare
  ● *vi* sapere (**of** di); **it** ~**s lovely** è ottimo; ~
**like sth** sapere di qcsa
**taste buds** *npl* papille *fpl* gustative
**tasteful** /'teɪs(t)ful/ *a* di [buon] gusto
**tastefully** /'teɪs(t)fulɪ/ *adv* con gusto
**tasteless** /'teɪs(t)lɪs/ *a* senza gusto
**tastelessly** /'teɪs(t)lɪslɪ/ *adv* con cattivo gusto
**taster** /'teɪstə(r)/ *n* (foretaste) assaggio *m*;
  (person) assaggiatore, -trice *mf*
**tasty** /'teɪstɪ/ *a* (**-ier, -iest**) saporito
**tat** /tæt/ *see* **tit²**
**tattered** /'tætəd/ *a* cencioso; ‹pages› stracciato

**tatters** /'tætəz/ *npl* **in** ~ a brandelli
**tattle** /'tætl/ *vi* spettegolare ● *n* pettegolezzo *m*
**tattoo¹** /tæ'tu:/ *n* tatuaggio *m* ● *vt* tatuare
**tattoo²** *n* Mil parata *f* militare
**tatty** /'tætɪ/ *a* (**-ier, -iest**) ‹clothes, person›
trasandato; ‹book› malandato
**taught** /tɔ:t/ *see* **teach**
**taunt** /tɔ:nt/ *n* scherno *m* ● *vt* schernire
**Taurus** /'tɔ:rəs/ *n* Astr Toro *m*
**taut** /tɔ:t/ *a* teso
**tauten** /'tɔ:tən/ *vt* tendere ● *vi* tendersi
**tautology** /tɔ:'tɒlədʒɪ/ *n* tautologia *f*
**tavern** /'tævən/ *n* liter taverna *f*
**tawdry** /'tɔ:drɪ/ *a* (**-ier, -iest**) pacchiano
**tawny** /'tɔ:nɪ/ *a* fulvo
**tax** /tæks/ *n* tassa *f*; (on income) imposte *fpl*;
**before** ~ ‹price› tasse escluse; ‹salary› lordo
  ● *vt* tassare; *fig* mettere alla prova; ~ **with**
accusare di
**taxable** /'tæksəbl/ *a* tassabile; ~ **income**
reddito *m* imponibile
**taxation** /tæk'seɪʃn/ *n* tasse *fpl*; ~ **at
source** ritenuta *f* alla fonte
**tax: tax allowance** *n* detrazione *f* di imposta. **tax avoidance** *n* elusione *f* fiscale. **tax
bracket** *n* scaglione *m* d'imposta. **tax break**
*n* agevolazione *f* fiscale. **tax burden** *n*
aggravio *m* fiscale. **tax code** *n* codice *m* fiscale. **tax consultant** *n* fiscalista *m*. **tax-
deductible** *a* detraibile. **tax disc** *n* Auto bollo *m*. **tax evader** *n* evasore *m* fiscale. **tax
evasion** *n* evasione *f* fiscale. **tax-free** *a* esentasse. **tax haven** *n* paradiso *m* fiscale. **tax
incentive** *n* incentivo *m* fiscale
**taxi** /'tæksɪ/ *n* taxi *m* *inv* ● *vi* (pt/pp **taxied**,
*pres p* **taxiing**) ‹aircraft:› rullare
**taxi driver** *n* tassista *mf*
**taxing** /'tæksɪŋ/ *a* (exhausting) sfiancante
**taxi rank** *n* posteggio *m* per taxi
**taxman** /'tæksmæn/ *n* **the** ~ il fisco
**tax: taxpayer** *n* contribuente *mf*. **tax
rebate** *n* rimborso *m* d'imposta. **tax return**
*n* dichiarazione *f* dei redditi. **tax shelter** *n*
paradiso *m* fiscale. **tax system** *n* regime *m*
fiscale
**TB** *n* abbr (**tuberculosis**) TBC *f*
**tbsp** *abbr* (**tablespoon**)
**tea** /ti:/ *n* tè *m* *inv*
**tea-bag** *n* bustina *f* di tè
**tea-break** *n* intervallo *m* per il tè
**teach** /ti:tʃ/ *vt/i* (pt/pp **taught**) insegnare; ~
**sb sth** insegnare qcsa a qcno; ~ **sb a lesson**
*fig* dare una lezione a qcno
**teacher** /'ti:tʃə(r)/ *n* insegnante *mf*;
  (primary) maestro, -a *mf*
**teaching** /'ti:tʃɪŋ/ *n* insegnamento *m*
**tea: teacloth** *n* (for drying) asciugapiatti *m*
*inv*. **tea cosy** *n* copriteiera *f*. **teacup** *n* tazza *f*
da tè
**teak** /ti:k/ *n* tek *m*
**tea leaves** *npl* tè *m* *inv* sfuso; (when
infused) fondi *mpl* di tè
**team** /ti:m/ *n* squadra *f*; *fig* équipe *f* *inv*
■ **team up** *vi* unirsi

**team: team captain** n caposquadra mf.
**team manager** n direttore m sportivo.
**team-mate** n compagno m di squadra. **team spirit** n spirito m di squadra. **teamwork** n lavoro m di squadra; fig lavoro m d'équipe
**teapot** /'ti:pɒt/ n teiera f
**tear¹** /teə(r)/ n strappo m ● v (pt **tore**, pp **torn**) ● vt strappare; ~ **to pieces** or **shreds** fare a pezzi; stroncare ⟨book, film⟩ ● vi strappare; ⟨material:⟩ strapparsi; (run) precipitarsi
■ **tear apart** vt (fig: criticize) fare a pezzi; (separate) dividere
■ **tear away** vt ~ **oneself away from** staccarsi da ⟨television⟩; abbandonare a malincuore ⟨party⟩
■ **tear into** vt fam (reprimand) attaccare duramente; (make a vigorous start on) dare dentro a
■ **tear open** vt aprire strappando
■ **tear out** vt staccare; ~ **one's hair out** mettersi le mani nei capelli
■ **tear up** vt strappare; rompere ⟨agreement⟩
**tear²** /tɪə(r)/ n lacrima f
**tearaway** /'teərəweɪ/ n giovane teppista mf
**tearful** /'tɪəful/ a ⟨person⟩ in lacrime; ⟨farewell⟩ lacrimevole
**tearfully** /'tɪəfʊlɪ/ adv in lacrime
**tear gas** /'tɪə/ n gas m lacrimogeno
**tearing** /'teərɪŋ/ a **be in a ~ hurry** avere una gran fretta
**tear-jerker** /'tɪədʒɜːkə(r)/ n fam **this film is a real ~** è davvero un film strappalacrime
**tease** /ti:z/ vt prendere in giro ⟨person⟩; tormentare ⟨animal⟩
**teasel** /'ti:zl/ n Bot cardo m
**teaset** /'ti:set/ n servizio m da tè
**tea shop** n sala f da tè
**teasing** /'ti:zɪŋ/ a canzonatorio
**tea: teaspoon** n cucchiaino m [da tè]. **teaspoon[ful]** n cucchiaino m. **tea-strainer** n colino m per il tè
**teat** /ti:t/ n capezzolo m; (on bottle) tettarella f
**tea towel** n strofinaccio m [per i piatti]
**technical** /'teknɪkl/ a tecnico
**technicality** /teknɪ'kælətɪ/ n tecnicismo m; Jur cavillo m giuridico
**technically** /'teknɪklɪ/ adv tecnicamente; (strictly) strettamente
**technician** /tek'nɪʃn/ n tecnico, -a mf
**technique** /tek'ni:k/ n tecnica f
**technocrat** /'teknəkræt/ n tecnocrate m
**technological** /teknə'lɒdʒɪkl/ a tecnologico
**technologically** /teknə'lɒdʒɪklɪ/ adv tecnologicamente
**technology** /tek'nɒlədʒɪ/ n tecnologia f
**teddy** /'tedɪ/ n ~ **[bear]** orsacchiotto m
**tedious** /'ti:dɪəs/ a noioso
**tedium** /'ti:dɪəm/ n tedio m
**tee** /ti:/ n (Golf) tee m inv
**teem** /ti:m/ vi (rain) piovere a dirotto; **be ~ing with** (full of) pullulare di
**teen** /ti:n/ a ⟨fashion, idol⟩ degli adolescenti

**teenage** /'ti:neɪdʒ/ a per ragazzi; ~ **boy/girl** adolescente mf
**teenager** /'ti:neɪdʒə(r)/ n adolescente mf
**teens** /ti:nz/ npl **the ~** l'adolescenza fsg; **be in one's ~** essere adolescente
**teeny** /'ti:nɪ/ a fam (-ier, -iest) piccolissimo
**teeny-weeny** /'ti:nɪ'wi:nɪ/ a fam minuscolo
**tee-shirt** n T-shirt f inv, maglietta f [a maniche corte]
**teeter** /'ti:tə(r)/ vi barcollare
**teeth** /ti:θ/ see **tooth**
**teethe** /ti:ð/ vi mettere i primi dent
**teething troubles** /'ti:ðɪŋ/ npl fig difficoltà fpl iniziali
**teetotal** /ti:'təʊtl/ a astemio
**teetotaller** /ti:'təʊt(ə)lə(r)/ n astemio, -a mf
**TEFL** /'tefl/ n insegnamento m dell'inglese come lingua straniera
**telebanking** /'telɪbæŋkɪŋ/ n servizi mpl bancari telematici
**telecast** /'telɪkɑːst/ n trasmissione f televisiva ● vt far vedere in televisione
**telecomms** /'telɪkɒmz/ npl telecomunicazioni fpl
**telecommunications** /telɪkəmju:nɪ'keɪʃnz/ npl telecomunicazioni fpl
**telecommuter** /telɪkə'mju:tə(r)/ n persona f che lavora da casa su computer
**telecommuting** /telɪkə'mju:tɪŋ/ n lavoro m su computer da casa
**teleconference** /'telɪkɒnf(ə)r(ə)ns/ n videoconferenza f
**telegenic** /telɪ'dʒenɪk/ a telegenico
**telegram** /'telɪgræm/ n telegramma m
**telegraph** /'telɪgrɑːf/ n telegrafo m
**telegraphic** /telɪ'græfɪk/ a telegrafico
**telegraph pole** n palo m del telegrafo
**telematics** /telɪ'mætɪks/ n telematica f
**telemessage** /'telɪmesɪdʒ/ n Br telegramma m
**telepathic** /telɪ'pæθɪk/ a telepatico
**telepathy** /tɪ'lepəθɪ/ n telepatia f; **by ~** per telepatia
**telephone** /'telɪfəʊn/ n telefono m; **be on the ~** avere il telefono; (be telephoning) essere al telefono ● vt telefonare a ● vi telefonare
**telephone: telephone answering service** n segreteria f telefonica. **telephone book** n elenco m telefonico. **telephone booking** n prenotazione f telefonica. **telephone booth** n, **telephone box** n cabina f telefonica. **telephone call** n telefonata f. **telephone conversation** n conversazione f telefonica. **telephone directory** n elenco m telefonico. **telephone helpline** n servizio m telefonico. **telephone message** n messaggio m telefonico. **telephone number** n numero m di telefono. **telephone tapping** n intercettazione f telefonica
**telephonist** /tɪ'lefənɪst/ n telefonista mf
**telephoto** /telɪ'fəʊtəʊ/ a ~ **lens** teleobiettivo m
**teleprinter** /'telɪprɪntə(r)/ n telescrivente f

329

**telerecording** /'telɪkrɪkɔːdɪŋ/ n programma m [televisivo] registrato
**telesales** /'telɪseɪlz/ n vendita f per telefono
**telescope** /'telɪskəup/ n telescopio m
**telescopic** /telɪ'skɒpɪk/ a telescopico
**teleshopping** /'telɪʃɒpɪŋ/ n acquisti mpl per telefono
**teletext** /'telɪtekst/ n televideo m
**telethon** /'telɪθɒn/ n telethon m inv
**televise** /'telɪvaɪz/ vt trasmettere per televisione
**television** /'telɪvɪʒn/ n televisione f; **watch ~** guardare la televisione; **on ~** alla televisione
**television: television channel** n rete f televisiva. **television licence** n abbonamento m alla televisione. **television licence fee** n costo m dell'abbonamento alla televisione. **television programme** n programma m televisivo. **television screen** n teleschermo m. **television serial** n sceneggiato m. **television set** n televisore m
**televisual** /telɪ'vɪʒʊəl/ a televisivo
**telex** /'teleks/ n telex m inv ● vt mandare via telex ‹message›; mandare un telex a ‹person›
**tell** /tel/ vt (pt/pp **told**) dire; raccontare ‹story›; ‹distinguish› distinguere (**from** da); **~ sb sth** dire qcsa a qcno; **~ sb to do sth** dire a qcno di fare qcsa; **~ the time** dire l'ora; **I couldn't ~ why...** non sapevo perché...; **you're ~ing me!** a chi lo dici! ● vi ‹produce an effect› avere effetto; **time will ~** il tempo ce lo dirà; **his age is beginning to ~** l'età comincia a farsi sentire [per lui]; **don't ~ me** non dirmelo; **you mustn't ~** non devi dire niente
■ **tell apart** vt distinguere
■ **tell off** vt sgridare
■ **tell on** vt ‹Sch: inform against› fare la spia a
**teller** /'telə(r)/ n ‹in bank› cassiere, -a mf
**telling** /'telɪŋ/ a significativo; ‹argument› efficace
**telling-off** n cicchetto m
**tell-tale** n spione, -a mf ● a rivelatore
**telly** /'telɪ/ n fam tv f inv, tele f inv
**temerity** /tɪ'merətɪ/ n audacia f
**temp** /temp/ fam n impiegato, -a mf temporaneo, -a ● vi lavorare come impiegato, -a temporaneo, -a
**temper** /'tempə(r)/ n ‹disposition› carattere m; ‹mood› umore m; ‹anger› collera f; **lose one's ~** arrabbiarsi; **be in a ~** essere arrabbiato; **keep one's ~** mantenere la calma ● vt fig temperare
**temperament** /'temprəmənt/ n temperamento m
**temperamental** /temprə'mentl/ a ‹moody› capriccioso
**temperamentally** /temprə'mentəlɪ/ adv **they are ~ unsuited** tra loro c'è incompatibilità di carattere
**temperance** /'tempərəns/ n ‹abstinence› astinenza f dal bere

**temperate** /'tempərət/ a ‹climate› temperato
**temperature** /'temprətʃə(r)/ n temperatura f; **have or run a ~** avere la febbre
**tempest** /'tempɪst/ n tempesta f
**tempestuous** /tem'pestjʊəs/ a tempestoso
**template** /'templɪt/ n sagoma f
**temple¹** /'templ/ n tempio m
**temple²** n Anat tempia f
**tempo** /'tempəʊ/ n ritmo m; Mus tempo m
**temporal** /'tempər(ə)l/ a temporale
**temporarily** /tempə'rerɪlɪ/ adv temporaneamente; ‹introduced, erected› provvisoriamente
**temporary** /'tempərərɪ/ a temporaneo; ‹measure, building› provvisorio
**tempt** /tempt/ vt tentare; sfidare ‹fate›; **~ sb to** indurre qcno a; **be ~ed** essere tentato (**to** di); **I am ~ed by the offer** l'offerta mi tenta
**temptation** /temp'teɪʃn/ n tentazione f
**tempting** /'temptɪŋ/ a allettante; ‹food, drink› invitante
**temptress** /'temptrɪs/ n seduttrice f
**ten** /ten/ a & n dieci m; **the T~ Commandments** i Dieci Comandamenti
**tenable** /'tenəbl/ a fig sostenibile
**tenacious** /tɪ'neɪʃəs/ a tenace
**tenacity** /tɪ'næsətɪ/ n tenacia f
**tenant** /'tenənt/ n inquilino, -a mf; Comm locatario, -a mf
**tend¹** /tend/ vt ‹look after› prendersi cura di
**tend²** vi **~ to do sth** tendere a far qcsa
**tendency** /'tendənsɪ/ n tendenza f
**tendentious** /ten'denʃəs/ a tendenzioso
**tender¹** /'tendə(r)/ n Comm offerta f; **put out to ~** dare in appalto; **be legal ~** avere corso legale ● vt offrire; presentare ‹resignation›
**tender²** a tenero; ‹painful› dolorante
**tender-hearted** /-'hɑːtɪd/ a dal cuore tenero
**tenderize** /'tendəraɪz/ vt rendere tenero ‹meat›
**tenderly** /'tendəlɪ/ adv teneramente
**tenderness** /'tendənɪs/ n tenerezza f; ‹painfulness› dolore m
**tendon** /'tendən/ n tendine m
**tendril** /'tendrɪl/ n ‹of plant› viticcio m
**tenement** /'tenəmənt/ n casamento m
**tenet** /'tenɪt/ n principio m
**tenner** /'tenə(r)/ n fam biglietto m da dieci sterline
**tennis** /'tenɪs/ n tennis m
**tennis: tennis ball** n palla f da tennis. **tennis-court** n campo m da tennis. **tennis match** n partita f di tennis. **tennis player** n tennista mf. **tennis racket** n racchetta f da tennis. **tennis shoes** npl scarpe fpl da tennis
**tenor** /'tenə(r)/ n tenore m
**tense¹** /tens/ n Gram tempo m
**tense²** a teso ● vt tendere ‹muscle›
■ **tense up** vi tendersi
**tension** /'tenʃn/ n tensione f
**tent** /tent/ n tenda f
**tentacle** /'tentəkl/ n tentacolo m

**tentative** /'tentətɪv/ *a* provvisorio; ‹*smile, gesture*› esitante

**tentatively** /'tentətɪvlɪ/ *adv* timidamente; ‹*accept*› provvisoriamente

**tent city** *n* tendopoli *f inv*

**tenterhooks** /'tentəhʊks/ *npl* **be on ~** essere sulle spine

**tenth** /tenθ/ *a & n* decimo, -a *mf*

**tenuous** /'tenjʊəs/ *a fig* debole

**tenure** /'tenjə/ *n* (*period of office*) permanenza *f* in carica; (*Univ: job security*) ruolo *m*; (*of land, property*) possesso *m*; **security of ~** (*of land, property*) diritto *m* di possesso

**tepid** /'tepɪd/ *a* tiepido

**tercentenary** /tɜːsen'tiːnərɪ/ *n* terzo centenario *m*

**term** /tɜːm/ *n* periodo *m*; *Sch Univ* trimestre *m*; (*in Italy*) *Sch* quadrimestre *m*; *Univ* semestre *m*; (*expression*) termine *m*; **~s** *pl* (*conditions*) condizioni *fpl*; **~ of office** carica *f*; **in the short/long ~** a breve/lungo termine; **be on good/bad ~s** essere in buoni/cattivi rapporti; **come to ~s with** accettare ‹*past, fact*›; **easy ~s** facilità *fpl* di pagamento; **~s of reference** *pl* (*of committee*) competenze *fpl*

**terminal** /'tɜːmɪnl/ *a* finale; *Med* terminale ● *n Aeron* terminal *m inv*; *Rail* stazione *f* di testa; (*of bus*) capolinea *m*; (*on battery*) morsetto *m*; *Comput* terminale *m*

**terminally** /'tɜːmɪnəlɪ/ *adv* **be ~ ill** essere in fase terminale

**terminate** /'tɜːmɪneɪt/ *vt* terminare; rescindere ‹*contract*›; interrompere ‹*pregnancy*› ● *vi* terminare; **~ in** finire in

**termination** /tɜːmɪ'neɪʃn/ *n* termine *m*; *Med* interruzione *f* di gravidanza

**terminologist** /tɜːmɪ'nɒlədʒɪst/ *n* linguista *mf* specializzato, -a in terminologia

**terminology** /tɜːmɪ'nɒlədʒɪ/ *n* terminologia *f*

**terminus** /'tɜːmɪnəs/ *n* (*pl* **-ni** /'tɜːmɪnaɪ/) (*for bus*) capolinea *m*; (*for train*) stazione *f* di testa

**term-time** *n* **during ~** durante il trimestre

**terrace** /'terəs/ *n* terrazza *f*; (*houses*) fila *f* di case a schiera; **the ~s** *pl Sport* le gradinate

**terraced house** /'terəsd/ *n* casa *f* a schiera

**terracotta** /terə'kɒtə/ *n* (*earthenware*) terracotta *f*; (*colour*) color *m* terracotta

**terrain** /te'reɪn/ *n* terreno *m*

**terrestrial** /tɪ'restrɪəl/ *n* terrestre *mf* ● *a* terrestre; **~ television** televisione *f* terrestre

**terrible** /'terəbl/ *a* terribile

**terribly** /'terəblɪ/ *adv* terribilmente; **I'm ~ sorry** sono infinitamente spiacente

**terrier** /'terɪə(r)/ *n* terrier *m inv*

**terrific** /tə'rɪfɪk/ *a fam* (*excellent*) fantastico; (*huge*) enorme

**terrifically** /tə'rɪfɪklɪ/ *adv fam* terribilmente

**terrify** /'terɪfaɪ/ *vt* (*pt/pp* **-ied**) atterrire; **be terrified** essere terrorizzato

**terrifying** /'terɪfaɪɪŋ/ *a* terrificante

**territorial** /terɪ'tɔːrɪəl/ *a* territoriale

**territorial waters** /wɔːtəz/ *npl* acque *fpl* territoriali

**territory** /'terɪtərɪ/ *n* territorio *m*

**terror** /'terə(r)/ *n* terrore *m*

**terrorism** /'terərɪzm/ *n* terrorismo *m*

**terrorist** /'terərɪst/ *n* terrorista *mf*

**terrorize** /'terəraɪz/ *vt* terrorizzare

**terror-stricken** *a* terrorizzato

**terry towelling** /terɪ'taʊəlɪŋ/ *n* tessuto *m* di spugna

**terse** /tɜːs/ *a* conciso

**tersely** /'tɜːslɪ/ *adv* concisamente

**tertiary** /'tɜːʃ(ə)rɪ/ *a* ‹*era, industry, sector*› terziario; ‹*education, college*› superiore

**Terylene®** /'terɪliːn/ *n* terilene ᴿ *m*

**test** /test/ *n* esame *m*; (*in laboratory*) esperimento *m*; (*of friendship, machine*) prova *f*; (*of intelligence, aptitude*) test *m inv*; **put to the ~** mettere alla prova; **pass one's ~** *Auto* passare l'esame di guida ● *vt* esaminare; provare ‹*machine*›

**testament** /'testəmənt/ *n* testamento *m*; **Old/New T~** Antico/Nuovo Testamento *m*

**test-drive** *vt* ‹*manufacturer:*› collaudare; ‹*buyer:*› provare ● *n* collaudo *m*; prova *f*

**tester** /'testə(r)/ *n* (*person*) collaudatore, -trice *mf*; (*device*) tester *m inv*; (*sample: of make-up, perfume*) campione *m*

**testicle** /'testɪkl/ *n* testicolo *m*

**testify** /'testɪfaɪ/ *vt/i* (*pt/pp* **-ied**) testimoniare

**testily** /'testɪlɪ/ *adv* ‹*say, reply*› in modo scontroso

**testimonial** /testɪ'məʊnɪəl/ *n* lettera *f* di referenze

**testimony** /'testɪmənɪ/ *n* testimonianza *f*

**test market** *n* mercato *m* di prova

**test match** *n* partita *f* internazionale

**testosterone** /tes'tɒstərəʊn/ *n* testosterone *m*

**test: test pilot** *n* pilota *mf* collaudatore, -trice. **test tube** *n* provetta *f*. **test tube baby** *n* fam bambino, -a *mf* in provetta

**testy** /'testɪ/ *a* irascibile

**tetanus** /'tetənəs/ *n* tetano *m*

**tetanus injection** *n* antitetanica *f*

**tetchy** /'tetʃɪ/ *a* facilmente irritabile

**tether** /'teðə(r)/ *n* **be at the end of one's ~** non poterne più ● *vt* legare

**Teutonic** /tju:'tɒnɪk/ *a* teutonico

**text** /tekst/ *n* testo *m*

**textbook** /'tekstbʊk/ *n* manuale *m*

**textile** /'tekstaɪl/ *a* tessile ● *n* stoffa *f*

**textual** /'tekstjʊəl/ *a* testuale

**texture** /'tekstʃə(r)/ *n* (*of skin*) grana *f*; (*of food*) consistenza *f*; **of a smooth ~** (*to the touch*) soffice al tatto

**Thai** /taɪ/ *a & n* tailandese *mf*; (*language*) tailandese *m*

**Thailand** /'taɪlænd/ *n* Tailandia *f*

**Thames** /temz/ *n* Tamigi *m*

**than** /ðən/ *accentato* /ðæn/ *conj* che; (*with numbers, names*) di; **older ~ me** più vecchio di me

**thank** /θæŋk/ *vt* ringraziare; **~ you [very much]** grazie [mille]

**thankful** /'θæŋkful/ *a* grato

**thankfully** /'θæŋkfulɪ/ *adv* con gratitudine; (*happily*) fortunatamente

**thankless** /'θæŋklɪs/ *a* ingrato

**thanks** /θæŋks/ *npl* ringraziamenti *mpl*; ~! *fam* grazie!; ~ **to** grazie a; **no** ~ **to you!** non certo grazie a te!

**thank-you letter** *n* lettera *f* di ringraziamento

**that** /ðæt/ *a & pron* (*pl* **those**) quel, quei *pl*; (*before s + consonant, gn, ps, z*) quello, quegli *pl*; (*before vowel*) quell' *mf*, quegli *mpl*, quelle *fpl*; ~ **shop** quel negozio; **those shops** quei negozi; ~ **mirror** quello specchio; ~ **man/woman** quell'uomo/quella donna; **those men/women** quegli uomini/quelle donne; ~ **one** quello; **I don't like those** quelli non mi piacciono; ~ **is** cioè; **is** ~ **you?** sei tu?; **who is** ~? chi è?; **what did you do after** ~? cosa hai fatto dopo?; **like** ~ in questo modo, così; **a man like** ~ un uomo così; ~ **is why** ecco perché; ~ **is the reason she gave me** questa è la ragione che mi ha dato; ~ **is the easiest thing to do** è la cosa più facile da fare; ~**'s it!** (*you've understood*) ecco!; (*I've finished*) ecco fatto!; (*I've had enough*) basta così!; (*there's nothing more*) tutto qui!; ~**'s** ~! (*with job*) ecco fatto!; (*with relationship*) è tutto finito!; **and** ~**'s** ~! punto e basta! ● *adv* così; **it wasn't** ~ **good** non era poi così buono ● *rel pron* che; **the man** ~ **I spoke to** l'uomo con cui ho parlato; **the day** ~ **I saw him** il giorno in cui l'ho visto; **all** ~ **I know** tutto quello che so ● *conj* che; **I think** ~**...** penso che...

**thatch** /θætʃ/ *n* tetto *m* di paglia

**thatched** /θætʃt/ *a* coperto di paglia

**thaw** /θɔː/ *n* disgelo *m* ● *vt* fare scongelare ⟨*food*⟩ ● *vi* ⟨*food:*⟩ scongelarsi; **it's** ~**ing** sta sgelando

**the** /ðə/ *di fronte a una vocale* /ðiː/ *def art* il *m*, la *f*; i *mpl*, le *fpl*; (*before s + consonant, gn, ps, z*) lo *m*, gli *mpl*; (*before vowel*) l'*mf*, gli *mpl*, le *fpl*; **at** ~ **cinema/station** al cinema/alla stazione; **from** ~ **cinema/station** dal cinema/dalla stazione ● *adv* ~ **more** ~ **better** più ce n'è meglio è; (*with reference to pl*) più ce ne sono, meglio è; **all** ~ **better** tanto meglio

**theatre** /'θɪətə(r)/ *n* teatro *m*; *Med* sala *f* operatoria

**theatregoer** /'θɪːətəgəʊə(r)/ *n* persona *f* che va a teatro

**theatregoing** /'θɪːətəgəʊɪŋ/ *n* l'andare *m* a teatro

**theatrical** /θɪ'ætrɪkl/ *a* teatrale; (*showy*) melodrammatico

**theft** /θeft/ *n* furto *m*

**theft-proof** *a* antiscippo

**their** /ðeə(r)/ *poss a* il loro *m*, la loro *f*, i loro *mpl*, le loro *fpl*; ~ **mother/father** la loro madre/il loro padre

**theirs** /ðeəz/ *poss pron* il loro *m*, la loro *f*, i loro *mpl*, le loro *fpl*; **a friend of** ~ un loro amico; **friends of** ~ dei loro amici; **those are** ~ quelli sono loro; (*as opposed to ours*) quelli sono i loro

**them** /ðem/ *pers pron* (*direct object*) li *m*, le *f*; (*indirect object*) gli, loro *fml*; (*after prep: with people*) loro; (*after preposition: with things*) essi; **we haven't seen** ~ non li/le abbiamo visti/viste; **give** ~ **the money** dai loro *or* dagli i soldi; **give it to** ~ daglielo; **I've spoken to** ~ ho parlato con loro; **it's** ~ sono loro

**theme** /θiːm/ *n* tema *m*

**theme: theme park** *n* parco *m* a tema.

**theme song** *n* motivo *m* conduttore

**themselves** /ðem'selvz/ *pron* (*reflexive*) si; (*emphatic*) se stessi; **they poured** ~ **a drink** si sono versati da bere; **they said so** ~ lo hanno detto loro stessi; **they kept it to** ~ se lo sono tenuti per sé; **by** ~ da soli

**then** /ðen/ *adv* allora; (*next*) poi; **by** ~ (*in the past*) ormai; (*in the future*) per allora; **since** ~ sin da allora; **before** ~ prima di allora; **from** ~ **on** da allora in poi; **now and** ~ ogni tanto; **there and** ~ all'istante ● *a* di allora

**thence** /ðens/ *adv* (*from there*) di là; (*therefore*) perciò

**theologian** /θɪə'ləʊdʒɪən/ *n* teologo, -a *mf*

**theological** /θɪə'lɒdʒɪkl/ *a* teologico

**theology** /θɪ'rɒlədʒɪ/ *n* teologia *f*

**theorem** /'θɪərəm/ *n* teorema *m*

**theoretical** /θɪə'retɪkl/ *a* teorico

**theoretically** /θɪə'retɪklɪ/ *adv* teoricamente

**theorist** /'θɪərɪst/ *n* teorico *m*

**theorize** /'θɪəraɪz/ *vi* teorizzare

**theory** /'θɪərɪ/ *n* teoria *f*; **in** ~ in teoria

**therapeutic** /θerə'pjuːtɪk/ *a* terapeutico

**therapist** /'θerəpɪst/ *n* terapista *mf*

**therapy** /'θerəpɪ/ *n* terapia *f*

**there** /ðeə(r)/ *adv* là, lì; **down/up** ~ laggiù/lassù; ~ **is/are** c'è/ci sono; ~ **he/she is** eccolo/eccola ● *int* ~, ~! dai, su!

**there: thereabouts** *adv* [*or*] ~**abouts** (*roughly*) all'incirca. **thereafter** *adv* dopo di che. **thereby** *adv* in tal modo. **therefore** /'ðeəfɔː(r)/ *adv* perciò. **therein** *adv* ~ **lies...** in ciò risiede...; **contained** ~ (*Jur: in contract*) contenuto nello stesso

**thermal** /'θɜːml/ *a* termico; ⟨*treatment*⟩ termale

**thermal: thermal paper** *n* carta *f* termica. **thermal printer** *n* stampante *f* termica. **thermal underwear** *n* biancheria *f* che mantiene la temperatura corporea

**thermometer** /θə'mɒmɪtə(r)/ *n* termometro *m*

**Thermos®** /'θɜːməs/ *n* ~ [**flask**] termos *m inv*

**thermostat** /'θɜːməstæt/ *n* termostato *m*

**thesaurus** /θɪ'sɔːrəs/ *n* (*of particular field*) dizionario *m* specialistico; (*of synonyms*) dizionario *m* dei sinonimi

**these** /ðiːz/ *see* **this**

**thesis** /'θiːsɪs/ *n* (*pl* **-ses** /-siːz/) tesi *f inv*

**they** /ðeɪ/ *pers pron* loro; ~ **are tired** sono stanchi; **we're going, but** ~ **are not** noi andiamo, ma loro no; ~ **say** (*generalizing*) si dice; ~ **are building a new road** stanno costruendo una nuova strada

**thick** /θɪk/ *a* spesso; ⟨*forest*⟩ fitto; ⟨*liquid*⟩

denso: ⟨*hair*⟩ folto; (*fam: stupid*) ottuso: (*fam: close*) molto unito; **be 5 mm ~** essere 5 mm di spessore; **give sb a ~ ear** *fam* dare uno schiaffone a qcno ● *adv* densamente ● **n in the ~ of** nel mezzo di

**thicken** /'θɪkn/ *vt* ispessire ⟨*sauce*⟩ ● *vi* ispessirsi; ⟨*fog:*⟩ infittirsi

**thicket** /'θɪkɪt/ *n* boscaglia *f*

**thickhead** /'θɪkhed/ *n fam* zuccone *mf*

**thickie** /'θɪkɪ/ *n fam* zucca *f* vuota

**thickly** /'θɪklɪ/ *adv* densamente; ⟨*cut*⟩ a fette spesse

**thickness** /'θɪknɪs/ *n* spessore *m*

**thicko** /'θɪkəʊ/ *n fam* zucca *f* vuota

**thickset** /'θɪkset/ *a* tozzo

**thick-skinned** /-'skɪnd/ *a fam* insensibile

**thief** /θi:f/ *n* (*pl* **thieves**) ladro, -a *mf*

**thieving** /'θi:vɪŋ/ *a* ladro ● *n* furti *mpl*

**thigh** /θaɪ/ *n* coscia *f*

**thimble** /'θɪmbl/ *n* ditale *m*

**thimbleful** /'θɪmbəlfʊl/ *n* (*of wine etc*) goccino *m*

**thin** /θɪn/ *a* (**thinner, thinnest**) sottile; ⟨*shoes, sweater*⟩ leggero; ⟨*liquid*⟩ liquido; ⟨*person*⟩ magro; ⟨*fig: excuse, plot*⟩ inconsistente; **be [going] ~ on top** (*be going bald*) perdere i capelli; **vanish into ~ air** volatilizzarsi ● *adv* = **thinly** ● *v* (*pt/pp* **thinned**) ● *vt* diluire ⟨*liquid*⟩ ● *vi* diradarsi

■ **thin down** *vt* diluire ⟨*paint etc*⟩ ● *vi* (*become slimmer*) dimagrire

■ **thin out** *vi* diradarsi

**thing** /θɪŋ/ *n* cosa *f*; **~s** *pl* (*belongings*) roba *fsg*; **for one ~** in primo luogo; **the right ~** la cosa giusta; **just the ~!** proprio quel che ci vuole!; **how are ~s?** come vanno le cose?; **the latest ~** *fam* l'ultima cosa; **the best ~ would be** la cosa migliore sarebbe; **poor ~!** poveretto!; **have a ~ about** (*be frightened of*) aver la fobia di; (*be attracted to*) avere un debole per

**thingumabob** /'θɪŋəməbɒb/ *n fam* coso *m*

**thingumajig** /'θɪŋəmədʒɪg/ *n fam* coso *m*

**think** /θɪŋk/ *vt/i* (*pt/pp* **thought**) pensare; (*believe*) credere; **I ~ so** credo di sì; **what do you ~?** (*what is your opinion?*) cosa ne pensi?; **~ of/about** pensare a; **what do you ~ of it?** cosa ne pensi di questo?; **~ of doing sth** pensare di fare qcsa; **~ better of it** ripensarci; **for oneself** pensare con la propria testa

■ **think again** *vi* pensarci su; **you can ~ again!** sei matto!

■ **think ahead** *vi* pensare al futuro; **~ ahead to sth** pensare in anticipo a qcsa

■ **think back** *vi* **~ back to sth** ripensare a qcsa

■ **think out** *vt* mettere a punto ⟨*strategy*⟩

■ **think over** *vt* riflettere su

■ **think through** *vt* riflettere bene su ⟨*problem*⟩

■ **think up** *vt* escogitare; trovare ⟨*name*⟩

**thinker** /'θɪŋkə(r)/ *n* pensatore, -trice *mf*

**thinking** /'θɪŋkɪŋ/ *n* (*opinion*) opinione *f*

**think-tank** *n* gruppo *m* d'esperti

**thinly** /'θɪnlɪ/ *adv* ⟨*populated*⟩ scarsamente; ⟨*disguised*⟩ leggermente; ⟨*cut*⟩ a fette sottili

**thinness** /'θɪnnɪs/ *n* (*of person*) magrezza *f*; (*of material*) finezza *f*

**thin-skinned** /-'skɪnd/ *a* (*sensitive*) permaloso

**third** /θɜ:d/ *a & n* terzo, -a *mf*

**third degree** *n* **give sb the ~ ~** fare il terzo grado a qcno

**third-degree burns** *npl* ustioni *fpl* di terzo grado

**thirdly** /'θɜ:dlɪ/ *adv* terzo

**third: third party** *n* (*in insurance, law*) terzi *mpl*. **third-party insurance** *n* assicurazione *f* contro terzi. **third person** *n* terzo *m*. **third-rate** *a* scadente. **Third World** *n* Terzo Mondo *m*

**thirst** /θɜ:st/ *n* sete *f*

**thirstily** /'θɜ:stɪlɪ/ *adv* con sete

**thirsty** /'θɜ:stɪ/ *a* assetato; **be ~** aver sete

**thirteen** /θɜ:'ti:n/ *a & n* tredici *m*

**thirteenth** /θɜ:'ti:nθ/ *a & n* tredicesimo, -a *mf*

**thirtieth** /'θɜ:tɪɪθ/ *a & n* trentesimo, -a *mf*

**thirty** /'θɜ:tɪ/ *a & n* trenta *m*

**this** /ðɪs/ *a* (*pl* **these**) questo; **~ man/woman** quest'uomo/questa donna; **these men/women** questi uomini/queste donne; **~ one** questo; **~ evening/morning** stamattina/stasera ● *pron* (*pl* **these**) questo; **we talked about ~ and that** abbiamo parlato del più e del meno; **like ~** così; **~ is Peter** questo è Peter; *Teleph* sono Peter; **who is ~?** chi è?; *Teleph* chi parla?; **~ is the happiest day of my life** è il giorno più felice della mia vita ● *adv* così; **~ big** così grande

**thistle** /'θɪsl/ *n* cardo *m*

**thong** /θɒŋ/ *n* (*on whip*) cinghia *f*; (*on shoe, garment*) laccetto *m*; (*underwear*) cache-sexe *m inv*; **~s** (*pl: sandals*) infradito *mpl or fpl*

**thorn** /θɔ:n/ *n* spina *f*

**thorny** /'θɔ:nɪ/ *a* spinoso

**thorough** /'θʌrə/ *a* completo; ⟨*knowledge*⟩ profondo; ⟨*clean, search, training*⟩ a fondo; ⟨*person*⟩ scrupoloso

**thorough: thoroughbred** *n* purosangue *m inv*. **thoroughfare** *n* via *f* principale; **'no ~'** 'strada non transitabile '

**thoroughly** /'θʌrəlɪ/ *adv* ⟨*clean, search, know sth*⟩ a fondo; (*extremely*) estremamente

**thoroughness** /'θʌrənɪs/ *n* completezza *f*

**those** /ðəʊz/ *see* **that**

**though** /ðəʊ/ *conj* sebbene; **as ~** come se ● *adv fam* tuttavia

**thought** /θɔ:t/ *see* **think** ● *n* pensiero *m*; (*idea*) idea *f*; **I've given this some ~** ci ho pensato su

**thoughtful** /'θɔ:tfʊl/ *a* pensieroso; (*considerate*) premuroso

**thoughtfully** /'θɔ:tfʊlɪ/ *adv* pensierosamente; (*considerately*) premurosamente

**thoughtfulness** /'θɔ:tfʊlnɪs/ *n* (*kindness*) considerazione *f*

**thoughtless** /'θɔ:tlɪs/ *a* (*inconsiderate*) sconsiderato

**thoughtlessness** /'θɔːtlɪsnɪs/ n sconsideratezza f

**thoughtlessly** /'θɔːtlɪslɪ/ adv con noncuranza

**thought-provoking** a ⟨book, film etc⟩ che fa riflettere

**thousand** /'θaʊznd/ a one/a ~ mille m inv ● n mille m inv; ~s of migliaia fpl di

**thousandth** /'θaʊzndθ/ a & n millesimo

**thrash** /θræʃ/ vt picchiare; (defeat) sconfiggere

■ **thrash about** vi dibattersi

■ **thrash out** vt mettere a punto

**thrashing** /'θræʃɪŋ/ n (defeat) sconfitta f; **give sb a ~** (beating) picchiare qcno

**thread** /θred/ n filo m; (of screw) filetto m ● vt infilare ⟨beads⟩; **~ one's way through** farsi strada fra

**threadbare** /'θredbeə/ a logoro

**threat** /θret/ n minaccia f

**threaten** /'θretn/ vt minacciare (**to do** if fare)● vi fig incalzare

**threatening** /'θretnɪŋ/ a minaccioso; ⟨sky, atmosphere⟩ sinistro

**threateningly** /'θretnɪŋlɪ/ adv minacciosamente

**three** /θriː/ a & n tre m

**three-dimensional** /-daɪ'menʃ(ə)nəl/ a tridimensionale

**threefold** /'θriːfəʊld/ a & adv triplo

**three: three-legged** /-'legɪd/ a con tre gambe. **three-piece suit** n vestito m da uomo con panciotto. **three-piece suite** n insieme m di divano e due poltrone coordinati. **three-quarter length** a ⟨portrait⟩ di tre quarti; ⟨sleeve⟩ a tre quarti. **three-quarters** adv ⟨empty, full, done⟩ per tre quarti

**threesome** /'θriːsəm/ n trio m

**three-wheeler** /-'wiːlə(r)/ n (car) auto f inv a tre ruote

**thresh** /θreʃ/ vt trebbiare

**threshold** /'θreʃəʊld/ n soglia f

**threw** /θruː/ see throw

**thrift** /θrɪft/ n economia f

**thrifty** /'θrɪftɪ/ a parsimonioso

**thrill** /θrɪl/ n emozione f; (of fear) brivido m ● vt entusiasmare; **be ~ed with** essere entusiasta di

**thriller** /'θrɪlə(r)/ n (book) [romanzo m] giallo m; (film) [film m inv] giallo m

**thrilling** /'θrɪlɪŋ/ a eccitante

**thrive** /θraɪv/ vi (pt thrived or throve, pp thrived) (business:) prosperare; ⟨child, plant:⟩ crescere bene; **I ~ on pressure** mi piace essere sotto tensione

**thriving** /'θraɪvɪŋ/ a fiorente

**throat** /θrəʊt/ n gola f; **sore ~** mal m di gola

**throaty** /'θrəʊtɪ/ a (husky) roco; (fam: with sore throat) rauco

**throb** /θrɒb/ n pulsazione f; (of heart) battito m ● vi (pt/pp throbbed) (vibrate) pulsare; ⟨heart:⟩ battere

**throes** /θrəʊz/ npl **in the ~ of** fig alle prese con

**thrombosis** /θrɒm'bəʊsɪs/ n trombosi f

**throne** /θrəʊn/ n trono m

**throng** /θrɒŋ/ n calca f

**throttle** /'θrɒtl/ n (on motorbike) manopola f di accelerazione ● vt strozzare

**through** /θruː/ prep attraverso; (during) durante; (by means of) tramite; (thanks to) grazie a; **Saturday ~ Tuesday** Am da sabato a martedì incluso ● adv attraverso; **~ and ~** fino in fondo; **wet ~** completamente bagnato; **read sth ~** dare una lettura a qcsa; **let ~** lasciar passare ⟨sb⟩ ● a ⟨train⟩ diretto; **be ~** (finished) aver finito; Teleph avere la comunicazione

**throughout** /θruː'aʊt/ prep per tutto ● adv completamente; (time) per tutto il tempo

**throve** /θrəʊv/ see thrive

**throw** /θrəʊ/ n tiro m ● vt (pt threw, pp thrown) lanciare; (throw away) gettare; azionare ⟨switch⟩; disarcionare ⟨rider⟩; (fam: disconcert) disorientare; fam dare ⟨party⟩

■ **throw about** vt spargere; **~ one's money about** sbandierare i propri soldi

■ **throw away** vt gettare via

■ **throw in** vt (include at no extra cost) aggiungere [gratuitamente]; (in football) rimettere in gioco; **~ the towel** or **the sponge** fig abbandonare il campo

■ **throw off** vt seminare ⟨pursuers⟩; liberarsi di ⟨cold, infection etc⟩

■ **throw together** vt (assemble hastily) mettere insieme; improvvisare ⟨meal⟩; (bring into contact) fare incontrare

■ **throw out** vt gettare via; rigettare ⟨plan⟩; buttare fuori ⟨person⟩

■ **throw up** vt alzare ● vi (vomit) vomitare

**throw: throwaway** a ⟨remark⟩ buttato lì; ⟨paper cup⟩ usa e getta inv. **throwback** n Biol atavismo m; fig regressione f. **throw-in** n Sport rimessa f laterale

**thrush** /θrʌʃ/ n tordo m; Med mughetto m; (in woman) candida f

**thrust** /θrʌst/ n spinta f● vt (pt/pp thrust) (push) spingere; (insert) conficcare; **~ [up]on** imporre a

**thud** /θʌd/ n tonfo m

**thug** /θʌg/ n deliquente m

**thuggish** /'θʌgɪʃ/ a violento

**thumb** /θʌm/ n pollice m; **as a rule of ~** come regola generale; **under sb's ~** succube di qcno ● vt **~ a lift** fare l'autostop

■ **thumb through** vt sfogliare

**thumb: thumb-index** n indice m a rubrica. **thumbnail sketch** n breve descrizione f. **thumbs down** n fam **get the ~ ~** non ottenere l'okay; **give sb/sth the ~ ~** non dare l'okay a qcno/qcsa. **thumbs up** n fam **get the ~ ~** ricevere l'okay; **give sb/sth the ~ ~** dare l'okay a qcno/qcsa. **thumbtack** n Am cimice f, puntina f [da disegno]

**thump** /θʌmp/ n colpo m; (noise) tonfo m ● vt battere su ⟨table, door⟩; battere ⟨fist⟩; colpire ⟨person⟩ ● vi battere (**on** su); ⟨heart:⟩ battere forte

■ **thump about** vi camminare pesantemente

**thumping** /'θʌmpɪŋ/ a (fam: very large) enorme; **a ~ headache** un mal di testa martellante

**thunder** /'θʌndə(r)/ n tuono m; (loud noise) rimbombo m ● vi tuonare; (make loud noise) rimbombare

**thunderbolt** /'θʌndəbəʊlt/ n folgore f

**thunderclap** /'θʌndəklæp/ n rombo m di tuono

**thundering** /'θʌndərɪŋ/ a (fam: very big or great) tremendo

**thunderous** /'θʌndərəs/ a (applause) scrosciante

**thunderstorm** /'θʌndəstɔːm/ n temporale m

**thunderstruck** /'θʌndəstrʌk/ a sbigottito

**thundery** /'θʌndəri/ a temporalesco

**Thursday** /'θɜːzdeɪ/ n giovedì m inv

**thus** /ðʌs/ adv così

**thwack** /θwæk/ vt colpire ● n colpo m

**thwart** /θwɔːt/ vt ostacolare

**thyme** /taɪm/ n timo m

**thyroid** /'θaɪrɔɪd/ n tiroide f

**tiara** /tɪ'ɑːrə/ n diadema m

**Tiber** /'taɪbə(r)/ n Tevere m

**tick¹** /tɪk/ n **on ~** fam a credito

**tick²** n (sound) ticchettio m; (mark) segno m; (fam: instant) attimo m ● vi ticchettare

■ **tick off** vt spuntare fam sgridare

■ **tick over** vi (engine:) andare al minimo

**ticket** /'tɪkɪt/ n biglietto m; (for item deposited, library) tagliando m; (label) cartellino m; (fine) multa f

**ticket: ticket-collector** n controllore m. **ticket-holder** n persona f munita di biglietto. **ticket-office** n biglietteria f. **ticket tout** n Br bagarino m

**tickle** /'tɪkl/ n solletico m ● vt fare il solletico a; (amuse) divertire ● vi fare prurito

**ticklish** /'tɪklɪʃ/ a che soffre il solletico; (problem) delicato

**tidal** /'taɪdl/ a (river, harbour) di marea

**tidal wave** n onda f di marea

**tiddly** /'tɪdlɪ/ a (Br fam: drunk) brillo

**tiddlywinks** /'tɪdlɪwɪŋks/ n gioco m delle pulci

**tide** /taɪd/ n marea f; (of events) corso m; **the ~ is in/out** c'è alta/bassa marea

■ **tide over** vt **~ sb over** aiutare qcno a andare avanti

**tidemark** /'taɪdmɑːk/ n linea f di marea; (Br fig: line of dirt) tracce fpl di sporco (nella vasca da bagno)

**tidily** /'taɪdɪlɪ/ adv in modo ordinato

**tidiness** /'taɪdɪnɪs/ n ordine m

**tidy** /'taɪdɪ/ a (-ier, -iest) ordinato; (fam: amount) bello ● vt ordinare

■ **tidy away** vt mettere a posto (toys, books)

■ **tidy out** vt mettere in ordine (drawer, cupboard)

■ **tidy up** vt ordinare; **~ oneself up** mettersi in ordine

**tie** /taɪ/ n cravatta f; (cord) legaccio m; (fig: bond) legame m; (restriction) impedimento m;

Sport pareggio m ● v (pres p **tying**) ● vt legare; fare (knot); **be ~d** (in competition) essere in parità ● vi pareggiare

■ **tie down** vt anche fig legare

■ **tie in with** vi corrispondere a

■ **tie on** vt attaccare

■ **tie up** vt legare; vincolare (capital); **be ~d up** (busy) essere occupato

**tie: tie-break[er]** n Tennis tie-break m inv; (in quiz) spareggio m. **tie-dye** vt tingere annodando. **tie-on** a (label) volante. **tiepin** n fermacravatta m

**tier** /tɪə(r)/ n fila f; (of cake) piano m; (in stadium) gradinata f

**tiff** /tɪf/ n battibecco m

**tiger** /'taɪgə(r)/ n tigre f

**tiger's-eye** /'taɪgəz/ n occhio m di tigre

**tight** /taɪt/ a stretto; (taut) teso; (fam: drunk) sbronzo; (fam: mean) spilorcio; **~ corner** fam brutta situazione f ● adv strettamente; (hold) forte; (closed) bene

**tighten** /'taɪtn/ vt stringere; avvitare (screw); intensificare (control); **~ one's belt** fig tirare la cinghia ● vi stringersi

■ **tighten up** vt stringere (screw); rendere più severo (security) ● vi (become stricter) diventare più severo

**tight: tight-fisted** /-'fɪstɪd/ a tirchio. **tight-fitting** /-'fɪtɪŋ/ a attillato. **tight-knit** a (fig: community, group) unito. **tight-lipped** /-'lɪpt/ a **they are remaining ~ about events** mantengono il riserbo riguardo all'accaduto

**tightly** /'taɪtlɪ/ adv strettamente; (hold) forte; (closed) bene

**tightrope** /'taɪtrəʊp/ n fune f (da funamboli)

**tights** /taɪts/ npl collant m inv

**tigress** /'taɪgrɪs/ n tigre f femmina

**tile** /taɪl/ n mattonella f; (on roof) tegola f ● vt rivestire di mattonelle (wall); coprire con tegole (roof)

**till¹** /tɪl/ prep & conj = **until**

**till²** n cassa f

**tiller** /'tɪlə(r)/ n barra f del timone

**tilt** /tɪlt/ n inclinazione f; **at full ~** a tutta velocità ● vt inclinare ● vi inclinarsi

**timber** /'tɪmbə(r)/ n legname m

**time** /taɪm/ n tempo m; (occasion) volta f; (by clock) ora f; **two ~s four** due volte quattro; **at any ~** in qualsiasi momento; **this ~** questa volta; **at ~s, from ~ to ~** ogni tanto; **~ and again** cento volte; **two at a ~** due alla volta; **on ~** in orario; **in ~** in tempo; (eventually) col tempo; **in no ~ at all** velocemente; **in a year's ~** fra un anno; **behind ~** in ritardo; **behind the ~s** antiquato; **for the ~ being** per il momento; **what is the ~?** che ora è?; **by the ~ we arrive** quando arriviamo; **do you have the ~?** (what ~ is it?) hai l'ora?; **did you have a nice ~?** ti sei divertito?; **have a good ~!** divertiti! ● vt scegliere il momento per; cronometrare (race); **be well ~d** essere ben calcolato

**time: time bomb** n bomba f a orologeria. **time-consuming** a che porta via molto tempo. **time-honoured** /-ɒnəd/ a venerando.

**timekeeper** n Sport cronometrista mf; **be a good ~** (be punctual) essere sempre puntuale. **time lag** n intervallo m [di tempo]

**timeless** /'taɪmlɪs/ a eterno

**time limit** n limite m di tempo

**timely** /'taɪmlɪ/ a opportuno

**time off** n (leave) permesso m; **take some ~ ~** prendere delle ferie

**time-out** n (break) pausa f; Sport time out m inv

**timer** /'taɪmə(r)/ n timer m inv

**time: timescale** n periodo m. **timeshare** n (apartment) appartamento m in multiproprietà; (house) casa f in multiproprietà. **time sheet** n foglio m di presenza. **time signal** n segnale m orario. **time span** n arco m di tempo. **time switch** n interruttore m a tempo. **timetable** n orario m. **time zone** n fuso m orario

**timid** /'tɪmɪd/ a (shy) timido; (fearful) timoroso

**timidly** /'tɪmɪdlɪ/ adv timidamente

**timidness** /'tɪmɪdnɪs/ n (shyness) timidezza f; (fear) paura f

**timing** /'taɪmɪŋ/ n Sport, Techn cronometraggio m; **the ~ of the election** il momento scelto per le elezioni; **have no sense of ~** non saper scegliere il momento opportuno

**timorous** /'tɪm(ə)rəs/ a timoroso

**timpani** /'tɪmpənɪ/ npl timpani mpl

**tin** /tɪn/ n stagno m; (container) barattolo m ● vt (pt/pp **tinned**) inscatolare

**tin foil** n [carta f] stagnola f

**tinge** /tɪndʒ/ n sfumatura f ● vt **~d with** fig misto a

**tingle** /'tɪŋgl/ vi pizzicare

**tinker** /'tɪŋkə(r)/ vi armeggiare

**tinkle** /'tɪŋkl/ n tintinnio m; (fam: phone call) colpo m di telefono ● vi tintinnare

**tinned** /tɪnd/ a in scatola

**tinnitus** /tɪnɪtəs/ n Med ronzio m auricolare

**tinny** /'tɪnɪ/ a (sound, music) metallico; (badly made) che sembra fatta di latta

**tin-opener** /-əʊpnə(r)/ n apriscatole m inv

**tinpot** /'tɪnpɒt/ a pej (firm) da due soldi

**tinsel** /'tɪnsl/ n filo m d'argento

**tint** /tɪnt/ n tinta f ● vt tingersi ⟨hair⟩; **~ed glasses** occhiali mpl colorati

**tiny** /'taɪnɪ/ a (-ier, -iest) minuscolo

**tip¹** /tɪp/ n (point, top) punta f

**tip²** n (money) mancia f; (advice) consiglio m; (for rubbish) discarica f ● v (pt/pp **tipped**) ● vt (tilt) inclinare; (overturn) capovolgere; (pour) versare; (reward) dare una mancia a ● vi inclinarsi; (overturn) capovolgersi

■ **tip off** vt **~ sb off** (inform) fare una soffiata a qcno

■ **tip out** vt rovesciare

■ **tip over** vt capovolgere ● vi capovolgersi

■ **tip up** vt sollevare ⟨seat⟩; (overturn) rovesciare

**tip-off** n soffiata f

**tipped** /tɪpt/ a (cigarette) col filtro

**tipple** /'tɪpl/ vi bere [alcool] ● n **have a ~** prendere un bicchierino; **my favourite ~** il mio liquore preferito

**tipster** /'tɪpstə(r)/ n esperto m che dà suggerimenti su cavalli da corsa, azioni ecc

**tipsy** /'tɪpsɪ/ a fam brillo

**tiptoe** /'tɪptəʊ/ n **on ~** in punta di piedi

**tip-top** a fam in condizioni perfette

**tirade** /taɪˈreɪd/ n filippica f

**tire** /'taɪə(r)/ vt stancare ● vi stancarsi

**tired** /'taɪəd/ a stanco; **~ of** stanco di; **~ out** stanco morto

**tiredness** /'taɪədnɪs/ n stanchezza f

**tireless** /'taɪəlɪs/ a instancabile

**tirelessly** /'taɪəlɪslɪ/ adv instancabilmente

**tiresome** /'taɪəsəm/ a fastidioso

**tiring** /'taɪərɪŋ/ a stancante

**tissue** /'tɪʃuː/ n tessuto m; (handkerchief) fazzolettino m di carta

**tissue-paper** n carta f velina

**tit¹** /tɪt/ n (bird) cincia f

**tit²** n **~ for tat** pan per focaccia

**tit³** n fam (breast) tetta f; (fool) stupido m

**titbit** /'tɪtbɪt/ n ghiottoneria f; (fig: of news) notizia f appetitosa

**titillate** /'tɪtɪleɪt/ vt titillare

**titivate** /'tɪtɪveɪt/ vt agghindare; **~ oneself** agghindarsi

**title** /'taɪtl/ n titolo m

**title: title deed** n atto m di proprietà. **title-holder** n detentore, -trice mf del titolo. **title-page** n frontespizio m. **title role** n ruolo m principale

**titter** /'tɪtə(r)/ vi ridere nervosamente ● n risatina f nervosa

**tittle-tattle** /'tɪtltætl/ n pettegolezzi mpl

**titular** /'tɪtjələ(r)/ a nominale

**tizzy** /'tɪzɪ/ n fam **in a ~** in grande agitazione

**to** /tuː/, atono /tə/ prep a; (to countries) in; (towards) verso; (up to, until) fino a; **I'm going to John's/the butcher's** vado da John/dal macellaio; **come/go to sb** venire/andare da qcno; **to Italy/Switzerland** in Italia/Svizzera; **I've never been to Rome** non sono mai stato a Roma; **go to the market** andare al mercato; **to the toilet/my room** in bagno/camera mia; **to an exhibition** a una mostra; **to university** all'università; **twenty/quarter to eight** le otto meno venti/un quarto; **5 to 6 kilos** da 5 a 6 chili; **to the end** alla fine; **to this day** fino a oggi; **to the best of my recollection** per quanto mi possa ricordare; **give/say sth to sb** dare/dire qcsa a qcno; **give it to me** dammelo; **there's nothing to it** è una cosa da niente ● verbal constructions **to go** andare; **learn to swim** imparare a nuotare; **I want to/have to go** voglio/devo andare; **it's easy to forget** è facile da dimenticare; **too ill/tired to go** troppo malato/stanco per andare; **you have to** devi; **I don't want to** non voglio; **he wants to be a teacher** vuole diventare un insegnante; **live to be 90** vivere fino a 90 anni; **he was the last to arrive** è stato l'ultimo ad arrivare; **to be honest,...** per essere sincero,.... ● adv **pull to** chiudere; **to and fro** avanti e indietro

**toad** /təʊd/ n rospo m

**toadstool** /'təʊdstuːl/ n fungo m velenoso

■ **toady to** /'təʊdɪ/ vi fare da leccapiedi a

**toast** /təʊst/ n pane m tostato; (drink) brindisi m inv ● vt tostare ⟨bread⟩; (drink a ~ to) brindare a·

**toaster** /'təʊstə(r)/ n tostapane m inv

**toastrack** /'təʊstræk/ n portatoast m inv

**tobacco** /tə'bækəʊ/ n tabacco m

**tobacconist's [shop]** /tə'bækənɪsts [ʃɒp]/ n tabaccheria f

**toboggan** /tə'bɒgən/ n toboga m inv ● vi andare in toboga

**today** /tə'deɪ/ a & adv oggi m; **a week ~** una settimana a oggi; **~'s paper** il giornale di oggi

**toddle** /'tɒdl/ vi ⟨child:⟩ cominciare a camminare; **~ into town** fam fare una passeggiata in centro; **I must be toddling** fam devo scappare

**toddler** /'tɒdlə(r)/ n bambino, -a mf piccolo, -a

**toddy** /'tɒdɪ/ n grog m inv

**to-do** /tə'duː/ n fam baccano m

**toe** /təʊ/ n dito m del piede; (of footwear) punta f; **on one's ~s** fig pronto ad agire; **big ~** alluce m; **little ~** mignolo m [del piede] ● vt **~ the line** rigar diritto

**toe-hold** n punto m d'appoggio

**toenail** n unghia f del piede

**toff** /tɒf/ n fam elegantone, -a mf

**toffee** /'tɒfɪ/ n caramella f al mou

**toffee apple** n mela f caramellata

**toffee-nosed** a Br fam con la puzza sotto il naso

**together** /tə'geðə(r)/ adv insieme; (at the same time) allo stesso tempo; **~ with** insieme a

**toggle** /'tɒgl/ n (fastening) olivetta f

**toil** /tɔɪl/ n duro lavoro m ● vi lavorare duramente

**toilet** /'tɔɪlɪt/ n (lavatory) gabinetto m

**toilet bag** n nécessaire m inv

**toilet paper** n carta f igienica

**toiletries** /'tɔɪlɪtrɪz/ npl articoli mpl da toilette

**toilet: toilet roll** n rotolo m di carta igienica. **toilet soap** n sapone m. **toilet tissue** n carta f igienica. **toilet-train** vt **~ a child** insegnare a un bambino a usare il vasino. **toilet water** n acqua f di colonia

**token** /'təʊkən/ n segno m; (counter) gettone m; (voucher) buono m ● attrib simbolico

**told** /təʊld/ see **tell** ● a **all ~** in tutto

**tolerable** /'tɒl(ə)rəbl/ a tollerabile; (not bad) discreto

**tolerably** /'tɒl(ə)rəblɪ/ adv discretamente

**tolerance** /'tɒl(ə)r(ə)ns/ n tolleranza f

**tolerant** /'tɒl(ə)r(ə)nt/ a tollerante

**tolerantly** /'tɒl(ə)r(ə)ntlɪ/ adv con tolleranza

**tolerate** /'tɒləreɪt/ vt tollerare

**toll¹** /təʊl/ n pedaggio m; **death ~** numero m di morti; **take a heavy ~** costare gravi perdite

**toll²** vi suonare a morto

**toll-booth** n casello m

**toll-free number** n Am Teleph numero m verde

**tom** /tɒm/ n (cat) gatto m maschio

**tomato** /tə'mɑːtəʊ/ n (pl **-es**) pomodoro m

**tomato: tomato ketchup** n ketchup m. **tomato purée** n concentrato m di pomodoro. **tomato sauce** n salsa f di pomodoro

**tomb** /tuːm/ n tomba f

**tomboy** /'tɒmbɔɪ/ n maschiaccio m

**tombstone** /'tuːmstəʊn/ n pietra f tombale

**tom-cat** n gatto m maschio

**tome** /təʊm/ n tomo m

**tomfoolery** /tɒm'fuːlərɪ/ n stupidaggini fpl

**tomorrow** /tə'mɒrəʊ/ a & adv domani; **~ morning** domani mattina; **the day after ~** dopodomani; **see you ~!** a domani!

**tom-tom** n tamtam m inv

**ton** /tʌn/ n tonnellata f (= 1,016 kg); **~s of** fam un sacco di

**tonal** /'təʊnl/ a tonale

**tonality** /təʊ'nælətɪ/ n tonalità f inv

**tone** /təʊn/ n tono m; (colour) tonalità f inv

■ **tone down** vt attenuare

■ **tone in** vi intonarsi

■ **tone up** vt tonificare ⟨muscles⟩

**tone-deaf** a **be ~** non avere orecchio

**toneless** /'təʊnlɪs/ a (unmusical) piatto

**toner** /'təʊnə(r)/ n toner m

**tongs** /tɒŋz/ npl pinze fpl

**tongue** /tʌŋ/ n lingua f; **~ in cheek** ⟨fam: say⟩ ironicamente

**tongue: tongue-lashing** n (severe reprimand) strigliata f. **tongue-tied** a senza parole. **tongue-twister** n scioglilingua m inv

**tonic** /'tɒnɪk/ n tonico m; (for hair) lozione f per i capelli; fig toccasana m inv; **~ [water]** acqua f tonica

**tonight** /tə'naɪt/ adv stanotte; (evening) stasera ● n questa notte f; (evening) questa sera f

**tonnage** /'tʌnɪdʒ/ n stazza f

**tonne** /tʌn/ n tonnellata f metrica

**tonsil** /'tɒnsl/ n Anat tonsilla f; **have one's ~s out** operarsi di tonsille

**tonsillitis** /tɒnsə'laɪtɪs/ n tonsillite f; **have ~** avere la tonsillite

**too** /tuː/ adv troppo; (also) anche; **~ many** troppi; **~ much** troppo; **~ little** troppo poco

**took** /tʊk/ see **take**

**tool** /tuːl/ n attrezzo m

**tool: tool-bag** n borsa f degli attrezzi. **tool bar** n Comput barra f strumenti. **toolbox** n cassetta f degli attrezzi. **tool kit** n astuccio m di attrezzi

**toot** /tuːt/ n suono m di clacson ● vi Auto clacsonare

**tooth** /tuːθ/ n (pl **teeth**) dente m

**tooth ache** /'tuːθeɪk/ n mal m di denti; **have ~** avere mal di denti

**toothbrush** /'tuːθbrʌʃ/ n spazzolino m da denti

**toothless** /'tuːθlɪs/ a sdentato

**toothpaste** /'tuːθpeɪst/ n dentifricio m

**toothpick** /'tuːθpɪk/ n stuzzicadenti m inv

**toothy** /'tu:θɪ/ a **give a ~ grin** fare un sorriso a trentadue denti

**top¹** /tɒp/ n (toy) trottola f

**top²** n cima f; Sch primo, -a mf; (upper part or half) parte f superiore; (of page, list, street) inizio m; (upper surface) superficie f; (lid) coperchio m; (of bottle) tappo m; (garment) maglia f; (blouse) camicia f; Auto marcia f più alta; **at the ~** fig al vertice; **at the ~ of one's voice** a squarciagola; **on ~/on ~ of** sopra; **on ~ of that** (besides) per di più; **from ~ to bottom** da cima a fondo; **blow one's ~** fam perdere le staffe; **over the ~** (fam: exaggerated, too much) eccessivo ● a in alto; (official, floor of building) superiore; (pupil, musician etc) migliore; (speed) massimo ● vt (pt/pp **topped**) essere in testa a (list); (exceed) sorpassare; **~ped with ice-cream** ricoperto di gelato; **~ oneself** sl suicidarsi

■ **top up** vt riempire

**topaz** /'təʊpæz/ n topazio m

**top: top brass** n fam pezzi mpl grossi. **topcoat** n (of paint) strato m finale. **top floor** n ultimo piano m. **top gear** n Auto marcia f più alta. **top hat** n cilindro m. **top-heavy** a con la parte superiore sovraccarica

**topic** /'tɒpɪk/ n soggetto m; (of conversation) argomento m

**topical** /'tɒpɪkl/ a d'attualità; **very ~** di grande attualità

**topless** /'tɒplɪs/ a & adv topless

**top-level** a ad alto livello

**topmost** /'tɒpməʊst/ a più alto

**top: top-notch** a fam eccellente. **top-of-the-range** a (model) della fascia più alta

**topping** /'tɒpɪŋ/ n **with a chocolate ~** ricoperto di cioccolato; **pizza with a ham and mushroom ~** pizza al prosciutto e funghi

**topple** /'tɒpl/ vt rovesciare ● vi rovesciarsi

■ **topple off** vi cadere

**top: top-ranking** a (official) di massimo grado. **top secret** a segretissimo, top secret inv. **top security** a di massima sicurezza. **topsoil** n strato m superficiale del terreno. **topspin** n topspin m inv

**topsy-turvy** /tɒpsɪ'tɜ:vɪ/ a & adv sottosopra

**top ten** npl primi dieci mpl in classifica

**top-up** n **would you like a ~?** ti riempio il bicchiere/la tazza?

**torch** /tɔ:tʃ/ n torcia f [elettrica]; (flaming) fiaccola f

**torchlight procession** /'tɔ:tʃlaɪt/ n fiaccolata f

**tore** /tɔ:(r)/ see **tear¹**

**torment¹** /'tɔ:ment/ n tormento m

**torment²** /tɔ:'ment/ vt tormentare

**tormentor** /tɔ:'mentə(r)/ n tormentatore, -trice mf

**torn** /tɔ:n/ see **tear¹** ● a bucato

**tornado** /tɔ:'neɪdəʊ/ n (pl -es) tornado m inv

**torpedo** /tɔ:'pi:dəʊ/ n (pl -es) siluro m ● vt silurare

**torpid** /'tɔ:pɪd/ a intorpidito

**torrent** /'tɒrənt/ n torrente m

**torrential** /tə'renʃl/ a (rain) torrenziale

**torrid** /'tɒrɪd/ a torrido

**torso** /'tɔ:səʊ/ n torso m; (in art) busto m

**tortoise** /'tɔ:təs/ n tartaruga f

**tortoiseshell** /'tɔ:təʃel/ n tartaruga f

**tortuous** /'tɔ:tʃʊəs/ a tortuoso

**tortuously** /'tɔ:tʃʊəslɪ/ adv tortuosamente

**torture** /'tɔ:tʃə(r)/ n tortura f ● vt torturare

**Tory** /'tɔ:rɪ/ Br n conservatore, -trice mf (appartenente al partito britannico dei conservatori) ● a del partito conservatore

**toss** /tɒs/ vt gettare; (into the air) lanciare in aria; (shake) scrollare; (horse:) disarcionare; mescolare (salad); rivoltare facendo saltare in aria (pancake); **~ a coin** fare testa o croce ● vi **~ and turn** (in bed) rigirarsi; **let's ~ for it** facciamo testa o croce

**toss-up** n fam **let's have a ~ to decide** facciamo testa o croce

**tot¹** /tɒt/ n bimbetto, -a mf; (fam: of liquor) goccio m

**tot²** vt (pt/pp **totted**) **~ up** fam fare la somma di

**total** /'təʊtl/ a totale ● n totale m ● vt (pt/pp **totalled**) ammontare a; (add up) sommare

**totalitarian** /təʊtælɪ'teərɪən/ a totalitario

**totally** /'təʊtəlɪ/ adv totalmente

**tote bag** /təʊt/ n sporta f

**totem pole** /'təʊtəm/ n totem m inv

**totter** /'tɒtə(r)/ vi barcollare; (government:) vacillare

**touch** /tʌtʃ/ n tocco m; (sense) tatto m; (contact) contatto m; (trace) traccia f; (of irony, humour) tocco m; **get/be in ~** mettersi/essere in contatto ● vt toccare; (lightly) sfiorare; (equal) eguagliare; (fig: move) commuovere ● vi toccarsi

■ **touch down** vi Aeron atterrare

■ **touch off** vi fig scatenare

■ **touch on** vt fig accennare a

■ **touch up** vt ritoccare (painting); **~ sb up** (sexually) allungare le mani su qcno

**touch-and-go** a incerto

**touchdown** /'tʌtʃdaʊn/ n Aeron atterraggio m; Sport meta f

**touché** /tu:'ʃeɪ/ int fig touché!

**touched** /tʌtʃt/ a (crazy) toccato

**touching** /'tʌtʃɪŋ/ a commovente

**touchingly** /'tʌtʃɪŋlɪ/ adv in modo commovente

**touch: touchline** n (in football) linea f laterale; (in rugby) touche nf inv. **touch[-sensitive] screen** n Comput schermo m a sfioramento. **touch-type** vi dattilografare a tastiera cieca. **touch-typing** n dattilografia f a tastiera cieca. **touch-up** n (of paintwork) ritocco m

**touchy** /'tʌtʃɪ/ a permaloso; (subject) delicato

**tough** /tʌf/ a duro; (severe, harsh) severo; (durable) resistente; (resilient) forte; **~!** (fam: too bad) peggio per te/lui!

**toughen** /'tʌfn/ vt rinforzare

■ **toughen up** vt rendere più forte (person)

**toupee** /'tu:peɪ/ n toupet m inv

**tour** /tʊə(r)/ n giro m; (of building, town) visita f; *Theat, Sport* tournée f *inv*; *(of duty)* servizio m ● *vt* visitare ● *vi* fare un giro turistico; *Theat* essere in tournée

**tour guide** n guida f turistica

**tourism** /'tʊərizm/ n turismo m

**tourist** /'tʊərist/ n turista mf ● *attrib* turistico

**tourist: tourist class** n classe f turistica. **tourist office** n ufficio m turistico. **tourist resort** n località f turistica. **tourist route** n itinerario m turistico. **tourist trap** n locale o località per turisti dove i prezzi sono molto alti

**touristy** /'tʊəristi/ a fam pej da turisti; **it's too ~ here** è troppo turistico qui

**tournament** /'tʊənəmənt/ n torneo m

**tourniquet** /'tʊənikei/ n laccio m emostatico

**tour operator** n tour operator mf *inv*, operatore, -trice mf turistico, -a

**tousle** /'taʊzl/ vt spettinare

**tout** /taʊt/ n *(ticket ~)* bagarino m; *(horse-racing)* informatore m ● *vi* **~ for** sollecitare

**tow** /təʊ/ n rimorchio m; **'on ~'** 'a rimorchio'; **in ~** fam al seguito ● *vt* rimorchiare

■ **tow away** vt portare via col carro attrezzi

**toward[s]** /tə'wɔːd(z)/ prep verso *(with respect to)* nei riguardi di

**tow bar** n barra f di rimorchio

**towel** /'taʊəl/ n asciugamano m

■ **towel down** vt asciugare

**towelling** /'taʊəliŋ/ n spugna f

**towelling robe** n accappatoio m

**towel rail** n portasciugamano m

**tower** /'taʊə(r)/ n torre f; **be a ~ of strength to sb** essere di grande conforto per qcno ● *vi* **~ above** dominare

**tower block** n palazzone m

**towering** /'taʊəriŋ/ a torreggiante; ⟨rage⟩ violento

**tow line** n cavo m da rimorchio

**town** /taʊn/ n città f *inv*; **in ~** nel centro

**town: town centre** n centro m della città. **town council** n municipalità f *inv*. **town hall** n municipio m. **town planner** n urbanista mf. **town planning** n urbanistica f

**towpath** /'təʊpɑːθ/ n strada f alzaia

**tow rope** n cavo m da rimorchio

**toxic** /'tɒksik/ a tossico

**toxicity** /tɒk'sisiti/ n tossicità f

**toxic waste** n rifiuti mpl tossici

**toxicologist** /tɒksi'kɒlədʒist/ n tossicologo, -a mf

**toxicology** /tɒksi'kɒlədʒi/ n tossicologia f

**toxin** /'tɒksin/ n tossina f

**toy** /tɔi/ n giocattolo m

■ **toy with** vt giocherellare con

**toyboy** /'tɔibɔi/ n Br fam uomo-oggetto m

**toyshop** /'tɔiʃɒp/ n negozio m di giocattoli

**trace** /treis/ n traccia f ● *vt* seguire le tracce di; *(find)* rintracciare; *(draw)* tracciare; *(with tracing-paper)* ricalcare

■ **trace back** vt trovare tracce di ⟨family⟩

■ **trace out** vt tracciare

**tracer** /'treisə(r)/ n Mil proiettile m tracciante

**tracing** /'treisiŋ/ n ricalco m

**tracing-paper** n carta f da ricalco

**track** /træk/ n traccia f; *(path, Sport)* pista f; *Rail* binario m; **keep ~ of** tenere d'occhio ● *vt* seguire le tracce di

■ **track down** vt scovare

**trackball** /'trækbɔːl/ n Comput trackball f *inv*

**tracker** /'trækə(r)/ n *(dog)* segugio m

**track record** n fig background m *inv*

**tracksuit** /'træksuːt/ n tuta f da ginnastica

**tract** /trækt/ n *(pamphlet)* opuscolo m

**tractable** /'træktəbl/ a trattabile; *(docile)* maneggevole

**traction** /'trækʃn/ n *(of wheel)* trazione f

**traction engine** n trattore m

**tractor** /'træktə(r)/ n trattore m

**trade** /treid/ n commercio m; *(line of business)* settore m; *(craft)* mestiere m; **by ~** di mestiere ● *vt* commerciare; **~ sth for sth** scambiare qcsa per qcsa ● *vi* commerciare

■ **trade in** vt *(give in part exchange)* dare in pagamento parziale

■ **trade off** vt scambiare

■ **trade on** vt approfittarsi di

**trade: trade deficit** n bilancio m commerciale in deficit. **trade discount** n sconto m commerciale. **trade fair** n fiera f commerciale. **trade-in** n permuta f come pagamento parziale. **trade mark** n marchio m di fabbrica. **trade-name** n nome m depositato. **trade-off** n compromesso m. **trade price** n prezzo m all'ingrosso

**trader** /'treidə(r)/ n commerciante mf

**trade secret** n segreto m commerciale

**tradesman** /'treidzmən/ n *(joiner etc)* operaio m

**trade: trade union** n sindacato m. **trade unionist** n sindacalista mf. **trade union representative** n rappresentante mf sindacale

**trading** /'treidiŋ/ n commercio m

**trading: trading estate** n zona f industriale. **trading floor** n Fin sala f delle contrattazioni. **trading stamp** n bollino m premio

**tradition** /trə'diʃn/ n tradizione f

**traditional** /trə'diʃnl/ a tradizionale

**traditionalist** /trə'diʃn(ə)list/ n tradizionalista mf

**traditionally** /trə'diʃn(ə)li/ adv tradizionalmente

**traffic** /'træfik/ n traffico m ● *vi* trafficare

**traffic: traffic calming measures** npl misure fpl per rallentare il traffico in città. **traffic circle** n Am isola f rotatoria. **traffic island** n isola f spartitraffico. **traffic jam** n ingorgo m. **traffic lights** npl semaforo msg. **traffic offence** n infrazione f al codice della strada. **traffic warden** n vigile m [urbano]; *(woman)* vigilessa f

**tragedy** /'trædʒədi/ n tragedia f

**tragic** /'trædʒik/ a tragico

**tragically** /'trædʒikli/ adv tragicamente

**trail** /treɪl/ n traccia f; ⟨path⟩ sentiero m ● vi strisciare; ⟨plant:⟩ arrampicarsi; ~ **[behind]** rimanere indietro; ⟨in competition⟩ essere in svantaggio ● vt trascinare

**trail bike** n moto f fuoristrada

**trailblazer** /'treɪlbleɪzə(r)/ n pioniere, -a mf

**trailblazing** /'treɪlbleɪzɪŋ/ a innovatore

**trailer** /'treɪlə(r)/ n Auto rimorchio m; ⟨Am: caravan⟩ roulotte f inv; ⟨film⟩ presentazione f ⟨di un film⟩

**train** /treɪn/ n treno m; ⟨of dress⟩ strascico m; **by** ~ in treno; ~ **of thought** filo m dei pensieri ● vt formare professionalmente; Sport allenare; ⟨aim⟩ puntare; educare ⟨child⟩; addestrare ⟨animal, soldier⟩; far crescere ⟨plant⟩ ● vi fare il tirocinio; Sport allenarsi

**trained** /treɪnd/ a ⟨animal⟩ addestrato (**to do** a fare)

**trainee** /treɪ'ni:/ n apprendista mf

**trainer** /'treɪnə(r)/ n Sport allenatore, -trice mf; ⟨in circus⟩ domatore, -trice mf; ⟨of dog, race-horse⟩ addestratore, -trice mf; ~**s** ⟨pl: shoes⟩ scarpe fpl da ginnastica

**training** /'treɪnɪŋ/ n tirocinio m; Sport allenamento m; ⟨of animal, soldier⟩ addestramento m

**training college** n istituto m professionale

**train set** n trenino m

**traipse** /treɪps/ vi ~ **around** fam andare in giro

**trait** /treɪt/ n caratteristica f

**traitor** /'treɪtə(r)/ n traditore, -trice mf

**trajectory** /trə'dʒekt(ə)rɪ/ n traiettoria f

**tram** /træm/ n tram m inv

**tram-lines** npl rotaie fpl del tram

**tramp** /træmp/ n ⟨hike⟩ camminata f; ⟨vagrant⟩ barbone, -a mf; ⟨of feet⟩ calpestio m ● vi camminare con passo pesante; ⟨hike⟩ percorrere a piedi

■ **trample on** /'træmpl/ vt calpestare

**trampoline** /'træmpəli:n/ n trampolino m

**trance** /trɑ:ns/ n trance f inv

**tranquil** /'træŋkwɪl/ a tranquillo

**tranquillity** /træŋ'kwɪlətɪ/ n tranquillità f

**tranquillizer** /'træŋkwɪlaɪzə(r)/ n tranquillante m

**transact** /træn'zækt/ vt trattare

**transaction** /træn'zækʃn/ n transazione f

**transatlantic** /trænzət'læntɪk/ a ⟨crossing, flight⟩ transatlantico; ⟨attitude, accent⟩ americano

**transceiver** /træn'si:və(r)/ n ricetrasmittente f

**transcend** /træn'send/ vt trascendere

**transcontinental** /trænzkɒntɪ'nent(ə)l/ a transcontinentale

**transcribe** /træn'skraɪb/ vt trascrivere

**transcript** /'trænskrɪpt/ n trascrizione f

**transcription** /træn'skrɪpʃn/ n trascrizione f

**transept** /'trænsept/ n transetto m

**transfer¹** /'trænsfɜ:(r)/ n trasferimento m; Sport cessione f; ⟨design⟩ decalcomania f

**transfer²** /træns'fɜ:(r)/ v ⟨pt/pp **trans-**

**ferred**⟩ ● vt trasferire; Sport cedere ● vi trasferirsi; ⟨when travelling⟩ cambiare

**transfer fee** n ⟨for footballer⟩ prezzo m d'acquisto

**transfer list** n ⟨in football⟩ lista f di giocatori da cedere

**transferable** /træns'fɜ:rəbl/ a trasferibile

**transfigure** /træns'fɪgə/ vt trasfigurare

**transfix** /træns'fɪks/ vt trafiggere; fig immobilizzare

**transfixed** /træns'fɪkst/ a ⟨with fascination⟩ folgorato; ⟨with horror⟩ paralizzato

**transform** /træns'fɔ:m/ vt trasformare

**transformation** /trænsfə'meɪʃn/ n trasformazione f

**transformer** /træns'fɔ:mə(r)/ n trasformatore m

**transfusion** /træns'fju:ʒn/ n trasfusione f

**transgression** /træns'greʃn/ n Jur trasgressione f; Relig peccato m

**transient** /'trænzɪənt/ a passeggero

**transistor** /træn'zɪstə(r)/ n transistor m inv; ⟨radio⟩ radiolina f a transistor

**transit** /'trænzɪt/ n transito m; **in** ~ ⟨goods⟩ in transito

**transition** /træn'zɪʃn/ n transizione f

**transitional** /træn'zɪʃənl/ a di transizione

**transitive** /'trænzɪtɪv/ a transitivo

**transitively** /'trænzɪtɪvlɪ/ adv transitivamente

**transit lounge** n sala f d'attesa transiti

**transitory** /'trænzɪtərɪ/ a transitorio

**transit passenger** n passeggero m in transito

**translate** /trænz'leɪt/ vt tradurre

**translation** /trænz'leɪʃn/ n traduzione f

**translation agency** n agenzia f di traduzioni

**translator** /trænz'leɪtə(r)/ n traduttore, -trice mf

**translucent** /trænz'lu:snt/ a liter traslucido

**transmissible** /trænz'mɪsəbl/ a trasmissibile

**transmission** /trænz'mɪʃn/ n trasmissione f

**transmit** /trænz'mɪt/ vt ⟨pt/pp **transmitted**⟩ trasmettere

**transmitter** /trænz'mɪtə(r)/ n trasmettitore m

**transparency** /træn'spærənsɪ/ n Phot diapositiva f

**transparent** /træn'spærənt/ a trasparente

**transpire** /træn'spaɪə(r)/ vi emergere; ⟨fam: happen⟩ accadere

**transplant¹** /'trænsplɑ:nt/ n trapianto m

**transplant²** /træns'plɑ:nt/ vt trapiantare

**transport¹** /'trænspɔ:t/ n trasporto m; **do you have** ~? hai un mezzo di trasporto?

**transport²** /træn'spɔ:t/ vt trasportare

**transportation** /trænspɔ:'teɪʃn/ n trasporto m

**transpose** /træns'pəʊz/ vt trasporre

**transsexual** /trænz'seksʃʊəl/ n transessuale mf ● a transessuale

**trans-shipment** /trænz'ʃɪpmənt/ n trasbordo m

**transverse** /trænz'vɜːs/ a trasversale

**transvestite** /trænz'vestaɪt/ n travestito, -a mf

**trap** /træp/ n trappola f; (fam: mouth) boccaccia f; (carriage) calesse m ● vt (pt/pp **trapped**) intrappolare; schiacciare ⟨finger in door⟩; **be ~ped** essere intrappolato

**trapdoor** /'træpdɔː(r)/ n botola f

**trapeze** /trə'piːz/ n trapezio m

**trappings** /'træpɪŋz/ npl (dress) ornamenti mpl; **the ~ of wealth/success** i segni esteriori della ricchezza/del successo

**trash** /træʃ/ n robaccia f; (rubbish) spazzatura f; (nonsense) schiocchezze fpl

**trashcan** /'træʃkæn/ n Am pattumiera f, secchio m della spazzatura

**trashy** /'træʃɪ/ a scadente

**trauma** /'trɔːmə/ n trauma m

**traumatic** /trɔː'mætɪk/ a traumatico

**traumatize** /'trɔːmətaɪz/ vt traumatizzare

**travel** /'trævl/ n viaggi mpl ● v (pt/pp **travelled**) vi viaggiare; (to work) andare ● vt percorrere ⟨distance⟩

**travel: travel agency** n agenzia f di viaggi. **travel agent** n agente mf di viaggio. **travel expenses** npl spese fpl di viaggio

**traveller** /'trævələ(r)/ n viaggiatore, -trice mf; Comm commesso m viaggiatore; **~s** pl (gypsies) zingari mpl

**traveller's cheque** n traveller's cheque m inv

**travelling salesman** /'trævəlɪŋ/ n commesso m viaggiatore

**travelogue** /'trævəlɒg/ n (film) documentario m di viaggio; (talk) conferenza f su un viaggio

**travel-sick** a be/get **~** (on plane) soffrire il mal d'aria; (in car) soffrire il mal d'auto; (on boat) soffrire il mal di mare

**travel-sickness** n (on plane) mal m d'aria; (in car) mal m d'auto; (on boat) mal m di mare ● attrib ⟨pills⟩ per il mal d'aria/d'auto/di mare

**traverse** /trə'vɜːs/ vt traversare

**travesty** /'trævɪstɪ/ n (fig: farce) farsa f; **a ~ of justice** una presa in giro della giustizia

**trawler** /'trɔːlə(r)/ n peschereccio m

**tray** /treɪ/ n vassoio m; (for baking) teglia f; (for documents) vaschetta f; (of printer, photocopier) vassoio m, cassetto m

**treacherous** /'tretʃərəs/ a traditore; ⟨weather, currents⟩ pericoloso

**treachery** /'tretʃ(ə)rɪ/ n tradimento m

**treacle** /'triːkl/ n melassa f

**tread** /tred/ n andatura f; (step) gradino m; (of tyre) battistrada m inv ● vi (pt **trod**, pp **trodden**) (walk) camminare

■ **tread on** vt calpestare ⟨grass⟩; pestare ⟨foot⟩

**treadmill** /'tredmɪl/ n fig solito tran tran m

**treason** /'triːzn/ n tradimento m

**treasonable** /'triːz(ə)nəbl/ a proditorio

**treasure** /'treʒə(r)/ n tesoro m ● vt tenere in gran conto

**treasurer** /'treʒərə(r)/ n tesoriere, -a mf

**treasury** /'treʒərɪ/ n **the T~** il Ministero del Tesoro

**treat** /triːt/ n piacere m; (present) regalo m; **give sb a ~** fare una sorpresa a qcno ● vt trattare; Med curare; **~ sb to sth** offrire qcsa a qcno; **~ sb for sth** Med sottoporre qcno ad una cura per qcsa

**treatise** /'triːtɪz/ n trattato m

**treatment** /'triːtmənt/ n trattamento m; Med cura f

**treaty** /'triːtɪ/ n trattato m

**treble** /'trebl/ a triplo; **~ the amount** il triplo ● n Mus (voice) voce f bianca ● vt triplicare ● vi triplicarsi

**treble clef** n chiave f di violino

**tree** /triː/ n albero m

**tree: tree house** n capanna f su un albero. **treetop** n cima f di un albero. **tree trunk** n tronco m d'albero

**trek** /trek/ n scarpinata f; (as holiday) trekking m inv ● vi (pt/pp **trekked**) farsi una scarpinata; (on holiday) fare trekking

**trekking** /'trekɪŋ/ n trekking m

**trellis** /'trelɪs/ n graticolato m

**tremble** /'trembl/ vi tremare (**with** di)

**trembling** /'tremblɪŋ/ a tremante

**tremendous** /trɪ'mendəs/ a (huge) enorme; (fam: excellent) formidabile

**tremendously** /trɪ'mendəslɪ/ adv (very) straordinariamente; (a lot) enormemente

**tremor** /'tremə(r)/ n tremito m; **[earth] ~** scossa f [sismica]

**tremulous** /'tremjʊləs/ a tremulo

**trench** /trentʃ/ n fosso m; Mil trincea f

**trenchant** /'trentʃənt/ a ⟨comment, criticism⟩ mordace

**trench coat** n trench m inv

**trend** /trend/ n tendenza f; (fashion) moda f

**trend-setter** n persona f che detta la moda

**trend-setting** a che detta la moda

**trendy** /'trendɪ/ a (-ier, -iest) fam di or alla moda

**trepidation** /trepɪ'deɪʃn/ n trepidazione f

**trespass** /'trespəs/ vi **~ on** introdursi abusivamente in; fig abusare di

**trespasser** /'trespəsə(r)/ n intruso, -a mf

**trestle** /'tresl/ n cavalletto m

**trestle table** n tavolo m a cavalletto

**trial** /'traɪəl/ n Jur processo m; (test, ordeal) prova f; **on ~** in prova; Jur in giudizio; **by ~ and error** per tentativi

**trial period** n periodo m di prova

**trial run** n (preliminary test) prova f

**triangle** /'traɪæŋgl/ n triangolo m

**triangular** /traɪ'æŋgjʊlə(r)/ a triangolare

**tribal** /'traɪbl/ a tribale

**tribe** /traɪb/ n tribù f inv

**tribulation** /trɪbjʊ'leɪʃn/ n tribolazione f

**tribunal** /traɪ'bjuːnl/ n tribunale m

**tributary** /'trɪbjʊtərɪ/ n affluente m

**tribute** /'trɪbjuːt/ n tributo m; **pay ~** rendere omaggio

**trice** /traɪs/ n **in a ~** in un attimo
**tricentenary** /traɪsen'tiːnərɪ/ n terzo centenario m ● a del terzo centenario
**trick** /trɪk/ n trucco m; (joke) scherzo m; (Cards) presa f; **do the ~** fam funzionare; **play a ~ on** fare uno scherzo a ● vt imbrogliare; **~ of the trade** trucco m del mestiere
■ **trick into** vt **~ sb into doing sth** convincere qcno a fare qcsa con l'inganno
■ **trick out** vt **~ sb out of sth** fregare qcno a qcsa
**trick cyclist** n (sl: psychiatrist) psichiatra mf
**trickle** /'trɪkl/ vi colare
■ **trickle in** vi fig entrare poco per volta
■ **trickle out** vi fig uscire poco per volta
**trickster** /'trɪkstə(r)/ n imbroglione, -a mf
**tricky** /'trɪkɪ/ a (-ier, -iest) a ⟨operation⟩ complesso; ⟨situation⟩ delicato
**tricolour** /'trɪkələ(r)/ n tricolore m
**tricycle** /'traɪsɪkl/ n triciclo m
**tried** /traɪd/ see **try**
**tried and tested** a ⟨method⟩ sperimentato
**trifle** /'traɪfl/ n inezia f; Culin zuppa f inglese
**trifling** /'traɪflɪŋ/ a insignificante
**trig** /trɪg/ n (fam: trigonometry) trigonometria f
**trigger** /'trɪgə(r)/ n grilletto m; fig causa f ● vt ~ [off] scatenare
**trigger-happy** a fam dalla pistola facile; fig impulsivo
**trigonometry** /trɪgə'nɒmɪtrɪ/ n trigonometria f
**trilateral** /traɪ'lætərəl/ a trilaterale
**trilby** /'trɪlbɪ/ n cappello m di feltro
**trill** /trɪl/ n Mus trillo m
**trilogy** /'trɪlədʒɪ/ n trilogia f
**trim** /trɪm/ a (trimmer, trimmest) curato; ⟨figure⟩ snello ● n (of hair, hedge) spuntata f; (decoration) rifinitura f; **in good ~** in buono stato; ⟨person⟩ in forma ● vt (pt/pp trimmed) spuntare ⟨hair etc⟩; (decorate) ornare; Naut orientare
■ **trim off** vt tagliare via
**trimming** /'trɪmɪŋ/ n bordo m; ~s pl (of pastry) ritagli mpl; (decorations) guarnizioni fpl; **with all the ~s** Culin guarnito
**Trinity** /'trɪmətɪ/ n **the [Holy] ~** la [Santissima] Trinità
**trinket** /'trɪŋkɪt/ n ninnolo m
**trio** /'triːəʊ/ n trio m
**trip** /trɪp/ n (excursion) gita f; (journey) viaggio m; (stumble) passo m falso ● v (pt/pp tripped) ● vt far inciampare ● vi inciampare (on/over in)
■ **trip up** vt far inciampare
**tripartite** /traɪ'pɑːtaɪt/ a tripartito
**tripe** /traɪp/ n trippa f; (sl: nonsense) fesserie fpl
**triple** /'trɪpl/ a triplo ● vt triplicare ● vi triplicarsi
**triplets** /'trɪplɪts/ npl tre gemelli mpl
**triplicate** /'trɪplɪkət/ n **in ~** in triplice copia
**tripod** /'traɪpɒd/ n treppiede m inv
**tripper** /'trɪpə(r)/ n gitante mf

**trite** /traɪt/ a banale
**triteness** /'traɪtnɪs/ n banalità f
**triumph** /'traɪʌmf/ n trionfo m ● vi trionfare (over su)
**triumphant** /traɪ'ʌmf(ə)nt/ a trionfante
**triumphantly** /traɪ'ʌmf(ə)ntlɪ/ adv ⟨exclaim⟩ con tono trionfante
**triumvirate** /traɪ'ʌmvɪrət/ n triumvirato m
**trivia** /'trɪvɪə/ npl cose fpl secondarie
**trivial** /'trɪvɪəl/ a insignificante
**triviality** /trɪvɪ'ælətɪ/ n banalità f inv
**trivialize** /'trɪvɪəlaɪz/ vt sminuire
**trod, trodden** /trɒd, 'trɒdn/ see **tread**
**trolley** /'trɒlɪ/ n carrello m; (Am: tram) tram m inv
**trolley bus** n filobus m inv
**trombone** /trɒm'bəʊn/ n trombone m
**trombonist** /trɒm'bəʊnɪst/ n trombonista mf
**troop** /truːp/ n gruppo m; ~s pl truppe fpl ● vi ~ **in/out** entrare/uscire in gruppo
**trooper** /'truːpə(r)/ n Mil soldato m di cavalleria; (Am: policeman) poliziotto m
**trophy** /'trəʊfɪ/ n trofeo m
**tropic** /'trɒpɪk/ n tropico m; ~s pl tropici mpl
**tropical** /'trɒpɪkl/ a tropicale
**tropical fruit** n frutta f inv esotica
**trot** /trɒt/ n trotto m ● vi (pt/pp trotted) trottare
■ **trot out** vt (fam: produce) tirar fuori
**trotter** /'trɒtə(r)/ n Culin piedino m di maiale
**trouble** /'trʌbl/ n guaio m; (difficulties) problemi mpl; (inconvenience, Med) disturbo m; (conflict) conflitto m; **be in ~** essere nei guai; ⟨swimmer, climber:⟩ essere in difficoltà; **get into ~** finire nei guai; **get sb into ~** mettere qcno nei guai; **take the ~ to do sth** darsi la pena di far qcsa; **it's no ~** nessun disturbo; **the ~ with you is...** il tuo problema è... ● vt (worry) preoccupare; (inconvenience) disturbare; ⟨conscience, old wound:⟩ tormentare ● vi **don't ~!** non ti disturbare!
**troubled** /'trʌbld/ a ⟨mind⟩ inquieto; ⟨person, expression⟩ preoccupato; ⟨times, area⟩ difficile; ⟨waters, sleep⟩ agitato
**troublemaker** /'trʌblmeɪkə(r)/ n **be a ~** seminare zizzania
**troublesome** /'trʌblsəm/ a fastidioso
**trouble spot** n zona f calda
**trough** /trɒf/ n trogolo m; (atmospheric) depressione f
**trounce** /traʊns/ vt (in competition) schiacciare
**troupe** /truːp/ n troupe f inv
**trouser press** n stiracalzoni m inv
**trousers** /'traʊzəz/ npl pantaloni mpl
**trouser suit** n tailleur m inv pantalone
**trousseau** /'truːsəʊ/ n corredo m
**trout** /traʊt/ n inv trota f
**trowel** /'traʊəl/ n (for gardening) paletta f; (for builder) cazzuola f
**truant** /'truːənt/ n **play ~** marinare la scuola
**truce** /truːs/ n tregua f

**truck** /trʌk/ *n* (*lorry*) camion *m inv*

**trucker** /'trʌkə(r)/ *n* (*fam: lorry driver*) camionista *mf*

**truck farmer** *n Am* ortofrutticoltore *m*, ortolano *m*

**truculent** /'trʌkjʊlənt/ *a* aggressivo

**truculently** /'trʌkjʊləntlɪ/ *adv* aggressivamente

**trudge** /trʌdʒ/ *n* camminata *f* faticosa ● *vi* arrancare

**true** /truː/ *a* vero; **come ~** avverarsi

**true-life** *a* ⟨*adventure. story*⟩ vero

**truffle** /'trʌfl/ *n* tartufo *m*

**truism** /'truːɪzm/ *n* truismo *m*

**truly** /'truːlɪ/ *adv* veramente; **Yours ~** Distinti saluti

**trump** /trʌmp/ *n* (*Cards*) atout *m inv* ● *vt* prendere con l'atout

■ **trump up** *vt fam* inventare

**trump card** *n fig* asso *m* nella manica

**trumpet** /'trʌmpɪt/ *n* tromba *f*

**trumpeter** /'trʌmpɪtə(r)/ *n* trombettista *mf*

**truncate** /'trʌŋkeɪt/ *vt* tagliare ⟨*text*⟩; interrompere ⟨*process, journey, event*⟩

**truncheon** /'trʌntʃn/ *n* manganello *m*

**trundle** /'trʌndl/ *vt* far rotolare ● *vi* rotolare

**trunk** /trʌŋk/ *n* (*of tree, body*) tronco *m*; (*of elephant*) proboscide *f*; (*for travelling, storage*) baule *m*; (*Am: of car*) bagagliaio *m*, portabagagli *m inv*

**trunk road** *n* statale *f*

**trunks** /trʌŋks/ *npl* calzoncini *mpl* da bagno

**truss** /trʌs/ *n Med* cinto *m* erniario

■ **truss up** *vt* legare

**trust** /trʌst/ *n* fiducia *f*; (*group of companies*) trust *m inv*; (*organization*) associazione *f*; **on ~** sulla parola ● *vt* fidarsi di; (*hope*) augurarsi ● *vi* ~ **in** credere in; ~ **to** affidarsi a

**trusted** /'trʌstɪd/ *a* fidato

**trustee** /trʌs'tiː/ *n* amministratore, -trice *mf* fiduciario, -a

**trustful** /'trʌstfʊl/ *a* fiducioso

**trustfully** /'trʌstfʊlɪ/ *adv* fiduciosamente

**trust fund** *n* fondo *m* fiduciario

**trusting** /'trʌstɪŋ/ *a* fiducioso

**trustworthiness** /'trʌstwɜːðɪnɪs/ *n* (*of person*) affidabilità *f*; (*of source*) attendibilità *f*

**trustworthy** /'trʌstwɜːðɪ/ *a* fidato

**trusty** /'trʌstɪ/ *a fam* fidato

**truth** /truːθ/ *n* (*pl* -**s** /truːðz/) verità *f inv*

**truthful** /'truːθfʊl/ *a* ⟨*person*⟩ sincero; ⟨*statement*⟩ veritiero

**truthfully** /'truːθfʊlɪ/ *adv* sinceramente

**truthfulness** /'truːθfʊlnɪs/ *n* (*of person*) sincerità *f*; (*of account*) veridicità *f*

**try** /traɪ/ *n* tentativo *m*, prova *f*; (*in rugby*) meta *f*; **I'll give it a ~** faccio un tentativo ● *v* (*pt/pp* **tried**) ● *vt* provare; (*be a strain on*) mettere a dura prova; *Jur* processare ⟨*person*⟩; discutere ⟨*case*⟩; ~ **to do sth** provare a fare qcsa ● *vi* provare

■ **try for** *vi* cercare di ottenere

■ **try on** *vt* provarsi ⟨*garment*⟩

■ **try out** *vt* provare

**trying** /'traɪɪŋ/ *a* duro; ⟨*person*⟩ irritante

**try-out** *n* **give sb a ~** mettere alla prova qcno

**tsar** /zɑː/ *n* zar *m inv*

**tsarina** /tsɑː'riːnə/ *n* zarina *f*

**tsarist** /'tsɑːrɪst/ *a* zarista

**T-shirt** *n* maglietta *f*

**tsp** *abbr* **teaspoonful**

**tub** /tʌb/ *n* tinozza *f*; (*carton*) vaschetta *f*; (*bath*) vasca *f* da bagno

**tuba** /'tjuːbə/ *n Mus* tuba *f*

**tubby** /'tʌbɪ/ *a* (-**ier**, -**iest**) tozzo

**tube** /tjuːb/ *n* tubo *m*; (*of toothpaste*) tubetto *m*; *Br Rail* metró *f*

**tuber** /'tjuːbə(r)/ *n* tubero *m*

**tuberculosis** /tjuːbɜːkjʊ'ləʊsɪs/ *n* tubercolosi *f*

**tubing** /'tjuːbɪŋ/ *n* tubi *mpl*

**tubular** /'tjuːbjʊlə(r)/ *a* tubolare

**tuck** /tʌk/ *n* piega *f* ● *vt* (*put*) infilare

■ **tuck away** *vt* (*put in a safe place*) mettere al sicuro; (*eat*) spolverare

■ **tuck in** *vt* rimboccare; ~ **sb in** rimboccare le coperte a qcno ● *vi* (*fam: eat*) mangiare con appetito

■ **tuck into** *vt* mangiare di gusto ⟨*meal*⟩: ~ **sth into one's pocket** infilarsi in tasca qcsa; ~ **sb into bed** rimboccare le coperte a qcno

■ **tuck up** *vt* rimboccarsi ⟨*sleeves*⟩; (*in bed*) rimboccare le coperte a

**Tuesday** /'tjuːzdeɪ/ *n* martedì *m inv*

**tuft** /tʌft/ *n* ciuffo *m*

**tug** /tʌg/ *n* strattone *m*; *Naut* rimorchiatore *m* ● *v* (*pt/pp* **tugged**) ● *vt* tirare ● *vi* dare uno strattone

**tug of war** *n* tiro *m* alla fune

**tuition** /tjuː'ɪʃn/ *n* lezioni *fpl*

**tulip** /'tjuːlɪp/ *n* tulipano *m*

**tumble** /'tʌmbl/ *n* ruzzolone *m* ● *vi* ruzzolare; ~ **to sth** (*fam: realize*) afferrare qcsa

**tumbledown** /'tʌmbldaʊn/ *a* cadente

**tumble-drier** *n* asciugabiancheria *f*

**tumbler** /'tʌmblə(r)/ *n* bicchiere *m* (*senza stelo*)

**tummy** /'tʌmɪ/ *n fam* pancia *f*

**tummy button** *n fam* ombelico *m*

**tumour** /'tjuːmə(r)/ *n* tumore *m*

**tumult** /'tjuːmʌlt/ *n* tumulto *m*

**tumultuous** /tjuː'mʌltjʊəs/ *a* tumultuoso

**tuna** /'tjuːnə/ *n* tonno *m*

**tune** /tjuːn/ *n* motivo *m*; **out of/in** ⟨*instrument*⟩ scordato/accordato; ⟨*person*⟩ stonato/intonato; **to the ~ of** *fam* per la modesta somma di ● *vt* accordare ⟨*instrument*⟩; sintonizzare ⟨*radio, TV*⟩; mettere a punto ⟨*engine*⟩

■ **tune in** *vt* sintonizzare ● *vi* sintonizzarsi (**to** su)

■ **tune up** *vi* ⟨*orchestra:*⟩ accordare gli strumenti

**tuneful** /'tjuːnfl/ *a* melodioso

**tuner** /'tjuːnə(r)/ *n* accordatore, -trice *mf*; *Radio, TV* sintonizzatore *m*

**tune-up** *n* (*of engine*) messa *f* a punto

**tungsten** /'tʌŋstən/ n tungsteno m
**tunic** /'tju:nɪk/ n tunica f; Mil giacca f; Sch ≈
  grembiule m
**tuning-fork** /'tu:nɪŋ/ n diapason m inv
**Tunisia** /tju:'nɪzɪə/ n Tunisia f
**Tunisian** /tju:'nɪzɪən/ a & n tunisino, -a mf
**tunnel** /'tʌnl/ n tunnel m inv ● vi (pt/pp
  **tunnelled**) scavare un tunnel
**tuppence** /'tʌpəns/ n due penny
**turban** /'tɜ:bən/ n turbante m
**turbine** /'tɜ:baɪn/ n turbina f
**turbo** /'tɜ:bəʊ/ n turbo m inv
**turbocharged** /'tɜ:bəʊtʃɑ:dʒd/ a con motore turbo
**turbocharger** /'tɜ:bəʊtʃɑ:dʒə(r)/ n turbo-
  compressore m
**turbot** /'tɜ:bət/ n rombo m gigante
**turbulence** /'tɜ:bjʊləns/ n turbolenza f
**turbulent** /'tɜ:bjʊlənt/ a turbolento
**turd** /tɜ:d/ n sl (excrement) stronzo m; (pej:
  person) stronzo, -a mf
**tureen** /tjʊ'ri:n/ n zuppiera f
**turf** /tɜ:f/ n erba f; (segment) zolla f erbosa
■ **turf out** vt fam buttar fuori
**turf accountant** n allibratore m
**turgid** /'tɜ:dʒɪd/ a (style, water) turgido
**Turin** /tjʊ'rɪn/ n Torino m
**Turk** /tɜ:k/ n turco, -a mf
**Turkey** /'tɜ:kɪ/ n Turchia f
**turkey** n tacchino m
**Turkish** /'tɜ:kɪʃ/ a turco
**Turkish bath** n bagno m turco
**Turkish delight** n cubetti mpl di gelatina
  ricoperti di zucchero a velo
**turmeric** /'tɜ:mərɪk/ n (spice) curcumina f;
  (plant) curcuma f
**turmoil** /'tɜ:mɔɪl/ n tumulto m
**turn** /tɜ:n/ n (rotation, short walk) giro m; (in
  road) svolta f, curva f; (development) svolta f;
  Theat numero m; (fam: attack) crisi f inv; **a ~
  for the better/worse** un miglioramento/
  peggioramento m; **do sb a good ~** rendere
  un servizio a qcno; **take ~s** fare a turno; **in
  ~** a turno; **out of ~** (speak) a sproposito; **it's
  your ~** tocca a te ● vt girare voltare (back,
  eyes); dirigere (gun, attention) ● vi girare;
  (person:) girarsi; (leaves:) ingiallire; (become)
  diventare; **~ right/left** girare a destra/sini-
  stra; **~ sour** inacidirsi; **~ to sb** girarsi verso
  qcno; fig rivolgersi a qcno
■ **turn against** vi diventare ostile a ● vt
  mettere contro
■ **turn around** vi (person:) girarsi; (car:) girare ● vt girare (object); risollevare
  (company)
■ **turn away** vt mandare via (people); girare
  dall'altra parte (head) ● vi girarsi dall'altra
  parte
■ **turn back** vi tornare indietro ● vt mandare indietro (people); ripiegare (covers, sheet
  etc)
■ **turn down** vt piegare (collar); abbassare
  (heat, gas, sound); respingere (person,
  proposal)
■ **turn in** vt ripiegare in dentro (edges); con-

segnare (lost object) ● vi (fam: go to bed) andare a letto; **~ in to the drive** entrare nel
  viale
■ **turn into** vt (become) diventare
■ **turn off** vt spegnere; chiudere (tap, water);
  **~ sb off** (fam: disgust) fare schifo a qcno ● vi
  (car:) girare
■ **turn on** vt accendere; aprire (tap, water);
  (fam: attract) eccitare ● vi (attack) attaccare
■ **turn out** vt (expel) mandar via; spegnere
  (light, gas); (produce) produrre; (empty) svuotare (room, cupboard) ● vi (transpire) risultare; (to see, do sth) venire; **~ out well/badly**
  (cake, dress:) riuscire bene/male; (situation:)
  andare bene/male
■ **turn over** vt girare; **~ sb over to the
  police** consegnare qcno alla polizia; **he ~ed
  the business over to her** le ha ceduto
  l'azienda ● vi girarsi; **please ~ over** vedi retro
■ **turn round** vi girarsi; (car:) girare
■ **turn up** vt tirare su (collar); alzare (heat,
  gas, sound, radio) ● vi farsi vedere
**turn: turn-about** n (fig: change of direction)
  cambiamento m. **turnaround** n (in attitude)
  dietrofront m inv; (of fortune) capovolgimento
  m; (for the better) ripresa f. **turncoat** n
  voltagabbana mf inv
**turning** /'tɜ:nɪŋ/ n svolta f
**turning-point** n svolta f decisiva
**turnip** /'tɜ:nɪp/ n rapa f
**turn: turn-off** n strada f laterale; **it's a real
  ~** fam ti fa davvero passar la voglia. **turn-on**
  n fam **be a real ~** essere veramente eccitante. **turnout** n (of people) affluenza f. **turnover**
  n Comm giro m d'affari, fatturato m; (of staff)
  ricambio m. **turnpike** n Am autostrada f.
  **turnround** n (in policy etc) cambiamento m.
  **turnstile** n cancelletto m girevole. **turntable**
  n piattaforma f girevole; (on record-player)
  piatto m. **turn-up** n (of trousers) risvolto m
**turpentine** /'tɜ:pəntaɪn/ n trementina f
**turquoise** /'tɜ:kwɔɪz/ a (colour) turchese ● n
  turchese m
**turret** /'tʌrɪt/ n torretta f
**turtle** /'tɜ:tl/ n tartaruga f acquatica
**turtle-dove** n tortora f
**turtleneck** /'tɜ:tlnek/ n collo m a lupetto;
  (sweater) maglia f a lupetto
**Tuscan** /'tʌskən/ a toscano
**Tuscany** /'tʌskənɪ/ n Toscana f
**tusk** /tʌsk/ n zanna f
**tussle** /'tʌsl/ n zuffa f ● vi azzuffarsi
**tussock** /'tʌsək/ n ciuffo m d'erba
**tut** /tʌt/ vi fare un'esclamazione di disapprovazione ● int ts!
**tutor** /'tju:tə(r)/ n insegnante mf privato, -a;
  Univ insegnante mf universitario, -a che segue
  individualmente un ristretto numero di studenti
**tutorial** /tju:'tɔ:rɪəl/ n discussione f col tutor
**tutorial package** n Comput software m di
  autoapprendimento
**tuxedo** /tʌk'si:dəʊ/ n Am smoking m inv
**TV** abbr (**television**) tv f inv, tivù f inv

**twaddle** /'twɒdl/ *n* scemenze *fpl*

**twain** /twein/ *npl* **the ~** i due; **and never the ~ shall meet** e mai i due si incontreranno

**twang** /twæŋ/ *n* (*in voice*) suono *m* nasale ● *vt* far vibrare

**tweak** /twi:k/ *vt* tirare ⟨*ear, nose*⟩; (*adjust*) apportare delle modifiche a ● *n* (*adjustment*) modifica *f*; **give sb's ears a ~** dare una tirata d'orecchie a qcno

**twee** /twi:/ *a Br fam* ⟨*manner*⟩ affettato

**tweed** /twi:d/ *n* tweed *m inv*

**tweezers** /'twi:zəz/ *npl* pinzette *f*

**twelfth** /twelfθ/ *a & n* dodicesimo, -a *mf*

**twelve** /twelv/ *a & n* dodici *m*

**twentieth** /'twentɪθ/ *a & n* ventesimo, -a *mf*

**twenty** /'twentɪ/ *a & n* venti *m*

**twerp** /twɜ:p/ *n fam* stupido, -a *mf*

**twice** /twais/ *adv* due volte; **she's done ~ as much as you** ha fatto il doppio di quanto hai fatto tu

**twiddle** /'twɪdl/ *vt* giocherellare con; **~ one's thumbs** *fig* girarsi i pollici

**twig**[1] /twɪg/ *n* ramoscello *m*

**twig**[2] *vt/i* (*pt/pp* **twigged**) *fam* intuire

**twilight** /'twailait/ *n* crepuscolo *m*

**twill** /twɪl/ *n* spigato *m*

**twin** /twɪn/ *n* gemello, -a *mf* ● *attrib* gemello

**twin beds** *npl* letti *mpl* gemelli

**twine** /twain/ *n* spago *m* ● *vi* intrecciarsi; ⟨*plant:*⟩ attorcigliarsi ● *vt* intrecciare

**twinge** /twɪndʒ/ *n* fitta *f*; **~ of conscience** rimorso *m* di coscienza

**twinkle** /'twɪŋkl/ *n* scintillio *m* ● *vi* scintillare

**twinning** /'twɪnɪŋ/ *n* (*of companies*) gemellaggio *m*

**twin town** *n* città *f inv* gemellata

**twirl** /twɜ:l/ *vt* far roteare ● *vi* volteggiare ● *n* piroetta *f*

**twist** /twɪst/ *n* torsione *f*; (*curve*) curva *f*; (*in rope*) attorcigliata *f*; (*in book, plot*) colpo *m* di scena; **round the ~** (*fam: crazy*) ammattito ● *vt* attorcigliare ⟨*rope*⟩; torcere ⟨*metal*⟩; girare ⟨*knob, cap*⟩; (*distort*) distorcere; **~ one's ankle** storcersi la caviglia ● *vi* attorcigliarsi; ⟨*road:*⟩ essere pieno di curve

**twister** /'twɪstə(r)/ *n fam* imbroglione, -a *mf*; (*tornado*) tornado *m inv*

**twit** /twɪt/ *n fam* cretino, -a *mf*

**twitch** /twɪtʃ/ *n* tic *m inv*; (*jerk*) strattone *m* ● *vi* contrarsi

**twitchy** /'twɪtʃɪ/ *a* (*fam: nervous*) nervosetto

**twitter** /'twɪtə(r)/ *n* cinguettio *m*; **in a ~** *fam* agitato ● *vi* cinguettare; ⟨*person:*⟩ cianciare

■ **twitter on about** *vt* parlare incessantemente di

**two** /tu:/ *a & n* due *m*; **put ~ and ~ together** fare due più due

**two:** **two-faced** /-'feist/ *a* falso. **two-piece** *a* (*swimsuit*) due pezzi *m inv*; (*suit*) completo *m*. **two-seater** /-si:tə(r)/ *n* biposto *m inv*. **twosome** /'tu:səm/ *n* coppia *f*. **two-time** *vt fam* fare le corna a. **two-tone** *a* (*in colour*) bicolore; (*in sound*) bitonale. **two-way** *a* ⟨*traffic*⟩ a doppio senso di marcia

**tycoon** /tai'ku:n/ *n* magnate *m*

**tying** /'taiiŋ/ *see* **tie**

**type** /taip/ *n* tipo *m*; (*printing*) carattere *m* [tipografico] ● *vt/i* scrivere a macchina

**type:** **typecast** *vt* Theat, *fig* far fare sempre la stessa parte a ⟨*person*⟩ ● *a* a ruolo fisso. **typeface** *n* carattere *m* tipografico. **typeset** *vt* comporre. **typesetter** *n* compositore *m*. **typewriter** *n* macchina *f* da scrivere. **typewritten** *a* dattiloscritto

**typhoid** /'taifoid/ *n* febbre *f* tifoidea

**typhoon** /tai'fu:n/ *n* tifone *m*

**typical** /'tɪpɪkl/ *a* tipico

**typically** /'tɪpɪklɪ/ *adv* tipicamente; (*as usual*) come al solito

**typify** /'tɪpɪfai/ *vt* (*pt/pp* **-ied**) essere tipico di

**typing** /'taipiŋ/ *n* dattilografia *f*

**typist** /'taipist/ *n* dattilografo, -a *mf*

**typo** /'taipəu/ *n* errore *m* di stampa; (*keying error*) errore *m* di battitura

**typography** /tai'pɒgrəfɪ/ *n* tipografia *f*

**tyrannical** /tɪ'rænɪkl/ *a* tirannico

**tyrannize** /'tɪrənaiz/ *vt* tiranneggiare

**tyranny** /'tɪrənɪ/ *n* tirannia *f*

**tyrant** /'tairənt/ *n* tiranno, -a *mf*

**tyre** /'taiə(r)/ *n* gomma *f*, pneumatico *m*

**tyre pressure** *n* pressione *f* delle gomme

**Tyrrhenian Sea** /tɪ'ri:nɪən/ *n* mar *m* Tirreno

**tzar** /za:/ *n* zar *m*

**tzarina** /tsa:'ri:nə/ *n* zarina *f*

# Uu

**u, U** /juː/ *n* (*letter*) u, U *f inv*
**u** *abbr Cinema* (**universal**) per tutti
**U-bend** *n* (*in pipe*) gomito *m*; (*in road*) curva *f* a gomito
**ubiquitous** /juːˈbɪkwɪtəs/ *a* onnipresente
**udder** /ˈʌdə(r)/ *n* mammella *f* (*di vacca, capra etc*)
**UFO** *abbr* (**unidentified flying object**) ufo *m inv*
**Uganda** /juːˈgændə/ *n* Uganda *f*
**Ugandan** /juːˈgændən/ *a & n* ugandese *mf*
**ugliness** /ˈʌglɪnɪs/ *n* bruttezza *f*
**ugly** /ˈʌglɪ/ *a* (**-ier, -iest**) brutto
**UK** *abbr* **United Kingdom**
**Ukraine** /juːˈkreɪn/ *n* Ucraina *f*
**Ukrainian** /juːˈkreɪnɪən/ *a & n* ucraino, -a *mf*; (*language*) ucraino *m*
**ulcer** /ˈʌlsə(r)/ *n* ulcera *f*
**ulterior** /ʌlˈtɪərɪə(r)/ *a* ~ **motive** secondo fine *m*
**ultimate** /ˈʌltɪmət/ *a* definitivo; (*final*) finale; (*fundamental*) fondamentale
**ultimately** /ˈʌltɪmətlɪ/ *adv* alla fine
**ultimatum** /ʌltɪˈmeɪtəm/ *n* ultimatum *m inv*
**ultramarine** /ʌltrəməˈriːn/ *a* oltremarino ● *n* azzurro *m* oltremarino
**ultrasound** /ˈʌltrəsaʊnd/ *n Med* ecografia *f*
**ultrasound scan** *n* ecografia *m*
**ultrasound scanner** *n* scanner *m inv* per ecografia
**ultraviolet** /ʌltrəˈvaɪələt/ *a* ultravioletto
**umbilical** /ʌmˈbɪlɪkl/ *a* ~ **cord** cordone *m* ombelicale
**umbrage** /ˈʌmbrɪdʒ/ *n* take ~ offendersi
**umbrella** /ʌmˈbrelə/ *n* ombrello *m*
**umbrella stand** *n* portaombrelli *m inv*
**umpire** /ˈʌmpaɪə(r)/ *n* arbitro *m* ● *vt/i* arbitrare
**umpteen** /ʌmpˈtiːn/ *a fam* innumerevole
**umpteenth** /ʌmpˈtiːnθ/ *a fam* ennesimo; **for the ~ time** per l'ennesima volta
**UN** *abbr* (**United Nations**) ONU *f*
**unabashed** /ʌnəˈbæʃt/ *a* spudorato
**unabated** /ʌnəˈbeɪtɪd/ *a* (*enthusiasm*) inalterato; **continue ~** (*gales:*) continuare con la stessa intensità
**unable** /ʌnˈeɪbl/ *a* **be ~ to do sth** non potere fare qcsa; (*not know how*) non sapere fare qcsa
**unabridged** /ʌnəˈbrɪdʒd/ *a* integrale
**unacceptable** /ʌnəkˈseptəbl/ *a* (*proposal, suggestion*) inaccettabile
**unaccompanied** /ʌnəˈkʌmpnɪd/ *a* non accompagnato; (*luggage*) incustodito

**unaccountable** /ʌnəˈkaʊntəbl/ *a* inspiegabile
**unaccountably** /ʌnəˈkaʊntəblɪ/ *adv* inspiegabilmente
**unaccounted** /ʌnəˈkaʊntɪd/ *a* **be ~ for** (*not explained*) non avere spiegazione; (*not found*) mancare
**unaccustomed** /ʌnəˈkʌstəmd/ *a* insolito; **be ~ to** non essere abituato a
**unadorned** /ʌnəˈdɔːnd/ *a* (*walls*) disadorno
**unadulterated** /ʌnəˈdʌltəreɪtɪd/ *a* (*water*) puro; (*wine*) non sofisticato; *fig* assoluto
**unadventurous** /ʌnədˈventʃ(ə)rəs/ *a* (*person, production*) poco avventuroso; (*meal*) poco fantasioso
**unaided** /ʌnˈeɪdɪd/ *a* senza aiuto
**unalloyed** /ʌnəˈlɔɪd/ *a fig* puro
**unanimity** /juːnəˈnɪmətɪ/ *n* unanimità *f*
**unanimous** /juːˈnænɪməs/ *a* unanime
**unanimously** /juːˈnænɪməslɪ/ *adv* all'unanimità
**unannounced** /ʌnəˈnaʊnst/ *a* inaspettato
**unanswerable** /ʌnˈɑːns(ə)rəbl/ *a* (*remark, case*) irrefutabile; (*question*) senza risposta
**unappealing** /ʌnəˈpiːlɪŋ/ *a* poco attraente
**unappetizing** /ʌnˈæpetaɪzɪŋ/ *a* poco appetitoso
**unappreciated** /ʌnəˈpriːʃɪeɪtɪd/ *a* (*work of art*) incompreso
**unappreciative** /ʌnəˈpriːʃ(ɪ)ətɪv/ *a* (*audience*) indifferente; (*person*) ingrato
**unapproachable** /ʌnəˈprəʊtʃəbl/ *a* (*person*) inavvicinabile
**unarmed** /ʌnˈɑːmd/ *a* disarmato
**unarmed combat** *n* lotta *f* senza armi
**unashamedly** /ʌnəˈʃeɪmd/ *adv* sfacciatamente
**unasked** /ʌnˈɑːskt/ *adv* **he came ~** è venuto senza che nessuno glielo chiedesse
**unassuming** /ʌnəˈsjuːmɪŋ/ *a* senza pretese
**unattached** /ʌnəˈtætʃd/ *a* staccato; (*person*) senza legami
**unattainable** /ʌnəˈteɪnəbl/ *a* irraggiungibile
**unattended** /ʌnəˈtendɪd/ *a* incustodito
**unattractive** /ʌnəˈtræktɪv/ *a* (*person*) poco attraente; (*proposition*) poco allettante; (*characteristic*) sgradevole; (*building, furniture*) brutto
**unauthorized** /ʌnˈɔːθəraɪzd/ *a* non autorizzato
**unavailable** /ʌnəˈveɪləbl/ *a* non disponibile
**unavoidable** /ʌnəˈvɔɪdəbl/ *a* inevitabile
**unavoidably** /ʌnəˈvɔɪdəblɪ/ *adv* inevitabil-

mente; **I was ~ detained** sono stato trattenuto da cause di forza maggiore

**unaware** /ʌnəˈweə/ a **be ~ of sth** non rendersi conto di qcsa

**unawares** /ʌnəˈweəz/ adv **catch sb ~** prendere qcno alla sprovvista

**unbalanced** /ʌnˈbælənst/ a non equilibrato; (*mentally*) squilibrato

**unbearable** /ʌnˈbeərəbl/ a insopportabile

**unbearably** /ʌnˈbeərəblɪ/ adv insopportabilmente

**unbeatable** /ʌnˈbiːtəbl/ a imbattibile

**unbeaten** /ʌnˈbiːtən/ a imbattuto

**unbecoming** /ʌnbɪˈkʌmɪŋ/ a (*garment*) che non dona

**unbeknown** /ʌnbɪˈnəʊn/ a *fam* **~ to me** a mia insaputa

**unbelievable** /ʌnbɪˈliːvəbl/ a incredibile

**unbend** /ʌnˈbend/ vi (*pt/pp* **-bent**) (*relax*) distendersi

**unbiased** /ʌnˈbaɪəst/ a obiettivo

**unblock** /ʌnˈblɒk/ vt sbloccare

**unbolt** /ʌnˈbəʊlt/ vt togliere il chiavistello di

**unborn** /ʌnˈbɔːn/ a non ancora nato

**unbreakable** /ʌnˈbreɪkəbl/ a infrangibile

**unbridled** /ʌnˈbraɪdld/ a sfrenato

**unbuckle** /ʌnˈbʌkl/ vt slacciare (*belt*)

**unburden** /ʌnˈbɜːdən/ vt **~ oneself** *fig* sfogarsi (**to** con)

**unbutton** /ʌnˈbʌtən/ vt sbottonare

**uncalled-for** /ʌnˈkɔːldfɔː(r)/ a fuori luogo

**uncannily** /ʌnˈkænɪlɪ/ adv incredibilmente

**uncanny** /ʌnˈkænɪ/ a sorprendente; (*silence, feeling*) inquietante

**uncared-for** /ʌnˈkeədfɔː(r)/ a (*house, pet*) trascurato

**uncaring** /ʌnˈkeərɪŋ/ a (*world*) indifferente

**unceasing** /ʌnˈsiːsɪŋ/ a incessante

**uncensored** /ʌnˈsensəd/ a (*film, book*) non censurato

**unceremonious** /ʌnserɪˈməʊnɪəs/ a (*abrupt*) brusco

**unceremoniously** /ʌnserɪˈməʊnɪəslɪ/ adv senza tante cerimonie

**uncertain** /ʌnˈsɜːtən/ a incerto; (*weather*) instabile; **in no ~ terms** senza mezzi termini

**uncertainty** /ʌnˈsɜːtəntɪ/ n incertezza f

**unchallenged** /ʌnˈtʃælɪmdʒd/ a (*statement, decision*) incontestato; **I can't let that go ~** non posso non contestarlo

**unchanged** /ʌnˈtʃeɪmdʒd/ a invariato

**uncharacteristic** /ʌnkærəktəˈrɪstɪk/ a (*generosity*) insolito

**uncharitable** /ʌnˈtʃærɪtəbl/ a duro

**uncivilized** /ʌnˈsɪvɪlaɪzd/ a (*people, nation*) non civilizzato; (*treatment, conditions*) incivile

**unclassified** /ʌnˈklæsɪfaɪd/ a (*document, information*) non riservato; (*road*) non classificato

**uncle** /ˈʌŋkl/ n zio m

**unclear** /ʌnˈkliːr/ a (*instructions, reason, voice, writing*) non chiaro; (*future*) incerto;

**be ~ about sth** (*person:*) non aver ben chiaro qcsa

**unclog** /ʌnˈklɒg/ vt sturare (*pipe*)

**uncoil** /ʌnˈkɔɪl/ vt srotolare

**uncomfortable** /ʌnˈkʌmftəbl/ a scomodo; imbarazzante (*silence, situation*); **feel ~** *fig* sentirsi a disagio

**uncomfortably** /ʌnˈkʌmftəblɪ/ adv (*sit*) scomodamente; (*causing alarm etc*) spaventosamente

**uncommon** /ʌnˈkɒmən/ a insolito

**uncommunicative** /ʌnkəˈmjuːnɪkətɪv/ a poco comunicativo

**uncompromising** /ʌnˈkɒmprəmaɪzɪŋ/ a intransigente

**unconditional** /ʌnkənˈdɪʃənl/ a incondizionato

**unconditionally** /ʌnkənˈdɪʃnəlɪ/ adv incondizionatamente

**unconscious** /ʌnˈkɒnʃəs/ a privo di sensi; (*unaware*) inconsapevole; **be ~ of sth** non rendersi conto di qcsa

**unconsciously** /ʌnˈkɒnʃəslɪ/ adv inconsapevolmente

**uncontested** /ʌnkənˈtestɪd/ a (*Pol: seat*) non disputato

**uncontrollable** /ʌnkənˈtrəʊləbl/ a incontrollabile; (*sobbing*) irrefrenabile

**uncontrollably** /ʌnkənˈtrəʊləblɪ/ adv (*increase*) incontrollatamente; (*laugh, sob*) senza potersi controllare

**unconventional** /ʌnkənˈvenʃəl/ a poco convenzionale

**unconvincing** /ʌnkənˈvɪnsɪŋ/ a poco convincente

**uncooked** /ʌnˈkʊkt/ a crudo

**uncooperative** /ʌnkəʊˈɒpr(ə)tɪv/ a poco cooperativo

**uncork** /ʌnˈkɔːk/ vt sturare

**uncorroborated** /ʌnkəˈrɒbəreɪtɪd/ a non convalidato

**uncouth** /ʌnˈkuːθ/ a zotico

**uncover** /ʌnˈkʌvə(r)/ vt scoprire; portare alla luce (*buried object*)

**uncross** /ʌnˈkrɒs/ vt disincrociare (*legs, arms*)

**unctuous** /ˈʌŋktjʊəs/ a untuoso

**uncultivated** /ʌnˈkʌltɪveɪtɪd/ a incolto

**undaunted** /ʌnˈdɔːntɪd/ a imperterrito; **~ by sth** per nulla intimidito da qcsa

**undecided** /ʌndɪˈsaɪdɪd/ a indeciso; (*not settled*) incerto

**undefined** /ʌndɪˈfaɪnd/ a (*objective, nature*) indeterminato

**undelivered** /ʌndɪˈlɪvəd/ a (*mail*) non recapitato

**undeniable** /ʌndɪˈnaɪəbl/ a innegabile

**undeniably** /ʌndɪˈnaɪəblɪ/ adv innegabilmente

**under** /ˈʌndə(r)/ prep sotto; (*less than*) al di sotto di; **~ there** lì sotto; **~ repair/ construction** in riparazione/costruzione; **~ way** *fig* in corso; ● adv (~ *water*) sott'acqua; (*unconscious*) sotto anestesia

**underachieve** /ʌndərə'tʃiːv/ *vi Sch* restare al di sotto delle proprie possibilità

**underarm** /'ʌndərɑːm/ *a* ⟨*deodorant*⟩ per le ascelle; ⟨*hair*⟩ sotto le ascelle; ⟨*service, throw*⟩ dal basso verso l'alto

**undercarriage** /'ʌndəkærɪdʒ/ *n Aeron* carrello *m*

**undercharge** /ʌndə'tʃɑːdʒ/ *vt* far pagare meno del dovuto a

**underclothes** /'ʌndəkləʊðz/ *npl* biancheria *fsg* intima

**undercoat** /'ʌndəkəʊt/ *n* prima mano *f*

**undercook** /ʌndə'kʊk/ *vt* non cuocere abbastanza

**undercover** /ʌndə'kʌvə(r)/ *a* clandestino

**undercurrent** /'ʌndəkʌrənt/ *n* corrente *f* sottomarina; *fig* sottofondo *m*

**undercut** /ʌndə'kʌt/ *vt* (*pt/pp* -**cut**) *Comm* vendere a minor prezzo di

**underdeveloped** /ʌndədɪ'veləpt/ *a* ⟨*country*⟩ sottosviluppato; *Phot* non completamente sviluppato

**underdog** /'ʌndədɒg/ *n* perdente *m*

**underdone** /ʌndə'dʌn/ *a* ⟨*meat*⟩ al sangue

**underemployed** /ʌndərɪm'plɔɪd/ *a* ⟨*person*⟩ sottoccupato; ⟨*resources, equipment etc*⟩ non sfruttato completamente

**underequipped** /ʌndərɪ'kwɪpt/ *a* ⟨*army, person*⟩ insufficientemente equipaggiato; ⟨*schools, gym*⟩ insufficientemente attrezzato

**underestimate** /ʌndər'estɪmeɪt/ *vt* sottovalutare

**underexpose** /ʌndərɪks'pəʊz/ *vt Phot* sottoesporre

**underfed** /ʌndə'fed/ *a* denutrito

**underfloor** /'ʌndəflɔː(r)/ *a* ⟨*pipes, wiring*⟩ sotto il pavimento

**underfoot** /ʌndə'fʊt/ *adv* sotto i piedi; **trample ~** calpestare

**underfunded** /ʌndə'fʌndɪd/ *a* insufficientemente finanziato

**underfunding** /ʌndə'fʌndɪŋ/ *n* finanziamento *m* insufficiente

**undergo** /ʌndə'gəʊ/ *vt* (*pt* -**went**, *pp* -**gone**) subire ⟨*operation, treatment*⟩; **~ repair** essere in riparazione

**undergraduate** /ʌndə'grædʒʊət/ *n* studente, -tessa *mf* universitario, -a

**underground¹** /ʌndə'graʊnd/ *adv* sottoterra

**underground²** /'ʌndəgraʊnd/ *a* sotterraneo; ⟨*secret*⟩ clandestino ● *n* ⟨*railway*⟩ metropolitana *f*

**underground car park** *n* parcheggio *m* sotterraneo

**undergrowth** /'ʌndəgrəʊθ/ *n* sottobosco *m*

**underhand** /ʌndə'hænd/ *a* subdolo

**underlay** /'ʌndəleɪ/ *n* strato *m* di gomma o feltro posto sotto la moquette

**underlie** /ʌndə'laɪ/ *vt* (*pt* -**lay**, *pp* -**lain**, *pres p* -**lying**) *fig* essere alla base di

**underline** /ʌndə'laɪn/ *vt* sottolineare

**underling** /'ʌndəlɪŋ/ *n pej* subalterno, -a *mf*

**underlying** /ʌndə'laɪɪŋ/ *a fig* fondamentale

**undermanned** /ʌndə'mænd/ *a* ⟨*factory*⟩ a corto di mano d'opera

**undermentioned** /ʌndə'menʃnd/ *a* sottoindicato

**undermine** /ʌndə'maɪn/ *vt fig* minare

**underneath** /ʌndə'niːθ/ *prep* sotto; **~ it** sotto ● *adv* sotto

**undernourished** /ʌndə'nʌrɪʃt/ *a* denutrito

**underpaid** /ʌndə'peɪd/ *a* mal pagato

**underpants** /'ʌndəpænts/ *npl* mutande *fpl*

**underpass** /'ʌndəpɑːs/ *n* sottopassaggio *m*

**underpay** /ʌndə'peɪ/ *vt* sottopagare ⟨*employee*⟩

**underpin** /ʌndə'pɪn/ *vt* puntellare ⟨*wall*⟩; rafforzare ⟨*currency, power, theory*⟩; essere alla base di ⟨*religion, society*⟩

**underpopulated** /ʌndə'pɒpjʊleɪtɪd/ *a* sottopopolato

**underprivileged** /ʌndə'prɪvɪlɪdʒd/ *a* non abbiente

**underrate** /ʌndə'reɪt/ *vt* sottovalutare

**underseal** /'ʌndəsiːl/ *n Auto* antiruggine *m inv*

**under-secretary** /ʌndə'sekrət(ə)rɪ/ *n Br Pol* sottosegretario *m*

**undersell** /ʌndə'sel/ *vt* vendere a prezzo inferiore rispetto a ⟨*competitor*⟩; pubblicizzare poco ⟨*product*⟩

**undersexed** /ʌndə'sekst/ *a* con scarsa libido

**undershirt** /'ʌndəʃɜːt/ *n Am* maglia *f* della pelle

**undersigned** /ʌndə'saɪnd/ *a* sottoscritto

**undersized** /ʌndə'saɪzd/ *a* ⟨*portion*⟩ scarso; ⟨*animal*⟩ troppo piccolo; ⟨*person*⟩ di statura inferiore alla media

**understaffed** /ʌndə'stɑːft/ *a* a corto di personale

**understand** /ʌndə'stænd/ *vt* (*pt/pp* -**stood**) capire; **I ~ that...** (*have heard*) mi risulta che... ● *vi* capire

**understandable** /ʌndə'stændəbl/ *a* comprensibile

**understandably** /ʌndə'stændəblɪ/ *adv* comprensibilmente

**understanding** /ʌndə'stændɪŋ/ *a* comprensivo ● *n* comprensione *f*; (*agreement*) accordo *m*; **reach an ~** trovare un accordo; **on the ~ that** a condizione che

**understatement** /'ʌndəsteɪtmənt/ *n* **that's an ~** non è dire abbastanza

**understudy** /'ʌndəstʌdɪ/ *n Theat* sostituto, -a *mf*

**undertake** /ʌndə'teɪk/ *vt* (*pt* -**took**, *pp* -**taken**) intraprendere; **~ to do sth** impegnarsi a fare qcsa

**undertaker** /'ʌndəteɪkə(r)/ *n* impresario *m* di pompe funebri; **[firm of] ~s** *n* impresa *f* di pompe funebri

**undertaking** /ʌndə'teɪkɪŋ/ *n* impresa *f*; (*promise*) promessa *f*

**under-the-counter** *a* ⟨*goods, supply, trade*⟩ comprato/venduto sottobanco

**undertone** /'ʌndətəʊn/ *n fig* sottofondo *m*; **in an ~** sottovoce

**undervalue** /ˌʌndə'væljuː/ vt sottovalutare; **the shares are ~d** le azioni si sono svalutate

**underwater¹** /'ʌndəwɔːtə(r)/ a subacqueo

**underwater²** /ʌndə'wɔːtə(r)/ adv sott'acqua

**under way** a be ~ ~ ⟨vehicle:⟩ essere in corsa; ⟨filming, talks:⟩ essere in corso; **get ~** ~ ⟨vehicle:⟩ mettersi in viaggio; ⟨preparations, season:⟩ avere inizio

**underwear** /'ʌndəweə(r)/ n biancheria f intima

**underweight** /ʌndə'weɪt/ a sotto peso

**underworld** /'ʌndəwɜːld/ n ⟨criminals⟩ malavita f

**underwriter** /'ʌndəraɪtə(r)/ n assicuratore m

**undeserved** /ʌndɪ'zɜːvd/ a ⟨praise, reward, win⟩ immeritato; ⟨blame, punish⟩ ingiusto

**undeservedly** /ʌndɪ'zɜːvɪdlɪ/ adv ⟨praise, reward, win⟩ immeritatamente; ⟨blame, punish⟩ ingiustamente

**undesirable** /ʌndɪ'zaɪərəbl/ a indesiderato; ⟨person⟩ poco raccomandabile

**undetected** /ʌndɪ'tektɪd/ a ⟨crime, cancer⟩ non scoperto; ⟨flaw, movement, intruder⟩ non visto; **go ~** ⟨cancer, crime:⟩ non essere scoperto; ⟨person:⟩ passare inosservato ● adv ⟨break in, listen⟩ senza essere scoperto

**undeveloped** /ʌndɪ'veləpt/ a non sviluppato; ⟨land⟩ non sfruttato

**undies** /'ʌndɪz/ npl fam biancheria f intima (da donna)

**undignified** /ʌn'dɪgnɪfaɪd/ a poco dignitoso

**undisciplined** /ʌn'dɪsɪplɪnd/ a indisciplinato

**undiscovered** /ʌndɪs'kʌvəd/ a ⟨secret⟩ non svelato; ⟨crime, document⟩ non scoperto; ⟨land⟩ inesplorato; ⟨species⟩ sconosciuto; ⟨talent⟩ non ancora scoperto

**undiscriminating** /ʌndɪs'krɪmɪneɪtɪŋ/ a che non sa fare distinzioni

**undisputed** /ʌndɪ'spjuːtd/ a indiscusso

**undisturbed** /ʌndɪ'stɜːbd/ a ⟨sleep, night⟩ indisturbato

**undivided** /ʌndɪ'vaɪdɪd/ a ⟨loyalty, attention⟩ assoluto

**undo** /ʌn'duː/ vt (pt -did, pp -done) disfare; slacciare ⟨dress, shoes⟩; sbottonare ⟨shirt⟩; fig, Comput annullare

**undone** /ʌn'dʌn/ a ⟨shirt, button⟩ sbottonato; ⟨shoes, dress⟩ slacciato; (not accomplished) non fatto; **leave ~** ⟨job⟩ tralasciare

**undoubted** /ʌn'daʊtɪd/ a indubbio

**undoubtedly** /ʌn'daʊtɪdlɪ/ adv senza dubbio

**undress** /ʌn'dres/ vt spogliare; **get ~ed** spogliarsi ● vi spogliarsi

**undrinkable** /ʌn'drɪŋkəbl/ a ⟨unpleasant⟩ imbevibile; ⟨dangerous⟩ non potabile

**undue** /ʌn'djuː/ a eccessivo

**undulating** /'ʌndjʊleɪtɪŋ/ a ondulato; ⟨country⟩ collinoso

**unduly** /ʌn'djuːlɪ/ adv eccessivamente

**undying** /ʌn'daɪɪŋ/ a eterno

**unearned** /ʌn'ɜːnd/ a immeritato; **~ income** rendita f

**unearth** /ʌn'ɜːθ/ vt dissotterrare; fig scovare; scoprire ⟨secret⟩

**unearthly** /ʌn'ɜːθlɪ/ a soprannaturale; **at an ~ hour** fam a un'ora impossibile

**unease** /ʌn'iːz/ n disagio m

**uneasy** /ʌn'iːzɪ/ a a disagio; ⟨person⟩ inquieto; ⟨feeling⟩ inquietante; ⟨truce⟩ precario

**uneatable** /ʌn'iːtəbl/ a immangiabile

**uneconomic** /ʌniːkə'nɒmɪk/ a poco remunerativo

**uneconomical** /ʌniːkə'nɒmɪkl/ a poco economico

**uneducated** /ʌn'edjʊkeɪtɪd/ a ⟨person⟩ non istruito; ⟨tastes⟩ non raffinato; ⟨accent, speech⟩ da persona non istruita

**unemployed** /ʌnem'plɔɪd/ a disoccupato ● npl **the ~** i disoccupati

**unemployment** /ʌnem'plɔɪmənt/ n disoccupazione f

**unemployment benefit** n sussidio m di disoccupazione

**unending** /ʌn'endɪŋ/ a senza fine

**unenthusiastic** /ʌnɪnθjuːzɪ'æstɪk/ a poco entusiasta

**unequal** /ʌn'iːkwəl/ a disuguale; ⟨struggle⟩ impari; **be ~ to a task** non essere all'altezza di un compito

**unequalled** /ʌn'iːkwəld/ a ⟨achievement, quality, record⟩ ineguagliato

**unequally** /ʌn'iːkwəlɪ/ adv in modo disuguale

**unequivocal** /ʌnɪ'kwɪvəkl/ a inequivocabile; ⟨person⟩ esplicito

**unequivocally** /ʌnɪ'kwɪvəklɪ/ adv inequivocabilmente

**unerring** /ʌn'ɜːrɪŋ/ a infallibile

**unethical** /ʌn'eθɪkl/ a immorale

**uneven** /ʌn'iːvən/ a irregolare; ⟨distribution⟩ ineguale; ⟨number⟩ dispari

**unevenly** /ʌn'iːvənlɪ/ adv irregolarmente; ⟨distributed⟩ inegualmente

**uneventful** /ʌnɪ'ventfʊl/ a senza avvenimenti di rilievo

**unexciting** /ʌnɪk'saɪtɪŋ/ a poco entusiasmante

**unexpected** /ʌnɪk'spektɪd/ a inaspettato

**unexpectedly** /ʌnɪk'spektɪdlɪ/ adv inaspettatamente

**unexplored** /ʌnɪk'splɔːd/ a inesplorato

**unfailing** /ʌn'feɪlɪŋ/ a infallibile

**unfair** /ʌn'feə/ a ingiusto

**unfair dismissal** n licenziamento m ingiustificato

**unfairly** /ʌn'feəlɪ/ adv ingiustamente

**unfairness** /ʌn'feənɪs/ n ingiustizia f

**unfaithful** /ʌn'feɪθfʊl/ a infedele

**unfamiliar** /ʌnfə'mɪljə(r)/ a sconosciuto; **be ~ with** non conoscere

**unfashionable** /ʌn'fæʃnəbl/ a fuori moda

**unfasten** /ʌn'fɑːsn/ vt slacciare; (detach) staccare

**unfathomable** /ʌnˈfæð(ə)məbl/ a imperscrutabile

**unfavourable** /ʌnˈfeɪv(ə)rəbl/ a sfavorevole; ⟨impression⟩ negativo

**unfeeling** /ʌnˈfiːlɪŋ/ a insensibile

**unfinished** /ʌnˈfɪnɪʃt/ a da finire; ⟨business⟩ in sospeso

**unfit** /ʌnˈfɪt/ a inadatto; (morally) indegno; *Sport* fuori forma; ~ **for work** non in grado di lavorare; ~ **for human consumption** non commestibile

**unflappable** /ʌnˈflæpəbl/ a fam calmo

**unflattering** /ʌnˈflæt(ə)rɪŋ/ a ⟨clothes, hairstyle⟩ che non dona; ⟨portrait, description⟩ poco lusinghiero

**unflinching** /ʌnˈflɪntʃɪŋ/ a risoluto

**unfold** /ʌnˈfəʊld/ vt spiegare; (spread out) aprire; fig rivelare ● vi ⟨view:⟩ spiegarsi

**unforeseeable** /ʌnfɔːˈsiːəbl/ a imprevedibile

**unforeseen** /ʌnfɔːˈsiːn/ a imprevisto

**unforgettable** /ʌnfəˈgetəbl/ a indimenticabile

**unforgivable** /ʌnfəˈgɪvəbl/ a imperdonabile

**unforgiving** /ʌnfəˈgɪvɪŋ/ a che non perdona

**unfortunate** /ʌnˈfɔːtʃənət/ a sfortunato; (regrettable) spiacevole; ⟨remark, choice⟩ infelice

**unfortunately** /ʌnˈfɔːtʃənətlɪ/ adv purtroppo

**unfounded** /ʌnˈfaʊndɪd/ a infondato

**unfriendly** /ʌnˈfrendlɪ/ a ⟨person, remark⟩ scortese, poco amichevole; ⟨place, climate, reception⟩ ostile; ⟨software⟩ difficile da usare

**unfulfilled** /ʌnfʊlˈfɪld/ a ⟨prophecy⟩ non avverato; ⟨promise⟩ non mantenuto; ⟨ambition⟩ non realizzato; ⟨desire, need⟩ non soddisfatto; ⟨condition⟩ non rispettato; **feel** ~ essere insoddisfatto

**unfurl** /ʌnˈfɜːl/ vt spiegare ● vi spiegarsi

**unfurnished** /ʌnˈfɜːnɪʃt/ a non ammobiliato

**ungainly** /ʌnˈgeɪnlɪ/ a sgraziato

**ungentlemanly** /ʌnˈdʒentlmənlɪ/ a non da gentiluomo

**ungodly** /ʌnˈgɒdlɪ/ a empio; ~ **hour** fam ora f impossibile

**ungracious** /ʌnˈgreɪʃəs/ a sgarbato

**ungrateful** /ʌnˈgreɪtfʊl/ a ingrato

**ungratefully** /ʌnˈgreɪtfʊlɪ/ adv senza riconoscenza

**unhappily** /ʌnˈhæpɪlɪ/ adv infelicemente; (unfortunately) purtroppo

**unhappiness** /ʌnˈhæpɪnɪs/ n infelicità f

**unhappy** /ʌnˈhæpɪ/ a infelice; (not content) insoddisfatto (**with** di)

**unharmed** /ʌnˈhɑːmd/ a incolume

**unhealthy** /ʌnˈhelθɪ/ a poco sano; (insanitary) malsano

**unheard-of** /ʌnˈhɜːdəv/ a ⟨actor, brand⟩ mai sentito; ⟨levels, price⟩ incredibile

**unheated** /ʌnˈhiːtɪd/ a senza riscaldamento

**unheeded** /ʌnˈhiːdɪd/ a ignorato; **go** ~ ⟨warning, plea:⟩ venir ignorato

**unhelpful** /ʌnˈhelpfʊl/ a ⟨person, attitude⟩ poco disponibile; ⟨witness⟩ che non collabora; ⟨remark⟩ di poco aiuto

**unholy** /ʌnˈhəʊlɪ/ a ⟨alliance, pact⟩ paradossale; ⟨fam: mess, hour⟩ indecente

**unhook** /ʌnˈhʊk/ vt sganciare; staccare ⟨picture⟩

**unhurt** /ʌnˈhɜːt/ a illeso

**unhygienic** /ʌnhaɪˈdʒiːnɪk/ a non igienico

**unicorn** /ˈjuːnɪkɔːn/ n unicorno m

**unidentified** /ʌnaɪˈdentɪfaɪd/ a non identificato

**unification** /juːnɪfɪˈkeɪʃn/ n unificazione f

**uniform** /ˈjuːnɪfɔːm/ a uniforme ● n uniforme f

**uniformly** /ˈjuːnɪfɔːmlɪ/ adv uniformemente

**unify** /ˈjuːnɪfaɪ/ vt (pt/pp **-ied**) unificare

**unilateral** /juːnɪˈlæt(ə)rəl/ a unilaterale

**unilaterally** /juːnɪˈlæt(ə)rəlɪ/ adv unilateralmente

**unimaginable** /ʌnɪˈmædʒɪnəbl/ a inimmaginabile

**unimaginative** /ʌnɪˈmædʒɪnətɪv/ a privo di fantasia

**unimportant** /ʌnɪmˈpɔːtənt/ a irrilevante

**uninformed** /ʌnɪnˈfɔːmd/ a ⟨person⟩ disinformato

**uninhabited** /ʌnɪnˈhæbɪtɪd/ a disabitato

**uninhibited** /ʌnɪnˈhɪbɪtɪd/ a ⟨person, attitude⟩ disinibito; ⟨performance, remarks⟩ disinvolto; **be** ~ **about doing sth** non avere problemi a fare qcsa

**uninitiated** /ʌnɪˈnɪʃɪeɪtɪd/ a ⟨person⟩ non iniziato ● npl **the** ~ i profani

**uninspired** /ʌnɪnˈspaɪəd/ a privo di immaginazione; ⟨performance⟩ piatto; ⟨times⟩ banale

**unintentional** /ʌnɪnˈtenʃənl/ a involontario

**unintentionally** /ʌnɪnˈtenʃənəlɪ/ adv involontariamente

**uninvited** /ʌnɪnˈvaɪtɪd/ a ⟨attentions⟩ non richiesto; ~ **guest** ospite mf senza invito

**union** /ˈjuːnɪən/ n unione f; (trade ~) sindacato m

**Union Jack** n bandiera f del Regno Unito

**unique** /juːˈniːk/ a unico

**uniquely** /juːˈniːklɪ/ adv unicamente

**unisex** /ˈjuːnɪseks/ a unisex inv

**unison** /ˈjuːnɪsn/ n **in** ~ all'unisono

**unit** /ˈjuːnɪt/ n unità f inv; (department) reparto m; (of furniture) elemento m

**unit cost** n costo m unitario

**unite** /juːˈnaɪt/ vt unire ● vi unirsi

**united** /juːˈnaɪtɪd/ a unito

**united: United Kingdom** n Regno m Unito. **United Nations** n [Organizzazione f delle] Nazioni Unite fpl. **United States [of America]** n Stati mpl Uniti [d'America]

**unit trust** n Fin fondo m comune di investimento aperto

**unity** /ˈjuːnətɪ/ n unità f; (agreement) accordo m

**universal** /juːnɪˈvɜːsl/ a universale

**universally** /juːnɪ'vɜːsəlɪ/ *adv* universalmente

**universe** /'juːnɪvɜːs/ *n* universo *m*

**university** /juːnɪ'vɜːsətɪ/ *n* università *f inv* ● *attrib* universitario

**unjust** /ʌn'dʒʌst/ *a* ingiusto

**unjustifiable** /ʌn'dʒʌstɪfaɪəbl/ *a* ingiustificato

**unjustifiably** /ʌn'dʒʌstɪfaɪəblɪ/ *adv* ‹*act*› senza giustificazione

**unjustified** /ʌn'dʒʌstɪfaɪd/ *a* ‹*suspicion*› ingiustificato

**unjustly** /ʌn'dʒʌstlɪ/ *adv* ingiustamente

**unkempt** /ʌn'kempt/ *a* trasandato; ‹*hair*› arruffato

**unkind** /ʌn'kaɪnd/ *a* scortese

**unkindly** /ʌn'kaɪndlɪ/ *adv* in modo scortese

**unkindness** /ʌn'kaɪndnɪs/ *n* mancanza *f* di gentilezza

**unknown** /ʌn'nəʊn/ *a* sconosciuto

**unlawful** /ʌn'lɔːfʊl/ *a* illecito, illegale

**unlawfully** /ʌn'lɔːfʊlɪ/ *adv* illegalmente

**unleaded** /ʌn'ledɪd/ *a* senza piombo

**unleash** /ʌn'liːʃ/ *vt fig* scatenare

**unless** /ən'les/ *conj* a meno che; **~ I am mistaken** se non mi sbaglio

**unlicensed** /ʌn'laɪsnst/ *a* ‹*transmitter, activity*› abusivo; ‹*vehicle*› senza bollo; ‹*restaurant*› non autorizzato a vendere alcolici

**unlike** /ʌn'laɪk/ *a* (*not the same*) diversi ● *prep* diverso da; **that's ~ him** non è da lui; **~ me, he...** diversamente da me, lui...

**unlikely** /ʌn'laɪklɪ/ *a* improbabile

**unlimited** /ʌn'lɪmɪtɪd/ *a* illimitato

**unlined** /ʌn'laɪnd/ *a* ‹*face*› senza rughe; ‹*paper*› senza righe; ‹*garment, curtain*› senza fodera

**unlit** /ʌn'lɪt/ *a* ‹*cigarette, fire*› spento; ‹*room, street*› non illuminato

**unload** /ʌn'ləʊd/ *vt* scaricare

**unlock** /ʌn'lɒk/ *vt* aprire (*con chiave*)

**unloved** /ʌn'lʌvd/ *a* **feel ~** ‹*person:*› non sentirsi amato

**unlucky** /ʌn'lʌkɪ/ *a* sfortunato; **it's ~ to...** porta sfortuna...

**unmade** /ʌn'meɪd/ *a* ‹*bed*› sfatto

**unmade-up** *a* ‹*road*› non asfaltato

**unmanageable** /ʌn'mænɪdʒəbl/ *a* ‹*number, company*› difficile da gestire; ‹*hair, child, animal*› ribelle; ‹*size*› ingombrante

**unmanly** /ʌn'mænlɪ/ *a* poco virile

**unmanned** /ʌn'mænd/ *a* senza equipaggio

**unmarked** /ʌn'mɑːkt/ *a Sport* smarcato; ‹*skin*› senza segni; ‹*container*› non contrassegnato; **~ police car** [auto *f inv*] civetta *f*

**unmarried** /ʌn'mærɪd/ *a* non sposato

**unmarried mother** *n* ragazza *f* madre

**unmask** /ʌn'mɑːsk/ *vt fig* smascherare

**unmentionable** /ʌn'menʃnəbl/ *a* innominabile

**unmistakable** /ʌnmɪ'steɪkəbl/ *a* inconfondibile

**unmistakably** /ʌnmɪ'steɪkəblɪ/ *adv* chiaramente

**unmitigated** /ʌn'mɪtɪgeɪtɪd/ *a* assoluto

**unmoved** /ʌn'muːvd/ *a fig* impassibile

**unnamed** /ʌn'neɪmd/ *a* (*not having a name*) senza nome; (*name not divulged*) di cui non si conosce il nome; **the as yet ~ winner...** il vincitore di cui ancora non si conosce il nome...

**unnatural** /ʌn'nætʃər(ə)l/ *a* innaturale; *pej* anormale

**unnaturally** /ʌn'nætʃər(ə)lɪ/ *adv* in modo innaturale; *pej* in modo anormale

**unnecessarily** /ʌn'nesəs(ə)rɪlɪ/ *adv* inutilmente

**unnecessary** /ʌn'nesəs(ə)rɪ/ *a* inutile

**unnerving** /ʌn'nɜːvɪŋ/ *a* inquietante

**unnoticed** /ʌn'nəʊtɪst/ *a* inosservato

**unobservant** /ʌnəb'zɜːvənt/ *a* senza spirito d'osservazione

**unobserved** /ʌnəb'zɜːvd/ *a* inosservato; **go ~** passare inosservato

**unobtainable** /ʌnəb'teɪnəbl/ *a* ‹*product*› introvabile; ‹*phone number*› non ottenibile

**unobtrusive** /ʌnəb'truːsɪf/ *a* discreto

**unobtrusively** /ʌnəb'truːsɪvlɪ/ *adv* in modo discreto

**unoccupied** /ʌn'ɒkjuːpaɪd/ *a* ‹*house, block, shop*› vuoto; ‹*table, seat*› libero

**unofficial** /ʌnə'fɪʃl/ *a* non ufficiale

**unofficially** /ʌnə'fɪʃ(ə)lɪ/ *adv* ufficiosamente

**unopened** /ʌn'əʊpənd/ *a* ‹*bottle, packet*› chiuso; ‹*package*› ancora incartato

**unorthodox** /ʌn'ɔːθədɒks/ *a* poco ortodosso

**unpack** /ʌn'pæk/ *vi* disfare le valigie ● *vt* svuotare ‹*parcel*›; spacchettare ‹*books*›; **~ one's case** disfare la valigia

**unpaid** /ʌn'peɪd/ *a* da pagare; (*work*) non retribuito

**unpalatable** /ʌn'pælətəbl/ *a* sgradevole

**unparalleled** /ʌn'pærəleld/ *a* senza pari

**unpasteurized** /ʌn'pɑːstʃəraɪzd/ *a* non pastorizzato

**unperturbed** /ʌnpə'tɜːbd/ *a* imperturbato

**unpick** /ʌn'pɪk/ *vt* disfare

**unplanned** /ʌn'plænd/ *a* ‹*stoppage, increase*› imprevisto

**unpleasant** /ʌn'plezənt/ *a* sgradevole; ‹*person*› maleducato

**unpleasantly** /ʌn'plezəntlɪ/ *adv* sgradevolmente; ‹*behave*› maleducatamente

**unpleasantness** /ʌn'plezəntnɪs/ *n* (*bad feeling*) tensioni *fpl*

**unplug** /ʌn'plʌg/ *vt* (*pt/pp* **-plugged**) staccare

**unpolluted** /ʌnpə'luːtɪd/ *a* ‹*water*› non inquinato; ‹*mind*› incontaminato

**unpopular** /ʌn'pɒpjʊlə(r)/ *a* impopolare

**unprecedented** /ʌn'presɪdntɪd/ *a* senza precedenti

**unpredictable** /ʌnprɪ'dɪktəbl/ *a* imprevedibile

**unprejudiced** /ʌn'predʒʊdɪst/ *a* ‹*person*› senza pregiudizi; ‹*opinion, judgement*› imparziale

**unpremeditated** /ʌnpriː'medɪteɪtɪd/ *a* involontario

# 351

## unprepared | unsuccessful

**unprepared** /ˌʌnprɪˈpeəd/ a impreparato

**unprepossessing** /ˌʌnpriːpəˈzesɪŋ/ a poco attraente

**unpretentious** /ˌʌnprɪˈtenʃəs/ a senza pretese

**unprincipled** /ʌnˈprɪnsɪpəld/ a senza principi; ⟨behaviour⟩ scorretto

**unprofessional** /ˌʌnprəˈfeʃnl/ a non professionale; **it's ~** è una mancanza di professionalità

**unprofitable** /ʌnˈprɒfɪtəbl/ a non redditizio

**unprompted** /ʌnˈprɒm(p)tɪd/ a ⟨offer⟩ spontaneo; ⟨answer⟩ non suggerito

**unpronounceable** /ˌʌnprəˈnaʊnsəbl/ a impronunciabile

**unprovoked** /ˌʌnprəˈvəʊkt/ a ⟨attack, aggression⟩ non provocato; **the attack was ~** l'attacco è avvenuto senza provocazione

**unqualified** /ʌnˈkwɒlɪfaɪd/ a non qualificato; (fig: absolute) assoluto

**unquestionable** /ʌnˈkwestʃənəbl/ a incontestabile

**unquote** /ʌnˈkwəʊt/ vi chiudere le virgolette

**unravel** /ʌnˈrævl/ vt (pt/pp -ravelled) districare; (in knitting) disfare

**unreal** /ʌnˈrɪəl/ a irreale; fam inverosimile

**unrealistic** /ˌʌnrɪəˈlɪstɪk/ a ⟨character, presentation⟩ poco realistico; ⟨expectation, aim⟩ irrealistico; ⟨person⟩ poco realista

**unreasonable** /ʌnˈriːz(ə)nəbl/ a irragionevole

**unrecognizable** /ʌnˈrekəgnaɪzəbl/ a irriconoscibile

**unrecorded** /ˌʌnrɪˈkɔːdɪd/ a non documentato; **go ~** non essere documentato

**unrefined** /ˌʌnrɪˈfaɪnd/ a ⟨person, manners, style⟩ rozzo; ⟨oil⟩ greggio; ⟨flour, sugar⟩ non raffinato

**unrehearsed** /ˌʌnrɪˈhɜːst/ a ⟨response, action⟩ imprevisto; ⟨speech⟩ improvvisato

**unrelated** /ˌʌnrɪˈleɪtɪd/ a ⟨facts⟩ senza rapporto (**to** con); ⟨person⟩ non imparentato (**to** con)

**unrelenting** /ˌʌnrɪˈlentɪŋ/ a ⟨person⟩ ostinato; ⟨stare⟩ insistente; ⟨pursuit⟩ continuo; ⟨heat, zeal⟩ costante

**unreliable** /ˌʌnrɪˈlaɪəbl/ a inattendibile; ⟨person⟩ inaffidabile, che non dà affidamento

**unremitting** /ˌʌnrɪˈmɪtɪŋ/ a costante; ⟨struggle⟩ continuo

**unrepeatable** /ˌʌnrɪˈpiːtəbl/ a ⟨offer, bargain⟩ unico; **his comment was ~** il commento che ha fatto è irripetibile

**unrepentant** /ˌʌnrɪˈpentənt/ a irriducibile; ⟨sinner⟩ impenitente

**unrequited** /ˌʌnrɪˈkwaɪtɪd/ a non corrisposto

**unreservedly** /ˌʌnrɪˈzɜːvɪdlɪ/ adv senza riserve; (frankly) francamente

**unresolved** /ˌʌnrɪˈzɒlvd/ a irrisolto

**unrest** /ʌnˈrest/ n fermenti mpl

**unripe** /ʌnˈraɪp/ a ⟨fruit⟩ acerbo; ⟨wheat⟩ non maturo

**unrivalled** /ʌnˈraɪvəld/ a ineguagliato

**unroll** /ʌnˈrəʊl/ vt srotolare ● vi srotolarsi

**unruffled** /ʌnˈrʌfld/ a ⟨person⟩ imperturbato; ⟨hair⟩ a posto; ⟨water⟩ non mosso; **be ~** ⟨person:⟩ rimanere imperturbato; ⟨person, hair:⟩ essere a posto

**unruly** /ʌnˈruːlɪ/ a indisciplinato

**unsafe** /ʌnˈseɪf/ a pericoloso

**unsaid** /ʌnˈsed/ a inespresso

**unsalaried** /ʌnˈsælərɪd/ a ⟨post⟩ non stipendiato

**unsalted** /ʌnˈsɔːltɪd/ a non salato

**unsatisfactory** /ˌʌnsætɪsˈfækt(ə)rɪ/ a poco soddisfacente

**unsavoury** /ʌnˈseɪvərɪ/ a equivoco

**unscathed** /ʌnˈskeɪðd/ a illeso

**unscheduled** /ʌnˈʃedjuːld/ a ⟨flight⟩ supplementare; ⟨appearance, speech⟩ fuori programma; ⟨stop⟩ non programmato

**unscramble** /ʌnˈskræmbl/ vt decifrare ⟨code, words⟩; sbrogliare ⟨ideas, thoughts⟩

**unscrew** /ʌnˈskruː/ vt svitare

**unscrupulous** /ʌnˈskruːpjʊləs/ a senza scrupoli

**unseasoned** /ʌnˈsiːznd/ a ⟨wood⟩ non stagionato; ⟨food⟩ scondito

**unseemly** /ʌnˈsiːmlɪ/ a indecoroso

**unselfish** /ʌnˈselfɪʃ/ a disinteressato

**unsettled** /ʌnˈsetld/ a in agitazione; ⟨weather⟩ variabile; ⟨bill⟩ non saldato

**unshakeable** /ʌnˈʃeɪkəbl/ a categorico

**unshaven** /ʌnˈʃeɪvn/ a non rasato

**unsightly** /ʌnˈsaɪtlɪ/ a brutto

**unsinkable** /ʌnˈsɪŋkəbl/ a ⟨ship, object⟩ inaffondabile; ⟨hum: personality⟩ che non si deprime

**unskilled** /ʌnˈskɪld/ a non specializzato

**unskilled worker** n manovale m

**unsmiling** /ʌnˈsmaɪlɪŋ/ a ⟨person⟩ serioso

**unsociable** /ʌnˈsəʊʃəbl/ a scontroso

**unsolicited** /ˌʌnsəˈlɪsɪtɪd/ a ⟨help, advice⟩ non richiesto; ⟨job application⟩ spontaneo

**unsophisticated** /ˌʌnsəˈfɪstɪkeɪtɪd/ a semplice

**unsound** /ʌnˈsaʊnd/ a ⟨building, reasoning⟩ poco solido; ⟨advice⟩ poco sensato; **of ~ mind** malato di mente

**unspeakable** /ʌnˈspiːkəbl/ a indicibile

**unspoiled** /ʌnˈspɔɪld/ a ⟨town⟩ non deturpato; ⟨landscape⟩ intatto; **she was ~ by fame** la fama non l'ha cambiata

**unstable** /ʌnˈsteɪbl/ a instabile; (mentally) squilibrato

**unsteadily** /ʌnˈstedɪlɪ/ adv ⟨walk, speak⟩ in modo malsicuro

**unsteady** /ʌnˈstedɪ/ a malsicuro

**unstoppable** /ʌnˈstɒpəbl/ a ⟨force, momentum⟩ inarrestabile

**unstressed** /ʌnˈstrest/ a ⟨vowel, word⟩ atono

**unstuck** /ʌnˈstʌk/ a **come ~** staccarsi; (fam: project) andare a monte

**unsuccessful** /ˌʌnsəkˈsesfʊl/ a fallimentare; **be ~** (in attempt) non aver successo

**unsuccessfully** /ʌnsək'sesfʊlɪ/ *adv* senza successo

**unsuitable** /ʌn'su:təbl/ *a* (*inappropriate*) inadatto; (*inconvenient*) inopportuno

**unsupervised** /ʌn'su:pəvaɪzd/ *a* (*activity*) non controllato

**unsuspecting** /ʌnsə'spektɪŋ/ *a* fiducioso

**unsweetened** /ʌn'swi:tənd/ *a* senza zucchero

**unsympathetic** /ʌnsɪmpə'θetɪk/ *a* (*person, attitude, manner, tone*) poco comprensivo; (*person, character*) antipatico; **she is ~ to the cause** non appoggia la causa

**untamed** /ʌn'teɪmd/ *a* (*lion*) non addomesticato; (*passion, person*) indomito

**untangle** /ʌn'tæŋgl/ *vt* sbrogliare (*threads*); risolvere (*difficulties, mystery*)

**unthinkable** /ʌn'θɪŋkəbl/ *a* impensabile

**unthought-of** /ʌn'θɔ:təv/ *a* impensato; **hitherto ~** finora impensato

**untidily** /ʌn'taɪdɪlɪ/ *adv* disordinatamente

**untidiness** /ʌn'taɪdɪnɪs/ *n* disordine *m*

**untidy** /ʌn'taɪdɪ/ *a* disordinato

**untie** /ʌn'taɪ/ *vt* slegare

**until** /ən'tɪl/ *prep* fino a; **not ~** non prima di; **~ the evening** fino alla sera; **~ his arrival** fino al suo arrivo ● *conj* finché, fino a quando; **not ~ you've seen it** non prima che tu l'abbia visto

**untimely** /ʌn'taɪmlɪ/ *a* inopportuno; (*premature*) prematuro

**untiring** /ʌn'taɪərɪŋ/ *a* instancabile

**untold** /ʌn'təʊld/ *a* (*wealth*) incalcolabile; (*suffering*) indescrivibile; (*story*) inedito

**untouched** /ʌn'tʌtʃt/ *a* (*unchanged, undisturbed*) intatto; (*unscathed*) incolume; (*unaffected*) non toccato; **leave one's dinner/a meal ~** non toccare cibo

**untoward** /ʌntə'wɔ:d/ *a* **if nothing ~ happens** se non capita un imprevisto

**untrained** /ʌn'treɪnd/ *a* (*voice*) non impostato; (*eye, artist, actor*) inesperto; **be ~** (*worker*:) non avere una formazione professionale

**untranslatable** /ʌntrænz'leɪtəbl/ *a* intraducibile

**untreated** /ʌn'tri:tɪd/ *a* (*sewage, water*) non depurato; (*illness*) non curato

**untrue** /ʌn'tru:/ *a* falso; **that's ~** non è vero

**unused[1]** /ʌn'ju:zd/ *a* non usato

**unused[2]** /ʌn'ju:st/ *a* **be ~ to** non essere abituato a

**unusual** /ʌn'ju:ʒʊəl/ *a* insolito

**unusually** /ʌn'ju:ʒʊəlɪ/ *adv* insolitamente

**unveil** /ʌn'veɪl/ *vt* scoprire

**unversed** /ʌn'vɜ:st/ *a* inesperto (**in** di)

**unwanted** /ʌn'wɒntɪd/ *a* (*child, pet, visitor*) indesiderato; (*goods, produce*) che non serve; **feel ~** sentirsi respinto

**unwarranted** /ʌn'wɒrəntɪd/ *a* ingiustificato

**unwelcome** /ʌn'welkəm/ *a* sgradito

**unwell** /ʌn'wel/ *a* indisposto

**unwieldy** /ʌn'wi:ldɪ/ *a* ingombrante

**unwilling** /ʌn'wɪlɪŋ/ *a* riluttante

**unwillingly** /ʌn'wɪlɪŋlɪ/ *adv* malvolentieri

**unwind** /ʌn'waɪnd/ *v* (*pt/pp* **unwound**) ● *vt* svolgere, srotolare ● *vi* svolgersi, srotolarsi; (*fam: relax*) rilassarsi

**unwise** /ʌn'waɪz/ *a* imprudente

**unwisely** /ʌn'waɪzlɪ/ *adv* imprudentemente

**unwitting** /ʌn'wɪtɪŋ/ *a* involontario; (*victim*) inconsapevole

**unwittingly** /ʌn'wɪtɪŋlɪ/ *adv* involontariamente

**unworldly** /ʌn'wɜ:ldlɪ/ *a* (*not materialistic*) poco materialista; (*naive*) ingenuo; (*spiritual*) non materialista

**unworthy** /ʌn'wɜ:ðɪ/ *a* non degno

**unwrap** /ʌn'ræp/ *vt* (*pt/pp* **-wrapped**) scartare (*present, parcel*)

**unwritten** /ʌn'rɪtn/ *a* tacito

**unyielding** /ʌn'ji:ldɪŋ/ *a* rigido

**unzip** /ʌn'zɪp/ *vt* aprire [la cerniera di] (*garment, bag*)

**up** /ʌp/ *adv* su; (*not in bed*) alzato; (*road*) smantellato; (*theatre curtain, blinds*) alzato; (*shelves, tent*) montato; (*notice*) affisso; (*building*) costruito; **prices are up** i prezzi sono aumentati; **be up for sale** essere in vendita; **up here/there** quassù/lassù; **time's up** tempo scaduto; **what's up?** *fam* cosa è successo?; **up to** (*as far as*) fino a; **be up to** essere all'altezza di (*task*); **what's he up to?** *fam* cosa sta facendo?; (*plotting*) cosa sta combinando?; **I'm up to page 100** sono arrivato a pagina 100; **feel up to it** sentirsela; **be one up on sb** *fam* essere in vantaggio su qcno; **go up** salire; **lift up** alzare; **up against** *fig* alle prese con ● *prep* su; **the cat ran/is up the tree** il gatto è salito di corsa/è sull'albero; **further up this road** più avanti su questa strada; **row up the river** risalire il fiume; **go up the stairs** salire su per le scale; **be up the pub** *fam* essere al pub; **be up on** *or* **in sth** essere bene informato su qcsa ● *npl* **ups and downs** alti *mpl* e bassi

**up-and-coming** *a* promettente

**upbeat** /'ʌpbi:t/ *a* ottimistico

**upbringing** /'ʌpbrɪŋɪŋ/ *n* educazione *f*

**update** /ʌp'deɪt/ *vt* aggiornare

**upfront** /ʌp'frʌnt/ *a* *fam* (*frank*) aperto; (*money*) anticipato ● *adv* (*pay*) in anticipo

**upgrade** /ʌp'greɪd/ *vt* promuovere (*person*); modernizzare (*equipment*) ● *n* aggiornamento *m*

**upheaval** /ʌp'hi:vl/ *n* scompiglio *m*

**uphill** /ʌp'hɪl/ *a* in salita; *fig* arduo ● *adv* in salita

**uphold** /ʌp'həʊld/ *vt* (*pt/pp* **upheld**) sostenere (*principle*); confermare (*verdict*)

**upholster** /ʌp'həʊlstə(r)/ *vt* tappezzare

**upholsterer** /ʌp'həʊlstərə(r)/ *n* tappezziere, -a *mf*

**upholstery** /ʌp'həʊlstərɪ/ *n* tappezzeria *f*

**upkeep** /'ʌpki:p/ *n* mantenimento *m*

**uplifting** /ʌp'lɪftɪŋ/ *a* (*morally*) edificante

**up-market** *a* di qualità

**upon** /ə'pɒn/ *prep* su; **~ arriving home** una volta arrivato a casa

**upper** /'ʌpə(r)/ *a* superiore ● *n* (*of shoe*) to-maia *f*

**upper: upper-case** *a* maiuscolo. **upper circle** *n* seconda galleria *f*. **upper class** *n* alta borghesia *f*. **upper crust** *a hum* aristo-cratico. **upper hand** *n* have the ~ ~ avere il sopravvento. **upper middle class** *n* ceto *m* medio-alto

**uppermost** /'ʌpəməʊst/ *a* più alto; **that's ~ in my mind** è la mia preoccupazione princi-pale

**upright** /'ʌpraɪt/ *a* dritto; ⟨*piano*⟩ verticale; ⟨*honest*⟩ retto ● *n* montante *m*

**upright freezer** *n* freezer *m inv* verticale

**uprising** /'ʌpraɪzɪŋ/ *n* rivolta *f*

**upriver** /ʌp'rɪvə/ *adv* ⟨*lie*⟩ a monte; ⟨*sail*⟩ controcorrente

**uproar** /'ʌprɔː(r)/ *n* tumulto *m*; **be in an ~** essere in trambusto

**uproot** /ʌp'ruːt/ *vt* sradicare

**upset**[1] /ʌp'set/ *vt* (*pt/pp* **upset**, *pres p* **upsetting**) rovesciare; sconvolgere ⟨*plan*⟩; ⟨*distress*⟩ turbare; **get ~ about sth** prender-sela per qcsa; **be very ~** essere sconvolto; **have an ~ stomach** avere l'intestino distur-bato

**upset**[2] /'ʌpset/ *n* scombussolamento *m*

**upshot** /'ʌpʃɒt/ *n* risultato *m*

**upside down** *adv* sottosopra; **turn ~ ~** ca-povolgere

**upstage** /ʌp'steɪdʒ/ *vt Theat, fig* distogliere l'attenzione del pubblico da ● *adv Theat* ⟨*stand*⟩ al fondo del palcoscenico; ⟨*move*⟩ ver-so il fondo del palcoscenico

**upstairs**[1] /ʌp'steəz/ *adv* [al piano] di sopra

**upstairs**[2] /'ʌpsteəz/ *a* del piano superiore

**upstart** /'ʌpstɑːt/ *n* arrivato, -a *mf*

**upstream** /ʌp'striːm/ *adv* controcorrente

**upsurge** /'ʌpsɜːdʒ/ *n* (*in sales*) aumento *m* improvviso; ⟨*of enthusiasm, crime*⟩ ondata *f*

**uptake** /'ʌpteɪk/ *n* **be slow on the ~** essere lento nel capire; **be quick on the ~** capire le cose al volo

**uptight** /ʌp'taɪt/ *a* teso

**up-to-date** *a* moderno; ⟨*news*⟩ ultimo; ⟨*person, information, records*⟩ aggiornato

**up-to-the-minute** *a* ⟨*information*⟩ dell'ul-timo minuto

**uptown** /'ʌptaʊn/ *a* (*Am: smart*) dei quartie-ri alti

**upturn** /'ʌptɜːn/ *n* ripresa *f*

**upward** /'ʌpwəd/ *a* verso l'alto, in su; ~ **slope** salita *f* ● *adv* ~[**s**] verso l'alto; **~s of** oltre

**upwardly mobile** /ʌpwədlɪ'məʊbaɪl/ *a* che sale nella scala sociale

**uranium** /jʊ'reɪnɪəm/ *n* uranio *m*

**urban** /'ɜːbən/ *a* urbano

**urban blight, urban decay** *n* degrado *m* urbano

**urbane** /ɜː'beɪn/ *a* cortese

**urban planning** *n* urbanistica *f*

**urge** /ɜːdʒ/ *n* forte desiderio *m* ● *vt* esortare (**to** a)

■ **urge on** *vt* spronare

**urgency** /'ɜːdʒənsɪ/ *n* urgenza *f*

**urgent** /'ɜːdʒənt/ *a* urgente

**urgently** /'ɜːdʒəntlɪ/ *adv* urgentemente

**urinal** /jʊ'raɪnl/ *n* (*fixture*) orinale *m*; (*place*) vespasiano *m*

**urinate** /'jʊərɪneɪt/ *vi* urinare

**urine** /'jʊərɪn/ *n* urina *f*

**urn** /ɜːn/ *n* urna *f*; (*for tea*) contenitore *m* mu-nito di cannella che si trova nei self-service, mense ecc

**US** *n abbr* (**United States**) U.S.A. *mpl*

**us** /ʌs/ *pers pron* ci; (*after prep*) noi; **they know us** ci conoscono; **give us the money** dateci i soldi; **give it to us** datecelo; **they showed it to us** ce l'hanno fatto vedere; **they meant us, not you** intendevano noi, non voi; **it's us** siamo noi; **she hates us** ci odia

**USA** *n abbr* (**United States of America**) U.S.A. *mpl*

**usable** /'juːzəbl/ *a* usabile

**usage** /'juːsɪdʒ/ *n* uso *m*

**use**[1] /juːs/ *n* uso *m*; **be of ~** essere utile; **be of no ~** essere inutile; **make ~ of** usare; ⟨*exploit*⟩ sfruttare; **it is no ~** è inutile; **what's the ~?** a che scopo?

**use**[2] /juːz/ *vt* usare

■ **use up** *vt* consumare

**used**[1] /juːzd/ *a* usato

**used**[2] /juːst/ *pt* **be ~ to sth** essere abituato a qcsa; **get ~ to** abituarsi a; **he ~ to say** dice-va; **he ~ to live here** viveva qui

**useful** /'juːsfl/ *a* utile

**usefulness** /'juːsflnɪs/ *n* utilità *f*

**useless** /'juːslɪs/ *a* inutile; ⟨*fam: person*⟩ in-capace; **you're ~!** sei un idiota!

**user** /'juːzə(r)/ *n* utente *mf*

**user: user-friendliness** *n* facilità *f* d'uso. **user-friendly** *a* facile da usare. **user manual** *n* manuale *m* d'uso

**usher** /'ʌʃə(r)/ *n Theat* maschera *f*; *Jur* uscie-re *m*; (*at wedding*) persona *f* che accompagna gli invitati a un matrimonio ai loro posti in chiesa

■ **usher in** *vt* fare entrare ⟨*person*⟩; inaugu-rare ⟨*new age*⟩

**usherette** /ʌʃə'ret/ *n* maschera *f*

**USSR** *n* URSS *f*

**usual** /'juːʒəl/ *a* usuale; **as ~** come al solito

**usually** /'juːʒʊəlɪ/ *adv* di solito

**usurp** /jʊ'zɜːp/ *vt* usurpare

**usurper** /jʊ'zɜːpə(r)/ *n* usurpatore, -trice *mf*

**utensil** /jʊ'tensl/ *n* utensile *m*

**uterus** /'juːtərəs/ *n* utero *m*

**utilitarian** /jʊtɪlɪ'teərɪən/ *a* funzionale

**utility** /jʊ'tɪlətɪ/ *n* utilità *f*; (*public*) servizio *m*

**utility: utility company** *n* servizio *m* pub-blico. **utility program** *n Comput* [programm-ma *m* di] utilità *f*. **utility room** *n stanza f* in casa privata per il lavaggio, la stiratura dei panni ecc

**utilize** /'juːtɪlaɪz/ *vt* utilizzare

**utmost** /'ʌtməʊst/ *a* estremo ● *n* one's ~ tutto il possibile

**Utopia** /juːˈtəʊpɪə/ n utopia f
**Utopian** /juːˈtəʊpɪən/ n utopista mf ● a utopistico
**utter**¹ /ˈʌtə(r)/ a totale
**utter**² vt emettere ⟨sigh, sound⟩; proferire ⟨word⟩

**utterance** /ˈʌtərəns/ n dichiarazione f
**utterly** /ˈʌtəlɪ/ adv completamente
**U-turn** n Auto inversione f a U; fig marcia f in dietro
**UV** abbr (**ultraviolet**) UVA mpl
**Uzbekistan** /ʌzbekɪˈstɑːn/ n Uzbekistan m

........................................

# Vv

........................................

**v, V** /viː/ n (letter) v, V f inv
**v** abbr (**versus**) contro; abbr (**volt**) V m
**vac** /væk/ n Br abbr (**vacation**) vacanze fpl
**vacancy** /ˈveɪk(ə)nsɪ/ n (job) posto m vacante; (room) stanza f disponibile
**vacant** /ˈveɪknt/ a libero; ⟨position⟩ vacante; ⟨look⟩ assente
**vacant possession** n Br Jur bene m immobile libero
**vacate** /vəˈkeɪt/ vt lasciare libero
**vacation** /vəˈkeɪʃn/ n Univ & Am vacanza f
**vaccinate** /ˈvæksɪneɪt/ vt vaccinare
**vaccination** /væksɪˈneɪʃn/ n vaccinazione f
**vaccine** /ˈvæksiːn/ n vaccino m
**vacillate** /ˈvæsɪleɪt/ vi tentennare
**vacuous** /ˈvækjʊəs/ a ⟨person, look, expression⟩ vacuo; ⟨person⟩ superficiale
**vacuum** /ˈvækjʊəm/ n vuoto m ● vt passare l'aspirapolvere in/su
**vacuum: vacuum cleaner** n aspirapolvere m inv. **vacuum flask** n thermos* m inv. **vacuum-packed** a confezionato sottovuoto
**vagabond** /ˈvæɡəbɒnd/ n vagabondo, -a mf
**vagaries** /ˈveɪɡərɪz/ npl capricci mpl
**vagina** /vəˈdʒaɪnə/ n Anat vagina f
**vagrancy** /ˈveɪɡrənsɪ/ n Jur vagabondaggio m
**vagrant** /ˈveɪɡrənt/ n vagabondo, -a mf
**vague** /veɪɡ/ a vago; ⟨outline⟩ impreciso; ⟨absent-minded⟩ distratto; **I'm still ~ about it** non ho ancora le idee chiare in proposito
**vaguely** /ˈveɪɡlɪ/ adv vagamente
**vagueness** /ˈveɪɡnɪs/ n (imprecision) vaghezza f; (of wording, proposals) indeterminatezza f; (of image) nebulosità f; (of thinking) imprecisione f
**vain** /veɪn/ a vanitoso; ⟨hope, attempt⟩ vano; **in ~** invano
**vainly** /ˈveɪnlɪ/ adv vanamente
**valance** /ˈvæləns/ n ⟨above curtains⟩ mantovana f; ⟨on bed base⟩ balza f
**vale** /veɪl/ n liter valle f
**valentine** /ˈvæləntaɪn/ n ⟨card⟩ biglietto m di San Valentino
**Valentine's Day** n giorno m di San Valentino
**valet** /ˈvæleɪ/ n servitore m personale
**valiant** /ˈvælɪənt/ a valoroso
**valiantly** /ˈvælɪəntlɪ/ adv coraggiosamente
**valid** /ˈvælɪd/ a valido

**validate** /ˈvælɪdeɪt/ vt (confirm) convalidare
**validity** /vəˈlɪdətɪ/ n validità f
**valley** /ˈvælɪ/ n valle f
**valour** /ˈvælə(r)/ n valore m
**valuable** /ˈvæljʊəbl/ a di valore; fig prezioso
**valuables** /ˈvæljʊəblz/ npl oggetti mpl di valore
**valuation** /væljʊˈeɪʃn/ n valutazione f
**value** /ˈvæljuː/ n valore m; (usefulness) utilità f ● vt valutare; ⟨cherish⟩ apprezzare
**value added tax** /ˈædɪd/ n imposta f sul valore aggiunto
**valued** /ˈvæljuːd/ a (appreciated) apprezzato
**valuer** /ˈvæljʊə(r)/ n stimatore, -trice mf
**valve** /vælv/ n valvola f
**vamp** /væmp/ n vamp f inv
**vampire** /ˈvæmpaɪə(r)/ n vampiro m
**van** /væn/ n furgone m
**vandal** /ˈvændl/ n vandalo, -a mf
**vandalism** /ˈvænd(ə)lɪzm/ n vandalismo m
**vandalize** /ˈvænd(ə)laɪz/ vt vandalizzare
**vane** /veɪn/ n banderuola f
**vanguard** /ˈvænɡɑːd/ n avanguardia f; **in the ~** all'avanguardia
**vanilla** /vəˈnɪlə/ n vaniglia f
**vanish** /ˈvænɪʃ/ vi svanire
**vanishing: vanishing cream** n crema f base per il trucco. **vanishing point** n punto m di fuga. **vanishing trick** n trucco m da illusionista per far sparire un oggetto; **he's done his ~ ~ again** fam è sparito come al solito
**vanity** /ˈvænɪtɪ/ n vanità f inv
**vanity bag, vanity case** n beauty-case m inv
**vanity mirror** n Auto specchietto m di cortesia
**vanquish** /ˈvæŋkwɪʃ/ vt sconfiggere ⟨enemy⟩
**vantage point** /ˈvɑːntɪdʒ/ n punto m d'osservazione; fig punto m di vista
**vaporize** /ˈveɪpəraɪz/ vt vaporizzare ⟨liquid⟩
**vapour** /ˈveɪpə(r)/ n vapore m
**vapour trail** n scia f
**variable** /ˈveərɪəbl/ a variabile; (adjustable) regolabile
**variance** /ˈveərɪəns/ n **be at ~** essere in disaccordo
**variant** /ˈveərɪənt/ n variante f
**variation** /veərɪˈeɪʃn/ n variazione f

**varicose** /'værɪkəʊs/ a ~ **veins** vene fpl varicose

**varied** /'veərɪd/ a vario; ⟨diet⟩ diversificato; ⟨life⟩ movimentato

**variegated** /'veərɪɡeɪtɪd/ a variegato

**variety** /və'raɪətɪ/ n varietà f inv

**various** /'veərɪəs/ a vario

**variously** /'veərɪəslɪ/ adv variamente

**varnish** /'vɑːnɪʃ/ n vernice f; (for nails) smalto m ● vt verniciare; ~ **one's nails** mettersi lo smalto

**vary** /'veərɪ/ vt/i (pt/pp -**ied**) variare

**varying** /'veərɪɪŋ/ a variabile; (different) diverso

**vascular** /'væskjʊlə/ a Anat, Bot vascolare

**vase** /vɑːz/ n vaso m

**vasectomy** /və'sektəmɪ/ n vasectomia f

**vast** /vɑːst/ a vasto; ⟨difference, amusement⟩ enorme

**vastly** /'vɑːstlɪ/ adv ⟨superior⟩ di gran lunga; ⟨different, amused⟩ enormemente

**VAT** /viːeɪ'tiː:, væt/ abbr (**value added tax**) I.V.A. f

**vat** /væt/ n tino m

**vaudeville** /'vɔːdəvɪl/ n Theat varietà m

**vault¹** /vɔːlt/ n (roof) volta f; (in bank) caveau m inv; (tomb) cripta f

**vault²** n salto m ● vt/i ~ [**over**] saltare

**VCR** n abbr (**video cassette recorder**) VCR m

**VD** abbr (**venereal disease**) malattia f venerea

**VDU** abbr (**visual display unit**) VDU m

**veal** /viːl/ n carne f di vitello ● attrib di vitello

**vector** /'vektə(r)/ n Biol, Math vettore m; Aeron rotta f

**veer** /vɪə(r)/ vi cambiare direzione; Naut, Auto virare

**vegan** /'viːɡn/ n vegetaliano, -a mf ● a vegetaliano

**vegetable** /'vedʒtəbl/ n (food) verdura f; (when growing) ortaggio m ● attrib ⟨oil, fat⟩ vegetale

**vegetarian** /vedʒɪ'teərɪən/ a & n vegetariano, -a mf

**vegetate** /'vedʒɪteɪt/ vi vegetare

**vegetation** /vedʒɪ'teɪʃn/ n vegetazione f

**vehemence** /'viːəməns/ n veemenza f

**vehement** /'viːəmənt/ a veemente

**vehemently** /'viːəməntlɪ/ adv con veemenza

**vehicle** /'viːɪkl/ n veicolo m; (fig: medium) mezzo m

**vehicular** /vɪ'hɪkjʊlə/ a no ~ **access**, no ~ **traffic** circolazione vietata

**veil** /veɪl/ n velo m ● vt velare

**vein** /veɪn/ n vena f; (mood) umore m; (manner) tenore m

**veined** /veɪnd/ a venato

**Velcro®** /'velkrəʊ/ n ~ **fastening** chiusura f con velcro

**vellum** /'veləm/ n pergamena f

**velocity** /vɪ'lɒsətɪ/ n velocità f inv

**velvet** /'velvɪt/ n velluto m

**velvety** /'velvətɪ/ a vellutato

**venal** /'viːnl/ a venale

**vendetta** /ven'detə/ n vendetta f

**vending machine** /'vendɪŋ/ n distributore m automatico

**vendor** /'vendə(r)/ n venditore, -trice mf

**veneer** /və'nɪə(r)/ n impiallacciatura f; fig vernice f

**veneered** /və'nɪərd/ a impiallacciato

**venerable** /'venərəbl/ a venerabile

**veneration** /venə'reɪʃn/ n venerazione f

**venereal** /vɪ'nɪərɪəl/ a ~ **disease** malattia f venerea

**Venetian** /və'niːʃn/ a & n veneziano, -a mf

**Venetian blind** n persiana f alla veneziana

**Venezuela** /venɪz'weɪlə/ n Venezuela m

**Venezuelan** /venɪz'weɪlən/ a & n venezuelano, -a mf

**vengeance** /'vendʒəns/ n vendetta f; **with a** ~ fam a più non posso

**Venice** /'venɪs/ n Venezia f

**venison** /'venɪsn/ n Culin carne f di cervo

**venom** /'venəm/ n veleno m

**venomous** /'venəməs/ a velenoso

**vent¹** /vent/ n presa f d'aria; **give** ~ **to** fig dar libero sfogo a ● vt fig sfogare ⟨anger⟩

**vent²** n (in jacket) spacco m

**ventilate** /'ventɪleɪt/ vt ventilare

**ventilation** /ventɪ'leɪʃn/ n ventilazione f; (installation) sistema m di ventilazione

**ventilator** /'ventɪleɪtə(r)/ n ventilatore m

**ventriloquist** /ven'trɪləkwɪst/ n ventriloquo, -a mf

**venture** /'ventʃə(r)/ n impresa f ● vt azzardare ● vi avventurarsi

**venture capital** n capitale m a rischio

**venue** /'venjuː/ n luogo m (di convegno, concerto ecc)

**veracity** /və'ræsətɪ/ n veridicità f

**veranda** /və'rændə/ n veranda f

**verb** /vɜːb/ n verbo m

**verbal** /'vɜːbl/ a verbale

**verbally** /'vɜːb(ə)lɪ/ adv verbalmente

**verbatim** /vɜː'beɪtɪm/ a letterale ● adv parola per parola

**verbose** /vɜː'bəʊs/ a prolisso

**verdict** /'vɜːdɪkt/ n verdetto m; (opinion) parere m

**verdigris** /'vɜːdɪɡriː/ n verderame m

**verge** /vɜːdʒ/ n orlo m; **be on the** ~ **of doing sth** essere sul punto di fare qcsa

■ **verge on** vt fig rasentare

**verger** /'vɜːdʒə(r)/ n sagrestano m

**verification** /verɪfɪ'keɪʃn/ n verifica f

**verify** /'verɪfaɪ/ vt (pt/pp -**ied**) verificare; (confirm) confermare

**veritable** /'verɪtəbl/ a vero

**vermicelli** /vɜːmɪ'tʃelɪ/ n (pasta) capelli mpl d'angelo; (chocolate) pezzettini mpl di cioccolato per decorazione

**vermilion** /və'mɪljən/ n rosso m vermiglio ● a vermiglio

**vermin** /'vɜːmɪn/ n animali mpl nocivi

**vermouth** /'vɜːməθ/ n vermut m inv

**vernacular** /və'nækjʊlə(r)/ n vernacolo m

**verruca** /vəˈruːkə/ n verruca f
**versatile** /ˈvɜːsətaɪl/ a versatile
**versatility** /vɜːsəˈtɪləti/ n versatilità f
**verse** /vɜːs/ n verso m; (of Bible) versetto m; (poetry) versi mpl
**versed** /vɜːst/ a ~ **in** versato in
**versifier** /ˈvɜːsɪfaɪə(r)/ n pej versificatore, -trice mf
**version** /ˈvɜːʃn/ n versione f; (translation) traduzione f
**versus** /ˈvɜːsəs/ prep contro
**vertebra** /ˈvɜːtɪbrə/ n (pl -brae /-briː/) Anat vertebra f
**vertebrate** /ˈvɜːtɪbrət/ n vertebrato m ● a vertebrato
**vertex** /ˈvɜːteks/ n Anat sommità f inv del capo; Math vertice m
**vertical** /ˈvɜːtɪkl/ a & n verticale m
**vertically** /ˈvɜːtɪklɪ/ adv verticalmente
**vertigo** /ˈvɜːtɪgəʊ/ n Med vertigine f
**verve** /vɜːv/ n verve f
**very** /ˈveri/ adv molto; ~ **much** molto; ~ **little** pochissimo; ~ **many** moltissimi; ~ **few** pochissimi; ~ **probably** molto probabilmente; ~ **well** benissimo; **at the** ~ **most** tutt'al più; **at the** ~ **latest** al più tardi ● a **the** ~ **first** il primissimo; **the** ~ **thing** proprio ciò che ci vuole; **at the** ~ **end/beginning** proprio alla fine/all'inizio; **that** ~ **day** proprio quel giorno; **the** ~ **thought** la sola idea; **only a** ~ **little** solo un pochino
**vespers** /ˈvespəz/ npl vespri mpl
**vessel** /ˈvesl/ n nave f; (receptacle) recipiente m; Anat vaso m
**vest** /vest/ n maglia f della pelle; (Am: waistcoat) gilè m inv ● vt ~ **sth in sb** investire qcno di qcsa
**vested interest** /vestɪdˈɪntrəst/ n interesse m personale
**vestige** /ˈvestɪdʒ/ n (of past) vestigio m
**vestment** /ˈvestmənt/ n Relig paramento m
**vestry** /ˈvestrɪ/ n sagrestia f
**vet** /vet/ n veterinario, -a mf ● vt (pt/pp **vetted**) controllare minuziosamente
**veteran** /ˈvetərən/ n veterano, -a mf
**veteran car** n auto f inv d'epoca (costruita prima del 1916)
**veterinary** /ˈvetərɪnəri/ a veterinario
**veterinary surgeon** n medico m veterinario
**veto** /ˈviːtəʊ/ n (pl -es) veto m ● vt proibire
**vetting** /ˈvetɪŋ/ n verifica f del passato di un individuo
**vex** /veks/ vt irritare
**vexation** /vekˈseɪʃn/ n irritazione f
**vexatious** /vekˈseɪʃəs/ a (person) fastidioso; (situation) spiacevole
**vexed** /vekst/ a irritato; ~ **question** questione f controversa
**vexing** /ˈveksɪŋ/ a irritante
**VHF** abbr (**very high frequency**) VHF
**via** /ˈvaɪə/ prep via; (by means of) attraverso
**viability** /vaɪəˈbɪlətɪ/ n probabilità f di sopravvivenza; (of proposition) attuabilità f
**viable** /ˈvaɪəbl/ a (life form, relationship,

company) in grado di sopravvivere; (proposition) attuabile
**viaduct** /ˈvaɪədʌkt/ n viadotto m
**vibes** /vaɪbz/ npl fam **I'm getting good/bad** ~ provo una sensazione gradevole/sgradevole
**vibrant** /ˈvaɪbrənt/ a fig che sprizza vitalità
**vibrate** /vaɪˈbreɪt/ vi vibrare
**vibration** /vaɪˈbreɪʃn/ n vibrazione f
**vicar** /ˈvɪkə(r)/ n parroco m (protestante)
**vicarage** /ˈvɪkərɪdʒ/ n casa f parrocchiale
**vicarious** /vɪˈkeərɪəs/ a indiretto
**vice¹** /vaɪs/ n vizio m
**vice²** n Techn morsa f
**vice: vice-captain** n Sport vicecapitano m.
**vice-chairman** n vicepresidente mf. **vice-chancellor** n Br Univ vicerettore m; Am Jur vicecancelliere m. **vice-president** n vicepresidente mf. **vice-principal** n (of senior school) vicepreside mf; (of junior school, college) vicedirettore, -trice mf
**vice squad** n buoncostume f
**vice versa** /vaɪsəˈvɜːsə/ adv viceversa
**vicinity** /vɪˈsɪnətɪ/ n vicinanza f; **in the** ~ **of** nelle vicinanze di
**vicious** /ˈvɪʃəs/ a cattivo; (attack) brutale; (animal) pericoloso
**vicious circle** n circolo m vizioso
**viciously** /ˈvɪʃəslɪ/ adv (attack) brutalmente
**victim** /ˈvɪktɪm/ n vittima f
**victimization** /vɪktɪmaɪˈzeɪʃn/ n vittimizzazione f
**victimize** /ˈvɪktɪmaɪz/ vt vittimizzare
**victor** /ˈvɪktə(r)/ n vincitore m
**Victorian** /vɪkˈtɔːrɪən/ n persona f vissuta in epoca vittoriana ● a (writer, poverty, age) vittoriano
**victorious** /vɪkˈtɔːrɪəs/ a vittorioso
**victory** /ˈvɪktəri/ n vittoria f
**video** /ˈvɪdɪəʊ/ n video m inv; (cassette) videocassetta f; (recorder) videoregistratore m ● attrib video ● vt registrare
**video: video camera** n videocamera f, telecamera f. **video card** n scheda f video. **video cassette** n videocassetta f. **video clip** n videoclip m inv. **videoconference** n videoconferenza f. **video game** n videogioco m. **video library** n videoteca f. **video nasty** n film m inv con scene violente o pornografiche. **video recorder** n videoregistratore m. **video shop** n negozio m che affitta o vende videocassette. **video surveillance** n videosorveglianza f. **videotape** n videocassetta f
**vie** /vaɪ/ vi (pres p **vying**) rivaleggiare
**Vienna** /vɪˈenə/ n Vienna f
**Viennese** /vɪəˈniːz/ a viennese
**Vietnam** /vɪetˈnæm/ n Vietnam m
**Vietnamese** /vɪetnæˈmiːz/ a & n vietnamita mf; (language) vietnamita m
**view** /vjuː/ n vista f; (photographed, painted) veduta f; (opinion) visione f; **look at the** ~ guardare il panorama; **in my** ~ secondo me; **in** ~ **of** in considerazione di; **on** ~ esposto; **with a** ~ **to** con l'intenzione di ● vt visitare

⟨*house*⟩; (*consider*) considerare ● *vi* TV guardare

**viewer** /'vju:ə(r)/ *n* TV telespettatore, -trice *mf*; *Phot* visore *m*

**viewfinder** /'vju:faɪndə(r)/ *n* Phot mirino *m*

**viewing** /'vju:ɪŋ/ *n* TV programmi *mpl* della televisione; (*of film*) proiezione *f*; (*of new range*) presentazione *f*; (*of exhibition, house*) visita *f*; **it makes good ~** TV vale la pena di vederlo; **what's tonight's ~?** cosa danno alla tv stasera? ● *attrib* ⟨*habits, preferences*⟩ dei telespettatori; **the ~ public** i telespettatori

**view phone** *n* videotelefono *m*

**viewpoint** /'vju:pɔɪnt/ *n* punto *m* di vista

**vigil** /'vɪdʒɪl/ *n* veglia *f*

**vigilance** /'vɪdʒɪləns/ *n* vigilanza *f*

**vigilant** /'vɪdʒɪlənt/ *a* vigile

**vigilante** /vɪdʒɪ'læntɪ/ *n* membro *m* di un'organizzazione privata per la prevenzione della criminalità

**vigorous** /'vɪg(ə)rəs/ *a* vigoroso

**vigorously** /'vɪg(ə)rəslɪ/ *adv* vigorosamente

**vigour** /'vɪgə(r)/ *n* vigore *m*

**vile** /vaɪl/ *a* disgustoso; ⟨*weather*⟩ orribile; ⟨*temper, mood*⟩ pessimo

**vilification** /vɪlɪfɪ'keɪʃn/ *n* denigrazione *f*

**villa** /'vɪlə/ *n* (*for holidays*) casa *f* di villeggiatura

**village** /'vɪlɪdʒ/ *n* paese *m*

**village green** *n* giardino *m* pubblico nel centro di un paese

**village hall** *n* sala *f* utilizzata per feste e altre attività

**villager** /'vɪlɪdʒə(r)/ *n* paesano, -a *mf*

**villain** /'vɪlən/ *n* furfante *m*; (*in story*) cattivo *m*

**villainous** /'vɪlənəs/ *a* infame

**vim** /vɪm/ *n fam* energia *f*

**vindicate** /'vɪndɪkeɪt/ *vt* (*from guilt*) discolpare; **you are ~d** ti sei dimostrato nel giusto

**vindictive** /vɪn'dɪktɪv/ *a* vendicativo

**vine** /vaɪn/ *n* vite *f*

**vinegar** /'vɪnɪgə(r)/ *n* aceto *m*

**vinegary** /'vɪnɪg(ə)rɪ/ *a* agro

**vineyard** /'vɪnjɑːd/ *n* vigneto *m*

**vintage** /'vɪntɪdʒ/ *a* ⟨*wine*⟩ d'annata ● *n* (*year*) annata *f*

**vintage car** *n* auto *f inv* d'epoca (costruita tra il 1917 e il 1930)

**vintage year** *n also fig* anno *m* memorabile

**vinyl** /'vaɪnɪl/ *n* vinile *m* ● *attrib* ⟨*paint*⟩ vinilico

**viola** /vɪ'əʊlə/ *n* Mus viola *f*

**violate** /'vaɪəleɪt/ *vt* violare

**violation** /vaɪə'leɪʃn/ *n* violazione *f*

**violence** /'vaɪələns/ *n* violenza *f*

**violent** /'vaɪələnt/ *a* violento

**violently** /'vaɪələntlɪ/ *adv* violentemente

**violet** /'vaɪələt/ *a* violetto ● *n* (*flower*) violetta *f*; (*colour*) violetto *m*

**violin** /vaɪə'lɪn/ *n* violino *m*

**violinist** /vaɪə'lɪnɪst/ *n* violinista *mf*

**VIP** *n abbr* (**very important person**) vip *mf*

**viper** /'vaɪpə(r)/ *n* vipera *f*

**virgin** /'vɜ:dʒɪn/ *a* vergine ● *n* vergine *f*

**virginal** /'vɜ:dʒɪn(ə)l/ *a* verginale

**virginals** /'vɜ:dʒɪn(ə)lz/ *npl* Mus spinetta *f*

**Virginia creeper** /vədʒɪnɪə'kri:pə(r)/ *n* vite *f* del Canada

**virginity** /və'dʒɪnətɪ/ *n* verginità *f*

**Virgo** /'vɜ:gəʊ/ *n* Astr Vergine *f*

**virile** /'vɪraɪl/ *a* virile

**virility** /vɪ'rɪlətɪ/ *n* virilità *f*

**virologist** /vaɪ'rɒlədʒɪst/ *n* virologo *m*

**virtual** /'vɜ:tjʊəl/ *a* effettivo

**virtually** /'vɜ:tjʊəlɪ/ *adv* praticamente

**virtual reality** *n* realtà *f* virtuale

**virtue** /'vɜ:tju:/ *n* virtù *f inv*; (*advantage*) vantaggio *m*; **by** *or* **in ~ of** a causa di

**virtuoso** /vɜ:tʊ'əʊzəʊ/ *n* (*pl* **-si** /-zi:/) virtuoso *m*

**virtuous** /'vɜ:tjʊəs/ *a* virtuoso

**virulent** /'vɪrʊlənt/ *a* virulento

**virus** /'vaɪərəs/ *n* virus *m inv*

**visa** /'vi:zə/ *n* visto *m*

**vis-à-vis** /vi:zɑ:'vi:/ *prep* rispetto a

**visceral** /'vɪs(ə)rəl/ *a* ⟨*power, performance*⟩ viscerale

**viscount** /'vaɪkaʊnt/ *n* visconte *m*

**viscous** /'vɪskəs/ *a* vischioso

**visibility** /vɪzə'bɪlətɪ/ *n* visibilità *f*

**visible** /'vɪzəbl/ *a* visibile

**visibly** /'vɪzəblɪ/ *adv* visibilmente

**vision** /'vɪʒn/ *n* visione *f*; (*sight*) vista *f*

**visionary** /'vɪʒn(ə)rɪ/ *a & n* visionario, -a *mf*

**vision mixer** *n* (*person*) tecnico *m* del mixaggio video; (*equipment*) mixaggio *m* video

**visit** /'vɪzɪt/ *n* visita *f* ● *vt* andare a trovare ⟨*person*⟩; andare da ⟨*doctor etc*⟩; visitare ⟨*town, building*⟩

**visiting** /'vɪzɪtɪŋ/: **visiting card** *n* biglietto *m* da visita. **visiting hours** *npl* orario *m* delle visite. **visiting lecturer** *n* conferenziere, -a *mf*. **visiting team** *n* squadra *f* ospite. **visiting time** *n* orario *m* delle visite

**visitor** /'vɪzɪtə(r)/ *n* ospite *mf*; (*of town, museum*) visitatore, -trice *mf*; (*in hotel*) cliente *mf*

**visitor centre** *n* centro *m* di accoglienza e di informazione per i visitatori

**visitors' book** *n* (*in exhibition*) albo *m* dei visitatori; (*in hotel*) registro *m* dei clienti

**visor** /'vaɪzə(r)/ *n* visiera *f*; Auto parasole *m*

**vista** /'vɪstə/ *n* (*view*) panorama *m*

**visual** /'vɪzjʊəl/ *a* visivo

**visual: visual aids** *npl* supporto *m* visivo. **visual arts** *npl* arti *fpl* visive. **visual display unit** *n* visualizzatore *m*

**visualize** /'vɪzjʊəlaɪz/ *vt* visualizzare

**visually** /'vɪzjʊəlɪ/ *adv* visualmente; **~ handicapped** non vedente

**vital** /'vaɪtl/ *a* vitale

**vitality** /vaɪ'tælətɪ/ *n* vitalità *f*

**vitally** /'vaɪtəlɪ/ *adv* estremamente

**vital statistics** *npl fam* misure *fpl*

**vitamin** /'vɪtəmɪn/ *n* vitamina *f*

**vitreous** /'vɪtrɪəs/ *a* vetroso; ⟨*enamel*⟩ vetrificato

**vitriolic** /vɪtrɪˈɒlɪk/ a Chem di vetriolo; fig al vetriolo

**vituperative** /vɪˈtjuːp(ə)rətɪv/ a ingiurioso

**viva** /ˈvaɪvə/ n Br Univ [esame m] orale m

**vivacious** /vɪˈveɪʃəs/ a vivace

**vivaciously** /vɪˈveɪʃəslɪ/ adv vivacemente

**vivacity** /vɪˈvæsətɪ/ n vivacità f

**vivid** /ˈvɪvɪd/ a vivido

**vividly** /ˈvɪvɪdlɪ/ adv in modo vivido

**vivisect** /ˈvɪvɪsekt/ vt vivisezionare

**vivisection** /vɪvɪˈsekʃn/ n vivisezione f

**vixen** /ˈvɪksn/ n volpe f femmina

**viz** /vɪz/ adv cioè

**vocabulary** /vəˈkæbjʊlərɪ/ n vocabolario m; (list) glossario m

**vocal** /ˈvəʊkl/ a vocale; (vociferous) eloquente

**vocal cords** npl corde fpl vocali

**vocalist** /ˈvəʊkəlɪst/ n vocalista mf

**vocalize** /ˈvəʊkəlaɪz/ vt (fig: express) esprimere a parole; articolare ‹sound›

**vocation** /vəˈkeɪʃn/ n vocazione f

**vocational** /vəˈkeɪʃ(ə)nl/ a di orientamento professionale

**vociferous** /vəˈsɪfərəs/ a vociante

**vodka** /ˈvɒdkə/ n vodka f inv

**vogue** /vəʊɡ/ n moda f; **in ~** in voga

**voice** /vɔɪs/ n voce f ● vt esprimere

**voice box** n Anat laringe f

**voiceless** /ˈvɔɪslɪs/ a ‹minority› silenzioso; ‹group› privo del diritto di parola

**voicemail** /ˈvɔɪsmeɪl/ n posta f elettronica vocale

**voice-over** n voce f fuori campo

**void** /vɔɪd/ a (not valid) nullo; **~ of** privo di ● n vuoto m

**vol** /vɒl/ abbr (volume) vol.

**volatile** /ˈvɒlətaɪl/ a volatile; ‹person› volubile

**volcanic** /vɒlˈkænɪk/ a vulcanico

**volcano** /vɒlˈkeɪnəʊ/ n vulcano m

**volition** /vəˈlɪʃn/ n **of his own ~** di sua spontanea volontà

**volley** /ˈvɒlɪ/ n (of gunfire) raffica f; (Tennis) volée f inv

**volleyball** /ˈvɒlɪbɔːl/ n pallavolo f

**volt** /vəʊlt/ n volt m inv

**voltage** /ˈvəʊltɪdʒ/ n Electr voltaggio m

**voluble** /ˈvɒljʊbl/ a loquace

**volume** /ˈvɒljuːm/ n volume m; (of work, traffic) quantità f inv

**volume control** n volume m

**voluntarily** /ˈvɒləntərɪlɪ/ adv volontariamente

**voluntary** /ˈvɒləntərɪ/ a volontario

**voluntary redundancy** n Br dimissioni fpl volontarie

**voluntary work** n volontariato m

**volunteer** /vɒlənˈtɪə(r)/ n volontario, -a mf ● vt offrire volontariamente ‹information› ● vi offrirsi volontario; Mil arruolarsi come volontario

**voluptuous** /vəˈlʌptjʊəs/ a voluttuoso

**vomit** /ˈvɒmɪt/ n vomito m ● vt/i vomitare

**voodoo** /ˈvuːduː/ n vudu m inv

**voracious** /vəˈreɪʃəs/ a vorace

**vortex** /ˈvɔːteks/ n vortice m; fig turbine m

**vote** /vəʊt/ n voto m; (ballot) votazione f; (right) diritto m di voto; **take a ~ on** votare su ● vi votare ● vt **~ sb president** eleggere qcno presidente

■ **vote down** vt (reject by vote) bocciare ai voti

■ **vote in** vt (elect) eleggere

**vote of confidence** n Pol, fig voto m di fiducia

**vote of thanks** n discorso m di ringraziamento

**voter** /ˈvəʊtə(r)/ n elettore, -trice mf

**voting** /ˈvəʊtɪŋ/ n votazione f

**voting age** n età f inv per votare

**voting booth** n cabina f elettorale

**vouch** /vaʊtʃ/ vi **~ for** garantire per

**voucher** /ˈvaʊtʃə(r)/ n buono m

**vow** /vaʊ/ n voto m ● vt giurare

**vowel** /ˈvaʊəl/ n vocale f

**vox pop** /vɒksˈpɒp/ n TV, Radio opinione f pubblica

**voyage** /ˈvɔɪdʒ/ n viaggio m [marittimo]; (in space) viaggio m [nello spazio]

**V-sign** n (offensive gesture) gestaccio m; (victory sign) segno m di vittoria

**VSO** abbr (**Voluntary Service Overseas**) servizio m civile volontario nei paesi in via di sviluppo

**vulgar** /ˈvʌlɡə(r)/ a volgare

**vulgar fraction** n Math frazione f ordinaria

**vulgarity** /vʌlˈɡærətɪ/ n volgarità f inv

**vulnerable** /ˈvʌlnərəbl/ a vulnerabile

**vulture** /ˈvʌltʃə(r)/ n avvoltoio m

**vying** /ˈvaɪɪŋ/ see **vie**

# Ww

**w, W** /'dʌblju:/ *n* (*letter*) w, W *f inv*
**W** *abbr* (**West**) O; *abbr Electr* (**watt**) w
**wad** /wɒd/ *n* batuffolo *m*; (*bundle*) rotolo *m*
**wadding** /'wɒdɪŋ/ *n* ovatta *f*
**waddle** /'wɒdl/ *vi* camminare ondeggiando
**wade** /weɪd/ *vi* guadare
■ **wade in** *vi* (*fam: start working*) mettersi al lavoro; (*take part*) prendere parte
■ **wade into** *vt* (*attack*) scagliarsi contro
■ **wade through** *vt fam* procedere faticosamente in (*book*)
**wader** /'weɪdə(r)/ *n Zool* trampoliere *m*; **~s** (*pl: boots*) stivaloni *mpl* di gomma
**wafer** /'weɪfə(r)/ *n* cialda *f*, wafer *m inv*; *Relig* ostia *f*
**wafer-thin** *a* sottilissimo
**waffle**¹ /'wɒfl/ *vi fam* blaterare
**waffle**² *n Culin* cialda *f*
**waft** /wɒft/ *vt* trasportare ● *vi* diffondersi
**wag** /wæg/ *v* (*pt/pp* **wagged**) ● *vt* agitare ● *vi* agitarsi
**wage**¹ /weɪdʒ/ *vt* dichiarare (*war*); lanciare (*campaign*)
**wage**² *n* & **~s** *pl* salario *msg*
**wage earner** *n* salariato, -a *mf*
**wage packet** *n* busta *f* paga
**wager** /'weɪdʒə(r)/ *n* scommessa *f*
**waggle** /'wægl/ *vt* dimenare ● *vi* dimenarsi
**wagon** /'wægən/ *n* carro *m*; *Rail* vagone *m* merci; **be on the ~** *fam* astenersi dall'alcol
**waif** /weɪf/ *n* trovatello, -a *mf*
**wail** /weɪl/ *n* piagnucolio *m*; (*of wind*) lamento *m*; (*of baby*) vagito *m* ● *vi* piagnucolare; (*wind:*) lamentarsi; (*baby:*) vagire
**Wailing Wall** /'weɪlɪŋ/ *n* Muro *m* del pianto
**waist** /weɪst/ *n* vita *f*
**waist:** **waistband** *n* cintura *f*. **waistcoat** *n* gilè *m inv*; (*of man's suit*) panciotto *m*. **waistline** *n* vita *f*. **waist measurement** *n* giro *m* vita
**wait** /weɪt/ *n* attesa *f*; **lie in ~ for** appostarsi per sorprendere ● *vi* aspettare; **~ at table** servire i tavoli; **~ for** aspettare ● *vt* **~ one's turn** aspettare il proprio turno
■ **wait about, wait around** *vi* aspettare
■ **wait behind** *vi* trattenersi
■ **wait in** *vi* rimanere a casa ad aspettare
■ **wait on** *vt* servire
■ **wait up** *vi* rimanere alzato ad aspettare; **don't ~ up for me** non mi aspettare alzato
**waiter** /'weɪtə(r)/ *n* cameriere *m*
**waiter service** *n* servizio *m* al tavolo
**waiting** /'weɪtɪŋ/: **waiting game** *n* **play a ~** *n* temporeggiare. **waiting list** *n* lista *f* d'attesa. **waiting room** *n* sala *f* d'aspetto
**waitress** /'weɪtrɪs/ *n* cameriera *f*

**waive** /weɪv/ *vt* rinunciare a (*claim*); non tener conto di (*rule*)
**waiver** /'weɪvə(r)/ *n Jur* rinuncia *f*
**wake**¹ /weɪk/ *n* veglia *f* funebre ● *v* (*pt* **woke**, *pp* **woken**) **~ [up]** ● *vt* svegliare ● *vi* svegliarsi
■ **wake up to** *vt* **~ up to the fact that...** (*realize*) aprire gli occhi di fronte al fatto che...
**wake**² *n Naut* scia *f*; **in the ~ of** *fig* nella scia di
**wakeful** /'weɪkfʊl/ *a* (*night*) insonne
**waken** /'weɪkn/ *vt* svegliare ● *vi* svegliarsi
**wake-up call** *n* sveglia *f* telefonica
**Wales** /weɪlz/ *n* Galles *m*
**walk** /wɔːk/ *n* passeggiata *f*; (*gait*) andatura *f*; (*path*) sentiero *m*; **go for a ~** andare a fare una passeggiata; **~ of life** livello *m* sociale ● *vi* camminare; (*as opposed to drive etc*) andare a piedi; (*ramble*) passeggiare; **'~'** *Am* (*at crossing*) 'avanti' ● *vt* portare a spasso (*dog*); percorrere (*streets*)
■ **walk into** *vt* entrare in (*room*); andare a sbattere contro (*door, lamp post*); cadere in (*trap*); trovare facilmente (*job*)
■ **walk off** *vi* (*leave*) andarsene
■ **walk off with** *vt* (*win easily*) riportare senza difficoltà; (*take, steal*) portarsi via
■ **walk out** *vi* (*husband, employee:*) andarsene; (*workers:*) scioperare
■ **walk out of** *vt* uscire da (*room*); abbandonare (*meeting*)
■ **walk out on** *vt* lasciare
■ **walk over** *vt* **~ all over sb** (*defeat*) stracciare qcno; (*treat badly*) trattare qcno come una pezza da piedi
■ **walk through** *vt* superare senza difficoltà (*exam, interview*)
■ **walk up** *vi* (*as opposed to taking the lift*) salire a piedi; (*approach*) avvicinarsi
**walkabout** /'wɔːkəbaʊt/ *n* escursione *f* periodica degli aborigeni australiani nell'entroterra; (*by royalty*) incontro *m* con la folla; **go ~** (*queen, politician:*) camminare tra la folla
**walker** /'wɔːkə(r)/ *n* camminatore, -trice *mf*; (*rambler*) escursionista *mf*
**walkie-talkie** /wɔːkɪ'tɔːkɪ/ *n* walkie-talkie *m inv*
**walk-in** *a* **~ closet** stanzino *m*
**walking** /'wɔːkɪŋ/ *n* camminare *m*; (*rambling*) fare *m* delle escursioni
**walking:** **walking boots** *npl* scarponi *mpl* [da trekking]. **walking distance** *n* **it's within ~** ci si arriva a piedi. **walking**

**frame** *n Med* deambulatore *m.* **walking pace** *n* passo *m.* **walking shoes** *npl* scarpe *fpl* da passeggio. **walking-stick** *n* bastone *m* da passeggio. **walking wounded** *npl feriti mpl in grado di camminare*

**walk: Walkman®** *n* Walkman *m inv.* **walk-on** *n Theat* comparsa *f* ● *a* ‹*role*› piccolo. **walkout** *n* sciopero *m.* **walkover** *n fig* vittoria *f* facile. **walkway** *n* passaggio *m* pedonale

**wall** /wɔːl/ *n* muro *m;* **go to the ~** *fam* andare a rotoli; **drive sb up the ~** *fam* far diventare matto qcno

■ **wall up** *vt* murare

**wallchart** /'wɔːltʃɑːt/ *n* tabellone *m*

**walled** /wɔːld/ *a* ‹*city*› fortificato

**wallet** /'wɒlɪt/ *n* portafoglio *m*

**wallflower** /'wɔːlflaʊə(r)/ *n* violaciocca *f*

**wall hanging** *n* decorazione *f* murale

**wallop** /'wɒləp/ *n fam* colpo *m* ● *vt* (*pt/pp* **walloped**) *fam* colpire

**walloping** /'wɒləpɪŋ/ *fam a* enorme ● *adv* ~ **great** (*very big*) enorme ● *n* **give sb a ~** suonarle a qcno

**wallow** /'wɒləʊ/ *vi* sguazzare; (*in self-pity, grief*) crogiolarsi

**wallpaper** /'wɔːlpeɪpə(r)/ *n* tappezzeria *f* ● *vt* tappezzare

**wall-to-wall** *a* che copre tutto il pavimento

**walnut** /'wɔːlnʌt/ *n* noce *f*

**waltz** /wɔːlts/ *n* valzer *m inv* ● *vi* ballare il valzer; **he came ~ing up and said** *fam* è arrivato e ha detto con nonchalance

■ **waltz off with** *vt* (*fam: take, win*) portarsi via

■ **waltz through** *vt* superare facilmente ‹*exam*›

**wan** /wɒn/ *a* esangue

**wand** /wɒnd/ *n* (*magic ~*) bacchetta *f* [magica]

**wander** /'wɒndə(r)/ *vi* girovagare; (*fig: digress*) divagare

■ **wander about** *vi* andare a spasso

■ **wander away** *vi* allontanarsi

■ **wander off** *vi* allontanarsi; **I'd better be ~ing off** *fam* è meglio che vada

**wanderer** /'wɒndərə(r)/ *n* vagabondo, -a *mf*

**wanderlust** /'wɒndəlʌst/ *n* smania *f* dei viaggi

**wane** /weɪn/ *n* **be on the ~** essere in fase calante ● *vi* calare

**wangle** /'wæŋgl/ *vt fam* rimediare ‹*invitation, holiday*›

**waning** /'weɪnɪŋ/ *n* (*of moon*) calare *m*; (*weakening*) declino *m* ● *a* ‹*moon*› calante; ‹*popularity*› in declino

**wannabee** /'wɒnəbiː/ *n fam* persona *f* che sogna di diventare famosa

**want** /wɒnt/ *n* (*hardship*) bisogno *m*; (*lack*) mancanza *f* ● *vt* volere; (*need*) aver bisogno di; ~ **[to have]** sth volere qcsa; ~ **to do** sth voler fare qcsa; **we ~ to stay** vogliamo rimanere; **I ~ you to go** voglio che tu vada; **it ~s painting** ha bisogno di essere dipinto; **you ~ to learn to swim** bisogna che impari a nuotare ● *vi* ~ **for** mancare di

**wanted** /'wɒntɪd/ *a* ricercato

**wanted list** *n* lista *f* dei ricercati

**wanting** /'wɒntɪŋ/ *a* **be ~** mancare; **be ~ in** mancare di

**wanton** /'wɒntən/ *a* ‹*cruelty, neglect*› gratuito; (*morally*) debosciato

**war** /wɔː(r)/ *n* guerra *f*; *fig* lotta *f* (**on** contro); **at ~** in guerra

**warble** /'wɔːbl/ *vt/i* trillare; ‹*singer:*› gorgheggiare

**war cabinet** *n* consiglio *m* di guerra

**war cry** *n* grido *m* di guerra

**ward** /wɔːd/ *n* (*in hospital*) reparto *m*; (*child*) minore *m* sotto tutela

■ **ward off** *vt* evitare; parare ‹*blow*›

**warden** /'wɔːdn/ *n* guardiano. -a *mf*

**warder** /'wɔːdə(r)/ *n* guardia *f* carceraria

**wardrobe** /'wɔːdrəʊb/ *n* guardaroba *m*

**wardrobe assistant** *n* costumista *mf*

**ward round** *n Med* giro *m* delle corsie

**ward sister** *n Br Med* caposala *f inv*

**warehouse** /'weəhaʊs/ *n* magazzino *m*

**wares** /weəz/ *npl* merci *mpl*

**warfare** /'wɔːfeə/ *n* guerra *f*

**war: war game** *n Mil* simulazione *f* di scontro militare. **warhead** *n* testata *f.* **warhorse** *n* cavallo *m* da battaglia; (*fig: campaigner*) veterano *m*

**warily** /'weərɪlɪ/ *adv* cautamente

**warlike** /'wɔːlaɪk/ *a* bellicoso

**warm** /wɔːm/ *a* caldo; ‹*welcome*› caloroso; **be ~** ‹*person:*› aver caldo; **it is ~** ‹*weather*› fa caldo ● *vt* scaldare

■ **warm up** *vt* scaldare ● *vi* scaldarsi; *fig* animarsi

**warm-blooded** /-'blʌdɪd/ *a Zool* con temperatura corporea costante

**war memorial** *n* monumento *m* ai caduti

**warm-hearted** /-'hɑːtɪd/ *a* espansivo

**warmly** /'wɔːmlɪ/ *adv* ‹*greet*› calorosamente; ‹*dress*› in modo pesante

**warmongering** /'wɔːmʌŋgərɪŋ/ *n* bellicismo *m* ● *a* ‹*article*› bellicistico; ‹*person*› guerrafondaio

**warmth** /wɔːmθ/ *n* calore *m*

**warm-up** *n Sport* riscaldamento *m*; (*of musicians*) prove *fpl*

**warn** /wɔːn/ *vt* avvertire

■ **warn off** *vt* dare un avvertimento a

**warning** /'wɔːnɪŋ/ *n* avvertimento *m*; (*advance notice*) preavviso *m*

**warp** /wɔːp/ *vt* deformare; *fig* distorcere ● *vi* deformarsi

**warpaint** /'wɔːpeɪnt/ *n Mil* pitture *fpl* di guerra

**warpath** /'wɔːpɑːθ/ *n* **on the ~** sul sentiero di guerra

**warped** /wɔːpt/ *a* deformato; ‹*personality*› contorto; ‹*sexuality*› deviato; ‹*view*› distorto

**warplane** /'wɔːpleɪn/ *n* aereo *m* da guerra

**warrant** /'wɒrənt/ *n* (*for arrest, search*) mandato *m* ● *vt* (*justify*) giustificare; (*guarantee*) garantire

**warranty** /'wɒrəntɪ/ *n* garanzia *f*

**warren** /'wɒr(ə)n/ *n* (*of rabbits*) area *f* piena

di tane di conigli: (*building, maze of streets*) labirinto *m*

**warring** /'wɔːrɪŋ/ *a* in guerra

**warrior** /'wɒrɪə(r)/ *n* guerriero, -a *mf*

**Warsaw** /'wɔːsɔː/ *n* Varsavia *f*

**warship** /'wɔːʃɪp/ *n* nave *f* da guerra

**wart** /wɔːt/ *n* porro *m*

**wartime** /'wɔːtaɪm/ *n* tempo *m* di guerra

**war-torn** /'wɔːtɔːn/ *a* logorato dalla guerra

**wary** /'weərɪ/ *a* (**-ier, -iest**) (*careful*) cauto; (*suspicious*) diffidente

**was** /wɒz/ *see* **be**

**wash** /wɒʃ/ *n* lavata *f*; (*clothes*) bucato *m*; (*in washing machine*) lavaggio *m*; **have a ~** darsi una lavata ● *vt* lavare; (*sea:*) bagnare; **~ one's hands** lavarsi le mani ● *vi* lavarsi

■ **wash away** *vt* (*rain:*) portare via; (*sea, floodwaters:*) spazzare via

■ **wash off** *vt* lavar via (*stain, mud*) ● *vi* andar via

■ **wash out** *vt* sciacquare (*soap*); sciacquarsi (*mouth*)

■ **wash up** *vt* lavare ● *vi* lavare i piatti; *Am* lavarsi

**washable** /'wɒʃəbl/ *a* lavabile

**wash: wash-and-wear** *a* che non si stira. **washbasin** *n* lavandino *m*. **wash cloth** *n* *Am* ≈ guanto *m* da bagno

**washed out** /wɒʃt'aʊt/ *a* (*faded*) scolorito; (*tired*) spossato

**washed up** *a fam* (*finished*) finito; (*tired*) distrutto

**washer** /'wɒʃə(r)/ *n Techn* guarnizione *f*; (*machine*) lavatrice *f*

**washer-dryer** /-'draɪə(r)/ *n* asciugabiancheria *m inv*

**washing** /'wɒʃɪŋ/ *n* bucato *m*

**washing: washing machine** *n* lavatrice *f*. **washing powder** *n* detersivo *m*. **washing soda** *n* soda *f* da bucato. **washing-up** *n* do the **~** lavare i piatti. **washing-up bowl** *n* bacinella *f* (*per i piatti*). **washing-up liquid** *n* detersivo *m* per i piatti. **washing-up water** *n* rigovernatura *f*

**wash: wash load** *n* carico *m* di lavatrice. **wash-out** *n* disastro *m*. **washroom** *n* bagno *m*

**wasp** /wɒsp/ *n* vespa *f*

**waspish** /'wɒspɪʃ/ *a* pungente

**wastage** /'weɪstɪdʒ/ *n* perdita *f*

**waste** /weɪst/ *n* spreco *m*; (*rubbish*) rifiuto *m*; **~s** *pl* distesa *fsg* desolata; **~ of time** perdita *f* di tempo ● *a* (*product*) di scarto; (*land*) desolato; **lay ~** devastare ● *vt* sprecare

■ **waste away** *vi* deperire

**waste: wastebasket** *n* cestino *m* della carta straccia. **waste bin** *n* (*for paper*) cestino *m* della carta straccia; (*for rubbish*) secchio *m* della spazzatura. **waste disposal unit** *n* eliminatore *m* di rifiuti

**wasteful** /'weɪstfʊl/ *a* dispendioso

**waste: waste paper** *n* carta *f* straccia. **waste-paper basket** *n* cestino *m* per la carta [straccia]. **waste pipe** *n* tubo *m* di scarico

**watch** /wɒtʃ/ *n* guardia *f*; (*period of duty*) turno *m* di guardia; (*timepiece*) orologio *m*; **be on the ~** stare all'erta ● *vt* guardare (*film, match, television*); (*be careful of, look after*) stare attento a ● *vi* guardare

■ **watch out** *vi* (*be careful*) stare attento (**for** a)

■ **watch out for** *vt* (*look for*) fare attenzione all'arrivo di (*person*)

**watchdog** /'wɒtʃdɒg/ *n* cane *m* da guardia

**watchful** /'wɒtʃfʊl/ *a* attento

**watchfully** /'wɒtʃfʊlɪ/ *adv* attentamente

**watch: watchmaker** *n* orologiaio, -a *mf*. **watchman** *n* guardiano *m*. **watch strap** *n* cinturino *m* dell'orologio. **watchtower** *n* torre *f* di guardia. **watchword** *n* motto *m*

**water** /'wɔːtə(r)/ *n* acqua *f*; **~s** *pl* acque *fpl* ● *vt* annaffiare (*garden, plant*); (*dilute*) annacquare; dare da bere a (*horse etc*) ● *vi* (*eyes:*) lacrimare; **my mouth was ~ing** avevo l'acquolina in bocca

■ **water down** *vt* diluire; *fig* attenuare

**water: water authority** *n* ente *m* dell'acqua. **waterbird** *n* uccello *m* acquatico. **water bottle** *n* borraccia *f*. **watercolour** *n* acquerello *m*. **water company** *n* società *f inv* dell'acqua. **watercress** *n* crescione *m*. **water-divining** *n* rabdomanzia *f*. **waterfall** *n* cascata *f*. **waterfront** *n* (*by lakeside, riverside*) riva *f*; (*on harbour*) zona *f* portuale. **waterhole** *n* pozza *f* d'acqua

**watering can** /'wɔːtərɪŋ/ *n* annaffiatoio *m*

**water: water lily** *n* ninfea *f*. **waterline** *n* linea *f* di galleggiamento. **waterlogged** *a* inzuppato. **water main** *n* conduttura *f* dell'acqua. **watermark** *n* filigrana *f*. **watermeadow** *n* marcita *f*. **watermelon** *n* cocomero *m*. **watermill** *n* mulino *m* ad acqua. **water polo** *n* pallanuoto *f*. **water-power** *n* energia *f* idraulica. **waterproof** *a* (*coat*) impermeabile; (*make-up*) water-proof *inv* ● *n* impermeabile *m*. **waterproofs** *npl* sovrapantaloni *mpl* e giacca impermeabili. **water rates** *mpl Br* tariffe *fpl* dell'acqua. **water-resistant** *a* (*sun cream*) resistente all'acqua; (*garment, watch*) impermeabile. **watershed** *n* spartiacque *m inv*; *fig* svolta *f*. **waterside** *n* riva *f* ● *attrib* (*cafe, hotel*) sulla riva. **water-skiing** *n* sci *m* nautico. **water softener** *n* (*equipment*) addolcitore *m*; (*substance*) anticalcare *m inv*. **water-soluble** *a* idrosolubile. **water sport** *n* sport *m inv* acquatico. **water-table** *n Geog* superficie *f* freatica. **watertight** *a* stagno; *fig* irrefutabile. **water tower** *n* serbatoio *m* idrico a torre. **waterway** *n* canale *m* navigabile. **waterwheel** *n* ruota *f* idraulica. **water wings** *npl* braccioli *mpl*. **waterworks** *n* impianto *m* idrico; **turn on the ~** *fam* mettersi a piangere come una fontana

**watery** /'wɔːtərɪ/ *a* acquoso; (*eyes*) lacrimoso

**watt** /wɒt/ *n* watt *m inv*

**wattage** /'wɒtɪdʒ/ *n* wattaggio *m*

**wave** /weɪv/ *n* onda *f*; (*gesture*) cenno *m*; *fig* ondata *f* ● *vt* agitare; **~ one's hand** agitare la mano ● *vi* far segno; (*flag:*) sventolare

■ **wave aside** *vt* respingere ⟨*criticism*⟩
■ **wave down** *vt* far segno di fermarsi a ⟨*vehicle*⟩
**waveband** /'weɪvbænd/ *n* gamma *f* d'onda
**wavelength** /'weɪvleŋθ/ *n* lunghezza *f* d'onda; **be on the same ~** *fig* essere sulla stessa lunghezza d'onda
**waver** /'weɪvə(r)/ *vi* vacillare; ⟨*hesitate*⟩ esitare
**wavy** /'weɪvɪ/ *a* ondulato
**wax¹** /wæks/ *vi* ⟨*moon:*⟩ crescere; (*fig: become*) diventare
**wax²** *n* cera *f*; (*in ear*) cerume *m* ● *vt* dare la cera a
**waxworks** /'wæksw3:ks/ *n* museo *m* delle cere
**waxy** /'wæksɪ/ *a* ⟨*skin, texture*⟩ cereo
**way** /weɪ/ *n* percorso *m*; (*direction*) direzione *f*; (*manner, method*) modo *m*; **~s** *pl* (*customs*) abitudini *fpl*; **be in the ~** essere in mezzo; **on the ~ to Rome** andando a Roma; **I'll do it on the ~** lo faccio mentre vado; **it's on my ~** è sul mio percorso; **a long ~ off** lontano; **this ~** da questa parte; (*like this*) così; **by the ~** a proposito; **by ~ of** come; (*via*) via; **either ~** (*whatever we do*) in un modo o nell'altro; **in some ~s** sotto certi aspetti; **in a ~** in un certo senso; **in a bad ~** ⟨*person*⟩ molto grave; **out of the ~** fuori mano; **under ~** in corso; **lead the ~** far strada; *fig* aprire la strada; **make ~** far posto (**for** a); **give ~** *Auto* dare la precedenza; **go out of one's ~** *fig* scomodarsi (**to** per); **get one's [own] ~** averla vinta ● *adv* **~ behind** molto indietro
**way in** *n* entrata *f*
**waylay** /weɪ'leɪ/ *vt* (*pt/pp* **-laid**) aspettare al varco ⟨*person*⟩; intercettare ⟨*letter*⟩
**way-out** *a fam* eccentrico
**way out** *n* uscita *f*; *fig* via *f* d'uscita
**wayside** /'weɪsaɪd/ *n* bordo *m*; **fall by the ~** (*morally*) smarrire la retta via; (*fail*) fallire
**wayward** /'weɪwəd/ *a* capriccioso
**WC** *abbr* WC; **the WC** il gabinetto
**we** /wi:/ *pers pron* noi; **we're the last** siamo gli ultimi; **they're going, but we're not** loro vanno, ma noi no
**weak** /wi:k/ *a* debole; ⟨*liquid*⟩ leggero; **go ~ at the knees** *fam* sentirsi piegare le ginocchia
**weaken** /'wi:kn/ *vt* indebolire ● *vi* indebolirsi
**weakling** /'wi:klɪŋ/ *n* smidollato, -a *mf*
**weakly** /'wi:klɪ/ *adv* debolmente
**weak-minded** /-'maɪndɪd/ *a* (*indecisive*) debole; (*simple*) poco intelligente
**weakness** /'wi:knɪs/ *n* debolezza *f*; (*liking*) debole *m*
**weak-willed** /-'wɪld/ *a* debole
**weal** /wi:l/ *n* piaga *f*
**wealth** /welθ/ *n* ricchezza *f*; *fig* gran quantità *f*
**wealthy** /'welθɪ/ *a* (**-ier, -iest**) ricco
**wean** /wi:n/ *vt* svezzare
**weapon** /'wepən/ *n* arma *f*
**wear** /weə(r)/ *n* (*clothing*) abbigliamento *m*;

**for everyday ~** da portare tutti i giorni; **~ [and tear]** usura *f* ● *v* (*pt* **wore**, *pp* **worn**) ● *vt* portare; (*damage*) consumare; **~ a hole in sth** logorare qcsa fino a fare un buco; **what shall I ~?** cosa mi metto? ● *vi* consumarsi; (*last*) durare
■ **wear away** *vt* consumare ● *vi* consumarsi
■ **wear down** *vt* estenuare ⟨*opposition etc*⟩
■ **wear off** *vi* scomparire; ⟨*effect:*⟩ finire
■ **wear out** *vt* consumare [fino in fondo]; (*exhaust*) estenuare ● *vi* estenuarsi
**wearable** /'weərəbl/ *a* portabile
**wearily** /'wɪərɪlɪ/ *adv* stancamente
**weariness** /'wɪərɪnɪs/ *n* stanchezza *f*
**weary** /'wɪərɪ/ *a* (**-ier, -iest**) sfinito ● *v* (*pt/pp* **wearied**) ● *vt* sfinire ● *vi* **~ of** stancarsi di
**weasel** /'wi:zl/ *n* donnola *f*
**weather** /'weðə(r)/ *n* tempo *m*; **in this ~** con questo tempo; **under the ~** *fam* giù di corda ● *vt* sopravvivere a ⟨*storm*⟩
**weather: weather balloon** *n* pallone *m* sonda. **weather-beaten** /-bi:tn/ *a* ⟨*face*⟩ segnato dalle intemperie. **weathercock** *n* gallo *m* segnavento. **weather forecast** *n* previsioni *fpl* del tempo. **weatherman** *n* TV meteorologo *m*. **weatherproof** *a* ⟨*garment, shoe*⟩ impermeabile; ⟨*shelter, door*⟩ resistente alle intemperie. **weather-vane** *n* banderuola *f*
**weave¹** /wi:v/ *vi* (*pt/pp* **weaved**) (*move*) zigzagare
**weave²** *n* (*Tex*) tessuto *m* ● *vt* (*pt* **wove**, *pp* **woven**) tessere; intrecciare ⟨*flowers etc*⟩; intrecciare le fila di ⟨*story etc*⟩
**weaver** /'wi:və(r)/ *n* tessitore, -trice *mf*
**web** /web/ *n* rete *f*; (*of spider*) ragnatela *f*
**webbed feet** /webd'fi:t/ *npl* piedi *mpl* palmati
**web page** *n Comput* pagina *f* web
**web site** *n Comput* sito *m* web
**wed** /wed/ *vt* (*pt/pp* **wedded**) sposare ● *vi* sposarsi
**wedding** /'wedɪŋ/ *n* matrimonio *m*
**wedding: wedding bells** *npl fig* marcia *f* nuziale. **wedding breakfast** *n* rinfresco *m* di nozze. **wedding cake** *n* torta *f* nuziale. **wedding day** *n* giorno *m* del matrimonio. **wedding dress** *n* vestito *m* da sposa. **wedding march** *n* marcia *f* nuziale. **wedding night** *n* prima notte *f* di nozze. **wedding reception** *n* ricevimento *m* di nozze. **wedding ring** *n* fede *f*. **wedding vows** *npl* voti *mpl* nuziali
**wedge** /wedʒ/ *n* zeppa *f*; (*for splitting wood*) cuneo *m*; (*of cheese*) fetta *f* ● *vt* (*fix*) fissare
**wedlock** /'wedlɒk/ *n* **born out of ~** nato fuori dal matrimonio
**Wednesday** /'wenzdeɪ/ *n* mercoledì *m inv*
**wee¹** /wi:/ *a fam* piccolo
**wee²** *n fam* **do a ~** fare la pipì ● *vi fam* fare la pipì
**weed** /wi:d/ *n* erbaccia *f*; (*fam: person*) mollusco *m* ● *vt* estirpare le erbacce da ● *vi* estirpare le erbacce

■ **weed out** *vt fig* eliminare

**weedkiller** /ˈwiːdkɪlə(r)/ *n* erbicida *m*

**weedy** /ˈwiːdɪ/ *a fam* mingherlino

**week** /wiːk/ *n* settimana *f*

**weekday** /ˈwiːkdeɪ/ *n* giorno *m* feriale

**weekend** /ˈwiːkend/ *n* fine *m* settimana

**weekly** /ˈwiːklɪ/ *a* settimanale ● *n* settimanale *m* ● *adv* settimanalmente

**weep** /wiːp/ *vi* (*pt/pp* **wept**) piangere

**weeping willow** /wiːpɪŋˈwɪləʊ/ *n* salice *m* piangente

**weepy** /ˈwiːpɪ/ *a* ⟨*film*⟩ strappalacrime *inv*

**weigh** /weɪ/ *vt/i* pesare; ~ **anchor** levare l'ancora

■ **weigh down** *vt fig* piegare

■ **weigh in** *vi* (*fam: join in discussion*) intromettersi

■ **weigh out** *vt* pesare ⟨*amount of flour etc*⟩

■ **weigh up** *vt fig* soppesare; valutare ⟨*person*⟩

**weighing machine** /ˈweɪɪŋ/ *n* bilancia *f*

**weight** /weɪt/ *n* peso *m*; **put on/lose ~** ingrassare/dimagrire

**weighting** /ˈweɪtɪŋ/ *n* ⟨*allowance*⟩ indennità *f inv*

**weightlessness** /ˈweɪtlɪsnɪs/ *n* assenza *f* di gravità

**weight: weightlifter** *n* sollevatore *m* di pesi. **weightlifting** *n* sollevamento *m* pesi. **weight training** *n* allenarsi con i pesi. **weight-watcher** *n* (*in group*) persona *f* che segue una dieta dimagrante

**weighty** /ˈweɪtɪ/ *a* (**-ier, -iest**) pesante; (*important*) di un certo peso

**weir** /wɪə(r)/ *n* chiusa *f*

**weird** /wɪəd/ *a* misterioso; (*bizarre*) bizzarro

**welcome** /ˈwelkəm/ *a* benvenuto; **you're ~!** prego!; **you're ~ to have it/to come** prendilo/vieni pure ● *n* accoglienza *f* ● *vt* accogliere; (*appreciate*) gradire

**welcoming** /ˈwelkəmɪŋ/ *a* ⟨*ceremony*⟩ di benvenuto; ⟨*committee, smile*⟩ di accoglienza; ⟨*house*⟩ accogliente

**weld** /weld/ *vt* saldare

**welder** /ˈweldə(r)/ *n* saldatore *m*

**welfare** /ˈwelfeə(r)/ *n* benessere *m*; (*aid*) assistenza *f*; *Am* previdenza *f* sociale

**welfare: welfare services** *n* servizi *mpl* sociali. **Welfare State** *n* Stato *m* assistenziale. **welfare work** *n* assistenza *m* sociale

**well**[1] /wel/ *n* pozzo *m*; (*oil ~*) pozzo *m*; (*of staircase*) tromba *f*

**well**[2] *adv* (**better, best**) bene; **as ~** anche; **as ~ as** (*in addition*) oltre a; **~ done!** bravo!; **very ~** benissimo ● *a* **he is not ~** non sta bene; **get ~ soon!** guarisci presto! ● *int* beh!; **~ I never!** ma va!

**well: well-attended** /-əˈtendɪd/ *a* ben frequentato. **well-behaved** /-bɪˈheɪvd/ *a* educato. **well-being** /ˈwelbɪɪŋ/ *n* benessere *m*. **well-bred** /welˈbred/ *a* beneducato. **well-defined** /-dɪˈfaɪnd/ *a* ⟨*role, boundary*⟩ ben definito; ⟨*outline, image*⟩ netto. **well-disposed** /-dɪˈspəʊzd/ *a* benevolo; **be ~ towards** essere bendisposto verso ⟨*person*⟩; essere favorevole

a ⟨*idea*⟩. **well done** /dʌn/ *a* ⟨*task*⟩ ben fatto; *Culin* ben cotto. **well-educated** *a* istruito; (*cultured*) colto. **well-founded** /-ˈfaʊndɪd/ *a* fondato. **well-heeled** /-ˈhiːld/ *a fam* danaroso. **well-informed** /-ɪnˈfɔːmd/ *a* beninformato

**wellingtons** /ˈwelɪŋtənz/ *npl* stivali *mpl* di gomma

**well: well-judged** /-ˈdʒʌdʒd/ *a* ⟨*performance*⟩ molto intelligente; ⟨*shot*⟩ ben assestato; ⟨*statement, phrase*⟩ ben ponderato. **well-kept** /-ˈkept/ *a* ⟨*garden*⟩ curato; ⟨*secret*⟩ ben custodito. **well-known** /-ˈnəʊn/ *a* famoso. **well-liked** /-ˈlaɪkt/ *a* popolare. **well-made** /-ˈmeɪd/ *a* benfatto. **well-mannered** /-ˈmænəd/ *a* educato. **well-meaning** *a* con buone intenzioni. **well-meant** /-ˈment/ *a* con le migliori intenzioni. **well-nigh** /ˈwelnaɪ/ *adv* quasi. **well-off** *a* benestante. **well-read** /-ˈred/ *a* colto. **well-spoken** /-ˈspəʊkən/ *a* ⟨*person*⟩ che parla bene. **well-thought-of** *a* stimato. **well-to-do** *a* ricco. **well-trodden** /-ˈtrɒdn/ *a also fig* battuto. **well-wisher** /ˈwelwɪʃə(r)/ *n* simpatizzante *mf*. **well-worn** /-ˈwɔːn/ *a* ⟨*steps, floorboards*⟩ consunto; ⟨*carpet, garment*⟩ logoro; ⟨*fig: argument*⟩ trito e ritrito

**Welsh** /welʃ/ *a & n* gallese *mf*; (*language*) gallese *m*; **the ~** *pl* i gallesi

**Welshman** /ˈwelʃmən/ *n* gallese *m*

**Welsh rabbit** *n* toast *m inv* al formaggio

**welt** /welt/ *n* (*on shoe*) rinforzo *m*; (*on skin*) segno *m* di frustata

**went** /went/ *see* **go**

**wept** /wept/ *see* **weep**

**were** /wɜː(r)/ *see* **be**

**west** /west/ *n* ovest *m*; **to the ~ of** a ovest di; **the W~** l'Occidente *m* ● *a* occidentale ● *adv* verso occidente; **go ~** *fam* andare in malora

**west: West Bank** *n* Cisgiordania *f*. **West Country** *n* sud-ovest *m* dell'Inghilterra. **West End** *n* zona *f* di Londra con un'alta concentrazione di teatri e negozi di lusso

**westerly** /ˈwestəlɪ/ *a* verso ovest; occidentale ⟨*wind*⟩

**western** /ˈwestən/ *a* occidentale ● *n* western *m inv*

**Westerner** /ˈwestənə(r)/ *n* occidentale *mf*

**West Germany** *n* Germania *f* Occidentale

**West Indian** *a & n* antillese *mf*

**West Indies** /ˈɪndɪz/ *npl* Antille *fpl*

**westward[s]** /ˈwestwəd[z]/ *adv* verso ovest

**wet** /wet/ *a* (**wetter, wettest**) bagnato; fresco ⟨*paint*⟩; (*rainy*) piovoso; ⟨*fam: person*⟩ smidollato; **get ~** bagnarsi ● *vt* (*pt/pp* **wet, wetted**) bagnare

**wet: wet blanket** *n* guastafeste *mf inv*. **wet fish** *n Br* pesce *m* fresco. **wet-look** ⟨*plastic, leather*⟩ lucido. **wet-nurse** *n* balia *f*. **wetsuit** *n* muta *f*

**whack** /wæk/ *n fam* colpo *m* ● *vt fam* dare un colpo a

**whacked** /wækt/ *a fam* stanco morto

**whacking** /ˈwækɪŋ/ *a* (*Br fam: enormous*) enorme ● *n fam* sculacciata *f*

**whacky** /'wækɪ/ a ⟨fam: joke, person etc⟩ demenziale

**whale** /weɪl/ n balena f; **have a ~ of a time** fam divertirsi un sacco

**wham** /wæm/ int bum!

**wharf** /wɔ:f/ n banchina f

**what** /wɒt/ pron che, [che] cosa; **~ for?** perché?; **~ is that for?** a che cosa serve?; **~ is it? (what do you want)** cosa c'è?; **~ is it like?** com'è?; **~ is your name?** come ti chiami?; **~ is the weather like?** com'è il tempo?; **~ is the film about?** di cosa parla il film?; **~ is he talking about?** di cosa sta parlando?; **he asked me ~ she had said** mi ha chiesto cosa ha detto; **~ about going to the cinema?** e se andassimo al cinema?; **~ about the children? (what will they do)** e i bambini?; **~ if it rains?** e se piove? ● a quale, che; **take ~ books you want** prendi tutti i libri che vuoi; **~ kind of a** che tipo di; **at ~ time?** a che ora? ● adv che; **~ a lovely day!** che bella giornata! ● int **~!** [che] cosa!; **~?** [che] cosa?

**whatever** /wɒt'evə(r)/ a qualunque ● pron qualsiasi cosa; **~ is it?** cos'è?; **~ he does** qualsiasi cosa faccia; **~ happens** qualunque cosa succeda; **nothing ~** proprio niente

**whatnot** /'wɒtnɒt/ n coso m; (stand) scaffaletto m; **and ~** (and so on) e così via

**what's-his-name** /'wɒtsɪzneɪm/ n fam coso m

**whatsit** /'wɒtsɪt/ n fam aggeggio m, coso m

**what's-its-name** n fam coso, -a mf

**whatsoever** /wɒtsəʊ'evə(r)/ a & pron = **whatever**

**wheat** /wi:t/ n grano m, frumento m

**wheatgerm** /'wi:tdʒɜ:m/ n germoglio m di grano

**wheatmeal** /'wi:tmi:l/ n farina f di frumento

**wheedle** /'wi:dl/ vt **~ sth out of sb** ottenere qcsa da qualcuno con le lusinghe

**wheel** /wi:l/ n ruota f; (steering ~) volante m; **at the ~** al volante ● vt (push) spingere ● vi (circle) ruotare; **~ round** ruotare

**wheel: wheelbarrow** n carriola f. **wheelchair** n sedia f a rotelle. **wheel clamp** n ceppo m bloccaruote

**wheeler-dealer** /wi:lə'di:lə(r)/ n trafficone, -a mf

**wheeze** /wi:z/ vi ansimare

**wheezy** /'wi:zɪ/ a ⟨voice, cough⟩ dal respiro affannato

**when** /wen/ adv & conj quando; **the day ~** il giorno in cui; **~ swimming/reading** nuotando/leggendo

**whence** /wens/ adv liter donde

**whenever** /wen'evə(r)/ adv & conj in qualsiasi momento; (every time that) ogni volta che; **~ did it happen?** quando è successo?

**where** /weə(r)/ adv & conj dove; **the street ~ I live** la via in cui abito; **~ do you come from?** da dove vieni?

**whereabouts[1]** /weərə'baʊts/ adv dove

**whereabouts[2]** /'weərəbaʊts/ n **nobody knows his ~** nessuno sa dove si trova

**whereas** /weər'æz/ conj dal momento che; (in contrast) mentre

**whereby** /weə'baɪ/ adv attraverso il quale

**whereupon** /weərə'pɒn/ adv dopo di che

**wherever** /weər'evə(r)/ adv & conj dovunque; **~ is he?** dov'è mai?; **~ possible** dovunque sia possibile

**wherewithal** /'weəwɪðɔ:l/ n mezzi mpl

**whet** /wet/ vt (pt/pp **whetted**) aguzzare ⟨appetite⟩

**whether** /'weðə(r)/ conj se: **~ you like it or not** che ti piaccia o no

**which** /wɪtʃ/ a & pron quale; **~ one?** quale?; **~ one of you?** chi di voi?; **~ way?** (direction) in che direzione? ● rel pron (object) che; **~ he does frequently** cosa che fa spesso; **after ~** dopo di che; **on/in ~** su/in cui

**whichever** /wɪtʃ'evə(r)/ a & pron qualunque; **~ it is** qualunque sia; **~ one of you** chiunque tra voi

**whiff** /wɪf/ n zaffata f; **have a ~ of sth** odorare qcsa

**while** /waɪl/ n **a long ~** un bel po'; **a little ~** un po' ● conj mentre; (as long as) finché; (although) sebbene; **he met her ~ in exile** l'ha incontrata mentre era in esilio

■ **while away** vt passare ⟨time⟩

**whilst** /waɪlst/ conj = **while**

**whim** /wɪm/ n capriccio m

**whimper** /'wɪmpə(r)/ vi piagnucolare; ⟨dog:⟩ mugolare

**whimsical** /'wɪmzɪkl/ a capriccioso; ⟨story⟩ fantasioso

**whine** /waɪn/ n lamento m; (of dog) guaito m ● vi lamentarsi; ⟨dog:⟩ guaire

**whinny** /'wɪnɪ/ n nitrito m ● vi ⟨horse:⟩ nitrire

**whip** /wɪp/ n frusta f; (Pol: person) parlamentare mf incaricato, -a di assicurarsi della presenza dei membri del suo partito alle votazioni ● vt (pt/pp **whipped**) frustare; Culin sbattere; (snatch) afferrare; (fam: steal) fregare

■ **whip up** vt (incite) stimolare; fam improvvisare ⟨meal⟩

**whiplash injury** /'wɪplæʃ/ n Med colpo m di frusta

**whipped cream** /wɪpt'kri:m/ n panna f montata

**whipping boy** /'wɪpɪŋ/ n capro m espiatorio

**whip-round** n fam colletta f; **have a ~** fare una colletta

**whirl** /wɜ:l/ n (movement) rotazione f; **my mind's in a ~** ho le idee confuse ● vi girare rapidamente ● vt far girare rapidamente

**whirlpool** /'wɜ:lpu:l/ n vortice m

**whirlwind** /'wɜ:lwɪnd/ n turbine m

**whirr** /wɜ:(r)/ vi ronzare

**whisk** /wɪsk/ n Culin frullino m ● vt Culin frullare

■ **whisk away** vt portare via

**whisker** /'wɪskə(r)/ n **~s** pl (of cat) baffi mpl; (on man's cheek) basette fpl; **by a ~** per un pelo

**whisky** /'wɪskɪ/ n whisky m inv

**whisper** /ˈwɪspə(r)/ n sussurro m; (rumour) diceria f ● vt/i sussurrare

**whispering gallery** /ˈwɪspərɪŋ/ n galleria f acustica

**whistle** /ˈwɪsl/ n fischio m; (instrument) fischietto m ● vt fischiettare ● vi fischiettare; (referee) fischiare

**whistle-stop tour** n Pol giro m elettorale

**white** /waɪt/ a bianco; **go ~** (pale) sbiancare ● n bianco m; (of egg) albume m; (person) bianco, -a mf

**white: whitebait** n bianchetti npl. **whiteboard** n lavagna f bianca. **white coffee** n caffè m inv macchiato. **white-collar worker** n colletto m bianco. **white elephant** n (public project) progetto m dispendioso e di scarsa efficacia; (building) cattedrale f nel deserto; (item, knicknack) oggetto m inutile. **white goods** n (linen) biancheria f per la casa; (appliances) elettrodomestici mpl. **Whitehall** n strada f di Londra, sede degli uffici del governo britannico; fig amministrazione f britannica. **white horses** npl cavalloni mpl. **white-hot** a (metal) arroventato. **white knight** n Fin white knight m inv. **white lie** n bugia f pietosa

**whiten** /ˈwaɪtn/ vt imbiancare ● vi sbiancare

**whitener** /ˈwaɪt(ə)nə(r)/ n (for shoes) bianchetto m; (for clothes) sbiancante m; (for coffee, tea) surrogato m del latte

**whiteness** /ˈwaɪtnɪs/ n bianchezza f

**white: white tie** n (tie) cravattino m bianco; (formal dress) frac m inv. **whitewash** n intonaco m; fig copertura f ● vt dare una mano d'intonaco a; fig coprire. **white water** n rapide fpl. **white wedding** n matrimonio m in bianco

**whither** /ˈwɪðə(r)/ adv liter dove

**whiting** /ˈwaɪtɪŋ/ n (fish) merlano m

**Whitsun** /ˈwɪtsn/ n Pentecoste f

■ **whittle away** /ˈwɪtl/ vt intaccare ⟨savings⟩; ridurre ⟨lead in race⟩

■ **whittle down** vt ridurre

**whiz[z]** /wɪz/ vi (pt/pp whizzed) sibilare

**whiz[z]-kid** n fam giovane m prodigio

**who** /huː/ inter pron chi ● rel pron che; **the children, ~ were all tired, ...** i bambini, che erano tutti stanchi,...

**whodunnit** /huːˈdʌnɪt/ n fam [romanzo m] giallo m

**whoever** /huːˈevə(r)/ pron chiunque; **~ he is** chiunque sia; **~ can that be?** chi può mai essere?

**whole** /həʊl/ a tutto; (not broken) intatto; **the ~ truth** tutta la verità; **the ~ world** il mondo intero; **the ~ lot** (everything) tutto; (pl) tutti; **the ~ lot of you** tutti voi ● n tutto m; **as a ~** nell'insieme; **on the ~** tutto considerato; **the ~ of Italy** tutta l'Italia

**whole: wholefood** n cibo m macrobiotico. **wholehearted** /ˈhəʊlhɑːtɪd/ a di tutto cuore. **wholemeal** a integrale. **whole milk** n latte m intero. **whole number** n numero m intero

**wholesale** /ˈhəʊlseɪl/ a & adv all'ingrosso; fig in massa

**wholesaler** /ˈhəʊlseɪlə(r)/ n grossista mf

**wholesome** /ˈhəʊlsəm/ a sano

**wholly** /ˈhəʊlɪ/ adv completamente

**wholly-owned subsidiary** n consociata f interamente controllata

**whom** /huːm/ rel pron che; **the man ~ I saw** l'uomo che ho visto; **to/with ~** a/con cui ● inter pron chi; **to ~ did you speak?** con chi hai parlato?

**whoop** /wuːp/ n (shout) grido m ● vi gridare

**whoopee** /ˈwʊpɪ/ int evviva! ● n hum **make ~** (have fun) fare baldoria; (make love) fare l'amore

**whooping cough** /ˈhuːpɪŋ/ n pertosse f

**whoosh** /wʊʃ/ int vuum!

**whopper** /ˈwɒpə(r)/ n fam (lie) balla f; **what a ~!** è veramente gigantesco!

**whopping** /ˈwɒpɪŋ/ a fam enorme

**whore** /hɔː(r)/ n puttana f vulg

**whorl** /wɜːl/ n (of cream, chocolate etc) ghirigoro m; (of fingerprint) spirale f

**whose** /huːz/ rel pron il cui; **people ~ name begins with D** le persone i cui nomi cominciano con la D ● inter pron di chi; **~ is that?** di chi è quello? ● a **~ car did you use?** di chi è la macchina che hai usato?

**Who's Who** n pubblicazione f annuale con l'elenco delle personalità di spicco

**why** /waɪ/ adv (inter) perché; **the reason ~** la ragione per cui; **that's ~** per questo ● int diamine!

**WI** abbr (**Women's Institute**); Am abbr **Wisconsin**

**wick** /wɪk/ n stoppino m

**wicked** /ˈwɪkɪd/ a cattivo; (mischievous) malizioso

**wicker** /ˈwɪkə(r)/ n vimini mpl ● attrib di vimini

**wicket** /ˈwɪkɪt/ n (field gate) cancelletto m; Sport porta f; (Am: of ticket office etc) sportello m; **be on a sticky ~** fam essere in una situazione difficile

**wide** /waɪd/ a largo; ⟨experience, knowledge⟩ vasto; ⟨difference⟩ profondo; (far from target) lontano; **10 cm ~** largo 10 cm; **how ~ is it?** quanto è largo? ● adv (off target) lontano dal bersaglio; **~ awake** del tutto sveglio; **~ open** spalancato; **open ~!** apri bene!; **far and ~** in lungo e in largo

**wide-angle lens** n grandangolo m

**wide-eyed** /-ˈaɪd/ a ⟨person, innocence⟩ ingenuo; (with fear, surprise) con gli occhi sbarrati

**widely** /ˈwaɪdlɪ/ adv largamente; ⟨known, accepted⟩ generalmente; ⟨different⟩ profondamente

**widen** /ˈwaɪdn/ vt allargare; **~ the gap** fig accentuare il contrasto ● vi allargarsi

**wide open** a ⟨door, window, eyes⟩ spalancato

**wide screen** n Cinema schermo m panoramico

**widespread** /ˈwaɪdspred/ a diffuso

**widow** /ˈwɪdəʊ/ n vedova f

**widowed** /ˈwɪdəʊd/ a vedovo

**widower** /ˈwɪdəʊə(r)/ n vedovo m

**width** /wɪdθ/ n larghezza f; (of material) altezza f

**widthways** /'wɪdθweɪz/ adv trasversalmente

**wield** /wi:ld/ vt maneggiare; esercitare ‹power›

**wife** /waɪf/ n (pl **wives**) moglie f

**wife battering** /'waɪfbæt(ə)rɪŋ/ n maltrattamento m della coniuge

**wig** /wɪg/ n parrucca f

**wiggle** /'wɪgl/ vi dimenarsi ● vt dimenare

**wild** /waɪld/ a selvaggio; ‹animal, flower› selvatico; ‹furious› furibondo; ‹applause› fragoroso; ‹idea› folle; ‹with joy› pazzo; ‹guess› azzardato; **be ~ about** (keen on) andare pazzo per ● adv **run ~** crescere senza controllo ● **in the ~** allo stato naturale; **the ~s** pl le zone sperdute

**wild: wild card** n jolly m inv; Comput carattere m jolly. **wildcat strike** n sciopero m selvaggio. **wild dog** n cane m randagio

**wilderness** /'wɪldənɪs/ n deserto m; ‹fig: garden› giungla f

**wild: wild-eyed** /-'aɪd/ a ‹distressed› dall'aria angosciata; ‹angry› dallo sguardo minaccioso. **wildfire** n **spread like ~** allargarsi a macchia d'olio. **wild flower** n fiore m di campo. **wildfowl** n ‹bird› uccello m selvatico; ‹birds collectively› uccelli mpl selvatici; ‹game› selvaggina f di penna. **wild-goose chase** n ricerca f inutile. **wildlife** n animali mpl selvatici. **wildlife park** n parco m naturale. **wildlife reserve** n riserva f naturale. **wildlife sanctuary** n riserva f naturale

**wildly** /'waɪldlɪ/ adv fig ‹exaggerated› estremamente; ‹speak› senza riflettere; ‹applaud› fragorosamente; ‹hit out› all'impazzata

**Wild West** n far west m

**wiles** /waɪlz/ npl astuzie fpl

**wilful** /'wɪlfʊl/ a intenzionale; ‹person, refusal› ostinato

**wilfully** /'wɪlfʊlɪ/ adv intenzionalmente; ‹refuse› ostinatamente

**will¹** /wɪl/ v aux **he ~ arrive tomorrow** arriverà domani; **I won't tell him** non glielo dirò; **you ~ be back soon, won't you?** tornerai presto, no?; **he ~ be there, won't he?** sarà là, no?; **she ~ be there by now** sarà là ormai; **~ you go?** (do you intend to go) pensi di andare?; **~ you go to the baker's and buy...?** puoi andare dal panettiere a comprare...?; **~ you be quiet!** vuoi stare calmo!; **~ you have some wine?** vuoi del vino?; **the engine won't start** la macchina non parte

**will²** n volontà f inv; ‹document› testamento m

**willing** /'wɪlɪŋ/ a disposto; ‹eager› volonteroso

**willingly** /'wɪlɪŋlɪ/ adv volentieri

**willingness** /'wɪlɪŋnɪs/ n buona volontà f

**willow** /'wɪləʊ/ n salice m

**willowy** /'wɪləʊɪ/ a ‹person, figure› slanciato

**will-power** n forza f di volontà

**willy-nilly** /wɪlɪ'nɪlɪ/ adv (at random) a casaccio; ‹wanting to or not› volente o nolente

**wilt** /wɪlt/ vi appassire

**wily** /'waɪlɪ/ a (-ier, -iest) astuto

**wimp** /wɪmp/ n rammollito, -a mf

**wimpish** /'wɪmpɪʃ/ a ‹fam: behaviour› da rammollito

**wimpy** /'wɪmpɪ/ a ‹fam: person› rammollito

**win** /wɪn/ n vittoria f; **have a ~** riportare una vittoria ● v (pt/pp won; pres p **winning**) ● vt vincere; conquistare ‹fame› ● vi vincere

■ **win back** vt recuperare

■ **win over** vt convincere

■ **win through** vi ‹fam: be successful› uscire vittorioso

**wince** /wɪns/ vi contrarre il viso

**winch** /wɪntʃ/ n argano m

■ **winch up** vt tirare con l'argano

**wind¹** /wɪnd/ n vento m; ‹breath› fiato m; ‹fam: flatulence› aria f; **get/have the ~ up** fam aver fifa; **get ~ of** aver sentore di; **in the ~** nell'aria ● vt ~ **sb** lasciare qcno senza fiato; ~ **a baby** far fare il ruttino a un neonato

**wind²** /waɪnd/ v (pt/pp **wound**) ● vt ‹wrap› avvolgere; (move by turning) far girare; ‹clock› caricare ● vi ‹road:› serpeggiare

■ **wind down** vi ‹relax› rilassarsi; (gradually come to an end) diminuire ● vt (gradually bring to an end) metter fine in modo graduale a

■ **wind up** /waɪnd/ vt caricare ‹clock›; concludere ‹proceedings›; fam sfottere ‹sb› ● vi (end up) ~ **up doing sth** finire per fare qcsa

**wind** /wɪnd/: **windbreak** n frangivento m. **windcheater** n Br giacca f a vento. **windchill factor** n fattore m di raffreddamento da vento. **wind energy** n forza f del vento. **windfall** n fig fortuna f inaspettata; ~**s** pl ‹fruit› frutta f abbattuta dal vento

**winder** /'waɪndə(r)/ n ‹for car window› manovella f alzacristalli; ‹for watch› bottone m di carica

**winding** /'waɪndɪŋ/ a tortuoso

**wind instrument** /'wɪnd/ n strumento m a fiato

**windmill** /'wɪn(d)mɪl/ n mulino m a vento

**window** /'wɪndəʊ/ n finestra f; ‹of car› finestrino m; ‹of shop› vetrina f

**window: window box** n cassetta f per i fiori. **window cleaner** n ‹person› lavavetri mf inv. **window display** n Comm esposizione f in vetrina. **window dresser** n vetrinista mf. **window dressing** n vetrinistica f; fig fumo m negli occhi. **window envelope** n busta f a finestra. **window frame** n telaio m di finestra. **window ledge** n davanzale m. **window pane** n vetro m. **window-shopping** n **go ~** andare in giro a vedere le vetrine. **window sill** n davanzale m

**wind** /wɪnd/: **windpipe** n trachea f. **windscreen** n, Am **windshield** n parabrezza m inv. **windscreen washer** n getto m d'acqua. **windscreen-wiper** n tergicristallo m. **wind-sleeve** n manica f a vento. **wind-sock** n manica f a vento. **wind surfing** n windsurf m inv. **windswept** a esposto al vento; ‹person› scompigliato

**windy** /'wɪndɪ/ a (-ier, -iest) ventoso

**wine** /waɪn/ n vino m

**wine: wine bar** n ≃ enoteca f. **wine box** n contenitore m di vino con rubinetto. **wine cooler** n (ice bucket) secchiello m del ghiaccio; (Am: drink) bibita f leggermente alcolica. **wineglass** n bicchiere m da vino. **wine list** n carta f dei vini. **wine merchant** n commerciante mf di vini. **wine producer** n produttore, -trice mf di vini. **wine rack** n portabottiglie m inv

**winery** /'waɪnərɪ/ n Am vigneto m

**wine tasting** /'waɪnteɪstɪŋ/ n degustazione f di vini

**wing** /wɪŋ/ n ala f; Auto parafango m; ~s pl Theat quinte fpl; **under sb's** ~ sotto l'ala [protettiva] di qcno

**wing: wing chair** n poltrona f con ampio schienale. **wing collar** n colletto m rigido. **wing commander** n tenente m colonnello delle forze aeree

**winger** /'wɪŋə(r)/ n Sport ala f

**wing: wing-half** n (in soccer) mediano m. **wing mirror** n Br specchietto m laterale. **wing nut** n dado m ad alette. **wingspan** n apertura f alare

**wink** /wɪŋk/ n strizzata f d'occhio; **not sleep a** ~ non chiudere occhio • vi strizzare l'occhio; (light:) lampeggiare

**winner** /'wɪnə(r)/ n vincitore, -trice mf

**winning** /'wɪnɪŋ/ a vincente; (smile) accattivante

**winning post** n linea f d'arrivo

**winnings** /'wɪnɪŋz/ npl vincite fpl

**winning streak** n periodo m fortunato; **be on a** ~ essere in un periodo fortunato

**winsome** /'wɪnsəm/ a accattivante

**winter** /'wɪntə(r)/ n inverno m

**winter sports** npl sport mpl invernali

**wintertime** /'wɪntətaɪm/ n inverno m

**wintry** /'wɪntrɪ/ a invernale

**wipe** /waɪp/ n passata f; (to dry) asciugata f • vt strofinare; (dry) asciugare

■ **wipe off** vt asciugare; (erase) cancellare

■ **wipe out** vt annientare; eliminare (village); estinguere (debt)

■ **wipe up** vt asciugare (dishes)

**wiper blade** /'waɪpə/ n Auto bordo f gommato del tergicristallo

**wire** /'waɪə(r)/ n fil m di ferro; (electrical) filo m elettrico

**wire: wire brush** n spazzola f metallica. **wire-cutters** n tronchese msg. **wire-haired** /-'heəd/ a dal pelo ispido

**wireless** /'waɪəlɪs/ n radio f inv

**wire: wire mesh** n rete f metallica. **wire netting** n rete f metallica. **wire wool** n lana f d'acciaio

**wiring** /'waɪərɪŋ/ n impianto m elettrico

**wiry** /'waɪərɪ/ a (-ier, -iest) (person) dal fisico asciutto; (hair) ispido

**wisdom** /'wɪzdəm/ n saggezza f; (of action) sensatezza f

**wisdom tooth** n dente m del giudizio

**wise** /waɪz/ a saggio; (prudent) sensato

■ **wise up** fam vi (become more aware) aprire gli occhi • vt aprire gli occhi a (**to** su)

**wisecrack** /'waɪzkræk/ fam n battuta f salace • vi far battute salaci

**wise guy** n fam sapientone m

**wisely** /'waɪzlɪ/ adv saggiamente; (act) sensatamente

**Wise Men** npl Re Magi mpl

**wish** /wɪʃ/ n desiderio m; **make a** ~ esprimere un desiderio; **with best** ~**es** con i miglia ri auguri • vt desiderare; ~ **sb well** fare tanti auguri a qcno; **I** ~ **you every success** ti auguro buona fortuna; **I** ~ **you could stay** vorrei che tu potessi rimanere; ~ **sth on sb** fam sbolognare qcsa a qcno • vi ~ **for sth** desiderare qcsa

**wishbone** /'wɪʃbəʊn/ n forcella f (di pollo o tacchino)

**wishful** /'wɪʃfʊl/ a ~ **thinking** illusione f

**wishy-washy** /'wɪʃɪwɒʃɪ/ a (colour) spento; (personality) insignificante

**wisp** /wɪsp/ n (of hair) ciocca f; (of smoke) filo m; (of grass) ciuffo m

**wisteria** /wɪs'tɪərɪə/ n glicine m

**wistful** /'wɪstfʊl/ a malinconico

**wistfully** /'wɪstfʊlɪ/ adv malinconicamente

**wit** /wɪt/ n spirito m; (person) persona f di spirito; **be at one's** ~**s' end** non saper che pesci pigliare; **scared out of one's** ~**s** spaventato a morte

**witch** /wɪtʃ/ n strega f

**witch: witchcraft** n magia f. **witch doctor** n stregone m. **witch-hunt** n caccia f alle streghe

**with** /wɪð/ prep con; (fear, cold, jealousy etc) di; **I'm not** ~ **you** fam non ti seguo; **can I leave it** ~ **you?** (task) puoi occupartene tu?; ~ **no regrets/money** senza rimpianti/soldi; **be** ~ **it** fam essere al passo coi tempi; (alert) essere concentrato

**withdraw** /wɪð'drɔː/ v (pt **-drew**, pp **-drawn**) • vt ritirare; prelevare (money) • vi ritirarsi

**withdrawal** /wɪð'drɔː(ə)l/ n ritiro m; (of money) prelevamento m; (from drugs) crisi f inv di astinenza; Psych chiusura f in se stessi

**withdrawal symptoms** npl sintomi mpl da crisi di astinenza

**withdrawn** /wɪð'drɔːn/ see **withdraw** • a (person) chiuso in se stesso

**wither** /'wɪðə(r)/ vi (flower:) appassire

**withering** /'wɪðərɪŋ/ a (look) fulminante

**withhold** /wɪð'həʊld/ vt (pt/pp **-held**) rifiutare (consent) (**from** a); nascondere (information) (**from** a); trattenere (smile)

**within** /wɪð'ɪn/ prep in; (before the end of) entro; ~ **the law** legale • adv all'interno

**without** /wɪð'aʊt/ prep senza; ~ **stopping** senza fermarsi; **how could it have happened** ~ **you noticing it?** come è potuto succedere senza che tu lo notassi?

**withstand** /wɪð'stænd/ vt (pt/pp **-stood**) resistere a

**witness** /'wɪtnɪs/ n testimone mf; **bear** ~ portare testimonianza • vt ≈ autenticare (signature); essere testimone di (accident)

**witness box,** *Am* **witness-stand** *n* banco *m* dei testimoni

**witticism** /'wɪtɪsɪzm/ *n* spiritosaggine *f*

**wittingly** /'wɪtɪŋlɪ/ *adv* consapevolmente

**witty** /'wɪtɪ/ *a* **(-ier, -iest)** spiritoso

**wives** /waɪvz/ *see* **wife**

**wizard** /'wɪzəd/ *n* mago *m*

**wizardry** /'wɪzədrɪ/ *n* stregoneria *f*

**wizened** /'wɪznd/ *a* raggrinzito

**wk** *abbr* **week**

**wobble** /'wɒbl/ *vi* traballare

**wobbly** /'wɒblɪ/ *a* traballante

**wodge** /wɒdʒ/ *n fam* mucchio *m*

**woe** /wəʊ/ *n* afflizione *f*; ~ **is me!** me meschino!

**woeful** /'wəʊful/ *a* ‹story, sight› triste; ‹lack› vergognoso

**woke, woken** /wəʊk, 'wəʊkn/ *see* **wake**[1]

**wolf** /wʊlf/ *n* (*pl* **wolves** /wʊlvz/) lupo *m*; (*fam:* womanizer) donnaiolo *m* ● *vt* ~ [**down**] divorare

**wolf: wolf cub** *n* cucciolo *m* di lupo. **wolfhound** *n Br* cane *m* lupo. **wolf whistle** *n* fischio *m* ● *vi* ~-**whistle at sb** fischiare dietro a qcno

**woman** /'wʊmən/ *n* (*pl* **women**) donna *f*

**womanizer** /'wʊmənaɪzə(r)/ *n* donnaiolo *m*

**womanly** /'wʊmənlɪ/ *a* femmineo

**womb** /wuːm/ *n* utero *m*

**women** /'wɪmɪn/ *see* **woman**

**women's: Women's Institute** *n* associazione *f* che si occupa dei problemi delle donne. **Women's Libber** /wɪmɪnz'lɪbə(r)/ *n* femminista *f*. **Women's Liberation** *n* movimento *m* femminista. **women's movement** *n* movimento *m* per l'emancipazione della donna. **women's studies** *npl* storia *f* dell'emancipazione femminile

**won** /wʌn/ *see* **win**

**wonder** /'wʌndə(r)/ *n* meraviglia *f*; (*surprise*) stupore *m*; **no ~!** non c'è da stupirsi!; **it's a ~ that...** è incredibile che... ● *vi* restare in ammirazione; (*be surprised*) essere sorpreso; **I ~** è quello che mi chiedo; **I ~ whether she is ill** mi chiedo se è malata?

**wonderful** /'wʌndəful/ *a* meraviglioso

**wonderfully** /'wʌndəfulɪ/ *adv* meravigliosamente

**wonderland** /'wʌndəlænd/ *n* paese *m* delle meraviglie

**wonky** /'wɒŋkɪ/ *a Br fam* (*faulty*) difettoso; ‹furniture› traballante; (*crooked*) storto

**wont** /wəʊnt/ *n* **as was his ~** come suo solito ● *a* **he was ~ to fall asleep** era solito addormentarsi

**won't** /wəʊnt/ = **will not**

**woo** /wuː/ *vt* corteggiare; *fig* cercare di accattivarsi ‹voters›; cercare di ottenere ‹fame, fortune›

**wood** /wʊd/ *n* legno *m*; (*for burning*) legna *f*; (*forest*) bosco *m*; **out of the ~** *fig* fuori pericolo; **touch ~!** tocca ferro!

**woodcarving** /'wʊdkɑːvɪŋ/ *n* scultura *f* di legno

**wooded** /'wʊdɪd/ *a* boscoso

**wooden** /'wʊdn/ *a* di legno; *fig* legnoso

**wooden horse** *n* cavallo *m* di Troia

**wooden spoon** *n* mestolo *m* di legno; *fig* premio *m* di consolazione

**wood: woodlouse** *n* onisco *m*. **woodpecker** *n* picchio *m*. **wood pigeon** *n* colombaccio *m*. **wood shavings** *npl* trucioli *mpl*. **woodshed** *n* legnaia *f*. **wood stove** *n* stufa *f* a legna. **woodwind** *n* strumenti *mpl* a fiato. **woodwork** *n* (*wooden parts*) parti *fpl* in legno; (*craft*) falegnameria *f*. **woodworm** *n* tarlo *m*

**woody** /'wʊdɪ/ *a* legnoso; ‹hill› boscoso

**wool** /wʊl/ *n* lana *f*; **pull the ~ over sb's eyes** gettar fumo negli occhi a qcno ● *attrib* di lana

**woollen** /'wʊlən/ *a* di lana

**woollens** /'wʊlənz/ *npl* capi *mpl* di lana

**woolly** /'wʊlɪ/ *a* **(-ier, -iest)** ‹sweater› di lana; *fig* confuso

**woozy** /'wuːzɪ/ *a* intontito

**word** /wɜːd/ *n* parola *f*; (*news*) notizia *f*; **by ~ of mouth** a viva voce; **have a ~ with** dire due parole a; **have ~s** bisticciare; **in other ~s** in altre parole; **go back on one's ~** rimangiarsi la parola

**word-for-word** *a* ‹translation› letterale ● *adv* parola per parola

**wording** /'wɜːdɪŋ/ *n* parole *fpl*

**word: word-perfect** *a* che sa a memoria. **word processing** *n Comput* word processing *m*, elaborazione *f* testi. **word processor** *n* sistema *m* di videoscrittura, word processor *m inv*

**wordy** /'wɜːdɪ/ *a* prolisso

**wore** /wɔː(r)/ *see* **wear**

**work** /wɜːk/ *n* lavoro *m*; (*of art*) opera *f*; ~**s** *pl* (*factory*) fabbrica *fsg*; (*mechanism*) meccanismo *msg*; **at ~** al lavoro; **out of ~** disoccupato ● *vi* lavorare; ‹machine, ruse:› funzionare; (*study*) studiare ● *vt* far funzionare ‹machine›; far lavorare ‹employee›; far studiare ‹student›; ~ **one's way through sth** (*read*) leggere attentamente

■ **work off** *vt* sfogare ‹anger›; lavorare per estinguere ‹debt›; fare sport per smaltire ‹weight›

■ **work out** *vt* elaborare ‹plan›; risolvere ‹problem›; calcolare ‹bill›; **I ~ed out how he did it** ho capito come l'ha fatto ● *vi* evolvere

■ **work up** *vt* **I've ~ed up an appetite** mi è venuto appetito; **don't get ~ed up** (*anxious*) non farti prendere dal panico; (*angry*) non arrabbiarti

**workable** /'wɜːkəbl/ *a* (*feasible*) fattibile

**workaday** /'wɜːkədeɪ/ *a* ‹clothes, life› ordinario

**workaholic** /wɜːkə'hɒlɪk/ *n* staccanovista *mf*

**work: workbench** *n* banco *m* da lavoro. **workbook** *n* (*blank*) quaderno *m*; (*with exercises*) libro *m* di esercizi. **workday** *n* giorno *m* lavorativo

**worker** /'wɜːkə(r)/ n lavoratore, -trice mf; (manual) operaio, -a mf

**work:** **work experience** n esperienza f professionale; (part of training programme) stage m inv. **workforce** n forza f lavoro. **workhorse** n fig lavoratore, -trice mf indefesso, -a

**working** /'wɜːkɪŋ/ a ⟨clothes etc⟩ da lavoro; ⟨day⟩ feriale; **in ~ order** funzionante

**working:** **working capital** n capitale m netto di esercizio. **working-class** a operaio; **be ~** appartenere alla classe operaia ● **working class** n classe f operaia. **working week** n settimana f lavorativa

**work:** **workload** n carico m di lavoro. **workman** n operaio m. **workmanlike** a fatto con competenza. **workmanship** n lavorazione f. **workmate** n collega mf. **work of art** n opera f d'arte. **workout** n allenamento m. **work permit** n permesso m di lavoro. **workplace** n posto m di lavoro. **work-sharing** n divisione f di un posto di lavoro tra più persone. **workshop** n officina f; (discussion) dibattito m. **work-shy** a pigro. **workstation** n stazione f di lavoro. **work surface** n piano m di lavoro. **worktop** n piano m di lavoro. **work-to-rule** n sciopero m bianco

**world** /wɜːld/ n mondo m; **a ~ of difference** una differenza abissale; **out of this ~** favoloso; **think the ~ of sb** andare matto per qcno

**world:** **world-class** a di livello internazionale. **World Cup** n (in football) Coppa f del Mondo. **world-famous** a di fama mondiale

**worldly** /'wɜːldlɪ/ a materiale; ⟨person⟩ materialista

**worldly-wise** a vissuto

**world war** n guerra f mondiale

**worldwide** /'wɜːldwaɪd/ a mondiale ● adv mondialmente

**worm** /wɜːm/ n verme m ● vt **~ one's way into sb's confidence** conquistarsi la fiducia di qcno in modo subdolo

■ **worm out** vt **~ sth out of sb** carpire qcsa a qcno

**worm-eaten** /'wɜːmiːtən/ a ⟨wood⟩ tarlato; ⟨fruit⟩ bacato

**wormhole** /'wɜːmhəʊl/ n (in wood) buco m di tarlo; (in fruit, plant) buco m del verme

**worn** /wɔːn/ see **wear** ● a sciupato

**worn-out** a consumato; ⟨person⟩ sfinito

**worried** /'wʌrɪd/ a preoccupato

**worrier** /'wʌrɪə(r)/ n ansioso, -a mf; **he's a terrible ~** è ansioso da morire

**worry** /'wʌrɪ/ n preoccupazione f ● v (pt/pp worried) ● vt preoccupare; (bother) disturbare ● vi preoccuparsi

**worrying** /'wʌrɪɪŋ/ a preoccupante

**worse** /wɜːs/ a peggiore ● adv peggio ● n peggio m

**worsen** /'wɜːsn/ vt/i peggiorare

**worse off** a be **~ ~ than** stare peggio di; **be £100 ~ ~** avere 100 sterline in meno

**worship** /'wɜːʃɪp/ n culto m; (service) funzione f; **Your/His W~** (to judge) signor giudice/il

giudice ● v (pt/pp **-shipped**) ● vt venerare ● vi andare a messa

**worst** /wɜːst/ a peggiore ● adv peggio ● n **the ~** il peggio; **get the ~ of it** avere la peggio; **if the ~ comes to the ~** nella peggiore delle ipotesi

**worsted** /'wʊstɪd/ n lana f pettinata

**worth** /wɜːθ/ n valore m; **£10 ~ of petrol** 10 sterline di benzina ● a **be ~** valere; **be ~ it** fig valerne la pena; **it is ~ trying** vale la pena di provare; **it's ~ my while** mi conviene; **I'll make it ~ your while** te ne ricompenserò

**worthless** /'wɜːθlɪs/ a senza valore

**worthwhile** /wɜːθ'waɪl/ a che vale la pena; ⟨cause⟩ lodevole

**worthy** /'wɜːðɪ/ a degno; ⟨cause, motive⟩ lodevole

**would** /wʊd/ v aux **I ~ do it** lo farei; **~ you go?** andresti?; **~ you mind if I opened the window?** ti dispiace se apro la finestra?; **he ~ come if he could** verrebbe se potesse; **he said he ~n't** ha detto di no; **he said he ~n't have** ha detto che non lo avrebbe fatto; **~ you like a drink?** vuoi qualcosa da bere?; **what ~ you like to drink?** cosa prendi da bere?; **you ~n't, ~ you?** non lo faresti, vero?

**would-be** a ⟨pej: actor, singer etc⟩ sedicente; ⟨investor, buyer⟩ aspirante

**wound**[1] /wuːnd/ n ferita f ● vt ferire

**wound**[2] /waʊnd/ see **wind**[2]

**wove, woven** /wəʊv, 'wəʊvn/ see **weave**[2]

**wow** /waʊ/ n (fam: success) successone m; (in sound system) wow m ● vt fam entusiasmare ⟨person⟩ ● int caspita!

**WP** abbr (**word processing**) elaborazione f testi

**wpm** abbr (**words per minute**) parole fpl al minuto

**wrangle** /'ræŋgl/ n litigio m ● vi litigare

**wrap** /ræp/ n (shawl) scialle m ● vt (pt/pp wrapped) **~ [up]** avvolgere; ⟨present⟩ incartare; **be ~ped up in fig** essere completamente preso da ● vi **~ up warmly** coprirsi bene

**wraparound** /'ræpəraʊnd/ a ⟨skirt⟩ a pareo; ⟨window, windscreen⟩ panoramico

**wrapper** /'ræpə(r)/ n (for sweet) carta f [di caramella]

**wrapping** /'ræpɪŋ/ n materiale m da imballaggio

**wrapping paper** n carta f da pacchi; (for gift) carta f da regalo

**wrath** /rɒθ/ n ira f

**wreak** /riːk/ vt **~ havoc with sth** scombussolare qcsa

**wreath** /riːθ/ n (pl **~s** /riːðz/) corona f

**wreathed** /riːðd/ a **~ in** avvolto in ⟨mists⟩; **her face was ~ in smiles** era raggiante

**wreck** /rek/ n (of ship) relitto m; (of car) carcassa f; ⟨person⟩ rottame m ● vt far naufragare; demolire ⟨car⟩

**wreckage** /'rekɪdʒ/ n rottami mpl; fig brandelli mpl

**wrecked** /rekt/ a ⟨ship, car⟩ distrutto;

‹*building*› demolito; (*fig: exhausted*) distrutto

**wren** /ren/ *n* scricciolo *m*

**wrench** /rentʃ/ *n* (*injury*) slogatura *f*; (*tool*) chiave *f* inglese; (*pull*) strattone *m*; **it was a ~ leaving home** *fig* è stato un passo difficile andarsene da casa ● *vt* (*pull*) strappare; slogarsi ‹*wrist, ankle etc*›

**wrest** /rest/ *vt* strappare (**from** a)

**wrestle** /'resl/ *vi* lottare corpo a corpo; *fig* lottare

**wrestler** /'reslə(r)/ *n* lottatore, -trice *mf*

**wrestling** /'reslɪŋ/ *n* lotta *f* libera; (*all-in*) catch *m*

**wretch** /retʃ/ *n* disgraziato, -a *mf*

**wretched** /'retʃɪd/ *a* odioso; ‹*weather*› orribile; **feel ~** (*unhappy*) essere triste; (*ill*) sentirsi malissimo

**wriggle** /'rɪgl/ *n* contorsione *f* ● *vi* contorcersi; (*move forward*) strisciare; **~ out of sth** *fam* sottrarsi a qcsa

**wriggly** /'rɪglɪ/ *a* ‹*person*› che si dimena; ‹*snake, worm*› che si contorce

**wring** /rɪŋ/ *vt* (*pt/pp* **wrung**) torcere ‹*sb's neck*›; strizzare ‹*clothes*›; **~ one's hands** torcersi le mani; **~ sth out of sb** *fig* estorcere qcsa a qcno; **~ing wet** inzuppato

**wrinkle** /'rɪŋkl/ *n* grinza *f*; (*on skin*) ruga *f* ● *vt/i* raggrinzire

**wrinkled** /'rɪŋkld/ *a* ‹*skin, face*› rugoso; ‹*clothes*› raggrinzito

**wrist** /rɪst/ *n* polso *m*

**wristband** /'rɪs(t)bænd/ *n* polsino *m*; (*on watch*) cinturino *m*

**wristwatch** /'rɪstwɒtʃ/ *n* orologio *m* da polso

**writ** /rɪt/ *n Jur* mandato *m*

**write** /raɪt/ *vt/i* (*pt* **wrote**, *pp* **written**, *pres p* **writing**) scrivere

■ **write away for** *vt* richiedere per posta ‹*information*›

■ **write back** *vi* rispondere

■ **write down** *vt* annotare

■ **write in** *vi* scrivere

■ **write off** *vt* cancellare ‹*debt*›; distruggere ‹*car*›

■ **write out** *vt* fare ‹*cheque, prescription*›; (*copy*) ricopiare

■ **write up** *vt* redigere; elaborare ‹*diary*›; elaborare ‹*notes*›

**write-off** *n* (*car*) rottame *m*

**writer** /'raɪtə(r)/ *n* autore, -trice *mf*; **she's a ~** è una scrittrice

**writer's block** *n* blocco *m* dello scrittore

**write-up** *n* (*review*) recensione *f*

**writhe** /raɪð/ *vi* contorcersi; **~ with embarrassment** vergognarsi a morte

**writing** /'raɪtɪŋ/ *n* (*occupation*) scrivere *m*; (*words*) scritte *fpl*; (*handwriting*) scrittura *f*; **~s** *pl* scritti *mpl*; **in ~** per iscritto

**writing: writing desk** *n* scrivania *f*. **writing pad** *n* (*for notes*) bloc-notes *m inv*; (*for letters*) blocco *m* di carta da lettere. **writing paper** *n* carta *f* da lettera

**written** /'rɪtn/ *see* **write**

**wrong** /rɒŋ/ *a* sbagliato; **be ~** ‹*person:*› sbagliare; **what's ~?** cosa c'è che non va? ● *adv* ‹*spelt*› in modo sbagliato; **go ~** ‹*person:*› sbagliare; ‹*machine:*› funzionare male; ‹*plan:*› andar male; **don't get me ~** non fraintendermi ● *n* ingiustizia *f*; **in the ~** dalla parte del torto; **know right from ~** distinguere il bene dal male ● *vt* fare torto a

**wrong-foot** *vt Sport, fig* prendere in contropiede

**wrongful** /'rɒŋfʊl/ *a* ingiusto

**wrongfully** /'rɒŋfʊlɪ/ *adv* ‹*accuse*› ingiustamente

**wrongly** /'rɒŋlɪ/ *adv* in modo sbagliato; ‹*accuse, imagine*› a torto; ‹*informed*› male

**wrote** /rəʊt/ *see* **write**

**wrought iron** /rɔːt'aɪən/ *n* ferro *m* battuto ● *attrib* di ferro battuto

**wrung** /rʌŋ/ *see* **wring**

**wry** /raɪ/ *a* (**-er, -est**) ‹*humour, smile*› beffardo

**WYSIWYG** /'wɪzɪwɪg/ *abbr Comput* (**what you see is what you get**) ciò che vedi è ciò che ottieni

# Xx

**x, X** /eks/ *n* (*letter*) x, X *f inv*; (*anonymous person, place etc*) X
**x** *n Math* x *f inv*
**X certificate** *a Br* vietato ai minori di 18 anni
**xenophobia** /zenəˈfəʊbɪə/ *n* xenofobia *f*
**xerox®** /ˈzɪərɒks/ *vt* xerocopiare ● *n* (*machine*) xerocopiatrice *f*; (*document*) xerocopia *f*

**Xmas** /ˈkrɪsməs/ *n fam* Natale *m*
**X-ray** *n* (*picture*) radiografia *f*; **have an ~** farsi fare una radiografia ● *vt* passare ai raggi X
**X-ray machine** *n* apparecchio *m* radiografico
**xxx** *n* (*at end of letter*) baci *mpl*

# Yy

**y, Y** /waɪ/ *n* (*letter*) y, Y *f inv*
**yacht** /jɒt/ *n* yacht *m inv*; (*for racing*) barca *f* a vela
**yachting** /ˈjɒtɪŋ/ *n* vela *f*
**yak** /jæk/ *n Zool* yak *m inv*
**Yale®** /jeɪl/ *n* (*lock*) serratura *f* di sicurezza
**yam** /jæm/ *n* (*tropical*) igname *m*; (*Am: sweet potato*) patata *f* dolce
**Yank** /jæŋk/ *n fam* americano, -a *mf*
**yank** *vt fam* tirare
**Yankee** /ˈjæŋkɪ/ *n* (*pej: American*) yankee *m inv*; (*soldier*) nordista *m*; (*Am: of Northern USA*) abitante *mf* degli USA settentrionali; (*Am: inhabitant of New England*) abitante *mf* della Nuova Inghilterra
**yap** /jæp/ *vi* (*pt/pp* **yapped**) (*dog:*) guaire
**yapping** /ˈjæpɪŋ/ *n* (*of dogs*) guaiti *mpl*; (*fam: of people*) ciance *fpl*
**yard¹** /jɑːd/ *n* cortile *m*; (*for storage*) deposito *m*; **the Y~** *fam* Scotland Yard *f* (*polizia londinese*)
**yard²** *n* iarda *f* (= *91,44 cm*)
**yardstick** /ˈjɑːdstɪk/ *n fig* pietra *f* di paragone
**yarn** /jɑːn/ *n* filo *m*; (*fam: tale*) storia *f*
**yashmak** /ˈjæʃmæk/ *n* velo *m* (*delle donne musulmane*)
**yawn** /jɔːn/ *n* sbadiglio *m* ● *vi* sbadigliare
**yawning** /ˈjɔːnɪŋ/ *a* **~ gap** sbadiglio *m*
**yd** *abbr* **yard**
**yeah** /je/ *adv fam* sì; **oh ~ ?** ma davvero?
**year** /jɪə(r)/ *n* anno *m*; (*of wine*) annata *f*; **for ~s** *fam* da secoli
**yearbook** /ˈjɪəbʊk/ *n* annuario *m*
**yearly** /ˈjɪəlɪ/ *a* annuale ● *adv* annualmente
**yearn** /jɜːn/ *vi* struggersi
**yearning** /ˈjɜːnɪŋ/ *n* desiderio *m* struggente
**year-round** *a* (*supply, source*) permanente

**yeast** /jiːst/ *n* lievito *m*
**yell** /jel/ *n* urlo *m* ● *vi* urlare
**yelling** /ˈjelɪŋ/ *n* urla *fpl*
**yellow** /ˈjeləʊ/ *a & n* giallo *m*
**yellow-belly** *n fam* fifone *m*
**yellow card** *n Sport* cartellino *m* giallo
**yellowish** /ˈjeləʊɪʃ/ *a* giallastro
**yellow pages** *npl* pagine *fpl* gialle
**yellowy** /ˈjeləʊɪ/ *a* giallastro
**yelp** /jelp/ *n* (*of dog*) guaito *m* ● *vi* (*dog:*) guaire
**Yemen** /ˈjemən/ *n* Yemen *m*
**Yemeni** /ˈjemənɪ/ *a & n* yemenita *mf*
**yen** /jen/ *n* forte desiderio *m* (**for** di)
**yeoman** /ˈjəʊmən/ *n Br* piccolo proprietario *m* terriero; **Y~ of the Guard** guardiano *m* della Torre di Londra
**yep** /jep/ *adv fam* sì
**yes** /jes/ *adv* sì ● *n* sì *m inv*
**yes-man** *n fam* tirapiedi *m inv*
**yesterday** /ˈjestədeɪ/ *n & adv* ieri *m inv*; **~'s paper** il giornale di ieri; **the day before ~** l'altroieri; **~ afternoon** ieri pomeriggio; **~ evening** ieri sera; **~ morning** ieri mattina
**yet** /jet/ *adv* ancora; **as ~** fino ad ora; **not ~** non ancora; **the best ~** il migliore finora ● *conj* eppure
**yew** /juː/ *n* tasso *m* (*albero*)
**Y-fronts** *npl Br* slip *m inv* da uomo con apertura
**YHA** *Br abbr* (**Youth Hostels Association**) associazione *f* degli ostelli della gioventù
**Yiddish** /ˈjɪdɪʃ/ *n* yiddish *m*
**yield** /jiːld/ *n* produzione *f*; (*profit*) reddito *m* ● *vt* produrre; fruttare (*profit*) ● *vi* cedere; *Am Auto* dare la precedenza
**yielding** /ˈjiːldɪŋ/ *a* (*submissive*) arrendevole; (*ground*) cedevole; (*person*) flessibile

**YMCA** *abbr* (**Young Men's Christian Association**) Associazione *f* Cristiana dei Giovani

**yodel** /'jəʊdl/ *vi* (*pt/pp* **yodelled**) cantare jodel

**yoga** /'jəʊgə/ *n* yoga *m*

**yoghurt** /'jɒgət/ *n* yogurt *m inv*

**yoke** /jəʊk/ *n* giogo *m*; (*of garment*) carré *m inv*

**yokel** /'jəʊkl/ *n* zotico, -a *mf*

**yolk** /jəʊk/ *n* tuorlo *m*

**yonder** /'jɒndə(r)/ *adv liter* laggiù

**yonks** /jɒŋks/ *npl fam* **I haven't seen him for ~** è un secolo che non lo vedo

**yore** /jɔ:(r)/ *n* **in days of ~** un tempo

**you** /ju:/ *pers pron* (*subject*) tu, voi *pl*; (*formal*) lei, voi *pl*; (*direct/indirect object*) ti, vi *pl*; (*formal: direct object*) la; (*formal: indirect object*) le; (*after prep*) te, voi *pl*; (*formal: after prep*) lei; **~ are very kind** (*sg*) sei molto gentile; (*formal*) è molto gentile; (*pl & formal pl*) siete molto gentili; **~ can stay, but he has to go** (*sg*) tu puoi rimanere, ma lui deve andarsene; (*pl*) voi potete rimanere, ma lui deve andarsene; **all of ~** tutti voi; **I'll give ~ the money** (*sg*) ti darò i soldi; (*pl*) vi darò i soldi; **I'll give it to ~** (*sg*) te/(*pl*) ve lo darò; **it does ~ good** (*sg*) ti/(*pl*) vi fa bene; **it was ~!** (*sg*) eri tu!; (*pl*) eravate voi!; **~ has to be careful these days** si deve fare attenzione di questi tempi; **~ can't tell the difference** non puoi vedere la differenza

**you'd** /ju:d/ *abbr* **you would; you had**

**you-know-what** *pron fam* sai cosa

**you-know-who** *pron fam* sai chi

**you'll** /ju:l/ *abbr* **you will**

**you're** /jʊə(r)/ *abbr* **you are**

**you've** /ju:v/ *abbr* **you have**

**young** /jʌŋ/ *a* giovane; **~ lady** signorina *f*; **~ man** giovanotto *m*; **her ~ man** (*boyfriend*) il suo ragazzo ● *npl* (*animals*) piccoli *mpl*; **the ~** (*people*) i giovani

**young blood** *n* nuove leve *fpl*

**youngish** /'jʌŋɪʃ/ *a* abbastanza giovane

**young-looking** *a* dall'aria giovanile

**young offender** *n* delinquente *mf* minorenne

**youngster** /'jʌŋstə(r)/ *n* ragazzo, -a *mf*; (*child*) bambino, -a *mf*

**your** /jɔ:(r)/ *poss a* tuo *m*, tua *f*, tuoi *mpl*, tue *fpl*; (*formal*) suo *m*, sua *f*, suoi *mpl*, sue *fpl*; (*pl & formal pl*) vostro *m*, vostra *f*, vostri *mpl*, vostre *fpl*; **~ task/house** il tuo compito/la tua casa; (*formal*) il suo compito/la sua casa; (*pl & formal pl*) il vostro compito/la vostra casa; **~ mother/father** tua madre/tuo padre; (*formal*) sua madre/suo padre; (*pl & formal pl*) vostra madre/vostro padre

**yours** /jɔ:z/ *poss pron* il tuo *m*, la tua *f*, i tuoi *mpl*, le tue *fpl*; (*formal*) il suo *m*, la sua *f*, i suoi *mpl*, le sue *fpl*; (*pl & formal pl*) il vostro *m*, la vostra *f*, i vostri *mpl*, le vostre *fpl*; **a friend of ~** un tuo/suo/vostro amico; **friends of ~** dei tuoi/vostri/suoi amici; **that is ~** quello è tuo/vostro/suo; (*as opposed to mine*) quello è il tuo/il vostro/il suo

**yourself** /jɔ:'self/ *pers pron* (*reflexive*) ti; (*formal*) si; (*emphatic*) te stesso/a, se stesso/a; **do pour ~ a drink** versati da bere; (*formal*) si versi da bere; **you said so ~** lo hai detto tu stesso; (*formal*) lo ha detto lei stesso; **you can be proud of ~** puoi essere fiero di te/di sé; **by ~** da solo

**yourselves** /jɔ:'selvz/ *pers pron* (*reflexive*) vi; (*emphatic*) voi stessi; **do pour ~ a drink** versatevi da bere; **you said so ~** lo avete detto voi stessi; **you can be proud of ~** potete essere fieri di voi; **by ~** da soli

**youth** /ju:θ/ *n* (*pl youths* /ju:ðz/) gioventù *f inv*; (*boy*) giovanetto *m*; **the ~** (*young people*) i giovani

**youthful** /'ju:θfʊl/ *a* giovanile

**youth:** **youth hostel** *n* ostello *m* [della gioventù]; **youth hostelling** *n* viaggiare *m* pernottando in ostelli della gioventù. **youth work** *n* lavoro *m* di educatore. **youth worker** *n* educatore, -trice *mf*

**yo-yo®** /'jəʊjəʊ/ *n* yo-yo *m inv* ● *vi* ⟨*prices, inflation:*⟩ andare su e giù

**Yugoslav** /'ju:gəslɑ:v/ *a & n* jugoslavo, -a *mf*

**Yugoslavia** /ju:gə'slɑ:vɪə/ *n* Jugoslavia *f*

**Yule log** /ju:l/ *n* tronchetto *m* natalizio

**yup** /jʌp/ *adv fam* sì

**yuppie** /'jʌpɪ/ *n* yuppie *mf inv*

**yuppie flu** *n* sindrome *f* da affaticamento cronico

**YWCA** *abbr* (**Young Women's Christian Association**) Associazione *f* Cristiana delle Giovani

**yr** *abbr* **year**

# Zz

**z, Z** /zed/ *n* (*letter*) z, Z *f inv*
**zany** /'zeɪnɪ/ *a* (**-ier, -iest**) demenziale
**zap** /zæp/ *n* (*fam: energy*) energia *f* ● *vt* (*pt/pp* **zapped**) *fam* (*destroy*) distruggere ‹*town*›; far fuori ‹*person, animal*›; (*fire at*) fulminare; (*Comput: delete*) cancellare
**zapper** /'zæpə(r)/ *n* (*fam: for TV*) telecomando *m*
**zeal** /ziːl/ *n* zelo *m*
**zealot** /'zelət/ *n fig* fanatico *m*
**zealous** /'zeləs/ *a* zelante
**zealously** /'zeləslɪ/ *adv* con zelo
**zebra** /'zebrə/ *n* zebra *f*
**zebra crossing** *n* passaggio *m* pedonale, zebre *fpl*
**zenith** /'zenɪθ/ *n* zenit *m inv*; *fig* apogeo *m*
**zero** /'zɪərəʊ/ *n* zero *m*
**zero: zero gravity** *n* assenza *f* di gravità. **zero hour** *n Mil, fig* ora *f* zero. **zero-rated** /-'reɪtɪd/ *a Br* esente [da] IVA
**zest** /zest/ *n* gusto *m*; (*peel*) scorza *f* (*di agrumi*)
**zigzag** /'zɪgzæg/ *n* zigzag *m inv* ● *vi* (*pt/pp* **-zagged**) zigzagare
**zilch** /zɪltʃ/ *n fam* un tubo; **I understood ~** non ho capito un tubo
**Zimbabwe** /zɪm'bæbweɪ/ *n* Zimbabwe *m*
**Zimmer®** /'zɪmə(r)/ *n Br* deambulatore *m*

**zinc** /zɪŋk/ *n* zinco *m*
**zinc oxide** *n* ossido *m* di zinco
**zing** /zɪŋ/ *n fam* (*energy*) brio *m*; (*sound*) sibilo *m* ● *vt* (*Am: criticize*) stroncare
**Zionism** /'zaɪənɪzm/ *n* sionismo *m*
**zip** /zɪp/ *n* ~ [**fastener**] cerniera *f* [lampo] ● *vt* (*pt/pp* **zipped**) ~ [**up**] chiudere con la cerniera [lampo]
■ **zip along** *vi* (*move quickly*) procedere velocemente
**zip code** *n Am* codice *m* [di avviamento] postale, C.A.P.
**zipper** /'zɪpə(r)/ *n Am* cerniera *f* [lampo]
**zippy** /'zɪpɪ/ *a* ‹*fam: vehicle*› scattante
**zither** /'zɪðə(r)/ *n* cetra *f*
**zodiac** /'zəʊdɪæk/ *n* zodiaco *m*
**zombie** /'zɒmbɪ/ *n fam* zombi *mf inv*
**zone** /zəʊn/ *n* zona *f*
**zoning** /'zəʊnɪŋ/ *n* zonazione *f*
**zonked** /zɒŋkt/ *a* (*fam: on drugs, drunk, tired*) fatto
**zoo** /zuː/ *n* zoo *m inv*
**zoological** /zəʊə'lɒdʒɪkl/ *a* zoologico
**zoologist** /zəʊ'ɒlədʒɪst/ *n* zoologo, -a *mf*
**zoology** /zəʊ'ɒlədʒɪ/ *n* zoologia *f*
**zoom** /zuːm/ *vi* sfrecciare
**zoom lens** *n* zoom *m inv*
**zucchini** /zʊ'kiːnɪ/ *n* zucchino *m*, zucchina *f*

# ITALIAN VERB TABLES

## REGULAR VERBS:

**1.** in **-are** (*eg* **compr|are**)

**Present** ~o, ~i, ~a, ~iamo, ~ate, ~ano
**Imperfect** ~avo, ~avi, ~ava, ~avamo, ~avate, ~avano
**Past historic** ~ai, ~asti, ~ò, ~ammo, ~aste, ~arono
**Future** ~erò, ~erai, ~erà, ~eremo, ~erete, ~eranno
**Present subjunctive** ~i, ~i, ~i, ~iamo, ~iate, ~ino
**Past subjunctive** ~assi, ~assi, ~asse, ~assimo, ~aste, ~assero
**Present participle** ~ando
**Past participle** ~ato
**Imperative** ~a (*fml* ~i), ~iamo, ~ate
**Conditional** ~erei, ~eresti, ~erebbe, ~eremmo, ~ereste, ~erebbero

**2.** in **-ere** (*eg* **vend|ere**)

**Pres** ~o, ~i, ~e, ~iamo, ~ete, ~ono
**Impf** ~evo, ~evi, ~eva, ~evamo, ~evate, ~evano
**Past hist** ~ei *or* ~etti, ~esti, ~è *or* ~ette, ~emmo, ~este, ~erono *or* ~ettero
**Fut** ~erò, ~erai, ~erà, ~eremo, ~erete, ~eranno
**Pres sub** ~a, ~a, ~a, ~iamo, ~iate, ~ano
**Past sub** ~essi, ~essi, ~esse, ~essimo, ~este, ~essero
**Pres part** ~endo
**Past part** ~uto
**Imp** ~i (*fml* ~a), ~iamo, ~ete
**Cond** ~erei, ~eresti, ~erebbe, ~eremmo, ~ereste, ~erebbero

**3.** in **-ire** (*eg* **dorm|ire**)

**Pres** ~o, ~i, ~e, ~iamo, ~ite, ~ono
**Impf** ~ivo, ~ivi, ~iva, ~ivamo, ~ivate, ~ivano
**Past hist** ~ii, ~isti, ~ì, ~immo, ~iste, ~irono
**Fut** ~irò, ~irai, ~irà, ~iremo, ~irete, ~iranno
**Pres sub** ~a, ~a, ~a, ~iamo, ~iate, ~ano
**Past sub** ~issi, ~issi, ~isse, ~issimo, ~iste, ~issero
**Pres part** ~endo
**Past part** ~ito
**Imp** ~i (*fml* ~a), ~iamo, ~ite
**Cond** ~irei, ~iresti, ~irebbe, ~iremmo, ~ireste, ~irebbero

## Notes

- Many verbs in the third conjugation take *isc* between the stem and the ending in the first, second, and third person singular and in the third person plural of the present, the present subjunctive, and the imperative: fin|ire **Pres** ~isco, ~isci, ~isce, ~iscono. **Pres sub** ~isca, ~iscano **Imp** ~isci.

- The three forms of the imperative are the same as the corresponding forms of the present for the second and third conjugation. In the first conjugation the forms are also the same except for the second person singular: present *compri*, imperative *compra*. The negative form of the second person singular is formed by putting *non* before the infinitive for all conjugations: *non comprare*. In polite forms the third person of the present subjunctive is used instead for all conjugations: *compri*.

## IRREGULAR VERBS:

Certain forms of all irregular verbs are regular (except for *essere*). These are: the second person plural of the present, the past subjunctive, and the present participle. All forms not listed below are regular and can be derived from the parts given. Only those irregular verbs considered to be the most useful are shown in the tables.

**accadere**   *as* **cadere**

**accendere**   • **Past hist** accesi, accendesti • **Past part** acceso

**affliggere**   • **Past hist** afflissi, affliggesti • **Past part** afflitto

**ammettere**   *as* **mettere**

**andare**   • **Pres** vado, vai, va, andiamo, andate, vanno • **Fut** andrò *etc* • **Pres sub** vada, vadano • **Imp** va', vada, vadano

**apparire**   • **Pres** appaio *or* apparisco, appari *or* apparisci, appare *or* apparisce, appaiono *or* appariscono • **Past hist** apparvi *or* apparsi, apparisti, apparve *or* apparì *or* apparse, apparvero *or* apparirono *or* apparsero • **Pres sub** appaia *or* apparisca

**aprire**   • **Pres** apro • **Past hist** aprii, apristi • **Pres sub** apra • **Past part** aperto

**avere**   • **Pres** ho, hai, ha, abbiamo, hanno • **Past hist** ebbi, avesti, ebbe, avemmo, aveste, ebbero • **Fut** avrò *etc* • **Pres sub** abbia *etc* • **Imp** abbi, abbia, abbiate, abbiano

**bere**   • **Pres** bevo *etc* • **Impf** bevevo *etc* • **Past hist** bevvi *or* bevetti, bevesti • **Fut** berrò *etc* • **Pres sub** beva *etc* • **Past sub** bevessi *etc* • **Pres part** bevendo • **Cond** berrei *etc*

**cadere**   • **Past hist** caddi, cadesti • **Fut** cadrò *etc*

**chiedere**   • **Past hist** chiesi, chiedesti • **Pres sub** chieda *etc* • **Past part** chiesto *etc*

**chiudere**   • **Past hist** chiusi, chiudesti • **Past part** chiuso

**cogliere**   • **Pres** colgo, colgono • **Past hist** colsi, cogliesti • **Pres sub** colga • **Past part** colto

**correre**   • **Past hist** corsi, corresti • **Past part** corso

**crescere**   • **Past hist** crebbi • **Past part** cresciuto

**cuocere**   • **Pres** cuocio, cuociamo, cuociono • **Past hist** cossi, cocesti • **Past part** cotto

**dare**   • **Pres** do, dai, da, diamo, danno • **Past hist** diedi *or* detti, desti • **Fut** darò *etc* • **Pres sub** dia *etc* • **Past sub** dessi *etc* • **Imp** da' (*fml* dia)

**dire**
- **Pres** dico, dici, dice, diciamo, dicono • **Impf** dicevo *etc* • **Past hist** dissi, dicesti • **Fut** dirò *etc* • **Pres sub** dica, diciamo, diciate, dicano • **Past sub** dicessi *etc* • **Pres part** dicendo • **Past part** detto • **Imp** di' (*fml* dica)

**dovere**
- **Pres** devo *or* debbo, devi, deve, dobbiamo, devono *or* debbono • **Fut** dovrò *etc* • **Pres sub** deva *or* debba, dobbiamo, dobbiate, devano *or* debbano • **Cond** dovrei *etc*

**essere**
- **Pres** sono, sei, è, siamo, siete, sono • **Impf** ero, eri, era, eravamo, eravate, erano • **Past hist** fui, fosti, fu, fummo, foste, furono • **Fut** sarò *etc* • **Pres sub** sia *etc* • **Past sub** fossi, fossi, fosse, fossimo, foste, fossero • **Past part** stato • **Imp** sii (*fml* sia), siate • **Cond** sarei *etc*

**fare**
- **Pres** faccio, fai, fa, facciamo, fanno • **Impf** facevo *etc* • **Past hist** feci, facesti • **Fut** farò *etc* • **Pres sub** faccia *etc* • **Past sub** facessi *etc* • **Pres part** facendo • **Past part** fatto • **Imp** fa' (*fml* faccia) • **Cond** farei *etc*

**fingere**
- **Past hist** finsi, fingesti, finsero • **Past part** finto

**giungere**
- **Past hist** giunsi, giungesti, giunsero • **Past part** giunto

**leggere**
- **Past hist** lessi, leggesti • **Past part** letto

**mettere**
- **Past hist** misi, mettesti • **Past part** messo

**morire**
- **Pres** muoio, muori, muore, muoiono • **Fut** morirò *or* morrò *etc* • **Pres sub** muoia • **Past part** morto

**muovere**
- **Past hist** mossi, movesti • **Past part** mosso

**nascere**
- **Past hist** nacqui, nascesti • **Past part** nato

**offrire**
- **Past hist** offersi *or* offrii, offristi • **Pres sub** offra • **Past part** offerto

**parere**
- **Pres** paio, pari, pare, pariamo, paiono • **Past hist** parvi *or* parsi, paresti • **Fut** parrò *etc* • **Pres sub** paia, paiamo *or* pariamo, pariate, paiano • **Past part** parso

**piacere**
- **Pres** piaccio, piaci, piace, piacciamo, piacciono • **Past hist** piacqui, piacesti, piacque, piacemmo, piaceste, piacquero • **Pres sub** piaccia *etc* • **Past part** piaciuto

**porre**
- **Pres** pongo, poni, pone, poniamo, ponete, pongono • **Impf** ponevo *etc* • **Past hist** posi, ponesti • **Fut** porrò *etc* • **Pres sub** ponga, poniamo, poniate, pongano • **Past sub** ponessi *etc*

**potere**
- **Pres** posso, puoi, può, possiamo, possono • **Fut** potrò *etc* • **Pres sub** possa, possiamo, possiate, possano • **Cond** potrei *etc*

**prendere**
- **Past hist** presi, prendesti • **Past part** preso

**ridere**
- **Past hist** risi, ridesti • **Past part** riso

**rimanere** • **Pres** rimango, rimani, rimane, rimaniamo, rimangono • **Past hist** rimasi, rimanesti • **Fut** rimarrò *etc* • **Pres sub** rimanga • **Past part** rimasto • **Cond** rimarrei

**salire** • **Pres** salgo, sali, sale, saliamo, salgono • **Pres sub** salga, saliate, salgano

**sapere** • **Pres** so, sai, sa, sappiamo, sanno • **Past hist** seppi, sapesti • **Fut** saprò *etc* • **Pres sub** sappia *etc* • **Imp** sappi (*fml* sappia), sappiate • **Cond** saprei *etc*

**scegliere** • **Pres** scelgo, scegli, sceglie, scegliamo, scelgono • **Past hist** scelsi, scegliesti *etc* • **Past part** scelto

**scrivere** • **Past hist** scrissi, scrivesti *etc* • **Past part** scritto

**sedere** • **Pres** siedo *or* seggo, siedi, siede, siedono • **Pres sub** sieda *or* segga

**spegnere** • **Pres** spengo, spengono • **Past hist** spensi, spegnesti • **Past part** spento

**stare** • **Pres** sto, stai, sta, stiamo, stanno • **Past hist** stetti, stesti • **Fut** starò *etc* • **Pres sub** stia *etc* • **Past sub** stessi *etc* • **Past part** stato • **Imp** sta' (*fml* stia)

**tacere** • **Pres** taccio, tacciono • **Past hist** tacqui, tacque, tacquero • **Pres sub** taccia

**tendere** • **Past hist** tesi • **Past part** teso

**tenere** • **Pres** tengo, tieni, tiene, tengono • **Past hist** tenni, tenesti • **Fut** terrò *etc* • **Pres sub** tenga

**togliere** • **Pres** tolgo, tolgono • **Past hist** tolsi, tolse, tolsero • **Pres sub** tolga, tolgano • **Past part** tolto • *Imp fml* tolga

**trarre** • **Pres** traggo, trai, trae, traiamo, traete, traggono • **Past hist** trassi, traesti • **Fut** trarrò *etc* • **Pres sub** tragga • **Past sub** traessi *etc* • **Past part** tratto

**uscire** • **Pres** esco, esci, esce, escono • **Pres sub** esca • **Imp** esci (*fml* esca)

**valere** • **Pres** valgo, valgono • **Past hist** valsi, valesti • **Fut** varrò *etc* • **Pres sub** valga, valgano • **Past part** valso • **Cond** varrei *etc*

**vedere** • **Past hist** vidi, vedesti • **Fut** vedrò *etc* • **Past part** visto *or* veduto • **Cond** vedrei *etc*

**venire** • **Pres** vengo, vieni, viene, vengono • **Past hist** venni, venisti • **Fut** verrò *etc*

**vivere** • **Past hist** vissi, vivesti • **Fut** vivrò *etc* • **Past part** vissuto • **Cond** vivrei *etc*

**volere** • **Pres** voglio, vuoi, vuole, vogliamo, volete, vogliono • **Past hist** volli, volesti • **Fut** vorrò *etc* • **Pres sub** voglia *etc* • **Imp** vogliate • **Cond** vorrei *etc*

# 379

# English irregular verbs

| Infinitive / *Infinito* | Past Tense / *Passato* | Past Participle / *Participio passato* | Infinitive / *Infinito* | Past Tense / *Passato* | Past Participle / *Participio passato* |
|---|---|---|---|---|---|
| arise | arose | arisen | feed | fed | fed |
| awake | awoke | awoken | feel | felt | felt |
| be | was | been | fight | fought | fought |
| bear | bore | borne | find | found | found |
| beat | beat | beaten | flee | fled | fled |
| become | became | become | fling | flung | flung |
| begin | began | begun | fly | flew | flown |
| behold | beheld | beheld | forbid | forbade | forbidden |
| bend | bent | bent | forget | forgot | forgotten |
| beseech | beseeched besought | beseeched besought | forgive | forgave | forgiven |
| | | | forsake | forsook | forsaken |
| bet | bet, betted | bet, betted | freeze | froze | frozen |
| bid | bade, bid | bidden, bid | get | got | got, gotten *Am* |
| bind | bound | bound | give | gave | given |
| bite | bit | bitten | go | went | gone |
| bleed | bled | bled | grind | ground | ground |
| blow | blew | blown | grow | grew | grown |
| break | broke | broken | hang | hung, hanged (*vt*) | hung, hanged |
| breed | bred | bred | have | had | had |
| bring | brought | brought | hear | heard | heard |
| build | built | built | hew | hewed | hewed, hewn |
| burn | burnt, burned | burnt, burned | hide | hid | hidden |
| burst | burst | burst | hit | hit | hit |
| bust | busted, bust | busted, bust | hold | held | held |
| buy | bought | bought | hurt | hurt | hurt |
| cast | cast | cast | keep | kept | kept |
| catch | caught | caught | kneel | knelt | knelt |
| choose | chose | chosen | know | knew | known |
| cling | clung | clung | lay | laid | laid |
| come | came | come | lead | led | led |
| cost | cost, costed (*vt*) | cost, costed | lean | leaned, leant | leaned, leant |
| creep | crept | crept | leap | leapt, leaped | leapt, leaped |
| cut | cut | cut | learn | learnt, learned | learnt, learned |
| deal | dealt | dealt | leave | left | left |
| dig | dug | dug | lend | lent | lent |
| do | did | done | let | let | let |
| draw | drew | drawn | lie | lay | lain |
| dream | dreamt, dreamed | dreamt, dreamed | light | lit, lighted | lit, lighted |
| drink | drank | drunk | lose | lost | lost |
| drive | drove | driven | make | made | made |
| dwell | dwelt | dwelt | mean | meant | meant |
| eat | ate | eaten | meet | met | met |
| fall | fell | fallen | | | |

| Infinitive | Past Tense | Past Participle | | Infinitive | Past Tense | Past Participle |
|---|---|---|---|---|---|---|
| Infinito | Passato | Participio passato | | Infinito | Passato | Participio passato |
| mow | mowed | mown, mowed | | spend | spent | spent |
| | | | | spill | spilt, spilled | spilt, spilled |
| overhang | overhung | overhung | | | | |
| pay | paid | paid | | spin | spun | spun |
| put | put | put | | spit | spat | spat |
| quit | quitted, quit | quitted, quit | | split | split | split |
| | | | | spoil | spoilt, spoiled | spoilt, spoiled |
| read | read /red/ | read /red/ | | | | |
| rid | rid | rid | | spread | spread | spread |
| ride | rode | ridden | | spring | sprang | sprung |
| ring | rang | rung | | stand | stood | stood |
| rise | rose | risen | | steal | stole | stolen |
| run | ran | run | | stick | stuck | stuck |
| saw | sawed | sawn, sawed | | sting | stung | stung |
| | | | | stink | stank | stunk |
| say | said | said | | strew | strewed | strewn, strewed |
| see | saw | seen | | | | |
| seek | sought | sought | | stride | strode | stridden |
| sell | sold | sold | | strike | struck | struck |
| send | sent | sent | | string | strung | strung |
| set | set | set | | strive | strove | striven |
| sew | sewed | sewn, sewed | | swear | swore | sworn |
| | | | | sweep | swept | swept |
| shake | shook | shaken | | swell | swelled | swollen, swelled |
| shear | sheared | shorn, sheared | | | | |
| | | | | swim | swam | swum |
| shed | shed | shed | | swing | swung | swung |
| shine | shone | shone | | take | took | taken |
| shit | shit | shit | | teach | taught | taught |
| shoe | shod | shod | | tear | tore | torn |
| shoot | shot | shot | | tell | told | told |
| show | showed | shown | | think | thought | thought |
| shrink | shrank | shrunk | | thrive | thrived, throve | thrived, thriven |
| shut | shut | shut | | | | |
| sing | sang | sung | | throw | threw | thrown |
| sink | sank | sunk | | thrust | thrust | thrust |
| sit | sat | sat | | tread | trod | trodden |
| slay | slew | slain | | understand | understood | understood |
| sleep | slept | slept | | undo | undid | undone |
| slide | slid | slid | | wake | woke | woken |
| sling | slung | slung | | wear | wore | worn |
| slit | slit | slit | | weave | wove | woven |
| smell | smelt, smelled | smelt, smelled | | weep | wept | wept |
| | | | | wet | wet, wetted | wet, wetted |
| sow | sowed | sown, sowed | | | | |
| | | | | win | won | won |
| speak | spoke | spoken | | wind | wound | wound |
| speed | sped, speeded | sped, speeded | | wring | wrung | wrung |
| | | | | write | wrote | written |
| spell | spelled, spelt | spelled, spelt | | | | |